Collins
Italian
Dictionary
& Grammar

HarperCollins Publishers
Westerhill Road
Bishopbriggs
Glasgow
G64 2QT

Third Edition 2014

Reprint 10 9 8 7 6 5 4 3 2 1 0

© HarperCollins Publishers 2008, 2010, 2014

ISBN 978-0-00-748437-9

www.collinsdictionary.com
www.collins.co.uk

A catalogue record for this book is available from the British Library

Typeset by Davidson Publishing Solutions

Printed in India by Gopsons Papers Ltd

Acknowledgements
We would like to thank those authors and publishers who kindly gave permission for copyright material to be used in the Collins Corpus. We would also like to thank Times Newspapers Ltd for providing valuable data.

EDITOR
Susie Beattie

CONTRIBUTORS
Phyllis Buchanan
Francesca Logi
Janice McNeillie
Helen Newstead

TECHNICAL SUPPORT
Thomas Callan
Agnieszka Urbanowicz
Dave Wark

FOR THE PUBLISHER
Gerry Breslin
Catherine Love
Evelyn Sword

Contributors to the previous edition
Gaëlle Amiot-Cadey, Gabriella Bacchelli, Donatella Boi, Michela Clari, Daphne Day, Genevieve Gerrard, Angela Jack, Joyce Littlejohn, Val McNulty, Elizabeth Potter, Maggie Seaton, Caroline Smart, Rachel Smith, Jill Williams

Indice

Contents

I MARCHI REGISTRATI
I termini che a nostro parere costituiscono un marchio registrato sono stati designati come tali. In ogni caso, né la presenza né l'assenza di tale designazione implicano alcuna valutazione del loro reale stato giuridico.

NOTE ON TRADEMARKS
Words which we have reason to believe constitute trademarks have been designated as such. However, neither the presence nor the absence of such designation should be regarded as affecting the legal status of any trademark.

Introduzione

Se desiderate imparare l'inglese o approfondire le conoscenze già acquisite, se volete leggere o redigere dei testi in inglese, oppure conversare con interlocutori di madrelingua inglese, se siete studenti, turisti, uomini o donne d'affari avete scelto il compagno di viaggio ideale per esprimervi e comunicare in inglese sia a voce che per iscritto. Strumento pratico e moderno, il vostro dizionario dà largo spazio al linguaggio quotidiano in campi quali l'attualità, gli affari, la gestione d'ufficio, l'informatica e il turismo. Come in tutti i nostri dizionari, grande importanza è stata data alla lingua contemporanea e alle espressioni idiomatiche.

Come usare il dizionario

Troverete qui di seguito alcune spiegazioni sul modo in cui le informazioni sono state presentate nel testo. L'obiettivo del dizionario è quello di darvi il maggior numero possibile di informazioni senza tuttavia sacrificare la chiarezza all'interno delle voci.

Le voci

Qui di seguito verranno descritti i vari elementi di cui si compone una voce tipo del vostro dizionario.

La trascrizione fonetica

Come regola generale è stata data la pronuncia di tutte le parole inglesi e quella delle parole italiane che potevano presentare qualche difficoltà per il parlante inglese. Nella parte inglese-italiano, tuttavia, per la pronuncia di nomi composti formati da due parole non unite dal trattino si dovrà cercare la trascrizione di ciascuna di queste parole alla rispettiva posizione alfabetica. La pronuncia si trova tra parentesi quadre, subito dopo il lemma. Come nella maggior parte dei dizionari moderni è stato adottato il sistema noto come "alfabeto fonetico internazionale". Troverete qui di seguito, a pagina xiii e xiv, un elenco completo dei caratteri utilizzati in questo sistema.

Le categorie grammaticali

Tutte le parole appartengono ad una categoria grammaticale, cioè possono essere sostantivi, verbi, aggettivi, avverbi, pronomi, articoli o congiunzioni.

I sostantivi possono essere singolari o plurali, sia in italiano che in inglese, e maschili o femminili in italiano. I verbi possono essere transitivi o intransitivi in entrambe le lingue, ma anche riflessivi o impersonali in italiano; nella sezione italiano-inglese, i verbi sono seguiti da un numero in grassetto che rimanda alle tavole dei verbi nelle pagine xviii-xxii. La categoria grammaticale appare in maiuscoletto subito dopo la pronuncia ed eventuali informazioni di tipo morfologico (plurali irregolari ecc.).

Numerose voci sono state suddivise in varie categorie grammaticali. Per esempio la parola italiana **bene** può essere sia un avverbio che un aggettivo o un sostantivo, e la parola inglese **sneeze** può essere sia un sostantivo ("starnuto") che un verbo intransitivo ("starnutire"). Analogamente il verbo italiano **correre** può essere usato sia come verbo intransitivo ("correre alla stazione") che come transitivo ("correre un rischio"). Per presentare la voce con maggiore chiarezza e permettervi di trovare rapidamente la traduzione che cercate, è stato introdotto un triangolino nero ▶ per contrassegnare il passaggio da una categoria grammaticale ad un'altra.

Suddivisioni semantiche

La maggior parte delle parole ha più di un significato. Per esempio, la parola **fiocco** può essere sia un'annodatura di un nastro che una falda di neve. Molte parole si traducono in modo diverso a seconda del contesto in cui sono usate: per esempio **scala** si tradurrà in inglese con "staircase" o "stairs" se si tratta di una scala con gradini, con "ladder" se è una scala a pioli. Per permettervi di scegliere la traduzione giusta per ciascuno dei contesti in cui la parola si può trovare, le voci sono state suddivise in categorie di significato. Ciascuna suddivisione è introdotta da un "indicatore d'uso" tra parentesi in *corsivo*. Le voci **fiocco** e **scala** compariranno quindi nel testo nel modo seguente:

> **fi'occo, -chi** SM (*di nastro*) bow; (*di stoffa, lana*) flock; (*di neve*) flake; ...

> **'scala** SF (*a gradini ecc*) staircase, stairs *pl*; (*a pioli, di corda*) ladder; ...

Per segnalare la traduzione appropriata sono stati introdotti anche degli indicatori d'ambito d'uso in *corsivo* con la prima lettera maiuscola, tra parentesi, spesso in forma abbreviata, come per esempio nel caso della voce **tromba**:

> **'tromba** SF (*Mus*) trumpet; (*Aut*) horn; ...

L'elenco completo delle abbreviazioni adottate nel dizionario è riportato alle pagine xiii e xiv.

Le traduzioni

Per la maggior parte delle parole inglesi ed italiane ci sono traduzioni precise a seconda del significato o del contesto, come risulta dagli esempi riportati fin qui. A volte, tuttavia, le parole non hanno un preciso equivalente nella lingua d'arrivo: in questi casi è stato fornito un equivalente approssimativo, preceduto dal segno ≈, come ad esempio per l'abbreviazione **RAC**, per cui è stato dato l'equivalente italiano "A.C.I.", dato che le due associazioni svolgono nei due paesi funzioni analoghe:

> **RAC** N ABBR (*Brit*: = *Royal Automobile Club*)
> ≈ A.C.I. *m* (= *Automobile Club d'Italia*)

A volte è persino impossibile trovare un equivalente approssimativo. Questo è il caso, per esempio, di piatti tipici di un certo paese, come ad esempio **pandoro**:

> **pan'doro** SM *type of sponge cake eaten at* Christmas

In questi casi, al posto della traduzione, che non esiste, comparirà una spiegazione: per maggiore chiarezza, questa spiegazione o glossa è stata messa in *corsivo*.

Molto spesso la traduzione di una parola può non funzionare all'interno di una data locuzione. Ad esempio alla voce **dare**, verbo spesso tradotto con "to give" in inglese, troviamo varie locuzioni per alcune delle quali la traduzione fornita all'inizio della voce non si può utilizzare: **quanti anni mi dai?** "how old do you think I am?" **danno ancora quel film?** "is that film still showing?", **dare per certo qc** "to consider sth certain", e così via. Ed è proprio in questi casi che potrete verificare l'utilità e la completezza del dizionario, che contiene una ricca gamma di composti, locuzioni e frasi idiomatiche.

Il registro linguistico

In italiano sapete istintivamente scegliere l'espressione corretta da usare a seconda del contesto in cui vi esprimete. Per esempio saprete quando dire **Non me ne importa!** e quando invece potete dire **Chi se ne frega?** Più difficile sarà farlo in inglese, dove avete minore consapevolezza delle sfumature di registro linguistico. Per questo motivo nella parte inglese-italiano le parole ed espressioni inglesi di uso più familiare sono segnalate dall'abbreviazione (*col*), mentre (*col!*) segnala le parole ed espressioni volgari. Nella parte italiano-inglese (*!*) dopo una traduzione segnala che si tratta di una parola od espressione volgare.

Parole chiave

Come vedrete, ad alcune voci è stato riservato un trattamento particolare sia dal punto di vista grafico che da quello linguistico. Si tratta di voci come **essere** o **fare**, o dei loro equivalenti inglesi **be** e **do**, che per la loro importanza e complessità meritano una strutturazione più articolata ed un maggior numero di locuzioni illustrative. Queste voci sono strutturate in diverse categorie di significato contrassegnate da numeri, e le costruzioni sintattiche e locuzioni che illustrano quel particolare significato sono riportate all'interno della relativa categoria.

Informazioni culturali

Le voci affiancate da una sbarra verticale digradante approfondiscono aspetti della cultura italiana o di quella dei paesi di lingua inglese in argomenti quali la politica, la scuola, i mass media e le festività nazionali.

Introduction

You may be starting to learn Italian, or you may wish to extend your knowledge of the language. Perhaps you want to read and study Italian books, newspapers and magazines, or perhaps simply have a conversation with Italian speakers. Whatever the reason, whether you're a student, a tourist or want to use Italian for business, this is the ideal book to help you understand and communicate. This modern, user-friendly dictionary gives priority to everyday vocabulary and the language of current affairs, business and tourism. As in all Collins dictionaries, the emphasis is firmly placed on contemporary language and expressions.

How to use the dictionary

Below you will find an outline of how information is presented in your dictionary. Our aim is to give you the maximum amount of detail in the clearest and most helpful way.

Entries

A typical entry in your dictionary will be made up of the following elements:

Phonetic transcription

Phonetics appear in square brackets immediately after the headword. They are shown using the International Phonetic Alphabet (IPA), and a complete list of the symbols used in this system can be found on pages xiii and xiv.

Grammatical information

All words belong to one of the following parts of speech: noun, verb, adjective, adverb, pronoun, article, conjunction, preposition.

Nouns can be singular or plural and, in Italian, masculine or feminine. Verbs can be transitive, intransitive, reflexive or impersonal: on the Italian side, each verb is followed by a number in bold, which corresponds to verb tables on pages xvi-xix. Parts of speech appear in SMALL CAPS immediately after the phonetic spelling of the headword.

Often a word can have more than one part of speech. Just as the English word **chemical** can be an adjective or a noun, the Italian word **fondo** can be an adjective ("deep") or a masculine noun ("bottom"). In the same way the verb **to walk** is sometimes transitive, ie it takes an object ("to walk the dog") and sometimes intransitive, ie it doesn't take an object ("to walk to school"). To help you find the meaning you are looking for quickly and for clarity of presentation, the different part of speech categories are separated by a solid black triangle ▶.

Meaning divisions

Most words have more than one meaning. Take, for example, **punch** which can be, amongst other things, a blow with the fist or an object used for making holes. Other words are translated differently depending on the context in which they are used. The transitive verb **to roll up**, for example, can be translated by "arrotolare" or "rimboccare" depending on what it is you are rolling up. To help you select the most appropriate translation in every context, entries are divided according to meaning. Each different meaning is introduced by an "indicator" in *italics* and in brackets. Thus, the examples given above will be shown as follows:

> **punch** [pʌntʃ] N (*blow*) pugno; (*fig: force*) forza;
> (*tool*) punzone *m*; ...

> ▶ **roll up** VI (*col: arrive*) arrivare ▶ VT (*carpet,
> cloth, map*) arrotolare; (*sleeves*) rimboccare ...

Likewise, some words can have a different meaning when used to talk about a specific subject area or field. For example, **bishop**, which is generally used to mean a high-ranking clergyman, is also the name of a chess piece. To show English speakers which translation to use, we have added "subject field labels" in *italics*, starting with a capital letter, and in brackets, in this case (*Chess*):

> **bishop** ['bɪʃəp] N vescovo; (*Chess*) alfiere *m*

Field labels are often shortened to save space. You will find a complete list of abbreviations used in the dictionary on pages xi and xii.

Translations

Most English words have a direct translation in Italian and vice versa, as shown in the examples given above. Sometimes, however, no exact equivalent exists in the target language. In such cases we have given an approximate equivalent, indicated by the sign ≈. Such is the case of **National Insurance**, the Italian equivalent of which is "Previdenza Sociale". This is not an exact translation since the systems of the two countries in question are quite different:

> **National Insurance** N (*BRIT*) ≈ Previdenza
> Sociale

On occasion it is impossible to find even an approximate equivalent. This may be the case, for example, with the names of types of food:

> **cottage pie** N *piatto a base di carne macinata in
> sugo e purè di patate*

Here the translation (which doesn't exist) is replaced by an explanation. For increased clarity the explanation, or "gloss", is shown in *italics*.

It is often the case that a word, or a particular meaning of a word, cannot be translated in isolation. The translation of **Dutch**, for example, is "olandese". However, the phrase **to go Dutch** is rendered by "fare alla romana". Even an expression as simple as **washing powder** needs a separate translation since it translates as "detersivo (in polvere)", not "polvere per lavare". This is where your dictionary will prove to be particularly informative and useful since it contains an abundance of compounds, phrases and idiomatic expressions.

Levels of formality and familiarity

In English you instinctively know when to say **I'm broke** *or* **I'm a bit short of cash** and when to say **I don't have any money**. When you are trying to understand someone who is speaking Italian, however, or when you yourself try to speak Italian, it is important to know what is polite and what is less so, and what you can say in a relaxed situation but not in a formal context. To help you with this, on the Italian-English side we have added the label (*col*) to show that an Italian word or expression is colloquial, while those words or expressions which are vulgar are given an exclamation mark (*col!*), warning you they can cause serious offence. Note also that on the English-Italian side, translations which are vulgar are followed by an exclamation mark in brackets.

Keywords

Words labelled in the text as KEYWORDS, such as **be** and **do** or their Italian equivalents **essere** and **fare**, have been given special treatment because they form the basic elements of the language. This extra help will ensure that you know how to use these complex words with confidence.

Cultural information

Entries which appear next to a fading vertical bar explain aspects of culture in Italy and English-speaking countries. Subject areas covered include politics, education, media and national festivals.

Abbreviazioni

Abbreviations

abbreviazione	ABBR	abbreviation
aggettivo	ADJ, AG	adjective
amministrazione	Admin	administration
avverbio	ADV	adverb
aeronautica, viaggi aerei	Aer	flying, air travel
aggettivo	AG	adjective
agricoltura	Agr	agriculture
amministrazione	Amm	administration
anatomia	Anat	anatomy
architettura	Archit	architecture
astronomia, astrologia	Astr	astronomy, astrology
l'automobile	Aut	the motor car and motoring
verbo ausiliare	AUX VB	auxiliary verb
avverbio	AV	adverb
aeronautica, viaggi aerei	Aviat	flying, air travel
biologia	Biol	biology
botanica	Bot	botany
inglese della Gran Bretagna	BRIT	British English
consonante	C	consonant
chimica	Chim, Chem	chemistry
familiare (! da evitare)	col(!)	colloquial usage (! particularly offensive)
commercio, finanza, banca	Comm	commerce, finance, banking
informatica	Comput	computing
congiunzione	CONG	conjunction
congiunzione	CONJ	conjunction
edilizia	Constr	building
sostantivo usato come aggettivo, non può essere usato nè come attributo, nè dopo il sostantivo qualificato	CPD	compound element: noun used as adjective and which cannot follow the noun it qualifies
cucina	Cus, Culin	cookery
davanti a	dav	before
determinante: articolo, aggettivo dimostrativo o indefinito etc	DET	determiner: article, demonstrative etc
diritto	Dir	law
economia	Econ	economics
edilizia	Edil	building
elettricità, elettronica	Elettr, Elec	electricity, electronics
esclamazione, interiezione	escl, excl	exclamation, interjection
specialmente	esp	especially
femminile	f	feminine
ferrovia	Ferr	railways
figurato	fig	figurative use
fisiologia	Fisiol	physiology
fotografia	Fot	photography
(verbo inglese) la cui particella è inseparabile dal verbo	VT FUS	(phrasal verb) where the particle cannot be separated from main verb
nella maggior parte dei sensi; generalmente	gen	in most or all senses; generally
geografia, geologia	Geo	geography, geology
geometria	Geom	geometry
impersonale	impers	impersonal
informatica	Inform	computing
insegnamento, sistema scolastico e universitario	Ins	schooling, schools and universities

invariabile	*inv*	invariable
irregolare	*irreg*	irregular
grammatica, linguistica	*Ling*	grammar, linguistics
maschile	*m*	masculine
matematica	*Mat(h)*	mathematics
termine medico, medicina	*Med*	medical term, medicine
il tempo, meteorologia	*Meteor*	the weather, meteorology
maschile o femminile	*m/f*	either masculine or feminine depending on sex
esercito, linguaggio militare	*Mil*	military matters
musica	*Mus*	music
sostantivo	N	noun
nautica	*Naut*	sailing, navigation
sostantivo che non si usa al plurale	*no pl*	uncountable noun: not used in the plural
numerale (aggettivo, sostantivo)	NUM	numeral adjective or noun
	o.s.	oneself
peggiorativo	*peg, pej*	derogatory, pejorative
fotografia	*Phot*	photography
fisiologia	*Physiol*	physiology
plurale	*pl*	plural
politica	*Pol*	politics
participio passato	*pp*	past participle
preposizione	PREP	preposition
pronome	PRON	pronoun
psicologia, psichiatria	*Psic, Psych*	psychology, psychiatry
tempo passato	*pt*	past tense
qualcosa	*qc*	
qualcuno	*qn*	
religione, liturgia	*Rel*	religions, church service
sostantivo	s	noun
	sb	somebody
insegnamento, sistema scolastico e universitario	*Scol*	schooling, schools and universities
singolare	*sg*	singular
soggetto (grammaticale)	*sog*	(grammatical) subject
	sth	something
congiuntivo	*sub*	subjunctive
soggetto (grammaticale)	*subj*	(grammatical) subject
termine tecnico, tecnologia	*Tecn, Tech*	technical term, technology
telecomunicazioni	*Tel*	telecommunications
tipografia	*Tip*	typography, printing
televisione	*TV*	television
tipografia	*Typ*	typography, printing
inglese degli Stati Uniti	*US*	American English
vocale	*v*	vowel
verbo (ausiliare)	VB (AUS)	(auxiliary) verb
verbo o gruppo verbale con funzione intransitiva	VI	verb or phrasal verb used intransitively
verbo riflessivo	VR	reflexive verb
verbo o gruppo verbale con funzione transitiva	VT	verb or phrasal verb used transitively
zoologia	*Zool*	zoology
marchio registrato	®	registered trademark
introduce un'equivalenza culturale	≈	introduces a cultural equivalent

Trascrizione fonetica

Consonanti

NB. **p, b, t, d, k, g** sono seguite
da un'aspirazione in inglese.

Consonants

NB. **p, b, t, d, k, g** are not
aspirated in Italian.

Italiano		Inglese
*p*adre	p	*p*u*pp*y
*b*am*b*ino	b	*b*a*b*y
*tutt*o	t	*t*en*t*
*d*a*d*o	d	*d*a*dd*y
*c*ane *ch*e	k	*c*ork *k*iss *ch*ord
*g*ola *gh*iro	g	*g*a*g g*uess
*s*ano	s	*s*o ri*c*e ki*ss*
*s*vago e*s*ame	z	cou*s*in bu*zz*
*sc*ena	ʃ	*sh*eep *s*ugar
	ʒ	plea*s*ure bei*g*e
pe*c*e lan*c*iare	tʃ	*ch*ur*ch*
*gi*ro *gi*oco	dʒ	*j*u*dg*e *g*eneral
a*f*a *f*aro	f	*f*arm ra*ff*le
*v*ero *b*ra*v*o	v	*v*ery re*v*
	θ	*th*in ma*th*s
	ð	*th*at o*th*er
*l*etto a*l*a	l	*l*itt*l*e ba*ll*
*gl*i	ʎ	
*r*ete a*r*co	r	*r*at b*r*at
*r*amo mad*r*e	m	*m*u*mm*y co*m*b
*n*o fuma*n*te	n	*n*o ra*n*
*gn*omo	ɲ	
	ŋ	si*ng*i*ng* ba*n*k
	h	*h*at re*h*eat
bu*i*o p*i*acere	j	*y*et
*u*omo g*u*aio	w	*w*all be*w*ail
	x	lo*ch*

Varie

per l'inglese: la "r" finale viene
pronunciata se seguita da una
vocale

ʳ

precede la sillaba accentata

ˈ

Miscellaneous

precedes the stressed syllable

Come regola generale, in tutte le voci la trascrizione fonetica in parentesi quadra
segue il termine cui si riferisce. Tuttavia, nella parte inglese-italiano del dizionario,
per la pronuncia di composti che sono formati da più parole non unite da trattino
che appaiono comunque nel dizionario, si veda la trascrizione fonetica di ciascuna di
queste parole alla rispettiva posizione alfabetica.

Phonetic transcription

Vocali

Vowels

NB. L'associazione di certi suoni indica solo una rassomiglianza approssimativa.

NB. The pairing of some vowel sounds only indicates approximate equivalence.

v*i*no *i*dea	i iː	h*ee*l b*ea*d
	ɪ	h*i*t p*i*ty
st*e*lla *e*dera	e	
*e*poca ecc*e*tto	ɛ	s*e*t t*e*nt
m*a*mma *a*more	a æ	*a*pple b*a*t
	ɑː	*a*fter c*a*r c*a*lm
	ʌ	f*u*n c*ou*sin
	ə	*o*ver *a*bove
	əː	*u*rn f*e*rn w*o*rk
r*o*sa *o*cchio	ɔ	w*a*sh p*o*t
	ɔː	b*o*rn c*o*rk
p*o*nte *o*gnun*o*	o	
*u*tile z*u*cca	u	f*u*ll s*oo*t
	uː	b*oo*n l*ew*d

Dittonghi

Diphthongs

ɪə	b*ee*r t*ie*r
ɛə	t*ea*r f*ai*r th*e*re
eɪ	d*a*te pl*ai*ce d*ay*
aɪ	l*i*fe b*uy* cr*y*
au	*ow*l f*ou*l n*ow*
əu	l*ow* n*o*
ɔɪ	b*oi*l b*oy* *oi*ly
uə	p*oo*r t*ou*r

In general, we give the pronunciation of each entry in square brackets after the word in question. However, on the English-Italian side, where the entry is composed of two or more unhyphenated words, each of which is given elsewhere in this dictionary, you will find the pronunciation of each word in its alphabetical position.

Italian pronunciation

Vowels

Where the vowel **e** or the vowel **o** appears in a stressed syllable it can be either open [ɛ], [ɔ] or closed [e], [o]. As the open or closed pronunciation of these vowels is subject to regional variation, the distinction is of little importance to the user of this dictionary. Phonetic transcription for headwords containing these vowels will therefore only appear where other pronunciation difficulties are present.

Consonants

c before "e" or "i" is pronounced *tch*.

ch is pronounced like the "k" in "kit".

g before "e" or "i" is pronounced like the "j" in "jet".

gh is pronounced like the "g" in "get".

gl before "e" or "i" is normally pronounced like the "lli" in "million", and in a few cases only like the "gl" in "glove".

gn is pronounced like the "ny" in "canyon".

sc before "e" or "i" is pronounced *sh*.

z is pronounced like the "ts" in "stetson", or like the "d's" in "bird's eye".

Headwords containing the above consonants and consonantal groups have been given full phonetic transcription in this dictionary.

NB. All double written consonants in Italian are fully sounded: e.g. the *tt* in "tutto" is pronounced as in "hat trick".

Italian verbs

1 Gerund 2 Past participle 3 Present 4 Imperfect 5 Past historic 6 Future 7 Conditional
8 Present subjunctive 9 Imperfect subjunctive 10 Imperative

1 abbattere **e** abbattei, abbattesti *(doesn't have alternative forms* -etti, -ette, -ettero*)*

2 accendere **b** acceso **e** accesi, accendesti

3 accludere **b** accluso **e** acclusi, accludesti

4 accorgersi **b** accorto **e** mi accorsi, ti accorgesti

5 aggiungere **b** aggiunto **e** aggiunsi, aggiungesti

6 andare **c** vado, vai, va, andiamo, andate, vanno **f** andrò *etc.* **h** vada **j** va'!, vada!, andate!, vadano!

7 apparire **b** apparso **c** appaio, appari *or* apparisci, appare *or* apparisce, appaiono *or* appariscono **e** apparvi *or* apparsi, apparisti, apparve *or* apparì *or* apparse, apparvero *or* apparirono *or* apparsero **h** appaia *or* apparisca

8 appendere **b** appeso **e** appesi, appendesti

9 aprire **b** aperto **c** apro **e** aprii, apristi **h** apra

10 ardere **b** arso **e** arsi, ardesti

11 assistere **b** assistito **e** assistei *or* assistetti, assistesti

12 assumere **b** assunto **e** assunsi, assumesti

13 AVERE **c** ho, hai, ha, abbiamo, avete, hanno **e** ebbi, avesti, ebbe, avemmo, aveste, ebbero **f** avrò *etc.* **h** abbia *etc.* **j** abbi!, abbia!, abbiate!, abbiano!

14 baciare *when the ending begins with* -e, *the* i *is dropped* → bacerò *(not* bacierò*)*

15 bagnare **c** bagniamo, bagniate **h** bagniamo, bagniate *(not* bagnamo, bagnate*)*

16 bere **a** bevendo **b** bevuto **c** bevo *etc.* **d** bevevo *etc.* **e** bevvi *or* -bevetti, bevesti **f** berrò *etc.* **h** beva *etc.* **i** bevessi *etc.*

17 bollire **c** bollo *or* bollisco, bolli *or* bollisci *etc.*

18 cadere **e** caddi, cadesti **f** cadrò *etc.*

19 cambiare *drops the* i *of the root if the ending*

starts with i (cambi, cambino *not* cambii, cambiino *(cf.* inviare)

20 caricare *when* c *in the root is* -i *followed by* -i *or* -e *an* h *should be inserted (ie* carichi, carichiamo, caricherò*)*

21 chiedere **b** chiesto **e** chiesi, chiedesti

22 chiudere **b** chiuso **e** chiusi, -chiudesti

23 cogliere **b** colto **c** colgo, colgono **e** colsi, cogliesti **h** colga

24 compiere **b** compiuto **e** compii, compisti

25 confondere **b** confuso **e** confusi, confondesti

26 conoscere **b** conosciuto **e** conobbi, conoscesti

27 consigliare *when the ending begins with* -i, *the* i *of the root is dropped* → consigli (*not* consiglii)

28 correre **b** corso **e** corsi, corresti

29 CREDERE **a** credendo **b** creduto **c** credo, credi, crede, crediamo, credete, credono **d** credevo, -credevi, credeva, credevamo, -credevate, credevano **e** credei *or* credetti, credesti, credé *or* -credette, credemmo, credeste, crederono *or* credettero **f** crederò, crederai, crederà, crederemo, crederete, crederanno **g** crederei, crederesti, crederebbe, -crederemmo, credereste, -crederebbero **h** creda, creda, creda, crediamo, crediate, credano **i** credessi, credessi, -credesse, credessimo, credeste, credessero **j** credi!, creda!, -credete!, credano!

30 :scere **b** cresciuto **e** crebbi, crescesti

31 cu cire *when* c *or* g *in the root is* -i *followed by* -o *or* -a *an* i *should be inserted (ie* cucio, cucia*)*

32 cuocere **b** cotto **c** cuocio, -cociamo, cuociono **e** cossi, -cocesti

33 dare **b** do, dai, dà, diamo, date, danno **e** diedi *or* detti, desti **f** darò *etc.* **h** dia *etc.* **i** dessi *etc.* **j** da'!, dai!, date!, diano!

34 decidere **b** deciso **e** decisi, decidesti
35 deludere **b** deluso **e** delusi, -deludesti
36 difendere **b** difeso **e** difesi, -difendesti
37 dipingere **b** dipinto **e** dipinsi, dipingesti
38 dire **a** dicendo **b** detto **c** dico, dici, dice, diciamo, dite, dicono **d** dicevo *etc.* e dissi, dicesti **f** dirò *etc.* **h** dica, diciamo, diciate, dicano **i** dicessi *etc.* **j** di'!, dica!, dite!, dicano!
39 dirigere **b** diretto **e** diressi, dirigesti
40 discutere **b** discusso **e** discussi, discutesti
41 disfare *like* fare *but* **c** disfo, dis' *etc.* **f** disferò, disferai *etc.* **i** dis', dis' *etc.* (*regular forms*)
42 distinguere **b** distinto **e** distinsi, distinguesti
43 dividere **b** diviso **e** divisi, dividesti
44 dolere **c** dolgo, duoli, duole, -dolgono e dolsi, dolesti **f** dorrò *etc.* **h** dolga
45 DORMIRE **a** dormendo **b** dormito **c** dormo, dormi, dorme, -dormiamo, dormite, dormono **d** dormivo, dormivi, dormiva, dormivamo, dormivate, -dormivano **e** dormii, dormisti, dormì, dormimmo, dormiste, dormirono **f** dormirò, dormirai, dormirà, dormiremo, dormirete, dormiranno **g** dormirei, dormiresti, dormirebbe, dormiremmo, dormireste, dormirebbero **h** dorma, dorma, dorma, dormiamo, dormiate, -dormano **i** dormissi, dormissi, dormisse, dormissimo, dormiste, dormissero **j** dormi!, dorma!, -dormite!, dormano!
46 dovere **c** devo *or* debbo, devi, deve, dobbiamo, dovete, devono *or* debbono **f** dovrò *etc.* **h** debba, dobbiamo, dobbiate, devano *or* debbano
47 esigere **b** esatto (*not common*) **e** esigei *or* esigetti, esigesti
48 espellere **b** espulso **e** espulsi, espellesti
49 esplodere **b** esploso **e** esplosi, esplodesti
50 esprimere **b** espresso **e** espressi, esprimesti

51 ESSERE **b** stato **c** sono, sei, è, siamo, siete, sono **d** ero, eri, era, eravamo, eravate, erano **e** fui, fosti, fu, fummo, foste, furono **f** sarò *etc.* **h** sia *etc.* i fossi, fossi, fosse, fossimo, foste, fossero **j** sii!, sia!, siate!, siano!
52 evadere **b** evaso **e** evasi, evadesti
53 fare **a** facendo **b** fatto **c** faccio, fai, fa, facciamo, fate, fanno **d** facevo *etc.* **e** feci, facesti **f** farò *etc.* **h** faccia *etc.* **i** facessi *etc.* **j** fa'!, faccia!, fate!, facciano!
54 fingere **b** 'nto **e** 'nsi, 'ngesti
55 FINIRE **a** 'nendo **b** 'nito **c** 'nisco, 'nisci, 'nisce, 'niamo, 'nite, 'niscono **d** 'nivo, 'nivi, 'niva, 'nivamo, 'nivate, 'nivano **e** 'nii, 'nisti, 'nì, 'nimmo, 'niste, 'nirono **f** 'nirò, 'nirai, 'nirà, 'niremo, 'nirete, 'niranno **g** 'nirei, 'niresti, 'nirebbe, -'niremmo, 'nireste, 'nirebbero **h** 'nisca, 'nisca, 'nisca, 'niamo, 'niate, 'niscano **i** 'nissi, 'nissi, 'nisse, 'nissimo, 'niste, 'nissero **j** 'nisci!, 'nisca!, 'nite!, 'niscano!
56 friggere **b** fritto **e** frissi, friggesti
57 giacere **b** giaciuto **e** giacqui, giacesti
58 godere **f** godrò, godrai *etc.* **g** godrei, godresti *etc.*
59 immergere **b** immerso **e** immersi, immergesti
60 inviare **c** (tu) invii **f** (essi) inviino
61 leggere **b** letto **e** lessi, leggesti
62 mangiare *when the ending begins with* -e, *the* i *is dropped* → mangerò (*not* mangierò)
63 mettere **b** messo **e** misi, mettesti
64 mordere **b** morso **e** morsi, mordesti
65 morire **b** morto **c** muoio, muori, muore, moriamo, morite, muoiono **f** morirò *or* morrò *etc.* **h** muoia
66 muovere **b** mosso **e** mossi, muovesti
67 nascere **b** nato **e** nacqui, nascesti
68 nascondere **b** nascosto **e** nascosi, nascondesti
69 nuocere **b** nuociuto **c** nuoccio, nuoci, nuoce, nociamo *or* -nuociamo, nuocete, nuocciono **d** nuocevo *etc.* **e** nocqui, nuocesti **f** nuocerò *etc.* **g** nuoccia
70 offrire **b** offerto **c** offro **e** offersi *or* offrii, offristi **h** offra

71 parere b parso c paio, paiamo, paiono
e parvi *or* parsi, paresti f parrò *etc.*
h paia, paiamo, paiate, paiano

72 PARLARE a parlando b parlato c parlo,
parli, parla, parliamo, -parlate, parlano
d parlavo, parlavi, parlava, parlavamo,
parlavate, parlavano e parlai, -parlasti,
parlò, parlammo, -parlaste, parlarono
f parlerò, -parlerai, parlerà, parleremo,
-parlerete, parleranno g parlerei,
parleresti, parlerebbe, -parleremmo,
parlereste, -parlerebbero h parli, parli,
parli, parliamo, parliate, parlino
i parlassi, parlassi, parlasse,
-parlassimo, parlaste, parlassero
j parla!, parli!, parlate!, parlino!

73 perdere b perso *or* perduto e persi,
perdesti

74 piacere b piaciuto c piaccio,
-piacciamo, piacciono e piacqui,
piacesti h piaccia *etc.*

75 piangere b pianto e piansi, piangesti

76 piovere b piovuto e piovve

77 porre a ponendo b posto c pongo,
poni, pone, poniamo, ponete, pongono
d ponevo *etc.* e posi, ponesti f porrò *etc.*
h ponga, -poniamo, poniate, pongano
i ponessi *etc.*

78 potere c posso, puoi, può, -possiamo,
potete, possono f potrò *etc.* h possa,
possiamo, possiate, possano

79 prefiggersi b pre'sso e mi -pre'ssi, ti
pre'ggesti

80 pregare *when* g *in the root is* -followed by -i
or -e *an* h *should be inserted* (ie preghi,
preghiàmo, pregherò)

81 prendere b preso e presi, -prendesti

82 prevedere *like* vedere *but* f prevederò,
prevederai *etc.* g prevederei *etc.*

83 proteggere b protetto e protessi,
proteggesti

84 pungere b punto e punsi, pungesti

85 radere b raso e rasi, radesti

86 redimere b redento e redensi,
redimesti

87 reggere b retto e ressi, reggesti

88 rendere b reso e resi, rendesti

89 ridere b riso e risi, ridesti

90 ridurre a riducendo b ridotto c riduco
etc. d riducevo *etc.* e ridussi, riducesti
f ridurrò *etc.* h riduca *etc.* i riducessi *etc.*

91 riempire a riempiendo c riempio,
riempi, riempie, riempiono

92 riflettere b ri.ettuto *or* ri.esso

93 rimanere b rimasto c rimango,
rimangono e rimasi, rimanesti
f rimarrò *etc.* h rimanga

94 risolvere b risolto e risolsi, risolvesti

95 rispondere b risposto e risposi,
rispondesti

96 rivolgere b rivolto e rivolsi, -rivolgesti

97 rompere b rotto e ruppi, rompesti

98 salire c salgo, sali, salgono h salga

99 sapere c so, sai, sa, sappiamo, sapete,
sanno e seppi, sapesti f saprò *etc.*
h sappia *etc.* j sappi!, sappia!, sappiate!,
sappiano!

100 scegliere b scelto c scelgo, scegli,
sceglie, scegliamo, -scegliete, scelgono
e scelsi, -scegliesti h scelga, scegliamo,
scegliate, scelgano j scegli!, -scelga!,
scegliamo!, scegliete!, scelgano!

101 scendere b sceso e scesi, -scendesti

102 scindere b scisso e scissi, scindesti

103 sciogliere b sciolto c sciolgo, sciogli,
scioglie, sciogliamo, sciogliete,
sciolgono e sciolsi, sciogliesti
h sciolga, sciogliamo, sciogliate,
sciolgano j sciogli!, -sciolga!,
sciogliamo!, sciogliete!, sciolgano!

104 sconfiggere b scon'tto e scon'ssi,
scon'ggesti

105 scrivere b scritto e scrissi, scrivesti

106 scuotere b scosso e scossi, scuotesti

107 sedere c siedo, siedi, siede, siedono
h sieda

108 solere b solito e soglio, suoli, suole,
sogliamo, solete, sogliono h soglia
(*regular imperfect, gerund, past participle; no
other verb forms*)

109 sorgere b sorto e sorse, sorsero

110 spandere b spanto e spansi,
spandesti

111 spargere b sorto e sorse, sorsero

112 sparire e sparii, sparisti

113 spegnere b spento c spengo, spengono e spensi, spegnesti h spenga

114 spingere b spinto e spinsi, spingesti

115 sporgere b sporto e sporsi, sporgesti

116 stare b stato c sto, stai, sta, -stiamo, state, stanno e stetti, stesti f starò *etc.* h stia *etc.* i stessi *etc.* j sta'!, stia!, state!, stiano!

117 stringere b stretto e strinsi, stringesti

118 succedere b successo e successi, succedesti

119 tacere b taciuto c taccio, -tacciono e tacqui, tacesti h taccia

120 tendere b teso e tesi, tendesti

121 tenere c tengo, tieni, tiene, -tengono e tenni, tenesti f terrò *etc.* h tenga

122 togliere b tolto c tolgo, togli, toglie, togliamo, togliete, tolgono e tolsi, togliesti h tolga j togli!, tolga!, togliamo!, togliete!, -tolgano!

123 trarre a traendo b tratto c traggo, trai, trae, traiamo, traete, traggono d traevo *etc.* e trassi, traesti f trarrò *etc.* h tragga i traessi *etc.*

124 udire c odo, odi, ode, odono h oda

125 uscire c esco, esci, esce, escono h esca

126 valere b valso c valgo, valgono e valsi, valesti f varrò *etc.* h valga

127 vedere b visto *or* veduto e vidi, vedesti f vedrò *etc.*

128 venire b venuto c vengo, vieni, viene, vengono e venni, venisti f verrò *etc.* h venga

129 vincere b vinto e vinsi, vincesti

130 vivere b vissuto e vissi, vivesti

131 volere c voglio, vuoi, vuole, vogliamo, volete, vogliono e volli, volesti f vorrò *etc.* h voglia *etc.* j *not common*

For additional information on Italian verb formation, see pp6–125 of the Grammar section.

Verbi inglesi

PRESENT	PT	PP	PRESENT	PT	PP
arise	arose	arisen	drink	drank	drunk
awake	awoke	awoken	drive	drove	driven
be (am, is,	was, were	been	dwell	dwelt	dwelt
are; being)			eat	ate	eaten
bear	bore	born(e)	fall	fell	fallen
beat	beat	beaten	feed	fed	fed
become	became	become	feel	felt	felt
befall	befell	befallen	fight	fought	fought
begin	began	begun	find	found	found
behold	beheld	beheld	flee	fled	fled
bend	bent	bent	fling	flung	flung
beset	beset	beset	fly	flew	flown
bet	bet, betted	bet, betted	forbid	forbad(e)	forbidden
bid (at auction,	bid	bid	forecast	forecast	forecast
cards)			forget	forgot	forgotten
bid (say)	bade	bidden	forgive	forgave	forgiven
bind	bound	bound	forsake	forsook	forsaken
bite	bit	bitten	freeze	froze	frozen
bleed	bled	bled	get	got	got, (US)
blow	blew	blown			gotten
break	broke	broken	give	gave	given
breed	bred	bred	go (goes)	went	gone
bring	brought	brought	grind	ground	ground
build	built	built	grow	grew	grown
burn	burnt,	burnt,	hang	hung	hung
	burned	burned	hang (execute)	hanged	hanged
burst	burst	burst	have	had	had
buy	bought	bought	hear	heard	heard
can	could	(been able)	hide	hid	hidden
cast	cast	cast	hit	hit	hit
catch	caught	caught	hold	held	held
choose	chose	chosen	hurt	hurt	hurt
cling	clung	clung	keep	kept	kept
come	came	come	kneel	knelt,	knelt,
cost	cost	cost		kneeled	kneeled
cost (work	costed	costed	know	knew	known
out price of)			lay	laid	laid
creep	crept	crept	lead	led	led
cut	cut	cut	lean	leant,	leant,
deal	dealt	dealt		leaned	leaned
dig	dug	dug	leap	leapt,	leapt,
do (3rd person:	did	done		leaped	leaped
he/she/			learn	learnt,	learnt,
it does)				learned	learned
draw	drew	drawn	leave	left	left
dream	dreamed,	dreamed,	lend	lent	lent
	dreamt	dreamt	let	let	let

PRESENT	PT	PP	PRESENT	PT	PP
lie (lying)	lay	lain	sow	sowed	sown, sowed
light	lit, lighted	lit, lighted			
lose	lost	lost	speak	spoke	spoken
make	made	made	speed	sped, speeded	sped, speeded
may	might	—			
mean	meant	meant	spell	spelt, spelled	spelt, spelled
meet	met	met			
mistake	mistook	mistaken	spend	spent	spent
mow	mowed	mown, mowed	spill	spilt, spilled	spilt, spilled
			spin	spun	spun
must	(had to)	(had to)	spit	spat	spat
pay	paid	paid	spoil	spoiled, spoilt	spoiled, spoilt
put	put	put			
quit	quit, quitted	quit, quitted	spread	spread	spread
			spring	sprang	sprung
read	read	read	stand	stood	stood
rid	rid	rid	steal	stole	stolen
ride	rode	ridden	stick	stuck	stuck
ring	rang	rung	sting	stung	stung
rise	rose	risen	stink	stank	stunk
run	ran	run	stride	strode	stridden
saw	sawed	sawed, sawn	strike	struck	struck
			strive	strove	striven
say	said	said	swear	swore	sworn
see	saw	seen	sweep	swept	swept
seek	sought	sought	swell	swelled	swollen, swelled
sell	sold	sold			
send	sent	sent	swim	swam	swum
set	set	set	swing	swung	swung
sew	sewed	sewn	take	took	taken
shake	shook	shaken	teach	taught	taught
shear	sheared	shorn, sheared	tear	tore	torn
			tell	told	told
shed	shed	shed	think	thought	thought
shine	shone	shone	throw	threw	thrown
shoot	shot	shot	thrust	thrust	thrust
show	showed	shown	tread	trod	trodden
shrink	shrank	shrunk	wake	woke, waked	woken, waked
shut	shut	shut			
sing	sang	sung	wear	wore	worn
sink	sank	sunk	weave	wove	woven
sit	sat	sat	weave (wind)	weaved	weaved
slay	slew	slain	wed	wedded, wed	wedded, wed
sleep	slept	slept			
slide	slid	slid	weep	wept	wept
sling	slung	slung	win	won	won
slit	slit	slit	wind	wound	wound
smell	smelt, smelled	smelt, smelled	wring	wrung	wrung
			write	wrote	written

I numeri

Numbers

uno(a)	1	one
due	2	two
tre	3	three
quattro	4	four
cinque	5	five
sei	6	six
sette	7	seven
otto	8	eight
nove	9	nine
dieci	10	ten
undici	11	eleven
dodici	12	twelve
tredici	13	thirteen
quattordici	14	fourteen
quindici	15	fifteen
sedici	16	sixteen
diciassette	17	seventeen
diciotto	18	eighteen
diciannove	19	nineteen
venti	20	twenty
ventuno	21	twenty-one
ventidue	22	twenty-two
ventitré	23	twenty-three
ventotto	28	twenty-eight
trenta	30	thirty
quaranta	40	forty
cinquanta	50	fifty
sessanta	60	sixty
settanta	70	seventy
ottanta	80	eighty
novanta	90	ninety
cento	100	a hundred, one hundred
centouno	101	a hundred and one
duecento	200	two hundred
mille	1 000	a thousand, one thousand
milleduecentodue	1 202	one thousand two hundred and two
cinquemila	5 000	five thousand
un milione	1 000 000	a million, one million

I numeri

Numbers

primo(a), 1°	first, 1st
secondo(a), 2°	second, 2nd
terzo(a), 3°	third, 3rd
quarto(a)	fourth, 4th
quinto(a)	fifth, 5th
sesto(a)	sixth, 6th
settimo(a)	seventh
ottavo(a)	eighth
nono(a)	ninth
decimo(a)	tenth
undicesimo(a)	eleventh
dodicesimo(a)	twelfth
tredicesimo(a)	thirteenth
quattordicesimo(a)	fourteenth
quindicesimo(a)	fifteenth
sedicesimo(a)	sixteenth
diciassettesimo(a)	seventeenth
diciottesimo(a)	eighteenth
diciannovesimo(a)	nineteenth
ventesimo(a)	twentieth
ventunesimo(a)	twenty-first
ventiduesimo(a)	twenty-second
ventitreesimo(a)	twenty-third
ventottesimo(a)	twenty-eighth
trentesimo(a)	thirtieth
centesimo(a)	hundredth
centunesimo(a)	hundred-and-first
millesimo(a)	thousandth
milionesimo(a)	millionth

L'ora

che ora è ?, che ore sono?
è ..., sono ...
mezzanotte
l'una (del mattino)
l'una e cinque
l'una e dieci
l'una e un quarto, l'una e quindici
l'una e venticinque
l'una e mezzo o mezza, l'una e trenta
l'una e trentacinque
le due meno venti, l'una e quaranta
le due meno un quarto, l'una e
    quarantacinque
le due meno dieci, l'una e cinquanta
mezzogiorno
le tre (del pomeriggio), le quindici
le sette (di sera), le diciannove

a che ora?
a mezzanotte
alle sette
fra venti minuti
venti minuti fa

The time

what time is it?
it's ...
midnight
one o'clock (in the morning), one (am)
five past one
ten past one
a quarter past one, one fifteen
twenty-five past one, one twenty-five
half past one, one thirty
twenty-five to two, one thirty-five
twenty to two, one forty
a quarter to two, one forty-five

ten to two, one fifty
twelve o'clock, midday, noon
three o'clock (in the afternoon), three (pm)
seven o'clock (in the evening), seven (pm)

at what time?
at midnight
at seven o'clock
in twenty minutes
twenty minutes ago

La data

oggi
domani
dopodomani
ieri
l'altro ieri
il giorno prima
il giorno dopo
la mattina
la sera
stamattina
stasera
questo pomeriggio

The date

today
tomorrow
the day after tomorrow
yesterday
the day before yesterday
the day before, the previous day
the next or following day
morning
evening
this morning
this evening
this afternoon

ieri mattina	yesterday morning
ieri sera	yesterday evening
domani mattina	tomorrow morning
domani sera	tomorrow evening
nella notte tra sabato e domenica	during Saturday night, during the night of Saturday to Sunday
viene sabato	he's coming on Saturday
il sabato	on Saturdays
tutti i sabati	every Saturday
sabato scorso, lo scorso sabato	last Saturday
il prossimo sabato	next Saturday
fra due sabati	a week on Saturday
fra tre sabati	a fortnight *or* two weeks on Saturday
da lunedì a sabato	from Monday to Saturday
tutti i lunedì	every day
una volta alla settimana	once a week
una volta al mese	once a month
due volte alla settimana	twice a week
una settimana fa	a week ago
quindici giorni fa	a fortnight *or* two weeks ago
l'anno scorso *or* passato	last year
fra due giorni	in two days
fra una settimana	in a week
fra quindici giorni	in a fortnight *or* two weeks
il mese prossimo	next month
l'anno prossimo	next year

che giorno è oggi?

il primo/24 ottobre 2013

what day is it?

the 1st/24th of October 2013, October 1st/24th 2013

nel 2013	in 2013
il millenovecentonovantacinque	nineteen ninety-five
44 a.C.	44 BC
14 d.C.	14 AD
nel diciannovesimo secolo, nel XIX secolo, nell'Ottocento	in the nineteenth century
negli anni trenta	in the thirties
c'era una volta ...	once upon a time ...

ITALIANO–INGLESE

ITALIAN–ENGLISH

Aa

A, a [a] SM O F INV (*lettera*) A, a; **A come Ancona** ≈ A for Andrew (BRIT), ≈ A for Able (US); **dalla a alla z** from a to z

A ABBR (= *altezza*) h; (= *area*) A; (= *autostrada*) ≈ M (BRIT)

[PAROLA CHIAVE]

a (*a+il* = **al**, *a+lo* = **allo**, *a+l'* = **all'**, *a+la* = **alla**, *a+i* = **ai**, *a+gli* = **agli**, *a+le* = **alle**) PREP **1** (*stato in luogo*) at; (: *in*) in; **essere alla stazione** to be at the station; **essere a casa/a scuola/a Roma** to be at home/at school/in Rome; **è a 10 km da qui** it's 10 km from here, it's 10 km away; **restare a cena** to stay for dinner

2 (*moto a luogo*) to; **andare a casa/a scuola/alla stazione** to go home/to school/to the station; **andare a Roma/al mare** to go to Rome/to the seaside

3 (*tempo*) at; (: *epoca, stagione*) in; **alle cinque** at five (o'clock); **a mezzanotte/Natale** at midnight/Christmas; **al mattino** in the morning; **a maggio/primavera** in May/spring; **a cinquant'anni** at fifty (years of age); **a domani!** see you tomorrow!; **a lunedì!** see you on Monday!; **a giorni** within (a few) days

4 (*complemento di termine*) to; **dare qc a qn** to give sb sth, give sth to sb; **l'ho chiesto a lui** I asked him

5 (*mezzo, modo*) with, by; **a piedi/cavallo** on foot/horseback; **viaggiare a 100 km all'ora** to travel at 100 km an *o* per hour; **alla televisione/radio** on television/the radio; **fatto a mano** made by hand, handmade; **una barca a motore** a motorboat; **una stufa a gas** a gas heater; **a uno a uno** one by one; **a fatica** with difficulty; **all'italiana** the Italian way, in the Italian fashion

6 (*rapporto*) a, per; (: *con prezzi*) at; **due volte al giorno/mese** twice a day/month; **prendo 2000 euro al mese** I get 2000 euro a *o* per month; **pagato a ore** paid by the hour; **vendere qc a 2 euro il chilo** to sell sth at 2 euros a *o* per kilo; **cinque a zero** (*punteggio*) five nil

AA SIGLA = **Alto Adige**

AAST SIGLA F = **Azienda Autonoma di Soggiorno e Turismo**

AA.VV. ABBR = **autori vari**

ab. ABBR = **abitante**

a'bate SM abbot

abbacchi'ato, -a [abbak'kjato] AG downhearted, in low spirits

abbacin'are [abbatʃi'nare] /**72**/ VT to dazzle

abbagli'ante [abbaʎ'ʎante] AG dazzling; **abbaglianti** SMPL (*Aut*): **accendere gli abbaglianti** to put one's headlights on full (BRIT) *o* high (US) beam

abbagli'are [abbaʎ'ʎare] /**27**/ VT to dazzle; (*illudere*) to delude

ab'baglio [ab'baʎʎo] SM blunder; **prendere un ~** to blunder, make a blunder

abbai'are /**19**/ VI to bark

abba'ino SM dormer window; (*soffitta*) attic room

abbando'nare /**72**/ VT to leave, abandon, desert; (*trascurare*) to neglect; (*rinunciare a*) to abandon, give up; **abbandonarsi** VPR to let o.s. go; **~ il campo** (*Mil*) to retreat; **~ la presa** to let go; **abbandonarsi a** (*ricordi, vizio*) to give o.s. up to

abbando'nato, -a AG (*casa*) deserted; (*miniera*) disused; (*trascurato: terreno, podere*) neglected; (: *bambino*) abandoned

abban'dono SM abandoning; neglecting; (*stato*) abandonment; neglect; (*Sport*) withdrawal; (*fig*) abandon; **in ~** (*edificio, giardino*) neglected

abbarbi'carsi /**61**/ VPR: **~ (a)** (*anche fig*) to cling (to)

abbassa'mento SM lowering; (*di pressione, livello dell'acqua*) fall; (*di prezzi*) reduction; **~ di temperatura** drop in temperature

abbas'sare /**72**/ VT to lower; (*radio*) to turn down; **abbassarsi** VPR (*chinarsi*) to stoop; (*livello, sole*) to go down; (*fig: umiliarsi*) to demean o.s.; **~ i fari** (*Aut*) to dip (BRIT) *o* dim (US) one's lights; **~ le armi** (*Mil*) to lay down one's arms

ab'basso ESCL: ~ **il re!** down with the king!
abbas'tanza [abbas'tantsa] AV (*a sufficienza*)
enough; (*alquanto*) quite, rather, fairly; **non
è ~ furbo** he's not shrewd enough; **un vino
~ dolce** quite a sweet wine, a fairly sweet
wine; **averne ~ di qn/qc** to have had enough
of sb/sth
ab'battere /1/ VT (*muro, casa, ostacolo*) to knock
down; (*albero*) to fell; (: *vento*) to bring down;
(*bestie da macello*) to slaughter; (*cane, cavallo*) to
destroy, put down; (*selvaggina, aereo*) to shoot
down; (*fig: malattia, disgrazia*) to lay low;
abbattersi VPR (*avvilirsi*) to lose heart;
abbattersi a terra o **al suolo** to fall to the
ground; **abbattersi su** (*maltempo*) to beat
down on; (*disgrazia*) to hit, strike
abbatti'mento SM knocking down; felling;
(*di casa*) demolition; (*prostrazione: fisica*)
exhaustion; (: *morale*) despondency
abbat'tuto, -a AG (*fig*) despondent,
depressed
abba'zia [abbat'tsia] SF abbey
abbece'dario [abbetʃe'darjo] SM primer
abbelli'mento SM embellishment
abbel'lire /55/ VT to make beautiful; (*ornare*)
to embellish
abbeve'rare /72/ VT to water; **abbeverarsi**
VPR to drink
abbevera'toio SM drinking trough
'abbi VB *vedi* **avere**
'abbia VB *vedi* **avere**
abbi'amo VB *vedi* **avere**
'abbiano VB *vedi* **avere**
abbi'ate VB *vedi* **avere**
abbicci [abbit'tʃi] SM INV alphabet; (*sillabario*)
primer; (*fig*) rudiments *pl*
abbi'ente AG well-to-do, well-off; **abbienti**
SMPL: **gli abbienti** the well-to-do
abbi'etto, -a AG = **abietto**
abbiezi'one [abbjet'tsjone] SF = **abiezione**
abbiglia'mento [abbiʎʎa'mento] SM dress *no
pl*; (*indumenti*) clothes *pl*; (*industria*) clothing
industry
abbigli'are [abbiʎ'ʎare] /27/ VT to dress up
abbina'mento SM combination; linking;
matching
abbi'nare /72/ VT: ~ **(con** o **a)** (*gen*) to combine
(with); (*nomi*) to link (with); ~ **qc a qc** (*colori
ecc*) to match sth with sth
abbindo'lare /72/ VT (*fig*) to cheat, trick
abbocca'mento SM (*colloquio*) talks *pl*,
meeting; (*Tecn: di tubi*) connection
abboc'care /20/ VT (*tubi, canali*) to connect,
join up ▶ VI (*pesce*) to bite; (*tubi*) to join;
~ **(all'amo)** (*fig*) to swallow the bait
abboc'cato, -a AG (*vino*) sweetish
abbona'mento SM subscription; (*alle ferrovie
ecc*) season ticket; **in ~** for subscribers only;
for season ticket holders only; **fare l'~ (a)** to

take out a subscription (to); to buy a season
ticket (for)
abbo'nare /72/ VT (*cifra*) to deduct; (*fig:
perdonare*) to forgive; **abbonarsi** VPR:
abbonarsi a un giornale to take out a
subscription to a newspaper; **abbonarsi al
teatro/alle ferrovie** to take out a season
ticket for the theatre/the train
abbo'nato, -a SM/F subscriber; season-
ticket holder; **elenco degli abbonati**
telephone directory
abbon'dante AG abundant, plentiful; (*giacca*)
roomy
abbon'danza [abbon'dantsa] SF abundance;
plenty
abbon'dare /72/ VI to abound, be plentiful;
~ **in** o **di** to be full of, abound in
abbor'dabile AG (*persona*) approachable;
(*prezzo*) reasonable
abbor'dare /72/ VT (*nave*) to board; (*persona*) to
approach; (*argomento*) to tackle; ~ **una curva**
to take a bend
abbotto'nare /72/ VT to button up, do up;
abbottonarsi VPR to button (up)
abbotto'nato, -a AG (*camicia ecc*) buttoned
(up); (*fig*) reserved
abbottona'tura SF buttons *pl*; **questo
cappotto ha l'~ da uomo/da donna** this
coat buttons on the man's/woman's side
abboz'zare [abbot'tsare] /72/ VT to sketch,
outline; (*Scultura*) to rough-hew; ~ **un
sorriso** to give a hint of a smile
ab'bozzo [ab'bottso] SM sketch, outline; (*Dir*)
draft
abbracci'are [abbrat'tʃare] /14/ VT to
embrace; (*persona*) to hug, embrace;
(*professione*) to take up; (*contenere*) to include;
abbracciarsi VPR to hug o embrace (one
another)
ab'braccio [ab'brattʃo] SM hug, embrace
abbrevi'are /19/ VT to shorten; (*parola*) to
abbreviate, shorten
abbreviazi'one [abbrevjat'tsjone] SF
abbreviation
abbron'zante [abbron'dzante] AG tanning,
sun *cpd*
abbron'zare [abbron'dzare] /72/ VT (*pelle*) to
tan; (*metalli*) to bronze; **abbronzarsi** VPR to
tan, get a tan
abbron'zato, -a [abbron'dzato] AG
(sun)tanned
abbronza'tura [abbrondza'tura] SF tan,
suntan
abbrusto'lire /55/ VT (*pane*) to toast; (*caffè*) to
roast; **abbrustolirsi** VPR to toast; (*fig: al sole*)
to soak up the sun
abbruti'mento SM exhaustion; degradation
abbru'tire /55/ VT (*snervare, stancare*) to
exhaust; (*degradare*) to degrade; **essere**

abbrutito dall'alcool to be ruined by drink
abbuffarsi /72/ VPR (col): ~ **(di qc)** to stuff o.s. (with sth)
abbuffata SF (col) nosh-up; (fig) binge; **farsi un'~** to stuff o.s.
abbuo'nare /72/ VT = **abbonare**
abbu'ono SM (Comm) allowance, discount; (Sport) handicap
abdi'care /20/ VI to abdicate; ~ **a** to give up, renounce
abdicazi'one [abdikat'tsjone] SF abdication
aberrazi'one [aberrat'tsjone] SF aberration
abe'taia SF fir wood
a'bete SM fir (tree); ~ **bianco** silver fir; ~ **rosso** spruce
abi'etto, -a AG despicable, abject
abiezi'one [abjet'tsjone] SF abjection
'abile AG (idoneo): ~ **(a qc/a fare qc)** fit (for sth/ to do sth); (capace) able; (astuto) clever; (accorto) skilful; ~ **al servizio militare** fit for military service
abilità SF INV ability; cleverness; skill
abili'tante AG qualifying; **corsi abilitanti** (Ins) ≈ teacher training sg
abili'tare /72/ VT: ~ **qn a qc/a fare qc** to qualify sb for sth/to do sth; **è stato abilitato all'insegnamento** he has qualified as a teacher
abili'tato, -a AG qualified; (Tel) which has an outside line
abilitazi'one [abilitat'tsjone] SF qualification
abis'sale AG abysmal; (fig: senza limiti) profound
abis'sino, -a AG, SM/F Abyssinian
a'bisso SM abyss, gulf
abitabilità SF: **licenza di ~** document stating that a property is fit for habitation
abi'tacolo SM (Aer) cockpit; (Aut) inside; (di camion) (driver's) cab
abi'tante SMF inhabitant
abi'tare /72/ VT to live in, dwell in ▶ VI: ~ **in campagna/a Roma** to live in the country/in Rome; **dove abita?** where do you live?
abi'tato, -a AG inhabited; lived in ▶ SM (anche: **centro abitato**) built-up area
abitazi'one [abitat'tsjone] SF residence; house
'abito SM dress no pl; (da uomo) suit; (da donna) dress; (abitudine, disposizione, Rel) habit; **abiti** SMPL (vestiti) clothes; **in ~ da cerimonia** in formal dress; **in ~ da sera** in evening dress; **"è gradito l'~ scuro"** "dress formal"; ~ **mentale** way of thinking
abitu'ale AG usual, habitual; (cliente) regular
abitual'mente AV usually, normally
abitu'are /72/ VT: ~ **qn a** to get sb used o accustomed to; **abituarsi a** to get used to, accustom o.s. to

abitudi'nario, -a AG of fixed habits ▶ SM/F creature of habit
abi'tudine SF habit; **aver l'~ di fare qc** to be in the habit of doing sth; **d'~** usually; **per ~** from o out of habit
abiu'rare /72/ VT to renounce
abla'tivo SM ablative
abnegazi'one [abnegat'tsjone] SF (self-) abnegation, self-denial
ab'norme AG (enorme) extraordinary; (anormale) abnormal
abo'lire /55/ VT to abolish; (Dir) to repeal
abolizi'one [abolit'tsjone] SF abolition; repeal
abomi'nevole AG abominable
abo'rigeno [abo'ridʒeno] SM aborigine
abor'rire /17/ VT to abhor, detest
abor'tire /55/ VI (Med: accidentalmente) to miscarry, have a miscarriage; (: deliberatamente) to have an abortion; (fig) to miscarry, fail
abor'tista, -i, -e AG pro-choice, pro-abortion ▶ SM/F pro-choicer
a'borto SM miscarriage; abortion; (fig) freak; ~ **clandestino** backstreet abortion
abrasi'one SF abrasion
abra'sivo, -a AG, SM abrasive
abro'gare /80/ VT to repeal, abrogate
abrogazi'one [abrogat'tsjone] SF repeal
abruz'zese [abrut'tsese] AG of (o from) the Abruzzi
A'bruzzo [a'bruttso] SM: **l'~, gli Abruzzi** the Abruzzi
ABS [abi'esse] SIGLA M (= Anti-Blockier System) ABS (= anti-lock braking system)
'abside SF apse
'Abu 'Dhabi SF Abu Dhabi
a'bulico, -a, -ci, -che AG lacking in willpower
abu'sare /72/ VI: ~ **di** to abuse, misuse; (approfittare, violare) to take advantage of; ~ **dell'alcool/dei cibi** to drink/eat to excess
abusi'vismo SM (anche: **abusivismo edilizio**) unlawful building, building without planning permission (BRIT)
abu'sivo, -a AG unauthorized, unlawful; (occupante) ~ (di una casa) squatter
a'buso SM abuse, misuse; excessive use; **fare ~ di** (stupefacenti, medicine) to abuse
a.C. ABBR (= avanti Cristo) BC
a'cacia, -cie [a'katʃa] SF (Bot) acacia
'acca SF letter H; **non capire un'~** not to understand a thing
ac'cadde VB vedi **accadere**
acca'demia SF (società) learned society; (scuola: d'arte, militare) academy; **A~ di Belle Arti** art school
acca'demico, -a, -ci, -che AG academic ▶ SM academician
acca'dere /18/ VB IMPERS to happen, occur

acca'duto SM event; **raccontare l'~** to describe what has happened

accalappia'cani SM INV dog-catcher

accalappi'are /19/ VT to catch; (*fig*) to trick, dupe

accal'care /20/ VT, **accal'carsi** VPR to crowd, throng

accal'darsi /61/ VPR to grow hot

accal'dato, -a AG hot

accalo'rarsi /61/ VPR (*fig*) to get excited

accampa'mento SM camp

accam'pare /72/ VT to encamp; (*fig*) to put forward, advance; **accamparsi** VPR to camp; **~ scuse** to make excuses

accani'mento SM fury; (*tenacia*) tenacity, perseverance

acca'nirsi /55/ VPR (*infierire*) to rage; (*ostinarsi*) to persist

accanita'mente AV fiercely; assiduously

acca'nito, -a AG (*odio, gelosia*) fierce, bitter; (*lavoratore*) assiduous; (*giocatore, fumatore*) inveterate; (*tifoso, sostenitore*) keen; **fumatore ~** chain smoker

ac'canto AV near, nearby; **~ a** prep near, beside, close to; **la casa ~** the house next door

accanto'nare /72/ VT (*problema*) to shelve; (*somma*) to set aside

accaparra'mento SM (*Comm*) cornering, buying up

accapar'rare /72/ VT (*Comm*) to corner, buy up; (*versare una caparra*) to pay a deposit on; **accaparrarsi** VPR: **accaparrarsi qc** (*fig: simpatia, voti*) to secure sth (for o.s.)

accapigli'arsi [akkapiʎ'ʎarsi] /27/ VPR to come to blows; (*fig*) to quarrel

accappa'toio SM bathrobe

accappo'nare /72/ VI: **far ~ la pelle a qn** (*fig*) to bring sb out in goosepimples

accarez'zare [akkaret'tsare] /72/ VT to caress, stroke, fondle; (*fig*) to toy with

accartocci'are [akkartot'tʃare] /14/ VT (*carta*) to roll up, screw up; **accartocciarsi** VPR (*foglie*) to curl up

acca'sarsi /27/ VPR to set up house; to get married

accasci'arsi [akkaʃ'ʃarsi] /14/ VPR to collapse; (*fig*) to lose heart

accatas'tare /72/ VT to stack, pile

accatto'naggio [akkatto'naddʒo] SM begging

accat'tone, -a SM/F beggar

accaval'lare /72/ VT (*gambe*) to cross; **accavallarsi** VPR (*sovrapporsi*) to overlap; (*addensarsi*) to gather

acce'care [attʃe'kare] /20/ VT to blind ▶ VI to go blind

ac'cedere [at'tʃɛdere] /29/ VI: **~ a** to enter; (*richiesta*) to grant, accede to; (*fonte*) to gain access to

accele'rare [attʃele'rare] /72/ VT to speed up ▶ VI (*Aut*) to accelerate; **~ il passo** to quicken one's pace

accele'rato, -a [attʃele'rato] AG quick, rapid ▶ SM (*Ferr*) local train, stopping train

accelera'tore [attʃelera'tore] SM (*Aut*) accelerator

accelerazi'one [attʃelerat'tsjone] SF acceleration

ac'cendere [at'tʃɛndere] /2/ VT (*fuoco, sigaretta*) to light; (*luce, televisione*) to put o switch o on; (*Aut: motore*) to switch on; (*Comm: conto*) to open; (*: debito*) to contract; (*: ipoteca*) to raise; (*fig: suscitare*) to inflame, stir up; **accendersi** VPR (*luce*) to come o go on; (*legna*) to catch fire, ignite; (*fig: lotta, conflitto*) to break out

accen'dino [attʃen'dino], **accendi'sigaro** [attʃendi'sigaro] SM (cigarette) lighter

accen'nare [attʃen'nare] /72/ VT to indicate, point out; (*Mus*) to pick out the notes of; to hum ▶ VI: **~ a** (*fig: alludere a*) to hint at; (*: far atto di*) to make as if; **~ un saluto** (*con la mano*) to make as if to wave; (*col capo*) to half nod; **~ un sorriso** to half smile; **accenna a piovere** it looks as if it's going to rain

ac'cenno [at'tʃenno] SM (*cenno*) sign; nod; (*allusione*) hint

accensi'one [attʃen'sjone] SF (*vedi accendere*) lighting; switching on; opening; (*Aut*) ignition

accen'tare [attʃen'tare] /72/ VT (*parlando*) to stress; (*scrivendo*) to accent

accentazi'one [attʃentat'tsjone] SF accentuation; stressing

ac'cento [at'tʃɛnto] SM accent; (*Fonetica, fig*) stress; (*inflessione*) tone (of voice)

accentra'mento [attʃentra'mento] SM centralization

accen'trare [attʃen'trare] /72/ VT to centralize

accentra'tore, -'trice [attʃentra'tore] AG (*persona*) unwilling to delegate; **politica accentratrice** policy of centralization

accentu'are [attʃentu'are] /72/ VT to stress, emphasize; **accentuarsi** VPR to become more noticeable

accerchi'are [attʃer'kjare] /19/ VT to surround, encircle

accerta'mento [attʃerta'mento] SM check; assessment

accer'tare [attʃer'tare] /72/ VT to ascertain; (*verificare*) to check; (*reddito*) to assess; **accertarsi** VPR: **accertarsi (di qc/che)** to make sure (of sth/that)

ac'ceso, -a [at'tʃeso] PP di **accendere** ▶ AG lit; on; open; (*colore*) bright; **~ di** (*ira, entusiasmo ecc*) burning with

acces'sibile [attʃes'sibile] AG (*luogo*)

accessible; (*persona*) approachable; (*prezzo*) reasonable; (*idea*): ~ **a qn** within the reach of sb

ac'cesso [at'tʃɛsso] SM (*anche Inform*) access; (*Med*) attack, fit; (*impulso violento*) fit, outburst; **programmi dell'-** (*TV*) educational programmes; **tempo di ~** (*Inform*) access time; **~ casuale/seriale/ sequenziale** (*Inform*) random/serial/ sequential access

accessori'ato, -a [attʃesso'rjato] AG with accessories

acces'sorio, -a [attʃes'sɔrjo] AG secondary, of secondary importance; **accessori** SMPL accessories

ac'cetta [at'tʃetta] SF hatchet

accet'tabile [attʃet'tabile] AG acceptable

accet'tare [attʃet'tare] /72/ VT to accept; **~ di fare qc** to agree to do sth

accettazi'one [attʃettat'tsjone] SF acceptance; (*locale di servizio pubblico*) reception; **~ bagagli** (*Aer*) check-in (desk); **~ con riserva** qualified acceptance

ac'cetto, -a [at'tʃetto] AG (*persona*) welcome; **(ben) ~ a tutti** well-liked by everybody

accezi'one [attʃet'tsjone] SF meaning

acchiap'pare [akkjap'pare] /72/ VT to catch; (*afferrare*) to seize

ac'chito [ak'kito] SM: **a primo ~** at first sight

acciac'cato, -a [attʃak'kato] AG (*persona*) full of aches and pains; (*abito*) crushed

acci'acco, -chi [at'tʃakko] SM ailment; **acciacchi** SMPL aches and pains

acciaie'ria [attʃaje'ria] SF steelworks *sg*

acci'aio [at'tʃajo] SM steel; **~ inossidabile** stainless steel

acciden'tale [attʃiden'tale] AG accidental

accidental'mente [attʃidental'mente] AV (*per caso*) by chance; (*non deliberatamente*) accidentally, by accident

acciden'tato, -a [attʃiden'tato] AG (*terreno ecc*) uneven

acci'dente [attʃi'dɛnte] SM (*caso imprevisto*) accident; (*disgrazia*) mishap; **accidenti!** (*col: per rabbia*) damn (it)!; (*: per meraviglia*) good heavens!; **accidenti a lui!** damn him!; **non vale un ~** it's not worth a damn; **non capisco un ~** it's as clear as mud to me; **mandare un ~ a qn** to curse sb

ac'cidia [at'tʃidja] SF (*Rel*) sloth

accigli'ato, -a [attʃiʎ'ʎato] AG frowning

ac'cingersi [at'tʃindʒersi] /54/ VPR: **~ a fare** to be about to do

acciotto'lato [attʃotto'lato] SM cobbles *pl*

acciuf'fare [attʃuf'fare] /72/ VT to seize, catch

acci'uga, -ghe [at'tʃuga] SF anchovy; **magro come un'~** as thin as a rake

accla'mare /72/ VT (*applaudire*) to applaud; (*eleggere*) to acclaim

acclamazi'one [akklamat'tsjone] SF applause; acclamation

acclima'tare /72/ VT to acclimatize; **acclimatarsi** VPR to become acclimatized

acclimatazi'one [akklimatat'tsjone] SF acclimatization

ac'cludere /3/ VT to enclose

ac'cluso, -a PP *di* **accludere** ▶ AG enclosed

accocco'larsi /72/ VPR to crouch

acco'darsi /72/ VPR to follow, tag on (behind)

accogli'ente [akkoʎ'ʎente] AG welcoming, friendly

accogli'enza [akkoʎ'ʎentsa] SF reception; welcome; **fare una buona ~ a qn** to welcome sb

ac'cogliere [ak'kɔʎʎere] /23/ VT (*ricevere*) to receive; (*dare il benvenuto*) to welcome; (*approvare*) to agree to, accept; (*contenere*) to hold, accommodate

ac'colgo *etc* VB *vedi* **accogliere**

accol'lare /72/ VT: **~ qc a qn** (*fig*) to force sth on sb; **accollarsi** VPR: **accollarsi qc** to take sth upon o.s., shoulder sth

accol'lato, -a AG (*vestito*) high-necked

ac'colsi *etc* VB *vedi* **accogliere**

accoltel'lare /72/ VT to knife, stab

ac'colto, -a PP *di* **accogliere**

accoman'dita SF (*Dir*) limited partnership

accomia'tare /72/ VT to dismiss; **accomiatarsi** VPR: **accomiatarsi (da)** to take one's leave (of)

accomoda'mento SM agreement, settlement

accomo'dante AG accommodating

accomo'dare /72/ VT (*aggiustare*) to repair, mend; (*riordinare*) to tidy; (*sistemare: questione, lite*) to settle; **accomodarsi** VPR (*sedersi*) to sit down; (*fig: risolversi: situazione*) to work out; **si accomodi!** (*venga avanti*) come in!; (*si sieda*) take a seat!

accompagna'mento [akkompaɲɲa'mento] SM (*Mus*) accompaniment; (*Comm*): **lettera di ~** accompanying letter

accompa'gnare [akkompaɲ'ɲare] /15/ VT to accompany, come *o* go with; (*Mus*) to accompany; (*unire*) to couple; **accompagnarsi** VPR (*armonizzarsi*) to go well together; **~ qn a casa** to see sb home; **~ qn alla porta** to show sb out; **~ un regalo con un biglietto** to put in *o* send a card with a present; **~ qn con lo sguardo** to follow sb with one's eyes; **~ la porta** to close the door gently; **accompagnarsi a** (*frequentare*) to frequent; (*colori*) to go with, match; (*cibi*) to go with

accompagna'tore, -'trice [akkompaɲɲa'tore] SM/F companion, escort; (*Mus*) accompanist; (*Sport*) team manager; **~ turistico** courier; tour guide

accomu'nare /**72**/ ᴠᴛ to pool, share; (*avvicinare*) to unite

acconcia'tura [akkontʃa'tura] sꜰ hairstyle

accondiscen'dente [akkondiʃʃen'dɛnte] ᴀɢ affable

accondi'scendere [akkondiʃʃendere] /**101**/ ᴠɪ: ~ **a** to agree ᴏ consent to

accondi'sceso, -a [akkondiʃʃeso] ᴘᴘ *di* **accondiscendere**

acconsen'tire /**17**/ ᴠɪ: ~ **(a)** to agree ᴏ consent (to); **chi tace acconsente** silence means consent

acconten'tare /**72**/ ᴠᴛ to satisfy; **accontentarsi** ᴠᴘʀ: **accontentarsi di** to be satisfied with, content o.s. with; **chi si accontenta gode** there's no point in complaining

ac'conto sᴍ part payment; **pagare una somma in** ~ to pay a sum of money as a deposit; ~ **di dividendo** interim dividend

accoppia'mento sᴍ pairing off; mating; (*Elettr, Inform*) coupling

accoppi'are /**19**/ ᴠᴛ to couple, pair off; (*Biol*) to mate; **accoppiarsi** ᴠᴘʀ to pair off; to mate

accoppia'tore sᴍ (*Tecn*) coupler; ~ **acustico** (*Inform*) acoustic coupler

acco'rato, -a ᴀɢ heartfelt

accorci'are [akkor'tʃare] /**14**/ ᴠᴛ to shorten; **accorciarsi** ᴠᴘʀ to become shorter; (*vestiti: nel lavaggio*) to shrink

accor'dare /**72**/ ᴠᴛ to reconcile; (*colori*) to match; (*Mus*) to tune; (*Ling*): ~ **qc con qc** to make sth agree with sth; (*Dir*) to grant; **accordarsi** ᴠᴘʀ to agree, come to an agreement; (*colori*) to match

ac'cordo sᴍ agreement; (*armonia*) harmony; (*Mus*) chord; **essere d'~** to agree; **andare d'~** to get on well together; **d'~!** all right!, agreed!; **mettersi d'~ (con qn)** to agree ᴏ come to an agreement (with sb); **prendere accordi con** to reach an agreement with; ~ **commerciale** trade agreement; **A~ generale sulle tariffe ed il commercio** General Agreement on Tariffs and Trade, GATT

ac'corgersi [ak'kɔrdʒersi] /**4**/ ᴠᴘʀ: ~ **di** to notice; (*fig*) to realize

accorgi'mento [akkordʒi'mento] sᴍ shrewdness *no pl*; (*espediente*) trick, device

ac'correre /**28**/ ᴠɪ to run up

ac'corsi ᴠʙ *vedi* **accorgersi**; **accorrere**

ac'corso, -a ᴘᴘ *di* **accorrere**

accor'tezza [akkor'tettsa] sꜰ (*avvedutezza*) good sense; (*astuzia*) shrewdness

ac'corto, -a ᴘᴘ *di* **accorgersi** ▶ ᴀɢ shrewd; **stare** ~ to be on one's guard

accosta'mento sᴍ (*di colori ecc*) combination

accos'tare /**72**/ ᴠᴛ (*avvicinarsi a*) to approach; (*socchiudere: imposte*) to half-close; (: *porta*) to leave ajar ▶ ᴠɪ: ~ **(a)** (*Naut*) to come alongside; (*Aut*) to draw up (at); **accostarsi** ᴠᴘʀ: **accostarsi a** to draw near, approach; (*somigliare*) to be like, resemble; (*fede, religione*) to turn to; (*idee politiche*) to come to agree with; ~ **qc a** (*avvicinare*) to bring sth near to, put sth near to; (*colori, stili*) to match sth with; (*appoggiare: scala ecc*) to lean sth against

accovacci'arsi [akkovat'tʃarsi] /**14**/ ᴠᴘʀ to crouch

accoz'zaglia [akkot'tsaʎʎa] sꜰ (*peg: di idee, oggetti*) jumble, hotchpotch; (: *di persone*) odd assortment

ac'crebbi *etc* ᴠʙ *vedi* **accrescere**

accredi'tare /**72**/ ᴠᴛ (*notizia*) to confirm the truth of; (*Comm*) to credit; (*diplomatico*) to accredit; **accreditarsi** ᴠᴘʀ (*fig*) to gain credit

ac'credito sᴍ (*Comm: atto*) crediting; (: *effetto*) credit

ac'crescere [ak'kreʃʃere] /**30**/ ᴠᴛ to increase; **accrescersi** ᴠᴘʀ to increase, grow

accresci'mento [akkreʃʃi'mento] sᴍ increase, growth

accresci'tivo, -a [akkreʃʃi'tivo] ᴀɢ, sᴍ (*Ling*) augmentative

accresci'uto, -a [akkreʃʃuto] ᴘᴘ *di* **accrescere**

accucci'arsi [akkut'tʃarsi] /**14**/ ᴠᴘʀ (*cane*) to lie down; (*persona*) to crouch down

accu'dire /**55**/ ᴠɪ: ~ **a** to attend to ▶ ᴠᴛ to look after

acculturazi'one [akkulturat'tsjone] sꜰ (*Sociologia*) integration

accumu'lare /**72**/ ᴠᴛ to accumulate; **accumularsi** ᴠᴘʀ to accumulate; (*Finanza*) to accrue

accumula'tore sᴍ (*Elettr*) accumulator

accumulazi'one [akkumulat'tsjone] sꜰ accumulation

ac'cumulo sᴍ accumulation

accurata'mente ᴀᴠ carefully

accura'tezza [akkura'tettsa] sꜰ care; accuracy

accu'rato, -a ᴀɢ (*diligente*) careful; (*preciso*) accurate

ac'cusa sꜰ accusation; (*Dir*) charge; **l'~, la pubblica** ~ (*Dir*) the prosecution; **mettere qn sotto** ~ to indict sb; **in stato di** ~ committed for trial

accu'sare /**72**/ ᴠᴛ (*sentire: dolore*) to feel; ~ **qn di qc** to accuse sb of sth; (*Dir*) to charge sb with sth; ~ **ricevuta di** (*Comm*) to acknowledge receipt of; ~ **la fatica** to show signs of exhaustion; **ha accusato il colpo** (*anche fig*) you could see that he had felt the blow

accusa'tivo sᴍ accusative

accu'sato, -a sᴍ/ꜰ accused

accusa'tore, -'trice ᴀɢ accusing ▶ sᴍ/ꜰ accuser ▶ sᴍ (*Dir*) prosecutor

a'cerbo, -a [a'tʃɛrbo] ᴀɢ bitter; (*frutta*) sour,

unripe; (*persona*) immature

'acero ['atʃero] SM maple

a'cerrimo, -a [a'tʃɛrrimo] AG very fierce

ace'tato [atʃe'tato] SM acetate

a'ceto [a'tʃeto] SM vinegar; **mettere sotto ~** to pickle

ace'tone [atʃe'tone] SM nail varnish remover

'A.C.I. ['atʃi] SIGLA M (= *Automobile Club d'Italia*) ≈ AA (BRIT), ≈ AAA (US)

acidità [atʃidi'ta] SF acidity; sourness; **~ (di stomaco)** heartburn

'acido, -a ['atʃido] AG (*sapore*) acid, sour; (*Chim, colore*) acid ▶ SM (*Chim*) acid

a'cidulo, -a [a'tʃidulo] AG slightly sour, slightly acid

'acino ['atʃino] SM berry; **~ d'uva** grape

'ACLI SIGLA FPL (= *Associazioni Cristiane dei Lavoratori Italiani*) Christian Trade Union Association

'acme SF (*fig*) acme, peak; (*Med*) crisis

'acne SF acne

ACNUR SIGLA M (= *Alto Commissariato delle Nazioni Unite per i Rifugiati*) UNHCR

'acqua SF water; (*pioggia*) rain; **acque** SFPL (*di mare, fiume ecc*) waters; **fare ~** (*Naut*) to leak, take in water; **essere con** o **avere l'~ alla gola** to be in great difficulty; **tirare ~ al proprio mulino** to feather one's own nest; **navigare in cattive acque** (*fig*) to be in deep water; **~ in bocca!** mum's the word!; **~ corrente** running water; **~ dolce** fresh water; **~ di mare** sea water; **~ minerale** mineral water; **~ ossigenata** hydrogen peroxide; **~ piovana** rain water; **~ potabile** drinking water; **~ salata** o **salmastra** salt water; **~ tonica** tonic water

acqua'forte (*pl* **acqueforti**) SF etching

a'cquaio SM sink

acqua'ragia [akkwa'radʒa] SF turpentine

a'cquario SM aquarium; **A~** Aquarius; **essere dell'A~** to be Aquarius

acquartie'rare /72/ VT (*Mil*) to quarter

acqua'santa SF holy water

acquas'cooter [akkwas'kuter] SM INV Jet Ski®

a'cquatico, -a, -ci, -che AG aquatic; (*sport, sci*) water *cpd*

acquat'tarsi /72/ VPR to crouch (down)

acqua'vite SF brandy

acquaz'zone [akkwat'tsone] SM cloudburst, heavy shower

acque'dotto SM aqueduct; waterworks *pl*, water system

'acqueo, -a AG: **vapore ~** water vapour (BRIT) o vapor (US); **umore ~** aqueous humour (BRIT) o humor (US)

acque'rello SM watercolour (BRIT), watercolor (US)

acque'rugiola [akkwe'rudʒola] SF drizzle

acquie'tare /72/ VT to appease; (*dolore*) to ease; **acquietarsi** VPR to calm down

acqui'rente SMF purchaser, buyer

acqui'sire /55/ VT to acquire

acquisizi'one [akkwizit'tsjone] SF acquisition

acquis'tare /72/ VT to purchase, buy; (*fig*) to gain ▶ VI to improve; **~ in bellezza** to become more beautiful; **ha acquistato in salute** his health has improved

a'cquisto SM purchase; **fare acquisti** to go shopping; **ufficio acquisti** (*Comm*) purchasing department; **~ rateale** instalment purchase, hire purchase (BRIT)

acqui'trino SM bog, marsh

acquo'lina SF: **far venire l'~ in bocca a qn** to make sb's mouth water

a'cquoso, -a AG watery

'acre AG acrid, pungent; (*fig*) harsh, biting

a'credine SF (*fig*) bitterness

a'crilico, -a, -ci, -che AG, SM acrylic

a'critico, -a, -ci, -che AG uncritical

a'crobata, -i, -e SM/F acrobat

acro'batico, -a, -ci, -che AG (*ginnastica*) acrobatic; (*Aer*) aerobatic ▶ SF acrobatics *sg*

acroba'zia [akrobat'tsia] SF acrobatic feat; **acrobazie aeree** aerobatics

a'cronimo SM acronym

a'cropoli SF INV: **l'A~** the Acropolis

acu'ire /55/ VT to sharpen; **acuirsi** VPR (*gen*) to increase; (*crisi*) to worsen

a'culeo SM (*Zool*) sting; (*Bot*) prickle

a'cume SM acumen, perspicacity

acumi'nato, -a AG sharp

a'custico, -a, -ci, -che AG acoustic ▶ SF (*scienza*) acoustics *sg*; (*di una sala*) acoustics *pl*; **apparecchio ~** hearing aid; **cornetto ~** ear trumpet

acu'tezza [aku'tettsa] SF sharpness; shrillness; acuteness; high pitch; intensity; keenness

acutiz'zare [akutid'dzare] /72/ VT (*fig*) to intensify; **acutizzarsi** VPR (*fig: crisi, malattia*) to become worse, worsen

a'cuto, -a AG (*appuntito*) sharp, pointed; (*suono, voce*) shrill, piercing; (*Mat, Ling, Med*) acute; (*Mus*) high-pitched; (*fig: dolore, desiderio*) intense; (: *perspicace*) acute, keen ▶ SM (*Mus*) high note

ad PREP (*dav V*) = **a**

adagi'are [ada'dʒare] /62/ VT to lay o set down carefully; **adagiarsi** VPR to lie down, stretch out

a'dagio [a'dadʒo] AV slowly ▶ SM (*Mus*) adagio; (*proverbio*) adage, saying

ada'mitico, -a, -ci, -che AG: **in costume ~** in one's birthday suit

adat'tabile AG adaptable

adattabilità SF adaptability

adatta'mento SM adaptation; **avere spirito di ~** to be adaptable

adat'tare /72/ VT to adapt; (*sistemare*) to fit; **adattarsi** VPR: **adattarsi (a)** (*ambiente, tempi*) to adapt (to); (*essere adatto*) to be suitable (for); **adattarsi a qc/a fare qc** (*accontentarsi*) to make the best of sth/of doing sth

adatta'tore SM (*Elettr*) adapter, adaptor

a'datto, -a AG: **~ (a)** suitable (for), right (for)

addebi'tare /72/ VT: **~ qc a qn** to debit sb with sth; (*fig: incolpare*) to blame sb for sth

ad'debito SM (*Comm*) debit

addensa'mento SM thickening; gathering

adden'sare /72/ VT to thicken; **addensarsi** VPR to thicken; (*nuvole*) to gather

adden'tare /72/ VT to bite into

adden'trarsi /72/ VPR: **~ in** to penetrate, go into

ad'dentro AV (*fig*): **essere molto ~ in qc** to be well-versed in sth

addestra'mento SM training; **~ aziendale** company training

addes'trare /72/ VT, **addes'trarsi** VPR to train; **addestrarsi in qc** to practise (*BRIT*) o practice (*US*) sth

ad'detto, -a AG: **~ a** (*persona*) assigned to; (*oggetto*) intended for ▶ SM employee; (*funzionario*) attaché; **~ commerciale/stampa** commercial/press attaché; **~ al telex** telex operator; **gli addetti ai lavori** authorized personnel; (*fig*) those in the know; **"vietato l'ingresso ai non addetti ai lavori"** "authorized personnel only"

addì AV (*Amm*): **~ 3 luglio 1989** on the 3rd of July 1989 (*BRIT*), on July 3rd 1989 (*US*)

addi'accio [ad'djattʃo] SM (*Mil*) bivouac; **dormire all'~** to sleep in the open

addi'etro AV (*indietro*) behind; (*nel passato, prima*) before, ago

ad'dio SM, ESCL goodbye, farewell

addirit'tura AV (*veramente*) really, absolutely; (*perfino*) even; (*direttamente*) directly, right away

ad'dirsi /38/ VPR: **~ a** to suit, be suitable for

'Addis A'beba SF Addis Ababa

addi'tare /72/ VT to point out; (*fig*) to expose

addi'tivo SM additive

addizio'nale [additsjo'nale] AG additional ▶ SF (*anche*: **imposta addizionale**) surtax

addizio'nare [additsjo'nare] /72/ VT (*Mat*) to add (up)

addizi'one [addit'tsjone] SF addition

addob'bare /72/ VT to decorate

ad'dobbo SM decoration

addol'cire [addol'tʃire] /55/ VT (*caffè ecc*) to sweeten; (*acqua, fig: carattere*) to soften; **addolcirsi** VPR (*fig*) to mellow, soften; **~ la pillola** (*fig*) to sugar the pill

addolo'rare /72/ VT to pain, grieve; **addolorarsi** VPR: **addolorarsi (per)** to be distressed (by)

addolo'rato, -a AG distressed, upset; **l'Addolorata** (*Rel*) Our Lady of Sorrows

ad'dome SM abdomen

addomesti'care /20/ VT to tame

addomi'nale AG abdominal; (**muscoli**) **addominali** stomach muscles

addormen'tare /72/ VT to put to sleep; **addormentarsi** VPR to fall asleep, go to sleep

addormen'tato, -a AG sleeping, asleep; (*fig: tardo*) stupid, dopey

addos'sare /72/ VT (*appoggiare*): **~ qc a qc** to lean sth against sth; (*fig*): **~ la colpa a qn** to lay the blame on sb; **addossarsi** VPR: **addossarsi qc** (*responsabilità ecc*) to shoulder sth

ad'dosso AV (*sulla persona*) on; **~ a** prep (*sopra*) on; (*molto vicino*) right next to; **mettersi ~ il cappotto** to put one's coat on; **andare** (*o* **venire**) **~ a** (*Aut: altra macchina*) to run into; (*: pedone*) to run over; **non ho soldi ~** I don't have any money on me; **stare ~ a qn** (*fig*) to breathe down sb's neck; **dare ~ a qn** (*fig*) to attack sb; **mettere gli occhi ~ a qn/qc** to take quite a fancy to sb/sth; **mettere le mani ~ a qn** (*picchiare*) to hit sb; (*catturare*) to seize sb; (*molestare: donna*) to touch sb up

ad'dotto, -a PP *di* **addurre**

ad'duco *etc* VB *vedi* **addurre**

ad'durre /90/ VT (*Dir*) to produce; (*citare*) to cite

ad'dussi *etc* VB *vedi* **addurre**

adegu'are /72/ VT: **~ qc a** to adjust sth to; **adeguarsi** VPR to adapt

adegua'tezza [adegwa'tettsa] SF adequacy; suitability; fairness

adegu'ato, -a AG adequate; (*conveniente*) suitable; (*equo*) fair

a'dempiere /24/ VT to fulfil (*BRIT*), fulfill (*US*), carry out; (*comando*) to carry out

adempi'mento SM fulfilment (*BRIT*), fulfillment (*US*); carrying out; **nell'~ del proprio dovere** in the performance of one's duty

adem'pire /17/ VT = **adempiere**

'Aden: **il golfo di ~** *sm* the Gulf of Aden

ade'noidi SFPL adenoids

a'depto SM disciple, follower

ade'rente AG adhesive; (*vestito*) close-fitting ▶ SMF follower

ade'renza [ade'rɛntsa] SF adhesion; **aderenze** SFPL (*fig*) connections, contacts

ade'rire /55/ VI (*stare attaccato*) to adhere, stick; **~ a** to adhere to, stick to; (*fig: società, partito*) to join (*: opinione*) to support; (*richiesta*) to agree to

ades'care /20/ VT (*attirare*) to lure, entice; (*Tecn: pompa*) to prime

adesi'one SF adhesion; (fig: assenso) agreement, acceptance; (appoggio) support

ade'sivo, -a AG, SM adhesive

a'desso AV (ora) now; (or ora, poco fa) just now; (tra poco) any moment now; **da ~ in poi** from now on; **per ~** for the moment, for now

adia'cente [adja'tʃɛnte] AG adjacent

adi'bire /55/ VT (usare): **~ qc a** to turn sth into

'Adige ['adidʒe] SM: **l'~** the Adige

'adipe SM fat

adi'poso, -a AG (tessuto, zona) adipose

adi'rarsi /72/ VPR: **~ (con o contro qn per qc)** to get angry (with sb over sth)

adi'rato, -a AG angry

a'dire /55/ VT (Dir): **~ le vie legali** to take legal proceedings; **~ un'eredità** to take legal possession of an inheritance

'adito SM: **dare ~ a** (sospetti) to give rise to

adocchi'are [adok'kjare] /19/ VT (scorgere) to catch sight of; (occhieggiare) to eye

adole'scente [adoleʃ'ʃɛnte] AG, SMF adolescent

adole'scenza [adoleʃ'ʃɛntsa] SF adolescence

adolescenzi'ale [adoleʃʃen'tsjale] AG adolescent

adom'brarsi /72/ VPR (cavallo) to shy; (persona) to grow suspicious; (: aversene a male) to be offended

adope'rare /72/ VT to use; **adoperarsi** VPR to strive; **adoperarsi per qn/qc** to do one's best for sb/sth

ado'rabile AG adorable

ado'rare /72/ VT to adore; (Rel) to adore, worship

adorazi'one [adorat'tsjone] SF adoration; worship

ador'nare /72/ VT to adorn

a'dorno, -a AG: **~ (di)** adorned (with)

adot'tare /72/ VT to adopt; (decisione, provvedimenti) to pass

adot'tivo, -a AG (genitori) adoptive; (figlio, patria) adopted

adozi'one [adot'tsjone] SF adoption; **~ a distanza** child sponsorship

adrena'linico, -a, -ci, -che AG (fig: vivace, eccitato) charged-up

adri'atico, -a, -ci, -che AG Adriatic ▶ SM: **l'A~, il mare A~** the Adriatic, the Adriatic Sea

ADSL SIGLA M ADSL (= asymmetric digital subscriber line)

adu'lare /72/ VT to flatter

adula'tore, -'trice SM/F flatterer

adula'torio, -a AG flattering

adulazi'one [adulat'tsjone] SF flattery

adulte'rare /72/ VT to adulterate

adul'terio SM adultery

a'dultero, -a AG adulterous ▶ SM/F adulterer (adulteress)

a'dulto, -a AG adult; (fig) mature ▶ SM adult, grown-up

adu'nanza [adu'nantsa] SF assembly, meeting

adu'nare /72/ VT, **adu'narsi** VPR to assemble, gather

adu'nata SF (Mil) parade, muster

a'dunco, -a, -chi, -che AG hooked

aerazi'one [aerat'tsjone] SF ventilation; (Tecn) aeration

a'ereo, -a AG air cpd; (radice) aerial ▶ SM aerial; (aeroplano) plane; **~ da caccia** fighter (plane); **~ di linea** airliner; **~ a reazione** jet (plane)

ae'robica SF aerobics sg

aerodi'namico, -a, -ci, -che AG aerodynamic; (affusolato) streamlined ▶ SF aerodynamics sg

aeromo'dello SM model aircraft

aero'nautica SF (scienza) aeronautics sg; **~ militare** air force

aerona'vale AG (forze, manovre) air and sea cpd

aero'plano SM (aero)plane (BRIT), (air)plane (US)

aero'porto SM airport

aeroportu'ale AG airport cpd

aeros'calo SM airstrip

aero'sol SM INV aerosol

aerospazi'ale [aerospat'tsjale] AG aerospace

aeros'tatico, -a, -ci, -che AG aerostatic; **pallone ~** air balloon

ae'rostato SM aerostat

A.F. ABBR (= alta frequenza) HF; (Amm) = **assegni familiari**

'afa SF sultriness

af'fabile AG affable

affabilità SF affability

affaccen'darsi [affattʃen'darsi] /72/ VPR: **~ intorno a qc** to busy o.s. with sth

affaccen'dato, -a [affattʃen'dato] AG (persona) busy

affacci'arsi [affat'tʃarsi] /14/ VPR: **~ (a)** to appear (at); **~ alla vita** to come into the world

affa'mato, -a AG starving; (fig): **~ (di)** eager (for)

affan'nare /72/ VT to leave breathless; (fig) to worry; **affannarsi** VPR: **affannarsi per qn/ qc** to worry about sb/sth

af'fanno SM breathlessness; (fig) anxiety, worry

affannosa'mente AV with difficulty; anxiously

affan'noso, -a AG (respiro) difficult; (fig) troubled, anxious

af'fare SM (faccenda) matter, affair; (Comm) piece of business, (business) deal; (occasione) bargain; (Dir) case; (col: cosa) thing; **affari** SMPL (Comm) business sg; **~ fatto!** done!, it's a deal!; **sono affari miei** that's my business;

bada agli affari tuoi! mind your own business!; **uomo d'affari** businessman; **ministro degli Affari Esteri** Foreign Secretary (BRIT), Secretary of State (US)

affa'rista, -i SM profiteer, unscrupulous businessman

affasci'nante [affaʃʃi'nante] AG fascinating

affasci'nare [affaʃʃi'nare] /72/ VT to bewitch; (fig) to charm, fascinate

affatica'mento SM tiredness

affati'care /20/ VT to tire; **affaticarsi** VPR (durar fatica) to tire o.s. out

affati'cato, -a AG tired

af'fatto AV completely; **non ... ~** not ... at all; **niente ~** not at all

affer'mare /72/ VI (dire di sì) to say yes ▶ VT (dichiarare) to maintain, affirm; **affermarsi** VPR to assert o.s., make one's name known

affermativa'mente AV in the affirmative, affirmatively

afferma'tivo, -a AG affirmative

affer'mato, -a AG established, well-known

affermazi'one [affermat'tsjone] SF affirmation, assertion; (successo) achievement

affer'rare /72/ VT to seize, grasp; (fig: idea) to grasp; **afferrarsi** VPR: **afferrarsi a** to cling to

Aff. Est. ABBR = **Affari Esteri**

affet'tare /72/ VT (tagliare a fette) to slice; (ostentare) to affect

affet'tato, -a AG sliced; affected ▶ SM sliced cold meat

affetta'trice [affetta'tritʃe] SF meat slicer

affettazi'one [affettat'tsjone] SF affectation

affet'tivo, -a AG emotional, affective

af'fetto, -a AG: **essere ~ da** to suffer from ▶ SM affection; **gli affetti familiari** one's nearest and dearest

affettuosa'mente AV affectionately; (nelle lettere): **(ti saluto) ~, Maria** love, Maria

affettuosità SF INV affection ▶ SFPL (manifestazioni) demonstrations of affection

affettu'oso, -a AG affectionate

affezio'narsi [affettsjo'narsi] /72/ VPR: **~ a** to grow fond of

affezio'nato, -a [affettsjo'nato] AG: **~ a qn/qc** fond of sb/sth; (attaccato) attached to sb/sth

affezi'one [affet'tsjone] SF (affetto) affection; (Med) ailment, disorder

affian'care /20/ VT to place side by side; (Mil) to flank; (fig) to support; **~ qc a qc** to place sth next to o beside sth; **affiancarsi** VPR: **affiancarsi a qn** to stand beside sb

affiata'mento SM understanding

affia'tato, -a AG: **essere affiatati** to work well together o get on; **formano una squadra affiatata** they make a good team

affibbi'are /19/ VT to buckle, do up; (fig: dare) to give

affi'dabile AG reliable

affidabilità SF reliability

affida'mento SM (Dir: di bambino) custody; (fiducia): **fare ~ su qn** to rely on sb; **non dà nessun ~** he's not to be trusted

affi'dare /72/ VT: **~ qc o qn a qn** to entrust sth o sb to sb; **affidarsi** VPR: **affidarsi a** to place one's trust in

affievo'lirsi /55/ VPR to grow weak

af'figgere [af'fiddʒere] /104/ VT to stick up, post up

affi'lare /72/ VT to sharpen

affi'lato, -a AG (gen) sharp; (volto, naso) thin

affili'are /19/ VT to affiliate; **affiliarsi** VPR: **affiliarsi a** to become affiliated to

affi'nare /72/ VT to sharpen

affin'ché [affin'ke] CONG in order that, so that

af'fine AG similar

affinità SF INV affinity

affio'rare /72/ VI to emerge

af'fissi etc VB vedi **affiggere**

affissi'one SF billposting

af'fisso, -a PP di **affiggere** ▶ SM bill, poster; (Ling) affix

affitta'camere SM INV/F INV landlord (landlady)

affit'tare /72/ VT (dare in affitto) to let, rent (out); (prendere in affitto) to rent

af'fitto SM rent; (contratto) lease; **dare in ~** to rent (out), let; **prendere in ~** to rent

affizi'one [afflit'tsjone] SF distress, torment

af'fliggere [af'fliddʒere] /104/ VT to torment; **affliggersi** VPR to grieve

af'flissi etc VB vedi **affliggere**

af'flitto, -a PP di **affliggere**

afflizi'one [afflit'tsjone] SF distress, torment

afflosci'arsi [affloʃ'ʃarsi] /14/ VPR to go limp; (frutta) to go soft

afflu'ente SM tributary

afflu'enza [afflu'entsa] SF flow; (di persone) crowd

afflu'ire /55/ VI to flow; (fig: merci, persone) to pour in

af'flusso SM influx

affo'gare /80/ VT, VI to drown; **affogarsi** VPR to drown; (deliberatamente) to drown o.s.

affo'gato, -a AG drowned; (Cuc: uova) poached

affolla'mento SM crowding; (folla) crowd

affol'lare /72/ VT, **affol'larsi** VPR to crowd

affol'lato, -a AG crowded

affonda'mento SM (di nave) sinking

affon'dare /72/ VT to sink

affran'care /20/ VT to free, liberate; (Amm) to redeem; (lettera) to stamp; (: meccanicamente) to frank (BRIT), meter (US); **affrancarsi** VPR to free o.s.

affranca'trice [affranka'tritʃe] SF franking machine (BRIT), postage meter (US)

affranca'tura sf (*di francobollo*) stamping; franking (*Brit*), metering (*US*); (*tassa di spedizione*) postage; **~ a carico del destinatario** postage paid

affranto, -a ag (*esausto*) worn out; (*abbattuto*) overcome

affresco, -schi sm fresco

affret'tare /**72**/ vt to quicken, speed up; **affrettarsi** vpr to hurry; **affrettarsi a fare qc** to hurry o hasten to do sth

affret'tato, -a ag (*veloce: passo, ritmo*) quick, fast; (*frettoloso: decisione*) hurried, hasty; (: *lavoro*) rushed

affron'tare /**72**/ vt (*pericolo ecc*) to face; (*assalire: nemico*) to confront; **affrontarsi** vpr (*reciproco*) to confront each other

af'fronto sm affront, insult; **fare un ~ a qn** to insult sb

affumi'care /**20**/ vt to fill with smoke; to blacken with smoke; (*alimenti*) to smoke

affumi'cato, -a ag (*prosciutto, aringa ecc*) smoked

affuso'lato, -a ag tapering

af'gano, -a ag, sm/f Afghan

Af'ghanistan [af'ganistan] sm: **l'~** Afghanistan

af'ghano, -a ag, sm/f = **afgano**

afo'risma, -i sm aphorism

a'foso, -a ag sultry, close

'Africa sf: **l'~** Africa

afri'cano, -a ag, sm/f African

afroasi'atico, -a, -ci, -che ag Afro-Asian

afrodi'siaco, -a, -ci, -che ag, sm aphrodisiac

AG sigla = **Agrigento**

a'genda [a'dʒɛnda] sf diary; **~ tascabile/da tavolo** pocket/desk diary

a'gente [a'dʒɛnte] sm agent; **~ di cambio** stockbroker; **~ di custodia** prison officer; **~ marittimo** shipping agent; **~ di polizia** police officer; **~ segreto** secret agent; **~ provocatore** agent provocateur; **~ delle tasse** tax inspector; **~ di vendita** sales agent; **resistente agli agenti atmosferici** weather-resistant

agen'zia [adʒen'tsia] sf agency; (*succursale*) branch; **~ di collocamento** employment agency; **~ immobiliare** estate agent's (office) (*Brit*), real estate office (*US*); **A~ Internazionale per l'Energia Atomica** International Atomic Energy Agency; **~ matrimoniale** marriage bureau; **~ pubblicitaria** advertising agency; **~ di stampa** press agency; **~ viaggi** travel agency

agevo'lare [adʒevo'lare] /**72**/ vt to facilitate, make easy

agevolazi'one [adʒevolat'tsjone] sf (*facilitazione economica*) facility; **~ di pagamento** payment on easy terms; **agevolazioni creditizie** credit facilities;

agevolazioni fiscali tax concessions

a'gevole [a'dʒevole] ag easy; (*strada*) smooth

agganci'are [aggan'tʃare] /**14**/ vt to hook up; (*Ferr*) to couple; **agganciarsi** vpr: **agganciarsi a** to hook up to; (*fig: pretesto*) to seize on

ag'gancio [ag'gantʃo] sm (*Tecn*) coupling; (*fig: conoscenza*) contact

ag'geggio [ad'dʒeddʒo] sm gadget, contraption

agget'tivo [addʒet'tivo] sm adjective

agghiacci'ante [aggjat'tʃante] ag (*fig*) chilling

agghiacci'are [aggjat'tʃare] /**14**/ vt to freeze; (*fig*) to make one's blood run cold; **agghiacciarsi** vpr to freeze

agghin'darsi [aggin'darsi] /**61**/ vpr to deck o.s. out

aggiorna'mento [addʒorna'mento] sm updating; revision; postponement; **corso di ~** refresher course

aggior'nare [addʒor'nare] /**72**/ vt (*opera, manuale*) to bring up-to-date; (: *rivedere*) to revise; (*listino*) to maintain, up-date; (*seduta ecc*) to postpone; **aggiornarsi** vpr to bring o keep o.s. up-to-date

aggior'nato, -a [addʒor'nato] ag up-to-date

aggio'taggio [addʒo'taddʒo] sm (*Econ*) rigging the market

aggi'rare [addʒi'rare] /**72**/ vt to go round; (*fig: ingannare*) to trick; **aggirarsi** vpr to wander about; **il prezzo s'aggira sul milione** the price is around the million mark

aggiudi'care [addʒudi'kare] /**20**/ vt to award; (*all'asta*) to knock down; **aggiudicarsi qc** to win sth

aggi'ungere [ad'dʒundʒere] /**5**/ vt to add; (*Inform*): **grazie per avermi aggiunto (come amico)** thanks for the add

aggi'unsi *etc* [ad'dʒunsi] vb *vedi* **aggiungere**

aggi'unto, -a [ad'dʒunto] pp *di* **aggiungere** ▶ ag assistant *cpd* ▶ sm assistant ▶ sf addition; **sindaco ~** deputy mayor; **in aggiunta ...** what's more ...

aggius'tare [addʒus'tare] /**72**/ vt (*accomodare*) to mend, repair; (*riassettare*) to adjust; (*fig: lite*) to settle; **aggiustarsi** vpr (*arrangiarsi*) to make do; (*con senso reciproco*) to come to an agreement; **ti aggiusto io!** I'll fix you!

agglome'rato sm (*di rocce*) conglomerate; (*di legno*) chipboard; **~ urbano** built-up area

aggrap'parsi /**72**/ vpr: **~ a** to cling to

aggrava'mento sm worsening

aggra'vante ag (*Dir*) aggravating ▶ sf aggravation

aggra'vare /**72**/ vt (*aumentare*) to increase; (*appesantire: anche fig*) to weigh down, make heavy; (*fig: pena*) to make worse; **aggravarsi** vpr (*fig*) to worsen, become worse

ag'gravio SM: ~ **di costi** increase in costs

aggrazi'ato, -a [aggrat'tsjato] AG graceful

aggre'dire /**55**/ VT to attack, assault

aggre'gare /**80**/ VT: ~ **qn a qc** to admit sb to sth; **aggregarsi** VPR to join; **aggregarersi a** to join, become a member of

aggre'gato, -a AG associated ▶ SM aggregate; ~ **urbano** built-up area

aggressi'one SF aggression; (atto) attack, assault; ~ **a mano armata** armed assault

aggressività SF aggressiveness

aggres'sivo, -a AG aggressive

aggres'sore SM aggressor, attacker

aggrot'tare /**72**/ VT: ~ **le sopracciglia** to frown

aggrovigli'are [aggroviʎ'ʎare] /**27**/ VT to tangle; **aggrovigliarsi** VPR (fig) to become complicated

agguan'tare /**72**/ VT to catch, seize

aggu'ato SM trap; (imboscata) ambush; **tendere un ~ a qn** to set a trap for sb

agguer'rito, -a AG (sostenitore, nemico) fierce

agia'tezza [adʒa'tettsa] SF prosperity

agi'ato, -a [a'dʒato] AG (vita) easy; (persona) well-off, well-to-do

'agile ['adʒile] AG agile, nimble

agilità [adʒili'ta] SF agility, nimbleness

'agio ['adʒo] SM ease, comfort; **agi** SMPL comforts; **mettersi a proprio ~** to make o.s. at home o comfortable; **dare ~ a qn di fare qc** to give sb the chance of doing sth

a'gire [a'dʒire] /**55**/ VI to act; (esercitare un'azione) to take effect; (Tecn) to work, function; ~ **contro qn** (Dir) to take action against sb

agi'tare [adʒi'tare] /**72**/ VT (bottiglia) to shake; (mano, fazzoletto) to wave; (fig: turbare) to disturb; (: incitare) to stir (up); (: dibattere) to discuss; **agitarsi** VPR (mare) to be rough; (malato, dormitore) to toss and turn; (bambino) to fidget; (emozionarsi) to get upset; (Pol) to agitate

agi'tato, -a [adʒi'tato] AG rough; restless; fidgety; upset, perturbed

agita'tore, -'trice [adʒita'tore] SM/F (Pol) agitator

agitazi'one [adʒitat'tsjone] SF agitation; (Pol) unrest, agitation; **mettere in ~ qn** to upset o distress sb

'agli ['aʎʎi] PREP + DET vedi **a**

'aglio ['aʎʎo] SM garlic

a'gnello [aɲ'ɲɛllo] SM lamb

a'gnostico, -a, -ci, -che [aɲ'ɲɔstiko] AG, SM/F agnostic

'ago (pl **aghi**) SM needle; ~ **da calza** knitting needle

ago. ABBR (= agosto) Aug.

ago'nia SF agony

ago'nistico, -a, -ci, -che AG athletic; (fig) competitive

agoniz'zante [agonid'dzante] AG dying

agoniz'zare [agonid'dzare] /**72**/ VI to be dying

agopun'tura SF acupuncture

agorafo'bia SF agoraphobia

a'gosto SM August; vedi anche **luglio**

a'grario, -a AG agrarian, agricultural; (riforma) land cpd ▶ SM landowner ▶ SF agriculture

a'gricolo, -a AG agricultural, farm cpd

agricol'tore SM farmer

agricol'tura SF agriculture, farming

agri'foglio [agri'fɔʎʎo] SM holly

agrimen'sore SM land surveyor

agritu'rismo SM farm holidays pl

agritu'ristico, -a, -ci, -che AG farm holiday cpd

'agro, -a AG sour, sharp

agro'dolce [agro'doltʃe] AG bittersweet; (salsa) sweet and sour

agrono'mia SF agronomy

a'gronomo SM agronomist

a'grume SM (spesso al pl: pianta) citrus; (: frutto) citrus fruit

agru'meto SM citrus grove

aguz'zare [agut'tsare] /**72**/ VT to sharpen; ~ **gli orecchi** to prick up one's ears; ~ **l'ingegno** to use one's wits

aguz'zino, -a [agud'dzino] SM/F jailer; (fig) tyrant

a'guzzo, -a [a'guttso] AG sharp

'ahi ESCL (dolore) ouch!

ahimè ESCL alas!

'ai PREP + DET vedi **a**

'Aia SF: **L'~** The Hague

'aia SF threshing floor

AIDDA SIGLA F (= Associazione Imprenditrici Donne Dirigenti d'Azienda) association of women entrepreneurs and managers

AIDS ['aids] ABBR M/ABBR F AIDS

AIE SIGLA F (= Associazione Italiana degli Editori) publishers' association

AIEA SIGLA F = **Agenzia Internazionale per l'Energia Atomica**

AIED SIGLA F (= Associazione Italiana Educazione Demografica) ≈ FPA (= Family Planning Association)

AIG SIGLA F (= Associazione Italiana Alberghi per la Gioventù) ≈ YHA (BRIT)

ai'ola SF = **aiuola**

airbag SM INV air bag

AIRC ABBR F = **Associazione Italiana per la Ricerca sul Cancro**

ai'rone SM heron

ai'tante AG robust

aiu'ola SF flower bed

aiu'tante SMF assistant ▶ SM (Mil) adjutant; (Naut) master-at-arms; ~ **di campo** aide-de-camp

aiu'tare /**72**/ VT to help; ~ **qn (a fare)** to help sb (to do); **aiutarsi** VPR to help each other;

~ **qn in qc/a fare qc** to help sb with sth/ to do sth; **può aiutarmi?** can you help me?

ai'uto SM help, assistance, aid; *(aiutante)* assistant; **venire in ~ di qn** to come to sb's aid; ~ **chirurgo** assistant surgeon

aiz'zare [ait'tsare] /**72**/ VT to incite; ~ **i cani contro qn** to set the dogs on sb

al PREP + DET *vedi* **a**

a.l. ABBR = **anno luce**

'ala *(pl* **ali**) SF wing; **fare ~** to fall back, make way; ~ **destra/sinistra** *(Sport)* right/left wing

ala'bastro SM alabaster

'alacre AG quick, brisk

alacrità SF promptness, speed

alam'bicco, -chi SM still *(Chim)*

a'lano SM Great Dane

a'lare AG wing *cpd*; **alari** SMPL firedogs

A'laska SF: **l'~** Alaska

a'lato, -a AG winged

'alba SF dawn; **all'~** at dawn

alba'nese AG, SMF Albanian

Alba'nia SF: **l'~** Albania

'albatro SM albatross

albeggi'are [albed'dʒare] /**62**/ VI, VB IMPERS to dawn

albe'rato, -a AG *(viale, piazza)* lined with trees, tree-lined

albera'tura SF *(Naut)* masts *pl*

alber'gare /**80**/ VT *(dare albergo)* to accommodate ▶ VI *(poetico)* to dwell

alberga'tore, -'trice SM/F hotelier, hotel owner

alberghi'ero, -a [alber'gjɛro] AG hotel *cpd*

al'bergo, -ghi SM hotel; ~ **diurno** *public toilets with washing and shaving facilities etc*; ~ **della gioventù** youth hostel

'albero SM tree; *(Naut)* mast; *(Tecn)* shaft; ~ **a camme** camshaft; ~ **genealogico** family tree; ~ **a gomiti** crankshaft; ~ **maestro** mainmast; ~ **di Natale** Christmas tree; ~ **di trasmissione** transmission shaft

albi'cocca, -che SF apricot

albi'cocco, -chi SM apricot tree

al'bino, -a AG, SM/F albino

'albo SM *(registro)* register, roll; *(Amm)* notice board

'album SM INV album; ~ **da disegno** sketch book

al'bume SM albumen; *(bianco d'uovo)* egg white

albu'mina SF albumin

'alce ['altʃe] SM elk

al'chimia [al'kimja] SF alchemy

alchi'mista, -i [alki'mista] SM alchemist

'alcol SM INV = **alcool**

alcolicità [alkolitʃi'ta] SF alcohol(ic) content

al'colico, -a, -ci, -che AG alcoholic ▶ SM alcoholic drink

alco'lismo SM alcoholism

alco'lista, -i, -e SM/F alcoholic

alcoliz'zato, -a [alkolid'dzato] SM/F alcoholic

'alcool SM INV alcohol; ~ **denaturato** methylated spirits *pl (BRIT)*, wood alcohol *(US)*; ~ **etilico** ethyl alcohol; ~ **metilico** methyl alcohol

alco'olico *etc vedi* **alcolico** *ecc*

alco'test SM INV Breathalyser® *(BRIT)*, Breathalyzer® *(US)*

al'cova SF alcove

al'cuno, -a DET *(dav sm:* **alcun** + C, V, **alcuno** + *s impura, gn, pn, ps, x, z; dav sf:* **alcuna** + C, **alcun'** + V: *nessuno)*: **non ... ~** no, not any; **alcuni, e** DET PL, PRON PL some, a few; **non c'è alcuna fretta** there's no hurry, there isn't any hurry; **senza alcun riguardo** without any consideration

aldilà SM INV: **l'~** the next life, the after-life

alea'torio, -a AG *(incerto)* uncertain

aleggi'are [aled'dʒare] /**62**/ VI *(fig: profumo, sospetto)* to be in the air

Ales'sandria SF *(anche:* **Alessandria d'Egitto)** Alexandria

a'letta SF *(Tecn)* fin; tab

alet'tone SM *(Aer)* aileron

Aleu'tine SFPL: **le isole ~** the Aleutian Islands

alfa'betico, -a, -ci, -che AG alphabetical

alfa'beto SM alphabet

alfanu'merico, -a, -ci, -che AG alphanumeric

alfi'ere SM standard-bearer; *(Scacchi)* bishop

al'fine AV finally, in the end

'alga, -ghe SF seaweed *no pl*, alga

'algebra ['aldʒebra] SF algebra

Al'geri [al'dʒeri] SF Algiers

Alge'ria [aldʒe'ria] SF: **l'~** Algeria

alge'rino, -a [aldʒe'rino] AG, SM/F Algerian

algo'ritmo SM algorithm

ALI SIGLA F *(= Associazione Librai Italiani) booksellers' association*

ali'ante SM *(Aer)* glider

'alibi SM INV alibi

a'lice [a'litʃe] SF anchovy

alie'nare /**72**/ VT *(Dir)* to transfer; *(rendere ostile)* to alienate; **alienarsi qn** to alienate sb

alie'nato, -a AG alienated; transferred; *(fuor di senno)* insane ▶ SM lunatic, insane person

alienazi'one [aljenat'tsjone] SF alienation; transfer; insanity

ali'eno, -a AG *(avverso):* ~ **(da)** opposed (to), averse (to) ▶ SM/F alien

alimen'tare /**72**/ VT to feed; *(Tecn)* to feed, supply; *(fig)* to sustain ▶ AG food *cpd*; **alimentari** SMPL foodstuffs; *(anche:* **negozio di alimentari)** grocer's shop; **regime ~** diet

alimenta'tore SM *(Elettr)* feeder

alimentazi'one [alimentat'tsjone] SF

feeding; supplying; sustaining; (*cibi*) diet; ~ **di fogli** (*Inform*) sheet feed

ali'mento SM food; **alimenti** SMPL food *sg*; (*Dir*) alimony

a'liquota SF share; ~ **d'imposta** tax rate; ~ **minima** (*Fisco*) basic rate

alis'cafo SM hydrofoil

'alito SM breath

all. ABBR (= *allegato*) enc., encl.

'alla PREP + DET *vedi* **a**

allaccia'mento [allattʃa'mento] SM (*Tecn*) connection

allacci'are [allat'tʃare] /**14**/ VT (*scarpe*) to tie, lace (up); (*cintura*) to do up, fasten; (*due località*) to link; (*luce, gas*) to connect; (*amicizia*) to form; **allacciarsi** VPR (*vestito*) to fasten; ~ *o* **allacciarsi la cintura** to fasten one's belt

allaccia'tura [allattʃa'tura] SF fastening

allaga'mento SM flooding *no pl*; flood

alla'gare /**80**/ VT, **alla'garsi** VPR to flood

allampa'nato, -a AG lanky

allar'gare /**80**/ VT to widen; (*vestito*) to let out; (*aprire*) to open; (*fig: dilatare*) to extend; **allargarsi** VPR (*gen*) to widen; (*scarpe, pantaloni*) to stretch; (*fig: problema, fenomeno*) to spread

allar'mare /**72**/ VT to alarm; **allarmarsi** VPR to become alarmed

al'larme SM alarm; **mettere qn in** ~ to alarm sb; ~ **aereo** air-raid warning

allar'mismo SM scaremongering

allar'mista, -i, -e SM/F scaremonger, alarmist

allat'tare /**72**/ VT (*donna*) to (breast-)feed; (: *animale*) to suckle; ~ **artificialmente** to bottle-feed

'alle PREP + DET *vedi* **a**

alle'anza [alle'antsa] SF alliance; **A~ Democratica** (*Pol*) moderate centre-left party; **A~ Nazionale** (*Pol*) party on the far right

alle'arsi /**72**/ VPR to form an alliance

alle'ato, -a AG allied ▶ SM/F ally

alleg. ABBR = **all.**

alle'gare /**80**/ VT (*accludere*) to enclose; (*Dir: citare*) to cite, adduce; (*denti*) to set on edge

alle'gato, -a AG enclosed ▶ SM enclosure; (*di e-mail*) attachment; **in** ~ enclosed; **in ~ Vi inviamo ...** please find enclosed ...

allegge'rire [alleddʒe'rire] /**55**/ VT to lighten, make lighter; (*fig: sofferenza*) to alleviate, lessen; (: *lavoro, tasse*) to reduce

allego'ria SF allegory

alle'gorico, -a, -ci, -che AG allegorical

alle'gria SF gaiety, cheerfulness

al'legro, -a AG cheerful, merry; (*un po' brillo*) merry, tipsy; (*vivace: colore*) bright ▶ SM (*Mus*) allegro

allena'mento SM training

alle'nare /**72**/ VT, **alle'narsi** VPR to train

allena'tore SM (*Sport*) trainer, coach

allen'tare /**72**/ VT to slacken; (*disciplina*) to relax; **allentarsi** VPR to become slack; (*ingranaggio*) to work loose

aller'gia, -'gie [aller'dʒia] SF allergy

al'lergico, -a, -ci, -che [al'lɛrdʒiko] AG allergic

allesti'mento SM preparation, setting up; **in** ~ in preparation

alles'tire /**55**/ VT (*cena*) to prepare; (*esercito, nave*) to equip, fit out; (*spettacolo*) to stage

allet'tante AG attractive, alluring

allet'tare /**72**/ VT to lure, entice

alleva'mento SM breeding, rearing; (*luogo*) stock farm; **pollo d'~** battery hen

alle'vare /**72**/ VT (*animale*) to breed, rear; (*bambino*) to bring up

alleva'tore SM breeder

allevi'are /**19**/ VT to alleviate

alli'bire /**55**/ VI to turn pale; (*essere turbato*) to be disconcerted

alli'bito, -a AG pale; disconcerted; astounded

allibra'tore SM bookmaker

allie'tare /**72**/ VT to cheer up, gladden

alli'evo SM pupil; (*apprendista*) apprentice; ~ **ufficiale** cadet

alliga'tore SM alligator

allinea'mento SM alignment

alline'are /**72**/ VT (*persone, cose*) to line up; (*Tip*) to align; (*fig: economia, salari*) to adjust, align; **allinearsi** VPR to line up; (*fig: a idee*) **allinearsi a** to come into line with

alline'ato, -a AG aligned, in line; **paesi non allineati** (*Pol*) non-aligned countries

'allo PREP + DET *vedi* **a**

allo'care /**20**/ VT to allocate

al'locco, -a, -chi, -che SM/F oaf ▶ SM tawny owl

allocuzi'one [allokut'tsjone] SF address, solemn speech

al'lodola SF (sky)lark

alloggi'are [allod'dʒare] /**62**/ VT to accommodate ▶ VI to live

al'loggio [al'lɔddʒo] SM lodging, accommodation (*Brit*), accommodations (*US*); (*appartamento*) flat (*Brit*), apartment (*US*)

allontana'mento SM removal; dismissal; estrangement

allonta'nare /**72**/ VT to send away, send off; (*impiegato*) to dismiss; (*pericolo*) to avert, remove; (*estraniare*) to alienate; **allontanarsi** VPR: **allontanarsi (da)** to go away (from); (*estraniarsi*) to become estranged (from)

al'lora AV (*in quel momento*) then ▶ CONG (*in questo caso*) well then; (*dunque*) well then, so; **la gente d'~** people then *o* in those days; **da ~ in poi** from then on; **e ~?** (*che fare?*) what now?; (*e con ciò?*) so what?

allor'ché [allor'ke] CONG (*formale*) when, as soon as

al'loro SM laurel; **riposare** *o* **dormire sugli allori** to rest on one's laurels

'alluce ['allutʃe] SM big toe

alluci'nante [allutʃi'nante] AG (*scena, spettacolo*) awful, terrifying; (*col: incredibile*) amazing

alluci'nato, -a [allutʃi'nato] AG terrified; (*fuori di sé*) bewildered, confused

allucinazi'one [allutʃinat'tsjone] SF hallucination

al'ludere /35/ VI: ~ **a** to allude to, hint at

allu'minio SM aluminium (BRIT), aluminum (US)

allu'naggio [allu'naddʒo] SM moon landing

allu'nare /72/ VI to land on the moon

allun'gare /80/ VT to lengthen; (*distendere*) to prolong, extend; (*diluire*) to water down; **allungarsi** VPR to lengthen; (*ragazzo*) to stretch, grow taller; (*sdraiarsi*) to lie down, stretch out; ~ **le mani** (*rubare*) to pick pockets; **gli allungò uno schiaffo** he took a swipe at him

al'lusi *etc* VB *vedi* **alludere**

allusi'one SF hint, allusion

al'luso, -a PP *di* **alludere**

alluvi'one SF flood

alma'nacco, -chi SM almanac

al'meno AV at least ▶ CONG: **(se)** ~ if only; **(se)** ~ **piovesse!** if only it would rain!

a'logeno, -a [a'lɔdʒeno] AG: **lampada alogena** halogen lamp

a'lone SM halo

al'pestre AG (*delle alpi*) alpine; (*montuoso*) mountainous

'Alpi SFPL: **le** ~ the Alps

alpi'nismo SM mountaineering, climbing

alpi'nista, -i, -e SM/F mountaineer, climber

al'pino, -a AG Alpine; mountain *cpd*; **alpini** SMPL (*Mil*) Italian Alpine troops

al'quanto AV rather, a little ▶ DET: ~(**-a**) a certain amount of, some ▶ PRON a certain amount, some; **alquanti, e** DET PL, PRON PL several, quite a few

Al'sazia [al'sattsja] SF Alsace

alt ESCL halt!, stop! ▶ SM: **dare l'**~ to call a halt

alta'lena SF (*a funi*) swing; (*in bilico, anche fig*) seesaw

alta'mente AV extremely, highly

al'tare SM altar

alte'rare /72/ VT to alter, change; (*cibo*) to adulterate; (*registro*) to falsify; (*persona*) to irritate; **alterarsi** VPR to alter; (*cibo*) to go bad; (*persona*) to lose one's temper

alterazi'one [alterat'tsjone] SF alteration, change; adulteration; falsification; annoyance

al'terco, -chi SM altercation, wrangle

alter'nanza [alter'nantsa] SF alternation; (*Agr*) rotation

alter'nare /72/ VT, **alter'narsi** VPR to alternate

alterna'tivo, -a AG alternative ▶ SF alternative; **non abbiamo alternative** we have no alternative

alter'nato, -a AG alternate; (*Elettr*) alternating

alterna'tore SM alternator

al'terno, -a AG alternate; **a giorni alterni** on alternate days, every other day; **circolazione a targhe alterne** (*Aut*) *system of restricting vehicle use to odd/even registrations on alternate days*

al'tero, -a AG proud

al'tezza [al'tettsa] SF (*di edificio, persona*) height; (*di tessuto*) width, breadth; (*di acqua, pozzo*) depth; (*di suono*) pitch; (*Geo*) latitude; (*titolo*) highness; (*fig: nobiltà*) greatness; **essere all'**~ **di** to be on a level with; (*fig*) to be up to *o* equal to; **all'**~ **della farmacia** near the chemist's

altez'zoso, -a [altet'tsoso] AG haughty

al'ticcio, -a, -ci, -ce [al'tittʃo] AG tipsy

altipi'ano SM = **altopiano**

altiso'nante AG (*fig*) high-sounding, pompous

alti'tudine SF altitude

'alto, -a AG high; (*persona*) tall; (*tessuto*) wide, broad; (*sonno, acque*) deep; (*suono*) high (-pitched); (*Geo*) upper; (*: settentrionale*) northern ▶ SM top (part) ▶ AV high; (*parlare*) aloud, loudly; **il palazzo è ~ 20 metri** the building is 20 metres high; **il tessuto è ~ 70 cm** the material is 70 cm wide; **ad alta voce** aloud; **a notte alta** in the dead of night; **in ~** up, upwards; at the top; **mani in ~!** hands up!; **dall'**~ **in** *o* **al basso** up and down; **degli alti e bassi** (*fig*) ups and downs; **andare a testa alta** (*fig*) to carry one's head high; **essere in ~ mare** (*fig*) to be far from a solution; **alta fedeltà** high fidelity, hi-fi; **alta finanza/società** high finance/society; **alta moda** haute couture; **l'A~ Medioevo** the Early Middle Ages; **l'~ Po** the upper reaches of the Po; **alta velocità** (*Ferr*) high speed rail system

altoate'sino, -a AG of (*o* from) the Alto Adige

alto'forno SM blast furnace

altolo'cato, -a AG of high rank, highly placed

altopar'lante SM loudspeaker

altopi'ano (*pl* **altipiani**) SM upland plain, plateau

'Alto 'Volta SM: **l'**~ Upper Volta

altret'tanto, -a AG, PRON as much; (*pl*) as many ▶ AV equally; **tanti auguri! — grazie, ~** all the best! — thank you, the same to you

'altri PRON INV (*qualcuno*) somebody; (: *in espressioni negative*) anybody; (*un'altra persona*) another (person)
altri'menti AV otherwise

(PAROLA CHIAVE)

'altro, -a DET 1 (*diverso*) other, different; questa è un'altra cosa that's another *o* a different thing; passami l'altra penna give me the other pen
2 (*supplementare*) other; prendi un altro cioccolatino have another chocolate; hai avuto altre notizie? have you had any more *o* any other news?; hai altro pane? have you got any more bread?
3 (*nel tempo*): l'altro giorno the other day; l'altr'anno last year; l'altro ieri the day before yesterday; domani l'altro the day after tomorrow; quest'altro mese next month
4: d'altra parte on the other hand
▶ PRON 1 (*persona: cosa diversa o supplementare*): un altro, un'altra another (one); lo farà un altro someone else will do it; altri, e others; gli altri (*la gente*) others, other people; l'uno e l'altro both (of them); aiutarsi l'un l'altro to help one another; prendine un altro have another (one); da un giorno all'altro from day to day; (*nel giro di 24 ore*) from one day to the next; (*da un momento all'altro*) any day now
2 (*sostantivato: solo maschile*) something else; (: *in espressioni interrogative*) anything else; non ho altro da dire I have nothing else *o* I don't have anything else to say; desidera altro? do you want anything else?; più che altro above all; se non altro if nothing else, at least; tra l'altro among other things; ci mancherebbe altro! that's all we need!; non faccio altro che lavorare I do nothing but work; contento? — altro che! are you pleased? — I certainly am!; *vedi anche* senza; noialtri; voialtri; tutto

altroché [altro'ke] ESCL certainly!, and how!
al'tronde AV: d'~ on the other hand
al'trove AV elsewhere, somewhere else
al'trui AG INV other people's ▶ SM: l'~ other people's belongings *pl*
altru'ismo SM altruism
altru'ista, -i, -e AG altruistic ▶ SM/F altruist
al'tura SF (*rialto*) height, high ground; (*alto mare*) open sea; pesca d'~ deep-sea fishing
a'lunno, -a SM/F pupil
alve'are SM hive
'alveo SM riverbed
alzaban'diera [altsaban'djera] SM INV (*Mil*): l'~ the raising of the flag
al'zare [al'tsare] /72/ VT to raise, lift; (*issare*) to hoist; (*costruire*) to build, erect; alzarsi VPR to rise; (*dal letto*) to get up; (*crescere*) to grow tall (*o* taller); ~ le spalle to shrug one's shoulders; ~ le carte to cut the cards; ~ il gomito to drink too much; ~ le mani su qn to raise one's hand to sb; ~ i tacchi to take to one's heels; alzarsi in piedi to stand up, get to one's feet; alzarsi col piede sbagliato to get out of bed on the wrong side
al'zata [al'tsata] SF lifting, raising; un'~ di spalle a shrug
A.M. ABBR = Aeronautica Militare
a'mabile AG lovable; (*vino*) sweet
'AMAC SIGLA F = Aeronautica Militare-Aviazione Civile
a'maca, -che SF hammock
amalga'mare /72/ VT, amalga'marsi VPR to amalgamate
a'mante AG: ~ di (*musica ecc*) fond of ▶ SMF lover (mistress)
amara'mente AV bitterly
ama'ranto SM (*Bot*) love-lies-bleeding ▶ AG INV: color ~ reddish purple
a'mare /72/ VT to love; (*amico, musica, sport*) to like; amarsi VPR to love each other
amareggi'are [amared'dʒare] /62/ VT to sadden, upset; amareggiarsi VPR to get upset; amareggiarsi la vita to make one's life a misery
amareggi'ato, -a [amared'dʒato] AG upset, saddened
ama'rena SF sour black cherry
ama'retto SM (*dolce*) macaroon; (*liquore*) bitter liqueur made with almonds
ama'rezza [ama'rettsa] SF bitterness
a'maro, -a AG bitter ▶ SM bitterness; (*liquore*) bitters *pl*
ama'rognolo, -a [ama'roɲɲolo] AG slightly bitter
a'mato, -a AG beloved, loved, dear ▶ SM/F loved one
ama'tore, -'trice SM/F (*amante*) lover; (*intenditore: di vini ecc*) connoisseur; (*dilettante*) amateur
a'mazzone [a'maddzone] SF (*Mitologia*) Amazon; (*cavallerizza*) horsewoman; (*abito*) riding habit; cavalcare all'~ to ride sidesaddle; il Rio delle Amazzoni the (river) Amazon
Amaz'zonia [amad'dzonja] SF Amazonia
amaz'zonico, -a, -ci, -che [amad'dzɔniko] AG Amazonian; Amazon *cpd*
ambasce'ria [ambaʃʃe'ria] SF embassy
ambasci'ata [ambaʃʃata] SF embassy; (*messaggio*) message
ambascia'tore, -'trice [ambaʃʃa'tore] SM/F ambassador (ambassadress)
ambe'due AG INV: ~ i ragazzi both boys ▶ PRON INV both

ambi'destro, -a AG ambidextrous

ambien'tale AG (*temperatura*) ambient *cpd*; (*problemi, tutela*) environmental

ambienta'lismo SM environmentalism

ambienta'lista, -i, -e AG environmental
▶ SM/F environmentalist

ambien'tare /72/ VT to acclimatize; (*romanzo, film*) to set; **ambientarsi** VPR to get used to one's surroundings

ambientazi'one [ambjentat'tsjone] SF setting

ambi'ente SM environment; (*fig: insieme di persone*) milieu; (*stanza*) room

ambiguità SF INV ambiguity

am'biguo, -a AG ambiguous; (*persona*) shady

am'bire /55/ VT (*anche: vi: ambire a*) to aspire to; **un premio molto ambito** a much sought-after prize

'ambito SM sphere, field

ambiva'lente AG ambivalent; **questo apparecchio è ~** this is a dual-purpose device

ambizi'one [ambit'tsjone] SF ambition

ambizi'oso, -a [ambit'tsjoso] AG ambitious

'ambo AG INV both ▶ SM (*al gioco*) double

'ambra SF amber; **~ grigia** ambergris

ambu'lante AG travelling, itinerant ▶ SM peddler

ambu'lanza [ambu'lantsa] SF ambulance; **chiamate un'~** call an ambulance

ambulatori'ale AG (*Med*) outpatients *cpd*; **operazione ~** operation as an outpatient; **visita ~** visit to the doctor's surgery (BRIT) o office (US)

ambula'torio SM (*studio medico*) surgery (BRIT), doctor's office (US)

'AMDI SIGLA F = **Associazione Medici Dentisti Italiani**

a'meba SF amoeba (BRIT), ameba (US)

amenità SF INV pleasantness *no pl*; (*facezia*) pleasantry

a'meno, -a AG pleasant; (*strano*) funny, strange; (*spiritoso*) amusing

A'merica SF: **l'~** America; **l'~ latina** Latin America; **l'~ del sud** South America

america'nata SF (*peg*): **le Olimpiadi sono state una vera ~** the Olympics were a typically vulgar American extravaganza

america'nismo SM Americanism; (*ammirazione*) love of America

ameri'cano, -a AG, SM/F American

ame'tista SF amethyst

ami'anto SM asbestos

a'mica SF *vedi* **amico**

ami'chevole [ami'kevole] AG friendly

ami'cizia [ami'tʃittsja] SF friendship; **amicizie** SFPL (*amici*) friends; **fare ~ con qn** to make friends with sb

a'mico, -a, -ci, -che SM/F friend; (*amante*)

boyfriend (girlfriend); **~ del cuore** o **intimo** bosom friend; **~ d'infanzia** childhood friend; **aggiungere come ~** (*Internet*) to friend

'amido SM starch

ammac'care /20/ VT (*pentola*) to dent; (*persona*) to bruise; **ammaccarsi** VPR to bruise

ammacca'tura SF dent; bruise

ammaes'trare /72/ VT (*animale*) to train; (*persona*) to teach

ammai'nare /72/ VT to lower, haul down

amma'larsi /72/ VPR to fall ill

amma'lato, -a AG ill, sick ▶ SM/F sick person; (*paziente*) patient

ammali'are /19/ VT (*fig*) to enchant, charm

ammalia'tore, -'trice SM/F enchanter (enchantress)

am'manco, -chi SM (*Econ*) deficit

ammanet'tare /72/ VT to handcuff

ammani'cato, -a, ammanigli'ato, -a [ammaniʎ'ʎato] AG (*fig*) with friends in high places

amman'sire /55/ VT (*animale*) to tame; (*fig: persona*) to calm down, placate

amman'tarsi /72/ VPR: **~ di** (*persona*) to wrap o.s. in; (*fig: prato ecc*) to be covered in

amma'raggio [amma'raddʒo] SM (sea) landing; splashdown

amma'rare /72/ VI (*Aer*) to make a sea landing; (*astronave*) to splash down

ammas'sare /72/ VT (*ammucchiare*) to amass; (*raccogliere*) to gather together; **ammassarsi** VPR to pile up; to gather

am'masso SM mass; (*mucchio*) pile, heap; (*Econ*) stockpile

ammat'tire /55/ VI to go mad

ammaz'zare [ammat'tsare] /72/ VT to kill; **ammazzarsi** VPR (*uccidersi*) to kill o.s.; (*rimanere ucciso*) to be killed; **ammazzarsi di lavoro** to work o.s. to death

am'menda SF amends *pl*; (*Dir, Sport*) fine; **fare ~ di qc** to make amends for sth

am'messo, -a PP *di* **ammettere** ▶ CONG: **~ che** supposing that

am'mettere /63/ VT to admit; (*riconoscere: fatto*) to acknowledge, admit; (*permettere*) to allow, accept; (*supporre*) to suppose; **ammettiamo che ...** let us suppose that ...

ammez'zato [ammed'dzato] SM (*anche:* **piano ammezzato**) entresol, mezzanine

ammic'care /20/ VI: **~ (a)** to wink (at)

amminis'trare /72/ VT to run, manage; (*Rel, Dir*) to administer

amministra'tivo, -a AG administrative

amministra'tore SM administrator; (*di condominio*) flats manager; (*Comm*) director; **~ aggiunto** associate director; **~ delegato** managing director; **~ fiduciario** trustee; **~ unico** sole director

amministrazi'one [amministrat'tsjone] SF management; administration; **consiglio d'~** board of directors; **l'~ comunale** local government; **~ fiduciaria** trust

ammi'raglia [ammi'raʎʎa] SF flagship

ammiragli'ato [ammiraʎ'ʎato] SM admiralty

ammi'raglio [ammi'raʎʎo] SM admiral

ammi'rare /**72**/ VT to admire

ammira'tore, -'trice SM/F admirer

ammirazi'one [ammirat'tsjone] SF admiration

am'misi etc VB vedi **ammettere**

ammis'sibile AG admissible, acceptable

ammissi'one SF admission; (approvazione) acknowledgment

Amm.ne ABBR = **amministrazione**

ammobili'are /**19**/ VT to furnish

ammobili'ato, -a AG (camera, appartamento) furnished

ammoder'nare /**72**/ VT to modernize

am'modo, a 'modo AV properly ▶ AG INV respectable, nice

ammogli'are [ammoʎ'ʎare] /**27**/ VT to find a wife for; **ammogliarsi** VPR to marry, take a wife

am'mollo SM: **lasciare in ~** to leave to soak

ammo'niaca SF ammonia

ammoni'mento SM warning; admonishment

ammo'nire /**55**/ VT (avvertire) to warn; (rimproverare) to admonish; (Dir) to caution

ammonizi'one [ammonit'tsjone] SF (monito: anche Sport) warning; (rimprovero) reprimand; (Dir) caution

ammon'tare /**72**/ VI: **~ a** to amount to ▶ SM (total) amount

ammonticchi'are [ammontik'kjare] /**19**/ VT to pile up, heap up

ammor'bare /**72**/ VT (diffondere malattia) to infect; (odore) to taint, foul

ammorbi'dente SM fabric softener

ammorbi'dire /**55**/ VT to soften

ammorta'mento SM redemption; amortization; **~ fiscale** capital allowance

ammor'tare /**72**/ VT (Finanza: debito) to pay off, redeem; (: spese d'impianto) to write off

ammortiz'zare [ammortid'dzare] /**72**/ VT (Finanza) to pay off, redeem; (: spese d'impianto) to write off; (Aut, Tecn) to absorb, deaden

ammortizza'tore [ammortiddza'tore] SM (Aut, Tecn) shock absorber

ammucchi'are [ammuk'kjare] /**19**/ VT, **ammucchi'arsi** VPR to pile up, accumulate

ammuf'fire /**55**/ VI to go mouldy (BRIT) o moldy (US)

ammutina'mento SM mutiny

ammuti'narsi /**72**/ VPR to mutiny

ammuti'nato, -a AG mutinous ▶ SM mutineer

ammuto'lire /**55**/ VI to be struck dumb

amne'sia SF amnesia

amnis'tia SF amnesty

'amo SM (Pesca) hook; (fig) bait

amo'rale AG amoral

a'more SM love; **amori** SMPL love affairs; **il tuo bambino è un ~** your baby's a darling; **fare l'~** o all'~ to make love; **andare d'~ e d'accordo con qn** to get on like a house on fire with sb; **per ~ o per forza** by hook or by crook; **amor proprio** self-esteem, pride

amoreggi'are [amored'dʒare] /**62**/ VI to flirt

amo'revole AG loving, affectionate

a'morfo, -a AG amorphous; (fig: persona) lifeless

amo'rino SM cupid

amo'roso, -a AG (affettuoso) loving, affectionate; (d'amore: sguardo) amorous; (: poesia, relazione) love cpd

am'pere [ã'pɛr] SM INV amp(ère)

ampi'ezza [am'pjettsa] SF width, breadth; spaciousness; (fig: importanza) scale, size; **~ di vedute** broad-mindedness

'ampio, -a AG wide, broad; (spazioso) spacious; (abbondante: vestito) loose; (: gonna) full; (: spiegazione) ample, full

am'plesso SM (sessuale) intercourse

amplia'mento SM (di strada) widening; (di aeroporto) expansion; (fig) broadening

ampli'are /**19**/ VT (ingrandire) to enlarge; (allargare) to widen; (fig: discorso) to enlarge on; **ampliarsi** VPR to grow, increase; **~ la propria cultura** to broaden one's mind

amplifi'care /**20**/ VT to amplify; (magnificare) to extol

amplifica'tore SM (Tecn, Mus) amplifier

amplificazi'one [amplifikat'tsjone] SF amplification

am'polla SF (vasetto) cruet

ampol'loso, -a AG bombastic, pompous

ampu'tare /**72**/ VT (Med) to amputate

amputazi'one [amputat'tsjone] SF amputation

'Amsterdam SF Amsterdam

amu'leto SM lucky charm

AN SIGLA = **Ancona**

A.N. SIGLA F (Pol) = **Alleanza Nazionale**

anabbagli'ante [anabbaʎ'ʎante] AG (Aut) dipped (BRIT), dimmed (US); **anabbaglianti** SMPL dipped or dimmed headlights

anaboliz'zante [anabolid'dzante] SM anabolic steroid ▶ AG anabolic

anacro'nismo SM anachronism

a'nagrafe SF (registro) register of births, marriages and deaths; (ufficio) registry office (BRIT), office of vital statistics (US)

ana'grafico, -a, -ci, -che AG (Amm): **dati**

anagrafici personal data; **comune di residenza anagrafica** district where resident

ana'gramma, -i SM anagram

anal'colico, -a, -ci, -che AG non-alcoholic ▸ SM soft drink; **bevanda analcolica** soft drink

a'nale AG anal

analfa'beta, -i, -e AG, SM/F illiterate

analfabe'tismo SM illiteracy

anal'gesico, -a, -ci, -che [anal'dʒɛziko] AG, SM analgesic

a'nalisi SF INV analysis; (Med: esame) test; **in ultima ~** in conclusion, in the final analysis; **~ grammaticale** parsing; **~ del sangue** blood test; **~ dei sistemi/costi** systems/cost analysis

ana'lista, -i, -e SM/F analyst; (Psic) (psycho)analyst; **~ finanziario** financial analyst; **~ di sistemi** systems analyst

ana'litico, -a, -ci, -che AG analytic(al)

analiz'zare [analid'dzare] /72/ VT to analyse (BRIT), analyze (US); (Med) to test

analo'gia, -'gie [analo'dʒia] SF analogy

ana'logico, -a, -ci, -che [ana'lɔdʒiko] AG analogical; (calcolatore, orologio) analog(ue)

a'nalogo, -a, -ghi, -ghe AG analogous

'ananas SM INV pineapple

anar'chia [anar'kia] SF anarchy

a'narchico, -a, -ci, -che [a'narkiko] AG anarchic(al) ▸ SM/F anarchist

anarco-insurreziona'lista [anarko,insurrettsjona'lista] AG anarcho-revolutionary

'A.N.A.S. SIGLA F (= Azienda Nazionale Autonoma delle Strade) national roads department

ana'tema, -i SM anathema

anato'mia SF anatomy

ana'tomico, -a, -ci, -che AG anatomical; (sedile) contoured

'anatra SF duck; **~ selvatica** mallard

ana'troccolo SM duckling

'ANCA SIGLA F = **Associazione Nazionale Cooperative Agricole**

'anca, -che SF (Anat) hip; (Zool) haunch

ANCC SIGLA F = **Associazione Nazionale Carabinieri**

'anche ['anke] CONG (inoltre, pure) also, too; (perfino) even; **vengo anch'io!** I'm coming too!; **~ se** even if; **~ volendo, non finiremmo in tempo** even if we wanted to, we wouldn't finish in time

ancheggi'are [anked'dʒare] /62/ VI to wiggle (one's hips)

anchilo'sato, -a [ankilo'zato] AG stiff

'ANCI ['antʃi] SIGLA F (= Associazione Nazionale dei Comuni Italiani) national confederation of local authorities

ancone'tano, -a AG of (o from) Ancona

an'cora¹ AV still; (di nuovo) again; (di più) some more; (persino): **~ più forte** even stronger; **non ~** not yet; **~ una volta** once more, once again; **~ un po'** a little more; (di tempo) a little longer

'ancora² SF anchor; **gettare/levare l'~** to cast/weigh anchor; **~ di salvezza** (fig) last hope

anco'raggio [anko'raddʒo] SM anchorage

anco'rare /72/ VT, **anco'rarsi** VPR to anchor

ANCR SIGLA F (= Associazione Nazionale Combattenti e Reduci) servicemen's and ex-servicemen's association

Andalu'sia SF: **l'~** Andalusia

anda'luso, -a AG, SM/F Andalusian

anda'mento SM (di strada, malattia) course; (del mercato) state

an'dante AG (corrente) current; (di poco pregio) cheap, second-rate ▸ SM (Mus) andante

an'dare /6/ SM: **a lungo ~** in the long run; **con l'andar del tempo** with the passing of time; **racconta storie a tutto ~** she's forever talking rubbish ▸ VI (gen) to go; **~ a** (essere adatto) to suit; **il suo comportamento non mi va** (piace) I don't like the way he behaves; **ti va di ~ al cinema?** do you feel like going to the cinema?; **~ a cavallo** to ride; **~ in macchina/aereo** to go by car/plane; **~ a fare qc** to go and do sth; **~ a pescare/sciare** to go fishing/skiing; **andarsene** to go away; **questa camicia va lavata** this shirt needs a wash o should be washed; **vado e vengo** I'll be back in a minute; **~ per i 50** (età) to be getting on for 50; **~ a male** to go bad; **~ fiero di qc/qn** to be proud of sth/sb; **~ perduto** to be lost; **come va?** (lavoro, progetto) how are things?; **come va? — bene, grazie!** how are you? — fine, thanks!; **va fatto entro oggi** it's got to be done today; **ne va della nostra vita** our lives are at stake; **se non vado errato** if I'm not mistaken; **le mele vanno molto** apples are selling well; **va da sé** (è naturale) it goes without saying; **per questa volta vada** let's say no more about it this time

an'data SF going; (viaggio) outward journey; **biglietto di sola ~** single (BRIT) o one-way ticket; **biglietto di ~ e ritorno** return (BRIT) o round-trip (US) ticket

anda'tura SF (modo di andare) walk, gait; (Sport) pace; (Naut) tack

an'dazzo [an'dattso] SM (peg): **prendere un brutto ~** to take a turn for the worse

'Ande SFPL: **le ~** the Andes

an'dino, -a AG Andean

andirivi'eni SM INV coming and going

'andito SM corridor, passage

An'dorra SF Andorra

andrò etc VB vedi **andare**

an'drone SM entrance hall

a'neddoto SM anecdote

ane'lare /**72**/ VI: ~ **a** (fig) to long for, yearn for

a'nelito SM (fig): ~ **di** longing o yearning for

a'nello SM ring; (di catena) link; **anelli** SMPL (Ginnastica) rings

ane'mia SF anaemia (BRIT), anemia (US)

a'nemico, -a, -ci, -che AG anaemic (BRIT), anemic (US)

a'nemone SM anemone

aneste'sia SF anaesthesia (BRIT), anesthesia (US)

aneste'sista, -i, -e SM/F anaesthetist (BRIT), anesthetist (US)

anes'tetico, -a, -ci, -che AG, SM anaesthetic (BRIT), anesthetic (US)

anestetiz'zare [anestetid'dzare] /**72**/ VT to anaesthetize (BRIT), anesthetize (US)

anfeta'mina SF amphetamine

anfeta'minico, -a, -ci, -che AG (fig) hyper

an'fibio, -a AG amphibious ▶ SM amphibian; (Aut) amphibious vehicle

anfite'atro SM amphitheatre (BRIT), amphitheater (US)

anfitri'one SM host

'anfora SF amphora

an'fratto SM ravine

an'gelico, -a, -ci, -che [an'dʒɛliko] AG angelic(al)

'angelo ['andʒelo] SM angel; ~ **custode** guardian angel; **l'~ del focolare** (fig) the perfect housewife

anghe'ria [ange'ria] SF vexation

an'gina [an'dʒina] SF tonsillitis; ~ **pectoris** angina

angli'cano, -a AG Anglican

angli'cismo [angli'tʃizmo] SM anglicism

an'glofilo, -a AG anglophilic ▶ SM/F anglophile

anglo'sassone AG Anglo-Saxon

An'gola SF: **l'~** Angola

ango'lano, -a AG, SM/F Angolan

ango'lare AG angular

angolazi'one [angolat'tsjone] SF (di angolo) angulation; (Fot, Cine, TV, fig) angle

'angolo SM corner; (Mat) angle; ~ **cottura** (di appartamento ecc) cooking area; **fare ~ con** (strada) to run into; **dietro l'~** (anche fig) round the corner

ango'loso, -a AG (oggetto) angular; (volto, corpo) angular, bony

'angora SF: **lana d'~** angora

an'goscia, -sce [an'gɔʃʃa] SF deep anxiety, anguish no pl

angosci'are [angoʃ'ʃare] /**14**/ VT to cause anguish to; **angosciarsi** VPR: **angosciarsi (per)** (preoccuparsi) to become anxious (about); (provare angoscia) to get upset (about o over)

angosci'oso, -a [angoʃ'ʃoso] AG (d'angoscia) anguished; (che dà angoscia) distressing, painful

angu'illa SF eel

an'guria SF watermelon

an'gustia SF (ansia) anguish, distress; (povertà) poverty, want

angusti'are /**19**/ VT to distress; **angustiarsi** VPR: **angustiarsi (per)** to worry (about)

an'gusto, -a AG (stretto) narrow; (fig) mean, petty

'anice ['anitʃe] SM (Cuc) aniseed; (Bot) anise; (liquore) anisette

ani'dride SF (Chim): ~ **carbonica/solforosa** carbon/sulphur dioxide

'anima SF soul; (abitante) inhabitant; ~ **gemella** soul mate; **un'~ in pena** (anche fig) a tormented soul; **non c'era ~ viva** there wasn't a living soul; **volere un bene dell'~ a qn** to be extremely fond of sb; **rompere l'~ a qn** to drive sb mad; **il nonno buon'~ ...** Grandfather, God rest his soul ...

ani'male SM, AG animal; ~ **domestico** pet

anima'lesco, -a, -schi, -sche AG (gesto, atteggiamento) animal-like

anima'lista, -i, -e AG animal rights cpd ▶ SM/F animal rights activist

ani'mare /**72**/ VT to give life to, liven (up); (incoraggiare) to encourage; **animarsi** VPR to become animated, come to life

ani'mato, -a AG animate; (vivace) lively, animated; (: strada) busy

anima'tore, -'trice SM/F guiding spirit; (Cine) animator; (di festa) life and soul

animazi'one [animat'tsjone] SF liveliness; (di strada) bustle; (Cine) animation; ~ **teatrale** amateur dramatics

'animo SM (mente) mind; (cuore) heart; (coraggio) courage; (disposizione) character, disposition; **avere in ~ di fare qc** to intend o have a mind to do sth; **farsi ~** to pluck up courage; **fare qc di buon/mal ~** to do sth willingly/unwillingly; **perdersi d'~** to lose heart

animosità SF animosity

A'NITA SIGLA F = **Associazione Naturista Italiana**

'anitra SF = **anatra**

'Ankara SF Ankara

ANM SIGLA F (= Associazione Nazionale dei Magistrati) national association of Magistrates

anna'cquare /**72**/ VT to water down, dilute

annaffi'are /**19**/ VT to water

annaffia'toio SM watering can

an'nali SMPL annals

annas'pare /**72**/ VI (nell'acqua) to flounder; (fig: nel buio, nell'incertezza) to grope

an'nata SF year; (importo annuo) annual amount; **vino d'~** vintage wine

annebbi'are /19/ VT (fig) to cloud; **annebbiarsi** VPR to become foggy; (vista) to become dim

annega'mento SM drowning

anne'gare /80/ VT, VI to drown; **annegarsi** VPR (accidentalmente) to drown; (deliberatamente) to drown o.s.

anne'rire /55/ VT to blacken ▶ VI to become black

annessi'one SF (Pol) annexation

an'nesso, -a PP di **annettere** ▶ AG attached; (Pol) annexed; ... **e tutti gli annessi e connessi** ... and so on and so forth

an'nettere /63/ VT (Pol) to annex; (accludere) to attach

annichi'lire [anniki'lire] /55/ VT to annihilate

anni'darsi /72/ VPR to nest

annienta'mento SM annihilation, destruction

annien'tare /72/ VT to annihilate, destroy

anniver'sario SM anniversary; **~ di matrimonio** wedding anniversary

'anno SM year; **quanti anni hai? — ho 40 anni** how old are you? — I'm 40 (years old); **gli anni 20** the 20s; **porta bene gli anni** she doesn't look her age; **porta male gli anni** she looks older than she is; **~ commerciale** business year; **~ giudiziario** legal year; **~ luce** light year; **gli anni di piombo** the Seventies in Italy, characterized by terrorist attacks and killings

anno'dare /72/ VT to knot, tie; (fig: rapporto) to form

annoi'are /19/ VT to bore; (seccare) to annoy; **annoiarsi** VPR to be bored; to be annoyed

an'noso, -a AG (albero) old; (fig: problema ecc) age-old

anno'tare /72/ VT (registrare) to note, note down (BRIT); (commentare) to annotate

annotazi'one [annotat'tsjone] SF note; annotation

annove'rare /72/ VT to number

annu'ale AG annual

annual'mente AV annually, yearly

annu'ario SM yearbook

annu'ire /55/ VI to nod; (acconsentire) to agree

annulla'mento SM annihilation, destruction; cancellation; annulment; quashing

annul'lare /72/ VT to annihilate, destroy; (contratto, francobollo) to cancel; (matrimonio) to annul; (sentenza) to quash; (risultati) to declare void

annunci'are [annun'tʃare] /14/ VT to announce; (dar segni rivelatori) to herald

annuncia'tore, -'trice [annuntʃa'tore] SM/F (Radio, TV) announcer

Annunciazi'one [annuntʃat'tsjone] SF (Rel): **l'~** the Annunciation

an'nuncio [an'nuntʃo] SM announcement; (fig) sign; **~ pubblicitario** advertisement; **annunci economici** classified advertisements, small ads; **piccoli annunci** small ads, classified ads; **annunci mortuari** (colonna) obituary column

'annuo, -a AG annual, yearly

annu'sare /72/ VT to sniff, smell; **~ tabacco** to take snuff

annuvola'mento SM clouding (over)

annuvo'lare /72/ VT to cloud; **annuvolarsi** VPR to become cloudy, cloud over

'ano SM anus

'anodo SM anode

anoma'lia SF anomaly

a'nomalo, -a AG anomalous

anoni'mato SM anonymity; **conservare l'~** to remain anonymous

a'nonimo, -a AG anonymous ▶ SM (autore) anonymous writer (o painter etc); **un tipo ~** (peg) a colourless (BRIT) o colorless (US) character; **società anonima** (Comm) joint stock company

anores'sia SF anorexia; **~ nervosa** anorexia nervosa

ano'ressico, -a, -ci, -che AG anorexic

anor'male AG abnormal ▶ SMF subnormal person; (eufemismo) homosexual

anormalità SF INV abnormality

'ANSA SIGLA F (= Agenzia Nazionale Stampa Associata) national press agency

'ansa SF (manico) handle; (di fiume) bend, loop

an'sante AG out of breath, panting

'ANSEA SIGLA F (= Associazione delle Nazioni del Sud-Est asiatico) ASEAN

'ansia SF anxiety; **stare in ~ (per qn/qc)** to be anxious (about sb/sth)

ansietà SF anxiety

ansi'mare /72/ VI to pant

ansi'oso, -a AG anxious

'anta SF (di finestra) shutter; (di armadio) door

antago'nismo SM antagonism

antago'nista, -i, -e SM/F antagonist

an'tartico, -a, -ci, -che AG Antarctic ▶ SM: **l'A~** the Antarctic

An'tartide SF: **l'~** Antarctica

ante'bellico, -a, -ci, -che AG prewar cpd

antece'dente [antetʃe'dɛnte] AG preceding, previous

ante'fatto SM previous events pl; previous history

ante'guerra SM pre-war period

ante'nato SM ancestor, forefather

an'tenna SF (Radio, TV) aerial; (Zool) antenna, feeler; (Naut) yard; **rizzare le antenne** (fig) to prick up one's ears; **~ parabolica** (TV) satellite dish

ante'porre /77/ VT: **~ qc a qc** to place o put sth before sth

ante'posto, -a PP *di* **anteporre**

ante'prima SF preview; **~ di stampa** (*Inform*) print preview

anteri'ore AG (*ruota, zampa*) front *cpd*; (*fatti*) previous, preceding

antesi'gnano [antesiɲˈɲano] SM (*Storia*) standard-bearer; (*fig*) forerunner

antiade'rente AG non-stick

antia'ereo, -a AG anti-aircraft *cpd*

antial'lergico, -a [antialˈlɛrdʒiko] AG, SM hypoallergenic

antia'tomico, -a, -ci, -che AG anti-nuclear; **rifugio ~** fallout shelter

antibi'otico, -a, -ci, -che AG, SM antibiotic

anti'caglia [antiˈkaʎʎa] SF junk *no pl*

antical'care AG (*prodotto, detersivo*) anti-limescale

anti'camera SF anteroom; **fare ~** to be kept waiting; **non mi passerebbe neanche per l'~ del cervello** it wouldn't even cross my mind

anti'carie AG INV which fights tooth decay

antichità [antikiˈta] SF INV antiquity; (*oggetto*) antique

antici'clone [antitʃiˈklone] SM anticyclone

antici'pare [antitʃiˈpare] /**72**/ VT (*consegna, visita*) to bring forward, anticipate; (*somma di denaro*) to pay in advance; (*notizia*) to disclose ▶ VI to be ahead of time

antici'pato, -a [antitʃiˈpato] AG (*prima del previsto*) early; **pagamento ~** payment in advance

anticipazi'one [antitʃipatˈtsjone] SF anticipation; (*di notizia*) advance information; (*somma di denaro*) advance

an'ticipo [anˈtitʃipo] SM anticipation; (*di denaro*) advance; **in ~** early, in advance; **con un sensibile ~** well in advance

anti'clan AG INV (*magistrato, processo*) anti-Mafia

an'tico, -a, -chi, -che AG (*quadro, mobili*) antique; (*dell'antichità*) ancient; **all'antica** old-fashioned

anticoncezio'nale [antikontʃettsjoˈnale] SM contraceptive

anticonfor'mista, -i, -e AG, SM/F nonconformist

anticonge'lante [antikondʒeˈlante] AG, SM antifreeze

anticongiuntu'rale [antikondʒuntuˈrale] AG (*Econ*): **misure anticongiunturali** measures to remedy the economic situation

anti'corpo SM antibody

anticostituzio'nale [antikostituttsjoˈnale] AG unconstitutional

antidepres'sivo, -a AG, SM antidepressant

antidiluvi'ano, -a AG (*fig: antiquato*) ancient

antidolo'rifico, -ci SM painkiller

anti'doping SM INV (*Sport*) dope test ▶ AG INV drug testing; **test ~** drugs (*BRIT*) *o* drug (*US*) test

an'tidoto SM antidote

anti'droga AG INV anti-drugs *cpd*

antie'stetico, -a, -ci, -che AG unsightly

an'tifona SF (*Mus, Rel*) antiphon; **capire l'~** (*fig*) to take the hint

anti'forfora AG INV anti-dandruff

anti'furto SM anti-theft device

anti'gelo [antiˈdʒɛlo] AG INV antifreeze *cpd* ▶ SM (*per motore*) antifreeze; (*per cristalli*) de-icer

an'tigene [anˈtidʒene] SM antigen

antigi'enico, -a, -ci, -che [antiˈdʒɛniko] AG unhygienic

antiglobalizza'zione [antiglobaliddzaˈtsjone] AG anti-globalization

An'tille SFPL: **le ~** the West Indies

an'tilope SF antelope

anti'mafia AG INV anti-mafia *cpd*

antin'cendio [antinˈtʃɛndjo] AG INV fire *cpd*; **bombola ~** fire extinguisher

anti'nebbia SM INV (*anche:* **faro antinebbia**: *Aut*) fog lamp

antine'vralgico, -a, -ci, -che [antineˈvraldʒiko] AG painkilling ▶ SM painkiller

antin'fiammatorio, -a AG, SM anti-inflammatory

antio'rario AG: **in senso ~** in an anticlockwise (*BRIT*) *o* counterclockwise (*US*) direction, anticlockwise, counterclockwise

anti'pasto SM hors d'œuvre

antipa'tia SF antipathy, dislike

anti'patico, -a, -ci, -che AG unpleasant, disagreeable

anti'placca AG INV (*dentifricio*) anti-plaque

an'tipodi SMPL: **essere agli ~** (*fig: di idee opposte*) to be poles apart

antipro'iettile AG INV bulletproof

antiquari'ato SM antique trade; **un pezzo d'~** an antique

anti'quario SM antique dealer

anti'quato, -a AG antiquated, old-fashioned

antirici'claggio [antiritʃiˈkladdʒo] AG INV (*attività, operazioni*) anti-laundering

antiri'flesso AG INV (*schermo*) non-glare *cpd*

anti'ruggine [antiˈruddʒine] AG INV anti-rust *cpd* ▶ SM INV rust-preventer

anti'rughe [antiˈruge] AG INV (*crema, prodotto*) anti-wrinkle

antise'mita, -i, -e AG anti-semitic

antisemi'tismo SM anti-semitism

anti'settico, -a, -ci, -che AG, SM antiseptic

antista'minico, -a, -ci, -che AG, SM antihistamine

anti'stante AG opposite

anti'tartaro AG INV anti-tartar

antiterro'rismo SM anti-terrorist measures *pl*

an'titesi SF antithesis

antitraspi'rante AG antiperspirant

anti'vipera AG INV: **siero** ~ remedy for snake bites

antivi'rale AG antiviral

anti'virus [anti'virus] SM INV antivirus software *no pl* ▶ AG INV antivirus

antolo'gia, -'gie [antolo'dʒia] SF anthology

antono'masia SF antonomasia; **per** ~ par excellence

antra'cite [antra'tʃite] SF anthracite

'antro SM cavern

antro'pofago, -gi SM cannibal

antropolo'gia [antropolo'dʒia] SF anthropology

antropo'logico, -a, -ci, -che [antropo'lɔdʒiko] AG anthropological

antro'pologo, -a, -gi, -ghe SM/F anthropologist

anu'lare AG ring *cpd* ▶ SM ring finger

An'versa SF Antwerp

'anzi ['antsi] AV (*invece*) on the contrary; (*o meglio*) or rather, or better still

anzianità [antsjani'ta] SF old age; (*Amm*) seniority

anzi'ano, -a [an'tsjano] AG old; (*Amm*) senior ▶ SM/F old person; senior member

anziché [antsi'ke] CONG rather than

anzi'tempo [antsi'tɛmpo] AV (*in anticipo*) early

anzi'tutto [antsi'tutto] AV first of all

AO SIGLA = **Aosta**

a'orta SF aorta

aos'tano, -a AG of (*o* from) Aosta

AP SIGLA = **Ascoli Piceno**

apar'titico, -a, -ci, -che AG (*Pol*) non-party *cpd*

apa'tia SF apathy, indifference

a'patico, -a, -ci, -che AG apathetic, indifferent

a.p.c. ABBR = **a pronta cassa**

'ape SF bee

aperi'tivo SM apéritif

aperta'mente AV openly

a'perto, -a PP *di* **aprire** ▶ AG open ▶ SM: **all'**~ in the open (air); **rimanere a bocca aperta** (*fig*) to be taken aback

aper'tura SF opening; (*ampiezza*) width, spread; (*Pol*) approach; (*Fot*) aperture; ~ **alare** wing span; ~ **mentale** open-mindedness; ~ **di credito** (*Comm*) granting of credit

API SIGLA F = **Associazione Piccole e Medie Industrie**

'apice ['apitʃe] SM apex; (*fig*) height

apicol'tore SM beekeeper

apicol'tura SF beekeeping

ap'nea SF: **immergersi in** ~ to dive without breathing apparatus

apoca'lisse SF apocalypse

apo'geo [apo'dʒɛo] SM (*Astr*) apogee; (*fig: culmine*) zenith

a'polide AG stateless

apo'litico, -a, -ci, -che AG (*neutrale*) nonpolitical; (*indifferente*) apolitical

apolo'gia, -gie [apolo'dʒia] SF (*difesa*) apologia; (*esaltazione*) praise; ~ **di reato** attempt to defend criminal acts

apoples'sia SF (*Med*) apoplexy

apop'lettico, -a, -ci, -che AG apoplectic; **colpo** ~ apoplectic fit

a'postolo SM apostle

apostro'fare /**72**/ VT (*parola*) to write with an apostrophe; (*persona*) to address

a'postrofo SM apostrophe

app. ABBR (= *appendice*) app.

appaga'mento SM satisfaction; fulfilment

appa'gare /**80**/ VT to satisfy; (*desiderio*) to fulfil; **appagarsi** VPR: **appagarsi di** to be satisfied with

appa'gato, -a AG satisfied

appai'are /**19**/ VT to couple, pair

ap'paio *etc* VB *vedi* **apparire**

appallotto'lare /**72**/ VT (*carta, foglio*) to screw into a ball; **appallottolarsi** VPR (*gatto*) to roll up into a ball

appalta'tore SM contractor

ap'palto SM (*Comm*) contract; **dare/prendere in** ~ **un lavoro** to let out/undertake a job on contract

appan'naggio [appan'naddʒo] SM (*compenso*) annuity; (*fig*) privilege, prerogative

appan'nare /**72**/ VT (*vetro*) to mist; (*metallo*) to tarnish; (*vista*) to dim; **appannarsi** VPR to mist over; to tarnish; to grow dim

appa'rato SM equipment, machinery; (*Anat*) apparatus; ~ **scenico** (*Teat*) props *pl*

apparecchi'are [apparek'kjare] /**19**/ VT to prepare; (*tavola*) to set ▶ VI to set the table

apparecchia'tura [apparekkja'tura] SF equipment; (*macchina*) machine, device

appa'recchio [appa'rekkjo] SM piece of apparatus, device; (*aeroplano*) aircraft *inv*; **apparecchi sanitari** bathroom *o* sanitary appliances; ~ **acustico** hearing aid; ~ **televisivo/telefonico** television set/ telephone

appa'rente AG apparent

apparente'mente AV apparently

appa'renza [appa'rentsa] SF appearance; **in** *o* **all'**~ apparently, to all appearances

appa'rire /**7**/ VI to appear; (*sembrare*) to seem, appear

appari'scente [appariʃ'ʃɛnte] AG (*colore*) garish, gaudy; (*bellezza*) striking

apparizi'one [apparit'tsjone] SF apparition

ap'parso, -a PP *di* **apparire**

apparta'mento SM flat (BRIT), apartment (US)

appar'tarsi /**72**/ VPR to withdraw
appar'tato, -a AG (*luogo*) secluded
apparte'nenza [apparte'nɛntsa] SF: ~ **(a)**
(*gen*) belonging (to); (*a un partito, club*)
membership (of)
apparte'nere /**121**/ VI: ~ **a** to belong to
ap'parvi *etc* VB *vedi* **apparire**
appassio'nante AG thrilling, exciting
appassio'nare /**72**/ VT to thrill; (*commuovere*)
to move; **appassionarsi** VPR: **appassionarsi**
a qc to take a great interest in sth; to be
deeply moved by sth
appassio'nato, -a AG passionate; (*entusiasta*):
~ **(di)** keen (on)
appas'sire /**55**/ VI to wither
appas'sito, -a AG dead
appel'larsi /**72**/ VPR (*ricorrere*): ~ **a** to appeal to;
(*Dir*) ~ **contro** to appeal against
ap'pello SM roll-call; (*implorazione, Dir*) appeal;
(*sessione d'esame*) exam session; **fare ~ a** to
appeal to; **fare l'~** (*Ins*) to call the register *o*
roll; (*Mil*) to call the roll
ap'pena AV (*a stento*) hardly, scarcely;
(*solamente, da poco*) just ▶ CONG as soon as;
(non) ~ furono arrivati ... as soon as they
had arrived ...; **~ ... che** *o* **quando** no sooner
... than; **basta ~ a sfamarli** it's scarcely
enough to feed them; **ho ~ finito** I've just
finished
ap'pendere /**8**/ VT to hang (up)
appendi'abiti SM INV hook, peg; (*mobile*) hall
stand (BRIT), hall tree (US)
appen'dice [appen'ditʃe] SF appendix;
romanzo d'~ popular serial
appendi'cite [appendi'tʃite] SF appendicitis
appen'dino SM (coat) hook
Appen'nini SMPL: **gli ~** the Apennines
appesan'tire /**55**/ VT to make heavy;
appesantirsi VPR to grow stout
ap'peso, -a PP *di* **appendere**
appe'tito SM appetite
appeti'toso, -a AG appetising; (*fig*)
attractive, desirable
appezza'mento [appettsa'mento] SM (*anche*:
appezzamento di terreno) plot, piece of
ground
appia'nare /**72**/ VT to level; (*fig*) to smooth
away, iron out; **appianarsi** VPR (*divergenze*) to
be ironed out
appiat'tire /**55**/ VT to flatten; **appiattirsi** VPR
to become flatter; (*farsi piatto*) to flatten o.s.;
appiattirsi al suolo to lie flat on the ground
appic'care /**20**/ VT: ~ **il fuoco a** to set fire to,
set on fire
appicci'care [appittʃi'kare] /**20**/ VT to stick;
(*fig*): ~ **qc a qn** to palm sth off on sb;
appiccicarsi VPR to stick; (*fig: persona*) to cling
appiccica'ticcio, -a, -ci, -ce
[appittʃika'tittʃo], **appicci'coso, -a**

[appittʃi'koso] AG sticky; (*fig: persona*): **essere**
~ to cling like a leech
appie'dato, -a AG: **rimanere** ~ to be left
without means of transport
appi'eno AV fully
appigli'arsi [appiʎ'ʎarsi] /**27**/ VPR: ~ **a**
(*afferrarsi*) to take hold of; (*fig*) to cling to
ap'piglio [ap'piʎʎo] SM hold; (*fig*) pretext
appiop'pare /**72**/ VT: ~ **qc a qn** (*nomignolo*) to
pin sth on sb; (*compito difficile*) to saddle sb
with sth; **gli ha appioppato un pugno sul**
muso he punched him in the face
appiso'larsi /**72**/ VPR to doze off
applau'dire /**45**/ VT, VI to applaud
ap'plauso SM applause *no pl*
appli'cabile AG: ~ **(a)** applicable (to)
appli'care /**20**/ VT to apply; (*regolamento*) to
enforce; **applicarsi** VPR to apply o.s.
appli'cato, -a AG (*arte, scienze*) applied ▶ SM
(*Amm*) clerk
applica'tore SM applicator
applicazi'one [applikat'tsjone] SF
application; enforcement; ~ **per il cellulare**
mobile app; **applicazioni tecniche** (*Ins*)
practical subjects
appoggi'are [appod'dʒare] /**62**/ VT (*fig:*
sostenere) to support; ~ **qc a qc** (*mettere contro*)
to lean *o* rest sth against sth; **appoggiarsi**
VPR: **appoggiarsi a** to lean against; (*fig*) to
rely upon
ap'poggio [ap'pɔddʒo] SM support
appollai'arsi /**72**/ VPR (*anche fig*) to perch
ap'pongo, ap'poni *etc* VB *vedi* **apporre**
ap'porre /**77**/ VT to affix
appor'tare /**72**/ VT to bring
ap'porto SM (*gen, Finanza*) contribution
ap'posi *etc* VB *vedi* **apporre**
apposita'mente AV (*apposta*) on purpose;
(*specialmente*) specially
ap'posito, -a AG appropriate
ap'posta AV on purpose, deliberately; **neanche**
a farlo ~, ... by sheer coincidence, ...
appos'tarsi /**72**/ VPR to lie in wait
ap'posto, -a PP *di* **apporre**
ap'prendere /**81**/ VT (*imparare*) to learn;
(*comprendere*) to grasp
apprendi'mento SM learning
appren'dista, -i, -e SM/F apprentice
apprendi'stato SM apprenticeship
apprensi'one SF apprehension
appren'sivo, -a AG apprehensive
ap'preso, -a PP *di* **apprendere**
ap'presso AV (*accanto, vicino*) close by, near;
(*dietro*) behind; (*dopo, più tardi*) after, later ▶ AG
INV (*dopo*): **il giorno ~** the next day; ~ **a** prep
(*vicino a*) near, close to
appres'tare /**72**/ VT to prepare, get ready;
apprestarsi VPR: **apprestarsi a fare qc** to
prepare *o* get ready to do sth

ap'pretto SM starch

apprez'zabile [appret'tsabile] AG (*notevole*) noteworthy, significant; (*percepibile*) appreciable

apprezza'mento [apprettsa'mento] SM appreciation; (*giudizio*) opinion; (*commento*) comment

apprez'zare [appret'tsare] /**72**/ VT to appreciate

ap'proccio [ap'prɔttʃo] SM approach

appro'dare /**72**/ VI (*Naut*) to land; (*fig*): **non ~ a nulla** to come to nothing

ap'prodo SM landing; (*luogo*) landing place

approfit'tare /**72**/ VI: **~ di** (*situazione*) to make the most of; (*persona*) to take advantage of; (*occasione, opportunità*) to make the most of, profit by

approfon'dire /**55**/ VT to deepen; (*fig*) to study in depth; **approfondirsi** VPR (*gen, fig*) to deepen; (*peggiorare*) to get worse

appron'tare /**72**/ VT to prepare, get ready

appropri'arsi /**19**/ VPR: **~ di qc** to appropriate sth, take possession of sth; **~ indebitamente di** to embezzle

appropri'ato, -a AG appropriate

appropriazi'one [approprjat'tsjone] SF appropriation; **~ indebita** (*Dir*) embezzlement

approssi'mare /**72**/ VT (*cifra*): **~ per eccesso/ per difetto** to round up/down; **approssimarsi** VPR: **approssimarsi a** to approach, draw near

approssima'tivo, -a AG approximate, rough; (*impreciso*) inexact, imprecise

approssimazi'one [approssimat'tsjone] SF approximation; **per ~** approximately, roughly

appro'vare /**72**/ VT (*condotta, azione*) to approve of; (*candidato*) to pass; (*progetto di legge*) to approve

approvazi'one [approvat'tsjone] SF approval

approvvigiona'mento [approvvidʒona'mento] SM supplying; stocking up; **approvvigionamenti** SMPL (*Mil*) supplies

approvvigio'nare [approvvidʒo'nare] /**72**/ VT to supply; **approvvigionarsi** VPR to lay in provisions, stock up; **~ qn di qc** to supply sb with sth

appunta'mento SM appointment; (*amoroso*) date; **darsi ~** to arrange to meet (one another); **ho un ~ con...** I have an appointment with ...; **vorrei prendere un ~** I'd like to make an appointment

appun'tare /**72**/ VT (*rendere aguzzo*) to sharpen; (*fissare*) to pin, fix; (*annotare*) to note down

appun'tato SM (*Carabinieri*) corporal

appun'tino AV perfectly

appun'tire /**55**/ VT to sharpen

ap'punto SM note; (*rimprovero*) reproach; (*Inform*): **Appunti** Clipboard *sg* ▶ AV (*proprio*) exactly, just; **per l'~!, ~!** exactly!

appu'rare /**72**/ VT to check, verify

apr. ABBR (= *aprile*) Apr.

apribot'tiglie [apribot'tiʎʎe] SM INV bottle opener

a'prile SM April; **pesce d'~!** April Fool!; *vedi anche* **luglio**

a'prire /**9**/ VT to open; (*via, cadavere*) to open up; (*gas, luce, acqua*) to turn on ▶ VI to open; **aprirsi** VPR to open; **~ le ostilità** (*Mil*) to start up o begin hostilities; **~ una sessione** (*Inform*) to log on; **aprirsi a qn** to confide in sb, open one's heart to sb; **mi si è aperto lo stomaco** I feel rather peckish; **apriti cielo!** heaven forbid!

apris'catole SM INV tin (*Brit*) o can opener

APT SIGLA F (= *Azienda di Promozione*) ≈ tourist board

AQ SIGLA = **L'Aquila**

aquagym [akwa'dʒim] SF aquarobics

a'quario SM = **acquario**

'aquila SF (*Zool*) eagle; (*fig*) genius

aqui'lino, -a AG aquiline

aqui'lone SM (*giocattolo*) kite; (*vento*) North wind

AR SIGLA = **Arezzo**

A/R ABBR (= *andata e ritorno: biglietto*) return (ticket) (*Brit*), round-trip ticket (*US*)

ara'besco, -schi SM (*decorazione*) arabesque

A'rabia Sau'dita SF: **l'~** Saudi Arabia

a'rabico, -a, -ci, -che AG: **il Deserto ~** the Arabian Desert

a'rabile AG arable

'arabo, -a AG, SM/F Arab ▶ SM (*Ling*) Arabic; **parlare ~** (*fig*) to speak double Dutch (*Brit*)

a'rachide [a'rakide] SF peanut

ara'gosta SF crayfish; spiny lobster

a'raldica SF heraldry

a'raldo SM herald

aran'ceto [aran'tʃeto] SM orange grove

a'rancia, -ce [a'rantʃa] SF orange

aranci'ata [aran'tʃata] SF orangeade

a'rancio [a'rantʃo] SM (*Bot*) orange tree; (*colore*) orange ▶ AG INV (*colore*) orange; **fiori di ~** orange blossom *sg*

aranci'one [aran'tʃone] AG INV: **(color) ~** bright orange

a'rare /**72**/ VT to plough (*Brit*), plow (*US*)

ara'tore SM ploughman (*Brit*), plowman (*US*)

a'ratro SM plough (*Brit*), plow (*US*)

ara'tura SF ploughing (*Brit*), plowing (*US*)

a'razzo [a'rattso] SM tapestry

arbi'traggio [arbi'traddʒo] SM (*Sport*) refereeing; umpiring; (*Dir*) arbitration; (*Comm*) arbitrage

arbi'trare /**72**/ VT (*Sport*) to referee; to umpire; (*Dir*) to arbitrate

arbi'trario, -a AG arbitrary

arbi'trato SM arbitration

ar'bitrio SM will; *(abuso, sopruso)* arbitrary act

'arbitro SM arbiter, judge; *(Dir)* arbitrator; *(Sport)* referee; *(: Tennis, Cricket)* umpire

ar'busto SM shrub

'arca, -che SF *(sarcofago)* sarcophagus; **l'~ di Noè** Noah's ark

ar'caico, -a, -ci, -che AG archaic

arca'ismo SM *(Ling)* archaism

ar'cangelo [ar'kandʒelo] SM archangel

ar'cano, -a AG arcane, mysterious ▶ SM mystery

ar'cata SF *(Archit, Anat)* arch; *(ordine di archi)* arcade

archeolo'gia [arkeolo'dʒia] SF arch(a)eology

archeo'logico, -a, -ci, -che [arkeo'lɔdʒiko] AG arch(a)eological

arche'ologo, -a, -gi, -ghe [arke'ɔlogo] SM/F arch(a)eologist

ar'chetipo [ar'kɛtipo] SM archetype

ar'chetto [ar'ketto] SM *(Mus)* bow

architet'tare [arkitet'tare] /**72**/ VT *(fig: ideare)* to devise; *(: macchinare)* to plan, concoct

archi'tetto [arki'tetto] SM architect

architet'tonico, -a, -ci, -che [arkitet'tɔniko] AG architectural

architet'tura [arkitet'tura] SF architecture

archivi'are [arki'vjare] /**19**/ VT *(documenti)* to file; *(Dir)* to dismiss

archiviazi'one [arkivjat'tsjone] SF filing; dismissal

ar'chivio [ar'kivjo] SM archives *pl*; *(Inform)* file; **~ principale** *(Inform)* master file

archi'vista, -i, -e [arki'vista] SM/F *(Amm)* archivist; *(in ufficio)* filing clerk

'ARCI ['artʃi] SIGLA F *(= Associazione Ricreativa Culturale Italiana)* cultural society

arci'duca, -chi [artʃi'duka] SM archduke

arci'ere [ar'tʃere] SM archer

ar'cigno, -a [ar'tʃiɲɲo] AG grim, severe

arci'pelago, -ghi [artʃi'pɛlago] SM archipelago

arci'vescovo [artʃi'veskovo] SM archbishop

'arco, -chi SM *(arma, Mus)* bow; *(Archit)* arch; *(Mat)* arc; **nell'~ di 3 settimane** within the space of 3 weeks; **~ costituzionale** *political parties involved in formulating Italy's post-war constitution*

arcoba'leno SM rainbow

arcu'ato, -a AG curved, bent; **dalle gambe arcuate** bow-legged

ar'dente AG burning; *(fig)* burning, ardent

'ardere /**10**/ VT, VI to burn; **legna da ~** firewood

ar'desia SF slate

ardi'mento SM daring

ar'dire /**55**/ VI to dare ▶ SM daring

ar'dito, -a AG brave, daring, bold; *(sfacciato)* bold

ar'dore SM blazing heat; *(fig)* ardour, fervour

'arduo, -a AG arduous, difficult

'area SF area; *(Edil)* land, ground; **nell'~ dei partiti di sinistra** among the parties of the left; **~ fabbricabile** building land; **~ di rigore** *(Sport)* penalty area; **~ di servizio** *(Aut)* service area

a'rena SF arena; *(per corride)* bullring; *(sabbia)* sand

are'naria SF sandstone

are'narsi /**72**/ VPR to run aground; *(fig: trattative)* to come to a standstill

areo'plano SM = **aeroplano**

are'tino, -a AG of *(o* from) Arezzo

'argano SM winch

argen'tato, -a [ardʒen'tato] AG silver-plated; *(colore)* silver, silvery; *(capelli)* silver(-grey)

ar'genteo, -a [ar'dʒɛnteo] AG silver, silvery

argente'ria [ardʒente'ria] SF silverware, silver

Argen'tina [ardʒen'tina] SF: **l'~** Argentina

argen'tino, -a [ardʒen'tino] AG, SM/F *(dell'Argentina)* Argentinian ▶ SF crewneck sweater

ar'gento [ar'dʒɛnto] SM silver; **~ vivo** quicksilver; **avere l'~ (vivo) addosso** *(fig)* to be fidgety

ar'gilla [ar'dʒilla] SF clay

argil'loso, -a [ardʒil'loso] AG *(contenente argilla)* clayey; *(simile ad argilla)* clay-like

argi'nare [ardʒi'nare] /**72**/ VT *(fiume, acque)* to embank; *(: con diga)* to dyke up; *(fig: inflazione, corruzione)* to check; *(: spese)* to limit

'argine ['ardʒine] SM embankment, bank; *(diga)* dyke, dike; **far ~ a, porre un ~ a** *(fig)* to check, hold back

argomen'tare /**72**/ VI to argue

argo'mento SM argument; *(motivo)* motive; *(materia, tema)* subject; **tornare sull'~** to bring the matter up again

argu'ire /**55**/ VT to deduce

ar'guto, -a AG sharp, quick-witted; *(spiritoso)* witty

ar'guzia [ar'guttsja] SF wit; *(battuta)* witty remark

'aria SF air; *(espressione, aspetto)* air, look; *(Mus: melodia)* tune; *(: di opera)* aria; **all'~ aperta** in the open (air); **manca l'~** it's stuffy; **andare all'~** *(piano, progetto)* to come to nothing; **mandare all'~ qc** to ruin *o* upset sth; **darsi delle arie** to put on airs and graces; **ha la testa per ~** his head is in the clouds; **che ~ tira?** *(fig: atmosfera)* what's the atmosphere like?

aridità SF aridity, dryness; *(fig)* lack of feeling

'arido, -a AG arid

arieggi'are [arjed'dʒare] /**62**/ VT *(cambiare aria)*

to air; (*imitare*) to imitate

ari'ete sm ram; (*Mil*) battering ram; **A~** Aries; **essere dell'A~** to be Aries

a'ringa, -ghe sf herring *inv*; **~ affumicata** smoked herring, kipper; **~ marinata** pickled herring

ari'oso, -a AG (*ambiente, stanza*) airy; (*Mus*) ariose

'arista sf (*Cuc*) chine of pork

aristo'cratico, -a, -ci, -che AG aristocratic

aristocra'zia [aristokrat'tsia] sf aristocracy

arit'metica sf arithmetic

arit'metico, -a, -ci, -che AG arithmetical

arlec'chino [arlek'kino] sm harlequin

'arma, -i sf weapon, arm; (*parte dell'esercito*) arm; **alle armi!** to arms!; **chiamare alle armi** to call up (*Brit*), draft (*US*); **sotto le armi** in the army (*o* forces); **combattere ad armi pari** (*anche fig*) to fight on equal terms; **essere alle prime armi** (*fig*) to be a novice; **passare qn per le armi** to execute sb; **~ a doppio taglio** (*anche fig*) double-edged weapon; **~ atomica/nucleare** atomic/ nuclear weapon; **~ da fuoco** firearm; **armi convenzionali/non convenzionali** conventional/unconventional weapons; **armi di distruzione di massa** weapons of mass destruction

arma'dietto sm (*di medicinali*) medicine cabinet; (*in palestra ecc*) locker; (*in cucina*) (kitchen) cupboard

ar'madio sm cupboard; (*per abiti*) wardrobe; **~ a muro** built-in cupboard

armamen'tario sm equipment, instruments *pl*

arma'mento sm (*Mil*) armament; (: *materiale*) arms *pl*, weapons *pl*; (*Naut*) fitting out; manning; **la corsa agli armamenti** the arms race

ar'mare /72/ vt to arm; (*arma da fuoco*) to cock; (*Naut: nave*) to rig, fit out; to man; (*Edil: volta, galleria*) to prop up, shore up; **armarsi** vpr to arm o.s.; (*Mil*) to take up arms

ar'mato, -a AG: **~ (di)** (*anche fig*) armed (with) ▶ sf (*Mil*) army; (*Naut*) fleet; **rapina a mano armata** armed robbery

arma'tore sm shipowner

arma'tura sf (*struttura di sostegno*) framework; (*impalcatura*) scaffolding; (*Storia*) armour *no pl* (*Brit*), armor *no pl* (*US*), suit of armour

armeggi'are [armed'dʒare] /62/ vi (*affaccendarsi*): **~ (intorno a qc)** to mess about (with sth)

ar'meno, -a AG, sm/f Armenian

arme'ria sf (*deposito*) armoury (*Brit*), armory (*US*); (*collezione*) collection of arms

armis'tizio [armis'tittsjo] sm armistice

armo'nia sf harmony

ar'monico, -a, -ci, -che AG harmonic;

(*fig*) harmonious ▶ sf (*Mus*) harmonica; **armonica a bocca** mouth organ

armoni'oso, -a AG harmonious

armoniz'zare [armonid'dzare] /72/ vt to harmonize; (*colori, abiti*) to match ▶ vi to be in harmony; to match

ar'nese sm tool, implement; (*oggetto indeterminato*) thing, contraption; **male in ~** (*malvestito*) badly dressed; (*di salute malferma*) in poor health; (*di condizioni economiche*) down-at-heel

'arnia sf hive

a'roma, -i sm aroma; fragrance; **aromi** smpl (*Cuc*) herbs and spices; **aromi naturali/ artificiali** natural/artificial flavouring *sg* (*Brit*) *o* flavoring *sg* (*US*)

aromatera'pia sf aromatherapy

aro'matico, -a, -ci, -che AG aromatic; (*cibo*) spicy

aromatiz'zare [aromatid'dzare] /72/ vt to season, flavour (*Brit*), flavor (*US*)

'arpa sf (*Mus*) harp

ar'peggio [ar'peddʒo] sm (*Mus*) arpeggio

ar'pia sf (*anche fig*) harpy

arpi'one sm (*gancio*) hook; (*cardine*) hinge; (*Pesca*) harpoon

arrabat'tarsi /72/ vpr to do all one can, strive

arrabbi'are /19/ vi (*cane*) to be affected with rabies; **arrabbiarsi** vpr (*essere preso dall'ira*) to get angry, fly into a rage

arrabbi'ato, -a AG (*cane*) rabid, with rabies; (*persona*) furious, angry

arrabbia'tura sf: **prendersi un'~ (per qc)** to become furious (over sth)

arraf'fare /72/ vt to snatch, seize; (*sottrarre*) to pinch

arrampi'carsi /20/ vpr to climb (up); **~ sui vetri** *o* **sugli specchi** (*fig*) to clutch at straws

arrampi'cata sf climb

arrampica'tore, -'trice sm/f (*gen, Sport*) climber; **~ sociale** (*fig*) social climber

arran'care /20/ vi to limp, hobble; (*fig*) to struggle along

arrangia'mento [arrandʒa'mento] sm (*Mus*) arrangement

arran'giare [arran'dʒare] /62/ vt to arrange; **arrangiarsi** vpr to manage, do the best one can

arre'care /20/ vt to bring; (*causare*) to cause

arreda'mento sm (*studio*) interior design; (*mobili ecc*) furnishings *pl*

arre'dare /72/ vt to furnish

arreda'tore, -'trice sm/f interior designer

ar'redo sm fittings *pl*, furnishings *pl*; **~ per uffici** office furnishings

arrem'baggio [arrem'baddʒo] sm (*Naut*) boarding

ar'rendersi /88/ vpr to surrender; **~ all'evidenza (dei fatti)** to face (the) facts

arren'devole AG (*persona*) yielding, compliant
arrendevo'lezza [arrendevo'lettsa] SF compliancy
ar'reso, -a PP *di* **arrendersi**
arres'tare /**72**/ VT (*fermare*) to stop, halt; (*catturare*) to arrest; **arrestarsi** VPR (*fermarsi*) to stop
arres'tato, -a SM/F person under arrest
ar'resto SM (*cessazione*) stopping; (*fermata*) stop; (*cattura, Med*) arrest; (*Comm: in produzione*) stoppage; **subire un ~** to come to a stop *o* standstill; **mettere agli arresti** to place under arrest; **arresti domiciliari** (*Dir*) house arrest *sg*
arre'trare /**72**/ VT, VI to withdraw
arre'trato, -a AG (*paese, bambino*) backward; (*numero di giornale*) back *cpd*; **arretrati** SMPL arrears; **gli arretrati dello stipendio** back pay *sg*
arricchi'mento [arrikki'mento] SM enrichment
arric'chire [arrik'kire] /**55**/ VT to enrich; **arricchirsi** VPR to become rich
arric'chito, -a [arrik'kito] SM/F nouveau riche
arricci'are [arrit'tʃare] /**14**/ VT to curl; **~ il naso** to turn up one's nose
ar'ridere /**89**/ VI: **~ a qn** (*fortuna, successo*) to smile on sb
ar'ringa, -ghe SF harangue; (*Dir*) address by counsel
arrischi'are [arris'kjare] /**19**/ VT to risk; **arrischiarsi** VPR to venture, dare
arrischi'ato, -a [arris'kjato] AG risky; (*temerario*) reckless, rash
ar'riso, -a PP *di* **arridere**
arri'vare /**72**/ VI to arrive; (*avvicinarsi*) to come; (*accadere*) to happen, occur; **~ a** (*livello, grado ecc*) to reach; **lui arriva a Roma alle 7** he gets to *o* arrives at Rome at 7; **~ a fare qc** to manage to do sth, succeed in doing sth; **non ci arrivo** I can't reach it; (*fig: non capisco*) I can't understand it
arri'vato, -a AG (*persona: di successo*) successful ▶ SM/F: **essere un ~** to have made it; **nuovo ~** newcomer; **ben ~!** welcome!; **non sono l'ultimo ~!** (*fig*) I'm no fool!
arrive'derci [arrive'dertʃi] ESCL goodbye!
arrive'derla ESCL (*forma di cortesia*) goodbye!
arri'vismo SM (*ambizione*) ambitiousness; (*sociale*) social climbing
arri'vista, -i, -e SM/F go-getter
ar'rivo SM arrival; (*Sport*) finish, finishing line
arro'gante AG arrogant
arro'ganza [arro'gantsa] SF arrogance
arro'gare /**80**/ VT: **arrogarsi il diritto di fare qc** to assume the right to do sth; **arrogarsi il merito di qc** to claim credit for sth

arrossa'mento SM reddening
arros'sare /**72**/ VT (*occhi, pelle*) to redden, make red; **arrossarsi** VPR to become red
arros'sire /**55**/ VI (*per vergogna, timidezza*) to blush; (*per gioia*) to flush, blush
arros'tire /**55**/ VT to roast; (*pane*) to toast; (*ai ferri*) to grill
ar'rosto SM, AG INV roast; **~ di manzo** roast beef
arro'tare /**72**/ VT to sharpen; (*investire con un veicolo*) to run over
arro'tino SM knife-grinder
arroto'lare /**72**/ VT to roll up
arroton'dare /**72**/ VT (*forma, oggetto*) to round; (*stipendio*) to add to; (*somma*) to round off
arrovel'larsi /**72**/ VPR (*anche*: **arrovellarsi il cervello**) to rack one's brains
arroven'tato, -a AG red-hot
arruf'fare /**72**/ VT to ruffle; (*fili*) to tangle; (*fig: questione*) to confuse
arruggi'nire [arruddʒi'nire] /**55**/ VT to rust; **arrugginirsi** VPR to rust; (*fig*) to become rusty
arruggi'nito, -a [arruddʒin'nito] AG rusty
arruola'mento SM (*Mil*) enlistment
arruo'lare /**72**/ VT (*Mil*) to enlist; **arruolarsi** VPR to enlist, join up
arse'nale SM (*Mil*) arsenal; (*cantiere navale*) dockyard
ar'senico SM arsenic
'arsi VB *vedi* **ardere**
'arso, -a PP *di* **ardere** ▶ AG (*bruciato*) burnt; (*arido*) dry
ar'sura SF (*calore opprimente*) burning heat; (*siccità*) drought
art. ABBR (= *articolo*) art.
'arte SF art; (*abilità*) skill; **a regola d'~** (*fig*) perfectly; **senz'~ né parte** penniless and out of a job; **arti figurative** visual arts
arte'fatto, -a AG (*stile, modi*) affected; (*cibo*) adulterated
ar'tefice [ar'tefitʃe] SMF craftsman(-woman); (*autore*) author
ar'teria SF artery; **~ stradale** main road
arterioscle'rosi SF arteriosclerosis, hardening of the arteries
arteri'oso, -a AG arterial
'artico, -a, -ci, -che AG Arctic ▶ SM: **l'A~** the Arctic; **il Circolo polare ~** the Arctic Circle; **l'Oceano ~** the Arctic Ocean
artico'lare /**72**/ AG (*Anat*) of the joints, articular ▶ VT to articulate; (*suddividere*) to divide, split up; **articolarsi** VPR: **articolarsi in** (*discorso, progetto*) to be divided into
artico'lato, -a AG (*linguaggio*) articulate; (*Aut*) articulated
articolazi'one [artikolat'tsjone] SF (*Anat, Tecn*) joint; (*di voce, concetto*) articulation
ar'ticolo SM article; **~ di fondo** (*Stampa*) leader, leading article; **articoli di marca**

branded goods; **un bell'~** (*fig*) a real character

'Artide SM: **l'~** the Arctic

artifici'ale [artifi'tʃale] AG artificial

artifici'ere [artifi'tʃɛre] SM (*Mil*) artificer; (: *per disinnescare bombe*) bomb-disposal expert

arti'ficio [arti'fitʃo] SM (*espediente*) trick, artifice; (*ricerca di effetto*) artificiality

artifici'oso, -a [artifi'tʃoso] AG cunning; (*non spontaneo*) affected

artigia'nale [artidʒa'nale] AG craft *cpd*

artigia'nato [artidʒa'nato] SM craftsmanship; craftsmen *pl*

artigi'ano, -a [arti'dʒano] SM/F craftsman(-woman)

artigli'ere [artiʎ'ʎɛre] SM artilleryman

artiglie'ria [artiʎʎe'ria] SF artillery

ar'tiglio [ar'tiʎʎo] SM claw; (*di rapaci*) talon; **sfoderare gli artigli** (*fig*) to show one's claws

ar'tista, -i, -e SM/F artist; **un lavoro da ~** (*fig*) a professional piece of work

ar'tistico, -a, -ci, -che AG artistic

'arto SM (*Anat*) limb

ar'trite SF (*Med*) arthritis

ar'trosi SF osteoarthritis

arzigogo'lato, -a [ardzigogo'lato] AG tortuous

ar'zillo, -a [ar'dzillo] AG lively, sprightly

a'scella [aʃ'ʃella] SF (*Anat*) armpit

ascen'dente [aʃʃen'dɛnte] SM ancestor; (*fig*) ascendancy; (*Astr*) ascendant

a'scendere [aʃ'ʃendere] /**101**/ VI: **~ al trono** to ascend the throne

ascensi'one [aʃʃen'sjone] SF (*Alpinismo*) ascent; (*Rel*): **l'A~** the Ascension; **isola dell'A~** Ascension Island

ascen'sore [aʃʃen'sore] SM lift

a'scesa [aʃ'ʃesa] SF ascent; (*al trono*) accession; (*al potere*) rise

a'scesi [aʃ'ʃezi] SF asceticism

a'sceso, -a [aʃ'ʃeso] PP *di* **ascendere**

a'scesso [aʃ'ʃɛsso] SM (*Med*) abscess

a'sceta, -i [aʃ'ʃeta] SM ascetic

'ascia ['aʃʃa] (*pl* **asce**) SF axe

asciugaca'pelli [aʃʃugaka'pelli] SM INV hair dryer

asciuga'mano [aʃʃuga'mano] SM towel

asciu'gare [aʃʃu'gare] /**80**/ VT to dry; **asciugarsi** VPR to dry o.s.; (*diventare asciutto*) to dry

asciuga'trice [aʃʃuga'tritʃe] SF spin-dryer

asciut'tezza [aʃʃut'tettsa] SF dryness; leanness; curtness

asci'utto, -a [aʃ'ʃutto] AG dry; (*fig: magro*) lean; (: *burbero*) curt ▶ SM: **restare all'~** (*fig*) to be left penniless; **restare a bocca asciutta** (*fig*) to be disappointed

asco'lano, -a AG of (*o* from) Ascoli

ascol'tare /**72**/ VT to listen to; **~ il consiglio di qn** to listen to *o* heed sb's advice

ascolta'tore, -'trice SM/F listener

as'colto SM: **essere** *o* **stare in ~** to be listening; **dare** *o* **prestare ~ (a)** to pay attention (to); **indice di ~** (*TV*, *Radio*) audience rating

AS. COM. SIGLA F = **Associazione Commercianti**

as'critto, -a PP *di* **ascrivere**

as'crivere /**105**/ VT (*attribuire*): **~ qc a qn** to attribute sth to sb; **~ qc a merito di qn** to give sb credit for sth

a'settico, -a, -ci, -che AG aseptic

asfal'tare /**72**/ VT to asphalt

as'falto SM asphalt

asfis'sia SF asphyxia, asphyxiation

asfissi'ante AG (*gas*) asphyxiating; (*fig: calore, ambiente*) stifling, suffocating; (: *persona*) tiresome

asfissi'are /**19**/ VT to asphyxiate, suffocate; (*fig: opprimere*) to stifle; (: *infastidire*) to get on sb's nerves ▶ VI to suffocate, asphyxiate

'Asia SF: **l'~** Asia

asi'atico, -a, -ci, -che AG, SM/F Asiatic, Asian

a'silo SM refuge, sanctuary; **~ (d'infanzia)** nursery(-school); **~ nido** day nursery, crèche (*for children aged 0 to 3*); **~ politico** political asylum

asim'metrico, -a, -ci, -che AG asymmetric(al)

'asino SM donkey, ass; **la bellezza dell'~** (*fig: di ragazza*) the beauty of youth; **qui casca l'~!** there's the rub!

ASL [azl] SIGLA F (= *Azienda Sanitaria Locale*) local health centre

'asma SF asthma

as'matico, -a, -ci, -che AG, SM/F asthmatic

asoci'ale [aso'tʃale] AG antisocial

'asola SF buttonhole

as'parago, -gi SM asparagus *no pl*

as'pergere [as'pɛrdʒere] /**59**/ VT: **~ (di** *o* **con)** to sprinkle (with)

asperità SF INV roughness *no pl*; (*fig*) harshness *no pl*

as'persi *etc* VB *vedi* **aspergere**

as'perso, -a PP *di* **aspergere**

aspet'tare /**72**/ VT to wait for; (*anche Comm*) to await; (*aspettarsi*) to expect; (*essere in serbo: notizia, evento ecc*) to be in store for, lie ahead of ▶ VI to wait; **aspettarsi qc** to expect sth; **~ un bambino** to be expecting (a baby); **questo non me l'aspettavo** I wasn't expecting this; **me l'aspettavo!** I thought as much!

aspetta'tiva SF expectation; **inferiore all'~** worse than expected; **essere/mettersi in ~** (*Amm*) to be on/take leave of absence

as'petto SM (*apparenza*) aspect, appearance,

look; (*punto di vista*) point of view; **di bell'~** good-looking

aspi'rante AG (*attore ecc*) aspiring ▶ SMF candidate, applicant

aspira'polvere SM INV vacuum cleaner

aspi'rare /72/ VT (*respirare*) to breathe in, inhale; (*apparecchi*) to suck (up) ▶ VI: **~ a** to aspire to

aspira'tore SM extractor fan

aspirazi'one [aspirat'tsjone] SF (*Tecn*) suction; (*anelito*) aspiration

aspi'rina SF aspirin

aspor'tare /72/ VT (*anche Med*) to remove, take away

as'prezza [as'prettsa] SF sourness, tartness; pungency; harshness; roughness; rugged nature

'aspro, -a AG (*sapore*) sour, tart; (*odore*) acrid, pungent; (*voce, clima, fig*) harsh; (*superficie*) rough; (*paesaggio*) rugged

Ass. ABBR = **assicurazione**; **assicurato**; **assegno**

assaggi'are [assad'dʒare] /62/ VT to taste

assag'gini [assad'dʒini] SMPL (*Cuc*) selection of first courses

as'saggio [as'saddʒo] SM tasting; (*piccola quantità*) taste; (*campione*) sample

as'sai AV (*molto*) a lot, much; (: *con ag*) very; (*a sufficienza*) enough ▶ AG INV (*quantità*) a lot of, much; (*numero*) a lot of, many; **~ contento** very pleased

as'salgo etc VB vedi **assalire**

assa'lire /98/ VT to attack, assail

assali'tore, -'trice SM/F attacker, assailant

assal'tare /72/ VT (*Mil*) to storm; (*banca*) to raid; (*treno, diligenza*) to hold up

as'salto SM attack, assault; **prendere d'~** (*fig: negozio, treno*) to storm; (: *personalità*) to besiege; **d'~** (*editoria, giornalista ecc*) aggressive

assapo'rare /72/ VT to savour (*BRIT*), savor (*US*)

assassi'nare /72/ VT to murder; (*Pol*) to assassinate; (*fig*) to ruin

assas'sinio SM murder; assassination

assas'sino, -a AG murderous ▶ SM/F murderer; assassin

'asse SM (*Tecn*) axle; (*Mat*) axis ▶ SF board; **~ da stiro** ironing board

assecon'dare /72/ VT: **~ qn (in qc)** to go along with sb (in sth); **~ i desideri di qn** to go along with sb's wishes; **~ i capricci di qn** to give in to sb's whims

assedi'are /19/ VT to besiege

as'sedio SM siege

asse'gnare [asseɲ'ɲare] /15/ VT to assign, allot; (*premio*) to award

assegna'tario [asseɲɲa'tarjo] SM (*Dir*) assignee; (*Comm*) recipient; **l'~ del premio** the person awarded the prize

assegnazi'one [asseɲɲat'tsjone] SF (*di casa, somma*) allocation; (*di carica*) assignment; (*di premio, borsa di studio*) awarding

as'segno [as'seɲɲo] SM allowance; (*anche:* **assegno bancario**) cheque (*BRIT*), check (*US*); **contro ~** cash on delivery; **~ circolare** bank draft; **~ di malattia** *o* **di invalidità** sick pay/ disability benefit; **~ post-datato** post-dated cheque; **~ sbarrato** crossed cheque; **~ non sbarrato** uncrossed cheque; **~ di studio** study grant; **"~ non trasferibile"** "account payee only"; **~ di viaggio** travel(l)er's cheque; **~ a vuoto** dud cheque; **assegni alimentari** alimony *sg*; **assegni familiari** ≈ child benefit *sg*

assem'blaggio [assem'bladdʒo] SM (*Industria*) assembly

assem'blare /72/ VT to assemble

assem'blea SF assembly; (*raduno, adunanza*) meeting

assembra'mento SM public gathering; **divieto di ~** ban on public meetings

assen'nato, -a AG sensible

as'senso SM assent, consent

assen'tarsi /72/ VPR to go out

as'sente AG absent; (*fig*) faraway, vacant ▶ SMF absentee

assente'ismo SM absenteeism

assente'ista, -i, -e SM/F (*dal lavoro*) absentee

assen'tire /45/ VI: **~ (a)** to agree (to), assent (to)

as'senza [as'sɛntsa] SF absence

asse'rire /55/ VT to maintain, assert

asserragli'arsi [asserraʎ'ʎarsi] /27/ VPR: **~ (in)** to barricade o.s. (in)

asser'vire /55/ VT to enslave; (*fig: animo, passioni*) to subdue; **asservirsi** VPR: **asservirsi (a)** to submit (to)

asserzi'one [asser'tsjone] SF assertion

assesso'rato SM councillorship

asses'sore SM councillor

assesta'mento SM (*sistemazione*) arrangement; (*Edil, Geo*) settlement

asses'tare /72/ VT (*mettere in ordine*) to put in order, arrange; **assestarsi** VPR to settle in; (*Geo*) to settle; **~ un colpo a qn** to deal sb a blow

asse'tato, -a AG thirsty, parched

as'setto SM order, arrangement; (*Naut, Aer*) trim; **in ~ di guerra** on a war footing; **~ territoriale** country planning

assicu'rare /72/ VT (*accertare*) to ensure; (*infondere certezza*) to assure; (*fermare, legare*) to make fast, secure; (*fare un contratto di assicurazione*) to insure; **assicurarsi** VPR: **assicurarsi (di)** (*accertarsi*) to make sure (of); **assicurarsi (contro)** (*il furto ecc*) to insure o.s. (against)

assicu'rato, -a AG insured ▶ SF (*anche:* **lettera assicurata**) registered letter

assicura'tore, -'trice AG insurance *cpd*
▶ SM/F insurance agent; **società
assicuratrice** insurance company
assicurazi'one [assikurat'tsjone] SF
assurance; insurance; ~ **multi-rischio**
comprehensive insurance
assidera'mento SM exposure
asside'rare /**72**/ VT to freeze; **assiderarsi** VPR
to freeze; **morire assiderato** to die of
exposure
as'siduo, -a AG (*costante*) assiduous; (*regolare*)
regular
assi'eme AV (*insieme*) together ▶ PREP: ~ **a**
(together) with
assil'lante AG (*dubbio, pensiero*) nagging;
(*creditore*) pestering
assil'lare /**72**/ VT to pester, torment
as'sillo SM (*fig*) worrying thought
assimi'lare /**72**/ VT to assimilate
assimilazi'one [assimilat'tsjone] SF
assimilation
assi'oma, -i SM axiom
assio'matico, -a, -ci, -che AG axiomatic
as'sise SFPL (*Dir*) assizes (*BRIT*); **corte d'~**
court of assizes, ≈ crown court (*BRIT*); *vedi
anche* **corte**
assis'tente SMF assistant; ~ **sociale** social
worker; ~ **universitario** (assistant) lecturer;
~ **di volo** (*Aer*) steward (stewardess)
assis'tenza [assis'tɛntsa] SF assistance;
~ **legale** legal aid; ~ **ospedaliera** free
hospital treatment; ~ **sanitaria** health
service; ~ **sociale** welfare services *pl*
assistenzi'ale [assisten'tsjale] AG (*ente,
organizzazione*) welfare *cpd*; (*opera*) charitable
assistenzia'lismo [assistentsja'lizmo] SM
(*peg*) excessive state aid
as'sistere /**11**/ VT (*aiutare*) to assist, help;
(*curare*) to treat ▶ VI: ~ **a qc** (*essere presente*) to
be present (at sth), attend (sth)
assis'tito, -a PP *di* **assistere**
'asso SM ace; **piantare qn in ~** to leave sb in
the lurch
associ'are [asso'tʃare] /**14**/ VT to associate;
(*rendere partecipe*): ~ **qn a** (*affari*) to take sb into
partnership in; (*partito*) to make sb a member
of; **associarsi** VPR to enter into partnership;
associarsi a to become a member of, join;
(*dolori, gioie*) to share in; ~ **qn alle carceri** to
take sb to prison
associazi'one [assotʃat'tsjone] SF
association; (*Comm*) association, society;
~ **di categoria** trade association; ~ **a** o **per
delinquere** (*Dir*) criminal association; **A~
Europea di Libero Scambio** European Free
Trade Association, EFTA; ~ **in
partecipazione** (*Comm*) joint venture
asso'dare /**72**/ VT (*muro, posizione*) to
strengthen; (*fatti, verità*) to ascertain

asso'dato, -a AG well-founded
assogget'tare [assoddʒet'tare] /**72**/ VT to
subject, subjugate; **assoggettarsi** VPR:
assoggettarsi a to submit to
asso'lato, -a AG sunny
assol'dare /**72**/ VT to recruit
as'solsi *etc* VB *vedi* **assolvere**
as'solto, -a PP *di* **assolvere**
assoluta'mente AV absolutely
asso'luto, -a AG absolute
assoluzi'one [assolut'tsjone] SF (*Dir*)
acquittal; (*Rel*) absolution
as'solvere /**94**/ VT (*Dir*) to acquit; (*Rel*) to
absolve; (*adempiere*) to carry out, perform
assomigli'are [assomiʎ'ʎare] /**27**/ VI: ~ **a** to
resemble, look like; **assomigliarsi** VPR to
look alike; (*nel carattere*) to be alike
asson'nato, -a AG sleepy
asso'pirsi /**55**/ VPR to doze off
assor'bente AG absorbent ▶ SM: ~ **igienico/
esterno** sanitary towel; ~ **interno** tampon
assor'bire /**17**/ VT to absorb; (*fig: far proprio*) to
assimilate
assor'dante AG (*rumore, musica*) deafening
assor'dare /**72**/ VT to deafen
assorti'mento SM assortment
assor'tire /**55**/ VT (*disporre*) to arrange
assor'tito, -a AG assorted; (*colori*) matched,
matching
as'sorto, -a AG absorbed, engrossed
assottigli'are [assottiʎ'ʎare] /**27**/ VT to make
thin, thin; (*aguzzare*) to sharpen; (*ridurre*) to
reduce; **assottigliarsi** VPR to grow thin; (*fig:
ridursi*) to be reduced
assue'fare /**41**/ VT to accustom; **assuefarsi**
VPR: **assuefarsi a** to get used to, accustom
o.s. to
assue'fatto, -a PP *di* **assuefare**
assuefazi'one [assuefat'tsjone] SF (*Med*)
addiction
as'sumere /**12**/ VT (*impiegato*) to take on,
engage; (*responsabilità*) to assume, take upon
o.s.; (*contegno, espressione*) to assume, put on;
(*droga*) to consume
as'sunsi *etc* VB *vedi* **assumere**
as'sunto, -a PP *di* **assumere** ▶ SM (*tesi*)
proposition
assunzi'one [assun'tsjone] SF (*di impiegati*)
employment, engagement; (*Rel*): **l'A~** the
Assumption
assurdità SF INV absurdity; **dire delle ~** to
talk nonsense
as'surdo, -a AG absurd
'asta SF pole; (*modo di vendita*) auction
as'tante SM bystander
astante'ria SF casualty department
as'temio, -a AG teetotal ▶ SM/F teetotaller
aste'nersi /**121**/ VPR: ~ **(da)** to abstain (from),
refrain (from); (*Pol*) to abstain (from)

astensi'one SF abstention

astensio'nista, -i, -e SM/F (Pol) abstentionist

aste'risco, -schi SM asterisk

aste'roide SM asteroid

'astice ['astitʃe] SM lobster

astigi'ano, -a [asti'dʒano] AG of (o from) Asti

astig'matico, -a, -ci, -che AG astigmatic

asti'nenza [asti'nɛntsa] SF abstinence;
essere in crisi di ~ to suffer from withdrawal symptoms

'astio SM rancour, resentment

asti'oso, -a AG resentful

astrat'tismo SM (Arte) abstract art

as'tratto, -a AG abstract

astrin'gente [astrin'dʒɛnte] AG, SM astringent

'astro SM star

'astro PREFISSO astro

astrolo'gia [astrolo'dʒia] SF astrology

astro'logico, -a, -ci, -che [astro'lɔdʒiko] AG astrological

as'trologo, -a, -ghi, -ghe SM/F astrologer

astro'nauta, -i, -e SM/F astronaut

astro'nautica SF astronautics sg

astro'nave SF space ship

astrono'mia SF astronomy

astro'nomico, -a, -ci, -che AG astronomic(al)

as'tronomo SM astronomer

as'truso, -a AG (discorso, ragionamento) abstruse

as'tuccio [as'tuttʃo] SM case, box, holder

as'tuto, -a AG astute, cunning, shrewd

as'tuzia [as'tuttsja] SF astuteness, shrewdness; (azione) trick

AT SIGLA = **Asti**

ATA SIGLA F = **Associazione Turistica Albergatori**

a'tavico, -a, -ci, -che AG atavistic

ate'ismo SM atheism

atelier [atə'lje] SM INV (laboratorio) workshop; (studio) studio; (sartoria) fashion house

A'tene SF Athens

ate'neo SM university

ateni'ese AG, SMF Athenian

'ateo, -a AG, SM/F atheist

a'tipico, -a, -ci, -che AG atypical

at'lante SM atlas; **i Monti dell'A~** the Atlas Mountains

at'lantico, -a, -ci, -che AG Atlantic ▶ SM:
l'A~, l'Oceano A~ the Atlantic, the Atlantic Ocean

at'leta, -i, -e SM/F athlete

at'letica SF athletics sg; **~ leggera** track and field events pl; **~ pesante** weightlifting and wrestling

atmos'fera SF atmosphere

atmos'ferico, -a, -ci, -che AG atmospheric

a'tollo SM atoll

a'tomico, -a, -ci, -che AG atomic;
(nucleare) atomic, atom cpd, nuclear

atomizza'tore [atomiddza'tore] SM (di acqua, lacca) spray; (di profumo) atomizer

'atomo SM atom

'atono, -a AG (Fonetica) unstressed

'atrio SM entrance hall, lobby

a'troce [a'trotʃe] AG (che provoca orrore) dreadful; (terribile) atrocious

atrocità [atrotʃi'ta] SF INV atrocity

atro'fia SF atrophy

attacca'brighe [attakka'brige] SM INV/F INV quarrelsome person

attacca'mento SM (fig) attachment, affection

attac'cante SMF (Sport) forward

attacca'panni SM hook, peg; (mobile) hall stand

attac'care /20/ VT (unire) to attach; (cucire) to sew on; (far aderire) to stick (on); (appendere) to hang (up); (assalire: anche fig) to attack; (iniziare) to begin, start; (fig: contagiare) to pass on ▶ VI to stick, adhere; **attaccarsi** VPR to stick, adhere; (trasmettersi per contagio) to be contagious; (afferrarsi) **attaccarsi (a)** to cling (to); (fig: affezionarsi) **attaccarsi (a)** to become attached (to); **~ discorso** to start a conversation; **con me non attacca!** that won't work with me!

attacca'ticcio, -a, -ci, -ce [attakka'tittʃo] AG sticky

attacca'tura SF (di manica) join; **~ (dei capelli)** hairline

at'tacco, -chi SM (azione offensiva: anche fig) attack; (Med) attack, fit; (Sci) binding; (Elettr) socket; **~ informatico** cyber attack

attanagli'are [attanaʎ'ʎare] /27/ VT (anche fig) to grip

attar'darsi /72/ VPR: **~ a fare qc** (fermarsi) to stop to do sth; (stare più a lungo) to stay behind to do sth

attec'chire [attek'kire] /55/ VI (pianta) to take root; (fig) to catch on

atteggia'mento [atteddʒa'mento] SM attitude

atteggi'arsi [atted'dʒarsi] /62/ VPR: **~ a** to pose as

attem'pato, -a AG elderly

atten'dente SM (Mil) orderly, batman

at'tendere /120/ VT to wait for, await ▶ VI: **~ a** to attend to

atten'dibile AG (scusa, storia) credible; (fonte, testimone, notizia) reliable; (persona) trustworthy

atte'nersi /121/ VPR: **~ a** to keep o stick to

atten'tare /72/ VI: **~ a** to make an attempt on

atten'tato SM attack; **~ alla vita di qn** attempt on sb's life

attenta'tore, -'trice SM/F bomber; **~ suicida** suicide bomber

at'tento, -a AG attentive; (*accurato*) careful, thorough ▶ ESCL be careful!; **stare ~ a qc** to pay attention to sth; **attenti!** (*Mil*) attention!; **attenti al cane** beware of the dog

attenu'ante SF (*Dir*) extenuating circumstance

attenu'are /**72**/ VT to alleviate, ease; (*diminuire*) to reduce; **attenuarsi** VPR to ease, abate

attenuazi'one [attenuat'tsjone] SF alleviation; easing; reduction

attenzi'one [atten'tsjone] SF attention ▶ ESCL watch out!, be careful!; **attenzioni** SFPL (*premure*) attentions; **fare ~ a** to watch out for; **coprire qn di attenzioni** to lavish attention on sb

atter'raggio [atter'raddʒo] SM landing; **~ di fortuna** emergency landing

atter'rare /**72**/ VT to bring down ▶ VI to land

atter'rire /**55**/ VT to terrify

at'tesa SF waiting; (*tempo trascorso aspettando*) wait; **essere in ~ di qc** to be waiting for sth; **in ~ di una vostra risposta** (*Comm*) awaiting your reply; **restiamo in ~ di Vostre ulteriori notizie** (*Comm*) we look forward to hearing (further) from you

at'tesi *etc* VB *vedi* **attendere**

at'teso, -a PP *di* **attendere**

attes'tare /**72**/ VT: **~ qc/che** to testify to sth/ (to the fact) that

attes'tato SM certificate

attestazi'one [attestat'tsjone] SF (*certificato*) certificate; (*dichiarazione*) statement

'attico, -ci SM attic

at'tiguo, -a AG adjacent, adjoining

attil'lato, -a AG (*vestito*) close-fitting, tight; (*persona*) dressed up

'attimo SM moment; **in un ~** in a moment

atti'nente AG: **~ a** relating to, concerning

atti'nenza [atti'nentsa] SF connection

at'tingere [at'tindʒere] /**37**/ VT: **~ a o da** (*acqua*) to draw from; (*denaro, notizie*) to obtain from

at'tinto, -a PP *di* **attingere**

atti'rare /**72**/ VT to attract; **attirarsi delle critiche** to incur criticism

atti'tudine SF (*disposizione*) aptitude; (*atteggiamento*) attitude

atti'vare /**72**/ VT to activate; (*far funzionare*) to set going, start

atti'vista, -i, -e SM/F activist

attività SF INV activity; (*Comm*) assets *pl*; **~ liquide** (*Comm*) liquid assets

at'tivo, -a AG active; (*Comm*) profit-making, credit *cpd* ▶ SM (*Comm*) assets *pl*; **in ~** in credit; **chiudere in ~** to show a profit; **avere qc al proprio ~** (*fig*) to have sth to one's credit

attiz'zare [attit'tsare] /**72**/ VT (*fuoco*) to poke; (*fig*) to stir up

attizza'toio [attittsa'tojo] SM poker

'atto, -a AG: **~ a** fit for, capable of ▶ SM act; (*azione, gesto*) action, act, deed; (*Dir: documento*) deed, document; **atti** SMPL (*di congressi ecc*) proceedings; **essere in ~** to be under way; **mettere in ~** to put into action; **fare ~ di fare qc** to make as if to do sth; **all'~ pratico** in practice; **dare ~ a qn di qc** to give sb credit for sth; **~ di nascita/morte** birth/ death certificate; **~ di proprietà** title deed; **~ pubblico** official document; **~ di vendita** bill of sale; **atti osceni (in luogo pubblico)** (*Dir*) indecent exposure; **atti verbali** transactions

at'tonito, -a AG dumbfounded, astonished

attorcigli'are [attortʃiʎ'ʎare] /**27**/ VT, **attorcigli'arsi** VPR to twist

at'tore, -'trice SM/F actor (actress)

attorni'are /**19**/ VT (*circondare*) to surround; **attorniarsi** VPR: **attorniarsi di** to surround o.s. with

at'torno AV round, around, about ▶ PREP: **~ a** round, around, about

attrac'care /**20**/ VT, VI (*Naut*) to dock, berth

at'tracco, -chi SM (*Naut: manovra*) docking, berthing; (: *luogo*) berth

at'trae *etc* VB *vedi* **attrarre**

attra'ente AG attractive

at'traggo *etc* VB *vedi* **attrarre**

at'trarre /**123**/ VT to attract

at'trassi *etc* VB *vedi* **attrarre**

attrat'tiva SF attraction, charm

at'tratto, -a PP *di* **attrarre**

attraversa'mento SM crossing; **~ pedonale** pedestrian crossing

attraver'sare /**72**/ VT to cross; (*città, bosco, fig: periodo*) to go through; (*fiume*) to run through

attra'verso PREP through; (*da una parte all'altra*) across

attrazi'one [attrat'tsjone] SF attraction

attrez'zare [attret'tsare] /**72**/ VT to equip; (*Naut*) to rig

attrezza'tura [attrettsa'tura] SF equipment *no pl*; rigging; **attrezzature per uffici** office equipment

at'trezzo [at'trettso] SM tool, instrument; (*Sport*) piece of equipment

attribu'ire /**55**/ VT: **~ qc a qn** (*assegnare*) to give *o* award sth to sb; (*quadro ecc*) to attribute sth to sb

attri'buto SM attribute

at'trice [at'tritʃe] SF *vedi* **attore**

at'trito SM (*anche fig*) friction

attu'abile AG feasible

attuabilità SF feasibility

attu'ale AG (*presente*) present; (*di attualità*) topical; (*che è in atto*) actual

attualità SF INV topicality; (*avvenimento*) current event; **notizie d'~** (*TV*) the news *sg*

attualiz'zare [attualid'dzare] /**72**/ VT to update, bring up to date

attual'mente AV at the moment, at present

attu'are /**72**/ VT to carry out; **attuarsi** VPR to be realized

attuazi'one [attuat'tsjone] SF carrying out

attu'tire /**55**/ VT to deaden, reduce; **attutirsi** VPR to die down

A.U. ABBR = **allievo ufficiale**

au'dace [au'datʃe] AG audacious, daring, bold; (*provocante*) provocative; (*sfacciato*) impudent, bold

au'dacia [au'datʃa] SF audacity, daring; boldness; (*provocatività*) impudence

'audio SM (*TV, Radio, Cine*) sound

audiocas'setta SF (audio) cassette

audio'leso, -a SM/F person who is hard of hearing

audiovi'sivo, -a AG audiovisual

audi'torio SM, **audi'torium** SM INV auditorium

audizi'one [audit'tsjone] SF hearing; (*Mus*) audition

'auge ['audʒe] SF (*della gloria, carriera*) height, peak; **essere in ~** to be at the top

augu'rale AG: **messaggio ~** greeting; **biglietto ~** greetings card

augu'rare /**72**/ VT to wish; **augurarsi qc** to hope for sth

au'gurio SM (*presagio*) omen; (*voto di benessere ecc*) (good) wish; **essere di buon/cattivo ~** to be of good omen/be ominous; **auguri** SMPL best wishes; **fare gli auguri a qn** to give sb one's best wishes; **tanti auguri!** best wishes!; (*per compleanno*) happy birthday!

'aula SF (*scolastica*) classroom; (*universitaria*) lecture theatre; (*di edificio pubblico*) hall; **~ magna** main hall; **~ del tribunale** courtroom

aumen'tare /**72**/ VT, VI to increase; **~ di peso** (*persona*) to put on weight; **la produzione è aumentata del 50%** production has increased by 50%

au'mento SM increase

'aureo, -a AG (*di oro*) gold *cpd*; (*fig: colore, periodo*) golden

au'reola SF halo

au'rora SF dawn

ausili'are AG, SMF auxiliary

au'silio SM aid

auspi'cabile AG desirable

auspi'care /**20**/ VT to call for, express a desire for

aus'picio [aus'pitʃo] SM omen; (*protezione*) patronage; **sotto gli auspici di** under the auspices of; **è di buon ~** it augurs well

austerità SF INV austerity

aus'tero, -a AG austere

aus'trale AG southern

Aus'tralia SF: **l'~** Australia

australi'ano, -a AG, SM/F Australian

'Austria SF: **l'~** Austria

aus'triaco, -a, -ci, -che AG, SM/F Austrian

au'tarchico, -a, -ci, -che [au'tarkiko] AG (*sistema*) self-sufficient, autarkic; (*prodotto*) home *cpd*, home-produced

'aut'aut SM INV ultimatum

autenti'care /**20**/ VT to authenticate

autenticità [autentitʃi'ta] SF authenticity

au'tentico, -a, -ci, -che AG (*quadro, firma*) authentic, genuine; (*fatto*) true, genuine

au'tista, -i SM driver; (*personale*) chauffeur

'auto SF INV car; **~ blu** official car

autoabbron'zante AG self-tanning

autoade'sivo, -a AG self-adhesive ▸ SM sticker

autoartico'lato SM articulated lorry (*BRIT*), semi (trailer) (*US*)

autobiogra'fia SF autobiography

autobio'grafico, -a, -ci, -che AG autobiographic(al)

auto'blinda SF armoured (*BRIT*) o armored (*US*) car

auto'bomba SF INV car carrying a bomb; **l'~ si trovava a pochi metri** the car bomb was a few metres away

auto'botte SF tanker

'autobus SM INV bus

autocari'cabile AG: **scheda ~** top-up card

auto'carro SM lorry (*BRIT*), truck

autocertificazi'one [autotʃertifikat'tsjone] SF self-declaration

autocis'terna [autotʃis'tɛrna] SF tanker

autoco'lonna SF convoy

autocon'trollo SM self-control

autocopia'tivo, -a AG: **carta autocopiativa** carbonless paper

autocorri'era SF coach, bus

auto'cratico, -a, -ci, -che AG autocratic

auto'critica, -che SF self-criticism

au'toctono, -a AG, SM/F native

autodemolizi'one [autodemolit'tsjone] SF breaker's yard (*BRIT*)

autodi'datta, -i, -e SM/F autodidact, self-taught person

autodi'fesa SF self-defence

autodistrut'tivo, -a AG self-destructive

autoferrotranvi'ario, -a AG public transport *cpd*

autogesti'one [autodʒes'tjone] SF worker management

autoges'tito, -a [autodʒes'tito] AG under worker management

auto'gol SM INV own goal

au'tografo, -a AG, SM autograph

auto'grill® sm inv motorway café (*Brit*), roadside restaurant (*US*)

autoim'mune ag autoimmune

autolesio'nismo sm (*fig*) self-destruction; (*Med*) self-harm

auto'linea sf bus route

au'toma, -i sm automaton

auto'matico, -a, -ci, -che ag automatic ▶ sm (*bottone*) snap fastener; (*fucile*) automatic; **selezione automatica** (*Tel*) direct dialling

automazi'one [automat'tsjone] sf: **~ delle procedure d'ufficio** office automation

automedicazi'one [automedikat'tsjone] sf (*medicine, farmaci*): **medicinale di ~** self-medication

auto'mezzo [auto'mɛddzo] sm motor vehicle

auto'mobile sf (*motor*) car; **~ da corsa** racing car (*Brit*), race car (*US*)

automobi'lismo sm (*gen*) motoring; (*Sport*) motor racing

automobi'lista, -i, -e sm/f motorist

automobi'listico, -a, -ci, -che ag car *cpd* (*Brit*), automobile *cpd* (*US*); (*sport*) motor *cpd*

autono'leggio [autono'leddʒo] sm car hire (*Brit*), car rental

autono'mia sf autonomy; (*di volo*) range

au'tonomo, -a ag autonomous; (*sindacato, pensiero*) independent

auto'parco, -chi sm (*parcheggio*) car park (*Brit*), parking lot (*US*); (*insieme di automezzi*) transport fleet

auto'pompa sf fire engine

autop'sia sf post-mortem (examination), autopsy

auto'radio sf inv (*apparecchio*) car radio; (*autoveicolo*) radio car

au'tore, -'trice sm/f author; **l'~ del furto** the person who committed the robbery; **diritti d'~** copyright *sg*; (*compenso*) royalties

autoreg'gente [autored'dʒɛnte] ag: **calze autoreggenti** hold ups

autoregolamentazi'one [autoregolamentat'tsjone] sf self-regulation

auto'revole ag authoritative; (*persona*) influential

autoricari'cabile ag: **scheda ~** top-up card

autori'messa sf garage

autorità sf inv authority

autori'tratto sm self-portrait

autoriz'zare [autorid'dzare] /**72**/ vt (*permettere*) to authorize, give permission for; (*giustificare*) to allow, sanction

autorizzazi'one [autoriddzat'tsjone] sf authorization; **~ a procedere** (*Dir*) authorization to proceed

autos'catto sm (*Fot*) timer

autos'contro sm dodgem car (*Brit*), bumper car (*US*)

autoscu'ola sf driving school

autosno'dato sm articulated vehicle

autos'tima sf self-esteem

autos'top sm hitchhiking

autostop'pista, -i, -e sm/f hitchhiker

autos'trada sf motorway (*Brit*), highway (*US*); **~ informatica** information superhighway

> You have to pay to use Italian motorways. They are indicated by an *A* followed by a number on a green sign. The speed limit on Italian motorways is 130 kph.

autosuffici'ente [autosuffi'tʃɛnte] ag self-sufficient

autosuffici'enza [autosuffi'tʃɛntsa] sf self-sufficiency

auto'treno sm articulated lorry (*Brit*), semi (trailer) (*US*)

autove'icolo sm motor vehicle

auto'velox® sm inv (*police*) speed camera

autovet'tura sf (*motor*) car

autun'nale ag (*di autunno*) autumn *cpd*; (*da autunno*) autumnal

au'tunno sm autumn

AV sigla = **Avellino**

aval'lare /**72**/ vt (*Finanza*) to guarantee; (*fig: sostenere*) to back; (*: confermare*) to confirm

a'vallo sm (*Finanza*) guarantee

avam'braccio [avam'brattʃo] (*pl(f)* **avambraccia**) sfpl forearm

avam'posto sm (*Mil*) outpost

A'vana sf: **l'~** Havana

a'vana sm inv (*sigaro*) Havana (cigar); (*colore*) Havana brown

avangu'ardia sf vanguard; (*Arte*) avant-garde

avansco'perta sf (*Mil*) reconnaissance; **andare in ~** to reconnoitre

a'vanti av (*stato in luogo*) in front; (*moto: andare, venire*) forward; (*tempo: prima*) before ▶ prep (*luogo*): **~ a** before, in front of; (*tempo*): **~ Cristo** before Christ ▶ escl (*entrate*) come (*o* go) in!; (*Mil*) forward!; (*coraggio*) come on! ▶ sm inv (*Sport*) forward; **il giorno ~** the day before; **~ e indietro** backwards and forwards; **andare ~** to go forward; (*continuare*) to go on; (*precedere*) to go (on) ahead; (*orologio*) to be fast; **essere ~ negli studi** to be well advanced with one's studies; **mandare ~ la famiglia** to provide for one's family; **mandare ~ un'azienda** to run a business; **~ il prossimo!** next please!

avan'treno sm (*Aut*) front chassis

avanza'mento [avantsa'mento] sm (*gen*) advance; (*fig*) progress; promotion

avan'zare [avan'tsare] /**72**/ vt (*spostare in avanti*) to move forward, advance; (*domanda*) to put forward; (*promuovere*) to promote; (*essere creditore*): **~ qc da qn** to be owed sth by sb ▶ vi (*andare avanti*) to move forward, advance; (*fig: progredire*) to make progress; (*essere d'avanzo*) to be left, remain; **basta e avanza** that's more than enough

avan'zato, -a [avan'tsato] AG (*teoria, tecnica*) advanced ▶ SF (*Mil*) advance; **in età avanzata** advanced in years, up in years

a'vanzo [a'vantso] SM (*residuo*) remains *pl*, left-overs *pl*; (*Mat*) remainder; (*Comm*) surplus; (*eccedenza di bilancio*) profit carried forward; **averne d'~ di qc** to have more than enough of sth; **~ di cassa** cash in hand; **~ di galera** (*fig*) jailbird

ava'ria SF (*guasto*) damage; (: *meccanico*) breakdown

avari'ato, -a AG (*merce*) damaged; (*cibo*) off

ava'rizia [ava'rittsja] SF avarice; **crepi l'~!** to hang with the expense!

a'varo, -a AG avaricious, miserly ▶ SM miser

a'vena SF oats *pl*

(PAROLA CHIAVE)

a'vere /13/ SM (*Comm*) credit; **gli averi** (*ricchezze*) wealth *sg*, possessions
▶ vt **1** (*possedere*) to have; **ha due bambini/ una bella casa** she has (got) two children/a lovely house; **ha i capelli lunghi** he has (got) long hair; **non ho da mangiare/bere** I've (got) nothing to eat/drink, I don't have anything to eat/drink
2 (*indossare*) to wear, have on; **aveva una maglietta rossa** he was wearing *o* he had on a red T-shirt; **ha gli occhiali** he wears *o* has glasses
3 (*ricevere*) to get; **hai avuto l'assegno?** did you get *o* have you had the cheque?
4 (*età, dimensione*) to be; **la stanza ha 3 metri di lunghezza** the room is 3 metres in length; **ha 9 anni** he is 9 (years old); *vedi* **fame; paura; sonno** *ecc*
5 (*tempo*): **quanti ne abbiamo oggi?** what's the date today?; **ne hai per molto?** will you be long?
6 (*fraseologia*): **avercela con qn** to be angry with sb; **cos'hai?** what's wrong *o* what's the matter (with you)?; **non ha niente a che vedere** *o* **fare con me** it's got nothing to do with me
▶ VB AUS **1** to have; **aver bevuto/mangiato** to have drunk/eaten; **l'ho già visto** I have seen it already; **l'ho visto ieri** I saw it yesterday; **ci ha creduto?** did he believe it?
2 (+ *da* + *infinito*): **avere da fare qc** to have to do sth; **non ho niente da dire** I have nothing to say; **non hai che da chiederlo** you only have to ask him

avi'ario, -a AG bird *cpd*; **influenza aviaria** bird flu

avia'tore, -'trice SM/F aviator, pilot

aviazi'one [avjat'tsjone] SF aviation; (*Mil*) air force; **~ civile** civil aviation

avicol'tura SF bird breeding; (*di pollame*) poultry farming

avidità SF eagerness; greed

'avido, -a AG eager; (*peg*) greedy

avi'ere SM (*Mil*) airman

avitami'nosi SF vitamin deficiency

'avo SM (*antenato*) ancestor; **i nostri avi** our ancestors

avo'cado SM avocado

a'vorio SM ivory

a'vulso, -a AG: **parole avulse dal contesto** words out of context; **~ dalla società** (*fig*) cut off from society

Avv. ABBR = **avvocato**

avva'lersi /126/ VPR: **~ di** to avail o.s. of

avvalla'mento SM sinking *no pl*; (*effetto*) depression

avvalo'rare /72/ VT to confirm

avvantaggi'are [avvantad'dʒare] /62/ VT to favour (BRIT), favor (US); **avvantaggiarsi** VPR (*trarre vantaggio*): **avvantaggiarsi di** to take advantage of; **avvantaggiarsi negli affari/ sui concorrenti** (*prevalere*) to get ahead in business/of one's competitors

avve'dersi /127/ VPR: **~ di qn/qc** to notice sb/ sth

avve'duto, -a AG (*accorto*) prudent; (*scaltro*) astute

avvelena'mento SM poisoning

avvele'nare /72/ VT to poison

avve'nente AG attractive, charming

avve'nenza [avve'nɛntsa] SF good looks *pl*

av'vengo *etc* VB *vedi* **avvenire**

avveni'mento SM event

avve'nire /128/ VI, VB IMPERS to happen, occur ▶ SM future

av'venni *etc* VB *vedi* **avvenire**

avven'tarsi /72/ VPR: **~ su** *o* **contro qn/qc** to hurl o.s. *o* rush at sb/sth

avven'tato, -a AG rash, reckless

avven'tizio, -a [avven'tittsjo] AG (*impiegato*) temporary; (*guadagno*) casual

av'vento SM advent, coming; (*Rel*): **l'A~** Advent

avven'tore SM customer

avven'tura SF adventure; (*amorosa*) affair; **avere spirito d'~** to be adventurous

avventu'rarsi /72/ VPR to venture

avventuri'ero, -a SM/F adventurer (adventuress)

avventu'roso, -a AG adventurous

avve'nuto, -a PP *di* **avvenire**

avve'rarsi /72/ VPR to come true

av'verbio SM adverb

avver'rò *etc* VB *vedi* **avvenire**

avver'sare /72/ VT to oppose

avver'sario, -a AG opposing ▶ SM opponent, adversary

avversi'one SF aversion

avversità SF INV adversity, misfortune

av'verso, -a AG (*contrario*) contrary; (*sfavorevole*) unfavourable (BRIT), unfavorable (US)

avver'tenza [avver'tɛntsa] SF (*ammonimento*) warning; (*cautela*) care; (*premessa*) foreword; **avvertenze** SF PL (*istruzioni per l'uso*) instructions

avverti'mento SM warning

avver'tire /45/ VT (*avvisare*) to warn; (*rendere consapevole*) to inform, notify; (*percepire*) to feel

av'vezzo, -a [av'vettso] AG: ~ **a** used to

avvia'mento SM (*atto*) starting; (*effetto*) start; (*Aut*) starting; (: *dispositivo*) starter; (*Comm*) goodwill

avvi'are /60/ VT (*mettere sul cammino*) to direct; (*impresa, trattative*) to begin, start; (*motore*) to start; **avviarsi** VPR to set off, set out

avvicenda'mento [avvitʃenda'mento] SM alternation; (*Agr*) rotation; **c'è molto ~ di personale** there is a high turnover of staff

avvicen'dare [avvitʃen'dare] /**72**/ VT, **avvicen'darsi** VPR to alternate

avvicina'mento [avvitʃina'mento] SM approach

avvici'nare [avvitʃi'nare] /**72**/ VT to bring near; (*trattare con: persona*) to approach; **avvicinarsi** VPR: **avvicinarsi (a qn/qc)** to approach (sb/sth), draw near (to sb/sth); (*somigliare*) to be similar (to sb/sth), be close (to sb/sth)

avvi'lente AG (*umiliante*) humiliating; (*scoraggiante*) discouraging, disheartening

avvili'mento SM humiliation; disgrace; discouragement

avvi'lire /55/ VT (*umiliare*) to humiliate; (*degradare*) to disgrace; (*scoraggiare*) to dishearten, discourage; **avvilirsi** VPR (*abbattersi*) to lose heart

avvi'lito, -a AG discouraged

avvilup'pare /72/ VT (*avvolgere*) to wrap up; (*ingarbugliare*) to entangle

avvinaz'zato, -a [avvinat'tsato] AG drunk

avvin'cente [avvin'tʃɛnte] AG (*film, racconto*) enthralling

av'vincere [av'vintʃere] /**129**/ VT to charm, enthral

avvinghi'are [avvin'gjare] /**19**/ VT to clasp; **avvinghiarsi** VPR: **avvinghiarsi a** to cling to

av'vinsi etc VB vedi **avvincere**

av'vinto, -a PP di **avvincere**

av'vio SM start, beginning; **dare l'~ a qc** to start sth off; **prendere l'~** to get going, get under way

avvi'saglia [avvi'zaʎʎa] SF (*sintomo: di*

temporale ecc) sign; (*di malattia*) manifestation, sign, symptom; (*scaramuccia*) skirmish

avvi'sare /72/ VT (*far sapere*) to inform; (*mettere in guardia*) to warn

avvisa'tore SM (*apparecchio d'allarme*) alarm; **~ acustico** horn; **~ d'incendio** fire alarm

av'viso SM warning; (*annuncio*) announcement; (*affisso*) notice; (*inserzione pubblicitaria*) advertisement; **a mio ~** in my opinion; **mettere qn sull'~** to put sb on their guard; **fino a nuovo ~** until further notice; **~ di chiamata** (*servizio*) call waiting; (*segnale*) call waiting signal; **~ di consegna/ spedizione** (*Comm*) delivery/consignment note; **~ di garanzia** (*Dir*) notification (*of impending investigation and of the right to name a defence laywer*); **~ di pagamento** (*Comm*) payment advice

avvista'mento SM sighting

avvis'tare /72/ VT to sight

avvi'tare /72/ VT to screw down (*o* in)

avviz'zire [avvit'tsire] /**55**/ VI to wither

avvo'cato, -'essa SM/F (*Dir*) barrister (BRIT), lawyer; (*fig*) defender, advocate; **~ del diavolo, fare l'~ del diavolo** to play devil's advocate; **~ difensore** counsel for the defence; **~ di parte civile** counsel for the plaintiff

av'volgere [av'vɔldʒere] /**96**/ VT to roll up; (*bobina*) to wind up; (*avviluppare*) to wrap up; **avvolgersi** VPR (*avvilupparsi*) to wrap o.s. up

avvol'gibile [avvol'dʒibile] SM roller blind (BRIT), blind

avvolgi'mento [avvoldʒi'mento] SM winding

av'volsi etc VB vedi **avvolgere**

av'volto, -a PP di **avvolgere**

avvol'toio SM vulture

aza'lea [addza'lɛa] SF azalea

Azerbaigi'an [addzɛrbai'dʒan] SM Azerbaijan

azerbaig'iano, -a [addzɛrbai'dʒano] AG Azerbaijani ▶ SM/F (*abitante*) Azerbaijani ▶ SM (*Ling*) Azerbaijani

a'zero, -a [ad'dzɛro] SM/F Azeri

azi'enda [ad'dzjɛnda] SF business, firm, concern; **~ agricola** farm; **~ (autonoma) di soggiorno** tourist board; **~ a partecipazione statale** business in which the State has a financial interest; **aziende pubbliche** public corporations

azien'dale [addzjen'dale] AG company cpd; **organizzazione ~** business administration

azio'nare [attsjo'nare] /**72**/ VT to activate

azio'nario, -a [attsjo'narjo] AG share cpd; **capitale ~** share capital; **mercato ~** stock market

azi'one [at'tsjone] SF action; (*Comm*) share; **~ sindacale** industrial action; **azioni**

preferenziali preference shares (BRIT), preferred stock sg (US)

azio'nista, -i, -e [attsjo'nista] SM/F (Comm) shareholder

a'zoto [ad'dzɔto] SM nitrogen

az'teco, -a, -ci, -che [as'tɛko] AG, SM/F Aztec

azzan'nare [attsan'nare] /72/ VT to sink one's teeth into

azzar'dare [addzar'dare] /72/ VT (soldi, vita) to risk, hazard; (domanda, ipotesi) to hazard, venture; **azzardarsi** VPR: **azzardarsi a fare** to dare (to) do

azzar'dato, -a [addzar'dato] AG (impresa) risky; (risposta) rash

az'zardo [ad'dzardo] SM risk; **gioco d'~** game of chance

azzec'care [attsek'kare] /20/ VT (bersaglio) to hit, strike; (risposta, pronostico) to get right; (fig: indovinare) to guess

azzera'mento [addzera'mento] SM (Inform) reset

azze'rare [addze'rare] /72/ VT (Mat, Fisica) to make equal to zero, reduce to zero; (Tecn: strumento) to (re)set to zero

'azzimo, -a ['addzimo] AG unleavened ▶ SM unleavened bread

azzop'pare [attsop'pare] /72/ VT to lame, make lame

Az'zorre [ad'dzorre] SFPL: **le ~** the Azores

azzuf'farsi [attsuf'farsi] /72/ VPR to come to blows

az'zurro, -a [ad'dzurro] AG blue ▶ SM (colore) blue; **gli azzurri** (Sport) the Italian national team

azzur'rognolo, -a [addzur'roɲɲolo] AG bluish

Bb

B, b [bi] SM O F INV (*lettera*) B, b; **B come Bologna** ≈ B for Benjamin (*BRIT*), ≈ B for Baker (*US*)

BA SIGLA = **Bari**

ba'bau SM INV ogre, bogey man

bab'beo SM simpleton

'babbo SM (*col*) dad, daddy; **B~ Natale** Father Christmas

bab'buccia, -ce [bab'buttʃa] SF slipper; (*per neonati*) bootee

babbu'ino SM baboon

babilo'nese AG, SMF Babylonian

Babi'lonia SF Babylonia

ba'bordo SM (*Naut*) port side

baby'sitter ['beɪbɪsɪtəʳ] SM INV/F INV baby-sitter

ba'cato, -a AG worm-eaten, rotten; (*fig: mente*) diseased; (: *persona*) corrupt

'bacca, -che SF berry

baccalà SM dried salted cod; (*fig: peg*) dummy

bac'cano SM din, clamour (*BRIT*), clamor (*US*)

bac'cello [bat'tʃello] SM pod

bac'chetta [bak'ketta] SF (*verga*) stick, rod; (*di direttore d'orchestra*) baton; (*di tamburo*) drumstick; **comandare a ~** to rule with a rod of iron; **~ magica** magic wand

ba'checa, -che [ba'kɛka] SF (*mobile*) showcase, display case; (*Università, in ufficio*) notice board (*BRIT*), bulletin board (*US*)

bacia'mano [batʃa'mano] SM: **fare il ~ a qn** to kiss sb's hand

baci'are [ba'tʃare] /14/ VT to kiss; **baciarsi** VPR to kiss (one another)

ba'cillo [ba'tʃillo] SM bacillus, germ

baci'nella [batʃi'nɛlla] SF basin

ba'cino [ba'tʃino] SM basin; (*Mineralogia*) field, bed; (*Anat*) pelvis; (*Naut*) dock; **~ carbonifero** coalfield; **~ di carenaggio** dry dock; **~ petrolifero** oilfield; **~ d'utenza** catchment area

'bacio ['batʃo] SM kiss

'baco, -chi SM worm; **~ da seta** silkworm

'bada SF: **tenere qn a ~** (*tener d'occhio*) to keep an eye on sb; (*tenere a distanza*) to hold sb at bay

ba'dante SMF care worker

ba'dare /72/ VI (*fare attenzione*) to take care, be careful; **~ a** (*occuparsi di*) to look after, take care of; (*dar ascolto*) to pay attention to; **è un tipo che non bada a spese** money is no object to him; **bada ai fatti tuoi!** mind your own business!

ba'dia SF abbey

ba'dile SM shovel

'baffi SMPL moustache *sg*, mustache *sg* (*US*); (*di animale*) whiskers; **leccarsi i ~** to lick one's lips; **ridere sotto i ~** to laugh up one's sleeve

bagagli'aio [bagaʎ'ʎajo] SM luggage van (*BRIT*) o car (*US*); (*Aut*) boot (*BRIT*), trunk (*US*)

ba'gaglio [ba'gaʎʎo] SM luggage *no pl*, baggage *no pl*; **fare/disfare i bagagli** to pack/unpack; **~ a mano** hand luggage

bagat'tella SF trifle, trifling matter

Bag'dad SF Baghdad

baggia'nata [baddʒa'nata] SF foolish action; **dire baggianate** to talk nonsense

bagli'ore [baʎ'ʎore] SM flash, dazzling light; **un ~ di speranza** a (sudden) ray of hope

ba'gnante [baɲ'ɲante] SMF bather

ba'gnare [baɲ'ɲare] /15/ VT to wet; (*inzuppare*) to soak; (*innaffiare*) to water; (*fiume*) to flow through; (: *mare*) to wash, bathe; (*brindare*) to drink to, toast; **bagnarsi** VPR to get wet; (*al mare*) to go swimming o bathing; (*in vasca*) to have a bath

ba'gnato, -a [baɲ'ɲato] AG wet; **era come un pulcino ~** he looked like a drowned rat

ba'gnino [baɲ'ɲino] SM lifeguard

'bagno ['baɲɲo] SM bath; (*locale*) bathroom; (*toilette*) toilet; **bagni** SMPL (*stabilimento*) baths; **fare il ~** to have a bath; (*nel mare*) to go swimming o bathing; **fare il ~ a qn** to give sb a bath; **mettere a ~** to soak

bagnoma'ria [baɲɲoma'ria] SM: **cuocere a ~** to cook in a double saucepan (*BRIT*) o double boiler (*US*)

bagnoschi'uma [baɲɲo'skjuma] SM INV bubble bath

Ba'hama [ba'ama] SFPL: **le ~** the Bahamas
Bah'rein [ba'rein] SM: **il ~** Bahrain o Bahrein
'**baia** SF bay
baio'netta SF bayonet
'**baita** SF mountain hut
balaus'trata SF balustrade
balbet'tare /72/ VI to stutter, stammer;
(*bimbo*) to babble ▶ VT to stammer out
bal'buzie [bal'buttsje] SF stammer
balbuzi'ente [balbut'tsjɛnte] AG stuttering,
stammering
Bal'cani SMPL: **i ~** the Balkans
bal'canico, -a, -ci, -che AG Balkan
bal'cone SM balcony
baldac'chino [baldak'kino] SM canopy;
letto a ~ four-poster (bed)
bal'danza [bal'dantsa] SF self-confidence;
boldness
'**baldo, -a** AG bold, daring
bal'doria SF: **fare ~** to have a riotous time
Bale'ari SFPL: **le isole ~** the Balearic Islands
ba'lena SF whale
bale'nare /72/ VB IMPERS: **balena** there's
lightning ▶ VI to flash; **mi balenò un'idea**
an idea flashed through my mind
baleni'era SF (*per la caccia*) whaler, whaling
ship
ba'leno SM flash of lightning; **in un ~** in a
flash
ba'lera SF (*locale*) dance hall; (*pista*) dance
floor
ba'lestra SF crossbow
'**balia**[1] SF wet-nurse; **~ asciutta** nanny
ba'lia[2] SF: **in ~ di** at the mercy of; **essere
lasciato in ~ di se stesso** to be left to one's
own devices
ba'lilla SM INV (*Storia*) member of Fascist youth
group
ba'listico, -a, -ci, -che AG ballistic ▶ SF
ballistics *sg*; **perito ~** ballistics expert
'**balla** SF (*di merci*) bale; (*fandonia*) (tall) story
bal'labile SM dance number, dance tune
bal'lare /72/ VT, VI to dance
bal'lata SF ballad
balla'toio SM (*terrazzina*) gallery
balle'rina SF dancer; ballet dancer; (*scarpa*)
pump, ballet shoe; **~ di rivista** chorus girl
balle'rino SM dancer; ballet dancer
bal'letto SM ballet
'**ballo** SM dance; (*azione*) dancing *no pl*; **~ in
maschera** o **mascherato** fancy-dress ball;
essere in ~ (*fig: persona*) to be involved; (: *cosa*)
to be at stake; **tirare in ~ qc** to bring sth up,
raise sth
ballot'taggio [ballot'taddʒo] SM (*Pol*) second
ballot
balne'are AG seaside *cpd*; (*stagione*) bathing
ba'locco, -chi SM toy
ba'lordo, -a AG stupid, senseless

bal'samico, -a, -ci, -che AG (*aria, brezza*)
balmy; **pomata balsamica** balsam
'**balsamo** SM (*aroma*) balsam; (*lenimento, fig*)
balm; (*per capelli*) conditioner
'**baltico, -a, -ci, -che** AG Baltic; **il (mar) B~**
the Baltic (Sea)
balu'ardo SM bulwark
'**balza** ['baltsa] SF (*dirupo*) crag; (*di stoffa*) frill
bal'zano, -a [bal'tsano] AG (*persona, idea*)
queer, odd
bal'zare [bal'tsare] **/72/** VI to bounce;
(*lanciarsi*) to jump, leap; **la verità balza agli
occhi** the truth of the matter is obvious
'**balzo** ['baltso] SM bounce; jump, leap; (*del
terreno*) crag; **prendere la palla al ~** (*fig*) to
seize one's opportunity
bam'bagia [bam'badʒa] SF (*ovatta*) cotton
wool (*BRIT*), absorbent cotton (*US*); (*cascame*)
cotton waste; **tenere qn nella ~** (*fig*) to
mollycoddle sb
bam'bina SF *vedi* **bambino**
bambi'naia SF nanny, nurse(maid)
bam'bino, -a SM/F child; **fare il ~** to behave
childishly
bam'boccio [bam'bɔttʃo] SM plump child;
(*pupazzo*) rag doll
'**bambola** SF doll
bambo'lotto SM male doll
bambù SM bamboo
ba'nale AG banal, commonplace
banalità SF INV banality
ba'nana SF banana
ba'nano SM banana tree
'**banca, -che** SF bank; **~ d'affari** merchant
bank; **~ (di) dati** data bank
banca'rella SF stall
ban'cario, -a AG banking, bank *cpd* ▶ SM bank
clerk
banca'rotta SF bankruptcy; **fare ~** to go
bankrupt
bancarotti'ere SM bankrupt
ban'chetto [ban'ketto] SM banquet
banchi'ere [ban'kjɛre] SM banker
ban'china [ban'kina] SF (*di porto*) quay; (*per
pedoni, ciclisti*) path; (*di stazione*) platform;
~ cedevole (*Aut*) soft verge (*BRIT*) o shoulder
(*US*); **~ spartitraffico** (*Aut*) central
reservation (*BRIT*), median (strip) (*US*)
ban'chisa [ban'kiza] SF pack ice
'**banco, -chi** SM bench; (*di negozio*) counter; (*di
mercato*) stall; (*di officina*) (work)bench; (*Geo,
banca*) bank; **sotto ~** (*fig*) under the counter;
tenere il ~ (*nei giochi*) to be (the) banker;
tener ~ (*fig*) to monopolize the conversation;
medicinali da ~ over-the-counter
medicines; **~ di chiesa** pew; **~ di corallo**
coral reef; **~ degli imputati** dock; **~ del
Lotto** lottery-ticket office; **~ di prova** (*fig*)
testing ground; **~ dei testimoni** witness

box (BRIT) o stand (US); **~ dei pegni** pawnshop; **~ di nebbia** bank of fog

banco'giro [banko'dʒiro] SM credit transfer

'Bancomat® SM INV automated banking; (tessera) cash card; (sportello automatico) cashpoint

banco'nota SF banknote

'banda SF band; (di stoffa) band, stripe; (lato, parte) side; (di calcolatore) tape; **~ larga** broadband; **~ perforata** punch tape

banderu'ola SF (Meteor) weathercock, weathervane; **essere una ~** (fig) to be fickle

bandi'era SF flag, banner; **battere ~ italiana** (nave ecc) to fly the Italian flag; **cambiare ~** (fig) to change sides; **~ di comodo** flag of convenience

ban'dire /55/ VT to proclaim; (esiliare) to exile; (fig) to dispense with

ban'dito SM outlaw, bandit

bandi'tore SM (di aste) auctioneer

'bando SM proclamation; (esilio) exile, banishment; **mettere al ~ qn** to exile sb; (fig) to freeze sb out; **~ alle ciance!** that's enough talk!; **~ di concorso** announcement of a competition

'bandolo SM (di matassa) end; **trovare il ~ della matassa** (fig) to find the key to the problem

Bang'kok [ban'kɔk] SF Bangkok

Bangla'desh [bangla'dɛʃ] SM: **il ~** Bangladesh

bar SM INV bar

'bara SF coffin

ba'racca, -che SF shed, hut; (peg) hovel; **mandare avanti la ~** to keep things going; **piantare ~ e burattini** to throw everything up

barac'cato, -a SM/F person living in temporary camp

barac'chino [barak'kino] SM (chiosco) stall; (apparecchio) CB radio

barac'cone SM booth, stall; **baracconi** SMPL (luna park) funfair sg (BRIT), amusement park; **fenomeno da ~** circus freak

barac'copoli SF INV shanty town

bara'onda SF hubbub, bustle

ba'rare /72/ VI to cheat

'baratro SM abyss

barat'tare /72/ VT: **~ qc con** to barter sth for, swap sth for

ba'ratto SM barter

ba'rattolo SM (di latta) tin; (di vetro) jar; (di coccio) pot

'barba SF beard; **farsi la ~** to shave; **farla in ~ a qn** (fig) to do sth to sb's face; **servire qn di ~ e capelli** (fig) to teach sb a lesson; **che ~!** what a bore!

barbabi'etola SF beetroot (BRIT), beet (US); **~ da zucchero** sugar beet

Bar'bados SF Barbados

bar'barico, -a, -ci, -che AG (invasione)

barbarian; (usanze, metodi) barbaric

bar'barie SF barbarity

'barbaro, -a AG barbarous ▶ SM barbarian; **i Barbari** the Barbarians

'barbecue ['ba:bikju:] SM INV barbecue

barbi'ere SM barber

barbi'turico, -a, -ci, -che AG barbituric ▶ SM barbiturate

bar'bone SM (cane) poodle; (vagabondo) tramp

bar'buto, -a AG bearded

'barca, -che SF boat; **una ~ di** (fig) heaps of, tons of; **mandare avanti la ~** (fig) to keep things going; **~ a motore** motorboat; **~ a remi** rowing boat (BRIT), rowboat (US); **~ a vela** sailing boat (BRIT), sailboat (US)

barcai'olo SM boatman

barcame'narsi /72/ VPR (nel lavoro) to get by; (a parole) to beat about the bush

Barcel'lona [bartʃel'lona] SF Barcelona

barcol'lare /72/ VI to stagger

bar'cone SM (per ponti di barche) pontoon

ba'rella SF (lettiga) stretcher

'Barents: il mar di ~ SM the Barents Sea

ba'rese AG of (o from) Bari

bari'centro [bari'tʃentro] SM centre (BRIT) o center (US) of gravity

ba'rile SM barrel, cask

ba'rista, -i, -e SM/F barman (barmaid); (proprietario) bar owner

ba'ritono SM baritone

bar'lume SM glimmer, gleam

'baro SM (Carte) cardsharp

ba'rocco, -a, -chi, -che AG, SM baroque

ba'rometro SM barometer

ba'rone SM baron; **i baroni della medicina** (fig: peg) the top brass in the medical faculty

baro'nessa SF baroness

'barra SF bar; (Naut) helm; (linea grafica) line, stroke

bar'rare /72/ VT to bar

barri'care /20/ VT to barricade; **barricarsi** VPR to barricade o.s.

barri'cata SF barricade; **essere dall'altra parte della ~** (fig) to be on the other side of the fence

barri'era SF barrier; (Geo) reef; **la Grande B~ Corallina** the Great Barrier Reef

bar'roccio [bar'rɔttʃo] SM cart

ba'ruffa SF scuffle; **fare ~** to squabble

barzel'letta [bardzel'letta] SF joke, funny story

basa'mento SM (parte inferiore, piedestallo) base; (Tecn) bed, base plate

ba'sare /72/ VT to base, found; **basarsi** VPR: **basarsi su** (fatti, prove) to be based o founded on; (persona) to base one's arguments on

'basco, -a, -schi, -sche AG Basque ▶ SM/F Basque ▶ SM (lingua) Basque; (copricapo) beret

bas'culla SF weighing machine, weighbridge

41

'**base** SF base; (*fig: fondamento*) basis; (*Pol*) rank and file; **di ~** basic; **in ~ a** on the basis of, according to; **in ~ a ciò ...** on that basis ...; **a ~ di caffè** coffee-based; **essere alla ~ di qc** to be at the root of sth; **gettare le basi per qc** to lay the basis *o* foundations for sth; **avere buone basi** (*Ins*) to have a sound educational background

'**baseball** ['beisbɔːl] SM baseball

ba'setta SF sideburn

basi'lare AG basic, fundamental

Basi'lea SF Basle

ba'silica, -che SF basilica

ba'silico SM basil

'**basket** ['basket] SM basketball

bas'sezza [bas'settsa] SF (*d'animo, di sentimenti*) baseness; (*azione*) base action

bas'sista, -i, -e SM/F bass player

'**basso, -a** AG low; (*di statura*) short; (*meridionale*) southern ▶ SM bottom, lower part; (*Mus*) bass; **a occhi bassi** with eyes lowered; **a ~ prezzo** cheap; **scendere da ~ to** go downstairs; **cadere in ~** (*fig*) to come down in the world; **la bassa Italia** southern Italy; **il ~ Medioevo** the late Middle Ages

basso'fondo (*pl* **bassifondi**) SM (*Geo*) shallows *pl*; **i bassifondi (della città)** the seediest parts of the town

bassorili'evo SM bas-relief

bas'sotto, -a AG squat ▶ SM (*cane*) dachshund

'**basta** ESCL (*that's*) enough!, that will do!

bas'tardo, -a AG (*animale, pianta*) hybrid, crossbreed; (*persona*) illegitimate, bastard (*peg*) ▶ SM/F illegitimate child, bastard (*peg*); (*cane*) mongrel

bas'tare /**72**/ VI, VB IMPERS to be enough, be sufficient; **~ a qn** to be enough for sb; **~ a se stesso** to be self-sufficient; **basta chiedere** *o* **che chieda a un vigile** you have only to *o* need only ask a policeman; **basti dire che ...** suffice it to say that ...; **basta!** that's enough!, that will do!; **basta così** (*al bar ecc*) will that be all?; **basta così, grazie** that's enough, thanks; **punto e basta!** and that's that!

basti'an SM: **~ contrario** awkward customer

basti'mento SM ship, vessel

basti'one SM bastion

basto'nare /**72**/ VT to beat, thrash; **avere l'aria di un cane bastonato** to look crestfallen

basto'nata SF blow (with a stick); **prendere qn a bastonate** to give sb a good beating

baston'cino [baston'tʃino] SM (*piccolo bastone*) small stick; (*Tecn*) rod; (*Sci*) ski pole; **bastoncini di pesce** (*Cuc*) fish fingers (BRIT), fish sticks (US)

bas'tone SM stick; **bastoni** SMPL (*Carte*) *suit in Neapolitan pack of cards*; **~ da passeggio** walking stick; **mettere i bastoni fra le ruote a qn** to put a spoke in sb's wheel

bat'tage [ba'taʒ] SM INV: **~ promozionale** *o* **pubblicitario** publicity campaign

bat'taglia [bat'taʎʎa] SF battle; fight

bat'taglio [bat'taʎʎo] SM (*di campana*) clapper; (*di porta*) knocker

battagli'one [battaʎ'ʎone] SM battalion

bat'tello SM boat

bat'tente SM (*imposta: di porta*) wing, flap; (: *di finestra*) shutter; (*batacchio: di porta*) knocker; (: *di orologio*) hammer; **chiudere i battenti** (*fig*) to shut up shop

'**battere** /**1**/ VT to beat; (*grano*) to thresh; (*percorrere*) to scour; (*rintoccare: le ore*) to strike ▶ VI (*bussare*) to knock; (*pioggia, sole*) to beat down; (*cuore*) to beat; (*Tennis*) to serve; (*urtare*): **~ contro** to hit *o* strike against; **battersi** VPR to fight; **~ le mani** to clap; **~ i piedi** to stamp one's feet; **~ su un argomento** to hammer home an argument; **~ a macchina** to type; **~ bandiera italiana** to fly the Italian flag; **~ il marciapiede** (*peg*) to walk the streets, be on the game; **~ un rigore** (*Calcio*) to take a penalty; **~ in testa** (*Aut*) to knock; **in un batter d'occhio** in the twinkling of an eye; **senza ~ ciglio** without batting an eyelid; **battersela** to run off

batte'ria SF battery; (*Mus*) drums *pl*; **~ da cucina** pots and pans *pl*

bat'terio SM bacterium; **batteri** SMPL bacteria

batteriolo'gia [batterjolo'dʒia] SF bacteriology

batte'rista, -i, -e SM/F drummer

bat'tesimo SM (*sacramento*) baptism; (*rito*) baptism; christening; **tenere qn a ~** to be godfather (*o* godmother) to sb

battez'zare [batted'dzare] /**72**/ VT to baptize; to christen

battiba'leno SM: **in un ~** in a flash

batti'becco, -chi SM squabble

batticu'ore SM palpitations *pl*; **avere il ~** to be frightened to death

bat'tigia [bat'tidʒa] SF water's edge

batti'mano SM applause

batti'panni SM INV carpet-beater

battis'tero SM baptistry

battis'trada SM INV (*di pneumatico*) tread; (*di gara*) pacemaker

battitap'peto SM INV upright vacuum cleaner

'**battito** SM beat, throb; **~ cardiaco** heartbeat; **~ della pioggia/dell'orologio** beating of the rain/ticking of the clock

batti'tore SM (*Cricket*) batsman; (*Baseball*) batter; (*Caccia*) beater

batti'tura SF (*anche:* **battitura a macchina**) typing (*del grano*) threshing

b

bat'tuta SF blow; (*di macchina da scrivere*) stroke; (*Mus*) bar; beat; (*Teat*) cue; (*frase spiritosa*) witty remark; (*di caccia*) beating; (*Polizia*) combing, scouring; (*Tennis*) service; **fare una ~** to crack a joke, make a witty remark; **aver la ~ pronta** (*fig*) to have a ready answer; **è ancora alle prime battute** it's just started

ba'tuffolo SM wad

ba'ule SM trunk; (*Aut*) boot (BRIT), trunk (US)

bau'xite [bauk'site] SF bauxite

'bava SF (*di animale*) slaver, slobber; (*di lumaca*) slime; (*di vento*) breath

bava'glino [bavaʎ'ʎino] SM bib

ba'vaglio [ba'vaʎʎo] SM gag

bava'rese AG, SMF Bavarian

'bavero SM collar

Bavi'era SF Bavaria

ba'zar [bad'dzar] SM INV bazaar

baz'zecola [bad'dzekola] SF trifle

bazzi'care [battsi'kare] /20/ VT (*persona*) to hang about with; (*posto*) to hang about
▶ VI: **~ in/con** to hang about/hang about with

BCE SIGLA F (= *Banca centrale europea*) ECB

be'arsi /72/ VPR: **~ di qc/a fare qc** to delight in sth/in doing sth; **~ alla vista di** to enjoy looking at

beati'tudine SF bliss

be'ato, -a AG blessed; (*fig*) happy; **~ te!** lucky you!

bebè SM INV baby

bec'caccia, -ce [bek'kattʃa] SF woodcock

bec'care /20/ VT to peck; (*fig: raffreddore*) to catch, pick up; **beccarsi** VPR (*fig*) to squabble; **beccarsi qc** to catch sth

bec'cata SF peck

beccheggi'are [bekked'dʒare] /62/ VI to pitch

beccherò *etc* [bekke'rɔ] VB *vedi* **beccare**

bec'chime [bek'kime] SM birdseed

bec'chino [bek'kino] SM gravedigger

'becco, -chi SM beak, bill; (*di caffettiera ecc*) spout; lip; (*fig: col*) cuckold; **mettere ~** (*col*) to butt in; **chiudi il ~!** (*col*) shut your mouth!, shut your trap!; **non ho il ~ di un quattrino** (*col*) I'm broke

Be'fana SF old woman who, according to legend, brings children their presents at the Epiphany; (*Epifania*) Epiphany; (*donna brutta*): **befana** hag, witch; *see note*

Marking the end of the traditional 12 days of Christmas on 6 January, the *Befana*, or the feast of the Epiphany, is a national holiday in Italy. It is named after the old woman who, legend has it, comes down the chimney the night before, bringing gifts to children who have been good during the year and leaving lumps of coal for those who have not.

'beffa SF practical joke; **farsi ~ o beffe di qn** to make a fool of sb

bef'fardo, -a AG scornful, mocking

bef'fare /72/ VT (*anche*: **beffarsi di**) to make a fool of, mock

'bega, -ghe SF quarrel

'begli ['beʎʎi], **'bei** AG *vedi* **bello**

beige [bɛʒ] AG INV beige

Bei'rut SF Beirut

bel AG *vedi* **bello**

be'lare /72/ VI to bleat

be'lato SM bleating

'belga, -gi, -ghe AG, SM/F Belgian

'Belgio ['bɛldʒo] SM: **il ~** Belgium

Bel'grado SF Belgrade

'bella SF (*Sport*) decider; *vedi* **bello**

bel'lezza [bel'lettsa] SF beauty; **chiudere o finire qc in ~** to finish sth with a flourish; **che ~!** fantastic!; **ho pagato la ~ di 300 euro** I paid 300 euro, no less

belli'coso, -a AG warlike

bellige'rante [bellidʒe'rante] AG belligerent

bellim'busto SM dandy

(PAROLA CHIAVE)

'bello, -a (*ag: dav sm* **bel** + C, **bell'** + V, **bello** + *s impura, gn, pn, ps, x, z, pl* **bei** + C, **begli** + *s impura ecc o* V) AG **1** (*oggetto, donna, paesaggio*) beautiful, lovely; (*uomo*) handsome; (*tempo*) beautiful, fine, lovely; **farsi bello di qc** to show off about sth; **fare la bella vita** to have an easy life; **le belle arti** fine arts

2 (*quantità*): **una bella cifra** a considerable sum of money; **un bel niente** absolutely nothing

3 (*rafforzativo*): **è una truffa bella e buona!** it's a real fraud!; **oh bella!, anche questa è bella!** (*ironico*) that's nice!; **è bell'e finito** it's already finished

▶ SM/F (*innamorato*) sweetheart

▶ SM **1** (*bellezza*) beauty; (*tempo*) fine weather
2: **adesso viene il bello** now comes the best bit; **sul più bello** at the crucial point; **cosa fai di bello?** are you doing anything interesting?

▶ SF **1** (*anche*: **bella copia**) fair copy
2 (*Sport, Carte*) decider

▶ AV: **fa bello** the weather is fine, it's fine; **alla bell'e meglio** somehow or other

---

bellu'nese AG of (*o* from) Belluno

'belva SF wild animal

belve'dere SM INV panoramic viewpoint

benché [ben'ke] CONG although

'benda SF bandage; (*per gli occhi*) blindfold

ben'daggio [ben'daddʒo] SM bandages; **fare un ~ a qc** to bandage sth up; **~ gastrico** gastric band surgery

ben'dare /72/ VT to bandage; to blindfold

bendis'posto, -a AG: ~ **a qn/qc** well disposed towards sb/sth

'**bene** AV well; (*completamente, affatto*): **è ben difficile** it's very difficult ▶ AG INV: **gente** ~ well-to-do people ▶ SM good; (*Comm*) asset; **beni** SMPL (*averi*) property *sg*, estate *sg*; **io sto** ~/**poco** ~ I'm well/not very well; **va** ~ all right; **ben più lungo/caro** much longer/more expensive; **lo spero** ~ I certainly hope so; **volere un** ~ **dell'anima a qn** to love sb very much; **un uomo per** ~ a respectable man; **fare** ~ to do the right thing; **fare** ~ **a** (*salute*) to be good for; **fare del** ~ **a qn** to do sb a good turn; **di** ~ **in meglio** better and better; **beni ambientali** environmental assets; **beni di consumo** consumer goods; **beni di consumo durevole** consumer durables; **beni culturali** cultural heritage; **beni immateriali** immaterial *o* intangible assets; **beni patrimoniali** fixed assets; **beni privati** private property *sg*; **beni pubblici** public property *sg*; **beni reali** tangible assets

bene'detto, -a PP *di* **benedire** ▶ AG blessed, holy

bene'dire /**38**/ VT to bless; to consecrate; **l'ho mandato a farsi** ~ (*fig*) I told him to go to hell

benedizi'one [benedit'tsjone] SF blessing

benedu'cato, -a AG well-mannered

benefat'tore, -'trice SM/F benefactor (benefactress)

benefi'cenza [benefi'tʃɛntsa] SF charity

benefici'are [benefi'tʃare] /**14**/ VI: ~ **di** to benefit by, benefit from

benefici'ario, -a [benefi'tʃarjo] AG, SM/F beneficiary

bene'ficio [bene'fitʃo] SM benefit; **con** ~ **d'inventario** (*fig*) with reservations

be'nefico, -a, -ci, -che AG beneficial; charitable

'**Benelux** SM: **il** ~ Benelux, the Benelux countries

beneme'renza [beneme'rɛntsa] SF merit

bene'merito, -a AG meritorious

bene'placito [bene'platʃito] SM (*approvazione*) approval; (*permesso*) permission

be'nessere SM well-being

benes'tante AG well-to-do

benes'tare SM consent, approval

benevo'lenza [benevo'lɛntsa] SF benevolence

be'nevolo, -a AG benevolent

ben'godi SM land of plenty

benia'mino, -a SM/F favourite (*BRIT*), favorite (*US*)

be'nigno, -a [be'niɲɲo] AG kind, kindly; (*critica ecc*) favourable (*BRIT*), favorable (*US*); (*Med*) benign

benintenzio'nato, -a [benintentsjo'nato] AG well-meaning

benin'teso AV of course; ~ **che** *cong* provided that

benpen'sante SMF conformist

benser'vito SM: **dare il** ~ **a qn** (*sul lavoro*) to give sb the sack, fire sb; (*fig*) to send sb packing

bensì CONG but (rather)

benve'nuto, -a AG, SM welcome; **dare il** ~ **a qn** to welcome sb

ben'visto, -a AG: **essere** ~ (**da**) to be well thought of (by)

benvo'lere /**131**/ VT: **farsi** ~ **da tutti** to win everybody's affection; **prendere a** ~ **qn/qc** to take a liking to sb/sth

ben'zina [ben'dzina] SF petrol (*BRIT*), gas (*US*); **fare** ~ to get petrol *o* gas; **rimanere senza** ~ to run out of petrol *o* gas; ~ **verde** unleaded petrol, lead-free petrol

benzi'naio [bendzi'najo] SM petrol (*BRIT*) *o* gas (*US*) pump attendant

be'one SM heavy drinker

'**bere** /**16**/ VT to drink; (*assorbire*) to soak up; **darla a** ~ **a qn** (*fig*) to fool sb; **questa volta non me la dai a** ~! I won't be taken in this time!

berga'masco, -a, -schi, -sche AG of (*o* from) Bergamo

'**Bering** ['beriŋ]: **il mar di** ~ *sm* the Bering Sea

ber'lina SF (*Aut*) saloon (car) (*BRIT*), sedan (*US*); **mettere alla** ~ (*fig*) to hold up to ridicule

Ber'lino SF Berlin; ~ **est/ovest** East/West Berlin

Ber'muda SFPL: **le** ~ Bermuda *sg*

ber'muda SMPL (*calzoncini*) Bermuda shorts

'**Berna** SF Bern

ber'noccolo SM bump; (*inclinazione*) flair

ber'retto SM cap

berrò *etc* VB *vedi* **bere**

bersagli'are [bersaʎ'ʎare] /**27**/ VT to shoot at; (*colpire ripetutamente, fig*) to bombard; **bersagliato dalla sfortuna** dogged by ill fortune

bersagli'ere [bersaʎ'ʎere] SM *member of rifle regiment in Italian army*

ber'saglio [ber'saʎʎo] SM target

bescia'mella [beʃʃa'mɛlla] SF béchamel sauce

bes'temmia SF curse; (*Rel*) blasphemy

bestemmi'are /**19**/ VI to curse, swear; to blaspheme ▶ VT to curse, swear at; to blaspheme; ~ **come un turco** to swear like a trooper

'**bestia** SF animal; **lavorare come una** ~ to work like a dog; **andare in** ~ (*fig*) to fly into a rage; **una** ~ **rara** (*fig: persona*) an oddball; ~ **da soma** beast of burden

besti'ale AG beastly; animal *cpd*; (*col*): **fa un**

caldo ~ it's terribly hot; **fa un freddo** ~ it's bitterly cold

bestialità SF INV (*qualità*) bestiality; **dire/ fare una** ~ **dopo l'altra** to say/do one idiotic thing after another

besti'ame SM livestock; (*bovino*) cattle *pl*

Bet'lemme SF Bethlehem

betoni'era SF cement mixer

'**bettola** SF (*peg*) dive

be'tulla SF birch

be'vanda SF drink, beverage; ~ **energetica** energy drink

bevi'tore, -'trice SM/F drinker

'**bevo** *etc* VB *vedi* **bere**

be'vuto, -a PP *di* **bere** ▶ SF drink

'**bevvi** *etc* VB *vedi* **bere**

BG SIGLA = **Bergamo**

BI SIGLA F = **Banca d'Italia** ▶ SIGLA = **Biella**

bi'ada SF fodder

bianche'ria [bjanke'ria] SF linen; ~ **intima** underwear; ~ **da donna** ladies' underwear, lingerie; ~ **femminile** lingerie

bi'anco, -a, -chi, -che AG white; (*non scritto*) blank ▶ SM white; (*intonaco*) whitewash ▶ SM/F white, white man(-woman); (*foglio, assegno*) blank; **in ~ e nero** (*TV, Fot*) black and white; **mangiare in** ~ to follow a bland diet; **pesce in** ~ boiled fish; **andare in** ~ (*non riuscire*) to fail; (*in amore*) to be rejected; **notte bianca** *o* **in** ~ sleepless night; **voce bianca** (*Mus*) treble (voice); **votare scheda bianca** to return a blank voting slip; ~ **dell'uovo** egg-white

bianco'segno [bjanko'seɲɲo] SM signature to a blank document

biancos'pino SM hawthorn

biasci'care [bjaʃʃi'kare] /**20**/ VT to mumble

biasi'mare /**72**/ VT to disapprove of, censure

bi'asimo SM disapproval, censure

'**bibbia** SF (*anche fig*) bible

bibe'ron SM INV feeding bottle

'**bibita** SF (soft) drink

bibliogra'fia SF bibliography

biblio'teca, -che SF library; (*mobile*) bookcase

bibliote'cario, -a SM/F librarian

bicame'rale AG (*Pol*) two-chamber *cpd*

bicarbo'nato SM: ~ **(di sodio)** bicarbonate (of soda)

bicchi'ere [bik'kjɛre] SM glass; **è (facile) come bere un bicchier d'acqua** it's as easy as pie

bici'cletta [bitʃi'kletta] SF bicycle; **andare in** ~ to cycle

bi'cipite [bi'tʃipite] SM bicep

bidè SM INV bidet

bi'dello, -a SM/F (*Ins*) janitor

bi'det SM INV = **bidè**

bidirezio'nale [bidirettsjo'nale] AG bidirectional

bido'nare /**72**/ VT (*col: piantare in asso*) to let down; (: *imbrogliare*) to cheat, swindle

bido'nata SF (*col*) swindle

bi'done SM drum, can; (*anche:* **bidone dell'immondizia**) (dust)bin; (*col: truffa*) swindle; **fare un** ~ **a qn** (*col*) to let sb down; to cheat sb

bidon'ville [bidɔ̃'vil] SF INV shanty town

bi'eco, -a, -chi, -che AG sinister

bi'ella SF (*Tecn*) connecting rod

Bielo'russia SF Belarussia

bielo'russo, -a AG, SM/F Belarussian, Belorussian

bien'nale AG biennial ▶ SF: **la B~ di Venezia** the Venice Arts Festival; *see note*

> Dating back to 1895, the *Biennale di Venezia* is an international festival of the contemporary arts. It takes place every two years in the *Giardini Pubblici*. The various countries taking part each put on exhibitions in their own pavilions. There is a section dedicated to the work of young artists, as well as a special exhibition organized around a specific theme for that year.

bi'ennio SM period of two years

bi'erre SMF *member of the Red Brigades*

bi'etola SF beet

bifami'liare AG (*villa, casetta*) semi-detached

bifo'cale AG bifocal

bi'folco, -a, -chi, -che SM/F (*peg*) bumpkin

'**bifora** SF (*Archit*) mullioned window

bifor'carsi /**20**/ VPR to fork

biforcazi'one [biforkat'tsjone] SF fork

bifor'cuto, -a AG (*anche fig*) forked

biga'mia SF bigamy

'**bigamo, -a** AG bigamous ▶ SM/F bigamist

bighello'nare [bigello'nare] /**72**/ VI to loaf (about)

bighel'lone, -a [bigel'lone] SM/F loafer

bigiotte'ria [bidʒotte'ria] SF costume jewellery (BRIT) *o* jewelry (US); (*negozio*) jeweller's (shop) (BRIT) *o* jewelry store (US: *selling only costume jewellery*)

bigli'ardo [biʎ'ʎardo] SM = **biliardo**

bigliet'taio, -a [biʎʎet'tajo] SM/F (*nei treni*) ticket inspector; (*in autobus ecc*) conductor (conductress); (*Cine, Teat*) box-office attendant

bigliette'ria [biʎʎette'ria] SF (*di stazione*) ticket office; booking office; (*di teatro*) box office

bigli'etto [biʎ'ʎetto] SM (*per viaggi, spettacoli ecc*) ticket; (*cartoncino*) card; ~ **di banca** (bank)note; (*anche:* **biglietto d'auguri/da visita**) greetings/visiting card; ~ **di andata e ritorno** return (BRIT) *o* round-trip (US) ticket; ~ **di sola andata** single (ticket); ~ **elettronico** e-ticket; ~ **omaggio** complimentary ticket

bignè [biɲ'ɲɛ] SM INV cream puff
bigo'dino SM roller, curler
bi'gotto, -a AG over-pious ▶ SM/F church
fiend
bi'kini SM INV bikini
bi'lancia, -ce [bi'lantʃa] SF (pesa) scales pl; (: di
precisione) balance; **B~** Libra; **essere della B~**
to be Libra; **~ commerciale/dei pagamenti**
balance of trade/payments
bilanci'are [bilan'tʃare] /14/ VT (pesare) to
weigh; (: fig) to weigh up; **~ le uscite e le
entrate** (Comm) to balance expenditure and
revenue
bi'lancio [bi'lantʃo] SM (Comm) balance
(sheet); (statale) budget; **far quadrare il ~** to
balance the books; **chiudere il ~ in attivo/
passivo** to make a profit/loss; **fare il ~ di**
(fig) to assess; **~ consolidato** consolidated
balance; **~ consuntivo** (final) balance;
~ preventivo budget; **~ pubblico** national
budget; **~ di verifica** trial balance
bilate'rale AG bilateral
'bile SF bile; (fig) rage, anger
biliar'dino SM pinball
bili'ardo SM billiards sg; (tavolo) billiard table
'bilico, -chi SM: **essere in ~** to be balanced;
(fig) to be undecided; **tenere qn in ~** to keep
sb in suspense
bi'lingue AG bilingual
bili'one SM (mille milioni) thousand million,
billion (US); (milione di milioni) billion (BRIT),
trillion (US)
bilo'cale SM two-room flat (BRIT) o apartment
(US)
'bimbo, -a SM/F little boy (girl)
bimen'sile AG fortnightly
bimes'trale AG two-monthly, bimonthly
bi'mestre SM two-month period; **ogni ~**
every two months
bi'nario, -a AG (sistema) binary ▶ SM (railway)
track o line; (piattaforma) platform; **~ morto**
dead-end track
bi'nocolo SM binoculars pl
bio... PREFISSO bio
biocarbu'rante SM biofuel
bio'chimica [bio'kimika] SF biochemistry
biodegra'dabile AG biodegradable
bio'diesel [bio'dizel] SM INV biodiesel
biodi'namico, -a, -ci, -che AG biodynamic
biodiversità SF biodiversity
bio'etica SF bioethics sg
bio'etico, -a, -ci, -che AG bioethical
bio'fabbrica SF factory producing biological
control agents
bio'fisica SF biophysics sg
biogra'fia SF biography
bio'grafico, -a, -ci, -che AG biographical
bi'ografo, -a SM/F biographer
biolo'gia [biolo'dʒia] SF biology

bio'logico, -a, -ci, -che [bio'lɔdʒiko] AG
(scienze, fenomeni ecc) biological; (agricoltura,
prodotti) organic; **guerra biologica**
biological warfare
bi'ologo, -a, -ghi, -ghe SM/F biologist
bi'ondo, -a AG blond, fair
bi'onico, -a, -ci, -che AG bionic
biop'sia SF biopsy
bio'ritmo SM biorhythm
bios'fera SF biosphere
biotecnolo'gia [bioteknolo'dʒia] SF
biotechnology
bipar'tito, -a AG (Pol) two-party cpd ▶ SM (Pol)
two-party alliance
'birba SF rascal, rogue
bir'bante SM rascal, rogue
birbo'nata SF naughty trick
bir'bone, -a AG (bambino) naughty ▶ SM/F
little rascal
biri'chino, -a [biri'kino] AG mischievous
▶ SM/F scamp, little rascal
bi'rillo SM skittle (BRIT), pin (US); **birilli** SMPL
(gioco) skittles sg (BRIT), bowling no pl (US)
Bir'mania SF: **la ~** Burma
bir'mano, -a AG, SM/F Burmese (inv)
'biro® SF INV biro®
'birra SF beer; **~ chiara/scura** lager/stout; **a
tutta ~** (fig) at top speed
birre'ria SF (locale) ≈ bierkeller; (fabbrica)
brewery
bis ESCL, SM INV encore ▶ AG INV (treno, autobus)
relief cpd (BRIT), additional; (numero): **12 ~** 12a
bi'saccia, -ce [bi'zattʃa] SF knapsack
Bi'sanzio [bi'zantsjo] SF Byzantium
bis'betico, -a, -ci, -che AG ill-tempered,
crabby
bisbigli'are [bizbiʎ'ʎare] /27/ VT, VI to
whisper
bis'biglio¹ [biz'biʎʎo] SM whisper; (notizia)
rumour (BRIT), rumor (US)
bisbi'glio² [bizbiʎ'ʎio] SM whispering
bis'boccia, -ce [biz'bɔttʃa] SF binge, spree;
fare ~ to have a binge
'bisca, -sche SF gambling house
Bis'caglia [bis'kaʎʎa] SF: **il golfo di ~** the Bay
of Biscay
'bischero ['biskero] SM (Mus) peg; (col: toscano)
fool, idiot
'biscia, -sce ['biʃʃa] SF snake; **~ d'acqua** water
snake
biscot'tato, -a AG crisp; **fette biscottate** rusks
bis'cotto SM biscuit
bisessu'ale AG, SMF bisexual
bises'tile AG: **anno ~** leap year
bisezi'one [biset'tsjone] SF dichotomy
bis'lacco, -a, -chi, -che AG odd, weird
bis'lungo, -a, -ghi, -ghe AG oblong
bis'nonno, -a SM/F great grandfather/
grandmother

biso'gnare [bizoɲ'ɲare] **/15/** VB IMPERS: **bisogna che tu parta/lo faccia** you'll have to go/do it; **bisogna parlargli** we'll (o I'll) have to talk to him ▶ VI (*esser utile*) to be necessary

bi'sogno [bi'zoɲɲo] SM need; **bisogni** SMPL (*necessità corporali*): **fare i propri bisogni** to relieve o.s.; **avere ~ di qc/di fare qc** to need sth/to do sth; **ha ~ di qualcosa?** do you need anything?; **al ~**, **in caso di ~** if need be

biso'gnoso, -a [bizoɲ'ɲoso] AG needy, poor; **~ di** in need of, needing

bi'sonte SM (*Zool*) bison

bis'tecca, -che SF steak, beefsteak; **~ al sangue/ai ferri** rare/grilled steak

bisticci'are [bistit'tʃare] **/14/** VI to quarrel, bicker; **bisticciarsi** VPR to quarrel, bicker

bis'ticcio [bis'tittʃo] SM quarrel, squabble; (*gioco di parole*) pun

bistrat'tare **/72/** VT to maltreat

'bisturi SM INV scalpel

bi'sunto, -a AG very greasy

bi'torzolo [bi'tortsolo] SM (*sulla testa*) bump; (*sul corpo*) lump

'bitter SM INV bitters pl

bi'tume SM bitumen

bivac'care **/20/** VI (*Mil*) to bivouac; (*fig*) to bed down

bi'vacco, -chi SM bivouac

'bivio SM fork; (*fig*) dilemma

bizan'tino, -a [biddzan'tino] AG Byzantine

'bizza ['biddza] SF tantrum; **fare le bizze** to throw a tantrum

biz'zarro, -a [bid'dzarro] AG bizarre, strange

biz'zeffe [bid'dzɛffe]: **a ~** av in plenty, galore

BL SIGLA = **Belluno**

blan'dire **/55/** VT to soothe; to flatter

'blando, -a AG mild, gentle

blas'femo, -a AG blasphemous ▶ SM/F blasphemer

bla'sone SM coat of arms

blate'rare **/72/** VI to chatter

'blatta SF cockroach

blin'dare **/72/** VT to armour (*BRIT*), armor (*US*)

blin'data SF (*macchina*) armoured car o limousine

blin'dato, -a AG armoured (*BRIT*), armored (*US*); **camera blindata** strongroom; **mezzo ~** armoured vehicle; **porta blindata** reinforced door; **vita blindata** life amid maximum security; **vetro ~** bulletproof glass

bloc'care **/20/** VT to block; (*isolare*) to isolate, cut off; (*porto*) to blockade; (*prezzi, beni*) to freeze; (*meccanismo*) to jam; **bloccarsi** VPR (*motore*) to stall; (*freni, porta*) to jam, stick; (*ascensore*) to get stuck, stop; **ha bloccato la macchina** (*Aut*) he jammed on the brakes

bloccas'terzo [blokkas'tɛrtso] SM (*Aut*) steering lock

bloccherò etc [blokke'rɔ] VB vedi **bloccare**

bloc'chetto [blok'ketto] SM notebook; (*di biglietti*) book

'blocco, -chi SM block; (*Mil*) blockade; (*dei fitti*) restriction; (*quadernetto*) pad; (*fig: unione*) coalition; (*il bloccare*) blocking; isolating, cutting-off; blockading; freezing; jamming; **in ~** (*nell'insieme*) as a whole; (*Comm*) in bulk; **~ cardiaco** cardiac arrest; **~ stradale** road block

bloc-'notes [blɔk'nɔt] SM INV notebook, notepad

blog [blog] SM INV blog

'bloggare **/80/** VI to blog

blogos'fera [blogos'fɛra] SF blogosphere

blu AG INV, SM INV dark blue

bluff [blɛf] SM INV bluff

bluf'fare **/72/** VI (*anche fig*) to bluff

'blusa SF (*camiciotto*) smock; (*camicetta*) blouse

BN SIGLA = **Benevento**

BO SIGLA = **Bologna**

'boa SM INV (*Zool*) boa constrictor; (*sciarpa*) feather boa ▶ SF buoy

bo'ato SM rumble, roar

bob [bɔb] SM INV bobsleigh

bo'bina SF reel, spool; (*di pellicola*) spool; (*di film*) reel; (*Elettr*) coil

'bocca, -che SF mouth; **essere di buona ~** to be a hearty eater; (*fig*) to be easily satisfied; **essere sulla ~ di tutti** (*persona, notizia*) to be the talk of the town; **rimanere a ~ asciutta** to have nothing to eat; (*fig*) to be disappointed; **in ~ al lupo!** good luck!; **~ di leone** (*Bot*) snapdragon

boc'caccia, -ce [bok'kattʃa] SF (*malalingua*) gossip; (*smorfia*): **fare le boccacce** to pull faces

boc'caglio [bok'kaʎʎo] SM (*Tecn*) nozzle; (*di respiratore*) mouthpiece

boc'cale SM jug; **~ da birra** tankard

bocca'scena [bokkaʃ'ʃena] SM INV proscenium

boc'cata SF mouthful; (*di fumo*) puff; **prendere una ~ d'aria** to go out for a breath of (fresh) air

boc'cetta [bot'tʃetta] SF small bottle

boccheggi'are [bokked'dʒare] **/62/** VI to gasp

boc'chino [bok'kino] SM (*di sigaretta, sigaro: cannella*) cigarette-holder; cigar-holder; (*di pipa, strumenti musicali*) mouthpiece

'boccia, -ce ['bottʃa] SF bottle; (*da vino*) decanter, carafe; (*palla di legno, metallo*) bowl; **gioco delle bocce** bowls sg

bocci'are [bot'tʃare] **/14/** VT (*proposta, progetto*) to reject; (*Ins*) to fail; (*Bocce*) to hit

boccia'tura [bottʃa'tura] SF failure

bocci'olo [bot'tʃɔlo] SM bud

'boccolo SM curl

boccon'cino [bokkon'tʃino] SM (*pietanza deliziosa*) delicacy

boc'cone SM mouthful, morsel; **mangiare un ~** to have a bite to eat

boc'coni AV face downwards

Bo'emia SF Bohemia

bo'emo, -a AG, SM/F Bohemian

bofonchi'are [bofon'kjare] /19/ VI to grumble

Bogotá SF Bogotá

'boia SM INV executioner; hangman; **fa un freddo ~** (*col*) it's cold as hell; **mondo ~!**, **~ d'un mondo ladro!** (*col*) damn!, blast!

boi'ata SF botch

boicot'taggio [boikot'taddʒo] SM boycott

boicot'tare /72/ VT to boycott

'bolgia, -ge ['bɔldʒa] SF (*fig*): **c'era una tale ~ al cinema** the cinema was absolutely mobbed

'bolide SM (*Astr*) meteor; (*macchina: da corsa*) racing car (BRIT), race car (US); (*: elaborata*) performance car; **come un ~** like a flash, at top speed; **entrare/uscire come un ~** to charge in/out

Bo'livia SF: **la ~** Bolivia

bolivi'ano, -a AG, SM/F Bolivian

'bolla SF bubble; (*Med*) blister; (*Comm*) bill, receipt; **finire in una ~ di sapone** (*fig*) to come to nothing; **~ di accompagnamento** waybill; **~ di consegna** (*Comm*) delivery note; **~ papale** papal bull

bol'lare /72/ VT to stamp; (*fig*) to brand

bol'lente AG boiling; boiling hot; **calmare i bollenti spiriti** to sober up, calm down

bol'letta SF bill; (*ricevuta*) receipt; **essere in ~** to be hard up; **~ di consegna** delivery note; **~ doganale** clearance certificate; **~ di trasporto aereo** air waybill

bollet'tino SM bulletin; (*Comm*) note; **~ meteorologico** weather forecast; **~ di ordinazione** order form; **~ di spedizione** consignment note

bolli'cina [bolli'tʃina] SF bubble; **acqua con le ~** fizzy water

bol'lire /17/ VT, VI to boil; **qualcosa bolle in pentola** (*fig*) there's something brewing

bol'lito SM (*Cuc*) boiled meat

bolli'tore SM (*Tecn*) boiler; (*Cuc: per acqua*) kettle; (*: per latte*) milk pan

bolli'tura SF boiling

'bollo SM stamp; **imposta di ~** stamp duty; **~ auto** road tax; **~ per patente** driving licence tax; **~ postale** postmark

bol'lore SM: **dare un ~ a qc** to bring sth to the boil (BRIT) o a boil (US); **i bollori della gioventù** youthful enthusiasm *sg*

Bo'logna [bo'lɔɲɲa] SF Bologna

bolo'gnese [bolɔɲ'ɲese] AG Bolognese; **spaghetti alla ~** spaghetti bolognese

'bomba SF bomb; **tornare a ~** (*fig*) to get back to the point; **sei stato una ~!** you were tremendous!; **~ atomica** atom bomb; **~ a mano** hand grenade; **~ ad orologeria** time bomb

bombarda'mento SM bombardment; bombing

bombar'dare /72/ VT to bombard; (*da aereo*) to bomb

bombardi'ere SM bomber

bom'betta SF bowler (hat) (BRIT), derby (US)

'bombola SF cylinder; **~ del gas** gas cylinder

bombo'letta SF spray can

bomboni'era SF box of sweets (*as souvenir at weddings, first communions etc*)

bo'naccia, -ce [bo'nattʃa] SF dead calm

bonacci'one, -a [bonat'tʃone] AG good-natured ▶ SM/F good-natured sort

bo'nario, -a AG good-natured, kind

bo'nifica, -che SF reclamation; reclaimed land

bo'nifico, -ci SM (*riduzione, abbuono*) discount; (*versamento a terzi*) credit transfer

Bonn SF Bonn

bontà SF goodness; (*cortesia*) kindness; **aver la ~ di fare qc** to be good o kind enough to do sth

'bonus-'malus SM INV ≈ no-claims bonus

bor'bonico, -a, -ci, -che AG Bourbon; (*fig*) backward, out of date

borbot'tare /72/ VI to mumble; (*stomaco*) to rumble

borbot'tio, -ii SM mumbling; rumbling

'borchia ['borkja] SF stud

borda'tura SF (*Sartoria*) border, trim

bor'deaux [bor'dɔ] AG INV maroon ▶ SM INV (*colore*) burgundy, maroon; (*vino*) Bordeaux

bor'dello SM brothel

'bordo SM (*Naut*) ship's side; (*orlo*) edge; (*striscia di guarnizione*) border, trim; **a ~ di** (*nave, aereo*) aboard, on board; (*macchina*) in; **sul ~ della strada** at the roadside; **persona d'alto ~** VIP

bor'dura SF border

bor'gata SF hamlet; (*a Roma*) working-class suburb

bor'ghese [bor'geze] AG (*spesso peg*) middle-class; bourgeois; **abito ~** civilian dress; **poliziotto in ~** plainclothes policeman

borghe'sia [borge'zia] SF middle classes *pl*; bourgeoisie

'borgo, -ghi SM (*paesino*) village; (*quartiere*) district; (*sobborgo*) suburb

'boria SF self-conceit, arrogance

bori'oso, -a AG arrogant

bor'lotto SM kidney bean

'Borneo SM: **il ~** Borneo

boro'talco SM talcum powder

bor'raccia, -ce [bor'rattʃa] SF canteen, water-bottle

'borsa SF bag; (anche: **borsa da signora**) handbag; (Econ) **la B~ (valori)** the Stock Exchange; **~ dell'acqua calda** hot-water bottle; **B~ merci** commodity exchange; **~ nera** black market; **~ della spesa** shopping bag; **~ di studio** grant

borsai'olo SM pickpocket

bor'seggio [bor'seddʒo] SM pickpocketing

borsel'lino SM purse

bor'sello SM gent's handbag

bor'setta SF handbag

bor'sista, -i, -e SM/F (Econ) speculator; (Ins) grant-holder

bos'caglia [bos'kaʎʎa] SF woodlands pl

boscai'olo, boscaiu'olo SM woodcutter; forester

bos'chetto [bos'ketto] SM copse, grove

'bosco, -schi SM wood

bos'coso, -a AG wooded

bos'niaco, -a, -ci, -che AG, SM/F Bosnian

'Bosnia-Erze'govina ['bɔsnja erdze'govina] SF: **la ~** Bosnia-Herzegovina

'bossolo SM cartridge case

Bot, bot SIGLA M INV (= buono ordinario del Tesoro) short-term Treasury bond

bo'tanico, -a, -ci, -che AG botanical ▶ SM botanist ▶ SF botany

'botola SF trap door

Bots'wana [bots'vana] SM: **il ~** Botswana

'botta SF blow; (rumore) bang; **dare (un sacco di) botte a qn** to give sb a good thrashing; **~ e risposta** (fig) cut and thrust

'botte SF barrel, cask; **essere in una ~ di ferro** (fig) to be as safe as houses; **volere la ~ piena e la moglie ubriaca** to want to have one's cake and eat it

bot'tega, -ghe SF shop; (officina) workshop; **stare a ~ da qn** to serve one's apprenticeship (with sb); **le Botteghe Oscure** headquarters of the DS, Italian left-wing party

botte'gaio, -a SM/F shopkeeper

botte'ghino [botte'gino] SM ticket office; (del lotto) public lottery office

bot'tiglia [bot'tiʎʎa] SF bottle

bottiglie'ria [bottiʎʎe'ria] SF wine shop

bot'tino SM (di guerra) booty; (di rapina, furto) loot; **fare ~ di qc** (anche fig) to make off with sth

'botto SM bang; crash; **di ~** suddenly; **d'un ~** (col) in a flash

bot'tone SM button; (Bot) bud; **stanza dei bottoni** control room; (fig) nerve centre; **attaccare (un) ~ a qn** to buttonhole sb

bo'vino, -a AG bovine; **bovini** SMPL cattle

box [bɔks] SM INV (per cavalli) horsebox; (per macchina) lock-up; (per macchina da corsa) pit; (per bambini) playpen

boxe [bɔks] SF boxing

'boxer ['bɔkser] SM INV (cane) boxer ▶ SMPL (mutande): **un paio di ~** a pair of boxer shorts

'bozza ['bɔttsa] SF draft; (Tip) proof; **~ di stampa/impaginata** galley/page proof

boz'zetto [bot'tsetto] SM sketch

'bozzolo ['bɔttsolo] SM cocoon

BR SIGLA FPL = **Brigate Rosse** ▶ SIGLA = **Brindisi**

'braca, -che SF (gamba di pantalone) trouser leg; **brache** SFPL (col) trousers, pants (US); (mutandoni) drawers; **calare le brache** (fig: col) to chicken out

brac'care /20/ VT to hunt

brac'cetto [brat'tʃetto] SM: **a ~** arm in arm

braccherò etc [brakke'rɔ] VB vedi **braccare**

bracci'ale [brat'tʃale] SM bracelet; (per nuotare, anche distintivo) armband

braccia'letto [brattʃa'letto] SM bracelet, bangle

bracci'ante [brat'tʃante] SM (Agr) day labourer

bracci'ata [brat'tʃata] SF armful; (nel nuoto) stroke

'braccio (Anat pl(f) **braccia**, di gru, fiume pl(m) **bracci**) ['brattʃo] SM arm; (di edificio) wing; **camminare sotto ~** to walk arm in arm; **è il suo ~ destro** he's his right-hand man; **~ di ferro** (anche fig) trial of strength; **~ di mare** sound

bracci'olo [brat'tʃolo] SM (appoggio) arm

'bracco, -chi SM hound

bracconi'ere SM poacher

'brace ['bratʃe] SF embers pl

braci'ere [bra'tʃere] SM brazier

braci'ola [bra'tʃɔla] SF (Cuc) chop

'bradipo SM (Zool) sloth

'brado, -a AG: **allo stato ~** in the wild o natural state

'brama SF: **~ (di/di fare)** longing (for/to do), yearning (for/to do)

bra'mare /72/ VT: **~ (qc/di fare qc)** to long (for sth/to do sth), yearn (for sth/to do sth)

bramo'sia SF: **~ (di)** longing (for), yearning (for)

'branca, -che SF branch

'branchia ['brankja] SF (Zool) gill

'branco, -chi SM (di cani, lupi) pack; (di uccelli, pecore) flock; (peg: di persone) gang, pack

branco'lare /72/ VI to grope, feel one's way

'branda SF camp bed

bran'dello SM scrap, shred; **a brandelli** in tatters, in rags; **fare a brandelli** to tear to shreds

bran'dina SF camp bed (BRIT), cot (US)

bran'dire /55/ VT to brandish

'brano SM piece; (di libro) passage

bra'sare /72/ VT to braise

bra'sato SM braised beef

Bra'sile SM: **il** ~ Brazil
Bra'silia SF Brasilia
brasili'ano, -a AG, SM/F Brazilian
bra'vata SF (*azione spavalda*) act of bravado
'bravo, -a AG (*abile*) clever, capable, skilful; (*buono*) good, honest; (*: bambino*) good; (*coraggioso*) brave; ~! well done!; (*al teatro*) bravo!; **su da** ~! (*col*) there's a good boy!; **mi sono fatto le mie brave 8 ore di lavoro** I put in a full 8 hours' work
bra'vura SF cleverness, skill
'breccia, -ce ['brettʃa] SF breach; **essere sulla** ~ (*fig*) to be going strong; **fare** ~ **nell'animo** *o* **nel cuore di qn** to find the way to sb's heart
'Brema SF Bremen
bre'saola SF kind of dried salted beef
bresci'ano, -a [breʃʃano] AG of (*o* from) Brescia
Bre'tagna [bre'taɲɲa] SF: **la** ~ Brittany
bre'tella SF (*Aut*) link; **bretelle** SFPL (*di calzoni*) braces
'bret(t)one AG, SMF Breton
'breve AG brief, short; **in** ~ in short; **per farla** ~ to cut a long story short; **a** ~ (*Comm*) short-term
brevet'tare /72/ VT to patent
bre'vetto SM patent; ~ **di pilotaggio** pilot's licence (*BRIT*) *o* license (*US*)
brevità SF brevity
'brezza ['breddza] SF breeze
'bricco, -chi SM jug; ~ **del caffè** coffeepot
bricco'nata SF mischievous trick
bric'cone, -a SM rogue, rascal
'briciola ['britʃola] SF crumb
'briciolo ['britʃolo] SM (*fig*) bit
bridge [bridʒ] SM bridge
'briga, -ghe SF (*fastidio*) trouble, bother; **attaccar** ~ to start a quarrel; **pigliarsi la** ~ **di fare qc** to take the trouble to do sth
brigadi'ere SM (*dei carabinieri ecc*) ≈ sergeant
bri'gante SM bandit
bri'gata SF (*Mil*) brigade; (*gruppo*) group, party; **le Brigate Rosse** (*Pol*) the Red Brigades
briga'tismo SM *phenomenon of the Red Brigades*
briga'tista, -i, -e SM/F (*Pol*) *member of the Red Brigades*
'briglia ['briʎʎa] SF rein; **a** ~ **sciolta** at full gallop; (*fig*) at full speed
bril'lante AG bright; (*anche fig*) brilliant; (*che luccica*) shining ▶ SM diamond
brillan'tina SF brilliantine
bril'lare /72/ VI to shine; (*mina*) to blow up ▶ VT (*mina*) to set off
'brillo, -a AG merry, tipsy
'brina SF hoarfrost
brin'dare /72/ VI: ~ **a qn/qc** to drink to *o* toast sb/sth

'brindisi SM INV toast
'brio SM liveliness, go
bri'oche [bri'ɔʃ] SF INV brioche (bun)
bri'oso, -a AG lively
'briscola SF *type of card game*; (*seme vincente*) trump(s); (*carta*) trump card
bri'tannico, -a, -ci, -che AG British ▶ SM/F Briton; **i Britannici** the British *pl*
'brivido SM shiver; (*di ribrezzo*) shudder; (*fig*) thrill; **racconti del** ~ suspense stories
brizzo'lato, -a [brittso'lato] AG (*persona*) going grey; (*barba, capelli*) greying
'brocca, -che SF jug
broc'cato SM brocade
'broccoli SMPL broccoli *sg*
bro'daglia [bro'daʎʎa] SF (*peg*) dishwater
'brodo SM broth; (*per cucinare*) stock; ~ **ristretto** consommé; **lasciare (cuocere) qn nel suo** ~ to let sb stew (in his own juice); **tutto fa** ~ every little bit helps
'broglio ['brɔʎʎo] SM: ~ **elettorale** gerrymandering; **brogli** SMPL (*Dir*) malpractices
'bromo SM (*Chim*) bromine
bron'chite [bron'kite] SF (*Med*) bronchitis
'broncio ['brontʃo] SM sulky expression; **tenere il** ~ to sulk
'bronco, -chi SM bronchial tube
bronto'lare /72/ VI to grumble; (*tuono, stomaco*) to rumble
bronto'lio SM grumbling, mumbling
bronto'lone, -a AG grumbling ▶ SM/F grumbler
bron'zina [bron'dzina] SF (*Tecn*) bush
'bronzo ['brondzo] SM bronze; **che faccia di** ~! what a brass neck!
bross. ABBR = **in brossura**
bros'sura SF: **in** ~ (*libro*) limpback
'browser ['brauzer] SM INV (*Inform*) browser
bru'care /20/ VT to browse on, nibble at
brucherà etc [bruke'ra] VB vedi **brucare**
bruciacchi'are [brutʃak'kjare] /19/ VT to singe, scorch; **bruciacchiarsi** VPR to become singed *o* scorched
brucia'pelo [brutʃa'pelo]: **a** ~ *av* point-blank
bruci'are [bru'tʃare] /14/ VT to burn; (*scottare*) to scald ▶ VI to burn; **bruciarsi** VPR to burn o.s.; (*fallire*) to ruin one's chances; ~ **gli avversari** (*Sport, fig*) to leave the rest of the field behind; ~ **le tappe** *o* **i tempi** (*Sport, fig*) to shoot ahead; **bruciarsi la carriera** to put an end to one's career
brucia'tore [brutʃa'tore] SM burner
brucia'tura [brutʃa'tura] SF (*atto*) burning *no pl*; (*segno*) burn; (*scottatura*) scald
bruci'ore [bru'tʃore] SM burning *o* smarting sensation
'bruco, -chi SM grub; (*di farfalla*) caterpillar
'brufolo SM pimple, spot

brughi'era [bru'gjɛra] SF heath, moor
bruli'care /20/ VI to swarm
bruli'chio, -ii [bruli'kio] SM swarming
'brullo, -a AG bare, bleak
'bruma SF mist
'bruno, -a AG brown, dark; (persona) dark(-haired)
brusca'mente AV (frenare, fermarsi) suddenly; (rispondere, reagire) sharply
'brusco, -a, -schi, -sche AG (sapore) sharp; (modi, persona) brusque, abrupt; (movimento) abrupt, sudden
bru'sio SM buzz, buzzing
bru'tale AG brutal
brutalità SF INV brutality
'bruto, -a AG (forza) brute cpd ▶ SM brute
'brutta SF vedi **brutto**
brut'tezza [brut'tettsa] SF ugliness
'brutto, -a AG ugly; (cattivo) bad; (malattia, strada, affare) nasty, bad ▶ SM: **guardare qn di ~** to give sb a nasty look ▶ SF rough copy, first draft; **~ tempo** bad weather; **passare un ~ quarto d'ora** to have a nasty time of it; **vedersela brutta** (per un attimo) to have a nasty moment; (per un periodo) to have a bad time of it
brut'tura SF (cosa brutta) ugly thing; (sudiciume) filth; (azione meschina) mean action
Bru'xelles [bry'sɛl] SF Brussels
BS SIGLA = **Brescia**
BSE [biɛssɛ'e] SIGLA F BSE (= bovine spongiform encephalopathy)
B.T. ABBR (= bassa tensione) LT ▶ SIGLA M INV = **buono del Tesoro**
btg ABBR = **battaglione**
Btp SIGLA M = **buono del Tesoro poliennale**; vedi **buono**
bub'bone SM swelling
'buca, -che SF hole; (avvallamento) hollow; **~ delle lettere** letterbox
buca'neve SM INV snowdrop
bu'care /20/ VT (forare) to make a hole (o holes) in; (pungere) to pierce; (biglietto) to punch; **bucarsi** VPR (con eroina) to mainline; **~ una gomma** to have a puncture; **avere le mani bucate** (fig) to be a spendthrift
'Bucarest SF Bucharest
bu'cato SM (operazione) washing; (panni) wash, washing
'buccia, -ce ['buttʃa] SF skin, peel; (corteccia) bark
bucherel'lare [bukerel'lare] /72/ VT to riddle with holes
bucherò etc [buke'rɔ] VB vedi **bucare**
'buco, -chi SM hole; **fare un ~ nell'acqua** to fail, draw a blank; **farsi un ~** (col: drogarsi) to have a fix; **~ nero** (anche fig) black hole
'Budapest SF Budapest
'Budda SM INV Buddha

bud'dismo SM Buddhism
bu'dello SM intestine; (fig: tubo) tube; (vicolo) alley; **budella** SFPL bowels, guts
bu'dino SM pudding
'bue (pl buoi) SM OX; (anche: **carne di bue**) beef; **uovo all'occhio di ~** fried egg
Bu'enos 'Aires SF Buenos Aires
'bufalo SM buffalo
bu'fera SF storm
buf'fetto SM flick
'buffo, -a AG funny; (Teat) comic
buffo'nata SF (azione) prank, jest; (parola) jest
buf'fone SM buffoon
bugge'rare [buddʒe'rare] /72/ VT to swindle, cheat
bu'gia, -'gie [bu'dʒia] SF lie; (candeliere) candleholder; **dire una ~** to tell a lie
bugi'ardo, -a [bu'dʒardo] AG lying, deceitful ▶ SM/F liar
bugi'gattolo [budʒi'gattolo] SM poky little room
'buio, -a AG dark ▶ SM dark, darkness; **fa ~ pesto** it's pitch-dark
'bulbo SM (Bot) bulb; **~ oculare** eyeball
Bulga'ria SF: **la ~** Bulgaria
'bulgaro, -a AG, SM/F Bulgarian
buli'mia SF bulimia
bu'limico, -a, -ci, -che AG bulimic
bul'lismo [bul'lizmo] SM bullying
'bullo SM (persona) tough
bul'lone SM bolt
bu'oi SMPL di **bue**
buona'fede SF good faith
buon'anima SF = **buon'anima**; vedi **anima**
buona'notte ESCL good night! ▶ SF: **dare la ~ a** to say good night to
buona'sera ESCL good evening!
buoncos'tume SM public morality; **la (squadra del) ~** (Polizia) the vice squad
buondì ESCL hello!
buongi'orno [bwon'dʒorno] ESCL good morning (o afternoon)!
buon'grado AV: **di ~** willingly
buongus'taio, -a SM/F gourmet
buon'gusto SM good taste

(**PAROLA CHIAVE**)

bu'ono, -a (ag: dav sm **buon** + C o V, **buono** + s impura, gn, pn, ps, z; dav sf **buon'** + V) AG **1** (gen) good; **un buon pranzo/ristorante** a good lunch/restaurant; (**stai**) **buono!** behave!; **che buono!** (cibo) this is nice!
2 (benevolo): **buono (con)** good (to), kind (to)
3 (giusto, valido) right; **al momento buono** at the right moment
4 (adatto): **buono a/da** fit for/to; **essere buono a nulla** to be no good o use at anything
5 (auguri): **buon anno!** happy New Year!; **buon appetito!** enjoy your meal!; **buon**

compleanno! happy birthday!; **buon divertimento!** have a nice time!; **buona fortuna!** good luck!; **buon riposo!** sleep well!; **buon viaggio!** bon voyage!, have a good trip!

6: **ad ogni buon conto** in any case; **tante buone cose!** all the best!; **di buon cuore** (*persona*) goodhearted; **di buon grado** willingly; **le buone maniere** good manners; **di buon mattino** early in the morning; **a buon mercato** cheap; **di buon'ora** early; **mettere una buona parola** to put in a good word; **di buon passo** at a good pace; **buon pro ti faccia!** much good may it do you!; **buon senso** common sense; **la buona società** the upper classes; **una buona volta** once and for all; **alla buona** *ag* simple

▶ *AV* in a simple way, without any fuss; **un tipo alla buona** an easy-going sort

▶ *SM/F*: **essere un buono/una buona** to be a good person; **buono a nulla** good for nothing; **i buoni e i cattivi** (*in storia, film*) the goodies and the baddies; **accetterà con le buone o con le cattive** one way or another he's going to agree to it

▶ *SM* **1** (*bontà*) goodness, good

2 (*Comm*) voucher, coupon; **buono d'acquisto** credit note; **buono di cassa** cash voucher; **buono di consegna** delivery note; **buono fruttifero** interest-bearing bond; **buono ordinario del Tesoro** short-term Treasury bond; **buono postale fruttifero** interest-bearing bond (*issued by Italian Post Office*); **buono del Tesoro** Treasury bill

buon'senso *SM* = **buon senso**
buontem'pone, -a *SM/F* jovial person
buonu'scita [bwonuʃʃita] *SF* (*Industria*) golden handshake; (*di affitti*) sum paid for the relinquishing of tenancy rights

buratti'naio *SM* puppeteer, puppet master
burat'tino *SM* puppet
'**burbero, -a** *AG* surly, gruff
'**burla** *SF* prank, trick
bur'lare /72/ *VT*: ~ **qc/qn**, **burlarsi di qc/qn** to make fun of sth/sb
bu'rocrate *SM* bureaucrat
buro'cratico, -a, -ci, -che *AG* bureaucratic
burocra'zia [burokrat'tsia] *SF* bureaucracy
bur'rasca, -sche *SF* storm
burras'coso, -a *AG* stormy
'**burro** *SM* butter
bur'rone *SM* ravine
bus'care /20/ *VT* (*raffreddore: anche*: **buscarsi**) to get, catch; **buscarle** (*col*) to get a hiding
buscherò *etc* [buske'rɔ] *VB vedi* **buscare**
bus'sare /72/ *VI* to knock; ~ **a quattrini** (*fig*) to ask for money
'**bussola** *SF* compass; **perdere la ~** (*fig*) to lose one's bearings
'**busta** *SF* (*da lettera*) envelope; (*astuccio*) case; **in ~ aperta/chiusa** in an unsealed/sealed envelope; ~ **paga** pay packet
busta'rella *SF* bribe, backhander
bus'tina *SF* (*piccola busta*) envelope; (*di cibi, farmaci*) sachet; (*Mil*) forage cap; ~ **di tè** tea bag
'**busto** *SM* bust; (*indumento*) corset, girdle; **a mezzo ~** (*fotografia, ritratto*) half-length
bu'tano *SM* butane
but'tare /72/ *VT* to throw; (*anche*: **buttare via**) to throw away; **buttarsi** *VPR* (*saltare*) to jump; ~ **giù** (*scritto*) to scribble down, dash off; (*cibo*) to gulp down; (*edificio*) to pull down, demolish; (*pasta, verdura*) to put into boiling water; **ho buttato là una frase** I mentioned it in passing; **buttiamoci!** (*saltiamo*) let's jump!; (*rischiamo*) let's have a go!; **buttarsi dalla finestra** to jump out of the window
'**buzzo** ['buddzo] *SM* (*col: pancia*) belly, paunch; **di ~ buono** (*con impegno*) with a will
byte ['bait] *SM INV* byte

Cc

C, c [tʃi] SM O F INV (*lettera*) C, c ▸ ABBR (*Geo*)
= **capo**; (= *Celsius, centigrado*) C; (= *conto*) a/c;
C come Como ≈ C for Charlie

CA SIGLA = **Cagliari**

c.a. ABBR (*Elettr*) *vedi* **corrente alternata**;
(*Comm*) = **corrente anno**

caba'ret [kaba'rɛ] SM INV cabaret

ca'bina SF (*di nave*) cabin; (*da spiaggia*) beach
hut; (*di autocarro, treno*) cab; (*di aereo*) cockpit;
(*di ascensore*) cage; **~ di pilotaggio** cockpit;
~ di proiezione (*Cine*) projection booth; **~ di
registrazione** recording booth;
~ telefonica callbox, (tele)phone box o booth

cabi'nato SM cabin cruiser

ca'blaggio [ka'bladdʒo] SM wiring

cablo'gramma SM cable(gram)

ca'cao SF cocoa

'cacca SF (*col: anche fig*) shit (!)

'caccia ['kattʃa] SF hunting; (*con fucile*)
shooting; (*inseguimento*) chase; (*cacciagione*)
game ▸ SM INV (*aereo*) fighter; (*nave*)
destroyer; **andare a ~** to go hunting;
andare a ~ di guai to be asking for trouble;
~ grossa big-game hunting; **~ all'uomo**
manhunt

cacciabombardi'ere [kattʃabombar'djɛre]
SM fighter-bomber

cacciagi'one [kattʃa'dʒone] SF game

cacci'are [kat'tʃare] /**14**/ VT to hunt; (*mandar
via*) to chase away; (*ficcare*) to shove, stick
▸ VI to hunt; **cacciarsi** VPR (*col: mettersi*):
cacciarsi tra la folla to plunge into the
crowd; **~ fuori qc** to whip o pull sth out;
~ un urlo to let out a yell; **dove s'è cacciata
la mia borsa?** where has my bag got to?;
cacciarsi nei guai to get into trouble

caccia'tora [kattʃa'tora] SF (*giacca*) hunting
jacket; (*Cuc*): **pollo** *etc* **alla ~** chicken *etc*
chasseur

caccia'tore [kattʃa'tore] SM hunter; **~ di
frodo** poacher; **~ di dote** fortune-hunter

cacciatorpedini'ere [kattʃatorpedi'njɛre]
SM destroyer

caccia'vite [kattʃa'vite] SM INV screwdriver

cache'mire [kaʃ'mir] SM INV cashmere

ca'chet [ka'ʃɛ] SM (*Med*) capsule; (: *compressa*)
tablet; (*compenso*) fee; (*colorante per capelli*) rinse

'cachi ['kaki] SM INV (*albero, frutto*) persimmon;
(*colore*) khaki ▸ AG INV khaki

'cacio ['katʃo] SM cheese; **essere come il ~
sui maccheroni** (*fig*) to turn up at the right
moment

'cactus SM INV cactus

ca'davere SM (dead) body, corpse

cada'verico, -a, -ci, -che AG (*fig*) deathly pale

'caddi *etc* VB *vedi* **cadere**

ca'dente AG falling; (*casa*) tumbledown;
(*persona*) decrepit

ca'denza [ka'dɛntsa] SF cadence; (*andamento
ritmico*) rhythm; (*Mus*) cadenza

ca'dere /**18**/ VI to fall; (*denti, capelli*) to fall out;
(*tetto*) to fall in; **questa gonna cade bene**
this skirt hangs well; **lasciar ~** (*anche fig*) to
drop; **~ dal sonno** to be falling asleep on
one's feet; **~ ammalato** to fall ill; **~ dalle
nuvole** (*fig*) to be taken aback

ca'detto SM cadet

cadrò *etc* VB *vedi* **cadere**

ca'duta SF fall; **la ~ dei capelli** hair loss

ca'duto, -a AG (*morto*) dead ▸ SM dead soldier
▸ SF fall; **monumento ai caduti** war
memorial; **caduta di temperatura** drop in
temperature; **la caduta dei capelli** hair
loss; **caduta del sistema** (*Inform*) system
failure

caffè SM INV coffee; (*locale*) café; **~ corretto**
coffee with liqueur; **~ in grani** coffee beans;
~ macchiato coffee with a dash of milk;
~ macinato ground coffee

caffe'ina SF caffeine

caffel'latte SM INV white coffee

caffette'ria SF coffee shop

caffetti'era SF coffeepot

ca'fone SM (*contadino*) peasant; (*peg*) boor

cagio'nare [kadʒo'nare] /**72**/ VT to cause, be
the cause of

cagio'nevole [kadʒo'nevole] AG delicate,
weak

cagli'are [kaʎ'ʎare] /**27**/ vi to curdle
cagliari'tano, -a [kaʎʎari'tano] AG of (o from)
  Cagliari
'**cagna** ['kaɲɲa] SF (Zool, peg) bitch
ca'gnara [kaɲ'ɲara] SF (fig) uproar
ca'gnesco, -a, -schi, -sche [kaɲ'ɲesko] AG
  (fig): **guardare qn in ~** to scowl at sb
CAI SIGLA M = **Club Alpino Italiano**
'**Cairo** SM: **il ~** Cairo
cala'brese AG, SMF Calabrian
cala'brone SM hornet
Cala'hari [kala'ari]: **il Deserto di ~** sm the
  Kalahari Desert
cala'maio SM inkpot; inkwell
cala'maro SM squid
cala'mita SF magnet
calamità SF INV calamity, disaster;
  ~ naturale natural disaster
ca'lare /**72**/ VT (far discendere) to lower; (Maglia)
  to decrease ▶ VI (discendere) to go (o come)
  down; (tramontare) to set, go down; **~ di peso**
  to lose weight
ca'lata SF (invasione) invasion
'**calca** SF throng, press
cal'cagno [kal'kaɲɲo] SM heel
cal'care /**20**/ SM limestone; (incrostazione)
  (lime)scale ▶ VT (premere coi piedi) to tread,
  press down; (premere con forza) to press down;
  (mettere in rilievo) to stress; **~ la mano** to
  overdo it, exaggerate; **~ le scene** (fig) to be on
  the stage; **~ le orme di qn** (fig) to follow in
  sb's footsteps
'**calce** ['kaltʃe] SM: **in ~** at the foot of the page
  ▶ SF lime; **~ viva** quicklime
calces'truzzo [kaltʃes'truttso] SM concrete
cal'cetto [kal'tʃetto] SM (calcio-balilla) table
  football; (calcio a cinque) five-a-side (football)
calcherò etc [kalke'rɔ] VB vedi **calcare**
calci'are [kal'tʃare] /**14**/ VT, VI to kick
calcia'tore [kaltʃa'tore] SM footballer (BRIT),
  (football) player
cal'cina [kal'tʃina] SF (lime) mortar
calci'naccio [kaltʃi'nattʃo] SM flake of
  plaster
'**calcio** ['kaltʃo] SM (pedata) kick; (sport)
  football, soccer; (di pistola, fucile) butt; (Chim)
  calcium; **~ d'angolo** (Sport) corner (kick);
  ~ di punizione (Sport) free kick; **~ di rigore**
  penalty
'**calco, -chi** SM (Arte) casting, moulding
  (BRIT), molding (US); cast, mo(u)ld
calco'lare /**72**/ VT to calculate, work out,
  reckon; (ponderare) to weigh (up)
calcola'tore, -'trice AG calculating ▶ SM
  calculator; (fig) calculating person ▶ SF
  (anche: **macchina calcolatrice**) calculator;
  ~ digitale digital computer; **~ elettronico**
  computer; **~ da tavolo** desktop computer
calcola'trice SF calculator

'**calcolo** SM (anche Mat) calculation;
  (infinitesimale ecc) calculus; (Med) stone; **fare
  il ~ di qc** to work sth out; **fare i propri
  calcoli** (fig) to weigh the pros and cons; **per
  ~** out of self-interest
cal'daia SF boiler
caldar'rosta SF roast chestnut
caldeggi'are [kalded'dʒare] /**62**/ VT to
  support
'**caldo, -a** AG warm; (molto caldo) hot; (fig:
  appassionato) keen; hearty ▶ SM heat; **ho ~**
  I'm warm; I'm hot; **fa ~** it's warm; it's hot;
  non mi fa né ~ né freddo I couldn't care
  less; **a ~** (fig) in the heat of the moment
caleidos'copio SM kaleidoscope
calen'dario SM calendar
ca'lende SFPL calends; **rimandare qc alle ~
  greche** to put sth off indefinitely
ca'lesse SM gig
'**calibro** SM (di arma) calibre, bore; (Tecn)
  callipers pl; (fig) calibre; **di grosso ~** (fig)
  prominent
'**calice** ['kalitʃe] SM goblet; (Rel) chalice
Cali'fornia SF California
californi'ano, -a AG Californian
ca'ligine [ka'lidʒine] SF fog; (mista con fumo)
  smog
calligra'fia SF (scrittura) handwriting; (arte)
  calligraphy
'**callo** SM callus; (ai piedi) corn; **fare il ~ a qc** to
  get used to sth
'**calma** SF calm; **faccia con ~** take your time
cal'mante SM sedative, tranquillizer
cal'mare /**72**/ VT to calm; (lenire) to soothe;
  calmarsi VPR to grow calm, calm down;
  (vento) to abate; (dolori) to ease
calmi'ere SM controlled price
'**calmo, -a** AG calm, quiet
'**calo** SM (Comm: di prezzi) fall; (: di volume)
  shrinkage; (: di peso) loss
ca'lore SM warmth; (intenso, Fisica) heat;
  essere in ~ (Zool) to be on heat
calo'ria SF calorie
calo'rifero SM radiator
calo'roso, -a AG warm; **essere ~** not to feel
  the cold
calpes'tare /**72**/ VT to tread on, trample on;
  "è vietato ~ l'erba" "keep off the grass"
ca'lunnia SF slander; (scritta) libel
calunni'are /**19**/ VT to slander
cal'vario SM (fig) affliction, cross
cal'vizie [kal'vittsje] SF baldness
'**calvo, -a** AG bald
'**calza** ['kaltsa] SF (da donna) stocking; (da
  uomo) sock; **fare la ~** to knit; **calze di nailon**
  nylons, (nylon) stockings
calza'maglia [kaltsa'maʎʎa] SF tights pl; (per
  danza, ginnastica) leotard
cal'zare [kal'tsare] /**72**/ VT (scarpe, guanti:

mettersi) to put on; (: portare) to wear ▸ vi to fit; ~ **a pennello** to fit like a glove

calza'tura [kaltsa'tura] sf footwear

calzaturi'ficio [kaltsaturi'fitʃo] sm shoe o footwear factory

cal'zetta [kal'tsetta] sf ankle sock; **una mezza ~** (fig) a nobody

calzet'tone [kaltset'tone] sm heavy knee-length sock

cal'zino [kal'tsino] sm sock

calzo'laio [kaltso'lajo] sm shoemaker; (che ripara scarpe) cobbler

calzole'ria [kaltsole'ria] sf (negozio) shoe shop; (arte) shoemaking

calzon'cini [kaltson'tʃini] smpl shorts; ~ **da bagno** (swimming) trunks

cal'zone [kal'tsone] sm trouser leg; (Cuc) savoury turnover made with pizza dough; **calzoni** smpl (pantaloni) trousers (BRIT), pants (US)

camale'onte sm chameleon

cambi'ale sf bill (of exchange); (pagherò cambiario) promissory note; ~ **di comodo** o **di favore** accommodation bill

cambia'mento sm change; **cambiamenti climatici** climate change sg

cambi'are /19/ vt to change; (modificare) to alter, change; (barattare): ~ **(qc con qn/qc)** to exchange (sth with sb/for sth) ▸ vi to change, alter; **cambiarsi** vpr (variare abito) to change; ~ **casa** to move (house); ~ **idea** to change one's mind; ~ **treno** to change trains; ~ **le carte in tavola** (fig) to change one's tune; ~ **(l')aria in una stanza** to air a room; **è ora di ~ aria** (andarsene) it's time to move on

cambiava'lute sm INV exchange office

'**cambio** sm change; (modifica) alteration, change; (scambio, Comm) exchange; (corso dei cambi) rate (of exchange); (Tecn, Aut) gears pl; **in ~ di** in exchange for; **dare il ~ a qn** to take over from sb; **fare il** o **un ~** to change (over); ~ **a termine** (Comm) forward exchange

'**Cambital** SIGLA M = **Ufficio Italiano dei Cambi**

Cam'bogia [kam'bɔdʒa] sf: **la ~** Cambodia

cambogi'ano, -a [kambo'dʒano] AG, SM/F Cambodian

cam'busa sf storeroom

'**camera** sf room; (anche: **camera da letto**) bedroom; (Pol) chamber, house; ~ **ardente** mortuary chapel; ~ **d'aria** inner tube; (di pallone) bladder; ~ **blindata** strongroom; **C~ di Commercio** Chamber of Commerce; **C~ dei Deputati** Chamber of Deputies, ≈ House of Commons (BRIT), ≈ House of Representatives (US); see note; ~ **a gas** gas chamber; ~ **del lavoro** trades union centre (BRIT), labor union center (US); ~ **a un letto/a due letti/matrimoniale** single/

twin-bedded/double room; ~ **oscura** (Fot) dark room; ~ **da pranzo** dining room

▌ The *Camera dei deputati* is the lower house of the Italian Parliament and is presided over by the *Presidente della Camera* who is chosen by the *deputati*. Elections to the Chamber are normally held every 5 years. Since the electoral reform of 1993 members have been voted in via a system which combines a first-past-the-post element with proportional representation. See also *Parlamento*.

came'rata, -i, -e sm/f companion, mate ▸ sf dormitory

camera'tismo sm comradeship

cameri'era sf (domestica) maid; (che serve a tavola) waitress; (che fa le camere) chambermaid

cameri'ere sm (man)servant; (di ristorante) waiter

came'rino sm (Teat) dressing room

'**Camerun** sm: **il ~** Cameroon

'**camice** ['kamitʃe] sm (Rel) alb; (per medici ecc) white coat

cami'cetta [kami'tʃetta] sf blouse

ca'micia, -cie [ka'mitʃa] sf (da uomo) shirt; (da donna) blouse; **nascere con la ~** (fig) to be born lucky; **sudare sette camicie** (fig) to have a hell of a time; ~ **di forza** straitjacket; ~ **da notte** (da donna) nightdress; (da uomo) nightshirt; **C~ nera** (fascista) Blackshirt

camici'aio, -a [kami'tʃajo] sm/f (sarto) shirtmaker; (che vende camicie) shirtseller

camici'ola [kami'tʃɔla] sf vest

camici'otto [kami'tʃɔtto] sm casual shirt; (per operai) smock

cami'netto sm hearth, fireplace

ca'mino sm chimney; (focolare) fireplace, hearth

'**camion** sm INV lorry (BRIT), truck (US)

camion'cino [kamjon'tʃino] sm van

camio'netta sf jeep

camio'nista, -i sm lorry driver (BRIT), truck driver (US)

'**camma** sf cam; **albero a camme** camshaft

cam'mello sm (Zool) camel; (tessuto) camel hair

cam'meo sm cameo

cammi'nare /72/ vi to walk; (funzionare) to work, go; ~ **a carponi** o **a quattro zampe** to go on all fours

cammi'nata sf walk; **fare una ~** to go for a walk

cam'mino sm walk; (sentiero) path; (itinerario, direzione, tragitto) way; **mettersi in ~** to set o start off; **cammin facendo** on the way; **riprendere il ~** to continue on one's way

camo'milla sf camomile; (infuso) camomile tea

ca'morra SF Camorra; (*fig*) racket
camor'rista, -i, -e SM/F member of the Camorra; (*fig*) racketeer
ca'moscio [ka'mɔʃʃo] SM chamois; **di ~** (*scarpe, borsa*) suede *cpd*
cam'pagna [kam'paɲɲa] SF country, countryside; (*Pol, Comm, Mil*) campaign; **in ~** in the country; **andare in ~** to go to the country; **fare una ~** to campaign; **~ promozionale vendite** sales campaign; **~ pubblicitaria** advertising campaign
campa'gnolo, -a [kampaɲ'ɲɔlo] AG country *cpd* ▶ SF (*Aut*) cross-country vehicle
cam'pale AG field *cpd*; (*fig*): **una giornata ~** a hard day
cam'pana SF bell; (*anche*: **campana di vetro**) bell jar; **sordo come una ~** as deaf as a doorpost; **sentire l'altra ~** (*fig*) to hear the other side of the story; **~ (per la raccolta del vetro)** bottle bank
campa'nella SF small bell; (*di tenda*) curtain ring
campa'nello SM (*all'uscio, da tavola*) bell
campa'nile SM bell tower, belfry
campani'lismo SM parochialism
cam'pano, -a AG of (*o* from) Campania
cam'pare /**72**/ VI to live; (*tirare avanti*) to get by, manage; **~ alla giornata** to live from day to day
cam'pato, -a AG: **~ in aria** unsound, unfounded
campeggi'are [kamped'dʒare] /**62**/ VI to camp; (*risaltare*) to stand out
campeggia'tore, -'trice [kampeddʒa'tore] SM/F camper
cam'peggio [kam'peddʒo] SM camping; (*terreno*) camp site; **fare (del) ~** to go camping
camper ['kamper] SM INV motor caravan (*BRIT*), motor home (*US*)
cam'pestre AG country *cpd*, rural; **corsa ~** cross-country race
Campi'doglio [kampi'dɔʎʎo] SM: **il ~** the Capitol; *see note*

The *Campidoglio*, one of the Seven Hills of Rome, is the home of the *Comune di Roma*.

'camping ['kæmpiŋ] SM INV camp site
campiona'mento SM sampling
campio'nario, -a AG: **fiera campionaria** trade fair ▶ SM collection of samples
campio'nato SM championship
campiona'tura SF (*Comm*) production of samples; (*Statistica*) sampling
campi'one, -'essa SM/F (*Sport*) champion ▶ SM (*Comm*) sample; **~ gratuito** free sample; **prelievi di ~** product samples
'campo SM (*gen*) field; (*Mil*) field; (: *accampamento*) camp; (*spazio delimitato*: *sportivo ecc*) ground; field; (*di quadro*)

background; **i campi** (*campagna*) the countryside; **padrone del ~** (*fig*) victor; **~ da aviazione** airfield; **~ di battaglia** (*Mil, fig*) battlefield; **~ di concentramento** concentration camp; **~ di golf** golf course; **~ profughi** refugee camp; **~ sportivo** sports ground; **~ lungo** (*Cine, TV, Fot*) long shot; **~ nomadi** travellers' camp; **~ da tennis** tennis court; **~ visivo** field of vision
campobas'sano, -a AG of (*o* from) Campobasso
campo'santo (*pl* **campisanti**) SM cemetery
camuf'fare /**72**/ VT to disguise; **camuffarsi** VPR: **camuffarsi (da)** to disguise o.s. (as); (*per ballo in maschera*) to dress up (as)
CAN ABBR (= *Costo, Assicurazione e Nolo*) CIF
Can. ABBR (*Geo*) = **canale**
'Canada SM: **il ~** Canada
cana'dese AG, SM/F Canadian ▶ SF (*anche*: **tenda canadese**) ridge tent
ca'naglia [ka'naʎʎa] SF rabble, mob; (*persona*) scoundrel, rogue
ca'nale SM (*anche fig*) channel; (*artificiale*) canal
'canapa SF hemp; **~ indiana** (*droga*) cannabis
Ca'narie SFPL: **le (isole) ~** the Canary Islands, the Canaries
cana'rino SM canary
Can'berra SF Canberra
cancel'lare [kantʃel'lare] /**72**/ VT (*con la gomma*) to rub out, erase; (*con la penna*) to strike out; (*annullare*) to annul, cancel; (*disdire*) to cancel
cancel'lata [kantʃel'lata] SF railing(s) *pl*
cancelle'ria [kantʃelle'ria] SF chancery; (*quanto necessario per scrivere*) stationery
cancelli'ere [kantʃel'ljɛre] SM chancellor; (*di tribunale*) clerk of the court
can'cello [kan'tʃello] SM gate
cance'rogeno, -a [kantʃe'rɔdʒeno] AG carcinogenic ▶ SM carcinogen
cance'rologo, -a, -gi, -ghe [kantʃe'rɔlogo] SM/F cancer specialist
cance'roso, -a [kantʃe'roso] AG cancerous ▶ SM/F cancer patient
can'crena SF gangrene
'cancro SM (*Med*) cancer; **C~** Cancer; **essere del C~** to be Cancer
candeggi'are [kanded'dʒare] /**62**/ VT to bleach
candeg'gina [kanded'dʒina] SF bleach
can'deggio [kan'deddʒo] SM bleaching
can'dela SF candle; **~ (di accensione)** (*Aut*) spark(ing) plug; **una lampadina da 100 candele** (*Elettr*) a 100 watt bulb; **a lume di ~** by candlelight; **tenere la ~** (*fig*) to play gooseberry (*BRIT*), act as chaperone
cande'labro SM candelabra
candeli'ere SM candlestick

cande'lotto SM candle; **~ di dinamite** stick of dynamite; **~ lacrimogeno** tear gas grenade

candi'dare /**72**/ VT to present as candidate; **candidarsi** VPR to present o.s. as candidate

candi'dato, -a SM/F candidate; (*aspirante a una carica*) applicant

candida'tura SF candidature; application

'candido, -a AG white as snow; (*puro*) pure; (*sincero*) sincere, candid

can'dito, -a AG candied

can'dore SM brilliant white; purity; sincerity, candour (BRIT), candor (US)

'cane SM dog; (*di pistola, fucile*) cock; **fa un freddo ~** it's bitterly cold; **non c'era un ~** there wasn't a soul; **quell'attore è un ~** he's a rotten actor; **~ da caccia** hunting dog; **~ da guardia** guard dog; **~ lupo** alsatian; **~ da salotto** lap dog; **~ da slitta** husky; **~ pastore** sheepdog

ca'nestro SM basket; **fare un ~** (*Sport*) to shoot a basket

'canfora SF camphor

cangi'ante [kan'dʒante] AG iridescent; **seta ~** shot silk

can'guro SM kangaroo

ca'nicola SF scorching heat

ca'nile SM kennel; (*di allevamento*) kennels *pl*; **~ municipale** dog pound

ca'nino, -a AG, SM canine

'canna SF (*pianta*) reed; (: *indica, da zucchero*) cane; (*bastone*) stick, cane; (*di fucile*) barrel; (*di organo*) pipe; (*col: Droga*) joint; **~ fumaria** chimney flue; **~ da pesca** (fishing) rod; **~ da zucchero** sugar cane

can'nella SF (*Cuc*) cinnamon; (*di conduttura, botte*) tap

cannel'loni SMPL *pasta tubes stuffed with sauce and baked*

can'neto SM bed of reeds

can'nibale SM cannibal

cannocchi'ale [kannok'kjale] SM telescope

canno'nata SF: **è una vera ~!** (*fig*) it's (o he's *etc*) fantastic!

can'none SM (*Mil*) gun; (: *Storia*) cannon; (*tubo*) pipe, tube; (*piega*) box pleat; (*fig*) ace; **donna ~** fat woman

cannoni'ere SM (*Naut*) gunner; (*Calcio*) goal scorer

can'nuccia, -ce [kan'nuttʃa] SF (drinking) straw

ca'noa SF canoe

'canone SM canon, criterion; (*mensile, annuo*) rent; fee; **legge dell'equo ~** fair rent act

ca'nonica, -che SF presbytery

ca'nonico, -ci SM (*Rel*) canon

canoniz'zare [kanonid'dzare] /**72**/ VT to canonize

ca'noro, -a AG (*uccello*) singing, song *cpd*

ca'notta SF vest

canot'taggio [kanot'taddʒo] SM rowing

canotti'era SF vest (BRIT), undershirt (US)

ca'notto SM small boat, dinghy; canoe

cano'vaccio [kano'vattʃo] SM (*tela*) canvas; (*strofinaccio*) duster; (*trama*) plot

can'tante SMF singer

can'tare /**72**/ VT, VI to sing; **~ vittoria** to crow; **fare ~ qn** (*fig*) to make sb talk

cantas'torie SM INV/F INV storyteller

cantau'tore, -'trice SM/F singer-composer

canterel'lare /**72**/ VT, VI to hum, sing to o.s.

canticchi'are [kantik'kjare] /**19**/ VT, VI to hum, sing to o.s.

canti'ere SM (*Edil*) (building) site; (*anche:* **cantiere navale**) shipyard

canti'lena SF (*filastrocca*) lullaby; (*fig*) singsong voice

can'tina SF (*locale*) cellar; (*bottega*) wine shop; **~ sociale** cooperative winegrowers' association

'canto SM song; (*arte*) singing; (*Rel*) chant; chanting; (*Poesia*) poem, lyric; (*parte di una poesia*) canto; (*parte, lato*): **da un ~** on the one hand; **d'altro ~** on the other hand

canto'nata SF (*di edificio*) corner; **prendere una ~** (*fig*) to blunder

can'tone SM (*in Svizzera*) canton

cantoni'era AG: **(casa) ~** road inspector's house

can'tuccio [kan'tuttʃo] SM corner, nook

ca'nuto, -a AG white, whitehaired

canzo'nare [kantso'nare] /**72**/ VT to tease

canzona'tura [kantsona'tura] SF teasing; (*beffa*) joke

can'zone [kan'tsone] SF song; (*Poesia*) canzone

canzoni'ere [kantsoɲ'ʃɛre] SM (*Mus*) songbook; (*Letteratura*) collection of poems

'caos SM INV chaos

ca'otico, -a, -ci, -che AG chaotic

CAP SIGLA M = **codice di avviamento postale**

cap. ABBR (= *capitolo*) ch.

ca'pace [ka'patʃe] AG able, capable; (*ampio, vasto*) large, capacious; **sei ~ di farlo?** can you o are you able to do it?; **~ d'intendere e di volere** (*Dir*) in full possession of one's faculties

capacità [kapatʃi'ta] SF INV ability; (*Dir, di recipiente*) capacity; **~ produttiva** production capacity

capaci'tarsi [kapatʃi'tarsi] /**72**/ VPR: **~ di** to make out, understand

ca'panna SF hut

capan'nello SM knot (of people)

ca'panno SM (*di cacciatori*) hide; (*da spiaggia*) bathing hut

capan'none SM (*Agr*) barn; (*fabbricato industriale*) (factory) shed

caparbietà SF stubbornness

ca'parbio, -a AG stubborn

ca'parra SF deposit, down payment

capa'tina SF: **fare una ~ da qn/in centro** to pop in on sb/into town

capeggi'are [kaped'dʒare] /62/ VT (*rivolta ecc*) to head, lead

ca'pello SM hair; **capelli** SMPL (*capigliatura*) hair *sg*; **averne fin sopra i capelli di qc/qn** to be fed up to the (back) teeth with sth/sb; **mi ci hanno tirato per i capelli** (*fig*) they dragged me into it; **tirato per i capelli** (*spiegazione*) far-fetched

capel'lone, -a SM/F hippie

capel'luto, -a AG: **cuoio ~** scalp

capez'zale [kapet'tsale] SM bolster; (*fig*) bedside

ca'pezzolo [ka'pettsolo] SM nipple

capi'ente AG capacious

capi'enza [ka'pjɛntsa] SF capacity

capiglia'tura [kapiʎʎa'tura] SF hair

capil'lare AG (*fig*) detailed ▶ SM (*Anat: anche:* **vaso capillare**) capillary

ca'pire /55/ VT to understand; **~ al volo** to catch on straight away; **si capisce!** (*certamente!*) of course!, certainly!

capi'tale AG (*mortale*) capital; (*fondamentale*) main *cpd*, chief *cpd* ▶ SF (*città*) capital ▶ SM (*Econ*) capital; **~ azionario** equity capital, share capital; **~ d'esercizio** working capital; **~ fisso** capital assets, fixed capital; **~ immobile** real estate; **~ liquido** cash assets *pl*; **~ mobile** movables *pl*; **~ di rischio** risk capital; **~ sociale** (*di società*) authorized capital; (*di club*) funds *pl*; **~ di ventura** venture capital, risk capital

capita'lismo SM capitalism

capita'lista, -i, -e AG, SM/F capitalist

capitaliz'zare [kapitalid'dzare] /72/ VT to capitalize

capitalizzazi'one [kapitaliddzat'tsjone] SF capitalization

capita'nare /72/ VT to lead; (*Calcio*) to captain

capitane'ria SF: **~ (di porto)** port authorities *pl*

capi'tano SM captain; **~ di lungo corso** master mariner; **~ di ventura** (*Storia*) mercenary leader

capi'tare /72/ VI (*giungere casualmente*) to happen to go, find o.s.; (*accadere*) to happen; (*presentarsi: cosa*) to turn up, present itself ▶ VB IMPERS to happen; **~ a proposito/bene/male** to turn up at the right moment/at a good time/at a bad time; **mi è capitato un guaio** I've had a spot of trouble

capi'tello SM (*Archit*) capital

capito'lare /72/ VI to capitulate

capitolazi'one [kapitolat'tsjone] SF capitulation

ca'pitolo SM chapter; **capitoli** SMPL (*Comm*) items; **non ho voce in ~** (*fig*) I have no say in the matter

capi'tombolo SM headlong fall, tumble

'capo SM (*Anat*) head; (*persona*) head, leader; (: *in ufficio*) head, boss; (: *in tribù*) chief; (*estremità: di tavolo, scale*) head, top; (: *di filo*) end; (*Geo*) cape; **andare a ~** to start a new paragraph; **"punto a ~"** "full stop — new paragraph"; **da ~** over again; **in ~ a** (*tempo*) within; **da un ~ all'altro** from one end to the other; **fra ~ e collo** (*all'improvviso*) out of the blue; **un discorso senza né ~ né coda** a senseless *o* meaningless speech; **~ d'accusa** (*Dir*) charge; **~ di bestiame** head *inv* of cattle; **C~ di Buona Speranza** Cape of Good Hope; **~ di vestiario** item of clothing

capo'banda (*pl* **capibanda**) SM (*Mus*) bandmaster; (*di malviventi, fig*) gang leader

ca'poccia [ka'pɔttʃa] SM INV (*di lavoranti*) overseer; (*peg: capobanda*) boss

capo'classe (*mpl* **capiclasse**, *fpl* **~**) SM/F (*Ins*) ≈ form captain (BRIT), class president (US)

capocu'oco, -chi SM head cook

Capo'danno SM New Year

capofa'miglia [kapofa'miʎʎa] (*mpl* **capifamiglia**, *fpl* **~**) SM/F head of the family

capo'fitto: a ~ AV headfirst, headlong

capo'giro [kapo'dʒiro] SM dizziness *no pl*; **da ~** (*fig*) astonishing, staggering

capo'gruppo (*mpl* **capigruppo**, *fpl* **~**) SM/F group leader

capola'voro, -i SM masterpiece

capo'linea (*pl* **capilinea**) SM terminus; (*fig*) end of the line

capo'lino SM: **far ~** to peep out (*o in etc*)

capo'lista (*mpl* **capilista**, *fpl* **~**) SM/F (*Pol*) top candidate on electoral list

capolu'ogo (**capoluoghi**, *pl* **capiluoghi**) SM chief town, administrative centre (BRIT) *o* center (US)

capo'mastro (**capomastri**, *pl* **capimastri**) SM master builder

capo'rale SM (*Mil*) lance corporal (BRIT), private first class (US)

capore'parto (*mpl* **capireparto**, *fpl* **~**) SM/F (*di operai*) foreman; (*di ufficio, negozio*) head of department

capo'sala SF INV (*Med*) ward sister

capo'saldo (*pl* **capisaldi**) SM stronghold; (*fig: fondamento*) basis, cornerstone

capo'squadra (*pl* **capisquadra**) SM (*di operai*) foreman, ganger; (*Mil*) squad leader; (*Sport*) team captain

capostazi'one [kapostat'tsjone] (*pl* **capistazione**) SM station master

capos'tipite SM progenitor; (*fig*) earliest example

capo'tavola (*mpl* **capitavola**, *fpl* ~) SM/F
(*persona*) head of the table; **sedere a** ~ to sit at
the head of the table

ca'pote [ka'pɔt] SF INV (*Aut*) hood (BRIT), soft
top

capo'treno (**capitreno**, *pl* **capotreni**) SM
guard

capouf'ficio [kapouf'fitʃo] SM INV/F INV head
clerk

'Capo 'Verde SM: **il** ~ Cape Verde

capo'verso SM (*di verso, periodo*) first line; (*Tip*)
indent; (*paragrafo*) paragraph; (*Dir*: *comma*)
section

capo'volgere [kapo'vɔldʒere] /**96**/ VT to
overturn; (*fig*) to reverse; **capovolgersi** VPR
to overturn; (*barca*) to capsize; (*fig*) to be
reversed

capovolgi'mento [kapovɔldʒi'mento] SM
(*fig*) reversal, complete change

capo'volto, -a PP *di* **capovolgere** ▶ AG upside
down; (*barca*) capsized

'cappa SF (*mantello*) cape, cloak; (*del camino*)
hood

cap'pella SF (*Rel*) chapel

cappel'lano SM chaplain

cap'pello SM hat; **Tanto di ~!** (*fig*) I take my
hat off to you!; ~ **a bombetta** bowler (hat),
derby (*US*); ~ **a cilindro** top hat; ~ **di paglia**
straw hat

'cappero SM caper

cap'pone SM capon

cappot'tare /**72**/ VI (*Aut*) to overturn

cap'potto SM (over)coat

cappuc'cino [kapput'tʃino] SM (*frate*)
Capuchin monk; (*bevanda*) cappuccino

cap'puccio [kap'puttʃo] SM (*copricapo*) hood;
(*della biro*) cap

'capra SF (she-)goat

ca'prese AG from (*o* of) Capri

ca'pretto SM kid

ca'priccio [ka'prittʃo] SM caprice, whim;
(*bizza*) tantrum; **fare i capricci** to be very
naughty; ~ **della sorte** quirk of fate

capricci'oso, -a [kaprit'tʃoso] AG capricious,
whimsical; naughty

Capri'corno SM Capricorn; **essere del** ~ (*dello
zodiaco*) to be Capricorn

capri'foglio [kapri'fɔʎʎo] SM honeysuckle

capri'ola SF somersault

capri'olo SM roe deer

'capro SM billy-goat; ~ **espiatorio** (*fig*)
scapegoat

ca'prone SM billy-goat

'capsula SF capsule; (*di arma, per bottiglie*) cap

cap'tare /**72**/ VT (*Radio, TV*) to pick up;
(*cattivarsi*) to gain, win

CAR SIGLA M = **Centro Addestramento
Reclute**

cara'bina SF rifle

carabini'ere SM *member of Italian military police
force*; *see note*

Originally part of the armed forces,
the *Carabinieri* are police who now have
civil as well as military duties, such as
maintaining public order. They include
paratroop units and mounted divisions
and report to either the Minister of the
Interior or the Minister of Defence,
depending on the function they are
performing.

Ca'racas SF Caracas

ca'raffa SF carafe

Ca'raibi SMPL: **il mar dei** ~ the Caribbean
(Sea)

cara'ibico, -a, -ci, -che AG Caribbean

cara'mella SF sweet

cara'mello SM caramel

ca'rato SM (*di oro, diamante ecc*) carat

ca'rattere SM character; (*caratteristica*)
characteristic, trait; **avere un buon** ~ to be
good-natured; **informazione di ~ tecnico/
confidenziale** information of a technical/
confidential nature; **essere in ~ con qc**
(*intonarsi*) to be in harmony with sth; ~ **jolly**
wild card

caratte'rino SM difficult nature *o* character

caratte'ristico, -a, -ci, -che AG
characteristic ▶ SF characteristic, feature,
trait; **segni caratteristici** (*su passaporto ecc*)
distinguishing marks

caratteriz'zare [karatterid'dzare] /**72**/ VT to
characterize, distinguish

carboi'drato SM carbohydrate

carbo'naio SM (*chi fa carbone*) charcoal-burner;
(*commerciante*) coalman, coal merchant

car'bone SM coal; ~ **fossile** (pit) coal; **essere
o stare sui carboni ardenti** to be like a cat
on hot bricks

car'bonio SM (*Chim*) carbon

carboniz'zare [karbonid'dzare] /**72**/ VT (*legna*)
to carbonize; (*: parzialmente*) to char; **morire
carbonizzato** to be burned to death

carbu'rante SM (motor) fuel

carbura'tore SM carburettor

car'cassa SF carcass; (*fig*: *peg*: *macchina ecc*)
(old) wreck

carce'rato, -a [kartʃe'rato] SM/F prisoner

'carcere ['kartʃere] SM prison; (*pena*)
imprisonment; ~ **di massima sicurezza**
top-security prison

carceri'ere, -a [kartʃe'rjɛre] SM/F (*anche fig*)
jailer

carci'ofo [kar'tʃɔfo] SM artichoke

cardel'lino SM goldfinch

car'diaco, -a, -ci, -che AG cardiac, heart *cpd*

cardi'nale AG, SM cardinal

'cardine SM hinge

cardiolo'gia [kardjolo'dʒia] SF cardiology

cardi'ologo, -gi SM heart specialist, cardiologist

'**cardo** SM thistle

ca'rente AG: ~ **di** lacking in

ca'renza [ka'rɛntsa] SF lack, scarcity; (*vitaminica*) deficiency

cares'tia SF famine; (*penuria*) scarcity, dearth

ca'rezza [ka'rettsa] SF caress; **dare** o **fare una ~ a** (*persona*) to caress; (*animale*) to stroke, pat

carez'zare [karet'tsare] /**20**/ VT to caress, stroke, fondle

carez'zevole [karet'tsevole] AG sweet, endearing

'**cargo, -ghi** SM (*nave*) cargo boat, freighter; (*aereo*) freighter

cari'are /**20**/ VT, **cari'arsi** VPR (*denti*) to decay

'**carica** SF *vedi* **carico**

caricabatte'ria SM INV (*Elettr*) battery charger

cari'care /**20**/ VT (*merce*) to load; (*aggravare: anche fig*) to weigh down; (*orologio*) to wind up; (*batteria, Mil*) to charge; (*Inform*) to load; **caricarsi** VPR: **caricarsi di** to burden o load o.s. with; (*fig: di responsabilità, impegni*) to burden o.s. with

carica'tura SF caricature

'**carico, -a, -chi, -che** AG (*fucile*) loaded; (*orologio*) wound up; (*batteria*) charged; (*colore*) deep; (*caffè, tè*) strong; **~ di** (*che porta un peso*) loaded o laden with ▶ SM (*il caricare*) loading; (*ciò che si carica*) load; (*Comm*) shipment; (*fig: peso*) burden, weight ▶ SF (*mansione ufficiale*) office, position; (*Mil, Tecn, Elettr*) charge; **~ di debiti** up to one's ears in debt; **persona a ~** dependent; **essere a ~ di qn** (*spese ecc*) to be charged to sb; (*accusa, prova*) to be against sb; **testimone a ~** witness for the prosecution; **farsi ~ di** (*problema, responsabilità*) to take on; **a ~ del cliente** at the customer's expense; **~ di lavoro** (*di ditta, reparto*) workload; **~ utile** payload; **capacità di ~** cargo capacity; **entrare/essere in carica** to come into/be in office; **ricoprire** o **rivestire una carica** to hold a position; **uscire di carica** to leave office; **dare la carica a** (*orologio*) to wind up; (*fig: persona*) to back up; **tornare alla carica** (*fig*) to insist, persist; **ha una forte carica di simpatia** he's very likeable

'**carie** SF (*dentaria*) decay

ca'rino, -a AG (*grazioso*) lovely, pretty, nice; (*simpatico*) nice

ca'risma [ka'rizma] SM charisma

caris'matico, -a, -ci, -che AG charismatic

carità SF charity; **per ~!** (*escl di rifiuto*) good heavens, no!

carita'tevole AG charitable

carnagi'one [karna'dʒone] SF complexion

car'nale AG (*amore*) carnal; (*fratello*) blood *cpd*

'**carne** SF flesh; (*bovina, ovina ecc*) meat; **in ~ e ossa** in the flesh, in person; **essere (bene) in ~** to be well padded, be plump; **non essere né ~ né pesce** (*fig*) to be neither fish nor fowl; **~ di manzo/maiale/pecora** beef/pork/mutton; **~ in scatola** tinned o canned meat; **~ tritata** o **macinata** mince (BRIT), hamburger meat (US), minced (BRIT) o ground (US) meat

car'nefice [kar'nefitʃe] SM executioner; hangman

carnefi'cina [karnefi'tʃina] SF carnage; (*fig*) disaster

carne'vale SM carnival; **C~** *see note*

Carnevale is the name given to the period between Epiphany (6 January) and the beginning of Lent, when people throw parties, put on processions with spectacular floats, build bonfires in the *piazze* and dress up in fabulous costumes and masks. Building to a peak just before Lent, *Carnevale* culminates in the festivities of *Martedì grasso* (Shrove Tuesday).

car'nivoro, -a AG carnivorous

car'noso, -a AG fleshy; (*pianta, frutto, radice*) pulpy; (*labbra*) full

'**caro, -a** AG (*amato*) dear; (*costoso*) dear, expensive; **se ti è cara la vita** if you value your life; **è troppo ~** it's too expensive

ca'rogna [ka'roɲɲa] SF carrion; (*fig: col*) swine

caro'sello SM merry-go-round

ca'rota SF carrot

caro'vana SF caravan

caro'vita SM high cost of living

'**carpa** SF carp

Car'pazi [kar'patsi] SMPL: **i ~** the Carpathian Mountains

carpente'ria SF carpentry

carpenti'ere SM carpenter

car'pire /**55**/ VT: **~ qc a qn** (*segreto ecc*) to get sth out of sb

car'poni AV on all fours

car'rabile AG suitable for vehicles; **"passo ~"** "keep clear"

car'raio, -a AG: **passo ~** vehicle entrance

carré SM (*acconciatura*) bob

carreggi'ata [karred'dʒata] SF carriageway (BRIT), roadway; **rimettersi in ~** (*fig: recuperare*) to catch up; **tenersi in ~** (*fig*) to keep to the right path

carrel'lata SF (*Cine, TV: tecnica*) tracking; (*: scena*) running shot; **~ di successi** medley of hit tunes

car'rello SM trolley; (*Aer*) undercarriage; (*Cine*) dolly; (*di macchina da scrivere*) carriage; (*Internet*) shopping basket (BRIT), shopping cart (US)

car'retta SF: **tirare la ~** (fig) to plod along
car'retto SM handcart
carri'era SF career; **fare ~** to get on; **ufficiale di ~** (Mil) regular officer; **a gran ~** at full speed
carri'ola SF wheelbarrow
'carro SM cart, wagon; **il Gran/Piccolo C~** (Astr) the Great/Little Bear; **mettere il ~ avanti ai buoi** (fig) to put the cart before the horse; **~ armato** tank; **~ attrezzi** (Aut) breakdown van (BRIT), tow truck (US); **~ funebre** hearse; **~ merci/bestiame** (Ferr) goods/animal wagon
car'roccio [kar'rɔtʃo] SM (Pol): **il C~** symbol of Lega Nord
car'rozza [kar'rɔttsa] SF carriage, coach; **~ letto** (Ferr) sleeper; **~ ristorante** (Ferr) dining car
carroz'zella [karrot'tsɛlla] SF (per bambini) pram (BRIT), baby carriage (US); (per invalidi) wheelchair
carrozze'ria [karrottse'ria] SF body, coachwork (BRIT); (officina) coachbuilder's workshop (BRIT), body shop
carrozzi'ere [karrot'tsjɛre] SM (Aut: progettista) car designer; (: meccanico) coachbuilder
carroz'zina [karrot'tsina] SF pram (BRIT), baby carriage (US)
carroz'zone [karrot'tsone] SM (da circo, di zingari) caravan
car'rucola SF pulley
'carta SF paper; (al ristorante) menu; (Geo) map; plan; (documento) card; (costituzione) charter; **carte** SFPL (documenti) papers, documents; **alla ~** (al ristorante) à la carte; **cambiare le carte in tavola** (fig) to shift one's ground; **fare carte false** (fig) to go to great lengths; **~ assegni** bank card; **~ assorbente** blotting paper; **~ bollata** o **da bollo** (Amm) official stamped paper; **~ (da gioco)** playing card; **~ di credito** credit card; **~ di debito** cash card; **~ fedeltà** loyalty card; **~ (geografica)** map; **~ d'identità** identity card; **~ igienica** toilet paper; **~ d'imbarco** (Aer, Naut) boarding card, boarding pass; **~ da lettere** writing paper; **~ libera** (Amm) unstamped paper; **~ stradale** road map; **~ millimetrata** graph paper; **~ oleata** waxed paper; **~ da pacchi**, **~ da imballo** wrapping paper, brown paper; **~ da parati** wallpaper; **~ verde** (Aut) green card; **~ vetrata** sandpaper; **~ da visita** visiting card
cartacar'bone (pl **cartecarbone**) SF carbon paper
car'taccia, -ce [kar'tattʃa] SF waste paper
cartamo'dello SM (Cucito) paper pattern
cartamo'neta SF paper money

carta'pecora SF parchment
carta'pesta SF papier-mâché
cartas'traccia [kartas'trattʃa] SF waste paper
car'teggio [kar'teddʒo] SM correspondence
car'tella SF (scheda) card; (custodia: di cartone, Inform) folder; (: di uomo d'affari ecc) briefcase; (: di scolaro) schoolbag, satchel; **~ clinica** (Med) case sheet
cartel'lino SM (etichetta) label; (su porta) notice; (scheda) card; **timbrare il ~** (all'entrata) to clock in; (all'uscita) to clock out; **~ di presenza** clock card, timecard
car'tello SM sign; (pubblicitario) poster; (stradale) sign, signpost; (in dimostrazioni) placard; (Econ) cartel; **~ stradale** sign
cartel'lone SM (della tombola) scoring frame; (Teat) playbill; **tenere il ~** (spettacolo) to have a long run; **~ pubblicitario** advertising poster
carti'era SF paper mill
carti'lagine [karti'ladʒine] SF cartilage
car'tina SF (Aut, Geo) map
car'toccio [kar'tɔttʃo] SM paper bag; **cuocere al ~** (Cuc) to bake in tinfoil
cartogra'fia SF cartography
carto'laio, -a SM/F stationer
cartolarizzazi'one [kartolariddza'tsjone] SF securitization
cartole'ria SF stationer's (shop (BRIT))
carto'lina SF postcard; **~ di auguri** greetings card; **~ precetto** o **rosa** (Mil) call-up card; **~ postale** ready-stamped postcard; **~ virtuale** e-card
carto'mante SMF fortune-teller (using cards)
carton'cino [karton'tʃino] SM (materiale) thin cardboard; (biglietto) card; **~ della società** compliments slip
car'tone SM cardboard; (del latte, dell'aranciata) carton; (Arte) cartoon; **cartoni animati** (Cine) cartoons
car'tuccia, -ce [kar'tuttʃa] SF cartridge; **~ a salve** blank cartridge; **mezza ~** (fig: persona) good-for-nothing
'casa SF house; (specialmente la propria casa) home; (Comm) firm, house; **essere a ~** to be at home; **vado a ~ mia/tua** I'm going home/ to your house; **~ di correzione** ≈ community home (BRIT), reformatory (US); **vino della ~** house wine; **~ di cura** nursing home; **~ editrice** publishing house; **C~ delle Libertà** House of Liberties, centre-right coalition; **~ di riposo** (old people's) home, care home; **~ dello studente** student hostel; **~ di tolleranza**, **~ d'appuntamenti** brothel; **case popolari** ≈ council houses (o flats) (BRIT), ≈ public housing units (US)
ca'sacca, -che SF military coat; (di fantino) blouse

ca'sale SM (*gruppo di case*) hamlet; (*casa di campagna*) farmhouse

casa'lingo, -a, -ghi, -ghe AG household, domestic; (*fatto a casa*) home-made; (*semplice*) homely; (*amante della casa*) home-loving ▶ SF housewife; **casalinghi** SMPL (*oggetti*) household articles; **cucina casalinga** plain home cooking

ca'sata SF family lineage

ca'sato SM family name

casca'morto SM woman-chaser; **fare il ~** to chase women

cas'care /20/ VI to fall; **~ bene/male** (*fig*) to land lucky/unlucky; **~ dalle nuvole** (*fig*) to be taken aback; **~ dal sonno** to be falling asleep on one's feet; **caschi il mondo** no matter what; **non cascherà il mondo se …** it won't be the end of the world if …

cas'cata SF fall; (*d'acqua*) cascade, waterfall

cascherò etc [kaske'rɔ] VB vedi **cascare**

ca'scina [kaʃ'ʃina] SF farmstead

casci'nale [kaʃʃi'nale] SM (*casolare*) farmhouse; (*cascina*) farmstead

'casco (*pl* **caschi**) SM helmet; (*del parrucchiere*) hair-dryer; (*di banane*) bunch; **~ blu** (*Mil*) blue helmet (UN *soldier*)

caseggi'ato [kased'dʒato] SM (*edificio*) large block of flats (BRIT) O apartment building (US); (*gruppo di case*) group of houses

casei'ficio [kazei'fitʃo] SM creamery

ca'sella SF pigeonhole; **~ email** mailbox; **~ di posta elettronica** mailbox; **~ postale** post office box

casel'lario SM (*mobile*) filing cabinet; (*raccolta di pratiche*) files *pl*; **~ giudiziale** court records *pl*; **~ penale** police files *pl*

ca'sello SM (*di autostrada*) tollgate

case'reccio, -a, -ci, -ce [kase'rettʃo] AG home-made

ca'serma SF barracks

caser'tano, -a AG of (O from) Caserta

ca'sino SM (*col*: *confusione*) row, racket; (*casa di prostituzione*) brothel

casinò SM INV casino

ca'sistica SF (*Med*) record of cases; **secondo la ~ degli incidenti stradali** according to road accident data

'caso SM chance; (*fatto, vicenda*) event, incident; (*possibilità*) possibility; (*Med, Ling*) case; **a ~** at random; **per ~** by chance, by accident; **in ogni ~**, **in tutti i casi** in any case, at any rate; **in ~ contrario** otherwise; **al ~** should the opportunity arise; **nel ~ che** in case; **~ mai** if by chance; **far ~ a qc/qn** to pay attention to sth/sb; **fare** O **porre** O **mettere il ~ che** to suppose that; **fa proprio al ~ nostro** it's just what we need; **guarda ~ …** strangely enough …; **è il ~ che ce ne andiamo** we'd better go; **~ limite** borderline case

caso'lare SM cottage

'Caspio SM: **il mar ~** the Caspian Sea

'caspita ESCL (*di sorpresa*) good heavens!; (*di impazienza*) for goodness' sake!

'cassa SF case, crate, box; (*bara*) coffin; (*mobile*) chest; (*involucro: di orologio ecc*) case; (*macchina*) cash register, till; (*luogo di pagamento*) cash desk, checkout (counter); (*fondo*) fund; (*istituto bancario*) bank; **battere ~** (*fig*) to come looking for money; **~ automatica prelievi** automatic telling machine, cash dispenser; **~ continua** night safe; **mettere in ~ integrazione** = to lay off; **C~ del Mezzogiorno** development fund for the South of Italy; **~ mutua** O **malattia** health insurance scheme; **~ di risonanza** (*Mus*) soundbox; (*fig*) platform; **~ di risparmio** savings bank; **~ rurale e artigiana** credit institution (*serving farmers and craftsmen*); **~ toracica** (*Anat*) chest

cassa'forte (*pl* **casseforti**) SF safe

cassa'panca (*pl* **cassapanche** O **cassepanche**) SF settle

casseru'ola, casse'rola SF saucepan

cas'setta SF box; (*per registratore*) cassette; (*Cine, Teat*) box-office takings *pl*; **pane a** O **in ~** toasting loaf; **film di ~** (*commerciale*) box-office draw; **far ~** to be a box-office success; **~ delle lettere** letterbox; **~ di sicurezza** strongbox

cas'setto SM drawer

casset'tone SM chest of drawers

cassi'ere, -a SM/F cashier; (*di banca*) teller

cassinte'grato, -a SM/F *person who has been laid off*

cas'sone SM (*cassa*) large case, large chest

casso'netto SM wheelie-bin

'casta SF caste

cas'tagna [kas'taɲɲa] SF chestnut; **prendere qn in ~** (*fig*) to catch sb in the act

cas'tagno [kas'taɲɲo] SM chestnut (tree)

cas'tano, -a AG chestnut (brown)

cas'tello SM castle; (*Tecn*) scaffolding

casti'gare /80/ VT to punish

casti'gato, -a AG (*casto, modesto*) pure, chaste; (*emendato: prosa, versione*) expurgated, amended

cas'tigo, -ghi SM punishment; **mettere/ essere in ~** to punish/be punished

castità SF chastity

'casto, -a AG chaste, pure

cas'toro SM beaver

cas'trante AG frustrating

cas'trare /72/ VT to castrate; to geld; to doctor (BRIT), fix (US); (*fig: iniziativa*) to frustrate

castrone'ria SF (*col*): **dire castronerie** to talk rubbish

casu'ale AG chance *cpd*; (*Inform*) random *cpd*

ca'supola SF simple little cottage

catac'lisma, -i SM (fig) catastrophe

cata'comba SF catacomb

cata'fascio [kata'faʃʃo] SM: **andare a ~** to collapse; **mandare a ~** to wreck

cata'litico, -a, -ci, -che AG: **marmitta catalitica** (Aut) catalytic converter

cataliz'zare [katalid'dzare] /72/ VT (fig) to act as a catalyst (up)on

cataliz'zato, -a [katalid'dzato] AG (Aut) with catalytic converter

catalizza'tore [kataliddza'tore] SM (anche fig) catalyst; (Aut) catalytic converter

Cata'logna [kata'loɲɲa] SF: **la ~** Catalonia

ca'talogo, -ghi SM catalogue; **~ dei prezzi** price list

cata'nese AG of (o from) Catania

catanza'rese [katandza'rese] AG of (o from) Catanzaro

cata'pecchia [kata'pekkja] SF hovel

cata'pulta SF catapult

catarifran'gente [katarifran'dʒɛnte] SM (Aut) reflector

ca'tarro SM catarrh

ca'tarsi SF INV catharsis

ca'tasta SF stack, pile

ca'tasto SM land register; land registry office

ca'tastrofe SF catastrophe, disaster

catas'trofico, -a, -ci, -che AG (evento) catastrophic; (persona, previsione) pessimistic

catastro'fista, -i, -e AG, SM/F doom-monger; **non fare il ~** don't be so pessimistic

cate'chismo [kate'kizmo] SM catechism

catego'ria SF category; (di albergo) class

cate'gorico, -a, -ci, -che AG categorical

ca'tena SF chain; **reazione a ~** chain reaction; **susseguirsi a ~** to happen in quick succession; **~ alimentare** food chain; **~ di montaggio** assembly line; **~ montuosa** mountain range; **catene da neve** (Aut) snow chains

cate'naccio [kate'nattʃo] SM bolt

cate'nella SF (ornamento) chain; (di orologio) watch chain; (di porta) door chain

cate'nina SF (gioiello) (thin) chain

cate'ratta SF cataract; (chiusa) sluice gate

ca'terva SF (di cose) loads pl, heaps pl; (di persone) horde

cate'tere SM (Med) catheter

cati'nella SF: **piovere a catinelle** to pour, rain cats and dogs

ca'tino SM basin

ca'todico, -a, -ci, -che AG: **tubo a raggi catodici** cathode-ray tube

ca'torcio [ka'tɔrtʃo] SM (peg) old wreck

ca'trame SM tar

'cattedra SF teacher's desk; (di università) chair; **salire** o **montare in ~** (fig) to pontificate

catte'drale SF cathedral

catte'dratico, -a, -ci, -che AG (insegnamento) university cpd; (ironico) pedantic ▸ SM/F professor

catti'veria SF (qualità) wickedness, malice; (di bambino) naughtiness; (azione) spiteful act; (parole) malicious o spiteful remark; **fare una ~** to do something wicked; to be naughty

cattività SF captivity

cat'tivo, -a AG bad; (malvagio) bad, wicked; (turbolento: bambino) bad, naughty; (: mare) rough; (odore, sapore) nasty, bad ▸ SM/F bad o wicked person; **farsi ~ sangue** to worry, get in a state; **farsi un ~ nome** to earn o.s. a bad reputation; **i cattivi** (nei film) the baddies (BRIT), the bad guys (US)

cattocomu'nista, -i, -e AG combining Catholic and communist ideas

cattoli'cesimo [kattoli'tʃezimo] SM Catholicism

cat'tolico, -a, -ci, -che AG, SM/F (Roman) Catholic

cat'tura SF capture

cattu'rare /72/ VT to capture

cau'casico, -a, -ci, -che AG, SM/F Caucasian

'Caucaso SM: **il ~** the Caucasus

caucciù [kaut'tʃu] SM rubber

'causa SF cause; (Dir) lawsuit, case, action; **a ~ di, per ~ di** because of; **per ~ sua** because of him; **fare** o **muovere ~ a qn** to take legal action against sb; **parte in ~** litigant

cau'sale AG (Ling) causal ▸ SF cause, reason

cau'sare /72/ VT to cause

'caustico, -a, -ci, -che AG caustic

cau'tela SF caution, prudence

caute'lare /72/ VT to protect; **cautelarsi** VPR: **cautelarsi (da** o **contro)** to take precautions (against)

'cauto, -a AG cautious, prudent

cauzio'nare [kauttsjo'nare] /72/ VT to guarantee

cauzi'one [kaut'tsjone] SF security; (Dir) bail; **rilasciare dietro ~** to release on bail

cav. ABBR = **cavaliere**

'cava SF quarry

caval'care /20/ VT (cavallo) to ride; (muro) to sit astride; (ponte) to span

caval'cata SF ride; (gruppo di persone) riding party

cavalca'via SM INV flyover

cavalci'oni [kaval'tʃoni]: **a ~ di** prep astride

cavali'ere SM rider; (feudale, titolo) knight; (soldato) cavalryman; (al ballo) partner

cavalleg'gero [kavalled'dʒero] SM (Mil) light cavalryman

cavalle'resco, -a, -schi, -sche AG chivalrous

cavalle'ria SF chivalry; (milizia a cavallo) cavalry

cavalle'rizzo, -a [kavalle'rittso] SM/F riding instructor; circus rider

caval'letta SF grasshopper; (*dannosa*) locust

caval'letto SM (*Fot*) tripod; (*da pittore*) easel

caval'lina SF (*Ginnastica*) horse; (*gioco*) leap-frog; **correre la ~** (*fig*) to sow one's wild oats

ca'vallo SM horse; (*Scacchi*) knight; (*Aut: anche:* **cavallo vapore**) horsepower; (*dei pantaloni*) crotch; **a ~** on horseback; **a ~ di** astride, straddling; **siamo a ~** (*fig*) we've made it; **da ~** (*fig: dose*) drastic; (*: febbre*) raging; **vivere a ~ tra due periodi** to straddle two periods; **~ di battaglia** (*Teat*) tour de force; (*fig*) hobbyhorse; **~ da corsa** racehorse; **~ a dondolo** rocking horse; **~ da sella** saddle horse; **~ da soma** packhorse

ca'vare /72/ VT (*togliere*) to draw out, extract, take out; (*: giacca, scarpe*) to take off; (*: fame, sete, voglia*) to satisfy; **cavarsi** VPR: **cavarsi da** (*guai, problemi*) to get out of; **cavarsela** to get away with it; to manage, get on all right; **non ci caverà un bel nulla** you'll get nothing out of it (*o him etc*)

cava'tappi SM INV corkscrew

ca'verna SF cave

caver'noso, -a AG (*luogo*) cavernous; (*fig: voce*) deep; (*: tosse*) raucous

ca'vezza [ka'vettsa] SF halter

'cavia SF guinea pig

cavi'ale SM caviar

ca'viglia [ka'viʎʎa] SF ankle

cavil'lare /72/ VI to quibble

ca'villo SM quibble

cavil'loso, -a AG quibbling, hair-splitting

cavità SF INV cavity

'cavo, -a AG hollow ▶ SM (*Anat*) cavity; (*grossa corda*) rope, cable; (*Elettr, Tel*) cable

cavo'lata SF (*col*) stupid thing

cavo'letto SM: **~ di Bruxelles** Brussels sprout

cavolfi'ore SM cauliflower

'cavolo SM cabbage; **non m'importa un ~** (*col*) I don't give a hoot; **che ~ vuoi?** (*col*) what the heck do you want?

caz'zata [kat'tsata] SF (*!: stupidaggine*) stupid thing, something stupid

'cazzo ['kattso] SM (*!: pene*) prick (*!*); **non gliene importa un ~** (*fig: !*) he doesn't give a damn about it; **fatti i cazzi tuoi** (*fig: !*) mind your own damn business

caz'zotto [kat'tsɔtto] SM punch; **fare a cazzotti** to have a punch-up

cazzu'ola [kat'tswɔla] SF trowel

CB SIGLA = **Campobasso**

CC ABBR = **Carabinieri**

cc ABBR (= *centimetro cubico*) cc

C.C. ABBR = **codice civile**

c.c. ABBR (= *conto corrente*) c/a, a/c; (*Elettr*) *vedi* **corrente continua**

c/c ABBR (= *conto corrente*) c/a, a/c

C.C.D. SIGLA M (*Pol*: = *Centro Cristiano Democratico*) *party originating from Democrazia Cristiana*

CCI SIGLA F (= *Camera di Commercio Internazionale*) ICC (= *International Chamber of Commerce*)

CCIAA ABBR = **Camera di Commercio Industria, Agricoltura e Artigianato**

CCT SIGLA M = **certificato di credito del Tesoro**

C.D. ABBR (= *Corpo Diplomatico*) CD ▶ SM INV (= *compact disc*) CD; (*lettore*) CD player

c.d. ABBR = **cosiddetto**

C.d.A. ABBR = **Consiglio di Amministrazione**

c.d.d. ABBR (= *come dovevasi dimostrare*) QED (= *quod erat demonstrandum*)

C.d.M. ABBR = **Cassa del Mezzogiorno**

CD-Rom [tʃidi'rɔm] SIGLA M INV (= *Compact Disc Read Only Memory*) CD-Rom

C.d.U. [tʃidi'u] SIGLA M (= *Cristiano Democratici Uniti*) United Christian Democrats (*Italian centre-right political party*)

CE SIGLA = **Caserta**

ce [tʃe] PRON, AV *vedi* **ci**

C.E. SIGLA = **Consiglio d'Europa**

cec'chino [tʃek'kino] SM sniper; (*Pol*) member of parliament who votes against his own party

'cece ['tʃetʃe] SM chickpea, garbanzo (*US*)

Ce'cenia [tʃe'tʃenja] SF Chechnya

ce'ceno, -a [tʃe'tʃeno] AG, SM/F Chechen

cecità [tʃetʃi'ta] SF blindness

'ceco, -a, -chi, -che ['tʃɛko] AG, SM/F, SM Czech; **la Repubblica Ceca** the Czech Republic

Cecoslo'vacchia [tʃekozlo'vakkja] SF (*Storia*): **la ~** Czechoslovakia

cecoslo'vacco, -a, -chi, -che [tʃekozlo'vakko] AG, SM/F (*Storia*) Czechoslovakian

CED [tʃɛd] SIGLA M = **centro elaborazione dati**

'cedere ['tʃedere] /29/ VT (*concedere: posto*) to give up; (*Dir*) to transfer, make over ▶ VI (*cadere*) to give way, subside; **~ (a)** to surrender (to), yield (to), give in (to); **~ il passo (a qn)** to let (sb) pass in front; **~ il passo a qc** (*fig*) to give way to sth; **~ la parola (a qn)** to hand over (to sb)

ce'devole [tʃe'devole] AG (*terreno*) soft; (*fig*) yielding

'cedola ['tʃedola] SF (*Comm*) coupon; voucher

ce'drata [tʃe'drata] SF citron juice

'cedro ['tʃedro] SM cedar; (*albero da frutto, frutto*) citron

'CEE ['tʃee] SIGLA F = **Comunità Economica Europea**

'ceffo ['tʃɛffo] SM (*peg*) ugly mug

ceffone [tʃef'fone] SM slap, smack

'ceko, -a ['tʃɛko] AG, SM/F = **ceco**

ce'lare [tʃe'lare] /**72**/ vt to conceal; **celarsi** vpr
to hide

cele'brare [tʃele'brare] /**72**/ vt to celebrate;
(cerimonia) to hold; **~ le lodi di qc/qn** to sing
the praises of sth/sb

celebrazi'one [tʃelebrat'tsjone] sf
celebration

'celebre ['tʃɛlebre] ag famous, celebrated

celebrità [tʃelebri'ta] sf inv fame; (persona)
celebrity

'celere ['tʃelere] ag fast, swift; (corso) crash cpd
▶ sf (Polizia) riot police

ce'leste [tʃe'lɛste] ag celestial; heavenly;
(colore) sky-blue

'celia [tʃɛlja] sf joke; **per ~** for a joke

celi'bato [tʃeli'bato] sm celibacy

'celibe ['tʃɛlibe] ag single, unmarried ▶ sm
bachelor

'cella ['tʃɛlla] sf cell; **~ di rigore** punishment
cell; **~ frigorifera** cold store

cello'phane® [sɛlo'fan] sm cellophane®

'cellula ['tʃɛllula] sf (Biol, Elettr, Pol) cell

cellu'lare [tʃellu'lare] ag cellular ▶ sm
(furgone) police van; (telefono) cellphone;
segregazione ~ (Dir) solitary confinement

cellu'lite [tʃellu'lite] sf cellulite

'celta ['tʃelta] smf Celt

'celtico, -a, -ci, -che ['tʃeltiko] ag, sm
Celtic

'cembalo ['tʃembalo] sm (Mus) harpsichord

cemen'tare [tʃemen'tare] /**72**/ vt (anche fig) to
cement

ce'mento [tʃe'mento] sm cement; **~ armato**
reinforced concrete

'cena ['tʃena] sf dinner; (leggera) supper

ce'nacolo [tʃe'nakolo] sm (circolo) coterie,
circle; (Rel, dipinto) Last Supper

ce'nare [tʃe'nare] /**72**/ vi to dine, have dinner

'cencio ['tʃentʃo] sm piece of cloth, rag; (per
spolverare) duster; **essere bianco come un ~**
to be as white as a sheet

'cenere ['tʃenere] sf ash

Cene'rentola [tʃene'rentola] sf (anche fig)
Cinderella

'cenno ['tʃenno] sm (segno) sign, signal; (gesto)
gesture; (col capo) nod; (con la mano) wave;
(allusione) hint, mention; (breve esposizione)
short account; **far ~ di sì/no** to nod (one's
head)/shake one's head; **~ d'intesa** sign of
agreement; **cenni di storia dell'arte** an
outline of the history of art

censi'mento [tʃensi'mento] sm census

cen'sire [tʃen'sire] /**55**/ vt to take a census of

'CENSIS ['tʃensis] sigla m (= Centro Studi
Investimenti Sociali) independent institute carrying
out research on Italy's social and cultural welfare

cen'sore [tʃen'sore] sm censor

cen'sura [tʃen'sura] sf censorship; censor's
office; (fig) censure

censu'rare [tʃensu'rare] /**72**/ vt to censor;
to censure

cent. abbr = **centesimo**

centelli'nare [tʃentelli'nare] /**72**/ vt to sip;
(fig) to savour (Brit), savor (US)

cente'nario, -a [tʃente'narjo] ag (che ha cento
anni) hundred-year-old; (che ricorre ogni cento
anni) centennial, centenary cpd ▶ sm/f
centenarian ▶ sm centenary

cen'tesimo, -a [tʃen'tɛzimo] ag, sm
hundredth; (di euro, dollaro) cent; **essere
senza un ~** to be penniless

cen'tigrado, -a [tʃen'tigrado] ag centigrade;
20 gradi centigradi 20 degrees centigrade

cen'tilitro [tʃen'tilitro] sm centilitre

cen'timetro [tʃen'timetro] sm centimetre
(Brit), centimeter (US); (nastro) measuring
tape (in centimetres)

centi'naio [tʃenti'najo] (pl(f) **centinaia**) sm:
un ~ (di) a hundred; about a hundred

'cento ['tʃento] num a hundred, one hundred;
per ~ per cent; **al ~ per ~** a hundred per cent;
~ di questi giorni! many happy returns (of
the day)!

centodi'eci [tʃento'djetʃi] num one hundred
and ten; **~ e lode** (Università) ≈ first-class
honours

cento'mila [tʃento'mila] num a 0 one
hundred thousand; **te l'ho detto ~ volte**
(fig) I've told you a thousand times

Cen'trafrica [tʃen'trafrika] sm: **il ~** the
Central African Republic

cen'trale [tʃen'trale] ag central ▶ sf:
~ elettrica electric power station; **~ eolica**
wind farm; **~ del latte** dairy; **~ di polizia**
police headquarters pl; **~ telefonica**
(telephone) exchange; **sede ~** head office

centrali'nista [tʃentrali'nista] smf operator

centra'lino [tʃentra'lino] sm (telephone)
exchange; (di albergo ecc) switchboard

centraliz'zare [tʃentralid'dzare] /**72**/ vt to
centralize

centraliz'zato, -a [tʃentralid'dzato] ag
central

cen'trare [tʃen'trare] /**72**/ vt to hit the centre
(Brit) o center (US) of; (Tecn) to centre; **~ una
risposta** to get the right answer; **ha
centrato il problema** you've hit the nail on
the head

centra'vanti [tʃentra'vanti] sm inv centre
forward

cen'trifuga [tʃen'trifuga] sf spin-dryer

centrifu'gare [tʃentrifu'gare] /**80**/ vt (Tecn)
to centrifuge; (biancheria) to spin-dry

'centro ['tʃentro] sm centre (Brit), center (US);
fare ~ to hit the bull's eye; (Calcio) to score;
(fig) to hit the nail on the head; **~ balneare**
seaside resort; **~ civico** civic centre;
~ commerciale shopping centre; (città)

commercial centre; ~ **di costo** cost centre;
~ **elaborazione dati** data-processing unit;
~ **ospedaliero** hospital complex; ~ **di
permanenza temporanea** reception
centre; ~ **sociale** community centre; **centri
vitali** (*anche fig*) vital organs

centro'destra [tʃentro'dɛstra] SM (*Pol*) centre
right

centromedi'ano [tʃentrome'djano] SM
(*Calcio*) centre half

centrosi'nistra [tʃentrosi'nistra] SM (*Pol*)
centre left

'**ceppo** ['tʃeppo] SM (*di albero*) stump; (*pezzo di
legno*) log

'**cera** ['tʃera] SF wax; (*aspetto*) appearance,
look; ~ **per pavimenti** floor polish

cera'lacca [tʃera'lakka] SF sealing wax

ce'ramica [tʃe'ramika] (*pl* **ceramiche**) SF
ceramic; (*Arte*) ceramics *sg*

cerbi'atto [tʃer'bjatto] SM (*Zool*) fawn

'**cerca** ['tʃerka] SF: **in** *o* **alla** ~ **di** in search of

cercaper'sone [tʃerkaper'sone] SM INV
bleeper

cer'care [tʃer'kare] /**20**/ VT to look for, search
for ▶ VI: ~ **di fare qc** to try to do sth

cercherò *etc* [tʃerke'rɔ] VB *vedi* **cercare**

'**cerchia** ['tʃerkja] SF circle

cerchi'ato, -a [tʃer'kjato] AG: **occhiali
cerchiati d'osso** horn-rimmed spectacles;
avere gli occhi cerchiati to have dark rings
under one's eyes

cer'chietto [tʃer'kjetto] SM (*per capelli*)
hairband

'**cerchio** ['tʃerkjo] SM circle; (*giocattolo, di botte*)
hoop; **dare un colpo al** ~ **e uno alla botte**
(*fig*) to keep two things going at the same
time

cerchi'one [tʃer'kjone] SM (wheel)rim

cere'ale [tʃere'ale] SM cereal

cere'brale [tʃere'brale] AG cerebral

ceri'monia [tʃeri'mɔnja] SF ceremony; **senza
tante cerimonie** (*senza formalità*) informally;
(*bruscamente*) unceremoniously, without so
much as a by-your-leave

cerimoni'ale [tʃerimo'njale] SM etiquette;
ceremonial

cerimoni'ere [tʃerimo'njɛre] SM master of
ceremonies

cerimoni'oso, -a [tʃerimo'njoso] AG formal,
ceremonious

ce'rino [tʃe'rino] SM wax match

CERN [tʃern] SIGLA M (= *Comitato Europeo di
Ricerche Nucleari*) CERN

'**cernia** ['tʃernja] SF (*Zool*) stone bass

cerni'era [tʃer'njɛra] SF hinge; ~ **lampo** zip
(fastener) (*BRIT*), zipper (*US*)

cernita ['tʃernita] SF selection; **fare una** ~ **di**
to select

'**cero** ['tʃero] SM (church) candle

ce'rone [tʃe'rone] SM (*trucco*) greasepaint

ce'rotto [tʃe'rɔtto] SM sticking plaster

certa'mente [tʃerta'mente] AV certainly,
surely

cer'tezza [tʃer'tettsa] SF certainty

certifi'care [tʃertifi'kare] /**20**/ VT to certify

certifi'cato [tʃertifi'kato] SM certificate;
~ **medico/di nascita/di morte** medical/
birth/death certificate; ~ **di credito del
Tesoro** treasury bill

certificazi'one [tʃertifikat'tsjone] SF
certification; ~ **di bilancio** (*Comm*) external
audit

(PAROLA CHIAVE)

'**certo, -a** ['tʃerto] AG (*sicuro*): **certo (di/che)**
certain *o* sure (of/that)
  ▶ DET **1** (*tale*) certain; **un certo signor
  Smith** a (certain) Mr Smith
  2 (*qualche: con valore intensivo*) some; **dopo un
  certo tempo** after some time; **un fatto di
  una certa importanza** a matter of some
  importance; **di una certa età** past one's
  prime, not so young
  ▶ PRON: **certi, e** (*pl*) some
  ▶ AV (*certamente*) certainly; (*senz'altro*) of
  course; **di certo** certainly; **no (di) certo!,
  certo che no!** certainly not!; **sì certo** yes
  indeed, certainly

certo'sino [tʃerto'zino] SM Carthusian
monk; (*liquore*) chartreuse; **è un lavoro da** ~
it's a pernickety job

cer'tuni [tʃer'tuni] PRON PL some (people)

ce'rume [tʃe'rume] SM (ear) wax

'**cerva** ['tʃerva] SF (female) deer, doe

cer'vello [tʃer'vɛllo] (*pl* **cervelli**, *pl(f)* **cervella**,
pl(f) **cervelle**) SM (*Anat*) brain; ~ **elettronico**
computer; **avere il** *o* **essere un** ~ **fino** to be
sharp-witted; **è uscito di** ~, **gli è dato di
volta il** ~ he's gone off his head

cervi'cale [tʃervi'kale] AG cervical

'**cervo, -a** ['tʃervo] SM/F stag (hind) ▶ SM deer;
~ **volante** stag beetle

cesel'lare [tʃezel'lare] /**72**/ VT to chisel;
(*incidere*) to engrave

ce'sello [tʃe'zɛllo] SM chisel

ce'soie [tʃe'zoje] SFPL shears

ces'puglio [tʃes'puʎʎo] SM bush

ces'sare [tʃes'sare] /**72**/ VI, VT to stop, cease;
~ **di fare qc** to stop doing sth; "**cessato
allarme**" "all clear"

ces'sate il fu'oco [tʃes'sate-] SM
ceasefire

cessazi'one [tʃessat'tsjone] SF cessation;
(*interruzione*) suspension

cessi'one [tʃes'sjone] SF transfer

'**cesso** ['tʃesso] SM (*col: gabinetto*) bog

'**cesta** ['tʃesta] SF (large) basket

ces'tello [tʃes'tɛllo] sm (*per bottiglie*) crate; (*di lavatrice*) drum

cesti'nare [tʃesti'nare] /**72**/ vt to throw away; (*fig: proposta*) to turn down; (: *romanzo*) to reject

ces'tino [tʃes'tino] sm basket; (*per la carta straccia*) wastepaper basket; (*Inform*) recycle bin; ~ **da viaggio** (*Ferr*) packed lunch (*o* dinner)

'cesto ['tʃesto] sm basket

ce'sura [tʃe'zura] sf caesura

ce'taceo [tʃe'tatʃeo] sm sea mammal

'ceto ['tʃeto] sm (social) class

'cetra ['tʃetra] sf zither; (*fig: di poeta*) lyre

cetrio'lino [tʃetrio'lino] sm gherkin

cetri'olo [tʃetri'ɔlo] sm cucumber

Cf., Cfr. abbr (= *confronta*) cf.

CFC [tʃiɛffe'tʃi] abbr mpl (= *clorofluorocarburi*) CFC

Cfr. abbr (= *confronta*) cf

CFS sigla m (= *Corpo Forestale dello Stato*) body responsible for the planting and management of forests

cg abbr (= *centigrammo*) cg

C.G.I.L. [tʃidʒi'ɛlle] sigla f (= *Confederazione Generale Italiana del Lavoro*) trades union organization

CH sigla = **Chieti**

cha'let [ʃa'lɛ] sm inv chalet

cham'pagne [ʃã'paɲ] sm inv champagne

chance [ʃãs] sf inv chance

charme [ʃarm] sm charm

'charter ['tʃa:tər] ag inv (*volo*) charter *cpd*; (*aereo*) chartered ▶ sm inv chartered plane

chat'line [tʃæt'laen] sf inv chat room

chat'tare [tʃat'tare] /**72**/ vi to chat; (*online*) to chat

chat'tata [tʃat'tata] sf chat

(PAROLA CHIAVE)

che [ke] pron **1** (*relativo: persona: soggetto*) who; (: *oggetto*) whom, that; (: *cosa, animale*) which, that; **il ragazzo che è venuto** the boy who came; **l'uomo che io vedo** the man (whom) I see; **il libro che è sul tavolo** the book which *o* that is on the table; **il libro che vedi** the book (which *o* that) you see; **la sera che ti ho visto** the evening I saw you

2 (*interrogativo, esclamativo*) what; **che (cosa) fai?** what are you doing?; **a che (cosa) pensi?** what are you thinking about?; **non sa che (cosa) fare** he doesn't know what to do; **sai di che si tratta?** do you know what it's about?; **che (cosa) succede?** what's happening?; **ma che dici!** what are you saying!

3 (*indefinito*): **quell'uomo ha un che di losco** there's something suspicious about that man; **un certo non so che** an indefinable

something; **non è un gran che** it's nothing much

▶ det **1** (*interrogativo: tra tanti*) what; (: *tra pochi*) which; **che tipo di film preferisci?** what sort of film do you prefer?; **che vestito ti vuoi mettere?** what (*o* which) dress do you want to put on?

2 (*esclamativo: seguito da aggettivo*) how; (: *seguito da sostantivo*) what; **che buono!** how delicious!; **che bel vestito!** what a lovely dress!; **che macchina!** what a car!

▶ cong **1** (*con proposizioni subordinate*) that; **credo che verrà** I think he'll come; **voglio che tu studi** I want you to study; **so che tu c'eri** I know (that) you were there; **non che sia sbagliato, ma …** not that it's wrong, but …

2 (*finale*) so that; **vieni qua, che ti veda** come here, so (that) I can see you; **stai attento che non cada** mind it doesn't fall

3 (*temporale*): **arrivai che eri già partito** you had already left when I arrived; **sono anni che non lo vedo** I haven't seen him for years

4 (*in frasi imperative, concessive*): **che venga pure!** let him come by all means!; **che tu sia benedetto!** may God bless you!; **che tu venga o no partiamo lo stesso** we're going whether you come or not

5 (*comparativo: con più, meno*) than; **è più lungo che largo** it's longer than it's wide; **più bella che mai** more beautiful than ever*vedi anche* **più**; **meno**

6 *vedi anche* **così** ecc

'checca, -che ['kekka] sf (*col: omosessuale*) fairy

chef [ʃɛf] sm inv chef

chemiotera'pia [kemjotera'pia] sf chemotherapy

chero'sene [kero'zɛne] sm kerosene

cheru'bino [keru'bino] sm cherub

che'tare [ke'tare] /**72**/ vt to hush, silence; **chetarsi** vpr to quieten down, fall silent

cheti'chella [keti'kɛlla]: **alla ~** av stealthily, unobtrusively; **andarsene alla ~** to slip away

'cheto, -a ['keto] ag quiet, silent

(PAROLA CHIAVE)

chi [ki] pron **1** (*interrogativo: soggetto*) who; (: *oggetto*) who, whom; **chi è?** who is it?; **di chi è questo libro?** whose book is this?, whose is this book?; **con chi parli?** who are you talking to?; **a chi pensi?** who are you thinking about?; **chi di voi?** which of you?; **non so a chi rivolgermi** I don't know who to ask

2 (*relativo*) whoever, anyone who; **dillo a chi vuoi** tell whoever you like; **portate chi**

volete bring anyone you like; **so io di chi parlo** I know who I'm talking about; **lo riferirò a chi di dovere** I'll pass it on to the relevant person

3 (*indefinito*): **chi … chi …** some … others …; **chi dice una cosa, chi dice un'altra** some say one thing, others say another

chiacchie'rare [kjakkje'rare] /**72**/ vi to chat; (*discorrere futilmente*) to chatter; (*far pettegolezzi*) to gossip

chiacchie'rata [kjakkje'rata] sf chat; **farsi una ~** to have a chat

chi'acchiere ['kjakkjere] sfpl chatter *no pl*; gossip *no pl*; **fare due** *o* **quattro ~** to have a chat; **perdersi in ~** to waste time talking

chiacchie'rone, -a [kjakkje'rone] ag talkative, chatty gossipy ▶ sm/f chatterbox; gossip

chia'mare [kja'mare] /**72**/ vt to call; (*rivolgersi a qn*) to call (in), send for; **chiamarsi** vpr (*aver nome*) to be called; **come ti chiami?** what's your name?; **mi chiamo Paolo** my name is Paolo, I'm called Paolo; **mandare a ~ qn** to send for sb, call sb in; **~ alle armi** to call up; **~ in giudizio** to summon; **~ qn da parte** to take sb aside

chia'mata [kja'mata] sf (*Tel*) call; (*Mil*) call-up; **~ interurbana** long-distance call; **~ con preavviso** person-to-person call; **~ alle urne** (*Pol*) election

chi'appa ['kjappa] sf (*col: natica*) cheek; **chiappe** sfpl bottom *sg*

chi'ara ['kjara] sf egg white

chia'rezza [kja'rettsa] sf clearness; clarity

chiarifi'care [kjarifi'kare] /**20**/ vt (*anche fig*) to clarify

chiarificazi'one [kjarifikat'tsjone] sf clarification

chiari'mento [kjari'mento] sm clarification *no pl*, explanation

chia'rire [kja'rire] /**55**/ vt to make clear; (*fig: spiegare*) to clear up, explain; **chiarirsi** vpr to become clear; **si sono chiariti** they've sorted things out

chi'aro, -a ['kjaro] ag clear; (*luminoso*) clear, bright; (*colore*) pale, light ▶ av (*parlare, vedere*) clearly; **si sta facendo ~** the day is dawning; **sia chiara una cosa** let's get one thing straight; **mettere in ~ qc** (*fig*) to clear sth up; **parliamoci ~** let's be frank; **trasmissione in ~** (*TV*) uncoded broadcast

chia'rore [kja'rore] sm (diffuse) light

chiaroveg'gente [kjaroved'dʒɛnte] smf clairvoyant

chi'asso ['kjasso] sm uproar, row; **far ~** to make a din; (*fig*) to make a fuss (: *notizia*) to cause a stir

chias'soso, -a [kjas'soso] ag noisy, rowdy; (*vistoso*) showy, gaudy

'chiatta ['kjatta] sf barge

chi'ave ['kjave] sf key ▶ ag inv key *cpd*; **chiudere a ~** to lock; **~ d'accensione** (*Aut*) ignition key; **~ a forcella** fork spanner; **~ inglese** monkey wrench; **in ~ politica** in political terms; **~ di volta** (*anche fig*) keystone; **chiavi in mano** (*contratto*) turn-key *cpd*; **prezzo chiavi in mano** (*di macchina*) on-the-road price; **~ hardware** (*Inform*) dongle; **~ USB** (*Inform*) USB key

chiavis'tello [kjavis'tɛllo] sm bolt

chi'azza ['kjattsa] sf stain, splash

chiaz'zare [kjat'tsare] /**72**/ vt to stain, splash

chic [ʃik] ag inv chic, elegant

chicches'sia [kikkes'sia] pron anyone, anybody

'chicco, -chi ['kikko] sm (*di cereale, riso*) grain; (*di caffè*) bean; **~ di grandine** hailstone; **~ d'uva** grape

chi'edere ['kjɛdere] /**21**/ vt (*per sapere*) to ask; (*per avere*) to ask for ▶ vi: **~ di qn** to ask after sb; (*al telefono*) to ask for *o* want sb; **chiedersi** vpr: **chiedersi (se)** to wonder (whether); **~ qc a qn** to ask sb sth; to ask sb for sth; **~ scusa a qn** to apologize to sb; **~ l'elemosina** to beg; **non chiedo altro** that's all I want

chieri'chetto [kjeri'ketto] sm altar boy

chi'erico, -ci ['kjɛriko] sm cleric; altar boy

chi'esa ['kjɛza] sf church

chi'esi *etc* ['kjɛzi] vb *vedi* **chiedere**

chi'esto, -a ['kjɛsto] pp *di* **chiedere**

'Chigi ['kidʒi]: **palazzo ~** sm (*Pol*) offices of the Italian Prime Minister

'chiglia ['kiʎʎa] sf keel

'chilo ['kilo] sm kilo

chilo'grammo [kilo'grammo] sm kilogram(me)

chilome'traggio [kilome'traddʒo] sm (*Aut*) ≈ mileage

chilo'metrico, -a, -ci, -che [kilo'mɛtriko] ag kilometric; (*fig*) endless

chi'lometro [ki'lɔmetro] sm kilometre (*Brit*), kilometer (*US*)

'chimico, -a, -ci, -che ['kimiko] ag chemical ▶ sm/f chemist ▶ sf chemistry

chi'mono [ki'mɔno] sm inv kimono

'china ['kina] sf (*pendio*) slope, descent; (*Bot*) cinchona; **(inchiostro di) ~** Indian ink; **risalire la ~** (*fig*) to be on the road to recovery

chi'nare [ki'nare] /**72**/ vt to lower, bend; **chinarsi** vpr to stoop, bend

chincaglie'ria [kinkaʎʎe'ria] sf fancy-goods shop; **chincaglierie** sfpl fancy goods, knick-knacks

chi'nino [ki'nino] sm quinine

'chino, -a ['kino] ag: **a capo ~**, **a testa china**

head bent o bowed

chi'occia, -ce ['kjɔttʃa] SF brooding hen

chi'occio, -a, -ci, -ce ['kjɔttʃo] AG (voce) clucking

chi'occiola ['kjɔttʃola] SF snail; (di indirizzo e-mail) at (symbol); **scala a ~** spiral staircase

chi'odo ['kjɔdo] SM nail; (fig) obsession; **~ scaccia ~** (proverbio) one problem drives away another; **roba da chiodi!** it's unbelievable!; **~ di garofano** (Cuc) clove

chi'oma ['kjɔma] SF (capelli) head of hair; (di albero) foliage

chi'osco, -schi ['kjɔsko] SM kiosk, stall

chi'ostro ['kjɔstro] SM cloister

chiro'mante [kiro'mante] SMF palmist; (indovino) fortune-teller

chirur'gia [kirur'dʒia] SF surgery; **~ estetica** cosmetic surgery

chi'rurgico, -a, -ci, -che [ki'rurdʒiko] AG (anche fig) surgical

chi'rurgo, -ghi, -gi [ki'rurgo] SM surgeon

chissà [kis'sa] AV who knows, I wonder

chi'tarra [ki'tarra] SF guitar

chitar'rista, -i, -e [kitar'rista] SM/F guitarist, guitar player

chi'udere ['kjudere] /22/ VT to close, shut; (luce, acqua) to put off, turn off; (definitivamente: fabbrica) to close down, shut down; (strada) to close; (recingere) to enclose; (porre termine a) to end ▶ VI to close, shut; to close down, shut down, to end; **chiudersi** VPR to shut, close; (ritirarsi: anche fig) to shut o.s. away; (ferita) to close; **~ un occhio su** (fig) to turn a blind eye to; **chiudi la bocca!** o **il becco!** (col) shut up!

chi'unque [ki'unkwe] PRON (relativo) whoever; (indefinito) anyone, anybody; **~ sia** whoever it is

'**chiusi** etc ['kjusi] VB vedi **chiudere**

chi'uso, -a ['kjuso] PP di **chiudere** ▶ AG (porta) shut, closed; (: a chiave) locked; (senza uscita: strada ecc) blocked off; (: rubinetto) off; (: persona) uncommunicative; (: ambiente, club) exclusive ▶ SM: **stare al ~** (fig) to be shut up ▶ SF (di corso d'acqua) sluice, lock; (recinto) enclosure; (di discorso ecc) conclusion, ending; "**~**" (negozio ecc) "closed"; "**~ al pubblico**" "no admittance to the public"

chiu'sura [kju'sura] SF closing; shutting; closing o shutting down; enclosing; putting o turning off; ending; (dispositivo) catch; fastening; fastener; **orario di ~** closing time; **~ lampo**® zip (fastener) (BRIT), zipper (US)

ci [tʃi] (dav lo, la, li, le, ne diventa **ce**) PRON
1 (personale: complemento oggetto) us; (: a noi: complemento di termine) (to) us; (: riflessivo) ourselves; (: reciproco) each other, one another; (: impersonale): **ci si veste** we get dressed; **ci ha visti** he's seen us; **non ci ha dato niente** he gave us nothing; **ci vestiamo** we get dressed; **ci amiamo** we love one another o each other; **ci siamo divertiti** we had a good time

2 (dimostrativo: di ciò, su ciò, in ciò ecc) about (o on o of) it; **non ci capisco nulla** I can't make head nor tail of it; **non so cosa farci** I don't know what to do about it; **che ci posso fare?** what can I do about it?; **che c'entro io?** what have I got to do with it?; **ci puoi giurare** you can bet on it; **ci puoi contare** you can depend on it; **ci sei?** (sei pronto?) are you ready?; (hai capito?) are you with me?

▶ AV (qui) here; (lì) there; (moto attraverso luogo): **ci passa sopra un ponte** a bridge passes over it; **non ci passa più nessuno** nobody comes this way any more; **qui ci abito da un anno** I've been living here for a year; **esserci** vedi **essere**

C.I. ABBR = **carta d'identità**

CIA ['tʃia] SIGLA F (= Central Intelligence Agency) CIA

C.ia ABBR (= compagnia) Co

cia'batta [tʃa'batta] SF mule, slipper; (pane) ciabatta

ciabat'tino [tʃabat'tino] SM cobbler

ciac [tʃak] SM (Cine) clapper board; **~, si gira!** action!

Ci'ad [tʃad] SM: **il ~** Chad

ci'alda ['tʃalda] SF (Cuc) wafer

cial'trone [tʃal'trone] SM good-for-nothing

ciam'bella [tʃam'bɛlla] SF (Cuc) ring-shaped cake; (salvagente) rubber ring

ci'ancia, -ce ['tʃantʃa] SF gossip no pl, tittle-tattle no pl

cianfru'saglie [tʃanfru'zaʎʎe] SFPL bits and pieces

cia'nuro [tʃa'nuro] SM cyanide

ci'ao ['tʃao] ESCL (all'arrivo) hello!; (alla partenza) cheerio! (BRIT), bye!

ciar'lare [tʃar'lare] /72/ VI to chatter; (peg) to gossip

ciarla'tano [tʃarla'tano] SM charlatan

cias'cuno, -a [tʃas'kuno] (dav sm: **ciascun** + C, V, **ciascuno** + s impura, gn, pn, ps, x, z; dav sf: **ciascuna** + C, **ciascun'** + V) DET every, each; (ogni) every ▶ PRON each (one); (tutti) everyone, everybody

ci'bare [tʃi'bare] /72/ VT to feed; **cibarsi** VPR: **cibarsi di** to eat

ci'barie [tʃi'barje] SFPL foodstuffs

ciber'nauta, -i, -e [tʃiber'nauta] SM/F Internet surfer

ciber'netica [tʃiber'nɛtika] SF cybernetics sg

ciber'spazio [tʃiber'spattsjo] SM cyberspace

'cibo ['tʃibo] SM food

ci'cala [tʃi'kala] SF cicada

cica'trice [tʃika'tritʃe] SF scar

cicatriz'zarsi [tʃikatrid'dzarsi] **/72/** VPR to form a scar, heal (up)

'cicca, -che ['tʃikka] SF cigarette end; (col: *sigaretta*) fag; **non vale una ~** (*fig*) it's worthless

'ciccia ['tʃittʃa] SF (col: *carne*) meat; (*grasso umano*) fat, flesh

cicci'one, -a [tʃit'tʃone] SM/F (col) fatty

cice'rone [tʃitʃe'rone] SM guide

cicla'mino [tʃikla'mino] SM cyclamen

ci'clismo [tʃi'klizmo] SM cycling

ci'clista, -i, -e [tʃi'klista] SM/F cyclist

'ciclo ['tʃiklo] SM cycle; (*di malattia*) course

ciclomo'tore [tʃiklomo'tore] SM moped

ci'clone [tʃi'klone] SM cyclone

ciclos'tile [tʃiklos'tile] SM cyclostyle (BRIT)

ci'cogna [tʃi'koɲɲa] SF stork

ci'coria [tʃi'kɔrja] SF chicory

ci'eco, -a, -chi, -che ['tʃɛko] AG blind ▶ SM/F blind man(-woman); **alla cieca** (*anche fig*) blindly

ciel'lino, -a [tʃiel'lino] SM/F (Pol) member of CL *movement*

ci'elo ['tʃɛlo] SM sky; (Rel) heaven; **toccare il ~ con un dito** (*fig*) to walk on air; **per amor del ~!** for heavens' sake!

'cifra ['tʃifra] SF (*numero*) figure, numeral; (*somma di denaro*) sum, figure; (*monogramma*) monogram, initials *pl*; (*codice*) code, cipher

ci'frare [tʃi'frare] **/72/** VT (*messaggio*) to code; (*lenzuola ecc*) to embroider with a monogram

'ciglio ['tʃiʎʎo] SM (*margine*) edge, verge; (*pl(f)* **ciglia**: *delle palpebre*) (eye)lash; (eye)lid; (*sopracciglio*) eyebrow; **non ha battuto ~** (*fig*) he didn't bat an eyelid

'cigno ['tʃiɲɲo] SM swan

cigo'lante [tʃigo'lante] AG squeaking, creaking

cigo'lare [tʃigo'lare] **/72/** VI to squeak, creak

'Cile ['tʃile] SM: **il ~** Chile

ci'lecca [tʃi'lekka] SF: **far ~** to fail

ci'leno, -a [tʃi'leno] AG, SM/F Chilean

cili'egia, -gie, -ge [tʃi'ljɛdʒa] SF cherry

cilie'gina [tʃilje'dʒina] SF glacé cherry; **la ~ sulla torta** (*fig*) the icing *o* cherry on the cake

cili'egio [tʃi'ljɛdʒo] SM cherry tree

cilin'drata [tʃilin'drata] SF (Aut) (cubic) capacity; **una macchina di grossa ~** a big-engined car

ci'lindro [tʃi'lindro] SM cylinder; (*cappello*) top hat

CIM [tʃim] SIGLA M = **centro d'igiene mentale**

'cima ['tʃima] SF (*sommità*) top; (*di monte*) top, summit; (*estremità*) end; (*fig: persona*) genius;

in ~ a at the top of; **da ~ a fondo** from top to bottom; (*fig*) from beginning to end

ci'melio [tʃi'mɛljo] SM relic

cimen'tarsi [tʃimen'tarsi] **/72/** VPR: **~ in** (*atleta, concorrente*) to try one's hand at

'cimice ['tʃimitʃe] SF (Zool) bug; (*puntina*) drawing pin (BRIT), thumbtack (US)

cimini'era [tʃimi'njɛra] SF chimney; (*di nave*) funnel

cimi'tero [tʃimi'tɛro] SM cemetery

ci'murro [tʃi'murro] SM (*di cani*) distemper

'Cina ['tʃina] SF: **la ~** China

cin'cin, cin cin [tʃin'tʃin] ESCL cheers!

cincischi'are [tʃintʃis'kjare] **/19/** VI to mess about

'cine ['tʃine] SM INV (col) cinema

cine'asta, -i, -e [tʃine'asta] SM/F person in the film industry; film-maker

cinegior'nale [tʃinedʒor'nale] SM newsreel

'cinema ['tʃinema] SM INV cinema; **~ muto** silent films; **~ d'essai** (*locale*) avant-garde cinema, experimental cinema

cinemato'grafico, -a, -ci, -che [tʃinemato'grafiko] AG (*attore, critica*) movie *cpd*, film *cpd*; (*festival*) film *cpd*; **sala cinematografica** cinema; **successo ~** box-office success

cinema'tografo [tʃinema'tɔgrafo] SM cinema

cine'presa [tʃine'presa] SF cine-camera

ci'nese [tʃi'nese] AG, SM F, SM Chinese *inv*

cine'teca, -che [tʃine'tɛka] SF (*collezione*) film collection; (*locale*) film library

ci'netico, -a, -ci, -che [tʃi'nɛtiko] AG kinetic

'cingere ['tʃindʒere] **/54/** VT (*attorniare*) to surround, encircle; **~ la vita con una cintura** to put a belt round one's waist; **~ d'assedio** to besiege, lay siege to

'cinghia ['tʃingja] SF strap; (*cintura, Tecn*) belt; **tirare la ~** (*fig*) to tighten one's belt

cinghi'ale [tʃin'gjale] SM wild boar

cinguet'tare [tʃingwet'tare] **/72/** VI to twitter

'cinico, -a, -ci, -che ['tʃiniko] AG cynical ▶ SM/F cynic

ci'nismo [tʃi'nizmo] SM cynicism

cin'quanta [tʃin'kwanta] NUM fifty

cinquante'nario [tʃinkwante'narjo] SM fiftieth anniversary

cinquan'tenne [tʃinkwan'tɛnne] SMF fifty-year-old man/woman

cinquan'tesimo, -a [tʃinkwan'tɛzimo] NUM fiftieth

cinquan'tina [tʃinkwan'tina] SF (*serie*): **una ~ (di)** about fifty; (*età*) **essere sulla ~** to be about fifty

'cinque ['tʃinkwe] NUM five; **avere ~ anni** to be five (years old); **il ~ dicembre 2008** the fifth of December 2008; **alle ~** (*ora*) at five (o'clock); **siamo in ~** there are five of us

cinquecen'tesco, -a, -schi, -sche
[tʃinkwetʃen'tesko] AG sixteenth-century
cinque'cento [tʃinkwe'tʃɛnto] NUM five
hundred ▶ SM: **il C~** the sixteenth century
cinque'mila [tʃinkwe'mila] NUM five
thousand
'cinsi *etc* ['tʃinsi] VB *vedi* **cingere**
'cinta ['tʃinta] SF (*anche*: **cinta muraria**) city
walls *pl*; **muro di ~** (*di giardino ecc*)
surrounding wall
cin'tare [tʃin'tare] **/72/** VT to enclose
'cinto, -a ['tʃinto] PP *di* **cingere**
'cintola ['tʃintola] SF (*cintura*) belt; (*vita*) waist
cin'tura [tʃin'tura] SF belt; **~ di salvataggio**
lifebelt (BRIT), life preserver (US); **~ di
sicurezza** (*Aut*, *Aer*) safety o seat belt
cintu'rino [tʃintu'rino] SM strap;
~ dell'orologio watch strap
CIO SIGLA M (= *Comitato Internazionale Olimpico*)
IOC (= *International Olympic Committee*)
ciò [tʃɔ] PRON this; that; **~ che** what;
~ nonostante *o* **nondimeno** nevertheless,
in spite of that; **con tutto ~** for all that, in
spite of everything
ci'occa, -che ['tʃɔkka] SF (*di capelli*) lock
ciocco'lata [tʃokko'lata] SF chocolate;
(*bevanda*) (hot) chocolate; **~ al latte/
fondente** milk/plain chocolate
cioccola'tino [tʃokkola'tino] SM chocolate
ciocco'lato [tʃokko'lato] SM chocolate
cio'è [tʃo'e] AV that is (to say)
ciondo'lare [tʃondo'lare] **/72/** VT (*far dondolare*)
to dangle, swing ▶ VI to dangle; (*fig*) to loaf
(about)
ci'ondolo ['tʃondolo] SM pendant;
~ portafortuna charm
ciondo'loni [tʃondo'loni] AV: **con le braccia/
gambe ~** with arms/legs dangling
ciononos'tante [tʃononos'tante] AV
nonetheless, nevertheless
ci'otola ['tʃotola] SF bowl
ci'ottolo ['tʃottolo] SM pebble; (*di strada*)
cobble(stone)
C.I.P. [tʃip] SIGLA M = **comitato
interministeriale prezzi**; *vedi* **comitato**
Cipe ['tʃipe] SIGLA M = **comitato
interministeriale per la programmazione
economica**; *vedi* **comitato**
'Cipi ['tʃipi] SIGLA M = **comitato
interministeriale per lo sviluppo
industriale**; *vedi* **comitato**
ci'piglio [tʃi'piʎʎo] SM frown
ci'polla [tʃi'polla] SF onion; (*di tulipano ecc*)
bulb
cipol'lina [tʃipol'lina] SF onion; **cipolline
sottaceto** pickled onions; **cipolline
sottolio** baby onions in oil
ci'presso [tʃi'pressso] SM cypress (tree)
'cipria ['tʃiprja] SF (face) powder

cipri'ota, -i, -e [tʃipri'ɔta] AG, SM/F Cypriot
'Cipro ['tʃipro] SM Cyprus
'circa ['tʃirka] AV about, roughly ▶ PREP about,
concerning; **a mezzogiorno ~** about midday
'circo, -chi ['tʃirko] SM circus
circo'lare [tʃirko'lare] **/72/** VI to circulate;
(*Aut*) to drive (along), move (along) ▶ AG
circular ▶ SF (*Amm*) circular; (*di autobus*)
circle (line); **circola voce che ...** there is a
rumour going about that ...; **assegno ~**
banker's draft
circolazi'one [tʃirkolat'tsjone] SF
circulation; (*Aut*): **la ~** (the) traffic; **libretto
di ~** log book, registration book; **tassa di ~**
road tax; **~ a targhe alterne** *see note*

Circolazione a targhe alterne was introduced
by some town councils to combat the
increase in traffic and pollution in town
centres. It stipulates that on days with an
even date, only cars whose number plate
ends in an even number or a zero may be
on the road; on days with an odd date,
only cars with odd registration numbers
may be used. Public holidays are
generally, but not always, exempt.

'circolo ['tʃirkolo] SM circle; **entrare in ~**
(*Anat*) to enter the bloodstream
circoncisi'one [tʃirkontʃi'zjone] SF
circumcision
circon'dare [tʃirkon'dare] **/72/** VT to
surround; **circondarsi** VPR: **circondarsi di**
to surround o.s. with
circondari'ale [tʃirkonda'rjale] AG: **casa di
pena** ~ district prison
circon'dario [tʃirkon'darjo] SM (*Dir*)
administrative district; (*zona circostante*)
neighbourhood (BRIT), neighborhood (US)
circonfe'renza [tʃirkonfe'rɛntsa] SF
circumference
circonvallazi'one [tʃirkonvallat'tsjone] SF
ring road (BRIT), beltway (US); (*per evitare una
città*) by-pass
circos'critto, -a [tʃirkos'kritto] PP *di*
circoscrivere
circos'crivere [tʃirkos'krivere] **/105/** VT to
circumscribe; (*fig*) to limit, restrict
circoscrizi'one [tʃirkoskrit'tsjone] SF (*Amm*)
district, area; **~ elettorale** constituency
circos'petto, -a [tʃirkos'pɛtto] AG
circumspect, cautious
circos'tante [tʃirkos'tante] AG surrounding,
neighbouring (BRIT), neighboring (US)
circos'tanza [tʃirkos'tantsa] SF
circumstance; (*occasione*) occasion; **parole
di ~** words suited to the occasion
circu'ire [tʃirku'ire] **/55/** VT (*fig*) to fool, take in
cir'cuito [tʃir'kuito] SM circuit; **andare in** *o*
fare corto ~ to short-circuit; **~ integrato**
integrated circuit

ci'rillico, -a, -ci, -che [tʃi'rilliko] AG Cyrillic

cir'rosi [tʃir'rɔzi] SF: ~ **epatica** cirrhosis (of the liver)

'C.I.S.A.L. ['tʃizal] SIGLA F (= *Confederazione Italiana Sindacati Autonomi dei Lavoratori*) *trades union organization*

C.I.S.L. [tʃizl] SIGLA F (= *Confederazione Italiana Sindacati Lavoratori*) *trades union organization*

'C.I.S.N.A.L. ['tʃiznal] SIGLA F (= *Confederazione Italiana Sindacati Nazionali dei Lavoratori*) *trades union organization*

'ciste ['tʃiste] SF = **cisti**

cis'terna [tʃis'tɛrna] SF tank, cistern

'cisti ['tʃisti] SF INV cyst

cis'tite [tʃis'tite] SF cystitis

cit. ABBR = **citato**; (= *citata*) cit.

C.I.T. [tʃit] SIGLA F = **Compagnia Italiana Turismo**

ci'tare [tʃi'tare] /**72**/ VT (*Dir*) to summon; (*autore*) to quote; (*a esempio, modello*) to cite; ~ **qn per danni** to sue sb

citazi'one [tʃitat'tsjone] SF summons *sg*; quotation; (*di persona*) mention

ci'tofono [tʃi'tɔfono] SM entry phone; (*in uffici*) intercom

cito'logico, -a, -ci, -che [tʃito'lɔdʒiko] AG: **esame** ~ *test for detection of cancerous cells*

'citrico, -a, -ci, -che ['tʃitriko] AG citric

città [tʃit'ta] SF INV town; (*importante*) city; ~ **giardino** garden city; ~ **mercato** shopping centre, mall; ~ **universitaria** university campus; **C~ del Capo** Cape Town

citta'della [tʃitta'dɛlla] SF citadel, stronghold

cittadi'nanza [tʃittadi'nantsa] SF citizens *pl*, inhabitants *pl* of a town (*o* city); (*Dir*) citizenship

citta'dino, -a [tʃitta'dino] AG town *cpd*; city *cpd* ► SM/F (*di uno Stato*) citizen; (*abitante di città*) town dweller, city dweller

ci'uccio ['tʃuttʃo] SM (*col*) comforter, dummy (BRIT), pacifier (US)

ci'uco, -a, -chi, -che ['tʃuko] SM/F ass

ci'uffo ['tʃuffo] SM tuft

ci'urma ['tʃurma] SF (*di nave*) crew

ci'vetta [tʃi'vetta] SF (*Zool*) owl; (*fig: donna*) coquette, flirt ► AG INV: **auto/nave** ~ decoy car/ship; **fare la** ~ **con qn** to flirt with sb

civet'tare [tʃivet'tare] /**72**/ VT to flirt

civette'ria [tʃivette'ria] SF coquetry, coquettishness

civettu'olo, -a [tʃivet'twɔlo] AG flirtatious

'civico, -a, -ci, -che ['tʃiviko] AG civic; (*museo*) municipal, town *cpd*; city *cpd*; **guardia civica** town policeman; **senso** ~ public spirit

ci'vile [tʃi'vile] AG civil; (*non militare*) civilian; (*nazione*) civilized ► SM civilian; **stato** ~ marital status; **abiti civili** civvies

civi'lista, -i, -e [tʃivi'lista] SM/F (*avvocato*) civil lawyer; (*studioso*) expert in civil law

civiliz'zare [tʃivilid'dzare] /**72**/ VT to civilize

civilizzazi'one [tʃiviliddzat'tsjone] SF civilization

civiltà [tʃivil'ta] SF civilization; (*cortesia*) civility

ci'vismo [tʃi'vizmo] SM public spirit

CL [tʃi'elle] SIGLA F (*Pol*: = *Comunione e Liberazione*) *Catholic youth movement* ► SIGLA = **Caltanissetta**

cl ABBR (= *centilitro*) cl

'clacson SM INV (*Aut*) horn

cla'more SM (*frastuono*) din, uproar, clamour (BRIT), clamor (US); (*fig*) outcry

clamo'roso, -a AG noisy; (*fig*) sensational

clan SM INV clan

clandestinità SF (*di attività*) secret nature; **vivere nella** ~ to live in hiding; (*ricercato politico*) to live underground

clandes'tino, -a AG clandestine; (*Pol*) underground, clandestine; (*immigrato*) illegal ► SM/F stowaway; (*anche*: **immigrato clandestino**) illegal immigrant

clari'netto SM clarinet

'classe SF class; **di** ~ (*fig*) with class; of excellent quality; ~ **operaia** working class; ~ **turistica** (*Aer*) economy class

classi'cismo [klassi'tʃizmo] SM classicism

'classico, -a, -ci, -che AG classical; (*tradizionale: moda*) classic(al) ► SM classic; classical author; (*anche*: **liceo classico**) *secondary school with emphasis on the humanities*

clas'sifica, -che SF classification; (*Sport*) placings *pl*; (*di dischi*) charts *pl*, hit parade

classifi'care /**20**/ VT to classify; (*candidato, compito*) to grade; **classificarsi** VPR to be placed

classifica'tore SM filing cabinet

classificazi'one [klassifikat'tsjone] SF classification; grading

clas'sista, -i, -e AG class-conscious ► SM/F class-conscious person

claudi'cante AG (*zoppo*) lame; (*fig: prosa*) halting

'clausola SF (*Dir*) clause

claustro'fobico, -a, -ci, -che AG claustrophobic

clau'sura SF (*Rel*): **monaca di** ~ nun belonging to an enclosed order; **fare una vita di** ~ (*fig*) to lead a cloistered life

'clava SF club

clavi'cembalo [klavi'tʃembalo] SM harpsichord

cla'vicola SF (*Anat*) collarbone

cle'mente AG merciful; (*clima*) mild

cle'menza [kle'mɛntsa] SF mercy, clemency; mildness

clep'tomane SMF kleptomaniac

cleri'cale AG clerical

'clero SM clergy

cles'sidra SF (*a sabbia*) hourglass; (*ad acqua*) water clock

clic'care /20/ VI (*Inform*): **~ su** to click on

cliché [kli'ʃe] SM INV (*Tip*) plate; (*fig*) cliché

cli'ente SMF customer, client

clien'tela SF customers *pl*, clientèle

cliente'lismo SM: **~ politico** political nepotism

'clima, -i SM climate

cli'matico, -a, -ci, -che AG climatic; **stazione climatica** health resort

climatizza'tore [klimatiddza'tore] SM air conditioner

climatizzazi'one [klimatiddzat'tsjone] SF air conditioning

'clinico, -a, -ci, -che AG clinical ▶ SM (*medico*) clinician ▶ SF (*scienza*) clinical medicine; (*casa di cura*) clinic, nursing home; (*settore d'ospedale*) clinic; **quadro ~** anamnesis; **avere l'occhio ~** (*fig*) to have an expert eye

clis'tere SM (*Med*) enema; (*: apparecchio*) device used to give an enema

clo'aca, -che SF sewer

cloche [klɔʃ] SF INV control stick, joystick; **cambio a ~** (*Aut*) floor-mounted gear lever

clo'nare /72/ VT to clone

clona'zione [klonat'tsjone] SF (*Biol, fig*) cloning

'cloro SM chlorine

cloro'filla SF chlorophyll

cloro'formio SM chloroform

cloud computing [klaud kom'pjutin] SM INV cloud computing

club SM INV club

cm ABBR (= *centimetro*) cm

c.m. ABBR (= *corrente mese*) inst.

CN SIGLA = **Cuneo**

c/n ABBR = **conto nuovo**

CNEN SIGLA M (= *Comitato Nazionale per l'Energia Nucleare*) ≈ AEA (*BRIT*), AEC (*US*)

CNIOP SIGLA M = **Centro Nazionale per l'Istruzione e l'Orientamento Professionale**

CNR SIGLA M (= *Consiglio Nazionale delle Ricerche*) science research council

CNRN SIGLA M = **Comitato Nazionale Ricerche Nucleari**

CO SIGLA = **Como**

Co. ABBR (= *compagnia*) Co.

c/o ABBR (= *care of*) c/o

coabi'tare /72/ VI to live together, live under the same roof

coagu'lare /72/ VT to coagulate ▶ VI (*anche*: **coagularsi**) to coagulate; (*: latte*) to curdle

coalizi'one [koalit'tsjone] SF coalition

co'atto, -a AG (*Dir*) compulsory, forced; **condannare al domicilio ~** to place under house arrest

'COBAS SIGLA M PL (= *Comitati di base*) independent trades unions

'cobra SM INV cobra

'coca SF (*bibita*) Coke®; (*droga*) cocaine

'coca 'cola® SF coca cola®

coca'ina SF cocaine

coc'carda SF cockade

cocchi'ere [kok'kjɛre] SM coachman

'cocchio ['kɔkkjo] SM (*carrozza*) coach; (*biga*) chariot

cocci'nella [kottʃi'nɛlla] SF ladybird (*BRIT*), ladybug (*US*)

'coccio ['kɔttʃo] SM earthenware; (*vaso*) earthenware pot; **cocci** SMPL fragments (of pottery)

cocciu'taggine [kottʃu'taddʒine] SF stubbornness, pig-headedness

cocci'uto, -a [kot'tʃuto] AG stubborn, pigheaded

'cocco, -chi SM (*pianta*) coconut palm; (*frutto*): **noce di ~** coconut ▶ SM/F (*col*) darling; **è il ~ della mamma** he's mummy's darling

cocco'drillo SM crocodile

cocco'lare /72/ VT to cuddle, fondle

co'cente [ko'tʃɛnte] AG (*anche fig*) burning

cocerò *etc* [kotʃe'rɔ] VB *vedi* **cuocere**

co'comero SM watermelon

co'cuzzolo [ko'kuttsolo] SM top; (*di capo, cappello*) crown

cod. ABBR = **codice**

'coda SF tail; (*fila di persone, auto*) queue (*BRIT*), line (*US*); (*di abiti*) train; **con la ~ dell'occhio** out of the corner of one's eye; **mettersi in ~** to queue (up) (*BRIT*), line up (*US*); to join the queue *o* line; **~ di cavallo** (*acconciatura*) ponytail; **avere la ~ di paglia** (*fig*) to have a guilty conscience; **~ di rospo** (*Cuc*) frogfish tail

codar'dia SF cowardice

co'dardo, -a AG cowardly ▶ SM/F coward

co'desto, -a AG, PRON (*poetico*) this; that

'codice ['kɔditʃe] SM code; (*manoscritto antico*) codex; **~ di avviamento postale** postcode (*BRIT*), zip code (*US*); **~ a barre** bar code; **~ civile** civil code; **~ fiscale** tax code; **~ penale** penal code; **~ segreto** (*di tessera magnetica*) PIN (number); **~ della strada** highway code

co'difica SF codification; (*Inform: di programma*) coding

codifi'care /20/ VT (*Dir*) to codify; (*cifrare*) to code

codificazi'one [kodifikat'tsjone] SF coding

coercizi'one [koertʃit'tsjone] SF coercion

coe'rente AG coherent

coe'renza [koe'rɛntsa] SF coherence

coesi'one SF cohesion

coe'sistere /11/ VI to coexist

coe'taneo, -a AG, SM/F contemporary;
essere ~ di qn to be the same age as sb
cofa'netto SM casket; **~ dei gioielli** jewel
case
'**cofano** SM (Aut) bonnet (BRIT), hood (US);
(forziere) chest
'**coffa** SF (Naut) top
'**cogli** ['koʎʎi] PREP + DET vedi **con**
'**cogliere** ['kɔʎʎere] /23/ VT (fiore, frutto) to pick,
gather; (sorprendere) to catch, surprise;
(bersaglio) to hit; (fig: momento opportuno ecc) to
grasp, seize, take; (: capire) to grasp;
~ l'occasione (per fare) to take the
opportunity (to do); **~ sul fatto** o **in
flagrante/alla sprovvista** to catch
red-handed/unprepared; **~ nel segno** (fig) to
hit the nail on the head
cogli'one [koʎˈʎone] SM (!: testicolo): **coglioni**
balls (!); (fig: persona sciocca) jerk; **rompere i
coglioni a qn** to get on sb's tits (!)
co'gnac [kɔˈɲak] SM INV cognac
co'gnato, -a [koɲˈɲato] SM/F brother-in-
law(-sister-in-law)
cogni'tivo, -a [koɲɲiˈtivo] AG cognitive
cognizi'one [koɲɲitˈtsjone] SF knowledge;
con ~ di causa with full knowledge of the
facts
co'gnome [koɲˈɲome] SM surname
'**coi** PREP + DET vedi **con**
coi'bente AG insulating
coinci'denza [kointʃiˈdɛntsa] SF coincidence;
(Ferr, Aer, di autobus) connection
coin'cidere [koinˈtʃidere] /34/ VI to coincide
coin'ciso, -a [koinˈtʃizo] PP di **coincidere**
coinqui'lino SM fellow tenant
cointeres'senza [kointeresˈsɛntsa] SF
(Comm): **avere una ~ in qc** to own shares in
sth; **~ dei lavoratori** profit-sharing
coin'volgere [koinˈvɔldʒere] /96/ VT: **~ in** to
involve in
coinvolgi'mento [koinvoldʒiˈmento] SM
involvement
coin'volto, -a PP di **coinvolgere**
col PREP + DET vedi **con**
Col. ABBR (= colonnello) Col.
colà AV there
cola'brodo SM INV strainer
cola'pasta SM INV colander
co'lare /72/ VT (liquido) to strain; (pasta) to
drain; (oro fuso) to pour ▶ VI (sudore) to drip;
(botte) to leak; (cera) to melt; **~ a picco** vt
(nave) to sink
co'lata SF (di lava) flow; (Industria) casting
colazi'one [kolatˈtsjone] SF (anche: **prima
colazione**) breakfast; (anche: **seconda
colazione**) lunch; **fare ~** to have breakfast (o
lunch); **~ di lavoro** working lunch
Coldi'retti ABBR F (= Confederazione nazionale
coltivatori diretti) federation of Italian farmers

co'lei PRON vedi **colui**
co'lera SM (Med) cholera
coleste'rolo SM cholesterol
colf ABBR F = **collaboratrice familiare**
'**colgo** etc VB vedi **cogliere**
colibrì SM hummingbird
'**colica** SF (Med) colic
co'lino SM strainer
'**colla** PREP + DET vedi **con** ▶ SF glue; (di farina)
paste
collabo'rare /72/ VI to collaborate; (con la
polizia) to co-operate; **~ a** to collaborate on;
(giornale) to contribute to
collabora'tore, -'trice SM/F collaborator; (di
giornale, rivista) contributor; **~ esterno**
freelance; **collaboratrice familiare** home
help; **~ di giustizia** = **pentito**
collaborazi'one [kollaboratˈtsjone] SF
collaboration; contribution
col'lana SF necklace; (collezione) collection,
series
col'lant [kɔˈlɑ̃] SM INV tights pl
col'lare SM collar
col'lasso SM (Med) collapse
collate'rale AG collateral; **effetti collaterali**
side effects
collau'dare /72/ VT to test, try out
col'laudo SM testing no pl; test
'**colle** PREP + DET vedi **con** ▶ SM hill
col'lega, -ghi, -ghe SM/F colleague
collega'mento SM connection; (Mil) liaison;
(Radio) link(-up); (Inform) link; **ufficiale di ~**
liaison officer; **~ ipertestuale** hyperlink
colle'gare /80/ VT to connect, join, link;
collegarsi VPR (Radio, TV) to link up;
collegarsi con (Tel) to get through to
collegi'ale [kolleˈdʒale] AG (riunione, decisione)
collective; (Ins) boarding school cpd ▶ SMF
boarder; (fig: persona timida e inesperta)
schoolboy(-girl)
col'legio [kolˈlɛdʒo] SM college; (convitto)
boarding school; **~ elettorale** (Pol)
constituency
'**collera** SF anger; **andare in ~** to get angry
col'lerico, -a, -ci, -che AG quick-tempered,
irascible
col'letta SF collection
collettività SF community
collet'tivo, -a AG collective; (interesse)
general, everybody's; (biglietto, visita ecc)
group cpd ▶ SM (Pol) political group;
società in nome ~ (Comm) partnership
col'letto SM collar; **colletti bianchi** (fig)
white-collar workers
collezio'nare [kollettsjoˈnare] /72/ VT to
collect
collezi'one [kolletˈtsjone] SF collection
collezio'nista [kollettsjoˈnista] SMF collector
colli'mare /72/ VI to correspond, coincide

col'lina SF hill

colli'nare AG hill *cpd*

col'lirio SM eyewash

collisi'one SF collision

'collo PREP + DET *vedi* **con** ▶ SM neck; *(di abito)* neck, collar; *(pacco)* parcel; **~ del piede** instep

colloca'mento SM *(impiego)* employment; *(disposizione)* placing, arrangement; **ufficio di ~** ≈ Jobcentre *(BRIT)*, state *(o federal)* employment agency *(US)*; **~ a riposo** retirement

collo'care /20/ VT *(libri, mobili)* to place; *(persona: trovare un lavoro per)* to find a job for, place; *(Comm: merce)* to find a market for; **~ qn a riposo** to retire sb

collocazi'one [kollokat'tsjone] SF placing; *(di libro)* classification

colloqui'ale AG *(termine ecc)* colloquial; *(tono)* informal

col'loquio SM conversation, talk; *(ufficiale, per un lavoro)* interview; *(Ins)* preliminary oral exam; **avviare un ~ con qn** *(Pol ecc)* to start talks with sb

col'loso, -a AG sticky

col'lottola SF nape *o* scruff of the neck; **afferrare qn per la ~** to grab sb by the scruff of the neck

collusi'one SF *(Dir)* collusion

colluttazi'one [kolluttat'tsjone] SF scuffle

col'mare /72/ VT: **~ di** *(anche fig)* to fill with; *(dare in abbondanza)* to load *o* overwhelm with; **~ un divario** *(fig)* to bridge a gap

'colmo, -a AG: **~ (di)** full (of) ▶ SM summit, top; *(fig)* height; **al ~ della disperazione** in the depths of despair; **è il ~!** it's the last straw!; **e per ~ di sfortuna ...** and to cap it all ...

co'lomba SF *vedi* **colombo**

Co'lombia SF: **la ~** Colombia

colombi'ano, -a AG, SM/F Colombian

co'lombo, -a SM/F dove; pigeon; **colombi** *(fig: col)* lovebirds

Co'lonia SF Cologne

co'lonia SF colony; *(per bambini)* holiday camp; **(acqua di) ~** (eau de) cologne

coloni'ale AG colonial ▶ SMF colonist, settler

co'lonico, -a, -ci, -che AG: **casa colonica** farmhouse

coloniz'zare [kolonid'dzare] /72/ VT to colonize

co'lonna SF column; **~ sonora** *(Cine)* sound track; **~ vertebrale** spine, spinal column

colon'nello SM colonel

co'lono SM *(coltivatore)* tenant farmer

colo'rante SM colouring *(BRIT)*, coloring *(US)*

colo'rare /72/ VT to colour *(BRIT)*, color *(US)*; *(disegno)* to colour in

co'lore SM colour *(BRIT)*, color *(US)*; *(Carte)* suit; **a colori** in colour, colour *cpd*; **la gente di ~** coloured people; **diventare di tutti i colori** to turn scarlet; **farne di tutti i colori** to get up to all sorts of mischief; **passarne di tutti i colori** to go through all sorts of problems

colo'rito, -a AG coloured *(BRIT)*, colored *(US)*; *(viso)* rosy, pink; *(linguaggio)* colourful *(BRIT)*, colorful *(US)* ▶ SM *(tinta)* colour *(BRIT)*, color *(US)*; *(carnagione)* complexion

co'loro PRON PL *vedi* **colui**

colos'sale AG colossal, enormous

co'losso SM colossus

'colpa SF fault; *(biasimo)* blame; *(colpevolezza)* guilt; *(azione colpevole)* offence; *(peccato)* sin; **di chi è la ~?** whose fault is it?; **è ~ sua** it's his fault; **per ~ di** through, owing to; **senso di ~** sense of guilt; **dare la ~ a qn di qc** to blame sb for sth

col'pevole AG guilty

colpevoliz'zare [kolpevolid'dzare] /72/ VT: **~ qn** to make sb feel guilty

col'pire /55/ VT to hit, strike; *(fig)* to strike; **rimanere colpito da qc** to be amazed *o* struck by sth; **è stato colpito da ordine di cattura** there is a warrant out for his arrest; **~ nel segno** *(fig)* to hit the nail on the head, be spot on *(BRIT)*

'colpo SM *(urto)* knock; *(fig: affettivo)* blow, shock; *(: aggressivo)* blow; *(di pistola)* shot; *(Med)* stroke; *(furto)* raid; **di ~, tutto d'un ~** suddenly; **fare ~** to make a strong impression; **il motore perde colpi** the engine is misfiring; **è morto sul ~** he died instantly; **mi hai fatto venire un ~!** what a fright you gave me!; **ti venisse un ~!** *(col)* drop dead!; **~ d'aria** chill; **~ in banca** bank job *o* raid; **~ basso** *(Pugilato, fig)* punch below the belt; **~ di fulmine** love at first sight; **~ di grazia** coup de grâce; *(fig)* finishing blow; **a ~ d'occhio** at a glance; **~ di scena** *(Teat)* coup de théâtre; *(fig)* dramatic turn of events; **~ di sole** sunstroke; **colpi di sole** *(nei capelli)* highlights; **~ di Stato** coup d'état; **~ di telefono** phone call; **~ di testa** (sudden) impulse *o* whim; **~ di vento** gust (of wind)

col'poso, -a AG: **omicidio ~** manslaughter

'colsi *etc vedi* **cogliere**

coltel'lata SF stab

col'tello SM knife; **avere il ~ dalla parte del manico** *(fig)* to have the whip hand; **~ a serramanico** clasp knife

colti'vare /72/ VT to cultivate; *(verdura)* to grow, cultivate

coltiva'tore SM farmer; **~ diretto** small independent farmer

coltivazi'one [koltivat'tsjone] SF cultivation; growing; **~ intensiva** intensive farming

'colto, -a PP di **cogliere** ▶ AG (*istruito*) cultured, educated

'coltre SF blanket

col'tura SF cultivation; ~ **alternata** crop rotation

co'lui (*f* **colei**, *pl* **coloro**) PRON the one; ~ **che parla** the one *o* the man *o* the person who is speaking; **colei che amo** the one *o* the woman *o* the person (whom) I love

com. ABBR = **comunale**; **commissione**

'coma SM INV coma

comanda'mento SM (*Rel*) commandment

coman'dante SM (*Mil*) commander, commandant; (*di reggimento*) commanding officer; (*Naut, Aer*) captain

coman'dare /72/ VI to be in command ▶ VT to command; (*imporre*) to order, command; ~ **a qn di fare** to order sb to do

co'mando SM (*ingiunzione*) order, command; (*autorità*) command; (*Tecn*) control; ~ **generale** general headquarters *pl*; ~ **a distanza** remote control

co'mare SF (*madrina*) godmother; (*donna pettegola*) gossip

co'masco, -a, -schi, -sche AG of (*o* from) Como

combaci'are [komba'tʃare] /14/ VI to meet; (*fig: coincidere*) to coincide, correspond

combat'tente AG fighting ▶ SM combatant; **ex-~** ex-serviceman

com'battere /1/ VT to fight; (*fig*) to combat, fight against ▶ VI to fight

combatti'mento SM fight; fighting *no pl*; (*di pugilato*) match; **mettere fuori ~** to knock out

combat'tivo, -a AG pugnacious

combat'tuto, -a AG (*incerto: persona*) uncertain, undecided; (*gara, partita*) hard fought

combi'nare /72/ VT to combine; (*organizzare*) to arrange; (*col: fare*) to make, cause ▶ VI (*corrispondere*): ~ **(con)** to correspond (with)

combinazi'one [kombinat'tsjone] SF combination; (*caso fortuito*) coincidence; **per ~** by chance

com'briccola SF (*gruppo*) party; (*banda*) gang

combus'tibile AG combustible ▶ SM fuel

combusti'one SF combustion

com'butta SF (*peg*) gang; **in ~** in league

'come AV **1** (*alla maniera di*) like; **ti comporti come lui** you behave like him *o* like he does; **bianco come la neve** (as) white as snow; **come se** as if, as though; **com'è vero Dio!** as God is my witness!

2 (*in qualità di*) as a; **lavora come autista** he works as a driver

3 (*interrogativo*) how; **come ti chiami?** what's your name?; **come sta?** how are you?; **com'è il tuo amico?** what is your friend like?; **come?** (*prego?*) pardon?, sorry?; **come mai?** how come?; **come mai non ci hai avvertiti?** how come you didn't warn us?

4 (*esclamativo*): **come sei bravo!** how clever you are!; **come mi dispiace!** I'm terribly sorry!

▶ CONG **1** (*in che modo*) how; **mi ha spiegato come l'ha conosciuto** he told me how he met him; **non so come sia successo** I don't know how it happened; **attento a come parli!** watch your mouth!

2 (*correlativo*) as; (: *con comparativi di maggioranza*) than; **non è bravo come pensavo** he isn't as clever as I thought; **è meglio di come pensassi** it's better than I thought

3 (*quasi se*) as; **è come se fosse ancora qui** it's as if he was still here; **come se niente fosse** as if nothing had happened; **come non detto!** let's forget it!

4 (*appena che, quando*) as soon as; **come arrivò, iniziò a lavorare** as soon as he arrived, he set to work

5 *vedi anche* **così**; **oggi**; **ora**; **tanto**

'COMECON ABBR M (= *Consiglio di Mutua Assistenza Economica*) COMECON

come'done SM blackhead

co'meta SF comet

'comico, -a, -ci, -che AG (*Teat*) comic; (*buffo*) comical ▶ SM (*attore*) comedian, comic actor; (*comicità*) comic spirit, comedy

co'mignolo [ko'miɲɲolo] SM chimney top

cominci'are [komin'tʃare] /14/ VT, VI to begin, start; ~ **a fare/col fare** to begin to do/by doing; **cominciamo bene!** (*ironico*) we're off to a fine start!

comi'tato SM committee; ~ **direttivo** steering committee; ~ **di gestione** works council; ~ **interministeriale prezzi** interdepartmental committee on prices; ~ **interministeriale per la programmazione economica** interdepartmental committee for economic planning; ~ **interministeriale per lo sviluppo industriale** interdepartmental committee for industrial development

comi'tiva SF party, group

co'mizio [ko'mittsjo] SM (*Pol*) meeting, assembly; ~ **elettorale** election rally

'comma, -i SM (*Dir*) subsection

com'mando SM INV commando (squad)

com'media SF comedy; (*opera teatrale*) play; (: *che fa ridere*) comedy; (*fig*) playacting *no pl*

commedi'ante SMF (*peg*) third-rate actor(-actress); (: *fig*) sham

commedi'ografo, -a SM/F (*autore*) comedy writer

commemo'rare /**72**/ vт to commemorate

commemorazi'one [kommemorat'tsjone] sF commemoration

commenda'tore sм *official title awarded for services to one's country*

commen'sale sмf table companion

commen'tare /**72**/ vт to comment on; (*testo*) to annotate; (*Radio, TV*) to give a commentary on

commenta'tore, -'trice sм/F commentator

com'mento sм comment; (*a un testo, Radio, TV*) commentary; **~ musicale** (*Cine*) background music

commerci'ale [kommer'tʃale] AG commercial, trading; (*peg*) commercial

commercia'lista, -i, -e [kommertʃa'lista] sм/F (*laureato*) graduate in economics and commerce; (*consulente*) business consultant

commercializ'zare [kommertʃalid'dzare] /**72**/ vт to market

commercializzazi'one [kommertʃaliddzat'tsjone] sF marketing

commerci'ante [kommer'tʃante] sмf trader, dealer; (*negoziante*) shopkeeper; **~ all'ingrosso** wholesaler; **~ in proprio** sole trader

commerci'are [kommer'tʃare] /**14**/ vi: **~ in** to deal *o* trade in ▶ vт to deal *o* trade in

com'mercio [kom'mɛrtʃo] sм trade, commerce; **essere in ~** (*prodotto*) to be on the market *o* on sale; **essere nel ~** (*persona*) to be in business; **~ all'ingrosso/al dettaglio** wholesale/retail trade

com'messo, -a PP *di* **commettere** ▶ sм/F shop assistant (*Brit*), sales clerk (*US*) ▶ sм (*impiegato*) clerk ▶ sF (*Comm*) order; **~ viaggiatore** commercial traveller

commes'tibile AG edible; **commestibili** sмPL foodstuffs

com'mettere /**63**/ vт to commit; (*ordinare*) to commission, order

commi'ato sм leave-taking; **prendere ~ da qn** to take one's leave of sb

commi'nare /**72**/ vт (*Dir*) to make provision for

commise'rare /**72**/ vт to sympathize with, commiserate with

commiserazi'one [kommizerat'tsjone] sF commiseration

com'misi *etc* vв *vedi* **commettere**

commissaria'mento sм temporary receivership

commissari'are /**19**/ vт to put under temporary receivership

commissari'ato sм (*Amm*) commissionership; (: *sede*) commissioner's office; (: *di polizia*) police station

commis'sario sм commissioner; (*di pubblica sicurezza*) ≈ (police) superintendent (*Brit*),

≈ (police) captain (*US*); (*Sport*) steward; (*membro di commissione*) member of a committee *o* board; **alto ~** high commissioner; **~ di bordo** (*Naut*) purser; **~ d'esame** member of an examining board; **~ di gara** race official; **~ tecnico** (*Sport*) national coach

commissio'nare /**72**/ vт to order, place an order for

commissio'nario sм (*Comm*) agent, broker

commissi'one sF (*incarico*) errand; (*comitato, percentuale*) commission; (*Comm: ordinazione*) order; **commissioni** sFPL (*acquisti*) shopping *sg*; **~ d'esame** examining board; **~ d'inchiesta** committee of enquiry; **~ permanente** standing committee; **commissioni bancarie** bank charges

commit'tente sмf (*Comm*) purchaser, customer

com'mosso, -a PP *di* **commuovere**

commo'vente AG moving

commozi'one [kommot'tsjone] sF emotion, deep feeling; **~ cerebrale** (*Med*) concussion

commu'overe /**66**/ vт to move, affect; **commuoversi** vPR to be moved

commu'tare /**72**/ vт (*pena*) to commute; (*Elettr*) to change *o* switch over

commutazi'one [kommutat'tsjone] sF (*Dir, Elettr*) commutation

comò sм inv chest of drawers

como'dino sм bedside table

comodità sF inv comfort; convenience

'comodo, -a AG comfortable; (*facile*) easy; (*conveniente*) convenient; (*utile*) useful, handy ▶ sм comfort; convenience; **con ~** at one's convenience *o* leisure; **fare il proprio ~** to do as one pleases; **far ~** to be useful *o* handy; **stia ~!** don't bother to get up!

'compact disc sм inv compact disc

compae'sano, -a sм/F fellow-countryman(-woman); person from the same town

com'pagine [kom'padʒine] sF (*squadra*) team

compa'gnia [kompaɲ'ɲia] sF company; (*gruppo*) gathering; **fare ~ a qn** to keep sb company; **essere di ~** to be sociable

com'pagno, -a [kom'paɲɲo] sм/F (*di classe, gioco*) companion; (*Pol*) comrade; **~ di lavoro** workmate; **~ di scuola** schoolfriend; **~ di viaggio** fellow traveller

com'paio *etc* vв *vedi* **comparire**

compa'rare /**72**/ vт to compare

compara'tivo, -a AG, sм comparative

comparazi'one [komparat'tsjone] sF comparison

com'pare sм (*padrino*) godfather; (*complice*) accomplice; (*col: amico*) old pal, old mate

compa'rire /**7**/ vi to appear; **~ in giudizio** (*Dir*) to appear before the court

comparizi'one [komparit'tsjone] SF (*Dir*) appearance; **mandato di** ~ summons *sg*

com'parso, -a PP *di* **comparire** ▶ SF appearance; (*Teat*) walk-on; (*Cine*) extra

comparteci'pare [kompartetʃi'pare] /**72**/ VI (*Comm*): ~ **a** to have a share in

compartecipazi'one [kompartetʃipat'tsjone] SF sharing; (*quota*) share; ~ **agli utili** profit-sharing; **in** ~ jointly

comparti'mento SM compartment; (*Amm*) district

com'parvi *etc* VB *vedi* **comparire**

compas'sato, -a AG (*persona*) composed; **freddo e** ~ cool and collected

compassi'one SF compassion, pity; **avere** ~ **di qn** to feel sorry for sb, pity sb; **fare** ~ to arouse pity

compassio'nevole AG compassionate

com'passo SM (pair of) compasses *pl*; callipers *pl*

compa'tibile AG (*scusabile*) excusable; (*conciliabile, Inform*) compatible

compati'mento SM compassion; indulgence; **con aria di** ~ with a condescending air

compa'tire /**55**/ VT (*aver compassione di*) to sympathize with, feel sorry for; (*scusare*) to make allowances for

compatri'ota, -i, -e SM/F compatriot

compat'tezza [kompat'tettsa] SF (*solidità*) compactness; (*fig: unità*) solidarity

com'patto, -a AG compact; (*roccia*) solid; (*folla*) dense; (*fig: gruppo, partito*) united, close-knit

com'pendio SM summary; (*libro*) compendium

compen'sare /**72**/ VT (*equilibrare*) to compensate for, make up for; **compensarsi** VPR (*reciproco*) to balance each other out; ~ **qn di** (*rimunerare*) to pay *o* remunerate sb for; (*risarcire*) to pay compensation to sb for; (*fig: fatiche, dolori*) to reward sb for

compen'sato SM (*anche:* **legno compensato**) plywood

com'penso SM compensation; payment, remuneration; reward; **in** ~ (*d'altra parte*) on the other hand

'**compera** SF purchase; **fare le compere** to do the shopping

compe'rare /**72**/ VT = **comprare**

'**compere** SFPL: **fare** ~ to do the shopping

compe'tente AG competent; (*mancia*) apt, suitable; (*capace*) qualified; **rivolgersi all'ufficio** ~ to apply to the office concerned

compe'tenza [kompe'tɛntsa] SF competence; (*Dir: autorità*) jurisdiction; (*Tecn, Comm*) expertise; **competenze** SFPL (*onorari*) fees; **definire le competenze**

to establish responsibilities

com'petere /**45**/ VI to compete, vie; (*Dir*): (*spettare*) ~ **a** to lie within the competence of

competitività SF INV competitiveness

competi'tivo, -a AG competitive

competi'tore, -'trice SM/F competitor

competizi'one [kompetit'tsjone] SF competition; **spirito di** ~ competitive spirit

compia'cente [kompja'tʃɛnte] AG courteous, obliging

compia'cenza [kompja'tʃɛntsa] SF courtesy

compia'cere [kompja'tʃere] /**74**/ VI: ~ **a** to gratify, please ▶ VT to please; **compiacersi** VPR: **compiacersi di** *o* **per qc** (*provare soddisfazione*) to be delighted at sth; **compiacersi con qn** (*rallegrarsi*) to congratulate sb; **compiacersi di fare** (*degnarsi*) to be so good as to do

compiaci'mento [kompjatʃi'mento] SM satisfaction

compiaci'uto, -a [kompja'tʃuto] PP *di* **compiacere**

compi'angere [kom'pjandʒere] /**75**/ VT to sympathize with, feel sorry for

compi'anto, -a PP *di* **compiangere** ▶ AG: **il** ~ **presidente** the late lamented president ▶ SM mourning, grief

'**compiere** /**24**/ VT (*concludere*) to finish, complete; (*adempiere*) to carry out, fulfil; **compiersi** VPR (*avverarsi*) to be fulfilled, come true; ~ **gli anni** to have one's birthday

compi'lare /**72**/ VT to compile; (*modulo*) to complete, fill in (*Brit*), fill out (*US*)

compila'tore, -'trice SM/F compiler

compilazi'one [kompilat'tsjone] SF compilation; completion

compi'mento SM (*termine, conclusione*) completion, fulfilment; **portare a** ~ **qc** to conclude sth, bring sth to a conclusion

com'pire /**92**/ VB = **compiere**

'**compito**[1] SM (*incarico*) task, duty; (*dovere*) duty; (*Ins*) exercise; (*: a casa*) piece of homework; **fare i compiti** to do one's homework

com'pito[2]**, -a** AG well-mannered, polite

compiu'tezza [kompju'tettsa] SF (*completezza*) completeness; (*perfezione*) perfection

compi'uto, -a PP *di* **compiere** ▶ AG: **a 20 anni compiuti** at 20 years of age, at age 20; **un fatto** ~ a fait accompli

comple'anno SM birthday

complemen'tare AG complementary; (*Ins: materia*) subsidiary

comple'mento SM complement; (*Mil*) reserve (troops); ~ **oggetto** (*Ling*) direct object

comples'sato, -a AG, SM/F: **essere (un)** ~ to be full of complexes *o* hang-ups (*col*)

complessità SF complexity
complessiva'mente AV (*nell'insieme*) on the whole; (*in tutto*) altogether
comples'sivo, -a AG (*globale*) comprehensive, overall; (*totale: cifra*) total; **visione complessiva** overview
com'plesso, -a AG complex ▶ SM (*Psic, Edil*) complex; (*Mus: corale*) ensemble; (: *orchestrina*) band; (: *di musica pop*) group; **in** o **nel ~** on the whole; **~ alberghiero** hotel complex; **~ edilizio** building complex; **~ vitaminico** vitamin complex
completa'mente AV completely
completa'mento SM completion
comple'tare /**72**/ VT to complete
com'pleto, -a AG complete; (*teatro, autobus*) full ▶ SM suit; **al ~** full; **essere al ~** (*teatro*) to be sold out; **~ da sci** ski suit
compli'care /**20**/ VT to complicate; **complicarsi** VPR to become complicated
complicazi'one [komplikat'tsjone] SF complication; **salvo complicazioni** unless any difficulties arise
'**complice** ['kɔmplitʃe] SMF accomplice
complicità [komplitʃi'ta] SF INV complicity; **un sorriso/uno sguardo di ~** a knowing smile/look
complimen'tarsi /**72**/ VPR: **~ con** to congratulate
compli'mento SM compliment; **complimenti** SMPL (*cortesia eccessiva*) ceremony sg; (*ossequi*) regards, compliments; **complimenti!** congratulations!; **senza complimenti!** don't stand on ceremony!; make yourself at home!; help yourself!
complot'tare /**72**/ VI to plot, conspire
com'plotto SM plot, conspiracy
com'pone etc VB vedi **comporre**
compo'nente SMF member ▶ SM component
com'pongo etc VB vedi **comporre**
compo'nibile AG (*mobili, cucina*) fitted
componi'mento SM (*Dir*) settlement; (*Ins*) composition; (*poetico, teatrale*) work
com'porre /**77**/ VT (*musica, testo*) to compose; (*mettere in ordine*) to arrange; (*Dir: lite*) to settle; (*Tip*) to set; (*Tel*) to dial; **comporsi** VPR: **comporsi di** to consist of, be composed of
comportamen'tale AG behavioural (BRIT), behavioral (US)
comporta'mento SM behaviour (BRIT), behavior (US); (*di prodotto*) performance
compor'tare /**72**/ VT (*implicare*) to involve, entail; (*consentire*) to permit, allow (of); **comportarsi** VPR (*condursi*) to behave
com'posi etc VB vedi **comporre**
composi'tore, -'trice SM/F composer; (*Tip*) compositor, typesetter
composizi'one [kompozit'tsjone] SF composition; (*Dir*) settlement

com'posta SF vedi **composto**
compos'tezza [kompos'tettsa] SF composure; decorum
com'posto, -a PP di **comporre** ▶ AG (*persona*) composed, self-possessed; (: *decoroso*) dignified; (*formato da più elementi*) compound cpd ▶ SM compound; (*Cuc ecc*) mixture ▶ SF (*Cuc*) stewed fruit *no pl*; (*Agr*) compost
com'prare /**72**/ VT to buy; (*corrompere*) to bribe
compra'tore, -'trice SM/F buyer, purchaser
compra'vendita SF (*Comm*) (contract of) sale; **un atto di ~** a deed of sale
com'prendere /**81**/ VT (*contenere*) to comprise, consist of; (*capire*) to understand
compren'donio SM: **essere duro di ~** to be slow on the uptake
compren'sibile AG understandable
comprensi'one SF understanding
compren'sivo, -a AG (*prezzo*): **~ di** inclusive of; (*indulgente*) understanding
compren'sorio SM area, territory; (*Amm*) district
com'preso, -a PP di **comprendere** ▶ AG (*incluso*) included; **tutto ~** all included, all-in (BRIT)
com'pressa SF vedi **compresso**
compressi'one SF compression
com'presso, -a PP di **comprimere** ▶ AG (vedi *comprimere*) pressed; compressed; repressed ▶ SF (*Med: garza*) compress; (: *pastiglia*) tablet
compres'sore SM compressor; (*anche:* **rullo compressore**) steamroller
compri'mario, -a SM/F (*Teat*) supporting actor(-actress)
com'primere /**50**/ VT (*premere*) to press; (*Fisica*) to compress; (*fig*) to repress
compro'messo, -a PP di **compromettere** ▶ SM compromise
compro'mettere /**63**/ VT to compromise; **compromettersi** VPR to compromise o.s.
compro'prietà SF (*Dir*) joint ownership
compro'vare /**72**/ VT to confirm
com'punto, -a AG contrite; **con fare ~** with a solemn air
compunzi'one [kompun'tsjone] SF contrition; solemnity
compu'tare /**72**/ VT to calculate; (*addebitare*): **~ qc a qn** to debit sb with sth
com'puter [kəm'pjuːtər] SM INV computer
computeriz'zato, -a [komputerid'dzato] AG computerized
computerizzazi'one [komputeriddzat'tsjone] SF computerization
computiste'ria SF accounting, book-keeping
'**computo** SM calculation; **fare il ~ di** to count
comu'nale AG municipal, town cpd; **consiglio/palazzo ~** town council/hall;

è un impiegato ~ he works for the local council

Co'mune SM (*Amm*) town council; (*sede*) town hall; *see note*

> The *Comune* is the smallest autonomous political and administrative unit. It keeps records of births, marriages and deaths and has the power to levy taxes and vet proposals for public works and town planning. It is run by a *Giunta comunale*, which is elected by the *Consiglio Comunale*. The *Comune* is headed by the *sindaco* (mayor) who since 1993 has been elected directly by the citizens.

co'mune AG common; (*consueto*) common, everyday; (*di livello medio*) average; (*ordinario*) ordinary ▶ SF (*di persone*) commune; **fuori del** ~ out of the ordinary; **avere in** ~ to have in common, share; **mettere in** ~ to share; **un nostro** ~ **amico** a mutual friend of ours; **fare cassa** ~ to pool one's money

comuni'care /20/ VT (*notizia*) to pass on, convey; (*malattia*) to pass on; (*ansia ecc*) to communicate; (*trasmettere: calore ecc*) to transmit, communicate; (*Rel*) to administer communion to ▶ VI to communicate; **comunicarsi** VPR (*propagarsi*): **comunicarsi a** to spread to; (*Rel*) to receive communion

comunica'tivo, -a AG (*sentimento*) infectious; (*persona*) communicative ▶ SF communicativeness

comuni'cato SM communiqué; ~ **stampa** press release

comunicazi'one [komunikat'tsjone] SF communication; (*annuncio*) announcement; (*Tel*): ~ **(telefonica)** (telephone) call; **dare la** ~ **a qn** to put sb through; **ottenere la** ~ to get through; **salvo comunicazioni contrarie da parte Vostra** unless we hear from you to the contrary

comuni'one SF communion; ~ **dei beni** (*Dir: tra coniugi*) joint ownership of property

comu'nismo SM communism

comu'nista, -i, -e AG, SM/F communist

comunità SF INV community; **C~ Economica Europea** European Economic Community; ~ **terapeutica** *rehabilitation centre run by voluntary organizations for people with drug, alcohol etc dependency*

comuni'tario, -a AG community *cpd*

co'munque CONG however, no matter how ▶ AV (*in ogni modo*) in any case; (*tuttavia*) however, nevertheless

con PREP (*nei seguenti casi* **con** *può fondersi con l'articolo definito:* con + il = **col**, con + la = **colla**, con + gli = **cogli**, con + I = **coi**, con + le = **colle**) with; **partire col treno** to leave by train; ~ **mio grande stupore** to my great astonishment; ~ **la forza** by force; ~ **questo freddo** in this

cold weather; ~ **il 1° di ottobre** as of October 1st; ~ **tutto ciò** in spite of that, for all that; ~ **tutto che era arrabbiato** even though he was angry, in spite of the fact that he was angry; **e ~ questo?** so what?

co'nato SM: ~ **di vomito** retching

'conca, -che SF (*Geo*) valley

concate'nare /72/ VT to link up, connect; **concatenarsi** VPR to be connected

'concavo, -a AG concave

con'cedere [kon'tʃɛdere] /29/ VT (*accordare*) to grant; (*ammettere*) to admit, concede; **concedersi qc** to treat o.s. to sth, allow o.s. sth

concentra'mento [kontʃentra'mento] SM concentration

concen'trare [kontʃen'trare] /72/ VT, **concen'trarsi** VPR to concentrate

concen'trato [kontʃen'trato] SM concentrate; ~ **di pomodoro** tomato purée

concentrazi'one [kontʃentrat'tsjone] SF concentration; ~ **orizzontale/verticale** (*Econ*) horizontal/vertical integration

con'centrico, -a, -ci, -che [kon'tʃɛntriko] AG concentric

conce'pibile [kontʃe'pibile] AG conceivable

concepi'mento [kontʃepi'mento] SM conception

conce'pire [kontʃe'pire] /55/ VT (*bambino*) to conceive; (*progetto, idea*) to conceive (of); (*metodo, piano*) to devise; (*situazione*) to imagine, understand

con'cernere [kon'tʃɛrnere] /45/ VT to concern; **per quanto mi concerne** as far as I'm concerned

concer'tare [kontʃer'tare] /72/ VT (*Mus*) to harmonize; (*ordire*) to devise, plan; **concertarsi** VPR to agree

concer'tista, -i, -e [kontʃer'tista] SM/F (*Mus*) concert performer

con'certo [kon'tʃɛrto] SM (*Mus*) concert; (: *componimento*) concerto

con'cessi *etc* [kon'tʃɛssi] VB *vedi* **concedere**

concessio'nario [kontʃessjo'narjo] SM (*Comm*) agent, dealer; ~ **esclusivo (di)** sole agent (for)

concessi'one [kontʃes'sjone] SF concession

con'cesso, -a [kon'tʃɛsso] PP *di* **concedere**

con'cetto [kon'tʃɛtto] SM (*pensiero, idea*) concept; (*opinione*) opinion; **è un impiegato di** ~ ≈ he's a white-collar worker

concezi'one [kontʃet'tsjone] SF conception; (*idea*) view, idea

con'chiglia [kon'kiʎʎa] SF shell

'concia ['kontʃa] SF (*di pelli*) tanning; (*di tabacco*) curing; (*sostanza*) tannin

conci'are [kon'tʃare] /14/ VT (*pelli*) to tan; (*tabacco*) to cure; (*fig: ridurre in cattivo stato*) to beat up; **conciarsi** VPR (*sporcarsi*) to get in a mess; (*vestirsi male*) to dress badly; **ti hanno conciato male** *o* **per le feste!** they've really beaten you up!

concili'abile [kontʃi'ljabile] AG compatible

concili'abolo [kontʃi'ljabolo] SM secret meeting

concili'ante [kontʃi'ljante] AG conciliatory

concili'are [kontʃi'ljare] /**19**/ VT to reconcile; (*contravvenzione*) to pay on the spot; (*favorire*: *sonno*) to be conducive to, induce; (*procurare*: *simpatia*) to gain; **conciliarsi qc** to gain *o* win sth (for o.s.); **conciliarsi qn** to win sb over; **conciliarsi con** to be reconciled with

conciliazi'one [kontʃiljat'tsjone] SF reconciliation; (*Dir*) settlement; **la C~** (*Storia*) the Lateran Pact

con'cilio [kon'tʃiljo] SM (*Rel*) council

conci'mare [kontʃi'mare] /**72**/ VT to fertilize; (*con letame*) to manure

con'cime [kon'tʃime] SM manure; (*chimico*) fertilizer

concisi'one [kontʃi'zjone] SF concision, conciseness

con'ciso, -a [kon'tʃizo] AG concise, succinct

conci'tato, -a [kontʃi'tato] AG excited, emotional

concitta'dino, -a [kontʃitta'dino] SM/F fellow citizen

con'clave SM conclave

con'cludere /**3**/ VT to conclude; (*portare a compimento*) to conclude, finish, bring to an end; (*operare positivamente*) to achieve ▶ VI (*essere convincente*) to be conclusive; **concludersi** VPR to come to an end, close

conclusi'one SF conclusion; (*risultato*) result

conclu'sivo, -a AG conclusive; (*finale*) final

con'cluso, -a PP *di* **concludere**

concomi'tanza [konkomi'tantsa] SF (*di circostanze, fatti*) combination

concor'danza [konkor'dantsa] SF (*anche Ling*) agreement

concor'dare /**72**/ VT (*prezzo*) to agree on; (*Ling*) to make agree ▶ VI to agree; **~ una tregua** to agree to a truce

concor'dato SM agreement; (*Rel*) concordat

con'corde AG (*d'accordo*) in agreement; (*simultaneo*) simultaneous

con'cordia SF harmony, concord

concor'rente AG competing; (*Mat*) concurrent ▶ SMF (*Sport, Comm*) competitor; (*Ins*) candidate; (*a un concorso di bellezza*) contestant

concor'renza [konkor'rɛntsa] SF competition; **~ sleale** unfair competition; **a prezzi di ~** at competitive prices

concorrenzi'ale [konkorren'tsjale] AG competitive

con'correre /**28**/ VI: **~ (in)** (*Mat*) to converge *o*

meet (in); **~ (a)** (*competere*) to compete (for); (*Ins: a una cattedra*) to apply (for); (*partecipare*: *a un'impresa*) to take part (in), contribute (to)

con'corso, -a PP *di* **concorrere** ▶ SM competition; (*esame*) competitive examination; **~ di bellezza** beauty contest; **~ di circostanze** combination of circumstances; **~ di colpa** (*Dir*) contributory negligence; **un ~ ippico** a showjumping event; **~ in reato** (*Dir*) complicity in a crime; **~ per titoli** competitive examination for qualified candidates

con'creto, -a AG concrete ▶ SM: **in ~** in reality

concu'bina SF concubine ▶ SM: **sono concubini** they are living together

concussi'one SF (*Dir*) extortion

con'danna SF condemnation; sentence; conviction; **a morte** death sentence

condan'nare /**72**/ VT (*disapprovare*) to condemn; (*Dir*): **~ a** to sentence to; **~ per** to convict of

condan'nato, -a SM/F convict

con'densa SF condensation

conden'sare /**72**/ VT, **conden'sarsi** VPR to condense

condensa'tore SM capacitor

condensazi'one [kondensat'tsjone] SF condensation

condi'mento SM seasoning; dressing

con'dire /**55**/ VT to season; (*insalata*) to dress

condiscen'dente [kondiʃʃen'dɛnte] AG obliging; compliant

condiscen'denza [kondiʃʃen'dɛntsa] SF (*disponibilità*) obligingness; (*arrendevolezza*) compliance

condi'scendere [kondiʃʃendere] /**101**/ VI: **~ a** to agree to

condi'sceso, -a [kondiʃʃeso] PP *di* **condiscendere**

condi'videre /**43**/ VT to share

condi'viso, -a PP *di* **condividere**

condizio'nale [kondittsjo'nale] AG conditional ▶ SM (*Ling*) conditional ▶ SF (*Dir*) suspended sentence

condiziona'mento [kondittsjona'mento] SM conditioning; **~ d'aria** air conditioning

condizio'nare [kondittsjo'nare] /**72**/ VT to condition; **ad aria condizionata** air-conditioned

condiziona'tore [kondittsjona'tore] SM air conditioner

condizi'one [kondit'tsjone] SF condition; **condizioni** SFPL (*di pagamento ecc*) terms, conditions; **a ~ che** on condition that, provided that; **a nessuna ~** on no account; **condizioni a convenirsi** terms to be arranged; **condizioni di lavoro** working conditions; **condizioni di vendita** sales terms

condogli'anze [kondoʎ'ʎantse] SFPL condolences

condomini'ale AG: **riunione ~** residents' meeting; **spese condominialei** common charges

condo'minio SM joint ownership; *(edificio)* jointly-owned building

con'domino SM joint owner

condo'nare /**72**/ VT *(Dir)* to remit

con'dono SM remission; **~ fiscale** *conditional amnesty for people evading tax*

con'dotta SF *vedi* **condotto**

con'dotto, -a PP *di* **condurre** ▸ AG: **medico ~** local authority doctor *(in country district)* ▸ SM *(canale, tubo)* pipe, conduit; *(Anat)* duct ▸ SF *(modo di comportarsi)* conduct, behaviour *(BRIT)*, behavior *(US)*; *(di un affare ecc)* handling; *(di acqua)* piping; *(incarico sanitario)* country medical practice controlled by a local authority

condu'cente [kondu'tʃɛnte] SM driver

con'duco *etc* VB *vedi* **condurre**

con'durre /**90**/ VT to conduct; *(azienda)* to manage; *(accompagnare: bambino)* to take; *(: automobile)* to drive; *(trasportare: acqua, gas)* to convey, conduct; *(fig)* to lead ▸ VI to lead; **condursi** VPR to behave, conduct o.s.; **~ a termine** to conclude

con'dussi *etc* VB *vedi* **condurre**

condut'tore, -'trice AG: **filo ~** *(fig)* thread; **motivo ~** leitmotiv ▸ SM *(di mezzi pubblici)* driver; *(Fisica)* conductor

condut'tura SF *(gen)* pipe; *(di acqua, gas)* main

conduzi'one [kondut'tsjone] SF *(di affari, ditta)* management; *(Dir: locazione)* lease; *(Fisica)* conduction

confabu'lare /**72**/ VI to confab

confa'cente [konfa'tʃɛnte] AG: **~ a qn/qc** suitable for sb/sth; **clima ~ alla salute** healthy climate

CONFAGRICOL'TURA ABBR F *(= Confederazione generale dell'Agricoltura Italiana)* confederation of Italian farmers

CON'FAPI SIGLA F = **Confederazione Nazionale della Piccola Industria**

con'farsi /**53**/ VPR: **~ a** to suit, agree with

CONFARTIGIA'NATO [konfartidʒa'nato] ABBR F = **Confederazione Generale dell'Artigianato Italiano**

con'fatto, -a PP *di* **confarsi**

CONFCOM'MERCIO [konfkom'mɛrtʃo] ABBR F = **Confederazione Generale del Commercio**

confederazi'one [konfederat'tsjone] SF confederation; **~ imprenditoriale** employers' association

confe'renza [konfe'rɛntsa] SF *(discorso)* lecture; *(riunione)* conference; **~ stampa** press conference

conferenzi'ere, -a [konferen'tsjɛre] SM/F lecturer

conferi'mento SM conferring, awarding

confe'rire /**55**/ VT: **~ qc a qn** to give sth to sb, confer sth on sb ▸ VI to confer

con'ferma SF confirmation

confer'mare /**72**/ VT to confirm

confes'sare /**72**/ VT, **confes'sarsi** VPR to confess; **andare a confessarsi** *(Rel)* to go to confession

confessio'nale AG, SM confessional

confessi'one SF confession; *(setta religiosa)* denomination

con'fesso, -a AG: **essere reo ~** to have pleaded guilty

confes'sore SM confessor

con'fetto SM sugared almond; *(Med)* pill

confet'tura SF *(gen)* jam; *(di arance)* marmalade

confezio'nare [konfettsjo'nare] /**72**/ VT *(vestito)* to make (up); *(merci, pacchi)* to package

confezi'one [konfet'tsjone] SF *(di abiti: da uomo)* tailoring; *(: da donna)* dressmaking; *(imballaggio)* packaging; **~ regalo** gift pack; **~ risparmio** economy size; **~ da viaggio** travel pack; **confezioni per signora** ladies' wear *no pl*; **confezioni da uomo** menswear *no pl*

confic'care /**20**/ VT: **~ qc in** to hammer o drive sth into; **conficcarsi** VPR to stick

confi'dare /**72**/ VI: **~ in** to confide in, rely on ▸ VT to confide; **confidarsi con qn** to confide in sb

confi'dente SMF *(persona amica)* confidant *(confidante)*; *(informatore)* informer

confi'denza [konfi'dɛntsa] SF *(familiarità)* intimacy, familiarity; *(fiducia)* trust, confidence; *(rivelazione)* confidence; **prendersi (troppe) confidenze** to take liberties; **fare una ~ a qn** to confide something to sb

confidenzi'ale [konfiden'tsjale] AG familiar, friendly; *(segreto)* confidential; **in via ~** confidentially

configu'rare /**72**/ VT *(Inform)* to set; **configurarsi** VPR: **configurarsi a** to assume the shape o form of

configurazi'one [konfigurat'tsjone] SF configuration; *(Inform)* setting

confi'nante AG neighbouring *(BRIT)*, neighboring *(US)*

confi'nare /**72**/ VI: **~ con** to border on ▸ VT *(Pol)* to intern; *(fig)* to confine; **confinarsi** VPR *(isolarsi)*: **confinarsi in** to shut o.s. up in

confi'nato, -a AG interned ▸ SM/F internee

CONFIN'DUSTRIA SIGLA F (= *Confederazione Generale dell'Industria Italiana)* employers' association, ≈ CBI *(BRIT)*

con'fine SM boundary; *(di paese)* border, frontier; **territorio di ~** border zone

con'fino SM internment

con'fisca SF confiscation

confis'care /**20**/ VT to confiscate

conflagrazi'one [konflagrat'tsjone] SF conflagration

con'flitto SM conflict; **essere in ~ con qc** to clash with sth; **essere in ~ con qn** to be at loggerheads with sb; **~ d'interessi** conflict of interests

conflittu'ale AG: **rapporto ~** relationship based on conflict

conflittualità SF conflicts *pl*

conflu'enza [konflu'ɛntsa] SF *(di fiumi)* confluence; *(di strade)* junction

conflu'ire /**55**/ VI *(fiumi)* to flow into each other, meet; *(strade)* to meet

con'fondere /**25**/ VT to mix up, confuse; *(imbarazzare)* to embarrass; **confondersi** VPR *(mescolarsi)* to mingle; *(turbarsi)* to be confused; *(sbagliare)* to get mixed up; **~ le idee a qn** to mix sb up, confuse sb

confor'mare /**72**/ VT *(adeguare)*: **~ a** to adapt *o* conform to; **conformarsi** VPR: **conformarsi (a)** to conform (to)

con'forme AG: **~ a** *(simile)* similar to; *(corrispondente)* in keeping with

conforme'mente AV accordingly; **~ a** in accordance with

confor'mismo SM conformity

confor'mista, -i, -e SM/F conformist

conformità SF conformity; **in ~ a** in conformity with

confor'tare /**72**/ VT to comfort, console

confor'tevole AG *(consolante)* comforting; *(comodo)* comfortable

con'forto SM *(consolazione, sollievo)* comfort, consolation; *(conferma)* support; **a ~ di qc** in support of sth; **i conforti (religiosi)** the last sacraments

confra'ternita SF brotherhood

confron'tare /**72**/ VT to compare; **confrontarsi** VPR *(scontrarsi)* to have a confrontation

con'fronto SM comparison; *(Dir, Mil, Pol)* confrontation; **in** *o* **a ~ di** in comparison with, compared to; **nei miei** *(o* **tuoi** *etc)* **confronti** towards me *(o* you *etc)*

con'fusi *etc* VB *vedi* **confondere**

confusi'one SF confusion; *(imbarazzo)* embarrassment; **far ~** *(disordine)* to make a mess; *(chiasso)* to make a racket; *(confondere)* to confuse things

con'fuso, -a PP *di* **confondere** ▶ AG *(vedi* **confondere***)* confused; embarrassed

confu'tare /**72**/ VT to refute

conge'dare [kondʒe'dare] /**72**/ VT to dismiss; *(Mil)* to demobilize; **congedarsi** VPR to take one's leave

con'gedo [kon'dʒedo] SM *(anche Mil)* leave;

prendere ~ da qn to take one's leave of sb; **~ assoluto** *(Mil)* discharge

conge'gnare [kondʒeɲ'ɲare] /**15**/ VT to construct, put together

con'gegno [kon'dʒeɲɲo] SM device, mechanism

congela'mento [kondʒela'mento] SM *(gen)* freezing; *(Med)* frostbite; **~ salariale** wage freeze

conge'lare [kondʒe'lare] /**72**/ VT, **conge'larsi** VPR to freeze

congela'tore [kondʒela'tore] SM freezer

con'genito, -a [kon'dʒɛnito] AG congenital

con'gerie [kon'dʒɛrje] SF INV *(di oggetti)* heap; *(di idee)* muddle, jumble

congestio'nare [kondʒestjo'nare] /**72**/ VT to congest; **essere congestionato** *(persona, viso)* to be flushed; *(zona: per traffico)* to be congested

congesti'one [kondʒes'tjone] SF congestion

conget'tura [kondʒet'tura] SF conjecture, supposition

con'giungere [kon'dʒundʒere] /**5**/ VT, **con'giungersi** VPR to join (together)

congiunti'vite [kondʒunti'vite] SF conjunctivitis

congiun'tivo [kondʒun'tivo] SM *(Ling)* subjunctive

congi'unto, -a [kon'dʒunto] PP *di* **congiungere** ▶ AG *(unito)* joined ▶ SM/F *(parente)* relative

congiun'tura [kondʒun'tura] SF *(giuntura)* junction, join; *(Anat)* joint; *(circostanza)* juncture; *(Econ)* economic situation

congiuntu'rale [kondʒuntu'rale] AG of the economic situation; **crisi ~** economic crisis

congiunzi'one [kondʒun'tsjone] SF *(Ling)* conjunction

congi'ura [kon'dʒura] SF conspiracy

congiu'rare [kondʒu'rare] /**72**/ VI to conspire

conglome'rato SM *(Geo)* conglomerate; *(fig)* conglomeration; *(Edil)* concrete

'Congo SM: **il ~** the Congo

congo'lese AG, SMF Congolese *inv*

congratu'larsi /**72**/ VPR: **~ con qn per qc** to congratulate sb on sth

congratulazi'oni [kongratulat'tsjoni] SFPL congratulations

con'grega, -ghe SF band, bunch

congregazi'one [kongregat'tsjone] SF congregation

congres'sista, -i, -e SM/F participant at a congress

con'gresso SM congress

'congruo, -a AG *(prezzo, compenso)* adequate, fair; *(ragionamento)* coherent, consistent

conguagli'are [kongwaʎ'ʎare] /**27**/ VT to balance; *(stipendio)* to adjust

congu'aglio [kon'gwaʎʎo] SM balancing; adjusting; *(somma di denaro)* balance;

fare il ~ di to balance; to adjust

C.O.N.I. SIGLA M (= *Comitato Olimpico Nazionale Italiano*) Italian Olympic Games Committee

coni'are /**19**/ VT to mint, coin; (*fig*) to coin

coniazi'one [konjat'tsjone] SF mintage

'**conico, -a, -ci, -che** AG conical

co'nifere SFPL conifers

conigli'era [koniʎ'ʎɛra] SF (*gabbia*) rabbit hutch; (*più grande*) rabbit run

conigli'etta [koniʎ'ʎetta] SF bunny girl

conigli'etto [koniʎ'ʎetto] SM bunny

co'niglio [ko'niʎʎo] SM rabbit; **sei un ~!** (*fig*) you're chicken!

coniu'gale AG (*amore, diritti*) conjugal; (*vita*) married, conjugal

coniu'gare /**80**/ VT to combine; (*Ling*) to conjugate; **coniugarsi** VPR to get married

coniu'gato, -a AG (*Amm*) married

coniugazi'one [konjugat'tsjone] SF (*Ling*) conjugation

'**coniuge** ['kɔnjudʒe] SMF spouse

connatu'rato, -a AG inborn

connazio'nale [konnattsjo'nale] SMF fellow-countryman(-woman)

connessi'one SF connection

con'nesso, -a PP *di* **connettere**

con'nettere /**63**/ VT to connect, join ▸ VI (*fig*) to think straight

connet'tore SM (*Elettr*) connector

conni'vente AG conniving

conno'tati SMPL distinguishing marks; **rispondere ai ~** to fit the description; **cambiare i ~ a qn** (*col*) to beat sb up

con'nubio SM (*matrimonio*) marriage; (*fig*) union

'**cono** SM cone; **~ gelato** ice-cream cone

co'nobbi *etc* VB **vedi conoscere**

cono'scente [konoʃ'ʃente] SMF acquaintance

cono'scenza [konoʃ'ʃentsa] SF (*il sapere*) knowledge *no pl*; (*persona*) acquaintance; (*facoltà sensoriale*) consciousness *no pl*; **essere a ~ di qc** to know sth; **portare qn a ~ di qc** to inform sb of sth; **per vostra ~** for your information; **fare la ~ di qn** to make sb's acquaintance; **perdere ~** to lose consciousness; **~ tecnica** know-how

co'noscere [ko'noʃʃere] /**26**/ VT to know; **ci siamo conosciuti a Firenze** we (first) met in Florence; **conoscersi** VPR to know o.s.; (*reciproco*) to know each other; (*incontrarsi*) to meet; **~ qn di vista** to know sb by sight; **farsi ~** (*fig*) to make a name for o.s.

conosci'tore, -'trice [konoʃʃi'tore] SM/F connoisseur

conosci'uto, -a [konoʃ'ʃuto] PP *di* **conoscere** ▸ AG well-known

con'quista SF conquest

conqui'stare /**72**/ VT to conquer; (*fig*) to gain, win

conquista'tore, -'trice SM/F (*in guerra*) conqueror ▸ SM (*seduttore*) lady-killer

cons. ABBR = **consiglio**

consa'crare /**72**/ VT (*Rel*) to consecrate; (: *sacerdote*) to ordain; (*dedicare*) to dedicate; (*fig: uso ecc*) to sanction; **consacrarsi a** to dedicate o.s. to

consangu'ineo, -a SM/F blood relation

consa'pevole AG **~ di** aware of

consapevo'lezza [konsapevo'lettsa] SF awareness, consciousness

conscia'mente [konʃa'mente] AV consciously

'**conscio, -a, -sci, -sce** ['kɔnʃo] AG **~ di** aware o conscious of

consecu'tivo, -a AG consecutive; (*successivo: giorno*) following, next

con'segna [kon'seɲɲa] SF delivery; (*merce consegnata*) consignment; (*custodia*) care, custody; (*Mil: ordine*) orders *pl*; (: *punizione*) confinement to barracks; **alla ~** on delivery; **dare qc in ~ a qn** to entrust sth to sb; **passare le consegne a qn** to hand over to sb; **~ a domicilio** home delivery; **~ in contrassegno, pagamento alla ~** cash on delivery; **~ sollecita** prompt delivery

conse'gnare [konseɲ'ɲare] /**15**/ VT to deliver; (*affidare*) to entrust, hand over; (*Mil*) to confine to barracks

consegna'tario [konseɲɲa'tarjo] SM consignee

consegu'ente AG consequent

conseguente'mente AV consequently

consegu'enza [konse'gwɛntsa] SF consequence; **per o di ~** consequently

consegui'mento SM (*di scopo, risultato ecc*) achievement, attainment; **al ~ della laurea** on graduation

consegu'ire /**17**/ VT to achieve ▸ VI to follow, result; **~ la laurea** to graduate, obtain one's degree

con'senso SM approval, consent; **~ informato** informed consent

consensu'ale AG (*Dir*) by mutual consent

consen'tire /**45**/ VI: **~ a** to consent o agree to ▸ VT to allow, permit; **mi si consenta di ringraziare …** I would like to thank …

consenzi'ente [konsen'tsjɛnte] AG (*gen, Dir*) consenting

con'serto, -a AG: **a braccia conserte** with one's arms folded

con'serva SF (*Cuc*) preserve; **~ di frutta** jam; **~ di pomodoro** tomato purée; **conserve alimentari** tinned (o canned o bottled) foods

conser'vante SM (*per alimenti*) preservative

conser'vare /**72**/ VT (*Cuc*) to preserve; (*custodire*) to keep; (: *dalla distruzione ecc*) to preserve, conserve; **conservarsi** VPR to keep

conserva'tore, -'trice AG, SM/F (*Pol*) conservative

conserva'torio SM (*di musica*) conservatory
conservato'rismo SM (*Pol*) conservatism
conservazi'one [konservat'tsjone] SF
preservation; conservation; **istinto di ~**
instinct for self-preservation; **a lunga ~**
(*latte, panna*) long-life *cpd*
con'sesso SM (*assemblea*) assembly; (*riunione*)
meeting
conside'rabile AG worthy of consideration
conside'rare /72/ VT to consider; (*reputare*) to
consider, regard; **~ molto qn** to think highly
of sb; **considerarsi** VPR to consider o.s.
conside'rato, -a AG (*prudente*) cautious,
careful; (*stimato*) highly thought of,
esteemed
considerazi'one [konsiderat'tsjone] SF
(*esame, riflessione*) consideration; (*stima*)
regard, esteem; (*pensiero, osservazione*)
observation; **prendere in ~** to take into
consideration
conside'revole AG considerable
consigli'abile [konsiʎ'ʎabile] AG advisable
consigli'are [konsiʎ'ʎare] /27/ VT (*persona*) to
advise; (*metodo, azione*) to recommend,
advise, suggest; **consigliarsi** VPR:
consigliarsi con qn to ask sb for advice
consigli'ere, -a [konsiʎ'ʎɛre] SM/F adviser
▶ SM: **~ d'amministrazione** board member;
~ comunale town councillor; **~ delegato**
(*Comm*) managing director
con'siglio [kon'siʎʎo] SM (*suggerimento*) advice
no pl, piece of advice; (*assemblea*) council;
~ d'amministrazione board; **C~ d'Europa**
Council of Europe; **~ di fabbrica** works
council; **il C~ dei Ministri** (*Pol*) ≈ the
Cabinet; **C~ di stato** *advisory body to the Italian
government on administrative matters and their
legal implications*; **C~ superiore della
magistratura** *state body responsible for judicial
appointments and regulations*; *see note*

> The *Consiglio dei Ministri*, the Italian
> Cabinet, is headed by the *Presidente del
> Consiglio*, the Prime Minister, who is the
> leader of the Government. The *Consiglio
> superiore della Magistratura*, the magistrates'
> governing body, ensures their autonomy
> and independence as enshrined in the
> Constitution. Chaired by the *Presidente
> della Repubblica*, it mainly deals with
> appointments and transfers, and can
> take disciplinary action as required.
> Of the 30 magistrates elected to the
> *Consiglio* for a period of four years, 20 are
> chosen by their fellow magistrates and
> 10 by Parliament. The *Presidente della
> Repubblica* and the *Vicepresidente* are
> ex-officio members.

con'simile AG similar
consis'tente AG thick; solid; (*fig*) sound, valid

consis'tenza [konsis'tɛntsa] SF (*di impasto*)
consistency; (*di stoffa*) texture; **senza ~**
(*sospetti, voci*) ill-founded, groundless; **~ di
cassa/di magazzino** cash/stock in hand;
~ patrimoniale financial solidity
con'sistere /11/ VI: **~ in** to consist of
consis'tito, -a PP *di* **consistere**
'CONSOB SIGLA F (= *Commissione nazionale
per le società e la borsa*) *regulatory body for the
Italian Stock Exchange*
consoci'arsi [konso'tʃarsi] /14/ VPR to go into
partnership
consociati'vismo [konsotʃati'vizmo] SM
(*Pol*) pact-building
consocia'tivo, -a [konsotʃa'tivo] AG (*Pol*:
democrazia) based on pacts
consoci'ato, -a [konso'tʃato] AG associated
▶ SM/F associate
conso'lante AG consoling, comforting
conso'lare /72/ AG consular ▶ VT (*confortare*) to
console, comfort; (*rallegrare*) to cheer up;
consolarsi VPR to be comforted; to cheer up
conso'lato SM consulate
consolazi'one [konsolat'tsjone] SF
consolation, comfort
'console¹ SM con'sul
console² [kɔ̃'sɔl] SF (*quadro di comando*) console
consolida'mento SM strengthening;
consolidation
consoli'dare /72/ VT to strengthen, reinforce;
(*Mil, terreno*) to consolidate; **consolidarsi** VPR
to consolidate
consolidazi'one [konsolidat'tsjone] SF
strengthening; consolidation
consommé [kɔ̃sɔ'me] SM INV consommé
conso'nante SF consonant
conso'nanza [konso'nantsa] SF consonance
'consono, -a AG: **~ a** consistent with,
consonant with
con'sorte SMF consort
con'sorzio [kon'sɔrtsjo] SM consortium;
~ agrario farmers' cooperative; **~ di
garanzia** (*Comm*) underwriting syndicate
con'stare /72/ VI: **~ di** to consist of ▶ VB
IMPERS: **mi consta che** it has come to my
knowledge that, it appears that; **a quanto
mi consta** as far as I know
consta'tare /72/ VT to establish, verify;
(*notare*) to notice, observe
constatazi'one [konstatat'tsjone] SF
observation; **~ amichevole** (*in incidenti*)
jointly-agreed statement for insurance purposes
consu'eto, -a AG habitual, usual ▶ SM: **come
di ~** as usual
consuetudi'nario, -a AG: **diritto ~** (*Dir*)
common law
consue'tudine SF habit; (*usanza*) custom
consu'lente SMF consultant; **~ aziendale/
tecnico** management/technical consultant

consu'lenza [konsu'lɛntsa] SF consultancy; ~ **medica/legale** medical/legal advice; **ufficio di ~ fiscale** tax consultancy office; ~ **tecnica** technical consultancy o advice

consul'tare /72/ VT to consult; **consultarsi** VPR: **consultarsi con qn** to seek the advice of sb

consultazi'one [konsultat'tsjone] SF consultation; **consultazioni** SFPL (Pol) talks, consultations; **libro di ~** reference book

consul'tivo, -a AG consultative

consul'torio SM: ~ **familiare** family planning clinic; ~ **matrimoniale** marriage guidance centre; ~ **pediatrico** children's clinic

consu'mare /72/ VT (logorare: abiti, scarpe) to wear out; (usare) to consume, use up; (mangiare, bere) to consume; (Dir) to consummate; **consumarsi** VPR to wear out; to be used up; (anche fig) to be consumed; (combustibile) to burn out

consu'mato, -a AG (vestiti, scarpe, tappeto) worn; (persona: esperto) accomplished

consuma'tore SM consumer

consumazi'one [konsumat'tsjone] SF (bibita) drink; (spuntino) snack; (Dir) consummation

consu'mismo SM consumerism

con'sumo SM consumption; wear; use; **generi** o **beni di ~** consumer goods; **beni di largo ~** basic commodities; **imposta sui consumi** tax on consumer goods

consun'tivo SM (Econ) final balance

con'sunto, -a AG worn-out; (viso) wasted

'conta SF (nei giochi): **fare la ~** to see who is going to be "it"

con'tabile AG accounts cpd, accounting ▶ SMF accountant

contabilità SF (attività, tecnica) accounting, accountancy; (insieme dei libri ecc) books pl, accounts pl; (ufficio) ~ accounts department; ~ **finanziaria** financial accounting; ~ **di gestione** management accounting

contachi'lometri [kontaki'lɔmetri] SM INV ≈ mileometer

conta'dino, -a SM/F countryman(-woman); farm worker; (peg) peasant

contagi'are [konta'dʒare] /62/ VT to infect

con'tagio [kon'tadʒo] SM infection; (per contatto diretto) contagion; (epidemia) epidemic

contagi'oso, -a [konta'dʒoso] AG infectious; contagious

conta'giri [konta'dʒiri] SM INV (Aut) rev counter

conta'gocce [konta'gottʃe] SM INV (Med) dropper

contami'nare /72/ VT to contaminate

contaminazi'one [kontaminat'tsjone] SF contamination

con'tante SM cash; **pagare in contanti** to pay cash; **non ho contanti** I haven't got any cash

con'tare /72/ VT to count; (considerare) to consider ▶ VI to count, be of importance; ~ **su qn** to count o rely on sb; ~ **di fare qc** to intend to do sth; **ha i giorni contati, ha le ore contate** his days are numbered; **la gente che conta** people who matter

contas'catti SM INV telephone meter

conta'tore SM meter

contat'tare /72/ VT to contact

con'tatto SM contact; **essere in ~ con qn** to be in touch with sb; **fare ~** (Elettr: fili) to touch

'conte SM count

con'tea SF (Storia) earldom; (Amm) county

conteggi'are [konted'dʒare] /62/ VT to charge, put on the bill

con'teggio [kon'teddʒo] SM calculation

con'tegno [kon'teɲɲo] SM (comportamento) behaviour (BRIT), behavior (US); (atteggiamento) attitude; **darsi un ~** (ostentare disinvoltura) to act nonchalant; (ricomporsi) to pull o.s. together

conte'gnoso, -a [konteɲ'ɲoso] AG reserved, dignified

contem'plare /72/ VT to contemplate, gaze at; (Dir) to make provision for

contempla'tivo, -a AG contemplative

contemplazi'one [kontemplat'tsjone] SF contemplation

con'tempo SM: **nel ~** meanwhile, in the meantime

contemporanea'mente AV simultaneously; at the same time

contempo'raneo, -a AG, SM/F contemporary

conten'dente SMF opponent, adversary

con'tendere /120/ VI (competere) to compete; (litigare) to quarrel ▶ VT: ~ **qc a qn** to contend with o be in competition with sb for sth

conte'nere /121/ VT to contain; **contenersi** VPR to contain o.s.

conteni'tore SM container

conten'tabile AG: **difficilmente ~** difficult to please

conten'tare /72/ VT to please, satisfy; **contentarsi** VPR: **contentarsi di** to be satisfied with, content o.s. with; **si contenta di poco** he is easily satisfied

conten'tezza [konten'tettsa] SF contentment

conten'tino SM sop

con'tento, -a AG pleased, glad; ~ **di** pleased with

conte'nuto AG (ira, entusiasmo) restrained, suppressed; (forza) contained ▶ SM contents pl; (argomento) content

contenzi'oso, -a [konten'tsjɔso] AG (*Dir*) contentious ▶ SM (*Amm: ufficio*) legal department

con'teso, -a PP *di* **contendere** ▶ SF dispute, argument

con'tessa SF countess

contes'tare /72/ VT (*Dir*) to notify; (*fig*) to dispute; **~ il sistema** to protest against the system

contesta'tore, -'trice AG anti-establishment ▶ SM/F protester

contestazi'one [kontestat'tsjone] SF (*Dir: disputa*) dispute; (: *notifica*) notification; (*Pol*) anti-establishment activity; **in caso di ~** if there are any objections

con'testo SM context

con'tiguo, -a AG: **~ (a)** adjacent (to)

continen'tale AG, SMF continental

conti'nente AG continent ▶ SM (*Geo*) continent; (: *terra ferma*) mainland

conti'nenza [konti'nɛntsa] SF continence

contin'gente [kontin'dʒɛnte] AG contingent ▶ SM (*Comm*) quota; (*Mil*) contingent

contin'genza [kontin'dʒɛntsa] SF circumstance; **(indennità di) ~** cost-of-living allowance

continua'mente AV (*senza interruzione*) continuously, nonstop; (*ripetutamente*) continually

continu'are /72/ VT to continue (with), go on with ▶ VI to continue, go on; **~ a fare qc** to go on *o* continue doing sth; **continua a nevicare/a fare freddo** it's still snowing/cold

continua'tivo, -a AG (*occupazione*) permanent; (*periodo*) consecutive

continuazi'one [kontinuat'tsjone] SF continuation

continuità SF continuity

con'tinuo, -a AG (*numerazione*) continuous; (*pioggia*) continual, constant; (*Elettr: corrente*) direct; **di ~** continually

'conto SM (*calcolo*) calculation; (*Comm, Econ*) account; (*di ristorante, albergo*) bill; (*fig: stima*) consideration, esteem; **avere un ~ in sospeso (con qn)** to have an outstanding account (with sb); (*fig*) to have a score to settle (with sb); **fare i conti con qn** to settle one's account with sb; **fare ~ su qn** to count *o* rely on sb; **fare ~ che** (*supporre*) to suppose that; **rendere ~ a qn di qc** to be accountable to sb for sth; **rendersi ~ di qc/che** to realize sth/that; **tener ~ di qn/qc** to take sb/sth into account; **tenere qc da ~** to take great care of sth; **ad ogni buon ~** in any case; **di poco/nessun ~** of little/no importance; **per ~ di** on behalf of; **per ~ mio** as far as I'm concerned; (*da solo*) on my own; **a conti fatti**, **in fin dei conti** all things considered;

mi hanno detto strane cose sul suo ~ I've heard some strange things about him; **~ capitale** capital account; **~ cifrato** numbered account; **~ corrente** current account (*BRIT*), checking account (*US*); **~ corrente postale** Post Office account; **~ economico** profit and loss account; **~ in partecipazione** joint account; **~ passivo** account payable; **~ profitti e perdite** profit and loss account; **~ alla rovescia** countdown; **~ valutario** foreign currency account

con'torcere [kon'tɔrtʃere] /106/ VT to twist; (*panni*) to wring (out); **contorcersi** VPR to twist, writhe

contor'nare /72/ VT to surround; **contornarsi** VPR: **contornarsi di** to surround o.s. with

con'torno SM (*linea*) outline, contour; (*ornamento*) border; (*Cuc*) vegetables *pl*; **fare da ~ a** to surround

contorsi'one SF contortion

con'torto, -a PP *di* **contorcere**

contrabban'dare /72/ VT to smuggle

contrabbandi'ere, -a SM/F smuggler

contrab'bando SM smuggling, contraband; **merce di ~** contraband, smuggled goods *pl*

contrab'basso SM (*Mus*) (double) bass

contraccambi'are /19/ VT (*favore ecc*) to return; **vorrei ~** I'd like to show my appreciation

contraccet'tivo, -a [kontrattʃet'tivo] AG, SM contraceptive

contrac'colpo SM rebound; (*di arma da fuoco*) recoil; (*fig*) repercussion

con'trada SF street; district; *vedi anche* **palio**

contrad'detto, -a PP *di* **contraddire**

contrad'dire /38/ VT to contradict; **contraddirsi** VPR to contradict o.s.; (*uso reciproco: persone*) to contradict each other *o* one another; (: *testimonianze ecc*) to be contradictory

contraddis'tinguere /42/ VT (*merce*) to mark; (*fig: atteggiamento, persona*) to distinguish

contraddis'tinto, -a PP *di* **contraddistinguere**

contraddit'torio, -a AG contradictory; (*sentimenti*) conflicting ▶ SM (*Dir*) cross-examination

contraddizi'one [kontraddit'tsjone] SF contradiction; **cadere in ~** to contradict o.s.; **essere in ~** (*tesi, affermazioni*) to contradict one another; **spirito di ~** argumentativeness

con'trae *etc* VB *vedi* **contrarre**

contra'ente SM contractor

contra'erea SF (*Mil*) anti-aircraft artillery

contra'ereo, -a AG anti-aircraft

contraf'fare /41/ VT (*persona*) to mimic; (*alterare: voce*) to disguise; (: *firma*) to forge, counterfeit

contraffatto, -a PP di **contraffare** ▶ AG counterfeit

contraffazi'one [kontraffat'tsjone] SF mimicking no pl; disguising no pl; forging no pl; (cosa contraffatta) forgery

contrafforte SM (Archit) buttress; (Geo) spur

con'traggo etc VB vedi **contrarre**

con'tralto SM (Mus) contralto

contrap'pello SM (Mil) second roll call

contrappe'sare /72/ VT to counterbalance; (fig: decisione) to weigh up

contrap'peso SM counterbalance, counterweight

contrap'porre /77/ VT: ~ qc a qc to counter sth with sth; (paragonare) to compare sth with sth; **contrapporsi** VPR: **contrapporsi a qc** to contrast with sth, be opposed to sth

contrap'posto, -a PP di **contrapporre**

contraria'mente AV: ~ **a** contrary to

contrari'are /19/ VT (contrastare) to thwart, oppose; (irritare) to annoy, bother; **contrariarsi** VPR to get annoyed

contrari'ato, -a AG annoyed

contrarietà SF adversity; (fig) aversion

con'trario, -a AG opposite; (sfavorevole) unfavourable (BRIT), unfavorable (US) ▶ SM opposite; **essere ~ a qc** (persona) to be against sth; **al ~** on the contrary; **in caso ~** otherwise; **avere qualcosa in ~** to have some objection; **non ho niente in ~** I have no objection

con'trarre /123/ VT (malattia, debito) to contract; (muscoli) to tense; (abitudine, vizio) to pick up; (accordo, patto) to enter into; **contrarsi** VPR to contract; ~ **matrimonio** to marry

contrasse'gnare [kontrasseɲ'ɲare] /15/ VT to mark

contras'segno [kontras'seɲɲo] SM (distintivo) distinguishing mark; **spedire in ~** (Comm) to send COD

con'trassi etc VB vedi **contrarre**

contras'tante AG contrasting

contras'tare /72/ VT (avversare) to oppose; (impedire) to bar; (negare: diritto) to contest, dispute ▶ VI: ~ **(con)** (essere in disaccordo) to contrast (with); (lottare) to struggle (with)

con'trasto SM contrast; (conflitto) conflict; (litigio) dispute

contrat'tacco SM counterattack; **passare al ~** (fig) to fight back

contrat'tare /72/ VT, VI to negotiate

contrat'tempo SM hitch

con'tratto, -a PP di **contrarre** ▶ SM contract; ~ **di acquisto** purchase agreement; ~ **di affitto**, ~ **di locazione** lease; ~ **collettivo di lavoro** collective agreement; ~ **di lavoro** contract of employment; ~ **a termine** forward contract

contrattu'ale AG contractual; **forza ~** (di sindacato) bargaining power

contravve'nire /128/ VI: ~ **a** (legge) to contravene; (obbligo) to fail to meet

contravven'tore, -'trice SM/F offender

contravve'nuto, -a PP di **contravvenire**

contravvenzi'one [kontravven'tsjone] SF contravention; (ammenda) fine

contrazi'one [kontrat'tsjone] SF contraction; (di prezzi ecc) reduction

contribu'ente SMF taxpayer; ratepayer (BRIT), property tax payer (US)

contribu'ire /55/ VI to contribute

contribu'tivo, -a AG contributory

contri'buto SM contribution; (sovvenzione) subsidy, contribution; (tassa) tax; **contributi previdenziali** = national insurance (BRIT) o welfare (US) contributions; **contributi sindacali** trade union dues

con'trito, -a AG contrite, penitent

'contro PREP against; ~ **di me/lui** against me/him; **pastiglie ~ la tosse** throat lozenges; ~ **pagamento** (Comm) on payment; ~ **ogni mia aspettativa** contrary to my expectations; **per ~** on the other hand

contro'battere /1/ VT (fig: a parole) to answer back; (: confutare) to refute

controbilanci'are [kontrobilan'tʃare] /14/ VT to counterbalance

controcor'rente AV: **andare ~** (anche fig) to swim against the tide

controcul'tura SF counterculture

contro'esodo SM return from holiday

contro'fax SM INV reply to a fax

controffen'siva SF counteroffensive

controfi'gura SF (Cine) double

controfir'mare /72/ VT to countersign

control'lare /72/ VT (accertare) to check; (sorvegliare) to watch, control; (tenere nel proprio potere, fig: dominare) to control; **controllarsi** VPR to control o.s.

control'lato, -a AG (persona) self-possessed; (reazioni) controlled ▶ SF (Comm: società) associated company

con'trollo SM check; watch; control; **base di ~** (Aer) ground control; **telefono sotto ~** tapped telephone; **visita di ~** (Med) checkup; ~ **doganale** customs inspection; ~ **di gestione** management control; ~ **delle nascite** birth control; ~ **di qualità** quality control

control'lore SM (Ferr, Aut) (ticket) inspector; ~ **di volo** o **del traffico aereo** air traffic controller

contro'luce [kontro'lutʃe] SF INV (Fot) backlit shot ▶ AV: **(in) ~** against the light; (fotografare) into the light

contro'mano AV: **guidare ~** to drive on the wrong side of the road; (*in un senso unico*) to drive the wrong way up a one-way street

contropar'tita SF (*fig: compenso*): **come ~** in return

contropi'ede SM (*Sport*): **azione di ~** sudden counter-attack; **prendere qn in ~** (*fig*) to catch sb off his (*o* her) guard

controprodu'cente [kontroprodu'tʃɛnte] AG counterproductive

con'trordine SM counter-order; **salvo ~** unless I (*o* you *etc*) hear to the contrary

contro'senso SM (*contraddizione*) contradiction in terms; (*assurdità*) nonsense

controspio'naggio [kontrospio'naddʒo] SM counterespionage

controva'lore SM equivalent (value)

contro'vento AV against the wind; **navigare ~** (*Naut*) to sail to windward

contro'versia SF controversy; (*Dir*) dispute; **~ sindacale** industrial dispute

contro'verso, -a AG controversial

contro'voglia [kontro'vɔʎʎa] AV unwillingly

contu'mace [kontu'matʃe] AG (*Dir*): **rendersi ~** to default, fail to appear in court ▶ SMF (*Dir*) defaulter

contu'macia [kontu'matʃa] SF (*Dir*) default

contun'dente AG: **corpo ~** blunt instrument

contur'bante AG (*sguardo, bellezza*) disturbing

contur'bare /**72**/ VT to disturb, upset

contusi'one SF (*Med*) bruise

convale'scente [konvaleʃʃɛnte] AG, SMF convalescent

convale'scenza [konvaleʃʃɛntsa] SF convalescence

con'valida SF (*Dir*) confirmation; (*di biglietto*) stamping

convali'dare /**72**/ VT (*Amm*) to validate; (*fig: sospetto, dubbio*) to confirm

con'vegno [kon'veɲɲo] SM (*incontro*) meeting; (*congresso*) convention, congress; (*luogo*) meeting place

conve'nevoli SMPL civilities

conveni'ente AG suitable; (*vantaggioso*) profitable; (*: prezzo*) cheap

conveni'enza [konve'njɛntsa] SF suitability; advantage; cheapness; **convenienze** SFPL social conventions

conve'nire /**128**/ VT to agree upon ▶ VI (*riunirsi*) to gather, assemble; (*concordare*) to agree; (*tornare utile*) to be worthwhile ▶ VB IMPERS: **conviene fare questo** it is advisable to do this; **conviene andarsene** we should go; **ne convengo** I agree; **come convenuto** as agreed; **in data da ~** on a date to be agreed; **come (si) conviene ad una signorina** as befits a young lady

conven'ticola SF (*cricca*) clique; (*riunione*) secret meeting

con'vento SM (*di frati*) monastery; (*di suore*) convent

conve'nuto, -a PP *di* **convenire** ▶ SM (*cosa pattuita*) agreement ▶ SM/F (*Dir*) defendant; **i convenuti** (*i presenti*) those present

convenzio'nale [konventsjo'nale] AG conventional

convenzio'nato, -a [konventsjo'nato] AG (*ospedale, clinica*) providing free health care, ≈ National Health Service *cpd* (BRIT)

convenzi'one [konven'tsjone] SF (*Dir*) agreement; (*nella società*) convention; **le convenzioni (sociali)** social conventions

conver'gente [konver'dʒɛnte] AG convergent

conver'genza [konver'dʒɛntsa] SF convergence

con'vergere [kon'vɛrdʒere] /**59**/ VI to converge

con'versa SF (*Rel*) lay sister

conver'sare /**72**/ VI to have a conversation, converse

conversazi'one [konversat'tsjone] SF conversation; **fare ~** (*chiacchierare*) to chat, have a chat

conversi'one SF conversion; **~ ad U** (*Aut*) U-turn

con'verso, -a PP *di* **convergere**; **per ~** conversely

conver'tire /**45**/ VT (*trasformare*) to change; (*Inform, Pol, Rel*) to convert; **convertirsi** VPR: **convertirsi (a)** to be converted (to)

conver'tito, -a SM/F convert

converti'tore SM (*Elettr*) converter

con'vesso, -a AG convex

convin'cente [konvin'tʃɛnte] AG convincing

con'vincere [kon'vintʃere] /**129**/ VT to convince; **convincersi** VPR: **convincersi (di qc)** to convince o.s. (of sth); **~ qn di qc** to convince sb of sth; (*Dir*) to prove sb guilty of sth; **~ qn a fare qc** to persuade sb to do sth

con'vinto, -a PP *di* **convincere** ▶ AG: **reo ~** (*Dir*) convicted criminal

convinzi'one [konvin'tsjone] SF conviction, firm belief

convis'suto, -a PP *di* **convivere**

convi'tato, -a SM/F guest

con'vitto SM (*Ins*) boarding school

convi'vente SMF common-law husband/ wife

convi'venza [konvi'vɛntsa] SF living together; (*Dir*) cohabitation

con'vivere /**130**/ VI to live together

convivi'ale AG convivial

convo'care /**20**/ VT to call, convene; (*Dir*) to summon

convocazi'one [konvokat'tsjone] SF meeting; summons *sg*; **lettera di ~** (letter of) notification to appear *o* attend

convogli'are [konvoʎ'ʎare] /**27**/ vt to convey; (*dirigere*) to direct, send

con'voglio [kon'vɔʎʎo] sm (*di veicoli*) convoy; (*Ferr*) train; ~ **funebre** funeral procession

convo'lare /**72**/ vi: ~ **a (giuste) nozze** (*scherzoso*) to tie the knot

convulsi'one sf convulsion

con'vulso, -a ag (*pianto*) violent, convulsive; (*attività*) feverish

COOP abbr f = **cooperativa**

coope'rare /**72**/ vi: ~ **(a)** to cooperate (in)

coopera'tiva sf cooperative

cooperazi'one [kooperat'tsjone] sf cooperation

coordina'mento sm coordination

coordi'nare /**72**/ vt to coordinate

coordi'nato, -a ag (*movimenti*) coordinated ▶ sf (*Ling, Geo, Mat*) coordinate ▶ smpl: **coordinati** (*Moda*) coordinates

coordinazi'one [koordinat'tsjone] sf coordination

co'perchio [ko'pɛrkjo] sm cover; (*di pentola*) lid

co'perta sf cover; (*di lana*) blanket; (*da viaggio*) rug; (*Naut*) deck

coper'tina sf (*Stampa*) cover, jacket

co'perto, -a pp di **coprire** ▶ ag covered; (*cielo*) overcast ▶ sm place setting; (*posto a tavola*) place; (*al ristorante*) cover charge; ~ **di** covered in o with

coper'tone sm (*telo impermeabile*) tarpaulin; (*Aut*) rubber tyre

coper'tura sf (*anche Econ, Mil*) cover; (*di edificio*) roofing; **fare un gioco di ~** (*Sport*) to play a defensive game; ~ **assicurativa** insurance cover

'copia sf copy; (*Fot*) print; **brutta/bella ~** rough/final copy; ~ **conforme** (*Dir*) certified copy; ~ **omaggio** presentation copy

copi'are /**19**/ vt to copy

copia'trice [kopja'tritʃe] sf copier, copying machine

copincol'lare /**72**/ vt to copy and paste

copin'collo sm copy and paste

copi'one sm (*Cine, Teat*) script

'coppa sf (*bicchiere*) goblet; (*per frutta, gelato*) dish; (*trofeo*) cup, trophy; **coppe** sfpl (*Carte*) suit in Neapolitan pack of cards; ~ **dell'olio** oil sump (*Brit*) o pan (*US*)

'coppia sf (*di persone*) couple; (*di animali, Sport*) pair

cop'rente ag (*colore, cosmetico*) covering; (*calze*) opaque

copri'capo sm headgear; (*cappello*) hat

coprifu'oco, -chi sm curfew

copri'letto sm bedspread

copripiu'mino sm inv duvet cover

co'prire /**9**/ vt to cover; (*occupare: carica, posto*) to hold; **coprirsi** vpr (*cielo*) to cloud over; (*vestirsi*) to wrap up, cover up; (*Econ*) to cover o.s.; **coprirsi di** (*macchie, muffa*) to become covered in; ~ **qn di baci** to smother sb with kisses; ~ **le spese** to break even; **coprirsi le spalle** (*fig*) to cover o.s.

coque [kɔk] sf: **uovo alla ~** boiled egg

co'raggio [ko'raddʒo] sm courage, bravery; ~! (*forza!*) come on!; (*animo!*) cheer up!; **farsi ~** to pluck up courage; **hai un bel ~!** (*sfacciataggine*) you've got a nerve o a cheek!

coraggi'oso, -a [korad'dʒoso] ag courageous, brave

co'rale ag choral; (*approvazione*) unanimous

co'rallo sm coral; **il mar dei Coralli** the Coral Sea

Co'rano sm (*Rel*) Koran

co'razza [ko'rattsa] sf armour (*Brit*), armor (*US*); (*di animali*) carapace, shell; (*Mil*) armour(-plating)

coraz'zato, -a [korat'tsato] ag (*Mil*) armoured (*Brit*), armored (*US*) ▶ sf battleship

corazzi'ere [korat'tsjɛre] sm (*Storia*) cuirassier; (*guardia presidenziale*) carabiniere of the President's guard

corbelle'ria sf stupid remark; **corbellerie** sfpl (*sciocchezze*) nonsense *no pl*

'corda sf cord; (*fune*) rope; (*spago, Mus*) string; **dare ~ a qn** (*fig*) to let sb have his (o her) way; **tenere sulla ~ qn** (*fig*) to keep sb on tenterhooks; **tagliare la ~** (*fig*) to slip away, sneak off; **essere giù di ~** to feel down; **corde vocali** vocal cords

cor'data sf (*Alpinismo*) roped party; (*fig*) alliance system in financial and business world

cordi'ale ag cordial, warm ▶ sm (*bevanda*) cordial

cordialità sf inv warmth, cordiality ▶ sfpl (*saluti*) best wishes

'cordless ['kɔːdlɪs] sm inv cordless phone

cor'doglio [kor'dɔʎʎo] sm grief; (*lutto*) mourning

cor'done sm cord, string; (*linea: di polizia*) cordon; ~ **ombelicale** umbilical cord; ~ **sanitario** quarantine line

Co'rea sf: **la ~** Korea; **la ~ del Nord/Sud** North/South Korea

core'ano, -a ag, sm/f Korean

coreogra'fia sf choreography

core'ografo, -a sm/f choreographer

cori'aceo, -a [ko'rjatʃeo] ag (*Bot, Zool*) coriaceous; (*fig*) tough

cori'andolo sm (*Bot*) coriander; **coriandoli** smpl (*per carnevale ecc*) confetti *no pl*

cori'care /**20**/ vt to put to bed; **coricarsi** vpr to go to bed

coricherò *etc* [korike'rɔ] vb *vedi* **coricare**

Co'rinto sf Corinth

co'rista, -i, -e sm/f (*Rel*) choir member, chorister; (*Teat*) member of the chorus '**corna** SFPL *vedi* **corno**

cor'nacchia [kor'nakkja] SF crow

corna'musa SF bagpipes *pl*

'**cornea** SF (*Anat*) cornea

'**corner** SM INV (*Calcio*) corner (kick);
salvarsi in ~ (*fig: in gara, esame ecc*) to get
through by the skin of one's teeth

cor'netta SF (*Mus*) cornet; (*Tel*) receiver

cor'netto SM (*Cuc*) croissant; (*gelato*) cone;
~ acustico ear trumpet

cor'nice [kor'nitʃe] SF frame; (*fig*)
background, setting

cornici'one [korni'tʃone] SM (*di edificio*) ledge;
(*Archit*) cornice

'**corno** SM (*pl(f)* **corna**: *Zool*) horn; (*pl(m)*
corni: *Mus*) horn; (*col*) **fare le corna a qn**
to be unfaithful to sb; **dire peste e corna
di qn** to call sb every name under the sun;
un ~! not on your life!

Corno'vaglia [korno'vaʎʎa] SF: **la ~**
Cornwall

cor'nuto, -a AG (*con corna*) horned; (*col: marito*)
cuckolded ▶ SM (*col*) cuckold; (: *insulto*)
bastard (!)

'**coro** SM chorus; (*Rel*) choir

corol'lario SM corollary

co'rona SF crown; (*di fiori*) wreath

corona'mento SM (*di impresa*) completion; (*di
carriera*) crowning achievement; **il ~ dei
propri sogni** the fulfilment of one's dreams

coro'nare /72/ VT to crown

coro'naria SF coronary artery

'**corpo** SM body; (*cadavere*) (dead) body;
(*militare, diplomatico*) corps INV; (*di opere*) corpus;
prendere ~ to take shape; **darsi anima e ~ a**
to give o.s. heart and soul to; **a ~ a ~**
hand-to-hand; **~ d'armata** army corps; **~ di
ballo** corps de ballet; **~ dei carabinieri**
≈ police force; **~ celeste** heavenly body; **~ di
guardia** (*soldati*) guard; (*locale*) guardroom;
~ insegnante teaching staff; **~ del reato**
material evidence

corpo'rale AG bodily; (*punizione*) corporal

corpora'tura SF build, physique

corporazi'one [korporat'tsjone] SF
corporation

cor'poreo, -a AG bodily, physical

cor'poso, -a AG (*vino*) full-bodied

corpu'lento, -a AG stout, corpulent

corpu'lenza [korpu'lɛntsa] SF stoutness,
corpulence

cor'puscolo SM corpuscle

corre'dare /72/ VT: **~ di** to provide *o* furnish
with; **domanda corredata dai seguenti
documenti** application accompanied by the
following documents

cor'redo SM equipment; (*di sposa*) trousseau

cor'reggere [kor'rɛddʒere] /87/ VT to correct;
(*compiti*) to correct, mark

cor'rente AG (*fiume*) flowing; (*acqua del
rubinetto*) running; (*moneta, prezzo*) current;
(*comune*) everyday ▶ SM: **essere al ~ (di)** to be
well-informed (about) ▶ SF (*movimento di
liquido*) current, stream; (*spiffero*) draught;
(*Elettr, Meteor*) current; (*fig*) trend, tendency;
mettere al ~ (di) to inform (of); **la vostra
lettera del 5 ~ mese** (*in lettere commerciali*)
in your letter of the 5th inst.; **articoli di
qualità ~** average-quality products;
~ alternata alternating current; **~ continua**
direct current

corrente'mente AV (*comunemente*)
commonly; **parlare una lingua ~** to speak a
language fluently

corren'tista, -i, -e SM/F (current (BRIT) *o*
checking (US)) account holder

cor'reo, -a SM/F (*Dir*) accomplice

'**correre** /28/ VI to run; (*precipitarsi*) to rush;
(*partecipare a una gara*) to race, run; (*fig:
diffondersi*) to go round ▶ VT (*Sport: gara*) to
compete in; (: *rischio*) to run; (: *pericolo*) to face;
~ dietro a qn to run after sb; **corre voce che
…** it is rumoured that …

corresponsabilità SF joint responsibility;
(*Dir*) joint liability

corresponsi'one SF payment

cor'ressi *etc* VB *vedi* **correggere**

corret'tezza [korret'tettsa] SF (*di
comportamento*) correctness; (*Sport*) fair play

cor'retto, -a PP *di* **correggere** ▶ AG
(*comportamento*) correct, proper; **caffè ~ al
cognac** coffee laced with brandy

corret'tore, -'trice SM/F: **~ di bozze**
proofreader ▶ SM: **(liquido) ~** correction
fluid

correzi'one [korret'tsjone] SF correction;
marking; **~ di bozze** proofreading

cor'rida SF bullfight

corri'doio SM corridor; (*in aereo, al cinema*)
aisle; **manovre di ~** (*Pol*) lobbying *sg*

corri'dore SM (*Sport*) runner; (: *su veicolo*) racer

corri'era SF coach (BRIT), bus

corri'ere SM (*diplomatico, di guerra, postale*)
courier; (*spedizioniere*) carrier

corri'mano SM handrail

corrispet'tivo SM amount due; **versare a qn
il ~ di una prestazione** to pay sb the
amount due for his (*o* her) services

corrispon'dente AG corresponding ▶ SMF
correspondent

corrispon'denza [korrispon'dɛntsa] SF
correspondence; **~ in arrivo/partenza**
incoming/outgoing mail

corris'pondere /95/ VI (*equivalere*): **~ (a)** to
correspond (to); (*per lettera*): **~ con** to
correspond with ▶ VT (*stipendio*) to pay; (*fig:
amore*) to return

corris'posto, -a PP *di* **corrispondere**

corrobo'rare /**72**/ VT to strengthen, fortify; (fig) to corroborate, bear out

cor'rodere /**49**/ VT, **cor'rodersi** VPR to corrode

cor'rompere /**97**/ VT to corrupt; (comprare) to bribe

corrosi'one SF corrosion

corro'sivo, -a AG corrosive

cor'roso, -a PP di **corrodere**

corrotta'mente AV corruptly

cor'rotto, -a PP di **corrompere** ▶ AG corrupt

corrucci'arsi [korrut'tʃarsi] /**14**/ VPR to grow angry o vexed

corru'gare /**80**/ VT to wrinkle; ~ **la fronte** to knit one's brows

cor'ruppi etc VB vedi **corrompere**

corrut'tela SF corruption, depravity

corruzi'one [korrut'tsjone] SF corruption; bribery; ~ **di minorenne** (Dir) corruption of a minor

'**corsa** SF running no pl; (gara) race; (di autobus, taxi) journey, trip; **fare una** ~ to run, dash; (Sport) to run a race; **andare** o **essere di** ~ to be in a hurry; ~ **automobilistica/ciclistica** motor/cycle race; ~ **campestre** cross-country race; ~ **ad ostacoli** (Ippica) steeplechase; (Atletica) hurdles race

cor'saro, -a AG: **nave corsara** privateer ▶ SM privateer

'**corsi** etc VB vedi **correre**

cor'sia SF (Aut, Sport) lane; (di ospedale) ward; ~ **di emergenza** (Aut) hard shoulder; ~ **preferenziale** ≈ bus lane; (fig) fast track; ~ **di sorpasso** (Aut) overtaking lane

'**Corsica** SF: **la** ~ Corsica

cor'sivo SM cursive (writing); (Tip) italics pl

'**corso, -a** PP di **correre** ▶ AG, SM/F Corsican ▶ SM course; (strada cittadina) main street; (di unità monetaria) circulation; (di titoli, valori) rate, price; **dar libero** ~ **a** to give free expression to; **in** ~ in progress, under way; (annata) current; ~ **d'acqua** river; stream; (artificiale) waterway; ~ **d'aggiornamento** refresher course; ~ **serale** evening class; **aver** ~ **legale** to be legal tender

'**corte** SF (court)yard; (Dir, regale) court; **fare la** ~ **a qn** to court sb; ~ **d'appello** court of appeal; ~ **di cassazione** final court of appeal; **C~ dei Conti** State audit court; **C~ Costituzionale** special court dealing with constitutional and ministerial matters; ~ **marziale** court-martial; see note

The Corte d'Appello hears appeals against sentences passed by courts in both civil and criminal cases and can modify sentences where necessary. The Corte d'Assise tries serious crimes such as manslaughter and murder; its judges include both legal professionals and members of the public. Similar in structure, the Corte d'Assise d'Appello hears appeals imposed by these two courts. The Corte di Cassazione is the highest judicial authority and ensures that the law is correctly applied by the other courts; it may call for a re-trial if required. The politically independent Corte Costituzionale decides whether laws comply with the principles of the Constitution, and has the power to impeach the "Presidente della Repubblica". The Corte dei Conti ensures the Government's compliance with the law and the Constitution. Reporting directly to Parliament, it oversees the financial aspects of the state budget.

cor'teccia, -ce [kor'tettʃa] SF bark

corteggia'mento [korteddʒa'mento] SM courtship

corteggi'are [korted'dʒare] /**62**/ VT to court

corteggia'tore [korteddʒa'tore] SM suitor

cor'teo SM procession; ~ **funebre** funeral cortège

cor'tese AG courteous

corte'sia SF courtesy; **fare una** ~ **a qn** to do sb a favour; **per** ~, **dov'è …?** excuse me, please, where is …?

cortigi'ano, -a [korti'dʒano] SM/F courtier ▶ SF courtesan

cor'tile SM (court)yard

cor'tina SF curtain; (anche fig) screen

corti'sone SM cortisone

'**corto, -a** AG short ▶ AV: **tagliare** ~ to come straight to the point; **essere a** ~ **di qc** to be short of sth; **essere a** ~ **di parole** to be at a loss for words; **la settimana corta** the 5-day week; ~ **circuito** short-circuit

cortocir'cuito [kortotʃir'kuito] SM = **corto circuito**

cortome'traggio [kortome'traddʒo] SM short (feature film)

cor'vino, -a AG (capelli) jet-black

'**corvo** SM raven

'**cosa** SF thing; (faccenda) affair, matter, business no pl; (che) ~? what?; (che) **cos'è?** what is it?; **a** ~ **pensi?** what are you thinking about?; **tante belle cose!** all the best!; **ormai è** ~ **fatta!** (positivo) it's in the bag!; (negativo) it's done now!; **a cose fatte** when it's all over

'**Cosa 'Nostra** SF Cosa Nostra

'**cosca, -sche** SF (di mafiosi) clan

'**coscia, -sce** ['kɔʃʃa] SF thigh; ~ **di pollo** (Cuc) chicken leg

cosci'ente [koʃʃɛnte] AG conscious; ~ **di** conscious o aware of

cosci'enza [koʃʃɛntsa] SF conscience; (consapevolezza) consciousness; ~ **politica** political awareness

coscienzi'oso, -a [koʃʃen'tsjoso] AG
conscientious
cosci'otto [koʃʃɔtto] SM (*Cuc*) leg
cos'critto SM (*Mil*) conscript
coscrizi'one [koskrit'tsjone] SF conscription

(PAROLA CHIAVE)

così AV **1** (*in questo modo*) like this, (in) this
way; (*in tal modo*) so; **le cose stanno così** this
is the way things stand; **non ho detto così!**
I didn't say that!; **come stai? — (e) così** how
are you? — so-so; **e così via** and so on; **per
così dire** so to speak; **così sia** amen
2 (*tanto*) so; **così lontano** so far away; **un
ragazzo così intelligente** such an
intelligent boy
▶ AG INV (*tale*): **non ho mai visto un film
così** I've never seen such a film
▶ CONG **1** (*perciò*) so, therefore; **e così ho
deciso di lasciarlo** so I decided to leave him
2: **così ... come** as ... as; **non è così bravo
come te** he's not as good as you; **così ... che**
so ... that

cosicché [kosik'ke] CONG so (that)
cosid'detto, -a AG so-called
cos'mesi SF (*scienza*) cosmetics *sg*; (*prodotti*)
cosmetics *pl*; (*trattamento*) beauty treatment
cos'metico, -a, -ci, -che AG, SM cosmetic
'cosmico, -a, -ci, -che AG cosmic
'cosmo SM cosmos
cosmo'nauta, -i, -e SM/F cosmonaut
cosmopo'lita, -i, -e AG cosmopolitan
'coso SM (*col: oggetto*) thing, thingumajig;
(*aggeggio*) contraption; (*persona*) what's his
name, thingumajig
cos'pargere [kos'pardʒere] /**111**/ VT: **~ di** to
sprinkle with
cos'parso, -a PP *di* **cospargere**
cos'petto SM: **al ~ di** in front of; in the
presence of
cospicuità SF vast quantity
cos'picuo, -a AG considerable, large
cospi'rare /**72**/ VI to conspire
cospira'tore, -'trice SM/F conspirator
cospirazi'one [kospirat'tsjone] SF
conspiracy
'cossi *etc* VB *vedi* **cuocere**
Cost. ABBR = **costituzione**
'costa SF (*tra terra e mare*) coast(line); (*litorale*)
shore; (*pendio*) slope; (*Anat*) rib; **la C~ Azzurra** the
French Riviera; **la C~ d'Avorio** the Ivory
Coast; **velluto a coste** corduroy
costà AV there
cos'tante AG constant; (*persona*) steadfast
▶ SF constant
cos'tanza [kos'tantsa] SF (*gen*) constancy;
(*fermezza*) constancy, steadfastness; **il Lago**

di C~ Lake Constance
cos'tare /**72**/ VI, VT to cost; **~ caro** to be
expensive, cost a lot; **~ un occhio della
testa** to cost a fortune; **costi quel che costi**
no matter what
'Costa 'Rica SF: **la ~** Costa Rica
cos'tata SF (*Cuc: di manzo*) large chop
cos'tato SM (*Anat*) ribs *pl*
costeggi'are [kosted'dʒare] /**62**/ VT to be
close to; to run alongside
cos'tei PRON *vedi* **costui**
costellazi'one [kostellat'tsjone] SF
constellation
coster'nare /**72**/ VT to dismay
coster'nato, -a AG dismayed
costernazi'one [kosternat'tsjone] SF
dismay, consternation
costi'ero, -a AG coastal, coast *cpd* ▶ SF stretch
of coast
costi'pato, -a AG (*stitico*) constipated
costitu'ire /**55**/ VT (*comitato, gruppo*) to set up,
form; (*collezione*) to put together, build up;
(*elementi, parati: comporre*) to make up,
constitute; (*rappresentare*) to constitute; (*Dir*)
to appoint; **costituirsi** VPR: **costituirsi (alla
polizia)** to give o.s. up (to the police);
costituirsi parte civile (*Dir*) *to associate in an
action with the public prosecutor for damages*; **il
fatto non costituisce reato** this is not a
crime
costitu'tivo, -a AG constituent, component;
atto ~ (*Dir: di società*) memorandum of
association
costituzio'nale [kostituttsjo'nale] AG
constitutional
costituzi'one [kostitut'tsjone] SF setting up;
building up; constitution
'costo SM cost; **sotto ~** for less than cost
price; **a ogni** *o* **qualunque ~**, **a tutti i costi**
at all costs; **costi di esercizio** running
costs; **costi fissi** fixed costs; **costi di
gestione** operating costs; **costi di
produzione** production costs
'costola SF (*Anat*) rib; **ha la polizia alle
costole** the police are hard on his heels
costo'letta SF (*Cuc*) cutlet
cos'toro PRON PL *vedi* **costui**
cos'toso, -a AG expensive, costly
cos'tretto, -a PP *di* **costringere**
cos'tringere [kos'trindʒere] /**117**/ VT: **~ qn a
fare qc** to force sb to do sth
costrit'tivo, -a AG coercive
costrizi'one [kostrit'tsjone] SF coercion
costru'ire /**55**/ VT to construct, build
costrut'tivo, -a AG (*Edil*) building *cpd*; (*fig*)
constructive
costruzi'one [kostrut'tsjone] SF
construction, building; **di ~ inglese**
British-made

C

cos'tui (*f* **costei**, *pl* **costoro**) PRON (*soggetto*) he (she); (*pl*) they; (*complemento*) him (her); (*pl*) them; **si può sapere chi è ~?** (*peg*) just who is that fellow?

cos'tume SM (*uso*) custom; (*foggia di vestire, indumento*) costume; **il buon ~** public morality; **donna di facili costumi** woman of easy morals; **~ da bagno** bathing *o* swimming costume (BRIT), swimsuit; (*da uomo*) bathing *o* swimming trunks *pl*

costu'mista, -i, -e SM/F costume maker, costume designer

co'tenna SF bacon rind

co'togna [ko'toɲɲa] SF quince

coto'letta SF (*di maiale, montone*) chop; (*di vitello, agnello*) cutlet

coto'nare /**72**/ VT (*capelli*) to backcomb

co'tone SM cotton; **~ idrofilo** cotton wool (BRIT), absorbent cotton (US)

cotoni'ficio [kotoni'fitʃo] SM cotton mill

'**cotta** SF (*Rel*) surplice; (*col: innamoramento*) crush

'**cottimo** SM: **lavorare a ~** to do piecework

'**cotto, -a** PP *di* **cuocere** ▶ AG cooked; (*col: innamorato*) head-over-heels in love ▶ SM brickwork; **~ a puntino** cooked to perfection; **dirne di cotte e di crude a qn** to call sb every name under the sun; **farne di cotte e di crude** to get up to all kinds of mischief; **mattone di ~** fired brick; **pavimento in ~** tile floor; **ben ~** (*carne*) well done

cot'tura SF cooking; (*in forno*) baking; (*in umido*) stewing; **~ a fuoco lento** simmering; **angolo (di) ~** cooking area

co'vare /**72**/ VT to hatch; (*fig: malattia*) to be sickening for; (*: odio, rancore*) to nurse ▶ VI (*fuoco, fig*) to smoulder (BRIT), smolder (US)

co'vata SF (*anche fig*) brood

'**covo** SM den; **~ di terroristi** terrorist base

co'vone SM sheaf

'**cozza** ['kottsa] SF mussel

coz'zare [kot'tsare] /**72**/ VI: **~ contro** to bang into, collide with

'**cozzo** ['kottso] SM collision

C.P. ABBR = *cartolina postale*) pc; (*Posta*) *vedi* **casella postale**; (*Naut*) = **capitaneria (di porto)**; (*Dir*) = **codice penale**

CPT SIGLA M INV = **Centro di Permanenza Temporanea**

crac'care /**20**/ VT (*Inform*) to crack

crack SM INV (*droga*) crack

Cra'covia SF Cracow

'**crampo** SM cramp; **ho un ~ alla gamba** I've got cramp in my leg

'**cranio** SM skull

cra'tere SM crater

cra'vatta SF tie; **~ a farfalla** bow tie

cravat'tino SM bow tie

cre'anza [kre'antsa] SF manners *pl*; **per buona ~** out of politeness

cre'are /**72**/ VT to create

creativi'tà SF creativity

cre'ato SM creation

crea'tore, -'trice AG creative ▶ SM/F creator; **un ~ di alta moda** fashion designer; **andare al C~** to go to meet one's maker

crea'tura SF creature; (*bimbo*) baby, infant

creazi'one [kreat'tsjone] SF creation; (*fondazione*) foundation, establishment

'**crebbi** *etc* VB *vedi* **crescere**

cre'dente SMF (*Rel*) believer

cre'denza [kre'dɛntsa] SF belief; (*armadio*) sideboard

credenzi'ali [kreden'tsjali] SFPL credentials

'**credere** /**29**/ VT to believe ▶ VI: **~ in, ~ a** to believe in; **~ qn onesto** to believe sb (to be) honest; **~ che** to believe *o* think that; **credersi furbo** to think one is clever; **lo credo bene!** I can well believe it!; **fai quello che credi** *o* **come credi** do as you please

cre'dibile AG credible, believable

credibili'tà SF credibility

credi'tizio, -a [kredi'tittsjo] AG credit

'**credito** SM (*anche Comm*) credit; (*reputazione*) esteem, repute; **comprare a ~** to buy on credit; **~ agevolato** easy credit terms; **~ d'imposta** tax credit

credi'tore, -'trice SM/F creditor

'**credo** SM INV creed

'**credulo, -a** AG credulous

credu'lone, -a SM/F simpleton, sucker (*col*)

'**crema** SF cream; (*con uova, zucchero ecc*) custard; **~ idratante** moisturizing cream; **~ pasticciera** confectioner's custard; **~ solare** sun cream

cre'mare /**72**/ VT to cremate

crema'torio SM crematorium

cremazi'one [kremat'tsjone] SF cremation

'**cremisi** AG INV, SM INV crimson

Crem'lino SM: **il ~** the Kremlin

cremo'nese AG *o* (*o from*) Cremona

cre'moso, -a AG creamy

'**crepa** SF crack

cre'paccio [kre'pattʃo] SM large crack, fissure; (*di ghiacciaio*) crevasse

crepacu'ore SM broken heart

crepa'pelle AV: **ridere a ~** to split one's sides laughing

cre'pare /**72**/ VI (*col: morire*) to snuff it (BRIT), kick the bucket; **~ dalle risa** to split one's sides laughing; **~ dall'invidia** to be green with envy

crêpe [krɛp] SF INV pancake

crepi'tare /**72**/ VI (*fuoco*) to crackle; (*pioggia*) to patter

crepi'tio, -ii SM crackling; pattering

cre'puscolo SM twilight, dusk

cre'scendo [kreʃʃendo] SM (*Mus*) crescendo
cre'scente [kreʃʃente] AG (*gen*) growing,
increasing; (*luna*) waxing
'crescere ['kreʃʃere] **/30/** VI to grow ▶ VT (*figli*)
to raise
cre'scione [kreʃʃone] SM watercress
'crescita ['kreʃʃita] SF growth
cresci'uto, -a [kreʃʃuto] PP *di* **crescere**
'cresima SF (*Rel*) confirmation
cresi'mare /72/ VT to confirm
'crespo, -a AG (*capelli*) frizzy; (*tessuto*)
puckered ▶ SM crêpe
'cresta SF crest; (*di polli, uccelli*) crest, comb;
alzare la ~ (*fig*) to become cocky; **abbassare
la ~** (*fig*) to climb down; **essere sulla ~
dell'onda** (*fig*) to be riding high
'Creta SF Crete
'creta SF (*gesso*) chalk; (*argilla*) clay
cre'tese AG, SMF Cretan
creti'nata SF (*col*): **dire/fare una ~** to say/do a
stupid thing
cre'tino, -a AG stupid ▶ SM/F idiot, fool
CRI SIGLA F = **Croce Rossa Italiana**
cric SM INV (*Tecn*) jack
'cricca, -che SF clique
'cricco, -chi SM = **cric**
cri'ceto [kri'tʃeto] SM hamster
crimi'nale AG, SMF criminal
criminalità SF crime; **~ organizzata**
organized crime
'Criminalpol ABBR = **polizia criminale**
'crimine SM (*Dir*) crime
criminolo'gia [kriminolo'dʒia] SF
criminology
crimi'noso, -a AG criminal
cri'nale SM ridge
'crine SM horsehair
crini'era SF mane
'cripta SF crypt
crip'tare /72/ VT (TV: *programma*) to encrypt
crip'tato, -a AG (*programma, messaggio*)
encrypted
crisan'temo SM chrysanthemum; *vedi anche*
giorno
'crisi SF INV crisis; (*Med*) attack, fit; **essere in
~** (*partito, impresa ecc*) to be in a state of crisis;
~ energetica energy crisis; **~ di nervi** attack
o fit of nerves
cristalle'ria SF (*fabbrica*) crystal glassworks *sg*;
(*oggetti*) crystalware
cristal'lino, -a AG (*Mineralogia*) crystalline;
(*fig: suono, acque*) crystal clear ▶ SM (*Anat*)
crystalline lens
cristalliz'zare [kristallid'dzare] **/72/** VI,
cristalliz'zarsi VPR to crystallize; (*fig*) to
become fossilized
cris'tallo SM crystal; **cristalli liquidi** liquid
crystals
cristia'nesimo SM Christianity

cristianità SF Christianity; (*i cristiani*)
Christendom
cristi'ano, -a AG, SM/F Christian; **un povero
~** (*fig*) a poor soul *o* beggar; **comportarsi da ~**
(*fig*) to behave in a civilized manner
'cristo SM: **C~** Christ; (**un**) **povero ~** (a) poor
beggar
cri'terio SM criterion; (*buon senso*)
(common) sense
'critica, -che SF *vedi* **critico**
criti'care /20/ VT to criticize
'critico, -a, -ci, -che AG critical ▶ SM critic
▶ SF criticism; **la critica** (*attività*) criticism;
(*persone*) the critics *pl*
criti'cone, -a SM/F faultfinder
crivel'lare /72/ VT: **~ (di)** to riddle (with)
cri'vello SM riddle
cro'ato, -a AG, SM/F Croatian, Croat
Cro'azia [kro'attsja] SF: **la ~** Croatia
croc'cante AG crisp, crunchy ▶ SM (*Cuc*)
almond crunch
'crocchia ['krɔkkja] SF chignon, bun
'crocchio ['krɔkkjo] SM (*di persone*) small
group, cluster
'croce ['krotʃe] SF cross; **in ~** (*di traverso*)
crosswise; (*fig*) on tenterhooks; **mettere in
~** (*anche fig: criticare*) to crucify (: *tormentare*) to
nag to death; **la C~ Rossa** the Red Cross;
~ uncinata swastika
croce'figgere *etc* [krotʃe'fiddʒere]
= **crocifiggere** *ecc*
croceros'sina [krotʃeros'sina] SF Red Cross
nurse
croce'via [krotʃe'via] SM INV crossroads *sg*
croci'ato, -a [kro'tʃato] AG cross-shaped ▶ SM
(*anche fig*) crusader ▶ SF crusade
cro'cicchio [kro'tʃikkjo] SM crossroads *sg*
croci'era [kro'tʃera] SF (*viaggio*) cruise; (*Archit*)
transept; **altezza di ~** (*Aer*) cruising height;
velocità di ~ (*Aer, Naut*) cruising speed
croci'figgere [krotʃi'fiddʒere] **/104/** VT to
crucify
crocifissi'one [krotʃifis'sjone] SF
crucifixion
croci'fisso, -a [krotʃi'fisso] PP *di* **crocifiggere**
▶ SM crucifix
crogio'larsi [krodʒo'larsi] **/72/** VPR: **~ al sole**
to bask in the sun
crogi'olo [kro'dʒɔlo], **crogiu'olo** [kro'dʒwɔlo]
SM crucible; (*fig*) melting pot
crol'lare /72/ VI to collapse
'crollo SM collapse; (*di prezzi*) slump, sudden
fall; **~ in Borsa** slump in prices on the Stock
Exchange
'croma SF (*Mus*) quaver (BRIT), eighth note
(US)
cro'mato, -a AG chromium-plated
'cromo SM chrome, chromium
cromo'soma, -i SM chromosome

'**cronaca, -che** SF chronicle; (*Stampa*) news *sg*; (: *rubrica*) column; (*TV*, *Radio*) commentary; **fatto** *o* **episodio di** ~ news item; ~ **nera** crime news *sg*; crime column

'**cronico, -a, -ci, -che** AG chronic

cro'nista, -i SM (*Stampa*) reporter, columnist

cronis'toria SF chronicle; (*fig: ironico*) blow-by-blow account

cro'nografo SM (*strumento*) chronograph

cronolo'gia [kronolo'dʒia] SF chronology

crono'nometrare /72/ VT to time

cro'nometro SM chronometer; (*a scatto*) stopwatch

'**crosta** SF crust; (*Med*) scab; (*Zool*) shell; (*di ghiaccio*) layer; (*fig: peg: quadro*) daub

cros'tacei [kros'tatʃei] SMPL shellfish

cros'tata SF (*Cuc*) tart

cros'tino SM (*Cuc*) croûton; (: *da antipasto*) canapé

crowd'sourcing [kraud'sursin(g)] SM crowdsourcing

crucci'are [krut'tʃare] /14/ VT to torment, worry; **crucciarsi** VPR: **crucciarsi per** to torment o.s. over

'**cruccio** ['kruttʃo] SM worry, torment

cruci'ale [kru'tʃale] AG crucial

cruci'verba [krutʃi'vɛrba] SM INV crossword (puzzle)

cru'dele AG cruel

crudeltà SF cruelty

'**crudo, -a** AG (*non cotto*) raw; (*aspro*) harsh, severe

cru'ento, -a AG bloody

cru'miro SM (*peg*) blackleg (BRIT), scab

'**cruna** SF eye (of a needle)

'**crusca** SF bran

crus'cotto SM (*Aut*) dashboard

CS SIGLA = **Cosenza**

c.s. ABBR = **come sopra**

CSI [tʃi'esse'i] SIGLA F (= *Comunità di Stati Indipendenti*) CIS

CSM [tʃi'esse'ɛmme] SIGLA M (= *consiglio superiore della magistratura*) Magistrates' Board of Supervisors

CT SIGLA = **Catania**

c.t. ABBR = **commissario tecnico**

'**Cuba** SF Cuba

cu'bano, -a AG, SM/F Cuban

cu'betto SM (small) cube; ~ **di ghiaccio** ice cube

'**cubico, -a, -ci, -che** AG cubic

cu'bista, -i, -e /a (*Arte*) Cubist ▶ SF podium dancer, *dancer who performs on stage in a club*

'**cubo, -a** AG cubic ▶ SM cube; **elevare al** ~ (*Mat*) to cube

cuc'cagna [kuk'kaɲɲa] SF: **paese della** ~ land of plenty; **albero della** ~ greasy pole (*fig*)

cuc'cetta [kut'tʃetta] SF (*Ferr*) couchette; (*Naut*) berth

cucchiai'ata [kukkja'jata] SF spoonful; tablespoonful

cucchia'ino [kukkja'ino] SM teaspoon; coffee spoon

cucchi'aio [kuk'kjajo] SM spoon; (*da tavola*) tablespoon; (*cucchiaiata*) spoonful; tablespoonful

'**cuccia, -ce** ['kuttʃa] SF dog's bed; **a** ~! down!

cuccio'lata [kuttʃo'lata] SF litter

'**cucciolo** ['kuttʃolo] SM cub; (*di cane*) puppy

cu'cina [ku'tʃina] SF (*locale*) kitchen; (*arte culinaria*) cooking, cookery; (*le vivande*) food, cooking; (*apparecchio*) cooker; **di** ~ (*libro, lezione*) cookery *cpd*; ~ **componibile** fitted kitchen; ~ **economica** kitchen range

cuci'nare [kutʃi'nare] /72/ VT to cook

cuci'nino [kutʃi'nino] SM kitchenette

cu'cire [ku'tʃire] /31/ VT to sew, stitch; ~ **la bocca a qn** (*fig*) to shut sb up

cu'cito, -a [ku'tʃito] SM sewing; (*Ins*) sewing, needlework

cuci'trice [kutʃi'tritʃe] SF (*Tip: per libri*) stitching machine; (*per fogli*) stapler

cuci'tura [kutʃi'tura] SF sewing, stitching; (*costura*) seam

cucù SM INV, **cu'culo** SM cuckoo

'**cuffia** SF bonnet, cap; (*da infermiera*) cap; (*da bagno*) (bathing) cap; (*per ascoltare*) headphones *pl*, headset

cu'gino, -a [ku'dʒino] SM/F cousin

| PAROLA CHIAVE |

'**cui** PRON **1** (*nei complementi indiretti: persona*) whom; (: *oggetto, animale*) which; **la persona/ le persone a cui accennavi** the person/ people you were referring to *o* to whom you were referring; **la penna con cui scrivo** the pen I'm writing with; **il paese da cui viene** the country he comes from; **i libri di cui parlavo** the books I was talking about *o* about which I was talking; **parla varie lingue, fra cui l'inglese** he speaks several languages, including English; **il quartiere in cui abito** the district where I live; **visto il modo in cui ti ha trattato** ... considering how he treated you ...; **la ragione per cui** the reason why; **per cui non so più che fare** that's why I don't know what to do **2** (*inserito tra articolo e sostantivo*) whose; **la donna i cui figli sono scomparsi** the woman whose children have disappeared; **il signore, dal cui figlio ho avuto il libro** the man from whose son I got the book

---

culi'naria SF cookery

culi'nario, -a AG culinary

'**culla** SF cradle

cul'lare /72/ VT to rock; (fig: idea, speranza) to cherish; **cullarsi** VPR (gen) to sway; **cullarsi in vane speranze** (fig) to cherish fond hopes; **cullarsi nel dolce far niente** (fig) to sit back and relax

culmi'nante AG: **posizione** ~ (Astr) highest point; **punto** o **momento** ~ (fig) climax

culmi'nare /72/ VI: ~ **in** o **con** to culminate in

'culmine SM top, summit

'culo SM (col) arse (BRIT!), ass (US!); (: fig: fortuna): **aver** ~ to have the luck of the devil; **prendere qn per il** ~ to take the piss out of sb (!)

'culto SM (religione) religion; (adorazione) worship, adoration; (venerazione: anche fig) cult

cul'tura SF (gen) culture; (conoscenza) education, learning; **di** ~ (persona) cultured; (istituto) cultural, of culture; ~ **generale** general knowledge; ~ **di massa** mass culture

cultu'rale AG cultural

cultu'rismo SM body-building

cumu'lare /72/ VT to accumulate, amass

cumula'tivo, -a AG cumulative; (prezzo) inclusive; (biglietto) group cpd

'cumulo SM (mucchio) pile, heap; (Meteor) cumulus; ~ **dei redditi** (Fisco) combined incomes; ~ **delle pene** (Dir) consecutive sentences

'cuneo SM wedge

cu'netta SF (di strada ecc) bump; (scolo: nelle strade di città) gutter; (: di campagna) ditch; (avvallamento) dip

cu'nicolo SM (galleria) tunnel; (di miniera) pit, shaft; (di talpa) hole

cu'oca SF vedi **cuoco**

cu'ocere ['kwɔtʃere] /32/ VT (alimenti) to cook; (mattoni ecc) to fire ▶ VI to cook; ~ **in umido/a vapore/in padella** to stew/steam/fry; ~ **al forno** (pane) to bake; (arrosto) to roast

cu'oco, -a, -chi, -che SM/F cook; (di ristorante) chef

cuoi'ame SM leather goods pl

cu'oio SM leather; ~ **capelluto** scalp; **tirare le cuoia** (col) to kick the bucket

cu'ore SM heart; **cuori** SMPL (Carte) hearts; **avere buon** ~ to be kind-hearted; **stare a** ~ **a qn** to be important to sb; **un grazie di** ~ heartfelt thanks; **ringraziare di** ~ to thank sincerely; **nel profondo del** ~ in one's heart of hearts; **avere la morte nel** ~ to be sick at heart; **club dei cuori solitari** lonely hearts club

cupi'digia [kupi'didʒa] SF greed, covetousness

'cupo, -a AG dark; (suono) dull; (fig) gloomy, dismal

'cupola SF dome; (più piccola) cupola; (fig) Mafia high command

'cura SF care; (Med: trattamento) (course of) treatment; **aver** ~ **di** (occuparsi di) to look after; **a** ~ **di** (libro) edited by; **fare una** ~ to follow a course of treatment; ~ **dimagrante** diet

cu'rabile AG curable

cu'rante AG: **medico** ~ doctor (in charge of a patient)

cu'rare /72/ VT (malato, malattia) to treat; (: guarire) to cure; (aver cura di) to take care of; (testo) to edit; **curarsi** VPR to take care of o.s.; (Med) to follow a course of treatment; **curarsi di** to pay attention to; (occuparsi di) to look after

cu'rato SM parish priest; (protestante) vicar, minister

cura'tore, -'trice SM/F (Dir) trustee; (di antologia ecc) editor; ~ **fallimentare** (official) receiver

'curdo, -a AG Kurdish ▶ SM/F Kurd

'curia SF (Rel): **la** ~ **romana** the Roman curia; ~ **notarile** notaries' association o guild

curio'saggine [kurjo'saddʒine] SF nosiness

curio'sare /72/ VI to look round, wander round; (tra libri) to browse; ~ **nei negozi** to look o wander round the shops; ~ **nelle faccende altrui** to poke one's nose into other people's affairs

curiosità SF INV curiosity; (cosa rara) curio, curiosity

curi'oso, -a AG (che vuol sapere) curious, inquiring; (ficcanaso) curious, inquisitive; (bizzarro) strange, curious ▶ SM/F busybody, nosy parker; **essere** ~ **di** to be curious about; **una folla di curiosi** a crowd of onlookers

cur'riculum SM INV: ~ (**vitae**) curriculum vitae

cur'sore SM (Inform) cursor

'curva SF curve; (stradale) bend, curve

cur'vare /72/ VT to bend ▶ VI (veicolo) to take a bend; (strada) to bend, curve; **curvarsi** VPR to bend; (legno) to warp

'curvo, -a AG curved; (piegato) bent

CUS SIGLA M = **Centro Universitario Sportivo**

cusci'netto [kuʃʃi'netto] SM pad; (Tecn) bearing ▶ AG INV: **stato** ~ buffer state; ~ **a sfere** ball bearing

cu'scino [kuʃʃino] SM cushion; (guanciale) pillow

'cuspide SF (Archit) spire

cus'tode SMF (di museo) keeper, custodian; (di parco) warden; (di casa) concierge; (di fabbrica, carcere) guard

cus'todia SF care; (Dir) custody; (astuccio) case, holder; **avere qc in** ~ to look after sth; **dare qc in** ~ **a qn** to entrust sth to sb's care;

agente di ~ prison warder; ~ **delle carceri** prison security; ~ **cautelare** (*Dir*) remand
custo'dire /55/ VT (*conservare*) to keep; (*assistere*) to look after, take care of; (*fare la guardia*) to guard
customiz'zare [kustomid'dzare] /72/ VT (*Inform*) to customize
'**cute** SF (*Anat*) skin
cu'ticola SF cuticle

C.V. ABBR (= *cavallo vapore*) h.p.
c.v.d. ABBR (= *come volevasi dimostrare*) QED (= *quod erat demonstrandum*)
c.vo ABBR = **corsivo**
cyberca'ffè [tʃiberka'fe] SM INV cybercafé
cyber'nauta, -i, -e SM/F Internet surfer
cyber'spazio SM cyberspace
cy'clette® [si'klɛt] SF INV exercise bike
CZ SIGLA = **Catanzaro**

Dd

D¹, d [di] SM O F INV (*lettera*) D, d; **D come Domodossola** ≈ D for David (*BRIT*), D for Dog (*US*)

D² ABBR (= *destra*) R; (*Ferr*) = **diretto**

(PAROLA CHIAVE)

da (*da* + *il* = **dal**, *da* + *lo* = **dallo**, *da* + *l'* = **dall'**, *da* + *la* = **dalla**, *da* + *i* = **dai**, *da* + *gli* = **dagli**, *da* + *le* = **dalle**) PREP **1** (*agente*) by; **dipinto da un grande artista** painted by a great artist
2 (*causa*) with; **tremare dalla paura** to tremble with fear
3 (*stato in luogo*) at; **abito da lui** I'm living at his house *o* with him; **sono dal giornalaio** I'm at the newsagent's; **era da Francesco** she was at Francesco's (house)
4 (*moto a luogo*) to; (*moto per luogo*) through; **vado da Pietro/dal giornalaio** I'm going to Pietro's (house)/to the newsagent's; **sono passati dalla finestra** they came in through the window
5 (*provenienza, allontanamento*) from; **da ... a** from ... to; **arrivare/partire da Milano** to arrive/depart from Milan; **scendere dal treno/dalla macchina** to get off the train/out of the car; **viene da una famiglia povera** he comes from a poor background; **viene dalla Scozia** he comes from Scotland; **ti chiamo da una cabina** I'm phoning from a call box; **si trova a 5 km da qui** it's 5 km from here
6 (*tempo: durata*) for; (: *a partire da: nel passato*) since; (: *nel futuro*) from; **vivo qui da un anno** I've been living here for a year; **è dalle 3 che ti aspetto** I've been waiting for you since 3 (o'clock); **da mattina a sera** from morning till night; **da oggi in poi** from today onwards; **da bambino** as a child, when I (*o* he *etc*) was a child
7 (*modo, maniera*) like; **comportarsi da uomo** to behave like a man; **l'ho fatto da me** I did it (by) myself; **non è da lui** it's not like him
8 (*descrittivo*): **una macchina da corsa** a racing car; **è una cosa da poco** it's nothing

special; **una ragazza dai capelli biondi** a girl with blonde hair; **sordo da un orecchio** deaf in one ear; **abbigliamento da uomo** menswear; **un vestito da 100 euro** a 100 euro dress; **qualcosa da bere/mangiare** something to drink/eat

dà VB *vedi* **dare**
dab'bene AG INV honest, decent
'Dacca SF Dacca
dac'capo, da 'capo AV (*di nuovo*) (once) again; (*dal principio*) all over again, from the beginning
dacché [dak'ke] CONG since
'dado SM (*da gioco*) dice *o* die; (*Cuc*) stock cube (*BRIT*), bouillon cube (*US*); (*Tecn*) (screw) nut; **dadi** SMPL (game of) dice; **giocare a dadi** to play dice
daffare, da 'fare SM work, toil; **avere un gran ~** to be very busy
'dagli ['daʎʎi], **'dai** PREP + DET *vedi* **da**
'daino SM (*fallow*) deer *inv*; (*pelle*) buckskin
Da'kar SF Dakar
dal¹ PREP + DET *vedi* **da**
dal² ABBR (= *decalitro*) dal
dall', **'dalla**, **'dalle**, **'dallo** PREP + DET *vedi* **da**
dal'tonico, -a, -ci, -che AG colour-blind (*BRIT*), colorblind (*US*)
dam ABBR (= *decametro*) dam
'dama SF lady; (*nei balli*) partner; (*gioco*) draughts *sg* (*BRIT*), checkers *sg* (*US*); **far ~** (*nel gioco*) to make a crown; **~ di compagnia** lady's companion; **~ di corte** lady-in-waiting
Da'masco SF Damascus
dami'gella [dami'dʒɛlla] SF (*Storia*) damsel; (: *titolo*) mistress; **~ d'onore** (*di sposa*) bridesmaid
damigi'ana [dami'dʒana] SF demijohn
dam'meno AG INV: **per non essere ~ di qn** so as not to be outdone by sb
DAMS SIGLA M: **Discipline delle Arti, della Musica, dello Spettacolo** *study of the performing arts*

da'naro SM = **denaro**

dana'roso, -a AG wealthy

da'nese AG Danish ▶ SMF Dane ▶ SM (*Ling*) Danish

Dani'marca SF: **la ~** Denmark

dan'nare /72/ VT (*Rel*) to damn; **dannarsi** VPR: **dannarsi per** (*fig: tormentarsi*) to be worried to death (by); **far ~ qn** to drive sb mad; **dannarsi l'anima per qc** (*affannarsi*) to work o.s. to death for sth; (*tormentarsi*) to worry o.s. to death over sth

dan'nato, -a AG damned

dannazi'one [dannat'tsjone] SF damnation

danneggi'are [danned'dʒare] /62/ VT to damage; (*rovinare*) to spoil; (*nuocere*) to harm; **la parte danneggiata** (*Dir*) the injured party

'danno VB *vedi* **dare** ▶ SM damage; (*a persona*) harm, injury; **danni** SMPL (*Dir*) damages; **a ~ di qn** to sb's detriment; **chiedere/risarcire i danni** to sue for/pay damages

dan'noso, -a AG: **~ (a o per)** harmful (to), bad (for)

dan'tesco, -a, -schi, -sche AG Dantesque; **l'opera dantesca** Dante's work

Da'nubio SM: **il ~** the Danube

'danza ['dantsa] SF: **la ~** dancing; **una ~** a dance

dan'zante [dan'tsante] AG dancing; **serata ~** dance

dan'zare [dan'tsare] /72/ VT, VI to dance

danza'tore, -'trice [dantsa'tore] SM/F dancer

dapper'tutto AV everywhere

dap'poco AG INV inept; worthless

dap'prima AV at first

Darda'nelli SMPL: **i ~** the Dardanelles

'dardo SM dart

'dare /33/ SM (*Comm*) debit ▶ VT to give; (*produrre: frutti, suono*) to produce ▶ VI (*guardare*): **~ su** to look (out) onto; **darsi** VPR: **darsi a** to dedicate o.s. to; **quanti anni mi dai?** how old do you think I am?; **danno ancora quel film?** is that film still showing?; **~ da mangiare a qn** to give sb something to eat; **~ per certo qc** to consider sth certain; **~ ad intendere a qn che ...** to lead sb to believe that ...; **~ per morto qn** to give sb up for dead; **~ qc per scontato** to take sth for granted; **darsi ammalato** to report sick; **darsi alla bella vita** to have a good time; **darsi al bere** to take to drink; **darsi al commercio** to go into business; **darsi da fare per fare qc** to go to a lot of bother to do sth; **darsi per vinto** to give in; **può darsi** maybe, perhaps; **si dà il caso che ...** it so happens that ...; **darsela a gambe** to take to one's heels; **il ~ e l'avere** (*Econ*) debits and credits *pl*

Dar-es-Sa'laam SF Dar-es-Salaam

'darsena SF dock

'data SF date; **in ~ da destinarsi** on a date still to be announced; **in ~ odierna** as of today; **amicizia di lunga o vecchia ~** long-standing friendship; **~ di emissione** date of issue; **~ di nascita** date of birth; **~ di scadenza** expiry date; **~ limite d'utilizzo o di consumo** (*Comm*) best-before date

da'tare /72/ VT to date ▶ VI: **~ da** to date from

da'tato, -a AG dated

da'tivo SM dative

'dato, -a AG (*stabilito*) given ▶ SM datum; **dati** SMPL data *pl*; **~ che** given that; **in dati casi** in certain cases; **è un ~ di fatto** it's a fact; **dati sensibili** sense data

da'tore, -'trice SM/F: **~ di lavoro** employer

'dattero SM date (*Bot*)

dattilogra'fare /72/ VT to type

dattilogra'fia SF typing

datti'lografo, -a SM/F typist

dattilos'critto SM typescript

da'vanti AV in front; (*dirimpetto*) opposite ▶ AG INV front ▶ SM front; **~ a** *prep* in front of; (*dirimpetto a*) facing, opposite; (*in presenza di*) before, in front of

davan'zale [davan'tsale] SM windowsill

da'vanzo, d'a'vanzo [da'vantso] AV more than enough

dav'vero AV really, indeed; **dico ~** I mean it

dazi'ario, -a [dat'tsjarjo] AG excise *cpd*

'dazio ['dattsjo] SM (*somma*) duty; (*luogo*) customs *pl*; **~ d'importazione** import duty

db ABBR (= *decibel*) dB

DC SIGLA F (*former political party*) = **la Democrazia Cristiana**

d.C. ABBR (= *dopo Cristo*) A.D.

D.D.T. ABBR M (= *dicloro-difenil-tricloroetano*) D.D.T.

'dea SF goddess

'debbo *etc* VB *vedi* **dovere**

debel'lare /72/ VT to overcome, conquer

debili'tare /72/ VT to debilitate

debita'mente AV duly, properly

'debito, -a AG due, proper ▶ SM debt; (*Comm: dare*) debit; **a tempo ~** at the right time; **portare a ~ di qn** to debit sb with; **~ consolidato** consolidated debt; **~ d'imposta** tax liability; **~ pubblico** national debt

debi'tore, -'trice SM/F debtor

'debole AG weak, feeble; (*suono*) faint; (*luce*) dim ▶ SM weakness

debo'lezza [debo'lettsa] SF weakness

debut'tante SMF (*gen*) beginner, novice; (*Teat*) actor (actress) (*at the beginning of his (or her) career*)

debut'tare /72/ VI to make one's début

de'butto SM début

'decade SF period of ten days

deca'dente AG decadent

deca'denza [deka'dɛntsa] sf decline; (*Dir*) loss, forfeiture

deca'dere /**18**/ vi to decline

deca'duto, -a ag (*persona*) impoverished; (*norma*) lapsed

decaffei'nato, -a ag decaffeinated

de'calogo sm (*fig*) rulebook

de'cano sm (*Rel*) dean

decan'tare /**72**/ vt (*virtù, bravura ecc*) to praise; (*persona*) to sing the praises of

decapi'tare /**72**/ vt to decapitate, behead

decappot'tabile ag, sf convertible

dece'duto, -a [detʃe'duto] ag deceased

decele'rare [detʃele'rare] /**72**/ vt, vi to decelerate, slow down

decen'nale [detʃen'nale] ag (*che dura 10 anni*) ten-year *cpd*; (*che ricorre ogni 10 anni*) ten-yearly, every ten years ▶ sm (*ricorrenza*) tenth anniversary

de'cenne [de'tʃɛnne] ag: **un bambino ~** a ten-year-old child, a child of ten

de'cennio [de'tʃɛnnjo] sm decade

de'cente [de'tʃɛnte] ag decent, respectable, proper; (*accettabile*) satisfactory, decent

decentraliz'zare [detʃentralid'dzare] /**72**/ vt (*Amm*) to decentralize

decentra'mento [detʃentra'mento] sm decentralization

decen'trare [detʃen'trare] /**72**/ vt to decentralize, move out of *o* away from the centre

de'cenza [de'tʃɛntsa] sf decency, propriety

de'cesso [de'tʃɛsso] sm death; **atto di ~** death certificate

de'cidere [de'tʃidere] /**34**/ vi to decide, make up one's mind ▶ vt: **~ qc** to decide on sth; (*questione, lite*) to settle sth; **decidersi** vpr: **decidersi (a fare)** to decide (to do), make up one's mind (to do); **~ di fare/che** to decide to do/that; **~ di qc** (*cosa*) to determine sth

deci'frare [detʃi'frare] /**72**/ vt to decode; (*fig*) to decipher, make out

de'cilitro [de'tʃilitro] sm decilitre (*Brit*), deciliter (*US*)

deci'male [detʃi'male] ag decimal

deci'mare [detʃi'mare] /**72**/ vt to decimate

de'cimetro [de'tʃimetro] sm decimetre

'decimo, -a ['dɛtʃimo] num tenth

de'cina [de'tʃina] sf ten; (*circa dieci*): **una ~ (di)** about ten

de'cisi *etc* [de'tʃizi] vb *vedi* **decidere**

decisio'nale [detʃizjo'nale] ag decision-making *cpd*

decisi'one [detʃi'zjone] sf decision; **prendere una ~** to make a decision; **con ~** decisively, resolutely

deci'sivo, -a [detʃi'zivo] ag (*gen*) decisive; (*fattore*) deciding

de'ciso, -a [de'tʃizo] pp *di* **decidere** ▶ ag (*persona, carattere*) determined; (*tono*) firm, resolute

declas'sare /**72**/ vt to downgrade; to lower in status; **1ª declassata** (*Ferr*) first-class carriage which may be used by second-class passengers

decli'nare /**72**/ vi (*pendio*) to slope down; (*fig: diminuire*) to decline; (: *tramontare*) to set, go down ▶ vt to decline; **~ le proprie generalità** (*fig*) to give one's particulars; **~ ogni responsabilità** to disclaim all responsibility

declinazi'one [deklinat'tsjone] sf (*Ling*) declension

de'clino sm decline

de'clivio sm (downward) slope

decodifi'care /**20**/ vt to decode

decodifica'tore sm (*Tel*) decoder

decol'lare /**72**/ vi (*Aer*) to take off

décolleté [dekol'te] ag *inv* (*abito*) low-necked, low-cut ▶ sm (*di abito*) low neckline; (*di donna*) cleavage

de'collo sm take-off

decolo'rare /**72**/ vt to bleach

decom'porre /**77**/ vt, **decomporsi** vpr to decompose

decomposizi'one [dekompozit'tsjone] sf decomposition

decom'posto, -a pp *di* **decomporre**

decompressi'one sf decompression

deconge'lare [dekondʒe'lare] /**72**/ vt to defrost

decongestio'nare [dekondʒestjo'nare] /**72**/ vt (*Med, traffico*) to relieve congestion in

deco'rare /**72**/ vt to decorate

decora'tivo, -a ag decorative

decora'tore, -'trice sm/f (interior) decorator

decorazi'one [dekorat'tsjone] sf decoration

de'coro sm decorum

deco'roso, -a ag decorous, dignified

decor'renza [dekor'rɛntsa] sf: **con ~ da** (as) from

de'correre /**28**/ vi to pass, elapse; (*avere effetto*) to run, have effect

de'corso, -a pp *di* **decorrere** ▶ sm (*evoluzione*: *anche Med*) course

de'crebbi *etc* vb *vedi* **decrescere**

de'crepito, -a ag decrepit

de'crescere [de'kreʃʃere] /**30**/ vi (*diminuire*) to decrease, diminish; (*acque*) to subside, go down; (*prezzi*) to go down

decresci'uto, -a [dekreʃ'ʃuto] pp *di* **decrescere**

decre'tare /**72**/ vt (*norma*) to decree; (*mobilitazione*) to order; **~ lo stato d'emergenza** to declare a state of emergency; **~ la nomina di qn** to decide on the appointment of sb

de'creto sm decree; **~ legge** *decree with the force of law*; **~ di sfratto** eviction order

decrip'tare [dekrip'tare] VT to decrypt

decur'tare /**72**/ VT (*debito, somma*) to reduce

decurtazi'one [dekurtat'tsjone] SF reduction

'dedalo SM maze, labyrinth

'dedica, -che SF dedication

dedi'care /**20**/ VT to dedicate; **dedicarsi** VPR: **dedicarsi a** (*votarsi*) to devote o.s. to

dedicherò *etc* [dedike'rɔ] VB *vedi* **dedicare**

'dedito, -a AG: ~ **a** (*studio ecc*) dedicated *o* devoted to; (*vizio*) addicted to

de'dotto, -a PP *di* **dedurre**

de'duco *etc* VB *vedi* **dedurre**

de'durre /**90**/ VT (*concludere*) to deduce; (*defalcare*) to deduct

de'dussi *etc* VB *vedi* **dedurre**

deduzi'one [dedut'tsjone] SF deduction

defal'care /**20**/ VT to deduct

defenes'trare /**72**/ VT to throw out of the window; (*fig*) to remove from office

defe'rente AG respectful, deferential

defe'rire /**55**/ VT (*Dir*): ~ **a** to refer to

defezi'one [defet'tsjone] SF defection, desertion

defici'ente [defi'tʃɛnte] AG (*insufficiente*) insufficient; ~ **di** (*mancante*) deficient in ▶ SMF mental defective; (*peg: cretino*) idiot

defici'enza [defi'tʃɛntsa] SF deficiency; (*carenza*) shortage; (*fig: lacuna*) weakness

'deficit ['dɛfitʃit] SM INV (*Econ*) deficit

defi'nire /**55**/ VT to define; (*risolvere*) to settle; (*questione*) to finalize

defini'tivo, -a AG definitive, final ▶ SF: **in definitiva** (*dopotutto*) when all is said and done; (*dunque*) hence

defi'nito, -a AG definite; **ben ~** clear, clear cut

definizi'one [definit'tsjone] SF (*gen*) definition; (*di disputa, vertenza*) settlement; (*di tempi, obiettivi*) establishment

deflagrazi'one [deflagrat'tsjone] SF explosion

deflazi'one [deflat'tsjone] SF (*Econ*) deflation

deflet'tore SM (*Aut*) quarterlight (*BRIT*), deflector (*US*)

deflu'ire /**55**/ VI: ~ **da** (*liquido*) to flow away from; (*fig: capitali*) to flow out of

de'flusso SM (*della marea*) ebb

defor'mare /**72**/ VT (*alterare*) to put out of shape; (*corpo*) to deform; (*pensiero, fatto*) to distort; **deformarsi** VPR to lose its shape

deformazi'one [deformat'tsjone] SF (*Med*) deformation; **questa è ~ professionale!** that's force of habit because of your (*o his etc*) job!

de'forme AG deformed; disfigured

deformità SF INV deformity

defrau'dare /**72**/ VT: ~ **qn di qc** to defraud sb of sth, cheat sb out of sth

de'funto, -a AG late *cpd* ▶ SM/F deceased

degene'rare [dedʒene'rare] /**72**/ VI to degenerate

degenerazi'one [dedʒenerat'tsjone] SF degeneration

de'genere [de'dʒɛnere] AG degenerate

de'gente [de'dʒɛnte] SMF bedridden person; (*ricoverato in ospedale*) in-patient

de'genza [de'dʒɛntsa] SF confinement to bed; ~ **ospedaliera** period in hospital

'degli [deʎʎi] PREP + DET *vedi* **di**

deglu'tire /**55**/ VT to swallow

de'gnare [deɲ'ɲare] /**15**/ VT: ~ **qn della propria presenza** to honour sb with one's presence; **degnarsi** VPR: **degnarsi di fare qc** to deign *o* condescend to do sth; **non mi ha degnato di uno sguardo** he wouldn't even look at me

'degno, -a ['deɲɲo] AG dignified; ~ **di** worthy of; ~ **di lode** praiseworthy

degra'dare /**72**/ VT (*Mil*) to demote; (*privare della dignità*) to degrade; **degradarsi** VPR to demean o.s

de'grado SM: ~ **urbano** urban decline

degus'tare /**72**/ VT to sample, taste

degustazi'one [degustat'tsjone] SF sampling, tasting; ~ **di vini** (*locale*) specialist wine bar; ~ **di caffè** (*locale*) specialist coffee shop

'dei SMPL *di* **dio** ▶ PREP + DET *vedi* **di**

del PREP + DET *vedi* **di**

dela'tore, -'trice SM/F police informer

delazi'one [delat'tsjone] SF informing

'delega, -ghe SF (*procura*) proxy; **per ~ notarile** ≈ through a solicitor (*BRIT*) *o* lawyer

dele'gare /**80**/ VT to delegate

dele'gato SM delegate

delegazi'one [delegat'tsjone] SF delegation

delegherò *etc* [delege'rɔ] VB *vedi* **delegare**

dele'terio, -a AG damaging; (*per salute ecc*) harmful

del'fino SM (*Zool*) dolphin; (*Storia*) dauphin; (*fig*) probable successor

'Delhi ['dɛli] SF Delhi

de'libera SF decision

delibe'rare /**72**/ VT to come to a decision on ▶ VI (*Dir*): ~ (**su qc**) to rule (on sth)

delica'tezza [delika'tettsa] SF delicacy; frailty; thoughtfulness; tactfulness

deli'cato, -a AG delicate; (*salute*) delicate, frail; (*fig: gentile*) thoughtful, considerate; (: *che dimostra tatto*) tactful

delimi'tare /**72**/ VT (*anche fig*) to delimit

deline'are /**72**/ VT to outline; **delinearsi** VPR to be outlined; (*fig*) to emerge

delin'quente SMF criminal, delinquent; ~ **abituale** regular offender, habitual offender

delin'quenza [delin'kwɛntsa] SF criminality, delinquency; ~ **minorile** juvenile delinquency

de'liquio SM (*Med*) swoon; **cadere in** ~ to swoon

deli'rante AG (*Med*) delirious; (*fig: folla*) frenzied; (*: discorso, mente*) insane

deli'rare /**72**/ VI to be delirious, rave; (*fig*) to rave

de'lirio SM delirium; (*ragionamento insensato*) raving; (*fig*): **andare/mandare in** ~ to go/ send into a frenzy

de'litto SM crime; ~ **d'onore** *crime committed to avenge one's honour*

delittu'oso, -a AG criminal

de'lizia [de'littsja] SF delight

delizi'are [delit'tsjare] /**19**/ VT to delight; **deliziarsi** VPR: **deliziarsi di qc/a fare qc** to take delight in sth/in doing sth

delizi'oso, -a [delit'tsjoso] AG delightful; (*cibi*) delicious

dell', 'della, 'delle, 'dello PREP + DET *vedi* **di**

'delta SM INV delta

delta'plano SM hang-glider; **volo col** ~ hang-gliding

delucidazi'one [delutʃidat'tsjone] SF clarification *no pl*

delu'dente AG disappointing

de'ludere /**35**/ VT to disappoint

delusi'one SF disappointment

de'luso, -a PP *di* **deludere** ▶ AG disappointed

dema'gogico, -a, -ci, -che [dema'gɔdʒiko] AG popularity-seeking, demagogic

dema'gogo, -ghi SM demagogue

de'manio SM state property

de'mente AG (*Med*) demented, mentally deranged; (*fig*) crazy, mad

de'menza [de'mɛntsa] SF dementia; madness; ~ **senile** senile dementia

demenzi'ale [demen'tsjale] AG (*fig*) off-the-wall

'demmo VB *vedi* **dare**

demo'cratico, -a, -ci, -che AG democratic

democra'zia [demokrat'tsia] SF democracy; **la D~ Cristiana** the Christian Democrat Party

democristi'ano, -a AG, SM/F Christian Democrat

demogra'fia SF demography

demo'grafico, -a, -ci, -che AG demographic; **incremento** ~ increase in population

demo'lire /**55**/ VT to demolish

demolizi'one [demolit'tsjone] SF demolition

'demone SM demon

de'monio SM demon, devil; **il D~** the Devil

demoniz'zare [demonid'dzare] /**72**/ VT to make a monster of

demonizzazi'one [demoniddzat'tsjone] SF demonizing, demonization

demoraliz'zare [demoralid'dzare] /**72**/ VT to demoralize; **demoralizzarsi** VPR to become demoralized

de'mordere /**64**/ VI: **non** ~ (**da**) to refuse to give up

demoti'vare /**72**/ VT: ~ **qn** to take away sb's motivation

demoti'vato, -a AG unmotivated, lacking motivation

de'naro SM money; **denari** SMPL (*Carte*) suit in Neapolitan pack of cards

denatu'rato, -a AG *vedi* **alcool**

deni'grare /**72**/ VT to denigrate, run down

denomi'nare /**72**/ VT to name; **denominarsi** VPR to be named *o* called

denomina'tore SM (*Mat*) denominator

denominazi'one [denominat'tsjone] SF name; denomination; ~ **di origine controllata** *label guaranteeing the quality and origin of a wine*

deno'tare /**72**/ VT to denote, indicate

densità SF INV density; (*di nebbia*) thickness, denseness; **ad alta/bassa** ~ **di popolazione** densely/sparsely populated

'denso, -a AG thick, dense

den'tale AG dental

den'tario, -a AG dental

denta'tura SF set of teeth, teeth *pl*; (*Tecn: di ruota*) serration

'dente SM tooth; (*di forchetta*) prong; (*Geo: cima*) jagged peak; **al** ~ (*Cuc: pasta*) al dente; **mettere i denti** to teethe; **mettere qc sotto i denti** to have a bite to eat; **avere il** ~ **avvelenato contro** *o* **con qn** to bear sb a grudge; ~ **di leone** (*Bot*) dandelion; **denti del giudizio** wisdom teeth; **denti da latte** milk teeth

'dentice ['dɛntitʃe] SM (*Zool*) sea bream

denti'era SF (set of) false teeth *pl*

denti'fricio [denti'fritʃo] SM toothpaste

den'tista, -i, -e SM/F dentist

'dentro AV inside; (*in casa*) indoors; (*fig: nell'intimo*) inwardly ▶ PREP: ~ (**a**) in; **piegato in** ~ folded over; **qui/là** ~ in here/ there; ~ **di sé** (*pensare, brontolare*) to oneself; **tenere tutto** ~ to keep everything bottled up (inside o.s.); **darci** ~ (*fig: col*) to slog away, work hard

denucleariz'zato, -a [denuklearid'dzato] AG denuclearized, nuclear-free

denu'dare /**72**/ VT (*persona*) to strip; (*parte del corpo*) to bare; **denudarsi** VPR to strip

de'nuncia [de'nuntʃa] (*pl* **-ce** *o* **-cie**), **de'nunzia** [de'nuntsja] SF denunciation; declaration; **fare una** ~ *o* **sporgere** ~ **contro qn** (*Dir*) to report sb to the police; ~ **del reddito** (income) tax return

denunci'are [denun'tʃare] /**14**/, **denunzi'are** [denun'tsjare] VT to denounce; (*dichiarare*) to declare; ~ **qn/qc (alla polizia)** to report sb/ sth to the police

denu'trito, -a AG undernourished

denutrizi'one [denutrit'tsjone] SF
malnutrition

deodo'rante SM deodorant

deontolo'gia [deontolo'dʒia] SF (*professionale*)
professional code of conduct

depenalizzazi'one [depenaliddzat'tsjone]
SF decriminalization

dépen'dance [depã'dãs] SF INV outbuilding

depe'ribile AG perishable; **merce ~**
perishables *pl*, perishable goods *pl*

deperi'mento SM (*di persona*) wasting away;
(*di merci*) deterioration

depe'rire /**55**/ VI to waste away

depi'lare /**72**/ VT to depilate; **depilarsi** VPR:
depilarsi (le gambe) (*con rasoio*) to shave
(one's legs); (*con ceretta*) to wax (one's legs)

depila'torio, -a AG hair-removing *cpd*,
depilatory ▶ SM hair remover, depilatory

depilazi'one [depilat'tsjone] SF hair
removal, depilation

depis'taggio [depis'taddʒo] SM diversion

depis'tare /**72**/ VT to set on the wrong track

dépli'ant [depli'ã] SM INV leaflet; (*opuscolo*)
brochure

deplo'rare /**72**/ VT to deplore; to lament

deplo'revole AG deplorable

de'pone, de'pongo *etc* VB *vedi* **deporre**

de'porre /**77**/ VT (*depositare*) to put down;
(*rimuovere: da una carica*) to remove; (: *re*) to
depose; (*Dir*) to testify; **~ le armi** (*Mil*) to lay
down arms; **~ le uova** to lay eggs

depor'tare /**72**/ VT to deport

depor'tato, -a SM/F deportee

deportazi'one [deportat'tsjone] SF
deportation

de'posi *etc* VB *vedi* **deporre**

deposi'tante SM (*Comm*) depositor

deposi'tare /**72**/ VT (*gen, Geo, Econ*) to deposit;
(*lasciare*) to leave; (*merci*) to store; **depositarsi**
VPR (*sabbia, polvere*) to settle

deposi'tario SM (*Comm*) depository

de'posito SM deposit; (*luogo*) warehouse;
depot; (: *Mil*) depot; **~ bagagli** left-luggage
office; **~ di munizioni** ammunition dump

deposizi'one [depozit'tsjone] SF deposition;
(*da una carica*) removal; **rendere una falsa ~**
to perjure o.s.

de'posto, -a PP *di* **deporre**

depra'vare /**72**/ VT to corrupt, pervert

depra'vato, -a AG depraved ▶ SM/F
degenerate

depre'care /**20**/ VT to deprecate, deplore

depre'dare /**72**/ VT to rob, plunder

depressi'one SF depression; **area** *o* **zona di ~**
(*Meteor*) area of low pressure; (*Econ*)
depressed area

de'presso, -a PP *di* **deprimere** ▶ AG depressed

deprezza'mento [deprettsa'mento] SM
depreciation

deprez'zare [depret'tsare] /**72**/ VT (*Econ*) to
depreciate

depri'mente AG depressing

de'primere /**50**/ VT to depress

depu'rare /**72**/ VT to purify

depura'tore SM: **~ d'acqua** water purifier;
~ di gas scrubber

depu'tato, -a SM/F (*Pol*) deputy, ≈ Member of
Parliament (*BRIT*), ≈ Congressman(-woman)
(*US*); *vedi anche* **Camera dei Deputati**

deputazi'one [deputat'tsjone] SF
deputation; (*Pol*) position of deputy,
≈ parliamentary seat (*BRIT*), ≈ seat in
Congress (*US*)

deraglia'mento [deraʎʎa'mento] SM
derailment

deragli'are [deraʎ'ʎare] /**27**/ VI to be derailed;
far ~ to derail

dera'pare /**72**/ VI (*veicolo*) to skid; (*Sci*) to
sideslip

derattizzazi'one [derattiddzat'tsjone] SF
rodent control

deregolamen'tare /**72**/ VT to deregulate

deregolamentazi'one
[deregolamentat'tsjone] SF deregulation

dere'litto, -a AG derelict

dere'tano SM (*col*) bottom, buttocks *pl*

de'ridere /**89**/ VT to mock, deride

de'risi *etc* VB *vedi* **deridere**

derisi'one SF derision, mockery

de'riso, -a PP *di* **deridere**

deri'sorio, -a AG (*gesto, tono*) mocking

de'riva SF (*Naut, Aer*) drift; (*dispositivo: Aer*) fin;
(: *Naut*) centre-board (*BRIT*), centerboard (*US*);
andare alla ~ (*anche fig*) to drift

deri'vare /**72**/ VI: **~ da** to derive from ▶ VT to
derive; (*corso d'acqua*) to divert

deri'vato, -a AG derived ▶ SM (*Chim, Ling*)
derivative; (*prodotto*) by-product

derivazi'one [derivat'tsjone] SF derivation;
diversion

derma'tite SF dermatitis

dermatolo'gia [dermatolo'dʒia] SF
dermatology

derma'tologo, -a, -gi, -ghe SM/F
dermatologist

dermoprotet'tivo, -a AG (*crema, azione*)
protecting the skin

'deroga, -ghe SF (special) dispensation;
in ~ a as a (special) dispensation to

dero'gare /**80**/ VI: **~ a** (*Dir*) to repeal in part

der'rate SFPL commodities; **~ alimentari**
foodstuffs

deru'bare /**72**/ VT to rob

des'critto, -a PP *di* **descrivere**

des'crivere /**105**/ VT to describe

descrizi'one [deskrit'tsjone] SF description

de'serto, -a AG deserted ▶ SM (*Geo*) desert;
isola deserta desert island

deside'rabile AG desirable

deside'rare /72/ VT to want, wish for; (*sessualmente*) to desire; ~ **fare/che qn faccia** to want *o* wish to do/sb to do; **desidera fare una passeggiata?** would you like to go for a walk?; **farsi** ~ (*fare il prezioso*) to play hard to get; (*farsi aspettare*) to take one's time; **lascia molto a** ~ it leaves a lot to be desired

desi'derio SM wish; (*più intenso, carnale*) desire

deside'roso, -a AG: ~ **di** longing *o* eager for

desi'gnare [desiɲ'ɲare] /15/ VT to designate, appoint; (*data*) to fix; **la vittima designata** the intended victim

designazi'one [desiɲɲat'tsjone] SF designation, appointment

desi'nare /72/ VI to dine, have dinner ▸ SM dinner

desi'nenza [dezi'nɛntsa] SF (*Ling*) ending, inflexion

de'sistere /11/ VI: ~ **da** to give up, desist from

desis'tito, -a PP *di* **desistere**

deso'lante AG distressing

deso'lato, -a AG (*paesaggio*) desolate; (*persona: spiacente*) sorry

desolazi'one [dezolat'tsjone] SF desolation

'despota, -i SM despot

'dessi *etc* VB *vedi* **dare**

destabiliz'zare [destabilid'dzare] /72/ VT to destabilize

des'tare /72/ VT to wake (up); (*fig*) to awaken, arouse; **destarsi** VPR to wake (up)

'deste *etc* VB *vedi* **dare**

desti'nare /72/ VT to destine; (*assegnare*) to appoint, assign; (*indirizzare*) to address; ~ **qc a qn** to intend to give sth to sb, intend sb to have sth

destina'tario, -a SM/F (*di lettera*) addressee; (*di merce*) consignee; (*di mandato*) payee

destinazi'one [destinat'tsjone] SF destination; (*uso*) purpose

des'tino SM destiny, fate

destitu'ire /55/ VT to dismiss, remove

destituzi'one [destitut'tsjone] SF dismissal, removal

'desto, -a AG (wide) awake

'destra SF *vedi* **destro**

destreggi'arsi [destred'dʒarsi] /62/ VPR to manoeuvre (*Brit*), maneuver (*US*)

des'trezza [des'trettsa] SF skill, dexterity

'destro, -a AG right, right-hand; (*abile*) skilful (*Brit*), skillful (*US*), adroit ▸ SF (*mano*) right hand; (*parte*) right (side); (*Pol*): **la destra** the right ▸ SM (*Pugilato*) right; **a destra** (*essere*) on the right; (*andare*) to the right; **tenere la destra** to keep to the right

de'sumere /12/ VT (*dedurre*) to infer, deduce; (*trarre: informazioni*) to obtain

de'sunto, -a PP *di* **desumere**

detas'sare /72/ VT to remove the duty (*o* tax) from

dete'nere /121/ VT (*incarico, primato*) to hold; (*proprietà*) to have, possess; (*in prigione*) to detain, hold

de'tengo, de'tenni *etc* VB *vedi* **detenere**

deten'tivo, -a AG: **mandato** ~ imprisonment order; **pena detentiva** prison sentence

deten'tore, -'trice SM/F (*di titolo, primato ecc*) holder

dete'nuto, -a SM/F prisoner

detenzi'one [deten'tsjone] SF holding; possession; detention

deter'gente [deter'dʒɛnte] AG (*crema, latte*) cleansing ▸ SM cleanser

de'tergere [de'tɛrdʒere] /111/ VT (*gen*) to clean; (*pelle, viso*) to cleanse; (*sudore*) to wipe (away)

deteriora'mento SM: ~ (**di**) deterioration (in)

deterio'rare /72/ VT to damage; **deteriorarsi** VPR to deteriorate

deteri'ore AG (*merce*) second-rate; (*significato*) pejorative; (*tradizione letteraria*) lesser, minor

determi'nante AG decisive, determining

determi'nare /72/ VT to determine

determina'tivo, -a AG determining; **articolo** ~ (*Ling*) definite article

determi'nato, -a AG (*gen*) certain; (*particolare*) specific; (*risoluto*) determined, resolute

determinazi'one [determinat'tsjone] SF determination; (*decisione*) decision

deter'rente AG, SM deterrent

deter'rò *etc* VB *vedi* **detenere**

deter'sivo SM detergent; (*per bucato: in polvere*) washing powder (*Brit*), soap powder

de'terso, -a PP *di* **detergere**

detes'tare /72/ VT to detest, hate

deti'ene *etc* VB *vedi* **detenere**

deto'nare /72/ VI to detonate

detona'tore SM detonator

detonazi'one [detonat'tsjone] SF (*di esplosivo*) detonation, explosion; (*di arma*) bang; (*di motore*) pinking (*Brit*), knocking

de'trae, de'traggo *etc* VB *vedi* **detrarre**

de'trarre /123/ VT: ~ (**da**) to deduct (from), take away (from)

de'trassi *etc* VB *vedi* **detrarre**

de'tratto, -a PP *di* **detrarre**

detrazi'one [detrat'tsjone] SF deduction; ~ **d'imposta** tax allowance

detri'mento SM detriment, harm; **a** ~ **di** to the detriment of

de'trito SM (*Geo*) detritus

detroniz'zare [detronid'dzare] /72/ VT to dethrone

'detta SF: **a** ~ **di** according to

dettagli'ante [dettaʎ'ʎante] SMF (*Comm*) retailer

dettagli'are [dettaʎ'ʎare] /**27**/ VT to detail, give full details of

dettagliata'mente [dettaʎʎata'mente] AV in detail

det'taglio [det'taʎʎo] SM detail; (Comm): **il ~** retail; **al ~** (Comm) retail; separately

det'tame SM dictate, precept

det'tare /**72**/ VT to dictate; **~ legge** (fig) to lay down the law

det'tato SM dictation

detta'tura SF dictation

'detto, -a PP di **dire** ▶ AG (soprannominato) called, known as; (già nominato) above-mentioned ▶ SM saying; **~ fatto** no sooner said than done; **presto ~!** it's easier said than done!

detur'pare /**72**/ VT to disfigure; (moralmente) to sully

devas'tante AG (anche fig) devastating

devas'tare /**72**/ VT to devastate; (fig) to ravage

devastazi'one [devastat'tsjone] SF devastation, destruction

devi'are /**19**/ VI: **~ (da)** to turn off (from) ▶ VT to divert

devi'ato, -a AG (fig: persona, organizzazione) corrupt, bent (col)

deviazi'one [devjat'tsjone] SF (anche Aut) diversion; **fare una ~** to make a detour

'devo etc VB vedi **dovere**

devo'luto, -a PP di **devolvere**

devoluzi'one [devolut'tsjone] SF (Dir) devolution, transfer

de'volvere /**94**/ VT (Dir) to transfer, devolve; **~ qc in beneficenza** to give sth to charity

de'voto, -a AG (Rel) devout, pious; (affezionato) devoted

devozi'one [devot'tsjone] SF devoutness; (anche Rel) devotion

dezip'pare [dedzip'pare] /**72**/ VT (Inform) to unzip

dg ABBR (= decigrammo) dg

(**PAROLA CHIAVE**)

di (di + il = **del**, di + lo = **dello**, di + l' = **dell'**, di + la = **della**, di + i = **dei**, di + gli = **degli**, di + le = **delle**) PREP **1** (possesso, specificazione) of; (composto da, scritto da) by; **la macchina di Paolo/di mio fratello** Paolo's/my brother's car; **un amico di mio fratello** a friend of my brother's, one of my brother's friends; **la grandezza della casa** the size of the house; **le foto delle vacanze** the holiday photos; **la città di Firenze** the city of Florence; **il nome di Maria** the name Mary; **un quadro di Botticelli** a painting by Botticelli

2 (caratterizzazione, misura) of; **una casa di mattoni** a brick house, a house made of bricks; **un orologio d'oro** a gold watch; **un bimbo di 3 anni** a child of 3, a 3-year-old

child; **una trota di un chilo** a trout weighing a kilo; **una strada di 10 km** a road 10 km long; **un quadro di valore** a valuable picture

3 (causa, mezzo, modo) with; **tremare di paura** to tremble with fear; **morire di cancro** to die of cancer; **spalmare di burro** to spread with butter

4 (argomento) about, of; **discutere di sport** to talk about sport; **parlare di politica/lavoro** to talk about politics/work

5 (luogo: provenienza) from; **essere di Roma** to be from Rome; out of; **uscire di casa** to come out o leave the house

6 (tempo) in; **d'estate/d'inverno** in (the) summer/winter; **di notte** by night, at night; **di mattina/sera** in the morning/evening; **di lunedì** on Mondays; **di ora in ora** by the hour

7 (partitivo) of; **alcuni di voi/noi** some of you/us; **il più bravo di tutti** the best of all; **il migliore del mondo** the best in the world; **non c'è niente di peggio** there's nothing worse

8 (paragone) than; **più veloce di me** faster than me; **guadagna meno di me** he earns less than me

▶ DET (una certa quantità di) some; (: negativo) any; (: interrogativo) any; some; **del pane** (some) bread; **delle caramelle** (some) sweets; **degli amici miei** some friends of mine; **vuoi del vino?** do you want some o any wine?

dì SM day; **buon dì!** hallo!; **a dì = addì**

DIA SIGLA F = **Direzione investigativa antimafia**

dia'bete SM diabetes sg

dia'betico, -a, -ci, -che AG, SM/F diabetic

dia'bolico, -a, -ci, -che AG diabolical

di'acono SM (Rel) deacon

dia'dema, -i SM diadem; (di donna) tiara

di'afano, -a AG (trasparente) diaphanous; (pelle) transparent

dia'framma, -i SM (divisione) screen; (Anat, Fot: contraccettivo) diaphragm

di'agnosi [di'aɲɲozi] SF diagnosis sg

diagnosti'care [diaɲɲosti'kare] /**20**/ VT to diagnose

dia'gnostico, -a, -ci, -che [diaɲ'ɲɔstiko] AG diagnostic; **aiuti diagnostici** (Inform) debugging aids

diago'nale AG, SF diagonal

dia'gramma, -i SM diagram; **~ a barre** bar chart; **~ di flusso** flow chart

dialet'tale AG dialectal; **poesia ~** poetry in dialect

dia'letto SM dialect

di'alisi SF dialysis sg

dialo'gante AG: **unità ~** (*Inform*) interactive terminal

dialo'gare /**8o**/ VI: **~ (con)** to have a dialogue (with); (*conversare*) to converse (with) ▶ VT (*scena*) to write the dialogue for

di'alogo, -ghi SM dialogue

dia'mante SM diamond

di'ametro SM diameter

di'amine ESCL: **che ~ ...?** what on earth ...?

diapo'rama [djapo'rama] SM INV slide show

diaposi'tiva SF transparency, slide

di'aria SF daily (expense) allowance

di'ario SM diary; **~ di bordo** (*Naut*) log(book); **~ di classe** (*Ins*) class register; **~ degli esami** (*Ins*) exam timetable

diar'rea SF diarrhoea

dia'triba SF diatribe

diavole'ria SF (*azione*) act of mischief; (*aggeggio*) weird contraption

di'avolo SM devil; **è un buon ~** he's a good sort; **avere un ~ per capello** to be in a foul temper; **avere una fame/un freddo del ~** to be ravenously hungry/frozen stiff; **mandare qn al ~** (*col*) to tell sb to go to hell; **fare il ~ a quattro** to kick up a fuss

di'battere /**1**/ VT to debate, discuss; **dibattersi** VPR to struggle

dibatti'mento SM (*dibattito*) debate, discussion; (*Dir*) hearing

di'battito SM debate, discussion

dic. ABBR (= *dicembre*) Dec

dicas'tero SM ministry

'dice ['ditʃe] VB *vedi* **dire**

di'cembre [di'tʃembre] SM December; *vedi anche* **luglio**

dice'ria [ditʃe'ria] SF rumour (*Brit*), rumor (*US*), piece of gossip

dichia'rare [dikja'rare] /**72**/ VT to declare; **dichiararsi** VPR to declare o.s.; (*innamorato*) to declare one's love; **si dichiara che ...** it is hereby declared that ...; **dichiararsi vinto** to admit defeat

dichia'rato, -a [dikja'rato] AG (*nemico, ateo*) avowed

dichiarazi'one [dikjarat'tsjone] SF declaration; **~ dei redditi** statement of income; (*modulo*) tax return

dician'nove [ditʃan'nove] NUM nineteen

dicianno'venne [ditʃanno'vɛnne] AG, SMF nineteen-year-old

dicias'sette [ditʃas'sɛtte] NUM seventeen

diciasset'tenne [ditʃasset'tɛnne] AG, SMF seventeen-year-old

diciot'tenne [ditʃot'tɛnne] AG, SMF eighteen-year-old

dici'otto [di'tʃotto] NUM eighteen ▶ SM INV (*Ins*) *minimum satisfactory mark awarded in Italian universities*

dici'tura [ditʃi'tura] SF words *pl*, wording

'dico *etc* VB *vedi* **dire**

didasca'lia SF (*di illustrazione*) caption; (*Cine*) subtitle; (*Teat*) stage directions *pl*

di'dattico, -a, -ci, -che AG didactic; (*metodo, programma*) teaching; (*libro*) educational ▶ SF didactics *sg*; teaching methodology

di'dentro AV inside, indoors

didi'etro AV behind ▶ AG INV (*ruota, giardino*) back, rear *cpd* ▶ SM (*di casa*) rear; (*col: sedere*) backside

di'eci ['djɛtʃi] NUM ten

dieci'mila [djɛtʃi'mila] NUM ten thousand

die'cina [dje'tʃina] SF = **decina**

di'edi *etc* VB *vedi* **dare**

di'eresi SF dieresis *sg*

'diesel ['di:zəl] SM INV diesel engine

dies'sino, -a AG (*Pol*) of o belonging to the Democrats of the Left (*Italian left-wing party*) ▶ SM/F *member of the DS political party*

di'eta SF diet; **essere a ~** to be on a diet

die'tetica SF dietetics *sg*

die'tologo, -a, -gi, -ghe SM/F dietician

di'etro AV behind; (*in fondo*) at the back ▶ PREP behind; (*tempo: dopo*) after ▶ SM (*di foglio, giacca*) back; (*di casa*) back, rear ▶ AG INV back *cpd*; **le zampe di ~** the hind legs; **~ ricevuta** against receipt; **~ richiesta** on demand; (*scritta*) on application; **andare ~ a** (*anche fig*) to follow; **stare ~ a qn** (*sorvegliare*) to keep an eye on sb; (*corteggiare*) to hang around sb; **portarsi ~ qn/qc** to bring sb/sth with one, bring sb/sth along; **gli hanno riso/parlato ~** they laughed at/talked about him behind his back

di'etro 'front ESCL about turn! (*Brit*), about face! (*US*) ▶ SM (*Mil*) about-turn, about-face; (*fig*) volte-face, about-turn, about-face; **fare ~** (*Mil, fig*) to about-turn, about-face; (*tornare indietro*) to turn round

di'fatti CONG in fact, as a matter of fact

di'fendere /**36**/ VT to defend; **difendersi** VPR (*cavarsela*) to get by; **difendersi da/contro** to defend o.s. from/against; **difendersi dal freddo** to protect o.s. from the cold; **sapersi ~** to know how to look after o.s.

difen'sivo, -a AG defensive ▶ SF: **stare sulla difensiva** (*anche fig*) to be on the defensive

difen'sore, -a SM/F defender; **avvocato ~** counsel for the defence (*Brit*) o defense (*US*)

di'fesa SF *vedi* **difeso**

di'fesi *etc* VB *vedi* **difendere**

di'feso, -a PP *di* **difendere** ▶ SF defence (*Brit*), defense (*US*); **prendere le difese di qn** to defend sb, take sb's part

difet'tare /**72**/ VI to be defective; **~ di** to be lacking in, lack

difet'tivo, -a AG defective

di'fetto SM (*mancanza*): **~ di** lack of; shortage of; (*di fabbricazione*) fault, flaw, defect; (*morale*)

fault, failing, defect; (*fisico*) defect; **far ~ to**
be lacking; **in ~** at fault; in the wrong
difet'toso, -a AG defective, faulty
diffa'mare /**72**/ VT (*a parole*) to slander; (*per
iscritto*) to libel
diffama'torio, -a AG slanderous; libellous
diffamazi'one [diffamat'tsjone] SF slander;
libel
diffe'rente AG different
diffe'renza [diffe'rɛntsa] SF difference;
a ~ di unlike; **non fare ~ (tra)** to make no
distinction (between)
differenzi'ale [differen'tsjale] AG, SM
differential; **classi differenziali** (*Ins*)
special classes (*for backward children*)
differenzi'are [differen'tsjare] /**19**/ VT to
differentiate; **differenziarsi da** to
differentiate o.s. from; to differ from
diffe'rire /**55**/ VT to postpone, defer ▶ VI to be
different
diffe'rita SF: **in ~** (*trasmettere*) prerecorded
diffi'cile [dif'fitʃile] AG difficult; (*persona*)
hard to please, difficult (to please); (*poco
probabile*): **è ~ che sia libero** it is unlikely that
he'll be free ▶ SMF: **fare il(la) ~** to be
difficult, be awkward ▶ SM difficult part;
difficulty; **essere ~ nel mangiare** to be
fussy about one's food
difficil'mente [diffitʃil'mente] AV (*con
difficoltà*) with difficulty; **~ verrà** he's
unlikely to come
difficoltà SF INV difficulty
difficol'toso, -a AG (*compito*) difficult, hard;
(*persona*) difficult, hard to please; **digestione
difficoltosa** poor digestion
dif'fida SF (*Dir*) warning, notice
diffi'dare /**72**/ VI: **~ di** to be suspicious *o*
distrustful of ▶ VT (*Dir*) to warn; **~ qn dal
fare qc** to warn sb not to do sth, caution sb
against doing sth
diffi'dente AG suspicious, distrustful
diffi'denza [diffi'dɛntsa] SF suspicion,
distrust
dif'fondere /**25**/ VT (*luce, calore*) to diffuse;
(*notizie*) to spread, circulate; **diffondersi** VPR
to spread
dif'fusi *etc* VB *vedi* **diffondere**
diffusi'one SF diffusion; spread; (*anche di
giornale*) circulation; (*Fisica*) scattering
dif'fuso, -a PP *di* **diffondere** ▶ AG (*Fisica*)
diffuse; (*fenomeno, notizia, malattia ecc*)
widespread; **è opinione diffusa che ...** it's
widely held that ....
difi'lato AV (*direttamente*) straight, directly;
(*subito*) straight away
difte'rite SF diphtheria
'**diga, -ghe** SF dam; (*portuale*) breakwater
dige'rente [didʒe'rɛnte] AG (*apparato*)
digestive

dige'rire [didʒe'rire] /**55**/ VT to digest
digesti'one [didʒes'tjone] SF digestion
diges'tivo, -a [didʒes'tivo] AG digestive
▶ SM (after-dinner) liqueur
Digi'one [di'dʒone] SF Dijon
digi'tale [didʒi'tale] AG digital; (*delle dita*)
finger *cpd*, digital ▶ SF (*Bot*) foxglove
digi'tare [didʒi'tare] /**72**/ VT (*dati*) to key (in);
(*tasto*) to press
digiu'nare [didʒu'nare] /**72**/ VI to starve o.s.;
(*Rel*) to fast
digi'uno, -a [di'dʒuno] AG: **essere ~** not to
have eaten ▶ SM fast; **a ~** on an empty
stomach
dignità [diɲɲi'ta] SF INV dignity
digni'tario [diɲɲi'tarjo] SM dignitary
digni'toso, -a [diɲɲi'toso] AG dignified
'**DIGOS** SIGLA F (= *Divisione Investigazioni Generali
e Operazioni Speciali*) police department dealing
with political security
digressi'one SF digression
digri'gnare [digriɲ'ɲare] /**15**/ VT: **~ i denti**
to grind one's teeth
dila'gare /**80**/ VI to flood; (*fig*) to spread
dilani'are /**19**/ VT to tear to pieces
dilapi'dare /**72**/ VT to squander, waste
dila'tare /**72**/ VT to dilate; (*gas*) to cause to
expand; (*passaggio, cavità*) to open (up);
dilatarsi VPR to dilate; (*Fisica*) to expand
dilatazi'one [dilatat'tsjone] SF (*Anat*)
dilation; (*di gas, metallo*) expansion
dilazio'nare [dilattsjo'nare] /**72**/ VT to delay,
defer
dilazi'one [dilat'tsjone] SF deferment
dileggi'are [diled'dʒare] /**62**/ VT to mock,
deride
dilegu'are /**72**/ VI, **dilegu'arsi** VPR to vanish,
disappear
di'lemma, -i SM dilemma
dilet'tante SMF dilettante; (*anche Sport*)
amateur
dilet'tare /**72**/ VT to give pleasure to, delight;
dilettarsi VPR: **dilettarsi di** to take pleasure
in, enjoy
dilet'tevole AG delightful
di'letto, -a AG dear, beloved ▶ SM pleasure,
delight
dili'gente [dili'dʒente] AG (*scrupoloso*) diligent;
(*accurato*) careful, accurate
dili'genza [dili'dʒentsa] SF diligence; care;
(*carrozza*) stagecoach
dilu'ire /**55**/ VT to dilute
dilun'garsi /**80**/ VPR (*fig*): **~ su** to talk at length
on *o* about
diluvi'are /**19**/ VB IMPERS to pour (down)
di'luvio SM downpour; (*inondazione, fig*) flood;
il ~ universale the Flood
dima'grante AG slimming *cpd*
dima'grire /**55**/ VI to get thinner, lose weight

dime'nare /**72**/ ᴠᴛ to wave, shake; **dimenarsi** ᴠᴘʀ to toss and turn; (*fig*) to struggle; **~ la coda** (*cane*) to wag its tail

dimensi'one sғ dimension; (*grandezza*) size; **considerare un discorso nella sua ~ politica** to look at a speech in terms of its political significance

dimenti'canza [dimenti'kantsa] sғ forgetfulness; (*errore*) oversight, slip; **per ~** inadvertently

dimenti'care /**20**/ ᴠᴛ to forget; **dimenticarsi** ᴠᴘʀ: **dimenticarsi di qc** to forget sth

dimentica'toio sᴍ (*scherzoso*): **cadere/ mettere nel ~** to sink into/consign to oblivion

di'mentico, -a, -chi, -che ᴀɢ: **~ di** (*che non ricorda*) forgetful of; (*incurante*) oblivious of, unmindful of

di'messo, -a ᴘᴘ *di* **dimettere** ▶ ᴀɢ (*voce*) subdued; (*uomo, abito*) modest, humble

dimesti'chezza [dimesti'kettsa] sғ familiarity

di'mettere /**63**/ ᴠᴛ: **~ qn da** to dismiss sb from; (*dall'ospedale*) to discharge sb from; **dimettersi** ᴠᴘʀ: **dimettersi (da)** to resign (from)

dimez'zare [dimed'dzare] /**72**/ ᴠᴛ to halve

diminu'ire /**55**/ ᴠᴛ to reduce, diminish; (*prezzi*) to bring down, reduce ▶ ᴠɪ to decrease, diminish; (*rumore*) to die down, die away; (*prezzi*) to fall, go down

diminu'tivo, -a ᴀɢ, sᴍ diminutive

diminuzi'one [diminut'tsjone] sғ decreasing, diminishing; **in ~** on the decrease; **~ della produttività** fall in productivity

di'misi *etc* ᴠʙ *vedi* **dimettere**

dimissio'nario, -a ᴀɢ outgoing, resigning

dimissi'oni sғᴘʟ resignation *sg*; **dare** *o* **presentare le ~** to resign, hand in one's resignation

di'mora sғ residence; **senza fissa ~** of no fixed address *o* abode

dimo'rare /**72**/ ᴠɪ to reside

dimos'trante sᴍғ (*Pol*) demonstrator

dimos'trare /**72**/ ᴠᴛ to demonstrate, show; (*provare*) to prove, demonstrate; **dimostrarsi** ᴠᴘʀ: **dimostrarsi molto abile** to show o.s. *o* prove to be very clever; **non dimostra la sua età** he doesn't look his age; **dimostra 30 anni** he looks about 30 (years old)

dimostra'tivo, -a ᴀɢ (*anche Ling*) demonstrative

dimostrazi'one [dimostrat'tsjone] sғ demonstration; proof

di'namico, -a, -ci, -che ᴀɢ dynamic ▶ sғ dynamics *sg*

dina'mismo sᴍ dynamism

dinami'tardo, -a ᴀɢ: **attentato ~** dynamite attack ▶ sᴍ/ғ dynamiter

dina'mite sғ dynamite

'dinamo sғ ɪɴᴠ dynamo

di'nanzi [di'nantsi]: **~ a** *prep* in front of

dinas'tia sғ dynasty

dini'ego, -ghi sᴍ (*rifiuto*) refusal; (*negazione*) denial

dinocco'lato, -a ᴀɢ lanky; **camminare ~** to walk with a slouch

dino'sauro sᴍ dinosaur

din'torno ᴀᴠ round, (round) about; **dintorni** sᴍᴘʟ outskirts; **nei dintorni di** in the vicinity *o* neighbourhood of

'dio (*pl* **dei**) sᴍ god; **D~** God; **gli dei** the gods; **si crede un ~** he thinks he's wonderful; **D~ mio!** my God!; **D~ ce la mandi buona** let's hope for the best; **D~ ce ne scampi e liberi!** God forbid!

di'ocesi [di'ɔtʃezi] sғ ɪɴᴠ diocese

dios'sina sғ dioxin

dipa'nare /**72**/ ᴠᴛ (*lana*) to wind into a ball; (*fig*) to disentangle, sort out

diparti'mento sᴍ department

dipen'dente ᴀɢ dependent ▶ sᴍғ employee; **~ statale** state employee

dipen'denza [dipen'dɛntsa] sғ dependence; **essere alle dipendenze di qn** to be employed by sb *o* in sb's employ

di'pendere /**8**/ ᴠɪ: **~ da** to depend on; (*finanziariamente*) to be dependent on; (*derivare*) to come from, be due to

di'pesi *etc* ᴠʙ *vedi* **dipendere**

di'peso, -a ᴘᴘ *di* **dipendere**

di'pingere [di'pindʒere] /**37**/ ᴠᴛ to paint

di'pinsi *etc* ᴠʙ *vedi* **dipingere**

di'pinto, -a ᴘᴘ *di* **dipingere** ▶ sᴍ painting

di'ploma, -i sᴍ diploma

diplo'mare /**72**/ ᴠᴛ to award a diploma to, graduate (*US*) ▶ ᴠɪ to obtain a diploma, graduate (*US*)

diplo'matico, -a, -ci, -che ᴀɢ diplomatic ▶ sᴍ diplomat

diplo'mato, -a ᴀɢ qualified ▶ sᴍ/ғ qualified person, holder of a diploma

diploma'zia [diplomat'tsia] sғ diplomacy

di'porto sᴍ: **imbarcazione da ~** pleasure craft

dira'dare /**72**/ ᴠᴛ to thin (out); (*visite*) to reduce, make less frequent; **diradarsi** ᴠᴘʀ to disperse; (*nebbia*) to clear (up)

dira'mare /**72**/ ᴠᴛ to issue ▶ ᴠɪ (*strade: anche*: **diramarsi**) to branch

'dire /**38**/ ᴠᴛ to say; (*segreto, fatto*) to tell; **~ qc a qn** to tell sb sth; **~ qn di fare qc** to tell sb to do sth; **~ di sì/no** to say yes/no; **si dice che ...** they say that ...; **mi si dice che ...** I am told that ...; **si direbbe che ...** it looks (*o* sounds) as though ...; **dica, signora?**

(in un negozio) yes, Madam, can I help you?; **sa quello che dice** he knows what he's talking about; **lascialo ~** *(esprimersi)* let him have his say; *(ignoralo)* just ignore him; **come sarebbe a ~?** what do you mean?; **che ne diresti di andarcene?** how about leaving?; **chi l'avrebbe mai detto!** who would have thought it!; **si dicono esperti** they say they are experts; **per così ~** so to speak; **a dir poco** to say the least; **non c'è che ~** there's no doubt about it; **non dico di no** I can't deny it; **il che è tutto ~** need I say more?

di'ressi *etc* VB *vedi* **dirigere**

di'retta SF: **in ~** *(trasmettere)* live; **un incontro di calcio in ~** a live football match; *vedi* **diretto**

diretta'mente AV *(immediatamente)* directly, straight; *(personalmente)* directly; *(senza intermediari)* direct, straight

diret'tissima SF *(tragitto)* most direct route; *(Dir)*: **processo per ~** summary trial

diret'tissimo SM *(Ferr)* fast (through) train

diret'tivo, -a AG *(Pol, Amm)* executive; *(Comm)* managerial, executive ▶ SM leadership, leaders *pl* ▶ SF directive, instruction

di'retto, -a PP *di* **dirigere** ▶ AG direct ▶ SM *(Ferr)* through train ▶ SF: **in (linea) diretta** *(Radio, TV)* live; **il mio ~ superiore** my immediate superior

diret'tore, -'trice SM/F *(di azienda)* director, manager (manageress); *(di scuola elementare)* head (teacher) *(BRIT)*, principal *(US)*; **~ amministrativo** company secretary *(BRIT)*, corporate executive secretary *(US)*; **~ del carcere** prison governor *(BRIT)* o warden *(US)*; **~ di filiale** branch manager; **~ d'orchestra** conductor; **~ di produzione** *(Cine)* producer; **~ sportivo** team manager; **~ tecnico** *(Sport)* trainer, coach; **~ vendite** sales director o manager

direzi'one [diret'tsjone] SF board of directors; management; *(senso: anche fig)* direction; *(conduzione: gen)* running; *(: di partito)* leadership; *(: di società)* management; *(: di giornale)* editorship; *(direttori)* management; **in ~ di** in the direction of, towards

diri'gente [diri'dʒente] AG managerial ▶ SMF executive; *(Pol)* leader ▶ AG: **classe ~** ruling class

diri'genza [diri'dʒentsa] SF management; *(Pol)* leadership

dirigenzi'ale [diridʒen'tsjale] AG managerial

di'rigere [di'ridʒere] /**39**/ VT to direct; *(impresa)* to run, manage; *(Mus)* to conduct; **dirigersi** VPR: **dirigersi verso** o **a** to make o head for; **~ i propri passi verso** to make one's way towards; **il treno era diretto a Pavia** the train was heading for Pavia

diri'gibile [diri'dʒibile] SM airship

dirim'petto AV opposite; **~ a** *prep* opposite, facing

di'ritto, -a AG straight; *(onesto)* straight, upright ▶ AV straight, directly ▶ SM right side; *(Tennis)* forehand; *(Maglia)* plain stitch, knit stitch; *(prerogativa)* right; *(leggi, scienza)*: **il ~** law; **diritti** SMPL *(tasse)* duty *sg*; **stare ~** to stand up straight; **aver ~ a qc** to be entitled to sth; **punto ~** plain (stitch); **andare ~** to go straight on; **a buon ~** quite rightly; **diritti (d'autore)** royalties; **~ di successione** right of succession

dirit'tura SF *(Sport)* straight; *(fig)* rectitude

diroc'cato, -a AG tumbledown, in ruins

dirom'pente AG *(anche fig)* explosive

dirotta'mento SM: **~ (aereo)** hijack

dirot'tare /**72**/ VT *(nave, aereo)* to change the course of; *(aereo: sotto minaccia)* to hijack; *(traffico)* to divert ▶ VI *(nave, aereo)* to change course

dirotta'tore, -'trice SM/F hijacker

di'rotto, -a AG *(pioggia)* torrential; *(pianto)* unrestrained; **piovere a ~** to pour, rain cats and dogs; **piangere a ~** to cry one's heart out

di'rupo SM crag, precipice

di'sabile SMF disabled person ▶ AG disabled; **i disabili** the disabled

disabi'tato, -a AG uninhabited

disabitu'arsi /**72**/ VPR: **~ a** to get out of the habit of

disac'cordo SM disagreement

disadat'tato, -a AG *(Psic)* maladjusted

disa'dorno, -a AG plain, unadorned

disaffezi'one [dizaffet'tsjone] SF disaffection

disa'gevole [disa'dʒevole] AG *(scomodo)* uncomfortable; *(difficile)* difficult

disagi'ato, -a [diza'dʒato] AG poor, needy; *(vita)* hard

di'sagio [di'zadʒo] SM discomfort; *(disturbo)* inconvenience; *(fig: imbarazzo)* embarrassment; **disagi** SMPL hardship *sg*, poverty *sg*; **essere a ~** to be ill at ease

di'samina SF close examination

disappro'vare /**72**/ VT to disapprove of

disapprovazi'one [dizapprovat'tsjone] SF disapproval

disap'punto SM disappointment

disarcio'nare [dizartʃo'nare] /**72**/ VT to unhorse

disar'mante AG *(fig)* disarming

disar'mare /**72**/ VT, VI to disarm

di'sarmo SM *(Mil)* disarmament

di'sastro SM disaster

disas'troso, -a AG disastrous

disat'tento, -a AG inattentive

disattenzi'one [dizatten'tsjone] SF carelessness, lack of attention

disatti'vare /**72**/ VT (*bomba*) to de-activate, defuse

disa'vanzo [diza'vantso] SM (*Econ*) deficit

disavven'tura SF misadventure, mishap

dis'brigo, -ghi SM (prompt) clearing up o settlement

dis'capito SM: **a ~ di** to the detriment of

dis'carica, -che SF (*di rifiuti*) rubbish tip o dump

discen'dente [diʃʃen'dɛnte] AG descending ▶ SMF descendant

di'scendere [diʃʃɛndere] /**101**/ VT to go (o come) down ▶ VI to go (o come) down; (*strada*) to go down; (*smontare*) to get off; **~ da** (*famiglia*) to be descended from; **~ dalla macchina/dal treno** to get out of the car/ out of o off the train; **~ da cavallo** to dismount, get off one's horse

di'scepolo, -a [diʃʃepolo] SM/F disciple

di'scernere [diʃʃernere] /**29**/ VT to discern

discerni'mento [diʃʃerni'mento] SM discernment

di'scesa [diʃʃesa] SF descent; (*pendio*) slope; **in ~** (*strada*) downhill *cpd*, sloping; **~ libera** (*Sci*) downhill (race)

disce'sista [diʃʃe'sista] SMF downhill skier

di'sceso, -a [diʃʃeso] PP di **discendere** ▶ SF descent; (*pendio*) slope; **in discesa** (*strada*) downhill *cpd*, sloping; **discesa libera** (*Sci*) downhill race

dischi'udere [dis'kjudere] /**22**/ VT (*aprire*) to open; (*fig: rivelare*) to disclose, reveal

dischi'usi *etc* [dis'kjusi] VB *vedi* **dischiudere**

dischi'uso, -a [dis'kjuso] PP di **dischiudere**

di'scinto, -a [diʃʃinto] AG (*anche*: **in abiti discinti**) half-undressed

disci'ogliere [diʃʃɔʎʎere] /**103**/ VT, **disci'ogliersi** VPR to dissolve; (*fondere*) to melt

disci'plina [diʃʃi'plina] SF discipline

discipli'nare [diʃʃipli'nare] /**72**/ AG disciplinary ▶ VT to discipline

'disco, -schi SM disc, disk; (*Sport*) discus; (*fonografico*) record; (*Inform*) disk; **~ magnetico** (*Inform*) magnetic disk; **~ orario** (*Aut*) parking disc; **~ rigido** (*Inform*) hard disk; **~ volante** flying saucer

discogra'fia SF (*tecnica*) recording, record-making; (*industria*) record industry

disco'grafico, -a, -ci, -che AG record *cpd*, recording *cpd* ▶ SM record producer; **casa discografica** record(ing) company

'discolo, -a AG (*bambino*) undisciplined, unruly ▶ SM/F rascal

discol'pare /**72**/ VT to clear of blame; **discolparsi** VPR to clear o.s., prove one's innocence; (*giustificarsi*) to excuse o.s.

disco'noscere [disko'noʃʃere] /**26**/ VT (*figlio*) to disown; (*meriti*) to ignore, disregard

disconosci'uto, -a [diskonoʃʃuto] PP di **disconoscere**

discon'tinuo, -a AG (*linea*) broken; (*rendimento, stile*) irregular; (*interesse*) sporadic

dis'corde AG conflicting, clashing

dis'cordia SF discord; (*dissidio*) disagreement, clash

dis'correre /**28**/ VI: **~ (di)** to talk (about)

dis'corso, -a PP di **discorrere** ▶ SM speech; (*conversazione*) conversation, talk

dis'costo, -a AG faraway, distant ▶ AV far away; **~ da** *prep* far from

disco'teca, -che SF (*raccolta*) record library; (*luogo di ballo*) disco(theque)

dis'count [dis'kaunt] SM INV (*supermercato*) cut-price supermarket

discre'panza [diskre'pantsa] SF discrepancy

dis'creto, -a AG discreet; (*abbastanza buono*) reasonable, fair

discrezi'one [diskret'tsjone] SF discretion; (*giudizio*) judgment, discernment; **a ~ di** at the discretion of

discrimi'nante AG (*fattore, elemento*) decisive ▶ SF (*Dir*) extenuating circumstance

discrimi'nare /**72**/ VT to discrimate

discriminazi'one [diskriminat'tsjone] SF discrimination

dis'cussi *etc* VB *vedi* **discutere**

discussi'one SF discussion; (*litigio*) argument; **mettere in ~** to bring into question; **fuori ~** out of the question

dis'cusso, -a PP di **discutere**

dis'cutere /**40**/ VT to discuss, debate; (*contestare*) to question, dispute ▶ VI (*litigare*) to argue; (*conversare*): **~ (di)** to discuss

discu'tibile AG questionable

disde'gnare [dizdeɲ'ɲare] /**15**/ VT to scorn

dis'degno [diz'deɲɲo] SM scorn, disdain

disde'gnoso, -a [dizdeɲ'ɲoso] AG disdainful, scornful

dis'detto, -a PP di **disdire** ▶ SF (*di prenotazione ecc*) cancellation; (*sfortuna*) bad luck

disdi'cevole [dizdi'tʃevole] AG improper, unseemly

dis'dire /**38**/ VT (*prenotazione*) to cancel; **~ un contratto d'affitto** (*Dir*) to give notice (to quit)

dise'gnare [diseɲ'ɲare] /**15**/ VT to draw; (*progettare*) to design; (*fig*) to outline

disegna'tore, -'trice [diseɲɲa'tore] SM/F designer

di'segno [di'zeɲɲo] SM drawing; (*su stoffa ecc*) design; (*fig: schema*) outline; **~ industriale** industrial design; **~ di legge** (*Dir*) bill

diser'bante SM weedkiller

disere'dare /**72**/ VT to disinherit

diser'tare /**72**/ VT, VI to desert

diser'tore SM (*Mil*) deserter

diserzi'one [dizer'tsjone] SF (*Mil*) desertion

disfaci'mento [disfatʃi'mento] SM (*di cadavere*) decay; (*fig: di istituzione, impero, società*) decline, decay; **in ~** in decay

dis'fare /41/ VT to undo; (*valigie*) to unpack; (*meccanismo*) to take to pieces; (*lavoro, paese*) to destroy; (*neve*) to melt; **disfarsi** VPR to come undone; (*neve*) to melt; **~ il letto** to strip the bed; **disfarsi di qn** (*liberarsi*) to get rid of sb

dis'fatta SF *vedi* **disfatto**

disfat'tista, -i, -e SM/F defeatist

dis'fatto, -a PP *di* **disfare ▸** AG (*gen*) undone, untied; (*letto*) unmade; (*persona: sfinito*) exhausted, worn-out; (: *addolorato*) grief-stricken **▸** SF (*sconfitta*) rout

disfunzi'one [disfun'tsjone] SF (*Med*) dysfunction; **~ cardiaca** heart trouble

disge'lare [dizdʒe'lare] /72/ VT, VI, **disge'larsi** VPR to thaw

dis'gelo [diz'dʒɛlo] SM thaw

dis'grazia [diz'grattsja] SF (*sventura*) misfortune; (*incidente*) accident, mishap

disgrazi'ato, -a [dizgrat'sjato] AG unfortunate **▸** SM/F wretch

disgre'gare /80/ VT, **disgre'garsi** VPR to break up

disgu'ido SM hitch; **~ postale** error in postal delivery

disgus'tare /72/ VT to disgust; **disgustarsi** VPR: **disgustarsi di** to be disgusted by

dis'gusto SM disgust

disgus'toso, -a AG disgusting

disidra'tare /72/ VT to dehydrate

disidra'tato, -a AG dehydrated

disil'ludere /35/ VT to disillusion, disenchant

disillusi'one SF disillusion, disenchantment

disimpa'rare /72/ VT to forget

disimpe'gnare [dizimpeɲ'ɲare] /15/ VT (*oggetto dato in pegno*) to redeem, get out of pawn; **~ da** (*persona: da obblighi*) to release from; **disimpegnarsi** VPR: **disimpegnarsi da** (*obblighi*) to release o.s. from, free o.s. from

disincagli'are [dizinkaʎ'ʎare] /27/ VT (*barca*) to refloat; **disincagliarsi** VPR to get afloat again

disincan'tato, -a AG disenchanted, disillusioned

disincenti'vare [dizintʃenti'vare] /72/ VT to discourage

disinfes'tare /72/ VT to disinfest

disinfestazi'one [dizinfestat'tsjone] SF disinfestation

disinfet'tante AG, SM disinfectant

disinfet'tare /72/ VT to disinfect

disinfezi'one [dizinfet'tsjone] SF disinfection

disingan'nare /72/ VT to disillusion

disin'ganno SM disillusion

disini'bito, -a AG uninhibited

disinnes'care /20/ VT to defuse

disinnes'tare /72/ VT (*marcia*) to disengage

disinqui'nare /72/ VT to free from pollution

disinstal'lare /72/ VT (*software*) to uninstall

disinte'grare /72/ VT, VI to disintegrate; **disintegrarsi** VPR to disintegrate

disinteres'sarsi /72/ VPR: **~ di** to take no interest in

disinte'resse SM indifference; (*generosità*) unselfishness

disintossi'care /20/ VT (*alcolizzato, drogato*) to treat for alcoholism (*o* drug addiction); **disintossicarsi** VPR to clear out one's system; (*alcolizzato, drogato*) to be treated for alcoholism (*o* drug addiction)

disintossicazi'one [dizintossikat'tsjone] SF treatment for alcoholism (*o* drug addiction)

disin'volto, -a AG casual, free and easy

disinvol'tura SF casualness, ease

disles'sia SF dyslexia

disli'vello SM difference in height; (*fig*) gap

dislo'care /20/ VT to station, position

dismi'sura SF excess; **a ~** to excess, excessively

disobbe'dire *etc* = **disubbidire** *ecc*

disoccu'pato, -a AG unemployed **▸** SM/F unemployed person

disoccupazi'one [dizokkupat'tsjone] SF unemployment

disonestà SF dishonesty

diso'nesto, -a AG dishonest

disono'rare /45/ VT to dishonour (*Brit*), dishonor (*US*), bring disgrace upon

diso'nore SM dishonour (*Brit*), dishonor (*US*), disgrace

di'sopra AV (*con contatto*) on top; (*senza contatto*) above; (*al piano superiore*) upstairs **▸** AG INV (*superiore*) upper **▸** SM INV top, upper part; **la gente ~** the people upstairs; **il piano ~** the floor above

disordi'nare /72/ VT to mess up, disarrange; (*Mil*) to throw into disorder

disordi'nato, -a AG untidy; (*privo di misura*) irregular, wild

di'sordine SM (*confusione*) disorder, confusion; (*sregolatezza*) debauchery; **disordini** SMPL (*Pol ecc*) disorder *sg*; (*tumulti*) riots

disor'ganico, -a, -ci, -che AG incoherent, disorganized

disorganiz'zato, -a [dizorganid'dzato] AG disorganized

disorienta'mento SM (*fig*) confusion, bewilderment

disorien'tare /72/ VT to disorientate; **disorientarsi** VPR (*fig*) to get confused, lose one's bearings

disorien'tato, -a AG disorientated

disos'sare /72/ VT (*Cuc*) to bone

di'sotto AV below, underneath; (*in fondo*) at the bottom; (*al piano inferiore*) downstairs

▶ AG INV (*inferiore*) lower; bottom *cpd* ▶ SM INV (*parte inferiore*) lower part; bottom; **la gente ~** the people downstairs; **il piano ~** the floor below

dis'paccio [dis'pattʃo] SM dispatch

dispa'rato, -a AG disparate

'dispari AG INV odd, uneven

disparità SF INV disparity

dis'parte: in ~ *av* (*da lato*) aside, apart; **tenersi** *o* **starsene in ~** to keep to o.s., hold aloof

dis'pendio SM (*di denaro, energie*) expenditure; (: *spreco*) waste

dispendi'oso, -a AG expensive

dis'pensa SF pantry, larder; (*mobile*) sideboard; (*Dir*) exemption; (*Rel*) dispensation; (*fascicolo*) number, issue

dispen'sare /72/ VT (*elemosine, favori*) to distribute; (*esonerare*) to exempt

dispe'rare /72/ VI: **~ (di)** to despair (of); **disperarsi** VPR to despair

dispe'rato, -a AG (*persona*) in despair; (*caso, tentativo*) desperate

disperazi'one [disperat'tsjone] SF despair

dis'perdere /73/ VT (*disseminare*) to disperse; (*Mil*) to scatter, rout; (*fig: consumare*) to waste, squander; **disperdersi** VPR to disperse; to scatter

dispersi'one SF dispersion, dispersal; (*Fisica, Chim*) dispersion

disper'sivo, -a AG (*lavoro ecc*) disorganized

dis'perso, -a PP *di* **disperdere** ▶ SM/F missing person; (*Mil*) missing soldier

dis'petto SM spite *no pl*, spitefulness *no pl*; **fare un ~ a qn** to play a (nasty) trick on sb; **a ~ di** in spite of; **con suo grande ~** much to his annoyance

dispet'toso, -a AG spiteful

dispia'cere [dispja'tʃere] **/74/** SM (*rammarico*) regret, sorrow; (*dolore*) grief ▶ VI: **~ a** to displease ▶ VB IMPERS: **mi dispiace (che)** I am sorry (that); **le dispiace se…?** do you mind if …?; **dispiaceri** SMPL (*preoccupazioni*) troubles, worries; **se non le dispiace, me ne vado adesso** if you don't mind, I'll go now

dispiaci'uto, -a [dispja'tʃuto] PP *di* **dispiacere** ▶ AG sorry

dis'pone, dis'pongo *etc* VB *vedi* **disporre**

dispo'nibile AG available; (*persona: solerte, gentile*) helpful

disponibilità SF INV availability; (*solerzia, gentilezza*) helpfulness ▶ SFPL (*economiche*) resources

dis'porre /77/ VT (*sistemare*) to arrange; (*preparare*) to prepare; (*Dir*) to order; (*persuadere*): **~ qn a** to incline *o* dispose sb towards ▶ VI (*decidere*) to decide; (*usufruire*): **~ di** to use, have at one's disposal; (*essere dotato*): **~ di** to have; **disporsi** VPR (*ordinarsi*) to

place o.s., arrange o.s.; **disporsi a fare** to get ready to do; **disporsi all'attacco** to prepare for an attack; **disporsi in cerchio** to form a circle

dis'posi *etc* VB *vedi* **disporre**

disposi'tivo SM (*meccanismo*) device; (*Dir*) pronouncement; **~ di controllo** *o* **di comando** control device; **~ di sicurezza** (*gen*) safety device; (*di arma da fuoco*) safety catch

disposizi'one [dispozit'tsjone] SF arrangement, layout; (*stato d'animo*) mood; (*tendenza*) bent, inclination; (*comando*) order; (*Dir*) provision, regulation; **a ~ di qn** at sb's disposal; **per ~ di legge** by law; **~ testamentaria** provisions of a will

dis'posto, -a PP *di* **disporre** ▶ AG (*incline*): **~ a fare** disposed *o* prepared to do

dis'potico, -a, -ci, -che AG despotic

dispo'tismo SM despotism

disprez'zare [dispret'tsare] **/72/** VT to despise

dis'prezzo [dis'prettso] SM contempt; **con ~ del pericolo** with a total disregard for the danger involved

'disputa SF dispute, quarrel

dispu'tare /72/ VT (*contendere*) to dispute, contest; (*Sport: partita*) to play; (: *gara*) to take part in ▶ VI to quarrel; **~ di** to discuss; **disputarsi qc** to fight for sth

disqui'sire /55/ VI to discourse on

disquisizi'one [diskwizit'tsjone] SF detailed analysis

dissa'crare /72/ VT to desecrate

dissangua'mento SM loss of blood

dissangu'are /72/ VT (*fig: persona*) to bleed white; (: *patrimonio*) to suck dry; **dissanguarsi** VPR (*Med*) to lose blood; (*fig*) to ruin o.s.; **morire dissanguato** to bleed to death

dissa'pore SM slight disagreement

'disse VB *vedi* **dire**

disse'care /20/ VT to dissect

dissec'care /20/ VT, **dissec'carsi** VPR to dry up

dissemi'nare /72/ VT to scatter; (*fig: notizie*) to spread

dissenna'tezza [dissenna'tettsa] SF foolishness

dis'senso SM dissent; (*disapprovazione*) disapproval

dissente'ria SF dysentery

dissen'tire /45/ VI: **~ (da)** to disagree (with)

disseppel'lire /55/ VT (*esumare: cadavere*) to disinter, exhume; (*dissotterrare: anche fig*) to dig up, unearth; (*rancori*) to resurrect

dissertazi'one [dissertat'tsjone] SF dissertation

disser'vizio [disser'vittsjo] SM inefficiency

disses'tare /72/ VT (*Econ*) to ruin

disses'tato, -a AG (*fondo stradale*) uneven; (*economia, finanze*) shaky; **"strada dissestata"**

d

(*per lavori in corso*) "road up" (BRIT), "road out" (US)

dis'sesto SM (financial) ruin

disse'tante AG refreshing

disse'tare /**72**/ VT to quench the thirst of; **dissetarsi** VPR to quench one's thirst

dissezi'one [disset'tsjone] SF dissection

'dissi VB *vedi* **dire**

dissi'dente AG, SMF dissident

dis'sidio SM disagreement

dis'simile AG different, dissimilar

dissimu'lare /**72**/ VT (*fingere*) to dissemble; (*nascondere*) to conceal

dissimula'tore, -'trice SM/F dissembler

dissimulazi'one [dissimulat'tsjone] SF dissembling; concealment

dissi'pare /**72**/ VT to dissipate; (*scialacquare*) to squander, waste

dissipa'tezza [dissipa'tettsa] SF dissipation

dissi'pato, -a AG dissolute, dissipated

dissipazi'one [dissipat'tsjone] SF squandering

dissoci'are [disso'tʃare] /**14**/ VT to dissociate

dis'solto, -a PP *di* **dissolvere**

disso'lubile AG soluble

dissolu'tezza [dissolu'tettsa] SF dissoluteness

dissolu'tivo, -a AG (*forza*) divisive; **processo ~** (*anche fig*) process of dissolution

disso'luto, -a PP *di* **dissolvere** ▶ AG dissolute, licentious

dissol'venza [dissol'vɛntsa] SF (*Cine*) fading

dis'solvere /**94**/ VT to dissolve; (*neve*) to melt; (*fumo*) to disperse; **dissolversi** VPR to dissolve; to melt; to disperse

disso'nante AG discordant

disso'nanza [disso'nantsa] SF (*fig: di opinioni*) clash

dissotter'rare /**72**/ VT (*cadavere*) to disinter, exhume; (*tesori, rovine*) to dig up, unearth; (*fig: sentimenti, odio*) to bring up again, resurrect

dissu'adere /**88**/ VT: **~ qn da** to dissuade sb from

dissuasi'one SF dissuasion

dissu'aso, -a PP *di* **dissuadere**

dissua'sore SM: **~ di velocità** (*Aut*) speed bump

distacca'mento SM (*Mil*) detachment

distac'care /**20**/ VT to detach, separate; (*Sport*) to leave behind; **distaccarsi** VPR to be detached; (*fig*) to stand out; **distaccarsi da** (*fig: allontanarsi*) to grow away from

dis'tacco, -chi SM (*separazione*) separation; (*fig: indifferenza*) detachment; (*Sport*): **vincere con un ~ di ...** to win by a distance of ...

dis'tante AV far away ▶ AG distant, far away; **essere ~ (da)** to be a long way (from); **è ~ da**

qui? is it far from here?; **essere ~ nel tempo** to be in the distant past

dis'tanza [dis'tantsa] SF distance; **comando a ~** remote control; **a ~ di 2 giorni** 2 days later; **tener qn a ~** to keep sb at arm's length; **prendere le distanze da qc/qn** to dissociate o.s. from sth/sb; **tenere** *o* **mantenere le distanze** to keep one's distance; **~ focale** focal length; **~ di sicurezza** safe distance; (*Aut*) braking distance; **~ di tiro** range; **~ di visibilità** visibility

distanzi'are [distan'tsjare] /**19**/ VT to space out, place at intervals; (*Sport*) to outdistance; (*fig: superare*) to outstrip, surpass

dis'tare /**72**/ VI: **distiamo pochi chilometri da Roma** we are only a few kilometres (away) from Rome; **dista molto da qui?** is it far (away) from here?; **non dista molto** it's not far (away); **quanto dista il centro da qui?** how far is the town centre?

dis'tendere /**120**/ VT (*coperta*) to spread out; (*gambe*) to stretch (out); (*mettere a giacere*) to lay; (*rilassare: muscoli, nervi*) to relax; **distendersi** VPR (*rilassarsi*) to relax; (*sdraiarsi*) to lie down

distensi'one SF stretching; relaxation; (*Pol*) détente

disten'sivo, -a AG (*gen*) relaxing, restful; (*farmaco*) tranquillizing; (*Pol*) conciliatory

dis'teso, -a PP *di* **distendere** ▶ AG (*allungato: persona, gamba*) stretched out; (*rilassato: persona, atmosfera*) relaxed ▶ SF expanse, stretch; **avere un volto ~** to look relaxed

distil'lare /**72**/ VT to distil

distil'lato SM distillate

distillazi'one [distillat'tsjone] SF distillation

distille'ria SF distillery

dis'tinguere /**42**/ VT to distinguish; **distinguersi** VPR (*essere riconoscibile*) to be distinguished; (*emergere*) to stand out, be conspicuous, distinguish o.s.; **un vino che si distingue per il suo aroma** a wine with a distinctive bouquet

dis'tinguo SM INV distinction

dis'tinta SF (*nota*) note; (*elenco*) list; **~ di pagamento** receipt; **~ di versamento** pay-in slip

distin'tivo, -a AG distinctive; distinguishing ▶ SM badge

dis'tinto, -a PP *di* **distinguere** ▶ AG (*dignitoso ed elegante*) distinguished; **distinti saluti** (*in lettera*) yours faithfully

distinzi'one [distin'tsjone] SF distinction; **non faccio distinzioni** (*tra persone*) I don't discriminate; (*tra cose*) it's all one to me; **senza ~ di razza/religione ...** no matter what one's race/creed ...

dis'togliere [dis'tɔʎʎere] /**122**/ VT: **~ da** to take away from; (*fig*) to dissuade from

dis'tolto, -a PP di **distogliere**

dis'torcere [dis'tortʃere] /**106**/ VT to twist; (fig) to twist, distort; **distorcersi** VPR (contorcersi) to twist

distorsi'one SF (Med) sprain; (Fisica, Ottica) distortion

dis'torto, -a PP di **distorcere**

dis'trarre /**123**/ VT to distract; (divertire) to entertain, amuse; **distrarsi** VPR (non fare attenzione) to be distracted, let one's mind wander; (svagarsi) to amuse o enjoy o.s.; **~ lo sguardo** to look away; **non distrarti!** pay attention!

distratta'mente AV absent-mindedly, without thinking

dis'tratto, -a PP di **distrarre** ▶ AG absent-minded; (disattento) inattentive

distrazi'one [distrat'tsjone] SF absent-mindedness; inattention; (svago) distraction, entertainment; **errori di ~** careless mistakes

dis'tretto SM district

distribu'ire /**55**/ VT to distribute; (Carte) to deal (out); (consegnare: posta) to deliver; (: lavoro) to allocate, assign; (ripartire) to share out

distribu'tore SM (di benzina) petrol (BRIT) o gas (US) pump; (Aut, Elettr) distributor; (automatico) vending machine

distribuzi'one [distribut'tsjone] SF distribution; delivery; allocation; assignment; sharing out

distri'care /**20**/ VT to disentangle, unravel; **districarsi** VPR (tirarsi fuori): **districarsi da** to get out of, disentangle o.s. from; (fig: cavarsela) to manage, get by

dis'truggere [dis'truddʒere] /**83**/ VT to destroy

distrut'tivo, -a AG destructive

dis'trutto, -a PP di **distruggere**

distruzi'one [distrut'tsjone] SF destruction

distur'bare /**72**/ VT to disturb, trouble; (sonno, lezioni) to disturb, interrupt; **disturbarsi** VPR to put o.s. out; **non si disturbi** please don't bother

dis'turbo SM trouble, bother, inconvenience; (indisposizione) (slight) disorder, ailment; **disturbi** SMPL (Radio, TV) static sg; **~ della quiete pubblica** (Dir) disturbance of the peace; **disturbi di stomaco** stomach trouble sg

disubbidi'ente AG disobedient

disubbidi'enza [dizubbi'djɛntsa] SF disobedience; **~ civile** civil disobedience

disubbi'dire /**55**/ VI: **~ (a qn)** to disobey (sb)

disuguagli'anza [dizugwaʎ'ʎantsa] SF inequality

disugu'ale AG unequal; (diverso) different; (irregolare) uneven

disumanità SF inhumanity

disu'mano, -a AG inhuman; **un grido ~** a terrible cry

disuni'one SF disunity

disu'nire /**55**/ VT to divide, disunite

di'suso SM: **andare** o **cadere in ~** to fall into disuse

'dita SFPL di **dito**

di'tale SM thimble

di'tata SF (colpo) jab (with one's finger); (segno) fingermark

'dito (pl(f) **dita**) SM finger; (misura) finger, finger's breadth; **~ (del piede)** toe; **mettersi le dita nel naso** to pick one's nose; **mettere il ~ sulla piaga** (fig) to touch a sore spot; **non ha mosso un ~ (per aiutarmi)** he didn't lift a finger (to help me); **ormai è segnato a ~** everyone knows about him now

'ditta SF firm, business; **macchina della ~** company car

dit'tafono SM Dictaphone®

ditta'tore SM dictator

ditta'tura SF dictatorship

dit'tongo, -ghi SM diphthong

di'urno, -a AG day cpd, daytime cpd; **ore diurne** daytime sg; **spettacolo ~** matinee; **turno ~** day shift; vedi anche **albergo**

'diva SF vedi **divo**

diva'gare /**80**/ VI to digress

divagazi'one [divagat'tsjone] SF digression; **divagazioni sul tema** variations on a theme

divam'pare /**72**/ VI to flare up, blaze up

di'vano SM sofa; (senza schienale) divan; **~ letto** bed settee, sofa bed

divari'care /**20**/ VT to open wide

di'vario SM difference

di'vengo etc VB vedi **divenire**

dive'nire /**128**/ VI = **diventare**

di'venni etc VB vedi **divenire**

diven'tare /**72**/ VI to become; **~ famoso/ professore** to become famous/a teacher; **~ vecchio** to grow old; **c'è da ~ matti** it's enough to drive you mad

dive'nuto, -a PP di **divenire**

di'verbio SM altercation

diver'gente [diver'dʒente] AG divergent

diver'genza [diver'dʒentsa] SF divergence; **~ d'opinioni** difference of opinion

di'vergere [di'vɛrdʒere] /**59**/ VI to diverge

diverrò etc VB vedi **divenire**

diversa'mente AV (in modo differente) differently; (altrimenti) otherwise; **~ da quanto stabilito** contrary to what had been decided

diversifi'care /**20**/ VT to diversify, vary; to differentiate; **diversificarsi** VPR: **diversificarsi (per)** to differ (in)

diversificazi'one [diversifikat'tsjone] SF
diversification; difference
diversi'one SF diversion
diversità SF INV difference, diversity; *(varietà)*
variety
diver'sivo, -a AG diversionary ▶ SM
diversion, distraction; **fare un'azione
diversiva** to create a diversion
di'verso, -a AG *(differente)*: ~ **(da)** different
(from) ▶ SM *(omosessuale)* homosexual;
diversi, e DET PL, PRON PL several, various;
(Comm) sundry; several people, many
(people)
diver'tente AG amusing
diverti'mento SM amusement, pleasure;
(passatempo) pastime, recreation; **buon ~!**
enjoy yourself!, have a nice time!
diver'tire /45/ VT to amuse, entertain;
divertirsi VPR to amuse o enjoy o.s.;
divertiti! enjoy yourself, have a good time!;
divertirsi alle spalle di qn to have a laugh
at sb's expense
diver'tito, -a AG amused
divi'dendo SM dividend
di'videre /43/ VT *(anche Mat)* to divide;
(distribuire, ripartire) to divide (up), split (up);
dividersi VPR *(persone)* to separate, part;
(coppia) to separate; *(ramificarsi)* to fork;
dividersi (in) *(scindersi)* to divide (into), split
up (into); **è diviso dalla moglie** he's
separated from his wife; **si divide tra casa
e lavoro** he divides his time between home
and work
divi'eto SM prohibition; **"~ di accesso"** "no
entry"; **"~ di caccia"** "no hunting"; **"~ di
parcheggio"** "no parking"; **"~ di sosta"**
(Aut) "no waiting"
divinco'larsi /72/ VPR to wriggle, writhe
divinità SF INV divinity
di'vino, -a AG divine
di'visa SF *(Mil ecc)* uniform; *(Comm)* foreign
currency
di'visi *etc* VB *vedi* **dividere**
divisi'one SF division; **~ in sillabe** syllable
division; *(a fine riga)* hyphenation
di'vismo SM *(esibizionismo)* playing to the
crowd
di'viso, -a PP *di* **dividere**
divi'sorio, -a AG *(siepe, muro esterno)* dividing;
(muro interno) dividing, partition *cpd* ▶ SM *(in
una stanza)* partition
'divo, -a SM/F star; **come una diva** like a
prima donna
divo'rare /72/ VT to devour; **~ qc con gli occhi**
to eye sth greedily
divorzi'are [divor'tsjare] /19/ VI: ~ **(da qn)** to
divorce (sb)
divorzi'ato, -a [divor'tsjato] AG divorced
▶ SM/F divorcee

di'vorzio [di'vɔrtsjo] SM divorce
divul'gare /80/ VT to divulge, disclose;
(rendere comprensibile) to popularize;
divulgarsi VPR to spread
divulgazi'one [divulgat'tsjone] SF *(vedi vb)*
disclosure; popularization; spread
dizio'nario [dittsjo'narjo] SM dictionary
dizi'one [dit'tsjone] SF diction;
pronunciation
DJ [di'dʒei] SIGLA M/SIGLA F (= *Disc Jockey*) DJ
Dja'karta [dʒa'karta] SF Djakarta
dl ABBR (= *decilitro*) dl
dm ABBR (= *decimetro*) dm
DNA [di'ennɛa] SIGLA M *(Biol*: = *acido
deossiribonucleico)* DNA ▶ SIGLA F = **direzione
nazionale antimafia**
do SM *(Mus)* C; (: *solfeggiando la scala*) do(h)
dobbi'amo VB *vedi* **dovere**
doc. ABBR = **documento**
D.O.C. [dɔk] SIGLA (= *denominazione di origine
controllata) label guaranteeing the quality of wine*
'doccia, -ce ['dottʃa] SF *(bagno)* shower;
(condotto) pipe; **fare la ~** to have a shower;
~ fredda *(fig)* slap in the face
docciaschi'uma [dottʃas'kjuma] SM INV
shower gel
do'cente [do'tʃɛnte] AG teaching ▶ SMF
teacher; *(di università)* lecturer; **personale
non ~** non-teaching staff
do'cenza [do'tʃɛntsa] SF university teaching
o lecturing; **ottenere la libera ~** to become
a lecturer
D.O.C.G. SIGLA (= *denominazione di origine
controllata e garantita) label guaranteeing the
quality and origin of a wine*
'docile ['dɔtʃile] AG docile
docilità [dotʃili'ta] SF docility
documen'tare /72/ VT to document;
documentarsi VPR: **documentarsi (su)** to
gather information o material (about)
documen'tario, -a AG, SM documentary
documentazi'one [dokumentat'tsjone] SF
documentation
docu'mento SM document; **documenti** SMPL
(d'identità ecc) papers
L   :an'neso SM: **le Isole del ~** the
Dodecanese Islands
do cenne [dodi'tʃenne] AG, SMF twelve-
year-old
dodi'cesimo, -a [dodi'tʃɛzimo] NUM twelfth
'dodici ['doditʃi] NUM twelve
do'gana SF *(ufficio)* customs *pl*; *(tassa)*
(customs) duty; **passare la ~** to go through
customs
doga'nale AG customs *cpd*
dogani'ere SM customs officer
'doglie ['dɔʎʎe] SFPL *(Med)* labour *sg* (BRIT),
labor *sg* (US), labour pains
'dogma, -i SM dogma

dog'matico, -a, -ci, -che AG dogmatic
'dolce ['doltʃe] AG sweet; (colore) soft; (carattere, persona) gentle, mild; (fig: mite: clima) mild; (non ripido: pendio) gentle ▶ SM (sapore dolce) sweetness, sweet taste; (Cuc: portata) sweet, dessert; (: torta) cake; **il ~ far niente** sweet idleness
dolcemente AV (baciare, trattare) gently; (sorridere, cantare) sweetly; (parlare) softly
dol'cezza [dol'tʃettsa] SF sweetness; softness; mildness; gentleness
dolci'ario, -a [dol'tʃarjo] AG confectionery cpd
dolci'astro, -a [dol'tʃastro] AG (sapore) sweetish
dolcifi'cante [doltʃifi'kante] AG sweetening ▶ SM sweetener
dolci'umi [dol'tʃumi] SMPL sweets
do'lente AG sorrowful, sad
do'lere /44/ VI to be sore, hurt, ache; **dolersi** VPR to complain; (essere spiacente) **dolersi di** to be sorry for; **mi duole la testa** my head aches, I've got a headache
'dolgo etc VB vedi **dolere**
'dollaro SM dollar
'dolo SM (Dir) malice; (frode) fraud, deceit
Dolo'miti SFPL: **le ~** the Dolomites
dolo'rante AG aching, sore
do'lore SM (fisico) pain; (morale) sorrow, grief; **se lo scoprono sono dolori!** if they find out there'll be trouble!
dolo'roso, -a AG painful; sorrowful, sad
do'loso, -a AG (Dir) malicious; **incendio ~** arson
'dolsi etc VB vedi **dolere**
dom. ABBR (= domenica) Sun
do'manda SF (interrogazione) question; (richiesta) demand; (: cortese) request; (Dir: richiesta scritta) application; (Econ): **la ~** demand; **fare una ~ a qn** to ask sb a question; **fare ~ (per un lavoro)** to apply (for a job); **far regolare ~ (di qc)** to apply through the proper channels (for sth); **fare ~ all'autorità giudiziaria** to apply to the courts; **~ di divorzio** divorce petition; **~ di matrimonio** proposal
doman'dare /72/ VT (per avere) to ask for; (per sapere) to ask; (esigere) to demand; **domandarsi** VPR to wonder; to ask o.s.; **~ qc a qn** to ask sb for sth; to ask sb sth
do'mani AV tomorrow ▶ SM (l'indomani) the next day, the following day; **il ~** (il futuro) the future; (il giorno successivo) the next day; **un ~** some day; **~ l'altro** the day after tomorrow; **~ (a) otto** tomorrow week, a week tomorrow; **a ~!** see you tomorrow!
do'mare /72/ VT to tame
doma'tore, -'trice SM/F (gen) tamer; **~ di cavalli** horsebreaker; **~ di leoni** lion tamer
domat'tina AV tomorrow morning

do'menica, -che SF Sunday; **di** o **la ~** on Sundays; vedi anche **martedì**
domeni'cale AG Sunday cpd
domeni'cano, -a AG, SM/F Dominican
do'mestica, -che SF vedi **domestico**
do'mestico, -a, -ci, -che AG domestic ▶ SM/F servant, domestic; **le pareti domestiche** one's own four walls; **animale ~** pet; **una domestica a ore** a daily (woman)
domicili'are [domitʃi'ljare] AG vedi **arresto**
domicili'arsi [domitʃi'ljarsi] **/19/** VPR to take up residence
domi'cilio [domi'tʃiljo] SM (Dir) domicile, place of residence; **visita a ~** (Med) house call; **"recapito a ~"** "deliveries"; **violazione di ~** (Dir) breaking and entering
domi'nante AG (colore, nota) dominant; (opinione) prevailing; (idea) main cpd, chief cpd; (posizione) dominating cpd; (classe, partito) ruling cpd
domi'nare /72/ VT to dominate; (fig: sentimenti) to control, master ▶ VI to be in the dominant position; **dominarsi** VPR (controllarsi) to control o.s.; **~ su** (fig) to surpass, outclass
domina'tore, -'trice AG ruling cpd ▶ SM/F ruler
dominazi'one [dominat'tsjone] SF domination
domini'cano, -a AG: **la Repubblica Dominicana** the Dominican Republic
do'minio SM dominion; (fig: campo) field, domain; **domini coloniali** colonies; **essere di ~ pubblico** (notizia ecc) to be common knowledge
don SM (Rel) Father
do'nare /72/ VT to give, present; (per beneficenza ecc) to donate ▶ VI (fig): **~ a** to suit, become; **~ sangue** to give blood
dona'tore, -'trice SM/F donor; **~ di sangue/ di organi** blood/organ donor
donazi'one [donat'tsjone] SF donation; **atto di ~** (Dir) deed of gift
'donde AV (poetico) whence
dondo'lare /72/ VT (cullare) to rock; **dondolarsi** VPR to swing, sway
'dondolo SM: **sedia/cavallo a ~** rocking chair/horse
dongio'vanni [dondʒo'vanni] SM Don Juan, ladies' man
'donna SF woman; (titolo) Donna; (Carte) queen; **figlio di buona ~!** (col) son of a bitch!; **~ di casa** housewife; home-loving woman; **~ a ore** daily (help o woman); **~ delle pulizie** cleaning lady, cleaner; **~ di servizio** maid; **~ di vita** o **di strada** prostitute, streetwalker
donnai'olo SM ladykiller
'donnola SF weasel
'dono SM gift
'doping SM doping

'**dopo** AV (*tempo*) afterwards; (: *più tardi*) later; (*luogo*) after, next ▶ PREP after ▶ CONG (*temporale*): ~ **aver studiato** after having studied ▶ AG INV: **il giorno** ~ the following day; ~ **mangiato va a dormire** after having eaten *o* after a meal he goes for a sleep; **un anno** ~ a year later; ~ **di me/lui** after me/him; ~, **a** ~! see you later!; ~ **che** = **dopoché**

dopo'barba SM INV after-shave

dopoché [dopo'ke] CONG after, when

dopodiché [dopodi'ke] AV after which

dopodo'mani AV the day after tomorrow

dopogu'erra SM postwar years *pl*

dopola'voro SM recreational club

dopo'pranzo [dopo'prandzo] AV after lunch (*o* dinner)

doposcì [dopoʃʃi] SM INV après-ski outfit

doposcu'ola SM INV *school club offering extra tuition and recreational facilities*

dopo'sole SM INV, AG INV: (**lozione/crema**) ~ aftersun (lotion/cream)

dopo'tutto AV (*tutto considerato*) after all

doppi'aggio [dop'pjaddʒo] SM (*Cine*) dubbing

doppi'are /19/ VT (*Naut*) to round; (*Sport*) to lap; (*Cine*) to dub

doppia'tore, -'trice SM/F dubber

doppi'etta SF (*fucile*) double-barrelled (BRIT) *o* double-barreled (US) shotgun; (*sparo*) shot from both barrels; (*Calcio*) double; (*Pugilato*) one-two; (*Aut*) double-declutch (BRIT), double-clutch (US)

doppi'ezza [dop'pjettsa] SF (*fig: di persona*) duplicity, double-dealing

'**doppio, -a** AG double; (*fig: falso*) double-dealing, deceitful ▶ SM (*quantità*) **il ~ (di)** twice as much (*o* many), double the amount (*o* number) of; (*Sport*) doubles *pl* ▶ AV double; **battere una lettera in doppia copia** to type a letter with a carbon copy; **fare il ~ gioco** (*fig*) to play a double game; **chiudere a doppia mandata** to double-lock; ~ **senso** double entendre; **frase a ~ senso** sentence with a double meaning; **un utensile a ~ uso** a dual-purpose utensil

doppio'fondo SM (*di valigia*) false bottom; (*Naut*) double hull

doppi'one SM duplicate (copy)

doppio'petto SM double-breasted jacket

dop'pista SMF (*Tennis*) doubles player

do'rare /72/ VT to gild; (*Cuc*) to brown; ~ **la pillola** (*fig*) to sugar the pill

do'rato, -a AG golden; (*ricoperto d'oro*) gilt, gilded

dora'tura SF gilding

dormicchi'are [dormik'kjare] /19/ VI to doze

dormi'ente AG sleeping ▶ SMF sleeper

dormigli'one, -a [dormiʎ'ʎone] SM/F sleepyhead

dor'mire /45/ VI to sleep; **andare a** ~ to go to bed; (*essere addormentato*) to be asleep, be sleeping; **il caffè non mi fa** ~ coffee keeps me awake; ~ **come un ghiro** to sleep like a log; ~ **della grossa** to sleep soundly, be dead to the world; ~ **in piedi** (*essere stanco*) to be asleep on one's feet

dor'mita SF: **farsi una** ~ to have a good sleep

dormi'torio SM dormitory; ~ **pubblico** doss house (BRIT) *o* flophouse (US: *run by local authority*)

dormi'veglia [dormi'veʎʎa] SM drowsiness

dorrò *etc* VB *vedi* **dolere**

dor'sale AG: **spina** ~ backbone, spine

'**dorso** SM back; (*di montagna*) ridge, crest; (*di libro*) spine; (*Nuoto*) backstroke; **a** ~ **di cavallo** on horseback

do'saggio [do'zaddʒo] SM (*atto*) measuring out; **sbagliare il** ~ to get the proportions wrong

do'sare /72/ VT to measure out; (*Med*) to dose

'**dose** SF quantity, amount; (*Med*) dose

dossi'er [do'sje] SM INV dossier, file

'**dosso** SM (*rilievo*) bump; (: *di strada*) bump; (*dorso*): **levarsi di** ~ **i vestiti** to take one's clothes off; **levarsi un peso di** ~ (*fig*) to take a weight off one's mind

do'tare /72/ VT: ~ **di** to provide *o* supply with; (*fig*) to endow with

do'tato, -a AG: ~ **di** (*attrezzature*) equipped with; (*bellezza, intelligenza*) endowed with; **un uomo** ~ a gifted man

dotazi'one [dotat'tsjone] SF (*insieme di beni*) endowment; (*di macchine ecc*) equipment; **dare qc in** ~ **a qn** to issue sb with sth, issue sth to sb; **i macchinari in** ~ **alla fabbrica** the machinery in use in the factory

'**dote** SF (*di sposa*) dowry; (*assegnata a un ente*) endowment; (*fig*) gift, talent

Dott. ABBR (= *dottore*) Dr

'**dotto, -a** AG (*colto*) learned ▶ SM (*sapiente*) scholar; (*Anat*) duct

dotto'rato SM degree; ~ **di ricerca** doctorate, doctor's degree

dot'tore, -'essa SM/F doctor

> In Italy, anyone who has a degree in any subject can use the title *dottore*. Thus a person who is addressed as *dottore* is not necessarily a doctor of medicine.

dot'trina SF doctrine

Dott.ssa ABBR (= *dottoressa*) Dr

double-'face [dubl'fas] AG INV reversible

'**dove** AV (*gen*) where; (*in cui*) where, in which; (*dovunque*) wherever ▶ CONG (*mentre, laddove*) whereas ▶ SM: **per ogni** ~ everywhere; ~ **sei?/vai?** where are you?/are you going?; **dimmi dov'è** tell me where it is; **di dov'è?** where are you from?; **da** ~ **abito vedo tutta la città** I can see the whole city from where

I live; **per ~ si passa?** which way should we go?; **le dò una mano fin ~ posso** I'll help you as much as I can; **la città ~ abito** the town where o in which I live; **siediti ~ vuoi** sit wherever you like

do'vere /46/ SM (obbligo) duty ▶ VT (essere debitore): **~ qc (a qn)** to owe (sb) sth ▶ VI (seguito dall'infinito: obbligo) to have to; **devo partire domani** (intenzione) I'm (due) to leave tomorrow; **dev'essere tardi** (probabilità) it must be late; **lui deve farlo** he has to do it, he must do it; **quanto le devo?** how much do I owe you?; **è dovuto partire** he had to leave; **ha dovuto pagare** he had to pay; **doveva accadere** it was bound to happen; **avere il senso del ~** to have a sense of duty; **rivolgersi a chi di ~** to apply to the appropriate authority o person; **a ~** (bene) properly; (debitamente) as he (o she etc) deserves; **come si deve** (bene) properly; (meritatamente) properly, as he (o she etc) deserves; **una persona come si deve** a respectable person

dove'roso, -a AG (right and) proper
do'vizia [do'vittsja] SF abundance
dovrò etc VB vedi **dovere**
do'vunque AV (in qualunque luogo) wherever; (dappertutto) everywhere; **~ io vada** wherever I go
dovuta'mente AV (debitamente: redigere, compilare) correctly; (: rimproverare) as he (o she etc) deserves
do'vuto, -a AG (causato): **~ a** due to ▶ SM due; **nel modo ~** in the proper way; **ho lavorato più del ~** I worked more than was necessary
doz'zina [dod'dzina] SF dozen; **una ~ di uova** a dozen eggs; **di** o **da ~** (scrittore, spettacolo) second-rate
dozzi'nale [doddzi'nale] AG cheap, second-rate
DP SIGLA F (= Democrazia Proletaria) political party
'draga, -ghe SF dredger
dra'gare /80/ VT to dredge
dragherò etc [drage'rɔ] VB vedi **dragare**
'drago, -ghi SM dragon; (fig: col) genius
'dramma, -i SM drama; **fare un ~ di qc** to make a drama out of sth
dram'matico, -a, -ci, -che AG dramatic
drammatiz'zare [drammatid'dzare] /72/ VT to dramatize
dramma'turgo, -ghi SM playwright
drappeggi'are [drapped'dʒare] /62/ VT to drape
drap'peggio [drap'peddʒo] SM (tessuto) drapery; (di abito) folds
drap'pello SM (Mil) squad; (gruppo) band, group
'drappo SM cloth
'drastico, -a, -ci, -che AG drastic

dre'naggio [dre'naddʒo] SM drainage
dre'nare /72/ VT to drain
'Dresda SF Dresden
drib'blare /72/ VI (Calcio) to dribble ▶ VT (avversario) to dodge, avoid
'dritto, -a AG, AV = **diritto** ▶ SM/F (col: furbo): **è un ~** he's a crafty o sly one ▶ SF (destra) right, right hand; (Naut) starboard; **a dritta e a manca** (fig) on all sides, right, left and centre
driz'zare [drit'tsare] /72/ VT (far tornare diritto) to straighten; (volgere: sguardo, occhi) to turn, direct; (innalzare: antenna, muro) to erect; **drizzarsi** VPR to stand up; **~ le orecchie** to prick up one's ears; **drizzarsi in piedi** to rise to one's feet; **drizzarsi a sedere** to sit up
'droga, -ghe SF (sostanza aromatica) spice; (stupefacente) drug; **droghe pesanti/leggere** hard/soft drugs
dro'gare /80/ VT to drug, dope; **drogarsi** VPR to take drugs
dro'gato, -a SM/F drug addict
droghe'ria [droge'ria] SF grocer's (shop) (BRIT), grocery (store) (US)
drogherò etc [droge'rɔ] VB vedi **drogare**
droghi'ere, -a [dro'gjere] SM/F grocer
drome'dario SM dromedary
DS [di'esse] SMPL (= Democratici di Sinistra) Democrats of the Left (Italian left-wing party)
'dubbio, -a AG (incerto) doubtful, dubious; (ambiguo) dubious ▶ SM (incertezza) doubt; **avere il ~ che** to be afraid that, suspect that; **essere in ~ fra** to hesitate between; **mettere in ~ qc** to question sth; **nutrire seri dubbi su qc** to have grave doubts about sth; **senza ~** doubtless, no doubt
dubbi'oso, -a AG doubtful, dubious
dubi'tare /72/ VI: **~ di** (onestà) to doubt; (risultato) to be doubtful of; **~ di qn** to mistrust sb; **~ di sé** to be unsure of o.s.
Du'blino SF Dublin
'duca, -chi SM duke
'duce ['dutʃe] SM (Storia) captain; (: del fascismo) duce
du'chessa [du'kessa] SF duchess
'due NUM two; **a ~ a ~** two at a time, two by two; **dire ~ parole** to say a few words; **ci metto ~ minuti** I'll have it done in a jiffy
duecen'tesco, -a, -schi, -sche [duetʃen'tesko] AG thirteenth-century
due'cento [due'tʃento] NUM two hundred ▶ SM: **il D~** the thirteenth century
duel'lare /72/ VI to fight a duel
du'ello SM duel
due'mila NUM two thousand ▶ SM INV: **il ~** the year two thousand
due'pezzi [due'pettsi] SM (costume da bagno) two-piece swimsuit; (abito femminile) two-piece suit

du'etto SM duet

'dulcis in 'fundo ['dultʃisin'fundo] AV to cap it all

'duna SF dune

'dunque CONG (*perciò*) so, therefore; (*riprendendo il discorso*) well (then) ▸ SM INV: **venire al ~** to come to the point

'duo SM INV (*Mus*) duet; (*Teat, Cine, fig*) duo

du'ole *etc* VB *vedi* **dolere**

du'omo SM cathedral

'duplex SM INV (*Tel*) party line

dupli'cato SM duplicate

'duplice ['duplitʃe] AG double, twofold; **in ~ copia** in duplicate

duplicità [duplitʃi'ta] SF (*fig*) duplicity

du'rante PREP during; **vita natural ~** for life

du'rare /72/ VI to last; **non può ~!** this can't go on any longer!; **~ fatica a** to have difficulty in; **~ in carica** to remain in office

du'rata SF length (of time); duration; **per tutta la ~ di** throughout; **~ media della vita** life expectancy

dura'turo, -a AG, **du'revole** AG (*ricordo*) lasting; (*materiale*) durable

du'rezza [du'rettsa] SF hardness; stubbornness; harshness; toughness

'duro, -a AG (*pietra, lavoro, materasso, problema*) hard; (*persona: ostinato*) stubborn, obstinate; (: *severo*) harsh, hard; (*voce*) harsh; (*carne*) tough ▸ SM/F hardness; (*difficoltà*) hard part; (*persona*) tough one ▸ AV: **tener ~** (*resistere*) to stand firm, hold out; **avere la pelle dura** (*fig: persona*) to be tough; **fare il ~** to act tough; **~ di comprendonio** slow-witted; **~ d'orecchi** hard of hearing

du'rone SM hard skin

'duttile AG (*sostanza*) malleable; (*fig: carattere*) docile, biddable; (: *stile*) adaptable

DVD [divu'di] SM INV DVD; (*lettore*) DVD player

Ee

E, e [e] SM O F INV (*lettera*) E, e; **E come Empoli** ≈ E for Edward (*BRIT*), E for Easy (*US*)

E ABBR (= *est*) E; (*Aut*) = **itinerario europeo**

e (*dav V spesso* **ed**) CONG and; (*avversativo*) but; (*eppure*) and yet; **e lui?** what about him?; **e compralo!** well buy it then!

è VB *vedi* **essere**

E.A.D. SIGLA F = **elaborazione automatica dei dati**

ebaniste'ria SF cabinet-making; (*negozio*) cabinet-maker's shop

'ebano SM ebony

eb'bene CONG well (then)

'ebbi *etc* VB *vedi* **avere**

eb'brezza [eb'brettsa] SF intoxication

'ebbro, -a AG drunk; **~ di** (*gioia ecc*) beside o.s. *o* wild with

'ebete AG stupid, idiotic

ebe'tismo SM stupidity

ebollizi'one [ebollit'tsjone] SF boiling; **punto di ~** boiling point

e'braico, -a, -ci, -che AG Hebrew, Hebraic ▶ SM (*Ling*) Hebrew

e'breo, -a AG Jewish ▶ SM/F Jewish person, Jew (Jewess)

'Ebridi SFPL: **le (isole) ~** the Hebrides

e'burneo, -a AG ivory *cpd*

EC ABBR (= *Eurocity*) fast train connecting Western European cities

E/C ABBR = **estratto conto**

eca'tombe SF (*strage*) slaughter, massacre

ecc. ABBR (= *eccetera*) etc

ecce'dente [ettʃe'dɛnte] SM surplus

ecce'denza [ettʃe'dɛntsa] SF excess, surplus; (*Inform*) overflow

ec'cedere [et'tʃɛdere] /29/ VT to exceed ▶ VI to go too far; **~ nel bere/mangiare** to indulge in drink/food to excess

eccel'lente [ettʃel'lɛnte] AG excellent; (*cadavere, arresto*) of a prominent person

eccel'lenza [ettʃe'lɛntsa] SF excellence; (*titolo*): **Sua E~** His Excellency

ec'cellere [et'tʃɛllere] /45/ VI: **~ (in)** to excel (at); **~ su tutti** to surpass everyone

ec'celso, -a [et'tʃɛlso] PP *di* **eccellere** ▶ AG (*cima, montagna*) high; (*fig: ingegno*) great, exceptional

ec'centrico, -a, -ci, -che [et'tʃɛntriko] AG eccentric

ecces'sivo, -a [ettʃes'sivo] AG excessive

ec'cesso [et'tʃɛsso] SM excess; **all'~** (*gentile, generoso*) to excess, excessively; **dare in eccessi** to fly into a rage; **~ di velocità** (*Aut*) speeding; **~ di zelo** overzealousness

ec'cetera [et'tʃɛtera] AV et cetera, and so on

ec'cetto [et'tʃɛtto] PREP except, with the exception of; **~ che** *cong* except, other than; **~ che (non)** unless

eccettu'are [ettʃettu'are] /72/ VT to except; **eccettuati i presenti** present company excepted

eccezio'nale [ettʃettsjo'nale] AG exceptional; **in via del tutto ~** in this instance, exceptionally

eccezi'one [ettʃet'tsjone] SF exception; (*Dir*) objection; **a ~ di** with the exception of, except for; **d'~** exceptional; **fare un'~ alla regola** to make an exception to the rule

ec'chimosi [ek'kimozi] SF INV bruise

ec'cidio [et'tʃidjo] SM massacre

ecci'tante [ettʃi'tante] AG (*gen*) exciting; (*sostanza*) stimulating ▶ SM stimulant

ecci'tare [ettʃi'tare] /72/ VT (*curiosità, interesse*) to excite, arouse; (*folla*) to incite; **eccitarsi** VPR to get excited; (*sessualmente*) to become aroused

eccitazi'one [ettʃitat'tsjone] SF excitement

ecclesi'astico, -a, -ci, -che AG ecclesiastical, church *cpd*; clerical ▶ SM ecclesiastic

'ecco AV (*per dimostrare*): **~ il treno!** here's *o* here comes the train!; (*dav pronome*) **eccomi!** here I am!; **eccone uno!** here's one (of them)!; (*dav pp*) **~ fatto!** there, that's it done!

ec'come AV rather; **ti piace? — ~!** do you like it? — I'll say! *o* and how! *o* rather! (*BRIT*)

ECG SIGLA M = **elettrocardiogramma**

echeggi'are [eked'dʒare] /62/ VI to echo

e'clettico, -a, -ci, -che AG, SM/F eclectic

eclet'tismo SM eclecticism
eclis'sare /72/ VT to eclipse; (fig) to eclipse, overshadow; **eclissarsi** VPR (persona: scherzoso) to slip away
e'clisse SF eclipse
e'clissi SF eclipse
'eco (pl(m) **echi**) SM O F echo; **suscitò** o **ebbe una profonda ~** it caused quite a stir
ecogra'fia SF (Med) ultrasound
ecolo'gia [ekolo'dʒia] SF ecology
eco'logico, -a, -ci, -che [eko'lɔdʒiko] AG ecological
ecolo'gista, -i, -e [ekolo'dʒista] AG ecological ▶ SM/F ecologist, environmentalist
e'cologo, -a, -gi, -ghe SM/F ecologist
eco'mafia SF mafia involved in crimes related to the environment, in particular the illegal disposal of waste
econo'mato SM (Ins) bursar's office
econo'mia SF economy; (scienza) economics sg; (risparmio: azione) saving; **fare ~** to economize, make economies; **l'~ sommersa** the black (BRIT) o underground (US) economy; **~ di mercato** market economy; **~ pianificata** planned economy
eco'nomico, -a, -ci, -che AG economic; (poco costoso) economical; **edizione economica** economy edition
econo'mista, -i SM economist
economiz'zare [ekonomid'dzare] /72/ VT, VI to save
e'conomo, -a AG thrifty ▶ SM/F (Ins) bursar
ecosis'tema, -i SM ecosystem
eco'tassa [eko'tassa] SF green tax
'ecstasy ['ɛkstasi] SF INV ecstasy
'Ecuador SM: **l'~** Ecuador
ecu'menico, -a, -ci, -che AG ecumenical
ec'zema [ek'dzɛma] SM eczema
ed CONG vedi **E**
Ed. ABBR = **editore**
ed. ABBR = **edizione**
'edera SF ivy
e'dicola SF newspaper kiosk o stand (US)
edico'lante SMF news vendor (in kiosk)
edifi'cante AG edifying
edifi'care /20/ VT to build; (fig: teoria, azienda) to establish; (indurre al bene) to edify
edi'ficio [edi'fitʃo] SM building; (fig) structure
e'dile AG building cpd
edi'lizio, -a [edi'littsjo] AG building cpd ▶ SF building, building trade
Edim'burgo SF Edinburgh
'edito, -a AG published
edi'tore, -'trice AG publishing cpd ▶ SM/F publisher
edito'ria SF publishing
editori'ale AG publishing cpd ▶ SM (articolo di fondo) editorial, leader

e'ditto SM edict
edizi'one [edit'tsjone] SF edition; (tiratura) printing; **~ a tiratura limitata** limited edition; **~ straordinaria** special edition
edo'nismo SM hedonism
e'dotto, -a AG informed; **rendere qn ~ su qc** to inform sb about sth
edu'canda SF boarder
edu'care /20/ VT to educate; (gusto, mente) to train; **~ qn a fare** to train sb to do
educa'tivo, -a AG educational
edu'cato, -a AG polite, well-mannered
educazi'one [edukat'tsjone] SF education; (familiare) upbringing; (comportamento) (good) manners pl; **per ~** out of politeness; **questa è pura mancanza d'~!** this is sheer bad manners!; **~ fisica** (Ins) physical training o education
educherò etc [eduke'rɔ] VB vedi **educare**
E.E.D. SIGLA F = **elaborazione elettronica dei dati**
EEG SIGLA M = **elettroencefalogramma**
e'felide SF freckle
effemi'nato, -a AG effeminate
effe'rato, -a AG brutal, savage
efferve'scente [efferveʃʃɛnte] AG effervescent
effettiva'mente AV (in effetti) in fact; (a dire il vero) really, actually
effet'tivo, -a AG (reale) real, actual; (impiegato, professore) permanent; (Mil) regular ▶ SM (Mil) strength; (di patrimonio ecc) sum total
ef'fetto SM effect; (Comm: cambiale) bill; (fig: impressione) impression; **far ~** (medicina) to take effect, (start to) work; **cercare l'~** to seek attention; **in effetti** in fact, actually; **effetti attivi** (Comm) bills receivable; **effetti passivi** (Comm) bills payable; **effetti personali** personal effects, personal belongings; **~ serra** greenhouse effect; **effetti speciali** (Cine) special effects
effettu'are /72/ VT to effect, carry out
effi'cace [effi'katʃe] AG effective
effi'cacia [effi'katʃa] SF effectiveness
effici'ente [effi'tʃɛnte] AG efficient
efficien'tismo [effitʃen'tizmo] SM maximum efficiency
effici'enza [effi'tʃɛntsa] SF efficiency
effigi'are [effi'dʒare] /62/ VT to represent, portray
ef'figie [ef'fidʒe] SF INV effigy
ef'fimero, -a AG ephemeral
ef'fluvio SM (anche peg, ironico) scent, perfume
effusi'one SF effusion
e.g. ABBR (= exempli gratia) e.g.
egemo'nia [edʒemo'nia] SF hegemony
E'geo [e'dʒɛo] SM: **l'~, il mare ~** the Aegean (Sea)
'egida ['ɛdʒida] SF: **sotto l'~ di** under the aegis of

E'gitto [e'dʒitto] SM: **l'~** Egypt

egizi'ano, -a [edʒit'tsjano] AG, SM/F Egyptian

e'gizio, -a [e'dʒittsjo] AG, SM/F (ancient) Egyptian

'egli ['eʎʎi] PRON he; **~ stesso** he himself

'ego SM INV (Psic) ego

ego'centrico, -a, -ci, -che [ego'tʃɛntriko] AG egocentric(al) ▶ SM/F self-centred (BRIT) o self-centered (US) person

egocen'trismo [egotʃen'trizmo] SM egocentricity

ego'ismo SM selfishness, egoism

ego'ista, -i, -e AG selfish, egoistic ▶ SM/F egoist

ego'istico, -a, -ci, -che AG egoistic, selfish

ego'tismo SM egotism

ego'tista, -i, -e AG egotistic ▶ SM/F egotist

Egr. ABBR = **egregio**

e'gregio, -a, -gi, -gie [e'grɛdʒo] AG distinguished; (nelle lettere): **E~ Signore** Dear Sir

eguagli'anza etc [egwaʎ'ʎantsa] vedi **uguaglianza** ecc

eguali'tario, -a AG, SM/F egalitarian

E.I. ABBR = **Esercito Italiano**

eiaculazi'one [ejakulat'tsjone] SF ejaculation; **~ precoce** premature ejaculation

elabo'rare /72/ VT (progetto) to work out, elaborate; (dati) to process; (digerire) to digest

elabora'tore SM (Inform): **~ elettronico** computer

elaborazi'one [elaborat'tsjone] SF elaboration; processing; digestion; **~ automatica dei dati** (Inform) automatic data processing; **~ elettronica dei dati** (Inform) electronic data processing; **~ testi** (Inform) text processing

elar'gire [elar'dʒire] /55/ VT to hand out

elargizi'one [elardʒit'tsjone] SF donation

elasticiz'zato, -a [elastitʃid'dzato] AG (tessuto) stretch cpd

e'lastico, -a, -ci, -che AG elastic; (fig: andatura) springy; (: decisione, vedute) flexible ▶ SM (gommino) rubber band; (per il cucito) elastic no pl

ele'fante SM elephant

ele'gante AG elegant

ele'ganza [ele'gantsa] SF elegance

e'leggere [e'lɛddʒere] /61/ VT to elect

elemen'tare AG elementary; **le (scuole) elementari** sfpl primary (BRIT) o grade (US) school; **prima ~** first year of primary school, ≈ infants' class (BRIT), ≈ 1st grade (US)

ele'mento SM element; (parte componente) element, component, part; **elementi** SMPL (della scienza ecc) elements, rudiments

ele'mosina SF charity, alms pl; **chiedere l'~** to beg

elemosi'nare /72/ VT to beg for, ask for ▶ VI to beg

elen'care /20/ VT to list

elencherò etc [elenke'rɔ] VB vedi **elencare**

e'lenco, -chi SM list; **~ nominativo** list of names; **~ telefonico** telephone directory

e'lessi etc VB vedi **eleggere**

elet'tivo, -a AG (carica ecc) elected

e'letto, -a PP di **eleggere** ▶ SM/F (nominato) elected member

eletto'rale AG electoral, election cpd

eletto'rato SM electorate

elet'tore, -'trice SM/F voter, elector

elet'trauto SM INV workshop for car electrical repairs; (tecnico) car electrician

elettri'cista, -i [elettri'tʃista] SM electrician

elettricità [elettritʃi'ta] SF electricity

e'lettrico, -a, -ci, -che AG electric(al)

elettrifi'care /20/ VT to electrify

elettriz'zante [elettrid'dzante] AG (fig) electrifying, thrilling

elettriz'zare [elettrid'dzare] /72/ VT to electrify; **elettrizzarsi** VPR to become charged with electricity; (fig: persona) to be thrilled

e'lettro... PREFISSO electro...

elettrocardio'gramma, -i SM electrocardiogram

e'lettrodo SM electrode

elettrodo'mestico, -a, -ci, -che AG: **apparecchi elettrodomestici** domestic (electrical) appliances

elettroencefalo'gramma, -i [elettroentʃefalo'gramma] SM electroencephalogram

elet'trogeno, -a [elet'trɔdʒeno] AG: **gruppo ~** generator

elet'trolisi SF electrolysis

elettroma'gnetico, -a, -ci, -che [elettromaɲ'ɲɛtiko] AG electromagnetic

elettromo'trice [elettromo'tritʃe] SF electric train

elet'trone SM electron

elet'tronico, -a, -ci, -che AG electronic ▶ SF electronics sg

elettro'shock [elettroʃ'ʃɔk] SM INV (electro)shock treatment

elettro'tecnico, -a, -ci, -che AG electrotechnical ▶ SM electrical engineer

ele'vare /72/ VT to raise; (edificio) to erect; (multa) to impose; **~ un numero al quadrato** to square a number

eleva'tezza [eleva'tettsa] SF (altezza) elevation; (di animo, pensiero) loftiness

ele'vato, -a AG (gen) high; (cime) high, lofty; (fig: stile, sentimenti) lofty

elevazi'one [elevat'tsjone] SF elevation; (l'elevare) raising

elezi'one [elet'tsjone] SF election; **elezioni** SFPL (Pol) election(s); **patria d'~** chosen country

'elica, -che SF propeller

eli'cottero SM helicopter

e'lidere /85/ VT (Fonetica) to elide; **elidersi** VPR (forze) to cancel each other out, neutralize each other

elimi'nare /72/ VT to eliminate

elimina'toria SF eliminating round

eliminazi'one [eliminat'tsjone] SF elimination

'elio SM helium

eli'porto SM heliport

elisabetti'ano, -a AG Elizabethan

eli'sir SM INV elixir

e'liso, -a PP di **elidere**

elisoc'corso SM helicopter ambulance

eli'tario, -a AG elitist

é'lite [e'lit] SF INV élite

'ella PRON she; (forma di cortesia) you; ~ **stessa** she herself; you yourself

el'lisse SF ellipse

el'littico, -a, -ci, -che AG elliptic(al)

el'metto SM helmet

'elmo SM helmet

elogi'are [elo'dʒare] /62/ VT to praise

elogia'tivo, -a [elodʒa'tivo] AG laudatory

e'logio [e'lɔdʒo] SM (discorso, scritto) eulogy; (lode) praise; ~ **funebre** funeral oration

elo'quente AG eloquent; **questi dati sono eloquenti** these facts speak for themselves

elo'quenza [elo'kwɛntsa] SF eloquence

e'loquio SM speech, language

elucu'brare /72/ VT to ponder about o over

elucubrazi'oni [elukubrat'tsjoni] SFPL (anche ironico) cogitations, ponderings

e'ludere /35/ VT to evade

e'lusi etc VB vedi **eludere**

elusi'one SF: ~ **d'imposta** tax evasion

elu'sivo, -a AG evasive

e'luso, -a PP di **eludere**

el'vetico, -a, -ci, -che AG Swiss

emaci'ato, -a [ema'tʃato] AG emaciated

e-'mail, email [e'meil] SF INV (messaggio, sistema) e-mail ▸ AG INV email; **indirizzo ~** email address

ema'nare /72/ VT to send out, give off; (fig: leggi) to promulgate; (: decreti) to issue ▸ VI: ~ **da** to come from

emanazi'one [emanat'tsjone] SF (di raggi, calore) emanation; (di odori) exhalation; (di legge) promulgation; (di ordine, circolare) issuing

emanci'pare [emantʃi'pare] /72/ VT to emancipate; **emanciparsi** VPR (fig) to become liberated o emancipated

emancipazi'one [emantʃipat'tsjone] SF emancipation

emargi'nare [emardʒi'nare] /72/ VT (fig: socialmente) to cast out

emargi'nato, -a [emardʒi'nato] SM/F outcast

emarginazi'one [emardʒinat'tsjone] SF marginalization

ematolo'gia [ematolo'dʒia] SF haematology (BRIT), hematology (US)

ema'toma, -i SM haematoma (BRIT), hematoma (US)

em'blema, -i SM emblem

emble'matico, -a, -ci, -che AG emblematic; (fig: atteggiamento, parole) symbolic

embo'lia SF embolism

embrio'nale, -i, -e AG embryonic, embryo cpd; **allo stadio ~** at the embryo stage

embri'one SM embryo

emenda'mento SM amendment

emen'dare /72/ VT to amend

emer'gente [emer'dʒɛnte] AG emerging

emer'genza [emer'dʒɛntsa] SF emergency; **in caso di ~** in an emergency

e'mergere [e'mɛrdʒere] /59/ VI to emerge; (sommergibile) to surface; (fig: distinguersi) to stand out

e'merito, -a AG (insigne) distinguished; **è un ~ cretino!** he's a complete idiot!

e'mersi etc VB vedi **emergere**

e'merso, -a PP di **emergere** ▸ AG (Geo): **terre emerse** lands above sea level

e'messo, -a PP di **emettere**

e'mettere /63/ VT (suono, luce) to give out, emit; (onde radio) to send out; (assegno, francobollo, ordine) to issue; (fig: giudizio) to express, voice; ~ **la sentenza** (Dir) to pass sentence

emi'crania SF migraine

emi'grante AG, SMF emigrant

emi'grare /72/ VI to emigrate

emi'grato, -a AG emigrant ▸ SM/F emigrant; (Storia) émigré

emigrazi'one [emigrat'tsjone] SF emigration

emili'ano, -a AG of (o from) Emilia

emi'nente AG eminent, distinguished

emi'nenza [emi'nɛntsa] SF eminence; ~ **grigia** (fig) éminence grise

emi'rato SM emirate; **gli Emirati Arabi Uniti** the United Arab Emirates

e'miro SM emir

emis'fero SM hemisphere; ~ **boreale/australe** northern/southern hemisphere

e'misi etc VB vedi **emettere**

emis'sario SM (Geo) outlet, effluent; (inviato) emissary

emissi'one SF (vedi emettere) emission; sending out; issue; (Radio) broadcast

emit'tente AG (banca) issuing; (Radio) broadcasting, transmitting ▸ SF (Radio) transmitter

emofi'lia SF haemophilia (BRIT), hemophilia (US)

emofi'liaco, -a, -ci, -che AG, SM/F haemophiliac (BRIT), hemophiliac (US)

emoglo'bina SF haemoglobin (BRIT), hemoglobin (US)

emolli'ente AG soothing

emorra'gia, -'gie [emorra'dʒia] SF haemorrhage (BRIT), hemorrhage (US)

emor'roidi SFPL haemorrhoids pl (BRIT), hemorrhoids pl (US)

emos'tatico, -a, -ci, -che AG haemostatic (BRIT), hemostatic (US); **laccio ~** tourniquet; **matita emostatica** styptic pencil

emotività SF emotionalism

emo'tivo, -a AG emotional

emozio'nante [emottsjo'nante] AG exciting, thrilling

emozio'nare [emottsjo'nare] /72/ VT (appassionare) to excite, thrill; (commuovere) to move; (agitare) to make nervous; (innervosire) to upset; **emozionarsi** VPR to be excited; to be moved; to be nervous; to be upset

emozio'nato, -a [emottsjo'nato] AG (commosso) moved; (agitato) nervous; (elettrizzato) excited

emozi'one [emot'tsjone] SF emotion; (agitazione) excitement

'empio, -a AG (sacrilego) impious; (spietato) cruel, pitiless; (malvagio) wicked, evil

em'pirico, -a, -ci, -che AG empirical

em'porio SM general store

emu'lare /72/ VT to emulate

'emulo, -a SM/F imitator

emulsi'one SF emulsion

EN SIGLA = **Enna**

en'ciclica, -che [en'tʃiklika] SF (Rel) encyclical

enciclope'dia [entʃiklope'dia] SF encyclop(a)edia

encomi'abile AG commendable, praiseworthy

encomi'are /19/ VT to commend, praise

en'comio SM commendation; **~ solenne** (Mil) mention in dispatches

endove'noso, -a AG (Med) intravenous ▶ SF intravenous injection

E'NEA SIGLA F = **Comitato nazionale per la ricerca e lo sviluppo dell'Energia Nucleare e delle Energie Alternative**

'E.N.E.L. SIGLA M = Ente Nazionale per l'Energia Elettrica) national electricity company

ener'getico, -a, -ci, -che [ener'dʒetiko] AG (risorse, crisi) energy cpd; (sostanza, alimento) energy-giving

ener'gia, -'gie [ener'dʒia] SF (Fisica) energy; (fig) energy, strength, vigour (BRIT), vigor (US); **~ eolica** wind power; **~ solare** solar energy, solar power

e'nergico, -a, -ci, -che [e'nɛrdʒiko] AG energetic, vigorous

'enfasi SF emphasis; (peg) bombast, pomposity

en'fatico, -a, -ci, -che AG emphatic; pompous

enfatiz'zare [enfatid'dzare] /72/ VT to emphasize, stress

enfi'sema SM emphysema

'ENI SIGLA M = **Ente Nazionale Idrocarburi**

e'nigma, -i SM enigma

enig'matico, -a, -ci, -che AG enigmatic

'ENIT SIGLA M (= Ente Nazionale Italiano per il Turismo) Italian tourist authority

en'nesimo, -a AG (Mat, fig) nth; **per l'ennesima volta** for the umpteenth time

enolo'gia [enolo'dʒia] SF oenology (BRIT), enology (US)

e'nologo, -gi SM wine expert

e'norme AG enormous, huge

enormità SF INV enormity, huge size; (assurdità) absurdity; **non dire ~!** don't talk nonsense!

eno'teca, -che SF (negozio) wine bar

'E.N.P.A. SIGLA M (= Ente Nazionale Protezione Animali) ≈ RSPCA (BRIT), ≈ SPCA (US)

'E.N.P.A.S. SIGLA M (= Ente Nazionale di Previdenza e Assistenza per i Dipendenti Statali) welfare organization for State employees

'ente SM (istituzione) body, board, corporation; (Filosofia) being; **~ locale** local authority (BRIT), local government (US); **~ pubblico** public body; **~ di ricerca** research organization

ente'rite SF enteritis

entità SF INV (Filosofia) entity; (di perdita, danni, investimenti) extent; (di popolazione) size; **di molta/poca ~** (avvenimento, incidente) of great/ little importance

en'trambi, -e PRON PL both (of them) ▶ AG PL: **~ i ragazzi** both boys, both of the boys

en'trante AG (prossimo: mese, anno) next, coming

en'trare /72/ VI to enter, go (o come) in; **~ in** (luogo) to enter, go (o come) into; (trovar posto, poter stare) to fit into; (essere ammesso a: club ecc) to join, become a member of; **~ in automobile** to get into the car; **far ~ qn** (visitatore ecc) to show sb in; **~ in società/in commercio con qn** to go into partnership/ business with sb; **questo non c'entra** (fig) that's got nothing to do with it

en'trata SF entrance, entry; **dov'è l'~?** where's the entrance?; **entrate** SFPL (Comm) receipts, takings; (Econ) income sg; **"~ libera"** "admission free"; **con l'~ in vigore dei nuovi provvedimenti …** once the new measures come into effect …; **entrate tributarie** tax revenue sg

'**entro** PREP (*temporale*) within; ~ **domani** by tomorrow; ~ **e non oltre il 25 aprile** no later than 25th April

entro'terra SM INV hinterland

entusias'mante AG exciting

entusias'mare /72/ VT to excite, fill with enthusiasm; **entusiasmarsi** VPR: **entusiasmarsi (per qc/qn)** to become enthusiastic (about sth/sb)

entusi'asmo SM enthusiasm

entusi'asta, -i, -e AG enthusiastic ▶ SM/F enthusiast

entusi'astico, -a, -ci, -che AG enthusiastic

enucle'are /72/ VT (*formale: chiarire*) to explain

enume'rare /72/ VT to enumerate, list

enunci'are [enun'tʃare] /14/ VT (*teoria*) to enunciate, set out

en'zima, -i SM enzyme

e'olico, -a, -chi, -che AG wind; **energia eolica** wind power

e'patico, -a, -ci, -che AG hepatic; **cirrosi epatica** cirrhosis of the liver

epa'tite SF hepatitis

'**epico, -a, -ci, -che** AG epic

epide'mia SF epidemic

epi'dermico, -a, -ci, -che AG (*Anat*) skin *cpd*; (*fig: interesse, impressioni*) superficial

epi'dermide SF skin, epidermis

Epifa'nia SF Epiphany

e'pigono SM imitator

e'pigrafe SF epigraph; (*su libro*) dedication

epiles'sia SF epilepsy

epi'lettico, -a, -ci, -che AG, SM/F epileptic

e'pilogo, -ghi SM conclusion

epi'sodico, -a, -ci, -che AG (*romanzo, narrazione*) episodic; (*fig: occasionale*) occasional

epi'sodio SM episode; **sceneggiato a episodi** serial

e'pistola SF epistle

episto'lare AG epistolary; **essere in rapporto** *o* **relazione ~ con qn** to correspond *o* be in correspondence with sb

e'piteto SM epithet

'**epoca, -che** SF (*periodo storico*) age, era; (*tempo*) time; (*Geo*) age; **mobili d'~** period furniture; **fare ~** (*scandalo*) to cause a stir; (*cantante, moda*) to mark a new era

epo'pea SF (*anche fig*) epic

ep'pure CONG and yet, nevertheless

EPT SIGLA M (= *Ente Provinciale per il Turismo*) district tourist bureau

epu'rare /72/ VT (*Pol*) to purge

equ'anime AG (*imparziale*) fair, impartial

equa'tore SM equator

equazi'one [ekwat'tsjone] SF (*Mat*) equation

e'questre AG equestrian

equi'latero, -a AG equilateral

equili'brare /72/ VT to balance

equili'brato, -a AG (*carico, fig: giudizio*) balanced; (*vita*) well-regulated; (*persona*) stable, well-balanced

equi'librio SM balance, equilibrium; **perdere l'~** to lose one's balance; **stare in ~ su** (*persona*) to balance on; (*oggetto*) to be balanced on

equili'brismo SM tightrope walking; (*fig*) juggling

e'quino, -a AG horse *cpd*, equine

equi'nozio [ekwi'nɔttsjo] SM equinox

equipaggia'mento [ekwipaddʒa'mento] SM (*operazione: di nave*) equipping, fitting out; (: *di spedizione, esercito*) equipping, kitting out; (*attrezzatura*) equipment

equipaggi'are [ekwipad'dʒare] /62/ VT (*di persone*) to man; (*di mezzi*) to equip; **equipaggiarsi** VPR to equip o.s.

equi'paggio [ekwi'paddʒo] SM crew

equipa'rare /72/ VT to make equal

é'quipe [e'kip] SF (*Sport, gen*) team

equità SF equity, fairness

equitazi'one [ekwitat'tsjone] SF (horse-) riding

equiva'lente AG, SM equivalent

equiva'lenza [ekwiva'lɛntsa] SF equivalence

equiva'lere /126/ VI: ~ **a** to be equivalent to; **equivalersi** VPR (*forze ecc*) to counterbalance each other; (*soluzioni*) to amount to the same thing; **equivale a dire che ...** that is the same as saying that ...

equi'valso, -a PP *di* **equivalere**

equivo'care /20/ VI to misunderstand

e'quivoco, -a, -ci, -che AG equivocal, ambiguous; (*sospetto*) dubious ▶ SM misunderstanding; **a scanso di equivoci** to avoid any misunderstanding; **giocare sull'~** to equivocate

'**equo, -a** AG fair, just

'**era** SF era

'**era** *etc* VB *vedi* **essere**

erari'ale AG: **ufficio ~** ≈ tax office; **imposte erariali** revenue taxes; **spese erariali** public expenditure *sg*

e'rario SM: **l'~** ≈ the Treasury

'**erba** SF grass; **in ~** (*fig*) budding; **fare di ogni ~ un fascio** (*fig*) to lump everything (*o* everybody) together; **erbe aromatiche** herbs; ~ **medica** lucerne

er'baccia, -ce [er'battʃa] SF weed

er'bivoro, -a AG herbivorous ▶ SM/F herbivore

erbo'rista, -i, -e SM/F herbalist

erboriste'ria SF (*scienza*) study of medicinal herbs; (*negozio*) herbalist's (shop)

er'boso, -a AG grassy

e'rede SMF heir(-ess); ~ **legittimo** heir-at-law

eredità SF (Dir) inheritance; (Biol) heredity; **lasciare qc in ~ a qn** to leave o bequeath sth to sb

eredi'tare /**72**/ VT to inherit

eredi'tario, -a AG hereditary

erediti'era SF heiress

ere'mita, -i SM hermit

eremi'taggio [eremi'taddʒo] SM hermitage

'eremo SM hermitage; (fig) retreat

ere'sia SF heresy

e'ressi etc VB vedi **erigere**

e'retico, -a, -ci, -che AG heretical ▶ SM/F heretic

e'retto, -a PP di **erigere** ▶ AG erect, upright

erezi'one [eret'tsjone] SF (Fisiol) erection

ergasto'lano, -a SM/F prisoner serving a life sentence, lifer (col)

er'gastolo SM (Dir: pena) life imprisonment; (: luogo di pena) prison (for those serving life sentences)

ergono'mia SF ergonomics sg

ergo'nomico, -a, -ci, -che AG ergonomic(al)

'erica SF heather

e'rigere [e'ridʒere] /**39**/ VT to erect, raise; (fig: fondare) to found

eri'tema SM (Med) inflammation, erythema; **~ solare** sunburn

Eri'trea SF Eritrea

ermel'lino SM ermine

er'metico, -a, -ci, -che AG hermetic

'ernia SF (Med) hernia; **~ del disco** slipped disc

'ero VB vedi **essere**

e'rodere /**49**/ VT to erode

e'roe SM hero

ero'gare /**80**/ VT (somme) to distribute; (gas, servizi) to supply

erogazi'one [erogat'tsjone] SF distribution; supply

e'roico, -a, -ci, -che AG heroic

ero'ina SF heroine; (droga) heroin

ero'ismo SM heroism

'eros SM Eros

erosi'one SF erosion

e'roso, -a PP di **erodere**

e'rotico, -a, -ci, -che AG erotic

ero'tismo SM eroticism

'erpete SM herpes sg

'erpice ['erpitʃe] SM (Agr) harrow

er'rare /**72**/ VI (vagare) to wander, roam; (sbagliare) to be mistaken

er'rato, -a AG wrong

er'roneo, -a AG erroneous, wrong

er'rore SM error, mistake; (morale) error; **per ~** by mistake; **ci dev'essere un ~** there must be some mistake; **~ giudiziario** miscarriage of justice

'erto, -a AG (very) steep ▶ SF steep slope; **stare all'erta** to be on the alert

eru'dire /**55**/ VT to teach, educate

eru'dito, -a AG learned, erudite

erut'tare /**72**/ VT (vulcano) to throw out, belch

eruzi'one [erut'tsjone] SF eruption; (Med) rash

es. ABBR (= esempio) e.g.

E.S. SIGLA M (= elettroshock) ECT

E.S.A. ['eza] SIGLA M (= European Space Agency) ESA

esacer'bare [ezatʃer'bare] /**72**/ VT to exacerbate

esage'rare [ezadʒe'rare] /**72**/ VT to exaggerate ▶ VI to exaggerate; (eccedere) to go too far; **senza ~** without exaggeration

esage'rato, -a [ezadʒe'rato] AG (notizia, proporzioni) exaggerated; (curiosità, pignoleria) excessive; (prezzo) exorbitant ▶ SM/F: **sei il solito ~** you are exaggerating as usual

esagerazi'one [ezadʒerat'tsjone] SF exaggeration

esago'nale AG hexagonal

e'sagono SM hexagon

esa'lare /**72**/ VT (odori) to give off ▶ VI: **~ (da)** to emanate (from); **~ l'ultimo respiro** (fig) to breathe one's last

esalazi'one [ezalat'tsjone] SF (emissione) exhalation; (odore) fumes pl

esal'tante AG exciting

esal'tare /**72**/ VT to exalt; (entusiasmare) to excite, stir; **esaltarsi** VPR: **esaltarsi (per qc)** to grow excited (about sth)

esal'tato, -a SM/F fanatic

esaltazi'one [ezaltat'tsjone] SF (elogio) extolling, exalting; (nervosa) intense excitement; (mistica) exaltation

e'same SM examination; (Ins) exam, examination; **fare o dare un ~** to sit o take an exam; **fare un ~ di coscienza** to search one's conscience; **~ di guida** driving test; **~ del sangue** blood test

esami'nare /**72**/ VT to examine

e'sangue AG bloodless; (fig: pallido) pale, wan; (: privo di vigore) lifeless

e'sanime AG lifeless

esaspe'rare /**72**/ VT to exasperate; (situazione) to exacerbate; **esasperarsi** VPR to become annoyed o exasperated

esasperazi'one [ezasperat'tsjone] SF exasperation

esatta'mente AV exactly; accurately, precisely

esat'tezza [ezat'tettsa] SF exactitude, accuracy, precision; **per l'~** to be precise

e'satto, -a PP di **esigere** ▶ AG (calcolo, ora) correct, right, exact; (preciso) accurate, precise; (puntuale) punctual

esat'tore SM (di imposte ecc) collector

esat'toria SF: **~ comunale** district rates office (BRIT) o assessor's office (US)

esau'dire /**55**/ VT to grant, fulfil (BRIT), fulfill (US)

esauri'ente AG exhaustive

esauri'mento SM exhaustion; **~ nervoso** nervous breakdown; **svendita (fino) ad ~ della merce** clearance sale

esau'rire /**55**/ VT (*stancare*) to exhaust, wear out; (*provviste, miniera*) to exhaust; **esaurirsi** VPR to exhaust o.s., wear o.s. out; (*provviste*) to run out

esau'rito, -a AG exhausted; (*merci*) sold out; (*libri*) out of print; **essere ~** (*persona*) to be run down; **registrare il tutto ~** (*Teat*) to have a full house

e'sausto, -a AG exhausted

esauto'rare /**72**/ VT (*dirigente, funzionario*) to deprive of authority

esazi'one [ezat'tsjone] SF collection (of taxes)

'esca (pl **esche**) SF bait

escamo'tage [εskamɔ'taʒ] SM subterfuge

escande'scenza [eskandeʃʃentsa] SF: **dare in escandescenze** to lose one's temper, fly into a rage

'esce ['εʃʃe] VB *vedi* **uscire**

eschi'mese [eski'mese] AG, SMF, SM Eskimo

'esci ['εʃʃi] VB *vedi* **uscire**

escl. ABBR (= *escluso*) excl

escla'mare /**72**/ VI to exclaim, cry out

esclama'tivo, -a AG: **punto ~** exclamation mark

esclamazi'one [esklamat'tsjone] SF exclamation

es'cludere /**3**/ VT to exclude

es'clusi etc VB *vedi* **escludere**

esclusi'one SF exclusion; **a ~ di, fatta ~ per** except (for), apart from; **senza ~ (alcuna)** without exception; **procedere per ~** to follow a process of elimination; **senza ~ di colpi** (*fig*) with no holds barred; **~ sociale** social exclusion

esclu'siva SF *vedi* **esclusivo**

esclusiva'mente AV exclusively, solely

esclu'sivo, -a AG exclusive ▶ SF (*Dir, Comm*) exclusive *o* sole rights *pl*

es'cluso, -a PP *di* **escludere** ▶ AG: **nessuno ~** without exception; **IVA esclusa** excluding VAT, exclusive of VAT

'esco VB *vedi* **uscire**

escogi'tare [eskodʒi'tare] /**72**/ VT to devise, think up

'escono VB *vedi* **uscire**

escoriazi'one [eskorjat'tsjone] SF abrasion, graze

escre'menti SMPL excrement *sg*, faeces

escursi'one SF (*gita*) excursion, trip; (: *a piedi*) hike, walk; (*Meteor*): **~ termica** temperature range

escursio'nista, -i, -e SM/F (*gitante*) (day) tripper; (*a piedi*) hiker, walker

ese'crare /**72**/ VT to loathe, abhor

esecu'tivo, -a AG, SM executive

esecu'tore, -'trice SM/F (*Mus*) performer; (*Dir*) executor

esecuzi'one [ezekut'tsjone] SF execution, carrying out; (*Mus*) performance; **~ capitale** execution

ese'geta, -i [eze'dʒɛta] SM commentator

esegu'ire /**45**/ VT to carry out, execute; (*Mus*) to perform, execute

e'sempio SM example; **per ~** for example, for instance; **fare un ~** to give an example

esem'plare AG exemplary ▶ SM example; (*copia*) copy; (*Bot, Zool, Geo*) specimen

esemplifi'care /**20**/ VT to exemplify

esen'tare /**72**/ VT: **~ qn/qc da** to exempt sb/ sth from

esen'tasse AG INV tax-free

e'sente AG: **~ da** (*dispensato da*) exempt from; (*privo di*) free from

esenzi'one [ezen'tsjone] SF exemption

e'sequie SFPL funeral rites; funeral service *sg*

eser'cente [ezer'tʃɛnte] SMF trader, dealer; shopkeeper

eserci'tare [ezertʃi'tare] /**72**/ VT (*professione*) to practise (BRIT), practice (US); (*allenare: corpo, mente*) to exercise, train; (: *diritto*) to exercise; (: *influenza, pressione*) to exert; **esercitarsi** VPR to practise; **esercitarsi nella guida** to practise one's driving

esercitazi'one [ezertʃitat'tsjone] SF (*scolastica, militare*) exercise; **esercitazioni di tiro** target practice *sg*

e'sercito [e'zɛrtʃito] SM army

eser'cizio [ezer'tʃittsjo] SM practice; (*compito, movimento*) exercise; (*azienda*) business, concern; exercising; (*fisico: di matematica*) exercise; (*Econ*): **~ finanziario** financial year; **in ~** (*medico ecc*) practising (BRIT), practicing (US); **nell'~ delle proprie funzioni** in the execution of one's duties

esfoli'ante SM exfoliator

esi'bire /**55**/ VT to exhibit, display; (*documenti*) to produce, present; **esibirsi** VPR (*attore*) to perform; (*fig*) to show off

esibizi'one [ezibit'tsjone] SF exhibition; (*di documento*) presentation; (*spettacolo*) show, performance

esibizio'nista, -i, -e [ezibittsjo'nista] SM/F exhibitionist

esi'gente [ezi'dʒɛnte] AG demanding

esi'genza [ezi'dʒɛntsa] SF demand, requirement

e'sigere [e'zidʒere] /**47**/ VT (*pretendere*) to demand; (*richiedere*) to demand, require; (*imposte*) to collect

esi'gibile [ezi'dʒibile] AG payable

e'siguo, -a AG small, slight

esila'rante AG hilarious; **gas ~** laughing gas

'esile AG (*persona*) slender, slim; (*stelo*) thin; (*voce*) faint

esili'are /**19**/ VT to exile

esili'ato, -a AG exiled ▶ SM/F exile

e'silio SM exile

e'simere /**29**/ VT: ~ **qn/qc da** to exempt sb/sth from; **esimersi** VPR: **esimersi da** to get out of

esis'tente AG existing; (*attuale*) present, current

esis'tenza [ezis'tɛntsa] SF existence

esistenzia'lismo [ezistentsja'lizmo] SM existentialism

e'sistere /**11**/ VI to exist; **esiste più di una versione dell'opera** there is more than one version of the work; **non esiste!** (*col*) no way!

esis'tito, -a PP *di* **esistere**

esi'tante AG hesitant; (*voce*) faltering

esi'tare /**72**/ VI to hesitate

esitazi'one [ezitat'tsjone] SF hesitation

'esito SM result, outcome

'eskimo SM (*giaccone*) parka

'esodo SM exodus

e'sofago, -gi SM oesophagus (BRIT), esophagus (US)

esone'rare /**72**/ VT: ~ **qn da** to exempt sb from

esorbi'tante AG exorbitant, excessive

esor'cismo [ezor'tʃizmo] SM exorcism

esor'cista, -i [ezor'tʃista] SM exorcist

esorciz'zare [ezortʃid'dzare] /**72**/ VT to exorcize

esordi'ente SMF beginner

e'sordio SM debut

esor'dire /**55**/ VI (*nel teatro*) to make one's debut; (*fig*) to start out, begin (one's career); **esordì dicendo che ...** he began by saying (that) ...

esor'tare /**72**/ VT: ~ **qn a fare** to urge sb to do

esortazi'one [ezortat'tsjone] SF exhortation

e'soso, -a AG (*prezzo*) exorbitant; (*persona: avido*) grasping

eso'terico, -a, -ci, -che AG esoteric

e'sotico, -a, -ci, -che AG exotic

es'pandere /**110**/ VT to expand; (*confini*) to extend; (*influenza*) to extend, spread; **espandersi** VPR to expand

espansi'one SF expansion; ~ **di memoria** (*Inform*) memory upgrade

espansività SF expansiveness

espan'sivo, -a AG expansive, communicative

es'panso, -a PP *di* **espandere**

espatri'are /**19**/ VI to leave one's country

es'patrio SM expatriation; **permesso di ~** authorization to leave the country

espedi'ente SM expedient; **vivere di espedienti** to live by one's wits

es'pellere /**48**/ VT to expel

esperi'enza [espe'rjɛntsa] SF experience; (*Sci: prova*) experiment; **parlare per ~** to speak from experience

esperi'mento SM experiment; **fare un ~** to carry out *o* do an experiment

es'perto, -a AG, SM/F expert

espi'anto SM (*Med*) removal

espi'are /**60**/ VT to atone for

espiazi'one [espiat'tsjone] SF: ~ **(di)** expiation (of), atonement (for)

espi'rare /**72**/ VT, VI to breathe out

espleta'mento SM (*Amm*) carrying out

esple'tare /**72**/ VT (*Amm*) to carry out

espli'care /**20**/ VT (*attività*) to carry out, perform

esplica'tivo, -a AG explanatory

es'plicito, -a [es'plitʃito] AG explicit

es'plodere /**49**/ VI (*anche fig*) to explode ▶ VT to fire

esplo'rare /**72**/ VT to explore

esplora'tore, -'trice SM/F explorer; (*anche: giovane esploratore*) (boy) scout/(girl) guide (BRIT) *o* scout (US) ▶ SM (*Naut*) scout (ship)

esplorazi'one [esplorat'tsjone] SF exploration; **mandare qn in ~** (*Mil*) to send sb to scout ahead

esplosi'one SF (*anche fig*) explosion

esplo'sivo, -a AG, SM explosive

es'ploso, -a PP *di* **esplodere**

es'pone *etc* VB *vedi* **esporre**

espo'nente SMF (*rappresentante*) representative

esponenzi'ale [esponen'tsjale] AG (*Mat*) exponential

es'pongo, es'poni *etc* VB *vedi* **esporre**

es'porre /**77**/ VT (*merci*) to display; (*quadro*) to exhibit, show; (*fatti, idee*) to explain, set out; (*porre in pericolo, Fot*) to expose; **esporsi** VPR: **esporsi a** (*sole, pericolo*) to expose o.s. to; (*critiche*) to lay o.s. open to

espor'tare /**72**/ VT to export

esporta'tore, -'trice AG exporting ▶ SM exporter

esportazi'one [esportat'tsjone] SF (*azione*) exportation, export; (*insieme di prodotti*) exports *pl*

es'pose *etc* VB *vedi* **esporre**

espo'simetro SM exposure meter

esposizi'one [espozit'tsjone] SF displaying; exhibiting; setting out; (*anche Fot*) exposure; (*mostra*) exhibition; (*narrazione*) explanation, exposition

es'posto, -a PP *di* **esporre** ▶ AG: ~ **a nord** facing north, north-facing ▶ SM (*Amm*) statement, account; (: *petizione*) petition

espressi'one SF expression

espres'sivo, -a AG expressive

es'presso, -a PP di **esprimere** ▶ AG express ▶ SM (lettera) express letter; (anche: **treno espresso**) express train; (anche: **caffè espresso**) espresso

es'primere /50/ VT to express; **esprimersi** VPR to express o.s.

espropri'are /19/ VT (terreni, edifici) to place a compulsory purchase order on; (persona) to dispossess

espropriazi'one [esproprjat'tsjone] SF, **es'proprio** SM expropriation; ~ **per pubblica utilità** compulsory purchase

espu'gnare [espuɲ'ɲare] /15/ VT to take by force, storm

es'pulsi etc VB vedi **espellere**

espulsi'one SF expulsion

es'pulso, -a PP di **espellere**

'essa PRON F (pl **esse**) vedi **esso**

es'senza [es'sɛntsa] SF essence

essenzi'ale [essen'tsjale] AG essential; (stile, linea) simple ▶ SM: **l'~** the main o most important thing

(PAROLA CHIAVE)

'essere /51/ SM being; **essere umano** human being

▶ VB COPULATIVO **1** (con attributo, sostantivo) to be; **sei giovane/simpatico** you are o you're young/nice; **è medico** he is o he's a doctor

2 (+ di: appartenere) to be; **di chi è la penna?** whose pen is it?; **è di Carla** it is o it's Carla's, it belongs to Carla

3 (+ di: provenire) to be; **è di Venezia** he is o he's from Venice

4 (data, ora): **è il 15 agosto** it is o it's the 15th of August; **è lunedì** it is o it's Monday; **che ora è, che ore sono?** what time is it?; **è l'una** it is o it's one o'clock; **sono le due** it is o it's two o'clock

5 (costare): **quant'è?** how much is it?; **sono 20 euro** it's 20 euros

▶ VB AUS **1** (attivo): **essere arrivato/venuto** to have arrived/come; **è già partita** she has already left

2 (passivo) to be; **essere fatto da** to be made by; **è stata uccisa** she has been killed

3 (riflessivo): **si sono lavati** they washed, they got washed

4 (+ da + infinito): **è da farsi subito** it must be done o is to be done immediately

▶ VI **1** (esistere, trovarsi) to be; **sono a casa** I'm at home; **essere in piedi/seduto** to be standing/sitting

2 (succedere): **sarà quel che sarà** what will be will be; **sia quel che sia, io me ne vado** come what may, I'm going now

3: **esserci**: **c'è** there is; **ci sono** there are; **che c'è?** what's the matter?, what is it?; **non c'è niente da fare** there's nothing we can do; **c'è da sperare che ...** one can only hope that ...; **ci sono!** (sono pronto) I'm ready; (ho capito) I get it!

▶ VB IMPERS: **è tardi/Pasqua** it's late/Easter; **è mezzanotte** it's midnight; **è bello/caldo/ freddo** it's nice/hot/cold; **è possibile che venga** he may come; **è così** that's the way it is

'essi PRON MPL vedi **esso**

essic'care /20/ VT (gen) to dry; (legname) to season; (cibi) to desiccate; (bacino, palude) to drain; **essiccarsi** VPR (fiume, pozzo) to dry up; (vernice) to dry (out)

'esso, -a PRON it; (riferito a persona: soggetto) he (she); (: complemento) him (her); **essi, e** PRON PL (soggetto) they; (complemento) them

est SM east; **i paesi dell'E~** the Eastern bloc sg

'estasi SF ecstasy

estasi'are /19/ VT to send into raptures; **estasiarsi** VPR: **estasiarsi (davanti a)** to go into ecstasies (over), go into raptures (over)

es'tate SF summer

es'tatico, -a, -ci, -che AG ecstatic

estempo'raneo, -a AG (discorso) extempore, impromptu; (brano musicale) impromptu

es'tendere /120/ VT to extend; **estendersi** VPR (diffondersi) to spread; (territorio, confini) to extend

estensi'one SF extension; (di superficie) expanse; (di voce) range

estenu'ante AG wearing, tiring

estenu'are /72/ VT (stancare) to wear out, tire out

esteri'ore AG outward, external

esteriorità SF INV outward appearance

esteriorizz'are [esterjorid'dzare] /72/ VT (gioia ecc) to show

ester'nare /72/ VT to express; **~ un sospetto** to voice a suspicion

es'terno, -a AG (porta, muro) outer, outside; (scala) outside; (alunno, impressione) external ▶ SM outside, exterior ▶ SM/F (allievo) day pupil; **esterni** SMPL (Cine) location shots; **"per uso ~"** "for external use only"; **all'~** outside; **gli esterni sono stati girati a Glasgow** the location shots were taken in Glasgow

'estero, -a AG foreign ▶ SM: **all'~** abroad; **Ministero degli Esteri, gli Esteri** Ministry for Foreign Affairs, ≈ Foreign Office (BRIT), ≈ State Department (US)

esterofi'lia SF excessive love of foreign things

esterre'fatto, -a AG (costernato) horrified; (sbalordito) astounded

es'tesi etc VB vedi **estendere**

es'teso, -a PP di **estendere** ▶ AG extensive, large; **scrivere per ~** to write in full

estetica'mente AV aesthetically
es'tetico, -a, -ci, -che AG aesthetic ▶ SF
(disciplina) aesthetics sg; (bellezza)
attractiveness; **chirurgia estetica** cosmetic
surgery; **cura estetica** beauty treatment
este'tista, -i, -e SM/F beautician
'**estimo** SM valuation; (disciplina) surveying
es'tinguere /42/ VT to extinguish, put out;
(debito) to pay off; (conto) to close; **estinguersi**
VPR to go out; (specie) to become extinct
es'tinsi etc VB vedi **estinguere**
es'tinto, -a PP di **estinguere**
estin'tore SM (fire) extinguisher
estinzi'one [estin'tsjone] SF putting out;
(di specie) extinction; (di debito) payment;
(di conto) closing
estir'pare /72/ VT (pianta) to uproot, pull up;
(dente) to extract; (tumore) to remove; (fig:
vizio) to eradicate
es'tivo, -a AG summer cpd
'**estone** AG, SMF, SM Estonian
Es'tonia SF: **l'~** Estonia
es'torcere [es'tɔrtʃere] **/106/** VT: **~ qc (a qn)**
to extort sth (from sb)
estorsi'one SF extortion
es'torto, -a PP di **estorcere**
estra'dare /72/ VT to extradite
estradizi'one [estradit'tsjone] SF extradition
es'trae, es'traggo etc VB vedi **estrarre**
es'traneo, -a AG foreign; (discorso)
extraneous, unrelated ▶ SM/F stranger;
rimanere ~ a qc to take no part in sth;
sentirsi ~ a (famiglia, società) to feel alienated
from; **"ingresso vietato agli estranei"**
"no admittance to unauthorized personnel"
estrani'arsi /19/ VPR: **~ (da)** to cut o.s. off
(from)
es'trarre /123/ VT to extract; (minerali) to mine;
(sorteggiare) to draw; **~ a sorte** to draw lots
es'trassi etc VB vedi **estrarre**
es'tratto, -a PP di **estrarre** ▶ SM extract;
(di documento) abstract; **~ conto** (bank)
statement; **~ di nascita** birth certificate
estrazi'one [estrat'tsjone] SF extraction;
mining; drawing no pl; draw
estrema'mente AV extremely
estre'mismo SM extremism
estre'mista, -i, -e SM/F extremist
estremità SF INV extremity, end ▶ SFPL (Anat)
extremities
es'tremo, -a AG extreme; (ultimo: ora, tentativo)
final, last ▶ SM extreme; (di pazienza, forza)
limit, end; **estremi** SMPL (Dir) essential
elements; (Amm: dati essenziali) details,
particulars; **l'E~ Oriente** the Far East
estrinse'care /20/ VT to express, show
'**estro** SM (capriccio) whim, fancy; (ispirazione
creativa) inspiration
estro'messo, -a PP di **estromettere**

estro'mettere /63/ VT: **~ (da)** (partito, club ecc)
to expel (from); (discussione) to exclude (from)
estromissi'one SF expulsion
es'troso, -a AG whimsical, capricious;
inspired
estro'verso, -a AG, SM extrovert
estu'ario SM estuary
esube'rante AG exuberant; (Comm)
redundant (BRIT)
esube'ranza [ezube'rantsa] SF (di persona)
exuberance; **~ di personale** (Comm)
overmanning (BRIT), over-staffing (US)
e'subero SM: **~ di personale** surplus staff;
in ~ redundant, due to be laid off
esu'lare /72/ VI: **~ da** (competenza) to be beyond;
(compiti) not to be part of
'**esule** SMF exile
esul'tanza [ezul'tantsa] SF exultation
esul'tare /72/ VI to exult
esu'mare /72/ VT (salma) to exhume, disinter;
(fig) to unearth
età SF INV age; **all'~ di 8 anni** at the age of 8,
at 8 years of age; **ha la mia ~** he (o she) is the
same age as me o as I am; **di mezza ~**
middle-aged; **raggiungere la maggiore ~**
to come of age; **essere in ~ minore** to be
under age; **in ~ avanzata** advanced in years
eta'nolo SM ethanol
etc. ABBR etc.
'**etere** SM ether; **via ~** on the airwaves
e'tereo, -a AG ethereal
eternità SF eternity
e'terno, -a AG eternal; (interminabile: lamenti,
attesa) never-ending; **in ~** for ever, eternally
etero'geneo, -a [etero'dʒɛneo] AG
heterogeneous
eterosessu'ale AG, SMF heterosexual
'**etica** SF vedi **etico**
eti'chetta [eti'ketta] SF label; (cerimoniale):
l'~ etiquette
'**etico, -a, -ci, -che** AG ethical ▶ SF ethics sg
eti'lometro SM Breathalyzer®
etimolo'gia, -'gie [etimolo'dʒia] SF
etymology
etimo'logico, -a, -ci, -che [etimo'lɔdʒiko] AG
etymological
e'tiope AG, SMF Ethiopian
Eti'opia SF: **l'~** Ethiopia
eti'opico, -a, -ci, -che AG, SM (Ling) Ethiopian
'**Etna** SM: **l'~** Etna
'**etnico, -a, -ci, -che** AG ethnic
e'trusco, -a, -schi, -sche AG, SM/F Etruscan
'**ettaro** SM hectare (10,000 m²)
'**etto** ABBR M (= ettogrammo) 100 grams
etto'grammo SM hectogram(me) (= 100 grams)
et'tolitro SM hectolitre (BRIT), hectoliter (US)
et'tometro SM hectometre
EU ABBR = **Europa**
euca'lipto SM eucalyptus

Eucaris'tia SF: **l'~** the Eucharist
eufe'mismo SM euphemism
eufe'mistico, -a, -ci, -che AG euphemistic
eufo'ria SF euphoria
eu'forico, -a, -ci, -che AG euphoric
Eu'rasia SF Eurasia
eurasi'atico, -a, -ci, -che AG, SM/F Eurasian
Eura'tom SIGLA F (= *Comunità Europea dell'Energia Atomica*) Euratom
eu'ristico, -a, -ci, -che AG heuristic
'euro SM INV (*divisa*) euro
euro'corpo SM European force
eurodepu'tato SM Euro MP
eurodi'visa SF Eurocurrency
euro'dollaro SM Eurodollar
Euro'landia SF Euroland
euromer'cato SM Euromarket
euro'missile SM Euro-missile
Eu'ropa SF: **l'~** Europe
europarlamen'tare SMF Member of the European Parliament, MEP
euro'peo, -a AG, SM/F European
euro'scettico, -a, -ci, -che [euroʃʃettiko] SM/F Euro-sceptic
eutana'sia SF euthanasia
E.V. ABBR = **Eccellenza Vostra**
evacu'are /**72**/ VT to evacuate
evacuazi'one [evakuat'tsjone] SF evacuation
e'vadere /**52**/ VI (*fuggire*): **~ da** to escape from ▶ VT (*sbrigare*) to deal with, dispatch; (*tasse*) to evade
evan'gelico, -a, -ci, -che [evan'dʒeliko] AG evangelical
evange'lista, -i [evandʒe'lista] SM evangelist
evapo'rare /**72**/ VI to evaporate
evaporazi'one [evaporat'tsjone] SF evaporation
e'vasi *etc* VB *vedi* **evadere**
evasi'one SF (*vedi evadere*) escape; dispatch; **dare ~ ad un ordine** to carry out *o* execute an order; **letteratura d'~** escapist literature; **~ fiscale** tax evasion
eva'sivo, -a AG evasive
e'vaso, -a PP *di* **evadere** ▶ SM escapee
eva'sore SM: **~ (fiscale)** tax evader
eveni'enza [eve'njentsa] SF: **nell'~ che ciò succeda** should that happen; **essere pronto ad ogni ~** to be ready for anything *o* any eventuality
e'vento SM event
eventu'ale AG possible

eventualità SF INV eventuality, possibility; **nell'~ di** in the event of
eventual'mente AV if need be, if necessary
'Everest SM: **l'~, il Monte ~** (Mount) Everest
eversi'one SF subversion
ever'sivo, -a AG subversive
evi'dente AG evident, obvious
evidente'mente AV evidently; (*palesemente*) obviously, evidently
evi'denza [evi'dɛntsa] SF obviousness; **mettere in ~** to point out, highlight; **tenere in ~ qc** to bear sth in mind
evidenzi'are [eviden'tsjare] /**19**/ VT (*sottolineare*) to emphasize, highlight; (*con evidenziatore*) to highlight
evidenzia'tore [evidentsja'tore] SM (*penna*) highlighter
evi'rare /**72**/ VT to castrate
evi'tabile AG avoidable
evi'tare /**72**/ VT to avoid; **~ di fare** to avoid doing; **~ qc a qn** to spare sb sth
'evo SM age, epoch
evo'care /**20**/ VT to evoke
evoca'tivo, -a AG evocative
evocherò *etc* [evoke'rɔ] VB *vedi* **evocare**
evolu'tivo, -a AG (*gen*, *Biol*) evolutionary; (*Med*) progressive
evo'luto, -a PP *di* **evolversi** ▶ AG (*popolo, civiltà*) (highly) developed, advanced; (*persona: emancipato*) independent; (*: senza pregiudizi*) broad-minded
evoluzi'one [evolut'tsjone] SF evolution
e'volversi /**94**/ VPR to evolve; **con l'~ della situazione** as the situation develops
ev'viva ESCL hurrah!; **~ il re!** long live the king!, hurrah for the king!
ex PREFISSO ex-, former ▶ SM INV/F INV ex-boyfriend/girlfriend
ex 'aequo [ɛg'zɛkwo] AV: **classificarsi primo ~** to come joint first, come equal first
'extra AG INV first-rate; top-quality ▶ SM INV extra
extracomuni'tario, -a AG non-EU ▶ SM/F non-EU citizen (*often referred to non-European immigrant*)
extraconiu'gale AG extramarital
extraparlamen'tare AG extraparliamentary
extrasensori'ale AG: **percezione ~** extrasensory perception
extrater'restre AG, SMF extraterrestrial
extraur'bano, -a AG suburban

Ff

F, f ['ɛffe] SM O F INV (*lettera*) F, f; **F come Firenze** ≈ F for Frederick (*BRIT*), F for Fox (*US*)

F ABBR (= *Fahrenheit*) F

F. ABBR (= *fiume*) R

fa VB *vedi* **fare** ▶ SM INV (*Mus*) F; (: *solfeggiando la scala*) fa ▶ AV: **10 anni fa** 10 years ago

fabbi'sogno [fabbi'zoɲɲo] SM needs *pl*, requirements *pl*; **il ~ nazionale di petrolio** the country's oil requirements; **~ del settore pubblico** public sector borrowing requirement (*BRIT*), government debt borrowing (*US*)

'fabbrica SF factory

fabbri'cante SM manufacturer, maker

fabbri'care /**20**/ VT to build; (*produrre*) to manufacture, make; (*fig*) to fabricate, invent

fabbri'cato SM building

fabbricazi'one [fabbrikat'tsjone] SF building, fabrication; making, manufacture, manufacturing

'fabbro SM (black)smith

fac'cenda [fat'tʃɛnda] SF matter, affair; (*cosa da fare*) task, chore; **le faccende domestiche** the housework *sg*

faccendi'ere [fattʃen'djɛre] SM wheeler-dealer, (shady) operator

fac'cetta [fat'tʃetta] SF (*di pietra preziosa*) facet

fac'chino [fak'kino] SM porter

'faccia, -ce ['fattʃa] SF face; (*di moneta, medaglia*) side; **~ a ~** face to face; **di ~** opposite, facing; **avere la ~ (tosta) di dire/ fare qc** to have the cheek o nerve to say/do sth; **fare qc alla ~ di qn** to do sth to spite sb; **leggere qc in ~ a qn** to see sth written all over sb's face

facci'ata [fat'tʃata] SF façade; (*di pagina*) side

fac'cina [fat'tʃina] SF (*Inform*) emoticon

'faccio *etc* ['fattʃo] VB *vedi* **fare**

Facebook® ['feisbuk] SM Facebook®

fa'cente [fa'tʃente]: **~ funzione** *sm* (*Amm*) deputy

fa'cessi *etc* [fa'tʃessi] VB *vedi* **fare**

fa'ceto, -a [fa'tʃeto] AG witty, humorous

fa'cevo *etc* [fa'tʃevo] VB *vedi* **fare**

fa'cezia [fa'tʃettsja] SF witticism, witty remark

fa'chiro [fa'kiro] SM fakir

'facile ['fatʃile] AG easy; (*affabile*) easy-going; (*disposto*): **~ a** inclined to, prone to; (*probabile*): **è ~ che piova** it's likely to rain; **donna di facili costumi** woman of easy virtue, loose woman

facilità [fatʃili'ta] SF easiness; (*disposizione, dono*) aptitude

facili'tare [fatʃili'tare] /**72**/ VT to make easier

facilitazi'one [fatʃilitat'tsjone] SF (*gen*) facilities *pl*; **facilitazioni di pagamento** easy terms, credit facilities

facil'mente [fatʃil'mente] AV (*gen*) easily; (*probabilmente*) probably

faci'lone, -a [fatʃi'lone] SM/F (*peg*) happy-go-lucky person

facino'roso, -a [fatʃino'roso] AG violent

facoltà SF INV faculty; (*Chim*) property; (*autorità*) power

facolta'tivo, -a AG optional; (*fermata d'autobus*) request *cpd*

facol'toso, -a AG wealthy, rich

fac'simile SM facsimile

'faggio ['faddʒo] SM beech

fagi'ano [fa'dʒano] SM pheasant

fagio'lino [fadʒo'lino] SM French (*BRIT*) o string bean

fagi'olo [fa'dʒɔlo] SM bean; **capitare a ~** to come at the right time

fagoci'tare [fagotʃi'tare] /**72**/ VT (*fig: industria ecc*) to absorb, swallow up; (*scherzoso: cibo*) to devour

fa'gotto SM bundle; (*Mus*) bassoon; **far ~** (*fig*) to pack up and go

'Fahrenheit ['fa:rənheit] SM Fahrenheit

'fai VB *vedi* **fare**

'faida SF feud

'fai-da-'te SM INV DIY, do-it-yourself

fa'ina SF (*Zool*) stone marten

fa'lange [fa'landʒe] SF (*Anat, Mil*) phalanx

fal'cata SF stride

'**falce** ['faltʃe] SF scythe; **~ e martello** (Pol) hammer and sickle

fal'cetto [fal'tʃetto] SM sickle

falci'are [fal'tʃare] /**14**/ VT to cut; (fig) to mow down

falcia'trice [faltʃa'tritʃe] SF (per fieno) reaping machine; (per erba) mowing machine

'**falco, -chi** SM (anche fig) hawk

fal'cone SM falcon

'**falda** SF (Geo) layer, stratum; (di cappello) brim; (di cappotto) tails pl; (di monte) lower slope; (di tetto) pitch; (di neve) flake; **abito a falde** tails pl

fale'gname [faleɲ'ɲame] SM joiner

fa'lena SF (Zool) moth

'**Falkland** ['fɔːklənd] SFPL: **le isole ~** the Falkland Islands

fal'lace [fal'latʃe] AG misleading, deceptive

'**fallico, -a, -ci, -che** AG phallic

fallimen'tare AG (Comm) bankruptcy cpd; **bilancio ~** negative balance, deficit; **diritto ~** bankruptcy law

falli'mento SM failure; bankruptcy

fal'lire /**55**/ VI (Dir) to go bankrupt; (non riuscire): **~ (in)** to fail (in) ▶ VT (colpo, bersaglio) to miss

fal'lito, -a AG unsuccessful; bankrupt ▶ SM/F bankrupt

'**fallo** SM error, mistake; (imperfezione) defect, flaw; (Sport) foul; fault; (Anat) phallus; **senza ~** without fail; **cogliere qn in ~** to catch sb out; **mettere il piede in ~** to slip

fal'locrate SM male chauvinist

falò SM INV bonfire

fal'sare /**72**/ VT to distort, misrepresent

falsa'riga, -ghe SF lined page, ruled page; **sulla ~ di ...** (fig) along the lines of ...

fal'sario SM forger; counterfeiter

falsifi'care /**20**/ VT to forge; (monete) to forge, counterfeit

falsità SF INV (di persona, notizia) falseness; (bugia) falsehood, lie

'**falso, -a** AG false; (errato) wrong; (falsificato) forged; fake; (: oro, gioielli) imitation cpd ▶ SM forgery; **essere un ~ magro** to be heavier than one looks; **giurare il ~** to commit perjury; **~ in atto pubblico** forgery (of a legal document)

'**fama** SF fame; (reputazione) reputation, name

'**fame** SF hunger; **aver ~** to be hungry; **fare la ~** (fig) to starve, exist at subsistence level

fa'melico, -a, -ci, -che AG ravenous

famige'rato, -a [famidʒe'rato] AG notorious, ill-famed

fa'miglia [fa'miʎʎa] SF family

famili'are AG (della famiglia) family cpd; (ben noto) familiar; (rapporti, atmosfera) friendly; (Ling) informal, colloquial ▶ SMF relative, relation; **una vettura ~** a family car

familiarità SF familiarity; friendliness; informality

familiariz'zare [familjarid'dzare] /**72**/ VI: **~ con qn** to get to know sb; **abbiamo familiarizzato subito** we got on well together from the start

fa'moso, -a AG famous, well-known

fa'nale SM (Aut) light, lamp (BRIT); (luce stradale, Naut) light; (di faro) beacon

fa'natico, -a, -ci, -che AG fanatical; (del teatro, calcio ecc): **~ di** o **per** mad o crazy about ▶ SM/F fanatic; (tifoso) fan

fana'tismo SM fanaticism

fanciul'lezza [fantʃul'lettsa] SF childhood

fanci'ullo, -a [fan'tʃullo] SM/F child

fan'donia SF tall story; **fandonie** SFPL nonsense sg

fan'fara SF brass band; (musica) fanfare

fanfa'rone SM braggart

fan'ghiglia [fan'giʎʎa] SF mire, mud

'**fango, -ghi** SM mud; **fare i fanghi** (Med) to take a course of mud baths

fan'goso, -a AG muddy

'**fanno** VB vedi **fare**

fannul'lone, -a SM/F idler, loafer

fantasci'enza [fantaʃʃentsa] SF science fiction

fanta'sia SF fantasy, imagination; (capriccio) whim, caprice ▶ AG INV: **vestito ~** patterned dress

fantasi'oso, -a AG (dotato di fantasia) imaginative; (bizzarro) fanciful, strange

fan'tasma, -i SM ghost, phantom

fantasti'care /**20**/ VI to daydream

fantasti'cheria [fantastike'ria] SF daydream

fan'tastico, -a, -ci, -che AG fantastic; (potenza, ingegno) imaginative

'**fante** SM infantryman; (Carte) jack, knave (BRIT)

fante'ria SF infantry

fan'tino SM jockey

fan'toccio [fan'tɔttʃo] SM puppet

fanto'matico, -a, -ci, -che AG (nave, esercito) phantom cpd; (personaggio) mysterious

FAO SIGLA F (= Food and Agriculture Organization) FAO

fara'butto SM crook

fara'ona SF guinea fowl

fara'one SM (Storia) Pharaoh

fara'onico, -a, -ci, -che AG of the Pharaohs; (fig) enormous, huge

far'cire [far'tʃire] /**55**/ VT (carni, peperoni ecc) to stuff; (torte) to fill

fard [far] SM INV blusher

far'dello SM bundle; (fig) burden

'fare /53/ SM **1** (*modo di fare*): **con fare distratto** absent-mindedly; **ha un fare simpatico** he has a pleasant manner **2**: **sul far del giorno/della notte** at daybreak/nightfall
▶ VT **1** (*fabbricare, creare*) to make; (: *casa*) to build; (: *assegno*) to make out; **fare un pasto/una promessa/un film** to make a meal/promise/a film; **fare rumore** to make a noise
2 (*effettuare: lavoro, attività, studi*) to do; (: *sport*) to play; **cosa fa?** (*adesso*) what are you doing?; (*di professione*) what do you do?; **fare psicologia/italiano** (*Ins*) to do psychology/Italian; **fare tennis** to play tennis; **fare un viaggio** to go on a trip *o* journey; **fare una passeggiata** to go for a walk; **fare la spesa** to do the shopping
3 (*funzione*) to be; (: *Teat*) to play, be; **fare il medico** to be a doctor; **fare il malato** (*fingere*) to act the invalid
4 (*suscitare: sentimenti*): **fare paura a qn** to frighten sb; **mi fa rabbia** it makes me angry; **(non) fa niente** (*non importa*) it doesn't matter
5 (*ammontare*): **3 più 3 fa 6** 3 and 3 are *o* make 6; **fanno 6 euro** that's 6 euros; **Roma fa oltre 2.000.000 di abitanti** Rome has over 2,000,000 inhabitants; **che ora fai?** what time do you make it?
6 (*+ infinito*): **far fare qc a qn** (*obbligare*) to make sb do sth; (*permettere*) to let sb do sth; **fare piangere/ridere qn** to make sb cry/laugh; **fare venire qn** to send for sb; **fammi vedere** let me see; **far partire il motore** to start (up) the engine; **far riparare la macchina/costruire una casa** to get *o* have the car repaired/a house built
7: **farsi**: **farsi una gonna** to make o.s. a skirt; **farsi un nome** to make a name for o.s.; **farsi la permanente** to get a perm; **farsi notare** to get o.s. noticed; **farsi tagliare i capelli** to get one's hair cut; **farsi operare** to have an operation
8 (*fraseologia*): **farcela** to succeed, manage; **non ce la faccio più** I can't go on; **ce la faremo** we'll make it; **me l'hanno fatta!** (*imbrogliare*) I've been done!; **lo facevo più giovane** I thought he was younger; **fare sì/no con la testa** to nod/shake one's head
▶ VI **1** (*agire*) to act, do; **fate come volete** do as you like; **fare presto** to be quick; **fare da** to act as; **non c'è niente da fare** it's no use; **saperci fare con qn/qc** to know how to deal with sb/sth; **ci sa fare** she's very good at it; **faccia pure!** go ahead!
2 (*dire*) to say; **"davvero?" fece** "really?" he said
3: **fare per** (*essere adatto*) to be suitable for;

fare per fare qc to be about to do sth; **fece per andarsene** he made as if to leave
4: **farsi**: **si fa così** you do it like this, this is the way it's done; **non si fa così!** (*rimprovero*) that's no way to behave!; **la festa non si fa** the party is off
5: **fare a gara con qn** to compete with sb; **fare a pugni** to come to blows; **fare in tempo a fare** to be in time to do
▶ VB IMPERS: **fa bel tempo** the weather is fine; **fa caldo/freddo** it's hot/cold; **fa notte** it's getting dark
▶ VPR **1** (*diventare*) to become; **farsi prete** to become a priest; **farsi grande/vecchio** to grow tall/old
2 (*spostarsi*): **farsi avanti/indietro** to move forward/back; **fatti più in là** move along a bit
3 (*col: drogarsi*) to be a junkie

fa'retra SF quiver

far'falla SF butterfly

farfugli'are [farfuʎˈʎare] /27/ VT, VI to mumble, mutter

fa'rina SF flour; **~ gialla** maize (*Brit*) *o* corn (*US*) flour; **~ integrale** wholemeal (*Brit*) *o* whole-wheat (*US*) flour; **questa non è ~ del tuo sacco** (*fig*) this isn't your own idea (*o* work)

fari'nacei [fariˈnatʃei] SMPL starches

fa'ringe [faˈrindʒe] SF (*Anat*) pharynx

farin'gite [farinˈdʒite] SF pharyngitis

fari'noso, -a AG (*patate*) floury; (*neve, mela*) powdery

farma'ceutico, -a, -ci, -che [farmaˈtʃeutiko] AG pharmaceutical

farma'cia, -'cie [farmaˈtʃia] SF pharmacy; (*negozio*) chemist's (shop) (*Brit*), pharmacy

farma'cista, -i, -e [farmaˈtʃista] SM/F chemist (*Brit*), pharmacist

'farmaco, -ci, -chi (SM drug, medicine

farneti'care /20/ VI to rave, be delirious

'faro SM (*Naut*) lighthouse; (*Aer*) beacon; (*Aut*) headlight, headlamp (*Brit*)

farragi'noso, -a [farradʒiˈnoso] AG (*stile*) muddled, confused

'farsa SF farce

far'sesco, -a, -schi, -sche AG farcical

fasc. ABBR = **fascicolo**

'fascia, -sce [ˈfaʃʃa] SF band, strip; (*Med*) bandage; (*di sindaco, ufficiale*) sash; (*parte di territorio*) strip, belt; (*di contribuenti ecc*) group, band; **essere in fasce** (*anche fig*) to be in one's infancy; **~ oraria** time band

fasci'are [faʃˈʃare] /14/ VT to bind; (*Med*) to bandage; (*bambino*) to put a nappy (*Brit*) *o* diaper (*US*) on

fascia'tura [faʃʃaˈtura] SF (*azione*) bandaging; (*fascia*) bandage

fa'scicolo [faʃʃikolo] SM (di documenti) file, dossier; (di rivista) issue, number; (opuscolo) booklet, pamphlet

'fascino ['faʃʃino] SM charm, fascination

'fascio ['faʃʃo] SM bundle, sheaf; (di fiori) bunch; (di luce) beam; (Pol): **il F~** the Fascist Party

fa'scismo [faʃʃizmo] SM fascism

fa'scista, -i, -e [faʃʃista] AG, SM/F fascist

'fase SF phase; (Tecn) stroke; **in ~ di espansione** in a period of expansion; **essere fuori ~** (motore) to be rough (BRIT), run roughly; (fig) to feel rough (BRIT) o rotten

fas'tidio SM bother, trouble; **dare ~ a qn** to bother o annoy sb; **sento ~ allo stomaco** my stomach's upset; **avere fastidi con la polizia** to have trouble o bother with the police

fastidi'oso, -a AG annoying, tiresome; (schifiltoso) fastidious

'fasto SM pomp, splendour (BRIT), splendor (US)

fas'toso, -a AG sumptuous, lavish

fa'sullo, -a AG (gen) fake; (dichiarazione, persona) false; (pretesto) bogus

'fata SF fairy

fa'tale AG fatal; (inevitabile) inevitable; (fig) irresistible

fata'lismo SM fatalism

fatalità SF INV inevitability; (avversità) misfortune; (fato) fate, destiny

fa'tato, -a AG (spada, chiave) magic; (castello) enchanted

fa'tica, -che SF hard work, toil; (sforzo) effort; (di metalli) fatigue; **a ~** with difficulty; **respirare a ~** to have difficulty (in) breathing; **fare ~ a fare qc** to find it difficult to do sth; **animale da ~** beast of burden

fati'caccia, -ce [fati'kattʃa] SF: **fu una ~** it was hard work, it was a hell of a job (col)

fati'care /20/ VI to toil; **~ a fare qc** to have difficulty doing sth

fati'cata SF hard work

fa'tichi etc ['fatiki] VB vedi **faticare**

fati'coso, -a AG (viaggio, camminata) tiring, exhausting; (lavoro) laborious

fa'tidico, -a, -ci, -che AG fateful

'fato SM fate, destiny

Fatt. ABBR (= fattura) inv

fat'taccio [fat'tattʃo] SM foul deed

fat'tezze [fat'tettse] SFPL features

fat'tibile AG feasible, possible

fattis'pecie [fattis'petʃe] SF: **nella** o **in ~** in this case o instance

'fatto, -a PP di **fare ▶** AG: **un uomo ~** a grown man **▶** SM fact; (azione) deed; (avvenimento) event, occurrence; (di romanzo, film) action, story; **~ a mano/in casa** hand-/home-made;

è ben fatta she has a nice figure; **cogliere qn sul ~** to catch sb red-handed; **il ~ sta** o **è che** the fact remains o is that; **in ~ di** as for, as far as ... is concerned; **fare i fatti propri** to mind one's own business; **è uno che sa il ~ suo** he knows what he's about; **gli ho detto il ~ suo** I told him what I thought of him; **porre qn di fronte al ~ compiuto** to present sb with a fait accompli; **coppia/unione ~** long-standing relationship

fat'tore SM (Agr) farm manager; (Mat: elemento costitutivo) factor; **~ di protezione** (di lozione solare) factor

fatto'ria SF farm; (casa) farmhouse

fatto'rino SM errand boy; (di ufficio) office boy; (d'albergo) porter

fattucchi'era [fattuk'kjɛra] SF witch

fat'tura SF (Comm) invoice; (di abito) tailoring; (malia) spell; **pagamento contro presentazione ~** payment on invoice

fattu'rare /72/ VT (Comm) to invoice; (prodotto) to produce; (vino) to adulterate

fattu'rato SM (Comm) turnover

fatturazi'one [fatturat'tsjone] SF billing, invoicing

'fatuo, -a AG vain, fatuous; **fuoco ~** (anche fig) will-o'-the-wisp

'fauci ['fautʃi] SFPL (di leone ecc) jaws; (di vulcano) mouth sg

'fauna SF fauna

'fausto, -a AG (formale) happy; **un ~ presagio** a good omen

fau'tore, -'trice SM/F advocate, supporter

'fava SF broad bean

fa'vella SF speech

fa'villa SF spark

'favo SM (di api) honeycomb

'favola SF (fiaba) fairy tale; (d'intento morale) fable; (fandonia) yarn; **essere la ~ del paese** (oggetto di critica) to be the talk of the town; (zimbello) to be a laughing stock

favo'loso, -a AG fabulous; (incredibile) incredible

fa'vore SM favour (BRIT), favor (US); **per ~** please; **prezzo/trattamento di ~** preferential price/treatment; **condizioni di ~** (Comm) favo(u)rable terms; **fare un ~ a qn** to do sb a favour; **col ~ delle tenebre** under cover of darkness

favoreggia'mento [favoreddʒa'mento] SM (Dir) aiding and abetting

favo'revole AG favourable (BRIT), favorable (US)

favo'rire /55/ VT to favour (BRIT), favor (US); (il commercio, l'industria, le arti) to promote, encourage; **vuole ~?** won't you help yourself?; **favorisca in salotto** please come into the sitting room; **mi favorisca i documenti** please may I see your papers?

favori'tismo SM favouritism (BRIT), favoritism (US)

favo'rito, -a AG, SM/F favourite (BRIT), favorite (US)

fax SM INV fax; **mandare qc via** ~ to fax sth

fa'xare /72/ VT to fax

fazi'one [fat'tsjone] SF faction

faziosità [fattsjosi'ta] SF sectarianism

fazzo'letto [fattso'letto] SM handkerchief; (per la testa) (head)scarf; ~ **di carta** tissue

F.B.I. SIGLA F (= Federal Bureau of Investigation) FBI

F.C. ABBR = **fuoricorso**

f.co ABBR = **franco**

FE SIGLA = **Ferrara**

febb. ABBR (= febbraio) Feb

feb'braio SM February; vedi anche **luglio**

'febbre SF fever; **aver la** ~ to have a high temperature; ~ **da fieno** hay fever

feb'brile AG (anche fig) feverish

'feccia, -ce ['fettʃa] SF dregs pl

'feci ['fetʃi] SFPL faeces, excrement sg

'feci etc ['fetʃi] VB vedi **fare**

'fecola SF potato flour

fecon'dare /72/ VT to fertilize

fecondazi'one [fekondat'tsjone] SF fertilization; ~ **artificiale** artificial insemination

fecondità SF fertility

fe'condo, -a AG fertile

'Fedcom SIGLA M = **Fondo Europeo di Cooperazione Monetaria**

'fede SF (credenza) belief, faith; (Rel) faith; (fiducia) faith, trust; (fedeltà) loyalty; (anello) wedding ring; (attestato) certificate; **aver ~ in qn** to have faith in sb; **tener ~ a** (ideale) to remain loyal to; (giuramento, promessa) to keep; **in buona/cattiva** ~ in good/bad faith; **"in ~"** (Dir) "in witness whereof"

fe'dele AG (leale, veritiero) true, accurate; ~ **(a)** faithful (to) ▶ SMF follower; **i fedeli** (Rel) the faithful

fedeltà SF faithfulness; (coniugale) fidelity; (esattezza: di copia, traduzione) accuracy; **alta ~** (Radio) high fidelity

'federa SF pillowslip, pillowcase

fede'rale AG federal

federa'lismo SM (Pol) federalism

federa'lista, -i, -e AG, SM/F (Pol) federalist

federazi'one [federat'tsjone] SF federation

Feder'caccia [feder'kattʃa] ABBR F (= Federazione Italiana della Caccia) hunting federation

Feder'calcio [feder'kaltʃo] ABBR M (= Federazione Italiana Gioco Calcio) Italian football association

Federcon'sorzi [federkon'sɔrtsi] ABBR F (= Federazione Italiana dei Consorzi Agrari) federation of farmers' cooperatives

fe'difrago, -a, -ghi, -ghe AG faithless, perfidious

fe'dina SF (Dir): ~ **(penale)** record; **avere la ~ penale sporca** to have a police record

'fegato SM liver; (fig) guts pl, nerve; **mangiarsi o rodersi il** ~ to be consumed with rage

'felce ['feltʃe] SF fern

fe'lice [fe'litʃe] AG happy; (fortunato) lucky

felicità [felitʃi'ta] SF happiness

felici'tarsi [felitʃi'tarsi] /72/ VPR (congratularsi): ~ **con qn per qc** to congratulate sb on sth

felicitazi'oni [felitʃitat'tsjoni] SFPL congratulations

fe'lino, -a AG, SM feline

'felpa SF sweatshirt

fel'pato, -a AG (tessuto) brushed; (passo) stealthy; **con passo** ~ stealthily

'feltro SM felt

'femmina SF (Zool, Tecn) female; (figlia) girl, daughter; (spesso peg) woman

femmi'nile AG feminine; (sesso) female; (lavoro, giornale) woman's, women's; (moda) women's ▶ SM (Ling) feminine

femminilità SF femininity

femmi'nismo SM feminism

femmi'nista, -i, -e AG, SM/F feminist

'femore SM thighbone, femur

'fendere /36/ VT to cut through

fendi'nebbia SM (Aut) fog lamp

fendi'tura SF (gen) crack; (di roccia) cleft, crack

fe'nomeno SM phenomenon

'feretro SM coffin

feri'ale AG: **giorno** ~ weekday, working day

'ferie SFPL holidays (BRIT), vacation sg (US); **andare in** ~ to go on holiday o vacation; **25 giorni di** ~ **pagate** 25 days' holiday o vacation with pay

feri'mento SM wounding

fe'rire /55/ VT to injure; (deliberatamente: Mil ecc) to wound; (colpire) to hurt; **ferirsi** VPR to hurt o.s., injure o.s.

fe'rito, -a SM/F wounded o injured man/woman ▶ SF injury; wound

feri'toia SF slit

'ferma SF (Mil) (period of) service; (Caccia): **cane da** ~ pointer

ferma'carte SM INV paperweight

fermacra'vatta SM INV tiepin (BRIT), tie tack (US)

fer'maglio [fer'maʎʎo] SM clasp; (gioiello) brooch; (per documenti) clip

ferma'mente AV firmly

fer'mare /72/ VT to stop, halt; (Polizia) to detain, hold; (bottone ecc) to fasten, fix ▶ VI to stop; **fermarsi** VPR to stop, halt; **fermarsi a fare qc** to stop to do sth

fer'mata SF stop; ~ **dell'autobus** bus stop

fermen'tare /72/ vi to ferment; (fig) to be in a ferment

fermentazi'one [fermentat'tsjone] sf fermentation

fer'mento sm (anche fig) ferment; (lievito) yeast; **fermenti lattici** probiotics, probiotic bacteria

fer'mezza [fer'mettsa] sf (fig) firmness, steadfastness

'fermo, -a ag still, motionless; (veicolo) stationary; (orologio) not working; (saldo: anche fig) firm; (voce, mano) steady ▶ escl stop!; keep still! ▶ sm (chiusura) catch, lock; (Dir): ~ **di polizia** police detention; ~ **restando che ...** it being understood that ...

'fermo 'posta av, sm inv poste restante (Brit), general delivery (US)

fe'roce [fe'rɔtʃe] ag (animale) wild, fierce, ferocious; (persona) cruel, fierce; (fame, dolore) raging; **le bestie feroci** wild animals

fe'rocia, -cie [fe'rɔtʃa] sf ferocity

Ferr. abbr = **ferrovia**

fer'raglia [fer'raʎʎa] sf scrap iron

ferra'gosto sm (festa) feast of the Assumption; (periodo) August holidays pl (Brit) o vacation (US); see note

> Ferragosto, 15 August, is a national holiday. Marking the feast of the Assumption, its origins are religious but in recent years it has simply become the most important public holiday of the summer season. Most people take some extra time off work and head out of town to the holiday resorts. Consequently, most of industry and commerce grinds to a standstill.

ferra'menta sfpl ironmongery sg (Brit), hardware sg; **negozio di** ~ ironmonger's (Brit), hardware shop o store (US)

fer'rare /72/ vt (cavallo) to shoe

fer'rato, -a ag (Ferr): **strada ferrata** railway line (Brit), railroad line (US); (fig) **essere ~ in** (materia) to be well up in

ferra'vecchio [ferra'vɛkkjo] sm scrap merchant

'ferreo, -a ag iron cpd

ferri'era sf ironworks inv

'ferro sm iron; **una bistecca ai ferri** a grilled steak; **mettere a ~ e fuoco** to put to the sword; **essere ai ferri corti** (fig) to be at daggers drawn; **tocca ~!** touch wood!; ~ **battuto** wrought iron; ~ **di cavallo** horseshoe; ~ **da stiro** iron; **ferri da calza** knitting needles; **i ferri del mestiere** the tools of the trade

ferrotranvi'ario, -a ag public transport cpd

Ferrotranvi'eri abbr f (= Federazione Nazionale Lavoratori Autoferrotranvieri e Internavigatori) transport workers' union

ferro'vecchio [ferro'vɛkkjo] sm = **ferravecchio**

ferro'via sf railway (Brit), railroad (US)

ferrovi'ario, -a ag railway cpd (Brit), railroad cpd (US)

ferrovi'ere sm railwayman (Brit), railroad man (US)

'fertile ag fertile

fertilità sf fertility

fertiliz'zante [fertilid'dzante] sm fertilizer

fertiliz'zare [fertilid'dzare] /72/ vt to fertilize

fer'vente ag fervent, ardent

'fervere /29/ vi: **fervono i preparativi per ...** they are making feverish preparations for ...

'fervido, -a ag fervent, ardent

fer'vore sm fervour (Brit), fervor (US), ardour (Brit), ardor (US); (punto culminante) height

'fesa sf (Cuc) rump of veal

fesse'ria sf stupidity; **dire fesserie** to talk nonsense

'fesso, -a pp di **fendere** ▶ ag (col: sciocco) crazy, cracked

fes'sura sf crack, split; (per gettone, moneta) slot

'festa sf (religiosa) feast; (pubblica) holiday; (compleanno) birthday; (onomastico) name day; (ricevimento) celebration, party; **far ~** to have a holiday; (far baldoria) to live it up; **far ~ a qn** to give sb a warm welcome; **essere vestito a ~** to be dressed up to the nines; ~ **comandata** (Rel) holiday of obligation; **la ~ della mamma/del papà** Mother's/Father's Day; **la F~ della Repubblica** see note

> The Festa della Repubblica, 2 June, celebrates the founding of the Italian Republic after the fall of the monarchy and the subsequent referendum in 1946. It is marked by military parades and political speeches.

festeggia'menti [festedd3a'menti] smpl celebrations

festeggi'are [fested'd3are] /62/ vt to celebrate; (persona) to have a celebration for

fes'tino sm party; (con balli) ball

fes'tivo, -a ag (atmosfera) festive; **giorno ~** holiday

fes'toso, -a ag merry, joyful

fe'tente ag (puzzolente) fetid; (comportamento) disgusting ▶ smf (col) stinker, rotter (Brit)

fe'ticcio [fe'tittʃo] sm fetish

'feto sm foetus (Brit), fetus (US)

fe'tore sm stench, stink

'fetta sf slice

fet'tuccia, -ce [fet'tuttʃa] sf tape, ribbon

fettuc'cine [fettut'tʃine] sfpl (Cuc) ribbon-shaped pasta

feu'dale ag feudal

'feudo sm (Storia) fief; (fig) stronghold

ff abbr (Amm) = **facente funzione**; (= fogli) pp

FF.AA ABBR = **forze armate**

FF.SS. ABBR = **Ferrovie dello Stato**

FG SIGLA = **Foggia**

FI SIGLA = **Firenze** ▶ ABBR (= *Forza Italia*) *Italian centre-right political party*

fi'aba SF fairy tale

fia'besco, -a, -schi, -sche AG fairy-tale *cpd*

fi'acca SF weariness; (*svogliatezza*) listlessness; **battere la ~** to shirk

fiac'care /20/ VT to weaken

fiaccherò *etc* [fjakke'rɔ] VB *vedi* **fiaccare**

fi'acco, -a, -chi, -che AG (*stanco*) tired, weary; (*svogliato*) listless; (*debole*) weak; (*mercato*) slack

fi'accola SF torch

fiacco'lata SF torchlight procession

fi'ala SF phial

fi'amma SF flame; (*Naut*) pennant

fiam'mante AG (*colore*) flaming; **nuovo ~** brand new

fiam'mata SF blaze

fiammeggi'are [fjammed'dʒare] **/62/** VI to blaze

fiam'mifero SM match

fiam'mingo, -a, -ghi, -ghe AG Flemish ▶ SM/F Fleming ▶ SM (*Ling*) Flemish; (*Zool*) flamingo; **i Fiamminghi** the Flemish

fian'cata SF (*di nave ecc*) side; (*Naut*) broadside

fiancheggi'are [fjanked'dʒare] **/62/** VT to border; (*fig*) to support, back (up); (*Mil*) to flank

fi'anco, -chi SM side; (*di persona*) hip; (*Mil*) flank; **di ~** sideways, from the side; **a ~ a ~** side by side; **prestare il proprio ~ alle critiche** to leave o.s. open to criticism; **~ destr/sinistr!** (*Mil*) right/left turn!

Fi'andre SFPL: **le ~** Flanders *sg*

fiaschette'ria [fjaskette'ria] SF wine shop

fi'asco, -schi SM flask; (*fig*) fiasco; **fare ~** to fail

fia'tare /72/ VI (*fig: parlare*): **senza ~** without saying a word

fi'ato SM breath; (*resistenza*) stamina; **fiati** SMPL (*Mus*) wind instruments; **avere il ~ grosso** to be out of breath; **prendere ~** to catch one's breath; **bere qc tutto d'un ~** to drink sth in one go *o* gulp

'fibbia SF buckle

'fibra SF fibre, fiber (*US*); (*fig*) constitution; **~ ottica** optical fibre; **~ di vetro** fibreglass (*BRIT*), fiberglass (*US*)

ficca'naso (*mpl* **ficcanasi**, *fpl* **~**) SM/F busybody, nos(e)y parker

fic'care /20/ VT to push, thrust, drive; **ficcarsi** VPR (*andare a finire*) to get to; **~ il naso negli affari altrui** (*fig*) to poke *o* stick one's nose into other people's business; **ficcarsi nei pasticci** *o* **nei guai** to get into hot water *o* a fix

ficcherò *etc* [fikke'rɔ] VB *vedi* **ficcare**

fiche [fiʃ] SF INV (*nei giochi d'azzardo*) chip

'fico, -chi SM (*pianta*) fig tree; (*frutto*) fig; **~ d'India** prickly pear; **~ secco** dried fig

fiction ['fikʃon] SF INV TV drama

fidanza'mento [fidantsa'mento] SM engagement

fidan'zarsi [fidan'tsarsi] **/72/** VPR to get engaged

fidan'zato, -a [fidan'tsato] SM/F fiancé (fiancée)

fi'darsi /72/ VPR: **~ di** to trust; **~ è bene non ~ è meglio** (*proverbio*) better safe than sorry

fi'dato, -a AG reliable, trustworthy

fide'ismo SM unquestioning belief

fide'istico, -a, -ci, -che AG (*atteggiamento, posizione*) totally uncritical

fideius'sore SM (*Dir*) guarantor

fideliz'zare [fidelid'dzare] **/72/** VT: **~ la clientela** to build customer loyalty; **fidelizzarsi** VPR to stay loyal

'fido, -a AG faithful, loyal ▶ SM (*Comm*) credit

fi'ducia [fi'dutʃa] SF confidence, trust; **incarico di ~** position of trust, responsible position; **persona di ~** reliable person; **è il mio uomo di ~** he is my right-hand man; **porre la questione di ~** (*Pol*) to ask for a vote of confidence

fiduci'oso, -a [fidu'tʃoso] AG trusting

fi'ele SM (*Med*) bile; (*fig*) bitterness

fie'nile SM barn; hayloft

fi'eno SM hay

fi'era SF fair; (*animale*) wild beast; **~ di beneficenza** charity bazaar; **~ campionaria** trade fair

fie'rezza [fje'rettsa] SF pride

fi'ero, -a AG proud; (*crudele*) fierce, cruel; (*audace*) bold

fi'evole AG (*luce*) dim; (*suono*) weak

'fifa SF (*col*): **aver ~** to have the jitters

F.I.F.A. SIGLA F (= *Féderation Internationale de Football Association*) FIFA

fi'fone, -a SM/F (*col, scherzoso*) coward

fig. ABBR (= *figura*) fig

FIGC SIGLA F (= *Federazione Italiana Gioco Calcio*) *Italian football association*

'Figi ['fidʒi] SFPL: **le isole ~** Fiji, the Fiji Islands

'figlia ['fiʎʎa] SF daughter; (*Comm*) counterfoil (*BRIT*), stub

figli'are [fiʎ'ʎare] **/27/** VI to give birth

figli'astro, -a [fiʎ'ʎastro] SM/F stepson(-daughter)

'figlio ['fiʎʎo] SM son; (*senza distinzione di sesso*) child; **~ d'arte: essere ~ d'arte** to come from a theatrical (*o* musical *etc*) family; **~ di puttana** (!) son of a bitch (!); **~ di papà** spoilt, wealthy young man; **~ unico** only child

figli'occio, -a, -ci, -ce [fiʎ'ʎɔttʃo] SM/F godchild, godson(-daughter)

figli'ola [fiʎ'ʎɔla] SF daughter; (fig: ragazza) girl

figli'olo [fiʎ'ʎɔlo] SM (anche fig: ragazzo) son

fi'gura SF figure; (forma, aspetto esterno) form, shape; (illustrazione) picture, illustration; **far ~ to** look smart; **fare una brutta ~** to make a bad impression; **che ~!** how embarrassing!

figu'raccia, -ce [figu'rattʃa] SF: **fare una ~** to create a bad impression

figu'rare /72/ VI to appear ▶ VT: **figurarsi qc** to imagine sth; **figurarsi** VPR: **figurati!** imagine that!; **ti do noia? — ma figurati!** am I disturbing you? — not at all!

figura'tivo, -a AG figurative

figu'rina SF (statuetta) figurine; (cartoncino) picture card

figuri'nista, -i, -e SM/F dress designer

figu'rino SM fashion sketch

fi'guro SM: **un losco ~** a suspicious character

figu'rone SM: **fare un ~** (persona, oggetto) to look terrific; (persona: con un discorso ecc) to make an excellent impression

'fila SF row, line; (coda) queue; (serie) series, string; **di ~** in succession; **fare la ~** to queue; **in ~ indiana** in single file

fila'mento SM filament

fi'lanca® SF stretch material

fi'landa SF spinning mill

fi'lante AG: **stella ~** (stella cadente) shooting star; (striscia di carta) streamer

filantro'pia SF philanthropy

filan'tropico, -a, -ci, -che AG philanthropic(al)

fi'lantropo SM philanthropist

fi'lare /72/ VT to spin; (Naut) to pay out ▶ VI (baco, ragno) to spin; (formaggio fuso) to go stringy; (liquido) to trickle; (discorso) to hang together; (col: amoreggiare) to go steady; (muoversi a forte velocità) to go at full speed; (andarsene lestamente) to make o.s. scarce ▶ SM (di alberi ecc) row, line; **~ diritto** (fig) to toe the line; **~ via** to dash off

filar'monico, -a, -ci, -che AG philharmonic

filas'trocca, -che SF nursery rhyme

filate'lia SF philately, stamp collecting

fi'lato, -a AG spun ▶ SM yarn ▶ AV: **vai dritto ~ a casa** go straight home; **3 giorni filati** 3 days running o on end

fila'tura SF spinning; (luogo) spinning mill

file' sharing [fail'ʃerin(g)] SM (Inform) file sharing

fi'letto SM (ornamento) braid, trimming; (di vite) thread; (di carne) fillet

fili'ale AG filial ▶ SF (di impresa) branch

filibusti'ere SM pirate; (fig) adventurer

fili'grana SF (in oreficeria) filigree; (su carta) watermark

fi'lippica SF invective

Filip'pine SFPL: **le ~** the Philippines

filip'pino, -a AG, SM/F Filipino

film SM INV film

fil'mare /72/ VT to film

fil'mato SM short film

fil'mina SF film strip

'filo SM (anche fig) thread; (filato) yarn; (metallico) wire; (di lama, rasoio) edge; **con un ~ di voce** in a whisper; **un ~ d'aria** (fig) a breath of air; **dare del ~ da torcere a qn** to create difficulties for sb, make life difficult for sb; **fare il ~ a qn** (corteggiare) to be after sb, chase sb; **per ~ e per segno** in detail; **~ d'erba** blade of grass; **~ interdentale** dental floss; **~ di perle** string of pearls; **~ di Scozia** fine cotton yarn; **~ spinato** barbed wire

filoameri'cano, -a AG pro-American

'filobus SM INV trolley bus

filodiffusi'one SF rediffusion

filodram'matico, -a, -ci, -che AG: **(compagnia) filodrammatica** amateur dramatic society ▶ SM/F amateur actor (actress)

filon'cino [filon'tʃino] SM ≈ French stick

fi'lone SM (di minerali) seam, vein; (pane) ≈ Vienna loaf; (fig) trend

filoso'fia SF philosophy

filo'sofico, -a, -ci, -che AG philosophical

fi'losofo, -a SM/F philosopher

filosovi'etico, -a, -ci, -che AG pro-Soviet

filo'via SF (linea) trolley line; (bus) trolley bus

fil'trare /72/ VT, VI to filter

'filtro SM filter; (pozione) potion; **~ dell'olio** (Aut) oil filter

'filza ['filtsa] SF (anche fig) string

FIN SIGLA F = **Federazione Italiana Nuoto**

fin AV, PREP = **fino**

fi'nale AG final ▶ SM (di libro, film) end, ending; (Mus) finale ▶ SF (Sport) final

fina'lista, -i, -e SM/F finalist

finalità SF (scopo) aim, purpose

finaliz'zare [finalid'dzare] /72/ VT: **~ a** to direct towards

final'mente AV finally, at last

fi'nanza [fi'nantsa] SF finance; **finanze** SFPL (di individuo, Stato) finances; **(Guardia di) ~** (di frontiera) ≈ Customs and Excise (BRIT), ≈ Customs Service (US); **(Intendenza di) ~** ≈ Inland Revenue (BRIT), ≈ Internal Revenue Service (US); **Ministro delle finanze** Minister of Finance, ≈ Chancellor of the Exchequer (BRIT), ≈ Secretary of the Treasury (US)

finanzia'mento [finantsja'mento] SM (azione) financing; (denaro fornito) funds pl

finanzi'are [finan'tsjare] /19/ VT to finance, fund

finanzi'ario, -a [finan'tsjarjo] AG financial ▶ SF (*anche*: **società finanziaria**) investment company; (*anche*: **legge finanziaria**) finance act, ≈ budget (BRIT)

finanzia'tore, -'trice AG: **ente ~** backer ▶ SM/F backer

finanzi'ere [finan'tsjɛre] SM financier; (*guardia di finanza: doganale*) customs officer; (: *tributaria*) Inland Revenue official (BRIT), Internal Revenue official (US)

finché [fin'ke] CONG (*per tutto il tempo che*) as long as; (*fino al momento in cui*) until; **~ vorrai** as long as you like; **aspetta ~ non esca** wait until he goes (*o* comes) out; **aspetta ~ io (non) sia ritornato** wait until I get back

'fine AG (*lamina, carta*) thin; (*capelli, polvere*) fine; (*vista, udito*) keen, sharp; (*persona: raffinata*) refined, distinguished; (*osservazione*) subtle ▶ SF end ▶ SM aim, purpose; (*esito*) result, outcome; **in** *o* **alla ~** in the end, finally; **alla fin ~** at the end of the day, in the end; **che ~ ha fatto?** what became of him?; **buona ~ e buon principio!** (*augurio*) happy New Year!; **a fin di bene** with the best of intentions; **al ~ di fare qc** (in order) to do sth; **condurre qc a buon ~** to bring sth to a successful conclusion; **secondo ~** ulterior motive

'fine setti'mana SM *O* F INV weekend

fi'nestra SF window

fines'trino SM (*di treno, auto*) window

fi'nezza [fi'nettsa] SF thinness; fineness; keenness, sharpness; refinement; subtlety

'fingere ['findʒere] /**54**/ VT to feign; (*supporre*) to imagine, suppose; **fingersi** VPR: **fingersi ubriaco/pazzo** to pretend to be drunk/crazy; **~ di fare** to pretend to do

fini'menti SMPL (*di cavallo ecc*) harness *sg*

fini'mondo SM pandemonium

fi'nire /**55**/ VT to finish ▶ VI to finish, end ▶ SM: **sul ~ della festa** towards the end of the party; **~ di fare** (*compiere*) to finish doing; (*smettere*) to stop doing; **~ in galera** to end up *o* finish up in prison; **farla finita** (*con la vita*) to put an end to one's life; **farla finita con qc** to have done with sth; **com'è andata a ~?** what happened in the end?; **finiscila!** stop it!

fini'tura SF finish

finlan'dese AG Finnish ▶ SMF Finn ▶ SM (*Ling*) Finnish

Fin'landia SF: **la ~** Finland

'fino, -a AG (*capelli, seta*) fine; (*oro*) pure; (*fig: acuto*) shrewd ▶ AV (*spesso troncato in fin: pure, anche*) even ▶ PREP (*spesso troncato in fin*): **fin quando?** till when?; **fin qui** as far as here; **~ a** (*tempo*) until, till; (*luogo*) as far as, (up) to; **fin da domani** from tomorrow onwards;

fin da ieri since yesterday; **fin dalla nascita** from *o* since birth

fi'nocchio [fi'nɔkkjo] SM fennel; (*col, peg: omosessuale*) queer

fi'nora AV up till now

'finsi *etc* VB *vedi* **fingere**

'finto, -a PP *di* **fingere** ▶ AG (*capelli, dente*) false; (*fiori*) artificial; (*cuoio, pelle*) imitation *cpd*; (*fig: simulato: pazzia ecc*) feigned, sham ▶ SF pretence (BRIT), pretense (US), sham; (*Sport*) feint; **far finta (di fare)** to pretend (to do); **l'ho detto per finta** I was only pretending; (*per scherzo*) I was only kidding

finzi'one [fin'tsjone] SF pretence (BRIT), pretense (US), sham

fioc'care /**20**/ VI (*neve*) to fall; (*fig: insulti ecc*) to fall thick and fast

fi'occo, -chi SM (*di nastro*) bow; (*di stoffa, lana*) flock; (*di neve*) flake; (*Naut*) jib; **coi fiocchi** (*fig*) first-rate; **fiocchi di avena** oatflakes; **fiocchi di granoturco** cornflakes

fi'ocina ['fjɔtʃina] SF harpoon

fi'oco, -a, -chi, -che AG faint, dim

fi'onda SF catapult

fio'raio, -a SM/F florist

fiorda'liso SM (*Bot*) cornflower

fi'ordo SM fjord

fi'ore SM flower; **fiori** SMPL (*Carte*) clubs; **nel ~ degli anni** in one's prime; **a fior d'acqua** on the surface of the water; **a fior di labbra** in a whisper; **aver i nervi a fior di pelle** to be on edge; **fior di latte** cream; **è costato fior di soldi** it cost a pretty penny; **il fior ~ della società** the cream of society; **~ all'occhiello** feather in the cap; **fiori di campo** wild flowers

fio'rente AG (*industria, paese*) flourishing; (*salute*) blooming; (*petto*) ample

fioren'tino, -a AG, SM/F Florentine ▶ SF (*Cuc*) T-bone steak

fio'retto SM (*Scherma*) foil

fio'rino SM florin

fio'rire /**55**/ VI (*rosa*) to flower; (*albero*) to blossom; (*fig*) to flourish

fio'rista, -i, -e SM/F florist

fiori'tura SF (*di pianta*) flowering, blooming; (*di albero*) blossoming; (*fig: di commercio, arte*) flourishing; (*insieme dei fiori*) flowers *pl*; (*Mus*) fioritura

fi'otto SM (*di lacrime*) flow, flood; (*di sangue*) gush, spurt

'FIPE SIGLA F = **Federazione Italiana Pubblici Esercizi**

Fi'renze [fi'rɛntse] SF Florence

'firma SF signature; (*reputazione*) name

firma'mento SM firmament

fir'mare /**72**/ VT to sign; **un abito firmato** a designer suit

firma'tario, -a SM/F signatory

fisar'monica, -che SF accordion

fis'cale AG fiscal, tax *cpd*; *(meticoloso)* punctilious; **medico ~** *doctor employed by Social Security to verify cases of sick leave*

fisca'lista, -i, -e SM/F tax consultant

fiscaliz'zare [fiskalid'dzare] /**72**/ VT to exempt from taxes

fischi'are [fis'kjare] /**19**/ VI to whistle ▶ VT to whistle; *(attore)* to boo, hiss; **mi fischian le orecchie** my ears are singing; *(fig)* my ears are burning

fischiet'tare [fiskjet'tare] /**72**/ VI, VT to whistle

fischi'etto [fis'kjetto] SM *(strumento)* whistle

'fischio ['fiskjo] SM whistle; **prendere fischi per fiaschi** to get hold of the wrong end of the stick

'fisco SM tax authorities *pl*, ≈ Inland Revenue (BRIT), ≈ Internal Revenue Service (US)

'fisica SF *vedi* **fisico**

fisica'mente AV physically

'fisico, -a, -ci, -che AG physical ▶ SM/F physicist ▶ SM physique ▶ SF physics *sg*

'fisima SF fixation

fisiolo'gia [fizjolo'dʒia] SF physiology

fisiono'mia SF face, physiognomy

fisiotera'pia SF physiotherapy

fisiotera'pista SMF physiotherapist

fis'saggio [fis'saddʒo] SM *(Fot)* fixing

fis'sante AG *(spray, lozione)* holding

fis'sare /**72**/ VT to fix, fasten; *(guardare intensamente)* to stare at; *(data, condizioni)* to fix, establish, set; *(prenotare)* to book; **fissarsi** VPR: **fissarsi su** *(sguardo, attenzione)* to focus on; *(fig: idea)* to become obsessed with

fissazi'one [fissat'tsjone] SF *(Psic)* fixation

fissi'one SF fission

'fisso, -a AG fixed; *(stipendio, impiego)* regular ▶ AV: **guardare ~ qn/qc** to stare at sb/sth; **avere un ragazzo ~** to have a steady boyfriend; **senza fissa dimora** of no fixed abode; **telefono ~** landline

fitoterma'lismo SM herbal hydrotherapy

'fitta SF *vedi* **fitto**

fit'tavolo SM tenant

fit'tizio, -a [fit'tittsjo] AG fictitious, imaginary

'fitto, -a AG thick, dense; *(pioggia)* heavy ▶ SM depths *pl*, middle; *(affitto, pigione)* rent ▶ SF sharp pain; **una fitta al cuore** *(fig)* a pang of grief; **nel ~ del bosco** in the heart *o* depths of the wood

fiu'mana SF torrent; *(fig)* stream, flood

fi'ume SM river ▶ AG INV: **processo ~** long-running trial; **scorrere a fiumi** *(acqua, sangue)* to flow in torrents

fiu'tare /**72**/ VT to smell, sniff; *(animale)* to scent; *(fig: inganno)* to get wind of, smell;

~ tabacco to take snuff; **~ cocaina** to snort cocaine

fi'uto SM (sense of) smell; *(fig)* nose

'flaccido, -a ['flattʃido] AG flabby

fla'cone SM bottle

flagel'lare [fladʒel'lare] /**72**/ VT to flog, scourge; *(onde)* to beat against

fla'gello [fla'dʒello] SM scourge

fla'grante AG flagrant; **cogliere qn in ~** to catch sb red-handed

fla'nella SF flannel

flash [flaʃ] SM INV *(Fot)* flash; *(giornalistico)* newsflash

flau'tista, -i SM/F flautist

'flauto SM flute

'flebile AG faint, feeble

fle'bite SF phlebitis

'flemma SF *(calma)* coolness, phlegm; *(Med)* phlegm

flem'matico, -a, -ci, -che AG phlegmatic, cool

fles'sibile AG pliable; *(fig: che si adatta)* flexible

flessibili'tà SF *(anche fig)* flexibility

flessi'one SF *(gen)* bending; *(Ginnastica: a terra)* sit-up; *(: in piedi)* forward bend; *(: sulle gambe)* knee-bend; *(diminuzione)* slight drop, slight fall; *(Ling)* inflection; **fare una ~** to bend; **una ~ economica** a downward trend in the economy

'flesso, -a PP *di* **flettere**

flessu'oso, -a AG supple, lithe; *(andatura)* flowing, graceful

'flettere /**92**/ VT to bend

'flipper ['flipper] SM INV pinball machine

flirt [fləːt] SM INV brief romance, flirtation

flir'tare /**72**/ VI to flirt

F.lli ABBR (= *fratelli*) Bros

'flora SF flora

'florido, -a AG flourishing; *(fig)* glowing with health

'floscio, -a, -sci, -sce ['floʃʃo] AG *(cappello)* floppy, soft; *(muscoli)* flabby

'flotta SF fleet

flo ̄ **'tante** SM *(Econ)*: **titoli a largo ~** blue chips, stocks on the market

' ̄ **, -a** AG, SM fluid

fl ̄ ̄ **/55/** VI to flow

flu ̄ **'e'scente** [fluoreʃʃɛnte] AG fluorescent

fluo'uro SM fluorine

fluo'ruro SM fluoride

'flusso SM flow; *(Fisica, Med)* flux; **~ e riflusso** ebb and flow; **~ di cassa** *(Comm)* cash flow

'flutti SMPL waves

fluttu'are /**72**/ VI to rise and fall; *(Econ)* to fluctuate

fluvi'ale AG river *cpd*, fluvial

FM ABBR *vedi* **modulazione di frequenza**

FMI SIGLA M (= *Fondo Monetario Internazionale*) IMF

FO SIGLA = **Forlì**

fo'bia SF phobia

'foca, -che SF (Zool) seal

fo'caccia, -ce [fo'kattʃa] SF kind of pizza; (dolce) bun; **rendere pan per ~** to get one's own back, give tit for tat

fo'cale AG focal

focaliz'zare [fokalid'dzare] /72/ VT (Fot: immagine) to get into focus; (fig: situazione) to get into perspective; **~ l'attenzione su** to focus one's attention on

'foce ['fotʃe] SF (Geo) mouth

fo'chista, -i [fo'kista] SM (Ferr) stoker, fireman

foco'laio SM (Med) centre (BRIT) o center (US) of infection; (fig) hotbed

foco'lare SM hearth, fireside; (Tecn) furnace

fo'coso, -a AG fiery; (cavallo) mettlesome, fiery

'fodera SF (di vestito) lining; (di libro, poltrona) cover

fode'rare /72/ VT to line; to cover

'fodero SM (di spada) scabbard; (di pugnale) sheath; (di pistola) holster

'foga SF enthusiasm, ardour (BRIT), ardor (US)

'foggia, -ge ['fɔddʒa] SF (maniera) style; (aspetto) form, shape; (moda) fashion, style

foggi'are [fod'dʒare] /62/ VT to shape; to style

'foglia ['fɔʎʎa] SF leaf; **ha mangiato la ~** (fig) he's caught on; **~ d'argento/d'oro** silver/gold leaf

fogli'ame [foʎ'ʎame] SM foliage, leaves pl

fogli'etto [foʎ'ʎetto] SM (piccolo foglio) slip of paper, piece of paper; (manifestino) leaflet, handout

'foglio ['fɔʎʎo] SM (di carta) sheet (of paper); (di metallo) sheet; (documento) document; (banconota) (bank)note; **~ di calcolo** (Inform) spreadsheet; **~ rosa** (Aut) provisional licence; **~ di via** (Dir) expulsion order; **~ volante** pamphlet

'fogna ['foɲɲa] SF drain, sewer

fogna'tura [foɲɲa'tura] SF drainage, sewerage

föhn [fø:n] SM INV hair-dryer

fo'lata SF gust

fol'clore SM folklore

folclo'ristico, -a, -ci, -che AG folk cpd

folgo'rare /72/ VT (fulmine) to strike down; (: alta tensione) to electrocute

folgorazi'one [folgorat'tsjone] SF electrocution; **ebbe una ~** (fig: idea) he had a brainwave

'folgore SF thunderbolt

folksono'mia SF (Inform) folksonomy

'folla SF crowd, throng

'folle AG mad, insane; (Tecn) idle; **in ~** (Aut) in neutral

folleggi'are [folled'dʒare] /62/ VI (divertirsi) to paint the town red

fol'letto SM elf

fol'lia SF folly, foolishness; foolish act; (pazzia) madness, lunacy; **amare qn alla ~** to love sb to distraction; **costare una ~** to cost the earth

'folto, -a AG thick

fomen'tare /72/ VT to stir up, foment

fon SM INV = **föhn**

fon'dale SM (del mare) bottom; (Teat) backdrop; **il ~ marino** the sea bed

fondamen'tale AG fundamental, basic

fondamenta'lista, -i, -e AG, SM/F (Rel) fundamentalist

fonda'mento SM foundation; **fondamenta** SFPL (Edil) foundations

fon'dare /72/ VT to found; (fig: dar base): **~ qc su** to base sth on; **fondarsi** VPR (teorie): **fondarsi (su)** to be based (on)

fonda'tezza [fonda'tettsa] SF (di ragioni) soundness; (di dubbio, sospetto) basis in fact

fon'dato, -a AG (ragioni) sound; (dubbio, sospetto) well-founded

fondazi'one [fondat'tsjone] SF foundation

fon'dente AG: **cioccolato ~** plain o dark chocolate

'fondere /25/ VT (neve) to melt; (metallo) to fuse, melt; (fig: colori) to merge, blend; (: imprese, gruppi) to merge ▶ VI to melt; **fondersi** VPR to melt; (fig: partiti, correnti) to unite, merge

fonde'ria SF foundry

fondi'ario, -a AG land cpd

fon'dina SF (piatto fondo) soup plate; (portapistola) holster

'fondo, -a AG deep ▶ SM (di recipiente, pozzo) bottom; (di stanza) back; (quantità di liquido che resta, deposito) dregs pl; (sfondo) background; (unità immobiliare) property, estate; (somma di denaro) fund; (Sport) long-distance race; **fondi** SMPL (denaro) funds; **a notte fonda** at dead of night; **in ~ a** at the bottom of; at the back of; (strada) at the end of; **laggiù in ~** (lontano) over there; (in profondità) down there; **in ~** (fig) after all, all things considered; **andare fino in ~ a** (fig) to examine thoroughly; **andare a ~** (nave) to sink; **conoscere a ~** to know inside out; **dar ~ a** (provviste, soldi) to use up; **toccare il ~** (fig) to plumb the depths; **a ~ perduto** (Comm) without security; **~ comune di investimento** investment trust; **F~ Monetario Internazionale** International Monetary Fund; **~ di previdenza** social insurance fund; **~ di riserva** reserve fund; **~ urbano** town property; **fondi di caffè** coffee grounds; **fondi d'esercizio** working capital sg; **fondi liquidi** ready money sg, liquid assets; **fondi di magazzino** old *o* unsold stock *sg*; **fondi neri** slush fund *sg*

fondo'tinta SM INV (*cosmetico*) foundation

fo'nema SM phoneme

fo'netica SF phonetics *sg*

fo'netico, -a, -ci, -che AG phonetic

fon'tana SF fountain

fonta'nella SF drinking fountain

'fonte SF spring, source; (*fig*) source ▶ SM: **~ battesimale** (*Rel*) font; **~ energetica** source of energy

fon'tina SM *full fat hard, sweet cheese*

'footing ['futiŋ] SM jogging

forag'giare [forad'dʒare] /62/ VT (*cavalli*) to fodder; (*fig: partito ecc*) to bankroll

fo'raggio [fo'raddʒo] SM fodder, forage

fo'rare /72/ VT to pierce, make a hole in; (*pallone*) to burst; (*pneumatico*) to puncture; (*biglietto*) to punch; **forarsi** VPR (*gen*) to develop a hole; (*Aut, pallone, timpano*) to burst; **~ una gomma** to burst a tyre (*BRIT*) *o* tire (*US*)

fora'tura SF piercing; bursting; puncturing; punching

'forbici ['fɔrbitʃi] SFPL scissors

forbi'cina [forbi'tʃina] SF earwig

for'bito, -a AG (*stile, modi*) polished

'forca, -che SF (*Agr*) fork, pitchfork; (*patibolo*) gallows *sg*

for'cella [for'tʃɛlla] SF (*Tecn*) fork; (*di monte*) pass

for'chetta [for'ketta] SF fork; **essere una buona ~** to enjoy one's food

for'cina [for'tʃina] SF hairpin

'forcipe ['fɔrtʃipe] SM forceps *pl*

for'cone SM pitchfork

fo'rense AG (*linguaggio*) legal; **avvocato ~** barrister (*BRIT*), lawyer

fo'resta SF forest; **la F~ Nera** the Black Forest

fores'tale AG forest *cpd*; **guardia ~** forester

foreste'ria SF (*di convento, palazzo ecc*) guest rooms *pl*, guest quarters *pl*

foresti'ero, -a AG foreign ▶ SM/F foreigner

for'fait [fɔr'fɛ] SM INV: (**prezzo a**) **~** fixed price, set price; **dichiarare ~** (*Sport*) to withdraw; (*fig*) to give up

forfe'tario, -a AG: **prezzo ~** (*da pagare*) fixed *o* set price; (*da ricevere*) lump sum

'forfora SF dandruff

'forgia, -ge ['fɔrdʒa] SF forge

forgi'are [for'dʒare] /62/ VT to forge

'forma SF form; (*aspetto esteriore*) form, shape; (*Dir: procedura*) procedure; (*per calzature*) last; (*stampo da cucina*) mould (*BRIT*), mold (*US*); **forme** SFPL (*del corpo*) figure, shape; **le forme** (*convenzioni*) appearances; **errori di ~** stylistic errors; **essere in ~** to be in good shape; **mantenersi in ~** to keep fit; **in ~ ufficiale/privata** officially/privately; **una ~ di formaggio** a (whole) cheese

formag'gino [formad'dʒino] SM processed cheese

for'maggio [for'maddʒo] SM cheese

for'male AG formal

formalità SF INV formality

formaliz'zare [formalid'dzare] /72/ VT to formalize

for'mare /72/ VT to form, shape, make; (*numero di telefono*) to dial; (*fig: carattere*) to form, mould (*BRIT*), mold (*US*); **formarsi** VPR to form, take shape; **il treno si forma a Milano** the train starts from Milan

for'mato SM format, size

format'tare /72/ VT (*Inform*) to format

formattazi'one [formattat'tsjone] SF (*Inform*) formatting

formazi'one [format'tsjone] SF formation; (*fig: educazione*) training; **~ continua** continuing education; **~ permanente** lifelong learning; **~ professionale** vocational training

for'mica¹, -che SF ant

formica²® ['fɔrmika] SF (*materiale*) Formica®

formi'caio SM anthill

formico'lare /72/ VI (*gamba, braccio*) to tingle; (*brulicare: anche fig*): **~ di** to be swarming with; **mi formicola la gamba** I've got pins and needles in my leg, my leg's tingling

formico'lio SM pins and needles *pl*; swarming

formi'dabile AG powerful, formidable; (*straordinario*) remarkable

for'moso, -a AG shapely

'formula SF formula; **~ di cortesia** (*nelle lettere*) letter ending

formu'lare /72/ VT to formulate; to express

for'nace [for'natʃe] SF (*per laterizi ecc*) kiln; (*per metalli*) furnace

for'naio SM baker

for'nello SM (*elettrico, a gas*) ring; (*di pipa*) bowl

for'nire /55/ VT: **~ qn di qc, ~ qc a qn** to provide *o* supply sb with sth, supply sth to sb; **fornirsi** VPR: **fornirsi di** (*procurarsi*) to provide o.s. with

for'nito, -a AG: **ben ~** (*negozio*) well-stocked

forni'tore, -'trice AG: **ditta fornitrice di ...** company supplying ... ▶ SM/F supplier

forni'tura SF supply

'forno SM (*di cucina*) oven; (*panetteria*) bakery; (*Tecn: per calce ecc*) kiln; (*: per metalli*) furnace; **fare i forni** (*Med*) to undergo heat treatment; **~ a microonde** microwave oven

'foro SM (*buco*) hole; (*Storia*) forum; (*tribunale*) (law) court

'forse AV perhaps, maybe; (*circa*) about; **essere in ~** to be in doubt

forsen'nato, -a AG mad, crazy, insane

'forte AG strong; (*suono*) loud; (*spesa*) considerable, great; (*passione, dolore*) great, deep ▶ AV strongly; (*velocemente*) fast; (*a voce alta*) loud(ly); (*violentemente*) hard ▶ SM (*edificio*) fort; (*specialità*) forte, strong point; **piatto ~** (*Cuc*) main dish; **avere un ~ mal di testa/raffreddore** to have a bad headache/cold; **essere ~ in qc** to be good at sth; **farsi ~ di qc** to make use of sth; **dare man ~ a qn** to back sb up, support sb; **usare le maniere forti** to use strong-arm tactics

for'tezza [for'tettsa] SF (*morale*) strength; (*luogo fortificato*) fortress

fortifi'care /**20**/ VT to fortify, strengthen

for'tuito, -a AG fortuitous, chance *cpd*

for'tuna SF (*destino*) fortune, luck; (*buona sorte*) success, fortune; (*eredità, averi*) fortune; **per ~** luckily, fortunately; **di ~** makeshift, improvised; **atterraggio di ~** emergency landing

fortu'nale SM storm

fortunata'mente AV luckily, fortunately

fortu'nato, -a AG lucky, fortunate; (*coronato da successo*) successful

fortu'noso, -a AG (*vita*) eventful; (*avvenimento*) unlucky

fo'runcolo SM (*Med*) boil

forvi'are /**19**/ VT, VI = **fuorviare**

'forza ['fortsa] SF strength; (*potere*) power; (*Fisica*) force ▶ ESCL come on!; **forze** SFPL (*fisiche*) strength *sg*; (*Mil*) forces; **per ~** against one's will; (*naturalmente*) of course; **per ~ di cose** by force of circumstances; **a viva ~** by force; **a ~ di** by dint of; **farsi ~** (*coraggio*) to pluck up one's courage; **bella ~!** (*ironico*) how clever of you (*o* him *etc*)!; **~ lavoro** work force, manpower; **per causa di ~ maggiore** (*Dir*) by reason of an act of God; (*per estensione*) due to circumstances beyond one's control; **la ~ pubblica** the police *pl*; **forze dell'ordine** the forces of law and order; **~ di pace** peacekeeping force; **~ di vendita** (*Comm*) sales force; **~ di volontà** willpower; **le forze armate** the armed forces; **F~ Italia** (*Pol*) moderate right-wing party

for'zare [for'tsare] /**72**/ VT to force; (*cassaforte, porta*) to force (open); (*voce*) to strain; **~ qn a fare** to force sb to do

for'zato, -a [for'tsato] AG forced ▶ SM (*Dir*) prisoner sentenced to hard labour (BRIT) *o* labor (US)

forzi'ere [for'tsjɛre] SM strongbox; (*di pirati*) treasure chest

for'zista, -i, -e [for'tsista] AG of Forza Italia ▶ SM/F member (*o* supporter) of Forza Italia

for'zuto, -a [for'tsuto] AG big and strong

fos'chia [fos'kia] SF mist, haze

'fosco, -a, -schi, -sche AG dark, gloomy; **dipingere qc a tinte fosche** (*fig*) to paint a gloomy picture of sth

fos'fato SM phosphate

fosfore'scente [fosforeʃʃɛnte] AG phosphorescent; (*lancetta dell'orologio ecc*) luminous

'fosforo SM phosphorous

'fossa SF pit; (*di cimitero*) grave; **~ comune** mass grave; **~ biologica** septic tank

fos'sato SM ditch; (*di fortezza*) moat

fos'setta SF dimple

'fossi *etc* VB *vedi* **essere**

'fossile AG, SM fossil (*cpd*)

'fosso SM ditch; (*Mil*) trench

'foste *etc* VB *vedi* **essere**

'foto SF INV photo ▶ PREFISSO: **~ ricordo** souvenir photo; **~ tessera** passport(-type) photo

foto... PREFISSO photo...

foto'camera SF: **~ digitale** digital camera

fotocomposi'tore SM filmsetter

fotocomposizi'one [fotokompozit'tsjone] SF film setting

foto'copia SF photocopy

fotocopi'are /**19**/ VT to photocopy

fotocopia'trice [fotokopja'tritʃe] SF photocopier

fotocopiste'ria SF photocopy shop

fotofo'nino SM camera phone

foto'genico, -a, -ci, -che [foto'dʒɛniko] AG photogenic

fotogra'fare /**72**/ VT to photograph

fotogra'fia SF (*procedimento*) photography; (*immagine*) photograph; **fare una ~** to take a photograph; **una ~ a colori/in bianco e nero** a colour/black and white photograph

foto'grafico, -a, -ci, -che AG photographic; **macchina fotografica** camera

fo'tografo, -a SM/F photographer

foto'gramma, -i SM (*Cine*) frame

fotomo'dello, -a SM/F fashion model

fotomon'taggio [fotomon'taddʒo] SM photomontage

fotore'porter SM INV/F INV newspaper (*o* magazine) photographer

fotoro'manzo [fotoro'mandzo] SM romantic picture story

foto'sintesi SF photosynthesis

fotovol'taico, -a, -ci, -che AG photovoltaic; **pannelli fotovoltaici** solar panels

'fottere /**1**/ VT (!: *avere rapporti sessuali*) to fuck (!), screw (!); (*rubare*) to pinch, swipe; (*fregare*): **mi hanno fottuto** they played a dirty trick on me; **vai a farti ~!** fuck off! (!)

fot'tuto, -a AG (!) bloody, fucking (!)

fou'lard [fu'lar] SM INV scarf

FR SIGLA = **Frosinone**

fra PREP = **tra**

fracas'sare /**72**/ VT to shatter, smash; **fracassarsi** VPR to shatter, smash; (*veicolo*) to crash

fra'casso SM smash; crash; (*baccano*) din, racket

'fradicio, -a, -ci, -ce ['fraditʃo] AG (*guasto*) rotten; (*molto bagnato*) soaking (wet); **ubriaco ~** blind drunk

'fragile ['fradʒile] AG fragile; (*fig: salute*) delicate; (*nervi, vetro*) brittle

fragilità [fradʒili'ta] SF (*vedi ag*) fragility; delicacy; brittleness

'fragola SF strawberry

fra'gore SM (*di cascate, carro armato*) roar; (*di tuono*) rumble

frago'roso, -a AG deafening; **ridere in modo ~** to roar with laughter

fra'grante AG fragrant

frain'tendere /120/ VT to misunderstand

fraintendi'mento SM misunderstanding

frain'teso, -a PP di **fraintendere**

fram'mento SM fragment

fram'misto, -a AG: **~ a** interspersed with

'frana SF landslide; (*fig: persona*): **essere una ~** to be useless, be a walking disaster area

fra'nare /72/ VI to slip, slide down

franca'mente AV frankly

fran'cese [fran'tʃeze] AG French ▶ SMF Frenchman(-woman) ▶ SM (*Ling*) French; **i Francesi** the French

fran'chezza [fran'kettsa] SF frankness, openness

fran'chigia, -gie [fran'kidʒa] SF (*Amm*) exemption; (*Dir*) franchise; (*Naut*) shore leave; **~ doganale** exemption from customs duty

'Francia ['frantʃa] SF: **la ~** France

franco, -a, -chi, -che AG (*Comm*) free; (*sincero*) frank, open, sincere ▶ SM (*moneta*) franc; **farla franca** (*fig*) to get off scot-free; **~ a bordo** free on board; **~ di dogana** duty-free; **~ a domicilio** delivered free of charge; **~ fabbrica** ex factory, ex works; **prezzo ~ fabbrica** ex-works price; **~ magazzino** ex warehouse; **~ di porto** carriage free; **~ vagone** free on rail; **~ tiratore** sniper (*Pol*) *member of parliament who votes against his own party*

franco'bollo SM (*postage*) stamp

franco-cana'dese AG, SMF French Canadian

Franco'forte SF Frankfurt

fran'gente [fran'dʒɛnte] SM (*onda*) breaker; (*scoglio emergente*) reef; (*circostanza*) situation, circumstance

'frangia, -ge ['frandʒa] SF fringe

frangi'flutti [frandʒi'flutti] SM INV breakwater

frangi'vento [frandʒi'vɛnto] SM windbreak

fran'toio SM (*Agr*) olive press; (*Tecn*) crusher

frantu'mare /72/ VT, **frantu'marsi** VPR to break into pieces, shatter

fran'tumi SMPL pieces, bits; (*schegge*) splinters; **andare in ~, mandare in ~** to shatter, smash to pieces *o* smithereens

frappé SM (*Cuc*) milk shake

fra'sario SM (*gergo*) vocabulary, language

'frasca, -sche SF (*leafy*) branch; **saltare di palo in ~** to jump from one subject to another

'frase SF (*Ling*) sentence; (*locuzione, espressione, Mus*) phrase; **~ fatta** set phrase

fraseolo'gia [frazeolo'dʒia] SF phraseology

'frassino SM ash (tree)

frastagli'ato, -a [frasta'ʎʎato] AG (*costa*) indented, jagged

frastor'nare /72/ VT (*intontire*) to daze; (*confondere*) to bewilder, befuddle

frastor'nato, -a AG dazed; bewildered

frastu'ono SM hubbub, din

'frate SM friar, monk

fratel'lanza [fratel'lantsa] SF brotherhood; (*associazione*) fraternity

fratel'lastro SM stepbrother; (*con genitore in comune*) half brother

fra'tello SM brother; **fratelli** SMPL brothers; (*nel senso di fratelli e sorelle*) brothers and sisters

fra'terno, -a AG fraternal, brotherly

fratri'cida, -i, -e [fratri'tʃida] AG fratricidal ▶ SM/F fratricide; **guerra ~** civil war

frat'taglie [frat'taʎʎe] SFPL (*Cuc: gen*) offal *sg*; (*: di pollo*) giblets

frat'tanto AV in the meantime, meanwhile

frat'tempo SM: **nel ~** in the meantime, meanwhile

frat'tura SF fracture; (*fig*) split, break

frattu'rare /72/ VT to fracture

fraudo'lento, -a AG fraudulent

fraziona'mento [frattsjona'mento] SM division, splitting up

frazio'nare [frattsjo'nare] /72/ VT to divide, split up

frazi'one [frat'tsjone] SF fraction; (*anche*: **frazione di comune**) hamlet

'freccia, -ce ['frettʃa] SF arrow; **~ di direzione** (*Aut*) indicator

frec'ciata [fret'tʃata] SF: **lanciare una ~** to make a cutting remark

fred'dare /72/ VT to shoot dead

fred'dezza [fred'dettsa] SF coldness

'freddo, -a AG, SM cold; **fa ~** it's cold; **aver ~** to be cold; **soffrire il ~** to feel the cold; **a ~** (*fig*) deliberately

freddo'loso, -a AG sensitive to the cold

fred'dura SF pun

'freezer ['frizer] SM INV fridge-freezer

fre'gare /80/ VT to rub; (*col: truffare*) to take in, cheat; (*: rubare*) to swipe, pinch; **fregarsene** (*col*): **chi se ne frega?** who gives a damn (about it)?

fre'gata SF rub; (*col*) swindle; (*Naut*) frigate

frega'tura SF (*col*: *imbroglio*) rip-off; (: *delusione*) let-down

fregherò *etc* [frege'rɔ] VB *vedi* **fregare**

'fregio ['fredʒo] SM (*Archit*) frieze; (*ornamento*) decoration

'fremere /29/ VI: ~ **di** to tremble o quiver with; ~ **d'impazienza** to be champing at the bit

'fremito SM tremor, quiver

fre'nare /72/ VT (*veicolo*) to slow down; (*cavallo*) to rein in; (*lacrime*) to restrain, hold back ▶ VI to brake; **frenarsi** VPR (*fig*) to restrain o.s., control o.s.

fre'nata SF: **fare una** ~ to brake

frene'sia SF frenzy

fre'netico, -a, -ci, -che AG frenetic

'freno SM brake; (*morso*) bit; **tenere a** ~ (*passioni ecc*) to restrain; **tenere a** ~ **la lingua** to hold one's tongue; ~ **a disco** disc brake; ~ **a mano** handbrake

'freon® SM INV (*Chim*) Freon®

frequen'tare /72/ VT (*scuola*, *corso*) to attend; (*locale*, *bar*) to go to, frequent; (*persone*) to see (often)

frequen'tato, -a AG (*locale*) busy

fre'quente AG frequent; **di** ~ frequently

fre'quenza [fre'kwɛntsa] SF frequency; (*Ins*) attendance

fre'sare /72/ VT (*Tecn*) to mill

fres'chezza [fres'kettsa] SF freshness

'fresco, -a, -schi, -sche AG fresh; (*temperatura*) cool; (*notizia*) recent, fresh ▶ SM: **godere il** ~ to enjoy the cool air; ~ **di bucato** straight from the wash, newly washed; **stare** ~ (*fig*) to be in for it; **mettere al** ~ to put in a cool place; (*fig: in prigione*) to put inside o in the cooler

fres'cura SF cool

'fresia SF freesia

'fretta SF hurry, haste; **in** ~ in a hurry; **in** ~ **e furia** in a mad rush; **aver** ~ to be in a hurry; **far** ~ **a qn** to hurry sb

frettolosa'mente AV hurriedly, in a rush

fretto'loso, -a AG (*persona*) in a hurry; (*lavoro ecc*) hurried, rushed

fri'abile AG (*terreno*) friable; (*pasta*) crumbly

'friggere ['friddʒere] **/56/** VT to fry ▶ VI (*olio ecc*) to sizzle; **vai a farti** ~! (*col*) get lost!

frigidità [fridʒidi'ta] SF frigidity

'frigido, -a ['fridʒido] AG (*Med*) frigid

fri'gnare [frin'nare] **/15/** VI to whine, snivel

fri'gnone, -a [frin'none] SM/F whiner, sniveller

'frigo, -ghi SM fridge

frigo'bar SM INV minibar

frigo'rifero, -a AG refrigerating ▶ SM refrigerator; **cella frigorifera** cold store

fringu'ello SM chaffinch

'frissi *etc* VB *vedi* **friggere**

frit'tata SF omelet(te); **fare una** ~ (*fig*) to make a mess of things

frit'tella SF (*Cuc*) pancake; (: *ripiena*) fritter

'fritto, -a PP *di* **friggere** ▶ AG ▶ SM fried food; **ormai siamo fritti!** (*fig: col*) now we've had it!; **è un argomento** ~ **e rifritto** that's old hat; ~ **misto** mixed fry

frit'tura SF (*cibo*) fried food; ~ **di pesce** mixed fried fish

friu'lano, -a AG of (*o* from) Friuli

frivo'lezza [frivo'lettsa] SF frivolity

'frivolo, -a AG frivolous

frizi'one [frit'tsjone] SF friction; (*di pelle*) rub, rub-down; (*Aut*) clutch

friz'zante [frid'dzante] AG (*anche fig*) sparkling

'frizzo ['friddzo] SM witticism

fro'dare /72/ VT to defraud, cheat

'frode SF fraud; ~ **fiscale** tax evasion

'frodo SM: **di** ~ illegal, contraband; **pescatore di** ~, **cacciatore di** ~ poacher

'frogia, -gie ['frɔdʒa] SF (*di cavallo ecc*) nostril

'frollo, -a AG (*carne*) tender; (: *selvaggina*) high; (*fig: persona*) soft; **pasta frolla** short(crust) pastry

'fronda SF (*leafy*) branch; (*di partito politico*) internal opposition; **fronde** SFPL (*di albero*) foliage *sg*

fron'tale AG frontal; (*scontro*) head-on

'fronte SF (*Anat*) forehead; (*di edificio*) front, façade ▶ SM (*Mil*, *Pol*, *Meteor*) front; **a** ~, **di** ~ facing, opposite; **di** ~ **a** (*posizione*) opposite, facing, in front of; (*a paragone di*) compared with; **far** ~ **a** (*nemico*, *problema*) to confront; (*responsabilità*) to face up to; (*spese*) to cope with

fronteggi'are [fronted'dʒare] **/62/** VT (*avversari*, *difficoltà*) to face, stand up to; (*spese*) to cope with

frontes'pizio [frontes'pittsjo] SM (*Archit*) frontispiece; (*di libro*) title page

fronti'era SF border, frontier

fron'tone SM pediment

'fronzolo ['frondzolo] SM frill

'frotta SF crowd; **in** ~, **a frotte** in their hundreds, in droves

'frottola SF fib; **raccontare un sacco di frottole** to tell a pack of lies

fru'gale AG frugal

fru'gare /80/ VI to rummage ▶ VT to search

frugherò *etc* [fruge'rɔ] VB *vedi* **frugare**

frui'tore SM user

fruizi'one [fruit'tsjone] SF use

frul'lare /72/ VT (*Cuc*) to whisk ▶ VI (*uccelli*) to flutter; **cosa ti frulla in mente?** what is going on in that mind of yours?

frul'lato SM (*Cuc*) milk shake; (: *con solo frutta*) fruit drink

frulla'tore SM electric mixer

frul'lino SM whisk

fru'mento SM wheat

frusci'are [fruʃʃare] /**14**/ VI to rustle

fru'scio [fruʃʃio] SM rustle; rustling; (*di acque*) murmur

'**frusta** SF whip; (*Cuc*) whisk

frus'tare /**72**/ VT to whip

frus'tata SF lash

frus'tino SM riding crop

frus'trare /**72**/ VT to frustrate

frus'trato, -a AG frustrated

frustrazi'one [frustrat'tsjone] SF frustration

'**frutta** SF fruit; (*portata*) dessert; **~ candita/ secca** candied/dried fruit

frut'tare /**72**/ VI (*investimenti, deposito*) to bear dividends, give a return; **il mio deposito in banca (mi) frutta il 10%** my bank deposits bring (me) in 10%; **quella gara gli fruttò la medaglia d'oro** he won the gold medal in that competition

frut'teto SM orchard

frutticol'tura SF fruit growing

frut'tifero, -a AG (*albero ecc*) fruit-bearing; (*fig: che frutta*) fruitful, profitable; **deposito ~** interest-bearing deposit

frutti'vendolo, -a SM/F greengrocer (BRIT), produce dealer (US)

'**frutto** SM fruit; (*fig: risultato*) result(s); (*Econ: interesse*) interest; (: *reddito*) income; **è ~ della tua immaginazione** it's a figment of your imagination; **frutti di mare** seafood *sg*; **frutti di bosco** berries

fruttu'oso, -a AG fruitful, profitable

FS ABBR (= *Ferrovie dello Stato*) Italian railways

f.t. ABBR = **fuori testo**

f.to ABBR (= *firmato*) signed

fu VB *vedi* **essere** ▶ AG INV: **il fu Paolo Bianchi** the late Paolo Bianchi

fuci'lare [futʃi'lare] /**72**/ VT to shoot

fuci'lata [futʃi'lata] SF rifle shot

fucilazi'one [futʃilat'tsjone] SF execution (by firing squad)

fu'cile [fu'tʃile] SM rifle, gun; (*da caccia*) shotgun, gun; **~ a canne mozze** sawn-off shotgun

fu'cina [fu'tʃina] SF forge

'**fuco, -chi** SM drone

'**fucsia** SF fuchsia

'**fuga, -ghe** SF escape, flight; (*di gas, liquidi*) leak; (*Mus*) fugue; **mettere qn in ~** to put sb to flight; **~ di cervelli** brain drain

fu'gace [fu'gatʃe] AG fleeting, transient

fu'gare /**80**/ VT (*dubbi, incertezze*) to dispel, drive out

fug'gevole [fud'dʒevole] AG fleeting

fuggi'asco, -a, -schi, -sche [fud'dʒasko] AG, SM/F fugitive

fuggi'fuggi [fuddʒi'fuddʒi] SM scramble, stampede

fug'gire [fud'dʒire] /**31**/ VI to flee, run away; (*fig: passar veloce*) to fly ▶ VT to avoid

fuggi'tivo, -a [fuddʒi'tivo] SM/F fugitive, runaway

'**fui** VB *vedi* **essere**

'**fulcro** SM (*Fisica*) fulcrum; (*fig: di teoria, questione*) central o key point

ful'gore SM brilliance, splendour (BRIT), splendor (US)

fu'liggine [fu'liddʒine] SF soot

fulmi'nare /**72**/ VT (*elettricità*) to electrocute; (*con arma da fuoco*) to shoot dead; **fulminarsi** VPR (*lampadina*) to go, blow; (*fig: con lo sguardo*) **mi fulminò (con uno sguardo)** he looked daggers at me

'**fulmine** SM bolt of lightning; **fulmini** SMPL lightning *sg*; **~ a ciel sereno** bolt from the blue

ful'mineo, -a AG (*fig: scatto*) rapid; (: *minaccioso*) threatening

'**fulvo, -a** AG tawny

fumai'olo SM (*di nave*) funnel; (*di fabbrica*) chimney

fu'mante AG (*piatto ecc*) steaming

fu'mare /**72**/ VI to smoke; (*emettere vapore*) to steam ▶ VT to smoke

fu'mario, -a AG: **canna fumaria** flue

fu'mata SF (*segnale*) smoke signal; **farsi una ~** to have a smoke; **~ bianca/nera** (*in Vaticano*) signal that a new pope has/has not been elected

fuma'tore, -'trice SM/F smoker

fu'metto SM comic strip; **giornale a fumetti** comic

'**fummo** VB *vedi* **essere**

'**fumo** SM smoke; (*vapore*) steam; (*il fumare tabacco*) smoking; **fumi** SMPL (*industriali ecc*) fumes; **vendere ~** to deceive, cheat; **è tutto ~ e niente arrosto** it has no substance to it; **i fumi dell'alcool** (*fig*) the after-effects of drink; **~ passivo** passive smoking

fu'mogeno, -a [fu'mɔdʒeno] AG (*candelotto*) smoke *cpd* ▶ SM smoke bomb; **cortina fumogena** smoke screen

fu'moso, -a AG smoky; (*fig*) muddled

fu'nambolo, -a SM/F tightrope walker

'**fune** SF rope, cord; (*più grossa*) cable

'**funebre** AG (*rito*) funeral; (*aspetto*) gloomy, funereal

fune'rale SM funeral

fu'nesto, -a AG (*incidente*) fatal; (*errore, decisione*) fatal, disastrous; (*atmosfera*) gloomy, dismal

'**fungere** ['fundʒere] /**5**/ VI: **~ da** to act as

'**fungo, -ghi** SM fungus; (*commestibile*) mushroom; **~ velenoso** toadstool; **crescere come i funghi** (*fig*) to spring up overnight

funico'lare SF funicular railway

funi'via SF cable railway

'**funsi** *etc* VB *vedi* **fungere**
'**funto, -a** PP *di* **fungere**
funzio'nare [funtsjo'nare] /**72**/ VI to work, function; (*fungere*): ~ **da** to act as
funzio'nario [funtsjo'narjo] SM official; ~ **statale** civil servant
funzi'one [fun'tsjone] SF function; (*carica*) post, position; (*Rel*) service; **in ~** (*meccanismo*) in operation; **in ~ di** (*come*) as; **vive in ~ dei figli** he lives for his children; **far ~ di** to act as; **fare la ~ di qn** (*farne le veci*) to take sb's place
fu'oco, -chi SM fire; (*fornello*) ring; (*Fot, Fisica*) focus; **dare ~ a qc** to set fire to sth; **far ~** (*sparare*) to fire; **prendere ~** to catch fire; **al ~!** fire!; ~ **d'artificio** firework; ~ **di paglia** flash in the pan; ~ **sacro** o **di Sant'Antonio** (*Med: col*) shingles *sg*
fuorché [fwor'ke] CONG, PREP except
FU'ORI SIGLA M (= *Fronte Unitario Omosessuale Rivoluzionario Italiano*) gay liberation movement
fu'ori AV outside; (*all'aperto*) outdoors, outside; (*fuori di casa, Sport*) out; (*esclamativo*) get out! ▶ PREP: ~ **(di)** out of, outside ▶ SM outside; **essere in ~** (*sporgere*) to stick out; **lasciar ~ qc/qn** to leave sth/sb out; **far ~** (*col: soldi*) to spend; (: *cioccolatini*) to eat up; (: *rubare*) to nick; **far ~ qn** (*col*) to kill sb, do sb in; **essere tagliato ~** (*da un gruppo, ambiente*) to be excluded; **essere ~ di sé** to be beside oneself; ~ **luogo** (*inopportuno*) out of place, uncalled for; ~ **mano** out of the way, remote; ~ **pasto** between meals; ~ **pericolo** out of danger; ~ **dai piedi!** get out of the way!; ~ **servizio** out of order; ~ **stagione** out of season; **illustrazione ~ testo** (*Stampa*) plate; ~ **uso** old-fashioned; obsolete
fuori'bordo SM INV speedboat (with outboard motor); outboard motor
fuori'busta SM INV unofficial payment
fuori'classe SM INV/F INV (undisputed) champion
fuori'corso AG INV (*moneta*) no longer in circulation; (*Ins*): **(studente)** ~ *undergraduate who has not completed a course in due time*
fuorigi'oco [fwori'dʒɔko] SM offside
fuori'legge [fwori'leddʒe] SM INV/F INV outlaw
fuoriprog'ramma SM INV (*TV, Radio*) unscheduled programme; (*fig*) change of plan o programme
fuori'serie AG INV (*auto ecc*) custom-built ▶ SF custom-built car

fuoris'trada SM (*Aut*) cross-country vehicle
fuoriu'scito, -a [fworuʃˈʃito], **fuoriu'scito, -a** [fworiuʃˈʃito] SM/F exile ▶ SF (*di gas*) leakage, escape; (*di sangue, linfa*) seepage
fuorvi'are /**60**/ VT to mislead; (*fig*) to lead astray ▶ VI to go astray
furbacchi'one, -a [furbak'kjone] SM/F cunning old devil
fur'bizia [fur'bittsja] SF (*vedi ag*) cleverness; cunning; **una ~** a cunning trick
'**furbo, -a** AG clever, smart; (*peg*) cunning ▶ SM/F: **fare il ~** to (try to) be clever o smart; **fatti ~!** show a bit of sense!
fu'rente AG: ~ **(contro)** furious (with)
fure'ria SF (*Mil*) orderly room
fu'retto SM ferret
fur'fante SM rascal, scoundrel
furgon'cino [furgon'tʃino] SM small van
fur'gone SM van
'**furia** SF (*ira*) fury, rage; (*fig: impeto*) fury, violence; (: *fretta*) rush; **a ~ di** by dint of; **andare su tutte le furie** to fly into a rage
furi'bondo, -a AG furious
furi'ere SM quartermaster
furi'oso, -a AG furious; (*mare, vento*) raging
'**furono** VB *vedi* **essere**
fu'rore SM fury; (*esaltazione*) frenzy; **far ~** to be all the rage
furtiva'mente AV furtively
fur'tivo, -a AG furtive
'**furto** SM theft; ~ **con scasso** burglary
'**fusa** SFPL: **fare le ~** to purr
fu'scello [fuʃˈʃello] SM twig
fu'seaux SMPL leggings
'**fusi** *etc* VB *vedi* **fondere**
fu'sibile SM (*Elettr*) fuse
fusi'one SF (*di metalli*) fusion, melting; (*colata*) casting; (*Comm*) merger; (*fig*) merging
'**fuso, -a** PP *di* **fondere** ▶ SM (*Filatura*) spindle; **diritto come un ~** as stiff as a ramrod; ~ **orario** time zone
fusoli'era SF (*Aer*) fusillage
fus'tagno [fus'taɲɲo] SM corduroy
fus'tella SF (*su scatola di medicinali*) tear-off tab
fusti'gare /**80**/ VT (*frustare*) to flog; (*fig: costumi*) to censure, denounce
fus'tino SM (*di detersivo*) tub
'**fusto** SM stem; (*Anat, di albero*) trunk; (*recipiente*) drum, can; (*col*) he-man
'**futile** AG vain, futile
futilità SF INV futility
futu'rismo SM futurism
fu'turo, -a AG, SM future

149

Gg

G, g [dʒi] SM O F INV (*lettera*) G, g; **G come Genova** ≈ G for George

g ABBR (= *grammo*) g

G8 [dʒi'otto] SM (= *Gruppo degli Otto*) G8

G20 [dʒi'venti] SM (= *Gruppo dei Venti*) G20

gabar'dine [gabar'din] SM (*tessuto*) gabardine; (*soprabito*) gabardine raincoat

gab'bare /72/ VT to take in, dupe; **gabbarsi** VPR: **gabbarsi di qn** to make fun of sb

'gabbia SF cage; (*Dir*) dock; (*da imballaggio*) crate; **la ~ degli accusati** (*Dir*) the dock; **~ dell'ascensore** lift (BRIT) o elevator (US) shaft; **~ toracica** (*Anat*) rib cage

gabbi'ano SM (sea)gull

gabi'netto SM (*Med ecc*) consulting room; (*Pol*) ministry; (*di decenza*) toilet, lavatory; (*Ins: di fisica ecc*) laboratory

Ga'bon SM: **il ~** Gabon

ga'elico, -a, -ci, -che AG, SM Gaelic

gaffe [gaf] SF INV blunder, boob (*col*)

gagli'ardo, -a [gaʎ'ʎardo] AG strong, vigorous

gai'ezza [ga'jettsa] SF gaiety, cheerfulness

'gaio, -a AG cheerful

'gala SF (*sfarzo*) pomp; (*festa*) gala

ga'lante AG gallant, courteous; (*avventura, poesia*) amorous

galante'ria SF gallantry

galantu'omo (*pl* **galantuomini**) SM gentleman

Ga'lapagos SFPL: **le (isole) ~** the Galapagos Islands

ga'lassia SF galaxy

gala'teo SM (good) manners *pl*, etiquette

gale'otto SM (*rematore*) galley slave; (*carcerato*) convict

ga'lera SF (*Naut*) galley; (*prigione*) prison

'galla SF: **a ~** afloat; **venire a ~** to surface, come to the surface; (*fig: verità*) to come out

galleggia'mento [galleddʒa'mento] SM floating; **linea di ~** (*di nave*) waterline

galleggi'ante [galled'dʒante] AG floating ▶ SM (*natante*) barge; (*di pescatore, lenza, Tecn*) float

galleggi'are [galled'dʒare] /62/ VI to float

galle'ria SF (*traforo*) tunnel; (*Archit, d'arte*) gallery; (*Teat*) circle; (*strada coperta con negozi*) arcade; **~ del vento** o **aerodinamica** (*Aer*) wind tunnel

'Galles SM: **il ~** Wales

gal'lese AG Welsh ▶ SMF Welshman(-woman) ▶ SM (*Ling*) Welsh; **i Gallesi** the Welsh

gal'letta SF cracker; (*Naut*) ship's biscuit

gal'letto SM young cock, cockerel; (*fig*) cocky young man; **fare il ~** to play the gallant

'Gallia SF: **la ~** Gaul

gal'lina SF hen; **andare a letto con le galline** to go to bed early

gal'lismo SM machismo

'gallo SM cock; **al canto del ~** at daybreak, at cockcrow; **fare il ~** to play the gallant

gal'lone SM piece of braid; (*Mil*) stripe; (*unità di misura*) gallon

galop'pare /72/ VI to gallop

galop'pino SM errand boy; (*Pol*) canvasser

ga'loppo SM gallop; **al** o **di ~** at a gallop

galvaniz'zare [galvanid'dzare] /72/ VT to galvanize

'gamba SF leg; (*asta: di lettera*) stem; **in ~** (*in buona salute*) well; (*bravo, sveglio*) bright, smart; **prendere qc sotto ~** (*fig*) to treat sth too lightly; **scappare a gambe levate** to take to one's heels; **gambe!** scatter!

gam'bale SM legging

gambe'retto SM shrimp

'gambero SM (*di acqua dolce*) crayfish; (*di mare*) prawn

'Gambia SF: **la ~** the Gambia

gambiz'zare [gambid'dzare] /72/ VT to kneecap

'gambo SM stem; (*di frutta*) stalk

ga'mella SF mess tin

'gamma SF (*Mus*) scale; (*di colori, fig*) range; **~ di prodotti** product range

ga'nascia, -sce [ga'naʃʃa] SF jaw; **ganasce del freno** (*Aut*) brake shoes

'gancio ['gantʃo] SM hook

'Gange ['gandʒe] SM: **il ~** the Ganges

'gangheri ['gangeri] SMPL: **uscire dai ~** (*fig*) to fly into a temper

gan'grena SF = **cancrena**

'gara SF competition; (*Sport*) competition; contest; match; (: *corsa*) race; **fare a** ~ to compete, vie; ~ **d'appalto** (*Comm*) tender

ga'rage [ga'raʒ] SM INV garage

ga'rante SMF guarantor

garan'tire /55/ VT to guarantee; (*debito*) to stand surety for; (*dare per certo*) to assure

garan'tismo SM protection of civil liberties

garan'tista, -i, -e AG concerned with civil liberties

garan'zia [garan'tsia] SF guarantee; (*pegno*) security; **in** ~ under guarantee

gar'bare /72/ VI: **non mi garba** I don't like it (*o him etc*)

garba'tezza [garba'tettsa] SF courtesy, politeness

gar'bato, -a AG courteous, polite

'garbo SM (*buone maniere*) politeness, courtesy; (*di vestito ecc*) grace, style

gar'buglio [gar'buʎʎo] SM tangle; (*fig*) muddle, mess

gareggi'are [gared'dʒare] **/62/** VI to compete

garga'nella SF: **a** ~ from the bottle

garga'rismo SM gargle; **fare i gargarismi** to gargle

ga'ritta SF (*di caserma*) sentry box

ga'rofano SM carnation; **chiodo di** ~ clove

gar'retto SM hock

gar'rire /55/ VI to chirp

'garrulo, -a AG (*uccello*) chirping; (*persona: loquace*) garrulous, talkative

'garza ['gardza] SF (*per bende*) gauze

gar'zone [gar'dzone] SM (*di negozio*) boy

gas SM INV gas; **a tutto** ~ at full speed; **dare** ~ (*Aut*) to accelerate; ~ **lacrimogeno** tear gas; ~ **naturale** natural gas

ga'sare *etc* **/72/** = **gassare** *ecc*

ga'sato, -a SM/F (*col: persona*) freak

gas'dotto SM gas pipeline

ga'solio SM diesel (oil)

ga's(s)are /72/ VT to aerate, carbonate; (*asfissiare*) to gas; **gas(s)arsi** VPR (*col*) to get excited

ga's(s)ato, -a AG (*bibita*) aerated, fizzy

gas'soso, -a AG gaseous; gassy ▶ SF fizzy drink

'gastrico, -a, -ci, -che AG gastric

gast'rite SF gastritis

gastroente'rite SF gastroenteritis

gastrono'mia SF gastronomy

gas'tronomo, -a SM/F gourmet, gastronome

G.A.T.T. SIGLA M (= *General Agreement on Tariffs and Trade*) GATT

'gatta SF cat, she-cat; **una** ~ **da pelare** (*col*) a thankless task; **qui** ~ **ci cova!** I smell a rat!, there's something fishy going on here!

gatta'buia SF (*col, scherzoso: prigione*) clink

gat'tino SM kitten

'gatto SM cat, tomcat; ~ **delle nevi** (*Aut, Sci*) snowcat; ~ **a nove code** cat-o'-nine-tails; ~ **selvatico** wildcat

gatto'pardo SM: ~ **africano** serval; ~ **americano** ocelot

gat'tuccio [gat'tuttʃo] SM dogfish

gau'dente SMF pleasure-seeker

'gaudio SM joy, happiness

ga'vetta SF (*Mil*) mess tin; **venire dalla** ~ (*Mil, fig*) to rise from the ranks

'gazza ['gaddza] SF magpie

gaz'zarra [gad'dzarra] SF racket, din

gaz'zella [gad'dzɛlla] SF gazelle; (*dei carabinieri*) (high-speed) police car

gaz'zetta [gad'dzetta] SF news sheet; **G~ Ufficiale** *official publication containing details of new laws*

gaz'zoso, -a [gad'dzoso] AG = **gassoso**

Gazz. Uff. ABBR = **Gazzetta Ufficiale**

GB SIGLA (= *Gran Bretagna*) GB

G.C. ABBR = **genio civile**

G.d.F. ABBR = **guardia di finanza**

GE SIGLA = **Genova**

gel [dʒɛl] SM INV gel

ge'lare [dʒe'lare] **/72/** VT, VI, VB IMPERS to freeze; **mi ha gelato il sangue** (*fig*) it made my blood run cold

ge'lata [dʒe'lata] SF frost

gela'taio, -a [dʒela'tajo] SM/F ice-cream vendor

gelate'ria [dʒelate'ria] SF ice-cream shop

gela'tina [dʒela'tina] SF gelatine; ~ **esplosiva** gelignite; ~ **di frutta** fruit jelly

gelati'noso, -a [dʒelati'noso] AG gelatinous, jelly-like

ge'lato, -a [dʒe'lato] AG frozen ▶ SM ice cream

'gelido, -a ['dʒɛlido] AG icy, ice-cold

'gelo ['dʒɛlo] SM (*temperatura*) intense cold; (*brina*) frost; (*fig*) chill

ge'lone [dʒe'lone] SM chilblain

gelo'sia [dʒelo'sia] SF jealousy

ge'loso, -a [dʒe'loso] AG jealous

'gelso ['dʒɛlso] SM mulberry (tree)

gelso'mino [dʒelso'mino] SM jasmine

gemel'laggio [dʒemel'laddʒo] SM twinning

gemel'lare [dʒemel'lare] **/72/** AG twin *cpd* ▶ VT (*città*) to twin

ge'mello, -a [dʒe'mɛllo] AG, SM/F twin; **gemelli** SMPL (*di camicia*) cufflinks; **Gemelli** Gemini *sg*; **essere dei Gemelli** to be Gemini

'gemere ['dʒɛmere] **/29/** VI to moan, groan; (*cigolare*) to creak; (*gocciolare*) to drip, ooze

'gemito ['dʒɛmito] SM moan, groan

'gemma ['dʒɛmma] SF (*Bot*) bud; (*pietra preziosa*) gem

Gen. ABBR (*Mil: = generale*) Gen

gen. ABBR (= *generale, generalmente*) gen

gen'darme [dʒen'darme] SM policeman; (*fig*) martinet

'gene ['dʒɛne] SM gene

genealo'gia, -'gie [dʒenealo'dʒia] SF genealogy

genea'logico, -a, -ci, -che [dʒenea'lɔdʒiko] AG genealogical; **albero ~** family tree

gene'rale [dʒene'rale] AG, SM general; **in ~** (per sommi capi) in general terms; (di solito) usually, in general; **a ~ richiesta** by popular request

generalità [dʒenerali'ta] SFPL (dati d'identità) particulars

generaliz'zare [dʒeneralid'dzare] /**72**/ VT, VI to generalize

generalizzazi'one [dʒeneraliddzat'tsjone] SF generalization

general'mente [dʒeneral'mente] AV generally

gene'rare [dʒene'rare] /**72**/ VT (dar vita) to give birth to; (produrre) to produce; (causare) to arouse; (Tecn) to produce, generate

genera'tore [dʒenera'tore] SM (Tecn) generator

generazi'one [dʒenerat'tsjone] SF generation

'genere ['dʒenere] SM kind, type, sort; (Biol) genus; (merce) article, product; (Ling) gender; (Arte, Letteratura) genre; **in ~** generally, as a rule; **cose del o di questo ~** such things; **il ~ umano** mankind; **generi alimentari** foodstuffs; **generi di consumo** consumer goods; **generi di prima necessità** basic essentials

ge'nerico, -a, -ci, -che [dʒe'nɛriko] AG generic; (vago) vague, imprecise; **medico ~** general practitioner

'genero ['dʒenero] SM son-in-law

generosità [dʒenerosi'ta] SF generosity

gene'roso, -a [dʒene'roso] AG generous

'genesi ['dʒɛnezi] SF genesis

ge'netico, -a, -ci, -che [dʒe'nɛtiko] AG genetic ▶ SF genetics sg

gen'giva [dʒen'dʒiva] SF (Anat) gum

ge'nia [dʒe'nia] SF (peg) mob, gang

geni'ale [dʒe'njale] AG (persona) of genius; (idea) ingenious, brilliant

'genio ['dʒɛnjo] SM genius; (attitudine, talento) talent, flair, genius; **andare a ~ a qn** to be to sb's liking, appeal to sb; **~ civile** civil engineers pl; **il ~ (militare)** the Engineers

geni'tale [dʒeni'tale] AG genital; **genitali** SMPL genitals

geni'tore [dʒeni'tore] SM parent, father o mother; **genitori** SMPL parents

genn. ABBR (= gennaio) Jan

gen'naio [dʒen'najo] SM January; vedi anche **luglio**

geno'cidio [dʒeno'tʃidjo] SM genocide

'Genova ['dʒɛnova] SF Genoa

geno'vese [dʒeno'vese] AG, SMF Genoese (pl inv)

gen'taglia [dʒen'taʎʎa] SF (peg) rabble

'gente ['dʒɛnte] SF people pl

gentil'donna [dʒentil'dɔnna] SF lady

gen'tile [dʒen'tile] AG (persona, atto) kind; (: garbato) courteous, polite; (nelle lettere): **G~ Signore** Dear Sir; **G~ Signor Fernando Villa** (sulla busta) Mr Fernando Villa

genti'lezza [dʒenti'lettsa] SF kindness; courtesy, politeness; **per ~** (per favore) please

gentilu'omo [dʒenti'lwɔmo] (pl **gentiluomini**) SM gentleman

genuflessi'one [dʒenufles'sjone] SF genuflection

genu'ino, -a [dʒenu'ino] AG (prodotto) natural; (persona, sentimento) genuine, sincere

geogra'fia [dʒeogra'fia] SF geography

geo'grafico, -a, -ci, -che [dʒeo'grafiko] AG geographical

ge'ografo, -a [dʒe'ɔgrafo] SM/F geographer

geolo'gia [dʒeolo'dʒia] SF geology

geo'logico, -a, -ci, -che [dʒeo'lɔdʒiko] AG geological

ge'ometra, -i, -e [dʒe'ɔmetra] SM/F (professionista) surveyor

geome'tria [dʒeome'tria] SF geometry

geo'metrico, -a, -ci, -che [dʒeo'mɛtriko] AG geometric(al)

geopo'litico, -a, -ci, -che [dʒeopo'litiko] AG geopolitical

Ge'orgia [dʒe'ɔrdʒa] SF Georgia

geor'giano, -a [dʒeor'dʒano] AG, SM/F Georgian

ge'ranio [dʒe'ranjo] SM geranium

ge'rarca, -chi [dʒe'rarka] SM (Storia: nel fascismo) party official

gerar'chia [dʒerar'kia] SF hierarchy

ge'rarchico, -a, -ci, -che [dʒe'rarkiko] AG hierarchical

ge'rente [dʒe'rɛnte] SMF manager (manageress)

ge'renza [dʒe'rɛntsa] SF management

ger'gale [dʒer'gale] AG slang cpd

'gergo, -ghi ['dʒɛrgo] SM jargon; slang

geria'tria [dʒerja'tria] SF geriatrics sg

geri'atrico, -a, -ci, -che [dʒe'rjatriko] AG geriatric

'gerla ['dʒɛrla] SF conical wicker basket

Ger'mania [dʒer'manja] SF: **la ~** Germany; **la ~ occidentale/orientale** West/East Germany

'germe ['dʒɛrme] SM germ; (fig) seed

germinazi'one [dʒerminat'tsjone] SF germination

germogli'are [dʒermoʎ'ʎare] /**27**/ VI (emettere germogli) to sprout; (germinare) to germinate

ger'moglio [dʒer'moʎʎo] SM shoot; (gemma) bud

gero'glifico, -ci [dʒero'glifiko] SM hieroglyphic

geron'tologo, -a, -gi, -ghe [dʒeron'tɔlogo] SM/F specialist in geriatrics

ge'rundio [dʒe'rundjo] SM gerund

Gerusa'lemme [dʒeruza'lɛmme] SF Jerusalem

'gesso ['dʒɛsso] SM chalk; (Scultura, Med, Edil) plaster; (statua) plaster figure; (minerale) gypsum

'gesta ['dʒɛsta] SFPL (letterario) deeds, feats

ges'tante [dʒes'tante] SF expectant mother

gestazi'one [dʒestat'tsjone] SF gestation

gestico'lare [dʒestiko'lare] /**72**/ VI to gesticulate

gestio'nale [dʒestjo'nale] AG administrative, management cpd

gesti'one [dʒes'tjone] SF management; **~ di magazzino** stock control; **~ patrimoniale** investment management

ges'tire [dʒes'tire] /**55**/ VT to run, manage

'gesto ['dʒɛsto] SM gesture

ges'tore [dʒes'tore] SM manager

Gesù [dʒe'zu] SM Jesus; **~ bambino** the Christ Child

gesu'ita, -i [dʒezu'ita] SM Jesuit

get'tare [dʒet'tare] /**72**/ VT to throw; (anche: **gettare via**) to throw away o out; (Scultura) to cast; (Edil) to lay; (acqua) to spout; (grido) to utter; **gettarsi** VPR: **gettarsi in** (impresa) to throw o.s. into; (mischia) to hurl o.s. into; (fiume) to flow into; **~ uno sguardo su** to take a quick look at

get'tata [dʒet'tata] SF (di cemento, gesso, metalli) cast; (diga) jetty

'gettito ['dʒettito] SM revenue

'getto ['dʒetto] SM (di gas, liquido, Aer) jet; (Bot) shoot; **a ~ continuo** uninterruptedly; **di ~** (fig) straight off, in one go

get'tone [dʒet'tone] SM token; (per giochi) counter; (: roulette ecc) chip; **~ di presenza** attendance fee; **~ telefonico** telephone token

gettoni'era [dʒetto'njɛra] SF telephone-token dispenser

'geyser ['gaizə] SM INV geyser

'Ghana ['gana] SM: **il ~** Ghana

'ghenga, -ghe ['gɛnga] SF (col) gang, crowd

ghe'pardo [ge'pardo] SM cheetah

gher'mire [ger'mire] /**55**/ VT to grasp, clasp, clutch

'ghetta ['getta] SF (gambale) gaiter

ghettiz'zare [gettid'dzare] /**72**/ VT to segregate

'ghetto ['getto] SM ghetto

ghiacci'aia [gjat'tʃaja] SF (anche fig) icebox

ghiacci'aio [gjat'tʃajo] SM glacier

ghiacci'are [gjat'tʃare] /**14**/ VT to freeze; (fig): **~ qn** to make sb's blood run cold ▶ VI to freeze, ice over

ghiacci'ato, -a [gjat'tʃato] AG frozen; (bevanda) ice-cold

ghi'accio ['gjattʃo] SM ice

ghiacci'olo [gjat'tʃolo] SM icicle; (tipo di gelato) ice lolly (BRIT), popsicle (US)

ghi'aia ['gjaja] SF gravel

ghi'anda ['gjanda] SF (Bot) acorn

ghi'andola ['gjandola] SF gland

ghiando'lare [gjando'lare] AG glandular

ghigliot'tina [giʎʎot'tina] SF guillotine

ghi'gnare [giɲ'ɲare] /**15**/ VI to sneer

'ghigno ['giɲɲo] SM (espressione) sneer; (risata) mocking laugh

'ghingheri ['gingeri] SMPL: **in ~** all dolled up; **mettersi in ~** to put on one's Sunday best

ghi'otto, -a ['gjotto] AG greedy; (cibo) delicious, appetizing

ghiot'tone, -a [gjot'tone] SM/F glutton

ghiotto'neria [gjottone'ria] SF greed, gluttony; (cibo) delicacy, titbit (BRIT), tidbit (US)

ghiri'goro [giri'goro] SM scribble, squiggle

ghir'landa [gir'landa] SF garland, wreath

'ghiro ['giro] SM dormouse

'ghisa ['giza] SF cast iron

G.I. ABBR = **giudice istruttore**

già [dʒa] AV already; (ex, in precedenza) formerly ▶ ESCL of course!, yes indeed!; **~ che ci sei ...** while you are at it ...

gi'acca, -che ['dʒakka] SF jacket; **~ a vento** windcheater (BRIT), windbreaker (US)

giacché [dʒak'ke] CONG since, as

giac'chetta [dʒak'ketta] SF (light) jacket

'giaccio etc ['dʒattʃo] VB vedi **giacere**

giac'cone [dʒak'kone] SM heavy jacket

gia'cenza [dʒa'tʃɛntsa] SF: **merce in ~** goods in stock; **capitale in ~** uninvested capital; **giacenze di magazzino** unsold stock

gia'cere [dʒa'tʃere] /**57**/ VI to lie

giaci'mento [dʒatʃi'mento] SM deposit

gia'cinto [dʒa'tʃinto] SM hyacinth

giaci'uto, -a [dʒa'tʃuto] PP di **giacere**

gi'acqui etc ['dʒakkwi] VB vedi **giacere**

gi'ada ['dʒada] SF jade

giaggi'olo [dʒad'dʒɔlo] SM iris

giagu'aro [dʒa'gwaro] SM jaguar

gial'lastro [dʒal'lastro] AG yellowish; (carnagione) sallow

gi'allo ['dʒallo] AG yellow; (carnagione) sallow ▶ SM yellow; (anche: **romanzo giallo**) detective novel; (anche: **film giallo**) detective film; **~ dell'uovo** yolk; **il mar G~** the Yellow Sea

gial'lognolo, -a [dʒal'loɲɲolo] AG yellowish, dirty yellow

Gia'maica [dʒa'maika] SF: **la ~** Jamaica

giamai'cano, -a [dʒamai'kano] AG, SM/F Jamaican

giam'mai [dʒam'mai] AV never

Giap'pone [dʒap'pone] SM: **il ~** Japan

giappo'nese [dʒappo'nese] AG, SMF, SM Japanese inv

gi'ara ['dʒara] SF jar

g

giardi'naggio [dʒardi'naddʒo] SM gardening

giardi'netta [dʒardi'netta] SF estate car (*BRIT*), station wagon (*US*)

giardini'ere, -a [dʒardi'njɛre] SM/F gardener ▶ SF (*misto di sottaceti*) mixed pickles *pl*; (*automobile*) = **giardinetta**

giar'dino [dʒar'dino] SM garden; ~ **d'infanzia** nursery school; ~ **pubblico** public gardens *pl*, (public) park; ~ **zoologico** zoo

giarretti'era [dʒarret'tjɛra] SF garter

Gi'ava ['dʒava] SF Java

giavel'lotto [dʒavel'lɔtto] SM javelin

gib'boso, -a [dʒib'boso] AG (*superficie*) bumpy; (*naso*) crooked

Gibil'terra [dʒibil'tɛrra] SF Gibraltar

giga SM INV (*Inform*) gig

giga'byte [dʒiga'bait] SM INV gigabyte

gi'gante, -'essa [dʒi'gante] SM/F giant ▶ AG giant, gigantic; (*Comm*) giant-size

gigan'tesco, -a, -schi, -sche [dʒigan'tesko] AG gigantic

gigantogra'fia [dʒigantogra'fia] SF (*Fot*) blow-up

'giglio ['dʒiʎʎo] SM lily

gilè [dʒi'lɛ] SM INV waistcoat

gin [dʒin] SM INV gin

gin'cana [dʒin'kana] SF gymkhana

ginecolo'gia [dʒinekolo'dʒia] SF gynaecology (*BRIT*), gynecology (*US*)

gine'cologo, -a, -gi, -ghe [dʒine'kɔlogo] SM/F gynaecologist (*BRIT*), gynecologist (*US*)

gi'nepro [dʒi'nepro] SM juniper

gi'nestra [dʒi'nɛstra] SF (*Bot*) broom

Gi'nevra [dʒi'nevra] SF Geneva; **il Lago di ~** Lake Geneva

gingil'larsi [dʒindʒil'larsi] /**72**/ VPR to fritter away one's time; (*giocare*): ~ **con** to fiddle with

gin'gillo [dʒin'dʒillo] SM plaything

gin'nasio [dʒin'nazjo] SM *the 4th and 5th year of secondary school in Italy*

gin'nasta, -i, -e [dʒin'nasta] SM/F gymnast

gin'nastica [dʒin'nastika] SF gymnastics *sg*; (*esercizio fisico*) keep-fit exercises *pl*; (*Ins*) physical education

'ginnico, -a, -ci, -che ['dʒinnko] AG gymnastic

gi'nocchio [dʒi'nɔkkjo] (*pl(m)* **ginocchi**, *pl(f)* **ginocchia**) SM knee; **stare in ~** to kneel, be on one's knees; **mettersi in ~** to kneel (down)

ginocchi'oni [dʒinok'kjoni] AV on one's knees

gio'care [dʒo'kare] /**20**/ VT to play; (*scommettere*) to stake, wager, bet; (*ingannare*) to take in ▶ VI to play; (*a roulette ecc*) to gamble; (*fig*) to play a part, be important; (*Tecn: meccanismo*) to be loose; ~ **a** (*gioco, sport*) to play; (*cavalli*) to bet on; ~ **d'astuzia** to be

crafty; **giocarsi la carriera** to put one's career at risk; **giocarsi tutto** to risk everything; **a che gioco giochiamo?** what are you playing at?

gioca'tore, -'trice [dʒoka'tore] SM/F player; gambler

gio'cattolo [dʒo'kattolo] SM toy

giocherel'lare [dʒokerel'lare] /**72**/ VI: ~ **con** (*giocattolo*) to play with; (*distrattamente*) to fiddle with

giocherò *etc* [dʒoke'rɔ] VB *vedi* **giocare**

gio'chetto [dʒo'ketto] SM (*gioco*) game; (*tranello*) trick; (*fig*): **è un ~** it's child's play

gi'oco, -chi ['dʒɔko] SM game; (*divertimento, Tecn*) play; (*al casinò*) gambling; (*Carte*) hand; (*insieme di pezzi ecc necessari per un gioco*) set; **per ~** for fun; **fare il doppio ~ con qn** to double-cross sb; **prendersi ~ di qn** to pull sb's leg; **stare al ~ di qn** to play along with sb; **è in ~ la mia reputazione** my reputation is at stake; ~ **d'azzardo** game of chance; ~ **della palla** ball game; ~ **degli scacchi** chess set; **i Giochi Olimpici** the Olympic Games

gioco'forza [dʒoko'fɔrtsa] SM: **essere ~** to be inevitable

giocoli'ere [dʒoko'ljɛre] SM juggler

gio'coso, -a [dʒo'koso] AG playful, jesting

gio'gaia [dʒo'gaja] SF (*Geo*) range of mountains

gi'ogo, -ghi ['dʒogo] SM yoke

gi'oia ['dʒɔja] SF joy, delight; (*pietra preziosa*) jewel, precious stone

gioielle'ria [dʒojelle'ria] SF jeweller's (*BRIT*) o jeweler's (*US*) craft; (*negozio*) jewel(l)er's (shop)

gioielli'ere, -a [dʒojel'ljɛre] SM/F jeweller (*BRIT*), jeweler (*US*)

gioi'ello [dʒo'jɛllo] SM jewel, piece of jewellery (*BRIT*) o jewelry (*US*); **gioielli** SMPL (*anelli, collane ecc*) jewellery *sg*; **i miei gioielli** my jewels o jewellery; **i gioielli della Corona** the crown jewels

gioi'oso, -a [dʒo'joso] AG joyful

Gior'dania [dʒor'danja] SF: **la ~** Jordan

Gior'dano [dʒor'dano] SM: **il ~** the Jordan

gior'dano, -a [dʒor'dano] AG, SM/F Jordanian

giorna'laio, -a [dʒorna'lajo] SM/F newsagent (*BRIT*), newsdealer (*US*)

gior'nale [dʒor'nale] SM (news)paper; (*diario*) journal, diary; (*Comm*) journal; ~ **di bordo** (*Naut*) ship's log; ~ **radio** radio news *sg*

giorna'letto [dʒorna'letto] SM (children's) comic

giornali'ero, -a [dʒorna'ljɛro] AG daily; (*che varia: umore*) changeable ▶ SM day labourer (*BRIT*) o laborer (*US*)

giorna'lino [dʒorna'lino] SM children's comic

giorna'lismo [dʒorna'lizmo] SM journalism

giorna'lista, -i, -e [dʒorna'lista] SM/F
journalist

giorna'listico, -a, -ci, -che [dʒorna'listiko]
AG journalistic; **stile ~** journalese

giornal'mente [dʒornal'mente] AV daily

gior'nata [dʒor'nata] SF day; (*paga*) day's
wages, day's pay; **durante la ~ di ieri**
yesterday; **fresco di ~** (*uovo*) freshly laid;
vivere alla ~ to live from day to day;
~ lavorativa working day

gi'orno ['dʒorno] SM day; (*opposto alla notte*)
day, daytime; (*luce del giorno*) daylight; **al ~**
per day; **di ~** by day; **~ per ~** day by day; **al ~
d'oggi** nowadays; **tutto il santo ~** all day
long; **il G~ dei Morti** *see note*

> Il *Giorno dei Morti*, All Souls' Day, falls on
> 2 November. At this time of year people
> visit cemeteries to lay flowers on the
> graves of their loved ones.

gi'ostra ['dʒɔstra] SF (*per bimbi*) merry-go-
round; (*torneo storico*) joust

gios'trare [dʒos'trare] /72/ VI (*Storia*) to joust,
tilt; **giostrarsi** VPR to manage

giov. ABBR (= *giovedì*) Thur(s)

giova'mento [dʒova'mento] SM benefit,
help

gi'ovane ['dʒovane] AG young; (*aspetto*)
youthful ▶ SM youth, young man ▶ SF girl,
young woman; **i giovani** young people;
è ~ del mestiere he's new to the job

giova'netto, -a [dʒova'netto] SM/F young
man(-woman)

giova'nile [dʒova'nile] AG youthful; (*scritti*)
early; (*errore*) of youth

giova'notto [dʒova'nɔtto] SM young man

gio'vare [dʒo'vare] /72/ VI: **~ a** (*essere utile*) to be
useful to; (*far bene*) to be good for ▶ VB IMPERS
(*essere bene, utile*) to be useful; **giovarsi** VPR:
giovarsi di qc to make use of sth; **a che
giova prendersela?** what's the point of
getting upset?

Gi'ove ['dʒɔve] SM (*Mitologia*) Jove; (*Astr*)
Jupiter

giovedì [dʒove'di] SM INV Thursday; **di** *o* **il ~**
on Thursdays; *vedi anche* **martedì**

gio'venca, -che [dʒo'vɛnka] SF heifer

gioventù [dʒoven'tu] SF (*periodo*) youth;
(*i giovani*) young people *pl*, youth

giovi'ale [dʒo'vjale] AG jovial, jolly

giovi'nastro [dʒovi'nastro] SM young thug

giovin'cello [dʒovin'tʃello] SM young lad

giovi'nezza [dʒovi'nettsa] SF youth

gip [dʒip] SIGLA M INV (= *giudice per le indagini
preliminari*) judge for preliminary enquiries

gira'dischi [dʒira'diski] SM INV record player

gi'raffa [dʒi'raffa] SF giraffe; (*TV, Cine, Radio*)
boom

gira'mento [dʒira'mento] SM: **~ di testa** fit
of dizziness

gira'mondo [dʒira'mondo] SM INV/F INV
globetrotter

gi'randola [dʒi'randola] SF (*fuoco d'artificio*)
Catherine wheel; (*giocattolo*) toy windmill;
(*banderuola*) weather vane, weathercock

gi'rante [dʒi'rante] SMF (*di assegno*) endorser

gi'rare [dʒi'rare] /72/ VT (*far ruotare*) to turn;
(*percorrere, visitare*) to go round; (*Cine*) to shoot;
(: *film: come regista*) to make; (*Comm*) to
endorse ▶ VI to turn; (*più veloce*) to spin;
(*andare in giro*) to wander, go around; **girarsi**
VPR to turn; **~ attorno a** to go round; to
revolve round; **si girava e rigirava nel
letto** he tossed and turned in bed; **far ~ la
testa a qn** to make sb dizzy; (*fig*) to turn
sb's head; **gira al largo** keep your
distance; **girala come ti pare** (*fig*) look at
it whichever way you like; **gira e rigira ...**
after a lot of driving (*o* walking) about ...;
(*fig*) whichever way you look at it; **cosa ti
gira?** (*col*) what's got into you?; **mi ha fatto
~ le scatole** (*col*) he drove me crazy

girar'rosto [dʒirar'rosto] SM (*Cuc*) spit

gira'sole [dʒira'sole] SM sunflower

gi'rata [dʒi'rata] SF (*passeggiata*) stroll; (*con
veicolo*) drive; (*Comm*) endorsement

gira'tario, -a [dʒira'tarjo] SM/F endorsee

gira'volta [dʒira'vɔlta] SF twirl, turn; (*curva*)
sharp bend; (*fig*) about-turn

gi'rello [dʒi'rɛllo] SM (*di bambino*) Babywalker®
(BRIT), go-cart (US); (*taglio di carne*) topside
(BRIT), top round (US)

gi'retto [dʒi'retto] SM (*passeggiata*) walk, stroll;
(: *in macchina*) drive, spin; (: *in bicicletta*) ride

gi'revole [dʒi'revole] AG revolving, turning

gi'rino [dʒi'rino] SM tadpole

'giro ['dʒiro] SM (*circuito, cerchio*) circle; (*di
chiave, manovella*) turn; (*viaggio*) tour,
excursion; (*passeggiata*) stroll, walk; (*in
macchina*) drive; (*in bicicletta*) ride; (*Sport: della
pista*) lap; (*di denaro*) circulation; (*Carte*) hand;
(*Tecn*) revolution; **fare un ~** to go for a walk
(*o* a drive *o* a ride); **fare il ~ di** (*parco, città*) to
go round; **andare in ~** (*a piedi*) to go about,
walk around; **guardarsi in ~** to look around;
prendere in ~ qn (*fig*) to take sb for a ride; **a
stretto ~ di posta** by return of post; **nel ~ di
un mese** in a month's time; **essere nel ~**
(*fig*) to belong to a circle (of friends);
~ d'affari (*viaggio*) business tour; (*Comm*)
turnover; **~ di parole** circumlocution; **~ di
prova** (*Aut*) test drive; **~ turistico**
sightseeing tour; **~ vita** waist measurement

giro'collo [dʒiro'kɔllo] SM: **a ~** crewneck *cpd*

giro'conto [dʒiro'konto] SM (*Econ*) credit
transfer

gi'rone [dʒi'rone] SM (*Sport*) series of games;
~ di andata/ritorno (*Calcio*) first/second half
of the season

gironzo'lare [dʒirondzo'lare] **/72/** vi to stroll about

giro'tondo [dʒiro'tondo] sm ring-a-ring-o'roses (BRIT), ring-around-the-rosey (US); **in ~** in a circle

girova'gare [dʒirova'gare] **/80/** vi to wander about

gi'rovago, -a, -ghi, -ghe [dʒi'rɔvago] sm/f (vagabondo) tramp; (venditore) peddler; **una compagnia di girovaghi** (attori) a company of strolling actors

'gita ['dʒita] sf excursion, trip; **fare una ~** to go for a trip, go on an outing

gi'tano, -a [dʒi'tano] sm/f gipsy

gi'tante [dʒi'tante] smf member of a tour

giù [dʒu] av down; (dabbasso) downstairs; **in ~** downwards, down; **la mia casa è un po' più in ~** my house is a bit further on; **~ di lì** (pressappoco) thereabouts; **bambini dai 6 anni in ~** children aged 6 and under; **~ per, cadere ~ per le scale** to fall down the stairs; **~ le mani!** hands off!; **essere ~** (fig: di salute) to be run down; (: di spirito) to be depressed; **quel tipo non mi va ~** I can't stand that guy

gi'ubba ['dʒubba] sf jacket

giub'botto [dʒub'bɔtto] sm jerkin; **~ antiproiettile** bulletproof vest; **~ salvagente** life jacket

giubi'lare [dʒubi'lare] **/72/** vi to rejoice

gi'ubilo ['dʒubilo] sm rejoicing

giudi'care [dʒudi'kare] **/20/** vt to judge; (accusato) to try; (lite) to arbitrate in; **~ qn/qc bello** to consider sb/sth (to be) beautiful

giudi'cato [dʒudi'kato] sm (Dir): **passare in ~** to pass final judgment

gi'udice ['dʒuditʃe] sm judge; **~ collegiale** member of the court; **~ conciliatore** justice of the peace; **~ istruttore** examining (BRIT) o committing (US) magistrate; **~ popolare** member of a jury

giudizi'ale [dʒudit'tsjale] ag judicial

giudizi'ario, -a [dʒudit'tsjarjo] ag legal, judicial

giu'dizio [dʒu'dittsjo] sm judgment; (opinione) opinion; (Dir) judgment, sentence; (: processo) trial; (: verdetto) verdict; **aver ~** to be wise o prudent; **essere in attesa di ~** to be awaiting trial; **citare in ~** to summons; **l'imputato è stato rinviato a ~** the accused has been committed for trial

giudizi'oso, -a [dʒudit'tsjoso] ag prudent, judicious

gi'uggiola ['dʒuddʒola] sf: **andare in brodo di giuggiole** (col) to be over the moon

gi'ugno ['dʒuɲɲo] sm June; vedi anche **luglio**

giu'livo, -a [dʒu'livo] ag merry

giul'lare [dʒul'lare] sm jester

giu'menta [dʒu'menta] sf mare

gi'unco, -chi ['dʒunko] sm (Bot) rush

gi'ungere ['dʒundʒere] **/5/** vi to arrive ▶ vt (mani ecc) to join; **~ a** to arrive at, reach; **~ nuovo a qn** to come as news to sb; **~ in porto** to reach harbour; (fig) to be brought to a successful outcome

gi'ungla ['dʒungla] sf jungle

gi'unsi etc ['dʒunsi] vb vedi **giungere**

gi'unto, -a ['dʒunto] pp di **giungere** ▶ sm (Tecn) coupling, joint ▶ sf addition; (organo esecutivo, amministrativo) council, board; **per giunta** into the bargain, in addition; **giunta militare** military junta; vedi anche **Comune; Provincia; Regione**

giun'tura [dʒun'tura] sf joint

giuo'care [dʒwo'kare] **/20/** vt, vi = **giocare**

giu'oco ['dʒwɔko] sm = **gioco**

giura'mento [dʒura'mento] sm oath; **~ falso** perjury

giu'rare [dʒu'rare] **/72/** vt to swear ▶ vi to swear, take an oath; **gliel'ho giurata** I swore I would get even with him

giu'rato, -a [dʒu'rato] ag: **nemico ~** sworn enemy ▶ sm/f juror, juryman(-woman)

giu'ria [dʒu'ria] sf jury

giu'ridico, -a, -ci, -che [dʒu'ridiko] ag legal

giurisdizi'one [dʒurizdit'tsjone] sf jurisdiction

giurispru'denza [dʒurispru'dɛntsa] sf jurisprudence

giu'rista, -i, -e [dʒu'rista] sm/f jurist

giustap'porre [dʒustap'porre] **/77/** vt to juxtapose

giustapposizi'one [dʒustappozit'tsjone] sf juxtaposition

giustap'posto, -a [dʒustap'posto] pp di **giustapporre**

giustifi'care [dʒustifi'kare] **/20/** vt to justify; **giustificarsi** vpr: **giustificarsi di** o **per qc** to justify o excuse o.s. for sth

giustifica'tivo, -a [dʒustifika'tivo] ag (Amm): **nota** o **pezza giustificativa** receipt

giustificazi'one [dʒustifikat'tsjone] sf justification; (Ins) (note of) excuse

gius'tizia [dʒus'tittsja] sf justice; **farsi ~ (da sé)** (vendicarsi) to take the law into one's own hands

giustizi'are [dʒustit'tsjare] **/19/** vt to execute, put to death

giustizi'ere [dʒustit'tsjere] sm executioner

gi'usto, -a ['dʒusto] ag (equo) fair, just; (vero) true, correct; (adatto) right, suitable; (preciso) exact, correct ▶ av (esattamente) exactly, precisely; (per l'appunto, appena) just; **arrivare ~** to arrive just in time; **ho ~ bisogno di te** you're just the person I need

'glabro, -a ag hairless

glaci'ale [gla'tʃale] ag glacial

gla'diolo sm gladiolus

'glandola sf = **ghiandola**

'glassa SF (*Cuc*) icing

glau'coma SM glaucoma

gli [ʎi] DET MPL (*dav V, s impura, gn, pn, ps, x, z*) the ▶ PRON (*a lui*) to him; (*a esso*) to it; (*in coppia con lo, la, li, le, ne: a lui, a lei, a loro ecc*): **gliele do** I'm giving them to him (*o* her *o* them); **gliene ho parlato** I spoke to him (*o* her *o* them) about it; *vedi anche* **il**

glice'mia [glitʃe'mia] SF glycaemia

glice'rina [glitʃe'rina] SF glycerine

'glicine ['glitʃine] SM wistaria

gli'ela *etc* ['ʎela] *vedi* **gli**

glo'bale AG overall; (*vista*) global

'globo SM globe

'globulo SM (*Anat*): **~ rosso/bianco** red/white corpuscle

glocalizzazi'one [glokaliddza'tsjone] SF glocalization

'gloria SF glory; **farsi ~ di qc** to pride o.s. on sth, take pride in sth

glori'arsi /72/ VPR: **~ di qc** to pride o.s. on sth, glory *o* take pride in sth

glorifi'care /20/ VT to glorify

glori'oso, -a AG glorious

glos'sario SM glossary

glu'cosio SM glucose

'gluteo SM gluteus; **glutei** SMPL buttocks

GM ABBR = **genio militare**

'gnocchi ['ɲɔkki] SMPL (*Cuc*) small dumplings made of semolina pasta or potato

'gnomo ['ɲɔmo] SM gnome

'gnorri ['ɲɔrri] SM INV/F INV: **non fare lo ~!** stop acting as if you didn't know anything about it!

GO SIGLA = **Gorizia**

'goal ['goul] SM INV (*Sport*) goal

'gobba SF (*Anat*) hump; (*protuberanza*) bump

'gobbo, -a AG hunchbacked; (*ricurvo*) round-shouldered ▶ SM/F hunchback

'Gobi SMPL: **il Deserto dei ~** the Gobi Desert

'goccia, -ce ['gottʃa] SF drop; **~ di rugiada** dewdrop; **somigliarsi come due gocce d'acqua** to be as like as two peas in a pod; **è la ~ che fa traboccare il vaso!** it's the last straw!

'goccio ['gottʃo] SM drop, spot

goccio'lare [gottʃo'lare] /72/ VI, VT to drip

goccio'lio [gottʃo'lio] SM dripping

go'dere /58/ VI: **~ (di)** (*compiacersi*) to be delighted (at), rejoice (at); **~ di** (*trarre vantaggio*) to enjoy, to benefit from ▶ VT to enjoy; **godersi la vita** to enjoy life; **godersela** to have a good time, enjoy o.s.

godi'mento SM enjoyment

godrò *etc* VB *vedi* **godere**

goffaggine [gof'faddʒine] SF clumsiness

'goffo, -a AG clumsy, awkward

'gogna ['goɲɲa] SF pillory

gol [gɔl] SM INV (*Sport*) = **goal**

'gola SF (*Anat*) throat; (*golosità*) gluttony, greed; (*di camino*) flue; (*di monte*) gorge; **fare ~** (*anche fig*) to tempt; **ricacciare il pianto** *o* **le lacrime in ~** to swallow one's tears

go'letta SF (*Naut*) schooner

golf SM INV (*Sport*) golf; (*maglia*) cardigan

'golfo SM gulf

goli'ardico, -a, -ci, -che AG (*canto, vita*) student *cpd*

go'loso, -a AG greedy

'golpe SM INV (*Pol*) coup

gomi'tata SF: **dare una ~ a qn** to elbow sb; **farsi avanti a (forza** *o* **furia di) gomitate** to elbow one's way through; **fare a gomitate per qc** to fight to get sth

'gomito SM elbow; (*di strada ecc*) sharp bend

go'mitolo SM ball

'gomma SF rubber; (*colla*) gum; (*per cancellare*) rubber, eraser; (*di veicolo*) tyre (BRIT), tire (US); **~ da masticare** chewing gum; **~ a terra** flat tyre

gommapi'uma® SF foam rubber

gom'mino SM rubber tip; (*rondella*) rubber washer

gom'mista, -i, -e SM/F tyre (BRIT) *o* tire (US) specialist; (*rivenditore*) tyre *o* tire merchant

gom'mone SM rubber dinghy

gom'moso, -a AG rubbery

'gondola SF gondola

gondoli'ere SM gondolier

gonfa'lone SM banner

gonfi'are /19/ VT (*pallone*) to blow up, inflate; (*dilatare, ingrossare*) to swell; (*fig: notizia*) to exaggerate; **gonfiarsi** VPR to swell; (*fiume*) to rise

'gonfio, -a AG swollen; (*stomaco*) bloated; (*palloncino, gomme*) inflated, blown up; (*con pompa*) pumped up; (*vela*) full; **occhi gonfi di pianto** eyes swollen with tears; **~ di orgoglio** (*persona*) puffed up (with pride); **avere il portafoglio ~** to have a bulging wallet

gonfi'ore SM swelling

gongo'lare /72/ VI to look pleased with o.s.; **~ di gioia** to be overjoyed

'gonna SF skirt; **~ pantalone** culottes *pl*

'gonzo ['gondzo] SM simpleton, fool

goo'glare [gu'glare] /72/ VT (*Inform*) to google

gorgheggi'are [gorged'dʒare] /62/ VI to warble; to trill

gor'gheggio [gor'geddʒo] SM (*Mus, di uccello*) trill

'gorgo, -ghi SM whirlpool

gorgogli'are [gorgoʎ'ʎare] /27/ VI to gurgle

gorgo'glio [gorgoʎ'ʎio] SM gurgling

go'rilla SM INV gorilla; (*guardia del corpo*) bodyguard

'Gotha SM INV (*del cinema, letteratura, industria*) leading lights *pl*

'gotico, -a, -ci, -che AG, SM Gothic

'gotta SF gout

gover'nante SMF ruler ▶ SF (di bambini) governess; (donna di servizio) housekeeper

gover'nare /72/ VT (stato) to govern, rule; (pilotare, guidare) to steer; (bestiame) to tend, look after

governa'tivo, -a AG (politica, decreto) government cpd, governmental; (stampa) pro-government

governa'tore SM governor

go'verno SM government; ~ **ombra** shadow cabinet

'gozzo ['gottso] SM (Zool) crop; (Med) goitre; (fig: col) throat

gozzovigli'are [gottsoviʎ'ʎare] /27/ VI to make merry, carouse

GPL [dʒipi'ɛlle] SIGLA M (= Gas di Petrolio Liquefatto) LPG (= Liquefied Petroleum Gas)

gpm ABBR (= giri per minuto) rpm

GPS [dʒipi'ɛsse] SIGLA M GPS (= Global Positioning System)

GR [dzi'erre] SIGLA = **Grosseto** ▶ SIGLA M (= giornale radio) radio news

gracchi'are [grak'kjare] /19/ VI to caw

graci'dare [gratʃi'dare] /72/ VI to croak

graci'dio, -ii [gratʃi'dio] SM croaking

'gracile ['gratʃile] AG frail, delicate

gra'dasso SM boaster

gradata'mente AV gradually, by degrees

gradazi'one [gradat'tsjone] SF (sfumatura) gradation; ~ **alcolica** alcoholic content, strength

gra'devole AG pleasant, agreeable

gradi'mento SM pleasure, satisfaction; **essere di mio** (o **tuo** etc) ~ to be to my (o your etc) liking

gradi'nata SF flight of steps; (in teatro, stadio) tiers pl

gra'dino SM step; (Alpinismo) foothold

gra'dire /55/ VT (accettare con piacere) to accept; (desiderare) to wish, like; **gradisce una tazza di tè?** would you like a cup of tea?

gra'dito, -a AG welcome

'grado SM (Mat, Fisica ecc) degree; (stadio) degree, level; (Mil, sociale) rank; **essere in ~ di fare** to be in a position to do; **di buon ~** willingly; **per gradi** by degrees; **un cugino di primo/secondo** ~ a first/second cousin; **subire il terzo** ~ (anche fig) to be given the third degree

gradu'ale AG gradual

gradu'are /72/ VT to grade

gradu'ato, -a AG (esercizi) graded; (scala, termometro) graduated ▶ SM (Mil) non-commissioned officer

gradua'toria SF (di concorso) list; (per la promozione) order of seniority

'graffa SF (gancio) clip; (segno grafico) brace

graf'fetta SF paper clip

graffi'are /19/ VT to scratch; **graffiarsi** VPR to get scratched; (con unghie) to scratch o.s.

graffia'tura SF scratch

'graffio SM scratch

graf'fiti SMPL graffiti

gra'fia SF spelling; (scrittura) handwriting

'grafico, -a, -ci, -che AG graphic ▶ SM graph; (persona) graphic designer ▶ SF graphic arts pl; ~ **a torta** pie chart

gra'migna [gra'miɲɲa] SF weed; couch grass

gram'matica, -che SF grammar

grammati'cale AG grammatical

'grammo SM gram(me)

gram'mofono SM gramophone

'gramo, -a AG (vita) wretched

gran AG vedi **grande**

'grana SF (granello, di minerali, corpi spezzati) grain; (col: seccatura) trouble; (: soldi) cash ▶ SM INV cheese similar to Parmesan

gra'naglie [gra'naʎʎe] SFPL corn sg, seed sg

gra'naio SM granary, barn

gra'nata SF (frutto) pomegranate; (pietra preziosa) garnet; (proiettile) grenade

granati'ere SM (Mil) grenadier; (fig) fine figure of a man

Gran Bre'tagna [granbre'taɲɲa] SF: **la** ~ Great Britain

gran'cassa SF (Mus) bass drum

'granchio ['grankjo] SM crab; (fig) blunder; **prendere un** ~ (fig) to blunder

grandango'lare SM wide-angle lens sg

gran'dangolo SM (Fot) wide-angle lens sg

'grande (qualche volta **gran** + C, **grand'** + V) AG (grosso, largo, vasto) big, large; (alto) tall; (lungo) long; (in sensi astratti) great ▶ SMF (persona adulta) adult, grown-up; (chi ha ingegno e potenza) great man(-woman); **mio fratello più** ~ my big o older brother; **il gran pubblico** the general public; **di gran classe** (prodotto) high-class; **cosa farai da ~?** what will you be o do when you grow up?; **fare le cose in** ~ to do things in style; **fare il** ~ (strafare) to act big; **una gran bella donna** a very beautiful woman; **non è una gran cosa** o **un gran che** it's nothing special; **non ne so gran che** I don't know very much about it

grandeggi'are [granded'dʒare] /62/ VI (emergere per grandezza): ~ **su** to tower over; (darsi arie) to put on airs

gran'dezza [gran'dettsa] SF (dimensione) size; magnitude; (fig) greatness; **in ~ naturale** lifesize; **manie di** ~ delusions of grandeur

grandi'nare /72/ VB IMPERS to hail

'grandine SF hail

grandi'oso, -a AG grand, grandiose

gran'duca, -chi SM grand duke

grandu'cato SM grand duchy

grandu'chessa [grandu'kessa] SF grand duchess

gra'nello SM (*di cereali, uva*) seed; (*di frutta*) pip; (*di sabbia, sale ecc*) grain

gra'nita SF *kind of water ice*

gra'nito SM granite

'grano SM (*in quasi tutti i sensi*) grain; (*frumento*) wheat; (*di rosario, collana*) bead; **~ di pepe** peppercorn

gran'turco SM maize

'granulo SM granule; (*Med*) pellet

'grappa SF *rough, strong brandy*

'grappolo SM bunch, cluster

'graspo SM bunch (of grapes)

gras'setto SM (*Tip*) bold (type) (*BRIT*), bold face

'grasso, -a AG fat; (*cibo*) fatty; (*pelle*) greasy; (*terreno*) rich; (*fig: guadagno, annata*) plentiful; (*: volgare*) coarse, lewd ▶ SM (*di persona, animale*) fat; (*sostanza che unge*) grease

gras'soccio, -a, -ci, -ce [gras'sɔttʃo] AG plump

gras'sone, -a SM/F (*col: persona*) dumpling

'grata SF grating

gra'ticcio [gra'tittʃo] SM trellis; (*stuoia*) mat

gra'ticola SF grill

gra'tifica, -che SF bonus; **~ natalizia** Christmas bonus

gratificazi'one [gratifikat'tsjone] SF (*soddisfazione*) satisfaction, reward

grati'nare /**72**/ VT (*Cuc*) to cook au gratin

'gratis AV free, for nothing

grati'tudine SF gratitude

'grato, -a AG grateful; (*gradito*) pleasant, agreeable

gratta'capo SM worry, headache

grattaci'elo [gratta'tʃɛlo] SM skyscraper

gratta e 'sosta SM INV *scratch card used to pay for parking*

gratta e 'vinci [grattae'vintʃi] SM (*lotteria*) lottery; (*biglietto*) scratchcard

grat'tare /**72**/ VT (*pelle*) to scratch; (*raschiare*) to scrape; (*pane, formaggio, carote*) to grate; (*col: rubare*) to pinch ▶ VI (*stridere*) to grate; (*Aut*) to grind; **grattarsi** VPR to scratch o.s.; **grattarsi la pancia** (*fig*) to twiddle one's thumbs

grat'tata SF scratch; **fare una ~** (*Aut: col*) to grind the gears

grat'tugia [grat'tudʒa], **-gie** SF grater

grattugi'are [grattu'dʒare] /**62**/ VT to grate; **pane grattugiato** breadcrumbs *pl*

gratuità SF (*fig*) gratuitousness

gra'tuito, -a AG free; (*fig*) gratuitous

gra'vame SM tax; (*fig*) burden, weight

gra'vare /**72**/ VT to burden ▶ VI: **~ su** to weigh on

'grave AG (*danno, pericolo, peccato ecc*) grave, serious; (*responsabilità*) heavy, grave; (*contegno*) grave, solemn; (*voce, suono*) deep, low-pitched; (*Ling*): **accento ~** grave accent ▶ SM (*Fisica*) (heavy) body; **un malato ~** a person who is seriously ill

grave'mente AV (*ammalato, ferito*) seriously

gravi'danza [gravi'dantsa] SF pregnancy

'gravido, -a AG pregnant

gravità SF seriousness; (*anche Fisica*) gravity

gravi'tare /**72**/ VI (*Fisica*): **~ intorno a** to gravitate round

gra'voso, -a AG heavy, onerous

'grazia ['grattsja] SF grace; (*favore*) favour (*BRIT*), favor (*US*) (*Dir*) pardon; **di ~** (*ironico*) if you please; **troppa ~!** (*ironico*) you're too generous!; **quanta ~ di Dio!** what abundance!; **entrare nelle grazie di qn** to win sb's favour; **Ministero di G~ e Giustizia** Ministry of Justice, ≈ Lord Chancellor's Office (*BRIT*), ≈ Department of Justice (*US*)

grazi'are [grat'tsjare] /**19**/ VT (*Dir*) to pardon

'grazie ['grattsje] ESCL thank you!; **~ mille!** *o* **tante!** *o* **infinite!** thank you very much!; **~ a** thanks to

grazi'oso, -a [grat'tsjoso] AG charming, delightful; (*gentile*) gracious

'Grecia ['grɛtʃa] SF: **la ~** Greece

'greco, -a, -ci, -che AG, SM/F, SM Greek

gre'gario SM (*Ciclismo*) supporting rider

'gregge ['greddʒe] (*pl(f)* **greggi**) SM flock

'greggio, -a, -gi, -ge ['greddʒo] AG raw, unrefined; (*diamante*) rough, uncut; (*tessuto*) unbleached ▶ SM (*anche:* **petrolio greggio**) crude (oil)

grembi'ule SM apron; (*sopravveste*) overall

'grembo SM lap; (*ventre della madre*) womb

gre'mito, -a AG: **~ (di)** packed *o* crowded (with)

'greto SM (exposed) gravel bed of a river

'gretto, -a AG mean, stingy; (*fig*) narrow-minded

'greve AG heavy

'grezzo, -a ['greddzo] AG = **greggio**

gri'dare /**72**/ VI (*per chiamare*) to shout, cry (out); (*strillare*) to scream, yell ▶ VT to shout (out), yell (out); **~ aiuto** to cry *o* shout for help

'grido (*pl(m)* **gridi**, *pl(f)* **grida**) SM shout, cry; scream, yell; (*di animale*) cry; **di ~** famous; **all'ultimo ~** in the latest style

'grigio ['gridʒo], **-a, -gi, -gie** AG, SM grey (*BRIT*), gray (*US*)

'griglia ['griʎʎa] SF (*per arrostire*) grill; (*Elettr*) grid; (*inferriata*) grating; **alla ~** (*Cuc*) grilled

grigli'ata [griʎ'ʎata] SF (*Cuc*) grill

gril'letto SM trigger

'grillo SM (*Zool*) cricket; (*fig*) whim; **ha dei grilli per la testa** his head is full of nonsense

grimal'dello SM picklock

'grinfia SF: **cadere nelle grinfie di qn** (*fig*) to fall into sb's clutches

'grinta SF grim expression; (*Sport*) fighting spirit; **avere molta ~** to be very determined

grintoso, -a AG forceful

'grinza ['grintsa] SF crease, wrinkle; (*ruga*) wrinkle; **il tuo ragionamento non fa una ~** your argument is faultless

grin'zoso, -a [grin'tsoso] AG wrinkled; creased

grip'pare /72/ VI (*Tecn*) to seize

gris'sino SM bread-stick

groenlan'dese AG Greenland *cpd* ▶ SMF Greenlander

Groen'landia SF: **la ~** Greenland

'gronda SF eaves *pl*

gron'daia SF gutter

gron'dante AG dripping

gron'dare /72/ VI to pour; (*essere bagnato*): **~ di** to be dripping with ▶ VT to drip with

'groppa SF (*di animale*) back, rump; (*col: dell'uomo*) back, shoulders *pl*

'groppo SM tangle; **avere un ~ alla gola** (*fig*) to have a lump in one's throat

'grossa SF (*unità di misura*) gross

gros'sezza [gros'settsa] SF size; thickness

gros'sista, -i, -e SM/F (*Comm*) wholesaler

'grosso, -a AG big, large; (*di spessore*) thick; (*grossolano: anche fig*) coarse; (*grave, insopportabile*) serious, great; (*tempo, mare*) rough ▶ SM: **il ~ di** the bulk of; **un pezzo ~** (*fig*) a VIP, a bigwig; **farla grossa** to do something very stupid; **dirle grosse** to tell tall stories (*BRIT*) *o* tales (*US*); **questa è grossa!** that's a good one!; **sbagliarsi di ~** to be completely wrong; **dormire della grossa** to sleep like a log

grossolanità SF coarseness

grosso'lano, -a AG rough, coarse; (*fig*) coarse, crude; (*: errore*) stupid

grosso'modo AV roughly

'grotta SF cave; grotto

grot'tesco, -a, -schi, -sche AG grotesque

grovi'era SM *o* F gruyère (cheese)

gro'viglio [gro'viʎʎo] SM tangle; (*fig*) muddle

gru SF INV crane

'gruccia, -ce ['gruttʃa] SF (*per camminare*) crutch; (*per abiti*) coat-hanger

gru'gnire [gruɲ'ɲire] /55/ VI to grunt

gru'gnito [gruɲ'ɲito] SM grunt

'grugno ['gruɲɲo] SM snout; (*col: faccia*) mug

'grullo, -a AG silly, stupid

'grumo SM (*di sangue*) clot; (*di farina ecc*) lump

gru'moso, -a AG lumpy

'gruppo SM group; **~ sanguigno** blood group

gruvi'era SM *o* F = **groviera**

'gruzzolo ['gruttsolo] SM (*di denaro*) hoard

GSM SIGLA M (= *Global System for Mobile Communication*) GSM

GT ABBR (*Aut*: = *gran turismo*) GT

G.U. ABBR = **Gazzetta Ufficiale**

guada'gnare [gwadaɲ'ɲare] /15/ VT (*ottenere*) to gain; (*soldi, stipendio*) to earn; (*vincere*) to win; (*raggiungere*) to reach; **tanto di guadagnato!** so much the better!

gua'dagno [gwa'daɲɲo] SM earnings *pl*; (*Comm*) profit; (*vantaggio, utile*) advantage, gain; **~ di capitale** capital gains *pl*; **~ lordo/netto** gross/net earnings *pl*

gu'ado SM ford; **passare a ~** to ford

gu'ai ESCL: **~ a te** (*o lui etc*)**!** woe betide you (*o him etc*)!

gua'ina SF (*fodero*) sheath; (*indumento per donna*) girdle

gu'aio SM trouble, mishap; (*inconveniente*) trouble, snag

gua'ire /55/ VI to whine, yelp

gua'ito SM (*di cane*) yelp, whine; (*il guaire*) yelping, whining

gu'ancia, -ce ['gwantʃa] SF cheek

guanci'ale [gwan'tʃale] SM pillow; **dormire fra due guanciali** (*fig*) to sleep easy, have no worries

gu'anto SM glove; **trattare qn con i guanti** (*fig*) to handle sb with kid gloves; **gettare/raccogliere il ~** (*fig*) to throw down/take up the gauntlet

guan'tone SM boxing glove

guarda'boschi [gwarda'bɔski] SM INV forester

guarda'caccia [gwarda'kattʃa] SM INV gamekeeper

guarda'coste SM INV coastguard; (*nave*) coastguard patrol vessel

guarda'linee SM INV (*Sport*) linesman

guarda'macchine [gwarda'makkine] SM INV/F INV car-park (*BRIT*) *o* parking lot (*US*) attendant

guar'dare /72/ VT (*con lo sguardo: osservare*) to look at; (*: film, televisione*) to watch; (*custodire*) to look after, take care of ▶ VI to look; (*badare*): **~ a** to pay attention to; (*luoghi: esser orientato*): **~ a** to face; **guardarsi** VPR to look at o.s.; **~ di** to try to; **guardarsi da** (*astenersi*) to refrain from; (*stare in guardia*) to beware of; **guardarsi dal fare** to take care not to do; **guarda di non sbagliare** try not to make a mistake; **ma guarda un po'!** good heavens!; **e guarda caso ...** as if by coincidence ...; **~ qn dall'alto in basso** to look down on sb; **non ~ in faccia a nessuno** (*fig*) to have no regard for anybody; **~ di traverso** to scowl *o* frown at; **~ a vista qn** to keep a close watch on sb

guarda'roba SM INV wardrobe; (*locale*) cloakroom

guardarobi'ere, -a SM/F cloakroom attendant

guardasi'gilli [gwardasi'dʒilli] SM INV ≈ Lord Chancellor (BRIT), ≈ Attorney General (US)

gu'ardia SF (individuo, corpo) guard; (sorveglianza) watch; **fare la ~ a qc/qn** to guard sth/sb; **stare in ~** (fig) to be on one's guard; **il medico di ~** the doctor on call; **il fiume ha raggiunto il livello di ~** the river has reached the high-water mark; **~ carceraria** (prison) warder (BRIT) o guard (US); **~ del corpo** bodyguard; **~ di finanza** (corpo) customs pl; (persona) customs officer; see note; **~ forestale** forest ranger; **~ giurata** security guard; **~ medica** emergency doctor service; **~ municipale** town policeman; **~ notturna** night security guard; **~ di pubblica sicurezza** policeman

The *Guardia di Finanza* is a military body which deals with infringements of the laws governing income tax and monopolies. It reports to the Ministers of Finance, Justice or Agriculture, depending on the function it is performing.

guardia'caccia [gwardja'kattʃa] SM INV = **guardacaccia**

guardi'ano, -a SM/F (di carcere) warder (BRIT), guard (US); (di villa ecc) caretaker; (di museo) custodian; (di zoo) keeper; **~ notturno** night watchman

guar'dina SF cell

guar'dingo, -a, -ghi, -ghe AG wary, cautious

guardi'ola SF porter's lodge; (Mil) look-out tower

guarigi'one [gwari'dʒone] SF recovery

gua'rire /55/ VT (persona, malattia) to cure; (ferita) to heal ▶ VI to recover, be cured; to heal (up)

guarnigi'one [gwarni'dʒone] SF garrison

guar'nire /55/ VT (ornare: abiti) to trim; (Cuc) to garnish

guarnizi'one [gwarnit'tsjone] SF trimming; garnish; (Tecn) gasket

guasta'feste SMF spoilsport

guas'tare /72/ VT to spoil, ruin; (meccanismo) to break; **guastarsi** VPR (cibo) to go bad; (meccanismo) to break down; (tempo) to change for the worse; (amici) to quarrel, fall out

gu'asto, -a AG (non funzionante) broken; (: telefono ecc) out of order; (andato a male) bad, rotten; (: dente) decayed, bad; (fig: corrotto) depraved ▶ SM breakdown; (avaria) failure; **~ al motore** engine failure

Guate'mala SM: **il ~** Guatemala

guatemal'teco, -a, -ci, -che AG, SM/F Guatemalan

gu'ercio, -a, -ci, -ce ['gwertʃo] AG cross-eyed

gu'erra SF war; (tecnica: atomica, chimica ecc)

warfare; **fare la ~ (a)** to wage war (against); **la ~ fredda** the Cold War; **~ mondiale** world war; **~ preventiva** preventive war; **la prima/seconda ~ mondiale** the First/Second World War

guerrafon'daio SM warmonger

guerreggi'are [gwerred'dʒare] **/62/** VI to wage war

guer'resco, -a, -schi, -sche AG (di guerra) war cpd; (incline alla guerra) warlike

guerri'ero, -a AG warlike ▶ SM warrior

guer'riglia [gwer'riʎʎa] SF guerrilla warfare

guerrigli'ero [gwerriʎ'ʎero] SM guerrilla

'gufo SM owl

'guglia ['guʎʎa] SF (Archit) spire; (di roccia) needle

Gui'ana SF: **la ~ francese** French Guiana

gu'ida SF (persona) guide; (libro) guide(book); (comando, direzione) guidance, direction; (Aut) driving; (: sterzo) steering; (tappeto: di tenda, cassetto) runner; **~ a destra/sinistra** (Aut) right-/left-hand drive; **essere alla ~ di** (governo) to head; (spedizione, paese) to lead; **far da ~ a qn** (mostrare la strada) to show sb the way; (in una città) to show sb (a)round; **~ telefonica** telephone directory; **~ turistica** tourist guide

gui'dare /72/ VT to guide; (squadra, rivolta) to lead; (auto) to drive; (aereo, nave) to pilot; **sa ~?** can you drive?

guida'tore, -'trice SM/F (conducente) driver

Gui'nea SF: **la Repubblica di ~** the Republic of Guinea; **la ~ Equatoriale** Equatorial Guinea

guin'zaglio [gwin'tsaʎʎo] SM leash, lead

gu'isa SF: **a ~ di** like, in the manner of

guiz'zare [gwit'tsare] **/72/** VI to dart; to flicker; to leap; **~ via** (fuggire) to slip away

gu'izzo ['gwittso] SM (di animali) dart; (di fulmine) flash

'guru SM INV (Rel, anche fig) guru

'guscio ['guʃʃo] SM shell

gus'tare /72/ VT (cibi) to taste; (: assaporare con piacere) to enjoy, savour (BRIT), savor (US); (fig) to enjoy, appreciate ▶ VI: **~ a** to please; **non mi gusta affatto** I don't like it at all

gusta'tivo, -a AG: **papille gustative** taste buds

'gusto SM (senso) taste; (sapore) taste, flavour (BRIT), flavor (US); (godimento) enjoyment; **al ~ di fragola** strawberry-flavoured; **di ~ barocco** in the baroque style; **mangiare di ~** to eat heartily; **prenderci ~: ci ha preso ~** he's acquired a taste for it, he's got to like it

gus'toso, -a AG tasty; (fig) agreeable

guttu'rale AG guttural

Gu'yana [gu'jana] SF: **la ~** Guyana

Hh

H, h ['akka] SM O F INV (*lettera*) H, h ▶ ABBR (= *ora*) hr; (= *etto, altezza*) h; **H come hotel** ≈ H for Harry (*BRIT*), H for How (*US*)

ha¹, 'hai [a, ai] VB *vedi* **avere**

ha² ABBR (= *ettaro*) ha

ha'cker ['haker] SM INV hacker

Ha'iti [a'iti] SF Haiti

haiti'ano, -a [ai'tjano] AG, SM/F Haitian

hall [hɔːl] SF INV hall, foyer

ham'burger [am'burger] SM INV (*carne*) hamburger; (*panino*) burger

'handicap ['handikap] SM INV handicap

handicap'pato, -a [andikap'pato] AG handicapped ▶ SM/F handicapped person, disabled person

'hanno ['anno] VB *vedi* **avere**

hard dis'count [ardis'kaunt] SM INV discount supermarket

hard 'disk [ar'disk] SM INV hard disk

'hardware ['ardwer] SM INV hardware

ha'scisc, hascisch [aʃʃiʃ] SM hashish

'hashtag ['aʃtag] SM INV (*Inform*) hashtag

hawai'ano, -a [ava'jano] AG, SM/F Hawaiian

Ha'waii [a'vai] SFPL: **le ~** Hawaii *sg*

help [ɛlp] SM INV (*Inform*) help

help' desk [ɛlp'dɛsk] SM INV (*Inform*) help desk

'Helsinki ['ɛlsinki] SF Helsinki

'herpes ['ɛrpes] SM (*Med*) herpes *sg*; **~ zoster** shingles *sg*

hg ABBR (= *ettogrammo*) hg

'hi-fi ['haifai] SM INV, AG INV hi-fi

Hima'laia [ima'laja] SM: **l' ~** the Himalayas *pl*

hl ABBR (= *ettolitro*) hl

ho [ɔ] VB *vedi* **avere**

'hobby ['hɔbi] SM INV hobby

'hockey ['hɔki] SM hockey; **~ su ghiaccio** ice hockey

'holding ['houldiŋ] SF INV holding company

'home page ['hom'pɛidʒ] SF INV home page

Hon'duras [on'duras] SM Honduras

'Hong Kong ['ɔkɔg] SF Hong Kong

Hono'lulu [ono'lulu] SF Honolulu

'hostess ['houstis] SF INV air hostess (*BRIT*) o stewardess

'hot dog ['hɔtdɔg] SM INV hot dog

ho'tel [o'tɛl] SM INV hotel

'humour ['jumor] SM INV (sense of) humour

'humus ['umus] SM humus

'husky ['aski] SM INV (*cane*) husky

Hz ABBR (= *hertz*) Hz

I i

I, i [i] SM O F INV (*lettera*) I, i; **I come Imola** ≈
 I for Isaac (*Brit*), I for Item (*US*)
i DET MPL the; *vedi anche* **il**
IACP SIGLA M (= *Istituto Autonomo per le Case
 Popolari*) *public housing association*
i'ato SM hiatus
i'berico, -a, -ci, -che AG Iberian; **la Penisola
 Iberica** the Iberian Peninsula
iber'nare /**72**/ VI to hibernate ▶ VT (*Med*) to
 induce hypothermia in
ibernazi'one [ibernat'tsjone] SF hibernation
ibid. ABBR (= *ibidem*) ib(id)
'ibrido, -a AG, SM hybrid
IC ABBR (= *Intercity*) Intercity
'ICE ['itʃe] SIGLA M (= *Istituto nazionale per il
 Commercio Estero*) *overseas trade board*
'ICI ['itʃi] SIGLA F (= *Imposta Comunale sugli
 Immobili*) ≈ Council Tax
i'cona SF (*Rel, Inform, anche fig*) icon
id ABBR (= *idem*) do.
Id'dio SM God
i'dea SF idea; (*opinione*) opinion, view; (*ideale*)
 ideal; **avere le idee chiare** to know one's
 mind; **cambiare ~** to change one's mind;
 dare l' ~ di to seem, look like; **neanche** *o*
 neppure per ~! certainly not!, no way!;
 ~ fissa obsession
ide'ale AG, SM ideal
idea'lismo SM idealism
idea'lista, -i, -e SM/F idealist
idea'listico, -a, -ci, -che AG idealistic
idealiz'zare [idealid'dzare] /**72**/ VT to idealize
ide'are /**72**/ VT (*immaginare*) to think up,
 conceive; (*progettare*) to plan
idea'tore, -'trice SM/F author
i'dentico, -a, -ci, -che AG identical
identifi'care /**20**/ VT to identify; **identificarsi**
 VPR: **identificarsi (con)** to identify o.s. (with)
identificazi'one [identifikat'tsjone] SF
 identification
identità SF INV identity
ideolo'gia, -'gie [ideolo'dʒia] SF ideology
ideo'logico, -a, -ci, -che [ideo'lɔdʒiko] AG
 ideological

idil'liaco, -a, -ci, -che AG = **idillico**
i'dillico, -a, -ci, -che AG idyllic
i'dillio SM idyll; **tra di loro è nato un ~**
 they have fallen in love
idi'oma, -i SM idiom, language
idio'matico, -a, -ci, -che AG idiomatic;
 frase idiomatica idiom
idiosincra'sia SF idiosyncrasy
idi'ota, -i, -e AG idiotic ▶ SM/F idiot
idio'zia [idjot'tsia] SF idiocy; (*atto, discorso*)
 idiotic thing to do (*o say*)
ido'latra, -i, -e AG idolatrous ▶ SM/F idolater
idola'trare /**72**/ VT to worship; (*fig*) to idolize
idola'tria SF idolatry
'idolo SM idol
idoneità SF suitability; **esame di ~**
 qualifying examination
i'doneo, -a AG: **~ a** suitable for, fit for; (*Mil*) fit
 for; (*qualificato*) qualified for
i'drante SM hydrant
idra'tante AG (*crema*) moisturizing ▶ SM
 moisturizer
idra'tare /**72**/ VT (*pelle*) to moisturize
idratazi'one [idrat'tsjone] SF moisturizing
i'draulico, -a, -ci, -che AG hydraulic ▶ SM
 plumber ▶ SF hydraulics *sg*
'idrico, -a, -ci, -che AG water *cpd*
idrocar'buro SM hydrocarbon
idroe'lettrico, -a, -ci, -che AG hydroelectric
i'drofilo, -a AG: **cotone ~** cotton wool (*Brit*),
 absorbent cotton (*US*)
idrofo'bia SF rabies *sg*
i'drofobo, -a AG rabid; (*fig*) furious
i'drogeno [i'drɔdʒeno] SM hydrogen
idroli'pidico, -a, -ci, -che AG hydrolipid
idro'porto SM (*Aer*) seaplane base
idrorepel'lente AG water-repellent
idros'calo SM = **idroporto**
idrovo'lante SM seaplane
i'ella SF bad luck
iel'lato, -a AG plagued by bad luck
i'ena SF hyena
ie'ratico, -a, -ci, -che AG (*Rel: scrittura*)
 hieratic; (*fig: atteggiamento*) solemn

i'eri AV, SM yesterday; **il giornale di ~** yesterday's paper; **~ l'altro** the day before yesterday; **~ sera** yesterday evening

ietta'tore, -'trice SM/F jinx

igi'ene [i'dʒɛne] SF hygiene; **norme d'~** sanitary regulations; **ufficio d'~** public health office; **~ mentale** mental health; **~ pubblica** public health

igi'enico, -a, -ci, -che [i'dʒɛniko] AG hygienic; (*salubre*) healthy

igloo [i'glu] SM INV igloo; (*tenda*) dome tent

IGM SIGLA M (= *Ispettorato Generale della Motorizzazione*) road traffic inspectorate

i'gnaro, -a [iɲ'ɲaro] AG: **~ di** unaware of, ignorant of

i'gnifugo, -a, -ghi, -ghe [iɲ'ɲifugo] AG flame-resistant, fireproof

i'gnobile [iɲ'ɲɔbile] AG despicable, vile

igno'minia [iɲɲo'minja] SF ignominy

igno'rante [iɲɲo'rante] AG ignorant

igno'ranza [iɲɲo'rantsa] SF ignorance

igno'rare [iɲɲo'rare] /**72**/ VT (*non sapere, conoscere*) to be ignorant o unaware of, not to know; (*fingere di non vedere, sentire*) to ignore

i'gnoto, -a [iɲ'ɲɔto] AG unknown ▶ SM/F: **figlio di ignoti** child of unknown parentage; **il Milite I~** the Unknown Soldier

---

(PAROLA CHIAVE)

il (*pl(m)* **i**; *diventa* **lo** (*pl* **gli**) *davanti a s impura, gn, pn, ps, x, z; f* **la** (*pl* **le**)) DET M **1** the; **il libro/lo studente/l'acqua** the book/the student/the water; **gli scolari** the pupils

2 (*astrazione*): **il coraggio/l'amore/la giovinezza** courage/love/youth

3 (*tempo*): **il mattino/la sera** in the morning/ evening; **il venerdì** (*abitualmente*) on Fridays; (*quel giorno*) on (the) Friday; **la settimana prossima** next week

4 (*distributivo*) a, an; **2 euro il chilo/paio** 2 euros a o per kilo/pair

5 (*partitivo*) some, any; **hai messo lo zucchero?** have you added sugar?; **hai comprato il latte?** did you buy (some o any) milk?

6 (*possesso*): **aprire gli occhi** to open one's eyes; **rompersi la gamba** to break one's leg; **avere i capelli neri/il naso rosso** to have dark hair/a red nose; **mettiti le scarpe** put your shoes on

7 (*con nomi propri*): **il Petrarca** Petrarch; **il Presidente Bush** President Bush; **dov'è la Francesca?** where's Francesca?

8 (*con nomi geografici*): **il Tevere** the Tiber; **l'Italia** Italy; **il Regno Unito** the United Kingdom; **l'Everest** Everest

---

'ilare AG cheerful

ilarità SF hilarity, mirth

ill. ABBR = **illustrazione**; (= *illustrato*) ill.

illangui'dire /**55**/ VI to grow weak o feeble

illazi'one [illat'tsjone] SF inference, deduction

il'lecito, -a [il'letʃito] AG illicit

ille'gale AG illegal

illegalità SF illegality

illeg'gibile [illed'dʒibile] AG illegible

illegittimità [illedʒittimi'ta] SF illegitimacy

ille'gittimo, -a [ille'dʒittimo] AG illegitimate

il'leso, -a AG unhurt, unharmed

illette'rato, -a AG illiterate

illiba'tezza [illiba'tettsa] SF (*di donna*) virginity

illi'bato, -a AG: **donna illibata** virgin

illimi'tato, -a AG boundless; unlimited

illivi'dire /**55**/ VI (*volto, mani*) to turn livid; (*cielo*) to grow leaden

ill.mo ABBR = **illustrissimo**

il'logico, -a, -ci, -che [il'lɔdʒiko] AG illogical

il'ludere /**35**/ VT to deceive, delude; **illudersi** VPR to deceive o.s., delude o.s.

illumi'nare /**72**/ VT to light up, illuminate; (*fig*) to enlighten; **illuminarsi** VPR to light up; **~ a giorno** (*con riflettori*) to floodlight

illumi'nato, -a AG (*fig: sovrano, spirito*) enlightened

illuminazi'one [illuminat'tsjone] SF lighting; illumination; floodlighting; (*fig*) flash of inspiration

illumi'nismo SM (*Storia*): **l'I~** the Enlightenment

il'lusi etc VB vedi **illudere**

illusi'one SF illusion; **farsi delle illusioni** to delude o.s.; **~ ottica** optical illusion

illusio'nismo SM conjuring

illusio'nista, -i, -e SM/F conjurer

il'luso, -a PP di **illudere**

illu'sorio, -a AG illusory

illus'trare /**72**/ VT to illustrate

illustra'tivo, -a AG illustrative

illustrazi'one [illustrat'tsjone] SF illustration

il'lustre AG eminent, renowned

illus'trissimo, -a AG (*negli indirizzi*) very revered

'ILOR SIGLA F = **imposta locale sui redditi**

IM SIGLA = **Imperia**

imbacuc'care /**20**/ VT, **imbacuc'carsi** VPR to wrap up

imbaldan'zire [imbaldan'tsire] /**55**/ VT to give confidence to; **imbaldanzirsi** VPR to grow bold

imbal'laggio [imbal'laddʒo] SM packing *no pl*

imbal'lare /**72**/ VT to pack; (*Aut*) to race; **imballarsi** VPR (*Aut*) to race

imbalsa'mare /**72**/ VT to embalm

imbalsa'mato, -a AG embalmed

imbambo'lato, -a AG (*sguardo, espressione*) vacant, blank

imban'dire /**55**/ VT: **~ un banchetto** to prepare a lavish feast

imban'dito, -a AG: **tavola imbandita** lavishly o sumptuously decked table

imbaraz'zante [imbarat'tsante] AG embarrassing, awkward

imbaraz'zare [imbarat'tsare] /**72**/ VT (*mettere a disagio*) to embarrass; (*ostacolare: movimenti*) to hamper; (: *stomaco*) to lie heavily on; **imbarazzarsi** VPR to become embarrassed

imbaraz'zato, -a [imbarat'tsato] AG embarrassed; **avere lo stomaco ~** to have an upset stomach

imba'razzo [imba'rattso] SM (*disagio*) embarrassment; (*perplessità*) puzzlement, bewilderment; **essere** *o* **trovarsi in ~** to be in an awkward situation *o* predicament; **mettere in ~** to embarrass; **~ di stomaco** indigestion

imbarbari'mento SM (*di civiltà, costumi*) barbarization

imbarca'dero SM landing stage

imbar'care /**20**/ VT (*passeggeri*) to embark; (*merci*) to load; **imbarcarsi** VPR: **imbarcarsi su** to board; **imbarcarsi per l'America** to sail for America; **imbarcarsi in** (*fig: affare*) to embark on

imbarcazi'one [imbarkat'tsjone] SF (small) boat, (small) craft *inv*; **~ di salvataggio** lifeboat

im'barco, -chi SM embarkation; loading; boarding; (*banchina*) landing stage; **carta d'~** boarding pass (BRIT), boarding card

imbastar'dire /**55**/ VT to bastardize, debase; **imbastardirsi** VPR to degenerate, become debased

imbas'tire /**55**/ VT (*cucire*) to tack; (*fig: abbozzare*) to sketch, outline

im'battersi /**72**/ VPR: **~ in** (*incontrare*) to bump *o* run into

imbat'tibile AG unbeatable, invincible

imbavagli'are [imbavaʎ'ʎare] /**27**/ VT to gag

imbec'care /**20**/ VT (*uccelli*) to feed; (*fig*) to prompt, put words into sb's mouth

imbec'cata SF (*Teat*) prompt; **dare l'~ a qn** to prompt sb; (*fig*) to give sb their cue

imbe'cille [imbe'tʃille] AG idiotic ▶ SMF idiot; (*Med*) imbecile

imbecillità [imbetʃilli'ta] SF INV (*Med, fig*) imbecility, idiocy; **dire ~** to talk nonsense

imbellet'tare /**72**/ VT (*viso*) to make up, put make-up on; **imbellettarsi** VPR to make o.s. up, put on one's make-up

imbel'lire /**55**/ VT to adorn, embellish ▶ VI to grow more beautiful

im'berbe AG beardless; **un giovanotto ~** a callow youth

imbestia'lire /**55**/ VT to infuriate; **imbestialirsi** VPR to become infuriated, fly into a rage

im'bevere /**16**/ VT to soak; **imbeversi** VPR: **imbeversi di** to soak up, absorb

imbe'vuto, -a AG: **~ (di)** soaked (in)

imbian'care /**20**/ VT to whiten; (*muro*) to whitewash ▶ VI to become *o* turn white

imbianca'tura SF (*di muro: con bianco di calce*) whitewashing; (: *con altre pitture*) painting

imbian'chino [imbjan'kino] SM (house) painter, painter and decorator

imbion'dire /**55**/ VT (*capelli*) to lighten; (*Cuc: cipolla*) to brown; **imbiondirsi** VPR (*capelli*) to lighten, go blonde, go fair; (*messi*) to turn golden, ripen

imbizzar'rirsi [imbiddzar'rirsi] /**55**/ VPR (*cavallo*) to become frisky

imboc'care /**20**/ VT (*bambino*) to feed; (*entrare: strada*) to enter, turn into ▶ VI: **~ in** (*strada*) to lead into (: *fiume*) to flow into

imbocca'tura SF mouth; (*di strada, porto*) entrance; (*Mus, del morso*) mouthpiece

im'bocco, -chi SM entrance

imboni'tore SM (*di spettacolo, circo*) barker

imborghe'sire [imborge'zire] /**55**/ VI, **imborghesirsi** VPR to become bourgeois

imbos'care /**20**/ VT to hide; **imboscarsi** VPR (*Mil*) to evade military service

imbos'cata SF ambush

imbos'cato SM draft dodger (US)

imboschi'mento [imboski'mento] SM afforestation

imbottigli'are [imbottiʎ'ʎare] /**27**/ VT to bottle; (*Naut*) to blockade; (*Mil*) to hem in; **imbottigliarsi** VPR to be stuck in a traffic jam

imbot'tire /**55**/ VT to stuff; (*giacca*) to pad; **imbottirsi** VPR (*rimpinzarsi*): **imbottirsi di** to stuff o.s. with

imbot'tito, -a AG stuffed; (*sedia*) upholstered; (*giacca*) padded ▶ SF quilt; **panino ~** filled roll

imbotti'tura SF stuffing; padding

imbracci'are [imbrat'tʃare] /**14**/ VT (*fucile*) to shoulder; (*scudo*) to grasp

imbra'nato, -a AG clumsy, awkward ▶ SM/F clumsy person

imbratta'carte SMF (*peg*) scribbler

imbrat'tare /**72**/ VT to dirty, smear, daub; **imbrattarsi** VPR: **imbrattarsi (di)** to dirty o.s. (with)

imbratta'tele SMF (*peg*) dauber

imbrigli'are [imbriʎ'ʎare] /**27**/ VT to bridle

imbroc'care /**20**/ VT (*fig*) to guess correctly

imbrogli'are [imbroʎ'ʎare] /**27**/ VT to mix up; (*fig: raggirare*) to deceive, cheat; (: *confondere*) to confuse, mix up; **imbrogliarsi** VPR to get tangled; (*fig*) to become confused

im'broglio [im'brɔʎʎo] SM (*groviglio*) tangle; (*situazione confusa*) mess; (*truffa*) swindle, trick

imbrogli'one, -a [imbroʎ'ʎone] SM/F cheat, swindler

imbronci'ato, -a [imbron'tʃato] AG (*persona*) sulky; (*cielo*) cloudy, threatening

imbru'nire /**55**/ VI, VB IMPERS to grow dark; **all'~** at dusk

imbrut'tire /55/ vt to make ugly ▶ vi
to become ugly

imbu'care /20/ vt to post

imbur'rare /72/ vt to butter

imbuti'forme AG funnel-shaped

im'buto SM funnel

I.M.C.T.C. SIGLA (= *Ispettorato Generale della Motorizzazione Civile e dei Trasporti in Concessione*) ≈ DVLA

i'mene SM hymen

imi'tare /72/ vt to imitate; (*riprodurre*) to copy; (*assomigliare*) to look like

imita'tore, -'trice SM/F (*gen*) imitator; (*Teat*) impersonator, impressionist

imitazi'one [imitat'tsjone] SF imitation

immaco'lato, -a AG spotless; immaculate

immagazzi'nare [immagaddzi'nare] **/72/** vt to store

immagi'nabile [immadʒi'nabile] AG imaginable

immagi'nare [immadʒi'nare] **/72/** vt to imagine; (*supporre*) to suppose; (*inventare*) to invent; **s'immagini!** don't mention it!, not at all!

immagi'nario, -a [immadʒi'narjo] AG imaginary

immagina'tiva [immadʒina'tiva] SF imagination

immaginazi'one [immadʒinat'tsjone] SF imagination; (*cosa immaginata*) fancy

im'magine [im'madʒine] SF image; (*rappresentazione grafica, mentale*) picture

immagi'noso, -a [immadʒi'noso] AG (*linguaggio, stile*) fantastic

immalinco'nire /55/ vt to sadden, depress; **immalinconirsi** VPR to become depressed, become melancholy

imman'cabile AG certain; unfailing

immancabil'mente AV without fail, unfailingly

im'mane AG (*smisurato*) huge; (*spaventoso, inumano*) terrible

imma'nente AG (*Filosofia*) inherent, immanent

immangi'abile [imman'dʒabile] AG inedible

immatrico'lare /72/ vt to register; **immatricolarsi** VPR (*Ins*) to matriculate, enrol

immatricolazi'one [immatrikolat'tsjone] SF registration; matriculation; enrolment

immaturità SF immaturity

imma'turo, -a AG (*frutto*) unripe; (*persona*) immature; (*prematuro*) premature

immedesi'marsi /72/ VPR: ~ **in** to identify with

immediata'mente AV immediately, at once

immedia'tezza [immedja'tettsa] SF immediacy

immedi'ato, -a AG immediate

immemo'rabile AG immemorial; **da tempo ~** from time immemorial

im'memore AG: ~ **di** forgetful of

immensità SF immensity

im'menso, -a AG immense

im'mergere [im'mɛrdʒere] **/59/** vt to immerse, plunge; **immergersi** VPR to plunge; (*sommergibile*) to dive, submerge; (*dedicarsi a*) **immergersi in** to immerse o.s. in

immeri'tato, -a AG undeserved

immeri'tevole AG undeserving, unworthy

immersi'one SF immersion; (*di sommergibile*) submersion, dive; (*di palombaro*) dive; **linea di ~** (*Naut*) water line

im'merso, -a PP di **immergere**

im'messo, -a PP di **immettere**

im'mettere /63/ vt: ~ **(in)** to introduce (into); ~ **dati in un computer** to enter data on a computer

immi'grante AG, SMF immigrant

immi'grare /72/ vi to immigrate

immi'grato, -a SM/F immigrant

immigrazi'one [immigrat'tsjone] SF immigration

immi'nente AG imminent

immi'nenza [immi'nɛntsa] SF imminence

immischi'are [immis'kjare] **/19/** vt: ~ **qn in** to involve sb in; **immischiarsi** VPR: **immischiarsi in** to interfere o meddle in

immiseri'mento SM impoverishment

immise'rire /55/ vt to impoverish

immis'sario SM (*Geo*) affluent, tributary

immissi'one SF (*gen*) introduction; (*di aria, gas*) intake; ~ **di dati** (*Inform*) data entry

im'mobile AG motionless, still; (**beni**) **immobili** real estate *sg*

immobili'are AG (*Dir*) property *cpd*; **patrimonio ~** real estate; **società ~** property company

immobi'lismo SM inertia

immobilità SF immobility

immobiliz'zare [immobilid'dzare] **/72/** vt to immobilize; (*Econ*) to lock up

immobi'lizzo [immobi'liddzo] SM: **spese d'~** capital expenditure

immo'destia SF immodesty

immo'desto, -a AG immodest

immo'lare /72/ vt to sacrifice

immondez'zaio [immondet'tsajo] SM rubbish dump

immon'dizia [immon'dittsja] SF dirt, filth; (*spesso al pl: spazzatura, rifiuti*) rubbish *no pl*, refuse *no pl*

immo'rale AG immoral

immoralità SF immorality

immorta'lare /72/ vt to immortalize

immor'tale AG immortal

immortalità SF immortality

im'mune AG (*esente*) exempt; (*Med, Dir*) immune

immunità SF immunity; ~ **diplomatica** diplomatic immunity; ~ **parlamentare** parliamentary privilege

immuniz'zare [immunid'dzare] /**72**/ VT (*Med*) to immunize

immunizzazi'one [immuniddzat'tsjone] SF immunization

immunodefi'cienza [immunodefi'tʃɛntsa] SF: ~ **acquisita** acquired immunodeficiency

immuno'logico, -a, -ci, -che [immuno'lɔdʒiko] AG immunological

immu'tabile AG immutable; unchanging

impac'care /**20**/ VT to pack

impacchet'tare [impakket'tare] /**72**/ VT to pack up

impacci'are [impat'tʃare] /**14**/ VT to hinder, hamper

impacci'ato, -a [impat'tʃato] AG awkward, clumsy; (*imbarazzato*) embarrassed

im'paccio [im'pattʃo] SM obstacle; (*imbarazzo*) embarrassment; (*situazione imbarazzante*) awkward situation

im'pacco, -chi SM (*Med*) compress

impadro'nirsi /**55**/ VPR: ~ **di** to seize, take possession of; (*fig: apprendere a fondo*) to master

impa'gabile AG priceless

impagi'nare [impadʒi'nare] /**72**/ VT (*Tip*) to paginate, page (up)

impaginazi'one [impadʒinat'tsjone] SF pagination

impagli'are [impaʎ'ʎare] /**27**/ VT to stuff (with straw)

impa'lato, -a AG (*fig*) stiff as a board

impalca'tura SF scaffolding; (*anche fig*) framework

impalli'dire /**55**/ VI to turn pale; (*fig*) to fade

impalli'nare /**72**/ VT to riddle with shot

impal'pabile AG impalpable

impa'nare /**72**/ VT (*Cuc*) to dip (*o* roll) in breadcrumbs, bread (*US*)

impa'nato, -a AG (*Cuc*) coated in breadcrumbs

impanta'narsi /**72**/ VPR to sink (in the mud); (*fig*) to get bogged down

impape'rarsi /**72**/ VPR to stumble over a word

impappi'narsi /**72**/ VPR to stammer, falter

impa'rare /**72**/ VT to learn; **così impari!** that'll teach you!

impara'ticcio [impara'tittʃo] SM half-baked notions *pl*

impareggi'abile [impared'dʒabile] AG incomparable

imparen'tarsi /**72**/ VPR: ~ **con** (*famiglia*) to marry into

'impari AG INV (*disuguale*) unequal; (*dispari*) odd

impar'tire /**55**/ VT to bestow, give

imparzi'ale [impar'tsjale] AG impartial, unbiased

imparzialità [impartsjali'ta] SF impartiality

impas'sibile AG impassive

impas'tare /**72**/ VT (*pasta*) to knead; (*colori*) to mix

impastic'carsi /**20**/ VPR to pop pills

im'pasto SM (*l'impastare*: *di pane*) kneading; (: *di cemento*) mixing; (*pasta*) dough; (*anche fig*) mixture

im'patto SM impact; ~ **ambientale** impact on the environment

impau'rire /**55**/ VT to scare, frighten ▶ VI (*anche*: **impaurirsi**) to become scared *o* frightened

im'pavido, -a AG intrepid, fearless

impazi'ente [impat'tsjɛnte] AG impatient

impazi'enza [impat'tsjɛntsa] SF impatience

impaz'zata [impat'tsata] SF: **all'~** (*precipitosamente*) at breakneck speed; (*colpire*) wildly

impaz'zire [impat'tsire] /**55**/ VI to go mad; ~ **per qn/qc** to be crazy about sb/sth

impec'cabile AG impeccable

impedi'mento SM obstacle, hindrance

impe'dire /**55**/ VT (*vietare*): ~ **a qn di fare** to prevent sb from doing; (*ostruire*) to obstruct; (*impacciare*) to hamper, hinder

impe'gnare [impeɲ'ɲare] /**15**/ VT (*dare in pegno*) to pawn; (*onore ecc*) to pledge; (*prenotare*) to book, reserve; (*obbligare*) to oblige; (*occupare*) to keep busy; (*Mil: nemico*) to engage; **impegnarsi** VPR (*vincolarsi*): **impegnarsi a fare** to undertake to do; (*mettersi risolutamente*): **impegnarsi in qc** to devote o.s. to sth; **impegnarsi con qn** (*accordarsi*) to come to an agreement with sb

impegna'tivo, -a [impeɲɲa'tivo] AG binding; (*lavoro*) demanding, exacting

impe'gnato, -a [impeɲ'ɲato] AG (*occupato*) busy; (*fig: romanzo, autore*) committed, engagé

im'pegno [im'peɲɲo] SM (*obbligo*) obligation; (*promessa*) promise, pledge; (*zelo*) diligence, zeal; (*compito: d'autore*) commitment; **impegni di lavoro** business commitments

impego'larsi /**72**/ VPR (*fig*): ~ **in** to get heavily involved in

impela'garsi /**80**/ VPR = **impegolarsi**

impel'lente AG pressing, urgent

impene'trabile AG impenetrable

impen'narsi /**72**/ VPR (*cavallo*) to rear up; (*Aer*) to go into a climb; (*fig*) to bridle

impen'nata SF (*di cavallo*) rearing up; (*di aereo*) climb, nose-up; (*fig: scatto d'ira*) burst of anger; (: *di prezzi ecc*) sudden increase

impen'sabile AG (*inaccettabile*) unthinkable; (*difficile da concepire*) inconceivable

impen'sato, -a AG unforeseen, unexpected

impensie'rirsi /**55**/ VT to worry; **impensierirsi** VPR to worry

impe'rante AG prevailing

impe'rare /**72**/ VI (*anche fig*) to reign, rule

impera'tivo, -a AG, SM imperative

impera'tore, -'trice SM/F emperor (empress)

impercet'tibile [impertʃet'tibile] AG imperceptible

imperdo'nabile AG unforgivable, unpardonable

imper'fetto, -a AG imperfect ▶ SM (*Ling*) imperfect (tense)

imperfezi'one [imperfet'tsjone] SF imperfection

imperi'ale AG imperial

imperia'lismo SM imperialism

imperia'lista, -i, -e AG imperialist

imperi'oso, -a AG (*persona*) imperious; (*motivo, esigenza*) urgent, pressing

imperi'turo, -a AG everlasting

impe'rizia [impe'rittsja] SF lack of experience

imperma'lirsi /55/ VPR to take offence

imperme'abile AG waterproof ▶ SM raincoat

imperni'are /19/ VT: ~ **qc su** to hinge sth on; (*fig: discorso, relazione ecc*) to base sth on; **imperniarsi** VPR (*fig*): **imperniarsi su** to be based on

im'pero SM empire; (*forza, autorità*) rule, control

imperscru'tabile AG inscrutable

imperso'nale AG impersonal

imperso'nare /72/ VT to personify; (*Teat*) to play, act (the part of); **impersonarsi** VPR: **impersonarsi in un ruolo** to get into a part, live a part

imper'territo, -a AG unperturbed, undaunted; impassive

imperti'nente AG impertinent

imperti'nenza [imperti'nentsa] SF impertinence

impertur'babile AG imperturbable

imperver'sare /72/ VI to rage

im'pervio, -a AG (*luogo*) inaccessible; (*strada*) impassable

'impeto SM (*moto, forza*) force, impetus; (*assalto*) onslaught; (*fig: impulso*) impulse; (: *slancio*) transport; **con ~** (*parlare*) forcefully, energetically, vehemently

impet'tito, -a AG stiff, erect; **camminare ~** to strut

impetu'oso, -a AG (*vento*) strong, raging; (*persona*) impetuous

impian'tare /72/ VT (*motore*) to install; (*azienda, discussione*) to establish, start

impian'tistica SF plant design and installation

impi'anto SM (*installazione*) installation; (*apparecchiature*) plant; (*sistema*) system; **~ elettrico** wiring; **~ di riscaldamento** heating system; **~ sportivo** sports complex; **impianti di risalita** (*Sci*) ski lifts

impias'trare /72/, impiastricci'are [impjastrit'tʃare] VT to smear, dirty

impi'astro SM poultice; (*fig: col: persona*) nuisance

impiccagi'one [impikka'dʒone] SF hanging

impic'care /20/ VT to hang; **impiccarsi** VPR to hang o.s.

impicci'are [impit'tʃare] /**14**/ VT to hinder, hamper; **impicciarsi** VPR (*immischiarsi*): **impicciarsi (in)** to meddle (in), interfere (in); **impicciati degli affari tuoi!** mind your own business!

im'piccio [im'pittʃo] SM (*ostacolo*) hindrance; (*seccatura*) trouble, bother; (*affare imbrogliato*) mess; **essere d'~** to be in the way; **cavare o togliere qn dagli impicci** to get sb out of trouble

impicci'one, -a [impit'tʃone] SM/F busybody

impie'gare /80/ VT (*usare*) to use, employ; (*assumere*) to employ, take on; (*spendere: denaro, tempo*) to spend; (*investire*) to invest; **impiegarsi** VPR to get a job, obtain employment; **impiego un quarto d'ora per andare a casa** it takes me o I take a quarter of an hour to get home

impiega'tizio, -a [impjega'tittsjo] AG clerical, white-collar *cpd*; **lavoro/ceto ~** clerical o white-collar work/workers *pl*

impie'gato, -a SM/F employee; **~ statale** state employee

impi'ego, -ghi SM (*uso*) use; (*occupazione*) employment; (*posto di lavoro*) (regular) job, post; (*Econ*) investment; **~ pubblico** job in the public sector

impieto'sire /55/ VT to move to pity; **impietosirsi** VPR to be moved to pity

impie'toso, -a AG pitiless, cruel

impie'trire /55/ VT (*anche fig*) to petrify

impigli'are [impiʎ'ʎare] /**27**/ VT to catch, entangle; **impigliarsi** VPR to get caught up o entangled

impi'grire /55/ VT to make lazy ▶ VI (*anche:* **impigrirsi**) to grow lazy

impingu'are /72/ VT (*maiale ecc*) to fatten; (*fig: tasche, casse dello Stato*) to stuff with money

impiom'bare /72/ VT (*pacco*) to seal (with lead); (*dente*) to fill

impla'cabile AG implacable

implemen'tare /72/ VT to implement

impli'care /20/ VT to imply; (*coinvolgere*) to involve; **implicarsi** VPR: **implicarsi (in)** to become involved (in)

implicazi'one [implikat'tsjone] SF implication

im'plicito, -a [im'plitʃito] AG implicit

implo'rare /72/ VT to implore; (*pietà ecc*) to beg for

implorazi'one [implorat'tsjone] SF plea, entreaty

impolli'nare /72/ VT to pollinate

impollinazi'one [impollinat'tsjone] SF pollination

impolve'rare /72/ VT to cover with dust; **impolverarsi** VPR to get dusty

impoma'tare /72/ VT (*pelle*) to put ointment on; (*capelli*) to pomade; (*baffi*) to wax; **impomatarsi** VPR (*col*) to get spruced up

imponde'rabile AG imponderable
im'pone etc VB vedi **imporre**
impo'nente AG imposing, impressive
im'pongo etc VB vedi **imporre**
impo'nibile AG taxable ▶ SM taxable income
impopo'lare AG unpopular
impopolarità SF unpopularity
im'porre /77/ VT to impose; (costringere) to force, make; (far valere) to impose, enforce; **imporsi** VPR (persona) to assert o.s.; (cosa: rendersi necessario) to become necessary; (aver successo: moda, attore) to become popular; ~ **a qn di fare** to force sb to do, make sb do
impor'tante AG important
impor'tanza [impor'tantsa] SF importance; **dare** ~ **a qc** to attach importance to sth; **darsi** ~ to give o.s. airs
impor'tare /72/ VT (introdurre dall'estero) to import ▶ VI to matter, be important ▶ VB IMPERS (essere necessario) to be necessary; (interessare) to matter; **non importa!** it doesn't matter!; **non me ne importa!** I don't care!
importa'tore, -'trice AG importing ▶ SM/F importer
importazi'one [importat'tsjone] SF importation; (merci importate) imports pl
im'porto SM (total) amount
importu'nare /72/ VT to bother
impor'tuno, -a AG irksome, annoying
im'posi etc VB vedi **imporre**
imposizi'one [impozit'tsjone] SF imposition; (ordine) order, command; (onere, imposta) tax
imposses'sarsi /72/ VPR: ~ **di** to seize, take possession of
impos'sibile AG impossible; **fare l'**~ to do one's utmost, do all one can
impossibilità SF impossibility; **essere nell'**~ **di fare qc** to be unable to do sth
impossibili'tato, -a AG: **essere** ~ **a fare qc** to be unable to do sth
im'posta SF (di finestra) shutter; (tassa) tax; ~ **indiretta sui consumi** excise duty o tax; ~ **locale sui redditi (ILOR)** tax on unearned income; ~ **patrimoniale** property tax; ~ **sul reddito** income tax; ~ **sul reddito delle persone fisiche** personal income tax; ~ **di successione** capital transfer tax (BRIT), inheritance tax (US); ~ **sugli utili** tax on profits; ~ **sul valore aggiunto** value added tax (BRIT), sales tax (US)
impos'tare /72/ VT (imbucare) to post; (servizio, organizzazione) to set up; (lavoro) to organize, plan; (resoconto, rapporto) to plan; (problema) to set out, formulate; (avviare) to begin, start off; (Tip: pagina) to lay out; ~ **la voce** (Mus) to pitch one's voice
impostazi'one [impostat'tsjone] SF (di lettera) posting (BRIT), mailing (US); (di problema, questione) formulation, statement; (di lavoro)

organization, planning; (di attività) setting up; (Mus: di voce) pitch; **impostazioni** SFPL (di computer) settings
im'posto, -a PP di **imporre**
impos'tore, -a SM/F impostor
impo'tente AG weak, powerless; (anche Med) impotent
impo'tenza [impo'tɛntsa] SF weakness, powerlessness; impotence
impove'rire /55/ VT to impoverish ▶ VI (anche: **impoverirsi**) to become poor
imprati'cabile AG (strada) impassable; (campo da gioco) unplayable
imprati'chire [imprati'kire] /55/ VT to train; **impratichirsi** VPR: **impratichirsi in qc** to practise (BRIT) o practice (US) sth
impre'care /20/ VI to curse, swear; ~ **contro** to hurl abuse at
imprecazi'one [imprekat'tsjone] SF abuse, curse
impreci'sato, -a [impretʃi'zato] AG (non preciso: quantità, numero) indeterminate
imprecisi'one [impretʃi'zjone] SF imprecision; inaccuracy
impre'ciso, -a [impre'tʃizo] AG imprecise, vague; (calcolo) inaccurate
impre'gnare [impreɲ'ɲare] /15/ VT: ~ **(di)** (imbevere) to soak o impregnate (with); (riempire: anche fig) to fill (with)
imprendi'tore SM (industriale) entrepreneur; (appaltatore) contractor; **piccolo** ~ small businessman
imprendito'ria SF enterprise; (imprenditori) entrepreneurs pl
imprenditori'ale AG (ceto, classe) entrepreneurial
imprepa'rato, -a AG: ~ **(a)** (gen) unprepared (for); (lavoratore) untrained (for); **cogliere qn** ~ to catch sb unawares
impreparazi'one [impreparat'tsjone] SF lack of preparation
im'presa SF (iniziativa) enterprise; (azione) exploit; (azienda) firm, concern; ~ **familiare** family firm; ~ **pubblica** state-owned enterprise
impre'sario SM (Teat) manager, impresario; ~ **di pompe funebri** funeral director
imprescin'dibile [impreʃʃin'dibile] AG not to be ignored
im'pressi etc VB vedi **imprimere**
impressio'nante AG impressive; upsetting
impressio'nare /72/ VT to impress; (turbare) to upset; (Fot) to expose; **impressionarsi** VPR to be easily upset
impressi'one SF impression; (fig: sensazione) sensation, feeling; (stampa) printing; **fare** ~ (colpire) to impress; (turbare) to frighten, upset; **fare buona/cattiva** ~ **a** to make a good/bad impression on

im'presso, -a PP *di* **imprimere**
impres'tare /72/ VT: ~ **qc a qn** to lend sth to sb
impreve'dibile AG unforeseeable; (*persona*) unpredictable
imprevi'dente AG lacking in foresight
imprevi'denza [imprevi'dɛntsa] SF lack of foresight
impre'visto, -a AG unexpected, unforeseen
▶ SM unforeseen event; **salvo imprevisti** unless anything unexpected happens
imprezio'sire [imprettsjo'sire] /55/ VT: ~ **di** to embellish with
imprigiona'mento [impridʒona'mento] SM imprisonment
imprigio'nare [impridʒo'nare] /72/ VT to imprison
im'primere /50/ VT (*anche fig*) to impress, stamp; (*comunicare: movimento*) to transmit, give
impro'babile AG improbable, unlikely
'improbo, -a AG (*fatica, lavoro*) hard, laborious
improdut'tivo, -a AG (*investimento*) unprofitable; (*terreno*) unfruitful; (*fig: sforzo*) fruitless
im'pronta SF imprint, impression, sign; (*di piede, mano*) print; (*fig*) mark, stamp; ~ **di carbonio** carbon footprint; ~ **digitale** fingerprint; **rilevamento delle impronte genetiche** genetic fingerprinting
impro'perio SM insult
impropo'nibile AG which cannot be proposed o suggested
im'proprio, -a AG improper; **arma impropria** offensive weapon
improro'gabile AG (*termine*) that cannot be extended
improvvisa'mente AV suddenly; unexpectedly
improvvi'sare /72/ VT to improvise; **improvvisarsi** VPR: **improvvisarsi cuoco** to (decide to) act as cook
improvvi'sata SF (pleasant) surprise
improvvisazi'one [improvvizat'tsjone] SF improvisation; **spirito d'~** spirit of invention
improv'viso, -a AG (*improvviso*) unexpected; (*subitaneo*) sudden; **all'~** unexpectedly; suddenly
impru'dente AG foolish, imprudent; (*osservazione*) unwise, rash
impru'denza [impru'dɛntsa] SF foolishness, imprudence; **è stata un'~** that was a foolish o an imprudent thing to do
impu'dente AG impudent
impu'denza [impu'dɛntsa] SF impudence
impudi'cizia [impudi'tʃittsja] SF immodesty
impu'dico, -a, -chi, -che AG immodest
impu'gnare [impuɲ'ɲare] /15/ VT to grasp, grip; (*Dir*) to contest
impugna'tura [impuɲɲa'tura] SF grip, grasp; (*manico*) handle; (: *di spada*) hilt

impulsività SF impulsiveness
impul'sivo, -a AG impulsive
im'pulso SM impulse; **dare un ~ alle vendite** to boost sales
impune'mente AV with impunity
impunità SF impunity
impun'tarsi /72/ VPR to stop dead, refuse to budge; (*fig*) to be obstinate
impun'tura SF stitching
impurità SF INV impurity
im'puro, -a AG impure
impu'tare /72/ VT (*ascrivere*): ~ **qc a** to attribute sth to; (*Dir: accusare*) ~ **qn di** to charge sb with, accuse sb of
impu'tato, -a SM/F (*Dir*) accused, defendant
imputazi'one [imputat'tsjone] SF (*Dir*) charge; (*di spese*) allocation
imputri'dire /55/ VI to rot

(PAROLA CHIAVE)

in (*in* + *il* = **nel**, *in* + *lo* = **nello**, *in* + *l'* = **nell'**, *in* + *la* = **nella**, *in* + *i* = **nei**, *in* + *gli* = **negli**, *in* + *le* = **nelle**)
PREP **1** (*stato in luogo*) in; **vivere in Italia/città** to live in Italy/town; **essere in casa/ufficio** to be at home/the office; **è nel cassetto/in salotto** it's in the drawer/in the sitting room; **se fossi in te** if I were you
2 (*moto a luogo*) to; (: *dentro*) into; **andare in Germania/città** to go to Germany/town; **andare in ufficio** to go to the office; **entrare in macchina/casa** to get into the car/go into the house
3 (*tempo*) in; **nel 1989** in 1989; **in giugno/estate** in June/summer; **l'ha fatto in sei mesi** he did it in six months; **in gioventù, io ...** when I was young, I ...
4 (*modo, maniera*) in; **in silenzio** in silence; **parlare in tedesco** to speak (in) German; **in abito da sera** in evening dress; **in guerra** at war; **in vacanza** on holiday; **Maria Bianchi in Rossi** Maria Rossi née Bianchi
5 (*mezzo*) by; **viaggiare in autobus/treno** to travel by bus/train
6 (*materia*) made of; **in marmo** made of marble, marble *cpd*; **una collana in oro** a gold necklace
7 (*misura*) in; **siamo in quattro** there are four of us; **in tutto** in all
8 (*fine*): **dare in dono** to give as a gift; **spende tutto in alcool** he spends all his money on drink; **in onore di** in honour of

i'nabile AG: ~ **a** incapable of; (*fisicamente, Mil*) unfit for
inabilità SF: ~ **(a)** unfitness (for)
inabis'sare /72/ VT (*nave*) to sink; **inabissarsi** VPR to go down
inabi'tabile AG uninhabitable
inabi'tato, -a AG uninhabited

inacces'sibile [inattʃes'sibile] AG (*luogo*) inaccessible; (*persona*) unapproachable; (*mistero*) unfathomable

inaccet'tabile [inattʃet'tabile] AG unacceptable

inacer'bire [inatʃer'bire] /**55**/ VT to exacerbate; **inacerbirsi** VPR (*persona*) to become embittered

inaci'dire [inatʃi'dire] /**55**/ VT (*persona, carattere*) to embitter; **inacidirsi** VPR (*latte*) to go sour; (*fig: persona, carattere*) to become sour, become embittered

ina'datto, -a AG: **~ (a)** unsuitable *o* unfit (for)

inadegu'ato, -a AG inadequate

inadempi'ente AG defaulting ▶ SMF defaulter

inadempi'enza [inadem'pjɛntsa] SF: **~ a un contratto** non-fulfilment of a contract; **dovuto alle inadempienze dei funzionari** due to negligence on the part of the officials

inadempi'mento SM non-fulfilment

inaffer'rabile AG elusive; (*concetto, senso*) difficult to grasp

inaffi'dabile AG unreliable

'INAIL SIGLA M (= *Istituto Nazionale per l'Assicurazione contro gli Infortuni sul Lavoro*) state body providing sickness benefit in the event of accidents at work

ina'lare /**72**/ VT to inhale

inala'tore SM inhaler

inalazi'one [inalat'tsjone] SF inhalation

inalbe'rare /**72**/ VT (*Naut*) to hoist, raise; **inalberarsi** VPR (*fig*) to flare up, fly off the handle

inalte'rabile AG unchangeable; (*colore*) fast, permanent; (*affetto*) constant

inalte'rato, -a AG unchanged

inami'dare /**72**/ VT to starch

inami'dato, -a AG starched

inammis'sibile AG inadmissible

inani'mato, -a AG inanimate; (*senza vita: corpo*) lifeless

inappa'gabile AG insatiable

inappel'labile AG (*decisione*) final, irrevocable; (*Dir*) final, not open to appeal

inappe'tenza [inappe'tɛntsa] SF (*Med*) lack of appetite

inappun'tabile AG irreproachable, flawless

inar'care /**20**/ VT (*schiena*) to arch; (*sopracciglia*) to raise; **inarcarsi** VPR to arch

inaridi'mento SM (*anche fig*) drying up ▶ VI

inari'dire /**55**/ VT to make arid, dry up ▶ VI (*anche:* **inaridirsi**) to dry up, become arid

inarres'tabile AG (*processo*) irreversible; (*emorragia*) that cannot be stemmed; (*corsa del tempo*) relentless

inascol'tato, -a AG unheeded, unheard

inaspettata'mente AV unexpectedly

inaspet'tato, -a AG unexpected

inas'prire /**55**/ VT (*disciplina*) to tighten up, make harsher; (*carattere*) to embitter; (*rapporti*) to make worse; **inasprirsi** VPR to become harsher; to become bitter; to become worse

inattac'cabile AG (*anche fig*) unassailable; (*alibi*) cast-iron

inatten'dibile AG unreliable

inat'teso, -a AG unexpected

inat'tivo, -a AG inactive, idle; (*Chim*) inactive

inattu'abile AG impracticable

inau'dito, -a AG unheard of

inaugu'rale AG inaugural

inaugu'rare /**72**/ VT to inaugurate, open; (*monumento*) to unveil

inaugurazi'one [inaugurat'tsjone] SF inauguration; unveiling

inavve'duto, -a AG careless, inadvertent

inavver'tenza [inavver'tɛntsa] SF carelessness, inadvertence

inavvertita'mente AV inadvertently, unintentionally

inavvici'nabile [inavvitʃi'nabile] AG unapproachable

'Inca AG INV, SM INV/F INV Inca

incagli'are [inkaʎ'ʎare] /**27**/ VI (*Naut: anche:* **incagliarsi**) to run aground

incalco'labile AG incalculable

incal'lito, -a AG calloused; (*fig*) hardened, inveterate; (*: insensibile*) hard

incal'zante [inkal'tsante] AG urgent, insistent; (*crisi*) imminent

incal'zare [inkal'tsare] /**72**/ VT to follow *o* pursue closely; (*fig*) to press ▶ VI (*urgere*) to be pressing; (*essere imminente*) to be imminent

incame'rare /**72**/ VT (*Dir*) to expropriate

incammi'nare /**72**/ VT (*fig: avviare*) to start up; **incamminarsi** VPR to set off

incana'lare /**72**/ VT (*anche fig*) to channel; **incanalarsi** VPR (*folla*): **incanalarsi verso** to converge on

incancre'nire /**55**/ VI, **incancre'nirsi** VPR to become gangrenous

incande'scente [inkandeʃ'ʃɛnte] AG incandescent, white-hot

incan'tare /**72**/ VT to enchant, bewitch; **incantarsi** VPR (*rimanere intontito*) to be spellbound; to be in a daze; (*meccanismo: bloccarsi*) to jam

incanta'tore, -'trice AG enchanting, bewitching ▶ SM/F enchanter (enchantress)

incan'tesimo SM spell, charm

incan'tevole AG charming, enchanting

in'canto SM spell, charm, enchantment; (*asta*) auction; **come per ~** as if by magic; **ti sta d'~!** (*vestito ecc*) it really suits you!; **mettere all'~** to put up for auction

incanu'tire /**55**/ VI to go white

inca'pace [inka'patʃe] AG incapable

incapacità [inkapatʃi'ta] SF inability; (Dir) incapacity; **~ d'intendere e di volere** diminished responsibility

incapo'nirsi /55/ VPR to be stubborn, be determined

incap'pare /72/ VI: **~ in qc/qn** (anche fig) to run into sth/sb

incappucci'are [inkapput'tʃare] /14/ VT to put a hood on; **incappucciarsi** VPR (persona) to put on a hood

incapricci'arsi [inkaprit'tʃarsi] /14/ VPR: **~ di** to take a fancy to o for

incapsu'lare /72/ VT (dente) to crown

incarce'rare [inkartʃe'rare] /72/ VT to imprison

incari'care /20/ VT: **~ qn di fare** to give sb the responsibility of doing; **incaricarsi di** to take care o charge of

incari'cato, -a AG: **~ (di)** in charge (of), responsible (for) ▶ SM/F delegate, representative; **docente ~** (di università) lecturer without tenure; **~ d'affari** (Pol) chargé d'affaires

in'carico, -chi SM task, job; (Ins) temporary post

incar'nare /72/ VT to embody; **incarnarsi** VPR to be embodied; (Rel) to become incarnate

incarnazi'one [inkarnat'tsjone] SF incarnation; (fig) embodiment

incarta'mento SM dossier, file

incartapeco'rito, -a AG (pelle) wizened, shrivelled (BRIT), shriveled (US)

incar'tare /72/ VT to wrap (in paper)

incasel'lare /72/ VT (posta) to sort; (fig: nozioni) to pigeonhole

incas'sare /72/ VT (merce) to pack (in cases); (gemma: incastonare) to set; (Econ: riscuotere) to collect; (Pugilato: colpi) to take, stand up to

in'casso SM cashing, encashment; (introito) takings pl

incasto'nare /72/ VT to set

incastona'tura SF setting

incas'trare /72/ VT to fit in, insert; (fig: intrappolare) to catch; **incastrarsi** VPR (combaciare) to fit together; (restare bloccato) to become stuck

in'castro SM slot, groove; (punto di unione) joint; **gioco a ~** interlocking puzzle

incate'nare /72/ VT to chain up

incatra'mare /72/ VT to tar

incatti'vire /55/ VT to make wicked; **incattivirsi** VPR to turn nasty

in'cauto, -a AG imprudent, rash

inca'vare /72/ VT to hollow out

inca'vato, -a AG hollow; (occhi) sunken

in'cavo SM hollow; (solco) groove

incavo'larsi /72/ VPR (col) to lose one's temper, get annoyed

incaz'zarsi [inkat'tsarsi] /72/ VPR (col) to get steamed up

in'cedere [in'tʃɛdere] /29/ VI (poetico) to advance solemnly ▶ SM solemn gait

incendi'are [intʃen'djare] /19/ VT to set fire to; **incendiarsi** VPR to catch fire, burst into flames

incendi'ario, -a [intʃen'djarjo] AG incendiary ▶ SM/F arsonist

in'cendio [in'tʃendjo] SM fire

incene'rire [intʃene'rire] /55/ VT to burn to ashes, incinerate; (cadavere) to cremate; **incenerirsi** VPR to be burnt to ashes

inceneri'tore [intʃeneri'tore] SM incinerator

in'censo [in'tʃenso] SM incense

incensu'rato, -a [intʃensu'rato] AG (Dir): **essere ~** to have a clean record

incenti'vare [intʃenti'vare] /72/ VT (produzione, vendite) to boost; (persona) to motivate

incen'tivo [intʃen'tivo] SM incentive

incen'trarsi [intʃen'trarsi] /72/ VPR: **~ su** (fig) to centre (BRIT) o center (US) on

incep'pare [intʃep'pare] /72/ VT to obstruct, hamper; **inceparsi** VPR to jam

ince'rata [intʃe'rata] SF (tela) tarpaulin; (impermeabile) oilskins pl

incer'tezza [intʃer'tettsa] SF uncertainty

in'certo, -a [in'tʃerto] AG uncertain; (irresoluto) undecided, hesitating ▶ SM uncertainty; **gli incerti del mestiere** the risks of the job

incespi'care [intʃespi'kare] /20/ VI: **~ (in qc)** to trip (over sth)

inces'sante [intʃes'sante] AG incessant

in'cesto [in'tʃesto] SM incest

incestu'oso, -a [intʃestu'oso] AG incestuous

in'cetta [in'tʃetta] SF buying up; **fare ~ di qc** to buy up sth

inchi'esta [in'kjɛsta] SF investigation, inquiry

inchi'nare [inki'nare] /72/ VT to bow; **inchinarsi** VPR to bend down; (per riverenza) to bow; (: donna) to curtsy

in'chino [in'kino] SM bow; curtsy

inchio'dare [inkjo'dare] /72/ VT to nail (down); **~ la macchina** (Aut) to jam on the brakes

inchi'ostro [in'kjɔstro] SM ink; **~ simpatico** invisible ink

inciam'pare [intʃam'pare] /72/ VI to trip, stumble

inci'ampo [in'tʃampo] SM obstacle; **essere d'~ a qn** (fig) to be in sb's way

inciden'tale [intʃiden'tale] AG incidental

incidental'mente [intʃidental'mente] AV (per caso) by chance; (per inciso) incidentally, by the way

inci'dente [intʃi'dɛnte] SM accident; (episodio) incident; **e con questo l'~ è chiuso** and that is the end of the matter; **~ automobilistico** o **d'auto** car accident; **~ diplomatico** diplomatic incident

inci'denza [intʃi'dɛntsa] SF incidence; **avere una forte ~ su qc** to affect sth greatly

in'cidere [in'tʃidere] /**34**/ vi: ~ **su** to bear upon, affect ▶ vt (*tagliare incavando*) to cut into; (*Arte*) to engrave; to etch; (*canzone*) to record

in'cinta [in'tʃinta] AG F pregnant

incipi'ente [intʃi'pjɛnte] AG incipient

incipri'are [intʃi'prjare] /**19**/ vt to powder; **incipriarsi** VPR to powder one's face

in'circa [in'tʃirka] AV: **all'**~ more or less, very nearly

in'cisi *etc* [in'tʃizi] VB *vedi* **incidere**

incisi'one [intʃi'zjone] SF cut; (*disegno*) engraving; etching; (*registrazione*) recording; (*Med*) incision

inci'sivo, -a [intʃi'zivo] AG incisive; (*Anat*): **(dente)** ~ incisor

in'ciso, -a [in'tʃizo] PP *di* **incidere** ▶ SM: **per** ~ incidentally, by the way

inci'sore [intʃi'zore] SM (*Arte*) engraver

incita'mento [intʃita'mento] SM incitement

inci'tare [intʃi'tare] /**72**/ vt to incite

inci'vile [intʃi'vile] AG uncivilized; (*villano*) impolite

incivi'lire [intʃivi'lire] /**55**/ vt to civilize

inciviltà [intʃivil'ta] SF (*di popolazione*) barbarism; (*fig: di trattamento*) barbarity; (: *maleducazione*) incivility, rudeness

incl. ABBR (= *incluso*) encl.

incle'mente AG (*giudice, sentenza*) severe, harsh; (*fig: clima*) harsh; (: *tempo*) inclement

incle'menza [inkle'mɛntsa] SF severity; harshness; inclemency

incli'nabile AG (*schienale*) reclinable

incli'nare /**72**/ vt to tilt ▶ vi (*fig*): ~ **a qc/a fare** to incline towards sth/doing; to tend towards sth/to do; **inclinarsi** VPR (*barca*) to list; (*aereo*) to bank

incli'nato, -a AG sloping

inclinazi'one [inklinat'tsjone] SF slope; (*fig*) inclination, tendency

in'cline AG: ~ **a** inclined to

in'cludere /**3**/ vt to include; (*accludere*) to enclose

inclusi'one SF inclusion

inclu'sivo, -a AG: ~ **di** inclusive of

in'cluso, -a PP *di* **includere** ▶ AG included; enclosed

incoe'rente AG incoherent; (*contraddittorio*) inconsistent

incoe'renza [inkoe'rɛntsa] SF incoherence; inconsistency

in'cognito, -a [in'kɔɲɲito] AG unknown ▶ SM: **in** ~ incognito ▶ SF (*Mat, fig*) unknown quantity

incol'lare /**72**/ vt to glue, gum; (*unire con colla*) to stick together; ~ **gli occhi addosso a qn** (*fig*) to fix one's eyes on sb

incolla'tura SF (*Ippica*): **vincere/perdere di un'**~ to win/lose by a head

incolon'nare /**72**/ vt to draw up in columns

inco'lore AG colourless (BRIT), colorless (US)

incol'pare /**72**/ vt: ~ **qn di** to charge sb with

in'colto, -a AG (*terreno*) uncultivated; (*trascurato: capelli*) neglected; (*persona*) uneducated

in'colume AG safe and sound, unhurt

incolumità SF safety

incom'bente AG (*pericolo*) imminent, impending

incom'benza [inkom'bɛntsa] SF duty, task

in'combere /**29**/ vi (*sovrastare minacciando*): ~ **su** to threaten, hang over

incominci'are [inkomin'tʃare] /**14**/ vi, vt to begin, start

incomo'dare /**72**/ vt to trouble, inconvenience; **incomodarsi** VPR to put o.s. out

in'comodo, -a AG uncomfortable; (*inopportuno*) inconvenient ▶ SM inconvenience, bother

incompa'rabile AG incomparable

incompa'tibile AG incompatible

incompatibilità SF incompatibility; ~ **di carattere** (mutual) incompatibility

incompe'tente AG incompetent

incompe'tenza [inkompe'tɛntsa] SF incompetence

incompi'uto, -a AG unfinished, incomplete

incom'pleto, -a AG incomplete

incompren'sibile AG incomprehensible

incomprensi'one SF incomprehension

incom'preso, -a AG not understood; misunderstood

inconce'pibile [inkontʃe'pibile] AG inconceivable

inconcili'abile [inkontʃi'ljabile] AG irreconcilable

inconclu'dente AG inconclusive; (*persona*) ineffectual

incondizio'nato, -a [inkondittsjo'nato] AG unconditional

inconfes'sabile AG (*pensiero, peccato*) unmentionable

inconfon'dibile AG unmistakable

inconfu'tabile AG irrefutable

incongru'ente AG inconsistent

incongru'enza [inkongru'ɛntsa] SF inconsistency

in'congruo, -a AG incongruous

inconsa'pevole AG: ~ **di** unaware of, ignorant of

inconsapevo'lezza [inkonsapevo'lettsa] SF ignorance, lack of awareness

in'conscio, -a, -sci, -sce [in'kɔnʃo] AG unconscious ▶ SM (*Psic*) **l'**~ the unconscious

inconsis'tente AG (*patrimonio*) insubstantial; (*dubbio*) unfounded; (*ragionamento, prove*) tenuous, flimsy

inconsis'tenza [inkonsis'tɛntsa] SF insubstantial nature; lack of foundation; flimsiness

inconso'labile AG inconsolable

inconsu'eto, -a AG unusual

incon'sulto, -a AG rash

inconte'nibile AG (*rabbia*) uncontrollable; (*entusiasmo*) irrepressible

inconten'tabile AG (*desiderio, avidità*) insatiable; (*persona: capriccioso*) hard to please, very demanding

incontes'tabile AG incontrovertible, indisputable

incontes'tato, -a AG undisputed

inconti'nenza [inkonti'nɛntsa] SF incontinence

incon'trare /**72**/ VT to meet; (*difficoltà*) to meet with; **incontrarsi** VPR to meet

incon'trario AV: **all'~** (*sottosopra*) upside down; (*alla rovescia*) back to front; (*all'indietro*) backwards; (*nel senso contrario*) the other way round

incontras'tabile AG incontrovertible, indisputable

incontras'tato, -a AG (*successo, vittoria, verità*) uncontested, undisputed

in'contro AV: **~ a** (*verso*) towards ▶ SM meeting; (*Sport*) match; meeting; (*fortuito*) encounter; **venire ~ a** (*richieste, esigenze*) to comply with; **~ di calcio** football match (BRIT), soccer game (US)

incontrol'labile AG uncontrollable

inconveni'ente SM drawback, snag

incoraggia'mento [inkoraddʒa'mento] SM encouragement; **premio d'~** consolation prize

incoraggi'are [inkorad'dʒare] /**62**/ VT to encourage

incor'nare /**72**/ VT to gore

incornici'are [inkorni'tʃare] /**14**/ VT to frame

incoro'nare /**72**/ VT to crown

incoronazi'one [inkoronat'tsjone] SF coronation

incorpo'rare /**72**/ VT to incorporate; (*fig: annettere*) to annex

incorreg'gibile [inkorred'dʒibile] AG incorrigible

in'correre /**28**/ VI: **~ in** to meet with, run into

incorrut'tibile AG incorruptible

in'corso, -a PP *di* **incorrere**

incosci'ente [inkoʃʃɛnte] AG (*inconscio*) unconscious; (*irresponsabile*) reckless, thoughtless

incosci'enza [inkoʃʃɛntsa] SF unconsciousness; recklessness, thoughtlessness

incos'tante AG (*studente, impiegato*) inconsistent; (*carattere*) fickle, inconstant; (*rendimento*) sporadic

incos'tanza [inkos'tantsa] SF inconstancy, fickleness

incostituzio'nale [inkostituttsjo'nale] AG unconstitutional

incre'dibile AG incredible, unbelievable

incredulità SF incredulity

in'credulo, -a AG incredulous, disbelieving

incremen'tare /**72**/ VT to increase; (*dar sviluppo a*) to promote

incre'mento SM (*sviluppo*) development; (*aumento numerico*) increase, growth

incresci'oso, -a [inkreʃʃoso] AG (*spiacevole*) unpleasant; (*incidente ecc*) regrettable

incres'pare /**72**/ VT (*capelli*) to curl; (*acque*) to ripple; **incresparsi** VPR (*vedi vt*) to curl; to ripple

incrimi'nare /**72**/ VT (*Dir*) to charge

incriminazi'one [inkriminat'tsjone] SF (*atto d'accusa*) indictment, charge

incri'nare /**72**/ VT to crack; (*fig: rapporti, amicizia*) to cause to deteriorate; **incrinarsi** VPR to crack; to deteriorate

incrina'tura SF crack; (*fig*) rift

incroci'are [inkro'tʃare] /**14**/ VT to cross; (*incontrare*) to meet ▶ VI (*Naut, Aer*) to cruise; **incrociarsi** VPR (*strade*) to cross, intersect; (*persone, veicoli*) to pass each other; **~ le braccia/le gambe** to fold one's arms/cross one's legs

incrocia'tore [inkrotʃa'tore] SM cruiser

in'crocio [in'krotʃo] SM (*anche Ferr*) crossing; (*di strade*) crossroads

incrol'labile AG (*fede*) unshakeable, firm

incros'tare /**72**/ VT to encrust; **incrostarsi** VPR: **incrostarsi di** to become encrusted with

incrostazi'one [inkrostat'tsjone] SF encrustation; (*di calcare*) scale; (*nelle tubature*) fur (BRIT), scale

incru'ento, -a AG (*battaglia*) without bloodshed, bloodless

incuba'trice [inkuba'tritʃe] SF incubator

incubazi'one [inkubat'tsjone] SF incubation

'incubo SM nightmare

in'cudine SF anvil; **trovarsi** *o* **essere tra l'~ e il martello** (*fig*) to be between the devil and the deep blue sea

incul'care /**20**/ VT: **~ qc in** to inculcate sth into, instill sth into

incune'are /**72**/ VT to wedge

incu'pire /**55**/ VT (*rendere scuro*) to darken; (*fig: intristire*) to fill with gloom ▶ VI (*vedi vt*) to darken; to become gloomy

incu'rabile AG incurable

incu'rante AG: **~ (di)** heedless (of), careless (of)

in'curia SF negligence

incurio'sire /**55**/ VT to make curious; **incuriosirsi** VPR to become curious

incursi'one SF raid

incur'vare /**72**/ VT to bend, curve; **incurvarsi** VPR to bend, curve in'cusso, -a PP di **incutere**

incusto'dito, -a AG unguarded, unattended; **passaggio a livello ~** unmanned level crossing

in'cutere /40/ VT to arouse; **~ timore/ rispetto a qn** to strike fear into sb/ command sb's respect

'indaco SM indigo

indaffa'rato, -a AG busy

inda'gare /80/ VT to investigate

indaga'tore, -'trice AG (sguardo, domanda) searching; (mente) inquiring

in'dagine [in'dadʒine] SF investigation, inquiry; (ricerca) research, study; **~ di mercato** market survey

indebita'mente AV (immeritatamente) undeservedly; (erroneamente) wrongfully

indebi'tare /72/ VT: **~ qn** to get sb into debt; **indebitarsi** VPR to run o get into debt

in'debito, -a AG undeserved; wrongful

indeboli'mento SM weakening; (debolezza) weakness

indebo'lire /55/ VT, VI (anche: **indebolirsi**) to weaken

inde'cente [inde'tʃɛnte] AG indecent

inde'cenza [inde'tʃɛntsa] SF indecency; **è un'~!** (vergogna) it's scandalous!, it's a disgrace!

indeci'frabile [indetʃi'frabile] AG indecipherable

indecisi'one [indetʃi'zjone] SF indecisiveness; indecision

inde'ciso, -a [inde'tʃizo] AG indecisive; (irresoluto) undecided

indeco'roso, -a AG (comportamento) indecorous, unseemly

inde'fesso, -a AG untiring, indefatigable

indefi'nibile AG indefinable

indefi'nito, -a AG (anche Ling) indefinite; (impreciso, non determinato) undefined

indefor'mabile AG crushproof

in'degno, -a [in'deɲɲo] AG (atto) shameful; (persona) unworthy

inde'lebile AG indelible

indelica'tezza [indelika'tettsa] SF tactlessness

indeli'cato, -a AG (domanda) indiscreet, tactless

indemoni'ato, -a AG possessed (by the devil)

in'denne AG unhurt, uninjured

indennità SF INV (rimborso: di spese) allowance; (: di perdita) compensation, indemnity; **~ di contingenza** cost-of-living allowance; **~ di fine rapporto** severance payment (on retirement, redundancy or when taking up other employment); **~ di trasferta** travel expenses pl

indenniz'zare [indennid'dzare] /72/ VT to compensate

inden'nizzo [inden'niddzo] SM (somma) compensation, indemnity

indero'gabile AG binding

indescri'vibile AG indescribable

indeside'rabile AG undesirable

indeside'rato, -a AG unwanted

indetermina'tezza [indetermina'tettsa] SF vagueness

indetermina'tivo, -a AG (Ling) indefinite

indetermi'nato, -a AG indefinite, indeterminate

in'detto, -a PP di **indire**

'India SF: **l'~** India; **le Indie occidentali** the West Indies

indi'ano, -a AG Indian ▶ SM/F (d'India) Indian; (d'America) Native American, (American) Indian; **l'Oceano I~** the Indian Ocean

indiavo'lato, -a AG possessed (by the devil); (vivace, violento) wild

indi'care /20/ VT (mostrare) to show, indicate; (: col dito) to point to, point out; (consigliare) to suggest, recommend

indica'tivo, -a AG indicative ▶ SM (Ling) indicative (mood)

indi'cato, -a AG (consigliato) advisable; (adatto): **~ per** suitable for, appropriate for

indica'tore, -'trice AG indicating ▶ SM (elenco) guide; directory; (Tecn) gauge; indicator; **cartello ~** sign; **~ della benzina** petrol (BRIT) o gas (US) gauge, fuel gauge; **~ di velocità** (Aut) speedometer; (Aer) airspeed indicator

indicazi'one [indikat'tsjone] SF indication; (informazione) piece of information; **indicazioni per l'uso** instructions for use

'indice ['inditʃe] SM (Anat: dito) index finger, forefinger; (lancetta) needle, pointer; (fig: indizio) sign; (Tecn, Mat, nei libri) index; **~ azionario** share index; **~ di gradimento** (Radio, TV) popularity rating; **~ dei prezzi al consumo** ≈ retail price index

indicherò etc [indike'rɔ] VB vedi **indicare**

indi'cibile [indi'tʃibile] AG inexpressible

indiciz'zare [inditʃid'dzare] /72/ VT: **~ al costo della vita** to index-link (BRIT), index (US)

indiciz'zato, -a [inditʃid'dzato] AG (polizza, salario ecc) index-linked (BRIT), indexed (US)

indicizzazi'one [inditʃiddzat'tsjone] SF indexing

indietreggi'are [indjetred'dʒare] /62/ VI to draw back, retreat

indi'etro AV back; (guardare) behind, back; (andare, cadere: anche: **all'indietro**) backwards; **rimanere ~** to be left behind; **essere ~** (col lavoro) to be behind; (orologio) to be slow; **rimandare qc** to send sth back; **non vado né avanti né ~** (fig) I'm not getting anywhere, I'm getting nowhere

indi'feso, -a AG (città, confine) undefended; (persona) defenceless (BRIT), defenseless (US), helpless

indiffe'rente AG indifferent ▸ SM: **fare l'~** to pretend to be indifferent, be *o* act casual; (*fingere di non vedere o sentire*) to pretend not to notice

indiffe'renza [indiffe'rɛntsa] SF indifference

in'digeno, -a [in'didʒeno] AG indigenous, native ▸ SM/F native

indi'gente [indi'dʒɛnte] AG poverty-stricken, destitute

indi'genza [indi'dʒɛntsa] SF extreme poverty

indigesti'one [indidʒes'tjone] SF indigestion

indi'gesto, -a [indi'dʒɛsto] AG indigestible

indi'gnare [indiɲ'ɲare] /15/ VT to fill with indignation; **indignarsi** VPR to be (*o* get) indignant

indignazi'one [indiɲɲat'tsjone] SF indignation

indimenti'cabile AG unforgettable

'**indio, -a** AG, SM/F (South American) Indian

indipen'dente AG independent

indipendente'mente AV independently; **~ dal fatto che gli piaccia o meno, verrà!** he's coming, whether he likes it or not!

indipen'denza [indipen'dɛntsa] SF independence

in'dire /38/ VT (*concorso*) to announce; (*elezioni*) to call

indi'retto, -a AG indirect

indiriz'zare [indirit'tsare] /72/ VT (*dirigere*) to direct; (*mandare*) to send; (*lettera*) to address; **~ la parola a qn** to address sb

indiriz'zario [indirit'tsarjo] SM mailing list

indi'rizzo [indi'rittso] SM address; (*direzione*) direction; (*avvio*) trend, course; **~ assoluto** (*Inform*) absolute address

indisci'plina [indiʃʃi'plina] SF indiscipline

indiscipli'nato, -a [indiʃʃipli'nato] AG undisciplined, unruly

indis'creto, -a AG indiscreet

indiscrezi'one [indiskret'tsjone] SF indiscretion

indiscrimi'nato, -a AG indiscriminate

indis'cusso, -a AG unquestioned

indiscu'tibile AG indisputable, unquestionable

indispen'sabile AG indispensable, essential

indispet'tire /55/ VT to irritate, annoy ▸ VI (*anche*: **indispettirsi**) to get irritated *o* annoyed

indispo'nente AG irritating, annoying

indis'porre /77/ VT to antagonize

indisposizi'one [indispozit'tsjone] SF (slight) indisposition

indis'posto, -a PP *di* **indisporre** ▸ AG indisposed, unwell

indisso'lubile AG indissoluble

indissolubil'mente AV indissolubly

indistinta'mente AV (*senza distinzioni*) indiscriminately, without exception; (*in modo indefinito: vedere, sentire*) vaguely, faintly

indis'tinto, -a AG indistinct

indistrut'tibile AG indestructible

in'divia SF endive

individu'ale AG individual

individua'lismo SM individualism

individua'lista, -i, -e SM/F individualist

individualità SF individuality

individual'mente AV individually

individu'are /72/ VT (*dar forma distinta a*) to characterize; (*determinare*) to locate; (*riconoscere*) to single out

indi'viduo SM individual

indivi'sibile AG indivisible; **quei due sono indivisibili** (*fig*) those two are inseparable

indizi'are [indit'tsjare] /19/ VT: **~ qn di qc** to cast suspicion on sb for sth

indizi'ato, -a [indit'tsjato] AG suspected ▸ SM/F suspect

in'dizio [in'dittsjo] SM (*segno*) sign, indication; (*Polizia*) clue; (*Dir*) piece of evidence

Indo'cina [indo'tʃina] SF: **l'~** Indochina

'**indole** SF nature, character

indo'lente AG indolent

indo'lenza [indo'lɛntsa] SF indolence

indolen'zire [indolen'tsire] /55/ VT (*gambe, braccia ecc*) to make stiff, cause to ache; (: *intorpidire*) to numb; **indolenzirsi** VPR to become stiff; to go numb

indolen'zito, -a [indolen'tsito] AG stiff, aching; (*intorpidito*) numb

indo'lore AG (*anche fig*) painless

indo'mani SM: **l'~** the next day, the following day

Indo'nesia SF: **l'~** Indonesia

indonesi'ano, -a AG, SM/F, SM Indonesian

indo'rare /72/ VT (*rivestire in oro*) to gild; (*Cuc*) to dip in egg yolk; **~ la pillola** (*fig*) to sugar the pill

indos'sare /72/ VT (*mettere indosso*) to put on; (*avere indosso*) to have on

indossa'tore, -'trice SM/F model

in'dotto, -a PP *di* **indurre**

indottri'nare /72/ VT to indoctrinate

indovi'nare /72/ VT (*scoprire*) to guess; (*immaginare*) to imagine, guess; (*il futuro*) to foretell; **tirare a ~** to make a shot in the dark

indovi'nato, -a AG successful; (*scelta*) inspired

indovi'nello SM riddle

indo'vino, -a SM/F fortuneteller

indù AG, SM F Hindu

indubbia'mente AV undoubtedly

in'dubbio, -a AG certain, undoubted

in'duco *etc* VB *vedi* **indurre**

indugi'are [indu'dʒare] /62/ VI to take one's time, delay

in'dugio [in'dudʒo] SM (*ritardo*) delay; **senza ~** without delay

indul'gente [indul'dʒɛnte] AG indulgent; (*giudice*) lenient

indul'genza [indul'dʒɛntsa] SF indulgence; leniency

in'dulgere [in'duldʒere] /**54**/ VI: ~ **a** (*accondiscendere*) to comply with; (*abbandonarsi*) to indulge in

in'dulto, -a PP *di* **indulgere** ► SM (*Dir*) pardon

indu'mento SM article of clothing, garment; **indumenti** SMPL (*vestiti*) clothes; **indumenti intimi** underwear *sg*

induri'mento SM hardening

indu'rire /**55**/ VT to harden ► VI (*anche*: **indurirsi**) to harden, become hard

in'durre /**90**/ VT: ~ **qn a fare qc** to induce *o* persuade sb to do sth; ~ **qn in errore** to mislead sb; ~ **in tentazione** to lead into temptation

in'dussi *etc* VB *vedi* **indurre**

in'dustria SF industry; **la piccola/grande ~** small/big business

industri'ale AG industrial ► SM industrialist

industrializ'zare [industrjalid'dzare] /**72**/ VT to industrialize

industrializzazi'one [industrjaliddzat'tsjone] SF industrialization

industri'arsi /**19**/ VPR to do one's best, try hard

industri'oso, -a AG industrious, hard-working

induzi'one [indut'tsjone] SF induction

inebe'tito, -a AG dazed, stunned

inebri'are /**19**/ VT (*anche fig*) to intoxicate; **inebriarsi** VPR to become intoxicated

inecce'pibile [inettʃe'pibile] AG unexceptionable

i'nedia SF starvation

i'nedito, -a AG unpublished

ineffabile AG ineffable

ineffi'cace [ineffi'katʃe] AG ineffective

ineffi'cacia [ineffi'katʃa] SF inefficacy, ineffectiveness

ineffici'ente [ineffi'tʃɛnte] AG inefficient

ineffici'enza [ineffi'tʃɛntsa] SF inefficiency

ineguagli'abile [inegwaʎ'ʎabile] AG incomparable, matchless

ineguagli'anza [inegwaʎ'ʎantsa] SF (*sociale*) inequality; (*di superficie, livello*) unevenness

inegu'ale AG unequal; (*irregolare*) uneven

inelut'tabile AG inescapable

ineluttabilità SF inescapability

inenar'rabile AG unutterable

inequivo'cabile AG unequivocal

ine'rente AG: ~ **a** concerning, regarding

i'nerme AG unarmed, defenceless (BRIT), defenseless (US)

inerpi'carsi /**72**/ VPR: ~ (**su**) to clamber (up)

i'nerte AG inert; (*inattivo*) indolent, sluggish

i'nerzia [i'nɛrtsja] SF inertia; indolence, sluggishness

inesat'tezza [inezat'tettsa] SF inaccuracy

ine'satto, -a AG (*impreciso*) inaccurate, inexact; (*erroneo*) incorrect; (*Amm: non riscosso*) uncollected

inesau'ribile AG inexhaustible

inesis'tente AG non-existent

ineso'rabile AG inexorable, relentless

inesorabil'mente AV inexorably

inesperi'enza [inespe'rjɛntsa] SF inexperience

ines'perto, -a AG inexperienced

inespli'cabile AG inexplicable

inesplo'rato, -a AG unexplored

ines'ploso, -a AG unexploded

inespres'sivo, -a AG (*viso*) expressionless, inexpressive

ines'presso, -a AG unexpressed

inespri'mibile AG inexpressible

inespu'gnabile [inespuɲ'ɲabile] AG (*fortezza, torre ecc*) impregnable

ineste'tismo SM beauty problem

inesti'mabile AG inestimable; (*valore*) incalculable

inestir'pabile AG ineradicable

inestri'cabile AG (*anche fig*) impenetrable

inetti'tudine SF ineptitude

i'netto, -a AG (*incapace*) inept; (*che non ha attitudine*): ~ (**a**) unsuited (to)

ine'vaso, -a AG (*ordine, corrispondenza*) outstanding

inevi'tabile AG inevitable

inevitabil'mente AV inevitably

i'nezia [i'nɛttsja] SF trifle, thing of no importance

infagot'tare /**72**/ VT to bundle up, wrap up; **infagottarsi** VPR to wrap up

infal'libile AG infallible

infallibilità SF infallibility

infa'mante AG (*accusa*) defamatory, slanderous

infa'mare /**72**/ VT to defame

in'fame AG infamous; (*fig: cosa, compito*) awful, dreadful

in'famia SF infamy

infan'gare /**80**/ VT (*sporcare*) to cover with mud; (*fig: nome, reputazione*) to sully; **infangarsi** VPR to get covered in mud; to be sullied

infan'tile AG child *cpd*; childlike; (*adulto, azione*) childish; **letteratura ~** children's books *pl*

in'fanzia [in'fantsja] SF childhood; (*bambini*) children *pl*; **prima ~** babyhood, infancy

infari'nare /**72**/ VT to cover with *o* sprinkle with *o* dip in) flour; ~ **di zucchero** to sprinkle with sugar

infarina'tura SF (*fig*) smattering

in'farto SM (Med): ~ (cardiaco) coronary

infasti'dire /55/ VT to annoy, irritate;
infastidirsi VPR to get annoyed o irritated

infati'cabile AG tireless, untiring

in'fatti CONG as a matter of fact, in fact,
actually

infatu'arsi /72/ VPR: ~ di o per to become
infatuated with, fall for

infatuazi'one [infatuat'tsjone] SF
infatuation

in'fausto, -a AG unpropitious, unfavourable
(BRIT), unfavorable (US)

infecondità SF infertility

infe'condo, -a AG infertile

infe'dele AG unfaithful

infedeltà SF infidelity

infe'lice [infe'litʃe] AG unhappy; (sfortunato)
unlucky, unfortunate; (inopportuno)
inopportune, ill-timed; (mal riuscito: lavoro)
bad, poor

infelicità [infelitʃi'ta] SF unhappiness

infel'trire /55/ VI, infeltrirsi VPR (lana) to
become matted

infe'renza [infe'rentsa] SF inference

inferi'ore AG lower; (per intelligenza, qualità)
inferior ▶ SMF inferior; ~ a (numero, quantità)
less o smaller than; (meno buono) inferior to;
~ alla media below average

inferiorità SF inferiority

infe'rire /55/ VT (dedurre) to infer, deduce

inferme'ria SF infirmary; (di scuola, nave) sick
bay

infermi'ere, -a SM/F nurse

infermità SF INV illness; infirmity;
~ mentale mental illness; (Dir) insanity

in'fermo, -a AG (ammalato) ill; (debole) infirm;
~ di mente mentally ill

infer'nale AG infernal; (proposito, complotto)
diabolical; un tempo ~ (col) hellish weather

in'ferno SM hell; soffrire le pene dell'~ (fig)
to go through hell

infero'cire [infero'tʃire] /55/ VT to make fierce
▶ VI (anche: inferocirsi) to become fierce

inferri'ata SF grating

infervo'rare /72/ VT to arouse enthusiasm in;
infervorarsi VPR to get excited, get carried
away

infes'tare /72/ VT to infest

infet'tare /72/ VT to infect; infettarsi VPR to
become infected

infet'tivo, -a AG infectious

in'fetto, -a AG infected; (acque) polluted,
contaminated

infezi'one [infet'tsjone] SF infection

infiac'chire [infjak'kire] /55/ VT to weaken
▶ VI (anche: infiacchirsi) to grow weak

infiam'mabile AG inflammable

infiam'mare /72/ VT to set alight; (fig, Med) to
inflame; infiammarsi VPR to catch fire;
(Med) to become inflamed; (fig)
infiammarsi di to be fired with

infiammazi'one [infjammat'tsjone] SF
(Med) inflammation

infias'care /20/ VT to bottle

infici'are [infi'tʃare] /14/ VT (Dir: atto,
dichiarazione) to challenge

in'fido, -a AG unreliable, treacherous

infie'rire /55/ VI: ~ su (fisicamente) to attack
furiously; (verbalmente) to rage at; (epidemia)
to rage over

in'figgere [in'fiddʒere] /104/ VT: ~ qc in to
thrust o drive sth into

infi'lare /72/ VT (ago) to thread; (mettere: chiave)
to insert; (: vestito) to slip o put on; (strada) to
turn into, take; infilarsi VPR: infilarsi in to
slip into; (indossare) to slip on; ~ un anello al
dito to slip a ring on one's finger; ~ l'uscio
to slip in; to slip out; infilarsi la giacca to
put on one's jacket

infil'trarsi /72/ VPR to penetrate, seep
through; (Mil) to infiltrate

infil'trato, -a SM/F infiltrator

infiltrazi'one [infiltrat'tsjone] SF
infiltration

infil'zare [infil'tsare] /72/ VT (infilare) to string
together; (trafiggere) to pierce

'infimo, -a AG lowest; un albergo di ~ ordine
a third-rate hotel

in'fine AV finally; (insomma) in short

infin'gardo, -a AG lazy ▶ SM/F slacker

infinità SF infinity; (in quantità): un'~ di an
infinite number of

infinitesi'male AG infinitesimal

infi'nito, -a AG infinite; (Ling) infinitive ▶ SM
infinity; (Ling) infinitive; all'~ (senza fine)
endlessly; (Ling) in the infinitive

infinocchi'are [infinok'kjare] /19/ VT (col) to
hoodwink

infiore'scenza [infjoreʃ'ʃentsa] SF
inflorescence

infir'mare /72/ VT (Dir) to invalidate

infischi'arsi [infis'kjarsi] /19/ VPR: ~ di not
to care about

in'fisso, -a PP di infiggere ▶ SM fixture; (di
porta, finestra) frame

infit'tire /55/ VT, VI (anche: infittirsi) to
thicken

inflazio'nare [inflattsjo'nare] /72/ VT to
inflate

inflazi'one [inflat'tsjone] SF inflation

inflazio'nistico, -a, -ci, -che
[inflattsjo'nistiko] AG inflationary

infles'sibile AG inflexible; (ferreo) unyielding

inflessi'one SF inflexion

in'fliggere [in'fliddʒere] /104/ VT to inflict

in'flissi etc VB vedi infliggere

in'flitto, -a PP di infliggere

influ'ente AG influential

influ'enza [influ'ɛntsa] SF influence; (*Med*) influenza, flu; **~ aviaria** bird flu; **~ suina** swine flu

influen'zare [influen'tsare] /**72**/ VT to influence, have an influence on

influ'ire /**55**/ VI: **~ su** to influence

in'flusso SM influence

INFN SIGLA M = **Istituto Nazionale di Fisica Nucleare**

info'cato, -a AG = **infuocato**

info'gnarsi [infoɲ'ɲarsi] /**15**/ VPR (*col*) to get into a mess; **~ in un mare di debiti** to be up to one's o the eyes in debt

infol'tire /**55**/ VT, VI to thicken

infon'dato, -a AG unfounded, groundless

in'fondere /**25**/ VT: **~ qc in qn** to instill sth in sb; **~ fiducia in qn** to inspire sb with confidence

infor'care /**20**/ VT to fork (up); (*bicicletta, cavallo*) to get on; (*occhiali*) to put on

infor'male AG informal

infor'mare /**72**/ VT to inform, tell; **informarsi** VPR: **informarsi (di o su)** to inquire (about); **tenere informato qn** to keep sb informed

infor'matico, -a, -ci, -che AG (*settore*) computer *cpd* ▶ SF computer science

informa'tivo, -a AG informative; **a titolo ~** for information only

informatiz'zare [informatid'dzare] /**72**/ VT to computerize

infor'mato, -a AG informed; **tenersi ~** to keep o.s. (well-)informed

informa'tore SM informer

informazi'one [informat'tsjone] SF piece of information; **informazioni** SFPL information *sg*; **chiedere un'~** to ask for (some) information; **~ di garanzia** (*Dir*) = **avviso di garanzia**

in'forme AG shapeless

informico'larsi /**72**/, **informico'lirsi** VPR: **mi si è informicolata una gamba** I've got pins and needles in my leg

infor'nare /**72**/ VT to put in the oven

infor'nata SF (*anche fig*) batch

infortu'narsi /**72**/ VPR to injure o.s., have an accident

infortu'nato, -a AG injured, hurt ▶ SM/F injured person

infor'tunio SM accident; **~ sul lavoro** industrial accident, accident at work

infortu'nistica SF study of (industrial) accidents

infos'sarsi /**72**/ VPR (*terreno*) to sink; (*guance*) to become hollow

infos'sato, -a AG hollow; (*occhi*) deep-set; (: *per malattia*) sunken

infradici'are [infradi'tʃare] /**14**/ VT (*inzuppare*) to soak, drench; (*marcire*) to rot; **infradiciarsi** VPR to get soaked, get drenched; to rot

infra'dito SM INV (*calzatura*) flip flop (*BRIT*), thong (*US*)

in'frangere [in'frandʒere] /**37**/ VT to smash; (*fig: legge, patti*) to break; **infrangersi** VPR to smash, break

infran'gibile [infran'dʒibile] AG unbreakable

in'franto, -a PP *di* **infrangere** ▶ AG broken

infra'rosso, -a AG, SM infrared

infrasettima'nale AG midweek *cpd*

infrastrut'tura SF infrastructure

infrazi'one [infrat'tsjone] SF: **~ a** breaking of, violation of

infredda'tura SF slight cold

infreddo'lito, -a AG cold, chilled

infre'quente AG infrequent, rare

infrol'lire /**55**/ VI, **infrol'lirsi** VPR (*selvaggina*) to become high

infruttu'oso, -a AG fruitless

infuo'cato, -a AG (*metallo*) red-hot; (*sabbia*) burning; (*fig: discorso*) heated, passionate

infu'ori AV out; **all'~** outwards; **all'~ di** (*eccetto*) except, with the exception of

infuri'are /**19**/ VI to rage; **infuriarsi** VPR to fly into a rage

infusi'one SF infusion

in'fuso, -a PP *di* **infondere** ▶ AG: **scienza infusa** (*anche ironico*) innate knowledge ▶ SM infusion; **~ di camomilla** camomile tea

Ing. ABBR = **ingegnere**

ingabbi'are /**19**/ VT to (put in a) cage

ingaggi'are [ingad'dʒare] /**62**/ VT (*assumere con compenso*) to take on, hire; (*Sport*) to sign on; (*Mil*) to engage

in'gaggio [in'gaddʒo] SM hiring; signing on

ingagliar'dire [ingaʎʎar'dire] /**55**/ VT to strengthen, invigorate ▶ VI (*anche*: **ingagliardirsi**) to grow stronger

ingan'nare /**72**/ VT to deceive; (*coniuge*) to be unfaithful to; (*fisco*) to cheat; (*eludere*) to dodge, elude; (*fig: tempo*) to while away ▶ VI (*apparenza*) to be deceptive; **ingannarsi** VPR to be mistaken, be wrong

inganna'tore, -'trice AG deceptive; (*persona*) deceitful

ingan'nevole AG deceptive

in'ganno SM deceit, deception; (*azione*) trick; (*menzogna, frode*) cheat, swindle; (*illusione*) illusion

ingarbugli'are [ingarbuʎ'ʎare] /**27**/ VT to tangle; (*fig*) to confuse, muddle; **ingarbugliarsi** VPR to become confused o muddled

ingarbu'gliato, -a [ingarbuʎ'ʎato] AG tangled; confused, muddled

inge'gnarsi [indʒeɲ'ɲarsi] /**15**/ VPR to do one's best, try hard; **~ per vivere** to live by one's wits; **basta ~ un po'** you just need a bit of ingenuity

inge'gnere [indʒeɲ'ɲere] SM engineer; **~ civile/navale** civil/naval engineer

ingegne'ria [indʒeɲɲe'ria] SF engineering; **~ genetica** genetic engineering

in'gegno [in'dʒeɲɲo] SM (*intelligenza*) intelligence, brains *pl*; (*capacità creativa*) ingenuity; (*disposizione*) talent

ingegnosità [indʒeɲɲosi'ta] SF ingenuity

inge'gnoso, -a [indʒeɲ'ɲoso] AG ingenious, clever

ingelo'sire [indʒelo'sire] /**55**/ VT to make jealous ▸ VI (*anche*: **ingelosirsi**) to become jealous

in'gente [in'dʒɛnte] AG huge, enormous

ingenti'lire [indʒenti'lire] /**55**/ VT to refine, civilize; **ingentilirsi** VPR to become more refined, become more civilized

ingenuità [indʒenui'ta] SF ingenuousness

in'genuo, -a [in'dʒɛnuo] AG naïve

inge'renza [indʒe'rɛntsa] SF interference

inge'rire [indʒe'rire] /**55**/ VT to ingest

inges'sare [indʒes'sare] /**72**/ VT (*Med*) to put in plaster

ingessa'tura [indʒessa'tura] SF plaster

Inghil'terra [ingil'tɛrra] SF: **l'~** England

inghiot'tire [ingjot'tire] /**17**/ VT to swallow

in'ghippo [in'gippo] SM trick

ingial'lire [indʒal'lire] /**55**/ VI to go yellow

ingigan'tire [indʒigan'tire] /**55**/ VT to enlarge, magnify ▸ VI to become gigantic *o* enormous

inginocchi'arsi [indʒinok'kjarsi] /**19**/ VPR to kneel (down)

inginocchia'toio [indʒinokkja'tojo] SM prie-dieu

ingioiel'lare [indʒojel'lare] /**72**/ VT to bejewel, adorn with jewels

ingiù [in'dʒu] AV down, downwards

ingi'ungere [in'dʒundʒere] /**5**/ VT: **~ a qn di fare qc** to enjoin *o* order sb to do sth

ingi'unto, -a [in'dʒunto] PP *di* **ingiungere**

ingiunzi'one [indʒun'tsjone] SF injunction, command; **~ di pagamento** final demand

ingi'uria [in'dʒurja] SF insult; (*fig: danno*) damage

ingiuri'are [indʒu'rjare] /**19**/ VT to insult, abuse

ingiuri'oso, -a [indʒu'rjoso] AG insulting, abusive

ingiusta'mente [indʒusta'mente] AV unjustly

ingiustifi'cabile [indʒustifi'kabile] AG unjustifiable

ingiustifi'cato, -a [indʒustifi'kato] AG unjustified

ingius'tizia [indʒus'tittsja] SF injustice

ingi'usto, -a [in'dʒusto] AG unjust, unfair

in'glese AG English ▸ SM/F Englishman(-woman) ▸ SM (*Ling*) English; **gli Inglesi** the English; **andarsene** *o* **filare all'~** to take French leave

inglori'oso, -a AG inglorious

ingob'bire /**55**/ VI, **ingob'birsi** VPR to become stooped

ingoi'are /**19**/ VT to gulp (down); (*fig*) to swallow (up); **ha dovuto ~ il rospo** (*fig*) he had to accept the situation

ingol'fare /**72**/ VT, **ingol'farsi** VPR (*motore*) to flood

ingolo'sire /**55**/ VT: **~ qn** to make sb's mouth water; (*fig*) to attract sb ▸ VI (*anche*: **ingolosirsi**): **~ (di)** (*anche fig*) to become greedy (for)

ingom'brante AG cumbersome

ingom'brare /**72**/ VT (*strada*) to block; (*stanza*) to clutter up

in'gombro, -a AG: **~ di** (*strada*) blocked by; (*stanza*) cluttered up with ▸ SM obstacle; **essere d'~** to be in the way; **per ragioni di ~** for reasons of space

ingor'digia [ingor'didʒa] SF: **~ (di)** greed (for); avidity (for)

in'gordo, -a AG: **~ di** greedy for; (*fig*) greedy *o* avid for ▸ SM/F glutton

ingor'gare /**80**/ VT to block; **ingorgarsi** VPR to be blocked up, be choked up

in'gorgo, -ghi SM blockage, obstruction; (*anche*: **ingorgo stradale**) traffic jam

ingoz'zare [ingot'tsare] /**72**/ VT (*animali*) to fatten; (*fig: persona*) to stuff; **ingozzarsi** VPR: **ingozzarsi (di)** to stuff o.s. (with)

ingra'naggio [ingra'naddʒo] SM (*Tecn*) gear; (*di orologio*) mechanism; **gli ingranaggi della burocrazia** the bureaucratic machinery

ingra'nare /**72**/ VI to mesh, engage ▸ VT to engage; **~ la marcia** to get into gear

ingrandi'mento SM enlargement; extension; magnification; growth; expansion

ingran'dire /**55**/ VT (*anche Fot*) to enlarge; (*estendere*) to extend; (*Ottica, fig*) to magnify ▸ VI (*anche*: **ingrandirsi**) to become larger *o* bigger; (*: aumentare*) to grow, increase; (*: espandersi*) to expand

ingrandi'tore SM (*Fot*) enlarger

ingras'saggio [ingras'saddʒo] SM greasing

ingras'sare /**72**/ VT to make fat; (*animali*) to fatten; (*Agr: terreno*) to manure; (*lubrificare*) to oil, lubricate ▸ VI (*anche*: **ingrassarsi**) to get fat, put on weight

ingrati'tudine SF ingratitude

in'grato, -a AG ungrateful; (*lavoro*) thankless, unrewarding

ingrazi'are [ingrat'tsjare] /**19**/ VT: **ingraziarsi qn** to ingratiate o.s. with sb

ingredi'ente SM ingredient

in'gresso SM (*porta*) entrance; (*atrio*) hall; (*l'entrare*) entrance, entry; (*facoltà di entrare*) admission; **"~ libero"** "admission free";

~ principale main entrance; **~ di servizio** tradesmen's entrance

ingros'sare /**72**/ VT to increase; (*folla, livello*) to swell ▶ VI (*anche:* **ingrossarsi**) to increase; to swell

in'grosso AV: **all'~** (*Comm*) wholesale; (*all'incirca*) roughly, about

ingru'gnato, -a [ingruɲˈɲato] AG grumpy

inguai'arsi /**19**/ VPR to get into trouble

inguai'nare /**72**/ VT to sheathe

ingual'cibile [ingwalˈtʃibile] AG crease-resistant

ingua'ribile AG incurable

'inguine SM (*Anat*) groin

ingurgi'tare [ingurdʒiˈtare] /**72**/ VT to gulp down

ini'bire /**55**/ VT to forbid, prohibit; (*Psic*) to inhibit; **inibirsi** VPR to restrain o.s.

ini'bito, -a AG inhibited ▶ SM/F inhibited person

inibi'torio, -a AG (*Psic*) inhibitory, inhibitive; (*provvedimento, misure*) restrictive

inibizi'one [inibitˈtsjone] SF prohibition; inhibition

iniet'tare /**72**/ VT to inject; **iniettarsi** VPR: **iniettarsi di sangue** (*occhi*) to become bloodshot

iniet'tore SM injector

iniezi'one [injetˈtsjone] SF injection

inimi'care /**20**/ VT to alienate, make hostile; **inimicarsi** VPR: **inimicarsi con qn** to fall out with sb; **si è inimicato gli amici di un tempo** he has alienated his old friends

inimi'cizia [inimiˈtʃittsja] SF animosity

inimi'tabile AG inimitable

inimmagi'nabile [inimmadʒiˈnabile] AG unimaginable

ininfiam'mabile AG non-flammable

inintelli'gibile [inintelliˈdʒibile] AG unintelligible

ininterrotta'mente AV non-stop, continuously

ininter'rotto, -a AG (*fila*) unbroken; (*rumore*) uninterrupted

iniquità SF INV iniquity; (*atto*) wicked action

i'niquo, -a AG iniquitous

inizi'ale [initˈtsjale] AG, SF initial

inizializ'zare [inittsjalidˈdzare] /**72**/ VT (*Inform*) to boot

inizial'mente [inittsjalˈmente] AV initially, at first

inizi'are [initˈtsjare] /**19**/ VI, VT to begin, start; **~ qn a** to initiate sb into; (*pittura ecc*) to introduce sb to; **~ a fare qc** to start doing sth

inizia'tiva [inittsjaˈtiva] SF initiative; **~ privata** private enterprise

inizia'tore, -'trice [inittsjaˈtore] SM/F initiator

i'nizio [iˈnittsjo] SM beginning; **all'~** at the beginning, at the start; **dare ~ a qc** to start

sth, get sth going; **essere agli inizi** (*progetto, lavoro ecc*) to be in the initial stages

innaffi'are *etc* = **annaffiare** *ecc*

innal'zare [innalˈtsare] /**72**/ VT (*sollevare, alzare*) to raise; (*rizzare*) to erect; **innalzarsi** VPR to rise

innamora'mento SM falling in love

innamo'rare /**72**/ VT to enchant, charm; **innamorarsi** VPR: **innamorarsi (di qn)** to fall in love (with sb)

innamo'rato, -a AG: **~ (di)** (*che nutre amore*) in love (with); **~ di** (*appassionato*) very fond of ▶ SM/F lover; (*anche scherzoso*) sweetheart

in'nanzi [inˈnantsi] AV (*stato in luogo*) in front, ahead; (*moto a luogo*) forward, on; (*tempo: prima*) before ▶ PREP (*prima*) before; **~ a** in front of; **d'ora ~** from now on; **farsi ~** to step forward; **~ tempo** ahead of time

innanzi'tutto [innantsiˈtutto] AV above all; (*per prima cosa*) first of all

in'nato, -a AG innate

innatu'rale AG unnatural

inne'gabile AG undeniable

inneggi'are [innedˈdʒare] /**62**/ VI: **~ a** to sing hymns to; (*fig*) to sing the praises of

innervo'sire /**55**/ VT: **~ qn** to get on sb's nerves; **innervosirsi** VPR to get irritated o upset

innes'care /**20**/ VT to prime

in'nesco, -schi SM primer

innes'tare /**72**/ VT (*Bot, Med*) to graft; (*Tecn*) to engage; (*inserire: presa*) to insert

in'nesto SM graft; grafting *no pl*; (*Tecn*) clutch; (*Elettr*) connection

'inno SM hymn; **~ nazionale** national anthem

inno'cente [innoˈtʃente] AG innocent

inno'cenza [innoˈtʃentsa] SF innocence

in'nocuo, -a AG innocuous, harmless

innomi'nato, -a AG unnamed

inno'vare /**72**/ VT to change, make innovations in

innova'tivo, -a AG innovative

innovazi'one [innovatˈtsjone] SF innovation

innume'revole AG innumerable

inocu'lare /**72**/ VT (*Med*) to inoculate

ino'doro, -a AG odourless (*BRIT*), odorless (*US*)

inoffen'sivo, -a AG harmless

inol'trare /**72**/ VT (*Amm*) to pass on, forward; **inoltrarsi** VPR (*addentrarsi*) to advance, go forward

inol'trato, -a AG: **a notte inoltrata** late at night; **a primavera inoltrata** late in the spring

i'noltre AV besides, moreover

i'noltro SM (*Amm*) forwarding

inon'dare /**72**/ VT to flood

inondazi'one [inondatˈtsjone] SF flooding *no pl*; flood

inope'roso, -a AG inactive, idle

inopi'nato, -a AG unexpected

inoppor'tuno, -a AG untimely, ill-timed; (*poco adatto*) inappropriate; (*momento*) inopportune

inoppu'gnabile [inoppuɲ'ɲabile] AG incontrovertible

inor'ganico, -a, -ci, -che AG inorganic

inorgo'glire [inorgoʎ'ʎire] /55/ VT to make proud ▶ VI (*anche*: **inorgoglirsi**) to become proud; **inorgoglirsi di qc** to pride o.s. on sth

inorri'dire /55/ VT to horrify ▶ VI to be horrified

inospi'tale AG inhospitable

inosser'vante AG: **essere ~ di** to fail to comply with

inosser'vato, -a AG (*non notato*) unobserved; (*non rispettato*) not observed, not kept; **passare ~** to go unobserved, escape notice

inossi'dabile AG stainless

INPS SIGLA M (= *Istituto Nazionale Previdenza Sociale*) social security service

inqua'drare /72/ VT (*foto, immagine*) to frame; (*fig*) to situate, set

inquadra'tura SF (*Cine, Fot: atto*) framing; (: *immagine*) shot; (: *sequenza*) sequence

inqualifi'cabile AG unspeakable

inquie'tante AG disturbing, worrying

inquie'tare /72/ VT (*turbare*) to disturb, worry; **inquietarsi** VPR to worry, become anxious; (*impazientirsi*) to get upset

inqui'eto, -a AG restless; (*preoccupato*) worried, anxious

inquie'tudine SF anxiety, worry

inqui'lino, -a SM/F tenant

inquina'mento SM pollution

inqui'nare /72/ VT to pollute

inqui'rente AG (*Dir*): **magistrato ~** examining (BRIT) *o* committing (US) magistrate; **commissione ~** commission of inquiry

inqui'sire /55/ VT, VI to investigate

inqui'sito, -a AG (*persona*) under investigation

inquisi'tore, -'trice AG (*sguardo*) inquiring

inquisizi'one [inkwizit'tsjone] SF inquisition

insabbia'mento SM (*fig*) shelving

insabbi'are /19/ VT (*fig: pratica*) to shelve; **insabbiarsi** VPR (*arenarsi: barca*) to run aground; (*fig: pratica*) to be shelved

insac'care /20/ VT (*grano, farina ecc*) to bag, put into sacks; (*carne*) to put into sausage skins

insac'cati SMPL (*Cuc*) sausages

insa'lata SF salad; (*pianta*) lettuce; **~ mista** mixed salad; **~ russa** (*Cuc*) Russian salad (*comprised of cold diced cooked vegetables in mayonnaise*)

insalati'era SF salad bowl

insa'lubre AG unhealthy

insa'nabile AG (*piaga*) which cannot be healed; (*situazione*) irremediable; (*odio*) implacable

insangui'nare /72/ VT to stain with blood

in'sania SF insanity

in'sano, -a AG (*pazzo, folle*) insane

insapo'nare /72/ VT to soap; **insaponarsi le mani** to soap one's hands

insapo'nata SF: **dare un'~ a qc** to give sth a (quick) soaping

insapo'rire /55/ VT to flavour (BRIT), flavor (US); (*con spezie*) to season; **insaporirsi** VPR to acquire flavo(u)r

insa'poro, -a AG tasteless, insipid

insa'puta SF: **all'~ di qn** without sb knowing

insazi'abile [insat'tsjabile] AG insatiable

inscato'lare /72/ VT (*frutta, carne*) to can

insce'nare [inʃe'nare] /72/ VT (*Teat*) to stage, put on; (*fig*) to stage

inscin'dibile [inʃin'dibile] AG (*fattori*) inseparable; (*legame*) indissoluble

insec'chire [insek'kire] /55/ VT (*seccare*) to dry up; (: *piante*) to wither ▶ VI to dry up, become dry; to wither

insedia'mento SM (*Amm: in carica, ufficio*) installation; (*villaggio, colonia*) settlement

insedi'are /19/ VT (*Amm*) to install; **insediarsi** VPR (*Amm*) to take up office; (*colonia, profughi ecc*) to settle; (*Mil*) to take up positions

in'segna [in'seɲɲa] SF sign; (*emblema*) sign, emblem; (*bandiera*) flag, banner; **insegne** SFPL (*decorazioni*) insignia *pl*

insegna'mento [inseɲɲa'mento] SM teaching; **trarre ~ da un'esperienza** to learn from an experience, draw a lesson from an experience; **che ti serva da ~** let this be a lesson to you

inse'gnante [inseɲ'ɲante] AG teaching ▶ SMF teacher; **~ di sostegno** teaching assistant

inse'gnare [inseɲ'ɲare] /15/ VT, VI to teach; **~ a qn qc** to teach sb sth; **~ a qn a fare qc** to teach sb (how) to do sth; **come lei ben m'insegna ...** (*ironico*) as you will doubtless be aware ...

insegui'mento SM pursuit, chase; **darsi all'~ di qn** to give chase to sb

insegu'ire /45/ VT to pursue, chase

insegui'tore, -'trice SM/F pursuer

insel'lare /72/ VT to saddle

inselvati'chire [inselvati'kire] /55/ VT (*persona*) to make unsociable ▶ VI (*anche*: **inselvatichirsi**) to grow wild; (: *persona*) to become unsociable

inseminazi'one [inseminat'tsjone] SF insemination

insena'tura SF inlet, creek

insen'sato, -a AG senseless, stupid

insen'sibile AG (*anche fig*) insensitive

insensibilità SF insensitivity, insensibility
insepa'rabile AG inseparable
inse'polto, -a AG unburied
inseri'mento SM (gen) insertion; **problemi di ~** (di persona) adjustment problems
inse'rire /55/ VT to insert; (Elettr) to connect; (allegare) to enclose; (annuncio) to put in, place; **inserirsi** VPR (fig): **inserirsi in** to become part of; **~ un annuncio sul giornale** to put o place an advertisement in the newspaper
in'serto SM (pubblicazione) insert; **~ filmato** (film) clip
inser'vibile AG useless
inservi'ente SMF attendant
inserzi'one [inser'tsjone] SF insertion; (avviso) advertisement; **fare un'~ sul giornale** to put an advertisement in the newspaper
inserzio'nista, -i, -e [insertsjo'nista] SM/F advertiser
insetti'cida, -i [insetti'tʃida] SM insecticide
in'setto SM insect
insicu'rezza [insiku'rettsa] SF insecurity
insi'curo, -a AG insecure
in'sidia SF snare, trap; (pericolo) hidden danger; **tendere un'~ a qn** to lay o set a trap for sb
insidi'are /19/ VT (Mil) to harass; **~ la vita di qn** to make an attempt on sb's life
insidi'oso, -a AG insidious
insi'eme AV together; (contemporaneamente) at the same time ▶ PREP: **~ a o con** together with ▶ SM whole; (Mat, servizio, assortimento) set; (Moda) ensemble, outfit; **tutti ~** all together; **tutto ~** all together; (in una volta) at one go; **nell'~** on the whole; **d'~** (veduta ecc) overall
in'signe [in'siɲɲe] AG (persona) famous, distinguished, eminent; (città, monumento) notable
insignifi'cante [insiɲɲifi'kante] AG insignificant
insi'gnire [insiɲ'ɲire] /55/ VT: **~ qn di** to honour (BRIT) o honor (US) sb with, decorate sb with
insin'cero, -a [insin'tʃεro] AG insincere
insinda'cabile AG unquestionable
insinu'ante AG (osservazione, sguardo) insinuating; (maniere) ingratiating
insinu'are /72/ VT (fig) to insinuate, imply; **~ qc in** (introdurre) to slip o slide sth into; **insinuarsi** VPR: **insinuarsi in** to seep into; (fig) to creep into; to worm one's way into
insinuazi'one [insinuat'tsjone] SF (fig) insinuation
in'sipido, -a AG insipid
insis'tente AG insistent; (pioggia, dolore) persistent

insistente'mente AV repeatedly
insis'tenza [insis'tɛntsa] SF insistence; persistence
in'sistere /11/ VI: **~ su qc** to insist on sth; **~ in qc/a fare** (perseverare) to persist in sth/in doing
insis'tito, -a PP di **insistere**
'insito, -a AG: **~ (in)** inherent (in)
insoddis'fatto, -a AG dissatisfied
insoddisfazi'one [insoddisfat'tsjone] SF dissatisfaction
insoffe'rente AG intolerant
insoffe'renza [insoffe'rɛntsa] SF impatience
insolazi'one [insolat'tsjone] SF (Med) sunstroke
inso'lente AG insolent
insolen'tire /55/ VI to grow insolent ▶ VT to insult, be rude to
inso'lenza [inso'lɛntsa] SF insolence
in'solito, -a AG unusual, out of the ordinary
inso'lubile AG insoluble
inso'luto, -a AG (non risolto) unsolved; (non pagato) unpaid, outstanding
insol'vente AG (Dir) insolvent
insol'venza [insol'vɛntsa] SF (Dir) insolvency
insol'vibile AG insolvent
in'somma AV (in breve, in conclusione) in short; (dunque) well ▶ ESCL for heaven's sake!
inson'dabile AG unfathomable
in'sonne AG sleepless
in'sonnia SF insomnia, sleeplessness
insonno'lito, -a AG sleepy, drowsy
insonorizzazi'one [insonoriddzat'tsjone] SF soundproofing
insoppor'tabile AG unbearable
insoppri'mibile AG insuppressible
insor'genza [insor'dʒɛntsa] SF (di malattia) onset
in'sorgere [in'sordʒere] /109/ VI (ribellarsi) to rise up, rebel; (apparire) to come up, arise
insormon'tabile AG (ostacolo) insurmountable, insuperable
in'sorsi etc VB vedi **insorgere**
in'sorto, -a PP di **insorgere** ▶ SM/F rebel, insurgent
insospet'tabile AG (al di sopra di ogni sospetto) above suspicion; (inatteso) unsuspected
insospet'tire /55/ VT to make suspicious ▶ VI (anche: **insospettirsi**) to become suspicious
insoste'nibile AG (posizione, teoria) untenable; (dolore, situazione) intolerable, unbearable; **le spese di manutenzione sono insostenibili** the maintenance costs are excessive
insostitu'ibile AG (persona) irreplaceable; (aiuto, presenza) invaluable
insoz'zare [insot'tsare] /72/ VT (pavimento) to make dirty; (fig: reputazione, memoria) to tarnish, sully; **insozzarsi** VPR to get dirty

inspe'rabile AG: **la guarigione/salvezza era**
~ there was no hope of a cure/of rescue;
abbiamo ottenuto risultati insperabili
the results we achieved were far better than
we had hoped
inspe'rato, -a AG unhoped-for
inspie'gabile AG inexplicable
inspi'rare /72/ VT to breathe in, inhale
in'stabile AG (carico, indole) unstable; (tempo)
unsettled; (equilibrio) unsteady
instabilità SF instability; (di tempo)
changeability
instal'lare /72/ VT to install; **installarsi** VPR
(sistemarsi): **installarsi in** to settle in
installazi'one [installat'tsjone] SF
installation
instan'cabile AG untiring, indefatigable
instau'rare /72/ VT to establish, introduce
instaurazi'one [instaurat'tsjone] SF
establishment
instil'lare /72/ VT to instil
instra'dare /72/ VT = **istradare**
insù AV up, upwards; **guardare all'~** to
look up o upwards; **naso all'~** turned-up
nose
insubordinazi'one [insubordinat'tsjone] SF
insubordination
insuc'cesso [insut't∫esso] SM failure, flop
insudici'are [insudi't∫are] **/14/** VT to dirty;
insudiciarsi VPR to get dirty
insuffici'ente [insuffi't∫ente] AG
insufficient; (compito, allievo) inadequate
insuffici'enza [insuffi't∫entsa] SF
insufficiency; inadequacy; (Ins) fail; **~ di
prove** (Dir) lack of evidence; **~ renale** renal
insufficiency
insu'lare AG insular
insu'lina SF insulin
in'sulso, -a AG (sciocco) inane, silly; (persona)
dull, insipid
insul'tare /72/ VT to insult, affront
in'sulto SM insult, affront
insupe'rabile AG (ostacolo, difficoltà)
insuperable, insurmountable; (eccellente:
qualità, prodotto) unbeatable; (: persona,
interpretazione) unequalled
insuper'bire /55/ VT to make proud, make
arrogant; **insuperbirsi** VPR to become
arrogant
insurrezi'one [insurret'tsjone] SF revolt,
insurrection
insussis'tente AG non-existent
intac'care /20/ VT (fare tacche) to cut into;
(corrodere) to corrode; (fig: cominciare ad usare:
risparmi) to break into; (: ledere) to damage
intagli'are [intaλ'λare] **/27/** VT to carve
intaglia'tore, -'trice [intaλλa'tore] SM/F
engraver
in'taglio [in'taλλo] SM carving

intan'gibile [intan'dʒibile] AG (bene,
patrimonio) untouchable; (fig: diritto)
inviolable
in'tanto AV (nel frattempo) meanwhile, in the
meantime; (per cominciare) just to begin with;
~ che cong while
intarsi'are /19/ VT to inlay
in'tarsio SM inlaying no pl, marquetry no pl;
inlay
intasa'mento SM (ostruzione) blockage,
obstruction; (Aut: ingorgo) traffic jam
inta'sare /72/ VT to choke (up), block (up);
(Aut) to obstruct, block; **intasarsi** VPR to
become choked o blocked
intas'care /20/ VT to pocket
in'tatto, -a AG intact; (puro) unsullied
intavo'lare /72/ VT to start, enter into
inte'gerrimo, -a [inte'dʒerrimo] AG honest,
upright
inte'grale AG complete; (pane, farina)
wholemeal (BRIT), wholewheat (US); **film in
versione ~** uncut version of a film; **calcolo ~**
(Mat) integral calculus; **edizione ~**
unabridged edition
inte'grante AG: **parte ~** integral part
inte'grare /72/ VT to complete; (Mat) to
integrate; **integrarsi** VPR (persona) to become
integrated
integra'tivo, -a AG (assegno) supplementary;
(Ins): **esame ~** assessment test sat when changing
schools
integra'tore SM: **integratori alimentari**
nutritional supplements
integrazi'one [integrat'tsjone] SF
integration
integrità SF integrity
'integro, -a AG (intatto, intero) complete,
whole; (retto) upright
intelaia'tura SF frame; (fig) structure,
framework
intel'letto SM intellect
intellettu'ale AG, SMF intellectual
intellettua'loide (peg) AG pseudo-
intellectual ▶ SMF pseudo-intellectual,
would-be intellectual
intelli'gente [intelli'dʒente] AG intelligent
intelli'genza [intelli'dʒentsa] SF intelligence
intelli'ghenzia [intelli'gentsja] SF
intelligentsia
intelli'gibile [intelli'dʒibile] AG intelligible
inteme'rato, -a AG (persona, vita) blameless,
irreproachable; (coscienza) clear; (fama)
unblemished
intempe'rante AG intemperate, immoderate
intempe'ranza [intempe'rantsa] SF
intemperance; **intemperanze** SFPL (eccessi)
excesses
intem'perie SFPL bad weather sg
intempes'tivo, -a AG untimely

inten'dente SM: **~ di Finanza** inland (BRIT) o internal (US) revenue officer

inten'denza [inten'dentsa] SF: **~ di Finanza** inland (BRIT) o internal (US) revenue office

in'tendere /120/ VT (comprendere) to understand; (udire) to hear; (significare) to mean; (avere intenzione): **~ fare qc** to intend o mean to do sth; **intendersi** VPR (conoscere): **intendersi di** to know a lot about, be a connoisseur of; (accordarsi) to get on (well); **intendersi con qn su qc** to come to an agreement with sb about sth; **intendersela con qn** (avere una relazione amorosa) to have an affair with sb; **mi ha dato a ~ che ...** he led me to believe that ...; **non vuole ~ ragione** he won't listen to reason; **s'intende!** naturally!, of course!; **intendiamoci** let's get it quite clear; **ci siamo intesi?** is that clear?, is that understood?

intendi'mento SM (intelligenza) understanding; (proposito) intention

intendi'tore, -'trice SM/F connoisseur, expert; **a buon intenditor poche parole** (proverbio) a word is enough to the wise

intene'rire /55/ VT (fig) to move (to pity); **intenerirsi** VPR (fig) to be moved

intensifi'care /20/ VT, **intensifi'carsi** VPR to intensify

intensità SF intensity; (del vento) force, strength

inten'sivo, -a AG intensive

in'tenso, -a AG (luce, profumo) strong; (colore) intense, deep

inten'tare /72/ VT (Dir): **~ causa contro qn** to start o institute proceedings against sb

inten'tato, -a AG: **non lasciare nulla d'~** to leave no stone unturned, try everything

in'tento, -a AG (teso, assorto): **~ (a)** intent (on), absorbed (in) ▶ SM aim, purpose; **fare qc con l'~ di** to do sth with the intention of; **riuscire nell'~** to achieve one's aim

intenzio'nale [intentsjo'nale] AG intentional; (Dir: omicidio) premeditated; **fallo ~** (Sport) deliberate foul

intenzio'nato, -a [intentsjo'nato] AG: **essere ~ a fare qc** to intend to do sth, have the intention of doing sth; **ben ~** well-meaning, well-intentioned; **mal ~** ill-intentioned

intenzi'one [inten'tsjone] SF intention; (Dir) intent; **avere ~ di fare qc** to intend to do sth, have the intention of doing sth

intera'gire [intera'dʒire] /55/ VI to interact

intera'mente AV entirely, completely

interat'tivo, -a AG interactive

interazi'one [interat'tsjone] SF interaction

interca'lare /72/ SM pet phrase, stock phrase ▶ VT to insert

interca'pedine SF gap, cavity

inter'cedere [inter'tʃɛdere] /29/ VI to intercede

intercessi'one [intertʃes'sjone] SF intercession

intercetta'mento [intertʃetta'mento] SM = **intercettazione**

intercet'tare [intertʃet'tare] /72/ VT to intercept

intercettazi'one [intertʃettat'tsjone] SF: **~ telefonica** telephone tapping

intercity [inter'siti] SM INV (Ferr) ≈ intercity (train)

intercon'nettere /63/ VT to interconnect

inter'correre /28/ VI (esserci) to exist; (passare: tempo) to elapse

inter'corso, -a PP di **intercorrere**

inter'detto, -a PP di **interdire** ▶ AG forbidden, prohibited; (sconcertato) dumbfounded ▶ SM (Rel) interdict; **rimanere ~** to be taken aback

inter'dire /38/ VT to forbid, prohibit, ban; (Rel) to interdict; (Dir) to deprive of civil rights

interdizi'one [interdit'tsjone] SF prohibition, ban

interessa'mento SM interest; (intervento) intervention, good offices pl

interes'sante AG interesting; **essere in stato ~** to be expecting (a baby)

interes'sare /72/ VT to interest; (concernere) to concern, be of interest to; (far intervenire): **~ qn a** to draw sb's attention to ▶ VI: **~ a** to interest, matter to; **interessarsi** VPR (mostrare interesse): **interessarsi a** to take an interest in, be interested in; (occuparsi): **interessarsi di** to take care of; **precipitazioni che interessano le regioni settentrionali** rainfall affecting the north; **si è interessato di farmi avere quei biglietti** he took the trouble to get me those tickets

interes'sato, -a AG (coinvolto) interested, involved; (peg): **essere ~** to act out of pure self-interest ▶ SM/F (coinvolto) person concerned; **a tutti gli interessati** to all those concerned, to all interested parties

inte'resse SM (anche Comm) interest; (tornaconto): **fare qc per ~** to do sth out of self-interest; **~ maturato** (Econ) accrued interest; **~ privato in atti di ufficio** (Amm) abuse of public office

interes'senza [interes'sɛntsa] SF (Econ) profit-sharing

inter'faccia, -ce [inter'fattʃa] SF (Inform) interface; **~ utente** user interface

interfacci'are [interfat'tʃare] /14/ VT (Inform) to interface

interfe'renza [interfe'rɛntsa] SF interference

interfe'rire /55/ VI to interfere

inter'fono SM intercom; (apparecchio) internal phone

interiezi'one [interjet'tsjone] SF exclamation, interjection '**interim** SM INV (*periodo*) interim, interval; (*incarico*) temporary appointment; **ministro ad** ~ acting o interim minister

interi'nale AG: **lavoro** ~ temporary work (*through an agency*); **lavoratore** ~ temporary worker

interi'ora SFPL entrails

interi'ore AG inner *cpd*; **parte** ~ inside

interiorità SF inner being

interioriz'zare [interjorid'dzare] /**72**/ VT to internalize

inter'linea SF (*Dattilografia*) spacing; (*Tip*) leading; **doppia** ~ double spacing

interlocu'tore, -'trice SM/F speaker

interlocu'torio, -a AG interlocutory

inter'ludio SM (*Mus*) interlude

intermedi'ario, -a AG, SM/F intermediary

intermediazi'one [intermedjat'tsjone] SF mediation

inter'medio, -a AG intermediate

inter'mezzo [inter'mɛddzo] SM (*intervallo*) interval; (*breve spettacolo*) intermezzo

intermi'nabile AG interminable, endless

intermit'tente AG intermittent

intermit'tenza [intermit'tɛntsa] SF: **ad** ~ intermittent

interna'mento SM internment; confinement (to a mental hospital)

inter'nare /**72**/ VT (*arrestare*) to intern; (*Med*) to commit (to a mental institution)

inter'nato, -a AG interned; confined (to a mental hospital) ▶ SM/F internee; inmate (of a mental hospital) ▶ SM (*collegio*) boarding school; (*Med*) period as a houseman (*BRIT*) o an intern (*US*)

inter'nauta SMF Internet user

internazio'nale [internattsjo'nale] AG international

'**Internet** ['internet] SF Internet; **in** ~ on the Internet

inter'nista, -i, -e SM/F specialist in internal medicine

in'terno, -a AG (*di dentro*) internal, interior, inner; (: *mare*) inland; (*nazionale*) domestic; (*allievo*) boarding ▶ SM inside, interior; (*di paese*) interior; (*fodera*) lining; (*di appartamento*) flat (*BRIT*) o apartment (*US*) (number); (*Tel*) extension ▶ SM/F (*Ins*) boarder; **interni** SMPL (*Cine*) interior shots; **commissione interna** (*Ins*) internal examination board; **"per uso ~"** (*Med*) "to be taken internally"; **all'**~ inside; **Ministero degli Interni** Ministry of the Interior, ≈ Home Office (*BRIT*), ≈ Department of the Interior (*US*); **notizie dall'**~ (*Stampa*) home news

in'tero, -a AG (*integro, intatto*) whole, entire; (*completo, totale*) complete; (*numero*) whole; (*non ridotto: biglietto*) full; (*latte*) full-cream

interpel'lanza [interpel'lantsa] SF: **presentare un'**~ (*Pol*) to ask a (parliamentary) question; ~ **parlamentare** interpellation

interpel'lare /**72**/ VT to consult; (*Pol*) to question

INTER'POL SIGLA F (= *International Criminal Police Organization*) INTERPOL

inter'porre /**77**/ VT (*influenza*) to use; (*ostacolo*): ~ **qc a qc** to put sth in the way of sth; **interporsi** VPR to intervene; (*Dir*) to appeal; **interporsi fra** (*mettersi in mezzo*) to come between

inter'posto, -a PP *di* **interporre**

interpre'tare /**72**/ VT (*spiegare, tradurre*) to interpret; (*Mus, Teat*) to perform; (*personaggio, sonata*) to play; (*canzone*) to sing

interpretari'ato SM interpreting

interpretazi'one [interpretat'tsjone] SF interpretation

in'terprete SMF interpreter; (*Teat*) actor (actress), performer; (*Mus*) performer; **farsi** ~ **di** to act as a spokesman for

interpunzi'one [interpun'tsjone] SF punctuation; **segni di** ~ punctuation marks

inter'rare /**72**/ VT (*seme, pianta*) to plant; (*tubature ecc*) to lay underground; (*Mil: pezzo d'artiglieria*) to dig in; (*riempire di terra: canale*) to fill in

interregio'nale [interredʒo'nale] SM train that travels between two or more regions of Italy

interro'gare /**80**/ VT to question; (*Ins*) to test

interroga'tivo, -a AG (*occhi, sguardo*) questioning, inquiring; (*Ling*) interrogative ▶ SM question; (*fig*) mystery

interroga'torio, -a AG interrogatory, questioning ▶ SM (*Dir*) questioning *no pl*

interrogazi'one [interrogat'tsjone] SF questioning *no pl*; (*Ins*) oral test; (*Pol*): ~ **(parlamentare)** question

inter'rompere /**97**/ VT to interrupt; (*studi, trattative*) to break off, interrupt; **interrompersi** VPR to break off, stop

inter'rotto, -a PP *di* **interrompere**

interrut'tore SM switch

interruzi'one [interrut'tsjone] SF (*vedi interrompere*) interruption; break; ~ **di gravidanza** termination of pregnancy

interse'care /**20**/ VT, **interse'carsi** VPR to intersect

inter'stizio [inter'stittsjo] SM interstice, crack

interur'bano, -a AG inter-city; (*Tel: chiamata, telefono*) long-distance ▶ SF long-distance call

inter'vallo SM interval; (*spazio*) space, gap; ~ **pubblicitario** (*TV*) commercial break

interve'nire /**128**/ VI (*partecipare*): ~ **a** to take part in; (*intromettersi: anche Pol*) to intervene; (*Med: operare*) to operate

interven'tista, -i, -e AG, SM/F interventionist
inter'vento SM participation; (*intromissione*) intervention; (*Med*) operation; (*breve discorso*) speech; **fare un ~ nel corso di** (*dibattito, programma*) to take part in
interve'nuto, -a PP *di* **intervenire** ▶ SM: **gli intervenuti** those present
inter'vista SF interview
intervis'tare /72/ VT to interview
intervista'tore, -'trice SM/F interviewer
in'teso, -a PP *di* **intendere** ▶ AG agreed ▶ SF understanding; (*accordo*) agreement, understanding; **resta ~ che ...** it is understood that ...; **non darsi per ~ di qc** to take no notice of sth; **uno sguardo d'intesa** a knowing look
in'tessere /1/ VT to weave together; (*fig: trama, storia*) to weave
intes'tare /72/ VT (*lettera*) to address; (*proprietà*): **~ a** to register in the name of; **~ un assegno a qn** to make out a cheque to sb
intesta'tario, -a SM/F holder
intestato, -a AG (*proprietà, casa, conto*) in the name of; (*assegno*) made out to; **carta intestata** headed paper
intestazi'one [intestat'tsjone] SF heading; (*su carta da lettere*) letterhead; (*registrazione*) registration
intesti'nale AG intestinal
intes'tino, -a AG (*lotte*) internal, civil ▶ SM (*Anat*) intestine
intiepi'dire /55/ VT (*riscaldare*) to warm (up); (*raffreddare*) to cool (down); (*fig: amicizia ecc*) to cool; **intiepidirsi** VPR to warm (up); to cool (down); to cool
Inti'fada SF Intifada
intima'mente AV intimately; **sono ~ convinto che ...** I'm firmly *o* deeply convinced that ...; **i due fatti sono ~ connessi** the two events are closely connected
inti'mare /72/ VT to order, command; **~ la resa a qn** (*Mil*) to call upon sb to surrender
intimazi'one [intimat'tsjone] SF order, command
intimida'torio, -a AG threatening
intimidazi'one [intimidat'tsjone] SF intimidation
intimi'dire /55/ VT to intimidate ▶ VI (*anche:* **intimidirsi**) to grow shy
intimità SF intimacy; privacy; (*familiarità*) familiarity
'intimo, -a AG intimate; (*affetti, vita*) private; (*fig: profondo*) inmost ▶ SM (*persona*) intimate *o* close friend; (*dell'animo*) bottom, depths *pl*; **parti intime** (*Anat*) private parts; **rapporti intimi** (*sessuali*) intimate relations
intimo'rire /55/ VT to frighten; **intimorirsi** VPR to become frightened

in'tingere [in'tindʒere] **/37/** VT to dip
in'tingolo SM sauce; (*pietanza*) stew
in'tinto, -a PP *di* **intingere**
intiriz'zire [intirid'dzire] **/55/** VT to numb ▶ VI (*anche:* **intirizzirsi**) to go numb
intiriz'zito, -a [intirid'dzito] AG numb (with cold)
intito'lare /72/ VT to give a title to; (*dedicare*) to dedicate; **intitolarsi** VPR (*libro, film*) to be called
intolle'rabile AG intolerable
intolle'rante AG intolerant
intolle'ranza [intolle'rantsa] SF intolerance
intona'care /20/ VT to plaster
in'tonaco (**intonaci** *o pl* **intonachi**) SM plaster
into'nare /72/ VT (*canto*) to start to sing; (*armonizzare*) to match; **intonarsi** VPR (*colori*) to go together; **intonarsi a** (*carnagione*) to suit; (*abito*) to go with, match
intonazi'one [intonat'tsjone] SF intonation
inton'tire /55/ VT to stun, daze ▶ VI (*anche:* **intontirsi**) to be stunned *o* dazed
inton'tito, -a AG stunned, dazed; **~ dal sonno** stupid with sleep
in'toppo SM stumbling block, obstacle
intorbi'dire /55/ VT (*liquido*) to make turbid; (*mente*) to cloud; **~ le acque** (*fig*) to muddy the waters
in'torno AV around; **~ a** prep (*attorno a*) around; (*riguardo, circa*) about
intorpi'dire /55/ VT to numb; (*fig*) to make sluggish ▶ VI (*anche:* **intorpidirsi**) to grow numb; (: *fig*) to become sluggish
intossi'care /20/ VT to poison
intossicazi'one [intossikat'tsjone] SF poisoning
intradu'cibile [intradu'tʃibile] AG untranslatable
intralci'are [intral'tʃare] **/14/** VT to hamper, hold up
in'tralcio [in'traltʃo] SM hitch
intrallaz'zare [intrallat'tsare] **/72/** VI to intrigue, scheme
intral'lazzo [intral'lattso] SM (*Pol*) intrigue, manoeuvre (*BRIT*), maneuver (*US*); (*traffico losco*) racket
intramon'tabile AG timeless
intramusco'lare AG intramuscular
'Intranet ['intranet] SF Intranet
intransi'gente [intransi'dʒente] AG intransigent, uncompromising
intransi'genza [intransi'dʒentsa] SF intransigence
intransi'tivo, -a AG, SM intransitive
intrappo'lare /72/ VT to trap; **rimanere intrappolato** to be trapped; **farsi ~** to get caught
intrapren'dente AG enterprising, go-ahead; (*con le donne*) forward, bold

intrapren'denza [intrapren'dɛntsa] SF
audacity, initiative; *(con le donne)* boldness

intra'prendere /81/ VT to undertake; *(carriera)*
to embark (up)on

intra'preso, -a PP *di* **intraprendere**

intrat'tabile AG intractable

intratte'nere /121/ VT *(divertire)* to entertain;
(chiacchierando) to engage in conversation;
(rapporti) to have, maintain; **intrattenersi**
VPR to linger; **intrattenersi su qc** to dwell
on sth

intratteni'mento SM entertainment

intrave'dere /127/ VT to catch a glimpse of;
(fig) to foresee

intrecci'are [intret'tʃare] /14/ VT *(capelli)* to
plait, braid; *(intessere: anche fig)* to weave,
interweave, intertwine; **intrecciarsi** VPR to
intertwine, become interwoven; ~ **le mani**
to clasp one's hands; ~ **una relazione
amorosa** *(fig)* to begin an affair

in'treccio [in'trettʃo] SM *(fig: trama)* plot, story

in'trepido, -a AG fearless, intrepid

intri'care /20/ VT *(fili)* to tangle; *(fig: faccenda)*
to complicate; **intricarsi** VPR to become
tangled; to become complicated

in'trico, -chi SM *(anche fig)* tangle

intri'gante AG scheming ▶ SMF schemer,
intriguer

intri'gare /80/ VI to manoeuvre *(BRIT)*,
maneuver *(US)*, scheme

in'trigo, -ghi SM plot, intrigue

in'trinseco, -a, -ci, -che AG intrinsic

in'triso, -a AG: ~ **(di)** soaked (in)

intris'tire /55/ VI *(persona: diventare triste)* to
grow sad; *(pianta)* to wilt

intro'dotto, -a PP *di* **introdurre**

intro'durre /90/ VT to introduce; *(chiave ecc)*:
~ **qc in** to insert sth into; *(persona: far entrare)*
to show in; **introdursi** VPR *(moda, tecniche)* to
be introduced; **introdursi in** *(persona:
penetrare)* to enter; *(: entrare furtivamente)* to
steal *o* slip into

introduzi'one SF introduction

in'troito SM income, revenue

intro'messo, -a PP *di* **intromettersi**

intro'mettersi /63/ VPR to interfere, meddle;
(interporsi) to intervene

intromissi'one SF interference, meddling;
intervention

introspezi'one [introspet'tsjone] SF
introspection

intro'vabile AG *(persona, oggetto)* who *(o* which)
cannot be found; *(libro ecc)* unobtainable

intro'verso, -a AG introverted ▶ SM/F
introvert

intrufo'larsi /72/ VPR: ~ **(in)** *(stanza)* to sneak
(into), slip (into); *(conversazione)* to butt in
(on)

in'truglio [in'truʎʎo] SM concoction

intrusi'one SF intrusion; interference

in'truso, -a SM/F intruder

intu'ire /55/ VT to perceive by intuition;
(rendersi conto) to realize

in'tuito SM intuition; *(perspicacia)*
perspicacity

intuizi'one [intuit'tsjone] SF intuition

inturgi'dire [inturdʒi'dire] /55/ VI,
inturgi'dirsi VPR to swell

inumanità SF INV inhumanity

inu'mano, -a AG inhuman

inu'mare /72/ VT *(seppellire)* to bury, inter

inumazi'one [inumat'tsjone] SF burial,
interment

inumi'dire /55/ VT to dampen, moisten;
inumidirsi VPR to become damp *o* wet

inurba'mento SM urbanization

inusi'tato, -a AG unusual

i'nutile AG useless; *(superfluo)* pointless,
unnecessary; **è stato tutto ~!** it was all in
vain!

inutilità SF uselessness; pointlessness

inutiliz'zabile [inutilid'dzabile] AG unusable

inutil'mente AV *(senza risultato)* in vain;
(senza utilità, scopo) unnecessarily, needlessly;
l'ho cercato ~ I looked for him in vain; **ti
preoccupi ~** there's nothing for you to
worry about, there's no need for you to
worry

inva'dente AG *(fig)* interfering, nosey

inva'denza [inva'dɛntsa] SF intrusiveness

in'vadere /52/ VT to invade; *(affollare)* to
swarm into, overrun; *(acque)* to flood

invadi'trice [invadi'tritʃe] AG F *vedi* **invasore**

inva'ghirsi [inva'girsi] /55/ VPR: ~ **di** to take a
fancy to

invali'cabile AG *(montagna)* impassable

invali'dare /72/ VT to invalidate

invalidità SF infirmity; disability; *(Dir)*
invalidity

in'valido, -a AG *(infermo)* infirm, invalid; *(al
lavoro)* disabled; *(Dir: nullo)* invalid ▶ SM/F
invalid; disabled person; ~ **di guerra**
disabled ex-serviceman; ~ **del lavoro**
industrially disabled person

in'valso, -a AG *(diffuso)* established

in'vano AV in vain

invari'abile AG invariable

invari'ato, -a AG unchanged

inva'sare /72/ VT *(pianta)* to pot

inva'sato, -a AG possessed (by the devil)
▶ SM/F person possessed by the devil; **urlare
come un ~** to shout like a madman

invasi'one SF invasion

in'vaso, -a PP *di* **invadere**

inva'sore, invadi'trice [invadi'tritʃe] AG
invading ▶ SMF invader

invecchia'mento [invekkja'mento] SM
growing old; ageing; **questo whisky ha**

un ~ di 12 anni this whisky has been matured for 12 years

invecchi'are [invek'kjare] /**19**/ VI (*persona*) to grow old; (*vino, popolazione*) to age; (*moda*) to become dated ▶ VT to age; (*far apparire più vecchio*) to make look older; **lo trovo invecchiato** I find he has aged

in'vece [in'vetʃe] AV instead; (*al contrario*) on the contrary; **~ di** *prep* instead of

inve'ire /**55**/ VI: **~ contro** to rail against

invele'nire /**55**/ VT to embitter; **invelenirsi** VPR to become bitter

inven'duto, -a AG unsold

inven'tare /**72**/ VT to invent; (*pericoli, pettegolezzi*) to make up, invent

inventari'are /**19**/ VT to make an inventory of, inventory

inven'tario SM inventory; (*Comm*) stocktaking *no pl*

inven'tivo, -a AG inventive ▶ SF inventiveness

inven'tore, -'trice SM/F inventor

invenzi'one [inven'tsjone] SF invention; (*bugia*) lie, story

invere'condia SF shamelessness, immodesty

inver'nale AG winter *cpd*; (*simile all'inverno*) wintry

in'verno SM winter; **d'~** in (the) winter

invero'simile AG unlikely ▶ SM: **ha dell'~** it's hard to believe, it's incredible

inversi'one SF inversion; reversal; **"divieto d'~"** (*Aut*) "no U-turns"

in'verso, -a AG opposite; (*Mat*) inverse ▶ SM contrary, opposite; **in senso ~** in the opposite direction; **in ordine ~** in reverse order

inverte'brato, -a AG, SM invertebrate

inver'tire /**45**/ VT to invert, reverse; (*disposizione, posti*) to change; (*ruoli*) to exchange; **~ la marcia** (*Aut*) to do a U-turn; **~ la rotta** (*Naut*) to go about; (*fig*) to do a U-turn

inver'tito, -a SM/F homosexual

investi'gare /**80**/ VT, VI to investigate

investiga'tivo, -a AG: **squadra investigativa** detective squad

investiga'tore, -'trice SM/F investigator, detective; **~ privato** private investigator

investigazi'one [investigat'tsjone] SF investigation, inquiry

investi'mento SM (*Econ*) investment; (*di veicolo*) crash, collision; (*di pedone*) knocking down

inves'tire /**45**/ VT (*denaro*) to invest; (*veicolo: pedone*) to knock down; (: *altro veicolo*) to crash into; (*apostrofare*) to assail; (*incaricare*): **~ qn di** to invest sb with; **investirsi** VPR (*fig*): **investirsi di una parte** to enter thoroughly into a role

investi'tore, -'trice SM/F driver responsible for an accident

investi'tura SF investiture

invete'rato, -a AG inveterate

invet'tiva SF invective

invi'are /**60**/ VT to send

invi'ato, -a SM/F envoy; (*Stampa*) correspondent; **~ speciale** (*Pol*) special envoy; (*di giornale*) special correspondent

in'vidia SF envy; **fare ~ a qn** to make sb envious

invidi'abile AG enviable

invidi'are /**19**/ VT: **~ qn (per qc)** to envy sb (for sth); **~ qc a qn** to envy sb sth; **non aver nulla da ~ a nessuno** to be as good as the next one

invidi'oso, -a AG envious

invin'cibile [invin'tʃibile] AG invincible

in'vio, -'vii SM sending; (*insieme di merci*) consignment; (*tasto*) Return (key), Enter (key)

invio'labile AG inviolable

invio'lato, -a AG (*diritto, segreto*) inviolate; (*foresta*) virgin *cpd*; (*montagna, vetta*) unscaled

invipe'rire /**55**/ VI, **invipe'rirsi** VPR to become furious, fly into a temper

invipe'rito, -a AG furious

invis'chiare [invis'kjare] /**19**/ VT (*fig*): **~ qn in qc** to involve sb in sth, mix sb up in sth; **invischiarsi** VPR: **invischiarsi (con qn/in qc)** to get mixed up *o* involved (with sb/in sth)

invi'sibile AG invisible

in'viso, -a AG: **~ a** unpopular with

invi'tante AG (*proposta, odorino*) inviting; (*sorriso*) appealing, attractive

invi'tare /**72**/ VT to invite; **~ qn a fare** to invite sb to do

invi'tato, -a SM/F guest

in'vito SM invitation; **dietro ~ del sig. Rossi** at Mr Rossi's invitation

invo'care /**20**/ VT (*chiedere: aiuto, pace*) to cry out for; (*appellarsi: la legge, Dio*) to appeal to, invoke

invogli'are [invoʎ'ʎare] /**27**/ VT: **~ qn a fare** to tempt sb to do, induce sb to do

involon'tario, -a AG (*errore*) unintentional; (*gesto*) involuntary

invol'tino SM (*Cuc*) roulade

in'volto SM (*pacco*) parcel; (*fagotto*) bundle

in'volucro SM cover, wrapping

involu'tivo, -a AG: **subire un processo ~** to regress

invo'luto, -a AG involved, intricate

involuzi'one [involut'tsjone] SF (*di stile*) convolutedness; (*regresso*): **subire un'~** to regress

invulne'rabile AG invulnerable

inzacche'rare [intsakke'rare] /**72**/ VT to spatter with mud; **inzaccherarsi** VPR to get muddy

inzup'pare [intsup'pare] /**72**/ VT to soak; **inzupparsi** VPR to get soaked; **inzuppò i biscotti nel latte** he dipped the biscuits in the milk

'io PRON I ▸ SM INV: **l'io** the ego, the self; **io stesso(a)** I myself; **sono io** it's me

i'odio SM iodine

i'ogurt SM INV = **yogurt**

i'one SM ion

I'onio SM: **lo ~**, **il mar ~** the Ionian (Sea)

ionizza'tore [joniddza'tore] SM ioniser

'iosa: **a ~** AV in abundance, in great quantity

'IPAB SIGLA FPL (= *Istituzioni pubbliche di Assistenza e Beneficenza*) charitable institutions

iPad® [ai'pad] SM INV iPad®

i'perbole SF (*Letteratura*) hyperbole; (*Mat*) hyperbola

iper'bolico, -a, -ci, -che AG (*Letteratura, Mat*) hyperbolic(al); (*fig: esagerato*) exaggerated

ipermer'cato SM hypermarket

ipersen'sibile AG (*persona*) hypersensitive; (*Fot: lastra, pellicola*) hypersensitized

ipertecno'logico, -a, -ci, -che [ipertekno'lɔdʒiko] AG hi-tech

ipertensi'one SF high blood pressure, hypertension

iper'testo SM hypertext

ipertestu'ale AG (*Inform*): **collegamento o link ~** hyperlink

iPhone® [ai'fon] SM INV iPhone®

ip'nosi SF hypnosis

ip'notico, -a, -ci, -che AG hypnotic

ipno'tismo SM hypnotism

ipnotiz'zare [ipnotid'dzare] /**72**/ VT to hypnotize

ipoaller'genico, -a, -ci, -che [ipoaller'dʒɛniko] AG hypoallergenic

ipocon'dria SF hypochondria

ipocon'driaco, -a, -ci, -che AG, SM/F hypochondriac

ipocri'sia SF hypocrisy

i'pocrita, -i, -e AG hypocritical ▸ SM/F hypocrite

ipo'sodico, -a, -ci, -che AG low sodium *cpd*

ipo'teca, -che SF mortgage

ipote'care /**20**/ VT to mortgage

ipote'nusa SF hypotenuse

i'potesi SF INV hypothesis; **facciamo l'~ che ...**, **ammettiamo per ~ che ...** let's suppose o assume that ...; **nella peggiore/migliore delle ~** at worst/best; **nell'~ che venga** should he come, if he comes; **se per ~ io partissi ...** just supposing I were to leave ....

ipo'tetico, -a, -ci, -che AG hypothetical

ipotiz'zare [ipotid'dzare] /**72**/ VT: **~ che** to form the hypothesis that

'ippico, -a, -ci, -che AG horse *cpd* ▸ SF horseracing

ippocas'tano SM horse chestnut

ip'podromo SM racecourse

ippo'potamo SM hippopotamus

'ipsilon SM O F INV (*lettera*) Y, y; (: *dell'alfabeto greco*) epsilon

IP'SOA SIGLA M (= *Istituto Post-Universitario per lo Studio dell'Organizzazione Aziendale*) postgraduate institute of business administration

IR ABBR (*Ferr*: = *Interregionale*) long distance train which stops frequently

IRA SIGLA F (= *Irish Republican Army*) IRA

'ira SF anger, wrath

ira'cheno, -a [ira'kɛno] AG, SM/F Iraqi

I'ran SM: **l'~** Iran

irani'ano, -a AG, SM/F Iranian

I'raq SM: **l'~** Iraq

iras'cibile [iraʃ'ʃibile] AG quick-tempered

'IRCE ['irtʃe] SIGLA M = **Istituto per le relazioni culturali con l'Estero**

'IRI SIGLA M (= *Istituto per la Ricostruzione Industriale*) state-controlled industrial investment office

'iride SF (*arcobaleno*) rainbow; (*Anat, Bot*) iris

'iris SM INV iris

Ir'landa SF: **l'~** Ireland; **l'~ del Nord** Northern Ireland, Ulster; **la Repubblica d'~** Eire, the Republic of Ireland; **il mar d'~** the Irish Sea

irlan'dese AG Irish ▸ SM F Irishman(-woman); **gli Irlandesi** the Irish

iro'nia SF irony

i'ronico, -a, -ci, -che AG ironic(al)

ironiz'zare [ironid'dzare] /**72**/ VT, VI: **~ su** to be ironical about

i'roso, -a AG (*sguardo, tono*) angry, wrathful; (*persona*) irascible

'IRPEF SIGLA F = **imposta sul reddito delle persone fisiche**

ir'pino, -a AG of (o from) Irpinia

irradi'are /**19**/ VT to radiate; (*raggi di luce: illuminare*) to shine on ▸ VI (*diffondersi: anche*: **irradiarsi**) to radiate

irradiazi'one [irradjat'tsjone] SF radiation

irraggiun'gibile [irraddʒun'dʒibile] AG unreachable; (*fig: meta*) unattainable

irragio'nevole [irradʒo'nevole] AG (*privo di ragione*) irrational; (*fig: persona, pretese, prezzo*) unreasonable

irrazio'nale [irrattsjo'nale] AG irrational

irre'ale AG unreal

irrealiz'zabile [irrealid'dzabile] AG (*sogno, desiderio*) unattainable, unrealizable; (*progetto*) unworkable, impracticable

irrealtà SF unreality

irrecupe'rabile AG (*gen*) irretrievable; (*fig: persona*) irredeemable

irrecu'sabile AG (*offerta*) not to be refused; (*prova*) irrefutable

irreden'tista, -i, -e AG, SM/F (*Storia*) Irredentist

irrefre'nabile AG uncontrollable
irrefu'tabile AG irrefutable
irrego'lare AG irregular; (*terreno*) uneven
irregolarità SF INV irregularity; unevenness *no pl*
irremo'vibile AG (*fig*) unshakeable, unyielding
irrepa'rabile AG irreparable; (*fig*) inevitable
irrepe'ribile AG nowhere to be found
irrepren'sibile AG irreproachable
irrequi'eto, -a AG restless
irresis'tibile AG irresistible
irreso'luto, -a AG irresolute
irrespi'rabile AG (*aria*) unbreathable; (*fig: opprimente*) stifling, oppressive; (: *malsano*) unhealthy
irrespon'sabile AG irresponsible
irrestrin'gibile [irrestrin'dʒibile] AG unshrinkable, non-shrink (BRIT)
irre'tire /55/ VT to seduce
irrever'sibile AG irreversible
irrevo'cabile AG irrevocable
irricono'scibile [irrikonoʃʃibile] AG unrecognizable
irridu'cibile [irridu'tʃibile] AG irreducible; (*fig*) unshakeable
irrifles'sivo, -a AG thoughtless
irri'gare /80/ VT (*annaffiare*) to irrigate; (*fiume ecc*) to flow through
irrigazi'one [irrigat'tsjone] SF irrigation
irrigidi'mento [irridʒidi'mento] SM stiffening; hardening; tightening
irrigi'dire [irridʒi'dire] **/55/** VT to stiffen; (*disciplina*) to tighten; **irrigidirsi** VPR to stiffen; (*posizione, atteggiamento*) to harden
irriguar'doso, -a AG disrespectful
irrile'vante AG (*trascurabile*) insignificant
irrimedi'abile AG: **un errore ~** a mistake which cannot be rectified; **non è ~!** we can do something about it!
irrinunci'abile [irrinun'tʃabile] AG vital; which cannot be abandoned
irripe'tibile AG unrepeatable
irri'solto, -a AG (*problema*) unresolved
irri'sorio, -a AG derisory
irrispet'toso, -a AG disrespectful
irri'tabile AG irritable
irri'tante AG (*atteggiamento*) irritating, annoying; (*Med*) irritant
irri'tare /72/ VT (*mettere di malumore*) to irritate, annoy; (*Med*) to irritate; **irritarsi** VPR (*stizzirsi*) to become irritated *o* annoyed; (*Med*) to become irritated
irritazi'one [irritat'tsjone] SF irritation; annoyance
irrive'rente AG irreverent
irrobus'tire /55/ VT (*persona*) to make stronger, make more robust; (*muscoli*) to strengthen; **irrobustirsi** VPR to become stronger

ir'rompere /97/ VI: **~ in** to burst into
irro'rare /72/ VT to sprinkle; (*Agr*) to spray
ir'rotto, -a PP *di* **irrompere**
irru'ente AG (*fig*) impetuous, violent
irru'enza [irru'ɛntsa] SF impetuousness; **con ~** impetuously
ir'ruppi *etc* VB *vedi* **irrompere**
irruvi'dire /55/ VT to roughen ▶ VI (*anche*: **irruvidirsi**) to become rough
irruzi'one [irrut'tsjone] SF: **fare ~ in** to burst into; (*polizia*) to raid
ir'suto, -a AG (*petto*) hairy; (*barba*) bristly
'irto, -a AG bristly; **~ di** bristling with
Is. ABBR (= *isola*) I
ISBN ABBR (= *International Standard Book Number*) ISBN
is'crissi *etc* VB *vedi* **iscrivere**
is'critto, -a PP *di* **iscrivere** ▶ SM/F member; **gli iscritti alla gara** the competitors; **per** *o* **in ~** in writing
is'crivere /105/ VT to register, enter; (*persona*): **~ (a)** to register (in), enrol (in); **iscriversi** VPR: **iscriversi (a)** (*club, partito*) to join; (*università*) to register *o* enrol (at); (*esame, concorso*) to register *o* enter (for)
iscrizi'one [iskrit'tsjone] SF (*epigrafe ecc*) inscription; (*a scuola, società ecc*) enrolment, registration; (*registrazione*) registration
'ISEF SIGLA M = **Istituto Superiore di Educazione Fisica**
Is'lam SM: **l'~** Islam
is'lamico, -a, -ci, -che AG Islamic
Is'landa SF: **l'~** Iceland
islan'dese AG Icelandic ▶ SMF Icelander ▶ SM (*Ling*) Icelandic
'isola SF island; **~ pedonale** (*Aut*) pedestrian precinct
isola'mento SM isolation; (*Tecn*) insulation; **essere in cella di ~** to be in solitary confinement; **~ acustico** soundproofing; **~ termico** thermal insulation
iso'lano, -a AG island *cpd* ▶ SM/F islander
iso'lante AG insulating ▶ SM insulator
iso'lare /72/ VT to isolate; (*Tecn*) to insulate; (: *acusticamente*) to soundproof; **isolarsi** VPR to isolate o.s.
iso'lato, -a AG isolated; insulated ▶ SM (*edificio*) block
isolazio'nismo [isolattsjo'nismo] SM isolationism
i'sotopo SM isotope
ispessi'mento SM thickening
ispes'sire /55/ VT to thicken; **ispessirsi** VPR to get thicker, thicken
ispetto'rato SM inspectorate
ispet'tore, -'trice SM/F inspector; (*Comm*) supervisor; **~ di zona** (*Comm*) area supervisor *o* manager; **~ di reparto** shop walker (BRIT), floor walker (US)

ispezio'nare [ispettsjo'nare] /**72**/ vt to inspect

ispezi'one [ispet'tsjone] sf inspection

'**ispido, -a** ag bristly, shaggy

ispi'rare /**72**/ vt to inspire; **ispirarsi** vpr: **ispirarsi a** to draw one's inspiration from; (*conformarsi*) to be based on; **l'idea m'ispira** the idea appeals to me

ispira'tore, -'trice ag inspiring ▸ sm/f inspirer; (*di ribellione*) instigator

ispirazi'one [ispirat'tsjone] sf inspiration; **secondo l'~ del momento** according to the mood of the moment

Isra'ele sm: **l'~** Israel

israeli'ano, -a ag, sm/f Israeli

israe'lita, -i, -e sm/f Jew (Jewess); (*Storia*) Israelite

israe'litico, -a, -ci, -che ag Jewish

is'sare /**72**/ vt to hoist; **~ l'ancora** to weigh anchor

'**Istanbul** sf Istanbul

istan'taneo, -a ag instantaneous ▸ sf (*Fot*) snapshot

is'tante sm instant, moment; **all'~, sull'~** instantly, immediately

is'tanza [is'tantsa] sf petition, request; **giudice di prima ~** (*Dir*) judge of the court of first instance; **giudizio di seconda ~** judgment on appeal; **in ultima ~** (*fig*) finally; **~ di divorzio** petition for divorce

'**ISTAT** sigla m = **Istituto Centrale di Statistica**

'**ISTEL** sigla f = **Indagine sull'ascolto delle televisioni in Italia**

is'terico, -a, -ci, -che ag hysterical

isteri'lire /**55**/ vt (*terreno*) to render infertile; (*fig: fantasia*) to dry up; **isterilirsi** vpr to become infertile; to dry up

iste'rismo sm hysteria

isti'gare /**80**/ vt to incite

istigazi'one [istigat'tsjone] sf instigation; **~ a delinquere** (*Dir*) incitement to crime

istin'tivo, -a ag instinctive

is'tinto sm instinct

istitu'ire /**55**/ vt (*fondare*) to institute, found; (*porre: confronto*) to establish; (*intraprendere: inchiesta*) to set up

isti'tuto sm institute; (*di università*) department; (*ente, Dir*) institution; **~ di bellezza** beauty salon; **~ di credito** bank, banking institution; **~ di ricerca** research institute; **~ tecnico commerciale** ≈ commercial college; **~ tecnico industriale statale** ≈ technical college

istitu'tore, -'trice sm/f (*fondatore*) founder; (*precettore*) tutor, governess

istituzi'one [istitut'tsjone] sf institution; **istituzioni** sfpl (*Dir*) institutes; **lotta alle istituzioni** struggle against the Establishment

'**istmo** sm (*Geo*) isthmus

isto'gramma, -i sm histogram

istra'dare /**72**/ vt (*fig: persona*): **~ (a/verso)** to direct (to/towards)

istri'ano, -a ag, sm/f Istrian

'**istrice** ['istritʃe] sm porcupine

istri'one sm (*peg*) ham (actor)

istru'ire /**55**/ vt (*insegnare*) to teach; (*ammaestrare*) to train; (*informare*) to instruct, inform; (*Dir*) to prepare

istru'ito, -a ag educated

istrut'tivo, -a ag instructive

istrut'tore, -'trice sm/f instructor ▸ ag: **giudice ~** examining (*Brit*) o committing (*US*) magistrate

istrut'toria sf (*Dir*) (preliminary) investigation and hearing; **formalizzare un'~** to proceed to a formal hearing

istruzi'one [istrut'tsjone] sf (*gen*) training; (*Ins, cultura*) education; (*direttiva*) instruction; (*Dir*) = **istruttoria**; **istruzioni** sfpl (*norme*) instructions; **Ministero della Pubblica I~** Ministry of Education; **istruzioni di spedizione** forwarding instructions; **istruzioni per l'uso** instructions (for use); **~ obbligatoria** (*Ins*) compulsory education

istupi'dire /**55**/ vt (*colpo*) to stun, daze; (*droga, stanchezza*) to stupefy; **istupidirsi** vpr to become stupid

'**ISVE** sigla m (= *Istituto di Studi per lo Sviluppo Economico*) *institute for research into economic development*

I'talia sf: **l'~** Italy

itali'ano, -a ag Italian ▸ sm/f Italian ▸ sm (*Ling*) Italian; **gli Italiani** the Italians

ITC sigla m = **istituto tecnico commerciale**

'**iter** sm passage, course; **l'~ burocratico** the bureaucratic process

itine'rante ag wandering, itinerant; **mostra ~** touring exhibition; **spettacolo ~** travelling (*Brit*) o traveling (*US*) show, touring show

itine'rario sm itinerary

'**ITIS** sigla m = **istituto tecnico industriale statale**

itte'rizia [itte'rittsja] sf (*Med*) jaundice

'**ittico, -a, -ci, -che** ag fish *cpd*; fishing *cpd*

IUD sigla m inv (= *intra-uterine device*) IUD

Iugos'lavia sf = **Jugoslavia**

iugos'lavo, -a ag, sm/f = **jugoslavo**

i'uta sf jute

'**I.V.A.** sigla f (= *imposta sul valore aggiunto*) VAT

'**ivi** av (*formale, poetico*) therein; (*nelle citazioni*) ibid

Jj

J, j [iˈlunga] SM O F INV (*lettera*) J, j;
J come Jersey ≈ J for Jack (BRIT),
J for Jig (US)

jazz [dʒaz] SM jazz

jazˈzista, -i [dʒadˈdzista] SM jazz player

jeans [dʒinz] SMPL jeans

jeep® [dʒip] SF INV jeep

ˈjersey [ˈdʒɛrzi] SM INV jersey (cloth)

ˈjockey [ˈdʒɔki] SM INV (*Carte*) jack; (*fantino*)
jockey

ˈjogging [ˈdʒɔɡiŋ] SM jogging; **fare ~**
to go jogging

ˈjolly [ˈdʒɔli] SM INV joker

joysˈtick [dʒoisˈtik] SM INV joystick

jr. ABBR (= *junior*) Jr., jr.

juˈdo [dʒuˈdɔ] SM judo

Jugosˈlavia [jugozˈlavja] SF (*Storia*): **la ~**
Yugoslavia; **la ex-~** former Yugoslavia

jugosˈlavo, -a AG, SM/F (*Storia*) Yugoslav(ian)

ˈjuke ˈbox [ˈdʒukˈbɔks] SM INV jukebox

Kk

K, k ['kappa] SM O F INV (*lettera*) K, k ▶ABBR
 (= *kilo-, chilo-*) k; (*Inform*) K; **K come Kursaal**
 ≈ K for King
kami'kaze [kami'kaddze] SM INV kamikaze
Kam'pala SF Kampala
kara'oke [kara'oke] SM INV karaoke
karatè [kara'tɛ] SM karate
'Kashmir ['kaʃmir] SM: **il** ~ Kashmir
ka'yak [ka'jak] SM INV kayak
Ka'zakistan [ka'dzakistan] SM
 Kazakhstan
ka'zako, -a [ka'dzako] AG, SM/F Kazakh
'Kenia ['kenja] SM: **il** ~ Kenya
keni'ano, -a AG, SM/F Kenyan
keni'ota, -i, -e AG, SM/F Kenyan
'Kenya ['kenja] SM: **il** ~ Kenya
kero'sene [kero'zɛne] SM = **cherosene**
kg ABBR (= *chilogrammo*) kg
kib'butz [kib'buts] SM INV kibbutz
Kilimangi'aro [kiliman'dʒaro] SM: **il** ~
 Kilimanjaro

'killer ['killer] SM INV gunman, hired gun
'kilo = **chilo** *ecc*
kilt [kilt] SM INV kilt
ki'mono [ki'mɔno] SM = **chimono**
Kindle® ['kindœl] SM INV Kindle®
kir'ghiso, -a [kir'gizo] AG, SM/F Kyrgyz
Kir'ghizistan [kir'gidzistan] SM Kyrgyzstan
kitsch [kitʃ] SM kitsch
'kiwi ['kiwi] SM INV kiwi (fruit)
km ABBR (= *chilometro*) km
kmq ABBR (= *chilometro quadrato*) km²
K.'O. [kappa'o] SM INV knockout
ko'ala [ko'ala] SM INV koala (bear)
koso'varo, -a AG, SM/F Kosovan
'Kosovo SM Kosovo
KR SIGLA = **Crotone**
'krapfen ['krapfən] (*Cuc*) SM INV doughnut
Ku'ala Lum'par SF Kuala Lumpur
Ku'wait [ku'vait] SM: **il** ~ Kuwait
kW ABBR (= *kilowatt, chilowatt*) kW
kWh ABBR (= *kilowattora*) kW/h

L l

L, l ['ɛlle] SM O F INV (*lettera*) L, l ► ABBR (= *lira*) L; **L come Livorno** ≈ L for Lucy (*BRIT*), L for Love (*US*)
l ABBR (= *litro*) l
l' DET *vedi* **la**; **lo**
la DET F (*dav V* **l'**) the ► PRON (*dav V* **l'**: *oggetto: persona*) her; (: *cosa*) it; (: *forma di cortesia*) you ► SM INV (*Mus*) A; (: *solfeggiando la scala*) la; *vedi anche* **il**
là AV there; **di là** (*da quel luogo*) from there; (*in quel luogo*) in there; (*dall'altra parte*) over there; **di là di** beyond; **per di là** that way; **più in là** further on; (*tempo*) later on; **fatti in là** move up; **là dentro/sopra/sotto** in/up o on/under there; **là per là** (*sul momento*) there and then; **essere in là con gli anni** to be getting on (in years); **essere più di là che di qua** to be more dead than alive; **va' là!** come off it!; **stavolta è andato troppo in là** this time he's gone too far; *vedi anche* **quello**
'labbro SM (*Anat: pl(f)* **labbra**) lip
'labile AG fleeting, ephemeral
labi'rinto SM labyrinth, maze
labora'torio SM (*di ricerca*) laboratory; (*di arti, mestieri*) workshop; **~ linguistico** language laboratory
labori'oso, -a AG (*faticoso*) laborious; (*attivo*) hard-working
labu'rista, -i, -e AG Labour *cpd* (*BRIT*) ► SM/F Labour Party member (*BRIT*)
'lacca, -che SF lacquer; (*per unghie*) nail varnish (*BRIT*), nail polish
lac'care /20/ VT (*mobili*) to varnish, lacquer
'laccio ['lattʃo] SM noose; (*legaccio, tirante*) lasso; (*di scarpa*) lace; **~ emostatico** (*Med*) tourniquet
lace'rante [latʃe'rante] AG (*suono*) piercing, shrill
lace'rare [latʃe'rare] /72/ VT to tear to shreds, lacerate; **lacerarsi** VPR to tear
lacerazi'one [latʃerat'tsjone] SF (*anche Med*) tear
'lacero, -a ['latʃero] AG (*logoro*) torn, tattered; (*Med*) lacerated; **ferita ~-contusa** injury with lacerations and bruising

la'conico, -a, -ci, -che AG laconic, brief
'lacrima SF tear; (*goccia*) drop; **in lacrime** in tears
lacri'mare /72/ VI to water
lacri'mevole AG heartrending, pitiful
lacri'mogeno, -a [lakri'mɔdʒeno] AG: **gas ~** tear gas
lacri'moso, -a AG tearful
la'cuna SF (*fig*) gap
la'custre AG lake *cpd*
lad'dove CONG whereas
'ladro SM thief; **al ~!** stop thief!
ladro'cinio [ladro'tʃinjo] SM theft, robbery
la'druncolo, -a SM/F petty thief
laggiù [lad'dʒu] AV down there; (*di là*) over there
'lagna ['laɲɲa] SF (*col: persona, cosa*) drag, bore; **fare la ~** to whine, moan
la'gnanza [laɲ'ɲantsa] SF complaint
la'gnarsi [laɲ'ɲarsi] /15/ VPR: **~ (di)** to complain (about)
'lago, -ghi SM lake
'Lagos ['lagos] SF Lagos
'lagrima *etc* = **lacrima** *ecc*
la'guna SF lagoon
lagu'nare AG lagoon *cpd*
'laico, -a, -ci, -che AG (*apostolato*) lay; (*vita*) secular; (*scuola*) non-denominational ► SM/F layman(-woman) ► SM lay brother
'laido, -a AG filthy, foul; (*fig: osceno*) obscene, filthy
'lama SF blade ► SM INV (*Zool*) llama; (*Rel*) lama
lambic'care /20/ VT to distil; **lambiccarsi il cervello** to rack one's brains
lam'bire /55/ VT (*fig: fiamme*) to lick; (*acqua*) to lap
lam'bretta® SF scooter
la'mella SF (*di metallo ecc*) thin sheet, thin strip; (*di fungo*) gill
lamen'tare /72/ VT to lament; **lamentarsi** VPR (*emettere lamenti*) to moan, groan; (*rammaricarsi*) **lamentarsi (di)** to complain (about)

lamen'tela SF complaining *no pl*
lamen'tevole AG (*voce*) complaining,
plaintive; (*stato*) lamentable, pitiful
la'mento SM moan, groan; (*per la morte di qn*)
lament
lamen'toso, -a AG plaintive
la'metta SF razor blade
lami'era SF sheet metal
'lamina SF (*lastra sottile*) thin sheet (*o* layer *o*
plate); **~ d'oro** gold leaf; gold foil
lami'nare /72/ VT to laminate
lami'nato, -a AG laminated; (*tessuto*) lamé
▶ SM laminate
'lampada SF lamp; **~ a petrolio/a gas** oil/gas
lamp; **~ a spirito** blowlamp (BRIT),
blowtorch; **~ a stelo** standard lamp (BRIT),
floor lamp; **~ da tavolo** table lamp
lampa'dario SM chandelier
lampa'dina SF light bulb; **~ tascabile** pocket
torch (BRIT), flashlight (US)
lam'pante AG (*fig: evidente*) crystal clear,
evident
lam'para SF fishing lamp; (*barca*) boat for
fishing by lamplight (*in Mediterranean*)
lampeggi'are [lamped'dʒare] /62/ VI (*luce,
fari*) to flash ▶ VB IMPERS: **lampeggia** there's
lightning
lampeggia'tore [lampeddʒa'tore] SM (*Aut*)
indicator
lampi'one SM street light *o* lamp (BRIT)
'lampo SM (*Meteor*) flash of lightning; (*di luce,
fig*) flash ▶ AG INV: **cerniera ~** zip (fastener)
(BRIT), zipper (US); **guerra ~** blitzkrieg;
lampi SMPL (*Meteor*) lightning *no pl*; **passare
come un ~** to flash past *o* by
lam'pone SM raspberry
'lana SF wool; **~ d'acciaio** steel wool; **pura ~
vergine** pure new wool; **~ di vetro** glass
wool
lan'cetta [lan'tʃetta] SF (*indice*) pointer,
needle; (*di orologio*) hand
'lancia, -ce ['lantʃa] SF (*arma*) lance; (: *picca*)
spear; (*di pompa antincendio*) nozzle;
(*imbarcazione*) launch; **partire ~ in resta** (*fig*)
to set off ready for battle; **spezzare una ~ in
favore di qn** (*fig*) to come to sb's defence;
~ di salvataggio lifeboat
lancia'bombe [lantʃa'bombe] SM INV (*Mil*)
mortar
lanciafi'amme [lantʃa'fjamme] SM INV
flamethrower
lancia'missili [lantʃa'missili] AG INV
missile-launching ▶ SM INV missile
launcher
lancia'razzi [lantʃa'raddzi] AG INV rocket-
launching ▶ SM INV rocket launcher
lanci'are [lan'tʃare] /14/ VT to throw, hurl,
fling; (*Sport*) to throw; (*far partire: automobile*)
to get up to full speed; (*bombe*) to drop; (*razzo,

prodotto, moda) to launch; (*emettere: grido*) to
give out; **lanciarsi** VPR: **lanciarsi contro/su**
to throw *o* hurl *o* fling o.s. against/on;
lanciarsi in (*fig*) to embark on; **~ un cavallo**
to give a horse his head; **~ il disco** (*Sport*) to
throw the discus; **~ il peso** (*Sport*) to put the
shot; **lanciarsi all'inseguimento di qn** to
set off in pursuit of sb; **lanciarsi col
paracadute** to parachute
lanci'ato, -a [lan'tʃato] AG (*affermato: attore,
prodotto*) well-known, famous; (: *veicolo*)
speeding along, racing along
lanci'nante [lantʃi'nante] AG (*dolore*)
shooting, throbbing; (*grido*) piercing
'lancio ['lantʃo] SM throwing *no pl*; throw;
dropping *no pl*; drop; launching *no pl*;
launch; **~ del disco** (*Sport*) throwing the
discus; **~ del peso** (*Sport*) putting the shot
'landa SF (*Geo*) moor
'languido, -a AG (*fiacco*) languid, weak;
(*tenero, malinconico*) languishing
langu'ire /17/ VI to languish; (*conversazione*)
to flag
langu'ore SM weakness, languor
lani'ero, -a AG wool *cpd*, woollen (BRIT),
woolen (US)
lani'ficio [lani'fitʃo] SM woollen (BRIT) *o*
woolen (US) mill
lano'lina SF lanolin(e)
la'noso, -a AG woolly
lan'terna SF lantern; (*faro*) lighthouse
lanter'nino SM: **cercarsele col ~** to be asking
for trouble
la'nugine [la'nudʒine] SF down
'Laos SM Laos
lapalissi'ano, -a AG self-evident
La 'Paz [la'pas] SF La Paz
lapi'dare /72/ VT to stone
lapi'dario, -a AG (*fig*) terse
'lapide SF (*di sepolcro*) tombstone;
(*commemorativa*) plaque
la'pin [la'pɛ̃] SM INV coney
'lapis SM INV pencil
lap'pone AG, SMF, SM Lapp
Lap'ponia SF: **la ~** Lapland
'lapsus SM INV slip
laptop ['læp tɔp] SM INV laptop (computer)
'lardo SM bacon fat, lard
lar'ghezza [lar'gettsa] SF width; breadth;
looseness; generosity; **~ di vedute**
broad-mindedness
lar'gire [lar'dʒire] /55/ VT to give generously
'largo, -a, -ghi, -ghe AG wide; broad;
(*maniche*) wide; (*abito: troppo ampio*) loose; (*fig*)
generous ▶ SM width; breadth; (*mare aperto*):
il ~ the open sea ▶ SF: **stare *o* tenersi alla
larga (da qn/qc)** to keep one's distance
(from sb/sth), keep away (from sb/sth);
~ due metri two metres wide; **~ di spalle**

broad-shouldered; **di larghe vedute** broad-minded; **in larga misura** to a great o large extent; **su larga scala** on a large scale; **di manica larga** generous, open-handed; **al ~ di Genova** off (the coast of) Genoa; **farsi ~ tra la folla** to push one's way through the crowd

'**larice** ['laritʃe] SM (*Bot*) larch

la'**ringe** [la'rindʒe] SF larynx

larin'**gite** [larin'dʒite] SF laryngitis

laringoi'**atra, -i, -e** SM/F (*medico*) throat specialist

'**larva** SF larva; (*fig*) shadow

la'**sagne** [la'zaɲɲe] SFPL lasagna *sg*

lasciapas'**sare** [laʃʃapas'sare] SM INV pass, permit

lasci'**are** [laʃʃare] /**14**/ VT to leave; (*abbandonare*) to leave, abandon, give up; (*cessare di tenere*) to let go of ▶ VB AUS: ~ **qn fare qc** to let sb do sth ▶ VI: ~ **di fare** (*smettere*) to stop doing; **lasciarsi** VPR (*persone*) to part; (*coppia*) to split up; ~ **andare** o **correre** o **perdere** to let things go their own way; ~ **stare qc/qn** to leave sth/sb alone; ~ **qn erede** to make sb one's heir; ~ **la presa** to lose one's grip; ~ **il segno (su qc)** to leave a mark (on sth); (*fig*) to leave one's mark (on sth); ~ **(molto) a desiderare** to leave much to be desired; **ci ha lasciato la vita** it cost him his life; **lasciarsi andare/truffare** to let o.s. go/be cheated

'**lascito** ['laʃʃito] SM (*Dir*) legacy

la'**scivia** [laʃʃivja] SF lust, lasciviousness

la'**scivo, -a** [laʃʃivo] AG lascivious

'**laser** ['lazer] AG, SM INV: (**raggio**) ~ laser (beam)

lassa'**tivo, -a** AG, SM laxative

las'**sismo** SM laxity

'**lasso** SM: ~ **di tempo** interval, lapse of time

las'**sù** AV up there

'**lastra** SF (*di pietra*) slab; (*di metallo, Fot*) plate; (*di ghiaccio, vetro*) sheet; (*radiografica*) X-ray (plate)

lastri'**care** /**20**/ VT to pave

lastri'**cato** SM paving

'**lastrico** (*pl* **lastrici** o **lastrichi**) SM paving; **essere sul ~** (*fig*) to be penniless; **gettare qn sul ~** (*fig*) to leave sb destitute

las'**trone** SM (*Alpinismo*) sheer rock face

la'**tente** AG latent

late'**rale** AG lateral, side *cpd*; (*uscita, ingresso ecc*) side *cpd* ▶ SM (*Calcio*) half-back

lateral'**mente** AV sideways

late'**rizio** [late'rittsjo] SM (perforated) brick

latifon'**dista, -i, -e** SM/F large agricultural landowner

lati'**fondo** SM large estate

la'**tino, -a** AG, SM Latin

la'**tinoameri'cano, -a** AG, SM/F Latin-American

lati'**tante** AG: **essere ~** to be on the run ▶ SMF fugitive (from justice)

lati'**tanza** [lati'tantsa] SF: **darsi alla ~** to go into hiding

lati'**tudine** SF latitude

'**lato, -a** AG (*fig*) wide, broad; **in senso ~** broadly speaking ▶ SM side; (*fig*) aspect, point of view; **d'altro ~** (*d'altra parte*) on the other hand

la'**trare** /**72**/ VI to bark

la'**trato** SM howling

la'**trina** SF public lavatory

latro'**cinio** [latro'tʃinjo] SM = **ladrocinio**

'**latta** SF tin (plate); (*recipiente*) tin, can

lat'**taio, -a** SM/F (*distributore*) milkman(-woman); (*commerciante*) dairyman(-woman)

lat'**tante** AG unweaned ▶ SMF breast-fed baby

'**latte** SM milk; **fratello di ~** foster brother; **avere ancora il ~ alla bocca** (*fig*) to be still wet behind the ears; **tutto ~ e miele** (*fig*) all smiles; ~ **detergente** cleansing milk o lotion; ~ **intero** full-cream milk; ~ **a lunga conservazione** UHT milk, long-life milk; ~ **magro** o **scremato** skimmed milk; ~ **secco** o **in polvere** dried o powdered milk; ~ **solare** suntan lotion

'**latteo, -a** AG milky; (*dieta, prodotto*) milk *cpd*

latte'**ria** SF dairy

latti'**cini** [latti'tʃini] SMPL dairy o milk products

lat'**tina** SF (*di birra ecc*) can

lat'**tuga, -ghe** SF lettuce

'**laurea** SF degree; ~ **in ingegneria** engineering degree; ~ **in lettere** ≈ arts degree; ~ **breve** *university degree awarded at the end of a three-year course*; **avere una ~ in chimica** to have a degree in chemistry o a chemistry degree; *see note*

> The *laurea* is awarded to students who successfully complete their degree courses. Traditionally, this takes between four and six years; a major element of the final examinations is the presentation and discussion of a dissertation. A shorter, more vocational course of study, taking from two to three years, is also available; at the end of this time students receive a diploma called the *laurea breve*.

laure'**ando, -a** SM/F final-year student

laure'**are** /**72**/ VT to confer a degree on; **laurearsi** VPR to graduate

laure'**ato, -a** AG, SM/F graduate

'**lauro** SM laurel

'**lauto, -a** AG (*pranzo, mancia*) lavish; **lauti guadagni** handsome profits

'**lava** SF lava

lavabianche'ria [lavabjanke'ria] SF INV washing machine

la'vabo SM washbasin

la'vaggio [la'vaddʒo] SM washing *no pl;* **~ del cervello** brainwashing *no pl;* **~ a secco** dry-cleaning

la'vagna [la'vaɲɲa] SF (*Geo*) slate; (*di scuola*) blackboard; **~ interattiva** interactive whiteboard; **~ luminosa** overhead projector

la'vanda SF (*anche Med*) wash; (*Bot*) lavender; **fare una ~ gastrica a qn** to pump sb's stomach

lavan'daia SF washerwoman

lavande'ria SF (*di ospedale, caserma ecc*) laundry; **~ automatica** launderette; **~ a secco** dry-cleaner's

lavan'dino SM sink; (*del bagno*) washbasin

lavapi'atti SM O F INV dishwasher

la'vare /**72**/ VT to wash; **lavarsi** VPR to wash, have a wash; **~ a secco** to dry-clean; **~ i panni sporchi in pubblico** (*fig*) to wash one's dirty linen in public; **lavarsi le mani/i denti** to wash one's hands/clean one's teeth

lava'secco SM O F INV dry-cleaner's

lavasto'viglie [lavasto'viʎʎe] SM O F INV (*macchina*) dishwasher

la'vata SF wash; (*fig*): **dare una ~ di capo a qn** to give sb a good telling-off

lava'tivo SM (*clistere*) enema; (*buono a nulla*) good-for-nothing, idler

lava'toio SM (*public*) washhouse

lava'trice [lava'tritʃe] SF washing machine

lava'tura SF washing *no pl;* **~ di piatti** dishwater

la'vello SM (*kitchen*) sink

la'vina SF snowslide

lavo'rante SMF worker

lavo'rare /**72**/ VI to work; (*fig: bar, studio ecc*) to do good business ▶ VT to work; **~ a** to work on; **~ a maglia** to knit; **~ di fantasia** (*suggestionarsi*) to imagine things; (*fantasticare*) to let one's imagination run free; **lavorarsi qn** (*fig: convincere*) to work on sb

lavora'tivo, -a AG working

lavora'tore, -'trice SM/F worker ▶ AG working

lavorazi'one [lavorat'tsjone] SF (*gen*) working; (*di legno, pietra*) carving; (*di film*) making; (*di prodotto*) manufacture; (*modo di esecuzione*) workmanship

lavo'rio SM intense activity

la'voro SM work; (*occupazione*) job, work *no pl;* (*opera*) piece of work, job; (*Econ*) labour (*BRIT*), labor (*US*); **che ~ fa?** what do you do?; **Ministero del L~** Department of Employment (*BRIT*), Department of Labor (*US*); **(fare) i lavori di casa** (to do) the housework *sg;* **lavori forzati** hard labour *sg;*

i lavori del parlamento the parliamentary session *sg;* **lavori pubblici** public works; **~ interinale** o **in affitto** temporary work

lazi'ale [lat'tsjale] AG of (o from) Lazio

lazza'retto [laddza'retto] SM leper hospital

lazza'rone [laddza'rone] SM scoundrel

'lazzo ['laddzo] SM jest

LC SIGLA = **Lecco**

LE SIGLA = **Lecce**

le DET FPL the ▶ PRON (*oggetto*) them; (*a lei, a essa*) (to) her; (*forma di cortesia*) (to) you; *vedi anche* **il**

le'ale AG loyal; (*sincero*) sincere; (*onesto*) fair

lea'lista, -i, -e SM/F loyalist

lealtà SF loyalty; sincerity; fairness

'leasing ['li:ziŋ] SM leasing; lease

'lebbra SF leprosy

lecca 'lecca SM INV lollipop

leccapi'edi SMF (*peg*) toady, bootlicker

lec'care /**20**/ VT to lick; (*gatto: latte ecc*) to lick o lap up; (*fig*) to flatter; **leccarsi** VPR (*fig*) to preen o.s.; **leccarsi i baffi** to lick one's lips

lec'cato, -a AG affected ▶ SF lick

leccherò *etc* [lekke'rɔ] VB *vedi* **leccare**

'leccio ['lettʃo] SM holm oak, ilex

leccor'nia SF titbit, delicacy

'lecito, -a ['lɛtʃito] AG permitted, allowed; **se mi è ~** if I may; **mi sia ~ far presente che ...** may I point out that ...

'ledere /**81**/ VT to damage, injure; **~ gli interessi di qn** to be prejudicial to sb's interests

'lega, -ghe SF (*anche Pol*) league; (*di metalli*) alloy; **metallo di bassa ~** base metal; **gente di bassa ~** common o vulgar people; **L~ Nord** (*Pol*) federalist party

le'gaccio [le'gattʃo] SM string, lace

le'gale AG legal ▶ SM lawyer; **corso ~ delle monete** official exchange rate; **medicina ~** forensic medicine; **studio ~** lawyer's office

legalità SF legality, lawfulness

legaliz'zare [legalid'dzare] /**72**/ VT to legalize; (*documento*) to authenticate

legalizzazi'one [legaliddzat'tsjone] SF (*vedi vt*) legalization; authentication

le'game SM (*corda, fig: affettivo*) tie, bond; (*nesso logico*) link, connection; **~ di sangue** o **di parentela** family tie

lega'mento SM (*Anat*) ligament

le'gare /**80**/ VT (*prigioniero, capelli, cane*) to tie (up); (*libro*) to bind; (*Chim*) to alloy; (*fig: collegare*) to bind, join ▶ VI (*far lega*) to unite; (*fig*) to get on well; **è pazzo da ~** (*col*) he should be locked up

lega'tario, -a SM/F (*Dir*) legatee

le'gato SM (*Rel*) legate; (*Dir*) legacy, bequest

legato'ria SF (*attività*) bookbinding; (*negozio*) bookbinder's

lega'tura SF (*di libro*) binding; (*Mus*) ligature

legazi'one [legat'tsjone] SF legation
le'genda [le'dʒɛnda] SF (di carta geografica ecc)
= **leggenda**
'**legge** ['leddʒe] SF law; **~ procedurale**
procedural law
leg'genda [led'dʒɛnda] SF (narrazione) legend;
(di carta geografica ecc) key, legend
leggen'dario, -a [leddʒen'darjo] AG
legendary
'**leggere** ['lɛddʒere] **/61/** VT, VI to read; **~ il**
pensiero di qn to read sb's mind o thoughts
legge'rezza [leddʒe'rettsa] SF lightness;
thoughtlessness; fickleness
leg'gero, -a [led'dʒero] AG light; (agile, snello)
nimble, agile, light; (tè, caffè) weak; (fig: non
grave, piccolo) slight; (: spensierato) thoughtless;
(: incostante) fickle; free and easy; **una**
ragazza leggera (fig) a flighty girl; **alla**
leggera thoughtlessly
leggi'adro, -a [led'dʒadro] AG pretty, lovely;
(movimenti) graceful
leg'gibile [led'dʒibile] AG legible; (libro)
readable, worth reading
leg'gio, -'gii [led'dʒio] SM lectern; (Mus)
music stand
legherò etc [lege'rɔ] VB vedi **legare**
le'ghismo [le'gismo] SM political movement
with federalist tendencies
le'ghista, -i, -e [le'gista] AG (Pol) of a "lega"
(especially Lega Nord) ▶ SM/F member (o
supporter) of a "lega" (especially Lega Nord)
legife'rare [ledʒife'rare] **/72/** VI to legislate
legio'nario [ledʒo'narjo] SM (romano)
legionary; (volontario) legionnaire
legi'one [le'dʒone] SF legion; **~ straniera**
foreign legion
legisla'tivo, -a [ledʒizla'tivo] AG legislative
legisla'tore [ledʒizla'tore] SM legislator
legisla'tura [ledʒizla'tura] SF legislature
legislazi'one [ledʒizlat'tsjone] SF legislation
legitti'mare [ledʒitti'mare] **/72/** VT (figlio) to
legitimize; (comportamento ecc) to justify
legittimità [ledʒittimi'ta] SF legitimacy
le'gittimo, -a [le'dʒittimo] AG legitimate;
(fig: giustificato, lecito) justified, legitimate;
legittima difesa (Dir) self-defence (BRIT),
self-defense (US)
'**legna** ['leɲɲa] SF firewood
le'gnaia [leɲ'ɲaja] SF woodshed
legnai'olo [leɲɲa'jɔlo] SM woodcutter
le'gname [leɲ'ɲame] SM wood, timber
le'gnata [leɲ'ɲata] SF blow with a stick;
dare a qn un sacco di legnate to give sb a
good hiding
'**legno** ['leɲɲo] SM wood; (pezzo di legno) piece
of wood; **di ~** wooden; **~ compensato**
plywood
le'gnoso, -a [leɲ'ɲoso] AG (di legno) wooden;
(come il legno) woody; (carne) tough

le'gume SM (Bot) pulse; **legumi** SMPL (fagioli,
piselli ecc) pulses
'**lei** PRON (soggetto) she; (oggetto: per dare rilievo,
con preposizione) her; (forma di cortesia: anche:
Lei) you ▶ SF INV: **la mia ~** my beloved ▶ SM:
dare del ~ a qn to address sb as "lei";
~ stessa she herself; you yourself; **è ~** it's her
> *lei* is the third person singular pronoun.
> It is used in Italian to address an adult
> whom you do not know or with whom
> you are on formal terms.

'**lembo** SM (di abito, strada) edge; (striscia sottile:
di terra) strip
'**lemma, -i** SM headword
'**lemme 'lemme** AV (very) very slowly
'**lena** SF (fig) energy, stamina; **di buona ~**
(lavorare, camminare) at a good pace
Lenin'grado SF Leningrad
le'nire **/55/** VT to soothe
lenta'mente AV slowly
'**lente** SF (Ottica) lens sg; **~ d'ingrandimento**
magnifying glass; **lenti** SFPL (occhiali) lenses;
lenti a contatto, lenti corneali contact
lenses; **lenti (a contatto) morbide/rigide**
soft/hard contact lenses
len'tezza [len'tettsa] SF slowness
len'ticchia [len'tikkja] SF (Bot) lentil
len'tiggine [len'tiddʒine] SF freckle
'**lento, -a** AG slow; (molle: fune) slack; (non
stretto: vite, abito) loose ▶ SM (ballo) slow dance
'**lenza** ['lentsa] SF fishing line
lenzu'olo [len'tswɔlo] SM sheet; **lenzuola**
SFPL pair of sheets; **~ funebre** shroud
leon'cino [leon'tʃino] SM lion cub
le'one SM lion; **L~** Leo; **essere del L~** to
be Leo
leo'pardo SM leopard
lepo'rino, -a AG: **labbro ~** harelip
'**lepre** SF hare
'**lercio, -a, -ci, -ce** ['lɛrtʃo] AG filthy
lerci'ume [ler'tʃume] SM filth
'**lesbico, -a, -ci, -che** AG, SF lesbian
'**lesi** etc VB vedi **ledere**
lesi'nare **/72/** VT to be stingy with ▶ VI: **~ (su)**
to skimp (on), be stingy (with)
lesi'one SF (Med) lesion; (Dir) injury, damage;
(Edil) crack
le'sivo, -a AG: **~ (di)** damaging (to),
detrimental (to)
'**leso, -a** PP di **ledere** ▶ AG (offeso) injured;
parte lesa (Dir) injured party; **lesa maestà**
lese-majesty
Le'sotho [le'soto] SM Lesotho
les'sare **/72/** VT (Cuc) to boil
'**lessi** etc VB vedi **leggere**
lessi'cale AG lexical
'**lessico, -ci** SM vocabulary; (dizionario) lexicon
lessicogra'fia SF lexicography
lessi'cografo, -a SM/F lexicographer

'**lesso, -a** AG boiled ▶ SM boiled meat
'**lesto, -a** AG quick; *(agile)* nimble; ~ **di mano** *(per rubare)* light-fingered; *(per picchiare)* free with one's fists
lesto'fante SM swindler, con man
le'tale AG lethal; fatal
leta'maio SM dunghill
le'tame SM manure, dung
le'targo, -ghi SM lethargy; *(Zool)* hibernation
le'tizia [le'tittsja] SF joy, happiness
'**letta** SF: **dare una ~ a qc** to glance o look through sth
'**lettera** SF letter; **lettere** SFPL *(letteratura)* literature *sg*; *(studi umanistici)* arts (subjects); **alla ~** literally; **in lettere** in words, in full; **diventar ~ morta** *(legge)* to become a dead letter; **restar ~ morta** *(consiglio, invito)* to go unheeded; **~ di accompagnamento** accompanying letter; **~ assicurata** registered letter; **~ di cambio** *(Comm)* bill of exchange; **~ di credito** *(Comm)* letter of credit; **~ di intenti** letter of intent; **~ di presentazione** o **raccomandazione** letter of introduction; **~ raccomandata** recorded delivery *(Brit)* o certified *(US)* letter; **~ di trasporto aereo** *(Comm)* air waybill
lette'rale AG literal
letteral'mente AV literally
lette'rario, -a AG literary
lette'rato, -a AG well-read, scholarly
lettera'tura SF literature
let'tiga, -ghe SF *(portantina)* litter; *(barella)* stretcher
let'tino SM cot *(Brit)*, crib *(US)*; *(per il sole)* sun lounger; **~ solare** sunbed
'**letto, -a** PP **di leggere** ▶ SM bed; **andare a ~** to go to bed; **~ a castello** bunk beds *pl*; **~ a una piazza/a due piazze** o **matrimoniale** single/double bed
'**lettone** AG, SMF Latvian ▶ SM *(Ling)* Latvian, Lettish
Let'tonia SF: **la ~** Latvia
lettorato SM *(Ins)* lectorship, assistantship; *(Rel)* lectorate
let'tore, -'trice SM/F reader; *(Ins)* (foreign language) assistant *(Brit)*, (foreign) teaching assistant *(US)* ▶ SM *(Tecn)*: **~ ottico (di caratteri)** optical character reader; **~ CD/DVD** CD/DVD player; **~ MP3/MP4** MP3/MP4 player
let'tura SF reading
leuce'mia [leutʃe'mia] SF leukaemia
'**leva** SF lever; *(Mil)* conscription; **far ~ su qn** to work on sb; **essere di ~** to be due for call-up; **~ del cambio** *(Aut)* gear lever
le'vante SM east; *(vento)* East wind; **il L~** the Levant
le'vare /**72**/ VT *(occhi, braccio)* to raise; *(sollevare, togliere: tassa, divieto)* to lift; *(: indumenti)* to take

off, remove; *(rimuovere)* to take away; *(: dal di sopra)* to take off; *(: dal di dentro)* to take out; **levarsi** VPR to get up; *(sole)* to rise; **~ le tende** *(fig)* to pack up and leave; **levarsi il pensiero** to put one's mind at rest; **levati di mezzo** o **di lì** o **di torno!** get out of my way!
le'vata SF *(di posta)* collection
leva'taccia, -ce [leva'tattʃa] SF early rise
leva'toio, -a AG: **ponte ~** drawbridge
leva'trice [leva'tritʃe] SF midwife
leva'tura SF intelligence, mental capacity
levi'gare /**80**/ VT to smooth; *(con carta vetrata)* to sand
levi'gato, -a AG *(superficie)* smooth; *(fig: stile)* polished; *(: viso)* flawless
levità SF lightness
levri'ere SM greyhound
lezi'one [let'tsjone] SF lesson; *(all'università, sgridata)* lecture; **fare ~** to teach; to lecture; **dare una ~ a qn** to teach sb a lesson; **lezioni private** private lessons
lezi'oso, -a [let'tsjoso] AG affected; simpering
'**lezzo** ['leddzo] SM stench, stink
LI SIGLA = **Livorno**
li PRON PL *(oggetto)* them
lì AV there; **di** o **da lì** from there; **per di lì** that way; **di lì a pochi giorni** a few days later; **lì per lì** there and then; at first; **essere lì (lì) per fare** to be on the point of doing, be about to do; **lì dentro** in there; **lì sotto** under there; **lì sopra** on there; up there; **tutto lì** that's all; *vedi anche* **quello**
libagi'one [liba'dʒone] SF libation
liba'nese AG, SMF Lebanese *inv*
Li'bano SM: **il ~** the Lebanon
'**libbra** SF *(peso)* pound
li'beccio [li'bettʃo] SM south-west wind
li'bello SM libel
li'bellula SF dragonfly
libe'rale AG, SMF liberal
liberaliz'zare [liberalid'dzare] /**72**/ VT to liberalize
libe'rare /**72**/ VT *(rendere libero: prigioniero)* to release; *(: popolo)* to free, liberate; *(sgombrare: passaggio)* to clear; *(: stanza)* to vacate; *(produrre: energia)* to release; **liberarsi** VPR: **liberarsi di qc/qn** to get rid of sth/sb
libera'tore, -'trice AG liberating ▶ SM/F liberator
liberazi'one [liberat'tsjone] SF *(di prigioniero)* release, freeing; *(di popolo)* liberation; rescuing; **che ~!** what a relief!; **la L~** *see note*

> The *Liberazione* is a national holiday which falls on 25 April. It commemorates the liberation of Italy in 1945 from German forces and Mussolini's government and marks the end of the war on Italian soil.

li'bercolo SM *(peg)* worthless book
Li'beria SF: **la ~** Liberia

liberi'ano, -a AG, SM/F Liberian

libe'rismo SM (*Econ*) laissez-faire

'libero, -a AG free; (*strada*) clear; (*non occupato*: *posto ecc*) vacant; free; not taken; empty; (: *Tel*) not engaged; **~ di fare qc** free to do sth; **~ da** free from; **una donna di liberi costumi** a woman of loose morals; **avere via libera** to have a free hand; **dare via libera a qn** to give sb the go-ahead; **via libera!** all clear!; **~ arbitrio** free will; **~ professionista** self-employed professional person; **~ scambio** free trade; **libera uscita** (*Mil*) leave

liberoscam'bismo SM (*Econ*) free trade

libertà SF INV freedom; (*tempo disponibile*) free time ▶ SFPL (*licenza*) liberties; **essere in ~ provvisoria/vigilata** to be released without bail/be on probation; **~ di riunione** right to hold meetings

liber'tario, -a AG libertarian

liber'tino, -a AG, SM/F libertine

'liberty ['liberti] AG INV, SM art nouveau

'Libia SF: **la ~** Libya

'libico, -a, -ci, -che AG, SM/F Libyan

li'bidine SF lust

libidi'noso, -a AG lustful, libidinous

li'bido SF libido

li'braio SM bookseller

li'brario, -a AG book *cpd*

li'brarsi /72/ VPR to hover

libre'ria SF (*bottega*) bookshop; (*stanza*) library; (*mobile*) bookcase

li'bretto SM booklet; (*taccuino*) notebook; (*Mus*) libretto; **~ degli assegni** chequebook (*BRIT*), checkbook (*US*); **~ di circolazione** (*Aut*) logbook; **~ di deposito** (bank) deposit book; **~ di risparmio** (savings) bankbook, passbook; **~ universitario** student's report book

'libro SM book; **~ bianco** (*Pol*) white paper; **~ di cassa** cash book; **~ di consultazione** reference book; **~ mastro** ledger; **~ paga** payroll; **~ tascabile** paperback; **~ di testo** textbook; **libri contabili** (account) books; **libri sociali** company records

li'cantropo SM werewolf

lice'ale [litʃe'ale] AG secondary school *cpd* (*BRIT*), high school *cpd* (*US*) ▶ SMF secondary school *o* high school pupil

li'cenza [li'tʃɛntsa] SF (*permesso*) permission, leave; (*di pesca, caccia, circolazione*) permit, licence (*BRIT*), license (*US*); (*Mil*) leave; (*Ins*) school-leaving certificate; (*libertà*) liberty; licence; (*sfrenatezza*) licentiousness; **andare in ~** (*Mil*) to go on leave; **su ~ di ...** (*Comm*) under licence from ...; **~ di esportazione** export licence; **~ di fabbricazione** manufacturer's licence; **~ poetica** poetic licence

licenzia'mento [litʃentsja'mento] SM dismissal

licenzi'are [litʃen'tsjare] /19/ VT (*impiegato*) to dismiss; (*Comm*: *per eccesso di personale*) to make redundant; (*Ins*) to award a certificate to; **licenziarsi** VPR (*impiegato*) to resign, hand in one's notice; (*Ins*) to obtain one's school-leaving certificate

licenziosità [litʃentsjosi'ta] SF licentiousness

licenzi'oso, -a [litʃen'tsjoso] AG licentious

li'ceo [li'tʃɛo] SM (*Ins*) secondary (*BRIT*) *o* high (*US*) school (*for 14- to 19-year-olds*); **~ classico/scientifico** secondary or high school specializing in classics/scientific subjects

li'chene [li'kɛne] SM (*Bot*) lichen

'lido SM beach, shore

'Liechtenstein ['liktənstain] SM: **il ~** Liechtenstein

li'eto, -a AG happy, glad; **"molto ~"** (*nelle presentazioni*) "pleased to meet you"; **a ~ fine** with a happy ending

li'eve AG light; (*di poco conto*) slight; (*sommesso*: *voce*) faint, soft

lievi'tare /72/ VI (*anche fig*) to rise ▶ VT to leaven

li'evito SM yeast; **~ di birra** brewer's yeast

'ligio, -a, -gi, -gie ['lidʒo] AG faithful, loyal

li'gnaggio [liɲ'naddʒo] SM descent, lineage

'ligure AG Ligurian; **la Riviera L~** the Italian Riviera

Li'kud [li'kud] SM Likud

'lilla, lillà SM INV lilac

'Lima SF Lima

'lima SF file; **~ da unghie** nail file

limacci'oso, -a [limat'tʃoso] AG slimy; muddy

li'mare /72/ VT to file (down); (*fig*) to polish

'limbo SM (*Rel*) limbo

li'metta SF nail file

limi'tare /72/ VT to limit, restrict; (*circoscrivere*) to bound, surround; **limitarsi** VPR: **limitarsi nel mangiare** to limit one's eating; **limitarsi a qc/a fare qc** to limit o.s. to sth/ to doing sth

limitata'mente AV to a limited extent; **~ alle mie possibilità** in so far as I am able

limi'tato, -a AG limited, restricted

limitazi'one [limitat'tsjone] SF limitation, restriction

'limite SM limit; (*confine*) border, boundary ▶ AG INV: **caso ~** extreme case; **al ~** if the worst comes to the worst (*BRIT*), if worst comes to worst (*US*); **~ di velocità** speed limit

li'mitrofo, -a AG neighbouring (*BRIT*), neighboring (*US*)

'limo SM mud, slime; (*Geo*) silt

limo'nata SF lemonade (BRIT), (lemon) soda (US); (*spremuta*) lemon squash (BRIT), lemonade (US)

li'mone SM (*pianta*) lemon tree; (*frutto*) lemon

limpi'dezza [limpi'dettsa] SF clearness; (*di discorso*) clarity

'limpido, -a AG (*acqua*) limpid, clear; (*cielo*) clear; (*fig: discorso*) clear, lucid

'lince ['lintʃe] SF lynx

linci'aggio [lin'tʃaddʒo] SM lynching

linci'are [lin'tʃare] /**14**/ VT to lynch

'lindo, -a AG tidy, spick and span; (*biancheria*) clean

'linea SF (*gen*) line; (*di mezzi pubblici di trasporto: itinerario*) route; (: *servizio*) service; (*di prodotto: collezione*) collection; (: *stile*) style; **a grandi linee** in outline; **mantenere la ~** to look after one's figure; **è caduta la ~** (*Tel*) I (*o you etc*) have been cut off; **di ~**, **aereo di ~** airliner; **nave di ~** liner; **volo di ~** scheduled flight; **in ~ diretta da** (*TV, Radio*) coming to you direct from; **~ aerea** airline; **~ continua** solid line; **~ di partenza/d'arrivo** (*Sport*) starting/finishing line; **~ punteggiata** dotted line; **~ di tiro** line of fire

linea'menti SMPL features; (*fig*) outlines

line'are AG linear; (*fig*) coherent, logical

line'etta SF (*trattino*) dash; (*d'unione*) hyphen

'linfa SF (*Bot*) sap; (*Anat*) lymph; **~ vitale** (*fig*) lifeblood

lin'gotto SM ingot, bar

'lingua SF (*Anat, Cuc*) tongue; (*idioma*) language; **mostrare la ~** to stick out one's tongue; **di ~ italiana** Italian-speaking; **~ madre** mother tongue; **una ~ di terra** a spit of land

lingu'accia [lin'gwattʃa] SF (*fig*) spiteful gossip

linguacci'uto, -a [lingwat'tʃuto] AG gossipy

lingu'aggio [lin'gwaddʒo] SM language; **~ giuridico** legal language; **~ macchina** (*Inform*) machine language; **~ di programmazione** (*Inform*) programming language

lingu'etta SF (*di strumento*) reed; (*di scarpa, Tecn*) tongue; (*di busta*) flap

lingu'ista, -i, -e SM/F linguist

lingu'istico, -a, -ci, -che AG linguistic ▶ SF linguistics *sg*

lini'mento SM liniment

'lino SM (*pianta*) flax; (*tessuto*) linen

li'noleum SM INV linoleum, lino

liofiliz'zare [liofilid'dzare] /**72**/ VT to freeze-dry

liofiliz'zati [liofilid'dzati] SMPL freeze-dried foods

Li'one SF Lyons

liposuzi'one [liposut'tsjone] SF liposuction

'LIPU SIGLA F (= *Lega Italiana Protezione Uccelli*) society for the protection of birds

liqu'ame SM liquid sewage

lique'fare /**41**/ VT (*render liquido*) to liquefy; (*fondere*) to melt; **liquefarsi** VPR to liquefy; to melt

lique'fatto, -a PP *di* **liquefare**

liqui'dare /**72**/ VT (*società, beni, persona: uccidere*) to liquidate; (*persona: sbarazzarsene*) to get rid of; (*conto, problema*) to settle; (*Comm: merce*) to sell off, clear

liquidazi'one [likwidat'tsjone] SF (*di società, persona*) liquidation; (*di conto*) settlement; (*di problema*) settling; (*Comm: di merce*) clearance sale; (*Amm*) severance pay (*on retirement, redundancy, or when taking up other employment*)

liquidità SF liquidity

'liquido, -a AG, SM liquid; **denaro ~** cash, ready money; **~ per freni** brake fluid

liqui'gas® SM INV Calor gas® (BRIT), butane

liqui'rizia [likwi'rittsja] SF liquorice

li'quore SM liqueur

liquo'roso, -a AG: **vino ~** dessert wine

'lira SF (*unità monetaria*) lira; (*Mus*) lyre; **~ sterlina** pound sterling

'lirico, -a, -ci, -che AG lyric(al); (*Mus*) lyric ▶ SF (*poesia*) lyric poetry; (*componimento poetico*) lyric; (*Mus*) opera; **cantante/teatro ~** opera singer/house

li'rismo SM lyricism

Lis'bona SF Lisbon

'lisca, -sche SF (*di pesce*) fishbone

lisci'are [liʃʃare] /**14**/ VT to smooth; (*fig*) to flatter; **lisciarsi i capelli** to straighten one's hair

'liscio, -a, -sci, -sce ['liʃʃo] AG smooth; (*capelli*) straight; (*mobile*) plain; (*bevanda alcolica*) neat; (*fig*) straightforward, simple ▶ AV: **andare ~** to go smoothly; **passarla liscia** to get away with it

'liso, -a AG worn out, threadbare

'lista SF (*striscia*) strip; (*elenco*) list; **~ elettorale** electoral roll; **~ delle spese** shopping list; **~ dei vini** wine list; **~ delle vivande** menu

lis'tare /**72**/ VT: **~ (di)** to edge (with), border (with)

lis'tato SM (*Inform*) list, listing

lis'tino SM list; **~ di borsa** the Stock Exchange list; **~ dei cambi** (foreign) exchange rate; **~ dei prezzi** price list

lita'nia SF litany

'lite SF quarrel, argument; (*Dir*) lawsuit

liti'gare /**80**/ VI to quarrel; (*Dir*) to litigate

li'tigio [li'tidʒo] SM quarrel

litigi'oso, -a [liti'dʒoso] AG quarrelsome; (*Dir*) litigious

litogra'fia SF (*sistema*) lithography; (*stampa*) lithograph lito'grafico, -a, -ci, -che AG lithographic

lito'rale AG coastal, coast *cpd* ▶ SM coast

lito'raneo, -a AG coastal

'litro SM litre (*BRIT*), liter (*US*)

lit'torio, -a AG (*Storia*) lictorial; **fascio** ~
fasces *pl*

Litu'ania SF: **la** ~ Lithuania

litu'ano, -a AG, SM/F, SM Lithuanian

litur'gia, -'gie [litur'dʒia] SF liturgy

li'uto SM lute

li'vella SF level; ~ **a bolla d'aria** spirit level

livel'lare /72/ VT to level, make level;
livellarsi VPR to become level; (*fig*) to
level out, balance out

livella'trice [livella'tritʃe] SF steamroller

li'vello SM level; (*fig*) level, standard; **ad alto**
~ (*fig*) high-level; **a** ~ **mondiale** world-wide;
a ~ **di confidenza** confidentially; ~ **di**
magazzino stock level; ~ **del mare** sea level;
sul ~ **del mare** above sea level;
~ **occupazionale** level of employment;
~ **retributivo** salary level

'livido, -a AG livid; (*per percosse*) bruised, black
and blue; (*cielo*) leaden ▶ SM bruise

li'vore SM malice, spite

Li'vorno SF Livorno, Leghorn

li'vrea SF livery

'lizza ['littsa] SF lists *pl*; **essere in** ~ **per** (*fig*) to
compete for; **scendere in** ~ (*anche fig*) to
enter the lists

LO SIGLA = **Lodi**

lo DET M (*dav s impura, gn, pn, ps, x, z; dav V l'*) the
▶ PRON (*dav V l'*: *oggetto: persona*) him; (: *cosa*) it;
lo sapevo I knew it; **lo so** I know; **sii buono,**
anche se lui non lo è be good, even if he
isn't; *vedi anche* **il**

lob'bista, -i, -e SM/F lobbyist

'lobby SF INV lobby

'lobo SM lobe; ~ **dell'orecchio** ear lobe

lo'cale AG local ▶ SM room; (*luogo pubblico*)
premises *pl*; ~ **notturno** nightclub

località SF INV locality

localiz'zare [lokalid'dzare] /72/ VT
(*circoscrivere*) to confine, localize; (*accertare*) to
locate, place

lo'canda SF inn

locandi'ere, -a SM/F innkeeper

locan'dina SF (*Teat*) poster

lo'care /20/ VT (*casa*) to rent out, let; (*macchina*)
to hire out (*BRIT*), rent (out)

loca'tario, -a SM/F tenant

loca'tivo, -a AG (*Dir*) rentable

loca'tore, -'trice SM/F landlord (lady)

locazi'one [lokat'tsjone] SF (*da parte del*
locatario) renting *no pl*; (*da parte del locatore*)
renting out *no pl*, letting *no pl*; (**contratto di**)
~ lease; (**canone di**) ~ rent; **dare in** ~ to rent
out, let

locomo'tiva SF locomotive

locomo'tore SM electric locomotive

locomot'rice [lokomo'tritʃe] SF = **locomotore**

locomozi'one [lokomot'tsjone] SF
locomotion; **mezzi di** ~ vehicles, means of
transport

'loculo SM burial recess

lo'custa SF locust

locuzi'one [lokut'tsjone] SF phrase,
expression

lo'dare /72/ VT to praise

'lode SF praise; (*Ins*): **laurearsi con 110 e** ~
≈ to graduate with first-class honours (*BRIT*),
≈ to graduate summa cum laude (*US*)

'loden SM INV (*stoffa*) loden; (*cappotto*) loden
overcoat

lo'devole AG praiseworthy

loga'ritmo SM logarithm

log'garsi /72/ VPR (*Inform*) to log in

'loggia, -ge ['lɔddʒa] SF (*Archit*) loggia; (*circolo*
massonico) lodge

loggi'one [lod'dʒone] SM (*di teatro*): **il** ~ the
Gods *sg*

logica'mente [lodʒika'mente] AV naturally,
obviously

logicità [lodʒitʃi'ta] SF logicality

'logico, -a, -ci, -che ['lɔdʒiko] AG logical
▶ SF logic

lo'gistica [lo'dʒistika] SF logistics *sg*

'logo SM INV logo

logora'mento SM (*di vestiti ecc*) wear

logo'rante AG exhausting

logo'rare /72/ VT to wear out; (*sciupare*) to
waste; **logorarsi** VPR to wear out; (*fig*) to
wear o.s. out

logo'rio SM wear and tear; (*fig*) strain

'logoro, -a AG (*stoffa*) worn out, threadbare;
(*persona*) worn out

'Loira SF: **la** ~ the Loire

lom'baggine [lom'baddʒine] SF lumbago

Lombar'dia SF: **la** ~ Lombardy

lom'bardo, -a AG, SM/F Lombard

lom'bare AG (*Anat, Med*) lumbar

lom'bata SF (*taglio di carne*) loin

'lombo SM (*Anat*) loin

lom'brico, -chi SM earthworm

londi'nese AG London *cpd* ▶ SMF Londoner

'Londra SF London

lon'ganime AG forbearing

longevità [londʒevi'ta] SF longevity

lon'gevo, -a [lon'dʒevo] AG long-lived

longi'lineo, -a [londʒi'lineo] AG long-limbed

longi'tudine [londʒi'tudine] SF longitude

lontana'mente AV remotely; **non ci**
pensavo neppure ~ it didn't even occur
to me

lonta'nanza [lonta'nantsa] SF distance;
absence

lon'tano, -a AG (*distante*) distant, faraway;
(*assente*) absent; (*vago: sospetto*) slight,

remote; (*tempo: remoto*) far-off, distant; (*parente*) distant, remote ▶ AV far; **è lontana la casa?** is it far to the house?, is the house far from here?; **è ~ un chilometro** it's a kilometre away *o* a kilometre from here; **più ~** farther; **da** *o* **di ~** from a distance; **~ da** a long way from; **è molto ~ da qui?** is it far from here?; **alla lontana** slightly, vaguely

'lontra SF otter

lo'quace [lo'kwatʃe] AG talkative, loquacious; (*fig: gesto ecc*) eloquent

loquacità [lokwatʃi'ta] SF talkativeness, loquacity

'lordo, -a AG dirty, filthy; (*peso, stipendio*) gross; **~ d'imposta** pre-tax

Lo'rena SF (*Geo*) Lorraine

'loro PRON PL (*oggetto, con preposizione*) them; (*complemento di termine*) to them; (*soggetto*) they; (*forma di cortesia: anche:* **Loro**) you; to you; **il (la) ~**, **i (le) ~** *det* their; (*forma di cortesia: anche:* **Loro**) your ▶ PRON theirs; (*forma di cortesia: anche:* **Loro**) yours ▶ SM INV: **il ~** their (*o* your) money ▶ SF INV: **la ~** (*opinione*) their (*o* your) view; **i ~** (*famiglia*) their (*o* your) family; (*amici ecc*) their (*o* your own) people; **un ~ amico** a friend of theirs; **è dalla ~** he's on their (*o* your) side; **ne hanno fatto un'altra delle ~** they've (*o* you've) done it again; **~ stessi(e)** they themselves; you yourselves

lo'sanga, -ghe SF diamond, lozenge

Lo'sanna SF Lausanne

'losco, -a, -schi, -sche AG (*fig*) shady, suspicious

'lotta SF struggle, fight; (*Sport*) wrestling; **essere in ~ (con)** to be in conflict (with); **fare la ~ (con)** to wrestle (with); **~ armata** armed struggle; **~ di classe** (*Pol*) class struggle; **~ libera** (*Sport*) all-in wrestling (BRIT), freestyle

lot'tare /72/ VI to fight, struggle; to wrestle

lotta'tore, -'trice SM/F wrestler

lotte'ria SF lottery; (*di gara ippica*) sweepstake

lottiz'zare [lottid'dzare] /72/ VT to divide into plots; (*fig*) to share out

lottizzazi'one [lottiddzat'tsjone] SF division into plots; (*fig*) share-out

'lotto SM (*gioco*) (state) lottery; (*parte*) lot; (*Edil*) site; **vincere un terno al ~** (*anche fig*) to hit the jackpot

> The *Lotto* is an official lottery run by the Italian Finance Ministry. It consists of a weekly draw of numbers and is very popular.

lozi'one [lot'tsjone] SF lotion

LT SIGLA = **Latina**

LU SIGLA = **Lucca**

lubrifi'cante SM lubricant

lubrifi'care /20/ VT to lubricate

lu'cano, -a AG of (*o* from) Lucania

luc'chetto [luk'ketto] SM padlock

lucci'care [luttʃi'kare] /20/ VI to sparkle; (*oro*) to glitter; (*stella*) to twinkle; (*occhi*) to glisten

lucci'chio [luttʃi'kio] SM sparkling; glittering; twinkling; glistening

lucci'cone [luttʃi'kone] SM: **avere i lucciconi agli occhi** to have tears in one's eyes

'luccio ['luttʃo] SM (*Zool*) pike

'lucciola ['luttʃola] SF (*Zool*) firefly; glow-worm; (*col: fig: prostituta*) girl (*o* woman) on the game

'luce ['lutʃe] SF light; (*finestra*) window; **alla ~ di** by the light of; **fare qc alla ~ del sole** (*fig*) to do sth in the open; **dare alla ~** (*bambino*) to give birth to; **fare ~ su qc** (*fig*) to shed *o* throw light on sth; **~ del sole/della luna** sun/moonlight

lu'cente [lu'tʃente] AG shining

lucen'tezza [lutʃen'tettsa] SF shine

lu'cerna [lu'tʃɛrna] SF oil lamp

lucer'nario [lutʃer'narjo] SM skylight

lu'certola [lu'tʃɛrtola] SF lizard

luci'dare [lutʃi'dare] /72/ VT to polish; (*ricalcare*) to trace

lucida'trice [lutʃida'tritʃe] SF floor polisher

lucidità [lutʃidi'ta] SF lucidity

'lucido, -a ['lutʃido] AG shining, bright; (*lucidato*) polished; (*fig*) lucid ▶ SM shine, lustre (BRIT), luster (US); (*per scarpe ecc*) polish; (*disegno*) tracing

lu'cignolo [lu'tʃiɲɲolo] SM wick

luc'rare /72/ VT to make money out of

lucra'tivo, -a AG lucrative; **a scopo ~** for gain

'lucro SM profit, gain; **a scopo di ~** for gain; **organizzazione senza scopo di ~** non-profit-making (BRIT) *o* non-profit (US) organization

lu'croso, -a AG lucrative, profitable

luculli'ano, -a AG (*pasto*) sumptuous

lu'dibrio SM mockery *no pl*; (*oggetto di scherno*) laughing stock

'lue SF syphilis

'luglio ['luʎʎo] SM July; **nel mese di ~** in July, in the month of July; **il primo ~** the first of July; **arrivare il 2 ~** to arrive on the 2nd of July; **all'inizio/alla fine di ~** at the beginning/at the end of July; **durante il mese di ~** during July; **a ~ del prossimo anno** in July of next year; **ogni anno a ~** every July; **che fai a ~?** what are you doing in July?; **ha piovuto molto a ~ quest'anno** July was very wet this year

'lugubre AG gloomy

'lui PRON (*soggetto*) he; (*oggetto: per dare rilievo, con preposizione*) him ▶ SM INV: **il mio ~** my beloved; **~ stesso** he himself; **è ~** it's him

lu'maca, -che SF slug; (*chiocciola*) snail

luma'cone SM (large) slug; (*fig*) slowcoach (BRIT), slowpoke (US)

'lume SM light; (*lampada*) lamp; **~ a olio** oil lamp; **chiedere lumi a qn** (*fig*) to ask sb for advice; **a ~ di naso** (*fig*) by rule of thumb

lumi'cino [lumi'tʃino] SM small o faint light; **essere (ridotto) al ~** (*fig*) to be at death's door

lumi'era SF chandelier

lumi'nare SM luminary

lumi'naria SF (*per feste*) illuminations *pl*

lumine'scente [lumineʃʃɛnte] AG luminescent

lu'mino SM small light; **~ da notte** night-light; **~ per i morti** candle for the dead

luminosità SF brightness; (*fig: di sorriso, volto*) radiance

lumi'noso, -a AG (*che emette luce*) luminous; (*cielo, colore, stanza*) bright; (*sorgente*) of light, light *cpd*; (*fig: sorriso*) bright, radiant; **insegna luminosa** neon sign

lun. ABBR (= *lunedì*) Mon.

'luna SF moon; **~ nuova/piena** new/full moon; **avere la ~** to be in a bad mood; **~ di miele** honeymoon

'luna park SM INV amusement park, funfair

lu'nare AG lunar, moon *cpd*

lu'nario SM almanac; **sbarcare il ~** to make ends meet

lu'natico, -a, -ci, -che AG whimsical, temperamental

lunedì SM INV Monday; **di o il ~** on Mondays; *vedi anche* **martedì**

lun'gaggine [lun'gaddʒine] SF slowness; **lungaggini della burocrazia** red tape

lunga'mente AV (*a lungo*) for a long time; (*estesamente*) at length

lun'garno SM embankment along the Arno

lun'ghezza [lun'gettsa] SF length; **~ d'onda** (*Fisica*) wavelength

'lungi ['lundʒi]: **~ da** *prep* far from

lungimi'rante [lundʒimi'rante] AG far-sighted

'lungo, -a, -ghi, -ghe AG long; (*lento: persona*) slow; (*diluito: caffè, brodo*) weak, watery, thin ▶ SM length ▶ PREP along; **~ 3 metri** 3 metres long; **avere la barba lunga** to be unshaven; **a ~** for a long time; **a ~ andare** in the long run; **di gran lunga** (*molto*) by far; **andare in ~ o per le lunghe** to drag on; **saperla lunga** to know what's what; **in ~ e in largo** far and wide, all over; **~ il corso dei secoli** throughout the centuries; **navigazione di ~ corso** ocean-going navigation

lungofi'ume SM embankment

lungo'lago SM road round a lake

lungo'mare SM promenade

lungome'traggio [lungome'traddʒo] SM (*Cine*) feature film

lungo'tevere SM embankment along the Tiber

lu'notto SM (*Aut*) rear o back window; **~ termico** heated rear window

lu'ogo, -ghi SM place; (*posto: di incidente ecc*) scene, site; (*punto, passo di libro*) passage; **in ~ di** instead of; **in primo ~** in the first place; **aver ~** to take place; **dar ~ a** to give rise to; **~ comune** commonplace; **~ del delitto** scene of the crime; **~ geometrico** locus; **~ di nascita** birthplace; (*Amm*) place of birth; **~ di pena** prison, penitentiary; **~ di provenienza** place of origin

luogote'nente SM (*Mil*) lieutenant

lupacchi'otto [lupak'kjɔtto] SM (*Zool*) (wolf) cub

lu'para SF sawn-off shotgun

lu'petto SM (*Zool*) (wolf) cub; (*negli scouts*) cub scout

'lupo, -a SM/F wolf/she-wolf; **cane ~** alsatian (dog) (*BRIT*), German shepherd (dog); **tempo da lupi** filthy weather

'luppolo SM (*Bot*) hop

'lurido, -a AG filthy

luri'dume SM filth

lu'singa, -ghe SF (*spesso al pl*) flattery *no pl*

lusin'gare /80/ VT to flatter

lusinghi'ero, -a [luzin'gjɛro] AG flattering, gratifying

lus'sare /72/ VT (*Med*) to dislocate

lussazi'one [lussat'tsjone] SF (*Med*) dislocation

lussembur'ghese [lussembur'gese] AG of (o from) Luxembourg ▶ SMF native (o inhabitant) of Luxembourg

Lussem'burgo SM (*stato*): **il ~** Luxembourg ▶ SF (*città*) Luxembourg

'lusso SM luxury; **di ~** luxury *cpd*

lussu'oso, -a AG luxurious

lussureggi'are [lussured'dʒare] /62/ VI to be luxuriant

lus'suria SF lust

lussuri'oso, -a AG lascivious, lustful

lus'trare /72/ VT to polish, shine

lustras'carpe SM INV/F INV shoeshine

lus'trino SM sequin

'lustro, -a AG shiny; (*pelliccia*) glossy ▶ SM shine, gloss; (*fig*) prestige, glory; (*quinquennio*) five-year period

lute'rano, -a AG, SM/F Lutheran

'lutto SM mourning; **essere in/portare il ~** to be in/wear mourning

Mm

M, m ['ɛmme] SM O F INV (lettera) M, m;
M come Milano M for Mary (BRIT), M for
Mike (US)

m. ABBR = **mese; metro; miglia; monte**

ma CONG but; **ma insomma!** for goodness
sake!; **ma no!** of course not!

'macabro, -a AG gruesome, macabre

ma'caco, -chi SM (Zool) macaque

macché [mak'ke] ESCL not at all!, certainly
not!

macche'roni [makke'roni] SMPL macaroni sg

'macchia ['makkja] SF stain, spot; (chiazza di
diverso colore) spot, splash, patch; (tipo di
boscaglia) scrub; **~ d'inchiostro** ink stain;
estendersi a ~ d'olio (fig) to spread rapidly;
darsi/vivere alla ~ (fig) to go into/live in
hiding

macchi'are [mak'kjare] /19/ VT (sporcare) to
stain, mark; **macchiarsi** VPR (persona) to get
o.s. dirty; (stoffa) to stain; to get stained o
marked; **macchiarsi di un delitto** to be
guilty of a crime

macchi'ato, -a [mak'kjato] AG (pelle, pelo)
spotted; **~ di** stained with; **caffè ~** coffee
with a dash of milk

macchi'etta [mak'kjetta] SF (disegno) sketch,
caricature; (Teat) caricature; (fig: persona)
character

'macchina ['makkina] SF machine; (motore,
locomotiva) engine; (automobile) car; (fig:
meccanismo) machinery; **andare in ~** (Aut) to
go by car; (Stampa) to go to press; **salire in ~**
to get into the car; **venire in ~** to come by
car; **sala macchine** (Naut) engine room;
~ da cucire sewing machine; **~ fotografica**
camera; **~ da presa** cine o movie camera;
~ da scrivere typewriter; **~ utensile**
machine tool; **~ a vapore** steam engine

macchinal'mente [makkinal'mente] AV
mechanically

macchi'nare [makki'nare] /72/ VT to plot

macchi'nario [makki'narjo] SM machinery

macchinazi'one [makkinat'tsjone] SF plot,
machination

macchi'netta [makki'netta] SF (col:
caffettiera) percolator; (: accendino) lighter

macchi'nista, -i [makki'nista] SM (di treno)
engine-driver; (di nave) engineer; (Teat, TV)
stagehand

macchi'noso, -a [makki'noso] AG complex,
complicated

ma'cedone [ma'tʃɛdone] AG, SMF Macedonian

Mace'donia [matʃe'dɔnja] SF Macedonia

mace'donia [matʃe'dɔnja] SF fruit salad

macel'laio [matʃel'lajo] SM butcher

macel'lare [matʃel'lare] /72/ VT to slaughter,
butcher

macellazi'one [matʃellat'tsjone] SF
slaughtering, butchering

macelle'ria [matʃelle'ria] SF butcher's (shop)

ma'cello [ma'tʃɛllo] SM (mattatoio)
slaughterhouse, abattoir (BRIT); (fig)
slaughter, massacre; (: disastro) shambles sg

mace'rare [matʃe'rare] /72/ VT to macerate;
(Cuc) to marinate; **macerarsi** VPR to waste
away; (fig) **macerarsi in** to be consumed
with

macerazi'one [matʃerat'tsjone] SF
maceration

ma'cerie [ma'tʃɛrje] SFPL rubble sg, debris sg

'macero ['matʃero] SM (operazione) pulping;
(stabilimento) pulping mill; **carta da ~** paper
for pulping

r   ia'vellico, -a, -ci, -che [makja'vɛlliko]
AG (anche fig) Machiavellian

n   gno [ma'tʃiɲɲo] SM (masso) rock,
boulder

mac i'lento, -a [matʃi'lɛnto] AG emaciated

'macina ['matʃina] SF (pietra) millstone;
(macchina) grinder

macinacaffè [matʃinakaf'fɛ] SM INV coffee
grinder

macina'pepe [matʃina'pepe] SM INV
peppermill

maci'nare [matʃi'nare] /72/ VT to grind;
(carne) to mince (BRIT), grind (US)

maci'nato [matʃi'nato] SM meal, flour;
(carne) minced (BRIT) o ground (US) meat

maci'nino [matʃi'nino] SM (per caffè) coffee grinder; (per pepe) peppermill; (scherzoso: macchina) old banger (BRIT), clunker (US)

maciul'lare [matʃul'lare] /**72**/ VT (canapa, lino) to brake; (fig: braccio ecc) to crush

'**macro ...** PREFISSO macro...

macrobi'otico, -a AG macrobiotic ▶ SF macrobiotics sg

macu'lato, -a AG (pelo) spotted

Ma'dama: palazzo ~ sm (Pol) seat of the Italian Chamber of Senators

made in Italy [meɪdɪ'nɪtəlɪ] SM: **il ~** Italian exports pl (especially fashion goods)

Ma'dera SF (Geo) Madeira ▶ SM INV (vino) Madeira

'**madido, -a** AG: **~ (di)** wet o moist (with)

Ma'donna SF (Rel) Our Lady

mador'nale AG enormous, huge

'**madre** SF mother; (matrice di bolletta) counterfoil ▶ AG INV mother cpd; **ragazza ~** unmarried mother; **scena ~** (Teat) principal scene; (fig) terrible scene

madre'lingua SF mother tongue, native language

madre'patria SF mother country, native land

madre'perla SF mother-of-pearl

Ma'drid SF Madrid

madri'gale SM madrigal

madri'leno, -a AG of (o from) Madrid ▶ SM/F person from Madrid

ma'drina SF godmother

maestà SF INV majesty; **Sua M~ la Regina** Her Majesty the Queen

maestosità SF majesty

maes'toso, -a AG majestic

ma'estra SF vedi **maestro**

maes'trale SM north-west wind, mistral

maes'tranze [maes'trantse] SFPL workforce sg

maes'tria SF mastery, skill

ma'estro, -a SM/F (Ins: anche: **maestro di scuola** o **elementare**) primary (BRIT) o grade school (US) teacher; (esperto) expert ▶ SM (artigiano, fig: guida) master; (Mus) maestro ▶ AG (principale) main; (di grande abilità) masterly, skilful (BRIT), skillful (US); **un colpo da ~** (fig) a masterly move; **muro ~** main wall; **strada maestra** main road; **maestra d'asilo** nursery teacher; **~ di ballo** dancing master; **~ di cerimonie** master of ceremonies; **~ d'orchestra** conductor, director (US); **~ di scherma** fencing master; **~ di sci** ski instructor

'**mafia** SF Mafia

mafi'oso SM member of the Mafia

'**maga, -ghe** SF sorceress

ma'gagna [ma'gaɲɲa] SF defect, flaw, blemish; (noia, guaio) problem

ma'gari ESCL (esprime desiderio): **~ fosse vero!** if only it were true!; **ti piacerebbe andare in Scozia? — ~!** would you like to go to Scotland? — I certainly would! ▶ AV (anche) even; (forse) perhaps

magazzi'naggio [magaddzi'naddʒo] SM: **(spese di) ~** storage charges pl, warehousing charges pl

magazzini'ere [magaddzi'njɛre] SM warehouseman

magaz'zino [magad'dzino] SM warehouse; **grande ~** department store; **~ doganale** bonded warehouse

'**maggio** ['maddʒo] SM May; vedi anche **luglio**

maggio'rana [maddʒo'rana] SF (Bot) (sweet) marjoram

maggio'ranza [maddʒo'rantsa] SF majority; **nella ~ dei casi** in most cases

maggio'rare [maddʒo'rare] /**72**/ VT to increase, raise

maggiorazi'one [maddʒorat'tsjone] SF (Comm) rise, increase

maggior'domo [maddʒor'dɔmo] SM butler

maggi'ore [mad'dʒore] AG (comparativo: più grande) bigger, larger; taller; greater; (: più vecchio: sorella, fratello) older, elder; (: di grado superiore) senior; (: più importante: Mil, Mus) major; (superlativo) biggest, largest; tallest; greatest; oldest, eldest ▶ SMF (di grado) superior; (di età) elder; (Mil) major; (: Aer) squadron leader; **la maggior parte** the majority; **andare per la ~** (cantante, attore ecc) to be very popular, be "in"

maggio'renne [maddʒo'rɛnne] AG of age ▶ SMF person who has come of age

maggiori'tario, -a [maddʒori'tarjo] AG majority cpd; (Pol: anche: **sistema maggioritario**) first-past-the-post system

maggior'mente [maddʒor'mente] AV much more; (con senso superlativo) most

ma'gia [ma'dʒia] SF magic

'**magico, -a, -ci, -che** ['madʒiko] AG magic; (fig) fascinating, charming, magical

'**magio** ['madʒo] SM (Rel): **i re Magi** the Magi, the Three Wise Men

magis'tero [madʒis'tɛro] SM teaching; (fig: maestria) skill; (Ins): **Facoltà di M~** ≈ teacher training college

magis'trale [madʒis'trale] AG primary (BRIT) o grade school (US) teachers', primary (BRIT) o grade school (US) teaching; (abile) skilful (BRIT), skillful (US); **istituto ~** secondary school for the training of primary teachers

magis'trato [madʒis'trato] SM magistrate

magistra'tura [madʒistra'tura] SF magistrature; (magistrati): **la ~** the Bench

'**maglia** ['maʎʎa] SF stitch; (lavoro ai ferri) knitting no pl; (tessuto, Sport) jersey; (maglione) jersey, sweater; (di catena) link; (di rete) mesh; **avviare/diminuire le maglie** to cast on/cast off; **lavorare a ~, fare la ~** to knit; **~ diritta/rovescia** plain/purl

m

maglie'ria [maʎʎe'ria] SF knitwear; (negozio) knitwear shop; **macchina per ~** knitting machine

magli'etta [maʎ'ʎetta] SF (canottiera) vest; (tipo camicia) T-shirt

magli'ficio [maʎʎi'fitʃo] SM knitwear factory

ma'glina [maʎ'ʎina] SF (tessuto) jersey

'**maglio** ['maʎʎo] SM mallet; (macchina) power hammer

magli'one [maʎ'ʎone] SM jumper, sweater

'**magma** SM magma; (fig) mass

ma'gnaccia [maɲ'ɲattʃa] SM INV (peg) pimp

magnanimità [maɲɲanimi'ta] SF magnanimity

ma'gnanimo, -a [maɲ'ɲanimo] AG magnanimous

ma'gnate [maɲ'ɲate] SM tycoon, magnate

ma'gnesia [maɲ'ɲɛzja] SF (Chim) magnesia

ma'gnesio [maɲ'ɲɛzjo] SM (Chim) magnesium; **al ~** (lampada, flash) magnesium cpd

ma'gnete [maɲ'ɲɛte] SM magnet

ma'gnetico, -a, -ci, -che [maɲ'ɲɛtiko] AG magnetic

magne'tismo [maɲɲe'tizmo] SM magnetism

magnetiz'zare [maɲɲetid'dzare] /72/ VT (Fisica) to magnetize; (fig) to mesmerize

magne'tofono [maɲɲe'tɔfono] SM tape recorder

magnifica'mente [maɲɲifika'mente] AV magnificently, extremely well

magnifi'cenza [maɲɲifi'tʃentsa] SF magnificence, splendour (BRIT), splendor (US)

ma'gnifico, -a, -ci, -che [maɲ'ɲifiko] AG magnificent, splendid; (ospite) generous

'**magno, -a** ['maɲɲo] AG: **aula magna** main hall

ma'gnolia [maɲ'ɲɔlja] SF magnolia

'**mago, -ghi** SM (stregone) magician, wizard; (illusionista) magician

ma'grezza [ma'grettsa] SF thinness

'**magro, -a** AG (very) thin, skinny; (carne) lean; (formaggio) low-fat; (fig: scarso, misero) meagre (BRIT), meager (US), poor; (: meschino: scusa) poor, lame; **mangiare di ~** not to eat meat

'**mai** AV (nessuna volta) never; (talvolta) ever; **non ... ~** never; **~ più** never again; **come ~?** why (o how) on earth?; **chi/dove/quando ~?** whoever/wherever/whenever?

mai'ale SM (Zool) pig; (carne) pork

mail ['meil] SF INV = **e-mail**

mai'olica SF majolica

maio'nese SF mayonnaise

Mai'orca SF Majorca

'**mais** SM maize (BRIT), corn (US)

mai'uscolo, -a AG (lettera) capital; (fig) enormous, huge ▶ SF capital letter ▶ SM capital letters pl; (Tip) upper case; **scrivere tutto (in) ~** to write everything in capitals o in capital letters

mal AV, SM vedi **male**

'**mala** SF (gergo) underworld

malac'corto, -a AG rash, careless

mala'fede SF bad faith

malaf'fare: di ~ ag (gente) shady, dishonest; **donna di ~** prostitute

mala'gevole [mala'dʒevole] AG difficult, hard

mala'grazia [mala'grattsja] SF: **con ~** with bad grace, impolitely

mala'lingua (pl malelingue) SF gossip (person)

mala'mente AV badly; (sgarbatamente) rudely

malan'dato, -a AG (persona: di salute) in poor health; (: di condizioni finanziarie) badly off; (trascurato) shabby

ma'lanimo SM ill will, malevolence; **di ~** unwillingly

ma'lanno SM (disgrazia) misfortune; (malattia) ailment

mala'pena SF: **a ~** hardly, scarcely

ma'laria SF (Med) malaria

ma'larico, -a, -ci, -che AG malarial

mala'sorte SF bad luck

mala'ticcio, -a [mala'tittʃo] AG sickly

ma'lato, -a AG ill, sick; (gamba) bad; (pianta) diseased ▶ SM/F sick person; (in ospedale) patient; **darsi ~** (sul lavoro ecc) to go sick

malat'tia SF (infettiva ecc) illness, disease; (cattiva salute) illness, sickness; (di pianta) disease; **mettersi in ~** to go on sick leave; **fare una ~ di qc** (fig: disperarsi) to get in a state about sth

malaugu'rato, -a AG ill-fated, unlucky

malau'gurio SM bad o ill omen; **uccello del ~** bird of ill omen

mala'vita SF underworld

malavi'toso, -a SM/F gangster

mala'voglia [mala'vɔʎʎa]: **di ~** av unwillingly, reluctantly

Ma'lawi [ma'lavi] SM: **il ~** Malawi

Mala'ysia SF Malaysia

malaysi'ano, -a AG, SM/F Malaysian

malcapi'tato, -a AG unlucky, unfortunate ▶ SM/F unfortunate person

mal'concio, -a, -ci, -ce [mal'kontʃo] AG in a sorry state

malcon'tento SM discontent

malcos'tume SM immorality

mal'destro, -a AG (inabile) inexpert, inexperienced; (goffo) awkward

maldi'cente [maldi'tʃente] AG slanderous

maldi'cenza [maldi'tʃentsa] SF malicious gossip

maldis'posto, -a AG: **~ (verso)** ill-disposed (towards)

Mal'dive SFPL: **le ~** the Maldives

'male AV badly ▶ SM (ciò che è ingiusto, disonesto) evil; (danno, svantaggio) harm; (sventura) misfortune; (dolore fisico, morale) pain, ache; **sentirsi ~** to feel ill; **aver mal di cuore/fegato** to have a heart/liver complaint; **aver mal di denti/d'orecchi/di testa** to have toothache/earache/a headache; **aver mal di gola** to have a sore throat; **aver ~ ai piedi** to have sore feet; **far ~** (dolere) to hurt; **far ~ alla salute** to be bad for one's health; **far del ~ a qn** to hurt o harm sb; **parlar ~ di qn** to speak ill of sb; **restare** o **rimanere ~** to be sorry; to be disappointed, to be hurt; **trattar ~ qn** to ill-treat sb; **andare a ~** to go off o bad; **come va? — non c'è ~** how are you? — not bad; **di ~ in peggio** from bad to worse; **per ~ che vada** however badly things go; **non avertene a ~**, **non prendertela a ~** don't take it to heart; **mal comune mezzo gaudio** (proverbio) a trouble shared is a trouble halved; **mal d'auto** carsickness; **mal di mare** seasickness

male'detto, -a PP di **maledire** ▶ AG cursed, damned; (fig: col) damned, blasted

male'dire /38/ VT to curse

maledizi'one [maledit'tsjone] SF curse; **~!** damn it!

maledu'cato, -a AG rude, ill-mannered

maleducazi'one [maledukat'tsjone] SF rudeness

male'fatta SF misdeed

male'ficio [male'fitʃo] SM witchcraft

ma'lefico, -a, -ci, -che AG (aria, cibo) harmful, bad; (influsso, azione) evil

ma'lese AG, SMF Malay(an) ▶ SM (Ling) Malay

Ma'lesia SF Malaya

ma'lessere SM indisposition, slight illness; (fig) uneasiness

malevo'lenza [malevo'lɛntsa] SF malevolence

ma'levolo, -a AG malevolent

malfa'mato, -a AG notorious

mal'fatto, -a AG (persona) deformed; (oggetto) badly made; (lavoro) badly done

malfat'tore, -'trice SM/F wrongdoer

mal'fermo, -a AG unsteady, shaky; (salute) poor, delicate

malformazi'one [malformat'tsjone] SF malformation

'malga, -ghe SF Alpine hut

malgo'verno SM maladministration

mal'grado PREP in spite of, despite ▶ CONG although; **mio** o **tuo** etc **~** against my (o your etc) will

ma'lia SF spell; (fig: fascino) charm

mali'ardo, -a AG (occhi, sorriso) bewitching ▶ SF enchantress

maligna'mente [maliɲɲa'mente] AV maliciously

mali'gnare [malin'ɲare] /15/ VI: **~ su** to malign, speak ill of

malignità [maliɲɲi'ta] SF INV (qualità) malice, spite; (osservazione) spiteful remark; **con ~** spitefully, maliciously

ma'ligno, -a [ma'liɲɲo] AG (malvagio) malicious, malignant; (Med) malignant

malinco'nia SF melancholy, gloom

malin'conico, -a, -ci, -che AG melancholy

malincu'ore: a ~ av reluctantly, unwillingly

malinfor'mato, -a AG misinformed

malintenzio'nato, -a [malintentsjo'nato] AG ill-intentioned

malin'teso, -a AG misunderstood; (riguardo, senso del dovere) mistaken, wrong ▶ SM misunderstanding; **c'è stato un ~** there's been a misunderstanding

ma'lizia [ma'littsja] SF (malignità) malice; (furbizia) cunning; (espediente) trick

malizi'oso, -a [malit'tsjoso] AG malicious; cunning; (vivace, birichino) mischievous

malle'abile AG malleable

mal'loppo SM (col: refurtiva) loot

malme'nare /72/ VT to beat up; (fig) to ill-treat

mal'messo, -a AG shabby

malnu'trito, -a AG undernourished

malnutrizi'one [malnutrit'tsjone] SF malnutrition

'malo, -a AG: **in ~ modo** badly

ma'locchio [ma'lɔkkjo] SM evil eye

ma'lora (col): **andare in ~** to go to the dogs; **va in ~!** go to hell!

ma'lore SM (sudden) illness

malri'dotto, -a AG (abiti, scarpe, persona) in a sorry state; (casa, macchina) dilapidated, in a poor state of repair

mal'sano, -a AG unhealthy

malsi'curo, -a AG unsafe

'Malta SF Malta

'malta SF (Edil) mortar

mal'tempo SM bad weather

'malto SM malt

mal'tolto SM ill-gotten gains pl

maltratta'mento SM ill treatment

maltrat'tare /72/ VT to ill-treat

malu'more SM bad mood; (irritabilità) bad temper; (discordia) ill feeling; **di ~** in a bad mood

'malva SF (Bot) mallow ▶ AG, SM INV mauve

mal'vagio, -a, -gi, -gie [mal'vadʒo] AG wicked, evil

malvagità [malvadʒi'ta] SF INV (qualità) wickedness; (azione) wicked deed

malva'sia SF Italian dessert wine

malversazi'one [malversat'tsjone] SF (Dir) embezzlement

malves'tito, -a AG badly dressed, ill-clad

mal'visto, -a AG: **~ (da)** disliked (by), unpopular (with)

malvi'vente SM criminal

malvolenti'eri AV unwillingly, reluctantly

malvo'lere /131/ VT: **farsi ~ da qn** to make o.s. unpopular with sb ▶ SM: **prendere qn a ~** to take a dislike to sb

'**malware** ['malwer] SM INV (*Inform*) malware (program)

'**mamma** SF mum(my) (*Brit*), mom (*US*); **~ mia!** my goodness!

mam'mario, -a AG (*Anat*) mammary

mam'mella SF (*Anat*) breast; (*di vacca, capra ecc*) udder

mam'mifero SM mammal

mam'mismo SM *excessive attachment to one's mother*

'**mammola** SF (*Bot*) violet

'**manager** ['mænidʒə] SM INV manager

manageri'ale [manadʒe'rjale] AG managerial

ma'nata SF (*colpo*) slap; (*quantità*) handful

'**manca** SF left (hand); **a destra e a ~** left, right and centre, on all sides

manca'mento SM (*di forze*) (feeling of) faintness, weakness

man'canza [man'kantsa] SF lack; (*carenza*) shortage, scarcity; (*fallo*) fault; (*imperfezione*) failing, shortcoming; **per ~ di tempo** through lack of time; **in ~ di meglio** for lack of anything better; **sentire la ~ di qc/qn** to miss sth/sb

man'care /20/ VI (*essere insufficiente*) to be lacking; (*venir meno*) to fail; (*sbagliare*) to be wrong, make a mistake; (*non esserci*) to be missing, not to be there; (*essere lontano*): **~ (da)** to be away (from) ▶ VT to miss; **~ di** to lack; **~ a** (*promessa*) to fail to keep; **tu mi manchi** I miss you; **mancò poco che morisse** he very nearly died; **mancano ancora 10 sterline** we're still £10 short; **manca un quarto alle 6** it's a quarter to 6; **non mancherò** I won't forget, I'll make sure I do; **ci mancherebbe altro!** of course I (*o you etc*) will!; **~ da casa** to be away from home; **~ di rispetto a *o* verso qn** to be lacking in respect towards sb, be disrespectful towards sb; **~ di parola** not to keep one's word, go back on one's word; **sentirsi ~** to feel faint

man'cato, -a AG (*tentativo*) unsuccessful; (*artista*) failed

manche [mãʃ] SF INV (*Sport*) heat

mancherò *etc* [manke'rɔ] VB *vedi* **mancare**

man'chevole [man'kevole] AG (*insufficiente*) inadequate, insufficient

manchevo'lezza [mankevo'lettsa] SF (*scorrettezza*) fault, shortcoming

'**mancia, -ce** ['mantʃa] SF tip; **~ competente** reward

manci'ata [man'tʃata] SF handful

man'cino, -a [man'tʃino] AG (*braccio*) left; (*persona*) left-handed; (*fig*) underhand

'**manco** AV (*nemmeno*): **~ per sogno *o* per idea!** not on your life!

man'dante SMF (*Dir*) principal; (*istigatore*) instigator

manda'rancio [manda'rantʃo] SM clementine

man'dare /72/ VT to send; (*far funzionare: macchina*) to drive; (*emettere*) to send out; (*: grido*) to give, utter, let out; **~ avanti** (*persona*) to send ahead; (*fig: famiglia*) to provide for; (*: ditta*) to look after, run; (*: fabbrica*) to run, look after; (*: pratica*) to attend to; **~ a chiamare qn** to send for sb; **~ giù** to send down; (*anche fig*) to swallow; **~ in onda** (*Radio, TV*) to broadcast; **~ in rovina** to ruin; **~ via** to send away; (*licenziare*) to fire

manda'rino SM mandarin (orange); (*cinese*) mandarin

man'data SF (*quantità*) lot, batch; (*di chiave*) turn; **chiudere a doppia ~** to double-lock

manda'tario SM (*Dir*) representative, agent

man'dato SM (*incarico*) commission; (*Dir: provvedimento*) warrant; (*di deputato ecc*) mandate; (*ordine di pagamento*) postal *o* money order; **~ d'arresto, ~ di cattura** warrant for arrest; **~ di comparizione** summons *sg*; **~ di perquisizione** search warrant

man'dibola SF mandible, jaw

mando'lino SM mandolin(e)

'**mandorla** SF almond

mandor'lato SM nut brittle

'**mandorlo** SM almond tree

'**mandria** SF herd

mandri'ano SM cowherd, herdsman

man'drino SM (*Tecn*) mandrel

maneg'gevole [maned'dʒevole] AG easy to handle

maneggi'are [maned'dʒare] /62/ VT (*creta, cera*) to mould (*Brit*), mold (*US*), work, fashion; (*arnesi, utensili*) to handle; (*: adoperare*) to use; (*fig: persone, denaro*) to handle, deal with

ma'neggio [ma'neddʒo] SM moulding (*Brit*), molding (*US*); handling; use; (*intrigo*) plot, scheme; (*per cavalli*) riding school

ma'nesco, -a, -schi, -sche AG free with one's fists

ma'nette SFPL handcuffs

manga'nello SM club

manga'nese SM manganese

mange'reccio, -a, -ci, -ce [mandʒe'rettʃo] AG edible

mangi'abile [man'dʒabile] AG edible, eatable

mangia'dischi [mandʒa'diski] SM INV record player

mangia'nastri [mandʒa'nastri] SM INV cassette-recorder

mangi'are [man'dʒare] /62/ VT to eat; (*intaccare*) to eat into o away; (*Carte, Scacchi ecc*) to take ▶ VI to eat ▶ SM eating; (*cibo*) food; (*cucina*) cooking; **fare da ~** to do the cooking; **mangiarsi le parole** to mumble; **mangiarsi le unghie** to bite one's nails

mangia'soldi [mandʒa'sɔldi] AG INV (*col*): **macchinetta ~** one-armed bandit

mangia'toia [mandʒa'toja] SF feeding-trough

man'gime [man'dʒime] SM fodder

mangiucchi'are [mandʒuk'kjare] /19/ VT to nibble

'mango, -ghi SM mango

ma'nia SF (*Psic*) mania; (*fig*) obsession, craze; **avere la ~ di fare qc** to have a habit of doing sth; **~ di persecuzione** persecution complex o mania

mania'cale AG (*Psic*) maniacal; (*fanatico*) fanatical

ma'niaco, -a, -ci, -che AG suffering from a mania; **~ (di)** obsessed (by), crazy (about)

'manica, -che SF sleeve; (*fig: gruppo*) gang, bunch; (*Geo*): **la M~, il Canale della M~** the (English) Channel; **senza maniche** sleeveless; **essere in maniche di camicia** to be in one's shirt sleeves; **essere di ~ larga/stretta** to be easy-going/strict; **~ a vento** (*Aer*) wind sock

manica'retto SM titbit (*BRIT*), tidbit (*US*)

mani'chetta [mani'ketta] SF (*Tecn*) hose

mani'chino [mani'kino] SM (*di sarto, vetrina*) dummy

'manico, -ci SM handle; (*Mus*) neck; **~ di scopa** broomstick

mani'comio SM mental hospital; (*fig*) madhouse

mani'cotto SM muff; (*Tecn*) coupling; sleeve

mani'cure SM o F INV manicure ▶ SF INV manicurist

mani'era SF way, manner; (*stile*) style, manner; **maniere** SFPL (*comportamento*) manners; **in ~ che** so that; **in ~ da** so as to; **alla ~ di** in o after the style of; **in una ~ o nell'altra** one way or another; **in tutte le maniere** at all costs; **usare buone maniere con qn** to be polite to sb; **usare le maniere forti** to use strong-arm tactics

manie'rato, -a AG affected

mani'ero SM manor

manifat'tura SF (*lavorazione*) manufacture; (*stabilimento*) factory

manifatturi'ero, -a AG manufacturing

manifes'tante SMF demonstrator

manifes'tare /72/ VT to show, display; (*esprimere*) to express; (*rivelare*) to reveal, disclose ▶ VI to demonstrate; **manifestarsi** VPR to show o.s.; **manifestarsi amico** to prove o.s. (to be) a friend

manifestazi'one [manifestat'tsjone] SF show, display, expression; (*sintomo*) sign, symptom; (*dimostrazione pubblica*) demonstration; (*cerimonia*) event

manifes'tino SM leaflet

mani'festo, -a AG obvious, evident ▶ SM poster, bill; (*scritto ideologico*) manifesto

ma'niglia [ma'niʎʎa] SF handle; (*sostegno: negli autobus ecc*) strap

Ma'nila SF Manila

manipo'lare /72/ VT to manipulate; (*alterare: vino*) to adulterate

manipolazi'one [manipolat'tsjone] SF manipulation; adulteration

ma'nipolo SM (*drappello*) handful

manis'calco, -chi SM blacksmith, farrier (*BRIT*)

'manna SF (*Rel*) manna

man'naia SF (*del boia*) (executioner's) axe o ax (*US*); (*per carni*) cleaver

man'naro, -a AG: **lupo ~** werewolf

'mano, -i SF hand; (*strato: di vernice ecc*) coat; **a ~** by hand; **cucito a ~** hand-sewn; **fatto a ~** handmade; **alla ~** (*persona*) easy-going; **fuori ~** out of the way; **di prima ~** (*notizia*) first-hand; **di seconda ~** second-hand; **man ~** little by little, gradually; **man ~ che** as; **a piene mani** (*fig*) generously; **avere le mani bucate** to spend money like water; **aver le mani in pasta** to be in the know; **avere qc per le mani** (*progetto, lavoro*) to have sth in hand; **dare una ~ a qn** to lend sb a hand; **dare una ~ di vernice a qc** to give sth a coat of paint; **darsi** o **stringersi la ~** to shake hands; **forzare la ~** to go too far; **mettere ~ a qc** to have a hand in sth; **mettere le mani avanti** (*fig*) to safeguard o.s.; **restare a mani vuote** to be left empty-handed; **venire alle mani** to come to blows; **mani in alto!** hands up!; **mani pulite** *see note*

> Mani pulite ("clean hands") is a term used to describe the judicial operation of the early 1990s to gather evidence against politicians and industrialists who were implicated in bribery and corruption scandals.

mano'dopera SF labour (*BRIT*), labor (*US*)

mano'messo, -a PP di **manomettere**

ma'nometro SM gauge, manometer

mano'mettere /63/ VT (*alterare*) to tamper with; (*aprire indebitamente*) to break open illegally

manomissi'one SF (*di prove ecc*) tampering; (*di lettera*) opening

ma'nopola SF (*dell'armatura*) gauntlet; (*guanto*) mitt; (*di impugnatura*) hand-grip; (*pomello*) knob

manos'critto, -a AG handwritten ▶ SM manuscript

manova'lanza [manova'lantsa] SF unskilled workers pl

mano'vale SM labourer (BRIT), laborer (US)

mano'vella SF handle; (Tecn) crank

ma'novra SF manoeuvre (BRIT), maneuver (US); (Ferr) shunting; **manovre di corridoio** palace intrigues

mano'vrare /72/ VT (veicolo) to manoeuvre (BRIT), maneuver (US); (macchina, congegno) to operate; (fig: persona) to manipulate ▶ VI to manoeuvre

manro'vescio [manro'veʃʃo] SM (with back of hand) slap

man'sarda SF attic

mansi'one SF task, duty, job

mansu'eto, -a AG (animale) tame; (persona) gentle, docile

mansue'tudine SF tameness gentleness, docility

man'tello SM cloak; (fig: di neve ecc) blanket, mantle; (Tecn: involucro) casing, shell; (Zool) coat

mante'nere /121/ VT to maintain; (adempiere: promesse) to keep, abide by; (provvedere a) to support, maintain; **mantenersi** VPR: **mantenersi calmo/giovane** to stay calm/ young; **~ i contatti con qn** to keep in touch with sb

manteni'mento SM maintenance

mante'nuto, -a SM/F gigolo/kept woman

'mantice ['mantitʃe] SM bellows pl; (di carrozza, automobile) hood

'manto SM cloak; **~ stradale** road surface

'Mantova SF Mantua

manto'vano, -a AG of (o from) Mantua

manu'ale AG manual ▶ SM (testo) manual, handbook

manua'listico, -a, -ci, -che AG textbook cpd

manual'mente AV manually, by hand

ma'nubrio SM handle; (di bicicletta ecc) handlebars pl; (Sport) dumbbell

manu'fatto SM manufactured article; **manufatti** SMPL manufactured goods

manutenzi'one SF [manuten'tsjone] SF maintenance, upkeep; (d'impianti) maintenance, servicing

'manzo ['mandzo] SM (Zool) steer; (carne) beef

Mao'metto SM Mohammed

'mappa SF (Geo) map

mappa'mondo SM map of the world; (globo girevole) globe

ma'rasma, -i SM (fig) decay, decline

mara'tona SF marathon

'marca, -che SF mark; (bollo) stamp; (Comm: di prodotti) brand; (contrassegno, scontrino) ticket, check; **prodotti di (gran) ~** high-class products; **~ da bollo** official stamp

mar'care /20/ VT (munire di contrassegno) to mark; (a fuoco) to brand; (Sport: gol) to score; (: avversario) to mark; (accentuare) to stress; **~ visita** (Mil) to report sick

mar'cato, -a AG (lineamenti, accento ecc) pronounced

'Marche ['marke] SFPL: **le ~** the Marches (region of central Italy)

marcherò etc [marke'rɔ] VB vedi **marcare**

mar'chese, -a [mar'keze] SM/F marquis o marquess/marchioness

marchi'ano, -a [mar'kjano] AG (errore) glaring, gross

marchi'are [mar'kjare] /19/ VT to brand

marchigi'ano, -a [marki'dʒano] AG of (o from) the Marches

'marchio ['markjo] SM (di bestiame: Comm: fig) brand; **~ depositato** registered trademark; **~ di fabbrica** trademark

'marcia, -ce ['martʃa] SF (anche Mus, Mil) march; (funzionamento) running; (il camminare) walking; (Aut) gear; **mettere in ~** to start; **mettersi in ~** to get moving; **far ~ indietro** (Aut) to reverse; (fig) to back-pedal; **~ forzata** forced march; **~ funebre** funeral march

marciapi'ede [martʃa'pjɛde] SM (di strada) pavement (BRIT), sidewalk (US); (Ferr) platform

marci'are [mar'tʃare] /14/ VI to march; (andare: treno, macchina) to go; (funzionare) to run, work

'marcio, -a, -ci, -ce ['martʃo] AG (frutta, legno) rotten, bad; (Med) festering; (fig) corrupt, rotten ▶ SM: **c'è del ~ in questa storia** (fig) there's something fishy about this business; **avere torto ~** to be utterly wrong

mar'cire [mar'tʃire] /55/ VI (andare a male) to go bad, rot; (suppurare) to fester; (fig) to rot, waste away

marci'ume [mar'tʃume] SM (parte guasta: di cibi ecc) rotten part, bad part; (: di radice, pianta) rot; (fig: corruzione) rottenness, corruption

'marco, -chi SM (unità monetaria) mark

'mare SM sea; **di ~** (brezza, acqua, uccelli, pesce) sea cpd; **in ~** at sea; **per ~** by sea; **sul ~** (barca) on the sea; (villaggio, località) by o beside the sea; **andare al ~** (in vacanza ecc) to go to the seaside; **il mar Caspio** the Caspian Sea; **il mar Morto** the Dead Sea; **il mar Nero** the Black Sea; **il ~ del Nord** the North Sea; **il mar Rosso** the Red Sea; **il mar dei Sargassi** the Sargasso Sea; **i mari del Sud** the South Seas

ma'rea SF tide; **alta/bassa ~** high/low tide

mareggi'ata [mared'dʒata] SF heavy sea

ma'remma SF (Geo) maremma, swampy coastal area

marem'mano, -a AG (zona, macchia) swampy; (della Maremma) of (o from) the Maremma

mare'moto SM seaquake

maresci'allo [mareʃʃallo] SM (*Mil*) marshal; (: *sottufficiale*) warrant officer

marez'zato, -a [mared'dzato] AG (*seta ecc*) watered, moiré; (*legno*) veined; (*carta*) marbled

marga'rina SF margarine

marghe'rita [marge'rita] SF (ox-eye) daisy, marguerite

margheri'tina [margeri'tina] SF daisy

margi'nale [mardʒi'nale] AG marginal

'margine ['mardʒine] SM margin; (*di bosco, via*) edge, border; **avere un buon ~ di tempo/denaro** to have plenty of time/money; **~ di guadagno** o **di utile** profit margin; **~ di sicurezza** safety margin

mariju'ana [mæri'waːnə] SF marijuana

ma'rina SF navy; (*costa*) coast; (*quadro*) seascape; **~ mercantile** merchant navy (*BRIT*) o marine (*US*); **~ militare** ≈ Royal Navy (*BRIT*), ≈ Navy (*US*)

mari'naio SM sailor

mari'nare /72/ VT (*Cuc*) to marinate; **~ la scuola** to play truant

mari'naro, -a AG (*tradizione, popolo*) seafaring; (*Cuc*) with seafood; **alla marinara** (*vestito, cappello*) sailor *cpd*; **borgo ~** district where fishing folk live

mari'nata SF marinade

ma'rino, -a AG sea *cpd*, marine

mario'netta SF puppet

mari'tare /72/ VT to marry; **maritarsi** VPR: **maritarsi a** o **con qn** to marry sb, get married to sb

mari'tato, -a AG married

ma'rito SM husband; **prendere ~** to get married; **ragazza (in età) da ~** girl of marriageable age

ma'rittimo, -a AG maritime, sea *cpd*

mar'maglia [mar'maʎʎa] SF mob, riff-raff

marmel'lata SF jam; (*di agrumi*) marmalade

mar'mitta SF (*recipiente*) pot; (*Aut*) silencer; **~ catalitica** catalytic converter

'marmo SM marble

mar'mocchio [mar'mɔkkjo] SM (*col*) (little) kid

mar'motta SF (*Zool*) marmot

maroc'chino, -a [marok'kino] AG, SM/F Moroccan

Ma'rocco SM: **il ~** Morocco

ma'roso SM breaker

'marra SF hoe

Marra'kesh [marra'keʃ] SF Marrakesh

mar'rone AG INV brown ▶ SM (*Bot*) chestnut

mar'sala SM INV (*vino*) Marsala (wine)

Mar'siglia [mar'siʎʎa] SF Marseilles

mar'sina SF tails *pl*, tail coat

mar'supio SM (*Zool*) pouch, marsupium

mart. ABBR (= *martedì*) Tue(s)

'Marte SM (*Astr, Mitologia*) Mars

martedì SM INV Tuesday; **di** o **il ~** on Tuesdays; **oggi è ~ 3 aprile** (the date) today is Tuesday 3rd April; **~ stavo male** I wasn't well on Tuesday; **il giornale di ~** Tuesday's newspaper; **~ grasso** Shrove Tuesday

martel'lante AG (*fig: dolore*) throbbing

martel'lare /72/ VT to hammer ▶ VI (*pulsare*) to throb; (: *cuore*) to thump

martel'letto SM (*di pianoforte*) hammer; (*di macchina da scrivere*) typebar; (*di giudice, nelle vendite all'asta*) gavel; (*Med*) percussion hammer

mar'tello SM hammer; (*di uscio*) knocker; **suonare a ~** (*fig: campane*) to sound the tocsin; **~ pneumatico** pneumatic drill

marti'netto SM (*Tecn*) jack

martin'gala SF (*di giacca*) half-belt; (*di cavallo*) martingale

'martire SMF martyr

mar'tirio SM martyrdom; (*fig*) agony, torture

martori'are /19/ VT to torment, torture

mar'xismo SM Marxism

mar'xista, -i, -e AG, SM/F Marxist

marza'pane [martsa'pane] SM marzipan

marzi'ale [mar'tsjale] AG martial

'marzo ['martso] SM March; *vedi* **luglio**

marzo'lino, -a [martso'lino] AG March *cpd*

mascalzo'nata [maskaltso'nata] SF dirty trick

mascal'zone [maskal'tsone] SM rascal, scoundrel

mas'cara SM INV mascara

mascar'pone SM *soft cream cheese often used in desserts*

ma'scella [maʃʃɛlla] SF (*Anat*) jaw

'maschera ['maskera] SF mask; (*travestimento*) disguise; (*per un ballo ecc*) fancy dress; (*Teat, Cine*) usher/usherette; (*personaggio del teatro*) stock character; **in ~** (*mascherato*) masked; **ballo in ~** fancy-dress ball; **gettare la ~** (*fig*) to reveal o.s.; **~ antigas/subacquea** gas/diving mask; **~ di bellezza** face pack

masche'rare [maske'rare] /72/ VT to mask; (*travestire*) to disguise; to dress up; (*fig: celare*) to hide, conceal; (*Mil*) to camouflage; **mascherarsi** VPR: **mascherarsi da** to disguise o.s. as; to dress up as; (*fig*) to masquerade as

masche'rina [maske'rina] SF (*piccola maschera*) mask; (*di animale*) patch; (*di scarpe*) toe-cap; (*Aut*) radiator grill

mas'chile [mas'kile] AG masculine; (*sesso, popolazione*) male; (*abiti*) men's; (*per ragazzi: scuola*) boys'

mas'chilista, -i, -e AG, SM/F (*uomo*) (male) chauvinist, sexist; (*donna*) sexist

m

'maschio, -a ['maskjo] AG (Biol) male; (virile) manly ▸ SM (anche Zool, Tecn) male; (uomo) man; (ragazzo) boy; (figlio) son

masco'lino, -a AG masculine

mas'cotte [mas'kɔt] SF INV mascot

maso'chismo [mazo'kizmo] SM masochism

maso'chista, -i, -e [mazo'kista] AG masochistic ▸ SM/F masochist

'massa SF mass; (di gente) mass, multitude; (Elettr) earth; **una ~ di** (di errori ecc) heaps of, masses of; **in ~** (Comm) in bulk; (tutti insieme) en masse; **adunata in ~** mass meeting; **manifestazione/cultura di ~** mass demonstration/culture; **produrre in ~** to mass-produce; **la ~ (del popolo)** the masses pl

massa'crante AG exhausting, gruelling

massa'crare /72/ VT to massacre, slaughter

mas'sacro SM massacre, slaughter; (fig) mess, disaster

massaggi'are [massad'dʒare] /62/ VT to massage

massaggia'tore, -'trice [massaddʒa'tore] SM/F masseur (masseuse)

mas'saggio [mas'saddʒo] SM massage; **~ cardiaco** cardiac massage

mas'saia SF housewife

masse'ria SF large farm

masse'rizie [masse'rittsje] SFPL (household) furnishings

massicci'ata [massit'tʃata] SF (di strada, ferrovia) ballast

mas'siccio, -a, -ci, -ce [mas'sittʃo] AG (oro, legno) solid; (palazzo) massive; (corporatura) stout ▸ SM (Geo) massif

'massima SF vedi **massimo**

massi'male SM maximum; (Comm) ceiling, limit

'massimo, -a AG, SM maximum ▸ SF (sentenza, regola) maxim; (Meteor) maximum temperature; **in linea di massima** generally speaking; **arrivare entro il tempo ~** to arrive within the time limit; **al ~** at (the) most; **sfruttare qc al ~** to make full use of sth; **arriverò al ~ alle 5** I'll arrive at 5 at the latest; **erano presenti le massime autorità** all the most important dignitaries were there; **il ~ della pena** (Dir) the maximum penalty

mas'sivo, -a AG (intervento) en masse; (emigrazione) mass; (emorragia) massive

'masso SM rock, boulder

mas'sone SM freemason

massone'ria SF freemasonry

mas'sonico, -a, -ci, -che AG masonic

mas'tello SM tub

masteriz'zare [masterid'dzare] /72/ VT (CD, DVD) to burn

masterizza'tore [masteriddza'tore] SM CD burner o writer

masti'care /20/ VT to chew

'mastice ['mastitʃe] SM mastic; (per vetri) putty

mas'tino SM mastiff

masto'dontico, -a, -ci, -che AG gigantic

mastur'barsi /72/ VPR to masturbate

masturbazi'one [masturbat'tsjone] SF masturbation

ma'tassa SF skein

mate'matico, -a, -ci, -che AG mathematical ▸ SM/F mathematician ▸ SF mathematics sg

materas'sino SM mat; **~ gonfiabile** air bed

mate'rasso SM mattress; **~ a molle** spring o interior-sprung mattress

ma'teria SF (Fisica) matter; (Tecn, Comm) material, matter no pl; (disciplina) subject; (argomento) subject matter, material; **in ~ di** (per quanto concerne) on the subject of; **prima di entrare in ~ …** before discussing the matter in hand …; **un esperto in ~ (di musica ecc)** an expert on the subject (of music etc); **sono ignorante in ~** I know nothing about it; **~ cerebrale** cerebral matter; **~ grassa** fat; **~ grigia** (anche fig) grey matter; **materie plastiche** plastics; **materie prime** raw materials

materi'ale AG material; (fig: grossolano) rough, rude ▸ SM material; (insieme di strumenti ecc) equipment no pl, materials pl; **~ da costruzione** building materials pl

materia'lista, -i, -e AG materialistic ▸ SM/F materialist

materializ'zarsi [materjalid'dzarsi] /72/ VPR to materialize

material'mente AV (fisicamente) materially; (economicamente) financially

maternità SF motherhood, maternity; (clinica) maternity hospital; (reparto) maternity ward; **in (congedo di) ~** on maternity leave

ma'terno, -a AG (amore, cura ecc) maternal, motherly; (nonno) maternal; (lingua, terra) mother cpd; vedi anche **scuola**

ma'tita SF pencil; **matite colorate** coloured pencils; **~ per gli occhi** eyeliner (pencil)

ma'trice [ma'tritʃe] SF matrix; (Comm) counterfoil; (fig: origine) background

ma'tricola SF (registro) register; (numero) registration number; (nell'università) freshman, fresher (BRIT col)

ma'trigna [ma'trinɲa] SF stepmother

matrimoni'ale AG matrimonial, marriage cpd; **camera/letto ~** double room/bed

matri'monio SM marriage, matrimony; (durata) marriage, married life; (cerimonia) wedding

ma'trona SF (fig) matronly woman

matta'toio SM abattoir (BRIT), slaughterhouse

mat'tina SF morning; **la** o **alla** o **di** ~ in the morning; **di prima** ~, **la** ~ **presto** early in the morning; **dalla** ~ **alla sera** (*continuamente*) from morning to night; (*improvvisamente*: *cambiare*) overnight

matti'nata SF morning; (*spettacolo*) matinée, afternoon performance; **in** ~ in the course of the morning; **nella** ~ in the morning; **nella tarda** ~ at the end of the morning; **nella tarda** ~ **di sabato** late on Saturday morning

mattini'ero, -a AG: **essere** ~ to be an early riser

mat'tino SM morning; **di buon** ~ early in the morning

'**matto, -a** AG mad, crazy; (*fig*: *falso*) false, imitation; (*opaco*) matt, dull ▶ SM/F madman/woman; **avere una voglia matta di qc** to be dying for sth; **far diventare** ~ **qn** to drive sb mad o crazy; **una gabbia di matti** (*fig*) a madhouse

mat'tone SM brick; (*fig*): **questo libro/film è un** ~ this book/film is heavy going

matto'nella SF tile

mattu'tino, -a AG morning *cpd*

matu'rare /72/ VI (*anche*: **maturarsi**: *frutta, grano*) to ripen; (*ascesso*) to come to a head; (*fig*: *persona, idea, Econ*) to mature ▶ VT to ripen, to (make) mature; ~ **una decisione** to come to a decision

maturità SF maturity; (*di frutta*) ripeness, maturity; (*Ins*) school-leaving examination, ≈ GCE A-levels (*BRIT*)

ma'turo, -a AG mature; (*frutto*) ripe, mature

ma'tusa SM INV/F INV (*scherzoso*) old fogey

Mauri'tania SF: **la** ~ Mauritania

Mau'rizio [mau'rittsjo] SF: (**l'isola di**) ~ Mauritius

mauso'leo SM mausoleum

max. ABBR (= *massimo*) max

'**maxi...** PREFISSO maxi...

maxipro'cesso [maksipro'tʃɛsso] SM *see note*

> A *maxiprocesso* is a criminal trial which is characterized by the large number of co-defendants. These people are usually members of terrorist or criminal organizations. The trials are often lengthy and many witnesses may be called to give evidence.

maxis'chermo [maksis'kermo] SM giant screen

'**mazza** ['mattsa] SF (*bastone*) club; (*martello*) sledge-hammer; (*Sport*: *da golf*) club; (: *da baseball, cricket*) bat

maz'zata [mat'tsata] SF (*anche fig*) heavy blow

maz'zetta [mat'tsetta] SF (*di banconote ecc*) bundle; (*fig*) rake-off

'**mazzo** ['mattso] SM (*di fiori, chiavi ecc*) bunch; (*di carte da gioco*) pack

MC SIGLA = **Macerata**

m.c.d. ABBR (= *minimo comune denominatore*) lcd

m.c.m. ABBR (= *minimo comune multiplo*) lcm

ME SIGLA = **Messina**

me PRON me; **me stesso, me stessa** myself; **sei bravo quanto me** you are as clever as I (am) o as me

me'andro SM meander

M.E.C. [mɛk] ABBR M = **Mercato Comune Europeo**

'**Mecca** SF (*anche fig*): **La** ~ Mecca

meccanica'mente AV mechanically

mec'canico, -a, -ci, -che AG mechanical ▶ SM mechanic ▶ SF mechanics *sg*; (*attività tecnologica*) mechanical engineering; (*meccanismo*) mechanism; **officina meccanica** garage

mecca'nismo SM mechanism

meccaniz'zare [mekkanid'dzare] /72/ VT to mechanize

meccanizzazi'one [mekkaniddzat'tsjone] SF mechanization

meccanogra'fia SF (*mechanical*) data processing

meccano'grafico, -a, -ci, -che AG: **centro** ~ data processing department

mece'nate [metʃe'nate] SM patron

mèche [mɛʃ] SF INV streak; **farsi le** ~ to have one's hair streaked

me'daglia [me'daʎʎa] SF medal; ~ **d'oro** (*oggetto*) gold medal; (*persona*) gold medallist (*BRIT*) o medalist (*US*)

medagli'one [medaʎ'ʎone] SM (*Archit*) medallion; (*gioiello*) locket

me'desimo, -a AG same; (*in persona*): **io** ~ I myself

'**media** SF *vedi* **medio**

media'mente AV on average

medi'ano, -a AG median; (*valore*) mean ▶ SM (*Calcio*) half-back

medi'ante PREP by means of

medi'are /19/ VT (*fare da mediatore*) to act as mediator in; (*Mat*) to average

medi'ato, -a AG indirect

media'tore, -'trice SM/F mediator; (*Comm*) middle man, agent; **fare da** ~ **fra** to mediate between

mediazi'one [medjat'tsjone] SF mediation; (*Comm*: *azione, compenso*) brokerage

medica'mento SM medicine, drug

medi'care /20/ VT to treat; (*ferita*) to dress

medi'cato, -a AG (*garza, shampoo*) medicated

medicazi'one [medikat'tsjone] SF treatment, medication dressing; **fare una** ~ **a qn** to dress sb's wounds

medi'cina [medi'tʃina] SF medicine; ~ **legale** forensic medicine

medici'nale [meditʃi'nale] AG medicinal ▶ SM drug, medicine

m

'**medico, -a, -ci, -che** AG medical ▶ SM doctor;
~ **di bordo** ship's doctor; ~ **di famiglia**
family doctor; ~ **fiscale** *doctor who examines
patients signed off sick for a lengthy period by their
private doctor*; ~ **generico** general
practitioner, GP
medie'vale AG medieval
'**medio, -a** AG average; (*punto, ceto*) middle;
(*altezza, statura*) medium ▶ SM (*dito*) middle
finger ▶ SF average; (*Mat*) mean; (*Ins: voto*)
end-of-term average; **medie** SFPL *vedi* **scuola
media**; **licenza media** *leaving certificate
awarded at the end of 3 years of secondary
education*; **in media** on average; **al di
sopra/sotto della media** above/below
average; **viaggiare ad una media di ...**
to travel at an average speed of ...; **il M~
Oriente** the Middle East
medi'ocre AG (*gen*) mediocre; (*qualità, stipendio*)
poor
mediocrità SF mediocrity; poorness
medioe'vale AG = **medievale**
Medio'evo SM Middle Ages *pl*
medita'bondo, -a AG thoughtful
medi'tare /**72**/ VT to ponder over, meditate
on; (*progettare*) to plan, think out ▶ VI to
meditate
medi'tato, -a AG (*gen*) meditated; (*parole*)
carefully-weighed; (*vendetta*) premeditated;
ben ~ (*piano*) well worked-out, neat
meditazi'one [meditat'tsjone] SF
meditation
mediter'raneo, -a AG Mediterranean;
il (mare) M~ the Mediterranean (Sea)
'**medium** SM INV/F INV medium
me'dusa SF (*Zool*) jellyfish
mega SM INV (*Inform*) meg
mega'byte SM INV (*Inform*) megabyte
me'gafono SM megaphone
mega'lomane AG, SMF megalomaniac
me'gera [me'dʒɛra] SF (*peg: donna*) shrew
'**meglio** ['mεʎʎo] AV, AG INV better; (*con senso
superlativo*) best ▶ SM (*la cosa migliore*): **il ~** the
best (thing); **faresti ~ ad andartene** you
had better leave; **alla ~** as best one can;
andar di bene in ~ to get better and better;
fare del proprio ~ to do one's best; **per il ~**
for the best; **aver la ~ su qn** to get the
better of sb
'**mela** SF apple; ~ **cotogna** quince
mela'grana SF pomegranate
melan'zana [melan'dzana] SF aubergine
(*BRIT*), eggplant (*US*)
me'lassa SF molasses *sg*, treacle
melato'nina SF melatonin
me'lenso, -a AG dull, stupid
me'lissa SF (*Bot*) balm
mel'lifluo, -a AG (*peg*) sugary, honeyed
'**melma** SF mud, mire

'**melo** SM apple tree
melo'dia SF melody
me'lodico, -a, -ci, -che AG melodic
melodi'oso, -a AG melodious
melo'dramma, -i SM melodrama
me'lone SM (musk) melon
'**membra** SFPL *vedi* **membro**
mem'brana SF membrane
'**membro** SM (*pl(m)* **membri**: *person*) member;
(*pl(f)* **membra**: *arto*) limb
memo'rabile AG memorable
memo'randum SM INV memorandum
'**memore** AG: ~ **di** (*ricordando*) mindful of;
(*riconoscente*) grateful for
me'moria SF (*anche Inform*) memory;
memorie SFPL (*opera autobiografica*) memoirs;
a ~ (*imparare, sapere*) by heart; **a ~ d'uomo**
within living memory; ~ **di sola lettura**
(*Inform*) read-only memory; ~ **tampone**
(*Inform*) buffer
memori'ale SM (*raccolta di memorie*) memoirs
pl; (*Dir*) memorial
memoriz'zare [memorid'dzare] /**72**/ VT (*gen*)
to memorize; (*Inform*) to store
memorizzazi'one [memoriddzat'tsjone] SF
memorization; storage
'**mena** SF scheme
mena'dito: **a** ~ *av* perfectly, thoroughly;
sapere qc a ~ to have sth at one's fingertips
mena'gramo SM INV/F INV jinx, Jonah
me'nare /**72**/ VT to lead; (*picchiare*) to hit, beat;
(*dare: colpi*) to deal; ~ **la coda** (*cane*) to wag
its tail; ~ **qc per le lunghe** to drag sth out;
~ **il can per l'aia** (*fig*) to beat about (*BRIT*) o
around (*US*) the bush
mendi'cante SMF beggar
mendi'care /**20**/ VT to beg for ▶ VI to beg
menefre'ghismo [menefre'gizmo] SM (*col*)
couldn't-care-less attitude
me'ninge [me'nindʒe] SF (*Med*) meninx;
spremersi le meningi to rack one's brains
menin'gite [menin'dʒite] SF meningitis
me'nisco SM (*Anat, Mat, Fisica*) meniscus

(PAROLA CHIAVE)

'**meno** AV **1** (*in minore misura*) less; **dovresti
mangiare meno** you should eat less, you
shouldn't eat so much; **è sempre meno
facile** it's getting less and less easy; **ne
voglio di meno** I don't want so much
2 (*comparativo*): **meno ... di** not as ..., less ...
than; **sono meno alto di te** I'm not as tall
as you (are), I'm less tall than you (are);
meno ... che not as ... as, less ... than; **meno
che mai** less than ever; **è meno
intelligente che ricco** he's more rich than
intelligent; **meno fumo più mangio** the
less I smoke the more I eat; **meno di quanto
pensassi** less than I thought

3 (*superlativo*) least; **il meno dotato degli studenti** the least gifted of the students; **è quello che compro meno spesso** it's the one I buy least often

4 (*Mat*) minus; **8 meno 5** 8 minus 5, 8 take away 5; **sono le 8 meno un quarto** it's a quarter to 8; **meno 5 gradi** 5 degrees below zero, minus 5 degrees; **mille euro in meno** a thousand euros less; **ha preso 6 meno** (*a scuola*) he scraped a pass; **cento euro meno le spese** a hundred euros minus *o* less expenses

5 (*fraseologia*): **quanto meno poteva telefonare** he could at least have phoned; **non so se accettare o meno** I don't know whether to accept or not; **non essere da meno di** not to be outdone by; **fare a meno di qc/qn** to do without sth/sb; **non potevo fare a meno di ridere** I couldn't help laughing; **meno male!** thank goodness!; **meno male che sei arrivato** it's a good job that you've come

▶ AG INV (*tempo, denaro*) less; (*errori, persone*) fewer; **ha fatto meno errori di tutti** he made fewer mistakes than anyone, he made the fewest mistakes of all

▶ SM INV **1**: **il meno** (*il minimo*) the least; **parlare del più e del meno** to talk about this and that; **era il meno che ti potesse succedere** it was the least you could have expected

2 (*Mat*) minus

▶ PREP (*eccetto*) except (for), apart from; **tutti meno lui** everybody apart from *o* except him; **a meno che, a meno di** unless; **a meno che non piova** unless it rains; **non posso, a meno di prendere ferie** I can't, unless I take some leave; *vedi anche* **più**

meno'mare /**72**/ VT (*danneggiare*) to maim, disable

meno'mato, -a AG (*persona*) disabled ▶ SM/F disabled person

menomazi'one [menomat'tsjone] SF disablement

meno'pausa SF menopause

'mensa SF (*locale*) canteen; (: *Mil*) mess; (: *nelle università*) refectory

men'sile AG monthly ▶ SM (*periodico*) monthly (magazine); (*stipendio*) monthly salary

mensil'mente AV (*ogni mese*) every month; (*una volta al mese*) monthly

'mensola SF bracket; (*ripiano*) shelf; (*Archit*) corbel

'menta SF mint; (*anche*: **menta piperita**) peppermint; (: *bibita*) peppermint cordial; (: *caramella*) mint, peppermint

men'tale AG mental

mentalità SF INV mentality

mental'mente AV mentally

'mente SF mind; **imparare/sapere qc a ~** to learn/know sth by heart; **avere in ~ qc** to have sth in mind; **avere in ~ di fare qc** to intend to do sth; **fare venire in ~ qc a qn** to remind sb of sth; **mettersi in ~ di fare qc** to make up one's mind to do sth; **passare di ~ a qn** to slip sb's mind; **tenere a ~ qc** to bear sth in mind; **a ~ fredda** objectively; **lasciami fare ~ locale** let me think

mente'catto, -a AG half-witted ▶ SM/F halfwit, imbecile

men'tire /**17**/ VI to lie

men'tito, -a AG: **sotto mentite spoglie** under false pretences (*BRIT*) *o* pretenses (*US*)

'mento SM chin; **doppio ~** double chin

men'tolo SM menthol

'mentre CONG (*temporale*) while; (*avversativo*) whereas ▶ SM: **in quel ~** at that very moment

menù SM INV (set) menu; **~ turistico** set *o* tourists' menu

menzio'nare [mentsjo'nare] /**72**/ VT to mention

menzi'one [men'tsjone] SF mention; **fare ~ di** to mention

men'zogna [men'tsɔɲɲa] SF lie

menzo'gnero, -a [mentsoɲ'ɲɛro] AG false, untrue

mera'viglia [mera'viʎʎa] SF amazement, wonder; (*persona, cosa*) marvel, wonder; **a ~** perfectly, wonderfully

meravigli'are [meraviʎ'ʎare] /**27**/ VT to amaze, astonish; **meravigliarsi** VPR: **meravigliarsi (di)** to marvel (at); (*stupirsi*) to be amazed (at), be astonished (at); **mi meraviglio di te!** I'm surprised at you!; **non c'è da meravigliarsi** it's not surprising

meravigli'oso, -a [meraviʎ'ʎoso] AG wonderful, marvellous (*BRIT*), marvelous (*US*)

merc. ABBR (= *mercoledì*) Wed

mer'cante SM merchant; **~ d'arte** art dealer; **~ di cavalli** horse dealer

mercanteggi'are [merkanted'dʒare] /**62**/ VT (*onore, voto*) to sell ▶ VI to bargain, haggle

mercan'tile AG commercial, mercantile; (*nave, marina*) merchant *cpd* ▶ SM (*nave*) merchantman

mercan'zia [merkan'tsia] SF merchandise, goods *pl*

merca'tino SM (*rionale*) local street market; (*Econ*) unofficial stock market

mer'cato SM market; **di ~** (*economia, prezzo, ricerche*) market *cpd*; **mettere** *o* **lanciare qc sul ~** to launch sth on the market; **a buon ~** cheap; **~ dei cambi** exchange market; **M~ Comune (Europeo)** (European) Common Market; **~ del lavoro** labour market, job market; **~ nero** black market; **~ al rialzo/al ribasso** (*Borsa*) sellers'/buyers' market

'**merce** ['mɛrtʃe] SF goods *pl*, merchandise; **~ deperibile** perishable goods *pl*

mercé [mer'tʃe] SF mercy; **essere alla ~ di qn** to be at sb's mercy

merce'nario, -a [mertʃe'narjo] AG, SM mercenary

merce'ria [mertʃe'ria] SF (*articoli*) haberdashery (*BRIT*), notions *pl* (*US*); (*bottega*) haberdasher's shop (*BRIT*), notions store (*US*)

mercoledì SM INV Wednesday; **di** *o* **il ~** on Wednesdays; **~ delle Ceneri** Ash Wednesday; *see notevedi anche* **martedì**

> In the Catholic church, *Mercoledì delle Ceneri* signals the beginning of Lent. Churchgoers are marked on the forehead with ash from the burning of the olive branch. Ash Wednesday is traditionally a day of fasting, abstinence and repentance.

mer'curio SM mercury

'**merda** SF (*col*) shit (*!*)

me'renda SF afternoon snack

meren'dina SF snack

meridi'ano, -a AG (*di mezzogiorno*) midday *cpd*, noonday ▶ SM meridian ▶ SF (*orologio*) sundial

meridio'nale AG southern ▶ SMF southerner

meridi'one SM south

me'ringa, -ghe SF (*Cuc*) meringue

meri'tare /**72**/ VT to deserve, merit ▶ VB IMPERS (*valere la pena*): **merita andare** it's worth going; **non merita neanche parlarne** it's not worth talking about; **per quel che merita** for what it's worth

meri'tevole AG worthy

'**merito** SM merit; (*valore*) worth; **dare ~ a qn di** to give sb credit for; **finire a pari ~** to finish joint first (*o* second *etc*); to tie; **in ~ a** as regards, with regard to; **entrare nel ~ di una questione** to go into a matter; **non so niente in ~** I don't know anything about it

meritocra'zia [meritokrat'tsia] SF meritocracy

meri'torio, -a AG praiseworthy

mer'letto SM lace

'**merlo** SM (*Zool*) blackbird; (*Archit*) battlement

mer'luzzo [mer'luttso] SM (*Zool*) cod

'**mescere** ['meʃʃere] /**29**/ VT to pour (out)

meschinità [meskini'ta] SF wretchedness; meagreness; meanness, narrow-mindedness

mes'chino, -a [mes'kino] AG wretched; (*scarso*) meagre (*BRIT*), meager (*US*), scanty, poor; (*persona: gretta*) mean; (*: limitata*) narrow-minded, petty; **fare una figura meschina** to cut a poor figure

'**mescita** ['meʃʃita] SF wine shop

mesci'uto, -a [meʃ'ʃuto] PP *di* **mescere**

mesco'lanza [mesko'lantsa] SF mixture

mesco'lare /**72**/ VT to mix; (*vini, colori*) to blend; (*mettere in disordine*) to mix up, muddle up; (*carte*) to shuffle; **mescolarsi** VPR to mix; to blend; to get mixed up; (*fig*) **mescolarsi in** to get mixed up in, meddle in

'**mese** SM month; **il ~ scorso** last month; **il corrente ~** this month

'**messa** SF (*Rel*) mass; (*il mettere*): **~ a fuoco** focusing; **~ in moto** starting; **~ in piega** (*acconciatura*) set; **~ a punto** (*Tecn*) adjustment; (*Aut*) tuning; (*fig*) clarification; **~ in scena** = **messinscena**

messagge'rie [messaddʒe'rie] SFPL (*ditta: di distribuzione*) distributors; (*: di trasporto*) freight company

messag'gero [messad'dʒero] SM messenger

messaggiare [messa'dzare] VI (*col*) to message ▶ VT to message; **~ con qn** to message sb; **~ qn su Facebook** to facebook sb

messaggi'arsi [messad'dʒarsi] /**72**/ VPR to text; **messaggiamoci** we'll text each other

messag'gino [messad'dʒino] SM (*di telefonino*) text (message)

mes'saggio [mes'saddʒo] SM message; **~ istantaneo** instant message

messag'gistica [messad'dʒistika] SF: **~ immediata** (*Inform*) instant messaging; **programma di ~ immediata** instant messenger

mes'sale SM (*Rel*) missal

'**messe** SF harvest

Mes'sia SM INV (*Rel*): **il ~** the Messiah

messi'cano, -a AG, SM/F Mexican

'**Messico** SM: **il ~** Mexico; **Città del ~** Mexico City

messin'scena [messin'ʃena] SF (*Teat*) production

'**messo, -a** PP *di* **mettere** ▶ SM messenger

mestie'rante SMF (*peg*) money-grubber; (*: scrittore*) hack

mesti'ere SM (*professione*) job; (*artigianale*) craft; (*manuale*) trade; (*fig: abilità nel lavoro*) skill, technique; **di ~** by *o* to trade; **essere del ~** to know the tricks of the trade

mes'tizia [mes'tittsja] SF sadness, melancholy

'**mesto, -a** AG sad, melancholy

'**mestolo** SM (*Cuc*) ladle

mestru'ale AG menstrual

mestruazi'one [mestruat'tsjone] SF menstruation; **avere le mestruazioni** to have one's period

'**meta** SF destination; (*fig*) aim, goal

metà SF INV half; (*punto di mezzo*) middle; **dividere qc a** *o* **per ~** to divide sth in half, halve sth; **fare a ~ (di qc con qn)** to go halves (with sb in sth); **a ~ prezzo** at half price; **a ~ settimana** midweek; **a ~ strada** halfway; **verso la ~ del mese** halfway through the month, towards the middle of the month; **dire le cose a ~** to leave some things unsaid; **fare le cose a ~** to leave things half-done; **la mia dolce ~** (*col, scherzoso*) my better half

metabo'lismo SM metabolism

meta'done SM methadone

meta'fisica SF metaphysics *sg*

me'tafora SF metaphor

meta'forico, -a, -ci, -che AG metaphorical

me'tallico, -a, -ci, -che AG (*di metallo*) metal *cpd*; (*splendore, rumore ecc*) metallic

metalliz'zato, -a [metallid'dzato] AG (*verniciatura*) metallic

me'tallo SM metal; **di ~** metal *cpd*

metallur'gia [metallur'dʒia] SF metallurgy

metalmec'canico, -a, -ci, -che AG engineering *cpd* ▶ SM engineering worker

meta'morfosi SF metamorphosis

me'tano SM methane

me'teora SF meteor

meteo'rite SM meteorite

meteorolo'gia [meteorolo'dʒia] SF meteorology

meteoro'logico, -a, -ci, -che [meteoro'lɔdʒiko] AG meteorological, weather *cpd*

meteo'rologo, -a, -ghi, -ghe SM/F meteorologist

me'ticcio, -a, -ci, -ce [me'tittʃo] SM/F half-caste, half-breed

meticolosità SF meticulousness

metico'loso, -a AG meticulous

me'todico, -a, -ci, -che AG methodical

'**metodo** SM method; (*manuale*) tutor (BRIT), manual; **far qc con/senza ~** to do sth methodically/unmethodically

me'traggio [me'traddʒo] SM (*Sartoria*) length; (*Cine*) footage; **film a lungo ~** feature film; **film a corto ~** short film

metra'tura SF length

'**metrico, -a, -ci, -che** AG metric; (*Poesia*) metrical ▶ SF metrics *sg*

'**metro** SM metre (BRIT), meter (US); (*nastro*) tape measure; (*asta*) (metre) rule

metrò SM INV underground (BRIT), subway (US)

metro'notte SM INV night security guard

me'tropoli SF metropolis

metropoli'tano, -a AG metropolitan ▶ SF underground (BRIT), subway (US); **metropolitana leggera** metro (*mainly on the surface*)

metroses'suale AG metrosexual

'**mettere** /63/ VT to put; (*abito*) to put on; (*: portare*) to wear; (*installare: telefono*) to put in;

~ fame/allegria a qn (*fig: provocare*) to make sb hungry/happy; (*supporre*): **mettiamo che … let's suppose** *o* say that …; **mettersi** VPR (*persona*) to put o.s.; (*oggetto*) to go; (*disporsi: faccenda*) to turn out; **mettersi a** (*cominciare*) to begin to, start to; **mettersi a piangere/ridere** to start crying/laughing, start *o* begin to cry/laugh; **mettersi a sedere** to sit down; **mettersi al lavoro** to set to work; **mettersi a letto** to get into bed; (*per malattia*) to take to one's bed; **mettersi il cappello** to put on one's hat; **mettersi sotto** to get down to things; **mettersi in società** to set up in business; **si sono messi insieme** (*coppia*) they've started going out together (BRIT) *o* dating (US); **mettersi con qn** (*in società*) to team up with sb; (*in coppia*) to start going out with sb; **metterci: metterci molta cura/molto tempo** to take a lot of care/a lot of time; **mettercela tutta** to do one's best; **ci ho messo 3 ore per venire** it's taken me 3 hours to get here; **~ un annuncio sul giornale** to place an advertisement in the paper; **~ a confronto** to compare; **~ in conto** (*somma ecc*) to put on account; **~ in luce** (*problemi, errori*) to stress, highlight; **~ a tacere qn/qc** to keep sb/sth quiet; **~ su casa** to set up house; **~ su un negozio** to start a shop; **~ su peso** to put on weight; **~ via** to put away

mez'zadro [med'dzadro] SM (*Agr*) sharecropper

mezza'luna [meddza'luna] (*pl* **mezzelune**) SF half-moon; (*dell'islamismo*) crescent; (*coltello*) (semicircular) chopping knife

mezza'nino [meddza'nino] SM mezzanine (floor)

mez'zano, -a [med'dzano] AG (*medio*) average, medium; (*figlio*) middle *cpd* ▶ SM/F (*intermediario*) go-between; (*ruffiano*) pimp

mezza'notte [meddza'nɔtte] SF midnight

'**mezzo, -a** ['mɛddzo] AG half; **un ~ litro/panino** half a litre/roll ▶ AV half-; **~ morto** half-dead ▶ SM (*metà*) half; (*parte centrale: di strada ecc*) middle; (*per raggiungere un fine*) means *sg*; (*veicolo*) vehicle; (*nell'indicare l'ora*): **le nove e ~** half past nine; **mezzogiorno e ~** half past twelve ▶ SF: **la mezza** half-past twelve (in the afternoon); **mezzi** SMPL (*possibilità economiche*) means; **di mezza età** middle-aged; **aver una mezza idea di fare qc** to have half a mind to do sth; **è stato un ~ scandalo** it almost caused a scandal; **un soprabito di mezza stagione** a spring (*o* autumn) coat; **a mezza voce** in an undertone; **una volta e ~ più grande** one and a half times bigger; **di ~** middle, in the middle; **andarci di ~** (*patir danno*) to suffer; **esserci di ~** (*ostacolo*) to be in the way;

m

levarsi o **togliersi di** ~ to get out of the way; **mettersi di** ~ to interfere; **togliere di** ~ *(persona, cosa)* to get rid of; *(col: uccidere)* to bump off; **non c'è una via di** ~ there's no middle course; **in** ~ **a** in the middle of; **nel bel** ~ **(di)** right in the middle (of); **per** o **a** ~ **di** by means of; **a** ~ **corriere** by carrier; **mezzi di comunicazione di massa** mass media *pl*; **mezzi pubblici** public transport *sg*; **mezzi di trasporto** means of transport

mezzogi'orno [meddzo'dʒorno] SM midday, noon; *(Geo)* south; **a** ~ at 12 (o'clock) o midday o noon; **il** ~ **d'Italia** southern Italy

mezz'ora [med'dzora] SF half-hour, half an hour

MI SIGLA = **Milano**

mi PRON *(dav lo, la, li, le, ne diventa* **me**: *oggetto)* me; *(complemento di termine)* (to) me; *(riflessivo)* myself ▶ SM *(Mus)* E; (: *solfeggiando la scala)* mi; **mi aiuti?** will you help me?; **me ne ha parlato** he spoke to me about it, he told me about it; **mi servo da solo** I'll help myself

'mia *vedi* **mio**

miago'lare /**72**/ VI to miaow, mew

Mib SIGLA M, AG (= *indice borsa Milano*) Milan Stock Exchange Index

'mica SF *(Chim)* mica ▶ AV *(col)*: **non ...** ~ not ... at all; **non sono** ~ **stanco** I'm not a bit tired; **non sarà** ~ **partito?** he wouldn't have left, would he?; ~ **male** not bad

'miccia, -ce ['mittʃa] SF fuse

micidi'ale [mitʃi'djale] AG fatal; *(dannosissimo)* deadly

'micio, -a, -ci, -cie ['mitʃo] SM/F pussy (cat)

microbiolo'gia [mikrobiolo'dʒia] SF microbiology

micro'blog [mikro'blɔg] SM INV microblog

'microbo SM microbe

microcir'cuito [mikrotʃir'kuito] SM microcircuit

micro'fibra SF microfibre

micro'film SM INV microfilm

mi'crofono SM microphone

microinfor'matica SF microcomputing

micro'onda SF microwave

microproces'sore [mikroprotʃes'sore] SM microprocessor

micros'copico, -a, -ci, -che AG microscopic

micros'copio SM microscope

micro'solco, -chi SM *(solco)* microgroove; *(disco: a 33 giri)* long-playing record, LP; (: *a 45 giri)* extended-play record, EP

micros'pia SF hidden microphone, bug *(col)*

mi'dollo *(pl(f)* **midolla**) SM *(Anat)* marrow; ~ **spinale** spinal cord; ~ **osseo** bone marrow

'mie *vedi* **mio**

mi'ele SM honey

mi'etere /**29**/ VT *(Agr)* to reap, harvest; *(fig: vite)* to take, claim

mietitrebbia'trice [mjetitrebbja'tritʃe] SF combine harvester

mieti'trice [mjeti'tritʃe] SF *(macchina)* harvester

mieti'tura SF *(raccolto)* harvest; *(lavoro)* harvesting; *(tempo)* harvest-time

'miglia ['miʎʎa] SFPL *di* **miglio¹**

migli'aio [miʎ'ʎajo] *(pl(f)* **migliaia**) SM thousand; **un** ~ **(di)** about a thousand; **a migliaia** by the thousand, in thousands

'miglio¹ ['miʎʎo] *(pl(f)* **miglia**) SM *(unità di misura)* mile; ~ **marino** o **nautico** nautical mile

'miglio² ['miʎʎo] SM *(Bot)* millet

migliora'mento [miʎʎora'mento] SM improvement

miglio'rare [miʎʎo'rare] /**72**/ VT, VI to improve

migli'ore [miʎ'ʎore] AG *(comparativo)* better; *(superlativo)* best ▶ SM: **il** ~ the best (thing) ▶ SMF: **il (la)** ~ the best (person); **il miglior vino di questa regione** the best wine in this area; **i migliori auguri** best wishes

miglio'ria [miʎʎo'ria] SF improvement

'mignolo ['miɲɲolo] SM *(Anat)* little finger, pinkie; (: *dito del piede)* little toe

mi'grare /**72**/ VI to migrate

migrazi'one [migrat'tsjone] SF migration

'mila PL *di* **mille**

mila'nese AG Milanese ▶ SMF person from Milan; **i milanesi** the Milanese; **cotoletta alla** ~ *(Cuc)* Wiener schnitzel; **risotto alla** ~ *(Cuc) risotto with saffron*

Mi'lano SF Milan

miliar'dario, -a AG, SM/F millionaire

mili'ardo SM thousand million *(BRIT)*, billion *(US)*

mili'are AG: **pietra** ~ milestone

milio'nario, -a AG, SM/F millionaire

mili'one SM million; **un** ~ **di euro** a million euros

mili'tante AG, SMF militant

mili'tanza [mili'tantsa] SF militancy

mili'tare /**72**/ VI *(Mil)* to be a soldier, serve; *(fig: in un partito)* to be a militant ▶ AG military ▶ SM serviceman; **fare il** ~ to do one's military service; ~ **di carriera** regular (soldier)

milita'resco, -a, -schi, -sche AG *(portamento)* military *cpd*

'milite SM soldier

mi'lizia [mi'littsja] SF *(corpo armato)* militia

milizi'ano [milit'tsjano] SM militiaman

millanta'tore, -'trice SM/F boaster

millante'ria SF *(qualità)* boastfulness

'mille *(pl* **mila**) NUM a o one thousand; **diecimila** ten thousand; ~ **euro** one thousand euros

mille'foglie [mille'fɔʎʎe] SM INV *(Cuc)* cream o vanilla slice

mil'lennio SM millennium
millepi'edi SM INV centipede
mil'lesimo, -a AG, SM thousandth
milli'grammo SM milligram(me)
mil'lilitro SM millilitre (BRIT), milliliter (US)
mil'limetro SM millimetre (BRIT), millimeter (US)
'milza ['miltsa] SF (Anat) spleen
mi'metico, -a, -ci, -che AG (arte) mimetic; **tuta mimetica** (Mil) camouflage
mime'tismo SM camouflage
mimetiz'zare [mimetid'dzare] /**72**/ VT to camouflage; **mimetizzarsi** VPR to camouflage o.s.
'mimica SF (arte) mime
'mimo SM (attore, componimento) mime
mi'mosa SF mimosa
min. ABBR (= minuto, minimo) min
'mina SF (esplosiva) mine; (di matita) lead
mi'naccia, -ce [mi'nattʃa] SF threat; **sotto la ~ di** under threat of
minacci'are [minat'tʃare] /**14**/ VT to threaten; **~ qn di morte** to threaten to kill sb; **~ di fare qc** to threaten to do sth; **minaccia di piovere** it looks like rain
minacci'oso, -a [minat'tʃoso] AG threatening
mi'nare /**72**/ VT (Mil) to mine; (fig) to undermine
mina'tore SM miner
mina'torio, -a AG threatening
minchi'one, -a [min'kjone] AG (col) idiotic ▶ SM/F idiot
mine'rale AG, SM mineral
mineralo'gia [mineralo'dʒia] SF mineralogy
mine'rario, -a AG (delle miniere) mining; (dei minerali) ore cpd
mi'nestra SF soup; **~ in brodo** noodle soup; **~ di verdura** vegetable soup
mines'trone SM thick vegetable and pasta soup
mingher'lino, -a [minger'lino] AG thin, slender
'mini AG INV mini ▶ SF INV miniskirt
minia'tura SF miniature
mini'bar SM INV minibar
minielabora'tore SM minicomputer
mini'era SF mine; **~ di carbone** coalmine; (impresa) colliery (BRIT), coalmine
mini'gonna SF miniskirt
minima'lista, -i, -e AG, SM/F minimalist
minimiz'zare [minimid'dzare] /**72**/ VT to minimize
'minimo, -a AG minimum, least, slightest; (piccolissimo) very small, slight; (il più basso) lowest, minimum ▶ SM minimum; **al ~** at least; **girare al ~** (Aut) to idle; **il ~ indispensabile** the bare minimum; **il ~ della pena** the minimum sentence

minis'tero SM (Pol, Rel) ministry; (governo) government; (Dir): **Pubblico M~** State Prosecutor; **M~ delle Finanze** Ministry of Finance, ≈ Treasury
mi'nistro SM (Pol, Rel) minister; **M~ delle Finanze** Minister of Finance, ≈ Chancellor of the Exchequer (BRIT)
mino'ranza [mino'rantsa] SF minority; **essere in ~** to be in the minority
mino'rato, -a AG handicapped ▶ SM/F physically (o mentally) handicapped person
minorazi'one [minorat'tsjone] SF handicap
Mi'norca SF Minorca
mi'nore AG (comparativo) less; (più piccolo) smaller; (numero) lower; (inferiore) lower, inferior; (meno importante) minor; (più giovane) younger; (superlativo) least; smallest; lowest, least important, youngest ▶ SMF = **minorenne; in misura ~** to a lesser extent; **questo è il male ~** this is the lesser evil
mino'renne AG under age ▶ SMF minor, person under age
mino'rile AG juvenile; **carcere ~** young offenders' institution; **delinquenza ~** juvenile delinquency
minori'tario, -a AG minority cpd
mi'nuscolo, -a AG (scrittura, carattere) small; (piccolissimo) tiny ▶ SF small letter ▶ SM small letters pl; (Tip) lower case; **scrivere tutto (in) ~** to write everything in small letters
mi'nuta SF rough copy, draft
mi'nuto, -a AG tiny, minute; (pioggia) fine; (corporatura) delicate, fine; (lavoro) detailed ▶ SM (unità di misura) minute; **al ~** (Comm) retail; **avere i minuti contati** to have very little time
mi'nuzia [mi'nuttsja] SF (cura) meticulousness; (particolare) detail
minuziosa'mente [minuttsjosa'mente] AV meticulously; in minute detail
minuzi'oso, -a [minut'tsjoso] AG (persona, descrizione) meticulous; (esame) minute
'mio, 'mia, 'miei, 'mie DET: **il ~, la mia** etc my ▶ PRON: **il ~, la mia** etc mine ▶ SM: **ho speso del ~** I spent my own money ▶ SF: **la mia** (opinione) my view; **i miei** my family; **un ~ amico** a friend of mine; **per amor ~** for my sake; **è dalla mia** he is on my side; **anch'io ho avuto le mie** (disavventure) I've had my problems too; **ne ho fatta una delle mie!** (sciocchezze) I've done it again!; **cerco di stare sulle mie** I try to keep myself to myself
'miope AG short-sighted
mio'pia SF short-sightedness, myopia; (fig) short-sightedness
'mira SF (anche fig) aim; **avere una buona/cattiva ~** to be a good/bad shot; **prendere la ~** to take aim; **prendere di ~ qn** (fig) to pick on sb

m

mi'rabile AG admirable, wonderful
mi'racolo SM miracle
miraco'loso, -a AG miraculous
mi'raggio [mi'raddʒo] SM mirage
mi'rare /72/ VI: ~ **a** to aim at
mi'rato, -a AG targeted
mi'riade SF myriad
mi'rino SM (Tecn) sight; (Fot) viewer, viewfinder
mir'tillo SM bilberry (BRIT), blueberry (US), whortleberry
'mirto SM myrtle
mi'santropo, -a SM/F misanthropist
mi'scela [miʃ'ʃela] SF mixture; (di caffè) blend
miscel'lanea [miʃʃel'lanea] SF miscellany
'mischia ['miskja] SF scuffle; (Rugby) scrum, scrummage
mischi'are [mis'kjare] /19/ VT, **mischi'arsi** VPR to mix, blend
misco'noscere [misko'noʃʃere] /26/ VT (qualità, coraggio ecc) to fail to appreciate
miscre'dente AG (Rel) misbelieving; (: incredulo) unbelieving ▶ SMF misbeliever; unbeliever
mis'cuglio [mis'kuʎʎo] SM mixture, hotchpotch, jumble
'mise VB vedi **mettere**
mise'rabile AG (infelice) miserable, wretched; (povero) poverty-stricken; (di scarso valore) miserable
mi'seria SF extreme poverty; (infelicità) misery; **miserie** SFPL (del mondo ecc) misfortunes, troubles; **costare una ~** to cost next to nothing; **piangere ~** to plead poverty; **ridursi in ~** to be reduced to poverty; **porca ~!** (col) (bloody) hell!
miseri'cordia SF mercy, pity
misericordi'oso, -a AG merciful
'misero, -a AG miserable, wretched; (povero) poverty-stricken; (insufficiente) miserable
mis'fatto SM misdeed, crime
'misi VB vedi **mettere**
mi'sogino [mi'zɔdʒino] SM misogynist
'missile SM missile; **~ cruise** o **di crociera** cruise missile; **~ terra-aria** surface-to-air missile
missio'nario, -a AG, SM/F missionary
missi'one SF mission
misteri'oso, -a AG mysterious
mis'tero SM mystery; **fare ~ di qc** to make a mystery out of sth; **quanti misteri!** why all the mystery?
'mistico, -a, -ci, -che AG mystic(al) ▶ SM mystic
mistifi'care /20/ VT to fool, bamboozle
'misto, -a AG mixed; (scuola) mixed, coeducational ▶ SM mixture; **un tessuto in ~ lino** a linen mix
mis'tura SF mixture

mi'sura SF measure; (misurazione, dimensione) measurement; (taglia) size; (provvedimento) measure, step; (moderazione) moderation; (Mus) time; (: divisione) bar; (fig: limite) bounds pl, limit; **in ~ di** in accordance with, according to; **nella ~ in cui** inasmuch as, insofar as; **in giusta ~** moderately; **oltre ~** beyond measure; **su ~** made to measure; **in ugual ~** equally, in the same way; **a ~ d'uomo** on a human scale; **passare la ~** to overstep the mark, go too far; **prendere le misure a qn** to take sb's measurements, measure sb; **prendere le misure di qc** to measure sth; **ho preso le mie misure** I've taken the necessary steps; **non ha il senso della ~** he doesn't know when to stop; **~ di lunghezza/capacità** measure of length/capacity; **misure di sicurezza/prevenzione** safety/precautionary measures
misu'rare /72/ VT (ambiente, stoffa) to measure; (terreno) to survey; (abito) to try on; (pesare) to weigh; (fig: parole ecc) to weigh up; (: spese, cibo) to limit ▶ VI to measure; **misurarsi** VPR: **misurarsi con qn** to have a confrontation with sb; (competere) to compete with sb
misu'rato, -a AG (ponderato) measured; (prudente) cautious; (moderato) moderate
misurazi'one [mizurat'tsjone] SF measuring; (di terreni) surveying
'mite AG mild; (prezzo) moderate, reasonable
'mitico, -a, -ci, -che AG mythical
miti'gare /80/ VT to mitigate, lessen; (lenire) to soothe, relieve; **mitigarsi** VPR (odio) to subside; (tempo) to become milder
'mitilo SM mussel
'mito SM myth
mitolo'gia, -'gie [mitolo'dʒia] SF mythology
mito'logico, -a, -ci, -che [mito'lɔdʒiko] AG mythological
'mitra SF (Rel) mitre (BRIT), miter (US) ▶ SM INV (arma) sub-machine gun
mitragli'are [mitraʎ'ʎare] /27/ VT to machine-gun
mitraglia'tore, -'trice [mitraʎʎa'tore] AG: **fucile ~** sub-machine gun ▶ SF machine gun
mitteleuro'peo, -a AG Central European
mit'tente SMF sender
ml ABBR (= millilitro) ml
MLD SIGLA M = **Movimento per la Liberazione della Donna**
MM ABBR = **Metropolitana Milanese**
mm ABBR (= millimetro) mm
M.M. ABBR = **marina militare**
mms ABBR M INV (= multimedia messaging service) (servizio) MMS (= multimedia messaging service); (messaggio) MMS message
MN SIGLA = **Mantova**

M/N, m/n ABBR (= *motonave*) MV

MO SIGLA = **Modena**

mo' SM: **a ~di** like; **a ~di esempio** by way of example

M.O. ABBR = **Medio Oriente**

'**mobile** AG mobile; (*parte di macchina*) moving; (*Dir: bene*) movable, personal ▶ SM (*arredamento*) piece of furniture; **mobili** SMPL (*mobilia*) furniture *sg*

mo'bilia SF furniture

mobili'are AG (*Dir*) personal, movable

mo'bilio SM = **mobilia**

mobilità SF mobility

mobili'tare /72/ VT to mobilize; **~ l'opinione pubblica** to rouse public opinion

mobilitazi'one [mobilitat'tsjone] SF mobilization

mocas'sino SM moccasin

mocci'oso, -a [mot'tʃoso] SM/F (*bambino piccolo*) little kid; (*peg*) snotty-nosed kid

'**moccolo** SM (*di candela*) candle end; (*col: bestemmia*) oath; (: *moccio*) snot; **reggere il ~** to play gooseberry (BRIT), act as chaperon(e)

'**moda** SF fashion; **alla ~, di ~** fashionable, in fashion

modalità SF INV formality; **seguire attentamente le ~ d'uso** to follow the instructions carefully; **~ giuridiche** legal procedures; **~ di pagamento** method of payment

mo'della SF model

model'lare /72/ VT (*creta*) to model, shape; **modellarsi** VPR: **modellarsi su** to model o.s. on

mo'dello SM model; (*stampo*) mould (BRIT), mold (US) ▶ AG INV model *cpd*

'**modem** SM INV modem

mode'nese AG of (*o* from) Modena

mode'rare /72/ VT to moderate; **moderarsi** VPR to restrain o.s.; **~ la velocità** to reduce speed; **~ i termini** to weigh one's words

mode'rato, -a AG moderate

modera'tore, -'trice SM/F moderator

moderazi'one [moderat'tsjone] SF moderation

moderniz'zare [modernid'dzare] /72/ VT to bring up to date, modernize; **modernizzarsi** VPR to get up to date

mo'derno, -a AG modern

mo'destia SF modesty; **~ a parte ...** in all modesty ..., though I say it myself ...

mo'desto, -a AG modest

'**modico, -a, -ci, -che** AG reasonable, moderate

mo'difica, -che SF modification; **subire delle modifiche** to undergo some modifications

modifi'cabile AG modifiable

modifi'care /20/ VT to modify, alter; **modificarsi** VPR to alter, change

mo'dista SF milliner

'**modo** SM way, manner; (*mezzo*) means, way; (*occasione*) opportunity; (*Ling*) mood; (*Mus*) mode; **modi** SMPL (*maniere*) manners; **a suo ~, a ~ suo** in his own way; **ad o in ogni ~** anyway; **di o in ~ ~ che** so that; **in ~ da** so as to; **in tutti i modi** at all costs; (*comunque sia*) anyway; (*in ogni caso*) in any case; **in un certo qual ~** in a way, in some ways; **in qualche ~** somehow or other; **oltre ~** extremely; **~ di dire** turn of phrase; **per ~ di dire** so to speak; **fare a ~ proprio** to do as one likes; **fare le cose a ~** to do things properly; **una persona a ~** a well-mannered person; **c'è ~ e ~ di farlo** there's a right way and a wrong way of doing it

modu'lare /72/ VT to modulate ▶ AG modular

modulazi'one [modulat'tsjone] SF modulation; **~ di frequenza** frequency modulation

'**modulo** SM (*modello*) form; (*Archit: lunare, di comando*) module; **~ di domanda** application form; **~ d'iscrizione** enrolment form; **~ di versamento** deposit slip

Moga'discio [moga'diʃʃo] SM Mogadishu

'**mogano** SM mahogany

'**mogio, -a, -gi, -gie** ['mɔdʒo] AG down in the dumps, dejected

'**moglie** ['moʎʎe] SF wife

mo'hair [mɔ'ɛr] SM mohair

mo'ine SFPL cajolery *sg*; (*leziosità*) affectation *sg*; **fare le ~ a qn** to cajole sb

'**mola** SF millstone; (*utensile abrasivo*) grindstone

mo'lare /72/ VT to grind ▶ AG (*pietra*) mill *cpd* ▶ SM (*dente*) molar

'**mole** SF mass; (*dimensioni*) size; (*edificio grandioso*) massive structure; **una ~ di lavoro** masses (BRIT) *o* loads of work

mo'lecola SF molecule

moles'tare /72/ VT to bother, annoy

mo'lestia SF annoyance, bother; **recar ~ a qn** to bother sb; **molestie sessuali** sexual harassment *sg*

mo'lesto, -a AG annoying

moli'sano, -a AG of (*o* from) Molise

'**molla** SF spring; **molle** SFPL (*per camino*) tongs; **prendere qn con le molle** to treat sb with kid gloves

mol'lare /72/ VT to release, let go; (*Naut*) to ease; (*fig: ceffone*) to give ▶ VI (*cedere*) to give in; **~ gli ormeggi** (*Naut*) to cast off; **~ la presa** to let go

'**molle** AG soft; (*muscoli*) flabby; (*fig: debole*) weak, feeble

molleggi'ato, -a [molled'dʒato] AG (*letto*) sprung; (*auto*) with good suspension

mol'leggio [mol'leddʒo] SM (per veicoli) suspension; (elasticità) springiness; (Ginnastica) knee-bends pl

mol'letta SF (per capelli) hairgrip; (per panni stesi) clothes peg (BRIT) o pin (US); **mollette** SFPL (per zucchero) tongs

mol'lezza [mol'lettsa] SF softness flabbiness weakness, feebleness; **mollezze** SFPL: **vivere nelle mollezze** to live in the lap of luxury

mol'lica, -che SF crumb, soft part

mol'liccio, -a, -ci, -ce [mol'littʃo] AG (terreno, impasto) soggy; (frutta) soft; (floscio: mano) limp; (: muscolo) flabby

mol'lusco, -schi SM mollusc

'molo SM breakwater; jetty, pier

mol'teplice [mol'teplitʃe] AG (formato di più elementi) complex; **molteplici** PL (svariati: interessi, attività) numerous, various

molteplicità [molteplitʃi'ta] SF multiplicity

moltipli'care /20/ VT to multiply; **moltiplicarsi** VPR to multiply; (richieste) to increase in number

moltiplicazi'one [moltiplikat'tsjone] SF multiplication

molti'tudine SF multitude; **una ~ di** a vast number o a multitude of

⸻ PAROLA CHIAVE ⸻

'molto, -a DET (quantità) a lot of, much; (numero) a lot of, many; **molto pane/carbone** a lot of bread/coal; **molta gente** a lot of people, many people; **molti libri** a lot of books, many books; **non ho molto tempo** I haven't got much time; **per molto (tempo)** for a long time; **ci vuole molto (tempo)?** will it take long?; **arriverà fra non molto** he'll arrive soon; **ne hai per molto?** will you be long?

▶ AV **1** a lot, (very) much; **viaggia molto** he travels a lot; **non viaggia molto** he doesn't travel much o a lot

2 (intensivo: con aggettivi, avverbi) very; (: con participio passato) (very) much; **molto buono** very good; **molto migliore, molto meglio** much o a lot better

▶ PRON much, a lot; **molti, e** (pl) many, a lot; **molti pensano che ...** many (people) think that ...; **molte sono rimaste a casa** a lot of them stayed at home; **c'era gente, ma non molta** there were people there, but not many

momentanea'mente AV at the moment, at present

momen'taneo, -a AG momentary, fleeting

mo'mento SM moment; **da un ~ all'altro** at any moment; (all'improvviso) suddenly; **al ~ di fare** just as I was (o you were o he was etc) doing; **a momenti** (da un momento all'altro)

any time o moment now; (quasi) nearly; **per il ~** for the time being; **dal ~ che** ever since; (dato che) since; **~ culminante** climax

'monaca, -che SF nun

'Monaco SF Monaco; **~ (di Baviera)** Munich

'monaco, -ci SM monk

mo'narca, -chi SM monarch

monar'chia [monar'kia] SF monarchy

mo'narchico, -a, -ci, -che [mo'narkiko] AG (stato, autorità) monarchic; (partito, fede) monarchist ▶ SM/F monarchist

monas'tero SM (di monaci) monastery; (di monache) convent

mo'nastico, -a, -ci, -che AG monastic

'monco, -a, -chi, -che AG maimed; (fig) incomplete; **~ d'un braccio** one-armed

mon'cone SM stump

mon'dana SF prostitute

mondanità SF (frivolezza) worldliness; **le ~** (piaceri) the pleasures of the world

mon'dano, -a AG (anche fig) worldly; (dell'alta società) society cpd; fashionable

mon'dare /72/ VT (frutta, patate) to peel; (piselli) to shell; (pulire) to clean

mondez'zaio [mondet'tsajo] SM rubbish (BRIT) o garbage (US) dump

mondi'ale AG (campionato, popolazione) world cpd; (influenza) world-wide; **di fama ~** world famous

'mondo SM world; (grande quantità): **un ~ di** lots of, a host of; **il gran** o **bel ~** high society; **per niente al ~, per nessuna cosa al ~** not for all the world; **da che ~ è ~** since time o the world began; **mandare qn all'altro ~** to kill sb; **mettere/venire al ~** to bring/come into the world; **vivere fuori dal ~** to be out of touch with the real world; **(sono) cose dell'altro ~!** it's incredible!; **com'è piccolo il ~!** it's a small world!

mone'gasco, -a, -schi, -sche AG, SM/F Monegasque

monelle'ria SF prank, naughty trick

mo'nello, -a SM/F street urchin; (ragazzo vivace) scamp, imp

mo'neta SF coin; (Econ: valuta) currency; (denaro spicciolo) (small) change; **~ estera** foreign currency; **~ legale** legal tender

mone'tario, -a AG monetary

mongol'fiera SF hot-air balloon

Mon'golia SF: **la ~** Mongolia

mon'golico, -a, -ci, -che AG Mongolian

mongo'lismo SM Down's syndrome

'mongolo, -a AG Mongolian ▶ SM/F, SM Mongol, Mongolian

mongo'loide AG, SMF (Med) mongol

'monito SM warning

'monitor SM INV (Tecn, TV) monitor

monito'raggio [monito'raddʒo] SM monitoring

monito'rare /**72**/ VT to monitor

mo'nocolo SM (*lente*) monocle, eyeglass

monoco'lore AG (*Pol*): **governo ~** one-party government

monoga'mia SF monogamy

mo'nogamo, -a AG monogamous ▶ SM monogamist

monogra'fia SF monograph

mono'gramma, -i SM monogram

mono'lingue AG monolingual

monolo'cale SM ≈ studio flat

mo'nologo, -ghi SM monologue

mono'pattino SM scooter

mono'polio SM monopoly; **~ di stato** government monopoly

monopoliz'zare [monopolid'dzare] /**72**/ VT to monopolize

mono'sillabo, -a AG monosyllabic ▶ SM monosyllable

monoto'nia SF monotony

mo'notono, -a AG monotonous

mono'uso AG INV disposable

monovo'lume SF INV (*anche*: **automobile monovolume**) people carrier, MPV

Mons. ABBR (= *Monsignore*) Mgr

monsi'gnore [monsiɲ'ɲore] SM (*Rel: titolo*) Your (*o* His) Grace

mon'sone SM monsoon

monta'carichi [monta'kariki] SM INV hoist, goods lift

mon'taggio [mon'taddʒo] SM (*Tecn*) assembly; (*Cine*) editing

mon'tagna [mon'taɲɲa] SF mountain; (*zona montuosa*): **la ~** the mountains *pl*; **andare in ~** to go to the mountains; **aria/strada di ~** mountain air/road; **casa di ~** house in the mountains; **montagne russe** roller coaster *sg*, big dipper *sg* (*BRIT*)

monta'gnoso, -a [montaɲ'ɲoso] AG mountainous

monta'naro, -a AG mountain *cpd* ▶ SM/F mountain dweller

mon'tano, -a AG mountain *cpd*; alpine

mon'tante SM (*di porta*) jamb; (*di finestra*) upright; (*Calcio: palo*) post; (*Pugilato*) upper cut; (*Comm*) total amount

mon'tare /**72**/ VT to go (*o* come) up; (*cavallo*) to ride; (*apparecchiatura*) to set up, assemble; (*Cuc*) to whip; (*Zool*) to cover; (*incastonare*) to mount, set; (*Cine*) to edit; (*Fot*) to mount ▶ VI to go (*o* come) up; (*aumentare di livello, volume*) to rise; (*a cavallo*): **~ bene/male** to ride well/badly; **montarsi** VPR to become big-headed; **~ qc** to exaggerate sth; **~ qn** *o* **la testa a qn** to turn sb's head; **montarsi la testa** to become big-headed; **montarsi la testa** to become big-headed; **~ in bicicletta/ macchina/treno** to get on a bicycle/ into a car/on a train; **~ a cavallo** to get on *o* mount a horse; **~ la guardia** (*Mil*) to mount guard

monta'tura SF assembling *no pl*; (*di occhiali*) frames *pl*; (*di gioiello*) mounting, setting; (*fig*): **~ pubblicitaria** publicity stunt

montavi'vande SM INV dumbwaiter

'monte SM mountain; **a ~** upstream; **andare a ~** (*fig*) to come to nothing; **mandare a ~ qc** (*fig*) to upset sth, cause sth to fail; **il M~ Bianco** Mont Blanc; **il M~ Everest** Mount Everest; **~ di pietà** pawnshop; **~ premi** prize

Monteci'torio [montetʃi'torjo] SM: **palazzo ~** (*Pol*) seat of the Italian Chamber of Deputies

montene'grino, -a AG, SM/F Montenegrin

Monte'negro SM Montenegro

mont'gomery [mənt'gʌməri] SM INV duffel coat

mon'tone SM (*Zool*) ram; (*anche*: **giacca di montone**) sheepskin (jacket); **carne di ~** mutton

montuosità SF mountainous nature

montu'oso, -a AG mountainous

monu'mento SM monument

mo'quette [mɔ'kɛt] SF fitted carpet

'mora SF (*del rovo*) blackberry; (*del gelso*) mulberry; (*Dir*) delay; (: *somma*) arrears *pl*

mo'rale AG moral ▶ SF (*scienza*) ethics *sg*, moral philosophy; (*complesso di norme*) moral standards *pl*, morality; (*condotta*) morals *pl*; (*insegnamento morale*) moral ▶ SM morale; **la ~ della favola** the moral of the tale; **essere giù di ~** to be feeling down; **aver il ~ alto/a terra** to be in good/low spirits

mora'lista, -i, -e AG moralistic ▶ SM/F moralist

moralità SF morality; (*condotta*) morals *pl*

moraliz'zare [moralid'dzare] /**72**/ VT (*costumi, vita pubblica*) to set moral standards for

moralizzazi'one [moraliddzat'tsjone] SF setting of moral standards

mora'toria SF (*Dir*) moratorium

morbi'dezza [morbi'dettsa] SF softness; smoothness; tenderness

'morbido, -a AG soft; (*pelle*) soft, smooth; (*carne*) tender

mor'billo SM (*Med*) measles *sg*

'morbo SM disease

mor'boso, -a AG (*fig*) morbid

'morchia ['mɔrkja] SF (*residuo grasso*) dregs *pl*; oily deposit

mor'dente SM (*fig: di satira, critica*) bite; (: *di persona*) drive

'mordere /**64**/ VT to bite; (*addentare*) to bite into; (*corrodere*) to eat into

mordicchi'are [mordik'kjare] /**19**/ VT (*gen*) to chew at

mo'rente AG dying ▶ SM/F dying man/woman

mor'fina SF morphine

mo'ria SF high mortality

mori'bondo, -a AG dying, moribund

morige'rato, -a [morid3e'rato] AG of good morals

mo'rire /65/ VI to die; (abitudine, civiltà) to die out; ~ **di dolore** to die of a broken heart; ~ **di fame** to die of hunger; (fig) to be starving; ~ **di freddo** to freeze to death; (fig) to be frozen; ~ **d'invidia** to be green with envy; ~ **di noia/paura** to be bored/scared to death; ~ **dalla voglia di fare qc** to be dying to do sth; **fa un caldo da** ~ it's terribly hot

mormo'rare /72/ VI to murmur; (brontolare) to grumble; **si mormora che …** it's rumoured (BRIT) o rumored (US) that …; **la gente mormora** people are talking

mormo'rio SM murmuring; grumbling

'moro, -a AG dark(-haired), dark(-complexioned); **i Mori** SMPL (Storia) the Moors

mo'roso, -a AG in arrears ▶ SM/F (col: innamorato) sweetheart

'morsa SF (Tecn) vice (BRIT), vise (US); (fig: stretta) grip

mor'setto SM (Tecn) clamp; (Elettr) terminal

morsi'care /20/ VT to nibble (at), gnaw (at); (insetto) to bite

'morso, -a PP di **mordere** ▶ SM bite; (di insetto) sting; (parte della briglia) bit; **dare un ~ a qc/qn** to bite sth/sb; **i morsi della fame** pangs of hunger

morta'della SF (Cuc) mortadella (type of salted pork meat)

mor'taio SM mortar

mor'tale AG, SM mortal

mortalità SF mortality; (Statistica) mortality, death rate

'morte SF death; **in punto di** ~ at death's door; **ferito a** ~ (soldato) mortally wounded; (in incidente) fatally injured; **essere annoiato a** ~ to be bored to death o to tears; **avercela a** ~ **con qn** to be bitterly resentful of sb; **avere la** ~ **nel cuore** to have a heavy heart

mortifi'care /20/ VT to mortify

'morto, -a PP di **morire** ▶ AG dead ▶ SM/F dead man/woman; **i morti** the dead; **fare il** ~ (nell'acqua) to float on one's back; **il Mar M~** the Dead Sea; **un ~ di fame** (fig peg) a down-and-out; **le campane suonavano a** ~ the funeral bells were tolling; vedi anche **il Giorno dei Morti**

mor'torio SM (anche fig) funeral

mo'saico, -ci SM mosaic; **l'ultimo tassello del** ~ (fig) the last piece of the puzzle

'Mosca SF Moscow

'mosca, -sche SF fly; **rimanere** o **restare con un pugno di mosche** (fig) to be left empty-handed; **non si sentiva volare una** ~ (fig) you could have heard a pin drop; ~ **cieca** blind-man's buff

mos'cato SM muscatel (wine)

mosce'rino [moʃʃe'rino] SM midge, gnat

mos'chea [mos'kɛa] SF mosque

mos'chetto [mos'ketto] SM musket

moschet'tone [mosket'tone] SM (gancio) spring clip; (Alpinismo) karabiner, snaplink

moschi'cida, -i, -e [moski'tʃida] AG fly cpd; **carta** ~ flypaper

'moscio, -a, -sci, -sce ['moʃʃo] AG (fig) lifeless; **ha la "r" moscia** he can't roll his "r"s

mos'cone SM (Zool) bluebottle; (barca) pedalo; (: a remi) kind of pedalo with oars

mosco'vita, -i, -e AG, SM/F Muscovite

'mossa SF movement; (nel gioco) move; **darsi una** ~ (fig) to give o.s. a shake; **prendere le mosse da qc** to come about as the result of sth

'mossi etc VB vedi **muovere**

'mosso, -a PP di **muovere** ▶ AG (mare) rough; (capelli) wavy; (Fot) blurred; (ritmo, prosa) animated

mos'tarda SF mustard; ~ **di Cremona** pickled fruit with mustard

'mosto SM must

'mostra SF exhibition, show; (ostentazione) show; **in** ~ on show; **far** ~ **di** (fingere) to pretend; **far** ~ **di sé** to show off; **mettersi in** ~ to draw attention to o.s.

mos'trare /72/ VT to show ▶ VI: ~ **di fare** to pretend to do; **mostrarsi** VPR to appear; ~ **la lingua** to stick out one's tongue

'mostro SM monster

mostru'oso, -a AG monstrous

mo'tel SM INV motel

moti'vare /72/ VT (causare) to cause; (giustificare) to justify, account for

motivazi'one [motivat'tsjone] SF justification; (Psic) motivation

mo'tivo SM (causa) reason, cause; (movente) motive; (letterario) (central) theme; (disegno) motif, design, pattern; (Mus) motif; **per quale ~?** why?, for what reason?; **per motivi di salute** for health reasons, on health grounds; **motivi personali** personal reasons

'moto SM (anche Fisica) motion; (movimento, gesto) movement; (esercizio fisico) exercise; (sommossa) rising, revolt; (commozione) feeling, impulse ▶ SF INV (motocicletta) motorbike; **fare del** ~ to take some exercise; **un** ~ **d'impazienza** an impatient gesture; **mettere in** ~ to set in motion; (Aut) to start up; ~ **d'acqua** Jet Ski®

moto'carro SM three-wheeler van

motoci'cletta [mototʃi'kletta] SF motorcycle

motoci'clismo [mototʃi'klizmo] SM motorcycling, motorcycle racing

motoci'clista, -i, -e [mototʃi'klista] SM/F motorcyclist

moto'nave SF motor vessel

motopesche'reccio [motopeske'rettʃo] SM
motor fishing vessel

mo'tore, -'trice AG motor; (Tecn) driving
▶ SM engine, motor ▶ SF (Tecn) engine,
motor; **albero ~** drive shaft; **forza motrice**
driving force; **a ~** motor cpd, power-driven;
~ a combustione interna/a reazione
internal combustion/jet engine; **~ di
ricerca** (Inform) search engine

moto'rino SM moped; **~ di avviamento** (Aut)
starter

motoriz'zato, -a [motorid'dzato] AG (truppe)
motorized; (persona) having a car o transport

motorizzazi'one [motoriddzat'tsjone] SF
(ufficio tecnico e organizzativo): **(ufficio della) ~**
road traffic office

motos'cafo SM motorboat

motove'detta SF motor patrol vessel

mo'trice [mo'tritʃe] SF vedi **motore**

mot'teggio [mot'teddʒo] SM banter

'motto SM (battuta scherzosa) witty remark;
(frase emblematica) motto, maxim

mountain bike SF INV mountain bike

'mouse ['maus] SM INV (Inform) mouse

mo'vente SM motive

mo'venza [mo'vɛntsa] SF movement

movimen'tare /72/ VT to liven up

movimen'tato, -a AG (festa, partita) lively;
(riunione) animated; (strada, vita) busy;
(soggiorno) eventful

movi'mento SM movement; (fig) activity,
hustle and bustle; (Mus) tempo, movement;
essere sempre in ~ to be always on the go;
fare un po' di ~ (esercizio fisico) to take some
exercise; **c'è molto ~ in città** the town is
very busy; **~ di capitali** movement of
capital; **M~ per la Liberazione della
Donna** Women's Movement

movi'ola SF moviola; **rivedere qc alla ~** to
see an action (BRIT) o instant (US) replay of
sth

Mozam'bico [moddzam'biko] SM: **il ~**
Mozambique

mozi'one [mot'tsjone] SF (Pol) motion;
~ d'ordine (Pol) point of order

mozzafi'ato [mottsa'fjato] AG INV
breathtaking

moz'zare [mot'tsare] /72/ VT to cut off; (coda)
to dock; **~ il fiato o il respiro a qn** (fig) to
take sb's breath away

mozza'rella [mottsa'rɛlla] SF mozzarella

mozzi'cone [mottsi'kone] SM stub, butt,
end; (anche: **mozzicone di sigaretta**)
cigarette end

'mozzo¹ ['mɔddzo] SM (Meccanica) hub

'mozzo² ['mottso] SM (Naut) ship's boy;
~ di stalla stable boy

mq ABBR (= metro quadro) sq.m

MS SIGLA = **Massa Carrara**

M.S.I. SIGLA M (= Movimento Sociale Italiano)
former right-wing political party

Mti ABBR = **monti**

'mucca, -che SF COW; **~ pazza** BSE; **(morbo
della) ~ pazza** mad cow disease, BSE;
l'emergenza ~ pazza the mad cow crisis

'mucchio ['mukkjo] SM pile, heap; (fig): **un ~
di** lots of, heaps of

mucil'lagine [mutʃil'ladʒine] SF (Bot)
mucilage (green slime produced by plants growing
in water)

'muco, -chi SM mucus

mu'cosa SF mucous membrane

'muesli ['mjusli] SM muesli

'muffa SF mould (BRIT), mold (US), mildew;
fare la ~ to go mouldy (BRIT) o moldy (US)

mugghi'are [mug'gjare] /19/ VI (fig: mare,
tuono) to roar; (: vento) to howl

mug'gire [mud'dʒire] /55/ VI (vacca) to low,
moo; (toro) to bellow; (fig) to roar

mug'gito [mud'dʒito] SM moo; bellow; roar

mu'ghetto [mu'getto] SM lily of the valley

mu'gnaio, -a [muɲ'ɲajo] SM/F miller

mugo'lare /72/ VI (cane) to whimper, whine;
(fig: persona) to moan

mugu'gnare [muguɲ'ɲare] /15/ VI (col) to
mutter, mumble

mulatti'era SF mule track

mu'latto, -a AG, SM/F mulatto

muli'nare /72/ VI to whirl, spin round
(and round)

muli'nello SM (moto vorticoso) eddy, whirl;
(di canna da pesca) reel; (Naut) windlass

mu'lino SM mill; **~ a vento** windmill

'mulo SM mule

'multa SF fine

mul'tare /72/ VT to fine

multico'lore AG multicoloured (BRIT),
multicolored (US)

multi'etnico, -a, -ci, -che AG multiethnic

multi'forme AG (paesaggio, attività, interessi)
varied; (ingegno) versatile

multimedi'ale AG multimedia cpd

multinazio'nale [multinattsjo'nale] AG, SF
multinational; **forza ~ di pace**
multinational peace-keeping force

'multiplo, -a AG, SM multiple

multiraz'ziale [multirat'tsjale] AG
multiracial

multi'sala AG INV multiscreen

multiu'tenza [multiu'tɛntsa] SF (Inform)
time sharing

multivitami'nico, -a, -ci, -che AG:
complesso ~ multivitamin

'mummia SF mummy

'mungere ['mundʒere] /5/ VT (anche fig)
to milk

mungi'tura [mundʒi'tura] SF milking

munici'pale [munitʃi'pale] AG (gen)

municipal; town *cpd*; **palazzo** ~ town hall;
autorità municipali local authorities
(*Brit*), local government *sg*
muni'cipio [muni't∫ipjo] sm town council,
corporation; (*edificio*) town hall; **sposarsi
in** ~ ≈ to get married in a registry office
(*Brit*), have a civil marriage
munifi'cenza [munifi't∫entsa] sf munificence
mu'nifico, -a, -ci, -che ag munificent,
generous
mu'nire /55/ vt: ~ **qc/qn di** to equip sth/sb
with; ~ **di firma** (*documento*) to sign
munizi'oni [munit'tsjoni] sfpl (*Mil*)
ammunition *sg*
'**munsi** *etc* vb *vedi* **mungere**
'**munto, -a** pp *di* **mungere**
mu'oio *etc* vb *vedi* **morire**
mu'overe /66/ vt to move; (*ruota, macchina*)
to drive; (*sollevare: questione, obiezione*) to raise,
bring up; (: *accusa*) to make, bring forward;
muoversi vpr to move; ~ **causa a qn** (*Dir*) to
take legal action against sb; ~ **a
compassione** to move to pity; ~ **guerra a**
o **contro qn** to wage war against sb; ~ **mari
e monti** to move heaven and earth; ~ **al
pianto** to move to tears; ~ **i primi passi** to
take one's first steps; (*fig*) to be starting out;
muoviti! hurry up!, get a move on!
'**mura** sfpl *vedi* **muro**
mu'raglia [mu'raʎʎa] sf (high) wall
mu'rale ag wall *cpd*; mural
mu'rare /72/ vt (*persona, porta*) to wall up
mu'rario, -a ag building *cpd*; **arte muraria**
masonry
mura'tore sm (*con pietre*) mason; (*con mattoni*)
bricklayer
mura'tura sf (*lavoro murario*) masonry; **casa
in** ~ (*di pietra*) stonebuilt house; (*di mattoni*)
brick house
'**muro** sm wall; **mura** sfpl (*cinta cittadina*)
walls; **a** ~ wall *cpd*; (*armadio ecc*) built-in;
mettere al ~ (*fucilare*) to shoot *o* execute (by
firing squad); ~ **di cinta** surrounding wall;
~ **divisorio** dividing wall; ~ **del suono**
sound barrier
'**musa** sf muse
'**muschio** ['muskjo] sm (*Zool*) musk; (*Bot*)
moss
musco'lare ag muscular, muscle *cpd*
muscola'tura sf muscle structure

'**muscolo** sm (*Anat*) muscle
musco'loso, -a ag muscular
mu'seo sm museum
museru'ola sf muzzle
'**musica** sf music; ~ **da ballo/camera** dance/
chamber music
musi'cale ag musical
musicas'setta sf (pre-recorded) cassette
musi'cista, -i, -e [muzi't∫ista] sm/f musician
musi'comane smf music lover
'**müsli** ['mysli] sm muesli
'**muso** sm muzzle; (*di auto, aereo*) nose; **tenere
il** ~ to sulk
mu'sone, -a sm/f sulky person
'**mussola** sf muslin
mus(s)ul'mano, -a ag, sm/f Muslim,
Moslem
'**muta** sf (*di animali*) moulting (*Brit*), molting
(*US*); (*di serpenti*) sloughing; (*per immersioni
subacquee*) diving suit; (*gruppo di cani*) pack
mu'tabile ag changeable
muta'mento sm change
mu'tande sfpl (*da uomo*) (under)pants
mutan'dine sfpl (*da donna, bambino*) pants
(*Brit*), briefs; ~ **di plastica** plastic pants
mu'tare /72/ vt, vi to change, alter
mutazi'one [mutat'tsjone] sf change,
alteration; (*Biol*) mutation
mu'tevole ag changeable
muti'lare /72/ vt to mutilate, maim; (*fig*) to
mutilate, deface
muti'lato, -a sm/f disabled person; (*through
loss of limbs*): ~ **di guerra** disabled ex-
serviceman (*Brit*) *o* war veteran (*US*)
mutilazi'one [mutilat'tsjone] sf mutilation
mu'tismo sm (*Med*) mutism; (*atteggiamento*)
(stubborn) silence
'**muto, -a** ag (*Med*) dumb; (*emozione, dolore:
Cine*) silent; (*Ling*) silent, mute; (*carta
geografica*) blank; ~ **per lo stupore** *etc*
speechless with amazement *etc*; **ha fatto
scena muta** he didn't utter a word
'**mutua** sf (*anche:* **cassa mutua**) health
insurance scheme; **medico della** ~
≈ National Health Service doctor (*Brit*)
mutu'are /72/ vt (*fig*) to borrow
mutu'ato, -a sm/f member of a health
insurance scheme
'**mutuo, -a** ag (*reciproco*) mutual ▶ sm (*Econ*)
(long-term) loan; ~ **ipotecario** mortgage

Nn

N, n ['ɛnne] SM O F (lettera) N, n; **N come Napoli** = N for Nellie (BRIT), N for Nan (US)
N ABBR (= nord) N
n ABBR (= numero) no.
NA SIGLA = **Napoli**
na'babbo SM (anche fig) nabob
'nacchere ['nakkere] SFPL castanets
NAD SIGLA M = **nucleo anti-droga**
na'dir SM (Astr) nadir
'nafta SF naphtha; (per motori diesel) diesel oil
nafta'lina SF (Chim) naphthalene; (tarmicida) mothballs pl
'naia SF (Zool) cobra; (Mil) slang term for national service
na'ïf [na'if] AG INV naïve
'nailon SM = **nylon**
Nai'robi SF Nairobi
'nanna SF (linguaggio infantile): **andare a ~** to go to beddy-byes
nano, -a AG, SM/F dwarf
napole'tano, -a AG, SM/F Neapolitan ▶ SF (macchinetta da caffè) Neapolitan coffee pot
'Napoli SF Naples
'nappa SF tassel
nar'ciso [nar'tʃizo] SM narcissus
narco'dollari SMPL drug money sg
'narcos SM INV (colombiano) Colombian drug trafficker
nar'cosi SF general anaesthesia, narcosis
nar'cotico, -ci SM narcotic
narcotraffi'cante SMF drug trafficker
narco'traffico SM drug trade
na'rice [na'ritʃe] SF nostril
nar'rare /72/ VT to tell the story of, recount
narra'tivo, -a AG narrative ▶ SF (branca) fiction
narra'tore, -'trice SM/F narrator
narrazi'one [narrat'tsjone] SF narration; (racconto) story, tale
N.A.S.A. ['naza] SIGLA F (= National Aeronautics and Space Administration) NASA
na'sale AG nasal
na'scente [naʃʃɛnte] AG (sole, luna) rising

'nascere ['naʃʃere] /67/ VI (bambino) to be born; (pianta) to come o spring up; (fiume) to rise, have its source; (sole) to rise; (dente) to come through; (fig: derivare, conseguire): **~ da** to arise from, be born out of; **è nata nel 1952** she was born in 1952; **da cosa nasce cosa** one thing leads to another
'nascita ['naʃʃita] SF birth
nasci'turo, -a [naʃʃi'turo] SM/F future child; **come si chiamerà il ~?** what's the baby going to be called?
nas'condere /68/ VT to hide, conceal; **nascondersi** VPR to hide
nascon'diglio [naskon'diʎʎo] SM hiding place
nascon'dino SM (gioco) hide-and-seek
nas'cosi etc VB vedi **nascondere**
nas'costo, -a PP di **nascondere** ▶ AG hidden; **di ~** secretly
na'sello SM (Zool) hake
'naso SM nose
Nas'sau SF Nassau
'nastro SM ribbon; (magnetico, isolante: Sport) tape; **~ adesivo** adhesive tape; **~ trasportatore** conveyor belt
nas'turzio [nas'turtsjo] SM nasturtium
na'tale AG of one's birth ▶ SM (Rel): **N~** Christmas; (giorno della nascita) birthday; **natali** SMPL: **di illustri/umili natali** of noble/humble birth
natalità SF birth rate
nata'lizio, -a [nata'littsjo] AG (del Natale) Christmas cpd
na'tante SM craft inv, boat
'natica, -che SF (Anat) buttock
na'tio, -a, -tii, -tie AG native
Nativ ità SF (Rel) Nativity
na'tivo, -a AG, SM/F native
'nato, -a PP di **nascere** ▶ AG: **un attore ~** a born actor; **nata Pieri** née Pieri
'N.A.T.O. SIGLA F NATO (= North Atlantic Treaty Organization)
na'tura SF nature; **pagare in ~** to pay in kind; **~ morta** still life

n

natu'rale AG natural ▶ SM: **al ~** (*alimenti*) served plain; (*ritratto*) life-size; **(ma) è ~!** (*in risposte*) of course!; **a grandezza ~** life-size; **acqua ~** spring water

natura'lezza [natura'lettsa] SF naturalness

natura'lista, -i, -e SM/F naturalist

naturaliz'zare [naturalid'dzare] /**72**/ VT to naturalize

natural'mente AV naturally; (*certamente, sì*) of course

natu'rismo SM naturism, nudism

natu'rista, -i, -e AG, SM/F naturist, nudist

naufra'gare /**8o**/ VI (*nave*) to be wrecked; (*persona*) to be shipwrecked; (*fig*) to fall through

nau'fragio [nau'fradʒo] SM shipwreck; (*fig*) ruin, failure

'naufrago, -ghi SM castaway, shipwreck victim

'nausea SF nausea; **avere la ~** to feel sick (BRIT) o ill (US); **fino alla ~** ad nauseam

nausea'bondo, -a AG, **nause'ante** AG (*sapore*) disgusting; nauseating, sickening

nause'are /**72**/ VT to nauseate, make (feel) sick (BRIT) o ill (US)

'nautico, -a, -ci, -che AG nautical ▶ SF (art of) navigation; **salone ~** (*mostra*) boat show

na'vale AG naval; **battaglia ~** naval battle; (*gioco*) battleships *pl*

na'vata SF (*anche*: **navata centrale**) nave; (*anche*: **navata laterale**) aisle

'nave SF ship, vessel; **~ da carico** cargo ship, freighter; **~ cisterna** tanker; **~ da guerra** warship; **~ di linea** liner; **~ passeggeri** passenger ship; **~ portaerei** aircraft carrier; **~ spaziale** spaceship

na'vetta SF shuttle; (*servizio di collegamento*) shuttle (service)

navi'cella [navi'tʃɛlla] SF (*di aerostato*) gondola; **~ spaziale** spaceship

navi'gabile AG navigable

navi'gante SM sailor, seaman

navi'gare /**8o**/ VI to sail; **~ in cattive acque** (*fig*) to be in deep water; **~ in Internet** to surf the Net

navi'gato, -a AG (*fig: esperto*) experienced

naviga'tore, -'trice SM: **~ satellitare** satnav, satellite navigator ▶ SM/F (*gen*) navigator; **~ solitario** single-handed sailor

navigazi'one [navigat'tsjone] SF navigation; **dopo una settimana di ~** after a week at sea

na'viglio [na'viʎʎo] SM fleet, ships *pl*; (*canale artificiale*) canal; **~ da pesca** fishing fleet

nazio'nale [nattsjo'nale] AG national ▶ SF (*Sport*) national team

naziona'lismo [nattsjona'lizmo] SM nationalism

naziona'lista, -i, -e [nattsjona'lista] AG, SM/F nationalist

nazionalità [nattsjonali'ta] SF INV nationality

nazionaliz'zare [nattsjonalid'dzare] /**72**/ VT to nationalize

nazionalizzazi'one [nattsjonaliddzat'tsjone] SF nationalization

nazi'one [nat'tsjone] SF nation

naziskin ['naːtsiskin] SM INV Nazi skinhead

na'zismo [nat'tsizmo] SM Nazism

na'zista, -i, -e [nat'tsista] AG, SM/F Nazi

NB ABBR (= *nota bene*) NB

N.d.A. ABBR (= *nota dell'autore*) author's note

N.d.D. ABBR = **nota della direzione**

N.d.E. ABBR (= *nota dell'editore*) publisher's note

N.d.R. ABBR (= *nota della redazione*) editor's note

'nd'rangheta [nd'rangeta] SF Calabrian Mafia

N.d.T. ABBR (= *nota del traduttore*) translator's note

(PAROLA CHIAVE)

ne PRON **1** (*di lui, lei, loro*) of him/her/them; about him/her/them; **ne riconosco la voce** I recognize his (*o* her) voice

2 (*di questa, quella cosa*) of it; about it; **ne voglio ancora** I want some more (of it *o* them); **non parliamone più!** let's not talk about it any more!

3 (*da ciò*) from this; **ne deduco che l'avete trovato** I gather you've found it; **ne consegue che ...** it follows therefore that ...

4 (*con valore partitivo*): **hai dei libri? — sì, ne ho** have you any books? — yes, I have (some); **hai del pane? — no, non ne ho** have you any bread? — no, I haven't any; **quanti anni hai? — ne ho 17** how old are you? — I'm 17

▶ AV (*moto da luogo: da lì*) from there; **ne vengo ora** I've just come from there

---

né CONG: **né ... né** neither ... nor; **né l'uno né l'altro lo vuole** neither of them wants it; **né più né meno** no more no less; **non parla né l'italiano né il tedesco** he speaks neither Italian nor German, he doesn't speak either Italian or German; **non piove né nevica** it isn't raining or snowing

N.E. ABBR (= *nordest*) NE

ne'anche [ne'anke] AV, CONG not even; **non ...** ~ not even; **~ se volesse potrebbe venire** he couldn't come even if he wanted to; **non l'ho visto — neanch'io** I didn't see him — neither did I *o* I didn't either; **~ per idea** *o* **sogno!** not on your life!; **non ci penso ~!** I wouldn't dream of it!; **~ a pagarlo lo farebbe** he wouldn't do it even if you paid him

'nebbia SF fog; (*foschia*) mist

nebbi'oso, -a AG foggy; misty

nebulizza'tore [nebuliddza'tore] SM atomizer

nebu'losa SF nebula

nebulosità SF haziness

nebu'loso, -a AG (*atmosfera, cielo*) hazy; (*fig*) hazy, vague

néces'saire [nesε'sεr] SM INV: ~ **da viaggio** overnight case o bag

necessaria'mente [netʃessarja'mente] AV necessarily

neces'sario, -a [netʃes'sarjo] AG necessary ▶ SM: **fare il ~** to do what is necessary; **lo stretto ~** the bare essentials *pl*

necessità [netʃessi'ta] SF INV necessity; (*povertà*) need, poverty; **trovarsi nella ~ di fare qc** to be forced o obliged to do sth, have to do sth

necessi'tare [netʃessi'tare] /**72**/ VT to require ▶ VI (*aver bisogno*): ~ **di** to need

necro'logio [nekro'lɔdʒo] SM obituary notice; (*registro*) register of deaths

ne'fando, -a AG infamous, wicked

ne'fasto, -a AG inauspicious, ill-omened

ne'gare /**80**/ VT to deny; (*rifiutare*) to deny, refuse; ~ **di aver fatto/che** to deny having done/that

negativa'mente AV negatively; **rispondere ~** to give a negative response

nega'tivo, -a AG, SF, SM negative

negazi'one [negat'tsjone] SF negation

negherò *etc* [nege'rɔ] VB *vedi* **negare**

ne'gletto, -a [ne'gletto] AG (*trascurato*) neglected

'negli ['neʎʎi] PREP + DET *vedi* **in**

négli'gé [negli'ʒe] SM INV negligee

negli'gente [negli'dʒεnte] AG negligent, careless

negli'genza [negli'dʒεntsa] SF negligence, carelessness

negozi'abile [negot'tsjabile] AG negotiable

negozi'ante [negot'tsjante] SMF trader, dealer; (*bottegaio*) shopkeeper (BRIT), storekeeper (US)

negozi'are [negot'tsjare] /**19**/ VT to negotiate ▶ VI: ~ **in** to trade o deal in

negozi'ato [negot'tsjato] SM negotiation

negozia'tore, -'trice [negottsja'tore] SM/F negotiator

ne'gozio [ne'gɔttsjo] SM (*locale*) shop (BRIT), store (US); (*affare*) (piece of) business *no pl*; (*Dir*): ~ **giuridico** legal transaction

negri'ere, -a, negri'ero, -a SM/F slave trader; (*fig*) slave driver

'negro, -a AG, SM/F Negro

negro'mante SMF necromancer

negroman'zia [negroman'tsia] SF necromancy

'nei, nel, nell', 'nella, 'nelle, 'nello PREP + DET *vedi* **in**

'nembo SM (*Meteor*) nimbus

ne'mico, -a, -ci, -che AG hostile; (*Mil*) enemy *cpd* ▶ SM/F enemy; **essere ~ di** to be strongly averse o opposed to

nem'meno AV, CONG = **neanche**

'nenia SF dirge; (*motivo monotono*) monotonous tune

'neo SM mole; (*fig*) (slight) flaw

'neo... PREFISSO neo...

neofa'scista, -i, -e [neofaʃ'ʃista] SM/F neofascist

neolo'gismo [neolo'dʒizmo] SM neologism

'neon SM (*Chim*) neon

neo'nato, -a AG newborn ▶ SM/F newborn baby

neozelan'dese [neoddzelan'dese] AG New Zealand *cpd* ▶ SMF New Zealander

Ne'pal SM: **il ~** Nepal

nepo'tismo SM nepotism

nep'pure AV, CONG = **neanche**

ner'bata SF (*colpo*) blow; (*sferzata*) whiplash

'nerbo SM lash; (*fig*) strength, backbone

nerbo'ruto, -a AG muscular; robust

ne'retto SM (*Tip*) bold type

'nero, -a AG black; (*scuro*) dark ▶ SM black; **nella miseria più nera** in utter o abject poverty; **essere di umore ~, essere ~** to be in a filthy mood; **mettere qc ~ su bianco** to put sth down in black and white; **vedere tutto ~** to look on the black side (of things); **il Mar N~** the Black Sea

nero'fumo SM lampblack

nerva'tura SF (*Anat*) nervous system; (*Bot*) veining; (*Archit, Tecn*) rib

'nervo SM (*Anat*) nerve; (*Bot*) vein; **avere i nervi** to be on edge; **dare sui nervi a qn** to get on sb's nerves; **tenere/avere i nervi saldi** to keep/be calm; **che nervi!** damn (it)!

nervo'sismo SM (*Psic*) nervousness; (*irritazione*) irritability

ner'voso, -a AG nervous; (*irritabile*) irritable ▶ SM (*col*): **far venire il ~ a qn** to get on sb's nerves; **farsi prendere dal ~** to let o.s. get irritated

'nespola SF (*Bot*) medlar; (*fig*) blow, punch

'nespolo SM medlar tree

'nesso SM connection, link

(PAROLA CHIAVE)

nes'suno, -a (*det: dav sm* **nessun** + C, V, **nessuno** + *s impura, gn, pn, ps, x, z; dav sf* **nessuna** + C, **nessun'** + V) DET **1** (*non uno*) no **2** (*espressione negativa*) + *any*; **non c'è nessun libro** there isn't any book, there is no book; **nessun altro** no one else, nobody else; **nessun'altra cosa** nothing else; **in nessun luogo** nowhere

n

3 (*qualche*) any; **hai nessuna obiezione?** do you have any objections?
▶ PRON **1** (*non uno*) no one, nobody; (*espressione negativa*) any(one); **nessuno è venuto, non è venuto nessuno** nobody came
2 (*cosa: espressione negativa*) none; (: *espressione negativa*) any
3 (*qualcuno*) anyone, anybody; **ha telefonato nessuno?** did anyone phone?

netta'mente AV clearly
net'tare¹ VT to clean
'nettare² ['nɛttare] SM nectar
net'tezza [net'tettsa] SF cleanness, cleanliness; **~ urbana** cleansing department (BRIT), department of sanitation (US)
'netto, -a AG (*pulito*) clean; (*chiaro*) clear, clear-cut; (*deciso*) definite; (*Econ*) net; **tagliare qc di ~** to cut sth clean off; **taglio ~ col passato** (*fig*) clean break with the past
nettur'bino SM dustman (BRIT), garbage collector (US)
'neuro... PREFISSO neuro...
neurochirur'gia [neurokirur'dʒia] SF neurosurgery
neurolo'gia [neurolo'dʒia] SF neurology
neuro'logico, -a, -ci, -che [neuro'lɔdʒiko] AG neurological
neu'rologo, -a, -gi, -ghe SM/F neurologist
neu'rosi SF INV = **nevrosi**
neu'trale AG neutral
neutralità SF neutrality
neutraliz'zare [neutralid'dzare] /**72**/ VT to neutralize
'neutro, -a AG neutral; (*Ling*) neuter ▶ SM (*Ling*) neuter
neu'trone SM neutron
ne'vaio SM snowfield
'neve SF snow; **montare a ~** (*Cuc*) to whip up; **~ carbonica** dry ice
nevi'care /**20**/ VB IMPERS to snow
nevi'cata SF snowfall
ne'vischio [ne'viskjo] SM sleet
ne'voso, -a AG snowy; snow-covered
nevral'gia [nevral'dʒia] SF neuralgia
ne'vralgico, -a, -ci, -che [ne'vraldʒiko] AG: **punto ~** (*Med*) nerve centre; (*fig*) crucial point
nevras'tenico, -a, -ci, -che AG (*Med*) neurasthenic; (*fig*) hot-tempered ▶ SM/F neurasthenic; hot-tempered person
ne'vrosi SF INV neurosis
ne'vrotico, -a, -ci, -che AG, SM/F (*anche fig*) neurotic
Nia'gara SM: **le cascate del ~** the Niagara Falls
'nibbio SM (*Zool*) kite
Nica'ragua SM: **il ~** Nicaragua
nicaragu'ense AG, SMF Nicaraguan

'nicchia ['nikkja] SF niche; (*naturale*) cavity, hollow; **~ di mercato** (*Comm*) niche market
nicchi'are [nik'kjare] /**19**/ VI to shilly-shally, hesitate
'nichel ['nikel] SM nickel
nichi'lismo [niki'lizmo] SM nihilism
Nico'sia SF Nicosia
nico'tina SF nicotine
nidi'ata SF (*di uccelli: anche fig: di bambini*) brood; (*di altri animali*) litter
nidifi'care /**20**/ VI to nest
'nido SM nest ▶ AG INV: **asilo ~** day nursery, crèche (*for children aged 0 to 3*); **a ~ d'ape** (*tessuto ecc*) honeycomb *cpd*

(PAROLA CHIAVE)

ni'ente PRON **1** (*nessuna cosa*) nothing; **niente può fermarlo** nothing can stop him; **niente di niente** absolutely nothing; **grazie! — di niente!** thank you! — not at all!; **nient'altro** nothing else; **nient'altro che** nothing but, just, only; **niente affatto** not at all, not in the least; **come se niente fosse** as if nothing had happened; **cose da niente** trivial matters; **per niente** (*gratis, invano*) for nothing; **non per niente, ma ...** not for any particular reason, but ...; **poco o niente** next to nothing; **un uomo da niente** a man of no consequence
2 (*qualcosa*): **hai bisogno di niente?** do you need anything?
3: **non ... niente** nothing; (*espressione negativa*) + anything; **non ho visto niente** I saw nothing, I didn't see anything; **non può farci niente** he can't do anything about it; **(non) fa niente** (*non importa*) it doesn't matter; **non ho niente da dire** I have nothing o haven't anything to say
▶ AG INV: **niente paura!** never fear!; **e niente scuse!** and I don't want to hear excuses!
▶ SM nothing; **un bel niente** absolutely nothing; **basta un niente per farla piangere** the slightest thing is enough to make her cry; **finire in niente** to come to nothing
▶ AV (*in nessuna misura*): **non ... niente** not ... at all; **non è (per) niente buono** it isn't good at all; **non ci penso per niente** (*non ne ho nessuna intenzione*) I wouldn't think of it; **niente male!** not bad at all!

nientedi'meno, niente'meno AV actually, even ▶ ESCL really!, I say!
'Niger ['nidʒer] SM: **il ~** Niger; (*fiume*) the Niger
Ni'geria [ni'dʒɛrja] SF: **la ~** Nigeria
nigeri'ano, -a [nidʒe'rjano] AG, SM/F Nigerian
'Nilo SM: **il ~** the Nile
'nimbo SM halo

'**ninfa** SF nymph

nin'fea SF water lily

nin'fomane SF nymphomaniac

ninna'nanna SF lullaby

'**ninnolo** SM (*balocco*) plaything; (*gingillo*) knick-knack

ni'pote SMF (*di zii*) nephew (niece); (*di nonni*) grandson (daughter), grandchild

nip'ponico, -a, -ci, -che AG Japanese

niti'dezza [niti'dettsa] SF (*gen*) clearness; (*di stile*) clarity; (*Fot, TV*) sharpness

'**nitido, -a** AG clear; (*immagine*) sharp; (*specchio*) bright

ni'trato SM nitrate

'**nitrico, -a, -ci, -che** AG nitric

ni'trire /55/ VI to neigh

ni'trito SM (*di cavallo*) neighing *no pl*; neigh; (*Chim*) nitrite

nitroglice'rina [nitroglit∫e'rina] SF nitroglycerine

'**niveo, -a** AG snow-white

'**Nizza** ['nittsa] SF Nice

nn ABBR (= *numeri*) nos

NO SIGLA = **Novara**

no AV (*risposta*) no; **vieni o no?** are you coming or not?; **come no!** of course!, certainly!; **perché no?** why not?; **lo conosciamo? — tu no ma io sì** do we know him? — you don't but I do; **verrai, no?** you'll come, won't you?

N.O. ABBR (= *nordovest*) NW

nobil'donna SF noblewoman

'**nobile** AG noble ▶ SMF noble, nobleman/woman

nobili'are AG noble

nobili'tare /72/ VT (*anche fig*) to ennoble; **nobilitarsi** VPR (*rendersi insigne*) to distinguish o.s.

nobiltà SF nobility; (*di azione ecc*) nobleness

nobilu'omo (*pl* **nobiluomini**) SM nobleman

'**nocca, -che** SF (*Anat*) knuckle

'**noccio** *etc* ['nɔttʃo] VB *vedi* **nuocere**

nocci'ola [not'tʃɔla] SF hazelnut ▶ AG INV (*anche: **color nocciola***) hazel, light brown

noccio'lina [nottʃo'lina] SF (*anche: **nocciolina americana***) peanut

'**nocciolo¹** [nɔt'tʃolo] SM (*di frutto*) stone; (*fig*) heart, core

nocci'olo² [not'tʃolo] SM (*albero*) hazel

'**noce** ['notʃe] SM (*albero*) walnut tree ▶ SF (*frutto*) walnut; **una ~ di burro** (*Cuc*) a knob of butter (*BRIT*), a dab of butter (*US*); **~ di cocco** coconut; **~ moscata** nutmeg

noce'pesca, -sche [notʃe'pɛska] SF nectarine

no'cevo *etc* [no'tʃevo] VB *vedi* **nuocere**

noci'uto [no'tʃuto] PP *di* **nuocere**

no'civo, -a [no'tʃivo] AG harmful, noxious

'**nocqui** *etc* VB *vedi* **nuocere**

'**nodo** SM (*di cravatta, legname, Naut*) knot; (*Aut, Ferr*) junction; (*Med, Astr, Bot*) node;

(*fig: legame*) bond, tie; (: *punto centrale*) heart, crux; **avere un ~ alla gola** to have a lump in one's throat; **tutti i nodi vengono al pettine** (*proverbio*) your sins will find you out

no'doso, -a AG (*tronco*) gnarled

'**nodulo** SM (*Anat, Bot*) nodule

no-'global [no-'global] SMF anti-globalization protester ▶ AG (*movimento, manifestante*) anti-globalization

'**noi** PRON (*soggetto*) we; (*oggetto: per dare rilievo, con preposizione*) us; **~ stessi(e)** we ourselves; (*oggetto*) ourselves; **da ~** (*nel nostro paese*) in our country, where we come from; (*a casa nostra*) at our house

'**noia** SF boredom; (*disturbo, impaccio*) bother *no pl*, trouble *no pl*; **avere qn/qc a ~** not to like sb/sth; **mi è venuto a ~** I'm tired of it; **dare ~** to annoy; **avere delle noie con qn** to have trouble with sb

noi'altri PRON we

noi'oso, -a AG boring; (*fastidioso*) annoying, troublesome

noleggi'are [noled'dʒare] /62/ VT (*prendere a noleggio*) to hire (*BRIT*), rent; (*dare a noleggio*) to hire out (*BRIT*), rent out; (*aereo, nave*) to charter

noleggia'tore, -'trice [noleddʒa'tore] SM/F hirer (*BRIT*), renter; charterer

no'leggio [no'leddʒo] SM hire (*BRIT*), rental; charter

no'lente AG: **volente o ~** whether one likes it or not, willy-nilly

'**nolo** SM hire (*BRIT*), rental charter; (*per trasporto merci*) freight; **prendere/dare a ~ qc** to hire/hire out sth (*BRIT*), rent/rent out sth

'**nomade** AG nomadic ▶ SMF nomad

noma'dismo SM nomadism

'**nome** SM name; (*Ling*) noun; **in** *o* **a ~ di** in the name of; **di** *o* **per ~** (*chiamato*) called, named; **conoscere qn di ~** to know sb by name; **fare il ~ di qn** to name sb; **faccia pure il mio ~** feel free to mention my name; **~ d'arte** stage name; **~ di battesimo** Christian name; **~ depositato** trade name; **~ di famiglia** surname; **~ da ragazza** maiden name; **~ da sposata** married name; **~ utente** login

no'mea SF notoriety

nomencla'tura SF nomenclature

nomenkla'tura SF (*di partito, stato*) nomenklatura

no'mignolo [no'miɲɲolo] SM nickname

'**nomina** SF appointment

nomi'nale AG nominal; (*Ling*) noun *cpd*

nomi'nare /72/ VT to name; (*eleggere*) to appoint; (*citare*) to mention; **non l'ho mai sentito ~** I've never heard of it (*o* him)

nomination [nomi'neʃʃon] SF INV (*in reality show*) nomination

n

nomina'tivo, -a AG (*intestato: titolo*) registered; (*: libretto*) personal; (*Ling*) nominative ▶ SM (*Amm: nome*) name; (*Ling*) nominative; **elenco ~** list of names

non AV not ▶ PREFISSO non-; **grazie — ~ c'è di che** thank you — don't mention it; **i ~ credenti** the unbelievers; **~ autosufficiente** (*persona anziana*) needing care; *vedi anche* **affatto; appena** *ecc*

nonché [non'ke] CONG (*tanto più, tanto meno*) let alone; (*e inoltre*) as well as

nonconfor'mista, -i, -e AG, SM/F nonconformist

noncu'rante AG: **~ (di)** careless (of), indifferent (to); **con fare ~** with a nonchalant air

noncu'ranza [nonku'rantsa] SF carelessness, indifference; **un'aria di ~** a nonchalant air

nondi'meno CONG (*tuttavia*) however; (*nonostante*) nevertheless

'nonno, -a SM/F grandfather/mother; (*in senso più familiare*) grandma/grandpa; **nonni** SMPL grandparents

non'nulla SM INV: **un ~** nothing, a trifle

'nono, -a NUM ninth

nonos'tante PREP in spite of, notwithstanding ▶ CONG although, even though

non plus 'ultra SM INV: **il ~ (di)** the last word (in)

nontiscordardimé SM INV (*Bot*) forget-me-not

nord SM north ▶ AG INV north; (*regione*) northern; **verso ~** north, northwards; **l'America del N~** North America; **il Mare del N~** the North Sea

nor'dest SM north-east

'nordico, -a, -ci, -che AG nordic, northern European

nor'dista, -i, -e AG, SM/F Yankee

nor'dovest SM north-west

Norim'berga SF Nuremberg

'norma SF (*principio*) norm; (*regola*) regulation, rule; (*consuetudine*) custom, rule; **di ~** normally; **a ~ di legge** according to law, as laid down by law; **al di sopra della ~** above average, above the norm; **per sua ~ e regola** for your information; **proporsi una ~ di vita** to set o.s. rules to live by; **norme di sicurezza** safety regulations; **norme per l'uso** instructions for use

nor'male AG normal; standard *cpd*

normalità SF normality

normaliz'zare [normalid'dzare] /72/ VT to normalize, bring back to normal

normal'mente AV normally

Norman'dia SF: **la ~** Normandy

nor'manno, -a AG, SM/F Norman

norma'tivo, -a AG normative ▶ SF regulations *pl*

norve'gese [norve'dʒese] AG, SMF, SM Norwegian

Nor'vegia [nor'vɛdʒa] SF: **la ~** Norway

noso'comio SM hospital

nostal'gia [nostal'dʒia] SF (*di casa, paese*) homesickness; (*del passato*) nostalgia

nos'talgico, -a, -ci, -che [nos'taldʒiko] AG homesick; nostalgic ▶ SM/F (*Pol*) person who hopes for the return of Fascism

nos'trano, -a AG local; national; (*pianta, frutta*) home-produced

'nostro, -a DET: **il (la) ~(nostra)** *etc* our ▶ PRON: **il (la) ~(nostra)** *etc* ours ▶ SM: **il ~** our money; our belongings ▶ SF: **la nostra** (*opinione*) our view; **abbiamo speso del ~** we spent our own money; **i nostri** our family; our own people; **è dei nostri** he's one of us; **è dalla nostra** (*parte*) he's on our side; **anche noi abbiamo avuto le nostre** (*disavventure*) we've had our problems too; **alla nostra!** (*brindisi*) to us!

nos'tromo SM boatswain

'nota SF (*segno*) mark; (*comunicazione scritta: Mus*) note; (*fattura*) bill; (*elenco*) list; **prendere ~ di qc** to note sth, make a note of sth, write sth down; (*fig: fare attenzione*) to note sth, take note of sth; **degno di ~** noteworthy, worthy of note; **note caratteristiche** distinguishing marks *o* features; **note a piè di pagina** footnotes

no'tabile AG notable; (*persona*) important ▶ SM prominent citizen

no'taio SM notary

no'tare /72/ VT (*segnare: errori*) to mark; (*registrare*) to note (down), write down; (*rilevare, osservare*) to note, notice; **farsi ~** to get o.s. noticed

nota'rile AG: **atto ~** legal document (*authorized by a notary*); **studio ~** notary's office

notazi'one [notat'tsjone] SF (*Mus*) notation

no'tevole AG (*talento*) notable, remarkable; (*peso*) considerable

no'tifica, -che SF notification

notifi'care /20/ VT (*Dir*): **~ qc a qn** to notify sb of sth, give sb notice of sth

notificazi'one [notifikat'tsjone] SF notification

no'tizia [no'tittsja] SF (piece of) news *sg*; (*informazione*) piece of information; **notizie** SFPL news *sg*; information *sg*

notizi'ario [notit'tsjarjo] SM (*Radio, TV, Stampa*) news *sg*

'noto, -a AG (well-)known

notorietà SF fame; notoriety

no'torio, -a AG well-known; (*peg*) notorious

not'tambulo, -a SM/F night-bird (*fig*)

not'tata SF night

'notte SF night; **di ~** at night; (*durante la notte*) in the night, during the night; **questa ~**

(passata) last night; *(che viene)* tonight; **nella ~ dei tempi** in the mists of time; **come va?** — **peggio che andar di ~** how are things? — worse than ever; **~ bianca** sleepless night

notte'tempo AV at night; during the night

'**nottola** SF *(Zool)* noctule

not'turno, -a AG nocturnal; *(servizio, guardiano)* night *cpd* ▶ SF *(Sport)* evening fixture *(BRIT)* o match

nov. ABBR *(= novembre)* Nov

no'vanta NUM ninety

novan'tenne AG, SMF ninety-year-old

novan'tesimo, -a NUM ninetieth

novan'tina SF: **una ~ (di)** about ninety

'**nove** NUM nine

novecen'tesco, -a, -schi, -sche [novetʃen'tesko] AG twentieth-century

nove'cento [nove'tʃento] NUM nine hundred ▶ SM: **il N~** the twentieth century

no'vella SF *(Letteratura)* short story

novel'lino, -a AG *(pivello)* green, inexperienced

novel'lista, -i, -e SM/F short-story writer

novel'listica SF *(arte)* short-story writing; *(insieme di racconti)* short stories *pl*

no'vello, -a AG *(piante, patate)* new; *(insalata, verdura)* early; *(sposo)* newly-married

no'vembre SM November; *vedi anche* **luglio**

novem'brino, -a AG November *cpd*

nove'mila NUM nine thousand

noven'nale AG *(che dura 9 anni)* nine-year *cpd*; *(ogni 9 anni)* nine-yearly

novi'lunio SM *(Astr)* new moon

novità SF INV novelty; *(innovazione)* innovation; *(cosa originale, insolita)* something new; *(notizia)* (piece of) news *sg*; **le ~ della moda** the latest fashions

novizi'ato [novit'tsjato] SM *(Rel)* novitiate; *(tirocinio)* apprenticeship

no'vizio, -a [no'vittsjo] SM/F *(Rel)* novice; *(tirocinante)* beginner, apprentice

nozi'one [not'tsjone] SF notion, idea; **nozioni** SFPL *(rudimenti)* basic knowledge *sg*, rudiments

nozio'nismo [nottsjo'nizmo] SM superficial knowledge

nozio'nistico, -a, -ci, -che [nottsjo'nistiko] AG superficial

'**nozze** ['nɔttse] SFPL wedding *sg*, marriage *sg*; **~ d'argento/d'oro** silver/golden wedding *sg*

ns . ABBR *(Comm)* = **nostro**

NU SIGLA = **Nuoro**

N.U. SIGLA *(= Nazioni Unite)* UN

'**nube** SF cloud

nubi'fragio [nubi'fradʒo] SM cloudburst

'**nubile** AG *(donna)* unmarried, single

'**nuca, -che** SF nape of the neck

nucle'are AG nuclear ▶ SM: **il ~** nuclear energy

'**nucleo** SM nucleus; *(gruppo)* team, unit, group; *(Mil, Polizia)* squad; **~ antidroga** anti-drugs squad; **il ~ familiare** the family unit

nu'dismo SM nudism

nu'dista, -i, -e SM/F nudist

nudità SF INV nudity, nakedness; *(di paesaggio)* bareness ▶ SFPL *(parti nude del corpo)* nakedness *sg*

'**nudo, -a** AG *(persona)* bare, naked, nude; *(membra)* bare, naked; *(montagna)* bare ▶ SM *(Arte)* nude; **a occhio ~** to the naked eye; **a piedi nudi** barefoot; **mettere a ~** *(cuore, verità)* to lay bare; **gli ha detto ~ e crudo che ...** he told him bluntly that ...

'**nugolo** SM: **un ~ di** a whole host of

'**nulla** PRON, AV = **niente** ▶ SM: **il ~** nothing; **svanire nel ~** to vanish into thin air; **basta un ~ per farlo arrabbiare** he gets annoyed over the slightest thing

nulla'osta SM INV authorization

nullate'nente AG: **essere ~** to own nothing ▶ SMF person with no property

nullità SF INV nullity; *(persona)* nonentity

'**nullo, -a** AG useless, worthless; *(Dir)* null (and void); *(Sport)*: **incontro ~** draw

nume'rale AG, SM numeral

nume'rare /72/ VT to number

numera'tore SM *(Mat)* numerator; *(macchina)* numbering device

numerazi'one [numerat'tsjone] SF numbering; *(araba, decimale)* notation

nu'merico, -a, -ci, -che AG numerical

'**numero** SM number; *(romano, arabo)* numeral; *(di spettacolo)* act, turn; **dare i numeri** *(farneticare)* not to be all there; **tanto per fare ~ invitiamo anche lui** why don't we invite him to make up the numbers?; **ha tutti i numeri per riuscire** he's got what it takes to succeed; **che ~ tuo fratello!** your brother is a real character!; **~ civico** house number; **~ chiuso** *(Università)* selective entry system; **~ doppio** *(di rivista)* issue with supplement; **~ di scarpe** shoe size; **~ di telefono** telephone number; **~ verde** *(Tel)* ≈ Freephone®

nume'roso, -a AG numerous, many; *(folla, famiglia)* large

numis'matica SF numismatics *sg*, coin collecting

'**nunzio** ['nuntsjo] SM *(Rel)* nuncio

nu'occio *etc* ['nwɔttʃo] VB *vedi* **nuocere**

nu'ocere ['nwɔtʃere] /69/ VI: **~ a** to harm, damage; **il tentar non nuoce** *(proverbio)* there's no harm in trying

nuoci'uto, -a [nwo'tʃuto] PP *di* **nuocere**

nu'ora SF daughter-in-law

nuo'tare /72/ VI to swim; *(galleggiare: oggetti)* to float; **~ a rana/sul dorso** to do the breast stroke/backstroke

nuo'tata SF swim

nuota'tore, -'trice SM/F swimmer

nu'oto SM swimming

nu'ova SF *vedi* **nuovo**

nuova'mente AV again

Nu'ova York SF New York

Nu'ova Ze'landa [-dze'landa] SF: **la ~** New Zealand

nu'ovo, -a AG new ▸ SF *(notizia)* (piece of) news *sg*; **come ~** as good as new; **di ~** again; **fino a ~ ordine** until further notice; **il suo volto non mi è ~** I know his face; **rimettere a ~** *(cosa, macchina)* to do up like new; **anno ~, vita nuova!** it's time to turn over a new leaf!; **~ fiammante** *o* **di zecca** brand-new; **la Nuova Guinea** New Guinea; **la Nuova Inghilterra** New England; **la Nuova Scozia** Nova Scotia

nu'trice [nu'tritʃe] SF wet nurse

nutri'ente AG nutritious, nourishing; *(crema, balsamo)* nourishing

nutri'mento SM food, nourishment

nu'trire /45/ VT to feed; *(fig: sentimenti)* to harbour *(BRIT)*, harbor *(US)*, nurse; **nutrirsi** VPR: **nutrirsi di** to feed on, to eat

nutri'tivo, -a AG nutritional; *(alimento)* nutritious

nu'trito, -a AG *(numeroso)* large; *(fitto)* heavy; **ben/mal ~** well/poorly fed

nutrizi'one [nutrit'tsjone] SF nutrition

'nuvolo, -a AG cloudy ▸ SF cloud

nuvolosità SF cloudiness

nuvo'loso, -a AG cloudy

nuzi'ale [nut'tsjale] AG nuptial; wedding *cpd*

'nylon ['nailən] SM nylon

Oo

O, o [ɔ] SM O F INV (*lettera*) O, o; **O come Otranto** = O for Oliver (BRIT), O for Oboe (US)
o CONG (*dav V spesso*): **od** or; **o … o** either … or; **o l'uno o l'altro** either (of them); **o meglio** or rather
O. ABBR (= *ovest*) W
'oasi SF INV oasis
obbedi'ente *etc vedi* **ubbidiente** *ecc*
obbiet'tare *etc vedi* **obbiettare** *ecc*
obbli'gare /80/ VT (*Dir*) to bind; (*costringere*): **~ qn a fare** to force o oblige sb to do; **obbligarsi** VPR: **obbligarsi a fare** to undertake to do; **obbligarsi per qn** (*Dir*) to stand surety for sb, act as guarantor for sb
obbliga'tissimo, -a AG (*ringraziamento*): **~!** much obliged!
obbli'gato, -a AG (*costretto, grato*) obliged; (*percorso, tappa*) set, fixed; **passaggio ~** (*fig*) essential requirement
obbliga'torio, -a AG compulsory, obligatory
obbligazi'one [obbligat'tsjone] SF obligation; (*Comm*) bond, debenture; **~ dello Stato** government bond; **obbligazioni convertibili** convertible loan stock, convertible debentures
obbligazio'nista, -i, -e [obbligattsjo'nista] SM/F bond-holder
'obbligo, -ghi SM obligation; (*dovere*) duty; **avere l'~ di fare, essere nell'~ di fare** to be obliged to do; **essere d'~** (*discorso, applauso*) to be called for; **avere degli obblighi con** o **verso qn** to be under an obligation to sb, be indebted to sb; **le formalità d'~** the necessary formalities
obb.mo ABBR = **obbligatissimo**
ob'brobrio SM disgrace; (*fig*) mess, eyesore
obe'lisco, -schi SM obelisk
obe'rato, -a AG: **~ di** (*lavoro*) overloaded o overburdened with; (*debiti*) crippled with
obesità SF obesity
o'beso, -a AG obese
obiet'tare /72/ VT: **~ che** to object that; **~ su qc** to object to sth, raise objections concerning sth

obiettiva'mente AV objectively
obiettività SF objectivity
obiet'tivo, -a AG objective ▶ SM (*Ottica, Fot*) lens *sg*, objective; (*Mil, fig*) objective
obiet'tore SM objector; **~ di coscienza** conscientious objector
obiezi'one [objet'tsjone] SF objection
obi'torio SM morgue
o'bliquo, -a AG oblique; (*inclinato*) slanting; (*fig*) devious, underhand; **sguardo ~** sidelong glance
oblite'rare /72/ VT (*francobollo*) to cancel; (*biglietto*) to stamp
oblitera'trice [oblitera'tritʃe] SF (*anche:* **macchina obliteratrice**) cancelling machine; stamping machine
oblò SM INV porthole
o'blungo, -a, -ghi, -ghe AG oblong
'oboe SM (*Mus*) oboe
'obolo SM (*elemosina*) (small) offering, mite
obsole'scenza [obsoleʃ'ʃentsa] SF (*Econ*) obsolescence
obso'leto, -a AG obsolete
OC ABBR (= *onde corte*) SW
'oca (*pl* **oche**) SF goose
o'caggine [o'kaddʒine] SF silliness, stupidity
occasio'nale AG (*incontro*) chance; (*cliente, guadagni*) casual, occasional
occasi'one SF (*caso favorevole*) opportunity; (*causa, motivo, circostanza*) occasion; (*Comm*) bargain; **all'~** should the need arise; **alla prima ~** at the first, opportunity; **d'~** (*a buon prezzo*) bargain *cpd*; (*usato*) secondhand
occhi'aia [ok'kjaja] SF eye socket; **occhiaie** SFPL (*sotto gli occhi*) shadows (under the eyes); **avere le occhiaie** to have shadows under one's eyes
occhi'ali [ok'kjali] SMPL glasses, spectacles; **~ da sole/da vista** sunglasses/(prescription) glasses
occhi'ata [ok'kjata] SF look, glance; **dare un'~ a** to have a look at
occhieggi'are [okkjed'dʒare] /62/ VI (*apparire qua e là*) to peep (out)

O

occhi'ello [ok'kjɛllo] SM buttonhole; (*asola*) eyelet

'**occhio** ['ɔkkjo] SM eye; ~! careful!, watch out!; **a ~ nudo** with the naked eye; **a quattr'occhi** privately, tête-à-tête, in private; **avere ~** to have a good eye; **chiudere un ~ (su)** (*fig*) to turn a blind eye (to), shut one's eyes (to); **costare un ~ della testa** to cost a fortune; **dare all'~** *o* **nell'~ a qn** to catch sb's eye; **fare l'~ a qc** to get used to sth; **tenere d'~ qn** to keep an eye on sb; **vedere di buon/mal ~ qc** to look favourably/unfavourably on sth

occhio'lino [okkjo'lino] SM: **fare l'~ a qn** to wink at sb

occiden'tale [ottʃiden'tale] AG western ▶ SMF Westerner

occi'dente [ottʃi'dɛnte] SM west; (*Pol*): **l'O~** the West; **a ~** in the west

oc'cipite [ot'tʃipite] SM back of the head, occiput (*Anat*)

oc'cludere /3/ VT to block

occlusi'one SF blockage, obstruction

oc'cluso, -a PP *di* **occludere**

occor'rente AG necessary ▶ SM all that is necessary

occor'renza [okkor'rɛntsa] SF necessity, need; **all'~** in case of need

oc'correre /28/ VI to be needed, be required ▶ VB IMPERS: **occorre farlo** it must be done; **occorre che tu parta** you must leave, you'll have to leave; **mi occorrono i soldi** I need the money

oc'corso, -a PP *di* **occorrere**

occulta'mento SM concealment

occul'tare /72/ VT to hide, conceal

oc'culto, -a AG hidden, concealed; (*scienze, forze*) occult

occu'pante SMF (*di casa*) occupier, occupant; **~ abusivo** squatter

occu'pare /72/ VT to occupy; (*manodopera*) to employ; (*ingombrare*) to occupy, take up; **occuparsi** VPR to occupy o.s., keep o.s. busy; (*impiegarsi*) to get a job; **occuparsi di** (*interessarsi*) to take an interest in; (*prendersi cura di*) to look after, take care of

occu'pato, -a AG (*Mil, Pol*) occupied; (*persona: affaccendato*) busy; (*posto, sedia*) taken; (*toilette, Tel*) engaged; **la linea è occupata** the line's engaged

occupazio'nale [okkupattsjo'nale] AG employment *cpd*, of employment

occupazi'one [okkupat'tsjone] SF occupation; (*impiego, lavoro*) job; (*Econ*) employment

Oce'ania [otʃe'anja] SF: **l'~** Oceania

o'ceano [o'tʃɛano] SM ocean

'**ocra** SF ochre

'**OCSE** SIGLA F (= *Organizzazione per la Cooperazione e lo Sviluppo Economico*) OECD (= *Organization for Economic Cooperation and Development*)

ocu'lare AG ocular, eye *cpd*; **testimone ~** eye witness

ocula'tezza [okula'tettsa] SF caution; shrewdness

ocu'lato, -a AG (*attento*) cautious, prudent; (*accorto*) shrewd

ocu'lista, -i, -e SM/F eye specialist, oculist

od CONG *vedi* **o**

'**ode** SF ode

'**ode** *etc* VB *vedi* **udire**

odi'are /19/ VT to hate, detest

odi'erno, -a AG today's, of today; (*attuale*) present; **in data odierna** (*formale*) today

'**odio** SM hatred; **avere in ~ qc/qn** to hate *o* detest sth/sb

odi'oso, -a AG hateful, odious; **rendersi ~ (a)** to make o.s. unpopular (with)

'**odo** *etc* VB *vedi* **udire**

odontoi'atra, -i, -e SM/F dentist, dental surgeon

odontoia'tria SF dentistry

odonto'tecnico, -ci SM dental technician

odo'rare /72/ VT (*annusare*) to smell; (*profumare*) to perfume, scent ▶ VI: **~ (di)** to smell (of)

odo'rato SM sense of smell

o'dore SM smell; **gli odori** (*Cuc*) (aromatic) herbs; **sentire ~ di qc** to smell sth; **morire in ~ di santità** (*Rel*) to die in the odour (*BRIT*) *o* odor (*US*) of sanctity

odo'roso, -a AG sweet-smelling

offen'dere /36/ VT to offend; (*violare*) to break, violate; (*insultare*) to insult; (*ferire*) to hurt; **offendersi** VPR (*con senso reciproco*) to insult one another; (*risentirsi*) **offendersi (di)** to take offence (at), be offended (by)

offen'sivo, -a AG, SF offensive

offen'sore SM offender; (*Mil*) aggressor

offe'rente SM (*in aste*): **al migliore ~** to the highest bidder

of'ferta, -a PP *di* **offrire** ▶ SF offer; (*donazione: anche Rel*) offering; (*in gara d'appalto*) tender; (*in aste*) bid; (*Econ*) supply; **fare un'offerta** to make an offer; (*per appalto*) to tender; (*ad un'asta*) to bid; **offerta pubblica d'acquisto** takeover bid; **offerta pubblica di vendita** public offer for sale; **offerta reale** tender; "**offerte d'impiego**" (*Stampa*) "situations vacant" (*BRIT*), "help wanted" (*US*); **offerta speciale** special offer

of'feso, -a PP *di* **offendere** ▶ AG offended; (*fisicamente*) hurt, injured ▶ SM/F offended party ▶ SF insult, affront; (*Mil*) attack; (*Dir*) offence (*BRIT*), offense (*US*); **essere ~ con qn** to be annoyed with sb; **parte offesa** (*Dir*) plaintiff

offi'ciare [offi'tʃare] /14/ VI (*Rel*) to officiate

offi'cina [offi'tʃina] SF workshop

of'frire /**70**/ VT to offer; **offrirsi** VPR (*proporsi*) to offer (o.s.), volunteer; (*occasione*) to present itself; (*esporsi*) **offrirsi a** to expose o.s. to; **ti offro da bere** I'll buy you a drink; **"offresi posto di segretaria"** "secretarial vacancy", "vacancy for secretary"; **"segretaria offresi"** "secretary seeks post"

offus'care /**20**/ VT to obscure, darken; (*fig: intelletto*) to dim, cloud; (: *fama*) to obscure, overshadow; **offuscarsi** VPR to grow dark; to cloud, grow dim; to be obscured

of'talmico, -a, -ci, -che AG ophthalmic

oggettività [oddʒettivi'ta] SF objectivity

ogget'tivo, -a [oddʒet'tivo] AG objective

og'getto [od'dʒetto] SM object; (*materia, argomento*) subject (matter); (*in lettere commerciali*): **~ ...** re ...; **essere ~ di** (*critiche, controversia*) to be the subject of; (*odio, pietà ecc*) to be the object of; **essere ~ di scherno** to be a laughing stock; **in ~ a quanto detto** (*in lettere*) as regards the matter mentioned above; **oggetti preziosi** valuables, articles of value; **oggetti smarriti** lost property *sg* (*BRIT*), lost and found *sg* (*US*)

'oggi ['ɔddʒi] AV, SM today; **~ stesso** today, this very day; **~ come ~** at present, as things stand; **dall' ~ al domani** from one day to the next; **a tutt'~** up till now, till today; **le spese a tutt'~ sono ...** expenses to date are ...; **~ a otto** a week today

oggigi'orno [oddʒi'dʒorno] AV nowadays

o'giva [o'dʒiva] SF ogive, pointed arch

OGM [ɔdʒi'ɛmme] SIGLA MPL (= *organismi geneticamente modificati*) GMO (= *genetically modified organisms*)

'ogni ['oɲɲi] DET every, each; (*tutti*) all; (*con valore distributivo*) every; **~ uomo è mortale** all men are mortal; **viene ~ due giorni** he comes every two days; **~ cosa** everything; **ad ~ costo** at all costs, at any price; **in ~ luogo** everywhere; **~ tanto** every so often; **~ volta che** every time that

Ognis'santi [oɲɲis'santi] SM All Saints' Day

o'gnuno [oɲ'ɲuno] PRON everyone, everybody

'ohi ESCL oh!; (*esprimente dolore*) ow!

ohimè ESCL oh dear!

'OIL SIGLA F (= *Organizzazione Internazionale del Lavoro*) ILO

OL ABBR (= *onde lunghe*) LW

O'landa SF: **l'~** Holland

olan'dese AG Dutch ▶ SM (*Ling*) Dutch ▶ SMF Dutchman/woman; **gli Olandesi** the Dutch

ole'andro SM oleander

ole'ato, -a AG: **carta oleata** greaseproof paper (*BRIT*), wax paper (*US*)

oleo'dotto SM oil pipeline

ole'oso, -a AG oily; (*che contiene olio*) oil *cpd*, oil-yielding

o'lezzo [o'leddzo] SM fragrance

ol'fatto SM sense of smell

oli'are /**19**/ VT to oil

olia'tore SM oil can, oiler

oli'era SF oil cruet

oligar'chia [oligar'kia] SF oligarchy

Olim'piadi SFPL Olympic Games

o'limpico, -a, -ci, -che AG Olympic

'olio SM oil; (*Pittura*): **un (quadro a) ~** an oil painting; **sott'~** (*Cuc*) in oil; **oli essenziali** essential oils; **~ di fegato di merluzzo** cod liver oil; **~ d'oliva** olive oil; **~ santo** holy oil; **~ di semi** vegetable oil; **~ solare** suntan oil; **oli essenziali** essential oils

o'liva SF olive

oli'vastro, -a AG olive(-coloured) (*BRIT*), olive(-colored) (*US*); (*carnagione*) sallow

oli'veto SM olive grove

o'livo SM olive tree

'olmo SM elm

olo'causto SM holocaust

OLP SIGLA F (= *Organizzazione per la Liberazione della Palestina*) PLO

oltraggi'are [oltrad'dʒare] /**62**/ VT to offend, insult

ol'traggio [ol'traddʒo] SM outrage; offence (*BRIT*), offense (*US*), insult; (*Dir*): **~ a pubblico ufficiale** insulting a public official; (*Dir*): **~ al pudore** indecent behaviour (*BRIT*) o behavior (*US*); **~ alla corte** contempt of court

oltraggi'oso, -a [oltrad'dʒoso] AG offensive

ol'tralpe AV beyond the Alps

ol'tranza [ol'trantsa] SF: **a ~** to the last, to the bitter end; **sciopero ad ~** all-out strike

oltran'zismo [oltran'tsizmo] SM (*Pol*) extremism

oltran'zista, -i, -e [oltran'tsista] SM/F (*Pol*) extremist

'oltre AV (*più in là*) further; (*di più: aspettare*) longer, more ▶ PREP (*di là da*) beyond, over, on the other side of; (*più di*) more than, over; (*in aggiunta a*) besides; (*eccetto*): **~ a** except, apart from; **~ a tutto** on top of all that

oltrecor'tina AV behind the Iron Curtain; **paesi d'~** Iron Curtain countries

oltre'manica AV across the Channel

oltre'mare AV overseas

oltre'modo AV extremely, greatly

oltreo'ceano [oltreo'tʃeano] AV overseas ▶ SM: **paesi d'~** overseas countries

oltrepas'sare /**72**/ VT to go beyond, exceed

oltre'tomba SM INV: **l'~** the hereafter

OM ABBR (= *onde medie*) MW; (*Mil*) = **ospedale militare**

o'maggio [o'maddʒo] SM (*dono*) gift; (*segno di rispetto*) homage, tribute; **omaggi** SMPL (*complimenti*) respects; **in ~** (*copia, biglietto*) complimentary; **rendere ~ a** to pay homage

239

o tribute to; **presentare i propri omaggi a qn** (*formale*) to pay one's respects to sb

'**Oman** SM: **l'~** Oman

ombeli'cale AG umbilical

ombe'lico, -chi SM navel

'**ombra** SF (*zona non assolata, fantasma*) shade; (*sagoma scura*) shadow ▶ AG INV: **bandiera ~** flag of convenience; **governo ~** (*Pol*) shadow cabinet; **sedere all'~** to sit in the shade; **nell'~** (*tramare, agire*) secretly; **restare nell'~** (*fig: persona*) to remain in obscurity; **senza ~ di dubbio** without the shadow of a doubt

ombreggi'are [ombred'dʒare] /**62**/ VT to shade

om'brello SM umbrella; **~ da sole** parasol, sunshade

ombrel'lone SM beach umbrella

om'bretto SM eyeshadow

om'broso, -a AG shady, shaded; (*cavallo*) nervous, skittish; (*persona*) touchy, easily offended

O.M.C. SIGLA F (= *Organizzazione Mondiale del Commercio*) WTO

ome'lette [ɔmə'lɛt] SF INV omelet(te)

ome'lia SF (*Rel*) homily, sermon

ome'opata SMF hom(o)eopath

omeopa'tia SF hom(o)eopathy

omeo'patico, -a, -ci, -che AG hom(o)eopathic ▶ SM hom(o)eopath

omertà SF conspiracy of silence

o'messo, -a PP *di* **omettere**

o'mettere /**63**/ VT to omit, leave out; **~ di fare** to omit *o* fail to do

omi'cida, -i, -e [omi'tʃida] AG homicidal, murderous ▶ SM/F murderer (murderess)

omi'cidio [omi'tʃidjo] SM murder; **~ colposo** (*Dir*) culpable homicide; **~ premeditato** (*Dir*) murder

o'misi *etc* VB *vedi* **omettere**

omissi'one SF omission; **reato d'~** criminal negligence; **~ di atti d'ufficio** negligence; **~ di denuncia** failure to report a crime; **~ di soccorso** (*Dir*) failure to stop and give assistance

omogeneiz'zato [omodʒeneid'dzato] SM baby food

omo'geneo, -a [omo'dʒɛneo] AG homogeneous

omolo'gare /**80**/ VT (*Dir*) to approve, recognize; (*ratificare*) to ratify

omologazi'one [omologat'tsjone] SF approval; ratification

o'mologo, -a, -ghi, -ghe AG homologous, corresponding ▶ SM/F opposite number

o'monimo, -a SM/F namesake ▶ SM (*Ling*) homonym

omosessu'ale AG, SMF homosexual

O.M.S. SIGLA F = **Organizzazione Mondiale della Sanità**

On. ABBR (*Pol*) = **onorevole**

'**oncia, -ce** ['ontʃa] SF ounce

'**onda** SF wave; **mettere** *o* **mandare in ~** (*Radio, TV*) to broadcast; **andare in ~** (*Radio, TV*) to go on the air; **onde corte/medie/lunghe** short/medium/long wave *sg*; **l'~ verde** (*Aut*) synchronized traffic lights *pl*

on'data SF wave, billow; (*fig*) wave, surge; **a ondate** in waves; **~ di caldo** heatwave; **~ di freddo** cold spell *o* snap

'**onde** CONG (*affinché: con il congiuntivo*) so that, in order that; (: *con l'infinito*) so as to, in order to

ondeggi'are [onded'dʒare] /**62**/ VI (*acqua*) to ripple; (*muoversi sulle onde: barca*) to rock, roll; (*fig: muoversi come le onde, barcollare*) to sway; (*essere incerto*) to waver

on'doso, -a AG (*moto*) of the waves

ondu'lato, -a AG (*capelli*) wavy; (*terreno*) undulating; **cartone ~** corrugated paper; **lamiera ondulata** sheet of corrugated iron

ondula'torio, -a AG undulating; (*Fisica*) undulatory, wave *cpd*

ondulazi'one [ondulat'tsjone] SF undulation; (*acconciatura*) wave

one'rato, -a AG: **~ di** burdened with, loaded with

'**onere** SM burden; **~ finanziario** financial charge; **oneri fiscali** taxes

one'roso, -a AG (*fig*) heavy, onerous

onestà SF honesty

onesta'mente AV honestly; fairly, virtuously; (*in verità*) honestly, frankly

o'nesto, -a AG (*probo, retto*) honest; (*giusto*) fair; (*casto*) chaste, virtuous

ONG SIGLA F INV (= *Organizzazione Non Governativa*) NGO

'**onice** ['ɔnitʃe] SF onyx

o'nirico, -a, -ci, -che AG dreamlike, dream *cpd*

onnipo'tente AG omnipotent

onnipre'sente AG omnipresent; (*scherzoso*) ubiquitous

onnisci'ente [onniʃ'ʃɛnte] AG omniscient

onniveg'gente [onnived'dʒɛnte] AG all-seeing

ono'mastico, -ci SM name day

onomato'pea SF onomatopoeia

onomato'peico, -a, -ci, -che AG onomatopoeic

ono'ranze [ono'rantse] SFPL honours (BRIT), honors (US)

ono'rare /**72**/ VT to honour (BRIT), honor (US); (*far onore a*) to do credit to; **onorarsi** VPR: **onorarsi di qc/di fare** to feel hono(u)red by sth/to do

ono'rario, -a AG honorary ▶ SM fee

onora'tissimo, -a AG (*in presentazioni*): **~!** delighted to meet you!

ono'rato, -a AG (*reputazione, famiglia, carriera*) distinguished; **essere ~ di fare qc** to have the honour to do sth *o* of doing sth; **~ di conoscerla!** (it is) a pleasure to meet you!

o'nore SM honour (BRIT), honor (US); **in ~ di** in hono(u)r of; **fare gli onori di casa** to play host (*o* hostess); **fare ~ a** to honour; (*pranzo*) to do justice to; (*famiglia*) to be a credit to; **farsi ~** to distinguish o.s.; **posto d'~** place of honour; **a onor del vero ...** to tell the truth ...

ono'revole AG honourable (BRIT), honorable (US) ▶ SMF (*Pol*) ≈ Member of Parliament (BRIT), ≈ Congressman/woman (US)

onorifi'cenza [onorifi'tʃɛntsa] SF honour (BRIT), honor (US); decoration

ono'rifico, -a, -ci, -che AG honorary

'onta SF shame, disgrace; **ad ~ di** despite, notwithstanding

on'tano SM (*Bot*) alder

'O.N.U. SIGLA F (= *Organizzazione delle Nazioni Unite*) UN, UNO

'OPA SIGLA F = **offerta pubblica d'acquisto**

o'paco, -a, -chi, -che AG (*vetro*) opaque; (*metallo*) dull, matt

o'pale SM O F opal

'O.P.E.C. SIGLA F (= *Organization of Petroleum Exporting Countries*) OPEC

'opera SF (*gen*) work; (*azione rilevante*) action, deed, work; (*Mus*) work; opus; (: *melodramma*) opera; (: *teatro*) opera house; (*ente*) institution, organization; **per ~ sua** thanks to him; **fare ~ di persuasione presso qn** to try to convince sb; **mettersi/essere all'~** to get down to/be at work; **~ d'arte** work of art; **~ buffa** comic opera; **~ lirica** (grand) opera; **~ pia** religious charity; **opere pubbliche** (**OO.PP.**) public works; **opere di restauro/ di scavo** restoration/excavation work *sg*

ope'raio, -a AG working-class; workers'; (*Zool: ape, formica*) worker *cpd* ▶ SM/F worker; **classe operaia** working class; **~ di fabbrica** factory worker; **~ a giornata** day labourer (BRIT) *o* laborer (US); **~ specializzato** *o* **qualificato** skilled worker; **~ non specializzato** semi-skilled worker

ope'rare /**72**/ VT to carry out, make; (*Med*) to operate on ▶ VI to operate, work; (*rimedio*) to act, work; (*Med*) to operate; **operarsi** VPR to occur, take place; (*Med*) to have an operation; **operarsi d'appendicite** to have one's appendix out; **~ qn d'urgenza** to perform an emergency operation on sb

opera'tivo, -a AG operative, operating; **piano ~** (*Mil*) plan of operations

ope'rato SM (*comportamento*) actions *pl*

opera'tore, -'trice SM/F operator; (*TV, Cine*) cameraman; **aperto solo agli operatori** (*Comm*) open to the trade only; **~ di borsa** dealer on the stock exchange; **~ ecologico** refuse collector; **~ economico** agent, broker; **~ del suono** sound recordist; **~ turistico** tour operator

opera'torio, -a AG (*Med*) operating

operazi'one [operat'tsjone] SF operation

ope'retta SF (*Mus*) operetta, light opera

operosità SF industry

ope'roso, -a AG industrious, hard-working

opi'ficio [opi'fitʃo] SM factory, works *pl*

opi'nabile AG (*discutibile*) debatable, questionable; **è ~** it is a matter of opinion

opini'one SF opinion; **avere il coraggio delle proprie opinioni** to have the courage of one's convictions; **l'~ pubblica** public opinion

opinio'nista, -i, -e SM/F (political) columnist

op là ESCL (*per far saltare*) hup!; (*a bimbo che è caduto*) upsy-daisy!

'oppio SM opium

oppi'omane SMF opium addict

oppo'nente AG opposing ▶ SMF opponent

op'pongo *etc* VB *vedi* **opporre**

op'porre /**77**/ VT to oppose; **opporsi** VPR: **opporsi (a qc)** to oppose (sth); to object (to sth); **~ resistenza/un rifiuto** to offer resistance/to refuse

opportu'nista, -i, -e SM/F opportunist

opportunità SF INV opportunity; (*convenienza*) opportuneness, timeliness

oppor'tuno, -a AG timely, opportune; (*giusto*) right, appropriate; **a tempo ~** at the right *o* the appropriate time

op'posi *etc* VB *vedi* **opporre**

opposi'tore, -'trice SM/F opposer, opponent

opposizi'one [oppozit'tsjone] SF opposition; (*Dir*) objection; **essere in netta ~** (*idee, opinioni*) to clash, be in complete opposition; **fare ~ a qn/qc** to oppose sb/sth

op'posto, -a PP *di* **opporre** ▶ AG opposite; (*opinioni*) conflicting ▶ SM opposite, contrary; **all'~** on the contrary

oppressi'one SF oppression

oppres'sivo, -a AG oppressive

op'presso, -a PP *di* **opprimere**

oppres'sore SM oppressor

oppri'mente AG (*caldo, noia*) oppressive; (*persona*) tiresome; (*deprimente*) depressing

op'primere /**50**/ VT (*premere, gravare*) to weigh down; (*estenuare: caldo*) to suffocate, oppress; (*tiranneggiare: popolo*) to oppress

oppu'gnare [oppuɲ'ɲare] /**15**/ VT (*fig*) to refute

op'pure CONG or (else)

op'tare /**72**/ VI: **~ per** (*scegliere*) to opt for, decide upon; (*Borsa*) to take (out) an option on

'optimum SM INV optimum

opu'lento, -a AG (*ricco*) rich, wealthy, affluent; (*arredamento ecc*) opulent

opu'lenza [opu'lɛntsa] SF (*vedi ag*) richness, wealth, affluence; opulence

o'puscolo SM booklet, pamphlet

OPV SIGLA F = **offerta pubblica di vendita**

opzio'nale [optsjo'nale] AG optional

opzi'one [op'tsjone] SF option

OR SIGLA = **Oristano**

'ora SF (*60 minuti*) hour; (*momento*) time ▶ AV (*adesso*) now; (*tra poco*) presently, in a minute; **è uscito proprio ~** (*poco fa*) he's just gone out; **~ ... ~** (*correlativo*) now ... now; **che ~ è?, che ore sono?** what time is it?; **domani a quest'~** this time tomorrow; **non veder l'~ di fare** to long to do, look forward to doing; **fare le ore piccole** to stay up till the early hours (of the morning) o the small hours; **è ~ di partire** it's time to go; **di buon'~** early; **alla buon'~!** at last!; **~ legale** o **estiva** summer time (BRIT), daylight saving time (US); **~ di cena** dinner time; **~ locale** local time; **~ di pranzo** lunchtime; **~ di punta** (*Aut*) rush hour; **d'~ in avanti** o **poi** from now on; **or ~** just now, a moment ago; **~ come ~** right now, at present; **10 anni or sono** 10 years ago

o'racolo SM oracle

'orafo SM goldsmith

o'rale AG, SM oral

oral'mente AV orally

ora'mai AV = **ormai**

o'rario, -a AG hourly; (*fuso, segnale*) time *cpd*; (*velocità*) per hour ▶ SM timetable, schedule; (*di ufficio, visite ecc*) hours *pl*; time(s); **~ di apertura/chiusura** opening/closing time; **~ di apertura degli sportelli** bank opening hours; **~ elastico** o **flessibile** (*Industria*) flexitime; **~ ferroviario** railway timetable; **~ di lavoro/d'ufficio** working/office hours; **in ~** on time

o'rata SF (*Zool*) sea bream

ora'tore, -'trice SM/F speaker; orator

ora'torio, -a AG oratorical ▶ SM (*Rel*) oratory; (*Mus*) oratorio ▶ SF (*arte*) oratory

orazi'one [orat'tsjone] SF (*Rel*) prayer; (*discorso*) speech, oration

or'bene CONG so, well (then)

'orbita SF (*Astr, Fisica*) orbit; (*Anat*) (eye-)socket

orbi'tare /72/ VI to orbit

'orbo, -a AG blind

'Orcadi SFPL: **le (isole) ~** the Orkney Islands, the Orkneys

or'chestra [or'kɛstra] SF orchestra

orches'trale [orkes'trale] AG orchestral ▶ SMF orchestra player

orches'trare [orkes'trare] /72/ VT to orchestrate; (*fig*) to stage-manage

orchi'dea [orki'dɛa] SF orchid

'orcio ['ortʃo] SM jar

'orco, -chi SM ogre

'orda SF horde

or'digno [or'diɲɲo] SM: **~ esplosivo** explosive device

ordi'nale AG, SM ordinal

ordina'mento SM order, arrangement; (*regolamento*) regulations *pl*, rules *pl*; **~ scolastico/giuridico** education/legal system

ordi'nanza [ordi'nantsa] SF (*Dir, Mil*) order; (*Amm: decreto*) decree; (*persona: Mil*) orderly, batman; **d'~** (*Mil*) regulation *cpd*; **ufficiale d'~** orderly; **~ municipale** by(e)-law

ordi'nare /72/ VT (*mettere in ordine*) to arrange, organize; (*Comm*) to order; (*prescrivere: medicina*) to prescribe; (*comandare*): **~ a qn di fare qc** to order o command sb to do sth; (*Rel*) to ordain

ordi'nario, -a AG (*comune*) ordinary; everyday; standard; (*grossolano*) coarse, common ▶ SM ordinary; (*Ins: di università*) full professor

ordina'tivo, -a AG regulating, governing ▶ SM (*Comm*) order

ordi'nato, -a AG tidy, orderly

ordinazi'one [ordinat'tsjone] SF (*Comm*) order; (*Rel*) ordination; **fare un'~ di qc** to put in an order for sth, order sth; **eseguire qc su ~** to make sth to order

'ordine SM order; (*carattere*): **d'~ pratico** of a practical nature; **all'~** (*Comm: assegno*) to order; **di prim'~** first-class; **fino a nuovo ~** until further notice; **essere in ~** (*documenti*) to be in order; (*persona, stanza*) to be tidy; **mettere in ~** to put in order, tidy (up); **richiamare all'~** to call to order; **le forze dell'~** the forces of law and order; **~ d'acquisto** purchase order; **l'~ degli avvocati** = the Bar; **~ del giorno** (*di seduta*) agenda; (*Mil*) order of the day; **l'~ dei medici** = the Medical Association; **~ di pagamento** standing order (BRIT), automatic payment (US); (*Comm*) order for payment; **l'~ pubblico** law and order; **ordini (sacri)** (*Rel*) holy orders

or'dire /55/ VT (*fig*) to plot, scheme

or'dito SM (*di tessuto*) warp

orecchi'abile [orek'kjabile] AG (*canzone*) catchy

orec'chino [orek'kino] SM earring

o'recchio [o'rekkjo] (*pl(f)* **orecchie**) SM (*Anat*) ear; **avere ~** to have a good ear (for music); **venire all'~ di qn** to come to sb's attention; **fare orecchie da mercante (a)** to turn a deaf ear (to)

orecchi'oni [orek'kjoni] SMPL (*Med*) mumps *sg*

o'refice [o'refitʃe] SM goldsmith; jeweller (BRIT), jeweler (US)

orefice'ria [orefitʃe'ria] SF (*arte*) goldsmith's art; (*negozio*) jeweller's (shop) (*BRIT*), jewelry store (*US*)

'**orfano, -a** AG orphan(ed) ▶ SM/F orphan; ~ **di padre/madre** fatherless/motherless

orfano'trofio SM orphanage

orga'netto SM barrel organ; (*col: armonica a bocca*) mouth organ; (*: fisarmonica*) accordion

or'ganico, -a, -ci, -che AG organic ▶ SM personnel, staff

organi'gramma, -i SM organization chart; (*Inform*) computer flow chart

orga'nismo SM (*Biol*) organism; (*Anat, Amm*) body, organism

orga'nista, -i, -e SM/F organist

organiz'zare [organid'dzare] /**72**/ VT to organize; **organizzarsi** VPR to get organized

organizza'tivo, -a [organiddza'tivo] AG organizational

organizza'tore, -'trice [organiddza'tore] AG organizing ▶ SM/F organizer

organizzazi'one [organiddzat'tsjone] SF (*azione*) organizing, arranging; (*risultato*) organization; **O~ Mondiale della Sanità** World Health Organization

'**organo** SM organ; (*di congegno*) part; (*portavoce*) spokesman/woman, mouthpiece; **organi di trasmissione** (*Tecn*) transmission (unit) *sg*

or'gasmo SM (*Fisiol*) orgasm; (*fig*) agitation, anxiety

'**orgia, -ge** ['ɔrdʒa] SF orgy

or'goglio [or'goʎʎo] SM pride

orgogli'oso, -a [orgoʎ'ʎoso] AG proud

orien'tabile AG adjustable

orien'tale AG (*paese, regione*) eastern; (*tappeti, lingua, civiltà*) oriental; east

orienta'mento SM positioning; orientation; direction; **senso di** ~ sense of direction; **perdere l'**~ to lose one's bearings; ~ **professionale** careers guidance

orien'tare /**72**/ VT (*situare*) to position; (*carta, bussola*) to orientate; (*fig*) to direct; **orientarsi** VPR to find one's bearings; (*fig: tendere*) to tend, lean; (*indirizzarsi*) **orientarsi verso** to take up, go in for

orienta'tivo, -a AG indicative, for guidance; **a scopo** ~ for guidance

ori'ente SM east; **l'O~** the East, the Orient; **il Medio/l'Estremo O~** the Middle/Far East; **a** ~ in the east

ori'ficio [ori'fitʃo], **ori'fizio** [ori'fittsjo] SM (*apertura*) opening; (*di tubo*) mouth; (*Anat*) orifice

o'rigano SM oregano

origi'nale [oridʒi'nale] AG original; (*bizzarro*) eccentric ▶ SM original

originalità [oridʒinali'ta] SF originality; eccentricity

origi'nare [oridʒi'nare] /**72**/ VT to bring about, produce ▶ VI: ~ **da** to arise o spring from

origi'nario, -a [oridʒi'narjo] AG original; **essere** ~ **di** to be a native of; (*provenire da*) to originate from; (*animale, pianta*) to be native to, be indigenous to

o'rigine [o'ridʒine] SF origin; **all'**~ originally; **d'**~ **inglese** of English origin; **avere** ~ **da** to originate from; **dare** ~ **a** to give rise to

origli'are [oriʎ'ʎare] /**27**/ VI: ~ **(a)** to eavesdrop (on)

o'rina SF urine

ori'nale SM chamberpot

ori'nare /**72**/ VI to urinate ▶ VT to pass

orina'toio SM (public) urinal

ori'undo, -a AG: **essere** ~ **di Milano** *etc* to be of Milanese *etc* extraction o origin ▶ SM/F person of foreign extraction o origin

orizzon'tale [oriddzon'tale] AG horizontal

oriz'zonte [orid'dzonte] SM horizon

ORL SIGLA F (*Med*: = *otorinolaringoiatria*) ENT

or'lare /**72**/ VT to hem

orla'tura SF (*azione*) hemming *no pl*; (*orlo*) hem

'**orlo** SM edge, border; (*di recipiente*) rim, brim; (*di vestito ecc*) hem; **pieno fino all'**~ full to the brim, brimful; **sull'**~ **della pazzia/della rovina** on the brink o verge of madness/ruin; ~ **a giorno** hemstitch

'**orma** SF (*di persona*) footprint; (*di animale*) track; (*impronta, traccia*) mark, trace; **seguire** o **calcare le orme di qn** to follow in sb's footsteps

or'mai AV by now, by this time; (*adesso*) now; (*quasi*) almost, nearly

ormeggi'are [ormed'dʒare] /**62**/ VT, **ormeggi'arsi** VPR (*Naut*) to moor

or'meggio [or'meddʒo] SM (*atto*) mooring *no pl*; (*luogo*) moorings *pl*; **posto d'**~ berth

ormo'nale AG hormonal; (*disfunzione, cura*) hormone *cpd*; **terapia** ~ hormone therapy

or'mone SM hormone

ornamen'tale AG ornamental, decorative

orna'mento SM ornament, decoration

or'nare /**72**/ VT to adorn, decorate; **ornarsi** VPR: **ornarsi (di)** to deck o.s. (out) (with)

or'nato, -a AG ornate

ornitolo'gia [ornitolo'dʒia] SF ornithology

orni'tologo, -a, -gi, -ghe SM/F ornithologist

'**oro** SM gold; **d'**~, **in** ~ gold *cpd*; **d'**~ (*colore, occasione*) golden; (*persona*) marvellous (*BRIT*), marvelous (*US*); **un affare d'**~ a real bargain; **prendere qc per** ~ **colato** to take sth as gospel (truth); ~ **nero** black gold; ~ **zecchino** pure gold

orologe'ria [orolodʒe'ria] SF watchmaking *no pl*; watchmaker's (shop), clockmaker's (shop); **bomba a** ~ time bomb

orologi'aio [orolo'dʒajo] SM watchmaker; clockmaker

243

oro'logio [oro'lɔdʒo] SM clock; (da tasca, da polso) watch; **~ biologico** biological clock; **~ da polso** wristwatch; **~ al quarzo** quartz watch; **~ a sveglia** alarm clock

o'roscopo SM horoscope

or'rendo, -a AG (spaventoso) horrible, awful; (bruttissimo) hideous

or'ribile AG horrible

'orrido, -a AG fearful, horrid

orripi'lante AG hair-raising, horrifying

or'rore SM horror; **avere in ~ qn/qc** to loathe o detest sb/sth; **mi fanno ~** I loathe o detest them

orsacchi'otto [orsak'kjɔtto] SM teddy bear

'orso SM bear; **~ bruno/bianco** brown/polar bear

orsù ESCL come now!

or'taggio [or'taddʒo] SM vegetable

or'tensia SF hydrangea

or'tica, -che SF (stinging) nettle

orti'caria SF nettle rash

orticol'tura SF horticulture

'orto SM vegetable garden, kitchen garden; (Agr) market garden (BRIT), truck farm (US); **~ botanico** botanical garden(s)

orto'dosso, -a AG orthodox

ortofrut'ticolo, -a AG fruit and vegetable cpd

ortogo'nale AG perpendicular

ortogra'fia SF spelling

orto'lano, -a SM/F (venditore) greengrocer (BRIT), produce dealer (US)

ortope'dia SF orthopaedics sg (BRIT), orthopedics sg (US)

orto'pedico, -a, -ci, -che AG orthopaedic (BRIT), orthopedic (US) ▶ SM orthopaedic specialist (BRIT), orthopedist (US)

orzai'olo [ordza'jɔlo], **orzaiu'olo** [ordza'jwɔlo] SM (Med) stye

or'zata [or'dzata] SF barley water

'orzo ['ɔrdzo] SM barley

'OSA SIGLA F (= Organizzazione degli Stati Americani) OAS (= Organization of American States)

o'sare /72/ VT, VI to dare; **~ fare** to dare (to) do; **come osi?** how dare you?

oscenità [oʃʃeni'ta] SF INV obscenity

o'sceno, -a [oʃʃɛno] AG obscene; (ripugnante) ghastly

oscil'lare [oʃʃil'lare] /72/ VI (pendolo) to swing; (dondolare: al vento ecc) to rock; (variare) to fluctuate; (Tecn) to oscillate; (fig): **~ fra** to waver o hesitate between

oscillazi'one [oʃʃillat'tsjone] SF oscillation; (di prezzi, temperatura) fluctuation

oscura'mento SM darkening; obscuring; (in tempo di guerra) blackout

oscu'rare /72/ VT to darken, obscure; (fig) to obscure; **oscurarsi** VPR (cielo) to darken, cloud over; (persona) **si oscurò in volto** his face clouded over

oscurità SF (vedi ag) darkness; obscurity, gloominess

os'curo, -a AG dark; (fig: incomprensibile) obscure; (umile: vita, natali) humble, lowly, obscure; (triste: pensiero) gloomy, sombre ▶ SM: **all'~** in the dark; **tenere qn all'~ di qc** to keep sb in the dark about sth

'Oslo SF Oslo

ospe'dale SM hospital

ospedali'ero, -a AG hospital cpd

ospi'tale AG hospitable

ospitalità SF hospitality

ospi'tare /72/ VT to give hospitality to; (albergo) to accommodate

'ospite SMF (persona che ospita) host/hostess; (persona ospitata) guest

os'pizio [os'pittsjo] SM (per vecchi ecc) home

'ossa SFPL vedi **osso**

os'sario SM (Mil) war memorial (with burial place)

ossa'tura SF (Anat) skeletal structure, frame; (Tecn: fig) framework

'osseo, -a AG bony; (tessuto ecc) bone cpd

osse'quente AG: **~ alla legge** law-abiding

os'sequio SM deference, respect; **ossequi** SMPL (saluto) respects, regards; **porgere i propri ossequi a qn** (formale) to pay one's respects to sb; **ossequi alla signora!** (give my) regards to your wife!

ossequi'oso, -a AG obsequious

osser'vanza [osser'vantsa] SF observance

osser'vare /72/ VT to observe, watch; (esaminare) to examine; (notare, rilevare) to notice, observe; (Dir: la legge) to observe, respect; (mantenere: silenzio) to keep, observe; **far ~ qc a qn** to point sth out to sb

osserva'tore, -'trice AG observant, perceptive ▶ SM/F observer

osserva'torio SM (Astr) observatory; (Mil) observation post

osservazi'one [osservat'tsjone] SF observation; (di legge ecc) observance; (considerazione critica) observation, remark; (rimprovero) reproof; **in ~** under observation; **fare un'~** to make a remark; to raise an objection; **fare un'~ a qn** to criticize sb

osses'sio'nare /72/ VT to obsess, haunt; (tormentare) to torment, harass

ossessi'one SF obsession; (seccatura) nuisance

osses'sivo, -a AG obsessive, haunting troublesome

os'sesso, -a AG (spiritato) possessed

os'sia CONG that is, to be precise

ossi'buchi [ossi'buki] SMPL di **ossobuco**

ossi'dare /72/ VT, **ossi'darsi** VPR to oxidize

ossidazi'one [ossidat'tsjone] SF oxidization, oxidation

'ossido SM oxide; **~ di carbonio** carbon monoxide

ossige'nare [ossidʒe'nare] /**72**/ VT to oxygenate; (*decolorare*) to bleach; **acqua ossigenata** hydrogen peroxide

os'sigeno [os'sidʒeno] SM oxygen

'osso SM (*pl(f)* **ossa**: *Anat*) bone; **d'~** (*bottone ecc*) of bone, bone *cpd*; **avere le ossa rotte** to be dead *o* dog tired; **bagnato fino all'~** soaked to the skin; **essere ridotto all'~** (*fig: magro*) to be just skin and bone; (: *senza soldi*) to be in dire straits; **rompersi l'~ del collo** to break one's neck; **rimetterci l'~ del collo** (*fig*) to ruin o.s., lose everything; **un ~ duro** (*persona, impresa*) a tough number; **~ di seppia** cuttlebone

osso'buco (*pl* **ossibuchi**) SM (*Cuc*) marrowbone; (*piatto*) *stew made with knuckle of veal in tomato sauce*

os'suto, -a AG bony

ostaco'lare /**72**/ VT to block, obstruct

os'tacolo SM obstacle; (*Equitazione*) hurdle, jump; **essere di ~ a qn/qc** (*fig*) to stand in the way of sb/sth

os'taggio [os'taddʒo] SM hostage

'oste, ostessa SM/F innkeeper

osteggi'are [osted'dʒare] /**62**/ VT to oppose, be opposed to

os'tello SM hostel; **~ della gioventù** youth hostel

osten'sorio SM (*Rel*) monstrance

osten'tare /**72**/ VT to make a show of, flaunt

ostentazi'one [ostentat'tsjone] SF ostentation, show

oste'ria SF inn

os'tessa SF *vedi* **oste**

os'tetrico, -a, -ci, -che AG obstetric ▶ SM obstetrician ▶ SF midwife

'ostia SF (*Rel*) host; (*per medicinali*) wafer

'ostico, -a, -ci, -che AG (*fig*) harsh; difficult, tough; unpleasant

os'tile AG hostile

ostilità SF hostility ▶ SFPL (*Mil*) hostilities

osti'narsi /**72**/ VPR to insist, dig one's heels in; **~ a fare** to persist (obstinately) in doing

osti'nato, -a AG (*caparbio*) obstinate; (*tenace*) persistent, determined

ostinazi'one [ostinat'tsjone] SF obstinacy; persistence

ostra'cismo [ostra'tʃizmo] SM ostracism

'ostrica, -che SF oyster

ostru'ire /**55**/ VT to obstruct, block

ostruzi'one [ostrut'tsjone] SF obstruction, blockage

ostruzio'nismo [ostruttsjo'nizmo] SM (*Pol*) obstructionism; (*Sport*) obstruction; **fare dell'~ a** (*progetto, legge*) to obstruct; **~ sindacale** work-to-rule (*BRIT*), slowdown (*US*)

o'tite SF ear infection

oto'rino(laringoi'atra), -i, -e SM/F ear, nose and throat specialist

'otre SM (*recipiente*) goatskin

ott. ABBR (= *ottobre*) Oct

ottago'nale AG octagonal

ot'tagono SM octagon

ot'tano SM octane; **numero di ottani** octane rating

ot'tanta NUM eighty

ottan'tenne AG eighty-year-old ▶ SMF octogenarian

ottan'tesimo, -a NUM eightieth

ottan'tina SF: **una ~ (di)** about eighty

ot'tavo, -a NUM eighth ▶ SF octave

ottempe'ranza [ottempe'rantsa] SF: **in ~ a** (*Amm*) in accordance with, in compliance with

ottempe'rare /**72**/ VI: **~ a** to comply with, obey

ottene'brare /**72**/ VT to darken; (*fig*) to cloud

otte'nere /**121**/ VT to obtain, get; (*risultato*) to achieve, obtain

'ottico, -a, -ci, -che AG (*della vista: nervo*) optic; (*dell'ottica*) optical ▶ SM optician ▶ SF (*scienza*) optics *sg*; (*Fot: lenti, prismi ecc*) optics *pl*

otti'male AG optimal, optimum

ottima'mente AV excellently, very well

otti'mismo SM optimism

otti'mista, -i, -e SM/F optimist

ottimiz'zare [ottimid'dzare] /**72**/ VT to optimize

ottimizzazi'one [ottimiddzat'tsjone] SF optimization

'ottimo, -a AG excellent, very good

ot'tobre SM October; *vedi anche* **luglio**

otto'brino, -a AG October *cpd*

ottocen'tesco, -a, -schi, -sche [ottotʃen'tesko] AG nineteenth-century

otto'cento [otto'tʃento] NUM eight hundred ▶ SM: **l'O~** the nineteenth century

otto'mila NUM eight thousand

ot'tone SM brass; **gli ottoni** (*Mus*) the brass

ottuage'nario, -a [ottuadʒe'narjo] AG, SM/F octogenarian

ot'tundere /**34**/ VT (*fig*) to dull

ottu'rare /**72**/ VT to close (up); (*dente*) to fill; **otturarsi** VPR to become *o* get blocked up

ottura'tore SM (*Fot*) shutter; (*nelle armi*) breechblock

otturazi'one [otturat'tsjone] SF closing (up); (*dentaria*) filling

ottusità SF (*vedi ag*) obtuseness; dullness

ot'tuso, -a PP *di* **ottundere** ▶ AG (*Mat: fig*) obtuse; (*suono*) dull

o'vaia SF, **o'vaio** SM (*Anat*) ovary

o'vale AG, SM oval

o'varico, -a AG ovarian

o'vatta SF cotton wool; (per imbottire) padding, wadding

ovat'tare /72/ VT (imbottire) to pad; (fig: smorzare) to muffle

ovazi'one [ovat'tsjone] SF ovation

'ovest SM west; **a ~ (di)** west (of); **verso ~** westward(s)

o'vile SM pen, enclosure; **tornare all'~** (fig) to return to the fold

o'vino, -a AG sheep cpd, ovine

'O.V.N.I. SIGLA M (= oggetto volante non identificato) UFO

ovulazi'one [ovulat'tsjone] SF ovulation

'ovulo SM (Fisiol) ovum

o'vunque AV = **dovunque**

ov'vero CONG (ossia) that is, to be precise; (oppure) or (else)

ovvi'are /19/ VI: **~ a** to obviate

'ovvio, -a AG obvious

ozi'are [ot'tsjare] /19/ VI to laze around, idle

'ozio ['ɔttsjo] SM idleness; (tempo libero) leisure; **ore d'~** leisure time; **stare in ~** to be idle

ozi'oso, -a [ot'tsjoso] AG idle

o'zono [od'dzɔno] SM ozone; **lo strato d'~** the ozone layer

ozonos'fera [oddzonos'fɛra] SF ozone layer

Pp

P, p [pi] SM O F INV (*lettera*) P, p; **P come Padova** ≈ P for Peter

P ABBR (= *peso*) wt; (= *parcheggio*) P; (*Aut*: = *principiante*) L

p. ABBR (= *pagina*) p

P2 ABBR F (= *la (loggia)* P2) the P2 masonic lodge

PA SIGLA = **Palermo**

P.A. ABBR = **pubblica amministrazione**

pa'care /**20**/ VT to calm; **pacarsi** VPR (*tempesta, disordini*) to subside

paca'tezza [paka'tettsa] SF quietness, calmness

pa'cato, -a AG quiet, calm

'pacca, -che SF slap

pac'chetto [pak'ketto] SM packet; **~ applicativo** (*Inform*) applications package; **~ azionario** (*Finanza*) shareholding; **~ software** (*Inform*) software package; **~ turistico** package holiday (*BRIT*) *o* tour

pacchi'ano, -a [pak'kjano] AG (*colori*) garish; (*abiti, arredamento*) vulgar, garish

'pacco, -chi SM parcel; (*involto*) bundle; **~ postale** parcel

paccot'tiglia [pakkot'tiʎʎa] SF trash, junk

'pace ['patʃe] SF peace; **darsi ~** to resign o.s.; **fare (la) ~ con qn** to make it up with sb

pachis'tano, -a [pakis'tano] AG, SM/F Pakistani

pacifi'care [patʃifi'kare] /**20**/ VT (*riconciliare*) to reconcile, make peace between; (*mettere in pace*) to pacify

pacificazi'one [patʃifikat'tsjone] SF (*vedi vt*) reconciliation; pacification

pa'cifico, -a, -ci, -che [pa'tʃifiko] AG (*persona*) peaceable; (*vita*) peaceful; (*fig: indiscusso*) indisputable; (: *ovvio*) obvious, clear ▶ SM: **il P~, l'Oceano P~** the Pacific (Ocean)

paci'fismo [patʃi'fizmo] SM pacifism

paci'fista, -i, -e [patʃi'fista] SM/F pacifist

PACS [paks] SIGLA MPL civil partnerships

pa'dano, -a AG of the Po; **la pianura padana** the Lombardy plain

pa'della SF frying pan; (*per infermi*) bedpan

padigli'one [padiʎ'ʎone] SM pavilion

'Padova SF Padua

pado'vano, -a AG of (*o* from) Padua

'padre SM father; **padri** SMPL (*antenati*) forefathers

Padre'terno SM: **il ~** God the Father

pa'drino SM godfather

padro'nale AG (*scala, entrata*) main, principal; **casa ~** country house

padro'nanza [padro'nantsa] SF command, mastery

padro'nato SM: **il ~** the ruling class

pa'drone, -a SM/F master/mistress; (*proprietario*) owner; (*datore di lavoro*) employer; **essere ~ di sé** to be in control of o.s.; **~/padrona di casa** master/mistress of the house; (*per gli inquilini*) landlord/lady

padroneggi'are [padroned'dʒare] /**62**/ VT (*fig: sentimenti*) to master, control; (*materia*) to master, know thoroughly; **padroneggiarsi** VPR to control o.s.

pae'saggio [pae'zaddʒo] SM landscape

paesag'gista, -i, -e [paezad'dʒista] SM/F (*pittore*) landscape painter

pae'sano, -a AG country *cpd* ▶ SM/F villager, countryman/woman

pa'ese SM (*nazione*) country, nation; (*terra*) country, land; (*villaggio*) village; **~ di provenienza** country of origin; **i Paesi Bassi** the Netherlands

paf'futo, -a AG chubby, plump

'paga, -ghe SF pay, wages *pl*; **giorno di ~** pay day

pa'gabile AG payable; **~ alla consegna/a vista** payable on delivery/on demand

pa'gaia SF paddle

paga'mento SM payment; **~ anticipato** payment in advance; **~ alla consegna** payment on delivery; **~ all'ordine** cash with order; **la TV a ~** pay TV

pa'gano, -a AG, SM/F pagan

pa'gare /**80**/ VT to pay; (*acquisto, fig, colpa*) to pay for; (*contraccambiare*) to repay, pay back ▶ VI to pay; **quanto l'ha pagato?** how much did you pay for it?; **~ con carta di credito**

to pay by credit card; **~ in contanti** to pay cash; **~ di persona** (*fig*) to suffer the consequences; **l'ho pagata cara** (*fig*) I paid dearly for it

pa'gella [pa'dʒella] SF (*Ins*) report card

'paggio ['paddʒo] SM page(boy)

pagherò [page'rɔ] VB *vedi* **pagare** ▶ SM INV acknowledgement of a debt, IOU; **~ cambiario** promissory note

'pagina ['padʒina] SF page; **Pagine bianche** phone book, telephone directory; **Pagine Gialle**® Yellow Pages®

'paglia ['paʎʎa] SF straw; **avere la coda di ~** (*fig*) to have a guilty conscience; **fuoco di ~** (*fig*) flash in the pan

pagliac'cetto [paʎʎat'tʃetto] SM (*per bambini*) rompers *pl*

pagliac'ciata [paʎʎat'tʃata] SF farce

pagli'accio [paʎ'ʎattʃo] SM clown

pagli'aio [paʎ'ʎajo] SM haystack

paglie'riccio [paʎʎe'rittʃo] SM straw mattress

paglie'rino, -a [paʎʎe'rino] AG: **giallo ~** pale yellow

pagli'etta [paʎ'ʎetta] SF (*cappello per uomo*) (straw) boater; (*per tegami ecc*) steel wool

pagli'uzza [paʎ'ʎuttsa] SF (blade of) straw; (*d'oro ecc*) tiny particle, speck

pa'gnotta [paɲ'ɲɔtta] SF round loaf

'pago, -a, -ghi, -ghe AG: **~ (di)** satisfied (with)

pa'goda SF pagoda

pail'lette [pa'jɛt] SF INV sequin

'paio (*pl(f)* **paia**) SM pair; **un ~ di** (*alcuni*) a couple of; **un ~ di occhiali** a pair of glasses; **è un altro ~ di maniche** (*fig*) that's another kettle of fish

'paio *etc* VB *vedi* **parere**

pai'olo, paiu'olo SM (copper) pot

'Pakistan SM: **il ~** Pakistan

pakis'tano, -a AG, SM/F = **pachistano**

pal. ABBR = **palude**

'pala SF shovel; (*di remo, ventilatore, elica*) blade; (*di ruota*) paddle

palan'drana SF (*scherzoso: abito lungo e largo*) tent

pa'lata SF shovelful; **fare soldi a palate** to make a mint

pala'tale AG (*Anat, Ling*) palatal

pa'lato SM palate

pa'lazzo [pa'lattso] SM (*reggia*) palace; (*edificio*) building; **~ di giustizia** courthouse; **~ dello sport** sports stadium; *see note*

> Several of the Roman *palazzi* now have political functions. The sixteenth-century *Palazzo Chigi*, in Piazza Colonna, was acquired by the state in 1919 and became the seat of the Ministry of Foreign Affairs; since 1961 it has housed the Prime Minister's office and hosted Cabinet meetings. *Palazzo Madama*, another sixteenth-century building which was originally built for the Medici family, has been the home of the Senate since 1871. *Palazzo di Montecitorio*, completed in 1694, has housed the *Camera dei deputati* since 1870.

pal'chetto [pal'ketto] SM shelf

'palco, -chi SM (*Teat*) box; (*tavolato*) platform, stand; (*ripiano*) layer

palco'scenico, -ci [palkoʃ'ʃɛniko] SM (*Teat*) stage

palermi'tano, -a AG of (*o from*) Palermo ▶ SM/F person from Palermo

Pa'lermo SF Palermo

pale'sare /72/ VT to reveal, disclose; **palesarsi** VPR to reveal *o* show o.s.

pa'lese AG clear, evident

Pales'tina SF: **la ~** Palestine

palesti'nese AG, SMF Palestinian

pa'lestra SF gymnasium; (*esercizio atletico*) exercise, training; (*fig*) training ground, school

paletot [pal'to] SM INV overcoat

pa'letta SF spade; (*per il focolare*) shovel; (*del capostazione*) signalling disc

pa'letto SM stake, peg; (*spranga*) bolt

palin'sesto SM (*Storia*) palimpsest; (*TV, Radio*) programme (*BRIT*) *o* program (*US*) schedule

'palio SM (*gara*): **il P~** horse race run at Siena; **mettere qc in ~** to offer sth as a prize; *see note*

> The *Palio* is a horse race which takes place in a number of Italian towns, the most famous being the *Palio di Siena*. The Tuscan race dates back to the thirteenth century; nowadays it is usually held twice a year, on 2 July and 16 August, in the Piazza del Campo. 10 of the 17 city districts or *contrade* take part; the winner is the first horse to complete the course, whether or not it still has its rider. The race is preceded by a procession of *contrada* members in historical dress.

palis'sandro SM rosewood

paliz'zata [palit'tsata] SF palisade

'palla SF ball; (*pallottola*) bullet; **~ di neve** snowball; **~ ovale** rugby ball

pallaca'nestro SF basketball

pallamano [palla'mano] SF handball

pallanu'oto SF water polo

palla'volo SF volleyball

palleggi'are [palled'dʒare] /62/ VI (*Calcio*) to practise (*BRIT*) *o* practice (*US*) with the ball; (*Tennis*) to knock up

pallia'tivo SM palliative; (*fig*) stopgap measure

'pallido, -a AG pale

pal'lina SF (*bilia*) marble

pal'lino SM (*Biliardo*) cue ball; (*Bocce*) jack; (*proiettile*) pellet; (*pois*) dot; **bianco a pallini blu** white with blue dots; **avere il ~ di** (*fig*) to be crazy about

pallon'cino [pallon'tʃino] SM balloon; (*lampioncino*) Chinese lantern

pal'lone SM (*palla*) ball; (*Calcio*) football; (*aerostato*) balloon; **gioco del ~** football

pal'lore SM pallor, paleness

pal'lottola SF pellet; (*proiettile*) bullet

'palma SF (*Anat*) = **palmo**; (*Bot, simbolo*) palm; **~ da datteri** date palm

pal'mato, -a AG (*Zool: piede*) webbed; (*Bot*) palmate

pal'mipede AG web-footed

pal'mizio [pal'mittsjo] SM (*palma*) palm tree; (*ramo*) palm

'palmo SM (*Anat*) palm; **essere alto un ~** (*fig*) to be tiny; **restare con un ~ di naso** (*fig*) to be badly disappointed

'palo SM (*legno appuntito*) stake; (*sostegno*) pole; **fare da o il ~** (*fig*) to act as look-out; **saltare di ~ in frasca** (*fig*) to jump from one topic to another

palom'baro SM diver

pa'lombo SM (*pesce*) dogfish

pal'pare /72/ VT to feel, finger

'palpebra SF eyelid

palpi'tare /72/ VI (*cuore, polso*) to beat; (*più forte*) to pound, throb; (*fremere*) to quiver

palpitazi'one [palpitat'tsjone] SF palpitation

'palpito SM (*del cuore*) beat; (*fig: d'amore ecc*) throb

pal'tò SM INV overcoat

pa'lude SF marsh, swamp

palu'doso, -a AG marshy, swampy

pa'lustre AG marsh *cpd*, swamp *cpd*

'pampino SM vine leaf

pana'cea [pana'tʃɛa] SF panacea

'Panama SF Panama; **il canale di ~** the Panama Canal

pana'mense AG, SMF Panamanian

'panca, -che SF bench

pancar'rè SM sliced bread

pan'cetta [pan'tʃetta] SF (*Cuc*) bacon

pan'chetto [pan'ketto] SM stool; footstool

pan'china [pan'kina] SF garden seat; (*di giardino pubblico*) (park) bench

'pancia, -ce ['pantʃa] SF belly, stomach; **mettere o fare ~** to be getting a paunch; **avere mal di ~** to have stomach ache o a sore stomach

panci'era [pan'tʃɛra] SF corset

panci'olle [pan'tʃɔlle] AV: **stare in ~** to lounge about (*Brit*) o around

panci'otto [pan'tʃɔtto] SM waistcoat

pan'ciuto, -a [pan'tʃuto] AG (*persona*) potbellied; (*vaso, bottiglia*) rounded

'pancreas SM INV pancreas

'panda SM INV panda

pande'mia SF pandemic

pande'monio SM pandemonium

pan'doro SM *type of sponge cake eaten at Christmas*

'pane SM bread; (*pagnotta*) loaf (of bread); (*forma*): **un ~ di burro/cera** *etc* a pat of butter/bar of wax *etc*; **guadagnarsi il ~** to earn one's living; **dire ~ al ~, vino al vino** (*fig*) to call a spade a spade; **rendere pan per focaccia** (*fig*) to give tit for tat; **~ casereccio** homemade bread; **~ a cassetta** sliced bread; **~ integrale** wholemeal bread; **~ di segale** rye bread; **~ di Spagna** sponge cake; **~ tostato** toast

pane'girico [pane'dʒiriko] SM (*fig*) panegyric

panette'ria SF (*forno*) bakery; (*negozio*) baker's (shop), bakery

panetti'ere, -a SM/F baker

panet'tone SM *a kind of spiced brioche with sultanas (eaten at Christmas)*

'panfilo SM yacht

pan'forte SM *Sienese nougat-type delicacy*

pangrat'tato SM breadcrumbs *pl*

'panico, -a, -ci, -che AG, SM panic; **essere in preda al ~** to be panic-stricken; **lasciarsi prendere dal ~** to panic

pani'ere SM basket

panifica'tore, -trice SM/F bread-maker, baker

pani'ficio [pani'fitʃo] SM (*forno*) bakery; (*negozio*) baker's (shop), bakery

pa'nino SM roll; **~ caldo** toasted sandwich; **~ imbottito** filled roll; sandwich

panino'teca, -che SF sandwich bar

'panna SF (*Cuc*) cream; (*Aut*) = **panne**; **~ da cucina** cooking cream; **~ montata** whipped cream

'panne [pan] SF INV (*Aut*) breakdown; : **essere in ~** to have broken down

pan'nello SM panel; **~ di controllo** control panel; **~ solare** solar panel

'panno SM cloth; **panni** SMPL (*abiti*) clothes; **mettiti nei miei panni** (*fig*) put yourself in my shoes

pan'nocchia [pan'nɔkkja] SF (*di mais ecc*) ear

panno'lino SM (*per bambini*) nappy (*Brit*), diaper (*US*)

panno'lone SM incontinence pad

pano'rama, -i SM panorama

pano'ramico, -a, -ci, -che AG panoramic; **strada panoramica** scenic route

pantacol'lant SMPL leggings

panta'loni SMPL trousers (*Brit*), pants (*US*), pair *sg* of trousers o pants

pan'tano SM bog

pan'tera SF panther

'pantheon ['panteon] SM INV pantheon

pan'tofola SF slipper
panto'mima SF pantomime
pan'zana [pan'tsana] SF fib, tall story
pao'nazzo, -a [pao'nattso] AG purple
'papa, -i SM pope
papà SM INV dad(dy); **figlio di ~** spoilt young man
pa'pale AG papal
pa'pato SM papacy
pa'pavero SM poppy
'papero, -a SM/F (*Zool*) gosling ▶ SF (*fig*) slip of the tongue, blunder
papi'llon [papi'jõ] SM INV bow tie
pa'piro SM papyrus
'pappa SF baby cereal; **~ reale** royal jelly
pappa'gallo SM parrot; (*fig: uomo*) Romeo, wolf
pappa'gorgia, -ge [pappa'gɔrdʒa] SF double chin
pappar'della SF (*fig*) rigmarole
pap'pare /72/ VT (*col: anche:* **papparsi**) to gobble up
par. ABBR (= *paragrafo*) par
'para SF: **suole di ~** crepe soles
parà ABBR M INV (= *paracadutista*) para
pa'rabola SF (*Mat*) parabola; (*Rel*) parable
para'bolico, -a, -ci, -che AG (*Mat*) parabolic; *vedi anche* **antenna**
para'brezza [para'breddza] SM INV (*Aut*) windscreen (*Brit*), windshield (*US*)
paracadu'tare /72/ VT, **paracadu'tarsi** VPR to parachute
paraca'dute SM INV parachute
paracadu'tismo SM parachuting
paracadu'tista, -i, -e SM/F parachutist; (*Mil*) paratrooper
para'carro SM kerbstone (*Brit*), curbstone (*US*)
paradi'siaco, -a, -ci, -che AG heavenly
para'diso SM paradise; **~ fiscale** tax haven
parados'sale AG paradoxical
para'dosso SM paradox
para'fango, -ghi SM mudguard
paraf'fina SF paraffin, paraffin wax
parafra'sare /72/ VT to paraphrase
pa'rafrasi SF INV paraphrase
para'fulmine SM lightning conductor
pa'raggi [pa'raddʒi] SMPL: **nei ~** in the vicinity, in the neighbourhood (*Brit*) o neighborhood (*US*)
parago'nare /72/ VT: **~ con/a** to compare with/to
para'gone SM comparison; (*esempio analogo*) analogy, parallel; **reggere al ~** to stand comparison
pa'ragrafo SM paragraph
paraguai'ano, -a AG, SM/F Paraguayan
Paragu'ay [para'gwai] SM: **il ~** Paraguay
pa'ralisi SF INV paralysis

para'litico, -a, -ci, -che AG, SM/F paralytic
paraliz'zare [paralid'dzare] /72/ VT to paralyze
parallela'mente AV in parallel
paralle'lismo SM (*Mat*) parallelism; (*fig: corrispondenza*) similarities pl
paral'lelo, -a AG parallel ▶ SM (*Geo*) parallel; (*comparazione*): **fare un ~ tra** to draw a parallel between ▶ SF parallel (line); **parallele** SFPL (*attrezzo ginnico*) parallel bars
para'lume SM lampshade
para'medico, -a, -ci, -che AG paramedical
para'menti SMPL (*Rel*) vestments
pa'rametro SM parameter
parami'litare AG paramilitary
pa'ranco, -chi SM hoist
para'noia SF paranoia; **andare/mandare in ~** (*col*) to freak/be freaked out
para'noico, -a, -ci, -che AG, SM/F paranoid; (*col: angosciato*) freaked (out)
paranor'male AG paranormal
para'occhi [para'ɔkki] SMPL blinkers (*Brit*), blinders (*US*)
paraolim'piadi SFPL paralympics
para'petto SM parapet
para'piglia [para'piʎʎa] SM commotion
parapsicolo'gia [parapsikolo'dʒia] SF parapsychology
pa'rare /72/ VT (*addobbare*) to adorn, deck; (*proteggere*) to shield, protect; (*scansare: colpo*) to parry; (*Calcio*) to save ▶ VI: **dove vuole andare a ~?** what are you driving at?; **pararsi** VPR (*presentarsi*) to appear, present o.s.
parasco'lastico, -a, -ci, -che AG (*attività*) extracurricular
para'sole SM INV parasol, sunshade
paras'sita, -i SM parasite
parassi'tario, -a AG parasitic
parasta'tale AG state-controlled
paras'tato SM *employees in the state-controlled sector*
pa'rata SF (*Sport*) save; (*Mil*) review, parade
pa'rati SMPL hangings pl; **carta da ~** wallpaper
para'tia SF (*di nave*) bulkhead
para'urti SM INV (*Aut*) bumper
para'vento SM folding screen; **fare da ~ a qn** (*fig*) to shield sb
par'cella [par'tʃɛlla] SF account, fee (*of lawyer etc*)
parcheggi'are [parked'dʒare] /62/ VT to park
parcheggia'tore, -'trice [parkedddʒa'tore] SM/F parking attendant
par'cheggio [par'kedddʒo] SM parking no pl; (*luogo*) car park (*Brit*), parking lot (*US*); (*singolo posto*) parking space; **~ di interscambio** park and ride
par'chimetro [par'kimetro] SM parking meter

'parco¹, -chi SM park; (*spazio per deposito*) depot; (*complesso di veicoli*) fleet

'parco², -a, -chi, -che AG: ~ **(in)** (*sobrio*) moderate (in); (*avaro*) sparing (with)

par'cometro SM (*Aut*) (Pay and Display) ticket machine

pa'recchio, -a [pa'rekkjo] DET quite a lot of; (*tempo*) quite a lot of, a long ▶ PRON quite a lot, quite a bit; (*tempo*) quite a while, a long time ▶ AV (*con ag*) quite, rather; (*con vb*) quite a lot, quite a bit; **parecchi, e** DET PL, PRON PL quite a lot of, several; quite a lot, several

pareggi'are [pared'dʒare] /**62**/ VT to make equal; (*terreno*) to level, make level; (*bilancio, conti*) to balance ▶ VI (*Sport*) to draw

pa'reggio [pa'reddʒo] SM (*Econ*) balance; (*Sport*) draw

paren'tado SM relatives *pl*, relations *pl*

pa'rente SMF relative, relation

paren'tela SF (*vincolo di sangue, fig*) relationship; (*insieme dei parenti*) relations *pl*, relatives *pl*

pa'rentesi SF (*segno grafico*) bracket, parenthesis; (*frase incisa*) parenthesis; (*digressione*) parenthesis, digression; **tra ~ in** brackets; (*fig*) incidentally

pa'rere /**71**/ SM (*opinione*) opinion; (*consiglio*) advice, opinion; **a mio ~** in my opinion ▶ VI to seem, appear ▶ VB IMPERS: **pare che** it seems *o* appears that, they say that; **mi pare che** it seems to me that; **mi pare di sì/no** I think so/don't think so; **fai come ti pare** do as you like; **che ti pare del mio libro?** what do you think of my book?

pa'rete SF wall

'pargolo, -a SM/F child

'pari AG INV (*uguale*) equal, same; (*in giochi*) equal, drawn, tied; (*Mat*) even ▶ SM INV (*Pol: di Gran Bretagna*) peer ▶ SM O F INV peer, equal; **copiato ~ ~** copied word for word; **siamo ~** (*fig*) we are quits *o* even; **alla ~** on the same level; (*Borsa*) at par; **ragazza alla ~** au pair (girl); **mettersi alla ~ con** to place o.s. on the same level as; **mettersi in ~ con** to catch up with; **andare di ~ passo con qn** to keep pace with sb

parifi'care /**20**/ VT (*scuola*) to recognize officially

parifi'cato, -a AG: **scuola parificata** *officially recognized private school*

Pa'rigi [pa'ridʒi] SF Paris

pari'gino, -a [pari'dʒino] AG, SM/F Parisian

pa'riglia [pa'riʎʎa] SF pair; **rendere la ~** to give tit for tat

parità SF parity, equality; (*Sport*) draw, tie

pari'tetico, -a, -ci, -che AG: **commissione paritetica** joint committee; **rapporto ~** equal relationship

parlamen'tare /**72**/ AG parliamentary ▶ SM/F ≈ Member of Parliament (*BRIT*), ≈ Congressman/woman (*US*) ▶ VI to negotiate, parley

parla'mento SM parliament; *see note*

> The Italian constitution, which came into force on 1 January 1948, states that the *Parlamento* has legislative power. It is made up of two chambers, the *Camera dei deputati* and the *Senato*. Parliamentary elections are held every 5 years.

parlan'tina SF (*col*) talkativeness; **avere ~** to have the gift of the gab

par'lare /**72**/ VI to speak, talk; (*confidare cose segrete*) to talk ▶ VT to speak; **~ (a qn) di** to speak *o* talk (to sb) about; **~ chiaro** to speak one's mind; **~ male di qn/qc** to speak ill of sb/sth; **~ del più e del meno** to talk of this and that; **ne ho sentito ~** I have heard it mentioned; **non parliamone più** let's just forget about it; **i dati parlano** (*fig*) the facts speak for themselves

par'lata SF (*dialetto*) dialect

parla'tore, -'trice SM/F speaker

parla'torio SM (*di carcere ecc*) visiting room; (*Rel*) parlour (*BRIT*), parlor (*US*)

parlot'tare /**72**/ VI to mutter

parmigi'ano, -a [parmi'dʒano] AG Parma *cpd* of (*o* from) Parma ▶ SM (*grana*) Parmesan (cheese); **alla parmigiana** (*Cuc*) with Parmesan cheese

paro'dia SF parody

parodi'are /**19**/ VT to parody

pa'rola SF word; (*facoltà*) speech; **parole** SFPL (*chiacchiere*) talk *sg*; **chiedere la ~** to ask permission to speak; **dare la ~ a qn** to call on sb to speak; **dare la propria ~ a qn** to give sb one's word; **mantenere la ~** to keep one's word; **mettere una buona ~ per qn** to put in a good word for sb; **passare dalle parole ai fatti** to get down to business; **prendere la ~** to take the floor; **rimanere senza parole** to be speechless; **rimangiarsi la ~** to go back on one's word; **non ho parole per ringraziarla** I don't know how to thank you; **rivolgere la ~ a qn** to speak to sb; **non è detta l'ultima ~** that's not the end of the matter; **è una persona di ~** he is a man of his word; **in parole povere** in plain English; **~ d'onore** word of honour; **~ d'ordine** (*Mil*) password; **parole incrociate** crossword (puzzle) *sg*

paro'laccia, -ce [paro'lattʃa] SF bad word, swearword

paros'sismo SM paroxysm

par'quet [par'kɛ] SM parquet (flooring)

parrò *etc* VB *vedi* **parere**

par'rocchia [par'rɔkkja] SF parish; (*chiesa*) parish church

P

parrocchi'ano, -a [parrok'kjano] SM/F parishioner

'parroco, -ci SM parish priest

par'rucca, -che SF wig

parrucchi'ere, -a [parruk'kjɛre] SM/F hairdresser ▶ SM barber

parruc'cone SM (peg) old fogey

parsi'monia SF frugality, thrift

parsimoni'oso, -a AG frugal, thrifty

'parso, -a PP di **parere**

'parte SF part; (lato) side; (quota spettante a ciascuno) share; (direzione) direction; (Pol) party; faction; (Dir) party; **a ~** ag separate ▶ AV separately; **scherzi a ~** joking aside; **a ~ ciò** apart from that; **inviare a ~** (campioni ecc) to send under separate cover; **da ~** (in disparte) to one side, aside; **mettere/ prendere da ~** to put/take aside; **d'altra ~** on the other hand; **da ~ di** (per conto di) on behalf of; **da ~ mia** as far as I'm concerned, as for me; **da ~ di madre** on his (o her etc) mother's side; **essere dalla ~ della ragione** to be in the right; **da ~ a ~** right through; **da qualche ~** somewhere; **da nessuna ~** nowhere; **da questa ~** (in questa direzione) this way; **da ogni ~** on all sides, everywhere; (moto da luogo) from all sides; **fare ~ di qc** to belong to sth; **prendere ~ a qc** to take part in sth; **prendere le parti di qn** to take sb's side; **mettere qn a ~ di qc** to inform sb of sth; **costituirsi ~ civile contro qn** (Dir) to associate in an action with the public prosecutor against sb; **la ~ lesa** (Dir) the injured party; **le parti in causa** the parties concerned; **parti sociali** representatives of workers and employers

parteci'pante [partetʃi'pante] SMF: **~ (a)** (a riunione, dibattito) participant (in); (a gara sportiva) competitor (in); (a concorso) entrant (to)

parteci'pare [partetʃi'pare] /72/ VI: **~ a** to take part in, participate in; (utili ecc) to share in; (spese ecc) to contribute to; (dolore, successo di qn) to share (in) ▶ VT: **~ le nozze (a)** to announce one's wedding (to)

partecipazi'one [partetʃipat'tsjone] SF participation; sharing; (Econ) interest; **~ a banda armata** (Dir) belonging to an armed gang; **~ di maggioranza/ minoranza** controlling/minority interest; **~ agli utili** profit-sharing; **partecipazioni di nozze** wedding announcement card; **ministro delle Partecipazioni statali** minister responsible for companies in which the state has a financial interest

par'tecipe [par'tetʃipe] AG participating; **essere ~ di** to take part in, participate in; (gioia, dolore) to share (in); (consapevole) to be aware of

parteggi'are [parted'dʒare] /62/ VI: **~ per** to side with, be on the side of

par'tenza [par'tɛntsa] SF departure; (Sport) start; **essere in ~** to be about to leave, be leaving; **passeggeri in ~ per** passengers travelling (BRIT) o traveling (US) to; **siamo tornati al punto di ~** (fig) we are back where we started; **falsa ~** (anche fig) false start

parti'cella [parti'tʃella] SF particle

parti'cipio [parti'tʃipjo] SM participle

partico'lare AG (specifico) particular; (proprio) personal, private; (speciale) special, particular; (caratteristico) distinctive, characteristic; (fuori dal comune) peculiar ▶ SM detail, particular; **in ~** in particular, particularly; **entrare nei particolari** to go into details

particolareggi'ato, -a [partikolared'dʒato] AG (extremely) detailed

particolarità SF INV (carattere eccezionale) peculiarity; (dettaglio) particularity, detail; (caratteristica) characteristic, feature

partigi'ano, -a [parti'dʒano] AG partisan ▶ SM (fautore) supporter, champion; (Mil) partisan

par'tire /45/ VI to go, leave; (allontanarsi) to go (o drive etc) away o off; (petardo, colpo) to go off; (fig: avere inizio, Sport) to start; **sono partita da Roma alle 7** I left Rome at 7; **il volo parte da Ciampino** the flight leaves from Ciampino; **a ~ da** from; **la seconda a ~ da destra** the second from the right; **~ in quarta** to drive off at top speed; (fig) to be very enthusiastic

par'tita SF (Comm) lot, consignment; (Econ: registrazione) entry, item; (Carte, Sport: gioco) game; (: competizione) match, game; **~ di caccia** hunting party; **numero di ~ IVA** VAT registration number; **~ semplice/ doppia** (Comm) single-/double-entry book-keeping

par'tito SM (Pol) party; (decisione) decision, resolution; (persona da maritare) match; **per ~ preso** on principle; **mettere la testa a ~** to settle down

partitocra'zia [partitokrat'tsia] SF hijacking of institutions by the party system

parti'tura SF (Mus) score

'parto SM (Med) labour (BRIT), labor (US), delivery, (child)birth; **sala ~** labo(u)r room; **morire di ~** to die in childbirth

partori'ente SF woman in labour (BRIT) o labor (US)

parto'rire /55/ VT to give birth to; (fig) to produce

par'venza [par'vɛntsa] SF semblance

'parvi etc VB vedi **parere**

parzi'ale [par'tsjale] AG (limitato) partial; (non obiettivo) biased, partial

parzialità [partsjali'ta] SF: ~ **a favore di** partiality (for), bias (towards); ~ **contro** bias (against)

'**pascere** ['paʃʃere] /**29**/ VI to graze ▶ VT (*brucare*) to graze on; (*far pascolare*) to graze, pasture

pasci'uto, -a [paʃʃuto] PP *di* **pascere** ▶ AG: **ben** ~ plump

pasco'lare /**72**/ VT, VI to graze

'**pascolo** SM pasture

'**Pasqua** SF Easter; **isola di** ~ Easter Island

pas'quale AG Easter *cpd*

Pasqu'etta SF Easter Monday

pas'sabile AG fairly good, passable

pas'saggio [pas'saddʒo] SM passing *no pl*, passage; (*traversata*) crossing *no pl*, passage; (*luogo, prezzo della traversata, brano di libro ecc*) passage; (*su veicolo altrui*) lift (BRIT), ride; (*Sport*) pass; **di** ~ (*persona*) passing through; ~ **pedonale/a livello** pedestrian/level (BRIT) *o* grade (US) crossing; ~ **di proprietà** transfer of ownership

passamane'ria SF braid, trimming

passamon'tagna [passamon'taɲɲa] SM INV balaclava

pas'sante SMF passer-by ▶ SM loop

passa'porto SM passport

pas'sare /**72**/ VI (*andare*) to go; (*veicolo, pedone*) to pass (by), go by; (*fare una breve sosta: postino ecc*) to come, call; (: *amico: per fare una visita*) to call *o* drop in; (*sole, aria, luce*) to get through; (*trascorrere: giorni, tempo*) to pass, go by; (*fig: proposta di legge*) to be passed; (: *dolore*) to pass, go away; (*Carte*) to pass ▶ VT (*attraversare*) to cross; (*trasmettere: messaggio*): ~ **qc a qn** to pass sth on to sb; (*dare*): ~ **qc a qn** to pass sth to sb, give sb sth; (*trascorrere: tempo*) to spend; (*superare: esame*) to pass; (*triturare: verdura*) to strain; (*approvare*) to pass; (*oltrepassare, sorpassare: anche fig*) to go beyond, pass; (*fig: subire*) to go through; ~ **da ... a** to pass from ... to; ~ **di padre in figlio** to be handed down *o* to pass from father to son; ~ **per** (*anche fig*) to go through; ~ **per stupido/un genio** to be taken for a fool/a genius; ~ **sopra** (*anche fig*) to pass over; ~ **attraverso** (*anche fig*) to go through; ~ **ad altro** to change the subject; (*in una riunione*) to discuss the next item; ~ **in banca/ufficio** to call (in) at the bank/office; ~ **alla storia** to pass into history; ~ **a un esame** to go up (to the next class) after an exam; ~ **inosservato** to go unnoticed; ~ **di moda** to go out of fashion; ~ **a prendere qc/qn** to call and pick sth/sb up; **le passo il Signor X** (*al telefono*) here is Mr X; I'm putting you through to Mr X; **farsi** ~ **per** to pass o.s. off as, pretend to be; **lasciar** ~ **qn/qc** to let sb/sth through; **col** ~ **degli anni** (*riferito al presente*) as time goes by; (*riferito al passato*) as time passed *o* went by; **il peggio è passato** the worst is over; **30 anni e passa** well over 30 years ago; ~ **una mano di vernice su qc** to give sth a coat of paint; **passarsela, come te la passi?** how are you getting on *o* along?

pas'sata SF: **dare una** ~ **di vernice a qc** to give sth a coat of paint; **dare una** ~ **al giornale** to have a look at the paper, skim through the paper

passa'tempo SM pastime, hobby

pas'sato, -a AG (*scorso*) last; (*finito: gloria, generazioni*) past; (*usanze*) out of date; (*sfiorito*) faded ▶ SM past; (*Ling*) past (tense); **l'anno** ~ last year; **nel corso degli anni passati** over the past years; **nei tempi passati** in the past; **sono le 8 passate** it's past *o* after 8 o'clock; **è acqua passata** (*fig*) it's over and done with; ~ **prossimo** (*Ling*) present perfect; ~ **remoto** (*Ling*) past historic; ~ **di verdura** (*Cuc*) vegetable purée

passa'tutto, passaver'dura SM INV vegetable mill

passeg'gero, -a [passed'dʒɛro] AG passing ▶ SM/F passenger

passeggi'are [passed'dʒare] /**62**/ VI to go for a walk; (*in veicolo*) to go for a drive

passeggi'ata [passed'dʒata] SF walk; drive; (*luogo*) promenade; **fare una** ~ to go for a walk (*o drive*)

passeg'gino [passed'dʒino] SM pushchair (BRIT), stroller (US)

pas'seggio [pas'seddʒo] SM walk, stroll; (*luogo*) promenade; **andare a** ~ to go for a walk *o* a stroll

passe'rella SF footbridge; (*di nave, aereo*) gangway; (*pedana*) catwalk

'**passero** SM sparrow

pas'sibile AG: ~ **di** liable to

passio'nale AG (*temperamento*) passionate; **delitto** ~ crime of passion

passi'one SF passion

passività SF (*qualità*) passivity, passiveness; (*Comm*) liability

pas'sivo, -a AG passive ▶ SM (*Ling*) passive; (*Econ*) debit; (*complesso dei debiti*) liabilities *pl*

'**passo** SM step; (*andatura*) pace; (*rumore*) (foot)step; (*orma*) footprint; (*passaggio, fig: brano*) passage; (*valico*) pass; ~ **a** ~ **d'uomo** at walking pace; (*Aut*) dead slow; ~ **(a)** ~ step by step; **fare due** *o* **quattro passi** to go for a walk *o* a stroll; **andare al** ~ **coi tempi** to keep up with the times; **di questo** ~ (*fig*) at this rate; **fare i primi passi** (*anche fig*) to take one's first steps; **fare il gran** ~ (*fig*) to take the plunge; **fare un** ~ **falso** (*fig*) to make the wrong move; **tornare sui propri passi** to retrace one's steps; "~ **carraio**" "vehicle entrance — keep clear"

'pasta SF (*Cuc*) dough; (: *impasto per dolce*) pastry; (*anche*: **pasta alimentare**) pasta; (*massa molle di materia*) paste; (*fig*: *indole*) nature; **paste** SFPL (*pasticcini*) pastries; **~ in brodo** noodle soup; **~ sfoglia** puff pastry *o* paste (US)

pastasci'utta [pastaʃˈʃutta] SF pasta

pasteggi'are [pastedˈdʒare] /**62**/ VI: **~ a vino/ champagne** to have wine/champagne with one's meal

pas'tella SF batter

pas'tello SM pastel

pas'tetta SF (*Cuc*) = **pastella**

pas'ticca, -che SF = **pastiglia**

pasticce'ria [pastittʃeˈria] SF (*pasticcini*) pastries *pl*, cakes *pl*; (*negozio*) cake shop; (*arte*) confectionery

pasticci'are [pastitˈtʃare] /**14**/ VT to mess up, make a mess of ▶ VI to make a mess

pasticci'ere, -a [pastitˈtʃɛre] SM/F pastrycook; confectioner

pastic'cino [pastitˈtʃino] SM petit four

pas'ticcio [pasˈtittʃo] SM (*Cuc*) pie; (*lavoro disordinato, imbroglio*) mess; **trovarsi nei pasticci** to get into trouble

pasti'ficio [pastiˈfitʃo] SM pasta factory

pas'tiglia [pasˈtiʎʎa] SF pastille, lozenge

pas'tina SF *small pasta shapes used in soup*

pasti'naca, -che SF parsnip

'pasto SM meal; **vino da ~** table wine

pas'toia SF (*fig*): **~ burocratica** red tape

pas'tone SM (*per animali*) mash; (*peg*) overcooked stodge

pasto'rale AG pastoral

pas'tore SM shepherd; (*Rel*) pastor, minister; (*anche*: **cane pastore**) sheepdog; **~ scozzese** (*Zool*) collie; **~ tedesco** (*Zool*) Alsatian (dog) (BRIT) German shepherd (dog)

pasto'rizia [pastoˈrittsja] SF sheep-rearing, sheep farming

pastoriz'zare [pastoridˈdzare] /**72**/ VT to pasteurize

pas'toso, -a AG doughy; pasty; (*fig*: *voce, colore*) mellow, soft

pas'trano SM greatcoat

pa'tacca, -che SF (*distintivo*) medal, decoration; (*fig*: *macchia*) grease spot, grease mark; (*articolo scadente*) bit of rubbish

pa'tata SF potato; **patate fritte** chips (BRIT), French fries

pata'tine SFPL (potato) crisps (BRIT) *o* chips (US); **~ fritte** chips

pata'trac SM (*crollo: anche fig*) crash

pâté [paˈte] SM INV pâté; **~ di fegato d'oca** pâté de foie gras

pa'tella SF (*Zool*) limpet

pa'tema, -i SM anxiety, worry

paten'tato, -a AG (*munito di patente*) licensed, certified; (*fig: scherzoso: qualificato*) utter, thorough

pa'tente SF licence (BRIT), license (US); (*anche*: **patente di guida**) driving licence (BRIT), driver's license (US); **~ a punti** *driving licence with penalty points*

paten'tino SM temporary licence (BRIT) *o* license (US)

paterna'lismo SM paternalism

paterna'lista SM paternalist

paterna'listico, -a, -ci, -che AG paternalistic

paternità SF paternity, fatherhood

pa'terno, -a AG (*affetto, consigli*) fatherly; (*casa, autorità*) paternal

pa'tetico, -a, -ci, -che AG pathetic; (*commovente*) moving, touching

'pathos [ˈpatos] SM pathos

pa'tibolo SM gallows *sg*, scaffold

pati'mento SM suffering

'patina SF (*su rame ecc*) patina; (*sulla lingua*) fur, coating

pa'tire /55/ VT, VI to suffer

pa'tito, -a SM/F enthusiast, fan, lover

patolo'gia [patoloˈdʒia] SF pathology

pato'logico, -a, -ci, -che [patoˈlɔdʒiko] AG pathological

pa'tologo, -a, -gi, -ghe SM/F pathologist

'patria SF homeland; **amor di ~** patriotism

patri'arca, -chi SM patriarch

pa'trigno [paˈtriɲɲo] SM stepfather

patrimoni'ale AG (*rendita*) from property ▶ SF (*anche*: **imposta patrimoniale**) property tax

patri'monio SM estate, property; (*fig*) heritage; **mi è costato un ~** (*fig*) it cost me a fortune, I paid a fortune for it; **~ spirituale/culturale** spiritual/cultural heritage; **~ ereditario** (*fig*) hereditary characteristics *pl*; **~ pubblico** public property

'patrio, -a, -ii, -ie AG (*di patria*) native *cpd*, of one's country; (*Dir*): **patria potestà** parental authority; **amor ~** love of one's country

patri'ota, -i, -e SM/F patriot

patri'ottico, -a, -ci, -che AG patriotic

patriot'tismo SM patriotism

patroci'nare [patrotʃiˈnare] /**72**/ VT (*Dir*: *difendere*) to defend; (*sostenere*) to sponsor, support

patro'cinio [patroˈtʃinjo] SM defence (BRIT), defense (US); support, sponsorship

patro'nato SM patronage; (*istituzione benefica*) charitable institution *o* society

pa'trono SM (*Rel*) patron saint; (*socio di patronato*) patron; (*Dir*) counsel

'patta SF flap; (*dei pantaloni*) fly

patteggia'mento [patteddʒaˈmento] SM (*Dir*) plea bargaining

patteggi'are [pattedˈdʒare] /**62**/ VT, VI to negotiate; (*Dir*) to plea-bargain

patti'naggio [pattiˈnaddʒo] SM skating; **~ a rotelle/sul ghiaccio** roller-/ice-skating

patti'nare /**72**/ vi to skate; ~ **sul ghiaccio** to ice-skate

pattina'tore, -'trice sm/f skater

'pattino[1] sm skate; *(di slitta)* runner; *(Aer)* skid; *(Tecn)* sliding block; **pattini (da ghiaccio)** (ice) skates; **pattini in linea** rollerblades®; **pattini a rotelle** roller skates

pat'tino[2] sm *(barca)* kind of *pedalo* with oars

pat'tista, -i, -e AG *(Pol)* of Patto per l'Italia ▶ sm/f *(Pol)* member *(o* supporter) of Patto per l'Italia

'patto sm *(accordo)* pact, agreement; *(condizione)* term, condition; **a ~ che** on condition that; **a nessun ~** under no circumstances; **venire** *o* **scendere a patti (con)** to come to an agreement (with); **P~ per l'Italia** *(Pol)* centrist party

pat'tuglia [pat'tuʎʎa] sf *(Mil)* patrol

pattugli'are [pattuʎ'ʎare] /**27**/ vt to patrol

pattu'ire /**55**/ vt to reach an agreement on

pattumi'era sf *(dust)bin (BRIT)*, ashcan *(US)*

pa'ura sf fear; **aver ~ di/di fare/che** to be frightened *o* afraid of/of doing/that; **far ~ a** to frighten; **per ~ di/che** for fear of/that; **ho ~ di sì/no** I am afraid so/not

pau'roso, -a AG *(che fa paura)* frightening; *(che ha paura)* fearful, timorous

'pausa sf *(sosta)* break; *(nel parlare: Mus)* pause

paven'tato, -a AG much-feared

pa'vese AG of *(o* from) Pavia

'pavido, -a AG *(letterario)* fearful

pavimen'tare /**72**/ vt *(stanza)* to floor; *(strada)* to pave

pavimentazi'one [pavimentat'tsjone] sf flooring; paving

pavi'mento sm floor

pa'vone sm peacock

pavoneggi'arsi [pavoned'dʒarsi] /**62**/ vpr to strut about, show off

'paywall ['peiwol] sm inv paywall

pazien'tare [pattsjen'tare] /**72**/ vi to be patient

pazi'ente [pat'tsjɛnte] AG, smf patient

pazi'enza [pat'tsjɛntsa] sf patience; **perdere la ~** to lose (one's) patience

pazza'mente [pattsa'mente] AV madly; **essere ~ innamorato** to be madly in love

paz'zesco, -a, -schi, -sche [pat'tsesko] AG mad, crazy

paz'zia [pat'tsia] sf *(Med)* madness, insanity; *(di azione, decisione)* madness, folly; **è stata una ~!** it was sheer madness!

'pazzo, -a ['pattso] AG *(Med)* mad, insane; *(strano)* wild, mad ▶ sm/f madman/woman; **~ di** *(gioia, amore ecc)* mad *o* crazy with; **~ per qc/qn** mad *o* crazy about sth/sb; **essere ~ da legare** to be raving mad *o* a raving lunatic

PC SIGLA = **Piacenza** ▶ SIGLA M INV [pi'tʃi] *(= personal computer)* PC; **PC portatile** laptop

p.c. ABBR = **per condoglianze; per conoscenza**

p.c.c. ABBR *(= per copia conforme)* cc

P.C.I. SIGLA M *(= Partito Comunista Italiano)* former political party

PCUS SIGLA M = **Partito Comunista dell'Unione Sovietica**

PD SIGLA = **Padova**

P.D . ABBR = **partita doppia**

PE SIGLA = **Pescara**

'pecca, -che sf defect, flaw, fault

peccami'noso, -a AG sinful

pec'care /**20**/ vi to sin; *(fig)* to err

pec'cato sm sin; **è un ~ che** it's a pity that; **che ~!** what a shame *o* pity!; **un ~ di gioventù** *(fig)* a youthful error *o* indiscretion

pecca'tore, -'trice sm/f sinner

pecche'rò *etc* [pekke'rɔ] vb *vedi* **peccare**

'pece ['petʃe] sf pitch

pechi'nese [peki'nese] AG, smf Pekin(g)ese inv ▶ sm *(anche:* **cane pechinese**) Pekin(g)ese inv, Peke

Pe'chino [pe'kino] sf Beijing, Peking

'pecora sf sheep; **~ nera** *(fig)* black sheep

peco'raio sm shepherd

peco'rella sf lamb; **la ~ smarrita** the lost sheep; **cielo a pecorelle** *(fig: nuvole)* mackerel sky

peco'rino sm sheep's milk cheese

pecu'lato sm *(Dir)* embezzlement

peculi'are AG: **~ di** peculiar to

peculiarità sf peculiarity

pecuni'ario, -a AG financial, money *cpd*

pe'daggio [pe'daddʒo] sm toll

pedago'gia [pedago'dʒia] sf pedagogy, educational methods *pl*

peda'gogico, -a, -ci, -che [peda'gɔdʒiko] AG pedagogic(al)

peda'gogo, -a, -ghi, -ghe sm/f pedagogue

peda'lare /**72**/ vi to pedal; *(andare in bicicletta)* to cycle

pe'dale sm pedal

pe'dana sf footboard; *(Sport: nel salto)* springboard; *(: nella scherma)* piste

pe'dante AG pedantic ▶ smf pedant

pedante'ria sf pedantry

pe'data sf *(impronta)* footprint; *(colpo)* kick; **prendere a pedate qn/qc** to kick sb/sth

pede'rasta, -i sm pederast

pe'destre AG prosaic, pedestrian

pedi'atra, -i, -e sm/f paediatrician *(BRIT)*, pediatrician *(US)*

pedia'tria sf paediatrics *sg (BRIT)*, pediatrics *sg (US)*

pedi'atrico, -a, -ci, -che AG pediatric

pedi'cure sm inv/f inv chiropodist *(BRIT)*, podiatrist *(US)*

pedigree sm inv pedigree

pedi'luvio sm footbath

pe'dina SF (*della dama*) draughtsman (BRIT), draftsman (US); (*fig*) pawn

pedi'nare /72/ VT to shadow, tail

pe'dofilo, -a AG, SM/F paedophile

pedo'nale AG pedestrian

pe'done, -a SM/F pedestrian ▶ SM (*Scacchi*) pawn

peeling ['piling] SM INV (*Cosmesi*) facial scrub

'peggio ['pɛddʒo] AV, AG INV worse ▶ SM O F: **il** *o* **la ~** the worst; **cambiare in ~** to get *o* become worse; **alla ~** at worst, if the worst comes to the worst; **tirare avanti alla meno ~** to get along as best one can; **avere la ~** to come off worse, get the worst of it

peggiora'mento [peddʒora'mento] SM worsening

peggio'rare [peddʒo'rare] /72/ VT to make worse, worsen ▶ VI to grow worse, worsen

peggiora'tivo, -a [peddʒora'tivo] AG pejorative

peggi'ore [ped'dʒore] AG (*comparativo*) worse; (*superlativo*) worst ▶ SM/F: **il (la) ~** the worst (person); **nel ~ dei casi** if the worst comes to the worst

'pegno ['peɲɲo] SM (*Dir*) security, pledge; (*nei giochi di società*) forfeit; (*fig*) pledge, token; **dare in ~ qc** to pawn sth; **in ~ d'amicizia** as a token of friendship; **banco dei pegni** pawnshop

pelapa'tate SM INV potato peeler

pe'lare /72/ VT (*spennare*) to pluck; (*spellare*) to skin; (*sbucciare*) to peel; (*fig*) to make pay through the nose; **pelarsi** VPR to go bald

pe'lato, -a AG (*sbucciato*) peeled; (*calvo*) bald; **(pomodori) pelati** peeled tomatoes

pel'lame SM skins *pl*, hides *pl*

'pelle SF skin; (*di animale*) skin, hide; (*cuoio*) leather; **essere ~ ed ossa** to be skin and bone; **avere la ~ d'oca** to have goose pimples *o* goose flesh; **avere i nervi a fior di ~** to be edgy; **non stare più nella ~ dalla gioia** to be beside o.s. with delight; **lasciarci la ~** to lose one's life; **amici per la ~** firm *o* close friends

pellegri'naggio [pellegri'naddʒo] SM pilgrimage

pelle'grino, -a SM/F pilgrim

pelle'rossa (*pl* **pellirosse**) SM/F (*peg*) Red Indian (*peg*)

pellette'ria SF (*articoli*) leather goods *pl*; (*negozio*) leather goods shop

pelli'cano SM pelican

pellicce'ria [pellittʃe'ria] SF (*negozio*) furrier's (shop); (*quantità di pellicce*) furs *pl*

pel'liccia, -ce [pel'littʃa] SF (*mantello di animale*) coat, fur; (*indumento*) fur coat; **~ ecologica** fake fur

pellicci'aio [pellit'tʃajo] SM furrier

pel'licola SF (*membrana sottile*) film, layer; (*Fot, Cine*) film

pelli'rossa SMF = **pellerossa**

'pelo SM hair; (*pelame*) coat, hair; (*pelliccia*) fur; (*di tappeto*) pile; (*di liquido*) surface; **per un ~**: **per un ~ non ho perduto il treno** I very nearly missed the train; **c'è mancato un ~ che affogasse** he narrowly escaped drowning; **cercare il ~ nell'uovo** (*fig*) to pick holes, split hairs; **non aver peli sulla lingua** (*fig*) to speak one's mind

pe'loso, -a AG hairy

'peltro SM pewter

pe'luche [pə'lyʃ] SM plush; **giocattoli di ~** soft toys

pe'luria SF down

'pelvi SF INV pelvis

'pelvico, -a, -ci, -che AG pelvic

'pena SF (*Dir*) sentence; (*punizione*) punishment; (*sofferenza*) sadness *no pl*, sorrow; (*fatica*) trouble *no pl*, effort; (*difficoltà*) difficulty; **far ~** to be pitiful; **mi fai ~** I feel sorry for you; **essere** *o* **stare in ~ (per qc/qn)** to worry *o* be anxious (about sth/sb); **prendersi** *o* **darsi la ~ di fare** to go to the trouble of doing; **vale la ~ farlo** it's worth doing, it's worth it; **non ne vale la ~** it's not worth the effort, it's not worth it; **~ di morte** death sentence; **~ pecuniaria** fine

pe'nale AG penal ▶ SF (*anche:* **clausola penale**) penalty clause; **causa ~** criminal trial; **diritto ~** criminal law; **pagare la ~** to pay the penalty

pena'lista, -i, -e SM/F (*avvocato*) criminal lawyer

penalità SF INV penalty

penaliz'zare [penalid'dzare] /72/ VT (*Sport*) to penalize

penalizzazi'one [penaliddzat'tsjone] SF (*Sport*) penalty

pe'nare /72/ VI (*patire*) to suffer; (*faticare*) to struggle

pen'dente AG hanging; leaning ▶ SM (*ciondolo*) pendant; (*orecchino*) drop earring

pen'denza [pen'dɛntsa] SF slope, slant; (*grado d'inclinazione*) gradient; (*Econ*) outstanding account

'pendere /8/ VI (*essere appeso*): **~ da** to hang from; (*essere inclinato*) to lean; (*fig: incombere*) **~ su** to hang over

pen'dice [pen'ditʃe] SF (*di monte*) slope

pen'dio, -ii SM slope, slant; (*luogo in pendenza*) slope

'pendola SF pendulum clock

pendo'lare AG pendulum *cpd*, pendular ▶ SMF commuter

pendola'rismo SM commuting

pendo'lino SM *high-speed train*

'**pendolo** SM (*peso*) pendulum; (*anche: orologio a pendolo*) pendulum clock

'**pene** SM penis

pene'trante AG piercing, penetrating

pene'trare /**72**/ VI to come *o* get in ▶ VT to penetrate; ~ **in** to enter; (*proiettile*) to penetrate (: *acqua, aria*) to go *o* come into

penetrazi'one [penetrat'tsjone] SF penetration

penicil'lina [penitʃil'lina] SF penicillin

peninsu'lare AG peninsular; **l'Italia** ~ mainland Italy

pe'nisola SF peninsula

peni'tente SMF penitent

peni'tenza [peni'tɛntsa] SF penitence; (*punizione*) penance

penitenzi'ario [peniten'tsjarjo] SM prison

'**penna** SF (*di uccello*) feather; (*per scrivere*) pen; **penne** SFPL (*Cuc*) quills (*type of pasta*); ~ **a feltro/stilografica/a sfera** felt-tip/fountain/ballpoint pen

penna'rello SM felt(-tip) pen

pennel'lare /**72**/ VI to paint

pennel'lata SF brushstroke

pen'nello SM brush; (*per dipingere*) (paint)brush; **a** ~ (*perfettamente*) to perfection, perfectly; ~ **per la barba** shaving brush

pennetta SF: ~ **USB** memory stick

Pen'nini SMPL: **i** ~ the Pennines

pen'nino SM nib

pen'none SM (*Naut*) yard; (*stendardo*) banner, standard

pen'nuto SM bird

pe'nombra SF half-light, dim light

pe'noso, -a AG painful, distressing; (*faticoso*) tiring, laborious

pen'sare /**72**/ VI to think ▶ VT to think; (*inventare, escogitare*) to think out; ~ **a** to think of; (*amico, vacanze*) to think of *o* about; (*problema*) to think about; ~ **di fare qc** to think of doing sth; ~ **bene/male di qn** to think well/badly of sb, have a good/bad opinion of sb; **penso di sì** I think so; **penso di no** I don't think so; **a pensarci bene ...** on second thoughts (*BRIT*) *o* thought (*US*)...; **non voglio nemmeno pensarci** I don't even want to think about it; **ci penso io** I'll see to *o* take care of it

pen'sata SF (*trovata*) idea, thought

pensa'tore, -'trice SM/F thinker

pensie'rino SM (*dono*) little gift; (*pensiero*): **ci farò un** ~ I'll think about it

pensi'ero SM thought *no pl*; (*modo di pensare, dottrina*) thinking *no pl*; (*preoccupazione*) worry, care, trouble; **darsi** ~ **per qc** to worry about

sth; **stare in** ~ **per qn** to be worried about sb; **un** ~ **gentile** (*anche fig: dono ecc*) a kind thought

pensie'roso, -a AG thoughtful

'**pensile** AG hanging ▶ SM (*in cucina*) wall cupboard

pensi'lina SF (*in stazione*) platform roof

pensiona'mento SM retirement; ~ **anticipato** early retirement

pensio'nante SMF (*presso una famiglia*) lodger; (*di albergo*) guest

pensio'nato, -a SM/F pensioner ▶ SM (*istituto*) hostel

pensi'one SF (*al prestatore di lavoro*) pension; (*vitto e alloggio*) board and lodging; (*albergo*) boarding house; **andare in** ~ to retire; **mezza** ~ half board; ~ **completa** full board; ~ **d'invalidità** disablement pension; ~ **per la vecchiaia** old-age pension

pensio'nistico, -a, -ci, -che AG pension *cpd*

pen'soso, -a AG thoughtful, pensive, lost in thought

pen'tagono SM pentagon; **il P~** the Pentagon

pentag'ramma, -i SM (*Mus*) staff, stave

pentapar'tito SM (*Pol*) five-party coalition government

'**pentathlon** ['pɛntatlon] SM (*Sport*) pentathlon

Pente'coste SF Pentecost, Whit Sunday (*BRIT*)

penti'mento SM repentance, contrition

pen'tirsi /**45**/ VPR: ~ **di** to repent of; (*rammaricarsi*) to regret, be sorry for

penti'tismo SM *confessions from terrorists and members of organized crime rackets; see note*

> The practice of *pentitismo* first emerged in Italy during the 1970s, a period marked by major terrorist activity. Once arrested, some members of terrorist groups would collaborate with the authorities by providing information in return for a reduced sentence, or indeed for their own reasons. In recent years it has become common practice for members of Mafia organizations to become *pentiti*, and special legislation has had to be introduced to provide for the sentencing and personal protection of these informants.

pen'tito, -a SM/F ≈ supergrass (*BRIT*), *terrorist/criminal who turns police informer*

'**pentola** SF pot; ~ **a pressione** pressure cooker

pe'nultimo, -a AG last but one (*BRIT*), next to last, penultimate

pe'nuria SF shortage

penzo'lare [pendzo'lare] /**72**/ VI to dangle, hang loosely

penzo'loni [pendzo'loni] AV dangling, hanging down; **stare ~** to dangle, hang down

pe'pato, -a AG (*condito con pepe*) peppery, hot; (*fig: pungente*) sharp

'pepe SM pepper; **~ macinato/in grani/nero** ground/whole/black pepper

pepero'nata SF *stewed peppers, tomatoes and onions*

peperon'cino [peperon'tʃino] SM chilli pepper

pepe'rone SM: **~ (rosso)** red pepper, capsicum; **~ (verde)** green pepper, capsicum; (*piccante*) chili; **rosso come un ~** as red as a beetroot (BRIT), fire-engine red (US); **peperoni ripieni** stuffed peppers

pe'pita SF nugget

PAROLA CHIAVE

per PREP **1** (*moto attraverso luogo*) through; **i ladri sono passati per la finestra** the thieves got in (*o* out) through the window; **l'ho cercato per tutta la casa** I've searched the whole house *o* all over the house for it

2 (*moto a luogo*) for, to; **partire per la Germania/il mare** to leave for Germany/the sea; **il treno per Roma** the Rome train, the train for *o* to Rome; **proseguire per Londra** to go on to London

3 (*stato in luogo*): **seduto/sdraiato per terra** sitting/lying on the ground

4 (*tempo*) for; **per anni/lungo tempo** for years/a long time; **per tutta l'estate** throughout the summer, all summer long; **lo rividi per Natale** I saw him again at Christmas; **lo faccio per lunedì** I'll do it for Monday

5 (*mezzo, maniera*) by; **per lettera/ferrovia/via aerea** by letter/rail/airmail; **prendere qn per un braccio** to take sb by the arm

6 (*causa, scopo*) for; **assente per malattia** absent because of *o* through *o* owing to illness; **ottimo per il mal di gola** excellent for sore throats; **per abitudine** out of habit, from habit

7 (*limitazione*) for; **è troppo difficile per lui** it's too difficult for him; **per quel che mi riguarda** as far as I'm concerned; **per poco che sia** however little it may be; **per questa volta ti perdono** I'll forgive you this time

8 (*prezzo, misura*) for; (*distributivo*) a, per; **venduto per 3 milioni** sold for 3 million; **la strada continua per 3 km** the street goes on for 3 km; **15 euro per persona** 15 euros a *o* per person; **uno per volta** one at a time; **uno per uno** one by one; **giorno per giorno** day by day; **due per parte** two either side; **5 per cento** 5 per cent; **3 per 4 fa 12** 3 times 4 equals 12; **dividere/moltiplicare**

12 per 4 to divide/multiply 12 by 4

9 (*in qualità di*) as; (*al posto di*) for; **avere qn per professore** to have sb as a teacher; **ti ho preso per Mario** I mistook you for Mario, I thought you were Mario; **dare per morto qn** to give sb up for dead; **lo prenderanno per pazzo** they'll think he's crazy

10 (*seguito da vb: finale*): **per fare qc** (so as) to do sth, in order to do sth; (*: causale*): **per aver fatto qc** for having done sth; **studia per passare l'esame** he's studying in order to *o* (so as) to pass his exam; **l'hanno punito per aver rubato i soldi** he was punished for having stolen the money; (*: consecutivo*): **è abbastanza grande per andarci da solo** he's big enough to go on his own

'pera SF pear

pe'raltro AV moreover, what's more

per'bacco ESCL by Jove!

per'bene AG INV respectable, decent ▶ AV (*con cura*) properly, well

perbe'nismo SM (*so-called*) respectability

percentu'ale [pertʃentu'ale] SF percentage; (*commissione*) commission

perce'pire [pertʃe'pire] /**55**/ VT (*sentire*) to perceive; (*ricevere*) to receive

percet'tibile [pertʃet'tibile] AG perceptible

percezi'one [pertʃet'tsjone] SF perception

PAROLA CHIAVE

perché [per'ke] AV why; **perché no?** why not?; **perché non vuoi andarci?** why don't you want to go?; **spiegami perché l'hai fatto** tell me why you did it

▶ CONG **1** (*causale*) because; **non posso uscire perché ho da fare** I can't go out because *o* as I've a lot to do

2 (*finale*) in order that, so that; **te lo do perché tu lo legga** I'm giving it to you so (that) you can read it

3 (*consecutivo*): **è troppo forte perché si possa batterlo** he's too strong to be beaten ▶ SM INV reason; **il perché di** the reason for; **non c'è un vero perché** there's no real reason for it

perciò [per'tʃɔ] CONG so, for this *o* that reason

per'correre /**28**/ VT (*luogo*) to go all over; (*paese*) to travel up and down, go all over; (*distanza*) to cover

percor'ribile AG (*strada*) which can be followed

per'corso, -a PP *di* **percorrere** ▶ SM (*tragitto*) journey; (*tratto*) route

per'cosso, -a PP *di* **percuotere** ▶ SF blow

percu'otere /**106**/ VT to hit, strike

percussi'one SF percussion; **strumenti a ~** (*Mus*) percussion instruments

per'dente AG losing ▶ SMF loser

'**perdere** /**73**/ VT to lose; (*lasciarsi sfuggire*) to miss; (*sprecare: tempo, denaro*) to waste; (*mandare in rovina: persona*) to ruin ▶ VI to lose; (*serbatoio ecc*) to leak; **perdersi** VPR (*smarrirsi*) to get lost; (*svanire*) to disappear, vanish; **saper ~** to be a good loser; **lascia ~!** forget it!, never mind!; **non ho niente da ~** (*fig*) I've got nothing to lose; **è un'occasione da non ~** it's a marvellous opportunity; (*affare*) it's a great bargain; **è fatica persa** it's a waste of effort; **~ al gioco** to lose money gambling; **~ di vista qn** (*anche fig*) to lose sight of sb; **perdersi di vista** to lose sight of each other; (*fig*) to lose touch; **perdersi alla vista** to disappear from sight; **perdersi in chiacchiere** to waste time talking

perdifi'ato: a ~ AV (*correre*) at breathtaking speed; (*gridare*) at the top of one's voice

perdigi'orno [perdi'dʒorno] SM INV/F INV idler, waster

'**perdita** SF loss; (*spreco*) waste; (*fuoriuscita*) leak; **siamo in ~** (*Comm*) we are running at a loss; **a ~ d'occhio** as far as the eye can see

perdi'tempo SM INV/F INV waster, idler

perdizi'one [perdit'tsjone] SF (*Rel*) perdition, damnation; **luogo di ~** place of ill repute

perdo'nare /**72**/ VT to pardon, forgive; (*scusare*) to excuse, pardon; **per farsi ~** in order to be forgiven; **perdona la domanda ...** if you don't mind my asking ...; **vogliate ~ il (mio) ritardo** my apologies for being late; **un male che non perdona** an incurable disease

per'dono SM forgiveness; (*Dir*) pardon; **chiedere ~ a qn (per)** to ask for sb's forgiveness (for); (*scusarsi*) to apologize to sb (for)

perdu'rare /**72**/ VI to go on, last; (*perseverare*) to persist

perduta'mente AV desperately, passionately

per'duto, -a PP di **perdere** ▶ AG (*gen*) lost; **sentirsi** o **vedersi ~** (*fig*) to realize the hopelessness of one's position; **una donna perduta** (*fig*) a fallen woman

peregri'nare /**72**/ VI to wander, roam

pe'renne AG eternal, perpetual, perennial; (*Bot*) perennial

peren'torio, -a AG peremptory; (*definitivo*) final

perfetta'mente AV perfectly; **sai ~ che ...** you know perfectly well that ...

per'fetto, -a AG perfect ▶ SM (*Ling*) perfect (tense)

perfeziona'mento [perfettsjona'mento] SM: **~ (di)** improvement (in), perfection (of); **corso di ~** proficiency course

perfezio'nare [perfettsjo'nare] /**72**/ VT to improve, perfect; **perfezionarsi** VPR to improve

perfezi'one [perfet'tsjone] SF perfection

perfezio'nismo [perfettsjo'nizmo] SM perfectionism

perfezio'nista, -i, -e [perfettsjo'nista] SM/F perfectionist

per'fidia SF perfidy

'**perfido, -a** AG perfidious, treacherous

per'fino AV even

perfo'rare /**72**/ VT to pierce; (*Med*) to perforate, to punch a hole (o holes) in; (*banda, schede*) to punch; (*trivellare*) to drill

perfora'tore, -'trice SM/F punch-card operator ▶ SM (*utensile*) punch; (*Inform*): **~ di schede** card punch ▶ SF (*Tecn*) boring o drilling machine; (*Inform*) card punch

perforazi'one [perforat'tsjone] SF piercing; perforation; punching drilling

perga'mena SF parchment

'**pergola** SF pergola

pergo'lato SM pergola

perico'lante AG precarious

pe'ricolo SM danger; **essere fuori ~** to be out of danger; (*Med*) to be off the danger list; **mettere in ~** to endanger, put in danger

perico'loso, -a AG dangerous

perife'ria SF (*anche fig*) periphery; (*di città*) outskirts *pl*

peri'ferico, -a, -ci, -che AG (*Anat, Inform*) peripheral; (*zona*) outlying

pe'rifrasi SF INV circumlocution

pe'rimetro SM perimeter

peri'odico, -a, -ci, -che AG periodic(al); (*Mat*) recurring ▶ SM periodical

pe'riodo SM period; **~ contabile** accounting period; **~ di prova** trial period

peripe'zie [peripet'tsie] SFPL ups and downs, vicissitudes

'**periplo** SM circumnavigation

pe'rire /**55**/ VI to perish, die

peris'copio SM periscope

pe'rito, -a AG expert, skilled ▶ SM/F expert; (*agronomo, navale*) surveyor; **un ~ chimico** a qualified chemist

perito'nite SF peritonitis

pe'rizia [pe'rittsja] SF (*abilità*) ability; (*giudizio tecnico*) expert opinion; expert's report; **~ psichiatrica** psychiatrist's report

peri'zoma, -i [peri'dzoma] SM G-string

'**perla** SF pearl

per'lina SF bead

perli'nato SM matchboarding

perlo'meno AV (*almeno*) at least

perlopiù AV (*quasi sempre*) in most cases, usually

perlus'trare /**72**/ VT to patrol

perlustrazi'one [perlustrat'tsjone] SF patrol, reconnaissance; **andare in ~** to go on patrol

perma'loso, -a AG touchy

perma'nente AG permanent ▶ SF permanent wave, perm

perma'nenza [perma'nɛntsa] SF permanence; (*soggiorno*) stay; **buona ~!** enjoy your stay!

perma'nere /93/ VI to remain

per'mango VB *vedi* **permanere**

per'masi *etc* VB *vedi* **permanere**

perme'abile AG permeable

perme'are /72/ VT to permeate

per'messo, -a PP *di* **permettere** ▶ SM (*autorizzazione*) permission, leave; (*dato a militare, impiegato*) leave; (*licenza*) licence (*BRIT*), license (*US*), permit; (*Mil: foglio*) pass; **~?, è ~?** (*posso entrare?*) may I come in?; (*posso passare?*) excuse me; **~ di lavoro/pesca** work/fishing permit; **~ di soggiorno** residence permit

per'mettere /63/ VT to allow, permit; **~ a qn qc/di fare qc** to allow sb sth/to do sth; **permettersi** VPR: **permettersi qc/di fare qc** (*concedersi*) to allow o.s. sth/to do sth; (*avere la possibilità*) to afford sth/to do sth; **permettete che mi presenti** let me introduce myself, may I introduce myself?; **mi sia permesso di sottolineare che …** may I take the liberty of pointing out that …

per'misi *etc* VB *vedi* **permettere**

permis'sivo, -a AG permissive

per'muta SF (*Dir*) transfer; (*Comm*) trade-in; **accettare qc in ~** to take sth as a trade-in; **valore di ~** (*di macchina ecc*) trade-in value

permu'tare /72/ VT to exchange; (*Mat*) to permute

per'nacchia [per'nakkja] SF (*col*): **fare una ~** to blow a raspberry

per'nice [per'nitʃe] SF partridge

'perno SM pivot

pernotta'mento SM overnight stay

pernot'tare /72/ VI to spend the night, stay overnight

'pero SM pear tree

però CONG (*ma*) but; (*tuttavia*) however, nevertheless

pero'rare /72/ VT (*Dir: fig*): **~ la causa di qn** to plead sb's case

perpendico'lare AG, SF perpendicular

perpen'dicolo SM: **a ~** perpendicularly

perpe'trare /72/ VT to perpetrate

perpetu'are /72/ VT to perpetuate

per'petuo, -a AG perpetual

perplessità SF INV perplexity

per'plesso, -a AG perplexed, puzzled; uncertain

perqui'sire /55/ VT to search

perquisizi'one [perkwizit'tsjone] SF (police) search; **mandato di ~** search warrant

'perse *etc* VB *vedi* **perdere**

persecu'tore SM persecutor

persecuzi'one [persekut'tsjone] SF persecution

persegu'ibile AG (*Dir*): **essere ~ per legge** to be liable to prosecution

persegu'ire /45/ VT to pursue; (*Dir*) to prosecute

persegui'tare /72/ VT to persecute

perseve'rante AG persevering

perseve'ranza [perseve'rantsa] SF perseverance

perseve'rare /72/ VI to persevere

'persi *etc* VB *vedi* **perdere**

'Persia SF: **la ~** Persia

persi'ano, -a AG, SM/F Persian ▶ SF shutter; **persiana avvolgibile** roller blind

'persico, -a, -ci, -che AG: **il golfo P~** the Persian Gulf; **pesce ~** perch

per'sino AV = **perfino**

persis'tente AG persistent

persis'tenza [persis'tɛntsa] SF persistence

per'sistere /11/ VI to persist; **~ a fare** to persist in doing

persis'tito, -a PP *di* **persistere**

'perso, -a PP *di* **perdere** ▶ AG (*smarrito: anche fig*) lost; (*sprecato*) wasted; **fare qc a tempo ~** to do sth in one's spare time; **~ per ~** I've (*o we've etc*) got nothing further to lose

per'sona SF person; (*qualcuno*): **una ~** someone, somebody; (*espressione*) anyone *o* anybody; **persone** SFPL people *pl*; **non c'è ~ che …** there's nobody who …, there isn't anybody who …; **in ~, di ~** in person; **per interposta ~** through an intermediary *o* a third party; **~ giuridica** (*Dir*) legal person

perso'naggio [perso'naddʒo] SM (*persona ragguardevole*) personality, figure; (*tipo*) character, individual; (*Letteratura*) character

perso'nale AG personal ▶ SM staff; personnel; (*figura fisica*) build ▶ SF (*mostra*) one-man *o* one-woman exhibition

personalità SF INV personality

personaliz'zare [personalid'dzare] /72/ VT (*arredamento, stile*) to personalize; (*adattare*) to customize

personaliz'zato, -a [personalid'dzato] AG personalized

personal'mente AV personally

personifi'care /20/ VT to personify; (*simboleggiare*) to embody

personificazi'one [personifikat'tsjone] SF (*vedi vb*) personification; embodiment

perspi'cace [perspi'katʃe] AG shrewd, discerning

perspi'cacia [perspi'katʃa] SF perspicacity, shrewdness

persu'adere /88/ VT: ~ **qn (di qc/a fare)** to persuade sb (of sth/to do)

persuasi'one SF persuasion

persua'sivo, -a AG persuasive

persu'aso, -a PP di **persuadere**

per'tanto CONG (quindi) so, therefore

'pertica, -che SF pole

perti'nace [perti'natʃe] AG determined; persistent

perti'nente AG: ~ **(a)** relevant (to), pertinent (to)

perti'nenza [perti'nɛntsa] SF (attinenza) pertinence, relevance; (competenza): **essere di ~ di qn** to be sb's business

per'tosse SF whooping cough

per'tugio [per'tudʒo] SM hole, opening

pertur'bare /72/ VT to disrupt; (persona) to disturb, perturb

perturbazi'one [perturbat'tsjone] SF disruption; disturbance; ~ **atmosferica** atmospheric disturbance

Perù SM: **il ~** Peru

peru'gino, -a [peru'dʒino] AG of (o from), Perugia

peruvi'ano, -a AG, SM/F Peruvian

per'vadere /52/ VT to pervade

per'vaso, -a PP di **pervadere**

perve'nire /128/ VI: ~ **a** to reach, arrive at, come to; (venire in possesso) **gli pervenne una fortuna** he inherited a fortune; **far ~ qc a** to have sth sent to

perve'nuto, -a PP di **pervenire**

perversi'one SF perversion

perversità SF perversity

per'verso, -a AG perverted; perverse

perver'tire /55/ VT to pervert

perver'tito, -a SM/F pervert

pervi'cace [pervi'katʃe] AG stubborn, obstinate

pervi'cacia [pervi'katʃa] SF stubbornness, obstinacy

per'vinca, -che SF periwinkle ▶ SM INV (colore) periwinkle (blue)

p.es. ABBR (= per esempio) e.g.

'pesa SF weighing no pl weighbridge

pe'sante AG heavy; (fig: noioso) dull, boring

pesan'tezza [pesan'tettsa] SF (anche fig) heaviness; **avere ~ di stomaco** to feel bloated

pesaper'sone AG INV: **(bilancia) ~** (weighing) scales pl; (automatica) weighing machine

pe'sare /72/ VT to weigh ▶ VI (avere un peso) to weigh; (essere pesante) to be heavy; (fig) to carry weight; ~ **su** (fig) to lie heavy on; to influence; to hang over; **mi pesa sgridarlo** I find it hard to scold him; **tutta la responsabilità pesa su di lui** all the responsibility rests on his shoulders; **è una situazione che mi pesa** it's a difficult situation for me; **il suo parere pesa molto** his opinion counts for a lot; ~ **le parole** to weigh one's words

'pesca (pl **pesche**) SF (frutto) peach; (il pescare) fishing; **andare a ~** to go fishing; ~ **di beneficenza** (lotteria) lucky dip; ~ **con la lenza** angling; ~ **subacquea** underwater fishing

pes'caggio [pes'kaddʒo] SM (Naut) draught (BRIT), draft (US)

pes'care /20/ VT (pesce) to fish for; to catch; (qc nell'acqua) to fish out; (fig: trovare) to get hold of, find; **andare a ~** to go fishing

pesca'tore SM fisherman; (con lenza) angler

'pesce ['peʃʃe] SM fish gen inv; **Pesci** (dello zodiaco) Pisces; **essere dei Pesci** to be Pisces; **non saper che pesci prendere** (fig) not to know which way to turn; ~ **d'aprile!** April Fool!; see note; ~ **martello** hammerhead; ~ **rosso** goldfish; ~ **spada** swordfish

> Il pesce d'aprile is a sort of April Fool's joke, played on 1 April. Originally it took its name from a paper fish which was secretly attached to a person's back but nowadays all sorts of practical jokes are popular.

pesce'cane [peʃʃe'kane] SM shark

pesche'reccio [peske'rettʃo] SM fishing boat

pesche'ria [peske'ria] SF fishmonger's (shop) (BRIT), fish store (US)

pescherò etc [peske'rɔ] VB vedi **pescare**

peschi'era [pes'kjɛra] SF fishpond

pesci'vendolo, -a [peʃʃi'vendolo] SM/F fishmonger (BRIT), fish merchant (US)

'pesco, -schi SM peach tree

pes'coso, -a AG teeming with fish

pe'seta SF peseta

'peso SM weight; (Sport) shot; **dar ~ a qc** to attach importance to sth; **essere di ~ a qn** (fig) to be a burden to sb; **rubare sul ~** to give short weight; **lo portarono via di ~** they carried him away bodily; **avere due pesi e due misure** (fig) to have double standards; ~ **lordo/netto** gross/net weight; ~ **piuma/ mosca/gallo/medio/massimo** (Pugilato) feather/fly/bantam/middle/heavyweight

pessi'mismo SM pessimism

pessi'mista, -i, -e AG pessimistic ▶ SM/F pessimist

'pessimo, -a AG very bad, awful; **di pessima qualità** of very poor quality

pes'tare /72/ VT to tread on, trample on; (sale, pepe) to grind; (uva, aglio) to crush; (fig: picchiare): ~ **qn** to beat sb up; ~ **i piedi** to stamp one's feet; ~ **i piedi a qn** (anche fig) to tread on sb's toes

'peste SF plague; (persona) nuisance, pest

pes'tello SM pestle

pesti'cida, -i [pesti'tʃida] SM pesticide

P

pes'tifero, -a AG (*anche fig*) pestilential, pestiferous; (*odore*) noxious

pesti'lenza [pesti'lɛntsa] SF pestilence; (*fetore*) stench

'pesto, -a AG: **c'è buio ~** it's pitch dark ▶ SM (*Cuc*) sauce made with basil, garlic, cheese and oil; **occhio ~** black eye

'petalo SM (*Bot*) petal

pe'tardo SM firecracker, banger (*BRIT*)

petizi'one [petit'tsjone] SF petition; **fare una ~ a** to petition

'peto SM (!) fart (!)

petro'dollaro SM petrodollar

petrol'chimica [petrol'kimika] SF petrochemical industry

petroli'era SF (*nave*) oil tanker

petroli'ere SM (*industriale*) oilman; (*tecnico*) worker in the oil industry

petroli'ero, -a AG oil *cpd*

petro'lifero, -a AG oil *cpd*

pe'trolio SM oil, petroleum; (*per lampada, fornello*) paraffin (*BRIT*), kerosene (*US*); **lume a ~** oil *o* paraffin *o* kerosene lamp; **~ grezzo** crude oil

pettego'lare /72/ VI to gossip

pettego'lezzo [pettego'leddzo] SM gossip *no pl*; **fare pettegolezzi** to gossip

pet'tegolo, -a AG gossipy ▶ SM/F gossip

petti'nare /72/ VT to comb (the hair of); **pettinarsi** VPR to comb one's hair

pettina'tura SF (*acconciatura*) hairstyle

'pettine SM comb; (*Zool*) scallop

petti'rosso SM robin

'petto SM chest; (*seno*) breast, bust; (*Cuc: di carne bovina*) brisket; (: *di pollo ecc*) breast; **prendere qn/qc di ~** to face up to sb/sth; **a doppio ~** (*abito*) double-breasted

petto'rale AG pectoral

petto'rina SF (*di grembiule*) bib

petto'ruto, -a AG broad-chested; full-breasted

petu'lante AG insolent

pe'tunia SF petunia

'pezza ['pɛttsa] SF piece of cloth; (*toppa*) patch; (*cencio*) rag, cloth; (*Amm*): **~ d'appoggio** *o* **giustificativa** voucher; **trattare qn come una ~ da piedi** to treat sb like a doormat

pez'zato, -a [pet'tsato] AG piebald

pez'zente [pet'tsɛnte] SMF beggar

'pezzo ['pɛttso] SM (*gen*) piece; (*brandello, frammento*) piece, bit; (*di macchina, arnese ecc*) part; (*Stampa*) article; **aspettare un ~** to wait quite a while *o* some time; **in** *o* **a pezzi** in pieces; **andare a pezzi** to break into pieces; **essere a pezzi** (*oggetto*) to be in pieces *o* bits; (*fig: persona*) to be shattered; **un bel ~ d'uomo** a fine figure of a man; **abito a due pezzi** two-piece suit; **essere tutto d'un ~**

(*fig*) to be a man (*o woman*) of integrity; **~ di cronaca** (*Stampa*) report; **~ grosso** (*fig*) bigwig; **~ di ricambio** spare part

PG SIGLA = **Perugia**

P.G. ABBR = **procuratore generale**

pH [pi'akka] SM INV (*Chim*) pH

PI SIGLA = **Pisa**

P.I. ABBR = **Pubblica Istruzione**

pi'accio *etc* ['pjattʃo] VB *vedi* **piacere**

pia'cente [pja'tʃɛnte] AG attractive, pleasant

pia'cere [pja'tʃere] /74/ VI to please ▶ SM pleasure; (*favore*) favour (*BRIT*), favor (*US*); **una ragazza che piace** (*piacevole*) a likeable girl; (*attraente*) an attractive girl; **mi piace** I like it; **quei ragazzi non mi piacciono** I don't like those boys; **gli piacerebbe andare al cinema** he would like to go to the cinema; **il suo discorso è piaciuto molto** his speech was well received; **"~!"** (*nelle presentazioni*) "pleased to meet you!"; **~ (di conoscerla)** nice to meet you; **con ~** certainly, with pleasure; **per ~** please; **fare un ~ a qn** to do sb a favour; **mi fa ~ per lui** I am pleased for him; **mi farebbe ~ rivederlo** I would like to see him again

pia'cevole [pja'tʃevole] AG pleasant, agreeable

piaci'mento [pjatʃi'mento] SM: **a ~** (*a volontà*) as much as one likes, at will; **lo farà a suo ~** he'll do it when it suits him

piaci'uto, -a [pja'tʃuto] PP *di* **piacere**

pi'acqui *etc* VB *vedi* **piacere**

pi'aga, -ghe SF (*lesione*) sore; (*ferita: anche fig*) wound; (*fig: flagello*) scourge, curse; (: *persona*) pest, nuisance

piagnis'teo [pjaɲɲis'tɛo] SM whining, whimpering

piagnuco'lare [pjaɲɲuko'lare] /72/ VI to whimper

piagnuco'lio, -ii [pjaɲɲuko'lio] SM whimpering

piagnuco'loso, -a [pjaɲɲuko'loso] AG whiny, whimpering, moaning

pi'alla SF (*arnese*) plane

pial'lare /72/ VT to plane

pialla'trice [pjalla'tritʃe] SF planing machine

pi'ana SF stretch of level ground; (*più esteso*) plain

pianeggi'ante [pjaned'dʒante] AG flat, level

piane'rottolo SM landing

pia'neta SM (*Astr*) planet

pi'angere [pjan'dʒere] /75/ VI to cry, weep; (*occhi*) to water ▶ VT to cry, weep; (*lamentare*) to bewail, lament; **~ la morte di qn** to mourn sb's death

pianifi'care /20/ VT to plan

pianificazi'one [pjanifikat'tsjone] SF (*Econ*) planning; **~ aziendale** corporate planning

pia'nista, -i, -e SM/F pianist

pi'ano, -a AG (*piatto*) flat, level; (*Mat*) plane; (*facile*) straightforward, simple; (*chiaro*) clear, plain ▶ AV (*adagio*) slowly; (*a bassa voce*) softly; (*con cautela*) slowly, carefully ▶ SM (*Mat*) plane; (*Geo*) plain; (*livello*) level, plane; (*di edificio*) floor; (*programma*) plan; (*Mus*) piano; **pian ~** very slowly; (*poco a poco*) little by little; **una casa di 3 piani** a 3-storey (*BRIT*) o 3-storied (*US*) house; **al ~ di sopra/di sotto** on the floor above/below; **all'ultimo ~** on the top floor; **al ~ terra** on the ground floor; **in primo/secondo ~** (*Fot, Cine ecc*) in the foreground/background; **fare un primo ~** (*Fot, Cine*) to take a close-up; **di primo ~** (*fig*) prominent, high-ranking; **un fattore di secondo ~** a secondary o minor factor; **passare in secondo ~** to become less important; **mettere tutto sullo stesso ~** to lump everything together, give equal importance to everything; **tutto secondo i piani** all according to plan; **~ di lavoro** (*superficie*) worktop; (*programma*) work plan; **~ regolatore** (*Urbanistica*) town-planning scheme; **~ stradale** road surface

piano'forte SM piano, pianoforte

piano'terra SM INV = **piano terra**

pi'ansi *etc* VB *vedi* **piangere**

pi'anta SF (*Bot*) plant; (*Anat: anche:* **pianta del piede**) sole (of the foot); (*grafico*) plan; (*cartina topografica*) map; **ufficio a ~ aperta** open-plan office; **in ~ stabile** on the permanent staff; **~ stradale** street map, street plan

piantagi'one [pjanta'dʒone] SF plantation

pianta'grane SM INV/F INV troublemaker

pian'tare /72/ VT to plant; (*conficcare*) to drive o hammer in; (*tenda*) to put up, pitch; (*fig: lasciare*) to leave, desert; **piantarsi** VPR: **piantarsi davanti a qn** to plant o.s. in front of sb; **~ qn in asso** to leave sb in the lurch; **~ grane** (*fig*) to cause trouble; **piantala!** (*col*) cut it out!

pian'tato, -a AG: **ben ~** (*persona*) well-built

pianta'tore SM planter

pianter'reno SM ground floor

pian'tina SF (*di edificio, città*) (small) map; (*Bot*) (small) plant

pi'anto, -a PP *di* **piangere** ▶ SM tears *pl*, crying

pianto'nare /72/ VT to guard, watch over

pian'tone SM (*vigilante*) sentry, guard; (*soldato*) orderly; (*Aut*) steering column

pia'nura SF plain

pi'astra SF plate; (*di pietra*) slab; (*di fornello*) hotplate; **panino alla ~** ≈ toasted sandwich; **~ di registrazione** tape deck

pias'trella SF tile

piastrel'lare /72/ VT to tile

pias'trina SF (*Anat*) platelet; (*Mil*) identity disc (*BRIT*) o tag (*US*)

piatta'forma SF (*anche fig*) platform; **~ continentale** (*Geo*) continental shelf; **~ girevole** (*Tecn*) turntable; **~ di lancio** (*Mil*) launching pad o platform; **~ rivendicativa** *document prepared by the unions in an industry, setting out their claims*

piat'tello SM clay pigeon; **tiro al ~** clay-pigeon shooting (*BRIT*), trapshooting

piat'tino SM (*di tazza*) saucer

pi'atto, -a AG flat; (*fig: scialbo*) dull ▶ SM (*recipiente, vivanda*) dish; (*portata*) course; (*parte piana*) flat (part); **piatti** SMPL (*Mus*) cymbals; **un ~ di minestra** a plate of soup; **~ fondo** soup dish; **~ forte** main course; **~ del giorno** dish of the day, plat du jour; **~ del giradischi** turntable; **piatti già pronti** (*Cuc*) ready-cooked dishes; **~ piano** dinner plate

pi'azza ['pjattsa] SF square; (*Comm*) market; (*letto, lenzuolo*): **a una ~** single; **a due piazze** double; **far ~ pulita** to make a clean sweep; **mettere in ~** (*fig: rendere pubblico*) to make public; **scendere in ~** (*fig*) to take to the streets, demonstrate; **~ d'armi** (*Mil*) parade ground

piazza'forte [pjattsa'forte] (*pl* **piazzeforti**) SF (*Mil*) stronghold

piaz'zale [pjat'tsale] SM (large) square

piazza'mento [pjattsa'mento] SM (*Sport*) place, placing

piaz'zare [pjat'tsare] /72/ VT to place; (*Comm*) to market, sell; **piazzarsi** VPR (*Sport*) to be placed; **piazzarsi bene** to finish with the leaders o in a good position

piaz'zista, -i [pjat'tsista] SM (*Comm*) commercial traveller

piaz'zola [pjat'tsɔla] SF (*Aut*) lay-by (*BRIT*), (roadside) stopping place; (*di tenda*) pitch

'picca, -che SF pike; **picche** SFPL (*Carte*) spades; **rispondere picche a qn** (*fig*) to give sb a flat refusal

pic'cante AG hot, pungent; (*fig*) racy; biting

pic'carsi /20/ VPR: **~ di fare** to pride o.s. on one's ability to do; **~ per qc** to take offence (*BRIT*) o offense (*US*) at sth

picchet'taggio [pikket'taddʒo] SM picketing

picchet'tare [pikket'tare] /72/ VT to picket

pic'chetto [pik'ketto] SM (*Mil, di scioperanti*) picket; (*di tenda*) peg

picchi'are [pik'kjare] /19/ VT (*persona: colpire*) to hit, strike; (: *prendere a botte*) to beat (up); (*battere*) to beat; (*sbattere*) to bang ▶ VI (*bussare*) to knock; (: *con forza*) to bang; (*colpire*) to hit, strike; (*sole*) to beat down

picchi'ata [pik'kjata] SF knock; bang; blow; (*percosse*) beating, thrashing; (*Aer*) dive; **scendere in ~** to (nose-)dive

picchiet'tare [pikkjet'tare] /72/ VT (*punteggiare*) to spot, dot; (*colpire*) to tap

'picchio ['pikkjo] SM woodpecker

pic'cino, -a [pit'tʃino] AG tiny, very small
picci'olo [pit'tʃolo] SM (Bot) stalk
piccio'naia [pittʃo'naja] SF pigeon-loft; (Teat): **la ~** the gods sg (BRIT), the gallery
picci'one [pit'tʃone] SM pigeon; **pigliare due piccioni con una fava** (fig) to kill two birds with one stone
'picco, -chi SM peak; **a ~** vertically; **colare a ~** (Naut, fig) to sink
picco'lezza [pikko'lettsa] SF (dimensione) smallness; (fig: grettezza) meanness, pettiness; (inezia) trifle
'piccolo, -a AG small; (oggetto, mano, di età: bambino) small, little; (dav sostantivo: di breve durata: viaggio) short; (fig) mean, petty ▶ SM/F child, little one ▶ SM: **nel mio ~** in my own small way; **piccoli** SMPL (di animale) young pl; **in ~** in miniature; **la piccola borghesia** the lower middle classes; (peg) the petty bourgeoisie
pic'cone SM pick(-axe)
pic'cozza [pik'kɔttsa] SF ice-axe
pic'nic SM INV picnic; **fare un ~** to have a picnic
pidies'sino, -a AG (Pol) of P.D.S ▶ SM/F member (o supporter) of P.D.S
pi'docchio [pi'dɔkkjo] SM louse
pidocchi'oso, -a [pidok'kjoso] AG (infestato) lousy; (fig: taccagno) mean, stingy, tight
pidu'ista, -i, -e AG P2 cpd (masonic lodge) ▶ SM member of the P2 masonic lodge
piè SM INV: **a ogni ~ sospinto** (fig) at every step; **saltare a ~ pari** (omettere) to skip; **a ~ di pagina** at the foot of the page; **note a ~ di pagina** footnotes
pi'ede SM foot; (di mobile) leg; **in piedi** standing; **a piedi** on foot; **a piedi nudi** barefoot; **su due piedi** (fig) at once; **mettere qc in piedi** (azienda ecc) to set sth up; **prendere ~** (fig) to gain ground, catch on; **puntare i piedi** (fig) to dig one's heels in; **sentirsi mancare la terra sotto i piedi** to feel lost; **non sta in piedi** (persona) he can't stand; (fig: scusa ecc) it doesn't hold water; **tenere in piedi** (persona) to keep on his (o her) feet; (fig: ditta ecc) to keep going; **a ~ libero** (Dir) on bail; **sul ~ di guerra** (Mil) ready for action; **~ di porco** crowbar
piedipi'atti SM INV (peg: poliziotto) cop
piedis'tallo, piedes'tallo SM pedestal
pi'ega, -ghe SF (piegatura, Geo) fold; (di gonna) pleat; (di pantaloni) crease; (grinza) wrinkle, crease; **prendere una brutta o cattiva ~** (fig: persona) to get into bad ways; (: situazione) to take a turn for the worse; **non fa una ~** (fig: ragionamento) it's faultless; **non ha fatto una ~** (fig: persona) he didn't bat an eye(lid) (BRIT) o an eye(lash) (US)

piega'mento SM folding; bending; **~ sulle gambe** (Ginnastica) kneebend
pie'gare /80/ VT to fold; (braccia, gambe, testa) to bend ▶ VI to bend; **piegarsi** VPR to bend; (fig) **piegarsi (a)** to yield (to), submit (to)
piega'tura SF folding no pl; bending no pl; fold bend
piegherò etc [pjege'rɔ] VB vedi **piegare**
pieghet'tare [pjeget'tare] /72/ VT to pleat
pie'ghevole [pje'gevole] AG pliable, flexible; (porta) folding; (fig) yielding, docile
Pie'monte SM: **il ~** Piedmont
piemon'tese AG, SMF Piedmontese
pi'ena SF vedi **pieno**
pie'nezza [pje'nettsa] SF fullness
pi'eno, -a AG full; (muro, mattone) solid ▶ SM (colmo) height, peak; (carico) full load ▶ SF (di fiume) flood, spate; (gran folla) crowd, throng; **~ di** full of; **a piene mani** abundantly; **a tempo ~** full-time; **a pieni voti** (eleggere) unanimously; **laurearsi a pieni voti** to graduate with full marks; **in ~ giorno** in broad daylight; **in ~ inverno** in the depths of winter; **in piena notte** in the middle of the night; **in piena stagione** at the height of the season; **in ~** (completamente: sbagliare) completely; (colpire, centrare) bang o right in the middle; **avere pieni poteri** to have full powers; **nel ~ possesso delle sue facoltà** in full possession of his faculties; **fare il ~ (di benzina)** to fill up (with petrol)
pie'none SM: **c'era il ~ al cinema/al teatro** the cinema/the theatre was packed
'piercing ['pirsing] SM: **farsi il ~ all'ombelico** to have one's navel pierced
pietà SF pity; (Rel) piety; **senza ~** (agire) ruthlessly; (persona) pitiless, ruthless; **avere ~ di** (compassione) to pity, feel sorry for; (misericordia) to have pity o mercy on; **far ~** to arouse pity; (peg) to be terrible
pie'tanza [pje'tantsa] SF dish, course
pie'toso, -a AG (compassionevole) pitying, compassionate; (che desta pietà) pitiful
pi'etra SF stone; **mettiamoci una ~ sopra** (fig) let bygones be bygones; **~ preziosa** precious stone, gem; **~ dello scandalo** (fig) cause of scandal
pie'traia SF (terreno) stony ground
pietrifi'care /20/ VT to petrify; (fig) to transfix, paralyze
piet'rina SF (per accendino) flint
pie'trisco, -schi SM crushed stone, road metal
pi'eve SF parish church
'piffero SM (Mus) pipe
pigi'ama [pi'dʒama] SM pyjamas pl
'pigia 'pigia ['pidʒa'pidʒa] SM crowd, press
pigi'are [pi'dʒare] /62/ VT to press
pigia'trice [pidʒa'tritʃe] SF (macchina) wine press

pigi'one [pi'dʒone] SF rent

pigli'are [piʎ'ʎare] **/27/** VT to take, grab; (*afferrare*) to catch

'piglio ['piʎʎo] SM look, expression

pig'mento SM pigment

pig'meo, -a SM/F pygmy

'pigna ['piɲɲa] SF pine cone

pignole'ria [piɲɲole'ria] SF fastidiousness, fussiness

pi'gnolo, -a [piɲ'ɲɔlo] AG pernickety

pigno'rare [piɲɲo'rare] **/72/** VT (*Dir*) to distrain

pigo'lare **/72/** VI to cheep, chirp

pigo'lio SM cheeping, chirping

pigra'mente AV lazily

pi'grizia [pi'grittsja] SF laziness

'pigro, -a AG lazy; (*fig: ottuso*) slow, dull

PIL SIGLA M (= *prodotto interno lordo*) GDP

'pila SF (*catasta, di ponte*) pile; (*Elettr*) battery; (*col: torcia*) torch (*BRIT*), flashlight; **a ~, a pile** battery-operated

pi'lastro SM pillar

'pile ['pail] SM INV fleece

'pillola SF pill; **prendere la ~** (*contraccettivo*) to be on the pill; **~ del giorno dopo** morning-after pill

pi'lone SM (*di ponte*) pier; (*di linea elettrica*) pylon

pi'lota, -i, -e SM/F pilot; (*Aut*) driver ▶ AG INV pilot *cpd*; **~ automatico** automatic pilot

pilo'taggio [pilo'taddʒo] SM: **cabina di ~** flight deck

pilo'tare **/72/** VT to pilot; to drive

piluc'care **/20/** VT to nibble at

pi'mento SM pimento, allspice

pim'pante AG lively, full of beans

pinaco'teca, -che SF art gallery

pi'neta SF pinewood

ping-'pong [piŋ'pɔŋ] SM table tennis

'pingue AG fat, corpulent

pingu'edine SF corpulence

pingu'ino SM (*Zool*) penguin

'pinna SF fin; (*di cetaceo, per nuotare*) flipper

pin'nacolo SM pinnacle

'pino SM pine (tree)

pi'nolo SM pine kernel

'pinta SF pint

'pinza ['pintsa] SF pliers *pl*; (*Med*) forceps *pl*; (*Zool*) pincer

pin'zette [pin'tsette] SFPL tweezers

'pio, -a, -'pii, -'pie AG pious; (*opere, istituzione*) charitable, charity *cpd*

piogge'rella [pjoddʒe'rɛlla] SF drizzle

pi'oggia, -ge ['pjɔddʒa] SF rain; (*fig: di regali, fiori*) shower; (*di insulti*) hail; **sotto la ~** in the rain; **~ acida** acid rain

pi'olo SM peg; (*di scala*) rung

piom'bare **/72/** VI to fall heavily; (*gettarsi con impeto*): **~ su** to fall upon, assail ▶ VT (*dente*) to fill

piomba'tura SF (*di dente*) filling

piom'bino SM (*sigillo*) (lead) seal; (*del filo a piombo*) plummet; (*Pesca*) sinker

pi'ombo SM (*Chim*) lead; (*sigillo*) (lead) seal; (*proiettile*) (lead) shot; **a ~** (*cadere*) straight down; (*muro ecc*) plumb; **andare con i piedi di ~** (*fig*) to tread carefully; **senza ~** (*benzina*) unleaded; **anni di ~** (*fig*) era of terrorist outrages

pioni'ere, -a SM/F pioneer

pi'oppo SM poplar

pio'vano, -a AG: **acqua piovana** rainwater

pi'overe **/76/** VB IMPERS to rain ▶ VI (*fig: scendere dall'alto*) to rain down; (*affluire in gran numero*): **~ in** to pour into; **non ci piove sopra** (*fig*) there's no doubt about it

pioviggi'nare [pjoviddʒi'nare] **/72/** VB IMPERS to drizzle

piovosità SF rainfall

pio'voso, -a AG rainy

pi'ovra SF octopus

pi'ovve *etc* VB *vedi* **piovere**

'pipa SF pipe

pipì SF (*col*): **fare ~** to have a wee (wee)

pipis'trello SM (*Zool*) bat

pi'ramide SF pyramid

pi'ranha SM INV piranha

pi'rata, -i SM pirate; **~ informatico** hacker; **~ della strada** hit-and-run driver

Pire'nei SMPL: **i ~** the Pyrenees

pi'retro SM pyrethrum

'pirico, -a, -ci, -che AG: **polvere pirica** gunpowder

pi'rite SF pyrite

piro'etta SF pirouette

pi'rofilo, -a AG heat-resistant ▶ SF heat-resistant glass; (*tegame*) heat-resistant dish

pi'roga, -ghe SF dug-out canoe

pi'romane SMF pyromaniac; arsonist

pi'roscafo SM steamer, steamship

'Pisa SF Pisa

pi'sano, -a AG Pisan

pisci'are [piʃʃare] **/14/** VI (*col*) to piss (!), pee (!)

pi'scina [piʃʃina] SF (swimming) pool

pi'sello SM pea

piso'lino SM nap; **fare un ~** to have a nap

'pista SF (*traccia*) track, trail; (*di stadio*) track; (*di pattinaggio*) rink; (*da sci*) run; (*Aer*) runway; (*di circo*) ring; **~ da ballo** dance floor; **~ ciclabile** cycle lane; **~ di lancio** launch(ing) pad; **~ di rullaggio** (*Aer*) taxiway; **~ di volo** (*Aer*) runway

pis'tacchio [pis'takkjo] SM pistachio (tree); pistachio (nut)

pis'tillo SM (*Bot*) pistil

pis'tola SF pistol, gun; **~ a spruzzo** spray gun; **~ a tamburo** revolver

pis'tone SM piston

pi'tocco, -chi SM skinflint, miser

pi'tone SM python

P

'**pittima** SF (*fig*) bore
pit'tore, -'trice SM/F painter
pitto'resco, -a, -schi, -sche AG picturesque
pit'torico, -a, -ci, -che AG of painting,
  pictorial
pit'tura SF painting; ~ **fresca** wet paint
pittu'rare /72/ VT to paint

[PAROLA CHIAVE]

più AV 1 (*in maggiore quantità*) more; **più del
  solito** more than usual; **in più, di più** more;
  ne voglio di più I want some more; **ci sono
  3 persone in** *o* **di più** there are 3 more *o* extra
  people; **costa di più** it's more expensive;
  una volta di più once more; **più o meno**
  more or less; **né più né meno** no more, no
  less; **per di più** (*inoltre*) what's more,
  moreover; **è sempre più difficile** it is
  getting more and more difficult; **chi più chi
  meno hanno tutti contribuito** everybody
  made a contribution of some sort; **più
  dormo e più dormirei** the more I sleep the
  more I want to sleep

2 (*comparativo*) more; (*: se monosillabo, spesso*) +
  ...er; **più ... di/che** more ... than; **più
  intelligente di lui** more intelligent than
  him; **più furbo di te** smarter than you; **più
  tardi di ...** later than ...; **lavoro più di te/di
  Paola** I work harder than you/than Paola; **è
  più intelligente che ricco** he's more
  intelligent than rich; **è più fortunato che
  bravo** he is lucky rather than skilled; **più di
  quanto pensassi** more than I thought; **più
  che altro** mainly; **più che mai** more than
  ever

3 (*superlativo*) most; (*: se monosillabico, spesso*) +
  ...est; **il più grande/intelligente** the
  biggest/most intelligent; **è quello che
  compro più spesso** that's the one I buy
  most often; **al più presto** as soon as
  possible; **al più tardi** at the latest

4 (*negazione*): **non ... più** no more, no longer;
  non ho più soldi I've got no more money,
  I don't have any more money; **non lavoro
  più** I'm no longer working, I don't work any
  more; **non ce n'è più** there isn't any left;
  non c'è più nessuno there's no one left;
  non c'è più niente da fare there's nothing
  more to be done; **a più non posso** (*gridare*)
  at the top of one's voice; (*correre*) as fast as
  one can

5 (*Mat*) plus; **4 più 5 fa 9** 4 plus 5 equals 9;
  più 5 gradi 5 degrees above freezing, plus 5;
  6 più (*a scuola*) just above a pass

▶ PREP plus; **500 più le spese** 500 plus
  expenses; **siamo in quattro più il nonno**
  there are four of us plus grandpa

▶ AG INV 1: **più ... (di)** more ... (than);
  più denaro/tempo more money/time;

più persone di quante ci aspettassimo
  more people than we expected

2 (*numerosi, diversi*) several; **l'aspettai per più
  giorni** I waited for it for several days

▶ SM 1 (*la maggior parte*): **il più è fatto** most of
  it is done; **il più delle volte** more often than
  not, generally; **parlare del più e del meno**
  to talk about this and that

2 (*Mat*) plus (sign)

3: **i più** the majority

piuccheper'fetto [pjukkeper'fɛtto] SM (*Ling*)
  pluperfect, past perfect
pi'uma SF feather; **piume** SFPL down *sg*;
  (*piumaggio*) plumage *sg*, feathers
piu'maggio [pju'maddʒo] SM plumage,
  feathers *pl*
piu'mino SM (eider)down; (*per letto*)
  eiderdown; (*: tipo danese*) duvet, continental
  quilt; (*giacca*) quilted jacket (*with goose-feather
  padding*); (*per cipria*) powder puff; (*per
  spolverare*) feather duster
piut'tosto AV rather; ~ **che** (*anziché*) rather
  than
'**piva** SF: **con le pive nel sacco** (*fig*) empty-
  handed
pi'vello, -a SM/F greenhorn
'**pizza** ['pittsa] SF (*Cuc*) pizza; (*Cine*) reel
pizze'ria [pittse'ria] SF *place where pizzas are
  made, sold or eaten*
pizzi'cagnolo, -a [pittsi'kaɲɲolo] SM/F
  specialist grocer
pizzi'care [pittsi'kare] /20/ VT (*stringere*) to
  nip, pinch; (*pungere*) to sting; to bite; (*Mus*) to
  pluck ▶ VI (*prudere*) to itch, be itchy; (*cibo*) to
  be hot *o* spicy
pizziche'ria [pittsike'ria] SF delicatessen
  (shop)
'**pizzico, -chi** ['pittsiko] SM (*pizzicotto*) pinch,
  nip; (*piccola quantità*) pinch, dash; (*d'insetto*)
  sting; bite
pizzi'cotto [pittsi'kotto] SM pinch, nip
'**pizzo** ['pittso] SM (*merletto*) lace; (*barbetta*)
  goatee beard; (*tangente*) protection money
pla'care /20/ VT to placate, soothe; **placarsi**
  VPR to calm down
'**placca, -che** SF plate; (*con iscrizione*) plaque;
  (*anche*: **placca dentaria**) (dental) plaque
plac'care /20/ VT to plate; **placcato in oro/
  argento** gold-/silver-plated
pla'centa [pla'tʃenta] SF placenta
placidità [platʃidi'ta] SF calm, peacefulness
'**placido, -a** ['platʃido] AG placid, calm
plafoni'era SF ceiling light
plagi'are [pla'dʒare] /62/ VT (*copiare*) to
  plagiarize; (*Dir: influenzare*) to coerce
'**plagio** ['pladʒo] SM plagiarism; (*Dir*) duress
plaid [plɛd] SM INV (travelling) rug (*BRIT*), lap
  robe (*US*)

pla'nare /**72**/ vi (Aer) to glide

'plancia, -ce ['plantʃa] sf (Naut) bridge; (Aut: cruscotto) dashboard

'plancton sm inv plankton

plane'tario, -a ag planetary ▶ sm (locale) planetarium

planis'fero sm planisphere

plan'tare sm arch support

'plasma sm plasma

plas'mare /**72**/ vt to mould (Brit), mold (US), shape

'plastico, -a, -ci, -che ag plastic ▶ sm (rappresentazione) relief model; (esplosivo): **bomba al ~** plastic bomb ▶ sf (arte) plastic arts pl; (Med) plastic surgery; (sostanza) plastic; **plastica facciale** face lift; **in materiale ~** plastic

plasti'lina® sf plasticine®

'platano sm plane tree

pla'tea sf (Teat) stalls pl (Brit), orchestra (US)

plate'ale ag (gesto, atteggiamento) theatrical

plateal'mente av theatrically

'platino sm platinum

pla'tonico, -a, -ci, -che ag platonic

plau'dire /**45**/ vi: **~ a** to applaud

plau'sibile ag plausible

'plauso sm (fig) approval

'playback ['plei bæk] sm: **cantare in ~** to mime

'playboy ['pleibɔi] sm inv playboy

'playmaker ['pleimeikəʳ] sm inv/f inv (Sport) playmaker

'play-off ['pleiɔf] sm inv (Sport) play-off

ple'baglia [ple'baʎʎa] sf (peg) rabble, mob

'plebe sf common people

ple'beo, -a ag plebeian; (volgare) coarse, common

plebi'scito [plebiʃ'ʃito] sm plebiscite

ple'nario, -a ag plenary

pleni'lunio sm full moon

plenipotenzi'ario, -a [plenipoten'tsjarjo] ag plenipotentiary

'plenum sm inv plenum

'plettro sm plectrum

'pleura sf (Anat) pleura

pleu'rite sf pleurisy

P.L.I. sigla m (= Partito Liberale Italiano) former political party

'plico, -chi sm (pacco) parcel; **in ~ a parte** (Comm) under separate cover

plissé [pli'se] ag inv plissé cpd ▶ sm inv (anche: **tessuto plissé**) plissé

plisset'tato, -a ag plissé cpd

plo'tone sm (Mil) platoon; **~ d'esecuzione** firing squad

plug-in [pla'gin] ag inv, sm inv (Inform) plug-in

'plumbeo, -a ag leaden

plu'rale ag, sm plural

plura'lismo sm pluralism

pluralità sf plurality; (maggioranza) majority

plusva'lenza [pluzva'lɛntsa] sf capital gain

plusva'lore sm (Econ) surplus

plu'tonio sm plutonium

pluvi'ale ag rain cpd

pluvi'ometro sm rain gauge

pm abbr = **peso molecolare**

P.M. abbr (Pol) = **Pubblico Ministero**; (= Polizia Militare) MP (= Military Police)

PMI sigla fpl (= Piccole e Medie Imprese) SME (= Small and Medium-sized Enterprises)

PN sigla = **Pordenone**

pneu'matico, -a, -ci, -che ag inflatable; (Tecn) pneumatic ▶ sm (Aut) tyre (Brit), tire (US)

PNL sigla m = **prodotto nazionale lordo**

PO sigla = **Prato**

Po sm: **il Po** the Po

po' av, sm vedi **poco**

P.O. abbr = **posta ordinaria**

po'chezza [po'kettsa] sf insufficiency, shortage; (fig: meschinità) meanness, smallness

---

(PAROLA CHIAVE)

'poco, -a, -chi, -che ag (quantità) little, not much; (numero) few, not many; **poco pane/denaro/spazio** little o not much bread/money/space; **con poca spesa** without spending much; **a poco prezzo** at a low price, cheap; **poco (tempo) fa** a short time ago; **poche persone/idee** few o not many people/ideas; **è un tipo di poche parole** he's a man of few words; **ci vediamo tra poco** (sottinteso: tempo) see you soon

▶ av **1** (in piccola quantità) little, not much **2** (numero limitato) few, not many; **guadagna poco** he doesn't earn much, he earns little **3** (con ag, av) (a) little, not very; **è poco più vecchia di lui** she's a little o slightly older than him; **è poco socievole** he's not very sociable; **sta poco bene** he isn't very well **4** (tempo): **poco dopo/prima** shortly afterwards/before; **il film dura poco** the film doesn't last very long; **ci vediamo molto poco** we don't see each other very often, we hardly ever see each other **5**: **un po'** a little, a bit; **è un po' corto** it's a little o a bit short; **arriverà fra un po'** he'll arrive shortly o in a little while **6**: **a dir poco** to say the least; **a poco a poco** little by little; **per poco non cadevo** I nearly fell; **è una cosa da poco** it's nothing, it's of no importance; **una persona da poco** a worthless person

▶ pron (a) little; **pochi, poche** pl (persone) few (people); (cose) few; **ci vediamo tra poco** see you soon; **pochi lo sanno** not many

people know it; **ci vuole tempo ed io ne ho poco** it takes time, and I haven't got much to spare
▶ SM **1** little; **vive del poco che ha** he lives on the little he has
2: **un po'** a little; **un po' di zucchero** a little sugar; **un bel po' di denaro** quite a lot of money; **un po' per ciascuno** a bit each

podcast ['pɔdkast] SM podcast
po'dere SM (*Agr*) farm
pode'roso, -a AG powerful
podestà SM INV (*nel fascismo*) podestà, mayor
'podio SM dais, platform; (*Mus*) podium
po'dismo SM (*Sport: marcia*) walking; (: *corsa*) running
po'dista, -i, -e SM/F walker; runner
po'ema, -i SM poem
poe'sia SF (*arte*) poetry; (*componimento*) poem
po'eta, -'essa SM/F poet (poetess)
poe'tare /**72**/ VI to write poetry
po'etico, -a, -ci, -che AG poetic(al)
poggi'are [pod'dʒare] /**62**/ VT to lean, rest; (*posare*) to lay, place
poggia'testa [poddʒa'tɛsta] SM INV (*Aut*) headrest
'poggio ['pɔddʒo] SM hillock, knoll
poggi'olo [pod'dʒɔlo] SM balcony
'poi AV then; (*alla fine*) finally, at last ▶ SM: **pensare al ~** to think of the future; **e ~** (*inoltre*) and besides; **questa ~ (è bella)!** (*ironico*) that's a good one!; **d'ora in ~** from now on; **da domani in ~** from tomorrow onwards
poi'ana SF buzzard
poiché [poi'ke] CONG since, as
pois [pwa] SM INV spot, (polka) dot; **a ~** spotted, polka-dot *cpd*
'poker SM poker
po'lacco, -a, -chi, -che AG Polish ▶ SM/F Pole
po'lare AG polar
polariz'zare [polarid'dzare] /**72**/ VT (*anche fig*) to polarize
'polca, -che SF polka
po'lemico, -a, -ci, -che AG polemical, controversial ▶ SF controversy; **fare polemiche** to be contentious
polemiz'zare [polemid'dzare] /**72**/ VI: **~ (su qc)** to argue (about sth)
po'lenta SF (*Cuc*) sort of thick porridge made with maize flour
polen'tone, -a SM/F slowcoach (*BRIT*), slowpoke (*US*)
pole'sano, -a AG of (*o* from) Polesine (*area between the Po and the Adige*)
POL'FER ABBR F = **Polizia Ferroviaria**
'poli... PREFISSO poly...
poliambula'torio SM (*Med*) health clinic
poli'clinico, -ci SM general hospital, polyclinic

poli'edro SM polyhedron
poli'estere SM polyester
poliga'mia SF polygamy
polig'lotta, -i, -e AG, SM/F polyglot
po'ligono SM polygon; **~ di tiro** rifle range
Poli'nesia SF: **la ~** Polynesia
polinesi'ano, -a AG, SM/F Polynesian
polio(mielite) SF polio(myelitis)
'polipo SM polyp
polisti'rolo SM polystyrene
poli'tecnico, -ci SM postgraduate technical college
po'litica, -che SF *vedi* **politico**
politica'mente AV politically; **~ corretto** politically correct
politi'cante SMF (*peg*) petty politician
politiciz'zare [polititʃid'dzare] /**72**/ VT to politicize
po'litico, -a, -ci, -che AG political ▶ SM/F politician ▶ SF politics *sg*; (*linea di condotta*) policy; **elezioni politiche** parliamentary (*BRIT*) *o* congressional (*US*) election(s); **uomo ~** politician; **darsi alla politica** to go into politics; **fare politica** (*militante*) to be a political activist; (*come professione*) to be in politics; **la politica del governo** the government's policies; **politica aziendale** company policy; **politica estera** foreign policy; **politica dei prezzi** prices policy; **politica dei redditi** incomes policy
poliva'lente AG multi-purpose
poli'zia [polit'tsia] SF police; **~ giudiziaria** ≈ Criminal Investigation Department (CID) (*BRIT*), Federal Bureau of Investigation (FBI) (*US*); **~ sanitaria/tributaria** health/tax inspectorate; **~ stradale** traffic police; **~ di stato** *see note*

> The remit of the *polizia di stato* is to maintain public order, to uphold the law, and to prevent and investigate crime. This is a civilian branch of the police force; male and female officers perform similar duties. The *polizia di stato* reports to the Minister of the Interior.

polizi'esco, -a, -schi, -sche [polit'tsjesko] AG police *cpd*; (*film, romanzo*) detective *cpd*
polizi'otto [polit'tsjɔtto] SM policeman; **cane ~** police dog; **donna ~** policewoman; **~ di quartiere** local police officer
'polizza ['pɔlittsa] SF (*Comm*) bill; **~ di assicurazione** insurance policy; **~ di carico** bill of lading
pol'laio SM henhouse
pollai'olo, -a SM/F poulterer (*BRIT*), poultryman
pol'lame SM poultry
pol'lastra SF pullet; (*fig: ragazza*) chick, wench
pol'lastro SM (*Zool*) cockerel

'**pollice** ['pɔllitʃe] sm thumb; (*unità di*) inch
'**polline** sm pollen
'**pollo** sm chicken; **far ridere i polli**
(*situazione, persona*) to be utterly ridiculous
polmo'nare ᴀɢ lung *cpd*, pulmonary
pol'mone sm lung; ~ **d'acciaio** (*Med*) iron
lung
polmo'nite sf pneumonia; ~ **atipica** SARS
'**Polo** sm (*Pol*) centre-right coalition
'**polo** sm (*Geo, Fisica*) pole; (*gioco*) polo ▶ sf ɪɴᴠ
(*maglia*) polo shirt; **il ~ sud/nord** the South/
North Pole
Po'lonia sf: **la ~** Poland
'**polpa** sf flesh, pulp; (*carne*) lean meat
pol'paccio [pol'pattʃo] sm (*Anat*) calf
polpas'trello sm fingertip
pol'petta sf (*Cuc*) meatball
polpet'tone sm (*Cuc*) meatloaf
'**polpo** sm octopus
pol'poso, -a ᴀɢ fleshy
pol'sino sm cuff
'**polso** sm (*Anat*) wrist; (*pulsazione*) pulse;
(*fig: forza*) drive, vigour (*Brit*), vigor (*US*);
avere ~ (*fig*) to be strong; **un uomo di ~**
a man of nerve
pol'tiglia [pol'tiʎʎa] sf (*composto*) mash,
mush; (*di fango e neve*) slush
pol'trire /55/ ᴠɪ to laze about
pol'trona sf armchair; (*Teat: posto*) seat in the
front stalls (*Brit*) o the orchestra (*US*)
poltron'cina [poltron'tʃina] sf (*Teat*) seat in
the back stalls (*Brit*) o the orchestra (*US*)
pol'trone ᴀɢ lazy, slothful
'**polvere** sf dust; (*sostanza ridotta minutissima*)
powder, dust; **caffè in ~** instant coffee;
latte in ~ dried o powdered milk; **sapone in**
~ soap powder; **~ d'oro** gold dust; **~ pirica** o
da sparo gunpowder; **polveri sottili**
particulates
polveri'era sf powder magazine
polve'rina sf (*gen, Med*) powder; (*gergo:
cocaina*) snow
polveriz'zare [polverid'dzare] **/72/** ᴠᴛ to
pulverize; (*nebulizzare*) to atomize; (*fig*) to
crush, pulverize; (*record*) to smash
polve'rone sm thick cloud of dust
polve'roso, -a ᴀɢ dusty
po'mata sf ointment, cream
po'mello sm knob
pomeridi'ano, -a ᴀɢ afternoon *cpd*; **nelle ore**
pomeridiane in the afternoon
pome'riggio [pome'riddʒo] sm afternoon;
nel primo/tardo ~ in the early/late
afternoon
'**pomice** ['pomitʃe] sf pumice
pomici'are [pomi'tʃare] **/14/** ᴠɪ (*col*) to neck
'**pomo** sm (*mela*) apple; (*ornamentale*) knob;
(*di sella*) pommel; **~ d'Adamo** (*Anat*) Adam's
apple

pomo'doro sm tomato; **pomodori pelati**
skinned tomatoes
'**pompa** sf pump; (*sfarzo*) pomp (and
ceremony); **~ antincendio** fire hose; **~ di**
benzina petrol (*Brit*) o gas (*US*) pump;
(*distributore*) filling o gas (*US*) station;
impresa di pompe funebri funeral parlour
sg (*Brit*), undertaker's *sg*, mortician's (*US*)
pom'pare /72/ ᴠᴛ to pump; (*trarre*) to pump
out; (*gonfiare d'aria*) to pump up
pompei'ano, -a ᴀɢ of (o from) Pompei
pom'pelmo sm grapefruit
pompi'ere sm fireman
pom'pon [pom'pɔn] sm ɪɴᴠ pompom,
pompon
pom'poso, -a ᴀɢ pompous
ponde'rare /72/ ᴠᴛ to ponder over, consider
carefully
ponde'roso, -a ᴀɢ (*anche fig*) weighty
po'nente sm west
'**pongo** ᴠʙ *vedi* **porre**
'**poni** ᴠʙ *vedi* **porre**
'**ponte** sm bridge; (*di nave*) deck; (*anche:* **ponte**
di comando) bridge; (*impalcatura*) scaffold;
vivere sotto i ponti to be a tramp; **fare il ~**
(*fig*) to take the extra day off (*between 2 public
holidays*); **governo ~** interim government;
~ aereo airlift; **~ di barche** (*Mil*) pontoon
bridge; **~ di coperta** (*Naut*) upper deck;
~ levatoio drawbridge; **~ radio** radio link;
~ sospeso suspension bridge
pon'tefice [pon'tefitʃe] sm (*Rel*) pontiff
ponti'cello [ponti'tʃello] sm (*di occhiali: Mus*)
bridge
pontifi'care /20/ ᴠɪ (*anche fig*) to pontificate
pontifi'cato sm pontificate
ponti'ficio, -a, -ci, -cie [ponti'fitʃo] ᴀɢ papal;
Stato P~ Papal State
pon'tile sm jetty
'**pony** ['pɔni] sm ɪɴᴠ pony
pool [puːl] sm ɪɴᴠ (*consorzio*) consortium;
(*organismo internazionale*) pool; (*di esperti,
ricercatori*) team; (*antimafia, antidroga*)
working party
pop [pɔp] ᴀɢ ɪɴᴠ pop *cpd*
'**popcorn** ['pɔpkɔːn] sm ɪɴᴠ popcorn
'**popeline** ['pɔpelin] sm poplin
popò sm ɪɴᴠ (*sedere*) botty
popo'lano, -a ᴀɢ popular, of the people
▶ sm/ғ man/woman of the people
popo'lare /72/ ᴀɢ popular; (*quartiere, clientela*)
working-class; (*Pol*) of P.P.I. ▶ sm/ғ (*Pol*)
member (o supporter) of P.P.I. ▶ ᴠᴛ (*rendere
abitato*) to populate; **popolarsi** ᴠᴘʀ to fill
with people, get crowded; **manifestazione**
~ mass demonstration; **repubblica ~**
people's republic
popolarità sf popularity
popolazi'one [popolat'tsjone] sf population

popolo SM people
popo'loso, -a AG densely populated
po'pone SM melon
poppa SF (di nave) stern; (col: mammella) breast; **a ~** aft, astern
pop'pante SMF unweaned infant; (fig) whippersnapper
pop'pare /72/ VT to suck
pop'pata SF (allattamento) feed
poppa'toio SM (feeding) bottle
popu'lista, -i, -e AG populist
por'caio SM (anche fig) pigsty
por'cata SF (libro, film ecc) load of rubbish; **fare una ~ a qn** to play a dirty trick on sb
porcel'lana [portʃel'lana] SF porcelain, china; (oggetto) piece of porcelain
porcel'lino, -a [portʃel'lino] SM/F piglet; **~ d'India** guinea pig
porche'ria [porke'ria] SF filth, muck; (fig: oscenità) obscenity; (: azione disonesta) dirty trick; (: cosa mal fatta) rubbish
por'chetta [por'ketta] SF roast sucking pig
por'cile [por'tʃile] SM pigsty
por'cino, -a [por'tʃino] AG of pigs, pork cpd ▶ SM (fungo) type of edible mushroom
porco, -ci SM pig; (carne) pork
porcos'pino SM porcupine
por'fido SM porphyry
porgere ['pɔrdʒere] /115/ VT to hand, give; (tendere) to hold out
porno AG INV porn, porno
pornogra'fia SF pornography
porno'grafico, -a, -ci, -che AG pornographic
poro SM pore
po'roso, -a AG porous
porpora SF purple
porre /77/ VT (mettere) to put; (collocare) to place; (posare) to lay (down), put (down); (fig: supporre): **poniamo (il caso) che ...** let's suppose that ...; **porsi** VPR (mettersi): **porsi a sedere/in cammino** to sit down/, set off; **~ le basi di** (fig) to lay the foundations of, establish; **~ una domanda a qn** to ask sb a question, put a question to sb; **~ la propria fiducia in** to place one's trust in sb; **~ fine o termine a qc** to put an end o a stop to sth; **posto che ...** supposing that ..., on the assumption that ...; **porsi in salvo** to save o.s.
porro SM (Bot) leek; (Med) wart
porsi etc VB vedi **porgere; porsi**
porta SF door; (Sport) goal; (Inform) port; **porte** SFPL (di città) gates; **mettere qn alla ~** to throw sb out; **sbattere o chiudere la ~ in faccia a qn** (anche fig) to slam the door in sb's face; **trovare tutte le porte chiuse** (fig) to find the way barred; **a porte chiuse** (Dir) in camera; **l'inverno è alle porte** (fig) winter is upon us; **vendita ~ a ~** door-to-door selling; **~ di servizio** tradesmen's entrance; **~ di sicurezza** emergency exit; **~ stagna** watertight door

portaba'gagli [portaba'gaʎʎi] SM INV (facchino) porter; (Aut, Ferr) luggage rack
portabandi'era SM INV standard bearer
porta'borse SM INV (peg) lackey
portabot'tiglie [portabot'tiʎʎe] SM INV bottle rack
porta-'CD [portatʃi'di] SM INV (mobile) CD rack; (astuccio) CD holder
porta'cenere [porta'tʃenere] SM INV ashtray
portachi'avi [porta'kjavi] SM INV keyring
porta'cipria [porta'tʃiprja] SM INV powder compact
porta'erei SF INV (nave) aircraft carrier ▶ SM INV (aereo) aircraft transporter
portafi'nestra (pl **portefinestre**) SF French window
porta'foglio [porta'fɔʎʎo] SM (busta) wallet; (cartella) briefcase; (Pol, Borsa) portfolio; **~ titoli** investment portfolio
portafor'tuna SM INV lucky charm; mascot
portagi'oie [porta'dʒoje], **portagioi'elli** [portadʒo'jɛlli] SM INV jewellery (BRIT) o jewelry (US) box
por'tale SM (di chiesa, Inform) portal
porta'lettere SM INV/F INV postman/woman (BRIT), mailman/woman (US)
porta'mento SM carriage, bearing
portamo'nete SM INV purse
por'tante AG (muro ecc) supporting, load-bearing
portan'tina SF sedan chair; (per ammalati) stretcher
portaog'getti [portaod'dʒetti] AG INV: **vano ~** (in macchina) glove compartment
portaom'brelli SM INV umbrella stand
porta'pacchi [porta'pakki] SM INV (di moto, bicicletta) luggage rack
porta'penne [porta'penne] SM INV pen holder; (astuccio) pencil case
por'tare /72/ VT (sostenere, sorreggere: peso, bambino, pacco) to carry; (indossare: abito, occhiali) to wear; (: capelli lunghi) to have; (avere: nome, titolo) to have, bear; (recare): **~ qc a qn** to take (o bring) sth to sb; (fig: sentimenti) to bear; **portarsi** VPR (recarsi) to go; **~ avanti** (discorso, idea) to pursue; **~ via** to take away; (rubare) to take; **~ i bambini a spasso** to take the children for a walk; **~ fortuna** to bring good luck; **~ qc alla bocca** to lift o put sth to one's lips; **porta bene i suoi anni** he's wearing well; **dove porta questa strada?** where does this road lead?, where does this road take you?; **il documento porta la tua firma** the document has o bears your signature; **non gli porto rancore** I don't bear him a grudge; **la polizia si è portata**

sul luogo del disastro the police went to the scene of the disaster

portarit'ratti SM INV photo(graph) frame

portari'viste SM INV magazine rack

portasa'pone SM INV soap dish

portasiga'rette SM INV cigarette case

portas'pilli SM INV pincushion

por'tata SF (*vivanda*) course; (*Aut*) carrying (o loading) capacity; (*di arma*) range; (*volume d'acqua*) (rate of) flow; (*fig: limite*) scope, capability; (: *importanza*) impact, import; **alla ~ di tutti** (*conoscenza*) within everybody's capabilities; (*prezzo*) within everybody's means; **a/fuori ~ (di)** within/ out of reach (of); **a ~ di mano** within (arm's) reach; **di grande ~** of great importance

por'tatile AG portable

por'tato, -a AG (*incline*): **~ a** inclined o apt to

porta'tore, -'trice SM/F (*anche Comm*) bearer; (*Med*) carrier; **pagabile al ~** payable to the bearer; **~ di handicap** disabled person

portatovagli'olo [portatovaʎ'ʎɔlo] SM napkin ring

portau'ovo SM INV eggcup

porta'voce [porta'votʃe] SM O F INV spokesman/woman

por'tello SM (*di portone*) door; (*Naut*) hatch

portel'lone SM (*Naut, Aer*) hold door

por'tento SM wonder, marvel

porten'toso, -a AG wonderful, marvellous (*BRIT*), marvelous (*US*)

porti'cato SM portico

'portico, -ci SM portico; (*riparo*) lean-to

porti'era SF (*Aut*) door

porti'ere SM (*portinaio*) concierge, caretaker; (*di hotel*) porter; (*nel calcio*) goalkeeper

porti'naio, -a SM/F concierge, caretaker

portine'ria SF caretaker's lodge

'porto, -a PP di **porgere** ▶ SM (*Naut*) harbour (*BRIT*), harbor (*US*), port; (*spesa di trasporto*) carriage ▶ SM INV port (wine); **andare** o **giungere in ~** (*fig*) to come to a successful conclusion; **condurre qc in ~** to bring sth to a successful conclusion; **~ d'armi** gun licence (*BRIT*) o license (*US*); **~ fluviale** river port; **~ franco** free port; **~ marittimo** seaport; **~ militare** naval base; **~ pagato** carriage paid, post free o paid; **~ di scalo** port of call

Porto'gallo SM: **il ~** Portugal

porto'ghese [porto'geze] AG, SMF, SM Portuguese *inv*

por'tone SM main entrance, main door

portori'cano, -a AG, SM/F Puerto Rican

Porto'rico SF Puerto Rico

portu'ale AG harbour *cpd* (*BRIT*), harbor *cpd* (*US*), port *cpd* ▶ SM dock worker

porzi'one [por'tsjone] SF portion, share; (*di cibo*) portion, helping

'posa SF (*Fot*) exposure; (*atteggiamento, di modello*) pose; (*riposo*): **lavorare senza ~** to work without a break; **mettersi in ~** to pose; **teatro di ~** photographic studio

posa'cenere [posa'tʃenere] SM INV ashtray

po'sare /72/ VT to put (down), lay (down) ▶ VI (*ponte, edificio, teoria*): **~ su** to rest on; (*Fot: atteggiarsi*) to pose; **posarsi** VPR (*ape, aereo*) to land; (*uccello*) to alight; (*sguardo*) to settle

po'sata SF piece of cutlery; **posate** SFPL cutlery *sg*

posa'tezza [posa'tettsa] SF (*di persona*) composure; (*di discorso*) balanced nature

po'sato, -a AG steady; (*discorso*) balanced

pos'critto SM postscript

'posi *etc* VB *vedi* **porre**

positiva'mente AV positively; (*rispondere*) in the affirmative, affirmatively

posi'tivo, -a AG positive

posizi'one [pozit'tsjone] SF position; **farsi una ~** to make one's way in the world; **prendere ~** (*fig*) to take a stand; **luci di ~** (*Aut*) sidelights

posolo'gia, -'gie [pozolo'dʒia] SF dosage, directions *pl* for use

pos'porre /77/ VT to place after; (*differire*) to postpone, defer

pos'posto, -a PP *di* **posporre**

posse'dere /107/ VT to own, possess; (*qualità, virtù*) to have, possess; (*conoscere a fondo: lingua ecc*) to have a thorough knowledge of; (*ira ecc*) to possess

possedi'mento SM possession

pos'sente AG strong, powerful

posses'sivo, -a AG possessive

pos'sesso SM ownership *no pl*; possession; **essere in ~ di** to be in possession of sth; **prendere ~** to take possession of sth; **entrare in ~** to come into one's inheritance

posses'sore SM owner

pos'sibile AG possible ▶ SM: **fare tutto il ~** to do everything possible; **nei limiti del ~** as far as possible; **al più tardi ~** as late as possible; **vieni prima ~** come as soon as possible

possibi'lista, -i, -e AG: **essere ~** to keep an open mind

possibilità SF INV possibility ▶ SFPL (*mezzi*) means; **aver la ~ di fare** to be in a position to do; to have the opportunity to do; **nei limiti delle nostre ~** in so far as we can

possibil'mente AV if possible

possi'dente SMF landowner

possi'edo *etc* VB *vedi* **possedere**

'posso *etc* VB *vedi* **potere**

post ... PREFISSO post...

'posta SF (*servizio*) post, postal service; (*corrispondenza*) post, mail; (*ufficio postale*) post office; (*nei giochi d'azzardo*) stake; (*Caccia*) hide

(BRIT), blind (US); **poste** SFPL (*amministrazione*) post office; **fare la ~ a qn** (*fig*) to lie in wait for sb; **la ~ in gioco è troppo alta** (*fig*) there's too much at stake; **a bella ~** (*apposta*) on purpose; **piccola ~** (*su giornale*) letters to the editor, letters page; **~ aerea** airmail; **~ elettronica** E-mail, e-mail, electronic mail; **~ in arrivo** inbox; **~ inviata** sent items; **~ in uscita** outbox; **~ ordinaria** ≈ second-class mail; **~ prioritaria** first class (post); **Poste e Telecomunicazioni** *postal and telecommunications service*; **ministro delle Poste e Telecomunicazioni** Postmaster General

posta'giro [posta'dʒiro] SM post office cheque (BRIT) o check (US), postal giro (BRIT)

pos'tale AG postal, post office *cpd* ▶ SM (*treno*) mail train; (*nave*) mail boat; (*furgone*) mail van; **timbro ~** postmark

postazi'one [postat'tsjone] SF (*Mil*) emplacement

post'bellico, -a, -ci, -che AG postwar

postda'tare /72/ VT to postdate

posteggi'are [posted'dʒare] /62/ VT, VI to park

posteggia'tore, -'trice [posteddʒa'tore] SM/F car-park attendant (BRIT), parking-lot attendant (US)

pos'teggio [pos'teddʒo] SM car park (BRIT), parking lot (US); (*di taxi*) rank (BRIT), stand (US)

postelegra'fonico, -a, -ci, -che AG postal and telecommunications *cpd*

'poster SM INV poster

'posteri SMPL posterity *sg*; **i nostri ~** our descendants

posteri'ore AG (*dietro*) back; (*dopo*) later ▶ SM (*col: sedere*) behind

posteri'ori: a posteri'ori *ag inv* after the event ▶ AV (*dopo sostantivo*) looking back

pos'ticcio, -a, -ci, -ce [pos'tittʃo] AG false ▶ SM hairpiece

postici'pare [postitʃi'pare] /72/ VT to defer, postpone

pos'tilla SF marginal note

pos'tino SM postman (BRIT), mailman (US)

'posto, -a PP *di* **porre** ▶ SM (*sito, posizione*) place; (*impiego*) job; (*spazio libero*) room, space; (*di parcheggio*) space; (*sedile: al teatro, in treno ecc*) seat; (*Mil*) post; **a ~** (*in ordine*) in place, tidy; (*fig*) settled (*: persona*) reliable; **mettere a ~** (*riordinare*) to tidy (up), put in order; (*faccende: sistemare*) to straighten out; **prender ~** to take a seat; **al ~ di** in place of; **sul ~** on the spot; **~ di blocco** roadblock; **~ di lavoro** job; **~ di polizia** police station; **~ telefonico pubblico** public telephone; **~ di villeggiatura** holiday (BRIT) o tourist spot; **posti in piedi** (*Teat, in autobus*) standing room

postopera'torio, -a AG (*Med*) postoperative

pos'tribolo SM brothel

post'scriptum SM INV postscript

'postumo, -a AG posthumous; (*tardivo*) belated; **postumi** SMPL (*conseguenze*) after-effects, consequences

po'tabile AG drinkable; **acqua ~** drinking water

po'tare /72/ VT to prune

po'tassio SM potassium

pota'tura SF pruning

po'tente AG (*nazione*) strong, powerful; (*veleno, farmaco*) potent, strong

poten'tino, -a AG of (o from) Potenza

Po'tenza [po'tentsa] SF Potenza

po'tenza [po'tentsa] SF power; (*forza*) strength; **all'ennesima ~** to the nth degree; **le Grandi Potenze** the Great Powers; **~ militare** military might o strength

potenzi'ale [poten'tsjale] AG, SM potential

potenzia'mento [potentsja'mento] SM development

potenzi'are [poten'tsjare] /19/ VT to develop

PAROLA CHIAVE

po'tere /78/ SM power; **al potere** (*partito ecc*) in power; **potere d'acquisto** purchasing power; **potere esecutivo** executive power; **potere giudiziario** legal power; **potere legislativo** legislative power

▶ VB AUS **1** (*essere in grado di*) can, be able to; **non ha potuto ripararlo** he couldn't o he wasn't able to repair it; **non è potuto venire** he couldn't o he wasn't able to come; **spiacente di non poter aiutare** sorry not to be able to help

2 (*avere il permesso*) can, may, be allowed to; **posso entrare?** can o may I come in?; **posso chiederti, dove sei stato?** where, may I ask, have you been?

3 (*eventualità*) may, might, could; **potrebbe essere vero** it might o could be true; **può aver avuto un incidente** he may o might o could have had an accident; **può darsi** perhaps; **può darsi** o **può essere che non venga** he may o might not come

4 (*augurio*): **potessi almeno parlargli!** if only I could speak to him!

5 (*suggerimento*): **potresti almeno scusarti!** you could at least apologize!

▶ VT can, be able to; **può molto per noi** he can do a lot for us; **non ne posso più** (*per stanchezza*) I'm exhausted; (*per rabbia*) I can't take any more

potestà SF (*potere*) power; (*Dir*) authority

potrò *etc* VB *vedi* **potere**

pove'raccio, -a, -ci, -ce [pove'rattʃo] SM/F poor devil

'povero, -a AG poor; *(disadorno)* plain, bare ► SM/F poor man/woman; **i poveri** the poor; **~ di** lacking in, having little; **minerale ~ di ferro** ore with a low iron content; **paese ~ di risorse** country short of *o* lacking in resources

povertà SF poverty; **~ energetica** fuel poverty

pozi'one [pot'tsjone] SF potion

'pozza ['pottsa] SF pool

poz'zanghera [pot'tsangera] SF puddle

'pozzo ['pottso] SM well; *(cava: di carbone)* pit; *(di miniera)* shaft; **~ nero** cesspit; **~ petrolifero** oil well

pp. ABBR *(= pagine)* pp

p.p. ABBR *(= per procura)* pp

P.P.I. SIGLA M *(Pol: Partito Popolare Italiano) party originating from D.C.*

PP.TT. ABBR = **Poste e Telecomunicazioni**

PR SIGLA = **Parma** ► SIGLA M *(Pol)* = **Partito Radicale**

P.R. ABBR = **piano regolatore; procuratore della Repubblica**

P.R.A. [pra] SIGLA M *(= Pubblico Registro Automobilistico)* ≈ DVLA

'Praga SF Prague

prag'matico, -a, -ci, -che AG pragmatic

pram'matica SF custom; **essere di ~** to be customary

pranotera'pia SF pranotherapy

pran'zare [pran'dzare] **/72/** VI to dine, have dinner, to lunch, have lunch

'pranzo ['prandzo] SM dinner; *(a mezzogiorno)* lunch

'prassi SF usual procedure

'pratica, -che SF practice; *(esperienza)* experience; *(conoscenza)* knowledge, familiarity; *(tirocinio)* training, practice; *(Amm: affare)* matter, case; *(: incartamento)* file, dossier; **in ~** *(praticamente)* in practice; **mettere in ~** to put into practice; **fare le pratiche per** *(Amm)* to do the paperwork for; **~ restrittiva** restrictive practice; **pratiche illecite** dishonest practices

prati'cabile AG *(progetto)* practicable, feasible; *(luogo)* passable, practicable

pratica'mente AV *(in modo pratico)* in a practical way, practically; *(quasi)* practically, almost

prati'cante SMF apprentice, trainee; *(Rel)* (regular) churchgoer

prati'care **/20/** VT to practise *(BRIT)*, practice *(US)*; *(Sport: tennis ecc)* to play; *(: nuoto, scherma ecc)* to go in for; *(eseguire: apertura, buco)* to make; **~ uno sconto** to give a discount

praticità [pratitʃi'ta] SF practicality, practicalness; **per ~** for practicality's sake

'pratico, -a, -ci, -che AG practical; **~ di** *(esperto)* experienced *o* skilled in; *(familiare)* familiar with; **all'atto ~** in practice; **è ~ del mestiere** he knows his trade; **mi è più ~ venire di pomeriggio** it's more convenient for me to come in the afternoon

'prato SM meadow; *(di giardino)* lawn

preal'larme SM warning (signal)

Pre'alpi SFPL: **le ~** (the) Pre-Alps

preal'pino, -a AG of the Pre-Alps

pre'ambolo SM preamble; **senza tanti preamboli** without beating about *(BRIT)* o around *(US)* the bush

preannunci'are [preannun'tʃare] **/14/**, **preannunzi'are** [preannun'tsjare] VT to give advance notice of

preavvi'sare **/72/** VT to give advance notice of

preav'viso SM notice; **telefonata con ~** personal *o* person to person call

pre'bellico, -a, -ci, -che AG prewar *cpd*

precari'ato SM temporary employment

precarietà SF precariousness

pre'cario, -a AG precarious; *(Ins)* temporary, without tenure

precauzio'nale [prekauttsjo'nale] AG precautionary

precauzi'one [prekaut'tsjone] SF caution, care; *(misura)* precaution; **prendere precauzioni** to take precautions

prece'dente [pretʃe'dɛnte] AG previous ► SM precedent; **il discorso/film ~** the previous *o* preceding speech/film; **senza precedenti** unprecedented; **precedenti penali** *(Dir)* criminal record *sg*

precedente'mente [pretʃedente'mente] AV previously

prece'denza [pretʃe'dɛntsa] SF priority, precedence; *(Aut)* right of way; **dare ~ assoluta a qc** to give sth top priority

pre'cedere [pre'tʃɛdere] **/29/** VT to precede, go *o* (come) before

precet'tare [pretʃet'tare] **/72/** VT *(lavoratori)* to order back to work *(via an injunction)*

precettazi'one [pretʃettat'tsjone] SF *(di lavoratori)* order to resume work

pre'cetto [pre'tʃetto] SM precept; *(Mil)* call-up notice

precet'tore [pretʃet'tore] SM (private) tutor

precipi'tare [pretʃipi'tare] **/72/** VI *(cadere)* to fall headlong; *(fig: situazione)* to get out of control ► VT *(gettare dall'alto in basso)* to hurl, fling; *(fig: affrettare)* to rush; **precipitarsi** VPR *(gettarsi)* to hurl *o* fling o.s.; *(affrettarsi)* to rush

precipi'tato, -a [pretʃipi'tato] AG hasty ► SM *(Chim)* precipitate

precipitazi'one [pretʃipitat'tsjone] SF *(Meteor)* precipitation; *(fig)* haste

precipi'toso, -a [pretʃipi'toso] AG *(caduta, fuga)* headlong; *(fig: avventato)* rash, reckless; *(: affrettato)* hasty, rushed

preci'pizio [pretʃi'pittsjo] SM precipice; **a ~** (*fig: correre*) headlong

pre'cipuo, -a [pre'tʃipuo] AG principal, main

precisa'mente [pretʃiza'mente] AV (*gen*) precisely; (*con esattezza*) exactly

preci'sare [pretʃi'zare] /**72**/ VT to state, specify; (*spiegare*) to explain (in detail); **vi preciseremo la data in seguito** we'll let you know the exact date later; **tengo a ~ che ...** I must point out that ...

precisazi'one [pretʃizat'tsjone] SF clarification

precisi'one [pretʃi'zjone] SF precision; accuracy; **strumenti di ~** precision instruments

pre'ciso, -a [pre'tʃizo] AG (*esatto*) precise; (*accurato*) accurate, precise; (*deciso: idea*) precise, definite; (*uguale*): **2 vestiti precisi** 2 dresses exactly the same; **sono le 9 precise** it's exactly 9 o'clock

pre'cludere /**3**/ VT to block, obstruct

pre'cluso, -a PP *di* **precludere**

pre'coce [pre'kɔtʃe] AG early; (*bambino*) precocious; (*vecchiaia*) premature

precocità [prekotʃi'ta] SF (*di morte*) untimeliness; (*di bambino*) precociousness

precon'cetto, -a [prekon'tʃetto] AG preconceived ▶ SM preconceived idea, prejudice

pre'correre /**28**/ VT to anticipate; **~ i tempi** to be ahead of one's time

precorri'tore, -'trice SM/F precursor, forerunner

pre'corso, -a PP *di* **precorrere**

precur'sore SM forerunner, precursor

'preda SF (*bottino*) booty; (*animale, fig*) prey; **essere ~ di** to fall prey to; **essere in ~ a** to be prey to

pre'dare /**72**/ VT to plunder

preda'tore SM predator

predeces'sore, -a [predetʃes'sore] SM/F predecessor

pre'della SF platform, dais, altar-step

predesti'nare /**72**/ VT to predestine

predestinazi'one [predestinat'tsjone] SF predestination

pre'detto, -a PP *di* **predire** ▶ AG aforesaid, aforementioned

'predica, -che SF sermon; (*fig*) lecture, talking-to

predi'care /**20**/ VT, VI to preach

predica'tivo, -a AG predicative

predi'cato SM (*Ling*) predicate

predi'letto, -a PP *di* **prediligere** ▶ AG, SM/F favourite (*Brit*), favorite (*US*)

predilezi'one [predilet'tsjone] SF fondness, partiality; **avere una ~ per qc/qn** to be partial to sth/fond of sb

predi'ligere [predi'lidʒere] /**117**/ VT to prefer, have a preference for

pre'dire /**38**/ VT to foretell, predict

predis'porre /**77**/ VT to get ready, prepare; **~ qn a qc** to predispose sb to sth

predisposizi'one [predispozit'tsjone] SF (*Med*) predisposition; (*attitudine*) bent, aptitude; **avere ~ alla musica** to have a bent for music

predis'posto, -a PP *di* **predisporre**

predizi'one [predit'tsjone] SF prediction

predomi'nante AG predominant

predomi'nare /**72**/ VI (*prevalere*) to predominate; (*eccellere*) to excel

predo'minio SM predominance; supremacy

preesis'tente AG pre-existent

pree'sistere /**11**/ VI to pre-exist

preesis'tito, -a PP *di* **preesistere**

prefabbri'cato, -a AG (*Edil*) prefabricated

prefazi'one [prefat'tsjone] SF preface, foreword

prefe'renza [prefe'rɛntsa] SF preference; **a ~ di** rather than; **di ~** preferably, by preference; **non ho preferenze** I have no preferences either way, I don't mind

preferenzi'ale [preferen'tsjale] AG preferential; **corsia ~** (*Aut*) bus and taxi lane

prefe'ribile AG: **~ (a)** preferable (to), better (than); **sarebbe ~ andarsene** it would be better to go

preferibil'mente AV preferably

prefe'rire /**55**/ VT to prefer, like better; **~ il caffè al tè** to prefer coffee to tea, like coffee better than tea

pre'fetto SM prefect

prefet'tura SF prefecture

pre'figgersi [pre'fiddʒersi] /**79**/ VPR: **~ uno scopo** to set o.s. a goal

prefigu'rare /**72**/ VT (*simboleggiare*) to foreshadow; (*prevedere*) to foresee

pre'fisso, -a PP *di* **prefiggersi** ▶ SM (*Ling*) prefix; (*Tel*) dialling (*Brit*) o dial (*US*) code

Preg. ABBR = **pregiatissimo**

pre'gare /**80**/ VI to pray ▶ VT (*Rel*) to pray to; (*implorare*) to beg; (*chiedere*): **~ qn di fare** to ask sb to do; **farsi ~** to need coaxing o persuading

pre'gevole [pre'dʒevole] AG valuable

pregherò *etc* [prege'rɔ] VB *vedi* **pregare**

preghi'era [pre'gjɛra] SF (*Rel*) prayer; (*domanda*) request

pregi'arsi [pre'dʒarsi] /**62**/ VPR: **mi pregio di farle sapere che ...** I am pleased to inform you that ...

pregia'tissimo, -a [predʒa'tissimo] AG (*in lettere*): **~ Signor G. Agnelli** G. Agnelli Esquire

pregi'ato, -a [pre'dʒato] AG (*opera*) valuable; (*tessuto*) fine; (*valuta*) strong; **vino ~** vintage wine

'pregio ['prɛdʒo] SM (*stima*) esteem, regard; (*qualità*) (good) quality, merit; (*valore*) value, worth; **il ~ di questo sistema è ...** the merit of this system is ...; **oggetto di ~** valuable object

pregiudi'care [predʒudi'kare] /**20**/ VT to prejudice, harm, be detrimental to

pregiudi'cato, -a [predʒudi'kato] SM/F (*Dir*) previous offender

pregiu'dizio [predʒu'dittsjo] SM (*idea errata*) prejudice; (*danno*) harm *no pl*

preg'nante [preɲ'ɲante] AG (*fig*) pregnant, meaningful

'pregno, -a ['preɲɲo] AG (*saturo*): **~ di** full of, saturated with

'prego ESCL (*a chi ringrazia*) don't mention it!; (*invitando qn ad accomodarsi*) please sit down!; (*invitando qn ad andare prima*) after you!

pregus'tare /**72**/ VT to look forward to

preis'toria SF prehistory

preis'torico, -a, -ci, -che AG prehistoric

pre'lato SM prelate

prela'vaggio [prela'vaddʒo] SM pre-wash

prelazi'one [prelat'tsjone] SF (*Dir*) pre-emption; **avere il diritto di ~ su qc** to have the first option on sth

preleva'mento SM (*Banca*) withdrawal; (*di merce*) picking up, collection

prele'vare /**72**/ VT (*denaro*) to withdraw; (*campione*) to take; (*merce*) to pick up, collect; (*polizia*) to take, capture

preli'evo SM (*Banca*) withdrawal; (*Med*): **fare un ~ (di)** to take a sample (of); **fare un ~ di sangue** to take a blood sample

prelimi'nare AG preliminary; **preliminari** SMPL preliminary talks; preliminaries

pre'ludere /**35**/ VI: **~ a** (*preannunciare: crisi, guerra, temporale*) to herald, be a sign of; (*introdurre: dibattito ecc*) to introduce, be a prelude to

pre'ludio SM prelude

pre'luso, -a PP *di* **preludere**

pre-ma'man [prema'mã] SM INV maternity dress

prematrimoni'ale AG premarital

prema'turo, -a AG premature

premedi'tare /**72**/ VT to premeditate, plan

premeditazi'one [premeditat'tsjone] SF (*Dir*) premeditation; **con ~** *ag* premeditated ▶ AV with intent

'premere /**29**/ VT to press ▶ VI: **~ su** to press down on; (*fig*) to put pressure on; **~ a** (*fig: importare*) to matter to; **~ il grilletto** to pull the trigger

pre'messo, -a PP *di* **premettere** ▶ SF introductory statement, introduction; **mancano le premesse per una buona riuscita** we lack the basis for a successful outcome

pre'mettere /**63**/ VT to put before; (*dire prima*) to start by saying, state first; **premetto che ...** I must say first of all that ...; **premesso che ...** given that ...; **ciò premesso ...** that having been said ...

premi'are /**19**/ VT to give a prize to; (*fig: merito, onestà*) to reward

premiazi'one [premjat'tsjone] SF prize giving

'premier ['prɛmjer] SM INV premier

premi'nente AG pre-eminent

'premio SM prize; (*ricompensa*) reward; (*Comm*) premium; (*Amm: indennità*) bonus; **in ~ per** as a prize (o reward) for; **~ d'ingaggio** (*Sport*) signing-on fee; **~ di produzione** productivity bonus

pre'misi *etc* VB *vedi* **premettere**

premoni'tore, -'trice AG premonitory

premonizi'one [premonit'tsjone] SF premonition

premu'nirsi /**55**/ VPR: **~ di** to provide o.s. with; **~ contro** to protect o.s. from, guard o.s. against

pre'mura SF (*fretta*) haste, hurry; (*riguardo*) attention, care; **premure** SFPL (*attenzioni, cure*) care *sg*; **aver ~** to be in a hurry; **far ~ a qn** to hurry sb; **usare ogni ~ nei riguardi di qn, circondare qn di premure** to be very attentive to sb

premu'roso, -a AG thoughtful, considerate

prena'tale AG antenatal

'prendere /**81**/ VT to take; (*andare a prendere*) to get, fetch; (*ottenere*) to get; (*guadagnare*) to get, earn; (*catturare: ladro, pesce*) to catch; (*: collaboratore, dipendente*) to take on; (*: passeggero*) to pick up; (*chiedere: somma, prezzo*) to charge, ask; (*trattare: persona*) to handle ▶ VI (*colla, cemento*) to set; (*pianta*) to take; (*fuoco: nel camino*) to catch; (*voltare*): **~ a destra** to turn (to the) right; **prendersi** VPR (*azzuffarsi*): **prendersi a pugni** to come to blows; **prende qualcosa?** (*da bere, da mangiare*) would you like something to eat (o drink)?; **prendo un caffè** I'll have a coffee; **~ a fare qc** to start doing sth; **~ qn/qc per** (*scambiare*) to take sb/sth for; **~ l'abitudine di** to get into the habit of; **~ fuoco** to catch fire; **~ le generalità di qn** to take down sb's particulars; **~ nota di** to take note of; **~ parte a** to take part in; **prendersi cura di qn/qc** to look after sb/sth; **prendersi un impegno** to take on a commitment; **prendersela** (*adirarsi*) to get annoyed; (*preoccuparsi*) to get upset, worry

prendi'sole SM INV sundress

preno'tare /**72**/ VT to book, reserve

prenotazi'one [prenotat'tsjone] SF booking, reservation

'prensile AG prehensile

preoccu'pante AG worrying
preoccu'pare /72/ VT to worry; to preoccupy;
  preoccuparsi VPR: **preoccuparsi di qn/qc**
  to worry about sb/sth; **preoccuparsi per qn**
  to be anxious for sb
preoccupazi'one [preokkupat'tsjone] SF
  worry, anxiety
preordi'nato, -a AG preordained
prepa'rare /72/ VT to prepare; (esame, concorso)
  to prepare for; **prepararsi** VPR (vestirsi) to get
  ready; **prepararsi a qc/a fare** to get ready o
  prepare (o.s.) for sth/to do; **~ da mangiare** to
  prepare a meal
prepara'tivi SMPL preparations
prepa'rato, -a AG (gen) prepared; (pronto)
  ready ▶ SM (prodotto) preparation
prepara'torio, -a AG preparatory
preparazi'one [preparat'tsjone] SF
  preparation; **non ha la necessaria ~ per
  svolgere questo lavoro** he lacks the
  qualifications necessary for the job
prepensiona'mento SM early retirement
preponde'rante AG predominant
pre'porre /77/ VT to place before; (fig) to prefer
preposizi'one [prepozit'tsjone] SF (Ling)
  preposition
pre'posto, -a PP di **preporre**
prepo'tente AG (persona) domineering,
  arrogant; (bisogno, desiderio) overwhelming,
  pressing ▶ SMF bully
prepo'tenza [prepo'tɛntsa] SF arrogance;
  (comportamento) arrogant behaviour (BRIT)
  o behavior (US)
pre'puzio [pre'puttsjo] SM (Anat) foreskin
preroga'tiva SF prerogative
'presa SF taking no pl; catching no pl; (di città)
  capture; (indurimento: di cemento) setting;
  (appiglio, Sport) hold; (di acqua, gas) (supply)
  point; (piccola quantità: di sale ecc) pinch;
  (Carte) trick; **~ (di corrente)** socket; (al muro)
  point; **far ~ (colla)** to set; **ha fatto ~ sul
  pubblico** (fig) it caught the public's
  imagination; **a ~ rapida** (cemento) quick-
  setting; **di forte ~** (fig) with wide appeal;
  essere alle prese con qc (fig) to be
  struggling with sth; **macchina da ~** (Cine)
  cine camera (BRIT), movie camera (US);
  ~ d'aria air inlet; **~ diretta** (Aut) direct drive;
  ~ in giro leg-pull (BRIT), joke; **~ di posizione**
  stand
pre'sagio [pre'zadʒo] SM omen
presa'gire [preza'dʒire] /55/ VT to foresee
presa'lario SM (Ins) grant
'presbite AG long-sighted
presbiteri'ano, -a AG, SM/F Presbyterian
presbi'terio SM presbytery
pre'scindere [preʃ'ʃindere] /102/ VI: **~ da** to
  leave out of consideration; **a ~ da** apart from
pre'scisso, -a [preʃ'ʃisso] PP di **prescindere**

presco'lastico, -a, -ci, -che AG pre-school cpd
pres'critto, -a PP di **prescrivere**
pres'crivere /105/ VT to prescribe
prescrizi'one [preskrit'tsjone] SF (Med, Dir)
  prescription; (norma) rule, regulation;
  cadere in ~ (Dir) to become statute-barred
'prese etc VB vedi **prendere**
presen'tare /72/ VT to present; (Amm: inoltrare)
  to submit; (far conoscere): **~ qn (a)** to introduce
  sb (to); **presentarsi** VPR (recarsi, farsi vedere) to
  present o.s., appear; (farsi conoscere) to
  introduce o.s.; (occasione) to arise; **~ qc in
  un'esposizione** to show o display sth at an
  exhibition; **~ qn in società** to introduce sb
  into society; **presentarsi come candidato**
  (Pol) to stand (BRIT) o run (US) as a candidate;
  presentarsi bene/male to have a good/poor
  appearance; **la situazione si presenta
  difficile** things aren't looking too good,
  things look a bit tricky
presentazi'one [prezentat'tsjone] SF
  presentation; introduction
pre'sente AG present; (questo) this ▶ SM
  present ▶ SF (lettera): **con la ~ vi comunico
  ...** this is to inform you that ... ▶ SMF person
  present; **i presenti** those present; **aver ~
  qc/qn** to remember sth/sb; **essere ~ a una
  riunione** to be present at o attend a
  meeting; **tener ~ qn/qc** to keep sb/sth in
  mind; **esclusi i presenti** present company
  excepted
presenti'mento SM premonition
pre'senza [pre'zɛntsa] SF presence; (aspetto
  esteriore) appearance; **in ~ di** in (the)
  presence of; **di bella ~** of good appearance;
  ~ di spirito presence of mind
presenzi'are [prezen'tsjare] /19/ VI: **~ a** to be
  present at, attend
pre'sepio, pre'sepe SM crib
preser'vare /72/ VT to protect; to save
preserva'tivo SM sheath, condom
'presi etc VB vedi **prendere**
'preside SMF (Ins) head (teacher) (BRIT),
  principal (US); (di facoltà universitaria) dean;
  ~ di facoltà (Università) dean of faculty
presi'dente SM (Pol) president; (di assemblea,
  Comm) chairman; **il P~ della Camera** (Pol)
  ≈ the Speaker; **P~ del Consiglio (dei
  Ministri)** ≈ Prime Minister; **P~ della
  Repubblica** President of the Republic;
  see note

  The Presidente del Consiglio, the Italian
  Prime Minister, is the leader of the
  Government. He or she submits
  nominations for ministerial posts to
  the Presidente della Repubblica, who then
  appoints them if approved. The Presidente
  del Consiglio is appointed by the Presidente
  della Repubblica, in consultation with the

leaders of the parliamentary parties, former heads of state, the *Presidente della Camera* and the *Presidente del Senato*. The *Presidente della Repubblica* is the head of state. He or she must be an Italian citizen of at least 50 years of age, and is elected by Parliament and by three delegates from each of the Italian regions. He or she has the power to suspend the implementation of legislation and to dissolve one or both chambers of Parliament, and presides over the magistrates' governing body (the *Consiglio Superiore della Magistratura*).

presiden'tessa SF president; (*moglie*) president's wife; (*di assemblea*, *Comm*) chairwoman

presi'denza [presi'dɛntsa] SF presidency; office of president; chairmanship; **assumere la ~** to become president; to take the chair; **essere alla ~** to be president (*o* chairman); **candidato alla ~** presidential candidate; candidate for the chairmanship

presidenzi'ale [presidɛn'tsjale] AG presidential

presidi'are /19/ VT to garrison

pre'sidio SM garrison

presi'edere /29/ VT to preside over ▶ VI: **~ a** to direct, be in charge of

'preso, -a PP *di* **prendere**

'pressa SF (*Tecn*) press

pres'sante AG (*bisogno*, *richiesta*) urgent, pressing

pressap'poco AV about, roughly, approximately

pres'sare /72/ VT (*anche fig*) to press; **~ qn con richieste** to pursue sb with demands

pressi'one SF pressure; **far ~ su qn** to put pressure on sb; **subire forti pressioni** to be under strong pressure; **~ sanguigna** blood pressure; **~ atmosferica** atmospheric pressure

'presso AV (*vicino*) nearby, close at hand ▶ PREP (*vicino a*) near; (*accanto a*) beside, next to; (*in casa di*): **~ qn** at sb's home; (*nelle lettere*) care of, c/o; (*alle dipendenze di*): **lavora ~ di noi** he works for *o* with us ▶ SMPL: **nei pressi di** near, in the vicinity of; **ha avuto grande successo ~ i giovani** it has been a hit with young people

pressoché [presso'ke] AV nearly, almost

pressuriz'zare [pressurid'dzare] /72/ VT to pressurize

prestabi'lire /55/ VT to arrange beforehand, arrange in advance

presta'nome SM INV/F INV (*peg*) figurehead

pres'tante AG good-looking

pres'tanza [pres'tantsa] SF (*robust*) good looks *pl*

pres'tare /72/ VT: **~ (qc a qn)** to lend (sb sth *o* sth to sb); **prestarsi** VPR (*offrirsi*): **prestarsi a fare** to offer to do; (*essere adatto*): **prestarsi a** to lend itself to, be suitable for; **~ aiuto** to lend a hand; **~ ascolto** *o* **orecchio** to listen; **~ attenzione** to pay attention; **~ fede a qc/ qn** to give credence to sth/sb; **~ giuramento** to take an oath; **la frase si presta a molteplici interpretazioni** the phrase lends itself to numerous interpretations

prestazi'one [prestat'tsjone] SF (*Tecn*, *Sport*) performance; **prestazioni** SFPL (*di persona*: *servizi*) services

prestigia'tore, -'trice [prestidʒa'tore] SM/F conjurer

pres'tigio [pres'tidʒo] SM (*potere*) prestige; (*illusione*): **gioco di ~** conjuring trick

prestigi'oso, -a [presti'dʒoso] AG prestigious

'prestito SM lending *no pl*; loan; **dar in ~** to lend; **prendere in ~** to borrow; **~ bancario** bank loan; **~ pubblico** public borrowing

'presto AV (*tra poco*) soon; (*in fretta*) quickly; (*di buon'ora*) early; **a ~** see you soon; **~ o tardi** sooner or later; **fare ~ a fare qc** to hurry up and do sth; (*non costare fatica*) to have no trouble doing sth; **si fa ~ a criticare** it's easy to criticize; **è ancora ~ per decidere** it's still too early *o* too soon to decide

pre'sumere /12/ VT to presume, assume

presu'mibile AG (*dati*, *risultati*) likely

pre'sunsi *etc* VB *vedi* **presumere**

pre'sunto, -a PP *di* **presumere** ▶ AG: **il ~ colpevole** the alleged culprit

presuntu'oso, -a AG presumptuous

presunzi'one [prezun'tsjone] SF presumption

presup'porre /77/ VT to suppose; to presuppose

presup'posto, -a PP *di* **presupporre** ▶ SM (*premessa*) supposition, premise; **partendo dal ~ che ...** assuming that ...; **mancano i presupposti necessari** the necessary conditions are lacking

'prete SM priest

preten'dente SMF pretender ▶ SM (*corteggiatore*) suitor

pre'tendere /120/ VT (*esigere*) to demand, require; (*sostenere*): **~ che** to claim that; **pretende di aver sempre ragione** he thinks he's always right

pretenzi'oso, -a [preten'tsjoso] AG pretentious

preterintenzio'nale [preterintentsjo'nale] AG (*Dir*): **omicidio ~** manslaughter

pre'teso, -a PP *di* **pretendere** ▶ SF (*esigenza*) claim, demand; (*presunzione*, *sfarzo*) pretentiousness ▶ AV unpretentiously; **avanzare una pretesa** to put forward a claim *o* demand; **senza pretese** *ag* unpretentious

P

pre'testo SM pretext, excuse; **con il ~ di** on the pretext of

pretestu'oso, -a AG (*data, motivo*) used as an excuse

pre'tore SM magistrate

pre'tura SF (*Dir: sede*) magistrate's court (*BRIT*), circuit o superior court (*US*); (: *magistratura*) magistracy

preva'lente AG prevailing

prevalente'mente AV mainly, for the most part

preva'lenza [preva'lɛntsa] SF predominance

preva'lere /126/ VI to prevail

pre'valso, -a PP *di* **prevalere**

prevari'care /20/ VI (*abusare del potere*) to abuse one's power

prevaricazi'one [prevarikat'tsjone] SF (*abuso di potere*) abuse of power

preve'dere /82/ VT (*indovinare*) to foresee; (*presagire*) to foretell; (*considerare*) to make provision for; **nulla lasciava ~ che ...** there was nothing to suggest o to make one think that ...; **come previsto** as expected; **spese previste** anticipated expenditure; **previsto per martedì** scheduled for Tuesday

prev'edibile AG predictable; **non era assolutamente ~ che ...** no one could have foreseen that ...

prevedibil'mente AV as one would expect

preve'nire /128/ VT (*anticipare: obiezione*) to forestall; (: *domanda*) to anticipate; (*evitare*) to avoid, prevent; (*avvertire*): **~ qn (di)** to warn sb (of); to inform sb (of)

preventi'vare /72/ VT (*Comm*) to estimate

preven'tivo, -a AG preventive ▶ SM (*Comm*) estimate; **fare un ~** to give an estimate; **bilancio ~** budget; **carcere ~** custody (*pending trial*)

preve'nuto, -a AG (*mal disposto*): **~ (contro qc/ qn)** prejudiced (against sth/sb)

prevenzi'one [preven'tsjone] SF prevention; (*preconcetto*) prejudice

previ'dente AG showing foresight; prudent

previ'denza [previ'dɛntsa] SF foresight; **istituto di ~** provident institution; **~ sociale** social security (*BRIT*), welfare (*US*)

pre'vidi *etc* VB *vedi* **prevedere**

'previo, -a AG (*Comm*): **~ avviso** upon notice; **~ pagamento** upon payment

previsi'one SF forecast, prediction; **previsioni meteorologiche** o **del tempo** weather forecast *sg*

pre'visto, -a PP *di* **prevedere** ▶ SM: **più/meno del ~** more/less than expected; **prima del ~** earlier than expected

prezi'oso, -a [pret'tsjoso] AG precious; (*aiuto, consiglio*) invaluable ▶ SM jewel; valuable

prez'zemolo [pret'tsemolo] SM parsley

'prezzo ['prɛttso] SM price; **a ~ di costo** at cost, at cost price (*BRIT*); **tirare sul ~** to bargain, haggle; **il ~ pattuito è di 1000 euro** the agreed price is 1000 euros; **~ d'acquisto/di vendita** purchase/selling price; **~ di fabbrica** factory price; **~ di mercato** market price; **~ scontato** reduced price; **~ unitario** unit price

P.R.I. SIGLA M (= *Partito Repubblicano Italiano*) *former political party*

prigi'one [pri'dʒone] SF prison

prigio'nia [pridʒo'nia] SF imprisonment

prigioni'ero, -a [pridʒo'njɛro] AG captive ▶ SM/F prisoner

'prima SF *vedi* **primo** ▶ AV before; (*in anticipo*) in advance, beforehand; (*per l'addietro*) at one time, formerly; (*più presto*) sooner, earlier; (*in primo luogo*) first ▶ CONG: **~ di fare/che parta** before doing/he leaves; **~ di** *prep* before; **~ o poi** sooner or later; **due giorni ~** two days before o earlier; **~ d'ora** before now

pri'mario, -a AG primary; (*principale*) chief, leading, primary ▶ SM/F (*medico*) head physician, chief physician

pri'mate SM (*Rel, Zool*) primate

prima'tista, -i, -e SM/F (*Sport*) record holder

pri'mato SM supremacy; (*Sport*) record

prima'vera SF spring

primave'rile AG spring *cpd*

primeggi'are [primed'dʒare] /62/ VI to excel, be one of the best

primi'tivo, -a AG (*gen*) primitive; (*significato*) original

pri'mizie [pri'mittsje] SFPL early produce *sg*

'primo, -a AG first; (*fig*) initial; basic; prime ▶ SM/F first (one) ▶ SM (*Cuc*) first course; (*in date*): **il ~ luglio** the first of July ▶ SF (*Teat*) first night; (*Cine*) première; (*Aut*) first (gear); **le prime ore del mattino** the early hours of the morning; **di prima mattina** early in the morning; **in prima pagina** (*Stampa*) on the front page; **ai primi freddi** at the first sign of cold weather; **ai primi di maggio** at the beginning of May; **i primi del Novecento** the early twentieth century; **viaggiare in prima** to travel first-class; **per prima cosa** firstly; **in ~ luogo** first of all, in the first place; **di prim'ordine** o **prima qualità** first-class, first-rate; **in un ~ tempo** o **momento** at first; **prima donna** leading lady; (*di opera lirica*) prima donna

primo'genito, -a [primo'dʒɛnito] AG, SM/F firstborn

pri'mordi SMPL beginnings

primordi'ale AG primordial

'primula SF primrose

princi'pale [printʃi'pale] AG main, principal ▶ SM manager, boss; **sede ~** head office

principal'mente [printʃipal'mente] AV
mainly, principally

princi'pato [printʃi'pato] SM principality

'principe ['printʃipe] SM prince; **~ ereditario**
crown prince

princi'pesco, -a, -schi, -sche [printʃi'pesko]
AG *(anche fig)* princely

princi'pessa [printʃi'pessa] SF princess

principi'ante [printʃi'pjante] SMF beginner

principi'are [printʃi'pjare] /19/ VT, VI to start,
begin

prin'cipio [prin'tʃipjo] SM *(inizio)* beginning,
start; *(origine)* origin, cause; *(concetto, norma)*
principle; **principi** SMPL *(concetti fondamentali)*
principles; **al** o **in** ~ at first; **fin dal** ~ right
from the start; **per** ~ on principle; **una
questione di** ~ a matter of principle;
~ attivo active ingredient; **una persona di
sani principi morali** a person of sound
moral principles

pri'ore SM *(Rel)* prior

pri'ori: a pri'ori *ag inv* prior; a priori ▶ AV at
first glance; initially; a priori

priorità SF priority; **avere la ~ (su)** to have
priority (over)

priori'tario, -a AG of utmost importance;
(scelta) first; *(interesse)* overriding; **posta
prioritaria** first class (post)

'prisma, -i SM prism

pri'vare /72/ VT: **~ qn di** to deprive sb of;
privarsi VPR: **privarsi di** to go o do without

priva'tiva SF *(Econ)* monopoly

privatiz'zare [privatid'dzare] /72/ VT to
privatize

privatizzazi'one [privatiddzat'tsjone] SF
privatization

pri'vato, -a AG private ▶ SM/F *(anche:* **privato
cittadino)** private citizen; **in** ~ in private;
diritto ~ *(Dir)* civil law; **ritirarsi a vita
privata** to withdraw from public life; **"non
vendiamo a privati"** "wholesale only"

privazi'one [privat'tsjone] SF privation,
hardship

privilegi'are [privile'dʒare] /62/ VT to favour
(BRIT), favor *(US)*, to grant a privilege to

privilegi'ato, -a [privile'dʒato] AG *(individuo,
classe)* privileged; *(trattamento, Comm: credito)*
preferential; **azioni privilegiate** preference
shares *(BRIT)*, preferred stock *(US)*

privi'legio [privi'lɛdʒo] SM privilege; **avere il
~ di fare** to have the privilege of doing, be
privileged to do

'privo, -a AG: **~ di** without, lacking

pro PREP for, on behalf of ▶ SM INV *(utilità)*
advantage, benefit; **a che ~?** what's the
use?; **il ~ e il contro** the pros and cons

pro'babile AG probable, likely

probabilità SF INV probability; **con molta ~**
very probably, in all probability

probabil'mente AV probably

pro'bante AG convincing

pro'blema, -i SM problem

proble'matico, -a, -ci, -che AG problematic;
(incerto) doubtful ▶ SF problems *pl*

pro'boscide [pro'bɔʃʃide] SF *(di elefante)* trunk

procacci'are [prokat'tʃare] /14/ VT to get, obtain

procaccia'tore [prokattʃa'tore] SM: **~ d'affari**
sales executive

pro'cace [pro'katʃe] AG *(donna, aspetto)*
provocative

pro'cedere [pro'tʃɛdere] /29/ VI to proceed;
(comportarsi) to behave; *(iniziare)*: **~ a** to start;
~ contro *(Dir)* to start legal proceedings
against; **~ oltre** to go on ahead; **prima di ~
oltre** before going any further; **gli affari
procedono bene** business is going well;
bisogna ~ con cautela we have to proceed
cautiously; **non luogo a ~** *(Dir)* nonsuit

procedi'mento [protʃedi'mento] SM *(modo di
condurre)* procedure; *(di avvenimenti)* course;
(Tecn) process; **~ penale** *(Dir)* criminal
proceedings *pl*

proce'dura [protʃe'dura] SF *(Dir)* procedure

proces'sare [protʃes'sare] /72/ VT *(Dir)* to try

processi'one [protʃes'sjone] SF procession

pro'cesso [pro'tʃɛsso] SM *(Dir)* trial;
proceedings *pl*; *(metodo)* process; **essere
sotto** ~ to be on trial; **mettere sotto** ~ *(anche
fig)* to put on trial; **~ di fabbricazione**
manufacturing process; **~ di pace** peace
process

processu'ale [protʃessu'ale] AG *(Dir)*: **atti
processuali** records of a trial; **spese
processuali** legal costs

Proc. Gen. ABBR = **procuratore generale**

pro'cinto [pro'tʃinto] SM: **in ~ di fare** about
to do, on the point of doing

pro'clama, -i SM proclamation

procla'mare /72/ VT to proclaim

proclamazi'one [proklamat'tsjone] SF
proclamation, declaration

procrasti'nare /72/ VT *(data)* to postpone;
(pagamento) to defer

procre'are /72/ VT to procreate

pro'cura SF *(Dir)* proxy, power of attorney;
(ufficio) attorney's office; **per** ~ by proxy;
la P~ della Repubblica the Public
Prosecutor's Office

procu'rare /72/ VT: **~ qc a qn** *(fornire)* to get o
obtain sth for sb; *(causare: noie ecc)* to bring o
give sb sth

procura'tore, -'trice SM/F *(Dir)* ≈ solicitor;
(: chi ha la procura) holder of power of attorney;
~ generale *(in corte d'appello)* public
prosecutor; *(in corte di cassazione)* Attorney
General; **~ legale** ≈ solicitor *(BRIT)*, lawyer;
~ della Repubblica *(in corte d'assise, tribunale)*
public prosecutor

P

prodi'gare /**8o**/ VT to be lavish with;
prodigarsi VPR: **prodigarsi per qn** to do all
one can for sb

pro'digio [pro'didʒo] SM marvel, wonder;
(*persona*) prodigy

prodigi'oso, -a [prodi'dʒoso] AG prodigious;
phenomenal

'prodigo, -a, -ghi, -ghe AG lavish,
extravagant

pro'dotto, -a PP *di* **produrre** ▶ SM product;
~ **di base** primary product; ~ **finale** end
product; ~ **interno lordo** gross domestic
product; ~ **nazionale lordo** gross national
product; **prodotti agricoli** farm produce *sg*;
prodotti di bellezza cosmetics; **prodotti
chimici** chemicals

pro'duco *etc* VB *vedi* **produrre**

pro'durre /**9o**/ VT to produce

pro'dussi *etc* VB *vedi* **produrre**

produttività SF productivity

produt'tivo, -a AG productive

produt'tore, -'trice AG producing *cpd* ▶ SM/F
producer; **paese ~ di petrolio** oil-producing
country

produzi'one [produt'tsjone] SF production;
(*rendimento*) output; ~ **in serie** mass
production

pro'emio SM introduction, preface

Prof. ABBR (= *professore*) Prof

profa'nare /**72**/ VT to desecrate

pro'fano, -a AG (*mondano*) secular, profane;
(*sacrilego*) profane

profe'rire /**55**/ VT to utter

profes'sare /**72**/ VT to profess; (*medicina ecc*)
to practise (*BRIT*), practice (*US*)

professio'nale AG professional; **scuola ~**
training college

professi'one SF profession; **di ~** professional,
by profession; **libera ~** profession

professio'nista, -i, -e SM/F professional

profes'sore, -'essa SM/F (*Ins*) teacher;
(: *di università*) lecturer; (: *titolare di cattedra*)
professor; ~ **d'orchestra** member of an
orchestra

pro'feta, -i SM prophet

pro'fetico, -a, -ci, -che AG prophetic

profetiz'zare [profetid'dzare] /**72**/ VT to
prophesy

profe'zia [profet'tsia] SF prophecy

pro'ficuo, -a AG useful, profitable

profi'lare /**72**/ VT to outline; (*ornare: vestito*) to
edge; **profilarsi** VPR to stand out, be
silhouetted; to loom up

profi'lassi SF (*Med*) preventive treatment,
prophylaxis

profi'lattico, -a, -ci, -che AG prophylactic
▶ SM (*anticoncezionale*) sheath, condom

pro'filo SM profile; (*breve descrizione*) sketch,
outline; **di ~** in profile

profit'tare /**72**/ VI: ~ **di** (*trarre profitto*) to profit
by; (*approfittare*) to take advantage of

pro'fitto SM advantage, profit, benefit; (*fig:
progresso*) progress; (*Comm*) profit; **ricavare
un ~ da** to make a profit from *o* out of;
vendere con ~ to sell at a profit; **conto
profitti e perdite** profit and loss account

pro'fondere /**25**/ VT (*lodi*) to lavish; (*denaro*) to
squander; **profondersi** VPR: **profondersi in**
to be profuse in

profondità SF INV depth

pro'fondo, -a AG deep; (*rancore, meditazione*)
profound ▶ SM depth(s), bottom; ~ **8 metri** 8
metres deep

pro'forma AG routine *cpd* ▶ SM INV formality
▶ AV: **fare qc ~** to do sth as a formality

'profugo, -a, -ghi, -ghe SM/F refugee

profu'mare /**72**/ VT to perfume ▶ VI to be
fragrant; **profumarsi** VPR to put on perfume
o scent

profumata'mente AV: **pagare qc ~** to pay
through the nose for sth

profu'mato, -a AG (*fiore, aria*) fragrant;
(*fazzoletto, saponetta*) scented; (*pelle*)
sweet-smelling; (*persona*) with perfume on

profume'ria SF perfumery; (*negozio*) perfume
shop

pro'fumo SM (*prodotto*) perfume, scent;
(*fragranza*) scent, fragrance

profusi'one SF profusion; **a ~** in plenty

pro'fuso, -a PP *di* **profondere**

progeni'tore, -'trice [prodʒeni'tore] SM/F
ancestor

proget'tare [prodʒet'tare] /**72**/ VT to plan;
(*Tecn: edificio*) to plan, design; ~ **di fare qc** to
plan to do sth

progettazi'one [prodʒettat'tsjone] SF
planning; **in corso di ~** at the planning
stage

proget'tista, -i, -e [prodʒet'tista] SM/F
designer

pro'getto [pro'dʒetto] SM plan; (*idea*) plan,
project; **avere in ~ di fare qc** to be planning
to do sth; ~ **di legge** (*Pol*) bill

'prognosi ['proɲɲozi] SF (*Med*) prognosis;
essere in ~ riservata to be on the danger list

pro'gramma, -i SM programme (*BRIT*),
program (*US*); (*TV, Radio*) programmes *pl*;
(*Ins*) syllabus, curriculum; (*Inform*) program;
avere in ~ di fare qc to be planning to do sth;
~ **applicativo** (*Inform*) application program

program'mare /**72**/ VT (*TV, Radio*) to put on;
(*Inform*) to program; (*Econ*) to plan

programma'tore, -'trice SM/F (*Inform*)
computer programmer (*BRIT*) *o* programer
(*US*)

programmazi'one [programmat'tsjone] SF
programming (*BRIT*), programing (*US*);
planning

progre'dire /55/ VI to progress, make progress
progressi'one SF progression
progres'sista, -i, -e AG, SM/F progressive
progressiva'mente AV progressively
progres'sivo, -a AG progressive
pro'gresso SM progress *no pl*; **fare progressi** to make progress
proi'bire /55/ VT to forbid, prohibit; **~ a qn di fare qc** (*vietare*) to forbid sb to do sth; (*impedire*) to prevent sb from doing sth
proibi'tivo, -a AG prohibitive
proi'bito, -a AG forbidden; **"è ~ l'accesso"** "no admittance"; **"è ~ fumare"** "no smoking"
proibizi'one [proibit'tsjone] SF prohibition
proibizio'nismo [proibittsjo'nizmo] SM prohibition
proiet'tare /72/ VT (*gen, Geom, Cine*) to project; (: *presentare*) to show, screen; (*luce, ombra*) to throw, cast, project
proi'ettile SM projectile, bullet, shell *etc*
proiet'tore SM (*Cine*) projector; (*Aut*) headlamp; (*Mil*) searchlight
proiezi'one [projet'tsjone] SF (*Cine*) projection; showing
'prole SF children *pl*, offspring
proletari'ato SM proletariat
prole'tario, -a AG, SM/F proletarian
prolife'rare /72/ VI (*fig*) to proliferate
pro'lifico, -a, -ci, -che AG prolific
pro'lisso, -a AG verbose
'prologo, -ghi SM prologue
pro'lunga, -ghe SF (*di cavo elettrico ecc*) extension
prolunga'mento SM (*gen*) extension; (*di strada*) continuation
prolun'gare /80/ VT (*discorso, attesa*) to prolong; (*linea, termine*) to extend
prome'moria SM INV memorandum
pro'messa SF promise; **fare/mantenere una ~** to make/keep a promise
pro'messo, -a PP *di* **promettere**
promet'tente AG promising
pro'mettere /63/ VT to promise ▶ VI to be *o* look promising; **~ a qn di fare** to promise sb that one will do
promi'nente AG prominent
promi'nenza [promi'nentsa] SF prominence
promiscuità SF promiscuousness
pro'miscuo, -a AG: **matrimonio ~** mixed marriage; **nome ~** (*Ling*) common-gender noun
pro'misi *etc* VB *vedi* **promettere**
promon'torio SM promontory, headland
pro'mosso, -a PP *di* **promuovere**
promo'tore, -'trice SM/F promoter, organizer
promozio'nale [promottsjo'nale] AG promotional; **"vendita ~"** "special offer"

promozi'one [promot'tsjone] SF promotion; **~ delle vendite** sales promotion
promul'gare /80/ VT to promulgate
promulgazi'one [promulgat'tsjone] SF promulgation
promu'overe /66/ VT to promote
proni'pote SMF (*di nonni*) great-grandchild, great-grandson/granddaughter; (*di zii*) great-nephew/niece; **pronipoti** SMPL (*discendenti*) descendants
pro'nome SM (*Ling*) pronoun
pronomi'nale AG pronominal
pronosti'care /20/ VT to foretell, predict
pro'nostico, -ci SM forecast
pron'tezza [pron'tettsa] SF readiness; quickness, promptness; **~ di riflessi** quick reflexes; **~ di spirito/mente** readiness of wit/mind
'pronto, -a AG ready; (*rapido*) fast, quick, prompt; **~!** (*Tel*) hello!; **essere ~ a fare qc** to be ready to do sth; **~ all'ira** quick-tempered; **a pronta cassa** (*Comm*) cash (*Brit*) *o* collect (*US*) on delivery; **pronta consegna** (*Comm*) prompt delivery; **~ soccorso** (*trattamento*) first aid; (*reparto*) A&E (*Brit*), ER (*US*)
prontu'ario SM manual, handbook
pro'nuncia [pro'nuntʃa] SF pronunciation
pronunci'are [pronun'tʃare] **/14/** VT (*parola, sentenza*) to pronounce; (*dire*) to utter; (*discorso*) to deliver; **pronunciarsi** VPR to declare one's opinion; **pronunciarsi a favore di/contro** to pronounce o.s. in favour of/against; **non mi pronuncio** I'm not prepared to comment
pronunci'ato, -a [pronun'tʃato] AG (*spiccato*) pronounced, marked; (*sporgente*) prominent
pro'nunzia *etc* [pro'nuntsja] = **pronuncia** *ecc*
propa'ganda SF propaganda
propagan'dare /72/ VT (*idea*) to propagandize; (*prodotto, invenzione*) to push, plug (*col*)
propa'gare /80/ VT (*Fisica, Biol*) to propagate; (*notizia, idea, malattia*) to spread; **propagarsi** VPR to propagate; to spread
propagazi'one [propagat'tsjone] SF (*vedi vb*) propagation; spreading
prope'deutico, -a, -ci, -che AG (*corso, trattato*) introductory
pro'pendere /8/ VI: **~ per** to favour (*Brit*), favor (*US*), lean towards
propensi'one SF inclination, propensity; **avere ~ a credere che ...** to be inclined to think that ...
pro'penso, -a PP *di* **propendere** ▶ AG: **essere ~ a qc** to be in favour (*Brit*) *o* favor (*US*) of sth; **essere ~ a fare qc** to be inclined to do sth
propi'nare /72/ VT to administer
pro'pizio, -a [pro'pittsjo] AG favourable (*Brit*), favorable (*US*)

P

pro'porre /77/ vt (*suggerire*): ~ **qc (a qn)** to suggest sth (to sb); (*candidato*) to put forward; (*legge, brindisi*) to propose; ~ **di fare** to suggest o propose doing; **proporsi di fare** to propose o intend to do; **proporsi una meta** to set o.s. a goal

proporzio'nale [proportsjo'nale] AG proportional; (**sistema**) ~ (*Pol*) proportional representation system

proporzio'nato, -a [proportsjo'nato] AG: ~ **a** proportionate to, proportional to; **ben** ~ well-proportioned

proporzi'one [propor'tsjone] SF proportion; **in** ~ **a** in proportion to; **proporzioni** SFPL (*dimensioni*) proportions; **di vaste proporzioni** huge

pro'posito SM (*intenzione*) intention, aim; (*argomento*) subject, matter; **a** ~ **di** regarding, with regard to; **a questo** ~ on this subject; **di** ~ (*apposta*) deliberately, on purpose; **a** ~ by the way; **capitare a** ~ (*cosa, persona*) to turn up at the right time

proposizi'one [propozit'tsjone] SF (*Ling*) clause; (: *periodo*) sentence

pro'posto, -a PP di **proporre** ▶ SF proposal; (*suggerimento*) suggestion; **fare una proposta** to put forward a proposal; to make a suggestion; **proposta di legge** (*Pol*) bill

propria'mente AV (*correttamente*) properly, correctly; (*in modo specifico*) specifically; ~ **detto** in the strict sense of the word

proprietà SF INV (*ciò che si possiede*) property, estate; (*caratteristica*) property; (*correttezza*) correctness; **essere di** ~ **di qn** to belong to sb; ~ **edilizia** (developed) property; ~ **privata** private property

proprie'tario, -a SM/F owner; (*di albergo ecc*) proprietor, owner; (*per l'inquilino*) landlord/lady; ~ **terriero** landowner

'proprio, -a AG (*possessivo*) own; (: *impersonale*) one's; (*esatto*) exact, correct, proper; (*senso, significato*) literal; (*Ling: nome*) proper; (*particolare*): ~ **di** characteristic of, peculiar to ▶ AV (*precisamente*) just, exactly; (*davvero*) really; (*affatto*): **non ...** ~ not ... at all ▶ SM (*Comm*): **mettersi in** ~ to set up on one's own; **l'ha visto con i (suoi) propri occhi** he saw it with his own eyes

propu'gnare [propun'nare] /15/ vt to support

propulsi'one SF propulsion; **a** ~ **atomica** atomic-powered

propul'sore SM (*Tecn*) propeller

'prora SF (*Naut*) bow(s), prow

'proroga, -ghe SF extension; postponement

proro'gare /80/ vt to extend; (*differire*) to postpone, defer

pro'rompere /97/ vi to burst out

pro'rotto, -a PP di **prorompere**

pro'ruppi etc VB vedi **prorompere**

'prosa SF prose; (*Teat*): **la stagione della** ~ the theatre season; **attore di** ~ theatre actor; **compagnia di** ~ theatrical company

pro'saico, -a, -ci, -che AG (*fig*) prosaic, mundane

pro'sciogliere [proʃ'ʃɔʎʎere] /103/ vt to release; (*Dir*) to acquit

prosciogli'mento [proʃʃoʎʎi'mento] SM acquittal

prosci'olto, -a [proʃ'ʃɔlto] PP di **prosciogliere**

prosciu'gare [proʃʃu'gare] /80/ vt (*terreni*) to drain, reclaim; **prosciugarsi** VPR to dry up

prosci'utto [proʃ'ʃutto] SM ham; ~ **cotto/crudo** cooked/cured ham

pros'critto, -a PP di **proscrivere** ▶ SM/F exile; outlaw

pros'crivere /105/ vt to exile, banish

proscrizi'one [proskrit'tsjone] SF (*esilio*) banishment, exile

prosecuzi'one [prosekut'tsjone] SF continuation

prosegui'mento SM continuation; **buon ~!** all the best!; (*a chi viaggia*) enjoy the rest of your journey!

prosegu'ire /45/ vt to carry on with, continue ▶ VI to carry on, go on

pro'selito SM (*Rel, Pol*) convert

prospe'rare /72/ vi to thrive

prosperità SF prosperity

'prospero, -a AG (*fiorente*) flourishing, thriving, prosperous

prospe'roso, -a AG (*robusto*) hale and hearty; (*ragazza*) buxom

prospet'tare /72/ vt (*esporre*) to point out, show; (*ipotesi*) to advance; (*affare*) to outline; **prospettarsi** VPR to look, appear

prospet'tiva SF (*Arte*) perspective; (*veduta*) view; (*fig: previsione, possibilità*) prospect

pros'petto SM (*Disegno*) elevation; (*veduta*) view, prospect; (*facciata*) façade, front; (*tabella*) table; (*sommario*) summary

prospici'ente [prospi'tʃente] AG: ~ **qc** facing o overlooking sth

prossima'mente AV soon

prossimità SF nearness, proximity; **in** ~ **di** near (to), close to; **in** ~ **delle feste natalizie** as Christmas approaches

'prossimo, -a AG (*che viene subito dopo*) next; (*parente*) close; (*vicino*): ~ **a** near (to), close to ▶ SM neighbour (*BRIT*), neighbor (*US*), fellow man; **nei prossimi giorni** in the next few days; **in un** ~ **futuro** in the near future; ~ **venturo (pv)** (*Amm*): **venerdì** ~ **venturo** next Friday

'prostata SF prostate (gland)

prostitu'irsi /55/ VPR to prostitute o.s.

prosti'tuta SF prostitute

prostituzi'one [prostitut'tsjone] SF prostitution

pros'trare /**72**/ VT (*fig*) to exhaust, wear out;
prostrarsi VPR (*fig*) to humble o.s.; **prostrato
dal dolore** overcome *o* prostrate with grief

prostrazi'one [prostrat'tsjone] SF
prostration

protago'nista, -i, -e SM/F protagonist

pro'teggere [pro'tɛddʒere] /**83**/ VT to protect

proteggi'slip [protɛddʒi'slip] SM INV panty
liner

pro'teico, -a, -ci, -che AG protein *cpd*;
altamente ~ high in protein

prote'ina SF protein

pro'tendere /**120**/ VT to stretch out

'**protesi** SF INV (*Med*) prosthesis

pro'teso, -a PP *di* **protendere**

pro'testa SF protest

protes'tante AG, SMF Protestant

protes'tare /**72**/ VT, VI to protest;
protestarsi VPR: **protestarsi innocente** *etc*
to protest one's innocence *o* that one is
innocent *etc*

pro'testo SM (*Dir*) protest; **mandare una
cambiale in ~** to dishonour (*Brit*) *o* dishonor
(*US*) a bill

protet'tivo, -a AG protective

pro'tetto, -a PP *di* **proteggere**

protetto'rato SM protectorate

protet'tore, -'trice SM/F protector;
(*sostenitore*) patron ▶ AG (*Rel*): **santo ~** patron
saint; **società protettrice dei
consumatori** consumer protection society

protezi'one [protet'tsjone] SF protection;
(*patrocinio*) patronage; **misure di ~**
protective measures; **~ civile** civil defence (*Brit*) *o*
defense (*US*)

protezio'nismo [protettsjo'nizmo] SM
protectionism

protocol'lare /**72**/ VT to register ▶ AG formal;
of protocol

proto'collo SM protocol; (*registro*) register of
documents ▶ AG INV: **foglio ~** foolscap;
numero di ~ reference number

pro'tone SM proton

pro'totipo SM prototype

pro'trarre /**123**/ VT (*prolungare*) to prolong;
protrarsi VPR to go on, continue

pro'tratto, -a PP *di* **protrarre**

protube'ranza [protube'rantsa] SF
protuberance, bulge

Prov. ABBR (= *provincia*) Prov

'**prova** SF (*esperimento, cimento*) test, trial;
(*tentativo*) attempt, try; (*Mat*) proof *no pl*;
(*Dir*) evidence *no pl*, proof *no pl*; (*Ins*) exam,
test; (*Teat*) rehearsal; (*di abito*) fitting; **a ~ di**
(*in testimonianza di*) as proof of; **a ~ di fuoco**
fireproof; **assumere in ~** (*per lavoro*) to
employ on a trial basis; **essere in ~** (*persona:
per lavoro*) to be on trial; **mettere alla ~** to put
to the test; **giro di ~** test *o* trial run; **fino a ~**

contraria until (it's) proved otherwise;
~ a carico/a discarico (*Dir*) evidence for the
prosecution/for the defence;
~ documentale (*Dir*) documentary evidence;
~ generale (*Teat*) dress rehearsal;
~ testimoniale (*Dir*) testimonial evidence

pro'vare /**72**/ VT (*sperimentare*) to test; (*tentare*)
to try, attempt; (*assaggiare*) to try, taste;
(*sperimentare in sé*) to experience; (*sentire*) to
feel; (*cimentare*) to put to the test; (*dimostrare*)
to prove; (*abito*) to try on; **provarsi** VPR:
provarsi (a fare) to try *o* attempt (to do);
~ a fare to try *o* attempt to do

proveni'enza [prove'njɛntsa] SF origin,
source

prove'nire /**128**/ VI: **~ da** to come from

pro'venti SMPL revenue *sg*

prove'nuto, -a PP *di* **provenire**

Pro'venza [pro'vɛntsa] SF: **la ~** Provence

proven'zale [proven'tsale] AG Provençal

pro'verbio SM proverb

pro'vetta SF test tube; **bambino in ~**
test-tube baby

pro'vetto, -a AG skilled, experienced

pro'vider [pro'vaider] SM INV (*Inform*) service
provider

pro'vincia [pro'vintʃa], **-ce** *o* **-cie** SF province;
see note

A *Provincia* is the autonomous political
and administrative unit which is on a
level between a *Comune* and a *Regione*;
there are 103 in the whole of Italy. The
Provincia is responsible for public health
and sanitation, for the maintenance of
major roads and public buildings such
as schools, and for agriculture and
fisheries. Situated in the *capoluogo*, or
chief town, each *Provincia* is run by a
Giunta provinciale, which is elected by the
Consiglio Provinciale; both of these bodies
are presided over by a *Presidente*.

provinci'ale [provin'tʃale] AG provincial;
(**strada**) **~** main road (*Brit*), highway (*US*)

pro'vino SM (*Cine*) screen test; (*campione*)
specimen

provo'cante AG (*attraente*) provocative

provo'care /**20**/ VT (*causare*) to cause, bring
about; (*eccitare: riso, pietà*) to arouse; (*irritare,
sfidare*) to provoke

provoca'tore, -'trice SM/F agitator ▶ AG:
agente ~ agent provocateur

provoca'torio, -a AG provocative

provocazi'one [provokat'tsjone] SF
provocation

provve'dere /**82**/ VI (*prendere un provvedimento*)
to take steps, act; (*disporre*): **~ (a)** to provide
(for) ▶ VT: **~ qc a qn** to supply sth to sb;
provvedersi VPR: **provvedersi di** to provide
o.s. with

provvedi'mento SM measure; (*di previdenza*) precaution; ~ **disciplinare** disciplinary measure

provvedito'rato SM (*Amm*): ~ **agli studi** divisional education offices *pl*

provvedi'tore SM (*Amm*): ~ **agli studi** divisional director of education

provvi'denza [provvi'dɛntsa] SF: **la ~** providence

provvidenzi'ale [provviden'tsjale] AG providential

provvigi'one [provvi'dʒone] SF (*Comm*) commission; **lavoro/stipendio a ~** job/salary on a commission basis

provvi'sorio, -a AG temporary; (*governo*) temporary, provisional

prov'vista SF (*riserva*) supply, stock; **fare ~ di** to stock up with

prov'visto, -a PP *di* **provvedere** ▶ SF provision, supply

pro'zia [prot'tsia] SF great-aunt

pro'zio, -zii [prot'tsio] SM great-uncle

'prua SF (*Naut*) bow(s), prow

pru'dente AG cautious, prudent; (*assennato*) sensible, wise

pru'denza [pru'dɛntsa] SF prudence, caution; wisdom; **per ~** as a precaution, to be on the safe side

'prudere /**29**/ VI to itch, be itchy

'prugna ['pruɲɲa] SF plum; ~ **secca** prune

prurigi'noso, -a [pruridʒi'noso] AG itchy

pru'rito SM itchiness *no pl*; itch

PS SIGLA = **Pesaro**

P.S. ABBR (= *postscriptum*) PS; (*Comm*) = **partita semplice** ▶ SIGLA F (*Polizia*) = **Pubblica Sicurezza**

P.S.D.I. SIGLA M (= *Partito Socialista Democratico Italiano*) *former political party*

pseu'donimo SM pseudonym

PSI SIGLA M (*Pol*) = **Partito Socialista Italiano**

psica'nalisi SF psychoanalysis

psicana'lista, -i, -e SM/F psychoanalyst

psicanaliz'zare [psikanalid'dzare] /**72**/ VT to psychoanalyse

'psiche ['psike] SF (*Psic*) psyche

psiche'delico, -a, -ci, -che [psike'dɛliko] AG psychedelic

psichi'atra, -i, -e [psi'kjatra] SM/F psychiatrist

psichia'tria [psikja'tria] SF psychiatry

psichi'atrico, -a, -ci, -che [psi'kjatriko] AG (*caso*) psychiatric; (*reparto, ospedale*) psychiatric, mental

'psichico, -a, -ci, -che ['psikiko] AG psychological

psico'farmaco, -ci SM (*Med*) *drug used in treatment of mental conditions*

psicolo'gia [psikolo'dʒia] SF psychology

psico'logico, -a, -ci, -che [psiko'lɔdʒiko] AG psychological

psi'cologo, -a, -gi, -ghe SM/F psychologist

psico'patico, -a, -ci, -che AG psychopathic ▶ SM/F psychopath

psi'cosi SF INV (*Med*) psychosis; (*fig*) obsessive fear

psicoso'matico, -a, -ci, -che AG psychosomatic

PT SIGLA = **Pistoia**

Pt. ABBR (*Geo*: = *punta*) Pt

P.T. ABBR (= *Posta e Telegrafi*) ≈ PO (= *Post Office*); (*Fisco*) = **polizia tributaria**

P.ta ABBR = **porta**

pubbli'care /**20**/ VT to publish

pubblicazi'one [pubblikat'tsjone] SF publication; ~ **periodica** periodical; **pubblicazioni (matrimoniali)** (marriage) banns

pubbli'cista, -i, -e [pubbli'tʃista] SM/F (*Stampa*) freelance journalist

pubblicità [pubblitʃi'ta] SF (*diffusione*) publicity; (*attività*) advertising; (*annunci nei giornali*) advertisements *pl*; **fare ~ a qc** to advertise sth

pubblici'tario, -a [pubblitʃi'tarjo] AG advertising *cpd*; (*trovata, film*) publicity *cpd* ▶ SM advertising agent; **annuncio** *o* **avviso ~** advertisement

'pubblico, -a, -ci, -che AG public; (*statale: scuola ecc*) state *cpd* ▶ SM public; (*spettatori*) audience; **in ~** in public; **la pubblica amministrazione** public administration; **un ~ esercizio** a catering (*o* hotel *o* entertainment) business; ~ **funzionario** civil servant; **Ministero della Pubblica Istruzione** ≈ Department of Education and Science (*BRIT*), ≈ Department of Health, Education and Welfare (*US*); **P~ Ministero** Public Prosecutor's Office; **la Pubblica Sicurezza** the police

'pube SM (*Anat*) pubis

pubertà SF puberty

'pudico, -a, -ci, -che AG modest

pu'dore SM modesty

puericul'tura SF infant care

pue'rile AG childish

pu'erpera SF *woman who has just given birth*

pugi'lato [pudʒi'lato] SM boxing

'pugile ['pudʒile] SM boxer

pugli'ese [puʎ'ʎese] AG of (*o* from) Puglia

pugna'lare [puɲɲa'lare] /**72**/ VT to stab

pu'gnale [puɲ'ɲale] SM dagger

'pugno ['puɲɲo] SM fist; (*colpo*) punch; (*quantità*) fistful; **avere qn in ~** to have sb in the palm of one's hand; **tenere la situazione in ~** to have control of the situation; **scrivere qc di proprio ~** to write sth in one's own hand

'pulce ['pultʃe] SF flea

pul'cino [pul'tʃino] SM chick

pu'ledro, -a SM/F colt/filly

pu'leggia, -ge [pu'leddʒa] SF pulley

pu'lire /55/ VT to clean; (*lucidare*) to polish; **far ~ qc** to have sth cleaned; **~ a secco** to dry-clean

pu'lito, -a AG (*anche fig*) clean; (*ordinato*) neat, tidy ▶ SF quick clean; **avere la coscienza pulita** to have a clear conscience

puli'tura SF cleaning; **~ a secco** dry-cleaning

puli'zia [pulit'tsia] SF (*atto*) cleaning; (*condizione*) cleanness; **fare le pulizie** to do the cleaning, do the housework; **~ etnica** ethnic cleansing

'pullman SM INV coach (BRIT), bus

pul'lover SM INV pullover, jumper

pullu'lare /72/ VI to swarm, teem

pul'mino SM minibus

'pulpito SM pulpit

pul'sante SM (push-)button

pul'sare /72/ VI to pulsate, beat

pulsazi'one [pulsat'tsjone] SF beat

pul'viscolo SM fine dust; **~ atmosferico** specks *pl* of dust

'puma SM INV puma

pun'gente [pun'dʒɛnte] AG prickly; stinging; (*anche fig*) biting

'pungere ['pundʒere] /84/ VT to prick; (*insetto, ortica*) to sting; (*freddo*) to bite; **~ qn sul vivo** (*fig*) to cut sb to the quick

pungigli'one [pundʒiʎ'ʎone] SM sting

pungo'lare /72/ VT to goad

pu'nire /55/ VT to punish

puni'tivo, -a AG punitive

punizi'one [punit'tsjone] SF punishment; (*Sport*) penalty

'punsi *etc* VB *vedi* **pungere**

'punta SF point; (*parte terminale*) tip, end; (*di monte*) peak; (*di costa*) promontory; (*minima parte*) touch, trace; **in ~ di piedi** on tiptoe; **ore di ~** peak hours; **uomo di ~** (*Sport, Pol*) front-rank *o* leading man; **doppie punte** split ends

pun'tare /72/ VT (*piedi a terra, gomiti sul tavolo*) to plant; (*dirigere: pistola*) to point; (*scommettere*): **~ su** to bet on ▶ VI (*mirare*): **~ a** to aim at; (*avviarsi*): **~ su** to head *o* make for; (*fig: contare*): **~ su** to count *o* rely on

puntas'pilli SM INV = **portaspilli**

pun'tata SF (*gita*) short trip; (*scommessa*) bet; (*parte di opera*) instalment (BRIT), installment (US); **farò una ~ a Parigi** I'll pay a flying visit to Paris; **romanzo a puntate** serial

punteggi'are [punted'dʒare] /62/ VT to punctuate

punteggia'tura [puntedʒa'tura] SF (*Ling*) punctuation

pun'teggio [pun'teddʒo] SM score

puntel'lare /72/ VT to support

pun'tello SM prop, support

punteru'olo SM (*Tecn*) punch; (*per stoffa*) bodkin

pun'tiglio [pun'tiʎʎo] SM obstinacy, stubbornness

puntigli'oso, -a [puntiʎ'ʎoso] AG punctilious

pun'tina SF: **~ da disegno** drawing pin (BRIT), thumb tack (US); **puntine** SFPL (*Aut*) points

pun'tino SM dot; **fare qc a ~** to do sth properly; **arrivare a ~** to arrive just at the right moment; **cotto a ~** cooked to perfection; **mettere i puntini sulle "i"** (*fig*) to dot the i's and cross the t's

'punto, -a PP *di* **pungere** ▶ SM point; (*segno, macchiolina*) dot; (*Ling*) full stop; (*di indirizzo e-mail*) dot; (*posto*) spot; (*a scuola*) mark; (*nel cucire, nella maglia, Med*) stitch ▶ AV: **non ... ~** not ... at all; **due punti** (*inv: Ling*) colon; **ad un certo ~** at a certain point; **fino ad un certo ~** (*fig*) to a certain extent; **sul ~ di fare** (just) about to do; **fare il ~** (*Naut*) to take a bearing; **fare il ~ della situazione** (*analisi*) to take stock of the situation; (*riassunto*) to sum up the situation; **alle 6 in ~** at 6 o'clock sharp *o* on the dot; **essere a buon ~** to have reached a satisfactory stage; **mettere a ~** to adjust; (*motore*) to tune; (*cannocchiale*) to focus; (*fig*) to settle; **venire al ~** to come to the point; **vestito di tutto ~** all dressed up; **di ~ in bianco** point-blank; **~ d'arrivo** arrival point; **~ cardinale** point of the compass, cardinal point; **~ debole** weak point; **~ esclamativo/interrogativo** exclamation/question mark; **~ d'incontro** meeting place, meeting point; **~ morto** standstill; **~ nero** (*comedone*) blackhead; **~ nevralgico** (*anche fig*) nerve centre (BRIT) *o* center (US); **~ di partenza** (*anche fig*) starting point; **~ di riferimento** landmark; (*fig*) point of reference; **~ di vendita** retail outlet; **~ e virgola** semicolon; **~ di vista** (*fig*) point of view; **punti di sospensione** suspension points

puntu'ale AG punctual

puntualità SF punctuality

puntualiz'zare [puntualid'dzare] /72/ VT to make clear

puntual'mente AV (*gen*) on time; (*ironico: al solito*) as usual

pun'tura SF (*di ago*) prick; (*di insetto*) sting, bite; (*Med*) puncture; (*: iniezione*) injection; (*dolore*) sharp pain

punzecchi'are [puntsek'kjare] /19/ VT to prick; (*fig*) to tease

punzo'nare [puntso'nare] /72/ VT (*Tecn*) to stamp

pun'zone [pun'tsone] SM (*per metalli*) stamp, die

285

può VB *vedi* **potere**

puoi VB *vedi* **potere**

'**pupa** SF doll

pu'pazzo [pu'pattso] SM puppet

pu'pillo, -a SM/F (*Dir*) ward; (*prediletto*) favourite (*BRIT*), favorite (*US*), pet ▶ SF (*Anat*) pupil

purché [pur'ke] CONG provided that, on condition that

'**pure** CONG (*tuttavia*) and yet, nevertheless; (*anche se*) even if ▶ AV (*anche*) too, also; **pur di** (*al fine di*) just to; **faccia ~!** go ahead!, please do!

purè SM, **pu'rea** SF (*Cuc*) purée; (*di patate*) mashed potatoes *pl*

pu'rezza [pu'rettsa] SF purity

'**purga, -ghe** SF purging *no pl*; purge

pur'gante SM (*Med*) purgative, purge

pur'gare /80/ VT (*Med, Pol*) to purge; (*pulire*) to clean

purga'torio SM purgatory

purifi'care /20/ VT to purify; (*metallo*) to refine

purificazi'one [purifikat'tsjone] SF purification; refinement

puri'tano, -a AG, SM/F puritan

'**puro, -a** AG pure; (*acqua*) clear, limpid; (*vino*) undiluted; **di razza pura** thoroughbred;

per ~ caso by sheer chance, purely by chance

puro'sangue SM INV/F INV thoroughbred

pur'troppo AV unfortunately

pus SM pus

pusil'lanime AG cowardly

'**pustola** SF pimple

puta'caso AV just supposing, suppose

puti'ferio SM rumpus, row

putre'fare /41/ VI to putrefy, rot

putre'fatto, -a PP *di* **putrefare**

putrefazi'one [putrefat'tsjone] SF putrefaction

'**putrido, -a** AG putrid, rotten

put'tana SF (*col*) whore (!)

'**putto** SM cupid

'**puzza** ['puttsa] SF = **puzzo**

puz'zare [put'tsare] /72/ VI to stink; **la faccenda puzza (d'imbroglio)** the whole business stinks

'**puzzo** ['puttso] SM stink, foul smell

'**puzzola** ['puttsola] SF polecat

puzzo'lente [puttso'lɛnte] AG stinking

PV SIGLA = **Pavia**

pv ABBR = **prossimo venturo**

P.V.C. [pivi'tʃi] SIGLA M (= *polyvinyl chloride*) PVC

PZ SIGLA = **Potenza**

p.za ABBR = **piazza**

Q q

Q, q [ku] SM O F INV *(lettera)* Q, q; **Q come Quarto** = Q for Queen

q ABBR (= *quintale*) q

Qa'tar [ka'tar] SM: **il ~** Qatar

q.b. ABBR (= *quanto basta*) as needed; (= *zucchero q.b.*) sugar to taste

Q.G. ABBR = **quartier generale**

Q.I. ABBR = **quoziente d'intelligenza**

qua AV here; **in ~** *(verso questa parte)* this way; **~ dentro/sotto** *etc* in/under here *etc*; **da un anno in ~** for a year now; **da quando in ~?** since when?; **per di ~** *(passare)* this way; **al di ~ di** *(fiume, strada)* on this side of; **~ dentro/ fuori** *ecc* in/out here *ecc*; *vedi anche* **questo**

'quacchero, -a ['kwakkero] SM/F Quaker

qua'derno SM notebook; *(per scuola)* exercise book

qua'drangolo SM quadrangle

qua'drante SM quadrant; *(di orologio)* face

qua'drare /72/ VI *(bilancio)* to balance, tally; *(fig: corrispondere)*: **~ (con)** to correspond (with) ▶ VT *(Mat)* to square; **far ~ il bilancio** to balance the books; **non mi quadra** I don't like it

qua'drato, -a AG square; *(fig: equilibrato)* level-headed, sensible; *(peg)* square ▶ SM *(Mat)* square; *(Pugilato)* ring; **5 al ~** 5 squared

quadret'tato, -a AG *(foglio)* squared; *(tessuto)* checked

qua'dretto SM: **a quadretti** *(tessuto)* checked; *(foglio)* squared

quadrien'nale AG *(che dura 4 anni)* four-year *cpd*; *(che avviene ogni 4 anni)* four-yearly

quadri'foglio [kwadri'fɔʎʎo] SM four-leaf clover

quadri'mestre SM *(periodo)* four-month period; *(Ins)* term

'quadro SM *(pittura)* painting, picture; *(quadrato)* square; *(tabella)* table, chart; *(Tecn)* board, panel; *(Teat)* scene; *(fig: scena, spettacolo)* sight; *(: descrizione)* outline, description; **quadri** SMPL *(Pol)* party organizers; *(Comm)* managerial staff; *(Mil)* cadres; *(Carte)* diamonds; **a quadri** *(disegno)* checked; **fare un ~ della situazione** to outline the situation; **~ clinico** *(Med)* case history; **~ di comando** control panel; **quadri intermedi** middle management *sg*

qua'drupede SM quadruped

quadrupli'care /20/ VT to quadruple

'quadruplo, -a AG, SM quadruple

quaggiù [kwad'dʒu] AV down here

'quaglia ['kwaʎʎa] SF quail

PAROLA CHIAVE

'qualche ['kwalke] DET **1** some, a few; *(in interrogative)* any; **ho comprato qualche libro** I've bought some *o* a few books; **qualche volta** sometimes; **hai qualche sigaretta?** have you any cigarettes?

2 *(uno)*: **c'è qualche medico?** is there a doctor?; **in qualche modo** somehow

3 *(un certo, parecchio)* some; **un personaggio di qualche rilievo** a figure of some importance

4: **qualche cosa** = **qualcosa**

---

qualche'duno [kwalke'duno] PRON = **qualcuno**

qual'cosa PRON something; *(in espressioni interrogative)* anything; **qualcos'altro** something else; anything else; **~ di nuovo** something new; anything new; **~ da mangiare** something to eat; anything to eat; **c'è ~ che non va?** is there something *o* anything wrong?

qual'cuno PRON *(persona)* someone, somebody; *(: in espressioni interrogative)* anyone, anybody; *(alcuni)* some; **~ è favorevole a noi** some are on our side; **qualcun altro** someone *o* somebody else; anyone *o* anybody else

---

PAROLA CHIAVE

'quale *(spesso troncato in* **qual***)* DET **1** *(interrogativo)* what; *(: scegliendo tra due o più cose o persone)* which; **quale uomo/denaro?**

what man/money?; which man/money?; **quali sono i tuoi programmi?** what are your plans?; **quale stanza preferisci?** which room do you prefer?

2 (*relativo: come*): **il risultato fu quale ci si aspettava** the result was as expected **3** (*in elenchi*) such as, like; **piante quali l'edera** plants such as *o* like ivy **4** (*esclamativo*) what; **quale disgrazia!** what bad luck!

5: **in un certo qual modo** in a way, in some ways; **per la qual cosa** for which reason

▶ PRON **1** (*interrogativo*) which; **quale dei due scegli?** which of the two do you want?

2 (*relativo*): **il (la) quale** (*persona: soggetto*) who; (*: oggetto, con preposizione*) whom; (*cosa*) which; (*possessivo*) whose; **suo padre, il quale è avvocato, ...** his father, who is a lawyer, ...; **a tutti coloro i quali fossero interessati ...** to whom it may concern ...; **il signore con il quale parlavo** the gentleman to whom I was speaking; **l'albergo al quale ci siamo fermati** the hotel where we stayed *o* which we stayed at; **la signora della quale ammiriamo la bellezza** the lady whose beauty we admire

▶ AV (*in qualità di, come*) as; **quale sindaco di questa città** as mayor of this town

qua'lifica, -che SF qualification; (*titolo*) title
qualifi'care /20/ VT to qualify; (*definire*): **~ qn/ qc come** to describe sb/sth as; **qualificarsi** VPR (*Sport*) to qualify; **qualificarsi a un concorso** to pass a competitive exam
qualifica'tivo, -a AG qualifying
qualifi'cato, -a AG (*dotato di qualifica*) qualified; (*esperto, abile*) skilled; **non mi ritengo ~ per questo lavoro** I don't think I'm qualified for this job; **è un medico molto ~** he is a very distinguished doctor
qualificazi'one [kwalifikat'tsjone] SF qualification; **gara di ~** (*Sport*) qualifying event
qualità SF INV quality; **di ottima** *o* **prima ~** top quality; **in ~ di** in one's capacity as; **in ~ di amica** as a friend; **articoli di ogni ~** all sorts of goods; **controllo (di) ~** quality control; **prodotto di ~** quality product
qualita'tivo, -a AG qualitative
qua'lora CONG in case, if
qual'siasi, qua'lunque DET *inv* any; (*quale che sia*) whatever; (*discriminativo*) whichever; (*posposto: mediocre*) poor, indifferent; ordinary; **mettiti un vestito ~** put on any old dress; **~ cosa** anything; **~ cosa accada** whatever happens; **a ~ costo** at any cost, whatever the cost; **l'uomo ~** the man in the street; **~ persona** anyone, anybody

qualunqu'ista, -i, -e SM/F person indifferent to politics
'quando CONG, AV when; **~ sarò ricco** when I'm rich; **da ~** (*dacché*) since; (*interrogativo*) **da ~ sei qui?** how long have you been here?; **di ~ in ~** from time to time; **quand'anche** even if
quantifi'care /20/ VT to quantify
quantità SF INV quantity; **una ~ di** (*gran numero*) a great deal of; a lot of; **in grande ~** in large quantities
quantita'tivo, -a AG quantitative ▶ SM (*Comm: di merce*) amount, quantity

(PAROLA CHIAVE)

'quanto, -a DET **1** (*interrogativo: quantità*) how much; (*: numero*) how many; **quanto pane/ denaro?** how much bread/money?; **quanti libri/ragazzi?** how many books/boys?; **quanto tempo?** how long?; **quanti anni hai?** how old are you?

2 (*esclamativo*): **quante storie!** what a lot of nonsense!; **quanto tempo sprecato!** what a waste of time!

3 (*relativo: quantità*) as much ... as; (*: numero*) as many ... as; **ho quanto denaro mi occorre** I have as much money as I need; **prendi quanti libri vuoi** take as many books as you like

▶ PRON **1** (*interrogativo: quantità*) how much; (*: numero*) how many; (*: tempo*) how long; **quanto mi dai?** how much will you give me?; **quanti me ne hai portati?** how many did you bring me?; **quanto starai via?** how long will you be away (for)?; **da quanto sei qui?** how long have you been here?; **quanti ne abbiamo oggi?** what's the date today?

2 (*relativo: quantità*) as much as; (*: numero*) as many as; **farò quanto posso** I'll do as much as I can; **a quanto dice lui** according to him; **in risposta a quanto esposto nella sua lettera ...** in answer to the points raised in your letter; **possono venire quanti sono stati invitati** all those who have been invited can come

▶ AV **1** (*interrogativo: con ag, av*) how; (*: con vb*) how much; **quanto stanco ti sembrava?** how tired did he seem to you?; **quanto corre la tua moto?** how fast can your motorbike go?; **quanto costa?** how much does it cost?; **quant'è?** how much is it?

2 (*esclamativo: con ag, av*) how; (*: con vb*) how much; **quanto sono felice!** how happy I am!; **sapessi quanto abbiamo camminato!** if you knew how far we've walked!; **studierò quanto posso** I'll study as much as *o* all I can; **quanto prima** as soon as possible; **quanto più ... tanto meno** the

more ... the less; **quanto più ... tanto più**
the more ... the more

3: **in quanto** (*in qualità di*) as; (*perché, per il fatto
che*) as, since; **in quanto legale della
signora** as the lady's lawyer; **non è
possibile in quanto non possiamo
permettercelo** it isn't possible, since we
can't afford it; (**in**) **quanto a** (*per ciò che
riguarda*) as for, as regards; (**in**) **quanto a lui**
as far as he's concerned

4: **per quanto** (*nonostante, anche se*) however;
per quanto si sforzi, non ce la farà try as
he may, he won't manage it; **per quanto
sia brava, fa degli errori** however good
she may be, she makes mistakes; **per
quanto io sappia** as far as I know

quan'tunque CONG although, though
qua'ranta NUM forty
quaran'tena SF quarantine
quaran'tenne AG, SMF forty-year-old
quaran'tennio SM (period of) forty years
quaran'tesimo, -a NUM fortieth
quaran'tina SF: **una ~ (di)** about forty
quaran'totto SM INV forty-eight; **fare un ~**
(*col*) to raise hell
Qua'resima SF: **la ~** Lent
'quarta SF *vedi* **quarto**
quar'tetto SM quartet(te)
quar'tiere SM district, area; (*Mil*) quarters *pl*;
~ generale headquarters *pl*; **~ residenziale**
residential area *o* district; **i quartieri alti**
the smart districts
'quarto, -a AG fourth ▶ SM fourth; (*quarta
parte*) quarter ▶ SF (*Aut*) fourth (gear); (*Ins:
elementare*) fourth year of primary school;
(: *superiore*) seventh year of secondary school; **un ~
di vino** a quarter-litre (BRIT) *o* quarter-liter
(US) bottle of wine; **le 6 e un ~** a quarter past
(BRIT) *o* after (US) 6; **~ d'ora** quarter of an
hour; **tre quarti d'ora** three quarters of an
hour; **le otto e tre quarti, le nove meno
un ~** (a) quarter to (BRIT) *o* of (US) nine;
passare un brutto ~ d'ora (*fig*) to have a bad
o nasty time of it; **quarti di finale** (*Sport*)
quarter finals
'quarzo ['kwartso] SM quartz
'quasi AV almost, nearly ▶ CONG (*anche*: **quasi
che**) as if; (**non**) **... ~ mai** hardly ever; **~ ~ me
ne andrei** I've half a mind to leave
quas'sù AV up here
'quatto, -a AG crouched, squatting; (*silenzioso*)
silent; **~ ~** very quietly; stealthily
quattordi'cenne [kwattordi'tʃɛnne] AG, SMF
fourteen-year-old
quat'tordici [kwat'torditʃi] NUM fourteen
quat'trini SMPL money *sg*, cash *sg*
'quattro NUM four; **in ~ e quattr'otto** in less
than no time; **dirne ~ a qn** to give sb a piece

of one's mind; **fare il diavolo a ~** to kick up
a rumpus; **fare ~ chiacchiere** to have a chat;
farsi in ~ per qn to go out of one's way for
sb, put o.s. out for sb; **~ per ~** four-by-four
quat'trocchi [kwat'trɔkki] SM INV (*fig*: *col*:
persona con occhiali) four-eyes; **a ~** *av* (*tra 2
persone*) face to face; (*privatamente*) in private
quattrocen'tesco, -a, -schi, -sche
[kwattrotʃen'tesko] AG fifteenth-century
quattro'cento [kwattro'tʃɛnto] NUM four
hundred ▶ SM: **il Q~** the fifteenth century
quattro'mila NUM four thousand

'quello, -a (*dav sm* **quel** + C, **quell'** + V, **quello** + *s
impura, gn, pn, ps, x, z; pl* **quei** + C, **quegli** + V *o s
impura, gn, pn, ps, x, z; dav sf* **quella** + C, **quell'** + V;
pl **quelle**) DET that; *pl* those; **quella casa** that
house; **quegli uomini** those men; **voglio
quella camicia** (**lì** *o* **là**) I want that shirt;
quello è mio fratello that's my brother
▶ PRON **1** (*dimostrativo*) that one; *pl* those
ones; (*ciò*) that; **conosci quella?** do you
know her?; **prendo quello bianco** I'll take
the white one; **chi è quello?** who's that?;
prendiamo quello (**lì** *o* **là**) let's take that
one (there); **in quel di Milano** in the Milan
area *o* region
2 (*relativo*): **quello(a) che** (*persona*) the one
(who); (*cosa*) the one (which), the one (that);
quelli(e) che (*persone*) those who; (*cose*) those
which; **è lui quello che non voleva venire**
he's the one who didn't want to come; **ho
fatto quello che potevo** I did what I could;
è quella che ti ho prestato that's the one
I lent you; **è proprio quello che gli ho
detto** that's exactly what I told him; **da
quello che ho sentito** from what I've heard

'quercia, -ce ['kwɛrtʃa] SF oak (tree); (*legno*)
oak; **la Q~** (*Pol*) symbol of P.D.S.
que'rela SF (*Dir*) (legal) action
quere'lare /72/ VT to bring an action against
que'sito SM question, query; problem
'questi PRON (*poetico*) this person
questio'nario SM questionnaire
questi'one SF problem, question;
(*controversia*) issue; (*litigio*) quarrel; **in ~** in
question; **il caso in ~** the matter at hand;
la persona in ~ the person involved; **non
voglio essere chiamato in ~** I don't want
to be dragged into the argument; **fuor di ~**
out of the question; **è ~ di tempo** it's a
matter *o* question of time

'questo, -a DET **1** (*dimostrativo*) this; *pl*
these; **questo libro** (**qui** *o* **qua**) this book;
io prendo questo cappotto, tu quello

q

I'll take this coat, you take that one; **quest'oggi** today; **questa sera** this evening **2** (*enfatico*): **non fatemi più prendere di queste paure** don't frighten me like that again

▶ PRON (*dimostrativo*) this (one); *pl* these (ones); (*ciò*) this; **prendo questo (qui** *o* **qua)** I'll take this one; **preferisci questi o quelli?** do you prefer these (ones) or those (ones)?; **questo intendevo io** this is what I meant; **vengono Paolo e Luca: questo da Roma, quello da Palermo** Paolo and Luca are coming: the former from Palermo, the latter from Rome; **questo non dovevi dirlo** you shouldn't have said that; **e con questo?** so what?; **e con questo se n'è andato** and with that he left; **con tutto questo** in spite of this, despite all this; **questo è quanto** that's all

ques'tore SM *public official in charge of the police in the provincial capital, reporting to the prefetto*, ≈ chief constable (*BRIT*), ≈ police commissioner (*US*)

'**questua** SF collection (of alms)
ques'tura SF police headquarters *pl*
questu'rino SM (*col: poliziotto*) cop
qui AV here; **da** *o* **di ~** from here; **di ~ in avanti** from now on; **di ~ a poco/una settimana** in a little while/a week's time; **~ dentro/sopra/vicino** in/up/near here; *vedi anche* **questo**
quie'scenza [kwjeʃʃɛntsa] SF (*Amm*): **porre qn in ~** to retire sb
quie'tanza [kwje'tantsa] SF receipt
quie'tare /**72**/ VT to calm, soothe
qui'ete SF quiet, quietness; calmness; stillness; peace; **turbare la ~ pubblica** (*Dir*) to disturb the peace
qui'eto, -a AG quiet; (*notte*) calm, still; (*mare*) calm; **l'ho fatto per il ~ vivere** I did it for a quiet life
'**quindi** AV then ▶ CONG therefore, so
quindi'cenne [kwindi'tʃɛnne] AG, SMF fifteen-year-old
'**quindici** ['kwinditʃi] NUM fifteen; **~ giorni** a fortnight (*BRIT*), two weeks

quindi'cina [kwindi'tʃina] SF (*serie*): **una ~ (di)** about fifteen; **fra una ~ di giorni** in a fortnight (*BRIT*) *o* two weeks
quindici'nale [kwinditʃi'nale] AG fortnightly (*BRIT*), semimonthly (*US*) ▶ SM (*rivista*) fortnightly magazine (*BRIT*), semimonthly (*US*)
quinquen'nale AG (*che dura 5 anni*) five-year *cpd*; (*che avviene ogni 5 anni*) five-yearly
quin'quennio SM period of five years
quinta SF *vedi* **quinto**
quin'tale SM quintal (*100 kg*)
quin'tetto SM quintet(te)
'**quinto, -a** NUM fifth ▶ SF (*Aut*) fifth (gear); (*Ins: elementare*) fifth year of primary school; (*: superiore*) final year of secondary school; (*Teat*) wing; **un ~ della popolazione** a fifth of the population; **tre quinti** three fifths; **in quinta pagina** on the fifth page, on page five
qui pro quo SM INV misunderstanding
Quiri'nale SM *see note*

> The *Quirinale* takes its name from one of the Seven Hills of Rome on which it stands. It is the official residence of the *Presidente della Repubblica*.

'**Quito** SF Quito
quiz [kwidz] SM INV (*domanda*) question; (*anche*: **gioco a quiz**) quiz game
'**quorum** SM quorum
'**quota** SF (*parte*) quota, share; (*Aer*) height, altitude; (*Ippica*) odds *pl*; **prendere/perdere ~** (*Aer*) to gain/lose height *o* altitude; **~ imponibile** taxable income; **~ d'iscrizione** (*Ins*) enrolment fee; (*ad una gara*) entry fee; (*ad un club*) membership fee; **~ di mercato** market share; **quote rosa** (*Pol*) quota for women
quo'tare /**72**/ VT (*Borsa*) to quote; (*valutare: anche fig*) to value; **è un pittore molto quotato** he is rated highly as a painter
quotazi'one [kwotat'tsjone] SF quotation
quotidiana'mente AV daily, every day
quotidi'ano, -a AG daily; (*banale*) everyday ▶ SM (*giornale*) daily (paper)
quozi'ente [kwot'tsjɛnte] SM (*Mat*) quotient; **~ di crescita zero** zero growth rate; **~ d'intelligenza** intelligence quotient, IQ

Rr

R, r ['ɛrre] SM O F (lettera) R, r; **R come Roma** ≈ R for Robert (BRIT), R for Roger (US)

R ABBR (Posta) = **raccomandato**; (Ferr) = **rapido**

RA SIGLA = **Ravenna**

ra'barbaro SM rhubarb

Ra'bat SF Rabat

rabberci'are [rabber't∫are] /**14**/ VT (anche fig) to patch up

'rabbia SF (ira) anger, rage; (accanimento, furia) fury; (Med: idrofobia) rabies sg

rab'bino SM rabbi

rabbi'oso, -a AG angry, furious; (facile all'ira) quick-tempered; (forze, acqua ecc) furious, raging; (Med) rabid, mad

rabbo'nire /**55**/ VT, **rabbo'nirsi** VPR to calm down

rabbrivi'dire /**55**/ VI to shudder, shiver

rabbui'arsi /**19**/ VPR to grow dark

rabdo'mante SM water diviner

racc. ABBR (Posta) = **raccomandato**

raccapez'zarsi [rakkapet'tsarsi] /**72**/ VPR: **non ~** to be at a loss

raccapricci'ante [rakkaprit't∫ante] AG horrifying

racca'priccio [rakka'pritt∫o] SM horror

raccatta'palle SM INV (Sport) ballboy

raccat'tare /**72**/ VT to pick up

rac'chetta [rak'ketta] SF (per tennis) racket; (per ping-pong) bat; **~ da neve** snowshoe; **~ da sci** ski stick

'racchio, -a ['rakkjo] AG (col) ugly

racchi'udere [rak'kjudere] /**22**/ VT to contain

racchi'uso, -a [rak'kjuso] PP di **racchiudere**

rac'cogliere [rak'koʎʎere] /**23**/ VT to collect; (raccattare) to pick up; (frutti, fiori) to pick, pluck; (Agr) to harvest; (approvazione, voti) to win; (profughi) to take in; (vele) to furl; (capelli) to put up; **raccogliersi** VPR to gather; (fig) to gather one's thoughts; to meditate; **non ha raccolto** (allusione) he didn't take the hint; (frecciata) he took no notice of it; **~ i frutti del proprio lavoro** (fig) to reap the benefits of one's work; **~ le idee** (fig) to gather one's thoughts

raccogli'mento [rakkoʎʎi'mento] SM meditation

raccogli'tore [rakkoʎʎi'tore] SM (cartella) folder, binder; **~ a fogli mobili** loose-leaf binder

rac'colta SF vedi **raccolto**

rac'colto, -a PP di **raccogliere** ▶ AG (persona: pensoso) thoughtful; (luogo: appartato) secluded, quiet ▶ SM (Agr) crop, harvest ▶ SF collecting no pl; collection; (Agr) harvesting no pl, gathering no pl; harvest, crop; (adunata) gathering; **fare la raccolta di qc** to collect sth; **chiamare a raccolta** to gather together; **raccolta differenziata** (dei rifiuti) separate collection of different kinds of household waste

raccoman'dabile AG (highly) commendable; **è un tipo poco ~** he is not to be trusted

raccoman'dare /**72**/ VT to recommend; (affidare) to entrust; **raccomandarsi** VPR: **raccomandarsi a qn** to commend o.s. to sb; **~ a qn di fare qc** to recommend that sb does sth; **~ a qn di non fare qc** to tell o warn sb not to do sth; **~ qn a qn/alle cure di qn** to entrust sb to sb/to sb's care; **mi raccomando!** don't forget!

raccoman'dato, -a AG (lettera, pacco) recorded-delivery (BRIT), certified (US); (candidato) recommended ▶ SM/F: **essere un(a) raccomandato(a) di ferro** to have friends in high places ▶ SF (anche: **lettera raccomandata**) recorded-delivery letter; **raccomandata con ricevuta di ritorno (Rr)** recorded-delivery letter with advice of receipt

raccomandazi'one [rakkomandat'tsjone] SF recommendation; **lettera di ~** letter of introduction

raccomo'dare /**72**/ VT (riparare) to repair, mend

raccon'tare /**72**/ VT: **~ (a qn)** (dire) to tell (sb); (narrare) to relate (to sb), tell (sb) about; **a me non la racconti** don't try and kid me; **cosa mi racconti di nuovo?** what's new?

r

rac'conto SM telling *no pl*, relating *no pl*; *(fatto raccontato)* story, tale; *(genere letterario)* short story; **racconti per bambini** children's stories

raccorci'are [rakkor'tʃare] /**14**/ VT to shorten

raccor'dare /**72**/ VT to link up, join

rac'cordo SM *(Tecn: giunzione)* connection, joint; *(Aut: di autostrada)* slip road (BRIT) entrance *(o exit)* ramp (US); **~ anulare** *(Aut)* ring road (BRIT), beltway (US); **~ autostradale** slip road (BRIT), entrance *(o exit)* ramp (US); **~ ferroviario** siding; **~ stradale** link road

ra'chitico, -a, -ci, -che [ra'kitiko] AG suffering from rickets; *(fig)* scraggy, scrawny

rachi'tismo [raki'tizmo] SM *(Med)* rickets *sg*

racimo'lare [ratʃimo'lare] /**72**/ VT *(fig)* to scrape together, glean

'rada SF *(natural)* harbour (BRIT) *o* harbor (US)

'radar SM INV radar

raddol'cire [raddol'tʃire] /**55**/ VT *(persona, carattere)* to soften; **raddolcirsi** VPR *(tempo)* to grow milder; *(persona)* to soften, mellow

raddoppia'mento SM doubling

raddoppi'are /**19**/ VT, VI to double

rad'doppio SM *(gen)* doubling; *(Biliardo)* double; *(Equitazione)* gallop

raddriz'zare [raddrit'tsare] /**72**/ VT to straighten; *(fig: correggere)* to put straight, correct

'radere /**85**/ VT *(barba)* to shave off; *(mento)* to shave; *(fig: rasentare)* to graze; to skim; **radersi** VPR to shave (o.s.); **~ al suolo** to raze to the ground

radi'ale AG radial

radi'ante AG *(calore, energia)* radiant

radi'are /**19**/ VT to strike off

radia'tore SM radiator

radiazi'one [radjat'tsjone] SF *(Fisica)* radiation; *(cancellazione)* striking off

'radica SF *(Bot)*: **~ di noce** walnut (wood)

radi'cale AG radical ▶ SM *(Ling)* root; *(Mat, Pol)* radical; **radicali liberi** free radicals

radi'cato, -a AG *(pregiudizio, credenza)* deep-seated, deeply-rooted

ra'dicchio [ra'dikkjo] SM *variety of chicory*

ra'dice [ra'ditʃe] SF root; **segno di ~** *(Mat)* radical sign; **colpire alla ~** *(fig)* to strike at the root; **mettere radici** *(idee, odio ecc)* to take root; *(persona)* to put down roots; **~ quadrata** *(Mat)* square root

'radio SF INV radio ▶ SM *(Chim)* radium; **trasmettere per ~** to broadcast; **stazione/ponte ~** radio station/link; **~ ricevente/trasmittente** receiver/transmitter

radioabbo'nato, -a SM/F radio subscriber

radioama'tore, -'trice SM/F amateur radio operator, ham *(col)*

radioascolta'tore, -'trice SM/F *(radio)* listener

radioattività SF radioactivity

radioat'tivo, -a AG radioactive

radiocoman'dare /**72**/ VT to operate by remote control

radiocoman'dato, -a AG remote-controlled

radioco'mando SM remote control

radiocomunicazi'one [radjokomunikat'tsjone] SF radio message

radio'cronaca, -che SF radio commentary

radiocro'nista, -i, -e SM/F radio commentator

radiodiffusi'one SF *(radio)* broadcasting

radio'fonico, -a, -ci, -che AG radio *cpd*

radiogra'fare /**72**/ VT to X-ray

radiogra'fia SF radiography; *(foto)* X-ray photograph

radio'lina SF portable radio, transistor *(radio)*

radiolo'gia [radjolo'dʒia] SF radiology

radi'ologo, -a, -gi, -ghe SM/F radiologist

radiorice'vente [radjoritʃe'vɛnte] SF *(anche:* **apparecchio radioricevente)** receiver

radi'oso, -a AG radiant

radiostazi'one [radjostat'tsjone] SF radio station

radios'veglia [radjoz'veʎʎa] SF radio alarm

radio'taxi SM INV radio taxi

radio'tecnico, -a, -ci, -che AG radio engineering *cpd* ▶ SM radio engineer

radiotelegra'fista, -i, -e SM/F radiotelegrapher

radiotera'pia SF radiotherapy

radiotrasmit'tente AG *(radio)* broadcasting *cpd* ▶ SF *(radio)* broadcasting station

'rado, -a AG *(capelli)* sparse, thin; *(visite)* infrequent; **di ~** rarely; **non di ~** not uncommonly

radu'nare /**72**/ VT, **radu'narsi** VPR to gather, assemble

radu'nata SF *(Mil)* muster

ra'duno SM gathering, meeting

ra'dura SF clearing

'rafano SM horseradish

raffazzo'nare [raffattso'nare] /**72**/ VT to patch up

raf'fermo, -a AG stale

'raffica, -che SF *(Meteor)* gust *(of wind)*; **~ di colpi** *(di fucile)* burst of gunfire

raffigu'rare /**72**/ VT to represent

raffigurazi'one [raffigurat'tsjone] SF representation, depiction

raffi'nare /**72**/ VT to refine

raffina'tezza [raffina'tettsa] SF refinement

raffi'nato, -a AG refined

raffinazi'one [raffinat'tsjone] SF *(di sostanza)* refining; **~ del petrolio** oil refining

raffine'ria SF refinery

raffor'zare [raffor'tsare] /**72**/ VT to reinforce

rafforza'tivo, -a [raffortsa'tivo] AG (Ling) intensifying ▶ SM (Ling) intensifier

raffredda'mento SM cooling

raffred'dare /**72**/ VT to cool; (fig) to dampen, have a cooling effect on; **raffreddarsi** VPR to grow cool o cold; (prendere un raffreddore) to catch a cold; (fig) to cool (off)

raffred'dato, -a AG (Med): **essere ~** to have a cold

raffred'dore SM (Med) cold

raffron'tare /**72**/ VT to compare

raffronto SM comparison

'rafia SF (fibra) raffia

'rafting ['rafting] SM white-water rafting

raga'nella SF (Zool) tree frog

ra'gazzo, -a [ra'gattso] SM/F boy/girl; (col: fidanzato) boyfriend/girlfriend; **ragazzi** SMPL (figli) kids; **nome da ragazza** maiden name; **ragazza madre** unmarried mother; **ragazza squillo** call girl; **ciao ragazzi!** (gruppo) hi guys!

ragge'lare [raddʒe'lare] /**72**/ VT, VI, **ragge'larsi** VPR to freeze

raggi'ante [rad'dʒante] AG radiant, shining; **~ di gioia** beaming o radiant with joy

raggi'era [rad'dʒɛra] SF (di ruota) spokes pl; **a ~** with a sunburst pattern

'raggio ['raddʒo] SM (di sole ecc) ray; (Mat, distanza) radius; (di ruota ecc) spoke; **nel ~ di 20 km** within a radius of 20 km o a 20-km radius; **a largo ~** (esplorazione, incursione) wide-ranging; **~ d'azione** range; **~ laser** laser beam; **raggi X** X-rays

raggi'rare [raddʒi'rare] /**72**/ VT to take in, trick

rag'giro [rad'dʒiro] SM trick

raggi'ungere [rad'dʒundʒere] /**5**/ VT to reach; (persona: riprendere) to catch up (with); (bersaglio) to hit; (fig: meta) to achieve; **~ il proprio scopo** to reach one's goal, achieve one's aim; **~ un accordo** to come to o reach an agreement

raggi'unto, -a [rad'dʒunto] PP di **raggiungere**

raggomito'larsi /**72**/ VPR to curl up

raggranel'lare /**72**/ VT to scrape together

raggrin'zare [raggrin'tsare] /**72**/ VT, VI (anche: **raggrinzarsi**) to wrinkle

raggrin'zire [raggrin'tsire] /**55**/ VT = **raggrinzare**

raggru'mare /**72**/ VT, **raggru'marsi** VPR (sangue, latte) to clot

raggruppa'mento SM (azione) grouping; (gruppo) group; (Mil) unit

raggrup'pare /**72**/ VT to group (together)

ragguagli'are [raggwaʎ'ʎare] /**72**/ VT (paragonare) to compare; (informare) to inform

raggu'aglio [rag'gwaʎʎo] SM comparison; (informazione, relazione) piece of information

ragguar'devole AG (degno di riguardo) distinguished, notable; (notevole: somma) considerable

'ragia ['radʒa] SF: **acqua ~** turpentine

ragiona'mento [radʒona'mento] SM reasoning no pl; arguing no pl; argument

ragio'nare [radʒo'nare] /**72**/ VI (usare la ragione) to reason; (discorrere): **~ (di)** to argue (about); **cerca di ~** try and be reasonable

ragi'one [ra'dʒone] SF reason; (dimostrazione, prova) argument, reason; (diritto) right; **aver ~** to be right; **aver ~ di qn** to get the better of sb; **dare ~ a qn** (persona) to side with sb; (fatto) to prove sb right; **farsi una ~ di qc** to accept sth, come to terms with sth; **in ~ di** at the rate of; to the amount of; according to; **a o con ~** rightly, justly; **perdere la ~** to become insane; (fig) to take leave of one's senses; **a ragion veduta** after due consideration; **per ragioni di famiglia** for family reasons; **~ di scambio** terms of trade; **~ sociale** (Comm) corporate name; **ragion di stato** reason of State

ragione'ria [radʒone'ria] SF accountancy; (ufficio) accounts department

ragio'nevole [radʒo'nevole] AG reasonable

ragioni'ere, -a [radʒo'njɛre] SM/F accountant

ragli'are [raʎ'ʎare] /**27**/ VI to bray

ragna'tela [raɲɲa'tela] SF cobweb, spider's web

'ragno ['raɲɲo] SM spider; **non cavare un ~ dal buco** (fig) to draw a blank

ragù SM INV (Cuc) meat sauce (for pasta); stew

RAI-TV [raiti'vu] SIGLA F (= Radio televisione italiana) Italian Broadcasting Company

rallegra'menti SMPL congratulations

ralle'grare /**72**/ VT to cheer up; **rallegrarsi** VPR to cheer up; (provare allegrezza) to rejoice; **rallegrarsi con qn** to congratulate sb

rallenta'mento SM slowing down; slackening

rallen'tare /**72**/ VT to slow down; (fig) to lessen, slacken ▶ VI to slow down; **~ il passo** to slacken one's pace

rallenta'tore SM (Cine) slow-motion camera; **al ~** (anche fig) in slow motion

raman'zina [raman'dzina] SF lecture, telling-off

ra'mare /**72**/ VT (superficie) to copper, coat with copper; (Agr: vite) to spray with copper sulphate

ra'marro SM green lizard

ra'mato, -a AG (oggetto: rivestito di rame) copper-coated, coppered; (capelli, barba) coppery, copper-coloured (BRIT), copper-colored (US)

'rame SM (Chim) copper; **di ~** copper cpd; **incisione su ~** copperplate

ramifi'care /**20**/ vi (*Bot*) to put out branches; **ramificarsi** VPR (*diramarsi*) to branch out; (*Med: tumore, vene*) to ramify; **ramificarsi in** (*biforcarsi*) to branch into

ramificazi'one [ramifikat'tsjone] SF ramification

ra'mingo, -a, -ghi, -ghe AG (*poetico*): **andare ~** to go wandering, wander

ra'mino SM (*Carte*) rummy

rammari'carsi /**20**/ VPR: **~ (di)** (*rincrescersi*) to be sorry (about), regret; (*lamentarsi*) to complain (about)

ram'marico, -chi SM regret

rammen'dare /**72**/ VT to mend; (*calza*) to darn

ram'mendo SM mending *no pl*; darning *no pl*; mend darn

rammen'tare /**72**/ VT to remember, recall; **rammentarsi** VPR: **rammentarsi (di qc)** to remember (sth); **~ qc a qn** to remind sb of sth

rammol'lire /**55**/ VT to soften ▶ VI (*anche*: **rammollirsi**) to go soft

rammol'lito, -a AG weak ▶ SM/F weakling

'ramo SM branch; (*di commercio*) field; **non è il mio ~** it's not my field *o* line

ramo'scello [ramoʃʃɛllo] SM twig

'rampa SF flight (of stairs); **~ di lancio** launching pad

rampi'cante AG (*Bot*) climbing

ram'pino SM (*gancio*) hook; (*Naut*) grapnel

ram'pollo SM (*di acqua*) spring; (*Bot: germoglio*) shoot; (*fig: discendente*) descendant

ram'pone SM harpoon; (*Alpinismo*) crampon

'rana SF frog; **~ pescatrice** angler fish

'rancido, -a ['rantʃido] AG rancid

'rancio ['rantʃo] SM (*Mil*) mess; **ora del ~** mess time

ran'core SM rancour (*Brit*), rancor (*US*), resentment; **portare ~ a qn, provare ~ per** *o* **verso qn** to bear sb a grudge

ran'dagio, -a, -gi, -gie *o* **-ge** [ran'dadʒo] AG (*gatto, cane*) stray

ran'dello SM club, cudgel

'rango, -ghi SM (*grado*) rank; (*condizione sociale*) station, social standing; **persone di ~ inferiore** people of lower standing; **uscire dai ranghi** to fall out; (*fig*) to step out of line

Ran'gun SF Rangoon

rannicchi'arsi [rannik'kjarsi] /**19**/ VPR to crouch, huddle

rannuvo'larsi /**72**/ VPR to cloud over, become overcast

ra'nocchio [ra'nɔkkjo] SM (edible) frog

ranto'lare /**72**/ VI to wheeze

ranto'lio SM (*il respirare affannoso*) wheezing; (*di agonizzante*) death rattle

'rantolo SM wheeze; death rattle

ra'nuncolo SM (*Bot*) buttercup

'rapa SF (*Bot*) turnip

ra'pace [ra'patʃe] AG (*animale*) predatory; (*fig*) rapacious, grasping ▶ SM bird of prey

ra'pare /**72**/ VT (*capelli*) to crop, cut very short

'rapida SF *vedi* **rapido**

rapida'mente AV quickly, rapidly

rapidità SF speed

'rapido, -a AG fast; (*esame, occhiata*) quick, rapid ▶ SM (*Ferr*) express (train) ▶ SF (*di fiume*) rapid

rapi'mento SM kidnapping; (*fig*) rapture

ra'pina SF robbery; **~ in banca** bank robbery; **~ a mano armata** armed robbery

rapi'nare /**72**/ VT to rob

ra'pire /**55**/ VT (*cose*) to steal; (*persone*) to kidnap; (*fig*) to enrapture, delight

ra'pito, -a AG (*persona*) kidnapped; (*fig: in estasi*): **ascoltare ~ qn** to be captivated by sb's words ▶ SM/F kidnapped person

rapi'tore, -'trice SM/F kidnapper

rappacifi'care [rappatʃifi'kare] /**20**/ VT (*riconciliare*) to reconcile; **rappacificarsi** VPR (*uso*) to be reconciled, make it up (*col*)

rappacificazi'one [rappatʃifikat'tsjone] SF reconciliation

rappez'zare [rappet'tsare] /**72**/ VT to patch

rappor'tare /**72**/ VT (*confrontare*) to compare; (*riprodurre*) to reproduce

rap'porto SM (*resoconto*) report; (*legame*) relationship; (*Mat, Tecn*) ratio; **rapporti** SMPL (*fra persone, paesi*) relations; **in ~ a quanto è successo** with regard to *o* in relation to what happened; **fare ~ a qn su qc** to report sth to sb; **andare a ~ da qn** to report to sb; **chiamare qn a ~** (*Mil*) to summon sb; **essere in buoni/cattivi rapporti con qn** to be on good/bad terms with sb; **~ d'affari, ~ di lavoro** business relations; **~ di compressione** (*Tecn*) pressure ratio; **~ coniugale** marital relationship; **~ di trasmissione** (*Tecn*) gear; **rapporti sessuali** sexual intercourse *sg*

rap'prendersi /**81**/ VPR to coagulate, clot; (*latte*) to curdle

rappre'saglia [rappre'saʎʎa] SF reprisal, retaliation

rappresen'tante SMF representative; **~ di commercio** sales representative, sales rep(*col*); **~ sindacale** union delegate *o* representative

rappresen'tanza [rapprezen'tantsa] SF delegation, deputation; (*Comm: ufficio, sede*) agency; **in ~ di qn** on behalf of sb; **spese di ~** entertainment expenses; **macchina di ~** official car; **avere la ~ di** to be the agent for; **~ esclusiva** sole agency; **avere la ~ esclusiva** to be sole agent

rappresen'tare /**72**/ VT to represent; (*Teat*) to perform; **farsi ~ dal proprio legale** to be represented by one's lawyer

rappresenta'tivo, -a AG representative ▶ SF (*di partito, sindacale*) representative group; (*Sport: squadra*) representative (team)

rappresentazi'one [rapprezentat'tsjone] SF representation; performing *no pl*; (*spettacolo*) performance; **prima ~ assoluta** world première

rap'preso, -a PP = **rapprendere**

rapso'dia SF rhapsody

'raptus SM INV: **~ di follia** fit of madness

rara'mente AV seldom, rarely

rare'fare /41/ VT, **rare'farsi** VPR to rarefy

rare'fatto, -a PP *di* **rarefare** ▶ AG rarefied

rarefazi'one [rarefat'tsjone] SF rarefaction

rarità SF INV rarity

'raro, -a AG rare

ra'sare /72/ VT (*barba ecc*) to shave off; (*siepi, erba*) to trim, cut; **rasarsi** VPR to shave (o.s.)

ra'sato, -a AG (*erba*) trimmed, cut; (*tessuto*) smooth; **avere la barba rasata** to be clean-shaven

rasa'tura SF shave

raschia'mento [raskja'mento] SM (*Med*) curettage; **~ uterino** D and C

raschi'are [ras'kjare] /19/ VT to scrape; (*macchia, fango*) to scrape off ▶ VI to clear one's throat

rasen'tare /72/ VT (*andar rasente*) to keep close to; (*sfiorare*) to skim along (*o* over); (*fig*) to border on

ra'sente PREP: **~ (a)** close to, very near

'raso, -a PP *di* **radere** ▶ AG (*barba*) shaved; (*capelli*) cropped; (*con misure di capacità*) level; (*pieno: bicchiere*) full to the brim ▶ SM (*tessuto*) satin; **~ terra** close to the ground; **volare ~ terra** to hedgehop; **un cucchiaio ~** a level spoonful

ra'soio SM razor; **~ elettrico** electric shaver *o* razor

ras'pare /72/ VT (*levigare*) to rasp; (*grattare*) to scratch

'raspo SM (*di uva*) grape stalk

ras'segna [ras'senna] SF (*Mil*) inspection, review; (*esame*) inspection; (*resoconto*) review, survey; (*pubblicazione letteraria ecc*) review; (*mostra*) exhibition, show; **passare in ~** (*Mil, fig*) to review

rasse'gnare [rassen'nare] /15/ VT: **~ le dimissioni** to resign, hand in one's resignation; **rassegnarsi** VPR (*accettare*): **rassegnarsi (a qc/a fare)** to resign o.s. (to sth/to doing)

rassegnazi'one [rassennat'tsjone] SF resignation

rasse're'nare /72/ VT (*persona*) to cheer up; **rasserenarsi** VPR (*tempo*) to clear up

rasset'tare /72/ VT to tidy, put in order; (*aggiustare*) to repair, mend

rassicu'rante AG reassuring

rassicu'rare /72/ VT to reassure; **rassicurarsi** VPR to take heart, recover one's confidence

rassicurazi'one [rassikurat'tsjone] SF reassurance

rasso'dare /72/ VT to harden, stiffen; (*fig*) to strengthen, consolidate; **rassodarsi** VPR to harden, to strengthen

rassomigli'anza [rassomiʎ'ʎantsa] SF resemblance

rassomigli'are [rassomiʎ'ʎare] /27/ VI: **~ a** to resemble, look like

rastrella'mento SM (*Mil: di polizia*) (thorough) search

rastrel'lare /72/ VT to rake; (*fig: perlustrare*) to comb

rastrelli'era SF rack; (*per piatti*) dish rack

ras'trello SM rake

'rata SF (*quota*) instalment, installment (US); **pagare a rate** to pay by instal(l)ments *o* on hire purchase (BRIT); **comprare/vendere a rate** to buy/sell on hire purchase (BRIT) *o* on the installment plan (US)

rate'ale AG: **pagamento ~** payment by instal(l)ments; **vendita ~** hire purchase (BRIT), installment plan (US)

rate'are /72/ VT to divide into instal(l)ments

rateazi'one [rateat'tsjone] SF division into instal(l)ments

rateiz'zare [rateid'dzare] /72/ VT = **rateare**

'rateo SM (*Comm*) accrual

ra'tifica, -che SF ratification

ratifi'care /20/ VT (*Dir*) to ratify

'ratto SM (*Dir*) abduction; (*Zool*) rat

rattop'pare /72/ VT to patch

rat'toppo SM patching *no pl*; patch

rattrap'pire /55/ VT to make stiff; **rattrappirsi** VPR to be stiff

rattris'tare /72/ VT to sadden; **rattristarsi** VPR to become sad

rau'cedine [rau'tʃedine] SF hoarseness

'rauco, -a, -chi, -che AG hoarse

rava'nello SM radish

raven'nate AG of (*o* from) Ravenna

ravi'oli SMPL ravioli *sg*

ravve'dersi /82/ VPR to mend one's ways

ravvi'are /60/ VT (*capelli*) to tidy; **ravviarsi i capelli** to tidy one's hair

ravvicina'mento [ravvitʃina'mento] SM (*tra persone*) reconciliation; (*Pol: tra paesi ecc*) rapprochement

ravvici'nare [ravvitʃi'nare] /72/ VT (*avvicinare: oggetti*) to bring closer together; (*fig: persone*) to reconcile, bring together; **~ qc a** to bring sth nearer to; **ravvicinarsi** VPR to be reconciled

ravvi'sare /72/ VT to recognize

ravvi'vare /72/ VT to revive; (*fig*) to brighten up, enliven; **ravvivarsi** VPR to revive; to brighten up

r

Rawal'pindi [raval'pindi] SF Rawalpindi

razio'cinio [rattsjo'tʃinjo] SM reasoning *no pl*; reason; (*buon senso*) common sense

razio'nale [rattsjo'nale] AG rational

razionalità [rattsjonali'ta] SF rationality; (*buon senso*) common sense

razionaliz'zare [rattsjonalid'dzare] /**72**/ VT (*metodo, lavoro, programma*) to rationalize; (*problema, situazione*) to approach rationally

raziona'mento [rattsjona'mento] SM rationing

razio'nare [rattsjo'nare] /**72**/ VT to ration

razi'one [rat'tsjone] SF ration; (*porzione*) portion, share

'razza ['rattsa] SF race; (*Zool*) breed; (*discendenza, stirpe*) stock, race; (*sorta*) sort, kind

raz'zia [rat'tsia] SF raid, foray

razzi'ale [rat'tsjale] AG racial

raz'zismo [rat'tsizmo] SM racism, racialism

raz'zista, -i, -e [rat'tsista] AG, SM/F racist, racialist

'razzo ['raddzo] SM rocket; **~ di segnalazione** flare; **~ vettore** vector rocket

razzo'lare [rattso'lare] /**72**/ VI (*galline*) to scratch about

RC SIGLA = **Reggio Calabria**; (= *partito della Rifondazione Comunista*) left-wing Italian political party

RDT SIGLA F *vedi* **la Repubblica Democratica Tedesca**

RE SIGLA = **Reggio Emilia**

re SM INV (*sovrano*) king; (*Mus*) D; (: *solfeggiando la scala*) re; **i Re Magi** the Three Wise Men, the Magi

rea'gente [rea'dʒɛnte] SM reagent

rea'gire [rea'dʒire] /**55**/ VI to react

re'ale AG real; (*di, da re*) royal ▶ SM: **il ~** reality; **i Reali** the Royal family

rea'lismo SM realism

rea'lista, -i, -e SM/F realist; (*Pol*) royalist

rea'listico, -a, -ci, -che AG realistic

reality [ri'aliti] SM INV reality show

realiz'zare [realid'dzare] /**72**/ VT (*progetto ecc*) to realize, carry out; (*sogno, desiderio*) to realize, fulfil; (*scopo*) to achieve; (*Comm: titoli ecc*) to realize; (*Calcio ecc*) to score; **realizzarsi** VPR to be realized

realizzazi'one [realiddzat'tsjone] SF realization; fulfilment; achievement; **~ scenica** stage production

rea'lizzo [rea'liddzo] SM (*conversione in denaro*) conversion into cash; (*vendita forzata*) clearance sale

real'mente AV really, actually

realtà SF INV reality; **in ~** (*in effetti*) in fact; (*a dire il vero*) really

re'ame SM kingdom, realm; (*fig*) realm

re'ato SM offence (BRIT), offense (US)

reat'tore SM (*Fisica*) reactor; (*Aer: aereo*) jet; (: *motore*) jet engine

reazio'nario, -a [reattsjo'narjo] AG, SM/F (*Pol*) reactionary

reazi'one [reat'tsjone] SF reaction; **motore/aereo a ~** jet engine/plane; **forze della ~** reactionary forces; **~ a catena** (*anche fig*) chain reaction

'rebbio SM prong

'rebus SM INV rebus; (*fig*) puzzle; enigma

recapi'tare /**72**/ VT to deliver

re'capito SM (*indirizzo*) address; (*consegna*) delivery; **~ telefonico** phone number; **ha un ~ telefonico?** do you have a telephone number where you can be reached?; **~ a domicilio** home delivery (service)

re'care /**20**/ VT (*portare*) to bring; (*avere su di sé*) to carry, bear; (*cagionare*) to cause, bring; **recarsi** VPR to go; **~ danno a qn** to harm sb, cause harm to sb; **recarsi in città/a scuola** to go into town/to school

re'cedere [re'tʃɛdere] /**29**/ VI to withdraw

recensi'one [retʃen'sjone] SF review

recen'sire [retʃen'sire] /**55**/ VT to review

recen'sore, -a [retʃen'sore] SM/F reviewer

re'cente [re'tʃɛnte] AG recent; **di ~** recently; **più ~** latest, most recent

recente'mente [retʃente'mente] AV recently

rece'pire [retʃe'pire] /**55**/ VT to understand, take in

recessi'one [retʃes'sjone] SF (*Econ*) recession

re'cesso [re'tʃɛsso] SM (*azione*) recession, receding; (*Dir*) withdrawal; (*luogo*) recess

recherò *etc* [reke'rɔ] VB *vedi* **recare**

re'cidere [re'tʃidere] /**34**/ VT to cut off, chop off

reci'divo, -a [retʃi'divo] SM/F (*Dir*) second (*o habitual*) offender, recidivist ▶ SF recidivism

recin'tare [retʃin'tare] /**72**/ VT to enclose, fence off

re'cinto [re'tʃinto] SM enclosure; (*ciò che recinge*) fence; surrounding wall

recinzi'one [retʃin'tsjone] SF (*azione*) enclosure, fencing-off; (*recinto: di legno*) fence; (: *di mattoni*) wall; (*reticolato*) wire fencing; (*a sbarre*) railings pl

recipi'ente [retʃi'pjɛnte] SM container

re'ciproco, -a, -ci, -che [re'tʃiproko] AG reciprocal

re'ciso, -a [re'tʃizo] PP *di* **recidere**

'recita ['rɛtʃita] SF performance

'recital ['rɛtʃital] SM INV recital

reci'tare [retʃi'tare] /**72**/ VT (*poesia, lezione*) to recite; (*dramma*) to perform; (*ruolo*) to play *o* act (the part of)

recitazi'one [retʃitat'tsjone] SF recitation; (*di attore*) acting; **scuola di ~** drama school

recla'mare /**72**/ vɪ to complain ▶ vᴛ (*richiedere*) to demand

ré'clame [re'klam] sꜰ ɪɴᴠ advertising *no pl* advertisement, advert (BRIT), ad (*col*)

reclamiz'zare [reklamid'dzare] /**72**/ vᴛ to advertise

re'clamo sᴍ complaint; **sporgere ~ a** to complain to, make a complaint to

recli'nabile ᴀɢ (*sedile*) reclining

recli'nare /**72**/ vᴛ (*capo*) to bow, lower; (*sedile*) to tilt

reclusi'one sꜰ (*Dir*) imprisonment

re'cluso, -a sᴍ/ꜰ prisoner

'recluta sꜰ recruit

recluta'mento sᴍ recruitment

reclu'tare /**72**/ vᴛ to recruit

re'condito, -a ᴀɢ secluded; (*fig*) secret, hidden

'record ᴀɢ ɪɴᴠ record *cpd* ▶ sᴍ ɪɴᴠ record; **in tempo ~, a tempo di ~** in record time; **detenere il ~ di** to hold the record for; **~ mondiale** world record

recrimi'nare /**72**/ vɪ: **~ (su qc)** to complain (about sth)

recriminazi'one [rekriminat'tsjone] sꜰ recrimination

recrude'scenza [rekrudeʃ'ʃɛntsa] sꜰ fresh outbreak

recupe'rare *etc* = **ricuperare** *ecc*

redargu'ire /**55**/ vᴛ to rebuke

re'dassi *etc* vʙ *vedi* **redigere**

re'datto, -a ᴘᴘ *di* **redigere**

redat'tore, -'trice sᴍ/ꜰ (*Stampa*) editor; (: *di articolo*) writer; (*di dizionario ecc*) compiler; **~ capo** chief editor

redazi'one [redat'tsjone] sꜰ editing; writing; (*sede*) editorial office(s); (*personale*) editorial staff; (*versione*) version

reddi'tizio, -a [reddi'tittsjo] ᴀɢ profitable

'reddito sᴍ income; (*dello Stato*) revenue; (*di un capitale*) yield; **~ complessivo** gross income; **~ disponibile** disposable income; **~ fisso** fixed income; **~ imponibile/non imponibile** taxable/non-taxable income; **~ da lavoro** earned income; **~ nazionale** national income; **~ pubblico** public revenue

re'densi *etc* vʙ *vedi* **redimere**

re'dento, -a ᴘᴘ *di* **redimere**

reden'tore sᴍ: **il R~** the Redeemer

redenzi'one [reden'tsjone] sꜰ redemption

re'digere [re'didʒere] /**47**/ vᴛ to write; (*contratto*) to draw up

re'dimere /**86**/ vᴛ to deliver; (*Rel*) to redeem

'redini sꜰᴘʟ reins

redi'vivo, -a ᴀɢ returned to life, reborn

'reduce ['redutʃe] ᴀɢ (*gen*): **~ da** returning from, back from ▶ sᴍꜰ survivor; (*veterano*) veteran; **essere ~ da** (*esame, colloquio*) to have been through; (*malattia*) to be just over

'refe sᴍ thread

refe'rendum sᴍ ɪɴᴠ referendum

refe'renza [refe'rɛntsa] sꜰ reference

re'ferto sᴍ medical report

refet'torio sᴍ refectory

refezi'one [refet'tsjone] sꜰ (*Ins*) school meal

refrat'tario, -a ᴀɢ refractory; (*fig*): **essere ~ alla matematica** to have no aptitude for mathematics

refrige'rante [refridʒe'rante] ᴀɢ (*Tecn*) cooling, refrigerating; (*bevanda*) refreshing ▶ sᴍ (*Chim: fluido*) coolant; (*Tecn: apparecchio*) refrigerator

refrige'rare [refridʒe'rare] /**72**/ vᴛ to refrigerate; (*rinfrescare*) to cool, refresh

refrigerazi'one [refridʒerat'tsjone] sꜰ refrigeration; (*Tecn*) cooling; **~ ad acqua** (*Aut*) water-cooling

refri'gerio [refri'dʒɛrjo] sᴍ: **trovare ~** to find somewhere cool

refur'tiva sꜰ stolen goods *pl*

Reg. ᴀʙʙʀ (= *reggimento*) Regt; (*Amm*) = **regolamento**

rega'lare /**72**/ vᴛ to give (as a present), make a present of

re'gale ᴀɢ regal

re'galo sᴍ gift, present ▶ ᴀɢ ɪɴᴠ: **confezione ~** gift pack; **fare un ~ a qn** to give sb a present; **"articoli da ~"** "gifts"

re'gata sꜰ regatta

reg'gente [red'dʒɛnte] ᴀɢ (*proposizione*) main; (*sovrano*) reigning ▶ sᴍꜰ regent; **principe ~** prince regent

reg'genza [red'dʒɛntsa] sꜰ regency

'reggere ['rɛddʒere] /**87**/ vᴛ (*tenere*) to hold; (*sostenere*) to support, bear, hold up; (*portare*) to carry, bear; (*resistere*) to withstand; (*dirigere: impresa*) to manage, run; (*governare*) to rule, govern; (*Ling*) to take, be followed by ▶ vɪ (*resistere*): **~ a** to stand up to, hold out against; (*sopportare*): **~ a** to stand; (*durare*) to last; (*fig: teoria ecc*) to hold water; **reggersi** vᴘʀ (*stare ritto*) to stand; (*fig: dominarsi*) to control o.s.; **reggersi sulle gambe** *o* **in piedi** to stand up

'reggia, -ge ['rɛddʒa] sꜰ royal palace

reggi'calze [reddʒi'kaltse] sᴍ ɪɴᴠ suspender belt

reggi'mento [reddʒi'mento] sᴍ (*Mil*) regiment

reggi'petto [reddʒi'pɛtto], **reggi'seno** [reddʒi'seno] sᴍ bra

re'gia, -'gie [re'dʒia] sꜰ (*TV, Cine ecc*) direction

re'gime [re'dʒime] sᴍ (*Pol*) regime; (*Dir: aureo, patrimoniale ecc*) system; (*Med*) diet; (*Tecn*) (engine) speed; **~ di giri** (*di motore*) revs *pl* per minute; **~ vegetariano** vegetarian diet

re'gina [re'dʒina] sꜰ queen

'regio, -a, -gi, -gie ['rɛdʒo] ᴀɢ royal

regio'nale [redʒo'nale] AG regional ▶ SM local train (*stopping frequently*)

regi'one [re'dʒone] SF (*gen*) region; (*territorio*) region, district, area; *see note*

> The *Regione* is the biggest administrative unit in Italy. Each of the 20 *Regioni* consists of a variable number of *Province*, which in turn are subdivided into *Comuni*. Each of the regions has a *capoluogo*, its chief province (for example, Florence is the chief province of the region of Tuscany). Five regions have special status and wider powers: Val d'Aosta, Friuli-Venezia Giulia, Trentino-Alto Adige, Sicily and Sardinia. A *Regione* is run by the *Giunta regionale*, which is elected by the *Consiglio regionale*; both are presided over by a *Presidente*. The *Giunta* has legislative powers within the region over the police, public health, schools, town planning and agriculture.

re'gista, -i, -e [re'dʒista] SM/F (TV, *Cine ecc*) director

regis'trare [redʒis'trare] /**72**/ VT (*Amm*) to register; (*Comm*) to enter; (*notare*) to report, note; (*canzone, conversazione, strumento di misura*) to record; (*mettere a punto*) to adjust, regulate; ~ **i bagagli** (*Aer*) to check in one's luggage; ~ **i freni** (*Tecn*) to adjust the brakes

registra'tore [redʒistra'tore] SM (*strumento*) recorder, register; (*magnetofono*) tape recorder; ~ **di cassa** cash register; ~ **a cassette** cassette recorder; ~ **di volo** (*Aer*) flight recorder, black box (*col*)

registrazi'one [redʒistrat'tsjone] SF registration; entry; reporting recording adjustment; ~ **bagagli** (*Aer*) check-in

re'gistro [re'dʒistro] SM register; (*Dir*) registry; (*Comm*): ~ (**di cassa**) ledger; **ufficio del** ~ registrar's office; ~ **di bordo** logbook; **registri contabili** (*account*) books

re'gnante [reɲ'ɲante] AG reigning, ruling ▶ SMF ruler

re'gnare [reɲ'ɲare] /**15**/ VI to reign, rule; (*fig*) to reign

'regno ['reɲɲo] SM kingdom; (*periodo*) reign; (*fig*) realm; **il** ~ **animale/vegetale** the animal/vegetable kingdom; **il R~ Unito** the United Kingdom

'regola SF rule; **a ~ d'arte** duly; perfectly; **essere in** ~ (*dipendente*) to be a registered employee; (*fig: essere pulito*) to be clean; **fare le cose in** ~ to do things properly; **avere le carte in** ~ (*gen*) to have one's papers in order; (*fig: essere adatto*) to be the right person; **per tua (norma e)** ~ for your information; **un'eccezione alla** ~ an exception to the rule

rego'labile AG adjustable

regolamen'tare /**72**/ AG (*distanza, velocità*) regulation *cpd*, proper; (*disposizione*) statutory ▶ VT (*gen*) to control; **entro il tempo** ~ within the time allowed, within the prescribed time

regola'mento SM (*complesso di norme*) regulations *pl*; (*di debito*) settlement; ~ **di conti** (*fig*) settling of scores

rego'lare /**72**/ AG regular; (*velocità*) steady; (*superficie*) even; (*passo*) steady, even; (*in regola: documento*) in order ▶ VT to regulate, control; (*apparecchio*) to adjust, regulate; (*questione, conto, debito*) to settle; **regolarsi** VPR (*comportarsi*) to behave, act; **regolarsi nel bere/nello spendere** (*moderarsi*) to control one's drinking/spending; **presentare** ~ **domanda** to apply through the proper channels; ~ **i conti** (*fig*) to settle old scores

regolarità SF INV regularity; steadiness; evenness; (*nel pagare*) punctuality

regolariz'zare [regolarid'dzare] /**72**/ VT (*posizione*) to regularize; (*debito*) to settle

rego'lata SF: **darsi una** ~ to pull o.s. together

regola'tezza [regola'tettsa] SF (*ordine*) orderliness; (*moderazione*) moderation

rego'lato, -a AG (*ordinato*) orderly; (*moderato*) moderate

regola'tore SM (*Tecn*) regulator; ~ **di frequenza/di volume** frequency/volume control

'regolo SM ruler; ~ **calcolatore** slide rule

regre'dire /**55**/ VI to regress

regressi'one SF regression

re'gresso SM (*fig: declino*) decline

rei'etto, -a SM/F outcast

reincarnazi'one [reinkarnat'tsjone] SF reincarnation

reinte'grare /**72**/ VT (*produzione*) to restore; (*energie*) to recover; (*dipendente*) to reinstate

reintegrazi'one [reintegrat'tsjone] SF (*di produzione*) restoration; (*di dipendente*) reinstatement

relativa'mente AV relatively

relatività SF relativity

rela'tivo, -a AG relative; (*attinente*) relevant; (*rispettivo*) respective; ~ **a** (*che concerne*) relating to, concerning; (*proporzionato*) in proportion to

rela'tore, -'trice SM/F (*gen*) spokesman/woman; (*Ins: di tesi*) supervisor

re'lax [re'laks] SM relaxation

relazi'one [relat'tsjone] SF (*fra cose, persone*) relation(ship); (*resoconto*) report, account; **relazioni** SFPL (*conoscenze*) connections; **essere in** ~ to be connected; **mettere in** ~ (*fatti, elementi*) to make the connection between; **in** ~ **a quanto detto prima** with regard to what has already been said; **essere in buone relazioni con qn** to be on good terms with sb; **fare una ~** to make a report, give an account; **relazioni pubbliche** public relations

rele'gare /80/ VT to banish; (fig) to relegate

religi'one [reli'dʒone] SF religion

religi'oso, -a [reli'dʒoso] AG religious ▸ SM/F monk/nun

re'liquia SF relic

re'litto SM wreck; (fig) down-and-out

re'mainder [ri'meindəʳ] SM INV (libro) remainder

're'make ['ri:'meik] SM INV (Cine) remake

re'mare /72/ VI to row

remini'scenze [reminiʃʃɛntse] SFPL reminiscences

remissi'one SF remission; (deferenza) submissiveness, compliance; **~ del debito** remission of debt; **~ di querela** (Dir) withdrawal of an action

remissività SF submissiveness

remis'sivo, -a AG submissive, compliant

'remo SM oar

'remora SF (poetico: indugio) hesitation

re'moto, -a AG remote

remune'rare etc = **rimunerare** ecc

'rena SF sand

re'nale AG kidney cpd

'rendere /88/ VT (ridare) to return, give back; (: saluto ecc) to return; (produrre) to yield, bring in; (esprimere, tradurre) to render; (far diventare): **~ qc possibile** to make sth possible ▸ VI (fruttare: ditta) to be profitable; (: investimento, campo) to yield, be productive; **~ grazie a qn** to thank sb; **~ omaggio a qn** to honour sb; **~ un servizio a qn** to do sb a service; **~ una testimonianza** to give evidence; **~ la visita** to pay a return visit; **non so se rendo l'idea** I don't know whether I'm making myself clear; **rendersi utile** to make o.s. useful; **rendersi conto di qc** to realize sth

rendi'conto SM (rapporto) report, account; (Amm, Comm) statement of account

rendi'mento SM (reddito) yield; (di manodopera, Tecn) efficiency; (capacità) output; (di studenti) performance

'rendita SF (di individuo) private o unearned income; (Comm) revenue; **~ annua** annuity; **~ vitalizia** life annuity

'rene SM kidney

'reni SFPL back sg

reni'tente AG reluctant, unwilling; **~ ai consigli di qn** unwilling to follow sb's advice; **essere ~ alla leva** (Mil) to fail to report for military service

'renna SF reindeer inv

'Reno SM: **il ~** the Rhine

'reo, -a SM/F (Dir) offender

re'parto SM department, section; (Mil) detachment; **~ acquisti** purchasing office

repel'lente AG repulsive; (Chim: insettifugo): **liquido ~** (liquid) repellent

repen'taglio [repen'taʎʎo] SM: **mettere a ~** to jeopardize, risk

repen'tino, -a AG sudden, unexpected

repe'ribile AG available

repe'rire /55/ VT to find, trace

re'perto SM (Archeologia) find; (Med) report; (anche: **reperto giudiziario**) exhibit

reper'torio SM (Teat) repertory; (elenco) index, (alphabetical) list

'replica, -che SF repetition; reply, answer; (obiezione) objection; (Teat, Cine) repeat performance; (copia) replica

repli'care /20/ VT (ripetere) to repeat; (rispondere) to answer, reply

repor'tage [rəpɔr'taʒ] SM INV (Stampa) report

repressi'one SF repression

repres'sivo, -a AG repressive

re'presso, -a PP di **reprimere**

re'primere /50/ VT to suppress, repress

re'pubblica, -che SF republic; **la R~ Democratica Tedesca** the German Democratic Republic; **la R~ Federale Tedesca** the Federal Republic of Germany; **la Prima/la Seconda R~** terms used to refer to Italy before and after the political changes resulting from the 1994 elections; vedi anche **Festa della Repubblica**

repubbli'cano, -a AG, SM/F republican

repu'tare /72/ VT to consider, judge

reputazi'one [reputat'tsjone] SF reputation; **farsi una cattiva ~** to get o.s. a bad name

'requie SF rest; **dare ~ a qn** to give sb some peace; **senza ~** unceasingly

'requiem SM INV (preghiera) requiem, prayer for the dead; (fig: ufficio funebre) requiem

requi'sire /55/ VT to requisition

requi'sito SM requirement; **avere i requisiti necessari per un lavoro** to have the necessary qualifications for a job

requisi'toria SF (Dir) closing speech (for the prosecution)

requisizi'one [rekwizit'tsjone] SF requisition

'resa SF (l'arrendersi) surrender; (restituzione, rendimento) return; **~ dei conti** rendering of accounts; (fig) day of reckoning

re'scindere [reʃʃindere] /102/ VT (Dir) to rescind, annul

re'scisso, -a [reʃʃisso] PP di **rescindere**

reset'tare /72/ VT (Inform) to reset

'resi etc VB vedi **rendere**

resi'dente AG resident

resi'denza [resi'dɛntsa] SF residence

residenzi'ale [residen'tsjale] AG residential

residu'ale AG residual

re'siduo, -a AG residual, remaining ▸ SM remainder; (Chim) residue; **residui industriali** industrial waste sg

'resina SF resin

resis'tente AG (*che resiste*): ~ **a** resistant to; (*forte*) strong; (*duraturo*) long-lasting, durable; ~ **all'acqua** waterproof; ~ **al caldo** heat-resistant; ~ **al fuoco** fireproof; ~ **al gelo** frost-resistant

resis'tenza [resis'tɛntsa] SF (*gen, Elettr*) resistance; (*di persona: fisica*) stamina, endurance; (: *mentale*) endurance, resistance; **opporre** ~ (**a**) to offer o put up resistance (to); (*decisione, scelta*) to show opposition (to); **la R~** *see note*

> The Italian *Resistenza* fought against both the Nazis and the Fascists during the Second World War. It was particularly active after the fall of the Fascist government on 25 July 1943, throughout the German occupation and during the period of Mussolini's Republic of Salò in northern Italy. Resistance members spanned the whole political spectrum and played a vital role in the Liberation and in the formation of the new democratic government.

re'sistere /11/ VI to resist; ~ **a** (*assalto, tentazioni*) to resist; (*dolore*) to withstand; (*non patir danno*) to be resistant to

resis'tito, -a PP *di* **resistere**

'reso, -a PP *di* **rendere**

reso'conto SM report, account

respin'gente [respin'dʒɛnte] SM (*Ferr*) buffer

res'pingere [res'pindʒere] /114/ VT to drive back, repel; (*rifiutare: pacco, lettera*) to return; (: *invito*) to refuse; (: *proposta*) to reject, turn down; (*Ins: bocciare*) to fail

res'pinto, -a PP *di* **respingere**

respi'rare /72/ VI to breathe; (*fig*) to get one's breath; to breathe again ▶ VT to breathe (in), inhale

respira'tore SM respirator

respira'torio, -a AG respiratory

respirazi'one [respirat'tsjone] SF breathing; ~ **artificiale** artificial respiration; ~ **bocca a bocca** mouth-to-mouth resuscitation, kiss of life (*col*)

res'piro SM breathing *no pl*; (*singolo atto*) breath; (*fig*) respite, rest; **mandare un ~ di sollievo** to give a sigh of relief; **trattenere il ~** to hold one's breath; **lavorare senza ~** to work non-stop; **di ampio ~** (*opera, lavoro*) far-reaching

respon'sabile AG responsible ▶ SMF person responsible; (*capo*) person in charge; ~ **di** responsible for; (*Dir*) liable for

responsabilità SF INV responsibility; (*legale*) liability; **assumere la ~ di** to take on the responsibility for; **affidare a qn la ~ di qc** to make sb responsible for sth; ~ **patrimoniale** debt liability; ~ **penale** criminal liability

responsabiliz'zare [responsabilid'dzare] /72/ VT: ~ **qn** to make sb feel responsible

res'ponso SM answer; (*Dir*) verdict

'ressa SF crowd, throng

'ressi *etc* VB *vedi* **reggere**

res'tare /72/ VI (*rimanere*) to remain, stay; (*avanzare*) to be left, remain; (*diventare*): ~ **orfano/cieco** to become o be left an orphan/become blind; (*trovarsi*): ~ **sorpreso** to be surprised; ~ **d'accordo** to agree; **non resta più niente** there's nothing left; **restano pochi giorni** there are only a few days left; **che resti tra di noi** this is just between ourselves; ~ **in buoni rapporti** to remain on good terms; ~ **senza parole** to be left speechless

restau'rare /72/ VT to restore

restaura'tore, -'trice SM/F restorer

restaurazi'one [restaurat'tsjone] SF (*Pol*) restoration

res'tauro SM (*di edifici ecc*) restoration; **in ~** under repair; **sotto ~** (*dipinto*) being restored; **chiuso per restauri** closed for repairs

res'tio, -a, -'tii, -'tie AG restive; (*persona*): ~ **a** reluctant to

restitu'ire /55/ VT to return, give back; (*energie, forze*) to restore

restituzi'one [restitut'tsjone] SF return; (*di soldi*) repayment

'resto SM remainder, rest; (*denaro*) change; (*Mat*) remainder; **resti** SMPL leftovers; (*di città*) remains; **del ~** moreover, besides; **tenga pure il ~** keep the change; **resti mortali** (*mortal*) remains

res'tringere [res'trindʒere] /117/ VT to reduce; (*vestito*) to take in; (*stoffa*) to shrink; (*fig*) to restrict, limit; **restringersi** VPR (*strada*) to narrow; (*stoffa*) to shrink

restrit'tivo, -a AG restrictive

restrizi'one [restrit'tsjone] SF restriction

resurrezi'one [resurret'tsjone] SF = **risurrezione**

resusci'tare [resuʃʃi'tare] /72/ VT, VI = **risuscitare**

re'tata SF (*Pesca*) haul, catch; **fare una ~ di** (*fig: persone*) to round up

'rete SF net; (*di recinzione*) wire netting; (*Aut, Ferr, di spionaggio ecc*) network; (*fig*) trap, snare; **segnare una ~** (*Calcio*) to score a goal; ~ **ferroviaria/stradale/di distribuzione** railway/road/distribution network; ~ **del letto** (*sprung*) bed base; ~ **da pesca** fishing net; ~ **sociale** social network; ~ (**televisiva**) (*sistema*) network; (*canale*) channel; **la R~** the web; **calze a ~** fishnet tights o stockings

reti'cente [reti'tʃɛnte] AG reticent

reti'cenza [reti'tʃɛntsa] SF reticence

retico'lato SM grid; (*rete metallica*) wire netting; (*di filo spinato*) barbed wire fence

'retina SF (*Anat*) retina

re'torico, -a, -ci, -che AG rhetorical ▶ SF rhetoric

retribu'ire /55/ VT to pay; (*premiare*) to reward; **un lavoro mal retribuito** a poorly-paid job

retribu'tivo, -a AG pay *cpd*

retribuzi'one [retribut'tsjone] SF payment; reward

re'trivo, -a AG (*fig*) reactionary

'retro SM INV back ▶ AV (*dietro*): **vedi ~** see over(leaf)

retroattività SF retroactivity

retroat'tivo, -a AG (*Dir: legge*) retroactive; (*Amm: salario*) backdated

retrobot'tega, -ghe SF back shop

retro'cedere [retro'tʃedere] /**29**/ VI to withdraw ▶ VT (*Calcio*) to relegate; (*Mil*) to degrade; (*Amm*) to demote

retrocessi'one [retrotʃes'sjone] SF (*di impiegato*) demotion

retro'cesso, -a [retro'tʃesso] PP *di* **retrocedere**

retroda'tare /72/ VT (*Amm*) to backdate

re'trogrado, -a AG (*fig*) reactionary, backward-looking

retrogu'ardia SF (*anche fig*) rearguard

retro'marcia [retro'martʃa] SF (*Aut*) reverse; (*: dispositivo*) reverse gear

retro'scena [retroʃ'ʃɛna] SF INV (*Teat*) backstage ▶ SM INV: **i ~** (*fig*) the behind-the-scenes activities

retrospet'tivo, -a AG retrospective ▶ SF (*Arte*) retrospective (exhibition)

retros'tante AG: **~ (a)** at the back (of)

retro'terra SM hinterland

retro'via SF (*Mil*) zone behind the front; **mandare nelle retrovie** to send to the rear

retrovi'sore SM (*Aut*) (rear-view) mirror

'retta SF (*Mat*) straight line; (*di convitto*) charge for bed and board; (*fig: ascolto*): **dar ~ a** to listen to, pay attention to

rettango'lare AG rectangular

ret'tangolo, -a AG right-angled ▶ SM rectangle

ret'tifica, -che SF rectification, correction

rettifi'care /20/ VT (*curva*) to straighten; (*fig*) to rectify, correct

'rettile SM reptile

retti'lineo, -a AG rectilinear

retti'tudine SF rectitude, uprightness

'retto, -a PP *di* **reggere** ▶ AG straight; (*onesto*) honest, upright; (*giusto, esatto*) correct, proper, right; **angolo ~** (*Mat*) right angle

ret'tore SM (*Rel*) rector; (*di università*) ≈ chancellor

re'tweet [ri'twit] SM INV (*su Twitter*) retweet

reuma'tismo SM rheumatism

Rev. ABBR (= *Reverendo*) Rev(d)

reve'rendo, -a AG: **il ~ padre Belli** the Reverend Father Belli

reve'rente AG = **riverente**

reve'renza [reve'rɛntsa] SF = **riverenza**

rever'sibile AG reversible

revisio'nare /72/ VT (*conti*) to audit; (*Tecn*) to overhaul, service; (*Dir: processo*) to review; (*componimento*) to revise

revisi'one SF auditing *no pl*; audit; servicing *no pl*; overhaul; review; revision; **~ di bilancio** audit; **~ di bozze** proofreading; **~ contabile interna** internal audit

revi'sore SM: **~ di conti/bozze** auditor/proofreader

re'vival [ri'vaivəl] SM INV revival

'revoca SF revocation

revo'care /20/ VT to revoke

re'volver SM INV revolver

revolve'rata SF revolver shot

'Reykjavik ['reikjavik] SF Reykjavik

RFT SIGLA F *vedi* **la Repubblica Federale Tedesca**

ri'abbia *etc* VB *vedi* **riavere**

riabili'tare /72/ VT to rehabilitate; (*fig*) to restore to favour (BRIT) *o* favor (US)

riabilitazi'one [riabilitat'tsjone] SF rehabilitation

riac'cendere [riat'tʃendere] /**2**/ VT (*sigaretta, fuoco, gas*) to light again; (*luce, radio, TV*) to switch on again; (*fig: sentimenti, interesse*) to rekindle, revive; **riaccendersi** VPR (*fuoco*) to catch again; (*luce, radio, TV*) to come back on again; (*fig: sentimenti*) to revive, be rekindled

riac'ceso, -a [riat'tʃeso] PP *di* **riaccendere**

riacqui'stare /72/ VT (*gen*) to buy again; (*ciò che si era venduto*) to buy back; (*fig: buonumore, sangue freddo, libertà*) to regain; **~ la salute** to recover (one's health); **~ le forze** to regain one's strength

Ri'ad SF Riyadh

riaddormen'tare /72/ VT to put to sleep again; **riaddormentarsi** VPR to fall asleep again

riallac'ciare [riallat'tʃare] /**14**/ VT (*cintura, cavo ecc*) to refasten, tie up *o* fasten again; (*fig: rapporti, amicizia*) to resume, renew; **riallacciarsi** VPR: **riallacciarsi a** (*fig: a discorso, tema*) to resume, take up again

rial'zare [rial'tsare] /**72**/ VT to raise, lift; (*alzare di più*) to heighten, raise; (*aumentare: prezzi*) to increase, raise ▶ VI (*prezzi*) to rise, increase

rial'zato, -a [rial'tsato] AG: **piano ~** mezzanine, entresol

rial'zista, -i [rial'tsista] SM (*Borsa*) bull

ri'alzo [ri'altso] SM (*di prezzi*) increase, rise; (*sporgenza*) rise; **giocare al ~** (*Borsa*) to bull

rian'dare /6/ VI: **~ (in), ~ (a)** to go back (to), return (to)

riani'mare /72/ VT (*Med*) to resuscitate; (*fig (rallegrare)* to cheer up; (*: dar coraggio*) to give

r

heart to; **rianimarsi** VPR to recover consciousness; to cheer up; to take heart

rianimazi'one [rianimat'tsjone] SF (*Med*) resuscitation; **centro di ~** intensive care unit

ria'perto, -a PP *di* **riaprire**

riaper'tura SF reopening

riappa'rire /7/ VI to reappear

riap'parso, -a PP *di* **riapparire**

riap'pendere /8/ VT to rehang; (*Tel*) to hang up

ria'prire /9/ VT, **ria'prirsi** VPR to reopen, open again

ri'armo SM (*Mil*) rearmament

ri'arso, -a AG (*terreno*) arid; (*gola*) parched; (*labbra*) dry

riasset'tare /72/ VT (*vedi sm*) to rearrange; to reorganize

rias'setto SM (*di stanza ecc*) rearrangement; (*ordinamento*) reorganization

rias'sumere /12/ VT (*riprendere*) to resume; (*impiegare di nuovo*) to re-employ; (*sintetizzare*) to summarize

rias'sunto, -a PP *di* **riassumere** ▶ SM summary

riattac'care /20/ VT (*attaccare di nuovo*): **~ (a)** (*manifesto, francobollo*) to stick back (on); (*bottone*) to sew back (on); (*quadro, chiavi*) to hang back up (on); **~ (il telefono** *o* **il ricevitore)** to hang up (the receiver)

riatti'vare /72/ VT to reactivate

ria'vere /13/ VT to have again; (*avere indietro*) to get back; (*riacquistare*) to recover; **riaversi** VPR to recover; (*da svenimento, stordimento*) to come round

riba'dire /55/ VT (*fig*) to confirm

ri'balta SF (*sportello*) flap; (*Teat: proscenio*) front of the stage; **luci della ~** footlights *pl*; (*fig*) limelight; **tornare alla ~** (*personaggio*) to make a comeback; (*problema*) to come up again

ribal'tabile AG (*sedile*) tip-up

ribal'tare /72/ VT, VI (*anche*: **ribaltarsi**) to turn over, tip over

ribas'sare /72/ VT to lower, bring down ▶ VI to come down, fall

ribas'sista, -i SM (*Borsa*) bear

ri'basso SM reduction, fall; **essere in ~** (*azioni, prezzi*) to be down; (*fig: popolarità*) to be on the decline; **giocare al ~** (*Borsa*) to bear

ri'battere /1/ VT (*battere di nuovo*) to beat again; (*con macchina da scrivere*) to type again; (*palla*) to return, hit back; (*confutare*) to refute; **~ che** to retort that

ribattez'zare [ribatted'dzare] /72/ VT to rename

ribel'larsi /72/ VPR: **~ (a)** to rebel (against)

ri'belle AG (*soldati*) rebel; (*ragazzo*) rebellious ▶ SMF rebel

ribelli'one SF rebellion

'ribes SM INV currant; **~ nero** blackcurrant; **~ rosso** redcurrant

ribol'lire /17/ VI (*fermentare*) to ferment; (*fare bolle*) to bubble, boil; (*fig*) to seethe

ri'brezzo [ri'breddzo] SM disgust, loathing; **far ~ a** to disgust

ribut'tante AG disgusting, revolting

ricacci'are [rikat'tʃare] /14/ VT (*respingere*) to drive back; **~ qn fuori** to throw sb out

rica'dere /18/ VI to fall again; (*scendere a terra: fig: nel peccato ecc*) to fall back; (*vestiti, capelli ecc*) to hang (down); (*riversarsi: fatiche: colpe*): **~ su** to fall on

rica'duta SF (*Med*) relapse

rical'care /20/ VT (*disegni*) to trace; (*fig*) to follow faithfully

ricalci'trare [rikaltʃi'trare] /72/ VI (*cavalli, asini, muli*) to kick

rica'mare /72/ VT to embroider

ricambi'are /19/ VT to change again; (*contraccambiare*) to return, repay

ri'cambio SM exchange, return; (*Fisiol*) metabolism; **ricambi** SMPL spare parts; **pezzi di ~** spare parts; **~ della manodopera** labour turnover

ri'camo SM embroidery; **senza ricami** (*fig*) without frills

ricapitalizzazione [rikapitaliddza'tsjone] SF bailout

ricapito'lare /72/ VT to recapitulate, sum up

ricapitolazi'one [rikapitolat'tsjone] SF recapitulation, summary

ricari'care /20/ VT (*arma, macchina fotografica*) to reload; (*penna, pipa*) to refill; (*orologio, giocattolo*) to rewind; (*Elettr*) to recharge

ricat'tare /72/ VT to blackmail

ricatta'tore, -'trice SM/F blackmailer

ri'catto SM blackmail; **fare un ~ a qn** to blackmail sb; **subire un ~** to be blackmailed

rica'vare /72/ VT (*estrarre*) to draw out, extract; (*ottenere*) to obtain, gain

rica'vato SM (*di vendite*) proceeds *pl*

ri'cavo SM proceeds *pl*; (*Contabilità*) revenue

ric'chezza [rik'kettsa] SF wealth; (*fig*) richness; **ricchezze** SFPL (*beni*) wealth *sg*, riches; **ricchezze naturali** natural resources

'riccio, -a, -ci, -ce ['rittʃo] AG curly ▶ SM (*Zool*) hedgehog; (*anche*: **riccio di mare**) sea urchin

'ricciolo ['rittʃolo] SM curl

ricci'uto, -a [rit'tʃuto] AG curly

'ricco, -a, -chi, -che AG rich; (*persona, paese*) rich, wealthy ▶ SM/F rich man/woman; **i ricchi** the rich; **~ di** (*idee, illustrazioni ecc*) full of; (*risorse, fauna ecc*) rich in

ri'cerca, -che [ri'tʃerka] SF search; (*indagine*) investigation, inquiry; (*studio*): **la ~** research; **una ~** a piece of research; **mettersi alla ~ di**

to go in search of, look o search o hunt for; **essere alla ~ di** to be searching for, be looking for; **~ di mercato** market research; **~ operativa** operational research

ricer'care [ritʃer'kare] /20/ vt (motivi, cause) to look for, try to determine; (successo, piacere) to pursue; (onore, gloria) to seek

ricerca'tezza [ritʃerka'tettsa] sf (raffinatezza) refinement; (peg) affectation

ricer'cato, -a [ritʃer'kato] AG (apprezzato) much sought-after; (affettato) studied, affected ▸ sm/f (Polizia) wanted man/woman

ricerca'tore, -'trice [ritʃerka'tore] sm/f (Ins) researcher

ricetrasmit'tente [ritʃetrazmit'tɛnte] sf two-way radio, transceiver

ri'cetta [ri'tʃetta] sf (Med) prescription; (Cuc) recipe; (fig: antidoto): **~ contro** remedy for

ricet'tacolo [ritʃet'takolo] sm (peg: luogo malfamato) den

ricet'tario [ritʃet'tarjo] sm (Med) prescription pad; (Cuc) recipe book

ricetta'tore, -'trice [ritʃetta'tore] sm/f (Dir) receiver (of stolen goods)

ricettazi'one [ritʃettat'tsjone] sf (Dir) receiving (stolen goods)

ricet'tivo, -a [ritʃet'tivo] AG receptive

rice'vente [ritʃe'vente] AG (Radio, TV) receiving ▸ smf (Comm) receiver

ri'cevere [ri'tʃevere] /29/ vt to receive; (stipendio, lettera) to get, receive; (accogliere: ospite) to welcome; (vedere: cliente, rappresentante ecc) to see; **"confermiamo di aver ricevuto tale merce"** (Comm) "we acknowledge receipt of these goods"

ricevi'mento [ritʃevi'mento] sm receiving no pl; (trattenimento) reception; **al ~ della merce** on receipt of the goods

ricevi'tore [ritʃevi'tore] sm (Tecn) receiver; **~ delle imposte** tax collector

ricevito'ria [ritʃevito'ria] sf (Fisco): **~ (delle imposte)** Inland Revenue(BRIT) Office, Internal Revenue (US) Office; **~ del lotto** lottery office

rice'vuta [ritʃe'vuta] sf receipt; **accusare ~ di qc** (Comm) to acknowledge receipt of sth; **~ fiscale** official receipt (for tax purposes); **~ di ritorno** (Posta) advice of receipt; **~ di versamento** receipt of payment

ricezi'one [ritʃet'tsjone] sf (Radio, TV) reception

richia'mare [rikja'mare] /72/ vt (chiamare indietro, ritelefonare) to call back; (ambasciatore, truppe) to recall; (rimproverare) to reprimand; (attirare) to attract, draw; **richiamarsi** vpr: **richiamarsi a** (riferirsi a) to refer to; **~ qn all'ordine** to call sb to order; **desidero ~ la vostra attenzione su ...** I would like to draw your attention to ...

richi'amo [ri'kjamo] sm call; recall reprimand; attraction

richie'dente [rikje'dɛnte] smf applicant

richi'edere [ri'kjedere] /21/ vt to ask again for; (chiedere: per sapere) to ask; (: per avere) to ask for; (Amm: documenti) to apply for; (esigere) to need, require; (chiedere indietro): **~ qc** to ask for sth back; **essere molto richiesto** to be in great demand

richi'esto, -a [ri'kjɛsto] pp di **richiedere** ▸ sf (domanda) request; (Amm) application, request; (esigenza) demand, request; **a richiesta** on request

rici'claggio [ritʃi'kladdʒo] sm (fig) laundering; **~ di materiale** recycling; **~ di denaro sporco** money laundering

rici'clare [ritʃi'klare] /72/ vt (vetro, carta, bottiglie) to recycle; (fig: personale) to retrain

'ricino ['ritʃino] sm: **olio di ~** castor oil

ricogni'tore [rikoɲɲi'tore] sm (Aer) reconnaissance aircraft

ricognizi'one [rikoɲɲit'tsjone] sf (Mil) reconnaissance; (Dir) recognition, acknowledgement

ricolle'gare /80/ vt (collegare nuovamente: gen) to join again, link again; (connettere: fatti): **~ (a, con)** to connect (with); **ricollegarsi** vpr: **ricollegarsi a** (fatti: connettersi) to be connected to; (persona: riferirsi) to refer to

ri'colmo, -a AG: **~ (di)** (bicchiere) full to the brim (with); (stanza) full (of)

ricominci'are [rikomin'tʃare] /14/ vt, vi to start again, begin again; **~ a fare qc** to begin doing o to do sth again, start doing o to do sth again

ricom'pensa sf reward

ricompen'sare /72/ vt to reward

ricom'porsi /77/ vpr to compose o.s., regain one's composure

ricom'posto, -a pp di **ricomporsi**

riconcili'are [rikontʃi'ljare] /19/ vt to reconcile; **riconciliarsi** vpr to be reconciled

riconciliazi'one [rikontʃiliat'tsjone] sf reconciliation

ricon'dotto, -a pp di **ricondurre**

ricon'durre /90/ vt to bring (o take) back

ricon'ferma sf reconfirmation

riconfer'mare /72/ vt to reconfirm

ricongiungi'mento [rikondʒundʒi'mento] sm (di famiglia, coniugi) reconciliation; **~ familiare** (Dir: di immigrati) family reunification

ricono'scente [rikonoʃʃɛnte] AG grateful

ricono'scenza [rikonoʃʃɛntsa] sf gratitude

rico'noscere [riko'noʃʃere] /26/ vt to recognize; (Dir: figlio, debito) to acknowledge; (ammettere: errore) to admit, acknowledge; **~ qn colpevole** to find sb guilty

r

303

riconosci'mento [rikonoʃʃi'mento] SM
recognition; acknowledgement;
(*identificazione*) identification; **come ~ dei**
servizi resi in recognition of services
rendered; **documento di ~** means of
identification; **segno di ~** distinguishing
mark; **programma per il ~ vocale** (*Inform*)
voice recognition program

riconosci'uto, -a [rikonoʃʃuto] PP *di*
riconoscere

riconquis'tare /72/ VT (*Mil*) to reconquer;
(*libertà, stima*) to win back

rico'perto, -a PP *di* **ricoprire**

ricopi'are /19/ VT to copy

rico'prire /9/ VT to re-cover; (*coprire*) to cover;
(*occupare: carica*) to hold

ricor'dare /72/ VT to remember, recall;
(*richiamare alla memoria*): **~ qc a qn** to remind
sb of sth; **ricordarsi** VPR: **ricordarsi (di)** to
remember; **ricordarsi di qc/di aver fatto** to
remember sth/having done

ri'cordo SM memory; (*regalo*) keepsake,
souvenir; (*di viaggio*) souvenir; **ricordi** SMPL
(*memorie*) memoirs

ricor'rente AG recurrent, recurring

ricor'renza [rikor'rɛntsa] SF recurrence;
(*festività*) anniversary

ri'correre /28/ VI (*ripetersi*) to recur; **~ a**
(*rivolgersi*) to turn to; (*Dir*) to appeal to;
(*servirsi di*) to have recourse to; **~ in appello**
to lodge an appeal

ri'corso, -a PP *di* **ricorrere** ▶ SM recurrence;
(*Dir*) appeal; **far ~ a** = **ricorrere a**

ricostitu'ente AG (*Med*): **cura ~** tonic
treatment, tonic ▶ SM (*Med*) tonic

ricostitu'ire /55/ VT (*società*) to build up again;
(*governo, partito*) to re-form; **ricostituirsi** VPR
(*gruppo ecc*) to re-form

ricostru'ire /55/ VT (*casa*) to rebuild; (*fatti*) to
reconstruct

ricostruzi'one [rikostrut'tsjone] SF
rebuilding *no pl*, reconstruction

ri'cotta SF soft white unsalted cheese made from
sheep's milk

ricove'rare /72/ VT to give shelter to; **~ qn in**
ospedale to admit sb to hospital

ricove'rato, -a SM/F patient

ri'covero SM shelter, refuge; (*Mil*) shelter;
(*Med*) admission (to hospital); **~ antiaereo**
air-raid shelter

ricre'are /72/ VT to recreate; (*rinvigorire*) to
restore; (*fig: distrarre*) to amuse

ricrea'tivo, -a AG recreational

ricreazi'one [rikreat'tsjone] SF recreation,
entertainment; (*Ins*) break

ri'credersi /29/ VPR to change one's mind

ricupe'rare /72/ VT (*rientrare in possesso di*) to
recover, get back; (*tempo perduto*) to make up
for; (*Naut*) to salvage; (*: naufraghi*) to rescue;

(*delinquente*) to rehabilitate; **~ lo svantaggio**
(*Sport*) to close the gap

ri'cupero SM (*gen*) recovery; (*di relitto ecc*)
salvaging; **capacità di ~** resilience

ricu'sare /72/ VT to refuse

ridacchi'are [ridak'kjare] /19/ VI to snigger

ri'dare /33/ VT to return, give back

'ridda SF (*di ammiratori ecc*) swarm; (*di pensieri*)
jumble

ri'dente AG (*occhi, volto*) smiling; (*paesaggio*)
delightful

'ridere /89/ VI to laugh; (*deridere, beffare*): **~ di**
to laugh at, make fun of; **non c'è niente**
da ~, c'è poco da ~ it's not a laughing
matter

rides'tare /72/ VT (*fig: ricordi, passioni*) to
reawaken

ri'detto, -a PP *di* **ridire**

ridico'laggine [ridiko'laddʒine] SF (*di*
situazione) absurdity; (*cosa detta o fatta*)
nonsense *no pl*

ridicoliz'zare [ridikolid'dzare] /72/ VT to
ridicule

ri'dicolo, -a AG ridiculous, absurd ▶ SM:
cadere nel ~ to become ridiculous;
rendersi ~ to make a fool of o.s.

ridimensiona'mento SM reorganization;
(*di fatto storico*) reappraisal

ridimensio'nare /72/ VT to reorganize; (*fig*)
to see in the right perspective

ri'dire /38/ VT to repeat; (*criticare*) to find fault
with; to object to; **trova sempre qualcosa**
da ~ he always manages to find fault

ridon'dante AG redundant

ri'dosso SM: **a ~ di** (*dietro*) behind; (*contro*)
against

ri'dotto, -a PP *di* **ridurre** ▶ AG (*biglietto*)
reduced; (*formato*) small

ri'duco *etc* VB *vedi* **ridurre**

ri'durre /90/ VT (*anche Chim, Mat*) to reduce;
(*prezzo, spese*) to cut, reduce; (*accorciare: opera*
letteraria) to abridge; (*Radio, TV*) to adapt;
ridursi VPR (*diminuirsi*) to be reduced, shrink;
ridursi a to be reduced to; **ridursi a pelle e**
ossa to be reduced to skin and bone

ri'dussi *etc* VB *vedi* **ridurre**

ridut'tore SM (*Tecn, Chim*) reducer; (*Elettr*)
adaptor

riduzi'one [ridut'tsjone] SF reduction;
abridgement; adaptation

ri'ebbi *etc* VB *vedi* **riavere**

riecheg'giare [rieked'dʒare] /62/ VI to
re-echo

riedu'care /20/ VT (*persona, arto*) to re-educate;
(*malato*) to rehabilitate

rieducazi'one [riedukat'tsjone] SF
re-education; rehabilitation; **centro di ~**
rehabilitation centre

rie'leggere [rie'lɛddʒere] /61/ VT to re-elect

rie'letto, -a PP di **rieleggere**

riempi'mento SM filling (up)

riem'pire /91/ VT to fill (up); (modulo) to fill in o out; **riempirsi** VPR to fill (up); (mangiare troppo) to stuff o.s.; **~ qc di** to fill sth (up) with

riempi'tivo, -a AG filling ▶ SM (anche fig) filler

rien'tranza [rien'trantsa] SF recess; indentation

rien'trare /72/ VI (entrare di nuovo) to go (o come) back in; (tornare) to return; (fare una rientranza) to go in, curve inwards; to be indented; (riguardare): **~ in** to be included among, form part of; **~ (a casa)** to get back home; **non rientriamo nelle spese** we are not within our budget

ri'entro SM (ritorno) return; (di astronave) re-entry; **è iniziato il grande ~** (estivo) people are coming back from their (summer) holidays

riepilo'gare /80/ VT to summarize ▶ VI to recapitulate

rie'pilogo, -ghi SM recapitulation; **fare un ~ di qc** to summarize sth

rie'same SM re-examination

riesami'nare /72/ VT to re-examine

ri'esco etc VB vedi **riuscire**

ri'essere /51/ VI: **ci risiamo!** (col) we're back to this again!

rievo'care /20/ VT (passato) to recall; (commemorare: figura, meriti) to commemorate

rievocazi'one [rievokat'tsjone] SF (vedi vt) recalling; commemoration

rifaci'mento [rifatʃi'mento] SM (di film) remake; (di opera letteraria) rehashing

ri'fare /53/ VT to do again; (ricostruire) to make again; (nodo) to tie again, do up again; (imitare) to imitate, copy; **rifarsi** VPR (risarcirsi): **rifarsi di** to make up for; (vendicarsi): **rifarsi di qc su qn** to get one's own back on sb for sth; (riferirsi): **rifarsi a** (periodo, fenomeno storico) to go back to; to follow; **~ il letto** to make the bed; **rifarsi una vita** to make a new life for o.s

ri'fatto, -a PP di **rifare**

riferi'mento SM reference; **in** o **con ~ a** with reference to; **far ~ a** to refer to

rife'rire /55/ VT (riportare) to report; (ascrivere): **~ qc a** to attribute sth to ▶ VI to do a report; **riferirsi** VPR: **riferirsi a** to refer to; **riferirò** I'll pass on the message

rifi'lare /72/ VT (tagliare a filo) to trim; (col: affibbiare): **~ qc a qn** to palm sth off on sb

rifi'nire /55/ VT to finish off, put the finishing touches to

rifini'tura SF finishing touch; **rifiniture** SFPL (di mobile, auto) finish sg

rifiu'tare /72/ VT to refuse; **~ di fare** to refuse to do

rifi'uto SM refusal; **rifiuti** SMPL (spazzatura) rubbish sg, refuse sg; **rifiuti solidi urbani** solid urban waste sg

riflessi'one SF (Fisica, meditazione) reflection; (il pensare) thought, reflection; (osservazione) remark

rifles'sivo, -a AG (persona) thoughtful, reflective; (Ling) reflexive

ri'flesso, -a PP di **riflettere** ▶ SM (di luce, allo specchio) reflection; (Fisiol) reflex; (su capelli) light; (fig) effect; **di** o **per ~** indirectly; **avere i riflessi pronti** to have quick reflexes

riflesso'gia [riflessolo'dʒia] SF: **~ (plantare)** reflexology

ri'flettere /92/ VT to reflect ▶ VI to think; **riflettersi** VPR to be reflected; (ripercuotersi) **riflettersi su** to have repercussions on; **~ su** to think over

riflet'tore SM reflector; (proiettore) floodlight; (Mil) searchlight

ri'flusso SM flowing back; (della marea) ebb; **un'epoca di ~** an era of nostalgia

rifocil'larsi [rifotʃil'larsi] /72/ VPR (poetico) to take refreshment

rifondazi'one [rifondat'tsjone] SF (Pol): **R~ Comunista** hard left party, originating from former P.C.I.

ri'fondere /25/ VT (rimborsare) to refund, repay; **~ le spese a qn** to refund sb's expenses; **~ i danni a qn** to compensate sb for damages

ri'forma SF reform; (Mil) declaration of unfitness for service; discharge (on health grounds); **la R~** (Rel) the Reformation

rifor'mare /72/ VT to re-form; (cambiare, innovare) to reform; (Mil: recluta) to declare unfit for service; (: soldato) to invalid out, discharge

riforma'tore, -'trice AG reforming ▶ SM/F reformer

riforma'torio SM (Dir) community home (BRIT), reformatory (US)

rifor'mista, -i, -e AG, SM/F reformist

riforni'mento SM supplying, providing; restocking; (di carburante) refuelling; **rifornimenti** SMPL (provviste) supplies, provisions; **fare ~ di** (viveri) to stock up with; (benzina) to fill up with; **posto di ~** filling o gas (US) station

rifor'nire /55/ VT (fornire di nuovo: casa ecc) to restock; (provvedere): **~ di** to supply o provide with; **rifornirsi** VPR: **rifornirsi di qc** to stock up on sth

ri'frangere [ri'frandʒere] /37/ VT to refract

ri'fratto, -a PP di **rifrangere**

rifrazi'one [rifrat'tsjone] SF refraction

rifug'gire [rifud'dʒire] /31/ VI to escape again; (fig): **~ da** to shun

rifugi'arsi [rifu'dʒarsi] /62/ VPR to take refuge

rifugi'ato, -a [rifu'dʒato] SM/F refugee

ri'fugio [ri'fudʒo] SM refuge, shelter; (*in montagna*) shelter; ~ **antiaereo** air-raid shelter

ri'fuso, -a PP *di* **rifondere**

'**riga, -ghe** SF line; (*striscia*) stripe; (*di persone, cose*) line, row; (*regolo*) ruler; (*scriminatura*) parting; **mettersi in** ~ to line up; **a righe** (*foglio*) lined; (*vestito*) striped; **buttare giù due righe** (*note*) to jot down a few notes; **mandami due righe appena arrivi** drop me a line as soon as you arrive

ri'gagnolo [ri'gaɲɲolo] SM rivulet

ri'gare /80/ VT (*foglio*) to rule ▶ VI: ~ **diritto** (*fig*) to toe the line

rigassifica'tore SM regasification terminal

riga'toni SMPL (*Cuc*) short, ridged pasta shapes

rigatti'ere SM junk dealer

riga'tura SF (*di pagina, quaderno*) lining, ruling; (*di fucile*) rifling

rigene'rare [ridʒene'rare] **/72/** VT (*gen, Tecn*) to regenerate; (*forze*) to restore; (*gomma*) to retread; **rigenerarsi** VPR (*gen*) to regenerate; (*ramo, tumore*) to regenerate, grow again; **gomma rigenerata** retread

rigenerazi'one [ridʒenerat'tsjone] SF regeneration

riget'tare [ridʒet'tare] **/72/** VT (*gettare indietro*) to throw back; (*fig: respingere*) to reject; (*vomitare*) to bring o throw up

ri'getto [ri'dʒetto] SM (*anche Med*) rejection

ri'ghello [ri'gɛllo] SM ruler

righerò etc [rige'rɔ] VB *vedi* **rigare**

rigi'dezza [ridʒi'dettsa], **rigidità** [ridʒidi'ta] SF rigidity, stiffness, severity, rigours *pl* (BRIT), rigors *pl* (US); strictness

'**rigido, -a** ['ridʒido] AG rigid, stiff; (*membra ecc: indurite*) stiff; (*Meteor*) harsh, severe; (*fig*) strict

rigi'rare [ridʒi'rare] **/72/** VT to turn; **rigirarsi** VPR to turn round; (*nel letto*) to turn over; ~ **qc tra le mani** to turn sth over in one's hands; ~ **il discorso** to change the subject

'**rigo, -ghi** SM line; (*Mus*) staff, stave

rigogli'oso, -a [rigoʎ'ʎoso] AG (*pianta*) luxuriant; (*fig: commercio, sviluppo*) thriving

rigonfia'mento SM (*Anat*) swelling; (*su legno, intonaco ecc*) bulge

ri'gonfio, -a AG swollen; (*grembiule, sporta*): ~ **di** bulging with

ri'gore SM (*Meteor*) harshness, rigours *pl* (BRIT), rigors *pl* (US); (*fig*) severity, strictness; (*anche*: **calcio di rigore**) penalty; **di** ~ compulsory; "**è di** ~ **l'abito da sera**" "evening dress"; **area di** ~ (*Calcio*) penalty box (BRIT); **a rigor di termini** strictly speaking

rigorosità SF strictness; rigour (BRIT), rigor (US)

rigo'roso, -a AG (*severo: persona, ordine*) strict; (*preciso*) rigorous

rigover'nare /72/ VT to wash (up)

riguar'dare /72/ VT to look at again; (*considerare*) to regard, consider; (*concernere*) to regard, concern; **riguardarsi** VPR (*aver cura di sé*) to look after o.s.; **per quel che mi riguarda** as far as I'm concerned; **sono affari che non ti riguardano** it's none of your business

rigu'ardo SM (*attenzione*) care; (*considerazione*) regard, respect; ~ **a** concerning, with regard to; **per** ~ **a** out of respect for; **ospite/ persona di** ~ very important guest/person; **non aver riguardi nell'agire/nel parlare** to act/speak freely

riguar'doso, -a AG (*rispettoso*) respectful; (*premuroso*) considerate, thoughtful

rigurgi'tare [rigurdʒi'tare] **/72/** VI (*liquido*): ~ **da** to gush out from; (*recipiente: traboccare*) ~ **di** to overflow with

ri'gurgito [ri'gurdʒito] SM (*Med*) regurgitation; (*fig: ritorno, risveglio*) revival

rilanci'are [rilan'tʃare] **/14/** VT (*lanciare di nuovo: gen*) to throw again; (*: moda*) to bring back; (*: prodotto*) to re-launch; ~ **un'offerta** (*asta*) to make a higher bid

ri'lancio [ri'lantʃo] SM (*Carte: di offerta*) raising

rilasci'are [rilaʃ'ʃare] **/14/** VT (*rimettere in libertà*) to release; (*Amm: documenti*) to issue; (*intervista*) to give; ~ **delle dichiarazioni** to make a statement

ri'lascio [ri'laʃʃo] SM release; issue

rilassa'mento SM (*gen, Med*) relaxation

rilas'sare /72/ VT to relax; **rilassarsi** VPR to relax; (*fig: disciplina*) to become slack

rilassa'tezza [rilassa'tettsa] SF (*fig: di costumi, disciplina*) laxity

rilas'sato, -a AG (*persona, muscoli*) relaxed; (*disciplina, costumi*) lax

rile'gare /80/ VT (*libro*) to bind

rilega'tura SF binding

ri'leggere [ri'lɛddʒere] **/61/** VT to reread, read again; (*rivedere*) to read over

ri'lento: a ~ *av* slowly

ri'letto, -a PP *di* **rileggere**

rilet'tura SF (*vedi vt*) rereading; reading over

rileva'mento SM (*topografico, statistico*) survey; (*Naut*) bearing

rile'vante AG considerable; important

rile'vanza [rile'vantsa] SF importance

rile'vare /72/ VT (*ricavare*) to find; (*notare*) to notice; (*mettere in evidenza*) to point out; (*venire a conoscere: notizia*) to learn; (*raccogliere: dati*) to gather, collect; (*Topografia*) to survey; (*Mil*) to relieve; (*Comm*) to take over

rilevazi'one [rilevat'tsjone] SF survey

rili'evo SM (*Arte, Geo*) relief; (*fig: rilevanza*) importance; (*osservazione*) point, remark; (*Topografia*) survey; **dar** ~ **a** o **mettere in** ~ **qc** (*fig*) to bring sth out, highlight sth; **di poco/**

nessun ~ (fig) of little/no importance; **un personaggio di ~** an important person

rilut'tante AG reluctant

rilut'tanza [rilut'tantsa] SF reluctance

'rima SF rhyme; (verso) verse; **far ~ con** to rhyme with; **rispondere a qn per le rime** to give sb tit for tat

riman'dare /72/ VT to send again; (restituire, rinviare) to send back, return; **~ qc (a)** (differire) to postpone sth o put sth off (till); **~ qn a** (fare riferimento) to refer sb to; **essere rimandato** (Ins) to have to resit one's exams

ri'mando SM (rinvio) return; (dilazione) postponement; (riferimento) cross-reference

rimaneggi'are [rimaned'dʒare] /62/ VT (testo) to reshape, recast; (Pol) to reshuffle

rima'nente AG remaining ▶ SM rest, remainder; **i rimanenti** (persone) the rest of them, the others

rima'nenza [rima'nentsa] SF rest, remainder; **rimanenze** SFPL (Comm) unsold stock sg

rima'nere /93/ VI (restare) to remain, stay; (avanzare) to be left, remain; (restare stupito) to be amazed; **rimangono poche settimane a Pasqua** there are only a few weeks left till Easter; **~ vedovo** to be left a widower; **~ confuso/sorpreso** to be confused/surprised; **rimane da vedere se** it remains to be seen whether

rimangi'are [riman'dʒare] /62/ VT to eat again; **rimangiarsi la parola/una promessa** (fig) to go back on one's word/one's promise

ri'mango etc VB vedi **rimanere**

ri'mare /72/ VT, VI to rhyme

rimargi'nare [rimardʒi'nare] /72/ VT, VI (anche: **rimarginarsi**) to heal

ri'masto, -a PP di **rimanere**

rima'sugli [rima'suʎʎi] SMPL leftovers

rimbal'zare [rimbal'tsare] /72/ VI to bounce back, rebound; (proiettile) to ricochet

rim'balzo [rim'baltso] SM rebound; ricochet

rimbam'bire /55/ VI to be in one's dotage; (rincretinire) to grow foolish

rimbam'bito, -a AG senile, in one's dotage; (col): **un vecchio ~** a doddering old man

rimbec'care /20/ VT (persona) to answer back; (offesa) to return

rimbecil'lire [rimbetʃil'lire] /55/ VI, **rimbecil'lirsi** VPR to become stupid

rimboc'care /20/ VT (orlo) to turn up; (coperta) to tuck in; (maniche, pantaloni) to turn o roll up

rimbom'bare /72/ VI to resound; (artiglieria) to boom; (tuono) to rumble

rim'bombo SM (vedi vi) boom; rumble

rimbor'sare /72/ VT to pay back, repay; **~ qc a qn** to reimburse sb for sth

rim'borso SM repayment; (di spese, biglietto) refund; **~ d'imposta** tax rebate

rimboschi'mento [rimboski'mento] SM reafforestation

rimbos'chire [rimbos'kire] /55/ VT to reafforest

rimbrot'tare /72/ VT to reproach

rim'brotto SM reproach

rimedi'are /19/ VI: **~ a** to remedy ▶ VT (col: procurarsi) to get o scrape together; **~ da vivere** to scrape a living

ri'medio SM (medicina) medicine; (cura, fig) remedy, cure; **porre ~ a qc** to remedy sth; **non c'è ~** there's no way out, there's nothing to be done about it

rimesco'lare /72/ VT to mix well, stir well; (carte) to shuffle; **sentirsi ~ il sangue** (per rabbia) to feel one's blood boil

ri'messa SF (locale: per veicoli) garage; (: per aerei) hangar; (Comm: di merce) consignment; (: di denaro) remittance; (Tennis) return; (Calcio: anche: **rimessa in gioco**) throw-in

ri'messo, -a PP di **rimettere**

rimes'tare /72/ VT (mescolare) to mix well, stir well; (fig: passato) to drag up again

ri'mettere /63/ VT (mettere di nuovo) to put back; (Comm: merci) to deliver; (: denaro) to remit; (vomitare) to bring up; (perdere: anche: **rimetterci**) to lose; (indossare di nuovo): **~ qc** to put sth back on, put sth on again; (restituire) to return, give back; (affidare) to entrust; (decisione) to refer; (condonare) to remit; **rimettersi** VPR: **rimettersi a** (affidarsi) to trust; **~ a nuovo** (casa ecc) to do up (BRIT) o over (US); **rimetterci di tasca propria** to be out of pocket; **rimettersi al bello** (tempo) to clear up; **rimettersi in cammino** to set off again; **rimettersi al lavoro** to start working again; **rimettersi in salute** to get better, recover one's health

rimi'nese AG of (o from) Rimini

ri'misi etc VB vedi **rimettere**

'rimmel® SM INV mascara

rimoderna'mento SM modernization

rimoder'nare /72/ VT to modernize

ri'monta SF (Sport: gen) recovery

rimon'tare /72/ VT (meccanismo) to reassemble; (tenda) to put up again ▶ VI (salire di nuovo): **~ in** (macchina, treno) to get back into; (Sport) to close the gap

rimorchi'are [rimor'kjare] /19/ VT to tow; (fig: ragazza) to pick up

rimorchia'tore [rimorkja'tore] SM (Naut) tug(boat)

ri'morchio [ri'morkjo] SM tow; (veicolo) trailer; **andare a ~** to be towed; **prendere a ~** to tow; **cavo da ~** towrope; **autocarro con ~** articulated lorry (BRIT), semi(trailer) (US)

ri'morso SM remorse; **avere il ~ di aver fatto qc** to deeply regret having done sth

ri'mosso, -a PP di **rimuovere**

r

rimos'tranza [rimos'trantsa] SF protest, complaint; **fare le proprie rimostranze a qn** to remonstrate with sb

rimozi'one [rimot'tsjone] SF removal; (*da un impiego*) dismissal; (*Psic*) repression; **"~ forzata"** "illegally parked vehicles will be removed at owner's expense"

rimpas'tare /**72**/ VT (*Pol: ministero*) to reshuffle

rim'pasto SM (*Pol*) reshuffle; **~ ministeriale** cabinet reshuffle

rimpatri'are /**19**/ VI to return home ▶ VT to repatriate

rim'patrio SM repatriation

rimpi'angere [rim'pjandʒere] /**75**/ VT to regret; (*persona*) to miss; **~ di (non) aver fatto qc** to regret (not) having done sth

rimpi'anto, -a PP di **rimpiangere** ▶ SM regret

rimpiat'tino SM hide-and-seek

rimpiaz'zare [rimpjat'tsare] /**72**/ VT to replace

rimpiccio'lire [rimpittʃo'lire] /**55**/ VT to make smaller ▶ VI (*anche:* **rimpicciolirsi**) to become smaller

rimpin'zare [rimpin'tsare] /**72**/ VT: **~ di** to cram o stuff with; **rimpinzarsi** VPR: **rimpinzarsi (di qc)** to stuff o.s. (with sth)

rimprove'rare /**72**/ VT to rebuke, reprimand

rim'provero SM rebuke, reprimand; **di ~** (*tono, occhiata*) reproachful; (*parole*) of reproach

rimugi'nare [rimudʒi'nare] /**72**/ VT (*fig*) to turn over in one's mind

rimune'rare /**72**/ VT (*retribuire*) to remunerate; (*ricompensare: sacrificio ecc*) to reward; **un lavoro ben rimunerato** a well-paid job

rimunera'tivo, -a AG (*lavoro, attività*) remunerative, profitable

rimunerazi'one [rimunerat'tsjone] SF remuneration; (*premio*) reward

rimu'overe /**66**/ VT to remove; (*destituire*) to dismiss; (*fig: distogliere*) to dissuade

rinascimen'tale [rinaʃʃimen'tale] AG Renaissance *cpd*, of the Renaissance

Rinasci'mento [rinaʃʃi'mento] SM: **il ~** the Renaissance

ri'nascita [ri'naʃʃita] SF rebirth, revival

rincal'zare [rinkal'tsare] /**72**/ VT (*palo, albero*) to support, prop up; (*lenzuola*) to tuck in

rin'calzo [rin'kaltso] SM support, prop; (*rinforzo*) reinforcement; (*Sport*) reserve (player); **rincalzi** SMPL (*Mil*) reserves

rinca'rare /**72**/ VT to increase the price of ▶ VI to go up, become more expensive; **~ la dose** (*fig*) to pile it on

rin'caro SM: **~ (di)** (*prezzi, costo della vita*) increase (in); (*prodotto*) increase in the price (of)

rinca'sare /**72**/ VI to go home

rinchi'udere [rin'kjudere] /**22**/ VT to shut (*o lock*) up; **rinchiudersi** VPR: **rinchiudersi**

in to shut o.s. up in; **rinchiudersi in se stesso** to withdraw into o.s.

rinchi'uso, -a [rin'kjuso] PP di **rinchiudere**

rincitrul'lirsi [rintʃitrul'lirsi] /**55**/ VPR to grow foolish

rin'correre /**28**/ VT to chase, run after

rin'corso, -a PP di **rincorrere** ▶ SF short run

rin'crescere [rin'kreʃʃere] /**30**/ VB IMPERS: **mi rincresce che/di non poter fare** I'm sorry that/I can't do, I regret that/being unable to do

rincresci'mento [rinkreʃʃi'mento] SM regret

rincresci'uto, -a [rinkreʃʃuto] PP di **rincrescere**

rincu'lare /**72**/ VI to draw back; (*arma*) to recoil

rinfacci'are [rinfat'tʃare] /**14**/ VT (*fig*): **~ qc a qn** to throw sth in sb's face

rinfoco'lare /**72**/ VT (*fig: odio, passioni*) to rekindle; (: *risentimento, rabbia*) to stir up

rinfor'zare [rinfor'tsare] /**72**/ VT to reinforce, strengthen ▶ VI (*anche:* **rinforzarsi**) to grow stronger

rin'forzo [rin'fortso] SM: **mettere un ~ a** to strengthen; **rinforzi** SMPL (*Mil*) reinforcements; **di ~** (*asse, sbarra*) strengthening; (*esercito*) supporting; (*personale*) extra, additional

rinfran'care /**20**/ VT to encourage, reassure

rinfres'cante AG (*bibita*) refreshing

rinfres'care /**20**/ VT (*atmosfera, temperatura*) to cool (down); (*abito, pareti*) to freshen up ▶ VI (*tempo*) to grow cooler; **rinfrescarsi** VPR (*ristorarsi*) to refresh o.s.; (*lavarsi*) to freshen up; **~ la memoria a qn** to refresh sb's memory

rin'fresco, -schi SM (*festa*) party; **rinfreschi** SMPL (*cibi e bevande*) refreshments

rin'fusa SF: **alla ~** in confusion, higgledy-piggledy

ringhi'are [rin'gjare] /**19**/ VI to growl, snarl

ringhi'era [rin'gjɛra] SF railing; (*delle scale*) banister(s)

'ringhio ['ringjo] SM growl, snarl

ringhi'oso, -a [rin'gjoso] AG growling, snarling

ringiova'nire [rindʒova'nire] /**55**/ VT: **~ qn** (*vestito, acconciatura ecc*) to make sb look younger; (*vacanze ecc*) to rejuvenate sb ▶ VI (*anche:* **ringiovanirsi**) to become (o look) younger

ringrazia'mento [ringrattsja'mento] SM thanks *pl*; **lettera/biglietto di ~** thank you letter/card

ringrazi'are [ringrat'tsjare] /**19**/ VT to thank; **~ qn di qc** to thank sb for sth; **~ qn per aver fatto qc** to thank sb for doing sth

rinne'gare /**80**/ VT (*fede*) to renounce; (*figlio*) to disown, repudiate

rinne'gato, -a SM/F renegade

rinno'vabile AG (*contratto, energia*) renewable

rinnova'mento SM renewal; (*economico*) revival

rinno'vare /**72**/ VT to renew; (*ripetere*) to repeat, renew; **rinnovarsi** VPR (*fenomeno*) to be repeated, recur

rin'novo SM (*di contratto*) renewal; **"chiuso per ~ (dei) locali"** (*negozio*) "closed for alterations"

rinoce'ronte [rinotʃe'ronte] SM rhinoceros

rino'mato, -a AG renowned, celebrated

rinsal'dare /**72**/ VT to strengthen

rinsa'vire /**55**/ VI to come to one's senses

rinsec'chito, -a [rinsek'kito] AG (*vecchio, albero*) thin, gaunt

rinta'narsi /**72**/ VPR (*animale*) to go into its den; (*persona: nascondersi*) to hide

rintoc'care /**20**/ VI (*campana*) to toll; (*orologio*) to strike

rin'tocco, -chi SM toll

rintracci'are [rintrat'tʃare] /**14**/ VT to track down; (*persona scomparsa, documento*) to trace

rintro'nare /**72**/ VI to boom, roar ▶ VT (*assordare*) to deafen; (*stordire*) to stun

rintuz'zare [rintut'tsare] /**72**/ VT (*fig: sentimento*) to check, repress; (*: accusa*) to refute

ri'nuncia [ri'nuntʃa] SF renunciation; ~ (*carica*) resignation from; (*eredità*) relinquishment of; **~ agli atti del giudizio** (*Dir*) abandonment of a claim

rinunci'are [rinun'tʃare] /**14**/ VI: **~ a** to give up, renounce; **~ a fare qc** to give up doing sth

rinuncia'tario, -a [rinuntʃa'tarjo] AG defeatist

ri'nunzia *etc* [ri'nuntsja] = **rinuncia** *ecc*

rinveni'mento SM (*ritrovamento*) recovery; (*scoperta*) discovery; (*Metallurgia*) tempering

rinve'nire /**128**/ VT to find, recover; (*scoprire*) to discover, find out ▶ VI (*riprendere i sensi*) to come round; (*riprendere l'aspetto naturale*) to revive

rinve'nuto, -a PP *di* **rinvenire**

rinver'dire /**55**/ VI (*bosco, ramo*) to become green again

rinvi'are /**60**/ VT (*rimandare indietro*) to send back, return; **~ qc (a)** (*differire*) to postpone sth *o* put sth off (till) (*: seduta*) to adjourn sth (till); **~ qn a** (*fare un rimando*) to refer sb to; **~ a giudizio** (*Dir*) to commit for trial

rinvigo'rire /**55**/ VT to strengthen

rin'vio, -'vii SM (*rimando*) return; (*differimento*) postponement; (*: di seduta*) adjournment; (*in un testo*) cross-reference; **~ a giudizio** (*Dir*) indictment

riò *etc* VB *vedi* **riavere**

'Rio de Ja'neiro ['riodedʒa'neiro] SF Rio de Janeiro

rio'nale AG (*mercato, cinema*) local, district *cpd*

ri'one SM district, quarter

riordina'mento SM (*di ente, azienda*) reorganization

riordi'nare /**72**/ VT (*rimettere in ordine*) to tidy; (*riorganizzare*) to reorganize

riorganiz'zare [riorganid'dzare] /**72**/ VT to reorganize

riorganizzazi'one [riorganiddzat'tsjone] SF reorganization

ripa'gare /**80**/ VT to repay

ripa'rare /**72**/ VT (*proteggere*) to protect, defend; (*correggere: male, torto*) to make up for; (*: errore*) to put right; (*aggiustare*) to repair ▶ VI (*mettere rimedio*): **~ a** to make up for; **ripararsi** VPR (*rifugiarsi*) to take refuge *o* shelter

ripa'rato, -a AG (*posto*) sheltered

riparazi'one [riparat'tsjone] SF (*di un torto*) reparation; (*di guasto, scarpe*) repairing *no pl*; repair; (*risarcimento*) compensation; (*Ins*): **esame di ~** resit (BRIT), test retake (US)

ri'paro SM (*protezione*) shelter, protection; (*rimedio*) remedy; **al ~ da** (*sole, vento*) sheltered from; **mettersi al ~** to take shelter; **correre ai ripari** (*fig*) to take remedial action

ripar'tire /**45**/ VT (*dividere*) to divide up; (*distribuire*) to share out, distribute ▶ VI to set off again; to leave again; (*motore*) to start again

ripartizi'one [ripartit'tsjone] SF division sharing out, distribution; (*Amm: dipartimento*) department

ripas'sare /**72**/ VI to come (*o* go) back ▶ VT (*scritto, lezione*) to go over (again)

ri'passo SM (*di lezione*) revision (BRIT), review (US)

ripensa'mento SM second thoughts *pl* (BRIT), change of mind; **avere un ~** to have second thoughts, change one's mind

ripen'sare /**72**/ VI to think; (*cambiare idea*) to change one's mind; (*tornare col pensiero*): **~ a** to recall; **a ripensarci ...** on thinking it over ...

riper'correre /**28**/ VT (*itinerario*) to travel over again; (*strada*) to go along again; (*fig: ricordi, passato*) to go back over

riper'corso, -a PP *di* **ripercorrere**

riper'cosso, -a PP *di* **ripercuotersi**

ripercu'otersi /**106**/ VPR: **~ su** (*fig*) to have repercussions on

ripercussi'one SF (*fig*): **avere una ~** *o* **delle ripercussioni su** to have repercussions on

ripes'care /**20**/ VT (*pesce*) to catch again; (*persona, cosa*) to fish out; (*fig: ritrovare*) to dig out

ripe'tente SMF student repeating the year, repeater (US)

ri'petere /**1**/ VT to repeat; (*ripassare*) to go over

ripeti'tore SM (*Radio, TV*) relay

r

ripetizi'one [ripetit'tsjone] SF repetition; (*di lezione*) revision; **ripetizioni** SFPL (*Ins*) private tutoring *o* coaching *sg*; **fucile a ~** repeating rifle

ripetuta'mente AV repeatedly, again and again

ripi'ano SM (*Geo*) terrace; (*di mobile*) shelf

ri'picca SF: **per ~** out of spite

'**ripido, -a** AG steep

ripiega'mento SM (*Mil*) retreat

ripie'gare /8o/ VT to refold; (*piegare più volte*) to fold (up) ▶ VI (*Mil*) to retreat, fall back; (*fig: accontentarsi*): **~ su** to make do with; **ripiegarsi** VPR to bend

ripi'ego, -ghi SM expedient; **una soluzione di ~** a makeshift solution

ripi'eno, -a AG full; (*Cuc*) stuffed; (*: panino*) filled ▶ SM (*Cuc*) stuffing

ri'pone VB *vedi* **riporre**

ri'pongo *etc* VB *vedi* **riporre**

ri'porre /77/ VT (*porre al suo posto*) to put back, replace; (*mettere via*) to put away; (*fiducia, speranza*): **~ qc in qn** to place *o* put sth in sb

ripor'tare /72/ VT (*portare indietro*) to bring (*o* take) back; (*riferire*) to report; (*citare*) to quote; (*ricevere*) to receive, get; (*vittoria*) to gain; (*successo*) to have; (*Mat*) to carry; (*Comm*) to carry forward; **riportarsi** VPR: **riportarsi a** (*anche fig*) to go back to; (*riferirsi a*) to refer to; **~ danni** to suffer damage; **ha riportato gravi ferite** he was seriously injured

ri'porto SM amount carried over; amount carried forward

ripo'sante AG (*gen*) restful; (*musica, colore*) soothing

ripo'sare /72/ VT (*bicchiere, valigia*) to put down; (*dare sollievo*) to rest ▶ VI to rest; **riposarsi** VPR to rest; **qui riposa ...** (*su tomba*) here lies ...

ripo'sato, -a AG (*viso, aspetto*) rested; (*mente*) fresh

ri'posi *etc* VB *vedi* **riporre**

ri'poso SM rest; (*Mil*): **~!** at ease!; **a ~** (*in pensione*) retired; **giorno di ~** day off; **"oggi ~"** (*Cine, Teat*) "no performance today"; (*ristorante*) "closed today"

ripos'tiglio [ripos'tiʎʎo] SM lumber room (*BRIT*), storage room (*US*)

ri'posto, -a PP *di* **riporre** ▶ AG (*fig: senso, significato*) hidden

ri'prendere /81/ VT (*prigioniero, fortezza*) to recapture; (*prendere indietro*) to take back; (*ricominciare: lavoro*) to resume; (*andare a prendere*) to fetch, come back for; (*assumere di nuovo: impiegati*) to take on again, re-employ; (*rimproverare*) to tell off; (*restringere: abito*) to take in; (*Cine*) to shoot; **riprendersi** VPR to recover; (*correggersi*) to correct o.s.; **~ a fare qc** to start doing sth again; **~ il cammino** to set

off again; **~ i sensi** to recover consciousness; **~ sonno** to go back to sleep

ripresen'tare /72/ VT (*certificato*) to submit again; (*domanda*) to put forward again; (*persona*) to introduce again; **ripresentarsi** VPR (*ritornare: persona*) to come back; (*: occasione*) to arise again; **ripresentarsi a** (*esame*) to sit (*BRIT*) *o* take (*US*) again; (*concorso*) to enter again; **ripresentarsi come candidato** (*Pol*) to stand (*BRIT*) *o* run (*US*) again (as a candidate)

ri'preso, -a PP *di* **riprendere** ▶ SF recapture; resumption; (*economica, da malattia, emozione*) recovery; (*Aut*) acceleration *no pl*; (*Teat, Cine*) rerun; (*Cine: presa*) shooting *no pl*; shot; (*Sport*) second half; (*Pugilato*) round; **a più riprese** on several occasions, several times; **ripresa cinematografica** shot

ripristi'nare /72/ VT to restore

ri'pristino SM (*gen*) restoration; (*di tradizioni*) revival

ripro'dotto, -a PP *di* **riprodurre**

ripro'durre /9o/ VT to reproduce; **riprodursi** VPR (*Biol*) to reproduce; (*riformarsi*) to form again

riprodut'tivo, -a AG reproductive

riprodut'tore, -'trice AG (*organo*) reproductive ▶ SM: **~ acustico** pick-up; **~ a cassetta** cassette player

riproduzi'one [riprodut'tsjone] SF reproduction; **~ vietata** all rights reserved

ripro'messo, -a PP *di* **ripromettersi**

ripro'mettersi /63/ VT (*aspettarsi*): **~ qc da** to expect sth from; (*intendere*) **~ di fare qc** to intend to do sth

ripro'porre /77/ VT: **riproporsi di fare qc** to intend to do sth

ripro'posto, -a PP *di* **riproporre**

ri'prova SF confirmation; **a ~ di** as confirmation of

ripro'vare /72/ VT (*provare di nuovo: gen*) to try again; (*: vestito*) to try on again; (*: sensazione*) to experience again ▶ VI (*tentare*): **~ (a fare qc)** to try (to do sth) again; **riproverò più tardi** I'll try again later

ripro'vevole AG reprehensible

ripudi'are /19/ VT to repudiate, disown

ri'pudio SM repudiation, disowning

ripu'gnante [ripuɲ'ɲante] AG disgusting, repulsive

ripu'gnanza [ripuɲ'ɲantsa] SF repugnance, disgust

ripu'gnare [ripuɲ'ɲare] /15/ VI: **~ a qn** to repel *o* disgust sb

ripu'lire /55/ VT to clean up; (*ladri*) to clean out; (*perfezionare*) to polish, refine

ripulsi'one SF (*Fisica, fig*) repulsion

ri'quadro SM square; (*Archit*) panel

RIS [ris] SIGLA M (= *Reparto Investigazioni Scientifiche*) ≈ CID, *branch of the Carabinieri*

ri'sacca, -che SF backwash

ri'saia SF paddy field

risa'lire /98/ VI (*ritornare in su*) to go back up; **~ a** (*ritornare con la mente*) to go back to; (*datare da*) to date back to, go back to

risa'lita SF: **mezzi di ~** (*Sci*) ski lifts

risal'tare /72/ VI (*fig: distinguersi*) to stand out; (*Archit*) to project, jut out

ri'salto SM prominence; (*sporgenza*) projection; **mettere** *o* **porre in ~ qc** to make sth stand out

risana'mento SM (*economico*) improvement; (*bonifica*) reclamation; **~ del bilancio** reorganization of the budget; **~ edilizio** building improvement

risa'nare /72/ VT (*guarire*) to heal, cure; (*palude*) to reclaim; (*economia*) to improve; (*bilancio*) to reorganize

risa'pere /99/ VT: **~ qc** to come to know of sth

risa'puto, -a AG: **è ~ che ...** everyone knows that ..., it's common knowledge that ...

risarci'mento [risartʃi'mento] SM: **~ (di)** compensation (for); **aver diritto al ~ dei danni** to be entitled to damages

risar'cire [risar'tʃire] **/55/** VT (*cose*) to pay compensation for; (*persona*): **~ qn di qc** to compensate sb for sth; **~ i danni a qn** to pay sb damages

ri'sata SF laugh

riscalda'mento SM heating; **~ centrale** central heating

riscal'dare /72/ VT (*scaldare*) to heat; (: *mani, persona*) to warm; (: *minestra*) to reheat; **riscaldarsi** VPR to warm up

ris'caldo SM (*col*) (slight) inflammation

riscat'tare /72/ VT (*prigioniero*) to ransom, pay a ransom for; (*Dir*) to redeem; **riscattarsi** VPR (*da disonore*) to redeem o.s.

ris'catto SM ransom; redemption

rischia'rare [riskja'rare] **/72/** VT (*illuminare*) to light up; (*colore*) to make lighter; **rischiararsi** VPR (*tempo*) to clear up; (*cielo*) to clear; (*fig: volto*) to brighten up; **rischiararsi la voce** to clear one's throat

rischi'are [ris'kjare] **/19/** VT to risk ▶ VI: **~ di fare qc** to risk *o* run the risk of doing sth

'rischio ['riskjo] SM risk; **a ~** (*zona, situazione*) at risk, vulnerable; **a proprio ~ e pericolo** at one's own risk; **correre il ~ di fare qc** to run the risk of doing sth; **~ del mestiere** occupational hazard

rischi'oso, -a [ris'kjoso] AG risky, dangerous

risciac'quare [riʃʃak'kware] **/72/** VT to rinse

risci'acquo [riʃʃakkwo] SM rinse

riscon'trare /72/ VT (*confrontare: due cose*) to compare; (*esaminare*) to check, verify; (*rilevare*) to find

ris'contro SM comparison check, verification; (*Amm: lettera di risposta*) reply; **mettere a ~** to compare; **in attesa di un vostro cortese ~** we look forward to your reply

risco'perto, -a PP *di* **riscoprire**

risco'prire /9/ VT to rediscover

riscossi'one SF collection

ris'cosso, -a PP *di* **riscuotere** ▶ SF (*riconquista*) recovery, reconquest

riscri'vibile AG (*CD, DVD*) rewritable

riscu'otere /106/ VT (*ritirare una somma dovuta*) to collect; (: *stipendio*) to draw, collect; (: *assegno*) to cash; (*fig: successo ecc*) to win, earn; **riscuotersi** VPR: **riscuotersi (da)** to shake o.s. (out of), rouse o.s. (from); **~ un assegno** to cash a cheque

'rise *etc* VB *vedi* **ridere**

risenti'mento SM resentment

risen'tire /45/ VT to hear again; (*provare*) to feel ▶ VI: **~ di** to feel (*o* show) the effects of; **risentirsi** VPR: **risentirsi di** *o* **per** to take offence (BRIT) *o* offense (US) at, resent

risen'tito, -a AG resentful

ri'serbo SM reserve

ri'serva SF reserve; (*di caccia, pesca*) preserve; (*restrizione, di indigeni*) reservation; (*Calcio*) substitute; **fare ~ di** (*cibo*) to get in a supply of; **tenere di ~** to keep in reserve; **con le dovute riserve** with certain reservations; **ha accettato con la ~ di potersi ritirare** he accepted with the proviso that he could pull out

riser'vare /72/ VT (*tenere in serbo*) to keep, put aside; (*prenotare*) to book, reserve; **riservarsi** VPR: **riservarsi di fare qc** to intend to do sth; **riservarsi il diritto di fare qc** to reserve the right to do sth

riserva'tezza [riserva'tettsa] SF reserve

riser'vato, -a AG (*prenotato: fig: persona*) reserved; (*confidenziale: lettera, informazione*) confidential

'risi *etc* VB *vedi* **ridere**

ri'sibile AG laughable

risi'cato, -a AG (*vittoria ecc*) very narrow

risi'edere /29/ VI: **~ a** *o* **in** to reside in

'risma SF (*di carta*) ream; (*fig*) kind, sort

'riso¹, -a PP *di* **ridere** ▶ SM (*pl(f)* **risa**) (*il ridere*): **un ~ a** laugh; **il ~** laughter; **uno scoppio di risa** a burst of laughter

'riso² SM (*pianta*) rice

riso'lino SM snigger

risolle'vare /72/ VT (*sollevare di nuovo: testa*) to raise again, lift up again; (*fig: questione*) to raise again, bring up again; (*morale*) to raise; **risollevarsi** VPR (*da terra*) to rise again; (*fig: da malattia*) to recover; **~ le sorti di qc** to improve the chances of sth

ri'solsi *etc* VB *vedi* **risolvere**

ri'solto, -a PP di **risolvere**

risolu'tezza [risolu'tettsa] SF determination

risolu'tivo, -a AG (*determinante*) decisive; (*che risolve*): **arrivare ad una formula risolutiva** to come up with a formula to resolve a situation

riso'luto, -a AG determined, resolute

risoluzi'one [risolut'tsjone] SF solving *no pl*; (*Mat*) solution; (*decisione, di schermo, immagine*) resolution; (*Dir: di contratto*) annulment, cancellation

ri'solvere /94/ VT (*difficoltà, controversia*) to resolve; (*problema*) to solve; (*decidere*): ~ **di fare** to resolve to do; **risolversi** VPR (*decidersi*): **risolversi a fare** to make up one's mind to do; (*andare a finire*): **risolversi in** to end up, turn out; **risolversi in nulla** to come to nothing

risol'vibile AG solvable

riso'nanza [riso'nantsa] SF resonance; **aver vasta** ~ (*fig: fatto ecc*) to be known far and wide; ~ **magnetica** magnetic resonance

riso'nare /72/ VT, VI = **risuonare**

ri'sorgere [ri'sordʒere] /109/ VI to rise again

risorgimen'tale [risordʒimen'tale] AG of the Risorgimento

risorgi'mento [risordʒi'mento] SM revival; **il R~** (*Storia*) the Risorgimento; *see note*

> The *Risorgimento*, the period stretching from the early nineteenth century to 1861 and the proclamation of the Kingdom of Italy, saw considerable upheaval and change. Political and personal freedom took on new importance as the events of the French Revolution unfolded. The *Risorgimento* paved the way for the unification of Italy in 1871.

ri'sorsa SF expedient, resort; **risorse** SFPL (*naturali, finanziarie ecc*) resources; **persona piena di risorse** resourceful person; **risorse umane** human resources

ri'sorsi *etc* VB *vedi* **risorgere**

ri'sorto, -a PP di **risorgere**

ri'sotto SM (*Cuc*) risotto

risparmi'are /19/ VT to save; (*non uccidere*) to spare ► VI to save; ~ **qc a qn** to spare sb sth; ~ **fatica/fiato** to save one's energy/breath; **risparmiati il disturbo** *o* **la fatica** (*anche ironico*) save yourself the trouble

risparmia'tore, -'trice SM/F saver

ris'parmio SM saving *no pl*; (*denaro*) savings *pl*; **risparmi** SMPL (*denaro*) savings

rispecchi'are [rispek'kjare] /19/ VT to reflect; **rispecchiarsi** VPR to be reflected

rispe'dire /55/ VT to send back; ~ **qc a qn** to send sth back to sb

rispet'tabile AG respectable; (*considerevole: somma*) sizeable, considerable

rispet'tare /72/ VT to respect; (*legge*) to obey, comply with, abide by; (*promessa*) to keep; **farsi** ~ to command respect; ~ **le distanze** to keep one's distance; ~ **i tempi** to keep to schedule; **ogni medico che si rispetti** every self-respecting doctor

rispettiva'mente AV respectively

rispet'tivo, -a AG respective

ris'petto SM respect; **rispetti** SMPL (*saluti*) respects, regards; ~ **a** (*in paragone a*) compared to; (*in relazione a*) as regards, as for; ~ (**di** *o* **per**) (*norme, leggi*) observance (of), compliance (with); **portare** ~ **a qn/qc** to have *o* feel respect for sb/sth; **mancare di** ~ **a qn** to be disrespectful to sb; **con** ~ **parlando** with respect, if you will excuse my saying so; **(porga) i miei rispetti alla signora** (give) my regards to your wife

rispet'toso, -a AG respectful

risplen'dente AG (*giornata, sole*) bright, shining; (*occhi*) sparkling

ris'plendere /29/ VI to shine

rispon'dente AG: ~ **a** in keeping *o* conformity with

rispon'denza [rispon'dɛntsa] SF correspondence

ris'pondere /95/ VI to answer, reply; (*freni*) to respond; ~ **a** (*domanda*) to answer, reply to; (*persona*) to answer; (*invito*) to reply to; (*provocazione, veicolo, apparecchio*) to respond to; (*corrispondere a*) to correspond to (*: speranze, bisogno*) to answer; ~ **a qn di qc** (*essere responsabile*) to be answerable to sb for sth

rispo'sarsi /72/ VPR to get married again, remarry

ris'posto, -a PP di **rispondere** ► SF answer, reply; **in risposta a** in reply to; **dare una risposta** to give an answer; **diamo risposta alla vostra lettera del ...** in reply to your letter of ...

'rissa SF brawl

ris'soso, -a AG quarrelsome

rist. ABBR = **ristampa**

ristabi'lire /55/ VT to re-establish, restore; (*persona, riposo ecc*) to restore to health; **ristabilirsi** VPR to recover

rista'gnare [ristaɲ'ɲare] /15/ VI (*acqua*) to become stagnant; (*sangue*) to cease flowing; (*fig: industria*) to stagnate

ris'tagno [ris'taɲɲo] SM stagnation; **c'è un** ~ **delle vendite** business is slack

ris'tampa SF reprinting *no pl*; reprint

ristam'pare /72/ VT to reprint

risto'rante SM restaurant

risto'rare /72/ VT (*persona, forze*) to revive, refresh; **ristorarsi** VPR (*rifocillarsi*) to have something to eat and drink; (*riposarsi*) to rest, have a rest

ristora'tore, -'trice AG refreshing, reviving ▶ SM (*gestore di ristorante*) restaurateur

ris'toro SM (*bevanda, cibo*) refreshment; **posto di ~** (Ferr) buffet, snack bar; **servizio di ~** (Ferr) refreshments *pl*

ristret'tezza [ristret'tettsa] SF (*strettezza*) narrowness; (*fig: scarsezza*) scarcity, lack; (: *meschinità*) meanness; **ristrettezze** SFPL (*povertà*) poverty *sg*

ris'tretto, -a PP *di* **restringere** ▶ AG (*racchiuso*) enclosed, hemmed in; (*angusto*) narrow; (*Cuc: brodo*) thick; (: *caffè*) extra strong; **~ (a)** (*limitato*) restricted o limited (to)

ristruttu'rare /72/ VT (*azienda*) to reorganize; (*edificio*) to restore; (*appartamento*) to alter; (*crema, balsamo*) to repair

ristrutturazi'one [ristrutturat'tsjone] SF reorganization; restoration; alteration

risucchi'are [risuk'kjare] /19/ VT to suck in

ri'succhio [ri'sukkjo] SM (*di acqua*) undertow, pull; (*di aria*) suction

risul'tare /72/ VI (*dimostrarsi*) to prove (to be), turn out (to be); (*riuscire*): **~ vincitore** to emerge as the winner; **~ da** (*provenire*) to result from, be the result of; **mi risulta che ...** I understand that ..., as far as I know ...; **(ne) risulta che ...** it follows that ...; **non mi risulta** not as far as I know

risul'tato SM result

risuo'nare /72/ VI (*rimbombare*) to resound

risurrezi'one [risurret'tsjone] SF (Rel) resurrection

risusci'tare [risuʃʃi'tare] /72/ VT to resuscitate, restore to life; (*fig*) to revive, bring back ▶ VI to rise (from the dead)

risvegli'are [rizveʎ'ʎare] /27/ VT (*gen*) to wake up, waken; (*fig: interesse*) to stir up, arouse; (: *curiosità*) to arouse; (: *dall'inerzia ecc*): **~ qn (da)** to rouse sb (from); **risvegliarsi** VPR to wake up, awaken; (*fig: interesse, curiosità*) to be aroused

ris'veglio [riz'veʎʎo] SM waking up; (*fig*) revival

ris'volto SM (*di giacca*) lapel; (*di pantaloni*) turn-up (Brit), cuff (US); (*di manica*) cuff; (*di tasca*) flap; (*di libro*) inside flap; (*fig*) implication

ritagli'are [ritaʎ'ʎare] /27/ VT (*tagliar via*) to cut out

ri'taglio [ri'taʎʎo] SM (*di giornale*) cutting, clipping; (*di stoffa ecc*) scrap; **nei ritagli di tempo** in one's spare time

ritar'dare /72/ VI (*persona, treno*) to be late; (*orologio*) to be slow ▶ VT (*rallentare*) to slow down; (*impedire*) to delay, hold up; (*differire*) to postpone, delay; **~ il pagamento** to defer payment

ritarda'tario, -a SM/F latecomer

ritar'dato, -a AG (Psic) retarded

ri'tardo SM delay; (*di persona aspettata*) lateness *no pl*; (*fig: mentale*) backwardness; **in ~** late

ri'tegno [ri'teɲɲo] SM restraint

ritem'prare /72/ VT (*forze, spirito*) to restore

rite'nere /121/ VT (*trattenere*) to hold back; (: *somma*) to deduct; (*giudicare*) to consider, believe

ri'tengo VB *vedi* **ritenere**

ri'tenni *etc* VB *vedi* **ritenere**

riten'tare /72/ VT to try again, make another attempt at

rite'nuta SF (*sul salario*) deduction; **~ d'acconto** advance deduction of tax; **~ alla fonte** (Fisco) taxation at source

riterrò *etc* VB *vedi* **ritenere**

ritiene *etc* VB *vedi* **ritenere**

riti'rare /72/ VT to withdraw; (Pol: *richiamare*) to recall; (*andare a prendere: pacco ecc*) to collect, pick up; **ritirarsi** VPR to withdraw; (*da un'attività*) to retire; (*stoffa*) to shrink; (*marea*) to recede; **gli hanno ritirato la patente** they disqualified him from driving (Brit), they took away his licence (Brit) o license (US); **ritirarsi a vita privata** to withdraw from public life

riti'rata SF (Mil) retreat; (*latrina*) lavatory

riti'rato, -a AG secluded; **fare vita ritirata** to live in seclusion

ri'tiro SM (*di truppe, candidati, soldi*) withdrawal; (*di pacchi*) collection; (*di passaporto*) confiscation; (*da attività*) retirement; (*luogo appartato*) retreat

rit'mato, -a AG rhythmic(al)

'ritmico, -a, -ci, -che AG rhythmic(al)

'ritmo SM rhythm; (*fig*) rate; (: *della vita*) pace, tempo; **al ~ di** at a speed o rate of; **ballare al ~ di valzer** to waltz

'rito SM rite; **di ~** = usual, customary

ritoc'care /20/ VT (*disegno, fotografia*) to touch up; (*testo*) to alter

ri'tocco, -chi SM touching up *no pl*; alteration

ri'torcere [ri'tɔrtʃere] /106/ VT (*filato*) to twist; (*fig: accusa, insulto*) to throw back; **ritorcersi** VPR (*tornare a danno di*): **ritorcersi contro** to turn against

ritor'nare /72/ VI to return, go (o come) back, get back; (*ripresentarsi*) to recur; (*ridiventare*): **~ ricco** to become rich again ▶ VT (*restituire*) to return, give back

ritor'nello SM refrain

ri'torno SM return; **durante il (viaggio di) ~** on the return trip, on the way back; **al ~** (*tornando*) on the way back; **essere di ~** to be back; **far ~** to return; **avere un ~ di fiamma** (Aut) to backfire; (*fig: persona*) to be back in love again

ritorsi'one SF (*rappresaglia*) retaliation

ri'torto, -a PP *di* **ritorcere** ▶ AG (*cotone, corda*) twisted

r

ri'trarre /123/ VT (*trarre indietro, via*) to withdraw; (*distogliere: sguardo*) to turn away; (*rappresentare*) to portray, depict; (*ricavare*) to get, obtain; **ritrarsi** VPR to move back

ritrat'tare /72/ VT (*disdire*) to retract, take back; (*trattare nuovamente*) to deal with again

ritrattazi'one [ritrattat'tsjone] SF withdrawal

ritrat'tista, -i, -e SM/F portrait painter

ri'tratto, -a PP di **ritrarre** ▶ SM portrait

ritro'sia SF (*riluttanza*) reluctance, unwillingness; (*timidezza*) shyness

ri'troso, -a AG (*restio*): ~ **(a)** reluctant (to); (*schivo*) shy; **andare a ~** to go backwards

ritrova'mento SM (*di cadavere, oggetto smarrito ecc*) finding; (*oggetto ritrovato*) find

ritro'vare /72/ VT to find; (*salute*) to regain; (*persona*) to find; to meet again; **ritrovarsi** VPR (*essere, capitare*) to find o.s.; (*raccapezzarsi*) to find one's way; (*con senso reciproco*) to meet (again)

ritro'vato SM discovery

ri'trovo SM meeting place; ~ **notturno** night club

'ritto, -a AG (*in piedi*) standing, on one's feet; (*levato in alto*) erect, raised; (*: capelli*) standing on end; (*posto verticalmente*) upright

ritu'ale AG, SM ritual

ritwit'tare [ritwit'tare] VT (*su Twitter*) to retweet

riuni'one SF (*adunanza*) meeting; (*riconciliazione*) reunion; **essere in ~** to be at a meeting

riu'nire /55/ VT (*ricongiungere*) to join (together); (*riconciliare*) to reunite, bring together (again); **riunirsi** VPR (*adunarsi*) to meet; (*tornare a stare insieme*) to be reunited; **siamo qui riuniti per festeggiare il vostro anniversario** we are gathered here to celebrate your anniversary

riu'scire [riuʃʃire] /125/ VI (*uscire di nuovo*) to go out again, go back out; (*aver esito: fatti, azioni*) to go, turn out; (*aver successo*) to succeed, be successful; (*essere, apparire*) to be, prove; (*raggiungere il fine*) to manage, succeed; ~ **a fare qc** to manage *o* be able to do sth; **questo mi riesce nuovo** this is new to me

riu'scita [riuʃʃita] SF (*esito*) result, outcome; (*buon esito*) success

riutiliz'zare [riutilid'dzare] /72/ VT to use again, re-use

'riva SF (*di fiume*) bank; (*di lago, mare*) shore; **in ~ al mare** on the (sea) shore

ri'vale AG rival *cpd* ▶ SMF rival; **non avere rivali** (*anche fig*) to be unrivalled

rivaleggi'are [rivaled'dʒare] /62/ VI to compete, vie

rivalità SF rivalry

ri'valsa SF (*rivincita*) revenge; (*risarcimento*) compensation; **prendersi una ~ su qn** to take revenge on sb

rivalu'tare /72/ VT (*Econ*) to revalue

rivalutazi'one [rivalutat'tsjone] SF (*Econ*) revaluation; (*fig*) re-evaluation

rivan'gare /80/ VT (*ricordi ecc*) to dig up (again)

rive'dere /127/ VT to see again; (*ripassare*) to revise; (*verificare*) to check

rivedrò etc VB vedi **rivedere**

rive'lare /72/ VT to reveal; (*divulgare*) to reveal, disclose; (*dare indizio*) to reveal, show; **rivelarsi** VPR (*manifestarsi*) to be revealed; **rivelarsi onesto** etc to prove to be honest etc

rivela'tore, -'trice AG revealing ▶ SM (*Tecn*) detector; (*Fot*) developer

rivelazi'one [rivelat'tsjone] SF revelation

ri'vendere /29/ VT (*vendere: di nuovo*) to resell, sell again; (*: al dettaglio*) to retail, sell retail

rivendi'care /20/ VT to claim, demand

rivendicazi'one [rivendikat'tsjone] SF claim; **rivendicazioni salariali** wage claims

ri'vendita SF (*bottega*) retailer's (shop); ~ **di tabacchi** tobacconist's (shop)

rivendi'tore, -'trice SM/F retailer; ~ **autorizzato** (*Comm*) authorized dealer

riverbe'rare /72/ VT to reflect

ri'verbero SM (*di luce, calore*) reflection; (*di suono*) reverberation

rive'rente AG reverent, respectful

rive'renza [rive'rentsa] SF reverence; (*inchino*) bow; curtsey

rive'rire /55/ VT (*rispettare*) to revere; (*salutare*) to pay one's respects to

river'sare /72/ VT (*anche fig*) to pour; **riversarsi** VPR (*fig: persone*) to pour out

rivesti'mento SM covering; coating

rives'tire /45/ VT to dress again; (*ricoprire*) to cover; (*con vernice*) to coat; (*fig: carica*) to hold; **rivestirsi** VPR to get dressed again, to change (one's clothes); ~ **di piastrelle** to tile

ri'vidi etc VB vedi **rivedere**

rivi'era SF coast; **la ~ italiana** the Italian Riviera

ri'vincita [ri'vintʃita] SF (*Sport*) return match; (*fig*) revenge; **prendersi la ~ (su qn)** to take *o* get one's revenge (on sb)

rivis'suto, -a PP di **rivivere**

ri'vista SF review; (*periodico*) magazine, review; (*Teat*) revue; variety show

ri'visto, -a PP di **rivedere**

rivitaliz'zante [rivitalid'dzante] AG revitalizing

rivitaliz'zare [rivitalid'dzare] /72/ VT to revitalize

ri'vivere /130/ VI (*riacquistare forza*) to come alive again; (*tornare in uso*) to be revived ▶ VT to relive '**rivo** SM stream

ri'volgere [ri'vɔldʒere] /**96**/ VT (attenzione, sguardo) to turn, direct; (parole) to address; **rivolgersi** VPR to turn round; **rivolgersi a** (fig: dirigersi per informazioni) to go and see, go and speak to (: ufficio) to enquire at; ~ **un'accusa/una critica a qn** to accuse/ criticize sb; **rivolgersi all'ufficio competente** to apply to the office concerned

rivolgi'mento [rivoldʒi'mento] SM upheaval

ri'volsi etc VB vedi **rivolgere**

ri'volta SF revolt, rebellion

rivol'tante AG revolting, disgusting

rivol'tare /**72**/ VT to turn over; (con l'interno all'esterno) to turn inside out; (disgustare: stomaco) to upset, turn; (: fig) to revolt, disgust; **rivoltarsi** VPR (ribellarsi): **rivoltarsi (a)** to rebel (against)

rivol'tella SF revolver

ri'volto, -a PP di **rivolgere**

rivol'toso, -a AG rebellious ▶ SM/F rebel

rivoluzio'nare [rivoluttsjo'nare] /**72**/ VT to revolutionize

rivoluzio'nario, -a [rivoluttsjo'narjo] AG, SM/F revolutionary

rivoluzi'one [rivolut'tsjone] SF revolution

riz'zare [rit'tsare] /**72**/ VT to raise, erect; **rizzarsi** VPR to stand up; (capelli) to stand on end; **rizzarsi in piedi** to stand up, get to one's feet

RN SIGLA = **Rimini**

RNA SIGLA M RNA (= ribonucleic acid)

RO SIGLA = **Rovigo**

'**roba** SF stuff, things pl; (possessi, beni) belongings pl, things pl, possessions pl; ~ **da mangiare** things to eat, food; ~ **da matti!** it's sheer madness o lunacy!

robi'vecchi [robi'vɛkki] SM INV/F INV junk dealer

'**robot** SM INV robot

ro'botica SF robotics sg

robus'tezza [robus'tettsa] SF (di persona, pianta) robustness, sturdiness; (di edificio, ponte) soundness

ro'busto, -a AG robust, sturdy; (solido: catena) strong; (: edificio, ponte) sound, solid; (: vino) full-bodied

'**rocca, -che** SF fortress

rocca'forte SF stronghold

roc'chetto [rok'ketto] SM reel, spool

'**roccia, -ce** ['rɔttʃa] SF rock; **fare** ~ (Sport) to go rock climbing

roccia'tore, -'trice [rottʃa'tore] SM/F rock climber

rocci'oso, -a [rot'tʃoso] AG rocky; **le Montagne Rocciose** the Rocky Mountains

'**roco, -a, -chi, -che** AG hoarse

ro'daggio [ro'daddʒo] SM running (BRIT) o breaking (US) in; **in** ~ running o breaking in; **periodo di** ~ (fig) period of adjustment

'**Rodano** SM: **il** ~ the Rhone

ro'dare /**72**/ VT (Aut, Tecn) to run (BRIT) o break (US) in

ro'deo SM rodeo

ro'dere /**49**/ VT to gnaw (at); (distruggere poco a poco) to eat into

'**Rodi** SF Rhodes

rodi'tore SM (Zool) rodent

rodo'dendro SM rhododendron

ro'gito ['rɔdʒito] SM (Dir) (notary's) deed

'**rogna** ['rɔɲɲa] SF (Med) scabies sg; (di animale) mange; (fig) bother, nuisance

ro'gnone [roɲ'ɲone] SM (Cuc) kidney

ro'gnoso, -a [roɲ'ɲoso] AG (persona) scabby; (animale) mangy; (fig) troublesome

'**rogo, -ghi** SM (per cadaveri) (funeral) pyre; (supplizio): **il** ~ the stake

rol'lare /**72**/ VI (Naut, Aer) to roll

rol'lino SM = **rullino**

rol'lio SM roll(ing)

'**Roma** SF Rome

roma'gnolo, -a [romaɲ'ɲɔlo] AG of (o from) Romagna

roma'nesco, -a, -schi, -sche AG Roman ▶ SM Roman dialect

Roma'nia SF: **la** ~ Romania

ro'manico, -a, -ci, -che AG Romanesque

ro'mano, -a AG, SM/F Roman; **fare alla romana** to go Dutch

romantiche'ria [romantike'ria] SF sentimentality

romanti'cismo [romanti'tʃizmo] SM romanticism

ro'mantico, -a, -ci, -che AG romantic

ro'manza [ro'mandza] SF (Mus, Letteratura) romance

roman'zare [roman'dzare] /**72**/ VT to romanticize

roman'zesco, -a, -schi, -sche [roman'dzesko] AG (stile, personaggi) fictional; (fig) storybook cpd

romanzi'ere [roman'dzjɛre] SM novelist

ro'manzo, -a [ro'mandzo] AG (Ling) romance cpd ▶ SM (medievale) romance; (moderno) novel; ~ **d'amore** love story; ~ **d'appendice** serial (story); ~ **cavalleresco** tale of chivalry; ~ **poliziesco**, ~ **giallo** detective story; ~ **rosa** romantic novel

rom'bare /**72**/ VI to rumble, thunder, roar

'**rombo** SM rumble, thunder, roar; (Mat) rhombus; (Zool) turbot; brill

ro'meno, -a AG, SM/F, SM = **rumeno**

'**rompere** /**97**/ VT to break; (conversazione, fidanzamento) to break off ▶ VI to break; **rompersi** VPR to break; **mi rompe le**

scatole (*col*) he (*o* she) is a pain in the neck;
rompersi un braccio to break an arm
rompi'capo SM worry, headache; (*indovinello*)
puzzle; (*in enigmistica*) brain-teaser
rompi'collo SM daredevil
rompighi'accio [rompi'gjattʃo] SM (*Naut*)
icebreaker
rompis'catole SM O F INV (*col*) pest, pain in
the neck
'**ronda** SF (*Mil*) rounds *pl*, patrol
ron'della SF (*Tecn*) washer
'**rondine** SF (*Zool*) swallow
ron'done SM (*Zool*) swift
ron'fare /72/ VI (*russare*) to snore
ron'zare [ron'dzare] /72/ VI to buzz, hum
ron'zino [ron'dzino] SM (*peg: cavallo*) nag
ron'zio, -ii [ron'dzio] SM buzzing, humming;
~ **auricolare** (*Med*) tinnitus *sg*
'**rosa** SF rose; (*fig: gruppo*): ~ **dei candidati** list
of candidates ▶ AG INV, SM pink
ro'saio SM (*pianta*) rosebush, rose tree;
(*giardino*) rose garden
ro'sario SM (*Rel*) rosary
ro'sato, -a AG pink, rosy ▶ SM (*vino*) rosé
(wine)
ro'seo, -a AG (*anche fig*) rosy
ro'seto SM rose garden
ro'setta SF (*diamante*) rose-cut diamond;
(*rondella*) washer
'**rosi** VB *vedi* **rodere**
rosicchi'are [rosik'kjare] /19/ VT to gnaw (at);
(*mangiucchiare*) to nibble (at)
rosma'rino SM rosemary
'**roso, -a** PP *di* **rodere**
roso'lare /72/ VT (*Cuc*) to brown
roso'lia SF (*Med*) German measles *sg*, rubella
ro'sone SM rosette; (*vetrata*) rose window
'**rospo** SM (*Zool*) toad; **mandar giù** *o* **ingoiare
un** *o* **il ~** (*fig*) to swallow a bitter pill; **sputa
il ~!** out with it!
ros'setto SM (*per labbra*) lipstick; (*per guance*)
rouge
ros'siccio, -a, -ci, -ce [ros'sittʃo] AG reddish
'**rosso, -a** AG, SM, SM/F red; **diventare ~
(per la vergogna)** to blush *o* go red (with *o*
for shame); **il mar R~** the Red Sea; **~ d'uovo**
egg yolk
ros'sore SM flush, blush
rosticce'ria [rostittʃe'ria] SF *shop selling roast
meat and other cooked food*
'**rostro** SM rostrum; (*becco*) beak
ro'tabile AG (*percorribile*): **strada** ~ roadway;
(*Ferr*) **materiale** ~ rolling stock
ro'taia SF rut, track; (*Ferr*) rail
ro'tare /72/ VT, VI to rotate
rota'tivo, -a AG rotating, rotation *cpd*
rotazi'one [rotat'tsjone] SF rotation
rote'are /72/ VT, VI to whirl; ~ **gli occhi** to roll
one's eyes

ro'tella SF small wheel; (*di mobile*) castor
roto'calco, -chi SM (*Tip*) rotogravure; (*rivista*)
illustrated magazine
roto'lare /72/ VT, VI to roll; **rotolarsi** VPR to
roll (about)
roto'lio SM rolling
'**rotolo** SM (*di carta, stoffa*) roll; (*di corda*) coil;
andare a rotoli (*fig*) to go to rack and ruin;
mandare a rotoli (*fig*) to ruin
ro'tondo, -a AG round ▶ SF rotunda
ro'tore SM rotor
'**rotta** SF (*Aer, Naut*) course, route; (*Mil*) rout;
a ~ di collo at breakneck speed; **essere in ~
con qn** to be on bad terms with sb; **fare ~ su**
o **per** *o* **verso** to head for *o* towards;
cambiare ~ (*anche fig*) to change course; **in ~
di collisione** on a collision course; **ufficiale
di ~** navigator, navigating officer
rotta'mare /72/ VT to scrap old vehicles in return
for incentives
rotta'zione [rottamat'tsjone] SF (*come
incentivo*) the scrapping of old vehicles in return for
incentives
rot'tame SM fragment, scrap, broken bit;
rottami SMPL (*di nave, aereo ecc*) wreckage *sg*;
rottami di ferro scrap iron *sg*
'**rotto, -a** PP *di* **rompere** ▶ AG broken; (*calzoni*)
torn, split; (*persona: pratico, resistente*): ~ **a**
accustomed *o* inured to ▶ SM: **per il ~ della
cuffia** by the skin of one's teeth; **rotti** SMPL:
20 euro e rotti 20-odd euros
rot'tura SF (*azione*) breaking *no pl*; break; (*di
rapporti*) breaking off; (*Med*) fracture, break
rou'lotte [ru'lɔt] SF INV caravan
ro'vente AG red-hot
'**rovere** SM oak
ro'vescia [ro'veʃʃa] SF: **alla ~** upside-down;
inside-out; **oggi mi va tutto alla ~**
everything is going wrong (for me) today
rovesci'are [roveʃ'ʃare] /14/ VT (*versare in giù*)
to pour; (: *accidentalmente*) to spill; (*capovolgere*) to
turn upside down; (*gettare a terra*) to knock
down; (*fig: governo*) to overthrow; (*piegare
all'indietro: testa*) to throw back; **rovesciarsi**
VPR (*sedia, macchina*) to overturn; (*barca*) to
capsize; (*liquido*) to spill; (*fig: situazione*) to be
reversed
ro'vescio, -sci [ro'veʃʃo] SM other side, wrong
side; (*della mano*) back; (*di moneta*) reverse;
(*pioggia*) sudden downpour; (*fig*) setback;
(*Maglia: anche*: **punto rovescio**) purl (stitch);
(*Tennis*) backhand (stroke); **a ~** (*sottosopra*)
upside-down; (*con l'esterno all'interno*)
inside-out; **capire qc a ~** to misunderstand
sth; **~ di fortuna** setback
ro'vina SF ruin; **rovine** SFPL (*ruderi*) ruins;
andare in ~ (*andare a pezzi*) to collapse; (*fig*) to
go to rack and ruin; **mandare qc/qn in ~** to
ruin sth/sb

rovi'nare /**72**/ VI to collapse, fall down ▶ VT (*far cadere giù: casa*) to demolish; (*danneggiare: fig*) to ruin; **rovinarsi** VPR (*persona*) to ruin o.s.; (*oggetto, vestito*) to be ruined

rovi'nato, -a AG ruined, damaged; (*fig: persona*) ruined

rovi'noso, -a AG ruinous

rovis'tare /**72**/ VT (*casa*) to ransack; (*tasche*) to rummage in (*o* through)

'rovo SM (*Bot*) blackberry *o* bramble bush

roz'zezza [rod'dzettsa] SF roughness, coarseness

'rozzo, -a ['roddzo] AG rough, coarse

RP SIGLA FPL *vedi* **relazioni pubbliche**

Rr ABBR (*Posta*) = **raccomandata con ricevuta di ritorno**

R.R. ABBR (*Posta*) = **ricevuta di ritorno**

RSVP ABBR (= *répondez s'il vous plaît*) RSVP

'ruba SF: **andare a ~** to sell like hot cakes

rubacu'ori SM INV ladykiller

ru'bare /**72**/ VT to steal; **~ qc a qn** to steal sth from sb

rubi'condo, -a AG ruddy

rubi'netto SM tap, faucet (*US*)

ru'bino SM ruby

ru'bizzo, -a [ru'bittso] AG lively, sprightly

'rublo SM rouble

ru'brica, -che SF (*di giornale: colonna*) column; (*: pagina*) page; (*quadernetto*) index book; address book; **~ d'indirizzi** address book; **~ telefonica** list of telephone numbers

'rude AG tough, rough

'rudere SM (*rovina*) ruins *pl*

rudimen'tale AG rudimentary, basic

rudi'menti SMPL rudiments; basic principles; basic knowledge *sg*

ruffi'ano SM pimp

'ruga, -ghe SF wrinkle

'ruggine ['ruddʒine] SF rust

rug'gire [rud'dʒire] /**55**/ VI to roar

rug'gito [rud'dʒito] SM roar

rugi'ada [ru'dʒada] SF dew

ru'goso, -a AG wrinkled; (*scabro: superficie ecc*) rough

rul'lare /**72**/ VI (*tamburo, nave*) to roll; (*aereo*) to taxi

rul'lino SM (*Fot*) (roll of) film, spool

rul'lio, -ii SM (*di tamburi*) roll

'rullo SM (*di tamburi*) roll; (*arnese cilindrico, Tip*) roller; **~ compressore** steam roller; **~ di pellicola** roll of film

rum SM rum

ru'meno, -a AG, SM/F, SM Romanian

rumi'nante SM (*Zool*) ruminant

rumi'nare /**72**/ VT (*Zool*) to ruminate; (*fig*) to ruminate on *o* over, chew over

ru'more SM: **un ~** a noise, a sound; **il ~** noise; **fare ~** to make a noise; **un ~ di passi** the sound of footsteps; **la notizia ha fatto molto ~** (*fig*) the news aroused great interest

rumoreggi'are [rumored'dʒare] /**62**/ VI (*tuono ecc*) to rumble; (*fig: folla*) to clamour (*BRIT*), clamor (*US*)

rumo'roso, -a AG noisy

ru'olo SM (*Teat, fig*) role, part; (*elenco*) roll, register, list; **di ~** permanent, on the permanent staff; **professore di ~** (*Ins*) ≈ lecturer with tenure; **fuori ~** (*personale, insegnante*) temporary

ru'ota SF wheel; **a ~** (*forma*) circular; **~ anteriore/posteriore** front/back wheel; **andare a ~ libera** to freewheel; **parlare a ~ libera** (*fig*) to speak freely; **~ di scorta** spare wheel

ruo'tare /**72**/ VT, VI to rotate

'rupe SF cliff, rock

ru'pestre AG rocky

ru'pia SF rupee

'ruppi *etc* VB *vedi* **rompere**

ru'rale AG rural, country *cpd*

ru'scello [ruʃʃello] SM stream

'ruspa SF excavator

rus'pante AG (*pollo*) free-range

rus'sare /**72**/ VI to snore

'Russia SF: **la ~** Russia

'russo, -a AG, SM/F, SM Russian

'rustico, -a, -ci, -che AG country *cpd*, rural; (*arredamento*) rustic; (*fig*) rough, unrefined ▶ SM (*fabbricato: per attrezzi*) shed; (*: per abitazione*) farm labourer's (*BRIT*) *o* farmhand's cottage

'ruta SF (*Bot*) rue

rut'tare /**72**/ VI to belch

'rutto SM belch

'ruvido, -a AG rough, coarse

ruzzo'lare [ruttso'lare] /**72**/ VI to tumble down

ruzzo'lone [ruttso'lone] SM tumble, fall

ruzzo'loni [ruttso'loni] AV: **cadere ~** to tumble down; **fare le scale ~** to tumble down the stairs

r

Ss

S, s ['ɛsse] SM O F (*lettera*) S, s; **S come Savona** ≈ S for Sugar

s ABBR (= *secondo*) sec.

S. ABBR (= *sud*) S; (= *santo*) St

SA SIGLA = **Salerno** ▶ ABBR = **società anonima**

sa VB *vedi* **sapere**

sab. ABBR (= *sabato*) Sat.

'sabato SM Saturday; **di** *o* **il ~** on Saturdays; *vedi anche* **martedì**

'sabbia SF sand; **sabbie mobili** quicksand(*s pl*)

sabbia'tura SF (*Med*) sand bath; (*Tecn*) sand-blasting; **fare le sabbiature** to take sand baths

sabbi'oso, -a AG sandy

sabo'taggio [sabo'taddʒo] SM sabotage

sabo'tare /**72**/ VT to sabotage

sabota'tore, -'trice SM/F saboteur

'sacca, -che SF bag; (*bisaccia*) haversack; (*insenatura*) inlet; **~ d'aria** air pocket; **~ da viaggio** travelling bag

sacca'rina SF saccharin(e)

sac'cente [sat'tʃɛnte] SMF know-all (*BRIT*), know-it-all (*US*)

saccheggi'are [sakked'dʒare] /**62**/ VT to sack, plunder

sac'cheggio [sak'keddʒo] SM sack(ing)

sac'chetto [sak'ketto] SM (small) bag; (small) sack; **~ di carta/di plastica** paper/ plastic bag

'sacco, -chi SM bag; (*per carbone ecc*) sack; (*Anat, Biol*) sac; (*tela*) sacking; (*saccheggio*) sack(ing); (*fig: grande quantità*): **un ~ di** lots of, heaps of; **cogliere** *o* **prendere qn con le mani nel ~** to catch sb red-handed; **vuotare il ~** to confess, spill the beans; **mettere qn nel ~** to cheat sb; **colazione al ~** packed lunch; **~ a pelo** sleeping bag; **~ per i rifiuti** bin bag (*BRIT*), garbage bag (*US*)

sacer'dote [satʃer'dote] SM priest

sacer'dozio [satʃer'dɔttsjo] SM priesthood

'Sacra Co'rona U'nita SF *the mafia in Puglia*

sacra'mento SM sacrament

sa'crario SM memorial chapel

sacres'tano SM = **sagrestano**

sacres'tia SF = **sagrestia**

sacrifi'care /**20**/ VT to sacrifice; **sacrificarsi** VPR to sacrifice o.s.; (*privarsi di qc*) to make sacrifices

sacrifi'cato, -a AG sacrificed; (*non valorizzato*) wasted; **una vita sacrificata** a life of sacrifice

sacri'ficio [sakri'fitʃo] SM sacrifice

sacri'legio [sakri'ledʒo] SM sacrilege

sa'crilego, -a, -ghi, -ghe AG (*Rel*) sacrilegious

'sacro, -a AG sacred

sacro'santo, -a AG sacrosanct

'sadico, -a, -ci, -che AG sadistic ▶ SM/F sadist

sa'dismo SM sadism

sadomaso'chismo [sadomazo'kismo] SM sadomasochism

sa'etta SF arrow; (*fulmine: anche fig*) thunderbolt; flash of lightning

sa'fari SM INV safari

sa'gace [sa'gatʃe] AG shrewd, sagacious

sa'gacia [sa'gatʃa] SF sagacity, shrewdness

sag'gezza [sad'dʒettsa] SF wisdom

saggi'are [sad'dʒare] /**62**/ VT (*metalli*) to assay; (*fig*) to test

'saggio, -a, -gi, -ge ['saddʒo] AG wise ▶ SM (*persona*) sage; (*operazione sperimentale*) test; (: *dell'oro*) assay; (*fig: prova*) proof; (*campione indicativo*) sample; (*scritto: letterario*) essay; (: *Ins*) written test; **dare ~ di** to give proof of; **in ~** as a sample

sag'gistica [sad'dʒistika] SF ≈ non-fiction

Sagit'tario [sadʒit'tarjo] SM Sagittarius; **essere del ~** to be Sagittarius

'sagoma SF (*profilo*) outline, profile; (*forma*) form, shape; (*Tecn*) template; (*bersaglio*) target; (*fig: persona*) character

'sagra SF festival

sa'grato SM churchyard

sagres'tano SM sacristan; sexton

sagres'tia SF sacristy; (*culto protestante*) vestry

Sa'hara [sa'ara] SM: **il (Deserto del) ~** the Sahara (Desert)

sahari'ana [saa'rjana] SF bush jacket

'sai VB vedi **sapere**

'saio SM (Rel) habit

'sala SF hall; (stanza) room; (Cine: di proiezione) cinema; ~ **d'aspetto** waiting room; ~ **da ballo** ballroom; ~ **(dei) comandi** control room; ~ **per concerti** concert hall; ~ **per conferenze** (Ins) lecture hall; (in aziende) conference room; ~ **corse** betting shop; ~ **giochi** amusement arcade; ~ **da gioco** gaming room; ~ **macchine** (Naut) engine room; ~ **operatoria** (Med) operating theatre (BRIT) o room (US); ~ **da pranzo** dining room; ~ **per ricevimenti** banqueting hall; ~ **delle udienze** (Dir) courtroom

sa'lace [sa'latʃe] AG (spinto, piccante) salacious, saucy; (mordace) cutting, biting

sala'mandra SF salamander

sa'lame SM salami no pl, salami sausage

sala'moia SF (Cuc) brine

sa'lare /72/ VT to salt

salari'ale AG wage cpd, pay cpd; **aumento ~** wage o pay increase (BRIT) o raise (US)

salari'ato, -a SM/F wage-earner

sa'lario SM pay, wages pl; ~ **base** basic wage; ~ **minimo garantito** guaranteed minimum wage

salas'sare /72/ VT (Med) to bleed

sa'lasso SM (Med) bleeding, bloodletting; (fig: forte spesa) drain

sala'tino SM cracker, salted biscuit

sa'lato, -a AG (sapore) salty; (Cuc) salted, salt cpd; (fig: discorso ecc) biting, sharp; (: prezzi) steep, stiff

sal'dare /72/ VT (congiungere) to join, bind; (parti metalliche) to solder; (: con saldatura autogena) to weld; (conto) to settle, pay

salda'tore SM (operaio) solderer; welder; (utensile) soldering iron

salda'trice [salda'tritʃe] SF (macchina) welder, welding machine; ~ **ad arco** arc welder

salda'tura SF soldering; welding; (punto saldato) soldered joint; weld; ~ **autogena** welding; ~ **dolce** soft soldering

sal'dezza [sal'dettsa] SF firmness, strength

'saldo, -a AG (resistente, forte) strong, firm; (fermo) firm, steady, stable; (fig) firm, steadfast ▶ SM (svendita) sale; (di conto) settlement; (Econ) balance; **saldi** SMPL (Comm) sales; **pagare a ~** to pay in full; ~ **attivo** credit; ~ **passivo** deficit; ~ **da riportare** balance carried forward; **essere ~ nella propria fede** (fig) to stick to one's guns

'sale SM salt; (fig) wit; **sali** SMPL (Med: da annusare) smelling salts; **sotto ~** salted; **restare di ~** (fig) to be dumbfounded; **ha poco ~ in zucca** he doesn't have much sense; ~ **da cucina**, ~ **grosso** cooking salt; ~ **da tavola**, ~ **fino** table salt; **sali da bagno** bath salts; **sali minerali** mineral salts; **sali e tabacchi** tobacconist's (shop)

sal'gemma [sal'dʒemma] SM rock salt

'salgo etc VB vedi **salire**

'salice ['salitʃe] SM willow; ~ **piangente** weeping willow

sali'ente AG (fig) salient, main

sali'era SF salt cellar

sa'lino, -a AG saline ▶ SF saltworks sg

sa'lire /98/ VI to go (o come) up; (aereo ecc) to climb, go up; (passeggero) to get on; (sentiero, prezzi, livello) to go up, rise ▶ VT (scale, gradini) to go (o come) up; ~ **su** to climb (up); ~ **sul treno/sull'autobus** to board the train/the bus; ~ **in macchina** to get into the car; ~ **a cavallo** to mount; ~ **al potere** to rise to power; ~ **al trono** to ascend the throne; ~ **alle stelle** (prezzi) to rocket

sali'scendi [saliʃ'ʃendi] SM INV latch

sa'lita SF climb, ascent; (erta) hill, slope; **in ~** ag, av uphill

sa'liva SF saliva

'salma SF corpse

sal'mastro, -a AG (acqua) salt cpd; (sapore) salty ▶ SM (sapore) salty taste; (odore) salty smell

salmì SM (Cuc) salmi; **lepre in ~** salmi of hare

'salmo SM psalm

sal'mone SM salmon

salmo'nella SF salmonella

Salo'mone: le isole ~ sfpl the Solomon Islands

sa'lone SM (stanza) sitting room, lounge; (in albergo) lounge; (di ricevimento) reception room; (su nave) lounge, saloon; (mostra) show, exhibition; (negozio: di parrucchiere) hairdresser's (salon); ~ **dell'automobile** motor show; ~ **di bellezza** beauty salon

salo'pette [salɔ'pɛt] SF INV dungarees pl

salotti'ero, -a AG mundane

sa'lotto SM lounge, sitting room; (mobilio) lounge suite

sal'pare /72/ VI (Naut) to set sail; (anche: **salpare l'ancora**) to weigh anchor

'salsa SF (Cuc) sauce; **in tutte le salse** (fig) in all kinds of ways; ~ **di pomodoro** tomato sauce

sal'sedine SF (del mare, vento) saltiness; (incrostazione) (dried) salt

sal'siccia, -ce [sal'sittʃa] SF pork sausage

salsi'era SF sauceboat (BRIT), gravy boat

'salso SM saltiness

sal'tare /72/ VI to jump, leap; (esplodere) to blow up, explode; (: valvola) to blow; (venir via) to pop off; (non aver luogo: corso ecc) to be cancelled ▶ VT to jump (over), leap (over); (fig: pranzo, capitolo) to skip, miss (out); (Cuc) to sauté; **far ~** to blow up; to burst open; (serratura: forzare) to break; **far ~ il banco** (Gioco) to break the bank; **farsi ~ le cervella** to blow one's brains out; **ma che ti salta in**

mente? what are you thinking of?; **~ da un argomento all'altro** to jump from one subject to another; **~ addosso a qn** (*aggredire*) to attack sb; **~ fuori** to jump out, leap out; (*venire trovato*) to turn up; **~ fuori con** (*frase, commento*) to come out with; **~ giù da qc** to jump off sth, jump down from sth

saltel'lare /**72**/ vi to skip; to hop

sal'tello sm hop, little jump

saltim'banco, -chi sm acrobat

'salto sm jump; (*Sport*) jumping; (*dislivello*) drop; **fare un ~** to jump, leap; **fare un ~ da qn** to pop over to sb's (place); **~ in alto/lungo** high/long jump; **~ con l'asta** pole vaulting; **~ mortale** somersault; **un ~ di qualità** (*miglioramento*) significant improvement

saltu'ario, -a ag occasional, irregular

sa'lubre ag healthy, salubrious

sa'lume sm (*Cuc*) cured pork; **salumi** smpl (*insaccati*) cured pork meats

salume'ria sf delicatessen

salumi'ere, -a sm/f ≈ delicatessen owner

salumi'ficio [salumi'fitʃo] sm cured pork meat factory

salu'tare /**72**/ ag healthy; (*fig*) salutary, beneficial ▶ vt (*per dire buon giorno, fig*) to greet; (*per dire addio*) to say goodbye to; (*Mil*) to salute; **mi saluti sua moglie** my regards to your wife

sa'lute sf health; **~!** (*a chi starnutisce*) bless you!; (*nei brindisi*) cheers!; **bere alla ~ di qn** to drink (to) sb's health; **la ~ pubblica** public welfare; **godere di buona ~** to be healthy, enjoy good health

sa'luto sm (*gesto*) wave; (*parola*) greeting; (*Mil*) salute; **gli ha tolto il ~** he no longer says hello to him; **cari saluti, tanti saluti** best regards; **vogliate gradire i nostri più distinti saluti** yours faithfully; **i miei saluti alla sua signora** my regards to your wife

'salva sf salvo

salvacon'dotto sm (*Mil*) safe-conduct

salva'naio sm moneybox, piggy bank

salvado'regno, -a [salvado'reɲɲo] ag, sm/f Salvadorean

salva'gente [salva'dʒɛnte] sm (*Naut*) lifebuoy; (*pl inv: stradale*) traffic island; **~ a ciambella** lifebelt; **~ a giubbotto** lifejacket (*Brit*), life preserver (*US*)

salvaguar'dare /**72**/ vt to safeguard

salvagu'ardia sf safeguard; **a ~ di** for the safeguard of

sal'vare /**72**/ vt to save; (*trarre da un pericolo*) to rescue; (*proteggere*) to protect; **salvarsi** vpr to save o.s.; to escape; **~ la vita a qn** to save sb's life; **~ le apparenze** to keep up appearances; **si salvi chi può!** every man for himself!

salvas'chermo [salvas'kermo] sm (*Inform*) screen saver

salva'slip® sm inv panty liner

salva'taggio [salva'taddʒo] sm rescue

salva'tore, -'trice sm/f saviour (*Brit*), savior (*US*)

salvazi'one [salvat'tsjone] sf (*Rel*) salvation

'salve escl (*col*) hi!

sal'vezza [sal'vettsa] sf salvation; (*sicurezza*) safety

'salvia sf (*Bot*) sage

salvi'etta sf napkin, serviette; **~ umidificata** baby wipe

'salvo, -a ag safe, unhurt, unharmed; (*fuori pericolo*) safe, out of danger ▶ sm: **in ~** safe ▶ prep (*eccetto*) except; **~ che** cong (*a meno che*) unless; (*eccetto che*) except (that); **mettere qc in ~** to put sth in a safe place; **mettersi in ~** to reach safety; **portare qn in ~** to lead sb to safety; **~ contrordini** barring instructions to the contrary; **~ errori e omissioni** errors and omissions excepted; **~ imprevisti** barring accidents

sam'buca sf (*liquore*) sambuca (*type of anisette*)

sam'buco sm elder (tree)

sa'nare /**72**/ vt to heal, cure; (*economia*) to put right

sana'toria sf (*Dir*) act of indemnity

sana'torio sm sanatorium (*Brit*), sanitarium (*US*)

san'cire [san'tʃire] /**55**/ vt to sanction

'sandalo sm (*Bot*) sandalwood; (*calzatura*) sandal

sang'ria [san'gria] sf (*bibita*) sangria

'sangue sm blood; **farsi cattivo ~** to fret, get worked up; **all'ultimo ~** (*duello, lotta*) to the death; **non corre buon ~ tra di loro** there's bad blood between them; **buon ~ non mente!** blood will out!; **~ freddo** (*fig*) sang-froid, calm; **a ~ freddo** in cold blood

sangu'igno, -a [san'gwiɲɲo] ag blood *cpd*; (*colore*) blood-red

sangui'nante ag bleeding

sangui'nare /**72**/ vi to bleed

sangui'nario, -a ag bloodthirsty

sangui'noso, -a ag bloody

sangui'suga, -ghe sf leech

sanità sf health; (*salubrità*) healthiness; **Ministero della S~** Department of Health; **~ mentale** sanity; **~ pubblica** public health

sani'tario, -a ag health *cpd*; (*condizioni*) sanitary ▶ sm (*Amm*) doctor; **Ufficiale S~** Health Officer; **sanitari** (*impianti*) bathroom *o* sanitary fittings

San Ma'rino sf: **la Repubblica di ~** the Republic of San Marino

'sanno vb *vedi* **sapere**

'sano, -a ag healthy; (*denti, costituzione*) healthy, sound; (*integro*) whole, unbroken;

(*fig: politica, consigli*) sound; **~ di mente** sane; **di sana pianta** completely, entirely; **~ e salvo** safe and sound

San Silvestro [san sil'vestro] SM (*giorno*) New Year's Eve

Santi'ago SF: **~ (del Cile)** Santiago (de Chile)

santifi'care /20/ VT to sanctify; (*feste*) to observe

san'tino SM holy picture

san'tissimo, -a AG: **il S~ Sacramento** the Holy Sacrament; **il Padre S~** (*papa*) the Holy Father

santità SF sanctity; holiness; **Sua/Vostra ~** (*titolo di papa*) His/Your Holiness

'santo, -a AG holy; (*fig*) saintly; (*seguito da nome proprio: dav sm* **san** + *C,* **sant'** + *V,* **santo** + *s impura, gn, pn, ps, x, z; dav sf* **santa** + *C,* **sant'** + *V*) saint ▶ SM/F saint; **parole sante!** very true!; **tutto il ~ giorno** the whole blessed day, all day long; **non c'è ~ che tenga!** that's no excuse!; **la Santa Sede** the Holy See

san'tone SM holy man

santu'ario SM sanctuary

sanzio'nare [santsjo'nare] **/72/** VT to sanction

sanzi'one [san'tsjone] SF sanction; (*penale, civile*) sanction, penalty; **sanzioni economiche** economic sanctions

sa'pere /99/ VT to know; (*essere capace di*): **so nuotare** I know how to swim, I can swim ▶ VI: **~ di** (*aver sapore*) to taste of; (*aver odore*) to smell of ▶ SM knowledge; **far ~ qc a qn** to inform sb about sth, let sb know sth; **venire a ~ qc (da qn)** to find out o hear about sth (from sb); **non ne vuole più ~ di lei** he doesn't want to have anything more to do with her; **mi sa che non sia vero** I don't think that's true; **non lo so** I don't know; **non so l'inglese** I don't speak English

sapi'ente AG (*dotto*) learned; (*che rivela abilità*) masterly ▶ SMF scholar

sapien'tone, -a SM/F (*peg*) know-all (BRIT), know-it-all (US)

sapi'enza [sa'pjentsa] SF wisdom

sa'pone SM soap; **~ da barba** shaving soap; **~ da bucato** washing soap; **~ liquido** liquid soap; **~ in scaglie** soapflakes *pl*

sapo'netta SF cake o bar o tablet of soap

sa'pore SM taste, flavour (BRIT), flavor (US)

sapo'rito, -a AG tasty; (*fig: arguto*) witty; (: *piccante*) racy

sappi'amo VB *vedi* **sapere**

saprò *etc* VB *vedi* **sapere**

sapu'tello, -a SM/F know-all (BRIT), know-it-all (US)

sarà *etc* VB *vedi* **essere**

sara'banda SF (*fig*) uproar

saraci'nesca, -sche [saratʃi'neska] SF (*serranda*) rolling shutter

sar'casmo SM sarcasm *no pl*; sarcastic remark

sar'castico, -a, -ci, -che AG sarcastic

sarchi'are [sar'kjare] /vb not found/ VT (*Agr*) to hoe

sar'cofago (*pl* **sarcofagi** o **sarcofaghi**) SM sarcophagus

Sar'degna [sar'deɲɲa] SF: **la ~** Sardinia

sar'dina SF sardine

'sardo, -a AG, SM/F Sardinian

sar'donico, -a, -ci, -che AG sardonic

sa'rei *etc* VB *vedi* **essere**

SARS SF (= *severe acute respiratory syndrome*) SARS

'sarta SF *vedi* **sarto**

'sartia SF (*Naut*) stay

'sarto, -a SM/F tailor/dressmaker; **~ d'alta moda** couturier

sarto'ria SF tailor's (shop); dressmaker's (shop); (*casa di moda*) fashion house; (*arte*) couture

sassai'ola SF hail of stones

sas'sata SF blow with a stone; **tirare una ~ contro** o **a qc/qn** to throw a stone at sth/sb

'sasso SM stone; (*ciottolo*) pebble; (*masso*) rock; **restare** o **rimanere di ~** to be dumbfounded

sassofo'nista, -i, -e SM/F saxophonist

sas'sofono SM saxophone

sas'sone AG, SMF, SM Saxon

sas'soso, -a AG stony; pebbly

'Satana SM Satan

sa'tanico, -a, -ci, -che AG satanic, fiendish

satelli'tare AG satellite *cpd*

sa'tellite SM, AG satellite

'satira SF satire

satireggi'are [satired'dʒare] /62/ VT to satirize ▶ VI (*fare della satira*) to be satirical; (*scrivere satire*) to write satires

sa'tirico, -a, -ci, -che AG satiric(al)

sa'tollo, -a AG full, replete

satu'rare /72/ VT to saturate

saturazi'one [saturat'tsjone] SF saturation

'saturo, -a AG saturated; (*fig*): **~ di** full of; **~ d'acqua** (*terreno*) waterlogged

'SAUB SIGLA F (= *Struttura Amministrativa Unificata di Base*) state welfare system

'sauna SF sauna; **fare la ~** to have o take a sauna

sa'vana SF savannah

'savio, -a AG wise, sensible ▶ SM wise man

Sa'voia SF: **la ~** Savoy

savoi'ardo, -a AG of Savoy, Savoyard ▶ SM (*biscotto*) sponge finger

sazi'are [sat'tsjare] /19/ VT to satisfy, satiate; **saziarsi** VPR (*riempirsi di cibo*): **saziarsi (di)** to eat one's fill (of); (*fig*): **saziarsi di** to grow tired o weary of

sazietà [sattsje'ta] SF satiety, satiation

'sazio, -a ['sattsjo] AG: **~ (di)** sated (with), full (of); (*fig: stufo*) fed up (with), sick (of); **sono ~** I'm full (up)

S

sbada'taggine [zbada'taddʒine] SF
(*sventatezza*) carelessness; (*azione*) oversight

sba'dato, -a AG careless, inattentive

sbadigli'are [zbadiʎ'ʎare] /**27**/ VI to yawn

sba'diglio [zba'diʎʎo] SM yawn; **fare uno ~**
to yawn

'sbafo SM: **a ~** at somebody else's expense

sbagli'are [zbaʎ'ʎare] /**27**/ VT to make a
mistake in, get wrong ▶ VI (*fare errori*) to
make a mistake (*o mistakes*), be mistaken;
(*ingannarsi*) to be wrong; (*operare in modo non
giusto*) to err; **sbagliarsi** VPR to make a
mistake, be mistaken, be wrong; **~ la
mira/strada** to miss one's target/take
the wrong road; **scusi, ho sbagliato
numero** (*Tel*) sorry, I've got the wrong
number; **non c'è da sbagliarsi** there can
be no mistake

sbagli'ato, -a [zbaʎ'ʎato] AG (*gen*) wrong;
(*compito*) full of mistakes; (*conclusione*)
erroneous

'sbaglio ['zbaʎʎo] SM mistake, error; (*morale*)
error; **fare uno ~** to make a mistake

sbales'trato, -a AG (*persona: scombussolato*)
unsettled

sbal'lare /**72**/ VT (*merce*) to unpack ▶ VI (*nel fare
un conto*) to overestimate; (*Droga: gergo*) to get
high

sbal'lato, -a AG (*calcolo*) wrong; (*col:
ragionamento, persona*) screwy

'sballo SM (*Droga: gergo*) trip

sballot'tare /**72**/ VT to toss (about)

sbalor'dire /**55**/ VT to stun, amaze ▶ VI to be
stunned, be amazed

sbalordi'tivo, -a AG amazing; (*prezzo*)
incredible, absurd

sbal'zare [zbal'tsare] /**72**/ VT to throw, hurl;
(*fig: da una carica*) to remove, dismiss ▶ VI
(*balzare*) to bounce; (*saltare*) to leap, bound

'sbalzo ['zbaltso] SM (*spostamento improvviso*)
jolt, jerk; **a sbalzi** jerkily; (*fig*) in fits and
starts; **uno ~ di temperatura** a sudden
change in temperature

sban'care /**20**/ VT (*nei giochi*) to break the bank
at (*o of it*); (*fig*) to ruin, bankrupt

sbanda'mento SM (*Naut*) list; (*Aut*) skid;
(*fig: di persona*) confusion; **ha avuto un
periodo di ~** he went off the rails for a bit

sban'dare /**72**/ VI (*Naut*) to list; (*Aut*) to skid;
(*Aer*) to bank; **sbandarsi** VPR (*folla*) to
disperse; (*truppe*) to scatter; (*fig: famiglia*) to
break up

sban'data SF (*Aut*) skid; (*Naut*) list; **prendere
una ~ per qn** (*fig*) to fall for sb

sban'dato, -a SM/F mixed-up person

sbandie'rare /**72**/ VT (*bandiera*) to wave; (*fig*) to
parade, show off

'sbando SM: **essere allo ~** to drift

sbarac'care /**20**/ VT (*libri, piatti ecc*) to clear (up)

sbaragli'are [zbaraʎ'ʎare] /**27**/ VT (*Mil*) to
rout; (*in gare sportive ecc*) to beat, defeat

sba'raglio [zba'raʎʎo] SM rout; defeat;
gettarsi allo ~ (*soldato*) to throw o.s. into the
fray; (*fig*) to risk everything

sbaraz'zarsi [zbarat'tsarsi] /**72**/ VPR: **~ di** to
get rid of, rid o.s. of

sbaraz'zino, -a [zbarat'tsino] AG impish,
cheeky

sbar'bare /**72**/ VT, **sbar'barsi** VPR to shave

sbarba'tello SM novice, greenhorn

sbar'care /**20**/ VT (*passeggeri*) to disembark;
(*merci*) to unload ▶ VI to disembark

'sbarco SM disembarkation; unloading; (*Mil*)
landing

'sbarra SF bar; (*di passaggio a livello*) barrier;
(*Dir*): **mettere/presentarsi alla ~** to bring/
appear before the court

sbarra'mento SM (*stradale*) barrier; (*diga*)
dam, barrage; (*Mil*) barrage; (*Pol*) cut-off
point (*level of support below which a political party
is excluded from representation in Parliament*)

sbar'rare /**72**/ VT (*bloccare: strada ecc*) to block,
bar; (*cancellare: assegno*) to cross (*BRIT*); **~ il
passo** to bar the way; **~ gli occhi** to open
one's eyes wide

sbar'rato, -a AG (*porta*) barred; (*passaggio*)
blocked, barred; (*strada*) blocked,
obstructed; (*occhi*) staring; (*assegno*)
crossed (*BRIT*)

'sbattere /**1**/ VT (*porta*) to bang, slam; (*tappeti,
ali, Cuc*) to beat; (*urtare*) to knock, hit ▶ VI
(*porta, finestra*) to bang; (*agitarsi: ali, vele ecc*) to
flap; **~ qn fuori/in galera** to throw sb out/
into prison; **me ne sbatto!** (*col*) I don't give a
damn!

sbat'tuto, -a AG (*viso, aria*) dejected, worn out;
(*uovo*) beaten

sba'vare /**72**/ VI to dribble; (*colore*) to smear,
smudge

sbava'tura SF (*di persone*) dribbling; (*di
lumache*) slime; (*di rossetto, vernice*) smear

sbelli'carsi /**20**/ VPR: **~ dalle risa** to split one's
sides laughing

'sberla SF slap

sber'leffo SM: **fare uno ~ a qn** to make a face
at sb

sbia'dire /**55**/ VI (*anche*: **sbiadirsi**) to fade ▶ VT
to fade

sbia'dito, -a AG faded; (*fig*) colourless (*BRIT*),
colorless (*US*), dull

sbian'care /**20**/ VT to whiten; (*tessuto*) to
bleach ▶ VI (*impallidire*) to grow pale *o* white

sbi'eco, -a, -chi, -che AG (*storto*) squint,
askew; **di ~**, **guardare qn di ~** (*fig*) to look
askance at sb; **tagliare una stoffa di ~** to
cut material on the bias

sbigot'tire /**55**/ VT to dismay, stun ▶ VI
(*anche*: **sbigottirsi**) to be dismayed

sbilanci'are [zbilan'tʃare] /**14**/ vт to throw off balance; **sbilanciarsi** vPR (*perdere l'equilibrio*) to overbalance, lose one's balance; (*fig: compromettersi*) to compromise o.s.

sbi'lenco, -a, -chi, -che AG (*persona*) crooked, misshapen; (*fig: idea, ragionamento*) twisted

sbirci'are [zbir'tʃare] /**14**/ vт to cast sidelong glances at, eye

sbirci'ata [zbir'tʃata] sF: **dare una ~ a qc** to glance at sth, have a look at sth

'sbirro sм (*peg*) cop

sbizzar'rirsi [zbiddzar'rirsi] /**55**/ vPR to indulge one's whims

sbloc'care /**20**/ vт to unblock, free; (*freno*) to release; (*prezzi, affitti*) to free from controls; **sbloccarsi** vPR (*gen*) to become unblocked; (*passaggio, strada*) to clear, become unblocked; **la situazione si è sbloccata** things are moving again

'sblocco, -chi sм (*vedi vt*) unblocking, freeing; release

sboc'care /**20**/ vɪ: **~ in** (*fiume*) to flow into; (*strada*) to lead into; (*persona*) to come (out) into; (*fig: concludersi*) to end (up) in

sboc'cato, -a AG (*persona*) foul-mouthed; (*linguaggio*) foul

sbocci'are [zbot'tʃare] /**14**/ vɪ (*fiore*) to bloom, open (out)

'sbocco, -chi sм (*di fiume*) mouth; (*di strada*) end; (*di tubazione, Comm*) outlet; (*uscita: anche fig*) way out; **una strada senza ~** a dead end; **siamo in una situazione senza sbocchi** there's no way out of this for us

sbocconcel'lare [zbokkontʃel'lare] /**72**/ vт: **~ (qc)** to nibble (at sth)

sbollen'tare /**72**/ vт (*Cuc*) to parboil

sbol'lire /**55**/ vɪ (*fig*) to cool down, calm down

'sbornia sF (*col*): **prendersi una ~** to get plastered

sbor'sare /**72**/ vт (*denaro*) to pay out

sbot'tare /**72**/ vɪ: **~ in una risata/per la collera** to burst out laughing/explode with anger

sbotto'nare /**72**/ vт to unbutton, undo

sbra'cato, -a AG slovenly

sbracci'arsi [zbrat'tʃarsi] /**14**/ vPR to wave (one's arms about)

sbracci'ato, -a [zbrat'tʃato] AG (*camicia*) sleeveless; (*persona*) bare-armed

sbrai'tare /**72**/ vɪ to yell, bawl

sbra'nare /**72**/ vт to tear to pieces

sbricio'lare [zbritʃo'lare] /**72**/ vт, **sbricio'larsi** vPR to crumble

sbri'gare /**80**/ vт to deal with, get through; (*cliente*) to attend to, deal with; **sbrigarsi** vPR to hurry (up)

sbriga'tivo, -a AG (*persona, modo*) quick, expeditious; (*giudizio*) hasty

sbrina'mento sм defrosting

sbri'nare /**72**/ vт to defrost

sbrindel'lato, -a AG tattered, in tatters

sbrodo'lare /**72**/ vт to stain, dirty

'sbronza ['zbrontsa] (*col*) sF (*ubriaco*): **prendersi una ~** to get plastered

sbron'zarsi [zbron'tsarsi] /**72**/ vPR (*col*) to get plastered

sbruf'fone, -a sм/ғ boaster, braggart

sbu'care /**20**/ vɪ to come out, emerge; (*improvvisamente*) to pop out (*o* up)

sbucci'are [zbut'tʃare] /**14**/ vт (*arancia, patata*) to peel; (*piselli*) to shell; **sbucciarsi un ginocchio** to graze one's knee

sbucherò *etc* [zbuke'rɔ] vв *vedi* **sbucare**

sbudel'larsi /**72**/ vPR: **~ dalle risa** to split one's sides laughing

sbuf'fare /**72**/ vɪ (*persona, cavallo*) to snort; (: *ansimare*) to puff, pant; (*treno*) to puff

'sbuffo sм (*di aria, fumo, vapore*) puff; **maniche a ~** puff(ed) sleeves

sc. ABBR (*Teat: = scena*) sc.

'scabbia sF (*Med*) scabies *sg*

'scabro, -a AG rough, harsh; (*fig*) concise, terse

sca'broso, -a AG (*fig: difficile*) difficult, thorny; (: *imbarazzante*) embarrassing; (: *sconcio*) indecent

scacchi'era [skak'kjɛra] sF chessboard

scacchiere [skak'kjɛre] sм (*Mil*) sector; **S~** (*in Gran Bretagna*) Exchequer

scaccia'cani [skattʃa'kani] sм o ғ ɪNV pistol with blanks

scacciapensi'eri [skattʃapen'sjɛri] sм ɪNV (*Mus*) jew's-harp

scacci'are [skat'tʃare] /**14**/ vт to chase away *o* out, drive away *o* out; **~ qn di casa** to turn sb out of the house

'scacco, -chi sм (*pezzo del gioco*) chessman; (*quadretto di scacchiera*) square; (*fig*) setback, reverse; **scacchi** sMPL (*gioco*) chess *sg*; **a scacchi** (*tessuto*) check(ed); **subire uno ~** (*fig: sconfitta*) to suffer a setback

scacco'matto sм checkmate; **dare ~ a qn** (*anche fig*) to checkmate sb

'scaddi *etc* vв *vedi* **scadere**

sca'dente AG shoddy, of poor quality

sca'denza [ska'dɛntsa] sF (*di cambiale, contratto*) maturity; (*di passaporto*) expiry date; **a breve/lunga ~** short-/long-term; **data di ~** expiry date; **~ a termine** fixed deadline

sca'dere /**18**/ vɪ (*contratto ecc*) to expire; (*debito*) to fall due; (*valore, forze, peso*) to decline, go down

sca'fandro sм (*di palombaro*) diving suit; (*di astronauta*) spacesuit

scaffala'tura sF shelving, shelves *pl*

scaffale sм shelf; (*mobile*) set of shelves

sca'fista sм (*di immigrati*) people smuggler (*by boat*) '**scafo** SM (*Naut*, *Aer*) hull

scagio'nare [skadʒo'nare] /**72**/ VT to exonerate, free from blame

'**scaglia** ['skaʎʎa] SF (*Zool*) scale; (*scheggia*) chip, flake

scagli'are [skaʎ'ʎare] /**27**/ VT (*lanciare: anche fig*) to hurl, fling; **scagliarsi** VPR: **scagliarsi su** *o* **contro** to hurl *o* fling o.s. at; (*fig*) to rail at

scagliona'mento [skaʎʎona'mento] SM (*Mil*) arrangement in echelons

scaglio'nare [skaʎʎo'nare] /**72**/ VT (*pagamenti*) to space out, spread out; (*Mil*) to echelon

scagli'one [skaʎ'ʎone] SM (*Mil*) echelon; (*Geo*) terrace; **a scaglioni** in groups

sca'gnozzo [skaɲ'ɲɔttso] SM (*peg*) lackey

'**Scala: la** ~ *see note*

> Milan's *la Scala* first opened its doors in 1778 with a performance of Salieri's opera, "L'Europa riconosciuta". Built on the site of the church of Santa Maria della Scala, the theatre suffered serious damage in the bombing campaigns of 1943 but reopened in 1946 with a concert conducted by Toscanini. Enjoying world-wide renown for its opera, *la Scala* also has a famous school of classical dance.

'**scala** SF (*a gradini ecc*) staircase, stairs *pl*; (*a pioli, di corda*) ladder; (*Mus, Geo, di colori, valori, fig*) scale; **scale** SFPL (*scalinata*) stairs; **su larga** *o* **vasta** ~ on a large scale; **su piccola** ~, **su** ~ **ridotta** on a small scale; **su** ~ **nazionale/mondiale** on a national/worldwide scale; **in** ~ **di 1 a 100.000** on a scale of 1 cm to 1 km; **riproduzione in** ~ reproduction to scale; ~ **a chiocciola** spiral staircase; ~ **a libretto** stepladder; ~ **di misure** system of weights and measures; ~ **mobile** escalator; (*Econ*) sliding scale; ~ **mobile (dei salari)** index-linked pay scale; ~ **di sicurezza** (*antincendio*) fire escape

sca'lare /**72**/ VT (*Alpinismo, muro*) to climb, scale; (*debito*) to scale down, reduce; **questa somma vi viene scalata dal prezzo originale** this sum is deducted from the original price

sca'lata SF scaling *no pl*, climbing *no pl*; (*arrampicata, fig*) climb; **dare la** ~ **a** (*fig*) to make a bid for

scala'tore, -'trice SM/F climber

scalca'gnato, -a [skalkaɲ'ɲato] AG (*logoro*) worn; (*persona*) shabby

scalci'are [skal'tʃare] /**14**/ VI to kick

scalci'nato, -a [skaltʃi'nato] AG (*fig: peg*) shabby

scalda'bagno [skalda'baɲɲo] SM water heater

scal'dare /**72**/ VT to heat; **scaldarsi** VPR to warm up, heat up; (*al fuoco, al sole*) to warm o.s.; (*fig*) to get excited; ~ **la sedia** (*fig*) to twiddle one's thumbs

scaldavi'vande SM INV dish warmer

scal'dino SM (*per mani*) hand-warmer; (*per piedi*) foot-warmer; (*per letto*) bedwarmer

scal'fire /**55**/ VT to scratch

scalfit'tura SF scratch

scali'nata SF staircase

sca'lino SM (*anche fig*) step; (*di scala a pioli*) rung

scal'mana SF (*hot*) flush

scalma'narsi /**72**/ VPR (*affaticarsi*) to rush about, rush around; (*agitarsi, darsi da fare*) to get all hot and bothered; (*arrabbiarsi*) to get excited, get steamed up

scalma'nato, -a SM/F hothead

'**scalo** SM (*Naut*) slipway; (: *porto d'approdo*) port of call; (*Aer*) stopover; **fare** ~ **(a)** (*Naut*) to call (at), put in (at); (*Aer*) to land (at), make a stop (at); **volo senza** ~ non-stop flight; ~ **merci** (*Ferr*) goods (BRIT) *o* freight yard

sca'logna [ska'loɲɲa] SF (*col*) bad luck

scalo'gnato, -a [skaloɲ'ɲato] AG (*col*) unlucky

scalop'pina SF (*Cuc*) escalope

scal'pello SM chisel

scalpi'tare /**72**/ VI (*cavallo*) to paw the ground; (*persona*) to stamp one's feet

scal'pore SM noise, row; **far** ~ (*notizia*) to cause a sensation *o* a stir

'**scaltro, -a** AG cunning, shrewd

scal'zare [skal'tsare] /**72**/ VT (*albero*) to bare the roots of; (*muro, fig: autorità*) to undermine

'**scalzo, -a** ['skaltso] AG barefoot

scambi'are /**19**/ VT to exchange; (*confondere*): ~ **qn/qc per** to take *o* mistake sb/sth for; **mi hanno scambiato il cappello** they've given me the wrong hat; **scambiarsi** VPR (*auguri, confidenze, visite*) to exchange

scambi'evole AG mutual, reciprocal

'**scambio** SM exchange; (*Comm*) trade; (*Ferr*) points *pl*; **fare (uno)** ~ to make a swap; **libero** ~ free trade; **scambi con l'estero** foreign trade

scamosci'ato, -a [skamoʃ'ʃato] AG suede

scampa'gnata [skampaɲ'ɲata] SF trip to the country

scampa'nare /**72**/ VI to peal

scam'pare /**72**/ VT (*salvare*) to rescue, save; (*evitare: morte, prigione*) to escape ▶ VI: ~ **(a qc)** to survive (sth), escape (sth); **scamparla bella** to have a narrow escape

'**scampo** SM (*salvezza*) escape; (*Zool*) prawn; **cercare** ~ **nella fuga** to seek safety in flight; **non c'è (via di)** ~ there's no way out

'**scampolo** SM remnant

scanala'tura SF (*incavo*) channel, groove

scandagli'are [skandaʎ'ʎare] /**27**/ VT (*Naut*) to sound; (*fig*) to sound out; to probe

scanda'listico, -a, -ci, -che AG (*settimanale ecc*) sensational

scandaliz'zare [skandalid'dzare] /**72**/ VT to shock, scandalize; **scandalizzarsi** VPR to be shocked

'**scandalo** SM scandal; **dare ~ to cause a scandal**

scanda'loso, -a AG scandalous, shocking

Scandi'navia SF: **la ~** Scandinavia

scandi'navo, -a AG, SM/F Scandinavian

scan'dire /**55**/ VT (*versi*) to scan; (*parole*) to articulate, pronounce distinctly; **~ il tempo** (*Mus*) to beat time

scan'nare /**72**/ VT (*animale*) to butcher, slaughter; (*persona*) to cut *o* slit the throat of

'**scanner** ['skanner] SM INV scanner

scanneriz'zare [skannerid'dzare] /**72**/ VT to scan

'**scanno** SM seat, bench

scansafa'tiche [skansafa'tike] SM O F INV idler, loafer

scan'sare /**72**/ VT (*rimuovere*) to move (aside), shift; (*schivare: schiaffo*) to dodge; (*sfuggire*) to avoid; **scansarsi** VPR to move aside

scan'sia SF shelves pl; (*per libri*) bookcase

'**scanso** SM: **a ~ di** in order to avoid, as a precaution against; **a ~ di equivoci** to avoid (any) misunderstanding

scanti'nato SM basement

scanto'nare /**72**/ VI to turn the corner; (*svignarsela*) to sneak off

scanzo'nato, -a [skantso'nato] AG easy-going

scapacci'one [skapat'tʃone] SM clout, slap

scapes'trato, -a AG dissolute

'**scapito** SM (*perdita*) loss; (*danno*) damage, detriment; **a ~ di** to the detriment of

'**scapola** SF shoulder blade

'**scapolo** SM bachelor

scappa'mento SM (*Aut*) exhaust

scap'pare /**72**/ VI (*fuggire*) to escape; (*andare via in fretta*) to rush off; **~ di prigione** to escape from prison; **~ di mano** (*oggetto*) to slip out of one's hands; **~ di mente a qn** to slip sb's mind; **lasciarsi ~** (*occasione, affare*) to let go by, miss; (*dettaglio*) to overlook; (*parola*) to let slip; (*prigioniero*) to let escape; **mi scappò detto** I let it slip

scap'pata SF quick visit *o* call

scappa'tella SF escapade

scappa'toia SF way out

scara'beo SM beetle

scarabocchi'are [skarabok'kjare] /**19**/ VT to scribble, scrawl

scara'bocchio [skara'bɔkkjo] SM scribble, scrawl

scara'faggio [skara'faddʒo] SM cockroach

scaraman'zia [skaraman'tsia] SF: **per ~** for luck

scara'muccia, -ce [skara'muttʃa] SF skirmish

scaraven'tare /**72**/ VT to fling, hurl; **scaraventarsi** VPR to fling o.s.

scarce'rare [skartʃe'rare] /**72**/ VT to release (from prison)

scarcerazi'one [skartʃerat'tsjone] SF release (from prison)

scardi'nare /**72**/ VT: **~ una porta** to take a door off its hinges

'**scarica, -che** SF (*di più armi*) volley of shots; (*di sassi, pugni*) hail, shower; (*Elettr*) discharge; **~ di mitra** burst of machine-gun fire

scari'care /**20**/ VT (*merci, camion ecc*) to unload; (*passeggeri*) to set down, put off; (*da Internet*) to download; (*arma*) to unload; (: *sparare, anche Elettr*) to discharge; (*corso d'acqua*) to empty, pour; (*fig: liberare da un peso*) to unburden, relieve; **scaricarsi** VPR (*orologio*) to run *o* wind down; (*batteria, accumulatore*) to go flat (BRIT) *o* dead; (*fig: rilassarsi*) to unwind; (: *sfogarsi*) to let off steam; **~ le proprie responsabilità su qn** to off-load one's responsibilities onto sb; **~ la colpa addosso a qn** to blame sb; **il fulmine si scaricò su un albero** the lightning struck a tree

scarica'tore SM loader; (*di porto*) docker

'**scarico, -a, -chi, -che** AG unloaded; (*orologio*) run down; (*batteria, accumulatore*) dead, flat (BRIT) ▶ SM (*di merci, materiali*) unloading; (*di immondizie*) dumping, tipping (BRIT); (: *luogo*) rubbish dump; (*Tecn: deflusso*) draining; (: *dispositivo*) drain; (*Aut*) exhaust; **~ del lavandino** waste outlet

scarlat'tina SF scarlet fever

scar'latto, -a AG scarlet

'**scarno, -a** AG thin, bony

'**scarpa** SF shoe; **fare le scarpe a qn** (*fig*) to double-cross sb; **scarpe da ginnastica** gym shoes; **scarpe coi tacchi (alti)** high-heeled shoes; **scarpe col tacco basso** low-heeled shoes; **scarpe senza tacco** flat shoes; **scarpe da tennis** tennis shoes

scar'pata SF escarpment

scarpi'era SF shoe rack

scar'pone SM boot; **scarponi da montagna** climbing boots; **scarponi da sci** ski-boots

scarroz'zare [skarrot'tsare] /**72**/ VT to drive around

scarseggi'are [skarsed'dʒare] /**62**/ VI to be scarce; **~ di** to be short of, lack

scar'sezza [skar'settsa] SF scarcity, lack

'**scarso, -a** AG (*insufficiente*) insufficient, meagre (BRIT), meager (US); (*povero: annata*) poor, lean; (*Ins: voto*) poor; **~ di** lacking in; **3 chili scarsi** just under 3 kilos, barely 3 kilos

scartabel'lare /**72**/ VT to skim through, glance through

S

scarta'faccio [skarta'fattʃo] SM notebook

scarta'mento SM (Ferr) gauge; **~ normale/ridotto** standard/narrow gauge

scar'tare /**72**/ VT (pacco) to unwrap; (idea) to reject; (Mil) to declare unfit for military service; (carte da gioco) to discard; (Calcio) to dodge (past) ▶ VI to swerve

'scarto SM (cosa scartata, anche Comm) reject; (di veicolo) swerve; (differenza) gap, difference; **~ salariale** wage differential

scar'toffie SFPL (peg) papers pl

scas'sare /**72**/ VT (col: rompere) to wreck

scassi'nare /**72**/ VT to break, force

'scasso SM vedi **furto**

scate'nare /**72**/ VT (fig) to incite, stir up; **scatenarsi** VPR (temporale) to break; (rivolta) to break out; (persona: infuriarsi) to rage

scate'nato, -a AG wild

'scatola SF box; (di latta) tin (BRIT), can; **cibi in ~** tinned (BRIT) o canned foods; **una ~ di cioccolatini** a box of chocolates; **comprare qc a ~ chiusa** to buy sth sight unseen; **~ cranica** cranium

scato'lone SM (big) box

scat'tante AG quick off the mark; (agile) agile

scat'tare /**72**/ VT (fotografia) to take ▶ VI (congegno, molla ecc) to be released; (balzare) to spring up; (Sport) to put on a spurt; (fig: per l'ira) to fly into a rage; (legge, provvedimento) to come into effect; **~ in piedi** to spring to one's feet; **far ~** to release

'scatto SM (dispositivo) release; (: di arma da fuoco) trigger mechanism; (rumore) click; (balzo) jump, start; (Sport) spurt; (fig: di ira ecc) fit; (: di stipendio) increment; **di ~** suddenly; **serratura a ~** spring lock

scatu'rire /**55**/ VI to gush, spring

scaval'care /**20**/ VT (ostacolo) to pass (o climb) over; (fig) to get ahead of, overtake

sca'vare /**72**/ VT (terreno) to dig; (legno) to hollow out; (pozzo, galleria) to bore; (città sepolta ecc) to excavate

scava'trice [skava'tritʃe] SF (macchina) excavator

scavezza'collo [skavettsa'kɔllo] SM daredevil

'scavo SM excavating no pl; excavation

scazzot'tare [skattsot'tare] /**72**/ VT (col) to beat up, give a thrashing to

'scegliere ['ʃeʎʎere] /**100**/ VT (gen) to choose; (candidato, prodotto) to choose, select; **~ di fare** to choose to do

sce'icco, -chi [ʃe'ikko] SM sheik

'scelgo etc ['ʃelgo] VB vedi **scegliere**

scelle'rato, -a [ʃelle'rato] AG wicked, evil

scel'lino [ʃel'lino] SM shilling

'scelto, -a ['ʃelto] PP di **scegliere** ▶ AG (gruppo) carefully selected; (frutta, verdura) choice, top quality; (Mil: specializzato) crack cpd,

highly skilled ▶ SF choice; (selezione) selection, choice; **frutta o formaggi a scelta** choice of fruit or cheese; **fare una scelta** to make a choice, choose; **non avere scelta** to have no choice o option; **di prima scelta** top grade o quality

sce'mare [ʃe'mare] /**72**/ VT, VI to diminish

sce'menza [ʃe'mentsa] SF stupidity no pl; stupid thing (to do o say)

'scemo, -a ['ʃemo] AG stupid, silly

'scempio ['ʃempjo] SM slaughter, massacre; (fig) ruin; **far ~ di** (fig) to play havoc with, ruin

'scena ['ʃena] SF (gen) scene; (palcoscenico) stage; **le scene** (fig: teatro) the stage; **andare in ~** to be staged o put on o performed; **mettere in ~** to stage; **uscire di ~** to leave the stage; (fig) to leave the scene; **fare una ~** (fig) to make a scene; **ha fatto ~ muta** (fig) he didn't open his mouth

sce'nario [ʃe'narjo] SM scenery; (di film) scenario

sce'nata [ʃe'nata] SF row, scene

'scendere ['ʃendere] /**101**/ VI to go (o come) down; (strada, sole) to go down; (notte) to fall; (passeggero: fermarsi) to get out, alight; (fig: temperatura, prezzi) to fall, drop ▶ VT (scale, pendio) to go (o come) down; **~ dalle scale** to go (o come) down the stairs; **~ dal treno** to get off o out of the train; **~ dalla macchina** to get out of the car; **~ da cavallo** to dismount, get off one's horse; **~ ad un albergo** to put up o stay at a hotel

sceneggi'ato [ʃened'dʒato] SM television drama

sceneggia'tore, -'trice [ʃeneddʒa'tore] SM/F script-writer

sceneggia'tura [ʃeneddʒa'tura] SF (Teat) scenario; (Cine) screenplay, scenario

'scenico, -a, -ci, -che ['ʃeniko] AG stage cpd

sceno'grafia [ʃenogra'fia] SF (Teat) stage design; (Cine) set design; (elementi scenici) scenery

sce'nografo, -a [ʃe'nɔgrafo] SM/F set designer

sce'riffo [ʃe'riffo] SM sheriff

scervel'larsi [ʃervel'larsi] /**72**/ VPR: **~ (su qc)** to rack one's brains (over sth)

scervel'lato, -a [ʃervel'lato] AG featherbrained

'sceso, -a ['ʃeso] PP di **scendere**

scetti'cismo [ʃetti'tʃizmo] SM scepticism (BRIT), skepticism (US)

'scettico, -a, -ci, -che ['ʃettiko] AG sceptical (BRIT), skeptical (US)

'scettro ['ʃettro] SM sceptre (BRIT), scepter (US)

'scheda ['skɛda] SF (index) card; (TV, Radio) (brief) report; **~ audio** (Inform) sound card;

~ **bianca/nulla** (*Pol*) unmarked/spoiled ballot paper; ~ **a circuito stampato** printed-circuit board; ~ **elettorale** ballot paper; ~ **madre** (*Inform*) motherboard; ~ **di memoria** (*Inform*) memory card; ~ **perforata** punch card; ~ **ricaricabile** (*Tel*) top-up card; ~ **telefonica** phone card; ~ **video** (*Inform*) video card

sche'dare [ske'dare] /**72**/ VT (*dati*) to file; (*libri*) to catalogue; (*registrare: anche Polizia*) to put on one's files

sche'dario [ske'darjo] SM file; (*mobile*) filing cabinet

sche'dato, -a [ske'dato] AG with a (police) record ▶ SM/F person with a (police) record

sche'dina [ske'dina] SF ≈ pools coupon (BRIT)

'scheggia, -ge ['skeddʒa] SF splinter, sliver; ~ **impazzita** (*fig*) maverick

sche'letrico, -a, -ci, -che [ske'lɛtriko] AG (*anche Anat*) skeletal; (*fig: essenziale*) skeleton *cpd*

'scheletro ['skɛletro] SM skeleton; **avere uno ~ nell'armadio** (*fig*) to have a skeleton in the cupboard

'schema, -i ['skɛma] SM (*diagramma*) diagram, sketch; (*progetto, abbozzo*) outline, plan; **ribellarsi agli schemi** to rebel against traditional values; **secondo gli schemi tradizionali** in accordance with traditional values

sche'matico, -a, -ci, -che [ske'matiko] AG schematic

schematiz'zare [skematid'dzare] /**72**/ VT to schematize

'scherma ['skerma] SF fencing

scher'maglia [sker'maʎʎa] SF (*fig*) skirmish

scher'mata [sker'mata] SF screenshot

scher'mirsi [sker'mirsi] /**55**/ VPR to defend o.s.

'schermo ['skermo] SM shield, screen; (*Cine, TV*) screen; **a ~ panoramico** (*TV*) widescreen

schermogra'fia [skermogra'fia] SF X-rays *pl*

scher'nire [sker'nire] /**55**/ VT to mock, sneer at

'scherno ['skerno] SM mockery, derision; **farsi ~ di** to sneer at; **essere oggetto di ~** to be a laughing stock

scher'zare [sker'tsare] /**72**/ VI to joke

'scherzo ['skertso] SM joke; (*tiro*) trick; (*Mus*) scherzo; **è uno ~!** (*una cosa facile*) it's child's play!, it's easy!; **per ~** in jest; for a joke *o* a laugh; **fare un brutto ~ a qn** to play a nasty trick on sb; **scherzi a parte** seriously, joking apart

scher'zoso, -a [sker'tsoso] AG (*tono, gesto*) playful; (*osservazione*) facetious; **è un tipo ~** he likes a joke

schiaccia'noci [skjattʃa'notʃi] SM INV nutcracker

schiacci'ante [skjat'tʃante] AG overwhelming

schiacci'are [skjat'tʃare] /**14**/ VT (*dito*) to crush; (*noci*) to crack; ~ **un pisolino** to have a nap; **schiacciarsi** VPR (*appiattirsi*) to get squashed; (*frantumarsi*) to get crushed

schiaffeggi'are [skjaffed'dʒare] /**62**/ VT to slap

schi'affo ['skjaffo] SM slap; **prendere qn a schiaffi** to slap sb's face; **uno ~ morale** a slap in the face, a rebuff

schiamaz'zare [skjamat'tsare] /**72**/ VI to squawk, cackle

schia'mazzo [skja'mattso] SM (*fig: chiasso*) din, racket

schian'tare [skjan'tare] /**72**/ VT to break, tear apart; **schiantarsi** VPR to break (up), shatter; **schiantarsi al suolo** (*aereo*) to crash (to the ground)

schi'anto ['skjanto] SM (*rumore*) crash; tearing sound; **è uno ~!** (*col*) it's (*o* he's *o* she's) terrific!; **di ~** all of a sudden

schia'rire [skja'rire] /**55**/ VT to lighten, make lighter ▶ VI (*anche*: **schiarirsi**) to grow lighter; (*tornar sereno*) to clear, brighten up; **schiarirsi la voce** to clear one's throat

schia'rita [skja'rita] SF (*Meteor*) bright spell; (*fig*) improvement, turn for the better

schiat'tare [skjat'tare] /**72**/ VI to burst; ~ **d'invidia** to be green with envy; ~ **di rabbia** to be beside o.s. with rage

schiavitù [skjavi'tu] SF slavery

schiaviz'zare [skjavid'dzare] /**72**/ VT to enslave

schi'avo, -a ['skjavo] SM/F slave

schi'ena ['skjɛna] SF (*Anat*) back

schie'nale [skje'nale] SM (*di sedia*) back

schi'era ['skjɛra] SF (*Mil*) rank; (*gruppo*) group, band; **villette a ~** ≈ terraced houses

schiera'mento [skjera'mento] SM (*Mil, Sport*) formation; (*fig*) alliance

schie'rare [skje'rare] /**72**/ VT (*esercito*) to line up, draw up, marshal; **schierarsi** VPR to line up; (*fig*) **schierarsi con** *o* **dalla parte di/ contro qn** to side with/oppose sb

schi'etto, -a ['skjetto] AG (*puro*) pure; (*fig*) frank, straightforward

schi'fare [ski'fare] /**72**/ VT to disgust

schi'fezza [ski'fettsa] SF: **essere una ~** (*cibo, bibita ecc*) to be disgusting; (*film, libro*) to be dreadful

schifil'toso, -a [skifil'toso] AG fussy, difficult

'schifo ['skifo] SM disgust; **fare ~** (*essere fatto male, dare pessimi risultati*) to be awful; **mi fa ~** it makes me sick, it's disgusting; **quel libro è uno ~** that book's rotten

schi'foso, -a [ski'foso] AG disgusting, revolting; (*molto scadente*) rotten, lousy

schioc'care [skjok'kare] /**20**/ VT (*frusta*) to crack; (*dita*) to snap; (*lingua*) to click; **~ le labbra** to smack one's lips

schioppet'tata [skjoppet'tata] SF gunshot

schi'oppo ['skjɔppo] SM rifle, gun

schi'udere ['skjudere] /**22**/ VT, **schi'udersi** VPR to open

schi'uma ['skjuma] SF foam; (*di sapone*) lather; (*di latte*) froth; (*fig: feccia*) scum

schiu'mare [skju'mare] /**72**/ VT to skim ▶ VI to foam

schi'uso, -a ['skjuso] PP *di* **schiudere**

schi'vare [ski'vare] /**72**/ VT to dodge, avoid

'schivo, -a ['skivo] AG (*ritroso*) stand-offish, reserved; (*timido*) shy

schizofre'nia [skiddzofre'nia] SF schizophrenia

schizo'frenico, -a, -ci, -che [skiddzo'frɛniko] AG schizophrenic

schiz'zare [skit'tsare] /**72**/ VT (*spruzzare*) to spurt, squirt; (*sporcare*) to splash, spatter; (*fig: abbozzare*) to sketch ▶ VI to spurt, squirt; (*saltar fuori*) to dart up (*o off etc*); **~ via** (*animale, persona*) to dart away; (*macchina, moto*) to accelerate away

schizzi'noso, -a [skittsi'noso] AG fussy, finicky

'schizzo ['skittso] SM (*di liquido*) spurt; splash, spatter; (*abbozzo*) sketch

sci [ʃi] SM INV (*attrezzo*) ski; (*attività*) skiing; **~ di fondo** cross-country skiing, ski touring (US); **~ d'acqua** *o* **nautico** water-skiing

'scia ['ʃia] (*pl* **scie**) SF (*di imbarcazione*) wake; (*di profumo*) trail

scià [ʃa] SM INV shah

sci'abola ['ʃabola] SF sabre (BRIT), saber (US)

scia'callo [ʃa'kallo] SM jackal; (*fig: peg: profittatore*) shark, profiteer; (: *ladro*) looter

sciac'quare [ʃak'kware] /**72**/ VT to rinse

scia'gura [ʃa'gura] SF disaster, calamity; misfortune

sciagu'rato, -a [ʃagu'rato] AG unfortunate; (*malvagio*) wicked

scialac'quare [ʃalak'kware] /**72**/ VT to squander

scia'lare [ʃa'lare] /**72**/ VI to throw one's money around

sci'albo, -a ['ʃalbo] AG pale, dull; (*fig*) dull, colourless (BRIT), colorless (US)

sci'alle ['ʃalle] SM shawl

sci'alo ['ʃalo] SM squandering, waste

scia'luppa [ʃa'luppa] SF (*Naut*) sloop; (*anche:* **scialuppa di salvataggio**) lifeboat

scia'mare [ʃa'mare] /**72**/ VI to swarm

sci'ame ['ʃame] SM swarm

scian'cato, -a [ʃan'kato] AG lame; (*mobile*) rickety

sci'are [ʃi'are] /**60**/ VI to ski; **andare a ~** to go skiing

sci'arpa ['ʃarpa] SF scarf; (*fascia*) sash

scia'tore, -'trice [ʃia'tore] SM/F skier

sciat'tezza [ʃat'tettsa] SF slovenliness

sci'atto, -a ['ʃatto] AG (*persona: nell'aspetto*) slovenly, unkempt; (: *nel lavoro*) sloppy, careless

'scibile ['ʃibile] SM knowledge

scien'tifico, -a, -ci, -che [ʃen'tifiko] AG scientific; **la (polizia) scientifica** the forensic department

sci'enza ['ʃɛntsa] SF science; (*sapere*) knowledge; **scienze** SFPL (*Ins*) science *sg*; **scienze naturali** natural sciences; **scienze politiche** political science *sg*

scienzi'ato, -a [ʃen'tsjato] SM/F scientist

'Scilly ['ʃilli]: **le isole ~** SFPL the Scilly Isles

'scimmia ['ʃimmja] SF monkey

scimmiot'tare [ʃimmjot'tare] /**72**/ VT to ape, mimic

scimpanzé [ʃimpan'tse] SM INV chimpanzee

scimu'nito, -a [ʃimu'nito] AG silly, idiotic

'scindere ['ʃindere] /**102**/ VT, **'scindersi** VPR to split (up)

scin'tilla [ʃin'tilla] SF spark

scintil'lare [ʃintil'lare] /**72**/ VI to spark; (*acqua, occhi*) to sparkle

scintil'lio [ʃintil'lio] SM sparkling

scioc'care [ʃok'kare] /**20**/ VT to shock

scioc'chezza [ʃok'kettsa] SF stupidity *no pl*; stupid *o* foolish thing; **dire sciocchezze** to talk nonsense

sci'occo, -a, -chi, -che ['ʃokko] AG stupid, foolish

sci'ogliere ['ʃɔʎʎere] /**103**/ VT (*nodo*) to untie; (*capelli*) to loosen; (*persona, animale*) to untie, release; (*nell'acqua: zucchero ecc*) to dissolve; (*fig: mistero*) to solve; (*porre fine a: contratto*) to cancel; (: *società, matrimonio*) to dissolve; (: *riunione*) to bring to an end; (*fig: persona*): **~ da** to release from; (*neve*) to melt; **sciogliersi** VPR to loosen, come untied; to melt; to dissolve; (*assemblea, corteo, duo*) to break up; **~ i muscoli** to limber up; **~ il ghiaccio** (*fig*) to break the ice; **~ le vele** (*Naut*) to set sail; **sciogliersi dai legami** (*fig*) to free o.s. from all ties

scioglilingua [ʃoʎʎi'lingwa] SM INV tongue-twister

sci'olgo *etc* ['ʃɔlgo] VB *vedi* **sciogliere**

sciol'tezza [ʃol'tettsa] SF agility; suppleness; ease

sci'olto, -a ['ʃɔlto] PP *di* **sciogliere** ▶ AG loose; (*agile*) agile, nimble; supple; (*disinvolto*) free and easy; **essere ~ nei movimenti** to be supple; **versi sciolti** (*Poesia*) blank verse

sciope'rante [ʃope'rante] SMF striker

sciope'rare [ʃope'rare] /**72**/ VI to strike, go on strike

sci'opero ['ʃopero] SM strike; **fare ~** to strike; **entrare in ~** to go on *o* come out on strike;

~ **bianco** work-to-rule (BRIT), slowdown (US); ~ **della fame** hunger strike; ~ **selvaggio** wildcat strike; ~ **a singhiozzo** on-off strike; ~ **di solidarietà** sympathy strike

sciori'nare [ʃori'nare] /**72**/ VT (ostentare) to show off, display

scio'via [ʃio'via] SF ski lift

sciovi'nismo [ʃovi'nizmo] SM chauvinism

sciovi'nista, -i, -e [ʃovi'nista] SM/F chauvinist

sci'pito, -a [ʃi'pito] AG insipid

scip'pare [ʃip'pare] /**72**/ VT: ~ **qn** to snatch sb's bag

scippa'tore [ʃippa'tore] SM bag-snatcher

'scippo ['ʃippo] SM bag-snatching

sci'rocco [ʃi'rɔkko] SM sirocco

sci'roppo [ʃi'rɔppo] SM syrup; ~ **per la tosse** cough syrup, cough mixture

'scisma, -i ['ʃizma] SM (Rel) schism

scissi'one [ʃis'sjone] SF (anche fig) split, division; (Fisica) fission

'scisso, -a ['ʃisso] PP di **scindere**

sciu'pare [ʃu'pare] /**72**/ VT (abito, libro, appetito) to spoil, ruin; (tempo, denaro) to waste; **sciuparsi** VPR to get spoilt o ruined; (rovinarsi la salute) to ruin one's health

scivo'lare [ʃivo'lare] /**72**/ VI to slide o glide along; (involontariamente) to slip, slide

'scivolo ['ʃivolo] SM slide; (Tecn) chute

scivo'loso, -a [ʃivo'loso] AG slippery

scle'rosi SF sclerosis

scoc'care /**20**/ VT (freccia) to shoot ▶ VI (guizzare) to shoot up; (battere: ora) to strike

scoccherò etc [skokke'rɔ] VB vedi **scoccare**

scocci'are [skot'tʃare] /**14**/ VT to bother, annoy; **scocciarsi** VPR to be bothered o annoyed

scoccia'tore, -'trice [skottʃa'tore] SM/F nuisance, pest (col)

scoccia'tura [skottʃa'tura] SF nuisance, bore

sco'della SF bowl

scodinzo'lare [skodintso'lare] /**72**/ VI to wag its tail

scogli'era [skoʎ'ʎɛra] SF reef; (rupe) cliff

'scoglio ['skɔʎʎo] SM (al mare) rock; (fig: ostacolo) difficulty, stumbling block

scogli'oso, -a [skoʎ'ʎoso] AG rocky

scoi'attolo SM squirrel

scola'pasta SM INV colander

scolapi'atti SM INV drainer (for plates)

sco'lare /**72**/ AG: **età** ~ school age ▶ VT to drain ▶ VI to drip

scola'resca SF schoolchildren pl, pupils pl

sco'laro, -a SM/F pupil, schoolboy(-girl)

sco'lastico, -a, -ci, -che AG (gen) scholastic; (libro, anno, divisa) school cpd

scol'lare /**72**/ VT (staccare) to unstick; **scollarsi** VPR to come unstuck

scol'lato, -a AG (vestito) low-cut, low-necked; (donna) wearing a low-cut dress (o blouse etc)

scolla'tura SF neckline

scolle'gare /**80**/ VT (fili, apparecchi) to disconnect; **scollegarsi** VPR (da Internet) to disconnect; (da chat-line) to log off

'scolo SM drainage; (sbocco) drain; (acqua) waste water; **canale di** ~ drain; **tubo di** ~ drainpipe

scolo'rire /**55**/ VT to fade; to discolour (BRIT), discolor (US) ▶ VI (anche: **scolorirsi**) to fade; to become discoloured; (impallidire) to turn pale

scol'pire /**55**/ VT to carve, sculpt

scombi'nare /**72**/ VT to mess up, upset

scombi'nato, -a AG confused, muddled

scombusso'lare /**72**/ VT to upset

scom'messo, -a PP di **scommettere** ▶ SF bet, wager; **fare una scommessa** to bet

scom'mettere /**63**/ VT, VI to bet

scomo'dare /**72**/ VT to trouble, bother, disturb; (fig: nome famoso) to involve, drag in; **scomodarsi** VPR to put o.s. out; **scomodarsi a fare** to go to the bother o trouble of doing

scomodità SF INV (di sedia, letto ecc) discomfort; (di orario, sistemazione ecc) inconvenience

'scomodo, -a AG uncomfortable; (sistemazione, posto) awkward, inconvenient

scompagi'nare [skompadʒi'nare] /**72**/ VT to upset, throw into disorder

scompag'nato, -a [skompaɲ'ɲato] AG (calzini, guanti) odd

scompa'rire /**7**/ VI (sparire) to disappear, vanish; (fig) to be insignificant

scom'parso, -a PP di **scomparire** ▶ SF disappearance; (fig: morte) passing away, death

scomparti'mento SM (Ferr) compartment; (sezione) division

scom'parto SM compartment, division

scom'penso SM imbalance, lack of balance

scompigli'are [skompiʎ'ʎare] /**27**/ VT (cassetto, capelli) to mess up, disarrange; (fig: piani) to upset

scom'piglio [skom'piʎʎo] SM mess, confusion

scom'porre /**77**/ VT (parola, numero) to break up; (Chim) to decompose; **scomporsi** VPR (Chim) to decompose; (fig) to get upset, lose one's composure; **senza scomporsi** unperturbed

scom'posto, -a PP di **scomporre** ▶ AG (gesto) unseemly; (capelli) ruffled, dishevelled

sco'munica, -che SF excommunication

scomuni'care /**20**/ VT to excommunicate

sconcer'tante [skontʃer'tante] AG disconcerting

sconcer'tare [skontʃer'tare] /**72**/ VT to disconcert, bewilder

'sconcio, -a, -ci, -ce ['skontʃo] AG (osceno) indecent, obscene ▶ SM (cosa riprovevole, mal fatta) disgrace

S

sconclusio'nato, -a AG incoherent, illogical
sconfes'sare /**72**/ VT to renounce, disavow;
to repudiate
scon'figgere [skon'fiddʒere] /**104**/ VT to
defeat, overcome
sconfi'nare /**72**/ VI to cross the border; (in
proprietà privata) to trespass; (fig): ~ **da** to stray
o digress from
sconfi'nato, -a AG boundless, unlimited
scon'fitto, -a PP di **sconfiggere** ▸ SF defeat
sconfor'tante, -a AG discouraging,
disheartening
sconfor'tare /**72**/ VT to discourage,
dishearten; **sconfortarsi** VPR to become
discouraged, become disheartened, lose
heart
scon'forto SM despondency
sconge'lare [skondʒe'lare] /**72**/ VT to defrost
scongiu'rare [skondʒu'rare] /**72**/ VT (implorare)
to beseech, entreat, implore; (eludere: pericolo)
to ward off, avert
scongi'uro [skon'dʒuro] SM (esorcismo)
exorcism; **fare gli scongiuri** to touch wood
(BRIT), knock on wood (US)
scon'nesso, -a AG (fig: discorso) incoherent,
rambling
sconosci'uto, -a [skonoʃʃuto] AG unknown;
new, strange ▸ SM/F stranger; unknown
person
sconquas'sare /**72**/ VT to shatter, smash
scon'quasso SM (danno) damage; (fig)
confusion
sconside'rato, -a AG thoughtless, rash
sconsigli'are [skonsiʎ'ʎare] /**27**/ VT: ~ **qc**
a qn to advise sb against sth; ~ **qn dal**
fare qc to advise sb not to do o against
doing sth
sconso'lato, -a AG inconsolable; desolate
scon'tare /**72**/ VT (Comm: detrarre) to deduct;
(: debito) to pay off; (: cambiale) to discount;
(pena) to serve; (colpa, errori) to pay for,
suffer for
scon'tato, -a AG (previsto) foreseen, taken for
granted; (prezzo, merce) discounted, at a
discount; **dare per ~ che** to take it for
granted that
sconten'tare /**72**/ VT to displease, dissatisfy
sconten'tezza [skonten'tettsa] SF
displeasure, dissatisfaction
scon'tento, -a AG: ~ **(di)** discontented o
dissatisfied (with) ▸ SM discontent,
dissatisfaction
'sconto SM discount; **fare** o **concedere uno ~**
to give a discount; **uno ~ del 10%** a 10%
discount
scon'trarsi /**72**/ VPR (treni ecc) to crash, collide;
(venire ad uno scontro: fig) to clash; ~ **con** to
crash into, collide with
scon'trino SM ticket; (di cassa) receipt

'scontro SM (Mil, fig) clash, encounter; (di
veicoli) crash, collision; ~ **a fuoco** shoot-out
scon'troso, -a AG sullen, surly; (permaloso)
touchy
sconveni'ente AG unseemly, improper
sconvol'gente [skonvol'dʒente] AG (notizia,
brutta esperienza) upsetting, disturbing;
(bellezza) amazing; (passione) overwhelming
scon'volgere [skon'vɔldʒere] /**96**/ VT to
throw into confusion, upset; (turbare) to
shake, disturb, upset
scon'volto, -a PP di **sconvolgere** ▸ AG (persona)
distraught, very upset
'scooter ['skuter] SM INV scooter
'scopa SF broom; (Carte) Italian card game
sco'pare /**72**/ VT to sweep; (!) to bonk (!)
sco'pata SF (!) bonk (!)
scoperchi'are [skoper'kjare] /**19**/ VT (pentola,
vaso) to take the lid off, uncover; (casa) to
take the roof off
sco'perto, -a PP di **scoprire** ▸ AG uncovered;
(capo) uncovered, bare; (macchina) open; (Mil)
exposed, without cover; (conto) overdrawn
▸ SF discovery ▸ SM: **allo ~** (dormire ecc) out in
the open; **assegno ~** uncovered cheque;
avere un conto ~ to be overdrawn
'scopo SM aim, purpose; **a che ~?** what for?;
adatto allo ~ fit for its purpose; **allo ~ di**
fare qc in order to do sth; **a ~ di lucro** for
gain o money; **senza ~** (fare, cercare)
pointlessly
scoppi'are /**19**/ VI (spaccarsi) to burst; (esplodere)
to explode; (fig) to break out; ~ **in pianto** o
a piangere to burst out crying; ~ **dalle risa**
o **dal ridere** to split one's sides laughing;
~ **dal caldo** to be boiling; ~ **di salute** to be
the picture of health
scoppiet'tare /**72**/ VI to crackle
'scoppio SM explosion; (di tuono, arma ecc)
crash, bang; (fig: di risa, ira) fit; (di pneumatico)
bang; (fig: di guerra) outbreak; **a ~ ritardato**
delayed-action; **reazione a ~ ritardato**
delayed o slow reaction; **uno ~ di risa** a
burst of laughter; **uno ~ di collera** an
explosion of anger
sco'prire /**9**/ VT to discover; (liberare da ciò che
copre) to uncover; (: monumento) to unveil;
scoprirsi VPR to put on lighter clothes; (fig) to
give o.s. away
scopri'tore, -'trice SM/F discoverer
scoraggi'are [skorad'dʒare] /**62**/ VT to
discourage; **scoraggiarsi** VPR to become
discouraged, lose heart
scor'butico, -a, -ci, -che AG (fig)
cantankerous
scorcia'toia [skortʃa'toja] SF short cut
'scorcio ['skortʃo] SM (Arte) foreshortening;
(di secolo, periodo) end, close; ~ **panoramico**
vista

scor'dare /**72**/ VT to forget; **scordarsi** VPR: **scordarsi di qc/di fare** to forget sth/to do

sco'reggia [sko'reddʒa] (!) SF fart (!)

scoreggi'are [skored'dʒare] /**62**/ (!) VI to fart (!)

'scorgere ['skɔrdʒere] /**59**/ VT to make out, distinguish, see

sco'ria SF (di metalli) slag; (vulcanica) scoria; **scorie radioattive** (Fisica) radioactive waste sg

'scorno SM ignominy, disgrace

scorpacci'ata [skorpat'tʃata] SF: **fare una ~ (di)** to stuff o.s. (with), eat one's fill (of)

scorpi'one SM scorpion; **S~** Scorpio; **essere dello S~** to be Scorpio

'scorporo SM (Pol) transfer of votes aimed at increasing the chances of representation for minority parties

scorraz'zare [skorrat'tsare] /**72**/ VI to run about

'scorrere /**28**/ VT (giornale, lettera) to run o skim through ▶ VI (liquido, fiume) to run, flow; (fune) to run; (cassetto, porta) to slide easily; (tempo) to pass (by)

scorre'ria SF raid, incursion

scorret'tezza [skorret'tettsa] SF incorrectness; lack of politeness, rudeness; unfairness; **commettere una ~** (essere sleale) to be unfair

scor'retto, -a AG (sbagliato) incorrect; (sgarbato) impolite; (sconveniente) improper; (sleale) unfair; (gioco) foul

scor'revole AG (porta) sliding; (fig: stile) fluent, flowing

scorri'banda SF (Mil) raid; (escursione) trip, excursion

'scorsi etc VB vedi **scorgere**

'scorso, -a PP di **scorrere** ▶ AG last ▶ SF quick look, glance; **lo ~ mese** last month

scor'soio, -a AG: **nodo ~** noose

'scorta SF (di personalità, convoglio) escort; (provvista) supply, stock; **sotto la ~ di due agenti** escorted by two policemen; **fare ~ di** to stock up with, get in a supply of; **di ~** (materiali) spare; **ruota di ~** spare wheel

scor'tare /**72**/ VT to escort

scor'tese AG discourteous, rude

scorte'sia SF discourtesy, rudeness; (azione) discourtesy

scorti'care /**20**/ VT to skin

'scorto, -a PP di **scorgere**

'scorza ['skɔrdza] SF (di albero) bark; (di agrumi) peel, skin

sco'sceso, -a [skoʃ'ʃeso] AG steep

'scosso, -a PP di **scuotere** ▶ AG (turbato) shaken, upset ▶ SF jerk, jolt, shake; (Elettr, fig) shock; **prendere la scossa** to get an electric shock; **scossa di terremoto** earth tremor

scos'sone SM: **dare uno ~ a qn** to give sb a shake; **procedere a scossoni** to jolt o jerk along

scos'tante AG (fig) off-putting (BRIT), unpleasant

scos'tare /**72**/ VT to move (away), shift; **scostarsi** VPR to move away

scostu'mato, -a AG immoral, dissolute

scotch [skɔtʃ] SM INV (whisky) Scotch®; (nastro adesivo) Scotch tape®, Sellotape®

scot'tante AG (fig: urgente) pressing; (: delicato) delicate

scot'tare /**72**/ VT (ustionare) to burn; (: con liquido bollente) to scald ▶ VI to burn; (caffè) to be too hot; **scottarsi** VPR to burn/scald o.s.; (fig) to have one's fingers burnt

scotta'tura SF burn; scald

'scotto, -a AG overcooked ▶ SM (fig): **pagare lo ~ (di)** to pay the penalty (for)

sco'vare /**72**/ VT to drive out, flush out; (fig) to discover

'Scozia ['skɔttsja] SF: **la ~** Scotland

scoz'zese [skot'tsese] AG Scottish ▶ SMF Scot

screan'zato, -a [skrean'tsato] AG ill-mannered ▶ SM/F boor

scredi'tare /**72**/ VT to discredit

'screen saver ['skriin'seivər] SM INV (Inform) screen saver

scre'mare /**72**/ VT to skim

scre'mato, -a AG skimmed; **parzialmente ~** semi-skimmed

screpo'lare /**72**/ VT, **screpo'larsi** VPR to crack

screpo'lato, -a AG (labbra) chapped; (muro) cracked

screpola'tura SF cracking no pl; crack

screzi'ato, -a [skret'tsjato] AG streaked

'screzio ['skrettsjo] SM disagreement

scribac'chino [skribak'kino] SM (peg: impiegato) penpusher; (: scrittore) hack

scricchio'lare [skrikkjo'lare] /**72**/ VI to creak, squeak

scricchio'lio [skrikkjo'lio] SM creaking

'scricciolo ['skrittʃolo] SM wren

'scrigno ['skriɲɲo] SM casket

scrimina'tura SF parting

'scrissi etc VB vedi **scrivere**

'scritto, -a PP di **scrivere** ▶ AG written ▶ SM writing; (lettera) letter, note ▶ SF inscription; **scritti** SMPL (letterari ecc) work(s), writings; **per o in ~** in writing

scrit'toio SM writing desk

scrit'tore, -'trice SM/F writer

scrit'tura SF writing; (Comm) entry; (contratto) contract; (Rel): **la Sacra S~** the Scriptures pl; **scritture** SFPL (Comm) accounts, books

scrittu'rare /**72**/ VT (Teat, Cine) to sign up, engage; (Comm) to enter

scriva'nia SF desk

scri'vano SM (*amanuense*) scribe; (*impiegato*) clerk

scri'vente SMF writer

'scrivere /105/ VT to write; **come si scrive?** how is it spelt?, how do you write it?; ~ **qc a qn** to write sth to sb; ~ **qc a macchina** to type sth; ~ **a penna/matita** to write in pen/pencil; ~ **qc maiuscolo/minuscolo** to write sth in capital/small letters

scroc'care /20/ VT (*col*) to scrounge, cadge

scroc'cone, -a SM/F scrounger

'scrofa SF (*Zool*) sow

scrol'lare /72/ VT to shake; **scrollarsi** VPR (*anche fig*) to give o.s. a shake; ~ **le spalle/il capo** to shrug one's shoulders/shake one's head; **scrollarsi qc di dosso** (*anche fig*) to shake sth off

scrol'lata SF shake; ~ **di spalle** shrug (of one's shoulders)

scrosci'ante [skroʃ'ʃante] AG (*pioggia*) pouring; (*fig: applausi*) thunderous

scrosci'are [skroʃ'ʃare] /14/ VI (*pioggia*) to pour down, pelt down; (*torrente, fig: applausi*) to thunder, roar

'scroscio ['skrɔʃʃo] SM pelting; thunder, roar; (*di applausi*) burst

scros'tare /72/ VT (*intonaco*) to scrape off, strip; **scrostarsi** VPR to peel off, flake off

'scrupolo SM scruple; (*meticolosità*) care, conscientiousness; **essere senza scrupoli** to be unscrupulous

scrupo'loso, -a AG scrupulous; conscientious

scru'tare /72/ VT to scrutinize; (*intenzioni, causa*) to examine, scrutinize

scruta'tore, -'trice SM/F (*Pol*) scrutineer

scruti'nare /72/ VT (*voti*) to count

scru'tinio SM (*votazione*) ballot; (*insieme delle operazioni*) poll; (*Ins*) meeting for assignment of marks at end of a term or year

scu'cire [sku'tʃire] /31/ VT (*orlo ecc*) to unpick, undo; **scucirsi** VPR to come unstitched

scude'ria SF stable

scu'detto SM (*Sport*) (championship) shield; (*distintivo*) badge

scu'discio [sku'diʃʃo] SM (riding) crop, (riding) whip

'scudo SM shield; **farsi ~ di** o **con qc** to shield o.s. with sth; ~ **aereo/missilistico** air/missile defence (BRIT) o defense (US); ~ **termico** heat shield

sculacci'are [skulat'tʃare] /14/ VT to spank

sculacci'one [skulat'tʃone] SM spanking

scul'tore, -'trice SM/F sculptor

scul'tura SF sculpture

scu'ola SF school; ~ **elementare** o **primaria** primary (BRIT) o grade (US) school (*for children from 6 to 11 years of age*); ~ **guida** driving school; ~ **materna** o **dell'infanzia** nursery school (*for children aged 3 to 6*); ~ **secondaria di**

primo grado *first 3 years of secondary school, for children from 11 to 14 years of age*; ~ **secondaria di secondo grado** secondary school (*for children aged 14 to 18*); ~ **media** secondary (BRIT) o high (US) school; ~ **dell'obbligo** compulsory education; ~ **privata/pubblica** private/state school; **scuole serali** evening classes, night school *sg*; ~ **tecnica** technical college; *see note*

> Italian children first go to school at the age of three. They remain at the *scuola materna* until they are six, when they move on to the *scuola primaria* for another five years. After this come three years of *scuola secondaria di primo grado*. Students who wish to continue their schooling attend *scuola secondaria di secondo grado*, choosing between several types of institution which specialize in different subject areas.

scu'otere /106/ VT to shake; **scuotersi** VPR to jump, be startled; (*fig: muoversi*) to rouse o.s., stir o.s.; (: *turbarsi*) to be shaken

'scure SF axe, ax (US)

scu'rire /55/ VT to darken, make darker

'scuro, -a AG dark; (*fig: espressione*) grim ▶ SM darkness; dark colour (BRIT) o color (US); (*imposta*) (window) shutter; **verde/rosso** *etc* ~ dark green/red *etc*

scur'rile AG scurrilous

'scusa SF excuse; **scuse** SFPL apology *sg*, apologies; **chiedere** ~ **a qn (per)** to apologize to sb (for); **chiedo** ~ I'm sorry; (*disturbando ecc*) excuse me; **vi prego di accettare le mie scuse** please accept my apologies

scu'sare /72/ VT to excuse; **scusarsi** VPR: **scusarsi (di)** to apologize (for); **(mi) scusi** I'm sorry; (*per richiamare l'attenzione*) excuse me

S.C.V. SIGLA = **Stato della Città del Vaticano**

sdebi'tarsi /72/ VPR: ~ **(con qn di** o **per qc)** (*anche fig*) to repay (sb for sth)

sde'gnare [zdeɲ'ɲare] /15/ VT to scorn, despise; **sdegnarsi** VPR (*adirarsi*) to get angry

sde'gnato, -a [zdeɲ'ɲato] AG indignant, angry

'sdegno ['zdeɲɲo] SM scorn, disdain

sdegnosa'mente [zdeɲɲosa'mente] AV scornfully, disdainfully

sde'gnoso, -a [zdeɲ'ɲoso] AG scornful, disdainful

sdilin'quirsi /55/ VPR (*illanguidirsi*) to become sentimental

sdoga'nare /72/ VT (*Comm*) to clear through customs

sdolci'nato, -a [zdoltʃi'nato] AG mawkish, oversentimental

sdoppia'mento SM (*Chim: di composto*) splitting; (*Psic*): ~ **della personalità** split personality

sdoppi'are /19/ VT (*dividere*) to divide o split in two

sdrai'arsi /19/ VPR to stretch out, lie down

'sdraio SM: **sedia a** ~ deck chair

sdrammatiz'zare [zdrammatid'dzare] /72/ VT to play down, minimize

sdruccio'lare [zdruttʃo'lare] /72/ VI to slip, slide

sdruccio'levole [zdruttʃo'levole] AG slippery

sdru'cito, -a [zdru'tʃito] AG (*strappato*) torn; (*logoro*) threadbare

PAROLA CHIAVE

se PRON *vedi* **si**

▶ CONG **1** (*condizionale, ipotetica*) if; **se nevica non vengo** I won't come if it snows; **se fossi in te** if I were you; **sarei rimasto se me l'avessero chiesto** I would have stayed if they'd asked me; **non puoi fare altro se non telefonare** all you can do is phone; **se mai** if, if ever; **siamo noi se mai che le siamo grati** it is we who should be grateful to you; **se no** (*altrimenti*) or (else), otherwise; **se non** (*anzi*) if not; (*tranne*) except; **se non altro** if nothing else, at least; **se solo** o **solamente** if only

2 (*in frasi dubitative, interrogative indirette*) if, whether; **non so se scrivere o telefonare** I don't know whether o if I should write or phone

sé PRON (*gen*) oneself; (*esso, essa, lui, lei, loro*) itself; himself; herself; themselves; **sé stesso(a)** *pron* oneself; itself; himself; herself; **sé stessi(e)** (*pl*) themselves; **di per sé non è un problema** it's no problem in itself; **parlare tra sé e sé** to talk to oneself; **va da sé che ...** it goes without saying that ..., it's obvious that ..., it stands to reason that ...; **è un caso a sé** o **a sé stante** it's a special case; **un uomo che s'è fatto da sé** a self-made man

S.E. ABBR (= *sud-est*) SE; (= *Sua Eccellenza*) HE

S.E.A.T.O. SIGLA F (= *Southeast Asia Treaty Organization*) SEATO

seb'bene CONG although, though

'sebo SM sebum

sec. ABBR (= *secolo*) c.

'SECAM SIGLA M (= *séquentiel couleur à mémoire*) SECAM

'secca SF *vedi* **secco**

secca'mente AV (*rispondere, rifiutare*) sharply, curtly

sec'care /20/ VT to dry; (*prosciugare*) to dry up; (*fig: importunare*) to annoy, bother ▶ VI to dry; to dry up; **seccarsi** VPR to dry; to dry up; (*fig*) to grow annoyed; **si è seccato molto** he was very annoyed

sec'cato, -a AG (*fig: infastidito*) bothered, annoyed; (: *stufo*) fed up

secca'tore, -'trice SM/F nuisance, bother

secca'tura SF (*fig*) bother *no pl*, trouble *no pl*

seccherò *etc* [sekke'rɔ] VB *vedi* **seccare**

'secchia ['sekkja] SF bucket, pail

secchi'ello [sek'kjɛllo] SM (*per bambini*) bucket, pail; ~ **del ghiaccio** ice bucket

'secchio ['sekkjo] SM bucket, pail; ~ **della spazzatura** o **delle immondizie** dustbin (BRIT), garbage can (US)

'secco, -a, -chi, -che AG dry; (*fichi, pesce*) dried; (*foglie, ramo*) withered; (*magro: persona*) thin, skinny; (*fig: risposta, modo di fare*) curt, abrupt; (: *colpo*) clean, sharp ▶ SM (*siccità*) drought ▶ SF (*del mare*) shallows *pl*; **restarci** ~ (*morire sul colpo*) to drop dead; **avere la gola secca** to feel dry, be parched; **lavare a** ~ to dry-clean; **tirare a** ~ (*barca*) to beach; **rimanere a** ~ (*fig*) to be left in the lurch

secen'tesco, -a, -schi, -sche [setʃen'tesko] AG = **seicentesco**

se'cernere [se'tʃɛrnere] /29/ VT to secrete

seco'lare AG age-old, centuries-old; (*laico, mondano*) secular

'secolo SM century; (*epoca*) age

se'conda SF *vedi* **secondo**; **la S~ Repubblica** *see note*

> Seconda Repubblica is the term used, especially by the Italian media, to refer to the government and the country in general since the 1994 elections. This is when the old party system collapsed, following the *Tangentopoli* scandals. New political parties were set up and the electoral system was reformed, a first-past-the-post element being introduced side by side with proportional representation.

secondaria'mente AV secondly

secon'dario, -a AG secondary; **scuola/ istruzione secondaria** secondary school/ education

secon'dino SM prison officer, warder (BRIT)

se'condo, -a AG second ▶ SM second; (*di pranzo*) main course ▶ SF (*Aut*) second (gear); (*Ferr*) second class ▶ PREP according to; (*nel modo prescritto*) in accordance with; **seconda classe** second-class; **di seconda classe** second-class; **di seconda mano** second-hand; **viaggiare in seconda** to travel second-class; **comandante in seconda** second-in-command; **a seconda di** *prep* according to; in accordance with; ~ **me** in my opinion, to my mind; ~ **la legge/ quanto si era deciso** in accordance with the law/the decision taken

secondo'genito, -a [sekondo'dʒɛnito] SM/F second-born

secrezi'one [sekret'tsjone] SF secretion

'**sedano** SM celery

se'**dare** /**72**/ VT (*dolore*) to soothe; (*rivolta*) to put down, suppress

seda'**tivo, -a** AG, SM sedative

'**sede** SF (*luogo di residenza*) (place of) residence; (*di ditta: principale*) head office; (: *secondaria*) branch (office); (*di organizzazione*) headquarters pl; (*di governo, parlamento*) seat; (*Rel*) see; **in ~ di** (*in occasione di*) during; **in altra ~** on another occasion; **in ~ legislativa** in legislative sitting; **prendere ~** to take up residence; **un'azienda con diverse sedi in città** a firm with several branches in the city; **~ centrale** head office; **~ sociale** registered office

seden'**tario, -a** AG sedentary

se'**dere** /**107**/ VI to sit, be seated; **sedersi** VPR, SM to sit down; (*deretano*) bottom; **posto a ~** seat

'**sedia** SF chair; **~ elettrica** electric chair; **~ a rotelle** wheelchair

sedi'**cenne** [sedi'tʃɛnne] AG, SMF sixteen-year-old

sedi'**cente** [sedi'tʃɛnte] AG self-styled

sedi'**cesimo, -a** [sedi'tʃɛzimo] NUM sixteenth

'**sedici** ['seditʃi] NUM sixteen

se'**dile** SM seat; (*panchina*) bench

sedimen'**tare** /**72**/ VI to leave a sediment

sedi'**mento** SM sediment

sedizi'**one** [sedit'tsjone] SF revolt, rebellion

sedizi'**oso, -a** [sedit'tsjoso] AG seditious

se'**dotto, -a** PP *di* **sedurre**

sedu'**cente** [sedu'tʃɛnte] AG seductive; (*proposta*) very attractive

se'**durre** /**90**/ VT to seduce

se'**duta** SF session, sitting; (*riunione*) meeting; **essere in ~** to be in session, be sitting; **~ stante** (*fig*) immediately; **~ spiritica** seance

sedut'**tore, -'trice** SM/F seducer/seductress

seduzi'**one** [sedut'tsjone] SF seduction; (*fascino*) charm, appeal

SEeO ABBR (= *salvo errori e omissioni*) E & OE

'**sega, -ghe** SF saw; **~ circolare** circular saw; **~ a mano** handsaw

'**segale** SF rye

se'**gare** /**80**/ VT to saw; (*recidere*) to saw off

sega'**tura** SF (*residuo*) sawdust

'**seggio** ['sɛddʒo] SM seat; **~ elettorale** polling station

'**seggiola** ['sɛddʒola] SF chair

seggio'**lino** [seddʒo'lino] SM seat; (*per bambini*) child's chair; **~ di sicurezza** (*Aut*) child safety seat

seggio'**lone** [seddʒo'lone] SM (*per bambini*) highchair

seggio'**via** [seddʒo'via] SF chairlift

seghe'**ria** [sege'ria] SF sawmill

seghe'**rò** etc [sege'rɔ] VB *vedi* **segare**

seghet'**tato, -a** [seget'tato] AG serrated

se'**ghetto** [se'getto] SM hacksaw

seg'**mento** SM segment

segna'**lare** [seɲɲa'lare] /**72**/ VT (*essere segno di*) to indicate, be a sign of; (*avvertire*) to signal; (*menzionare*) to indicate; (: *fatto, risultato, aumento*) to report; (: *errore, dettaglio*) to point out; (: *persona*) to single out; (*Aut*) to signal, indicate; **segnalarsi** VPR (*distinguersi*) to distinguish o.s.; **~ qn a qn** (*per lavoro ecc*) to bring sb to sb's attention

segnalazi'**one** [seɲɲalat'tsjone] SF (*azione*) signalling; (*segnale*) signal; (*annuncio*) report; (*raccomandazione*) recommendation

se'**gnale** [seɲ'ɲale] SM signal; (*cartello*): **~ stradale** road sign; **~ acustico** acoustic o sound signal; (*di segreteria telefonica*) tone; **~ d'allarme** alarm; (*Ferr*) communication cord; **~ di linea libera** (*Tel*) dialling (BRIT) o dial (US) tone; **~ luminoso** light signal; **~ di occupato** (*Tel*) engaged tone (BRIT), busy signal (US); **~ orario** (*Radio*) time signal

segna'**letica** [seɲɲa'lɛtika] SF signalling, signposting; **~ stradale** road signs pl

segna'**libro** [seɲɲa'libro] SM (*anche Inform*) bookmark

segna'**punti** [seɲɲa'punti] SM INV/F INV scorer, scorekeeper

se'**gnare** [seɲ'ɲare] /**15**/ VT to mark; (*prendere nota*) to note; (*indicare*) to indicate, mark; (*Sport: goal*) to score; **segnarsi** VPR (*Rel*) to make the sign of the cross, cross o.s.

'**segno** ['seɲɲo] SM sign; (*impronta, contrassegno*) mark; (*limite*) limit, bounds pl; (*bersaglio*) target; **fare ~ di sì/no** to nod (one's head)/shake one's head; **fare ~ a qn di fermarsi** to motion (to) sb to stop; **cogliere** o **colpire nel ~** (*fig*) to hit the mark; **in** o **come ~ d'amicizia** as a mark o token of friendship; "**segni particolari**" (*su documento ecc*) "distinguishing marks"; **~ zodiacale** star sign

segre'**gare** /**80**/ VT to segregate, isolate

segregazi'**one** [segregat'tsjone] SF segregation

se'**greta** SF *vedi* **segreto**

segre'**tario, -a** SM/F secretary; **~ comunale** town clerk; **~ del partito** party leader; **S~ di Stato** Secretary of State

segrete'**ria** SF (*di ditta, scuola*) (secretary's) office; (*d'organizzazione internazionale*) secretariat; (*Pol ecc: carica*) office of Secretary; **~ telefonica** answering machine

segre'**tezza** [segre'tettsa] SF secrecy; **notizie della massima ~** confidential information; **in tutta ~** in secret; (*confidenzialmente*) in confidence se'greto, -a AG secret ▶ SM secret; secrecy *no pl* ▶ SF dungeon; **in ~** in secret, secretly; **il ~ professionale** professional secrecy; **un ~ professionale** a professional secret

segu'ace [se'gwatʃe] SMF follower, disciple

segu'ente AG following, next; **nel modo ~** as follows, in the following way

se'gugio [se'gudʒo] SM hound, hunting dog; (*fig*) private eye, sleuth

segu'ire /45/ VT to follow; (*frequentare: corso*) to attend ▶ VI to follow; (*continuare: testo*) to continue; **~ i consigli di qn** to follow *o* to take sb's advice; **~ gli avvenimenti di attualità** to follow *o* keep up with current events; **come segue** as follows; **"segue"** "to be continued"

segui'tare /72/ VT to continue, carry on with ▶ VI to continue, carry on

'seguito SM (*scorta*) suite, retinue; (*discepoli*) followers *pl*; (*favore*) following; (*serie*) sequence, series *sg*; (*continuazione*) continuation; (*conseguenza*) result; **di ~** at a stretch, on end; **in ~** later on; **in ~ a, a ~ di** following; (*a causa di*) as a result of, owing to; **essere al ~ di qn** to be among sb's suite, be one of sb's retinue; **non aver ~** (*conseguenze*) to have no repercussions; **facciamo ~ alla lettera del …** further to *o* in answer to your letter of …

'sei VB *vedi* **essere** ▶ NUM six

Sei'celle [sei'tʃɛlle] SFPL: **le ~** the Seychelles

seicen'tesco, -a, -schi, -sche [seitʃen'tesko] AG seventeenth-century

sei'cento [sei'tʃɛnto] NUM six hundred ▶ SM: **il S~** the seventeenth century

sei'mila NUM six thousand

'selce ['seltʃe] SF flint, flintstone

selci'ato [sel'tʃato] SM cobbled surface

selet'tivo, -a AG selective

selet'tore SM (*Tecn*) selector

selezio'nare [selettsjo'nare] /72/ VT to select

selezi'one [selet'tsjone] SF selection; **fare una ~** to make a selection *o* choice

'sella SF saddle

sel'lare /72/ VT to saddle

sel'lino SM saddle

seltz SM INV soda (water)

'selva SF (*bosco*) wood; (*foresta*) forest

selvag'gina [selvad'dʒina] SF (*animali*) game

sel'vaggio, -a, -gi, -ge [sel'vaddʒo] AG wild; (*tribù*) savage, uncivilized; (*fig: brutale*) savage, brutal; (: *incontrollato: fenomeno, aumento ecc*) uncontrolled ▶ SM/F savage; **inflazione selvaggia** runaway inflation

sel'vatico, -a, -ci, -che AG wild

S.Em. ABBR (= *Sua Eminenza*) HE

se'maforo SM (*Aut*) traffic lights *pl*

se'mantico, -a AG semantic ▶ SF semantics *sg*

sembi'anza [sem'bjantsa] SF (*poetico: aspetto*) appearance; **sembianze** SFPL (*fig: lineamenti*) features; (*falsa apparenza*) semblance *sg*

sem'brare /72/ VI to seem ▶ VB IMPERS: **sembra che** it seems that; **mi sembra che** it seems to me that; (*penso che*) I think (that); **~ di essere** to seem to be; **non mi sembra vero!** I can't believe it!

'seme SM seed; (*sperma*) semen; (*Carte*) suit

se'mente SF seed

semes'trale AG (*che dura 6 mesi*) six-month *cpd*; (*che avviene ogni 6 mesi*) six-monthly

se'mestre SM half-year, six-month period

'semi ... PREFISSO semi ...

semi'cerchio [semi'tʃerkjo] SM semicircle

semicondut'tore SM semiconductor

semidetenzi'one [semideten'tsjone] SF *custodial sentence whereby individual must spend a minimum of 10 hours per day in prison*

semifi'nale SF semifinal

semi'freddo, -a AG (*Cuc*) chilled ▶ SM ice-cream dessert

semilibertà SF *custodial sentence which allows prisoner to study or work outside prison for part of the day*

'semina SF (*Agr*) sowing

semi'nare /72/ VT to sow

semi'nario SM seminar; (*Rel*) seminary

semi'nato SM: **uscire dal ~** (*fig*) to wander off the point

seminter'rato SM basement; (*appartamento*) basement flat (BRIT) *o* apartment (US)

semi'ologo, -a, -gi, -ghe SM/F semiologist

semi'otica SF semiotics *sg*

se'mitico, -a, -ci, -che AG semitic

semivu'oto, -a AG half-empty

sem'mai = **se mai**

'semola SF bran; **~ di grano duro** durum wheat

semo'lato AG: **zucchero ~** caster sugar

semo'lino SM semolina

'semplice ['semplitʃe] AG simple; (*di un solo elemento*) single; **è una ~ formalità** it's a mere formality

semplice'mente [semplitʃe'mente] AV simply

sempli'cistico, -a, -ci, -che [sempli'tʃistiko] AG simplistic

semplicità [semplitʃi'ta] SF simplicity

semplifi'care /20/ VT to simplify

semplificazi'one [semplifikat'tsjone] SF simplification; **fare una ~ di** to simplify

'sempre AV always; (*ancora*) still; **posso ~ tentare** I can always *o* still try; **da ~** always; **per ~** forever; **una volta per ~** once and for all; **~ che** *cong* as long as, provided (that); **~ più** more and more; **~ meno** less and less; **va ~ meglio** things are getting better and better; **è ~ più giovane** she gets younger and younger; **è ~ meglio che niente** it's better than nothing; **è (pur) ~ tuo fratello** he is still your brother (however); **c'è ~ la possibilità che ...** there's still a chance that ..., there's always the possibility that ...

sempre'verde AG, SM O F (*Bot*) evergreen

Sen. ABBR (= *senatore*) Sen.

'senape SF (*Cuc*) mustard

se'nato SM senate; **il S~** *see note*

> The *Senato* is the upper house of the Italian parliament, with similar functions to the *Camera dei deputati*. Candidates must be at least 40 years of age and electors must be 25 or over. Elections are held every five years. Former heads of state become senators for life, as do five distinguished members of the public who are chosen by the head of state for their scientific, social, artistic or literary achievements. the chamber is presided over by the *Presidente del Senato*, who is elected by the senators.

sena'tore, -'trice SM/F senator

'Senegal SM: **il ~** Senegal

senega'lese AG, SMF Senegalese *inv*

se'nese AG of (*o* from) Siena

se'nile AG senile

'Senna SF: **la ~** the Seine

'senno SM judgment, (common) sense; **col ~ di poi** with hindsight

sennò AV = **se no**

'seno SM (*Anat: petto, mammella*) breast; (: *grembo, anche fig*) womb; (: *cavità*) sinus; (*Geo*) inlet, creek; (*Mat*) sine; **in ~ al partito/all'organizzazione** within the party/the organization

sen'sale SM (*Comm*) agent

sensa'tezza [sensa'tettsa] SF good sense, good judgment

sen'sato, -a AG sensible

sensazio'nale [sensattsjo'nale] AG sensational

sensazi'one [sensat'tsjone] SF feeling, sensation; **fare ~** to cause a sensation, create a stir; **avere la ~ che** to have a feeling that

sen'sibile AG sensitive; (*ai sensi*) perceptible; (*rilevante, notevole*) appreciable, noticeable; **~ a** sensitive to

sensibilità SF sensitivity

sensibiliz'zare [sensibilid'dzare] /72/ VT (*fig*) to make aware, awaken

'senso SM (*Fisiol, istinto*) sense; (*impressione, sensazione*) feeling, sensation; (*significato*) meaning, sense; (*direzione*) direction; **sensi** SMPL (*coscienza*) consciousness *sg*; (*sensualità*) senses; **perdere/riprendere i sensi** to lose/regain consciousness; **avere ~ pratico** to be practical; **avere un sesto ~** to have a sixth sense; **fare ~ a** (*ripugnare*) to disgust, repel;

ciò non ha ~ that doesn't make sense; **senza** *o* **privo di ~** meaningless; **nel ~ che** in the sense that; **nel vero ~ della parola** in the true sense of the word; **nel ~ della lunghezza** lengthwise, lengthways; **nel ~ della larghezza** widthwise; **ho dato disposizioni in quel ~** I've given instructions to that end *o* effect; **~ comune** common sense; **~ del dovere** sense of duty; **in ~ opposto** in the opposite direction; **in ~ orario/antiorario** clockwise/anticlockwise; **~ dell'umorismo** sense of humour; **~ di colpa** sense of guilt; **a ~ unico** one-way; **"~ vietato"** (*Aut*) "no entry"

sensu'ale AG sensual; sensuous

sensualità SF sensuality; sensuousness

sen'tenza [sen'tentsa] SF (*Dir*) sentence; (*massima*) maxim

sentenzi'are [senten'tsjare] /19/ VI (*Dir*) to pass judgment

senti'ero SM path

sentimen'tale AG sentimental; (*vita, avventura*) love *cpd*

senti'mento SM feeling

senti'nella SF sentry

sen'tire /45/ VT (*percepire al tatto, fig*) to feel; (*udire*) to hear; (*ascoltare*) to listen to; (*odore*) to smell; (*avvertire con il gusto, assaggiare*) to taste ▶ VI: **~ di** (*avere sapore*) to taste of; (*avere odore*) to smell of; **sentirsi** VPR (*uso reciproco*) to be in touch; **sentirsi bene/male** to feel well/unwell *o* ill; **sentirsi di fare qc** (*essere disposto*) to feel like doing sth; **~ la mancanza di qn** to miss sb; **ho sentito dire che ...** I have heard that ...; **a ~ lui ...** to hear him talk ...; **fatti ~** keep in touch; **intendo ~ il mio legale/il parere di un medico** I'm going to consult my lawyer/a doctor

sentita'mente AV sincerely; **ringraziare ~** to thank sincerely

sen'tito, -a AG (*sincero*) sincere, warm; **per ~ dire** by hearsay

sen'tore SM rumour (*BRIT*), rumor (*US*), talk; **aver ~ di qc** to hear about sth

'senza ['sentsa] PREP, CONG without; **~ dir nulla** without saying a word; **~ dire che ...** not to mention the fact that ...; **~ contare che ...** without considering that ...; **fare ~ qc** to do without sth; **~ di me** without me; **~ che io lo sapessi** without me *o* my knowing; **~ amici** friendless; **senz'altro** of course, certainly; **~ dubbio** no doubt; **~ scrupoli** unscrupulous; **i ~ lavoro** the jobless, the unemployed; **i ~ tetto** the homeless

senza'tetto [sentsa'tetto] SM INV/F INV homeless person; **i ~** the homeless

sepa'rare /72/ VT to separate; (*dividere*) to divide; (*tenere distinto*) to distinguish;

separarsi VPR (coniugi) to separate, part; (amici) to part, leave each other; **separarsi da** (coniuge) to separate o part from; (amico, socio) to part company with; (oggetto) to part with

separata'mente AV separately

sepa'rato, -a AG (letti, conto ecc) separate; (coniugi) separated

separazi'one [separat'tsjone] SF separation; **~ dei beni** division of property

séparé [sepa're] SM INV screen

se'polcro SM sepulchre (BRIT), sepulcher (US)

se'polto, -a PP di **seppellire**

sepol'tura SF burial; **dare ~ a qn** to bury sb

seppel'lire /55/ VT to bury

'seppi etc VB vedi **sapere**

'seppia SF cuttlefish ▶ AG INV sepia

sep'pure CONG even if

se'quela SF (di avvenimenti) series, sequence; (di offese, ingiurie) string

se'quenza [se'kwentsa] SF sequence

sequenzi'ale [sekwen'tsjale] AG sequential

seques'trare /72/ VT (Dir) to impound; (rapire) to kidnap; (costringere in un luogo) to keep, confine

se'questro SM (Dir) impoundment; **~ di persona** kidnapping

se'quoia SF sequoia

'sera SF evening; **di ~** in the evening; **domani ~** tomorrow evening, tomorrow night; **questa ~** this evening, tonight

se'rale AG evening cpd; **scuola ~** evening classes pl, night school

se'rata SF evening; (ricevimento) party

ser'bare /72/ VT to keep; (mettere da parte) to put aside; **~ rancore/odio verso qn** to bear sb a grudge/hate sb

serba'toio SM tank; (cisterna) cistern

'Serbia SF: **la ~** Serbia

'serbo, -a AG Serbian ▶ SM/F Serbian, Serb ▶ SM (Ling) Serbian; (il serbare): **mettere/ tenere** o **avere in ~ qc** to put/keep sth aside

serbocro'ato, -a AG, SM Serbo-Croat

serena'mente AV serenely, calmly

sere'nata SF (Mus) serenade

serenità SF serenity

se'reno, -a AG (tempo, cielo) clear; (fig) serene, calm ▶ SM (tempo) good weather; **un fulmine a ciel ~** (fig) a bolt from the blue

serg. ABBR (= sergente) Sgt.

ser'gente [ser'dʒɛnte] SM (Mil) sergeant

seri'ale AG (Inform) serial

seria'mente AV (con serietà, in modo grave) seriously; **lavorare ~** to take one's job seriously

'serie SF INV (successione) series inv; (gruppo, collezione di chiavi ecc) set; (Sport) division; league; (Comm): **modello di ~/fuori ~** standard/custom-built model; **in ~** in

quick succession; (Comm) mass cpd; **tutta una ~ di problemi** a whole string o series of problems

serietà SF seriousness; reliability

'serio, -a AG serious; (impiegato) responsible, reliable; (ditta, cliente) reliable, dependable; **sul ~** (davvero) really, truly; (seriamente) seriously, in earnest; **dico sul ~** I'm serious; **faccio sul ~** I mean it; **prendere qc/qn sul ~** to take sth/sb, seriously

seri'oso, -a AG (persona, modi): **un po' ~** a bit too serious

ser'mone SM sermon

'serpe SF snake; (fig: peg) viper

serpeggi'are [serped'dʒare] /62/ VI to wind; (fig) to spread

ser'pente SM snake; **~ a sonagli** rattlesnake

'serra SF greenhouse; hothouse; (Geo) sierra

serra'manico SM: **coltello a ~** jack-knife

ser'randa SF roller shutter

ser'rare /72/ VT to close, shut; (a chiave) to lock; (stringere) to tighten; (premere: nemico) to close in on; **~ i pugni/i denti** to clench one's fists/teeth; **~ le file** to close ranks

ser'rata SF (Industria) lockout

ser'rato, -a AG (veloce): **a ritmo ~** quickly, fast

serra'tura SF lock

'serva SF vedi **servo**

'server ['server] SM INV (Inform) server

ser'vigio [ser'vidʒo] SM favour (BRIT), favor (US), service

ser'vire /45/ VT to serve; (clienti: al ristorante) to wait on; (: al negozio) to serve, attend to; (fig: giovare) to aid, help; (Carte) to deal ▶ VI (Tennis) to serve; (essere utile): **~ a qn** to be of use to sb; **servirsi** VPR (usare): **servirsi di** to use; (prendere: cibo): **servirsi (di)** to help o.s. (to); (essere cliente abituale): **servirsi da** to be a regular customer at, go to; **non mi serve più** I don't need it any more; **non serve che lei vada** you don't need to go; **~ a qc/ a fare** (utensile ecc) to be used for sth/for doing; **~ (a qn) da** to serve as (for sb); **serviti pure!** help yourself!

servitù SF servitude; slavery; (personale di servizio) servants pl, domestic staff

servizi'evole [servit'tsjevole] AG obliging, willing to help

ser'vizio [ser'vittsjo] SM service; (al ristorante: sul conto) service (charge); (Stampa, TV, Radio) report; (da tè, caffè ecc) set, service; **servizi** SMPL (di casa) kitchen and bathroom; (Econ) services; **essere di ~** to be on duty; **fuori ~** (telefono ecc) out of order; **~ compreso/ escluso** service included/not included; **entrata di ~** service o tradesman's (BRIT) entrance; **casa con doppi servizi** house with two bathrooms; **~ assistenza clienti** customer service; **~ civile** ≈ community

S

service; **~ in diretta** (TV, Radio) live coverage; **~ fotografico** (Stampa) photo feature; **~ di posate** set of cutlery; **~ militare** military service; **~ d'ordine** (Polizia) police patrol; (di manifestanti) team of stewards (responsible for crowd control); **servizi segreti** secret service sg; **servizi di sicurezza** security forces

'servo, -a SM/F servant

servo'freno SM (Aut) servo brake

servos'terzo [servos'tɛrtso] SM (Aut) power steering

'sesamo SM (Bot) sesame

ses'santa NUM sixty

sessan'tenne AG, SMF sixty-year-old

sessan'tesimo, -a NUM sixtieth

sessan'tina SF: **una ~ (di)** about sixty

sessantot'tino, -a SM/F a person who took part in the events of 1968

sessan'totto SM see note

> Sessantotto refers to the year 1968, the year of student protests. Originating in France, unrest soon spread to other industrialized countries including Italy. What began as a purely student concern gradually came to include other parts of society and led to major political and social change. Among the changes that resulted from the protests were reform of schools and universities and the referendum on divorce.

sessi'one SF session

'sesso SM sex; **il ~ debole/forte** the weaker/stronger sex

sessu'ale AG sexual, sex cpd

sessualità SF sexuality

sessu'ologo, -a, -gi, -ghe SM/F sexologist, sex specialist

ses'tante SM sextant

'sesto, -a NUM sixth ▶ SM: **rimettere in ~** (aggiustare) to put back in order; (fig: persona) to put back on his (o her) feet; **rimettersi in ~** (riprendersi) to recover, get well; (riassettarsi) to tidy o.s. up

'seta SF silk

setacci'are [setat'tʃare] /14/ VT to sift, sieve; (fig: zona) to search, comb

se'taccio [se'tattʃo] SM sieve; **passare al ~** (fig) to search, comb

'sete SF thirst; **avere ~** to be thirsty; **~ di potere** thirst for power

seti'ficio [seti'fitʃo] SM silk factory

'setola SF bristle

sett. ABBR (= settembre) Sept.

'setta SF sect

set'tanta NUM seventy

settan'tenne AG, SMF seventy-year-old

settan'tesimo, -a NUM seventieth

settan'tina SF: **una ~ (di)** about seventy

set'tare /72/ VT (Inform) to set up

'sette NUM seven

settecen'tesco, -a, -schi, -sche [settetʃen'tesko] AG eighteenth-century

sette'cento [sette'tʃento] NUM seven hundred ▶ SM: **il S~** the eighteenth century

set'tembre SM September; vedi anche **luglio**

sette'mila NUM seven thousand

settentrio'nale AG northern ▶ SMF northerner

settentri'one SM north

'settico, -a, -ci, -che AG (Med) septic

setti'mana SF week; **la ~ scorsa/prossima** last/next week; **a metà ~** in the middle of the week; **~ bianca** winter-sport holiday

> Settimana bianca is the name given to a week-long winter-sports holiday taken by many Italians some time in the skiing season.

settima'nale AG, SM weekly

'settimo, -a NUM seventh

set'tore SM sector; **~ privato/pubblico** private/public sector; **~ terziario** service industries pl

Se'ul SF Seoul

severità SF severity

se'vero, -a AG severe

sevizi'are [sevit'tsjare] /19/ VT to torture

se'vizie [se'vittsje] SFPL torture sg

'sexy ['seksi] AG INV sexy

sez. ABBR = **sezione**

sezio'nare [settsjo'nare] /72/ VT to divide into sections; (Med) to dissect

sezi'one [set'tsjone] SF section; (Med) dissection

sfaccen'dato, -a [sfattʃen'dato] AG idle

sfacceta'tura [sfattʃetta'tura] SF (azione) faceting; (parte sfaccettata, fig) facet

sfacchi'nare [sfakki'nare] /72/ VI (col) to toil, drudge

sfacchi'nata [sfakki'nata] SF (col) chore, drudgery no pl

sfaccia'taggine [sfattʃa'taddʒine] SF insolence, cheek

sfacci'ato, -a [sfat'tʃato] AG (maleducato) cheeky, impudent; (vistoso) gaudy

sfa'celo [sfa'tʃɛlo] SM (fig) ruin, collapse

sfal'darsi /72/ VPR to flake (off)

sfal'sare /72/ VT to offset

sfa'mare /72/ VT (nutrire) to feed; (cibo) to fill; (soddisfare la fame): **~ qn** to satisfy sb's hunger; **sfamarsi** VPR to satisfy one's hunger, fill o.s. up

sfarfal'lio SM (Cine, TV) flickering

'sfarzo ['sfartso] SM pomp, splendour (BRIT), splendor (US)

sfar'zoso, -a [sfar'tsoso] AG splendid, magnificent

sfasa'mento SM (Elettr) phase displacement; (fig) confusion, bewilderment

sfa'sato, -a AG (*Elettr, motore*) out of phase; (*fig: persona*) confused, bewildered

sfasci'are [sfaʃʃare] /**14**/ VT (*ferita*) to unbandage; (*distruggere: porta*) to smash, shatter; **sfasciarsi** VPR (*rompersi*) to smash, shatter

sfa'tare /**72**/ VT (*leggenda*) to explode

sfati'cato, -a SM/F idler, loafer

'sfatto, -a AG (*letto*) unmade; (*orlo ecc*) undone; (*gelato, neve*) melted; (*frutta*) overripe; (*riso, pasta ecc*) overdone, overcooked; (*col: persona, corpo*) flabby

sfavil'lare /**72**/ VI to spark, send out sparks; (*risplendere*) to sparkle

sfa'vore SM disfavour (BRIT), disfavor (US), disapproval

sfavo'revole AG unfavourable (BRIT), unfavorable (US)

sfega'tato, -a AG fanatical

'sfera SF sphere

'sferico, -a, -ci, -che AG spherical

sfer'rare /**72**/ VT (*fig: colpo*) to land, deal; (: *attacco*) to launch

sfer'zante [sfer'tsante] AG (*critiche, parole*) stinging

sfer'zare [sfer'tsare] /**72**/ VT to whip; (*fig*) to lash out at

sfian'care /**20**/ VT to wear out, exhaust; **sfiancarsi** VPR to exhaust o.s., wear o.s. out

sfia'tare /**72**/ VI to allow air (*o gas etc*) to escape

sfiata'toio SM blowhole; (*Tecn*) vent

sfi'brante AG exhausting, energy-sapping

sfi'brare /**72**/ VT (*indebolire*) to exhaust, enervate

sfi'brato, -a AG exhausted, worn out

'sfida SF challenge

sfi'dante AG challenging ▶ SMF challenger

sfi'dare /**72**/ VT to challenge; (*fig*) to defy, brave; **~ qn a fare qc** to challenge sb to do sth; **~ un pericolo** to brave a danger; **sfido che ...** I dare say (that) ...

sfi'ducia [sfi'dutʃa] SF distrust, mistrust; **avere ~ in qn/qc** to distrust sb/sth

sfiduci'ato, -a [sfidu'tʃato] AG lacking confidence

sfi'gato, -a (*col*) AG: **essere ~** (*sfortunato*) to be unlucky ▶ SM/F (*fallito, sfortunato*) loser; (*fuori moda*) dork

sfigu'rare /**72**/ VT (*persona*) to disfigure; (*quadro, statua*) to deface ▶ VI (*far cattiva figura*) to make a bad impression

sfilacci'are [sfilat'tʃare] /**14**/ VT, VI, **sfilacci'arsi** VPR to fray

sfi'lare /**72**/ VT (*ago*) to unthread; (*abito, scarpe*) to slip off ▶ VI (*truppe*) to march past, parade; (*atleti*) to parade; (*manifestanti*) to march; **sfilarsi** VPR (*perle ecc*) to come unstrung; (*orlo, tessuto*) to fray; (*calza*) to run, ladder

sfi'lata SF (*Mil*) parade; (*di manifestanti*) march; **~ di moda** fashion show

'sfilza ['sfiltsa] SF (*di case*) row; (*di errori*) series *inv*

'sfinge ['sfindʒe] SF sphinx

sfini'mento SM exhaustion

sfi'nito, -a AG exhausted

sfio'rare /**72**/ VT to brush (against); (*argomento*) to touch upon; **~ la velocità di 150 km/h** to touch 150 km/h

sfio'rire /**55**/ VI to wither, fade

'sfitto, -a AG vacant, empty

sfo'cato, -a AG (*Fot*) out of focus

sfoci'are [sfo'tʃare] /**14**/ VI: **~ in** to flow into; (*fig: malcontento*) to develop into

sfode'rato, -a AG (*vestito*) unlined

sfo'gare /**80**/ VT to vent, pour out; **sfogarsi** VPR (*sfogare la propria rabbia*) to give vent to one's anger; (*confidarsi*) **sfogarsi (con)** to pour out one's feelings (to); **non sfogarti su di me!** don't take your bad temper out on me!

sfoggi'are [sfod'dʒare] /**62**/ VT, VI to show off

'sfoggio ['sfoddʒo] SM show, display; **fare ~ di** to show off, display

sfogherò *etc* [sfoge'rɔ] VB *vedi* **sfogare**

'sfoglia ['sfoʎʎa] SF sheet of pasta dough; **pasta ~** (*Cuc*) puff pastry

sfogli'are [sfoʎ'ʎare] /**27**/ VT (*libro*) to leaf through

'sfogo, -ghi SM outlet; (*eruzione cutanea*) rash; (*fig*) outburst; **dare ~ a** (*fig*) to give vent to

sfolgo'rante AG (*luce*) blazing; (*fig: vittoria*) brilliant

sfolgo'rare /**72**/ VI to blaze

sfolla'gente [sfolla'dʒɛnte] SM INV truncheon (BRIT), billy (US)

sfol'lare /**72**/ VT to empty, clear ▶ VI to disperse; **~ da** (*città*) to evacuate

sfol'lato, -a AG evacuated ▶ SM/F evacuee

sfol'tire /**55**/ VT, **sfol'tirsi** VPR to thin (out)

sfon'dare /**72**/ VT (*porta*) to break down; (*scarpe*) to wear a hole in; (*cesto, scatola*) to burst, knock the bottom out of; (*Mil*) to break through ▶ VI (*riuscire*) to make a name for o.s.

sfon'dato, -a AG (*scarpe*) worn out; (*scatola*) burst; (*sedia*) broken, damaged; **essere ricco ~** to be rolling in it

'sfondo SM background

sfo'rare /**72**/ VI to overrun

sfor'mare /**72**/ VT to put out of shape, knock out of shape; **sformarsi** VPR to lose shape, get out of shape

sfor'mato, -a AG (*che ha perso forma*) shapeless ▶ SM (*Cuc*) type of soufflé

sfor'nare /**72**/ VT (*pane*) to take out of the oven; (*fig*) to churn out

sfor'nito, -a AG: ~ **di** lacking in, without; (*negozio*) out of

sfor'tuna SF misfortune, ill luck *no pl*; **avere** ~ to be unlucky; **che** ~! how unfortunate!

sfortu'nato, -a AG unlucky; (*impresa, film*) unsuccessful

sfor'zare [sfor'tsare] /**72**/ VT to force; (*voce, occhi*) to strain; **sforzarsi** VPR: **sforzarsi di** o **a** o **per fare** to try hard to do

'sforzo ['sfɔrtso] SM effort; (*tensione eccessiva, Tecn*) strain; **fare uno** ~ to make an effort; **essere sotto** ~ (*motore, macchina, fig: persona*) to be under stress

'sfottere /**1**/ VT (*col*) to tease

sfracel'lare [sfratʃel'lare] /**72**/ VT, **sfracel'larsi** VPR to smash

sfrat'tare /**72**/ VT to evict

'sfratto SM eviction; **dare lo** ~ **a qn** to give sb notice to quit

sfrecci'are [sfret'tʃare] /**14**/ VI to shoot o flash past

sfre'gare /**80**/ VT (*strofinare*) to rub; (*graffiare*) to scratch; **sfregarsi le mani** to rub one's hands; ~ **un fiammifero** to strike a match

sfregi'are [sfre'dʒare] /**62**/ VT to slash, gash; (*persona*) to disfigure; (*quadro*) to deface

'sfregio ['sfredʒo] SM gash; scar; (*fig*) insult

sfre'nato, -a AG (*fig*) unrestrained, unbridled

sfron'dare /**72**/ VT (*albero*) to prune, thin out; (*fig: discorso, scritto*) to prune (down)

sfronta'tezza [sfronta'tettsa] SF impudence, cheek

sfron'tato, -a AG impudent, cheeky; shameless

sfrutta'mento SM exploitation

sfrut'tare /**72**/ VT (*terreno*) to overwork, exhaust; (*miniera*) to exploit, work; (*fig: operai, occasione, potere*) to exploit

sfrutta'tore, -'trice SM/F exploiter

sfug'gente [sfud'dʒɛnte] AG (*fig: sguardo*) elusive; (*mento*) receding

sfug'gire [sfud'dʒire] /**31**/ VI to escape; ~ **a** (*custode*) to escape (from); (*morte*) to escape; ~ **a qn** (*dettaglio, nome*) to escape sb; ~ **di mano a qn** to slip out of sb's hand (o hands); **lasciarsi** ~ **un'occasione** to let an opportunity go by; ~ **al controllo** (*macchina*) to go out of control; (*situazione*) to be no longer under control

sfug'gita [sfud'dʒita] SF: **di** ~ (*rapidamente, in fretta*) in passing

sfu'mare /**72**/ VT (*colori, contorni*) to soften, shade off ▶ VI to shade (off), fade; (*fig: svanire*) to vanish, disappear; (: *speranze*) to come to nothing

sfuma'tura SF shading off *no pl*; (*tonalità*) shade, tone; (*fig*) touch, hint

sfuo'cato, -a AG = **sfocato**

sfuri'ata SF (*scatto di collera*) fit of anger; (*rimprovero*) sharp rebuke

'sfuso, -a AG (*caramelle ecc*) loose, unpacked; (*vino*) unbottled; (*birra*) draught (BRIT), draft (US)

sg. ABBR = **seguente**

sga'bello SM stool

sgabuz'zino [zgabud'dzino] SM lumber room

sgambet'tare /**72**/ VI to kick one's legs about

sgam'betto SM: **far lo** ~ **a qn** to trip sb up; (*fig*) to oust sb

sganasci'arsi [zganaʃ'ʃarsi] /**14**/ VPR: ~ **dalle risa** to roar with laughter

sganci'are [zgan'tʃare] /**14**/ VT to unhook; (*chiusura*) to unfasten, undo; (*Ferr*) to uncouple; (*bombe: da aereo*) to release, drop; (*fig: col: soldi*) to fork out; **sganciarsi** VPR to come unhooked; to come unfastened, come undone; to uncouple; (*fig*) **sganciarsi (da)** to get away (from)

sganghe'rato, -a [zgange'rato] AG (*porta*) off its hinges; (*auto*) ramshackle; (*riso*) wild, boisterous

sgar'bato, -a AG rude, impolite

'sgarbo SM: **fare uno** ~ **a qn** to be rude to sb

sgargi'ante [zgar'dʒante] AG gaudy, showy

sgar'rare /**72**/ VI (*persona*) to step out of line; (*orologio: essere avanti*) to gain; (: *essere indietro*) to lose

'sgarro SM inaccuracy

sgattaio'lare /**72**/ VI to sneak away o off

sge'lare [zdʒe'lare] /**72**/ VI, VT to thaw

'sghembo, -a ['zgembo] AG (*obliquo*) slanting; (*storto*) crooked

sghignaz'zare [zgiɲɲat'tsare] /**72**/ VI to laugh scornfully

sghignaz'zata [zgiɲɲat'tsata] SF scornful laugh

sgob'bare /**72**/ VI (*col: scolaro*) to swot; (: *operaio*) to slog

sgoccio'lare [zgottʃo'lare] /**72**/ VT (*vuotare*) to drain (to the last drop) ▶ VI (*acqua*) to drip; (*recipiente*) to drain

'sgoccioli ['zgottʃoli] SMPL: **essere agli** ~ (*lavoro, provviste ecc*) to be nearly finished; (*periodo*) to be nearly over; **siamo agli** ~ we've nearly finished, the end is in sight

sgo'larsi /**72**/ VPR to talk (o shout o sing) o.s. hoarse

sgombe'rare /**72**/, **sgomb'rare** VT (*tavolo, stanza*) to clear; (*andarsene da: stanza*) to vacate; (*evacuare: piazza, città*) to evacuate ▶ VI to move

'sgombero SM *vedi* **sgombro**

'sgombro, -a AG: ~ **(di)** clear (of), free (from) ▶ SM (*Zool*) mackerel; (*anche*: **sgombero**) clearing; vacating; evacuation; (*trasloco*) removal

sgomen'tare /**72**/ VT to dismay; **sgomentarsi** VPR to be dismayed

sgo'mento, -a AG dismayed ▶ SM dismay, consternation

sgomi'nare /**72**/ VT (*nemico*) to rout; (*avversario*) to defeat; (*fig: epidemia*) to overcome

sgonfi'are /**19**/ VT to let down, deflate; **sgonfiarsi** VPR to go down

'sgonfio, -a AG (*pneumatico, pallone*) flat

'sgorbio SM blot; scribble

sgor'gare /**80**/ VI to gush (out)

sgoz'zare [zgot'tsare] /**72**/ VT to cut the throat of

sgra'devole AG unpleasant, disagreeable

sgra'dito, -a AG unpleasant, unwelcome

sgraffi'gnare [zgraffiɲ'ɲare] /**15**/ VT (*col*) to pinch, swipe

sgrammati'cato, -a AG ungrammatical

sgra'nare /**72**/ VT (*piselli*) to shell; **~ gli occhi** to open one's eyes wide

gran'chirsi [zgran'kire] /**55**/ VT (*anche*: **sgranchirsi**) to stretch; **~ le gambe** to stretch one's legs

sgranocchi'are [zgranok'kjare] /**19**/ VT to munch

sgras'sare /**72**/ VT to remove the grease from

'sgravio SM: **~ fiscale** *o* **contributivo** tax relief

sgrazi'ato, -a [zgrat'tsjato] AG clumsy, ungainly

sgreto'lare /**72**/ VT to cause to crumble; **sgretolarsi** VPR to crumble

sgri'dare /**72**/ VT to scold

sgri'data SF scolding

sguai'ato, -a AG coarse, vulgar

sguai'nare /**72**/ VT to draw, unsheathe

sgual'cire [zgwal'tʃire] /**55**/ VT to crumple (up), crease

sgual'drina SF (*peg*) slut

sgu'ardo SM (*occhiata*) look, glance; (*espressione*) look (in one's eyes); **dare uno ~ a qc** to glance at sth, cast a glance *o* an eye over sth; **alzare** *o* **sollevare lo ~** to raise one's eyes, look up; **cercare qc/qn con lo ~** to look around for sth/sb

'sguattero, -a SM/F scullery boy(-maid)

sguaz'zare [zgwat'tsare] /**72**/ VI (*nell'acqua*) to splash about; (*nella melma*) to wallow; **~ nell'oro** to be rolling in money

sguinzagli'are [zgwintsaʎ'ʎare] /**27**/ VT to let off the leash; (*fig: persona*): **~ qn dietro a qn** to set sb on sb

sgusci'are [zguʃʃare] /**14**/ VT to shell ▶ VI (*sfuggire di mano*) to slip; **~ via** to slip *o* slink away

'shaker ['ʃeikəʳ] SM INV (cocktail) shaker

'shampoo ['ʃampo] SM INV shampoo

'shiatsu ['tʃiatsu] SM INV, AG INV shiatsu

shoc'care [ʃok'kare] /**20**/ VT = **shockare**

shock [ʃɔk] SM INV shock

shoc'kare [ʃok'kare] /**72**/ VT to shock

SI SIGLA = **Siena**

(PAROLA CHIAVE)

si (*dav lo, la, li, le, ne diventa* **se**) PRON **1** (*riflessivo: maschile*) himself; (: *femminile*) herself; (: *neutro*) itself; (: *impersonale*) oneself; *pl* themselves; **lavarsi** to wash (oneself); **si è tagliato** he has cut himself; **si credono importanti** they think a lot of themselves **2** (*riflessivo: con complemento oggetto*): **lavarsi le mani** to wash one's hands; **sporcarsi i pantaloni** to get one's trousers dirty; **si sta lavando i capelli** he (*o* she) is washing his (*o* her) hair

3 (*reciproco*) one another, each other; **si amano** they love one another *o* each other

4 (*passivo*): **si ripara facilmente** it is easily repaired; **affittasi camera** room to let

5 (*impersonale*): **si dice che ...** they *o* people say that ...; **si vede che è vecchio** one *o* you can see that it's old; **non si fa credito** we do not give credit; **ci si sbaglia facilmente** it's easy to make a mistake

6 (*noi*) we; **tra poco si parte** we're leaving soon

sì AV yes ▶ SM: **non mi aspettavo un sì** I didn't expect him (*o* her *etc*) to say yes; **per me è sì** I should think so, I expect so; **saranno stati sì e no in 20** there must have been about 20 of them; **uno sì e uno no** every other one; **un giorno sì e uno no** every other day; **dire di sì** to say yes; **spero/penso di sì** I hope/think so; **fece di sì col capo** he nodded (his head); **e sì che ...** and to think that ...

'sia¹ CONG: **~ ... ~**: (*o ... o*) **~ che lavori, ~ che non lavori** whether he works or not; (*tanto ... quanto*) **verranno ~ Luigi ~ suo fratello** both Luigi and his brother will be coming

'sia² *etc* VB *vedi* **essere**

SIAE SIGLA F = **Società Italiana Autori ed Editori**

Si'am SM: **il ~** Siam

sia'mese AG, SM/F siamese *inv*

si'amo VB *vedi* **essere**

Si'beria SF: **la ~** Siberia

siberi'ano, -a AG, SM/F Siberian

sibi'lare /**72**/ VI to hiss; (*fischiare*) to whistle

'sibilo SM hiss; whistle

si'cario SM hired killer

sicché [sik'ke] CONG (*perciò*) so (that), therefore; (*e quindi*) (and) so

siccità [sittʃi'ta] SF drought

sic'come CONG since, as

Si'cilia [si'tʃilja] SF: **la ~** Sicily

sicili'ano, -a [sitʃi'ljano] AG, SM/F Sicilian

sico'moro SM sycamore

'siculo, -a AG, SM/F Sicilian

si'cura SF (*di arma, spilla*) safety catch; (*Aut: di portiera*) safety lock

sicura'mente AV certainly

sicu'rezza [siku'rettsa] SF safety; security; confidence; certainty; **di** ~ safety *cpd*; **la** ~ **stradale** road safety; **avere la** ~ **di qc** to be sure *o* certain of sth; **lo so con** ~ I am quite certain; **ha risposto con molta** ~ he answered very confidently; ~ **informatica** cybersecurity

si'curo, -a AG safe; (*ben difeso*) secure; (*fiducioso*) confident; (*certo*) sure, certain; (*notizia, amico*) reliable; (*esperto*) skilled ▶ AV (*anche*: **di sicuro**) certainly ▶ SM: **andare sul** ~ to play safe; **essere/mettere al** ~ to be safe/put in a safe place; ~ **di sé** self-confident, sure of o.s.; **sentirsi** ~ to feel safe *o* secure; **essere** ~ **di/che** to be sure of/that; **da fonte sicura** from reliable sources

siderur'gia [siderur'dʒia] SF iron and steel industry

side'rurgico, -a, -ci, -che [side'rurdʒiko] AG iron and steel *cpd*

'sidro SM cider

si'edo *etc* VB *vedi* **sedere**

si'epe SF hedge

si'ero SM (*Med*) serum; ~ **antivipera** snake bite serum; ~ **del latte** whey

sieronegatività SF INV HIV-negative status

sieronega'tivo, -a AG HIV-negative ▶ SM/F HIV-negative person

sieropositività SF INV HIV-positive status

sieroposi'tivo, -a AG HIV-positive ▶ SM/F HIV-positive person

si'erra SF (*Geo*) sierra

Si'erra Le'one SF: **la** ~ Sierra Leone

si'esta SF siesta, (afternoon) nap

si'ete VB *vedi* **essere**

si'filide SF syphilis

si'fone SM siphon

Sig. ABBR (= *signore*) Mr

siga'retta SF cigarette

'sigaro SM cigar

Sigg. ABBR (= *signori*) Messrs

sigil'lare [sidʒil'lare] /**72**/ VT to seal

si'gillo [si'dʒillo] SM seal

'sigla SF (*iniziali*) initials *pl*; (*abbreviazione*) acronym, abbreviation; ~ **automobilistica** *abbreviation of province on vehicle number plate*; ~ **musicale** signature tune

si'glare /**72**/ VT to initial

Sig.na ABBR (= *signorina*) Miss

signifi'care [siɲɲifi'kare] /**20**/ VT to mean; **cosa significa?** what does this mean?

significa'tivo, -a [siɲɲifika'tivo] AG significant

signifi'cato [siɲɲifi'kato] SM meaning

si'gnora [siɲ'ɲora] SF lady; **la** ~ **X** Mrs X; **buon giorno S~/Signore/Signorina** good morning; (*deferente*) good morning Madam/Sir/Madam; (*quando si conosce il nome*) good morning Mrs/Mr/Miss X; **Gentile S~/Signore/Signorina** (*in una lettera*) Dear Madam/Sir/Madam; **Gentile** (*o Cara*) **S~ Rossi** Dear Mrs Rossi; **Gentile S~ Anna Rossi** (*sulle buste*) Mrs Anna Rossi; **il signor Rossi e** ~ Mr Rossi and his wife; **signore e signori** ladies and gentlemen; **le presento la mia** ~ may I introduce my wife?

si'gnore [siɲ'ɲore] SM gentleman; (*padrone*) lord, master; (*Rel*): **il S~** the Lord; **il signor X** Mr X; **signor Presidente** Mr Chairman; **Gentile** (*o Caro*) **Signor Rossi** (*in lettere*) Dear Mr Rossi; **Gentile Signor Paolo Rossi** (*sulle buste*) Mr Paolo Rossi; **i signori Bianchi** (*coniugi*) Mr and Mrs Bianchi; *vedi anche* **signora**

signo'ria [siɲɲo'ria] SF (*Storia*) seignory, signoria; **S~ Vostra** (*Amm*) you

signo'rile [siɲɲo'rile] AG refined

signorilità [siɲɲorili'ta] SF (*raffinatezza*) refinement; (*eleganza*) elegance

signo'rina [siɲɲo'rina] SF young lady; **la** ~ **X** Miss X; **Gentile** (*o Cara*) **S~ Rossi** (*in lettere*) Dear Miss Rossi; **Gentile S~ Anna Rossi** (*sulle buste*) Miss Anna Rossi; *vedi anche* **signora**

signo'rino [siɲɲo'rino] SM young master

Sig.ra ABBR (= *signora*) Mrs

silenzia'tore [silentsja'tore] SM silencer

si'lenzio [si'lɛntsjo] SM silence; **fare** ~ to be quiet, stop talking; **far passare qc sotto** ~ to keep quiet about sth, hush sth up

silenzi'oso, -a [silen'tsjoso] AG silent, quiet

'silice ['silitʃe] SF silica

si'licio [si'litʃo] SM silicon; **piastrina di** ~ silicon chip

sili'cone SM silicone

'sillaba SF syllable

silu'rare /**72**/ VT to torpedo; (*fig: privare del comando*) to oust

si'luro SM torpedo

SIM [sim] SIGLA F INV (*Tel*): ~ **card** SIM card

simbi'osi SF (*Biol, fig*) symbiosis

simboleggi'are [simboled'dʒare] /**62**/ VT to symbolize

sim'bolico, -a, -ci, -che AG symbolic(al)

simbo'lismo SM symbolism

'simbolo SM symbol

simi'lare AG similar

'simile AG (*analogo*) similar; (*di questo tipo*): **un uomo** ~ such a man, a man like this ▶ SM (*persona*) fellow man; **libri simili** such books; ~ **a** similar to; **non ho mai visto niente di** ~ I've never seen anything like that; **è insegnante o qualcosa di** ~ he's a teacher or something like that; **vendono vasi e simili** they sell vases and things like that; **i suoi simili** one's fellow men; one's peers

simili'tudine SF (Ling) simile

simme'tria SF symmetry

sim'metrico, -a, -ci, -che AG symmetric(al)

simpa'tia SF (qualità) pleasantness; (inclinazione) liking; **avere ~ per qn** to like sb, have a liking for sb; **con ~** (su lettera ecc) with much affection

sim'patico, -a, -ci, -che AG (persona) nice, pleasant, likeable; (casa, albergo ecc) nice, pleasant

simpatiz'zante [simpatid'dzante] SMF sympathizer

simpatiz'zare [simpatid'dzare] /72/ VI: **~ con** to take a liking to

sim'posio SM symposium

simu'lacro SM (monumento, statua) image; (fig) semblance

simu'lare /72/ VT to sham, simulate; (Tecn) to simulate

simulazi'one [simulat'tsjone] SF shamming; simulation

simul'taneo, -a AG simultaneous

sin. ABBR (= sinistra) L

sina'goga, -ghe SF synagogue

sincera'mente [sintʃera'mente] AV (gen) sincerely; (francamente) honestly, sincerely

since'rarsi [sintʃe'rarsi] /72/ VPR: **~ (di qc)** to make sure (of sth)

sincerità [sintʃeri'ta] SF sincerity

sin'cero, -a [sin'tʃero] AG (genuino) sincere; (onesto) genuine; heartfelt

'**sincope** SF syncopation; (Med) blackout

sincro'nia SF (di movimento) synchronism

sin'cronico, -a, -ci, -che AG synchronic

sincroniz'zare [sinkronid'dzare] /72/ VT to synchronize

sinda'cale AG (trade-)union cpd

sindaca'lista, -i, -e SM/F trade unionist

sinda'care /20/ VT (controllare) to inspect; (fig: criticare) to criticize

sinda'cato SM (di lavoratori) (trade) union; (Amm, Econ, Dir) syndicate, trust, pool; **~ dei datori di lavoro** employers' association

'**sindaco, -ci** SM mayor

'**sindrome** SF (Med) syndrome

siner'gia, -gie [siner'dʒia] SF (anche fig) synergy

sinfo'nia SF (Mus) symphony

sin'fonico, -a, -ci, -che AG symphonic; (orchestra) symphony cpd

singa'lese AG, SMF Sin(g)halese inv

Singa'pore SF Singapore

singhioz'zare [singjot'tsare] /72/ VI to sob; to hiccup

singhi'ozzo [sin'gjottso] SM (di pianto) sob; (Med) hiccup; **avere il ~** to have the hiccups; **a ~** (fig) by fits and starts

'**single** ['singol] AG INV, SM O F INV single

singo'lare AG (insolito) remarkable, singular; (Ling) singular ▶ SM (Ling) singular; (Tennis): **~ maschile/femminile** men's(-women's) singles

singolar'mente AV (separatamente) individually, one at a time; (in modo strano) strangely, peculiarly, oddly

'**singolo, -a** AG single, individual ▶ SM (persona) individual; (Tennis) = **singolare**; **ogni ~ individuo** each individual; **camera singola** single room

sinis'trato, -a AG damaged ▶ SM/F disaster victim; **zona sinistrata** disaster area

si'nistro, -a AG left, left-hand; (fig) sinister ▶ SM (incidente) accident ▶ SF (Pol) left (wing); **a sinistra** on the left; (direzione) to the left; **a sinistra di** to the left of; **di sinistra** left-wing; **tenere la sinistra** to keep to the left; **guida a sinistra** left-hand drive

'**sino** PREP = **fino**

si'nonimo, -a AG synonymous ▶ SM synonym; **~ di** synonymous with

sin'tassi SF syntax

sin'tattico, -a, -ci, -che AG syntactic

'**sintesi** SF synthesis; (riassunto) summary, résumé; **in ~** in brief, in short

sin'tetico, -a, -ci, -che AG synthetic; (conciso) brief, concise

sintetiz'zare [sintetid'dzare] /72/ VT to synthesize; (riassumere) to summarize

sintetizza'tore [sintetiddza'tore] SM (Mus) synthesizer; **~ di voce** voice synthesizer

sinto'matico, -a, -ci, -che AG symptomatic

'**sintomo** SM symptom

sinto'nia SF (Radio) tuning; **essere in ~ con qn** (fig) to be on the same wavelength as sb

sintoniz'zare [sintonid'dzare] /72/ VT to tune (in); **sintonizzarsi** VPR: **sintonizzarsi su** to tune in to

sintonizza'tore [sintoniddza'tore] SM tuner

sinu'oso, -a AG (strada) winding

sinu'site SF sinusitis

SIP SIGLA F (= Società Italiana per l'esercizio telefonico) former name of Italian telephone company

si'pario SM (Teat) curtain

si'rena SF (apparecchio) siren; (nella mitologia, fig) siren, mermaid; **~ d'allarme** (per incendio) fire alarm; (per furto) burglar alarm

'**Siria** SF: **la ~** Syria

siri'ano, -a AG, SM/F Syrian

si'ringa, -ghe SF syringe

'**sisma, -i** SM earthquake

'**SISMI** SIGLA M (= Servizio per l'Informazione e la Sicurezza Militari) military security service

'**sismico, -a, -ci, -che** AG seismic; (zona) earthquake cpd

sis'mografo SM seismograph

S

sissi'gnore [sissiɲˈɲore] AV (*a un superiore*) yes, sir; (*enfatico*) yes indeed, of course

sis'tema, -i SM system; (*metodo*) method, way; **trovare il ~ per fare qc** to find a way to do sth; **~ decimale/metrico** decimal/ metric system; **~ nervoso** nervous system; **~ operativo** (*Inform*) operating system; **~ solare** solar system; **~ di vita** way of life

siste'mare /**72**/ VT (*mettere a posto*) to tidy, put in order; (*risolvere: questione*) to sort out, settle; (*procurare un lavoro a*) to find a job for; (*dare un alloggio a*) to settle, find accommodation (BRIT) *o* accommodations (US) for; **sistemarsi** VPR (*problema*) to be settled; (*persona: trovare alloggio*) to find accommodation(s); (*: trovarsi un lavoro*) to get fixed up with a job; **ti sistemo io!** I'll soon sort you out!; **~ qn in un albergo** to fix sb up with a hotel

sistematica'mente AV systematically

siste'matico, -a, -ci, -che AG systematic

sistemazi'one [sistematˈtsjone] SF arrangement; order; settlement; employment; accommodation (BRIT), accommodations (US)

'sito, -a AG (*Amm*) situated ▶ SM (*letterario*) place; **~ Internet** website

situ'are /**72**/ VT to site, situate

situ'ato, -a AG: **~ a/su** situated at/on

situazi'one [situatˈtsjone] SF situation; **vista la sua ~ familiare** given your family situation *o* circumstances; **nella sua ~** in your position *o* situation; **mi trovo in una ~ critica** I'm in a very difficult situation *o* position

'skai® SM Leatherette®

ski-lift [skiˈlift] SM INV ski tow

ski pass [skiˈpaːs] SM INV ski pass

slacci'are [zlatˈtʃare] /**14**/ VT to undo, unfasten

slanci'arsi [zlanˈtʃarsi] /**14**/ VPR to dash, fling o.s.

slanci'ato, -a [zlanˈtʃato] AG slender

'slancio [ˈzlantʃo] SM dash, leap; (*fig*) surge; **in uno ~ d'affetto** in a burst *o* rush of affection; **di ~** impetuously

sla'vato, -a AG faded, washed out; (*fig: viso, occhi*) pale, colourless (BRIT), colorless (US)

sla'vina SF snowslide

'slavo, -a AG Slav(onic), Slavic

sle'ale AG disloyal; (*concorrenza ecc*) unfair

slealtà SF disloyalty; unfairness

sle'gare /**80**/ VT to untie

slip [zlip] SM INV (*mutandine*) briefs pl; (*da bagno: per uomo*) (swimming) trunks pl; (*: per donna*) bikini bottoms pl

'slitta SF sledge; (*trainata*) sleigh

slitta'mento SM slipping; skidding; postponement; **~ salariale** wage drift

slit'tare /**72**/ VI to slip, slide; (*Aut*) to skid; (*incontro, conferenza*) to be put off, be postponed

s.l.m. ABBR (= *sul livello del mare*) a.s.l.

slo'gare /**80**/ VT (*Med*) to dislocate; (*: caviglia, polso*) to sprain

sloga'tura SF dislocation; sprain

sloggi'are [zlodˈdʒare] /**62**/ VT (*inquilino*) to turn out; (*nemico*) to drive out, dislodge ▶ VI to move out

Slo'vacchia [zloˈvakkja] SF Slovakia

slo'vacco, -a, -ci, -che AG, SM/F Slovak, Slovakian; **la Repubblica Slovacca** the Slovak Republic

Slo'venia SF Slovenia

slo'veno, -a AG, SM/F Slovene, Slovenian ▶ SM (*Ling*) Slovene

S.M. ABBR (*Mil*) = **Stato Maggiore**; (= *Sua Maestà*) HM

smac'cato, -a AG (*fig*) excessive

smacchi'are [zmakˈkjare] /**19**/ VT to remove stains from

smacchia'tore [zmakkjaˈtore] SM stain remover

'smacco, -chi SM humiliating defeat

smagli'ante [zmaʎˈʎante] AG brilliant, dazzling

smagli'are [zmaʎˈʎare] /**27**/ VT, **smagli'arsi** VPR (*calza*) to ladder

smaglia'tura [zmaʎʎaˈtura] SF (*su maglia, calza*) ladder (BRIT), run; (*Med: sulla pelle*) stretch mark

sma'grire /**55**/ VT to make thin ▶ VI to get *o* grow thin, lose weight

sma'grito, -a AG: **essere ~** to have lost a lot of weight

smalizi'ato, -a [zmalitˈtsjato] AG shrewd, cunning

smal'tare /**72**/ VT to enamel; (*ceramica*) to glaze; (*unghie*) to varnish

smalti'mento SM (*di rifiuti*) disposal

smal'tire /**55**/ VT (*merce*) to sell off; (*rifiuti*) to dispose of; (*cibo*) to digest; (*peso*) to lose; (*rabbia*) to get over; **~ la sbornia** to sober up

'smalto SM (*anche di denti*) enamel; (*per ceramica*) glaze; **~ per unghie** nail varnish

smance'rie [zmantʃeˈrie] SFPL mawkishness sg

'smania SF agitation, restlessness; (*fig*): **~ di** thirst for, craving for; **avere la ~ addosso** to have the fidgets; **avere la ~ di fare** to long *o* yearn to do

smani'are /**19**/ VI (*agitarsi*) to be restless *o* agitated; (*fig*): **~ di fare** to long *o* yearn to do

smantella'mento SM dismantling

smantel'lare /**72**/ VT to dismantle

smar'carsi /**20**/ VPR (*Sport*) to get free of marking

smargi'asso [zmarˈdʒasso] SM show-off

smarri'mento SM loss; (fig) bewilderment; dismay

smar'rire /55/ VT to lose; (non riuscire a trovare) to mislay; **smarrirsi** VPR (perdersi) to lose one's way, get lost; (: oggetto) to go astray

smar'rito, -a AG (oggetto) lost; (fig: confuso: persona) bewildered, nonplussed; (: sguardo) bewildered; **ufficio oggetti smarriti** lost property office (BRIT), lost and found (US)

smasche'rare [zmaske'rare] /72/ VT to unmask

SME ABBR = **Stato Maggiore Esercito** ▶ SIGLA M (= Sistema Monetario Europeo) EMS (= European Monetary System)

smem'brare /72/ VT (gruppo, partito ecc) to split; **smembrarsi** VPR to split up

smemo'rato, -a AG forgetful

smen'tire /55/ VT (negare) to deny; (testimonianza) to refute; (reputazione) to give the lie to; **smentirsi** VPR to be inconsistent

smen'tita SF denial; refutation

sme'raldo SM, AG INV emerald

smerci'are [zmer'tʃare] /14/ VT (Comm) to sell; (: svendere) to sell off

'smercio ['zmɛrtʃo] SM sale; **avere poco/molto ~** to have poor/good sales

smerigli'ato, -a [zmeriʎ'ʎato] AG: **carta smerigliata** emery paper; **vetro ~** frosted glass

sme'riglio [zme'riʎʎo] SM emery

'smesso, -a PP di **smettere** ▶ AG: **abiti smessi** cast-offs

'smettere /63/ VT to stop; (vestiti) to stop wearing ▶ VI to stop, cease; **~ di fare** to stop doing

smidol'lato, -a AG spineless ▶ SM/F spineless person

smilitarizzazi'one [zmilitariddzat'tsjone] SF demilitarization

'smilzo, -a ['zmiltso] AG thin, lean

sminu'ire /72/ VT to diminish, lessen; (fig) to belittle; **~ l'importanza di qc** to play sth down

sminuz'zare [zminut'tsare] /72/ VT to break into small pieces; to crumble

'smisi etc VB vedi **smettere**

smista'mento SM (di posta) sorting; (Ferr) shunting

smis'tare /72/ VT (pacchi ecc) to sort; (Ferr) to shunt

smisu'rato, -a AG boundless, immeasurable; (grandissimo) immense, enormous

smitiz'zare [zmitid'dzare] /72/ VT to debunk

smobili'tare /72/ VT to demobilize

smobilitazi'one [zmobilitat'tsjone] SF demobilization

smobi'lizzo [zmobi'liddzo] SM (Comm) disinvestment

smo'dato, -a AG excessive, unrestrained

smode'rato, -a AG immoderate

smog [zmɔg] SM INV smog

'smoking ['smoukɪŋ] SM INV dinner jacket (BRIT), tuxedo (US)

smon'tare /72/ VT (mobile, macchina ecc) to take to pieces, dismantle; (fig: scoraggiare) to dishearten ▶ VI (scendere: da cavallo) to dismount; (: da treno) to get off; (terminare il lavoro) to stop (work); **smontarsi** VPR to lose heart; to lose one's enthusiasm

'smorfia SF grimace; (atteggiamento lezioso) simpering; **fare smorfie** to make faces; to simper

smorfi'oso, -a AG simpering

'smorto, -a AG (viso) pale, wan; (colore) dull

smor'zare [zmor'tsare] /72/ VT (suoni) to deaden; (colori) to tone down; (luce) to dim; (sete) to quench; (entusiasmo) to dampen; **smorzarsi** VPR (suono, luce) to fade; (entusiasmo) to dampen

'smosso, -a PP di **smuovere**

smotta'mento SM landslide

sms ['ɛsse'ɛmme'ɛsse] SM INV text (message)

'smunto, -a AG haggard, pinched

smu'overe /66/ VT to move, shift; (fig: commuovere) to move; (: dall'inerzia) to rouse, stir; **smuoversi** VPR to move, shift

smus'sare /72/ VT (angolo) to round off, smooth; (lama ecc) to blunt; **smussarsi** VPR to become blunt

s.n. ABBR = **senza numero**

snatu'rato, -a AG inhuman, heartless

snazionaliz'zare [znattsjonalid'dzare] /72/ VT to denationalize

snelli'mento SM (di traffico) speeding up; (di procedura) streamlining

snel'lire /55/ VT (persona) to make slim; (traffico) to speed up; (procedura) to streamline; **snellirsi** VPR (persona) to (get) slim; (traffico) to speed up

'snello, -a AG (agile) agile; (svelto) slender, slim

sner'vante AG (attesa, lavoro) exasperating

sner'vare /72/ VT to enervate, wear out; **snervarsi** VPR to become enervated

sni'dare /72/ VT to drive out, flush out

snif'fare [znif'fare] /72/ VT (col: cocaina) to snort

snob'bare /72/ VT to snub

sno'bismo SM snobbery

snoccio'lare [znottʃo'lare] /72/ VT (frutta) to stone; (fig: orazioni) to rattle off; (: verità) to blab; (: col: soldi) to shell out

sno'dabile AG (lampada) adjustable; (tubo, braccio) hinged; **rasoio con testina ~** swivel-head razor

sno'dare /72/ VT to untie, undo; (rendere agile, mobile) to loosen; **snodarsi** VPR to come loose; (articolarsi) to bend; (strada, fiume) to wind

sno'dato, -a AG (articolazione, persona) flexible; (fune ecc) undone

S

'snowboard ['znobord] SM INV (*tavola*) snowboard; (*sport*) snowboarding; **fare ~** to go snowboarding

SO SIGLA = **Sondrio**

so VB *vedi* **sapere**

S.O. ABBR (= *sudovest*) SW

so'ave AG (*voce, maniera*) gentle; (*volto*) delicate, sweet; (*musica*) soft, sweet; (*profumo*) delicate

soavità SF gentleness; delicacy; sweetness; softness

sobbal'zare [sobbal'tsare] /**72**/ VI to jolt, jerk; (*trasalire*) to jump, start

sob'balzo [sob'baltso] SM jerk, jolt; jump, start

sobbar'carsi /**20**/ VPR: **~ a** to take on, undertake

sob'borgo, -ghi SM suburb

sobil'lare /**72**/ VT to stir up, incite

'sobrio, -a AG sober

Soc. ABBR (= *società*) Soc.

socchi'udere [sok'kjudere] /**22**/ VT (*porta*) to leave ajar; (*occhi*) to half-close

socchi'uso, -a [sok'kjuso] PP *di* **socchiudere** ▸ AG (*porta, finestra*) ajar; (*occhi*) half-closed

soc'combere /**29**/ VI to succumb, give way

soc'correre /**28**/ VT to help, assist

soccorri'tore, -'trice SM/F rescuer

soc'corso, -a PP *di* **soccorrere** ▸ SM help, aid, assistance; **soccorsi** SMPL relief *sg*, aid *sg*; **prestare ~ a qn** to help *o* assist sb; **venire in ~ di qn** to help sb, come to sb's aid; **operazioni di ~** rescue operations; **~ stradale** breakdown service

socialdemo'cratico, -a, -ci, -che [sotʃaldemo'kratiko] SM/F Social Democrat

soci'ale [so'tʃale] AG social; (*di associazione*) club *cpd*, association *cpd*

socia'lismo [sotʃa'lizmo] SM socialism

socia'lista, -i, -e [sotʃa'lista] AG, SM/F socialist

socializ'zare [sotʃalid'dzare] /**72**/ VI to socialize

società [sotʃe'ta] SF INV society; (*sportiva*) club; (*Comm*) company; **in ~ con qn** in partnership with sb; **mettersi in ~ con qn** to go into business with sb; **l'alta ~** high society; **~ anonima** ≈ limited (BRIT) *o* incorporated (US) company; **~ per azioni** joint-stock company; **~ di comodo** shell company; **~ fiduciaria** trust company; **~ di mutuo soccorso** friendly society (BRIT), benefit society (US); **~ a responsabilità limitata** *type of limited liability company*

soci'evole [so'tʃevole] AG sociable

socievo'lezza [sotʃevo'lettsa] SF sociableness

'socio ['sɔtʃo] SM (*Dir, Comm*) partner; (*membro di associazione*) member

sociolo'gia [sotʃolo'dʒia] SF sociology

soci'ologo, -a, -gi, -ghe [so'tʃɔlogo] SM/F sociologist

'soda SF (*Chim*) soda; (*acqua gassata*) soda (water)

soda'lizio [soda'littsjo] SM association, society

soddisfa'cente [soddisfa'tʃɛnte] AG satisfactory

soddis'fare /**41**/ VT, VI: **~ (a)** to satisfy; (*impegno*) to fulfil; (*debito*) to pay off; (*richiesta*) to meet, comply with; (*offesa*) to make amends for

soddis'fatto, -a PP *di* **soddisfare** ▸ AG satisfied, pleased; **essere ~ di** to be satisfied *o* pleased with

soddisfazi'one [soddisfat'tsjone] SF satisfaction

'sodio SM (*Chim*) sodium

'sodo, -a AG firm, hard; (*uovo*) hard-boiled ▸ SM: **venire al ~** to come to the point ▸ AV (*picchiare, lavorare*) hard; **dormire ~** to sleep soundly

sofà SM INV sofa

soffe'renza [soffe'rentsa] SF suffering; (*Comm*): **in ~** unpaid

sof'ferto, -a PP *di* **soffrire** ▸ AG (*vittoria*) hard-fought; (*distacco, decisione*) painful

soffi'are /**19**/ VT to blow; (*notizia, segreto*) to whisper ▸ VI to blow; (*sbuffare*) to puff (and blow); **soffiarsi il naso** to blow one's nose; **~ qc/qn a qn** (*fig*) to pinch *o* steal sth/sb from sb; **~ via qc** to blow sth away

soffi'ata SF (*col*) tip-off; **fare una ~ alla polizia** to tip off the police

'soffice ['sɔffitʃe] AG soft

soffi'etto SM (*Mus, per fuoco*) bellows *pl*; **porta a ~** folding door

'soffio SM (*di vento*) breath; (*di fumo*) puff; (*Med*) murmur

soffi'one SM (*Bot*) dandelion

sof'fitta SF attic

sof'fitto SM ceiling

soffo'cante AG suffocating, stifling

soffo'care /**20**/ VI (*anche*: **soffocarsi**) to suffocate, choke ▸ VT to suffocate, choke; (*fig*) to stifle, suppress

soffocazi'one [soffokat'tsjone] SF suffocation

sof'friggere [sof'friddʒere] /**56**/ VT to fry lightly

sof'frire /**70**/ VT to suffer, endure; (*sopportare*) to bear, stand ▸ VI to suffer; to be in pain; **~ (di) qc** (*Med*) to suffer from sth

sof'fritto, -a PP *di* **soffriggere** ▸ SM (*Cuc*) fried mixture of herbs, bacon and onions

sof'fuso, -a AG (*di luce*) suffused

So'fia SF (*Geo*) Sofia

sofisti'care /**20**/ VT (*vino, cibo*) to adulterate

sofisti'cato, -a AG sophisticated; (*vino*) adulterated

sofisticazi'one [sofistikat'tsjone] SF
adulteration

'software ['sɔftwɛə] SM: **~ applicativo**
applications package

sogget'tivo, -a [soddʒet'tivo] AG subjective

sog'getto, -a [sod'dʒɛtto] AG: **~ a** (sottomesso)
subject to; (esposto: a variazioni, danni ecc)
subject o liable to ▶ SM subject; **~ a tassa**
taxable; **recitare a ~** (Teat) to improvise

soggezi'one [soddʒet'tsjone] SF subjection;
(timidezza) awe; **avere ~ di qn** to stand in awe
of sb; to be ill at ease in sb's presence

sogghi'gnare [soggiɲ'ɲare] /15/ VI to sneer

sog'ghigno [sog'giɲɲo] SM sneer

soggia'cere [soddʒa'tʃere] /57/ VI: **~ a** to be
subjected to

soggio'gare [soddʒo'gare] /80/ VT to subdue,
subjugate

soggior'nare [soddʒor'nare] /72/ VI to stay

soggi'orno [sod'dʒorno] SM (permanenza) stay;
(stanza) living room

soggi'ungere [sod'dʒundʒere] /5/ VT to add

soggi'unto, -a [sod'dʒunto] PP di **soggiungere**

'soglia ['sɔʎʎa] SF doorstep; (anche fig)
threshold

'sogliola ['sɔʎʎola] SF (Zool) sole

so'gnante [soɲ'ɲante] AG dreamy

so'gnare [soɲ'ɲare] /15/ VT, VI to dream;
~ a occhi aperti to daydream

sogna'tore, -'trice [soɲɲa'tore] SM/F
dreamer

'sogno ['soɲɲo] SM dream

'soia SF (Bot) soya

sol SM (Mus) G; (: solfeggiando la scala) so(h)

so'laio SM (soffitta) attic

sola'mente AV only, just

so'lare AG solar, sun cpd

sol'care /20/ VT (terreno, fig: mari) to plough
(BRIT), plow (US)

'solco, -chi SM (scavo, fig: ruga) furrow; (incavo)
rut, track; (di disco) groove; (scia) wake

sol'dato SM soldier; **~ di leva** conscript;
~ semplice private

'soldo SM (fig): **non avere un ~** to be
penniless; **: non vale un ~** it's not worth a
penny; **soldi** SMPL (denaro) money sg; **non ho
soldi** I haven't got any money

'sole SM sun; (luce) sun(light); (tempo assolato)
sun(shine); **prendere il ~** to sunbathe;
il S~ che ride (Pol) symbol of the Italian
Green party

soleggi'ato, -a [soled'dʒato] AG sunny

so'lenne AG solemn

solennità SF solemnity; (festività) holiday,
feast day

so'lere /108/ VT: **~ fare qc** to be in the habit of
doing sth ▶ VB IMPERS: **come suole
accadere** as is usually the case, as usually
happens; **come si suol dire** as they say

so'lerte AG diligent

so'lerzia [so'lɛrtsja] SF diligence

so'letta SF (per scarpe) insole

sol'fato SM sulphate (BRIT), sulfate (US)

sol'forico, -a, -ci, -che AG sulphuric (BRIT),
sulfuric (US); **acido ~** sulphuric o sulfuric
acid

sol'furo SM sulphur (BRIT), sulfur (US)

soli'dale AG in agreement; **essere ~ con qn**
(essere d'accordo) to be in agreement with sb;
(appoggiare) to be behind sb

solidarietà SF solidarity

solidifi'care /20/ VT, VI (anche: **solidificarsi**) to
solidify

solidità SF solidity

'solido, -a AG solid; (forte, robusto) sturdy, solid;
(fig: ditta) sound, solid ▶ SM (Mat) solid

soli'loquio SM soliloquy

so'lista, -i, -e AG solo ▶ SM/F soloist

solita'mente AV usually, as a rule

soli'tario, -a AG (senza compagnia) solitary,
lonely; (solo, isolato) solitary, lone; (deserto)
lonely ▶ SM (gioiello, gioco) solitaire

'solito, -a AG usual; **essere ~ fare** to be in the
habit of doing; **di ~** usually; **più tardi del ~**
later than usual; **come al ~** as usual; **siamo
alle solite!** (col) here we go again!

soli'tudine SF solitude

sollaz'zare [sollat'tsare] /72/ VT to entertain;
sollazzarsi VPR to amuse o.s.

sol'lazzo [sol'lattso] SM amusement

solleci'tare [solletʃi'tare] /72/ VT (lavoro) to
speed up; (persona) to urge on; (chiedere con
insistenza) to press for, request urgently;
(Tecn) to stress; (stimolare): **~ qn a fare** to urge
sb to do

sollecitazi'one [solletʃitat'tsjone] SF
entreaty, request; (fig) incentive; (Tecn)
stress; **lettera di ~** (Comm) reminder

sol'lecito, -a [sol'letʃito] AG prompt, quick
▶ SM (Comm) reminder; **~ di pagamento**
payment reminder

solleci'tudine [solletʃi'tudine] SF
promptness, speed

solleti'care /20/ VT to tickle

sol'letico SM tickling; **soffrire il ~** to be
ticklish

solleva'mento SM raising; lifting; (ribellione)
revolt; **~ pesi** (Sport) weight-lifting

solle'vare /72/ VT to lift, raise; (fig: persona:
alleggerire): **~ (da)** to relieve (of); (: dar conforto)
to comfort, relieve; (questione) to raise; (far
insorgere) to stir (to revolt); **sollevarsi** VPR to
rise; (fig: riprendersi) to recover; (: ribellarsi) to
rise up; **sollevarsi da terra** (persona) to get
up from the ground; (aereo) to take off;
sentirsi sollevato to feel relieved

solli'evo SM relief; (conforto) comfort; **con
mio grande ~** to my great relief

S

'**solo, -a** AG alone; (*in senso spirituale: isolato*) lonely; (*unico*): **un ~ libro** only one book, a single book; (*con ag numerale*): **veniamo noi tre soli** just o only the three of us are coming ▶ AV (*soltanto*) only, just; **~ che** *cong* but; **è il ~ proprietario** he's the sole proprietor; **l'incontrò due sole volte** he only met him twice; **non ~ ... ma anche** not only ... but also; **fare qc da ~** to do sth (all) by oneself; **vive (da) ~** he lives on his own; **possiamo vederci da soli?** can I see you in private?

sol'stizio [sol'stittsjo] SM solstice

sol'tanto AV only

so'lubile AG (*sostanza*) soluble; **caffè ~** instant coffee

soluzi'one [solut'tsjone] SF solution; **senza ~ di continuità** uninterruptedly

sol'vente AG, SM solvent; **~ per unghie** nail polish remover; **~ per vernici** paint remover

sol'venza [sol'vɛntsa] SF (*Comm*) solvency

'**soma** SF load, burden; **bestia da ~** beast of burden

So'malia SF: **la ~** Somalia

'**somalo, -a** AG, SM/F, SM Somali

so'maro SM ass, donkey

so'matico, -a, -ci, -che AG somatic

somigli'anza [somiʎ'ʎantsa] SF resemblance

somigli'are [somiʎ'ʎare] /27/ VI: **~ a** to be like, resemble; (*nell'aspetto fisico*) to look like; **somigliarsi** VPR to be (o look) alike

'**somma** SF (*Mat*) sum; (*di denaro*) sum (of money); (*complesso di varie cose*) whole amount, sum total; **tirare le somme** (*fig*) to sum up; **tirate le somme** (*fig*) all things considered

som'mare /72/ VT to add up; (*aggiungere*) to add; **tutto sommato** all things considered

som'mario, -a AG (*racconto, indagine*) brief; (*giustizia*) summary ▶ SM summary

som'mergere [som'mɛrdʒere] /59/ VT to submerge

sommer'gibile [sommer'dʒibile] SM submarine

som'merso, -a PP *di* **sommergere**

som'messo, -a AG (*voce*) soft, subdued

somminis'trare /72/ VT to give, administer

sommità SF INV summit, top; (*fig*) height

'**sommo, -a** AG highest; (*rispetto*) highest, greatest; (*poeta, artista*) great, outstanding ▶ SM (*fig*) height; **per sommi capi** in short, in brief

som'mossa SF uprising

sommozza'tore [sommottsa'tore] SM (deep-sea) diver; (*Mil*) frogman

so'naglio [so'naʎʎo] SM (*di mucche ecc*) bell; (*per bambini*) rattle

so'nante AG: **denaro** o **moneta ~** (ready) cash

so'nare *etc* = **suonare** *ecc*

'**sonda** SF (*Med, Meteor, Aer*) probe; (*Mineralogia*) drill ▶ AG INV: **pallone** *m* **~** weather balloon

son'daggio [son'daddʒo] SM sounding; probe; boring, drilling; (*indagine*) survey; **~ d'opinioni** opinion poll

son'dare /72/ VT (*Naut*) to sound; (*atmosfera, piaga*) to probe; (*Mineralogia*) to bore, drill; (*fig: opinione ecc*) to survey, poll

so'netto SM sonnet

son'nambulo, -a SM/F sleepwalker

sonnecchi'are [sonnek'kjare] /19/ VI to doze, nod

sonnel'lino SM nap

son'nifero SM sleeping drug (o pill)

'**sonno** SM sleep; **aver ~** to be sleepy; **prendere ~** to fall asleep

sonno'lento, -a AG sleepy, drowsy; (*movimenti*) sluggish

sonno'lenza [sonno'lɛntsa] SF sleepiness, drowsiness

'**sono** VB *vedi* **essere**

sonoriz'zare [sonorid'dzare] /72/ VT (*Ling*) to voice; (*Cine*) to add a sound-track to

so'noro, -a AG (*ambiente*) resonant; (*voce*) sonorous, ringing; (*onde, Cine*) sound *cpd* ▶ SM: **il ~** (*Cine*) the talkies *pl*

sontu'oso, -a AG sumptuous; lavish

so'pire /55/ VT (*fig: dolore, tensione*) to soothe

so'pore SM drowsiness

sopo'rifero, -a AG soporific

sop'palco, -chi SM mezzanine

soppe'rire /55/ VI: **~ a** to provide for; **~ alla mancanza di qc** to make up for the lack of sth

soppe'sare /72/ VT to weigh in one's hand(s), feel the weight of; (*fig*) to weigh up

soppian'tare /72/ VT to supplant

soppi'atto AV: **di ~** secretly; furtively

soppor'tabile AG tolerable, bearable

soppor'tare /72/ VT (*reggere*) to support; (*subire: perdita, spese*) to bear, sustain; (*soffrire: dolore*) to bear, endure; (*cosa: freddo*) to withstand; (*persona: freddo, vino*) to take; (*tollerare*) to put up with, tolerate

sopportazi'one [sopportat'tsjone] SF patience; **avere spirito di ~, avere capacità di ~** to be long-suffering

soppressi'one SF abolition; withdrawal; suppression; deletion; elimination, liquidation

sop'presso, -a PP *di* **sopprimere**

sop'primere /50/ VT (*carica, privilegi ecc*) to do away with, abolish; (*servizio*) to withdraw; (*pubblicazione*) to suppress; (*parola, frase*) to delete; (*uccidere*) to eliminate, liquidate

'**sopra** PREP (*gen*) on; (*al di sopra di, più in alto di*) above; over; (*riguardo a*) on, about ▶ AV on top;

(*attaccato, scritto*) on it; (*al di sopra*) above; (*al piano superiore*) upstairs; **donne ~ i 30 anni** women over 30 (years of age); **100 metri ~ il livello del mare** 100 metres above sea level; **5 gradi ~ lo zero** 5 degrees above zero; **abito di ~** I live upstairs; **essere al di ~ di ogni sospetto** to be above suspicion; **per i motivi ~ illustrati** for the above-mentioned reasons, for the reasons shown above; **dormirci ~** (*fig*) to sleep on it; **passar ~ a qc** (*anche fig*) to pass over sth

so'prabito SM overcoat

sopraccen'nato, -a [soprattʃen'nato] AG above-mentioned

soprac'ciglio [soprat'tʃiʎʎo] (*pl(f)* **sopracciglia**) SM eyebrow

sopracco'perta SF (*di letto*) bedspread; (*di libro*) jacket

soprad'detto, -a /41/ AG aforesaid

sopraf'fare /41/ VT to overcome, overwhelm

sopraf'fatto, -a PP *di* **sopraffare**

sopraffazi'one [sopraffat'tsjone] SF overwhelming, overpowering

sopraf'fino, -a AG (*pranzo, vino*) excellent; (*fig*) masterly

sopraggi'ungere [soprad'dʒundʒere] /5/ VI (*giungere all'improvviso*) to arrive (unexpectedly); (*accadere*) to occur (unexpectedly)

sopraggi'unto, -a [soprad'dʒunto] PP *di* **sopraggiungere**

soprallu'ogo, -ghi SM (*di esperti*) inspection; (*di polizia*) on-the-spot investigation

sopram'mobile SM ornament

soprannatu'rale AG supernatural

sopran'nome SM nickname

soprannomi'nare /72/ VT to nickname

sopran'numero AV: **in ~** in excess

so'prano, -a SM/F (*persona*) soprano ▶ SM (*voce*) soprano

soprappensi'ero AV lost in thought

soprappiù SM surplus, extra; **in ~** extra, surplus; (*per giunta*) besides, in addition

sopras'salto SM: **di ~** with a start, with a jump; suddenly

soprasse'dere /107/ VI: **~ a** to delay, put off

soprat'tassa SF surtax

soprat'tutto AV (*anzitutto*) above all; (*specialmente*) especially

sopravvalu'tare /72/ VT (*persona, capacità*) to overestimate

sopravve'nire /128/ VI to arrive, appear; (*fatto*) to occur

soprav'vento SM: **avere/prendere il ~ su qn** to have/get the upper hand over sb

sopravvis'suto, -a PP *di* **sopravvivere** ▶ SM/F survivor

sopravvi'venza [sopravvi'vɛntsa] SF survival

soprav'vivere /130/ VI to survive; (*continuare a vivere*): **~ (in)** to live on (in); **~ a** (*incidente ecc*) to survive; (*persona*) to outlive

soprele'vata SF (*di strada, ferrovia*) elevated section

soprinten'dente SMF supervisor; (*statale: di belle arti ecc*) keeper

soprinten'denza [soprinten'dɛntsa] SF supervision; (*ente*): **~ alle Belle Arti** government department responsible for monuments and artistic treasures

soprin'tendere /120/ VI: **~ a** to superintend, supervise

soprin'teso, -a PP *di* **soprintendere**

so'pruso SM abuse of power; **subire un ~** to be abused

soq'quadro SM: **mettere a ~** to turn upside-down

sor'betto SM sorbet, water ice (BRIT)

sor'bire /17/ VT to sip; (*fig*) to put up with

'**sorcio** ['sortʃo] SM mouse

'**sordido, -a** AG sordid; (*fig: gretto*) stingy

sor'dina SF: **in ~** softly; (*fig*) on the sly

sordità SF deafness

'**sordo, -a** AG deaf; (*rumore*) muffled; (*dolore*) dull; (*lotta*) silent, hidden; (*odio, rancore*) veiled ▶ SM/F deaf person

sordo'muto, -a AG deaf-and-dumb ▶ SM/F deaf-mute

so'rella SF sister

sorel'lastra SF stepsister; (*con genitore in comune*) half sister

sor'gente [sor'dʒɛnte] SF (*acqua che sgorga*) spring; (*di fiume, Fisica, fig*) source; **acqua di ~** spring water; **~ di calore** source of heat; **~ termale** thermal spring

'**sorgere** ['sordʒere] /109/ VI to rise; (*scaturire*) to spring, rise; (*fig: difficoltà*) to arise ▶ SM: **al ~ del sole** at sunrise

sori'ano, -a AG, SM/F tabby

sormon'tare /72/ VT (*fig*) to overcome, surmount

sorni'one, -a AG sly

sorpas'sare /72/ VT (*Aut*) to overtake; (*fig*) to surpass; (: *eccedere*) to exceed, go beyond; **~ in altezza** to be higher than; (*persona*) to be taller than

sorpas'sato, -a AG (*metodo, moda*) outmoded, old-fashioned; (*macchina*) obsolete

sor'passo SM (*Aut*) overtaking

sorpren'dente AG surprising; (*eccezionale, inaspettato*) astonishing, amazing

sor'prendere /81/ VT (*cogliere: in flagrante ecc*) to catch; (*stupire*) to surprise; **sorprendersi** VPR: **sorprendersi (di)** to be surprised (at)

sor'preso, -a PP *di* **sorprendere** ▶ SF surprise; **fare una sorpresa a qn** to give sb a surprise; **prendere qn di sorpresa** to take sb by surprise *o* unawares

S

sor'reggere [sor'rɛddʒere] /**87**/ vт to support, hold up; (*fig*) to sustain; **sorreggersi** vpr (*tenersi ritto*) to stay upright

sor'retto, -a pp *di* **sorreggere**

sor'ridere /**89**/ vi to smile

sor'riso, -a pp *di* **sorridere** ▶ sm smile

sor'sata sf gulp; **bere a sorsate** to gulp

sorseggi'are [sorsed'dʒare] /**62**/ vт to sip

'sorsi *etc* vв *vedi* **sorgere**

'sorso sm sip; **d'un ~, in un ~ solo** at one gulp

'sorta sf sort, kind; **di ~** whatever, of any kind at all; **ogni ~ di** all sorts of; **di ogni ~** of every kind

'sorte sf (*fato*) fate, destiny; (*evento fortuito*) chance; **tirare a ~** to draw lots; **tentare la ~** to try one's luck

sorteggi'are [sorted'dʒare] /**62**/ vт to draw for

sor'teggio [sor'teddʒo] sm draw

sorti'legio [sorti'lɛdʒo] sm witchcraft *no pl*; (*incantesimo*) spell; **fare un ~ a qn** to cast a spell on sb

sor'tire /**55**/ vт (*ottenere*) to produce

sor'tita sf (*Mil*) sortie

'sorto, -a pp *di* **sorgere**

sorvegli'ante [sorveʎ'ʎante] smf (*di carcere*) guard, warder (Brıт); (*di fabbrica ecc*) supervisor

sorvegli'anza [sorveʎ'ʎantsa] sf watch; supervision; (*Polizia, Mil*) surveillance

sorvegli'are [sorveʎ'ʎare] /**27**/ vт (*bambino, bagagli, prigioniero*) to watch, keep an eye on; (*malato*) to watch over; (*territorio, casa*) to watch *o* keep watch over; (*lavori*) to supervise

sorvo'lare /**72**/ vт (*territorio*) to fly over ▶ vi: **~ su** (*fig*) to skim over

S.O.S. sigla m mayday, SOS

'sosia sm inv double

sos'pendere /**8**/ vт (*appendere*) to hang (up); (*interrompere, privare di una carica*) to suspend; (*rimandare*) to defer; (*appendere*) to hang; **~ un quadro al muro/un lampadario al soffitto** to hang a picture on the wall/a chandelier from the ceiling; **~ qn dal suo incarico** to suspend sb from office

sospensi'one sf (*anche Chim, Aut*) suspension; deferment; **~ condizionale della pena** (*Dir*) suspended sentence

sos'peso, -a pp *di* **sospendere** ▶ ag (*appeso*): **~ a** hanging on (*o* from); (*treno, autobus*) cancelled; **in ~** in abeyance; (*conto*) outstanding; **tenere in ~** (*fig*) to keep in suspense; **col fiato ~** with bated breath

sospet'tare /**72**/ vт to suspect ▶ vi: **~ di** to suspect; (*diffidare*) to be suspicious of

sos'petto, -a ag suspicious ▶ sm suspicion; **destare sospetti** to arouse suspicion

sospet'toso, -a ag suspicious

sos'pingere [sos'pindʒere] /**114**/ vт to drive, push

sos'pinto, -a pp *di* **sospingere**

sospi'rare /**72**/ vi to sigh ▶ vт to long for, yearn for

sos'piro sm sigh; **~ di sollievo** sigh of relief

'sosta sf (*fermata*) stop, halt; (*pausa*) pause, break; **senza ~** non-stop, without a break

sostanti'vato, -a ag (*Ling*): **aggettivo ~** adjective used as a noun

sostan'tivo sm noun, substantive

sos'tanza [sos'tantsa] sf substance; **sostanze** sfpl (*ricchezze*) wealth *sg*, possessions; **in ~** in short, to sum up; **la ~ del discorso** the essence of the speech

sostanzi'ale [sostan'tsjale] ag substantial

sostanzi'oso, -a [sostan'tsjoso] ag (*cibo*) nourishing, substantial

sos'tare /**72**/ vi (*fermarsi*) to stop (for a while), stay; (*fare una pausa*) to take a break

sos'tegno [sos'teɲɲo] sm support; **a ~ di** in support of; **muro di ~** supporting wall

soste'nere /**121**/ vт to support; (*prendere su di sé*) to take on, bear; (*resistere*) to withstand, stand up to; (*affermare*): **~ che** to maintain that; **sostenersi** vpr to hold o.s. up, support o.s.; (*fig*) to keep up one's strength; **~ qn** (*moralmente*) to be a support to sb; (*difendere*) to stand up for sb, take sb's part; **~ gli esami** to sit exams; **~ il confronto** to bear *o* stand comparison

soste'nibile ag (*tesi*) tenable; (*spese*) bearable; (*sviluppo*) sustainable

soste'nitore, -'trice sm/f supporter

sostenta'mento sm maintenance, support; **mezzi di ~** means of support

soste'nuto, -a ag (*stile*) elevated; (*velocità, ritmo*) sustained; (*prezzo*) high ▶ sm/f: **fare il(la) ~(a)** to be standoffish, keep one's distance

sostitu'ire /**55**/ vт (*mettere al posto di*): **~ qn/qc a** to substitute sb/sth for; (*prendere il posto di*) to replace, take the place of

sostitu'tivo, -a ag (*Amm: documento, certificato*) equivalent

sosti'tuto, -a sm/f substitute; **~ procuratore della Repubblica** (*Dir*) deputy public prosecutor

sostituzi'one [sostitut'tsjone] sf substitution; **in ~ di** as a substitute for, in place of

sotta'ceti [sotta'tʃeti] smpl pickles

sot'tana sf (*sottoveste*) underskirt; (*gonna*) skirt; (*Rel*) soutane, cassock

sot'tecchi [sot'tekki] av: **guardare di ~** to steal a glance at

sotter'fugio [sotter'fudʒo] sm subterfuge

sotter'raneo, -a ag underground ▶ sm cellar

sotter'rare /**72**/ vт to bury

sottigli'ezza [sottiʎ'ʎettsa] SF thinness; slimness; (fig: acutezza) subtlety; shrewdness; **sottigliezze** SFPL (pedanteria) quibbles

sot'tile AG thin; (figura, caviglia) thin, slim, slender; (fine: polvere, capelli) fine; (fig: leggero) light; (: vista) sharp, keen; (: olfatto) fine, discriminating; (: mente) subtle; shrewd ▶ SM: **non andare per il ~** not to mince matters

sottiliz'zare [sottilid'dzare] /72/ VI to split hairs

sottin'tendere /120/ VT (intendere qc non espresso) to understand; (implicare) to imply; **lasciare ~ che** to let it be understood that

sottin'teso, -a PP di **sottintendere** ▶ SM allusion; **parlare senza sottintesi** to speak plainly

'sotto PREP (gen) under; (più in basso di) below ▶ AV underneath, beneath; below; (al piano inferiore): **(al piano) di ~** downstairs; **~ il monte** at the foot of the mountain; **~ la pioggia/il sole** in the rain/sun(shine); **tutti quelli ~ i 18 anni** all those under 18 (years of age) (BRIT) o under age 18 (US); **~ il livello del mare** below sea level; **~ il chilo** under o less than a kilo; **ha 5 impiegati ~ di sé** he has 5 clerks under him; **siamo ~ Natale/Pasqua** it's nearly Christmas/Easter; **~ un certo punto di vista** in a sense; **~ forma di** in the form of; **~ falso nome** under a false name; **~ terra** underground; **~ voce** in a low voice; **chiuso ~ vuoto** vacuum packed

sotto'banco AV (di nascosto: vendere, comprare) under the counter; (: agire) in an underhand way

sottobicchi'ere [sottobik'kjɛre] SM mat, coaster

sotto'bosco, -schi SM undergrowth no pl

sotto'braccio [sotto'brattʃo] AV by the arm; **prendere qn ~** to take sb by the arm; **camminare ~ a qn** to walk arm in arm with sb

sottochi'ave [sotto'kjave] AV under lock and key

sottoco'perta AV (Naut) below deck

sotto'costo AV below cost (price)

sottocu'taneo, -a AG subcutaneous

sottoes'posto, -a AG (fotografia, pellicola) underexposed

sotto'fondo SM background; **~ musicale** background music

sotto'gamba AV: **prendere qc ~** not to take sth seriously

sotto'gonna SF underskirt

sottogo'verno SM political patronage

sotto'gruppo SM subgroup; (di partito) faction

sottoline'are /72/ VT to underline; (fig) to emphasize, stress

sot't'olio AV, AG INV in oil

sotto'mano AV (a portata di mano) within reach, to hand; (di nascosto) secretly

sottoma'rino, -a AG (flora) submarine; (cavo, navigazione) underwater ▶ SM (Naut) submarine

sotto'messo, -a PP di **sottomettere** ▶ AG submissive

sotto'mettere /63/ VT to subdue, subjugate; **sottomettersi** VPR to submit

sottomissi'one SF submission

sottopas'saggio [sottopas'saddʒo] SM (Aut) underpass; (pedonale) subway, underpass

sotto'porre /77/ VT (costringere) to subject; (fig: presentare) to submit; **sottoporsi** VPR to submit; **sottoporsi a** (subire) to undergo

sotto'posto, -a PP di **sottoporre**

sottopro'dotto SM by-product

sottoproduzi'one [sottoprodut'tsjone] SF underproduction

sottoproletari'ato SM: **il ~** the underprivileged class

sot'tordine AV: **passare in ~** to become of minor importance

sottos'cala SM INV (ripostiglio) cupboard (BRIT) o closet (US) under the stairs; (stanza) room under the stairs

sottos'critto, -a PP di **sottoscrivere** ▶ SM/F: **io ~, il ~** the undersigned

sottos'crivere /105/ VT to sign ▶ VI: **~ a** to subscribe to

sottoscrizi'one [sottoskrit'tsjone] SF signing; subscription

sottosegre'tario SM: **S~ di Stato** undersecretary of state (BRIT), assistant secretary of state (US)

sotto'sopra AV upside-down

sottos'tante AG (piani) lower; **nella valle ~** in the valley below

sottos'tare /116/ VI: **~ a** (assoggettarsi a) to submit to; (: richieste) to give in to; (subire: prova) to undergo

sottosu'olo SM subsoil

sottosvilup'pato, -a AG underdeveloped

sottosvi'luppo SM underdevelopment

sottote'nente SM (Mil) second lieutenant

sotto'terra AV underground

sotto'tetto SM attic

sotto'titolo SM subtitle

sottovalu'tare /72/ VT (persona, prova) to underestimate, underrate

sotto'vento AV (Naut) leeward(s) ▶ AG INV (lato) leeward, lee

sotto'veste SF underskirt

sotto'voce [sotto'votʃe] AV in a low voice

sottovu'oto AV: **confezionare ~** to vacuum-pack ▶ AG: **confezione f ~** vacuum pack

sot'trarre /123/ VT (*Mat*) to subtract, take away; **sottrarsi** VPR: **sottrarsi a** (*sfuggire*) to escape; (*evitare*) to avoid; **~ qn/qc a** (*togliere*) to remove sb/sth from; (*salvare*) to save o rescue sb/sth from; **~ qc a qn** (*rubare*) to steal sth from sb; **sottratte le spese** once expenses have been deducted

sot'tratto, -a PP *di* **sottrarre**

sottrazi'one [sottrat'tsjone] SF (*Mat*) subtraction; (*furto*) removal

sottuffici'ale [sottuffi'tʃale] SM (*Mil*) non-commissioned officer; (*Naut*) petty officer

soufflé [su'fle] SM INV (*Cuc*) soufflé

souve'nir [suvə'nir] SM INV souvenir

so'vente AV often

soverchi'are [sover'kjare] /19/ VT to overpower, overwhelm

soverchie'ria [soverkje'ria] SF (*prepotenza*) abuse (of power)

sovi'etico, -a, -ci, -che AG Soviet ▶ SM/F Soviet citizen

sovrabbon'dante AG overabundant

sovrabbon'danza [sovrabbon'dantsa] SF overabundance; **in ~** in excess

sovraccari'care /20/ VT to overload

sovrac'carico, -a, -chi, -che AG: **~ (di)** overloaded (with) ▶ SM excess load; **~ di lavoro** extra work

sovraesposizi'one [sovraespozit'tsjone] SF (*Fot*) overexposure

sovraffol'lato, -a AG overcrowded

sovraimmagazzi'nare [sovraimmagaddzi'nare] /72/ VT to overstock

sovranità SF sovereignty; (*fig: superiorità*) supremacy

sovrannatu'rale AG = **soprannaturale**

so'vrano, -a AG sovereign; (*fig: sommo*) supreme ▶ SM/F sovereign, monarch

sovrappopolazi'one [sovrappopolat'tsjone] SF overpopulation

sovrap'porre /77/ VT to place on top of, put on top of; (*Fot, Geom*) to superimpose; **sovrapporsi** VPR (*fig: aggiungersi*) to be added; (*Fot*) to be superimposed

sovrapposizi'one [sovrapposit'tsjone] SF superimposition

sovrap'posto, -a PP *di* **sovrapporre**

sovrapproduzi'one [sovrapprodut'tsjone] SF overproduction

sovras'tante AG overhanging; (*fig*) imminent

sovras'tare /72/ VT (*vallata, fiume*) to overhang; (*fig*) to hang over, threaten

sovrastrut'tura SF superstructure

sovrecci'tare [sovrettʃi'tare] /72/ VT to overexcite

sovrimpressi'one SF (*Fot, Cine*) double exposure; **immagini in ~** superimposed images

sovrinten'dente *etc* = **soprintendente** *ecc*

sovru'mano, -a AG superhuman

sovve'nire /128/ VI (*venire in mente*): **~ a** to occur to

sovvenzio'nare [sovventsjo'nare] /72/ VT to subsidize

sovvenzi'one [sovven'tsjone] SF subsidy, grant

sovver'sivo, -a AG subversive

sovverti'mento SM subversion, undermining

sovver'tire /45/ VT (*Pol: ordine, stato*) to subvert, undermine

'sozzo, -a ['sottso] AG filthy, dirty

SP SIGLA = **La Spezia**

S.P. ABBR = **strada provinciale**; *vedi* **provinciale**

S.p.A. ABBR *vedi* **società per azioni**

spac'care /20/ VT to split, break; (*legna*) to chop; (*fig*) to divide; **spaccarsi** VPR to split, break

spacca'tura SF split

spaccherò *etc* [spakke'rɔ] VB *vedi* **spaccare**

spacci'are [spat'tʃare] /14/ VT (*vendere*) to sell (off); (*mettere in circolazione*) to circulate; (*droga*) to peddle, push; **spacciarsi** VPR: **spacciarsi per** (*farsi credere*) to pass o.s. off as, pretend to be

spacci'ato, -a [spat'tʃato] AG (*col: malato, fuggiasco*): **essere ~** to be done for

spaccia'tore, -'trice [spattʃa'tore] SM/F (*di droga*) pusher; (*di denaro falso*) dealer

'spaccio ['spattʃo] SM: **~ (di)** (*di merce rubata, droga*) trafficking (in); (*di denaro falso*) passing (of); (*vendita*) sale; (*bottega*) shop

'spacco, -chi SM (*fenditura*) split, crack; (*strappo*) tear; (*di gonna*) slit

spac'cone SMF boaster, braggart

'spada SF sword

spadroneggi'are [spadroned'dʒare] /62/ VI to swagger

spae'sato, -a AG disorientated, lost

spaghet'tata [spaget'tata] SF spaghetti meal

spa'ghetti [spa'getti] SMPL (*Cuc*) spaghetti *sg*

'Spagna ['spaɲɲa] SF: **la ~** Spain

spa'gnolo, -a [spaɲ'ɲɔlo] AG Spanish ▶ SM/F Spaniard ▶ SM (*Ling*) Spanish; **gli Spagnoli** the Spanish

'spago, -ghi SM string, twine; **dare ~ a qn** (*fig*) to let sb have his (o her) way

spai'ato, -a AG (*calza, guanto*) odd

spalan'care /20/ VT, **spalan'carsi** VPR to open wide

spa'lare /72/ VT to shovel

'spalla SF shoulder; (*fig: Teat*) stooge; **spalle** SFPL (*dorso*) back; **di spalle** from behind; **seduto alle mie spalle** sitting behind me; **prendere/colpire qn alle spalle** to take/hit sb from behind; **mettere qn con le spalle al muro** (*fig*) to put sb with his (*o* her) back to the wall; **vivere alle spalle di qn** (*fig*) to live off sb

spal'lata SF (*urto*) shove *o* push with the shoulder; **dare una ~ a qc** to give sth a push *o* shove with one's shoulder

spalleggi'are [spalled'dʒare] /**62**/ VT to back up, support

spal'letta SF (*parapetto*) parapet

spalli'era SF (*di sedia ecc*) back; (*di letto: da capo*) head(board); (*: da piedi*) foot(board); (*Ginnastica*) wall bars *pl*

spal'lina SF (*Mil*) epaulette; (*di sottoveste, maglietta*) strap; (*imbottitura*) shoulder pad; **senza spalline** strapless

spal'mare /**72**/ VT to spread

'spalti SMPL (*di stadio*) terraces (*BRIT*), ≈ bleachers (*US*)

spamming ['spammiŋ] SM (*Internet*) spamming

'spandere /**110**/ VT to spread; (*versare*) to pour (out); **spandersi** VPR to spread; **~ lacrime** to shed tears

'spanto, -a PP *di* **spandere**

spa'rare /**72**/ VT to fire ▶ VI (*far fuoco*) to fire; (*tirare*) to shoot; **~ a qn/qc** to shoot sb/sth, fire at sb/sth

spa'rato SM (*di camicia*) dicky

spara'tore SM gunman

spara'toria SF exchange of shots

sparecchi'are [sparek'kjare] /**19**/ VT: **~ (la tavola)** to clear the table

spa'reggio [spa'reddʒo] SM (*Sport*) play-off

'spargere ['spardʒere] /**111**/ VT (*spargagliare*) to scatter; (*versare: vino*) to spill; (*: lacrime, sangue*) to shed; (*diffondere*) to spread; (*emanare*) to give off (*o* out); **spargersi** VPR (*voce, notizia*) to spread; (*persone*) to scatter; **si è sparsa una voce sul suo conto** there is a rumour going round about him

spargi'mento [spardʒi'mento] SM scattering; spilling; shedding; **~ di sangue** bloodshed

spa'rire /**112**/ VI to disappear, vanish; **~ dalla circolazione** (*fig: col*) to lie low, keep a low profile

sparizi'one [sparit'tsjone] SF disappearance

spar'lare /**72**/ VI: **~ di** to run down, speak ill of

'sparo SM shot

sparpagli'are [sparpaʎ'ʎare] /**27**/ VT, **sparpagli'arsi** VPR to scatter

'sparso, -a PP *di* **spargere** ▶ AG scattered; (*sciolto*) loose; **in ordine ~** (*Mil*) in open order

sparti'acque SM (*Geo*) watershed

sparti'neve SM INV snowplough (*BRIT*), snowplow (*US*)

spar'tire /**55**/ VT (*eredità, bottino*) to share out; (*avversari*) to separate

spar'tito SM (*Mus*) score

sparti'traffico SM INV (*Aut*) central reservation (*BRIT*), median (strip) (*US*)

spartizi'one [spartit'tsjone] SF division

spa'ruto, -a AG (*viso ecc*) haggard

sparvi'ero SM (*Zool*) sparrowhawk

spasi'mante SM suitor

spasi'mare /**72**/ VI to be in agony; **~ di fare** (*fig*) to yearn to do; **~ per qn** to be madly in love with sb

'spasimo SM pang

'spasmo SM (*Med*) spasm

spas'modico, -a, -ci, -che AG (*angoscioso*) agonizing; (*Med*) spasmodic

spas'sarsela /**72**/ VI to enjoy o.s., have a good time

spassio'nato, -a AG dispassionate, impartial

'spasso SM (*divertimento*) amusement, enjoyment; **andare a ~** to go out for a walk; **essere a ~** (*fig*) to be out of work; **mandare qn a ~** (*fig*) to give sb the sack

spas'soso, -a AG amusing, entertaining

'spastico, -a, -ci, -che AG, SM/F spastic

'spatola SF spatula; (*di muratore*) trowel

spau'racchio [spau'rakkjo] SM scarecrow

spau'rire /**55**/ VT to frighten, terrify

spavalde'ria SF boldness, arrogance

spa'valdo, -a AG arrogant, bold

spaventa'passeri SM INV scarecrow

spaven'tare /**72**/ VT to frighten, scare; **spaventarsi** VPR to become frightened, become scared; to get a fright

spa'vento SM fear, fright; **far ~ a qn** to give sb a fright

spaven'toso, -a AG frightening, terrible; (*fig: col*) tremendous, fantastic

spazi'ale [spat'tsjale] AG (*volo, nave, tuta*) space *cpd*; (*Archit, Geom*) spatial

spazia'tura [spattsja'tura] SF (*Tip*) spacing

spazien'tirsi [spattsjen'tirsi] /**55**/ VPR to lose one's patience

'spazio ['spattsjo] SM space; (*posto*) room, space; **fare ~ per qc/qn** to make room for sth/sb; **nello ~ di un'ora** within an hour, in the space of an hour; **dare ~ a** (*fig*) to make room for; **~ aereo** airspace

spazi'oso, -a [spat'tsjoso] AG spacious

spazzaca'mino [spattsaka'mino] SM chimney sweep

spazza'neve [spattsa'neve] SM INV (*spartineve, Sci*) snowplough (*BRIT*), snowplow (*US*)

spaz'zare [spat'tsare] /**72**/ VT to sweep; (*foglie ecc*) to sweep up; (*cacciare*) to sweep away

spazza'tura [spattsa'tura] SF sweepings *pl*; (*immondizia*) rubbish

spaz'zino [spat'tsino] SM street sweeper

'spazzola ['spattsola] SF brush; **capelli a ~** crew cut *sg*; **~ per abiti** clothesbrush; **~ da capelli** hairbrush

S

spazzo'lare [spattso'lare] /**72**/ VT to brush
spazzo'lino [spattso'lino] SM (small) brush;
~ **da denti** toothbrush
specchi'arsi [spek'kjarsi] /**19**/ VPR to look at
o.s. in a mirror; (*riflettersi*) to be mirrored, be
reflected
specchi'era [spek'kjɛra] SF large mirror;
(*mobile*) dressing table
specchi'etto [spek'kjetto] SM (*tabella*) table,
chart; ~ **da borsetta** pocket mirror;
~ **retrovisore** (*Aut*) rear-view mirror
specchio [ˈspɛkkjo] SM mirror; (*tabella*)
table, chart; **uno ~ d'acqua** a sheet of water
speci'ale [spe'tʃale] AG special; **in special
modo** especially; **inviato ~** (*Radio, TV,
Stampa*) special correspondent; **offerta ~**
special offer; **poteri/leggi speciali** (*Pol*)
emergency powers/legislation
specia'lista, -i, -e [spetʃa'lista] SM/F
specialist
specia'listico, -a, -ci, -che [spetʃa'listiko]
AG (*conoscenza, preparazione*) specialized
specialità [spetʃali'ta] SF INV speciality;
(*branca di studio*) special field, speciality
specializ'zare [spetʃalid'dzare] /**72**/ VT
(*industria*) to make more specialized;
specializzarsi VPR: **specializzarsi (in)** to
specialize (in)
specializ'zato, -a [spetʃalid'dzato] AG
(*manodopera*) skilled; **operaio non ~**
semiskilled worker; **essere ~ in** to be a
specialist in
specializzazi'one [spetʃaliddzat'tsjone] SF
specialization; **prendere la ~ in** to
specialize in
special'mente [spetʃal'mente] AV especially,
particularly
specie [ˈspɛtʃe] SF INV (*Biol, Bot, Zool*) species
inv; (*tipo*) kind, sort ▶ AV especially,
particularly; **una ~ di** a kind of; **fare ~ a qn**
to surprise sb; **la ~ umana** mankind
spe'cifica, -che [spe'tʃifika] SF specification
specifi'care [spetʃifi'kare] /**20**/ VT to specify,
state
specificata'mente [spetʃifikata'mente] AV
in detail
spe'cifico, -a, -ci, -che [spe'tʃifiko] AG
specific
speck [ʃpɛk] SM INV *kind of smoked ham*
specu'lare /**72**/ VI: ~ **su** (*Comm*) to speculate in;
(*sfruttare*) to exploit; (*meditare*) to speculate on
specula'tore, -'trice SM/F (*Comm*) speculator
speculazi'one [spekulat'tsjone] SF
speculation
spe'dire /**55**/ VT to send; (*Comm*) to dispatch,
forward; ~ **per posta** to post (*BRIT*), mail
(*US*); ~ **per mare** to ship
spedita'mente AV quickly; **camminare ~**
to walk at a brisk pace

spe'dito, -a AG (*gen*) quick; **con passo ~** at a
brisk pace
spedizi'one [spedit'tsjone] SF sending; (*collo*)
consignment; (*scientifica ecc*) expedition;
(*Comm*) forwarding; shipping; **fare una ~**
to send a consignment; **agenzia di ~**
forwarding agency; **spese di ~** postal
charges; (*Comm*) forwarding charges
spedizioni'ere [spedittsjo'njɛre] SM
forwarding agent, shipping agent
spegnere [ˈspɛɲɲere] /**113**/ VT (*fuoco, sigaretta*)
to put out, extinguish; (*apparecchio elettrico*) to
turn o switch off; (*gas*) to turn off; (*fig: suoni,
passioni*) to stifle; (*debito*) to cancel; **spegnersi**
VPR to go out; to go off; (*morire*) to pass away;
puoi ~ la luce? could you switch off the
light?
speleolo'gia [speleolo'dʒia] SF (*studio*)
speleology; (*pratica*) potholing (*BRIT*),
speleology
spele'ologo, -a, -gi, -ghe SM/F speleologist;
potholer
spel'lare /**72**/ VT (*scuoiare*) to skin; (*scorticare*) to
graze; **spellarsi** VPR to peel
spendacci'one, -a [spendat'tʃone] SM/F
spendthrift
spendere /**8**/ VT to spend; ~ **una buona
parola per qn** (*fig*) to put in a good word
for sb
spengo etc VB vedi **spegnere**
spen'nare /**72**/ VT to pluck
spensi etc VB vedi **spegnere**
spensiera'tezza [spensjera'tettsa] SF
carefreeness, lightheartedness
spensie'rato, -a AG carefree
spento, -a PP di **spegnere** ▶ AG (*suono*)
muffled; (*colore*) dull; (*sigaretta*) out; (*civiltà,
vulcano*) extinct
spe'ranza [spe'rantsa] SF hope; **nella ~ di
rivederti** hoping to see o in the hope of
seeing you again; **pieno di speranze**
hopeful; **senza ~** (*situazione*) hopeless; (*amare*)
without hope
speran'zoso, -a [speran'tsoso] AG hopeful
spe'rare /**72**/ VT to hope for ▶ VI: ~ **in** to trust
in; ~ **che/di fare** to hope that/to do; **lo
spero, spero di sì** I hope so; **tutto fa ~ per
il meglio** everything leads one to hope for
the best
sper'duto, -a AG (*isolato*) out-of-the-way;
(*persona: smarrita, a disagio*) lost
spergi'uro, -a [sper'dʒuro] SM/F perjurer
▶ SM perjury
sperico'lato, -a AG fearless, daring;
(*guidatore*) reckless
sperimen'tale AG experimental; **fare qc in
via ~** to try sth out
sperimen'tare /**72**/ VT to experiment with,
test; (*fig*) to test, put to the test

sperimentazi'one [sperimentat'tsjone] SF experimentation

'**sperma, -i** SM (Biol) sperm

spermato'zoo, -i [spermatod'dzɔo] SM spermatozoon

spe'rone SM spur

sperpe'rare /72/ VT to squander

'**sperpero** SM (di denaro) squandering, waste; (di cibo, materiali) waste

'**spesa** SF (soldi spesi) expense; (costo) cost; (acquisto) purchase; (col: acquisto del cibo quotidiano) shopping; **spese** SFPL expenses; (Comm) costs; charges; **ridurre le spese** (gen) to cut down; (Comm) to reduce expenditure; **fare la ~** to do the shopping; **fare le spese di qc** (fig) to pay the price for sth; **a spese di** (a carico di) at the expense of; **con la modica ~ di 200 euro** for the modest sum o outlay of 200 euros; **~ pubblica** public expenditure; **spese accessorie** incidental · expenses; **spese generali** overheads; **spese di gestione** operating expenses; **spese d'impianto** initial outlay; **spese legali** legal costs; **spese di manutenzione, spese di mantenimento** maintenance costs; **spese postali** postage sg; **spese di sbarco e sdoganamento** landing charges; **spese di trasporto** handling charge; **spese di viaggio** travelling (BRIT) o traveling (US) expenses

spe'sare /72/ VT: **viaggio tutto spesato** all-expenses-paid trip

'**speso, -a** PP di **spendere**

'**spesso, -a** AG (fitto) thick; (frequente) frequent ▶ AV often; **spesse volte** frequently, often

spes'sore SM thickness; **ha uno ~ di 20 cm** it is 20 cm thick

Spett. ABBR vedi **spettabile**

spet'tabile AG (in lettere: abbr Spett.): **~ ditta X** Messrs X and Co; **avvertiamo la ~ clientela · ...** we inform our customers ...

spettaco'lare AG spectacular

spet'tacolo SM (rappresentazione) performance, show; (vista, scena) sight; **dare ~ di sé** to make an exhibition o a spectacle of o.s.

spettaco'loso, -a AG spectacular

spet'tanza [spet'tantsa] SF (competenza) concern; **non è di mia ~** it's no concern of mine

spet'tare /72/ VI: **~ a** (decisione) to be up to; (stipendio) to be due to; **spetta a lei decidere** it's up to you to decide

spetta'tore, -'trice SM/F (Cine, Teat) member of the audience; (di avvenimento) onlooker, witness

spettego'lare /72/ VI to gossip

spetti'nare /72/ VT: **~ qn** to ruffle sb's hair; **spettinarsi** VPR to get one's hair in a mess

spetti'nato, -a AG dishevelled

spet'trale AG spectral, ghostly

'**spettro** SM (fantasma) spectre (BRIT), specter (US); (Fisica) spectrum

'**spezie** ['spettsje] SFPL (Cuc) spices

spez'zare [spet'tsare] /72/ VT (rompere) to break; (fig: interrompere) to break up; **spezzarsi** VPR to break

spezza'tino [spettsa'tino] SM (Cuc) stew

spez'zato, -a [spet'tsato] AG (unghia, ramo, braccio) broken ▶ SM (abito maschile) coordinated jacket and trousers (BRIT) o pants (US); **fare orario ~** to work a split shift

spezzet'tare [spettset'tare] /72/ VT to break up (o chop) into small pieces

spez'zino, -a [spet'tsino] AG of (o from) La Spezia

spez'zone [spet'tsone] SM (Cine) clip

'**spia** SF spy; (confidente della polizia) informer; (Elettr) indicating light; warning light; (fessura) peephole; (fig: sintomo) sign, indication; **~ dell'olio** (Aut) oil warning light

spiacci'care [spjattʃi'kare] /20/ VT to squash, crush

spia'cente [spja'tʃɛnte] AG sorry; **essere ~ di qc/di fare qc** to be sorry about sth/for doing sth; **siamo spiacenti di dovervi annunciare che ...** we regret to announce that ...

spia'cevole [spja'tʃevole] AG unpleasant, disagreeable

spi'aggia, -ge ['spjaddʒa] SF beach; **~ libera** public beach

spia'nare /72/ VT (terreno) to level, make level; (edificio) to raze to the ground; (pasta) to roll out; (rendere liscio) to smooth (out)

spi'ano SM: **a tutto ~** (lavorare) non-stop, without a break; (spendere) lavishly

spian'tato, -a AG penniless, ruined

spi'are /60/ VT to spy on; (occasione ecc) to watch o wait for

spi'ata SF tip-off

spiattel'lare /72/ VT (col: verità, segreto) to blurt out

spi'azzo ['spjattso] SM open space; (radura) clearing

spic'care /20/ VT (assegno, mandato di cattura) to issue ▶ VI (risaltare) to stand out; **~ il volo** to fly off; (fig) to spread one's wings; **~ un balzo** to jump, leap

spic'cato, -a AG (marcato) marked, strong; (notevole) remarkable

spiccherò etc [spikke'rɔ] VB vedi **spiccare**

'**spicchio** ['spikkjo] SM (di agrumi) segment; (di aglio) clove; (parte) piece, slice

spicci'are [spit'tʃare] /14/ VT (faccenda, impegno) to finish off; **spicciarsi** VPR (fare in fretta) to hurry up, get a move on

S

'spiccio, -a, -ci, -ce ['spittʃo] AG (*modi, mezzi*) quick; **andare per le spicce** to be quick off the mark, waste no time

spiccio'lata [spittʃo'lata] AV: **alla ~** in dribs and drabs, a few at a time

'spicciolo, -a ['spittʃolo] AG: **moneta spicciola** (small) change; **spiccioli** SMPL (small) change

'spicco, -chi SM: **fare ~** to stand out; **di ~** outstanding, prominent; (*tema*) main, principal

spie'dino SM (*utensile*) skewer; (*cibo*) kebab

spi'edo SM (*Cuc*) spit; **pollo allo ~** spit-roasted chicken

spiega'mento SM (*Mil*): **~ di forze** deployment of forces

spie'gare /8o/ VT (*far capire*) to explain; (*tovaglia*) to unfold; (*vele*) to unfurl; **spiegarsi** VPR to explain o.s., make o.s. clear; **~ qc a qn** to explain sth to sb; **il problema si spiega** one can understand the problem; **non mi spiego come ...** I can't understand how ...

spiegazi'one [spjegat'tsjone] SF explanation; **avere una ~ con qn** to have it out with sb

spiegaz'zare [spjegat'tsare] /72/ VT to crease, crumple

spiegherò *etc* [spjege'rɔ] VB *vedi* **spiegare**

spie'tato, -a AG ruthless, pitiless

spiffe'rare /72/ VT (*col*) to blurt out, blab

'spiffero SM draught (BRIT), draft (US)

'spiga, -ghe SF (*Bot*) ear

spigli'ato, -a [spiʎ'ʎato] AG self-possessed, self-confident

spigo'lare /72/ VT (*anche fig*) to glean

'spigolo SM corner; (*Geom*) edge

spigo'loso, -a AG (*mobile*) angular; (*persona, carattere*) difficult

'spilla SF brooch; (*da cravatta, cappello*) pin; **~ di sicurezza** *o* **da balia** safety pin

spil'lare /72/ VT (*vino, fig*) to tap; **~ denaro/ notizie a qn** to tap sb for money/ information

'spillo SM pin; (*spilla*) brooch; **tacco a ~** stiletto heel (BRIT), spike heel (US); **~ di sicurezza** *o* **da balia** safety pin; **~ di sicurezza** (*Mil*) (safety) pin

spilorce'ria [spilortʃe'ria] SF meanness, stinginess

spi'lorcio, -a, -ci, -ce [spi'lortʃo] AG mean, stingy

spilun'gone SMF beanpole

'spina SF (*Bot*) thorn; (*Zool*) spine, prickle; (*di pesce*) bone; (*Elettr*) plug; (*di botte*) bunghole; **birra alla ~** draught beer; **stare sulle spine** (*fig*) to be on tenterhooks; **~ dorsale** (*Anat*) backbone

spi'nacio [spi'natʃo] SM spinach *no pl*; (*Cuc*): **spinaci** spinach *sg*

spi'nale AG (*Anat*) spinal

spi'nato, -a AG (*fornito di spine*): **filo ~** barbed wire; (*tessuto*) herringbone *cpd*

spi'nello SM (*Droga: gergo*) joint

'spingere ['spindʒere] /114/ VT to push; (*condurre: anche fig*) to drive; (*stimolare*): **~ qn a fare** to urge *o* press sb to do; **spingersi** VPR (*inoltrarsi*) to push on, carry on; **spingersi troppo lontano** (*anche fig*) to go too far

'spino SM (*Bot*) thorn bush

spi'noso, -a AG thorny, prickly

'spinsi *etc* VB *vedi* **spingere**

spinte'rogeno [spinte'rɔdʒeno] SM (*Aut*) coil ignition

'spinto, -a PP *di* **spingere** ▶ SF (*urto*) push; (*Fisica*) thrust; (*fig: stimolo*) incentive, spur; (: *appoggio*) string-pulling *no pl*; **dare una spinta a qn** (*fig*) to pull strings for sb

spinto'nare /72/ VT to shove, push

spin'tone SM push, shove

spio'naggio [spio'naddʒo] SM espionage, spying

spion'cino [spion'tʃino] SM peephole

spi'one, -a SM/F (*spia*) informer; (*ragazzino, collega*) telltale, sneak

spio'nistico, -a, -ci, -che AG (*organizzazione*) spy *cpd*; **rete spionistica** spy ring

spi'overe /76/ VI (*scorrere*) to flow down; (*ricadere*) to hang down, fall

'spira SF coil

spi'raglio [spi'raʎʎo] SM (*fessura*) chink, narrow opening; (*raggio di luce, fig*) glimmer, gleam

spi'rale SF spiral; (*contraccettivo*) coil; **a ~** spiral(-shaped); **~ inflazionistica** inflationary spiral

spi'rare /72/ VI (*vento*) to blow; (*morire*) to expire, pass away

spiri'tato, -a AG possessed; (*fig: persona, espressione*) wild

spiri'tismo SM spiritualism

'spirito SM (*Rel, Chim, disposizione d'animo, di legge ecc, fantasma*) spirit; (*pensieri, intelletto*) mind; (*arguzia*) wit; (*umorismo*) humour, wit; **in buone condizioni di ~** in the right frame of mind; **è una persona di ~** he has a sense of humour (BRIT) *o* humor (US); **battuta di ~** joke; **~ di classe** class consciousness; **non ha ~ di parte** he never takes sides; **lo S~ Santo** the Holy Spirit *o* Ghost

spirito'saggine [spirito'saddʒine] SF witticism; (*peg*) wisecrack

spiri'toso, -a AG witty

spiritu'ale AG spiritual

splen'dente AG (*giornata*) bright, sunny; (*occhi*) shining; (*pavimento*) shining, gleaming

'splendere /29/ VI to shine

'**splendido, -a** AG splendid; (*splendente*) shining; (*sfarzoso*) magnificent, splendid

splen'dore SM splendour (BRIT), splendor (US); (*luce intensa*) brilliance, brightness

spodes'tare /**72**/ VT to deprive of power; (*sovrano*) to depose

'**spoglia** ['spɔʎʎa] SF *vedi* **spoglio**

spogli'are [spoʎ'ʎare] /**27**/ VT (*svestire*) to undress; (*privare, fig: depredare*): ~ **qn di qc** to deprive sb of sth; (*togliere ornamenti: anche fig*): ~ **qn/qc di** to strip sb/sth of; **spogliarsi** VPR to undress, strip; **spogliarsi di** (*ricchezze ecc*) to deprive o.s. of, give up; (*pregiudizi*) to rid o.s. of

spoglia'rello [spoʎʎa'rɛllo] SM striptease

spoglia'toio [spoʎʎa'tojo] SM dressing room; (*di scuola ecc*) cloakroom; (*Sport*) changing room

'**spoglio, -a** ['spɔʎʎo] AG (*pianta, terreno*) bare; (*privo*): ~ **di** stripped of; lacking in, without ▶ SM (*di voti*) counting ▶ SF (*Zool*) skin, hide; (*di rettile*) slough; **spoglie** SFPL (*salma*) remains; (*preda*) spoils, booty *sg*

'**spola** SF shuttle; (*bobina*) spool; **fare la ~ (fra)** to go to and fro *o* shuttle (between)

spo'letta SF (*Cucito: bobina*) spool; (*di bomba*) fuse

spol'pare /**72**/ VT to strip the flesh off

spolve'rare /**72**/ VT (*anche Cuc*) to dust; (*con spazzola*) to brush; (*con battipanni*) to beat; (*fig: mangiare*) to polish off ▶ VI to dust

spolve'rino SM (*soprabito*) dust coat

'**sponda** SF (*di fiume*) bank; (*di mare, lago*) shore; (*bordo*) edge

sponsoriz'zare [sponsorid'dzare] /**72**/ VT to sponsor

sponsorizzazi'one [sponsoriddzat'tsjone] SF sponsorship

spontanea'mente AV (*comportarsi*) naturally; (*agire*) spontaneously; (*reagire*) instinctively, spontaneously

spon'taneo, -a AG spontaneous; (*persona*) unaffected, natural; **di sua spontanea volontà** of his own free will

spopo'lare /**72**/ VT to depopulate ▶ VI (*attirare folla*) to draw the crowds; **spopolarsi** VPR to become depopulated

spo'radico, -a, -ci, -che AG sporadic

sporcacci'one, -a [sporkat'tʃone] SM/F (*peg*) pig, filthy person

spor'care /**20**/ VT to dirty, make dirty; (*fig*) to sully, soil; **sporcarsi** VPR to get dirty

spor'cizia [spor'tʃittsja] SF (*stato*) dirtiness; (*sudiciume*) dirt, filth; (*cosa sporca*) dirt *no pl*, something dirty; (*fig: cosa oscena*) obscenity

'**sporco, -a, -chi, -che** AG dirty, filthy; **avere la coscienza sporca** to have a guilty conscience

spor'genza [spor'dʒɛntsa] SF projection

'**sporgere** ['spɔrdʒere] /**115**/ VT to put out, stretch out ▶ VI (*venire in fuori*) to stick out; **sporgersi** VPR to lean out; ~ **querela contro qn** (*Dir*) to take legal action against sb

'**sporsi** *etc* VB *vedi* **sporgere**

sport SM INV sport

'**sporta** SF shopping bag

spor'tello SM (*di treno, auto ecc*) door; (*di banca, ufficio*) window, counter; ~ **automatico** (*Banca*) cash dispenser, automated telling machine

spor'tivo, -a AG (*gara, giornale*) sports *cpd*; (*persona*) sporty; (*abito*) casual; (*spirito, atteggiamento*) sporting ▶ SM/F sportsman(-woman); **campo ~** playing field; **giacca sportiva** sports (BRIT) *o* sport (US) jacket

'**sporto, -a** PP *di* **sporgere**

'**sposa** SF bride; (*moglie*) wife; **abito** *o* **vestito da ~** wedding dress

sposa'lizio [spoza'littsjo] SM wedding

spo'sare /**72**/ VT to marry; (*fig: idea, fede*) to espouse; **sposarsi** VPR to get married, marry; **sposarsi con qn** to marry sb, get married to sb

spo'sato, -a AG married

'**sposo** SM (*bride*)groom; (*marito*) husband; **gli sposi** the newlyweds

spos'sante AG exhausting

spos'satezza [spossa'tettsa] SF exhaustion

spos'sato, -a AG exhausted, weary

sposta'mento SM movement, change of position

spos'tare /**72**/ VT to move, shift; (*cambiare: orario*) to change; **spostarsi** VPR to move; **hanno spostato la partenza di qualche giorno** they postponed *o* put off their departure by a few days

spot [spɔt] SM INV (*faretto*) spotlight, spot; (*TV*) advert, commercial, ad

'**spranga, -ghe** SF (*sbarra*) bar; (*catenaccio*) bolt

spran'gare /**80**/ VT to bar; to bolt

spray ['spraɪ] SM INV (*dispositivo, sostanza*) spray ▶ AG INV (*bombola, confezione*) spray *cpd*

'**sprazzo** ['sprattso] SM (*di sole ecc*) flash; (*fig: di gioia ecc*) burst

spre'care /**20**/ VT to waste; **sprecarsi** VPR (*persona*) to waste one's energy

'**spreco, -chi** SM waste

spre'gevole [spre'dʒevole] AG contemptible, despicable

'**spregio** ['spredʒo] SM scorn, disdain

spregiudi'cato, -a [spredʒudi'kato] AG unprejudiced, unbiased; (*peg*) unscrupulous

spre'mere /**62**/ VT to squeeze; **spremersi le meningi** (*fig*) to rack one's brains

spremia'grumi SM INV lemon squeezer

spre'muta SF fresh fruit juice; ~ **d'arancia** fresh orange juice

sprez'zante [spret'tsante] AG scornful, contemptuous

'**sprezzo** ['sprettso] SM contempt, scorn, disdain

sprigio'nare [sprid3o'nare] /**72**/ VT to give off, emit; **sprigionarsi** VPR to emanate; (*uscire con impeto*) to burst out

spriz'zare [sprit'tsare] /**72**/ VT, VI to spurt; **~ gioia/salute** to be bursting with joy/ health

sprofon'dare /**72**/ VI to sink; (*casa*) to collapse; (*suolo*) to give way, subside; **sprofondarsi** VPR: **sprofondarsi in** (*poltrona*) to sink into; (*fig*) to become immersed o absorbed in

sproloqui'are /**19**/ VI to ramble on

spro'loquio SM rambling speech

spro'nare /**72**/ VT to spur (on)

'**sprone** SM (*sperone, fig*) spur

sproporzio'nato, -a [sproportsjo'nato] AG disproportionate, out of all proportion

sproporzi'one [sropor'tsjone] SF disproportion

sproposi'tato, -a AG (*lettera, discorso*) full of mistakes; (*fig: costo*) excessive, enormous

spro'posito SM blunder; **a ~** at the wrong time; (*rispondere, parlare*) irrelevantly

sprovve'duto, -a AG inexperienced, naïve

sprov'visto, -a AG (*mancante*): **~ di** lacking in, without; **ne siamo sprovvisti** (*negozio*) we are out of it (o them); **alla sprovvista** unawares

spruz'zare [sprut'tsare] /**72**/ VT (*a nebulizzazione*) to spray; (*aspergere*) to sprinkle; (*inzaccherare*) to splash

spruzza'tore [spruttsa'tore] SM (*per profumi*) spray, atomizer; (*per biancheria*) sprinkler, spray

'**spruzzo** ['spruttso] SM spray; splash; **verniciatura a ~** spray painting

spudora'tezza [spudora'tettsa] SF shamelessness

spudo'rato, -a AG shameless

'**spugna** ['spuɲɲa] SF (*Zool*) sponge; (*tessuto*) towelling

spu'gnoso, -a [spuɲ'ɲoso] AG spongy

spulci'are [spul'tʃare] /**14**/ VT (*animali*) to rid of fleas; (*fig: testo, compito*) to examine thoroughly

'**spuma** SF (*schiuma*) foam; (*bibita*) fizzy drink

spu'mante SM sparkling wine

spumeggi'ante [spumed'dʒante] AG (*vino, fig*) sparkling; (*birra, mare*) foaming

spu'mone SM (*Cuc*) mousse

spun'tare /**72**/ SM : **allo ~ del sole** at sunrise; : **allo ~ del giorno** at daybreak ▶ VT (*coltello*) to break the point of; (*capelli*) to trim; (*elenco*) to tick off (BRIT), check off (US) ▶ VI (*uscire: germogli*) to sprout; (*: capelli*) to begin to grow;

(*: denti*) to come through; (*apparire*) to appear (suddenly); **spuntarsi** VPR to become blunt, lose its point; **spuntarla** (*fig*) to make it, win through

spun'tino SM snack

'**spunto** SM (*Teat, Mus*) cue; (*fig*) starting point; **dare lo ~ a** (*fig*) to give rise to; **prendere ~ da qc** to take sth as one's starting point

spur'gare /**80**/ VT (*fogna*) to clean, clear; **spurgarsi** VPR (*Med*) to expectorate

spu'tare /**72**/ VT to spit out; (*fig*) to belch (out) ▶ VI to spit

'**sputo** SM spittle *no pl*, spit *no pl*

sputta'nare /**72**/ VT (*col*) to bad-mouth

spyware ['spaiwer] SM INV (*Inform*) spyware (program)

'**squadra** SF (*strumento*) (set) square; (*gruppo*) team, squad; (*di operai*) gang, squad; (*Mil*) squad; (*: Aer, Naut*) squadron; (*Sport*) team; **lavoro a squadre** teamwork; **~ mobile/del buon costume** (*Polizia*) flying/vice squad

squa'drare /**72**/ VT to square, make square; (*osservare*) to look at closely

squa'driglia [skwa'driʎʎa] SF (*Aer*) flight; (*Naut*) squadron

squa'drone SM squadron

squagli'arsi [skwaʎ'ʎarsi] /**27**/ VPR to melt; (*fig*) to sneak off

squa'lifica, -che SF disqualification

squalifi'care /**20**/ VT to disqualify

'**squallido, -a** AG wretched, bleak

squal'lore SM wretchedness, bleakness

'**squalo** SM shark

'**squama** SF scale

squa'mare /**72**/ VT to scale; **squamarsi** VPR to flake o peel (off)

squarcia'gola [skwartʃa'gola]: **a ~** AV at the top of one's voice

squarci'are [skwar'tʃare] /**14**/ VT (*muro, corpo*) to rip open; (*tessuto*) to rip; (*fig: tenebre, silenzio*) to split; (*: nuvole*) to pierce

'**squarcio** ['skwartʃo] SM (*ferita*) gash; (*in lenzuolo, abito*) rip; (*in un muro*) breach; (*in una nave*) hole; (*brano*) passage, excerpt; **uno ~ di sole** a burst of sunlight

squar'tare /**72**/ VT to quarter, cut up; (*cadavere*) to dismember

squattri'nato, -a AG penniless ▶ SM/F pauper

squili'brare /**72**/ VT to unbalance

squili'brato, -a AG (*Psic*) unbalanced ▶ SM/F deranged person

squi'librio SM (*differenza, sbilancio*) imbalance; (*Psic*) derangement

squil'lante AG (*suono*) shrill, sharp; (*voce*) shrill

squil'lare /**72**/ VI (*campanello, telefono*) to ring (out); (*tromba*) to blare

'squillo SM ring, ringing *no pl*; blare ▶ SF INV (*anche:* **ragazza squillo**) call girl

squi'sito, -a AG exquisite; (*cibo*) delicious; (*persona*) delightful

squit'tire /**55**/ VI (*uccello*) to squawk; (*topo*) to squeak

SR SIGLA = **Siracusa**

sradi'care /**20**/ VT to uproot; (*fig*) to eradicate

sragio'nare [zradʒo'nare] /**72**/ VI to talk nonsense, rave

srego'latezza [zregola'tettsa] SF (*nel mangiare, bere*) lack of moderation; (*di vita*) dissoluteness, dissipation

srego'lato, -a AG (*senza ordine: vita*) disorderly; (*smodato*) immoderate; (*dissoluto*) dissolute

Sri 'Lanka [sri'lanka] SM: **lo ~** Sri Lanka

S.r.l. ABBR *vedi* **società a responsabilità limitata**

sroto'lare /**72**/ VT, **sroto'larsi** VPR to unroll

SS SIGLA = **Sassari**

S.S. ABBR (*Rel*) = **Sua Santità**; **Santa Sede**; **santi, santissimo**; (*Aut*) = **strada statale**; *vedi* **statale**

S.S.N. ABBR (= *Servizio Sanitario Nazionale*) ≈ NHS

sta *etc* VB *vedi* **stare**

'stabbio SM (*recinto*) pen, fold; (*di maiali*) pigsty; (*letame*) manure

'stabile AG stable, steady; (*tempo: non variabile*) settled; (*Teat: compagnia*) resident ▶ SM (*edificio*) building; **teatro ~** civic theatre

stabili'mento SM (*edificio*) establishment; (*fabbrica*) plant, factory; **~ balneare** bathing establishment; **~ tessile** textile mill

stabi'lire /**55**/ VT to establish; (*fissare: prezzi, data*) to fix; (*decidere*) to decide; **stabilirsi** VPR (*prendere dimora*) to settle; **resta stabilito che …** it is agreed that …

stabilità SF stability

stabiliz'zare [stabilid'dzare] /**72**/ VT to stabilize

stabilizza'tore [stabiliddza'tore] SM stabilizer; (*fig*) stabilizing force

stabilizzazi'one [stabiliddzat'tsjone] SF stabilization

stacano'vista, -i, -e SM/F (*ironico*) eager beaver

stac'care /**20**/ VT (*levare*) to detach, remove; (*separare: anche fig*) to separate, divide; (*strappare*) to tear off (*o out*); (*scandire: parole*) to pronounce clearly; (*Sport*) to leave behind; **staccarsi** VPR (*bottone ecc*) to come off; (*scostarsi*) **staccarsi (da)** to move away (from); (*fig: separarsi*) **staccarsi da** to leave; **non ~ gli occhi da qn** not to take one's eyes off sb; **~ la televisione/il telefono** to disconnect the television/the phone; **~ un assegno** to write a cheque

staccio'nata [stattʃo'nata] SF (*gen*) fence; (*Ippica*) hurdle

'stacco, -chi SM (*intervallo*) gap; (: *tra due scene*) break; (*differenza*) difference; (*Sport: nel salto*) takeoff

sta'dera SF lever scales *pl*

'stadio SM (*Sport*) stadium; (*periodo, fase*) phase, stage

'staffa SF (*di sella, Tecn*) stirrup; **perdere le staffe** (*fig*) to fly off the handle

staf'fetta SF (*messo*) dispatch rider; (*Sport*) relay race

stagflazi'one [stagflat'tsjone] SF (*Econ*) stagflation

stagio'nale [stadʒo'nale] AG seasonal ▶ SMF seasonal worker

stagio'nare [stadʒo'nare] /**72**/ VT (*legno*) to season; (*formaggi, vino*) to mature

stagio'nato, -a [stadʒo'nato] AG seasoned; matured; (*scherzoso: attempato*) getting on in years

stagi'one [sta'dʒone] SF season; **alta/bassa ~** high/low season

sta'gista, -i, -e [sta'dʒista] SM/F trainee, intern (*US*)

stagli'arsi [staʎ'ʎarsi] /**27**/ VPR to stand out, be silhouetted

sta'gnante [staɲ'ɲante] AG stagnant

sta'gnare [staɲ'ɲare] /**15**/ VT (*vaso, tegame*) to tin-plate; (*barca, botte*) to make watertight; (*sangue*) to stop ▶ VI to stagnate

sta'gnino [staɲ'ɲino] SM tinsmith

'stagno, -a ['staɲɲo] AG (*a tenuta d'acqua*) watertight; (*a tenuta d'aria*) airtight ▶ SM (*acquitrino*) pond; (*Chim*) tin

sta'gnola [staɲ'ɲɔla] SF tinfoil

stalag'mite SF stalagmite

stalat'tite SF stalactite

stali'nismo SM (*Pol*) Stalinism

'stalla SF (*per bovini*) cowshed; (*per cavalli*) stable

stalli'ere SM groom, stableboy

'stallo SM stall, seat; (*Scacchi*) stalemate; (*Aer*) stall; **situazione di ~** (*fig*) stalemate

stal'lone SM stallion

sta'mani, stamat'tina AV this morning

stam'becco, -chi SM ibex

stam'berga, -ghe SF hovel

stami'nale AG: **cellula ~** stem cell; **ricerca sulle cellule staminali** stem-cell research

'stampa SF (*Tip, Fot: tecnica*) printing; (*impressione, copia fotografica*) print; (*insieme di quotidiani, giornalisti ecc*): **la ~** the press; **andare in ~** to go to press; **mandare in ~** to pass for press; **errore di ~** printing error; **prova di ~** print sample; **libertà di ~** freedom of the press; **"stampe"** "printed matter"

stam'pante SF (*Inform*) printer; **~ seriale/termica** serial/thermal printer

stam'pare /**72**/ vt to print; (*pubblicare*) to publish; (*coniare*) to strike, coin; (*imprimere*: *anche fig*) to impress

stampa'tello sm block letters *pl*

stam'pato, -a ag printed ▶ sm (*opuscolo*) leaflet; (*modulo*) form; **stampati** smpl printed matter *sg*

stam'pella sf crutch

stampigli'are [stampiʎ'ʎare] /**27**/ vt to stamp

stampiglia'tura [stampiʎʎa'tura] sf (*atto*) stamping; (*marchio*) stamp

'stampo sm mould; (*fig*: *indole*) type, kind, sort

sta'nare /**72**/ vt to drive out

stan'care /**20**/ vt to tire, make tired; (*annoiare*) to bore; (*infastidire*) to annoy; **stancarsi** vpr to get tired, tire o.s. out; **stancarsi (di)** (*stufarsi*) to grow weary (of), grow tired (of)

stan'chezza [stan'kettsa] sf tiredness, fatigue

'stanco, -a, -chi, -che ag tired; ~ **di** tired of, fed up with

stand [stand] sm inv (*in fiera*) stand

'standard ['standard] sm inv (*livello*) standard

standardiz'zare [standardid'dzare] /**72**/ vt to standardize

stan'dista, -i, -e sm/f (*in una fiera ecc*) person responsible for a stand

'stanga, -ghe sm bar; (*di carro*) shaft

stan'gare /**80**/ vt (*fig*: *cliente*) to overcharge; (: *studente*) to fail

stan'gata sf (*colpo*: *anche fig*) blow; (*cattivo risultato*) poor result; (*Calcio*) shot

stan'ghetta [stan'getta] sf (*di occhiali*) leg; (*Mus*, *di scrittura*) bar

'stanno vb *vedi* **stare**

sta'notte av tonight; (*notte passata*) last night

'stante prep owing to, because of; **a sé ~** (*appartamento, casa*) independent, separate

stan'tio, -a, -'tii, -'tie ag stale; (*burro*) rancid; (*fig*) old

stan'tuffo sm piston

'stanza ['stantsa] sf room; (*Poesia*) stanza; **essere di ~ a** (*Mil*) to be stationed in; ~ **da bagno** bathroom; ~ **da letto** bedroom

stanzia'mento [stantsja'mento] sm allocation

stanzi'are [stan'tsjare] /**19**/ vt to allocate

stan'zino [stan'tsino] sm (*ripostiglio*) storeroom; (*spogliatoio*) changing room (*Brit*), locker room (*US*)

stap'pare /**72**/ vt to uncork; (*tappo a corona*) to uncap

star [star] sf (*attore, attrice ecc*) star

'stare /**116**/ vi (*restare in un luogo*) to stay, remain; (*abitare*) to stay, live; (*essere situato*) to be, be situated; (*anche*: **stare in piedi**) to stand; (*essere, trovarsi*) to be; (*seguito da gerundio*): **sta studiando** he's studying; **se stesse in me** if it were up to me, if it depended on me; ~ **per fare qc** to be about to do sth; **starci** (*esserci spazio*): **nel baule non ci sta più niente** there's no more room in the boot; (*accettare*) to accept; **ci stai?** is that okay with you?; ~ **a** (*attenersi a*) to follow, stick to; (*seguito dall'infinito*): ~ **a sentire** to listen; **staremo a vedere** let's wait and see; **stiamo a discutere** we're talking; (*toccare a*): **sta a te giocare** it's your turn to play; **sta a te decidere** it's up to you to decide; ~ **a qn** (*abiti ecc*) to fit sb; **queste scarpe mi stanno strette** these shoes are tight for me; **il rosso ti sta bene** red suits you; **come sta?** how are you?; **io sto bene/male** I'm very well/not very well; ~ **fermo** to keep o stay still; ~ **seduto** to sit, be sitting; ~ **zitto** to keep quiet; **stando così le cose** given the situation; **stando a ciò che dice lui** according to him o to his version

starnaz'zare [starnat'tsare] /**72**/ vi to squawk

starnu'tire /**55**/ vi to sneeze

star'nuto sm sneeze

sta'sera av this evening, tonight

'stasi sf (*Med*, *fig*) stasis

sta'tale ag state *cpd*, government *cpd* ▶ smf state employee, local authority employee; (*nell'amministrazione*) ≈ civil servant; **bilancio ~** national budget; **strada ~** ≈ trunk (*Brit*) o main road

statalizz'zare [statalid'dzare] /**72**/ vt to nationalize, put under state control

'statico, -a, -ci, -che ag (*Elettr*, *fig*) static

sta'tista, -i sm statesman

sta'tistico, -a, -ci, -che ag statistical ▶ sf statistic; (*scienza*) statistics *sg*; **fare una statistica** to carry out a statistical examination

'stato, -a pp *di* **essere**; **stare** ▶ sm (*condizione*) state, condition; (*Pol*) state; (*Dir*) status; **essere in ~ d'accusa** (*Dir*) to be committed for trial; **essere in ~ d'arresto** (*Dir*) to be under arrest; **essere in ~ interessante** to be pregnant; ~ **d'assedio/d'emergenza** state of siege/emergency; ~ **civile** (*Amm*) marital status; ~ **di famiglia** (*Amm*) certificate giving details of a household and its dependents; ~ **d'animo** mood; ~ **maggiore** (*Mil*) general staff; ~ **patrimoniale** (*Comm*) statement of assets and liabilities; **gli Stati Uniti (d'America)** the United States (of America)

'statua sf statue

statuni'tense ag United States *cpd*, of the United States

sta'tura sf (*Anat*) height, stature; (*fig*) stature; **essere alto/basso di ~** to be tall/short o small

sta'tuto SM (*Dir*) statute; constitution;
regione a ~ speciale *Italian region with political autonomy in certain matters*; **~ della società** (*Comm*) articles *pl* of association

sta'volta AV this time

staziona'mento [stattsjona'mento] SM (*Aut*) parking; (: *sosta*) waiting; **freno di ~** handbrake

stazio'nare [stattsjo'nare] /**72**/ VI (*veicoli*) to be parked

stazio'nario, -a [stattsjo'narjo] AG stationary; (*fig*) unchanged

stazi'one [stat'tsjone] SF station; (*balneare, invernale ecc*) resort; **~ degli autobus** bus station; **~ balneare** seaside resort; **~ climatica** health resort; **~ ferroviaria** railway (*BRIT*) o railroad (*US*) station; **~ invernale** winter sports resort; **~ di lavoro** work station; **~ di polizia** police station (*in small town*); **~ di servizio** service o petrol (*BRIT*) o filling station; **~ termale** spa; **~ radio base** mobile phone mast (*BRIT*), cell tower (*US*)

'stazza ['stattsa] SF tonnage

st. civ. ABBR = **stato civile**

'stecca, -che SF stick; (*di ombrello*) rib; (*di sigarette*) carton; (*Med*) splint; (*stonatura*): **fare una ~** to sing (o play) a wrong note

stec'cato SM fence

stec'chito, -a [stek'kito] AG dried up; (*persona*) skinny; **lasciar ~ qn** (*fig*) to leave sb flabbergasted; **morto ~** stone dead

'stella SF star; **~ alpina** (*Bot*) edelweiss; **~ cadente** o **filante** shooting star; **~ di mare** (*Zool*) starfish; **~ di Natale** (*Bot*) poinsettia

stel'lato, -a AG (*cielo, notte*) starry

'stelo SM stem; (*asta*) rod; **lampada a ~** standard lamp (*BRIT*), floor lamp

'stemma, -i SM coat of arms

'stemmo VB *vedi* **stare**

stempe'rare /**72**/ VT (*calce, colore*) to dissolve

stempi'ato, -a AG with a receding hairline

stempia'tura SF receding hairline

sten'dardo SM standard

'stendere /**120**/ VT (*braccia, gambe*) to stretch (out); (*tovaglia*) to spread (out); (*bucato*) to hang out; (*mettere a giacere*) to lay (down); (*spalmare: colore*) to spread; (*mettere per iscritto*) to draw up; **stendersi** VPR (*coricarsi*) to stretch out, lie down; (*estendersi*) to extend, stretch

stendibianche'ria [stendibjanke'ria] SM INV clotheshorse

stendi'toio SM (*locale*) drying room; (*stendibiancheria*) clotheshorse

stenodattilogra'fia SF shorthand typing (*BRIT*), stenography (*US*)

stenodatti'lografo, -a SM/F shorthand typist (*BRIT*), stenographer (*US*)

stenogra'fare /**72**/ VT to take down in shorthand

stenogra'fia SF shorthand

ste'nografo, -a SM/F stenographer

sten'tare /**72**/ VI: **~ a fare** to find it hard to do, have difficulty doing

sten'tato, -a AG (*compito, stile*) laboured (*BRIT*), labored (*US*); (*sorriso*) forced

'stento SM (*fatica*) difficulty; **stenti** SMPL (*privazioni*) hardship *sg*, privation *sg*; **a ~** av with difficulty, barely

'steppa SF steppe

'sterco SM dung

'stereo AG INV stereo ▶ SM INV (*impianto*) stereo

stereofo'nia SF stereophony

'stereo('fonico), -a, -ci, -che AG stereo(phonic)

stereoti'pato, -a AG stereotyped

stere'otipo SM stereotype; **pensare per stereotipi** to think in clichés

'sterile AG sterile; (*terra*) barren; (*fig*) futile, fruitless

sterilità SF sterility

steriliz'zare [sterilid'dzare] /**72**/ VT to sterilize

sterilizzazi'one [steriliddzat'tsjone] SF sterilization

ster'lina SF pound (sterling)

stermi'nare /**72**/ VT to exterminate, wipe out

stermi'nato, -a AG immense; endless

ster'minio SM extermination, destruction; **campo di ~** death camp

'sterno SM (*Anat*) breastbone

ste'roide SM steroid

ster'paglia [ster'paʎʎa] SF brushwood

'sterpo SM dry twig

ster'rare /**72**/ VT to excavate

ster'zare [ster'tsare] /**72**/ VT, VI (*Aut*) to steer

'sterzo ['stertso] SM steering; (*volante*) steering wheel

'steso, -a PP *di* **stendere**

'stessi *etc* VB *vedi* **stare**

'stesso, -a AG same; (*rafforzativo: in persona, proprio*): **il re ~** the king himself o in person ▶ PRON: **lo(la) ~(a)** the same (one); **quello ~ giorno** that very day; **i suoi stessi avversari lo ammirano** even his enemies admire him; **fa lo ~** it doesn't matter; **parto lo ~** I'm going all the same; **per me è lo ~** it's all the same to me, it doesn't matter to me; *vedi* **io**; **tu** *ecc*

ste'sura SF (*azione*) drafting *no pl*, drawing up *no pl*; (*documento*) draft

stetos'copio SM stethoscope

'stetti *etc* VB *vedi* **stare**

'stia¹ SF hutch

'stia² *etc* VB *vedi* **stare**

'stigma, -i SM stigma

'stigmate SFPL (*Rel*) stigmata

sti'lare /**72**/ VT to draw up, draft

S

'stile SM style; (classe) style, class; (Sport):
~ **libero** freestyle; **mobili in** ~ period
furniture; **in grande** ~ in great style;
è proprio nel suo ~ (fig) it's just like him
sti'lismo SM concern for style
sti'lista, -i, -e SM/F designer
sti'listico, -a, -ci, -che AG stylistic
stiliz'zato, -a [stilid'dzato] AG stylized
stil'lare /72/ VI (trasudare) to ooze; (gocciolare)
to drip
stilli'cidio [stilli'tʃidjo] SM (fig) continual
pestering (o moaning etc)
stilo'grafica, -che SF (anche: **penna**
stilografica) fountain pen
Stim. ABBR = **stimata**
'stima SF esteem; valuation; assessment,
estimate; **avere** ~ **di qn** to have respect for
sb; **godere della** ~ **di qn** to enjoy sb's
respect; **fare la** ~ **di qc** to estimate the value
of sth
sti'mare /72/ VT (persona) to esteem, hold in
high regard; (terreno, casa ecc) to value;
(stabilire in misura approssimativa) to estimate,
assess; (ritenere): ~ **che** to consider that;
stimarsi fortunato to consider o.s. (to be)
lucky
Stim.ma ABBR = **stimatissima**
stimo'lante AG stimulating ▶ SM (Med)
stimulant
stimo'lare /72/ VT to stimulate; (incitare):
~ **qn (a fare)** to spur sb on (to do)
stimolazi'one [stimolat'tsjone] SF
stimulation
'stimolo SM (anche fig) stimulus
'stinco, -chi SM shin; shinbone
'stingere ['stindʒere] /37/ VT, VI (anche:
stingersi) to fade
'stinto, -a PP di **stingere**
sti'pare /72/ VT to cram, pack; **stiparsi** VPR
(accalcarsi) to crowd, throng
stipendi'are /19/ VT (pagare) to pay (a
salary to)
stipendi'ato, -a AG salaried ▶ SM/F salaried
worker
sti'pendio SM salary
'stipite SM (di porta, finestra) jamb
stipu'lare /72/ VT (redigere) to draw up
stipulazi'one [stipulat'tsjone] SF (di contratto:
stesura) drafting; (: firma) signing
stiracchi'are [stirak'kjare] /19/ VT (fig:
significato di una parola) to stretch, force;
stiracchiarsi VPR (persona) to stretch
stira'mento SM (Med) sprain
sti'rare /72/ VT (abito) to iron; (distendere) to
stretch; (strappare: muscolo) to strain; **stirarsi**
VPR (col) to stretch (o.s.)
stira'tura SF ironing
'stirpe SF birth, stock; descendants pl
stiti'chezza [stiti'kettsa] SF constipation

'stitico, -a, -ci, -che AG constipated
'stiva SF (di nave) hold
sti'vale SM boot
stiva'letto SM ankle boot
sti'vare /72/ VT to stow, load
'stizza ['stittsa] SF anger, vexation
stiz'zire [stit'tsire] /55/ VT to irritate ▶ VI
(anche: **stizzirsi**) to become irritated,
become vexed
stiz'zoso, -a [stit'tsoso] AG (persona)
quick-tempered, irascible; (risposta) angry
stocca'fisso SM stockfish, dried cod
Stoc'carda SF Stuttgart
stoc'cata SF (colpo) stab, thrust; (fig) gibe,
cutting remark
Stoc'colma SF Stockholm
stock [stɔk] SM INV (Comm) stock
'stoffa SF material, fabric; (fig): **aver la** ~ **di** to
have the makings of; **avere della** ~ to have
what it takes
stoi'cismo [stoi'tʃizmo] SM stoicism
'stoico, -a, -ci, -che AG stoic(al)
sto'ino SM doormat
'stola SF stole
stol'tezza [stol'tettsa] SF stupidity; (azione)
foolish action
'stolto, -a AG stupid, foolish
'stomaco, -chi SM stomach; **dare di** ~ to
vomit, be sick
sto'nare /72/ VT to sing (o play) out of tune
▶ VI to be out of tune, sing (o play) out of
tune; (fig) to be out of place, jar; (: colori)
to clash
sto'nato, -a AG (persona) off-key; (strumento)
off-key, out of tune
stona'tura SF (suono) false note
stop SM INV (Telegrafia) stop; (Aut: cartello) stop
sign; (: fanalino d'arresto) brake-light (BRIT),
stoplight
'stoppa SF tow
'stoppia SF (Agr) stubble
stop'pino SM (di candela) wick; (miccia) fuse
'storcere ['stɔrtʃere] /106/ VT to twist;
storcersi VPR to writhe, twist; ~ **il naso** (fig)
to turn up one's nose; **storcersi la caviglia**
to twist one's ankle
stordi'mento SM (gen) dizziness; (da droga)
stupefaction
stor'dire /55/ VT (intontire) to stun, daze;
stordirsi VPR: **stordirsi col bere** to dull one's
senses with drink
stor'dito, -a AG stunned; (sventato)
scatterbrained, heedless
'storia SF (scienza, avvenimenti) history;
(racconto, bugia) story; (faccenda, questione)
business no pl; (pretesto) excuse, pretext;
storie SFPL (smancerie) fuss sg; **passare alla** ~
to go down in history; **non ha fatto storie**
he didn't make a fuss

storicità [storitʃi'ta] SF historical authenticity

'storico, -a, -ci, -che AG historic(al) ▶ SM/F historian

storiogra'fia SF historiography

stori'one SM (Zool) sturgeon

stor'mire /55/ VI to rustle

'stormo SM (di uccelli) flock

stor'nare /72/ VT (Comm) to transfer

stor'nello SM kind of folk song

'storno SM starling

storpi'are /19/ VT to cripple, maim; (fig: parole) to mangle; (: significato) to twist

storpia'tura SF (fig: di parola) twisting, distortion

'storpio, -a AG crippled, maimed

'storsi etc VB vedi **storcere**

'storto, -a PP di **storcere** ▶ AG (chiodo) twisted, bent; (gamba, quadro) crooked; (fig: ragionamento) false, wrong ▶ SF (distorsione) sprain, twist; (recipiente) retort ▶ AV: **guardare ~ qn** (fig) to look askance at sb; **andar ~** to go wrong

sto'viglie [sto'viʎʎe] SFPL dishes pl, crockery sg

str. ABBR (Geo) = **stretto**

'strabico, -a, -ci, -che AG squint-eyed; (occhi) squint

strabili'ante AG astonishing, amazing

strabili'are /19/ VI to astonish, amaze

stra'bismo SM squinting

strabuz'zare [strabud'dzare] /72/ VT: **~ gli occhi** to open one's eyes wide

stra'carico, -a, -chi, -che AG overloaded

strac'chino [strak'kino] SM type of soft cheese

stracci'are [strat'tʃare] /14/ VT to tear; **stracciarsi** VPR to tear

'straccio, -a, -ci, -ce ['strattʃo] AG: **carta straccia** waste paper ▶ SM rag; (per pulire) cloth, duster; **stracci** SMPL (indumenti) rags; **si è ridotto a uno ~** he's worn himself out; **non ha uno ~ di lavoro** he's not got a job of any sort

stracci'one, -a [strat'tʃone] SM/F ragamuffin

stracci'vendolo [strattʃi'vendolo] SM ragman

'stracco, -a, -chi, -che AG: **~ (morto)** exhausted, dead tired

stra'cotto, -a AG overcooked ▶ SM (Cuc) beef stew

'strada SF road; (di città) street; (cammino, via, fig) way; **~ facendo** on the way; **tre ore di ~ (a piedi)/(in macchina)** three hours' walk/drive; **essere sulla buona ~** (nella vita) to be on the right road o path; (con indagine ecc) to be on the right track; **essere fuori ~** (fig) to be on the wrong track; **fare ~ a qn** to show sb the way; **fare o farsi ~** (fig: persona) to get on in life; **portare qn sulla cattiva ~** to lead sb astray; **donna di ~** (fig: peg) streetwalker;

ragazzo di ~ (fig: peg) street urchin; **~ ferrata** railway (BRIT), railroad (US); **~ principale** main road; **~ senza uscita** dead end, cul-de-sac

stra'dale AG road cpd; (polizia, regolamento) traffic cpd

stra'dario SM street guide

stra'dino SM road worker

strafalci'one [strafal'tʃone] SM blunder, howler

stra'fare /53/ VI to overdo it

stra'fatto, -a PP di **strafare**

stra'foro: di ~ AV (di nascosto) on the sly

strafot'tente AG: **è ~** he doesn't give a damn, he couldn't care less

strafot'tenza [strafot'tentsa] SF arrogance

'strage ['stradʒe] SF massacre, slaughter

stra'grande AG: **la ~ maggioranza** the overwhelming majority

stralci'are [stral'tʃare] /14/ VT to remove

'stralcio ['straltʃo] SM (Comm): **vendere in ~** to sell off (at bargain prices) ▶ AG INV: **legge ~** abridged version of an act

stralu'nato, -a AG (occhi) rolling; (persona) beside o.s., very upset

stramaz'zare [stramat'tsare] /72/ VI to fall heavily

strambe'ria SF eccentricity

'strambo, -a AG strange, queer

strampa'lato, -a AG odd, eccentric

strana'mente AV oddly, strangely; **e lui, ~, ha accettato** and surprisingly, he agreed

stra'nezza [stra'nettsa] SF strangeness

strango'lare /72/ VT to strangle; **strangolarsi** VPR to choke

strani'ero, -a AG foreign ▶ SM/F foreigner

stra'nito, -a AG dazed

'strano, -a AG strange, odd

straordi'nario, -a AG extraordinary; (treno ecc) special ▶ SM (lavoro) overtime

strapaz'zare [strapat'tsare] /72/ VT to ill-treat; **strapazzarsi** VPR to tire o.s. out, overdo things

strapaz'zato, -a [strapat'tsato] AG: **uova strapazzate** scrambled eggs

stra'pazzo [stra'pattso] SM strain, fatigue; **da ~** (fig) third-rate

strapi'eno, -a AG full to overflowing

strapi'ombo SM overhanging rock; **a ~** overhanging

strapo'tere SM excessive power

strappa'lacrime AG INV (col): **romanzo** (o film etc) **~** tear-jerker

strap'pare /72/ VT (gen) to tear, rip; (pagina ecc) to tear off, tear out; (sradicare) to pull up; (fig) to wrest sth from sb; (togliere): **~ qc a qn** to snatch sth from sb; **strapparsi** VPR (lacerarsi) to rip, tear; (rompersi) to break; **strapparsi un muscolo** to tear a muscle

S

strap'pato, -a AG torn, ripped
'**strappo** SM (*strattone*) pull, tug; (*lacerazione*) tear, rip; (*fig: col: passaggio*) lift (BRIT), ride (US); **fare uno ~ alla regola** to make an exception to the rule; **~ muscolare** torn muscle
strapun'tino SM jump o foldaway seat
strari'pare /72/ VI to overflow
Stras'burgo SF Strasbourg
strasci'care [straʃʃi'kare] /20/ VT to trail; (*piedi*) to drag; **~ le parole** to drawl
strascico, -chi ['straʃʃiko] SM (*di abito*) train; (*conseguenza*) after-effect
strata'gemma, -i [strata'dʒɛmma] SM stratagem
stra'tega, -ghi SM strategist
strate'gia, -'gie [strate'dʒia] SF strategy
stra'tegico, -a, -ci, -che [stra'tɛdʒiko] AG strategic
'**strato** SM layer; (*rivestimento*) coat, coating; (*Geo, fig*) stratum; (*Meteor*) stratus; **~ d'ozono** ozone layer
stratos'fera SF stratosphere
strat'tone SM tug, jerk; **dare uno ~ a qc** to tug o jerk sth, give sth a tug o jerk
stravac'cato, -a AG sprawling
strava'gante AG odd, eccentric
strava'ganza [strava'gantsa] SF eccentricity
stra'vecchio, -a [stra'vɛkkjo] AG very old
strave'dere /127/ VI: **~ per qn** to dote on sb
stra'visto, -a PP di **stravedere**
stra'vizio [stra'vittsjo] SM excess
stra'volgere [stra'vɔldʒere] /96/ VT (*volto*) to contort; (*fig: animo*) to trouble deeply; (: *verità*) to twist, distort
stra'volto, -a PP di **stravolgere** ▶ AG (*persona: per stanchezza ecc*) in a terrible state; (: *per sofferenza*) distraught
strazi'ante [strat'tsjante] AG (*scena*) harrowing; (*urlo*) bloodcurdling; (*dolore*) excruciating
strazi'are [strat'tsjare] /19/ VT to torture, torment
'**strazio** ['strattsjo] SM torture; (*fig: cosa fatta male*): **essere uno ~** to be appalling; **fare ~ di** (*corpo, vittima*) to mutilate
'**strega, -ghe** SF witch
stre'gare /80/ VT to bewitch
stre'gone SM (*mago*) wizard; (*di tribù*) witch doctor
stregone'ria SF (*pratica*) witchcraft; **fare una ~** to cast a spell
'**stregua** SF: **alla ~ di** by the same standard as
stre'mare /72/ VT to exhaust
'**stremo** SM: **essere allo ~** to be at the end of one's tether
'**strenna** SF: **~ natalizia** (*regalo*) Christmas present; (*libro*) book published for the Christmas market

'**strenuo, -a** AG brave, courageous
strepi'tare /72/ VI to yell and shout
'**strepito** SM (*di voci, folla*) clamour (BRIT), clamor (US); (*di catene*) clanking, rattling
strepi'toso, -a AG clamorous, deafening; (*fig: successo*) resounding
stres'sante AG stressful
stres'sare /72/ VT to put under stress
stres'sato, -a AG under stress
stretch [stretʃ] AG INV stretch
'**stretta** SF vedi **stretto**
stretta'mente AV tightly; (*rigorosamente*) strictly
stret'tezza [stret'tettsa] SF narrowness; **strettezze** SFPL (*povertà*) poverty sg, straitened circumstances
'**stretto, -a** PP di **stringere** ▶ AG (*corridoio, limiti*) narrow; (*gonna, scarpe, nodo, curva*) tight; (*intimo: parente, amico*) close; (*rigoroso: osservanza*) strict; (*preciso: significato*) precise, exact ▶ SM (*braccio di mare*) strait ▶ SF (*di mano*) grasp; (*finanziaria*) squeeze; (*fig: dolore, turbamento*) pang; **a denti stretti** with clenched teeth; **lo ~ necessario** the bare minimum; **una stretta di mano** a handshake; **una stretta al cuore** a sudden sadness; **essere alle strette** to have one's back to the wall
stret'toia SF bottleneck; (*fig*) tricky situation
stri'ato, -a AG streaked
stria'tura SF (*atto*) streaking; (*effetto*) streaks pl
stric'nina SF strychnine
'**strida** SFPL screaming sg
stri'dente AG strident
stri'dere /89/ VI (*porta*) to squeak; (*animale*) to screech, shriek; (*colori*) to clash
'**strido** (*pl(f)* **strida**) SM screech, shriek
stri'dore SM screeching, shrieking
stri'dulo, -a AG shrill
'**striglia** ['striʎʎa] SF currycomb
strigli'are [striʎ'ʎare] /27/ VT (*cavallo*) to curry
strigli'ata [striʎ'ʎata] SF (*di cavallo*) currying; (*fig*): **dare una ~ a qn** to give sb a scolding
stril'lare /72/ VT, VI to scream, shriek
'**strillo** SM scream, shriek
stril'lone SM newspaper seller
strimin'zito, -a [strimin'tsito] AG (*misero*) shabby; (*molto magro*) skinny
strimpel'lare /72/ VT (*Mus*) to strum
'**stringa, -ghe** SF lace; (*Inform*) string
strin'gare /80/ VT (*fig: discorso*) to condense
strin'gato, -a AG (*fig*) concise
'**stringere** ['strindʒere] /117/ VT (*avvicinare due cose*) to press (together), squeeze (together); (*tenere stretto*) to hold tight, clasp, clutch; (*pugno, mascella, denti*) to clench; (*labbra*) to compress; (*avvitare*) to tighten; (*abito*) to take in; (*scarpe*) to pinch, be tight for; (*fig: concludere: patto*) to make; (: *accelerare: passo*)

to quicken ▶ VI (*essere stretto*) to be tight; (*tempo: incalzare*) to be pressing; **stringersi** VPR (*accostarsi*): **stringersi a** to press o.s. up against; **~ la mano a qn** to shake sb's hand; **~ gli occhi** to screw up one's eyes; **~ amicizia con qn** to make friends with sb; **stringi stringi** in conclusion; **il tempo stringe** time is short

'**strinsi** *etc* VB *vedi* **stringere**

'**striscia, -sce** ['striʃʃa] SF (*di carta, tessuto ecc*) strip; (*riga*) stripe; **strisce (pedonali)** zebra crossing *sg*; **a strisce** striped

strisci'**ante** [striʃʃante] AG (*fig: peg*) unctuous; (*Econ: inflazione*) creeping

strisci'**are** [striʃʃare] /**14**/ VT (*piedi*) to drag; (*muro, macchina*) to graze ▶ VI to crawl, creep

'**striscio** ['striʃʃo] SM graze; (*Med*) smear; **colpire di ~** to graze

strisci'**one** [striʃʃone] SM banner

strito'**lare** /**72**/ VT to grind

striz'**zare** [strit'tsare] /**72**/ VT (*arancia*) to squeeze; (*panni*) to wring (out); **~ l'occhio** to wink

striz'**zata** [strit'tsata] SF: **dare una ~ a qc** to give sth a wring; **una ~ d'occhio** a wink

'**strofa** SF, '**strofe** SF INV strophe

strofi'**naccio** [strofi'nattʃo] SM duster, cloth; (*per piatti*) dishcloth; (*per pavimenti*) floorcloth

strofi'**nare** /**72**/ VT to rub

stron'**care** /**20**/ VT to break off; (*fig: ribellione*) to suppress, put down; (: *film, libro*) to tear to pieces

'**stronzo** ['strontso] SM (*sterco*) turd; (*col: persona*) shit (!)

stropicci'**are** [stropit'tʃare] /**14**/ VT to rub

stroz'**zare** [strot'tsare] /**72**/ VT (*soffocare*) to choke, strangle; **strozzarsi** VPR to choke

strozza'**tura** [strottsa'tura] SF (*restringimento*) narrowing; (*di strada ecc*) bottleneck

stroz'**zino, -a** [strot'tsino] SM/F (*usuraio*) usurer; (*fig*) shark

struc'**care** /**20**/ VT to remove make-up from; **struccarsi** VPR to remove one's make-up

'**struggere** ['struddʒere] /**39**/ VT (*fig*) to consume; **struggersi** VPR (*fig*): **struggersi di** to be consumed with

struggi'**mento** [struddʒi'mento] SM (*desiderio*) yearning

strumen'**tale** AG (*Mus*) instrumental

strumentaliz'**zare** [strumentalid'dzare] /**72**/ VT to exploit, use to one's own ends

strumentalizzazi'**one** [strumentaliddzat'tsjone] SF exploitation

strumentazi'**one** [strumentat'tsjone] SF (*Mus*) orchestration; (*Tecn*) instrumentation

stru'**mento** SM (*arnese, fig*) instrument, tool; (*Mus*) instrument; **~ a corda** *o* **ad arco/a fiato** string(ed)/wind instrument

'**strussi** *etc* VB *vedi* **struggere**

'**strutto** SM lard

strut'**tura** SF structure

struttu'**rare** /**72**/ VT to structure

'**struzzo** ['struttso] SM ostrich; **fare lo ~, fare la politica dello ~** to bury one's head in the sand

stuc'**care** /**20**/ VT (*muro*) to plaster; (*vetro*) to putty; (*decorare con stucchi*) to stucco

stucca'**tore, -'trice** SM/F plasterer; (*artista*) stucco worker

stuc'**chevole** [stuk'kevole] AG nauseating; (*fig*) tedious, boring

'**stucco, -chi** SM plaster; (*da vetri*) putty; (*ornamentale*) stucco; **rimanere di ~** (*fig*) to be dumbfounded

stu'**dente, -'essa** SM/F student; (*scolaro*) pupil, schoolboy(-girl)

studen'**tesco, -a, -schi, -sche** AG student *cpd*

studi'**are** /**19**/ VT to study; **studiarsi** VPR (*sforzarsi*): **studiarsi di fare** to try *o* endeavour (BRIT) *o* endeavor (US) to do

studi'**ato, -a** AG (*modi, sorriso*) affected

'**studio** SM studying; (*ricerca, saggio, stanza*) study; (*di professionista*) office; (*di artista, Cine, TV, Radio*) studio; (*di medico*) surgery (BRIT), office (US); **studi** SMPL (*Ins*) studies; **alla fine degli studi** at the end of one's course (of studies); **secondo recenti studi, appare che ...** recent research indicates that ...; **la proposta è allo ~** the proposal is under consideration; **~ legale** lawyer's office

studi'**oso, -a** AG studious, hardworking ▶ SM/F scholar

'**stufa** SF stove; **~ elettrica** electric fire *o* heater; **~ a legna/carbone** wood-burning/coal stove

stu'**fare** /**72**/ VT (*Cuc*) to stew; (*fig: col*) to bore; **stufarsi** VPR (*col*): **stufarsi (di)** (*fig*) to get fed up (with)

stu'**fato** SM (*Cuc*) stew

'**stufo, -a** AG (*col*): **essere ~ di** to be fed up with, be sick and tired of

stu'**oia** SF mat

stu'**olo** SM crowd, host

stupefa'**cente** [stupefa'tʃɛnte] AG stunning, astounding ▶ SM drug, narcotic

stupe'**fare** /**53**/ VT to stun, astound

stupe'**fatto, -a** PP *di* **stupefare**

stupefazi'**one** [stupefat'tsjone] SF astonishment

stu'**pendo, -a** AG marvellous, wonderful

stupi'**daggine** [stupi'daddʒine] SF stupid thing (to do *o* say)

stupi'**dità** SF stupidity

'**stupido, -a** AG stupid

stu'**pire** /**55**/ VT to amaze, stun ▶ VI (*anche*: **stupirsi**): **~ (di)** to be amazed (at), be stunned (by); **non c'è da stupirsi** that's not surprising

S

stu'pore SM amazement, astonishment
stu'prare /**72**/ VT to rape
stupra'tore SM rapist
'stupro SM rape
stu'rare /**72**/ VT (*lavandino*) to clear
stuzzica'denti [stuttsika'dɛnti] SM toothpick
stuzzi'cante [stuttsi'kante] AG (*gen*) stimulating; (*appetitoso*) appetizing
stuzzi'care [stuttsi'kare] /**20**/ VT (*ferita ecc*) to poke (at), prod (at); (*fig*) to tease; (: *appetito*) to whet; (: *curiosità*) to stimulate; **~ i denti** to pick one's teeth

[PAROLA CHIAVE]

su (*su* + *il* = **sul**, *su* + *lo* = **sullo**, *su* + *l'* = **sull'**, *su* + *la* = **sulla**, *su* + *i* = **sui**, *su* + *gli* = **sugli**, *su* + *le* = **sulle**) PREP **1** (*gen*) on; (*moto*) on(to); (*in cima a*) on (top of); **mettilo sul tavolo** put it on the table; **salire sul treno** to get on the train; **un paesino sul mare** a village by the sea; **è sulla destra** it's on the right; **cento metri sul livello del mare** a hundred metres above sea level; **fecero rotta su Palermo** they set out for Palermo; **sul vestito portava un golf rosso** she was wearing a red sweater over her dress
2 (*argomento*) about, on; **un libro su Cesare** a book on *o* about Caesar
3 (*circa*) about; **costerà sui 3 milioni** it will cost about 3 million; **una ragazza sui 17 anni** a girl of about 17 (years of age)
4: **su misura** made to measure; **su ordinazione** to order; **su richiesta** on request; **3 casi su dieci** 3 cases out of 10
▶ AV **1** (*in alto, verso l'alto*) up; **vieni su** come on up; **guarda su** look up; **andare su e giù** to go up and down; **su le mani!** hands up!; **in su** (*verso l'alto*) up(wards); (*in poi*) onwards; **vieni su da me?** are you going to come up?; **dai 20 anni in su** from the age of 20 onwards
2 (*addosso*) on; **cos'hai su?** what have you got on?
▶ ESCL come on!; **su avanti, muoviti!** come on, hurry up!; **su coraggio!** come on, cheer up!

'sua *vedi* **suo**
sua'dente AG persuasive
sub SM INV/F INV skin-diver
su'bacqueo, -a AG underwater ▶ SM skin-diver
subaffit'tare /**72**/ VT to sublet
subaf'fitto SM (*contratto*) sublet
subal'terno, -a AG, SM subordinate; (*Mil*) subaltern
subappal'tare /**72**/ VT to subcontract
subap'palto SM subcontract

sub'buglio [sub'buʎʎo] SM confusion, turmoil; **essere/mettere in ~** to be in/ throw into a turmoil
sub'conscio, -a [sub'kɔnʃo] AG, SM subconscious
subcosci'ente [subkoʃʃɛnte] SM subconscious
'subdolo, -a AG underhand, sneaky
suben'trare /**72**/ VI: **~ a qn in qc** to take over sth from sb; **sono subentrati altri problemi** other problems arose
su'bire /**55**/ VT to suffer, endure
subis'sare /**72**/ VT (*fig*): **~ di** to overwhelm with, load with
subi'taneo, -a AG sudden
'subito AV immediately, at once, straight away
subli'mare /**72**/ VT (*Psic*) to sublimate; (*Chim*) to sublime
su'blime AG sublime
sublo'care /**20**/ VT to sublease
sublocazi'one [sublokat'tsjone] SF sublease
subnor'male AG subnormal ▶ SMF mentally handicapped person
subodo'rare /**72**/ VT (*insidia ecc*) to smell, suspect
subordi'nare /**72**/ VT to subordinate
subordi'nato, -a AG subordinate; (*dipendente*): **~ a** dependent on, subject to
subordinazi'one [subordinat'tsjone] SF subordination
su'bordine SM: **in ~** secondarily
sub'prime [sab'praim] AG INV subprime; **mutuo ~** subprime mortgage ▶ SM subprime lending
subur'bano, -a AG suburban
succe'daneo [suttʃe'daneo] SM substitute
suc'cedere [sut'tʃedere] /**118**/ VI (*accadere*) to happen; **~ a** (*prendere il posto di*) to succeed; (*venire dopo*) to follow; **succedersi** VPR to follow each other; **~ al trono** to succeed to the throne; **sono cose che succedono** these things happen; **cos'è successo?** what happened?
successi'one [suttʃes'sjone] SF succession; **tassa di ~** death duty (*BRIT*), inheritance tax (*US*)
successiva'mente [suttʃessiva'mente] AV subsequently
succes'sivo, -a [suttʃes'sivo] AG successive; **il giorno ~** the following day; **in un momento ~** subsequently
suc'cesso, -a [sut'tʃɛsso] PP *di* **succedere** ▶ SM (*esito*) outcome; (*buona riuscita*) success; **di ~** (*libro, personaggio*) successful; **avere ~** (*persona*) to be successful; (*idea*) to be well received
succes'sore [suttʃes'sore] SM successor
succhi'are [suk'kjare] /**19**/ VT to suck (up)
succhi'otto [suk'kjɔtto] SM dummy (*BRIT*), pacifier (*US*), comforter (*US*)

suc'cinto, -a [sut'tʃinto] AG (*discorso*) succinct; (*abito*) brief

'**succo, -chi** SM juice; (*fig*) essence, gist; **~ di frutta/pomodoro** fruit/tomato juice

suc'coso, -a AG juicy; (*fig*) pithy

'**succube** SMF victim; **essere ~ di qn** to be dominated by sb

succur'sale SF branch (office)

sud SM south ▶ AG INV south; (*regione*) southern; **verso ~** south, southwards; **l'Italia del S~** Southern Italy; **l'America del S~** South America

Su'dafrica SM: **il ~** South Africa

sudafri'cano, -a AG, SM/F South African

Suda'merica SM: **il ~** South America

sudameri'cano, -a AG, SM/F South American

Su'dan SM: **il ~** (the) Sudan

suda'nese AG, SMF Sudanese *inv*

su'dare /**72**/ VI to perspire, sweat; **~ freddo** to come out in a cold sweat

su'dato, -a AG (*persona, mani*) sweaty; (*fig: denaro*) hard-earned ▶ SF (*anche fig*) sweat; **una vittoria sudata** a hard-won victory; **ho fatto una bella sudata per finirlo in tempo** it was a real sweat to get it finished in time

sud'detto, -a AG above-mentioned

suddi'tanza [suddi'tantsa] SF subjection; (*cittadinanza*) citizenship

sud'dito, -a SM/F subject

suddi'videre /**43**/ VT to subdivide

suddivisi'one SF subdivision

suddi'viso, -a PP *di* **suddividere**

su'dest SM south-east; **vento di ~** south-easterly wind; **il ~ asiatico** South-East Asia

sudice'ria [sudit ʃe'ria] SF (*qualità*) filthiness, dirtiness; (*cosa sporca*) dirty thing

'**sudicio, -a, -ci, -ce** ['suditʃo] AG dirty, filthy

sudici'ume [sudi'tʃume] SM dirt, filth

su'doku SM INV sudoku

su'dore SM perspiration, sweat

su'dovest SM south-west; **vento di ~** south-westerly wind

'**sue** *vedi* **suo**

'**Suez** ['suez] SM: **il Canale di ~** the Suez Canal

suffici'ente [suffi'tʃɛnte] AG enough, sufficient; (*borioso*) self-important; (*Ins*) satisfactory

sufficiente'mente [suffitʃente'mente] AV sufficiently, enough; (*guadagnare, darsi da fare*) enough

suffici'enza [suffi'tʃɛntsa] SF self-importance; (*Ins*) pass mark; **con un'aria di ~** (*fig*) with a condescending air; **a ~** enough; **ne ho avuto a ~!** I've had enough of this!

suf'fisso SM (*Ling*) suffix

suffra'gare /**80**/ VT to support

suf'fragio [suf'fradʒo] SM (*voto*) vote; **~ universale** universal suffrage

suggel'lare [suddʒel'lare] /**72**/ VT (*fig*) to seal

suggeri'mento [suddʒeri'mento] SM suggestion; (*consiglio*) piece of advice, advice *no pl*; **dietro suo ~** on his advice

sugge'rire [suddʒe'rire] /**55**/ VT (*risposta*) to tell; (*consigliare*) to advise; (*proporre*) to suggest; (*Teat*) to prompt; **~ a qn di fare qc** to suggest to sb that he (*o* she) do sth

suggeri'tore, -'trice [suddʒeri'tore] SM/F (*Teat*) prompter

suggestio'nare [suddʒestjo'nare] /**72**/ VT to influence

suggesti'one [suddʒes'tjone] SF (*Psic*) suggestion; (*istigazione*) instigation

sugges'tivo, -a [suddʒes'tivo] AG (*paesaggio*) evocative; (*teoria*) interesting, attractive

'**sughero** ['sugero] SM cork

'**sugli** ['suʎʎi] PREP + DET *vedi* **su**

'**sugo, -ghi** SM (*succo*) juice; (*di carne*) gravy; (*condimento*) sauce; (*fig*) gist, essence

su'goso, -a (*frutto*) juicy; (*fig: articolo ecc*) pithy

'**sui** PREP + DET *vedi* **su**

sui'cida, -i, -e [sui'tʃida] AG suicidal ▶ SMF suicide

suici'darsi [suitʃi'darsi] /**72**/ VPR to commit suicide

sui'cidio [sui'tʃidjo] SM suicide

su'ino, -a AG: **carne suina** pork ▶ SM pig; **suini** SMPL swine *pl*

sul, sull', 'sulla, 'sulle, 'sullo PREP + DET *vedi* **su**

sulfa'midico, -a, -ci, -che AG, SM (*Med*) sulphonamide

sulta'nina SF: (**uva**) **~** sultana

sul'tano, -a SM/F sultan (sultana)

Su'matra SF Sumatra

'**summit** ['summit] SM INV summit

S.U.N.I.A. SIGLA M (= *sindacato unitario nazionale inquilini e assegnatari*) national association of tenants

sunnomi'nato, -a AG aforesaid *cpd*

'**sunto** SM summary

'**suo** (*f* **sua**, *pl* **sue, suoi**) DET: **il ~, la sua** *etc* (*di lui*) his; (*di lei*) her; (*di esso*) its; (*con valore indefinito*) one's, his/her; (*forma di cortesia: anche:* **Suo**) your ▶ PRON: **il ~, la sua** *etc* his; hers; yours ▶ SM: **ha speso del ~** he (*o* she *etc*) spent his (*o* her *etc*) own money ▶ SF: **la sua** (*opinione*) his (*o* her *etc*) view; **i suoi** (*parenti*) his (*o* hers *etc*) family; **un ~ amico** a friend of his (*o* hers *etc*); **è dalla sua** he's on his (*o* her *etc*) side; **anche lui ha avuto le sue** (*disavventure*) he's had his problems too; **sta sulle sue** he keeps himself to himself

su'ocero, -a ['swɔtʃero] SM/F father-in-law (mother-in-law); **i suoceri** (*pl*) father- and mother-in-law

su'oi *vedi* **suo**

su'ola SF (*di scarpa*) sole

su'olo SM (*terreno*) ground; (*terra*) soil

suo'nare /72/ VT (*Mus*) to play; (*campana*) to ring; (*ore*) to strike; (*clacson, allarme*) to sound ▶ VI to play; (*telefono, campana*) to ring; (*ore*) to strike; (*clacson, fig: parole*) to sound

suo'nato, -a AG (*compiuto*): **ha cinquant'anni suonati** he is well over fifty

suona'tore, -'trice SM/F player; **~ ambulante** street musician

suone'ria SF (*di sveglia*) alarm; (*di telefono*) ringtone

su'ono SM sound

su'ora SF (*Rel*) nun; **Suor Maria** Sister Maria

'super AG INV: **(benzina)** ~ ≈ four-star (petrol) (*BRIT*), ≈ premium (*US*)

supera'mento SM (*di ostacolo*) overcoming; (*di montagna*) crossing

supe'rare /72/ VT (*oltrepassare: limite*) to exceed, surpass; (*percorrere*) to cover; (*attraversare: fiume*) to cross; (*sorpassare: veicolo*) to overtake; (*fig: essere più bravo di*) to surpass, outdo; (: *difficoltà*) to overcome; (: *esame*) to get through; **~ qn in altezza/peso** to be taller/heavier than sb; **ha superato la cinquantina** he's over fifty (years of age); **~ i limiti di velocità** to exceed the speed limit; **stavolta ha superato se stesso** this time he has surpassed himself

supe'rato, -a AG outmoded

supe'rattico, -ci SM penthouse

su'perbia SF pride

su'perbo, -a AG proud; (*fig*) magnificent, superb

supercondut'tore SM superconductor

superena'lotto SM *Italian national lottery*

superfici'ale [superfi'tʃale] AG superficial

superficialità [superfitʃali'ta] SF superficiality

super'ficie, -ci [super'fitʃe] SF surface; **tornare in ~** (*a galla*) to return to the surface; (*fig: problemi ecc*) to resurface; **~ alare** (*Aer*) wing area; **~ velica** (*Naut*) sail area

su'perfluo, -a AG superfluous

superi'ora SF (*Rel: anche:* **madre superiora**) mother superior

superi'ore AG (*piano, arto, classi*) upper; (*più elevato: temperatura, livello*): **~ (a)** higher (than); (*migliore*): **~ (a)** superior (to) ▶ SFPL: **le superiori** (*Ins*) *vedi* **scuola media superiore**; **il corso ~ di un fiume** the upper reaches of a river; **scuola media ~** ≈ senior comprehensive school (*BRIT*), ≈ senior high (school) (*US*)

superiorità SF superiority

superla'tivo, -a AG, SM superlative

superla'voro SM overwork

super'market [super'market] SM INV = **supermercato**

supermer'cato SM supermarket

super'nova SF supernova

superpo'tenza [superpo'tentsa] SF (*Pol*) superpower

super'sonico, -a, -ci, -che AG supersonic

su'perstite AG surviving ▶ SMF survivor

superstizi'one [superstit'tsjone] SF superstition

superstizi'oso, -a [superstit'tsjoso] AG superstitious

super'strada SF ≈ expressway

supervisi'one SF supervision

supervi'sore SM supervisor

su'pino, -a AG supine; **accettazione supina** (*fig*) blind acceptance

suppel'lettile SF furnishings *pl*

suppergiù [supper'dʒu] AV more or less, roughly

suppl. ABBR (= *supplemento*) supp(l)

supplemen'tare AG extra; (*treno*) relief *cpd*; (*entrate*) additional

supple'mento SM supplement

sup'plente AG temporary; (*insegnante*) supply *cpd* (*BRIT*), substitute *cpd* (*US*) ▶ SMF temporary member of staff; supply (*o* substitute) teacher

supp'lenza [sup'plɛntsa] SF: **fare ~** to do supply (*BRIT*) *o* substitute (*US*) teaching

supple'tivo, -a AG (*gen*) supplementary; (*sessione d'esami*) extra

'supplica, -che SF (*preghiera*) plea; (*domanda scritta*) petition, request

suppli'care /20/ VT to implore, beseech

suppli'chevole [suppli'kevole] AG imploring

sup'plire /45/ VI: **~ a** to make up for, compensate for

sup'plizio [sup'plittsjo] SM torture

sup'pongo, sup'poni *etc* VB *vedi* **supporre**

sup'porre /77/ VT to suppose; **supponiamo che ...** let's *o* just suppose that ...

sup'porto SM (*sostegno*) support

supposizi'one [suppozit'tsjone] SF supposition

sup'posta SF (*Med*) suppository

sup'posto, -a PP *di* **supporre**

suppu'rare /72/ VI to suppurate

suprema'zia [supremat'tsia] SF supremacy

su'premo, -a AG supreme; **Suprema Corte (di Cassazione)** Supreme Court

surclas'sare /72/ VT to outclass

surge'lare [surdʒe'lare] /72/ VT to (deep-)freeze

surge'lato, -a [surdʒe'lato] AG (deep-)frozen ▶ SMPL: **i surgelati** frozen food *sg*

surme'nage [syrmə'naʒ] SM (*fisico*) overwork; (*mentale*) mental strain; (*Sport*) overtraining

sur'plus SM INV (*Econ*) surplus; **~ di manodopera** overmanning

surre'ale AG surrealistic

surriscalda'mento SM (*gen*, *Tecn*)
overheating
surriscal'dare /**72**/ VT to overheat
surro'gato SM substitute
suscet'tibile [suʃʃet'tibile] AG (*sensibile*)
touchy, sensitive; (*soggetto*): **~ di
miglioramento** that can be improved, open
to improvement
suscettibilità [suʃʃettibili'ta] SF touchiness;
urtare la ~ di qn to hurt sb's feelings
susci'tare [suʃʃi'tare] /**72**/ VT to provoke,
arouse
su'sina SF plum
su'sino SM plum (tree)
sussegu'ire /**45**/ VT to follow; **susseguirsi** VPR
to follow one another
sussidi'ario, -a AG subsidiary; (*treno*) relief
cpd; (*fermata*) extra
sus'sidio SM subsidy; (*aiuto*) aid; **sussidi
didattici/audiovisivi** teaching/audiovisual
aids; **~ di disoccupazione** unemployment
benefit (*BRIT*) *o* benefits (*US*); **~ per malattia**
sickness benefit
sussi'ego SM haughtiness; **con aria di ~**
haughtily
sussis'tenza [sussis'tɛntsa] SF subsistence
sus'sistere /**11**/ VI to exist; (*essere fondato*) to be
valid *o* sound
sussul'tare /**72**/ VI to shudder
sus'sulto SM start
sussur'rare /**72**/ VT, VI to whisper, murmur;
si sussurra che ... it's rumoured (*BRIT*) *o*
rumored (*US*) that ...
sus'surro SM whisper, murmur
su'tura SF (*Med*) suture
sutu'rare /**72**/ VT to stitch up, suture
suv'via ESCL come on!
SV SIGLA = **Savona**
S.V. ABBR = **Signoria Vostra**
sva'gare /**80**/ VT (*divertire*) to amuse; (*distrarre*):
~ qn to take sb's mind off things; **svagarsi**
VPR to amuse o.s.; to take one's mind off
things
sva'gato, -a AG (*persona*) absent-minded;
(*scolaro*) inattentive
'svago, -ghi SM (*riposo*) relaxation; (*ricreazione*)
amusement; (*passatempo*) pastime
svaligi'are [zvali'dʒare] /**62**/ VT to rob, burgle
(*BRIT*), burglarize (*US*)
svaligia'tore, -'trice [zvalidʒa'tore] SM/F
(*di banca*) robber; (*di casa*) burglar
svalu'tare /**72**/ VT (*Econ*) to devalue; (*fig*) to
belittle; **svalutarsi** VPR (*Econ*) to be devalued
svalutazi'one [zvalutat'tsjone] SF
devaluation
svam'pito, -a AG absent-minded ▶ SM/F
absent-minded person
sva'nire /**55**/ VI to disappear, vanish
sva'nito, -a AG (*fig: persona*) absent-minded

svantaggi'ato, -a [zvantad'dʒato] AG at a
disadvantage
svan'taggio [zvan'taddʒo] SM
disadvantage; (*inconveniente*) drawback,
disadvantage; **tornerà a suo ~** it will
work against you
svantaggi'oso, -a [zvantad'dʒoso] AG
disadvantageous; **è un'offerta
svantaggiosa per me** it's not in my interest
to accept this offer; **è un prezzo ~** it is not
an attractive price
svapo'rare /**72**/ VI to evaporate
svapo'rato, -a AG (*bibita*) flat
svari'ato, -a AG (*vario, diverso*) varied;
(*numeroso*) various
'svastica, -che SF swastika
sve'dese AG Swedish ▶ SMF Swede ▶ SM (*Ling*)
Swedish
'sveglia ['zveʎʎa] SF waking up; (*orologio*)
alarm (clock); **suonare la ~** (*Mil*) to sound
the reveille; **~ telefonica** alarm call
svegli'are [zveʎ'ʎare] /**27**/ VT to wake up; (*fig*)
to awaken, arouse; **svegliarsi** VPR to wake
up; (*fig*) to be revived, reawaken
'sveglio, -a ['zveʎʎo] AG awake; (*fig*) alert,
quick-witted
sve'lare /**72**/ VT to reveal
svel'tezza [zvel'tettsa] SF (*gen*) speed;
(*mentale*) quick-wittedness
svel'tire /**55**/ VT (*gen*) to speed up; (*procedura*) to
streamline
'svelto, -a AG (*passo*) quick; (*mente*) quick,
alert; (*linea*) slim, slender; **alla svelta**
quickly
'svendere /**29**/ VT to sell off, clear
'svendita SF (*Comm*) (clearance) sale
sve'nevole AG mawkish
'svengo *etc* VB *vedi* **svenire**
sveni'mento SM fainting fit, faint
sve'nire /**128**/ VI to faint
sven'tare /**72**/ VT to foil, thwart
sventa'tezza [zventa'tettsa] SF (*distrazione*)
absent-mindedness; (*mancanza di prudenza*)
rashness
sven'tato, -a AG (*distratto*) scatterbrained;
(*imprudente*) rash
'sventola SF (*colpo*) slap; **orecchie a ~**
sticking-out ears
svento'lare /**72**/ VT, VI to wave, flutter
sven'trare /**72**/ VT to disembowel
sven'tura SF misfortune
sventu'rato, -a AG unlucky, unfortunate
sve'nuto, -a PP *di* **svenire**
svergo'gnare [zvergoɲ'ɲare] /**15**/ VT to
shame
svergo'gnato, -a [zvergoɲ'ɲato] AG
shameless ▶ SM/F shameless person
sver'nare /**72**/ VI to spend the winter
sverrò *etc* VB *vedi* **svenire**

S

sves'tire /45/ VT to undress; **svestirsi** VPR to get undressed

'Svezia ['zvɛttsja] SF: **la ~** Sweden

svez'zare [zvet'tsare] /72/ VT to wean

svi'are /60/ VT to divert; (fig) to lead astray; **sviarsi** VPR to go astray

svico'lare /72/ VI to slip down an alley; (fig) to sneak off

svi'gnarsela [zviɲ'ɲarsela] /72/ VPR to slip away, sneak off

svili'mento SM debasement

svi'lire /55/ VT to debase

svilup'pare /72/ VT, **svilup'parsi** VPR to develop

sviluppa'tore, -trice SM/F (Inform) developer

svi'luppo SM development; (di industria) expansion; **in via di ~** in the process of development; **paesi in via di ~** developing countries

svinco'lare /72/ VT to free, release; (merce) to clear

'svincolo SM (Comm) clearance; (stradale) motorway (BRIT) o expressway (US) intersection

svisce'rare [zviʃʃe'rare] /72/ VT (fig: argomento) to examine in depth

svisce'rato, -a [zviʃʃe'rato] AG (amore, odio) passionate

'svista SF oversight

svi'tare /72/ VT to unscrew

'Svizzera ['zvittsera] SF: **la ~** Switzerland

'svizzero, -a ['zvittsero] AG, SM/F Swiss

svoglia'tezza [zvoʎʎa'tettsa] SF listlessness; indolence

svogli'ato, -a [zvoʎ'ʎato] AG listless; (pigro) lazy, indolent

svolaz'zare [zvolat'tsare] /72/ VI to flutter

'svolgere ['zvɔldʒere] /96/ VT to unwind; (srotolare) to unroll; (fig: argomento) to develop; (: piano, programma) to carry out; **svolgersi** VPR to unwind; to unroll; (fig: aver luogo) to take place; (: procedere) to go on; **tutto si è svolto secondo i piani** everything went according to plan

svolgi'mento [zvoldʒi'mento] SM development; carrying out; (andamento) course

'svolsi etc VB vedi **svolgere**

'svolta SF (atto) turning no pl; (curva) turn, bend; (fig) turning-point; **essere ad una ~ nella propria vita** to be at a crossroads in one's life

svol'tare /72/ VI to turn

'svolto, -a PP di **svolgere**

svuo'tare /72/ VT to empty (out)

'Swaziland ['swadziland] SM: **lo ~** Swaziland

Tt

T, t [ti] SM O F INV (*lettera*) T, t; **T come Taranto** ≈ T for Tommy

T ABBR = **tabaccheria**

t ABBR = **tara; tonnellata**

TA SIGLA = **Taranto**

tabac'caio, -a SM/F tobacconist

tabacche'ria [tabakke'ria] SF tobacconist's (shop)

> *Tabaccherie* sell cigarettes and tobacco and can easily be identified by their sign, a large white "T" on a black background. You can buy postage stamps and bus tickets at a *tabaccheria* and some also sell newspapers.

tabacchi'era [tabak'kjɛra] SF snuffbox

ta'bacco, -chi SM tobacco

ta'bella SF (*tavola*) table; (*elenco*) list; **~ di marcia** schedule; **~ dei prezzi** price list

tabel'lone SM (*per pubblicità*) billboard; (*per informazioni*) notice board (BRIT), bulletin board (US); (: *in stazione*) timetable board

taber'nacolo SM tabernacle

tabù AG, SM INV taboo

'tabula 'rasa SF tabula rasa; **fare ~** (*fig*) to make a clean sweep

tabu'lare /**72**/ VT to tabulate

tabu'lato SM (*Inform*) printout

tabula'tore SM tabulator

TAC SIGLA F (*Med*: = *Tomografia Assiale Computerizzata*) CAT

'tacca, -che SF notch, nick; **di mezza ~** (*fig*) mediocre

taccagne'ria [takkaɲɲe'ria] SF meanness, stinginess

tac'cagno, -a [tak'kaɲɲo] AG mean, stingy

tac'cheggio [tak'keddʒo] SM shoplifting

tac'chino [tak'kino] SM turkey

'taccia, -ce ['tattʃa] SF bad reputation

tacci'are [tat'tʃare] /**14**/ VT: **~ qn di** (*vigliaccheria ecc*) to accuse sb of

'taccio *etc* ['tattʃo] VB *vedi* **tacere**

'tacco, -chi SM heel; **tacchi a spillo** stiletto heels

taccu'ino SM notebook

ta'cere [ta'tʃere] /**119**/ VI to be silent *o* quiet; (*smettere di parlare*) to fall silent ▶ VT to keep to oneself, say nothing about; **far ~ qn** to make sb be quiet; (*fig*) to silence sb; **mettere a ~ qc** to hush sth up

tachicar'dia [takikar'dia] SF (*Med*) tachycardia

ta'chimetro [ta'kimetro] SM speedometer

'tacito, -a ['tatʃito] AG silent; (*sottinteso*) tacit, unspoken

taci'turno, -a [tatʃi'turno] AG taciturn

taci'uto, -a [ta'tʃuto] PP *di* **tacere**

'tacqui *etc* VB *vedi* **tacere**

ta'fano SM horsefly

taffe'ruglio [taffe'ruʎʎo] SM brawl, scuffle

taffettà SM taffeta

'taglia ['taʎʎa] SF (*statura*) height; (*misura*) size; (*riscatto*) ransom; (*ricompensa*) reward; **taglie forti** (*Abbigliamento*) outsize

taglia'boschi [taʎʎa'bɔski] SM INV woodcutter

taglia'carte [taʎʎa'karte] SM INV paperknife

taglia'legna [taʎʎa'leɲɲa] SM INV woodcutter

tagli'ando [taʎ'ʎando] SM coupon

tagli'are [taʎ'ʎare] /**27**/ VT to cut; (*recidere, interrompere*) to cut off; (*intersecare*) to cut across, intersect; (*carne*) to carve; (*vini*) to blend ▶ VI to cut; (*prendere una scorciatoia*) to take a short-cut; **tagliarsi** VPR to cut o.s.; **~ la strada a qn** to cut across in front of sb; **~ corto** (*fig*) to cut short; **~ la corda** (*fig*) to sneak off; **~ i ponti (con)** (*fig*) to break off relations (with); **mi sono tagliato** I've cut myself

taglia'telle [taʎʎa'tɛlle] SFPL tagliatelle *pl*

tagli'ato, -a [taʎ'ʎato] AG: **essere ~ per qc** (*fig*) to be cut out for sth

taglia'trice [taʎʎa'tritʃe] SF (*Tecn*) cutter

taglia'unghie [taʎʎa'ungje] SM INV nail clippers *pl*

tagliaggi'are [taʎʎed'dʒare] /**62**/ VT to exact a tribute from

tagli'ente [taʎ'ʎɛnte] AG sharp

tagli'ere [taʎˈʎɛre] SM chopping board; (per il pane) bread board

'taglio [ˈtaʎʎo] SM (anche fig) cut; (azione) cutting no pl; (di carne) piece; (parte tagliente) cutting edge; (di abito) cut, style; (di stoffa) length; (di vini) blending; **di ~** on edge, edgeways; **banconote di piccolo/grosso ~** notes of small/large denomination; **un bel ~ di capelli** a nice haircut o hairstyle; **pizza al ~** pizza by the slice; **~ cesareo** Caesarean section

tagli'ola [taʎˈʎɔla] SF trap, snare

tagli'one [taʎˈʎone] SM: **la legge del ~** the concept of an eye for an eye and a tooth for a tooth

tagliuz'zare [taʎʎutˈtsare] /**72**/ VT to cut into small pieces

Ta'hiti [taˈiti] SF Tahiti

tailan'dese AG, SMF, SM Thai

Tai'landia SF: **la ~** Thailand

tai'lleur [taˈjœr] SM INV lady's suit

'talamo SM (poetico) marriage bed

'talco SM talcum powder

'tale DET **1** (simile, così grande) such; **un(a) tale ...** such a ...; **non accetto tali discorsi** I won't allow such talk; **è di una tale arroganza** he is so arrogant; **fa una tale confusione!** he makes such a mess!
2 (persona o cosa indeterminata) such-and-such; **il giorno tale all'ora tale** on such-and-such a day at such-and-such a time; **la tal persona** that person; **ha telefonato una tale Giovanna** somebody called Giovanna phoned
3 (nelle similitudini): **tale ... tale** like ... like; **tale padre tale figlio** like father, like son; **hai il vestito tale quale il mio** your dress is just o exactly like mine
▶ PRON (indefinito: persona): **un(a) tale** someone; **quel** (o **quella**) **tale** that person, that man (o woman); **il tal dei tali** what's-his-name

tale'bano SM Taliban

ta'lento SM talent

talis'mano SM talisman

talk-'show [tɔlkˈʃo] SM INV talk o chat show

tallo'nare /**72**/ VT to pursue; **~ il pallone** (Calcio, Rugby) to heel the ball

tallon'cino [tallonˈtʃino] SM counterfoil (BRIT), stub; **~ del prezzo** (di medicinali) tear-off tag

tal'lone SM heel

tal'mente AV so

ta'lora AV = **talvolta**

'talpa SF (Zool: anche fig) mole

tal'volta AV sometimes, at times

tambu'rello SM tambourine

tambu'rino SM drummer boy

tam'buro SM drum; **freni a ~** drum brakes; **pistola a ~** revolver; **a ~ battente** (fig) immediately, at once

Ta'migi [taˈmidʒi] SM: **il ~** the Thames

tampona'mento SM (Aut) collision; **~ a catena** pile-up

tampo'nare /**72**/ VT (otturare) to plug; (urtare: macchina) to crash o ram into

tam'pone SM (Med) wad, pad; (per timbri) ink-pad; (respingente) buffer; **~ assorbente** tampon

'tamtam SM INV (fig) grapevine

'tana SF lair, den; (fig) den, hideout

'tanfo SM (di muffa) musty smell; (puzza) stench

'tanga SM INV G-string

tan'gente [tanˈdʒɛnte] AG (Mat): **~ a** tangential to ▶ SF tangent; (quota) share; (denaro estorto) rake-off (col), cut

tangen'topoli [tandʒenˈtopoli] SF (Pol, Media) Bribesville; see note

> Tangentopoli refers to the corruption scandal of the early 1990s which involved a large number of politicians from all parties, including government ministers, as well as leading industrialists and business people. Subsequent investigations unearthed a complex series of illegal payments and bribes involving both public and private money. The scandal began in Milan, which came to be known as Tangentopoli, or "Bribesville".

tangenzi'ale [tandʒenˈtsjale] SF (strada) bypass

Tan'geri [ˈtandʒeri] SF Tangiers

tan'gibile [tanˈdʒibile] AG tangible

tangibil'mente [tandʒibilˈmente] AV tangibly

'tango, -ghi SM tango

'tanica, -che SF (contenitore) jerry can

tan'nino SM tannin

tan'tino: **un ~** av (un po') a little, a bit; (alquanto) rather

'tanto, -a DET **1** (molto: quantità) a lot of, much; (: numero) a lot of, many; **tanto pane/latte** a lot of bread/milk; **tanto tempo** a lot of time, a long time; **tanti auguri!** all the best!; **tante grazie** many thanks; **tanto persone** a lot of people, many people; **tante volte** many times, often; **ogni tanti chilometri** every so many kilometres
2 (così tanto: quantità) so much, such a lot of; (: numero) so many, such a lot of; **tanta fatica per niente!** a lot of trouble for nothing!;

ha tanto coraggio che ... he's got so much courage that ..., he's so brave that ...; **ho aspettato per tanto tempo** I waited so long *o* for such a long time
3: **tanto ... quanto** (*quantità*) as much ... as; (*numero*) as many ... as; **ho tanta pazienza quanta ne hai tu** I have as much patience as you have *o* as you; **ha tanti amici quanti nemici** he has as many friends as he has enemies
▶ PRON **1** (*molto*) much, a lot; (*così tanto*) so much, such a lot; **tanti/tante** many, a lot; so many; such a lot; **credevo ce ne fosse tanto** I thought there was (such) a lot, I thought there was plenty; **una persona come tante** a person just like any other; **è passato tanto** (*tempo*) it's been so long; **è tanto che aspetto** I've been waiting for a long time; **tanto di guadagnato!** so much the better!
2: **tanto quanto** (*denaro*) as much as; (*cioccolatini*) as many as; **ne ho tanto quanto basta** I have as much as I need; **due volte tanto** twice as much
3 (*indeterminato*) so much; **tanto per l'affitto, tanto per il gas** so much for the rent, so much for the gas; **costa un tanto al metro** it costs so much per metre; **di tanto in tanto, ogni tanto** every so often; **tanto vale che ...** I (*o we etc*) may as well ...; **tanto meglio!** so much the better!; **tanto peggio per lui!** so much the worse for him!; **se tanto mi dà tanto** if that's how things are; **guardare qc con tanto d'occhi** to gaze wide-eyed at sth
▶ AV **1** (*molto*) very; **vengo tanto volentieri** I'd be very glad to come; **non ci vuole tanto a capirlo** it doesn't take much to understand it
2 (*così tanto: con ag, av*) so; (: *con vb*) so much, such a lot; **è tanto bella!** she's so beautiful!; **non urlare tanto** (*forte*) don't shout so much; **sto tanto meglio adesso** I'm so much better now; **era tanto bella da non credere** she was incredibly beautiful; **tanto ... che** so ... (that); **tanto ... da** so ... as
3: **tanto ... quanto** as ... as; **conosco tanto Carlo quanto suo padre** I know both Carlo and his father; **non è poi tanto complicato quanto sembra** it's not as difficult as it seems; **è tanto bella quanto buona** she is as good as she is beautiful; **tanto più insisti, tanto più non mollerà** the more you insist, the more stubborn he'll be; **quanto più ... tanto meno** the more ... the less; **quanto più lo conosco tanto meno mi piace** the better I know him the less I like him

4 (*solamente*) just; **tanto per cambiare/scherzare** just for a change/a joke; **una volta tanto** for once
5 (*a lungo*) (for) long
▶ CONG after all; **non insistere, tanto è inutile** don't keep on, it's no use; **lascia stare, tanto è troppo tardi** forget it, it's too late

Tanza'nia [tandza'nia] SF: **la ~** Tanzania
tapi'oca SF tapioca
ta'piro SM (*Zool*) tapir
'tappa SF (*luogo di sosta, fermata*) stop, halt; (*parte di un percorso*) stage, leg; (*Sport*) lap; **a tappe** in stages; **bruciare le tappe** (*fig*) to be a whizz kid
tappa'buchi [tappa'buki] SM INV stopgap; **fare da ~** to act as a stopgap
tap'pare /72/ VT to plug, stop up; (*bottiglia*) to cork; **tapparsi** VPR: **tapparsi in casa** to shut o.s. up at home; **tapparsi la bocca** to shut up; **tapparsi il naso** to hold one's nose; **tapparsi le orecchie** to turn a deaf ear; **tapparsi gli occhi** to turn a blind eye
tappa'rella SF rolling shutter
tappe'tino SM (*per auto*) car mat; **~ antiscivolo** (*da bagno*) non-slip mat; **~ del mouse** mouse mat
tap'peto SM carpet; (*anche*: **tappetino**) rug; (*di tavolo*) cloth; (*Sport*): **andare al ~** to go down for the count; **mettere sul ~** (*fig*) to bring up for discussion
tappez'zare [tappet'tsare] /72/ VT (*con carta*) to paper; (*rivestire*): **~ qc (di)** to cover sth (with)
tappez'zeria [tappettse'ria] SF (*arredamento*) soft furnishings *pl*; (*tessuto*) tapestry; (*carta da parati*) wallpaper, wall covering; (*arte, di automobile*) upholstery; **far da ~** (*fig*) to be a wallflower
tappezzi'ere [tappet'tsjɛre] SM upholsterer
'tappo SM stopper; (*in sughero*) cork; **~ a corona** bottle top; **~ a vite** screw top
TAR SIGLA M = **Tribunale Amministrativo Regionale**
'tara SF (*peso*) tare; (*Med*) hereditary defect; (*difetto*) flaw
taran'tella SF tarantella
ta'rantola SF tarantula
ta'rare /72/ VT (*Comm*) to tare; (*Tecn*) to calibrate
ta'rato, -a AG (*Comm*) tared; (*Med*) with a hereditary defect
tara'tura SF (*Comm*) taring; (*Tecn*) calibration
tarchi'ato, -a [tar'kjato] AG stocky, thickset
tar'dare /72/ VI to be late ▶ VT to delay; **~ a fare** to delay doing
'tardi AV late; **più ~** later (on); **al più ~** at the latest; **sul ~** (*verso sera*) late in the day; **far ~**

to be late; (*restare alzato*) to stay up late; **è troppo ~** it's too late

tar'divo, -a AG (*primavera*) late; (*rimedio*) belated, tardy; (*fig: bambino*) retarded

'tardo, -a AG (*lento, fig: ottuso*) slow; (*tempo: avanzato*) late

tar'dona SF (*peg*): **essere una ~** to be mutton dressed as lamb

'targa, -ghe SF plate; (*Aut*) number (BRIT) o license (US) plate; *vedi anche* **circolazione**

tar'gare /80/ VT (*Aut*) to register

targ'hetta [tar'getta] SF (*con nome: su porta*) nameplate; (: *su bagaglio*) name tag

ta'riffa SF (*gen*) rate, tariff; (*di trasporti*) fare; (*elenco*) price list; tariff; **la ~ in vigore** the going rate; **~ normale/ ridotta** standard/reduced rate; (*su mezzi di trasporto*) full/concessionary fare; **~ salariale** wage rate; **~ unica** flat rate; **tariffe doganali** customs rates o tariff; **tariffe postali/telefoniche** postal/telephone charges

tarif'fario, -ii AG: **aumento ~** increase in charges o rates ▸ SM tariff, table of charges

'tarlo SM woodworm

'tarma SF moth

tarmi'cida, -i [tarmi'tʃida] AG, SM moth-killer

ta'rocco, -chi SM tarot card; **tarocchi** SMPL (*gioco*) tarot sg

tar'pare /72/ VT (*fig*): **~ le ali a qn** to clip sb's wings

tartagli'are [tartaʎ'ʎare] /27/ VI to stutter, stammer

'tartaro, -a AG, SM (*in tutti i sensi*) tartar

tarta'ruga, -ghe SF tortoise; (*di mare*) turtle; (*materiale*) tortoiseshell

tartas'sare /72/ VT (*col*): **~ qn** to give sb the works; **~ qn a un esame** to give sb a grilling at an exam

tar'tina SF canapé

tar'tufo SM (*Bot*) truffle

'tasca, -sche SF pocket; **da ~** pocket *cpd*; **fare i conti in ~ a qn** (*fig*) to meddle in sb's affairs

tas'cabile AG (*libro*) pocket *cpd*

tasca'pane SM haversack

tas'chino [tas'kino] SM breast pocket

Tas'mania SF: **la ~** Tasmania

'tassa SF (*imposta*) tax; (*doganale*) duty; (*per iscrizione: a scuola ecc*) fee; **~ di circolazione/di soggiorno** road/tourist tax

tas'sametro SM taximeter

tas'sare /72/ VT to tax; to levy a duty on

tassa'tivo, -a AG peremptory

tassazi'one [tassat'tsjone] SF taxation; **soggetto a ~** taxable

tas'sello SM (*di legno, pietra*) plug; (*assaggio*) wedge

tassì SM INV = **taxi**

tas'sista, -i, -e SM/F taxi driver

'tasso SM (*di natalità, d'interesse ecc*) rate; (*Bot*) yew; (*Zool*) badger; **~ di cambio/d'interesse** rate of exchange/interest; **~ di crescita** growth rate

tas'tare /72/ VT to feel; **~ il terreno** (*fig*) to see how the land lies

tasti'era SF keyboard

tastie'rino SM: **~ numerico** numeric keypad

'tasto SM key; (*tatto*) touch, feel; **toccare un ~ delicato** (*fig*) to touch on a delicate subject; **toccare il ~ giusto** (*fig*) to strike the right note; **~ funzione** (*Inform*) function key; **~ delle maiuscole** (*su macchina da scrivere ecc*) shift key

tas'toni AV: **procedere (a) ~** to grope one's way forward

'tata SF (*linguaggio infantile*) nanny

'tattico, -a, -ci, -che AG tactical ▸ SF tactics *pl*

'tatto SM (*senso*) touch; (*fig*) tact; **duro al ~** hard to the touch; **aver ~** to be tactful, have tact

tatu'aggio [tatu'addʒo] SM tattooing; (*disegno*) tattoo

tatu'are /72/ VT to tattoo

tauma'turgico, -a, -ci, -che [tauma'turdʒiko] AG (*fig*) miraculous

TAV [tav] SM o F INV (= *treno alta velocità*) high-speed train; (*sistema*) high-speed rail system

ta'verna SF (*osteria*) tavern

'tavola SF table; (*asse*) plank, board; (*lastra*) tablet; (*quadro*) panel (painting); (*illustrazione*) plate; **~ calda** snack bar; **~ pieghevole** folding table; **~ rotonda** (*fig*) round table; **~ a vela** windsurfer

tavo'lata SF company at table

tavo'lato SM boarding; (*pavimento*) wooden floor

tavo'letta SF tablet, bar; **a ~** (*Aut*) flat out

tavo'lino SM small table; (*scrivania*) desk; **~ da tè/gioco** coffee/card table; **mettersi a ~** to get down to work; **decidere qc a ~** (*fig*) to decide sth on a theoretical level

'tavolo SM table; **~ da disegno** drawing board; **~ da lavoro** desk; (*Tecn*) workbench; **~ operatorio** (*Med*) operating table

tavo'lozza [tavo'lɔttsa] SF (*Arte*) palette

'taxi SM INV taxi

'tazza ['tattsa] SF cup; **~ da caffè/tè** coffee/ tea cup; **una ~ di caffè/tè** a cup of coffee/tea

taz'zina [tat'tsina] SF coffee cup

TBC ABBR F (= *tubercolosi*) TB

TCI SIGLA M = **Touring Club Italiano**

TE SIGLA = **Teramo**

te PRON (*soggetto: in forme comparative, oggetto*) you

tè SM INV tea; (*trattenimento*) tea party

tea'trale AG theatrical

te'atro SM theatre; ~ **comico** comedy; ~ **di posa** film studio

techno ['tɛkno] AG INV (*musica*) techno

'tecnico, -a, -ci, -che AG technical ▶ SM/F technician ▶ SF technique; (*tecnologia*) technology

tecnolo'gia [teknolo'dʒia] SF technology; **alta** ~ high technology, hi-tech; **tecnologie ambientali** clean technology

tecno'logico, -a, -ci, -che [tekno'lɔdʒiko] AG technological

te'desco, -a, -schi, -sche AG, SM/F, SM German; ~ **orientale/occidentale** East/West German

tedi'are /19/ VT (*infastidire*) to bother, annoy; (*annoiare*) to bore

'tedio SM tedium, boredom

tedi'oso, -a AG tedious, boring

te'game SM (*Cuc*) pan; **al** ~ fried

'teglia ['teʎʎa] SF (*Cuc: per dolci*) (baking) tin (BRIT), cake pan (US); (*: per arrosti*) (roasting) tin

'tegola SF tile

Teh'ran SF Tehran

tei'era SF teapot

te'ina SF (*Chim*) theine

tel. ABBR (= *telefono*) tel.

'tela SF (*tessuto*) cloth; (*per vele, quadri*) canvas; (*dipinto*) canvas, painting; **di** ~ (*calzoni*) (heavy) cotton *cpd*; (*scarpe, borsa*) canvas *cpd*; ~ **cerata** oilcloth; ~ **di ragno** spider's web

te'laio SM (*apparecchio*) loom; (*struttura*) frame

Tel A'viv SF Tel Aviv

tele... PREFISSO tele...

teleabbo'nato SM television licence holder

tele'camera SF television camera; ~ **TVCC** CCTV camera

telecoman'dare /72/ VT to operate by remote control

teleco'mando SM remote control; (*dispositivo*) remote-control device

telecomunicazi'oni [telekomunikat'tsjoni] SFPL telecommunications

teleconfe'renza SF teleconferencing

tele'cronaca, -che SF television report

telecro'nista, -i, -e SM/F (television) commentator

tele'ferica, -che SF cableway

tele'film SM INV television film

telefo'nare /72/ VI to telephone, ring; (*fare una chiamata*) to make a phone call ▶ VT to telephone; ~ **a qn** to phone o ring o call sb (up)

telefo'nata SF (telephone) call; ~ **urbana/interurbana** local/long-distance call; ~ **a carico del destinatario** reverse charge (BRIT) o collect (US) call; ~ **con preavviso** person-to-person call

telefonica'mente AV by (tele)phone

tele'fonico, -a, -ci, -che AG (tele)phone *cpd*

telefo'nino SM (*cellulare*) mobile phone

telefo'nista, -i, -e SM/F telephonist; (*d'impresa*) switchboard operator

te'lefono SM telephone; **essere al** ~ to be on the (tele)phone; ~ **a gettoni** ≈ pay phone; ~ **azzurro** ≈ Childline; ~ **fisso** landline; ~ **interno** internal phone; ~ **pubblico** public phone, call box (BRIT); ~ **rosa** ≈ rape crisis

telegior'nale [teledʒor'nale] SM television news (programme)

telegra'fare /41/ VT, VI to telegraph, cable

telegra'fia SF telegraphy

tele'grafico, -a, -ci, -che AG telegraph *cpd*, telegraphic

telegra'fista, -i, -e SM/F telegraphist, telegraph operator

te'legrafo SM telegraph; (*ufficio*) telegraph office

tele'gramma, -i SM telegram

telela'voro SM teleworking

tele'matica SF data transmission; telematics *sg*

teleno'vela SF soap opera

teleobiet'tivo SM telephoto lens *sg*

Tele'pass® SM INV *automatic payment card for use on Italian motorways*

telepa'tia SF telepathy

tele'quiz [tele'kwits] SM INV (TV) game show

teles'chermo [teles'kɛrmo] SM television screen

teles'copio SM telescope

telescri'vente SF teleprinter (BRIT), teletypewriter (US)

teleselet'tivo, -a AG: **prefisso** ~ dialling code (BRIT), dial code (US)

teleselezi'one [teleselet'tsjone] SF direct dialling

telespetta'tore, -'trice SM/F (television) viewer

tele'text SM INV teletext

tele'vendita [tele'vendita] SF teleshopping

tele'video SM *videotext service*

televisi'one SF television; *see note*

Three state-owned channels, RAI 1, 2 and 3, and a large number of private companies broadcast television programmes in Italy. Some of the latter function at purely local level, while others are regional; some form part of a network, while others remain independent. As a public corporation, RAI reports to the Post and Telecommunications Ministry. Both RAI and the private-sector channels compete for advertising revenues.

televi'sore SM television set

'telex SM INV telex

'telo SM length of cloth

te'lone SM (*per merci ecc*) tarpaulin; (*sipario*) drop curtain

'tema, -i SM theme; (*Ins*) essay, composition

te'matica SF basic themes *pl*

teme'rario, -a AG rash, reckless

te'mere /29/ VT to fear, be afraid of; (*essere sensibile a: freddo, calore*) to be sensitive to ► VI to be afraid; (*essere preoccupato*): ~ **per** to worry about, fear for; ~ **di/che** to be afraid of/that

'tempera SF (*pittura*) tempera; (*dipinto*) painting in tempera

temperama'tite SM INV pencil sharpener

tempera'mento SM temperament

tempe'rante AG moderate

tempe'rare /72/ VT (*aguzzare*) to sharpen; (*fig*) to moderate, control, temper

tempe'rato, -a AG moderate, temperate; (*clima*) temperate

tempera'tura SF temperature; ~ **ambiente** room temperature

tempe'rino SM penknife

tem'pesta SF storm; ~ **di sabbia/neve** sand/snowstorm

tempes'tare /72/ VT (*percuotere*): ~ **qn di colpi** to rain blows on sb; (*bombardare*) ~ **qn di domande** to bombard sb with questions; (*ornare*) to stud

tempestività SF timeliness

tempes'tivo, -a AG timely

tempes'toso, -a AG stormy

'tempia SF (*Anat*) temple

'tempio SM (*edificio*) temple

tem'pismo SM sense of timing

tem'pistiche [tem'pistike] SFPL (*Comm*) time and motion

'tempo SM (*Meteor*) weather; (*cronologico*) time; (*epoca*) time, times *pl*; (*di film, gioco: parte*) part; (*Mus*) time; (*: battuta*) beat; (*Ling*) tense; **che ~ fa?** what's the weather like?; **un ~** once; **da ~** for a long time now; ~ **fa** some time ago; **poco ~ dopo** not long after; **a ~ e luogo** at the right time and place; **ogni cosa a suo ~** we'll (*o* you'll *etc*) deal with it in due course; **al ~ stesso** *o* **a un ~** at the same time; **per ~** early; **per qualche ~** for a while; **trovare il ~ di fare qc** to find the time to do sth; **aver fatto il proprio ~** to have had its (*o* his *etc*) day; **primo/secondo ~** (*Teat*) first/second part; (*Sport*) first/second half; **rispettare i tempi** to keep to the timetable; **stringere i tempi** to speed things up; **con i tempi che corrono** these days; **in questi ultimi tempi** of late; **ai miei tempi** in my day; ~ **di cottura** cooking time; **in ~ utile** in due time *o* course; **a ~ pieno** full-time; ~ **libero** free time; **tempi di esecuzione** (*Comm*) time scale *sg*; **tempi di lavorazione** (*Comm*) throughput time *sg*; **tempi morti** (*Comm*) downtime *sg*, idle time *sg*

tempo'rale AG temporal ► SM (*Meteor*) (thunder)storm

tempora'lesco, -a, -schi, -sche AG stormy

tempo'raneo, -a AG temporary

temporeggi'are [tempored'dʒare] /62/ VI to play for time, temporize

'tempra SF (*Tecn: atto*) tempering, hardening; (*: effetto*) temper; (*fig: costituzione fisica*) constitution; (*: intellettuale*) temperament

tem'prare /72/ VT to temper

te'nace [te'natʃe] AG strong, tough; (*fig*) tenacious

te'nacia [te'natʃa] SF tenacity

te'naglie [te'naʎʎe] SFPL pincers *pl*

'tenda SF (*riparo*) awning; (*di finestra*) curtain; (*per campeggio ecc*) tent

ten'daggio [ten'daddʒo] SM curtaining, curtains *pl*, drapes *pl* (US)

ten'denza [ten'dɛntsa] SF tendency; (*orientamento*) trend; **avere ~ a** *o* **per qc** to have a bent for sth; ~ **al rialzo/ribasso** (*Borsa*) upward/downward trend

tendenziosità [tendentsjosi'ta] SF tendentiousness

tendenzi'oso, -a [tenden'tsjoso] AG tendentious, bias(s)ed

'tendere /120/ VT (*allungare al massimo*) to stretch, draw tight; (*porgere: mano*) to hold out; (*fig: trappola*) to lay, set ► VI: ~ **a qc/a fare** to tend towards sth/to do; **tutti i nostri sforzi sono tesi a ...** all our efforts are geared towards ...; ~ **l'orecchio** to prick up one's ears; **il tempo tende al caldo** the weather is getting hot; **un blu che tende al verde** a greenish blue

ten'dina SF curtain

'tendine SM tendon, sinew

ten'done SM (*da circo*) big top

ten'dopoli SF INV (large) camp

'tenebre SFPL darkness *sg*

tene'broso, -a AG dark, gloomy

te'nente SM lieutenant

te'nere /121/ VT to hold; (*conservare, mantenere*) to keep; (*ritenere, considerare*) to consider; (*occupare: spazio*) to take up, occupy; (*seguire: strada*) to keep to; (*dare: lezione, conferenza*) to give ► VI to hold; (*colori*) to be fast; (*dare importanza*): ~ **a** to care about; ~ **a fare** to want to do, be keen to do; **tenersi** VPR (*stare in una determinata posizione*) to stand; (*stimarsi*) to consider o.s.; (*aggrapparsi*): **tenersi a** to hold on to; (*attenersi*): **tenersi a** to stick to; ~ **in gran conto** *o* **considerazione qn** to have a high regard for sb, think highly of sb; ~ **una conferenza** to give a lecture; ~ **conto di qc** to take sth into consideration; ~ **presente qc** to bear sth in mind; **non ci sono scuse che tengano** I'll take no excuses; **tenersi**

per la mano (*uso reciproco*) to hold hands; **tenersi in piedi** to stay on one's feet

tene'rezza [tene'rettsa] SF tenderness

'**tenero, -a** AG tender; (*pietra, cera, colore*) soft; (*fig*) tender, loving ▶ SM: **tra quei due c'è del ~** there's a romance budding between those two

'**tengo** *etc* VB *vedi* **tenere**

'**tenia** SF tapeworm

'**tenni** *etc* VB *vedi* **tenere**

'**tennis** SM tennis; **~ da tavolo** table tennis

ten'nista, -i, -e SM/F tennis player

te'nore SM (*tono*) tone; (*Mus*) tenor; **~ di vita** way of life; (*livello*) standard of living

tensi'one SF tension; **ad alta ~** (*Elettr*) high-voltage *cpd*, high-tension *cpd*

tentaco'lare AG tentacular; (*fig: città*) magnet-like

ten'tacolo SM tentacle

ten'tare /**72**/ VT (*indurre*) to tempt; (*provare*): **~ qc/di fare** to attempt *o* try to sth/to do; **~ la sorte** to try one's luck

tenta'tivo SM attempt

tentazi'one [tentat'tsjone] SF temptation; **aver la ~ di fare** to be tempted to do

tentenna'mento SM (*fig*) hesitation, wavering; **dopo molti tentennamenti** after much hesitation

tenten'nare /**72**/ VI to shake, be unsteady; (*fig*) to hesitate, waver ▶ VT: **~ il capo** to shake one's head

ten'toni AV: **andare a ~** (*anche fig*) to grope one's way

'**tenue** AG (*sottile*) fine; (*colore*) soft; (*fig*) slender, slight

te'nuta SF (*capacità*) capacity; (*divisa*) uniform; (*abito*) dress; (*Agr*) estate; **a ~ d'aria** airtight; **~ di strada** roadholding power; **in ~ da lavoro** in one's working clothes; **in ~ da sci** in a skiing outfit

teolo'gia [teolo'dʒia] SF theology

teo'logico, -a, -ci, -che [teo'lɔdʒiko] AG theological

te'ologo, -gi SM theologian

teo'rema, -i SM theorem

teo'ria SF theory; **in ~** in theory, theoretically

te'orico, -a, -ci, -che AG theoretic(al) ▶ SM theorist, theoretician; **a livello ~**, **in linea teorica** theoretically

teoriz'zare [teorid'dzare] /**72**/ VT to theorize

'**tepido, -a** AG = **tiepido**

te'pore SM warmth

'**teppa** SF mob, hooligans *pl*

tep'paglia [tep'paʎʎa] SF hooligans *pl*

tep'pismo SM hooliganism

tep'pista, -i SM hooligan

tera'peutico, -a, -ci, -che AG therapeutic

tera'pia SF therapy; **~ di gruppo** group therapy; **~ intensiva** intensive care

tera'pista, -i, -e SM/F therapist

tergicris'tallo [terdʒikris'tallo] SM windscreen (BRIT) *o* windshield (US) wiper

tergiver'sare [terdʒiver'sare] /**72**/ VI to shilly-shally

'**tergo** SM: **a ~** behind; **vedi a ~** please turn over

'**terital**® SM INV Terylene®

ter'male AG thermal; **stazione** *sf* **~** spa

'**terme** SFPL thermal baths

'**termico, -a, -ci, -che** AG thermal; **centrale termica** thermal power station

termi'nale AG (*fase, parte*) final; (*Med*) terminal ▶ SM terminal; **tratto ~** (*di fiume*) lower reaches *pl*

termi'nare /**72**/ VT to end; (*lavoro*) to finish ▶ VI to end

terminazi'one [terminat'tsjone] SF (*fine*) end; (*Ling*) ending; **terminazioni nervose** (*Anat*) nerve endings

'**termine** SM term; (*fine, estremità*) end; (*di territorio*) boundary, limit; **fissare un ~** to set a deadline; **portare a ~ qc** to bring sth to a conclusion; **contratto a ~** (*Comm*) forward contract; **a breve/lungo ~** short-/long-term; **ai termini di legge** by law; **in altri termini** in other words; **parlare senza mezzi termini** to talk frankly, not to mince one's words

terminolo'gia [terminolo'dʒia] SF terminology

'**termite** SF termite

termoco'perta SF electric blanket

ter'mometro SM thermometer

termonucle'are AG thermonuclear

'**termos** SM INV = **thermos**

termosi'fone SM radiator; (*riscaldamento* **a**) **~** central heating

ter'mostato SM thermostat

'**terna** SF set of three; (*lista di tre nomi*) list of three candidates

'**terno** SM (*al lotto ecc*) (set of) three winning numbers; **vincere un ~ al lotto** (*fig*) to hit the jackpot

'**terra** SF (*gen, Elettr*) earth; (*sostanza*) soil, earth; (*opposto al mare*) land *no pl*; (*regione, paese*) land; (*argilla*) clay; **terre** SFPL (*possedimento*) lands, land *sg*; **a** *o* **per ~** (*stato*) on the ground (*o* floor); (*moto*) to the ground, down; **mettere a ~** (*Elettr*) to earth; **essere a ~** (*fig: depresso*) to be at rock bottom; **via ~** (*viaggiare*) by land, overland; **strada in ~ battuta** dirt track; **~ di nessuno** no man's land; **la T~ Santa** the Holy Land; **~ di Siena** sienna; **~ ~** (*fig: persona, argomento*) prosaic, pedestrian

terra-'aria AG INV (*Mil*) ground-to-air

terra'cotta SF terracotta; **vasellame di ~** earthenware

t

terra'ferma SF dry land, terra firma; *(continente)* mainland

ter'raglia [ter'raʎʎa] SF pottery; **terraglie** SFPL *(oggetti)* crockery *sg*, earthenware *sg*

Terra'nova SF: **la ~** Newfoundland

terrapi'eno SM embankment, bank

'terra-'terra AG INV *(Mil)* surface-to-surface

ter'razza [ter'rattsa] SF, **ter'razzo** [ter'rattso] SM terrace

terremo'tato, -a AG *(zona)* devastated by an earthquake ▶ SM/F earthquake victim

terre'moto SM earthquake

ter'reno, -a AG *(vita, beni)* earthly ▶ SM *(suolo, fig)* ground; *(Comm)* land *no pl*, plot (of land); site; *(Sport, Mil)* field; **perdere ~** *(anche fig)* to lose ground; **un ~ montuoso** a mountainous terrain; **~ alluvionale** *(Geo)* alluvial soil

'terreo, -a AG *(viso, colorito)* wan

ter'restre AG *(superficie)* of the earth, earth's; *(di terra: battaglia, animale)* land *cpd*; *(Rel)* earthly, worldly

ter'ribile AG terrible, dreadful

ter'riccio [ter'rittʃo] SM soil

terri'ero, -a AG: **proprietà terriera** landed property; **proprietario ~** landowner

terrifi'cante AG terrifying

ter'rina SF *(zuppiera)* tureen

territori'ale AG territorial

terri'torio SM territory

ter'rone, -a SM/F derogatory term used by Northern Italians to describe Southern Italians

ter'rore SM terror; **avere il ~ di qc** to be terrified of sth

terro'rismo SM terrorism

terro'rista, -i, -e SM/F terrorist

terroriz'zare [terrorid'dzare] /**72**/ VT to terrorize

'terso, -a AG clear

'terza ['tɛrtsa] SF *vedi* **terzo**

ter'zetto [ter'tsetto] SM *(Mus)* trio, terzetto; *(di persone)* trio

terzi'ario, -a [ter'tsjarjo] AG *(Geo, Econ)* tertiary

ter'zino [ter'tsino] SM *(Calcio)* fullback, back

'terzo, -a ['tɛrtso] AG third ▶ SM *(frazione)* third; *(Dir)* third party ▶ SF *(gen)* third; *(Aut)* third (gear); *(di trasporti)* third class; *(Ins: elementare)* third year at primary school; *(: media)* third year at secondary school; *(: superiore)* sixth year at secondary school; **terzi** SMPL *(altri)* others, other people; **agire per conto di terzi** to act on behalf of a third party; **assicurazione contro terzi** third-party insurance (BRIT), liability insurance (US); **la terza età** old age; **il ~ mondo** the Third World; **di terz'ordine** third rate; **la terza pagina** *(Stampa)* the Arts page

'tesa SF brim; **a larghe tese** wide-brimmed

'teschio ['tɛskjo] SM skull

'tesi¹ SF INV thesis; **~ di laurea** degree thesis

'tesi² *etc* VB *vedi* **tesi**

'teso, -a PP *di* **tendere** ▶ AG *(tirato)* taut, tight; *(fig)* tense

tesore'ria SF treasury

tesori'ere SM treasurer

te'soro SM treasure; **il Ministero del T~** the Treasury; **far ~ dei consigli di qn** to take sb's advice to heart

'tessera SF *(documento)* card; *(di abbonato)* season ticket; *(di giornalista)* pass; **ha la ~ del partito** he's a party member; **~ elettorale** ballot paper

tesse'rare /**72**/ VT *(iscrivere)* to give a membership card to

tesse'rato, -a SM/F *(di società sportiva ecc)* (fully paid-up) member; *(Pol)* (card-carrying) member

'tessere /**1**/ VT to weave; **~ le lodi di qn** *(fig)* to sing sb's praises

'tessile AG, SM textile

tessi'tore, -'trice SM/F weaver

tessi'tura SF weaving

tes'suto SM fabric, material; *(Biol)* tissue; *(fig)* web

'test ['tɛst] SM INV test

'testa SF head; *(di cose: estremità, parte anteriore)* head, front; **50 euro a ~** 50 euros apiece *o* a head *o* per person; **a ~ alta** with one's head held high; **a ~ bassa** *(correre)* headlong; *(con aria dimessa)* with head bowed; **di ~** *ag (vettura ecc)* front; **dare alla ~** to go to one's head; **fare di ~ propria** to go one's own way; **in ~** *(Sport)* in the lead; **essere in ~ alla classifica** *(corridore)* to be number one; *(squadra)* to be at the top of the league table; *(disco)* to be top of the charts, be number one; **essere alla ~ di qc** *(società)* to be the head of; *(esercito)* to be at the head of; **tenere ~ a qn** *(nemico ecc)* to stand up to sb; **una ~ d'aglio** a bulb of garlic; **~ o croce?** heads or tails?; **avere la ~ dura** to be stubborn; **~ di serie** *(Tennis)* seed, seeded player

'testa-'coda SM INV *(Aut)* spin

testamen'tario, -a AG *(Dir)* testamentary; **le sue disposizioni testamentarie** the provisions of his will

testa'mento SM *(atto)* will, testament; **l'Antico/il Nuovo T~** *(Rel)* the Old/New Testament; **~ biologico** living will

testar'daggine [testar'daddʒine] SF stubbornness, obstinacy

tes'tardo, -a AG stubborn, pig-headed

tes'tare /**72**/ VT to test

tes'tata SF *(parte anteriore)* head; *(intestazione)* heading; **missile a ~ nucleare** missile with a nuclear warhead

'teste SMF witness

tes'ticolo SM testicle

testi'era SF (*del letto*) headboard; (*di cavallo*) headpiece

testi'mone SMF (*Dir*) witness; **fare da ~ alle nozze di qn** to be a witness at sb's wedding; **~ oculare** eye witness

testimoni'anza [testimo'njantsa] SF (*atto*) deposition; (*effetto*) evidence; (*fig: prova*) proof; **accusare qn di falsa ~** to accuse sb of perjury; **rilasciare una ~** to give evidence

testimoni'are /19/ VT to testify; (*fig*) to bear witness to, testify to ▶ VI to give evidence, testify; **~ il vero** to tell the truth; **~ il falso** to perjure o.s.

tes'tina SF (*di giradischi, registratore*) head

'testo SM text; **fare ~** (*opera, autore*) to be authoritative; (*fig: dichiarazione*) to carry weight; **questo libro non fa ~** this book is not essential reading

testoste'rone SM testosterone

testu'ale AG textual; **le sue parole testuali** his (*o* her) actual words

tes'tuggine [tes'tuddʒine] SF tortoise; (*di mare*) turtle

'tetano SM (*Med*) tetanus

'tetro, -a AG gloomy

'tetta SF (*col*) boob, tit

tetta'rella SF teat

'tetto SM roof; **abbandonare il ~ coniugale** to desert one's family; **~ a cupola** dome

tet'toia SF roofing; canopy

tet'tuccio [tet'tuttʃo] SM: **~ apribile** (*Aut*) sunroof

'Tevere SM: **il ~** the Tiber

TG [tid'dʒi], **tg** ABBR M (= *telegiornale*) TV news *sg*

'thermos® ['tɛrmos] SM INV vacuum *o* Thermos® flask

'thriller ['θrilə], **'thrilling** ['θriliŋ] SM INV thriller

ti PRON (*dav lo, la, li, le, ne diventa* **te**: *oggetto*) you; (*complemento di termine*) (to) you; (*riflessivo*) yourself; **ti aiuto?** can I give you a hand?; **te lo ha dato?** did he give it to you?; **ti sei lavato?** have you washed?

ti'ara SF (*Rel*) tiara

'Tibet SM: **il ~** Tibet

tibe'tano, -a AG, SM/F Tibetan

'tibia SF tibia, shinbone

tic SM INV tic, (*nervous*) twitch; (*fig*) mannerism

ticchet'tio [tikket'tio] SM (*di macchina da scrivere*) clatter; (*di orologio*) ticking; (*della pioggia*) patter

'ticchio ['tikkjo] SM (*ghiribizzo*) whim; (*tic*) tic, (*nervous*) twitch

'ticket SM INV (*Med*) prescription charge (BRIT)

ti'ene *etc* VB *vedi* **tenere**

ti'epido, -a AG lukewarm, tepid

ti'fare /72/ VI: **~ per** to be a fan of; (*parteggiare*) to side with

'tifo SM (*Med*) typhus; (*fig*): **fare il ~ per** to be a fan of

tifoi'dea SF typhoid

ti'fone SM typhoon

ti'foso, -a SM/F (*Sport ecc*) fan

tight ['tait] SM INV morning suit

tigì [ti'dʒi] SM INV TV news

'tiglio ['tiʎʎo] SM lime (tree), linden (tree)

'tigna ['tiɲɲa] SF (*Med*) ringworm

ti'grato, -a AG striped

'tigre SF tiger

tilt SM: **andare in ~** (*fig*) to go haywire

tim'ballo SM (*strumento*) kettledrum; (*Cuc*) timbale

tim'brare /72/ VT to stamp; (*annullare: francobolli*) to postmark; **~ il cartellino** to clock in

'timbro SM stamp; (*Mus*) timbre, tone

timi'dezza [timi'dettsa] SF shyness, timidity

'timido, -a AG shy; timid

'timo SM thyme

ti'mone SM (*Naut*) rudder

timoni'ere SM helmsman

timo'rato, -a AG conscientious; **~ di Dio** God-fearing

ti'more SM (*paura*) fear; (*rispetto*) awe; **avere ~ di qc/qn** (*paura*) to be afraid of sth/sb

timo'roso, -a AG timid, timorous

'timpano SM (*Anat*) eardrum; (*Mus*): **timpani** kettledrums, timpani

'tinca, -che SF (*Zool*) tench

ti'nello SM small dining room

'tingere ['tindʒere] /37/ VT to dye

'tino SM vat

ti'nozza [ti'nɔttsa] SF tub

'tinsi *etc* VB *vedi* **tingere**

'tinta SF (*materia colorante*) dye; (*colore*) colour (BRIT), color (US), shade

tinta'rella SF (*col*) (sun)tan

tintin'nare /72/ VI to tinkle

tintin'nio SM tinkling

'tinto, -a PP *di* **tingere**

tinto'ria SF (*officina*) dyeworks *sg*; (*lavasecco*) dry cleaner's (shop)

tin'tura SF (*operazione*) dyeing; (*colorante*) dye; **~ di iodio** tincture of iodine

'tipico, -a, -ci, -che AG typical

'tipo SM type; (*genere*) kind, type; (*col*) chap, fellow; **che ~ di...?** what kind of ...?; **vestiti di tutti i tipi** all kinds of clothes; **sul ~ di questo** of this sort; **sei un bel ~!** you're a fine one!

tipogra'fia SF typography; (*procedimento*) letterpress (printing); (*officina*) printing house

tipo'grafico, -a, -ci, -che AG typographic(al)

ti'pografo SM typographer

tip 'tap [tip'tap] SM (*ballo*) tap dancing

T.I.R. SIGLA M (= *Transports Internationaux Routiers*) International Heavy Goods Vehicle

'tira e 'molla SM INV tug-of-war

ti'raggio [ti'raddʒo] SM (*di camino ecc*) draught (BRIT), draft (US)

Ti'rana SF Tirana

tiranneggi'are [tiranned'dʒare] /62/ VT to tyrannize

tiran'nia SF tyranny

ti'ranno, -a AG tyrannical ▶ SM tyrant

ti'rante SM (*Naut, di tenda ecc*) guy; (*Edil*) brace

tirapi'edi SM INV/F INV hanger-on

tira'pugni [tira'puɲɲi] SM INV knuckle-duster

ti'rare /72/ VT (*gen*) to pull; (*chiudere: tenda ecc*) to draw, pull; (*tracciare, disegnare*) to draw, trace; (*lanciare: sasso, palla*) to throw; (*stampare*) to print; (*pistola, freccia*) to fire; (*estrarre*): ~ **qc da** to take *o* pull sth out of; to get sth out of; to extract sth from ▶ VI (*pipa, camino*) to draw; (*vento*) to blow; (*abito*) to be tight; (*fare fuoco*) to fire; (*fare del tiro, Calcio*) to shoot; ~ **qn da parte** to take *o* draw sb aside; ~ **un sospiro (di sollievo)** to heave a sigh (of relief); ~ **a indovinare** to take a guess; ~ **sul prezzo** to bargain; ~ **avanti** vi to struggle on, to keep going; vt (*: famiglia*) to provide for; (*: ditta*) to look after; ~ **fuori** (*estrarre*) to take out, pull out; ~ **giù** to pull down; (*abbassare*) to bring down, to lower; (*da scaffale ecc*) to take down; ~ **su** to pull up; (*capelli*) to put up; (*fig: bambino*) to bring up; **tirar dritto** to keep right on going; ~ **via** (*togliere*) to take off; **tirarsi indietro** to move back; (*fig*) to back out; **tirarsi su** to pull o.s. up; (*fig*) to cheer o.s. up; **tirati su!** cheer up!

ti'rato, -a AG (*teso*) taut; (*fig: teso, stanco*) drawn

tira'tore SM gunman; **un buon** ~ a good shot; ~ **scelto** marksman

tira'tura SF (*azione*) printing; (*di libro*) (print) run; (*di giornale*) circulation

tirchie'ria [tirkje'ria] SF meanness, stinginess

'tirchio, -a ['tirkjo] AG mean, stingy

tiri'tera SF drivel, hot air

'tiro SM shooting *no pl*, firing *no pl*; (*colpo, sparo*) shot; (*di palla: lancio*) throwing *no pl*; throw; (*fig*) trick; **essere a** ~ to be in range; **giocare un brutto** ~ *o* **un** ~ **mancino a qn** to play a dirty trick on s.b.; **cavallo da** ~ draught (BRIT) *o* draft (US) horse; ~ **a segno** target shooting; (*luogo*) shooting range; ~ **con l'arco** archery

tiroci'nante [tirotʃi'nante] AG, SMF apprentice *cpd*; trainee *cpd*

tiro'cinio [tiro'tʃinjo] SM apprenticeship; (*professionale*) training

ti'roide SF thyroid (gland)

tiro'lese AG, SMF Tyrolean, Tyrolese *inv*

Ti'rolo SM: **il** ~ the Tyrol

tir'rennico, -a, -ci, -che AG Tyrrhenian

Tir'reno SM: **il (mar)** ~ the Tyrrhenian Sea

ti'sana SF herb tea

'tisi SF (*Med*) consumption

'tisico, -a, -ci, -che AG (*Med*) consumptive; (*fig: gracile*) frail ▶ SM/F consumptive (person)

ti'tanico, -a, -ci, -che AG gigantic, enormous

ti'tano SM (*Mitologia, fig*) titan

tito'lare AG appointed; (*sovrano*) titular ▶ SMF incumbent; (*proprietario*) owner; (*Calcio*) regular player

tito'lato, -a AG (*persona*) titled

'titolo SM title; (*di giornale*) headline; (*diploma*) qualification; (*Comm*) security; (*: azione*) share; **a che ~?** for what reason?; **a ~ di amicizia** out of friendship; **a ~ di cronaca** for your information; **a ~ di premio** as a prize; ~ **di credito** share; ~ **obbligazionario** bond; ~ **al portatore** bearer bond; ~ **di proprietà** title deed; **titoli di stato** government securities; **titoli di testa** (*Cine*) credits

titu'bante AG hesitant, irresolute

tivù SF INV (*col*) telly (BRIT), TV

'tizio, -a ['tittsjo] SM/F fellow, chap

tiz'zone [tit'tsone] SM brand

T.M.G. ABBR (= *tempo medio di Greenwich*) GMT

TN SIGLA = **Trento**

TNT SIGLA M (= *trinitrotoluolo*) TNT

TO SIGLA = **Torino**

toast [toust] SM INV toasted sandwich (*generally with ham and cheese*)

toc'cante AG touching

toc'care /20/ VT to touch; (*tastare*) to feel; (*fig: riguardare*) to concern; (*commuovere*) to touch, move; (*pungere*) to hurt, wound; (*far cenno a: argomento*) to touch on, mention ▶ VI: ~ **a** (*accadere*) to happen to; (*spettare*) to be up to; **tocca a te difenderci** it's up to you to defend us; **a chi tocca?** whose turn is it?; **mi toccò pagare** I had to pay; ~ **il fondo** (*in acqua*) to touch the bottom; (*fig*) to touch rock bottom; ~ **con mano** (*fig*) to find out for o.s.; ~ **qn sul vivo** to cut sb to the quick

tocca'sana SM INV cure-all, panacea

toccherò etc [tokke'rɔ] VB vedi **toccare**

'tocco, -chi SM touch; (*Arte*) stroke, touch

toe'letta SF = **toilette**

'toga, -ghe SF toga; (*di magistrato, professore*) gown

'togliere ['tɔʎʎere] /122/ VT (*rimuovere*) to take away (*o* off), remove; (*riprendere, non concedere più*) to take away, remove; (*Mat*) to take away, subtract; (*liberare*) to free; ~ **qc a qn** to take sth (away) from sb; **ciò non toglie che ...** nevertheless ..., be that as it may ...; **togliersi il cappello** to take off one's hat

'Togo SM: **il** ~ Togo

toilette [twa'lɛt] SF INV (*gabinetto*) toilet; (*cosmesi*) make-up; (*abbigliamento*) gown, dress; (*mobile*) dressing table; **fare ~** to get made up, make o.s. beautiful

'Tokyo SF Tokyo

to'letta SF = **toilette**

'tolgo *etc* VB *vedi* **togliere**

tolle'rante AG tolerant

tolle'ranza [tolle'rantsa] SF tolerance; **casa di ~** brothel

tolle'rare /72/ VT to tolerate; **non tollero repliche** I won't stand for objections; **non sono tollerati i ritardi** lateness will not be tolerated

To'losa SF Toulouse

'tolsi *etc* VB *vedi* **togliere**

'tolto, -a PP *di* **togliere**

to'maia SF (*di scarpa*) upper

'tomba SF tomb

tom'bale AG: **pietra ~** tombstone, gravestone

tom'bino SM manhole cover

'tombola SF (*gioco*) tombola; (*ruzzolone*) tumble

'tomo SM volume

tomogra'fia SF (*Med*) tomography; **~ assiale computerizzata** computerized axial tomography

'tonaca, -che SF (*Rel*) habit

to'nare /72/ VI = **tuonare**

'tondo, -a AG round

'tonfo SM splash; (*rumore sordo*) thud; (*caduta*): **fare un ~** to take a tumble

'tonico, -a, -ci, -che AG tonic ▶ SM tonic; (*cosmetico*) toner

tonifi'cante AG invigorating, bracing

tonifi'care /20/ VT (*muscoli, pelle*) to tone up; (*irrobustire*) to invigorate, brace

ton'nara SF tuna-fishing nets *pl*

ton'nato, -a AG (*Cuc*): **salsa tonnata** tuna fish sauce; **vitello ~** veal with tuna fish sauce

tonnel'laggio [tonnel'laddʒo] SM (*Naut*) tonnage

tonnel'lata SF ton

'tonno SM tuna (fish)

'tono SM (*gen, Mus*) tone; (: *di pezzo*) key; (*di colore*) shade, tone; **rispondere a ~** (*a proposito*) to answer to the point; (*nello stesso modo*) to answer in kind; (*per le rime*) to answer back

ton'silla SF tonsil

tonsil'lite SF tonsillitis

ton'sura SF tonsure

'tonto, -a AG dull, stupid ▶ SM/F blockhead, dunce; **fare il finto ~** to play dumb

top [tɔp] SM INV (*vertice, camicetta*) top

to'paia SF (*di topo*) mousehole; (*di ratto*) rat's nest; (*fig*: *casa ecc*) hovel, dump

to'pazio [to'pattsjo] SM topaz

topi'cida, -i [topi'tʃida] SM rat poison

'topless ['tɔplis] SM INV topless bathing costume

'topo SM mouse; **~ d'albergo** (*fig*) hotel thief; **~ di biblioteca** (*fig*) bookworm

topogra'fia SF topography

topo'grafico, -a, -ci, -che AG topographic, topographical

to'ponimo SM place name

'toppa SF (*serratura*) keyhole; (*pezza*) patch

to'race [to'ratʃe] SM chest

'torba SF peat

'torbido, -a AG (*liquido*) cloudy; (*fiume*) muddy; (*fig*) dark; troubled ▶ SM: **pescare nel ~** (*fig*) to fish in troubled waters

'torcere ['tɔrtʃere] /106/ VT to twist; (*biancheria*) to wring (out); **torcersi** VPR to twist, writhe; **dare del filo da ~ a qn** to make life o things difficult for sb

torchi'are [tor'kjare] /19/ VT to press

'torchio ['tɔrkjo] SM press; **mettere qn sotto il ~** (*fig*: *col*: *interrogare*) to grill sb; **~ tipografico** printing press

'torcia, -ce ['tɔrtʃa] SF torch; **~ elettrica** torch (BRIT), flashlight (US)

torci'collo [tortʃi'kɔllo] SM stiff neck

'tordo SM thrush

to'rero SM bullfighter, toreador

tori'nese AG of (o from) Turin ▶ SMF person from Turin

To'rino SF Turin

tor'menta SF snowstorm

tormen'tare /72/ VT to torment; **tormentarsi** VPR to fret, worry o.s.

tor'mento SM torment

torna'conto SM advantage, benefit

tor'nado SM tornado

tor'nante SM hairpin bend (BRIT) o curve (US)

tor'nare /72/ VI to return, go (o come) back; (*ridiventare*: *anche fig*) to become (again); (*riuscire giusto, esatto*: *conto*) to work out; (*risultare*) to turn out (to be), prove (to be); **~ al punto di partenza** to start again; **~ a casa** to go (o come) home; **i conti tornano** the accounts balance; **~ utile** to prove o turn out (to be) useful; **torno a casa martedì** I'm going home on Tuesday

torna'sole SM INV litmus

tor'neo SM tournament

'tornio SM lathe

tor'nire /55/ VT (*Tecn*) to turn (on a lathe); (*fig*) to shape, polish

tor'nito, -a AG (*gambe, caviglie*) well-shaped

'toro SM bull; **T~** Taurus; **essere del T~** to be Taurus

tor'pedine SF torpedo

torpedini'era SF torpedo boat

tor'pore SM torpor

'torre SF tower; (*Scacchi*) rook, castle; **~ di controllo** (*Aer*) control tower

torrefazi'one [torrefat'tsjone] SF roasting

torreggi'are [torred'dʒare] /**62**/ VI: ~ **(su)** to tower (over)

tor'rente SM torrent

torren'tizio, -a [torren'tittsjo] AG torrential

torrenzi'ale [torren'tsjale] AG torrential

tor'retta SF turret

'torrido, -a AG torrid

torri'one SM keep

tor'rone SM nougat

'torsi etc VB vedi **torcere**

torsi'one SF twisting; (Tecn) torsion

'torso SM torso, trunk; (Arte) torso; **a ~ nudo** bare-chested

'torsolo SM (di cavolo ecc) stump; (di frutta) core

'torta SF cake

tortel'lini SMPL (Cuc) tortellini

torti'era SF cake tin (BRIT), cake pan (US)

'torto, -a PP di **torcere** ▶ AG (ritorto) twisted; (storto) twisted, crooked ▶ SM (ingiustizia) wrong; (colpa) fault; **a ~** wrongly; **a ~ o a ragione** rightly or wrongly; **aver ~** to be wrong; **fare un ~ a qn** to wrong sb; **essere/ passare dalla parte del ~** to be/put o.s. in the wrong; **lui non ha tutti i torti** there's something in what he says

'tortora SF turtle dove

tortu'oso, -a AG (strada) twisting; (fig) tortuous

tor'tura SF torture

tortu'rare /**72**/ VT to torture

'torvo, -a AG menacing, grim

tosa'erba SM O F INV (lawn)mower

to'sare /**72**/ VT (pecora) to shear; (cane) to clip; (siepe) to clip, trim

tosa'tura SF (di pecore) shearing; (di cani) clipping; (di siepi) trimming, clipping

Tos'cana SF: **la ~** Tuscany

tos'cano, -a AG, SM/F Tuscan ▶ SM (anche: **sigaro toscano**) strong Italian cigar

'tosse SF cough; **ho la ~** I've got a cough

tossicità [tossitʃi'ta] SF toxicity

'tossico, -a, -ci, -che AG toxic; (Econ): **titolo ~** toxic asset

tossicodipen'dente SMF drug addict

tossicodipen'denza [tossikodipen'dɛntsa] SF drug addiction

tossi'comane SMF drug addict

tossicoma'nia SF drug addiction

tos'sina SF toxin

tos'sire /**55**/ VI to cough

tosta'pane SM INV toaster

tos'tare /**72**/ VT to toast; (caffè) to roast

tosta'tura SF (di pane) toasting; (di caffè) roasting

'tosto, -a AG: **faccia tosta** cheek ▶ AV at once, immediately; **~ che** as soon as

to'tale AG, SM total

totalità SF: **la ~ di** all of, the total amount (o number) of; the whole (+ n sg)

totali'tario, -a AG totalitarian; (totale) complete, total; **adesione totalitaria** complete support

totalita'rismo SM (Pol) totalitarianism

totaliz'zare [totalid'dzare] /**72**/ VT to total; (Sport: punti) to score

totalizza'tore [totaliddza'tore] SM (Tecn) totalizator; (Ippica) totalizator, tote (col)

to'tip SM gambling pool betting on horse racing

toto'calcio [toto'kaltʃo] SM gambling pool betting on football results, ≈ (football) pools pl (BRIT)

tou'pet [tu'pɛ] SM INV toupee

tour [tur] SM INV (giro) tour; (Ciclismo) tour de France

tour de 'force ['tur də 'fɔrs] SM INV (Sport: anche fig) tour de force

tour'née [tur'ne] SF tour; **essere in ~** to be on tour

to'vaglia [to'vaʎʎa] SF tablecloth

tovagli'olo [tovaʎ'ʎɔlo] SM napkin

'tozzo, -a ['tɔttso] AG squat ▶ SM: ~ **di pane** crust of bread

TP SIGLA = **Trapani**

TR SIGLA = **Terni**

Tr ABBR (Comm) = **tratta**

tra PREP (di due persone, cose) between; (di più persone, cose) among(st); (tempo: entro) within, in; **prendere qn ~ le braccia** to take sb in one's arms; **litigano ~ (di) loro** they're fighting amongst themselves; ~ **5 giorni** in 5 days' time; ~ **breve** o **poco** soon; ~ **sé e sé** (parlare ecc) to oneself; **sia detto ~ noi ...** between you and me ...; ~ **una cosa e l'altra** what with one thing and another

trabal'lante AG shaky

trabal'lare /**72**/ VI to stagger, totter

tra'biccolo SM (peg: auto) old banger (BRIT), jalopy

traboc'care /**20**/ VI to overflow

traboc'chetto [trabok'ketto] SM (fig) trap ▶ AG INV trap cpd; **domanda ~** trick question

traca'gnotto, -a [trakaɲ'ɲɔtto] AG dumpy ▶ SM/F dumpy person

tracan'nare /**72**/ VT to gulp down

'traccia, -ce ['trattʃa] SF (segno, striscia) trail, track; (orma) tracks pl; (residuo, testimonianza) trace, sign; (abbozzo) outline; **essere sulle tracce di qn** to be on sb's trail

tracci'are [trat'tʃare] /**14**/ VT to trace, mark (out); (disegnare) to draw; (fig: abbozzare) to outline; ~ **un quadro della situazione** to outline the situation

tracci'ato [trat'tʃato] SM (grafico) layout, plan; ~ **di gara** (Sport) race route

tra'chea [tra'kɛa] SF windpipe, trachea

tra'colla SF shoulder strap; **portare qc a ~** to carry sth over one's shoulder; **borsa a ~** shoulder bag tra'collo SM (*fig*) collapse, ruin; ~ **finanziario** crash; **avere un ~** (*Med*) to have a setback; (*Comm*) to collapse

traco'tante AG overbearing, arrogant

traco'tanza [trako'tantsa] SF arrogance

trad. ABBR = **traduzione**

tradi'mento SM betrayal; (*Dir*, *Mil*) treason; **a ~** by surprise; **alto ~** high treason

tra'dire /**55**/ VT to betray; (*coniuge*) to be unfaithful to; (*doveri: mancare*) to fail in; (*rivelare*) to give away, reveal; **ha tradito le attese di tutti** he let everyone down

tradi'tore, -trice SM/F traitor

tradizio'nale [tradittsjo'nale] AG traditional

tradizi'one [tradit'tsjone] SF tradition

tra'dotto, -a PP *di* **tradurre** ▶ SF (*Mil*) troop train

tra'durre /**90**/ VT to translate; (*spiegare*) to render, convey; (*Dir*): ~ **qn in carcere/tribunale** to take sb to prison/court; ~ **in cifre** to put into figures; ~ **in atto** (*fig*) to put into effect

tradut'tore, -'trice SM/F translator

traduzi'one [tradut'tsjone] SF translation; (*Dir*) transfer

'trae VB *vedi* **trarre**

tra'ente SMF (*Econ*) drawer

trafe'lato, -a AG out of breath

traffi'cante SMF dealer; (*peg*) trafficker

traffi'care /**20**/ VI (*affaccendarsi*) to busy o.s.; (*commerciare*): ~ (**in**) to trade (in), deal (in) ▶ VT (*peg*) to traffic in

traffi'cato, -a AG (*strada, zona*) busy

'traffico, -ci SM traffic; (*commercio*) trade, traffic; ~ **aereo/ferroviario** air/rail traffic; ~ **di armi/droga** arms/drug trafficking; ~ **stradale** traffic

tra'figgere [tra'fiddʒere] /**104**/ VT to run through, stab; (*fig*) to pierce

tra'fila SF procedure

trafi'letto SM (*di giornale*) short article

tra'fitto, -a PP *di* **trafiggere**

trafo'rare /**72**/ VT to bore, drill

tra'foro SM (*azione*) boring, drilling; (*galleria*) tunnel

trafu'gare /**80**/ VT to purloin

tra'gedia [tra'dʒɛdja] SF tragedy

'traggo *etc* VB *vedi* **trarre**

traghet'tare [traget'tare] /**72**/ VT to ferry

tra'ghetto [tra'getto] SM crossing; (*barca*) ferry(boat)

tragicità [tradʒitʃi'ta] SF tragedy

'tragico, -a, -ci, -che ['tradʒiko] AG tragic ▶ SM (*autore*) tragedian; **prendere tutto sul ~** (*fig*) to take everything far too seriously

tragi'comico, -a, -ci, -che [tradʒi'kɔmiko] AG tragicomic

tra'gitto [tra'dʒitto] SM (*passaggio*) crossing; (*viaggio*) journey

tragu'ardo SM (*Sport*) finishing line; (*fig*) goal, aim

'trai *etc* VB *vedi* **trarre**

traiet'toria SF trajectory

trai'nante AG (*cavo, fune*) towing; (*fig: persona, settore*) driving

trai'nare /**72**/ VT to drag, haul; (*rimorchiare*) to tow

'training ['treiniŋ] SM INV training

'traino SM (*carro*) wagon; (*slitta*) sledge; (*carico*) load

tralasci'are [tralaʃʃare] /**14**/ VT (*studi*) to neglect; (*dettagli*) to leave out, omit

'tralcio ['traltʃo] SM (*Bot*) shoot

tra'liccio [tra'littʃo] SM (*tela*) ticking; (*struttura*) trellis; (*Elettr*) pylon

tram SM INV tram (*BRIT*), streetcar (*US*)

'trama SF (*filo*) weft, woof; (*fig: argomento, maneggio*) plot

traman'dare /**72**/ VT to pass on, hand down

tra'mare /**72**/ VT (*fig*) to scheme, plot

tram'busto SM turmoil

trames'tio SM bustle

tramez'zino [tramed'dzino] SM sandwich

tra'mezzo [tra'mɛddzo] SM partition

'tramite PREP through ▶ SM means *pl*; **agire/fare da ~** to act as/be a go-between

tramon'tana SF (*Meteor*) north wind

tramon'tare /**72**/ VI to set, go down

tra'monto SM setting; (*del sole*) sunset

tramor'tire /**55**/ VI to faint ▶ VT to stun

trampo'lino SM (*per tuffi*) springboard, diving board; (*per lo sci*) ski-jump

'trampolo SM stilt

tramu'tare /**72**/ VT: ~ **in** to change into

trance [traːns] SF INV (*di medium*) trance; **cadere in ~** to fall into a trance

'trancia, -ce ['trantʃa] SF slice; (*cesoia*) shearing machine

tranci'are [tran'tʃare] /**14**/ VT (*Tecn*) to shear

'trancio ['trantʃo] SM slice

tra'nello SM trap; **tendere un ~ a qn** to set a trap for sb; **cadere in un ~** to fall into a trap

trangugi'are [trangu'dʒare] /**62**/ VT to gulp down

'tranne PREP except (for), but (for); ~ **che** *cong* unless; **tutti i giorni ~ il venerdì** every day except *o* with the exception of Friday

tranquil'lante SM (*Med*) tranquillizer

tranquillità SF calm, stillness; quietness; peace of mind

tranquilliz'zare [trankwillid'dzare] /**72**/ VT to reassure

tran'quillo, -a AG calm, quiet; (*bambino, scolaro*) quiet; (*sereno*) with one's mind at rest; **sta' ~** don't worry

transat'lantico, -a, -ci, -che AG transatlantic ▶ SM transatlantic liner; (*Pol*) *corridor used as a meeting place by members of the lower chamber of the Italian Parliament; see note*

The *transatlantico* is a room in the Palazzo di Montecitorio which is used by *deputati* between parliamentary sessions for relaxation and conversation. It is also used for media interviews and press conferences.

tran'satto, -a PP *di* **transigere**

transazi'one [transat'tsjone] SF compromise; (*Dir*) settlement; (*Comm*) transaction, deal

tran'senna SF barrier

tran'setto SM transept

trans'genico, -a, -ci, -che [trans'dʒɛniko] AG genetically modified, GM; **pianta transgenica** GM crop; **cibo ~** GM food

transiberi'ano, -a AG trans-Siberian

tran'sigere [tran'sidʒere] /47/ VI (*Dir*) to reach a settlement; (*venire a patti*) to compromise, come to an agreement

tran'sistor SM INV, **transis'tore** SM transistor

transi'tabile AG passable

transi'tare /72/ VI to pass

transi'tivo, -a AG transitive

'transito SM transit; **di ~** (*merci*) in transit; (*stazione*) transit *cpd*; **"divieto di ~"** "no entry"; **"~ interrotto"** "road closed"

transi'torio, -a AG transitory, transient; (*provvisorio*) provisional

transizi'one [transit'tsjone] SF transition

tran 'tran SM routine; **il solito ~** the same old routine

tran'via SF tramway (*BRIT*), streetcar line (*US*)

tranvi'ario, -a AG tram *cpd* (*BRIT*), streetcar *cpd* (*US*); **linea tranviaria** tramline, streetcar line

tranvi'ere SM (*conducente*) tram driver (*BRIT*), streetcar driver (*US*); (*bigliettaio*) tram *o* streetcar conductor

trapa'nare /72/ VT (*Tecn*) to drill

'trapano SM (*utensile*) drill; (*Med*) trepan

trapas'sare /72/ VT to pierce

trapas'sato SM (*Ling*) past perfect

tra'passo SM passage; **~ di proprietà** (*di case*) conveyancing; (*di auto ecc*) legal transfer

trape'lare /72/ VI to leak, drip; (*fig*) to leak out

tra'pezio [tra'pɛttsjo] SM (*Mat*) trapezium; (*attrezzo ginnico*) trapeze

trape'zista, -i, -e [trapet'tsista] SM/F trapeze artist

trapian'tare /72/ VT to transplant

trapi'anto SM transplanting; (*Med*) transplant; **~ cardiaco** heart transplant

'trappola SF trap

tra'punta SF quilt

'trarre /123/ VT to draw, pull; (*portare*) to take; (*prendere, tirare fuori*) to take (out), draw; (*derivare*) to obtain; **~ beneficio** *o* **profitto** **da qc** to benefit from sth; **~ le conclusioni** to draw one's own conclusions; **~ esempio da qn** to follow sb's example; **~ guadagno** to make a profit; **~ qn d'impaccio** to get sb out of an awkward situation; **~ origine da qc** to have its origins *o* originate in sth; **~ in salvo** to rescue

trasa'lire /55/ VI to start, jump

trasan'dato, -a AG shabby

trasbor'dare /72/ VT to transfer; (*Naut*) to tran(s)ship ▶ VI (*Naut*) to change ship; (*Aer*) to change plane; (*Ferr*) to change (trains)

trascenden'tale [traʃʃenden'tale] AG transcendental

tra'scendere [traʃ'ʃendere] /101/ VT (*Filosofia, Rel*) to transcend; (*fig: superare*) to surpass, go beyond

tra'sceso, -a [traʃ'ʃeso] PP *di* **trascendere**

trasci'nare [traʃʃi'nare] /72/ VT to drag; **trascinarsi** VPR to drag o.s. along; (*fig*) to drag on

tras'correre /28/ VT (*tempo*) to spend, pass ▶ VI to pass

tras'corso, -a PP *di* **trascorrere** ▶ AG past ▶ SM mistake

tras'critto, -a PP *di* **trascrivere**

tras'crivere /105/ VT to transcribe

trascrizi'one [traskrit'tsjone] SF transcription

trascu'rare /72/ VT to neglect; (*non considerare*) to disregard

trascura'tezza [traskura'tettsa] SF carelessness, negligence

trascu'rato, -a AG (*casa*) neglected; (*persona*) careless, negligent

traseco'lato, -a AG astounded, amazed

trasferi'mento SM transfer; (*trasloco*) removal, move; **~ di chiamata** (*Tel*) call forwarding

trasfe'rire /55/ VT to transfer; **trasferirsi** VPR to move

tras'ferta SF transfer; (*indennità*) travelling expenses *pl*; (*Sport*) away game

trasfigu'rare /72/ VT to transfigure

trasfor'mare /72/ VT to transform, change; **trasformarsi** VPR to be transformed; **trasformarsi in qc** to turn into sth

trasforma'tore SM (*Elettr*) transformer

trasformazi'one [trasformat'tsjone] SF transformation

trasfusi'one SF (*Med*) transfusion

trasgre'dire /55/ VT to break, infringe; (*ordini*) to disobey, contravene

trasgressi'one SF breaking, infringement; disobeying

trasgres'sivo, -a AG (*personaggio, atteggiamento*) rule-breaking

trasgres'sore, trasgredi'trice [trazgredi'tritʃe] SM/F (*Dir*) transgressor

tras'lato, -a AG metaphorical, figurative

traslo'care /20/ VT to move, transfer; **traslocarsi** VPR to move

tras'loco, -chi SM removal

tras'messo, -a PP di **trasmettere**

tras'mettere /63/ VT (passare): ~ **qc a qn** to pass sth on to sb; (mandare) to send; (Tecn, Tel, Med) to transmit; (TV, Radio) to broadcast

trasmetti'tore SM transmitter

trasmissi'one SF (gen, Fisica, Tecn) transmission; (passaggio) transmission, passing on; (TV, Radio) broadcast

trasmit'tente SF transmitting o broadcasting station

traso'gnato, -a [trasoɲˈɲato] AG dreamy

traspa'rente AG transparent

traspa'renza [traspaˈrɛntsa] SF transparency; **guardare qc in** ~ to look at sth against the light

traspa'rire /112/ VI to show (through)

tras'parso, -a PP di **trasparire**

traspi'rare /72/ VI to perspire; (fig) to come to light, leak out

traspirazi'one [traspiratˈtsjone] SF perspiration

tras'porre /77/ VT to transpose

traspor'tare /72/ VT to carry, move; (merce) to transport, convey; **lasciarsi ~ (da qc)** (fig) to let o.s. be carried away (by sth)

tras'porto SM transport; (fig) rapture, passion; **con ~** passionately; **compagnia di ~** carriers pl; (per strada) hauliers pl (BRIT), haulers pl (US); **mezzi di ~** means of transport; **nave/aereo da ~** transport ship/aircraft inv; ~ **(funebre)** funeral procession; ~ **marittimo/aereo** sea/air transport; ~ **stradale** (road) haulage; **i trasporti pubblici** public transport

tras'posto, -a PP di **trasporre**

'trassi etc VB vedi **trarre**

trastul'lare /72/ VT to amuse; **trastullarsi** VPR to amuse o.s.

tras'tullo SM game

trasu'dare /72/ VI (filtrare) to ooze; (sudare) to sweat ▶ VT to ooze with

trasver'sale AG (taglio, sbarra) cross(-); (retta) transverse; running at right angles; **via ~** side street

trasvo'lare /72/ VT to fly over

'tratta SF (Econ) draft; **la ~ delle bianche** the white slave trade; ~ **documentaria** documentary bill of exchange

tratta'mento SM treatment; (servizio) service; **ricevere un buon ~** (cliente) to get good service; ~ **di bellezza** beauty treatment; ~ **di fine rapporto** (Comm) severance pay

trat'tare /72/ VT (gen) to treat; (commerciare) to deal in; (svolgere: argomento) to discuss, deal

with; (negoziare) to negotiate ▶ VI: ~ **di** to deal with; ~ **con** (persona) to deal with; **si tratta di ...** it's about ...; **si tratterebbe solo di poche ore** it would just be a matter of a few hours

tratta'tiva SF negotiation; **trattative** SFPL (tra governi, stati) talks; **essere in ~ con** to be in negotiation with

trat'tato SM (testo) treatise; (accordo) treaty; ~ **commerciale** trade agreement; ~ **di pace** peace treaty

trattazi'one [trattatˈtsjone] SF treatment

tratteggi'are [trattedˈdʒare] /62/ VT (disegnare: a tratti) to sketch, outline; (: col tratteggio) to hatch

trat'teggio [tratˈteddʒo] SM hatching

tratte'nere /121/ VT (far rimanere: persona) to detain; (intrattenere: ospiti) to entertain; (tenere, frenare, reprimere) to hold back, keep back; (astenersi dal consegnare) to hold, keep; (detrarre: somma) to deduct; **trattenersi** VPR (astenersi) to restrain o.s., stop o.s.; (soffermarsi) to stay, remain; **sono stato trattenuto in ufficio** I was delayed at the office

tratteni'mento SM entertainment; (festa) party

tratte'nuta SF deduction

trat'tino SM dash; (in parole composte) hyphen

'tratto, -a PP di **trarre** ▶ SM (di penna, matita) stroke; (parte) part, piece; (di strada) stretch; (di mare, cielo) expanse; (di tempo) period (of time); **tratti** SMPL (caratteristiche) features; (modo di) ways, manners; **a un ~, d'un ~** suddenly

trat'tore SM tractor

tratto'ria SF (small) restaurant

'trauma, -i SM trauma; ~ **cranico** concussion

trau'matico, -a, -ci, -che AG traumatic

traumatiz'zare [traumatidˈdzare] /72/ VT (Med) to traumatize; (fig: impressionare) to shock

tra'vaglio [traˈvaʎʎo] SM (angoscia) pain, suffering; (Med) pains pl; ~ **di parto** labour pains

trava'sare /72/ VT to pour; (vino) to decant

tra'vaso SM pouring; decanting

trava'tura SF beams pl

'trave SF beam

tra'veggole SFPL: **avere le ~** to be seeing things

tra'versa SF (trave) crosspiece; (via) sidestreet; (Ferr) sleeper (BRIT), (railroad) tie (US); (Calcio) crossbar

traver'sare /72/ VT to cross

traver'sata SF crossing; (Aer) flight, trip

traver'sie SFPL mishaps, misfortunes

traver'sina SF (Ferr) sleeper (BRIT), (railroad) tie (US)

t

tra'verso, -a AG oblique; **di ~** ag askew ▶ AV sideways; **andare di ~** (cibo) to go down the wrong way; **messo di ~** sideways on; **guardare di ~** to look askance at; **via traversa** side road; **ottenere qc per vie traverse** (fig) to obtain sth in an underhand way

travesti'mento SM disguise

traves'tire /45/ VT to disguise; **travestirsi** VPR to disguise o.s.

traves'tito SM transvestite

travi'are /19/ VT (fig) to lead astray

travi'sare /72/ VT (fig) to distort, misrepresent

travol'gente [travol'dʒɛnte] AG overwhelming

tra'volgere [tra'vɔldʒere] /96/ VT to sweep away, carry away; (fig) to overwhelm

tra'volto, -a PP di **travolgere**

trazi'one [trat'tsjone] SF traction; **~ anteriore/posteriore** (Aut) front-wheel/rear-wheel drive

tre NUM three

tre'alberi SM INV (Naut) three-master

'trebbia SF (Agr: operazione) threshing; (: stagione) threshing season

trebbi'are /19/ VT to thresh

trebbia'trice [trebbja'tritʃe] SF threshing machine

trebbia'tura SF threshing

'treccia, -ce ['trettʃa] SF plait, braid; **lavorato a trecce** (pullover ecc) cable-knit

trecen'tesco, -a, -schi, -sche [tretʃen'tesko] AG fourteenth-century

tre'cento [tre'tʃɛnto] NUM three hundred ▶ SM: **il T~** the fourteenth century

tredi'cenne [tredi'tʃɛnne] AG, SMF thirteen-year-old

tredi'cesimo, -a [tredi'tʃɛzimo] NUM thirteenth ▶ SF Christmas bonus of a month's pay

'tredici ['treditʃi] NUM thirteen ▶ SM INV: **fare ~** (Totocalcio) to win the pools (BRIT)

'tregua SF truce; (fig) respite; **senza ~** non-stop, without stopping, uninterruptedly

tre'mante AG trembling, shaking

tre'mare /72/ VI to tremble, shake; **~ di** (freddo ecc) to shiver o tremble with; (paura, rabbia) to shake o tremble with

trema'rella SF shivers pl

tre'mendo, -a AG terrible, awful

tremen'tina SF turpentine

tre'mila NUM three thousand

'tremito SM trembling no pl; shaking no pl; shivering no pl

tremo'lare /72/ VI to tremble; (luce) to flicker; (foglie) to quiver

tremo'lio SM (vedi vi) tremble; flicker; quiver

tre'more SM tremor

'treno SM train; (Aut): **~ di gomme** set of tyres o (BRIT) o tires (US); **~ locale/diretto/**

espresso local/fast/express train; **~ merci** goods (BRIT) o freight train; **~ rapido** express (train) (for which supplement must be paid); **~ straordinario** special train; **~ viaggiatori** passenger train; see note

> There are several different types of train in Italy. Regionali and interregionali are local trains which stop at every small town and village; the former operate within regional boundaries, while the latter may cross them. Diretti are ordinary trains for which passengers do not pay a supplement; the main difference from espressi is that the latter are long-distance and mainly run at night. Intercity and eurocity are faster and entail a supplement. Rapidi only contain first-class seats, and the high-speed pendolino, which offers both first- and second-class travel, runs between the major cities.

'trenta NUM thirty ▶ SM INV (Ins): **~ e lode** full marks plus distinction o cum laude

tren'tenne AG, SMF thirty-year-old

tren'tennio SM period of thirty years

tren'tesimo, -a NUM thirtieth

tren'tina SF: **una ~ (di)** thirty or so, about thirty

tren'tino, -a AG of (o from) Trento

trepi'dante AG anxious

trepi'dare /72/ VI to be anxious; **~ per qn** to be anxious about sb

'trepido, -a AG anxious

treppi'ede SM tripod; (Cuc) trivet

tre'quarti SM INV three-quarter-length coat

'tresca, -sche SF (fig) intrigue; (: relazione amorosa) affair

'trespolo SM trestle

trevigi'ano, -a [trevi'dʒano] AG of (o from) Treviso

triango'lare AG triangular

tri'angolo SM triangle

tribo'lare /72/ VI (patire) to suffer; (fare fatica) to have a lot of trouble

tribolazi'one [tribolat'tsjone] SF suffering, tribulation

tri'bordo SM (Naut) starboard

tribù SF INV tribe

tri'buna SF (podio) platform; (in aule ecc) gallery; (di stadio) stand; **~ della stampa/riservata al pubblico** press/public gallery

tribu'nale SM court; **presentarsi o comparire in ~** to appear in court; **~ militare** military tribunal; **~ supremo** supreme court

tribu'tare /72/ VT to bestow; **~ gli onori dovuti a qn** to pay tribute to sb

tribu'tario, -a AG (imposta) fiscal, tax cpd; (Geo): **essere ~ di** to be a tributary of

tri'buto SM tax; *(fig)* tribute
tri'checo, -chi [tri'kɛko] SM *(Zool)* walrus
tri'ciclo [tri'tʃiklo] SM tricycle
trico'lore AG three-coloured *(BRIT)*,
   three-colored *(US)* ▶ SM tricolo(u)r; *(bandiera
   italiana)* Italian flag
tri'dente SM trident
trien'nale AG *(che dura 3 anni)* three-year *cpd*;
   (che avviene ogni 3 anni) three-yearly
tri'ennio SM period of three years
tries'tino, -a AG of *(o* from*)* Trieste
tri'fase AG *(Elettr)* three-phase
tri'foglio [tri'fɔʎʎo] SM clover
trifo'lato, -a AG *(Cuc)* cooked in oil, garlic and parsley
'triglia ['triʎʎa] SF red mullet
trigonome'tria SF trigonometry
tril'lare /72/ VI *(Mus)* to trill
'trillo SM trill
tri'mestre SM period of three months; *(Ins)*
   term, quarter *(US)*; *(Comm)* quarter
trimo'tore SM *(Aer)* three-engined plane
'trina SF lace
trin'cea [trin'tʃea] SF trench
trince'rare [trintʃe'rare] /72/ VT to entrench
trinci'are [trin'tʃare] /14/ VT to cut up
'Trinidad SM: **~ e Tobago** Trinidad and Tobago
Trinità SF *(Rel)* Trinity
'trio *(pl* **trii)** SM trio
trion'fale AG triumphal, triumphant
trion'fante AG triumphant
trion'fare /72/ VI to triumph, win; **~ su** to
   triumph over, overcome
tri'onfo SM triumph
tripli'care /20/ VT to triple
'triplice ['triplitʃe] AG triple; **in ~ copia** in
   triplicate
'triplo, -a AG triple; treble ▶ SM: **il ~ (di)** three
   times as much (as); **la spesa è tripla** it costs
   three times as much
'tripode SM tripod
'Tripoli SF Tripoli
'trippa SF *(Cuc)* tripe
tri'pudio SM triumph, jubilation; *(fig: di colori)*
   galaxy
tris SM INV *(Carte)*: **~ d'assi/di re** *etc* three aces/
   kings *etc*
'triste AG sad; *(luogo)* dreary, gloomy
tris'tezza [tris'tettsa] SF sadness;
   gloominess
'tristo, -a AG *(cattivo)* wicked, evil; *(meschino)*
   sorry, poor
trita'carne SM INV mincer, grinder *(US)*
trita'ghiaccio [trita'gjattʃo] SM INV ice
   crusher
tri'tare /72/ VT to mince, grind *(US)*
trita'tutto SM INV mincer, grinder *(US)*
'trito, -a AG *(tritato)* minced, ground *(US)*; **~ e
   ritrito** *(idee, argomenti, frasi)* trite, hackneyed
tri'tolo SM trinitrotoluene

tri'tone SM *(Zool)* newt
'trittico, -ci SM *(Arte)* triptych
tritu'rare /72/ VT to grind
tri'vella SF drill
trivel'lare /72/ VT to drill
trivellazi'one [trivellat'tsjone] SF drilling;
   torre di ~ derrick
trivi'ale AG vulgar, low
trivialità SF INV *(volgarità)* coarseness,
   crudeness; *(: osservazione)* coarse *o* crude
   remark
tro'feo SM trophy
'trogolo SM *(per maiali)* trough
'troia SF *(Zool)* sow; *(fig: peg)* whore
troll [trɔl] SM INV *(anche Internet)* troll
'tromba SF *(Mus)* trumpet; *(Aut)* horn;
   ~ d'aria whirlwind; **~ delle scale** stairwell
trombet'tista, -i, -e SM/F trumpeter,
   trumpet (player)
trom'bone SM trombone
trom'bosi SF thrombosis
tron'care /20/ VT to cut off; *(spezzare)* to break
   off
'tronco, -a, -chi, -che AG cut off; broken off;
   (Ling) truncated; *(fig)* cut short ▶ SM *(Bot,
   Anat)* trunk; *(fig: tratto)* section; *(: pezzo: di
   lancia)* stump; **licenziare qn in ~** *(fig)* to fire
   sb on the spot
troneggi'are [troned'dʒare] /62/ VI: **~ (su)** to
   tower (over)
'tronfio, -a AG conceited
'trono SM throne
tropi'cale AG tropical
'tropico, -ci SM tropic; **~ del Cancro/
   Capricorno** Tropic of Cancer/Capricorn;
   i tropici the tropics

PAROLA CHIAVE

'troppo, -a DET *(in eccesso: quantità)* too much;
   (: numero) too many; **ho messo troppo
   zucchero** I put too much sugar in; **c'era
   troppa gente** there were too many people;
   fa troppo caldo it's too hot
   ▶ PRON *(in eccesso: quantità)* too much;
   (: numero) too many; **ne hai messo troppo**
   you've put in too much; **meglio troppi che
   pochi** better too many than too few
   ▶ AV *(eccessivamente: con ag, av)* too; *(: con vb)* too
   much; **troppo amaro/tardi** too bitter/late;
   lavora troppo he works too much; **costa
   troppo** it costs too much; **troppo buono da
   parte tua!** *(anche ironico)* you're too kind!; **di
   troppo** too much; too many; **qualche tazza
   di troppo** a few cups too many; **5 euro di
   troppo** 5 euros too much; **essere di troppo**
   to be in the way

'trota SF trout
trot'tare /72/ VI to trot

trotterel'lare /72/ VI to trot along; (*bambino*) to toddle

'trotto SM trot

'trottola SF spinning top

tro'vare /72/ VT to find; (*giudicare*): **trovo che** I find o think that; **trovarsi** VPR (*reciproco: incontrarsi*) to meet; (*essere, stare*) to be; (*arrivare, capitare*) to find o.s.; **andare a ~ qn** to go and see sb; **~ qn colpevole** to find sb guilty; **trovo giusto/sbagliato che ...** I think/don't think it's right that ...; **trovarsi bene/male** (*in un luogo, con qn*) to get on well/badly; **trovarsi d'accordo con qn** to be in agreement with sb

tro'vata SF good idea; **~ pubblicitaria** advertising gimmick

trova'tello, -a SM/F foundling

truc'care /20/ VT (*falsare*) to fake; (*attore ecc*) to make up; (*travestire*) to disguise; (*Sport*) to fix; (*Aut*) to soup up; **truccarsi** VPR to make up (one's face)

trucca'tore, -'trice SM/F (*Cine, Teat*) make-up artist

'trucco, -chi SM trick; (*cosmesi*) make-up; **i trucchi del mestiere** the tricks of the trade

'truce ['trutʃe] AG fierce

truci'dare [trutʃi'dare] /72/ VT to slaughter

'truciolo ['trutʃolo] SM shaving

'truffa SF fraud, swindle

truf'fare /72/ VT to swindle, cheat

truffa'tore, -'trice SM/F swindler, cheat

'truppa SF troop

TS SIGLA = **Trieste**

tu PRON you; **tu stesso(a)** you yourself; **dare del tu a qn** to address sb as "tu"; **trovarsi a tu per tu con qn** to find o.s. face to face with sb

'tua *vedi* **tuo**

'tuba SF (*Mus*) tuba; (*cappello*) top hat

tu'bare /72/ VI to coo

tuba'tura, tubazi'one [tubat'tsjone] SF piping *no pl*, pipes *pl*

tuberco'losi SF tuberculosis

'tubero SM (*Bot*) tuber

tu'betto SM tube

tu'bino SM (*cappello*) bowler (BRIT), derby (US); (*abito da donna*) sheath dress

'tubo SM tube; (*per conduttore*) pipe; **~ digerente** (*Anat*) alimentary canal, digestive tract; **~ di scappamento** (*Aut*) exhaust pipe

tubo'lare AG tubular ▶ SM tubeless tyre (BRIT) o tire (US)

'tue *vedi* **tuo**

tuf'fare /72/ VT to plunge; (*intingere*) to dip; **tuffarsi** VPR to plunge, dive

tuffa'tore, -'trice SM/F (*Sport*) diver

'tuffo SM dive; (*breve bagno*) dip

tu'gurio SM hovel

tuli'pano SM tulip

'tulle SM (*tessuto*) tulle

tume'fare /42/ VT to cause to swell; **tumefarsi** VPR to swell

'tumido, -a AG swollen

tu'more SM (*Med*) tumour (BRIT), tumor (US)

tumulazi'one [tumulat'tsjone] SF burial

tu'multo SM uproar, commotion; (*sommossa*) riot; (*fig*) turmoil

tumultu'oso, -a AG rowdy, unruly; (*fig*) turbulent, stormy

tungs'teno SM tungsten

'tunica, -che SF tunic

'Tunisi SF Tunis

Tuni'sia SF: **la ~** Tunisia

tuni'sino, -a AG, SM/F Tunisian

'tunnel SM INV tunnel

'tuo (*f* **tua**, *pl* **tue, tuoi**) DET: **il ~, la tua** *etc* your ▶ PRON: **il ~, la tua** *etc* yours ▶ SM: **hai speso del ~?** did you spend your own money? ▶ SF: **la tua** (*opinione*) your view; **i tuoi** (*genitori, famiglia*) your family; **una tua amica** a friend of yours; **è dalla tua** he is on your side; **alla tua!** (*brindisi*) your health!; **ne hai fatta una delle tue!** (*sciocchezze*) you've done it again!

tuo'nare /72/ VI to thunder; **tuona** it is thundering, there's some thunder

tu'ono SM thunder

tu'orlo SM yolk

tu'racciolo [tu'rattʃolo] SM cap, top; (*di sughero*) cork

tu'rare /72/ VT to stop, plug; (*con sughero*) to cork; **turarsi il naso** to hold one's nose

'turba SF (*folla*) crowd, throng; (: *peg*) mob; **turbe** SFPL disorder(s); **soffrire di turbe psichiche** to suffer from a mental disorder

turba'mento SM disturbance; (*di animo*) anxiety, agitation

tur'bante SM turban

tur'bare /72/ VT to disturb, trouble; **~ la quiete pubblica** (*Dir*) to disturb the peace

tur'bato, -a AG upset; (*preoccupato, ansioso*) anxious

tur'bina SF turbine

turbi'nare /72/ VI to whirl

'turbine SM whirlwind; **~ di neve** swirl of snow; **~ di polvere/sabbia** dust/sandstorm

turbi'noso, -a AG (*vento, danza ecc*) whirling

turbo'lento, -a AG turbulent; (*ragazzo*) boisterous, unruly

turbo'lenza [turbo'lentsa] SF turbulence

turboreat'tore SM turbojet engine

tur'chese [tur'kese] AG, SM, SF turquoise

Tur'chia [tur'kia] SF: **la ~** Turkey

tur'chino, -a [tur'kino] AG deep blue

'turco, -a, -chi, -che AG Turkish ▶ SM/F Turk (Turkish woman) ▶ SM (*Ling*) Turkish; **parlare ~** (*fig*) to talk double Dutch

'turgido, -a ['turdʒido] AG swollen
tu'rismo SM tourism; tourist industry;
~ sessuale sex tourism
tu'rista, -i, -e SM/F tourist
tu'ristico, -a, -ci, -che AG tourist cpd
tur'nista, -i, -e SM/F shift worker
'turno SM turn; (di lavoro) shift; **di ~** (soldato, medico, custode) on duty; **a ~** (rispondere) in turn; (lavorare) in shifts; **fare a ~ a fare qc** to take turns to do sth; **è il suo ~** it's your (o his etc) turn
'turpe AG filthy, vile
turpi'loquio SM obscene language
'tuta SF overalls pl; (Sport) tracksuit; **~ mimetica** (Mil) camouflage clothing; **~ spaziale** spacesuit; **~ subacquea** wetsuit
tu'tela SF (Dir: di minore) guardianship; (: protezione) protection; (difesa) defence (BRIT), defense (US); **~ dell'ambiente** environmental protection; **~ del consumatore** consumer protection
tute'lare /72/ VT to protect, defend ▶ AG (Dir): **giudice ~** judge with responsibility for guardianship cases
tutor ['tiutor] SM INV (Aut) speed monitoring system
tu'tore, -'trice SM/F (Dir) guardian
tutta'via CONG nevertheless, yet

(PAROLA CHIAVE)

'tutto, -a DET **1** (intero) all; **tutto il latte** all the milk; **tutta la notte** all night, the whole night; **tutto il libro** the whole book; **tutta una bottiglia** a whole bottle; **in tutto il mondo** all over the world
2 (pl, collettivo) all; every; **tutti i libri** all the books; **tutte le notti** every night; **tutti i venerdì** every Friday; **tutti gli uomini** all the men; (collettivo) all men; **tutto l'anno** all year long; **tutte le volte che** every time (that); **tutti e due** both o each of us (o them o you); **tutti e cinque** all five of us (o them o you)
3 (completamente): **era tutta sporca** she was

all dirty; **tremava tutto** he was trembling all over; **è tutta sua madre** she's just o exactly like her mother
4: **a tutt'oggi** so far, up till now; **a tutta velocità** at full o top speed
▶ PRON **1** (ogni cosa) everything, all; (qualsiasi cosa) anything; **ha mangiato tutto** he's eaten everything; **dimmi tutto** tell me all about it; **tutto compreso** all included, all-in (BRIT); **tutto considerato** all things considered; **con tutto che** (malgrado) although; **del tutto** completely; **100 euro in tutto** 100 euros in all; **in tutto eravamo 50** there were 50 of us in all; **in tutto e per tutto** completely; **il che è tutto dire** and that's saying a lot
2: **tutti, e** (ognuno) all, everybody; **vengono tutti** they are all coming, everybody's coming; **tutti sanno che** everybody knows that; **tutti quanti** all and sundry
▶ AV (completamente) entirely, quite; **è tutto il contrario** it's quite o exactly the opposite; **tutt'al più: saranno stati tutt'al più una cinquantina** there were about fifty of them at (the very) most; **tutt'al più possiamo prendere un treno** if the worst comes to the worst we can take a train; **tutt'altro** on the contrary; **è tutt'altro che felice** he's anything but happy; **tutt'intorno** all around; **tutt'a un tratto** suddenly
▶ SM: **il tutto** the whole lot, all of it; **il tutto si è svolto senza incidenti** it all went off without incident; **il tutto le costerà due milioni** the whole thing will cost you two million

tutto'fare AG INV: **domestica ~** general maid; : **ragazzo ~** office boy ▶ SM INV/F INV handyman(-woman)
tut'tora AV still
tutù SM INV tutu, ballet skirt
TV [ti'vu] SF INV (= televisione) TV ▶ SIGLA = **Treviso**

U u

U, u [u] SM O F INV (*lettera*) U, u; **U come Udine** ≈ U for Uncle; **inversione ad U** U-turn

ub'bia SF (*letterario*) irrational fear

ubbidi'ente AG obedient

ubbidi'enza [ubbi'djɛntsa] SF obedience

ubbi'dire /55/ VI to obey; **~ a** to obey; (*veicolo, macchina*) to respond to

ubicazi'one [ubikat'tsjone] SF site, location

ubiquità SF: **non ho il dono dell'~** I can't be everywhere at once

ubria'care /20/ VT: **~ qn** to get sb drunk; (*alcool*) to make sb drunk; (*fig*) to make sb's head spin *o* reel; **ubriacarsi** VPR to get drunk; **ubriacarsi di** (*fig*) to become intoxicated with

ubria'chezza [ubria'kettsa] SF drunkenness

ubri'aco, -a, -chi, -che AG, SM/F drunk

ubria'cone SM drunkard

uccellagi'one [uttʃella'dʒone] SF bird catching

uccelli'era [uttʃel'ljɛra] SF aviary

uccel'lino [uttʃel'lino] SM baby bird, chick

uc'cello [ut'tʃello] SM bird

uc'cidere [ut'tʃidere] /34/ VT to kill; **uccidersi** VPR (*suicidarsi*) to kill o.s.; (*perdere la vita*) to be killed

uccisi'one [uttʃi'zjone] SF killing

uc'ciso, -a [ut'tʃizo] PP *di* **uccidere**

ucci'sore [uttʃi'zore] SM killer

U'craina SF Ukraine

u'craino, -a AG, SM/F Ukrainian

UD SIGLA = **Udine**

U.D.C. SIGLA F (*Pol*: = *Unione di Centro*) centre party

u'dente SMF: **i non udenti** the hard of hearing

u'dibile AG audible

udi'enza [u'djɛntsa] SF audience; (*Dir*) hearing; **dare ~ (a)** to grant an audience (to); **~ a porte chiuse** hearing in camera

u'dire /124/ VT to hear

udi'tivo, -a AG auditory

u'dito SM (sense of) hearing

udi'tore, -'trice SM/F listener; (*Ins*) unregistered student (*attending lectures*)

udi'torio SM (*persone*) audience

UE SIGLA F (= *Unione Europea*) EU

U.E. ABBR = **uso esterno**

UEFA SIGLA F UEFA (= *Union of European Football Associations*)

UEM SIGLA F (= *Unione economica e monetaria*) EMU

'uffa ESCL tut!

uffici'ale [uffi'tʃale] AG official ▶ SM (*Amm*) official, officer; (*Mil*) officer; **pubblico ~** public official; **~ giudiziario** clerk of the court; **~ di marina** naval officer; **~ sanitario** health inspector; **~ di stato civile** registrar

ufficializ'zare [uffitʃalid'dzare] /72/ VT to make official

uf'ficio [uf'fitʃo] SM (*gen*) office; (*dovere*) duty; (*mansione*) task, function, job; (*agenzia*) agency, bureau; (*Rel*) service; **d'~** *ag* office *cpd*; official ▶ AV officially; **provvedere d'~** to act officially; **convocare d'~** (*Dir*) to summons; **difensore** *o* **avvocato d'~** (*Dir*) court-appointed counsel for the defence; **~ brevetti** patent office; **~ di collocamento** employment office; **~ informazioni** information bureau; **~ oggetti smarriti** lost property office (*BRIT*), lost and found (*US*); **~ postale** post office; **~ vendite/del personale** sales/personnel department

uffici'oso, -a [uffi'tʃoso] AG unofficial

'UFO SM INV (= *unidentified flying object*) UFO

'ufo: a ~ *av* free, for nothing

U'ganda SF: **l'~** Uganda

'uggia ['uddʒa] SF (*noia*) boredom; (*fastidio*) bore; **avere/prendere qn in ~** to dislike/take a dislike to sb

uggi'oso, -a [ud'dʒoso] AG tiresome; (*tempo*) dull

'ugola SF uvula

uguagli'anza [ugwaʎ'ʎantsa] SF equality

uguagli'are [ugwaʎ'ʎare] /27/ VT to make equal; (*essere uguale*) to equal, be equal to; (*livellare*) to level; **uguagliarsi** VPR:

uguagliarsi a *o* **con qn** (*paragonarsi*) to compare o.s. to sb

ugu'ale AG equal; (*identico*) identical, the same; (*uniforme*) level, even ▶ AV: **costano ~** they cost the same; **sono bravi ~** they're equally good

ugual'mente AV equally; (*lo stesso*) all the same

U.I. ABBR = **uso interno**

UIL SIGLA F (= *Unione Italiana del Lavoro*) trade union federation

'ulcera ['ultʃera] SF ulcer

ulcerazi'one [ultʃerat'tsjone] SF ulceration

u'liva *etc* = **oliva** *ecc*

U'livo SM (*Pol*) centre-left coalition

ulteri'ore AG further

ultima'mente AV lately, of late

ulti'mare /72/ VT to finish, complete

ulti'matum SM INV ultimatum

ulti'missime SFPL latest news *sg*

'ultimo, -a AG (*finale*) last; (*estremo*) farthest, utmost; (*recente: notizia, moda*) latest; (*fig: sommo, fondamentale*) ultimate ▶ SM/F last (one); **fino all'~** to the last, until the end; **da ~, in ~** in the end; **per ~** (*entrare, arrivare*) last; **abitare all'~ piano** to live on the top floor; **in ultima pagina** (*di giornale*) on the back page; **negli ultimi tempi** recently; **all'~ momento** at the last minute; **… la vostra lettera del 7 aprile ~ scorso** … your letter of April 7th last; **in ultima analisi** in the final *o* last analysis; **in ~ luogo** finally

ultrà SMF ultra

ultrasi'nistra SF (*Pol*) extreme left

ultrasu'ono SM ultrasound

ultravio'letto, -a AG ultraviolet

ulu'lare /72/ VI to howl

ulu'lato SM howling *no pl*; howl

umana'mente AV (*con umanità*) humanely; (*nei limiti delle capacità umane*) humanly

uma'nesimo SM humanism

umanità SF humanity

umani'tario, -a AG humanitarian

umaniz'zare [umanid'dzare] **/72/** VT to humanize

u'mano, -a AG human; (*comprensivo*) humane

umbi'lico SM = **ombelico**

'umbro, -a AG of (*o* from) Umbria

umet'tare /72/ VT to dampen, moisten

umi'diccio, -a, -ci, -ce [umi'dittʃo] AG (*terreno*) damp; (*mano*) moist, clammy

umidifi'care /20/ VT to humidify

umidifica'tore SM humidifier

umidità SF dampness; moistness; humidity

'umido, -a AG damp; (*mano, occhi*) moist; (*clima*) humid ▶ SM dampness, damp; **carne in ~** stew

'umile AG humble

umili'ante AG humiliating

umili'are /19/ VT to humiliate; **umiliarsi** VPR to humble o.s.

umiliazi'one [umiljat'tsjone] SF humiliation

umiltà SF humility, humbleness

u'more SM (*disposizione d'animo*) mood; (*carattere*) temper; **di buon/cattivo ~** in a good/bad mood

umo'rismo SM humour (BRIT), humor (US); **avere il senso dell'~** to have a sense of humour

umo'rista, -i, -e SM/F humorist

umo'ristico, -a, -ci, -che AG humorous, funny

un, un', una *vedi* **uno**

u'nanime AG unanimous

unanimità SF unanimity; **all'~** unanimously

'una 'tantum AG one-off *cpd* ▶ SF (*imposta*) one-off tax

unci'nato, -a [untʃi'nato] AG (*amo*) barbed; (*ferro*) hooked; **croce uncinata** swastika

unci'netto [untʃi'netto] SM crochet hook

un'cino [un'tʃino] SM hook

undi'cenne [undi'tʃɛnne] AG, SMF eleven-year-old

undi'cesimo, -a [undi'tʃɛzimo] AG eleventh

'undici ['unditʃi] NUM eleven

U'NESCO SIGLA F (= *United Nations Educational, Scientific and Cultural Organization*) UNESCO

'ungere ['undʒere] **/5/** VT to grease, oil; (*Rel*) to anoint; (*fig*) to flatter, butter up; **ungersi** VPR (*sporcarsi*) to get covered in grease; **ungersi con la crema** to put on cream

unghe'rese [unge'rese] AG, SMF, SM Hungarian

Unghe'ria [unge'ria] SF: **l'~** Hungary

'unghia ['ungja] SF (*Anat*) nail; (*di animale*) claw; (*di rapace*) talon; (*di cavallo*) hoof; **pagare sull'~** (*fig*) to pay on the nail

unghi'ata [un'gjata] SF (*graffio*) scratch

ungu'ento SM ointment

unica'mente AV only

'UNICEF ['unitʃɛf] SIGLA M (= *United Nations International Children's Emergency Fund*) UNICEF

'unico, -a, -ci, -che AG (*solo*) only; (*ineguagliabile*) unique; (*singolo: binario*) single; **è figlio ~** he's an only child; **atto ~** (*Teat*) one-act play; **agente ~** (*Comm*) sole agent

uni'corno SM unicorn

unifi'care /20/ VT to unite, unify; (*sistemi*) to standardize

unificazi'one [unifikat'tsjone] SF uniting; unification; standardization

unifor'mare /72/ VT (*terreno, superficie*) to level; **uniformarsi** VPR: **uniformarsi a** to conform to; **~ qc a** to adjust *o* relate sth to

uni'forme AG uniform; (*superficie*) even ▶ SF (*divisa*) uniform; **alta ~** dress uniform

uniformità SF uniformity; evenness

unilate'rale AG one-sided; (*Dir, Pol*) unilateral

uninomi'nale AG (*Pol: collegio, sistema*) single-candidate *cpd*

uni'one SF union; (*fig: concordia*) unity, harmony; **l'U~** (*Pol*) *coalition of centre-left parties*; **U~ economica e monetaria** economic and monetary union; **U~ Europea** European Union; **ex U~ Sovietica** former Soviet Union

u'nire /**55**/ VT to unite; (*congiungere*) to join, connect; (*ingredienti, colori*) to combine; (*in matrimonio*) to unite, join together; **unirsi** VPR to unite; (*in matrimonio*) to be joined together; **~ qc a** to unite sth with; to join *o* connect sth with; to combine sth with; **unirsi a** (*gruppo, società*) to join

u'nisono SM: **all'~** in unison

unità SF INV (*unione, concordia*) unity; (*Mat, Mil, Comm, di misura*) unit; **~ centrale (di elaborazione)** (*Inform*) central processing unit; **~ disco** (*Inform*) disk drive; **~ monetaria** monetary unit; **~ di misura** unit of measurement

uni'tario, -a AG unitary; **prezzo ~** price per unit

u'nito, -a AG (*paese*) united; (*amici, famiglia*) close; **in tinta unita** plain, self-coloured (*BRIT*), self-colored (*US*)

univer'sale AG universal; general

universalità SF universality

universal'mente AV universally

università SF INV university

universi'tario, -a AG university *cpd* ▶ SM/F (*studente*) university student; (*insegnante*) academic, university lecturer

uni'verso SM universe

u'nivoco, -a, -ci, -che AG unambiguous

(PAROLA CHIAVE)

'uno, -a (*dav sm* **un** + C, V, **uno** + *s impura, gn, pn, ps, x, z; dav sf* **un'** + V, **una** + C) DET **1** a; (*dav vocale*) an; **un bambino** a child; **una strada** a street; **uno zingaro** a gypsy
2 (*intensivo*): **ho avuto una paura!** I got such a fright!
▶ PRON **1** one; **ce n'è uno qui** there's one here; **prendine uno** take one (of them); **l'uno o l'altro** either (of them); **l'uno e l'altro** both (of them); **aiutarsi l'un l'altro** to help one another *o* each other; **sono entrati l'uno dopo l'altro** they came in one after the other; **a uno a uno** one by one; **metà per uno** half each
2 (*un tale*) someone, somebody; **ho incontrato uno che ti conosce** I met somebody who knows you
3 (*con valore impersonale*) one, you; **se uno vuole** if one wants, if you want; **cosa fa uno in quella situazione?** what does one do in that situation?
▶ NUM one; **una mela e due pere** one apple and two pears; **uno più uno fa due** one plus one equals two, one and one are two
▶ SF: **è l'una** it's one (o'clock)

'unsi *etc* VB *vedi* **ungere**

'unto, -a PP *di* **ungere** ▶ AG greasy, oily ▶ SM grease

untu'oso, -a AG greasy, oily

unzi'one [un'tsjone] SF: **l'Estrema U~** (*Rel*) Extreme Unction

u'omo (*pl* **uomini**) SM man; **da ~** (*abito, scarpe*) men's, for men; **a memoria d'~** since the world began; **a passo d'~** at walking pace; **~ d'affari** businessman; **~ d'azione** man of action; **~ di fiducia** right-hand man; **~ di mondo** man of the world; **~ di paglia** stooge; **~ politico** politician; **~ rana** frogman; **l'~ della strada** the man in the street

u'opo SM: **all'~** if necessary

u'ovo (*pl(f)* **uova**) SM egg; **cercare il pelo nell'~** (*fig*) to split hairs; **~ affogato** *o* **in camicia** poached egg; **~ bazzotto/sodo** soft-/hard-boiled egg; **~ alla coque** boiled egg; **~ di Pasqua** Easter egg; **~ al tegame** *o* **all'occhio di bue** fried egg; **uova strapazzate** scrambled eggs

ura'gano SM hurricane

U'rali SMPL: **gli ~**, **i Monti ~** the Urals, the Ural Mountains

u'ranio SM uranium; **~ impoverito** depleted uranium

urba'nista, -i, -e SM/F town planner

urba'nistica SF town planning

urbanità SF urbanity

ur'bano, -a AG urban, city *cpd*, town *cpd*; (*Tel: chiamata*) local; (*fig*) urbane

ur'gente [ur'dʒɛnte] AG urgent

ur'genza [ur'dʒɛntsa] SF urgency; **in caso d'~** in (case of) an emergency; **d'~** *ag* emergency; *av* urgently, as a matter of urgency; **non c'è ~** there's no hurry; **questo lavoro va fatto con ~** this work is urgent

'urgere ['urdʒere] /**5**/ VI to be needed urgently

u'rina *etc* = **orina** *ecc*

ur'lare /**72**/ VI (*persona*) to scream, yell; (*animale, vento*) to howl ▶ VT to scream, yell

'urlo (*pl(m)* **urli**, *pl(f)* **urla**) SM scream, yell; howl

'urna SF urn; (*elettorale*) ballot box; **andare alle urne** to go to the polls

URP [urp] SIGLA M (= *Ufficio Relazioni con il Pubblico*) PR Office

urrà ESCL hurrah!

U.R.S.S. SIGLA F = **Unione delle Repubbliche Socialiste Sovietiche**; **l'U.R.S.S.** the USSR

ur'tare /72/ VT to bump into, knock against, crash into; (*fig: irritare*) to annoy ▶ VI: ~ **contro** *o* **in** to bump into, knock against; (*fig: imbattersi*) to come up against; **urtarsi** VPR (*reciproco: scontrarsi*) to collide; (: *fig*) to clash; (*irritarsi*) to get annoyed

'urto SM (*colpo*) knock, bump; (*scontro*) crash, collision; (*fig*) clash; **terapia d'**~ (*Med*) shock treatment

uruguai'ano, -a AG, SM/F Uruguayan

Urugu'ay SM: l'~ Uruguay

u.s. ABBR = **ultimo scorso**

'USA SMPL: **gli** ~ the USA

u'sanza [u'zantsa] SF custom; (*moda*) fashion

u'sare /72/ VT to use, employ ▶ VI (*essere di moda*) to be fashionable; (*servirsi*): ~ **di** to use (*diritto*) to exercise; (*essere solito*): ~ **fare** to be in the habit of doing, be accustomed to doing ▶ VB IMPERS: **qui usa così** it's the custom round here; **fare la massima cura nel fare qc** to exercise great care when doing sth

u'sato, -a AG used; (*consumato*) worn; (*di seconda mano*) used, second-hand ▶ SM second-hand goods *pl*

u'scente [uʃʃɛnte] AG (*Amm*) outgoing

usci'ere [uʃʃɛre] SM usher

'uscio ['uʃʃo] SM door

u'scire [uʃʃire] /125/ VI (*gen*) to come out; (*partire, andare a passeggio, a uno spettacolo ecc*) to go out; (*essere sorteggiato: numero*) to come up; ~ **da** (*gen*) to leave; (*posto*) to go (*o* come) out of, leave; (*solco, vasca ecc*) to come out of; (*muro*) to stick out of; (*competenza ecc*) to be outside; (*infanzia, adolescenza*) to leave behind; (*famiglia nobile ecc*) to come from; ~ **da** *o* **di casa** to go out; (*fig*) to leave home; ~ **in automobile** to go out in the car, go for a drive; ~ **di strada** (*Aut*) to go off *o* leave the road

u'scita [uʃʃita] SF (*passaggio, varco*) exit, way out; (*per divertimento*) outing; (*Econ: somma*) expenditure; (*Teat*) entrance; (*fig: battuta*) witty remark; **"vietata l'~"** "no exit"; ~ **di sicurezza** emergency exit

user'name [juzer'neim] SM INV username

usi'gnolo [uziɲ'ɲɔlo] SM nightingale

'uso SM (*utilizzazione*) use; (*esercizio*) practice (BRIT), practise (US); (*abitudine*) custom; **fare** ~ **di qc** to use sth; **con l'**~ with practice;

a ~ **di** for (the use of); **d'**~ (*corrente*) in use; **fuori** ~ out of use; **essere in** ~ to be in common *o* current use; **per** ~ **esterno** for external use only

ustio'nare /72/ VT to burn; **ustionarsi** VPR to burn o.s.

usti'one SF burn

usu'ale AG common, everyday

usufru'ire /55/ VI: ~ **di** (*giovarsi di*) to take advantage of, make use of

usu'frutto SM (*Dir*) usufruct

u'sura SF usury; (*logoramento*) wear (and tear)

usu'raio SM usurer

usur'pare /72/ VT to usurp

usurpa'tore, -'trice SM/F usurper

uten'sile SM tool, implement ▶ AG: **macchina** ~ machine tool; **utensili da cucina** kitchen utensils

utensile'ria SF (*utensili*) tools *pl*; (*reparto*) tool room

u'tente SMF user; (*di gas ecc*) consumer; (*del telefono*) subscriber; ~ **finale** end user

'utero SM uterus, womb; ~ **in affitto** host womb

'utile AG useful ▶ SM (*vantaggio*) advantage, benefit; (*Econ: profitto*) profit; **rendersi** ~ to be helpful; **in tempo** ~ **per** in time for; **unire l'**~ **al dilettevole** to combine business with pleasure; **partecipare agli utili** (*Econ*) to share in the profits

utilità SF usefulness *no pl*; use; (*vantaggio*) benefit; **essere di grande** ~ to be very useful

utili'tario, -a AG utilitarian ▶ SF (*Aut*) economy car

utiliz'zare [utilid'dzare] /72/ VT to use, make use of, utilize

utilizzazi'one [utiliddzat'tsjone] SF utilization, use

uti'lizzo [uti'liddzo] SM (*Amm*) utilization; (*Banca: di credito*) availment

util'mente AV usefully, profitably

uto'pia SF utopia; **è pura** ~ that's sheer utopianism

uto'pistico, -a, -ci, -che AG utopian

UVA ABBR (= *ultravioletto prossimo*) UVA

'uva SF grapes *pl*; ~ **passa** raisins *pl*; ~ **spina** gooseberry

UVB ABBR (= *ultravioletto lontano*) UVB

Vv

V, v [vi, vu] SM O F INV (*lettera*) V, v; **V come Venezia** ≈ V for Victor

V ABBR (= *volt*) V

v. ABBR (= *vedi*) v.; (= *verso*) v.; (= *versetto*) v.

VA SIGLA = **Varese**

va, va' VB *vedi* **andare**

va'cante AG vacant

va'canza [va'kantsa] SF (*l'essere vacante*) vacancy; (*riposo, ferie*) holiday(s pl) (BRIT), vacation (US); (*giorno di permesso*) day off, holiday; **vacanze** SFPL (*periodo di ferie*) holidays, vacation *sg*; **essere/andare in ~** to be/go on holiday *o* vacation; **far ~** to have a holiday; **vacanze estive** summer holiday(s) *o* vacation; **vacanze natalizie** Christmas holidays *o* vacation

'vacca, -che SF COW

vacci'nare [vattʃi'nare] /**72**/ VT to vaccinate; **farsi ~** to have a vaccination, get vaccinated

vaccinazi'one [vattʃinat'tsjone] SF vaccination

vac'cino [vat'tʃino] SM (*Med*) vaccine

vacil'lante [vatʃil'lante] AG (*edificio, vecchio*) shaky, unsteady; (*fiamma*) flickering; (*salute, memoria*) shaky, failing

vacil'lare [vatʃil'lare] /**72**/ VI to sway, wobble; (*fiamma, luce*) to flicker; (*fig: memoria, coraggio*) to be failing, falter

'vacuo, -a AG (*fig*) empty, vacuous ▶ SM vacuum

'vado *etc* VB *vedi* **andare**

vagabon'daggio [vagabon'daddʒo] SM wandering, roaming; (*Dir*) vagrancy

vagabon'dare /**72**/ VI to roam, wander

vaga'bondo, -a SM/F tramp, vagrant; (*fannullone*) idler, loafer

va'gare /**80**/ VI to wander

vagheggi'are [vaged'dʒare] /**62**/ VT to long for, dream of

vagherò *etc* [vage'rɔ] VB *vedi* **vagare**

va'ghezza [va'gettsa] SF vagueness

va'gina [va'dʒina] SF vagina

va'gire [va'dʒire] /**55**/ VI to whimper

va'gito [va'dʒito] SM cry, wailing

'vaglia ['vaʎʎa] SM INV money order; **~ cambiario** promissory note; **~ postale** postal order

vagli'are [vaʎ'ʎare] /**27**/ VT to sift; (*fig*) to weigh up

'vaglio ['vaʎʎo] SM sieve; **passare al ~** (*fig*) to examine closely

'vago, -a, -ghi, -ghe AG vague

va'gone SM (*Ferr: per passeggeri*) coach, carriage (BRIT), car (US); (: *per merci*) truck, wagon; **~ letto** sleeper, sleeping car; **~ ristorante** dining *o* restaurant car

'vai VB *vedi* **andare**

vai'olo SM smallpox

val. ABBR = **valuta**

va'langa, -ghe SF avalanche

va'lente AG able, talented

va'lenza [va'lɛntsa] SF (*fig: significato*) content; (*Chim*) valency

va'lere /**126**/ VI (*avere forza, potenza*) to have influence; (*essere valido*) to be valid; (*avere vigore, autorità*) to hold, apply; (*essere capace: poeta, studente*) to be good, be able ▶ VT (*prezzo, sforzo*) to be worth; (*corrispondere*) to correspond to; (*procurare*): **~ qc a qn** to earn sb sth; **valersi** VPR: **valersi di** to make use of, take advantage of; **far ~** (*autorità ecc*) to assert; **far ~ le proprie ragioni** to make o.s. heard; **farsi ~** to make o.s. appreciated *o* respected; **vale a dire** that is to say; **~ la pena** to be worth the effort *o* worth it; **l'uno vale l'altro** the one is as good as the other, they amount to the same thing; **non vale niente** it's worthless; **valersi dei consigli di qn** to take *o* act upon sb's advice

valeri'ana SF (*Bot, Med*) valerian

va'levole AG valid

'valgo *etc* VB *vedi* **valere**

vali'care /**20**/ VT to cross

'valico, -chi SM (*passo*) pass

validità SF validity

'valido, -a AG valid; (*rimedio*) effective; (*aiuto*) real; (*persona*) worthwhile; **essere di ~ aiuto a qn** to be a great help to sb

vali'ge'ria [valid3e'ria] SF (*assortimento*) leather goods *pl*; (*fabbrica*) leather goods factory; (*negozio*) leather goods shop

vali'getta [vali'd3ɛtta] SF briefcase; **~ ventiquattrore** overnight bag *o* case

va'ligia, -gie, -ge [va'lid3a] SF (suit)case; **fare le valigie** to pack (up); **~ diplomatica** diplomatic bag

val'lata SF valley

'valle SF valley; **a ~** (*di fiume*) downstream; **scendere a ~** to go downhill

val'letto SM valet

valligi'ano, -a [valli'd3ano] SM/F inhabitant of a valley

va'lore SM (*gen, Comm*) value; (*merito*) merit, worth; (*coraggio*) valour (*BRIT*), valor (*US*), courage; (*Finanza: titolo*) security; **valori** SMPL (*oggetti preziosi*) valuables; **crescere/ diminuire di ~** to go up/down in value, gain/lose in value; **è di gran ~** it's worth a lot, it's very valuable; **privo di ~** worthless; **~ contabile** book value; **~ effettivo** real value; **~ nominale** *o* **facciale** nominal value; **~ di realizzo** break-up value; **~ di riscatto** surrender value; **valori bollati** (revenue) stamps

valoriz'zare [valorid'dzare] **/72/** VT (*terreno*) to develop; (*fig*) to make the most of

valo'roso, -a AG courageous

'valso, -a PP *di* **valere**

va'luta SF currency, money; (*Banca*): **~ 15 gennaio** interest to run from January 15th; **~ estera** foreign currency

valu'tare **/72/** VT (*casa, gioiello, fig*) to value; (*stabilire: peso, entrate, fig*) to estimate

valu'tario, -a AG (*Finanza: norme*) currency *cpd*

valutazi'one [valutat'tsjone] SF valuation; estimate

'valva SF (*Zool, Bot*) valve

'valvola SF (*Tecn, Anat*) valve; (*Elettr*) fuse; **~ a farfalla del carburatore** (*Aut*) throttle; **~ di sicurezza** safety valve

'valzer ['valtser] SM INV waltz

vam'pata SF (*di fiamma*) blaze; (*di calore*) blast; (: *al viso*) flush

vam'piro SM vampire

vana'gloria SF boastfulness

van'dalico, -a, -ci, -che AG vandal *cpd*; **atto ~** act of vandalism

vanda'lismo SM vandalism

'vandalo SM vandal

vaneggia'mento [vanedd3a'mento] SM raving, delirium

vaneggi'are [vaned'd3are] **/62/** VI to rave

va'nesio, -a AG vain, conceited

'vanga, -ghe SF spade

van'gare **/80/** VT to dig

van'gelo [van'd3ɛlo] SM gospel

vanifi'care **/20/** VT to nullify

va'niglia [va'niʎʎa] SF vanilla

vanigli'ato, -a [vaniʎ'ʎato] AG: **zucchero ~** (*Cuc*) vanilla sugar

vanità SF vanity; (*di promessa*) emptiness; (*di sforzo*) futility

vani'toso, -a AG vain, conceited

'vanno VB *vedi* **andare**

'vano, -a AG vain ▶ SM (*spazio*) space; (*apertura*) opening; (*stanza*) room; **il ~ della porta** the doorway; **il ~ portabagagli** (*Aut*) the boot (*BRIT*), the trunk (*US*)

van'taggio [van'tadd3o] SM advantage; **trarre ~ da qc** to benefit from sth; **essere/portarsi in ~** (*Sport*) to be in/take the lead

vantaggi'oso, -a [vantad'd3oso] AG advantageous, favourable (*BRIT*), favorable (*US*)

van'tare **/72/** VT to praise, speak highly of; **vantarsi** VPR: **vantarsi (di/di aver fatto)** to boast *o* brag (about/about having done)

vante'ria SF boasting

'vanto SM boasting; (*merito*) virtue, merit; (*gloria*) pride

'vanvera SF: **a ~** haphazardly; **parlare a ~** to talk nonsense

va'pore SM vapour (*BRIT*), vapor (*US*); (*anche*: **vapore acqueo**) steam; (*nave*) steamer; **a ~** (*turbina ecc*) steam *cpd*; **al ~** (*Cuc*) steamed

vapo'retto SM steamer

vapori'era SF (*Ferr*) steam engine

vaporiz'zare [vaporid'dzare] **/72/** VT to vaporize

vaporizza'tore [vaporiddza'tore] SM spray

vaporizzazi'one [vaporiddzat'tsjone] SF vaporization

vapo'roso, -a AG (*tessuto*) filmy; (*capelli*) soft and full

va'rare **/72/** VT (*Naut, fig*) to launch; (*Dir*) to pass

var'care **/20/** VT to cross

'varco, -chi SM passage; **aprirsi un ~ tra la folla** to push one's way through the crowd

vare'china [vare'kina] SF bleach

vari'abile AG variable; (*tempo, umore*) changeable, variable ▶ SF (*Mat*) variable

vari'ante SF (*gen*) variation, change; (*di piano*) modification; (*Ling*) variant; (*Sport*) alternative route

vari'are **/19/** VT, VI to vary; **~ di opinione** to change one's mind

variazi'one [varjat'tsjone] SF variation, change; (*Mus*) variation; **una ~ di programma** a change of plan

va'rice [va'ritʃe] SF varicose vein

vari'cella [vari'tʃella] SF chickenpox

vari'coso, -a AG varicose

varie'gato, -a AG variegated

varietà SF INV variety ▶ SM INV variety show

V

'vario, -a AG varied; (*parecchi: col sostantivo al pl*) various; (*mutevole: umore*) changeable; **varie** SFPL: **varie ed eventuali** (*nell'ordine del giorno*) any other business

vario'pinto, -a AG multicoloured (BRIT), multicolored (US)

'varo SM (*Naut, fig*) launch; (*di leggi*) passing

varrò *etc* VB *vedi* **valere**

Var'savia SF Warsaw

va'saio SM potter

'vasca, -sche SF basin; (*anche:* **vasca da bagno**) bathtub, bath

va'scello [vaʃ'ʃɛllo] SM (*Naut*) vessel, ship

vas'chetta [vas'ketta] SF (*per gelato*) tub; (*per sviluppare fotografie*) dish

vase'lina SF vaseline

vasel'lame SM (*stoviglie*) crockery; (: *di porcellana*) china; ~ **d'oro/d'argento** gold/silver plate

'vaso SM (*recipiente*) pot; (: *barattolo*) jar; (: *decorativo*) vase; (*Anat*) vessel; ~ **da fiori** vase; (*per piante*) flowerpot

vas'sallo SM vassal

vas'soio SM tray

vastità SF vastness

'vasto, -a AG vast, immense; **di vaste proporzioni** (*incendio*) huge; (*fenomeno, rivolta*) widespread; **su vasta scala** on a vast *o* huge scale

Vati'cano SM: **il** ~ the Vatican; **la Città del** ~ the Vatican City

VB SIGLA = **Vibo Valenza**

VC SIGLA = **Vercelli**

VE SIGLA = **Venezia** ▶ ABBR = **Vostra Eccellenza**

ve PRON, AV *vedi* **vi**

vecchi'aia [vek'kjaja] SF old age

'vecchio, -a ['vɛkkjo] AG old ▶ SM/F old man(-woman); **i vecchi** the old; **è un mio ~ amico** he's an old friend of mine; **è un uomo ~ stile** *o* **stampo** he's an old-fashioned man; **è ~ del mestiere** he's an old hand at the job

'vece ['vetʃe] SF: **in ~ di** in the place of, for; **fare le veci di qn** to take sb's place; **firma del padre o di chi ne fa le veci** signature of the father or guardian

ve'dere /127/ VT, VI to see; **vedersi** VPR to meet, see one another; ~ **di fare qc** to see (to it) that sth is done, make sure that sth is done; **avere a che ~ con** to have to do with; **far ~ qc a qn** to show sb sth; **farsi ~** to show o.s.; (*farsi vivo*) to show one's face; **vedi di non farlo** make sure *o* see you don't do it; **farsi ~ da un medico** to go and see a doctor; **modo di ~** outlook, view of things; **vedi pagina 8** (*rimando*) see page 8; **è da ~ se …** it remains to be seen whether …; **non vedo la ragione di farlo** I can't see any reason to do

it; **si era visto costretto a …** he found himself forced to …; **non (ci) si vede** (*è buio ecc*) you can't see a thing; **ci vediamo domani!** see you tomorrow!; **non lo posso ~** (*fig*) I can't stand him

ve'detta SF (*sentinella, posto*) look-out; (*Naut*) patrol boat

ve'dette [və'dɛt] SF INV (*attrice*) star

'vedovo, -a SM/F widower (widow); **rimaner ~** to be widowed

vedrò *etc* VB *vedi* **vedere**

ve'duta SF view; **vedute** SFPL (*fig: opinioni*) views; **di larghe** *o* **ampie vedute** broad-minded; **di vedute limitate** narrow-minded

vee'mente AG (*discorso, azione*) vehement; (*assalto*) vigorous; (*passione*) overwhelming

vee'menza [vee'mɛntsa] SF vehemence; **con ~** vehemently

vege'tale [vedʒe'tale] AG, SM vegetable

vege'tare [vedʒe'tare] /72/ VI (*fig*) to vegetate

vegetari'ano, -a [vedʒeta'rjano] AG, SM/F vegetarian

vegeta'tivo, -a AG vegetative

vegetazi'one [vedʒetat'tsjone] SF vegetation

'vegeto, -a ['vedʒeto] AG (*pianta*) thriving; (*persona*) strong, vigorous

veg'gente [ved'dʒɛnte] SMF (*indovino*) clairvoyant

'veglia ['veʎʎa] SF wakefulness; (*sorveglianza*) watch; (*trattenimento*) evening gathering; **tra la ~ e il sonno** half awake; **fare la ~ a un malato** to watch over a sick person; **~ funebre** wake

vegli'ardo, -a [veʎ'ʎardo] SM/F venerable old man/woman

vegli'are [veʎ'ʎare] /27/ VI to stay *o* sit up; (*stare vigile*) to keep watch ▶ VT (*malato, morto*) to watch over, sit up with

vegli'one [veʎ'ʎone] SM ball, dance; **~ di Capodanno** New Year's Eve party

ve'icolo SM vehicle; **~ spaziale** spacecraft *inv*

'vela SF (*Naut: tela*) sail; (: *sport*) sailing; **tutto va a gonfie vele** (*fig*) everything is going perfectly

ve'lare /72/ VT to veil; **velarsi** VPR (*occhi, luna*) to mist over; (*voce*) to become husky; **velarsi il viso** to cover one's face (with a veil)

ve'lato, -a AG veiled

vela'tura SF (*Naut*) sails *pl*

veleggi'are [veled'dʒare] /62/ VI to sail; (*Aer*) to glide

ve'leno SM poison

vele'noso, -a AG poisonous

ve'letta SF (*di cappello*) veil

veli'ero SM sailing ship

ve'lina SF: **carta ~** (*per imballare*) tissue paper; (: *per copie*) flimsy paper; (*copia*) carbon copy

ve'lista, -i, -e SM/F yachtsman(-woman)

ve'livolo SM aircraft
velleità SF INV vain ambition, vain desire
vellei'tario, -a AG unrealistic
'vello SM fleece
vellu'tato, -a AG (*stoffa, pesca, colore*) velvety; (*voce*) mellow
vel'luto SM velvet; ~ **a coste** cord
'velo SM veil; (*tessuto*) voile
ve'loce [ve'lotʃe] AG fast, quick ▶ AV fast, quickly
velo'cista, -i, -e [velo'tʃista] SM/F (*Sport*) sprinter
velocità [velotʃi'ta] SF speed; **a forte** ~ at high speed; ~ **di crociera** cruising speed
ve'lodromo SM velodrome
ven. ABBR (= *venerdì*) Fri.
'vena SF (*gen*) vein; (*filone*) vein, seam; (*fig: ispirazione*) inspiration; (: *umore*) mood; **essere in** ~ **di qc** to be in the mood for sth
ve'nale AG (*prezzo, valore*) market *cpd*; (*fig*) venal; mercenary
venalità SF venality
ve'nato, -a AG (*marmo*) veined, streaked; (*legno*) grained
vena'torio, -a AG hunting; **la stagione venatoria** the hunting season
vena'tura SF (*di marmo*) vein, streak; (*di legno*) grain
ven'demmia SF (*raccolta*) grape harvest; (*quantità d'uva*) grape crop, grapes *pl*; (*vino ottenuto*) vintage
vendemmi'are /19/ VT to harvest ▶ VI to harvest the grapes
'vendere /29/ VT to sell; ~ **all'ingrosso/al dettaglio** *o* **minuto** to sell wholesale/retail; ~ **all'asta** to auction, sell by auction; **"vendesi"** "for sale"
ven'detta SF revenge
vendi'care /20/ VT to avenge; **vendicarsi** VPR: **vendicarsi (di)** to avenge o.s. (for); (*per rancore*) to take one's revenge (for); **vendicarsi su qn** to revenge o.s. on sb
vendica'tivo, -a AG vindictive
'vendita SF sale; **la** ~ (*attività*) selling; (*smercio*) sales *pl*; **in** ~ on sale; **mettere in** ~ to put on sale; **in** ~ **presso** on sale at; **contratto di** ~ sales agreement; **reparto vendite** sales department; ~ **all'asta** sale by auction; ~ **per telefono** telesales *sg*; ~ **al dettaglio** *o* **minuto** retail; ~ **all'ingrosso** wholesale
vendi'tore, -'trice SM/F seller, vendor; (*gestore di negozio*) trader, dealer
ven'duto, -a AG (*merce*) sold; (*fig: corrotto*) corrupt
ve'nefico, -a, -ci, -che AG poisonous
vene'rabile, vene'rando, -a AG venerable
vene'rare /72/ VT to venerate
venerazi'one [venerat'tsjone] SF veneration

venerdì SM INV Friday; **di** *o* **il** ~ on Fridays; **V~ Santo** Good Friday; *vedi anche* **martedì**
'Venere SM F Venus
ve'nereo, -a AG venereal
'veneto, -a AG of (*o* from) the Veneto
'veneto-giuli'ano, -a ['vɛnetodʒu'ljano] AG of (*o* from) Venezia-Giulia
Ve'nezia [ve'nɛttsja] SF Venice
venezi'ano, -a [venet'tsjano] AG, SM/F Venetian
Venezu'ela [venettsu'ela] SM: **il** ~ Venezuela
venezue'lano, -a [venettsue'lano] AG, SM/F Venezuelan
'vengo *etc* VB *vedi* **venire**
veni'ale AG venial
ve'nire /128/ VI to come; (*riuscire: dolce, fotografia*) to turn out; (*come ausiliare: essere*): **viene ammirato da tutti** he is admired by everyone; ~ **da** to come from; **quanto viene?** how much does it cost?; **far** ~ (*mandare a chiamare*) to send for; (*medico*) to call, send for; ~ **a capo di qc** to unravel sth, sort sth out; ~ **al dunque** *o* **nocciolo** *o* **fatto** to come to the point; ~ **fuori** to come out; ~ **giù** to come down; ~ **meno** (*svenire*) to faint; ~ **meno a qc** not to fulfil sth; ~ **su** to come up; ~ **via** to come away; ~ **a sapere qc** to learn sth; ~ **a trovare qn** to come and see sb; **negli anni a** ~ in the years to come, in future; **è venuto il momento di …** the time has come to …
'venni *etc* VB *vedi* **venire**
ven'taglio [ven'taʎʎo] SM fan
ven'tata SF gust (of wind)
venten'nale AG (*che dura 20 anni*) twenty-year *cpd*; (*che ricorre ogni 20 anni*) which takes place every twenty years
ven'tenne AG: **una ragazza** ~ a twenty-year-old girl, a girl of twenty ▶ SM F twenty-year-old
ven'tennio SM period of twenty years; **il** ~ **fascista** the Fascist period
ven'tesimo, -a NUM twentieth
'venti NUM twenty
venti'lare /72/ VT (*stanza*) to air, ventilate; (*fig: idea, proposta*) to air
venti'lato, -a AG (*camera, zona*) airy; **poco** ~ airless
ventila'tore SM fan; (*su parete, finestra*) ventilator, fan
ventilazi'one [ventilat'tsjone] SF ventilation
ven'tina SF: **una** ~ **(di)** around twenty, twenty or so
ventiquattr'ore SFPL (*periodo*) twenty-four hours ▶ SF INV (*Sport*) twenty-four-hour race; (*valigetta*) overnight case
venti'sette NUM twenty-seven; **il** ~ (*giorno di paga*) (monthly) pay day

V

ventitré NUM twenty-three ▶ SFPL: **portava il cappello sulle ~** he wore his hat at a jaunty angle

'**vento** SM wind; **c'è ~** it's windy; **un colpo di ~** a gust of wind; **contro ~** against the wind; **~ contrario** (*Naut*) headwind

'**ventola** SF (*Aut, Tecn*) fan

ven'tosa SF (*Zool*) sucker; (*di gomma*) suction pad

ven'toso, -a AG windy

ven'totto NUM twenty-eight

'**ventre** SM stomach

ven'triloquo SM ventriloquist

ven'tuno NUM twenty-one

ven'tura SF: **andare alla ~** to trust to luck; **soldato di ~** mercenary

ven'turo, -a AG next, coming

ve'nuto, -a PP *di* **venire** ▶ SM/F: **il(la) primo(a) ~(a)** the first person who comes along ▶ SF coming, arrival

ver. ABBR = **versamento**

'**vera** SF wedding ring

ve'race [ve'ratʃe] AG (*testimone*) truthful; (*testimonianza*) accurate; (*cibi*) real, genuine

vera'mente AV really

ve'randa SF veranda(h)

ver'bale AG verbal ▶ SM (*di riunione*) minutes *pl*; **accordo ~** verbal agreement; **mettere a ~** to place in the minutes *o* on record

'**verbo** SM (*Ling*) verb; (*parola*) word; (*Rel*): **il V~** the Word

ver'boso, -a AG verbose, wordy

ver'dastro, -a AG greenish

'**verde** AG, SM green; **~ bottiglia/oliva** (*inv*) bottle/olive green; **benzina ~** lead-free *o* unleaded petrol; **i Verdi** (*Pol*) the Greens; **essere al ~** (*fig*) to be broke

verdeggi'ante [verded'dʒante] AG green, verdant

verde'rame SM verdigris

ver'detto SM verdict

ver'dura SF vegetables *pl*

vere'condia SF modesty

vere'condo, -a AG modest

'**verga, -ghe** SF rod

ver'gato, -a AG (*foglio*) ruled

vergi'nale [verdʒi'nale] AG virginal

'**vergine** ['verdʒine] SF virgin; **V~** Virgo ▶ AG virgin; (*ragazza*): **essere ~** to be a virgin; **essere della V~** (*dello zodiaco*) to be Virgo; **pura lana ~** pure new wool; **olio ~ d'oliva** unrefined olive oil

verginità [verdʒini'ta] SF virginity

ver'gogna [ver'goɲɲa] SF shame; (*timidezza*) shyness, embarrassment

vergo'gnarsi [vergoɲ'narsi] /15/ VPR: **~ (di)** to be *o* feel ashamed (of); to be shy (about), be embarrassed (about)

vergo'gnoso, -a [vergoɲ'ɲoso] AG ashamed; (*timido*) shy, embarrassed; (*causa di vergogna: azione*) shameful

veridicità [veriditʃi'ta] SF truthfulness

ve'ridico, -a, -ci, -che AG truthful

ve'rifica, -che SF checking *no pl*; check; **fare una ~ di** (*freni, testimonianza, firma*) to check; **~ contabile** (*Finanza*) audit

verifi'care /20/ VT (*controllare*) to check; (*confermare*) to confirm, bear out; (*Finanza*) to audit

verità SF INV truth; **a dire la ~, per la ~** truth to tell, actually

veriti'ero, -a AG (*che dice la verità*) truthful; (*conforme a verità*) true

'**verme** SM worm

vermi'celli [vermi'tʃelli] SMPL vermicelli *sg*

ver'miglio [ver'miʎʎo] SM vermilion, scarlet

'**vermut** SM INV vermouth

ver'nacolo SM vernacular

ver'nice [ver'nitʃe] SF (*colorazione*) paint; (*trasparente*) varnish; (*pelle*) patent leather; **"~ fresca"** "wet paint"

vernici'are [verni'tʃare] /14/ VT to paint; to varnish

vernicia'tura [vernitʃa'tura] SF painting; varnishing

'**vero, -a** AG (*veridico: fatti, testimonianza*) true; (*autentico*) real ▶ SM (*verità*) truth; (*realtà*) (real) life; **un ~ e proprio delinquente** a real criminal, an out and out criminal; **tant'è ~ che ...** so much so that ...; **a onor del ~, a dire il ~** to tell the truth

Ve'rona SF Verona

vero'nese AG of (*o* from) Verona

vero'simile AG likely, probable

verrò *etc* VB *vedi* **venire**

ver'ruca, -che SF wart

versa'mento SM (*pagamento*) payment; (*deposito di denaro*) deposit

ver'sante SM slopes *pl*, side

ver'sare /72/ VT (*fare uscire: vino, farina*) to pour (out); (*spargere: lacrime, sangue*) to shed; (*rovesciare*) to spill; (*Econ*) to pay; (: *depositare*) to deposit, pay in ▶ VI: **~ in gravi difficoltà** to find o.s. with serious problems; **versarsi** VPR (*rovesciarsi*) to spill; (*fiume, folla*) **versarsi (in)** to pour (into)

ver'satile AG versatile

ver'satilità SF versatility

ver'sato, -a AG: **~ in** to be (well-)versed in

ver'setto SM (*Rel*) verse

versi'one SF version; (*traduzione*) translation

'**verso** SM (*di poesia*) verse, line; (*di animale, uccello, venditore ambulante*) cry; (*direzione*) direction; (*modo*) way; (*di foglio di carta*) verso; (*di moneta*) reverse; **versi** SMPL (*poesia*) verse *sg* ▶ PREP (*in direzione di*) toward(s); (*nei pressi di*) near, around (about); (*in senso temporale*) about, around; (*nei confronti di*) for; **per un ~ o** per l'altro one way or another; **prendere qn/qc per il ~ giusto** to approach sb/sth the right wa; **rifare il ~ a qn** (*imitare*) to mimic sb; **non c'è ~ di persuaderlo** there's no way of persuading him, he can't be persuaded; **~ di me** towards me; **~ l'alto** upwards; **~ il basso** downwards; **~ sera** towards evening

'**vertebra** SF vertebra

verte'brale AG vertebral; **colonna ~** spinal column, spine

verte'brato, -a AG, SM vertebrate

ver'tenza [ver'tɛntsa] SF (*lite*) lawsuit, case; (*sindacale*) dispute

'**vertere** /vb not found/ VI: ~ **su** to deal with, be about

verti'cale AG, SF vertical

'**vertice** ['vertitʃe] SM summit, top; (*Mat*) vertex; **conferenza al ~** (*Pol*) summit conference

ver'tigine [ver'tidʒine] SF dizziness *no pl*; dizzy spell; (*Med*) vertigo; **avere le vertigini** to feel dizzy

vertigi'noso, -a [vertidʒi'noso] AG (*altezza*) dizzy; (*fig*) breathtakingly high (*o deep etc*)

'**verza** ['verdza] SF Savoy cabbage

ve'scica, -che [veʃʃika] SF (*Anat*) bladder; (*Med*) blister

vesco'vile AG episcopal

'**vescovo** SM bishop

'**vespa** SF wasp; ® (*veicolo*) (motor) scooter

ves'paio SM wasps' nest; **suscitare un ~** (*fig*) to stir up a hornets' nest

vespasi'ano SM urinal

'**vespro** SM (*Rel*) vespers *pl*

ves'sare /72/ VT to oppress

vessazi'one [vessat'tsjone] SF oppression

ves'sillo SM standard; (*bandiera*) flag

ves'taglia [ves'taʎʎa] SF dressing gown, robe (*US*)

'**veste** SF garment; (*rivestimento*) covering; (*qualità, facoltà*) capacity; **vesti** SFPL clothes, clothing *sg*; **in ~ ufficiale** (*fig*) in an official capacity; **in ~ di** in the guise of, as; **~ da camera** dressing gown, robe (*US*); **~ editoriale** layout

vesti'ario SM wardrobe, clothes *pl*; **capo di ~** article of clothing, garment

ves'tibolo SM (entrance) hall

ves'tigia [ves'tidʒa] SFPL (*tracce*) vestiges, traces; (*rovine*) ruins, remains

ves'tire /45/ VT (*bambino, malato*) to dress; (*avere indosso*) to have on, wear; **vestirsi** VPR to dress, get dressed; **vestirsi da** (*negozio, sarto*) to buy *o* get one's clothes at

ves'tito, -a AG dressed ▶ SM garment; (*da donna*) dress; (*da uomo*) suit; **vestiti** SMPL (*indumenti*) clothes; **~ di bianco** dressed in white

Ve'suvio SM: **il ~** Vesuvius

vete'rano, -a AG, SM/F veteran

veteri'nario, -a AG veterinary ▶ SM veterinary surgeon (*BRIT*), veterinarian (*US*), vet ▶ SF veterinary medicine

'**veto** SM INV veto; **porre il ~ a qc** to veto sth

ve'traio SM glassmaker; (*per finestre*) glazier

ve'trato, -a AG (*porta, finestra*) glazed; (*che contiene vetro*) glass *cpd* ▶ SF glass door (*o* window); (*di chiesa*) stained glass window; **carta vetrata** sandpaper

vetre'ria SF (*stabilimento*) glassworks *sg*; (*oggetti di vetro*) glassware

ve'trina SF (*di negozio*) (shop) window; (*armadio*) display cabinet

vetri'nista, -i, -e SM/F window dresser

ve'trino SM slide

vetri'olo SM vitriol

'**vetro** SM glass; (*per finestra, porta*) pane (of glass); **~ blindato** bulletproof glass; **~ infrangibile** shatterproof glass; **~ di sicurezza** safety glass; **i vetri di Murano** Murano glassware *sg*

ve'troso, -a AG vitreous

'**vetta** SF peak, summit, top

vet'tore SM (*Mat, Fisica*) vector; (*chi trasporta*) carrier

vetto'vaglie [vetto'vaʎʎe] SFPL supplies

vet'tura SF (*carrozza*) carriage; (*Ferr*) carriage (*BRIT*), car (*US*); (*auto*) car (*BRIT*), automobile (*US*); **~ di piazza** hackney carriage

vettu'rino SM coach driver, coachman

vezzeggi'are [vettsed'dʒare] /62/ VT to fondle, caress

vezzeggia'tivo [vettseddʒa'tivo] SM (*Ling*) term of endearment

'**vezzo** ['vettso] SM habit; **vezzi** SMPL (*smancerie*) affected ways; (*leggiadria*) charms

vez'zoso, -a [vet'tsoso] AG (*grazioso*) charming, pretty; (*lezioso*) affected

V.F. ABBR = **vigili del fuoco**

V.G. ABBR = **Vostra Grazia**

VI SIGLA = **Vicenza**

vi (*dav lo, la, li, le, ne diventa* **ve**) PRON (*oggetto*) you; (*complemento di termine*) (to) you; (*riflessivo*) yourselves; (*reciproco*) each other ▶ AV (*lì*) there; (*qui*) here; (*per questo/quel luogo*) through here/there; **vi è/sono** there is/are

'**via** SF (*gen*) way; (*strada*) street; (*sentiero, pista*) path, track; (*Amm: procedimento*) channels *pl* ▶ PREP (*passando per*) via, by way of ▶ AV away ▶ ESCL go away!; (*suvvia*) come on!; (*Sport*) go! ▶ SM (*Sport*) starting signal; **per ~ di** (*a causa di*) because of, on account of; **in *o* per ~** on the way; **in ~ di guarigione** (*fig*) on the road to recovery; **per ~ aerea** by air; (*lettere*) by airmail; **~ satellite** by satellite; **andare/essere ~** to go/be away; **~ ~** (*pian piano*) gradually; **~ ~ che** (*a mano a mano*) as; **e ~ dicendo, e ~ di questo passo** and so on (and so forth); **dare il ~** (*Sport*) to give the starting signal; **dare il ~ a** (*fig*) to start; **dare il ~ a un progetto** to give the green light to a project; **hanno dato il ~ ai lavori** they've begun *o* started work; **in ~ amichevole** in a friendly manner; **comporre una disputa in ~ amichevole** (*Dir*) to settle a dispute out of court; **in ~ eccezionale** as an exception; **in ~ privata** *o* **confidenziale** (*dire ecc*) in confidence; **in ~ provvisoria** provisionally; **V~ lattea** (*Astr*) Milky Way; **~ di mezzo** middle course; **non c'è ~ di scampo** *o* **d'uscita** there's no way out; **vie di comunicazione** communication routes

viabilità SF (*di strada*) practicability; (*rete stradale*) roads pl, road network

via'dotto SM viaduct

viaggi'are [viad'dʒare] /**62**/ VI to travel; **le merci viaggiano via mare** the goods go by sea

viaggia'tore, -'trice [viaddʒa'tore] AG travelling (*BRIT*), traveling (*US*) ▶ SM traveller (*BRIT*), traveler (*US*), passenger

vi'aggio [vi'addʒo] SM travel(ling); (*tragitto*) journey, trip; **buon ~!** have a good trip!; **~ d'affari** business trip; **~ di nozze** honeymoon; **~ organizzato** package tour *o* holiday

vi'ale SM avenue

vian'dante SMF vagrant

vi'atico, -ci SM (*Rel*) viaticum; (*fig*) encouragement

via'vai SM coming and going, bustle

vi'brare /**72**/ VI to vibrate; (*agitarsi*): **~ (di)** to quiver (with)

vibra'tore SM vibrator

vibrazi'one [vibrat'tsjone] SF vibration

vi'cario SM (*apostolico ecc*) vicar

'vice ['vitʃe] SMF deputy ▶ PREFISSO vice

vice'console [vitʃe'kɔnsole] SM vice-consul

vicediret'tore, -'trice [vitʃediret'tore] SM/F assistant manager(-manageress); (*di giornale ecc*) deputy editor

vi'cenda [vi'tʃɛnda] SF event; **vicende** SFPL (*sorte*) fortunes; **a ~** in turn; **con alterne vicende** with mixed fortunes

vicen'devole [vitʃen'devole] AG mutual, reciprocal

vicen'tino, -a [vitʃen'tino] AG of (*o* from) Vicenza

vicepresi'dente [vitʃepresi'dɛnte] SM vice-president, vice-chairman

vice'versa [vitʃe'vɛrsa] AV vice versa; **da Roma a Pisa e ~** from Rome to Pisa and back

vi'chingo, -a, -ghi, -ghe [vi'kingo] AG, SM/F Viking

vici'nanza [vitʃi'nantsa] SF nearness, closeness; **vicinanze** SFPL (*paraggi*)

neighbourhood (*BRIT*), neighborhood (*US*), vicinity

vici'nato [vitʃi'nato] SM neighbourhood (*BRIT*), neighborhood (*US*); (*vicini*) neighbo(u)rs pl

vi'cino, -a [vi'tʃino] AG (*gen*) near; (*nello spazio*) near, nearby; (*accanto*) next; (*nel tempo*) near, close at hand ▶ SM/F neighbour (*BRIT*), neighbor (*US*) ▶ AV near, close; **da ~** (*guardare*) close up; (*esaminare, seguire*) closely; (*conoscere*) well, intimately; **~ a** prep near (to), close to; (*accanto a*) beside; **mi sono stati molto vicini** (*fig*) they were very supportive towards me; **~ di casa** neighbour

vicissi'tudini [vitʃissi'tudini] SFPL trials and tribulations

'vicolo SM alley; **~ cieco** blind alley

'video SM INV (*TV: schermo*) screen

video'camera SF camcorder

videocas'setta SF videocassette

videochia'mare [videokja'mare] /**72**/ VT to video call

video'clip [video'klip] SM INV videoclip

videodipen'dente SMF telly addict ▶ AG: **un pigrone ~** a couch potato

videofo'nino SM video mobile

videogi'oco, -chi [video'dʒɔko] SM video game

videono'leggio [videono'leddʒo] SM video rental

videoregistra'tore [videoredʒistra'tore] SM (*apparecchio*) video (recorder)

video'teca, -che SF video shop

videote'lefono SM videophone

videotermi'nale SM visual display unit

'vidi *etc* VB *vedi* **vedere**

vidi'mare /**72**/ VT (*Amm*) to authenticate

vidimazi'one [vidimat'tsjone] SF (*Amm*) authentication

Vi'enna SF Vienna

vien'nese AG, SMF Viennese *inv*

vie'tare /**72**/ VT to forbid; (*Amm*) to prohibit; (*libro*) to ban; **~ a qn di fare** to forbid sb to do; to prohibit sb from doing

vie'tato, -a AG (*vedi vb*) forbidden; prohibited; banned; **"~ fumare/l'ingresso"** "no smoking/admittance"; **~ ai minori di 14/18 anni** prohibited to children under 14/18; **"senso ~"** (*Aut*) "no entry"; **"sosta vietata"** (*Aut*) "no parking"

Viet'nam SM: **il ~** Vietnam

vietna'mita, -i, -e AG, SM/F, SM Vietnamese *inv*

vi'eto, -a AG worthless

vi'gente [vi'dʒente] AG in force

'vigere ['vidʒere] VI (*difettivo: si usa solo alla terza persona*) to be in force; **in casa mia vige l'abitudine di ...** at home we are in the habit of ...

vigi'lante [vidʒi'lante] AG vigilant, watchful
vigi'lanza [vidʒi'lantsa] SF vigilance; (*sorveglianza: di operai, alunni*) supervision; (: *di sospetti, criminali*) surveillance; **~ notturna** night-watchman service
vigi'lare [vidʒi'lare] /**72**/ VT to watch over, keep an eye on; **~ che** to make sure that, see to it that
vigi'lato, -a [vidʒi'lato] SM/F (*Dir*) person under police surveillance
vigila'trice [vidʒila'tritʃe] SF: **~ d'infanzia** nursery-school teacher; **~ scolastica** school health officer
'vigile ['vidʒile] AG watchful ▶ SM (*anche:* **vigile urbano**) policeman (*in towns*); **~ del fuoco** fireman; *see note*

┃ The *vigili urbani* are a municipal police
┃ force attached to the *Comune*. Their duties
┃ involve everyday aspects of life such as
┃ traffic, public works and services, and
┃ commerce.

vigi'lessa [vidʒi'lessa] SF (traffic) policewoman
vi'gilia [vi'dʒilja] SF (*giorno antecedente*) eve; **la ~ di Natale** Christmas Eve
vigliacche'ria [viʎʎakke'ria] SF cowardice
vigli'acco, -a, -chi, -che [viʎ'ʎakko] AG cowardly ▶ SM/F coward
'vigna ['viɲɲa] SF, **vi'gneto** [viɲ'ɲeto] SM vineyard
vi'gnetta [viɲ'ɲetta] SF cartoon; (*Aut: anche:* **vignetta autostradale**: *tassa*) car tax (*for motorways*); (: *adesivo*) *sticker showing that this tax has been paid*
vi'gogna [vi'goɲɲa] SF vicuña
vi'gore SM vigour (*Brit*), vigor (*US*); (*Dir*): **essere/entrare in ~** to be in/come into force; **non è più in ~** it is no longer in force, it no longer applies
vigo'roso, -a AG vigorous
'vile AG (*spregevole*) low, mean, base; (*codardo*) cowardly
vili'pendere /**8**/ VT to despise, scorn
vili'pendio SM contempt, scorn
vili'peso, -a PP *di* **vilipendere**
'villa SF villa
vil'laggio [vil'laddʒo] SM village; **~ turistico** holiday village
villa'nia SF rudeness, lack of manners; **fare** (*o* **dire**) **una ~ a qn** to be rude to sb
vil'lano, -a AG rude, ill-mannered ▶ SM/F boor
villeggi'ante [villed'dʒante] SMF holiday-maker (*Brit*), vacationer (*US*)
villeggi'are [villed'dʒare] /**62**/ VI to holiday, spend one's holidays, vacation (*US*)
villeggia'tura [villeddʒa'tura] SF holiday(s *pl*) (*Brit*), vacation (*US*); **luogo di ~** (holiday) resort

vil'letta SF, **vil'lino** SM small house (with a garden), cottage
vil'loso, -a AG hairy
viltà SF cowardice *no pl*; (*gesto*) cowardly act
Vimi'nale SM *see note*

┃ The *Viminale*, which takes its name from
┃ one of the famous Seven Hills of Rome on
┃ which it stands, is home to the Ministry
┃ of the Interior.

'vimini SMPL wicker; **mobili di ~** wicker furniture *sg*
vi'naio SM wine merchant
'vincere ['vintʃere] /**129**/ VT (*in guerra, al gioco, a una gara*) to defeat, beat; (*premio, guerra, partita*) to win; (*fig*) to overcome, conquer ▶ VI to win; **~ qn in** (*abilità, bellezza*) to surpass sb in
'vincita ['vintʃita] SF win; (*denaro vinto*) winnings *pl*
vinci'tore, -'trice [vintʃi'tore] SM/F winner; (*Mil*) victor
vinco'lante AG binding
vinco'lare /**72**/ VT to bind; (*Comm: denaro*) to tie up
vinco'lato, -a AG: **deposito ~** (*Comm*) fixed deposit
'vincolo SM (*fig*) bond, tie; (*Dir*) obligation
vi'nicolo, -a AG wine *cpd*; **regione vinicola** wine-producing area
vinificazi'one [vinifikat'tsjone] SF wine-making
'vino SM wine; **~ bianco/rosato/rosso** white/rosé/red wine; **~ da pasto** table wine
'vinsi *etc* VB *vedi* **vincere**
'vinto, -a PP *di* **vincere** ▶ AG: **darla vinta a qn** to let sb have his (*o* her) way; **darsi per ~** to give up, give in
vi'ola SF (*Bot*) violet; (*Mus*) viola ▶ AG, SM INV (*colore*) purple
vio'lare /**72**/ VT (*chiesa*) to desecrate, violate; (*giuramento, legge*) to violate
violazi'one [violat'tsjone] SF desecration; violation; **~ di domicilio** (*Dir*) breaking and entering
violen'tare /**72**/ VT to use violence on; (*donna*) to rape
vio'lento, -a AG violent
vio'lenza [vio'lentsa] SF violence; **~ carnale** rape
vio'letto, -a AG, SM (*colore*) violet ▶ SF (*Bot*) violet
violi'nista, -i, -e SM/F violinist
vio'lino SM violin
violoncel'lista, -i, -e [violontʃel'lista] SM/F cellist, cello player
violon'cello [violon'tʃello] SM cello
vi'ottolo SM path, track
VIP [vip] SM INV/F INV (= *Very Important Person*) VIP

┃ **V**

'**vipera** SF viper, adder

vi'raggio [vi'raddʒo] SM (Naut, Aer) turn; (Fot) toning

vi'rale AG viral

vi'rare /72/ VI (Naut, Aer) to turn; (Fot) to tone; ~ **di bordo** to change course; (Naut) to tack

vi'rata SF coming about; turning; change of course

'**virgola** SF (Ling) comma; (Mat) point

virgo'lette SFPL inverted commas, quotation marks

vi'rile AG (proprio dell'uomo) masculine; (non puerile, da uomo) manly, virile

virilità SF masculinity; manliness; (sessuale) virility

virtù SF INV virtue; **in** o **per ~ di** by virtue of, by

virtu'ale AG virtual

virtu'oso, -a AG virtuous ▶ SM/F (Mus ecc) virtuoso

viru'lento, -a AG virulent

'**virus** SM INV (anche Inform) virus

visa'gista, -i, -e [viza'dʒista] SM/F beautician

visce'rale [viʃʃe'rale] AG (Med) visceral; (fig) profound, deep-rooted

'**viscere** ['viʃʃere] SM (Anat) internal organ ▶ SFPL (di animale) entrails pl; (fig) depths pl, bowels pl

'**vischio** ['viskjo] SM (Bot) mistletoe; (pania) birdlime

vischi'oso, -a [vis'kjoso] AG sticky

viscidità [viʃʃidi'ta] SF sliminess

'**viscido, -a** ['viʃʃido] AG slimy

vis'conte, -'essa SM/F viscount (viscountess)

viscosità SF viscosity

vis'coso, -a AG viscous

vi'sibile AG visible

visi'bilio SM: **andare in ~** to go into raptures

visibilità SF visibility

visi'era SF (di elmo) visor; (di berretto) peak

visio'nare /72/ VT (gen) to look at, examine; (Cine) to screen

visio'nario, -a AG, SM/F visionary

visi'one SF vision; **prendere ~ di qc** to examine sth, look sth over; **prima/seconda ~** (Cine) first/second showing

'**visita** SF visit; (Med) visit, call; (: esame) examination; **far ~ a qn, andare in ~ da qn** to visit sb, pay sb a visit; **in ~ ufficiale in Italia** on an official visit to Italy; **orario di visite** (ospedale) visiting hours; **~ di controllo** (Med) checkup; **~ medica** medical examination; **~ a domicilio** house call; **~ guidata** guided tour; **~ sanitaria** sanitary inspection

visi'tare /72/ VT to visit; (Med) to visit, call on; (: esaminare) to examine

visita'tore, -'trice SM/F visitor

vi'sivo, -a AG visual

'**viso** SM face; **fare buon ~ a cattivo gioco** to make the best of things

vi'sone SM mink

vi'sore SM (Fot) viewer

'**vispo, -a** AG quick, lively

'**vissi** etc VB vedi **vivere**

vis'suto, -a PP di **vivere** ▶ AG (aria, modo di fare) experienced

'**vista** SF (facoltà) (eye)sight; (veduta) view; (fatto di vedere): **la ~ di** the sight of; **con ~ sul lago** with a view over the lake; **sparare a ~** to shoot on sight; **pagabile a ~** payable on demand; **in ~** in sight; **avere in ~ qc** to have sth in view; **mettersi in ~** to draw attention to o.s.; (peg) to show off; **perdere qn di ~** to lose sight of sb; (fig) to lose touch with sb; **far ~ di fare** to pretend to do; **a ~ d'occhio** as far as the eye can see; (fig) before one's very eyes

vis'tare /72/ VT to approve; (Amm: passaporto) to visa

'**visto, -a** PP di **vedere** ▶ SM visa; **~ che** cong seeing (that); **~ d'ingresso/di transito** entry/transit visa; **~ permanente/di soggiorno** permanent/tourist visa

vis'toso, -a AG gaudy, garish; (ingente) considerable

visu'ale AG visual

visualiz'zare [vizualid'dzare] /72/ VT to visualize

visualizza'tore [vizualiddza'tore] SM (Inform) visual display unit, VDU

visualizzazi'one [vizualiddzat'tsjone] SF (Inform) display

'**vita** SF life; (Anat) waist; **essere in ~** to be alive; **pieno di ~** full of life; **a ~** for life; **membro a ~** life member

vi'tale AG vital

vitalità SF vitality

vita'lizio, -a [vita'littsjo] AG life cpd ▶ SM life annuity

vita'mina SF vitamin

'**vite** SF (Bot) vine; (Tecn) screw; **giro di ~** (anche fig) turn of the screw

vi'tello SM (Zool) calf; (carne) veal; (pelle) calfskin

vi'ticcio [vi'tittʃo] SM (Bot) tendril

viticol'tore SM wine grower

viticol'tura SF wine growing

'**vitreo, -a** AG vitreous; (occhio, sguardo) glassy

'**vittima** SF victim

vitti'mismo SM self-pity

'**vitto** SM food; (in un albergo ecc) board; **~ e alloggio** board and lodging

vit'toria SF victory

vittori'ano, -a AG Victorian

vittori'oso, -a AG victorious

vitupe'rare /72/ VT to rail at o against

vi'uzza [vi'uttsa] SF (in città) alley

'**viva** ESCL: **~ il re!** long live the king!

vivacchi'are [vivak'kjare] /**19**/ VI to scrape a living

vi'vace [vi'vatʃe] AG (*vivo, animato*) lively; (*mente*) lively, sharp; (*colore*) bright

vivacità [vivatʃi'ta] SF liveliness; brightness

vivaciz'zare [vivatʃid'dzare] /**72**/ VT to liven up

vi'vaio SM (*di pesci*) hatchery; (*Agr*) nursery

viva'mente AV (*commuoversi*) deeply, profoundly; (*ringraziare ecc*) sincerely, warmly

vi'vanda SF food; (*piatto*) dish

viva'voce [viva'votʃe] SM INV (*dispositivo*) loudspeaker ▸ AG INV: **telefono ~** speakerphone; **mettere in ~** to switch on the loudspeaker

vi'vente AG living, alive; **i viventi** the living

'vivere /**130**/ VI to live ▸ VT to live; (*passare: brutto momento*) to live through, go through; (*sentire: gioie, pene di qn*) to share ▸ SM life; (*anche: **modo di vivere***) way of life; **viveri** SMPL (*cibo*) food *sg*, provisions; **~ di** to live on

vi'veur [vi'vœr] SM INV pleasure-seeker

'vivido, -a AG (*colore*) vivid, bright

vivifi'care /**20**/ VT to enliven, give life to; (*piante ecc*) to revive

vivisezi'one [viviset'tsjone] SF vivisection

'vivo, -a AG (*vivente*) alive, living; (*: animale*) live; (*fig*) lively; (*: colore*) bright, brilliant ▸ SM: **entrare nel ~ di una questione** to get to the heart of a matter; **i vivi** the living; **esperimenti su animali vivi** experiments on live *o* living animals; **~ e vegeto** hale and hearty; **farsi ~** (*fig*) to show one's face; to keep in touch; **con ~ rammarico** with deep regret; **congratulazioni vivissime** heartiest congratulations; **con i più vivi ringraziamenti** with deepest *o* warmest thanks; **ritrarre dal ~** to paint from life; **pungere qn nel ~** (*fig*) to cut sb to the quick

vivrò etc VB vedi **vivere**

vizi'are [vit'tsjare] /**19**/ VT (*bambino*) to spoil; (*corrompere moralmente*) to corrupt; (*Dir*) to invalidate

vizi'ato, -a [vit'tsjato] AG spoilt; (*aria, acqua*) polluted; (*Dir*) invalid, invalidated

'vizio ['vittsjo] SM (*morale*) vice; (*cattiva abitudine*) bad habit; (*imperfezione*) flaw, defect; (*errore*) fault, mistake; **~ di forma** legal flaw *o* irregularity; **~ procedurale** procedural error

vizi'oso, -a [vit'tsjoso] AG depraved; (*inesatto*) incorrect; **circolo ~** vicious circle

V.le ABBR = **viale**

vocabo'lario SM (*dizionario*) dictionary; (*lessico*) vocabulary

vo'cabolo SM word

vo'cale AG vocal ▸ SF vowel

vocazi'one [vokat'tsjone] SF vocation; (*fig*) natural bent

'voce ['votʃe] SF voice; (*diceria*) rumour (BRIT), rumor (US); (*di un elenco: in bilancio*) item; (*di dizionario*) entry; **parlare a alta/bassa ~** to speak in a loud/low *o* soft voice; **fare la ~ grossa** to raise one's voice; **dar ~ a qc** to voice sth, give voice to sth; **a gran ~** in a loud voice, loudly; **te lo dico a ~** I'll tell you when I see you; **a una ~** unanimously; **aver ~ in capitolo** (*fig*) to have a say in the matter; **voci di corridoio** rumours

voci'are [vo'tʃare] /**14**/ VI to shout, yell

vocife'rante [votʃife'rante] AG noisy

vo'cio [vo'tʃio] SM shouting

'vodka SF INV vodka

'voga SF (*Naut*) rowing; (*usanza*): **essere in ~** to be in fashion *o* in vogue

vo'gare /**80**/ VI to row

voga'tore, -'trice SM/F oarsman(-woman) ▸ SM rowing machine

vogherò etc VB vedi **vogare**

'voglia ['vɔʎʎa] SF desire, wish; (*macchia*) birthmark; **aver ~ di qc/di fare** to feel like sth/like doing; (*più forte*) to want sth/to do; **di buona ~** willingly

'voglio etc ['vɔʎʎo] VB vedi **volere**

vogli'oso, -a [voʎ'ʎoso] AG (*sguardo ecc*) longing; (*più forte*) full of desire

'voi PRON you; **~ stessi(e)** you yourselves

voi'altri PRON you

vol. ABBR (= *volume*) vol.

vo'lano SM (*Sport*) shuttlecock; (*Tecn*) flywheel

vo'lant [vo'lã] SM INV frill

vo'lante AG flying ▸ SM (steering) wheel ▸ SF (*Polizia: anche: **squadra volante***) flying squad

volanti'naggio [volanti'naddʒo] SM leafleting

volanti'nare /**72**/ VT (*distribuire volantini*) to leaflet, hand out leaflets

volan'tino SM leaflet

vo'lare /**72**/ VI (*uccello, aereo, fig*) to fly; (*cappello*) to blow away *o* off, fly away *o* off; **~ via** to fly away *o* off

vo'lata SF flight; (*d'uccelli*) flock, flight; (*corsa*) rush; (*Sport*) final sprint; **passare di ~ da qn** to drop in on sb briefly

vo'latile AG (*Chim*) volatile ▸ SM (*Zool*) bird

volatiliz'zarsi [volatilid'dzarsi] /**61**/ VPR (*Chim*) to volatilize; (*fig*) to vanish, disappear

vo'lente AG: **verrai ~ o nolente** you'll come whether you like it or not

volente'roso, -a AG willing, keen

volenti'eri AV willingly; **"~"** "with pleasure", "I'd be glad to"

(PAROLA CHIAVE)

vo'lere /**131**/ SM will, wish(es); **contro il volere di** against the wishes of; **per volere di qn** in obedience to sb's will *o* wishes ▸ VT **1** (*esigere, desiderare*) to want; **volere**

403

fare qc to want to do sth; **volere che qn faccia qc** to want sb to do sth; **vorrei andarmene** I'd like to go; **vorrei che se ne andasse** I'd like him to go; **vorrei questo/fare** I would *o* I'd like this/to do; **volevo parlartene** I meant to talk to you about it; **come vuoi** as you like; **la vogliono al telefono** there's a call for you; **che tu lo voglia o no** whether you like it or not; **vuoi un caffè?** would you like a coffee?; **senza volere** (*inavvertitamente*) without meaning to, unintentionally; **te la sei voluta** you asked for it; **la tradizione vuole che ...** custom requires that ...; **la leggenda vuole che ...** legend has it that ...
2 (*consentire*): **vogliate attendere, per piacere** please wait; **vogliamo andare?** shall we go?; **vuole essere così gentile da ...?** would you be so kind as to ...?; **non ha voluto ricevermi** he wouldn't see me
3: **volerci** (*essere necessario: materiale, attenzione*) to be needed; (: *tempo*) to take; **quanta farina ci vuole per questa torta?** how much flour do you need for this cake?; **ci vuole un'ora per arrivare a Venezia** it takes an hour to get to Venice; **è quel che ci vuole** it's just what is needed
4: **voler bene a qn** (*amore*) to love sb; (*affetto*) to be fond of sb, like sb very much; **voler male a qn** to dislike sb; **volerne a qn** to bear sb a grudge; **voler dire** to mean; **voglio dire ...** I mean ...; **volevo ben dire!** I thought as much!

vol'gare AG vulgar
volgarità SF vulgarity
volgariz'zare [volgarid'dzare] /**72**/ VT to popularize
volgar'mente AV (*in modo volgare*) vulgarly, coarsely; (*del popolo*) commonly, popularly
'volgere ['vɔldʒere] /**96**/ VT to turn ▶ VI to turn; (*tendere*): **~ a: il tempo volge al brutto/al bello** the weather is breaking/is setting fair; **un rosso che volge al viola** a red verging on purple; **volgersi** VPR to turn; **~ al peggio** to take a turn for the worse; **~ al termine** to draw to an end
'volgo SM common people
voli'era SF aviary
voli'tivo, -a AG strong-willed
'volli *etc* VB *vedi* **volere**
'volo SM flight; **ci sono due ore di ~ da Londra a Milano** it's a two-hour flight between London and Milan; **colpire qc al ~** to hit sth as it flies past; **prendere al ~** (*autobus, treno*) to catch at the last possible moment; (*palla*) to catch as it flies past; (*occasione*) to seize; **capire al ~** to understand straight away; **veduta a ~ d'uccello**

bird's-eye view; **~ charter** charter flight; **~ di linea** scheduled flight
volontà SF INV will; **a ~** (*mangiare, bere*) as much as one likes; **buona/cattiva ~** goodwill/lack of goodwill; **le sue ultime ~** (*testamento*) his last will and testament *sg*
volontaria'mente AV voluntarily
volontari'ato SM (*Mil*) voluntary service; (*lavoro*) voluntary work
volon'tario, -a AG voluntary ▶ SM (*Mil*) volunteer
'volpe SF fox
vol'pino, -a AG (*pelo, coda*) fox's; (*aspetto, astuzia*) fox-like ▶ SM (*cane*) Pomeranian
vol'pone SM/F (*fig*) old fox
'volsi *etc* VB *vedi* **volgere**
volt SM INV (*Elettr*) volt
'volta SF (*momento, circostanza*) time; (*turno, giro*) turn; (*curva*) turn, bend; (*Archit*) vault; (*direzione*): **partire alla ~ di** to set off for; **a mia** (*o* **tua** *etc*) **~** in turn; **una ~** once; **una ~ sola** only once; **c'era una ~** once upon a time there was; **le cose di una ~** the things of the past; **due volte** twice; **tre volte** three times; **una cosa per ~** one thing at a time; **una ~ o l'altra** one of these days; **una ~ per tutte** once and for all; **una ~ tanto** just for once; **lo facciamo un'altra ~** we'll do it another time *o* some other time; **a volte** at times, sometimes; **di ~ in ~** from time to time; **una ~ che** (*temporale*) once; (*causale*) since; **3 volte 4** 3 times 4; **ti ha dato di ~ il cervello?** have you gone out of your mind?
volta'faccia [volta'fattʃa] SM INV (*fig*) volte-face
vol'taggio [vol'taddʒo] SM (*Elettr*) voltage
vol'tare /**72**/ VT to turn; (*girare: moneta*) to turn over; (*rigirare*) to turn round ▶ VI to turn; **voltarsi** VPR to turn; to turn over; to turn round
voltas'tomaco SM nausea; (*fig*) disgust
volteggi'are [volted'dʒare] /**62**/ VI (*volare*) to circle; (*in equitazione*) to do trick riding; (*in ginnastica*) to vault
'volto, -a PP *di* **volgere** ▶ AG (*inteso a*): **il mio discorso è ~ a spiegare ...** in my speech I intend to explain ... ▶ SM face
vo'lubile AG changeable, fickle
vo'lume SM volume
volumi'noso, -a AG voluminous, bulky
vo'luta SF (*gen*) spiral; (*Archit*) volute
voluttà SF sensual pleasure *o* delight
voluttu'oso, -a AG voluptuous
vomi'tare /**72**/ VT, VI to vomit
'vomito SM vomiting *no pl*; vomit; **ho il ~** I feel sick
'vongola SF clam
vo'race [vo'ratʃe] AG voracious, greedy

voracità [voratʃi'ta] SF voracity,
voraciousness

vo'ragine [vo'radʒine] SF abyss, chasm

vorrò etc VB vedi **volere**

'**vortice** ['vɔrtitʃe] SM whirlwind; whirlpool;
(fig) whirl

vorti'coso, -a AG whirling

'**vostro, -a** DET: **il (la) ~(a)** etc your ▶ PRON:
il (la) ~(a) etc yours ▶ SM: **avete speso del ~?**
did you spend your own money? ▶ SF: **la
vostra** (opinione) your view; **i vostri** (famiglia)
your family; **un ~ amico** a friend of yours;
è dei vostri, è dalla vostra he's on your
side; **l'ultima vostra** (Comm: lettera) your
most recent letter; **alla vostra!** (brindisi)
here's to you!, your health!

vo'tante SMF voter

vo'tare /72/ VI to vote ▶ VT (sottoporre a
votazione) to take a vote on; (approvare) to vote
for; (Rel): **~ qc a** to dedicate sth to; **votarsi**
VPR to devote o.s. to

votazi'one [votat'tsjone] SF vote, voting;
votazioni SFPL (Pol) votes; (Ins) marks

'**voto** SM (Pol) vote; (Ins) mark (BRIT), grade
(US); (Rel) vow; (: offerta) votive offering; **aver
voti belli/brutti** (Ins) to get good/bad marks
o grades; **prendere i voti** to take one's vows;
~ di fiducia vote of confidence

V.P. ABBR (= vicepresidente) VP

VR SIGLA = **Verona**

v.r. ABBR (= vedi retro) PTO

vs. ABBR (= vostro) yr

v.s. ABBR = **vedi sopra**

VT SIGLA = **Viterbo**

V.U. ABBR = **vigile urbano**

vul'canico, -a, -ci, -che AG volcanic

vulcanizzazi'one [vulkaniddzat'tsjone] SF
vulcanization

vul'cano SM volcano

vulne'rabile AG vulnerable

vulnerabilità SF vulnerability

vu'oi, vu'ole VB vedi **volere**

vuo'tare /72/ VT, **vuo'tarsi** VPR to empty

vu'oto, -a AG empty; (fig: privo): **~ di** (senso ecc)
devoid of ▶ SM empty space, gap; (spazio in
bianco) blank; (Fisica) vacuum; (fig: mancanza)
gap, void; **a mani vuote** empty-handed;
assegno a ~ dud cheque (BRIT), bad check
(US); **~ d'aria** air pocket; **"~ a perdere"** "no
deposit"; **"~ a rendere"** "returnable bottle"

Ww

W, w ['dɔppjovu] SM O F INV (*lettera*) W, w;
  W come Washington ≈ W for William
W ABBR = **viva, evviva**
'**wafer** ['vafer] SM INV (*Cuc, Elettr*) wafer
wagon-'lit [vagɔ̃'li] SM INV (*Ferr*) sleeping
  car
'**walkman**® ['wɔ:kmən] SM INV Walkman®
'**water** ['wɔ:təʳ] SM INV toilet
'**water 'closet** ['wɔ:tə'klɔzɪt] SM INV toilet,
  lavatory
watt [vat] SM INV (*Elettr*) watt
wat'tora [vat'tora] SM INV (*Elettr*) watt-hour
WC SM INV WC
web [ueb] SM: **il ~** the web ▶ AG INV: **pagina ~**
  webpage; **cercare nel ~** to search the web

webcam [web'kam] SF INV (*Inform*) webcam
'**webinar** ['wɛbinar] SM INV (*Inform*) webinar
web'mail [wɛb'meil] SF webmail; **delle ~**
  (*Inform*) webmail services
'**weekend** ['wi:kend] SM INV weekend
'**western** ['wɛstern] AG (*Cine*) cowboy *cpd*
  ▶ SM INV western, cowboy film;
  ~ all'italiana spaghetti western
'**whisky** ['wiski] SM INV whisky
Wi-Fi [uai'fai] (*Inform*) SM Wi-Fi ▶ AG INV
  Wi-Fi
'**wiki** ['wiki] SM INV (*Internet*) wiki
'**windsurf** ['windsə:f] SM INV (*tavola*)
  windsurfer, sailboard; (*sport*) windsurfing
'**würstel** ['vyrstəl] SM INV frankfurter

Xx

X, x [iks] SM O F INV (*lettera*) X, x; **X come Xeres** ≈ X for Xmas
xenofo'bia [ksenofo'bia] SF xenophobia
xe'nofobo, -a [kse'nɔfobo] AG xenophobic
▶ SM/F xenophobe
'xeres ['ksɛres] SM INV sherry

xero'copia [ksero'kɔpja] SF xerox®, photocopy
xerocopi'are [kseroko'pjare] /**19**/ VT to photocopy
xi'lofono [ksi'lɔfono] SM xylophone

Yy

Y, y ['ipsilon] SM O F INV (*lettera*) Y, y; **Y come Yacht** ≈ Y for Yellow (*BRIT*), ≈ Y for Yoke (*US*)

yacht [jɔt] SM INV yacht

'yankee ['jæŋki] SM INV/F INV Yank, Yankee

Y.C.I. ABBR = **Yacht Club d'Italia**

'Yemen ['jemen] SM: **lo ~** Yemen

yen [jen] SM INV (*moneta*) yen

'yiddish ['jidiʃ] AG INV, SM INV Yiddish

'yoga ['jɔga] AG INV, SM yoga (*cpd*)

yogurt ['jɔgurt] SM INV yog(h)urt

Zz

Z, z ['dzɛta] SM O F INV (*lettera*) Z, z; **Z come Zara** = Z for Zebra
zabaione [dzaba'jone] SM *dessert made of egg yolks, sugar and marsala*
zaffata [tsafˈfata] SF (*tanfo*) stench
zafferano [dzaffeˈrano] SM saffron
zaffiro [dzafˈfiro] SM sapphire
'zagara ['dzagara] SF orange blossom
zaiˈnetto [dzaiˈnetto] SM (small) rucksack
'zaino ['dzaino] SM rucksack
Zaˈire [dzaˈire] SM: **lo ~** Zaire
'Zambia ['dzambja] SM: **lo ~** Zambia
'zampa ['tsampa] SF (*di animale: gamba*) leg; (: *piede*) paw; **a quattro zampe** on all fours; **zampe di gallina** (*calligrafia*) scrawl; (*rughe*) crow's feet
zamˈpata [tsamˈpata] SF (*di cane, gatto*) blow with a paw
zampetˈtare [tsampetˈtare] /**72**/ VI to scamper
zampilˈlare [tsampilˈlare] /**72**/ VI to gush, spurt
zamˈpillo [tsamˈpillo] SM gush, spurt
zamˈpino [tsamˈpino] SM paw; **qui c'è sotto il suo ~** (*fig*) he's had a hand in this
zamˈpogna [tsamˈpoɲɲa] SF *instrument similar to bagpipes*
'zanna ['tsanna] SF (*di elefante*) tusk; (*di carnivori*) fang
zanˈzara [dzanˈdzara] SF mosquito
zanzariˈera [dzandzaˈrjɛra] SF mosquito net
'zappa ['tsappa] SF hoe
zapˈpare [tsapˈpare] /**72**/ VT to hoe
zappaˈtore [tsappaˈtore] SM (*Agr*) hoer
zappaˈtura [tsappaˈtura] SF (*Agr*) hoeing
'zapping ['tsapɪn] SM (*TV*) channel-hopping
zar, zaˈrina [tsar, tsaˈrina] SM/F tsar (tsarina)
'zattera ['dzattera] SF raft
zaˈvorra [dzaˈvɔrra] SF ballast
'zazzera ['tsattsera] SF shock of hair
'zebra ['dzɛbra] SF zebra; **zebre** SFPL (*Aut*) zebra crossing *sg* (BRIT), crosswalk *sg* (US)
zeˈbrato, -a [dzeˈbrato] AG with black and white stripes; **strisce zebrate,**
attraversamento ~ (*Aut*) zebra crossing (BRIT), crosswalk (US)
'zecca, -che ['tsekka] SF (*Zool*) tick; (*officina di monete*) mint
zecˈchino [tsekˈkino] SM gold coin; **oro ~** pure gold
zeˈlante [dzeˈlante] AG zealous
'zelo ['dzɛlo] SM zeal
'zenit ['dzɛnit] SM zenith
'zenzero ['dzendzero] SM ginger
'zeppa ['tseppa] SF wedge
'zeppo, -a ['tseppo] AG: **~ di** crammed *o* packed with
zerˈbino [dzerˈbino] SM doormat
'zero ['dzɛro] SM zero, nought; **vincere per tre a ~** (*Sport*) to win three-nil
'zeta ['dzɛta] SM O F zed, (the letter) z
'zia ['tsia] SF aunt
zibelˈlino [dzibelˈlino] SM sable
ziˈgano, -a [tsiˈgano] AG, SM/F gypsy
'zigomo ['dzigomo] SM cheekbone
zigriˈnare [dzigriˈnare] /**72**/ VT (*gen*) to knurl; (*pellame*) to grain; (*monete*) to mill
zigˈzag [dzigˈdzag] SM INV zigzag; **andare a ~** to zigzag
Zimˈbabwe [tsimˈbabwe] SM: **lo ~** Zimbabwe
zimˈbello [dzimˈbɛllo] SM (*oggetto di burle*) laughing-stock
'zinco ['dzinko] SM zinc
zingaˈresco, -a, -schi, -sche [dzingaˈresko] AG gypsy *cpd*
'zingaro, -a ['dzingaro] SM/F gipsy
'zio ['tsio] (*pl* **zii**) SM uncle; **zii** SMPL (*zio e zia*) uncle and aunt
zipˈpare [dzipˈpare] /**72**/ VT (*Inform: file*) to zip
ziˈtella [dziˈtɛlla] SF spinster; (*peg*) old maid
zitˈtire [tsitˈtire] /**55**/ VT to silence, hush *o* shut up ▶ VI to hiss
'zitto, -a ['tsitto] AG quiet, silent; **sta' ~!** be quiet!
zizˈzania [dzidˈdzanja] SF (*Bot*) darnel; (*fig*) discord; **gettare** *o* **seminare ~** to sow discord

Z

'zoccolo ['tsɔkkolo] SM (*calzatura*) clog; (*di cavallo ecc*) hoof; (*Archit*) plinth; (*di parete*) skirting (board); (*di armadio*) base

zodia'cale [dzodia'kale] AG zodiac *cpd*; **segno ~** sign of the zodiac

zo'diaco [dzo'diako] SM zodiac

zolfa'nello [tsolfa'nɛllo] SM (sulphur) match

'zolfo ['tsolfo] SM sulphur (BRIT), sulfur (US)

'zolla ['dzolla] SF clod (of earth)

zol'letta [dzol'letta] SF sugar lump

'zona ['dzɔna] SF zone, area; **~ di depressione** (*Meteor*) trough of low pressure; **~ disco** (*Aut*) ≈ meter zone; **~ industriale** industrial estate; **~ erogena** erogenous zone; **~ pedonale** pedestrian precinct; **~ verde** (*di abitato*) green area

'zonzo ['dzondzo]: **a ~** *av*: **andare a ~** to wander about, stroll about

'zoo ['dzɔo] SM INV zoo

zoolo'gia [dzoolo'dʒia] SF zoology

zoo'logico, -a, -ci, -che [dzoo'lɔdʒiko] AG zoological

zo'ologo, -a, -gi, -ghe [dzo'ɔlogo] SM/F zoologist

zoosa'fari [dzoosa'fari] SM INV safari park

zoo'tecnico, -a, -ci, -che [dzoo'tɛkniko] AG zootechnical; **il patrimonio ~ di un paese** a country's livestock resources

zoppi'care [tsoppi'kare] /**20**/ VI to limp; (*fig: mobile*) to be shaky, rickety

'zoppo, -a ['tsɔppo] AG lame; (*fig: mobile*) shaky, rickety

zoti'cone [dzoti'kone] SM lout

ZTL [dzetati'ɛlle] SIGLA F (= *Zona a Traffico Limitato*) *controlled traffic zone*

zu'ava [dzu'ava] SF: **pantaloni alla ~** knickerbockers

'zucca, -che ['tsukka] SF (*Bot*) marrow (BRIT), vegetable marrow (US); pumpkin; (*scherzoso*) head

zucche'rare [tsukke'rare] /**72**/ VT to put sugar in

zucche'rato, -a [tsukke'rato] AG sweet, sweetened

zuccheri'era [tsukke'rjɛra] SF sugar bowl

zuccheri'ficio [tsukkeri'fitʃo] SM sugar refinery

zucche'rino, -a [tsukke'rino] AG sugary, sweet

'zucchero ['tsukkero] SM sugar; **~ di canna** cane sugar; **~ caramellato** caramel; **~ filato** candy floss, cotton candy (US); **~ a velo** icing sugar (BRIT), confectioner's sugar (US)

zucche'roso, -a [tsukke'roso] AG sugary

zuc'china [tsuk'kina] SF, **zuc'chino** [tsuk'kino] SM courgette (BRIT), zucchini (US)

zuc'cotto [tsuk'kɔtto] SM ice-cream sponge

'zuffa ['tsuffa] SF brawl

zufo'lare [tsufo'lare] /**72**/ VT, VI to whistle

'zufolo ['tsufolo] SM (*Mus*) flageolet

'zuppa ['tsuppa] SF soup; (*fig*) mixture, muddle; **~ inglese** (*Cuc*) dessert made with sponge cake, custard and chocolate, ≈ trifle (BRIT)

zuppi'era [tsup'pjɛra] SF soup tureen

'zuppo, -a ['tsuppo] AG: **~ (di)** drenched (with), soaked (with)

Zu'rigo [dzu'rigo] SF Zurich

ENGLISH–ITALIAN

INGLESE–ITALIANO

Aa

A, a [eɪ] N (letter) A, a f inv or m inv; (Scol: mark) ≈ 10 (ottimo); (Mus): **A** la m; **A for Andrew**, (US) **A for Able** ≈ A come Ancona; **from A to Z** dall'A alla Z; **A road** n (BRIT Aut) ≈ strada statale; **A shares** npl (BRIT Stock Exchange) azioni fpl senza diritto di voto; **A to Z**® n stradario

(KEYWORD)

a [ə] (before vowel or silent h: an) INDEF ART **1** un, uno (+ s impure, gn, pn, ps, x, z), una f, un' + vowel; **a book** un libro; **a mirror** uno specchio; **an apple** una mela; **she's a doctor** è medico
2 (instead of the number "one") un(o), una f; **a year ago** un anno fa; **a hundred/thousand pounds** cento/mille sterline
3 (in expressing ratios, prices etc) a, per; **3 a day/week** 3 al giorno/alla settimana; **10 km an hour** 10 km all'ora; **£5 a person** 5 sterline a persona or per persona

a. ABBR = **acre**
A2 N ABBR (BRIT Scol) seconda parte del diploma di studi superiori chiamato "A level"
AA N ABBR (BRIT: = Automobile Association) ≈ A.C.I. m (= Automobile Club d'Italia); (US: = Associate in/of Arts) titolo di studio; (= Alcoholics Anonymous) A.A. f (= Anonima Alcolisti); (Mil) = **anti-aircraft**
AAA N ABBR (= American Automobile Association) ≈ A.C.I. m (= Automobile Club d'Italia); (BRIT) = **Amateur Athletics Association**
A & R N ABBR (Mus) = **artists and repertoire**; **~ man** talent scout m inv
AAUP N ABBR (= American Association of University Professors) associazione dei professori universitari
AB ABBR (BRIT) = **able-bodied seaman**; (CANADA) = **Alberta**
aback [ə'bæk] ADV: **to be taken ~** essere sbalordito(-a)
abacus ['æbəkəs] (pl **abaci** [-saɪ]) N pallottoliere m, abaco
abandon [ə'bændən] VT abbandonare ▶ N abbandono; **to ~ ship** abbandonare la nave;

with ~ sfrenatamente, spensieratamente
abandoned [ə'bændənd] ADJ (child, house etc) abbandonato(-a); (unrestrained: manner) disinvolto(-a)
abase [ə'beɪs] VT: **to ~ o.s. (so far as to do)** umiliarsi or abbassarsi (al punto di fare)
abashed [ə'bæʃt] ADJ imbarazzato(-a)
abate [ə'beɪt] VI calmarsi
abatement [ə'beɪtmənt] N (of pollution, noise) soppressione f, eliminazione f; **noise ~ society** associazione f per la lotta contro i rumori
abattoir ['æbətwɑːʳ] N (BRIT) mattatoio
abbey ['æbɪ] N abbazia, badia
abbot ['æbət] N abate m
abbreviate [ə'briːvɪeɪt] VT abbreviare
abbreviation [əbriːvɪ'eɪʃən] N abbreviazione f
ABC N ABBR (= American Broadcasting Company) rete televisiva americana
abdicate ['æbdɪkeɪt] VT abdicare a ▶ VI abdicare
abdication [æbdɪ'keɪʃən] N abdicazione f
abdomen ['æbdəmən] N addome m
abdominal [æb'dɔmɪnl] ADJ addominale
abduct [æb'dʌkt] VT rapire
abduction [æb'dʌkʃən] N rapimento
Aberdonian [æbə'dəʊnɪən] ADJ di Aberdeen ▶ N abitante mf di Aberdeen, originario(-a) di Aberdeen
aberration [æbə'reɪʃən] N aberrazione f
abet [ə'bɛt] VT see **aid**
abeyance [ə'beɪəns] N: **in ~** in sospeso
abhor [əb'hɔːʳ] VT aborrire
abhorrent [əb'hɔrənt] ADJ odioso(-a)
abide [ə'baɪd] VT sopportare; **I can't ~ it/him** non lo posso soffrire or sopportare ▶ **abide by** VT FUS conformarsi a
abiding [ə'baɪdɪŋ] ADJ (memory etc) persistente, duraturo(-a)
ability [ə'bɪlɪtɪ] N abilità f inv; **to the best of my ~** con il massimo impegno
abject ['æbdʒɛkt] ADJ (poverty) abietto(-a); (apology) umiliante; (coward) indegno(-a), vile

ablaze [ə'bleɪz] ADJ in fiamme; **~ with light** risplendente di luce

able ['eɪbl] ADJ capace; **to be ~ to do sth** essere capace di fare qc, poter fare qc

able-bodied ['eɪbl'bɔdɪd] ADJ robusto(-a)

able-bodied seaman N (BRIT) marinaio scelto

ably ['eɪblɪ] ADV abilmente

ABM N ABBR (= anti-ballistic missile) ABM m

abnormal [æb'nɔːməl] ADJ anormale

abnormality [æbnɔːˈmælɪtɪ] N (condition) anormalità; (instance) anomalia

aboard [ə'bɔːd] ADV a bordo ▶ PREP a bordo di; **~ the train** in or sul treno

abode [ə'bəud] N (old) dimora; (Law) domicilio, dimora; **of no fixed ~** senza fissa dimora

abolish [ə'bɔlɪʃ] VT abolire

abolition [æbəu'lɪʃən] N abolizione f

abominable [ə'bɔmɪnəbl] ADJ abominevole

aborigine [æbə'rɪdʒɪnɪ] N aborigeno(-a)

abort [ə'bɔːt] VT (Med, fig) abortire; (Comput) interrompere l'esecuzione di

abortion [ə'bɔːʃən] N aborto; **to have an ~** avere un aborto, abortire

abortionist [ə'bɔːʃənɪst] N abortista mf

abortive [ə'bɔːtɪv] ADJ abortivo(-a)

abound [ə'baund] VI abbondare; **to ~ in** abbondare di

(KEYWORD)

about [ə'baut] ADV **1** (approximately) circa, quasi; **about a hundred/thousand** un centinaio/migliaio, circa cento/mille; **it takes about 10 hours** ci vogliono circa 10 ore; **at about 2 o'clock** verso le 2; **I've just about finished** ho quasi finito; **it's about here** è qui intorno, è qui vicino

2 (referring to place) qua e là, in giro; **to leave things lying about** lasciare delle cose in giro; **to run about** correre qua e là; **to walk about** camminare; **is Paul about?** (BRIT) hai visto Paul in giro?; **it's the other way about** (BRIT) è il contrario

3: **to be about to do sth** stare per fare qc; **I'm not about to do all that for nothing** non ho intenzione di fare tutto questo per niente

▶ PREP **1** (relating to) su, di; **a book about London** un libro su Londra; **what is it about?** di che si tratta?; (book, film etc) di cosa tratta?; **we talked about it** ne abbiamo parlato; **do something about it!** fai qualcosa!; **what** or **how about doing this?** che ne dici di fare questo?

2 (referring to place): **to walk about the town** camminare per la città; **her clothes were scattered about the room** i suoi vestiti erano sparsi or in giro per tutta la stanza

about-face [ə'baut'feɪs], **about-turn** [ə'baut'tɜːn] N (Mil) dietro front m inv

above [ə'bʌv] ADV, PREP sopra; **mentioned ~** suddetto; **costing ~ £10** più caro di 10 sterline; **he's not ~ a bit of blackmail** non rifuggirebbe dal ricatto; **~ all** soprattutto

aboveboard [ə'bʌv'bɔːd] ADJ aperto(-a); onesto(-a)

abrasion [ə'breɪʒən] N abrasione f

abrasive [ə'breɪzɪv] ADJ abrasivo(-a)

abreast [ə'brɛst] ADV di fianco; **3 ~** per 3 di fronte; **to keep ~ of** tenersi aggiornato su

abridge [ə'brɪdʒ] VT ridurre

abroad [ə'brɔːd] ADV all'estero; **there is a rumour ~ that ...** (fig) si sente dire in giro che ..., circola la voce che ...

abrupt [ə'brʌpt] ADJ (steep) erto(-a); (sudden) improvviso(-a); (gruff, blunt) brusco(-a)

abscess ['æbsɪs] N ascesso

abscond [əb'skɔnd] VI scappare

absence ['æbsəns] N assenza; **in the ~ of** (person) in assenza di; (thing) in mancanza di

absent ['æbsənt] ADJ assente; **to be ~ without leave** (Mil etc) essere assente ingiustificato

absentee [æbsən'tiː] N assente mf

absenteeism [æbsən'tiːɪzəm] N assenteismo

absent-minded ['æbsənt'maɪndɪd] ADJ distratto(-a)

absent-mindedness ['æbsənt'maɪndɪdnɪs] N distrazione f

absolute ['æbsəluːt] ADJ assoluto(-a)

absolutely [æbsə'luːtlɪ] ADV assolutamente

absolve [əb'zɔlv] VT: **to ~ sb (from)** (sin etc) assolvere qn (da); **to ~ sb from** (oath) sciogliere qn da

absorb [əb'sɔːb] VT assorbire; **to be absorbed in a book** essere immerso(-a) in un libro

absorbent [əb'sɔːbənt] ADJ assorbente

absorbent cotton [əb'zɔːbənt-] N (US) cotone m idrofilo

absorbing [əb'sɔːbɪŋ] ADJ avvincente, molto interessante

absorption [əb'sɔːpʃən] N assorbimento

abstain [əb'steɪn] VI: **to ~ (from)** astenersi (da)

abstemious [əb'stiːmɪəs] ADJ astemio(-a)

abstention [əb'stɛnʃən] N astensione f

abstinence ['æbstɪnəns] N astinenza

abstract ['æbstrækt] ADJ astratto(-a) ▶ N (summary) riassunto ▶ VT [æb'strækt] estrarre

absurd [əb'sɜːd] ADJ assurdo(-a)

absurdity [əb'sɜːdɪtɪ] N assurdità f inv

ABTA ['æbtə] N ABBR = **Association of British Travel Agents**

Abu Dhabi ['æbuː'dɑːbɪ] N Abu Dhabi f

abundance [ə'bʌndəns] N abbondanza

abundant [ə'bʌndənt] ADJ abbondante
abuse N [ə'bju:s] abuso; *(insults)* ingiurie *fpl*
  ▶ VT [ə'bju:z] abusare di; **open to ~** che si
  presta ad abusi
abusive [ə'bju:sɪv] ADJ ingiurioso(-a)
abysmal [ə'bɪzməl] ADJ spaventoso(-a)
abyss [ə'bɪs] N abisso
AC N ABBR *(US)* = **athletic club**
a/c ABBR *(Banking etc)* = **account**; *(= account current)* c
academic [ækə'dɛmɪk] ADJ accademico(-a);
  (pej: issue) puramente formale ▶ N
  universitario(-a)
academic year N anno accademico
academy [ə'kædəmɪ] N *(learned body)*
  accademia; *(school)* scuola privata; **military/
  naval ~** scuola militare/navale; **~ of music**
  conservatorio
ACAS ['eɪkæs] N ABBR *(BRIT:* = *Advisory,
  Conciliation and Arbitration Service)* comitato
  governativo per il miglioramento della
  contrattazione collettiva
accede [æk'si:d] VI: **to ~ to** *(request)* accedere
  a; *(throne)* ascendere a
accelerate [æk'sɛləreɪt] VT, VI accelerare
acceleration [æksɛlə'reɪʃən] N
  accelerazione *f*
accelerator [æk'sɛləreɪtəʳ] N acceleratore *m*
accent ['æksɛnt] N accento
accentuate [æk'sɛntjueɪt] VT *(syllable)*
  accentuare; *(need, difference etc)* accentuare,
  mettere in risalto *or* in evidenza
accept [ək'sɛpt] VT accettare
acceptable [ək'sɛptəbl] ADJ accettabile
acceptance [ək'sɛptəns] N accettazione *f*; **to
  meet with general ~** incontrare il favore *or*
  il consenso generale
access ['æksɛs] N accesso ▶ VT *(Comput)*
  accedere a; **to have ~ to** avere accesso a; **the
  burglars gained ~ through a window** i
  ladri sono riusciti a penetrare da *or*
  attraverso una finestra
accessible [æk'sɛsəbl] ADJ accessibile
accession [æk'sɛʃən] N *(addition)* aggiunta;
  (to library) accessione *f*, acquisto; *(of king)*
  ascesa *or* salita al trono
accessory [æk'sɛsərɪ] N accessorio; *(Law)*:
  ~ to complice *mf* di; **toilet accessories** *npl*
  (BRIT) articoli *mpl* da toilette
access road N strada d'accesso; *(to motorway)*
  raccordo di entrata
access time N *(Comput)* tempo di accesso
accident ['æksɪdənt] N incidente *m*; *(chance)*
  caso; **to meet with** *or* **to have an ~** avere un
  incidente; **I've had an ~** ho avuto un
  incidente; **accidents at work** infortuni *mpl*
  sul lavoro; **by ~** per caso
accidental [æksɪ'dɛntl] ADJ accidentale
accidentally [æksɪ'dɛntəlɪ] ADV per caso

Accident and Emergency Department N
  (BRIT) pronto soccorso
accident insurance N assicurazione *f* contro
  gli infortuni
accident-prone ['æksɪdənt'prəun] ADJ:
  he's very ~ è un vero passaguai
acclaim [ə'kleɪm] VT acclamare ▶ N
  acclamazione *f*
acclamation [æklə'meɪʃən] N *(approval)*
  acclamazione *f*; *(applause)* applauso
acclimatize [ə'klaɪmətaɪz], *(US)* **acclimate**
  [ə'klaɪmeɪt] VT: **to become acclimatized**
  acclimatarsi
accolade ['ækəleɪd] N encomio
accommodate [ə'kɔmədeɪt] VT alloggiare;
  (oblige, help) favorire; **this car
  accommodates 4 people comfortably**
  quest'auto può trasportare comodamente
  4 persone
accommodating [ə'kɔmədeɪtɪŋ] ADJ
  compiacente
accommodation [əkɔmə'deɪʃən] N, *(US)*
  accommodations [əkɔmə'deɪʃənz] NPL
  alloggio; **seating ~** *(BRIT)* posti a sedere;
  "~ to let" *(BRIT)* "camere in affitto"; **have
  you any ~?** avete posto?
accompaniment [ə'kʌmpənɪmənt] N
  accompagnamento
accompanist [ə'kʌmpənɪst] N *(Mus)*
  accompagnatore(-trice)
accompany [ə'kʌmpənɪ] VT accompagnare
accomplice [ə'kʌmplɪs] N complice *mf*
accomplish [ə'kʌmplɪʃ] VT compiere;
  (achieve) ottenere; *(goal)* raggiungere
accomplished [ə'kʌmplɪʃt] ADJ *(person)*
  esperto(-a)
accomplishment [ə'kʌmplɪʃmənt] N
  compimento; realizzazione *f*; *(thing achieved)*
  risultato; **accomplishments** NPL *(skills)* doti
  fpl
accord [ə'kɔ:d] N accordo ▶ VT accordare; **of
  his own ~** di propria iniziativa; **with one ~**
  all'unanimità, di comune accordo
accordance [ə'kɔ:dəns] N: **in ~ with** in
  conformità con
according [ə'kɔ:dɪŋ]: **~ to** *prep* secondo; **it
  went ~ to plan** è andata secondo il previsto
accordingly [ə'kɔ:dɪŋlɪ] ADV in conformità
accordion [ə'kɔ:dɪən] N fisarmonica
accost [ə'kɔst] VT avvicinare
account [ə'kaunt] N *(Comm)* conto; *(report)*
  descrizione *f*; **accounts** NPL *(Comm)* conti
  mpl; **"~ payee only"** *(BRIT)* "assegno non
  trasferibile"; **to keep an ~ of** tenere nota di;
  **to bring sb to ~ for sth/for having done
  sth** chiedere a qn di render conto di qc/per
  aver fatto qc; **by all accounts** a quanto si
  dice; **of little ~** di poca importanza; **on ~** in
  acconto; **to buy sth on ~** comprare qc a

credito; **on no** ~ per nessun motivo; **on** ~ **of** a causa di; **to take into** ~, **take** ~ **of** tener conto di

▸ **account for** VT FUS (*explain*) spiegare; giustificare; **all the children were accounted for** nessun bambino mancava all'appello

accountability [ə'kauntə'bılıtı] N responsabilità

accountable [ə'kauntəbl] ADJ responsabile; **to be held** ~ **for sth** dover rispondere di qc; ~ **(to)** responsabile (verso)

accountancy [ə'kauntənsı] N ragioneria

accountant [ə'kauntənt] N ragioniere(-a)

accounting [ə'kauntıŋ] N contabilità

accounting period N esercizio finanziario, periodo contabile

account number N numero di conto

account payable N conto passivo

account receivable N conto da esigere

accredited [ə'kredıtıd] ADJ accreditato(-a)

accretion [ə'kri:ʃən] N accrescimento

accrue [ə'kru:] VI (*mount up*) aumentare; **to** ~ **to** derivare a; **accrued charges** ratei *mpl* passivi; **accrued interest** interesse *m* maturato

accumulate [ə'kju:mjuleıt] VT accumulare ▸ VI accumularsi

accumulation [əkju:mju'leıʃən] N accumulazione *f*

accuracy ['ækjurəsı] N precisione *f*

accurate ['ækjurıt] ADJ preciso(-a)

accurately ['ækjurıtlı] ADV precisamente

accusation [ækju'zeıʃən] N accusa

accusative [ə'kju:zətıv] N (*Ling*) accusativo

accuse [ə'kju:z] VT accusare

accused [ə'kju:zd] N accusato(-a)

accuser [ə'kju:zə'] N accusatore(-trice)

accustom [ə'kʌstəm] VT abituare; **to** ~ **o.s. to sth** abituarsi a qc

accustomed [ə'kʌstəmd] ADJ (*usual*) abituale; ~ **to** abituato(-a) a

AC/DC ABBR (= *alternating current/direct current*) c.a./c.c.

ACE [eıs] N ABBR = **American Council on Education**

ace [eıs] N asso; **within an** ~ **of** (*BRIT*) a un pelo da

acerbic [ə'sə:bık] ADJ (*also fig*) acido(-a)

acetate ['æsıteıt] N acetato

ache [eık] N male *m*, dolore *m* ▸ VI (*be sore*) far male, dolere; (*yearn*): **to** ~ **to do sth** morire dalla voglia di fare qc; **I've got stomach** ~ *or* (*US*) **a stomach** ~ ho mal di stomaco; **my head aches** mi fa male la testa; **I'm aching all over** mi duole dappertutto

achieve [ə'tʃi:v] VT (*aim*) raggiungere; (*victory, success*) ottenere; (*task*) compiere

achievement [ə'tʃi:vmənt] N compimento; successo

Achilles heel [ə'kıli:z-] N tallone *m* d'Achille

acid ['æsıd] ADJ acido(-a) ▸ N acido

acidity [ə'sıdıtı] N acidità

acid rain N pioggia acida

acid test N (*fig*) prova del fuoco

acknowledge [ək'nɔlıdʒ] VT (*fact*) riconoscere; (*letter: also:* **acknowledge receipt of**) accusare ricevuta di

acknowledgement [ək'nɔlıdʒmənt] N riconoscimento; (*of letter*) conferma; **acknowledgements** NPL (*in book*) ringraziamenti *mpl*

ACLU N ABBR (= *American Civil Liberties Union*) unione americana per le libertà civili

acme ['ækmı] N culmine *m*, acme *m*

acne ['æknı] N acne *f*

acorn ['eıkɔ:n] N ghianda

acoustic [ə'ku:stık] ADJ acustico(-a); *see also* **acoustics**

acoustic coupler [-'kʌplə'] N (*Comput*) accoppiatore *m* acustico

acoustics [ə'ku:stıks] N, NPL acustica

acquaint [ə'kweınt] VT: **to** ~ **sb with sth** far sapere qc a qn; **to be acquainted with** (*person*) conoscere

acquaintance [ə'kweıntəns] N conoscenza; (*person*) conoscente *mf*; **to make sb's** ~ fare la conoscenza di qn

acquiesce [ækwı'ɛs] VI (*agree*): **to** ~ **(in)** acconsentire (a)

acquire [ə'kwaıə'] VT acquistare

acquired [ə'kwaıəd] ADJ acquisito(-a); **it's an** ~ **taste** è una cosa che si impara ad apprezzare

acquisition [ækwı'zıʃən] N acquisto

acquisitive [ə'kwızıtıv] ADJ a cui piace accumulare le cose

acquit [ə'kwıt] VT assolvere; **to** ~ **o.s. well** comportarsi bene

acquittal [ə'kwıtl] N assoluzione *f*

acre ['eıkə'] N acro (= 4047 m^2)

acreage ['eıkərıdʒ] N superficie *f* in acri

acrid ['ækrıd] ADJ (*smell*) acre, pungente; (*fig*) pungente

acrimonious [ækrı'məunıəs] ADJ astioso(-a)

acrobat ['ækrəbæt] N acrobata *mf*

acrobatic [ækrə'bætık] ADJ acrobatico(-a)

acrobatics [ækrə'bætıks] N acrobatica ▸ NPL acrobazie *fpl*

acronym ['ækrənım] N acronimo

Acropolis [ə'krɔpəlıs] N: **the** ~ l'Acropoli *f*

across [ə'krɔs] PREP (*on the other side*) dall'altra parte di; (*crosswise*) attraverso ▸ ADV dall'altra parte; in larghezza; **to walk** ~ **(the road)** attraversare (la strada); **to run/swim** ~ attraversare di corsa/a nuoto; **to take sb** ~ **the road** far attraversare la strada a qn;

~ **from** di fronte a; **the lake is 12 km** ~ il lago ha una larghezza di 12 km *or* è largo 12 km; **to get sth** ~ **to sb** (*fig*) far capire qc a qn

acrylic [ə'krɪlɪk] ADJ acrilico(-a) ▶ N acrilico

ACT N ABBR (= *American College Test*) esame di ammissione a college

act [ækt] N atto; (*in music-hall etc*) numero; (*Law*) decreto ▶ VI agire; (*Theat*) recitare; (*pretend*) fingere ▶ VT (*part*) recitare; **to catch sb in the** ~ cogliere qn in flagrante *or* sul fatto; **it's only an** ~ è tutta scena, è solo una messinscena; ~ **of God** (*Law*) calamità *f inv* naturale; **to** ~ **Hamlet** (BRIT) recitare la parte di Amleto; **to** ~ **the fool** (BRIT) fare lo stupido; **to** ~ **as** agire da; **it acts as a deterrent** serve da deterrente; **acting in my capacity as chairman, I ...** in qualità di presidente, io ...

▶ **act on** VT: **to** ~ **on sth** agire in base a qc

▶ **act out** VT (*event*) ricostruire; (*fantasies*) dare forma concreta a

▶ **act up** (*col*) VI (*person*) comportarsi male; (*knee, back, injury*) fare male; (*machine*) non funzionare

acting ['æktɪŋ] ADJ che fa le funzioni di ▶ N (*of actor*) recitazione *f*; **to do some** ~ fare del teatro (*or* del cinema); **he is the** ~ **manager** fa le veci del direttore

action ['ækʃən] N azione *f*; (*Mil*) combattimento; (*Law*) processo ▶ VT (*Comm: request*) evadere; (*tasks*) portare a termine; **to take** ~ agire; **to put a plan into** ~ realizzare un piano; **out of** ~ fuori combattimento; (*machine etc*) fuori servizio; **killed in** ~ (*Mil*) ucciso in combattimento; **to bring an** ~ **against sb** (*Law*) intentare causa contro qn

action replay N (BRIT TV) replay *m inv*

activate ['æktɪveɪt] VT (*mechanism*) fare funzionare, attivare; (*Chem, Physics*) rendere attivo(-a)

active ['æktɪv] ADJ attivo(-a); **to play an** ~ **part in** partecipare attivamente a

active duty N (US Mil) = **active service**

actively ['æktɪvlɪ] ADV (*participate*) attivamente; (*discourage, dislike*) vivamente

active partner N (*Comm*) socio effettivo

active service N (BRIT Mil): **to be on** ~ prestar servizio in zona di operazioni

activist ['æktɪvɪst] N attivista *mf*

activity [æk'tɪvɪtɪ] N attività *f inv*

activity holiday N vacanza attiva (*in bici, a cavallo, in barca, a vela ecc.*)

actor ['æktər] N attore *m*

actress ['æktrɪs] N attrice *f*

actual ['æktjuəl] ADJ reale, vero(-a)

actually ['æktjuəlɪ] ADV veramente; (*even*) addirittura

actuary ['æktjuərɪ] N attuario(-a)

actuate ['æktjueɪt] VT attivare

acuity [ə'kjuːɪtɪ] N acutezza

acumen ['ækjumən] N acume *m*; **business** ~ fiuto negli affari

acupuncture ['ækjupʌŋktʃər] N agopuntura

acute [ə'kjuːt] ADJ acuto(-a); (*mind, person*) perspicace

AD ADV ABBR (= *Anno Domini*) d. C. ▶ N ABBR (US Mil) = **active duty**

ad [æd] N ABBR = **advertisement**

adamant ['ædəmənt] ADJ irremovibile

Adam's apple ['ædəmz-] N pomo di Adamo

adapt [ə'dæpt] VT adattare ▶ VI: **to** ~ (**to**) adattarsi (a)

adaptability [ədæptə'bɪlɪtɪ] N adattabilità

adaptable [ə'dæptəbl] ADJ (*device*) adattabile; (*person*) che sa adattarsi

adaptation [ædæp'teɪʃən] N adattamento

adapter, adaptor [ə'dæptər] N (*Elec*) adattatore *m*

ADC N ABBR (Mil) = **aide-de-camp**; (*US: = Aid to Dependent Children*) sussidio per figli a carico

add [æd] VT aggiungere; (*figures*) addizionare ▶ VI: **to** ~ **to** (*increase*) aumentare ▶ N (*Internet*): **thanks for the** ~ grazie per avermi aggiunto (come amico)

▶ **add on** VT aggiungere

▶ **add up** VT (*figures*) addizionare ▶ VI (*fig*): **it doesn't** ~ **up** non ha senso; **it doesn't** ~ **up to much** non è un granché

adder ['ædər] N vipera

addict ['ædɪkt] N tossicomane *mf*; (*fig*) fanatico(-a); **heroin** ~ eroinomane *mf*; **drug** ~ tossicodipendente *mf*, tossicomane *mf*

addicted [ə'dɪktɪd] ADJ: **to be** ~ **to** (*drink etc*) essere dedito(-a) a; (*fig: football etc*) essere tifoso(-a) di

addiction [ə'dɪkʃən] N (*Med*) tossicodipendenza

addictive [ə'dɪktɪv] ADJ che dà assuefazione

adding machine ['ædɪŋ-] N addizionatrice *f*

Addis Ababa ['ædɪs'æbəbə] N Addis Abeba *f*

addition [ə'dɪʃən] N addizione *f*; (*thing added*) aggiunta; **in** ~ inoltre; **in** ~ **to** oltre

additional [ə'dɪʃənl] ADJ supplementare

additive ['ædɪtɪv] N additivo

address [ə'drɛs] N (*gen, Comput*) indirizzo; (*talk*) discorso ▶ VT indirizzare; (*speak to*) fare un discorso a; (*issue*) affrontare; **my** ~ **is ...** il mio indirizzo è ...; **form of** ~ (*gen*) formula di cortesia; (*in letters*) formula d'indirizzo *or* di intestazione; **to** ~ **o.s. to sth** indirizzare le proprie energie verso qc; **absolute/relative** ~ (*Comput*) indirizzo assoluto/relativo

address book N rubrica

addressee [ædrɛ'siː] N destinatario(-a)

Aden ['eɪdən] N: **the Gulf of** ~ il golfo di Aden

adenoids ['ædɪnɔɪdz] NPL adenoidi *fpl*

adept ['ædɛpt] ADJ: ~ **at** esperto(-a) in

adequate ['ædɪkwɪt] ADJ (*description, reward*)

adeguato(-a); (*amount*) sufficiente; **to feel ~ to a task** sentirsi all'altezza di un compito

adequately ['ædɪkwɪtlɪ] ADV adeguatamente; sufficientemente

adhere [əd'hɪə^r] VI: **to ~ to** aderire a; (*fig: rule, decision*) seguire

adhesion [əd'hi:ʒən] N adesione *f*

adhesive [əd'hi:zɪv] ADJ adesivo(-a) ▸ N adesivo; **~ tape** (*BRIT: for parcels etc*) nastro adesivo; (*US Med*) cerotto adesivo

ad hoc [æd'hɔk] ADJ (*decision*) ad hoc *inv*; (*committee*) apposito(-a)

ad infinitum ['ædɪnfɪ'naɪtəm] ADV all'infinito

adjacent [ə'dʒeɪsənt] ADJ adiacente; **~ to** accanto a

adjective ['ædʒɛktɪv] N aggettivo

adjoin [ə'dʒɔɪn] VT essere contiguo(-a) *or* attiguo(-a)

adjoining [ə'dʒɔɪnɪŋ] ADJ accanto *inv*, adiacente ▸ PREP accanto a

adjourn [ə'dʒə:n] VT rimandare, aggiornare; (*US: end*) sospendere ▸ VI essere aggiornato(-a); (*Parliament*) sospendere i lavori; (*go*) spostarsi; **to ~ a meeting till the following week** aggiornare *or* rinviare un incontro alla settimana seguente; **they adjourned to the pub** (*col*) si sono trasferiti al pub

adjournment [ə'dʒə:nmənt] N rinvio, aggiornamento; sospensione *f*

Adjt ABBR (*Mil*) = **adjutant**

adjudicate [ə'dʒu:dɪkeɪt] VT (*contest*) giudicare; (*claim*) decidere su

adjudication [ədʒu:dɪ'keɪʃən] N decisione *f*

adjust [ə'dʒʌst] VT aggiustare; (*Comm: change*) rettificare ▸ VI: **to ~ (to)** adattarsi (a)

adjustable [ə'dʒʌstəbl] ADJ regolabile

adjuster [ə'dʒʌstə^r] N *see* **loss adjuster**

adjustment [ə'dʒʌstmənt] N (*Psych*) adattamento; (*of machine*) regolazione *f*; (*of prices, wages*) aggiustamento

adjutant ['ædʒətənt] N aiutante *m*

ad-lib [æd'lɪb] VT, VI improvvisare ▸ N improvvisazione *f* ▸ ADV: **ad lib** a piacere, a volontà

adman ['ædmæn] N (*irreg*) (*col*) pubblicitario

admin [æd'mɪn] N ABBR (*col*) = **administration**

administer [əd'mɪnɪstə^r] VT amministrare; (*justice*) somministrare

administration [ədmɪnɪs'treɪʃən] N amministrazione *f*; **the A~** (*US*) il Governo

administrative [əd'mɪnɪstrətɪv] ADJ amministrativo(-a)

administrator [əd'mɪnɪstreɪtə^r] N amministratore(-trice)

admirable ['ædmərəbl] ADJ ammirevole

admiral ['ædmərəl] N ammiraglio

Admiralty ['ædmərəltɪ] N (*BRIT: also*: **Admiralty Board**) Ministero della Marina

admiration [ædmə'reɪʃən] N ammirazione *f*

admire [əd'maɪə^r] VT ammirare

admirer [əd'maɪərə^r] N ammiratore(-trice)

admiring [əd'maɪərɪŋ] ADJ (*glance etc*) di ammirazione

admissible [əd'mɪsəbl] ADJ ammissibile

admission [əd'mɪʃən] N ammissione *f*; (*to exhibition, nightclub etc*) ingresso; (*confession*) confessione *f*; **by his own ~** per sua ammissione; **"~ free"**, **"free ~"** "ingresso gratuito"

admit [əd'mɪt] VT ammettere; far entrare; (*agree*) riconoscere; **"children not admitted"** "vietato l'ingresso ai bambini"; **this ticket admits two** questo biglietto è valido per due persone; **I must ~ that ...** devo ammettere *or* confessare che ...
▸ **admit of** VT FUS lasciare adito a
▸ **admit to** VT FUS riconoscere

admittance [əd'mɪtəns] N ingresso; **"no ~"** "vietato l'ingresso"

admittedly [əd'mɪtɪdlɪ] ADV bisogna pur riconoscere (che)

admonish [əd'mɔnɪʃ] VT ammonire

ad nauseam [æd'nɔ:zɪæm] ADV fino alla nausea, a non finire

ado [ə'du:] N: **without (any) more ~** senza più indugi

adolescence [ædəu'lɛsns] N adolescenza

adolescent [ædəu'lɛsnt] ADJ, N adolescente *mf*

adopt [ə'dɔpt] VT adottare

adopted [ə'dɔptɪd] ADJ adottivo(-a)

adoption [ə'dɔpʃən] N adozione *f*

adore [ə'dɔ:^r] VT adorare

adoring [ə'dɔ:rɪŋ] ADJ adorante; **his ~ wife** sua moglie che lo adora

adoringly [ə'dɔ:rɪŋlɪ] ADV con adorazione

adorn [ə'dɔ:n] VT ornare

adornment [ə'dɔ:nmənt] N ornamento

ADP N ABBR = **automatic data processing**

adrenalin [ə'drɛnəlɪn] N adrenalina; **it gets the ~ going** ti dà una carica

Adriatic [eɪdrɪ'ætɪk] N: **the ~ (Sea)** il mare Adriatico, l'Adriatico

adrift [ə'drɪft] ADV alla deriva; **to come ~** (*boat*) andare alla deriva; (*wire, rope etc*) essersi staccato(-a) *or* sciolto(-a)

adroit [ə'drɔɪt] ADJ abile, destro(-a)

ADSL N ABBR (= *asymmetric digital subscriber line*) ADSL *m*

ADT ABBR (*US*: = *Atlantic Daylight Time*) ora legale di New York

adult ['ædʌlt] N adulto(-a) ▸ ADJ adulto(-a); (*work, education*) per adulti

adult education N scuola per adulti

adulterate [ə'dʌltəreɪt] VT adulterare

adulterer [ə'dʌltərəʳ] N adultero
adulteress [ə'dʌltərɪs] N adultera
adultery [ə'dʌltərɪ] N adulterio
adulthood ['ædʌlthud] N età adulta
advance [əd'vɑːns] N avanzamento; *(money)* anticipo ▸ ADJ *(booking etc)* in anticipo ▸ VT avanzare; *(date, money)* anticipare ▸ VI avanzare; **in ~** in anticipo; **to make advances to sb** *(gen)* fare degli approcci a qn; *(amorously)* fare delle avances a qn; **do I need to book in ~?** occorre che prenoti in anticipo?
advanced [əd'vɑːnst] ADJ avanzato(-a); *(Scol: studies)* superiore; **~ in years** avanti negli anni
advancement [əd'vɑːnsmənt] N avanzamento
advance notice N preavviso
advantage [əd'vɑːntɪdʒ] N *(also Tennis)* vantaggio; **to take ~ of** approfittarsi di; **it's to our ~** è nel nostro interesse, torna a nostro vantaggio
advantageous [ædvən'teɪdʒəs] ADJ vantaggioso(-a)
advent ['ædvənt] N avvento; **A~** *(Rel)* Avvento
Advent calendar N calendario dell'Avvento
adventure [əd'vɛntʃəʳ] N avventura
adventure playground N *area attrezzata di giochi per bambini con funi, strutture in legno ecc*
adventurous [əd'vɛntʃərəs] ADJ avventuroso(-a)
adverb ['ædvəːb] N avverbio
adversary ['ædvəsərɪ] N avversario(-a)
adverse ['ædvəːs] ADJ avverso(-a); **in ~ circumstances** nelle avversità; **~ to** contrario(-a) a
adversity [əd'vəːsɪtɪ] N avversità
advert ['ædvəːt] N ABBR *(BRIT)* = **advertisement**
advertise ['ædvətaɪz] VI, VT fare pubblicità *or* réclame (a), fare un'inserzione (per vendere); **to ~ for** *(staff)* cercare tramite annuncio
advertisement [əd'vəːtɪsmənt] N *(Comm)* réclame *f inv*, pubblicità *f inv*; *(in classified ads)* inserzione *f*
advertiser ['ædvətaɪzəʳ] N azienda che reclamizza un prodotto; *(in newspaper)* inserzionista *mf*
advertising ['ædvətaɪzɪŋ] N pubblicità
advertising agency N agenzia pubblicitaria *or* di pubblicità
advertising campaign N campagna pubblicitaria
advice [əd'vaɪs] N consigli *mpl*; *(notification)* avviso; **piece of ~** consiglio; **to ask (sb) for ~** chiedere il consiglio (di qn), chiedere un consiglio (a qn); **legal ~** consulenza legale; **to take legal ~** consultare un avvocato

advice note N *(BRIT)* avviso di spedizione
advisable [əd'vaɪzəbl] ADJ consigliabile
advise [əd'vaɪz] VT consigliare; **to ~ sb of sth** informare qn di qc; **to ~ sb against sth/ against doing sth** sconsigliare qc a qn/ a qn di fare qc; **you will be well/ill advised to go** fareste bene/male ad andare
advisedly [əd'vaɪzɪdlɪ] ADV *(deliberately)* deliberatamente
adviser [əd'vaɪzəʳ] N consigliere(-a); *(in business)* consulente *mf*, consigliere(-a)
advisory [-ərɪ, əd'vaɪzərɪ] ADJ consultivo(-a); **in an ~ capacity** in veste di consulente
advocate N ['ædvəkɪt] *(upholder)* sostenitore(-trice); *(Law)* avvocato (difensore) ▸ VT ['ædvəkeɪt] propugnare; **to be an ~ of** essere a favore di
advt. ABBR = **advertisement**
AEA N ABBR *(BRIT: = Atomic Energy Authority)* ente di controllo sulla ricerca e lo sviluppo dell'energia atomica
AEC N ABBR *(US: = Atomic Energy Commission)* ente di controllo sulla ricerca e lo sviluppo dell'energia atomica
Aegean (Sea) [iː'dʒiːən-] N *(mare m)* Egeo
aegis ['iːdʒɪs] N: **under the ~ of** sotto gli auspici di
aeon ['iːən] N eternità *f inv*
aerial ['ɛərɪəl] N antenna ▸ ADJ aereo(-a)
aerobatics ['ɛərəu'bætɪks] NPL acrobazia *sg* aerea; *(stunts)* acrobazie *fpl* aeree
aerobics [ɛə'rəubɪks] N aerobica
aerodrome ['ɛərədrəum] N *(BRIT)* aerodromo
aerodynamic ['ɛərəudaɪ'næmɪk] ADJ aerodinamico(-a)
aeronautics [ɛərə'nɔːtɪks] N aeronautica
aeroplane ['ɛərəpleɪn] *(BRIT)* N aeroplano
aerosol ['ɛərəsɔl] *(BRIT)* N aerosol *m inv*
aerospace industry ['ɛərəuspeɪs-] N industria aerospaziale
aesthetic [ɪs'θɛtɪk] ADJ estetico(-a)
afar [ə'fɑːʳ] ADV lontano; **from ~** da lontano
AFB N ABBR *(US)* = **Air Force Base**
AFDC N ABBR *(US: = Aid to Families with Dependent Children)* ≈ A.F. (= assegni familiari)
affable ['æfəbl] ADJ affabile
affair [ə'fɛəʳ] N affare *m*; *(also:* **love affair**) relazione *f* amorosa; **affairs** NPL *(business)* affari; **the Watergate ~** il caso Watergate
affect [ə'fɛkt] VT *(influence)* influire su, incidere su; *(feign)* fingere
affectation [æfɛk'teɪʃən] N affettazione *f*
affected [ə'fɛktɪd] ADJ affettato(-a)
affection [ə'fɛkʃən] N affetto
affectionate [ə'fɛkʃənɪt] ADJ affettuoso(-a)
affectionately [ə'fɛkʃənɪtlɪ] ADV affettuosamente
affidavit [æfɪ'deɪvɪt] N *(Law)* affidavit *m inv*

417

affiliated [əˈfɪlieɪtɪd] ADJ affiliato(-a);
~ **company** filiale f
affinity [əˈfɪnɪtɪ] N affinità f inv
affirm [əˈfəːm] VT affermare, asserire
affirmation [æfəˈmeɪʃən] N affermazione f
affirmative [əˈfəːmətɪv] ADJ affermativo(-a)
▶ N: **in the** ~ affermativamente
affix [əˈfɪks] VT apporre; attaccare
afflict [əˈflɪkt] VT affliggere
affliction [əˈflɪkʃən] N afflizione f
affluence [ˈæfluəns] N ricchezza
affluent [ˈæfluənt] ADJ ricco(-a); **the ~
society** la società del benessere
afford [əˈfɔːd] VT permettersi; (provide)
fornire; **I can't ~ the time** non ho
veramente il tempo; **can we ~ a car?**
possiamo permetterci un'automobile?
affordable [əˈfɔːdəbl] ADJ (che ha un prezzo)
abbordabile
affray [əˈfreɪ] N (BRIT Law) rissa
affront [əˈfrʌnt] N affronto
affronted [əˈfrʌntɪd] ADJ insultato(-a)
Afghan [ˈæfgæn] ADJ, N afgano(-a)
Afghanistan [æfˈgænɪstɑːn] N Afganistan m
afield [əˈfiːld] ADV: **far** ~ lontano
AFL-CIO N ABBR (= American Federation of Labor
and Congress of Industrial Organizations)
confederazione sindacale
afloat [əˈfləʊt] ADJ, ADV a galla
afoot [əˈfʊt] ADV: **there is something** ~ si sta
preparando qualcosa
aforementioned [əˈfɔːmɛnʃənd] ADJ
suddetto(-a)
aforesaid [əˈfɔːsɛd] ADJ suddetto(-a),
predetto(-a)
afraid [əˈfreɪd] ADJ impaurito(-a); **to be ~ of**
aver paura di; **to be ~ of doing** or **to do** aver
paura di fare; **to be ~ that** aver paura che; **I
am ~ that I'll be late** mi dispiace, ma farò
tardi; **I'm ~ so!** ho paura di sì!, temo proprio
di sì!; **I'm ~ not** no, mi dispiace, purtroppo
no
afresh [əˈfrɛʃ] ADV di nuovo
Africa [ˈæfrɪkə] N Africa
African [ˈæfrɪkən] ADJ, N africano(-a)
African-American ADJ, N afroamericano(-a)
Afrikaans [æfrɪˈkɑːns] N afrikaans m
Afrikaner [æfrɪˈkɑːnəʳ] N africaner m inv
Afro-American [ˈæfrəʊəˈmɛrɪkən] ADJ
afroamericano(-a)
Afro-Caribbean [ˈæfrəʊkærɪˈbɪən] ADJ
afrocaraibico(-a)
AFT N ABBR (= American Federation of Teachers)
sindacato degli insegnanti
aft [ɑːft] ADV a poppa, verso poppa
after [ˈɑːftəʳ] PREP, ADV dopo ▶ CONJ dopo che;
~ **dinner** dopo cena; **the day ~ tomorrow**
dopodomani; **what/who are you ~?** che/chi
cerca?; **the police are ~ him** è ricercato

dalla polizia; ~ **he left/having done** dopo
che se ne fu andato/dopo aver fatto; **to
name sb ~ sb** dare a qn il nome di qn; **it's
twenty ~ eight** (US) sono le otto e venti; **to
ask ~ sb** chiedere di qn; ~ **you!** prima lei!,
dopo di lei!; ~ **all** dopo tutto
afterbirth [ˈɑːftəbəːθ] N placenta
aftercare [ˈɑːftəkɛəʳ] N (BRIT Med) assistenza
medica post-degenza
after-effects [ˈɑːftərɪfɛkts] NPL conseguenze
fpl; (of illness) postumi mpl
afterlife [ˈɑːftəlaɪf] N vita dell'al di là
aftermath [ˈɑːftəmæθ] N conseguenze fpl; **in
the ~ of** nel periodo dopo
afternoon [ˈɑːftəˈnuːn] N pomeriggio; **good
~!** buon giorno!
afterparty [ˈɑːftəpɑːtɪ] N after-party m inv
afters [ˈɑːftəz] N (BRIT col: dessert) dessert m inv
after-sales service [ɑːftəˈseɪlz-] N servizio
assistenza clienti
after-shave [ˈɑːftəʃeɪv], **after-shave lotion**
[ˈɑːftəʃeɪv-] N dopobarba m inv
aftershock [ˈɑːftəʃɔk] N scossa di
assestamento
aftersun [ˈɑːftəsʌn] ADJ: ~ **(lotion/cream)**
(lozione f/crema) doposole m inv
aftertaste [ˈɑːftəteɪst] N retrogusto
afterthought [ˈɑːftəθɔːt] N: **as an** ~ come
aggiunta
afterwards [ˈɑːftəwədz], (US) **afterward**
ADV dopo
again [əˈgɛn] ADV di nuovo; **to begin/see** ~
ricominciare/rivedere; **he opened it** ~ l'ha
aperto di nuovo, l'ha riaperto; **not ...** ~ non
... più; ~ **and** ~ ripetutamente; **now and** ~ di
tanto in tanto, a volte
against [əˈgɛnst] PREP contro; ~ **a blue
background** su uno sfondo azzurro;
leaning ~ **the desk** appoggiato alla
scrivania; **(as)** ~ (BRIT) in confronto a, contro
age [eɪdʒ] N età f inv ▶ VT, VI invecchiare;
what ~ is he? quanti anni ha?; **he is 20
years of** ~ ha 20 anni; **aged 10** di 10 anni;
under ~ minorenne; **to come of** ~ diventare
maggiorenne; **it's been ages since ...** sono
secoli che ...; **the aged** gli anziani
aged [ˈeɪdʒd] ADJ: ~ **10** di 10 anni ▶ NPL
[ˈeɪdʒɪd]: **the** ~ gli anziani
age group N generazione f; **the 40 to 50** ~ le
persone fra i 40 e i 50 anni
ageing [ˈeɪdʒɪŋ] ADJ che diventa vecchio(-a);
an ~ **film star** una diva stagionata
ageless [ˈeɪdʒlɪs] ADJ senza età
age limit N limite m d'età
agency [ˈeɪdʒənsɪ] N agenzia; **through** or **by
the** ~ **of** grazie a
agenda [əˈdʒɛndə] N ordine m del giorno; **on
the** ~ all'ordine del giorno
agent [ˈeɪdʒənt] N agente m

aggravate ['ægrəveɪt] VT aggravare, peggiorare; (*annoy*) esasperare

aggravation [ægrə'veɪʃən] N peggioramento; esasperazione f

aggregate ['ægrɪgeɪt] N aggregato; **on ~** (*Sport*) con punteggio complessivo

aggression [ə'grɛʃən] N aggressione f

aggressive [ə'grɛsɪv] ADJ aggressivo(-a)

aggressiveness [ə'grɛsɪvnɪs] N aggressività

aggressor [ə'grɛsəʳ] N aggressore m

aggrieved [ə'gri:vd] ADJ addolorato(-a)

aggro ['ægrəʊ] N (*Brit col: behaviour*) aggressività f inv; (*hassle*) rottura

aghast [ə'gɑ:st] ADJ sbigottito(-a)

agile ['ædʒaɪl] ADJ agile

agility [ə'dʒɪlɪtɪ] N agilità f inv

agitate ['ædʒɪteɪt] VT turbare; agitare ▶ VI: **to ~ for** agitarsi per

agitated ['ædʒɪteɪtɪd] ADJ agitato(-a), turbato(-a)

agitator ['ædʒɪteɪtəʳ] N agitatore(-trice)

AGM N ABBR = **annual general meeting**

agnostic [æg'nɔstɪk] ADJ, N agnostico(-a)

ago [ə'gəʊ] ADV: **2 days ~** 2 giorni fa; **not long ~** poco tempo fa; **as long ~ as 1960** già nel 1960; **how long ~?** quanto tempo fa?

agog [ə'gɔg] ADJ: **(all) ~ (for)** ansioso(-a) (di), impaziente (di)

agonize ['ægənaɪz] VI: **to ~ (over)** angosciarsi (per)

agonizing ['ægənaɪzɪŋ] ADJ straziante

agony ['ægənɪ] N dolore m atroce; **I was in ~** avevo dei dolori atroci

agony aunt N (*Brit col*) chi tiene la rubrica della posta del cuore

agony column N posta del cuore

agree [ə'gri:] VT (*price*) pattuire ▶ VI: **to ~ (with)** essere d'accordo (con); (*Ling*) concordare (con); **to ~ to sth/to do sth** accettare qc/di fare qc; **to ~ that** (*admit*) ammettere che; **to ~ on sth** accordarsi su qc; **it was agreed that ...** è stato deciso (di comune accordo) che ...; **garlic doesn't ~ with me** l'aglio non mi va

agreeable [ə'gri:əbl] ADJ gradevole; (*willing*) disposto(-a); **are you ~ to this?** è d'accordo con questo?

agreed [ə'gri:d] ADJ (*time, place*) stabilito(-a); **to be ~** essere d'accordo

agreement [ə'gri:mənt] N accordo; **in ~** d'accordo; **by mutual ~** di comune accordo

agricultural [ægrɪ'kʌltʃərəl] ADJ agricolo(-a)

agriculture ['ægrɪkʌltʃəʳ] N agricoltura

aground [ə'graʊnd] ADV: **to run ~** arenarsi

ahead [ə'hɛd] ADV avanti; davanti; **~ of** davanti a; (*fig: schedule etc*) in anticipo su; **~ of time** in anticipo; **go ~!** avanti!; **go right** or **straight ~** tiri diritto; **they were (right) ~ of us** erano (proprio) davanti a noi

AI N ABBR = **Amnesty International**; (*Comput*) = **artificial intelligence**

AIB N ABBR (*Brit*: = *Accident Investigation Bureau*) ufficio d'inchiesta per incidenti aerei e simili

AID N ABBR = **artificial insemination by donor**; (*US*: = *Agency for International Development*) A.I.D. f

aid [eɪd] N aiuto ▶ VT aiutare; **with the ~ of** con l'aiuto di; **in ~ of** a favore di; **to ~ and abet** (*Law*) essere complice di

aide [eɪd] N (*person*) aiutante mf

aide-de-camp ['eɪddə'kɔŋ] N (*Mil*) aiutante m di campo

AIDS [eɪdz] N ABBR (= *acquired immune deficiency or immunodeficiency syndrome*) AIDS f

AIH N ABBR = **artificial insemination by husband**

ailing ['eɪlɪŋ] ADJ sofferente; (*fig: economy, industry etc*) in difficoltà

ailment ['eɪlmənt] N indisposizione f

aim [eɪm] VT: **to ~ sth at** (*gun*) mirare qc a, puntare qc a; (*camera, remark*) rivolgere qc a; (*missile*) lanciare qc contro; (*blow etc*) tirare qc a ▶ VI (*also*: **take aim**) prendere la mira ▶ N mira; **to ~ at** mirare; **to ~ to do** aver l'intenzione di fare

aimless ['eɪmlɪs] ADJ senza scopo

aimlessly ['eɪmlɪslɪ] ADV senza scopo

ain't [eɪnt] (*col*) = **am not; aren't; isn't**

air [ɛəʳ] N aria ▶ VT (*room, bed*) arieggiare; (*clothes*) far prendere aria a; (*idea, grievance*) esprimere pubblicamente, manifestare; (*views*) far conoscere ▶ CPD (*currents*) d'aria; (*attack*) aereo(-a); **to throw sth into the ~** lanciare qc in aria; **by ~** (*travel*) in aereo; **to be on the ~** (*Radio, TV: station*) trasmettere; (*: programme*) essere in onda

air bag N airbag m inv

air base N base f aerea

airbed ['ɛəbed] N (*Brit*) materassino

airborne ['ɛəbɔ:n] ADJ (*plane*) in volo; (*troops*) aerotrasportato(-a); **as soon as the plane was ~** appena l'aereo ebbe decollato

air cargo N carico trasportato per via aerea

air-conditioned ['ɛəkən'dɪʃənd] ADJ con or ad aria condizionata

air conditioning N condizionamento d'aria

air-cooled ['ɛəku:ld] ADJ raffreddato(-a) ad aria

aircraft ['ɛəkrɑ:ft] N pl inv apparecchio

aircraft carrier N portaerei f inv

air cushion N cuscino gonfiabile; (*Tech*) cuscino d'aria

airfield ['ɛəfi:ld] N campo d'aviazione

Air Force N aviazione f militare

air freight N spedizione f di merci per via aerea; (*goods*) carico spedito per via aerea

airgun ['ɛəgʌn] N fucile m ad aria compressa

air hostess N (*Brit*) hostess f inv

airily ['ɛərɪlɪ] ADV con disinvoltura

airing ['ɛərɪŋ] N: **to give an ~ to** (linen) far prendere aria a; (room) arieggiare; (fig: ideas etc) ventilare

airing cupboard ['ɛərɪŋ-] N armadio riscaldato per asciugare panni.

air letter N (BRIT) aerogramma m

airlift ['ɛəlɪft] N ponte m aereo

airline ['ɛəlaɪn] N linea aerea

airliner ['ɛəlaɪnəʳ] N aereo di linea

airlock ['ɛəlɔk] N cassa d'aria

airmail N posta aerea; **by ~** per via or posta aerea

air mattress N materassino gonfiabile

airplane ['ɛəpleɪn] N (US) aeroplano

air pocket N vuoto d'aria

airport ['ɛəpɔːt] N aeroporto

air rage N comportamento aggressivo dei passeggeri di un aereo

air raid N incursione f aerea

air rifle N fucile m ad aria compressa

airsick ['ɛəsɪk] ADJ: **to be ~** soffrire di mal d'aereo

airspace ['ɛəspeɪs] N spazio aereo

airspeed ['ɛəspiːd] N velocità f inv di crociera (Aer)

airstrip ['ɛəstrɪp] N pista d'atterraggio

air terminal N air-terminal m inv

airtight ['ɛətaɪt] ADJ ermetico(-a)

air time N (Radio) spazio radiofonico; (TV) spazio televisivo

air traffic control N controllo del traffico aereo

air traffic controller N controllore m del traffico aereo

airway ['ɛəweɪ] N (Aviat) rotte fpl aeree; (Anat) vie fpl respiratorie

airy ['ɛərɪ] ADJ arioso(-a); (manners) noncurante

aisle [aɪl] N (of church) navata laterale; navata centrale; (of plane) corridoio

aisle seat N (on plane) posto sul corridoio

ajar [ə'dʒɑːʳ] ADJ socchiuso(-a)

AK ABBR (US) = **Alaska**

aka ABBR (= also known as) alias

akin [ə'kɪn] PREP: **~ to** simile a

AL ABBR (US) = **Alabama**

ALA N ABBR = **American Library Association**

Ala. ABBR (US) = **Alabama**

à la carte [ɑːlɑː'kɑːt] ADV alla carta

alacrity [ə'lækrɪtɪ] N: **with ~** con prontezza

alarm [ə'lɑːm] N allarme m ▸ VT allarmare

alarm call N (in hotel etc) sveglia; **could I have an ~ at 7 am, please?** vorrei essere svegliato alle 7, per favore

alarm clock N sveglia

alarmed [ə'lɑːmd] ADJ (person) allarmato(-a); (house, car etc) dotato(-a) di allarme

alarming [ə'lɑːmɪŋ] ADJ allarmante, preoccupante

alarmingly [ə'lɑːmɪŋlɪ] ADV in modo allarmante; **~ close** pericolosamente vicino

alarmist [ə'lɑːmɪst] N allarmista mf

alas [ə'læs] EXCL ohimè!, ahimè!

Alas. ABBR (US) = **Alaska**

Alaska [ə'læskə] N Alasca

Albania [æl'beɪnɪə] N Albania

Albanian [æl'beɪnɪən] ADJ albanese ▸ N albanese mf; (Ling) albanese m

albatross ['ælbətrɔs] N albatro, albatros m inv

albeit [ɔːl'biːɪt] CONJ sebbene + sub, benché + sub

album ['ælbəm] N album m inv; (L.P.) 33 giri m inv, L.P. m inv

albumen ['ælbjumɪn] N albume m

alchemy ['ælkɪmɪ] N alchimia

alcohol ['ælkəhɔl] N alcool m

alcohol-free ['ælkəhɔl'friː] ADJ analcolico(-a)

alcoholic [ælkə'hɔlɪk] ADJ alcolico(-a) ▸ N alcolizzato(-a)

alcoholism ['ælkəhɔlɪzəm] N alcolismo

alcove ['ælkəuv] N alcova

Ald. ABBR = **alderman**

alderman ['ɔːldəmən] N (irreg) consigliere m comunale

ale [eɪl] N birra

alert [ə'lɜːt] ADJ vivo(-a); (watchful) vigile ▸ N allarme m ▸ VT: **to ~ sb (to sth)** avvisare qn (di qc), avvertire qn (di qc); **to ~ sb to the dangers of sth** mettere qn in guardia contro qc; **on the ~** all'erta

Aleutian Islands [ə'luːʃən-] NPL isole fpl Aleutine

A level N (BRIT) diploma di studi superiori

Alexandria [ælɪg'zændrɪə] N Alessandria (d'Egitto)

alfresco [æl'freskəu] ADJ, ADV all'aperto

algebra ['ældʒɪbrə] N algebra

Algeria [æl'dʒɪərɪə] N Algeria

Algerian [æl'dʒɪərɪən] ADJ, N algerino(-a)

Algiers [æl'dʒɪəz] N Algeri f

algorithm ['ælgərɪðəm] N algoritmo

alias ['eɪlɪəs] ADV alias ▸ N pseudonimo, falso nome m

alibi ['ælɪbaɪ] N alibi m inv

alien ['eɪlɪən] N straniero(-a); (extraterrestrial) alieno(-a) ▸ ADJ: **~ (to)** estraneo(-a) (a)

alienate ['eɪlɪəneɪt] VT alienare

alienation [eɪlɪə'neɪʃən] N alienazione f

alight [ə'laɪt] ADJ acceso(-a) ▸ VI scendere; (bird) posarsi

align [ə'laɪn] VT allineare

alignment [ə'laɪnmənt] N allineamento; **out of ~ (with)** non allineato (con)

alike [ə'laɪk] ADJ simile ▸ ADV allo stesso modo; **to look ~** assomigliarsi; **winter and summer ~** sia d'estate che d'inverno

alimony ['ælɪmənɪ] N (*payment*) alimenti *mpl*

alive [ə'laɪv] ADJ vivo(-a); (*active*) attivo(-a); **~ with** pieno(-a) di; **~ to** conscio(-a) di

alkali ['ælkəlaɪ] N alcali *m inv*

(KEYWORD)

all [ɔːl] ADJ tutto(-a); **all day** tutto il giorno; **all night** tutta la notte; **all men** tutti gli uomini; **all five girls** tutt'e cinque le ragazze; **all five came** sono venuti tutti e cinque; **all the books** tutti i libri; **all the food** tutto il cibo; **all the time** tutto il tempo; (*always*) sempre; **all his life** tutta la vita; **for all their efforts** nonostante tutti i loro sforzi

▶ PRON **1** tutto(-a); **is that all?** non c'è altro?; (*in shop*) basta così?; **all of them** tutti(-e); **all of it** tutto(-a); **I ate it all**, I ate all of it l'ho mangiato tutto; **all of us went** tutti noi siamo andati; **all of the boys went** tutti i ragazzi sono andati

2 (*in phrases*): **above all** soprattutto; **after all** dopotutto; **at all: not at all** (*in answer to question*) niente affatto; (*in answer to thanks*) prego!, di niente!, s'immagini!; **I'm not at all tired** non sono affatto stanco; **anything at all will do** andrà bene qualsiasi cosa; **all in all** tutto sommato

▶ ADV: **all alone** tutto(-a) solo(-a); **to be/feel all in** (BRIT *col*) essere/sentirsi sfinito(-a) *or* distrutto(-a); **all out** *adv*: **to go all out** mettercela tutta; **it's not as hard as all that** non è poi così difficile; **all the more/ the better** tanto più/meglio; **all but** quasi; **the score is two all** il punteggio è di due a due *or* è due pari

Allah ['ælə] N Allah *m*

allay [ə'leɪ] VT (*fears*) dissipare

all clear N (Mil) cessato allarme *m inv*; (*fig*) okay *m*

allegation [ælɪ'geɪʃən] N asserzione *f*

allege [ə'lɛdʒ] VT asserire; **he is alleged to have said ...** avrebbe detto che ...

alleged [ə'lɛdʒd] ADJ presunto(-a)

allegedly [ə'lɛdʒɪdlɪ] ADV secondo quanto si asserisce

allegiance [ə'liːdʒəns] N fedeltà

allegory ['ælɪɡərɪ] N allegoria

all-embracing ['ɔːlɪm'breɪsɪŋ] ADJ universale

allergic [ə'lə:dʒɪk] ADJ: **~ to** allergico(-a) a

allergy ['ælədʒɪ] N allergia

alleviate [ə'liːvɪeɪt] VT alleviare, sollevare

alley ['ælɪ] N vicolo; (*in garden*) vialetto

alleyway ['ælɪweɪ] N vicolo

alliance [ə'laɪəns] N alleanza

allied ['ælaɪd] ADJ alleato(-a)

alligator ['ælɪgeɪtər] N alligatore *m*

all-important ['ɔːlɪm'pɔːtənt] ADJ importantissimo(-a)

all-in ['ɔːlɪn] ADJ, ADV (BRIT: *charge*) tutto compreso

all-in wrestling N (BRIT) lotta americana

alliteration [əlɪtə'reɪʃən] N allitterazione *f*

all-night ['ɔːl'naɪt] ADJ aperto(-a) (*or* che dura) tutta la notte

allocate ['æləkeɪt] VT (*share out*) distribuire; (*duties, sum, time*): **to ~ sth to** assegnare qc a; **to ~ sth for** stanziare qc per

allocation [æləu'keɪʃən] N: **~ (of money)** stanziamento

allot [ə'lɔt] VT (*share out*) spartire; **to ~ sth to** (*time*) dare qc a; (*duties*) assegnare qc a; **in the allotted time** nel tempo fissato *or* prestabilito

allotment [ə'lɔtmənt] N (*share*) spartizione *f*; (*garden*) lotto di terra

all-out ['ɔːl'laut] ADJ (*effort etc*) totale ▶ ADV: **to go all out for** mettercela tutta per

allow [ə'lau] VT (*practice, behaviour*) permettere; (*sum to spend etc*) accordare; (*sum, time estimated*) dare; (*concede*): **to ~ that** ammettere che; **to ~ sb to do** permettere a qn di fare; **he is allowed to (do it)** lo può fare; **smoking is not allowed** è vietato fumare, non è permesso fumare; **we must ~ 3 days for the journey** dobbiamo calcolare 3 giorni per il viaggio

▶ **allow for** VT FUS tener conto di

allowance [ə'lauəns] N (*money received*) assegno; (*for travelling, accommodation*) indennità *f inv*; (*Tax*) detrazione *f* di imposta; **to make ~(s) for** tener conto di; (*person*) scusare

alloy ['ælɔɪ] N lega

all right ADV (*feel, work*) bene; (*as answer*) va bene

all-round ['ɔːl'raund] ADJ completo(-a)

all-rounder [ɔːl'raundər] N (BRIT): **to be a good ~** essere bravo(-a) in tutto

allspice ['ɔːlspaɪs] N pepe *m* della Giamaica

all-time ['ɔːl'taɪm] ADJ (*record*) assoluto(-a)

allude [ə'luːd] VI: **to ~ to** alludere a

alluring [ə'ljuərɪŋ] ADJ seducente

allusion [ə'luːʒən] N allusione *f*

alluvium [ə'luːvɪəm] N materiale *m* alluvionale

ally N ['ælaɪ] alleato ▶ VT [ə'laɪ]: **to ~ o.s. with** allearsi con

almighty [ɔːl'maɪtɪ] ADJ onnipotente; (*row etc*) colossale

almond ['ɑːmənd] N mandorla

almost ['ɔːlmoust] ADV quasi; **he ~ fell** per poco non è caduto

alms [ɑːmz] N elemosina

aloft [ə'lɔft] ADV in alto; (*Naut*) sull'alberatura

alone [əˈləʊn] ADJ, ADV solo(-a); **to leave sb ~** lasciare qn in pace; **to leave sth ~** lasciare stare qc; **let ~ ...** figuriamoci poi ..., tanto meno ...

along [əˈlɒŋ] PREP lungo ▶ ADV: **is he coming ~?** viene con noi?; **he was hopping/limping ~** veniva saltellando/zoppicando; **~ with** insieme con; **all ~** (all the time) sempre, fin dall'inizio

alongside [əˈlɒŋˈsaɪd] PREP accanto a; lungo ▶ ADV accanto; (Naut) sottobordo; **we brought our boat ~** (of a pier/shore etc) abbiamo accostato la barca (al molo/alla riva etc)

aloof [əˈluːf] ADJ distaccato(-a) ▶ ADV a distanza, in disparte; **to stand ~** tenersi a distanza or in disparte

aloofness [əˈluːfnɪs] N distacco, riserbo

aloud [əˈlaʊd] ADV ad alta voce

alphabet [ˈælfəbet] N alfabeto

alphabetical [ælfəˈbetɪkəl] ADJ alfabetico(-a); **in ~ order** in ordine alfabetico

alphanumeric [ælfənjuːˈmerɪk] ADJ alfanumerico(-a)

alpine [ˈælpaɪn] ADJ alpino(-a); **~ hut** rifugio alpino; **~ pasture** pascolo alpestre; **~ skiing** sci alpino

Alps [ælps] NPL: **the ~** le Alpi

already [ɔːlˈredɪ] ADV già

alright [ˈɔːlˈraɪt] ADV (BRIT) = **all right**

Alsatian [ælˈseɪʃən] N (BRIT: dog) pastore m tedesco, (cane m) lupo

also [ˈɔːlsəʊ] ADV anche

Alta. ABBR (CANADA) = **Alberta**

altar [ˈɔltəʳ] N altare m

alter [ˈɔltəʳ] VT, VI alterare

alteration [ɔltəˈreɪʃən] N modificazione f, alterazione f; **alterations** (Sewing, Archit) modifiche fpl; **timetable subject to ~** orario soggetto a variazioni

altercation [ɔːltəˈkeɪʃən] N alterco, litigio

alternate ADJ [ɔlˈtəːnɪt] alterno(-a); (US: plan etc) alternativo(-a) ▶ VI [ˈɔltəneɪt] alternare; **to ~ (with)** alternarsi (a); **on ~ days** ogni due giorni

alternately [ɔlˈtəːnɪtlɪ] ADV alternatamente

alternating current [ˈɔltəneɪtɪŋ-] N corrente f alternata

alternative [ɔlˈtəːnətɪv] ADJ (solutions) alternativo(-a); (solution) altro(-a) ▶ N (choice) alternativa; (other possibility) altra possibilità

alternatively [ɔlˈtəːnətɪvlɪ] ADV altrimenti, come alternativa

alternative medicine N medicina alternativa

alternator [ˈɔltəːneɪtəʳ] N (Aut) alternatore m

although [ɔːlˈðəʊ] CONJ benché + sub, sebbene + sub

altitude [ˈæltɪtjuːd] N altitudine f

alto [ˈæltəʊ] N contralto

altogether [ɔːltəˈgeðəʳ] ADV del tutto, completamente; (on the whole) tutto considerato; (in all) in tutto; **how much is that ~?** quant'è in tutto?

altruism [ˈæltruɪzəm] N altruismo

altruistic [æltruˈɪstɪk] ADJ altruistico(-a)

aluminium [æljuˈmɪnɪəm], (US) **aluminum** [əˈluːmɪnəm] N alluminio

always [ˈɔːlweɪz] ADV sempre

Alzheimer's [ˈæltshaɪməz] N (also: **Alzheimer's disease**) morbo di Alzheimer

AM ABBR (= amplitude modulation) AM ▶ N ABBR (= Assembly Member) deputato gallese

am [æm] VB see **be**

a.m. ADV ABBR (= ante meridiem) della mattina

AMA N ABBR = **American Medical Association**

amalgam [əˈmælgəm] N amalgama m

amalgamate [əˈmælgəmeɪt] VT amalgamare ▶ VI amalgamarsi

amalgamation [əmælgəˈmeɪʃən] N amalgamazione f; (Comm) fusione f

amass [əˈmæs] VT ammassare

amateur [ˈæmətəʳ] N dilettante mf ▶ ADJ (Sport) dilettante; **~ dramatics** n filodrammatica

amateurish [ˈæmətərɪʃ] ADJ (pej) da dilettante

amaze [əˈmeɪz] VT stupire

amazed ADJ sbalordito(-a); **to be ~ (at)** essere sbalordito(-a) (da)

amazement [əˈmeɪzmənt] N stupore m

amazing [əˈmeɪzɪŋ] ADJ sorprendente, sbalorditivo(-a); (bargain, offer) sensazionale

amazingly [əˈmeɪzɪŋlɪ] ADV incredibilmente, sbalorditivamente

Amazon [ˈæməzən] N (Mythology) Amazzone f; **the ~** il Rio delle Amazzoni ▶ CPD (basin, jungle) amazzonico(-a)

Amazonian [æməˈzəʊnɪən] ADJ amazzonico(-a)

ambassador [æmˈbæsədəʳ] N ambasciatore(-trice)

amber [ˈæmbəʳ] N ambra; **at ~** (BRIT Aut) giallo

ambidextrous [æmbɪˈdekstrəs] ADJ ambidestro(-a)

ambience [ˈæmbɪəns] N ambiente m

ambiguity [æmbɪˈgjuɪtɪ] N ambiguità f inv

ambiguous [æmˈbɪgjuəs] ADJ ambiguo(-a)

ambition [æmˈbɪʃən] N ambizione f; **to achieve one's ~** realizzare le proprie aspirazioni or ambizioni

ambitious [æmˈbɪʃəs] ADJ ambizioso(-a)

ambivalent [æmˈbɪvələnt] ADJ ambivalente

amble [ˈæmbl] VI (also: **amble along**) camminare tranquillamente

ambulance [ˈæmbjuləns] N ambulanza

ambush ['æmbʊʃ] N imboscata ▶ VT fare un'imboscata a

ameba [ə'mi:bə] N (US) = **amoeba**

ameliorate [ə'mi:lɪəreɪt] VT migliorare

amen ['ɑ:'mɛn] EXCL così sia, amen

amenable [ə'mi:nəbl] ADJ: ~ **to** (advice etc) ben disposto(-a) a

amend [ə'mɛnd] VT (law) emendare; (text) correggere ▶ VI emendarsi; **to make amends** fare ammenda

amendment [ə'mɛndmənt] N emendamento; correzione f

amenities [ə'mi:nɪtɪz] NPL attrezzature fpl ricreative e culturali

amenity [ə'mi:nɪtɪ] N amenità f inv

America [ə'mɛrɪkə] N America

American [ə'mɛrɪkən] ADJ, N americano(-a)

American football N (BRIT) football m americano

americanize [ə'mɛrɪkənaɪz] VT americanizzare

amethyst ['æmɪθɪst] N ametista

Amex ['æmɛks] N ABBR = **American Stock Exchange**

amiable ['eɪmɪəbl] ADJ amabile, gentile

amicable ['æmɪkəbl] ADJ amichevole

amicably ['æmɪkəblɪ] ADV: **to part** ~ lasciarsi senza rancori

amid [ə'mɪd], **amidst** [ə'mɪdst] PREP fra, tra, in mezzo a

amiss [ə'mɪs] ADJ, ADV: **there's something** ~ c'è qualcosa che non va bene; **don't take it** ~ non avertene a male

ammo ['æməʊ] N ABBR (col) = **ammunition**

ammonia [ə'məʊnɪə] N ammoniaca

ammunition [æmju'nɪʃən] N munizioni fpl; (fig) arma

ammunition dump N deposito di munizioni

amnesia [æm'ni:zɪə] N amnesia

amnesty ['æmnɪstɪ] N amnistia; **to grant an** ~ **to** concedere l'amnistia a, amnistiare

Amnesty International N Amnesty International f

amoeba, (US) **ameba** [ə'mi:bə] N ameba

amok [ə'mɔk] ADV: **to run** ~ diventare pazzo(-a) furioso(-a)

among [ə'mʌŋ], **amongst** [ə'mʌŋst] PREP fra, tra, in mezzo a

amoral [eɪ'mɔrəl] ADJ amorale

amorous ['æmərəs] ADJ amoroso(-a)

amorphous [ə'mɔ:fəs] ADJ amorfo(-a)

amortization [əmɔ:taɪ'zeɪʃən] N (Comm) ammortamento

amount [ə'maʊnt] N (sum of money) somma; ammontare m; (of bill etc) importo; (quantity) quantità f inv ▶ VI: **to** ~ **to** (total) ammontare a; (be same as) essere come; **this amounts to a refusal** questo equivale a un rifiuto

amp ['æmp], **ampère** ['æmpɛər] N ampere m inv; **a 13** ~ **plug** una spina con fusibile da 13 ampere

ampersand ['æmpəsænd] N e f commerciale

amphetamine [æm'fɛtəmi:n] N anfetamina

amphibian [æm'fɪbɪən] N anfibio

amphibious [æm'fɪbɪəs] ADJ anfibio(-a)

amphitheatre, (US) **amphitheater** ['æmfɪθɪətər] N anfiteatro

ample ['æmpl] ADJ ampio(-a); spazioso(-a); (enough): **this is** ~ questo è più che sufficiente; **to have** ~ **time/room** avere assai tempo/posto

amplifier ['æmplɪfaɪər] N amplificatore m

amplify ['æmplɪfaɪ] VT amplificare

amply ['æmplɪ] ADV ampiamente

ampoule, (US) **ampule** ['æmpu:l] N (Med) fiala

amputate ['æmpjuteɪt] VT amputare

amputee [æmpju'ti:] N mutilato(-a), chi ha subito un'amputazione

Amsterdam [æmstə'dæm] N Amsterdam f

amt ABBR = **amount**

Amtrak ['æmtræk] (US) N società ferroviaria americana

amuck [ə'mʌk] ADV = **amok**

amuse [ə'mju:z] VT divertire; **to** ~ **o.s. with sth/by doing sth** divertirsi con qc/a fare qc; **to be amused at** essere divertito da; **he was not amused** non l'ha trovato divertente

amusement [ə'mju:zmənt] N divertimento; **much to my** ~ con mio grande spasso

amusement arcade N sala giochi (solo con macchinette a gettoni)

amusement park N luna park m inv

amusing [ə'mju:zɪŋ] ADJ divertente

an [æn, ən, n] INDEF ART see **a**

ANA N ABBR = **American Newspaper Association; American Nurses Association**

anachronism [ə'nækrənɪzəm] N anacronismo

anaemia [ə'ni:mɪə] N anemia

anaemic [ə'ni:mɪk] ADJ anemico(-a)

anaesthetic [ænɪs'θɛtɪk] ADJ anestetico(-a) ▶ N anestetico; **local/general** ~ anestesia locale/totale; **under the** ~ sotto anestesia

anaesthetist [æ'ni:sθɪtɪst] N anestesista mf

anagram ['ænəgræm] N anagramma m

anal ['eɪnl] ADJ anale

analgesic [ænæl'dʒi:sɪk] ADJ analgesico(-a) ▶ N analgesico

analog, analogue ['ænəlɔg] ADJ (watch, computer) analogico(-a)

analogous [ə'næləgəs] ADJ: ~ **to** or **with** analogo(-a) a

analogy [ə'nælədʒɪ] N analogia; **to draw an** ~ **between** fare un'analogia tra

analyse, (US) **analyze** ['ænəlaɪz] VT analizzare

analysis [ə'næləsɪs] (*pl* **analyses** [-siːz]) N
analisi *f inv*; **in the last ~** in ultima analisi

analyst ['ænəlɪst] N (*political analyst etc*)
analista *mf*; (US) (psic)analista *mf*

analytic [ænə'lɪtɪk], **analytical** [ænə'lɪtɪkl]
ADJ analitico(-a)

analyze ['ænəlaɪz] VT (US) = **analyse**

anarchic [æ'nɑːkɪk] ADJ anarchico(-a)

anarchist ['ænəkɪst] ADJ, N anarchico(-a)

anarchy ['ænəkɪ] N anarchia

anathema [ə'næθɪmə] N: **it is ~ to him** non
ne vuol neanche sentir parlare

anatomical [ænə'tɔmɪkl] ADJ anatomico(-a)

anatomy [ə'nætəmɪ] N anatomia

ANC N ABBR = **African National Congress**

ancestor ['ænsɪstə^r] N antenato(-a)

ancestral [æn'sɛstrəl] ADJ avito(-a)

ancestry ['ænsɪstrɪ] N antenati *mpl*;
ascendenza

anchor ['æŋkə^r] N ancora ▶ VI (*also*: **to drop
anchor**) gettare l'ancora ▶ VT ancorare; **to
weigh ~** salpare *or* levare l'ancora

anchorage ['æŋkərɪdʒ] N ancoraggio

anchor man N (*irreg*) (TV, *Radio*) anchorman
m inv

anchor woman N (*irreg*) (TV, *Radio*)
anchorwoman *f inv*

anchovy ['æntʃəvɪ] N acciuga

ancient ['eɪnʃənt] ADJ antico(-a); (*person, car*)
vecchissimo(-a); **~ monument** monumento
storico

ancillary [æn'sɪlərɪ] ADJ ausiliario(-a)

and [ænd] CONJ e (*often 'ed' before vowel*); **~ so
on** e così via; **try ~ do it** prova a farlo; **try ~
come** cerca di venire; **he talked ~ talked**
non la finiva di parlare; **come ~ sit here**
vieni a sedere qui; **better ~ better** sempre
meglio; **more ~ more** sempre di più

Andes ['ændiːz] NPL: **the ~** le Ande

Andorra [æn'dɔːrə] N Andorra

anecdote ['ænɪkdəut] N aneddoto

anemia *etc* [ə'niːmɪə] (US) = **anaemia** *etc*

anemone [ə'nɛmənɪ] N (*Bot*) anemone *m*;
(*sea anemone*) anemone *m* di mare, attinia

anesthetic *etc* [ænɪs'θɛtɪk] (US) = **anaesthetic**
etc

anew [ə'njuː] ADV di nuovo

angel ['eɪndʒəl] N angelo

angel dust N *sedativo usato a scopo
allucinogeno*

anger ['æŋgə^r] N rabbia ▶ VT arrabbiare

angina [æn'dʒaɪnə] N angina pectoris

angle ['æŋgl] N angolo ▶ VI: **to ~ for** (*fig*)
cercare di avere; **from their ~** dal loro punto
di vista

angler ['æŋglə^r] N pescatore *m* con la lenza

Anglican ['æŋglɪkən] ADJ, N anglicano(-a)

anglicize ['æŋglɪsaɪz] VT anglicizzare

angling ['æŋglɪŋ] N pesca con la lenza

Anglo- ['æŋgləu] PREFIX, N anglo...; **~Italian**
adj italobritannico(-a)

Anglo-Saxon ['æŋgləu'sæksən] ADJ, N
anglosassone *mf*

Angola [æŋ'gəulə] N Angola

Angolan [æŋ'gəulən] ADJ, N angolano(-a)

angrily ['æŋgrɪlɪ] ADV con rabbia

angry ['æŋgrɪ] ADJ arrabbiato(-a), furioso(-a);
(*wound*) infiammato(-a); **to be ~ with sb/
sth** essere in collera con qn/per qc; **to get ~**
arrabbiarsi; **to make sb ~** fare arrabbiare qn

anguish ['æŋgwɪʃ] N angoscia

anguished ['æŋgwɪʃt] ADJ angosciato(-a),
pieno(-a) d'angoscia

angular ['æŋgjulə^r] ADJ angolare

animal ['ænɪməl] ADJ animale ▶ N animale *m*

animal rights NPL diritti *mpl* degli animali

animate VT ['ænɪmeɪt] animare ▶ ADJ
['ænɪmɪt] animato(-a)

animated ['ænɪmeɪtɪd] ADJ animato(-a)

animation [ænɪ'meɪʃən] N animazione *f*

animosity [ænɪ'mɔsɪtɪ] N animosità

aniseed ['ænɪsiːd] N semi *mpl* di anice

Ankara ['æŋkərə] N Ankara

ankle ['æŋkl] N caviglia

ankle socks NPL calzini *mpl*

annex N ['ænɛks] (BRIT: *also*: **annexe**) edificio
annesso ▶ VT [ə'nɛks] annettere

annexation [ænɛk'seɪʃən] N annessione *f*

annihilate [ə'naɪəleɪt] VT annientare

annihilation [ənaɪə'leɪʃən] N
annientamento

anniversary [ænɪ'vəːsərɪ] N anniversario

anniversary dinner N cena commemorativa

annotate ['ænəuteɪt] VT annotare

announce [ə'nauns] VT annunciare; **he
announced that he wasn't going** ha
dichiarato che non (ci) sarebbe andato

announcement [ə'naunsmənt] N annuncio;
(*letter, card*) partecipazione *f*; **I'd like to
make an ~** ho una comunicazione da fare

announcer [ə'naunsə^r] N (*Radio*, TV: *between
programmes*) annunciatore(-trice); (: *in a
programme*) presentatore(-trice)

annoy [ə'nɔɪ] VT dare fastidio a; **to be
annoyed (at sth/with sb)** essere seccato *or*
irritato (per qc/con qn); **don't get annoyed!**
non irritarti!

annoyance [ə'nɔɪəns] N fastidio; (*cause of
annoyance*) noia

annoying [ə'nɔɪɪŋ] ADJ irritante, seccante

annual ['ænjuəl] ADJ annuale ▶ N (*Bot*)
pianta annua; (*book*) annuario

annual general meeting N (BRIT) assemblea
generale

annually ['ænjuəlɪ] ADV annualmente

annual report N relazione *f* annuale

annuity [ə'njuːɪtɪ] N annualità *f inv*; **life ~**
vitalizio

annul [ə'nʌl] VT annullare; (law) rescindere
annulment [ə'nʌlmənt] N annullamento;
rescissione f
annum ['ænəm] N see **per annum**
Annunciation [ənʌnsɪ'eɪʃən] N
Annunciazione f
anode ['ænəud] N anodo
anoint [ə'nɔɪnt] VT ungere
anomalous [ə'nɔmələs] ADJ anomalo(-a)
anomaly [ə'nɔməlɪ] N anomalia
anon. [ə'nɔn] ABBR = **anonymous**
anonymity [ænə'nɪmɪtɪ] N anonimato
anonymous [ə'nɔnɪməs] ADJ anonimo(-a);
to remain ~ mantenere l'anonimato
anorak ['ænəræk] N giacca a vento
anorexia [ænə'rɛksɪə] N (Med: also: **anorexia
nervosa**) anoressia
anorexic [ænə'rɛksɪk] ADJ, N anoressico(-a)
another [ə'nʌðəʳ] ADJ: **~ book** (one more)
un altro libro, ancora un libro; (a different one)
un altro libro ▶ PRON un altro (un'altra),
ancora uno(-a); **~ drink?** ancora qualcosa
da bere?; **in ~ 5 years** fra altri 5 anni;
see also **one**
ANSI N ABBR (= American National Standards
Institution) Istituto americano di standardizzazione
answer ['ɑ:nsəʳ] N risposta; soluzione f ▶ VI
rispondere ▶ VT (reply to) rispondere a;
(problem) risolvere; (prayer) esaudire; **in ~ to
your letter** in risposta alla sua lettera; **to ~
the phone** rispondere (al telefono); **to ~ the
bell** rispondere al campanello; **to ~ the
door** aprire la porta
▶ **answer back** VI ribattere
▶ **answer for** VT FUS essere responsabile di
▶ **answer to** VT FUS (description)
corrispondere a
answerable ['ɑ:nsərəbl] ADJ: **~ (to sb/for
sth)** responsabile (verso qn/di qc); **I am ~ to
no-one** non devo rispondere a nessuno
answering machine ['ɑ:nsərɪŋ-] N
segreteria (telefonica) automatica
answerphone N (esp BRIT) segreteria
telefonica
ant [ænt] N formica
ANTA N ABBR = **American National Theater
and Academy**
antagonism [æn'tægənɪzəm] N
antagonismo
antagonist [æn'tægənɪst] N antagonista mf
antagonistic [æntægə'nɪstɪk] ADJ
antagonistico(-a)
antagonize [æn'tægənaɪz] VT provocare
l'ostilità di
Antarctic [ænt'ɑ:ktɪk] N: **the ~** l'Antartide f
▶ ADJ antartico(-a)
Antarctica [ænt'ɑ:ktɪkə] N Antartide f
Antarctic Circle N Circolo polare
antartico

Antarctic Ocean N Oceano antartico
ante ['æntɪ] N (Cards, fig): **to up the ~** alzare la
posta in palio
ante... ['æntɪ] PREFIX anti..., ante..., pre...
anteater ['æntɪ:təʳ] N formichiere m
antecedent [æntɪ'si:dənt] N antecedente m,
precedente m
antechamber ['æntɪtʃeɪmbəʳ] N anticamera
antelope ['æntɪləup] N antilope f
antenatal ['æntɪ'neɪtl] ADJ prenatale
antenatal clinic N assistenza medica
preparto
antenna [æn'tɛnə] (pl **antennae** [-ni:]) N
antenna
anthem ['ænθəm] N antifona; **national ~**
inno nazionale
ant-hill ['ænthɪl] N formicaio
anthology [æn'θɔlədʒɪ] N antologia
anthrax ['ænθræks] N antrace m
anthropologist [ænθrə'pɔlədʒɪst] N
antropologo(-a)
anthropology [ænθrə'pɔlədʒɪ] N
antropologia
anti- ['æntɪ] PREFIX anti...
anti-aircraft ['æntɪ'ɛəkrɑ:ft] ADJ
antiaereo(-a)
anti-aircraft defence N difesa antiaerea
antiballistic ['æntɪbə'lɪstɪk] ADJ
antibalistico(-a)
antibiotic ['æntɪbaɪ'ɔtɪk] ADJ antibiotico(-a)
▶ N antibiotico
antibody ['æntɪbɔdɪ] N anticorpo
anticipate [æn'tɪsɪpeɪt] VT prevedere;
pregustare; (wishes, request) prevenire; **as
anticipated** come previsto; **this is worse
than I anticipated** è peggio di quel che
immaginavo or pensavo
anticipation [æntɪsɪ'peɪʃən] N anticipazione
f; (expectation) aspettative fpl; **thanking you
in ~** vi ringrazio in anticipo
anticlimax ['æntɪ'klaɪmæks] N: **it was an ~**
fu una completa delusione
anticlockwise ['æntɪ'klɔkwaɪz] ADJ, ADV in
senso antiorario
antics ['æntɪks] NPL buffonerie fpl
anticyclone ['æntɪ'saɪkləun] N anticiclone m
antidote ['æntɪdəut] N antidoto
antifreeze ['æntɪfri:z] N anticongelante m
anti-globalization [æntɪgləubəlaɪ'zeɪʃən]
ADJ antiglobalizzazione inv ▶ N
antiglobalizzazione f
antihistamine [æntɪ'hɪstəmɪn] N
antistaminico
Antilles [æn'tɪli:z] NPL: **the ~** le Antille
antipathy [æn'tɪpəθɪ] N antipatia
antiperspirant ['æntɪ'pə:spərənt] ADJ
antitraspirante
Antipodean [æntɪpə'di:ən] ADJ degli
Antipodi

Antipodes [æn'tɪpədiːz] NPL: **the ~ gli** Antipodi

antiquarian [æntɪ'kwɛərɪən] ADJ: **~ bookshop** libreria antiquaria ► N antiquario(-a)

antiquated ['æntɪkweɪtɪd] ADJ antiquato(-a)

antique [æn'tiːk] N antichità f inv ► ADJ antico(-a)

antique dealer N antiquario(-a)

antique shop N negozio d'antichità

antiquity [æn'tɪkwɪtɪ] N antichità f inv

anti-semitic ['æntɪsɪ'mɪtɪk] ADJ antisemitico(-a), antisemita

anti-semitism ['æntɪ'sɛmɪtɪzəm] N antisemitismo

antiseptic [æntɪ'sɛptɪk] ADJ antisettico(-a) ► N antisettico

antisocial ['æntɪ'səuʃəl] ADJ asociale; (against society) antisociale

antitank [æntɪ'tæŋk] ADJ anticarro inv

antithesis [æn'tɪθɪsɪs] (pl **antitheses** [-siːz]) N antitesi f inv; (contrast) carattere m antitetico

anti-trust [æntɪ'trʌst] ADJ (Comm): **~ legislation** legislazione f antitrust inv

antiviral [æntɪ'vaɪərəl] ADJ (Med) antivirale

antivirus [æntɪ'vaɪərəs] ADJ (Comput) antivirus inv; **~ program** antivirus m inv

antivirus software N antivirus m inv

antlers ['æntləz] NPL palchi mpl

Antwerp ['æntwɜːp] N Anversa

anus ['eɪnəs] N ano

anvil ['ænvɪl] N incudine f

anxiety [æŋ'zaɪətɪ] N ansia; (keenness): **~ to do** smania di fare

anxious ['æŋkʃəs] ADJ ansioso(-a), inquieto(-a); (worrying) angosciante; (keen): **~ to do/that** impaziente di fare/che + sub; **I'm very ~ about you** sono molto preoccupato or in pensiero per te

anxiously ['æŋkʃəslɪ] ADV ansiosamente, con ansia

(KEYWORD)

any ['ɛnɪ] ADJ **1** (in questions etc): **have you any butter?** hai del burro?, hai un po' di burro?; **have you any children?** hai bambini?; **if there are any tickets left** se ci sono ancora (dei) biglietti, se c'è ancora qualche biglietto
2 (with negative): **I haven't any money/books** non ho soldi/libri; **without any difficulty** senza nessuna or alcuna difficoltà
3 (no matter which) qualsiasi, qualunque; **choose any book you like** scegli un libro qualsiasi
4 (in phrases): **in any case** in ogni caso; **any day now** da un giorno all'altro; **at any moment** in qualsiasi momento, da un momento all'altro; **at any rate** ad ogni modo
► PRON **1** (in questions: with negative): **have you got any?** ne hai?; **can any of you sing?** qualcuno di voi sa cantare?; **I haven't any (of them)** non ne ho
2 (no matter which one(s)): **take any of those books (you like)** prendi uno qualsiasi di quei libri
► ADV **1** (in questions etc): **do you want any more soup/sandwiches?** vuoi ancora un po' di minestra/degli altri panini?; **are you feeling any better?** ti senti meglio?
2 (with negative): **I can't hear him any more** non lo sento più; **don't wait any longer** non aspettare più

anybody ['ɛnɪbɔdɪ] PRON qualsiasi persona; (in interrogative sentences) qualcuno; (in negative sentences) nessuno; (no matter who) chiunque; **can you see ~?** vedi qualcuno or nessuno?; **if ~ should phone ...** se telefona qualcuno ...; **I don't see ~** non vedo nessuno; **~ could do it** chiunque potrebbe farlo

anyhow ['ɛnɪhau] ADV in qualsiasi modo; (haphazardly) come capita; (at any rate) ad ogni modo, comunque; (haphazard): **do it ~ you like** fallo come ti pare; **I shall go ~** ci andrò lo stesso or comunque; **she leaves things just ~** lascia tutto come capita

anyone ['ɛnɪwʌn] PRON = **anybody**

anyplace ['ɛnɪpleɪs] ADV (US col) = **anywhere**

anything ['ɛnɪθɪŋ] PRON qualsiasi cosa; (in interrogative sentences) qualcosa, niente; (with negative) niente; **you can say ~ you like** (no matter what) puoi dire quello che ti pare; **can you see ~?** vedi niente or qualcosa?; **if ~ happens to me ...** se mi dovesse succedere qualcosa ...; **I can't see ~** non vedo niente; **~ will do** va bene qualsiasi cosa or tutto; **~ else?** (in shop) basta (così)?; **it can cost ~ between £15 and £20** può costare qualcosa come 15 o 20 sterline

anytime ['ɛnɪtaɪm] ADV in qualunque momento; quando vuole

anyway ['ɛnɪweɪ] ADV (at any rate) ad ogni modo, comunque; (besides) ad ogni modo

anywhere ['ɛnɪwɛə'] ADV da qualsiasi parte; (in interrogative sentences) da qualche parte; (with negative) da nessuna parte; (no matter where) da qualsiasi or qualunque parte, dovunque; **can you see him ~?** lo vedi da qualche parte?; **I don't see him ~** non lo vedo da nessuna parte; **~ in the world** dovunque nel mondo

Anzac ['ænzæk] N ABBR (= Australia-New Zealand Army Corps) A.N.Z.A.C. m; (soldier) soldato dell'A.N.Z.A.C.

Anzac Day N vedi nota

L' *Anzac Day* è una festa nazionale australiana e neozelandese che cade il 25 aprile e commemora il famoso sbarco delle forze armate congiunte dei due paesi a Gallipoli nel 1915, durante la prima guerra mondiale.

apart [ə'pɑːt] ADV (*to one side*) a parte; (*separately*) separatamente; **with one's legs ~** con le gambe divaricate; **10 miles/a long way ~** a 10 miglia di distanza/molto lontani l'uno dall'altro; **they are living ~** sono separati; **to take ~** smontare; **~ from** *prep* a parte, eccetto

apartheid [ə'pɑːteɪt] N apartheid f

apartment [ə'pɑːtmənt] N (*US*) appartamento; (*room*) locale m; **apartments** NPL appartamento ammobiliato

apartment building N (*US*) stabile m, caseggiato

apathetic [æpə'θɛtɪk] ADJ apatico(-a)

apathy ['æpəθɪ] N apatia

APB N ABBR (*US: police expression: = all points bulletin*) espressione della polizia che significa "trovate e arrestate il sospetto"

ape [eɪp] N scimmia ▶ VT scimmiottare

Apennines ['æpənaɪnz] NPL: **the ~** gli Apennini

aperitif [ə'pɛrɪtiːf] N aperitivo

aperture ['æpətfjuə'] N apertura

APEX ['eɪpɛks] N ABBR (*Aviat: = advance purchase excursion*) APEX m inv

apex ['eɪpɛks] N apice m

aphid ['æfɪd] N afide f

aphrodisiac [æfrəu'dɪzɪæk] ADJ afrodisiaco(-a) ▶ N afrodisiaco

API N ABBR = **American Press Institute**

apiece [ə'piːs] ADV ciascuno(-a)

aplomb [ə'plɔm] N disinvoltura

APO N ABBR (*US: = Army Post Office*) ufficio postale dell'esercito

apocalypse [ə'pɔkəlɪps] N apocalisse f

apolitical [eɪpə'lɪtɪkl] ADJ apolitico(-a)

apologetic [əpɔlə'dʒɛtɪk] ADJ (*tone, letter*) di scusa; **to be very ~ about** scusarsi moltissimo di

apologetically [əpɔlə'dʒɛtɪkəlɪ] ADV per scusarsi

apologize [ə'pɔlədʒaɪz] VI: **to ~ (for sth to sb)** scusarsi (di qc a qn), chiedere scusa (a qn per qc)

apology [ə'pɔlədʒɪ] N scuse *fpl*; **please accept my apologies** la prego di accettare le mie scuse

apoplectic [æpə'plɛktɪk] ADJ (*Med*) apoplettico(-a); **~ with rage** (*col*) livido(-a) per la rabbia

apoplexy ['æpəplɛksɪ] N apoplessia

apostle [ə'pɔsl] N apostolo

apostrophe [ə'pɔstrəfɪ] N (*sign*) apostrofo

app N ABBR (*col: Comput: = application*) applicazione f

appal, (*US*) **appall** [ə'pɔːl] VT atterrire; sconvolgere

Appalachian Mountains [æpə'leɪʃən-] NPL: **the ~** i Monti Appalachi

appalling [ə'pɔːlɪŋ] ADJ spaventoso(-a); **she's an ~ cook** è un disastro come cuoca

apparatus [æpə'reɪtəs] N apparato; (*in gymnasium*) attrezzatura

apparel [ə'pærl] N (*US*) abbigliamento, confezioni *fpl*

apparent [ə'pærənt] ADJ evidente

apparently [ə'pærəntlɪ] ADV evidentemente, a quanto pare

apparition [æpə'rɪʃən] N apparizione f

appeal [ə'piːl] VI (*Law*) appellarsi alla legge ▶ N (*Law*) appello; (*request*) richiesta; (*charm*) attrattiva; **to ~ for** chiedere (con insistenza); **to ~ to** (*person*) appellarsi a; (*thing*) piacere a; **to ~ to sb for mercy** chiedere pietà a qn; **it doesn't ~ to me** mi dice poco; **right of ~** diritto d'appello

appealing [ə'piːlɪŋ] ADJ (*moving*) commovente; (*attractive*) attraente

appear [ə'pɪə'] VI apparire; (*Law*) comparire; (*publication*) essere pubblicato(-a); (*seem*) sembrare; **it would ~ that** sembra che; **to ~ in Hamlet** recitare nell'Amleto; **to ~ on TV** presentarsi in televisione

appearance [ə'pɪərəns] N apparizione f; apparenza; (*look, aspect*) aspetto; **to put in** or **make an ~** fare atto di presenza; **by order of ~** (*Theat*) in ordine di apparizione; **to keep up appearances** salvare le apparenze; **to all appearances** a giudicar dalle apparenze

appease [ə'piːz] VT calmare, appagare

appeasement [ə'piːzmənt] N (*Pol*) appeasement m inv

append [ə'pɛnd] VT (*Comput*) aggiungere in coda

appendage [ə'pɛndɪdʒ] N aggiunta

appendicitis [əpɛndɪ'saɪtɪs] N appendicite f

appendix [ə'pɛndɪks] (*pl* **appendices** [-siːz]) N appendice f; **to have one's ~ out** operarsi or farsi operare di appendicite

appetite ['æpɪtaɪt] N appetito; **that walk has given me an ~** la passeggiata mi ha messo appetito

appetizer ['æpɪtaɪzə'] N (*food*) stuzzichino; (*drink*) aperitivo

appetizing ['æpɪtaɪzɪŋ] ADJ appetitoso(-a)

applaud [ə'plɔːd] VT, VI applaudire

applause [ə'plɔːz] N applauso

apple ['æpl] N mela; (*also*: **apple tree**) melo; **the ~ of one's eye** la pupilla dei propri occhi

apple pie N torta di mele

apple turnover N sfogliatella alle mele

appliance [ə'plaɪəns] N apparecchio; **electrical appliances** elettrodomestici *mpl*

applicable [ə'plɪkəbl] ADJ applicabile; **to be ~ to** essere valido per; **the law is ~ from January** la legge entrerà in vigore in gennaio

applicant ['æplɪkənt] N candidato(-a); (*Admin: for benefit etc*) chi ha fatto domanda *or* richiesta

application [æplɪ'keɪʃən] N applicazione *f*; (*for a job, a grant etc*) domanda; (*Comput*) applicazione *f*; **on ~** su richiesta

application form N modulo per la domanda

application program N (*Comput*) programma applicativo

applications package N (*Comput*) software *m inv* applicativo

applied [ə'plaɪd] ADJ applicato(-a); **~ arts** arti *fpl* applicate

apply [ə'plaɪ] VT: **to ~ (to)** (*paint, ointment*) dare (a); (*theory, technique*) applicare (a) ▶ VI: **to ~ to** (*ask*) rivolgersi a; (*be suitable for, relevant to*) riguardare, riferirsi a; **to ~ (for)** (*permit, grant, job*) fare domanda (per); **to ~ the brakes** frenare; **to ~ o.s. to** dedicarsi a

appoint [ə'pɔɪnt] VT nominare

appointee [əpɔɪn'tiː] N incaricato(-a)

appointment [ə'pɔɪntmənt] N nomina; (*arrangement to meet*) appuntamento; **by ~** su *or* per appuntamento; **to make an ~ with sb** prendere un appuntamento con qn; **I have an ~ (with)** … ho un appuntamento (con) …; **"appointments (vacant)"** (*Press*) "offerte *fpl* di impiego"

apportion [ə'pɔːʃən] VT attribuire

appraisal [ə'preɪzl] N valutazione *f*

appraise [ə'preɪz] VT (*value*) valutare, fare una stima di; (*situation etc*) fare il bilancio di

appreciable [ə'priːʃəbl] ADJ apprezzabile

appreciably [ə'priːʃəblɪ] ADV notevolmente, sensibilmente

appreciate [ə'priːʃɪeɪt] VT (*like*) apprezzare; (*be grateful for*) essere riconoscente di; (*be aware of*) rendersi conto di ▶ VI (*Comm*) aumentare; **I'd ~ your help** ti sono grato per l'aiuto

appreciation [əpriːʃɪ'eɪʃən] N apprezzamento; (*Finance*) aumento del valore

appreciative [ə'priːʃɪətɪv] ADJ (*person*) sensibile; (*comment*) elogiativo(-a)

apprehend [æprɪ'hɛnd] VT (*arrest*) arrestare; (*understand*) comprendere

apprehension [æprɪ'hɛnʃən] N (*fear*) inquietudine *f*

apprehensive [æprɪ'hɛnsɪv] ADJ apprensivo(-a)

apprentice [ə'prɛntɪs] N apprendista *mf*

▶ VT: **to be apprenticed to** lavorare come apprendista presso

apprenticeship [ə'prɛntɪʃɪp] N apprendistato; **to serve one's ~** fare il proprio apprendistato *or* tirocinio

appro. ['æprəu] ABBR (*BRIT Comm: col*) = **approval**

approach [ə'prəutʃ] VI avvicinarsi ▶ VT (*come near*) avvicinarsi a; (*ask, apply to*) rivolgersi a; (*subject, passer-by*) avvicinare ▶ N approccio; accesso; (*to problem*) modo di affrontare; **to ~ sb about sth** rivolgersi a qn per qc

approachable [ə'prəutʃəbl] ADJ accessibile

approach road N strada d'accesso

approbation [æprə'beɪʃən] N approvazione *f*, benestare *m*

appropriate VT [ə'prəuprɪeɪt] (*take*) appropriarsi di ▶ ADJ [ə'prəuprɪɪt] appropriato(-a), adatto(-a); **it would not be ~ for me to comment** non sta a me fare dei commenti

appropriately [ə'prəuprɪɪtlɪ] ADV in modo appropriato

appropriation [əprəuprɪ'eɪʃən] N stanziamento

approval [ə'pruːvəl] N approvazione *f*; **on ~** (*Comm*) in prova, in esame; **to meet with sb's ~** soddisfare qn, essere di gradimento di qn

approve [ə'pruːv] VT, VI approvare ▶ **approve of** VT FUS approvare

approved school N (*BRIT old*) riformatorio

approvingly [ə'pruːvɪŋlɪ] ADV in approvazione

approx. ABBR = **approximately**

approximate ADJ [ə'prɒksɪmɪt] approssimativo(-a) ▶ VT [ə'prɒksɪmeɪt] essere un'approssimazione di, avvicinarsi a

approximately [ə'prɒksɪmətlɪ] ADV circa

approximation [əprɒksɪ'meɪʃən] N approssimazione *f*

apr N ABBR (= *annual percentage rate*) tasso di percentuale annuo

Apr. ABBR (= *April*) apr.

apricot ['eɪprɪkɔt] N albicocca

April ['eɪprəl] N aprile *m*; **~ fool!** pesce d'aprile!; *see also* **July**

April Fools' Day N *vedi nota*

> April Fools' Day è il primo aprile, il giorno degli scherzi e delle burle. Il nome deriva dal fatto che, se una persona cade nella trappola che gli è stata tesa, fa la figura del fool, cioè dello sciocco. Di recente gli scherzi stanno diventando sempre più elaborati, e persino i giornalisti a volte inventano vicende incredibili per burlarsi dei lettori.

apron ['eɪprən] N grembiule *m*; (*Aviat*) area di stazionamento

apse [æps] N (*Archit*) abside f
APT N ABBR (*BRIT*: = *advanced passenger train*) treno ad altissima velocità
apt [æpt] ADJ (*suitable*) adatto(-a); (*able*) capace; (*likely*): **to be ~ to do** avere tendenza a fare
Apt. ABBR = **apartment**
aptitude ['æptɪtjuːd] N abilità f inv
aptitude test N test m inv attitudinale
aptly ['æptlɪ] ADV appropriatamente, in modo adatto
aqualung ['ækwəlʌŋ] N autorespiratore m
aquarium [ə'kwɛərɪəm] N acquario
Aquarius [ə'kwɛərɪəs] N Acquario; **to be ~** essere dell'Acquario
aquatic [ə'kwætɪk] ADJ acquatico(-a)
aqueduct ['ækwɪdʌkt] N acquedotto
AR ABBR (*US*) = **Arkansas**
ARA N ABBR (*BRIT*) = **Associate of the Royal Academy**
Arab ['ærəb] ADJ, N arabo(-a)
Arabia [ə'reɪbɪə] N Arabia
Arabian [ə'reɪbɪən] ADJ arabo(-a)
Arabian Desert N Deserto arabico
Arabian Sea N mare m Arabico
Arabic ['ærəbɪk] ADJ arabico(-a), arabo(-a) ▶ N arabo
Arabic numerals NPL numeri mpl arabi, numerazione f araba
arable ['ærəbl] ADJ arabile
ARAM N ABBR (*BRIT*) = **Associate of the Royal Academy of Music**
arbiter ['ɑːbɪtəʳ] N arbitro
arbitrary ['ɑːbɪtrərɪ] ADJ arbitrario(-a)
arbitrate ['ɑːbɪtreɪt] VI arbitrare
arbitration [ɑːbɪ'treɪʃən] N (*Law*) arbitrato; (*Industry*) arbitraggio
arbitrator ['ɑːbɪtreɪtəʳ] N arbitro
ARC N ABBR (= *American Red Cross*) C.R.I. f (= *Croce Rossa Italiana*)
arc [ɑːk] N arco
arcade [ɑː'keɪd] N portico; (*passage with shops*) galleria
arch [ɑːtʃ] N arco; (*of foot*) arco plantare ▶ VT inarcare ▶ PREFIX: **~(-)** grande (*before n*); per eccellenza
archaeological [ɑːkɪə'lɔdʒɪkəl] ADJ archeologico(-a)
archaeologist [ɑːkɪ'ɔlədʒɪst] N archeologo(-a)
archaeology [ɑːkɪ'ɔlədʒɪ] N archeologia
archaic [ɑː'keɪɪk] ADJ arcaico(-a)
archangel ['ɑːkeɪndʒəl] N arcangelo
archbishop [ɑːtʃ'bɪʃəp] N arcivescovo
arched [ɑːtʃt] ADJ arcuato(-a), ad arco
arch-enemy ['ɑːtʃ'ɛnɪmɪ] N arcinemico(-a)
archeology *etc* [ɑːkɪ'ɔlədʒɪ] = **archaeology** *etc*
archer ['ɑːtʃəʳ] N arciere m
archery ['ɑːtʃərɪ] N tiro all'arco

archetypal ['ɑːkɪtaɪpəl] ADJ tipico(-a)
archetype ['ɑːkɪtaɪp] N archetipo
archipelago [ɑːkɪ'pɛlɪgəu] N arcipelago
architect ['ɑːkɪtɛkt] N architetto
architectural [ɑːkɪ'tɛktʃərəl] ADJ architettonico(-a)
architecture ['ɑːkɪtɛktʃəʳ] N architettura
archive ['ɑːkaɪv] N (*also Comput*) archivio; **archives** NPL archivi mpl
archive file N (*Comput*) file m inv di archivio
archivist ['ɑːkɪvɪst] N archivista mf
archway ['ɑːtʃweɪ] N arco
ARCM N ABBR (*BRIT*) = **Associate of the Royal College of Music**
Arctic ['ɑːktɪk] ADJ artico(-a) ▶ N: **the ~** l'Artico
Arctic Circle N Circolo polare artico
Arctic Ocean N Oceano artico
ARD N ABBR (*US Med*) = **acute respiratory disease**
ardent ['ɑːdənt] ADJ ardente
ardour, (*US*) **ardor** ['ɑːdəʳ] N ardore m
arduous ['ɑːdjuəs] ADJ arduo(-a)
are [ɑːʳ] VB *see* **be**
area ['ɛərɪə] N (*Geom*) area; (*zone*) zona; (*: smaller*) settore m; **dining ~** zona pranzo; **the London ~** la zona di Londra
area code N (*US Tel*) prefisso
arena [ə'riːnə] N arena
aren't [ɑːnt] = **are not**
Argentina [ɑːdʒən'tiːnə] N Argentina
Argentinian [ɑːdʒən'tɪnɪən] ADJ, N argentino(-a)
arguable ['ɑːgjuəbl] ADJ discutibile; **it is ~ whether ...** è una cosa discutibile se ... + *sub*
arguably ['ɑːgjuəblɪ] ADV: **it is ~ ...** si può sostenere che sia ...
argue ['ɑːgjuː] VI (*quarrel*) litigare; (*reason*) ragionare ▶ VT (*debate: case, matter*) dibattere; **to ~ that** sostenere che; **to ~ about sth (with sb)** litigare per *or* a proposito di qc (con qn)
argument ['ɑːgjumənt] N (*reasons*) argomento; (*quarrel*) lite f; (*debate*) discussione f; **~ for/against** argomento a *or* in favore di/contro
argumentative [ɑːgju'mɛntətɪv] ADJ litigioso(-a)
aria ['ɑːrɪə] N aria
ARIBA N ABBR (*BRIT*) = **Associate of the Royal Institute of British Architects**
arid ['ærɪd] ADJ arido(-a)
aridity [ə'rɪdɪtɪ] N aridità
Aries ['ɛərɪz] N Ariete m; **to be ~** essere dell'Ariete
arise [ə'raɪz] (*pt* **arose** [ə'rəuz], *pp* **arisen** [ə'rɪzn]) VI alzarsi; (*opportunity, problem*) presentarsi; **to ~ from** risultare da; **should the need ~** dovesse presentarsi la necessità, in caso di necessità

aristocracy [ærɪs'tɔkrəsɪ] N aristocrazia
aristocrat ['ærɪstəkræt] N aristocratico(-a)
aristocratic [ærɪstə'krætɪk] ADJ
aristocratico(-a)
arithmetic [ə'rɪθmətɪk] N aritmetica
arithmetical [ærɪθ'mɛtɪkəl] ADJ
aritmetico(-a)
Ariz. ABBR (US) = **Arizona**
ark [ɑːk] N: **Noah's A~** l'arca di Noè
Ark. ABBR (US) = **Arkansas**
arm [ɑːm] N braccio; (Mil: branch) arma ▶ VT
armare; **~ in ~** a braccetto; see also **arms**
armaments ['ɑːməmənts] NPL (weapons)
armamenti mpl
armband ['ɑːmbænd] N bracciale m
armchair ['ɑːmtʃɛəʳ] N poltrona
armed [ɑːmd] ADJ armato(-a)
armed forces NPL forze fpl armate
armed robbery N rapina a mano armata
Armenia [ɑː'miːnɪə] N Armenia
Armenian [ɑː'miːnɪən] ADJ armeno(-a) ▶ N
armeno(-a); (Ling) armeno
armful ['ɑːmful] N bracciata
armistice ['ɑːmɪstɪs] N armistizio
armour, (US) **armor** ['ɑːməʳ] N armatura;
(also: **armour-plating**) corazza, blindatura;
(Mil: tanks) mezzi mpl blindati
armoured car, (US) **armored car** N
autoblinda f inv
armoury, (US) **armory** ['ɑːmərɪ] N
arsenale m
armpit ['ɑːmpɪt] N ascella
armrest ['ɑːmrɛst] N bracciolo
arms [ɑːmz] NPL (weapons) armi fpl; (Heraldry)
stemma m
arms control N controllo degli armamenti
arms race N corsa agli armamenti
army ['ɑːmɪ] N esercito
aroma [ə'rəumə] N aroma
aromatherapy [ərəumə'θɛrəpɪ] N
aromaterapia
aromatic [ærə'mætɪk] ADJ aromatico(-a)
arose [ə'rəuz] PT of **arise**
around [ə'raund] ADV attorno, intorno ▶ PREP
intorno a; (fig: about): **~ £5/3 o'clock** circa 5
sterline/le 3; **is he ~?** è in giro?
arousal [ə'rauzəl] N (sexual etc) eccitazione f;
(awakening) risveglio
arouse [ə'rauz] VT (sleeper) svegliare; (curiosity,
passions) suscitare
arrange [ə'reɪndʒ] VT sistemare; (programme)
preparare ▶ VI: **we have arranged for a taxi
to pick you up** la faremo venire a prendere
da un taxi; **it was arranged that ...** è stato
deciso or stabilito che ...; **to ~ to do sth**
mettersi d'accordo per fare qc
arrangement [ə'reɪndʒmənt] N
sistemazione f; (agreement) accordo;
arrangements NPL (plans etc) progetti mpl,

piani mpl; **by ~** su richiesta; **to come to an ~
(with sb)** venire ad un accordo (con qn),
mettersi d'accordo or accordarsi (con qn); **I'll
make arrangements for you to be met**
darò disposizioni or istruzioni perché ci sia
qualcuno ad incontrarla
arrant ['ærənt] ADJ: **~ nonsense** colossali
sciocchezze fpl
array [ə'reɪ] N fila; (Comput) array m inv,
insiemi mpl; **~ of** fila di
arrears [ə'rɪəz] NPL arretrati mpl; **to be in ~
with one's rent** essere in arretrato con
l'affitto
arrest [ə'rɛst] VT arrestare; (sb's attention)
attirare ▶ N arresto; **under ~** in arresto
arresting [ə'rɛstɪŋ] ADJ (fig) che colpisce
arrival [ə'raɪvəl] N arrivo; (person)
arrivato(-a); **a new ~** un nuovo venuto; (baby)
un neonato
arrive [ə'raɪv] VI arrivare
▶ **arrive at** VT FUS arrivare a
arrogance ['ærəgəns] N arroganza
arrogant ['ærəgənt] ADJ arrogante
arrow ['ærəu] N freccia
arse [ɑːs] N (BRIT col!) culo (!)
arsenal ['ɑːsɪnl] N arsenale m
arsenic ['ɑːsnɪk] N arsenico
arson ['ɑːsn] N incendio doloso
art [ɑːt] N arte f; (craft) mestiere m; **work of ~**
opera d'arte; see also **arts**
art college N scuola di belle arti
artefact, (US) **artifact** ['ɑːtɪfækt] N
manufatto
arterial [ɑː'tɪərɪəl] ADJ (Anat) arterioso(-a);
(road etc) di grande comunicazione; **~ roads**
le (grandi or principali) arterie
artery ['ɑːtərɪ] N arteria
artful ['ɑːtful] ADJ furbo(-a)
art gallery N galleria d'arte
arthritis [ɑː'θraɪtɪs] N artrite f
artichoke ['ɑːtɪtʃəuk] N carciofo; **Jerusalem
~** topinambur m inv
article ['ɑːtɪkl] N articolo; **articles** NPL (BRIT
Law: training) contratto di tirocinio; **articles
of clothing** indumenti mpl
articles of association NPL (Comm) statuto
sociale
articulate ADJ [ɑː'tɪkjulɪt] (person) che si
esprime forbitamente; (speech) articolato(-a)
▶ VI [ɑː'tɪkjuleɪt] articolare
articulated lorry N (BRIT) autotreno
artifact ['ɑːtɪfækt] N (US) = **artefact**
artifice ['ɑːtɪfɪs] N (cunning) abilità, destrezza;
(trick) artificio
artificial [ɑːtɪ'fɪʃəl] ADJ artificiale
artificial insemination [-ɪnsɛmɪ'neɪʃən] N
fecondazione f artificiale
artificial intelligence N intelligenza
artificiale

artificial respiration N respirazione f artificiale

artillery [ɑːˈtɪləri] N artiglieria

artisan [ˈɑːtɪzæn] N artigiano(-a)

artist [ˈɑːtɪst] N artista mf

artistic [ɑːˈtɪstɪk] ADJ artistico(-a)

artistry [ˈɑːtɪstri] N arte f

artless [ˈɑːtlɪs] ADJ semplice, ingenuo(-a)

arts [ɑːts] NPL (Scol) lettere fpl

art school N scuola d'arte

artwork [ˈɑːtwəːk] N materiale m illustrativo

ARV N ABBR (= American Revised Version) traduzione della Bibbia

AS N ABBR (US Scol: = Associate in Science) titolo di studio

(KEYWORD)

as [æz] CONJ **1** (referring to time) mentre; **as the years went by** col passare degli anni; **he came in as I was leaving** arrivò mentre stavo uscendo; **as from tomorrow** da domani

2 (in comparisons): **as big as** grande come; **twice as big as** due volte più grande di; **as much/many as** tanto quanto/tanti quanti; **as soon as possible** prima possibile

3 (since, because) dal momento che, siccome

4 (referring to manner, way) come; **big as it is** grande com'è; **much as I like them, …** per quanto mi siano simpatici, …; **do as you wish** fa' come vuoi; **as she said** come ha detto lei

5 (concerning): **as for** or **to that** per quanto riguarda or quanto a quello

6: **as if** or **though** come se; **he looked as if he was ill** sembrava stare male; see also **long**; **such**; **well**

▶ PREP: **he works as a driver** fa l'autista; **as chairman of the company, he …** come presidente della compagnia, lui …; **he gave me it as a present** me lo ha regalato

ASA N ABBR (= American Standards Association) associazione per la normalizzazione; (BRIT: = Advertising Standards Association) ≈ Istituto di Autodisciplina Pubblicitaria

a.s.a.p. ABBR (= as soon as possible) prima possibile

asbestos [æzˈbɛstəs] N asbesto, amianto

ASBO [ˈæzbəu] N ABBR (BRIT: = antisocial behaviour order) provvedimento restrittivo per comportamento antisociale

ascend [əˈsɛnd] VT salire

ascendancy [əˈsɛndənsɪ] N ascendente m

ascendant [əˈsɛndənt] N: **to be in the ~** essere in auge

ascension [əˈsɛnʃən] N: **the A~** (Rel) l'Ascensione f

Ascension Island N isola dell'Ascensione

ascent [əˈsɛnt] N salita

ascertain [æsəˈteɪn] VT accertare

ascetic [əˈsɛtɪk] ADJ ascetico(-a)

asceticism [əˈsɛtɪsɪzəm] N ascetismo

ASCII [ˈæskiː] N ABBR (= American Standard Code for Information Interchange) ASCII m

ascribe [əˈskraɪb] VT: **to ~ sth to** attribuire qc a

ASCU N ABBR (US) = **Association of State Colleges and Universities**

ASE N ABBR = **American Stock Exchange**

ASH [æʃ] N ABBR (BRIT: = Action on Smoking and Health) iniziativa contro il fumo

ash [æʃ] N (dust) cenere f; **~ (tree)** frassino

ashamed [əˈʃeɪmd] ADJ vergognoso(-a); **to be ~ of** vergognarsi di; **to be ~ (of o.s.) for having done** vergognarsi di aver fatto

ashen [ˈæʃən] ADJ (pale) livido(-a)

ashore [əˈʃɔːʳ] ADV a terra; **to go ~** sbarcare

ashtray [ˈæʃtreɪ] N portacenere m

Ash Wednesday N Mercoledì m inv delle Ceneri

Asia [ˈeɪʃə] N Asia

Asia Minor N Asia minore

Asian [ˈeɪʃən] ADJ, N asiatico(-a)

Asiatic [eɪsɪˈætɪk] ADJ asiatico(-a)

aside [əˈsaɪd] ADV da parte ▶ N a parte m; **to take sb ~** prendere qn da parte; **~ from** (as well as) oltre a; (except for) a parte

ask [ɑːsk] VT (request) chiedere; (question) domandare; (invite) invitare; **to ~ about sth** informarsi su or di qc; **to ~ sb sth/sb to do sth** chiedere qc a qn/a qn di fare qc; **to ~ sb about sth** chiedere a qn di qc; **to ~ (sb) a question** fare una domanda (a qn); **to ~ sb the time** chiedere l'ora a qn; **to ~ sb out to dinner** invitare qn a mangiare fuori; **you should ~ at the information desk** dovreste rivolgervi all'ufficio informazioni

▶ **ask after** VT FUS chiedere di

▶ **ask for** VT FUS chiedere; **it's just asking for trouble** or **for it** è proprio (come) andarsele a cercare

askance [əˈskɑːns] ADV: **to look ~ at sb** guardare qn di traverso

askew [əˈskjuː] ADV di traverso, storto

asking price [ˈɑːskɪŋ-] N prezzo di partenza

asleep [əˈsliːp] ADJ addormentato(-a); **to be ~** dormire; **to fall ~** addormentarsi

ASLEF [ˈæzlɛf] N ABBR (BRIT: = Associated Society of Locomotive Engineers and Firemen) sindacato dei conducenti dei treni e dei macchinisti

AS level N ABBR (= Advanced Subsidiary level) prima parte del diploma di studi superiori chiamato "A level"

asp [æsp] N cobra m inv egiziano

asparagus [əsˈpærəgəs] N asparagi mpl

asparagus tips NPL punte fpl d'asparagi

ASPCA N ABBR (= *American Society for the Prevention of Cruelty to Animals*) ≈ E.N.P.A. *m* (= *Ente Nazionale per la Protezione degli Animali*)

aspect ['æspɛkt] N aspetto

aspersions [əs'pə:ʃənz] NPL: **to cast ~ on** diffamare

asphalt ['æsfælt] N asfalto

asphyxiate [æs'fɪksɪeɪt] VT asfissiare

asphyxiation [æsfɪksɪ'eɪʃən] N asfissia

aspiration [æspə'reɪʃən] N aspirazione *f*; **aspirations** NPL aspirazioni *fpl*

aspire [əs'paɪər] VI: **to ~ to** aspirare a

aspirin ['æsprɪn] N aspirina

aspiring [əs'paɪərɪŋ] ADJ aspirante

ass [æs] N asino; (*col*) scemo(-a); (*US col!*) culo (!)

assail [ə'seɪl] VT assalire

assailant [ə'seɪlənt] N assalitore *m*

assassin [ə'sæsɪn] N assassino

assassinate [ə'sæsɪneɪt] VT assassinare

assassination [əsæsɪ'neɪʃən] N assassinio

assault [ə'sɔ:lt] N (*Mil*) assalto; (*gen: attack*) aggressione *f*; (*Law*): **~ (and battery)** minacce e vie di fatto *fpl* ▶ VT assaltare; aggredire; (*sexually*) violentare

assemble [ə'sɛmbl] VT riunire; (*Tech*) montare ▶ VI riunirsi

assembly [ə'sɛmblɪ] N (*meeting*) assemblea; (*construction*) montaggio

assembly language N (*Comput*) linguaggio assemblativo

assembly line N catena di montaggio

assent [ə'sɛnt] N assenso, consenso ▶ VI assentire; **to ~ (to sth)** approvare (qc)

assert [ə'sə:t] VT asserire; (*insist on*) far valere; **to ~ o.s.** farsi valere

assertion [ə'sə:ʃən] N asserzione *f*

assertive [ə'sə:tɪv] ADJ che sa imporsi

assess [ə'sɛs] VT valutare

assessment [ə'sɛsmənt] N valutazione *f*; (*judgment*): **~ (of)** giudizio (su)

assessor [ə'sɛsər] N perito; funzionario del fisco

asset ['æsɛt] N vantaggio; (*person*) elemento prezioso; **assets** NPL (*Comm: of individual*) beni *mpl*; disponibilità *fpl* (*of company*) attivo

asset-stripping ['æsɛt'strɪpɪŋ] N (*Comm*) *acquisto di una società in fallimento con lo scopo di rivenderne le attività*

assiduous [ə'sɪdjuəs] ADJ assiduo(-a)

assign [ə'saɪn] VT: **to ~ (to)** (*task*) assegnare (a); (*resources*) riservare (a); (*cause, meaning*) attribuire (a); **to ~ a date to sth** fissare la data di qc

assignment [ə'saɪnmənt] N compito

assimilate [ə'sɪmɪleɪt] VT assimilare

assimilation [əsɪmɪ'leɪʃən] N assimilazione *f*

assist [ə'sɪst] VT assistere, aiutare

assistance [ə'sɪstəns] N assistenza, aiuto

assistant [ə'sɪstənt] N assistente *mf*; (BRIT: *also*: **shop assistant**) commesso(-a)

assistant manager N vicedirettore *m*

assizes [ə'saɪzɪz] NPL assise *fpl*

associate ADJ [ə'səuʃɪɪt] associato(-a); (*member*) aggiunto(-a) ▶ N [ə'səuʃɪɪt] collega *mf*; (*in business*) socio(-a) ▶ VT [ə'səuʃɪeɪt] associare ▶ VI [ə'səuʃɪeɪt]: **to ~ with sb** frequentare qn

associated company [ə'səusɪ'eɪtɪd-] N società collegata

associate director N amministratore *m* aggiunto

association [əsəusɪ'eɪʃən] N associazione *f*; **in ~ with** in collaborazione con

association football N (BRIT) (gioco del) calcio

assorted [ə'sɔ:tɪd] ADJ assortito(-a); **in ~ sizes** in diverse taglie

assortment [ə'sɔ:tmənt] N assortimento

Asst. ABBR = **assistant**

assuage [ə'sweɪdʒ] VT alleviare

assume [ə'sju:m] VT supporre; (*responsibilities etc*) assumere; (*attitude, name*) prendere

assumed name N nome *m* falso

assumption [ə'sʌmpʃən] N supposizione *f*, ipotesi *f inv*; (*of power*) assunzione *f*; **on the ~ that ...** partendo dal presupposto che ...

assurance [ə'ʃuərəns] N assicurazione *f*; (*self-confidence*) fiducia in se stesso; **I can give you no assurances** non posso assicurarle *or* garantirle niente

assure [ə'ʃuər] VT assicurare

assured [ə'ʃuəd] ADJ (*confident*) sicuro(-a); (*certain: promotion etc*) assicurato(-a)

AST ABBR (US: = *Atlantic Standard Time*) ora invernale di New York

asterisk ['æstərɪsk] N asterisco

astern [ə'stə:n] ADV a poppa

asteroid ['æstərɔɪd] N asteroide *m*

asthma ['æsmə] N asma

asthmatic [æs'mætɪk] ADJ, N asmatico(-a)

astigmatism [ə'stɪgmətɪzəm] N astigmatismo

astir [ə'stə:r] ADV in piedi; (*excited*) in fermento

astonish [ə'stɔnɪʃ] VT stupire

astonished ADJ stupito(-a), sorpreso(-a); **to be ~ (at)** essere stupito(-a) (da)

astonishing [ə'stɔnɪʃɪŋ] ADJ sorprendente, stupefacente; **I find it ~ that ...** mi stupisce che ...

astonishingly [ə'stɔnɪʃɪŋlɪ] ADV straordinariamente, incredibilmente

astonishment [ə'stɔnɪʃmənt] N stupore *m*; **to my ~** con mia gran meraviglia, con mio grande stupore

astound [ə'staund] VT sbalordire

astray [ə'streɪ] ADV: **to go ~** smarrirsi; (*fig*)

traviarsi; **to lead ~** portare sulla cattiva strada; **to go ~ in one's calculations** sbagliare i calcoli

astride [ə'straɪd] ADV a cavalcioni ▶ PREP a cavalcioni di

astringent [əs'trɪndʒənt] ADJ, N astringente *m*

astrologer [əs'trɔlədʒər] N astrologo(-a)

astrology [əs'trɔlədʒɪ] N astrologia

astronaut ['æstrənɔ:t] N astronauta *mf*

astronomer [əs'trɔnəmər] N astronomo(-a)

astronomical [æstrə'nɔmɪkl] ADJ astronomico(-a)

astronomy [əs'trɔnəmɪ] N astronomia

astrophysics ['æstrəu'fɪzɪks] N astrofisica

astute [əs'tju:t] ADJ astuto(-a)

asunder [ə'sʌndər] ADV: **to tear ~** strappare

ASV N ABBR (= *American Standard Version*) *traduzione della Bibbia*

asylum [ə'saɪləm] N asilo; (*lunatic asylum*) manicomio; **to seek political ~** chiedere asilo politico

asymmetric [eɪsɪ'mɛtrɪk], **asymmetrical** [eɪsɪ'mɛtrɪkəl] ADJ asimmetrico(-a)

(KEYWORD)

at [æt] PREP **1** (*referring to position, direction*) a; **at the top** in cima; **at the desk** al banco, alla scrivania; **at home/school** a casa/scuola; **at Paolo's** da Paolo; **at the baker's** dal panettiere; **to look at sth** guardare qc; **to throw sth at sb** lanciare qc a qn

2 (*referring to time*) a; **at 4 o'clock** alle 4; **at night** di notte; **at Christmas** a Natale; **at times** a volte

3 (*referring to rates, speed etc*) a; **at £1 a kilo** a 1 sterlina al chilo; **two at a time** due alla volta, due per volta; **at 50 km/h** a 50 km/h; **at full speed** a tutta velocità

4 (*referring to manner*): **at a stroke** d'un solo colpo; **at peace** in pace

5 (*referring to activity*): **to be at work** essere al lavoro; **to play at cowboys** giocare ai cowboy; **to be good at sth/doing sth** essere bravo in qc/a fare qc

6 (*referring to cause*): **shocked/surprised/ annoyed at sth** colpito da/sorpreso da/ arrabbiato per qc; **I went at his suggestion** ci sono andato dietro suo consiglio

▶ N (*Comput*: @ *symbol*) chiocciola

ate [eɪt] PT *of* **eat**

atheism ['eɪθɪɪzəm] N ateismo

atheist ['eɪθɪɪst] N ateo(-a)

Athenian [ə'θi:nɪən] ADJ, N ateniese *mf*

Athens ['æθɪnz] N Atene *f*

athlete ['æθli:t] N atleta *mf*

athletic [æθ'lɛtɪk] ADJ atletico(-a)

athletics [æθ'lɛtɪks] N atletica

Atlantic [ət'læntɪk] ADJ atlantico(-a)
▶ N: **the ~ (Ocean)** l'Atlantico, l'Oceano Atlantico

atlas ['ætləs] N atlante *m*

Atlas Mountains NPL: **the ~** i Monti dell'Atlante

ATM ABBR (= *automated telling machine*) (sportello) Bancomat® *m inv*

atmosphere ['ætməsfɪər] N atmosfera; (*air*) aria

atmospheric [ætməs'fɛrɪk] ADJ atmosferico(-a)

atmospherics [ætməs'fɛrɪks] NPL (*Radio*) scariche *fpl*

atoll ['ætɔl] N atollo

atom ['ætəm] N atomo

atom bomb, atomic bomb N bomba atomica

atomic [ə'tɔmɪk] ADJ atomico(-a)

atomizer ['ætəmaɪzər] N atomizzatore *m*

atone [ə'təun] VI: **to ~ for** espiare

atonement [ə'təunmənt] N espiazione *f*

ATP N ABBR = **Association of Tennis Professionals**

atrocious [ə'trəuʃəs] ADJ atroce, pessimo(-a)

atrocity [ə'trɔsɪtɪ] N atrocità *f inv*

atrophy ['ætrəfɪ] N atrofia ▶ VI atrofizzarsi

attach [ə'tætʃ] VT attaccare; (*document, letter*) allegare; (*importance etc*) attribuire; (*Mil: troops*) assegnare; **to be attached to sb/sth** (*to like*) essere affezionato(-a) a qn/qc; **the attached letter** la lettera acclusa *or* allegata

attaché [ə'tæʃeɪ] N addetto

attaché case N valigetta per documenti

attachment [ə'tætʃmənt] N (*tool*) accessorio; (*Comput*) allegato; (*love*): ~ **(to)** affetto (per)

attack [ə'tæk] VT attaccare; (*person*) aggredire; (*task etc*) iniziare; (*problem*) affrontare ▶ N attacco; (*also*: **heart attack**) infarto

attacker [ə'tækər] N aggressore *m*, assalitore(-trice)

attain [ə'teɪn] VT (*also*: **attain to**) arrivare a, raggiungere

attainments [ə'teɪnmənts] NPL cognizioni *fpl*

attempt [ə'tɛmpt] N tentativo ▶ VT tentare; **attempted murder** (*Law*) tentato omicidio; **to make an ~ on sb's life** attentare alla vita di qn; **he made no ~ to help** non ha (neanche) tentato *or* cercato di aiutare

attend [ə'tɛnd] VT frequentare; (*meeting, talk*) andare a; (*patient*) assistere
▶ **attend to** VT FUS (*needs, affairs etc*) prendersi cura di; (*customer*) occuparsi di

attendance [ə'tɛndəns] N (*being present*) presenza; (*people present*) gente *f* presente

attendant [ə'tɛndənt] N custode *mf*; persona di servizio ▶ ADJ concomitante

433

attention [ə'tɛnʃən] N attenzione f;
attentions premure fpl, attenzioni fpl; **~!**
(Mil) attenti!; **at ~** (Mil) sull'attenti; **for the
~ of** (Admin) per l'attenzione di; **it has come
to my ~ that ...** sono venuto a conoscenza
(del fatto) che ...
attentive [ə'tɛntɪv] ADJ attento(-a); (kind)
premuroso(-a)
attentively [ə'tɛntɪvlɪ] ADV attentamente
attenuate [ə'tɛnjueɪt] VT attenuare ▶ VI
attenuarsi
attest [ə'tɛst] VI: **to ~ to** attestare
attic ['ætɪk] N soffitta
attire [ə'taɪər] N abbigliamento
attitude ['ætɪtjuːd] N (behaviour)
atteggiamento; (posture) posa; (view): **~ (to)**
punto di vista (nei confronti di)
attorney [ə'təːnɪ] N (US: lawyer) avvocato;
(having proxy) mandatario; **power of ~**
procura
Attorney General N (BRIT) Procuratore m
Generale; (US) Ministro della Giustizia
attract [ə'trækt] VT attirare
attraction [ə'trækʃən] N (gen pl: pleasant
things) attrattiva; (Physics, fig: towards sth)
attrazione f
attractive [ə'træktɪv] ADJ attraente; (idea,
offer, price) allettante, interessante
attribute N ['ætrɪbjuːt] attributo ▶ VT
[ə'trɪbjuːt]: **to ~ sth to** attribuire qc a
attrition [ə'trɪʃən] N: **war of ~** guerra di
logoramento
Atty. Gen. ABBR = **Attorney General**
atypical [eɪ'tɪpɪkl] ADJ atipico(-a)
AU N ABBR (= African Union) Unione Africana
aubergine ['əubəʒiːn] N melanzana
auburn ['ɔːbən] ADJ tizianesco(-a)
auction ['ɔːkʃən] N (also: **sale by auction**) asta
▶ VT (also: **sell by auction**) vendere all'asta;
(also: **put up for auction**) mettere all'asta
auctioneer [ɔːkʃə'nɪər] N banditore m
auction room N sala dell'asta
audacious [ɔː'deɪʃəs] ADJ (bold) audace;
(impudent) sfrontato(-a)
audacity [ɔː'dæsɪtɪ] N audacia
audible ['ɔːdɪbl] ADJ udibile
audience ['ɔːdɪəns] N (people) pubblico;
spettatori mpl; ascoltatori mpl; (interview)
udienza
audio-typist ['ɔːdɪəu'taɪpɪst] N
dattilografo(-a) che trascrive da nastro
audiovisual [ɔːdɪəu'vɪzjuəl] ADJ
audiovisivo(-a); **~ aids** sussidi mpl
audiovisivi
audit ['ɔːdɪt] N revisione f, verifica ▶ VT
rivedere, verificare
audition [ɔː'dɪʃən] N (Theat) audizione f;
(Cine) provino ▶ VI fare un'audizione (or un
provino)

auditor ['ɔːdɪtər] N revisore m
auditorium [ɔːdɪ'tɔːrɪəm] N sala, auditorio
Aug. ABBR (= August) ago., ag.
augment [ɔːg'mɛnt] VT, VI aumentare
augur ['ɔːgər] VT (be a sign of) predire ▶ VI: **it
augurs well** promette bene
August ['ɔːgəst] N agosto; see also **July**
august [ɔː'gʌst] ADJ augusto(-a)
aunt [ɑːnt] N zia
auntie, aunty ['ɑːntɪ] N zietta
au pair ['əu'pɛər] N (also: **au pair girl**) (ragazza
f) alla pari inv
aura ['ɔːrə] N aura
auspices ['ɔːspɪsɪz] NPL: **under the ~ of** sotto
gli auspici di
auspicious [ɔːs'pɪʃəs] ADJ propizio(-a)
austere [ɔs'tɪər] ADJ austero(-a)
austerity [ɔs'tɛrɪtɪ] N austerità f inv
Australasia [ɔstrə'leɪzɪə] N Australasia
Australia [ɔs'treɪlɪə] N Australia
Australian [ɔs'treɪlɪən] ADJ, N australiano(-a)
Austria ['ɔstrɪə] N Austria
Austrian ['ɔstrɪən] ADJ, N austriaco(-a)
AUT N ABBR (BRIT: = Association of University
Teachers) associazione dei docenti universitari
authentic [ɔː'θɛntɪk] ADJ autentico(-a)
authenticate [ɔː'θɛntɪkeɪt] VT autenticare
authenticity [ɔːθɛn'tɪsɪtɪ] N autenticità
author ['ɔːθər] N autore(-trice)
authoritarian [ɔːθɔrɪ'tɛərɪən] ADJ
autoritario(-a)
authoritative [ɔː'θɔrɪtətɪv] ADJ (account etc)
autorevole; (manner) autoritario(-a)
authority [ɔː'θɔrɪtɪ] N autorità f inv;
(permission) autorizzazione f; **the authorities**
NPL (government etc) le autorità; **to have ~ to
do sth** avere l'autorizzazione a fare or il
diritto di fare qc
authorization [ɔːθəraɪ'zeɪʃən] N
autorizzazione f
authorize ['ɔːθəraɪz] VT autorizzare
authorized capital N capitale m nominale
authorship ['ɔːθəʃɪp] N paternità (letteraria
ecc)
autistic [ɔː'tɪstɪk] ADJ autistico(-a)
auto ['ɔːtəu] N (US) auto f inv
autobiography [ɔːtəbaɪ'ɔgrəfɪ] N
autobiografia
autocratic [ɔːtə'krætɪk] ADJ autocratico(-a)
Autocue® ['ɔːtəukjuː] N (BRIT) gobbo (TV)
autograph ['ɔːtəgrɑːf] N autografo ▶ VT
firmare
autoimmune [ɔːtəʊɪ'mjuːn] ADJ
autoimmune
automat ['ɔːtəmæt] N (US) tavola calda fornita
esclusivamente di distributori automatici
automated ['ɔːtəmeɪtɪd] ADJ
automatizzato(-a)
automatic [ɔːtə'mætɪk] ADJ automatico(-a)

▶ N (*gun*) arma automatica; (*car*) automobile f con cambio automatico; (*washing machine*) lavatrice f automatica

automatically [ɔːtə'mætɪklɪ] ADV automaticamente

automatic data processing N elaborazione f automatica dei dati

automation [ɔːtə'meɪʃən] N automazione f

automaton [ɔː'tɔmətən] (*pl* **automata** [-tə]) N automa m

automobile ['ɔːtəməbiːl] N (*US*) automobile f

autonomous [ɔː'tɔnəməs] ADJ autonomo(-a)

autonomy [ɔː'tɔnəmɪ] N autonomia

autopsy ['ɔːtɔpsɪ] N autopsia

autumn ['ɔːtəm] N autunno

auxiliary [ɔːg'zɪlɪərɪ] ADJ ausiliario(-a) ▶ N ausiliare mf

AV N ABBR (= *Authorized Version*) traduzione inglese della Bibbia ▶ ABBR = **audiovisual**

Av. ABBR = **avenue**

avail [ə'veɪl] VT: **to ~ o.s. of** servirsi di; approfittarsi di ▶ N: **to no ~** inutilmente

availability [əveɪlə'bɪlɪtɪ] N disponibilità

available [ə'veɪləbl] ADJ disponibile; **every ~ means** tutti i mezzi disponibili; **to make sth ~ to sb** mettere qc a disposizione di qn; **is the manager ~?** è libero il direttore?

avalanche ['ævəlɑːnʃ] N valanga

avant-garde ['ævɑ̃'gɑːd] ADJ d'avanguardia

avarice ['ævərɪs] N avarizia

avaricious [ævə'rɪʃəs] ADJ avaro(-a)

avdp. ABBR (= *avoirdupois*) sistema ponderale anglosassone basato su libbra, oncia e multipli

Ave. ABBR = **avenue**

avenge [ə'vɛndʒ] VT vendicare

avenue ['ævənjuː] N viale m; (*fig*) strada, via

average ['ævərɪdʒ] N media ▶ ADJ medio(-a) ▶ VT (*also:* **average out at**) aggirarsi in media su, essere in media di; **on ~** in media; **above/below (the) ~** sopra/sotto la media

averse [ə'vəːs] ADJ: **to be ~ to sth/doing** essere contrario(-a) a qc/a fare; **I wouldn't be ~ to a drink** non avrei nulla in contrario a bere qualcosa

aversion [ə'vəːʃən] N avversione f

avert [ə'vəːt] VT evitare, prevenire; (*one's eyes*) distogliere

avian flu ['eɪvɪən-] N influenza aviaria

aviary ['eɪvɪərɪ] N voliera, uccelliera

aviation [eɪvɪ'eɪʃən] N aviazione f

avid ['ævɪd] ADJ avido(-a); (*supporter etc*) accanito(-a)

avidly ['ævɪdlɪ] ADV avidamente

avocado [ævə'kɑːdəu] N (*BRIT: also:* **avocado pear**) avocado m inv

avoid [ə'vɔɪd] VT evitare

avoidable [ə'vɔɪdəbl] ADJ evitabile

avoidance [ə'vɔɪdəns] N l'evitare m

avowed [ə'vaud] ADJ dichiarato(-a)

AVP N ABBR (*US*) = **assistant vice-president**

AWACS ['eɪwæks] N ABBR (= *airborne warning and control system*) sistema di allarme e controllo in volo

await [ə'weɪt] VT aspettare; **awaiting attention** (*Comm: letter*) in attesa di risposta; (: *order*) in attesa di essere evaso; **long awaited** tanto atteso(-a)

awake [ə'weɪk] (*pt* **awoke**, *pp* **awoken** *or* **awaked**) VT svegliare ▶ VI svegliarsi ▶ ADJ sveglio(-a); **~ to** consapevole di

awakening [ə'weɪknɪŋ] N risveglio

award [ə'wɔːd] N premio; (*Law*) decreto; (*sum*) risarcimento ▶ VT assegnare; (*Law: damages*) decretare

aware [ə'wɛər] ADJ: **~ of** (*conscious*) conscio(-a) di; (*informed*) informato(-a) di; **to become ~ of** accorgersi di; **politically/socially ~** politicamente/socialmente preparato; **I am fully ~ that ...** mi rendo perfettamente conto che ...

awareness [ə'wɛənɪs] N consapevolezza; coscienza; **to develop people's ~ (of)** sensibilizzare la gente (a)

awash [ə'wɔʃ] ADJ: **~ (with)** inondato(-a) (da)

away [ə'weɪ] ADJ, ADV via; lontano(-a); **two kilometres ~** a due chilometri di distanza; **two hours ~ by car** a due ore di distanza in macchina; **the holiday was two weeks ~** mancavano due settimane alle vacanze; **~ from** lontano da; **he's ~ for a week** è andato via per una settimana; **he's ~ in Milan** è (andato) a Milano; **to take ~** vt portare via; **he was working/pedalling ~** lavorava/pedalava più che poteva; **to fade ~** scomparire

away game N (*Sport*) partita fuori casa

awe [ɔː] N timore m

awe-inspiring ['ɔːɪnspaɪərɪŋ], **awesome** ['ɔːsəm] ADJ imponente

awestruck ['ɔːstrʌk] ADJ sgomento(-a)

awful ['ɔːfəl] ADJ terribile; **an ~ lot of** (*people, cars, dogs*) un numero incredibile di; (*jam, flowers*) una quantità incredibile di

awfully ['ɔːflɪ] ADV (*very*) terribilmente

awhile [ə'waɪl] ADV (per) un po'

awkward ['ɔːkwəd] ADJ (*clumsy*) goffo(-a); (*inconvenient*) scomodo(-a); (*embarrassing*) imbarazzante; (*difficult*) delicato(-a), difficile

awkwardness ['ɔːkwədnɪs] N goffaggine f; scomodità; imbarazzo; delicatezza, difficoltà

awl ['ɔːl] N punteruolo

awning ['ɔːnɪŋ] N (*of tent*) veranda; (*of shop, hotel etc*) tenda

awoke [ə'wəuk] PT *of* **awake**

awoken [ə'wəukən] PP *of* **awake**

AWOL ['eɪwɔl] ABBR (*Mil etc*) = **absent without leave**

awry [əˈraɪ] ADV di traverso ▸ ADJ storto(-a);
  to go ~ andare a monte
axe, (US) **ax** [æks] N scure f ▸ VT (project etc)
  abolire; (jobs) sopprimere; **to have an ~ to
  grind** (fig) fare i propri interessi or il proprio
  tornaconto
axiom [ˈæksɪəm] N assioma m
axiomatic [æksɪəuˈmætɪk] ADJ
  assiomatico(-a)
axis [ˈæksɪs] (pl **axes** [-siːz]) N asse m
axle [ˈæksl] N (also: **axle-tree**) asse m

ay, aye [aɪ] EXCL (yes) sì
AYH N ABBR = **American Youth Hostels**
AZ ABBR (US) = **Arizona**
azalea [əˈzeɪlɪə] N azalea
Azerbaijan [æzəbaɪˈdʒɑːn] N Azerbaigian m
Azerbaijani [æzəbaɪˈdʒɑːnɪ], **Azeri** [əˈzɛərɪ]
  ADJ, N azerbaigiano(-a), azero(-a)
Azores [əˈzɔːz] NPL: **the ~** le Azzorre
AZT N ABBR (= azidothymidine) AZT m
Aztec [ˈæztɛk] ADJ, N azteco(-a)
azure [ˈeɪʒər] ADJ azzurro(-a)

Bb

B, b [biː] N (*letter*) B, b f *inv or* m *inv*; (*Scol: mark*)
≈ 8 (*buono*); (*Mus*): **B** si m; **B for Benjamin**,
(*US*) **B for Baker** ≈ B come Bologna; **B road** n
(*BRIT Aut*) ≈ strada secondaria

b. ABBR = **born**

BA N ABBR = **British Academy**; (*Scol*)
= **Bachelor of Arts**

babble ['bæbl] VI cianciare; mormorare ▶ N
ciance fpl mormorio

babe [beɪb] N (*col*): **she's a real** ~ è uno
schianto di ragazza

baboon [bə'buːn] N babbuino

baby ['beɪbɪ] N bambino(-a)

baby carriage N (*US*) carrozzina

baby grand N (*also*: **baby grand piano**)
pianoforte m a mezza coda

babyhood ['beɪbɪhʊd] N prima infanzia

babyish ['beɪbɪʃ] ADJ infantile

baby-minder ['beɪbɪ'maɪndə^r] N (*BRIT*)
bambinaia (*che tiene i bambini mentre la madre
lavora*)

baby-sit ['beɪbɪsɪt] VI fare il (*or* la) babysitter

baby-sitter ['beɪbɪsɪtə^r] N baby-sitter mf

baby wipe N salvietta umidificata

bachelor ['bætʃələ^r] N scapolo; **B~ of Arts/
Science (BA/BSc)** ≈ laureato(-a) in lettere/
scienze; **B~ of Arts/Science degree (BA/
BSc)** n ≈ laurea in lettere/scienze; *vedi nota*

> Il *Bachelor's degree* è il riconoscimento che
> viene conferito a chi ha completato un
> corso di laurea di tre o quattro anni
> all'università. I *Bachelor's degree* più
> importanti sono il *BA* (*Bachelor of Arts*), il
> *BSc* (*Bachelor of Science*), il *BEd* (*Bachelor of
> Education*), e il *LLB* (*Bachelor of Laws*); *vedi
> anche* **Master's degree**, **doctorate**.

bachelorhood ['bætʃələhʊd] N celibato

bachelor party N (*US*) festa di addio al
celibato

back [bæk] N (*of person, horse*) dorso, schiena;
(*as opposed to front*) dietro; (*of hand*) dorso; (*of
house, car*) didietro; (*of train*) coda; (*of chair*)
schienale m; (*of page*) rovescio; (*of book*) retro;
(*Football*) difensore m ▶ VT (*financially*)

finanziare; (*candidate: also*: **back up**)
appoggiare; (*horse: at races*) puntare su; (*car*)
guidare a marcia indietro ▶ VI indietreggiare;
(*car etc*) fare marcia indietro ▶ ADJ (*in
compounds*) posteriore, di dietro; arretrato(-a)
▶ ADV (*not forward*) indietro; (*returned*): **he's** ~ è
tornato; ~ **to front** all'incontrario; **to break
the** ~ **of a job** (*BRIT*) fare il grosso *or* il peggio
di un lavoro; **to have one's** ~ **to the wall** (*fig*)
essere *or* trovarsi con le spalle al muro; **when
will you be** ~? quando torni?; **he ran** ~ tornò
indietro di corsa; **throw the ball** ~
(*restitution*) ritira la palla; **can I have it** ~?
posso riaverlo?; **he called** ~ (*again*) ha
richiamato; ~ **seats/wheels** (*Aut*) sedili mpl/
ruote fpl posteriori; **to take a** ~ **seat** (*fig*)
restare in secondo piano; ~ **payments/rent**
arretrati mpl; ~ **garden/room** giardino/
stanza sul retro (della casa)
  ▶ **back down** VI (*fig*) fare marcia indietro
  ▶ **back on to** VT FUS: **the house backs on to
  the golf course** il retro della casa dà sul
  campo da golf
  ▶ **back out** VI (*of promise*) tirarsi indietro
  ▶ **back up** VT (*support*) appoggiare, sostenere;
  (*Comput*) fare una copia di riserva di

backache ['bækeɪk] N mal m di schiena

backbencher ['bæk'bentʃə^r] N (*BRIT*)
*parlamentare che non ha incarichi né al governo né
all'opposizione*

back benches NPL *posti in Parlamento occupati
dai backbencher*; *vedi nota*

> Nella *House of Commons*, una delle camere
> del Parlamento britannico, sono
> chiamati *back benches* gli scanni dove
> siedono i *backbenchers*, parlamentari che
> non hanno incarichi né al governo né
> all'opposizione. Nelle file davanti ad essi
> siedono i *frontbencher*; *vedi anche* **front
> bench**.

backbiting ['bækbaɪtɪŋ] N maldicenza

backbone ['bækbəʊn] N spina dorsale; **the** ~
of the organization l'anima
dell'organizzazione

backchat ['bæktʃæt] N (BRIT col) impertinenza

backcloth ['bækklɔθ] N (BRIT) scena di sfondo

backcomb ['bækkəum] VT (BRIT) cotonare

backdate [bæk'deit] VT (letter) retrodatare; **backdated pay rise** aumento retroattivo

back door N porta sul retro

backdrop ['bækdrɔp] N = **backcloth**

backer ['bækər] N sostenitore(-trice); (Comm) fautore m

backfire ['bæk'faiər] VI (Aut) dar ritorni di fiamma; (plans) fallire

backgammon ['bækgæmən] N tavola reale

background ['bækgraund] N sfondo; (of events, Comput) background m inv; (basic knowledge) base f; (experience) esperienza ▶ CPD (noise, music) di fondo; ~ **reading** letture fpl sull'argomento; **family** ~ ambiente m familiare

backhand ['bækhænd] N (Tennis: also: **backhand stroke**) rovescio

backhanded [bæk'hændid] ADJ (fig) ambiguo(-a)

backhander ['bækhændər] N (BRIT: bribe) bustarella

backing ['bækiŋ] N (Comm) finanziamento; (Mus) accompagnamento; (fig) appoggio

backlash ['bæklæʃ] N contraccolpo, ripercussione f

backlog ['bæklɔg] N: ~ **of work** lavoro arretrato

back number N (of magazine etc) numero arretrato

backpack ['bækpæk] N zaino

backpacker ['bækpækər] N chi viaggia con zaino e sacco a pelo

back pay N arretrato di paga

backpedal ['bækpɛdl] VI pedalare all'indietro; (fig) far marcia indietro

backseat driver ['bæksi:t-] N passeggero che dà consigli non richiesti al guidatore

backside [bæk'said] N (col) sedere m

backslash ['bækslæʃ] N backslash m inv, barra obliqua inversa

backslide ['bækslaid] VI ricadere

backspace ['bækspeis] VI (in typing) battere il tasto di ritorno

backstage [bæk'steidʒ] ADV nel retroscena

back street N vicolo

back-street ['bækstri:t] ADJ: ~ **abortionist** praticante mf di aborti clandestini

backstroke ['bækstrəuk] N nuoto sul dorso

backtrack ['bæktræk] VI = **backpedal**

backup ['bækʌp] ADJ (train, plane) supplementare; (Comput) di riserva ▶ N (support) appoggio, sostegno; (Comput: also: **backup file**) file m inv di riserva

backward ['bækwəd] ADJ (movement) indietro inv; (person) tardivo(-a); (country) arretrato(-a); ~ **and forward movement** movimento avanti e indietro

backwards ['bækwədz] ADV indietro; (fall, walk) all'indietro; **to know sth** ~ or (US) ~ **and forwards** (col) sapere qc a menadito

backwater ['bækwɔ:tər] N (fig) posto morto

back yard N cortile m sul retro

bacon ['beikən] N pancetta

bacteria [bæk'tiəriə] NPL batteri mpl

bacteriology [bæktiəri'ɔlədʒi] N batteriologia

bad [bæd] ADJ cattivo(-a); (child) cattivello(-a); (meat, food) andato(-a) a male; **his** ~ **leg** la sua gamba malata; **to go** ~ (meat, food) andare a male; **to have a** ~ **time of it** passarsela male; **I feel** ~ **about it** (guilty) mi sento un po' in colpa; ~ **debt** credito difficile da recuperare; ~ **faith** malafede f

baddie, baddy ['bædi] N (col: Cine etc) cattivo(-a)

bade [bæd] PT of **bid**

badge [bædʒ] N insegna; (of policeman) stemma m; (stick-on) adesivo

badger ['bædʒər] N tasso ▶ VT tormentare

badly ['bædli] ADV (work, dress etc) male; **things are going** ~ le cose vanno male; ~ **wounded** gravemente ferito; **he needs it** ~ ne ha gran bisogno; ~ **off** adj povero(-a)

bad-mannered [bæd'mænəd] ADJ maleducato(-a), sgarbato(-a)

badminton ['bædmintən] N badminton m

bad-tempered [bæd'tɛmpəd] ADJ irritabile; (in bad mood) di malumore

baffle ['bæfl] VT (puzzle) confondere

baffling ['bæfliŋ] ADJ sconcertante

bag [bæg] N sacco; (handbag etc) borsa; (of hunter) carniere m; bottino ▶ VT (col: take) mettersi in tasca; prendersi; **bags of** (col: lots of) un sacco di; **to pack one's bags** fare le valigie; **bags under the eyes** borse sotto gli occhi

bagful ['bægful] N sacco (pieno)

baggage ['bægidʒ] N bagagli mpl

baggage allowance N peso bagaglio consentito

baggage car N (US) bagagliaio

baggage claim, baggage reclaim N ritiro m bagaglio inv

baggy ['bægi] ADJ largo(-a), sformato(-a)

Baghdad [bæg'dæd] N Bagdad f

bag lady N (col) stracciona, barbona

bagpipes ['bægpaips] NPL cornamusa

bag-snatcher ['bægsnætʃər] N (BRIT) scippatore(-trice)

bag-snatching ['bægsnætʃiŋ] N (BRIT) scippo

Bahamas [bə'hɑ:məz] NPL: **the** ~ le isole Bahama

Bahrain [bɑ:'rein] N Bahrein m

bail [beɪl] N cauzione f ▶ VT (prisoner: also: **grant bail to**) concedere la libertà provvisoria su cauzione a; (Naut: also: **bail out**) aggottare; **on ~** in libertà provvisoria su cauzione; **to be released on ~** essere rilasciato(-a) su cauzione
▶ **bail out** VT (prisoner) ottenere la libertà provvisoria su cauzione di; (fig) tirare fuori dai guai ▶ VI see **bale out**

bailiff ['beɪlɪf] N usciere m; fattore m

bailout ['beɪlaʊt] N ricapitalizzazione f; **government bailouts of large corporations** ricapitalizzazioni di grosse società da parte del governo

bait [beɪt] N esca ▶ VT (hook) innescare; (trap) munire di esca; (fig) tormentare

bake [beɪk] VT cuocere al forno ▶ VI cuocersi al forno

baked beans [-bi:nz] NPL fagioli mpl in salsa di pomodoro

baked potato N patata (con la buccia) cotta al forno

baker ['beɪkəʳ] N fornaio(-a), panettiere(-a)

bakery ['beɪkərɪ] N panetteria

baking ['beɪkɪŋ] N cottura (al forno)

baking powder N lievito in polvere

baking tin N stampo, tortiera

baking tray N teglia

balaclava [bælə'klɑ:və] N (also: **balaclava helmet**) passamontagna m inv

balance ['bæləns] N equilibrio; (Comm: sum) bilancio; (remainder) resto; (scales) bilancia
▶ VT tenere in equilibrio; (pros and cons) soppesare; (budget) far quadrare; (account) pareggiare; (compensate) contrappesare; **~ of trade/payments** bilancia commerciale/dei pagamenti; **~ brought forward** saldo riportato; **~ carried forward** saldo da riportare; **to ~ the books** fare il bilancio

balanced ['bælənst] ADJ (personality, diet) equilibrato(-a)

balance sheet N bilancio

balcony ['bælkənɪ] N balcone m; (in theatre) balconata

bald [bɔ:ld] ADJ calvo(-a); (tyre) liscio(-a)

baldness ['bɔ:ldnɪs] N calvizie f

bale [beɪl] N balla
▶ **bale out** VT (Naut: water) vuotare; (: boat) aggottare ▶ VI (of a plane) gettarsi col paracadute

Balearic Islands NPL: **the Balearics** le Baleari fpl

baleful ['beɪlful] ADJ funesto(-a)

balk [bɔ:lk] VI: **to ~ (at)** tirarsi indietro (davanti a); (horse) recalcitrare (davanti a)

Balkan ['bɔ:lkən] ADJ balcanico(-a) ▶ N: **the Balkans** i Balcani

ball [bɔ:l] N palla; (football) pallone m; (for golf) pallina; (of wool, string) gomitolo; (dance)

ballo; **to play ~ (with sb)** giocare a palla (con qn); (fig) stare al gioco (di qn); **to be on the ~** (fig: competent) essere in gamba (: alert) stare all'erta; **to start the ~ rolling** (fig) fare la prima mossa; **the ~ is in your court** (fig) a lei la prossima mossa; see also **balls**

ballad ['bæləd] N ballata

ballast ['bæləst] N zavorra

ball bearing N cuscinetto a sfere

ball cock N galleggiante m

ballerina [bælə'ri:nə] N ballerina

ballet ['bæleɪ] N balletto

ballet dancer N ballerino(-a) classico(-a)

ballistic [bə'lɪstɪk] ADJ balistico(-a)

ballistics [bə'lɪstɪks] N balistica

balloon [bə'lu:n] N pallone m; (in comic strip) fumetto ▶ VI gonfiarsi

balloonist [bə'lu:nɪst] N aeronauta mf

ballot ['bælət] N scrutinio

ballot box N urna (per le schede)

ballot paper N scheda

ballpark ['bɔ:lpɑ:k] N (US) stadio di baseball

ballpark figure N (col) cifra approssimativa

ball-point pen ['bɔ:lpɔɪnt-] N penna a sfera

ballroom ['bɔ:lrum] N sala da ballo

balls [bɔ:lz] NPL (col!) coglioni mpl (!)

balm [bɑ:m] N balsamo

balmy ['bɑ:mɪ] ADJ (breeze, air) balsamico(-a); (BRIT col) = **barmy**

BALPA ['bælpə] N ABBR (= British Airline Pilots' Association) sindacato dei piloti

balsa ['bɔ:lsə], **balsa wood** N (legno di) balsa

balsam ['bɔ:lsəm] N balsamo

Baltic ['bɔ:ltɪk] ADJ, N: **the ~ Sea** il (mar) Baltico

balustrade [bæləs'treɪd] N balaustrata

bamboo [bæm'bu:] N bambù m

bamboozle [bæm'bu:zl] VT (col) infinocchiare

ban [bæn] N interdizione f ▶ VT interdire; **he was banned from driving** (BRIT) gli hanno ritirato la patente

banal [bə'nɑ:l] ADJ banale

banana [bə'nɑ:nə] N banana

band [bænd] N banda; (at a dance) orchestra; (Mil) fanfara
▶ **band together** VI collegarsi

bandage ['bændɪdʒ] N benda, fascia

Band-Aid® ['bændeɪd] N (US) cerotto

B & B N ABBR = **bed and breakfast**

bandit ['bændɪt] N bandito

bandstand ['bændstænd] N palco dell'orchestra

bandwagon ['bændwægən] N: **to jump on the ~** (fig) seguire la corrente

bandy ['bændɪ] VT (jokes, insults) scambiare
▶ **bandy about** VT far circolare

bandy-legged ['bændɪ'lɛgɪd] ADJ dalle gambe storte

bane [beɪn] N: **it** (or **he** etc) **is the ~ of my life** è la mia rovina

bang [bæŋ] N botta; (of door) lo sbattere; (blow) colpo ▶ VT battere (violentemente); (door) sbattere ▶ VI scoppiare; sbattere ▶ ADV (BRIT col): **to be ~ on time** spaccare il secondo; **to ~ at the door** picchiare alla porta; **to ~ into sth** sbattere contro qc; see also **bangs**

banger [ˈbæŋəʳ] N (BRIT col: car: also: **old banger**) macinino; (: sausage) salsiccia; (firework) mortaretto

Bangkok [ˈbæŋkɔk] N Bangkok f

Bangladesh [bɑːŋgləˈdɛʃ] N Bangladesh m

bangle [ˈbæŋgl] N braccialetto

bangs [bæŋz] NPL (US: fringe) frangia, frangetta

banish [ˈbænɪʃ] VT bandire

banister [ˈbænɪstəʳ] N, **banisters** [ˈbænɪstəz] NPL ringhiera

banjo [ˈbændʒəu] (pl **banjoes** or **banjos**) N banjo m inv

bank [bæŋk] N (for money) banca, banco; (of river, lake) riva, sponda; (of earth) banco ▶ VI (Aviat) inclinarsi in virata; (Comm): **they ~ with Pitt's** sono clienti di Pitt's
▶ **bank on** VT FUS contare su

bank account N conto in banca

bank balance N saldo; **a healthy ~** un solido conto in banca

bank card N carta f assegni inv

bank charges NPL (BRIT) spese fpl bancarie

bank draft N assegno circolare or bancario

banker [ˈbæŋkəʳ] N banchiere m; **~'s card** (BRIT) carta f assegni inv; **~'s order** (BRIT) ordine m di banca

bank giro N bancogiro

bank holiday N (BRIT) giorno di festa; vedi nota

> Una bank holiday, in Gran Bretagna, è una giornata in cui le banche e molti negozi sono chiusi. Generalmente le bank holiday cadono di lunedì e molti ne approfittano per fare una breve vacanza fuori città. Di conseguenza, durante questi fine settimana lunghi (bank holiday weekend) si verifica un notevole aumento del traffico sulle strade, negli aeroporti e nelle stazioni e molte località turistiche registrano il tutto esaurito.

banking [ˈbæŋkɪŋ] N attività bancaria; professione f di banchiere

banking hours NPL orario di sportello

bank loan N prestito bancario

bank manager N direttore m di banca

banknote [ˈbæŋknəut] N banconota

bank rate N tasso bancario

bankrupt [ˈbæŋkrʌpt] ADJ, N fallito(-a); **to go ~** fallire

bankruptcy [ˈbæŋkrʌptsɪ] N fallimento

bank statement N estratto conto

banned substance N sostanza al bando (nello sport)

banner [ˈbænəʳ] N striscione m

bannister [ˈbænɪstə] N, **bannisters** [ˈbænɪstəz] NPL see **banister**

banns [bænz] NPL pubblicazioni fpl di matrimonio

banquet [ˈbæŋkwɪt] N banchetto

bantam-weight [ˈbæntəmweɪt] N peso gallo

banter [ˈbæntəʳ] N scherzi mpl bonari

baptism [ˈbæptɪzəm] N battesimo

Baptist [ˈbæptɪst] ADJ, N battista (mf)

baptize [bæpˈtaɪz] VT battezzare

bar [bɑːʳ] N (rod) barra; (of window etc) sbarra; (of chocolate) tavoletta; (fig) ostacolo; restrizione f; (pub) bar m inv; (counter: in pub) banco; (Mus) battuta ▶ VT (road, window) sbarrare; (person) escludere; (activity) interdire; **~ of soap** saponetta; **the B~** (Law) l'Ordine m degli avvocati; **behind bars** (prisoner) dietro le sbarre; **~ none** senza eccezione

Barbados [bɑːˈbeɪdɔs] N Barbados fsg

barbaric [bɑːˈbærɪk], **barbarous** [ˈbɑːbərəs] ADJ barbaro(-a), barbarico(-a)

barbecue [ˈbɑːbɪkjuː] N barbecue m inv

barbed wire [ˈbɑːbd-] N filo spinato

barber [ˈbɑːbəʳ] N barbiere m

barber's (shop), (US) **barber shop** N barbiere m

barbiturate [bɑːˈbɪtjurɪt] N barbiturico

Barcelona [bɑːsɪˈləunə] N Barcellona

bar chart N diagramma m di frequenza

bar code N codice m a barre

bare [bɛəʳ] ADJ nudo(-a) ▶ VT scoprire, denudare; (teeth) mostrare; **the ~ essentials**, **the ~ necessities** lo stretto necessario

bareback [ˈbɛəbæk] ADV senza sella

barefaced [ˈbɛəfeɪst] ADJ sfacciato(-a)

barefoot [ˈbɛəfut] ADJ, ADV scalzo(-a)

bareheaded [bɛəˈhɛdɪd] ADJ, ADV a capo scoperto

barely [ˈbɛəlɪ] ADV appena

Barents Sea [ˈbærənts-] N: **the ~** il mar di Barents

bargain [ˈbɑːgɪn] N (transaction) contratto; (good buy) affare m ▶ VI (haggle) tirare sul prezzo; (trade) contrattare; **into the ~** per giunta
▶ **bargain for** VT FUS (col): **to ~ for sth** aspettarsi qc; **he got more than he bargained for** gli è andata peggio di quel che si aspettasse

bargaining [ˈbɑːgənɪŋ] N contrattazione f

bargaining position N: **to be in a weak/ strong ~** non avere/avere potere contrattuale

barge [bɑːdʒ] N chiatta
▶ **barge in** VI (*walk in*) piombare dentro; (*interrupt talk*) intromettersi a sproposito
▶ **barge into** VT FUS urtare contro
baritone ['bærɪtəun] N baritono
barium meal ['bɛərɪəm-] N (*pasto di*) bario
bark [bɑːk] N (*of tree*) corteccia; (*of dog*) abbaio
▶ VI abbaiare
barley ['bɑːlɪ] N orzo
barley sugar N zucchero d'orzo
barmaid ['bɑːmeɪd] N cameriera al banco
barman ['bɑːmən] N (*irreg*) barista *m*
barmy ['bɑːmɪ] ADJ (*BRIT col*) tocco(-a)
barn [bɑːn] N granaio; (*for animals*) stalla
barnacle ['bɑːnəkl] N cirripede *m*
barn owl N barbagianni *m inv*
barometer [bə'rɔmɪtə^r] N barometro
baron ['bærən] N barone *m*; (*fig*) magnate *m*; **the oil barons** i magnati del petrolio; **the press barons** i baroni della stampa
baroness ['bærənɪs] N baronessa
baronet ['bærənɪt] N baronetto
barrack ['bærək] VT (*BRIT*): **to ~ sb** subissare qn di grida e fischi
barracking ['bærəkɪŋ] N (*BRIT*): **to give sb a ~** subissare qn di grida e fischi
barracks ['bærəks] NPL caserma
barrage ['bærɑːʒ] N (*Mil*, *dam*) sbarramento; (*fig*) fiume *m*; **a ~ of questions** una raffica di *or* un fuoco di fila di domande
barrel ['bærəl] N barile *m*; (*of gun*) canna
barrel organ N organetto a cilindro
barren ['bærən] ADJ sterile; (*soil*) arido(-a)
barrette [bə'rɛt] N (*US*) fermaglio per capelli
barricade [bærɪ'keɪd] N barricata ▶ VT barricare
barrier ['bærɪə^r] N barriera; (*BRIT*: *also*: **crash barrier**) guardrail *m inv*
barrier cream N (*BRIT*) crema protettiva
barring ['bɑːrɪŋ] PREP salvo
barrister ['bærɪstə^r] N (*BRIT*) avvocato(-essa); *vedi nota*

Il *barrister* è un membro della più prestigiosa delle due branche della professione legale (l'altra è quella dei *solicitor*); la sua funzione è quella di rappresentare i propri clienti in tutte le corti (*magistrates' court*, *crown court* e *Court of Appeal*), generalmente seguendo le istruzioni del caso preparate dai *solicitor*.

barrow ['bærəu] N (*cart*) carriola
barstool ['bɑːstuːl] N sgabello
Bart. ABBR (*BRIT*) = **baronet**
bartender ['bɑːtɛndə^r] N (*US*) barista *m*
barter ['bɑːtə^r] N baratto ▶ VT: **to ~ sth for** barattare qc con
base [beɪs] N base *f* ▶ ADJ vile ▶ VT: **to ~ sth on** basare qc su; **to ~ at** (*troops*) mettere di stanza a; **coffee-based** a base di caffè; **a**

Paris-based firm una ditta con sede centrale a Parigi; **I'm based in London** sono di base *or* ho base a Londra
baseball ['beɪsbɔːl] N baseball *m*
baseball cap N berretto da baseball
baseboard ['beɪsbɔːd] N (*US*) zoccolo, battiscopa *m inv*
base camp N campo *m* base *inv*
Basel [bɑːl] N = **Basle**
baseline ['beɪslaɪn] N (*Tennis*) linea di fondo
basement ['beɪsmənt] N seminterrato; (*of shop*) piano interrato
base rate N tasso di base
bases ['beɪsiːz] NPL *of* **basis**
bash [bæʃ] VT (*col*) picchiare ▶ N: **I'll have a ~ (at it)** (*BRIT col*) ci proverò; **bashed in** adj sfondato(-a)
▶ **bash up** VT (*col*: *car*) sfasciare; (: *BRIT*: *person*) riempire di *or* prendere a botte
bashful ['bæʃful] ADJ timido(-a)
bashing ['bæʃɪŋ] N: **Paki-/queer-~** atti *mpl* di violenza contro i pachistani/gli omosessuali
BASIC ['beɪsɪk] N (*Comput*) BASIC *m*
basic ['beɪsɪk] ADJ (*principles*, *precautions*, *rules*) elementare; (*salary*) base *inv* (*after n*)
basically ['beɪsɪklɪ] ADV fondamentalmente, sostanzialmente
basic rate N (*of tax*) aliquota minima
basics NPL: **the ~** l'essenziale *m*
basil ['bæzl] N basilico
basin ['beɪsn] N (*vessel*, *also Geo*) bacino; (*also*: **washbasin**) lavabo; (*BRIT*: *for food*) terrina
basis ['beɪsɪs] (*pl* **bases** [-siːz]) N base *f*; **on a part-time ~** part-time; **on a trial ~** in prova; **on the ~ of what you've said** in base alle sue asserzioni
bask [bɑːsk] VI: **to ~ in the sun** crogiolarsi al sole
basket ['bɑːskɪt] N cesta; (*smaller*) cestino; (*with handle*) paniere *m*
basketball ['bɑːskɪtbɔːl] N pallacanestro *f*
basketball player N cestista *mf*
Basle [bɑːl] N Basilea
basmati rice [bəz'mætɪ-] N riso basmati
Basque [bæsk] ADJ, N basco(-a)
bass [beɪs] N (*Mus*) basso
bass clef N chiave *f* di basso
bassoon [bə'suːn] N fagotto
bastard ['bɑːstəd] N bastardo(-a); (*col!*) stronzo (!)
baste [beɪst] VT (*Culin*) ungere con grasso; (*Sewing*) imbastire
bastion ['bæstɪən] N bastione *m*; (*fig*) baluardo
bat [bæt] N pipistrello; (*for baseball etc*) mazza; (*BRIT*: *for table tennis*) racchetta; **off one's own ~** di propria iniziativa ▶ VT: **he didn't ~ an eyelid** non battè ciglio

batch [bætʃ] N (of bread) infornata; (of papers) cumulo; (of applicants, letters) gruppo; (of work) sezione f; (of goods) partita, lotto

batch processing N (Comput) elaborazione f a blocchi

bated ['beɪtɪd] ADJ: **with ~ breath** col fiato sospeso

bath [bɑːθ] (pl **baths** [bɑːðz]) N bagno; (bathtub) vasca da bagno ▶ VT far fare il bagno a; **to have a ~** fare un bagno; see also **baths**

bathchair ['bɑːθtʃɛəʳ] N (BRIT) poltrona a rotelle

bathe [beɪð] VI fare il bagno ▶ VT bagnare; (wound etc) lavare

bather ['beɪðəʳ] N bagnante mf

bathing ['beɪðɪŋ] N bagni mpl

bathing cap N cuffia da bagno

bathing costume, (US) **bathing suit** N costume m da bagno

bathmat ['bɑːθmæt] N tappetino da bagno

bathrobe ['bɑːθrəub] N accappatoio

bathroom ['bɑːθrum] N stanza da bagno

baths [bɑːðz] NPL bagni mpl pubblici

bath towel N asciugamano da bagno

bathtub ['bɑːθtʌb] N (vasca da) bagno

batman ['bætmən] N (irreg) (BRIT Mil) attendente m

baton ['bætən] N bastone m; (Mus) bacchetta; (Athletics) testimone m; (club) manganello

battalion [bə'tælɪən] N battaglione m

batten ['bætən] N (Carpentry) assicella, correntino; (for flooring) tavola per pavimenti; (Naut) serretta; (: on sail) stecca
▶ **batten down** VT (Naut): **to ~ down the hatches** chiudere i boccaporti

batter ['bætəʳ] VT battere ▶ N pastetta

battered ['bætəd] ADJ (hat) sformato(-a); (pan) ammaccato(-a); **~ wife/baby** consorte f/bambino(-a) maltrattato(-a)

battering ram ['bætərɪŋ-] N ariete m

battery ['bætərɪ] N batteria; (of torch) pila

battery charger N caricabatterie m inv

battery farming N allevamento in batteria

battle ['bætl] N battaglia ▶ VI battagliare, lottare; **to fight a losing ~** (fig) battersi per una causa persa; **that's half the ~** (col) è già una mezza vittoria

battle dress N uniforme f da combattimento

battlefield ['bætlfiːld] N campo di battaglia

battlements ['bætlmənts] NPL bastioni mpl

battleship ['bætlʃɪp] N nave f da guerra

batty ['bætɪ] ADJ (col: person) svitato(-a), strambo(-a); (behaviour, idea) strampalato(-a)

bauble ['bɔːbl] N ninnolo

baud [bɔːd] N (Comput) baud m inv

baulk [bɔːlk] VI = **balk**

bauxite ['bɔːksaɪt] N bauxite f

Bavaria [bə'vɛərɪə] N Bavaria

Bavarian [bə'vɛərɪən] ADJ, N bavarese (mf)

bawdy ['bɔːdɪ] ADJ piccante

bawl [bɔːl] VI urlare

bay [beɪ] N (of sea) baia; (BRIT: for parking) piazzola di sosta; (: for loading) piazzale m di (sosta e) carico; **to hold sb at ~** tenere qn a bada

bay leaf N foglia d'alloro

bayonet ['beɪənɪt] N baionetta

bay tree N alloro

bay window N bovindo

bazaar [bə'zɑːʳ] N bazar m inv; vendita di beneficenza

bazooka [bə'zuːkə] N bazooka m inv

BB N ABBR (BRIT: = Boys' Brigade) organizzazione giovanile a fine educativo

BBB N ABBR (US: = Better Business Bureau) organismo per la difesa dei consumatori

BBC N ABBR (= British Broadcasting Corporation) vedi nota

La BBC è l'azienda statale che fornisce il servizio radiofonico e televisivo in Gran Bretagna. Pur dovendo rispondere al Parlamento del proprio operato, la BBC non è soggetta al controllo dello stato per scelte e programmi, anche perché si autofinanzia con il ricavato dei canoni d'abbonamento. La BBC ha canali televisivi digitali e terrestri, oltre a diverse emittenti radiofoniche nazionali e locali. Fornisce un servizio di informazione internazionale, il BBC World Service, trasmesso in tutto il mondo.

BBE N ABBR (US: = Benevolent and Protective Order of Elks) organizzazione filantropica

BC ADV ABBR (= before Christ) a.C. ▶ ABBR (CANADA) = **British Columbia**

BCG N ABBR (= Bacillus Calmette-Guérin) vaccino antitubercolare

BD N ABBR (= Bachelor of Divinity) titolo di studio

B/D ABBR = **bank draft**

BDS N ABBR (= Bachelor of Dental Surgery) titolo di studio

(KEYWORD)

be [biː] (pt **was, were**, pp **been**) AUX VB **1** (with present participle: forming continuous tenses): **what are you doing?** che fai?, che stai facendo?; **they're coming tomorrow** vengono domani; **I've been waiting for her for hours** sono ore che l'aspetto

2 (with pp: forming passives) essere; **to be killed** essere or venire ucciso(-a); **the box had been opened** la scatola era stata aperta; **the thief was nowhere to be seen** il ladro non si trovava da nessuna parte

3 (in tag questions): **it was fun, wasn't it?** è stato divertente, no?; **he's good-looking, isn't he?** è un bell'uomo, vero?; **she's back, is she?** così è tornata, eh?

4 (+ to + infinitive): **the house is to be sold** abbiamo (or hanno etc) intenzione di vendere casa; **you're to be congratulated for all your work** dovremo farvi i complimenti per tutto il vostro lavoro; **am I to understand that ...?** devo dedurre che ...?; **he's not to open it** non deve aprirlo; **he was to have come yesterday** sarebbe dovuto venire ieri

▶ VB + COMPLEMENT **1** (gen) essere; **I'm English** sono inglese; **I'm tired** sono stanco(-a); **I'm hot/cold** ho caldo/freddo; **he's a doctor** è medico; **2 and 2 are 4** 2 più 2 fa 4; **be careful!** sta attento(-a)!; **be good** sii buono(-a); **if I were you ...** se fossi in te ... **2** (of health) stare; **how are you?** come sta?; **he's very ill** sta molto male

3 (of age): **how old are you?** quanti anni hai?; **I'm sixteen (years old)** ho sedici anni **4** (cost) costare; **how much was the meal?** quant'era or quanto costava il pranzo?; **that'll be £5, please** (sono) 5 sterline, per favore

▶ VI **1** (exist, occur etc) essere, esistere; **the best singer that ever was** il migliore cantante mai esistito or di tutti tempi; **be that as it may** comunque sia, sia come sia; **so be it** sia pure, e sia **2** (referring to place) essere, trovarsi; **I won't be here tomorrow** non ci sarò domani; **Edinburgh is in Scotland** Edimburgo si trova in Scozia

3 (referring to movement): **where have you been?** dove sei stato?; **I've been to China** sono stato in Cina

▶ IMPERS VB **1** (referring to time, distance) essere; **it's 5 o'clock** sono le 5; **it's the 28th of April** è il 28 aprile; **it's 10 km to the village** di qui al paese sono 10 km **2** (referring to the weather) fare; **it's too hot/cold** fa troppo caldo/freddo; **it's windy** c'è vento

3 (emphatic): **it's me** sono io; **it's only me** sono solo io; **it was Maria who paid the bill** è stata Maria che ha pagato il conto

B/E ABBR = **bill of exchange**
beach [biːtʃ] N spiaggia ▶ VT tirare in secco
beach buggy N dune buggy f inv
beachcomber ['biːtʃkəʊmə^r] N vagabondo (che s'aggira sulla spiaggia)
beachwear ['biːtʃwɛə^r] N articoli mpl da spiaggia
beacon ['biːkən] N (lighthouse) faro; (marker) segnale m; (also: **radio beacon**) radiofaro
bead [biːd] N perlina; (of dew, sweat) goccia; **beads** NPL (necklace) collana
beady ['biːdɪ] ADJ: ~ **eyes** occhi mpl piccoli e penetranti

beagle ['biːgl] N cane m da lepre
beak [biːk] N becco
beaker ['biːkə^r] N coppa
beam [biːm] N trave f; (of light) raggio; (Radio) fascio (d'onde) ▶ VI brillare; (smile): **to ~ at sb** rivolgere un radioso sorriso a qn; **to drive on full** or **main ~** or (US) **high ~** guidare con gli abbaglianti accesi
beaming ['biːmɪŋ] ADJ (sun, smile) raggiante
bean [biːn] N fagiolo; (coffee bean) chicco; **runner ~** fagiolino
beanpole ['biːnpəʊl] N (col) spilungone(-a)
beansprouts ['biːnsprauts] NPL germogli mpl di soia
bear [bɛə^r] (pt **bore** [bɔː^r], pp **borne** [bɔːn]) N orso; (Stock Exchange) ribassista mf ▶ VT (gen) portare; (produce) generare; (: fruit) produrre, dare; (: traces, signs) mostrare; (Comm: interest) fruttare; (endure) sopportare ▶ VI: **to ~ right/left** piegare a destra/sinistra; **to ~ the responsibility of** assumersi la responsabilità di; **to ~ comparison with** reggere al paragone con; **I can't ~ him** non lo posso soffrire or sopportare; **to bring pressure to ~ on sb** fare pressione su qn
▶ **bear out** VT (theory, suspicion) confermare, convalidare
▶ **bear up** VI farsi coraggio; **he bore up well under the strain** ha sopportato bene lo stress
▶ **bear with** VT FUS (sb's moods, temper) sopportare (con pazienza); ~ **with me a minute** solo un attimo, prego
bearable ['bɛərəbl] ADJ sopportabile
beard [bɪəd] N barba
bearded ['bɪədɪd] ADJ barbuto(-a)
bearer ['bɛərə^r] N portatore m; (of passport) titolare mf
bearing ['bɛərɪŋ] N portamento; (connection) rapporto; **bearings** NPL (also: **ball bearings**) cuscinetti mpl a sfere; **to take a ~** fare un rilevamento; **to find one's bearings** orientarsi
beast [biːst] N bestia
beastly ['biːstlɪ] ADJ meschino(-a); (weather) da cani
beat [biːt] (pt ~, pp **beaten**) N colpo; (of heart) battito; (Mus) tempo; battuta; (of policeman) giro ▶ VT battere; (eggs, cream) sbattere; **off the beaten track** fuori mano; **to ~ about the bush** menare il cane per l'aia; **to ~ time** battere il tempo; **that beats everything!** (col) questo è il colmo!; ~ **it!** (col) fila!, fuori dai piedi!
▶ **beat down** VT (door) abbattere, buttare giù; (price) far abbassare; (seller) far scendere ▶ VI (rain) scrosciare; (sun) picchiare
▶ **beat off** VT respingere
▶ **beat up** VT (col: person) picchiare; (eggs) sbattere

beater ['biːtə'] N (*for eggs, cream*) frullino
beating ['biːtɪŋ] N botte *fpl*; (*defeat*) batosta;
 to take a ~ prendere una (bella) batosta
beat-up [biːt'ʌp] ADJ (*col*) scassato(-a)
beautician [bjuː'tɪʃən] N estetista *mf*
beautiful ['bjuːtɪful] ADJ bello(-a)
beautifully ADV splendidamente
beautify ['bjuːtɪfaɪ] VT abbellire
beauty ['bjuːtɪ] N bellezza; (*concept*) bello;
 the ~ of it is that … il bello è che …
beauty contest N concorso di bellezza
beauty parlour [-'pɑːlə'], (*US*) **beauty
 parlor** N salone *m* di bellezza
beauty queen N miss *f inv*, reginetta di
 bellezza
beauty salon N istituto di bellezza
beauty sleep N: **to get one's ~** farsi un
 sonno ristoratore
beauty spot N neo; (*BRIT Tourism*) luogo
 pittoresco
beaver ['biːvə'] N castoro
becalmed [bɪ'kɑːmd] ADJ in bonaccia
became [bɪ'keɪm] PT of **become**
because [bɪ'kɔz] CONJ perché; **~ of** *prep* a
 causa di
beck [bɛk] N: **to be at sb's ~ and call** essere a
 completa disposizione di qn
beckon ['bɛkən] VT (*also:* **beckon to**)
 chiamare con un cenno
become [bɪ'kʌm] VT (*irreg: like* **come**)
 diventare; **to ~ fat/thin** ingrassarsi/
 dimagrire; **to ~ angry** arrabbiarsi; **it
 became known that …** si è venuto a sapere
 che …; **what has ~ of him?** che gli è
 successo?
becoming [bɪ'kʌmɪŋ] ADJ (*behaviour*) che si
 conviene; (*clothes*) grazioso(-a)
BECTU ['bɛktuː] N ABBR (*BRIT*) = **Broadcasting
 Entertainment Cinematographic and
 Theatre Union**
BEd N ABBR (= *Bachelor of Education*) laurea con
 abilitazione all'insegnamento
bed [bɛd] N letto; (*of flowers*) aiuola; (*of coal,
 clay*) strato; (*of sea, lake*) fondo; **to go to ~**
 andare a letto
 ▶ **bed down** VI sistemarsi (per dormire)
bed and breakfast N (*terms*) camera con
 colazione; (*place*) ≈ pensione *f* familiare;
 vedi nota

 I *bed and breakfasts*, anche *B & Bs*, sono
 piccole pensioni a conduzione familiare,
 in case private o fattorie, dove si affittano
 camere e viene servita al mattino la
 tradizionale colazione all'inglese. Queste
 pensioni offrono un servizio di camera
 con prima colazione, appunto *bed and
 breakfast*, a prezzi più contenuti rispetto
 agli alberghi.

bedbug ['bɛdbʌg] N cimice *f*

bedclothes ['bɛdkləuðz] NPL coperte e
 lenzuola *fpl*
bedcover ['bɛdkʌvə'] N copriletto
bedding ['bɛdɪŋ] N coperte e lenzuola *fpl*
bedevil [bɪ'dɛvl] VT (*person*) tormentare;
 (*plans*) ostacolare continuamente
bedfellow ['bɛdfɛləu] N: **they are strange
 bedfellows** (*fig*) fanno una coppia ben
 strana
bedlam ['bɛdləm] N baraonda
bed linen N biancheria da letto
bedpan ['bɛdpæn] N padella
bedpost ['bɛdpəust] N colonnina del letto
bedraggled [bɪ'drægld] ADJ sbrindellato(-a);
 (*wet*) fradicio(-a)
bedridden ['bɛdrɪdən] ADJ costretto(-a) a
 letto
bedrock ['bɛdrɔk] N (*Geo*) basamento; (*fig*)
 fatti *mpl* di base
bedroom ['bɛdrum] N camera da letto
Beds ABBR (*BRIT*) = **Bedfordshire**
bed settee N divano *m* letto *inv*
bedside ['bɛdsaɪd] N: **at sb's ~** al capezzale di
 qn
bedside lamp N lampada da comodino
bedside table N comodino
bedsit ['bɛdsɪt], **bedsitter** ['bɛdsɪtə'] N (*BRIT*)
 monolocale *m*
bedspread ['bɛdsprɛd] N copriletto
bedtime ['bɛdtaɪm] N: **it's ~** è ora di andare a
 letto
bee [biː] N ape *f*; **to have a ~ in one's bonnet
 (about sth)** avere la fissazione (di qc)
beech [biːtʃ] N faggio
beef [biːf] N manzo; **roast ~** arrosto di manzo
 ▶ **beef up** VT (*col*) rinforzare
beefburger ['biːfbəːgə'] N hamburger *m inv*
Beefeater ['biːfiːtə'] N guardia della Torre di
 Londra
beehive ['biːhaɪv] N alveare *m*
bee-keeping ['biːkiːpɪŋ] N apicoltura
beeline ['biːlaɪn] N: **to make a ~ for** buttarsi
 a capo fitto verso
been [biːn] PP of **be**
beep [biːp] N (*of horn*) colpo di clacson; (*of
 phone etc*) segnale *m* (acustico), bip *m inv* ▶ VI
 suonare
beeper ['biːpə'] N (*of doctor etc*) cercapersone *m
 inv*
beer [bɪə'] N birra
beer belly N (*col*) stomaco da bevitore
beer can N lattina di birra
beer garden N (*BRIT*) giardino (*di pub*)
beet [biːt] (*US*) N (*also:* **red beet**) barbabietola
 rossa
beetle ['biːtl] N scarafaggio; coleottero
beetroot ['biːtruːt] N (*BRIT*) barbabietola
befall [bɪ'fɔːl] VI, VT (*irreg: like* **fall**) accadere (a)
befit [bɪ'fɪt] VT addirsi a

before [bɪ'fɔːʳ] PREP (*in time*) prima di; (*in space*) davanti a ▸ CONJ prima che + *sub*; prima di ▸ ADV prima; ~ **going** prima di andare; ~ **she goes** prima che vada; **the week** ~ la settimana prima; **I've seen it** ~ l'ho già visto; **I've never seen it** ~ è la prima volta che lo vedo

beforehand [bɪ'fɔːhænd] ADV in anticipo

befriend [bɪ'frɛnd] VT assistere; mostrarsi amico a

befuddled [bɪ'fʌdld] ADJ confuso(-a)

beg [bɛg] VI chiedere l'elemosina ▸ VT (*also:* **beg for**) chiedere in elemosina; (: *favour*) chiedere; (: *entreat*) pregare; **I** ~ **your pardon** (*apologising*) mi scusi; (*not hearing*) scusi?; **this begs the question of …** questo presuppone che sia già risolto il problema di …; **to** ~ **sb to do** pregare qn di fare

began [bɪ'gæn] PT *of* **begin**

beggar ['bɛgəʳ] N (*also:* **beggarman,** **beggarwoman**) mendicante *mf*

begin [bɪ'gɪn] (*pt* **began** [bɪ'gæn], *pp* **begun** [bɪ'gʌn]) VT, VI cominciare; **to** ~ **doing** *or* **to do sth** incominciare *or* iniziare a fare qc; **I can't** ~ **to thank you** non so proprio come ringraziarla; **to** ~ **with, I'd like to know …** tanto per cominciare vorrei sapere …; **beginning from Monday** a partire da lunedì

beginner [bɪ'gɪnəʳ] N principiante *mf*

beginning [bɪ'gɪnɪŋ] N inizio, principio; **right from the** ~ fin dall'inizio

begrudge [bɪ'grʌdʒ] VT: **to** ~ **sb sth** dare qc a qn a malincuore; invidiare qn per qc

beguile [bɪ'gaɪl] VT (*enchant*) incantare

beguiling [bɪ'gaɪlɪŋ] ADJ (*charming*) allettante; (*deluding*) ingannevole

begun [bɪ'gʌn] PP *of* **begin**

behalf [bɪ'hɑːf] N: **on** ~ **of,** (*US*) **in** ~ **of** per conto di; a nome di

behave [bɪ'heɪv] VI comportarsi; (*well: also:* **behave o.s.**) comportarsi bene

behaviour, (*US*) **behavior** [bɪ'heɪvjəʳ] N comportamento, condotta

behead [bɪ'hɛd] VT decapitare

beheld [bɪ'hɛld] PT, PP *of* **behold**

behind [bɪ'haɪnd] PREP dietro; (*followed by pronoun*) dietro di; (*time*) in ritardo con ▸ ADV dietro; in ritardo; (*leave, stay*) indietro ▸ N didietro; **we're** ~ **them in technology** siamo più indietro *or* più arretrati di loro nella tecnica; ~ **the scenes** dietro le quinte; **to be** ~ **(schedule) with sth** essere indietro con qc; (*payments*) essere in arretrato con qc; **to leave sth** ~ dimenticare di prendere qc

behold [bɪ'həuld] VT (*irreg: like* **hold**) vedere, scorgere

beige [beɪʒ] ADJ beige *inv*

Beijing [beɪ'dʒɪŋ] N Pechino *f*

being ['biːɪŋ] N essere *m*; **to come into** ~ cominciare ad esistere

Beirut [beɪ'ruːt] N Beirut *f*

Belarus ['bɛlærus] N Bielorussia

Belarussian [bɛlə'rʌʃən] ADJ bielorusso(-a) ▸ N bielorusso(-a); (*Ling*) bielorusso

belated [bɪ'leɪtɪd] ADJ tardo(-a)

belch [bɛltʃ] VI ruttare ▸ VT (*gen: also:* **belch out:** *smoke etc*) eruttare

beleaguered [bɪ'liːgəd] ADJ (*city*) assediato(-a); (*army*) accerchiato(-a); (*fig*) assillato(-a)

Belfast ['bɛlfɑːst] N Belfast *f*

belfry ['bɛlfrɪ] N campanile *m*

Belgian ['bɛldʒən] ADJ, N belga *mf*

Belgium ['bɛldʒəm] N Belgio

Belgrade [bɛl'greɪd] N Belgrado *f*

belie [bɪ'laɪ] VT smentire; (*give false impression of*) nascondere

belief [bɪ'liːf] N (*opinion*) opinione *f*, convinzione *f*; (*trust, faith*) fede *f*; (*acceptance as true*) credenza; **in the** ~ **that** nella convinzione che; **it's beyond** ~ è incredibile

believe [bɪ'liːv] VT, VI credere; **to** ~ **in** (*God*) credere in; (*ghosts*) credere a; (*method*) avere fiducia in; **I don't** ~ **in corporal punishment** sono contrario alle punizioni corporali; **he is believed to be abroad** si pensa (che) sia all'estero

believer [bɪ'liːvəʳ] N (*Rel*) credente *mf*; (*in idea, activity*): **to be a** ~ **in** credere in

belittle [bɪ'lɪtl] VT sminuire

Belize [bɛ'liːz] N Belize *m*

bell [bɛl] N campana; (*small, on door, electric*) campanello; **that rings a** ~ (*fig*) mi ricorda qualcosa

bell-bottoms ['bɛlbɔtəmz] NPL calzoni *mpl* a zampa d'elefante

bellboy ['bɛlbɔɪ], (*US*) **bellhop** ['bɛlhɔp] N ragazzo d'albergo, fattorino d'albergo

belligerent [bɪ'lɪdʒərənt] ADJ (*at war*) belligerante; (*fig*) bellicoso(-a)

bellow ['bɛləu] VI muggire; (*cry*) urlare (a squarciagola) ▸ VT (*orders*) urlare (a squarciagola)

bellows ['bɛləuz] NPL soffietto

bell pepper (*esp US*) N peperone *m*

bell push N (*BRIT*) pulsante *m* del campanello

belly ['bɛlɪ] N pancia

bellyache ['bɛlɪeɪk] N mal *m* di pancia ▸ VI (*col*) mugugnare

bellybutton ['bɛlɪbʌtn] N ombelico

bellyful ['bɛlɪful] N (*col*): **to have had a** ~ **of** (*fig*) averne piene le tasche (di)

belong [bɪ'lɔŋ] VI: **to** ~ **to** appartenere a; (*club etc*) essere socio di; **this book belongs here** questo libro va qui

belongings [bɪ'lɔŋɪŋz] NPL cose *fpl*, roba; **personal** ~ effetti *mpl* personali

Belorussia [bɛləu'rʌʃə] N Bielorussia
Belorussian [bɛləu'rʌʃən] ADJ, N
= **Belarussian**
beloved [bɪ'lʌvɪd] ADJ adorato(-a)
below [bɪ'ləu] PREP sotto, al di sotto di ▶ ADV
sotto, di sotto; giù; **see** ~ vedi sotto or oltre;
temperatures ~ normal temperature al di
sotto del normale
belt [bɛlt] N cintura; (Tech) cinghia ▶ VT
(thrash) picchiare ▶ VI (BRIT col) filarsela;
industrial ~ zona industriale
▶ **belt out** VT (song) cantare a squarciagola
▶ **belt up** VI (BRIT col) chiudere la boccaccia
beltway ['bɛltweɪ] N (US: Aut: ring road)
circonvallazione f; (: motorway) autostrada
bemoan [bɪ'məun] VT lamentare
bemused [bɪ'mju:zd] ADJ perplesso(-a),
stupito(-a)
bench [bɛntʃ] N panca; (in workshop, Pol)
banco; **the B~** (Law) la Corte
bench mark N banco di prova
bend [bɛnd] (pt, pp **bent** [bɛnt]) VT curvare;
(leg, arm) piegare ▶ VI curvarsi; piegarsi ▶ N
(in road) curva; (in pipe, river) gomito
▶ **bend down** VI chinarsi
▶ **bend over** VI piegarsi
bends [bɛndz] NPL (Med) embolia
beneath [bɪ'ni:θ] PREP sotto, al di sotto di;
(unworthy of) indegno(-a) di ▶ ADV sotto, di
sotto
benefactor ['bɛnɪfæktəʳ] N benefattore m
benefactress ['bɛnɪfæktrɪs] N benefattrice f
beneficial [bɛnɪ'fɪʃəl] ADJ che fa bene;
vantaggioso(-a); ~ **to** che giova a
beneficiary [bɛnɪ'fɪʃərɪ] N (Law)
beneficiario(-a)
benefit ['bɛnɪfɪt] N beneficio, vantaggio;
(allowance of money) indennità f inv ▶ VT far
bene a ▶ VI: **he'll ~ from it** ne trarrà
beneficio or profitto
benefit performance N spettacolo di
beneficenza
Benelux ['bɛnɪlʌks] N Benelux m
benevolent [bɪ'nɛvələnt] ADJ benevolo(-a)
BEng N ABBR (= Bachelor of Engineering) laurea in
ingegneria
benign [bɪ'naɪn] ADJ (person, smile)
benevolo(-a); (Med) benigno(-a)
bent [bɛnt] PT, PP of **bend** ▶ N inclinazione f
▶ ADJ (wire, pipe) piegato(-a), storto(-a); (col:
dishonest) losco(-a); **to be ~ on** essere
deciso(-a) a
bequeath [bɪ'kwi:ð] VT lasciare in eredità
bequest [bɪ'kwɛst] N lascito
bereaved [bɪ'ri:vd] ADJ in lutto ▶ NPL: **the ~** i
familiari in lutto
bereavement [bɪ'ri:vmənt] N lutto
beret ['bɛreɪ] N berretto
Bering Sea ['bɛrɪŋ-] N: **the ~** il mar di Bering

berk [bə:k] N (BRIT col!) coglione(-a) (!)
Berks ABBR (BRIT) = **Berkshire**
Berlin [bə:'lɪn] N Berlino f; **East/West ~**
Berlino est/ovest
berm [bə:m] N (US Aut) corsia d'emergenza
Bermuda [bə:'mju:də] N le Bermude
Bermuda shorts NPL bermuda mpl
Bern [bə:n] N Berna f
berry ['bɛrɪ] N bacca
berserk [bə'sə:k] ADJ: **to go ~** montare su
tutte le furie
berth [bə:θ] N (bed) cuccetta; (for ship)
ormeggio ▶ VI (in harbour) entrare in porto;
(at anchor) gettare l'ancora; **to give sb a wide
~** (fig) tenersi alla larga da qn
beseech [bɪ'si:tʃ] (pt, pp **besought** [bɪ'sɔ:t]) VT
implorare
beset [bɪ'sɛt] (pt, pp **~**) VT assalire ▶ ADJ: **a
policy ~ with dangers** una politica irta or
piena di pericoli
besetting [bɪ'sɛtɪŋ] ADJ: **his ~ sin** il suo più
grande difetto
beside [bɪ'saɪd] PREP accanto a; (compared
with) rispetto a, in confronto a; **to be ~ o.s.
(with anger)** essere fuori di sé; **that's ~ the
point** non c'entra
besides [bɪ'saɪdz] ADV inoltre, per di più
▶ PREP oltre a; (except) a parte
besiege [bɪ'si:dʒ] VT (town) assediare; (fig)
tempestare
besotted [bɪ'sɔtɪd] ADJ (BRIT): **~ with**
infatuato(-a) di
besought [bɪ'sɔ:t] PT, PP of **beseech**
bespectacled [bɪ'spɛktɪkld] ADJ
occhialuto(-a)
bespoke [bɪ'spəuk] ADJ (BRIT: garment) su
misura; **~ tailor** sarto
best [bɛst] ADJ migliore ▶ ADV meglio; **the ~
thing to do is ...** la cosa migliore da fare or
farsi è ...; **the ~ part of** (quantity) la maggior
parte di; **at ~** tutt'al più; **to make the ~ of
sth** cavare il meglio possibile da qc; **to do
one's ~** fare del proprio meglio; **to the ~ of
my knowledge** per quel che ne so; **to the ~
of my ability** al massimo delle mie capacità;
he's not exactly patient at the ~ of times
non è mai molto paziente
best-before date N (Comm): **"~: ..."** da
consumarsi preferibilmente entro il...
best man N (irreg) testimone m dello sposo
bestow [bɪ'stəu] VT: **to ~ sth on sb** conferire
qc a qn
bestseller ['bɛst'sɛləʳ] N bestseller m inv
bet [bɛt] (pt, pp **~** or **betted**) N scommessa
▶ VT, VI scommettere; **to ~ sb sth**
scommettere qc con qn; **it's a safe ~** (fig) è
molto probabile
Bethlehem ['bɛθlɪhɛm] N Betlemme f
betray [bɪ'treɪ] VT tradire

betrayal [bɪ'treɪəl] N tradimento
better ['bɛtə^r] ADJ migliore ► ADV meglio
► VT migliorare ► N: **to get the ~ of** avere la
meglio su; **you had ~ do it** è meglio che lo
faccia; **he thought ~ of it** cambiò idea; **to
get ~** migliorare; **a change for the ~** un
cambiamento in meglio; **that's ~!** così va
meglio!; **I had ~ go** dovrei andare; **~ off** adj
più ricco(-a); (fig) **you'd be ~ off this way**
starebbe meglio così
betting ['bɛtɪŋ] N scommesse fpl
betting shop N (BRIT) ufficio dell'allibratore
between [bɪ'twiːn] PREP tra ► ADV in mezzo,
nel mezzo; **the road ~ here and London** la
strada da qui a Londra; **we only had £5 ~ us**
fra tutti e due avevamo solo 5 sterline
bevel ['bɛvl] N (also: **bevel(led) edge**) profilo
smussato
beverage ['bɛvərɪdʒ] N bevanda
bevy ['bɛvɪ] N: **a ~ of** una banda di
bewail [bɪ'weɪl] VT lamentare
beware [bɪ'wɛə^r] VT, VI: **to ~ (of)** stare
attento(-a) (a); **"~ of the dog"** "attenti al
cane"
bewildered [bɪ'wɪldəd] ADJ sconcertato(-a),
confuso(-a)
bewildering [bɪ'wɪldərɪŋ] ADJ sconcertante,
sbalorditivo(-a)
bewitching [bɪ'wɪtʃɪŋ] ADJ affascinante
beyond [bɪ'jɔnd] PREP (in space) oltre;
(exceeding) al di sopra di ► ADV di là; **~ doubt**
senza dubbio; **~ repair** irreparabile
b/f ABBR = **brought forward**
BFPO N ABBR (= British Forces Post Office) recapito
delle truppe britanniche all'estero
bhp N ABBR (Aut: = brake horsepower) c.v. (= cavallo
vapore)
bi... [baɪ] PREFIX bi...
biannual [baɪ'ænjuəl] ADJ semestrale
bias ['baɪəs] N (prejudice) pregiudizio;
(preference) preferenza
biased, biassed ['baɪəst] ADJ parziale; **to be
bias(s)ed against** essere prevenuto(-a)
contro
biathlon [baɪ'æθlən] N biathlon m
bib [bɪb] N bavaglino
Bible ['baɪbl] N Bibbia
bibliography [bɪblɪ'ɔɡrəfɪ] N bibliografia
bicarbonate of soda [baɪ'kɑːbənɪt-] N
bicarbonato (di sodio)
bicentenary [baɪsɛn'tiːnərɪ], **bicentennial**
[baɪsɛn'tɛnɪəl] N bicentenario
biceps ['baɪsɛps] N bicipite m
bicker ['bɪkə^r] VI bisticciare
bicycle ['baɪsɪkl] N bicicletta
bicycle path, bicycle track N sentiero
ciclabile
bicycle pump N pompa della bicicletta
bid [bɪd] N offerta; (attempt) tentativo

► VI (pt, pp ~) fare un'offerta ► VT (pt **bade**
[bæd], pp **bidden** ['bɪdn]) fare un'offerta di;
to ~ sb good day dire buon giorno a qn
bidder ['bɪdə^r] N: **the highest ~** il maggior
offerente
bidding ['bɪdɪŋ] N offerte fpl
bide [baɪd] VT: **to ~ one's time** aspettare il
momento giusto
bidet ['biːdeɪ] N bidè m inv
bidirectional ['baɪdɪ'rɛkʃənl] ADJ
bidirezionale
biennial [baɪ'ɛnɪəl] ADJ biennale ► N (pianta)
biennale f
bier [bɪə^r] N bara
bifocals [baɪ'fəuklz] NPL occhiali mpl bifocali
big [bɪg] ADJ grande; grosso(-a); **my ~
brother** mio fratello maggiore; **to do
things in a ~ way** fare le cose in grande
bigamy ['bɪgəmɪ] N bigamia
Big Apple N vedi nota

> Tutti sanno che The Big Apple, la Grande
> Mela, è New York ("apple" in gergo
> significa grande città), ma sicuramente
> i soprannomi di altre città americane
> non sono così conosciuti. Chicago è
> soprannominata the Windy City perché è
> ventosa, New Orleans si chiama the Big
> Easy per il modo di vivere tranquillo e
> rilassato dei suoi abitanti, e l'industria
> automobilistica ha fatto sì che Detroit
> fosse soprannominata Motown.

big dipper [-'dɪpə^r] N montagne fpl russe,
otto m inv volante
big end N (Aut) testa di biella
biggish ['bɪgɪʃ] ADJ see **big** piuttosto grande,
piuttosto grosso(-a); **a ~ rent** un affitto
piuttosto alto
bigheaded ['bɪg'hɛdɪd] ADJ presuntuoso(-a)
big-hearted ['bɪg'hɑːtɪd] ADJ generoso(-a)
bigot ['bɪgət] N persona gretta
bigoted ['bɪgətɪd] ADJ gretto(-a)
bigotry ['bɪgətrɪ] N grettezza
big toe N alluce m
big top N tendone m del circo
big wheel N (at fair) ruota (panoramica)
bigwig ['bɪgwɪg] N (col) pezzo grosso
bike [baɪk] N bici f inv
bike lane N pista ciclabile
bikini [bɪ'kiːnɪ] N bikini m inv
bilateral [baɪ'lætərl] ADJ bilaterale
bile [baɪl] N bile f
bilingual [baɪ'lɪŋgwəl] ADJ bilingue
bilious ['bɪlɪəs] ADJ biliare; (fig) bilioso(-a)
bill [bɪl] N (in hotel, restaurant) conto; (Comm)
fattura; (for gas, electricity) bolletta, conto;
(Pol) atto; (US: banknote) banconota; (notice)
avviso; (of bird) becco; (of show) locandina;
(Theat): **on the ~** in cartellone ► VT mandare
il conto a; **may I have the ~ please?** posso

avere il conto per piacere?; **"stick** or **post no bills"** "divieto di affissione"; **to fit** or **fill the ~** (fig) fare al caso; **~ of exchange** cambiale f, tratta; **~ of lading** polizza di carico; **~ of sale** atto di vendita

billboard ['bɪlbɔ:d] N tabellone m

billet ['bɪlɪt] N alloggio ▸ VT (troops etc) alloggiare

billfold ['bɪlfəuld] N (US) portafoglio

billiards ['bɪljədz] N biliardo

billion ['bɪljən] N (BRIT) bilione m; (US) miliardo

billow ['bɪləu] N (of smoke) nuvola; (of sail) rigonfiamento ▸ VI (smoke) alzarsi in volute; (sail) gonfiarsi

bills payable NPL effetti mpl passivi

bills receivable NPL effetti mpl attivi

billy goat ['bɪlɪgəut] N caprone m, becco

bimbo ['bɪmbəu] N (col) pollastrella, svampitella

bin [bɪn] N (for coal, rubbish) bidone m; (for bread) cassetta; (BRIT: also: **dustbin**) pattumiera; (also: **litter bin**) cestino

binary ['baɪnərɪ] ADJ binario(-a)

bind [baɪnd] (pt, pp **bound** [baund]) VT legare; (oblige) obbligare ▸ N (col) scocciatura
  ▸ **bind over** VT (Law) dare la condizionale a
  ▸ **bind up** VT (wound) fasciare, bendare; **to be bound up in** (work, research etc) essere completamente assorbito da; **to be bound up with** (person) dedicarsi completamente a

binder ['baɪndər] N (file) classificatore m

binding ['baɪndɪŋ] N (of book) legatura ▸ ADJ (contract) vincolante

binge [bɪndʒ] N (col): **to go on a ~** fare baldoria

binge drinker N persona che di norma beve troppo

bingo ['bɪŋgəu] N gioco simile alla tombola

bin liner N sacchetto per l'immondizia

binoculars [bɪ'nɔkjuləz] NPL binocolo

bio... [baɪə...] PREFIX bio

biochemistry [baɪəu'kɛmɪstrɪ] N biochimica

biodegradable ['baɪəudɪ'greɪdəbl] ADJ biodegradabile

biodiesel ['baɪəudi:zl] N biodiesel m

biodiversity ['baɪəudaɪ'və:sɪtɪ] N biodiversità f inv

biofuel ['baɪəufjuəl] N biocarburante m

biographer [baɪ'ɔgrəfər] N biografo(-a)

biographic [baɪə'græfɪk], **biographical** [baɪə'græfɪkl] ADJ biografico(-a)

biography [baɪ'ɔgrəfɪ] N biografia

biological [baɪə'lɔdʒɪkl] ADJ biologico(-a)

biological clock N orologio biologico

biologist [baɪ'ɔlədʒɪst] N biologo(-a)

biology [baɪ'ɔlədʒɪ] N biologia

biometric [baɪəu'mɛtrɪk] ADJ biometrico(-a)

biophysics [baɪəu'fɪzɪks] N biofisica

biopic ['baɪəupɪk] N film m inv biografia inv

biopsy ['baɪɔpsɪ] N biopsia

biosphere ['baɪəusfɪər] N biosfera

biotechnology [baɪəutɛk'nɔlədʒɪ] N biotecnologia

bioterrorism [baɪəu'tɛrərɪzəm] N bioterrorismo

birch [bə:tʃ] N betulla

bird [bə:d] N uccello; (BRIT col: girl) bambola

bird flu N influenza aviaria

bird of prey N (uccello) rapace m

bird's-eye view ['bə:dzaɪ-] N veduta a volo d'uccello

bird watcher N ornitologo(-a) dilettante

birdwatching N birdwatching m

Biro® ['baɪrəu] N biro® f inv

birth [bə:θ] N nascita; **to give ~ to** dare alla luce, partorire; (fig) dare inizio a

birth certificate N certificato di nascita

birth control N controllo delle nascite; contraccezione f

birthday ['bə:θdeɪ] N compleanno ▸ CPD di compleanno

birthmark ['bə:θmɑ:k] N voglia

birthplace ['bə:θpleɪs] N luogo di nascita

birth rate N indice m di natalità

Biscay ['bɪskeɪ] N: **the Bay of ~** il golfo di Biscaglia

biscuit ['bɪskɪt] N (BRIT) biscotto; (US) panino al latte

bisect [baɪ'sɛkt] VT tagliare in due (parti); (Math) bisecare

bisexual [baɪ'sɛksjuəl] ADJ, N bisessuale (mf)

bishop ['bɪʃəp] N vescovo; (Chess) alfiere m

bistro ['bi:strəu] N bistrò m inv

bit [bɪt] PT of **bite** ▸ N pezzo; (of tool) punta; (of horse) morso; (Comput) bit m inv; (US: coin) ottavo di dollaro; **a ~ of** un po' di; **a ~ mad/dangerous** un po' matto/pericoloso; **~ by ~** a poco a poco; **to do one's ~** fare la propria parte; **to come to bits** (break) andare a pezzi; **bring all your bits and pieces** porta tutte le tue cose

bitch [bɪtʃ] N (dog) cagna; (col!) puttana (!)

bite [baɪt] (pt **bit**, pp **bitten**) VT, VI mordere; (insect) pungere ▸ N morso; (insect bite) puntura; (mouthful) boccone m; **let's have a ~ to eat** mangiamo un boccone; **to ~ one's nails** mangiarsi le unghie

biting ['baɪtɪŋ] ADJ pungente

bit part N (Theat) particina

bitten ['bɪtn] PP of **bite**

bitter ['bɪtər] ADJ amaro(-a); (wind, criticism) pungente; (icy: weather) gelido(-a)
  ▸ N (BRIT: beer) birra amara; **to the ~ end** a oltranza

bitterly ['bɪtəlɪ] ADV (disappoint, complain, weep) amaramente; (oppose, criticise) aspramente; (jealous) profondamente; **it's ~ cold** fa un freddo gelido

bitterness ['bɪtənɪs] N amarezza; gusto amaro

bittersweet ['bɪtəswi:t] ADJ agrodolce

bitty ['bɪtɪ] ADJ (BRIT col) frammentario(-a)

bitumen ['bɪtjumɪn] N bitume *m*

bivouac ['bɪvuæk] N bivacco

bizarre [bɪ'zɑːᵣ] ADJ bizzarro(-a)

bk ABBR = **bank**; **book**

BL N ABBR = **Bachelor of Law(s)**; (= *Bachelor of Letters*) titolo di studio; (US: = *Bachelor of Literature*) titolo di studio

B/L ABBR = **bill of lading**

blab [blæb] VI parlare troppo ▶ VT (*also*: **blab out**) spifferare

black [blæk] ADJ nero(-a) ▶ N nero ▶ VT (BRIT *Industry*) boicottare; **B~** negro(-a); **~ coffee** caffè *m inv* nero; **to give sb a ~ eye** fare un occhio nero a qn; **in the ~** (*in credit*) in attivo; **there it is in ~ and white** (*fig*) eccolo nero su bianco; **~ and blue** *adj* tutto(-a) pesto(-a) ▶ **black out** VI (*faint*) svenire

black belt N (*Sport*) cintura nera; (*US: area*): **the ~** zona abitata principalmente da negri

blackberry ['blækbərɪ] N mora

blackbird ['blækbə:d] N merlo

blackboard ['blækbɔ:d] N lavagna

black box N (*Aviat*) scatola nera

Black Country N (BRIT): **the ~** zona carbonifera del centro dell'Inghilterra

blackcurrant [blæk'kʌrənt] N ribes *m inv*

black economy N (BRIT) economia sommersa

blacken ['blækn] VT annerire

Black Forest N: **the ~** la Foresta Nera

blackhead ['blækhɛd] N punto nero, comedone *m*

black hole N (*Astron*) buco nero

black ice N strato trasparente di ghiaccio

blackjack ['blækdʒæk] N (*Cards*) ventuno; (*US: truncheon*) manganello

blackleg ['blæklɛg] N (BRIT) crumiro

blacklist ['blæklɪst] N lista nera ▶ VT mettere sulla lista nera

blackmail ['blækmeɪl] N ricatto ▶ VT ricattare

blackmailer ['blækmeɪləᵣ] N ricattatore(-trice)

black market N mercato nero

blackout ['blækaut] N oscuramento; (*fainting*) svenimento; (*TV*) interruzione *f* delle trasmissioni

black pepper N pepe *m* nero

black pudding N sanguinaccio

Black Sea N: **the ~** il mar Nero

black sheep N pecora nera

blacksmith ['blæksmɪθ] N fabbro ferraio

black spot N (*Aut*) luogo famigerato per gli incidenti

bladder ['blædəᵣ] N vescica

blade [bleɪd] N lama; (*of oar*) pala; **~ of grass** filo d'erba

blame [bleɪm] N colpa ▶ VT: **to ~ sb/sth for sth** dare la colpa di qc a qn/qc; **who's to ~?** chi è colpevole?; **I'm not to ~** non è colpa mia

blameless ['bleɪmlɪs] ADJ irreprensibile

blanch [blɑ:ntʃ] VI (*person*) sbiancare in viso ▶ VT (*Culin*) scottare

bland [blænd] ADJ mite; (*taste*) blando(-a)

blank [blæŋk] ADJ bianco(-a); (*look*) distratto(-a) ▶ N spazio vuoto; (*cartridge*) cartuccia a salve; **to draw a ~** (*fig*) non aver nessun risultato

blank cheque, (US) **blank check** N assegno in bianco; **to give sb a ~ to do** (*fig*) dare carta bianca a qn per fare

blanket ['blæŋkɪt] N coperta ▶ ADJ (*statement, agreement*) globale

blanket cover N: **to give ~** (*insurance policy*) coprire tutti i rischi

blare [blɛəᵣ] VI strombettare; (*radio*) suonare a tutto volume

blasé ['blɑːzeɪ] ADJ blasé *inv*

blasphemous ['blæsfɪməs] ADJ blasfemo(-a)

blasphemy ['blæsfɪmɪ] N bestemmia

blast [blɑ:st] N (*of wind*) raffica; (*of air, steam*) getto; (*bomb blast*) esplosione *f* ▶ VT far saltare ▶ EXCL (BRIT *col*) mannaggia!; **(at) full ~** a tutta forza ▶ **blast off** VI (*Space*) essere lanciato(-a)

blast-off ['blɑ:stɔf] N (*Space*) lancio

blatant ['bleɪtənt] ADJ flagrante

blatantly ['bleɪtəntlɪ] ADV: **it's ~ obvious** è lampante

blaze [bleɪz] N (*fire*) incendio; (*glow: of fire, sun etc*) bagliore *m*; (*fig*) vampata; splendore *m* ▶ VI (*fire*) ardere, fiammeggiare; (*fig*) infiammarsi; (*guns*) sparare senza sosta; (*fig: eyes*) ardere ▶ VT: **to ~ a trail** (*fig*) tracciare una via nuova; **in a ~ of publicity** circondato da grande pubblicità

blazer ['bleɪzəᵣ] N blazer *m inv*

bleach [bli:tʃ] N (*also*: **household bleach**) varechina ▶ VT (*material*) candeggiare

bleached ['bli:tʃt] ADJ (*hair*) decolorato(-a)

bleachers ['bli:tʃəz] NPL (*US Sport*) posti *mpl* di gradinata

bleak [bli:k] ADJ (*prospect, future*) tetro(-a); (*landscape*) desolato(-a); (*weather*) gelido(-a) e cupo(-a); (*smile*) pallido(-a)

bleary-eyed ['blɪərɪ'aɪd] ADJ dagli occhi offuscati

bleat [bli:t] VI belare

bled [blɛd] PT, PP *of* **bleed**

bleed [bli:d] (*pt, pp* **bled** [blɛd]) VT dissanguare; (*brakes, radiator*) spurgare ▶ VI sanguinare; **my nose is bleeding** mi viene fuori sangue dal naso

449

bleep [bli:p] N breve segnale *m* acustico, bip *m inv* ▶ VI suonare ▶ VT (*doctor*) chiamare con il cercapersone

bleeper ['bli:pəʳ] N (*of doctor etc*) cercapersone *m inv*

blemish ['blɛmɪʃ] N macchia

blend [blɛnd] N miscela ▶ VT mescolare ▶ VI (*colours etc: also:* **blend in**) armonizzare

blender ['blɛndəʳ] N (*Culin*) frullatore *m*

bless [blɛs] (*pt, pp* **blessed** *or* **blest** [blɛst]) VT benedire; **~ you!** (*sneezing*) salute!; **to be blessed with** godere di

blessed ['blɛsɪd] ADJ (*Rel: holy*) benedetto(-a); (*happy*) beato(-a); **every ~ day** tutti i santi giorni

blessing ['blɛsɪŋ] N benedizione *f*; fortuna; **to count one's blessings** ringraziare Iddio, ritenersi fortunato; **it was a ~ in disguise** in fondo è stato un bene

blest [blɛst] PT, PP *of* **bless**

blew [blu:] PT *of* **blow**

blight [blaɪt] N (*of plants*) golpe *f* ▶ VT (*hopes etc*) deludere; (*life*) rovinare

blimey ['blaɪmɪ] EXCL (*BRIT col*) accidenti!

blind [blaɪnd] ADJ cieco(-a) ▶ N (*for window*) avvolgibile *m*; (*Venetian blind*) veneziana ▶ VT accecare; **the blind** NPL i ciechi; **to turn a ~ eye (on** *or* **to)** chiudere un occhio (su)

blind alley N vicolo cieco

blind corner N (*BRIT*) svolta cieca

blind date N appuntamento combinato (*tra due persone che non si conoscono*)

blinders ['blaɪndəz] NPL (*US*) = **blinkers**

blindfold ['blaɪndfəuld] N benda ▶ ADJ, ADV bendato(-a) ▶ VT bendare gli occhi a

blinding ['blaɪndɪŋ] ADJ (*flash, light*) accecante; (*pain*) atroce

blindly ['blaɪndlɪ] ADV ciecamente

blindness ['blaɪndnɪs] N cecità

blind spot N (*Aut etc*) punto cieco; (*fig*) punto debole

bling [blɪŋ] N *gioielli vistosi*

blink [blɪŋk] VI battere gli occhi; (*light*) lampeggiare ▶ N: **to be on the ~** (*col*) essere scassato(-a)

blinkers ['blɪŋkəz] NPL (*BRIT*) paraocchi *mpl*

blinking ['blɪŋkɪŋ] ADJ (*BRIT col*): **this ~ ...** questo(-a) maledetto(-a) ...

blip [blɪp] N (*on radar etc*) segnale *m* intermittente; (*on graph*) piccola variazione *f*; (*fig*) momentanea battuta d'arresto

bliss [blɪs] N estasi *f*

blissful ['blɪsfəl] ADJ (*event, day*) stupendo(-a), meraviglioso(-a); (*smile*) beato(-a); **in ~ ignorance** nella (più) beata ignoranza

blissfully ['blɪsfəlɪ] ADV (*sigh, smile*) beatamente; **~ happy** magnificamente felice

blister ['blɪstəʳ] N (*on skin*) vescica; (*on paintwork*) bolla ▶ VI (*paint*) coprirsi di bolle

BLit, BLitt N ABBR (= *Bachelor of Literature*) titolo di studio

blithe [blaɪð] ADJ gioioso(-a), allegro(-a)

blithely ['blaɪðlɪ] ADV allegramente

blithering ['blɪðərɪŋ] ADJ (*col*): **this ~ idiot** questa razza d'idiota

blitz [blɪts] N blitz *m*; **to have a ~ on sth** (*fig*) prendere d'assalto qc

blizzard ['blɪzəd] N bufera di neve

bloated ['bləutɪd] ADJ gonfio(-a)

blob [blɔb] N (*drop*) goccia; (*stain, spot*) macchia

bloc [blɔk] N (*Pol*) blocco

block [blɔk] N (*gen, Comput*) blocco; (*in pipes*) ingombro; (*toy*) cubo; (*of buildings*) isolato ▶ VT (*gen, Comput*) bloccare; **the sink is blocked** il lavandino è otturato; **~ of flats** caseggiato; **3 blocks from here** a 3 isolati di distanza da qui; **mental ~** blocco mentale ▶ **block up** VT bloccare; (*pipe*) ingorgare, intasare

blockade [blɔ'keɪd] N blocco ▶ VT assediare

blockage ['blɔkɪdʒ] N ostacolo

block and tackle N (*Tech*) paranco

block booking N prenotazione *f* in blocco

blockbuster ['blɔkbʌstəʳ] N grande successo

block capitals NPL stampatello

blockhead ['blɔkhɛd] N testa di legno

block letters NPL stampatello

block release N (*BRIT*) periodo pagato concesso al tirocinante per effettuare studi superiori

block vote N voto per delega

blog [blɔg] N blog *m inv* ▶ VI scrivere blog, bloggare

blogger [blɔgəʳ] N (*Comput*) blogger *mf*

blogging ['blɔgɪŋ] N blogging *m* ▶ ADJ: **~ website** sito di blogging

blogosphere ['blɔgəsfɪəʳ] N blogosfera *f*

bloke [bləuk] N (*BRIT col*) tizio

blond, blonde [blɔnd] N (*man*) biondo; (*woman*) bionda ▶ ADJ biondo(-a)

blood [blʌd] N sangue *m*; **new ~** (*fig*) nuova linfa

blood bank N banca del sangue

blood count N conteggio di globuli rossi e bianchi

bloodcurdling ['blʌdkəːdlɪŋ] ADJ raccapricciante, da far gelare il sangue

blood donor N donatore(-trice) di sangue

blood group N gruppo sanguigno

bloodhound ['blʌdhaund] N segugio

bloodless ['blʌdlɪs] ADJ (*pale*) smorto(-a), esangue; (*coup*) senza spargimento di sangue

bloodletting ['blʌdlɛtɪŋ] N (*Med*) salasso; (*fig*) spargimento di sangue

blood poisoning N setticemia

blood pressure N pressione f sanguigna; **to have high/low ~** avere la pressione alta/bassa

bloodshed ['blʌdʃɛd] N spargimento di sangue

bloodshot ['blʌdʃɔt] ADJ: **~ eyes** occhi iniettati di sangue

bloodstained ['blʌdsteɪnd] ADJ macchiato(-a) di sangue

bloodstream ['blʌdstriːm] N flusso del sangue

blood test N analisi f inv del sangue

bloodthirsty ['blʌdθəːstɪ] ADJ assetato(-a) di sangue

blood transfusion N trasfusione f di sangue

blood type N gruppo sanguigno

blood vessel N vaso sanguigno

bloody ['blʌdɪ] ADJ (fight) sanguinoso(-a); (nose) sanguinante; (BRIT col!): **this ~ ...** questo maledetto ...; **~ awful/good** (col!) veramente terribile/buono; **a ~ awful day** (col!) una giornata di merda (!)

bloody-minded ['blʌdɪ'maɪndɪd] ADJ (BRIT col) indisponente

bloom [bluːm] N fiore m ▶ VI essere in fiore

blooming ['bluːmɪŋ] ADJ (col): **this ~ ...** questo(-a) dannato(-a) ...

blossom ['blɔsəm] N fiore m; (with pl sense) fiori mpl ▶ VI essere in fiore; **to ~ into** (fig) diventare

blot [blɔt] N macchia ▶ VT macchiare; **to be a ~ on the landscape** rovinare il paesaggio; **to ~ one's copy book** (fig) farla grossa
▶ **blot out** VT (memories) cancellare; (view) nascondere; (nation, city) annientare

blotchy ['blɔtʃɪ] ADJ (complexion) coperto(-a) di macchie

blotter ['blɔtər] N tampone m (di carta assorbente)

blotting paper ['blɔtɪŋ-] N carta assorbente

blotto ['blɔtəu] ADJ (col) sbronzo(-a)

blouse [blauz] N camicetta

blow [bləu] (pt **blew**, pp **blown**) N colpo ▶ VI soffiare ▶ VT (fuse) far saltare; (wind) spingere; (instrument) suonare; **to come to blows** venire alle mani; **to ~ one's nose** soffiarsi il naso; **to ~ a whistle** fischiare
▶ **blow away** VI volare via ▶ VT portare via
▶ **blow down** VT abbattere
▶ **blow off** VT far volare via; **to ~ off course** far uscire di rotta
▶ **blow out** VI scoppiare
▶ **blow over** VI calmarsi
▶ **blow up** VI saltare in aria ▶ VT far saltare in aria; (tyre) gonfiare; (Phot) ingrandire

blow-dry ['bləudraɪ] N (hairstyle) messa in piega a föhn ▶ VT asciugare con il föhn

blowlamp ['bləulæmp] N (BRIT) lampada a benzina per saldare

blown [bləun] PP of **blow**

blowout ['bləuaut] N (of tyre) scoppio; (col: big meal) abbuffata

blowtorch ['bləutɔːtʃ] N lampada a benzina per saldare

blowzy ['blauzɪ] ADJ trasandato(-a)

BLS N ABBR (US) = **Bureau of Labor Statistics**

blubber ['blʌbər] N grasso di balena ▶ VI (pej) piangere forte

bludgeon ['blʌdʒən] VT prendere a randellate

blue [bluː] ADJ azzurro(-a), celeste; (darker) blu inv; (depressed) giù inv; **~ film/joke** film/barzelletta pornografico(a); **(only) once in a ~ moon** a ogni morte di papa; **out of the ~** (fig) all'improvviso; see also **blues**

blue baby N neonato cianotico

bluebell ['bluːbɛl] N giacinto di bosco

blueberry N mirtillo

bluebottle ['bluːbɔtl] N moscone m

blue cheese N formaggio tipo gorgonzola

blue-chip ['bluːtʃɪp] ADJ: **~ investment** investimento sicuro

blue-collar worker ['bluːkɔlər-] N operaio(-a)

blue jeans NPL blue-jeans mpl

blueprint ['bluːprɪnt] N cianografia; (fig): **~ (for)** formula (di)

blues [bluːz] NPL: **the ~** (Mus) il blues; **to have the ~** (col: feeling) essere a terra

bluetit N cinciarella

bluff [blʌf] VI bluffare ▶ N bluff m inv; (promontory) promontorio scosceso ▶ ADJ (person) brusco(-a); **to call sb's ~** mettere alla prova il bluff di qn

blunder ['blʌndər] N abbaglio ▶ VI prendere un abbaglio; **to ~ into sb/sth** andare a sbattere contro qn/qc

blunt [blʌnt] ADJ (edge) smussato(-a); (point) spuntato(-a); (knife) che non taglia; (person) brusco(-a) ▶ VT smussare; spuntare; **this pencil is ~** questa matita non ha più la punta; **~ instrument** (Law) corpo contundente

bluntly ['blʌntlɪ] ADV (speak) senza mezzi termini

bluntness ['blʌntnɪs] N (of person) brutale franchezza

blur [bləːr] N forma indistinta ▶ VT offuscare

blurb [bləːb] N trafiletto pubblicitario

blurred [bləːd] ADJ (photo) mosso(-a); (TV) sfuocato(-a)

blurt out [bləːt-] VT lasciarsi sfuggire

blush [blʌʃ] VI arrossire ▶ N rossore m

blusher ['blʌʃər] N fard m inv

bluster ['blʌstər] N spacconate fpl; (threats) vuote minacce fpl ▶ VI fare lo spaccone; minacciare a vuoto

blustering ['blʌstərɪŋ] ADJ (tone etc) da spaccone

blustery ['blʌstərɪ] ADJ (weather) burrascoso(-a)
Blvd ABBR = **boulevard**
BM N ABBR = **British Museum**; (Scol: = Bachelor of Medicine) titolo di studio
BMA N ABBR = **British Medical Association**
BMJ N ABBR = **British Medical Journal**
BMus N ABBR (= Bachelor of Music) titolo di studio
BMX N ABBR (= bicycle motocross) BMX f inv; **~ bike** mountain bike f inv per cross
bn ABBR = **billion**
BO N ABBR (col: = body odour) odori mpl sgradevoli (del corpo); = **box office**
boar [bɔːʳ] N cinghiale m
board [bɔːd] N tavola; (on wall) tabellone m; (for chess etc) scacchiera; (committee) consiglio, comitato; (in firm) consiglio d'amministrazione; (Naut, Aviat): **on ~** a bordo ▶ VT (ship) salire a bordo di; (train) salire su; **full ~** (BRIT) pensione f completa; **half ~** (BRIT) mezza pensione; **~ and lodging** vitto e alloggio; **above ~** (fig) regolare; **across the ~** (fig) adv per tutte le categorie; adj generale; **to go by the ~** venir messo(-a) da parte
▶ **board up** VT (door) chiudere con assi
boarder ['bɔːdəʳ] N pensionante mf; (Scol) convittore(-trice)
board game N gioco da tavolo
boarding card ['bɔːdɪŋ-] N (Aviat, Naut) carta d'imbarco
boarding house N pensione f
boarding party N squadra di ispezione (del carico di una nave)
boarding pass N (BRIT) = **boarding card**
boarding school N collegio
board meeting N riunione f di consiglio
board room N sala del consiglio
boardwalk ['bɔːdwɔːk] N (US) passeggiata a mare
boast [bəust] VI: **to ~ (about** or **of)** vantarsi (di) ▶ VT vantare ▶ N vanteria; vanto
boastful ['bəustful] ADJ vanaglorioso(-a)
boastfulness ['bəustfulnɪs] N vanagloria
boat [bəut] N nave f; (small) barca; **to go by ~** andare in barca or in nave; **we're all in the same ~** (fig) siamo tutti nella stessa barca
boater ['bəutəʳ] N (hat) paglietta
boating ['bəutɪŋ] N canottaggio
boat people N boat people mpl
boatswain ['bəusn] N nostromo
bob [bɔb] VI (boat, cork on water: also: **bob up and down)** andare su e giù ▶ N (BRIT col) = **shilling**
▶ **bob up** VI saltare fuori
bobbin ['bɔbɪn] N bobina; (of sewing machine) rocchetto
bobby ['bɔbɪ] N (BRIT col) ≈ poliziotto

bobby pin ['bɔbɪ-] (US) N fermaglio per capelli
bobsleigh ['bɔbsleɪ] N bob m inv
bode [bəud] VI: **to ~ well/ill (for)** essere di buon/cattivo auspicio (per)
bodice ['bɔdɪs] N corsetto
bodily ['bɔdɪlɪ] ADJ (comfort, needs) materiale; (pain) fisico(-a) ▶ ADV (carry) in braccio; (lift) di peso
body ['bɔdɪ] N corpo; (of car) carrozzeria; (of plane) fusoliera; (fig: group) gruppo; (: organization) associazione f, organizzazione f; (quantity) quantità f inv; (of speech, document) parte f principale; (also: **body stocking**) body m inv; **in a ~** in massa; **ruling ~** direttivo; **a wine with ~** un vino corposo
body blow N (fig) duro colpo
body-building ['bɔdɪˈbɪldɪŋ] N culturismo
bodyguard ['bɔdɪgaːd] N guardia del corpo
body language N linguaggio del corpo
body repairs NPL (Aut) lavori mpl di carrozzeria
body search N perquisizione f personale; **to submit to** or **undergo a ~** essere sottoposto(-a) a perquisizione personale
bodywork ['bɔdɪwəːk] N carrozzeria
boffin ['bɔfɪn] N scienziato
bog [bɔg] N palude f ▶ VT: **to get bogged down** (fig) impantanarsi
bogey ['bəugɪ] N (worry) spauracchio; (also: **bogey man**) babau m inv
boggle ['bɔgl] VI: **the mind boggles** è incredibile
Bogotá [bəugə'taː] N Bogotà f
bogus ['bəugəs] ADJ falso(-a); finto(-a)
Bohemia [bəu'hiːmɪə] N Boemia
Bohemian [bəu'hiːmɪən] ADJ, N boemo(-a)
boil [bɔɪl] VT, VI bollire ▶ N (Med) foruncolo; **to come to the** or (US) **a ~** raggiungere l'ebollizione; **to bring to the** or (US) **a ~** portare a ebollizione; **boiled egg** uovo alla coque; **boiled potatoes** patate fpl bollite or lesse
▶ **boil down** VI (fig): **to ~ down to** ridursi a
▶ **boil over** VI traboccare (bollendo)
boiler ['bɔɪləʳ] N caldaia
boiler suit N (BRIT) tuta
boiling ['bɔɪlɪŋ] ADJ bollente; **I'm ~ (hot)** (col) sto morendo di caldo
boiling point N punto di ebollizione
boil-in-the-bag [bɔɪlɪnðə'bæg] ADJ (rice etc) da bollire nel sacchetto
boisterous ['bɔɪstərəs] ADJ chiassoso(-a)
bold [bəuld] ADJ audace; (child) impudente; (outline) chiaro(-a); (colour) deciso(-a)
boldness ['bəuldnɪs] N audacia; impudenza
bold type N (Typ) neretto, grassetto
Bolivia [bə'lɪvɪə] N Bolivia
Bolivian [bə'lɪvɪən] ADJ, N boliviano(-a)

bollard ['bɔləd] N (Naut) bitta; (BRIT Aut) colonnina luminosa

Bollywood ['bɔlɪwud] N Bollywood f

bolshy ['bɔlʃɪ] ADJ (BRIT col) piantagrane, ribelle; **to be in a ~ mood** essere in vena di piantar grane

bolster ['bəulstə^r] N capezzale m
▶ **bolster up** VT sostenere

bolt [bəult] N chiavistello; (with nut) bullone m ▶ ADV: **~ upright** diritto(-a) come un fuso ▶ VT serrare; (also: **bolt together**) imbullonare; (food) mangiare in fretta ▶ VI scappare via; **a ~ from the blue** (fig) un fulmine a ciel sereno

bomb [bɔm] N bomba ▶ VT bombardare

bombard [bɔm'bɑːd] VT bombardare

bombardment [bɔm'bɑːdmənt] N bombardamento

bombastic [bɔm'bæstɪk] ADJ ampolloso(-a)

bomb disposal N: **~ expert** artificiere m; **~ unit** corpo degli artificieri

bomber ['bɔmə^r] N (Aviat) bombardiere m; (terrorist) dinamitardo(-a)

bombing ['bɔmɪŋ] N bombardamento

bomb scare N stato di allarme (per sospetta presenza di una bomba)

bombshell ['bɔmʃel] N (fig) notizia bomba

bomb site N luogo bombardato

bona fide ['bəunə'faɪdɪ] ADJ sincero(-a); (offer) onesto(-a)

bonanza [bə'nænzə] N cuccagna

bond [bɔnd] N legame m; (binding promise, Finance) obbligazione f; (Comm): **in ~** (of goods) in attesa di sdoganamento

bondage ['bɔndɪdʒ] N schiavitù f

bonded warehouse ['bɔndɪd-] N magazzino doganale

bone [bəun] N osso; (of fish) spina, lisca ▶ VT disossare; togliere le spine a

bone china N porcellana fine

bone-dry ['bəun'draɪ] ADJ asciuttissimo(-a)

bone idle ADJ: **to be ~** essere un(a) fannullone(-a)

bone marrow N midollo osseo

boner ['bəunə^r] N (US) gaffe f inv

bonfire ['bɔnfaɪə^r] N falò m inv

bonk [bɔŋk] VT, VI (humorous, col) scopare (!)

bonkers ['bɔŋkəz] ADJ (BRIT col) suonato(-a)

Bonn [bɔn] N Bonn f

bonnet ['bɔnɪt] N cuffia; (BRIT: of car) cofano

bonny ['bɔnɪ] ADJ (esp SCOTTISH) bello(-a), carino(-a)

bonus ['bəunəs] N premio; (on wages) gratifica; (fig) sovrappiù m inv

bony ['bəunɪ] ADJ (thin: person) ossuto(-a), angoloso(-a); (arm, face, Med: tissue) osseo(-a); (meat) pieno(-a) di ossi; (fish) pieno(-a) di spine

boo [bu:] EXCL ba! ▶ VT fischiare ▶ N fischio

boob [bu:b] N (col: breast) tetta; (: BRIT: mistake) gaffe f inv

booby prize ['bu:bɪ-] N premio per il peggior contendente

booby trap ['bu:bɪ-] N trabocchetto; (bomb) congegno che esplode al contatto

booby-trapped ['bu:bɪtræpt] ADJ: **a ~ car** una macchina con dell'esplosivo a bordo

book [buk] N libro; (of stamps etc) blocchetto ▶ VT (ticket, seat, room) prenotare; (driver) multare; (football player) ammonire; **books** NPL (Comm) conti mpl; **to keep the books** (Comm) tenere la contabilità; **by the ~** secondo le regole; **to throw the ~ at sb** incriminare qn seriamente or con tutte le aggravanti
▶ **book in** VI (BRIT: at hotel) prendere una camera
▶ **book up** VT riservare, prenotare; **the hotel is booked up** l'albergo è al completo; **all seats are booked up** è tutto esaurito

bookable ['bukəbl] ADJ: **seats are ~** si possono prenotare i posti

bookcase ['bukkeɪs] N libreria

book ends NPL reggilibri mpl

booking ['bukɪŋ] N (BRIT) prenotazione f

booking office N (BRIT Rail) biglietteria; (Theat) botteghino

book-keeping ['buk'ki:pɪŋ] N contabilità

booklet ['buklɪt] N opuscolo, libriccino

bookmaker ['bukmeɪkə^r] N allibratore m

bookmark ['bukmɑːk] (also Comput) N segnalibro ▶ VT (Comput) mettere un segnalibro a; (Internet) aggiungere a "Preferiti"

bookseller ['buksɛlə^r] N libraio

bookshelf ['bukʃɛlf] N mensola (per libri); **bookshelves** NPL (bookcase) libreria

bookshop ['bukʃɔp] N libreria

bookstall ['bukstɔːl] N bancarella di libri

bookstore ['bukstɔː^r] N = **bookshop**

book token N buono m libri inv

book value N valore m contabile

bookworm ['bukwə:m] N (fig) topo di biblioteca

boom [bu:m] N (noise) rimbombo; (busy period) boom m inv ▶ VI rimbombare; andare a gonfie vele

boomerang ['bu:məræŋ] N boomerang m inv ▶ VI (fig) avere effetto contrario; **to ~ on sb** (fig) ritorcersi contro qn

boom town N città f inv in rapidissima espansione

boon [bu:n] N vantaggio

boorish ['buərɪʃ] ADJ maleducato(-a)

boost [bu:st] N spinta ▶ VT spingere; (increase: sales, production) incentivare; **to give a ~ to** (morale) tirar su; **it gave a ~ to his**

confidence è stata per lui un'iniezione di fiducia

booster ['buːstə^r] N (*Elec*) amplificatore *m*; (*TV*) amplificatore *m* di segnale; (*also:* **booster rocket**) razzo vettore; (*Med*) richiamo

booster seat N (*Aut: for children*) seggiolino di sicurezza

boot [buːt] N stivale *m*; (*ankle boot*) stivaletto; (*for hiking*) scarpone *m* da montagna; (*for football etc*) scarpa; (*Brit: of car*) portabagagli *m inv* ▶ VT (*Comput*) inizializzare; **to ~** (*in addition*) per giunta, in più; **to give sb the ~** (*col*) mettere qn alla porta

booth [buːð] N (*at fair*) baraccone *m*; (*of cinema, telephone etc*) cabina; (*also:* **voting booth**) cabina (elettorale)

bootleg ['buːtlɛg] ADJ di contrabbando; **~ record** registrazione *f* pirata *inv*

booty ['buːtɪ] N bottino

booze [buːz] (*col*) N alcool *m* ▶ VI trincare

boozer ['buːzə^r] N (*col: person*) beone *m*; (*Brit col: pub*) osteria

border ['bɔːdə^r] N orlo; margine *m*; (*of a country*) frontiera; (*for flowers*) aiuola (laterale) ▶ VT (*road*) costeggiare; **the B~** *la frontiera tra l'Inghilterra e la Scozia*; **the Borders** *la zona di confine tra l'Inghilterra e la Scozia*

  ▶ **border on** VT FUS confinare con

borderline ['bɔːdəlaɪn] N (*fig*) linea di demarcazione ▶ ADJ: **~ case** caso limite; **on the ~** incerto(-a)

bore [bɔː^r] PT *of* **bear** ▶ VT (*hole*) scavare; (*person*) annoiare ▶ N (*person*) seccatore(-trice); (*of gun*) calibro

bored ADJ annoiato(-a); **to be ~** annoiarsi; **he's ~ to tears** *or* **~ to death** *or* **~ stiff** è annoiato a morte, si annoia da morire

boredom ['bɔːdəm] N noia

boring ['bɔːrɪŋ] ADJ noioso(-a)

born [bɔːn] ADJ: **to be ~** nascere; **I was ~ in 1960** sono nato nel 1960; **~ blind** cieco dalla nascita; **a ~ comedian** un comico nato

born-again [bɔːnə'gɛn] ADJ: **~ Christian** convertito(-a) alla chiesa evangelica

borne [bɔːn] PP *of* **bear**

Borneo ['bɔːnɪəu] N Borneo

borough ['bʌrə] N comune *m*

borrow ['bɔrəu] VT: **to ~ sth (from sb)** prendere in prestito qc (da qn); **may I ~ your car?** può prestarmi la macchina?

borrower ['bɔrəuə^r] N (*gen*) chi prende a prestito; (*Econ*) mutuatario(-a)

borrowing ['bɔrəuɪŋ] N prestito

borstal ['bɔːstl] N (*Brit*) riformatorio

Bosnia ['bɔznɪə] N Bosnia

Bosnia-Herzegovina ['bɔznɪəhɛrtsə'gəuviːnə] N (*also:* **Bosnia-Hercegovina**) Bosnia-Erzegovina

Bosnian ['bɔznɪən] ADJ, N bosniaco(-a)

bosom ['buzəm] N petto; (*fig*) seno

bosom friend N amico(-a) del cuore

boss [bɔs] N capo ▶ VT (*also:* **boss about** *or* **around**) comandare a bacchetta; **stop bossing everyone about!** smettila di dare ordini a tutti!

bossy ['bɔsɪ] ADJ prepotente

bosun ['bəusn] N nostromo

botanical [bə'tænɪkl] ADJ botanico(-a)

botanist ['bɔtənɪst] N botanico(-a)

botany ['bɔtənɪ] N botanica

botch [bɔtʃ] VT fare un pasticcio di

both [bəuθ] ADJ entrambi(-e), tutt'e due

  ▶ PRON: **~ of them** entrambi(-e) ▶ ADV: **they sell ~ meat and poultry** vendono insieme la carne ed il pollame; **~ of us went, we ~ went** ci siamo andati tutt'e due

bother ['bɔðə^r] VT (*worry*) preoccupare; (*annoy*) infastidire ▶ VI (*gen: also:* **bother o.s.**) preoccuparsi ▶ N: **it is a ~ to have to do** è una seccatura dover fare ▶ EXCL uffa!, accidenti!; **it was no ~** non c'era problema; **to ~ doing sth** darsi la pena di fare qc; **I'm sorry to ~ you** mi dispiace disturbarla; **please don't ~** non si scomodi; **it's no ~** non c'è problema

Botswana [bɔt'swɑːnə] N Botswana *m*

bottle ['bɔtl] N bottiglia; (*of perfume, shampoo etc*) flacone *m*; (*baby's*) biberon *m* ▶ VT imbottigliare; **~ of wine/milk** bottiglia di vino/latte; **wine/milk ~** bottiglia da vino/del latte

  ▶ **bottle up** VT contenere

bottle bank N contenitore *m* per la raccolta del vetro

bottle-fed ['bɔtlfɛd] ADJ allattato(-a) artificialmente

bottleneck ['bɔtlnɛk] N ingorgo

bottle-opener ['bɔtləupnə^r] N apribottiglie *m inv*

bottom ['bɔtəm] N fondo; (*of mountain, tree, hill*) piedi *mpl*; (*buttocks*) sedere *m* ▶ ADJ più basso(-a), ultimo(-a); **at the ~ of** in fondo a; **to get to the ~ of sth** (*fig*) andare al fondo di *or* in fondo a qc

bottomless ['bɔtəmlɪs] ADJ senza fondo

bottom line N: **the ~ is …** in ultima analisi ....

botulism ['bɔtjulɪzəm] N botulismo

bough [bau] N ramo

bought [bɔːt] PT, PP *of* **buy**

boulder ['bəuldə^r] N masso (tondeggiante)

boulevard ['buːlvɑːd] N viale *m*

bounce [bauns] VI (*ball*) rimbalzare; (*cheque*) essere restituito(-a) ▶ VT far rimbalzare ▶ N (*rebound*) rimbalzo; **to ~ in** entrare di slancio *or* con foga; **he's got plenty of ~** (*fig*) è molto esuberante

bouncer ['baʊnsəʳ] (col) N buttafuori m inv
bouncy castle® ['baʊnsɪ-] N grande castello gonfiabile per giocare
bound [baʊnd] PT, PP of **bind** ▶ N (gen pl) limite m; (leap) salto ▶ VI saltare ▶ VT (leap) saltare; (limit) delimitare ▶ ADJ: ~ **by law** obbligato(-a) per legge; **to be ~ to do sth** (obliged) essere costretto(-a) a fare qc; **he's ~ to fail** (likely) fallirà di certo; **~ for** diretto(-a) a; **out of bounds** il cui accesso è vietato
boundary ['baʊndrɪ] N confine m
boundless ['baʊndlɪs] ADJ illimitato(-a)
bountiful ['baʊntɪful] ADJ (person) munifico(-a); (God) misericordioso(-a); (supply) abbondante
bounty ['baʊntɪ] N (generosity) liberalità, munificenza; (reward) taglia
bounty hunter N cacciatore m di taglie
bouquet ['bukeɪ] N bouquet m inv
bourbon ['buəbən] N (US: also: **bourbon whiskey**) bourbon m inv
bourgeois ['buəʒwaː] ADJ, N borghese (mf)
bout [baʊt] N periodo; (of malaria etc) attacco; (Boxing etc) incontro
boutique [buːˈtiːk] N boutique f inv
bow¹ [bəʊ] N nodo; (weapon) arco; (Mus) archetto
bow² [bau] N (with body) inchino; (Naut: also: **bows**) prua ▶ VI inchinarsi; (yield): **to ~ to** or **before** sottomettersi a; **to ~ to the inevitable** rassegnarsi all'inevitabile
bowels [baʊəlz] NPL intestini mpl; (fig) viscere fpl
bowl [bəʊl] N (for eating) scodella; (for washing) bacino; (ball) boccia; (of pipe) fornello; (US: stadium) stadio ▶ VI (Cricket) servire (la palla); see also **bowls**
  ▶ **bowl over** VT (fig) sconcertare
bow-legged ['bəʊˈlɛgɪd] ADJ dalle gambe storte
bowler ['bəʊləʳ] N giocatore m di bocce; (Cricket) lanciatore m; (BRIT: also: **bowler hat**) bombetta
bowling ['bəʊlɪŋ] N (game) gioco delle bocce; bowling m
bowling alley N pista da bowling
bowling green N campo di bocce
bowls [bəʊlz] N gioco delle bocce
bow tie N cravatta a farfalla
box [bɔks] N scatola; (also: **cardboard box**) (scatola di) cartone m; (crate: also for money) cassetta; (Theat) palco; (BRIT Aut) area d'incrocio ▶ VI fare pugilato ▶ VT mettere in (una) scatola, inscatolare; (Sport) combattere contro
boxer ['bɔksəʳ] N (person) pugile m; (dog) boxer m inv
boxer shorts ['bɔksəʃɔːts] NPL boxer; **a pair of ~** un paio di boxer

boxing ['bɔksɪŋ] N (Sport) pugilato
Boxing Day N (BRIT) ≈ Santo Stefano; vedi nota

Il Boxing Day è un giorno di festa e cade in genere il 26 dicembre. Prende il nome dall'usanza di donare pacchi regalo natalizi, un tempo chiamati Christmas boxes, a fornitori e dipendenti.

boxing gloves NPL guantoni mpl da pugile
boxing ring N ring m inv
box number N (for advertisements) casella
box office N biglietteria
box room N ripostiglio
boy [bɔɪ] N ragazzo; (small) bambino; (son) figlio; (servant) servo
boy band N gruppo pop di soli ragazzi maschi creato per far presa su un pubblico giovane
boycott ['bɔɪkɔt] N boicottaggio ▶ VT boicottare
boyfriend ['bɔɪfrɛnd] N ragazzo
boyish ['bɔɪʃ] ADJ di or da ragazzo
bp ABBR = **bishop**
bra [braː] N reggipetto, reggiseno
brace [breɪs] N sostegno; (on teeth) apparecchio correttore; (tool) trapano; (Typ: also: **brace bracket**) graffa ▶ VT rinforzare, sostenere; **to ~ o.s.** (fig) farsi coraggio; see also **braces**
bracelet ['breɪslɪt] N braccialetto
braces ['breɪsɪz] NPL (BRIT) bretelle fpl
bracing ['breɪsɪŋ] ADJ invigorante
bracken ['brækən] N felce f
bracket ['brækɪt] N (Tech) mensola; (group) gruppo; (Typ) parentesi f inv ▶ VT mettere fra parentesi; (fig: also: **bracket together**) mettere insieme; **in brackets** tra parentesi; **round/square brackets** parentesi tonde/quadre; **income ~** fascia di reddito
brackish ['brækɪʃ] ADJ (water) salmastro(-a)
brag [bræg] VI vantarsi
braid [breɪd] N (trimming) passamano; (of hair) treccia
Braille [breɪl] N braille m
brain [breɪn] N cervello; **brains** NPL (intelligence) cervella fpl; **he's got brains** è intelligente
brainchild ['breɪntʃaɪld] N creatura, creazione f
braindead ['breɪndɛd] ADJ (Med) che ha subito morte cerebrale; (col) cerebroleso(-a), deficiente
brainless ['breɪnlɪs] ADJ deficiente, stupido(-a)
brainstorm ['breɪnstɔːm] N (fig) attacco di pazzia; (US) = **brainwave**
brainwash ['breɪnwɔʃ] VT fare un lavaggio di cervello a
brainwave ['breɪnweɪv] N lampo di genio
brainy ['breɪnɪ] ADJ intelligente
braise [breɪz] VT brasare

brake [breɪk] N (*on vehicle*) freno ▶ VT, VI
frenare
brake light N (fanalino dello) stop *m inv*
brake pedal N pedale *m* del freno
bramble ['bræmbl] N rovo; (*fruit*) mora
bran [bræn] N crusca
branch [brɑ:ntʃ] N ramo; (*Comm*) succursale
f, filiale *f*
▶ **branch off** VI diramarsi
▶ **branch out** VI: **to ~ out into**
intraprendere una nuova attività nel
ramo di
branch line N (*Rail*) linea secondaria
branch manager N direttore *m* di filiale
brand [brænd] N marca; (*fig*) tipo ▶ VT (*cattle*)
marcare (a ferro rovente); (*fig: pej*): **to ~ sb**
a communist *etc* definire qn come
comunista *etc*
brandish ['brændɪʃ] VT brandire
brand name N marca
brand-new ['brænd'nju:] ADJ nuovo(-a) di
zecca
brandy ['brændɪ] N brandy *m inv*
brash [bræʃ] ADJ sfacciato(-a)
Brasilia [brə'zɪljə] N Brasilia
brass [brɑ:s] N ottone *m*; **the ~** (*Mus*) gli
ottoni
brass band N fanfara
brassière ['bræsɪəʳ] N reggipetto, reggiseno
brass tacks NPL: **to get down to ~** (*col*) venire
al sodo
brat [bræt] N (*pej*) marmocchio, monello(-a)
bravado [brə'vɑ:dəʊ] N spavalderia
brave [breɪv] ADJ coraggioso(-a) ▶ N guerriero
m pellerossa *inv* ▶ VT affrontare
bravery ['breɪvərɪ] N coraggio
bravo [brɑ:'vəʊ] EXCL bravo!, bene!
brawl [brɔ:l] N rissa ▶ VI azzuffarsi
brawn [brɔ:n] N muscolo; (*meat*) carne *f* di
testa di maiale
brawny ['brɔ:nɪ] ADJ muscoloso(-a)
bray [breɪ] N raglio ▶ VI ragliare
brazen ['breɪzn] ADJ svergognato(-a) ▶ VT: **to**
~ it out fare lo sfacciato
brazier ['breɪzɪəʳ] N braciere *m*
Brazil [brə'zɪl] N Brasile *m*
Brazilian [brə'zɪljən] ADJ, N brasiliano(-a)
Brazil nut N noce *f* del Brasile
breach [bri:tʃ] VT aprire una breccia in ▶ N
(*gap*) breccia, varco; (*estrangement*) rottura; (*of
duty*) abuso; (*breaking*): **~ of contract** rottura
di contratto; **~ of the peace** violazione *f*
dell'ordine pubblico; **~ of trust** abuso di
fiducia
bread [brɛd] N pane *m*; (*col: money*) grana;
to earn one's daily ~ guadagnarsi il pane;
to know which side one's ~ is buttered on
saper fare i propri interessi; **~ and butter** *n*
pane e burro; (*fig*) mezzi *mpl* di sussistenza

breadbin ['brɛdbɪn] N (*BRIT*) cassetta *f*
portapane *inv*
breadboard ['brɛdbɔ:d] N tagliere *m* (*per il
pane*); (*Comput*) pannello per esperimenti
breadbox ['brɛdbɔks] N (*US*) cassetta *f*
portapane *inv*
breadcrumbs ['brɛdkrʌmz] NPL briciole *fpl*;
(*Culin*) pangrattato
breadline ['brɛdlaɪn] N: **to be on the ~** avere
appena denaro per vivere
breadth [brɛtθ] N larghezza; (*fig: of knowledge
etc*) ampiezza
breadwinner ['brɛdwɪnəʳ] N chi guadagna il
pane per tutta la famiglia
break [breɪk] (*pt* **broke**, *pp* **broken**) VT
rompere; (*law*) violare; (*promise*) mancare a
▶ VI rompersi; (*storm*) scoppiare; (*weather*)
cambiare; (*dawn*) spuntare; (*news*) saltare
fuori ▶ N (*gap*) breccia; (*fracture*) rottura;
(*rest, also Scol*) intervallo; (: *short*) pausa;
(*chance*) possibilità *f inv*; (*holiday*) vacanza; **to**
~ one's leg *etc* rompersi la gamba *etc*; **to ~ a**
record battere un primato; **to ~ the news to**
sb comunicare per primo la notizia a qn; **to**
~ with sb (*fig*) rompere con qn; **to ~ even** vi
coprire le spese; **to ~ free** *or* **loose** liberarsi;
without a ~ senza una pausa; **to have** *or*
take a ~ (*few minutes*) fare una pausa; (*holiday*)
prendere un po' di riposo; **a lucky ~** un colpo
di fortuna
▶ **break down** VT (*figures, data*) analizzare;
(*door etc*) buttare giù, abbattere; (*resistance*)
stroncare ▶ VI crollare; (*Med*) avere un
esaurimento (nervoso); (*Aut*) guastarsi
▶ **break in** VT (*horse etc*) domare ▶ VI (*burglar*)
fare irruzione
▶ **break into** VT FUS (*house*) fare irruzione in
▶ **break off** VI (*speaker*) interrompersi;
(*branch*) troncarsi ▶ VT (*talks, engagement*)
rompere
▶ **break open** VT (*door etc*) sfondare
▶ **break out** VI evadere; **to ~ out in spots**
coprirsi di macchie
▶ **break through** VI: **the sun broke through**
il sole ha fatto capolino tra le nuvole ▶ VT
(*defences, barrier*) sfondare, penetrare in;
(*crowd*) aprirsi un varco in *or* tra, aprirsi un
passaggio in *or* tra
▶ **break up** VI (*partnership*) sciogliersi; (*friends*)
separarsi; **the line's** *or* **you're breaking up**
la linea è disturbata ▶ VT fare in pezzi,
spaccare; (*fight etc*) interrompere, far cessare;
(*marriage*) finire
breakable ['breɪkəbl] ADJ fragile; **breakables**
NPL oggetti *mpl* fragili
breakage ['breɪkɪdʒ] N rottura; **to pay for**
breakages pagare i danni
breakaway ['breɪkəweɪ] ADJ (*group etc*)
scissionista, dissidente

break-dancing ['breɪkdɑ:nsɪŋ] N
breakdance f
breakdown ['breɪkdaun] N (*Aut*) guasto; (*in
communications*) interruzione f; (*of marriage*)
rottura; (*Med: also:* **nervous breakdown**)
esaurimento nervoso; (*of payments, statistics
etc*) resoconto
breakdown service N (*BRIT*) servizio
riparazioni
breakdown truck, breakdown van N carro
m attrezzi *inv*
breakdown van N *see* **breakdown truck**
breaker ['breɪkəʳ] N frangente m
breakeven ['breɪk'i:vn] CPD: ~ **chart**
diagramma m del punto di rottura *or*
pareggio; ~ **point** punto di rottura *or*
pareggio
breakfast ['brɛkfəst] N colazione f
breakfast cereal N fiocchi *mpl* d'avena *or* di
mais *etc*
break-in ['breɪkɪn] N irruzione f
breaking point ['breɪkɪŋ-] N punto di rottura
breakthrough ['breɪkθru:] N (*Mil*) breccia;
(*fig*) passo avanti
break-up ['breɪkʌp] N (*of partnership, marriage*)
rottura
break-up value N (*Comm*) valore m di realizzo
breakwater ['breɪkwɔ:təʳ] N frangiflutti m
inv
breast [brɛst] N (*of woman*) seno; (*chest, Culin*)
petto
breast-feed ['brɛstfi:d] VT, VI (*irreg: like* **feed**)
allattare (al seno)
breast pocket N taschino
breast-stroke ['brɛststrəuk] N nuoto a rana
breath [brɛθ] N respiro; **out of ~** senza fiato;
to go out for a ~ of air andare a prendere
una boccata d'aria
Breathalyser® ['brɛθəlaɪzəʳ] (*BRIT*) N
alcoltest m *inv*
breathe [bri:ð] VT, VI respirare; **I won't ~ a
word about it** non fiaterò
▶ **breathe in** VI inspirare ▶ VT respirare
▶ **breathe out** VT, VI espirare
breather ['bri:ðəʳ] N attimo di respiro
breathing ['bri:ðɪŋ] N respiro, respirazione f
breathing space N (*fig*) attimo di respiro
breathless ['brɛθlɪs] ADJ senza fiato; (*with
excitement*) con il fiato sospeso
breath-taking ['brɛθteɪkɪŋ] ADJ mozzafiato
inv
breath test N ≈ prova del palloncino
bred [brɛd] PT, PP *of* **breed**
-bred [brɛd] SUFFIX: **to be well/ill~** essere ben
educato(-a)/maleducato(-a)
breed [bri:d] (*pt, pp* **bred**) VT allevare; (*fig:
hate, suspicion*) generare, provocare ▶ VI
riprodursi ▶ N razza; (*type, class*) varietà f *inv*
breeder ['bri:dəʳ] N (*Physics: also:* **breeder**

reactor) reattore m autofertilizzante
breeding ['bri:dɪŋ] N riproduzione f;
allevamento
breeze [bri:z] N brezza
breeze block N (*BRIT*) mattone composto di scorie
di coke
breezy ['bri:zɪ] ADJ (*day*) ventilato(-a);
(*person*) allegro(-a)
Breton ['brɛtən] ADJ, N bretone (*mf*)
brevity ['brɛvɪtɪ] N brevità
brew [bru:] VT (*tea*) fare un infuso di; (*beer*)
fare; (*plot*) tramare ▶ VI (*tea*) essere in
infusione; (*beer*) essere in fermentazione;
(*storm, fig: trouble etc*) prepararsi
brewer ['bru:əʳ] N birraio
brewery ['bru:ərɪ] N fabbrica di birra
briar ['braɪəʳ] N (*thorny bush*) rovo; (*wild rose*)
rosa selvatica
bribe [braɪb] N bustarella ▶ VT comprare; **to
~ sb to do sth** pagare qn sottobanco perché
faccia qc
bribery ['braɪbərɪ] N corruzione f
bric-a-brac ['brɪkəbræk] N bric-a-brac m
brick [brɪk] N mattone m
bricklayer ['brɪkleɪəʳ] N muratore m
brickwork ['brɪkwə:k] N muratura in
mattoni
brickworks ['brɪkwə:ks] N fabbrica di
mattoni
bridal ['braɪdl] ADJ nuziale; ~ **party** corteo
nuziale
bride [braɪd] N sposa
bridegroom ['braɪdgru:m] N sposo
bridesmaid ['braɪdzmeɪd] N damigella
d'onore
bridge [brɪdʒ] N ponte m; (*Naut*) ponte di
comando; (*of nose*) dorso; (*Cards, Dentistry*)
bridge m *inv* ▶ VT (*river*) fare un ponte sopra;
(*fig: gap*) colmare
bridging loan ['brɪdʒɪŋ-] N (*BRIT*)
anticipazione f sul mutuo
bridle ['braɪdl] N briglia ▶ VT tenere a freno;
(*horse*) mettere la briglia a ▶ VI (*in anger etc*)
adombrarsi, adontarsi
bridle path N sentiero (per cavalli)
brief [bri:f] ADJ breve ▶ N (*Law*) comparsa;
(*gen*) istruzioni *fpl* ▶ VT (*Mil etc*) dare
istruzioni a; **in ~ ...** in breve ..., a farla breve
...; **to ~ sb (about sth)** mettere qn al
corrente (di qc); *see also* **briefs**
briefcase ['bri:fkeɪs] N cartella
briefing ['bri:fɪŋ] N istruzioni *fpl*, briefing m
inv
briefly ['bri:flɪ] ADV (*speak, visit, explain, say*)
brevemente; (*glimpse, glance*) di sfuggita
briefness ['bri:fnɪs] N brevità
briefs [bri:fs] NPL mutande *fpl*
Brig. ABBR = **brigadier**
brigade [brɪ'geɪd] N (*Mil*) brigata

brigadier [ˌbrɪɡəˈdɪər] N generale m di brigata

bright [braɪt] ADJ luminoso(-a); (person) sveglio(-a); (colour) vivace; **to look on the ~ side** vedere il lato positivo delle cose

brighten [ˈbraɪtn], **brighten up** VT (room) rendere luminoso(-a); rallegrare ▶ VI schiarirsi; (person) rallegrarsi

brightly [ˈbraɪtlɪ] ADV (shine) vivamente, intensamente; (smile) radiosamente; (talk) con animazione

brill [brɪl] EXCL (BRIT col) stupendo!, fantastico!

brilliance [ˈbrɪljəns] N splendore m; (fig: of person) genialità, talento

brilliant [ˈbrɪljənt] ADJ brillante; (sunshine) sfolgorante; (light, smile) radioso(-a); (col) splendido(-a)

brim [brɪm] N orlo

brimful [ˈbrɪmˈful] ADJ pieno(-a) or colmo(-a) fino all'orlo; (fig) pieno(-a)

brine [braɪn] N acqua salmastra; (Culin) salamoia

bring [brɪŋ] (pt, pp **brought** [brɔːt]) VT portare; **to ~ sth to an end** mettere fine a qc; **I can't ~ myself to sack him** non so risolvermi a licenziarlo
▶ **bring about** VT causare
▶ **bring back** VT riportare
▶ **bring down** VT (lower) far scendere; (shoot down) abbattere; (government) far cadere
▶ **bring forward** VT portare avanti; (in time) anticipare; (Book-keeping) riportare
▶ **bring in** VT (person) fare entrare; (object) portare; (Pol: bill) presentare; (: legislation) introdurre; (Law: verdict) emettere; (produce: income) rendere
▶ **bring off** VT (task, plan) portare a compimento; (deal) concludere
▶ **bring on** VT (illness, attack) causare, provocare; (player, substitute) far scendere in campo
▶ **bring out** VT (meaning) mettere in evidenza; (new product) lanciare; (book) pubblicare, fare uscire
▶ **bring round, bring to** VT (unconscious person) far rinvenire
▶ **bring up** VT allevare; (question) introdurre

brink [brɪŋk] N orlo; **on the ~ of doing sth** sul punto di fare qc; **she was on the ~ of tears** era lì lì per piangere

brisk [brɪsk] ADJ (person, tone) spiccio(-a), sbrigativo(-a); (: abrupt) brusco(-a); (wind) fresco(-a); (trade etc) vivace, attivo(-a); (pace) svelto(-a); **to go for a ~ walk** fare una camminata di buon passo; **business is ~** gli affari vanno bene

bristle [ˈbrɪsl] N setola ▶ VI rizzarsi; **bristling with** irto(-a) di

bristly [ˈbrɪslɪ] ADJ (chin) ispido(-a); (beard, hair) irsuto(-a), setoloso(-a)

Brit [brɪt] N ABBR (col: = British person) britannico(-a)

Britain [ˈbrɪtən] N (also: **Great Britain**) Gran Bretagna

British [ˈbrɪtɪʃ] ADJ britannico(-a); **the British** NPL i Britannici; **the ~ Isles** npl le Isole Britanniche

British Summer Time N ora legale (in Gran Bretagna)

Briton [ˈbrɪtən] N britannico(-a)

Brittany [ˈbrɪtənɪ] N Bretagna

brittle [ˈbrɪtl] ADJ fragile

Br(o) ABBR (Rel) = **brother**

broach [brəutʃ] VT (subject) affrontare

broad [brɔːd] ADJ largo(-a); (distinction) generale; (accent) spiccato(-a) ▶ N (US col) bellona; **~ hint** allusione f esplicita; **in ~ daylight** in pieno giorno; **the ~ outlines** le grandi linee

broadband [ˈbrɔːdbænd] ADJ (Comput) a banda larga, ADSL ▶ N banda larga, ADSL m inv

broad bean N fava

broadcast [ˈbrɔːdkɑːst] (pt, pp **~**) N trasmissione f ▶ VT trasmettere per radio (or per televisione) ▶ VI fare una trasmissione

broadcaster [ˈbrɔːdkɑːstər] N annunciatore(-trice) radiotelevisivo(-a) (or radiofonico(-a))

broadcasting [ˈbrɔːdkɑːstɪŋ] N radiodiffusione f; televisione f

broadcasting station N stazione f trasmittente

broaden [ˈbrɔːdn] VT allargare ▶ VI allargarsi

broadly [ˈbrɔːdlɪ] ADV (fig) in generale

broad-minded [ˈbrɔːdˈmaɪndɪd] ADJ di mente aperta

broadsheet [ˈbrɔːdʃiːt] N (BRIT) giornale m (si contrappone al tabloid che è di formato più piccolo)

broccoli [ˈbrɔkəlɪ] N (Bot) broccolo; (Culin) broccoli mpl

brochure [ˈbrəuʃjuər] N dépliant m inv

brogue [brəuɡ] N (shoe) scarpa rozza in cuoio; (accent) accento irlandese

broil [brɔɪl] VT cuocere a fuoco vivo

broiler [ˈbrɔɪlər] (US) N (grill) griglia

broke [brəuk] PT of **break** ▶ ADJ (col) squattrinato(-a); **to go ~** fare fallimento

broken [ˈbrəukən] PP of **break** ▶ ADJ (gen) rotto(-a); (stick, promise, vow) spezzato(-a); (marriage) fallito(-a); **a ~ leg** una gamba rotta; **he comes from a ~ home** i suoi sono divisi; **in ~ French/English** in un francese/inglese stentato

broken-down [ˈbrəukənˈdaun] ADJ (car) in panne, rotto(-a); (machine) guasto(-a), fuori uso; (house) abbandonato(-a), in rovina

broken-hearted ['brəʊkən'hɑ:tɪd] ADJ: **to be ~** avere il cuore spezzato
broker ['brəʊkəʳ] N agente *m*
brokerage ['brəʊkərɪdʒ] N (*Comm*) commissione *f* di intermediazione
brolly ['brɒlɪ] N (*BRIT col*) ombrello
bronchitis [brɒŋ'kaɪtɪs] N bronchite *f*
bronze [brɒnz] N bronzo
bronzed [brɒnzd] ADJ abbronzato(-a)
brooch [brəʊtʃ] N spilla
brood [bru:d] N covata ▸ VI (*hen*) covare; (*person*) rimuginare
broody ['bru:dɪ] ADJ (*fig*) cupo(-a) e taciturno(-a)
brook [brʊk] N ruscello
broom [brum] N scopa; (*Bot*) ginestra
broomstick ['brʊmstɪk] N manico di scopa
Bros. ABBR (*Comm*: = *brothers*) F.lli (= *Fratelli*)
broth [brɒθ] N brodo
brothel ['brɒθl] N bordello
brother ['brʌðəʳ] N fratello
brotherhood ['brʌðəhʊd] N fratellanza; confraternità *f inv*
brother-in-law ['brʌðərɪnlɔ:] N cognato
brotherly ['brʌðəlɪ] ADJ fraterno(-a)
brought [brɔ:t] PT, PP *of* **bring**
brought forward ADJ (*Comm*) riportato(-a)
brow [braʊ] N fronte *f*; (*rare, gen: also:* **eyebrow**) sopracciglio; (*of hill*) cima
browbeat ['braʊbi:t] VT (*irreg: like* **beat**) intimidire
brown [braʊn] ADJ bruno(-a), marrone; (*hair*) castano(-a); (*tanned*) abbronzato(-a) ▸ N (*colour*) color *m* bruno *or* marrone ▸ VT (*Culin*) rosolare; **to go ~** (*person*) abbronzarsi; (*leaves*) ingiallire
brown bread N pane *m* integrale, pane nero
Brownie ['braʊnɪ] N giovane esploratrice *f*
brown paper N carta da pacchi *or* da imballaggio
brown rice N riso greggio
brown sugar N zucchero greggio
browse [braʊz] VI (*animal*) brucare; (*in bookshop etc*) curiosare; (*Comput*) navigare (in Internet) ▸ VT: **to ~ the web** navigare in Internet ▸ N: **to have a ~ (around)** dare un'occhiata (in giro); **to ~ through a book** sfogliare un libro
browser ['braʊzəʳ] N (*Comput*) browser *m inv*
bruise [bru:z] N ammaccatura; (*on person*) livido ▸ VT ammaccare; (*one's leg etc*) farsi un livido a; (*fig: feelings*) urtare ▸ VI (*fruit*) ammaccarsi
Brum [brʌm], **Brummagem** ['brʌmədʒəm] N (*col*) = **Birmingham**
Brummie ['brʌmɪ] N (*BRIT col*) abitante *mf* di Birmingham, originario(-a) di Birmingham
brunch [brʌntʃ] N *ricca colazione consumata in tarda mattinata*

brunette [bru:'nɛt] N bruna
brunt [brʌnt] N: **the ~ of** (*attack, criticism etc*) il peso maggiore di
brush [brʌʃ] N spazzola; (*for painting, shaving*) pennello; (*quarrel*) schermaglia ▸ VT spazzolare; (*also:* **brush past, brush against**) sfiorare; **to have a ~ with sb** (*verbally*) avere uno scontro con qn; (*physically*) venire a diverbio *or* alle mani con qn; **to have a ~ with the police** avere delle noie con la polizia
 ▸ **brush aside** VT scostare
 ▸ **brush up** VT (*knowledge*) rinfrescare
brushed [brʌʃt] ADJ (*Tech: steel, chrome etc*) sabbiato(-a); (*nylon, denim etc*) pettinato(-a)
brush-off ['brʌʃɔf] N: **to give sb the ~** dare il ben servito a qn
brushwood ['brʌʃwʊd] N macchia
brusque [bru:sk] ADJ (*person, manner*) brusco(-a); (*tone*) secco(-a)
Brussels ['brʌslz] N Bruxelles *f*
Brussels sprout [-spraʊt] N cavolo di Bruxelles
brutal ['bru:tl] ADJ brutale
brutality [bru:'tælɪtɪ] N brutalità
brutalize ['bru:təlaɪz] VT (*harden*) abbrutire; (*ill-treat*) brutalizzare
brute [bru:t] N bestia; **by ~ force** con la forza, a viva forza
brutish ['bru:tɪʃ] ADJ da bruto
BS N ABBR (*US:* = *Bachelor of Science*) titolo di studio
bs ABBR = **bill of sale**
BSA N ABBR (*US*) = **Boy Scouts of America**
BSc N ABBR (*Univ*) = **Bachelor of Science**
BSE N ABBR (= *bovine spongiform encephalopathy*) encefalite *f* bovina spongiforme
BSI N ABBR (= *British Standards Institution*) *associazione per la normalizzazione*
BST ABBR (= *British Summer Time*) ora legale
Bt. ABBR (*BRIT*) = **baronet**
btu N ABBR (= *British thermal unit*) Btu *m* (= 1054.2 *joules*)
bubble ['bʌbl] N bolla ▸ VI ribollire; (*sparkle: fig*) essere effervescente
bubble bath N bagno *m* schiuma *inv*
bubble gum N gomma americana
bubble jet printer ['bʌbldʒɛt-] N stampante *f* a getto d'inchiostro
bubbly ['bʌblɪ] ADJ (*also fig*) frizzante ▸ N (*col: champagne*) spumante *m*
Bucharest [bu:kə'rɛst] N Bucarest *f*
buck [bʌk] N maschio (*di camoscio, caprone, coniglio ecc*); (*US col*) dollaro ▸ VI sgroppare; **to pass the ~ (to sb)** scaricare (su di qn) la propria responsabilità
 ▸ **buck up** VI (*cheer up*) rianimarsi ▸ VT: **to ~ one's ideas up** mettere la testa a partito
bucket ['bʌkɪt] N secchio ▸ VI (*BRIT col*): **the rain is bucketing (down)** piove a catinelle

b

Buckingham Palace ['bʌkɪŋəm-] N *vedi nota*

Buckingham Palace è la residenza ufficiale a Londra del sovrano britannico. Costruita nel 1703 per il duca di Buckingham, fu acquistata nel 1762 dal re Giorgio III e ricostruita tra il 1821 e il 1838 sotto la guida dell'architetto John Nash. All'inizio del Novecento alcune sue parti sono state ulteriormente modificate.

buckle ['bʌkl] N fibbia ▶ VT allacciare; (*warp*) deformare ▶ VI (*wheel etc*) piegarsi
  ▶ **buckle down** VI mettersi sotto

Bucks [bʌks] ABBR (*BRIT*) = **Buckinghamshire**

bud [bʌd] N gemma; (*of flower*) bocciolo ▶ VI germogliare; (*flower*) sbocciare

Budapest [bju:də'pɛst] N Budapest f

Buddha ['budə] N Budda m

Buddhism ['budɪzəm] N buddismo

Buddhist ['budɪst] ADJ, N buddista (*mf*)

budding ['bʌdɪŋ] ADJ (*flower*) in boccio; (*poet etc*) in erba

buddy ['bʌdɪ] N (*US*) compagno

budge [bʌdʒ] VT scostare; (*fig*) smuovere
  ▶ VI spostarsi; smuoversi

budgerigar ['bʌdʒərɪgɑːʳ] N pappagallino

budget ['bʌdʒɪt] N bilancio preventivo ▶ VI: **to ~ for sth** fare il bilancio per qc; **I'm on a tight ~** devo contare la lira; **she works out her ~ every month** fa il preventivo delle spese ogni mese

budgie ['bʌdʒɪ] N = **budgerigar**

Buenos Aires ['bweɪnɔs'aɪrɪz] N Buenos Aires f

buff [bʌf] ADJ color camoscio *inv* ▶ N (*col: enthusiast*) appassionato(-a)

buffalo ['bʌfələu] (*pl ~ or* **buffaloes**) N bufalo; (*US*) bisonte m

buffer ['bʌfəʳ] N respingente m; (*Comput*) memoria tampone, buffer m *inv* ▶ VI (*Comput*) fare il buffering, trasferire nella memoria tampone

buffering ['bʌfərɪŋ] N buffering m *inv*, trasferimento nella memoria tampone

buffer state N stato cuscinetto

buffer zone N zona f cuscinetto *inv*

buffet N ['bufeɪ] (*food, BRIT: bar*) buffet m *inv*
  ▶ VT ['bʌfɪt] sferzare; urtare

buffet car N (*BRIT Rail*) ≈ servizio ristoro

buffet lunch N pranzo in piedi

buffoon [bə'fu:n] N buffone m

bug [bʌg] N (*insect*) cimice f; (*: gen*) insetto; (*fig: germ*) virus m *inv*; (*spy device*) microfono spia; (*Comput*) bug m *inv*, errore m nel programma ▶ VT mettere sotto controllo; (*room*) installare microfoni spia in; (*annoy*) scocciare; **I've got the travel ~** (*fig*) mi è presa la mania dei viaggi

bugbear ['bʌgbɛəʳ] N spauracchio

bugger ['bʌgəʳ] (*col!*) N bastardo (*!*)
  ▶ VI: **~ off!** vaffanculo! (*!*) ▶ VT: **~ (it)!** merda! (*!*)

buggy ['bʌgɪ] N (*baby buggy*) passeggino

bugle ['bju:gl] N tromba

build [bɪld] (*pt, pp* **built**) N (*of person*) corporatura ▶ VT costruire
  ▶ **build on** VT FUS (*fig*) prendere il via da
  ▶ **build up** VT (*establish: business*) costruire; (*: reputation*) fare, consolidare; (*increase: production*) allargare, incrementare; **don't ~ your hopes up too soon** non sperarci troppo

builder ['bɪldəʳ] N costruttore m

building ['bɪldɪŋ] N costruzione f; edificio; (*also:* **building trade**) edilizia

building contractor N costruttore m, imprenditore m (edile)

building industry N industria edilizia

building site N cantiere m di costruzione

building society N società immobiliare e finanziaria; *vedi nota*

Le building societies sono società immobiliari e finanziarie che forniscono anche numerosi servizi bancari ai clienti che vi investono i risparmi, e in particolare concedono mutui per l'acquisto della casa.

building trade N = **building industry**

build-up ['bɪldʌp] N (*of gas etc*) accumulo; (*publicity*): **to give sb/sth a good ~** fare buona pubblicità a qn/qc

built [bɪlt] PT, PP *of* **build**; **well-~** robusto(-a)

built-in ['bɪlt'ɪn] ADJ (*cupboard*) a muro; (*device*) incorporato(-a)

built-up area ['bɪltʌp-] N abitato

bulb [bʌlb] N (*Bot*) bulbo; (*Elec*) lampadina

bulbous ['bʌlbəs] ADJ bulboso(-a)

Bulgaria [bʌl'gɛərɪə] N Bulgaria

Bulgarian [bʌl'gɛərɪən] ADJ bulgaro(-a)
  ▶ N bulgaro(-a); (*Ling*) bulgaro

bulge [bʌldʒ] N rigonfiamento; (*in birth rate, sales*) punta ▶ VI essere protuberante *or* rigonfio(-a); **to be bulging with** essere pieno(-a) *or* zeppo(-a) di

bulimia [bə'lɪmɪə] N bulimia

bulimic [bju:'lɪmɪk] ADJ, N bulimico(-a)

bulk [bʌlk] N massa, volume m; **the ~ of** il grosso di; (**to buy**) **in ~** (comprare) in grande quantità; (*Comm*) (comprare) all'ingrosso

bulk buying N acquisto di merce in grande quantità

bulk carrier N grossa nave f da carico

bulkhead ['bʌlkhɛd] N paratia

bulky ['bʌlkɪ] ADJ grosso(-a); voluminoso(-a)

bull [bul] N toro; (*male elephant, whale*) maschio; (*Stock Exchange*) rialzista mf; (*Rel*) bolla (papale)

bulldog ['buldɔg] N bulldog m *inv*

bulldoze ['buldəuz] VT aprire or spianare col bulldozer; **I was bulldozed into doing it** (fig: col) mi ci hanno costretto con la prepotenza

bulldozer ['buldəuzəʳ] N bulldozer m inv

bullet ['bulɪt] N pallottola

bulletin ['bulɪtɪn] N bollettino

bulletin board N (Comput) bulletin board m inv

bullet point N punto; **bullet points** elenco sg puntato

bullet-proof ['bulɪtpru:f] ADJ a prova di proiettile; **~ vest** giubbotto antiproiettile

bullfight ['bulfaɪt] N corrida

bullfighter ['bulfaɪtəʳ] N torero

bullfighting ['bulfaɪtɪŋ] N tauromachia

bullion ['buljən] N oro or argento in lingotti

bullock ['bulək] N giovenco

bullring ['bulrɪŋ] N arena (per corride)

bull's-eye ['bulzaɪ] N centro del bersaglio

bullshit ['bulʃɪt] (col!) EXCL, N stronzate fpl (!)
▶ VI raccontare stronzate (!) ▶ VT raccontare stronzate a (!)

bully ['bulɪ] N prepotente m ▶ VT angariare; (frighten) intimidire

bullying ['bulɪɪŋ] N prepotenze fpl

bum [bʌm] N (col: backside) culo; (tramp) vagabondo(-a); (US: idler) fannullone(-a)
▶ **bum around** VI (col) fare il vagabondo

bumblebee ['bʌmblbi:] N (Zool) bombo

bumf [bʌmf] N (col: forms etc) scartoffie fpl

bump [bʌmp] N (blow) colpo; (in car) piccolo tamponamento; (jolt) scossa; (noise) botto; (on road etc) protuberanza; (on head) bernoccolo ▶ VT battere; (car) urtare, sbattere
▶ **bump along** VI procedere sobbalzando
▶ **bump into** VT FUS scontrarsi con; (col: meet) imbattersi in, incontrare per caso

bumper ['bʌmpəʳ] N (BRIT) paraurti m inv
▶ ADJ: **~ harvest** raccolto eccezionale

bumper cars NPL (US) autoscontri mpl

bumph [bʌmf] N = **bumf**

bumptious ['bʌmpʃəs] ADJ presuntuoso(-a)

bumpy ['bʌmpɪ] ADJ (road) dissestato(-a); (journey, flight) movimentato(-a)

bun [bʌn] N focaccia; (of hair) crocchia

bunch [bʌntʃ] N (of flowers, keys) mazzo; (of bananas) casco; (of people) gruppo; **~ of grapes** grappolo d'uva; **bunches** NPL (in hair) codine fpl

bundle ['bʌndl] N fascio ▶ VT (also: **bundle up**) legare in un fascio; (put): **to ~ sth/sb into** spingere qc/qn in
▶ **bundle off** VT (person) mandare via in gran fretta
▶ **bundle out** VT far uscire (senza tante cerimonie)

bun fight N (BRIT col) tè m inv (ricevimento)

bung [bʌŋ] N tappo ▶ VT (BRIT: throw: also: **bung into**) buttare; (also: **bung up**: pipe, hole) tappare, otturare; **my nose is bunged up** (col) ho il naso otturato

bungalow ['bʌŋgələu] N bungalow m inv

bungee jumping ['bʌndʒi:'dʒʌmpɪŋ] N salto nel vuoto da ponti, grattacieli ecc con un cavo fissato alla caviglia

bungle ['bʌŋgl] VT abborracciare

bunion ['bʌnjən] N callo (al piede)

bunk [bʌŋk] N cuccetta
▶ **bunk off** VI (BRIT col): **to ~ off school** marinare la scuola; **I'll ~ off at 3 this afternoon** oggi me la filo dal lavoro alle 3

bunk beds NPL letti mpl a castello

bunker ['bʌŋkəʳ] N (coal store) ripostiglio per il carbone; (Mil, Golf) bunker m inv

bunny ['bʌnɪ] N (also: **bunny rabbit**) coniglietto

bunny girl N coniglietta

bunny hill N (US Ski) pista per principianti

bunting ['bʌntɪŋ] N pavesi mpl, bandierine fpl

buoy [bɔɪ] N boa
▶ **buoy up** VT tenere a galla; (fig) sostenere

buoyancy ['bɔɪənsɪ] N (of ship) galleggiabilità

buoyant ['bɔɪənt] ADJ galleggiante; (fig) vivace; (Comm: market) sostenuto(-a); (: prices, currency) stabile

burden ['bə:dn] N carico, fardello ▶ VT caricare; (oppress) opprimere; **to ~ sb with** caricare qn di; **to be a ~ to sb** essere di peso a qn

bureau ['bjuərəu] (pl **bureaux** [-z]) N (BRIT: writing desk) scrivania; (US: chest of drawers) cassettone m; (office) ufficio, agenzia

bureaucracy [bjuə'rɔkrəsɪ] N burocrazia

bureaucrat ['bjuərəkræt] N burocrate mf

bureaucratic [bjuərə'krætɪk] ADJ burocratico(-a)

bureau de change [-də'ʃãʒ] (pl **bureaux de change**) N cambiavalute m inv

bureaux [bjuə'rəuz] NPL of **bureau**

burgeon ['bə:dʒən] VI svilupparsi rapidamente

burger ['bə:gəʳ] N hamburger m inv

burglar ['bə:gləʳ] N scassinatore m

burglar alarm N (allarme m) antifurto m inv

burglarize ['bə:gləraɪz] VT (US) svaligiare

burglary ['bə:glərɪ] N furto con scasso

burgle ['bə:gl] VT svaligiare

Burgundy ['bə:gəndɪ] N Borgogna

burial ['bɛrɪəl] N sepoltura

burial ground N cimitero

burly ['bə:lɪ] ADJ robusto(-a)

Burma ['bə:mə] N Birmania; see **Myanmar**

Burmese [bə:'mi:z] ADJ birmano(-a) ▶ N (pl inv) birmano(-a); (Ling) birmano

burn [bə:n] (pt, pp **burned** or **burnt**) VT, VI bruciare ▶ N bruciatura, scottatura; (Med)

ustione f; **I've burnt myself!** mi sono bruciato!; **the cigarette burnt a hole in her dress** si è fatta un buco nel vestito con la sigaretta
▶ **burn down** VT distruggere col fuoco
▶ **burn out** VT (writer etc): **to ~ o.s. out** esaurirsi
burner ['bə:nə^r] N fornello
burning ['bə:nɪŋ] ADJ (building, forest) in fiamme; (sand) che scotta; (ambition) bruciante; (issue, question) scottante
burnish ['bə:nɪʃ] VT brunire
Burns Night N vedi nota

> Burns Night è la festa celebrata il 25 gennaio per commemorare il poeta scozzese Robert Burns (1759–1796). Gli scozzesi festeggiano questa data con una cena, Burns supper a base de haggis e whisky, spesso al suono di una cornamusa durante la cena vengono recitate le poesie di Robert Burns e vengono letti discorsi alla sua memoria.

burnt [bə:nt] PT, PP of **burn**
burnt sugar N (BRIT) caramello
burp [bə:p] (col) N rutto ▶ VI ruttare
burrow ['bʌrəu] N tana ▶ VT scavare
bursar ['bə:sə^r] N economo(-a); (BRIT: student) borsista mf
bursary ['bə:sərɪ] N (BRIT) borsa di studio
burst [bə:st] (pt, pp ~) VT far scoppiare or esplodere ▶ VI esplodere; (tyre) scoppiare ▶ N scoppio; (also: **burst pipe**) rottura nel tubo, perdita; ~ **of energy/laughter** scoppio d'energia/di risa; **a ~ of applause** uno scroscio d'applausi; **a ~ of speed** uno scatto (di velocità); ~ **blood vessel** rottura di un vaso sanguigno; **the river has ~ its banks** il fiume ha rotto gli argini or ha straripato; **to ~ into flames/tears** scoppiare in fiamme/lacrime; **to be bursting with** essere pronto a scoppiare di; **to ~ out laughing** scoppiare a ridere; **to ~ open** vi aprirsi improvvisamente; (door) spalancarsi
▶ **burst into** VT FUS (room etc) irrompere in
▶ **burst out of** VT FUS precipitarsi fuori da
bury ['bɛrɪ] VT seppellire; **to ~ one's face in one's hands** nascondere la faccia tra le mani; **to ~ one's head in the sand** (fig) fare (la politica del)lo struzzo; **to ~ the hatchet** (fig) seppellire l'ascia di guerra
bus [bʌs] (pl **buses** ['bʌsɪz]) N autobus m inv
bus boy N (US) aiuto inv cameriere(-a)
bus conductor N autista mf (dell'autobus)
bush [buʃ] N cespuglio; (scrub land) macchia; **to beat about the ~** menare il cane per l'aia
bushed [buʃt] ADJ (col) distrutto(-a)
bushel ['buʃl] N staio
bushfire ['buʃfaɪə^r] N grande incendio in aperta campagna

bushy ['buʃɪ] ADJ (plant, tail, beard) folto(-a); (eyebrows) irsuto(-a)
busily ['bɪzɪlɪ] ADV con impegno, alacremente
business ['bɪznɪs] N (matter) affare m; (trading) affari mpl; (firm) azienda; (job, duty) lavoro; **to be away on ~** essere andato via per affari; **I'm here on ~** sono qui per affari; **to do ~ with sb** fare affari con qn; **he's in the insurance ~** lavora nel campo delle assicurazioni; **it's none of my ~** questo non mi riguarda; **he means ~** non scherza
business address N indirizzo di lavoro or d'ufficio
business card N biglietto da visita della ditta
business class N (Aviat) business class f
businesslike ['bɪznɪslaɪk] ADJ serio(-a); efficiente
businessman ['bɪznɪsmən] N (irreg) uomo d'affari
business trip N viaggio d'affari
businesswoman ['bɪznɪswumən] N (irreg) donna d'affari
busker ['bʌskə^r] N (BRIT) suonatore(-trice) ambulante
bus lane N (BRIT) corsia riservata agli autobus
bus pass N tessera dell'autobus
bus shelter N pensilina (alla fermata dell'autobus)
bus station N stazione f delle corriere, autostazione f
bus stop N fermata d'autobus
bust [bʌst] N (Art) busto; (Anat: bosom) seno ▶ ADJ (col: broken) rotto(-a) ▶ VT (col: Police: arrest) pizzicare, beccare; **to go ~** fallire
bustle ['bʌsl] N movimento, attività ▶ VI darsi da fare
bustling ['bʌslɪŋ] ADJ (person) indaffarato(-a); (town) animato(-a)
bust-up ['bʌstʌp] N (BRIT col) lite f
busty ['bʌstɪ] ADJ (col) tettone(-a)
busy ['bɪzɪ] ADJ occupato(-a); (shop, street) molto frequentato(-a) ▶ VT: **to ~ o.s.** darsi da fare; **he's a ~ man** (normally) è un uomo molto occupato; (temporarily) ha molto da fare, è molto occupato
busybody ['bɪzɪbɔdɪ] N ficcanaso mf
busy signal N (US Tel) segnale m di occupato

(KEYWORD)

but [bʌt] CONJ ma; **I'd love to come, but I'm busy** vorrei tanto venire, ma ho da fare
▶ PREP (apart from, except) eccetto, tranne, meno; **nothing but** nient'altro che; **he was nothing but trouble** non dava altro che guai; **no-one but him** solo lui; **no-one but him can do it** nessuno può farlo tranne lui; **the last but one** (BRIT) il penultimo(-a);

but for you/your help se non fosse per te/per il tuo aiuto; **anything but that** tutto ma non questo; **anything but finished** tutt'altro che finito

▶ ADV *(just, only)* solo, soltanto; **she's but a child** è solo una bambina; **had I but known** se solo avessi saputo; **I can but try** tentar non nuoce; **all but finished** quasi finito

butane ['bju:teɪn] N *(also:* **butane gas)** butano
butch [butʃ] ADJ *(col: woman: pej)* mascolino(-a); *(man)* macho *inv*
butcher ['butʃəʳ] N macellaio ▶ VT macellare; **~'s (shop)** macelleria
butler ['bʌtləʳ] N maggiordomo
butt [bʌt] N *(cask)* grossa botte *f*; *(thick end)* estremità *f inv* più grossa; *(of gun)* calcio; *(of cigarette)* mozzicone *m*; *(BRIT fig: target)* oggetto ▶ VT cozzare
▶ **butt in** VI *(interrupt)* interrompere
butter ['bʌtəʳ] N burro ▶ VT imburrare
buttercup ['bʌtəkʌp] N ranuncolo
butter dish N burriera
butterfingers ['bʌtəfɪŋɡəz] N *(col)* mani *fpl* di ricotta
butterfly ['bʌtəflaɪ] N farfalla; *(Swimming: also:* **butterfly stroke)** (nuoto a) farfalla
buttocks ['bʌtəks] NPL natiche *fpl*
button ['bʌtn] N bottone *m*; *(US: badge)* distintivo ▶ VT *(also:* **button up)** abbottonare ▶ VI abbottonarsi
buttonhole ['bʌtnhəul] N asola, occhiello ▶ VT *(person)* attaccar bottone a
buttress ['bʌtrɪs] N contrafforte *m*
buxom ['bʌksəm] ADJ formoso(-a)
buy [baɪ] *(pt, pp* **bought)** VT comprare, acquistare ▶ N acquisto; **a good/bad ~** un buon/cattivo acquisto *or* affare; **to ~ sb sth/sth from sb** comprare qc per qn/qc da qn; **to ~ sb a drink** offrire da bere a qn
▶ **buy back** VT riprendersi, prendersi indietro
▶ **buy in** VT *(BRIT: goods)* far provvista di
▶ **buy into** VT FUS *(BRIT Comm)* acquistare delle azioni di
▶ **buy off** VT *(col: bribe)* comprare
▶ **buy out** VT *(business)* rilevare
▶ **buy up** VT accaparrare
buyer ['baɪəʳ] N compratore(-trice); **~'s market** mercato favorevole ai compratori
buy-out ['baɪaut] N *(Comm)* acquisto di una *società da parte dei suoi dipendenti*
buzz [bʌz] N ronzio; *(col: phone call)* colpo di telefono ▶ VI ronzare ▶ VT *(call on intercom)* chiamare al citofono; *(: with buzzer)* chiamare col cicalino; *(Aviat: plane, building)* passare rasente; **my head is buzzing** mi gira la testa

▶ **buzz off** VI *(BRIT col)* filare, levarsi di torno
buzzard ['bʌzəd] N poiana
buzzer ['bʌzəʳ] N cicalino
buzz word N *(col)* termine *m* in voga

(KEYWORD)

by [baɪ] PREP **1** *(referring to cause, agent)* da; **killed by lightning** ucciso da un fulmine; **surrounded by a fence** circondato da uno steccato; **a painting by Picasso** un quadro di Picasso
2 *(referring to method: manner: means)*: **by bus/car/train** in autobus/macchina/treno, con l'autobus/la macchina/il treno; **to pay by cheque** pagare con (un) assegno; **by moonlight** al chiaro di luna; **by saving hard, he ...** risparmiando molto, lui ...
3 *(via, through)* per; **we came by Dover** siamo venuti via Dover
4 *(close to, past)* accanto a; **the house by the river** la casa sul fiume; **a holiday by the sea** una vacanza al mare; **she sat by his bed** si sedette accanto al suo letto; **she rushed by me** mi è passata accanto correndo; **I go by the post office every day** passo davanti all'ufficio postale ogni giorno
5 *(not later than)* per, entro; **by 4 o'clock** per *or* entro le 4; **by this time tomorrow** domani a quest'ora; **by the time I got here it was too late** quando sono arrivato era ormai troppo tardi
6 *(during)*: **by day/night** di giorno/notte
7 *(amount)* a; **by the kilo** a chili; **paid by the hour** pagato all'ora; **to increase by the hour** aumentare di ora in ora; **one by one** uno per uno; **little by little** a poco a poco
8 *(Math: measure)*: **to divide/multiply by 3** dividere/moltiplicare per 3; **a room 3 metres by 4** una stanza di 3 metri per 4; **it's broader by a metre** è un metro più largo, è più largo di un metro
9 *(according to)* per; **to play by the rules** attenersi alle regole; **it's all right by me** per me va bene
10: **(all) by oneself** (tutto(-a)) solo(-a); **he did it (all) by himself** lo ha fatto (tutto) da solo
11: **by the way** a proposito; **this wasn't my idea by the way** tra l'altro l'idea non è stata mia

▶ ADV **1** *see* **go**; **pass** *etc*
2: **by and by** *(in past)* poco dopo; *(in future)* fra breve; **by and large** nel complesso

bye ['baɪ], **bye-bye** ['baɪ'baɪ] EXCL ciao!, arrivederci!
bye-law ['baɪlɔ:] N legge *f* locale
by-election ['baɪɪlɛkʃən] N *(BRIT)* elezione *f* straordinaria; *vedi nota*

Una *by-election* in Gran Bretagna e in alcuni paesi del *Commonwealth* è un'elezione che si tiene per coprire un posto in Parlamento resosi vacante, a governo ancora in carica. é importante in quanto serve a misurare il consenso degli elettori in vista delle successive elezioni politiche.

Byelorussia [bjɛləu'rʌʃə] N Bielorussia, Belorussia

Byelorussian [bjɛləu'rʌʃən] ADJ, N = **Belarussian**

bygone ['baɪgɔn] ADJ passato(-a) ▶ N: **let bygones be bygones** mettiamoci una pietra sopra

by-law ['baɪlɔ:] N legge *f* locale

bypass ['baɪpɑːs] N circonvallazione *f*; (*Med*) by-pass *m inv* ▶ VT fare una deviazione intorno a

by-product ['baɪprɔdʌkt] N sottoprodotto; (*fig*) conseguenza secondaria

byre ['baɪəʳ] N (*BRIT*) stalla

bystander ['baɪstændəʳ] N spettatore(-trice)

byte [baɪt] N (*Comput*) byte *m inv*, bicarattere *m*

byway ['baɪweɪ] N strada secondaria

byword ['baɪwəːd] N: **to be a ~ for** essere sinonimo di

by-your-leave ['baɪjɔː'liːv] N: **without so much as a ~** senza nemmeno chiedere il permesso

Cc

C, c [si:] N (*letter*) C, c *f inv* or *m inv*; (*Scol: mark*) ≈ 6 (*sufficiente*); (*Mus*): **C** do; **C for Charlie** ≈ C come Como

C ABBR = **Celsius**; (= *centigrade*) C

c. ABBR (= *century*) sec.; (*US etc*) = **cent**; (= *circa*) c

CA ABBR = **Central America**; (*US*) = **California** ▶ N ABBR (*BRIT*) = **chartered accountant**

ca. ABBR (= *circa*) ca

c/a ABBR = **capital account; credit account; current account**

CAA N ABBR *BRIT*: = **Civil Aviation Authority**; (*US*: = *Civil Aeronautics Authority*) *organismo di controllo e di sviluppo dell'aviazione civile*

CAB N ABBR (*BRIT*: = *Citizens' Advice Bureau*) *organizzazione per la tutela del consumatore*

cab [kæb] N taxi *m inv*; (*of train, truck*) cabina; (*horsedrawn*) carrozza

cabaret ['kæbəreɪ] N cabaret *m inv*

cabbage ['kæbɪdʒ] N cavolo

cabbie, cabby ['kæbɪ] N (*col*) tassista *mf*

cab driver N tassista *mf*

cabin ['kæbɪn] N capanna; (*on ship*) cabina

cabin crew N equipaggio

cabin cruiser N cabinato

cabinet ['kæbɪnɪt] N (*Pol*) consiglio dei ministri; (*furniture*) armadietto; (*also*: **display cabinet**) vetrinetta; **cocktail ~** mobile *m* bar *inv*

cabinet-maker ['kæbɪnɪt'meɪkə^r] N stipettaio

cabinet minister N ministro (*membro del Consiglio*)

cable ['keɪbl] N cavo; fune *f*; (*Tel*) cablogramma *m* ▶ VT telegrafare

cable-car ['keɪblkɑ:^r] N funivia

cablegram ['keɪblgræm] N cablogramma *m*

cable railway N funicolare *f*

cable television N televisione *f* via cavo

cache [kæʃ] N nascondiglio; **a ~ of food** *etc* un deposito segreto di viveri *etc*

cackle ['kækl] VI schiamazzare

cactus ['kæktəs] (*pl* **cacti** [-taɪ]) N cactus *m inv*

CAD N ABBR (= *computer-aided design*) progettazione *f* con l'ausilio dell'elaboratore

caddie ['kædɪ] N caddie *m inv*

cadet [kə'dɛt] N (*Mil*) cadetto; **police ~** allievo poliziotto

cadge [kædʒ] VT (*col*) scroccare; **to ~ a meal (off sb)** scroccare un pranzo (a qn)

cadre ['kædrɪ] N quadro

Caesarean, (*US*) **Cesarean** [si:'zɛərɪən] ADJ: **~ (section)** (*taglio*) cesareo

CAF ABBR (*BRIT*: = *cost and freight*) Caf *m*

café ['kæfeɪ] N caffè *m inv*

cafeteria [kæfɪ'tɪərɪə] N self-service *m inv*

caffein, caffeine ['kæfi:n] N caffeina

cage [keɪdʒ] N gabbia ▶ VT mettere in gabbia

cagey ['keɪdʒɪ] ADJ (*col*) chiuso(-a); guardingo(-a)

cagoule [kə'gu:l] N K-way® *m inv*

cahoots [kə'hu:ts] N: **to be in ~ (with sb)** essere in combutta (con qn)

CAI N ABBR (= *computer-aided instruction*) istruzione *f* assistita dall'elaboratore

Cairo ['kaɪərəu] N il Cairo

cajole [kə'dʒəul] VT allettare

cake [keɪk] N (*large*) torta; (*small*) pasticcino; **~ of soap** saponetta; **it's a piece of ~** (*col*) è una cosa da nulla; **he wants to have his ~ and eat it (too)** (*fig*) vuole la botte piena e la moglie ubriaca

caked [keɪkt] ADJ: **~ with** incrostato(-a) di

cake shop N pasticceria

Cal. ABBR (*US*) = **California**

calamitous [kə'læmɪtəs] ADJ disastroso(-a)

calamity [kə'læmɪtɪ] N calamità *f inv*

calcium ['kælsɪəm] N calcio

calculate ['kælkjuleɪt] VT calcolare; (*estimate: chances, effect*) valutare ▶ **calculate on** VT FUS: **to ~ on sth/on doing sth** contare su qc/di fare qc

calculated ['kælkjuleɪtɪd] ADJ calcolato(-a), intenzionale; **a ~ risk** un rischio calcolato

calculating ['kælkjuleɪtɪŋ] ADJ calcolatore(-trice)

calculation [kælkju'leɪʃən] N calcolo

calculator ['kælkjuleɪtə^r] N calcolatrice *f*

calculus ['kælkjuləs] N calcolo; **integral/ differential** ~ calcolo integrale/ differenziale

calendar ['kæləndəʳ] N calendario

calendar year N anno civile

calf [kɑːf] (pl **calves** [kɑːvz]) N (of cow) vitello; (of other animals) piccolo; (also: **calfskin**) (pelle f di) vitello; (Anat) polpaccio

caliber ['kælɪbəʳ] N (US) = **calibre**

calibrate ['kælɪbreɪt] VT (gun etc) calibrare; (scale of measuring instrument) tarare

calibre, (US) **caliber** ['kælɪbəʳ] N calibro

calico ['kælɪkəu] N tela grezza, cotone m grezzo; (US) cotonina stampata

Calif. ABBR (US) = **California**

California [kælɪ'fɔːnɪə] N California

calipers ['kælɪpəz] NPL (US) = **callipers**

call [kɔːl] VT (gen, also Tel) chiamare; (announce: flight) annunciare; (: meeting, strike) indire, proclamare ▶ VI chiamare; (visit: also: **call in, call round**) passare ▶ N (shout) grido, urlo; (visit) visita; (summons: for flight etc) chiamata; (fig: lure) richiamo; (also: **telephone call**) telefonata; **to be called** (person, object) chiamarsi; **to be on** ~ essere a disposizione; **to make a** ~ telefonare, fare una telefonata; **please give me a ~ at 7** per piacere mi chiami alle 7; **to pay a ~ on sb** fare (una) visita a qn; **there's not much ~ for these items** non c'è molta richiesta di questi articoli; **she's called Jane** si chiama Jane; **who is calling?** (Tel) chi parla?; **London calling** (Radio) qui Londra

▶ **call at** VT FUS (ship) fare scalo a; (train) fermarsi a

▶ **call back** VI (return) ritornare; (Tel) ritelefonare, richiamare ▶ VT (Tel) ritelefonare a, richiamare; **can you ~ back later?** può richiamare più tardi?

▶ **call for** VT FUS (demand: action etc) richiedere; (collect: person) passare a prendere; (: goods) ritirare

▶ **call in** VT (doctor, expert, police) chiamare, far venire

▶ **call off** VT (meeting, race) disdire; (deal) cancellare; (dog) richiamare; **the strike was called off** lo sciopero è stato revocato

▶ **call on** VT FUS (visit) passare da; (request): **to ~ sb to do** chiedere a qn di fare

▶ **call out** VI (in pain) urlare; (to person) chiamare ▶ VT (doctor, police, troops) chiamare

▶ **call up** VT (Mil) richiamare; (Tel) telefonare a

Callanetics® [kælə'nɛtɪks] NSG tipo di ginnastica basata sulla ripetizione di piccoli movimenti

callbox ['kɔːlbɔks] N (BRIT) cabina telefonica

call centre, (US) **call center** N centro informazioni telefoniche

caller ['kɔːləʳ] N persona che chiama; visitatore(-trice); **hold the line, ~!** (Tel) rimanga in linea, signore (or signora)!

call girl N ragazza f squillo inv

call-in ['kɔːlɪn] N (US) = **phone-in**

calling ['kɔːlɪŋ] N vocazione f

calling card N (US) biglietto da visita

callipers, (US) **calipers** ['kælɪpəz] NPL (Med) gambale m; (Math) calibro

callous ['kæləs] ADJ indurito(-a), insensibile

callousness ['kæləsnɪs] N insensibilità

callow ['kæləu] ADJ immaturo(-a)

calm [kɑːm] ADJ calmo(-a) ▶ N calma ▶ VT calmare

▶ **calm down** VI calmarsi ▶ VT calmare

calmly ['kɑːmlɪ] ADV con calma

calmness ['kɑːmnɪs] N calma

Calor gas® ['kælə'-] N (BRIT) butano

calorie ['kælərɪ] N caloria; **low-~ product** prodotto a basso contenuto di calorie

calve [kɑːv] VI figliare

calves [kɑːvz] NPL of **calf**

CAM N ABBR (= computer-aided manufacturing) fabbricazione f con l'ausilio dell'elaboratore

camber ['kæmbəʳ] N (of road) bombatura

Cambodia [kæm'bəudjə] N Cambogia

Cambodian [kæm'bəudɪən] ADJ, N cambogiano(-a)

Cambs ABBR (BRIT) = **Cambridgeshire**

camcorder ['kæmkɔːdəʳ] N videocamera

came [keɪm] PT of **come**

camel ['kæməl] N cammello

cameo ['kæmɪəu] N cammeo

camera ['kæmərə] N macchina fotografica; (Cine, TV) telecamera; (also: **cinecamera, movie camera**) cinepresa; **in ~** a porte chiuse

cameraman ['kæmərəmæn] N (irreg) cameraman m inv

camera phone N telefono cellulare con fotocamera integrata

Cameroon, Cameroun ['kæməruːn] N Camerun m

camouflage ['kæməflɑːʒ] N (feeling) camuffamento; (Mil, Zool) mimetizzazione f ▶ VT (feeling) camuffare; mimetizzare

camp [kæmp] N campeggio; (Mil) campo ▶ VI campeggiare; accamparsi; **to go camping** andare in campeggio ▶ ADJ effeminato(-a)

campaign [kæm'peɪn] N (Mil, Pol etc) campagna ▶ VI: **to ~ (for/against)** (also fig) fare una campagna (per/contro)

campaigner [kæm'peɪnəʳ] N: ~ **for** fautore(-trice) di; ~ **against** oppositore(-trice) di

campbed ['kæmp'bɛd] N (BRIT) brandina

camper ['kæmpəʳ] N campeggiatore(-trice); (vehicle) camper m inv

campground N (US) campeggio

camping ['kæmpɪŋ] N campeggio; **to go ~** andare in campeggio

camp site ['kæmpsaɪt], **camping site** N campeggio

campus ['kæmpəs] N campus *m inv*

camshaft ['kæmʃɑːft] N albero a camme

can[1] [kæn] N (*of milk*) scatola; (*of oil*) bidone *m*; (*of water*) tanica; (*tin*) scatola ▶ VT mettere in scatola; **a ~ of beer** una lattina di birra; **to carry the ~** (*BRIT col*) prendere la colpa

(KEYWORD)

can[2] [kæn] (*negative* **cannot**, **can't**, *pt*, *conditional* **could**) AUX VB **1** (*be able to*) potere; **I can't go any further** non posso andare oltre; **you can do it if you try** sei in grado di farlo - basta provarci; **I'll help you all I can** ti aiuterò come potrò; **I can't see you** non ti vedo; **can you hear me?** mi senti?, riesci a sentirmi?

2 (*know how to*) sapere, essere capace di; **I can swim** so nuotare; **can you speak French?** parla francese?

3 (*may*) potere; **could I have a word with you?** posso parlarle un momento?

4 (*expressing disbelief: puzzlement etc*): **it can't be true!** non può essere vero!; **what CAN he want?** cosa può mai volere?

5 (*expressing possibility: suggestion etc*): **he could be in the library** può darsi che sia in biblioteca; **they could have forgotten** potrebbero essersene dimenticati; **she could have been delayed** può aver avuto un contrattempo

Canada ['kænədə] N Canada *m*

Canadian [kə'neɪdɪən] ADJ, N canadese (*mf*)

canal [kə'næl] N canale *m*

canary [kə'nɛərɪ] N canarino

Canary Islands, Canaries [kə'nɛərɪz] NPL: **the ~** le (isole) Canarie ˙

Canberra ['kænbərə] N Camberra

cancel ['kænsəl] VT annullare; (*train*) sopprimere; (*cross out*) cancellare ▶ **cancel out** VT (*Math*) semplificare; (*fig*) annullare; **they ~ each other out** (*also fig*) si annullano a vicenda

cancellation [kænsə'leɪʃən] N annullamento; soppressione *f*; cancellazione *f*; (*Tourism*) prenotazione *f* annullata

cancer ['kænsə[r]] N cancro; **C~** (*sign*) Cancro; **to be C~** essere del Cancro

cancerous ['kænsərəs] ADJ canceroso(-a)

cancer patient N malato(-a) di cancro

cancer research N ricerca sul cancro

C and F ABBR (*BRIT*: = *cost and freight*) Caf *m*

candid ['kændɪd] ADJ onesto(-a)

candidacy ['kændɪdəsɪ] N candidatura

candidate ['kændɪdeɪt] N candidato(-a)

candidature ['kændɪdətʃə[r]] N (*BRIT*) = **candidacy**

candied ['kændɪd] ADJ candito(-a); **~ apple** (*US*) mela caramellata

candle ['kændl] N candela; (*in church*) cero

candlelight ['kændl'laɪt] N: **by ~** a lume di candela

candlestick ['kændlstɪk] N (*also*: **candle holder**) bugia; (*bigger, ornate*) candeliere *m*

candour, (*US*) **candor** ['kændə[r]] N sincerità

C & W N ABBR = **country and western (music)**

candy ['kændɪ] N zucchero candito; (*US*) caramella; **caramelle** *fpl*

candy bar (*US*) N *lungo biscotto, in genere ricoperto di cioccolata*

candy-floss ['kændɪflɔs] N (*BRIT*) zucchero filato

candy store N (*US*) = pasticceria

cane [keɪn] N canna; (*for baskets, chairs etc*) bambù *m*; (*Scol*) verga; (*for walking*) bastone *m* (da passeggio) ▶ VT (*BRIT Scol*) punire a colpi di verga

canine ['keɪnaɪn] ADJ canino(-a)

canister ['kænɪstə[r]] N scatola metallica

cannabis ['kænəbɪs] N canapa indiana

canned ['kænd] ADJ (*food*) in scatola; (*col: recorded: music*) registrato(-a); (*BRIT col: drunk*) sbronzo(-a); (*US col: worker*) licenziato(-a)

cannibal ['kænɪbəl] N cannibale *mf*

cannibalism ['kænɪbəlɪzəm] N cannibalismo

cannon ['kænən] (*pl ~ or* **cannons**) N (*gun*) cannone *m*

cannonball ['kænənbɔːl] N palla di cannone

cannon fodder N carne *f* da macello

cannot ['kænɔt] = **can not**

canny ['kænɪ] ADJ furbo(-a)

canoe [kə'nuː] N canoa; (*Sport*) canotto

canoeing [kə'nuːɪŋ] N (*Sport*) canottaggio

canoeist [kə'nuːɪst] N canottiere *m*

canon ['kænən] N (*clergyman*) canonico; (*standard*) canone *m*

canonize ['kænənaɪz] VT canonizzare

can opener [-əupnə[r]] N apriscatole *m inv*

canopy ['kænəpɪ] N baldacchino

cant [kænt] N gergo ▶ VT inclinare ▶ VI inclinarsi

can't [kænt] = **can not**

Cantab. ABBR (*BRIT*: = *cantabrigiensis*) *of Cambridge*

cantankerous [kæn'tæŋkərəs] ADJ stizzoso(-a)

canteen [kæn'tiːn] N mensa; (*BRIT: of cutlery*) portaposate *m inv*

canter ['kæntə[r]] N piccolo galoppo ▶ VI andare al piccolo galoppo

cantilever ['kæntɪliːvə[r]] N trave *f* a sbalzo

canvas ['kænvəs] N tela; **under ~** (*camping*) sotto la tenda; (*Naut*) sotto la vela

canvass ['kænvəs] VI (*Pol*): **to ~ for** raccogliere voti per ▶ VT (*Comm: district*) fare un'indagine di mercato in; (: *citizens, opinions*) fare un sondaggio di; (*Pol: district*) fare un giro elettorale di; (: *person*) fare propaganda elettorale a

canvasser ['kænvəsəʳ] N (*Comm*) agente *m* viaggiatore, piazzista *m*; (*Pol*) propagandista *mf* (elettorale)

canvassing ['kænvəsıŋ] N sollecitazione *f*

canyon ['kænjən] N canyon *m inv*

CAP N ABBR (= *Common Agricultural Policy*) PAC *f*

cap [kæp] N (*also BRIT Football: hat*) berretto; (*of pen*) coperchio; (*of bottle*) tappo; (*for swimming*) cuffia; (*BRIT: contraceptive: also*: **Dutch cap**) diaframma *m* ▶ VT tappare; (*outdo*) superare; (*limit*) fissare un tetto (a); **capped with** ricoperto(-a) di; **and to ~ it all, he ...** (*BRIT*) e per completare l'opera, lui ...

capability [keɪpə'bılıtı] N capacità *f inv*, abilità *f inv*

capable ['keɪpəbl] ADJ capace; **~ of** capace di; suscettibile di

capacious [kə'peɪʃəs] ADJ capace

capacity [kə'pæsıtı] N capacità *f inv*; (*of lift etc*) capienza; **in his ~ as** nella sua qualità di; **to work at full ~** lavorare al massimo delle proprie capacità; **this work is beyond my ~** questo lavoro supera le mie possibilità; **filled to ~** pieno zeppo; **in an advisory ~** a titolo consultativo

cape [keɪp] N (*garment*) cappa; (*Geo*) capo

Cape of Good Hope N Capo di Buona Speranza

caper ['keɪpəʳ] N (*Culin: also*: **capers**) cappero; (*leap*) saltello; (*escapade*) birichinata; (*prank*) scherzetto

Cape Town N Città del Capo

capita ['kæpıtə] *see* **per capita**

capital ['kæpıtl] N (*also*: **capital city**) capitale *f*; (*money*) capitale *m*; (*also*: **capital letter**) (lettera) maiuscola

capital account N conto capitale

capital allowance N ammortamento fiscale

capital assets NPL capitale *m* fisso

capital expenditure N spese *fpl* in capitale

capital gains tax N imposta sulla plusvalenza

capital goods N beni *mpl* d'investimento, beni *mpl* capitali

capital-intensive ['kæpıtlın'tɛnsıv] ADJ ad alta intensità di capitale

capitalism ['kæpıtəlızəm] N capitalismo

capitalist ['kæpıtəlıst] ADJ, N capitalista (*mf*)

capitalize ['kæpıtəlaɪz] VT (*provide with capital*) capitalizzare

▶ **capitalize on** VT FUS (*fig*) trarre vantaggio da

capital punishment N pena capitale

capital transfer tax N (*BRIT*) imposta sui trasferimenti di capitali

Capitol ['kæpıtl] N: **the ~** il Campidoglio; *vedi nota*

Il *Capitol* è l'edificio che ospita le riunioni del Congresso degli Stati Uniti. è situato sull'omonimo colle, *Capitol Hill*, a Washington DC. In molti stati americani il termine *Capitol* viene usato per indicare l'edificio dove si riuniscono i rappresentanti dello stato.

capitulate [kə'pıtjuleɪt] VI capitolare

capitulation [kəpıtju'leɪʃən] N capitolazione *f*

capricious [kə'prıʃəs] ADJ capriccioso(-a)

Capricorn ['kæprıkɔːn] N Capricorno; **to be ~** essere del Capricorno

caps [kæps] ABBR = **capital letters**

capsize [kæp'saız] VT capovolgere ▶ VI capovolgersi

capstan ['kæpstən] N argano

capsule ['kæpsjuːl] N capsula

Capt. ABBR (= *captain*) Cap.

captain ['kæptın] N capitano ▶ VT capitanare

caption ['kæpʃən] N leggenda

captivate ['kæptıveɪt] VT avvincere

captive ['kæptıv] ADJ, N prigioniero(-a)

captivity [kæp'tıvıtı] N prigionia; **in ~** (*animal*) in cattività

captor ['kæptəʳ] N (*lawful*) chi ha catturato; (*unlawful*) rapitore *m*

capture ['kæptʃəʳ] VT catturare, prendere; (*attention*) attirare; (*Comput*) registrare ▶ N cattura; (*data capture*) registrazione *f or* rilevazione *f* di dati

car [kɑːʳ] N macchina, automobile *f*; (*US Rail*) vagone *m*; **by ~** in macchina

Caracas [kə'rækəs] N Caracas *f*

carafe [kə'ræf] N caraffa

carafe wine N (*in restaurant*) ≈ vino sfuso

caramel ['kærəməl] N caramello

carat ['kærət] N carato; **18 ~ gold** oro a 18 carati

caravan ['kærəvæn] N (*BRIT*) roulotte *f inv*; (*of camels*) carovana

caravan site N (*BRIT*) campeggio per roulotte

caraway ['kærəweɪ] N: **~ seed** seme *m* di cumino

carb [kɑːb] N (*col*) cibo *m* ad alto contenuto di carboidrati

carbohydrate [kɑːbəu'haɪdreɪt] N carboidrato

carbolic acid [kɑː'bɔlık-] N acido fenico, fenolo

car bomb N *ordigno esplosivo collocato in una macchina*; **a ~ went off yesterday** ieri è esplosa un'autobomba

carbon ['kɑːbən] N carbonio

carbonated ['kɑ:bəneɪtəd] ADJ (drink) gassato(-a)

carbon copy N copia f carbone inv

carbon credit N quota f di emissione

carbon dioxide [-daɪˈɔksaɪd] N diossido di carbonio

carbon footprint N impronta di carbonio

carbon monoxide [-mɔˈnɔksaɪd] N monossido di carbonio

carbon-neutral ADJ a zero emissioni di gas serra

carbon offset N riduzione f delle emissioni di gas serra

carbon paper N carta carbone

carbon ribbon N nastro carbonato

car boot sale N vedi nota

> Il car boot sale è un mercatino dell'usato molto popolare in Gran Bretagna. Normalmente ha luogo in un parcheggio o in un grande spiazzo, e la merce viene in genere esposta nei bagagliai, in inglese appunto boots, aperti delle macchine.

carburettor, (US) **carburetor** [kɑ:bjuˈrɛtəʳ] N carburatore m

carcass ['kɑ:kəs] N carcassa

carcinogenic [kɑ:sɪnəˈdʒɛnɪk] ADJ cancerogeno(-a)

card [kɑ:d] N carta; (thin cardboard) cartoncino; (visiting card etc) biglietto; (membership card) tessera; (Christmas card etc) cartolina; **to play cards** giocare a carte

cardamom ['kɑ:dəməm] N cardamomo

cardboard ['kɑ:dbɔ:d] N cartone m

cardboard box N (scatola di) cartone m

cardboard city N luogo dove dormono in scatole di cartone emarginati senzatetto

card-carrying member ['kɑ:d'kærɪɪŋ-] N tesserato(-a)

card game N gioco di carte

cardiac ['kɑ:dɪæk] ADJ cardiaco(-a)

cardigan ['kɑ:dɪgən] N cardigan m inv

cardinal ['kɑ:dɪnl] ADJ, N cardinale (m)

card index N schedario

cardphone ['kɑ:dfəun] N telefono a scheda (magnetica)

cardsharp ['kɑ:dʃɑ:p] N baro

card vote N (BRIT) voto (palese) per delega

CARE [kɛəʳ] N ABBR = **Cooperative for American Relief Everywhere**

care [kɛəʳ] N cura, attenzione f; (worry) preoccupazione f ▶ VI: **to ~ about** curarsi di; (thing, idea) interessarsi di; **would you ~ to/ for …?** le piacerebbe …?; **I wouldn't ~ to do it** non lo vorrei fare; **in sb's ~** alle cure di qn; **to take ~** fare attenzione; **to take ~ of** curarsi di; (details, arrangements, bill, problem) occuparsi di; **I don't ~** non me ne importa; **I couldn't ~ less** non me ne importa un bel

niente; **~ of (c/o)** (on letter) presso; **"with ~"** "fragile"; **the child has been taken into ~** il bambino è stato preso in custodia

> ▶ **care for** VT FUS aver cura di; (like) voler bene a

careen [kəˈri:n] VI (ship) sbandare ▶ VT carenare

career [kəˈrɪəʳ] N carriera; (occupation) professione f ▶ VI (also: **career along**) andare di (gran) carriera

career girl N donna dedita alla carriera

careers officer N consulente mf d'orientamento professionale

carefree ['kɛəfri:] ADJ sgombro(-a) di preoccupazioni

careful ['kɛəful] ADJ attento(-a); (cautious) cauto(-a); **(be) ~!** attenzione!; **he's very ~ with his money** bada molto alle spese

carefully ['kɛəfəlɪ] ADV con cura; cautamente

caregiver (US) N (professional) badante mf; (unpaid) persona che si prende cura di un parente malato o anziano

careless ['kɛəlɪs] ADJ negligente; (remark) privo(-a) di tatto; (heedless) spensierato(-a)

carelessly ['kɛəlɪslɪ] ADV negligentemente; senza tatto; (without thinking) distrattamente

carelessness ['kɛəlɪsnɪs] N negligenza; mancanza di tatto

carer ['kɛərəʳ] N chi si occupa di un familiare anziano o invalido

caress [kəˈrɛs] N carezza ▶ VT accarezzare

caretaker ['kɛəteɪkəʳ] N custode m

caretaker government N (BRIT) governo m ponte inv

car-ferry ['kɑ:fɛrɪ] N traghetto

cargo ['kɑ:gəu] (pl **cargoes**) N carico

cargo boat N cargo

cargo plane N aereo di linea da carico

car hire N (BRIT) autonoleggio

Caribbean [kærɪˈbi:ən] ADJ caraibico(-a); **the ~ (Sea)** il Mar dei Caraibi

caricature ['kærɪkətjuəʳ] N caricatura

caring ['kɛərɪŋ] ADJ (person) premuroso(-a); (society, organization) umanitario(-a)

carnage ['kɑ:nɪdʒ] N carneficina

carnal ['kɑ:nl] ADJ carnale

carnation [kɑ:ˈneɪʃən] N garofano

carnival ['kɑ:nɪvəl] N (public celebration) carnevale m; (US: funfair) luna park m inv

carnivorous [kɑ:ˈnɪvərəs] ADJ carnivoro(-a)

carol ['kærəl] N: **(Christmas) ~** canto di Natale

carouse [kəˈrauz] VI far baldoria

carousel [kærəˈsɛl] N (US) giostra

carp [kɑ:p] N (fish) carpa

> ▶ **carp at** VT FUS trovare a ridire su

car park N (BRIT) parcheggio

carpenter ['kɑ:pɪntəʳ] N carpentiere m

carpentry ['kɑ:pɪntrɪ] N carpenteria

carpet ['kɑ:pɪt] N tappeto; (BRIT: *fitted carpet*) moquette *f inv* ▸ VT coprire con tappeto

carpet bombing N bombardamento a tappeto

carpet slippers NPL pantofole *fpl*

carpet sweeper N scopatappeti *m inv*

car phone N telefonino per auto

car rental N (US) autonoleggio

carriage ['kærɪdʒ] N vettura; (*of goods*) trasporto; (*of typewriter*) carrello; (*bearing*) portamento; **~ forward** porto assegnato; **~ free** franco di porto; **~ paid** porto pagato

carriage return N (*on typewriter etc*) leva (*or* tasto) del ritorno a capo

carriageway ['kærɪdʒweɪ] N (BRIT: *part of road*) carreggiata

carrier ['kærɪəʳ] N (*of disease*) portatore(-trice); (*Comm*) impresa di trasporti; (*Naut*) portaerei *f inv*

carrier bag N (BRIT) sacchetto

carrier pigeon N colombo viaggiatore

carrion ['kærɪən] N carogna

carrot ['kærət] N carota

carry ['kærɪ] VT (*person*) portare; (*vehicle*) trasportare; (*a motion, bill*) far passare; (*involve: responsibilities etc*) comportare; (*Med*) essere portatore(-trice) di; (*Comm: goods*) tenere; (: *interest*) avere; (*Math: figure*) riportare ▸ VI (*sound*) farsi sentire; **this loan carries 10% interest** questo prestito è sulla base di un interesse del 10%; **to be** *or* **get carried away** (*fig*) farsi trascinare
▸ **carry forward** VT (*Math, Comm*) riportare
▸ **carry on** VI: **to ~ on with sth/doing** continuare qc/a fare ▸ VT mandare avanti
▸ **carry out** VT (*orders*) eseguire; (*investigation*) svolgere; (*accomplish etc: plan*) realizzare; (*perform, implement: idea, threat*) mettere in pratica

carrycot ['kærɪkɔt] N (BRIT) culla portabile

carry-on [kærɪ'ɔn] N (*col: fuss*) casino, confusione *f*; (: *annoying behaviour*): **I've had enough of your ~!** mi hai proprio scocciato!

cart [kɑ:t] N carro ▸ VT (*col*) trascinare, scarrozzare

carte blanche ['kɑ:t'blɒnʃ] N: **to give sb ~** dare carta bianca a qn

cartel [kɑ:'tɛl] N (*Comm*) cartello

cartilage ['kɑ:tɪlɪdʒ] N cartilagine *f*

cartographer [kɑ:'tɔgrəfəʳ] N cartografo(-a)

cartography [kɑ:'tɔgrəfɪ] N cartografia

carton ['kɑ:tən] N (*box*) scatola di cartone; (*of yogurt*) cartone *m*; (*of cigarettes*) stecca

cartoon [kɑ:'tu:n] N (*in newspaper etc*) vignetta; (*comic strip*) fumetto; (*Cine, TV*) cartone *m* animato; (*Art*) cartone

cartoonist [kɑ:'tu:nɪst] N vignettista *mf*; cartonista *mf*

cartridge ['kɑ:trɪdʒ] N (*for gun, pen*) cartuccia; (*for camera*) caricatore *m*; (*music tape*) cassetta; (*of record player*) testina

cartwheel ['kɑ:twi:l] N: **to turn a ~** (*Sport etc*) fare la ruota

carve [kɑ:v] VT (*meat*) trinciare; (*wood, stone*) intagliare
▸ **carve up** VT (*meat*) tagliare; (*fig: country*) suddividere

carving ['kɑ:vɪŋ] N (*in wood etc*) scultura

carving knife N trinciante *m*

car wash N lavaggio auto

Casablanca [kæsə'blæŋkə] N Casablanca

cascade [kæs'keɪd] N cascata ▸ VI scendere a cascata

case [keɪs] N caso; (*Law*) causa, processo; (*box*) scatola; (BRIT: *also*: **suitcase**) valigia; (*Typ*): **lower/upper ~** (carattere *m*) minuscolo/maiuscolo; **to have a good ~** avere pretese legittime; **there's a strong ~ for reform** ci sono validi argomenti a favore della riforma; **in ~ of** in caso di; **in ~ he** caso mai lui; **in any ~** in ogni caso; **just in ~** in caso di bisogno

case history N (*Med*) cartella clinica

case-sensitive ['keɪs'sɛnsɪtɪv] ADJ (*Comput*) sensibile alle maiuscole o minuscole

case study N studio di un caso

cash [kæʃ] N (*coins, notes*) soldi *mpl*, denaro ▸ VT incassare; **I haven't got any ~** non ho contanti; **to pay (in) ~** pagare in contanti; **to be short of ~** essere a corto di soldi; **~ with order/on delivery (COD)** (*Comm*) pagamento all'ordinazione/alla consegna
▸ **cash in** VT (*insurance policy etc*) riscuotere, riconvertire
▸ **cash in on** VT FUS: **to ~ in on sth** sfruttare qc

cash account N conto *m* cassa *inv*

cash-and-carry ['kæʃənd'kærɪ] N cash and carry *m inv*

cashback N (*discount*) sconto; (*at supermarket etc*) anticipo di contanti ottenuto presso la cassa di un negozio tramite una carta di debito

cashbook ['kæʃbuk] N giornale *m* di cassa

cash box N cassetta per il denaro spicciolo

cash card N (BRIT) carta per prelievi automatici

cash desk N (BRIT) cassa

cash discount N sconto per contanti

cash dispenser N (BRIT) sportello automatico

cashew [kæ'ʃu:] N (*also*: **cashew nut**) anacardio

cash flow N cash-flow *m inv*, liquidità *f inv*

cashier [kæ'ʃɪəʳ] N cassiere(-a) ▸ VT (*esp Mil*) destituire

cashmere ['kæʃmɪəʳ] N cachemire *m*

cash payment N pagamento in contanti

cash point N sportello bancario automatico, Bancomat® *m inv*

cash price N prezzo per contanti
cash register N registratore *m* di cassa
cash sale N vendita per contanti
casing ['keɪsɪŋ] N rivestimento
casino [kə'si:nəu] N casinò *m inv*
cask [kɑ:sk] N botte *f*
casket ['kɑ:skɪt] N cofanetto; (*US: coffin*) bara
Caspian Sea ['kæspɪən-] N: **the ~** il mar Caspio
casserole ['kæsərəul] N casseruola; **chicken ~** pollo in casseruola
cassette [kæ'sɛt] N cassetta
cassette deck N piastra di registrazione
cassette player N riproduttore *m* a cassette
cassette recorder N registratore *m* a cassette
cast [kɑ:st] (*pt, pp ~*) VT (*throw*) gettare; (*shed*) perdere; spogliarsi di; (*metal*) gettare, fondere; (*Theat*): **to ~ sb as Hamlet** scegliere qn per la parte di Amleto ▸ N (*Theat*) cast *m inv*; (*mould*) forma; (*also*: **plaster cast**) ingessatura; **to ~ one's vote** votare, dare il voto
▸ **cast aside** VT (*reject*) mettere da parte
▸ **cast off** VI (*Naut*) salpare ▸ VT (*Naut*) disormeggiare; (*Knitting*) diminuire, calare
▸ **cast on** (*Knitting*) VT avviare ▸ VI avviare (le maglie)
castanets [kæstə'nɛts] NPL castagnette *fpl*
castaway ['kɑ:stəwəɪ] N naufrago(-a)
caste [kɑ:st] N casta
caster sugar ['kɑ:stə-] N (*BRIT*) zucchero semolato
casting vote ['kɑ:stɪŋ-] N (*BRIT*) voto decisivo
cast iron N ghisa ▸ ADJ: **cast-iron** (*lit*) di ghisa; (*fig: will, alibi*) di ferro, d'acciaio
castle ['kɑ:sl] N castello; (*fortified*) rocca
castor ['kɑ:stə'] N (*wheel*) rotella
castor oil N olio di ricino
castrate [kæs'treɪt] VT castrare
casual ['kæʒjul] ADJ (*chance*) casuale, fortuito(-a); (*irregular: work etc*) avventizio(-a); (*unconcerned*) noncurante, indifferente; **~ wear** casual *m*
casual labour N manodopera avventizia
casually ['kæʒjulɪ] ADV con disinvoltura; (*by chance*) casualmente
casualty ['kæʒjultɪ] N ferito(-a); (*dead*) morto(-a), vittima; (*Med: department*) pronto soccorso; **heavy casualties** grosse perdite *fpl*
casualty ward N (*BRIT*) pronto soccorso (*reparto*)
cat [kæt] N gatto
catacombs ['kætəku:mz] NPL catacombe *fpl*
catalogue, (*US*) **catalog** ['kætəlɒg] N catalogo ▸ VT catalogare
catalyst ['kætəlɪst] N catalizzatore *m*
catalytic converter [kætə'lɪtɪk kən'vɜ:tə'] N marmitta catalitica, catalizzatore *m*

catapult ['kætəpʌlt] N catapulta; fionda
cataract ['kætərækt] N (*also Med*) cateratta
catarrh [kə'tɑ:'] N catarro
catastrophe [kə'tæstrəfɪ] N catastrofe *f*
catastrophic [kætə'strɒfɪk] ADJ catastrofico(-a)
catcall ['kætkɔ:l] N (*at meeting etc*) fischio
catch [kætʃ] (*pt, pp caught* [kɔ:t]) VT prendere; (*train, thief, cold*) acchiappare; (*ball*) afferrare; (*person: by surprise*) sorprendere; (*understand*) comprendere; (*get entangled*) impigliare; (*attention*) attirare; (*comment, whisper*) cogliere; (*person*) raggiungere ▸ VI (*fire*) prendere ▸ N (*fish etc caught*) retata; (*of ball*) presa; (*trick*) inganno; (*Tech*) gancio; (*game*) catch *m inv*; **to ~ fire** prendere fuoco; **to ~ sight of** scorgere
▸ **catch on** VI (*become popular*) affermarsi, far presa; (*understand*): **to ~ on (to sth)** capire (qc)
▸ **catch out** VT (*BRIT fig: with trick question*) cogliere in fallo
▸ **catch up** VI mettersi in pari ▸ VT (*also*: **catch up with**) raggiungere
catching ['kætʃɪŋ] ADJ (*Med*) contagioso(-a)
catchment area ['kætʃmənt-] N (*BRIT Scol*) circoscrizione *f* scolare; (*Geo*) bacino pluviale
catch phrase N slogan *m inv*; frase *f* fatta
catch-22 ['kætʃtwɛntɪ'tu:] N: **it's a ~ situation** non c'è via d'uscita
catchy ['kætʃɪ] ADJ orecchiabile
catechism ['kætɪkɪzəm] N catechismo
categoric [kætɪ'gɒrɪk], **categorical** [kætɪ'gɒrɪkl] ADJ categorico(-a)
categorize ['kætɪgəraɪz] VT categorizzare
category ['kætɪgərɪ] N categoria
cater ['keɪtə']
▸ **cater for** VT FUS (*BRIT: needs*) provvedere a; (*: readers, consumers*) incontrare i gusti di; (*Comm: provide food*) provvedere alla ristorazione di
caterer ['keɪtərə'] N fornitore *m*
catering ['keɪtərɪŋ] N approvvigionamento
catering trade N settore *m* ristoranti
caterpillar ['kætəpɪlə'] N (*Zool*) bruco ▸ CPD (*vehicle*) cingolato(-a); **~ track** cingolo
cat flap N gattaiola
cathedral [kə'θi:drəl] N cattedrale *f*, duomo
cathode ['kæθəud] N catodo
cathode ray tube N tubo a raggi catodici
Catholic ['kæθəlɪk] ADJ, N (*Rel*) cattolico(-a)
catholic ['kæθəlɪk] ADJ (*wide-ranging*) universale; aperto(-a); eclettico(-a)
CAT scanner [kæt-] N (*Med: = computerized axial tomography scanner*) (rilevatore *m* per la) TAC *f inv*
Catseye® ['kætsˈaɪ] N (*BRIT Aut*) catarifrangente *m*
catsup ['kætsəp] N (*US*) ketchup *m inv*
cattle ['kætl] NPL bestiame *m*, bestie *fpl*

catty ['kætɪ] ADJ maligno(-a), dispettoso(-a)
catwalk ['kætwɔːk] N passerella
Caucasian [kɔːˈkeɪzɪən] ADJ, N caucasico(-a)
Caucasus ['kɔːkəsəs] N Caucaso
caucus ['kɔːkəs] N (US Pol) (riunione f del) comitato elettorale; (BRIT Pol: group) comitato di dirigenti; vedi nota

> Caucus è il termine usato, specialmente negli Stati Uniti, per indicare una riunione informale dei rappresentanti di spicco di un partito politico che precede una riunione ufficiale. Con uso estensivo, la parola indica il nucleo direttivo di un partito politico.

caught [kɔːt] PT, PP of **catch**
cauliflower ['kɔlɪflauəʳ] N cavolfiore m
cause [kɔːz] N causa ▶ VT causare; **there is no ~ for concern** non c'è ragione di preoccuparsi; **to ~ sb to do sth** far fare qc a qn; **to ~ sth to be done** far fare qc
causeway ['kɔːzweɪ] N strada rialzata
caustic ['kɔːstɪk] ADJ caustico(-a)
caution ['kɔːʃən] N prudenza; (warning) avvertimento ▶ VT avvertire; ammonire
cautious ['kɔːʃəs] ADJ cauto(-a), prudente
cautiously ['kɔːʃəslɪ] ADV prudentemente
cautiousness ['kɔːʃəsnɪs] N cautela
cavalier [kævəˈlɪəʳ] N (knight) cavaliere m ▶ ADJ (pej: offhand) brusco(-a)
cavalry ['kævəlrɪ] N cavalleria
cave [keɪv] N caverna, grotta ▶ VI: **to go caving** fare speleologia
  ▶ **cave in** VI (roof etc) crollare
caveman ['keɪvmæn] N (irreg) uomo delle caverne
cavern ['kævən] N caverna
caviar, caviare ['kævɪɑːʳ] N caviale m
cavity ['kævɪtɪ] N cavità f inv
cavity wall insulation N isolamento per pareti a intercapedine
cavort [kəˈvɔːt] VI far capriole
cayenne [keɪˈɛn], **cayenne pepper** [keɪˈɛn-] N pepe m di Caienna
CB N ABBR (BRIT: = Companion (of the Order) of the Bath) titolo; (= Citizens' Band (Radio)) C.B m; **CB radio (set)** baracchino
CBC N ABBR = **Canadian Broadcasting Corporation**
CBE N ABBR (BRIT: = Companion (of the Order) of the British Empire) titolo
CBI N ABBR (= Confederation of British Industry) ≈ CONFINDUSTRIA (= Confederazione Generale dell'Industria Italiana)
CBS N ABBR (US) = **Columbia Broadcasting System**
CC ABBR (BRIT) = **county council**
cc ABBR (= cubic centimetre) cc; (on letter etc) = **carbon copy**
CCA N ABBR (US: = Circuit Court of Appeals) corte f

d'appello itinerante
CCTV N ABBR (= closed-circuit television) televisione f a circuito chiuso
CCTV camera N telecamera f TVCC
CCU N ABBR (US: = coronary care unit) unità coronarica
CD N ABBR (= compact disk) CD m inv; (player) lettore m CD inv; (Mil: BRIT) = **Civil Defence (Corps)**; (: US) = **Civil Defense** ▶ ABBR (BRIT: = Corps Diplomatique) C.D.
CD burner N masterizzatore m (di) CD
CDC N ABBR (US) = **center for disease control**
CD-I® N CD-I m inv, compact disc m inv interattivo
CD player N lettore m CD
Cdr. ABBR (= commander) Com
CD-ROM ['siːˈdiːˈrɔm] N ABBR (= compact disc read-only memory) CD-ROM m inv
CDT ABBR (US: = Central Daylight Time) ora legale del centro; (BRIT Scol: = Craft, Design and Technology) educazione tecnica
CDW N ABBR = **collision damage waiver**
CD writer N masterizzatore m
cease [siːs] VT, VI cessare
ceasefire ['siːsfaɪəʳ] N cessate il fuoco m inv
ceaseless ['siːslɪs] ADJ incessante, continuo(-a)
CED N ABBR (US) = **Committee for Economic Development**
cedar ['siːdəʳ] N cedro
cede [siːd] VT cedere
CEEB N ABBR (US: = College Entrance Examination Board) commissione per l'esame di ammissione al college
ceilidh ['keɪlɪ] N festa con musiche e danze popolari scozzesi o irlandesi
ceiling ['siːlɪŋ] N soffitto; (fig: upper limit) tetto, limite m massimo
celebrate ['sɛlɪbreɪt] VT, VI celebrare
celebrated ['sɛlɪbreɪtɪd] ADJ celebre
celebration [sɛlɪˈbreɪʃən] N celebrazione f
celebrity [sɪˈlɛbrɪtɪ] N celebrità f inv
celeriac [səˈlɛrɪæk] N sedano m rapa inv
celery ['sɛlərɪ] N sedano
celestial [sɪˈlɛstɪəl] ADJ celeste
celibacy ['sɛlɪbəsɪ] N celibato
cell [sɛl] N cella; (of revolutionaries, Biol) cellula; (Elec) elemento (di batteria)
cellar ['sɛləʳ] N sottosuolo; cantina
cellist ['tʃɛlɪst] N violoncellista mf
cello ['tʃɛləu] N violoncello
cellophane® ['sɛləfeɪn] N cellophane® m
cellphone ['sɛlfəun] N cellulare m
cell tower N (US Tel) stazione f radio base
cellular ['sɛljuləʳ] ADJ cellulare
celluloid ['sɛljulɔɪd] N celluloide f
cellulose ['sɛljuləus] N cellulosa
Celsius ['sɛlsɪəs] ADJ Celsius inv
Celt [kɛlt, sɛlt] N celta mf

Celtic ['kɛltɪk, 'sɛltɪk] ADJ celtico(-a) ▶ N (Ling) celtico

cement [sə'mɛnt] N cemento ▶ VT cementare

cement mixer N betoniera

cemetery ['sɛmɪtrɪ] N cimitero

cenotaph ['sɛnətɑːf] N cenotafio

censor ['sɛnsə^r] N censore m ▶ VT censurare

censorship ['sɛnsəʃɪp] N censura

censure ['sɛnʃə^r] VT censurare

census ['sɛnsəs] N censimento

cent [sɛnt] N (of dollar, euro) centesimo; see also **per cent**

centenary [sɛn'tiːnərɪ], (US) **centennial** [sɛn'tɛnɪəl] N centenario

center ['sɛntə^r] N, VT (US) = **centre**

centigrade ['sɛntɪgreɪd] ADJ centigrado(-a)

centilitre, (US) **centiliter** ['sɛntɪliːtə^r] N centilitro

centimetre, (US) **centimeter** ['sɛntɪmiːtə^r] N centimetro

centipede ['sɛntɪpiːd] N centopiedi m inv

central ['sɛntrəl] ADJ centrale

Central African Republic N Repubblica centrafricana

Central America N America centrale

central heating N riscaldamento centrale

centralize ['sɛntrəlaɪz] VT accentrare

central processing unit N (Comput) unità f inv centrale di elaborazione

central reservation N (Brit Aut) banchina f spartitraffico inv

centre, (US) **center** ['sɛntə^r] N centro ▶ VT centrare; (concentrate): **to ~ (on)** concentrare (su)

centrefold, (US) **centerfold** ['sɛntəfəuld] N (Press) poster m (all'interno di rivista)

centre-forward ['sɛntə'fɔːwəd] N (Sport) centroavanti m inv

centre-half ['sɛntə'hɑːf] N (Sport) centromediano

centrepiece, (US) **centerpiece** ['sɛntəpiːs] N centrotavola m; (fig) punto centrale

centre spread N (Brit) pubblicità a doppia pagina

centre-stage [sɛntə'steɪdʒ] N: **to take ~** porsi al centro dell'attenzione

centrifugal [sɛn'trɪfjugəl] ADJ centrifugo(-a)

centrifuge ['sɛntrɪfjuːʒ] N centrifuga

century ['sɛntjurɪ] N secolo; **in the twentieth ~** nel ventesimo secolo

CEO N ABBR = **chief executive officer**

ceramic [sɪ'ræmɪk] ADJ ceramico(-a)

cereal ['siːrɪəl] N cereale m

cerebral ['sɛrɪbrəl] ADJ cerebrale

ceremonial [sɛrɪ'məunɪəl] N cerimoniale m; (rite) rito

ceremony ['sɛrɪmənɪ] N cerimonia; **to stand on ~** fare complimenti

cert [səːt] N (Brit col): **it's a dead ~** non c'è alcun dubbio

certain ['səːtən] ADJ certo(-a); **to make ~ of** assicurarsi di; **for ~** per certo, di sicuro

certainly ['səːtənlɪ] ADV certamente, certo

certainty ['səːtəntɪ] N certezza

certificate [sə'tɪfɪkɪt] N certificato; diploma m

certified letter ['səːtɪfaɪd-] N (US) lettera raccomandata

certified public accountant ['səːtɪfaɪd-] N (US) ≈ commercialista mf

certify ['səːtɪfaɪ] VT certificare; (award diploma to) conferire un diploma a; (declare insane) dichiarare pazzo(-a) ▶ VI: **to ~ to** attestare a

cervical ['səːvɪkl] ADJ: **~ cancer** cancro della cervice, tumore m al collo dell'utero; **~ smear** Pap-test m inv

cervix ['səːvɪks] N cervice f

Cesarean [siː'zɛərɪən] ADJ, N (US) = **Caesarean**

cessation [sə'seɪʃən] N cessazione f; arresto

cesspit ['sɛspɪt] N pozzo nero

CET ABBR (= Central European Time) fuso orario

Ceylon [sɪ'lɔn] N Ceylon f

cf. ABBR (= compare) cfr

c/f ABBR (Comm) = **carried forward**

CFC N ABBR (= chlorofluorocarbon) CFC m inv

CG N ABBR (US) = **coastguard**

cg ABBR (= centigram) cg

CH N ABBR (Brit: = Companion of Honour) titolo

ch. ABBR (= chapter) cap

Chad [tʃæd] N Chad m

chafe [tʃeɪf] VT fregare, irritare ▶ VI (fig): **to ~ against** scontrarsi con

chaffinch ['tʃæfɪntʃ] N fringuello

chagrin ['ʃægrɪn] N disappunto, dispiacere m

chain [tʃeɪn] N catena ▶ VT (also: **chain up**) incatenare

chain reaction N reazione f a catena

chain-smoke ['tʃeɪnsməuk] VI fumare una sigaretta dopo l'altra

chain store N negozio a catena

chair [tʃɛə^r] N sedia; (armchair) poltrona; (of university) cattedra; (of meeting) presidenza ▶ VT (meeting) presiedere; **the ~** (US: electric chair) la sedia elettrica

chairlift ['tʃɛəlɪft] N seggiovia

chairman ['tʃɛəmən] N (irreg) presidente m

chairperson ['tʃɛəpəːsn] N presidente(-essa)

chairwoman ['tʃɛəwumən] N (irreg) presidentessa

chalet ['ʃæleɪ] N chalet m inv

chalice ['tʃælɪs] N calice m

chalk [tʃɔːk] N gesso ▶ **chalk up** VT scrivere col gesso; (fig: success) ottenere; (: victory) riportare

chalkboard (US) N lavagna

challenge ['tʃælɪndʒ] N sfida ▶ VT sfidare; (statement, right) mettere in dubbio; **to ~ sb to**

a fight/game sfidare qn a battersi/ad una partita; **to ~ sb to do** sfidare qn a fare

challenger ['tʃælɪndʒər] N (Sport) sfidante mf

challenging ['tʃælɪndʒɪŋ] ADJ (task) impegnativo(-a); (remark) provocatorio(-a); (look) di sfida

chamber ['tʃeɪmbər] N camera; **~ of commerce** camera di commercio

chambermaid ['tʃeɪmbəmeɪd] N cameriera

chamber music N musica da camera

chamberpot ['tʃeɪmbəpɔt] N vaso da notte

chameleon [kə'miːlɪən] N camaleonte m

chamois ['ʃæmwɑː] N camoscio

chamois leather ['ʃæmɪ-] N pelle f di camoscio

champagne [ʃæm'peɪn] N champagne m inv

champers ['ʃæmpəz] NSG (col) sciampagna

champion ['tʃæmpɪən] N campione(-essa); (of cause) difensore m ▶ VT difendere, lottare per

championship ['tʃæmpɪənʃɪp] N campionato

chance [tʃɑːns] N caso; (opportunity) occasione f; (likelihood) possibilità f inv ▶ VT: **to ~ it** rischiare, provarci ▶ ADJ fortuito(-a); **there is little ~ of his coming** è molto improbabile che venga; **to take a ~** rischiare; **by ~** per caso; **it's the ~ of a lifetime** è un'occasione unica; **the chances are that ...** probabilmente ..., è probabile che ... + sub; **to ~ to do sth** (formal: happen) fare per caso qc

  ▶ **chance (up)on** VT FUS (person) incontrare per caso, imbattersi in; (thing) trovare per caso

chancel ['tʃɑːnsəl] N coro

chancellor ['tʃɑːnsələr] N cancelliere m; (of university) rettore m (onorario); **C~ of the Exchequer** (BRIT) Cancelliere m dello Scacchiere

chandelier [ʃændə'lɪər] N lampadario

change [tʃeɪndʒ] VT cambiare; (transform): **to ~ sb into** trasformare qn in ▶ VI cambiare; (change one's clothes) cambiarsi; (be transformed): **to ~ into** trasformarsi in ▶ N cambiamento; (money) resto; **to ~ one's mind** cambiare idea; **to ~ gear** (Aut) cambiare (marcia); **she changed into an old skirt** si è cambiata e ha messo una vecchia gonna; **a ~ of clothes** un cambio (di vestiti); **for a ~** tanto per cambiare; **small ~** spiccioli mpl, moneta; **keep the ~** tenga il resto; **can you give me ~ for £1?** mi può cambiare una sterlina?; **sorry, I don't have any ~** mi dispiace, non ho spiccioli

  ▶ **change over** VI (from sth to sth) passare; (players etc) scambiarsi (di posto o di campo) ▶ VT cambiare

changeable ['tʃeɪndʒəbl] ADJ (weather) variabile; (person) mutevole

change machine N distributore m automatico di monete

changeover ['tʃeɪndʒəuvər] N cambiamento, passaggio

changing ['tʃeɪndʒɪŋ] ADJ che cambia; (colours) cangiante

changing room N (BRIT: in shop) camerino; (Sport) spogliatoio

channel ['tʃænl] N canale m; (of river, sea) alveo ▶ VT canalizzare; (fig: interest, energies): **to ~ into** concentrare su, indirizzare verso; **through the usual channels** per le solite vie; **the (English) C~** la Manica; **green/red ~** (Customs) uscita "niente da dichiarare"/"merci da dichiarare"

channel-hopping ['tʃænlhɔpɪŋ] N (TV) zapping m

Channel Islands NPL: **the ~** le Isole Normanne

Channel Tunnel N: **the ~** il tunnel sotto la Manica

chant [tʃɑːnt] N canto; salmodia; (of crowd) slogan m inv ▶ VT cantare; salmodiare; **the demonstrators chanted their disapproval** i dimostranti lanciavano slogan di protesta

chaos ['keɪɔs] N caos m

chaos theory N teoria del caos

chaotic [keɪ'ɔtɪk] ADJ caotico(-a)

chap [tʃæp] N (BRIT col: man) tipo ▶ VT (skin) screpolare; **old ~** vecchio mio

chapel ['tʃæpl] N cappella

chaperone ['ʃæpərəun] N accompagnatore(-trice) ▶ VT accompagnare

chaplain ['tʃæplɪn] N cappellano

chapped [tʃæpt] ADJ (skin, lips) screpolato(-a)

chapter ['tʃæptər] N capitolo

char [tʃɑːr] VT (burn) carbonizzare ▶ VI (BRIT: cleaner) lavorare come domestica (a ore) ▶ N (BRIT) = **charlady**

character ['kærɪktər] N (gen, Comput) carattere m; (in novel, film) personaggio; (eccentric) originale m; **a person of good ~** una persona a modo

character code N (Comput) codice m di carattere

characteristic ['kærɪktə'rɪstɪk] ADJ caratteristico(-a) ▶ N caratteristica; **~ of** tipico(-a) di

characterize ['kærɪktəraɪz] VT caratterizzare; (describe): **to ~ (as)** descrivere (come)

charade [ʃə'rɑːd] N sciarada

charcoal ['tʃɑːkəul] N carbone m di legna

charge [tʃɑːdʒ] N accusa; (cost) prezzo; (of gun, battery, Mil: attack) carica; (responsibility) responsabilità ▶ VT (gun, battery, Mil: enemy) caricare; (customer) fare pagare a; (sum) fare pagare; (Law): **to ~ sb (with)** accusare qn (di)

▶ VI (*gen with*: *up, along etc*) lanciarsi; **charges** NPL: **bank charges** commissioni *fpl* bancarie; **labour charges** costi *mpl* del lavoro; **to reverse the charges** (*Tel*) fare una telefonata a carico del destinatario; **to ~ in/out** precipitarsi dentro/fuori; **to ~ up/down** lanciarsi su/giù per; **is there a ~?** c'è da pagare?; **there's no ~** non c'è niente da pagare; **extra ~** supplemento; **to take ~ of** incaricarsi di; **to be in ~ of** essere responsabile per; **to have ~ of sb** aver cura di qn; **how much do you ~ for this repair?** quanto chiede per la riparazione?; **to ~ an expense (up) to sb** addebitare una spesa a qn; **~ it to my account** lo metta *or* addebiti sul mio conto

charge account N conto

charge card N (*of shop*) carta *f* clienti *inv*

chargé d'affaires ['ʃɑ:ʒeɪdæ'fɛəʳ] N incaricato d'affari

chargehand ['tʃɑ:dʒhænd] N (*Brit*) caposquadra *mf*

charger ['tʃɑ:dʒəʳ] N (*also*: **battery charger**) caricabatterie *m inv*; (*old*: *warhorse*) destriero

chariot ['tʃærɪət] N carro

charismatic [kærɪz'mætɪk] ADJ carismatico(-a)

charitable ['tʃærɪtəbl] ADJ caritatevole

charity ['tʃærɪtɪ] N carità; (*organization*) opera pia

charity shop N (*Brit*) *negozi che vendono articoli di seconda mano e devolvono il ricavato in beneficenza*

charlady ['tʃɑ:leɪdɪ] N (*Brit*) domestica a ore

charlatan ['ʃɑ:lətən] N ciarlatano

charm [tʃɑ:m] N fascino; (*on bracelet*) ciondolo ▶ VT affascinare, incantare

charm bracelet N braccialetto con ciondoli

charming ['tʃɑ:mɪŋ] ADJ affascinante

chart [tʃɑ:t] N tabella; grafico; (*map*) carta nautica; (*weather chart*) carta del tempo ▶ VT fare una carta nautica di; (*sales, progress*) tracciare il grafico di; **to be in the charts** (*record, pop group*) essere in classifica; **charts** NPL (*Mus*) hit parade *f*

charter ['tʃɑ:təʳ] VT (*plane*) noleggiare ▶ N (*document*) carta; **on ~** a nolo

chartered accountant ['tʃɑ:təd-] N (*Brit*) ragioniere(-a) professionista

charter flight N volo *m* charter *inv*

charwoman ['tʃɑ:wumən] N (*irreg*) = **charlady**

chase [tʃeɪs] VT inseguire; (*also*: **chase away**) cacciare ▶ N caccia
▶ **chase down** VT (*US*) = **chase up**
▶ **chase up** VT (*Brit*: *person*) scovare; (*information*) scoprire, raccogliere

chasm ['kæzəm] N abisso

chassis ['ʃæsɪ] N telaio

chastened ['tʃeɪsnd] ADJ abbattuto(-a), provato(-a)

chastening ['tʃeɪsnɪŋ] ADJ che fa riflettere

chastise [tʃæs'taɪz] VT punire, castigare

chastity ['tʃæstɪtɪ] N castità

chat [tʃæt] VI (*also*: **have a chat**) chiacchierare; (*on the internet*) chattare
▶ N chiacchierata; (*on the internet*) chat *f inv*
▶ **chat up** VT (*Brit col*: *girl, boy*) abbordare

chatline ['tʃætlaɪn] N *servicio telefonico che permette a più utenti di conversare insieme*

chat room N (*Internet*) chat *f inv*

chat show N (*Brit*) talk show *m inv*, conversazione *f* televisiva

chattel ['tʃætl] N *see* **goods**

chatter ['tʃætəʳ] VI (*person*) ciarlare; (*bird*) cinguettare; (*teeth*) battere ▶ N ciarle *fpl*; cinguettio; **her teeth were chattering** batteva i denti

chatterbox ['tʃætəbɔks] N chiacchierone(-a)

chattering classes ['tʃætərɪŋ-] NPL: **the ~** (*col, pej*) ≈ gli intellettuali da salotto

chatty ['tʃætɪ] ADJ (*style*) familiare; (*person*) chiacchierino(-a)

chauffeur ['ʃəufəʳ] N autista *m*

chauvinism ['ʃəuvɪnɪzəm] N (*also*: **male chauvinism**) maschilismo; (*nationalism*) sciovinismo

chauvinist ['ʃəuvɪnɪst] N (*also*: **male chauvinist**) maschilista *m*; (*nationalist*) sciovinista *mf*

chauvinistic [ʃəuvɪ'nɪstɪk] ADJ sciovinistico(-a)

chav [tʃæv] N (*Brit pej*) *giovane della periferia urbana poco colto che indossa abiti sportivi di particolari marche*

ChE ABBR = **chemical engineer**

cheap [tʃi:p] ADJ a buon mercato, economico(-a); (*reduced*: *fare, ticket*) ridotto(-a); (*joke*) grossolano(-a); (*poor quality*) di cattiva qualità ▶ ADV a buon mercato; **cheaper** meno caro; **~ money** denaro a basso tasso di interesse

cheap day return N *biglietto ridotto di andata e ritorno valido in giornata*

cheapen ['tʃi:pn] VT ribassare; (*fig*) avvilire

cheaply ['tʃi:plɪ] ADV a buon prezzo, a buon mercato

cheat [tʃi:t] VI imbrogliare; (*at school*) copiare ▶ VT ingannare; (*rob*) defraudare ▶ N imbroglione *m*; copione *m*; (*trick*) inganno; **to ~ sb out of sth** defraudare qn di qc
▶ **cheat on** VT FUS (*husband, wife*) tradire; **he's been cheating on his wife** ha tradito sua moglie

cheating ['tʃi:tɪŋ] N imbrogliare *m*; copiare *m*

Chechnya [tʃɪtʃ'njɑ:] N Cecenia

check [tʃɛk] VT verificare; (*passport, ticket*) controllare; (*halt*) fermare; (*restrain*)

C

contenere ▸ vɪ (*official etc*) informarsi ▸ N
verifica; controllo; (*curb*) freno; (*US: bill*)
conto; (*pattern: gen pl*) quadretti *mpl*; (*US*)
= **cheque** ▸ ADJ (*pattern, cloth: also:* **checked**) a
scacchi, a quadretti; **to ~ with sb** chiedere a
qn; **to keep a ~ on sb/sth** controllare qn/qc,
fare attenzione a qn/qc
▸ **check in** vɪ (*in hotel*) registrare; (*at airport*)
presentarsi all'accettazione ▸ VT (*luggage*)
depositare
▸ **check off** VT segnare
▸ **check out** vɪ (*from hotel*) saldare il conto
▸ VT (*luggage*) ritirare; (*investigate: story*)
controllare, verificare; (*: person*) prendere
informazioni su
▸ **check up** vɪ: **to ~ up (on sth)** investigare
(qc); **to ~ up on sb** informarsi sul conto di qn
checkbook ['tʃɛkbʊk] N (*US*) = **chequebook**
checkered ['tʃɛkəd] ADJ (*US*) = **chequered**
checkers ['tʃɛkəz] N (*US*) dama
check guarantee card N (*US*) carta *f* assegni
inv
check-in ['tʃɛkɪn] N (*at airport: also:* **check-in
desk**) check-in *m inv*, accettazione *f* (bagagli
inv)
checking account ['tʃɛkɪŋ-] N (*US*) conto
corrente
checklist ['tʃɛklɪst] N lista di controllo
checkmate ['tʃɛkmeɪt] N scaccomatto
checkout ['tʃɛkaʊt] N (*in supermarket*) cassa
checkpoint ['tʃɛkpɔɪnt] N posto di blocco
checkroom ['tʃɛkrʊm] N (*US*) deposito *m*
bagagli *inv*
checkup ['tʃɛkʌp] N (*Med*) controllo medico
cheddar ['tʃɛdə^r] N formaggio duro di latte di
mucca di colore bianco o arancione
cheek [tʃiːk] N guancia; (*impudence*) faccia
tosta
cheekbone ['tʃiːkbəʊn] N zigomo
cheeky ['tʃiːkɪ] ADJ sfacciato(-a)
cheep [tʃiːp] N (*of bird*) pigolio ▸ vɪ pigolare
cheer [tʃɪə^r] VT applaudire; (*gladden*)
rallegrare ▸ vɪ applaudire ▸ N grido (di
incoraggiamento); **cheers** NPL (*of approval,
encouragement*) applausi *mpl*; evviva *mpl*;
cheers! salute!
▸ **cheer on** VT (*person etc*) incitare
▸ **cheer up** vɪ rallegrarsi, farsi animo ▸ VT
rallegrare
cheerful ['tʃɪəful] ADJ allegro(-a)
cheerfulness ['tʃɪəfulnɪs] N allegria
cheerio ['tʃɪərɪ'əʊ] EXCL (*BRIT*) ciao!
cheerleader ['tʃɪərliːdə^r] N cheerleader *f inv*
cheerless ['tʃɪəlɪs] ADJ triste
cheese [tʃiːz] N formaggio
cheeseboard ['tʃiːzbɔːd] N piatto del (*or* per
il) formaggio
cheeseburger ['tʃiːzbəːgə^r] N cheeseburger *m*
inv

cheesecake ['tʃiːzkeɪk] N specie di torta di
ricotta, a volte con frutta
cheetah ['tʃiːtə] N ghepardo
chef [ʃɛf] N capocuoco
chemical ['kɛmɪkl] ADJ chimico(-a) ▸ N
prodotto chimico
chemical engineering N ingegneria
chimica
chemist ['kɛmɪst] N (*BRIT: pharmacist*)
farmacista *mf*; (*scientist*) chimico(-a); **~'s
shop** *n* (*BRIT*) farmacia
chemistry ['kɛmɪstrɪ] N chimica
chemo [kiːməʊ] N chemio *f inv*
chemotherapy [kiːməʊ'θɛrəpɪ] N
chemioterapia
cheque, (*US*) **check** [tʃɛk] N assegno;
to pay by ~ pagare per assegno *or* con un
assegno
chequebook, (*US*) **checkbook** ['tʃɛkbʊk] N
libretto degli assegni
cheque card N (*BRIT*) carta *f* assegni *inv*
chequered, (*US*) **checkered** ['tʃɛkəd] ADJ (*fig*)
movimentato(-a)
cherish ['tʃɛrɪʃ] VT aver caro; (*hope etc*) nutrire
cheroot [ʃə'ruːt] N sigaro spuntato
cherry ['tʃɛrɪ] N ciliegia; (*also:* **cherry tree**)
ciliegio
Ches ABBR (*BRIT*) = **Cheshire**
chess [tʃɛs] N scacchi *mpl*
chessboard ['tʃɛsbɔːd] N scacchiera
chessman ['tʃɛsmæn] N (*irreg*) pezzo degli
scacchi
chessplayer ['tʃɛspleɪə^r] N scacchista *mf*
chest [tʃɛst] N petto; (*box*) cassa; **to get sth
off one's ~** (*col*) sputare il rospo
chest measurement N giro *m* torace *inv*
chestnut ['tʃɛsnʌt] N castagna; (*also:*
chestnut tree) castagno ▸ ADJ castano(-a)
chest of drawers N cassettone *m*
chesty ['tʃɛstɪ] ADJ: **~ cough** tosse *f* bronchiale
chew [tʃuː] VT masticare
chewing gum ['tʃuːɪŋ-] N chewing gum *m*
chic [ʃiːk] ADJ elegante
chick [tʃɪk] N pulcino; (*US col*) pollastrella
chicken ['tʃɪkɪn] N pollo; (*col: coward*) coniglio
▸ **chicken out** vɪ (*col*) avere fifa; **to ~ out of
sth** tirarsi indietro da qc per fifa *or* paura
chicken feed N (*fig*) miseria
chickenpox ['tʃɪkɪnpɔks] N varicella
chick flick N (*col*) filmetto rosa
chickpea ['tʃɪkpiː] N cece *m*
chicory ['tʃɪkərɪ] N cicoria
chide [tʃaɪd] VT rimproverare
chief [tʃiːf] N capo ▸ ADJ principale; **C~ of
Staff** (*Mil*) Capo di Stato Maggiore
chief constable N (*BRIT*) ≈ questore *m*
chief executive, (*US*) **chief executive
officer** N direttore *m* generale
chiefly ['tʃiːflɪ] ADV per lo più, soprattutto

chief operating officer N direttore(-trice) operativo(-a)

chiffon ['ʃɪfɒn] N chiffon *m inv*

chilblain ['tʃɪlbleɪn] N gelone *m*

child [tʃaɪld] (*pl* **children** ['tʃɪldrən]) N bambino(-a)

child abuse N molestie *fpl* a minori

child abuser [-ə'bjuːzəʳ] N molestatore(-trice) di minori

child benefit N (BRIT) ≈ assegni *mpl* familiari

childbirth ['tʃaɪldbəːθ] N parto

childcare N servizio *m* di custodia dei bambini

childhood ['tʃaɪldhud] N infanzia

childish ['tʃaɪldɪʃ] ADJ puerile

childless ['tʃaɪldlɪs] ADJ senza figli

childlike ['tʃaɪldlaɪk] ADJ fanciullesco(-a)

child minder [-'maɪndəʳ] N (BRIT) bambinaia

child prodigy N bambino *m* prodigio *inv*

children ['tʃɪldrən] NPL *of* **child**

children's home N istituto per l'infanzia

Chile ['tʃɪlɪ] N Cile *m*

Chilean ['tʃɪlɪən] ADJ, N cileno(-a)

chill [tʃɪl] N freddo; (*Med*) infreddatura ▶ ADJ freddo(-a), gelido(-a) ▶ VT raffreddare; (*Culin*) mettere in fresco; **"serve chilled"** "servire fresco"

▶ **chill out** VI (*esp US col*) darsi una calmata

chilli, (*US*) **chili** ['tʃɪlɪ] N peperoncino

chilling ['tʃɪlɪŋ] ADJ agghiacciante; (*wind*) gelido(-a)

chilly ['tʃɪlɪ] ADJ freddo(-a), fresco(-a); (*sensitive to cold*) freddoloso(-a); **to feel ~** sentirsi infreddolito(-a)

chime [tʃaɪm] N carillon *m inv* ▶ VI suonare, scampanare

chimney ['tʃɪmnɪ] N camino

chimney sweep N spazzacamino

chimpanzee [tʃɪmpæn'ziː] N scimpanzé *m inv*

chin [tʃɪn] N mento

China ['tʃaɪnə] N Cina

china ['tʃaɪnə] N porcellana

Chinese [tʃaɪ'niːz] ADJ cinese ▶ N (*pl inv*) cinese *mf*; (*Ling*) cinese *m*

chink [tʃɪŋk] N (*opening*) fessura; (*noise*) tintinnio

chinwag ['tʃɪnwæg] N (*col*): **to have a ~** fare una chiacchierata

chip [tʃɪp] N (*gen pl: Culin*) patatina fritta; (: *US: also*: **potato chip**) patatina; (*of wood, glass, stone*) scheggia; (*in gambling*) fiche *f inv*; (*Comput: microchip*) chip *m inv* ▶ VT (*cup, plate*) scheggiare; **when the chips are down** (*fig*) al momento critico

▶ **chip in** VI (*col: contribute*) contribuire; (*interrupt*) intromettersi

chip and PIN N sistema *m* chip e PIN; **~ machine** lettore *m* di carte chip e PIN; **~ card** carta chip e PIN

chipboard ['tʃɪpbɔːd] N agglomerato

chipmunk ['tʃɪpmʌŋk] N tamia *m* striato

chippings ['tʃɪpɪŋz] NPL: **loose ~** brecciame *m*

chip shop N (BRIT); *vedi nota*

I *chip shops*, anche chiamati *fish-and-chip shops*, sono friggitorie che vendono principalmente filetti di pesce impanati e patatine fritte che un tempo venivano serviti ai clienti avvolti in carta di giornale.

chiropodist [kɪ'rɔpədɪst] N (BRIT) pedicure *mf*

chiropody [kɪ'rɔpədɪ] N (BRIT) pedicure *f inv*

chirp [tʃəːp] N cinguettio; (*of crickets*) cri cri *m* ▶ VI cinguettare

chirpy ['tʃəːpɪ] ADJ (*col*) frizzante

chisel ['tʃɪzl] N cesello

chit [tʃɪt] N biglietto

chitchat ['tʃɪttʃæt] N (*col*) chiacchiere *fpl*

chivalrous ['ʃɪvəlrəs] ADJ cavalleresco(-a)

chivalry ['ʃɪvəlrɪ] N cavalleria; cortesia

chives [tʃaɪvz] NPL erba cipollina

chloride ['klɔːraɪd] N cloruro

chlorinate ['klɔːrɪneɪt] VT clorare

chlorine ['klɔːriːn] N cloro

choc-ice ['tʃɔkaɪs] N (BRIT) gelato ricoperto al cioccolato

chock [tʃɔk] N zeppa

chock-a-block ['tʃɔkə'blɔk], **chockfull** ['tʃɔk'ful] ADJ pieno(-a) zeppo(-a)

chocolate ['tʃɔklɪt] N (*substance*) cioccolato, cioccolata; (*drink*) cioccolata; (*a sweet*) cioccolatino

choice [tʃɔɪs] N scelta ▶ ADJ scelto(-a); **a wide ~** un'ampia scelta; **I did it by** *or* **from ~** l'ho fatto di mia volontà *or* per mia scelta

choir ['kwaɪəʳ] N coro

choirboy ['kwaɪəbɔɪ] N corista *m* fanciullo

choke [tʃəuk] VI soffocare ▶ VT soffocare; (*block*) ingombrare ▶ N (*Aut*) valvola dell'aria; **to be choked with** essere intasato(-a)

cholera ['kɔlərə] N colera *m*

cholesterol [kə'lɛstərɔl] N colesterolo

chook [tʃuk] N (AUSTRALIA, NEW ZEALAND *col*) gallina

choose [tʃuːz] (*pt* **chose** [tʃəuz], *pp* **chosen** ['tʃəuzn]) VT scegliere; **to ~ to do** decidere di fare; preferire fare; **to ~ between** scegliere tra; **to ~ from** scegliere da *or* tra

choosy ['tʃuːzɪ] ADJ: **(to be) ~** (fare lo) schizzinoso(-a)

chop [tʃɔp] VT (*wood*) spaccare; (*Culin: also*: **chop up**) tritare ▶ N colpo netto; (*Culin*) costoletta; **to get the ~** (BRIT *col: project*) essere bocciato(-a); (*person: be sacked*) essere licenziato(-a); *see also* **chops**

▶ **chop down** VT (*tree*) abbattere

▶ **chop off** VT tagliare

choppy ['tʃɔpɪ] ADJ (*sea*) mosso(-a)

chops [tʃɔps] NPL (*jaws*) mascelle *fpl*

chopsticks ['tʃɔpstɪks] NPL bastoncini *mpl* cinesi

choral ['kɔ:rəl] ADJ corale

chord [kɔ:d] N (*Mus*) accordo

chore [tʃɔ:ʳ] N faccenda; **household chores** faccende *fpl* domestiche

choreographer [kɔrɪ'ɔgrəfəʳ] N coreografo(-a)

choreography [kɔrɪ'ɔgrəfɪ] N coreografia

chorister ['kɔrɪstəʳ] N corista *mf*

chortle ['tʃɔ:tl] VI ridacchiare

chorus ['kɔ:rəs] N coro; (*repeated part of song, also fig*) ritornello

chose [tʃəuz] PT *of* **choose**

chosen ['tʃəuzn] PP *of* **choose**

chowder ['tʃaudəʳ] N zuppa di pesce

Christ [kraɪst] N Cristo

christen ['krɪsn] VT battezzare

christening ['krɪsnɪŋ] N battesimo

Christian ['krɪstɪən] ADJ, N cristiano(-a)

Christianity [krɪstɪ'ænɪtɪ] N cristianesimo

Christian name N nome *m* di battesimo

Christmas ['krɪsməs] N Natale *m*; **happy** or **merry ~!** Buon Natale!

Christmas card N cartolina di Natale

Christmas carol N canto natalizio

Christmas Day N il giorno di Natale

Christmas Eve N la vigilia di Natale

Christmas Island N isola di Christmas

Christmas pudding N (*esp BRIT*) specie di budino con frutta secca, spezie e brandy

Christmas tree N albero di Natale

chrome [krəum] N cromo

chromium ['krəumɪəm] N cromo; (*also:* **chromium plating**) cromatura

chromosome ['krəuməsəum] N cromosoma *m*

chronic ['krɔnɪk] ADJ cronico(-a); (*fig: liar, smoker*) incallito(-a)

chronicle ['krɔnɪkl] N cronaca

chronological [krɔnə'lɔdʒɪkl] ADJ cronologico(-a)

chrysanthemum [krɪ'sænθəməm] N crisantemo

chubby ['tʃʌbɪ] ADJ paffuto(-a)

chuck [tʃʌk] VT buttare, gettare; **to ~ (up** or **in)** (*BRIT: job, person*) piantare
▶ **chuck out** VT buttar fuori

chuckle ['tʃʌkl] VI ridere sommessamente

chuffed [tʃʌft] ADJ (*col*): **to be ~ about sth** essere arcicontento(-a) di qc

chug [tʃʌg] VI (*also:* **chug along**: *train*) muoversi sbuffando

chum [tʃʌm] N compagno(-a)

chump [tʃʌmp] N (*col*) idiota *mf*

chunk [tʃʌŋk] N pezzo; (*of bread*) tocco

chunky [tʃʌŋkɪ] ADJ (*furniture etc*) basso(-a) e largo(-a); (*person*) ben piantato(-a); (*knitwear*) di lana grossa

Chunnel ['tʃʌnəl] N = **Channel Tunnel**

church [tʃə:tʃ] N chiesa; **the C~ of England** la Chiesa anglicana

churchyard ['tʃə:tʃjɑ:d] N sagrato

churlish ['tʃə:lɪʃ] ADJ rozzo(-a), sgarbato(-a)

churn [tʃə:n] N (*for butter*) zangola; (*also:* **milk churn**) bidone *m*
▶ **churn out** VT sfornare

chute [ʃu:t] N cascata; (*also:* **rubbish chute**) canale *m* di scarico; (*BRIT: children's slide*) scivolo

chutney ['tʃʌtnɪ] N salsa piccante (di frutta, zucchero e spezie)

CIA N ABBR (*US:* = *Central Intelligence Agency*) C.I.A. *f*

CID N ABBR (*BRIT:* = *Criminal Investigation Department*) ≈ polizia giudiziaria

cider ['saɪdəʳ] N sidro

CIF ABBR (= *cost, insurance, and freight*) C.I.F. *m*

cigar [sɪ'gɑ:ʳ] N sigaro

cigarette [sɪgə'ret] N sigaretta

cigarette case N portasigarette *m inv*

cigarette end N mozzicone *m*

cigarette holder N bocchino

cigarette lighter N accendino

C-in-C ABBR = **commander-in-chief**

cinch [sɪntʃ] N (*col*): **it's a ~** è presto fatto; (*sure thing*) è una cosa sicura

cinder ['sɪndəʳ] N cenere *f*

Cinderella [sɪndə'relə] N Cenerentola

cine-camera ['sɪnɪ'kæmərə] N (*BRIT*) cinepresa

cine-film ['sɪnɪfɪlm] N (*BRIT*) pellicola

cinema ['sɪnəmə] N cinema *m inv*

cine-projector ['sɪnɪprə'dʒɛktəʳ] N (*BRIT*) proiettore *m*

cinnamon ['sɪnəmən] N cannella

cipher ['saɪfəʳ] N cifra; (*fig: faceless employee etc*) persona di nessun conto; **in ~** in codice

circa ['sə:kə] PREP circa

circle ['sə:kl] N cerchio; (*of friends etc*) circolo; (*in cinema*) galleria ▶ VI girare in circolo
▶ VT (*surround*) circondare; (*move round*) girare intorno a

circuit ['sə:kɪt] N circuito

circuit board N (*Comput*) tavola dei circuiti

circuitous [sə:'kjuɪtəs] ADJ indiretto(-a)

circular ['sə:kjuləʳ] ADJ circolare ▶ N (*letter*) circolare *f*; (*as advertisement*) volantino pubblicitario

circulate ['sə:kjuleɪt] VI circolare; (*person: socially*) girare e andare un po' da tutti
▶ VT far circolare

circulating capital ['sə:kjuleɪtɪŋ-] N (*Comm*) capitale *m* d'esercizio

circulation [sə:kju'leɪʃən] N circolazione *f*; (*of newspaper*) tiratura

circumcise ['sə:kəmsaɪz] VT circoncidere

circumference [sə'kʌmfərəns] N circonferenza

circumflex ['sə:kəmflɛks] N (also: **circumflex accent**) accento circonflesso

circumscribe ['sə:kəmskraɪb] VT circoscrivere; (fig: limit) limitare

circumspect ['sə:kəmspɛkt] ADJ circospetto(-a)

circumstances ['sə:kəmstənsɪz] NPL circostanze fpl; (financial condition) condizioni fpl finanziarie; **in the ~** date le circostanze; **under no ~** per nessun motivo

circumstantial ['sə:kəm'stænʃəl] ADJ (report, statement) circostanziato(-a), dettagliato(-a); **~ evidence** prova indiretta

circumvent [sə:kəm'vɛnt] VT (rule etc) aggirare

circus ['sə:kəs] N circo; (also: **Circus**: in place names) piazza (di forma circolare)

cirrhosis [sɪ'rəusɪs] N (also: **cirrhosis of the liver**) cirrosi f inv (epatica)

CIS N ABBR (= Commonwealth of Independent States) CSI f

cissy ['sɪsɪ] N = **sissy**

cistern ['sɪstən] N cisterna; (in toilet) serbatoio d'acqua

citation [saɪ'teɪʃən] N citazione f

cite [saɪt] VT citare

citizen ['sɪtɪzn] N (Pol: of country) cittadino(-a); (: of town) abitante mf; **the citizens of this town** gli abitanti di questa città

Citizens' Advice Bureau N (BRIT) organizzazione di volontari che offre gratuitamente assistenza su questioni legali e finanziarie

citizenship ['sɪtɪznʃɪp] N cittadinanza

citric acid ['sɪtrɪk] N acido citrico

citrus fruit ['sɪtrəs-] N agrume m

city ['sɪtɪ] N città f inv; **the C~** la Città di Londra (centro commerciale)

city centre N centro della città

City Hall N (US) ≈ Comune m

City Technology College N (BRIT) istituto tecnico superiore (finanziato dall'industria)

civic ['sɪvɪk] ADJ civico(-a)

civic centre N (BRIT) centro civico

civil ['sɪvɪl] ADJ civile; (polite) educato(-a), gentile

civil disobedience N disubbidienza civile

civil engineer N ingegnere m civile

civil engineering N ingegneria civile

civilian [sɪ'vɪlɪən] ADJ, N borghese (mf)

civilization [sɪvɪlaɪ'zeɪʃən] N civiltà f inv

civilized ['sɪvɪlaɪzd] ADJ civilizzato(-a); (fig) cortese

civil law N codice m civile; (study) diritto civile

civil liberties NPL libertà fpl civili

civil rights NPL diritti mpl civili

civil servant N impiegato(-a) statale

Civil Service N amministrazione f statale

civil war N guerra civile

civvies ['sɪvɪz] NPL (col): **in ~** in borghese

CJD N ABBR (= Creutzfeld-Jakob disease) malattia di Creutzfeldt-Jakob

cl ABBR (= centilitre) cl

clad [klæd] ADJ: **~ (in)** vestito(-a) (di)

claim [kleɪm] VT (rights etc) rivendicare; (damages) richiedere; (assert) sostenere, pretendere ▶ VI (for insurance) fare una domanda d'indennizzo ▶ N rivendicazione f; pretesa; richiesta; (right) diritto; **to ~ that/ to be** sostenere che/di essere; **(insurance) ~** domanda d'indennizzo; **to put in a ~ for sth** fare una richiesta di qc

claimant ['kleɪmənt] N (Admin, Law) richiedente mf

claim form N (gen) modulo di richiesta; (for expenses) modulo di rimborso spese

clairvoyant [klɛə'vɔɪənt] N chiaroveggente mf

clam [klæm] N vongola
▶ **clam up** VI (col) azzittirsi

clamber ['klæmbə^r] VI arrampicarsi

clammy ['klæmɪ] ADJ (weather) caldo(-a) umido(-a); (hands) viscido(-a)

clamour, (US) clamor ['klæmə^r] N (noise) clamore m; (protest) protesta ▶ VI: **to ~ for sth** chiedere a gran voce qc

clamp [klæmp] N pinza; morsa ▶ VT stringere con una morsa; (Aut: wheel) applicare le ganasce a
▶ **clamp down** VT FUS (fig): **to ~ down (on)** dare un giro di vite (a)

clampdown ['klæmpdaun] N stretta, giro di vite; **a ~ on sth/sb** un giro di vite a qc/qn

clan [klæn] N clan m inv

clandestine [klæn'dɛstɪn] ADJ clandestino(-a)

clang [klæŋ] N fragore m, suono metallico

clanger ['klæŋə^r] N: **to drop a ~** (BRIT col) fare una gaffe

clansman ['klænzmən] N (irreg) membro di un clan

clap [klæp] VI applaudire ▶ VT: **to ~ one's hands** battere le mani ▶ N: **a ~ of thunder** un tuono

clapping ['klæpɪŋ] N applausi mpl

claptrap ['klæptræp] N (col) stupidaggini fpl

claret ['klærət] N vino di Bordeaux

clarification [klærɪfɪ'keɪʃən] N (fig) chiarificazione f, chiarimento

clarify ['klærɪfaɪ] VT chiarificare, chiarire

clarinet [klærɪ'nɛt] N clarinetto

clarity ['klærɪtɪ] N chiarezza

clash [klæʃ] N frastuono; (fig) scontro ▶ VI (Mil, fig: have an argument) scontrarsi; cozzare; (colours) stridere; (dates, events) coincidere

clasp [klɑ:sp] N (hold) stretta; (of necklace, bag) fermaglio, fibbia ▶ VT stringere

C

class [klɑːs] N classe f; (group, category) tipo, categoria ▶ vt classificare

class-conscious ['klɑːskɔnʃəs] ADJ che ha coscienza di classe

class consciousness N coscienza di classe

classic ['klæsɪk] ADJ classico(-a) ▶ N classico

classical ['klæsɪkəl] ADJ classico(-a)

classics ['klæsɪks] NPL (Scol) studi mpl umanistici

classification [klæsɪfɪ'keɪʃən] N classificazione f

classified ['klæsɪfaɪd] ADJ (information) segreto(-a), riservato(-a); ~ **ads** annunci economici

classify ['klæsɪfaɪ] vt classificare

classless society ['klɑːslɪs-] N società f inv senza distinzioni di classe

classmate ['klɑːsmeɪt] N compagno(-a) di classe

classroom ['klɑːsrum] N aula

classroom assistant N assistente mf in classe dell'insegnante

classy ['klɑːsɪ] ADJ (col) chic inv, elegante

clatter ['klætə'] N tintinnio; scalpitio ▶ vi tintinnare; scalpitare

clause [klɔːz] N clausola; (Ling) proposizione f

claustrophobia [klɔːstrə'fəubɪə] N claustrofobia

claustrophobic [klɔːstrə'fəubɪk] ADJ claustrofobico(-a)

claw [klɔː] N tenaglia; (of bird of prey) artiglio; (of lobster) pinza ▶ vt graffiare; afferrare

clay [kleɪ] N argilla

clean [kliːn] ADJ pulito(-a); (outline, break, movement) netto(-a) ▶ vt pulire ▶ ADV: **he ~ forgot** si è completamente dimenticato; **to come ~** (col: admit guilt) confessare; **to have a ~ driving licence or record** (US) non aver mai preso contravvenzioni; **to ~ one's teeth** (BRIT) lavarsi i denti
  ▶ **clean off** vt togliere
  ▶ **clean out** vt ripulire
  ▶ **clean up** vi far pulizia ▶ vt (also fig) ripulire; (fig: make profit): **to ~ up on** fare una barca di soldi con

clean-cut ['kliːn'kʌt] ADJ (man) curato(-a); (situation etc) ben definito(-a)

cleaner ['kliːnə'] N (person) uomo (donna) delle pulizie; (also: **dry cleaner**) tintore(-a) (product) smacchiatore m

cleaner's N (also: **dry cleaner's**) tintoria

cleaning ['kliːnɪŋ] N pulizia

cleaning lady N donna delle pulizie

cleanliness ['klɛnlɪnɪs] N pulizia

cleanly ['kliːnlɪ] ADV in modo netto

cleanse [klɛnz] vt pulire; purificare

cleanser ['klɛnzə'] N detergente m; (cosmetic) latte m detergente

clean-shaven ['kliːn'ʃeɪvn] ADJ sbarbato(-a)

cleansing department ['klɛnzɪŋ-] N (BRIT) nettezza urbana

clean sweep N: **to make a ~ (of)** fare piazza pulita (di)

clean technology N tecnologie fpl ambientali

clean-up ['kliːnʌp] N pulizia

clear [klɪə'] ADJ chiaro(-a); (glass etc) trasparente; (road, way) libero(-a); (profit, majority) netto(-a); (conscience) pulito(-a) ▶ vt sgombrare; liberare; (table) sparecchiare; (site, woodland) spianare; (Comm: goods) liquidare; (Law: suspect) discolpare; (obstacle) superare; (cheque) fare la compensazione di ▶ vi (weather) rasserenarsi; (fog) andarsene ▶ ADV: ~ **of** distante da ▶ N: **to be in the ~** (out of debt) essere in attivo; (out of suspicion) essere a posto; (out of danger) essere fuori pericolo; **to ~ the table** sparecchiare (la tavola); **to ~ one's throat** schiarirsi la gola; **to ~ a profit** avere un profitto netto; **to make o.s. ~** spiegarsi bene; **to make it ~ to sb that ...** far capire a qn che ...; **I have a ~ day tomorrow** (BRIT) non ho impegni domani; **to keep ~ of sb/sth** tenersi lontano da qn/ qc, stare alla larga da qn/qc
  ▶ **clear away** vt (things, clothes, etc) mettere a posto; **to ~ away the dishes** sparecchiare la tavola
  ▶ **clear off** vi (col: leave) svignarsela
  ▶ **clear up** vi schiarirsi ▶ vt mettere in ordine; (mystery) risolvere

clearance ['klɪərəns] N (removal) sgombro; (free space) spazio; (permission) autorizzazione f, permesso

clearance sale N vendita di liquidazione

clear-cut ['klɪə'kʌt] ADJ ben delineato(-a), distinto(-a)

clearing ['klɪərɪŋ] N radura; (BRIT Banking) clearing m

clearing bank N (BRIT) banca che fa uso della camera di compensazione

clearing house N (Comm) camera di compensazione

clearly ['klɪəlɪ] ADV chiaramente

clearway ['klɪəweɪ] N (BRIT) strada con divieto di sosta

cleavage ['kliːvɪdʒ] N (of woman) scollatura

cleaver ['kliːvə'] N mannaia

clef [klɛf] N (Mus) chiave f

cleft [klɛft] N (in rock) crepa, fenditura

clemency ['klɛmənsɪ] N clemenza

clement ['klɛmənt] ADJ (weather) mite, clemente

clench [klɛntʃ] vt stringere

clergy ['kləːdʒɪ] N clero

clergyman ['kləːdʒɪmən] N (irreg) ecclesiastico

clerical ['klɛrɪkl] ADJ d'impiegato; (Rel) clericale

clerk [klɑːk, (US) kləːrk] N (BRIT)
impiegato(-a); (US: salesman/woman)
commesso(-a); **C~ of the Court** (Law)
cancelliere m

clever ['klɛvər] ADJ (mentally) intelligente;
(deft, skilful) abile; (device, arrangement)
ingegnoso(-a)

cleverly ['klɛvəlɪ] ADV abilmente

clew [kluː] N (US) = **clue**

cliché ['kliːʃeɪ] N cliché m inv

click [klɪk] VI scattare ▶ VT: **to ~ one's tongue**
schioccare la lingua; **to ~ one's heels**
battere i tacchi

clickable ['klɪkəbl] ADJ cliccabile

client ['klaɪənt] N cliente mf

clientele [kliːɑːnˈtɛl] N clientela

cliff [klɪf] N scogliera scoscesa, rupe f

cliffhanger ['klɪfhæŋər] N (TV, fig) episodio
(or situazione etc) ricco(-a) di suspense

climactic [klaɪˈmæktɪk] ADJ culminante

climate ['klaɪmɪt] N clima m

climate change N cambiamenti mpl
climatici

climax ['klaɪmæks] N culmine m; (of play etc)
momento più emozionante; (sexual) orgasmo

climb [klaɪm] VI salire; (clamber)
arrampicarsi; (plane) prendere quota ▶ VT
salire; (Climbing) scalare ▶ N salita;
arrampicata; scalata; **to ~ over a wall**
scavalcare un muro
▶ **climb down** VI scendere; (BRIT fig) far
marcia indietro

climbdown ['klaɪmdaun] N (BRIT) ritirata

climber ['klaɪmər] N (also: **rock climber**)
rocciatore(-trice); alpinista mf

climbing ['klaɪmɪŋ] N (also: **rock climbing**)
alpinismo

clinch [klɪntʃ] VT (deal) concludere

clincher ['klɪntʃər] N (col): **that was the ~**
quello è stato il fattore decisivo

cling [klɪŋ] (pt, pp **clung** [klʌŋ]) VI: **to ~ (to)**
tenersi stretto(-a) (a), aggrapparsi (a);
(clothes) aderire strettamente (a)

clingfilm® ['klɪŋfɪlm] N pellicola trasparente
(per alimenti)

clinic ['klɪnɪk] N clinica; (session) seduta; serie
f di sedute

clinical ['klɪnɪkəl] ADJ clinico(-a); (fig)
freddo(-a), distaccato(-a)

clink [klɪŋk] VI tintinnare

clip [klɪp] N (for hair) forcina; (also: **paper clip**)
graffetta; (TV, Cine) sequenza; (BRIT: also:
bulldog clip) fermafogli m inv; (holding hose
etc) anello d'attacco ▶ VT (also: **clip together**:
papers) attaccare insieme; (hair, nails) tagliare;
(hedge) tosare

clippers ['klɪpəz] NPL macchinetta per
capelli; (also: **nail clippers**) forbicine fpl per le
unghie

clipping ['klɪpɪŋ] N (from newspaper) ritaglio

clique [kliːk] N cricca

cloak [kləuk] N mantello ▶ VT avvolgere

cloakroom ['kləukrum] N (for coats etc)
guardaroba m inv; (BRIT: W.C.) gabinetti mpl

clock [klɔk] N orologio; (of taxi) tassametro;
around the ~ ventiquattr'ore su
ventiquattro; **to sleep round the ~** or **the ~
round** dormire un giorno intero; **to work
against the ~** lavorare in gara col tempo;
30,000 on the ~ (BRIT Aut) 30.000 sul
contachilometri
▶ **clock in, clock on** VI (BRIT) timbrare il
cartellino (all'entrata)
▶ **clock off, clock out** VI (BRIT) timbrare il
cartellino (all'uscita)
▶ **clock up** VT (miles, hours etc) fare

clockwise ['klɔkwaɪz] ADV in senso orario

clockwork ['klɔkwəːk] N movimento or
meccanismo a orologeria ▶ ADJ (toy, train) a
molla

clog [klɔg] N zoccolo ▶ VT intasare ▶ VI (also:
clog up) intasarsi, bloccarsi

cloister ['klɔɪstər] N chiostro

clone [kləun] N clone m ▶ VT clonare

close¹ [kləus] ADJ vicino(-a); (writing, texture)
fitto(-a); (watch) stretto(-a); (examination)
attento(-a); (contest) combattuto(-a);
(weather) afoso(-a) ▶ ADV vicino, dappresso;
~ to prep vicino a; **~ by, ~ at hand** qui (or lì)
vicino; **how ~ is Edinburgh to Glasgow?**
quanto dista Edimburgo da Glasgow?; **a ~
friend** un amico intimo; **to have a ~ shave**
(fig) scamparla bella; **at ~ quarters** da vicino

close² [kləuz] VT chiudere; (bargain, deal)
concludere ▶ VI (shop etc) chiudere; (lid, door
etc) chiudersi; (end) finire ▶ N (end) fine f; **to
bring sth to a ~** terminare qc
▶ **close down** VT chiudere (definitivamente)
▶ VI cessare (definitivamente)
▶ **close in** VI (hunters) stringersi attorno;
(evening, night, fog) calare; **to ~ in on sb**
accerchiare qn; **the days are closing in** le
giornate si accorciano
▶ **close off** VT (area) chiudere

closed [kləuzd] ADJ chiuso(-a)

closed-circuit ['kləuzd'səːkɪt] ADJ:
~ television televisione f a circuito chiuso

closed shop N azienda o fabbrica che impiega solo
aderenti ai sindacati

close-knit ['kləus'nɪt] ADJ (family, community)
molto unito(-a)

closely ['kləuslɪ] ADV (examine, watch) da
vicino; **we are ~ related** siamo parenti
stretti; **a ~ guarded secret** un assoluto
segreto

close season ['kləuz-] N (Football) periodo di
vacanza del campionato; (Hunting) stagione f
di chiusura (di caccia, pesca ecc)

closet ['klɔzɪt] N (*cupboard*) armadio
close-up ['kləusʌp] N primo piano
closing ['kləuzɪŋ] ADJ (*stages, remarks*)
conclusivo(-a), finale; **~ price** (*Stock Exchange*)
prezzo di chiusura
closing time N orario di chiusura
closure ['kləuʒəʳ] N chiusura
clot [klɔt] N (*also:* **blood clot**) coagulo; (*col:
idiot*) scemo(-a) ▶ VI coagularsi
cloth [klɔθ] N (*material*) tessuto, stoffa;
(*BRIT: also:* **teacloth**) strofinaccio; (*also:*
tablecloth) tovaglia
clothe [kləuð] VT vestire
clothes [kləuðz] NPL abiti *mpl*, vestiti *mpl*; **to
put one's ~ on** vestirsi; **to take one's ~ off**
togliersi i vestiti, svestirsi
clothes brush N spazzola per abiti
clothes line N corda (per stendere il bucato)
clothes peg, (US) **clothes pin** N molletta
clothing ['kləuðɪŋ] N = **clothes**
clotted cream ['klɔtɪd-] N (*BRIT*) panna
rappresa
cloud [klaud] N nuvola; (*of dust, smoke, gas*)
nube *f* ▶ VT (*liquid*) intorbidire; **to ~ the issue**
distogliere dal problema; **every ~ has a
silver lining** (*proverb*) non tutto il male vien
per nuocere
▶ **cloud over** VI rannuvolarsi; (*fig*)
offuscarsi
cloudburst ['klaudbə:st] N acquazzone *m*
cloud computing N cloud computing *m inv*
cloud-cuckoo-land ['klaud'kuku:'lænd] N
(*BRIT*) mondo dei sogni
cloudy ['klaudɪ] ADJ nuvoloso(-a); (*liquid*)
torbido(-a)
clout [klaut] N (*blow*) colpo; (*fig*) influenza
▶ VT dare un colpo a
clove [kləuv] N chiodo di garofano
clove of garlic N spicchio d'aglio
clover ['kləuvəʳ] N trifoglio
cloverleaf ['kləuvəli:f] N foglia di trifoglio;
(*Aut*) raccordo (a quadrifoglio)
clown [klaun] N pagliaccio ▶ VI (*also:* **clown
about, clown around**) fare il pagliaccio
cloying ['klɔɪɪŋ] ADJ (*taste, smell*)
nauseabondo(-a)
club [klʌb] N (*society*) club *m inv*, circolo;
(*weapon, Golf*) mazza ▶ VT bastonare ▶ VI: **to ~
together** associarsi; **clubs** NPL (*Cards*) fiori
mpl
club car N (*US Rail*) carrozza *or* vagone *m*
ristorante
club class N (*Aviat*) classe *f* club *inv*
clubhouse ['klʌbhaus] N sede *f* del circolo
club soda N (US) = **soda**
cluck [klʌk] VI chiocciare
clue [klu:] N indizio; (*in crosswords*)
definizione *f*; **I haven't a ~** non ho la
minima idea

clued up, (US) **clued in** [klu:d-] ADJ (*col*) (ben)
informato(-a)
clump [klʌmp] N (*of flowers, trees*) gruppo; (*of
grass*) ciuffo
clumsy ['klʌmzɪ] ADJ (*person*) goffo(-a),
maldestro(-a); (*object*) malfatto(-a), mal
costruito(-a)
clung [klʌŋ] PT, PP *of* **cling**
cluster ['klʌstəʳ] N gruppo ▶ VI raggrupparsi
clutch [klʌtʃ] N (*grip, grasp*) presa, stretta;
(*Aut*) frizione *f* ▶ VT afferrare, stringere forte;
to ~ at aggrapparsi a
clutter ['klʌtəʳ] VT (*also:* **clutter up**)
ingombrare ▶ N confusione *f*, disordine *m*
cm ABBR (= *centimetre*) cm
CNAA N ABBR (*BRIT*: = *Council for National
Academic Awards*) *organizzazione che conferisce
premi accademici*
CND N ABBR (*BRIT*) = **Campaign for Nuclear
Disarmament**
CO N ABBR (= *commanding officer*) Com.; (*BRIT*)
= **Commonwealth Office** ▶ ABBR (*US*)
= **Colorado**
Co. ABBR = **county**; (= *company*) C., C.ia
c/o ABBR (= *care of*) presso
coach [kəutʃ] N (*bus*) pullman *m inv*;
(*horse-drawn, of train*) carrozza; (*Sport*)
allenatore(-trice); (*tutor*) chi dà ripetizioni
▶ VT allenare; dare ripetizioni a
coach station (*BRIT*) N stazione *f* delle
corriere
coach trip N viaggio in pullman
coagulate [kəu'ægjuleɪt] VT coagulare ▶ VI
coagularsi
coal [kəul] N carbone *m*
coalface ['kəulfeɪs] N fronte *f*
coalfield ['kəulfi:ld] N bacino carbonifero
coalition [kəuə'lɪʃən] N coalizione *f*
coalman ['kəulmən] N (*irreg*) negoziante *m* di
carbone
coalmine ['kəulmaɪn] N miniera di carbone
coalminer ['kəulmaɪnəʳ] N minatore *m*
coalmining ['kəulmaɪnɪŋ] N estrazione *f* del
carbone
coarse [kɔ:s] ADJ (*salt, sand etc*) grosso(-a);
(*cloth, person*) rozzo(-a); (*vulgar: character, laugh*)
volgare
coast [kəust] N costa ▶ VI (*with cycle etc*)
scendere a ruota libera
coastal ['kəustəl] ADJ costiero(-a)
coaster ['kəustəʳ] N (*Naut*) nave *f* da
cabotaggio; (*for glass*) sottobicchiere *m*
coastguard ['kəustgɑ:d] N guardia costiera
coastline ['kəustlaɪn] N linea costiera
coat [kəut] N cappotto; (*of animal*) pelo; (*of
paint*) mano *f* ▶ VT coprire; **~ of arms** *n*
stemma *m*
coat hanger N attaccapanni *m inv*
coating ['kəutɪŋ] N rivestimento

co-author ['kəʊ'ɔːθə^r] N coautore(-trice)

coax [kəʊks] VT indurre (con moine)

cob [kɔb] N see **corn**

cobbled ['kɔbld] ADJ: ~ **street** strada pavimentata a ciottoli

cobbler ['kɔblə^r] N calzolaio

cobbles ['kɔblz], **cobblestones** ['kɔblstəʊnz] NPL ciottoli mpl

COBOL ['kəʊbɔl] N COBOL m

cobra ['kəʊbrə] N cobra m inv

cobweb ['kɔbwɛb] N ragnatela

cocaine [kə'keɪn] N cocaina

cock [kɔk] N (rooster) gallo; (male bird) maschio ▶ VT (gun) armare; **to ~ one's ears** (fig) drizzare le orecchie

cock-a-hoop [kɔkə'huːp] ADJ euforico(-a)

cockerel ['kɔkərəl] N galletto

cock-eyed ['kɔkaɪd] ADJ (fig) storto(-a); strampalato(-a)

cockle ['kɔkl] N cardio

cockney ['kɔknɪ] N cockney mf (abitante dei quartieri popolari dell'East End di Londra)

cockpit ['kɔkpɪt] N abitacolo

cockroach ['kɔkrəʊtʃ] N blatta

cocktail ['kɔkteɪl] N cocktail m inv; **prawn ~**, (US) **shrimp ~** cocktail m inv di gamberetti

cocktail cabinet N mobile m bar inv

cocktail party N cocktail m inv

cocktail shaker N shaker m inv

cocky ['kɔkɪ] ADJ spavaldo(-a), arrogante

cocoa ['kəʊkəʊ] N cacao

coconut ['kəʊkənʌt] N noce f di cocco

cocoon [kə'kuːn] N bozzolo

COD ABBR = **cash on delivery**; (US) = **collect on delivery**

cod [kɔd] N merluzzo

C.O.D. ABBR = **cash on delivery**

code [kəʊd] N codice m; ~ **of behaviour** regole fpl di condotta; ~ **of practice** codice professionale

codeine ['kəʊdiːn] N codeina

codger ['kɔdʒə^r] N (BRIT col): **an old ~** un simpatico nonnetto

codicil ['kɔdɪsɪl] N codicillo

codify ['kəʊdɪfaɪ] VT codificare

cod-liver oil ['kɔdlɪvə^r-] N olio di fegato di merluzzo

co-driver ['kəʊ'draɪvə^r] N (in race) copilota m; (of lorry) secondo autista m

co-ed ['kəʊ'ɛd] ADJ ABBR = **coeducational** ▶ N ABBR (US: female student) studentessa presso un'università mista; (BRIT: school) scuola mista

coeducational ['kəʊɛdju'keɪʃənl] ADJ misto(-a)

coerce [kəʊ'əːs] VT costringere

coercion [kəʊ'əːʃən] N coercizione f

coexistence ['kəʊɪg'zɪstəns] N coesistenza

C. of C. N ABBR = **chamber of commerce**

C of E ABBR = **Church of England**

coffee ['kɔfɪ] N caffè m inv; **white ~**, (US) **~ with cream** caffellatte m

coffee bar N (BRIT) caffè m inv

coffee bean N grano or chicco di caffè

coffee break N pausa per il caffè

coffeecake ['kɔfɪkeɪk] N (US) panino dolce all'uva

coffee cup N tazzina da caffè

coffee maker N bollitore m per il caffè

coffeepot ['kɔfɪpɔt] N caffettiera

coffee shop N ≈ caffè m inv

coffee table N tavolino

coffin ['kɔfɪn] N bara

C of I ABBR = **Church of Ireland**

C of S ABBR = **Church of Scotland**

cog [kɔg] N dente m

cogent ['kəʊdʒənt] ADJ convincente

cognac ['kɔnjæk] N cognac m inv

cognitive ['kɔgnɪtɪv] ADJ cognitivo(-a)

cogwheel ['kɔgwiːl] N ruota dentata

cohabit [kəʊ'hæbɪt] VI (formal): **to ~ (with sb)** coabitare (con qn)

coherent [kəʊ'hɪərənt] ADJ coerente

cohesion [kəʊ'hiːʒən] N coesione f

cohesive [kəʊ'hiːsɪv] ADJ (fig) unificante, coesivo(-a)

COI N ABBR (BRIT) = **Central Office of Information**

coil [kɔɪl] N rotolo; (one loop) anello; (Aut, Elec) bobina; (contraceptive) spirale f; (of smoke) filo ▶ VT avvolgere

coin [kɔɪn] N moneta ▶ VT (word) coniare

coinage ['kɔɪnɪdʒ] N sistema m monetario

coin-box ['kɔɪnbɔks] N (BRIT) cabina telefonica

coincide [kəʊɪn'saɪd] VI coincidere

coincidence [kəʊ'ɪnsɪdəns] N combinazione f

coin-operated ['kɔɪn'ɔpəreɪtɪd] ADJ (machine) (che funziona) a monete

Coke® [kəʊk] N (Coca-Cola) coca f inv

coke [kəʊk] N coke m

Col. ABBR = **colonel**; (US) = **Colorado**

COLA N ABBR (US: = cost-of-living adjustment) ≈ scala mobile

colander ['kɔləndə^r] N colino

cold [kəʊld] ADJ freddo(-a) ▶ N freddo; (Med) raffreddore m; **it's ~** fa freddo; **to be ~** (person) aver freddo; (object) essere freddo(-a); **to catch ~** prendere freddo; **to catch a ~** prendere un raffreddore; **in ~ blood** a sangue freddo; **to have ~ feet** avere i piedi freddi; (fig) aver la fifa; **to give sb the ~ shoulder** ignorare qn

cold-blooded [kəʊld'blʌdɪd] ADJ (Zool) a sangue freddo

cold call N chiamata pubblicitaria non richiesta

cold cream N crema emolliente

coldly ['kəuldlɪ] ADV freddamente

cold sore N erpete m

cold sweat N: **to be in a ~ (about sth)** sudare freddo (per qc)

cold turkey N (col): **to go ~** avere la scimmia (drogato)

Cold War N: **the ~** la guerra fredda

coleslaw ['kəulslɔ:] N insalata di cavolo bianco

colic ['kɔlɪk] N colica

colicky ['kɔlɪkɪ] ADJ che soffre di coliche

collaborate [kə'læbəreɪt] VI collaborare

collaboration [kəlæbə'reɪʃən] N collaborazione f

collaborator [kə'læbəreɪtə^r] N collaboratore(-trice)

collage [kɔ'lɑ:ʒ] N (Art) collage m inv

collagen ['kɔlədʒən] N collageno

collapse [kə'læps] VI (gen) crollare; (government) cadere; (Med) avere un collasso; (plans) fallire ▶ N crollo; caduta; (Med) collasso; fallimento

collapsible [kə'læpsəbl] ADJ pieghevole

collar ['kɔlə^r] N (of coat, shirt) colletto; (for dog) collare m; (Tech) anello, fascetta ▶ VT (col: person, object) beccare

collarbone ['kɔləbəun] N clavicola

collate [kɔ'leɪt] VT collazionare

collateral [kɔ'lætərəl] N garanzia

collation [kɔ'leɪʃən] N collazione f

colleague ['kɔli:g] N collega mf

collect [kə'lɛkt] VT (gen) raccogliere; (as a hobby) fare collezione di; (BRIT: call for) prendere; (money owed, pension) riscuotere; (donations, subscriptions) fare una colletta di ▶ VI (people) adunarsi, riunirsi; (rubbish etc) ammucchiarsi ▶ ADV (US Tel): **to call ~** fare una chiamata a carico del destinatario; **to ~ one's thoughts** raccogliere le idee; **~ on delivery** (US Comm) pagamento alla consegna

collected [kə'lɛktɪd] ADJ: **~ works** opere fpl raccolte

collection [kə'lɛkʃən] N collezione f; raccolta; (for money) colletta; (Post) levata

collective [kə'lɛktɪv] ADJ collettivo(-a) ▶ N collettivo

collective bargaining N trattative fpl (sindacali) collettive

collector [kə'lɛktə^r] N collezionista mf; (of taxes) esattore m; **~'s item** or **piece** pezzo da collezionista

college ['kɔlɪdʒ] N (Scol) college m inv; (of technology, agriculture etc) istituto superiore; (body) collegio; **~ of education** ≈ facoltà f inv di Magistero

collide [kə'laɪd] VI: **to ~ (with)** scontrarsi (con)

collie ['kɔlɪ] N (dog) collie m inv

colliery ['kɔlɪərɪ] N (BRIT) miniera di carbone

collision [kə'lɪʒən] N collisione f, scontro; **to be on a ~ course** (also fig) essere in rotta di collisione

collision damage waiver N (Insurance) copertura per i danni alla vettura

colloquial [kə'ləukwɪəl] ADJ familiare

collusion [kə'lu:ʒən] N collusione f; **in ~ with** in accordo segreto con

Colo. ABBR (US) = **Colorado**

Cologne [kə'ləun] N Colonia

cologne [kə'ləun] N (also: **eau de cologne**) acqua di colonia

Colombia [kə'lɔmbɪə] N Colombia

Colombian [kə'lɔmbɪən] ADJ, N colombiano(-a)

colon ['kəulən] N (sign) due punti mpl; (Med) colon m inv

colonel ['kə:nl] N colonnello

colonial [kə'ləunɪəl] ADJ coloniale

colonize ['kɔlənaɪz] VT colonizzare

colony ['kɔlənɪ] N colonia

color etc ['kʌlə^r] (US) = **colour** etc

Colorado beetle [kɔlə'rɑ:dəu-] N dorifora

colossal [kə'lɔsl] ADJ colossale

colour, (US) **color** ['kʌlə^r] N colore m ▶ VT colorare; (tint, dye) tingere; (fig: affect) influenzare ▶ VI (blush) arrossire ▶ CPD (film, photograph, television) a colori; **colours** NPL (of party, club) emblemi mpl ▶ **colour in** VT colorare

colour bar, (US) **color bar** N discriminazione f razziale (in locali ecc)

colour-blind, (US) **color-blind** ['kʌləblaɪnd] ADJ daltonico(-a)

coloured, (US) **colored** ['kʌləd] ADJ colorato(-a); (photo) a colori; (person) di colore ▶ N: **colo(u)reds** gente f di colore

colour film, (US) **color film** N (for camera) pellicola a colori

colourful, (US) **colorful** ['kʌləful] ADJ pieno(-a) di colore, a vivaci colori; (personality) colorato(-a)

colouring, (US) **coloring** ['kʌlərɪŋ] N colorazione f; (substance) colorante m; (complexion) colorito

colour scheme, (US) **color scheme** N combinazione f di colori

colour supplement N (BRIT Press) supplemento a colori

colour television, (US) **color television** N televisione f a colori

colt [kəult] N puledro

column ['kɔləm] N colonna; (fashion column, sports column etc) rubrica; **the editorial ~** l'articolo di fondo

columnist ['kɔləmnɪst] N articolista mf

coma ['kəumə] N coma m inv

comb [kəum] N pettine m ▶ VT (hair) pettinare; (area) battere a tappeto

combat ['kɔmbæt] N combattimento ▶ VT combattere, lottare contro

combination [kɔmbɪ'neɪʃən] N combinazione *f*

combination lock N serratura a combinazione

combine¹ [kəm'baɪn] VT: **to ~ (with)** combinare (con); *(one quality with another)* **to ~ sth with sth** unire qc a qc ▶ VI unirsi; *(Chem)* combinarsi ▶ N ['kɔmbaɪn] lega; *(Econ)* associazione *f*; **a combined effort** uno sforzo collettivo

combine², **combine harvester** N mietitrebbia

combo ['kɔmbəʊ] N *(Jazz etc)* gruppo

combustible [kəm'bʌstɪbl] ADJ combustibile

combustion [kəm'bʌstʃən] N combustione *f*

come [kʌm] *(pt* came [keɪm], *pp ~* [kʌm]) VI venire; *(arrive)* venire, arrivare; **~ with me** vieni con me; **we've just ~ from Paris** siamo appena arrivati da Parigi; **nothing came of it** non è saltato fuori niente; **to ~ into sight** *or* **view** apparire; **to ~ to** *(decision etc)* raggiungere; **I've ~ to like him** ha cominciato a piacermi; **to ~ undone/loose** slacciarsi/allentarsi; **coming!** vengo!; **if it comes to it** nella peggiore delle ipotesi

▶ **come about** VI succedere

▶ **come across** VT FUS trovare per caso ▶ VI: **to ~ across well/badly** fare una buona/cattiva impressione

▶ **come along** VI *(pupil, work)* fare progressi; **~ along!** avanti!, andiamo!, forza!

▶ **come apart** VI andare in pezzi; *(become detached)* staccarsi

▶ **come away** VI venire via; *(become detached)* staccarsi

▶ **come back** VI ritornare; *(reply: col)*: **can I ~ back to you on that one?** possiamo riparlarne più tardi?

▶ **come by** VT FUS *(acquire)* ottenere; procurarsi

▶ **come down** VI scendere; *(prices)* calare; *(buildings)* essere demolito(-a)

▶ **come forward** VI farsi avanti; presentarsi

▶ **come from** VT FUS venire da; provenire da

▶ **come in** VI entrare

▶ **come in for** VT FUS *(criticism etc)* ricevere

▶ **come into** VT FUS *(money)* ereditare

▶ **come off** VI *(button)* staccarsi; *(stain)* andar via; *(attempt)* riuscire

▶ **come on** VI *(lights)* accendersi; *(electricity)* entrare in funzione; *(pupil, undertaking)* fare progressi; **~ on!** avanti!, andiamo!, forza!

▶ **come out** VI uscire; *(strike)* entrare in sciopero; *(stain)* andare via

▶ **come over** VT FUS: **I don't know what's ~ over him!** non so cosa gli sia successo!

▶ **come round** VI *(after faint, operation)* riprendere conoscenza, rinvenire

▶ **come through** VI *(survive)* sopravvivere, farcela; **the call came through** ci hanno passato la telefonata

▶ **come to** VI rinvenire ▶ VT *(add up to: amount)*: **how much does it ~ to?** quanto costa?, quanto viene?

▶ **come under** VT FUS *(heading)* trovarsi sotto; *(influence)* cadere sotto, subire

▶ **come up** VI venire su; *(sun)* salire; *(problem)* sorgere; *(event)* essere in arrivo; *(in conversation)* saltar fuori

▶ **come up against** VT FUS *(resistance, difficulties)* urtare contro

▶ **come up to** VT FUS arrivare (fino) a; **the film didn't ~ up to our expectations** il film ci ha delusi

▶ **come up with** VT FUS: **he came up with an idea** venne fuori con un'idea

▶ **come upon** VT FUS trovare per caso

comeback ['kʌmbæk] N *(Theat etc)* ritorno; *(reaction)* reazione *f*; *(response)* risultato, risposta

comedian [kə'mi:dɪən] N comico

comedienne [kəmi:dɪ'ɛn] N attrice *f* comica

comedown ['kʌmdaʊn] N rovescio

comedy ['kɔmɪdɪ] N commedia

comet ['kɔmɪt] N cometa

comeuppance [kʌm'ʌpəns] N: **to get one's ~** ricevere ciò che si merita

comfort ['kʌmfət] N comodità *f inv*, benessere *m*; *(relief)* consolazione *f*, conforto ▶ VT consolare, confortare

comfortable ['kʌmfətəbl] ADJ comodo(-a); *(financially)* agiato(-a); *(income, majority)* più che sufficiente; **I don't feel very ~ about it** non mi sento molto tranquillo

comfortably ['kʌmfətəblɪ] ADV *(sit)* comodamente; *(live)* bene

comforter ['kʌmfətəʳ] N *(US)* trapunta

comforts ['kʌmfəts] NPL comforts *mpl*, comodità *fpl*

comfort station N *(US)* gabinetti *mpl*

comic ['kɔmɪk] ADJ *(also: **comical**)* comico(-a), divertente ▶ N comico; *(Brit: magazine)* giornaletto

comic book N *(US)* giornalino (a fumetti)

comic strip N fumetto

coming ['kʌmɪŋ] N arrivo ▶ ADJ *(next)* prossimo(-a); *(future)* futuro(-a); **in the ~ weeks** nelle prossime settimane

comings and goings NPL, **coming and going** N andirivieni *m inv*

Comintern ['kɔmɪntə:n] N KOMINTERN *m*

comma ['kɔmə] N virgola

command [kə'mɑ:nd] N ordine *m*, comando; *(Mil: authority)* comando; *(mastery)* padronanza; *(Comput)* command *m inv*, comando ▶ VT comandare; **to ~ sb to do**

ordinare a qn di fare; **to have/take ~ of** avere/prendere il comando di; **to have at one's ~** (*money, resources etc*) avere a propria disposizione

command economy N = **planned economy**

commandeer [kɔmən'dɪər] VT requisire

commander [kə'mɑːndər] N capo; (*Mil*) comandante *m*

commander-in-chief [kə'mɑːndərɪn'tʃiːf] N (*Mil*) comandante *m* in capo

commanding [kə'mɑːndɪŋ] ADJ (*appearance*) imponente; (*voice, tone*) autorevole; (*lead, position*) dominante

commanding officer N comandante *m*

commandment [kə'mɑːndmənt] N (*Rel*) comandamento

command module N (*Space*) modulo di comando

commando [kə'mɑːndəu] N commando *m* inv; membro di un commando

commemorate [kə'mɛməreɪt] VT commemorare

commemoration [kəmɛmə'reɪʃən] N commemorazione *f*

commemorative [kə'mɛmərətɪv] ADJ commemorativo(-a)

commence [kə'mɛns] VT, VI cominciare

commencement (*US*) N (*Univ*) cerimonia di consegna dei diplomi

commend [kə'mɛnd] VT lodare; raccomandare

commendable [kə'mɛndəbl] ADJ lodevole

commendation [kɔmɛn'deɪʃən] N lode *f*; raccomandazione *f*; (*for bravery etc*) encomio

commensurate [kə'mɛnʃərɪt] ADJ: **~ with** proporzionato(-a) a

comment ['kɔmɛnt] N commento ▶ VI: **to ~ (on)** fare commenti (su); **to ~ that** osservare che; **"no ~"** "niente da dire"

commentary ['kɔməntərɪ] N commentario; (*Sport*) radiocronaca; telecronaca

commentator ['kɔmənteɪtər] N commentatore(-trice); (*Sport*) radiocronista *mf*; telecronista *mf*

commerce ['kɔmɜːs] N commercio

commercial [kə'mɜːʃəl] ADJ commerciale ▶ N (*TV, Radio*) pubblicità *f* inv

commercial bank N banca commerciale

commercial break N intervallo pubblicitario

commercial college N ≈ istituto commerciale

commercialism [kə'mɜːʃəlɪzəm] N affarismo

commercial television N televisione *f* commerciale

commercial traveller N commesso viaggiatore

commercial vehicle N veicolo commerciale

commiserate [kə'mɪzəreɪt] VI: **to ~ with** condolersi con

commission [kə'mɪʃən] N commissione *f*; (*for salesman*) commissione, provvigione *f* ▶ VT (*Mil*) nominare (al comando); (*work of art*) commissionare; **I get 10% ~** ricevo il 10% sulle vendite; **out of ~** (*Naut*) in disarmo; (*machine*) fuori uso; **to ~ sb to do sth** incaricare qn di fare qc; **to ~ sth from sb** (*painting etc*) commissionare qc a qn; **~ of inquiry** (*Brit*) commissione *f* d'inchiesta

commissionaire [kəmɪʃə'nɛər] N (*Brit: at shop, cinema etc*) portiere *m* in livrea

commissioner [kə'mɪʃənər] N commissionario; (*Police*) questore *m*

commit [kə'mɪt] VT (*act*) commettere; (*to sb's care*) affidare; **to ~ o.s. (to do)** impegnarsi (a fare); **to ~ suicide** suicidarsi; **to ~ sb for trial** rinviare qn a giudizio

commitment [kə'mɪtmənt] N impegno; promessa

committed [kə'mɪtɪd] ADJ (*writer*) impegnato(-a); (*Christian*) convinto(-a)

committee [kə'mɪtɪ] N comitato, commissione *f*; **to be on a ~** far parte di un comitato *or* di una commissione

committee meeting N riunione *f* di comitato *or* di commissione

commodity [kə'mɔdɪtɪ] N prodotto, articolo; (*food*) derrata

commodity exchange N borsa *f* merci inv

common ['kɔmən] ADJ comune; (*pej*) volgare; (*usual*) normale ▶ N terreno comune; **in ~** in comune; **in ~ use** di uso comune; **it's ~ knowledge that** è di dominio pubblico che; **to the ~ good** nell'interesse generale, per il bene comune; *see also* **Commons**

common cold N: **the ~** il raffreddore

common denominator N denominatore *m* comune

commoner ['kɔmənər] N cittadino(-a) (non nobile)

common ground N (*fig*) terreno comune

common land N terreno di uso pubblico

common law N diritto consuetudinario

common-law ['kɔmənlɔː] ADJ: **~ wife** convivente *f* more uxorio

commonly ['kɔmənlɪ] ADV comunemente, usualmente

Common Market N Mercato Comune

commonplace ['kɔmənpleɪs] ADJ banale, ordinario(-a)

common room ['kɔmənrum] N sala di riunione; (*Scol*) sala dei professori

Commons ['kɔmənz] NPL (*Brit Pol*): **the (House of) ~** la Camera dei Comuni

common sense N buon senso

Commonwealth ['kɔmənwɛlθ] N: **the ~** il Commonwealth; *vedi nota*

Il *Commonwealth* è un'associazione di stati sovrani indipendenti e di alcuni territori annessi che facevano parte dell'antico Impero Britannico. Ancora oggi molti stati del *Commonwealth* riconoscono simbolicamente il sovrano brittanico come capo di stato, e i loro rappresentanti si riuniscono per discutere questioni di comune interesse.

commotion [kə'məʊʃən] N confusione *f*, tumulto

communal ['kɔmjuːnl] ADJ (*life*) comunale; (*for common use*) pubblico(-a)

commune N ['kɔmjuːn] (*group*) comune *f* ▶ VI [kə'mjuːn]: **to ~ with** mettersi in comunione con

communicate [kə'mjuːnɪkeɪt] VT comunicare, trasmettere ▶ VI: **to ~ (with)** comunicare (con)

communication [kəmjuːnɪ'keɪʃən] N comunicazione *f*

communication cord N (*BRIT*) segnale *m* d'allarme

communications network N rete *f* delle comunicazioni

communications satellite N satellite *m* per telecomunicazioni

communicative [kə'mjuːnɪkətɪv] ADJ (*gen*) loquace

communion [kə'mjuːnɪən] N (*also:* **Holy Communion**) comunione *f*

communiqué [kə'mjuːnɪkeɪ] N comunicato

communism ['kɔmjunɪzəm] N comunismo

communist ['kɔmjunɪst] ADJ, N comunista (*mf*)

community [kə'mjuːnɪtɪ] N comunità *f inv*

community centre, (*US*) **community center** N circolo ricreativo

community chest N (*US*) fondo di beneficenza

community health centre N centro socio-sanitario

community home N (*BRIT*) riformatorio

community service N (*BRIT*) ≈ lavoro sostitutivo

community spirit N spirito civico

commutation ticket [kɔmjuː'teɪʃən-] N (*US*) biglietto di abbonamento

commute [kə'mjuːt] VI fare il pendolare ▶ VT (*Law*) commutare

commuter [kə'mjuːtə'] N pendolare *mf*

compact ADJ [kəm'pækt] compatto(-a) ▶ N ['kɔmpækt] (*also:* **powder compact**) portacipria *m inv*

compact disc N compact disc *m inv*

compact disc player N lettore *m* CD *inv*

companion [kəm'pænjən] N compagno(-a)

companionship [kəm'pænjənʃɪp] N compagnia

companionway [kəm'pænjənweɪ] N (*Naut*) scala

company ['kʌmpənɪ] N (*also Comm, Mil, Theat*) compagnia; **he's good** ~ è di buona compagnia; **we have** ~ abbiamo ospiti; **to keep sb** ~ tenere compagnia a qn; **to part ~ with** separarsi da; **Smith and C~** Smith e soci

company car N macchina (di proprietà) della ditta

company director N amministratore *m*, consigliere *m* di amministrazione

company secretary N (*BRIT Comm*) segretario(-a) generale

comparable ['kɔmpərəbl] ADJ simile; ~ **to** *or* **with** paragonabile a

comparative [kəm'pærətɪv] ADJ (*freedom, cost*) relativo(-a); (*adjective, adverb etc*) comparativo(-a); (*literature*) comparato(-a)

comparatively [kəm'pærətɪvlɪ] ADV relativamente

compare [kəm'pɛə'] VT: **to ~ sth/sb with/to** confrontare qc/qn con/a ▶ VI: **to ~ (with)** reggere il confronto (con); **compared with** *or* **to** a paragone di, rispetto a; **how do the prices ~?** che differenza di prezzo c'è?

comparison [kəm'pærɪsn] N confronto; **in ~ with** confronto a

compartment [kəm'pɑːtmənt] N compartimento; (*Rail*) scompartimento

compass ['kʌmpəs] N bussola; **(a pair of) compasses** (*Math*) compasso; **within the ~ of** entro i limiti di

compassion [kəm'pæʃən] N compassione *f*

compassionate [kəm'pæʃənɪt] ADJ compassionevole; **on ~ grounds** per motivi personali

compassionate leave N congedo straordinario (*per gravi motivi di famiglia*)

compatibility [kəmpætɪ'bɪlɪtɪ] N compatibilità

compatible [kəm'pætɪbl] ADJ compatibile

compel [kəm'pɛl] VT costringere, obbligare

compelling [kəm'pɛlɪŋ] ADJ (*fig: argument*) irresistibile

compendium [kəm'pɛndɪəm] N compendio

compensate ['kɔmpənseɪt] VT risarcire ▶ VI: **to ~ for** compensare

compensation [kɔmpən'seɪʃən] N compensazione *f*; (*money*) risarcimento

compère ['kɔmpɛə'] N presentatore(-trice)

compete [kəm'piːt] VI (*take part*) concorrere; (*vie*): **to ~ (with)** fare concorrenza (a)

competence ['kɔmpɪtəns] N competenza

competent ['kɔmpɪtənt] ADJ competente

competing [kəm'piːtɪŋ] ADJ (*theories, ideas*) opposto(-a); (*companies*) in concorrenza; **three ~ explanations (of)** tre spiegazioni contrastanti tra di loro (di)

competition [kɔmpɪˈtɪʃən] N gara; concorso; (*Sport*) gara; (*Econ*) concorrenza; **in ~ with** in concorrenza con

competitive [kəmˈpɛtɪtɪv] ADJ (*sports*) agonistico(-a); (*person*) che ha spirito di competizione; che ha spirito agonistico; (*Econ*) concorrenziale

competitive examination N concorso

competitor [kəmˈpɛtɪtəʳ] N concorrente *mf*

compile [kəmˈpaɪl] VT compilare

complacency [kəmˈpleɪsnsɪ] N compiacenza di sé

complacent [kəmˈpleɪsnt] ADJ compiaciuto(-a) di sé

complain [kəmˈpleɪn] VI lagnarsi, lamentarsi; **to ~ (about)** lagnarsi (di); (*in shop etc*) reclamare (per)
 ▶ **complain of** VT FUS (*Med*) accusare

complaint [kəmˈpleɪnt] N lamento; (*in shop etc*) reclamo; (*Med*) malattia

complement N [ˈkɒmplɪmənt] complemento; (*especially of ship's crew etc*) effettivo ▶ VT [ˈkɒmplɪmɛnt] (*enhance*) accompagnarsi bene a

complementary [kɒmplɪˈmɛntərɪ] ADJ complementare

complete [kəmˈpliːt] ADJ completo(-a) ▶ VT completare; (*form*) riempire; **it's a ~ disaster** è un vero disastro

completely [kəmˈpliːtlɪ] ADV completamente

completion [kəmˈpliːʃən] N completamento; **to be nearing ~** essere in fase di completamento; **on ~ of contract** alla firma del contratto

complex [ˈkɒmplɛks] ADJ complesso(-a) ▶ N (*Psych, buildings etc*) complesso

complexion [kəmˈplɛkʃən] N (*of face*) carnagione *f*; (*of event etc*) aspetto

complexity [kəmˈplɛksɪtɪ] N complessità *f inv*

compliance [kəmˈplaɪəns] N acquiescenza; **in ~ with** (*orders, wishes etc*) in conformità con

compliant [kəmˈplaɪənt] ADJ acquiescente, arrendevole

complicate [ˈkɒmplɪkeɪt] VT complicare

complicated [ˈkɒmplɪkeɪtɪd] ADJ complicato(-a)

complication [kɒmplɪˈkeɪʃən] N complicazione *f*

compliment N [ˈkɒmplɪmənt] complimento ▶ VT [ˈkɒmplɪmɛnt] fare un complimento a; **compliments** NPL complimenti *mpl*; rispetti *mpl*; **to pay sb a ~** fare un complimento a qn; **to ~ sb (on sth/on doing sth)** congratularsi *or* complimentarsi con qn (per qc/per aver fatto qc)

complimentary [kɒmplɪˈmɛntərɪ] ADJ complimentoso(-a), elogiativo(-a); (*free*) in omaggio

complimentary ticket N biglietto d'omaggio

compliments slip N cartoncino della società

comply [kəmˈplaɪ] VI: **to ~ with** assentire a; conformarsi a

component [kəmˈpəunənt] ADJ, N componente (*m*)

compose [kəmˈpəuz] VT (*music, poem etc*) comporre; **to ~ o.s.** ricomporsi; **composed of** composto(-a) di

composed [kəmˈpəuzd] ADJ calmo(-a)

composer [kəmˈpəuzəʳ] N (*Mus*) compositore(-trice)

composite [ˈkɒmpəzɪt] ADJ composito(-a); (*Math*) composto(-a)

composition [kɒmpəˈzɪʃən] N composizione *f*

compost [ˈkɒmpɒst] N composta, concime *m*

composure [kəmˈpəuʒəʳ] N calma

compound [ˈkɒmpaund] N (*Chem, Ling*) composto; (*enclosure*) recinto ▶ ADJ composto(-a) ▶ VT [kəmˈpaund] (*fig: problem, difficulty*) peggiorare

compound fracture N frattura esposta

compound interest N interesse *m* composto

comprehend [kɒmprɪˈhɛnd] VT comprendere, capire

comprehension [kɒmprɪˈhɛnʃən] N comprensione *f*

comprehensive [kɒmprɪˈhɛnsɪv] ADJ completo(-a) ▶ N (*BRIT: also:* **comprehensive school**) *scuola secondaria aperta a tutti*

comprehensive insurance policy N polizza multi-rischio *inv*

compress VT [kəmˈprɛs] comprimere ▶ N [ˈkɒmprɛs] (*Med*) compressa

compression [kəmˈprɛʃən] N compressione *f*

comprise [kəmˈpraɪz] VT (*also:* **be comprised of**) comprendere

compromise [ˈkɒmprəmaɪz] N compromesso ▶ VT compromettere ▶ VI venire a un compromesso ▶ CPD (*decision, solution*) di compromesso

compulsion [kəmˈpʌlʃən] N costrizione *f*; **under ~** sotto pressioni

compulsive [kəmˈpʌlsɪv] ADJ (*Psych*) incontrollabile; (*liar, gambler*) che non riesce a controllarsi; (*viewing, reading*) cui non si può fare a meno

compulsory [kəmˈpʌlsərɪ] ADJ obbligatorio(-a)

compulsory purchase N espropriazione *f*

compunction [kəmˈpʌŋkʃən] N scrupolo; **to have no ~ about doing sth** non farsi scrupoli a fare qc

computer [kəmˈpjuːtəʳ] N computer *m inv*, elaboratore *m* elettronico

computer game N gioco per computer

computer-generated ADJ realizzato(-a) al computer

computerization [kəmpju:təraɪ'zeɪʃən] N computerizzazione f

computerize [kəm'pju:təraɪz] VT computerizzare

computer language N linguaggio m macchina inv

computer literate ADJ: **to be ~** essere in grado di usare il computer

computer peripheral N unità periferica

computer program N programma m di computer

computer programmer N programmatore(-trice)

computer programming N programmazione f di computer

computer science N informatica

computer scientist N informatico(-a)

computer studies NPL informatica

computing [kəm'pju:tɪŋ] N informatica

comrade ['kɔmrɪd] N compagno(-a)

comradeship ['kɔmrɪdʃɪp] N cameratismo

Comsat® ['kɔmsæt] N ABBR = **communications satellite**

con [kɔn] VT (col) truffare ▶ N truffa; **to ~ sb into doing sth** indurre qn a fare qc con raggiri

concave ['kɔn'keɪv] ADJ concavo(-a)

conceal [kən'si:l] VT nascondere

concede [kən'si:d] VT concedere; (admit) ammettere ▶ VI cedere

conceit [kən'si:t] N presunzione f, vanità

conceited [kən'si:tɪd] ADJ presuntuoso(-a), vanitoso(-a)

conceivable [kən'si:vəbl] ADJ concepibile; **it is ~ that ...** può anche darsi che ...

conceivably [kən'si:vəblɪ] ADV: **he may ~ be right** può anche darsi che abbia ragione

conceive [kən'si:v] VT concepire ▶ VI concepire un bambino; **to ~ of sth/of doing sth** immaginare qc/di fare qc

concentrate ['kɔnsəntreɪt] VI concentrarsi ▶ VT concentrare

concentration [kɔnsən'treɪʃən] N concentrazione f

concentration camp N campo di concentramento

concentric [kɔn'sɛntrɪk] ADJ concentrico(-a)

concept ['kɔnsɛpt] N concetto

conception [kən'sɛpʃən] N concezione f; (idea) idea, concetto

concern [kən'sə:n] N affare m; (Comm) azienda, ditta; (anxiety) preoccupazione f ▶ VT riguardare; **to be concerned (about)** preoccuparsi (di); **to be concerned with** occuparsi di; **as far as I am concerned** per quanto mi riguarda; **"to whom it may ~"** "a tutti gli interessati"; **the department**

concerned (under discussion) l'ufficio in questione; (relevant) l'ufficio competente

concerning [kən'sə:nɪŋ] PREP riguardo a, circa

concert ['kɔnsət] N concerto; **in ~** di concerto

concerted [kən'sə:tɪd] ADJ concertato(-a)

concert hall N sala da concerti

concertina [kɔnsə'ti:nə] N piccola fisarmonica ▶ VI ridursi come una fisarmonica

concerto [kən'tʃə:təu] N concerto

concession [kən'sɛʃən] N concessione f

concessionaire [kənsɛʃə'nɛər] N concessionario

concessionary [kən'sɛʃənərɪ] ADJ (ticket, fare) a prezzo ridotto

conciliation [kənsɪlɪ'eɪʃən] N conciliazione f

conciliatory [kən'sɪlɪətrɪ] ADJ conciliativo(-a)

concise [kən'saɪs] ADJ conciso(-a)

conclave ['kɔnkleɪv] N riunione f segreta; (Rel) conclave m

conclude [kən'klu:d] VT concludere ▶ VI (speaker) concludere; (events): **to ~ (with)** concludersi (con)

concluding [kən'klu:dɪŋ] ADJ (remarks etc) conclusivo(-a), finale

conclusion [kən'klu:ʒən] N conclusione f; **to come to the ~ that ...** concludere che ..., arrivare alla conclusione che ...

conclusive [kən'klu:sɪv] ADJ conclusivo(-a)

concoct [kən'kɔkt] VT inventare

concoction [kən'kɔkʃən] N (food, drink) miscuglio

concord ['kɔnkɔ:d] N (harmony) armonia, concordia; (treaty) accordo

concourse ['kɔnkɔ:s] N (hall) atrio

concrete ['kɔnkri:t] N calcestruzzo ▶ ADJ concreto(-a); (Constr) di calcestruzzo

concrete mixer N betoniera

concur [kən'kə:r] VI concordare

concurrently [kən'kʌrntlɪ] ADV simultaneamente

concussion [kən'kʌʃən] N (Med) commozione f cerebrale

condemn [kən'dɛm] VT condannare; (building) dichiarare pericoloso(-a)

condemnation [kɔndɛm'neɪʃən] N condanna

condensation [kɔndɛn'seɪʃən] N condensazione f

condense [kən'dɛns] VI condensarsi ▶ VT condensare

condensed milk N latte m condensato

condescend [kɔndɪ'sɛnd] VI condiscendere; **to ~ to do sth** degnarsi di fare qc

condescending [kɔndɪ'sɛndɪŋ] ADJ condiscendente

condition [kən'dɪʃən] N condizione f; (disease)

C

malattia ▸ vᴛ condizionare, regolare; **in good/poor ~** in buone/cattive condizioni; **to have a heart ~** soffrire di (mal di) cuore; **weather conditions** condizioni meteorologiche; **on ~ that** a condizione che + *sub*, a condizione di

conditional [kən'dɪʃənl] ᴀᴅᴊ condizionale; **to be ~ upon** dipendere da

conditioner [kən'dɪʃənəʳ] ɴ (*for hair*) balsamo; (*for fabrics*) ammorbidente *m*

condo ['kɔndəu] ɴ ᴀʙʙʀ (*US col*) = **condominium**

condolences [kən'dəulənsɪz] ɴᴘʟ condoglianze *fpl*

condom ['kɔndəm] ɴ preservativo

condominium [kɔndə'mɪnɪəm] ɴ (*US*) condominio

condone [kən'dəun] vᴛ condonare

conducive [kən'dju:sɪv] ᴀᴅᴊ: **~ to** favorevole a

conduct ɴ ['kɔndʌkt] condotta ▸ vᴛ [kən'dʌkt] condurre; (*manage*) dirigere; amministrare; (*Mus*) dirigere; **to ~ o.s.** comportarsi

conducted tour [kən'dʌktɪd-] ɴ gita accompagnata

conductor [kən'dʌktəʳ] ɴ (*of orchestra*) direttore *m* d'orchestra; (*on bus*) bigliettaio; (*US Rail*) controllore *m*; (*Elec*) conduttore *m*

conductress [kən'dʌktrɪs] ɴ (*on bus*) bigliettaia

conduit ['kɔndɪt] ɴ condotto; tubo

cone [kəun] ɴ cono; (*Bot*) pigna; (*traffic cone*) birillo

confectioner [kən'fɛkʃənəʳ] ɴ: **~'s (shop)** = pasticceria

confectionery [kən'fɛkʃənərɪ] ɴ dolciumi *mpl*

confederate [kən'fɛdərɪt] ᴀᴅᴊ confederato(-a) ▸ ɴ (*pej*) complice *mf*; (*US Hist*) confederato

confederation [kənfɛdə'reɪʃən] ɴ confederazione *f*

confer [kən'fəːʳ] vᴛ: **to ~ sth on** conferire qc a ▸ vɪ conferire; **to ~ (with sb about sth)** consultarsi (con qn su qc)

conference ['kɔnfərns] ɴ congresso; **to be in ~** essere in riunione

conference room ɴ sala *f* conferenze *inv*

confess [kən'fɛs] vᴛ confessare, ammettere ▸ vɪ confessarsi

confession [kən'fɛʃən] ɴ confessione *f*

confessional [kən'fɛʃənl] ɴ confessionale *m*

confessor [kən'fɛsəʳ] ɴ confessore *m*

confetti [kən'fɛtɪ] ɴ coriandoli *mpl*

confide [kən'faɪd] vɪ: **to ~ in** confidarsi con

confidence ['kɔnfɪdns] ɴ confidenza; (*trust*) fiducia; (*also:* **self-confidence**) sicurezza di sé; **in ~** (*speak, write*) in confidenza, confidenzialmente; **to tell sb sth in strict ~** dire qc a qn in via strettamente confidenziale; **to have (every) ~ that ...** essere assolutamente certo(-a) che ...; **motion of no ~** mozione *f* di sfiducia

confidence trick ɴ truffa

confident ['kɔnfɪdənt] ᴀᴅᴊ sicuro(-a); (*also:* **self-confident**) sicuro(-a) di sé

confidential [kɔnfɪ'dɛnʃəl] ᴀᴅᴊ riservato(-a), confidenziale; (*secretary*) particolare

confidentiality ['kɔnfɪdɛnʃɪ'ælɪtɪ] ɴ riservatezza, carattere *m* confidenziale

configuration [kən'fɪgju'reɪʃən] ɴ (*Comput*) configurazione *f*

confine [kən'faɪn] vᴛ limitare; (*shut up*) rinchiudere; **to ~ o.s. to doing sth** limitarsi a fare qc; *see also* **confines**

confined [kən'faɪnd] ᴀᴅᴊ (*space*) ristretto(-a)

confinement [kən'faɪnmənt] ɴ prigionia; (*Mil*) consegna; (*Med*) parto

confines ['kɔnfaɪnz] ɴᴘʟ confini *mpl*

confirm [kən'fəːm] vᴛ confermare; (*Rel*) cresimare

confirmation [kɔnfə'meɪʃən] ɴ conferma; (*Rel*) cresima

confirmed [kən'fəːmd] ᴀᴅᴊ inveterato(-a)

confiscate ['kɔnfɪskeɪt] vᴛ confiscare

confiscation [kɔnfɪs'keɪʃən] ɴ confisca

conflagration [kɔnflə'greɪʃən] ɴ conflagrazione *f*

conflict ɴ ['kɔnflɪkt] conflitto ▸ vɪ [kən'flɪkt] essere in conflitto

conflicting [kən'flɪktɪŋ] ᴀᴅᴊ contrastante; (*reports, evidence, opinions*) contraddittorio(-a)

conform [kən'fɔːm] vɪ: **to ~ (to)** conformarsi (a)

conformist [kən'fɔːmɪst] ɴ conformista *mf*

confound [kən'faund] vᴛ confondere; (*amaze*) sconcertare

confounded [kən'faundɪd] ᴀᴅᴊ maledetto(-a)

confront [kən'frʌnt] vᴛ confrontare; (*enemy, danger*) affrontare

confrontation [kɔnfrən'teɪʃən] ɴ scontro

confrontational [kɔnfrən'teɪʃənəl] ᴀᴅᴊ polemico(-a), aggressivo(-a)

confuse [kən'fju:z] vᴛ imbrogliare; (*one thing with another*) confondere

confused [kən'fju:zd] ᴀᴅᴊ confuso(-a); **to get ~** confondersi

confusing [kən'fju:zɪŋ] ᴀᴅᴊ che fa confondere

confusion [kən'fju:ʒən] ɴ confusione *f*

congeal [kən'dʒi:l] vɪ (*blood*) congelarsi

congenial [kən'dʒi:nɪəl] ᴀᴅᴊ (*person*) simpatico(-a); (*place, work, company*) piacevole

congenital [kən'dʒɛnɪtl] ᴀᴅᴊ congenito(-a)

conger eel ['kɔŋgər-] ɴ grongo

congested [kən'dʒɛstɪd] ᴀᴅᴊ congestionato(-a); (*telephone lines*) sovraccarico(-a)

quence ['kɔnsɪkwəns] N conseguenza,
tato; importanza; **in ~** di conseguenza

quently ['kɔnsɪkwəntlɪ] ADV di
eguenza, dunque

rvation [kɔnsə'veɪʃən] N
ervazione f; (also: **nature conservation**)
la dell'ambiente; **energy ~** risparmio
getico

rvationist [kɔnsə'veɪʃnɪst] N
ɔre(-trice) della tutela dell'ambiente

rvative [kən'sə:vətɪv] ADJ, N
ervatore(-trice); (cautious) cauto(-a); **C~**
(BRIT Pol) conservatore(-trice); **the C~**
ty il partito conservatore

rvatory [kən'sə:vətrɪ] N (greenhouse)
a; (Mus) conservatorio

rve [kən'sə:v] VT conservare ▶ N
serva

ider [kən'sɪdəʳ] VT considerare; (take into
unt) tener conto di; **to ~ doing sth**
siderare la possibilità di fare qc; **all**
ngs considered tutto sommato or
siderato; **~ yourself lucky** puoi dirti
unato

iderable [kən'sɪdərəbl] ADJ
siderevole, notevole

iderably [kən'sɪdərəblɪ] ADV
evolmente, decisamente

iderate [kən'sɪdərɪt] ADJ premuroso(-a)

ideration [kənsɪdə'reɪʃən] N
siderazione f; (reward) rimunerazione f;
of ~ for per riguardo a; **under ~** in
me; **my first ~ is my family** il mio primo
siero è per la mia famiglia

idered [kən'sɪdəd] ADJ: **it is my ~**
nion that ... dopo lunga riflessione il
o parere è che ...

idering [kən'sɪdərɪŋ] PREP in
siderazione di; **~ (that)** se si considera
e)

ign [kən'saɪn] VT consegnare; (send:
ds) spedire

ignee [kɔnsaɪ'ni:] N consegnatario(-a),
tinatario(-a)

ignment [kən'saɪnmənt] N (of goods)
segna; spedizione f

ignment note N (Comm) nota di
dizione

ignor [kən'saɪnəʳ] N mittente mf

ist [kən'sɪst] VI: **to ~ of** constare di,
re composto(-a) di

istency [kən'sɪstənsɪ] N consistenza;
coerenza

istent [kən'sɪstənt] ADJ coerente;
tant) costante; **~ with** compatibile con

olation [kɔnsə'leɪʃən] N consolazione f

ole VT [kən'səul] consolare ▶ N
səul] quadro di comando

lidate [kən'sɔlɪdeɪt] VT consolidare

consols ['kɔnsɔlz] NPL (Stock Exchange) titoli
mpl del debito consolidato

consommé [kən'sɔmeɪ] N consommé m inv,
brodo ristretto

consonant ['kɔnsənənt] N consonante f

consort ['kɔnsɔ:t] N consorte mf; **prince ~**
principe m consorte ▶ VI [kən'sɔ:t] (often pej):
to ~ with sb frequentare qn

consortium [kən'sɔ:tɪəm] N consorzio

conspicuous [kən'spɪkjuəs] ADJ cospicuo(-a);
to make o.s. ~ farsi notare

conspiracy [kən'spɪrəsɪ] N congiura,
cospirazione f

conspiratorial [kənspɪrə'tɔ:rɪəl] ADJ
cospiratorio(-a)

conspire [kən'spaɪəʳ] VI congiurare,
cospirare

constable ['kʌnstəbl] N (BRIT: also: **police**
constable) ≈ poliziotto, agente m di polizia;
chief ~ ≈ questore m

constabulary [kən'stæbjulərɪ] N forze fpl
dell'ordine

constant ['kɔnstənt] ADJ costante;
continuo(-a)

constantly ['kɔnstəntlɪ] ADV costantemente;
continuamente

constellation [kɔnstə'leɪʃən] N
costellazione f

consternation [kɔnstə'neɪʃən] N
costernazione f

constipated ['kɔnstɪpeɪtɪd] ADJ stitico(-a)

constipation [kɔnstɪ'peɪʃən] N stitichezza

constituency [kən'stɪtjuənsɪ] N collegio
elettorale; (people) elettori mpl (del collegio);
vedi nota

> Con il termine constituency viene indicato
> sia un collegio elettorale che i suoi
> elettori. In Gran Bretagna ogni collegio
> elegge un rappresentante che in seguito
> incontra regolarmente i propri elettori in
> riunioni chiamate surgeries per discutere
> questioni di interesse locale.

constituency party N sezione f locale (del
partito)

constituent [kən'stɪtjuənt] N
elettore(-trice); (part) elemento componente

constitute ['kɔnstɪtju:t] VT costituire

constitution [kɔnstɪ'tju:ʃən] N costituzione f

constitutional [kɔnstɪ'tju:ʃənl] ADJ
costituzionale

constitutional monarchy N monarchia
costituzionale

constrain [kən'streɪn] VT costringere

constrained [kən'streɪnd] ADJ costretto(-a)

constraint [kən'streɪnt] N (restraint)
limitazione f, costrizione f; (embarrassment)
imbarazzo, soggezione f

constrict [kən'strɪkt] VT comprimere;
opprimere

congestion [kən'dʒɛstʃən] N congestione f

congestion charge N pedaggio da pagare per poter circolare in automobile nel centro di alcune città, introdotto per la prima volta a Londra nel 2002

conglomerate [kən'glɔmərɪt] N (Comm) conglomerato

conglomeration [kənglɔmə'reɪʃən] N conglomerazione f

Congo ['kɔŋgəu] N Congo

congratulate [kən'grætjuleɪt] VT: **to ~ sb (on)** congratularsi con qn (per or di)

congratulations [kəngrætju'leɪʃənz] NPL auguri mpl; (on success) complimenti mpl; **~ (on)** congratulazioni fpl (per) ▶ EXCL congratulazioni!, rallegramenti!

congregate ['kɔŋgrɪgeɪt] VI congregarsi, riunirsi

congregation [kɔŋgrɪ'geɪʃən] N congregazione f

congress ['kɔŋgrɛs] N congresso; (US Pol): **C~** il Congresso; vedi nota

> Il Congress è l'assemblea statunitense che si riunisce a Washington D.C. nel Capitol per elaborare e discutere le leggi federali. é costituita dalla House of Representatives (435 membri, eletti nei vari stati in base al numero degli abitanti) e dal Senate (100 senatori, due per ogni stato). Sia i membri della House of Representatives che quelli del Senate sono eletti direttamente dal popolo.

congressman ['kɔŋgrɛsmən] N (irreg) (US) membro del Congresso

congresswoman ['kɔŋgrɛswumən] N (irreg) (US) (donna) membro del Congresso

conical ['kɔnɪkl] ADJ conico(-a)

conifer ['kɔnɪfə'] N conifero

coniferous [kə'nɪfərəs] ADJ (forest) di conifere

conjecture [kən'dʒɛktʃə'] N congettura ▶ VT, VI congetturare

conjoined twin [kən'dʒɔɪnd-] N fratello (or sorella) siamese

conjugal ['kɔndʒugl] ADJ coniugale

conjugate ['kɔndʒugeɪt] VT coniugare

conjugation [kɔndʒə'geɪʃən] N coniugazione f

conjunction [kən'dʒʌŋkʃən] N congiunzione f; **in ~ with** in accordo con, insieme con

conjunctivitis [kəndʒʌŋktɪ'vaɪtɪs] N congiuntivite f

conjure ['kʌndʒə'] VI fare giochi di prestigio ▶ **conjure up** VT (ghost, spirit) evocare; (memories) rievocare

conjurer ['kʌndʒərə'] N prestigiatore(-trice), prestidigitatore(-trice)

conjuring trick ['kʌndʒərɪŋ-] N gioco di prestigio

conker ['kɔŋkə'] N (BRIT col) castagna (d'ippocastano)

conk out [kɔŋk-] VI (col) andare

conman ['kɔnmæn] N (irreg) tru

Conn. ABBR (US) = **Connecticut**

connect [kə'nɛkt] VT connettere (Elec) collegare; (fig) associare ▶ **with** essere in coincidenza con; **connected with** (associated) ave con; essere imparentato(-a) con **trying to ~ you** (Tel) sto cercando linea

connecting flight N volo in coin

connection [kə'nɛkʃən] N relazi rapporto; (Elec) connessione f; (collegamento; (train, plane etc) co **in ~ with** con riferimento a, a p **what is the ~ between them?** i sono legati?; **business connect** rapporti d'affari; **to miss/get o** etc) perdere/prendere la coincid

connexion [kə'nɛkʃən] N (BRIT) =

conning tower ['kɔnɪŋ-] N torre comando

connive [kə'naɪv] VI: **to ~ at** esse connivente in

connoisseur [kɔnɪ'sə:'] N conos

connotation [kɔnə'teɪʃən] N cor

connubial [kə'nju:bɪəl] ADJ coni

conquer ['kɔŋkə'] VT conquistar vincere

conqueror ['kɔŋkərə'] N conqui

conquest ['kɔŋkwɛst] N conqui

cons [kɔnz] NPL see **pro**; **conveni**

conscience ['kɔnʃəns] N coscie onestamente, in coscienza

conscientious [kɔnʃɪ'ɛnʃəs] AD coscienzioso(-a)

conscientious objector N obi coscienza

conscious ['kɔnʃəs] ADJ consaj cosciente; (deliberate: insult, err intenzionale, voluto(-a); **to b sth/that** rendersi conto di qc

consciousness ['kɔnʃəsnɪs] consapevolezza; (Med) coscie **regain ~** perdere/riprendere

conscript ['kɔnskrɪpt] N cosc

conscription [kən'skrɪpʃən]

consecrate ['kɔnsɪkreɪt] VT

consecutive [kən'sɛkjutɪv] consecutivo(-a); **on 3 ~ occ** fila

consensus [kən'sɛnsəs] N c **opinion** l'opinione f unan

consent [kən'sɛnt] N conse acconsentire (a); **age of ~** avere rapporti sessuali); **b** comune accordo

consenting adults [kən's mpl consenzienti

construct [kən'strʌkt] VT costruire

construction [kən'strʌkʃən] N costruzione f; (fig: interpretation) interpretazione f; **under ~** in costruzione

construction industry N edilizia, industria edile

constructive [kən'strʌktɪv] ADJ costruttivo(-a)

construe [kən'stru:] VT interpretare

consul ['kɔnsl] N console m

consulate ['kɔnsjulɪt] N consolato

consult [kən'sʌlt] VT: **to ~ sb (about sth)** consultare qn (su or riguardo a qc)

consultancy [kən'sʌltənsɪ] N consulenza

consultancy fee N onorario di consulenza

consultant [kən'sʌltənt] N (Med) consulente m medico; (other specialist) consulente ▶ CPD: **~ engineer** n ingegnere m consulente; **~ paediatrician** n specialista mf in pediatria; **legal/management ~** consulente legale/gestionale

consultation [kɔnsəl'teɪʃən] N (discussion) consultazione f; (Med, Law) consulto; **in ~ with** consultandosi con

consultative [kən'sʌltətɪv] ADJ di consulenza

consulting room [kən'sʌltɪŋ-] N (Brit) ambulatorio

consume [kən'sju:m] VT consumare

consumer [kən'sju:mə[r]] N consumatore(-trice); (of electricity, gas etc) utente mf

consumer credit N credito al consumatore

consumer durables NPL prodotti mpl di consumo durevole

consumer goods NPL beni mpl di consumo

consumerism [kən'sju:mərɪzəm] N (consumer protection) tutela del consumatore; (Econ) consumismo

consumer society N società dei consumi

consumer watchdog N comitato di difesa dei consumatori

consummate ['kɔnsʌmeɪt] VT consumare

consumption [kən'sʌmpʃən] N consumo; (Med) consunzione f; **not fit for human ~** non commestibile

cont. ABBR (= continued) segue

contact ['kɔntækt] N contatto; (person) conoscenza ▶ VT mettersi in contatto con; **to be in ~ with sb/sth** essere in contatto con qn/qc; **business contacts** contatti mpl d'affari

contact lenses NPL lenti fpl a contatto

contagious [kən'teɪdʒəs] ADJ (also fig) contagioso(-a)

contain [kən'teɪn] VT contenere; **to ~ o.s.** contenersi

container [kən'teɪnə[r]] N recipiente m; (for shipping etc) container m inv

containerize [kən'teɪnəraɪz] VT mettere in container

container ship N nave f container inv

contaminate [kən'tæmɪneɪt] VT contaminare

contamination [kəntæmɪ'neɪʃən] N contaminazione f

cont'd ABBR (= continued) segue

contemplate ['kɔntəmpleɪt] VT contemplare; (consider) pensare a (or di)

contemplation [kɔntəm'pleɪʃən] N contemplazione f

contemporary [kən'tempərərɪ] ADJ contemporaneo(-a); (design) moderno(-a) ▶ N contemporaneo(-a); (of the same age) coetaneo(-a)

contempt [kən'tempt] N disprezzo; **~ of court** (Law) oltraggio alla Corte

contemptible [kən'temptəbl] ADJ spregevole, vergognoso(-a)

contemptuous [kən'temptjuəs] ADJ sdegnoso(-a)

contend [kən'tend] VT: **to ~ that** sostenere che ▶ VI: **to ~ with** lottare contro; **he has a lot to ~ with** ha un sacco di guai

contender [kən'tendə[r]] N contendente mf; concorrente mf

content[1] ['kɔntent] N contenuto; **contents** NPL (of box, case etc) contenuto; (of barrel etc: capacity) capacità f inv; **(table of) contents** indice m

content[2] [kən'tent] ADJ contento(-a), soddisfatto(-a) ▶ VT contentare, soddisfare; **to be ~ with** essere contento di; **to ~ o.s. with sth/with doing sth** accontentarsi di qc/di fare qc

contented [kən'tentɪd] ADJ contento(-a), soddisfatto(-a)

contentedly [kən'tentɪdlɪ] ADV con soddisfazione

contention [kən'tenʃən] N contesa; (assertion) tesi f inv; **bone of ~** pomo della discordia

contentious [kən'tenʃəs] ADJ polemico(-a)

contentment [kən'tentmənt] N contentezza

contest N ['kɔntest] lotta; (competition) gara, concorso ▶ VT [kən'test] contestare; (Law) impugnare; (compete for) contendersi

contestant [kən'testənt] N concorrente mf; (in fight) avversario(-a)

context ['kɔntekst] N contesto; **in/out of ~** nel/fuori dal contesto

continent ['kɔntɪnənt] N continente m; **the C~** (Brit) l'Europa continentale; **on the C~** in Europa

continental [kɔntɪ'nentl] ADJ continentale ▶ N (Brit) abitante mf dell'Europa continentale

continental breakfast N colazione f all'europea (*senza piatti caldi*)
continental quilt N (BRIT) piumino
contingency [kən'tɪndʒənsɪ] N eventualità f inv
contingency plan N misura d'emergenza
contingent [kən'tɪndʒənt] N contingenza ▶ADJ: **to be ~ upon** dipendere da
continual [kən'tɪnjuəl] ADJ continuo(-a)
continually [kən'tɪnjuəlɪ] ADV di continuo
continuation [kəntɪnju'eɪʃən] N continuazione f; (*after interruption*) ripresa; (*of story*) seguito
continue [kən'tɪnjuː] VI continuare ▶VT continuare; (*start again*) riprendere; **to be continued** (*story*) continua; **continued on page 10** segue *or* continua a pagina 10
continuing education [kən'tɪnjuɪŋ-] N corsi mpl per adulti
continuity [kɒntɪ'njuːɪtɪ] N continuità; (*Cine*) (ordine m della) sceneggiatura
continuity girl N (*Cine*) segretaria di edizione
continuous [kən'tɪnjuəs] ADJ continuo(-a), ininterrotto(-a); **~ performance** (*Cine*) spettacolo continuato; **~ stationery** (*Comput*) carta a moduli continui
continuous assessment N (BRIT) valutazione f continua
continuously [kən'tɪnjuəslɪ] ADV (*repeatedly*) continuamente; (*uninterruptedly*) ininterrottamente
contort [kən'tɔːt] VT contorcere
contortion [kən'tɔːʃən] N contorcimento; (*of acrobat*) contorsione f
contortionist [kən'tɔːʃənɪst] N contorsionista mf
contour ['kɒntuər] N contorno, profilo; (*also*: **contour line**) curva di livello
contraband ['kɒntrəbænd] N contrabbando ▶ADJ di contrabbando
contraception [kɒntrə'sɛpʃən] N contraccezione f
contraceptive [kɒntrə'sɛptɪv] ADJ contraccettivo(-a) ▶N contraccettivo
contract N ['kɒntrækt] contratto ▶CPD ['kɒntrækt] (*price, date*) del contratto; (*work*) a contratto ▶VI [kən'trækt] (*become smaller*) contrarsi; (*Comm*): **to ~ to do sth** fare un contratto per fare qc ▶VT [kən'trækt] (*illness*) contrarre; **to be under ~ to do sth** aver stipulato un contratto per fare qc; **~ of employment** contratto di lavoro ▶**contract in** VI impegnarsi (con un contratto); (*BRIT Admin*) scegliere di pagare i contributi per una pensione ▶**contract out** VI: **to ~ out (of)** ritirarsi (da); (*BRIT Admin*) (*scegliere di*) non pagare i contributi per una pensione
contraction [kən'trækʃən] N contrazione f

contractor [kən'træktər] N imprenditore m
contractual [kən'træktjuəl] ADJ contrattuale
contradict [kɒntrə'dɪkt] VT contraddire
contradiction [kɒntrə'dɪkʃən] N contraddizione f; **to be in ~ with** discordare con
contradictory [kɒntrə'dɪktərɪ] ADJ contraddittorio(-a)
contralto [kən'træltəu] N contralto
contraption [kən'træpʃən] N (*pej*) aggeggio
contrary¹ ['kɒntrərɪ] ADJ contrario(-a); (*unfavourable*) avverso(-a), contrario(-a) ▶N contrario; **on the ~** al contrario; **unless you hear to the ~** salvo contrordine; **~ to what we thought** a differenza di *or* contrariamente a quanto pensavamo
contrary² [kən'trɛərɪ] ADJ (*perverse*) bisbetico(-a)
contrast N ['kɒntrɑːst] contrasto ▶VT [kən'trɑːst] mettere in contrasto; **in ~ to** *or* **with** a differenza di, contrariamente a
contrasting [kən'trɑːstɪŋ] ADJ contrastante, di contrasto
contravene [kɒntrə'viːn] VT contravvenire
contravention [kɒntrə'vɛnʃən] N: **~ (of)** contravvenzione f (a), infrazione f (di)
contribute [kən'trɪbjuːt] VI contribuire ▶VT: **to ~ £10/an article to** dare 10 sterline/un articolo a; **to ~ to** contribuire a; (*newspaper*) scrivere per; (*discussion*) partecipare a
contribution [kɒntrɪ'bjuːʃən] N contributo
contributor [kən'trɪbjutər] N (*to newspaper*) collaboratore(-trice)
contributory [kən'trɪbjutərɪ] ADJ (*cause*) che contribuisce; **it was a ~ factor in ...** quello ha contribuito a ...
contributory pension scheme N (BRIT) sistema di pensionamento finanziato congiuntamente dai contributi del lavoratore e del datore di lavoro
contrite ['kɒntraɪt] ADJ contrito(-a)
contrivance [kən'traɪvəns] N congegno; espediente m
contrive [kən'traɪv] VT inventare; escogitare ▶VI: **to ~ to do** fare in modo di fare
control [kən'trəul] VT dominare; (*firm, operation etc*) dirigere; (*check*) controllare; (*disease, fire*) arginare, limitare ▶N controllo; **controls** NPL (*of vehicle etc*) comandi mpl; **to take ~ of** assumere il controllo di; **to be in ~ of** avere il controllo di; essere responsabile di; controllare; **to ~ o.s.** controllarsi; **everything is under ~** tutto è sotto controllo; **to go out of ~** (*car*) non rispondere ai comandi; (*situation*) sfuggire di mano; **circumstances beyond our ~** circostanze fpl che non dipendono da noi
control key N (*Comput*) tasto di controllo

controlled substance [kən'trəuld-] N sostanza stupefacente

controller [kən'trəulə^r] N controllore m

controlling interest [kən'trəulɪŋ-] N (Comm) maggioranza delle azioni

control panel N (on aircraft, ship, TV etc) quadro dei comandi

control point N punto di controllo

control room N (Naut, Mil) sala di comando; (Radio, TV) sala di regia

control tower N (Aviat) torre f di controllo

control unit N (Comput) unità f inv di controllo

controversial [kɔntrə'və:ʃl] ADJ controverso(-a), polemico(-a)

controversy ['kɔntrəvə:sɪ] N controversia, polemica

conurbation [kɔnə:'beɪʃən] N conurbazione f

convalesce [kɔnvə'lɛs] VI rimettersi in salute

convalescence [kɔnvə'lɛsns] N convalescenza

convalescent [kɔnvə'lɛsnt] ADJ, N convalescente (mf)

convector [kən'vɛktə^r] N convettore m

convene [kən'vi:n] VT convocare; (meeting) organizzare ▶ VI convenire, adunarsi

convenience [kən'vi:nɪəns] N comodità f inv; **at your ~** a suo comodo; **at your earliest ~** (Comm) appena possibile; **all modern conveniences**, (BRIT) **all mod cons** tutte le comodità moderne

convenience foods NPL cibi mpl precotti

convenient [kən'vi:nɪənt] ADJ comodo(-a); **if it is ~ to you** se per lei va bene, se non la incomoda

conveniently [kən'vi:nɪəntlɪ] ADV (happen) a proposito; (situated) in un posto comodo

convent ['kɔnvənt] N convento

convention [kən'vɛnʃən] N convenzione f; (meeting) convegno

conventional [kən'vɛnʃənl] ADJ convenzionale

convent school N scuola retta da suore

converge [kən'və:dʒ] VI convergere

conversant [kən'və:snt] ADJ: **to be ~ with** essere al corrente di; essere pratico(-a) di

conversation [kɔnvə'seɪʃən] N conversazione f

conversational [kɔnvə'seɪʃənl] ADJ non formale; (Comput) conversazionale; **~ Italian** l'italiano parlato

conversationalist [kɔnvə'seɪʃnəlɪst] N conversatore(-trice)

converse N ['kɔnvə:s] contrario, opposto ▶ VI [kən'və:s]: **to ~ (with sb about sth)** conversare (con qn su qc)

conversely [kɔn'və:slɪ] ADV al contrario, per contro

conversion [kən'və:ʃən] N conversione f; (BRIT: of house) trasformazione f, rimodernamento

conversion table N tavola di equivalenze

convert VT [kən'və:t] (Rel, Comm) convertire; (alter) trasformare ▶ N ['kɔnvə:t] convertito(-a)

convertible [kən'və:təbl] N macchina decappottabile

convex ['kɔnvɛks] ADJ convesso(-a)

convey [kən'veɪ] VT trasportare; (thanks) comunicare; (idea) dare

conveyance [kən'veɪəns] N (of goods) trasporto; (vehicle) mezzo di trasporto

conveyancing [kən'veɪənsɪŋ] N (Law) redazione f di transazioni di proprietà

conveyor belt [kən'veɪə^r-] N nastro trasportatore

convict VT [kən'vɪkt] dichiarare colpevole ▶ N ['kɔnvɪkt] carcerato(-a)

conviction [kən'vɪkʃən] N condanna; (belief) convinzione f

convince [kən'vɪns] VT: **to ~ sb (of sth/that)** convincere qn (di qc/che), persuadere qn (di qc/che)

convinced ADJ: **~ of/that** convinto(-a) di/che

convincing [kən'vɪnsɪŋ] ADJ convincente

convincingly [kən'vɪnsɪŋlɪ] ADV in modo convincente

convivial [kən'vɪvɪəl] ADJ allegro(-a)

convoluted ['kɔnvəlu:tɪd] ADJ (shape) attorcigliato(-a), avvolto(-a); (argument) involuto(-a)

convoy ['kɔnvɔɪ] N convoglio

convulse [kən'vʌls] VT sconvolgere; **to be convulsed with laughter** contorcersi dalle risa

convulsion [kən'vʌlʃən] N convulsione f

COO N ABBR = **chief operating officer**

coo [ku:] VI tubare

cook [kuk] VT cucinare, cuocere; (meal) preparare ▶ VI cuocere; (person) cucinare ▶ N cuoco(-a)
▶ **cook up** VT (col: excuse, story) improvvisare, inventare

cookbook ['kukbuk] N = **cookery book**

cooker ['kukə^r] N fornello, cucina

cookery N cucina

cookery book N (BRIT) libro di cucina

cookie ['kukɪ] N (US) biscotto; (Comput) cookie m inv

cooking ['kukɪŋ] N cucina ▶ CPD (apples, chocolate) da cuocere; (utensils, salt, foil) da cucina

cookout ['kukaut] N (US) pranzo (cucinato) all'aperto

cool [ku:l] ADJ fresco(-a); (not afraid) calmo(-a); (unfriendly) freddo(-a); (impertinent) sfacciato(-a) ▶ VT raffreddare; (room)

rinfrescare ▸ VI (water) raffreddarsi; (air) rinfrescarsi; **it's ~** (weather) fa fresco; **to keep sth ~** or **in a ~ place** tenere qc in fresco
▸ **cool down** VI raffreddarsi; (fig: person, situation) calmarsi
▸ **cool off** VI (become calmer) calmarsi; (lose enthusiasm) perdere interesse
coolant ['ku:lənt] N (liquido) refrigerante m
cool box, (US) **cooler** ['ku:lə'] N borsa termica
cooling ['ku:lɪŋ] ADJ (breeze) fresco(-a)
cooling tower N torre f di raffreddamento
coolly ['ku:lɪ] ADV (calmly) con calma, tranquillamente; (audaciously) come se niente fosse; (unenthusiastically) freddamente
coolness ['ku:lnɪs] N freschezza; sangue m freddo, calma
coop [ku:p] N stia ▸ VT: **to ~ up** (fig) rinchiudere
co-op ['kəuɔp] N ABBR (= cooperative (society)) coop f
cooperate [kəu'ɔpəreɪt] VI cooperare, collaborare
cooperation [kəuɔpə'reɪʃən] N cooperazione f, collaborazione f
cooperative [kəu'ɔpərətɪv] ADJ cooperativo(-a) ▸ N cooperativa
coopt [kəu'ɔpt] VT: **to ~ sb into sth** cooptare qn per qc
coordinate VT [kəu'ɔ:dɪneɪt] coordinare ▸ N [kəu'ɔ:dɪnət] (Math) coordinata; **coordinates** NPL (clothes) coordinati mpl
coordination [kəuɔ:dɪ'neɪʃən] N coordinazione f
coot [ku:t] N folaga
co-ownership [kəu'əunəʃɪp] N comproprietà
cop [kɔp] N (col) sbirro
cope [kəup] VI farcela; **to ~ with** (problems) far fronte a
Copenhagen [kəupən'heɪgən] N Copenhagen f
copier ['kɔpɪə'] N (also: **photocopier**) (foto)copiatrice f
co-pilot ['kəupaɪlət] N secondo pilota m
copious ['kəupɪəs] ADJ copioso(-a), abbondante
copper ['kɔpə'] N rame m; (col: policeman) sbirro; **coppers** NPL spiccioli mpl
coppice ['kɔpɪs], **copse** [kɔps] N bosco ceduo
copulate ['kɔpjuleɪt] VI accoppiarsi
copy ['kɔpɪ] N copia; (book etc) esemplare m; (material: for printing) materiale m, testo ▸ VT (gen, Comput) copiare; (imitate) imitare; **rough/fair ~** brutta/bella (copia); **to make good ~** (fig) fare notizia
▸ **copy out** VT ricopiare, trascrivere
copycat ['kɔpɪkæt] N (pej) copione m
copyright ['kɔpɪraɪt] N diritto d'autore; **~ reserved** tutti i diritti riservati

copy typist N dattilografo(-a)
copywriter ['kɔpɪraɪtə'] N redattore m pubblicitario
coral ['kɔrəl] N corallo
coral reef N barriera corallina
Coral Sea N: **the ~** il mar dei Coralli
cord [kɔ:d] N corda; (Elec) filo; (fabric) velluto a coste; **cords** NPL (trousers) calzoni mpl (di velluto) a coste
cordial ['kɔ:dɪəl] ADJ, N cordiale (m)
cordless ['kɔ:dlɪs] ADJ senza cavo
cordon ['kɔ:dn] N cordone m
▸ **cordon off** VT fare cordone intorno a
corduroy ['kɔ:dərɔɪ] N fustagno
CORE [kɔ:'] N ABBR (US) = **Congress of Racial Equality**
core [kɔ:'] N (of fruit) torsolo; (Tech) centro; (of earth, nuclear reactor) nucleo; (of organization etc) cuore m; (of problem etc) cuore m, nocciolo ▸ VT estrarre il torsolo da; **rotten to the ~** marcio fino al midollo
Corfu [kɔ:'fu:] N Corfù f
coriander [kɔrɪ'ændə'] N coriandolo
cork [kɔ:k] N sughero; (of bottle) tappo
corkage ['kɔ:kɪdʒ] N somma da pagare se il cliente porta il proprio vino
corked [kɔ:kt], (US) **corky** ['kɔ:kɪ] ADJ (wine) che sa di tappo
corkscrew ['kɔ:kskru:] N cavatappi m inv
cormorant ['kɔ:mərnt] N cormorano
corn [kɔ:n] N (Brit: wheat) grano; (US: maize) granturco; (on foot) callo; **~ on the cob** (Culin) pannocchia cotta
cornea ['kɔ:nɪə] N cornea
corned beef ['kɔ:nd-] N carne f di manzo in scatola
corner ['kɔ:nə'] N angolo; (Aut) curva; (Football: also: **corner kick**) corner m inv, calcio d'angolo ▸ VT intrappolare; mettere con le spalle al muro; (Comm: market) accaparrare ▸ VI prendere una curva; **to cut corners** (fig) prendere una scorciatoia
corner flag N (Football) bandierina d'angolo
corner kick N (Football) calcio d'angolo
corner shop N (Brit) piccolo negozio di generi alimentari
cornerstone ['kɔ:nəstəun] N pietra angolare
cornet ['kɔ:nɪt] N (Mus) cornetta; (Brit: of ice-cream) cono
cornflakes ['kɔ:nfleɪks] NPL fiocchi mpl di granturco
cornflour ['kɔ:nflauə'] N (Brit) farina finissima di granturco
cornice ['kɔ:nɪs] N cornicione m; cornice f
Cornish ['kɔ:nɪʃ] ADJ della Cornovaglia
corn oil N olio di mais
cornstarch ['kɔ:nstɑ:tʃ] N (US) = **cornflour**
cornucopia [kɔ:nju'kəupɪə] N grande abbondanza

Cornwall ['kɔːnwəl] N Cornovaglia
corny ['kɔːnɪ] ADJ (col) trito(-a)
corollary [kə'rɔlərɪ] N corollario
coronary ['kɔrənərɪ] N: ~ **(thrombosis)** trombosi f coronaria
coronation [kɔrə'neɪʃən] N incoronazione f
coroner ['kɔrənəʳ] N magistrato incaricato di indagare la causa di morte in circostanze sospette
coronet ['kɔrənɪt] N diadema m
Corp. ABBR = **corporation**
corporal ['kɔːprəl] N caporalmaggiore m
▶ ADJ: ~ **punishment** pena corporale
corporate ['kɔːpərɪt] ADJ comune; (Comm) costituito(-a) (in corporazione)
corporate hospitality N omaggi mpl ai clienti (come biglietti per spettacoli, cene ecc)
corporate identity, corporate image N (of organization) immagine f di marca
corporation [kɔːpə'reɪʃən] N (of town) consiglio comunale; (Comm) ente m
corporation tax N ≈ imposta societaria
corps [kɔː] (pl ~ [kɔːz]) N corpo; **press ~** ufficio m stampa inv
corpse [kɔːps] N cadavere m
corpuscle ['kɔːpʌsl] N corpuscolo
corral [kə'rɑːl] N recinto
correct [kə'rɛkt] ADJ (accurate) corretto(-a), esatto(-a); (proper) corretto(-a) ▶ VT correggere; **you are ~** ha ragione
correction [kə'rɛkʃən] N correzione f
correlate ['kɔrɪleɪt] VT mettere in correlazione ▶ VI: **to ~ with** essere in rapporto con
correlation [kɔrɪ'leɪʃən] N correlazione f
correspond [kɔrɪs'pɔnd] VI corrispondere
correspondence [kɔrɪs'pɔndəns] N corrispondenza
correspondence course N corso per corrispondenza
correspondent [kɔrɪs'pɔndənt] N corrispondente mf
corresponding ADJ corrispondente
corridor ['kɔrɪdɔː] N corridoio
corroborate [kə'rɔbəreɪt] VT corroborare, confermare
corrode [kə'rəud] VT corrodere ▶ VI corrodersi
corrosion [kə'rəuʒən] N corrosione f
corrosive [kə'rəuzɪv] ADJ corrosivo(-a)
corrugated ['kɔrəgeɪtɪd] ADJ increspato(-a), ondulato(-a)
corrugated iron N lamiera di ferro ondulata
corrupt [kə'rʌpt] ADJ corrotto(-a); (Comput) alterato(-a) ▶ VT corrompere; ~ **practices** (dishonesty, bribery) pratiche fpl illecite
corruption [kə'rʌpʃən] N corruzione f
corset ['kɔːsɪt] N busto
Corsica ['kɔːsɪkə] N Corsica
Corsican ['kɔːsɪkən] ADJ, N corso(-a)

cortège [kɔː'teɪʒ] N corteo
cortisone ['kɔːtɪzəun] N cortisone m
coruscating ['kɔrəskeɪtɪŋ] ADJ scintillante
cosh [kɔʃ] N (BRIT) randello (corto)
cosignatory [kəu'sɪgnətərɪ] N cofirmatario(-a)
cosiness ['kəuzɪnɪs] N intimità
cos lettuce ['kɔs-] N lattuga romana
cosmetic [kɔz'mɛtɪk] N cosmetico ▶ ADJ (preparation) cosmetico(-a); (fig: reforms, measures) apparente
cosmetic surgery N chirurgia plastica
cosmic ['kɔzmɪk] ADJ cosmico(-a)
cosmonaut ['kɔzmənɔːt] N cosmonauta mf
cosmopolitan [kɔzmə'pɔlɪtn] ADJ cosmopolita
cosmos ['kɔzmɔs] N cosmo
cosset ['kɔsɪt] VT vezzeggiare
cost [kɔst] (pt, pp ~) N costo ▶ VI costare ▶ VT stabilire il prezzo di; **costs** NPL (Law) spese fpl; **it costs £5/too much** costa 5 sterline/troppo; **it ~ him his life/job** gli costò la vita/il suo lavoro; **how much does it ~?** quanto costa?, quanto viene?; **what will it ~ to have it repaired?** quanto costerà farlo riparare?; ~ **of living** costo della vita; **at all costs** a ogni costo
cost accountant N analizzatore m dei costi
co-star ['kəustɑː] N attore/trice della stessa importanza del protagonista
Costa Rica ['kɔstə'riːkə] N Costa Rica
cost centre N centro di costo
cost control N controllo dei costi
cost-effective ['kɔstɪ'fɛktɪv] ADJ (gen) conveniente, economico(-a); (Comm) redditizio(-a), conveniente
cost-effectiveness ['kɔstɪ'fɛktɪvnɪs] N convenienza
costing ['kɔstɪŋ] N (determinazione f dei) costi mpl
costly ['kɔstlɪ] ADJ costoso(-a), caro(-a)
cost-of-living ['kɔstəv'lɪvɪŋ] ADJ: ~ **allowance** indennità f inv di contingenza; ~ **index** indice m della scala mobile
cost price N (BRIT) prezzo all'ingrosso
costume ['kɔstjuːm] N costume m; (lady's suit) tailleur m inv; (BRIT: also: **swimming costume**) costume da bagno
costume jewellery N bigiotteria
cosy, (US) **cozy** ['kəuzɪ] ADJ intimo(-a); (room, atmosphere) accogliente; **I'm very ~ here** sto proprio bene qui
cot [kɔt] N (BRIT: child's) lettino; (US: folding bed) brandina
cot death N improvvisa e inspiegabile morte nel sonno di un neonato
Cotswolds ['kɔtswəuldz] NPL: **the ~** zona collinare del Gloucestershire
cottage ['kɔtɪdʒ] N cottage m inv

497

cottage cheese N fiocchi *mpl* di latte magro
cottage industry N industria artigianale basata sul lavoro a cottimo
cottage pie N piatto a base di carne macinata in sugo e purè di patate
cotton ['kɔtn] N cotone *m*; ~ **dress** *etc* vestito *etc* di cotone
▶ **cotton on** VI (*col*): **to ~ on (to sth)** afferrare (qc)
cotton bud N (BRIT) cotton fioc® *m inv*
cotton candy (US) N zucchero filato
cotton wool N (BRIT) cotone *m* idrofilo
couch [kautʃ] N sofà *m inv*; (*in doctor's surgery*) lettino ▶ VT esprimere
couchette [kuːˈʃɛt] N cuccetta
couch potato N (*col*) pigrone(-a) teledipendente
cough [kɔf] VI tossire ▶ N tosse *f*; **I've got a ~** ho la tosse
cough drop N pasticca per la tosse
cough mixture, cough syrup N sciroppo per la tosse
could [kud] PT *of* **can²**
couldn't ['kudnt] = **could not**
council ['kaunsl] N consiglio; **city** *or* **town ~** consiglio comunale; **C~ of Europe** Consiglio d'Europa
council estate N (BRIT) quartiere *m* di case popolari
council house N (BRIT) casa popolare
council housing N alloggi *mpl* popolari
councillor ['kaunsələʳ] N consigliere(-a)
council tax N (BRIT) tassa comunale sulla proprietà
counsel ['kaunsl] N avvocato; consultazione *f* ▶ VT: **to ~ sth/sb to do sth** consigliare qc/a qn di fare qc; ~ **for the defence/the prosecution** avvocato difensore/di parte civile
counselling, (US) counseling N (*Psych*) assistenza psicologica
counsellor, (US) counselor ['kaunsləʳ] N consigliere(-a); (*US: lawyer*) avvocato(-essa)
count [kaunt] VT, VI contare ▶ N conto; (*nobleman*) conte *m*; **to ~ (up) to 10** contare fino a 10; **to ~ the cost of** calcolare il costo di; **not counting the children** senza contare i bambini; **10 counting him** 10 compreso lui; ~ **yourself lucky** considerati fortunato; **it counts for very little** non conta molto, non ha molta importanza; **to keep ~ of sth** tenere il conto di qc
▶ **count in** VT (*col*) includere; ~ **me in** ci sto anch'io
▶ **count on** VT FUS contare su; **to ~ on doing sth** contare di fare qc
▶ **count up** VT addizionare
countdown ['kauntdaun] N conto alla rovescia

countenance ['kauntinəns] N volto, aspetto ▶ VT approvare
counter ['kauntəʳ] N banco; (*position: in post office, bank*) sportello; (*in game*) gettone *m*; (*Tech*) contatore *m* ▶ VT opporsi a; (*blow*) parare ▶ ADV: ~ **to** contro; in opposizione a; **to buy under the ~** (*fig*) comperare sottobanco; **to ~ sth with sth/by doing sth** rispondere a qc con qc/facendo qc
counteract [kauntər'ækt] VT agire in opposizione a; (*poison etc*) annullare gli effetti di
counterattack ['kauntərətæk] N contrattacco ▶ VI contrattaccare
counterbalance ['kauntəbæləns] VT contrappesare
counter-clockwise ['kauntə'klɔkwaiz] (US) ADV in senso antiorario
counter-espionage [kauntər'ɛspiɑnɑːʒ] N controspionaggio
counterfeit ['kauntəfit] N contraffazione *f*, falso ▶ VT contraffare, falsificare ▶ ADJ falso(-a)
counterfoil ['kauntəfɔil] N matrice *f*
counterintelligence ['kauntərin'tɛlidʒəns] N = **counter-espionage**
countermand ['kauntəmɑːnd] VT annullare
countermeasure ['kauntəmɛʒəʳ] N contromisura
counteroffensive ['kauntərə'fɛnsiv] N controffensiva
counterpane ['kauntəpein] N copriletto *m inv*
counterpart ['kauntəpɑːt] N (*of document etc*) copia; (*of person*) corrispondente *mf*
counterproductive ['kauntəprə'dʌktiv] ADJ controproducente
counterproposal ['kauntəprə'pəuzl] N controproposta
countersign ['kauntəsain] VT controfirmare
countersink ['kauntəsiŋk] VT (*hole*) svasare
counterterrorism ['kauntə'terərizəm] N antiterrorismo
countess ['kauntis] N contessa
countless ['kauntlis] ADJ innumerevole
countrified ['kʌntrifaid] ADJ rustico(-a), campagnolo(-a)
country ['kʌntri] N paese *m*; (*native land*) patria; (*as opposed to town*) campagna; (*region*) regione *f*; **in the ~** in campagna; **mountainous ~** territorio montagnoso
country and western, country and western music N musica country e western, country *m*
country dancing N (BRIT) danza popolare
country house N villa in campagna
countryman ['kʌntrimən] N (*irreg*) (*national*) compatriota *m*; (*rural*) contadino
countryside ['kʌntrisaid] N campagna

country-wide [ˈkʌntrɪˈwaɪd] ADJ diffuso(-a) in tutto il paese ▶ ADV in tutto il paese
county [ˈkaʊntɪ] N contea
county council N (BRIT) consiglio di contea
county town N (BRIT) capoluogo
coup [kuː] (pl **coups** [kuːz]) N colpo; (also: **coup d'état**) colpo di Stato; (triumph) bel colpo
coupé [kuːˈpeɪ] N coupé m inv
couple [ˈkʌpl] N coppia ▶ VT (carriages) agganciare; (Tech) accoppiare; (ideas, names) associare; **a ~ of** un paio di
couplet [ˈkʌplɪt] N distico
coupling [ˈkʌplɪŋ] N (Rail) agganciamento
coupon [ˈkuːpɔn] N (voucher) buono; (Comm) coupon m inv
courage [ˈkʌrɪdʒ] N coraggio
courageous [kəˈreɪdʒəs] ADJ coraggioso(-a)
courgette [kuəˈʒɛt] N (BRIT) zucchina
courier [ˈkʊrɪər] N corriere m; (for tourists) guida
course [kɔːs] N corso; (of ship) rotta; (for golf) campo; (part of meal) piatto; **first ~** primo piatto; **of ~** adv senz'altro, naturalmente; **(no) of ~ not!** certo che no!, no di certo!; **in the ~ of the next few days** nel corso dei prossimi giorni; **in due ~** a tempo debito; **~ (of action)** modo d'agire; **the best ~ would be to …** la cosa migliore sarebbe …; **we have no other ~ but to …** non possiamo far altro che …; **~ of lectures** corso di lezioni; **a ~ of treatment** (Med) una cura
court [kɔːt] N corte f; (Tennis) campo ▶ VT (woman) fare la corte a; (fig: favour, popularity) cercare di conquistare; (: death, disaster) sfiorare, rasentare; **out of ~** (Law: settle) in via amichevole; **to take to ~** citare in tribunale; **C~ of Appeal** corte d'appello
courteous [ˈkəːtɪəs] ADJ cortese
courtesan [kɔːtɪˈzæn] N cortigiana
courtesy [ˈkəːtəsɪ] N cortesia; **by ~ of** per gentile concessione di
courtesy bus, courtesy coach N navetta gratuita (di hotel, aeroporto)
courtesy car N vettura sostitutiva
courtesy light N (Aut) luce f interna
court-house [ˈkɔːthaʊs] N (US) palazzo di giustizia
courtier [ˈkɔːtɪər] N cortigiano(-a)
court martial (pl **courts martial**) N corte f marziale
courtroom [ˈkɔːtrum] N tribunale m
court shoe N scarpa f décolleté inv
courtyard [ˈkɔːtjɑːd] N cortile m
cousin [ˈkʌzn] N cugino(-a); **first ~** cugino di primo grado
cove [kəʊv] N piccola baia
covenant [ˈkʌvənənt] N accordo ▶ VT: **to ~ to do sth** impegnarsi (per iscritto) a fare qc

Coventry [ˈkɔvəntrɪ] N: **to send sb to ~** (fig) dare l'ostracismo a qn
cover [ˈkʌvər] VT (gen) coprire; (distance) coprire, percorrere; (book, table) rivestire; (include) comprendere; (Press: report on) fare un servizio su ▶ N (of pan) coperchio; (over furniture) fodera; (of bed) copriletto; (of book) copertina; (shelter) riparo; (Comm, Insurance, of spy) copertura; **covers** NPL (on bed) lenzuola e coperte fpl; **to take ~** mettersi al riparo; **under ~** al riparo; **under ~ of darkness** protetto dall'oscurità; **under separate ~** (Comm) a parte, in plico separato; **£10 will ~ everything** 10 sterline saranno sufficienti ▶ **cover up** VT (hide: truth, facts) nascondere; (child, object): **to ~ up (with)** coprire (di) ▶ VI: **to ~ up for sb** (fig) coprire qn
coverage [ˈkʌvərɪdʒ] N (Press, TV, Radio): **to give full ~** to fare un ampio servizio su
coveralls [ˈkʌvərɔːlz] NPL (US) tuta
cover charge N coperto
covering [ˈkʌvərɪŋ] N copertura
covering letter, (US) cover letter N lettera d'accompagnamento
cover note N (Insurance) polizza (di assicurazione) provvisoria
cover price N prezzo di copertina
covert [ˈkʌvət] ADJ nascosto(-a); (glance) di sottecchi, furtivo(-a)
cover-up [ˈkʌvərʌp] N occultamento (di informazioni)
covet [ˈkʌvɪt] VT bramare
cow [kaʊ] N vacca ▶ CPD femmina ▶ VT (person) intimidire; **~ elephant** n elefantessa
coward [ˈkaʊəd] N vigliacco(-a)
cowardice [ˈkaʊədɪs] N vigliaccheria
cowardly [ˈkaʊədlɪ] ADJ vigliacco(-a)
cowboy [ˈkaʊbɔɪ] N cow-boy m inv
cower [ˈkaʊər] VI acquattarsi
cowshed [ˈkaʊʃɛd] N stalla
cowslip [ˈkaʊslɪp] N (Bot) primula (odorata)
coxswain [ˈkɔksn] N (also: **cox**) timoniere m
coy [kɔɪ] ADJ falsamente timido(-a)
coyote [kɔɪˈəʊtɪ] N coyote m inv
cozy [ˈkəʊzɪ] ADJ (US) = **cosy**
CP N ABBR (= Communist Party) P.C. m
cp. ABBR (= compare) cfr.
CPA N ABBR (US) = **certified public accountant**
CPI N ABBR (US: = Consumer Price Index) indice dei prezzi al consumo
Cpl. ABBR = **corporal**
CP/M N ABBR (= Control Program for Microcomputers) CP/M m
c.p.s. ABBR (= characters per second) c.p.s.
CPSA N ABBR (BRIT: = Civil and Public Services Association) sindacato dei servizi pubblici
CPU N ABBR = **central processing unit**
cr. ABBR = **credit; creditor**
crab [kræb] N granchio

crab apple N mela selvatica
crack [kræk] N (split, slit) fessura, crepa; incrinatura; (noise) schiocco; (: of gun) scoppio; (joke) battuta; (col: attempt): **to have a ~ at sth** tentare qc; (Drugs) crack m inv ▶ VT spaccare; incrinare; (whip) schioccare; (nut) schiacciare; (solve: problem, case) risolvere; (: code) decifrare ▶ CPD (athlete) di prim'ordine; (troops) fuori classe; **to ~ jokes** (col) dire battute, scherzare; **to get cracking** (col) darsi una mossa
▶ **crack down on** VT FUS prendere serie misure contro, porre freno a
▶ **crack up** VI crollare
crackdown ['krækdaun] N repressione f
cracked [krækt] ADJ (col) matto(-a)
cracker ['krækə'] N cracker m inv; (firework) petardo; (Christmas cracker) mortaretto natalizio (con sorpresa); **a ~ of a ...** (BRIT col) un(-a) ... formidabile; **he's crackers** (BRIT col) è tocco
crackle ['krækl] VI crepitare
crackling ['kræklɪŋ] N crepitio m; (on radio, telephone) disturbo; (of pork) cotenna croccante (del maiale)
crackpot ['krækpot] N (col) imbecille mf con idee assurde, assurdo(-a)
cradle ['kreɪdl] N culla ▶ VT (child) tenere fra le braccia; (object) reggere tra le braccia
craft [krɑ:ft] N mestiere m; (cunning) astuzia; (boat) naviglio
craftsman ['krɑ:ftsmən] N (irreg) artigiano
craftsmanship ['krɑ:ftsmənʃɪp] N abilità
crafty ['krɑ:ftɪ] ADJ furbo(-a), astuto(-a)
crag [kræg] N roccia
cram [kræm] VI (for exams) prepararsi (in gran fretta) ▶ VT (fill): **to ~ sth with** riempire qc di; (put): **to ~ sth into** stipare qc in
cramming ['kræmɪŋ] N (fig: pej) sgobbare m
cramp [kræmp] N crampo ▶ VT soffocare, impedire; **I've got ~ in my leg** ho un crampo alla gamba
cramped [kræmpt] ADJ ristretto(-a)
crampon ['kræmpən] N (Climbing) rampone m
cranberry ['krænbərɪ] N mirtillo
crane [kreɪn] N gru f inv ▶ VT, VI: **to ~ forward, to ~ one's neck** allungare il collo
cranium ['kreɪnɪəm] (pl crania ['kreɪnɪə]) N cranio
crank [kræŋk] N manovella; (person) persona stramba
crankshaft ['kræŋkʃɑ:ft] N albero a gomiti
cranky ['kræŋkɪ] ADJ eccentrico(-a); (bad-tempered): **to be ~** avere i nervi
cranny ['krænɪ] N see **nook**
crap [kræp] N (col!) fesserie fpl; **to have a ~** cacare (!)
crappy ['kræpɪ] ADJ (col) di merda (!)
crash [kræʃ] N fragore m; (of car) incidente m;

(of plane) caduta; (of business) fallimento; (Stock Exchange) crollo ▶ VT fracassare ▶ VI (plane) fracassarsi; (car) avere un incidente; (two cars) scontrarsi; (fig: business etc) fallire, andare in rovina; **to ~ into** scontrarsi con; **he crashed the car into a wall** andò a sbattere contro un muro con la macchina
crash barrier N (BRIT Aut) guardrail m inv
crash course N corso intensivo
crash helmet N casco
crash landing N atterraggio di fortuna
crass [kræs] ADJ crasso(-a)
crate [kreɪt] N cassa
crater ['kreɪtə'] N cratere m
cravat, cravate [krə'væt] N fazzoletto da collo
crave [kreɪv] VT, VI: **to ~ (for)** desiderare ardentemente
craving ['kreɪvɪŋ] N: **~ (for)** (for food, cigarettes etc) (gran) voglia (di)
crawl [krɔ:l] VI strisciare carponi; (child) andare a gattoni; (vehicle) avanzare lentamente ▶ N (Swimming) crawl m; **to ~ to sb** (col: suck up) arruffianarsi qn
crawler lane ['krɔ:lə'-] N (BRIT Aut) corsia riservata al traffico lento
crayfish ['kreɪfɪʃ] N INV (freshwater) gambero (d'acqua dolce); (saltwater) gambero
crayon ['kreɪən] N matita colorata
craze [kreɪz] N mania
crazed [kreɪzd] ADJ (look, person) folle, pazzo(-a); (pottery, glaze) incrinato(-a)
crazy ['kreɪzɪ] ADJ matto(-a); (col: keen): **to be ~ about sb** essere pazzo di qn; **to be ~ about sth** andare matto per qc; **to go ~** uscir di senno, impazzire
crazy paving N (BRIT) lastricato a mosaico irregolare
creak [kri:k] VI cigolare, scricchiolare
cream [kri:m] N crema; (fresh) panna ▶ ADJ (colour) color crema inv; **whipped ~** panna montata
▶ **cream off** VT (best talents, part of profits) portarsi via
cream cake N torta alla panna
cream cheese N formaggio fresco
creamery ['kri:mərɪ] N (shop) latteria; (factory) caseificio
creamy ['kri:mɪ] ADJ cremoso(-a)
crease [kri:s] N grinza; (deliberate) piega ▶ VT sgualcire ▶ VI sgualcirsi
crease-resistant ['kri:srɪzɪstənt] ADJ ingualcibile
create [kri:'eɪt] VT creare; (fuss, noise) fare
creation [kri:'eɪʃən] N creazione f
creative [kri:'eɪtɪv] ADJ creativo(-a)
creativity [kri:eɪ'tɪvɪtɪ] N creatività
creator [kri:'eɪtə'] N creatore(-trice)
creature ['kri:tʃə'] N creatura

crèche, creche [krɛʃ] N asilo infantile
credence ['kri:dns] N credenza, fede f
credentials [krɪ'dɛnʃlz] NPL (*papers*)
  credenziali *fpl*; (*letters of reference*) referenze *fpl*
credibility [krɛdɪ'bɪlɪtɪ] N credibilità
credible ['krɛdɪbl] ADJ credibile; (*witness, source*) attendibile
credit ['krɛdɪt] N credito; onore *m*; (*Scol: esp US*) certificato del compimento di una parte del corso universitario ▶ VT (*Comm*) accreditare; (*believe: also:* **give credit to**) credere, prestar fede a; **to ~ £5 to sb** accreditare 5 sterline a qn; **to ~ sb with sth** (*fig*) attribuire qc a qn; **on ~** a credito; **to one's ~** a proprio onore; **to take the ~ for** farsi il merito di; **to be in ~** (*person*) essere creditore(-trice); (*bank account*) essere coperto(-a); **he's a ~ to his family** fa onore alla sua famiglia; *see also* **credits**
creditable ['krɛdɪtəbl] ADJ che fa onore, degno(-a) di lode
credit account N conto di credito
credit agency N (*BRIT*) agenzia di analisi di credito
credit balance N saldo attivo
credit bureau N (*US*) agenzia di analisi di credito
credit card N carta di credito
credit control N controllo dei crediti
credit crunch N improvvisa stretta di credito
credit facilities NPL agevolazioni *fpl* creditizie
credit limit N limite *m* di credito
credit note N (*BRIT*) nota di credito
creditor ['krɛdɪtər] N creditore(-trice)
credits ['krɛdɪts] NPL (*Cine*) titoli *mpl*
credit transfer N bancogiro, postagiro
creditworthy ['krɛdɪt'wə:ðɪ] ADJ autorizzabile al credito
credulity [krɪ'dju:lɪtɪ] N credulità
creed [kri:d] N credo; dottrina
creek [kri:k] N insenatura; (*US*) piccolo fiume *m*
creel [kri:l] N cestino per il pesce; (*also:* **lobster creel**) nassa
creep [kri:p] N (*pt, pp* **crept** [krɛpt]) VI avanzare furtivamente (*or* pian piano); (*plant*) arrampicarsi ▶ N (*col*): **he's a ~** è un tipo viscido; **it gives me the creeps** (*col*) mi fa venire la pelle d'oca; **to ~ up on sb** avvicinarsi quatto quatto a qn; (*fig: old age etc*) cogliere qn alla sprovvista
creeper ['kri:pər] N pianta rampicante
creepers ['kri:pəz] NPL (*US: rompers*) tutina
creepy ['kri:pɪ] ADJ (*frightening*) che fa accapponare la pelle
creepy-crawly ['kri:pɪ'krɔ:lɪ] N (*col*) bestiolina, insetto
cremate [krɪ'meɪt] VT cremare
cremation [krɪ'meɪʃən] N cremazione *f*

crematorium [krɛmə'tɔ:rɪəm] (*pl* **crematoria** [-'tɔ:rɪə]) N forno crematorio
creosote ['krɪəsəut] N creosoto
crêpe [kreɪp] N crespo
crêpe bandage N (*BRIT*) fascia elastica
crêpe paper N carta crespa
crêpe sole N suola di para
crept [krɛpt] PT, PP *of* **creep**
crescendo [krɪ'ʃɛndəu] N crescendo
crescent ['krɛsnt] N (*shape*) mezzaluna; (*street*) strada semicircolare
cress [krɛs] N crescione *m*
crest [krɛst] N cresta; (*of helmet*) pennacchiera; (*of coat of arms*) cimiero
crestfallen ['krɛstfɔ:lən] ADJ mortificato(-a)
Crete ['kri:t] N Creta
crevasse [krɪ'væs] N crepaccio
crevice ['krɛvɪs] N fessura, crepa
crew [kru:] N equipaggio; (*Cine*) troupe *f inv*; (*gang*) banda, compagnia
crew-cut ['kru:kʌt] N: **to have a ~** avere i capelli a spazzola
crew-neck ['kru:nɛk] N girocollo
crib [krɪb] N culla; (*Rel*) presepio ▶ VT (*col*) copiare
cribbage ['krɪbɪdʒ] N tipo di gioco di carte
crick [krɪk] N crampo; **~ in the neck** torcicollo
cricket ['krɪkɪt] N (*insect*) grillo; (*game*) cricket *m*
cricketer ['krɪkɪtər] N giocatore *m* di cricket
crime [kraɪm] N (*in general*) criminalità; (*instance*) crimine *m*, delitto
crime wave N ondata di criminalità
criminal ['krɪmɪnl] ADJ, N criminale (*mf*); **C~ Investigation Department (CID)** ≈ polizia giudiziaria
crimp [krɪmp] VT arricciare
crimson ['krɪmzn] ADJ color cremisi *inv*
cringe [krɪndʒ] VI acquattarsi; (*fig*) essere servile; (*in embarrassment*) sentirsi sprofondare
crinkle ['krɪŋkl] VT arricciare, increspare
cripple ['krɪpl] N zoppo(-a) ▶ VT azzoppare; (*ship, plane*) avariare; (*production, exports*) rovinare; **crippled with arthritis** sciancato(-a) per l'artrite
crippling ['krɪplɪŋ] ADJ (*taxes, debts*) esorbitante; (*disease*) molto debilitante
crisis ['kraɪsɪs] (*pl* **crises** [-si:z]) N crisi *f inv*
crisp [krɪsp] ADJ croccante; (*fig*) frizzante; vivace; deciso(-a)
crisps [krɪsps] NPL (*BRIT*) patatine *fpl* fritte
crispy ADJ croccante
criss-cross ['krɪskrɔs] ADJ incrociato(-a) ▶ VT incrociarsi
criterion [kraɪ'tɪərɪən] (*pl* **criteria** [-'tɪərɪə]) N criterio
critic ['krɪtɪk] N critico(-a)

critical ['krɪtɪkl] ADJ critico(-a); **to be ~ of sb/ sth** criticare qn/qc, essere critico verso qn/qc

critically ['krɪtɪklɪ] ADV criticamente; **~ ill** gravemente malato

criticism ['krɪtɪsɪzəm] N critica

criticize ['krɪtɪsaɪz] VT criticare

critique [krɪ'ti:k] N critica, saggio critico

croak [krəuk] VI gracchiare

Croat ['krəuæt] ADJ, N = **Croatian**

Croatia [krəu'eɪʃə] N Croazia

Croatian [krəu'eɪʃən] ADJ croato(-a) ▶ N croato(-a); (Ling) croato

crochet ['krəuʃeɪ] N lavoro all'uncinetto

crock [krɔk] N coccio; (col: person: also: **old crock**) rottame m; (car etc) caffettiera, rottame m

crockery ['krɔkərɪ] N vasellame m; (plates, cups etc) stoviglie fpl

crocodile ['krɔkədaɪl] N coccodrillo

crocus ['krəukəs] N croco

croft [krɔft] N (BRIT) piccolo podere m

crofter ['krɔftər] N (BRIT) affittuario di un piccolo podere

croissant ['krwasã] N brioche f inv, croissant m inv

crone [krəun] N strega

crony ['krəunɪ] N (col) amicone(-a)

crook [kruk] N (col) truffatore m; (of shepherd) bastone m

crooked ['krukɪd] ADJ curvo(-a), storto(-a); (person, action) disonesto(-a)

crop [krɔp] N raccolto; (produce) coltivazione f; (amount produced) raccolto; (riding crop) frustino; (of bird) gozzo, ingluvie f ▶ VT (cut: hair) tagliare, rapare; (animals: grass) brucare ▶ **crop up** VI presentarsi

cropper ['krɔpər] N: **to come a ~** (col) fare fiasco

crop spraying N spruzzatura di antiparassitari

croquet ['krəukeɪ] N croquet m

croquette [krə'kɛt] N crocchetta

cross [krɔs] N croce f; (Biol) incrocio ▶ VT (street etc) attraversare; (arms, legs, Biol) incrociare; (cheque) sbarrare; (thwart: person, plan) contrastare, ostacolare ▶ VI: **the boat crosses from ... to ...** la barca fa la traversata da ... a ... ▶ ADJ di cattivo umore; **to ~ o.s.** fare il segno della croce, segnarsi; **we have a crossed line** (BRIT: on telephone) c'è un'interferenza; **they've got their lines crossed** (fig) si sono fraintesi; **to be/get ~ with sb (about sth)** essere arrabbiato(-a)/ arrabbiarsi con qn (per qc)
▶ **cross off** VT cancellare (tirando una riga con la penna)
▶ **cross out** VT cancellare
▶ **cross over** VI attraversare

crossbar ['krɔsba:r] N traversa

crossbow ['krɔsbəu] N balestra

crossbreed ['krɔsbri:d] N incrocio

cross-Channel ferry ['krɔs'tʃænl-] N traghetto che attraversa la Manica

cross-check ['krɔstʃɛk] N controprova ▶ VI fare una controprova

crosscountry [krɔs'kʌntrɪ], **crosscountry race** [krɔs'kʌntrɪ-] N cross-country m inv

cross-dressing [krɔs'drɛsɪŋ] N travestitismo

cross-examination ['krɔsɪgzæmɪ'neɪʃən] N (Law) controinterrogatorio

cross-examine ['krɔsɪg'zæmɪn] VT (Law) sottoporre a controinterrogatorio

cross-eyed ['krɔsaɪd] ADJ strabico(-a)

crossfire ['krɔsfaɪər] N fuoco incrociato

crossing ['krɔsɪŋ] N incrocio; (sea-passage) traversata; (also: **pedestrian crossing**) passaggio pedonale

crossing guard (US) N dipendente comunale che aiuta i bambini ad attraversare la strada

crossing point N valico di frontiera

cross-purposes ['krɔs'pə:pəsɪz] NPL: **to be at ~ with sb** (misunderstand) fraintendere qn; **to talk at ~** fraintendersi

cross-question [krɔs'kwɛstʃən] VT (Law) = **cross-examine**; (fig) sottoporre ad un interrogatorio

cross-reference ['krɔs'rɛfərəns] N rinvio, rimando

crossroads ['krɔsrəudz] N incrocio

cross section N (Biol) sezione f trasversale; (in population) settore m rappresentativo

crosswalk ['krɔswɔ:k] N (US) strisce fpl pedonali, passaggio pedonale

crosswind ['krɔswɪnd] N vento di traverso

crosswise ['krɔswaɪz] ADV di traverso

crossword ['krɔswə:d] N cruciverba m inv

crotch [krɔtʃ] N (Anat) inforcatura; (of garment) pattina

crotchet ['krɔtʃɪt] N (Mus) semiminima

crotchety ['krɔtʃɪtɪ] ADJ (person) burbero(-a)

crouch [krautʃ] VI acquattarsi; rannicchiarsi

croup [kru:p] N (Med) croup m

crouton ['kru:tɔn] N crostino

crow [krəu] N (bird) cornacchia; (of cock) canto del gallo ▶ VI (cock) cantare; (fig) vantarsi; cantar vittoria

crowbar ['krəuba:r] N piede m di porco

crowd [kraud] N folla ▶ VT affollare, stipare ▶ VI affollarsi; **crowds of people** un sacco di gente; **to ~ round/in** affollarsi intorno a/in

crowded ['kraudɪd] ADJ affollato(-a); **~ with** stipato(-a) di

crowd scene N (Cine, Theat) scena di massa

crowdsource ['kraudsɔ:s] VT ricorrere al crowdsourcing per

crowdsourcing ['kraudsɔ:sɪŋ] N crowdsourcing m

crown [kraun] N corona; (*of head*) calotta cranica; (*of hat*) cocuzzolo; (*of hill*) cima ▶ VT incoronare; (*tooth*) incapsulare; (*fig: career*) coronare; **and to ~ it all ...** (*fig*) e per giunta ..., e come se non bastasse ...; *vedi nota*

> Nel sistema legale inglese, la *crown court* è un tribunale penale che si sposta da una città all'altra. È formata da una giuria locale ed è presieduta da un giudice che si sposta assieme alla *court*. Vi si discutono i reati più gravi, mentre dei reati minori si occupano le *magistrates' courts*, presiedute da un giudice di pace, ma senza giuria. è il giudice di pace che decide se passare o meno un caso alla *crown court*.

crowning ['kraunɪŋ] ADJ (*achievement, glory*) supremo(-a)
crown jewels NPL gioielli *mpl* della Corona
crown prince N principe *m* ereditario
crow's-feet ['krəuzfiːt] NPL zampe *fpl* di gallina
crow's-nest ['krəuznɛst] N (*on sailing-ship*) coffa
crucial ['kruːʃl] ADJ cruciale, decisivo(-a); **~ to** essenziale per
crucifix ['kruːsɪfɪks] N crocifisso
crucifixion [kruːsɪ'fɪkʃən] N crocifissione *f*
crucify ['kruːsɪfaɪ] VT crocifiggere, mettere in croce; (*fig*) distruggere, fare a pezzi
crude [kruːd] ADJ (*materials*) greggio(-a); non raffinato(-a); (*fig: basic*) crudo(-a), primitivo(-a); (: *vulgar*) rozzo(-a), grossolano(-a) ▶ N (*also*: **crude oil**) (petrolio) greggio
cruel ['kruəl] ADJ crudele
cruelty ['kruəltɪ] N crudeltà *f inv*
cruet ['kruːɪt] N ampolla
cruise [kruːz] N crociera ▶ VI andare a velocità di crociera; (*taxi*) circolare
cruise missile N missile *m* cruise *inv*
cruiser ['kruːzəʳ] N incrociatore *m*
cruising speed ['kruːzɪŋ-] N velocità *f inv* di crociera
crumb [krʌm] N briciola
crumble ['krʌmbl] VT sbriciolare ▶ VI sbriciolarsi; (*plaster etc*) sgretolarsi; (*land, earth*) franare; (*building, fig*) crollare
crumbly ['krʌmblɪ] ADJ friabile
crummy ['krʌmɪ] ADJ (*col: cheap*) di infima categoria; (: *depressed*) giù *inv*
crumpet ['krʌmpɪt] N *specie di frittella*
crumple ['krʌmpl] VT raggrinzare, spiegazzare
crunch [krʌntʃ] VT sgranocchiare; (*underfoot*) scricchiolare ▶ N (*fig*) punto *or* momento cruciale
crunchy ['krʌntʃɪ] ADJ croccante
crusade [kruː'seɪd] N crociata ▶ VI (*fig*): **to ~ for/against** fare una crociata per/contro

crusader [kruː'seɪdəʳ] N crociato; (*fig*): **~ (for)** sostenitore(-trice) (di)
crush [krʌʃ] N folla; (*love*): **to have a ~ on sb** avere una cotta per qn; (*drink*): **lemon ~** spremuta di limone ▶ VT schiacciare; (*crumple*) sgualcire; (*grind, break up: garlic, ice*) tritare; (: *grapes*) pigiare
crush barrier N (BRIT) transenna
crushing ['krʌʃɪŋ] ADJ schiacciante
crust [krʌst] N crosta
crustacean [krʌs'teɪʃən] N crostaceo
crusty ['krʌstɪ] ADJ (*bread*) croccante; (*person*) brontolone(-a); (*remark*) brusco(-a)
crutch [krʌtʃ] N (*Med*) gruccia; (*support*) sostegno; (*also*: **crotch**) pattina
crux [krʌks] N nodo
cry [kraɪ] VI piangere; (*shout: also*: **cry out**) urlare ▶ N urlo, grido; (*of animal*) verso; **to ~ for help** gridare aiuto; **what are you crying about?** perché piangi?; **she had a good ~** si è fatta un bel pianto; **it's a far ~ from ...** (*fig*) è tutt'un'altra cosa da ...
  ▶ **cry off** VI ritirarsi
  ▶ **cry out** VI, VT gridare
crying ['kraɪɪŋ] ADJ (*fig*) palese; urgente
crypt [krɪpt] N cripta
cryptic ['krɪptɪk] ADJ ermetico(-a)
crystal ['krɪstl] N cristallo
crystal-clear ['krɪstl'klɪəʳ] ADJ cristallino(-a); (*fig*) chiaro(-a) (come il sole)
crystallize ['krɪstəlaɪz] VI cristallizzarsi ▶ VT (*fig*) concretizzare, concretare; **crystallized fruits** (BRIT) frutta candita
CSA N ABBR (US) = **Confederate States of America**; (BRIT: = *Child Support Agency*) istituto a difesa dei figli di coppie separate, che si adopera affinché venga rispettato l'obbligo del mantenimento
CSC N ABBR (= *Civil Service Commission*) commissione per il reclutamento dei funzionari statali
CS gas N (BRIT) tipo di gas lacrimogeno
CST ABBR (US: = *Central Standard Time*) fuso orario
CT ABBR (US) = **Connecticut**
ct ABBR = **cent; court**
CTC N ABBR (BRIT: = *city technology college*) istituto tecnico superiore
cu. ABBR = **cubic**
cub [kʌb] N cucciolo; (*also*: **cub scout**) lupetto
Cuba ['kjuːbə] N Cuba
Cuban ['kjuːbən] ADJ, N cubano(-a)
cubbyhole ['kʌbɪhəul] N angolino
cube [kjuːb] N cubo ▶ VT (*Math*) elevare al cubo
cube root N radice *f* cubica
cubic ['kjuːbɪk] ADJ cubico(-a); **~ metre** *etc* metro *etc* cubo; **~ capacity** (*Aut*) cilindrata
cubicle ['kjuːbɪkl] N scompartimento separato; cabina

cuckoo ['kuku:] N cucù *m inv*
cuckoo clock N orologio a cucù
cucumber ['kju:kʌmbə*r*] N cetriolo
cud [kʌd] N: **to chew the ~** ruminare
cuddle ['kʌdl] VT abbracciare, coccolare
 ▶ VI abbracciarsi
cuddly ['kʌdlɪ] ADJ (*person*) coccolone(-a);
 (*col*) paffuto(-a); **~ toy** (animale *m* di)
 peluche *m inv*
cudgel ['kʌdʒl] N randello ▶ VT: **to ~ one's
 brains** scervellarsi, spremere le meningi
cue [kju:] N stecca; (*Theat etc*) segnale *m*
cuff [kʌf] N (*Brit: of shirt, coat etc*) polsino;
 (*US: on trousers*) risvolto; (*blow*) schiaffo
 ▶ VT dare uno schiaffo a; **off the ~** adv
 improvvisando
cufflink ['kʌflɪŋk] N gemello
cu. ft. ABBR = **cubic feet**
cu. in. ABBR = **cubic inches**
cuisine [kwɪ'zi:n] N cucina
cul-de-sac ['kʌldəsæk] N vicolo cieco
culinary ['kʌlɪnərɪ] ADJ culinario(-a)
cull [kʌl] VT (*kill selectively: animals*) selezionare
 e abbattere; (*: ideas etc*) scegliere ▶ N (*of
 animals*) abbattimento selettivo
culminate ['kʌlmɪneɪt] VI: **to ~ in** culminare
 con
culmination [kʌlmɪ'neɪʃən] N culmine *m*
culottes [kju:'lɔts] NPL gonna *f* pantalone *inv*
culpable ['kʌlpəbl] ADJ colpevole
culprit ['kʌlprɪt] N colpevole *mf*
cult [kʌlt] N culto
cult figure N idolo
cultivate ['kʌltɪveɪt] VT (*also fig*) coltivare
cultivation [kʌltɪ'veɪʃən] N coltivazione *f*
cultural ['kʌltʃərəl] ADJ culturale
culture ['kʌltʃə*r*] N (*also fig*) cultura
cultured ['kʌltʃəd] ADJ colto(-a)
cumbersome ['kʌmbəsəm] ADJ ingombrante
cumin ['kʌmɪn] N (*spice*) cumino
cumulative ['kju:mjulətɪv] ADJ
 cumulativo(-a)
cunning ['kʌnɪŋ] N astuzia, furberia ▶ ADJ
 astuto(-a), furbo(-a); (*clever: device, idea*)
 ingegnoso(-a)
cunt [kʌnt] N (*col!*) figa (!); (*insult*) stronzo(-a)
 (!)
cup [kʌp] N tazza; (*prize, of bra*) coppa; **a ~ of
 tea** una tazza di tè
cupboard ['kʌbəd] N armadio
cup final N (*Brit Football*) finale *f* di coppa
Cupid ['kju:pɪd] N Cupido; **cupid** cupido
cupidity [kju:'pɪdɪtɪ] N cupidigia
cupola ['kju:pələ] N cupola
cuppa ['kʌpə] N (*Brit col*) tazza di tè
cup-tie ['kʌptaɪ] N (*Brit Football*) partita di
 coppa
curable ['kjuərəbl] ADJ curabile
curate ['kjuərɪt] N cappellano

curator [kjuə'reɪtə*r*] N direttore *m* (*di museo ecc*)
curb [kə:b] VT tenere a freno; (*expenditure*)
 limitare ▶ N freno; (*US*) bordo del
 marciapiede
curd cheese [kə:d-] N cagliata
curdle ['kə:dl] VI cagliare
curds [kə:dz] NPL latte *m* cagliato
cure [kjuə*r*] VT guarire; (*Culin*) trattare;
 affumicare; essiccare ▶ N rimedio; **to be
 cured of sth** essere guarito(-a) da qc
cure-all ['kjuərɔ:l] N (*also fig*) panacea,
 toccasana *m inv*
curfew ['kə:fju:] N coprifuoco
curio ['kjuərɪəu] N curiosità *f inv*
curiosity [kjuərɪ'ɔsɪtɪ] N curiosità
curious ['kjuərɪəs] ADJ curioso(-a); **I'm ~
 about him** m'incuriosisce
curiously ['kjuərɪəslɪ] ADV con curiosità;
 (*strangely*) stranamente; **~ enough, ...** per
 quanto possa sembrare strano, ...
curl [kə:l] N riccio; (*of smoke etc*) anello ▶ VT
 ondulare; (*tightly*) arricciare ▶ VI arricciarsi
 ▶ **curl up** VI avvolgersi a spirale;
 rannicchiarsi
curler ['kə:lə*r*] N bigodino; (*Sport*)
 giocatore(-trice) di curling
curlew ['kə:lu:] N chiurlo
curling ['kə:lɪŋ] N (*Sport*) curling *m*
curling tongs, (*US*) **curling irons** NPL (*for
 hair*) arricciacapelli *m inv*
curly ['kə:lɪ] ADJ ricciuto(-a)
currant ['kʌrnt] N (*dried*) uvetta; (*bush, fruit*)
 ribes *m inv*
currency ['kʌrnsɪ] N moneta; **foreign ~**
 divisa estera; **to gain ~** (*fig*) acquistare larga
 diffusione
current ['kʌrnt] ADJ corrente; (*tendency, price,
 event*) attuale ▶ N corrente *f*; **in ~ use** in uso
 corrente, d'uso comune; **the ~ issue of a
 magazine** l'ultimo numero di una rivista;
 direct/alternating ~ (*Elec*) corrente
 continua/alternata
current account N (*Brit*) conto corrente
current affairs NPL attualità *fpl*
current assets NPL (*Comm*) attivo
 realizzabile e disponibile
current liabilities NPL (*Comm*) passività *fpl*
 correnti
currently ['kʌrntlɪ] ADV attualmente
curriculum [kə'rɪkjuləm] (*pl* **curriculums** *or*
 curricula [-lə]) N curriculum *m inv*
curriculum vitae [-'vi:taɪ] N curriculum
 vitae *m inv*
curry ['kʌrɪ] N curry *m inv* ▶ VT: **to ~ favour
 with** cercare di attirarsi i favori di; **chicken
 ~** pollo al curry
curry powder N curry *m*
curse [kə:s] VT maledire ▶ VI bestemmiare
 ▶ N maledizione *f*; bestemmia

cursor ['kə:sə'] N (*Comput*) cursore *m*
cursory ['kə:sərɪ] ADJ superficiale
curt [kə:t] ADJ secco(-a)
curtail [kə:'teɪl] VT (*visit etc*) accorciare; (*expenses etc*) ridurre, decurtare
curtain ['kə:tn] N tenda; (*Theat*) sipario; **to draw the curtains** (*together*) chiudere *or* tirare le tende; (*apart*) aprire le tende
curtain call N (*Theat*) chinata alla ribalta
curtsy, curtsey ['kə:tsɪ] N inchino, riverenza ▶ VI fare un inchino *or* una riverenza
curvature ['kə:vətʃə'] N curvatura
curve [kə:v] N curva ▶ VT curvare ▶ VI curvarsi; (*road*) fare una curva
curved [kə:vd] ADJ curvo(-a)
cushion ['kuʃən] N cuscino ▶ VT (*shock*) fare da cuscinetto a
cushy ['kuʃɪ] ADJ (*col*): **a ~ job** un lavoro di tutto riposo; **to have a ~ time** spassarsela
custard ['kʌstəd] N (*for pouring*) crema
custard powder N (*BRIT*) crema pasticcera in polvere
custodial sentence [kʌs'təudɪəl-] N condanna a pena detentiva
custodian [kʌs'təudɪən] N custode *mf*; (*of museum etc*) soprintendente *mf*
custody ['kʌstədɪ] N (*of child*) custodia; (*for offenders*) arresto; **to take sb into ~** mettere qn in detenzione preventiva; **in the ~ of** alla custodia di
custom ['kʌstəm] N costume *m*, usanza; (*Law*) consuetudine *f*; (*Comm*) clientela; *see also* **customs**
customary ['kʌstəmərɪ] ADJ consueto(-a); **it is ~ to do** è consuetudine fare
custom-built ['kʌstəm'bɪlt] ADJ *see* **custom-made**
customer ['kʌstəmə'] N cliente *mf*; **he's an awkward ~** (*col*) è un tipo incontentabile
customer profile N profilo del cliente
customize ['kʌstəmaɪz] VT customizzare
customized ['kʌstəmaɪzd] ADJ personalizzato(-a); (*car*) fuoriserie *inv*
custom-made ['kʌstəm'meɪd] ADJ (*clothes*) fatto(-a) su misura; (*other goods: also:* **custom-built**) fatto(-a) su ordinazione
customs ['kʌstəmz] NPL dogana; **to go through (the) ~** passare la dogana
Customs and Excise N (*BRIT*) Ufficio Dazi e Dogana
customs officer N doganiere *m*
cut [kʌt] (*pt, pp* **~**) VT tagliare; (*shape, make*) intagliare; (*reduce*) ridurre; (*col: avoid: class, lecture, appointment*) saltare ▶ VI tagliare; (*intersect*) tagliarsi ▶ N taglio; (*in salary etc*) riduzione *f*; **cold cuts** *npl* (*US*) affettati *mpl*; **power ~** mancanza di corrente elettrica; **to ~ one's finger** tagliarsi un dito; **I've ~**

myself mi sono tagliato; **to get one's hair ~** farsi tagliare i capelli; **to ~ a tooth** mettere un dente; **to ~ sb/sth short** interrompere qn/qc; **to ~ sb dead** ignorare qn completamente
▶ **cut back** VT (*plants*) tagliare; (*production, expenditure*) ridurre
▶ **cut down** VT (*tree*) abbattere; (*consumption, expenses*) ridurre; **to ~ sb down to size** (*fig*) sgonfiare *or* ridimensionare qn
▶ **cut down on** VT FUS ridurre
▶ **cut in** VI: **to ~ in (on)** (*interrupt conversation*) intromettersi (in); (*Aut*) tagliare la strada (a)
▶ **cut off** VT tagliare; (*fig*) isolare; **we've been ~ off** (*Tel*) è caduta la linea
▶ **cut out** VT tagliare; eliminare; (*picture*) ritagliare
▶ **cut up** VT (*gen*) tagliare a pezzi
cut-and-dried ['kʌtən'draɪd] ADJ (*also:* **cut-and-dry**) assodato(-a)
cutaway ['kʌtəweɪ] ADJ, N: **~ (drawing)** spaccato
cutback ['kʌtbæk] N riduzione *f*
cute [kju:t] ADJ carino(-a); (*clever*) astuto(-a)
cut glass N cristallo
cuticle ['kju:tɪkl] N (*on nail*) pellicina, cuticola
cutlery ['kʌtlərɪ] N posate *fpl*
cutlet ['kʌtlɪt] N costoletta; (*nut cutlet*) cotoletta vegetariana
cutoff ['kʌtɔf] N (*also:* **cutoff point**) limite *m*
cutoff switch N interruttore *m*
cutout ['kʌtaut] N (*switch*) interruttore *m*; (*paper, cardboard figure*) ritaglio
cut-price ['kʌt'praɪs], (*US*) **cut-rate** ['kʌt'reɪt] ADJ a prezzo ridotto
cutthroat ['kʌtθrəut] N assassino ▶ ADJ: **~ competition** concorrenza spietata
cutting ['kʌtɪŋ] ADJ tagliente; (*fig*) pungente ▶ N (*BRIT: Press*) ritaglio (di giornale); (*: Rail*) trincea; (*Cine*) montaggio; (*from plant*) talea
cutting edge N (*of knife*) taglio, filo; **on** *or* **at the ~ of sth** all'avanguardia di qc
cutting-edge [kʌtɪŋ'edʒ] ADJ d'avanguardia
cuttlefish ['kʌtlfɪʃ] N seppia
cut-up ['kʌtʌp] ADJ stravolto(-a)
CV N ABBR = **curriculum vitae**
CWO ABBR = **cash with order**
cwt. ABBR = **hundredweight**
cyanide ['saɪənaɪd] N cianuro
cyber attack N attacco *m* informatico
cyberbullying ['saɪbəbulɪŋ] N bullismo informatico
cybercafé ['saɪbəkæfeɪ] N cybercaffè *m inv*
cybercrime ['saɪbəkraɪm] N delinquenza informatica
cybernetics [saɪbə'nɛtɪks] N cibernetica
cybersecurity [saɪbəsɪ'kjurɪtɪ] N sicurezza *f* informatica
cyberspace ['saɪbəspeɪs] N ciberspazio

C

cyberterrorism [saɪbə'terərɪzəm] N ciberterrorismo

cyclamen ['sɪkləmən] N ciclamino

cycle ['saɪkl] N ciclo; (bicycle) bicicletta ▶ VI andare in bicicletta

cycle hire N noleggio m biciclette inv

cycle lane N pista ciclabile

cycle path N pista ciclabile

cycle race N gara or corsa ciclistica

cycle rack N portabiciclette m inv

cycle track N percorso ciclabile; (in velodrome) pista

cycling ['saɪklɪŋ] N ciclismo; **to go on a ~ holiday** (BRIT) fare una vacanza in bicicletta

cyclist ['saɪklɪst] N ciclista mf

cyclone ['saɪkləun] N ciclone m

cygnet ['sɪɡnɪt] N cigno giovane

cylinder ['sɪlɪndə'] N cilindro

cylinder capacity N cilindrata

cylinder head N testata

cylinder head gasket N guarnizione f della testata del cilindro

cymbals ['sɪmblz] NPL piatti mpl

cynic ['sɪnɪk] N cinico(-a)

cynical ['sɪnɪkl] ADJ cinico(-a)

cynicism ['sɪnɪsɪzəm] N cinismo

cypress ['saɪprɪs] N cipresso

Cypriot ['sɪprɪət] ADJ, N cipriota (mf)

Cyprus ['saɪprəs] N Cipro

cyst [sɪst] N cisti f inv

cystitis [sɪ'staɪtɪs] N cistite f

CZ N ABBR (US: = Canal Zone) zona del Canale di Panama

czar [zɑːʳ] N zar m inv

Czech [tʃɛk] ADJ ceco(-a) ▶ N ceco(-a); (Ling) ceco

Czechoslovak [tʃɛkə'sləuvæk] ADJ, N (Hist) = **Czechoslovakian**

Czechoslovakia [tʃɛkəslə'vækɪə] N (Hist) Cecoslovacchia

Czechoslovakian [tʃɛkəslə'vækɪən] (Hist) ADJ, N cecoslovacco(-a)

Czech Republic N: **the ~** la Repubblica Ceca

Dd

D, d [di:] N (*letter*) D, d *f inv or m inv*; (*Mus*):
D re *m*; **D for David**, (*US*) **D for Dog** = D come
Domodossola

D ABBR (*US Pol*) = **democrat**

d ABBR (*BRIT old*) = **penny**

d. ABBR = **died**

DA N ABBR (*US*) = **district attorney**

dab [dæb] VT (*eyes, wound*) tamponare;
(*paint, cream*) applicare (con leggeri colpetti);
a ~ of paint un colpetto di vernice

dabble ['dæbl] VI: **to ~ in** occuparsi (da
dilettante) di

Dacca ['dækə] N Dacca *f*

dachshund ['dækshund] N bassotto

dad [dæd], **daddy** ['dædɪ] N babbo, papà *m inv*

daddy-long-legs [dædɪ'lɔŋlɛgz] N tipula,
zanzarone *m*

daffodil ['dæfədɪl] N trombone *m*,
giunchiglia

daft [dɑ:ft] ADJ sciocco(-a); **to be ~ about sb**
perdere la testa per qn; **to be ~ about sth**
andare pazzo per qc

dagger ['dægə'] N pugnale *m*

dahlia ['deɪljə] N dalia

daily ['deɪlɪ] ADJ quotidiano(-a), giornaliero(-a)
▶ N quotidiano; (*BRIT: servant*) donna di
servizio ▶ ADV tutti i giorni; **twice ~** due
volte al giorno

dainty ['deɪntɪ] ADJ delicato(-a),
grazioso(-a)

dairy ['dɛərɪ] N (*shop*) latteria; (*on farm*)
caseificio ▶ CPD caseario(-a)

dairy cow N mucca da latte

dairy farm N caseificio

dairy produce N latticini *mpl*

dais ['deɪɪs] N pedana, palco

daisy ['deɪzɪ] N margherita

daisy wheel N (*on printer*) margherita

daisy-wheel printer ['deɪzɪwi:l-] N
stampante *f* a margherita

Dakar ['dækə'] N Dakar *f*

dale [deɪl] N valle *f*

dally ['dælɪ] VI trastullarsi

dalmatian [dæl'meɪʃən] N (*dog*) dalmata *m*

dam [dæm] N diga; (*reservoir*) bacino
artificiale ▶ VT sbarrare; costruire dighe su

damage ['dæmɪdʒ] N danno, danni *mpl*; (*fig*)
danno ▶ VT danneggiare; (*fig*) recar danno a;
~ to property danni materiali

damages NPL (*Law*) danni *mpl*; **to pay £5000
in ~** pagare 5000 sterline di indennizzo

damaging ['dæmɪdʒɪŋ] ADJ: **~ (to)** nocivo(-a)
(a)

Damascus [də'mɑ:skəs] N Damasco *f*

dame [deɪm] N (*title, US col*) donna; (*Theat*)
vecchia signora (*ruolo comico di donna recitato da
un uomo*)

damn [dæm] VT condannare; (*curse*) maledire
▶ N (*col*): **I don't give a ~** non me ne frega
niente ▶ ADJ (*col: also*: **damned**): **this ~ ...**
questo maledetto ...; **~ (it)!** accidenti!

damnable ['dæmnəbl] ADJ (*col: behaviour*)
vergognoso(-a); (*weather*) schifoso(-a)

damnation [dæm'neɪʃən] N (*Rel*) dannazione
f ▶ EXCL (*col*) dannazione!, diavolo!

damning ['dæmɪŋ] ADJ (*evidence*) schiacciante

damp [dæmp] ADJ umido(-a) ▶ N umidità,
umido ▶ VT (*also*: **dampen**: *cloth, rag*)
inumidire, bagnare; (: *enthusiasm etc*)
spegnere

dampcourse ['dæmpkɔːs] N strato *m*
isolante antiumido *inv*

damper ['dæmpə'] N (*Mus*) sordina; (*of fire*)
valvola di tiraggio; **to put a ~ on sth** (*fig*:
atmosphere) gelare; (*enthusiasm*) far sbollire

dampness ['dæmpnɪs] N umidità, umido

damson ['dæmzən] N susina damaschina

dance [dɑːns] N danza, ballo; (*ball*) ballo ▶ VI
ballare; **to ~ about** saltellare

dance floor N pista da ballo

dance hall N dancing *m inv*, sala da ballo

dancer ['dɑːnsə'] N danzatore(-trice);
(*professional*) ballerino(-a)

dancing ['dɑːnsɪŋ] N danza, ballo

D and C N ABBR (*Med:* = *dilation and curettage*)
raschiamento

dandelion ['dændɪlaɪən] N dente *m* di leone

dandruff ['dændrəf] N forfora

D & T N ABBR (*Brit Scol*) = **design and technology**

dandy ['dændɪ] N dandy *m inv*, elegantone *m*
▶ ADJ (*US col*) fantastico(-a)

Dane [deɪn] N danese *mf*

danger ['deɪndʒə^r] N pericolo; **there is a ~ of fire** c'è pericolo di incendio; **in ~** in pericolo; **out of ~** fuori pericolo; **he was in ~ of falling** rischiava di cadere

danger list N (*Med*): **on the ~** in prognosi riservata

dangerous ['deɪndʒrəs] ADJ pericoloso(-a)

dangerously ['deɪndʒrəslɪ] ADV: **~ ill** in pericolo di vita

danger zone N area di pericolo

dangle ['dæŋgl] VT dondolare; (*fig*) far balenare ▶ VI pendolare

Danish ['deɪnɪʃ] ADJ danese ▶ N (*Ling*) danese *m*

Danish pastry N dolce *m* di pasta sfoglia

dank [dæŋk] ADJ freddo(-a) e umido(-a)

Danube ['dænjuːb] N: **the ~** il Danubio

dapper ['dæpə^r] ADJ lindo(-a)

Dardanelles [dɑːdə'nɛlz] NPL Dardanelli *mpl*

dare [dɛə^r] VT: **to ~ sb to do** sfidare qn a fare ▶ VI: **to ~ (to) do sth** osare fare qc; **I daren't tell him** (*Brit*) non oso dirglielo; **I ~ say** (*I suppose*) immagino (che); **I ~ say he'll turn up** immagino che spunterà

daredevil ['dɛədɛvl] N scavezzacollo *mf*

Dar-es-Salaam ['dɑːrɛssə'lɑːm] N Dar-es-Salaam *f*

daring ['dɛərɪŋ] ADJ audace, ardito(-a) ▶ N audacia

dark [dɑːk] ADJ (*night, room*) buio(-a), scuro(-a); (*colour, complexion*) scuro(-a); (*fig*) cupo(-a), tetro(-a), nero(-a) ▶ N: **in the ~** al buio; **it is/is getting ~** è/si sta facendo buio; **in the ~ about** (*fig*) all'oscuro di; **after ~** a notte fatta; **~ chocolate** cioccolata amara

darken ['dɑːkən] VT (*room*) oscurare; (*photo, painting*) far scuro(-a); (*colour*) scurire ▶ VI (*sky, room*) oscurarsi; imbrunirsi

dark glasses NPL occhiali *mpl* scuri

dark horse N (*fig*) incognita

darkly ['dɑːklɪ] ADV (*gloomily*) cupamente, con aria cupa; (*in a sinister way*) minacciosamente

darkness ['dɑːknɪs] N oscurità, buio

darkroom ['dɑːkruːm] N camera oscura

darling ['dɑːlɪŋ] ADJ caro(-a) ▶ N tesoro

darn [dɑːn] VT rammendare

dart [dɑːt] N freccetta; (*Sewing*) pince *f inv* ▶ VI: **to ~ towards** (*also*: **make a dart towards**) precipitarsi verso; **to ~ along** passare come un razzo; **to ~ away/along** sfrecciare via/lungo; *see also* **darts**

dartboard ['dɑːtbɔːd] N bersaglio (per freccette)

darts [dɑːts] N tiro al bersaglio (con freccette)

dash [dæʃ] N (*sign*) lineetta; (*small quantity: of liquid*) goccio, goccino; (: *of soda*) spruzzo ▶ VT (*missile*) gettare; (*hopes*) infrangere ▶ VI: **to ~ towards** (*also*: **make a dash towards**) precipitarsi verso
▶ **dash away** VI scappare via

dashboard ['dæʃbɔːd] N (*Aut*) cruscotto

dashing ['dæʃɪŋ] ADJ ardito(-a)

dastardly ['dæstədlɪ] ADJ vile

DAT N ABBR (= *digital audio tape*) cassetta *f* digitale audio *inv*

data ['deɪtə] NPL dati *mpl*

database ['deɪtəbeɪs] N database *m inv*, base *f* di dati

data capture N registrazione *f or* rilevazione *f* di dati

data processing N elaborazione *f* (elettronica) dei dati

data transmission N trasmissione *f* di dati

date [deɪt] N data; (*appointment*) appuntamento; (*fruit*) dattero ▶ VT datare; (*person*) uscire con; **what's the ~ today?** quanti ne abbiamo oggi?; **~ of birth** data di nascita; **closing ~** scadenza, termine *m*; **to ~** *adv* (*until now*) fino a oggi; **out of ~** scaduto(-a); (*old-fashioned*) passato(-a) di moda; **up to ~** moderno(-a), aggiornato(-a); **to bring up to ~** (*correspondence, information*) aggiornare; (*method*) modernizzare; (*person*) aggiornare, mettere al corrente; **dated the 13th** datato il 13; **thank you for your letter dated 5th July** *or* **July 5th** (*US*) la ringrazio per la sua lettera in data 5 luglio

dated ['deɪtɪd] ADJ passato(-a) di moda

dateline ['deɪtlaɪn] N linea del cambiamento di data

date rape N *stupro perpetrato da persona conosciuta*

date stamp N timbro datario

daub [dɔːb] VT imbrattare

daughter ['dɔːtə^r] N figlia

daughter-in-law ['dɔːtərɪnlɔː] N nuora

daunt [dɔːnt] VT intimidire

daunting ['dɔːntɪŋ] ADJ non invidiabile

dauntless ['dɔːntlɪs] ADJ intrepido(-a)

dawdle ['dɔːdl] VI bighellonare; **to ~ over one's work** gingillarsi con il lavoro

dawn [dɔːn] N alba ▶ VI (*day*) spuntare; (*fig*) venire in mente; **at ~** all'alba; **from ~ to dusk** dall'alba al tramonto; **it dawned on him that** ... gli è venuto in mente che ...

dawn chorus N (*Brit*) coro mattutino degli uccelli

day [deɪ] N giorno; (*as duration*) giornata; (*period of time, age*) tempo, epoca; **the ~ before** il giorno avanti *or* prima; **the ~ after, the following ~** il giorno dopo, il giorno seguente; **the ~ before yesterday** l'altro ieri; **the ~ after tomorrow** dopodomani; **(on) that ~** quel giorno; **(on) the ~ that** ... il giorno che or in cui ...; **to work an 8-hour ~** avere una giornata lavorativa di 8 ore; **by ~** di giorno; **~ by ~** giorno per giorno; **paid by the ~** pagato(-a) a giornata; **these days, in the present ~** di questi tempi, oggigiorno

daybook ['deɪbuk] N (BRIT) brogliaccio

day boy N (Scol) alunno esterno

daybreak ['deɪbreɪk] N spuntar m del giorno

day care centre N scuola materna

daydream ['deɪdriːm] N sogno a occhi aperti ▶ VI sognare a occhi aperti

day girl N (Scol) alunna esterna

daylight ['deɪlaɪt] N luce f del giorno

daylight robbery N: **it's ~!** (BRIT col) è un vero furto!

Daylight Saving Time N (US) ora legale

day release N: **to be on ~** avere un giorno di congedo alla settimana per formazione professionale

day return, day return ticket N (BRIT) biglietto giornaliero di andata e ritorno

day shift N turno di giorno

daytime ['deɪtaɪm] N giorno

day-to-day ['deɪtə'deɪ] ADJ (routine, life, organization) quotidiano(-a); (expenses) giornaliero(-a); **on a ~ basis** a giornata

day trader N (Stock Exchange) day dealer mf, operatore che compra e vende titoli nel corso della stessa giornata

day trip N gita (di un giorno)

day tripper N gitante mf

daze [deɪz] VT (drug) inebetire; (blow) stordire ▶ N: **in a ~** inebetito(-a), stordito(-a)

dazed [deɪzd] ADJ stordito(-a)

dazzle ['dæzl] VT abbagliare

dazzling ['dæzlɪŋ] ADJ (light) abbagliante; (colour) violento(-a); (smile) smagliante

dB ABBR (= decibel) db

DC ABBR (Elec: = direct current) c.c.; (US) = District of Columbia

DCC® N ABBR = **digital compact cassette**

DD N ABBR (= Doctor of Divinity) titolo di studio

DD ABBR = **direct debit**

dd. ABBR (Comm) = **delivered**

D-day ['diːdeɪ] N giorno dello sbarco alleato in Normandia

DDS N ABBR US: = **Doctor of Dental Science**; (= Doctor of Dental Surgery) titoli di studio

DDT N ABBR (= dichlorodiphenyl trichloroethane) D.D.T. m

DE ABBR (US) = **Delaware**

deacon ['diːkən] N diacono

dead [dɛd] ADJ morto(-a); (numb) intirizzito(-a); (telephone) muto(-a); (battery) scarico(-a) ▶ ADV assolutamente, perfettamente; **the dead** NPL i morti; **he was shot ~** fu colpito a morte; **~ on time** in perfetto orario; **~ tired** stanco(-a) morto(-a); **to stop ~** fermarsi di colpo; **the line has gone ~** (Tel) è caduta la linea

dead beat ADJ (col) stanco(-a) morto(-a)

deaden ['dɛdn] VT (blow, sound) ammortire; (make numb) intirizzire

dead end N vicolo cieco

dead-end ['dɛdɛnd] ADJ: **a ~ job** un lavoro senza sbocchi

dead heat N (Sport): **to finish in a ~** finire alla pari

dead-letter office [dɛd'lɛtə-] N ufficio della posta in giacenza

deadline ['dɛdlaɪn] N scadenza; **to work to a ~** avere una scadenza

deadlock ['dɛdlɔk] N punto morto

dead loss N (col): **to be a ~** (person, thing) non valere niente

deadly ['dɛdlɪ] ADJ mortale; (weapon, poison) micidiale ▶ ADV: **~ dull** di una noia micidiale

deadpan ['dɛdpæn] ADJ a faccia impassibile

Dead Sea N: **the ~** il mar Morto

deaf [dɛf] ADJ sordo(-a); **to turn a ~ ear to sth** fare orecchi da mercante a qc

deaf-aid ['dɛfeɪd] N apparecchio per la sordità

deaf-and-dumb ['dɛfən'dʌm] ADJ (person) sordomuto(-a); (alphabet) dei sordomuti

deafen ['dɛfn] VT assordare

deafening ['dɛfnɪŋ] ADJ fragoroso(-a), assordante

deaf-mute ['dɛfmjuːt] N sordomuto(-a)

deafness ['dɛfnɪs] N sordità

deal [diːl] (pt, pp **dealt** [dɛlt]) N accordo; (business deal) affare m ▶ VT (blow, cards) dare; **to strike a ~ with sb** fare un affare con qn; **it's a ~!** (col) affare fatto!; **he got a bad/fair ~ from them** l'hanno trattato male/bene; **a good ~ of, a great ~ of** molto(-a)
▶ **deal in** VT FUS (Comm) occuparsi di
▶ **deal with** VT FUS (Comm) fare affari con, trattare con; (handle) occuparsi di; (be about: book etc) trattare di

dealer ['diːləʳ] N commerciante mf

dealership ['diːləʃɪp] N rivenditore m

dealings ['diːlɪŋz] NPL (Comm) relazioni fpl; (relations) rapporti mpl; (in goods, shares) transazioni fpl

dealt [dɛlt] PT, PP of **deal**

dean [diːn] N (Rel) decano; (Scol) preside m di facoltà (or di collegio)

dear [dɪəʳ] ADJ caro(-a) ▶ N: **my ~** caro mio/cara mia ▶ EXCL: **~ me!** Dio mio!; **D~ Sir/Madam** (in letter) Egregio Signore/Egregia Signora, **D~ Mr/Mrs X** Gentile Signor/Signora X

dearly ['dɪəlɪ] ADV (love) moltissimo; (pay) a caro prezzo

dear money N (Comm) denaro ad alto interesse

dearth [dəːθ] N scarsità, carestia

death [dɛθ] N morte f; (Admin) decesso

deathbed ['dɛθbɛd] N letto di morte
death certificate N atto di decesso
death duty N (BRIT) imposta or tassa di successione
deathly ['dɛθlɪ] ADJ di morte ▶ ADV come un cadavere
death penalty N pena di morte
death rate N indice m di mortalità
death row [-rəu] N (US): **to be on ~** essere nel braccio della morte
death sentence N condanna a morte
death squad N squadra della morte
deathtrap ['dɛθtræp] N trappola mortale
deb [dɛb] N ABBR (col) = **debutante**
debacle [deɪ'bɑːkl] N (defeat) disfatta; (collapse) sfacelo
debar [dɪ'bɑːʳ] VT: **to ~ sb from a club** etc escludere qn da un club etc; **to ~ sb from doing** vietare a qn di fare
debase [dɪ'beɪs] VT (currency) adulterare; (person) degradare
debatable [dɪ'beɪtəbl] ADJ discutibile; **it is ~ whether ...** è in dubbio se ...
debate [dɪ'beɪt] N dibattito ▶ VT dibattere; discutere ▶ VI (consider): **to ~ whether** riflettere se
debauchery [dɪ'bɔːtʃərɪ] N dissolutezza
debenture [dɪ'bɛntʃəʳ] N (Comm) obbligazione f
debilitate [dɪ'bɪlɪteɪt] VT debilitare
debit ['dɛbɪt] N debito ▶ VT: **to ~ a sum to sb** or **to sb's account** addebitare una somma a qn
debit balance N saldo debitore
debit card N carta di debito
debit note N nota di addebito
debonair [dɛbə'nɛəʳ] ADJ gioviale e disinvolto(-a)
debrief [diː'briːf] VT chiamare a rapporto (a operazione ultimata)
debriefing [diː'briːfɪŋ] N rapporto
debris ['dɛbriː] N detriti mpl
debt [dɛt] N debito; **to be in ~** essere indebitato(-a); **debts of £5000** debiti per 5000 sterline; **bad ~** debito insoluto
debt collector N agente m di recupero crediti
debtor ['dɛtəʳ] N debitore(-trice)
debug [diː'bʌg] VT (Comput) localizzare e rimuovere errori in
debunk [diː'bʌŋk] VT (col: theory) demistificare; (claim) smentire; (person, institution) screditare
debut ['deɪbjuː] N debutto
debutante ['dɛbjutɑːnt] N debuttante f
Dec. ABBR (= December) dic.
decade ['dɛkeɪd] N decennio
decadence ['dɛkədəns] N decadenza
decadent ['dɛkədənt] ADJ decadente
de-caff ['diːkæf] N (col) decaffeinato

decaffeinated [dɪ'kæfɪneɪtɪd] ADJ decaffeinato(-a)
decamp [dɪ'kæmp] VI (col) filarsela, levare le tende
decant [dɪ'kænt] VT (wine) travasare
decanter [dɪ'kæntəʳ] N caraffa
decarbonize [diː'kɑːbənaɪz] VT (Aut) decarburare
decathlon [dɪ'kæθlən] N decathlon m
decay [dɪ'keɪ] N decadimento; imputridimento; (fig) rovina; (also: **tooth decay**) carie f ▶ VI (rot) imputridire; (fig) andare in rovina
decease [dɪ'siːs] N decesso
deceased [dɪ'siːst] N: **the ~** il(la) defunto(a)
deceit [dɪ'siːt] N inganno
deceitful [dɪ'siːtful] ADJ ingannevole, perfido(-a)
deceive [dɪ'siːv] VT ingannare; **to ~ o.s.** illudersi, ingannarsi
decelerate [diː'sɛləreɪt] VT, VI rallentare
December [dɪ'sɛmbəʳ] N dicembre m; see also **July**
decency ['diːsənsɪ] N decenza
decent ['diːsənt] ADJ decente; (respectable) per bene; (kind) gentile; **they were very ~ about it** si sono comportati da signori riguardo a ciò
decently ['diːsəntlɪ] ADV (respectably) decentemente, convenientemente; (kindly) gentilmente
decentralization [diːsɛntrəlaɪ'zeɪʃən] N decentramento
decentralize [diː'sɛntrəlaɪz] VT decentrare
deception [dɪ'sɛpʃən] N inganno
deceptive [dɪ'sɛptɪv] ADJ ingannevole
decibel ['dɛsɪbɛl] N decibel m inv
decide [dɪ'saɪd] VT (person) far prendere una decisione a; (question, argument) risolvere, decidere ▶ VI decidere, decidersi; **to ~ to do/that** decidere di fare/che; **to ~ on** decidere per; **to ~ against doing sth** decidere di non fare qc
decided [dɪ'saɪdɪd] ADJ (resolute) deciso(-a); (clear, definite) netto(-a), chiaro(-a)
decidedly [dɪ'saɪdɪdlɪ] ADV indubbiamente; decisamente
deciding [dɪ'saɪdɪŋ] ADJ decisivo(-a)
deciduous [dɪ'sɪdjuəs] ADJ deciduo(-a)
decimal ['dɛsɪməl] ADJ, N decimale (m); **to 3 ~ places** al terzo decimale
decimalize ['dɛsɪmələɪz] VT (BRIT) convertire al sistema metrico decimale
decimal point N ≈ virgola
decimate ['dɛsɪmeɪt] VT decimare
decipher [dɪ'saɪfəʳ] VT decifrare
decision [dɪ'sɪʒən] N decisione f; **to make a ~** prendere una decisione
decisive [dɪ'saɪsɪv] ADJ (victory, factor) decisivo(-a); (influence) determinante;

(*manner, person*) risoluto(-a), deciso(-a); (*reply*) deciso(-a), categorico(-a)

deck [dɛk] N (*Naut*) ponte *m*; (*of cards*) mazzo; **top ~** imperiale *m*; **to go up on ~** salire in coperta; **below ~** sotto coperta; **cassette ~** piastra (di registrazione); **record ~** piatto (giradischi); (*of cards*) mazzo

deckchair ['dɛktʃɛəʳ] N sedia a sdraio

deck hand N marinaio

declaration [dɛklə'reɪʃən] N dichiarazione *f*

declare [dɪ'klɛəʳ] VT dichiarare

declassify [di:'klæsɪfaɪ] VT rendere accessibile al pubblico

decline [dɪ'klaɪn] N (*decay*) declino; (*lessening*) ribasso ▶ VT declinare; rifiutare ▶ VI declinare; diminuire; **~ in living standards** abbassamento del tenore di vita; **to ~ to do sth** rifiutar(si) di fare qc

declutch [di:'klʌtʃ] VI (*BRIT*) premere la frizione

decode [di:'kəud] VT decifrare

decoder [di:'kəudəʳ] N (*Comput, TV*) decodificatore *m*

decompose [di:kəm'pəuz] VI decomporre

decomposition [di:kɔmpə'zɪʃən] N decomposizione *f*

decompression [di:kəm'prɛʃən] N decompressione *f*

decompression chamber N camera di decompressione

decongestant [di:kən'dʒɛstənt] N decongestionante *m*

decontaminate [di:kən'tæmɪneɪt] VT decontaminare

decontrol [di:kən'trəul] VT (*trade*) liberalizzare; (*prices*) togliere il controllo governativo a

decor ['deɪkɔːʳ] N decorazione *f*

decorate ['dɛkəreɪt] VT (*adorn, give a medal to*) decorare; (*paint and paper*) tinteggiare e tappezzare

decoration [dɛkə'reɪʃən] N (*medal etc, adornment*) decorazione *f*

decorative ['dɛkərətɪv] ADJ decorativo(-a)

decorator ['dɛkəreɪtəʳ] N decoratore(-trice)

decorum [dɪ'kɔːrəm] N decoro

decoy ['di:kɔɪ] N zimbello; **they used him as a ~ for the enemy** l'hanno usato come esca per il nemico

decrease N ['di:kri:s] diminuzione *f* ▶ VT, VI [di:'kri:s] diminuire; **to be on the ~** essere in diminuzione

decreasing [di:'kri:sɪŋ] ADJ sempre meno *inv*

decree [dɪ'kri:] N decreto ▶ VT: **to ~ (that)** decretare (che + *sub*); **~ absolute** sentenza di divorzio definitiva; **~ nisi** sentenza provvisoria di divorzio

decrepit [dɪ'krɛpɪt] ADJ decrepito(-a); (*building*) cadente

decry [dɪ'kraɪ] VT condannare, deplorare

decrypt [di:'krɪpt] VT (*Comput, Tel*) decriptare

dedicate ['dɛdɪkeɪt] VT consacrare; (*book etc*) dedicare

dedicated ['dɛdɪkeɪtɪd] ADJ coscienzioso(-a); (*Comput*) specializzato(-a), dedicato(-a)

dedication [dɛdɪ'keɪʃən] N (*devotion*) dedizione *f*; (*in book*) dedica

deduce [dɪ'dju:s] VT dedurre

deduct [dɪ'dʌkt] VT: **to ~ sth (from)** dedurre qc (da); (*from wage etc*) trattenere qc (da)

deduction [dɪ'dʌkʃən] N (*deducting*) deduzione *f*; (*from wage etc*) trattenuta; (*deducing*) deduzione *f*, conclusione *f*

deed [di:d] N azione *f*, atto; (*Law*) atto; **~ of covenant** atto di donazione

deem [di:m] VT (*formal*) giudicare, ritenere; **to ~ it wise to do** ritenere prudente fare

deep [di:p] ADJ profondo(-a) ▶ ADV: **~ in snow** affondato(-a) nella neve; **spectators stood 20 ~** c'erano 20 file di spettatori; **knee-~ in water** in acqua fino alle ginocchia; **4 metres ~** profondo(a) 4 metri; **he took a ~ breath** fece un respiro profondo; **how ~ is the water?** quanto è profonda l'acqua?

deepen ['di:pn] VT (*hole*) approfondire ▶ VI approfondirsi; (*darkness*) farsi più intenso(-a)

deep-freeze [di:p'fri:z] N congelatore *m* ▶ VT congelare

deep-fry ['di:p'fraɪ] VT friggere in olio abbondante

deeply ['di:plɪ] ADV profondamente; **to regret sth ~** rammaricarsi sinceramente di qc

deep-rooted ['di:p'ru:tɪd] ADJ (*prejudice*) profondamente radicato(-a); (*affection*) profondo(-a); (*habit*) inveterato(-a)

deep-sea diver ['di:p'si:-] N palombaro

deep-sea diving N immersione *f* in alto mare

deep-sea fishing N pesca d'alto mare

deep-seated ['di:p'si:tɪd] ADJ (*beliefs*) radicato(-a)

deep-set ['di:psɛt] ADJ (*eyes*) infossato(-a)

deep-vein thrombosis ['di:pveɪn-] N trombosi *f* inv venosa profonda

deer [dɪəʳ] N (*pl inv*): **the ~** i cervidi (*Zool*); **(red) ~** cervo; **(fallow) ~** daino; **(roe) ~** capriolo

deerskin ['dɪəskɪn] N pelle *f* di daino

deerstalker ['dɪəstɔːkəʳ] N berretto da cacciatore

deface [dɪ'feɪs] VT imbrattare

defamation [dɛfə'meɪʃən] N diffamazione *f*

defamatory [dɪ'fæmətərɪ] ADJ diffamatorio(-a)

default [dɪ'fɔːlt] VI (*Law*) essere contumace; (*gen*) essere inadempiente ▶ N (*Comput: also:* **default value**) default *m inv*; **by ~** (*Law*) in

d

contumacia; (*Sport*) per abbandono; **to ~ on a debt** non onorare un debito

defaulter [dɪˈfɔːltə^r] N (*on debt*) inadempiente *mf*

default option N (*Comput*) opzione *f* di default

defeat [dɪˈfiːt] N sconfitta ▶ VT (*team, opponents*) sconfiggere; (*fig: plans, efforts*) frustrare

defeatism [dɪˈfiːtɪzəm] N disfattismo

defeatist [dɪˈfiːtɪst] ADJ, N disfattista (*mf*)

defecate [ˈdɛfəkeɪt] VI defecare

defect N [ˈdiːfɛkt] difetto ▶ VI [dɪˈfɛkt]: **to ~ to the enemy/the West** passare al nemico/all'Ovest; **physical ~** difetto fisico; **mental ~** anomalia mentale

defective [dɪˈfɛktɪv] ADJ difettoso(-a)

defector [dɪˈfɛktə^r] N rifugiato(-a) politico(-a)

defence, (*US*) **defense** [dɪˈfɛns] N difesa; **in ~ of** in difesa di; **the Ministry of D~**, (*US*) **the Department of Defense** il Ministero della Difesa; **witness for the ~** teste *mf* a difesa

defenceless [dɪˈfɛnslɪs] ADJ senza difesa

defend [dɪˈfɛnd] VT difendere; (*decision, action*) giustificare; (*opinion*) sostenere

defendant [dɪˈfɛndənt] N imputato(-a)

defender [dɪˈfɛndə^r] N difensore(-a)

defending champion N (*Sport*) campione(-essa) in carica

defending counsel N (*Law*) avvocato difensore

defense [dɪˈfɛns] N (*US*) = **defence**

defensive [dɪˈfɛnsɪv] ADJ difensivo(-a) ▶ N difensiva; **on the ~** sulla difensiva

defer [dɪˈfəː^r] VT (*postpone*) differire, rinviare ▶ VI (*submit*): **to ~ to sb/sth** rimettersi a qn/qc

deference [ˈdɛfərəns] N deferenza; riguardo; **out of** *or* **in ~ to** per riguardo a

defiance [dɪˈfaɪəns] N sfida; **in ~ of** a dispetto di

defiant [dɪˈfaɪənt] ADJ (*attitude*) di sfida; (*person*) ribelle

defiantly [dɪˈfaɪəntlɪ] ADV con aria di sfida

deficiency [dɪˈfɪʃənsɪ] N deficienza; carenza; (*Comm*) ammanco

deficiency disease N malattia da carenza

deficient [dɪˈfɪʃənt] ADJ deficiente; insufficiente; **to be ~ in** mancare di

deficit [ˈdɛfɪsɪt] N disavanzo, deficit *m inv*

defile [dɪˈfaɪl] VT contaminare ▶ VI sfilare ▶ N [ˈdiːfaɪl] gola, stretta

define [dɪˈfaɪn] VT (*gen, Comput*) definire

definite [ˈdɛfɪnɪt] ADJ (*fixed*) definito(-a), preciso(-a); (*clear, obvious*) ben definito(-a), esatto(-a); (*Ling*) determinativo(-a); **he was ~ about it** ne era sicuro

definitely [ˈdɛfɪnɪtlɪ] ADV indubbiamente

definition [dɛfɪˈnɪʃən] N definizione *f*

definitive [dɪˈfɪnɪtɪv] ADJ definitivo(-a)

deflate [diːˈfleɪt] VT sgonfiare; (*Econ*) deflazionare; (*pompous person*) fare abbassare la cresta a

deflation [diːˈfleɪʃən] N (*Econ*) deflazione *f*

deflationary [diːˈfleɪʃənrɪ] ADJ (*Econ*) deflazionistico(-a)

deflect [dɪˈflɛkt] VT deflettere, deviare

defog [ˈdiːˈfɔɡ] VT (*US Aut*) sbrinare

defogger [ˈdiːˈfɔɡə^r] N (*US Aut*) sbrinatore *m*

deform [dɪˈfɔːm] VT deformare

deformed [dɪˈfɔːmd] ADJ deforme

deformity [dɪˈfɔːmɪtɪ] N deformità *f inv*

Defra N ABBR (*Brit*) = **Department for Environment, Food and Rural Affairs**

defraud [dɪˈfrɔːd] VT: **to ~ (of)** defraudare (di)

defray [dɪˈfreɪ] VT: **to ~ sb's expenses** sostenere le spese di qn

defriend [diːˈfrɛnd] VT (*Internet*) cancellare dagli amici

defrost [diːˈfrɔst] VT (*fridge*) disgelare; (*frozen food*) scongelare

deft [dɛft] ADJ svelto(-a), destro(-a)

defunct [dɪˈfʌŋkt] ADJ defunto(-a)

defuse [diːˈfjuːz] VT disinnescare; (*fig*) distendere

defy [dɪˈfaɪ] VT sfidare; (*efforts etc*) resistere a; (*refuse to obey: person*) rifiutare di obbedire a; **it defies description** supera ogni descrizione

degenerate VI [dɪˈdʒɛnəreɪt] degenerare ▶ ADJ [dɪˈdʒɛnərɪt] degenere

degradation [dɛɡrəˈdeɪʃən] N degradazione *f*

degrade [dɪˈɡreɪd] VT degradare

degrading [dɪˈɡreɪdɪŋ] ADJ degradante

degree [dɪˈɡriː] N grado; (*Scol*) laurea (universitaria); **10 degrees below freezing** 10 gradi sotto zero; **a (first) ~ in maths** una laurea in matematica; **a considerable ~ of risk** una grossa percentuale di rischio; **by degrees** (*gradually*) gradualmente, a poco a poco; **to some ~, to a certain ~** fino a un certo punto, in certa misura

dehydrated [diːhaɪˈdreɪtɪd] ADJ disidratato(-a); (*milk, eggs*) in polvere

dehydration [diːhaɪˈdreɪʃən] N disidratazione *f*

de-ice [diːˈaɪs] VT (*windscreen*) disgelare

de-icer [ˈdiːˈaɪsə^r] N sbrinatore *m*

deign [deɪn] VI: **to ~ to do** degnarsi di fare

deity [ˈdiːɪtɪ] N divinità *f inv*; dio (dea)

déjà vu [deɪʒɑːˈvuː] N déjà vu *m inv*

dejected [dɪˈdʒɛktɪd] ADJ abbattuto(-a), avvilito(-a)

dejection [dɪˈdʒɛkʃən] N abbattimento, avvilimento

Del. ABBR (*US*) = **Delaware**

delay [dɪˈleɪ] VT (*journey, operation*) ritardare, rinviare; (*travellers, trains*) ritardare; (*payment*) differire ▶ VI: **to ~ (in doing sth)** ritardare (a fare qc) ▶ N ritardo; **without ~** senza ritardo; **to be delayed** subire un ritardo; (*person*) essere trattenuto(-a)

delayed-action [dɪ'leɪd'ækʃən] ADJ a azione ritardata

delectable [dɪ'lɛktəbl] ADJ delizioso(-a)

delegate N ['dɛlɪgɪt] delegato(-a) ▶ VT ['dɛlɪgeɪt] delegare; **to ~ sth/sb to do sth** delegare qc a qn/qn a fare qc

delegation [dɛlɪ'geɪʃən] N delegazione f; (*of work etc*) delega

delete [dɪ'liːt] VT (*gen, Comput*) cancellare

Delhi ['dɛlɪ] N Delhi f

deli ['dɛlɪ] N = delicatessen

deliberate ADJ [dɪ'lɪbərɪt] (*intentional*) intenzionale; (*slow*) misurato(-a) ▶ VI [dɪ'lɪbəreɪt] deliberare, riflettere

deliberately [dɪ'lɪbərɪtlɪ] ADV (*on purpose*) deliberatamente

deliberation [dɪlɪbə'reɪʃən] N (*consideration*) riflessione f; (*discussion*) discussione f, deliberazione f

delicacy ['dɛlɪkəsɪ] N delicatezza

delicate ['dɛlɪkɪt] ADJ delicato(-a)

delicately ['dɛlɪkɪtlɪ] ADV (*gen*) delicatamente; (*act, express*) con delicatezza

delicatessen [dɛlɪkə'tɛsn] N = salumeria

delicious [dɪ'lɪʃəs] ADJ delizioso(-a), squisito(-a)

delight [dɪ'laɪt] N delizia, gran piacere m ▶ VT dilettare; **it is a ~ to the eyes** è un piacere guardarlo; **to take ~ in** divertirsi a; **to be the ~ of** essere la gioia di

delighted [dɪ'laɪtɪd] ADJ: **~ (at or with sth)** contentissimo(-a) (di qc), felice (di qc); **to be ~ to do sth/that** essere felice di fare qc/che + sub; **I'd be ~** con grande piacere

delightful [dɪ'laɪtful] ADJ (*person, place, meal*) delizioso(-a); (*smile, manner*) incantevole

delimit [diː'lɪmɪt] VT delimitare

delineate [dɪ'lɪnɪeɪt] VT delineare

delinquency [dɪ'lɪŋkwənsɪ] N delinquenza

delinquent [dɪ'lɪŋkwənt] ADJ, N delinquente (*mf*)

delirious [dɪ'lɪrɪəs] ADJ (*Med, fig*) delirante, in delirio; **to be ~** delirare; (*fig*) farneticare

delirium [dɪ'lɪrɪəm] N delirio

deliver [dɪ'lɪvə^r] VT (*mail*) distribuire; (*goods*) consegnare; (*speech*) pronunciare; (*free*) liberare; (*Med*) far partorire; **to ~ a message** fare un'ambasciata; **to ~ the goods** (*fig*) partorire

deliverance [dɪ'lɪvrəns] N liberazione f

delivery [dɪ'lɪvrɪ] N distribuzione f; consegna; (*of speaker*) dizione f; (*Med*) parto; **to take ~ of** prendere in consegna

delivery note N bolla di consegna

delivery van, (*US*) **delivery truck** N furgoncino (per le consegne)

delta ['dɛltə] N delta m

delude [dɪ'luːd] VT deludere, illudere

deluge ['dɛljuːdʒ] N diluvio ▶ VT (*fig*): **to ~ (with)** subissare (di), inondare (di)

delusion [dɪ'luːʒən] N illusione f

de luxe [də'lʌks] ADJ di lusso

delve [dɛlv] VI: **to ~ into** frugare in; (*subject*) far ricerche in

Dem. ABBR (*US Pol*) = **democrat**

demagogue ['dɛməgɔg] N demagogo

demand [dɪ'maːnd] VT richiedere; (*rights*) rivendicare ▶ N richiesta; (*Econ*) domanda; (*claim*) rivendicazione f; **to ~ sth (from or of sb)** pretendere qc (da qn), esigere qc (da qn); **in ~** ricercato(-a), richiesto(-a); **on ~** a richiesta

demand draft N (*Comm*) tratta a vista

demanding [dɪ'maːndɪŋ] ADJ (*boss*) esigente; (*work*) impegnativo(-a)

demarcation [diːmaː'keɪʃən] N demarcazione f

demarcation dispute N (*Industry*) controversia settoriale (*or di categoria*)

demean [dɪ'miːn] VT: **to ~ o.s.** umiliarsi

demeanour, (*US*) **demeanor** [dɪ'miːnə^r] N comportamento; contegno

demented [dɪ'mɛntɪd] ADJ demente, impazzito(-a)

demilitarized zone [diː'mɪlɪtəraɪzd-] N zona smilitarizzata

demise [dɪ'maɪz] N decesso

demist [diː'mɪst] VT (*BRIT Aut*) sbrinare

demister [diː'mɪstə^r] N (*BRIT Aut*) sbrinatore m

demo ['dɛməu] N ABBR (*col*: = **demonstration**) manifestazione f

demobilize [diː'məubɪlaɪz] VT smobilitare

democracy [dɪ'mɔkrəsɪ] N democrazia

democrat ['dɛməkræt] N democratico(-a)

democratic [dɛmə'krætɪk] ADJ democratico(-a); **the D~ Party** (*US*) il partito democratico

demography [dɪ'mɔgrəfɪ] N demografia

demolish [dɪ'mɔlɪʃ] VT demolire

demolition [dɛmə'lɪʃən] N demolizione f

demon ['diːmən] N (*also fig*) demonio ▶ CPD: **a ~ squash player** un mago dello squash; **a ~ driver** un guidatore folle

demonstrate ['dɛmənstreɪt] VT dimostrare, provare ▶ VI: **to ~ (for/against)** dimostrare (per/contro), manifestare (per/contro)

demonstration [dɛmən'streɪʃən] N dimostrazione f; (*Pol*) manifestazione f, dimostrazione; **to hold a ~** (*Pol*) tenere una manifestazione, fare una dimostrazione

demonstrative [dɪ'mɔnstrətɪv] ADJ dimostrativo(-a)

demonstrator ['dɛmənstreɪtə^r] N (*Pol*) dimostrante *mf*; (*Comm: sales person*)

d

dimostratore(-trice); (: *car, computer etc*) modello per dimostrazione

demoralize [dɪ'mɔrəlaɪz] vт demoralizzare

demote [dɪ'məut] vт far retrocedere

demotion [dɪ'məuʃən] ɴ retrocessione f, degradazione f

demur [dɪ'mə:ʳ] vı (*formal*): **to ~ (at)** sollevare obiezioni (a *or* su) ▶ ɴ: **without ~** senza obiezioni

demure [dɪ'mjuəʳ] ᴀᴅᴊ contegnoso(-a)

demurrage [dɪ'mʌrɪdʒ] ɴ diritti *mpl* di immagazzinaggio; spese *fpl* di controstallia

den [dɛn] ɴ tana, covo; (*room*) buco

denationalization ['di:næʃnəlaɪ'zeɪʃən] ɴ denazionalizzazione f

denationalize [di:'næʃnəlaɪz] vт snazionalizzare

denial [dɪ'naɪəl] ɴ diniego; rifiuto

denier ['dɛnɪəʳ] ɴ denaro (*di filati, calze*)

denigrate ['dɛnɪɡreɪt] vт denigrare

denim ['dɛnɪm] ɴ tessuto di cotone ritorto; *see also* **denims**

denim jacket ɴ giubbotto di jeans

denims ['dɛnɪmz] ɴᴘʟ blue jeans *mpl*

denizen ['dɛnɪzən] ɴ (*inhabitant*) abitante *mf*; (*foreigner*) straniero(-a) naturalizzato(-a)

Denmark ['dɛnmɑ:k] ɴ Danimarca

denomination [dɪnɔmɪ'neɪʃən] ɴ (*of money*) valore *m*; (*Rel*) confessione f

denominator [dɪ'nɔmɪneɪtəʳ] ɴ denominatore *m*

denote [dɪ'nəut] vт denotare

denounce [dɪ'nauns] vт denunciare

dense [dɛns] ᴀᴅᴊ fitto(-a); (*smoke*) denso(-a); (*col: stupid*) ottuso(-a), duro(-a)

densely ['dɛnslɪ] ᴀᴅᴠ: **~ wooded** fittamente boscoso(-a); **~ populated** densamente popolato(-a)

density ['dɛnsɪtɪ] ɴ densità f inv; **single/double ~ disk** (*Comput*) disco a singola/doppia densità di registrazione

dent [dɛnt] ɴ ammaccatura ▶ vт (*also*: **make a dent in**) ammaccare; (: *fig*) intaccare

dental ['dɛntl] ᴀᴅᴊ dentale

dental floss [-flɔs] ɴ filo interdentale

dental surgeon ɴ medico(-a) dentista

dental surgery ɴ studio dentistico

dentist ['dɛntɪst] ɴ dentista *mf*; **~'s surgery** (Bʀɪт) studio dentistico

dentistry ['dɛntɪstrɪ] ɴ odontoiatria

dentures ['dɛntʃəz] ɴᴘʟ dentiera

denunciation [dɪnʌnsɪ'eɪʃən] ɴ denuncia

deny [dɪ'naɪ] vт negare; (*refuse*) rifiutare; **he denies having said it** nega di averlo detto

deodorant [di:'əudərənt] ɴ deodorante *m*

depart [dɪ'pɑ:t] vı partire; **to ~ from** (*leave*) allontanarsi da, partire da; (*fig*) deviare da

departed [dɪ'pɑ:tɪd] ᴀᴅᴊ estinto(-a) ▶ ɴ: **the ~** il caro estinto/la cara estinta

department [dɪ'pɑ:tmənt] ɴ (*Comm*) reparto; (*Scol*) sezione f, dipartimento; (*Pol*) ministero; **that's not my ~** (*also fig*) questo non è di mia competenza; **D~ of State** (US) Dipartimento di Stato

departmental [di:pɑ:t'mɛntl] ᴀᴅᴊ (*dispute*) settoriale; (*meeting*) di sezione; **~ manager** caporeparto *mf*

department store ɴ grande magazzino

departure [dɪ'pɑ:tʃəʳ] ɴ partenza; (*fig*): **~ from** deviazione f da; **a new ~** una svolta (decisiva)

departure lounge ɴ sala d'attesa

depend [dɪ'pɛnd] vı: **to ~ (up)on** dipendere da; (*rely on*) contare su; (*be dependent on*) dipendere (economicamente) da, essere a carico di; **it depends** dipende; **depending on the result ...** a seconda del risultato ...

dependable [dɪ'pɛndəbl] ᴀᴅᴊ fidato(-a); (*car etc*) affidabile

dependant [dɪ'pɛndənt] ɴ persona a carico

dependence [dɪ'pɛndəns] ɴ dipendenza

dependent [dɪ'pɛndənt] ᴀᴅᴊ: **to be ~ (on)** (*gen*) dipendere (da); (*child, relative*) essere a carico (di) ▶ ɴ = **dependant**

depict [dɪ'pɪkt] vт (*in picture*) dipingere; (*in words*) descrivere

depilatory [dɪ'pɪlətərɪ] ɴ (*also*: **depilatory cream**) crema depilatoria

depleted [dɪ'pli:tɪd] ᴀᴅᴊ diminuito(-a)

deplorable [dɪ'plɔ:rəbl] ᴀᴅᴊ deplorevole, lamentevole

deplore [dɪ'plɔ:ʳ] vт deplorare

deploy [dɪ'plɔɪ] vт dispiegare

depopulate [di:'pɔpjuleɪt] vт spopolare

depopulation ['di:pɔpju'leɪʃən] ɴ spopolamento

deport [dɪ'pɔ:t] vт deportare; espellere

deportation [di:pɔ:'teɪʃən] ɴ deportazione f

deportation order ɴ foglio di via obbligatorio

deportee [di:pɔ:'ti:] ɴ deportato(-a)

deportment [dɪ'pɔ:tmənt] ɴ portamento

depose [dɪ'pəuz] vт deporre

deposit [dɪ'pɔzɪt] ɴ (*Comm, Geo*) deposito; (*of ore, oil*) giacimento; (*Chem*) sedimento; (*part payment*) acconto; (*for hired goods etc*) cauzione f ▶ vт depositare; dare in acconto; (*luggage etc*) mettere *or* lasciare in deposito; **to put down a ~ of £50** versare una caparra di 50 sterline

deposit account ɴ conto vincolato

depositor [dɪ'pɔzɪtəʳ] ɴ depositante *mf*

depository [dɪ'pɔzɪtərɪ] ɴ (*person*) depositario(-a); (*place*) deposito

depot ['dɛpəu] ɴ deposito; (US) stazione f ferroviaria

depraved [dɪ'preɪvd] ᴀᴅᴊ depravato(-a)

depravity [dɪ'prævɪtɪ] ɴ depravazione f

deprecate ['dɛprɪkeɪt] VT deprecare
deprecating ['dɛprɪkeɪtɪŋ] ADJ (disapproving) di biasimo; (apologetic): **a ~ smile** un sorriso di scusa
depreciate [dɪ'priːʃɪeɪt] VT svalutare ▸ VI svalutarsi
depreciation [dɪpriːʃɪ'eɪʃən] N svalutazione f
depress [dɪ'prɛs] VT deprimere; (price, wages) abbassare; (press down) premere
depressant [dɪ'prɛsnt] N (Med) sedativo
depressed [dɪ'prɛst] ADJ (person) depresso(-a), abbattuto(-a); (area) depresso(-a); (Comm: market, trade) stagnante, in ribasso; (: industry) in crisi; **to get ~** deprimersi
depressing [dɪ'prɛsɪŋ] ADJ deprimente
depression [dɪ'prɛʃən] N depressione f
deprivation [dɛprɪ'veɪʃən] N privazione f; (state) indigenza; (Psych) carenza affettiva
deprive [dɪ'praɪv] VT: **to ~ sb of** privare qn di
deprived [dɪ'praɪvd] ADJ disgraziato(-a)
dept. ABBR = **department**
depth [dɛpθ] N profondità f inv; **at a ~ of 3 metres** a una profondità di 3 metri, a 3 metri di profondità; **in the depths of** nel profondo di; nel cuore di; **in the depths of winter** in pieno inverno; **to study sth in ~** studiare qc in profondità; **to be out of one's ~** (BRIT: swimmer) essere dove non si tocca; (fig) non sentirsi all'altezza della situazione
depth charge N carica di profondità
deputation [dɛpju'teɪʃən] N deputazione f, delegazione f
deputize ['dɛpjutaɪz] VI: **to ~ for** svolgere le funzioni di
deputy ['dɛpjutɪ] N (replacement) supplente mf; (second in command) vice mf; (US: also: **deputy sheriff**) vice-sceriffo ▸ CPD: **~ chairman** vicepresidente m; **~ head** (BRIT: Scol) vicepreside mf; **~ leader** (BRIT Pol) sottosegretario
derail [dɪ'reɪl] VT far deragliare; **to be derailed** deragliare
derailment [dɪ'reɪlmənt] N deragliamento
deranged [dɪ'reɪndʒd] ADJ: **to be (mentally) ~** essere pazzo(a)
derby ['dəːbɪ] N (US) bombetta
deregulate [dɪ'rɛgjuleɪt] VT eliminare la regolamentazione di
deregulation ['diːrɛgju'leɪʃən] N eliminazione f della regolamentazione
derelict ['dɛrɪlɪkt] ADJ abbandonato(-a)
deride [dɪ'raɪd] VT deridere
derision [dɪ'rɪʒən] N derisione f
derisive [dɪ'raɪsɪv] ADJ di derisione
derisory [dɪ'raɪsərɪ] ADJ (sum) irrisorio(-a)
derivation [dɛrɪ'veɪʃən] N derivazione f
derivative [dɪ'rɪvətɪv] N derivato ▸ ADJ derivato(-a)

derive [dɪ'raɪv] VT: **to ~ sth from** derivare qc da; trarre qc da ▸ VI: **to ~ from** derivare da
dermatitis [dəːmə'taɪtɪs] N dermatite f
dermatology [dəːmə'tɔlədʒɪ] N dermatologia
derogatory [dɪ'rɔgətərɪ] ADJ denigratorio(-a)
derrick ['dɛrɪk] N gru f inv; (for oil) derrick m inv
derv [dəːv] N (BRIT) gasolio
desalination [diːsælɪ'neɪʃən] N desalinizzazione f, dissalazione f
descend [dɪ'sɛnd] VT, VI discendere, scendere; **to ~ from** discendere da; **to ~ to** (lying, begging) abbassarsi a; **in descending order of importance** in ordine decrescente d'importanza
▸ **descend on** VT FUS (enemy, angry person) assalire, piombare su; (misfortune) arrivare addosso a; (fig: gloom, silence) scendere su; **visitors descended (up)on us** ci sono arrivate visite tra capo e collo
descendant [dɪ'sɛndənt] N discendente mf
descent [dɪ'sɛnt] N discesa; (origin) discendenza, famiglia
describe [dɪs'kraɪb] VT descrivere
description [dɪs'krɪpʃən] N descrizione f; (sort) genere m, specie f; **of every ~** di ogni genere e specie
descriptive [dɪs'krɪptɪv] ADJ descrittivo(-a)
desecrate ['dɛsɪkreɪt] VT profanare
desert N ['dɛzət] deserto ▸ VT [dɪ'zəːt] lasciare, abbandonare ▸ VI [dɪ'zəːt] (Mil) disertare; see also **deserts**
deserted [dɪ'zəːtɪd] ADJ deserto(-a)
deserter [dɪ'zəːtə^r] N disertore m
desertion [dɪ'zəːʃən] N diserzione f
desert island N isola deserta
deserts [dɪ'zəːts] NPL: **to get one's just ~** avere ciò che si merita
deserve [dɪ'zəːv] VT meritare
deservedly [dɪ'zəːvɪdlɪ] ADV meritatamente, giustamente
deserving [dɪ'zəːvɪŋ] ADJ (person) meritevole, degno(-a); (cause) meritorio(-a)
desiccated ['dɛsɪkeɪtɪd] ADJ essiccato(-a)
design [dɪ'zaɪn] N (sketch) disegno; (: of dress, car) modello; (layout, shape) linea; (pattern) fantasia; (Comm) disegno tecnico; (intention) intenzione f ▸ VT disegnare; progettare; **to have designs on** aver mire su; **well-designed** ben concepito; **industrial ~** disegno industriale
design and technology N (BRIT Scol) progettazione f e tecnologie fpl
designate VT ['dɛzɪgneɪt] designare ▸ ADJ ['dɛzɪgnɪt] designato(-a)
designation [dɛzɪg'neɪʃən] N designazione f
designer [dɪ'zaɪnə^r] N (Tech) disegnatore(-trice), progettista mf; (of furniture) designer mf; (fashion designer)

d

disegnatore(-trice) di moda; *(of theatre sets)* scenografo(-a)

designer baby N *bambino progettato geneticamente prima della nascita*

desirability [dızaıərə'bılıtı] N desiderabilità; vantaggio

desirable [dı'zaıərəbl] ADJ desiderabile; **it is ~ that** è opportuno che + *sub*

desire [dı'zaıər] N desiderio, voglia ▶ VT desiderare, volere; **to ~ sth/to do sth/that** desiderare qc/di fare qc/che + *sub*

desirous [dı'zaıərəs] ADJ: **~ of** desideroso(-a) di

desk [dɛsk] N *(in office)* scrivania; *(for pupil)* banco; *(BRIT: in shop, restaurant)* cassa; *(in hotel)* ricevimento; *(at airport)* accettazione *f*

desk job N lavoro d'ufficio

desktop N computer *m inv* desktop

desktop computer ['dɛsktɔp-] N personal *m inv*, personal computer *m inv*

desktop publishing N desktop publishing *m*

desolate ['dɛsəlıt] ADJ desolato(-a)

desolation [dɛsə'leıʃən] N desolazione *f*

despair [dıs'pɛər] N disperazione *f* ▶ VI: **to ~ of** disperare di; **in ~** disperato(-a)

despatch [dıs'pætʃ] N, VT = **dispatch**

desperate ['dɛspərıt] ADJ disperato(-a); *(measures)* estremo(-a); *(fugitive)* capace di tutto; **to be ~ for sth/to do** volere disperatamente qc/fare; **we are getting ~** siamo sull'orlo della disperazione

desperately ['dɛspərıtlı] ADV disperatamente; *(very)* terribilmente, estremamente; **~ ill** in pericolo di vita

desperation [dɛspə'reıʃən] N disperazione *f*; **in ~** per disperazione

despicable [dıs'pıkəbl] ADJ disprezzabile

despise [dıs'paız] VT disprezzare, sdegnare

despite [dıs'paıt] PREP malgrado, a dispetto di, nonostante

despondent [dıs'pɔndənt] ADJ abbattuto(-a), scoraggiato(-a)

despot ['dɛspɔt] N despota *m*

dessert [dı'zə:t] N dolce *m*; frutta

dessertspoon [dı'zə:tspu:n] N cucchiaio da dolci

destabilize [di:'steıbılaız] VT privare di stabilità; *(fig)* destabilizzare

destination [dɛstı'neıʃən] N destinazione *f*

destine ['dɛstın] VT destinare

destined ['dɛstınd] ADJ: **to be ~ to do sth** essere destinato(a) a fare qc; **~ for London** diretto a Londra, con destinazione Londra

destiny ['dɛstını] N destino

destitute ['dɛstıtju:t] ADJ indigente, bisognoso(-a); **~ of** privo(a) di

destroy [dıs'trɔı] VT distruggere

destroyer [dıs'trɔıər] N *(Naut)* cacciatorpediniere *m*

destruction [dıs'trʌkʃən] N distruzione *f*

destructive [dıs'trʌktıv] ADJ distruttivo(-a)

desultory ['dɛsəltərı] ADJ *(reading)* disordinato(-a); *(conversation)* sconnesso(-a); *(contact)* saltuario(-a), irregolare

detach [dı'tætʃ] VT staccare, distaccare

detachable [dı'tætʃəbl] ADJ staccabile

detached [dı'tætʃt] ADJ *(attitude)* distante

detached house N villa

detachment [dı'tætʃmənt] N *(Mil)* distaccamento; *(fig)* distacco

detail ['di:teıl] N particolare *m*, dettaglio; *(Mil)* piccolo distaccamento ▶ VT dettagliare, particolareggiare; *(Mil)*: **to ~ sb (for)** assegnare qn (a); **in ~** nei particolari; **to go into ~(s)** scendere nei particolari

detailed ['di:teıld] ADJ particolareggiato(-a)

detain [dı'teın] VT trattenere; *(in captivity)* detenere

detainee [di:teı'ni:] N detenuto(-a)

detect [dı'tɛkt] VT scoprire, scorgere; *(Med, Police, Radar etc)* individuare

detection [dı'tɛkʃən] N scoperta; individuazione *f*; **crime ~** indagini *fpl* criminali; **to escape ~** *(criminal)* eludere le ricerche; *(mistake)* passare inosservato(-a)

detective [dı'tɛktıv] N investigatore(-trice); **private ~** investigatore *m* privato

detective story N giallo

detector [dı'tɛktər] N rivelatore *m*

détente [deı'tɑ:nt] N distensione *f*

detention [dı'tɛnʃən] N detenzione *f*; *(Scol)* permanenza forzata per punizione

deter [dı'tə:r] VT dissuadere

detergent [dı'tə:dʒənt] N detersivo

deteriorate [dı'tıərıəreıt] VI deteriorarsi

deterioration [dıtıərıə'reıʃən] N deterioramento

determination [dıtə:mı'neıʃən] N determinazione *f*

determine [dı'tə:mın] VT determinare; **to ~ to do sth** decidere di fare qc

determined [dı'tə:mınd] ADJ *(person)* risoluto(-a), deciso(-a); **to be ~ to do sth** essere determinato or deciso a fare qc; **a ~ effort** uno sforzo di volontà

deterrence [dı'tɛrəns] N deterrenza

deterrent [dı'tɛrənt] N deterrente *m*; **to act as a ~** fungere da deterrente

detest [dı'tɛst] VT detestare

detestable [dı'tɛstəbl] ADJ detestabile, abominevole

detonate ['dɛtəneıt] VI detonare ▶ VT far detonare

detonator ['dɛtəneıtər] N detonatore *m*

detour ['di:tuər] N deviazione *f*

detox ['di:tɔks] VT disintossicare ▶ VI disintossicarsi ▶ N disintossicazione *f*

detoxification [diːtɔksɪfɪ'keɪʃən] N
disintossicazione f

detoxify [diː'tɔksɪfaɪ] VT disintossicare ▸ VI
disintossicarsi

detract [dɪ'trækt] VI: **to ~ from** detrarre da

detractor [dɪ'træktər] N detrattore(-trice)

detriment ['dɛtrɪmənt] N: **to the ~ of**
detrimento di; **without ~ to** senza danno a

detrimental [dɛtrɪ'mɛntl] ADJ: **~ to**
dannoso(-a) a, nocivo(-a) a

deuce [djuːs] N (Tennis) quaranta pari m inv

devaluation [diːvæljuˈeɪʃən] N
svalutazione f

devalue ['diːvæljuː] VT svalutare

devastate ['dɛvəsteɪt] VT devastare; **he was
devastated by the news** la notizia fu per lui
un colpo terribile

devastating ['dɛvəsteɪtɪŋ] ADJ
devastatore(-trice), sconvolgente

devastation [dɛvəˈsteɪʃən] N devastazione f

develop [dɪ'vɛləp] VT sviluppare; (habit)
prendere (gradualmente) ▸ VI svilupparsi;
(facts, symptoms: appear) manifestarsi,
rivelarsi; **to ~ a taste for sth** imparare a
gustare qc; **to ~ into** diventare

developer [dɪ'vɛləpər] N (Phot) sviluppatore
m; **property ~** costruttore m (edile)

developing country [dɪ'vɛləpɪŋ-] N paese m
in via di sviluppo

development [dɪ'vɛləpmənt] N sviluppo

development area N area di sviluppo
industriale

deviant ['diːvɪənt] ADJ deviante

deviate ['diːvɪeɪt] VI: **to ~ (from)** deviare (da)

deviation [diːvɪ'eɪʃən] N deviazione f

device [dɪ'vaɪs] N (apparatus) congegno;
(explosive device) ordigno esplosivo

devil ['dɛvl] N diavolo; demonio

devilish ['dɛvlɪʃ] N diabolico(-a)

devil-may-care ['dɛvlmeɪ'kɛər] ADJ
impudente

devil's advocate N: **to play ~** fare l'avvocato
del diavolo

devious ['diːvɪəs] ADJ (means) indiretto(-a),
tortuoso(-a); (person) subdolo(-a)

devise [dɪ'vaɪz] VT escogitare, concepire

devoid [dɪ'vɔɪd] ADJ: **~ of** privo(-a) di

devolution [diːvə'luːʃən] N (Pol)
decentramento

devolve [dɪ'vɔlv] VI: **to ~ (up)on** ricadere su

devote [dɪ'vəut] VT: **to ~ sth to** dedicare qc a

devoted [dɪ'vəutɪd] ADJ devoto(-a); **to be ~ to**
essere molto affezionato(-a) a

devotee [dɛvəu'tiː] N (Rel) adepto(-a); (Mus,
Sport) appassionato(-a)

devotion [dɪ'vəuʃən] N devozione f,
attaccamento; (Rel) atto di devozione,
preghiera

devour [dɪ'vauər] VT divorare

devout [dɪ'vaut] ADJ pio(-a), devoto(-a)

dew [djuː] N rugiada

dexterity [dɛks'tɛrɪtɪ] N destrezza

dexterous, dextrous ['dɛkstrəs] ADJ (skilful)
destro(-a), abile; (movement) agile

DfEE N ABBR (BRIT: = Department for Education and
Employment) Ministero della pubblica
istruzione e dell'occupazione

dg ABBR (= decigram) dg

diabetes [daɪə'biːtiːz] N diabete m

diabetic [daɪə'bɛtɪk] ADJ diabetico(-a);
(chocolate, jam) per diabetici ▸ N diabetico(-a)

diabolical [daɪə'bɔlɪkl] ADJ diabolico(-a); (col:
dreadful) infernale, atroce

diaerisis [daɪ'ɛrɪsɪs] N dieresi f inv

diagnose [daɪəg'nəuz] VT diagnosticare

diagnosis [daɪəg'nəusɪs] (pl **diagnoses** [-siːz])
N diagnosi f inv

diagonal [daɪ'ægənl] ADJ, N diagonale (f)

diagram ['daɪəgræm] N diagramma m

dial ['daɪəl] N quadrante m; (on radio) lancetta;
(on telephone) disco combinatore ▸ VT (number)
fare; **to ~ a wrong number** sbagliare
numero; **can I ~ London direct?** si può
chiamare Londra in teleselezione?

dial. ABBR = **dialect**

dialect ['daɪəlɛkt] N dialetto

dialling code ['daɪəlɪŋ-], (US) **area code** N
prefisso

dialling tone ['daɪəlɪŋ-], (US) **dial tone** N
segnale m di linea libera

dialogue, (US) **dialog** ['daɪəlɔg] N dialogo

dialysis [daɪ'ælɪsɪs] N dialisi f

diameter [daɪ'æmɪtər] N diametro

diametrically [daɪə'mɛtrɪklɪ] ADV: **~ opposed
(to)** diametralmente opposto(-a) (a)

diamond ['daɪəmənd] N diamante m; (shape)
rombo; **diamonds** NPL (Cards) quadri mpl

diamond ring N anello di brillanti; (with one
diamond) anello con brillante

diaper ['daɪəpər] N (US) pannolino

diaphragm ['daɪəfræm] N diaframma m

diarrhoea, (US) **diarrhea** [daɪə'riːə] N
diarrea

diary ['daɪərɪ] N (daily account) diario; (book)
agenda; **to keep a ~** tenere un diario

diatribe ['daɪətraɪb] N diatriba

dice [daɪs] N (pl inv) dado ▸ VT (Culin) tagliare a
dadini

dicey ['daɪsɪ] ADJ (col): **it's a bit ~** è un po' un
rischio

dichotomy [daɪ'kɔtəmɪ] N dicotomia

dickhead ['dɪkhɛd] N (BRIT col!) testa m di
cazzo (!)

Dictaphone® ['dɪktəfəun] N dittafono

dictate VT [dɪk'teɪt] dettare ▸ VI: **to ~ to**
(person) dare ordini a, dettar legge a ▸ N
['dɪkteɪt] dettame m; **I won't be dictated to**
non ricevo ordini

dictation [dɪk'teɪʃən] N (to secretary etc) dettatura; (Scol) dettato; **at ~ speed** a velocità di dettatura

dictator [dɪk'teɪtə^r] N dittatore m

dictatorship [dɪk'teɪtəʃɪp] N dittatura

diction ['dɪkʃən] N dizione f

dictionary ['dɪkʃənrɪ] N dizionario

did [dɪd] PT of **do**

didactic [daɪ'dæktɪk] ADJ didattico(-a)

didn't [dɪdnt]= **did not**

die [daɪ] N (pl **dies**) conio; matrice f; stampo ▶ VI morire; **to be dying** star morendo; **to be dying for sth/to do sth** morire dalla voglia di qc/di fare qc; **to ~ (of or from)** morire (di)
  ▶ **die away** VI spegnersi a poco a poco
  ▶ **die down** VI abbassarsi
  ▶ **die out** VI estinguersi

diehard ['daɪhɑːd] N reazionario(-a)

diesel ['diːzl] N (vehicle) diesel m inv

diesel engine N motore m diesel inv

diesel fuel, diesel oil N gasolio (per motori diesel)

diet ['daɪət] N alimentazione f; (restricted food) dieta ▶ VI (also: **be on a diet**) stare a dieta; **to live on a ~ of** nutrirsi di

dietician [daɪə'tɪʃən] N dietologo(-a)

differ ['dɪfə^r] VI: **to ~ from sth** differire da qc; essere diverso(-a) da qc; **to ~ from sb over sth** essere in disaccordo con qn su qc

difference ['dɪfrəns] N differenza; (quarrel) screzio; **it makes no ~ to me** per me è lo stesso; **to settle one's differences** risolvere la situazione

different ['dɪfrənt] ADJ diverso(-a)

differential [dɪfə'rɛnʃəl] N (Aut, in wages) differenziale m

differentiate [dɪfə'rɛnʃɪeɪt] VI differenziarsi; **to ~ between** discriminare fra, fare differenza fra

differently ['dɪfrəntlɪ] ADV diversamente

difficult ['dɪfɪkəlt] ADJ difficile; **~ to understand** difficile da capire

difficulty ['dɪfɪkəltɪ] N difficoltà f inv; **to have difficulties with** (police, landlord etc) avere noie con; **to be in ~** essere or trovarsi in difficoltà

diffidence ['dɪfɪdəns] N mancanza di sicurezza

diffident ['dɪfɪdənt] ADJ sfiduciato(-a)

diffuse ADJ [dɪ'fjuːs] diffuso(-a) ▶ VT [dɪ'fjuːz] diffondere, emanare

dig [dɪg] (pt, pp **dug** [dʌg]) VT (hole) scavare; (garden) vangare ▶ VI scavare ▶ N (prod) gomitata; (fig) frecciata; (Archaeology) scavo, scavi mpl; **to ~ into** (snow, soil) scavare; **to ~ into one's pockets for sth** frugarsi le tasche cercando qc; **to ~ one's nails into** conficcare le unghie in; see also **digs**
  ▶ **dig in** VI (col: eat) attaccare a mangiare;

(also: **dig o.s. in**: Mil) trincerarsi; (: fig) insediarsi, installarsi ▶ VT (compost) interrare; (knife, claw) affondare; **to ~ in one's heels** (fig) impuntarsi
  ▶ **dig out** VT (survivors, car from snow) tirar fuori (scavando), estrarre (scavando)
  ▶ **dig up** VT scavare; (tree etc) sradicare; (information) scavare fuori

digest VT [daɪ'dʒɛst] digerire ▶ N ['daɪdʒɛst] compendio

digestible [dɪ'dʒɛstəbl] ADJ digeribile

digestion [dɪ'dʒɛstʃən] N digestione f

digestive [dɪ'dʒɛstɪv] ADJ digestivo(-a); **~ system** apparato digerente

digit ['dɪdʒɪt] N cifra; (finger) dito

digital ['dɪdʒɪtəl] ADJ digitale

digital camera N fotocamera digitale

digital compact cassette N piastra digitale per CD

digital radio N radio digitale

digital TV N televisione f digitale

dignified ['dɪgnɪfaɪd] ADJ dignitoso(-a)

dignitary ['dɪgnɪtərɪ] N dignitario

dignity ['dɪgnɪtɪ] N dignità

digress [daɪ'grɛs] VI: **to ~ from** divagare da

digression [daɪ'grɛʃən] N digressione f

digs [dɪgz] NPL (BRIT col) camera ammobiliata

dilapidated [dɪ'læpɪdeɪtɪd] ADJ cadente

dilate [daɪ'leɪt] VT dilatare ▶ VI dilatarsi

dilatory ['dɪlətərɪ] ADJ dilatorio(-a)

dilemma [daɪ'lɛmə] N dilemma m; **to be in a ~** essere di fronte a un dilemma

diligent ['dɪlɪdʒənt] ADJ diligente

dill [dɪl] N aneto

dilly-dally ['dɪlɪdælɪ] VI gingillarsi

dilute [daɪ'luːt] VT diluire; (with water) annacquare ▶ ADJ diluito(-a)

dim [dɪm] ADJ (light, eyesight) debole; (memory, outline) vago(-a); (room) in penombra; (col: stupid) ottuso(-a), tonto(-a) ▶ VT (light: also US Aut) abbassare; **to take a ~ view of sth** non vedere di buon occhio qc

dime [daɪm] N (US) = **10 cents**

dimension [dɪ'mɛnʃən] N dimensione f

-dimensional [dɪ'mɛnʃənl] ADJ SUFFIX: **two~** bi-dimensionale

diminish [dɪ'mɪnɪʃ] VT, VI diminuire

diminished [dɪ'mɪnɪʃt] ADJ: **~ responsibility** (Law) incapacità d'intendere e di volere

diminutive [dɪ'mɪnjutɪv] ADJ minuscolo(-a) ▶ N (Ling) diminutivo

dimly ['dɪmlɪ] ADV debolmente; indistintamente

dimmer ['dɪmə^r] N (also: **dimmer switch**) dimmer m inv, interruttore m a reostato; **dimmers** NPL (US Aut) anabbaglianti mpl; (parking lights) luci fpl di posizione

dimple ['dɪmpl] N fossetta

dim-witted ['dɪm'wɪtɪd] ADJ (col) sciocco(-a), stupido(-a)

din [dɪn] N chiasso, fracasso ▸ VT: **to ~ sth into sb** (col) ficcare qc in testa a qn

dine [daɪn] VI pranzare

diner ['daɪnə^r] N (person: in restaurant) cliente mf; (Rail) carrozza or vagone m ristorante; (US: eating place) tavola calda

dinghy ['dɪŋgɪ] N gommone m; (also: **sailing dinghy**) dinghy m inv

dingy ['dɪndʒɪ] ADJ grigio(-a)

dining area ['daɪnɪŋ-] N zona pranzo inv

dining car ['daɪnɪŋ-] (BRIT) N vagone m ristorante

dining room N sala da pranzo

dining table N tavolo da pranzo

dinkum ['dɪŋkʌm] ADJ (AUSTRALIA, NEW ZEALAND col) genuino(-a)

dinner ['dɪnə^r] N (lunch) pranzo; (evening meal) cena; (public) banchetto; **~'s ready!** a tavola!

dinner jacket N smoking m inv

dinner party N cena

dinner service N servizio da tavola

dinner time N ora di pranzo (or cena)

dinosaur ['daɪnəsɔː^r] N dinosauro

dint [dɪnt] N: **by ~ of (doing) sth** a forza di (fare) qc

diocese ['daɪəsɪs] N diocesi f inv

dioxide [daɪ'ɔksaɪd] N biossido

dip [dɪp] N (slope) discesa; (in sea) bagno; (Culin) salsetta ▸ VT immergere; bagnare; (BRIT Aut: lights) abbassare ▸ VI (road) essere in pendenza; (bird, plane) abbassarsi

Dip. ABBR (BRIT) = **diploma**

diphtheria [dɪf'θɪərɪə] N difterite f

diphthong ['dɪfθɔŋ] N dittongo

diploma [dɪ'pləumə] N diploma m

diplomacy [dɪ'pləuməsɪ] N diplomazia

diplomat ['dɪpləmæt] N diplomatico

diplomatic [dɪplə'mætɪk] ADJ diplomatico(-a); **to break off ~ relations** rompere le relazioni diplomatiche

diplomatic corps N corpo diplomatico

diplomatic immunity N immunità f inv diplomatica

dipstick ['dɪpstɪk] N (Aut) indicatore m di livello dell'olio

dipswitch ['dɪpswɪtʃ] N (BRIT Aut) levetta dei fari

dire [daɪə^r] ADJ terribile; estremo(-a)

direct [daɪ'rɛkt] ADJ diretto(-a); (manner, person) franco(-a), esplicito(-a) ▸ VT dirigere; (order): **to ~ sb to do sth** dare direttive a qn di fare qc ▸ ADV direttamente; **can you ~ me to ...?** mi può indicare la strada per ...?

direct cost N (Comm) costo diretto

direct current N (Elec) corrente f continua

direct debit N (Banking) addebito effettuato per ordine di un cliente di banca

direct dialling N (Tel) = teleselezione f

direct hit N (Mil) colpo diretto

direction [dɪ'rɛkʃən] N direzione f; (of play, film, programme) regia; **directions** NPL (advice) chiarimenti mpl; (instructions: to a place) indicazioni fpl; **directions for use** istruzioni fpl; **to ask for directions** chiedere la strada; **sense of ~** senso dell'orientamento; **in the ~ of** in direzione di

directive [dɪ'rɛktɪv] N direttiva, ordine m; **a government ~** una disposizione governativa

direct labour N manodopera diretta

directly [dɪ'rɛktlɪ] ADV (in straight line) direttamente; (at once) subito

direct mail N pubblicità diretta

direct mailshot N (BRIT) materiale m pubblicitario ad approccio diretto

directness [daɪ'rɛktnɪs] N (of person, speech) franchezza

director [dɪ'rɛktə^r] N direttore(-trice), amministratore(-trice); (Theat, Cine, TV) regista mf; **D~ of Public Prosecutions** (BRIT) = Procuratore m della Repubblica

directory [dɪ'rɛktərɪ] N elenco; (street directory) stradario; (trade directory) repertorio del commercio; (Comput) directory m inv

directory enquiries, (US) **directory assistance** N (Tel) servizio informazioni, informazioni fpl elenco abbonati

dirt [dəːt] N sporcizia; immondizia; (earth) terra; **to treat sb like ~** trattare qn come uno straccio

dirt-cheap ['dəːt'tʃiːp] ADJ da due soldi

dirt road N strada non asfaltata

dirty ['dəːtɪ] ADJ sporco(-a) ▸ VT sporcare; **~ bomb** bomba convenzionale contenente materiale radioattivo; **~ story** storia oscena; **~ trick** brutto scherzo

disability [dɪsə'bɪlɪtɪ] N invalidità f inv; (Law) incapacità f inv

disability allowance N pensione f d'invalidità

disable [dɪs'eɪbl] VT (illness, accident) rendere invalido(-a); (tank, gun) mettere fuori uso

disabled [dɪs'eɪbld] ADJ invalido(-a); (maimed) mutilato(-a); (mentally) ritardato(-a); (through illness, old age) inabile ▸ NPL: **the ~** gli invalidi

disadvantage [dɪsəd'vɑːntɪdʒ] N svantaggio

disadvantaged [dɪsəd'vɑːntɪdʒd] ADJ (person) svantaggiato(-a)

disadvantageous [dɪsædvɑːn'teɪdʒəs] ADJ svantaggioso(-a)

disaffected [dɪsə'fɛktɪd] ADJ: **~ (to or towards)** scontento(-a) di, insoddisfatto(-a) di

disaffection [dɪsə'fɛkʃən] N malcontento, insoddisfazione f

d

disagree [dɪsə'griː] vɪ (differ) discordare; (be against, think otherwise): **to ~ (with)** essere in disaccordo (con), dissentire (da); **I ~ with you** non sono d'accordo con lei; **garlic disagrees with me** l'aglio non mi va

disagreeable [dɪsə'griːəbl] ADJ sgradevole; (person) antipatico(-a)

disagreement [dɪsə'griːmənt] N disaccordo; (quarrel) dissapore m; **to have a ~ with sb** litigare con qn

disallow ['dɪsə'lau] vᴛ respingere; (Bʀɪᴛ Football: goal) annullare

disappear [dɪsə'pɪər] vɪ scomparire

disappearance [dɪsə'pɪərəns] N scomparsa

disappoint [dɪsə'pɔɪnt] vᴛ deludere

disappointed [dɪsə'pɔɪntɪd] ADJ deluso(-a)

disappointing [dɪsə'pɔɪntɪŋ] ADJ deludente

disappointment [dɪsə'pɔɪntmənt] N delusione f

disapproval [dɪsə'pruːvəl] N disapprovazione f

disapprove [dɪsə'pruːv] vɪ: **to ~ of** disapprovare

disapproving [dɪsə'pruːvɪŋ] ADJ di disapprovazione

disarm [dɪs'ɑːm] vᴛ disarmare

disarmament [dɪs'ɑːməmənt] N disarmo

disarming [dɪs'ɑːmɪŋ] ADJ (smile) disarmante

disarray [dɪsə'reɪ] N: **in ~** (troops) in rotta; (thoughts) confuso(-a); (clothes) in disordine; **to throw into ~** buttare all'aria

disaster [dɪ'zɑːstər] N disastro

disaster area N zona disastrata

disastrous [dɪ'zɑːstrəs] ADJ disastroso(-a)

disband [dɪs'bænd] vᴛ sbandare; (Mil) congedare ▶ vɪ sciogliersi

disbelief ['dɪsbə'liːf] N incredulità; **in ~** incredulo(-a)

disbelieve ['dɪsbə'liːv] vᴛ (person, story) non credere a, mettere in dubbio; **I don't ~ you** vorrei poterle credere

disc [dɪsk] N disco; (Comput) = **disk**

disc. ABBR (Comm) = **discount**

discard [dɪs'kɑːd] vᴛ (old things) scartare; (fig) abbandonare

disc brake N freno a disco

discern [dɪ'səːn] vᴛ discernere, distinguere

discernible [dɪ'səːnəbl] ADJ percepibile

discerning [dɪ'səːnɪŋ] ADJ perspicace

discharge vᴛ [dɪs'tʃɑːdʒ] (duties) compiere; (settle: debt) pagare, estinguere; (Elec, waste etc) scaricare; (Med) emettere; (patient) dimettere; (employee) licenziare; (soldier) congedare; (defendant) liberare ▶ N ['dɪstʃɑːdʒ] (Elec) scarica; (Med, of gas, chemicals) emissione f; (vaginal discharge) perdite fpl (bianche); (dismissal) licenziamento; congedo; liberazione f; **to ~ one's gun** fare fuoco

discharged bankrupt [dɪs'tʃɑːdʒd-] N fallito cui il tribunale ha concesso la riabilitazione

disciple [dɪ'saɪpl] N discepolo

disciplinary ['dɪsɪplɪnərɪ] ADJ disciplinare; **to take ~ action against sb** prendere un provvedimento disciplinare contro qn

discipline ['dɪsɪplɪn] N disciplina ▶ vᴛ disciplinare; (punish) punire; **to ~ o.s. to do sth** imporsi di fare qc

disc jockey N disc jockey m inv

disclaim [dɪs'kleɪm] vᴛ negare, smentire

disclaimer [dɪs'kleɪmər] N smentita; **to issue a ~** pubblicare una smentita

disclose [dɪs'kləuz] vᴛ rivelare, svelare

disclosure [dɪs'kləuʒər] N rivelazione f

disco ['dɪskəu] N ABBR discoteca

discolour, (US) **discolor** [dɪs'kʌlər] vᴛ scolorire; (sth white) ingiallire ▶ vɪ sbiadire, scolorirsi; (sth white) ingiallire

discolouration, (US) **discoloration** [dɪskʌlə'reɪʃən] N scolorimento

discoloured, (US) **discolored** [dɪs'kʌləd] ADJ scolorito(-a), ingiallito(-a)

discomfort [dɪs'kʌmfət] N disagio; (lack of comfort) scomodità f inv

disconcert [dɪskən'səːt] vᴛ sconcertare

disconnect [dɪskə'nɛkt] vᴛ sconnettere, staccare; (Elec, Radio) staccare; (gas, water) chiudere

disconnected [dɪskə'nɛktɪd] ADJ (speech, thought) sconnesso(-a)

disconsolate [dɪs'kɔnsəlɪt] ADJ sconsolato(-a)

discontent [dɪskən'tɛnt] N scontentezza

discontented [dɪskən'tɛntɪd] ADJ scontento(-a)

discontinue [dɪskən'tɪnjuː] vᴛ smettere, cessare; **"discontinued"** (Comm) "fuori produzione"

discord ['dɪskɔːd] N disaccordo; (Mus) dissonanza

discordant [dɪs'kɔːdənt] ADJ discordante; dissonante

discothèque ['dɪskəutɛk] N discoteca

discount N ['dɪskaunt] sconto ▶ vᴛ [dɪs'kaunt] scontare; (report, idea etc) non badare a; **at a ~** con uno sconto; **to give sb a ~ on sth** fare uno sconto a qn su qc; **~ for cash** sconto m cassa inv

discount house N (Finance) casa di sconto, discount house f inv; (Comm: also: **discount store**) discount m inv

discount rate N tasso di sconto

discourage [dɪs'kʌrɪdʒ] vᴛ scoraggiare; (dissuade, deter) tentare di dissuadere

discouragement [dɪs'kʌrɪdʒmənt] N (dissuasion) disapprovazione f; (depression) scoraggiamento; **to act as a ~ to** ostacolare

discouraging [dɪs'kʌrɪdʒɪŋ] ADJ scoraggiante

discourteous [dɪs'kə:tɪəs] ADJ scortese
discover [dɪs'kʌvə^r] VT scoprire
discovery [dɪs'kʌvərɪ] N scoperta
discredit [dɪs'krɛdɪt] VT screditare; mettere in dubbio ▶ N discredito
discreet [dɪ'skri:t] ADJ discreto(-a)
discreetly [dɪ'skri:tlɪ] ADV con discrezione
discrepancy [dɪ'skrɛpənsɪ] N discrepanza
discretion [dɪ'skrɛʃən] N discrezione f; **use your own ~** giudichi lei
discretionary [dɪs'krɛʃənərɪ] ADJ (*powers*) discrezionale
discriminate [dɪ'skrɪmɪneɪt] VI: **to ~ between** distinguere tra; **to ~ against** discriminare contro
discriminating [dɪs'krɪmɪneɪtɪŋ] ADJ (*ear, taste*) fine, giudizioso(-a); (*person*) esigente; (*tax, duty*) discriminante
discrimination [dɪskrɪmɪ'neɪʃən] N discriminazione f; (*judgement*) discernimento; **racial/sexual ~** discriminazione razziale/sessuale
discus ['dɪskəs] N disco
discuss [dɪ'skʌs] VT discutere; (*debate*) dibattere
discussion [dɪ'skʌʃən] N discussione f; **under ~** in discussione
discussion forum N (*Comput*) forum m inv di discussione
disdain [dɪs'deɪn] N disdegno
disease [dɪ'zi:z] N malattia
diseased [dɪ'zi:zd] ADJ malato(-a)
disembark [dɪsɪm'bɑ:k] VT, VI sbarcare
disembarkation [dɪsɛmbɑ:'keɪʃən] N sbarco
disembodied [dɪsɪm'bɔdɪd] ADJ disincarnato(-a)
disembowel [dɪsɪm'bauəl] VT sbudellare, sventrare
disenchanted [dɪsɪn'tʃɑ:ntɪd] ADJ disincantato(-a); **~ (with)** deluso(-a) (da)
disenfranchise [dɪsɪn'fræntʃaɪz] VT privare del diritto di voto; (*Comm*) revocare una condizione di privilegio commerciale a
disengage [dɪsɪn'geɪdʒ] VT disimpegnare; (*Tech*) distaccare; (*Aut*) disinnestare
disentangle [dɪsɪn'tæŋgl] VT sbrogliare
disfavour, (*US*) **disfavor** [dɪs'feɪvə^r] N sfavore m; disgrazia
disfigure [dɪs'fɪgə^r] VT sfigurare
disgorge [dɪs'gɔ:dʒ] VT (*river*) riversare
disgrace [dɪs'greɪs] N vergogna; (*disfavour*) disgrazia ▶ VT disonorare, far cadere in disgrazia
disgraceful [dɪs'greɪsful] ADJ scandaloso(-a), vergognoso(-a)
disgruntled [dɪs'grʌntld] ADJ scontento(-a), di cattivo umore
disguise [dɪs'gaɪz] N travestimento ▶ VT travestire; (*voice*) contraffare; (*feelings etc*) mascherare; **to ~ o.s. as** travestirsi da; **in ~** travestito(-a); **there's no disguising the fact that ...** non si può nascondere (il fatto) che ...
disgust [dɪs'gʌst] N disgusto, nausea ▶ VT disgustare, far schifo a
disgusted [dɪs'gʌstɪd] ADJ indignato(-a)
disgusting [dɪs'gʌstɪŋ] ADJ disgustoso(-a), ripugnante
dish [dɪʃ] N piatto; **to do** or **wash the dishes** fare i piatti
▶ **dish out** VT (*food*) servire; (*advice*) elargire; (*money*) tirare fuori; (*exam papers*) distribuire
▶ **dish up** VT (*food*) servire; (*facts, statistics*) presentare
dishcloth ['dɪʃklɔθ] N strofinaccio dei piatti
dishearten [dɪs'hɑ:tn] VT scoraggiare
dishevelled, (*US*) **disheveled** [dɪ'ʃɛvəld] ADJ arruffato(-a), scapigliato(-a)
dishonest [dɪs'ɔnɪst] ADJ disonesto(-a)
dishonesty [dɪs'ɔnɪstɪ] N disonestà
dishonour, (*US*) **dishonor** [dɪs'ɔnə^r] N disonore m
dishonourable, (*US*) **dishonorable** [dɪs'ɔnərəbl] ADJ disonorevole
dish soap N (*US*) detersivo liquido (per stoviglie)
dishtowel ['dɪʃtauəl] N strofinaccio dei piatti
dishwasher ['dɪʃwɔʃə^r] N lavastoviglie f inv; (*person*) sguattero(-a)
dishy ['dɪʃɪ] ADJ (*BRIT col*) figo(-a)
disillusion [dɪsɪ'lu:ʒən] VT disilludere, disingannare ▶ N disillusione f; **to become disillusioned (with)** perdere le illusioni (su)
disillusionment [dɪsɪ'lu:ʒənmənt] N disillusione f
disincentive [dɪsɪn'sɛntɪv] N: **to act as a ~ (to)** agire da freno (su); **to be a ~ to** scoraggiare
disinclined [dɪsɪn'klaɪnd] ADJ: **to be ~ to do sth** essere poco propenso(-a) a fare qc
disinfect [dɪsɪn'fɛkt] VT disinfettare
disinfectant [dɪsɪn'fɛktənt] N disinfettante m
disinflation [dɪsɪn'fleɪʃən] N disinflazione f
disinformation [dɪsɪnfə'meɪʃən] N disinformazione f
disinherit [dɪsɪn'hɛrɪt] VT diseredare
disintegrate [dɪs'ɪntɪgreɪt] VI disintegrarsi
disinterested [dɪs'ɪntrəstɪd] ADJ disinteressato(-a)
disjointed [dɪs'dʒɔɪntɪd] ADJ sconnesso(-a)
disk [dɪsk] N (*Comput*) disco; **double-sided ~** disco a doppia faccia
disk drive N disk drive m inv
diskette [dɪs'kɛt] N (*Comput*) dischetto
disk operating system N sistema m operativo a disco

dislike [dɪs'laɪk] N antipatia, avversione f; (gen pl) cosa che non piace ▶ VT: **he dislikes it** non gli piace; **I ~ the idea** l'idea non mi va; **to take a ~ to sb/sth** prendere in antipatia qn/qc

dislocate ['dɪsləkeɪt] VT (Med) slogare; (fig) disorganizzare; **he dislocated his shoulder** si è lussato una spalla

dislodge [dɪs'lɒdʒ] VT rimuovere, staccare; (enemy) sloggiare

disloyal [dɪs'lɔɪəl] ADJ sleale

dismal ['dɪzml] ADJ triste, cupo(-a)

dismantle [dɪs'mæntl] VT (machine) smantellare, smontare; (fort, warship) disarmare

dismast [dɪs'mɑːst] VT disalberare

dismay [dɪs'meɪ] N costernazione f ▶ VT sgomentare; **much to my ~** con mio gran stupore

dismiss [dɪs'mɪs] VT congedare; (employee) licenziare; (idea) scacciare; (Law) respingere ▶ VI (Mil) rompere i ranghi

dismissal [dɪs'mɪsəl] N congedo; licenziamento

dismount [dɪs'maunt] VI scendere ▶ VT (rider) disarcionare

disobedience [dɪsə'biːdɪəns] N disubbidienza

disobedient [dɪsə'biːdɪənt] ADJ disubbidiente

disobey [dɪsə'beɪ] VT disubbidire a; (rule) trasgredire a

disorder [dɪs'ɔːdəʳ] N disordine m; (rioting) tumulto; (Med) disturbo; **civil ~** disordini mpl interni

disorderly [dɪs'ɔːdəlɪ] ADJ disordinato(-a), tumultuoso(-a)

disorderly conduct N (Law) comportamento atto a turbare l'ordine pubblico

disorganize [dɪs'ɔːgənaɪz] VT disorganizzare

disorganized [dɪs'ɔːgənaɪzd] ADJ (person, life) disorganizzato(-a); (system, meeting) male organizzato(-a)

disorientated [dɪs'ɔːrɪenteɪtɪd] ADJ disorientato(-a)

disown [dɪs'əun] VT rinnegare, disconoscere

disparaging [dɪs'pærɪdʒɪŋ] ADJ spregiativo(-a), sprezzante; **to be ~ about sb/sth** denigrare qn/qc

disparate ['dɪspərɪt] ADJ disparato(-a)

disparity [dɪs'pærɪtɪ] N disparità f inv

dispassionate [dɪs'pæʃənət] ADJ calmo(-a), freddo(-a); imparziale

dispatch [dɪs'pætʃ] VT spedire, inviare; (deal with: business) sbrigare ▶ N spedizione f, invio; (Mil, Press) dispaccio

dispatch department N reparto spedizioni

dispatch rider N (Mil) corriere m, portaordini m inv

dispel [dɪs'pɛl] VT dissipare, scacciare

dispensary [dɪs'pɛnsərɪ] N farmacia; (in chemist's) dispensario

dispense [dɪs'pɛns] VT distribuire, amministrare; (medicine) preparare e dare; **to ~ sb from** dispensare qn da
▶ **dispense with** VT FUS fare a meno di; (make unnecessary) rendere superfluo(-a)

dispenser [dɪs'pɛnsəʳ] N (container) distributore m

dispensing chemist N (Brit) farmacista mf

dispersal [dɪs'pəːsl] N dispersione f

disperse [dɪs'pəːs] VT disperdere; (knowledge) disseminare ▶ VI disperdersi

dispirited [dɪs'pɪrɪtɪd] ADJ scoraggiato(-a), abbattuto(-a)

displace [dɪs'pleɪs] VT spostare

displaced person N (Pol) profugo(-a)

displacement [dɪs'pleɪsmənt] N spostamento

display [dɪs'pleɪ] N mostra; esposizione f; (of feeling etc) manifestazione f; (military display) parata (militare); (computer display) display m inv; (pej) ostentazione f; (screen) schermo ▶ VT mostrare; (goods) esporre; (pej) ostentare; (results) affiggere; (departure times) indicare; **on ~** (gen) in mostra; (goods) in vetrina

display advertising N pubblicità tabellare

displease [dɪs'pliːz] VT dispiacere a, scontentare; **displeased with** scontento(-a) di

displeasure [dɪs'plɛʒəʳ] N dispiacere m

disposable [dɪs'pəuzəbl] ADJ (pack etc) a perdere; (income) disponibile; **~ nappy** (Brit) pannolino di carta

disposal [dɪs'pəuzl] N (of rubbish) smaltimento; (of property etc: by selling) vendita; (: by giving away) cessione f; **at one's ~** alla sua disposizione; **to put sth at sb's ~** mettere qc a disposizione di qn

dispose [dɪs'pəuz] VT disporre
▶ **dispose of** VT FUS (time, money) disporre di; (Comm: sell) vendere; (unwanted goods) sbarazzarsi di; (problem) eliminare

disposed [dɪs'pəuzd] ADJ: **~ to do** disposto(-a) a fare

disposition [dɪspə'zɪʃən] N disposizione f; (temperament) carattere m

dispossess ['dɪspə'zɛs] VT: **to ~ sb (of)** spossessare qn (di)

disproportion [dɪsprə'pɔːʃən] N sproporzione f

disproportionate [dɪsprə'pɔːʃənət] ADJ sproporzionato(-a)

disprove [dɪs'pruːv] VT confutare

dispute [dɪs'pjuːt] N disputa; (also: **industrial dispute**) controversia (sindacale) ▶ VT contestare; (matter) discutere; (victory) disputare; **to be in** or **under ~** (matter) essere in discussione; (*territory*) essere oggetto di contesa

disqualification [dɪskwɔlɪfɪ'keɪʃən] N squalifica; **~ (from driving)** (BRIT) ritiro della patente

disqualify [dɪs'kwɔlɪfaɪ] VT (*Sport*) squalificare; **to ~ sb from sth/from doing** rendere qn incapace a qc/a fare; squalificare qn da qc/da fare; **to ~ sb from driving** (BRIT) ritirare la patente a qn

disquiet [dɪs'kwaɪət] N inquietudine f

disquieting [dɪs'kwaɪətɪŋ] ADJ inquietante, allarmante

disregard [dɪsrɪ'gɑːd] VT non far caso a, non badare a ▶ N (*indifference*): **~ (for)** (*feelings*) insensibilità (a), indifferenza (verso); (*danger*) noncuranza (di); (*money*) disprezzo (di)

disrepair [dɪsrɪ'pɛə^r] N cattivo stato; **to fall into ~** (*building*) andare in rovina; (*street*) deteriorarsi

disreputable [dɪs'rɛpjutəbl] ADJ (*person*) di cattiva fama; (*area*) malfamato(-a), poco raccomandabile

disrepute ['dɪsrɪ'pjuːt] N disonore *m*, vergogna; **to bring into ~** rovinare la reputazione di

disrespectful [dɪsrɪ'spɛktful] ADJ che manca di rispetto

disrupt [dɪs'rʌpt] VT (*meeting, lesson*) disturbare, interrompere; (*public transport*) creare scompiglio in; (*plans*) scombussolare

disruption [dɪs'rʌpʃən] N disordine *m*; interruzione f

disruptive [dɪs'rʌptɪv] ADJ (*influence*) negativo(-a), deleterio(-a); (*strike action*) paralizzante

dissatisfaction [dɪssætɪs'fækʃən] N scontentezza, insoddisfazione f

dissatisfied [dɪs'sætɪsfaɪd] ADJ: **~ (with)** scontento(a) *or* insoddisfatto(a) (di)

dissect [dɪ'sɛkt] VT sezionare; (*fig*) sviscerare

disseminate [dɪ'sɛmɪneɪt] VT disseminare

dissent [dɪ'sɛnt] N dissenso

dissenter [dɪ'sɛntə^r] N (*Rel, Pol etc*) dissidente *mf*

dissertation [dɪsə'teɪʃən] N (*Scol*) tesi f inv, dissertazione f

disservice [dɪs'səːvɪs] N: **to do sb a ~** fare un cattivo servizio a qn

dissident ['dɪsɪdnt] ADJ dissidente; (*speech, voice*) di dissenso ▶ N dissidente *mf*

dissimilar [dɪ'sɪmɪlə^r] ADJ: **~ (to)** dissimile *or* diverso(a) (da)

dissipate ['dɪsɪpeɪt] VT dissipare

dissipated ['dɪsɪpeɪtɪd] ADJ dissipato(-a)

dissociate [dɪ'səuʃɪeɪt] VT dissociare; **to ~ o.s. from** dichiarare di non avere niente a che fare con

dissolute ['dɪsəluːt] ADJ dissoluto(-a), licenzioso(-a)

dissolve [dɪ'zɔlv] VT dissolvere, sciogliere; (*Comm, Pol, marriage*) sciogliere ▶ VI dissolversi, sciogliersi; (*fig*) svanire

dissuade [dɪ'sweɪd] VT: **to ~ sb (from)** dissuadere qn (da)

distaff side ['dɪstɑːf-] N *ramo femminile di una famiglia*

distance ['dɪstns] N distanza; **in the ~** in lontananza; **what's the ~ to London?** quanto dista Londra?; **it's within walking ~** ci si arriva a piedi; **at a ~ of 2 metres** a 2 metri di distanza

distant ['dɪstnt] ADJ lontano(-a), distante; (*manner*) riservato(-a), freddo(-a)

distaste [dɪs'teɪst] N ripugnanza

distasteful [dɪs'teɪstful] ADJ ripugnante, sgradevole

Dist. Atty. ABBR (*US*) = **district attorney**

distemper [dɪs'tɛmpə^r] N (*paint*) tempera; (*of dogs*) cimurro

distend [dɪs'tɛnd] VT dilatare ▶ VI dilatarsi

distended [dɪs'tɛndɪd] ADJ (*stomach*) dilatato(-a)

distil, (*US*) **distill** [dɪs'tɪl] VT distillare

distillery [dɪs'tɪlərɪ] N distilleria

distinct [dɪs'tɪŋkt] ADJ distinto(-a); (*preference, progress*) definito(-a); **as ~ from** a differenza di

distinction [dɪs'tɪŋkʃən] N distinzione f; (*in exam*) lode f; **to draw a ~ between** fare distinzione tra; **a writer of ~** uno scrittore di notevoli qualità

distinctive [dɪs'tɪŋktɪv] ADJ distintivo(-a)

distinctly [dɪs'tɪŋktlɪ] ADV distintamente; (*remember*) chiaramente; (*unhappy, better*) decisamente

distinguish [dɪs'tɪŋgwɪʃ] VT distinguere; discernere ▶ VI: **to ~ (between)** distinguere (tra); **to ~ o.s.** distinguersi

distinguished [dɪs'tɪŋgwɪʃt] ADJ (*eminent*) eminente; (*career*) brillante; (*refined*) distinto(-a), signorile

distinguishing [dɪs'tɪŋgwɪʃɪŋ] ADJ (*feature*) distinto(-a), caratteristico(-a)

distort [dɪs'tɔːt] VT (*also fig*) distorcere; (*account, news*) falsare; (*Tech*) deformare

distortion [dɪs'tɔːʃən] N (*gen*) distorsione f; (*of truth etc*) alterazione f; (*of facts*) travisamento; (*Tech*) deformazione f

distract [dɪs'trækt] VT distrarre

distracted [dɪs'træktɪd] ADJ distratto(-a)

distraction [dɪs'trækʃən] N distrazione f; **to drive sb to ~** spingere qn alla pazzia

distraught [dɪs'trɔːt] ADJ stravolto(-a)

distress [dɪs'trɛs] N angoscia; (*pain*) dolore *m* ▶ VT affliggere; **in ~** (*ship etc*) in pericolo, in difficoltà; **distressed area** (BRIT) zona sinistrata

distressing [dɪs'trɛsɪŋ] ADJ doloroso(-a), penoso(-a)

distress signal N segnale *m* di pericolo

distribute [dɪs'trɪbjuːt] VT distribuire

distribution [dɪstrɪ'bjuːʃən] N distribuzione *f*

distribution cost N costo di distribuzione

distributor [dɪs'trɪbjutəʳ] N distributore *m*; (*Comm*) concessionario

district ['dɪstrɪkt] N (*of country*) regione *f*; (*of town*) quartiere *m*; (*Admin*) distretto

district attorney N (*US*) ≈ sostituto procuratore *m* della Repubblica

district council N *organo di amministrazione regionale*; *vedi nota*

> In Inghilterra e in Galles, il *district council* è l'organo responsabile dell'amministrazione dei paesi più piccoli e dei distretti di campagna. È finanziato tramite una tassa locale e riceve un contributo da parte del governo. I district councils vengono eletti a livello locale ogni quattro anni. L'organo amministrativo nelle città è invece il *city council*.

district nurse N (*BRIT*) infermiera di quartiere

distrust [dɪs'trʌst] N diffidenza, sfiducia ▶ VT non aver fiducia in

distrustful [dɪs'trʌstful] ADJ diffidente

disturb [dɪs'təːb] VT disturbare; (*inconvenience*) scomodare; **sorry to ~ you** scusi se la disturbo

disturbance [dɪs'təːbəns] N disturbo; (*political etc*) tumulto; (*by drunks etc*) disordini *mpl*; **~ of the peace** disturbo della quiete pubblica; **to cause a ~** provocare disordini

disturbed [dɪs'təːbd] ADJ (*worried, upset*) turbato(-a); **to be emotionally ~** avere turbe emotive; **to be mentally ~** essere malato(-a) di mente

disturbing [dɪs'təːbɪŋ] ADJ sconvolgente

disuse [dɪs'juːs] N: **to fall into ~** cadere in disuso

disused [dɪs'juːzd] ADJ abbandonato(-a)

ditch [dɪtʃ] N fossa ▶ VT (*col*) piantare in asso

dither ['dɪðəʳ] VI vacillare

ditto ['dɪtəu] ADV idem

divan [dɪ'væn] N divano

divan bed N divano letto *inv*

dive [daɪv] N tuffo; (*of submarine*) immersione *f*; (*Aviat*) picchiata; (*pej*) buco ▶ VI tuffarsi; immergersi

diver ['daɪvəʳ] N tuffatore(-trice); (*deep-sea diver*) palombaro

diverge [daɪ'vəːdʒ] VI divergere

divergent [daɪ'vəːdʒənt] ADJ divergente

diverse [daɪ'vəːs] ADJ vario(-a)

diversification [daɪvəːsɪfɪ'keɪʃən] N diversificazione *f*

diversify [daɪ'vəːsɪfaɪ] VT diversificare

diversion [daɪ'vəːʃən] N (*BRIT Aut*) deviazione *f*; (*distraction*) divertimento

diversionary tactics [daɪ'vəːʃənrɪ-] NPL tattica *fsg* diversiva

diversity [daɪ'vəːsɪtɪ] N diversità *f inv*, varietà *f inv*

divert [daɪ'vəːt] VT (*traffic, river*) deviare; (*train, plane*) dirottare; (*amuse*) divertire

divest [daɪ'vɛst] VT: **to ~ sb of** spogliare qn di

divide [dɪ'vaɪd] VT dividere; (*separate*) separare ▶ VI dividersi; **to ~ (between** or **among)** dividere (tra), ripartire (tra); **40 divided by 5** 40 diviso 5
▶ **divide out** VT: **to ~ out (between** or **among)** (*sweets etc*) distribuire (tra); (*tasks*) distribuire or ripartire (tra)

divided [dɪ'vaɪdɪd] ADJ (*country*) diviso(-a); (*opinions*) discordi

divided highway N (*US*) strada a doppia carreggiata

divided skirt N gonna *f* pantalone *inv*

dividend ['dɪvɪdɛnd] N dividendo

dividend cover N rapporto dividendo profitti

dividers [dɪ'vaɪdəz] NPL compasso a punte fisse

divine [dɪ'vaɪn] ADJ divino(-a) ▶ VT (*future*) divinare, predire; (*truth*) indovinare; (*water, metal*) individuare tramite radioestesia

diving ['daɪvɪŋ] N tuffo

diving board N trampolino

diving suit N scafandro

divinity [dɪ'vɪnɪtɪ] N divinità *f inv*; teologia

division [dɪ'vɪʒən] N divisione *f*; separazione *f*; (*BRIT Football*) serie *f inv*; **~ of labour** divisione *f* del lavoro

divisive [dɪ'vaɪsɪv] ADJ che è causa di discordia

divorce [dɪ'vɔːs] N divorzio ▶ VT divorziare da; (*dissociate*) separare

divorced [dɪ'vɔːst] ADJ divorziato(-a)

divorcee [dɪvɔː'siː] N divorziato(-a)

divot ['dɪvət] N (*Golf*) zolla di terra (*sollevata accidentalmente*)

divulge [daɪ'vʌldʒ] VT divulgare, rivelare

D.I.Y. ADJ, N ABBR (*BRIT*) = **do-it-yourself**

dizziness ['dɪzɪnɪs] N vertigini *fpl*

dizzy ['dɪzɪ] ADJ (*height*) vertiginoso(-a); **to feel ~** avere il capogiro; **I feel ~** mi gira la testa, ho il capogiro; **to make sb ~** far girare la testa a qn

DJ N ABBR = **disc jockey**

dj N ABBR = **dinner jacket**

Djakarta [dʒə'kɑːtə] N Giakarta

DJIA N ABBR (*US Stock Exchange*: = *Dow-Jones Industrial Average*) indice *m* Dow-Jones

dl ABBR (= *decilitre*) dl

DLit, DLitt N ABBR = **Doctor of Literature**; **Doctor of Letters**

dm ABBR (= *decimetre*) dm

DMus N ABBR = **Doctor of Music**

DMZ N ABBR (= *demilitarized zone*) zona smilitarizzata

DNA N ABBR (= *deoxyribonucleic acid*) DNA *m*

DNA test N test *m inv* del DNA

(KEYWORD)

do [duː] (*pt* **did**, *pp* **done**) AUX VB **1** (*in negative constructions*) non tradotto; **I don't understand** non capisco

2 (*to form questions*) non tradotto; **didn't you know?** non lo sapevi?; **why didn't you come?** perché non sei venuto?

3 (*for emphasis: in polite expressions*): **she does seem rather late** sembra essere piuttosto in ritardo; **I DO wish I could …** magari potessi …; **but I DO like it!** sì che mi piace!; **do sit down** si accomodi la prego, prego si sieda; **do take care!** mi raccomando, stai attento!

4 (*used to avoid repeating vb*): **she swims better than I do** lei nuota meglio di me; **do you agree? — yes, I do/no, I don't** sei d'accordo? — sì/no; **she lives in Glasgow — so do I** lei vive a Glasgow — anch'io; **he asked me to help him and I did** mi ha chiesto di aiutarlo ed io l'ho fatto; **they come here often — do they?** vengono qui spesso — ah sì?, davvero?

5 (*in question tags*): **you like him, don't you?** ti piace, vero?; **I don't know him, do I?** non lo conosco, vero?

▶ VT (*gen: carry out, perform etc*) fare; **what are you doing tonight?** che fai stasera?; **what can I do for you?** (*in shop*) desidera?; **I'll do all I can** farò tutto il possibile; **to do the cooking** cucinare; **to do the washing-up** fare i piatti; **to do one's teeth** lavarsi i denti; **to do one's hair/nails** farsi i capelli/le unghie; **the car was doing 100** la macchina faceva i 100 all'ora; **how do you like your steak done?** come preferisce la bistecca?; **well done** ben cotto(-a)

▶ VI **1** (*act, behave*) fare; **do as I do** faccia come me, faccia come faccio io; **what did he do with the cat?** che ne ha fatto del gatto?

2 (*get on, fare*) andare; **he's doing well/badly at school** va bene/male a scuola; **how do you do?** piacere!

3 (*suit*) andare bene; **this room will do** questa stanza va bene

4 (*be sufficient*) bastare; **will £10 do?** basteranno 10 sterline?; **that'll do** basta così; **that'll do!** (*in annoyance*) ora basta!; **to make do (with)** arrangiarsi (con)

▶ N (*col: party etc*) festa; **it was rather a grand do** è stato un ricevimento piuttosto importante

▶ **do away with** VT FUS (*col: kill*) far fuori; (*abolish*) abolire

▶ **do for** VT FUS (*BRIT col: clean for*) fare i servizi per

▶ **do out of** VT FUS: **to do sb out of sth** fregare qc a qn

▶ **do up** VT (*laces*) allacciare; (*dress, buttons*) abbottonare; (*renovate: room, house*) rimettere a nuovo, rifare; **to do o.s. up** farsi bello(-a)

▶ **do with** VT FUS (*need*) aver bisogno di; **I could do with some help/a drink** un aiuto/un bicchierino non guasterebbe; **it could do with a wash** una lavata non gli farebbe male; (*be connected*): **what has it got to do with you?** e tu che c'entri?; **I won't have anything to do with it** non voglio avere niente a che farci; **it has to do with money** si tratta di soldi

▶ **do without** VI fare senza ▶ VT FUS fare a meno di

do. ABBR = **ditto**

DOA ABBR (= *dead on arrival*) morto(a) durante il trasporto

d.o.b. ABBR = **date of birth**

doc [dɔk] N (*col*) dottore(-essa)

docile ['dəʊsaɪl] ADJ docile

dock [dɔk] N (*Naut*) bacino; (*wharf*) molo; (*Law*) banco degli imputati ▶ VI entrare in bacino; (*Space*) agganciarsi; **docks** NPL, VT (*Naut*) dock *m inv*; (*pay etc*) decurtare

dock dues NPL diritti *mpl* di banchina

docker ['dɔkə^r] N scaricatore *m*

docket ['dɔkɪt] N (*on parcel etc*) etichetta, cartellino

dockyard ['dɔkjɑːd] N cantiere *m* navale

doctor ['dɔktə^r] N medico(-a), dottore(-essa); (*PhD etc*) dottore(-essa) ▶ VT (*interfere with: food, drink*) adulterare; (: *text, document*) alterare, manipolare; **~'s office** (*US*) gabinetto medico, ambulatorio

doctorate ['dɔktərɪt] N dottorato di ricerca; *vedi nota*

Il *doctorate* è il riconoscimento accademico più prestigioso in tutti i campi del sapere e viene conferito in seguito alla presentazione di una tesi originale di fronte ad una commissione di esperti. Generalmente tale tesi è un compendio del lavoro svolto durante più anni di studi; *vedi anche* **Bachelor's degree**, **Master's degree**.

Doctor of Philosophy, PhD N dottorato di ricerca; (*person*) titolare *mf* di un dottorato di ricerca

doctrine ['dɔktrɪn] N dottrina

docudrama [dɔkjuˈdrɑːmə] N (*TV*) ricostruzione *f* filmata

document N ['dɔkjumənt] documento ▶ VT ['dɔkjumɛnt] documentare
documentary [dɔkju'mɛntərɪ] ADJ documentario(-a); (evidence) documentato(-a) ▶ N documentario
documentation [dɔkjumən'teɪʃən] N documentazione f
DOD N ABBR (US) = **Department of Defense**
doddering ['dɔdərɪŋ] ADJ traballante
doddery ['dɔdərɪ] ADJ malfermo(-a)
doddle ['dɔdl] N: **it's a ~** (col) è un gioco da ragazzi
Dodecanese Islands [dəudɪkə'niːz-] NPL Isole fpl del Dodecanneso
dodge [dɔdʒ] N trucco; schivata ▶ VT schivare, eludere ▶ VI scansarsi; (Sport) fare una schivata; **to ~ out of the way** scansarsi; **to ~ through the traffic** destreggiarsi nel traffico
Dodgems® ['dɔdʒəmz] NPL (BRIT) autoscontri mpl
dodgy ['dɔdʒɪ] ADJ (BRIT col: uncertain) rischioso(-a); (untrustworthy) sospetto(-a)
DOE N ABBR (US) = **Department of Energy**
doe [dəu] N (deer) femmina di daino; (rabbit) coniglia
does [dʌz] see **do**
doesn't ['dʌznt] = **does not**
dog [dɔg] N cane m ▶ VT (follow closely) pedinare; (fig: memory etc) perseguitare; **to go to the dogs** (person) ridursi male, lasciarsi andare; (nation etc) andare in malora
dog biscuits NPL biscotti mpl per cani
dog collar N collare m di cane; (fig) collarino
dog-eared ['dɔgɪəd] ADJ (book) con orecchie
dog food N cibo per cani
dogged ['dɔgɪd] ADJ ostinato(-a), tenace
doggie, doggy ['dɔgɪ] N (col) cane m, cagnolino
doggy bag N sacchetto per gli avanzi (da portare a casa)
dogma ['dɔgmə] N dogma m
dogmatic [dɔg'mætɪk] ADJ dogmatico(-a)
do-gooder [duː'gudər] N (col, pej): **to be a ~** fare il filantropo
dogsbody ['dɔgzbɔdɪ] N (BRIT) factotum m inv
doily ['dɔɪlɪ] N centrino di carta sottopiatto
doing ['duːɪŋ] N: **this is your ~** è opera tua, sei stato tu
doings ['duːɪŋz] NPL attività fpl
do-it-yourself ['duːɪtjɔː'sɛlf] N il far da sé
doldrums ['dɔldrəmz] NPL (fig): **to be in the ~** essere giù; (business) attraversare un momento difficile
dole [dəul] N (BRIT) sussidio di disoccupazione; **to be on the ~** vivere del sussidio
▶ **dole out** VT distribuire
doleful ['dəulful] ADJ triste, doloroso(-a)

doll [dɔl] N bambola
▶ **doll up** VT: **to ~ o.s. up** farsi bello(a)
dollar ['dɔlər] N dollaro
dollop ['dɔləp] N (of food) cucchiaiata
dolly ['dɔlɪ] N bambola
dolphin ['dɔlfɪn] N delfino
domain [də'meɪn] N dominio; (fig) campo, sfera
dome [dəum] N cupola
domestic [də'mɛstɪk] ADJ (duty, happiness, animal) domestico(-a); (policy, affairs, flights) nazionale; (news) dall'interno
domestic appliance N elettrodomestico
domesticated [də'mɛstɪkeɪtɪd] ADJ addomesticato(-a); (person) casalingo(-a)
domesticity [dəumɛs'tɪsɪtɪ] N vita di famiglia
domestic servant N domestico(-a)
domicile ['dɔmɪsaɪl] N domicilio
dominant ['dɔmɪnənt] ADJ dominante
dominate ['dɔmɪneɪt] VT dominare
domination [dɔmɪ'neɪʃən] N dominazione f
domineering [dɔmɪ'nɪərɪŋ] ADJ dispotico(-a), autoritario(-a)
Dominican Republic [də'mɪnɪkən-] N Repubblica Dominicana
dominion [də'mɪnɪən] N dominio; sovranità; (BRIT Pol) dominion m inv
domino ['dɔmɪnəu] (pl **dominoes**) N domino; **dominoes** NPL (game) gioco del domino
don [dɔn] N (BRIT) docente mf universitario(-a) ▶ VT indossare
donate [də'neɪt] VT donare
donation [də'neɪʃən] N donazione f
done [dʌn] PP of **do**
dongle ['dɔŋgl] N (Comput) dongle m inv; chiave f hardware
donkey ['dɔŋkɪ] N asino
donkey-work ['dɔŋkɪwaːk] N (BRIT col) lavoro ingrato
donor ['dəunər] N donatore(-trice)
donor card N tessera di donatore di organi
don't [dəunt] = **do not**
donut ['dəunʌt] N (US) = **doughnut**
doodle ['duːdl] N scarabocchio ▶ VI scarabocchiare
doom [duːm] N destino; rovina ▶ VT: **to be doomed (to failure)** essere predestinato(-a) (a fallire)
doomsday ['duːmzdeɪ] N il giorno del Giudizio
door [dɔːr] N porta; (of vehicle) sportello, portiera; **from ~ to ~** di porta in porta
doorbell ['dɔːbɛl] N campanello
door handle N maniglia
doorknob ['dɔːnɔb] N pomello, maniglia
doorman ['dɔːmæn] N (irreg) (in hotel) portiere m in livrea; (in block of flats) portinaio
doormat ['dɔːmæt] N stuoia della porta

doorstep ['dɔːstɛp] N gradino della porta

door-to-door ['dɔːtə'dɔːʳ] ADJ: ~ **selling** vendita porta a porta

doorway ['dɔːweɪ] N porta; **in the ~** nel vano della porta

dope [dəup] N (col: drugs) roba; (: information) dati mpl ▶ VT (horse etc) drogare

dopey ['dəupɪ] ADJ (col) inebetito(-a)

dormant ['dɔːmənt] ADJ inattivo(-a); (fig) latente

dormer ['dɔːməʳ] N (also: **dormer window**) abbaino

dormice ['dɔːmaɪs] N PL of **dormouse**

dormitory ['dɔːmɪtrɪ] N dormitorio; (US: hall of residence) casa dello studente

dormouse ['dɔːmaus] (pl **dormice** [-maɪs]) N ghiro

DOS [dɔs] N ABBR (= disk operating system) DOS m

dosage ['dəusɪdʒ] N (on medicine bottle) posologia

dose [dəus] N dose f; (BRIT: bout) attacco ▶ VT: **to ~ sb with sth** somministrare qc a qn; **a ~ of flu** una bella influenza

dosser ['dɔsəʳ] N (BRIT col) barbone(-a)

doss house ['dɔs-] N (BRIT) asilo notturno

dossier ['dɔsɪeɪ] N dossier m inv

DOT N ABBR (US) = **Department of Transportation**

dot [dɔt] N punto; macchiolina ▶ VT: **dotted with** punteggiato(a) di; **on the ~** in punto

dotcom [dɔt'kɔm] N azienda che opera in Internet

dot command N (Comput) dot command m inv

dote [dəut]: **to ~ on** vt fus essere infatuato(a) di

dot-matrix printer [dɔt'meɪtrɪks-] N stampante f a matrice a punti

dotted line ['dɔtɪd-] N linea punteggiata; **to sign on the ~** firmare (nell'apposito spazio); (fig) accettare

dotty ['dɔtɪ] ADJ (col) strambo(-a)

double ['dʌbl] ADJ doppio(-a) ▶ ADV (fold) in due, doppio; (twice): **to cost ~ sth** costare il doppio (di qc) ▶ N sosia m inv; (Cine) controfigura ▶ VT raddoppiare; (fold) piegare doppio or in due ▶ VI raddoppiarsi; **spelt with a ~ "l"** scritto con due elle or con doppia elle; **~ five two six (5526)** (BRIT Tel) cinque cinque due sei; **on the ~**, (BRIT) **at the ~** a passo di corsa; **to ~ as** (have two uses etc) funzionare or servire anche da; see also **doubles**

▶ **double back** VI (person) tornare sui propri passi

▶ **double up** VI (bend over) piegarsi in due; (share room) dividere la stanza

double bass N contrabbasso

double bed N letto matrimoniale

double-breasted ['dʌbl'brɛstɪd] ADJ a doppio petto

double-check ['dʌbl'tʃɛk] VT, VI ricontrollare

double-click VI (Comput) fare doppio click

double-clutch ['dʌbl'klʌtʃ] VI (US) fare la doppietta

double cream N (BRIT) doppia panna

double-cross ['dʌbl'krɔs] VT fare il doppio gioco con

doubledecker ['dʌbl'dɛkəʳ] N autobus m inv a due piani

double declutch VI (BRIT) fare la doppietta

double exposure N (Phot) sovrimpressione f

double glazing N (BRIT) doppi vetri mpl

double-page ['dʌblpeɪdʒ] ADJ: ~ **spread** pubblicità a doppia pagina

double parking N parcheggio in doppia fila

double room N camera matrimoniale

doubles ['dʌblz] N (Tennis) doppio

double time N tariffa doppia per lavoro straordinario

double whammy [-'wæmɪ] N doppia mazzata (fig)

double yellow lines NPL (BRIT Aut) linea gialla doppia continua che segnala il divieto di sosta

doubly ['dʌblɪ] ADV doppiamente

doubt [daut] N dubbio ▶ VT dubitare di; **to ~ that** dubitare che + sub; **without (a)** ~ senza dubbio; **beyond ~** fuor di dubbio; **I ~ it very much** ho i miei dubbi, nutro seri dubbi in proposito

doubtful ['dautful] ADJ dubbioso(-a), incerto(-a); (person) equivoco(-a); **to be ~ about sth** avere dei dubbi su qc, non essere convinto di qc; **I'm a bit ~** non ne sono sicuro

doubtless ['dautlɪs] ADV indubbiamente

dough [dəu] N pasta, impasto; (col: money) grana

doughnut, (US) **donut** ['dəunʌt] N bombolone m

dour [duəʳ] ADJ arcigno(-a)

douse [daus] VT (with water) infradiciare; (flames) spegnere

dove [dʌv] N colombo(-a)

Dover ['dəuvəʳ] N Dover f

dovetail ['dʌvteɪl] N: ~ **joint** incastro a coda di rondine ▶ VI (fig) combaciare

dowager ['dauədʒəʳ] N vedova titolata

dowdy ['daudɪ] ADJ trasandato(-a), malvestito(-a)

Dow-Jones average ['dau'dʒəunz-] N (US) indice m Dow-Jones

down [daun] N (fluff) piumino; (hill) collina, colle m ▶ ADV giù, di sotto ▶ PREP giù per ▶ VT (col: drink) scolarsi; ~ **there** laggiù, là in fondo; ~ **here** quaggiù; **I'll be ~ in a minute** scendo tra un minuto; **the price of meat is** ~ il prezzo della carne è sceso; **I've got it ~ in**

my diary ce l'ho sulla mia agenda; **to pay £2 ~** dare 2 sterline in acconto *or* di anticipo; **I've been ~ with flu** sono stato a letto con l'influenza; **England is two goals ~** l'Inghilterra sta perdendo per due goal; **to ~ tools** (BRIT) incrociare le braccia; **~ with X!** abbasso X!

down-and-out ['daunəndaut] N (*tramp*) barbone *m*

down-at-heel ['daunət'hi:l] ADJ scalcagnato(-a); (*fig*) trasandato(-a)

downbeat ['daunbi:t] N (*Mus*) tempo in battere ▸ ADJ (*col*) volutamente distaccato(-a)

downcast ['daunka:st] ADJ abbattuto(-a)

downer ['daunə^r] N (*col: drug*) farmaco depressivo; **to be on a ~** (*depressed*) essere giù

downfall ['daunfɔ:l] N caduta; rovina

downgrade ['daungreid] VT (*job, hotel*) declassare; (*employee*) degradare

downhearted [daun'hɑ:tid] ADJ scoraggiato(-a)

downhill ['daun'hil] ADV verso il basso; **to go ~** andare in discesa; (*business*) lasciarsi andare; andare a rotoli ▸ N (*Ski: also:* **downhill race**) discesa libera

Downing Street ['daunɪŋ-] N: **10 ~** *residenza del primo ministro inglese; vedi nota*

> *Downing Street* è la via di Westminster che porta da Whitehall al parco di St James dove, al numero 10, si trova la residenza del primo ministro inglese. Nella stessa via, al numero 11, si trova la residenza del Cancelliere dello Scacchiere. Spesso si usa *Downing Street* per indicare il governo britannico.

download ['daunləud] VT (*Comput*) scaricare ▸ N (*Comput*) file *m inv* da scaricare

downloadable ADJ (*Comput*) scaricabile

down-market ['daun'mɑ:kit] ADJ rivolto(-a) ad una fascia di mercato inferiore

down payment N acconto

downplay ['daunpleı] VT (*US*) minimizzare

downpour ['daunpɔ:^r] N scroscio di pioggia

downright ['daunraɪt] ADJ franco(-a); (*refusal*) assoluto(-a)

Downs [daunz] NPL (BRIT): **the ~** *colline ricche di gesso nella sud-est dell'Inghilterra*

downsize ['daun'saɪz] VT (*workforce*) ridurre

Down's syndrome N sindrome *f* di Down

downstairs ['daun'stɛəz] ADV di sotto; al piano inferiore; **to come ~, go ~** scendere giù

downstream ['daun'stri:m] ADV a valle

downtime ['dauntaim] N (*Comm*) tempi *mpl* morti

down-to-earth ['dauntu'ə:θ] ADJ pratico(-a)

downtown ['daun'taun] ADV in città ▸ ADJ (*US*): **~ Chicago** il centro di Chicago

downtrodden ['dauntrɔdn] ADJ oppresso(-a)

down under ADV (*Australia etc*) agli antipodi

downward ['daunwəd] ADJ in giù, in discesa; **a ~ trend** una diminuzione progressiva ▸ ADV in giù, in discesa

downwards ['daunwədz] ADV in giù, in discesa

dowry ['dauri] N dote *f*

doz. ABBR = **dozen**

doze [dəuz] VI sonnecchiare ▸ **doze off** VI appisolarsi

dozen ['dʌzn] N dozzina; **a ~ books** una dozzina di libri; **80p a ~** 80 pence la dozzina; **dozens of times** centinaia *or* migliaia di volte

DPh, DPhil N ABBR (= *Doctor of Philosophy*) ≈ dottorato di ricerca

DPP N ABBR (BRIT) = **Director of Public Prosecutions**

DPT N ABBR (*Med: = diphtheria, pertussis, tetanus*) vaccino

Dr, Dr. ABBR (= *doctor*) Dr, Dott./Dott.ssa; (*in street names*) = **drive**

dr ABBR (*Comm*) = **debtor**

drab [dræb] ADJ tetro(-a), grigio(-a)

draft [drɑ:ft] N abbozzo; (*Pol*) bozza; (*Comm*) tratta; (*US Mil*) contingente *m*; (: *call-up*) leva ▸ VT abbozzare; (*document, report*) stendere (in versione preliminare); *see also* **draught**

drag [dræg] VT trascinare; (*river*) dragare ▸ VI trascinarsi ▸ N (*Aviat, Naut*) resistenza (aerodinamica); (*col: person*) noioso(-a); (: *task*) noia; (*women's clothing*): **in ~** travestito (da donna)
▸ **drag away** VT: **to ~ away (from)** tirare via (da)
▸ **drag on** VI tirar avanti lentamente

dragnet ['drægnɛt] N giacchio; (*fig*) rastrellamento

dragon ['drægən] N drago

dragonfly ['drægənflaı] N libellula

dragoon [drə'gu:n] N (*cavalryman*) dragone *m* ▸ VT: **to ~ sb into doing sth** (BRIT) costringere qn a fare qc

drain [dreın] N canale *m* di scolo; (*for sewage*) fogna; (*on resources*) salasso ▸ VT (*land, marshes*) prosciugare; (*vegetables*) scolare; (*reservoir etc*) vuotare ▸ VI (*water*) defluire; **to feel drained** sentirsi svuotato(-a), sentirsi sfinito(-a)

drainage ['dreınıdʒ] N prosciugamento; fognatura

draining board ['dreınıŋ-], (*US*) **drainboard** ['dreınbɔ:d] N piano del lavello

drainpipe ['dreınpaıp] N tubo di scarico

drake [dreık] N maschio dell'anatra

dram [dræm] N bicchierino (di whisky *etc*)

drama ['drɑ:mə] N (*art*) dramma *m*, teatro; (*play*) commedia; (*event*) dramma

dramatic [drə'mætık] ADJ drammatico(-a)

dramatically [drə'mætɪklɪ] ADV in modo spettacolare

dramatist ['dræmətɪst] N drammaturgo(-a)

dramatize ['dræmətaɪz] VT (events etc) drammatizzare; (adapt: novel: for TV) ridurre or adattare per la televisione; (: for cinema) ridurre or adattare per lo schermo

drank [dræŋk] PT of **drink**

drape [dreɪp] VT drappeggiare; see also **drapes**

draper ['dreɪpər] N (BRIT) negoziante mf di stoffe

drapes [dreɪps] NPL (US: curtains) tende fpl

drastic ['dræstɪk] ADJ drastico(-a)

drastically ['dræstɪklɪ] ADV drasticamente

draught, (US) **draft** [drɑːft] N corrente f d'aria; (Naut) pescaggio; **on ~** (beer) alla spina; see also **draughts**

draught beer N birra alla spina

draughtboard ['drɑːftbɔːd] N scacchiera

draughts [drɑːfts] N (BRIT) (gioco della) dama

draughtsman, (US) **draftsman** ['drɑːftsmən] N (irreg) disegnatore m

draughtsmanship, (US) **draftsmanship** ['drɑːftsmənʃɪp] N disegno tecnico; (skill) arte f del disegno

draw [drɔː] (pt **drew** [druː], pp **drawn** [drɔːn]) VT tirare; (take out) estrarre; (attract) attirare; (picture) disegnare; (line, circle) tracciare; (money) ritirare; (formulate: conclusion) trarre, ricavare; (: comparison, distinction): **to ~ (between)** fare (tra) ▶ VI (Sport) pareggiare ▶ N (Sport) pareggio; (in lottery) estrazione f; (attraction) attrazione f; **to ~ to a close** avvicinarsi alla conclusione; **to ~ near** vi avvicinarsi

▶ **draw back** VI: **to ~ back (from)** indietreggiare (di fronte a), tirarsi indietro (di fronte a)

▶ **draw in** VI (BRIT: car) accostarsi; (train) entrare in stazione

▶ **draw on** VT (resources) attingere a; (imagination, person) far ricorso a

▶ **draw out** VI (lengthen) allungarsi ▶ VT (money) ritirare

▶ **draw up** VI (stop) arrestarsi, fermarsi ▶ VT (chair) avvicinare; (document) compilare; (plans) formulare

drawback ['drɔːbæk] N svantaggio, inconveniente m

drawbridge ['drɔːbrɪdʒ] N ponte m levatoio

drawee [drɔː'iː] N trattario

drawer [drɔːr] N cassetto ['drɔːər]; (of cheque) riscuotitore(-trice)

drawing ['drɔːɪŋ] N disegno

drawing board N tavola da disegno

drawing pin N (BRIT) puntina da disegno

drawing room N salotto

drawl [drɔːl] N pronuncia strascicata

drawn [drɔːn] PP of **draw** ▶ ADJ (haggard: with tiredness) tirato(-a); (: with pain) contratto(-a) (dal dolore)

drawstring ['drɔːstrɪŋ] N laccio (per stringere maglie, sacche ecc)

dread [drɛd] N terrore m ▶ VT tremare all'idea di

dreadful ['drɛdful] ADJ terribile; **I feel ~!** (ill) mi sento uno straccio!; (ashamed) vorrei scomparire (dalla vergogna)!

dream [driːm] (pt, pp **dreamed** or **dreamt** [drɛmt]) N sogno ▶ VT, VI sognare; **to have a ~ about sb/sth** fare un sogno su qn/qc; **sweet dreams!** sogni d'oro!

▶ **dream up** VT (reason, excuse) inventare; (plan, idea) escogitare

dreamer ['driːmər] N sognatore(-trice)

dreamt [drɛmt] PT, PP of **dream**

dreamy ['driːmɪ] ADJ (look, voice) sognante; (person) distratto(-a), sognatore(-trice)

dreary ['drɪərɪ] ADJ tetro(-a); monotono(-a)

dredge [drɛdʒ] VT dragare

▶ **dredge up** VT tirare alla superficie; (fig: unpleasant facts) rivangare

dredger ['drɛdʒər] N draga; (BRIT: also: **sugar dredger**) spargizucchero m inv

dregs [drɛgz] NPL feccia

drench [drɛntʃ] VT inzuppare; **drenched to the skin** bagnato(a) fino all'osso, bagnato(a) fradicio(a)

dress [drɛs] N vestito; (no pl: clothing) abbigliamento ▶ VT vestire; (wound) fasciare; (food) condire; preparare; (shop window) allestire ▶ VI vestirsi; **to ~ o.s., to get dressed** vestirsi; **she dresses very well** veste molto bene

▶ **dress up** VI vestirsi a festa; (in fancy dress) vestirsi in costume

dress circle (BRIT) N prima galleria

dress designer N disegnatore(-trice) di moda

dresser ['drɛsər] N (Theat) assistente mf del camerino; (also: **window dresser**) vetrinista mf (furniture) credenza; (US) cassettone m

dressing ['drɛsɪŋ] N (Med) benda; (Culin) condimento

dressing gown N (BRIT) vestaglia

dressing room N (Theat) camerino; (Sport) spogliatoio

dressing table N toilette f inv

dressmaker ['drɛsmeɪkər] N sarta

dressmaking ['drɛsmeɪkɪŋ] N sartoria; confezioni fpl per donna

dress rehearsal N prova generale

dress shirt N camicia da sera

dressy ['drɛsɪ] ADJ (col) elegante

drew [druː] PT of **draw**

dribble ['drɪbl] VI gocciolare; (baby) sbavare; (Football) dribblare ▶ VT (ball) dribblare

d

dried [draɪd] ADJ *(fruit, beans)* secco(-a); *(eggs, milk)* in polvere

drier ['draɪəʳ] N = **dryer**

drift [drɪft] N *(of current etc)* direzione *f*; forza; *(of sand, snow)* cumulo; turbine *m*; *(general meaning)* senso ▶ VI *(boat)* essere trasportato(-a) dalla corrente; *(sand, snow)* ammucchiarsi; **to catch sb's ~** capire dove qn vuole arrivare; **to let things ~** lasciare che le cose vadano come vogliono; **to ~ apart** *(friends)* perdersi di vista; *(lovers)* allontanarsi l'uno dall'altro

drifter ['drɪftəʳ] N *persona che fa una vita da zingaro*

driftwood ['drɪftwud] N resti *mpl* della mareggiata

drill [drɪl] N trapano; *(Mil)* esercitazione *f* ▶ VT trapanare; *(soldiers)* esercitare, addestrare; *(pupils: in grammar)* fare esercitare ▶ VI *(for oil)* fare trivellazioni

drilling ['drɪlɪŋ] N *(for oil)* trivellazione *f*

drilling rig N *(on land)* torre *f* di perforazione; *(at sea)* piattaforma (per trivellazioni subacquee)

drily ['draɪlɪ] ADV = **dryly**

drink [drɪŋk] *(pt* **drank** [dræŋk], *pp* **drunk** [drʌŋk]) N bevanda, bibita; *(alcoholic drink)* bicchierino; *(sip)* sorso ▶ VT, VI bere; **to have a ~** bere qualcosa; **a ~ of water** un po' d'acqua; **would you like something to ~?** vuole qualcosa da bere?; **we had drinks before lunch** abbiamo preso l'aperitivo

▶ **drink in** VT *(person: fresh air)* aspirare; *(: story)* ascoltare avidamente; *(: sight)* ammirare, bersi con gli occhi

drinkable ['drɪŋkəbl] ADJ *(not poisonous)* potabile; *(palatable)* bevibile

drink-driving ['drɪŋk'draɪvɪŋ] N guida in stato di ebbrezza

drinker ['drɪŋkəʳ] N bevitore(-trice)

drinking ['drɪŋkɪŋ] N *(drunkenness)* il bere, alcoolismo

drinking fountain N fontanella

drinking water N acqua potabile

drip [drɪp] N goccia; *(dripping)* sgocciolio; *(Med)* fleboclisi *f* inv; *(col: spineless person)* lavativo ▶ VI gocciolare; *(washing, tap)* sgocciolare; *(wall)* trasudare

drip-dry ['drɪp'draɪ] ADJ *(shirt)* che non si stira

drip-feed ['drɪpfi:d] VT alimentare mediante fleboclisi

dripping ['drɪpɪŋ] N *(Culin)* grasso d'arrosto ▶ ADJ: **~ wet** fradicio(a)

drive [draɪv] *(pt* **drove** [drəuv], *pp* **driven** ['drɪvn]) N passeggiata *or* giro in macchina; *(also:* **driveway**) viale *m* d'accesso; *(energy)* energia; *(Psych)* impulso; bisogno; *(push)* sforzo eccezionale; *(campaign)* campagna; *(Sport)* drive *m inv*; *(Tech)* trasmissione *f*;

(Comput: also: **disk drive**) disk drive *m inv* ▶ VT *(vehicle)* guidare; *(nail)* piantare; *(push)* cacciare, spingere; *(Tech: motor)* azionare; far funzionare ▶ VI *(Aut: at controls)* guidare; *(: travel)* andare in macchina; **to go for a ~** andare a fare un giro in macchina; **it's 3 hours' ~ from London** è a 3 ore di macchina da Londra; **left-/right-hand ~** *(Aut)* guida a sinistra/destra; **front-/rear-wheel ~** *(Aut)* trazione *f* anteriore/posteriore; **to ~ sb to (do) sth** spingere qn a (fare) qc; **to ~ sb mad** far impazzire qn; **he drives a taxi** fa il tassista; **to ~ at 50 km an hour** guidare *or* andare a 50 km all'ora

▶ **drive at** VT FUS *(fig: intend, mean)* mirare a, voler dire

▶ **drive on** VI proseguire, andare (più) avanti ▶ VT *(incite, encourage)* sospingere, spingere

▶ **drive out** VT *(force out)* cacciare, mandare via

drive-by ['draɪvbaɪ] N *(also:* **drive-by shooting**) sparatoria dalla macchina; **he was killed in a ~ shooting** lo hanno ammazzato sparandogli da una macchina in corsa

drive-in ['draɪvɪn] ADJ, N *(esp US)* drive-in *(m inv)*

drive-in window N *(US)* sportello di drive-in

drivel ['drɪvl] N *(col: nonsense)* ciance *fpl*

driven ['drɪvn] PP of **drive**

driver ['draɪvəʳ] N conducente *mf*; *(of taxi)* tassista *m*; *(chauffeur: of bus)* autista *mf*; *(Comput)* driver *m inv*

driver's license N *(US)* patente *f* di guida

driveway ['draɪvweɪ] N viale *m* d'accesso

driving ['draɪvɪŋ] ADJ: **~ rain** pioggia sferzante ▶ N guida

driving force N forza trainante

driving instructor N istruttore(-trice) di scuola guida

driving lesson N lezione *f* di guida

driving licence N *(BRIT)* patente *f* di guida

driving school N scuola *f* guida *inv*

driving test N esame *m* di guida

drizzle ['drɪzl] N pioggerella ▶ VI piovigginare

droll [drəul] ADJ buffo(-a)

dromedary ['drɔmədərɪ] N dromedario

drone [drəun] N ronzio; *(male bee)* fuco ▶ VI *(bee, aircraft, engine)* ronzare; *(also:* **drone on**: *person)* continuare a parlare (in modo monotono); *(: voice)* continuare a ronzare

drool [dru:l] VI sbavare; **to ~ over sb/sth** *(fig)* andare in estasi per qn/qc

droop [dru:p] VI abbassarsi; languire; *(flower)* appassire; *(head, shoulders)* chinarsi

drop [drɔp] N *(of water)* goccia; *(lessening)* diminuzione *f*; *(fall)* caduta; *(: in price)* calo, ribasso; *(: in salary)* riduzione *f*, taglio; *(also:*

parachute drop) lancio; (*steep incline*) salto
▶ VT lasciar cadere; (*voice, eyes, price*)
abbassare; (*set down from car*) far scendere;
(*name from list*) lasciare fuori ▶ VI cascare;
(*decrease: wind, temperature, price*) calare,
abbassarsi; (: *numbers, attendance*) diminuire;
(*voice*) abbassarsi; **drops** NPL (*Med*) gocce *fpl*;
cough drops pastiglie *fpl* per la tosse; **a ~ of
10%** un calo del 10%; **to ~ sb a line** mandare
due righe a qn; **to ~ anchor** gettare l'ancora
▶ **drop in** VI (*col: visit*): **to ~ in (on)** fare un
salto (da), passare (da)
▶ **drop off** VI (*sleep*) addormentarsi ▶ VT: **to ~
sb off** far scendere qn
▶ **drop out** VI (*withdraw*) ritirarsi; (*student etc*)
smettere di studiare
droplet ['drɔplɪt] N gocciolina
dropout ['drɔpaut] N (*from society/university*)
chi ha abbandonato (la società/gli studi)
dropper ['drɔpəʳ] N (*Med*) contagocce *m inv*
droppings ['drɔpɪŋz] NPL sterco
dross [drɔs] N scoria; scarto
drought [draut] N siccità *f inv*
drove [drəuv] PT *of* **drive** ▶ N: **droves of
people** una moltitudine di persone
drown [draun] VT affogare; (*fig: noise*)
soffocare; (*also*: **drown out**: *sound*) coprire
▶ VI affogare
drowse [drauz] VI sonnecchiare
drowsy ['drauzɪ] ADJ sonnolento(-a),
assonnato(-a)
drudge [drʌdʒ] N (*person*) uomo (donna) di
fatica; (*job*) faticaccia
drudgery ['drʌdʒərɪ] N fatica improba;
housework is sheer ~ le faccende
domestiche sono alienanti
drug [drʌg] N farmaco; (*narcotic*) droga ▶ VT
drogare; **to be on drugs** drogarsi; (*Med*)
prendere medicinali; **hard/soft drugs**
droghe pesanti/leggere
drug abuser [-ə'bjuːzəʳ] N chi fa uso di
droghe
drug addict N tossicomane *mf*
drug dealer N trafficante *mf* di droga
drug driving N guida *f* sotto l'effetto di
droghe
druggist ['drʌgɪst] N (*US*) farmacista *mf*
drug peddler N spacciatore(-trice) di droga
drugstore ['drʌgstɔːʳ] N (*US*) negozio di generi
vari e di articoli di farmacia con un bar
drum [drʌm] N tamburo; (*for oil, petrol*) fusto
▶ VT: **to ~ one's fingers on the table**
tamburellare con le dita sulla tavola ▶ VI
tamburellare; **drums** NPL (*Mus: set of drums*)
batteria
▶ **drum up** VT (*enthusiasm, support*)
conquistarsi
drummer ['drʌməʳ] N batterista *mf*
drum roll N rullio di tamburi

drumstick ['drʌmstɪk] N (*Mus*) bacchetta;
(*chicken leg*) coscia di pollo
drunk [drʌŋk] PP *of* **drink** ▶ ADJ ubriaco(-a),
ebbro(-a) ▶ N ubriacone(-a); **to get ~**
ubriacarsi, prendere una sbornia
drunkard ['drʌŋkəd] N ubriacone(-a)
drunken ['drʌŋkən] ADJ ubriaco(-a), da
ubriaco; **~ driving** guida in stato di ebbrezza
drunkenness ['drʌŋkənnɪs] N ubriachezza;
ebbrezza
dry [draɪ] ADJ secco(-a); (*day, clothes: fig:
humour*) asciutto(-a); (*uninteresting: lecture,
subject*) poco avvincente ▶ VT seccare; (*clothes,
hair, hands*) asciugare ▶ VI asciugarsi; **on ~
land** sulla terraferma; **to ~ one's hands/
hair/eyes** asciugarsi le mani/i capelli/gli
occhi
▶ **dry off** VI asciugarsi ▶ VT asciugare
▶ **dry up** VI seccarsi; (*source of supply*)
esaurirsi; (*fig: imagination etc*) inaridirsi;
(*fall silent: speaker*) azzittirsi
dry-clean [draɪ'kliːn] VT pulire *or* lavare a
secco
dry-cleaner's [draɪ'kliːnəz] N lavasecco *m inv*
dry-cleaning [draɪ'kliːnɪŋ] N pulitura a
secco
dry dock N (*Naut*) bacino di carenaggio
dryer ['draɪəʳ] N (*for hair*) föhn *m inv*,
asciugacapelli *m inv*; (*for clothes*)
asciugabiancheria *m inv*; (*US: spin-dryer*)
centrifuga
dry goods NPL (*Comm*) tessuti *mpl* e mercerie
fpl
dry goods store N (*US*) negozio di stoffe
dry ice N ghiaccio secco
dryly ['draɪlɪ] ADV con fare asciutto
dryness ['draɪnɪs] N secchezza; (*of ground*)
aridità
dry rot N fungo del legno
dry run N (*fig*) prova
dry ski slope N pista artificiale
DSc N ABBR (= *Doctor of Science*) titolo di studio
DSS N ABBR (*BRIT*: = *Department of Social Security*)
ministero della Previdenza sociale
DST ABBR = **Daylight Saving Time**
DTI N ABBR (*BRIT*) = **Department of Trade and
Industry**; *see* **trade**
DTP N ABBR (= *desk-top publishing*) desktop
publishing *m inv*; (*Med*: = *diphtheria, tetanus,
pertussis*) vaccino
DT's N ABBR (*col*) = **delirium tremens**
dual ['djuəl] ADJ doppio(-a)
dual carriageway N (*BRIT*) strada a doppia
carreggiata
dual-control ['djuəlkən'trəul] ADJ con doppi
comandi
dual nationality N doppia nazionalità
dual-purpose ['djuəl'pə:pəs] ADJ
a doppio uso

d

dubbed [dʌbd] ADJ (*Cine*) doppiato(-a); (*nicknamed*) soprannominato(-a)

dubious ['djuːbɪəs] ADJ dubbio(-a); (*character, manner*) ambiguo(-a), equivoco(-a); **I'm very ~ about it** ho i miei dubbi in proposito

Dublin ['dʌblɪn] N Dublino f

Dubliner ['dʌblɪnər] N dublinese mf

duchess ['dʌtʃɪs] N duchessa

duck [dʌk] N anatra ▶ VI abbassare la testa ▶ VT spingere sotto (acqua)

duckling ['dʌklɪŋ] N anatroccolo

duct [dʌkt] N condotto; (*Anat*) canale m

dud [dʌd] N (*shell*) proiettile m che fa cilecca; (*object, tool*): **it's a ~** è inutile, non funziona ▶ ADJ (*cheque*) a vuoto; (*note, coin*) falso(-a)

due [djuː] ADJ dovuto(-a); (*expected*) atteso(-a); (*fitting*) giusto(-a) ▶ N dovuto ▶ ADV: **~ north** diritto verso nord; **dues** NPL (*for club, union*) quota; (*in harbour*) diritti mpl di porto; **in ~ course** a tempo debito; finalmente; **~ to** dovuto a; a causa di; **the rent's ~ on the 30th** l'affitto scade il 30; **the train is ~ at 8** il treno è atteso per le 8; **she is ~ back tomorrow** dovrebbe essere di ritorno domani; **I am ~ 6 days' leave** mi spettano 6 giorni di ferie

due date N data di scadenza

duel ['djuəl] N duello

duet [djuːˈɛt] N duetto

duff [dʌf] ADJ (*BRIT col*) barboso(-a)

duffelbag, duffle bag ['dʌflbæg] N sacca da viaggio di tela

duffelcoat, duffle coat ['dʌflkəut] N montgomery m inv

duffer ['dʌfər] N (*col*) schiappa

dug [dʌg] PT, PP of **dig**

dugout ['dʌgaut] N (*Football*) panchina

duke [djuːk] N duca m

dull [dʌl] ADJ (*light*) debole; (*boring*) noioso(-a); (*slow-witted*) ottuso(-a); (*sound, pain*) sordo(-a); (*weather, day*) fosco(-a), scuro(-a); (*blade*) smussato(-a) ▶ VT (*pain, grief*) attutire; (*mind, senses*) intorpidire

duly ['djuːlɪ] ADV (*on time*) a tempo debito; (*as expected*) debitamente

dumb [dʌm] ADJ muto(-a); (*stupid*) stupido(-a); **to be struck ~** (*fig*) ammutolire, restare senza parole

dumbbell ['dʌmbel] N (*Sport*) manubrio, peso

dumbfounded [dʌmˈfaundɪd] ADJ stupito(-a), stordito(-a)

dummy ['dʌmɪ] N (*tailor's model*) manichino; (*Sport*) finto; (*Tech, Comm*) riproduzione f; (*BRIT: for baby*) tettarella ▶ ADJ falso(-a), finto(-a)

dummy run N giro di prova

dump [dʌmp] N (*also:* **rubbish dump**) mucchio di rifiuti (*place*) discarica; (*Mil*) deposito; (*Comput*) scaricamento, dump m inv ▶ VT (*put down*) scaricare; mettere giù; (*get rid of*) buttar via; (*Comm: goods*) svendere; (*Comput*) scaricare; **to be (down) in the dumps** (*col*) essere giù di corda

dumping ['dʌmpɪŋ] N (*Econ*) dumping m; **"no ~"** "vietato lo scarico"

dumpling ['dʌmplɪŋ] N *specie di gnocco*

dumpy ['dʌmpɪ] ADJ tracagnotto(-a)

dunce [dʌns] N asino

dune [djuːn] N duna

dung [dʌŋ] N concime m

dungarees [dʌŋɡəˈriːz] NPL tuta

dungeon ['dʌndʒən] N prigione f sotterranea

dunk [dʌŋk] VT inzuppare

duo ['djuːəu] N (*gen, Mus*) duo m inv

duodenal [djuːəuˈdiːnl] ADJ (*ulcer*) duodenale

duodenum [djuːəuˈdiːnəm] N duodeno

dupe [djuːp] VT gabbare, ingannare

duplex ['djuːplɛks] N (*US: house*) casa con muro divisorio in comune con un'altra; (*also:* **duplex apartment**) appartamento su due piani

duplicate N ['djuːplɪkət] doppio; (*copy of letter etc*) duplicato ▶ VT ['djuːplɪkeɪt] duplicare; (*on machine*) ciclostilare ▶ ADJ (*copy*) conforme, esattamente uguale; **in ~** in duplice copia; **~ key** duplicato (della chiave)

duplicity [djuːˈplɪsɪtɪ] N doppiezza, duplicità

Dur. ABBR (*BRIT*) = **Durham**

durability [djuərəˈbɪlɪtɪ] N durevolezza; resistenza

durable ['djuərəbl] ADJ durevole; (*clothes, metal*) resistente

duration [djuəˈreɪʃən] N durata

duress [djuəˈrɛs] N: **under ~** sotto costrizione

Durex® ['djuərɛks] N (*BRIT*) preservativo

during ['djuərɪŋ] PREP durante, nel corso di

dusk [dʌsk] N crepuscolo

dusky ['dʌskɪ] ADJ scuro(-a)

dust [dʌst] N polvere f ▶ VT (*furniture*) spolverare; (*cake etc*): **to ~ with** cospargere con

▶ **dust off** VT rispolverare

dustbin ['dʌstbɪn] N (*BRIT*) pattumiera

duster ['dʌstər] N straccio per la polvere

dust jacket N sopraccoperta

dustman ['dʌstmən] N (*irreg*) (*BRIT*) netturbino

dustpan ['dʌstpæn] N pattumiera

dusty ['dʌstɪ] ADJ polveroso(-a)

Dutch [dʌtʃ] ADJ olandese ▶ N (*Ling*) olandese m ▶ ADV: **to go ~** or **dutch** (*col*) fare alla romana; **the ~** gli Olandesi

Dutch auction N asta all'olandese

Dutchman ['dʌtʃmən], **Dutchwoman** ['dʌtʃwumən] N (*irreg*) olandese mf

dutiable ['djuːtɪəbl] ADJ soggetto(-a) a dazio

dutiful ['djuːtɪful] ADJ (*child*) rispettoso(-a); (*husband*) premuroso(-a); (*employee*) coscienzioso(-a)

duty ['dju:tɪ] N dovere m; (tax) dazio, tassa; **duties** NPL mansioni fpl; **on ~** di servizio; (Med: in hospital) di guardia; **off ~** libero(a), fuori servizio; **to make it one's ~ to do sth** assumersi l'obbligo di fare qc; **to pay ~ on sth** pagare il dazio su qc

duty-free ['dju:tɪ'fri:] ADJ esente da dazio; **~ shop** duty free m inv

duty officer N (Mil etc) ufficiale m di servizio

duvet ['du:veɪ] (BRIT) N piumino, piumone m

DV ABBR (= Deo volente) D.V.

DVD N ABBR (= digital versatile or video disc) DVD m inv

DVD burner N masterizzatore m (di) DVD

DVD player N lettore m DVD

DVD writer N masterizzatore m (di) DVD

DVLA N ABBR (BRIT: = Driver and Vehicle Licensing Agency) ≈ I.M.C.T.C. m (= Ispettorato Generale della Motorizzazione Civile e dei Trasporti in Concessione)

DVM N ABBR (US: = Doctor of Veterinary Medicine) titolo di studio

DVT N ABBR = **deep-vein thrombosis**

dwarf [dwɔ:f] N nano(-a) ▶ VT far apparire piccolo

dwell [dwɛl] (pt, pp **dwelt** [dwɛlt]) VI dimorare
▶ **dwell on** VT FUS indugiare su

dweller ['dwɛlər] N abitante mf; **city ~** cittadino(-a)

dwelling ['dwɛlɪŋ] N dimora

dwelt [dwɛlt] PT, PP of **dwell**

dwindle ['dwɪndl] VI diminuire, decrescere

dwindling ['dwɪndlɪŋ] ADJ (strength, interest) che si affievolisce; (resources, supplies) in diminuzione

dye [daɪ] N colore m; (chemical) colorante m, tintura ▶ VT tingere; **hair ~** tinta per capelli

dyestuffs ['daɪstʌfs] NPL coloranti mpl

dying ['daɪɪŋ] ADJ morente, moribondo(-a)

dyke [daɪk] N diga; (channel) canale m di scolo; (causeway) sentiero rialzato

dynamic [daɪ'næmɪk] ADJ dinamico(-a)

dynamics [daɪ'næmɪks] N, NPL dinamica

dynamite ['daɪnəmaɪt] N dinamite f
▶ VT far saltare con la dinamite

dynamo ['daɪnəməu] N dinamo f inv

dynasty ['dɪnəstɪ] N dinastia

dysentery ['dɪsntrɪ] N dissenteria

dyslexia [dɪs'lɛksɪə] N dislessia

dyslexic [dɪs'lɛksɪk] ADJ, N dislessico(-a)

dyspepsia [dɪs'pɛpsɪə] N dispepsia

dystrophy ['dɪstrəfɪ] N distrofia; **muscular ~** distrofia muscolare

d

Ee

E, e [iː] N (letter) E, e f inv or m inv; (Mus): **E** mi m;
E for Edward, (US) **E for Easy** ≈ E come
Empoli
E ABBR (= east) E ▶ N ABBR (= Ecstasy) ecstasy f
inv
e- [iː] PREFIX e-
E111 N ABBR (formerly: also: **form E111**) E111
(modulo UE per rimborso spese mediche)
ea. ABBR = **each**
each [iːtʃ] ADJ ogni, ciascuno(-a) ▶ PRON
ciascuno(-a), ognuno(-a); **~ one** ognuno(a);
~ other si (or ci etc); **they hate ~ other** si
odiano (l'un l'altro); **you are jealous of ~
other** siete gelosi l'uno dell'altro; **~ day**
ogni giorno; **they have 2 books ~** hanno 2
libri ciascuno; **they cost £5 ~** costano 5
sterline l'uno; **~ of us** ciascuno or ognuno di
noi
eager ['iːgəʳ] ADJ impaziente; desideroso(-a);
ardente; (keen: pupil) appassionato(-a),
attento(-a); **to be ~ to do sth** non veder l'ora
di fare qc; essere desideroso di fare qc; **to be
~ for** essere desideroso di, aver gran voglia di
eagle ['iːgl] N aquila
E & OE ABBR (= errors and omissions excepted)
S.E.O.
ear [ɪəʳ] N orecchio; (of corn) pannocchia; **up
to the ears in debt** nei debiti fino al collo
earache ['ɪəreɪk] N mal m d'orecchi
eardrum ['ɪədrʌm] N timpano
earful ['ɪəful] N: **to give sb an ~** fare una
ramanzina a qn
earl [əːl] (BRIT) N conte m
earlier ['əːlɪəʳ] ADJ (date etc) anteriore; (edition
etc) precedente, anteriore ▶ ADV prima; **I
can't come any ~** non posso venire prima
early ['əːlɪ] ADV presto, di buon'ora; (ahead of
time) in anticipo ▶ ADJ primo(-a);
anticipato(-a); (man) primitivo(-a); (quick:
reply) veloce; **~ in the morning/afternoon**
nelle prime ore del mattino/del pomeriggio;
you're ~! sei in anticipo!; **at an ~ hour** di
buon'ora; **have an ~ night/start** vada a
letto/parta presto; **in the ~ or ~ in the**

spring/19th century all'inizio della
primavera/dell'Ottocento; **she's in her ~
forties** ha appena passato la quarantina;
at your earliest convenience (Comm) non
appena possibile
early retirement N prepensionamento
early warning system N sistema m di
preallarme
earmark ['ɪəmɑːk] VT: **to ~ sth for** destinare
qc a
earn [əːn] VT guadagnare; (rest, reward)
meritare; (Comm: yield) maturare; **to ~ one's
living** guadagnarsi da vivere; **this earned
him much praise, he earned much praise
for this** si è attirato grandi lodi per questo
earned income N reddito da lavoro
earnest ['əːnɪst] ADJ serio(-a) ▶ N (also:
earnest money) caparra; **in ~** adv sul serio
earnings ['əːnɪŋz] NPL guadagni mpl; (of
company etc) proventi mpl; (salary) stipendio
ear, nose and throat specialist N
otorinolaringoiatra mf
earphones ['ɪəfəunz] NPL cuffia
earplugs ['ɪəplʌgz] NPL tappi mpl per le
orecchie
earring ['ɪərɪŋ] N orecchino
earshot ['ɪəʃɔt] N: **out of/within ~** fuori
portata/a portata d'orecchio
earth [əːθ] N (gen: also BRIT Elec) terra; (of fox
etc) tana ▶ VT (BRIT Elec) mettere a terra
earthenware ['əːθənwɛəʳ] N terracotta;
stoviglie fpl di terracotta ▶ ADJ di terracotta
earthly ['əːθlɪ] ADJ terreno(-a); **~ paradise**
paradiso terrestre; **there is no ~ reason to
think ...** non vi è ragione di pensare ...
earthquake ['əːθkweɪk] N terremoto
earth-shattering ['əːθʃætərɪŋ] ADJ
stupefacente
earth tremor N scossa sismica
earthworks ['əːθwəːks] NPL lavori mpl di
sterro
earthworm ['əːθwəːm] N lombrico
earthy ['əːθɪ] ADJ (fig) grossolano(-a)
earwax ['ɪəwæks] N cerume m

earwig ['ɪəwɪg] N forbicina

ease [i:z] N agio, comodo ▶ VT (*soothe*) calmare; (*loosen*) allentare ▶ VI (*situation*) allentarsi, distendersi; **life of** ~ vita comoda; **with** ~ senza difficoltà; **at** ~ a proprio agio; (*Mil*) a riposo; **to feel at** ~/**ill at** ~ sentirsi a proprio agio/a disagio; **to** ~ **sth out/in** tirare fuori/infilare qc con delicatezza; facilitare l'uscita/l'entrata di qc
▶ **ease off, ease up** VI diminuire; (*slow down*) rallentarsi; (*fig*) rilassarsi

easel ['i:zl] N cavalletto

easily ['i:zɪlɪ] ADV facilmente

easiness ['i:zɪnɪs] N facilità, semplicità; (*of manners*) disinvoltura

east [i:st] N est *m* ▶ ADJ dell'est ▶ ADV a oriente; **the E~** l'Oriente *m*; (*Pol*) i Paesi dell'Est

eastbound ['i:stbaund] ADJ (*traffic*) diretto(-a) a est; (*carriageway*) che porta a est

Easter ['i:stə'] N Pasqua ▶ ADJ (*holidays*) pasquale, di Pasqua

Easter egg N uovo di Pasqua

Easter Island N isola di Pasqua

easterly ['i:stəlɪ] ADJ dall'est, d'oriente

Easter Monday N Pasquetta

eastern ['i:stən] ADJ orientale, d'oriente; (*Pol*) dell'est; **E~ Europe** l'Europa orientale; **the E~ bloc** (*Pol*) i Paesi dell'Est

Easter Sunday N domenica di Pasqua

East Germany N (*formerly*) Germania dell'Est

eastward ['i:stwəd], **eastwards** ['i:stwədz] ADV verso est, verso levante

easy ['i:zɪ] ADJ facile; (*manner*) disinvolto(-a); (*carefree: life*) agiato(-a), tranquillo(-a) ▶ ADV: **to take it** *or* **things** ~ prendersela con calma; **I'm** ~ (*col*) non ho problemi; **easier said than done** tra il dire e il fare c'è di mezzo il mare; **payment on** ~ **terms** (*Comm*) facilitazioni *fpl* di pagamento

easy chair N poltrona

easy-going ['i:zɪ'gəuɪŋ] ADJ accomodante

eat [i:t] (*pt* **ate** [eɪt], *pp* **eaten** ['i:tn]) VT mangiare
▶ **eat away** VT (*sea*) erodere; (*acid*) corrodere
▶ **eat away at, eat into** VT FUS rodere
▶ **eat out** VI mangiare fuori
▶ **eat up** VT (*meal etc*) finire di mangiare; **it eats up electricity** consuma un sacco di corrente

eatable ['i:təbl] ADJ mangiabile; (*safe to eat*) commestibile

eaten ['i:tn] PP *of* **eat**

eau de Cologne ['əudəkə'ləun] N acqua di colonia

eaves [i:vz] NPL gronda

eavesdrop ['i:vzdrɔp] VI: **to** ~ **(on a conversation)** origliare (una conversazione)

ebb [ɛb] N riflusso ▶ VI rifluire; (*fig: also:* **ebb away**) declinare; ~ **and flow** flusso e riflusso; **to be at a low** ~ (*fig: person, spirits*) avere il morale a terra; (: *business*) andar male

ebb tide N marea discendente

ebony ['ɛbənɪ] N ebano

e-book ['i:buk] N libro elettronico

ebullient [ɪ'bʌlɪənt] ADJ esuberante

e-business ['i:bɪznɪs] N (*company*) azienda che opera in Internet; (*commerce*) commercio elettronico

EC N ABBR (= *European Community*) CE *f*

e-card ['i:kɑ:d] N e-card *f inv*, cartolina virtuale

ECB N ABBR (= *European Central Bank*) BCE *f*

eccentric [ɪk'sɛntrɪk] ADJ, N eccentrico(-a)

ecclesiastic [ɪkli:zɪ'æstɪk] N ecclesiastico ▶ ADJ ecclesiastico(-a)

ecclesiastical [ɪkli:zɪ'æstɪkəl] ADJ ecclesiastico(-a)

ECG N ABBR = **electrocardiogram**

echo ['ɛkəu] (*pl* **echoes**) N eco *m or f* ▶ VT ripetere; fare eco a ▶ VI echeggiare; dare un eco

éclair ['eɪklɛə'] N ≈ bignè *m inv*

eclipse [ɪ'klɪps] N eclissi *f inv* ▶ VT eclissare

eco... ['i:kəu] PREFIX eco...

eco-friendly [i:kəu'frɛndlɪ] ADJ ecologico(-a)

ecological [i:kə'lɔdʒɪkəl] ADJ ecologico(-a)

ecologist [ɪ'kɔlədʒɪst] N ecologo(-a)

ecology [ɪ'kɔlədʒɪ] N ecologia

e-commerce [i:'kɔmə:s] N commercio elettronico, e-commerce *m inv*

economic [i:kə'nɔmɪk] ADJ economico(-a); (*profitable: price*) vantaggioso(-a); (: *business*) che rende

economical [i:kə'nɔmɪkəl] ADJ economico(-a); (*person*) economo(-a)

economically [i:kə'nɔmɪklɪ] ADV con economia; (*regarding economics*) dal punto di vista economico

economics [i:kə'nɔmɪks] N economia ▶ NPL (*financial aspect*) lato finanziario

economist [ɪ'kɔnəmɪst] N economista *mf*

economize [ɪ'kɔnəmaɪz] VI risparmiare, fare economia

economy [ɪ'kɔnəmɪ] N economia; **economies of scale** (*Comm*) economie *fpl* di scala

economy class N (*Aviat etc*) classe *f* turistica

economy class syndrome N sindrome *f* della classe economica

economy size N confezione *f* economica

ecosystem ['i:kəusɪstəm] N ecosistema *m*

eco-tourism [i:kəu'tuərɪzəm] N ecoturismo

ECSC N ABBR (= *European Coal & Steel Community*) C.E.C.A. *f* (= *Comunità Europea del Carbone e dell'Acciaio*)

e

ecstasy ['ɛkstəsɪ] N estasi *f inv*; **to go into ecstasies over** andare in estasi davanti a; **E~** (*drug*) ecstasy *f inv*

ecstatic [ɛks'tætɪk] ADJ estatico(-a), in estasi

ECT N ABBR = **electroconvulsive therapy**

ECU, ecu ['eɪkjuː] N ABBR (= *European Currency Unit*) ECU *f inv*, ecu *f inv*

Ecuador ['ɛkwədɔːʳ] N Ecuador *m*

ecumenical [iːkjuː'mɛnɪkl] ADJ ecumenico(-a)

eczema ['ɛksɪmə] N eczema *m*

eddy ['ɛdɪ] N mulinello

edge [ɛdʒ] N margine *m*; (*of table, plate, cup*) orlo; (*of knife etc*) taglio ▶ VT bordare ▶ VI: **to ~ away from** sgattaiolare da; **to ~ past** passar rasente; **to ~ forward** avanzare a poco a poco; **on ~** (*fig*) = **edgy; to have the ~ on** essere in vantaggio su; **to ~ away from** sgattaiolare da

edgeways ['ɛdʒweɪz] ADV di fianco; **he couldn't get a word in ~** non riuscì a dire una parola

edging ['ɛdʒɪŋ] N bordo

edgy ['ɛdʒɪ] ADJ nervoso(-a)

edible ['ɛdɪbl] ADJ commestibile; (*meal*) mangiabile

edict ['iːdɪkt] N editto

edifice ['ɛdɪfɪs] N edificio

edifying ['ɛdɪfaɪɪŋ] ADJ edificante

Edinburgh ['ɛdɪnbərə] N Edimburgo *f*

edit ['ɛdɪt] VT curare; (*newspaper, magazine*) dirigere; (*Comput*) correggere e modificare, editare

edition [ɪ'dɪʃən] N edizione *f*

editor ['ɛdɪtəʳ] N (*in newspaper*) redattore(-trice); redattore(-trice) capo; (*of sb's work*) curatore(-trice); (*film editor*) responsabile *mf* del montaggio

editorial [ɛdɪ'tɔːrɪəl] ADJ redazionale, editoriale ▶ N editoriale *m*; **the ~ staff** la redazione

EDP N ABBR = **electronic data processing**

EDT ABBR (*US*: = *Eastern Daylight Time*) ora legale di New York

educate ['ɛdjukeɪt] VT istruire; educare

educated ADJ istruito(-a)

educated guess ['ɛdjukeɪtɪd-] N ipotesi *f* ben fondata

education [ɛdju'keɪʃən] N (*teaching*) insegnamento; (*schooling*) istruzione *f*; (*knowledge, culture*) cultura; (*Scol: subject etc*) pedagogia; **primary** *or* (*US*) **elementary/secondary ~** scuola primaria/secondaria

educational [ɛdju'keɪʃənl] ADJ pedagogico(-a); scolastico(-a); istruttivo(-a); **~ technology** tecnologie *fpl* applicate alla didattica

Edwardian [ɛd'wɔːdɪən] ADJ edoardiano(-a)

EE ABBR = **electrical engineer**

EEG N ABBR = **electroencephalogram**

eel [iːl] N anguilla

EENT N ABBR (*US Med*) = **eye, ear, nose and throat**

EEOC N ABBR (*US*) = **Equal Employment Opportunity Commission**

eerie ['ɪərɪ] ADJ che fa accapponare la pelle

EET ABBR (= *Eastern European Time*) fuso orario

effect [ɪ'fɛkt] N effetto ▶ VT effettuare; **to take ~** (*law*) entrare in vigore; (*drug*) fare effetto; **to have an ~ on sb/sth** avere *or* produrre un effetto su qn/qc; **to put into ~** (*plan*) attuare; **in ~** effettivamente; **his letter is to the ~ that ...** il contenuto della sua lettera è che ...; *see also* **effects**

effective [ɪ'fɛktɪv] ADJ efficace; (*actual*) effettivo(-a); (*striking: display, outfit*) che fa colpo; **~ date** data d'entrata in vigore; **to become ~** (*law*) entrare in vigore

effectively [ɪ'fɛktɪvlɪ] ADV (*efficiently*) efficacemente; effettivamente; (*strikingly*) ad effetto; (*in reality*) di fatto; (*in effect*) in effetti

effectiveness [ɪ'fɛktɪvnɪs] N efficacia

effects [ɪ'fɛkts] NPL (*Theat*) effetti *mpl* scenici; (*property*) effetti *mpl*

effeminate [ɪ'fɛmɪnɪt] ADJ effeminato(-a)

effervescent [ɛfə'vɛsnt] ADJ effervescente

efficacy ['ɛfɪkəsɪ] N efficacia

efficiency [ɪ'fɪʃənsɪ] N efficienza; rendimento effettivo

efficiency apartment N (*US*) miniappartamento

efficient [ɪ'fɪʃənt] ADJ efficiente; (*remedy, product, system*) efficace; (*machine, car*) che ha un buon rendimento

efficiently [ɪ'fɪʃəntlɪ] ADV efficientemente; efficacemente

effigy ['ɛfɪdʒɪ] N effigie *f*

effluent ['ɛfluənt] N effluente *m*

effort ['ɛfət] N sforzo; **to make an ~ to do sth** sforzarsi di fare qc

effortless ['ɛfətlɪs] ADJ senza sforzo, facile

effrontery [ɪ'frʌntərɪ] N sfrontatezza

effusive [ɪ'fjuːsɪv] ADJ (*person*) espansivo(-a); (*welcome, letter*) caloroso(-a); (*thanks, apologies*) interminabile

EFL N ABBR (*Scol*) = **English as a foreign language**

EFTA ['ɛftə] N ABBR (= *European Free Trade Association*) E.F.T.A. *f*

e.g. ADV ABBR (= *exempli gratia*) per esempio, p.es.

egalitarian [ɪgælɪ'tɛərɪən] ADJ egualitario(-a)

egg [ɛg] N uovo; **hard-boiled/soft-boiled ~** uovo sodo/alla coque
▶ **egg on** VT incitare

eggcup ['ɛgkʌp] N portauovo *m inv*

eggplant ['ɛgplɑːnt] N (*esp US*) melanzana

eggshell ['ɛgʃɛl] N guscio d'uovo ▸ ADJ (*colour*) guscio d'uovo *inv*

egg-timer ['ɛgtaɪmə'] N clessidra (*per misurare il tempo di cottura delle uova*)

egg white N albume *m*, bianco d'uovo

egg yolk N tuorlo, rosso (d'uovo)

ego ['i:gəu] N ego *m inv*

egoism ['ɛgəuɪzəm] N egoismo

egoist ['ɛgəuɪst] N egoista *mf*

egotism ['ɛgəutɪzəm] N egotismo

egotist ['ɛgəutɪst] N egotista *mf*

ego trip N: **to be on an ~** gasarsi

Egypt ['i:dʒɪpt] N Egitto

Egyptian [ɪ'dʒɪpʃən] ADJ, N egiziano(-a)

eiderdown ['aɪdədaun] N piumino

eight [eɪt] NUM otto

eighteen ['eɪ'ti:n] NUM diciotto

eighteenth NUM diciottesimo(-a)

eighth [eɪtθ] NUM ottavo(-a)

eightieth ['eɪtɪɪθ] NUM ottantesimo(-a)

eighty [eɪtɪ] NUM ottanta

Eire ['ɛərə] N Repubblica d'Irlanda

EIS N ABBR (= *Educational Institute of Scotland*) *principale sindacato degli insegnanti in Scozia*

either ['aɪðə'] ADJ l'uno(-a) o l'altro(-a); (*both, each*) ciascuno(-a); **on ~ side** su ciascun lato ▸ PRON: **~ (of them)** (o) l'uno(a) o l'altro(a); **I don't like ~** non mi piace né l'uno né l'altro ▸ ADV neanche; **no, I don't ~** no, neanch'io ▸ CONJ: **~ good or bad** o buono o cattivo; **I haven't seen ~ one or the other** non ho visto né l'uno né l'altro

ejaculation [ɪdʒækju'leɪʃən] N (*Physiol*) eiaculazione *f*

eject [ɪ'dʒɛkt] VT espellere; lanciare ▸ VI (*pilot*) catapultarsi

ejector seat [ɪ'dʒɛktə-] N sedile *m* eiettabile

eke [i:k]: **to ~ out** VT far durare; aumentare

EKG N ABBR (*US*) = **electrocardiogram**

el [ɛl] N ABBR (*US col*) = **elevated railroad**

elaborate ADJ [ɪ'læbərɪt] elaborato(-a), minuzioso(-a) ▸ VT [ɪ'læbəreɪt] elaborare ▸ VI [ɪ'læbəreɪt] fornire i dettagli

elapse [ɪ'læps] VI trascorrere, passare

elastic [ɪ'læstɪk] ADJ elastico(-a) ▸ N elastico

elastic band N (*Brit*) elastico

elasticity [ɪlæs'tɪsɪtɪ] N elasticità

elated [ɪ'leɪtɪd] ADJ pieno(-a) di gioia

elation [ɪ'leɪʃən] N gioia

elbow ['ɛlbəu] N gomito ▸ VT: **to ~ one's way through the crowd** farsi largo tra la folla a gomitate

elbow grease N: **to use a bit of ~** usare un po' di olio di gomiti

elbowroom ['ɛlbəurum] N spazio

elder ['ɛldə'] ADJ maggiore, più vecchio(-a) ▸ N (*tree*) sambuco; **one's elders** i più anziani

elderly ['ɛldəlɪ] ADJ anziano(-a) ▸ NPL: **the ~** gli anziani

elder statesman N (*irreg*) anziano uomo politico in pensione, ma ancora influente; (*of company*) anziano(-a) consigliere(-a)

eldest ['ɛldɪst] ADJ, N: **the ~ (child)** il(la) maggiore (dei bambini)

elect [ɪ'lɛkt] VT eleggere; (*choose*): **to ~ to do** decidere di fare ▸ ADJ: **the president ~** il presidente designato

election [ɪ'lɛkʃən] N elezione *f*; **to hold an ~** indire un'elezione

election campaign N campagna elettorale

electioneering [ɪlɛkʃə'nɪərɪŋ] N propaganda elettorale

elector [ɪ'lɛktə'] N elettore(-trice)

electoral [ɪ'lɛktərəl] ADJ elettorale

electoral college N collegio elettorale

electoral roll N (*Brit*) registro elettorale

electoral system N sistema *m* elettorale

electorate [ɪ'lɛktərɪt] N elettorato

electric [ɪ'lɛktrɪk] ADJ elettrico(-a)

electrical [ɪ'lɛktrɪkəl] ADJ elettrico(-a)

electrical engineer N ingegnere *m* elettrotecnico

electrical failure N guasto all'impianto elettrico

electric blanket N coperta elettrica

electric chair N sedia elettrica

electric cooker N cucina elettrica

electric current N corrente *f* elettrica

electric fire N (*Brit*) stufa elettrica

electrician [ɪlɛk'trɪʃən] N elettricista *m*

electricity [ɪlɛk'trɪsɪtɪ] N elettricità; **to switch on/off the ~** attaccare/staccare la corrente

electricity board N (*Brit*) ente *m* regionale per l'energia elettrica

electric light N luce *f* elettrica

electric shock N scossa (elettrica)

electrify [ɪ'lɛktrɪfaɪ] VT (*Rail*) elettrificare; (*audience*) elettrizzare

electro... [ɪ'lɛktrəu] PREFIX elettro...

electrocardiogram [ɪ'lɛktrə'ka:dɪəgræm] N elettrocardiogramma *m*

electroconvulsive therapy [ɪ'lɛktrəkən'vʌlsɪv-] N elettroshockterapia

electrocute [ɪ'lɛktrəkju:t] VT fulminare

electrode [ɪ'lɛktrəud] N elettrodo

electroencephalogram [ɪ'lɛktrəuɛn'sɛfələgræm] N (*Med*) elettroencefalogramma *m*

electrolysis [ɪlɛk'trɔlɪsɪs] N elettrolisi *f*

electromagnetic [ɪ'lɛktrəumæg'nɛtɪk] N elettromagnetico(-a)

electron [ɪ'lɛktrɔn] N elettrone *m*

electronic [ɪlɛk'trɔnɪk] ADJ elettronico(-a); *see also* **electronics**

electronic data processing N elaborazione *f* elettronica di dati

electronic mail N posta elettronica

e

electronics [ɪlɛk'trɒnɪks] N elettronica
electron microscope N microscopio elettronico
electroplated [ɪ'lɛktrəu'pleɪtɪd] ADJ galvanizzato(-a)
electrotherapy [ɪ'lɛktrəu'θɛrəpɪ] N elettroterapia
elegance ['ɛlɪɡəns] N eleganza
elegant ['ɛlɪɡənt] ADJ elegante
element ['ɛlɪmənt] N elemento; (*of heater, kettle etc*) resistenza
elementary [ɛlɪ'mɛntərɪ] ADJ elementare
elementary school N (*US*) scuola elementare; *vedi nota*

> Negli Stati Uniti e in Canada, i bambini frequentano la *elementary school* per almeno sei anni, a volte anche per otto. Negli Stati Uniti si chiama anche *grade school* o *grammar school*.

elephant ['ɛlɪfənt] N elefante(-essa)
elevate ['ɛlɪveɪt] VT elevare
elevated railroad, el N (*US*) (ferrovia) soprelevata
elevation [ɛlɪ'veɪʃən] N elevazione f; (*height*) altitudine f
elevator ['ɛlɪveɪtə'] N elevatore m; (*US: lift*) ascensore m
eleven [ɪ'lɛvn] NUM undici
elevenses [ɪ'lɛvnzɪz] NPL (*BRIT*) caffè m a metà mattina
eleventh [ɪ'lɛvnθ] ADJ undicesimo(-a); **at the ~ hour** (*fig*) all'ultimo minuto
elf [ɛlf] (*pl* **elves** [ɛlvz]) N elfo
elicit [ɪ'lɪsɪt] VT: **to ~ (from)** trarre (da), cavare fuori (da); **to ~ sth (from sb)** strappare qc (a qn)
eligible ['ɛlɪdʒəbl] ADJ eleggibile; (*for membership*) che ha i requisiti; **to be ~ for a pension** essere pensionabile
eliminate [ɪ'lɪmɪneɪt] VT eliminare
elimination [ɪlɪmɪ'neɪʃən] N eliminazione f; **by process of ~** per eliminazione
élite [eɪ'liːt] N élite f inv
elitist [eɪ'liːtɪst] ADJ (*pej*) elitario(-a)
elixir [ɪ'lɪksə'] N elisir m inv
Elizabethan [ɪlɪzə'biːθən] N elisabettiano(-a)
ellipse [ɪ'lɪps] N ellisse f
elliptical [ɪ'lɪptɪkl] ADJ ellittico(-a)
elm [ɛlm] N olmo
elocution [ɛlə'kjuːʃən] N elocuzione f
elongated ['iːlɒŋɡeɪtɪd] ADJ allungato(-a)
elope [ɪ'ləup] VI (*lovers*) scappare
elopement [ɪ'ləupmənt] N fuga romantica
eloquence ['ɛləkwəns] N eloquenza
eloquent ['ɛləkwənt] ADJ eloquente
else [ɛls] ADV altro; **something ~** qualcos'altro; **somewhere ~** altrove; **everywhere ~** in qualsiasi altro luogo; **nobody ~** nessun altro; **where ~?** in quale

altro luogo?; **little ~** poco altro; **everyone ~** tutti gli altri; **nothing ~** nient'altro; **or ~** (*otherwise*) altrimenti; **is there anything ~ I can do?** posso fare qualcos'altro?
elsewhere [ɛls'wɛə'] ADV altrove
ELT N ABBR (*Scol*) = **English Language Teaching**
elucidate [ɪ'luːsɪdeɪt] VT delucidare
elude [ɪ'luːd] VT eludere
elusive [ɪ'luːsɪv] ADJ elusivo(-a); (*answer*) evasivo(-a); **he is very ~** è proprio inafferrabile *or* irraggiungibile
elves [ɛlvz] NPL *of* **elf**
emaciated [ɪ'meɪsɪeɪtɪd] ADJ emaciato(-a)
email ['iːmeɪl] N ABBR (= *electronic mail*) posta elettronica, e-mail m inv ▶ VT mandare un messaggio di posta elettronica *or* un e-mail a; **to ~ sb** comunicare con qn mediante posta elettronica; **~ account** account m inv di posta elettronica
email address N indirizzo di posta elettronica
emanate ['ɛməneɪt] VI: **to ~ from** emanare da
emancipate [ɪ'mænsɪpeɪt] VT emancipare
emancipation [ɪmænsɪ'peɪʃən] N emancipazione f
emasculate [ɪ'mæskjuleɪt] VT (*fig*) rendere impotente
embalm [ɪm'bɑːm] VT imbalsamare
embankment [ɪm'bæŋkmənt] N (*of road, railway*) massicciata; (*riverside*) argine m; (*dyke*) diga
embargo [ɪm'bɑːɡəu] (*pl* **embargoes**) N (*Comm, Naut*) embargo ▶ VT mettere l'embargo su; **to put an ~ on sth** mettere l'embargo su qc
embark [ɪm'bɑːk] VI: **to ~ (on)** imbarcarsi (su) ▶ VT imbarcare; **to ~ on** (*fig*) imbarcarsi in; (*journey*) intraprendere
embarkation [ɛmbɑː'keɪʃən] N imbarco
embarkation card N carta d'imbarco
embarrass [ɪm'bærəs] VT imbarazzare
embarrassed ADJ imbarazzato(-a); **to be ~** essere imbarazzato(-a)
embarrassing [ɪm'bærəsɪŋ] ADJ imbarazzante
embarrassment [ɪm'bærəsmənt] N imbarazzo
embassy ['ɛmbəsɪ] N ambasciata; **the Italian E~** l'ambasciata d'Italia
embed [ɪm'bɛd] VT conficcare; incastrare
embellish [ɪm'bɛlɪʃ] VT abbellire; **to ~ (with)** (*fig: story, truth*) infiorare (con)
embers ['ɛmbəz] NPL braci fpl
embezzle [ɪm'bɛzl] VT appropriarsi indebitamente di
embezzlement [ɪm'bɛzlmənt] N appropriazione f indebita, malversazione f

embezzler [ɪm'bɛzlə^r] N malversatore(-trice)
embitter [ɪm'bɪtə^r] VT amareggiare; inasprire
emblem ['ɛmbləm] N emblema *m*
embodiment [ɪm'bɔdɪmənt] N personificazione *f*, incarnazione *f*
embody [ɪm'bɔdɪ] VT (*features*) racchiudere, comprendere; (*ideas*) dar forma concreta a, esprimere
embolden [ɪm'bəuldn] VT incitare
embolism ['ɛmbəlɪzəm] N embolia
embossed [ɪm'bɔst] ADJ in rilievo; goffrato(-a); **~ with** ... con in rilievo ...
embrace [ɪm'breɪs] VT abbracciare; (*include*) comprendere ▶ VI abbracciarsi ▶ N abbraccio
embroider [ɪm'brɔɪdə^r] VT ricamare; (*fig: story*) abbellire
embroidery [ɪm'brɔɪdərɪ] N ricamo
embroil [ɪm'brɔɪl] VT: **to become embroiled (in sth)** restare invischiato(a) (in qc)
embryo ['ɛmbrɪəu] N (*also fig*) embrione *m*
emcee [ɛm'siː] N ABBR = **master of ceremonies**
emend [ɪ'mɛnd] VT (*text*) correggere, emendare
emerald ['ɛmərəld] N smeraldo
emerge [ɪ'məːdʒ] VI apparire, emergere; **it emerges that** (BRIT) risulta che
emergence [ɪ'məːdʒəns] N apparizione *f*; (*of nation*) nascita
emergency [ɪ'məːdʒənsɪ] N emergenza; **in an ~** in caso di emergenza; **to declare a state of ~** dichiarare lo stato di emergenza
emergency brake (US) N freno a mano
emergency exit N uscita di sicurezza
emergency landing N atterraggio forzato
emergency lane N (US Aut) corsia d'emergenza
emergency road service N (US) servizio riparazioni
emergency room (US Med) N pronto soccorso
emergency service N servizio di pronto intervento
emergency stop N (BRIT Aut) frenata improvvisa
emergent [ɪ'məːdʒənt] ADJ: **~ nation** paese *m* in via di sviluppo
emery board ['ɛmərɪ-] N limetta di carta smerigliata
emery paper N carta smerigliata
emetic [ɪ'mɛtɪk] N emetico
emigrant ['ɛmɪgrənt] N emigrante *mf*
emigrate ['ɛmɪgreɪt] VI emigrare
emigration [ɛmɪ'greɪʃən] N emigrazione *f*
émigré ['ɛmɪgreɪ] N emigrato(-a)
eminence ['ɛmɪnəns] N eminenza
eminent ['ɛmɪnənt] ADJ eminente
eminently ['ɛmɪnəntlɪ] ADV assolutamente, perfettamente

emirate [ɛ'mɪərɪt] N emirato
emission [ɪ'mɪʃən] N (*of gas, radiation*) emissione *f*
emit [ɪ'mɪt] VT emettere
emolument [ɪ'mɔljumənt] N (*often pl: formal*) emolumento
emoticon [ɪ'məutɪkən] N (*Comput*) faccina
emotion [ɪ'məuʃən] N emozione *f*; (*love, jealousy etc*) sentimento
emotional [ɪ'məuʃənl] ADJ (*person*) emotivo(-a); (*scene*) commovente; (*tone, speech*) carico(-a) d'emozione
emotionally [ɪ'məuʃnəlɪ] ADV (*behave, be involved*) sentimentalmente; (*speak*) con emozione; **~ disturbed** con turbe emotive
emotive [ɪ'məutɪv] ADJ emotivo(-a); **~ power** capacità di commuovere
empathy ['ɛmpəθɪ] N immedesimazione *f*; **to feel ~ with sb** immedesimarsi con i sentimenti di qn
emperor ['ɛmpərə^r] N imperatore *m*
emphasis ['ɛmfəsɪs] (*pl* **emphases** [-siːz]) N enfasi *f inv*; importanza; **to lay** *or* **place ~ on sth** (*fig*) mettere in risalto *or* in evidenza qc; **the ~ is on sport** si dà molta importanza allo sport
emphasize ['ɛmfəsaɪz] VT (*word, point*) sottolineare; (*feature*) mettere in evidenza
emphatic [ɪm'fætɪk] ADJ (*strong*) vigoroso(-a); (*unambiguous, clear*) netto(-a), categorico(-a)
emphatically [ɪm'fætɪkəlɪ] ADV vigorosamente; nettamente
emphysema [ɛmfɪ'siːmə] N (*Med*) enfisema *m*
empire ['ɛmpaɪə^r] N impero
empirical [ɛm'pɪrɪkl] ADJ empirico(-a)
employ [ɪm'plɔɪ] VT (*make use of: thing, method, person*) impiegare, servirsi di; (*give job to*) dare lavoro a, impiegare; **he's employed in a bank** lavora in banca
employee [ɪmplɔɪ'iː] N impiegato(-a)
employer [ɪm'plɔɪə^r] N principale *mf*, datore *m* di lavoro
employment [ɪm'plɔɪmənt] N impiego; **to find ~** trovare impiego *or* lavoro; **without ~** disoccupato(a); **place of ~** posto di lavoro
employment agency N agenzia di collocamento
employment exchange N (BRIT) ufficio *m* collocamento *inv*
empower [ɪm'pauə^r] VT: **to ~ sb to do** concedere autorità a qn di fare
empress ['ɛmprɪs] N imperatrice *f*
emptiness ['ɛmptɪnɪs] N vuoto
empty ['ɛmptɪ] ADJ vuoto(-a); (*street, area*) deserto(-a); (*threat, promise*) vano(-a) ▶ N (*bottle*) vuoto ▶ VT vuotare ▶ VI vuotarsi; (*liquid*) scaricarsi; **on an ~ stomach** a stomaco vuoto; **to ~ into** (*river*) gettarsi in

empty-handed [ɛmptɪ'hændɪd] ADJ a mani vuote

empty-headed [ɛmptɪ'hɛdɪd] ADJ sciocco(-a)

EMS N ABBR (= European Monetary System) S.M.E. m

EMT N ABBR (US) = **emergency medical technician**

EMU N ABBR (= European Monetary Union) Unità f monetaria europea; (= economic and monetary union) UEM f

emulate ['ɛmjuleɪt] VT emulare

emulsion [ɪ'mʌlʃən] N emulsione f; (also: **emulsion paint**) colore m a tempera

enable [ɪ'neɪbl] VT: **to ~ sb to do** permettere a qn di fare

enact [ɪn'ækt] VT (law) emanare; (play, scene) rappresentare

enamel [ɪ'næməl] N smalto

enamel paint N vernice f a smalto

enamoured [ɪ'næməd] ADJ: **~ of** innamorato(a) di

enc. ABBR (on letters etc: = enclosed, enclosure) all., alleg.

encampment [ɪn'kæmpmənt] N accampamento

encased [ɪn'keɪst] ADJ: **~ in** racchiuso(a) in, rivestito(a) di

enchant [ɪn'tʃɑ:nt] VT incantare; (magic spell) catturare

enchanting [ɪn'tʃɑ:ntɪŋ] ADJ incantevole, affascinante

encircle [ɪn'sə:kl] VT accerchiare

encl. ABBR (on letters etc: = enclosed, enclosure) all., alleg.

enclose [ɪn'kləuz] VT (land) circondare, recingere; (letter etc): **to ~ (with)** allegare (con); **please find enclosed** trovi qui accluso

enclosure [ɪn'kləuʒər] N recinto; (Comm) allegato

encoder [ɪn'kəudər] N (Comput) codificatore m

encompass [ɪn'kʌmpəs] VT comprendere

encore [ɔŋ'kɔ:r] EXCL, N bis (m inv)

encounter [ɪn'kauntər] N incontro ▶ VT incontrare

encourage [ɪn'kʌrɪdʒ] VT incoraggiare; (industry, growth etc) favorire; **to ~ sb to do sth** incoraggiare qn a fare qc

encouragement [ɪn'kʌrɪdʒmənt] N incoraggiamento

encouraging [ɪn'kʌrɪdʒɪŋ] ADJ incoraggiante

encroach [ɪn'krəutʃ] VI: **to ~ (up)on** (rights) usurpare; (time) abusare di; (land) oltrepassare i limiti di

encrusted [ɪn'krʌstɪd] ADJ: **~ with** incrostato(a) di

encrypt [ɪn'krɪpt] VT (Comput, Tel) criptare

encumbered [ɪn'kʌmbəd] ADJ: **to be ~ (with)** essere carico(a) di

encyclopedia, encyclopaedia [ɛnsaɪkləu'pi:dɪə] N enciclopedia

end [ɛnd] N fine f; (aim) fine m; (of table) bordo estremo; (of line, rope etc) estremità f inv; (of pointed object) punta; (of town) parte f ▶ VT finire; (also: **bring to an end, put an end to**) mettere fine a ▶ VI finire; **from ~ to ~** da un'estremità all'altra; **to come to an ~** arrivare alla fine, finire; **to be at an ~** essere finito; **in the ~** alla fine; **at the ~ of the street** in fondo alla strada; **at the ~ of the day** (BRIT fig) in fin dei conti; **on ~** (object) ritto(a); **to stand on ~** (hair) rizzarsi; **for 5 hours on ~** per 5 ore di fila; **for hours on ~** per ore e ore; **to this ~, with this ~ in view** a questo fine; **to ~ (with)** concludere (con)
▶ **end up** VI: **to ~ up in** finire in

endanger [ɪn'deɪndʒər] VT mettere in pericolo; **an endangered species** una specie in via di estinzione

endear [ɪn'dɪər] VT: **to ~ o.s. to sb** accattivarsi le simpatie di qn

endearing [ɪn'dɪərɪŋ] ADJ accattivante

endearment [ɪn'dɪəmənt] N: **to whisper endearments** sussurrare tenerezze; **term of ~** vezzeggiativo, parola affettuosa

endeavour, (US) **endeavor** [ɪn'dɛvər] N sforzo, tentativo ▶ VI: **to ~ to do** cercare or sforzarsi di fare

endemic [ɛn'dɛmɪk] ADJ endemico(-a)

ending ['ɛndɪŋ] N fine f, conclusione f; (Ling) desinenza

endive ['ɛndaɪv] N (curly) indivia (riccia); (smooth, flat) indivia belga

endless ['ɛndlɪs] ADJ senza fine; (patience, resources) infinito(-a); (possibilities) illimitato(-a)

endorse [ɪn'dɔ:s] VT (cheque) girare; (approve) approvare, appoggiare

endorsee [ɪndɔ:'si:] N giratario(-a)

endorsement [ɪn'dɔ:smənt] N (approval) approvazione f; (signature) firma; (BRIT: on driving licence) contravvenzione registrata sulla patente

endorser [ɪn'dɔ:sər] N girante mf

endow [ɪn'dau] VT (prize) istituire; (hospital) fondare; (provide with money) devolvere denaro a; (equip): **to ~ with** fornire di, dotare di

endowment [ɪn'daumənt] N istituzione f; fondazione f; (amount) donazione f

endowment mortgage N mutuo che viene ripagato sotto forma di un'assicurazione a vita

endowment policy N polizza-vita mista

end product N (Industry) prodotto finito; (fig) risultato

end result N risultato finale

endurable [ɪn'djuərəbl] ADJ sopportabile

endurance [ɪn'djuərəns] N resistenza; pazienza

endurance test N prova di resistenza
endure [ɪn'djuə^r] VT sopportare, resistere a
▶ VI durare
enduring [ɪn'djuərɪŋ] ADJ duraturo(-a)
end user N (Comput) consumatore(-trice)
effettivo(-a)
enema ['ɛnɪmə] N (Med) clistere m
enemy ['ɛnəmɪ] ADJ, N nemico(-a); **to make
an ~ of sb** inimicarsi qn
energetic [ɛnə'dʒɛtɪk] ADJ energico(-a),
attivo(-a)
energy ['ɛnədʒɪ] N energia; **Department of
E~** (US) Ministero dell'Energia
energy crisis N crisi f energetica
energy drink N bevanda energetica
energy-saving ['ɛnədʒɪ'seɪvɪŋ] ADJ (policy) del
risparmio energetico; (device) che risparmia
energia
enervating ['ɛnə:veɪtɪŋ] ADJ debilitante
enforce [ɪn'fɔːs] VT (Law) applicare, far
osservare
enforced [ɪn'fɔːst] ADJ forzato(-a)
enfranchise [ɪn'fræntʃaɪz] VT (give vote to)
concedere il diritto di voto a; (set free)
affrancare
engage [ɪn'geɪdʒ] VT (hire) assumere; (lawyer)
incaricare; (attention, interest) assorbire; (Mil)
attaccare; (Tech): **to ~ gear/the clutch**
innestare la marcia/la frizione ▶ VI (Tech)
ingranare; **to ~ in** impegnarsi in; **he is
engaged in research/a survey** si occupa di
ricerca/di un'inchiesta; **to ~ sb in
conversation** attaccare conversazione con
qn
engaged [ɪn'geɪdʒd] ADJ (BRIT: busy, in use)
occupato(-a); (betrothed) fidanzato(-a); **the
line's ~** (BRIT) la linea è occupata; **to get ~**
fidanzarsi
engaged tone N (BRIT Tel) segnale m di
occupato
engagement [ɪn'geɪdʒmənt] N impegno,
obbligo; appuntamento; (to marry)
fidanzamento; (Mil) combattimento; **I have
a previous ~** ho già un impegno
engagement ring N anello di fidanzamento
engaging [ɪn'geɪdʒɪŋ] ADJ attraente
engender [ɪn'dʒɛndə^r] VT produrre, causare
engine ['ɛndʒɪn] N (Aut) motore m; (Rail)
locomotiva
engine driver N (BRIT: of train) macchinista m
engineer [ɛndʒɪ'nɪə^r] N ingegnere m; (BRIT:
for domestic appliances) tecnico; (US Rail)
macchinista m; **civil/mechanical ~**
ingegnere civile/meccanico
engineering [ɛndʒɪ'nɪərɪŋ] N ingegneria
▶ CPD (works, factory, worker etc)
metalmeccanico(-a)
engine failure N guasto al motore
engine trouble N panne f

England ['ɪŋglənd] N Inghilterra
English ['ɪŋglɪʃ] ADJ inglese ▶ N (Ling) inglese
m; **the English** NPL gli Inglesi; **to be an ~
speaker** essere anglofono(a)
English Channel N: **the ~** il Canale della
Manica
Englishman ['ɪŋglɪʃmən] N (irreg) inglese m
English-speaking ['ɪŋglɪʃspiːkɪŋ] ADJ di
lingua inglese
Englishwoman ['ɪŋglɪʃwumən] N (irreg)
inglese f
engrave [ɪn'greɪv] VT incidere
engraving [ɪn'greɪvɪŋ] N incisione f
engrossed [ɪn'grəust] ADJ: **~ in** assorbito(a)
da, preso(a) da
engulf [ɪn'gʌlf] VT inghiottire
enhance [ɪn'hɑːns] VT accrescere; (position,
reputation) migliorare
enigma [ɪ'nɪgmə] N enigma m
enigmatic [ɛnɪg'mætɪk] ADJ enigmatico(-a)
enjoy [ɪn'dʒɔɪ] VT godere; (have: success,
fortune) avere; (have benefit of: health) godere
(di); **I ~ dancing** mi piace ballare; **to ~ o.s.**
godersela, divertirsi
enjoyable [ɪn'dʒɔɪəbl] ADJ piacevole
enjoyment [ɪn'dʒɔɪmənt] N piacere m,
godimento
enlarge [ɪn'lɑːdʒ] VT ingrandire ▶ VI: **to ~ on**
(subject) dilungarsi su
enlarged [ɪn'lɑːdʒd] ADJ (edition) ampliato(-a);
(Med: organ, gland) ingrossato(-a)
enlargement [ɪn'lɑːdʒmənt] N (Phot)
ingrandimento
enlighten [ɪn'laɪtn] VT illuminare; dare
chiarimenti a
enlightened [ɪn'laɪtnd] ADJ illuminato(-a)
enlightening [ɪn'laɪtnɪŋ] ADJ istruttivo(-a)
enlightenment [ɪn'laɪtnmənt] N progresso
culturale; chiarimenti mpl; (Hist): **the E~**
l'Illuminismo
enlist [ɪn'lɪst] VT arruolare; (support)
procurare ▶ VI arruolarsi; **enlisted man** (US
Mil) soldato semplice
enliven [ɪn'laɪvn] VT (people) rallegrare;
(events) ravvivare
enmity ['ɛnmɪtɪ] N inimicizia
ennoble [ɪ'nəubl] VT nobilitare; (with title)
conferire un titolo nobiliare a
enormity [ɪ'nɔːmɪtɪ] N enormità f inv
enormous [ɪ'nɔːməs] ADJ enorme
enormously [ɪ'nɔːməslɪ] ADV enormemente
enough [ɪ'nʌf] ADJ, N: **~ time/books** assai
tempo/libri; **have you got ~?** ne ha
abbastanza or a sufficienza? ▶ ADV: **big ~**
abbastanza grande; **he has not worked ~**
non ha lavorato abbastanza; **~! basta!; it's
hot ~ (as it is)!** fa abbastanza caldo così!;
will £5 be ~? bastano 5 sterline?; **that's ~,
thanks** basta così, grazie; **I've had ~!** non ne

posso più!; **I've had ~ of him** ne ho abbastanza di lui; **he was kind ~ to lend me the money** è stato così gentile da prestarmi i soldi; ... **which, funnily ~** ... che, strano a dirsi

enquire [ɪnˈkwaɪəʳ] VT, VI (esp BRIT) = **inquire**

enquiry [ɪnˈkwaɪərɪ] N (esp BRIT) = **inquiry**

enrage [ɪnˈreɪdʒ] VT fare arrabbiare

enrich [ɪnˈrɪtʃ] VT arricchire

enrol, (US) **enroll** [ɪnˈrəʊl] VT iscrivere; (at university) immatricolare ▸ VI iscriversi

enrolment, (US) **enrollment** [ɪnˈrəʊlmənt] N iscrizione f

en route [ɔnˈruːt] ADV: **~ for/from/to** in viaggio per/da/a

ensconced [ɪnˈskɔnst] ADJ: **~ in** ben sistemato(a) in

ensemble [ɑ̃ːnˈsɑ̃ːmbl] N (Mus) ensemble m inv

enshrine [ɪnˈʃraɪn] VT conservare come una reliquia

ensign N (Naut) [ˈɛnsən] bandiera; (Mil) [ˈɛnsaɪn] portabandiera m inv

enslave [ɪnˈsleɪv] VT fare schiavo

ensue [ɪnˈsjuː] VI seguire, risultare

en suite [ɔnˈswiːt] ADJ: **room with ~ bathroom** camera con bagno

ensure [ɪnˈʃuəʳ] VT assicurare; garantire; **to ~ that** assicurarsi che

ENT N ABBR (Med: = ear, nose and throat) O.R.L.

entail [ɪnˈteɪl] VT comportare

entangle [ɪnˈtæŋgl] VT (thread etc) impigliare; **to become entangled in sth** (fig) rimanere impegolato in qc

enter [ˈɛntəʳ] VT (gen) entrare in; (club) associarsi a; (profession) intraprendere; (army) arruolarsi in; (competition) partecipare a; (sb for a competition) iscrivere; (write down) registrare; (Comput: data) introdurre, inserire ▸ VI entrare
  ▸ **enter for** VT FUS iscriversi a
  ▸ **enter into** VT FUS (explanation) cominciare a dare; (debate) partecipare a; (agreement) concludere; (negotiations) prendere parte a
  ▸ **enter (up)on** VT FUS cominciare

enteritis [ɛntəˈraɪtɪs] N enterite f

enterprise [ˈɛntəpraɪz] N (undertaking, company) impresa; (spirit) iniziativa; **free ~** liberalismo economico; **private ~** iniziativa privata

enterprising [ˈɛntəpraɪzɪŋ] ADJ intraprendente

entertain [ɛntəˈteɪn] VT divertire; (invite) ricevere; (idea, plan) nutrire

entertainer [ɛntəˈteɪnəʳ] N comico(-a)

entertaining [ɛntəˈteɪnɪŋ] ADJ divertente
  ▸ N: **to do a lot of ~** avere molti ospiti

entertainment [ɛntəˈteɪnmənt] N (amusement) divertimento; (show) spettacolo

entertainment allowance N spese fpl di rappresentanza

enthral [ɪnˈθrɔːl] VT affascinare, avvincere

enthralled [ɪnˈθrɔːld] ADJ affascinato(-a)

enthralling [ɪnˈθrɔːlɪŋ] ADJ avvincente

enthuse [ɪnˈθuːz] VI: **to ~ (about or over)** entusiasmarsi (per)

enthusiasm [ɪnˈθuːzɪæzəm] N entusiasmo

enthusiast [ɪnˈθuːzɪæst] N entusiasta mf; **a jazz etc ~** un appassionato di jazz etc

enthusiastic [ɪnθuːzɪˈæstɪk] ADJ entusiasta, entusiastico(-a); **to be ~ about sth/sb** essere appassionato di qc/entusiasta di qn

entice [ɪnˈtaɪs] VT allettare, sedurre

enticing [ɪnˈtaɪsɪŋ] ADJ allettante

entire [ɪnˈtaɪəʳ] ADJ intero(-a)

entirely [ɪnˈtaɪəlɪ] ADV completamente, interamente

entirety [ɪnˈtaɪərətɪ] N: **in its ~** nel suo complesso

entitle [ɪnˈtaɪtl] VT (give right): **to ~ sb to sth/ to do** dare diritto a qn a qc/a fare

entitled [ɪnˈtaɪtld] ADJ (book) che si intitola; **to be ~ to sth** avere diritto a qc; **to be ~ to do sth** avere il diritto di fare qc

entity [ˈɛntɪtɪ] N entità f inv

entrails [ˈɛntreɪlz] NPL interiora fpl

entrance N [ˈɛntrns] entrata, ingresso; (of person) entrata ▸ VT [ɪnˈtrɑːns] incantare, rapire; **to gain ~ to** (university etc) essere ammesso a

entrance examination N (to school) esame m di ammissione

entrance fee N (to museum etc) prezzo d'ingresso

entrance ramp N (US Aut) rampa di accesso

entrancing [ɪnˈtrɑːnsɪŋ] ADJ incantevole

entrant [ˈɛntrnt] N partecipante mf; concorrente mf; (BRIT: in exam) candidato(-a)

entreat [ɛnˈtriːt] VT supplicare

entreaty [ɪnˈtriːtɪ] N supplica, preghiera

entrée [ˈɔntreɪ] N (Culin) prima portata

entrenched [ɛnˈtrɛntʃt] ADJ radicato(-a)

entrepreneur [ˈɔntrəprəˈnəːʳ] N imprenditore m

entrepreneurial [ˈɔntrəprəˈnəːrɪəl] ADJ imprenditoriale

entrust [ɪnˈtrʌst] VT: **to ~ sth to** affidare qc a

entry [ˈɛntrɪ] N entrata; (way in) entrata, ingresso; (item: on list) iscrizione f; (in dictionary) voce f; (in diary, ship's log) annotazione f; (in account book, ledger, list) registrazione f; **"no ~"** "vietato l'ingresso"; (Aut) "divieto di accesso"; **single/double ~ book-keeping** partita semplice/doppia

entry form N modulo d'iscrizione

entry phone N (BRIT) citofono

entwine [ɪnˈtwaɪn] VT intrecciare

E number N sigla di additivo alimentare

enumerate [ɪˈnjuːməreɪt] vt enumerare
enunciate [ɪˈnʌnsɪeɪt] vt enunciare; pronunciare
envelop [ɪnˈvɛləp] vt avvolgere, avviluppare
envelope [ˈɛnvələup] n busta
enviable [ˈɛnvɪəbl] adj invidiabile
envious [ˈɛnvɪəs] adj invidioso(-a)
environment [ɪnˈvaɪərənmənt] n ambiente m; **Department of the E~** (BRIT) ≈ Ministero dell'Ambiente
environmental [ɪnvaɪərənˈmɛntl] adj ecologico(-a); ambientale; **~ studies** (in school etc) ecologia
environmentalist [ɪnˈvaɪərənˈmɛntəlɪst] n studioso(-a) della protezione dell'ambiente
environmentally [ɪnvaɪərənˈmɛntəlɪ] adv: **~ sound/friendly** che rispetta l'ambiente
Environmental Protection Agency n (US) ≈ Ministero dell'Ambiente
envisage [ɪnˈvɪzɪdʒ] vt immaginare; prevedere
envision [ɪnˈvɪʒən] vt concepire, prevedere
envoy [ˈɛnvɔɪ] n inviato(-a)
envy [ˈɛnvɪ] n invidia ▶ vt invidiare; **to ~ sb sth** invidiare qn per qc
enzyme [ˈɛnzaɪm] n enzima m
EPA n ABBR (US) = **Environmental Protection Agency**
ephemeral [ɪˈfɛmərəl] adj effimero(-a)
epic [ˈɛpɪk] n poema m epico ▶ adj epico(-a)
epicentre, (US) **epicenter** [ˈɛpɪsɛntər] n epicentro
epidemic [ɛpɪˈdɛmɪk] n epidemia
epilepsy [ˈɛpɪlɛpsɪ] n epilessia
epileptic [ɛpɪˈlɛptɪk] adj, n epilettico(-a)
epileptic fit n attacco epilettico
epilogue [ˈɛpɪlɔg] n epilogo
Epiphany [ɪˈpɪfənɪ] n Epifania
episcopal [ɪˈpɪskəpəl] adj episcopale
episode [ˈɛpɪsəud] n episodio
epistle [ɪˈpɪsl] n epistola
epitaph [ˈɛpɪtɑːf] n epitaffio
epithet [ˈɛpɪθɛt] n epiteto
epitome [ɪˈpɪtəmɪ] n epitome f; quintessenza
epitomize [ɪˈpɪtəmaɪz] vt (fig) incarnare
epoch [ˈiːpɔk] n epoca
epoch-making [ˈiːpɔkmeɪkɪŋ] adj che fa epoca
eponymous [ɪˈpɔnɪməs] adj dello stesso nome
equable [ˈɛkwəbl] adj uniforme; (climate) costante; (character) equilibrato(-a)
equal [ˈiːkwl] adj, n pari (mf) ▶ vt uguagliare; **~ to** (task) all'altezza di
equality [iːˈkwɔlɪtɪ] n uguaglianza
equalize [ˈiːkwəlaɪz] vt, vi pareggiare
equalizer [ˈiːkwəlaɪzər] n punto del pareggio
equally [ˈiːkwəlɪ] adv ugualmente; **they are**

~ clever sono intelligenti allo stesso modo
Equal Opportunities Commission, (US) **Equal Employment Opportunity Commission** n commissione contro discriminazioni sessuali o razziali nel mondo del lavoro
equal sign, equals sign n segno d'uguaglianza
equanimity [ɛkwəˈnɪmɪtɪ] n serenità
equate [ɪˈkweɪt] vt: **to ~ sth with** considerare qc uguale a; (compare) paragonare qc con; **to ~ A to B** mettere in equazione A e B
equation [ɪˈkweɪʃən] n (Math) equazione f
equator [ɪˈkweɪtər] n equatore m
Equatorial Guinea [ɛkwəˈtɔːrɪəl-] n Guinea Equatoriale
equestrian [ɪˈkwɛstrɪən] adj equestre ▶ n cavaliere (amazzone)
equilibrium [iːkwɪˈlɪbrɪəm] n equilibrio
equinox [ˈiːkwɪnɔks] n equinozio
equip [ɪˈkwɪp] vt equipaggiare, attrezzare; **to ~ sb/sth with** fornire qn/qc di; **equipped with** (machinery etc) dotato(a) di; **to be well equipped** (office etc) essere ben attrezzato(-a); **he is well equipped for the job** ha i requisiti necessari per quel lavoro
equipment [ɪˈkwɪpmənt] n attrezzatura; (electrical etc) apparecchiatura
equitable [ˈɛkwɪtəbl] adj equo(-a), giusto(-a)
equities [ˈɛkwɪtɪz] npl (BRIT Comm) azioni fpl ordinarie
equity [ˈɛkwɪtɪ] n equità
equity capital n capitale m azionario
equivalent [ɪˈkwɪvələnt] adj, n equivalente (m); **to be ~ to** equivalere a
equivocal [ɪˈkwɪvəkl] adj equivoco(-a); (open to suspicion) dubbio(-a)
equivocate [ɪˈkwɪvəkeɪt] vi esprimersi in modo equivoco
equivocation [ɪkwɪvəˈkeɪʃən] n parole fpl equivoche
ER ABBR BRIT: = **Elizabeth Regina;** (US Med) = **emergency room**
ERA n ABBR (US Pol) = **Equal Rights Amendment**
era [ˈɪərə] n era, età f inv
eradicate [ɪˈrædɪkeɪt] vt sradicare
erase [ɪˈreɪz] vt cancellare
eraser [ɪˈreɪzər] n gomma
e-reader [ˈiːriːdər] n lettore m di e-book
erect [ɪˈrɛkt] adj eretto(-a) ▶ vt costruire; (assemble) montare; (monument, tent) alzare
erection [ɪˈrɛkʃən] n (also Physiol) erezione f; (of building) costruzione f; (of machinery) montaggio
ergonomics [əːgəˈnɔmɪks] n ergonomia
ERISA n ABBR (US: = Employee Retirement Income Security Act) legge relativa al pensionamento statale

Eritrea [ɛɪɪ'treɪə] N Eritrea

ERM N ABBR (= *Exchange Rate Mechanism*)
ERM *m*, meccanismo dei tassi di cambio

ermine ['ə:mɪn] N ermellino

ERNIE ['ə:nɪ] N ABBR (*BRIT*: = *Electronic Random Number Indicator Equipment*) *sistema che seleziona i numeri vincenti di buoni del Tesoro*

erode [ɪ'rəud] VT erodere; (*metal*) corrodere

erogenous zone [ɪ'rɔdʒənəs-] N zona erogena

erosion [ɪ'rəuʒən] N erosione *f*

erotic [ɪ'rɔtɪk] ADJ erotico(-a)

eroticism [ɪ'rɔtɪsɪzəm] N erotismo

err [ə:ʳ] VI errare; (*Rel*) peccare

errand ['ɛrənd] N commissione *f*; (*also*: **run errands**) fare commissioni; **~ of mercy** atto di carità

errand boy N fattorino

erratic [ɪ'rætɪk] ADJ imprevedibile; (*person, mood*) incostante

erroneous [ɪ'rəunɪəs] ADJ erroneo(-a)

error ['ɛrəʳ] N errore *m*; **typing/spelling ~** errore di battitura/di ortografia; **in ~** per errore; **errors and omissions excepted** salvo errori ed omissioni

error message N (*Comput*) messaggio di errore

erstwhile ['ə:stwaɪl] ADV allora, un tempo ▸ ADJ di allora

erudite ['ɛrjudaɪt] ADJ erudito(-a)

erupt [ɪ'rʌpt] VI erompere; (*volcano*) mettersi (*or essere*) in eruzione; (*war, crisis*) scoppiare

eruption [ɪ'rʌpʃən] N eruzione *f*; (*of anger, violence*) esplosione *f*; scoppio

ESA N ABBR (= *European Space Agency*) ESA *f*

escalate ['ɛskəleɪt] VI intensificarsi; (*costs*) salire

escalation [ɛskə'leɪʃən] N escalation *f*; (*of prices*) aumento

escalation clause N clausola di revisione

escalator ['ɛskəleɪtəʳ] N scala mobile

escapade [ɛskə'peɪd] N scappatella; avventura

escape [ɪ'skeɪp] N evasione *f*, fuga; (*of gas etc*) fuga, fuoriuscita ▸ VI fuggire; (*from jail*) evadere, scappare; (*fig*) sfuggire; (*leak*) uscire ▸ VT sfuggire a; **to ~ from** (*place*) fuggire da; (*person*) sfuggire a; **to ~ to** (*another place*) fuggire in; (*freedom, safety*) fuggire verso; **to ~ notice** passare inosservato(a)

escape artist N mago della fuga

escape clause N clausola scappatoia

escapee [ɪskeɪ'pi:] N evaso(-a)

escape hatch N (*in submarine, space rocket*) portello di sicurezza

escape key N (*Comput*) tasto di escape, tasto per cambio di codice

escape route N percorso della fuga

escapism [ɪs'keɪpɪzəm] N evasione *f* (dalla realtà)

escapist [ɪs'keɪpɪst] ADJ d'evasione ▸ N persona che cerca di evadere dalla realtà

escapologist [ɛskə'pɔlədʒɪst] N (*BRIT*) = **escape artist**

escarpment [ɪs'kɑ:pmənt] N scarpata

eschew [ɪs'tʃu:] VT evitare

escort N ['ɛskɔ:t] scorta; (*to dance etc*): **her ~** il suo cavaliere; **his ~** la sua dama ▸ VT [ɪ'skɔ:t] scortare; accompagnare

escort agency N agenzia di hostess

Eskimo ['ɛskɪməu] ADJ eschimese ▸ N eschimese *mf*; (*Ling*) eschimese *m*

ESL N ABBR (*Scol*) = **English as a Second Language**

esophagus [i:'sɔfəgəs] N (*US*) = **oesophagus**

esoteric [ɛsəu'tɛrɪk] ADJ esoterico(-a)

ESP N ABBR = **extrasensory perception**; (*Scol*) = **English for Specific Purposes**; = **English for Special Purposes**

esp. ABBR (= *especially*) spec.

especially [ɪ'spɛʃlɪ] ADV specialmente; (*above all*) soprattutto; (*specifically*) espressamente; (*particularly*) particolarmente

espionage ['ɛspɪənɑ:ʒ] N spionaggio

esplanade [ɛsplə'neɪd] N lungomare *m*

espouse [ɪ'spauz] VT abbracciare

Esquire [ɪ'skwaɪəʳ] N (*BRIT*): **J. Brown, ~** Signor J. Brown

essay ['ɛseɪ] N (*Scol*) composizione *f*; (*Literature*) saggio

essence ['ɛsns] N essenza; **in ~** in sostanza; **speed is of the ~** la velocità è di estrema importanza

essential [ɪ'sɛnʃəl] ADJ essenziale; (*basic*) fondamentale ▸ N elemento essenziale; **it is ~ that** è essenziale che + *sub*

essentially [ɪ'sɛnʃəlɪ] ADV essenzialmente

essentials NPL **the ~** l'essenziale *msg*

EST ABBR (*US*: = *Eastern Standard Time*) *fuso orario*

est. ABBR (= *established*) = **estimate**

establish [ɪ'stæblɪʃ] VT stabilire; (*business*) mettere su; (*one's power etc*) affermare; (*prove: fact, identity, sb's innocence*) dimostrare

establishment [ɪs'tæblɪʃmənt] N stabilimento; (*business*) azienda; **the E~** la classe dirigente; l'establishment *m*; **a teaching ~** un istituto d'istruzione

estate [ɪ'steɪt] N proprietà *f inv*; (*Law*) beni *mpl*, patrimonio; (*BRIT: also*: **housing estate**) complesso edilizio

estate agency N (*BRIT*) agenzia immobiliare

estate agent N (*BRIT*) agente *m* immobiliare

estate car N (*BRIT*) giardiniera

esteem [ɪ'sti:m] N stima ▸ VT considerare; stimare; **I hold him in high ~** gode di tutta la mia stima

esthetic [ɪs'θɛtɪk] ADJ (*US*) = **aesthetic**

estimate N ['ɛstɪmət] stima; (*Comm*) preventivo ▸ VT ['ɛstɪmeɪt] stimare, valutare

▶ VI (BRIT Comm): **to ~ for** fare il preventivo per; **to give sb an ~ of** fare a qn una valutazione approssimativa (or un preventivo) di; **at a rough ~** approssimativamente

estimation [ɛstɪˈmeɪʃən] N stima; opinione f; **in my ~** a mio giudizio, a mio avviso

Estonia [ɛˈstəʊnɪə] N Estonia

Estonian [ɛˈstəʊnɪən] ADJ estone inv ▶ N estone mf; (Ling) estone m

estranged [ɪˈstreɪndʒd] ADJ separato(-a)

estrangement [ɪsˈtreɪndʒmənt] N alienazione f

estrogen [ˈiːstrəʊdʒən] N (US) = **oestrogen**

estuary [ˈɛstjuərɪ] N estuario

ET ABBR (= Eastern Time) fuso orario; (BRIT: = Employment Training) corso di formazione professionale per disoccupati

ETA N ABBR (= estimated time of arrival) ora di arrivo prevista

e-tailer [ˈiːteɪlər] N venditore(-trice) in Internet

e-tailing [ˈiːteɪlɪŋ] N commercio in Internet

et al. ABBR (= et alii: and others) ed altri

etc. ABBR (= et cetera) ecc., etc.

etch [ɛtʃ] VT incidere all'acquaforte

etching [ˈɛtʃɪŋ] N acquaforte f

ETD N ABBR (= estimated time of departure) ora di partenza prevista

eternal [ɪˈtəːnl] ADJ eterno(-a)

eternity [ɪˈtəːnɪtɪ] N eternità

ether [ˈiːθər] N etere m

ethereal [ɪˈθɪərɪəl] ADJ etereo(-a)

ethical [ˈɛθɪkl] ADJ etico(-a), morale

ethics [ˈɛθɪks] N etica ▶ NPL morale f

Ethiopia [iːθɪˈəʊpɪə] N Etiopia

Ethiopian [iːθɪˈəʊpɪən] ADJ, N etiope (mf)

ethnic [ˈɛθnɪk] ADJ etnico(-a)

ethnic cleansing [-ˈklɛnzɪŋ] N pulizia etnica

ethnic minority N minoranza etnica

ethnology [ɛθˈnɔlədʒɪ] N etnologia

ethos [ˈiːθɔs] N (of culture, group) norma di vita

e-ticket [ˈiːtɪkɪt] N e-ticket m inv, biglietto elettronico

etiquette [ˈɛtɪkɛt] N etichetta

ETV N ABBR (US) = **Educational Television**

etymology [ɛtɪˈmɔlədʒɪ] N etimologia

EU N ABBR (= European Union) UE f

eucalyptus [juːkəˈlɪptəs] N eucalipto

eulogy [ˈjuːlədʒɪ] N elogio

euphemism [ˈjuːfəmɪzəm] N eufemismo

euphemistic [juːfəˈmɪstɪk] ADJ eufemistico(-a)

euphoria [juːˈfɔːrɪə] N euforia

Eurasia [juəˈreɪʃə] N Eurasia

Eurasian [juəˈreɪʃən] ADJ, N eurasiano(-a)

Euratom [juəˈrætəm] N ABBR (= European Atomic Energy Community) EURATOM f

euro [ˈjuərəʊ] N (currency) euro m inv

Euro- [ˈjuərəʊ] PREFIX euro-

Eurocheque [ˈjuərəʊtʃɛk] N eurochèque m inv

Eurocrat [ˈjuərəʊkræt] N eurocrate mf

Eurodollar [ˈjuərəʊdɔlər] N eurodollaro

Euroland [ˈjuərəʊlænd] N Eurolandia

Europe [ˈjuərəp] N Europa

European [juərəˈpiːən] ADJ, N europeo(-a)

European Community N Comunità Europea

European Court of Justice N Corte f di Giustizia della Comunità Europea

European Union N Unione f europea

Europol [ˈjuərəʊpɔl] N Europol f

Euro-sceptic [ˈjuərəʊskɛptɪk] N euroscettico(-a)

Eurostar® [ˈjuərəʊstɑːr] N Eurostar® m inv

Eurozone [ˈjuərəʊzəʊn] N zona euro

euthanasia [juːθəˈneɪzɪə] N eutanasia

evacuate [ɪˈvækjueɪt] VT evacuare

evacuation [ɪvækjuˈeɪʃən] N evacuazione f

evacuee [ɪvækjuˈiː] N sfollato(-a)

evade [ɪˈveɪd] VT eludere; (tax) evadere; (duties etc) sottrarsi a; (person) schivare

evaluate [ɪˈvæljueɪt] VT valutare

evangelist [ɪˈvændʒəlɪst] N evangelista m

evangelize [ɪˈvændʒəlaɪz] VT evangelizzare

evaporate [ɪˈvæpəreɪt] VI evaporare ▶ VT far evaporare

evaporated milk N latte m concentrato

evaporation [ɪvæpəˈreɪʃən] N evaporazione f

evasion [ɪˈveɪʒən] N evasione f

evasive [ɪˈveɪsɪv] ADJ evasivo(-a)

eve [iːv] N: **on the ~ of** alla vigilia di

even [ˈiːvn] ADJ regolare; (number) pari inv ▶ ADV anche, perfino; **~ if**, **~ though** anche se; **~ more** ancora di più; **he loves her ~ more** la ama anche di più; **~ faster** ancora più veloce; **~ so** ciò nonostante; **not ~ ...** nemmeno ...; **to break ~** finire in pari o alla pari; **to get ~ with sb** dare la pari a qn ▶ **even out** VI pareggiare

even-handed [ˈiːvnˈhændɪd] ADJ imparziale, equo(-a)

evening [ˈiːvnɪŋ] N sera; (as duration, event) serata; **in the ~** la sera; **this ~** stasera, questa sera; **tomorrow/yesterday ~** domani/ieri sera

evening class N corso serale

evening dress N (woman's) abito da sera; **in ~** (man) in abito scuro; (woman) in abito lungo

evenly [ˈiːvnlɪ] ADV (distribute, space, spread) uniformemente; (divide) in parti uguali

evensong [ˈiːvnsɔŋ] N ≈ vespro

event [ɪˈvɛnt] N avvenimento; (Sport) gara; **in the ~ of** in caso di; **at all events**, (BRIT) **in any ~** in ogni caso; **in the ~** in realtà, di fatto; **in the course of events** nel corso degli eventi

eventful [ɪˈvɛntful] ADJ denso(-a) di eventi

eventing [ɪˈvɛntɪŋ] N (*Horseriding*) concorso ippico

eventual [ɪˈvɛntʃuəl] ADJ finale

eventuality [ɪvɛntʃuˈælɪtɪ] N possibilità *f* inv, eventualità *f* inv

eventually [ɪˈvɛntʃuəlɪ] ADV alla fine

ever [ˈɛvəʳ] ADV mai; (*at all times*) sempre; **for ~** per sempre; **the best ~** il migliore che ci sia mai stato; **hardly ~** non ... quasi mai; **have you ~ seen it?** l'ha mai visto?; **have you ~ been there?** c'è mai stato?; **~ so pretty** così bello(a); **thank you ~ so much** grazie mille; **yours ~** (BRIT: *in letters*) sempre tuo; **~ since** *adv* da allora; *conj* sin da quando

Everest [ˈɛvərɪst] N (*also*: **Mount Everest**) Everest *m*

evergreen [ˈɛvəgriːn] N sempreverde *m*

everlasting [ɛvəˈlɑːstɪŋ] ADJ eterno(-a)

every [ˈɛvrɪ] ADJ ogni; **~ day** tutti i giorni, ogni giorno; **~ other/third day** ogni due/tre giorni; **~ other car** una macchina su due; **~ now and then** ogni tanto, di quando in quando; **I have ~ confidence in him** ho piena fiducia in lui

everybody [ˈɛvrɪbɔdɪ] PRON ognuno, tutti *pl*; **~ else** tutti gli altri; **~ knows about it** lo sanno tutti

everyday [ˈɛvrɪdeɪ] ADJ quotidiano(-a); di ogni giorno; (*use, occurrence, experience*) comune; (*expression*) di uso corrente

everyone [ˈɛvrɪwʌn] = **everybody**

everything [ˈɛvrɪθɪŋ] PRON tutto, ogni cosa; **~ is ready** è tutto pronto; **he did ~ possible** ha fatto tutto il possibile

everywhere [ˈɛvrɪwɛəʳ] ADV in ogni luogo, dappertutto; (*wherever*) ovunque; **~ you go you meet ...** ovunque si vada si trova ...

evict [ɪˈvɪkt] VT sfrattare

eviction [ɪˈvɪkʃən] N sfratto

eviction notice N avviso di sfratto

evidence [ˈɛvɪdəns] N (*proof*) prova; (*of witness*) testimonianza; **to show ~ of** (*sign*) dare segni di; **to give ~** deporre; **in ~** (*obvious*) in evidenza; in vista

evident [ˈɛvɪdənt] ADJ evidente

evidently [ˈɛvɪdəntlɪ] ADV evidentemente

evil [ˈiːvl] ADJ cattivo(-a), maligno(-a) ▶ N male *m*

evince [ɪˈvɪns] VT manifestare

evocative [ɪˈvɔkətɪv] ADJ evocativo(-a)

evoke [ɪˈvəuk] VT evocare; (*admiration*) suscitare

evolution [iːvəˈluːʃən] N evoluzione *f*

evolve [ɪˈvɔlv] VT elaborare ▶ VI svilupparsi, evolversi

ewe [juː] N pecora

ex [ɛks] N (*col*): **my ex** il mio(-a) ex

ex- [ɛks] PREFIX ex; (*out of*): **the price ~works** il prezzo franco fabbrica

exacerbate [ɪkˈsæsəbeɪt] VT (*pain*) aggravare; (*fig: relations, situation*) esacerbare, esasperare

exact [ɪgˈzækt] ADJ esatto(-a) ▶ VT: **to ~ sth (from)** estorcere qc (da); esigere qc (da)

exacting [ɪgˈzæktɪŋ] ADJ esigente; (*work*) faticoso(-a)

exactitude [ɪgˈzæktɪtjuːd] N esattezza, precisione *f*

exactly [ɪgˈzæktlɪ] ADV esattamente; **~!** esatto!

exaggerate [ɪgˈzædʒəreɪt] VT, VI esagerare

exaggeration [ɪgzædʒəˈreɪʃən] N esagerazione *f*

exalt [ɪgˈzɔːlt] VT esaltare; elevare

exalted [ɪgˈzɔːltɪd] ADJ (*rank, person*) elevato(-a); (*elated*) esaltato(-a)

exam [ɪgˈzæm] N ABBR (*Scol*) = **examination**

examination [ɪgzæmɪˈneɪʃən] N (*Scol*) esame *m*; (*Med*) controllo; **to take** *or* **sit an ~** (BRIT) sostenere *or* dare un esame; **the matter is under ~** la questione è all'esame

examine [ɪgˈzæmɪn] VT esaminare; (*Scol: orally, Law: person*) interrogare; (*inspect: machine, premises*) ispezionare; (: *luggage, passport*) controllare; (*Med*) visitare

examiner [ɪgˈzæmɪnəʳ] N esaminatore(-trice)

example [ɪgˈzɑːmpl] N esempio; **for ~** ad *or* per esempio; **to set a good/bad ~** dare il buon/cattivo esempio

exasperate [ɪgˈzɑːspəreɪt] VT esasperare; **exasperated by** (*or* **at** *or* **with**) esasperato da

exasperated [ɪgˈzɑːspəreɪtɪd] ADJ esasperato(-a)

exasperating [ɪgˈzɑːspəreɪtɪŋ] ADJ esasperante

exasperation [ɪgzɑːspəˈreɪʃən] N esasperazione *f*

excavate [ˈɛkskəveɪt] VT scavare

excavation [ɛkskəˈveɪʃən] N escavazione *f*

excavator [ˈɛkskəveɪtəʳ] N scavatore *m*, scavatrice *f*

exceed [ɪkˈsiːd] VT superare; (*one's powers, time limit*) oltrepassare

exceedingly [ɪkˈsiːdɪŋlɪ] ADV eccessivamente

excel [ɪkˈsɛl] VI eccellere ▶ VT sorpassare; **to ~ o.s.** (BRIT) superare se stesso

excellence [ˈɛksələns] N eccellenza

Excellency [ˈɛksələnsɪ] N: **His ~** Sua Eccellenza

excellent [ˈɛksələnt] ADJ eccellente

except [ɪkˈsɛpt] PREP (*also*: **except for, excepting**) salvo, all'infuori di, eccetto ▶ VT escludere; **~ if/when** salvo se/quando; **~ that** salvo che

exception [ɪkˈsɛpʃən] N eccezione *f*; **to take ~ to** trovare a ridire su; **with the ~ of** ad eccezione di

exceptional [ɪkˈsɛpʃənl] ADJ eccezionale

exceptionally [ɪk'sepʃənəlɪ] ADV eccezionalmente

excerpt ['ɛksəːpt] N estratto

excess [ɪk'sɛs] N eccesso; **in ~ of** al di sopra di

excess baggage N bagaglio in eccedenza

excess fare N supplemento

excessive [ɪk'sɛsɪv] ADJ eccessivo(-a)

excess supply N eccesso di offerta

exchange [ɪks'tʃeɪndʒ] N scambio; *(also:* **telephone exchange**) centralino ▶ VT: **to ~ (for)** scambiare (con); **in ~ for** in cambio di; **foreign ~** *(Comm)* cambio

exchange control N controllo sui cambi

exchange market N mercato dei cambi

exchange rate N tasso di cambio

Exchequer [ɪks'tʃekər] N: **the ~** *(Brit)* lo Scacchiere, ≈ il ministero delle Finanze

excisable [ɪk'saɪzəbl] ADJ soggetto(-a) a dazio

excise N ['ɛksaɪz] imposta, dazio ▶ VT [ɛk'saɪz] recidere

excise duties NPL dazi *mpl*

excitable [ɪk'saɪtəbl] ADJ eccitabile

excite [ɪk'saɪt] VT eccitare; **to get excited** eccitarsi

excited ADJ: **to get ~** essere elettrizzato(-a)

excitement [ɪk'saɪtmənt] N eccitazione *f*; agitazione *f*

exciting [ɪk'saɪtɪŋ] ADJ avventuroso(-a); *(film, book)* appassionante

excl. ABBR (= *excluding, exclusive (of)*) escl.

exclaim [ɪk'skleɪm] VI esclamare

exclamation [ɛksklə'meɪʃən] N esclamazione *f*

exclamation mark, *(US)* **exclamation point** N punto esclamativo

exclude [ɪk'skluːd] VT escludere

excluding [ɪk'skluːdɪŋ] PREP: **~ VAT** IVA esclusa

exclusion [ɪk'skluːʒən] N esclusione *f*; **to the ~ of** escludendo

exclusion clause N clausola di esclusione

exclusion zone N area interdetta

exclusive [ɪk'skluːsɪv] ADJ esclusivo(-a); *(club)* selettivo(-a); *(district)* snob *inv* ▶ ADV *(Comm)* non compreso; **~ of VAT** IVA esclusa; **~ of postage** spese postali escluse; **~ of service** servizio escluso; **from 1st to 15th March ~** dal 1° al 15 marzo esclusi; **~ rights** *npl (Comm)* diritti *mpl* esclusivi

exclusively [ɪk'skluːsɪvlɪ] ADV esclusivamente

excommunicate [ɛkskə'mjuːnɪkeɪt] VT scomunicare

excrement ['ɛkskrəmənt] N escremento

excruciating [ɪk'skruːʃɪeɪtɪŋ] ADJ straziante, atroce

excursion [ɪk'skəːʃən] N escursione *f*, gita

excursion ticket N biglietto a tariffa escursionistica

excusable [ɪk'skjuːzəbl] ADJ scusabile

excuse N [ɪk'skjuːs] scusa ▶ VT [ɪk'skjuːz] scusare; *(justify)* giustificare; **to make excuses for sb** trovare giustificazioni per qn; **to ~ sb from** *(activity)* dispensare qn da; **~ me!** mi scusi!; **now if you will ~ me, ...** ora, mi scusi ma ...; **to ~ o.s. (for (doing) sth)** giustificarsi (per (aver fatto) qc)

ex-directory ['ɛksdɪ'rɛktərɪ] ADJ *(Brit)*: **to be ~** non essere sull'elenco; **~ (phone) number** numero non compreso nell'elenco telefonico

execrable ['ɛksɪkrəbl] ADJ *(gen)* pessimo(-a); *(manners)* esecrabile

execute ['ɛksɪkjuːt] VT *(prisoner)* giustiziare; *(plan etc)* eseguire

execution [ɛksɪ'kjuːʃən] N esecuzione *f*

executioner [ɛksɪ'kjuːʃnər] N boia *m inv*

executive [ɪg'zɛkjutɪv] N *(Comm)* dirigente *m*; *(Pol)* esecutivo *m* ▶ ADJ esecutivo(-a); *(secretary)* di direzione; *(offices, suite)* della direzione; *(car, plane)* dirigenziale; *(position, job, duties)* direttivo(-a)

executive director N amministratore(-trice)

executor [ɪg'zɛkjutər] N esecutore(-trice) testamentario(-a)

exemplary [ɪg'zɛmplərɪ] ADJ esemplare

exemplify [ɪg'zɛmplɪfaɪ] VT esemplificare

exempt [ɪg'zɛmpt] ADJ: **~ (from)** *(person: from tax)* esentato(-a) (da); (: *from military service etc)* esonerato(-a) (da); *(goods)* esente (da) ▶ VT: **to ~ sb from** esentare qn da

exemption [ɪg'zɛmpʃən] N esenzione *f*

exercise [ɪk'sɛsəsaɪz] N *(keep fit)* moto; *(Scol, Mil etc)* esercizio ▶ VT esercitare; *(patience)* usare; *(dog)* portar fuori ▶ VI *(also:* **take exercise**) fare del movimento *or* moto

exercise bike N cyclette® *f inv*

exercise book N quaderno

exert [ɪg'zəːt] VT esercitare; *(strength, force)* impiegare; **to ~ o.s.** sforzarsi

exertion [ɪg'zəːʃən] N sforzo

ex gratia ['ɛks'greɪʃə] ADJ: **~ payment** gratifica

exhale [ɛks'heɪl] VT, VI espirare

exhaust [ɪg'zɔːst] N *(also:* **exhaust fumes**) scappamento; *(also:* **exhaust pipe**) tubo di scappamento ▶ VT esaurire; **to ~ o.s.** sfiancarsi

exhausted [ɪg'zɔːstɪd] ADJ esaurito(-a)

exhausting [ɪg'zɔːstɪŋ] ADJ estenuante

exhaustion [ɪg'zɔːstʃən] N esaurimento; **nervous ~** sovraffaticamento mentale

exhaustive [ɪg'zɔːstɪv] ADJ esauriente

exhibit [ɪg'zɪbɪt] N *(Art)* oggetto esposto; *(Law)* documento *or* oggetto esibito ▶ VT esporre; *(courage, skill)* dimostrare

exhibition [ɛksɪ'bɪʃən] N mostra, esposizione *f*; *(of rudeness etc)* spettacolo; **to make an ~ of o.s.** dare spettacolo di sé

exhibitionist [ɛksɪ'bɪʃənɪst] N esibizionista mf

exhibitor [ɪg'zɪbɪtər] N espositore(-trice)

exhilarating [ɪg'zɪləreɪtɪŋ] ADJ esilarante; stimolante

exhilaration [ɪgzɪlə'reɪʃən] N esaltazione f, ebbrezza

exhort [ɪg'zɔːt] VT esortare

exile ['ɛksaɪl] N esilio; (person) esiliato(-a) ► VT esiliare; **in ~** in esilio

exist [ɪg'zɪst] VI esistere

existence [ɪg'zɪstəns] N esistenza; **to be in ~** esistere

existentialism [ɛgzɪs'tɛnʃəlɪzəm] N esistenzialismo

existing [ɪg'zɪstɪŋ] ADJ esistente; (laws, regime) attuale

exit ['ɛksɪt] N uscita ► VI (Comput, Theat) uscire

exit poll N exit poll m inv, sondaggio all'uscita dei seggi

exit ramp N (US Aut) rampa di uscita

exit visa N visto d'uscita

exodus ['ɛksədəs] N esodo

ex officio ['ɛksə'fɪʃɪəu] ADJ, ADV d'ufficio

exonerate [ɪg'zɔnəreɪt] VT: **to ~ from** discolpare da

exorbitant [ɪg'zɔːbɪtənt] ADJ (price) esorbitante; (demands) spropositato(-a)

exorcize ['ɛksɔːsaɪz] VT esorcizzare

exotic [ɪg'zɔtɪk] ADJ esotico(-a)

expand [ɪk'spænd] VT (chest, economy etc) sviluppare; (market, operations) espandere; (influence) estendere; (horizons) allargare ► VI svilupparsi; (gas) espandersi; (metal) dilatarsi; **to ~ on** (notes, story etc) ampliare

expanse [ɪk'spæns] N distesa, estensione f

expansion [ɪk'spænʃən] N (gen) espansione f; (of town, economy) sviluppo; (of metal) dilatazione f

expansionism [ɪk'spænʃənɪzəm] N espansionismo

expansionist [ɪk'spænʃənɪst] ADJ espansionistico(-a)

expatriate N [ɛks'pætrɪət] espatriato(-a) ► VT [ɛks'pætrɪeɪt] espatriare

expect [ɪk'spɛkt] VT (anticipate) prevedere, aspettarsi, prevedere or aspettarsi che + sub; (count on) contare su; (hope for) sperare; (require) richiedere, esigere; (suppose) supporre; (await, also baby) aspettare ► VI: **to be expecting** essere in stato interessante; **to ~ sb to do** aspettarsi che qn faccia; **to ~ to do sth** pensare or contare di fare qc; **as expected** come previsto; **I ~ so** credo di sì

expectancy [ɪk'spɛktənsɪ] N attesa; **life ~** probabilità fpl di vita

expectant [ɪk'spɛktənt] ADJ pieno(-a) di aspettative

expectantly [ɪk'spɛktəntlɪ] ADV (look, listen) con un'aria d'attesa

expectant mother N gestante f

expectation [ɛkspɛk'teɪʃən] N aspettativa; speranza; **in ~ of** in previsione di; **against** or **contrary to all ~(s)** contro ogni aspettativa; **to come** or **live up to sb's expectations** rispondere alle attese di qn

expedience [ɪk'spiːdɪəns], **expediency** [ɪk'spiːdɪənsɪ] N convenienza; **for the sake of ~** per una questione di comodità

expedient [ɪk'spiːdɪənt] ADJ conveniente; vantaggioso(-a) ► N espediente m

expedite ['ɛkspədaɪt] VT sbrigare; facilitare

expedition [ɛkspə'dɪʃən] N spedizione f

expeditionary force [ɛkspə'dɪʃənərɪ-] N corpo di spedizione

expeditious [ɛkspə'dɪʃəs] ADJ sollecito(-a), rapido(-a)

expel [ɪk'spɛl] VT espellere

expend [ɪk'spɛnd] VT spendere; (use up) consumare

expendable [ɪk'spɛndəbl] ADJ sacrificabile

expenditure [ɪk'spɛndɪtʃər] N spesa; (of time, effort) dispendio

expense [ɪk'spɛns] N spesa; (high cost) costo; **expenses** NPL (Comm) spese fpl, indennità fpl; **to go to the ~ of** sobbarcarsi la spesa di; **at great ~** con grande impiego di mezzi; **at the ~ of** a spese di

expense account N conto m spese inv

expensive [ɪk'spɛnsɪv] ADJ caro(-a), costoso(-a); **she has ~ tastes** le piacciono le cose costose

experience [ɪk'spɪərɪəns] N esperienza ► VT (pleasure) provare; (hardship) soffrire; **to learn by ~** imparare per esperienza

experienced [ɪk'spɪərɪənst] ADJ esperto(-a)

experiment N [ɪk'spɛrɪmənt] esperimento, esperienza ► VI [ɪk'spɛrɪment] fare esperimenti; **to perform** or **carry out an ~** fare un esperimento; **as an ~** a titolo di esperimento; **to ~ with a new vaccine** sperimentare un nuovo vaccino

experimental [ɪkspɛrɪ'mɛntl] ADJ sperimentale; **at the ~ stage** in via di sperimentazione

expert ['ɛkspəːt] ADJ, N esperto(-a); **~ witness** (Law) esperto(-a); **~ in** or **at doing sth** esperto nel fare qc; **an ~ on sth** un esperto di qc

expertise [ɛkspəː'tiːz] N competenza

expire [ɪk'spaɪər] VI (period of time, licence) scadere

expiry [ɪk'spaɪərɪ] N scadenza

expiry date N (of medicine, food item) data di scadenza

explain [ɪk'spleɪn] VT spiegare
  ► **explain away** VT dar ragione di

explanation [ɛksplə'neɪʃən] N spiegazione f; **to find an ~ for sth** trovare la spiegazione di qc

explanatory [ɪk'splænətrɪ] ADJ esplicativo(-a)

expletive [ɪk'spliːtɪv] N imprecazione f

explicit [ɪk'splɪsɪt] ADJ esplicito(-a); (definite) netto(-a)

explode [ɪk'spləud] VI esplodere ▶ VT (fig: theory) demolire; **to ~ a myth** distruggere un mito

exploit N ['ɛksplɔɪt] impresa ▶ VT [ɪk'splɔɪt] sfruttare

exploitation [ɛksplɔɪ'teɪʃən] N sfruttamento

exploration [ɛksplə'reɪʃən] N esplorazione f

exploratory [ɪk'splɔrətrɪ] ADJ (fig: talks) esplorativo(-a); **~ operation** (Med) intervento d'esplorazione

explore [ɪk'splɔːʳ] VT esplorare; (possibilities) esaminare

explorer [ɪk'splɔːrəʳ] N esploratore(-trice)

explosion [ɪk'spləuʒən] N esplosione f

explosive [ɪk'spləusɪv] ADJ esplosivo(-a) ▶ N esplosivo

exponent [ɪk'spəunənt] N esponente mf

export VT [ɛk'spɔːt] esportare ▶ N ['ɛkspɔːt] esportazione f; articolo di esportazione ▶ CPD d'esportazione

exportation [ɛkspɔː'teɪʃən] N esportazione f

exporter [ɪk'spɔːtəʳ] N esportatore m

export licence N licenza d'esportazione

expose [ɪk'spəuz] VT esporre; (unmask) smascherare; **to ~ o.s.** (Law) oltraggiare il pudore

exposed [ɪk'spəuzd] ADJ (land, house) esposto(-a); (Elec: wire) scoperto(-a); (: pipe, beam) a vista

exposition [ɛkspə'zɪʃən] N esposizione f

exposure [ɪk'spəuʒəʳ] N esposizione f; (Phot) posa; (Med) assideramento; **to die of ~** morire assiderato(-a)

exposure meter N esposimetro

expound [ɪk'spaund] VT esporre; (theory, text) spiegare

express [ɪk'sprɛs] ADJ (definite) chiaro(-a), espresso(-a); (BRIT: letter etc) espresso inv ▶ N (train) espresso ▶ ADV: **to send sth ~** spedire qc per espresso ▶ VT esprimere; **to ~ o.s.** esprimersi

expression [ɪk'sprɛʃən] N espressione f

expressionism [ɪk'sprɛʃənɪzəm] N espressionismo

expressive [ɪk'sprɛsɪv] ADJ espressivo(-a)

expressly [ɪk'sprɛslɪ] ADV espressamente

expressway [ɪk'sprɛsweɪ] N (US: urban motorway) autostrada che attraversa la città

expropriate [ɛks'prəuprɪeɪt] VT espropriare

expulsion [ɪk'spʌlʃən] N espulsione f

exquisite [ɛk'skwɪzɪt] ADJ squisito(-a)

ex-serviceman ['ɛks'səːvɪsmən] N (irreg) ex combattente m

ext. ABBR (Tel: = extension) int. (= interno)

extemporize [ɪk'stɛmpəraɪz] VI improvvisare

extend [ɪk'stɛnd] VT (visit) protrarre; (road, deadline) prolungare; (building) ampliare; (offer) offrire, porgere; (Comm: credit) accordare ▶ VI (land) estendersi

extension [ɪk'stɛnʃən] N (of road, term) prolungamento; (of contract, deadline) proroga; (building) annesso; (to wire, table) prolunga; (telephone) interno; (: in private house) apparecchio supplementare; **~ 3718** (Tel) interno 3718

extension cable, extension lead N (Elec) prolunga

extensive [ɪk'stɛnsɪv] ADJ esteso(-a), ampio(-a); (damage) su larga scala; (alterations) notevole; (inquiries, coverage, discussion) esauriente; (use) grande

extensively [ɪk'stɛnsɪvlɪ] ADV (altered, damaged etc) radicalmente; **he's travelled ~** ha viaggiato molto

extent [ɪk'stɛnt] N estensione f; (of knowledge, activities, power) portata; (degree: of damage, loss) proporzioni fpl; **to some ~** fino a un certo punto; **to a certain/large ~** in certa/larga misura; **to what ~?** fino a che punto?; **to such an ~ that ...** a tal punto che ...; **to the ~ of ...** fino al punto di ...

extenuating [ɪk'stɛnjueɪtɪŋ] ADJ: **~ circumstances** attenuanti fpl

exterior [ɛk'stɪərɪəʳ] ADJ esteriore, esterno(-a) ▶ N esteriore m, esterno; aspetto (esteriore)

exterminate [ɪk'stəːmɪneɪt] VT sterminare

extermination [ɪkstəːmɪ'neɪʃən] N sterminio

external [ɛk'stəːnl] ADJ esterno(-a), esteriore ▶ N: **the externals** le apparenze; **for ~ use only** (Med) solo per uso esterno; **~ affairs** (Pol) affari mpl esteri

externally [ɛk'stəːnəlɪ] ADV esternamente

extinct [ɪk'stɪŋkt] ADJ estinto(-a)

extinction [ɪk'stɪŋkʃən] N estinzione f

extinguish [ɪk'stɪŋgwɪʃ] VT estinguere

extinguisher [ɪk'stɪŋgwɪʃəʳ] N estintore m

extol, (US) **extoll** [ɪk'stəul] VT (merits, virtues) magnificare; (person) celebrare

extort [ɪk'stɔːt] VT: **to ~ sth from** estorcere qc (da)

extortion [ɪk'stɔːʃən] N estorsione f

extortionate [ɪk'stɔːʃənɪt] ADJ esorbitante

extra ['ɛkstrə] ADJ extra inv, supplementare ▶ ADV (in addition) di più ▶ N extra m inv; (surcharge) supplemento; (Theat) comparso; **wine will cost ~** il vino è extra; **~ large sizes** taglie fpl forti

extra... ['ɛkstrə] PREFIX extra...

extract VT [ɪk'strækt] estrarre; (money, promise) strappare ▶ N ['ɛkstrækt] estratto; (passage) brano

extraction [ɪk'strækʃən] N estrazione f; (descent) origine f

extractor fan [ɪk'stræktə'-] N aspiratore m

extracurricular [ɛkstrəkə'rɪkjulə'] ADJ (Scol) parascolastico(-a)

extradite ['ɛkstrədaɪt] VT estradare

extradition [ɛkstrə'dɪʃən] N estradizione f

extramarital [ɛkstrə'mærɪtl] ADJ extraconiugale

extramural [ɛkstrə'mjuərl] ADJ fuori dell'università

extraneous [ɛk'streɪnɪəs] ADJ: ~ **to** estraneo(a) a

extraordinary [ɪk'strɔ:dnrɪ] ADJ straordinario(-a); **the ~ thing is that ...** la cosa strana è che ...

extraordinary general meeting N assemblea straordinaria

extrapolation [ɪkstræpə'leɪʃən] N estrapolazione f

extrasensory perception [ɛkstrə'sɛnsərɪ-] N percezione f extrasensoriale

extra time N (Football) tempo supplementare

extravagance [ɪk'strævəgəns] N (excessive spending) sperpero; (thing bought) stravaganza

extravagant [ɪk'strævəgənt] ADJ (in spending: person) prodigo(-a); (: tastes) dispendioso(-a); (behaviour) esagerato(-a)

extreme [ɪk'stri:m] ADJ estremo(-a) ▶ N estremo; **extremes of temperature** eccessivi sbalzi mpl di temperatura; **the ~ left/right** (Pol) l'estrema sinistra/destra

extremely [ɪk'stri:mlɪ] ADV estremamente

extremist [ɪk'stri:mɪst] ADJ, N estremista (mf)

extremity [ɪk'strɛmɪtɪ] N estremità f inv

extricate ['ɛkstrɪkeɪt] VT: **to ~ sth from** districare qc (da)

extrovert ['ɛkstrəvə:t] N estroverso(-a)

exuberance [ɪg'zu:bərəns] N esuberanza

exuberant [ɪg'zju:bərənt] ADJ esuberante

exude [ɪg'zju:d] VT trasudare; (fig) emanare

exult [ɪg'zʌlt] VI esultare, gioire

exultant [ɪg'zʌltənt] ADJ (person, smile) esultante; (shout, expression) di giubilo

exultation [ɛgzʌl'teɪʃən] N giubilo; **in ~** per la gioia

eye [aɪ] N occhio; (of needle) cruna ▶ VT osservare; **to keep an ~ on** tenere d'occhio; **in the public ~** esposto(a) al pubblico; **as far as the ~ can see** a perdita d'occhio; **with an ~ to doing sth** (BRIT) con l'idea di far qc; **to have an ~ for sth** avere occhio per qc; **there's more to this than meets the ~** non è così semplice come sembra

eyeball ['aɪbɔ:l] N globo dell'occhio

eyebath ['aɪbɑ:θ] N occhino

eyebrow ['aɪbrau] N sopracciglio

eyebrow pencil N matita per le sopracciglia

eye-catching ['aɪkætʃɪŋ] ADJ che colpisce l'occhio

eye cup N (US) = **eyebath**

eyedrops ['aɪdrɔps] NPL gocce fpl oculari, collirio

eyeful ['aɪful] N: **to get an ~ (of sth)** (col) avere l'occasione di dare una bella sbirciata (a qc)

eyeglass ['aɪglɑ:s] N monocolo

eyelash ['aɪlæʃ] N ciglio

eyelet ['aɪlɪt] N occhiello

eye-level ['aɪlɛvl] ADJ all'altezza degli occhi

eyelid ['aɪlɪd] N palpebra

eyeliner ['aɪlaɪnə'] N eye-liner m inv

eye-opener ['aɪəupnə'] N rivelazione f

eyeshadow ['aɪʃædəu] N ombretto

eyesight ['aɪsaɪt] N vista

eyesore ['aɪsɔ:'] N pugno nell'occhio

eyestrain ['aɪstreɪn] N: **to get ~** stancarsi gli occhi

eye-tooth ['aɪtu:θ] (pl **eye-teeth** [-ti:θ]) N canino superiore; **to give one's eye-teeth for sth/to do sth** (fig) dare non so che cosa per qc/per fare qc

eyewash ['aɪwɔʃ] N collirio; (fig) sciocchezze fpl

eye witness N testimone mf oculare

eyrie ['ɪərɪ] N nido (d'aquila)

Ff

F, f [ɛf] N (letter) F, f inv or m inv; (Mus): **F** fa m; **F for Frederick**, (US) **F for Fox** ≈ F come Firenze

F. ABBR (= Fahrenheit) F

FA N ABBR (BRIT) = **Football Association**

FAA N ABBR (US) = **Federal Aviation Administration**

fable ['feɪbl] N favola

fabric ['fæbrɪk] N stoffa, tessuto; (Archit) struttura

fabricate ['fæbrɪkeɪt] VT fabbricare

fabrication [fæbrɪ'keɪʃən] N fabbricazione f

fabric ribbon N (for typewriter) dattilonastro di tessuto

fabulous ['fæbjuləs] ADJ favoloso(-a); (col: super) favoloso(-a), fantastico(-a)

façade [fə'sɑ:d] N facciata; (fig) apparenza

face [feɪs] N faccia, viso, volto; (expression) faccia; (grimace) smorfia; (of clock) quadrante m; (of building) facciata; (side, surface) faccia; (of mountain, cliff) parete f ▶ VT fronteggiare; (fig) affrontare; **~ down** (person) bocconi; (object) a faccia in giù; **to lose/save ~** perdere/salvare la faccia; **to pull a ~** fare una smorfia; **in the ~ of** (difficulties etc) di fronte a; **on the ~ of it** a prima vista; **~ to ~** faccia a faccia; **to ~ the fact that ...** riconoscere or ammettere che ...

▶ **face up to** VT FUS affrontare, far fronte a

Facebook® ['feɪs,bʊk] N Facebook® m

facebook® ['feɪs,bʊk] VB messaggiare vt su Facebook/facebook

face cloth N (BRIT) guanto di spugna

face cream N crema per il viso

faceless ['feɪslɪs] ADJ anonimo(-a)

face lift N lifting m inv; (of façade etc) ripulita

face pack N (BRIT) maschera di bellezza

face powder N cipria

face-saving ['feɪs'seɪvɪŋ] ADJ che salva la faccia

facet ['fæsɪt] N faccetta, sfaccettatura; (fig) sfaccettatura

facetious [fə'si:ʃəs] ADJ faceto(-a)

face-to-face ['feɪstə'feɪs] ADV faccia a faccia

face value ['feɪs'vælju:] N (of coin) valore m facciale or nominale; **to take sth at ~** (fig) giudicare qc dalle apparenze

facia ['feɪʃɪə] N = **fascia**

facial ['feɪʃəl] ADJ facciale, del viso ▶ N trattamento del viso

facile ['fæsaɪl] ADJ facile; superficiale

facilitate [fə'sɪlɪteɪt] VT facilitare

facility [fə'sɪlɪtɪ] N facilità; **facilities** NPL attrezzature fpl; **credit facilities** facilitazioni fpl di credito

facing ['feɪsɪŋ] N (of wall etc) rivestimento; (Sewing) paramontura

facsimile [fæk'sɪmɪlɪ] N facsimile m inv

facsimile machine N telecopiatrice f

fact [fækt] N fatto; **in ~** in effetti; **to know for a ~ that ...** sapere per certo che ...; **the ~ (of the matter) is that ...** la verità è che ...; **the facts of life** (sex) i fatti riguardanti la vita sessuale; (fig) le realtà della vita

fact-finding ['fæktfaɪndɪŋ] ADJ: **a ~ tour/ mission** un viaggio/una missione d'inchiesta

faction ['fækʃən] N fazione f

factional ['fækʃnl] ADJ: **~ fighting** scontri mpl tra fazioni

factor ['fæktər] N fattore m; (Comm: company) organizzazione specializzata nell'incasso di crediti per conto terzi; (: agent) agente m depositario ▶ VI incassare crediti per conto terzi; **human ~** elemento umano; **safety ~** coefficiente m di sicurezza

factory ['fæktərɪ] N fabbrica, stabilimento

factory farming N (BRIT) allevamento su scala industriale

factory floor N: **the ~** (workers) gli operai; (area) il reparto produzione; **on the ~** nel reparto produzione

factory ship N nave f fattoria inv

factual ['fæktjuəl] ADJ che si attiene ai fatti

faculty ['fækəltɪ] N facoltà f inv; (US: teaching staff) corpo insegnante

fad [fæd] N mania; capriccio

fade [feɪd] vɪ sbiadire, sbiadirsi; (light, sound, hope) attenuarsi, affievolirsi; (flower) appassire
▶ **fade away** vɪ (sound) affievolirsi
▶ **fade in** vᴛ (picture) aprire in dissolvenza; (sound) aumentare gradualmente d'intensità
▶ **fade out** vᴛ (picture) chiudere in dissolvenza; (sound) diminuire gradualmente d'intensità
faeces, (US) **feces** ['fiːsiːz] NPL feci fpl
fag [fæg] N (BRIT: col: cigarette) cicca; (: chore) sfacchinata; (US col: homosexual) frocio
fag end N (BRIT col) mozzicone m
fagged out ['fægd-] ADJ (BRIT col) stanco(-a) morto(-a)
Fahrenheit ['fɑːrənhaɪt] N Fahrenheit m inv
fail [feɪl] vᴛ (exam) non superare; (candidate) bocciare; (courage, memory) mancare a ▶ vɪ fallire; (student) essere respinto(-a); (supplies) mancare; (eyesight, health, light: also: **be failing**) venire a mancare; (: brakes) non funzionare; **to ~ to do sth** (neglect) mancare di fare qc; (be unable) non riuscire a fare qc; **without ~** senza fallo; certamente
failing ['feɪlɪŋ] N difetto ▶ PREP in mancanza di; **~ that** se questo non è possibile
failsafe ['feɪlseɪf] ADJ (device etc) di sicurezza
failure ['feɪljəʳ] N fallimento; (person) fallito(-a); (mechanical etc) guasto; (in exam) insuccesso, bocciatura; (of crops) perdita; **his ~ to come** il fatto che non sia venuto; **it was a complete ~** è stato un vero fiasco
faint [feɪnt] ADJ debole; (recollection) vago(-a); (mark) indistinto(-a); (smell, breeze, trace) leggero(-a) ▶ N (Med) svenimento ▶ vɪ svenire; **to feel ~** sentirsi svenire
faintest ['feɪntɪst] ADJ: **I haven't the ~ idea** non ho la più pallida idea
faint-hearted [feɪnt'hɑːtɪd] ADJ pusillanime
faintly ['feɪntlɪ] ADV debolmente; vagamente
faintness ['feɪntnɪs] N debolezza
fair [fɛəʳ] ADJ (person, decision) giusto(-a), equo(-a); (quite large, quite good) discreto(-a); (hair etc) biondo(-a); (skin, complexion) chiaro(-a); (weather) bello(-a), clemente; (good enough) assai buono(-a); (sizeable) bello(-a) ▶ ADV: **to play ~** giocare correttamente ▶ N fiera; (BRIT: funfair) luna park m inv; (also: **trade fair**) fiera campionaria; **it's not ~!** non è giusto!; **a ~ amount of** un bel po' di
fair copy N bella copia
fair game N: **to be ~** (person) essere bersaglio legittimo
fairground ['fɛəgraʊnd] N luna park m inv
fair-haired [fɛə'hɛəd] ADJ (person) biondo(-a)
fairly ['fɛəlɪ] ADV equamente; (quite) abbastanza

fairness ['fɛənɪs] N equità, giustizia; **in all ~** per essere giusti, a dire il vero
fair play N correttezza
fair trade N commercio equo e solidale
fairway N (Golf) fairway m inv
fairy ['fɛərɪ] N fata
fairy godmother N fata buona
fairy lights NPL (BRIT) lanternine fpl colorate
fairy tale N fiaba
faith [feɪθ] N fede f; (trust) fiducia; (sect) religione f, fede f; **to have ~ in sb/sth** avere fiducia in qn/qc
faithful ['feɪθfʊl] ADJ fedele
faithfully ['feɪθfəlɪ] ADV fedelmente; **yours ~** (BRIT: in letters) distinti saluti
faith healer N guaritore(-trice)
fake [feɪk] N imitazione f; (picture) falso; (person) impostore(-a) ▶ ADJ falso(-a) ▶ vᴛ (accounts) falsificare; (illness) fingere; (painting) contraffare; **his illness is a ~** fa finta di essere malato
falcon ['fɔːlkən] N falco, falcone m
Falkland Islands ['fɔːlklənd-] NPL: **the ~** le isole Falkland
fall [fɔːl] (pt **fell** [fɛl], pp **fallen** ['fɔːlən]) N caduta; (decrease) diminuzione f, calo; (in temperature) abbassamento; (in price) ribasso; (US: autumn) autunno ▶ vɪ cadere; (temperature, price) scendere; **a ~ of earth** uno smottamento; **a ~ of snow** (BRIT) una nevicata; **to ~ in love (with sb/sth)** innamorarsi (di qn/qc); **to ~ short of** (sb's expectations) non corrispondere a; **to ~ flat** vɪ (on one's face) cadere bocconi; (joke) fare cilecca; (plan) fallire; see also **falls**
▶ **fall apart** vɪ cadere a pezzi
▶ **fall back** vɪ indietreggiare; (Mil) ritirarsi
▶ **fall back on** vᴛ ꜰᴜs ripiegare su; **to have sth to ~ back on** avere qc di riserva
▶ **fall behind** vɪ rimanere indietro; (fig: with payments) essere in arretrato
▶ **fall down** vɪ (person) cadere; (building, hopes) crollare
▶ **fall for** vᴛ ꜰᴜs (person) prendere una cotta per; **to ~ for a trick** (or **a story** etc) cascarci
▶ **fall in** vɪ crollare; (Mil) mettersi in riga
▶ **fall in with** vᴛ ꜰᴜs (sb's plans etc) trovarsi d'accordo con
▶ **fall off** vɪ cadere; (diminish) diminuire, abbassarsi
▶ **fall out** vɪ (hair, teeth) cadere; (friends etc) litigare
▶ **fall over** vɪ cadere
▶ **fall through** vɪ (plan, project) fallire
fallacy ['fæləsɪ] N errore m
fallback ['fɔːlbæk] ADJ: **~ position** posizione f di ripiego
fallen ['fɔːlən] PP of **fall**
fallible ['fælɪbl] ADJ fallibile

falling ['fɔːlɪŋ] ADJ: **~ market** (*Comm*) mercato in ribasso
falling-off ['fɔːlɪŋ'ɔf] N calo
fallopian tube [fə'ləʊpɪən-] N (*Anat*) tuba di Falloppio
fallout ['fɔːlaut] N fall-out *m*
fallout shelter N rifugio antiatomico
fallow ['fæləʊ] ADJ incolto(-a); a maggese
falls [fɔːlz] NPL (*waterfall*) cascate *fpl*
false [fɔːls] ADJ falso(-a); **under ~ pretences** con l'inganno
false alarm N falso allarme *m*
falsehood ['fɔːlshud] N menzogna
falsely ['fɔːlslɪ] ADV (*accuse*) a torto
false teeth NPL (*BRIT*) denti *mpl* finti
falsify ['fɔːlsɪfaɪ] VT falsificare; (*figures*) alterare
falter ['fɔːltəʳ] VI esitare, vacillare
fame [feɪm] N fama, celebrità
familiar [fə'mɪlɪəʳ] ADJ familiare; (*common*) comune; (*close*) intimo(-a); **to be ~ with** (*subject*) conoscere; **to make o.s. ~ with** familiarizzarsi con; **to be on ~ terms with** essere in confidenza con
familiarity [fəmɪlɪ'ærɪtɪ] N familiarità; intimità
familiarize [fə'mɪlɪəraɪz] VT: **to ~ sb with sth** far conoscere qc a qn; **to ~ o.s. with** familiarizzare con
family ['fæmɪlɪ] N famiglia
family allowance N (*BRIT*) assegni *mpl* familiari
family business N impresa familiare
family credit N (*BRIT*) ≈ assegni *mpl* familiari
family doctor N medico di famiglia
family life N vita familiare
family man N (*irreg*) padre *m* di famiglia
family planning N pianificazione *f* familiare
family planning clinic N consultorio familiare
family tree N albergo genealogico
famine ['fæmɪn] N carestia
famished ['fæmɪʃt] ADJ affamato(-a); **I'm ~!** (*col*) ho una fame da lupo!
famous ['feɪməs] ADJ famoso(-a)
famously ['feɪməslɪ] ADV (*get on*) a meraviglia
fan [fæn] N (*folding*) ventaglio; (*machine*) ventilatore *m*; (*person*) ammiratore(-trice); (*Sport*) tifoso(-a) ▶ VT far vento a; (*fire, quarrel*) alimentare
▶ **fan out** VI spargersi (a ventaglio)
fanatic [fə'nætɪk] N fanatico(-a)
fanatical [fə'nætɪkl] ADJ fanatico(-a)
fan belt N cinghia del ventilatore
fancied ['fænsɪd] ADJ immaginario(-a)
fanciful ['fænsɪful] ADJ fantasioso(-a); (*object*) di fantasia
fan club N fan club *m inv*
fancy ['fænsɪ] N immaginazione *f*, fantasia; (*whim*) capriccio ▶ CPD (di) fantasia *inv* ▶ ADJ (*hat*) stravagante; (*hotel, food*) speciale ▶ VT (*feel like, want*) aver voglia di; (*imagine*) immaginare, credere; **to take a ~ to** incapricciarsi di; **it took** *or* **caught my ~** mi è piaciuto; **when the ~ takes him** quando ne ha voglia; **to ~ that** immaginare che; **he fancies her** gli piace
fancy dress N costume *m* (per maschera)
fancy-dress ball N ballo in maschera
fancy goods NPL articoli *mpl* di ogni genere
fanfare ['fænfɛəʳ] N fanfara
fanfold paper ['fænfəuld-] N carta a moduli continui
fang [fæŋ] N zanna; (*of snake*) dente *m*
fan heater N (*BRIT*) stufa ad aria calda
fanlight ['fænlaɪt] N lunetta
fanny ['fænɪ] N (*BRIT col!*) figa (*!*); (*US col*) culo (*!*)
fantasize ['fæntəsaɪz] VI fantasticare, sognare
fantastic [fæn'tæstɪk] ADJ fantastico(-a)
fantasy ['fæntəsɪ] N fantasia, immaginazione *f*; fantasticheria; chimera
fanzine ['fænziːn] N rivista specialistica (*per appassionati*)
FAO N ABBR (= *Food and Agriculture Organization*) FAO *f*
FAQ ABBR (= *free alongside quay*) franco lungo banchina; (*Comput*: = *frequently asked question(s)*) FAQ
far [fɑːʳ] ADJ lontano(-a) ▶ ADV lontano; (*much, greatly*) molto; **is it ~ from here?** è molto lontano da qui?; **it's not ~ (from here)** non è lontano (da qui); **how ~?** quanto lontano?; (*referring to activity etc*) fino a dove?; **how ~ is the town centre?** quanto dista il centro da qui?; **~ away, ~ off** lontano, distante; **the ~ side/end** l'altra parte/l'altro capo; **the ~ left/right** (*Pol*) l'estrema sinistra/destra; **~ better** assai migliore; **~ from** lontano da; **by ~** di gran lunga; **as ~ back as the 13th century** già nel duecento; **go as ~ as the farm** vada fino alla fattoria; **as ~ as I know** per quel che so; **as ~ as possible** nei limiti del possibile; **how ~ have you got with your work?** dov'è arrivato con il suo lavoro?
faraway ['fɑːrəweɪ] ADJ lontano(-a); (*voice, look*) assente
farce [fɑːs] N farsa
farcical ['fɑːsɪkəl] ADJ farsesco(-a)
fare [fɛəʳ] N (*on trains, buses*) tariffa; (*in taxi*) prezzo della corsa; (*food*) vitto, cibo ▶ VI passarsela; **half ~** metà tariffa; **full ~** tariffa intera
Far East N: **the ~** l'Estremo Oriente *m*
farewell [fɛə'wɛl] EXCL, N addio ▶ CPD (*party etc*) d'addio

far-fetched ['fɑː'fɛtʃt] ADJ (explanation) stiracchiato(-a), forzato(-a); (idea, scheme, story) inverosimile

farm [fɑːm] N fattoria, podere m ▶ VT coltivare
▶ **farm out** VT (work) dare in consegna

farmer ['fɑːmə'] N coltivatore(-trice), agricoltore(-trice)

farmhand ['fɑːmhænd] N bracciante m agricolo

farmhouse ['fɑːmhaus] N fattoria

farming ['fɑːmɪŋ] N (gen) agricoltura; (of crops) coltivazione f; (of animals) allevamento; **intensive ~** coltura intensiva; **sheep ~** allevamento di pecore

farm labourer N = **farmhand**

farmland ['fɑːmlænd] N terreno da coltivare

farm produce N prodotti mpl agricoli

farm worker N = **farmhand**

farmyard ['fɑːmjɑːd] N aia

Faroe Islands ['fɛərəu-], **Faroes** ['fɛərəuz] NPL: **the ~** le isole Faeroer

far-reaching ['fɑː'riːtʃɪŋ] ADJ di vasta portata

far-sighted ['fɑː'saɪtɪd] ADJ presbite; (fig) lungimirante

fart [fɑːt] (col!) N scoreggia (!) ▶ VI scoreggiare (!)

farther ['fɑːðə'] ADV più lontano ▶ ADJ più lontano(-a)

farthest ['fɑːðɪst] ADV SUPERLATIVE of **far**

FAS ABBR (BRIT: = free alongside ship) franco banchina nave

fascia ['feɪʃɪə] N (Aut) cruscotto; (of mobile phone) cover f inv

fascinate ['fæsɪneɪt] VT affascinare

fascinated ADJ affascinato(-a)

fascinating ['fæsɪneɪtɪŋ] ADJ affascinante

fascination [fæsɪ'neɪʃən] N fascino

fascism ['fæʃɪzəm] N fascismo

fascist ['fæʃɪst] ADJ, N fascista (mf)

fashion ['fæʃən] N moda; (manner) maniera, modo ▶ VT foggiare, formare; **in ~** alla moda; **out of ~** passato(a) di moda; **after a ~** (finish, manage etc) così così; **in the Greek ~** alla greca

fashionable ['fæʃənəbl] ADJ alla moda, di moda; (writer) di grido

fashion designer N disegnatore(-trice) di moda

fashionista [fæʃə'nɪstə] N fashionista mf, maniaco(-a) della moda

fashion show N sfilata di moda

fast [fɑːst] ADJ rapido(-a), svelto(-a), veloce; (clock): **to be ~** andare avanti; (dye, colour) solido(-a) ▶ ADV rapidamente; (stuck, held) saldamente ▶ N digiuno ▶ VI digiunare; **~ asleep** profondamente addormentato; **as ~ as I can** più in fretta possibile; **my watch is 5 minutes ~** il mio orologio va avanti di 5

minuti; **to make a boat ~** (BRIT) ormeggiare una barca

fasten ['fɑːsn] VT chiudere, fissare; (coat) abbottonare, allacciare ▶ VI chiudersi, fissarsi; abbottonarsi, allacciarsi
▶ **fasten (up)on** VT FUS (idea) cogliere al volo

fastener ['fɑːsnə'], **fastening** ['fɑːsnɪŋ] N fermaglio, chiusura; (BRIT: zip fastener) chiusura lampo

fast food N fast food m inv

fastidious [fæs'tɪdɪəs] ADJ esigente, difficile

fast lane N (Aut) ≈ corsia di sorpasso

fat [fæt] ADJ grasso(-a); (book, profit etc) grosso(-a) ▶ N grasso; **to live off the ~ of the land** vivere nel lusso, avere ogni ben di Dio

fatal ['feɪtl] ADJ fatale; mortale; disastroso(-a)

fatalism ['feɪtəlɪzəm] N fatalismo

fatality [fə'tælɪtɪ] N (road death etc) morto(-a), vittima

fatally ['feɪtəlɪ] ADV a morte

fate [feɪt] N destino; (of person) sorte f; **to meet one's ~** trovare la morte

fated ['feɪtɪd] ADJ (governed by fate) destinato(-a); (person, project etc) destinato(-a) a finire male

fateful ['feɪtful] ADJ fatidico(-a)

fat-free ['fæt'friː] ADJ senza grassi

father ['fɑːðə'] N padre m

Father Christmas N Babbo Natale

fatherhood ['fɑːðəhuːd] N paternità

father-in-law ['fɑːðərɪnlɔː] N suocero

fatherland ['fɑːðəlænd] N patria

fatherly ['fɑːðəlɪ] ADJ paterno(-a)

fathom ['fæðəm] N braccio (= 1828 mm) ▶ VT (mystery) penetrare, sondare

fatigue [fə'tiːg] N stanchezza; (Mil) corvé f; **metal ~** fatica del metallo

fatness ['fætnɪs] N grassezza

fatten ['fætn] VT, VI ingrassare; **chocolate is fattening** la cioccolata fa ingrassare

fattening ['fætnɪŋ] ADJ (food) che fa ingrassare

fatty ['fætɪ] ADJ (food) grasso(-a) ▶ N (col) ciccione(-a)

fatuous ['fætjuəs] ADJ fatuo(-a)

faucet ['fɔːsɪt] N (US) rubinetto

fault [fɔːlt] N colpa; (Tennis) fallo; (defect) difetto; (Geo) faglia ▶ VT criticare; **it's my ~** è colpa mia; **to find ~ with** trovare da ridire su; **at ~** in fallo; **generous to a ~** eccessivamente generoso

faultless ['fɔːltlɪs] ADJ perfetto(-a); senza difetto; impeccabile

faulty ['fɔːltɪ] ADJ difettoso(-a)

fauna ['fɔːnə] N fauna

faux pas [fəu'pɑː] N gaffe f inv

favour, (US) **favor** ['feɪvə'] N favore m ▶ VT (proposition) favorire, essere favorevole a;

(*pupil etc*) favorire; (*team, horse*) dare per vincente; **to do sb a ~** fare un favore *or* una cortesia a qn; **in ~ of** in favore di; **to be in ~ of sth/of doing sth** essere favorevole a qc/a fare qc; **to find ~ with sb** (*person*) entrare nelle buone grazie di qn; (*suggestion*) avere l'approvazione di qn

favourable, (*US*) **favorable** ['feɪvərəbl] ADJ favorevole

favourably, (*US*) **favorably** ['feɪvərəblɪ] ADV favorevolmente

favourite, (*US*) **favorite** ['feɪvrɪt] ADJ, N favorito(-a)

favouritism, (*US*) **favoritism** ['feɪvrɪtɪzəm] N favoritismo

fawn [fɔːn] N daino ▶ ADJ (*also:* **fawn-coloured**) marrone chiaro *inv* ▶ VI: **to ~ (up)on** adulare servilmente

fax [fæks] N (*document, machine*) facsimile *m inv*, telecopia; (*machine*) telecopiatrice *f* ▶ VT teletrasmettere, spedire via fax

FBI N ABBR (*US: = Federal Bureau of Investigation*) FBI *f*

FCC N ABBR (*US*) = **Federal Communications Commission**

FCO N ABBR (*BRIT: = Foreign and Commonwealth Office*) ≈ Ufficio affari esteri

FD N ABBR (*US*) = **fire department**

FDA N ABBR (*US*) = **Food and Drug Administration**

FE N ABBR = **further education**

fear [fɪər] N paura, timore *m* ▶ VT aver paura di, temere ▶ VI: **to ~ for** temere per, essere in ansia per; **~ of heights** vertigini *fpl*; **for ~ of** per paura di; **to ~ that** avere paura di (*or* che +*sub*), temere di (*or* che +*sub*)

fearful ['fɪəful] ADJ pauroso(-a); (*sight, noise*) terribile, spaventoso(-a); (*frightened*): **to be ~ of** temere

fearfully ['fɪəfəlɪ] ADV (*timidly*) timorosamente; (*col: very*) terribilmente, spaventosamente

fearless ['fɪəlɪs] ADJ intrepido(-a), senza paura

fearsome ['fɪəsəm] ADJ (*opponent*) formidabile, terribile; (*sight*) terrificante

feasibility [fiːzə'bɪlɪtɪ] N praticabilità

feasibility study N studio delle possibilità di realizzazione

feasible ['fiːzəbl] ADJ fattibile, realizzabile

feast [fiːst] N festa, banchetto; (*Rel: also:* **feast day**) festa ▶ VI banchettare; **to ~ on** godersi, gustare

feat [fiːt] N impresa, fatto insigne

feather ['fɛðər] N penna ▶ CPD (*mattress, bed, pillow*) di piume ▶ VT: **to ~ one's nest** (*fig*) arricchirsi

feather-weight ['fɛðəweɪt] N peso *m* piuma *inv*

feature ['fiːtʃər] N caratteristica; (*article*) articolo ▶ VT (*film*) avere come protagonista ▶ VI figurare; **features** NPL (*of face*) fisionomia; **a (special) ~ on sth/sb** un servizio speciale su qc/qn; **it featured prominently in …** ha avuto un posto di prima importanza in …

feature film N film *m inv* principale

featureless ['fiːtʃəlɪs] ADJ anonimo(-a), senza caratteri distinti

Feb. [fɛb] ABBR (= *February*) feb.

February ['fɛbruərɪ] N febbraio; *see also* **July**

feces ['fiːsiːz] NPL (*US*) = **faeces**

feckless ['fɛklɪs] ADJ irresponsabile, incosciente

Fed [fɛd] ABBR (*US*) = **federal; federation**

fed [fɛd] PT, PP *of* **feed**

Fed. [fɛd] N ABBR (*US col*) = **Federal Reserve Board**

federal ['fɛdərəl] ADJ federale

Federal Republic of Germany N Repubblica Federale Tedesca

Federal Reserve Board N (*US*) *organo di controllo del sistema bancario statunitense*

Federal Trade Commission N (*US*) *organismo di protezione contro le pratiche commerciali abusive*

federation [fɛdə'reɪʃən] N federazione *f*

fed up ADJ: **to be ~** essere stufo(-a)

fee [fiː] N pagamento; (*of doctor, lawyer*) onorario; (*for examination*) tassa d'esame; **school fees** tasse *fpl* scolastiche; **entrance ~, membership ~** quota d'iscrizione; **for a small ~** per una somma modesta

feeble ['fiːbl] ADJ debole

feeble-minded [fiːbl'maɪndɪd] ADJ deficiente

feed [fiːd] [*pt, pp* **fed**] N (*of baby*) pappa; (*of animal*) mangime *m*; (*on printer*) meccanismo di alimentazione ▶ VT nutrire; (*baby*) allattare; (*horse etc*) dare da mangiare a; (*fire, machine*) alimentare ▶ VI (*baby, animal*) mangiare; **to ~ material into sth** introdurre materiale in qc; **to ~ data/information into sth** inserire dati/informazioni in qc

▶ **feed back** VT (*results*) riferire

▶ **feed on** VT FUS nutrirsi di

feedback ['fiːdbæk] N feed-back *m*; (*from person*) reazioni *fpl*

feeder ['fiːdər] N (*bib*) bavaglino

feeding bottle ['fiːdɪŋ-] N (*BRIT*) biberon *m inv*

feel [fiːl] [*pt, pp* **felt**] N sensazione *f*; (*sense of touch*) tatto; (*of substance*) consistenza ▶ VT toccare; palpare; tastare; (*cold, pain, anger*) sentire; (*grief*) provare; (*think, believe*): **to ~ that** pensare che; **I ~ that you ought to do it** penso che dovreste farlo; **to ~ hungry/cold** aver fame/freddo; **to ~ lonely/better**

sentirsi solo/meglio; **I don't ~ well** non mi sento bene; **to ~ sorry for** dispiacersi per; **it feels soft** è morbido al tatto; **it feels colder out here** sembra più freddo qui fuori; **it feels like velvet** sembra velluto (al tatto); **to ~ like** (*want*) aver voglia di; **to ~ about** *or* **around for** cercare a tastoni; **to ~ about** *or* **around in one's pocket for** frugarsi in tasca per cercare; **I'm still feeling my way** (*fig*) sto ancora tastando il terreno; **to get the ~ of sth** (*fig*) abituarsi a qc

feeler ['fiːləʳ] N (*of insect*) antenna; **to put out feelers** (*fig*) fare un sondaggio

feelgood ['fiːlgud] ADJ (*film, song*) allegro(-a) e a lieto fine

feeling ['fiːlɪŋ] N sensazione *f*; (*emotion*) sentimento; (*impression*) senso, impressione *f*; **to hurt sb's feelings** offendere qn; **what are your feelings about the matter?** che cosa ne pensa?; **my ~ is that ...** ho l'impressione che ...; **I got the ~ that ...** ho avuto l'impressione che ...; **feelings ran high about it** la cosa aveva provocato grande eccitazione

fee-paying school ['fiːpeɪɪŋ-] N scuola privata

feet [fiːt] NPL *of* **foot**

feign [feɪn] VT fingere, simulare

felicitous [fɪ'lɪsɪtəs] ADJ felice

fell [fɛl] PT *of* **fall** ▶ VT (*tree*) abbattere; (*person*) atterrare ▶ ADJ: **with one ~ blow** con un colpo terribile; **at one ~ swoop** in un colpo solo ▶ N (*BRIT: mountain*) monte *m*; (: *moorland*): **the fells** la brughiera

fellow ['fɛləu] N individuo, tipo; (*comrade*) compagno; (*of learned society*) membro *cpd*; (*of university*) ≈ docente *mf* ▶ CPD: **their ~ prisoners/students** i loro compagni di prigione/studio

fellow citizen N concittadino(-a)

fellow countryman N (*irreg*) compatriota *m*

fellow feeling N simpatia

fellow men NPL simili *mpl*

fellowship ['fɛləuʃɪp] N associazione *f*; compagnia; (*Scol*) specie di borsa di studio universitaria

fellow traveller N compagno(-a) di viaggio; (*Pol*) simpatizzante *mf*

fell-walking ['fɛlwɔːkɪŋ] N (*BRIT*) passeggiate *fpl* in montagna

felon ['fɛlən] N (*Law*) criminale *mf*

felony ['fɛlənɪ] N (*Law*) reato, crimine *m*

felt [fɛlt] PT, PP *of* **feel** ▶ N feltro

felt-tip pen ['fɛlttɪp-] N pennarello

female ['fiːmeɪl] N (*Zool*) femmina; (*pej: woman*) donna, femmina ▶ ADJ (*sex, character*) femminile; (*Biol, Elec*) femmina *inv*; (*vote etc*) di donne; **male and ~ students** studenti e studentesse

female impersonator N (*Theat*) attore comico che fa parti da donna

feminine ['fɛmɪnɪn] ADJ, N femminile (*m*)

femininity [fɛmɪ'nɪnɪtɪ] N femminilità

feminism ['fɛmɪnɪzəm] N femminismo

feminist ['fɛmɪnɪst] N femminista *mf*

fen [fɛn] N (*BRIT*): **the Fens** la regione delle Fen

fence [fɛns] N recinto; (*Sport*) ostacolo; (*col: person*) ricettatore(-trice) ▶ VT (*also*: **fence in**) recingere ▶ VI schermire; **to sit on the ~** (*fig*) rimanere neutrale; (*Sport*) tirare di scherma

fencing ['fɛnsɪŋ] N (*Sport*) scherma

fend [fɛnd] VI: **to ~ for o.s.** arrangiarsi
▶ **fend off** VT (*attack, attacker*) respingere, difendersi da; (*blow*) parare; (*awkward question*) eludere

fender ['fɛndəʳ] N parafuoco; (*on boat*) parabordo; (*US*) parafango; paraurti *m inv*

fennel ['fɛnl] N finocchio

ferment VI [fə'mɛnt] fermentare ▶ N ['fəːmɛnt] (*fig*) agitazione *f*, eccitazione *f*

fermentation [fəːmɛn'teɪʃən] N fermentazione *f*

fern [fəːn] N felce *f*

ferocious [fə'rəuʃəs] ADJ feroce

ferocity [fə'rɔsɪtɪ] N ferocità

ferret ['fɛrɪt] N furetto
▶ **ferret about, ferret around** VI frugare
▶ **ferret out** VT (*person*) scovare, scoprire; (*secret, truth*) scoprire

ferry ['fɛrɪ] N (*small*) traghetto; (*large: also*: **ferryboat**) nave *f* traghetto *inv* ▶ VT traghettare; **to ~ sth/sb across** *or* **over** traghettare qc/qn da una parte all'altra

ferryman ['fɛrɪmən] N (*irreg*) traghettatore *m*

fertile ['fəːtaɪl] ADJ fertile; (*Biol*) fecondo(-a); **~ period** periodo di fecondità

fertility [fə'tɪlɪtɪ] N fertilità; fecondità

fertility drug N farmaco fecondativo

fertilize ['fəːtɪlaɪz] VT fertilizzare; fecondare

fertilizer ['fəːtɪlaɪzəʳ] N fertilizzante *m*

fervent ['fəːvənt] ADJ ardente, fervente

fervour, (*US*) **fervor** ['fəːvəʳ] N fervore *m*, ardore *m*

fester ['fɛstəʳ] VI suppurare

festival ['fɛstɪvəl] N (*Rel*) festa; (*Art, Mus*) festival *m inv*

festive ['fɛstɪv] ADJ di festa; **the ~ season** (*BRIT: Christmas*) il periodo delle feste

festivities [fɛs'tɪvɪtɪz] NPL festeggiamenti *mpl*

festoon [fɛ'stuːn] VT: **to ~ with** ornare di; decorare con

fetch [fɛtʃ] VT andare a prendere; (*sell for*) essere venduto(-a) per; **how much did it ~?** a *or* per quanto lo ha venduto?
▶ **fetch up** VI (*BRIT*) andare a finire

fetching ['fɛtʃɪŋ] ADJ attraente

fête [feɪt] N festa
fetid ['fɛtɪd] ADJ fetido(-a)
fetish ['fɛtɪʃ] N feticcio
fetter ['fɛtə^r] VT (person) incatenare; (horse) legare; (fig) ostacolare
fetters ['fɛtəz] NPL catene fpl
fettle ['fɛtl] N (BRIT): **in fine ~** in gran forma
fetus ['fiːtəs] N (US) = **foetus**
feud [fjuːd] N contesa, lotta ▸ VI essere in lotta; **a family ~** una lite in famiglia
feudal ['fjuːdl] ADJ feudale
feudalism ['fjuːdəlɪzəm] N feudalesimo
fever ['fiːvə^r] N febbre f; **he has a ~** ha la febbre
feverish ['fiːvərɪʃ] ADJ (also fig) febbrile; (person) febbricitante
few [fjuː] ADJ pochi(-e) ▸ PRON alcuni(-e); **~ succeed** pochi ci riescono; **they were ~** erano pochi; **a ~ ...** qualche ...; **I know a ~** ne conosco alcuni; **a good ~, quite a ~** parecchi; **in the next ~ days** nei prossimi giorni; **in the past ~ days** negli ultimi giorni, in questi ultimi giorni; **every ~ days/ months** ogni due o tre giorni/mesi; **a ~ more days** qualche altro giorno
fewer ['fjuːə^r] ADJ meno inv; meno numerosi(-e) ▸ PRON meno; **they are ~ now** adesso ce ne sono di meno
fewest ['fjuːɪst] ADJ il minor numero di
FFA N ABBR = **Future Farmers of America**
FH ABBR (BRIT) = **fire hydrant**
FHA N ABBR (US) = **Federal Housing Administration**
fiancé [fɪ'ɑːŋseɪ] N fidanzato
fiancée [fɪ'ɑːŋseɪ] N fidanzata
fiasco [fɪ'æskəu] N fiasco
fib [fɪb] N piccola bugia
fibre, (US) **fiber** ['faɪbə^r] N fibra
fibreboard, (US) **fiberboard** ['faɪbəbɔːd] N pannello di fibre
fibreglass, (US) **fiberglass** N fibra di vetro
fibrositis [faɪbrə'saɪtɪs] N cellulite f
FICA N ABBR (US) = **Federal Insurance Contributions Act**
fickle ['fɪkl] ADJ incostante, capriccioso(-a)
fiction ['fɪkʃən] N narrativa, romanzi mpl; (sth made up) finzione f
fictional ['fɪkʃənl] ADJ immaginario(-a)
fictionalize ['fɪkʃənəlaɪz] VT romanzare
fictitious [fɪk'tɪʃəs] ADJ fittizio(-a)
fiddle ['fɪdl] N (Mus) violino; (cheating) imbroglio; truffa ▸ VT (BRIT: accounts) falsificare, falsare; **tax ~** frode f fiscale; **to work a ~** fare un imbroglio
▸ **fiddle with** VT FUS gingillarsi con
fiddler ['fɪdlə^r] N violinista mf
fiddly ['fɪdlɪ] ADJ (task) da certosino; (object) complesso(-a)

fidelity [fɪ'dɛlɪtɪ] N fedeltà; (accuracy) esattezza
fidget ['fɪdʒɪt] VI agitarsi
fidgety ['fɪdʒɪtɪ] ADJ agitato(-a)
fiduciary [fɪ'duːʃɪərɪ] N fiduciario
field [fiːld] N (gen, Comput) campo; **to lead the ~** (Sport, Comm) essere in testa, essere al primo posto; **to have a ~ day** (fig) divertirsi, spassarsela
field glasses NPL binocolo (da campagna)
field hospital N ospedale m da campo
field marshal N feldmaresciallo
fieldwork ['fiːldwəːk] N ricerche fpl esterne; (Archaeology, Geo) lavoro sul campo
fiend [fiːnd] N demonio
fiendish ['fiːndɪʃ] ADJ demoniaco(-a)
fierce [fɪəs] ADJ (look) fiero(-a); (fighting) accanito(-a); (wind) furioso(-a); (heat) intenso(-a); (animal, person, attack) feroce; (enemy) acerrimo(-a)
fiery ['faɪərɪ] ADJ ardente; infocato(-a)
FIFA ['fiːfə] N ABBR (= Fédération Internationale de Football Association) F.I.F.A. f
fifteen [fɪf'tiːn] NUM quindici
fifteenth NUM quindicesimo(-a)
fifth [fɪfθ] NUM quinto(-a)
fiftieth ['fɪftɪɪθ] NUM cinquantesimo(-a)
fifty ['fɪftɪ] NUM cinquanta
fifty-fifty ['fɪftɪ'fɪftɪ] ADJ: **a ~ chance** una possibilità su due ▸ ADV: **to go ~ with sb** fare a metà con qn
fig [fɪg] N fico
fight [faɪt] (pt, pp **fought** [fɔːt]) N zuffa, rissa; (Mil) battaglia, combattimento; (against cancer etc) lotta ▸ VT (person) azzuffarsi con; (enemy: also Mil) combattere; (cancer, alcoholism, emotion) lottare contro, combattere; (election) partecipare a; (Law: case) difendere ▸ VI battersi, combattere; (quarrel): **to ~ (with sb)** litigare (con qn); (fig): **to ~ (for/against)** lottare (per/contro)
▸ **fight back** VI difendersi; (Sport, after illness) riprendersi ▸ VT (tears) ricacciare
▸ **fight down** VT (anger, anxiety) vincere; (urge) reprimere
▸ **fight off** VT (attack, attacker) respingere; (disease, sleep, urge) lottare contro
▸ **fight out** VT: **to ~ it out** risolvere la questione a pugni
fighter ['faɪtə^r] N combattente m; (plane) aeroplano da caccia
fighter-bomber ['faɪtəbɔmə^r] N cacciabombardiere m
fighter pilot N pilota m di caccia
fighting ['faɪtɪŋ] N combattimento; (in streets) scontri mpl
figment ['fɪgmənt] N: **a ~ of the imagination** un parto della fantasia
figurative ['fɪgjurətɪv] ADJ figurato(-a)

557

figure ['fɪgə^r] N (Drawing, Geom, person) figura; (number, cipher) cifra; (body, outline) forma ▶ VT (think: esp US) pensare ▶ VI (appear) figurare; (US: make sense) spiegarsi; essere logico(-a) ▶ VT (US: think, calculate) pensare, immaginare; **public ~** personaggio pubblico; **~ of speech** figura retorica
▶ **figure on** VT FUS (US) contare su
▶ **figure out** VT riuscire a capire; calcolare
figurehead ['fɪgəhɛd] N (Naut) polena; (pej) prestanome mf
figure skating N pattinaggio artistico
Fiji ['fi:dʒi:] N, **Fiji Islands** NPL le (isole) Figi
filament ['fɪləmənt] N filamento
filch [fɪltʃ] VT (col: steal) grattare
file [faɪl] N (tool) lima; (for nails) limetta; (dossier) incartamento; (in cabinet) scheda; (folder) cartellina; (for loose leaf) raccoglitore m; (row) fila; (Comput) archivio, file m inv ▶ VT (nails, wood) limare; (papers) archiviare; (Law: claim) presentare; passare agli atti ▶ VI: **to ~ in/out** entrare/uscire in fila; **to ~ past** marciare in fila davanti a; **to ~ a suit against sb** intentare causa contro qn
file name N (Comput) nome m del file
file sharing [-ʃɛərɪŋ] N (Comput) file sharing m, condivisione f di file
filibuster ['fɪlɪbʌstə^r] (esp US Pol) N (also: **filibusterer**) ostruzionista mf ▶ VI fare ostruzionismo
filing ['faɪlɪŋ] N archiviare m; see also **filings**
filing cabinet ['faɪlɪŋ-] N casellario
filing clerk N archivista mf
filings ['faɪlɪŋz] NPL limatura
Filipino [fɪlɪ'pi:nəu] N filippino(-a); (Ling) tagal m
fill [fɪl] VT riempire; (tooth) otturare; (job) coprire; (supply: order, requirements, need) soddisfare ▶ N: **to eat one's ~** mangiare a sazietà; **we've already filled that vacancy** abbiamo già assunto qualcuno per quel posto
▶ **fill in** VT (hole) riempire; (form) compilare; (details, report) completare ▶ VI: **to ~ in for sb** sostituire qn; **to ~ sb in on sth** (col) mettere qn al corrente di qc
▶ **fill out** VT (form, receipt) riempire
▶ **fill up** VT riempire ▶ VI (Aut) fare il pieno; **~ it up, please** (Aut) il pieno, per favore
fillet ['fɪlɪt] N filetto
fillet steak N bistecca di filetto
filling ['fɪlɪŋ] N (Culin) impasto, ripieno; (for tooth) otturazione f
filling station N stazione f di rifornimento
fillip ['fɪlɪp] N incentivo, stimolo
filly ['fɪlɪ] N puledra
film [fɪlm] N (Cine) film m inv; (Phot) pellicola, rullino; (of powder, liquid) sottile strato; (thin layer) velo ▶ VT (scene) filmare ▶ VI girare

film script N copione m
film star N divo(-a) dello schermo
filmstrip ['fɪlmstrɪp] N filmina
film studio N studio cinematografico
Filofax® ['faɪləufæks] N agenda ad anelli
filter ['fɪltə^r] N filtro ▶ VT filtrare
▶ **filter in, filter through** VI (news) trapelare
filter coffee N caffè m da passare al filtro
filter lane N (BRIT Aut) corsia di svincolo
filter tip N filtro
filth [fɪlθ] N sporcizia; (fig) oscenità
filthy ['fɪlθɪ] ADJ lordo(-a), sozzo(-a); (language) osceno(-a)
fin [fɪn] N (of fish) pinna
final ['faɪnl] ADJ finale, ultimo(-a); definitivo(-a) ▶ N (Sport) finale f; **finals** NPL (Scol) esami mpl finali; **~ demand** ingiunzione f di pagamento
finale [fɪ'nɑ:lɪ] N finale m
finalist ['faɪnəlɪst] N (Sport) finalista mf
finality [faɪ'nælɪtɪ] N irrevocabilità; **with an air of ~** con risolutezza
finalize ['faɪnəlaɪz] VT mettere a punto
finally ['faɪnəlɪ] ADV (lastly) alla fine; (eventually) finalmente; (once and for all) definitivamente
finance [faɪ'næns] N finanza; (funds) fondi mpl; (capital) capitale m ▶ VT finanziare; **finances** NPL (funds) finanze fpl
financial [faɪ'nænʃəl] ADJ finanziario(-a); **~ statement** estratto conto finanziario
financial adviser N consulente mf finanziario(-a)
financially [faɪ'nænʃəlɪ] ADV finanziariamente
financial year N anno finanziario, esercizio finanziario
financier [faɪ'nænsɪə^r] N finanziatore m
find [faɪnd] (pt, pp **found** [faund]) VT trovare; (lost object) ritrovare ▶ N trovata, scoperta; **to ~ (some) difficulty in doing sth** trovare delle difficoltà nel fare qc; **to ~ sb guilty** (Law) giudicare qn colpevole
▶ **find out** VT informarsi di; (truth, secret) scoprire; (person) cogliere in fallo ▶ VI: **to ~ out about** informarsi su; (by chance) venire a sapere
findings ['faɪndɪŋz] NPL (Law) sentenza, conclusioni fpl; (of report) conclusioni
fine [faɪn] ADJ bello(-a); ottimo(-a); (thin, subtle) fine ▶ ADV (well) molto bene; (small) finemente ▶ N (Law) multa ▶ VT (Law) multare; **to be ~** (person) stare bene; (weather) far bello; **you're doing ~** te la cavi benissimo; **to cut it ~** (with time, money) farcela per un pelo
fine arts NPL belle arti fpl
finely ['faɪnlɪ] ADV (splendidly) in modo stupendo; (chop) finemente; (adjust) con precisione

fine print N: **the ~** i caratteri minuti
finery ['faɪnərɪ] N abiti *mpl* eleganti
finesse [fɪ'nɛs] N finezza
fine-tooth comb ['faɪntu:θ-] N: **to go through sth with a ~** (*fig*) passare qc al setaccio
finger ['fɪŋgər] N dito ▶ VT toccare, tastare; **little/index ~** mignolo/(dito) indice *m*
fingernail ['fɪŋgəneɪl] N unghia
fingerprint ['fɪŋgəprɪnt] N impronta digitale ▶ VT (*person*) prendere le impronte digitali di
fingerstall ['fɪŋgəstɔ:l] N ditale *m*
fingertip ['fɪŋgətɪp] N punta del dito; **to have sth at one's fingertips** (*fig*) avere qc sulla punta delle dita
finicky ['fɪnɪkɪ] ADJ esigente, pignolo(-a); minuziosoa(-a)
finish ['fɪnɪʃ] N fine *f*; (*Sport: place*) traguardo; (: *polish etc*) finitura ▶ VT finire; (*use up*) esaurire ▶ VI finire; (*session*) terminare; **to ~ doing sth** finire di fare qc; **to ~ first/second** (*Sport*) arrivare primo/secondo; **she's finished with him** ha chiuso con lui ▶ **finish off** VT compiere; (*kill*) uccidere ▶ **finish up** VI, VT finire
finished ['fɪnɪʃt] ADJ (*product*) finito(-a); (*performance*) perfetto(-a); (*col: tired*) sfinito(-a)
finishing line ['fɪnɪʃɪŋ-] N linea d'arrivo
finishing school N scuola privata di perfezionamento (*per signorine*)
finishing touches NPL ultimi ritocchi *mpl*
finite ['faɪnaɪt] ADJ limitato(-a); (*verb*) finito(-a)
Finland ['fɪnlənd] N Finlandia
Finn [fɪn] N finlandese *mf*
Finnish ['fɪnɪʃ] ADJ finlandese ▶ N (*Ling*) finlandese *m*
fiord [fjɔ:d] N fiordo
fir [fə:r] N abete *m*
fire [faɪər] N fuoco; (*destructive*) incendio; (*gas fire, electric fire*) stufa ▶ VT (*discharge*): **to ~ a gun** fare fuoco; (*arrow*) sparare; (*fig*) infiammare; (*dismiss*) licenziare ▶ VI sparare, far fuoco; **~!** al fuoco!; **on ~** in fiamme; **insured against ~** assicurato contro gli incendi; **electric/gas ~** stufa elettrica/a gas; **to set ~ to sth, set sth on ~** dar fuoco a qc, incendiare qc; **to be/come under ~ (from)** essere/finire sotto il fuoco *or* il tiro (di)
fire alarm N allarme *m* d'incendio
firearm ['faɪərɑ:m] N arma da fuoco
fire brigade [-brɪ'geɪd], (*US*) **fire department** N (*BRIT*) (corpo dei) pompieri *mpl*
fire chief N (*US*) = **fire master**
fire department N = **fire brigade**
fire door N porta *f* rompifuoco *inv*
fire drill N esercitazione *f* antincendio
fire engine N autopompa

fire escape N scala di sicurezza
fire exit N uscita di sicurezza
fire extinguisher [-ɪk'stɪŋgwɪʃər] N estintore *m*
fireguard ['faɪəgɑ:d] N (*BRIT*) parafuoco
fire hazard N: **that's a ~** comporta rischi in caso d'incendio
fire hydrant N idrante *m*
fire insurance N assicurazione *f* contro gli incendi
fireman ['faɪəmən] N (*irreg*) pompiere *m*
fire master N (*BRIT*) comandante *m* dei vigili del fuoco
fireplace ['faɪəpleɪs] N focolare *m*
fireplug ['faɪəplʌg] N (*US*) = **fire hydrant**
fire practice N = **fire drill**
fireproof ['faɪəpru:f] ADJ resistente al fuoco
fire regulations NPL norme *fpl* antincendio
fire screen N parafuoco
fireside ['faɪəsaɪd] N angolo del focolare
fire station N caserma dei pompieri
firetruck (*US*) N = **fire engine**
firewall ['faɪəwɔ:l] N (*Internet*) firewall *m inv*
firewood ['faɪəwud] N legna
fireworks NPL fuochi *mpl* d'artificio
firing ['faɪərɪŋ] N (*Mil*) spari *mpl*, tiro
firing line N linea del fuoco; **to be in the ~** (*fig*) essere sotto tiro
firing squad N plotone *m* d'esecuzione
firm [fə:m] ADJ fermo(-a); (*offer, decision*) definitivo(-a) ▶ N ditta, azienda; **to be a ~ believer in sth** credere fermamente in qc
firmly ['fə:mlɪ] ADV fermamente
firmness ['fə:mnɪs] N fermezza
first [fə:st] ADJ primo(-a) ▶ ADV (*before others*) il primo, la prima; (*before other things*) per primo; (*for the first time*) per la prima volta; (*when listing reasons etc*) per prima cosa ▶ N (*person: in race*) primo(-a); (*BRIT Scol*) laurea con lode; (*Aut*) prima; **at ~** dapprima, all'inizio; **~ of all** prima di tutto; **in the ~ instance** prima di tutto, in primo luogo; **I'll do it ~ thing tomorrow** lo farò per prima cosa domani; **from the (very) ~** fin dall'inizio, fin dal primo momento; **the ~ of January** il primo (di) gennaio
first aid N pronto soccorso
first-aid kit ['fə:st'eɪd-] N cassetta pronto soccorso
first-class ['fə:st'klɑ:s] ADJ di prima classe
first-class mail N ≈ espresso
first-hand ['fə:st'hænd] ADJ di prima mano; diretto(-a)
first lady N (*US*) moglie *f* del presidente
firstly ['fə:stlɪ] ADV in primo luogo
first name N prenome *m*
first night N (*Theat*) prima
first-rate ['fə:st'reɪt] ADJ di prima qualità, ottimo(-a)

first-time buyer ['fə:sttaɪm-] N acquirente
  mf di prima casa
First World War N: **the** ~ la prima guerra
  mondiale
fir tree N abete *m*
fiscal ['fɪskəl] ADJ fiscale; ~ **year** anno fiscale
fish [fɪʃ] N (*pl inv*) pesce *m* ▶ VT (*river, area*)
  pescare in ▶ VI pescare; **to go fishing**
  andare a pesca
  ▶ **fish out** VT (*from water*) ripescare; (*from box
  etc*) tirare fuori
fish-and-chip shop [fɪʃən'tʃɪp-] N
  ≈ friggitoria; *see* **chip shop**
fishbone ['fɪʃbəun] N lisca, spina
fisherman ['fɪʃəmən] N (*irreg*) pescatore *m*
fishery ['fɪʃərɪ] N zona da pesca
fish factory N (*BRIT*) fabbrica per la
  lavorazione del pesce
fish farm N vivaio
fish fingers NPL (*BRIT*) bastoncini *mpl* di pesce
  (surgelati)
fish hook N amo
fishing N pesca
fishing boat ['fɪʃɪŋ-] N barca da pesca
fishing industry N industria della pesca
fishing line N lenza
fishing net N rete *f* da pesca
fishing rod N canna da pesca
fishing tackle N attrezzatura da pesca
fish market N mercato del pesce
fishmonger ['fɪʃmʌŋgəʳ] N pescivendolo; ~**'s
  (shop)** pescheria
fish slice N (*BRIT*) posata per servire il pesce
fish sticks NPL (*US*) = **fish fingers**
fishy ['fɪʃɪ] ADJ (*fig: tale, story*) sospetto(-a)
fission ['fɪʃən] N fissione *f*; **atomic/nuclear** ~
  fissione atomica/nucleare
fissure ['fɪʃəʳ] N fessura
fist [fɪst] N pugno
fistfight ['fɪstfaɪt] N scazzottata
fit [fɪt] ADJ (*Med, Sport*) in forma; (*proper*)
  adatto(-a), appropriato(-a); conveniente ▶ VT
  (*clothes*) stare bene a; (*match: facts etc*)
  concordare con; (: *description*) corrispondere a;
  (*adjust*) aggiustare; (*put in, attach*) mettere;
  installare; (*equip*) fornire, equipaggiare ▶ VI
  (*clothes*) stare bene; (*parts*) andare bene,
  adattarsi; (*in space, gap*) entrare ▶ N (*Med*)
  accesso, attacco; ~ **to** in grado di; ~ **for**
  adatto(-a) a; degno(-a) di; **to keep** ~ tenersi
  in forma; ~ **for work** (*after illness*) in grado di
  riprendere il lavoro; **do as you think** *or* **see** ~
  faccia come meglio crede; **this dress is a
  tight/good** ~ questo vestito è stretto/sta
  bene; ~ **of anger/enthusiasm** accesso
  d'ira/d'entusiasmo; **to have a** ~ (*col*) avere
  un attacco di convulsioni; (*col*) andare su
  tutte le furie; **by fits and starts** a sbalzi
  ▶ **fit in** VI accordarsi; adattarsi ▶ VT (*object*)

far entrare; (*fig: appointment, visitor*) trovare il
  tempo per; **to** ~ **in with sb's plans** adattarsi
  ai progetti di qn
  ▶ **fit out** VT (*BRIT: also:* **fit up**) equipaggiare
fitful ['fɪtful] ADJ saltuario(-a)
fitment ['fɪtmənt] N componibile *m*
fitness ['fɪtnɪs] N (*Med*) forma fisica; (*of
  remark*) appropriatezza
fitness instructor N instruttore(-trice) di
  fitness
fitted ['fɪtɪd] ADJ: ~ **carpet** moquette *f inv*;
  ~ **cupboards** armadi *mpl* a muro; ~ **kitchen**
  (*BRIT*) cucina componibile
fitter ['fɪtəʳ] N aggiustatore *m or* montatore *m*
  meccanico; (*Dress*) sarto(-a)
fitting ['fɪtɪŋ] ADJ appropriato(-a) ▶ N (*of dress*)
  prova; (*of piece of equipment*) montaggio,
  aggiustaggio; *see also* **fittings**
fitting room N (*in shop*) camerino
fittings ['fɪtɪŋz] NPL (*in building*) impianti *mpl*
five [faɪv] NUM cinque
five-day week ['faɪvdeɪ-] N settimana di 5
  giorni (lavorativi)
fiver ['faɪvəʳ] N (*col: BRIT*) biglietto da cinque
  sterline; (: *US*) biglietto da cinque dollari
fix [fɪks] VT fissare; (*mend*) riparare; (*make
  ready: meal, drink*) preparare ▶ N: **to be in a** ~
  essere nei guai; **the fight was a** ~ (*col*)
  l'incontro è stato truccato
  ▶ **fix up** VT (*arrange: date, meeting*) fissare,
  stabilire; **to** ~ **sb up with sth** procurare qc a
  qn
fixation [fɪk'seɪʃən] N (*Psych, fig*) fissazione *f*,
  ossessione *f*
fixed [fɪkst] ADJ (*prices etc*) fisso(-a); **there's a**
  ~ **charge** c'è una quota fissa; **how are you** ~
  for money? (*col*) a soldi come stai?
fixed assets NPL beni *mpl* patrimoniali
fixed penalty, fixed penalty fine N
  contravvenzione *f* a importo fisso
fixture ['fɪkstʃəʳ] N impianto (fisso); (*Sport*)
  incontro (del calendario sportivo)
fizz [fɪz] VI frizzare
fizzle ['fɪzl] VI frizzare; (*also:* **fizzle out**:
  enthusiasm, interest) smorzarsi, svanire; (: *plan*)
  fallire
fizzy ['fɪzɪ] ADJ frizzante; gassato(-a)
fjord [fjɔ:d] N = **fiord**
FL, Fla. ABBR (*US*) = **Florida**
flabbergasted ['flæbəgɑ:stɪd] ADJ
  sbalordito(-a)
flabby ['flæbɪ] ADJ flaccido(-a)
flag [flæg] N bandiera; (*also:* **flagstone**)
  pietra da lastricare ▶ VI stancarsi;
  affievolirsi; ~ **of convenience** bandiera di
  convenienza
  ▶ **flag down** VT fare segno (di fermarsi) a
flagon ['flægən] N bottiglione *m*
flagpole ['flægpəul] N albero

flagrant ['fleɪgrənt] ADJ flagrante

flag stop N (*US: for bus*) fermata facoltativa, fermata a richiesta

flair [flɛə^r] N (*for business etc*) fiuto; (*for languages etc*) facilità; (*style*) stile *m*

flak [flæk] N (*Mil*) fuoco d'artiglieria; (*col: criticism*) critiche *fpl*

flake [fleɪk] N (*of rust, paint*) scaglia; (*of snow, soap powder*) fiocco ▶ VI (*also:* **flake off**) sfaldarsi

flaky ['fleɪkɪ] ADJ (*paintwork*) scrostato(-a); (*skin*) squamoso(-a); ~ **pastry** (*Culin*) pasta sfoglia

flamboyant [flæm'bɔɪənt] ADJ sgargiante

flame [fleɪm] N fiamma; **old ~** (*col*) vecchia fiamma

flamingo [flə'mɪŋgəu] N fenicottero, fiammingo

flammable ['flæməbl] ADJ infiammabile

flan [flæn] N (*BRIT*) flan *m inv*

Flanders ['flɑːndəz] N Fiandre *fpl*

flange [flændʒ] N flangia; (*on wheel*) suola

flank [flæŋk] N fianco ▶ VT fiancheggiare

flannel ['flænl] N (*BRIT: also:* **face flannel**) guanto di spugna; (*fabric*) flanella; **flannels** NPL pantaloni *mpl* di flanella

flannelette [flænə'lɛt] N flanella di cotone

flap [flæp] N (*of pocket*) patta; (*of envelope*) lembo; (*Aviat*) flap *m inv* ▶ VT (*wings*) battere ▶ VI (*sail, flag*) sbattere; (*col: also:* **be in a flap**) essere in agitazione

flapjack ['flæpdʒæk] N (*US: pancake*) frittella; (*BRIT: biscuit*) biscotto di avena

flare [flɛə^r] N razzo; (*in skirt etc*) svasatura; **flares** (*trousers*) pantaloni *mpl* a zampa d'elefante
▶ **flare up** VI andare in fiamme; (*fig: person*) infiammarsi di rabbia; (*: revolt*) scoppiare

flared ['flɛəd] ADJ (*trousers*) svasato(-a)

flash [flæʃ] N vampata; (*also:* **news flash**) notizia *f* lampo *inv*; (*: Phot*) flash *m inv*; (*: US: torch*) torcia elettrica, lampadina tascabile
▶ VT accendere e spegnere; (*send: message*) trasmettere; (*: look, smile*) lanciare; (*flaunt*) ostentare ▶ VI brillare; (*light on ambulance, eyes etc*) lampeggiare; **in a ~** in un lampo; **~ of inspiration** lampo di genio; **to ~ one's headlights** lampeggiare; **he flashed by** or **past** ci passò davanti come un lampo

flashback ['flæʃbæk] N flashback *m inv*

flashbulb ['flæʃbʌlb] N cubo *m* flash *inv*

flash card N (*Scol*) scheda didattica

flashcube ['flæʃkjuːb] N flash *m inv*

flash drive N (*Comput*) chiavetta USB

flasher ['flæʃə^r] N (*Aut*) lampeggiatore *m*

flashlight ['flæʃlaɪt] N (*torch*) lampadina tascabile

flashpoint ['flæʃpɔɪnt] N punto di infiammabilità; (*fig*) livello critico

flashy ['flæʃɪ] ADJ (*pej*) vistoso(-a)

flask [flɑːsk] N fiasco; (*Chem*) beuta; (*also:* **vacuum flask**) thermos® *m inv*

flat [flæt] ADJ piatto(-a); (*tyre*) sgonfio(-a), a terra; (*battery*) scarico(-a); (*beer*) svampito(-a); (*denial*) netto(-a); (*Mus*) bemolle *inv*; (*: voice*) stonato(-a); (*: instrument*) scordato(-a) ▶ N (*BRIT: rooms*) appartamento; (*Mus*) bemolle *m*; (*Aut*) pneumatico sgonfio
▶ ADV: **(to work) ~ out** (lavorare) a più non posso; **~ rate of pay** tariffa unica di pagamento

flat-footed ['flæt'futɪd] ADJ: **to be ~** avere i piedi piatti

flatly ['flætlɪ] ADV categoricamente, nettamente

flatmate ['flætmeɪt] N (*BRIT*): **he's my ~** divide l'appartamento con me

flatness ['flætnɪs] N (*of land*) assenza di rilievi

flat-pack ['flætpæk] ADJ: **~ furniture** mobili *mpl* in kit ▶ N: **flat pack** kit *m inv*

flat-screen ['flætskriːn] ADJ a schermo piatto

flatten ['flætn] VT (*also:* **flatten out**) appiattire; (*: house, city*) abbattere, radere al suolo

flatter ['flætə^r] VT lusingare; (*show to advantage*) donare a

flatterer ['flætərə^r] N adulatore(-trice)

flattering ['flætərɪŋ] ADJ lusinghiero(-a); (*clothes etc*) che dona, che abbellisce

flattery ['flætərɪ] N adulazione *f*

flatulence ['flætjuləns] N flatulenza

flaunt [flɔːnt] VT fare mostra di

flavour, (*US*)**flavor** ['fleɪvə^r] N gusto, sapore *m* ▶ VT insaporire, aggiungere sapore a; **what flavours do you have?** che gusti avete?; **vanilla-flavoured** al gusto di vaniglia

flavouring, (*US*)**flavoring** ['fleɪvərɪŋ] N essenza (artificiale)

flaw [flɔː] N difetto

flawless ['flɔːlɪs] ADJ senza difetti

flax [flæks] N lino

flaxen ['flæksən] ADJ biondo(-a)

flea [fliː] N pulce *f*

flea market N mercato delle pulci

fleck [flɛk] N (*of mud, paint, colour*) macchiolina; (*of dust*) granello ▶ VT (*with blood, mud etc*) macchiettare; **brown flecked with white** marrone screziato di bianco

fled [flɛd] PT, PP *of* **flee**

fledgeling, fledgling ['flɛdʒlɪŋ] N uccellino

flee [fliː] (*pt, pp* **fled** [flɛd]) VT fuggire da ▶ VI fuggire, scappare

fleece [fliːs] N vello; (*garment*) pile *m inv* ▶ VT (*col*) pelare

fleecy ['fliːsɪ] ADJ (*blanket*) soffice; (*cloud*) come ovatta

fleet [fliːt] N flotta; (*of lorries etc*) convoglio; (*of cars*) parco

fleeting ['fliːtɪŋ] ADJ fugace, fuggitivo(-a); (visit) volante

Flemish ['flɛmɪʃ] ADJ fiammingo(-a) ▶ N (Ling) fiammingo; **the Flemish** NPL i Fiamminghi

flesh [flɛʃ] N carne f; (of fruit) polpa

flesh wound N ferita superficiale

flew [fluː] PT of **fly**

flex [flɛks] N filo (flessibile) ▶ VT flettere; (muscles) contrarre

flexibility [flɛksɪ'bɪlɪtɪ] N flessibilità

flexible ['flɛksəbl] ADJ flessibile

flexitime ['flɛksɪtaɪm] N orario flessibile

flick [flɪk] N colpetto; scarto ▶ VT dare un colpetto a; see also **flicks**
  ▶ **flick through** VT FUS sfogliare

flicker ['flɪkə'] VI tremolare ▶ N tremolio; **a ~ of light** un breve bagliore

flick knife N (BRIT) coltello a serramanico

flicks NPL: **the ~** (col) il cine

flier ['flaɪə'] N aviatore m

flies [flaɪz] NPL of **fly**

flight [flaɪt] N volo m; (escape) fuga; (also: **flight of steps**) scalinata; **to take ~** darsi alla fuga; **to put to ~** mettere in fuga

flight attendant N (US) steward m, hostess f inv

flight crew N equipaggio

flight deck N (Aviat) cabina di controllo; (Naut) ponte m di comando

flight path N (of aircraft) rotta di volo; (of rocket, projectile) traiettoria

flight recorder N registratore m di volo

flimsy ['flɪmzɪ] ADJ (fabric) leggero(-a); (building) poco solido(-a); (excuse) debole

flinch [flɪntʃ] VI ritirarsi; **to ~ from** tirarsi indietro di fronte a

fling [flɪŋ] (pt, pp **flung** [flʌŋ]) VT lanciare, gettare ▶ N (love affair) avventura

flint [flɪnt] N selce f; (in lighter) pietrina

flip [flɪp] N colpetto ▶ VT dare un colpetto a; (switch) far scattare; (coin) lanciare in aria; (US: pancake) far saltare (in aria) ▶ VI: **to ~ for sth** (US) fare a testa e croce per qc
  ▶ **flip through** VT FUS (book, records) dare una scorsa a

flip-flops ['flɪpflɒps] NPL (esp BRIT: sandals) infradito mpl

flippant ['flɪpənt] ADJ senza rispetto, irriverente

flipper ['flɪpə'] N pinna

flip side N (of record) retro

flirt [fləːt] VI flirtare ▶ N civetta

flirtation [fləː'teɪʃən] N flirt m inv

flit [flɪt] VI svolazzare

float [fləut] N galleggiante m; (in procession) carro; (sum of money) somma ▶ VI galleggiare; (bather) fare il morto; (Comm: currency) fluttuare ▶ VT far galleggiare; (loan, business) lanciare; **to ~ an idea** ventilare un'idea

floating ['fləutɪŋ] ADJ a galla; **~ vote** voto oscillante; **~ voter** elettore m indeciso

flock [flɒk] N (of sheep, Rel) gregge m; (of people) folla; (of birds) stormo ▶ VI: **to ~ to** accorrere in massa a

floe [fləu] N (also: **ice floe**) banchisa

flog [flɒg] VT flagellare

flood [flʌd] N alluvione f; (of words, tears etc) diluvio; (of letters etc) marea ▶ VT inondare, allagare; (people) invadere; (Aut: carburettor) ingolfare ▶ VI (place) allagarsi; (people): **to ~ into** riversarsi in; **in ~** in pieno; **to ~ the market** (Comm) inondare il mercato

flooding ['flʌdɪŋ] N inondazione f

floodlight ['flʌdlaɪt] N riflettore m ▶ VT (irreg: like **light**) illuminare a giorno

floodlit ['flʌdlɪt] PT, PP of **floodlight** ▶ ADJ illuminato(-a) a giorno

flood tide N alta marea, marea crescente

floodwater ['flʌdwɔːtə'] N acque fpl (di inondazione)

floor [flɔː'] N pavimento; (storey) piano; (of sea, valley) fondo; (fig: at meeting): **the ~** il pubblico ▶ VT pavimentare; (knock down) atterrare; (baffle) confondere; (silence) far tacere; **on the ~** sul pavimento, per terra; **ground ~**, (US) **first ~** pianterreno; **first ~**, (US) **second ~** primo piano; **top ~** ultimo piano; **to have the ~** (speaker) prendere la parola

floorboard ['flɔːbɔːd] N tavellone m di legno

flooring ['flɔːrɪŋ] N (floor) pavimento; (material) materiale m per pavimentazioni

floor lamp N (US) lampada a stelo

floor show N spettacolo di varietà

floorwalker ['flɔːwɔːkə'] N (esp US) ispettore m di reparto

flop [flɒp] N fiasco ▶ VI (fail) far fiasco; (fall) lasciarsi cadere

floppy ['flɒpɪ] ADJ floscio(-a), molle ▶ N (Comput) = **floppy disk**; **~ hat** cappello floscio

floppy disk N floppy disk m inv

flora ['flɔːrə] N flora

floral ['flɔːrl] ADJ floreale

Florence ['flɔrəns] N Firenze f

Florentine ['flɔrəntaɪn] ADJ fiorentino(-a)

florid ['flɔrɪd] ADJ (complexion) florido(-a); (style) fiorito(-a)

florist ['flɔrɪst] N fioraio(-a)

florist's, florist's shop N fioraio(-a); **at the ~ (shop)** dal fioraio

flotation [fləu'teɪʃən] N (Comm) lancio

flounce [flauns] N balzo
  ▶ **flounce out** VI uscire stizzito(-a)

flounder ['flaundə'] VI annaspare ▶ N (Zool) passera di mare

flour ['flauə'] N farina

flourish ['flʌrɪʃ] VI fiorire ▶ VT brandire ▶ N

abbellimento; svolazzo; (*of trumpets*) fanfara; (*bold gesture*): **with a ~** con ostentazione

flourishing ['flʌrɪʃɪŋ] ADJ prosperoso(-a), fiorente

flout [flaut] VT (*order*) contravvenire a; (*convention*) sfidare

flow [fləu] N flusso; circolazione *f*; (*of river, also Elec*) corrente *f* ▶ VI fluire; (*traffic, blood in veins*) circolare; (*hair*) scendere

flow chart N schema *m* di flusso

flow diagram N organigramma *m*

flower ['flauə^r] N fiore *m* ▶ VI fiorire; **in ~** in fiore

flower bed N aiuola

flowerpot ['flauəpɒt] N vaso da fiori

flowery ['flauərɪ] ADJ fiorito(-a)

flown [fləun] PP *of* **fly**

fl. oz. ABBR = **fluid ounce**

flu [fluː] N influenza

fluctuate ['flʌktjueɪt] VI fluttuare, oscillare

fluctuation [flʌktju'eɪʃən] N fluttuazione *f*, oscillazione *f*

flue [fluː] N canna fumaria

fluency ['fluːənsɪ] N facilità, scioltezza; **his ~ in English** la sua scioltezza nel parlare l'inglese

fluent ['fluːənt] ADJ (*speech*) facile, sciolto(-a); corrente; **he's a ~ speaker/reader** si esprime/legge senza difficoltà; **he speaks ~ Italian, he's ~ in Italian** parla l'italiano correntemente

fluently ['fluːəntlɪ] ADV con facilità; correntemente

fluff [flʌf] N lanugine *f*

fluffy ['flʌfɪ] ADJ lanuginoso(-a); (*toy*) di peluche

fluid ['fluːɪd] ADJ fluido(-a) ▶ N fluido; (*in diet*) liquido

fluid ounce N (*BRIT*) = 0.028 l; 0.05 *pints*

fluke [fluːk] N (*col*) colpo di fortuna

flummox ['flʌməks] VT rendere perplesso(-a)

flung [flʌŋ] PT, PP *of* **fling**

flunky ['flʌŋkɪ] N tirapiedi *mf*

fluorescent [fluə'rɛsnt] ADJ fluorescente

fluoride ['fluəraɪd] N fluoruro

fluorine ['fluəriːn] N fluoro

flurry ['flʌrɪ] N (*of snow*) tempesta; **a ~ of activity/excitement** un'intensa attività/un'improvvisa agitazione

flush [flʌʃ] N rossore *m*; (*fig*) ebbrezza; (*fig: of youth, beauty etc*) rigoglio, pieno vigore ▶ VT ripulire con un getto d'acqua; (*also:* **flush out**: *birds*) far alzare in volo; (: *animals, fig: criminal*) stanare ▶ VI arrossire ▶ ADJ: **~ with** a livello di, pari a; **~ against** aderente a; **hot flushes** (*Med*) vampate *fpl* di calore; **to ~ the toilet** tirare l'acqua

flushed [flʌʃt] ADJ tutto(-a) rosso(-a)

fluster ['flʌstə^r] N agitazione *f*

flustered ['flʌstəd] ADJ sconvolto(-a)

flute [fluːt] N flauto

flutter ['flʌtə^r] N agitazione *f*; (*of wings*) battito ▶ VI (*bird*) battere le ali

flux [flʌks] N: **in a state of ~** in continuo mutamento

fly [flaɪ] (*pt* **flew** [fluː], *pp* **flown** [fləun]) N (*insect*) mosca; (*on trousers: also:* **flies**) patta ▶ VT pilotare; (*passengers, cargo*) trasportare (in aereo); (*distances*) percorrere ▶ VI volare; (*passengers*) andare in aereo; (*escape*) fuggire; (*flag*) sventolare; **to ~ open** spalancarsi all'improvviso; **to ~ off the handle** perdere le staffe, uscire dai gangheri

▶ **fly away** VI volar via

▶ **fly in** VI (*plane*) arrivare; (*person*) arrivare in aereo

▶ **fly off** VI volare via

▶ **fly out** VI (*plane*) partire; (*person*) partire in aereo

fly-drive N: **~ holiday** fly and drive *m inv*

fly-fishing ['flaɪfɪʃɪŋ] N pesca con la mosca

flying ['flaɪɪŋ] N (*activity*) aviazione *f*; (*action*) volo ▶ ADJ: **~ visit** visita volante; **with ~ colours** con risultati brillanti; **he doesn't like ~** non gli piace viaggiare in aereo

flying buttress N arco rampante

flying picket N picchetto (*proveniente da fabbriche non direttamente coinvolte nello sciopero*)

flying saucer N disco volante

flying squad N (*Police*) (squadra) volante *f*

flying start N: **to get off to a ~** partire come un razzo

flyleaf ['flaɪliːf] N risguardo

flyover ['flaɪəuvə^r] N (*BRIT: bridge*) cavalcavia *m inv*

flypast ['flaɪpɑːst] N esibizione *f* della pattuglia aerea

flysheet ['flaɪʃiːt] N (*for tent*) sopratetto

flyweight ['flaɪweɪt] N (*Sport*) peso *m* mosca *inv*

flywheel ['flaɪwiːl] N volano

FM ABBR = **frequency modulation**; (*BRIT Mil*) = **Field Marshal**

FMB N ABBR (*US*) = **Federal Maritime Board**

FMCS N ABBR (*US*: = *Federal Mediation and Conciliation Services*) organismo di conciliazione in caso di conflitti sul lavoro

FO N ABBR (*BRIT*) = **Foreign Office**

foal [fəul] N puledro

foam [fəum] N schiuma; (*also:* **foam rubber**) gommapiuma® ▶ VI schiumare; (*soapy water*) fare la schiuma

foam rubber N gommapiuma®

FOB ABBR (= *free on board*) franco a bordo

fob [fɔb] VT: **to ~ sb off with** appioppare qn con; sbarazzarsi di qn con ▶ N (*also:* **watch fob**: *chain*) catena per orologio; (: *band of cloth*) nastro per orologio

foc ABBR (BRIT) = **free of charge**

focal ['fəukəl] ADJ focale

focal point N punto focale

focus ['fəukəs] N (pl **focuses**) fuoco; (of interest) centro ▶ VT (field glasses etc) mettere a fuoco; (light rays) far convergere ▶ VI: **to ~ on** (with camera) mettere a fuoco; (person) fissare lo sguardo su; **in ~** a fuoco; **out of ~** sfocato(-a)

focus group N (Pol) gruppo di discussione, focus group m inv

fodder ['fɔdə'] N foraggio

FOE N ABBR (= Friends of the Earth) Amici mpl della Terra; (US: = Fraternal Order of Eagles) organizzazione filantropica

foe [fəu] N nemico

foetus, (US) **fetus** ['fi:təs] N feto

fog [fɔg] N nebbia

fogbound ['fɔgbaund] ADJ fermo(-a) a causa della nebbia

foggy ['fɔgɪ] ADJ nebbioso(-a); **it's ~** c'è nebbia

fog lamp, (US) **fog light** N (Aut) faro m antinebbia inv

foible ['fɔɪbl] N debolezza, punto debole

foil [fɔɪl] VT confondere, frustrare ▶ N lamina di metallo; (also: **kitchen foil**) foglio di alluminio; (: Fencing) fioretto; **to act as a ~ to** (fig) far risaltare

foist [fɔɪst] VT: **to ~ sth on sb** rifilare qc a qn

fold [fəuld] N (bend, crease) piega; (Agr) ovile m; (fig) gregge m ▶ VT piegare; **to ~ one's arms** incrociare le braccia
▶ **fold up** VI (map etc) piegarsi; (business) crollare ▶ VT (map etc) piegare, ripiegare

folder ['fəuldə'] N (for papers) cartella; cartellina; (binder) raccoglitore m

folding ['fəuldɪŋ] ADJ (chair, bed) pieghevole

foliage ['fəulɪɪdʒ] N fogliame m

folk [fəuk] NPL gente f ▶ CPD popolare; **folks** NPL: **my folks** i miei

folklore ['fəuklɔ:'] N folclore m

folk music N musica folk inv

folk singer N cantante mf folk inv

folksong ['fəuksɔŋ] N canto popolare

follow ['fɔləu] VT seguire ▶ VI seguire; (result) conseguire, risultare; **to ~ sb's advice** seguire il consiglio di qn; **I don't quite ~ you** non ti capisco or seguo affatto; **to ~ in sb's footsteps** seguire le orme di qn; **it follows that ...** ne consegue che ...; **he followed suit** lui ha fatto lo stesso
▶ **follow on** VI (continue): **to ~ on from** seguire
▶ **follow out** VT (implement: idea, plan) eseguire, portare a termine
▶ **follow through** VT = **follow out**
▶ **follow up** VT (victory) sfruttare; (letter, offer) fare seguito a; (case) seguire

follower ['fɔləuə'] N seguace mf, discepolo(-a)

following ['fɔləuɪŋ] ADJ seguente, successivo(-a) ▶ N seguito, discepoli mpl

follow-up ['fɔləuʌp] N seguito

folly ['fɔlɪ] N pazzia, follia

fond [fɔnd] ADJ (memory, look) tenero(-a), affettuoso(-a); **to be ~ of** volere bene a; **she's ~ of swimming** le piace nuotare

fondle ['fɔndl] VT accarezzare

fondly ['fɔndlɪ] ADV (lovingly) affettuosamente; (naïvely): **he ~ believed that ...** ha avuto l'ingenuità di credere che ...

fondness ['fɔndnɪs] N affetto; **~ (for sth)** predilezione f (per qc)

font [fɔnt] N (Rel) fonte m (battesimale); (Typ) stile m di carattere

food [fu:d] N cibo

food chain N catena alimentare

food mixer N frullatore m

food poisoning N intossicazione f alimentare

food processor [-'prəusesə] N tritatutto m inv elettrico

food stamp N (US) buono alimentare dato agli indigenti

foodstuffs ['fu:dstʌfs] NPL generi fpl alimentari

fool [fu:l] N sciocco(-a); (Hist: of king) buffone m; (Culin) frullato ▶ VT ingannare ▶ VI (gen): **~ around** fare lo sciocco; **to make a ~ of sb** prendere in giro qn; **to make a ~ of o.s.** coprirsi di ridicolo; **you can't ~ me** non mi inganna
▶ **fool about, fool around** VI (waste time) perdere tempo

foolhardy ['fu:lhɑ:dɪ] ADJ avventato(-a)

foolish ['fu:lɪʃ] ADJ scemo(-a), stupido(-a); imprudente

foolishly ['fu:lɪʃlɪ] ADV stupidamente

foolishness ['fu:lɪʃnɪs] N stupidità

foolproof ['fu:lpru:f] ADJ (plan etc) sicurissimo(-a)

foolscap ['fu:lskæp] N carta protocollo

foot [fut] N (pl **feet** [fi:t]) N piede m; (measure) piede (= 304 mm; = 12 inches); (of animal) zampa; (of page, stairs etc) fondo ▶ VT (bill) pagare; **on ~** a piedi; **to put one's ~ down** (Aut) schiacciare l'accelleratore; (say no) imporsi; **to find one's feet** ambientarsi

footage ['futɪdʒ] N (Cine: length) ≈ metraggio; (: material) sequenza

foot and mouth, foot and mouth disease N afta epizootica

football ['futbɔ:l] N pallone m; (sport: BRIT) calcio; (: US) football m americano

footballer ['futbɔ:lə'] N (BRIT) = **football player**

football ground N campo di calcio

football match N (BRIT) partita di calcio
football player N (BRIT: also: **footballer**)
calciatore m; (US) giocatore m di football
americano
footbrake ['fuːtbreɪk] N freno a pedale
footbridge ['futbrɪdʒ] N passerella
foothills ['futhɪlz] NPL contrafforti fpl
foothold ['futhəuld] N punto d'appoggio
footing ['futɪŋ] N (fig) posizione f; **to lose
one's ~** mettere un piede in fallo; **on an
equal ~** in condizioni di parità
footlights ['futlaɪts] NPL luci fpl della ribalta
footman ['futmən] N (irreg) lacchè m inv
footnote ['futnəut] N nota (a piè di pagina)
footpath ['futpɑːθ] N sentiero; (in street)
marciapiede m
footprint ['futprɪnt] N orma, impronta
footrest ['futrɛst] N poggiapiedi m inv
Footsie ['futsɪ], **Footsie index** ['futsɪ-] N
(col) = **Financial Times Stock Exchange 100
Index**
footsie ['futsɪ] N (col): **to play ~ with sb** fare
piedino a qn
footsore ['futsɔːʳ] ADJ: **to be ~** avere mal di
piedi
footstep ['futstɛp] N passo
footwear ['futwɛəʳ] N calzatura
FOR ABBR (= free on rail) franco vagone

(KEYWORD)

for [fɔːʳ] PREP **1** (indicating destination, intention,
purpose) per; **the train for London** il treno
per Londra; **he went for the paper** è andato
a prendere il giornale; **it's time for lunch** è
ora di pranzo; **what's it for?** a che serve?;
what for? (why) perché?
2 (on behalf of, representing) per; **to work for sb/
sth** lavorare per qn/qc; **I'll ask him for you**
glielo chiederò a nome tuo; **G for George** ≈ G
come George
3 (because of) per, a causa di; **for this reason**
per questo motivo
4 (with regard to) per; **it's cold for July** è
freddo per luglio; **for everyone who voted
yes, 50 voted no** per ogni voto a favore ce
n'erano 50 contro
5 (in exchange for) per; **I sold it for £5** l'ho
venduto per 5 sterline
6 (in favour of) per, a favore di; **are you for or
against us?** sei con noi o contro di noi?; **I'm
all for it** sono completamente a favore
7 (referring to distance, time) per; **there are
roadworks for 5 km** ci sono lavori in corso
per 5 km; **he was away for 2 years** è stato
via per 2 anni; **she will be away for a
month** starà via un mese; **it hasn't rained
for 3 weeks** non piove da 3 settimane; **can
you do it for tomorrow?** può farlo per
domani?

8 (with infinitive clauses): **it is not for me to
decide** non sta a me decidere; **it would be
best for you to leave** sarebbe meglio che lei
se ne andasse; **there is still time for you to
do it** ha ancora tempo per farlo; **for this to
be possible ...** perché ciò sia possibile ...
9 (in spite of) nonostante; **for all his
complaints, he's very fond of her**
nonostante tutte le sue lamentele, le vuole
molto bene
▶ CONJ (since, as: formal) dal momento che,
poiché

forage ['fɔrɪdʒ] VI foraggiare
forage cap N bustina
foray ['fɔreɪ] N incursione f
forbad, forbade [fə'bæd] PT of **forbid**
forbearing [fɔː'bɛərɪŋ] ADJ paziente,
tollerante
forbid [fə'bɪd] (pt **forbad(e)** [-'bæd], pp
forbidden [-'bɪdn]) VT vietare, interdire;
to ~ sb to do sth proibire a qn di fare qc
forbidden PT of **forbid** ▶ ADJ (food) proibito(-a);
(area, territory) vietato(-a); (word, subject) tabù inv
forbidding [fə'bɪdɪŋ] ADJ arcigno(-a),
d'aspetto minaccioso
force [fɔːs] N forza ▶ VT forzare; (obtain by
force: smile, confession) strappare; **the Forces**
NPL (BRIT) le forze armate; **in ~** (in large
numbers) in gran numero; (law) in vigore;
to come into ~ entrare in vigore; **a ~ 5 wind**
un vento forza 5; **to join forces** unire le
forze; **the sales ~** (Comm) l'effettivo dei
rappresentanti; **to ~ sb to do sth**
costringere qn a fare qc
▶ **force back** VT (crowd, enemy) respingere;
(tears) ingoiare
▶ **force down** VT (food) sforzarsi di mangiare
forced [fɔːst] ADJ forzato(-a)
force-feed ['fɔːsfiːd] VT sottoporre ad
alimentazione forzata
forceful ['fɔːsful] ADJ forte, vigoroso(-a)
forcemeat ['fɔːsmiːt] N (BRIT Culin) ripieno
forceps ['fɔːsɪps] NPL forcipe m
forcibly ['fɔːsəblɪ] ADV con la forza; (vigorously)
vigorosamente
ford [fɔːd] N guado ▶ VT guadare
fore [fɔːʳ] N: **to the ~** in prima linea; **to come
to the ~** mettersi in evidenza
forearm ['fɔːrɑːm] N avambraccio
forebear ['fɔːbɛəʳ] N antenato
foreboding [fɔː'bəudɪŋ] N presagio di male
forecast ['fɔːkɑːst] N (irreg: like **cast**)
previsione f; (weather forecast) previsioni fpl
del tempo ▶ VT (irreg: like **cast**) prevedere
foreclose [fɔː'kləuz] VT (Law: also: **foreclose
on**) sequestrare l'immobile ipotecato di
foreclosure [fɔː'kləuʒəʳ] N sequestro di
immobile ipotecato

forecourt ['fɔːkɔːt] N (of garage) corte f esterna
forefathers ['fɔːfɑːðəz] NPL antenati mpl, avi mpl
forefinger ['fɔːfɪŋgəʳ] N (dito) indice m
forefront ['fɔːfrʌnt] N: **in the ~ of** all'avanguardia di
forego [fɔː'gəu] VT = **forgo**
foregoing ['fɔːgəuɪŋ] ADJ precedente
foregone ['fɔːgɔn] PP of **forego** ▶ ADJ: **it's a ~ conclusion** è una conclusione scontata
foreground ['fɔːgraund] N primo piano
▶ CPD (Comput) foreground inv, di primo piano
forehand ['fɔːhænd] N (Tennis) diritto
forehead ['fɔrɪd] N fronte f
foreign ['fɔrən] ADJ straniero(-a); (trade) estero(-a); (object, matter) estraneo(-a)
foreign body N corpo estraneo
foreign currency N valuta estera
foreigner ['fɔrənəʳ] N straniero(-a)
foreign exchange N cambio di valuta; (currency) valuta estera
foreign exchange market N mercato delle valute
foreign exchange rate N cambio
foreign investment N investimento all'estero
foreign minister N ministro degli Affari esteri
Foreign Office N (BRIT) Ministero degli Esteri
foreign secretary N (BRIT) ministro degli Affari esteri
foreleg ['fɔːlɛg] N zampa anteriore
foreman ['fɔːmən] N (irreg) caposquadra m; (Law: of jury) portavoce m della giuria
foremost ['fɔːməust] ADJ principale; più in vista ▶ ADV: **first and ~** innanzitutto
forename ['fɔːneɪm] N nome m di battesimo
forensic [fə'rɛnsɪk] ADJ: ~ **medicine** medicina legale; ~ **expert** esperto della (polizia) scientifica
foreplay ['fɔːpleɪ] N preliminari mpl
forerunner ['fɔːrʌnəʳ] N precursore m
foresee [fɔː'siː] (pt **foresaw** [-'sɔː], pp **foreseen** [-'siːn]) VT (irreg: like **see**) prevedere
foreseeable [fɔː'siːəbl] ADJ prevedibile
foreseen [fɔː'siːn] PP of **foresee**
foreshadow [fɔː'ʃædəu] VT presagire, far prevedere
foreshorten [fɔː'ʃɔːtn] VT (figure, scene) rappresentare in scorcio
foresight ['fɔːsaɪt] N previdenza
foreskin ['fɔːskɪn] N (Anat) prepuzio
forest ['fɔrɪst] N foresta
forestall [fɔː'stɔːl] VT prevenire
forestry ['fɔrɪstrɪ] N silvicoltura
foretaste ['fɔːteɪst] N pregustazione f
foretell [fɔː'tɛl] VT (irreg: like **tell**) predire
forethought ['fɔːθɔːt] N previdenza

foretold [fɔː'təuld] PT, PP of **foretell**
forever [fə'rɛvəʳ] ADV per sempre; (fig: endlessly) sempre, di continuo
forewarn [fɔː'wɔːn] VT avvisare in precedenza
forewent [fɔː'wɛnt] PT of **forego**
foreword ['fɔːwəːd] N prefazione f
forfeit ['fɔːfɪt] N ammenda, pena ▶ VT perdere; (one's happiness, health) giocarsi
forgave [fə'geɪv] PT of **forgive**
forge [fɔːdʒ] N fucina ▶ VT falsificare; (signature) contraffare, falsificare; (wrought iron) fucinare, foggiare
▶ **forge ahead** VI tirare avanti
forger ['fɔːdʒəʳ] N contraffattore m
forgery ['fɔːdʒərɪ] N falso; (activity) contraffazione f
forget [fə'gɛt] (pt **forgot** [-'gɔt], pp **forgotten** [-'gɔtn]) VT, VI dimenticare
forgetful [fə'gɛtful] ADJ di corta memoria; ~ **of** dimentico(a) di
forgetfulness [fə'gɛtfulnɪs] N smemoratezza; (oblivion) oblio
forget-me-not [fə'gɛtmɪnɔt] N nontiscordardimé m inv
forgive [fə'gɪv] (pt **forgave** [-'geɪv], pp **forgiven** [-'gɪvn]) VT perdonare; **to ~ sb for sth/for doing sth** perdonare qc a qn/a qn di aver fatto qc
forgiveness [fə'gɪvnɪs] N perdono
forgiving [fə'gɪvɪŋ] ADJ indulgente
forgo [fɔː'gəu] (pt **forwent** [-'wɛnt], pp **forgone** [-'gɔn]) VT rinunciare a
forgot [fə'gɔt] PT of **forget**
forgotten [fə'gɔtn] PP of **forget**
fork [fɔːk] N (for eating) forchetta; (for gardening) forca; (of roads, railways) bivio, biforcazione f ▶ VI (road) biforcarsi
▶ **fork out** (col: pay) VT sborsare ▶ VI pagare
forked [fɔːkt] (lightning) a zigzag
fork-lift truck ['fɔːklɪft-] N carrello elevatore
forlorn [fə'lɔːn] ADJ (person) sconsolato(-a); (deserted: cottage) abbandonato(-a); (desperate: attempt) disperato(-a); (: hope) vano(-a)
form [fɔːm] N forma; (Scol) classe f; (questionnaire) modulo ▶ VT formare; (circle, queue etc) fare; **in the ~ of** a forma di, sotto forma di; **to be in good ~** (Sport, fig) essere in forma; **in top ~** in gran forma; **to ~ part of sth** far parte di qc
formal ['fɔːməl] ADJ formale; (gardens) simmetrico(-a), regolare; (offer, receipt) vero(-a) e proprio(-a); (person) cerimonioso(-a); (occasion, dinner) formale, ufficiale; (Art, Philosophy) formale; ~ **dress** abito da cerimonia; (evening dress) abito da sera
formality [fɔː'mælɪtɪ] N formalità f inv
formalize ['fɔːməlaɪz] VT rendere ufficiale

formally ['fɔːməlɪ] ADV ufficialmente; formalmente; cerimoniosamente; **to be ~ invited** ricevere un invito ufficiale

format ['fɔːmæt] N formato ▶ VT (*Comput*) formattare

formation [fɔː'meɪʃən] N formazione f

formative ['fɔːmətɪv] ADJ: **~ years** anni mpl formativi

former ['fɔːmər] ADJ vecchio(-a) (*before n*), ex inv (*before n*); **the ~ president** l'ex presidente; **the ~ ... the latter** quello ... questo; **the ~ Yugoslavia/Soviet Union** l'ex Jugoslavia/Unione Sovietica

formerly ['fɔːməlɪ] ADV in passato

form feed N (*on printer*) alimentazione f modulo

formidable ['fɔːmɪdəbl] ADJ formidabile

formula ['fɔːmjulə] N formula; **F~ One** (*Aut*) formula uno

formulate ['fɔːmjuleɪt] VT formulare

fornicate ['fɔːnɪkeɪt] VI fornicare

forsake [fə'seɪk] (*pt* **forsook** [-'suk], *pp* **forsaken** [-'seɪkən]) VT abbandonare

fort [fɔːt] N forte m; **to hold the ~** (*fig*) prendere le redini (della situazione)

forte ['fɔːtɪ] N forte m

forth [fɔːθ] ADV in avanti; **to go back and ~** andare avanti e indietro; **and so ~** e così via

forthcoming [fɔːθ'kʌmɪŋ] ADJ (*event*) prossimo(-a); (*help*) disponibile; (*character*) aperto(-a), comunicativo(-a)

forthright ['fɔːθraɪt] ADJ franco(-a), schietto(-a)

forthwith [fɔːθ'wɪθ] ADV immediatamente, subito

fortieth ['fɔːtɪɪθ] NUM quarantesimo(-a)

fortification [fɔːtɪfɪ'keɪʃən] N fortificazione f

fortified wine N vino ad alta gradazione alcolica

fortify ['fɔːtɪfaɪ] VT (*city*) fortificare; (*person*) armare

fortitude ['fɔːtɪtjuːd] N forza d'animo

fortnight ['fɔːtnaɪt] N (*BRIT*) quindici giorni mpl, due settimane fpl; **it's a ~ since ...** sono due settimane da quando ...

fortnightly ['fɔːtnaɪtlɪ] ADJ bimensile ▶ ADV ogni quindici giorni

FORTRAN ['fɔːtræn] N FORTRAN m

fortress ['fɔːtrɪs] N fortezza, rocca

fortuitous [fɔː'tjuːɪtəs] ADJ fortuito(-a)

fortunate ['fɔːtʃənɪt] ADJ fortunato(-a); **he is ~ to have ...** ha la fortuna di avere ...; **it is ~ that** è una fortuna che + *sub*

fortunately ['fɔːtʃənɪtlɪ] ADV fortunatamente

fortune ['fɔːtʃən] N fortuna; **to make a ~** farsi una fortuna

fortune-teller ['fɔːtʃəntɛlər] N indovino(-a)

forty ['fɔːtɪ] NUM quaranta

forum ['fɔːrəm] N foro; (*fig*) luogo di pubblica discussione

forward ['fɔːwəd] ADJ (*ahead of schedule*) in anticipo; (*movement, position*) in avanti; (*not shy*) sfacciato(-a); (*Comm: delivery, sales, exchange*) a termine ▶ ADV avanti ▶ N (*Sport*) avanti m inv ▶ VT (*letter*) inoltrare; (*parcel, goods*) spedire; (*fig: career, plans*) promuovere, appoggiare; **to move ~** avanzare; **"please ~"** "si prega di inoltrare"; **~ planning** programmazione f in anticipo

forwarding address N nuovo recapito cui spedire la posta

forwards ['fɔːwədz] ADV avanti

forward slash N barra obliqua

forwent [fɔː'wɛnt] PT of **forgo**

fossick ['fɔsɪk] VI (*AUSTRALIA, NEW ZEALAND col*) cercare; **to ~ in a drawer** rovistare in un cassetto

fossil ['fɔsl] ADJ, N fossile (m); **~ fuel** combustibile m fossile

foster ['fɔstər] VT incoraggiare, nutrire; (*child*) avere in affidamento

foster brother N fratello addottivo (*in affidamento temporaneo presso la propria famiglia*)

foster child N (*irreg*) bambino(-a) preso(-a) in affidamento

foster mother N madre f affidataria

foster sister N sorella addottiva (*in affidamento temporaneo presso la propria famiglia*)

fought [fɔːt] PT, PP of **fight**

foul [faul] ADJ (*smell, food*) cattivo(-a); (*weather*) brutto(-a), orribile; (*language*) osceno(-a); (*deed*) infame ▶ N (*Football*) fallo ▶ VT sporcare; (*football player*) commettere un fallo su; (*entangle: anchor, propeller*) impigliarsi in

foul play N (*Sport*) gioco scorretto; **~ is not suspected** si è scartata l'ipotesi dell'atto criminale

found [faund] PT, PP of **find** ▶ VT (*establish*) fondare

foundation [faun'deɪʃən] N (*act*) fondazione f; (*base*) base f; (*also:* **foundation cream**) fondo tinta; **foundations** NPL (*of building*) fondamenta fpl; **to lay the foundations** gettare le fondamenta

foundation stone N prima pietra

founder ['faundər] N fondatore(-trice) ▶ VI affondare

founding ['faundɪŋ] ADJ: **~ fathers** (*US*) padri mpl fondatori; **~ member** socio fondatore

foundry ['faundrɪ] N fonderia

fount [faunt] N fonte f; (*Typ*) stile m di carattere

fountain ['fauntɪn] N fontana

fountain pen N penna stilografica

four [fɔːr] NUM quattro; **on all fours** a carponi

four-by-four [fɔːbaɪ'fɔːr] N quattro per quattro f inv

four-letter word ['fɔːlɛtə-] N parolaccia
four-poster ['fɔːˈpəustəʳ] N (also: **four-poster bed**) letto a quattro colonne
foursome ['fɔːsəm] N partita a quattro; uscita in quattro
fourteen ['fɔːˈtiːn] NUM quattordici
fourteenth NUM quattordicesimo(-a)
fourth [fɔːθ] NUM quarto(-a) ▶ N (Aut: also: **fourth gear**) quarta
four-wheel drive ['fɔːwiːl-] N (Aut): **with** ~ con quattro ruote motrici
fowl [faul] N pollame m; volatile m
fox [fɔks] N volpe f ▶ VT confondere
fox fur N volpe f, pelliccia di volpe
foxglove ['fɔksglʌv] N (Bot) digitale f
fox-hunting ['fɔkshʌntɪŋ] N caccia alla volpe
foyer ['fɔɪeɪ] N atrio; (Theat) ridotto
FPA N ABBR (BRIT: = Family Planning Association) ≈ A.I.E.D. f (= Associazione Italiana Educazione Demografica)
Fr. ABBR (Rel) = **father; friar**
fr. ABBR (= franc) fr.
fracas ['frækɑː] N rissa, lite f
fraction ['frækʃən] N frazione f
fractionally ['frækʃnəlɪ] ADV un tantino, minimamente
fractious ['frækʃəs] ADJ irritabile
fracture ['fræktʃəʳ] N frattura ▶ VT fratturare
fragile ['frædʒaɪl] ADJ fragile
fragment ['frægmənt] N frammento
fragmentary ['frægməntərɪ] ADJ frammentario(-a)
fragrance ['freɪgrəns] N fragranza, profumo
fragrant ['freɪgrənt] ADJ fragrante, profumato(-a)
frail [freɪl] ADJ debole, delicato(-a)
frame [freɪm] N (of building) armatura; (of human, animal) ossatura, corpo; (of picture) cornice f; (of door, window) telaio; (of spectacles: also: **frames**) montatura ▶ VT (picture) incorniciare; **to** ~ **sb** (col) incastrare qn; ~ **of mind** stato d'animo
framework ['freɪmwəːk] N struttura
France [frɑːns] N Francia
franchise ['fræntʃaɪz] N (Pol) diritto di voto; (Comm) concessione f
franchisee [fræntʃaɪˈziː] N concessionaria
franchiser ['fræntʃaɪzəʳ] N concedente m
frank [fræŋk] ADJ franco(-a), aperto(-a) ▶ VT (letter) affrancare
Frankfurt ['fræŋkfəːt] N Francoforte f
frankfurter ['fræŋkfəːtəʳ] N würstel m inv
franking machine ['fræŋkɪŋ-] N macchina affrancatrice
frankly ['fræŋklɪ] ADV francamente, sinceramente
frankness ['fræŋknɪs] N franchezza
frantic ['fræntɪk] ADJ (activity, pace) frenetico(-a); (desperate: need, desire) pazzo(-a), sfrenato(-a); (: search) affannoso(-a); (person) fuori di sé
frantically ['fræntɪklɪ] ADV freneticamente; affannosamente
fraternal [frəˈtəːnl] ADJ fraterno(-a)
fraternity [frəˈtəːnɪtɪ] N (club) associazione f; (spirit) fratellanza
fraternize ['frætənaɪz] VI fraternizzare
fraud [frɔːd] N truffa; (Law) frode f; (person) impostore(-a)
fraudulent ['frɔːdjulənt] ADJ fraudolento(-a)
fraught [frɔːt] ADJ (tense) teso(-a); ~ **with** pieno(a) di, intriso(a) da
fray [freɪ] N baruffa ▶ VT logorare ▶ VI logorarsi; **to return to the** ~ tornare nella mischia; **tempers were getting frayed** cominciavano ad innervosirsi; **her nerves were frayed** aveva i nervi a pezzi
FRB N ABBR (US) = **Federal Reserve Board**
FRCM N ABBR (BRIT) = **Fellow of the Royal College of Music**
FRCO N ABBR (BRIT) = **Fellow of the Royal College of Organists**
FRCP N ABBR (BRIT) = **Fellow of the Royal College of Physicians**
FRCS N ABBR (BRIT) = **Fellow of the Royal College of Surgeons**
freak [friːk] N fenomeno, mostro; (col: enthusiast) fanatico(-a) ▶ ADJ (storm, conditions) anormale; (victory) inatteso(-a)
▶ **freak out** VI (col) andare fuori di testa
freakish ['friːkɪʃ] ADJ (result, appearance) strano(-a), bizzarro(-a); (weather) anormale
freckle ['frɛkl] N lentiggine f
free [friː] ADJ libero(-a); (gratis) gratuito(-a); (liberal) generoso(-a) ▶ VT (prisoner, jammed person) liberare; (jammed object) districare; ~ **(of charge)** gratuitamente; **admission** ~ entrata libera; **to give sb a** ~ **hand** dare carta bianca a qn; ~ **and easy** rilassato
freebie ['friːbɪ] N (col): **it's a** ~ è in omaggio
freedom ['friːdəm] N libertà
freedom fighter N combattente mf per la libertà
free enterprise N liberalismo economico
Freefone® ['friːfəun] N (BRIT) ≈ numero verde
free-for-all ['friːfərɔːl] N parapiglia m generale
free gift N regalo, omaggio
freehold ['friːhəuld] N proprietà assoluta
free kick N (Sport) calcio libero
freelance ['friːlɑːns] ADJ indipendente; ~ **work** collaborazione f esterna
freeloader ['friːləudəʳ] N (pej) scroccone(-a)
freely ['friːlɪ] ADV liberamente; (liberally) liberalmente
free-market economy [friːˈmɑːkɪt-] N economia di libero mercato
freemason ['friːmeɪsn] N massone m

freemasonry ['fri:meɪsnrɪ] N massoneria
Freepost® ['fri:pəʊst] N affrancatura a carica del destinatario
free-range ['fri:'reɪndʒ] ADJ (hen) ruspante; (eggs) di gallina ruspante
free sample N campione m gratuito
free speech N libertà di parola
freestyle ['fri:staɪl] N (in swimming) stile m libero
free trade N libero scambio
freeway ['fri:weɪ] N (US) superstrada
freewheel [fri:'wi:l] VI andare a ruota libera
freewheeling [fri:'wi:lɪŋ] ADJ a ruota libera
free will N libero arbitrio; **of one's own** ~ di spontanea volontà
freeze [fri:z] (pt **froze** [frəʊz], pp **frozen** ['frəʊzn]) VI gelare ▸ VT gelare; (food) congelare; (prices, salaries) bloccare ▸ N gelo; blocco
▸ **freeze over** VI (lake, river) ghiacciarsi; (windows, windscreen) coprirsi di ghiaccio
▸ **freeze up** VI gelarsi
freeze-dried ['fri:zdraɪd] ADJ liofilizzato(-a)
freezer ['fri:zə'] N congelatore m
freezing ['fri:zɪŋ] ADJ (wind, weather) gelido(-a); **I'm** ~ mi sto congelando ▸ N (also: **freezing point**) punto di congelamento; **3 degrees below** ~ 3 gradi sotto zero
freight [freɪt] N (goods) merce f, merci fpl; (money charged) spese fpl di trasporto; ~ **forward** spese a carico del destinatario; ~ **inward** spese di trasporto sulla merce in entrata
freight car N (US) carro m merci inv
freighter ['freɪtə'] N (Naut) nave f da carico
freight forwarder [-'fɔ:wədə'] N spedizioniere m
freight train N (US) treno m merci inv
French [frentʃ] ADJ francese ▸ N (Ling) francese m; **the French** NPL i Francesi
French bean N fagiolino
French bread N baguette f inv
French Canadian ADJ, N franco-canadese (mf)
French dressing N (Culin) condimento per insalata
French fried potatoes, (US) **French fries** NPL patate fpl fritte
French Guiana [-gaɪ'ænə] N Guiana francese
French loaf N ≈ filoncino
Frenchman ['frentʃmən] N (irreg) francese m
French Riviera N: **the** ~ la Costa Azzurra
French stick N baguette f inv
French window N portafinestra
Frenchwoman ['frentʃwumən] N (irreg) francese f
frenetic [frə'nɛtɪk] ADJ frenetico(-a)
frenzy ['frɛnzɪ] N frenesia
frequency ['fri:kwənsɪ] N frequenza

frequency modulation N modulazione f di frequenza
frequent ADJ ['fri:kwənt] frequente ▸ VT [frɪ'kwɛnt] frequentare
frequently ['fri:kwəntlɪ] ADV frequentemente, spesso
fresco ['frɛskəʊ] N affresco
fresh [frɛʃ] ADJ fresco(-a); (new) nuovo(-a); (cheeky) sfacciato(-a); **to make a** ~ **start** cominciare da capo
freshen ['frɛʃən] VI (wind, air) rinfrescare ▸ **freshen up** VI rinfrescarsi
freshener ['frɛʃnə'] N: **skin** ~ tonico rinfrescante; **air** ~ deodorante m per ambienti
fresher ['frɛʃə'] N (Brit Scol: col) = **freshman**
freshly ['frɛʃlɪ] ADV di recente, di fresco
freshman ['frɛʃmən] N (irreg) (Scol) matricola
freshness ['frɛʃnɪs] N freschezza
freshwater ['frɛʃwɔ:tə'] ADJ (fish) d'acqua dolce
fret [frɛt] VI agitarsi, affliggersi
fretful ['frɛtful] ADJ (child) irritabile
Freudian ['frɔɪdɪən] ADJ freudiano(-a); ~ **slip** lapsus m inv freudiano
FRG N ABBR = **Federal Republic of Germany**
Fri. ABBR (= Friday) ven.
friar ['fraɪə'] N frate m
friction ['frɪkʃən] N frizione f, attrito
friction feed N (on printer) trascinamento ad attrito
Friday ['fraɪdɪ] N venerdì m inv; see also **Tuesday**
fridge [frɪdʒ] N (Brit) frigo, frigorifero
fridge-freezer ['frɪdʒ'fri:zə'] N freezer m inv
fried [fraɪd] PT, PP of **fry** ▸ ADJ fritto(-a); ~ **egg** uovo fritto
friend [frɛnd] N amico(-a); **to make friends with** fare amicizia con ▸ VT (Internet) aggiungere tra gli amici
friendliness ['frɛndlɪnɪs] N amichevolezza
friendly ['frɛndlɪ] ADJ amichevole ▸ N (also: **friendly match**) partita amichevole; **to be** ~ **with** essere amico di; **to be** ~ **to** essere cordiale con
friendly fire N fuoco amico
friendly society N società f inv di mutuo soccorso
friendship ['frɛndʃɪp] N amicizia
fries [fraɪz] NPL (esp US) patate fpl fritte
frieze [fri:z] N fregio
frigate ['frɪgɪt] N (Naut: modern) fregata
fright [fraɪt] N paura, spavento; **to take** ~ spaventarsi; **she looks a** ~! guarda com'è conciata!
frighten ['fraɪtn] VT spaventare, far paura a
▸ **frighten away, frighten off** VT (birds, children etc) scacciare (facendogli paura)
frightened ['fraɪtnd] ADJ spaventato(-a); **to be** ~ **(of)** avere paura (di)

frightening ['fraɪtnɪŋ] ADJ spaventoso(-a), pauroso(-a)

frightful ['fraɪtful] ADJ orribile

frightfully ['fraɪtfulɪ] ADV terribilmente; **I'm ~ sorry** mi dispiace moltissimo

frigid ['frɪdʒɪd] ADJ (woman) frigido(-a)

frigidity [frɪ'dʒɪdɪtɪ] N frigidità

frill [frɪl] N balza; **without frills** (fig) senza fronzoli

frilly ['frɪlɪ] ADJ (clothes, lampshade) pieno(-a) di fronzoli

fringe [frɪndʒ] N (BRIT: of hair) frangia; (edge: of forest etc) margine m; (fig): **on the ~** al margine

fringe benefits NPL vantaggi mpl

fringe theatre N teatro d'avanguardia

Frisbee® ['frɪzbɪ] N frisbee® m inv

frisk [frɪsk] VT perquisire

frisky ['frɪskɪ] ADJ vivace, vispo(-a)

fritter ['frɪtə'] N frittella
  ▶ **fritter away** VT sprecare

frivolity [frɪ'vɔlɪtɪ] N frivolezza

frivolous ['frɪvələs] ADJ frivolo(-a)

frizzy ['frɪzɪ] ADJ crespo(-a)

fro [frəʊ] ADV: **to and ~** avanti e indietro

frock [frɔk] N vestito

frog [frɔg] N rana; **to have a ~ in one's throat** avere la voce rauca

frogman ['frɔgmən] N (irreg) uomo m rana inv

frogmarch ['frɔgmɑːtʃ] VT (BRIT): **to ~ sb in/out** portar qn dentro/fuori con la forza

frolic ['frɔlɪk] VI sgambettare

(KEYWORD)

from [frɔm] PREP **1** (indicating starting place, origin etc) da; **where do you come from?**, **where are you from?** da dove viene?, di dov'è?; **where has he come from?** da dove arriva?; **from London to Glasgow** da Londra a Glasgow; **a letter from my sister** una lettera da mia sorella; **tell him from me that ...** gli dica da parte mia che ...
2 (indicating time) da; **from one o'clock to** or **until** or **till two** dall'una alle due; **(as) from Friday** a partire da venerdì; **from January (on)** da gennaio, a partire da gennaio
3 (indicating distance) da; **the hotel is 1 km from the beach** l'albergo è a 1 km dalla spiaggia
4 (indicating price, number etc) da; **from a pound** da una sterlina in su; **from £10 to £50** i prezzi vanno dalle 10 alle 50 sterline
5 (indicating difference) da; **he can't tell red from green** non sa distinguere il rosso dal verde
6 (because of, on the basis of): **from what he says** da quanto dice lui; **weak from hunger** debole per la fame

frond [frɔnd] N fronda

front [frʌnt] N (of house, dress) davanti m inv; (of train) testa; (of book) copertina; (promenade: also: **sea front**) lungomare m; (Mil, Pol, Meteor) fronte m; (fig: appearances) fronte f
  ▶ ADJ primo(-a); anteriore, davanti inv ▶ VI: **to ~ onto sth** dare su qc, guardare verso qc; **in ~ (of)** davanti (a)

frontage ['frʌntɪdʒ] N facciata

frontal ['frʌntl] ADJ frontale

front bench N posti in Parlamento occupati dai frontbenchers; vedi nota

> Nel Parlamento britannico, si chiamano *front bench* gli scanni della *House of Commons* che si trovano alla sinistra e alla destra dello *Speaker* davanti ai *backbenches*. I *front bench* sono occupati dai *frontbenchers*, parlamentari che ricoprono una carica di governo o che fanno parte dello *shadow cabinet* dell'opposizione.

frontbencher ['frʌnt'bentʃə'] N (BRIT) parlamentare con carica al governo o all'opposizione

front desk N (US: in hotel) reception f inv; (: at doctor's) accettazione f

front door N porta d'entrata; (of car) sportello anteriore

frontier ['frʌntɪə'] N frontiera

frontispiece ['frʌntɪspiːs] N frontespizio

front page N prima pagina

front room N (BRIT) salotto

front runner N (fig) favorito(-a)

front-wheel drive ['frʌntwiːl-] N trasmissione f anteriore

frost [frɔst] N gelo; (also: **hoarfrost**) brina

frostbite ['frɔstbaɪt] N congelamento

frosted ['frɔstɪd] ADJ (glass) smerigliato(-a); (US: cake) glassato(-a)

frosting ['frɔstɪŋ] N (US: on cake) glassa

frosty ['frɔstɪ] ADJ (window) coperto(-a) di ghiaccio; (weather, look, welcome) gelido(-a)

froth [frɔθ] N spuma; schiuma

frown [fraʊn] N cipiglio ▶ VI accigliarsi
  ▶ **frown on** VT FUS (fig) disapprovare

froze [frəʊz] PT of **freeze**

frozen ['frəʊzn] PP of **freeze** ▶ ADJ (food) congelato(-a); (Comm: assets) bloccato(-a)

FRS N ABBR (BRIT) = **Fellow of the Royal Society**; (US: = Federal Reserve System) sistema bancario degli Stati Uniti

frugal ['fruːgəl] ADJ frugale; (person) economo(-a)

fruit [fruːt] N (pl inv) frutto; (collectively) frutta

fruiterer ['fruːtərə'] N fruttivendolo; **at the ~'s (shop)** dal fruttivendolo

fruit fly N mosca della frutta

fruitful ['fruːtful] ADJ fruttuoso(-a); (plant) fruttifero(-a); (soil) fertile

fruition [fruː'ɪʃən] N: **to come to ~** realizzarsi

fruit juice N succo di frutta

fruitless ['fru:tlɪs] ADJ *(fig)* vano(-a), inutile
fruit machine N *(BRIT)* macchina *f* mangiasoldi *inv*
fruit salad N macedonia
frump [frʌmp] N: **to feel a ~** sentirsi infagottato (a)
frustrate [frʌsˈtreɪt] VT frustrare
frustrated [frʌsˈtreɪtɪd] ADJ frustrato(-a)
frustrating [frʌsˈtreɪtɪŋ] ADJ *(job)* frustrante; *(day)* disastroso(-a)
frustration [frʌsˈtreɪʃən] N frustrazione *f*
fry [fraɪ] *(pt, pp* **fried** [-d]*)* VT friggere ▶ NPL: **the small ~** i pesci piccoli
frying pan ['fraɪɪŋ-] N padella
FT N ABBR *(BRIT: = Financial Times)* giornale finanziario; **the FT index** l'indice FT
ft. ABBR = **foot; feet**
FTC N ABBR *(US)* = **Federal Trade Commission**
FT-SE 100 Index N ABBR = **Financial Times Stock Exchange 100 Index**
fuchsia ['fju:ʃə] N fucsia
fuck [fʌk] VT, VI *(col!)* fottere *(!)*; **~ off!** vaffanculo! *(!)*
fuddled ['fʌdld] ADJ *(muddled)* confuso(-a); *(col: tipsy)* brillo(-a)
fuddy-duddy ['fʌdɪdʌdɪ] N *(pej)* parruccone *m*
fudge [fʌdʒ] N *(Culin) specie di caramella a base di latte, burro e zucchero* ▶ VT *(issue, problem)* evitare
fuel [fjuəl] N *(for heating)* combustibile *m*; *(for propelling)* carburante *m* ▶ VT *(furnace etc)* alimentare; *(aircraft, ship etc)* rifornire di carburante
fuel oil N nafta
fuel poverty N povertà energetica
fuel pump N *(Aut)* pompa del carburante
fuel tank N deposito *m* nafta *inv*; *(on vehicle)* serbatoio (della benzina)
fug [fʌg] N *(BRIT)* aria viziata
fugitive ['fju:dʒɪtɪv] N fuggitivo(-a), profugo(-a); *(from prison)* evaso(-a)
fulfil, *(US)* **fulfill** [fulˈfɪl] VT *(function)* compiere; *(order)* eseguire; *(wish, desire)* soddisfare, appagare
fulfilled [fulˈfɪld] ADJ *(person)* realizzato(-a), soddisfatto(-a)
fulfilment, *(US)* **fulfillment** [fulˈfɪlmənt] N *(of wishes)* soddisfazione *f*, appagamento
full [ful] ADJ pieno(-a); *(details, skirt)* ampio(-a); *(price)* intero(-a) ▶ ADV: **to know ~ well that** sapere benissimo che; **~ (up)** *(hotel etc)* al completo; **I'm ~ (up)** sono sazio; **a ~ two hours** due ore intere; **at ~ speed** a tutta velocità; **in ~** per intero; **to pay in ~** pagare tutto; **~ name** nome *m* e cognome *m*; **~ employment** piena occupazione; **~ fare** tariffa completa
fullback ['fulbæk] N *(Rugby, Football)* terzino
full-blooded ['ful'blʌdɪd] ADJ *(vigorous: attack)* energico(-a); *(virile: male)* virile

full-cream ['ful'kri:m] ADJ: **~ milk** *(BRIT)* latte *m* intero
full-grown ['ful'grəun] ADJ maturo(-a)
full-length ['ful'lɛŋθ] ADJ *(portrait)* in piedi; *(film)* a lungometraggio; *(coat, novel)* lungo(-a)
full moon N luna piena
full-scale ['fulskeɪl] ADJ *(plan, model)* in grandezza naturale; *(attack, search, retreat)* su vasta scala
full-sized ['ful'saɪzd] ADJ *(portrait etc)* a grandezza naturale
full stop N punto
full-time ['ful'taɪm] ADJ, ADV *(work)* a tempo pieno ▶ N *(Sport)* fine *f* partita
fully ['fulɪ] ADV interamente, pienamente, completamente; *(at least)*: **~ as big** almeno così grosso
fully-fledged ['fulɪ'flɛdʒd] ADJ *(bird)* adulto(-a); *(fig: teacher, member etc)* a tutti gli effetti
fulsome ['fulsəm] ADJ *(pej: praise)* esagerato(-a), eccessivo(-a); *(manner)* insincero
fumble ['fʌmbl] VI brancolare, andare a tentoni ▶ VT *(ball)* lasciarsi sfuggire
▶ **fumble with** VT FUS trafficare con
fume [fju:m] VI essere furioso(-a); **fumes** NPL esalazioni *fpl*, vapori *mpl*
fumigate ['fju:mɪgeɪt] VT suffumicare
fun [fʌn] N divertimento, spasso; **to have ~** divertirsi; **for ~** per scherzo; **it's not much ~** non è molto divertente; **to make ~ of** prendersi gioco di
function ['fʌŋkʃən] N funzione *f*; cerimonia, ricevimento ▶ VI funzionare; **to ~ as** fungere da, funzionare da
functional ['fʌŋkʃənl] ADJ funzionale
function key N *(Comput)* tasto di funzioni
fund [fʌnd] N fondo, cassa; *(source)* fondo; *(store)* riserva; **funds** NPL *(money)* fondi *mpl*
fundamental [fʌndə'mɛntl] ADJ fondamentale; **fundamentals** NPL basi *fpl*
fundamentalism [fʌndə'mɛntəlɪzəm] N fondamentalismo
fundamentalist [fʌndə'mɛntəlɪst] N fondamentalista *mf*
fundamentally [fʌndə'mɛntəlɪ] ADV essenzialmente, fondamentalmente
funding ['fʌndɪŋ] N finanziamento
fund-raising ['fʌndreɪzɪŋ] N raccolta di fondi
funeral ['fju:nərəl] N funerale *m*
funeral director N impresario di pompe funebri
funeral parlour [-'pɑːlər] N impresa di pompe funebri
funeral service N ufficio funebre
funereal [fju:'nɪərɪəl] ADJ funereo(-a), lugubre

fun fair ['fʌnfɛəʳ] N luna park m inv
fungus ['fʌŋgəs] (pl **fungi** [-gaɪ]) N fungo; (mould) muffa
funicular [fjuːˈnɪkjuləʳ] ADJ (also: **funicular railway**) funicolare f
funky ['fʌŋkɪ] ADJ (music) funky inv; (col: excellent) figo(-a)
funnel ['fʌnl] N imbuto; (of ship) ciminiera
funnily ['fʌnɪlɪ] ADV in modo divertente; (oddly) stranamente
funny ['fʌnɪ] ADJ divertente, buffo(-a); (strange) strano(-a), bizzarro(-a)
funny bone N osso cubitale
fun run N marcia non competitiva
fur [fəːʳ] N pelo; pelliccia; pelle f; (BRIT: in kettle etc) deposito calcare
fur coat N pelliccia
furious ['fjuərɪəs] ADJ furioso(-a); (effort) accanito(-a); (argument) violento(-a)
furiously ['fjuərɪəslɪ] ADV furiosamente; accanitamente
furl [fəːl] VT (sail) piegare
furlong ['fəːlɔŋ] N 201.17 m (termine ippico)
furlough ['fəːləu] N (US) congedo, permesso
furnace ['fəːnɪs] N fornace f
furnish ['fəːnɪʃ] VT ammobiliare; (supply) fornire; **furnished flat** or (US) **apartment** appartamento ammobiliato
furnishings ['fəːnɪʃɪŋz] NPL mobili mpl, mobilia
furniture ['fəːnɪtʃəʳ] N mobili mpl; **piece of ~** mobile m
furore [fjuəˈrɔːrɪ] N (protests) scalpore m; (enthusiasm) entusiasmo
furrier ['fʌrɪəʳ] N pellicciaio(-a)
furrow ['fʌrəu] N solco ▶ VT (forehead) segnare di rughe
furry ['fəːrɪ] ADJ (animal) peloso(-a); (toy) di peluche
further ['fəːðəʳ] ADJ supplementare, altro(-a); nuovo(-a); più lontano(-a) ▶ ADV più lontano; (more) di più; (moreover) inoltre ▶ VT favorire, promuovere; **until ~ notice** fino a nuovo avviso; **how much ~ is it?** quanto manca or dista?; **~ to your letter of ...** (Comm) con riferimento alla vostra lettera del ...; **to ~ one's interests** fare i propri interessi
further education N ≈ corsi mpl di formazione; **college of ~** istituto statale con corsi specializzati (di formazione professionale, aggiornamento professionale ecc)
furthermore [fəːðəˈmɔːʳ] ADV inoltre, per di più
furthermost ['fəːðəməust] ADJ più lontano(-a)
furthest ['fəːðɪst] ADV SUPERLATIVE of **far**
furtive ['fəːtɪv] ADJ furtivo(-a)
fury ['fjuərɪ] N furore m
fuse, (US) **fuze** [fjuːz] N fusibile m; (for bomb etc) miccia, spoletta ▶ VT fondere; (Elec): **to ~ the lights** far saltare i fusibili ▶ VI fondersi; **a ~ has blown** è saltato un fusibile
fuse box N cassetta dei fusibili
fuselage ['fjuːzəlɑːʒ] N fusoliera
fuse wire N filo (di fusibile)
fusillade [fjuːzɪˈleɪd] N scarica di fucileria; (fig) fuoco di fila, serie f inv incalzante
fusion ['fjuːʒən] N fusione f
fuss [fʌs] N agitazione f, trambusto, confusione f; (complaining) storie fpl ▶ VT (person) infastidire, scocciare ▶ VI agitarsi; **to make a ~** fare delle storie; **to make a ~ of sb** coprire qn di attenzioni
▶ **fuss over** VT FUS (person) circondare di premure
fusspot ['fʌspɔt] N (col): **he's such a ~** fa sempre tante storie
fussy ['fʌsɪ] ADJ (person) puntiglioso(-a), esigente; che fa le storie; (dress) carico(-a) di fronzoli; (style) elaborato(-a); **I'm not ~** (col) per me è lo stesso
fusty ['fʌstɪ] ADJ (pej: archaic) stantio(-a); (: smell) che sa di stantio
futile ['fjuːtaɪl] ADJ futile
futility [fjuːˈtɪlɪtɪ] N futilità
futon ['fuːtɔn] N futon m inv, letto giapponese
future ['fjuːtʃəʳ] ADJ futuro(-a) ▶ N futuro, avvenire m; (Ling) futuro; **futures** NPL (Comm) operazioni fpl a termine; **in ~** in futuro; **in the near ~** in un prossimo futuro; **in the immediate ~** nell'immediato futuro
futuristic [fjuːtʃəˈrɪstɪk] ADJ futuristico(-a)
fuze [fjuːz] N, VT, VI (US) = **fuse**
fuzzy ['fʌzɪ] ADJ (Phot) indistinto(-a), sfocato(-a); (hair) crespo(-a)
fwd. ABBR = **forward**
fwy ABBR (US) = **freeway**
FY ABBR = **fiscal year**
FYI ABBR = **for your information**

Gg

G, g [dʒiː] N (letter) G, g f inv or m inv; (Mus): **G** sol m; **G for George** ≈ G come Genova

G N ABBR (BRIT Scol: mark: = good) ≈ buono; (US Cine: = general audience) per tutti

g ABBR (= gram, gravity) g

G7 N ABBR (Pol: = Group of Seven) G7 mpl

G8 N ABBR (Pol: = Group of Eight) G8 m

G20 N ABBR (Pol: = Group of Twenty) G20 m

GA ABBR (US Post) = **Georgia**

gab [gæb] N (col): **to have the gift of the ~** avere parlantina

gabble ['gæbl] VI borbottare; farfugliare

gaberdine [gæbə'diːn] N gabardine m inv

gable ['geɪbl] N frontone m

Gabon [gə'bɔn] N Gabon m

gad about [gæd-] VI (col) svolazzare (qua e là)

gadget ['gædʒɪt] N aggeggio

Gaelic ['geɪlɪk] ADJ gaelico(-a) ▶ N (language) gaelico

gaffe [gæf] N gaffe f inv

gaffer ['gæfəʳ] N (BRIT col) capo

gag [gæg] N bavaglio; (joke) facezia, scherzo ▶ VT (prisoner etc) imbavagliare ▶ VI (choke) soffocare

gaga ['gaːgaː] ADJ: **to go ~** rimbambirsi

gage [geɪdʒ] N, VT (US) = **gauge**

gaiety ['geɪɪtɪ] N gaiezza

gaily ['geɪlɪ] ADV allegramente

gain [geɪn] N guadagno, profitto ▶ VT guadagnare ▶ VI (watch) andare avanti; (benefit): **to ~ (from)** trarre beneficio (da); **to ~ in/by** aumentare di/con; **to ~ 3lbs (in weight)** aumentare di 3 libbre; **to ~ ground** guadagnare terreno

▶ **gain (up)on** VT FUS guadagnare terreno su, accorciare le distanze da

gainful ['geɪnful] ADJ profittevole, lucrativo(-a)

gainfully ['geɪnfəlɪ] ADV: **to be ~ employed** avere un lavoro retribuito

gainsay [geɪn'seɪ] VT (irreg: like **say**) contraddire; negare

gait [geɪt] N andatura

gal. ABBR = **gallon**

gala ['gɑːlə] N gala; **swimming ~** manifestazione f di nuoto

Galapagos Islands [gə'læpəgəs-] NPL: **the ~** le isole Galapagos

galaxy ['gæləksɪ] N galassia

gale [geɪl] N vento forte; burrasca; **~ force 10** vento forza 10

gall [gɔːl] N (Anat) bile f; (fig: impudence) fegato, faccia ▶ VT urtare (i nervi a)

gall. ABBR = **gallon**

gallant ['gælənt] ADJ valoroso(-a); (towards ladies) galante, cortese

gallantry ['gæləntrɪ] N valore m militare; galanteria, cortesia

gall bladder ['gɔːl-] N cistifellea

galleon ['gælɪən] N galeone m

gallery ['gælərɪ] N galleria; loggia; (for spectators) tribuna; (in theatre) loggione m, balconata; (also: **art gallery**: state-owned) museo; (: private) galleria

galley ['gælɪ] N (ship's kitchen) cambusa; (ship) galea; (also: **galley proof**) bozza in colonna

Gallic ['gælɪk] ADJ gallico(-a); (French) francese

galling ['gɔːlɪŋ] ADJ irritante

gallon ['gælən] N gallone m (Brit = 4.543 l; 8 pints; US = 3.785 l)

gallop ['gæləp] N galoppo ▶ VI galoppare; **galloping inflation** inflazione f galoppante

gallows ['gæləuz] N forca

gallstone ['gɔːlstəun] N calcolo biliare

Gallup Poll ['gæləp-] N sondaggio a campione

galore [gə'lɔːʳ] ADV a iosa, a profusione

galvanize ['gælvənaɪz] VT galvanizzare; **to ~ sb into action** (fig) galvanizzare qn, spronare qn all'azione

Gambia ['gæmbɪə] N Gambia m

gambit ['gæmbɪt] N (fig): (opening) **~** prima mossa

gamble ['gæmbl] N azzardo, rischio calcolato ▶ VT, VI giocare; **to ~ on** (fig) giocare su; **to ~ on the Stock Exchange** giocare in Borsa

gambler ['gæmbləʳ] N giocatore(-trice) d'azzardo

gambling ['gæmblɪŋ] N gioco d'azzardo
gambol ['gæmbəl] VI saltellare
game [geɪm] N gioco; (event) partita; (Tennis) game m inv; (Hunting, Culin) selvaggina ▶ ADJ coraggioso(-a); (ready): **to be ~ (for sth/to do)** essere pronto(-a) (a qc/a fare); **games** NPL (Scol) attività fpl sportive; **big ~** selvaggina grossa
game bird N uccello selvatico
gamekeeper ['geɪmkiːpər] N guardacaccia m inv
gamely ['geɪmlɪ] ADV coraggiosamente
gamer ['geɪmər] N chi gioca con i videogame
game reserve N riserva di caccia
games console [geɪmz-] N console f inv dei videogame
gameshow ['geɪmʃəu] N gioco a premi
gamesmanship ['geɪmzmənʃɪp] N abilità
gaming ['geɪmɪn] N gioco d'azzardo; (Comput) il giocare con i videogame
gammon ['gæmən] N (bacon) quarto di maiale; (ham) prosciutto affumicato
gamut ['gæmət] N gamma
gang [gæŋ] N banda, squadra ▶ VI: **to ~ up on sb** far combutta contro qn
Ganges ['gændʒiːz] N: **the ~** il Gange
gangland ['gæŋlænd] ADJ della malavita; **~ killer** sicario
gangling ['gæŋlɪŋ] ADJ allampanato(-a)
gangly ['gæŋglɪ] ADJ = **gangling**
gangplank ['gæŋplæŋk] N passerella
gangrene ['gæŋgriːn] N cancrena
gangster ['gæŋstər] N gangster m inv
gangway ['gæŋweɪ] N passerella; (BRIT: of bus) passaggio
gantry ['gæntrɪ] N (for crane, railway signal) cavalletto; (for rocket) torre f di lancio
GAO N ABBR (US: = General Accounting Office) ≈ Corte f dei Conti
gaol [dʒeɪl] N, VT (BRIT) = **jail**
gap [gæp] N (space) buco; (in time) intervallo; (fig) lacuna; vuoto; (difference): **~ (between)** divario (tra)
gape [geɪp] VI (person) restare a bocca aperta; (shirt, hole) essere spalancato(-a)
gaping ['geɪpɪŋ] ADJ (hole) squarciato(-a)
gap year N (Scol) anno di pausa preso prima di iniziare l'università, per lavorare o viaggiare
garage ['gæraːʒ] N garage m inv
garage sale N vendita di oggetti usati nel garage di un privato
garb [gaːb] N abiti mpl, veste f
garbage ['gaːbɪdʒ] (US) N immondizie fpl, rifiuti mpl; (col) sciocchezze fpl; (fig: film, book) porcheria, robaccia; (: nonsense) fesserie fpl
garbage can N (US) bidone m della spazzatura
garbage collector N (US) spazzino(-a)
garbage disposal unit N tritarifiuti m inv

garbage truck N (US) camion m inv della spazzatura
garbled ['gaːbld] ADJ deformato(-a); ingarbugliato(-a)
garden ['gaːdn] N giardino ▶ VI lavorare nel giardino; **gardens** NPL (public) giardini pubblici; (private) parco
garden centre N vivaio
garden city N (BRIT) città f inv giardino inv
gardener ['gaːdnər] N giardiniere(-a)
gardening ['gaːdnɪŋ] N giardinaggio
gargle ['gaːgl] VI fare gargarismi ▶ N gargarismo
gargoyle ['gaːgɔɪl] N gargouille f inv
garish ['gɛərɪʃ] ADJ vistoso(-a)
garland ['gaːlənd] N ghirlanda; corona
garlic ['gaːlɪk] N aglio
garment ['gaːmənt] N indumento
garner ['gaːnər] VT ammucchiare, raccogliere
garnish ['gaːnɪʃ] VT (food) guarnire
garret ['gærɪt] N soffitta
garrison ['gærɪsn] N guarnigione f ▶ VT guarnire
garrulous ['gærjuləs] ADJ ciarliero(-a), loquace
garter ['gaːtər] N giarrettiera; (US: suspender) gancio (di reggicalze)
garter belt N (US) reggicalze m inv
gas [gæs] N gas m inv; (used as anaesthetic) etere m; (US: gasoline) benzina ▶ VT asfissiare con il gas; (Mil) gasare
gas cooker N (BRIT) cucina a gas
gas cylinder N bombola del gas
gaseous ['gæsɪəs] ADJ gassoso(-a)
gas fire N (BRIT) radiatore m a gas
gas-fired ['gæsfaɪəd] ADJ (alimentato(-a)) a gas
gash [gæʃ] N sfregio ▶ VT sfregiare
gasket ['gæskɪt] N (Aut) guarnizione f
gas mask N maschera f antigas inv
gas meter N contatore m del gas
gasoline ['gæsəliːn] N (US) benzina
gasp [gaːsp] N respiro affannoso, ansito ▶ VI ansimare, boccheggiare; (in surprise) restare senza fiato
▶ **gasp out** VT dire affannosamente
gas pedal N (esp US) pedale m dell'acceleratore
gas ring N fornello a gas
gas station N (US) distributore m di benzina
gas stove N cucina a gas
gassy ['gæsɪ] ADJ gassoso(-a)
gas tank N (US Aut) serbatoio (di benzina)
gas tap N (on cooker) manopola del gas; (on pipe) rubinetto del gas
gastric ['gæstrɪk] ADJ gastrico(-a)
gastric band N (Med) sistema m di bendaggio gastrico

gastric ulcer N ulcera gastrica
gastroenteritis ['gæstrəυεntə'raɪtɪs] N gastroenterite f
gastronomy [gæs'trɔnəmɪ] N gastronomia
gasworks ['gæswəːks] N, NPL impianto di produzione del gas
gate [geɪt] N cancello; (*of castle, town*) porta; (*at airport*) uscita; (*at level crossing*) barriera
gâteau ['gætəυ] (*pl* **gâteaux** [-z]) N torta
gatecrash ['geɪtkræʃ] (BRIT) VT partecipare senza invito a
gatecrasher ['geɪtkræʃəʳ] N intruso(-a), ospite *mf* non invitato(-a)
gated community ['geɪtɪd-] N quartiere residenziale autonomo, recintato e sorvegliato, con accesso limitato
gatehouse ['geɪthaυs] N casetta del custode (*all'entrata di un parco*)
gateway ['geɪtweɪ] N porta
gather ['gæðəʳ] VT (*flowers, fruit*) cogliere; (*pick up*) raccogliere; (*assemble*) radunare; raccogliere; (*understand*) capire; (*Sewing*) increspare ▸ VI (*assemble*) radunarsi; (*dust*) accumularsi; (*clouds*) addensarsi; **to ~ speed** acquistare velocità; **to ~ (from/that)** comprendere (da/che), dedurre (da/che); **as far as I can ~** da quel che ho potuto capire
gathering ['gæðərɪŋ] N adunanza
GATT [gæt] N ABBR (= *General Agreement on Tariffs and Trade*) G.A.T.T *m*
gauche [gəυʃ] ADJ goffo(-a), maldestro(-a)
gaudy ['gɔːdɪ] ADJ vistoso(-a)
gauge [geɪdʒ] N (*standard measure*) calibro; (*Rail*) scartamento; (*instrument*) indicatore *m* ▸ VT misurare; (*fig: sb's capabilities, character*) valutare, stimare; **to ~ the right moment** calcolare il momento giusto; **petrol ~**, (US) **gas ~** indicatore *m or* spia della benzina
gaunt [gɔːnt] ADJ scarno(-a); (*grim, desolate*) desolato(-a)
gauntlet ['gɔːntlɪt] N (*fig*): **to run the ~ through an angry crowd** passare sotto il fuoco di una folla ostile; **to throw down the ~** gettare il guanto
gauze [gɔːz] N garza
gave [geɪv] PT *of* **give**
gawky ['gɔːkɪ] ADJ goffo(-a), sgraziato(-a)
gawp [gɔːp] VI: **to ~ at** guardare a bocca aperta
gay [geɪ] ADJ (*homosexual*) omosessuale; (*cheerful*) gaio(-a), allegro(-a); (*colour*) vivace, vivo(-a)
gaze [geɪz] N sguardo fisso ▸ VI: **to ~ at** guardare fisso
gazelle [gə'zεl] N gazzella
gazette [gə'zεt] N (*newspaper*) gazzetta; (*official publication*) gazzetta ufficiale
gazetteer [gæzə'tɪəʳ] N (*book*) dizionario dei nomi geografici; (*section of book*) indice *m* dei nomi geografici

gazump [gə'zʌmp] VT (BRIT): **to ~ sb** nella compravendita di immobili, venire meno all'impegno preso con un acquirente accettando un'offerta migliore fatta da altri
GB ABBR (= *Great Britain*) GB
GBH N ABBR (BRIT Law: col) = **grievous bodily harm**
GC N ABBR (BRIT: = *George Cross*) decorazione al valore
GCE N ABBR (BRIT: = *General Certificate of Education*) ≈ diploma *m* di maturità
GCHQ N ABBR (BRIT: = *Government Communications Headquarters*) centro per l'intercettazione delle telecomunicazioni straniere
GCSE N ABBR (BRIT: = *General Certificate of Secondary Education*) diploma di istruzione secondaria conseguito a 16 anni in Inghilterra e Galles
Gdns. ABBR = **gardens**
GDP N ABBR = **gross domestic product**
GDR N ABBR (*Hist*) = **German Democratic Republic**
gear [gɪəʳ] N attrezzi *mpl*, equipaggiamento; (*belongings*) roba; (*Tech*) ingranaggio; (*Aut*) marcia ▸ VT (*fig: adapt*): **to ~ sth to** adattare qc a; **top** *or* **high/low/bottom ~** (US) quinta (*or* sesta)/seconda/prima; **in ~** in marcia; **out of ~** in folle; **our service is geared to meet the needs of the disabled** la nostra organizzazione risponde espressamente alle esigenze degli handicappati
▸ **gear up** VI: **to ~ up (to do)** prepararsi (a fare)
gear box N scatola del cambio
gear lever, (US) **gear shift** N leva del cambio
GED N ABBR (US Scol) = **general educational development**
geese [giːs] NPL *of* **goose**
geezer ['giːzəʳ] N (BRIT col) tizio
Geiger counter ['gaɪgə-] N geiger *m inv*
gel [dʒεl] N gel *m inv*
gelatin, gelatine ['dʒεləti:n] N gelatina
gelignite ['dʒεlɪgnaɪt] N nitroglicerina
gem [dʒεm] N gemma
Gemini ['dʒεmɪnaɪ] N Gemelli *mpl*; **to be ~** essere dei Gemelli
gen [dʒεn] N (BRIT col): **to give sb the ~ on sth** mettere qn al corrente di qc
Gen. ABBR (Mil: = *General*) Gen.
gen. ABBR = **general**; (= *generally*) gen.
gender ['dʒεndəʳ] N genere *m*
gene [dʒiːn] N (Biol) gene *m*
genealogy [dʒiːnɪ'ælədʒɪ] N genealogia
general ['dʒεnərl] N generale *m* ▸ ADJ generale; **in ~** in genere; **the ~ public** il grande pubblico
general anaesthetic, (US) **general anesthetic** N anestesia totale
general delivery N (US) fermo posta *m*

575

general election N elezioni *fpl* generali
generalization ['dʒɛnrəlaɪ'zeɪʃən] N
generalizzazione *f*
generalize ['dʒɛnrəlaɪz] VI generalizzare
generally ['dʒɛnrəlɪ] ADV generalmente
general manager N direttore *m* generale
general practitioner N medico generico
general store N emporio
general strike N sciopero generale
generate ['dʒɛnəreɪt] VT generare
generation [dʒɛnə'reɪʃən] N generazione *f*;
(*of electricity etc*) produzione *f*
generator ['dʒɛnəreɪtə ⁱ] N generatore *m*
generic [dʒɪ'nɛrɪk] ADJ generico(-a)
generosity [dʒɛnə'rɔsɪtɪ] N generosità
generous ['dʒɛnərəs] ADJ generoso(-a);
(*copious*) abbondante
genesis ['dʒɛnɪsɪs] N genesi *f*
genetic [dʒɪ'nɛtɪk] ADJ genetico(-a);
~ **engineering** ingegneria genetica
genetically modified [dʒɪ'nɛtɪklɪ'mɔdɪfaɪd]
ADJ geneticamente modificato(-a),
transgenico(-a); ~ **organism** organismo
geneticamente modificato
genetic fingerprinting [-fɪŋɡəprɪntɪŋ] N
rilevamento delle impronte genetiche
genetics [dʒɪ'nɛtɪks] N genetica
Geneva [dʒɪ'niːvə] N Ginevra; **Lake ~** il lago
di Ginevra
genial ['dʒiːnɪəl] ADJ geniale, cordiale
genitals ['dʒɛnɪtlz] NPL genitali *mpl*
genitive ['dʒɛnɪtɪv] N genitivo
genius ['dʒiːnɪəs] N genio
Genoa ['dʒɛnəuə] N Genova
genocide ['dʒɛnəusaɪd] N genocidio
Genoese [dʒɛnəu'iːz] ADJ, N (*pl inv*) genovese
(*mf*)
genome ['dʒiːnəum] N (*Biol*) genoma *m*
gent [dʒɛnt] N ABBR (*BRIT col*) = **gentleman**
genteel [dʒɛn'tiːl] ADJ raffinato(-a),
distinto(-a)
gentle ['dʒɛntl] ADJ delicato(-a); (*person*) dolce
gentleman ['dʒɛntlmən] N (*irreg*) signore *m*;
(*well-bred man*) gentiluomo; ~**'s agreement**
impegno sulla parola
gentlemanly ['dʒɛntlmənlɪ] ADJ da
gentiluomo
gentleness ['dʒɛntlnɪs] N delicatezza;
dolcezza
gently ['dʒɛntlɪ] ADV delicatamente
gentry ['dʒɛntrɪ] N nobiltà minore
gents [dʒɛnts] N W.C. *m* (per signori)
genuine ['dʒɛnjuɪn] ADJ autentico(-a);
sincero(-a)
genuinely ['dʒɛnjuɪnlɪ] ADV genuinamente
geographer [dʒɪ'ɔɡrəfə ⁱ] N geografo(-a)
geographic [dʒɪə'ɡræfɪk], **geographical**
[dʒɪə'ɡræfɪkl] ADJ geografico(-a)
geography [dʒɪ'ɔɡrəfɪ] N geografia

geological [dʒɪə'lɔdʒɪkl] ADJ geologico(-a)
geologist [dʒɪ'ɔlədʒɪst] N geologo(-a)
geology [dʒɪ'ɔlədʒɪ] N geologia
geometric [dʒɪə'mɛtrɪk], **geometrical**
[dʒɪə'mɛtrɪkl] ADJ geometrico(-a)
geometry [dʒɪ'ɔmətrɪ] N geometria
Geordie ['dʒɔːdɪ] N (*col*) abitante *mf* del
Tyneside; originario(-a) del Tyneside
Georgia ['dʒɔːdʒə] N Georgia
Georgian ['dʒɔːdʒən] ADJ georgiano(-a) ▶ N
georgiano(-a); (*Ling*) georgiano
geranium [dʒɪ'reɪnɪəm] N geranio
geriatric [dʒɛrɪ'ætrɪk] ADJ geriatrico(-a)
germ [dʒəːm] N (*Med*) microbo; (*Biol, fig*)
germe *m*
German ['dʒəːmən] ADJ tedesco(-a) ▶ N
tedesco(-a); (*Ling*) tedesco
German Democratic Republic N
Repubblica Democratica Tedesca
germane [dʒəː'meɪn] ADJ (*formal*): **to be ~ to
sth** essere attinente a qc
German measles (*BRIT*) N rosolia
Germany ['dʒəːmənɪ] N Germania
germination [dʒəːmɪ'neɪʃən] N
germinazione *f*
germ warfare N guerra batteriologica
gerrymandering ['dʒɛrɪmændərɪŋ] N
manipolazione *f* dei distretti elettorali.
gestation [dʒɛs'teɪʃən] N gestazione *f*
gesticulate [dʒɛs'tɪkjuleɪt] VI gesticolare
gesture ['dʒɛstjə ⁱ] N gesto; **as a ~ of
friendship** in segno d'amicizia

(KEYWORD)

get [ɡɛt] (*pt, pp* **got**, *US pp* **gotten**) VI **1** (*become,
be*) diventare, farsi; **to get drunk** ubriacarsi;
to get killed venire *or* rimanere ucciso(-a);
it's getting late si sta facendo tardi; **to get
old** invecchiare; **to get paid** venire
pagato(-a); **when do I get paid?** quando mi
pagate?; **to get ready** prepararsi; **to get
shaved** farsi la barba; **to get tired** stancarsi;
to get washed lavarsi
2 (*go*): **to get to/from** andare a/da; **to get
home** arrivare *or* tornare a casa; **how did
you get here?** come sei venuto?; **he got
across the bridge** ha attraversato il ponte;
he got under the fence è passato sotto il
recinto
3 (*begin*) mettersi a, cominciare a; **to get to
know sb** incominciare a conoscere qn; **let's
get going** *or* **started** muoviamoci
4 (*modal aux vb*): **you've got to do it** devi farlo
▶ VT **1**: **to get sth done** (*do*) fare qc; (*have done*)
far fare qc; **to get sth/sb ready** preparare
qc/qn; **to get one's hair cut** tagliarsi *or* farsi
tagliare i capelli; **to get sb to do sth** far fare
qc a qn
2 (*obtain: money, permission, results*) ottenere;

(find: job, flat) trovare; (fetch: person, doctor) chiamare; **get me Mr Jones, please** (Tel) mi passi il signor Jones, per favore; (: object) prendere; **to get sth for sb** prendere or procurare qc a qn; **can I get you a drink?** le posso offrire da bere?

3 (receive: present, letter, prize) ricevere; (: acquire: reputation) farsi; **how much did you get for the painting?** quanto le hanno dato per il quadro?

4 (catch) prendere; **to get sb by the arm/ throat** afferrare qn per un braccio/alla gola; **get him!** prendetelo!; **he really gets me** (fig: annoy) mi dà proprio sui nervi

5 (hit: target etc) colpire

6 (take, move) portare; **to get sth to sb** far avere qc a qn; **do you think we'll get it through the door?** pensi che riusciremo a farlo passare per la porta?

7 (catch, take: plane, bus etc) prendere; **he got the last bus** ha preso l'ultimo autobus; **she got the morning flight to Milan** ha preso il volo per Milano del mattino; **where do we get the ferry to …?** dove si prende il traghetto per …?

8 (understand) afferrare; **I've got it!** ci sono arrivato!, ci sono!

9 (hear) sentire; **I'm sorry, I didn't get your name** scusi, non ho capito (or sentito) come si chiama

10 (have, possess): **to have got** avere; **how many have you got?** quanti ne ha?

▶ **get about** vi muoversi; (news) diffondersi
▶ **get across** vt: **to get across (to)** (message, meaning) comunicare (a) ▶ vi: **to get across to** (speaker) comunicare con
▶ **get along** vi (agree) andare d'accordo; (depart) andarsene; (manage) = **get by**
▶ **get at** vt fus (attack) prendersela con; (reach) raggiungere, arrivare a; **what are you getting at?** dove vuoi arrivare?
▶ **get away** vi partire, andarsene; (escape) scappare
▶ **get away with** vt fus cavarsela; farla franca; **he'll never get away with it!** non riuscirà a farla franca!
▶ **get back** vi (return) ritornare, tornare ▶ vt riottenere, riavere; **to get back to** (start again) ritornare a; (contact again) rimettersi in contatto con; **when do we get back?** quando ritorniamo?
▶ **get back at** vt fus (col): **to get back at sb (for sth)** rendere pan per focaccia a qn (per qc)
▶ **get by** vi (pass) passare; (manage) farcela; **I can get by in Dutch** mi arrangio in olandese
▶ **get down** vi, vt fus scendere ▶ vt far scendere; (depress) buttare giù

▶ **get down to** vt fus (work) mettersi a (fare); **to get down to business** venire al dunque
▶ **get in** vi entrare; (train) arrivare; (arrive home) ritornare, tornare ▶ vt (bring in: harvest) raccogliere; (: coal, shopping, supplies) fare provvista di; (insert) far entrare, infilare
▶ **get into** vt fus entrare in; **to get into a rage** incavolarsi; **to get into bed** mettersi a letto
▶ **get off** vi (from train etc) scendere; (depart: person, car) andare via; (escape) cavarsela ▶ vt (remove: clothes, stain) levare; (send off) spedire; (have as leave: days, time): **we got 2 days off** abbiamo avuto 2 giorni liberi ▶ vt fus (train, bus) scendere da; **to get off to a good start** (fig) cominciare bene
▶ **get on** vi: **how did you get on?** com'è andata?; **he got on quite well** ha fatto bene, (gli) è andata bene; **to get on (with sb)** andare d'accordo (con qn); **how are you getting on?** come va la vita? ▶ vt fus montare in; (horse) montare su
▶ **get on to** vt fus (BRIT col: contact: on phone etc) contattare, rintracciare; (deal with) occuparsi di
▶ **get out** vi uscire; (of vehicle) scendere ▶ vt tirar fuori, far uscire; **to get out (of)** (money from bank etc) ritirare (da)
▶ **get out of** vt fus uscire da; (duty etc) evitare; **what will you get out of it?** cosa ci guadagni?
▶ **get over** vt fus (illness) riaversi da; (communicate: idea etc) comunicare, passare; **let's get it over (with)** togliamoci il pensiero
▶ **get round** vt fus aggirare; (fig: person) rigirare ▶ vi: **to get round to doing sth** trovare il tempo di fare qc
▶ **get through** vi (Tel) avere la linea ▶ vt fus (finish: work) sbrigare; (: book) finire
▶ **get through to** vt fus (Tel) parlare a
▶ **get together** vi riunirsi ▶ vt raccogliere; (people) adunare
▶ **get up** vi (rise) alzarsi ▶ vt fus salire su per
▶ **get up to** vt fus (reach) raggiungere; (prank etc) fare

getaway ['gɛtəweɪ] N fuga
getaway car N macchina per la fuga
get-together ['gɛttəgɛðəʳ] N (piccola) riunione f; (party) festicciola
get-up ['gɛtʌp] N (col: outfit) tenuta
get-well card [gɛt'wɛl-] N cartolina di auguri di pronta guarigione
geyser ['giːzəʳ] N scaldabagno; (Geo) geyser m inv
Ghana ['gɑːnə] N Ghana m
Ghanaian [gɑː'neɪən] ADJ, N ganaense (mf)
ghastly ['gɑːstlɪ] ADJ orribile, orrendo(-a); (pale) spettrale

gherkin ['gə:kɪn] N cetriolino

ghetto ['gɛtəu] N ghetto

ghetto blaster [-'blɑ:stəʳ] N maxistereo portatile

ghost [gəust] N fantasma *m*, spettro ▶ VT (*book*) fare lo scrittore ombra per

ghostly ['gəustlɪ] ADJ spettrale

ghostwriter ['gəustraɪtəʳ] N scrittore(-trice) ombra *inv*

ghoul [gu:l] N vampiro che si nutre di cadaveri

ghoulish ['gu:lɪʃ] ADJ (*tastes etc*) macabro(-a)

GHQ N ABBR (*Mil*: = *general headquarters*) ≈ comando di Stato maggiore

GI N ABBR (*US*: *col*: = *government issue*) G.I. *m*, soldato americano

giant ['dʒaɪənt] N gigante(-essa) ▶ ADJ gigantesco(-a), enorme; **~ (size) packet** confezione *f* gigante

giant killer N (*Sport*) *piccola squadra che riesce a batterne una importante*

gibber ['dʒɪbəʳ] VI (*monkey*) squittire confusamente; (*idiot*) farfugliare

gibberish ['dʒɪbərɪʃ] N parole *fpl* senza senso

gibe [dʒaɪb] N frecciata ▶ VI: **to ~ at** lanciare frecciate a

giblets ['dʒɪblɪts] NPL frattaglie *fpl*

Gibraltar [dʒɪ'brɔ:ltəʳ] N Gibilterra

giddiness ['gɪdɪnɪs] N vertigine *f*

giddy ['gɪdɪ] ADJ (*dizzy*): **to be ~** aver le vertigini; (*height*) vertiginoso(-a); **I feel ~** mi gira la testa

gift [gɪft] N regalo; (*donation, ability*) dono; (*Comm*: *also*: **free gift**) omaggio; **to have a ~ for sth** (*talent*) avere il dono di qc

gifted ['gɪftɪd] ADJ dotato(-a)

gift shop, (*US*) **gift store** N negozio di souvenir

gift token, gift voucher N buono (acquisto)

gig [gɪg] N (*col*: *of musician*) serata

gigabyte [gi:gəbaɪt] N gigabyte *m inv*

gigantic [dʒaɪ'gæntɪk] ADJ gigantesco(-a)

giggle ['gɪgl] VI ridere scioccamente ▶ N risolino (sciocco)

GIGO ['gaɪgəu] ABBR (*Comput*: *col*: = *garbage in, garbage out*) qualità di input = qualità di output

gild [gɪld] VT dorare

gill [dʒɪl] N (*measure*) = 0.25 pints (*Brit* = 0.148 *l*; *US* = 0.118 *l*)

gills [gɪlz] NPL (*of fish*) branchie *fpl*

gilt [gɪlt] N doratura ▶ ADJ dorato(-a)

gilt-edged ['gɪltɛdʒd] ADJ (*stocks, securities*) della massima sicurezza

gimlet ['gɪmlɪt] N succhiello

gimmick ['gɪmɪk] N trucco; **sales ~** trovata commerciale

gin [dʒɪn] N (*liquor*) gin *m inv*

ginger ['dʒɪndʒəʳ] N zenzero

▶ **ginger up** VT scuotere; animare

ginger ale, ginger beer N bibita gassosa allo zenzero

gingerbread ['dʒɪndʒəbrɛd] N pan *m* di zenzero

ginger group N (*BRIT*) gruppo di pressione

ginger-haired ['dʒɪndʒə'hɛəd] ADJ rossiccio(-a)

gingerly ['dʒɪndʒəlɪ] ADV cautamente

gingham ['gɪŋəm] N percalle *m* a righe (*or* quadretti)

ginseng ['dʒɪnsɛŋ] N ginseng *m*

gipsy ['dʒɪpsɪ] N zingaro(-a) ▶ ADJ degli zingari

giraffe [dʒɪ'rɑ:f] N giraffa

girder ['gə:dəʳ] N trave *f*

girdle ['gə:dl] N (*corset*) guaina

girl [gə:l] N ragazza; (*young unmarried woman*) signorina; (*daughter*) figlia, figliola; **a little ~** una bambina

girl band N *gruppo pop di sole ragazze creato per far presa su un pubblico giovane*

girlfriend ['gə:lfrɛnd] N (*of girl*) amica; (*of boy*) ragazza

girlish ['gə:lɪʃ] ADJ da ragazza

Girl Scout N (*US*) Giovane Esploratrice *f*

Giro ['dʒaɪrəu] N: **the National ~** (*BRIT*) ≈ la *or* il Bancoposta

giro ['dʒaɪrəu] N (*bank giro*) versamento bancario; (*post office giro*) postagiro

girth [gə:θ] N circonferenza; (*of horse*) cinghia

gist [dʒɪst] N succo

give [gɪv] (*pt* **gave** [geɪv], *pp* **given** ['gɪvn]) N (*of fabric*) elasticità ▶ VT dare ▶ VI cedere; **to ~ sb sth, ~ sth to sb** dare qc a qn; **I'll ~ you £5 for it** te lo pago 5 sterline; **to ~ a cry/sigh** emettere un grido/sospiro; **to ~ a speech** fare un discorso; **how much did you ~ for it?** quanto (l')hai pagato?; **12 o'clock, ~ or take a few minutes** mezzogiorno, minuto più minuto meno; **to ~ way** VI cedere; (*BRIT Aut*) dare la precedenza

▶ **give away** VT dare via; (*give free*) fare dono di; (*betray*) tradire; (*disclose*) rivelare; (*bride*) condurre all'altare

▶ **give back** VT rendere

▶ **give in** VI cedere ▶ VT consegnare

▶ **give off** VT emettere

▶ **give out** VT distribuire; annunciare ▶ VI (*be exhausted*: *supplies*) esaurirsi, venir meno; (*fail*: *engine*) fermarsi; (: *strength*) mancare

▶ **give up** VI rinunciare ▶ VT rinunciare a; **to ~ up smoking** smettere di fumare; **to ~ o.s. up** arrendersi

give-and-take [gɪvən'teɪk] N (*col*) elasticità (da ambo le parti), concessioni *fpl* reciproche

giveaway ['gɪvəweɪ] N (*col*): **her expression was a ~** le si leggeva tutto in volto; **the exam was a ~!** l'esame è stato uno scherzo! ▶ CPD:

~ prices prezzi stracciati

given ['gɪvn] PP of **give** ▶ ADJ (fixed: time, amount) dato(-a), determinato(-a) ▶ CONJ: **~ (that)** ... dato che ...; **~ the circumstances** ... date le circostanze ...

glacial ['gleɪsɪəl] ADJ glaciale

glacier ['glæsɪəʳ] N ghiacciaio

glad [glæd] ADJ lieto(-a), contento(-a); **to be ~ about sth/that** essere contento or lieto di qc/che + sub; **I was ~ of his help** gli sono stato grato del suo aiuto

gladden ['glædn] VT rallegrare, allietare

glade [gleɪd] N radura

gladioli [glædɪ'əʊlaɪ] NPL gladioli mpl

gladly ['glædlɪ] ADV volentieri

glamorous ['glæmərəs] ADJ (gen) favoloso(-a); (person) affascinante, seducente; (occasion) brillante, elegante

glamour, (US) **glamor** ['glæməʳ] N fascino

glance [glɑːns] N occhiata, sguardo ▶ VI: **to ~ at** dare un'occhiata a
▶ **glance off** VT FUS (bullet) rimbalzare su

glancing ['glɑːnsɪŋ] ADJ (blow) che colpisce di striscio

gland [glænd] N ghiandola

glandular ['glændjʊləʳ] ADJ: **~ fever** (BRIT) mononucleosi f

glare [glɛəʳ] N (of anger) sguardo furioso; (of light) riverbero, luce f abbagliante; (of publicity) chiasso ▶ VI abbagliare; **to ~ at** guardare male

glaring ['glɛərɪŋ] ADJ (mistake) madornale

glasnost ['glæznɔst] N glasnost f

glass [glɑːs] N (substance) vetro; (tumbler) bicchiere m; (also: **looking glass**) specchio; see also **glasses**

glass-blowing ['glɑːsbləʊɪŋ] N soffiatura del vetro

glass ceiling N (fig) barriera invisibile

glasses ['glɑːsɪz] NPL (spectacles) occhiali mpl

glass fibre N fibra di vetro

glasshouse ['glɑːshaʊs] N serra

glassware ['glɑːswɛəʳ] N vetrame m

glassy ['glɑːsɪ] ADJ (eyes) vitreo(-a)

Glaswegian [glæs'wiːdʒən] ADJ di Glasgow ▶ N abitante mf di Glasgow, originario(-a) di Glasgow

glaze [gleɪz] VT (door) fornire di vetri; (pottery) smaltare; (Culin) glassare ▶ N smalto; glassa

glazed ['gleɪzd] ADJ (eye) vitreo(-a); (tiles, pottery) smaltato(-a)

glazier ['gleɪzɪəʳ] N vetraio

gleam [gliːm] N barlume m; raggio ▶ VI luccicare; **a ~ of hope** un barlume di speranza

gleaming ['gliːmɪŋ] ADJ lucente

glean [gliːn] VT (information) racimolare

glee [gliː] N allegrezza, gioia

gleeful ['gliːful] ADJ allegro(-a), gioioso(-a)

glen [glɛn] N valletta

glib [glɪb] ADJ dalla parola facile; facile

glide [glaɪd] VI scivolare; (Aviat, birds) planare ▶ N scivolata; planata

glider ['glaɪdəʳ] N (Aviat) aliante m

gliding ['glaɪdɪŋ] N (Aviat) volo a vela

glimmer ['glɪməʳ] VI luccicare ▶ N barlume m

glimpse [glɪmps] N impressione f fugace ▶ VT vedere di sfuggita; **to catch a ~ of** vedere di sfuggita

glint [glɪnt] N luccichio ▶ VI luccicare

glisten ['glɪsn] VI luccicare

glitter ['glɪtəʳ] VI scintillare ▶ N scintillio

glitz [glɪts] N (col) vistosità, chiassosità

gloat [gləʊt] VI: **to ~ (over)** gongolare di piacere (per)

global ['gləʊbl] ADJ globale; (world-wide) mondiale

globalization [gləʊbəlaɪˈzeɪʃən] N globalizzazione f

global warming N riscaldamento globale

globe [gləʊb] N globo, sfera

globetrotter ['gləʊbtrɔtəʳ] N giramondo mf

globule ['glɔbjuːl] N (Anat) globulo; (of water etc) gocciolina

gloom [gluːm] N oscurità, buio; (sadness) tristezza, malinconia

gloomy ['gluːmɪ] ADJ scuro(-a), fosco(-a), triste; **to feel ~** sentirsi giù or depresso

glorification [glɔːrɪfɪ'keɪʃən] N glorificazione f

glorify ['glɔːrɪfaɪ] VT glorificare; celebrare, esaltare

glorious ['glɔːrɪəs] ADJ glorioso(-a), magnifico(-a)

glory ['glɔːrɪ] N gloria; splendore m ▶ VI: **to ~ in** gloriarsi di or in

glory hole N (col) ripostiglio

Glos ABBR (BRIT) = **Gloucestershire**

gloss [glɔs] N (shine) lucentezza; (also: **gloss paint**) vernice f a olio
▶ **gloss over** VT FUS scivolare su

glossary ['glɔsərɪ] N glossario

glossy ['glɔsɪ] ADJ lucente ▶ N (also: **glossy magazine**) rivista di lusso

glove [glʌv] N guanto

glove compartment N (Aut) vano portaoggetti

glow [gləʊ] VI ardere; (face) essere luminoso(-a) ▶ N bagliore m; (of face) colorito acceso

glower ['glaʊəʳ] VI: **to ~ (at sb)** guardare (qn) in cagnesco

glowing ['gləʊɪŋ] ADJ (fire) ardente; (complexion) luminoso(-a); (fig: report, description etc) entusiasta

glow-worm ['gləʊwəːm] N lucciola

glucose ['gluːkəʊs] N glucosio

glue [gluː] N colla ▶ VT incollare

glue-sniffing ['glu:snɪfɪŋ] N sniffare m (colla)

glum [glʌm] ADJ abbattuto(-a)

glut [glʌt] N eccesso ▶ VT saziare; (*market*) saturare

glutinous ['glu:tɪnəs] ADJ colloso(-a), appiccicoso(-a)

glutton ['glʌtn] N ghiottone(-a); **a ~ for work** un(-a) patito(-a) del lavoro

gluttonous ['glʌtənəs] ADJ ghiotto(-a), goloso(-a)

gluttony ['glʌtənɪ] N ghiottoneria; (*sin*) gola

glycerin, glycerine ['glɪsəri:n] N glicerina

GM ADJ ABBR (= *genetically modified*) geneticamente modificato(-a)

gm ABBR = **gram**

GMAT N ABBR (US: = *Graduate Management Admissions Test*) esame di ammissione all'ultimo biennio di scuola superiore

GMB N ABBR (BRIT) = **General, Municipal, and Boilermakers (Union)**

GM crop N pianta transgenica

GM food N cibo transgenico

GM-free [dʒi:ɛm'fri:] ADJ privo(-a) di OGM

GMO N ABBR (= *genetically modified organism*) OGM m inv

GMT ABBR (= *Greenwich Mean Time*) T.M.G.

gnarled [nɑ:ld] ADJ nodoso(-a)

gnash [næʃ] VT: **to ~ one's teeth** digrignare i denti

gnat [næt] N moscerino

gnaw [nɔ:] VT rodere

gnome [nəum] N gnomo

GNP N ABBR = **gross national product**

go [gəu] VI (*pt* **went** [wɛnt], *pp* **gone** [gɔn]) andare; (*depart*) partire, andarsene; (*work*) funzionare; (*time*) passare; (*break etc*) cedere; (*be sold*): **to go for £10** essere venduto per 10 sterline; (*fit, suit*): **to go with** andare bene con; (*become*): **to go pale** diventare pallido(-a); **to go mouldy** ammuffire ▶ N (*pl* **goes**): **to have a go (at)** provare; **to be on the go** essere in moto; **whose go is it?** a chi tocca?; **to go by car/on foot** andare in macchina/a piedi; **he's going to do** sta per fare; **to go for a walk** andare a fare una passeggiata; **to go dancing/shopping** andare a ballare/fare la spesa; **just then the bell went** proprio allora suonò il campanello; **to go looking for sb/sth** andare in cerca di qn/qc; **to go to sleep** addormentarsi; **to go and see sb, to go to see sb** andare a trovare qn; **how is it going?** come va (la vita)?; **how did it go?** com'è andato?; **to go round the back/by the shop** passare da dietro/davanti al negozio; **my voice has gone** m'è andata via la voce; **the cake is all gone** il dolce è finito tutto; **I'll take whatever is going** (BRIT) prendo quello

che c'è; **... to go** (US: *food*) ... da portar via; **the money will go towards our holiday** questi soldi li mettiamo per la vacanza

▶ **go about** VI (*also:* **go around**) aggirarsi; (: *rumour*) correre, circolare ▶ VT FUS: **how do I go about this?** qual è la prassi per questo?; **to go about one's business** occuparsi delle proprie faccende

▶ **go after** VT FUS (*pursue*) correr dietro a, rincorrere; (*job, record etc*) mirare a

▶ **go against** VT FUS (*be unfavourable to*) essere contro; (*be contrary to*) andare contro

▶ **go ahead** VI andare avanti; **go ahead!** faccia pure!

▶ **go along** VI andare, avanzare ▶ VT FUS percorrere; **to go along with** (*accompany*) andare con, accompagnare; (*agree with: idea*) sottoscrivere, appoggiare

▶ **go away** VI partire, andarsene

▶ **go back** VI tornare, ritornare; (*go again*) andare di nuovo

▶ **go back on** VT FUS (*promise*) non mantenere

▶ **go by** VI (*years, time*) scorrere ▶ VT FUS attenersi a, seguire (alla lettera); prestar fede a

▶ **go down** VI scendere; (*ship*) affondare; (*sun*) tramontare ▶ VT FUS scendere; **that should go down well with him** dovrebbe incontrare la sua approvazione

▶ **go for** VT FUS (*fetch*) andare a prendere; (*like*) andar matto(-a) per; (*attack*) attaccare; saltare addosso a

▶ **go in** VI entrare

▶ **go in for** VT FUS (*competition*) iscriversi a; (*be interested in*) interessarsi di

▶ **go into** VT FUS entrare in; (*investigate*) indagare, esaminare; (*embark on*) lanciarsi in

▶ **go off** VI partire, andar via; (*food*) guastarsi; (*explode*) esplodere, scoppiare; (*lights etc*) spegnersi; (*event*) passare ▶ VT FUS: **I've gone off chocolate** la cioccolata non mi piace più; **the gun went off** il fucile si scaricò; **the party went off well** la festa è andata *or* è riuscita bene; **to go off to sleep** addormentarsi

▶ **go on** VI continuare; (*happen*) succedere; (*lights*) accendersi ▶ VT FUS (*be guided by: evidence etc*) basarsi su, fondarsi su; **to go on doing** continuare a fare; **what's going on here?** che succede *or* che sta succedendo qui?

▶ **go on at** VI (*nag*) assillare

▶ **go on with** VT FUS continuare, proseguire

▶ **go out** VI uscire; (*fire, light*) spegnersi; (*ebb: tide*) calare; **to go out with sb** uscire con qn; **they went out for 3 years** (*couple*) sono stati insieme per 3 anni

▶ **go over** VI (*ship*) ribaltarsi ▶ VT FUS (*check*) esaminare; **to go over sth in one's mind** pensare bene a qc

▶ **go past** VI passare ▶ VT FUS passare davanti a

▶ **go round** VI (*circulate: news, rumour*) circolare; (*revolve*) girare; (*suffice*) bastare (per tutti); **to go round (to sb's)** (*visit*) passare (da qn); **to go round (by)** (*make a detour*) passare (per)

▶ **go through** VT FUS (*town etc*) attraversare; (*search through: files, papers*) vagliare attentamente; (*examine: list, book*) leggere da cima a fondo; (*perform*) fare

▶ **go through with** VT FUS (*plan, crime*) mettere in atto, eseguire; **I couldn't go through with it** non sono riuscito ad andare fino in fondo

▶ **go under** VI (*sink: ship*) affondare, colare a picco; (*: person*) andare sotto; (*fig: business, firm*) fallire

▶ **go up** VI salire ▶ VT FUS salire su per; **to go up in flames** andare in fiamme

▶ **go with** VT FUS (*accompany*) accompagnare

▶ **go without** VT FUS fare a meno di

goad [gəud] VT spronare

go-ahead ['gəuəhɛd] ADJ intraprendente

▶ N: **to give sb/sth the ~** dare il via libera a qn/qc

goal [gəul] N (*Sport*) gol *m*, rete *f*; (*: place*) porta; (*fig: aim*) fine *m*, scopo

goal difference N differenza *f* reti *inv*

goalie ['gəuli] N (*col*) portiere *m*

goalkeeper ['gəulkiːpəʳ] N portiere *m*

goalpost ['gəulpəust] N palo (della porta)

goat [gəut] N capra

gobble ['gɔbl] VT (*also*: **gobble down, gobble up**) ingoiare

go-between ['gəubitwiːn] N intermediario(-a)

Gobi Desert ['gəubɪ-] N: **the ~** il Deserto dei Gobi

goblet ['gɔblɪt] N calice *m*, coppa

goblin ['gɔblɪn] N folletto

go-cart ['gəukɑːt] N go-kart *m inv* ▶ CPD: **~ racing** *n* kartismo

god [gɔd] N dio; **G~** Dio

god-awful [gɔd'ɔːfəl] ADJ (*col*) di merda (!)

godchild ['gɔdtʃaɪld] N (*irreg*) figlioccio(-a)

goddamn ['gɔddæm], (*US*) **goddamned** ['gɔddæmd] (*esp col*) EXCL: **~!** porca miseria! ▶ ADJ fottuto(-a) (!), maledetto(-a) ▶ ADV maledettamente

goddaughter ['gɔddɔːtəʳ] N figlioccia

goddess ['gɔdɪs] N dea

godfather ['gɔdfɑːðəʳ] N padrino

god-fearing ['gɔdfɪərɪŋ] ADJ timorato(-a) di Dio

god-forsaken ['gɔdfəseɪkən] ADJ desolato(-a), sperduto(-a)

godmother ['gɔdmʌðəʳ] N madrina

godparents ['gɔdpɛərənts] NPL: **the ~** il padrino e la madrina

godsend ['gɔdsɛnd] N dono del cielo

godson ['gɔdsʌn] N figlioccio

goes [gəuz] *see* **go**

gofer ['gəufəʳ] N (*col*) tuttofare *mf*, tirapiedi *mf*

go-getter ['gəugɛtəʳ] N arrivista *mf*

goggle ['gɔgl] VI: **to ~ (at)** stare con gli occhi incollati *or* appiccicati (a *or* addosso a)

goggles ['gɔglz] NPL occhiali *mpl* (di protezione)

going ['gəuɪŋ] N (*conditions*) andare *m*, stato del terreno ▶ ADJ: **the ~ rate** la tariffa in vigore; **a ~ concern** un'azienda avviata; **it was slow ~** si andava a rilento

going-over [gəuɪŋ'əuvəʳ] N (*col*) controllata; (*violent attack*) pestaggio

goings-on ['gəuɪŋz'ɔn] NPL (*col*) fatti *mpl* strani, cose *fpl* strane

go-kart ['gəukɑːt] N = **go-cart**

gold [gəuld] N oro ▶ ADJ d'oro; (*reserves*) aureo(-a)

golden ['gəuldən] ADJ (*made of gold*) d'oro; (*gold in colour*) dorato(-a)

golden age N età d'oro

golden handshake N (*BRIT*) gratifica di fine servizio

golden rule N regola principale

goldfish ['gəuldfɪʃ] N pesce *m* dorato *or* rosso

gold leaf N lamina d'oro

gold medal N (*Sport*) medaglia d'oro

goldmine ['gəuldmaɪn] N (*also fig*) miniera d'oro

gold-plated ['gəuld'pleɪtɪd] ADJ placcato(-a) oro *inv*

goldsmith ['gəuldsmɪθ] N orefice *m*, orafo

gold standard N tallone *m* aureo

golf [gɔlf] N golf *m*

golf ball N (*for game*) pallina da golf; (*on typewriter*) pallina

golf club N circolo di golf; (*stick*) bastone *m or* mazza da golf

golf course N campo di golf

golfer ['gɔlfəʳ] N giocatore(-trice) di golf

golfing ['gɔlfɪŋ] N il giocare a golf

gondola ['gɔndələ] N gondola

gondolier [gɔndə'lɪəʳ] N gondoliere *m*

gone [gɔn] PP *of* **go** ▶ ADJ partito(-a)

goner ['gɔnəʳ] N (*col*): **I thought you were a ~** pensavo che ormai fossi spacciato

gong [gɔŋ] N gong *m inv*

good [gud] ADJ buono(-a); (*kind*) buono(-a), gentile; (*child*) buono(-a) ▶ N bene *m*; **~!** bene!, ottimo!; **to be ~ at** essere bravo(-a) in; **to be ~ for** andare bene per; **it's ~ for you** fa bene; **it's a ~ thing you were there** meno male che c'era; **she is ~ with children/her hands** ci sa fare coi bambini/è abile nei lavori manuali; **to feel ~** sentirsi bene; **it's ~ to see you** che piacere vederla; **to make ~**

(*loss, damage*) compensare; **he's up to no ~** ne sta combinando qualcuna; **it's no ~ complaining** brontolare non serve a niente; **for the common ~** nell'interesse generale, per il bene comune; **for ~** (*for ever*) per sempre, definitivamente; **would you be ~ enough to …?** avrebbe la gentilezza di …?; **that's very ~ of you** è molto gentile da parte sua; **is this any ~?** (*will it do?*) va bene questo?; (*what's it like?*) com'è?; **a ~ deal (of)** molto(-a), una buona quantità (di); **a ~ many** molti(-e); **~ morning!** buon giorno!; **~ afternoon/evening!** buona sera!; **~ night!** buona notte!; *see also* **goods**

goodbye [gud'baɪ] EXCL arrivederci!; **to say ~ to** (*person*) salutare

good faith N buona fede

good-for-nothing ['gudfənʌθɪŋ] N buono(-a) a nulla, vagabondo(-a)

Good Friday N Venerdì Santo

good-humoured [gud'hju:məd] ADJ (*person*) di buon umore; (*remark, joke*) bonario(-a)

good-looking [gud'lukɪŋ] ADJ bello(-a)

good-natured [gud'neɪtʃəd] ADJ (*person*) affabile; (*discussion*) amichevole, cordiale

goodness ['gudnɪs] N (*of person*) bontà; **for ~ sake!** per amor di Dio!; **~ gracious!** santo cielo!, mamma mia!

goods [gudz] NPL (*Comm etc*) merci *fpl*, articoli *mpl*; **~ and chattels** beni *mpl* e effetti *mpl*

goods train N (*BRIT*) treno *m* merci *inv*

goodwill [gud'wɪl] N amicizia, benevolenza; (*Comm*) avviamento

goody-goody ['gudɪgudɪ] N (*pej*) santarellino(-a)

gooey ['gu:ɪ] ADJ (*col: sticky*) appiccicoso(-a); (*cake, dessert*) troppo zuccherato(-a)

Google® ['gu:gl] VT, VI cercare su Google®

goose [gu:s] (*pl* **geese** [gi:s]) N oca

gooseberry ['guzbərɪ] N uva spina; **to play ~** (*BRIT*) tenere la candela

goose bumps ['gu:sbʌmpz] NPL, **gooseflesh** ['gu:sflɛʃ] N, **goosepimples** ['gu:spɪmplz] NPL pelle *f* d'oca

goose step N (*Mil*) passo dell'oca

GOP N ABBR (*US Pol: col:* = *Grand Old Party*) partito repubblicano

gopher ['gəufəʳ] N = **gofer**

gore [gɔːʳ] VT incornare ▶ N sangue *m* (coagulato)

gorge [gɔːdʒ] N gola ▶ VT: **to ~ o.s. (on)** ingozzarsi (di)

gorgeous ['gɔːdʒəs] ADJ magnifico(-a)

gorilla [gə'rɪlə] N gorilla *m inv*

gormless ['gɔːmlɪs] ADJ (*BRIT: col*) tonto(-a); (*: stronger*) deficiente

gorse [gɔːs] N ginestrone *m*

gory ['gɔːrɪ] ADJ sanguinoso(-a)

gosh [gɔʃ] EXCL (*col*) perdinci!

go-slow ['gəu'sləu] N (*BRIT*) rallentamento dei lavori (*per agitazione sindacale*)

gospel ['gɔspl] N vangelo

gossamer ['gɔsəməʳ] N (*cobweb*) fili *mpl* della Madonna *or* di ragnatela; (*light fabric*) stoffa sottilissima

gossip ['gɔsɪp] N chiacchiere *fpl*; pettegolezzi *mpl*; (*person*) pettegolo(-a) ▶ VI chiacchierare; (*maliciously*) pettegolare; **a piece of ~** un pettegolezzo

gossip column N cronaca mondana

got [gɔt] PT, PP *of* **get**

Gothic ['gɔθɪk] ADJ gotico(-a)

gotten ['gɔtn] (*US*) PP *of* **get**

gouge [gaudʒ] VT (*also:* **gouge out**: *hole etc*) scavare; (*: initials*) scolpire; (*: sb's eyes*) cavare

gourd [guəd] N zucca

gourmet ['guəmeɪ] N buongustaio(-a)

gout [gaut] N gotta

govern ['gʌvən] VT governare; (*Ling*) reggere

governess ['gʌvənɪs] N governante *f*

governing ['gʌvənɪŋ] ADJ (*Pol*) al potere, al governo; **~ body** consiglio di amministrazione

government ['gʌvnmənt] N governo; (*BRIT: ministers*) ministero ▶ CPD statale; **local ~** amministrazione *f* locale

governmental [gʌvn'mɛntl] ADJ governativo(-a)

government housing N (*US*) alloggi *mpl* popolari

government stock N titoli *mpl* di stato

governor ['gʌvənəʳ] N (*of state, bank*) governatore *m*; (*of school, hospital*) amministratore *m*; (*BRIT: of prison*) direttore(-trice)

Govt ABBR = **government**

gown [gaun] N vestito lungo; (*of teacher, judge: BRIT*) toga

GP N ABBR (*Med*) = **general practitioner**; **who's your GP?** qual è il suo medico di fiducia?

GPMU N ABBR (*BRIT*) = **Graphical, Paper and Media Union**

GPO N ABBR (*BRIT old*) = **General Post Office**; (*US:* = *Government Printing Office*) ≈ Poligrafici dello Stato

GPS N ABBR (= *global positioning system*) GPS *m*

gr. ABBR (*Comm*) = **gross**

grab [græb] VT afferrare, arraffare; (*property, power*) impadronirsi di ▶ VI: **to ~ at** cercare di afferrare

grace [greɪs] N grazia; (*graciousness*) garbo, cortesia ▶ VT onorare; **5 days' ~** dilazione *f* di 5 giorni; **to say ~** dire il benedicite; **with a good/bad ~** volentieri/malvolentieri; **his sense of humour is his saving ~** il suo senso dell'umorismo è quello che lo salva

graceful ['greɪsful] ADJ elegante, aggraziato(-a)

gracious ['greɪʃəs] ADJ grazioso(-a), misericordioso(-a) ▶ EXCL: **(good)** ~! madonna (mia)!

gradation [grə'deɪʃən] N gradazione f

grade [greɪd] N (Comm) qualità f inv; classe f; categoria; (in hierarchy) grado; (US Scol: mark) voto; classe; (gradient) pendenza, gradiente m ▶ VT classificare; ordinare; graduare; **to make the** ~ (fig) farcela

grade crossing N (US) passaggio a livello

grade school N (US) scuola elementare or primaria

gradient ['greɪdɪənt] N pendenza, inclinazione m

gradual ['grædjuəl] ADJ graduale

gradually ['grædjuəlɪ] ADV man mano, a poco a poco

graduate N ['grædjuɪt] laureato(-a); (US Scol) diplomato(-a), licenziato(-a) ▶ VI ['grædjueɪt] laurearsi; diplomarsi

graduated pension ['grædjueɪtɪd-] N pensione calcolata sugli ultimi stipendi

graduation [grædju'eɪʃən] N cerimonia del conferimento della laurea; (US Scol) consegna dei diplomi

graffiti [grə'fi:tɪ] NPL graffiti mpl

graft [grɑ:ft] N (Agr, Med) innesto; (col: bribery) corruzione f; (BRIT col): **hard** ~ duro lavoro ▶ VT innestare; **it's hard** ~ (BRIT col) è un lavoraccio

grain [greɪn] N (no pl: cereals) cereali mpl; (US: corn) grano; (of sand) granello; (of wood) venatura; **it goes against the** ~ (fig) va contro la mia (or la sua etc) natura

gram [græm] N grammo

grammar ['græmə'] N grammatica

grammar school N (BRIT) ≈ liceo; (US) ≈ scuola elementare

grammatical [grə'mætɪkl] ADJ grammaticale

gramme [græm] N = **gram**

gramophone ['græməfəun] N (BRIT) grammofono

gran [græn] N (col: BRIT) nonna

granary ['grænərɪ] N granaio

grand [grænd] ADJ grande, magnifico(-a); grandioso(-a) ▶ N (col: thousand) mille dollari mpl (or sterline fpl)

grandad ['grændæd] N (col) = **granddad**

grandchild ['græntʃaɪld] (pl **-children** [-tʃɪldrən]) N nipote m

granddad ['grændæd] N (col) nonno

granddaughter ['grændɔ:tə'] N nipote f

grandeur ['grændjə'] N (of style, house) splendore m; (of occasion, scenery etc) grandiosità, maestà

grandfather ['grændfɑ:ðə'] N nonno

grandiose ['grændɪəus] ADJ grandioso(-a); (pej) pomposo(-a)

grand jury N (US) giuria (formata da 12 a 23 membri)

grandma ['grænmɑ:] N (col) nonna

grandmother ['grænmʌðə'] N nonna

grandpa ['grænpɑ:] N (col) = **granddad**

grandparent ['grænpɛərənt] N nonno(-a)

grand piano N pianoforte m a coda

Grand Prix ['grɑ̃:'pri:] N (Aut) Gran Premio, Grand Prix m inv

grandson ['grænsʌn] N nipote m

grandstand ['grændstænd] N (Sport) tribuna

grand total N somma complessiva

granite ['grænɪt] N granito

granny ['grænɪ] N (col) nonna

grant [grɑ:nt] VT accordare; (a request) accogliere; (admit) ammettere, concedere ▶ N (Scol) borsa; (Admin) sussidio, sovvenzione f; **to take sth for granted** dare qc per scontato; **to take sb for granted** dare per scontata la presenza di qn

granulated ['grænjuleɪtɪd] ADJ: ~ **sugar** zucchero cristallizzato

granule ['grænju:l] N granello

grape [greɪp] N chicco d'uva, acino; **a bunch of grapes** un grappolo d'uva

grapefruit ['greɪpfru:t] N pompelmo

grapevine ['greɪpvaɪn] N vite f; **I heard it on the** ~ (fig) me l'ha detto l'uccellino

graph [grɑ:f] N grafico

graphic ['græfɪk] ADJ grafico(-a); (vivid) vivido(-a); see also **graphics**

graphic designer N grafico(-a)

graphic equalizer N equalizzatore m grafico

graphics ['græfɪks] N (art, process) grafica ▶ NPL (drawings) illustrazioni fpl

graphite ['græfaɪt] N grafite f

graph paper N carta millimetrata

grapple ['græpl] VI: **to** ~ **with** essere alle prese con

grappling iron ['græplɪŋ-] N (Naut) grappino

grasp [grɑ:sp] VT afferrare ▶ N (grip) presa; (fig) potere m; comprensione f; **to have sth within one's** ~ avere qc a portata di mano; **to have a good** ~ **of** (subject) avere una buona padronanza di
▶ **grasp at** VT FUS (rope etc) afferrarsi a, aggrapparsi a; (fig: opportunity) non farsi sfuggire, approfittare di

grasping ['grɑ:spɪŋ] ADJ avido(-a)

grass [grɑ:s] N erba; (pasture) pascolo, prato; (BRIT col: informer) informatore(-trice); (ex-terrorist) pentito(-a)

grasshopper ['grɑ:shɒpə'] N cavalletta

grassland ['grɑ:slænd] N prateria

grass roots NPL (fig) base f

grass snake N natrice f

grassy ['grɑ:sɪ] ADJ erboso(-a)

grate [greɪt] N graticola (del focolare) ▶ VI
cigolare, stridere ▶ VT (Culin) grattugiare

grateful ['greɪtful] ADJ grato(-a),
riconoscente

gratefully ['greɪtfulɪ] ADV con gratitudine

grater ['greɪtəʳ] N grattugia

gratification [grætɪfɪ'keɪʃən] N
soddisfazione f

gratify ['grætɪfaɪ] VT appagare; (whim)
soddisfare

gratifying ['grætɪfaɪɪŋ] ADJ gradito(-a),
soddisfacente

grating ['greɪtɪŋ] N (iron bars) grata ▶ ADJ
(noise) stridente, stridulo(-a)

gratitude ['grætɪtjuːd] N gratitudine f

gratuitous [grə'tjuːɪtəs] ADJ gratuito(-a)

gratuity [grə'tjuːɪtɪ] N mancia

grave [greɪv] N tomba ▶ ADJ grave, serio(-a)

gravedigger ['greɪvdɪgəʳ] N becchino

gravel ['grævl] N ghiaia

gravely ['greɪvlɪ] ADV gravemente,
solennemente; ~ **ill** in pericolo di vita

gravestone ['greɪvstəun] N pietra tombale

graveyard ['greɪvjɑːd] N cimitero

gravitate ['grævɪteɪt] VI gravitare

gravity ['grævɪtɪ] N (Physics) gravità;
pesantezza; (seriousness) gravità, serietà

gravy ['greɪvɪ] N intingolo della carne; salsa

gravy boat N salsiera

gravy train N: **the ~** (col) l'albero della
cuccagna

gray [greɪ] ADJ (US) = **grey**

graze [greɪz] VI pascolare, pascere ▶ VT (touch
lightly) sfiorare; (scrape) escoriare ▶ N (Med)
escoriazione f

grazing ['greɪzɪŋ] N pascolo

grease [griːs] N (fat) grasso; (lubricant)
lubrificante m ▶ VT ingrassare; lubrificare;
to ~ the skids (US fig) spianare la strada

grease gun N ingrassatore m

greasepaint ['griːspeɪnt] N cerone m

greaseproof paper ['griːspruː f-] N (BRIT)
carta oleata

greasy ['griːsɪ] ADJ grasso(-a), untuoso(-a);
(BRIT: road, surface) scivoloso(-a); (hands,
clothes) unto(-a)

great [greɪt] ADJ grande; (pain, heat) forte,
intenso(-a); (col) magnifico(-a),
meraviglioso(-a); **they're ~ friends** sono
grandi amici; **the ~ thing is that ...** il bello
è che ...; **it was ~!** è stato fantastico!; **we had
a ~ time** ci siamo divertiti un mondo

Great Barrier Reef N: **the ~** la Grande
Barriera Corallina

Great Britain N Gran Bretagna

great-grandchild [greɪt'græntʃaɪld] (pl
-children [-tʃɪldrən]) N pronipote mf

great-grandfather [greɪt'grændfɑːðəʳ] N
bisnonno

great-grandmother [greɪt'grænmʌðəʳ] N
bisnonna

Great Lakes NPL: **the ~** i Grandi Laghi

greatly ['greɪtlɪ] ADV molto

greatness ['greɪtnɪs] N grandezza

Grecian ['griːʃən] ADJ greco(-a)

Greece [griːs] N Grecia

greed [griːd] N (also: **greediness**) avarizia;
(: for food) golosità, ghiottoneria

greedily ['griːdɪlɪ] ADV avidamente;
golosamente

greedy ['griːdɪ] ADJ avido(-a); goloso(-a),
ghiotto(-a)

Greek [griːk] ADJ greco(-a) ▶ N greco(-a);
(Ling) greco; **ancient/modern ~** greco
antico/moderno

green [griːn] ADJ (also Pol) verde; (inexperienced)
inesperto(-a), ingenuo(-a) ▶ N verde m;
(stretch of grass) prato; (also: **village green**)
≈ piazza del paese (of golf course) green m inv;
greens NPL (vegetables) verdura; **to have ~
fingers** or (US) **a ~ thumb** (fig) avere il pollice
verde; **the G~ Party** (BRIT Pol) i Verdi

green belt N (round town) cintura di verde

green card N (BRIT Aut) carta verde; (US
Admin) permesso di soggiorno e di lavoro

greenery ['griːnərɪ] N verde m

greenfly ['griːnflaɪ] N afide f

greengage ['griːngeɪdʒ] N susina Regina
Claudia

greengrocer ['griːngrəusəʳ] N (BRIT)
fruttivendolo(-a), erbivendolo(-a)

greenhouse ['griːnhaus] N serra

greenhouse effect N: **the ~** l'effetto serra

greenhouse gas N gas m inv responsabile
dell'effetto serra

greenish ['griːnɪʃ] ADJ verdastro(-a)

Greenland ['griːnlənd] N Groenlandia

Greenlander ['griːnləndəʳ] N groenlandese
mf

green light N: **to give sb the ~** dare via libera
a qn

green pepper N peperone m verde

green salad N insalata verde

green tax N ecotassa

greet [griːt] VT salutare

greeting ['griːtɪŋ] N saluto; **Christmas/
birthday greetings** auguri mpl di Natale/di
compleanno; **Season's greetings** Buone
Feste

greetings card N cartolina d'auguri

gregarious [grə'gɛərɪəs] ADJ gregario(-a),
socievole

grenade [grə'neɪd] N (also: **hand grenade**)
granata

grew [gruː] PT of **grow**

grey, (US) **gray** [greɪ] ADJ grigio(-a); **to go ~**
diventar grigio

grey-haired ADJ dai capelli grigi

greyhound ['greɪhaund] N levriere m
grey vote N elettori mpl senior
grid [grɪd] N grata; (Elec) rete f; (US Aut) area d'incrocio
griddle ['grɪdl] N piastra
gridiron ['grɪdaɪən] N graticola
gridlock ['grɪdlɔk] N (traffic jam) paralisi f inv del traffico; **gridlocked** adj paralizzato(-a) dal traffico; (talks etc) in fase di stallo
grief [gri:f] N dolore m; **to come to ~** (plan) naufragare; (person) finire male
grievance ['gri:vəns] N doglianza, lagnanza; (cause for complaint) motivo di risentimento
grieve [gri:v] VI affliggersi ▶ VT addolorare; **to ~ for sb** compiangere qn; (dead person) piangere qn
grievous bodily harm ['gri:vəs-] N (Law) aggressione f
grill [grɪl] N (on cooker) griglia; (also: **mixed grill**) grigliata mista ▶ VT (BRIT) cuocere ai ferri; (col: question) interrogare senza sosta; **grilled meat** (BRIT) carne f ai ferri or alla griglia; see **grillroom**
grille [grɪl] N grata; (Aut) griglia
grillroom ['grɪlrum], **grill** ['grɪl] N rosticceria
grim [grɪm] ADJ sinistro(-a), brutto(-a)
grimace [grɪ'meɪs] N smorfia ▶ VI fare smorfie
grime [graɪm] N sudiciume m
grimy ['graɪmɪ] ADJ sudicio(-a)
grin [grɪn] N sorriso smagliante ▶ VI: **to ~ (at)** sorridere (a), fare un gran sorriso (a)
grind [graɪnd] (pt, pp **ground** [graund]) VT macinare; (US: meat) tritare, macinare; (make sharp) arrotare; (polish: gem, lens) molare ▶ VI (car gears) grattare ▶ N (work) sgobbata; **to ~ one's teeth** digrignare i denti; **to ~ to a halt** (vehicle) arrestarsi con uno stridio di freni; (fig: talks, scheme) insabbiarsi (: work, production) cessare del tutto; **the daily ~** (col) il tran tran quotidiano
grinder ['graɪndə^r] N (machine: for coffee) macinino
grindstone ['graɪndstəun] N: **to keep one's nose to the ~** darci sotto
grip [grɪp] N impugnatura; presa; (holdall) borsa da viaggio ▶ VT (object) afferrare; (attention) catturare; **to come to grips with** affrontare; cercare di risolvere; **to ~ the road** (tyres) far presa sulla strada; (car) tenere bene la strada; **to lose one's ~** perdere or allentare la presa; (fig) perdere la grinta
gripe [graɪp] N (Med) colica; (col: complaint) lagna ▶ VI (col) brontolare
gripping ['grɪpɪŋ] ADJ avvincente
grisly ['grɪzlɪ] ADJ macabro(-a), orrido(-a)
grist [grɪst] N (fig): **it's (all) ~ to the mill** tutto aiuta
gristle ['grɪsl] N cartilagine f

grit [grɪt] N ghiaia; (courage) fegato ▶ VT (road) coprire di sabbia; **to ~ one's teeth** stringere i denti; **I've got a piece of ~ in my eye** ho un bruscolino nell'occhio
grits [grɪts] NPL (US) macinato grosso (di avena etc)
grizzle ['grɪzl] VI (BRIT) piagnucolare
grizzly ['grɪzlɪ] N (also: **grizzly bear**) orso grigio, grizzly m inv
groan [grəun] N gemito ▶ VI gemere
grocer ['grəusə^r] N negoziante m di generi alimentari; **~'s (shop)** negozio di alimentari
groceries ['grəusərɪz] NPL provviste fpl
grocery ['grəusərɪ] N (shop) (negozio di) alimentari
grog [grɔg] N grog m inv
groggy ['grɔgɪ] ADJ barcollante
groin [grɔɪn] N inguine m
groom [gru:m] N palafreniere m; (also: **bridegroom**) sposo ▶ VT (horse) strigliare; (fig): **to ~ sb for** avviare qn a; **well-groomed** (person) curato(-a)
groove [gru:v] N scanalatura, solco
grope [grəup] VI andare a tentoni; **to ~ for sth** cercare qc a tastoni
gross [grəus] ADJ grossolano(-a); (Comm) lordo(-a) ▶ N (pl inv: twelve dozen) grossa ▶ VT (Comm) incassare, avere un incasso lordo di
gross domestic product N prodotto interno lordo
grossly ['grəuslɪ] ADV (greatly) molto
gross national product N prodotto nazionale lordo
grotesque [grəu'tɛsk] ADJ grottesco(-a)
grotto ['grɔtəu] N grotta
grotty ['grɔtɪ] ADJ (BRIT col) squallido(-a)
grouch [grautʃ] (col) VI brontolare ▶ N (person) brontolone(-a)
ground [graund] PT, PP of **grind** ▶ ADJ (coffee etc) macinato(-a) ▶ N suolo, terra; (land) terreno; (Sport) campo; (reason: gen pl) ragione f; (US: also: **ground wire**) (presa a) terra ▶ VT (plane) tenere a terra; (US Elec) mettere la presa a terra a ▶ VI (ship) arenarsi; **grounds** NPL (of coffee etc) fondi mpl; (gardens etc) terreno, giardini mpl; **on/to the ~** per/a terra; **below ~** sottoterra; **common ~** terreno comune; **to gain/lose ~** guadagnare/perdere terreno; **he covered a lot of ~ in his lecture** ha toccato molti argomenti nel corso della conferenza
ground cloth N (US) = **groundsheet**
ground control N (Aviat, Space) base f di controllo
ground floor N pianterreno
grounding ['graundɪŋ] N (in education) basi fpl
groundless ['graundlɪs] ADJ infondato(-a)
groundnut ['graundnʌt] N arachide f

g

ground rent N (*BRIT*) canone *m* di affitto di un terreno

ground rules NPL regole *fpl* fondamentali

groundsheet ['graundʃi:t] N (*BRIT*) telone *m* impermeabile

groundsman ['graundzmən] (*irreg*), (*US*) **groundskeeper** ['graundzki:pə*r*] N (*Sport*) custode *m* (di campo sportivo)

ground staff N personale *m* di terra

groundswell ['graundswɛl] N maremoto; (*fig*) movimento

ground-to-air ['graundtu'ɛə*r*] ADJ terra-aria *inv*

ground-to-ground ['grauntə'graund] ADJ: **~ missile** missile *m* terra-terra

groundwork ['graundwə:k] N preparazione *f*

group [gru:p] N gruppo; (*Mus: pop group*) complesso, gruppo ▶ VT (*also:* **group together**) raggruppare ▶ VI (*also:* **group together**) raggrupparsi

groupie ['gru:pɪ] N groupie *mf*, fan *m inv/f inv* scatenato(-a)

group therapy N terapia di gruppo

grouse [graus] N (*pl inv: bird*) tetraone *m* ▶ VI (*complain*) brontolare

grove [grəuv] N boschetto

grovel ['grɔvl] VI (*fig*): **to ~ (before)** strisciare (di fronte a)

grow [grəu] (*pt* **grew** [gru:], *pp* **grown** [grəun]) VI crescere; (*increase*) aumentare; (*develop*) svilupparsi; (*become*): **to ~ rich/weak** arricchirsi/indebolirsi ▶ VT coltivare, far crescere; **to ~ tired of waiting** stancarsi di aspettare

▶ **grow apart** VI (*fig*) estraniarsi

▶ **grow away from** VT FUS (*fig*) allontanarsi da, staccarsi da

▶ **grow on** VT FUS: **that painting is growing on me** quel quadro più lo guardo più mi piace

▶ **grow out of** VT FUS (*clothes*) diventare troppo grande per indossare; (*habit*) perdere (col tempo); **he'll ~ out of it** gli passerà

▶ **grow up** VI farsi grande, crescere

grower ['grəuə*r*] N coltivatore(-trice)

growing ['grəuɪŋ] ADJ (*fear, amount*) crescente; **~ pains** (*also fig*) problemi *mpl* di crescita

growl [graul] VI ringhiare

grown [grəun] PP *of* **grow** ▶ ADJ adulto(-a), maturo(-a)

grown-up [grəun'ʌp] N adulto(-a), grande *mf*

growth [grəuθ] N crescita, sviluppo; (*what has grown*) crescita; (*Med*) escrescenza, tumore *m*

growth rate N tasso di crescita

grub [grʌb] N larva; (*col: food*) roba (da mangiare)

grubby ['grʌbɪ] ADJ sporco(-a)

grudge [grʌdʒ] N rancore *m* ▶ VT: **to ~ sb sth** dare qc a qn di malavoglia; invidiare qc a qn; **to bear sb a ~ (for)** serbar rancore a qn (per)

grudgingly ['grʌdʒɪŋlɪ] ADV di malavoglia, di malincuore

gruelling, (*US*) **grueling** ['gruəlɪŋ] ADJ estenuante

gruesome ['gru:səm] ADJ orribile

gruff [grʌf] ADJ rozzo(-a)

grumble ['grʌmbl] VI brontolare, lagnarsi

grumpy ['grʌmpɪ] ADJ scorbutico(-a)

grunge [grʌndʒ] N (*Mus*) grunge *m inv*; (*style*) moda *f* grunge *inv*

grunt [grʌnt] VI grugnire ▶ N grugnito

G-string ['dʒi:strɪŋ] N (*garment*) tanga *m inv*

GT ABBR (*Aut: = gran turismo*) GT

GU ABBR (*US Post*) = **Guam**

guarantee [gærən'ti:] N garanzia ▶ VT garantire; **he can't ~ (that) he'll come** non può garantire che verrà

guarantor [gærən'tɔ:*r*] N garante *mf*

guard [gɑ:d] N guardia; (*protection*) riparo, protezione *f*; (*Boxing*) difesa; (*one man*) guardia, sentinella; (*BRIT Rail*) capotreno; (*safety device: on machine*) schermo protettivo; (*also:* **fire guard**) parafuoco ▶ VT fare la guardia a; **to ~ (against** *or* **from)** proteggere (da), salvaguardare (da); **to be on one's ~** (*fig*) stare in guardia

▶ **guard against** VI: **to ~ against doing sth** guardarsi dal fare qc

guard dog N cane *m* da guardia

guarded ['gɑ:dɪd] ADJ (*fig*) cauto(-a), guardingo(-a)

guardian ['gɑ:dɪən] N custode *m*; (*of minor*) tutore(-trice)

guard's van N (*BRIT Rail*) vagone *m* di servizio

Guatemala [gwɑ:tə'mɑ:lə] N Guatemala *m*

Guernsey ['gə:nzɪ] N Guernesey *f*

guerrilla [gə'rɪlə] N guerrigliero

guerrilla warfare N guerriglia

guess [gɛs] VI indovinare ▶ VT indovinare; (*US*) credere, pensare ▶ N congettura; **to take** *or* **have a ~** provare a indovinare; **my ~ is that ...** suppongo che ...; **to keep sb guessing** tenere qn in sospeso *or* sulla corda; **I ~ you're right** mi sa che hai ragione

guesstimate ['gɛstɪmɪt] N (*col*) stima approssimativa

guesswork ['gɛswə:k] N: **I got the answer by ~** ho azzeccato la risposta

guest [gɛst] N ospite *mf*; (*in hotel*) cliente *mf*; **be my ~** (*col*) fai come (se fossi) a casa tua

guest-house ['gɛsthaus] N pensione *f*

guest room N camera degli ospiti

guff [gʌf] N (*col*) stupidaggini *fpl*, assurdità *fpl*

guffaw [gʌ'fɔ:] N risata sonora ▶ VI scoppiare di una risata sonora

guidance ['gaɪdəns] N guida, direzione f;
marriage/vocational ~ consulenza
matrimoniale/per l'avviamento
professionale

guide [gaɪd] N (*person, book etc*) guida;
(*BRIT: also*: **girl guide**) giovane esploratrice f
▶ VT guidare; **to be guided by sb/sth** farsi
or lasciarsi guidare da qn/qc ·

guidebook ['gaɪdbʊk] N guida

guided missile N missile m telecomandato

guide dog N (*BRIT*) cane m guida *inv*

guided tour N visita guidata; **what time
does the ~ start?** a che ora comincia la
visita guidata?

guidelines ['gaɪdlaɪnz] NPL (*fig*) indicazioni
fpl, linee fpl direttive

guild [gɪld] N arte f, corporazione f;
associazione f

guildhall ['gɪldhɔːl] N (*BRIT*) palazzo
municipale

guile [gaɪl] N astuzia

guileless ['gaɪllɪs] ADJ candido(-a)

guillotine ['gɪləti:n] N ghigliottina

guilt [gɪlt] N colpevolezza

guilty ['gɪltɪ] ADJ colpevole; **to feel ~ (about)**
sentirsi in colpa (per); **to plead ~/not ~**
dichiararsi colpevole/innocente

Guinea ['gɪnɪ] N: **Republic of ~** Repubblica di
Guinea

guinea ['gɪnɪ] N (*BRIT*) ghinea (= *21 shillings:
valuta ora fuori uso*)

guinea pig ['gɪnɪ-] N cavia

guise [gaɪz] N maschera

guitar [gɪ'tɑːʳ] N chitarra

guitarist [gɪ'tɑːrɪst] N chitarrista mf

gulch [gʌltʃ] N (*US*) burrone m

gulf [gʌlf] N golfo; (*abyss*) abisso; **the
(Persian) G~** il Golfo Persico

Gulf States NPL: **the ~** i paesi del Golfo
Persico

Gulf Stream N: **the ~** la corrente del Golfo

gull [gʌl] N gabbiano

gullet ['gʌlɪt] N gola

gullibility [gʌlɪ'bɪlɪtɪ] N semplicioneria

gullible ['gʌlɪbl] ADJ credulo(-a)

gully ['gʌlɪ] N burrone m; gola; canale m

gulp [gʌlp] VI deglutire; (*from emotion*)
avere il nodo in gola ▶ VT (*also*: **gulp down**)
tracannare, inghiottire ▶ N (*of liquid*) sorso;
(*of food*) boccone m; **in** or **at one ~** in un sorso,
d'un fiato

gum [gʌm] N (*Anat*) gengiva; (*glue*) colla;
(*sweet*) caramella gommosa; (*also*: **chewing-
gum**) chewing-gum m ▶ VT incollare
▶ **gum up** VT: **to ~ up the works** (*col*) mettere
il bastone tra le ruote

gumboil ['gʌmbɔɪl] N ascesso (dentario)

gumboots ['gʌmbu:ts] NPL (*BRIT*) stivali mpl
di gomma

gumption ['gʌmpʃən] N buon senso, senso
pratico

gun [gʌn] N fucile m; (*small*) pistola,
rivoltella; (*rifle*) carabina; (*shotgun*) fucile da
caccia; (*cannon*) cannone m ▶ VT (*also*: **gun
down**) abbattere a colpi di pistola or fucile;
to stick to one's guns (*fig*) tener duro

gunboat ['gʌnbəʊt] N cannoniera

gun dog N cane m da caccia

gunfire ['gʌnfaɪəʳ] N spari mpl

gung-ho [gʌŋ'həʊ] ADJ (*col*) stupidamente
entusiasta

gunk [gʌŋk] N porcherie fpl

gunman ['gʌnmən] N (*irreg*) bandito armato

gunner ['gʌnəʳ] N artigliere m

gunpoint ['gʌnpɔɪnt] N: **at ~** sotto minaccia
di fucile

gunpowder ['gʌnpaʊdəʳ] N polvere f da sparo

gunrunner ['gʌnrʌnəʳ] N contrabbandiere
d'armi

gunrunning ['gʌnrʌnɪŋ] N contrabbando
d'armi

gunshot ['gʌnʃɔt] N sparo; **within ~** a
portata di fucile

gunsmith ['gʌnsmɪθ] N armaiolo

gurgle ['gəːgl] N gorgoglio ▶ VI gorgogliare

guru ['guru:] N guru m inv

gush [gʌʃ] N fiotto, getto ▶ VI sgorgare; (*fig*)
abbandonarsi ad effusioni

gushing ['gʌʃɪŋ] ADJ che fa smancerie,
smorfioso(-a)

gusset ['gʌsɪt] N gherone m; (*in tights, pants*)
rinforzo

gust [gʌst] N (*of wind*) raffica; (*of smoke*)
buffata

gusto ['gʌstəʊ] N entusiasmo

gusty ['gʌstɪ] ADJ (*wind*) a raffiche; (*day*)
tempestoso(-a)

gut [gʌt] N intestino, budello; (*Mus etc*)
minugia ▶ VT (*poultry, fish*) levare le interiora
a, sventrare; (*building*) svuotare; (: *fire*)
divorare l'interno di; **guts** NPL (*col: innards*)
budella fpl; (: *of animals*) interiora fpl; (*courage*)
fegato; **to hate sb's guts** odiare qn a morte

gut reaction N reazione f istintiva

gutsy ['gʌtsɪ] ADJ (*col, style*) che ha mordente;
(*plucky*) coraggioso(-a)

gutted ['gʌtɪd] ADV (*col: upset*) scioccato(-a)

gutter ['gʌtəʳ] N (*of roof*) grondaia; (*in street*)
cunetta

gutter press N: **the ~** la stampa
scandalistica

guttural ['gʌtərl] ADJ gutturale

guy [gaɪ] N (*also*: **guyrope**) cavo or corda di
fissaggio; (: *col: man*) tipo, elemento; (: *figure*)
effigie di Guy Fawkes

Guyana [gaɪ'ænə] N Guayana f

Guy Fawkes Night [-'fɔ:ks-] N (*BRIT*);
vedi nota

La sera del 5 novembre, in occasione della *Guy Fawkes Night*, altrimenti chiamata *Bonfire Night*, viene commemorato con falò e fuochi d'artificio il fallimento della Congiura delle Polveri contro Giacomo I nel 1605. La festa prende il nome dal principale congiurato della cospirazione, Guy Fawkes, la cui effigie viene bruciata durante i festeggiamenti.

guzzle ['gʌzl] vi gozzovigliare ▶ vt trangugiare

gym [dʒɪm] n (*also:* **gymnasium**) palestra; (*also:* **gymnastics**) ginnastica

gymkhana [dʒɪm'kɑːnə] n gimkana

gymnasium [dʒɪm'neɪzɪəm] n palestra

gymnast ['dʒɪmnæst] n ginnasta *mf*

gymnastics [dʒɪm'næstɪks] n, npl ginnastica

gym shoes npl scarpe *fpl* da ginnastica

gym slip n (*Brit*) grembiule *m* da scuola (*per ragazze*)

gynaecologist, (*US*) **gynecologist** [gaɪnɪ'kɒlədʒɪst] n ginecologo(-a)

gynaecology, (*US*) **gynecology** [gaɪnə'kɒlədʒɪ] n ginecologia

gypsy ['dʒɪpsɪ] n = **gipsy**

gyrate [dʒaɪ'reɪt] vi girare

gyroscope ['dʒaɪərəskəup] n giroscopio

Hh

H, h [eɪtʃ] N (*letter*) H, h *f inv or m inv*; **H for Harry,** (*US*) **H for How** = H come Hotel

habeas corpus [ˈheɪbɪəsˈkɔːpəs] N (*Law*) habeas corpus *m inv*

haberdashery [ˈhæbədæʃərɪ] (BRIT) N merceria

habit [ˈhæbɪt] N abitudine *f*; (*costume*) abito; (*Rel*) tonaca; **to get out of/into the ~ of doing sth** perdere/prendere l'abitudine di fare qc

habitable [ˈhæbɪtəbl] ADJ abitabile

habitat [ˈhæbɪtæt] N habitat *m inv*

habitation [hæbɪˈteɪʃən] N abitazione *f*

habitual [həˈbɪtjuəl] ADJ abituale; (*drinker, liar*) inveterato(-a)

habitually [həˈbɪtjuəlɪ] ADV abitualmente, di solito

hack [hæk] VT tagliare, fare a pezzi ▶ N (*cut*) taglio; (*blow*) colpo; (*old horse*) ronzino; (*pej: writer*) scribacchino(-a)

hacker [ˈhækəʳ] N (*Comput*) pirata *m* informatico

hackles [ˈhæklz] NPL: **to make sb's ~ rise** (*fig*) rendere qn furioso

hackney cab [ˈhæknɪ-] N carrozza a nolo

hackneyed [ˈhæknɪd] ADJ comune, trito(-a)

hacksaw [ˈhæksɔː] N seghetto (per metallo)

had [hæd] PT, PP *of* **have**

haddock [ˈhædək] (*pl* ~ *or* **haddocks**) N eglefino

hadn't [ˈhædnt]= **had not**

haematology, (*US*) **hematology** [hiːməˈtɔlədʒɪ] N ematologia

haemoglobin, (*US*) **hemoglobin** [hiːməʊˈɡləʊbɪn] N emoglobina

haemophilia, (*US*) **hemophilia** [hiːməʊˈfɪlɪə] N emofilia

haemorrhage, (*US*) **hemorrhage** [ˈhɛmərɪdʒ] N emorragia

haemorrhoids, (*US*) **hemorrhoids** [ˈhɛmərɔɪdz] NPL emorroidi *fpl*

hag [hæg] N (*ugly*) befana; (*nasty*) megera; (*witch*) strega

haggard [ˈhægəd] ADJ smunto(-a)

haggis [ˈhægɪs] N (SCOTTISH) insaccato a base di frattaglie di pecora e avena

haggle [ˈhægl] VI mercanteggiare; **to ~ (over)** contrattare (su); (*argue*) discutere (su)

haggling [ˈhæglɪŋ] N contrattazioni *fpl*

Hague [heɪɡ] N: **The ~** L'Aia

hail [heɪl] N grandine *f*; (*of criticism etc*) pioggia ▶ VT (*call*) chiamare; (*flag down: taxi*) fermare; (*greet*) salutare ▶ VI grandinare; **to ~ (as)** acclamare (come); **he hails from Scotland** viene dalla Scozia

hailstone [ˈheɪlstəʊn] N chicco di grandine

hailstorm [ˈheɪlstɔːm] N grandinata

hair [hɛəʳ] N capelli *mpl*; (*single hair: on head*) capello; (: *on body*) pelo; **to do one's ~** pettinarsi

hairband [ˈhɛəbænd] N (*elastic*) fascia per i capelli; (*rigid*) cerchietto

hairbrush [ˈhɛəbrʌʃ] N spazzola per capelli

haircut [ˈhɛəkʌt] N taglio di capelli; **I need a ~** devo tagliarmi i capelli

hairdo [ˈhɛəduː] N acconciatura, pettinatura

hairdresser [ˈhɛədrɛsəʳ] N parrucchiere(-a)

hairdresser's N parrucchiere(-a)

hair-dryer [ˈhɛədraɪəʳ] N asciugacapelli *m inv*

-haired [hɛəd] SUFFIX: **fair/long~** dai capelli biondi/lunghi

hair gel N gel *m inv* per capelli

hairgrip [ˈhɛəɡrɪp] N forcina

hairline [ˈhɛəlaɪn] N attaccatura dei capelli

hairline fracture N incrinatura

hairnet [ˈhɛənɛt] N retina (per capelli)

hair oil N brillantina

hairpiece [ˈhɛəpiːs] N toupet *m inv*

hairpin [ˈhɛəpɪn] N forcina

hairpin bend, (*US*) **hairpin curve** N tornante *m*

hair-raising [ˈhɛəreɪzɪŋ] ADJ orripilante

hair remover N crema depilatoria

hair spray N lacca per capelli

hairstyle [ˈhɛəstaɪl] N pettinatura, acconciatura

hairy [ˈhɛərɪ] ADJ irsuto(-a); peloso(-a); (*col: frightening*) spaventoso(-a)

Haiti ['heɪtɪ] N Haiti f

haka ['hɑːkə] N (NEW ZEALAND) danza eseguita dai giocatori prima di una partita

hake [heɪk] (pl ~ or **hakes**) N nasello

halal [hə'lɑːl] N: ~ **meat** carne macellata secondo la legge mussulmana

halcyon ['hælsɪən] ADJ sereno(-a)

hale [heɪl] ADJ: ~ **and hearty** che scoppia di salute

half [hɑːf] N (pl **halves** [hɑːvz]) mezzo, metà f inv; (Sport: of match) tempo; (: of ground) metà campo ▶ ADJ mezzo(-a) ▶ ADV a mezzo, a metà; ~ **an hour** mezz'ora; ~ **a dozen** mezza dozzina; ~ **a pound** mezza libbra; **two and a** ~ due e mezzo; **a week and a** ~ una settimana e mezza; ~ (**of it**) la metà; ~ (**of**) la metà di; ~ **the amount of** la metà di; **to cut sth in** ~ tagliare qc in due; ~ **empty/closed** mezzo vuoto/chiuso, semivuoto/ semichiuso; ~ **past 3** le 3 e mezza; **to go halves (with sb)** fare a metà (con qn); ~ **asleep** mezzo(-a) addormentato(-a)

half-back ['hɑːfbæk] N (Sport) mediano

half-baked [hɑːf'beɪkt] ADJ (col: idea, scheme) mal combinato(-a), che non sta in piedi

half board (BRIT) N mezza pensione

half-breed ['hɑːfbriːd] N = **half-caste**

half-brother ['hɑːfbrʌðəʳ] N fratellastro

half-caste ['hɑːfkɑːst] N (pej) meticcio(-a)

half day N mezza giornata

half fare N tariffa a metà prezzo

half-hearted [hɑːf'hɑːtɪd] ADJ tiepido(-a)

half-hour [hɑːf'auəʳ] N mezz'ora

half-mast ['hɑːf'mɑːst] N: **at** ~ (flag) a mezz'asta

halfpenny ['heɪpnɪ] N mezzo penny m inv

half-price ['hɑːf'praɪs] ADJ a metà prezzo ▶ ADV (also: **at half-price**) a metà prezzo

half-sister ['hɑːfsɪstəʳ] N sorellastra

half term N (BRIT Scol) vacanza a or di metà trimestre

half-time [hɑːf'taɪm] N (Sport) intervallo

halfway [hɑːf'weɪ] ADV a metà strada; **to meet sb** ~ (fig) arrivare a un compromesso con qn

halfway house N (hostel) ostello dove possono alloggiare temporaneamente ex detenuti; (fig) via di mezzo

half-wit ['hɑːfwɪt] N (col) idiota mf

half-yearly [hɑːf'jɪəlɪ] ADV semestralmente, ogni sei mesi ▶ ADJ semestrale

halibut ['hælɪbət] N (pl inv) ippoglosso

halitosis [hælɪ'təʊsɪs] N alitosi f

hall [hɔːl] N sala, salone m; (entrance way) entrata; (corridor) corridoio; (mansion) grande villa, maniero; ~ **of residence** n (BRIT) casa dello studente

hallmark ['hɔːlmɑːk] N marchio di garanzia; (fig) caratteristica

hallo [hə'ləʊ] EXCL = **hello**

hall of residence (BRIT) N casa dello studente

Halloween ['hæləʊ'iːn] N vigilia d'Ognissanti

Secondo la tradizione anglosassone, durante la notte di Halloween, il 31 di ottobre, è possibile vedere le streghe e i fantasmi. I bambini, travestiti da fantasmi, streghe, mostri o simili, vanno di porta in porta e raccolgono dolci e piccoli doni.

hallucination [həluːsɪ'neɪʃən] N allucinazione f

hallucinogenic [həluːsɪnəʊ'dʒenɪk] ADJ allucinogeno(-a)

hallway ['hɔːlweɪ] N ingresso; corridoio

halo ['heɪləʊ] N (of saint etc) aureola; (of sun) alone m

halt [hɔːlt] N fermata ▶ VT fermare ▶ VI fermarsi; **to call a** ~ (**to sth**) (fig) mettere or porre fine (a qc)

halter ['hɔːltəʳ] N (for horse) cavezza

halterneck ['hɔːltənɛk] ADJ allacciato(-a) dietro il collo

halve [hɑːv] VT (apple etc) dividere a metà; (expense) ridurre di metà

halves [hɑːvz] NPL of **half**

ham [hæm] N prosciutto; (col: also: **radio ham**) radioamatore(-trice); (also: **ham actor**) attore(-trice) senza talento

Hamburg ['hæmbəːg] N Amburgo f

hamburger ['hæmbəːgəʳ] N hamburger m inv

ham-fisted ['hæm'fɪstɪd], (US) **ham-handed** ['hæm'hændɪd] ADJ maldestro(-a)

hamlet ['hæmlɪt] N paesetto

hammer ['hæməʳ] N martello ▶ VT martellare; (fig) sconfiggere duramente ▶ VI (at door) picchiare; **to** ~ **a point home to sb** cacciare un'idea in testa a qn; **to** ~ **on** or **at the door** picchiare alla porta ▶ **hammer out** VT (metal) spianare (a martellate); (fig: solution, agreement) mettere a punto

hammock ['hæmək] N amaca

hamper ['hæmpəʳ] VT impedire ▶ N cesta

hamster ['hæmstəʳ] N criceto

hamstring ['hæmstrɪŋ] N (Anat) tendine m del ginocchio

hand [hænd] N mano f; (of clock) lancetta; (handwriting) scrittura; (at cards) mano; (: game) partita; (worker) operaio(-a); (measurement, of horse) ≈ dieci centimetri ▶ VT dare, passare; **to give sb a** ~ dare una mano a qn; **at** ~ a portata di mano; **in** ~ a disposizione; (work) in corso; **we have the matter in** ~ ci stiamo occupando della cosa; **we have the situation in** ~ abbiamo la situazione sotto controllo; **to be on** ~ (person) essere disponibile; (emergency services) essere pronto(-a) a intervenire; **to** ~ (information etc)

a portata di mano; **to force sb's ~** forzare la mano a qn; **to have a free ~** avere carta bianca; **to have in one's ~** (*also fig*) avere in mano *or* in pugno; **on the one ~ ..., on the other ~** da un lato ..., dall'altro
▶ **hand down** VT passare giù; (*tradition, heirloom*) tramandare; (*US: sentence, verdict*) emettere
▶ **hand in** VT consegnare
▶ **hand out** VT (*leaflets*) distribuire; (*advice*) elargire
▶ **hand over** VT passare; cedere
▶ **hand round** VT (*BRIT: information, papers*) far passare; (*distribute: chocolates etc*) far girare; (*hostess*) offrire
handbag ['hændbæg] N borsetta
hand baggage N bagaglio a mano
handball ['hændbɔːl] N pallamano f
handbasin ['hændbeɪsn] N lavandino
handbook ['hændbuk] N manuale m
handbrake ['hændbreɪk] N freno a mano
h & c ABBR (*BRIT*) = **hot and cold (water)**
hand cream N crema per le mani
handcuffs ['hændkʌfs] NPL manette fpl
handful ['hændful] N manciata, pugno
hand-held ['hænd'held] ADJ portatile
handicap ['hændɪkæp] N handicap m inv ▶ VT handicappare; **to be mentally handicapped** essere un handicappato mentale; **to be physically handicapped** essere handicappato
handicraft ['hændɪkrɑːft] N lavoro d'artigiano
handiwork ['hændɪwəːk] N lavorazione f a mano; **this looks like his ~** (*pej*) qui c'è il suo zampino
handkerchief ['hæŋkətʃɪf] N fazzoletto
handle ['hændl] N (*of door etc*) maniglia; (*of cup etc*) ansa; (*of knife etc*) impugnatura; (*of saucepan*) manico; (*for winding*) manovella ▶ VT toccare, maneggiare; manovrare; (*deal with*) occuparsi di; (*treat: people*) trattare; **"~ with care"** "fragile"; **to fly off the ~** (*fig*) perdere le staffe, uscire dai gangheri
handlebar ['hændlbɑːʳ] N, **handlebars** ['hændlbɑːz] NPL manubrio
handling ['hændlɪŋ] N (*Aut*) maneggevolezza; (*of issue*) modo di affrontare
handling charges NPL commissione f per la prestazione; (*for goods*) spese fpl di trasporto; (*Banking*) spese fpl bancarie
hand luggage ['hændlʌgɪdʒ] N bagagli mpl a mano
handmade [hænd'meɪd] ADJ fatto(-a) a mano; (*biscuits etc*) fatto(-a) in casa
handout ['hændaut] N (*money, food*) elemosina; (*leaflet*) volantino; (*at lecture*) prospetto; (*press handout*) comunicato stampa

hand-picked [hænd'pɪkt] ADJ (*produce*) scelto(-a), selezionato(-a); (*staff etc*) scelto(-a)
handrail ['hændreɪl] N (*on staircase etc*) corrimano
handset ['hændset] N (*Tel*) ricevitore m
hands-free ['hændzfriː] N, ADJ (*telephone*) con auricolare; (*microphone*) vivavoce inv
handshake ['hændʃeɪk] N stretta di mano; (*Comput*) colloquio
handsome ['hænsəm] ADJ bello(-a); (*reward*) generoso(-a); (*profit, fortune*) considerevole
hands-on ['hændz'ɔn] ADJ: **~ experience** esperienza diretta *or* pratica
handstand ['hændstænd] N: **to do a ~** fare la verticale
hand-to-mouth ['hændtə'mauθ] ADJ (*existence*) precario(-a)
handwriting ['hændraɪtɪŋ] N scrittura
handwritten ['hændrɪtn] ADJ scritto(-a) a mano, manoscritto(-a)
handy ['hændɪ] ADJ (*person*) bravo(-a); (*close at hand*) a portata di mano; (*convenient*) comodo(-a); (*useful: machine etc*) pratico(-a), utile; **to come in ~** servire
handyman ['hændɪmæn] N (*irreg*) tuttofare m inv; **tools for the ~** arnesi per il fatelo-da-voi
hang [hæŋ] (*pt, pp* **hung** [hʌŋ]) VT appendere; (*pt, pp* **hanged**: *criminal*) impiccare ▶ VI pendere; (*painting*) essere appeso(-a); (*hair*) scendere; (*drapery*) cadere; **to get the ~ of (doing) sth** (*col*) cominiciare a capire (come si fa) qc
▶ **hang about** VI bighellonare, ciondolare
▶ **hang back** VI (*hesitate*): **to ~ back (from doing)** essere riluttante (a fare)
▶ **hang down** VI ricadere
▶ **hang on** VI (*wait*) aspettare ▶ VT FUS (*depend on: decision etc*) dipendere da; **to ~ on to** (*keep hold of*) aggrapparsi a, attaccarsi a; (*keep*) tenere
▶ **hang out** VT (*washing*) stendere (fuori); (*col: live*) stare ▶ VI penzolare, pendere
▶ **hang round** VI = **hang around**
▶ **hang together** VI (*argument etc*) stare in piedi
▶ **hang up** VI (*Tel*) riattaccare ▶ VT appendere; **to ~ up on sb** (*Tel*) metter giù il ricevitore a qn
hangar ['hæŋəʳ] N hangar m inv
hangdog ['hæŋdɔg] ADJ (*guilty: look, expression*) da cane bastonato
hanger ['hæŋəʳ] N gruccia
hanger-on [hæŋər'ɔn] N parassita m
hang-glider ['hæŋglaɪdəʳ] N deltaplano
hang-gliding ['hæŋglaɪdɪŋ] N volo col deltaplano
hanging ['hæŋɪŋ] N (*execution*) impiccagione f
hangman ['hæŋmən] N (*irreg*) boia m, carnefice m

hangover ['hæŋəuvə'] N (after drinking) postumi mpl di sbornia

hang-up ['hæŋʌp] N complesso

hank [hæŋk] N matassa

hanker ['hæŋkə'] VI: **to ~ after** bramare

hankering ['hæŋkərɪŋ] N: **to have a ~ for sth/to do sth** avere una gran voglia di qc/di fare qc

hankie, hanky ['hæŋkɪ] N ABBR = **handkerchief**

Hants ABBR (BRIT) = **Hampshire**

haphazard [hæp'hæzəd] ADJ a casaccio, alla carlona

hapless ['hæplɪs] ADJ disgraziato(-a); (unfortunate) sventurato(-a)

happen ['hæpən] VI accadere, succedere; **she happened to be free** per caso era libera; **to ~ to do sth** fare qc per caso; **if anything happened to him** se dovesse succedergli qualcosa; **as it happens** guarda caso; **what's happening?** cosa succede?, cosa sta succedendo?

▶ **happen (up)on** VT FUS capitare su

happening ['hæpnɪŋ] N avvenimento

happily ['hæpɪlɪ] ADV felicemente; fortunatamente

happiness ['hæpɪnɪs] N felicità, contentezza

happy ['hæpɪ] ADJ felice, contento(-a); ~ (arrangements etc) soddisfatto(-a) di; **to be ~ to do** (willing) fare volentieri; **yes, I'd be ~ to** (certo,) con piacere, (ben) volentieri; **~ birthday!** buon compleanno!; **~ Christmas/New Year!** buon Natale/anno!

happy-go-lucky ['hæpɪgəu'lʌkɪ] ADJ spensierato(-a)

happy hour N orario in cui i pub hanno prezzi ridotti

harangue [hə'ræŋ] VT arringare

harass ['hærəs] VT molestare

harassed ['hærəst] ADJ assillato(-a)

harassment ['hærəsmənt] N molestia

harbour, (US) **harbor** ['hɑ:bə'] N porto ▶ VT (hope) nutrire; (fear) avere; (grudge) covare; (criminal) dare rifugio a

harbour dues, (US) **harbor dues** NPL diritti mpl portuali

harbour master, (US) **harbor master** N capitano di porto

hard [hɑ:d] ADJ duro(-a) ▶ ADV (work) sodo; (think, try) bene; **to look ~ at** guardare fissamente; esaminare attentamente; **to drink ~** bere forte; **~ luck!** peccato!; **no ~ feelings!** senza rancore!; **to be ~ of hearing** essere duro(-a) d'orecchio; **to be ~ on sb** essere severo con qn; **to be ~ done by** essere trattato(-a) ingiustamente; **I find it ~ to believe that ...** stento or faccio fatica a credere che ... +sub

hard-and-fast ['hɑ:dən'fɑ:st] ADJ ferreo(-a)

hardback ['hɑ:dbæk] N libro rilegato

hardboard ['hɑ:dbɔ:d] N legno precompresso

hard-boiled egg ['hɑ:d'bɔɪld-] N uovo sodo

hard cash N denaro in contanti

hard copy N (Comput) hard copy f inv, terminale m di stampa

hard-core ['hɑ:d'kɔ:'] ADJ (pornography) hardcore inv; (supporters) irriducibile

hard court N (Tennis) campo in terra battuta

hard disk N (Comput) hard disk m inv, disco rigido

hard drive N (Comput) hard drive m inv

harden ['hɑ:dn] VT indurire; (steel) temprare; (fig: determination) rafforzare ▶ VI (substance) indurirsi

hardened ['hɑ:dnd] ADJ (criminal) incallito(-a); **to be ~ to sth** essere (diventato) insensibile a qc

hard graft N: **by sheer ~** lavorando da matti

hard-headed ['hɑ:d'hɛdɪd] ADJ pratico(-a)

hard-hearted ['hɑ:d'hɑ:tɪd] ADJ che non si lascia commuovere, dal cuore duro

hard-hitting ['hɑ:d'hɪtɪŋ] ADJ molto duro(-a); **a ~ documentary** un documentario m verità inv

hard labour N lavori forzati mpl

hardliner [hɑ:d'laɪnə'] N fautore(-trice) della linea dura

hard-luck story [hɑ:d'lʌk-] N storia lacrimosa (con un fine ben preciso)

hardly ['hɑ:dlɪ] ADV (scarcely) appena, a mala pena; **it's ~ the case** non è proprio il caso; **~ anyone/anywhere** quasi nessuno/da nessuna parte; **~ ever** quasi mai; **I can ~ believe it** stento a crederci

hardness ['hɑ:dnɪs] N durezza

hard-nosed ['hɑ:d'nəuzd] ADJ (people) con i piedi per terra

hard-pressed ['hɑ:d'prɛst] ADJ in difficoltà

hard sell N (Comm) intensa campagna promozionale

hardship ['hɑ:dʃɪp] N avversità f inv; privazioni fpl

hard shoulder N (BRIT Aut) corsia d'emergenza

hard-up [hɑ:d'ʌp] ADJ (col) al verde

hardware ['hɑ:dwɛə'] N ferramenta fpl; (Comput) hardware m; (Mil) armamenti mpl

hardware shop, (US) **hardware store** N (negozio di) ferramenta fpl

hard-wearing [hɑ:d'wɛərɪŋ] ADJ resistente, robusto(-a)

hard-won ['hɑ:d'wʌn] ADJ sudato(-a)

hard-working [hɑ:d'wə:kɪŋ] ADJ lavoratore(-trice)

hardy ['hɑ:dɪ] ADJ robusto(-a); (plant) resistente al gelo

hare [hɛə'] N lepre f

hare-brained ['hɛəbreɪnd] ADJ folle; scervellato(-a)

harelip ['hɛəlɪp] N (Med) labbro leporino

harem [hɑː'riːm] N harem m inv

hark back [hɑːk-] VI: **to ~ to** (former days) rievocare; (earlier occasion) ritornare a or su

harm [hɑːm] N male m; (wrong) danno ▶ VT (person) fare male a; (reputation) danneggiare; **to mean no ~** non avere l'intenzione d'offendere; **out of ~'s way** al sicuro; **there's no ~ in trying** tentar non nuoce

harmful ['hɑːmful] ADJ dannoso(-a)

harmless ['hɑːmlɪs] ADJ innocuo(-a); inoffensivo(-a)

harmonic [hɑː'mɔnɪk] ADJ armonico(-a)

harmonica [hɑː'mɔnɪkə] N armonica

harmonics [hɑː'mɔnɪks] NPL armonia

harmonious [hɑː'məunɪəs] ADJ armonioso(-a)

harmonium [hɑː'məunɪəm] N armonium m inv

harmonize ['hɑːmənaɪz] VT, VI armonizzare

harmony ['hɑːmənɪ] N armonia

harness ['hɑːnɪs] N (for horse) bardatura, finimenti mpl; (for child) briglie fpl; (safety harness) imbracatura ▶ VT (horse) bardare; (resources) sfruttare

harp [hɑːp] N arpa ▶ VI: **to ~ on about** insistere tediosamente su

harpist ['hɑːpɪst] N arpista mf

harpoon [hɑː'puːn] N arpione m

harpsichord ['hɑːpsɪkɔːd] N clavicembalo

harrow ['hærəu] N (Agr) erpice m

harrowing ['hærəuɪŋ] ADJ straziante

harry ['hærɪ] VT (Mil) saccheggiare; (person) assillare

harsh [hɑːʃ] ADJ (life, winter) duro(-a); (judge, criticism) severo(-a); (sound) rauco(-a); (colour) chiassoso(-a); (light) violento(-a)

harshly ['hɑːʃlɪ] ADV duramente; severamente

harshness ['hɑːʃnɪs] N durezza; severità

harvest ['hɑːvɪst] N raccolto; (of grapes) vendemmia ▶ VT fare il raccolto di, raccogliere; vendemmiare ▶ VI fare il raccolto; vendemmiare

harvester ['hɑːvɪstər] N (machine) mietitrice f; (also: **combine harvester**) mietitrebbia (person) mietitore(-trice)

has [hæz] see **have**

has-been ['hæzbiːn] N (col: person): **he's/she's a ~** ha fatto il suo tempo

hash [hæʃ] N (Culin) specie di spezzatino fatto con carne già cotta; (fig: mess) pasticcio ▶ N ABBR (col) = **hashish**

hashish ['hæʃɪʃ] N hascisc m

hashtag ['hæʃtæg] N (on Twitter) hashtag m inv; cancelletto

hasn't ['hæznt] = **has not**

hassle ['hæsl] N (col) sacco di problemi

haste [heɪst] N fretta; precipitazione f

hasten ['heɪsn] VT affrettare ▶ VI: **to ~ (to)** affrettarsi (a); **I ~ to add that** ... mi preme di aggiungere che ...

hastily ['heɪstɪlɪ] ADV in fretta, precipitosamente

hasty ['heɪstɪ] ADJ affrettato(-a), precipitoso(-a)

hat [hæt] N cappello

hatbox ['hætbɔks] N cappelliera

hatch [hætʃ] N (Naut: also: **hatchway**) boccaporto; (BRIT: also: **service hatch**) portello di servizio ▶ VI (bird) uscire dal guscio; (egg) schiudersi ▶ VT covare; (fig: scheme, plot) elaborare, mettere a punto

hatchback ['hætʃbæk] N (Aut) tre (or cinque) porte f inv

hatchet ['hætʃɪt] N accetta

hatchet job N (col) attacco spietato; **to do a ~ on sb** fare a pezzi qn

hatchet man N (irreg) (col) tirapiedi m inv, scagnozzo

hate [heɪt] VT odiare, detestare ▶ N odio; **to ~ to do** or **doing** detestare fare; **I ~ to trouble you, but** ... mi dispiace disturbarla, ma ...

hateful ['heɪtful] ADJ odioso(-a), detestabile

hater ['heɪtər] N: **cop-~** persona che odia i poliziotti; **woman-~** misogino(-a)

hatred ['heɪtrɪd] N odio

hat trick N (BRIT Sport, also fig): **to get a ~** segnare tre punti consecutivi (or vincere per tre volte consecutive)

haughty ['hɔːtɪ] ADJ altero(-a), arrogante

haul [hɔːl] VT trascinare, tirare ▶ N (of fish) pescata; (of stolen goods etc) bottino

haulage ['hɔːlɪdʒ] N trasporto; autotrasporto

haulage contractor N (BRIT: firm) impresa di trasporti; (: person) autotrasportatore m

haulier ['hɔːlɪər], (US) **hauler** ['hɔːlər] N autotrasportatore m

haunch [hɔːntʃ] N anca; **a ~ of venison** una coscia di cervo

haunt [hɔːnt] VT (fear) pervadere; (person) frequentare ▶ N rifugio; **this house is haunted** questa casa è abitata da un fantasma

haunted ['hɔːntɪd] ADJ (castle etc) abitato(-a) dai fantasmi or dagli spiriti; (look) ossessionato(-a), tormentato(-a)

haunting ['hɔːntɪŋ] ADJ (sight, music) ossessionante, che perseguita

Havana [hə'vænə] N l'Avana

(KEYWORD)

have [hæv] (pt, pp **had**) AUX VB **1** (gen) avere; essere; **to have arrived/gone** essere arrivato(-a)/andato(-a); **to have eaten/slept** avere mangiato/dormito; **he has been kind/promoted** è stato gentile/promosso; **having finished** or **when he had finished**,

he left dopo aver finito, se n'è andato
2 (in tag questions): **you've done it, haven't
you?** l'hai fatto, (non è) vero?; **he hasn't
done it, has he?** non l'ha fatto, vero?
3 (in short answers and questions): **you've made a
mistake — no I haven't/so I have** ha fatto
un errore — ma no, niente affatto/sì, è vero;
we haven't paid — yes we have! non
abbiamo pagato — ma sì che abbiamo
pagato!; **I've been there before, have you?**
ci sono già stato, e lei?
▶ MODAL AUX VB (be obliged): **to have (got) to
do sth** dover fare qc; **I haven't got** or **I don't
have to wear glasses** non ho bisogno di
portare gli occhiali; **I had better leave** è
meglio che io vada
▶ VT 1 (possess, obtain) avere; **he has (got)
blue eyes/dark hair** ha gli occhi azzurri/i
capelli scuri; **have you got** or **do you have a
car/phone?** ha la macchina/il telefono?;
may I have your address? potrebbe darmi il
suo indirizzo?; **you can have it for £5** te lo
do per 5 sterline
2 (+ noun: take, hold etc): **to have breakfast/a
swim/a bath** fare colazione/una nuotata/un
bagno; **to have a cigarette** fumare una
sigaretta; **to have dinner** cenare; **to have a
drink** bere qualcosa; **to have lunch**
pranzare; **to have a party** dare or fare una
festa; **to have an operation** avere or subire
un'operazione; **I'll have a coffee** prendo un
caffè; **let me have a try** fammi or lasciami
provare
3: **to have sth done** far fare qc; **to have
one's hair cut** tagliarsi or farsi tagliare i
capelli; **he had a suit made** si fece fare un
abito; **to have sb do sth** far fare qc a qn; **he
had me phone his boss** mi ha fatto
telefonare al suo capo
4 (experience, suffer) avere; **to have a cold/flu**
avere il raffreddore/l'influenza; **she had
her bag stolen** le hanno rubato la borsa
5 (phrases): (col) **you've been had!** ci sei
cascato!; **I won't have it!** (accept) non mi sta
affatto bene!; see also **haves**
▶ **have in** VT: **to have it in for sb** (col)
avercela con qn
▶ **have on** VT (garment) avere addosso; (be busy
with) avere da fare; **I don't have any money
on me** non ho soldi con me; **have you
anything on tomorrow?** (BRIT) ha qualcosa
in programma per domani?; **to have sb on**
(BRIT col) prendere in giro qn
▶ **have out** VT: **to have it out with sb** (settle a
problem etc) mettere le cose in chiaro con qn

haven ['heɪvn] N porto; (fig) rifugio
haven't ['hævnt] = **have not**
haversack ['hævəsæk] N zaino

haves [hævz] NPL (col): **the ~ and the
have-nots** gli abbienti e i non abbienti
havoc ['hævək] N gran subbuglio; **to play ~
with sth** scombussolare qc; **to wreak ~ on
sth** mettere in subbuglio qc
Hawaii [hə'waɪ:] N le Hawaii
Hawaiian [hə'waɪjən] ADJ hawaiano(-a)
▶ N hawaiano(-a); (Ling) lingua hawaiana
hawk [hɔ:k] N falco ▶ VT (goods for sale)
vendere per strada
hawker ['hɔ:kə*] N venditore m ambulante
hawkish ['hɔ:kɪʃ] ADJ violento(-a)
hawthorn ['hɔ:θɔ:n] N biancospino
hay [heɪ] N fieno
hay fever N febbre f da fieno
haystack ['heɪstæk] N pagliaio
haywire ['heɪwaɪə*] ADJ (col): **to go ~** perdere
la testa; impazzire
hazard ['hæzəd] N (chance) azzardo, ventura;
(: risk) pericolo, rischio ▶ VT (one's life)
rischiare, mettere a repentaglio; (guess,
remark) azzardare; **to be a health/fire ~**
essere pericoloso per la salute/in caso
d'incendio; **to ~ a guess** tirare a indovinare
hazardous ['hæzədəs] ADJ pericoloso(-a),
rischioso(-a)
hazard pay N (US) indennità di rischio
hazard warning lights NPL (Aut) luci fpl di
emergenza
haze [heɪz] N foschia
hazel ['heɪzl] N (tree) nocciolo ▶ ADJ (eyes)
(color) nocciola inv
hazelnut ['heɪzlnʌt] N nocciola
hazy ['heɪzɪ] ADJ fosco(-a); (idea) vago(-a);
(photograph) indistinto(-a)
H-bomb ['eɪtʃbɔm] N bomba H
HD ABBR (= high definition) HD, alta definizione
HDTV N ABBR (= high definition television)
televisore m HD, TV f inv ad alta definizione
HE ABBR = **high explosive**; (Rel, Diplomacy: = His
(or Her) Excellency) S.E.
he [hi:] PRON lui, egli; **it is he who ...** è lui
che ...; **here he is** eccolo; **he-bear** etc orso etc
maschio
head [hɛd] N testa, capo; (leader) capo; (of
school) preside mf; (on tape recorder, computer etc)
testina ▶ VT (list) essere in testa a; (group)
essere a capo di; **heads (or tails)** testa (o
croce), pari (o dispari); **~ first** a capofitto, di
testa; **~ over heels in love** pazzamente
innamorato(-a); **£10 a** or **per ~** 10 sterline a
testa; **to sit at the ~ of the table** sedersi a
capotavola; **to have a ~ for business** essere
tagliato per gli affari; **to have no ~ for
heights** soffrire di vertigini; **to lose/keep
one's ~** perdere/non perdere la testa; **to
come to a ~** (fig: situation etc) precipitare; **to ~
the ball** (Sport) dare di testa alla palla
▶ **head for** VT FUS dirigersi verso

▶ **head off** VT (*threat, danger*) sventare

headache ['hɛdeɪk] N mal *m* di testa;
to have a ~ aver mal di testa

headband ['hɛdbænd] N fascia per i capelli

headboard ['hɛdbɔːd] N testiera (del letto)

head cold N raffreddore *m* di testa

headdress ['hɛddrɛs] N (*of Indian etc*)
copricapo; (*of bride*) acconciatura

headed notepaper ['hɛdɪd-] N carta
intestata

header ['hɛdə^r] N (*BRIT: col: Football*) colpo di
testa; (*: fall*) caduta di testa

head-first ['hɛd'fəːst] ADV a testa in giù;
(*fig*) senza pensare

headhunt ['hɛdhʌnt] VT: **to be headhunted**
avere un'offerta di lavoro da un cacciatore di
teste

headhunter ['hɛdhʌntə^r] N cacciatore *m*
di teste

heading ['hɛdɪŋ] N titolo; intestazione *f*

headlamp ['hɛdlæmp] N (*BRIT*) = **headlight**

headland ['hɛdlənd] N promontorio

headlight ['hɛdlaɪt] N fanale *m*

headline ['hɛdlaɪn] N titolo

headlong ['hɛdlɔŋ] ADV (*fall*) a capofitto;
(*rush*) precipitosamente

headmaster [hɛd'mɑːstə^r] N preside *m*

headmistress [hɛd'mɪstrɪs] N preside *f*

head office N sede *f* (centrale)

head-on [hɛd'ɔn] ADJ (*collision*) frontale

headphones ['hɛdfəunz] NPL cuffia

headquarters [hɛd'kwɔːtəz] NPL ufficio
centrale; (*Mil*) quartiere *m* generale

head-rest ['hɛdrɛst] N poggiacapo

headroom ['hɛdrum] N (*in car*) altezza
dell'abitacolo; (*under bridge*) altezza limite

headscarf ['hɛdskɑːf] N foulard *m inv*

headset ['hɛdsɛt] N = **headphones**

headstone ['hɛdstəun] N (*on grave*) lapide *f*,
pietra tombale

headstrong ['hɛdstrɔŋ] ADJ testardo(-a)

headteacher N (*of primary school*)
direttore(-trice); (*of secondary school*) preside
mf

head waiter N capocameriere *m*

headway ['hɛdweɪ] N: **to make ~** fare
progressi *or* passi avanti

headwind ['hɛdwɪnd] N controvento

heady ['hɛdɪ] ADJ che dà alla testa; inebriante

heal [hiːl] VT, VI guarire

health [hɛlθ] N salute *f*; **Department of H~**
≈ Ministero della Sanità

health care N assistenza sanitaria

health centre N (*BRIT*) poliambulatorio

health food N, **health foods** NPL alimenti
mpl macrobiotici

health hazard N pericolo per la salute

Health Service N: **the ~** (*BRIT*) ≈ il Servizio
Sanitario Statale

healthy ['hɛlθɪ] ADJ (*person*) sano(-a), in
buona salute; (*climate*) salubre; (*food*)
salutare; (*appetite, attitude etc*) sano(-a);
(*economy*) florido(-a); (*bank balance*) solido(-a)

heap [hiːp] N mucchio ▶ VT (*stones, sand*): **to ~
(up)** ammucchiare; **heaps (of)** (*col: lots*) un
sacco (di), un mucchio (di); **to ~ favours/
praise/gifts** *etc* **on sb** ricolmare qn di favori/
lodi/regali *etc*

hear [hɪə^r] (*pt, pp* **heard** [həːd]) VT sentire;
(*news*) ascoltare; (*lecture*) assistere a; (*Law:
case*) esaminare ▶ VI sentire; **to ~ about**
avere notizie di; sentire parlare di; (*have news
of*) avere notizie di; **did you ~ about the
move?** ha sentito del trasloco?; **to ~ from sb**
ricevere notizie da qn
▶ **hear out** VT ascoltare senza interrompere

hearing ['hɪərɪŋ] N (*sense*) udito; (*of witnesses*)
audizione *f*; (*of a case*) udienza; **to give sb a ~**
dare ascolto a qn

hearing aid N apparecchio acustico

hearsay ['hɪəseɪ] N dicerie *fpl*, chiacchiere *fpl*;
by ~ *adv* per sentito dire

hearse [həːs] N carro funebre

heart [hɑːt] N cuore *m*; **hearts** NPL (*Cards*)
cuori *mpl*; **at ~** in fondo; **by ~** (*learn, know*) a
memoria; **to take ~** farsi coraggio *or* animo;
to lose ~ perdere coraggio, scoraggiarsi; **to
have a weak ~** avere il cuore debole; **to set
one's ~ on sth/on doing sth** tenere molto a
qc/a fare qc; **the ~ of the matter** il nocciolo
della questione

heartache ['hɑːteɪk] N pene *fpl*, dolori *mpl*

heart attack N attacco di cuore

heartbeat ['hɑːtbiːt] N battito del cuore

heartbreak ['hɑːtbreɪk] N immenso dolore *m*

heartbreaking ['hɑːtbreɪkɪŋ] ADJ straziante

heartbroken ['hɑːtbrəukən] ADJ affranto(-a);
to be ~ avere il cuore spezzato

heartburn ['hɑːtbəːn] N bruciore *m* di stomaco

heart disease N malattia di cuore

-hearted ['hɑːtɪd] SUFFIX: **a kind~ person**
una persona molto gentile

heartening ['hɑːtnɪŋ] ADJ incoraggiante

heart failure N (*Med*) arresto cardiaco

heartfelt ['hɑːtfɛlt] ADJ sincero(-a)

hearth [hɑːθ] N focolare *m*

heartily ['hɑːtɪlɪ] ADV (*laugh*) di cuore; (*eat*) di
buon appetito; (*agree*) in pieno,
completamente; **to be ~ sick of** (*BRIT*) essere
veramente stufo di, essere arcistufo di

heartland ['hɑːtlænd] N zona centrale;
Italy's industrial ~ il cuore dell'industria
italiana

heartless ['hɑːtlɪs] ADJ senza cuore,
insensibile; crudele

heartstrings ['hɑːtstrɪŋz] NPL: **to tug at sb's
~** toccare il cuore a qn, toccare qn nel
profondo

heart-throb ['hɑːtθrɔb] N rubacuori *m inv*
heart-to-heart ['hɑːttə'hɑːt] ADJ, ADV a cuore aperto
heart transplant N trapianto del cuore
heartwarming ['hɑːtwɔːmɪŋ] ADJ confortante, che scalda il cuore
hearty ['hɑːtɪ] ADJ caloroso(-a); robusto(-a), sano(-a); vigoroso(-a)
heat [hiːt] N calore *m*; (*fig*) ardore *m*; fuoco; (*Sport: also*: **qualifying heat**) prova eliminatoria ▸ VT scaldare; **in** *or* (*BRIT*) **on ~** in calore
  ▸ **heat up** VI (*liquids*) scaldarsi; (*room*) riscaldarsi ▸ VT riscaldare
heated ['hiːtɪd] ADJ riscaldato(-a); (*fig*) appassionato(-a); (*argument*) acceso(-a)
heater ['hiːtər] N radiatore *m*; (*stove*) stufa
heath [hiːθ] N (*BRIT*) landa
heathen ['hiːðn] ADJ, N pagano(-a)
heather ['hɛðər] N erica
heating ['hiːtɪŋ] N riscaldamento
heat-resistant ['hiːtrɪzɪstənt] ADJ termoresistente
heat-seeking ['hiːtsiːkɪŋ] ADJ che cerca fonti di calore
heatstroke ['hiːtstrəuk] N colpo di sole
heatwave ['hiːtweɪv] N ondata di caldo
heave [hiːv] VT sollevare (con forza) ▸ VI sollevarsi ▸ N (*push*) grande spinta; **to ~ a sigh** emettere *or* mandare un sospiro
  ▸ **heave to** (*pt, pp* **hove**) VI (*Naut*) mettersi in cappa
heaven ['hɛvn] N paradiso, cielo; **~ forbid!** Dio ce ne guardi!; **for ~'s sake!** (*pleading*) per amor del cielo!, per carità!; (*protesting*) santo cielo!, in nome del cielo!; **thank ~!** grazie al cielo!
heavenly ['hɛvnlɪ] ADJ divino(-a), celeste
heavily ['hɛvɪlɪ] ADV pesantemente; (*drink, smoke*) molto
heavy ['hɛvɪ] ADJ pesante; (*sea*) grosso(-a); (*rain*) forte; (*weather*) afoso(-a); (*drinker, smoker*) gran (*before noun*); **it's ~ going** è una gran fatica; **~ industry** industria pesante
heavy cream N (*US*) doppia panna
heavy-duty ['hɛvɪ'djuːtɪ] ADJ molto resistente
heavy goods vehicle N (*BRIT*) veicolo per trasporti pesanti
heavy-handed ['hɛvɪ'hændɪd] ADJ (*clumsy, tactless*) pesante
heavy metal N (*Mus*) heavy metal *m*
heavy-set ['hɛvɪ'sɛt] ADJ (*esp US*) tarchiato(-a)
heavyweight ['hɛvɪweɪt] N (*Sport*) peso massimo
Hebrew ['hiːbruː] ADJ ebreo(-a) ▸ N (*Ling*) ebraico
Hebrides ['hɛbrɪdiːz] NPL: **the ~** le Ebridi
heck [hɛk] (*col*) EXCL: **oh ~!** oh no!

▸ N: **a ~ of a lot of** un gran bel po' di
heckle ['hɛkl] VT interpellare e dare noia a (*un oratore*)
heckler ['hɛklər] N agitatore(-trice)
hectare ['hɛktɑːr] N (*BRIT*) ettaro
hectic ['hɛktɪk] ADJ movimentato(-a); (*busy*) frenetico(-a)
hector ['hɛktər] VT usare le maniere forti con
he'd [hiːd] = **he would**; **he had**
hedge [hɛdʒ] N siepe *f* ▸ VI essere elusivo(-a); **as a ~ against inflation** per cautelarsi contro l'inflazione; **to ~ one's bets** (*fig*) coprirsi dai rischi
  ▸ **hedge in** VT recintare con una siepe
hedgehog ['hɛdʒhɔg] N riccio
hedgerow ['hɛdʒrəu] N siepe *f*
hedonism ['hiːdənɪzəm] N edonismo
heed [hiːd] VT (*also*: **take heed of**) badare a, far conto di ▸ N: **to pay (no) ~ to, to take (no) ~ of** (non) ascoltare, (non) tener conto di
heedless ['hiːdlɪs] ADJ sbadato(-a)
heel [hiːl] N (*Anat*) calcagno; (*of shoe*) tacco ▸ VT (*shoe*) rifare i tacchi a; **to bring to ~** addomesticare; **to take to one's heels** (*col*) darsela a gambe, alzare i tacchi
hefty ['hɛftɪ] ADJ (*person*) solido(-a); (*parcel*) pesante; (*piece, price, profit*) grosso(-a)
heifer ['hɛfər] N giovenca
height [haɪt] N altezza; (*high ground*) altura; (*fig: of glory*) apice *m*; (: *of stupidity*) colmo; **what ~ are you?** quanto sei alto?; **of average ~** di statura media; **to be afraid of heights** soffrire di vertigini; **it's the ~ of fashion** è l'ultimo grido della moda
heighten ['haɪtn] VT innalzare; (*fig*) accrescere
heinous ['heɪnəs] ADJ nefando(-a), atroce
heir [ɛər] N erede *m*
heir apparent N erede *mf* legittimo(-a)
heiress ['ɛərɛs] N erede *f*
heirloom ['ɛəluːm] N mobile *m* (*or* gioiello *or* quadro) di famiglia
heist [haɪst] N (*US col*) rapina
held [hɛld] PT, PP *of* **hold**
helicopter ['hɛlɪkɔptər] N elicottero
heliport ['hɛlɪpɔːt] N eliporto
helium ['hiːlɪəm] N elio
hell [hɛl] N inferno; **a ~ of a ...** (*col*) un(-a) maledetto(-a) ...; **oh ~!** (*col*) porca miseria!, accidenti!
he'll [hiːl] = **he will**; **he shall**
hell-bent [hɛl'bɛnt] ADJ (*col*): **to be ~ on doing sth** voler fare qc a tutti i costi
hellish ['hɛlɪʃ] ADJ infernale
hello [hə'ləu] EXCL buon giorno!; ciao! (*to sb one addresses as "tu"*); (*surprise*) ma guarda!
helm [hɛlm] N (*Naut*) timone *m*
helmet ['hɛlmɪt] N casco
helmsman ['hɛlmzmən] N (*irreg*) timoniere *m*

help [hɛlp] N aiuto; *(charwoman)* donna di servizio; *(assistant etc)* impiegato(-a) ▸ VT aiutare; ~! aiuto!; **with the ~ of** con l'aiuto di; **to be of ~ to sb** essere di aiuto *or* essere utile a qn; **to ~ sb (to) do sth** aiutare qn a far qc; **can you ~ me?** può aiutarmi?; **can I ~ you?** *(in shop)* desidera?; ~ **yourself (to bread)** si serva (del pane); **I can't ~ saying** non posso evitare di dire; **he can't ~ it** non ci può far niente
▸ **help out** VI aiutare ▸ VT: **to ~ sb out** aiutare qn

help desk N *(esp Comput)* help desk *m inv*
helper ['hɛlpəʳ] N aiutante *mf*, assistente *mf*
helpful ['hɛlpful] ADJ di grande aiuto; *(useful)* utile
helping ['hɛlpɪŋ] N porzione *f*
helping hand N: **to give sb a ~** dare una mano a qn
helpless ['hɛlplɪs] ADJ impotente; debole; *(baby)* indifeso(-a)
helplessly ['hɛlplɪslɪ] ADV *(watch)* senza poter fare nulla
helpline ['hɛlplaɪn] N ≈ telefono amico; *(Comm)* servizio *m* informazioni *inv (a pagamento)*
Helsinki ['hɛlsɪŋkɪ] N Helsinki *f*
helter-skelter ['hɛltə'skɛltəʳ] N *(BRIT: in funfair)* scivolo (a spirale)
hem [hɛm] N orlo ▸ VT fare l'orlo a
▸ **hem in** VT cingere; **to feel hemmed in** *(fig)* sentirsi soffocare
he-man ['hi:mæn] N *(irreg) (col)* fusto
hematology [hi:mə'tɔlədʒɪ] N *(US)*
= **haematology**
hemisphere ['hɛmɪsfɪəʳ] N emisfero
hemlock ['hɛmlɔk] N cicuta
hemoglobin [hi:məu'gləubɪn] N *(US)*
= **haemoglobin**
hemophilia [hi:məu'fɪlɪə] N *(US)*
= **haemophilia**
hemorrhage ['hɛmərɪdʒ] N *(US)*
= **haemorrhage**
hemorrhoids ['hɛmərɔɪdz] NPL *(US)*
= **haemorrhoids**
hemp [hɛmp] N canapa
hen [hɛn] N gallina; *(female bird)* femmina
hence [hɛns] ADV *(therefore)* dunque; **2 years ~** di qui a 2 anni
henceforth [hɛns'fɔ:θ] ADV d'ora in poi
henchman ['hɛntʃmən] N *(irreg) (pej)* caudatario
henna ['hɛnə] N henna
hen night N *(col)* addio al nubilato
hen party N *(col)* festa di sole donne
henpecked ['hɛnpɛkt] ADJ dominato dalla moglie
hepatitis [hɛpə'taɪtɪs] N epatite *f*
her [hə:ʳ] PRON *(direct)* la, l' + *vowel; (indirect)* le;

(stressed, after prep) lei ▸ ADJ il (la) suo(-a), i (le) suoi (sue); **I see ~** la vedo; **give ~ a book** le dia un libro; **after ~** dopo (di) lei; *see also* **me**; **my**

herald ['hɛrəld] N araldo ▸ VT annunciare
heraldic [hɛ'rældɪk] ADJ araldico(-a)
heraldry ['hɛrəldrɪ] N araldica
herb [hə:b] N erba; **herbs** NPL *(Culin)* erbette *fpl*
herbaceous [hə:'beɪʃəs] ADJ erbaceo(-a)
herbal ['hə:bəl] ADJ di erbe; ~ **tea** tisana
herbicide ['hə:bɪsaɪd] N erbicida *m*
herd [hə:d] N mandria; *(of wild animals, swine)* branco ▸ VT *(drive, gather: animals)* guidare; *(: people)* radunare; **herded together** ammassati *(come bestie)*
here [hɪəʳ] ADV qui, qua ▸ EXCL ehi!; ~! *(at roll call)* presente!; ~ **is**, ~ **are** ecco; ~'**s my sister** ecco mia sorella; ~ **he/she is** eccolo/eccola; ~ **she comes** eccola che viene; **come ~!** vieni qui!; ~ **and there** qua e là
hereabouts ['hɪərəbauts] ADV da queste parti
hereafter [hɪər'ɑ:ftəʳ] ADV in futuro; dopo questo ▸ N: **the ~** l'al di là *m*
hereby [hɪə'baɪ] ADV *(in letter)* con la presente
hereditary [hɪ'rɛdɪtrɪ] ADJ ereditario(-a)
heredity [hɪ'rɛdɪtɪ] N eredità
heresy ['hɛrəsɪ] N eresia
heretic ['hɛrətɪk] N eretico(-a)
heretical [hɪ'rɛtɪkl] ADJ eretico(-a)
herewith [hɪə'wɪð] ADV qui accluso
heritage ['hɛrɪtɪdʒ] N eredità; *(of country, nation)* retaggio; **our national ~** il nostro patrimonio nazionale
hermetically [hə:'mɛtɪklɪ] ADV ermeticamente; ~ **sealed** ermeticamente chiuso
hermit ['hə:mɪt] N eremita *m*
hernia ['hə:nɪə] N ernia
hero ['hɪərəu] *(pl* **heroes)** N eroe *m*
heroic [hɪ'rəuɪk] ADJ eroico(-a)
heroin ['hɛrəuɪn] N eroina *(droga)*
heroin addict N eroinomane *mf*
heroine ['hɛrəuɪn] N eroina *(donna)*
heroism ['hɛrəuɪzəm] N eroismo
heron ['hɛrən] N airone *m*
hero worship N divismo
herring ['hɛrɪŋ] N aringa
hers [hə:z] PRON il (la) suo(-a), i (le) suoi (sue); **a friend of ~** un suo amico; **this is ~** questo è (il) suo; *see also* **mine'**
herself [hə:'sɛlf] PRON *(reflexive)* si; *(emphatic)* lei stessa; *(after prep)* se stessa, sé; *see also* **oneself**
Herts ABBR *(BRIT)* = **Hertfordshire**
he's [hi:z] = **he is**; **he has**
hesitant ['hɛzɪtənt] ADJ esitante, indeciso(-a); **to be ~ about doing sth** esitare a fare qc

h

hesitate ['hɛzɪteɪt] VI: **to ~ (about/to do)** esitare (su/a fare); **don't ~ to ask (me)** non aver timore or paura di chiedermelo

hesitation [hɛzɪ'teɪʃən] N esitazione f; **I have no ~ in saying (that)** ... non esito a dire che ...

hessian ['hɛsɪən] N tela di canapa

heterogeneous [hɛtərəʊ'dʒiːnɪəs] ADJ eterogeneo(-a)

heterosexual [hɛtərəʊ'sɛksjuəl] ADJ, N eterosessuale (mf)

het up [hɛt'ʌp] ADJ agitato(-a)

HEW N ABBR (US: = Department of Health, Education, and Welfare) ministero della sanità, della pubblica istruzione e della previdenza sociale

hew [hjuː] VT tagliare (con l'accetta)

hex [hɛks] (US) N stregoneria ▶ VT stregare

hexagon ['hɛksəgən] N esagono

hexagonal [hɛk'sægənl] ADJ esagonale

hey [heɪ] EXCL ehi!

heyday ['heɪdeɪ] N: **the ~ of** i bei giorni di, l'età d'oro di

HF N ABBR (= high frequency) AF

HGV N ABBR = **heavy goods vehicle**

HI ABBR (US) = **Hawaii**

hi [haɪ] EXCL ciao!

hiatus [haɪ'eɪtəs] N vuoto; (Ling) iato

hibernate ['haɪbəneɪt] VI ibernare

hibernation [haɪbə'neɪʃən] N letargo, ibernazione f

hiccough, hiccup ['hɪkʌp] VI singhiozzare ▶ N singhiozzo; **to have (the) hiccoughs** avere il singhiozzo

hick [hɪk] N (US col) buzzurro(-a)

hid [hɪd] PT of **hide**

hidden ['hɪdn] PP of **hide** ▶ ADJ nascosto(-a); **there are no ~ extras** è veramente tutto compreso nel prezzo; **~ agenda** programma m occulto

hide [haɪd] (pt **hid**, pp **hidden**) N (skin) pelle f ▶ VT: **to ~ sth (from sb)** nascondere qc (a qn) ▶ VI: **to ~ (from sb)** nascondersi (da qn)

hide-and-seek ['haɪdən'siːk] N rimpiattino

hideaway ['haɪdəweɪ] N nascondiglio

hideous ['hɪdɪəs] ADJ laido(-a); orribile

hide-out ['haɪdaut] N nascondiglio

hiding ['haɪdɪŋ] N (beating) bastonata; **to be in ~** (concealed) tenersi nascosto(-a)

hiding place N nascondiglio

hierarchy ['haɪərɑːkɪ] N gerarchia

hieroglyphic [haɪərə'glɪfɪk] ADJ geroglifico(-a); **hieroglyphics** NPL geroglifici mpl

hi-fi ['haɪfaɪ] ADJ, N ABBR (= high fidelity) hi-fi (m) inv

higgledy-piggledy ['hɪgldɪ'pɪgldɪ] ADV alla rinfusa

high [haɪ] ADJ alto(-a); (speed, respect, number) grande; (wind) forte; (voice) acuto(-a); (BRIT: Culin: meat, game) frollato(-a); (: spoilt) andato(-a) a male; (col: on drugs) fatto(-a); (: on drink) su di giri ▶ ADV alto, in alto ▶ N: **exports have reached a new ~** le esportazioni hanno toccato un nuovo record; **20m ~** alto(-a) 20m; **to pay a ~ price for sth** pagare (molto) caro qc

highball ['haɪbɔːl] N (US: drink) whisky (or brandy) e soda con ghiaccio

highboy ['haɪbɔɪ] N (US) cassettone m

highbrow ['haɪbrau] ADJ, N intellettuale (mf)

highchair ['haɪtʃɛəʳ] N seggiolone m

high-class ['haɪ'klɑːs] ADJ (neighbourhood) elegante; (hotel) di prim'ordine; (person) di gran classe; (food) raffinato(-a)

High Court N alta corte f; vedi nota

Nel sistema legale inglese e gallese, la High Court e la Court of Appeal compongono la Supreme Court of Judicature, e si occupa di casi più importanti e complessi. In Scozia, invece, la High Court è la corte che si occupa dei reati più gravi e corrisponde alla crown court inglese.

higher ['haɪəʳ] ADJ (form of life, study etc) superiore ▶ ADV più in alto, più in su

higher education N istruzione f superiore or universitaria

highfalutin [haɪfə'luːtɪn] ADJ (col) pretenzioso(-a)

high finance N alta finanza

high-flier, high-flyer [haɪ'flaɪəʳ] N (giovane) promessa (fig)

high-flying [haɪ'flaɪɪŋ] ADJ (fig) promettente

high-handed [haɪ'hændɪd] ADJ prepotente

high-heeled [haɪ'hiːld] ADJ a tacchi alti

high heels NPL (heels) tacchi mpl alti; (shoes) scarpe fpl con i tacchi alti

highjack ['haɪdʒæk] VT, N = **hijack**

high jump N (Sport) salto in alto

highlands ['haɪləndz] NPL zona montuosa; **the H~** le Highlands scozzesi

high-level ['haɪlɛvl] ADJ (talks etc, Comput) ad alto livello

highlight ['haɪlaɪt] N (fig: of event) momento culminante; (in hair) colpo di sole ▶ VT mettere in evidenza; **highlights** NPL (in hair) colpi mpl di sole

highlighter ['haɪlaɪtəʳ] N (pen) evidenziatore m

highly ['haɪlɪ] ADV molto; **~ paid** pagato molto bene; **to speak ~ of** parlare molto bene di

highly-strung ['haɪlɪ'strʌŋ] ADJ teso(-a) di nervi, eccitabile

High Mass N messa cantata or solenne

highness ['haɪnɪs] N altezza; **Her H~** Sua Altezza

high-pitched [haɪ'pɪtʃt] ADJ acuto(-a)

high point N: **the ~** il momento più importante

high-powered ['haɪ'pauəd] ADJ (engine) molto potente, ad alta potenza; (fig: person) di prestigio

high-pressure ['haɪprɛʃəʳ] ADJ ad alta pressione; (fig) aggressivo(-a)

high-rise N (also: **high-rise block, high-rise building**) palazzone m

high-rise block ['haɪraɪz-] N palazzone m

high school N (BRIT) scuola secondaria; (US) istituto d'istruzione secondaria; vedi nota

> Negli Stati Uniti la high school è un istituto di istruzione secondaria. Si suddivide in junior high school (dal settimo al nono anno di corso) e senior high school (dal decimo al dodicesimo), dove vengono impartiti sia insegnamenti scolastici che di formazione professionale. In Gran Bretagna molte scuole secondarie si chiamano high school.

high season N (BRIT) alta stagione

high spirits NPL buonumore m, euforia; **to be in ~** essere euforico(-a)

high street N (BRIT) strada principale

high-tech ADJ (col) high-tech inv

highway ['haɪweɪ] N strada maestra; **the information ~** l'autostrada telematica

Highway Code N (BRIT) codice m della strada

highwayman ['haɪweɪmən] N (irreg) bandito

hijack ['haɪdʒæk] VT dirottare ▶ N dirottamento; (also: **hijacking**) pirateria aerea

hijacker ['haɪdʒækəʳ] N dirottatore(-trice)

hike [haɪk] VI fare un'escursione a piedi ▶ N escursione f a piedi; (col: in prices etc) aumento ▶ VT (col) aumentare

hiker ['haɪkəʳ] N escursionista mf

hiking ['haɪkɪŋ] N escursioni fpl a piedi

hilarious [hɪ'lɛərɪəs] ADJ che fa schiantare dal ridere; (behaviour, event) spassosissimo(-a)

hilarity [hɪ'lærɪtɪ] N ilarità

hill [hɪl] N collina, colle m; (fairly high) montagna; (on road) salita

hillbilly ['hɪlbɪlɪ] N (US) montanaro(-a) dal sud degli Stati Uniti; (pej) zotico(-a)

hillock ['hɪlək] N collinetta, poggio

hillside ['hɪlsaɪd] N fianco della collina

hill start N (Aut) partenza in salita

hill walking N escursioni fpl in collina

hilly ['hɪlɪ] ADJ collinoso(-a)

hilt [hɪlt] N (of sword) elsa; **to the ~** (fig: support) fino in fondo

him [hɪm] PRON (direct) lo, l' +vowel; (indirect) gli; (stressed, after prep) lui; **I see ~** lo vedo; **give ~ a book** gli dia un libro; **after ~** dopo (di) lui

Himalayas [hɪmə'leɪəz] NPL: **the ~** l'Himalaia m

himself [hɪm'sɛlf] PRON (reflexive) si; (emphatic) lui stesso; (after prep) se stesso, sé; see also **oneself**

hind [haɪnd] ADJ posteriore ▶ N cerva

hinder ['hɪndəʳ] VT ostacolare; (delay) tardare; (prevent): **to ~ sb from doing** impedire a qn di fare

hindquarters ['haɪndkwɔːtəz] NPL (Zool) posteriore m

hindrance ['hɪndrəns] N ostacolo, impedimento

hindsight ['haɪndsaɪt] N senno di poi; **with (the benefit of) ~** con il senno di poi

Hindu ['hɪnduː] N indù mf

Hinduism N (Rel) induismo

hinge [hɪndʒ] N cardine m ▶ VI (fig): **to ~ on** dipendere da

hint [hɪnt] N (suggestion) allusione f; (advice) consiglio; (sign) accenno ▶ VT: **to ~ that** lasciar capire che ▶ VI: **to ~ at** accennare a, alludere a; **to drop a ~** lasciar capire; **give me a ~** (clue) dammi almeno un'idea, dammi un'indicazione

hip [hɪp] N anca, fianco; (Bot) frutto della rosa canina

hip flask N fiaschetta da liquore tascabile

hip hop N hip-hop m

hippie ['hɪpɪ] N hippy mf

hippo ['hɪpəu] (pl **hippos**) N ippopotamo

hip pocket N tasca posteriore dei calzoni

hippopotamus [hɪpə'pɔtəməs] (pl **hippopotamuses** or **hippopotami** [-'pɔtəmaɪ]) N ippopotamo

hippy ['hɪpɪ] N = **hippie**

hire ['haɪəʳ] VT (BRIT: car, equipment) noleggiare; (worker) assumere, dare lavoro a ▶ N nolo, noleggio; **for ~** da nolo; (taxi) libero(-a); **on ~** a nolo

> ▶ **hire out** VT noleggiare, dare a nolo or noleggio, affittare

hire car, hired car N (BRIT) macchina a nolo

hire purchase N (BRIT) acquisto (or vendita) rateale; **to buy sth on ~** comprare qc a rate

his [hɪz] ADJ, PRON il (la) suo (sua), i (le) suoi (sue); **this is ~** questo è (il) suo; see also **my**; **mine**[1]

Hispanic [hɪs'pænɪk] ADJ ispanico(-a)

hiss [hɪs] VI fischiare; (cat, snake) sibilare ▶ N fischio; sibilo

histogram ['hɪstəgræm] N istogramma m

historian [hɪ'stɔːrɪən] N storico(-a)

historic [hɪ'stɔrɪk], **historical** [hɪ'stɔrɪkl] ADJ storico(-a)

history ['hɪstərɪ] N storia; **there's a long ~ of that illness in his family** ci sono molti precedenti (della malattia) nella sua famiglia

histrionics [hɪstrɪ'ɔnɪks] N istrionismo

hit [hɪt] (pt, pp ~) VT colpire, picchiare; (knock against) battere; (reach: target) raggiungere; (collide with: car) urtare contro; (fig: affect) colpire; (find: problem) incontrare ▶ N colpo;

(*success, song*) successo; **to ~ the headlines** far titolo; **to ~ the road** (*col*) mettersi in cammino; **to ~ it off with sb** andare molto d'accordo con qn; **to get a ~/10,000 hits** (*Comput*) trovare una pagina Web/10.000 pagine Web; **our web page had 10,000 hits last month** lo scorso mese il nostro sito ha avuto 10.000 visitatori

▶ **hit back** vi: **to ~ back at sb** restituire il colpo a qn

▶ **hit out at** vt fus sferrare dei colpi contro; (*fig*) attaccare

▶ **hit (up)on** vt fus (*answer*) imbroccare, azzeccare; (*solution*) trovare (per caso)

hit-and-run driver ['hɪtænd'rʌn-] n pirata m della strada

hitch [hɪtʃ] vt (*fasten*) attaccare; (*also:* **hitch up**) tirare su ▶ n (*difficulty*) intoppo, difficoltà f inv; **technical ~** difficoltà tecnica; **to ~ a lift** fare l'autostop

▶ **hitch up** vt (*horse, cart*) attaccare

hitch-hike ['hɪtʃhaɪk] vi fare l'autostop

hitch-hiker ['hɪtʃhaɪkər] n autostoppista mf

hitch-hiking n autostop m

hi-tech ['haɪ'tɛk] adj high-tech inv, a tecnologia avanzata

hitherto ['hɪðə'tu:] adv finora

hit list n libro nero

hitman ['hɪtmæn] n (*irreg*) (*col*) sicario

hit-or-miss ['hɪtə'mɪs] adj casuale; **it's ~ whether ...** è in dubbio se ...; **the service in this hotel is very ~** il servizio dell'albergo lascia a desiderare

hit parade n hit-parade f

HIV n abbr (= *human immunodeficiency virus*) virus m inv di immunodeficienza; **~-negative/-positive** adj sieronegativo(-a)/sieropositivo(-a)

hive [haɪv] n alveare m; **the shop was a ~ of activity** (*fig*) c'era una grande attività nel negozio

▶ **hive off** vt (*col*) separare

hl abbr (= *hectolitre*) hl

HM abbr (= *His (or Her) Majesty*) S.M. (= *Sua Maestà*)

HMG abbr (*Brit*) = **Her Majesty's Government; His Majesty's Government**

HMI n abbr (*Brit Scol:* = *His (or Her) Majesty's Inspector*) ≈ ispettore m scolastico

HMO n abbr (*US:* = *Health Maintenance Organization*) organo per la salvaguardia della salute pubblica

HMS abbr (*Brit*) = **His Majesty's Ship; Her Majesty's Ship**

HNC n abbr (*Brit:* = *Higher National Certificate*) diploma di istituto tecnico o professionale

HND n abbr (*Brit:* = *Higher National Diploma*) diploma in materie tecniche equivalente ad una laurea

hoard [hɔ:d] n (*of food*) provviste fpl; (*of money*) gruzzolo ▶ vt ammassare

hoarding ['hɔ:dɪŋ] n (*Brit*) tabellone m per affissioni

hoarfrost ['hɔ:frɔst] n brina

hoarse [hɔ:s] adj rauco(-a)

hoax [həuks] n scherzo; falso allarme

hob [hɔb] n piastra (con fornelli)

hobble ['hɔbl] vi zoppicare

hobby ['hɔbɪ] n hobby m inv, passatempo

hobby-horse ['hɔbɪhɔ:s] n cavallo a dondolo; (*fig*) chiodo fisso

hobnail boots ['hɔbneɪl-], **hobnailed boots** ['hɔbneɪld-] n scarponi mpl chiodati

hobnob ['hɔbnɔb] vi: **to ~ (with)** mescolarsi (con)

hobo ['həubəu] n (*US*) vagabondo

hock [hɔk] n (*Brit: wine*) vino del Reno; (*of animal, Culin*) garretto; (*col*): **to be in ~** avere debiti

hockey ['hɔkɪ] n hockey m

hockey stick n bastone m da hockey

hocus-pocus ['həukəs'pəukəs] n (*trickery*) trucco; (*words: of magician*) abracadabra m inv; (: *jargon*) parolone fpl

hod [hɔd] n (*Tech*) cassetta per portare i mattoni

hodgepodge ['hɔdʒpɔdʒ] n = **hotchpotch**

hoe [həu] n zappa ▶ vt (*ground*) zappare

hog [hɔg] n maiale m ▶ vt (*fig*) arraffare; **to go the whole ~** farlo fino in fondo

Hogmanay [hɔgmə'neɪ] n (*Scottish*) ≈ San Silvestro

hogwash ['hɔgwɔʃ] n (*col*) stupidaggini fpl

hoist [hɔɪst] n paranco ▶ vt issare

hoity-toity [hɔɪtɪ'tɔɪtɪ] adj (*col*) altezzoso(-a)

hold [həuld] (*pt, pp* **held**) vt tenere; (*contain*) contenere; (*keep back*) trattenere; (*believe*) mantenere; considerare; (*possess*) avere, possedere; detenere ▶ vi (*withstand pressure*) tenere; (*be valid*) essere valido(-a) ▶ n presa; (*fig*) potere m; (*control*): **to have a ~ over** avere controllo su; (*Naut*) stiva; **~ the line!** (*Tel*) resti in linea!; **to ~ office** (*Pol*) essere in carica; **to ~ sb responsible for sth** considerare *or* ritenere qn responsabile di qc; **to ~ one's own** (*fig*) difendersi bene; **he holds the view that ...** è del parere che ...; **to ~ firm** *or* **fast** resistere bene, tenere; **to catch** *or* **get (a) ~ of** afferrare; **to get ~ of** (*fig*) trovare; **to get ~ of o.s.** trattenersi

▶ **hold back** vt trattenere; (*secret*) tenere celato(-a); **to ~ sb back from doing sth** impedire a qn di fare qc

▶ **hold down** vt (*person*) tenere a terra; (*job*) tenere

▶ **hold forth** vi fare *or* tenere una concione

▶ **hold off** vt tener lontano ▶ vi (*rain*): **if the rain holds off** se continua a non piovere

▶ hold on VI tener fermo; (*wait*) aspettare; **~ on!** (*Tel*) resti in linea!

▶ hold on to VT FUS tenersi stretto(-a) a; (*keep*) conservare

▶ hold out VT offrire ▶ VI (*resist*): **to ~ out (against)** resistere (a)

▶ hold over VT (*meeting etc*) rimandare, rinviare

▶ hold up VT (*raise*) alzare; (*support*) sostenere; (*delay*) ritardare; (*traffic*) rallentare; (*rob: bank*) assaltare

holdall ['həʊldɔːl] N (BRIT) borsone *m*

holder ['həʊldə^r] N (*container*) contenitore *m*; (*of ticket, title*) possessore (posseditrice); (*of office etc*) incaricato(-a); (*of passport, post*) titolare; (*of record*) detentore(-trice)

holding ['həʊldɪŋ] N (*share*) azioni *fpl*, titoli *mpl*; (*farm*) podere *m*, tenuta

holding company N holding *f inv*

holdup ['həʊldʌp] N (*robbery*) rapina a mano armata; (*delay*) ritardo; (BRIT: *in traffic*) blocco

hole [həʊl] N buco, buca ▶ VT bucare; **~ in the heart** (*Med*) morbo blu; **to pick holes in** (*fig*) trovare da ridire su

▶ hole up VI nascondersi, rifugiarsi

holiday ['hɔlədɪ] N vacanza; (*from work*) ferie *fpl*; (*day off*) giorno di vacanza; (*public*) giorno festivo; **to be on ~** essere in vacanza; **tomorrow is a ~** domani è festa

holiday camp N (BRIT: *for children*) colonia (di villeggiatura); (*also*: **holiday centre**) ≈ villaggio (di vacanze)

holiday home N seconda casa (*per le vacanze*)

holiday job N (BRIT) ≈ lavoro estivo

holiday-maker ['hɔlədɪmeɪkə^r] N (BRIT) villeggiante *mf*

holiday pay N stipendio delle ferie

holiday resort N luogo di villeggiatura

holiday season N stagione *f* delle vacanze

holiness ['həʊlɪnɪs] N santità

holistic [həʊ'lɪstɪk] ADJ olistico(-a)

Holland ['hɔlənd] N Olanda

holler ['hɔlə^r] VI gridare, urlare

hollow ['hɔləʊ] ADJ cavo(-a); (*container, claim*) vuoto(-a); (*laugh*) forzato(-a), falso(-a); (*sound*) cavernoso(-a) ▶ N cavità *f inv*; (*in land*) valletta, depressione *f*

▶ hollow out VT scavare

holly ['hɔlɪ] N agrifoglio

hollyhock ['hɔlɪhɔk] N malvone *m*

Hollywood ['hɔlɪwʊd] N Hollywood *f*

holocaust ['hɔləkɔːst] N olocausto

hologram ['hɔləgræm] N ologramma *m*

hols [hɔlz] NPL: **the ~** le vacanze

holster ['həʊlstə^r] N fondina (di pistola)

holy ['həʊlɪ] ADJ santo(-a); (*bread*) benedetto(-a), consacrato(-a); (*ground*) consacrato(-a); **the H~ Father** il Santo Padre

Holy Communion N la Santa Comunione

Holy Ghost, Holy Spirit N Spirito Santo

Holy Land N: **the ~** la Terra Santa

holy orders NPL ordini *mpl* (sacri)

homage ['hɔmɪdʒ] N omaggio; **to pay ~ to** rendere omaggio a

home [həʊm] N casa; (*country*) patria; (*institution*) casa, ricovero ▶ CPD (*life*) familiare; (*cooking etc*) casalingo(-a); (*Econ, Pol*) nazionale, interno(-a); (*Sport: team*) di casa; (: *match, win*) in casa ▶ ADV a casa; in patria; (*right in: nail etc*) fino in fondo; **at ~** a casa; (*in situation*) a proprio agio; **to go** (*or* **come**) **~** tornare a casa (*or* in patria); **it's near my ~** è vicino a casa mia; **make yourself at ~** si metta a suo agio

▶ home in on VT FUS (*missiles*) dirigersi (automaticamente) verso

home address N indirizzo di casa

home-brew [həʊm'bruː] N birra *or* vino fatto(-a) in casa

homecoming ['həʊmkʌmɪŋ] N ritorno

home computer N home computer *m inv*

Home Counties NPL contee *fpl* intorno a Londra

home economics N economia domestica

home ground N (*fig*): **to be on ~** essere sul proprio terreno

home-grown [həʊm'grəʊn] ADJ nostrano(-a), di produzione locale

home help N (BRIT) *collaboratore familiare per persone bisognose stipendiato dal comune*

homeland ['həʊmlænd] N patria

homeless ['həʊmlɪs] ADJ senza tetto; **the homeless** NPL i senzatetto

home loan N prestito con garanzia immobiliare

homely ['həʊmlɪ] ADJ semplice, alla buona; accogliente

home-made [həʊm'meɪd] ADJ casalingo(-a)

home match N partita in casa

Home Office N (BRIT) ministero degli Interni

homeopathy *etc* [həʊmɪ'ɔpəθɪ] (US) = **homoeopathy** *etc*

home owner N proprietario(-a) di casa

home page N (*Comput*) home page *f inv*

home rule N autogoverno

Home Secretary N (BRIT) ministro degli Interni

homesick ['həʊmsɪk] ADJ: **to be ~** avere la nostalgia

homestead ['həʊmstɛd] N fattoria e terreni

home town N città *f inv* natale

home truth N: **to tell sb a few home truths** dire a qn qualche amara verità

homeward ['həʊmwəd] ADJ (*journey*) di ritorno ▶ ADV verso casa

homewards ['həʊmwədz] ADV verso casa

homework ['həʊmwəːk] N compiti *mpl* (per casa)

homicidal [hɒmɪ'saɪdl] ADJ omicida

homicide ['hɒmɪsaɪd] N (US) omicidio

homily ['hɒmɪlɪ] N omelia

homing ['həʊmɪŋ] ADJ (device, missile) autocercante; ~ **pigeon** piccione m viaggiatore

homoeopath, (US) homeopath ['həʊmɪəʊpæθ] N omeopatico

homoeopathic, (US) homeopathic ['həʊmɪəʊ'pæθɪk] ADJ omeopatico(-a)

homoeopathy, (US) homeopathy [həʊmɪ'ɒpəθɪ] N omeopatia

homogeneous [hɒməʊ'dʒiːnɪəs] ADJ omogeneo(-a)

homogenize [hə'mɒdʒənaɪz] VT omogenizzare

homosexual [hɒməʊ'sɛksjʊəl] ADJ, N omosessuale (mf)

Hon. ABBR = **honourable; honorary**

Honduras [hɒn'djʊərəs] N Honduras m

hone [həʊn] VT (sharpen) affilare; (fig) affinare

honest ['ɒnɪst] ADJ onesto(-a); sincero(-a); **to be quite ~ with you** ... se devo dirle la verità ...

honestly ['ɒnɪstlɪ] ADV onestamente; sinceramente

honesty ['ɒnɪstɪ] N onestà

honey ['hʌnɪ] N miele m; (US col) tesoro, amore m

honeycomb ['hʌnɪkəʊm] N favo ▶ VT (fig): **honeycombed with tunnels** etc pieno(-a) di gallerie etc

honeymoon ['hʌnɪmuːn] N luna di miele, viaggio di nozze

honeysuckle ['hʌnɪsʌkl] N (Bot) caprifoglio

Hong Kong ['hɒŋ'kɒŋ] N Hong Kong f

honk [hɒŋk] N (Aut) colpo di clacson ▶ VI suonare il clacson

Honolulu [hɒnə'luːluː] N Honolulu f

honorary ['ɒnərərɪ] ADJ onorario(-a); (duty, title) onorifico(-a)

honour, (US) honor ['ɒnəʳ] VT onorare ▶ N onore m; **in ~ of** in onore di

honourable, (US) honorable ['ɒnərəbl] ADJ onorevole

honour-bound, (US) honor-bound ['ɒnə'baʊnd] ADJ: **to be hono(u)r-bound to do** dover fare per una questione di onore

honours degree N (Scol) laurea (con corso di studi di 4 o 5 anni); vedi nota

> In Gran Bretagna esistono titoli universitari di diverso livello. Gli studenti che conseguono ottimi risultati e che approfondiscono una o più materie possono ottenere l' honours degree. Questo titolo, abbreviato in Hons., viene posto dopo il titolo ottenuto (ad esempio BA Hons); vedi anche **ordinary degree**.

honours list N (BRIT) elenco ufficiale dei destinati al conferimento di onorificenze; vedi nota

> La honours list è un elenco di cittadini britannici e del Commonwealth che si sono distinti in campo imprenditoriale, militare, sportivo ecc, meritando il conferimento di un titolo o di una decorazione da parte del sovrano. Ogni anno vengono redatte dal primo ministro due honours lists, una a Capodanno e una in occasione del compleanno del sovrano.

Hons. [ɒnz] ABBR (Scol) = **hono(u)rs degree**

hood [hʊd] N cappuccio; (on cooker) cappa; (BRIT Aut) capote f; (US Aut) cofano; (col) malvivente mf

hooded ['hʊdɪd] ADJ (robber) mascherato(-a)

hoodie ['hʊdɪ] N felpa con cappuccio

hoodlum ['huːdləm] N malvivente mf

hoodwink ['hʊdwɪŋk] VT infinocchiare

hoof [huːf] (pl **hoofs** or **hooves** [huːvz]) N zoccolo

hook [hʊk] N gancio; (for fishing) amo ▶ VT uncinare; (dress) agganciare; **to be hooked on** (col) essere fanatico di; **hooks and eyes** gancetti; **by ~ or by crook** in un modo o nell'altro

▶ **hook up** VT (Radio, TV etc) allacciare, collegare

hooligan ['huːlɪɡən] N giovinastro, teppista m

hooliganism ['huːlɪɡənɪzəm] N teppismo

hoop [huːp] N cerchio

hooray [huː'reɪ] EXCL = **hurrah**

hoot [huːt] VI (Aut) suonare il clacson; (siren) ululare; (owl) gufare ▶ N colpo di clacson; **to ~ with laughter** farsi una gran risata

hooter ['huːtəʳ] N (Aut) clacson m inv; (Naut, at factory) sirena

hoover® ['huːvəʳ] N (BRIT) aspirapolvere m inv ▶ VT pulire con l'aspirapolvere

hooves [huːvz] NPL of **hoof**

hop [hɒp] VI saltellare, saltare; (on one foot) saltare su una gamba ▶ N salto; **hops** npl luppoli mpl

hope [həʊp] VT: **to ~ that/to do** sperare che/di fare ▶ VI sperare ▶ N speranza; **I ~ so/not** spero di sì/no

hopeful ['həʊpful] ADJ (person) pieno(-a) di speranza; (situation) promettente; **I'm ~ that she'll manage to come** ho buone speranze che venga

hopefully ['həʊpfulɪ] ADV con speranza; ~ **he will recover** speriamo che si riprenda

hopeless ['həʊplɪs] ADJ senza speranza, disperato(-a); (useless) inutile

hopelessly ['həʊplɪslɪ] ADV (live etc) senza speranza; (involved, complicated) spaventosamente; (late) disperatamente, irrimediabilmente; **I'm ~ confused/lost**

sono completamente confuso/perso

hopper ['hɔpəʳ] N (chute) tramoggia

hops [hɔps] NPL luppoli mpl

horde [hɔːd] N orda

horizon [hə'raızn] N orizzonte m

horizontal [hɔrɪ'zɔntl] ADJ orizzontale

hormone ['hɔːməun] N ormone m

hormone replacement therapy N terapia ormonale (usata in menopausa)

horn [hɔːn] N (Zool, Mus) corno; (Aut) clacson m inv

horned [hɔːnd] ADJ (animal) cornuto(-a)

hornet ['hɔːnɪt] N calabrone m

horny ['hɔːnɪ] ADJ corneo(-a); (hands) calloso(-a)

horoscope ['hɔrəskəup] N oroscopo

horrendous [hɔ'rɛndəs] ADJ orrendo(-a)

horrible ['hɔrɪbl] ADJ orribile, tremendo(-a)

horrid ['hɔrɪd] ADJ orrido(-a); (person) odioso(-a)

horrific [hɔ'rɪfɪk] ADJ (accident) spaventoso(-a); (film) orripilante

horrify ['hɔrɪfaɪ] VT lasciare inorridito(-a)

horrifying ['hɔrɪfaɪɪŋ] ADJ terrificante

horror ['hɔrəʳ] N orrore m

horror film N film m inv dell'orrore

horror-struck ['hɔrəstrʌk], **horror-stricken** ['hɔrəstrɪkn] ADJ inorridito(-a)

hors d'œuvre [ɔː'dəːvrə] N antipasto

horse [hɔːs] N cavallo

horseback ['hɔːsbæk]: **on ~** adj, adv a cavallo

horsebox ['hɔːsbɔks] N carro or furgone m per il trasporto dei cavalli

horse chestnut N ippocastano

horse-drawn ['hɔːsdrɔːn] ADJ tirato(-a) da cavallo

horsefly ['hɔːsflaɪ] N tafano, mosca cavallina

horseman ['hɔːsmən] N (irreg) cavaliere m

horsemanship ['hɔːsmənʃɪp] N equitazione f

horseplay ['hɔːspleɪ] N giochi mpl scatenati

horsepower ['hɔːspauəʳ] N cavallo (vapore), c/v

horse-racing ['hɔːsreɪsɪŋ] N ippica

horseradish ['hɔːsrædɪʃ] N rafano

horse riding N (BRIT) equitazione f

horseshoe ['hɔːsʃuː] N ferro di cavallo

horse show N concorso ippico, gare fpl ippiche

horse-trading ['hɔːstreɪdɪŋ] N mercanteggiamento

horse trials NPL = **horse show**

horsewhip ['hɔːswɪp] VT frustare

horsewoman ['hɔːswumən] N (irreg) amazzone f

horsey ['hɔːsɪ] ADJ (col: person) che adora i cavalli; (appearance) cavallino(-a), da cavallo

horticulture ['hɔːtɪkʌltʃəʳ] N orticoltura

hose [həuz] N (also: **hosepipe**) tubo; (also: **garden hose**) tubo per annaffiare

▶ **hose down** VT lavare con un getto d'acqua

hosepipe ['həuzpaɪp] N see **hose**

hosiery ['həuzɪərɪ] N (in shop) (reparto di) calze fpl e calzini mpl

hospice ['hɔspɪs] N ricovero, ospizio

hospitable [hɔ'spɪtəbl] ADJ ospitale

hospital ['hɔspɪtl] N ospedale m; **in ~**, (US) **in the ~** all'ospedale

hospitality [hɔspɪ'tælɪtɪ] N ospitalità

hospitalize ['hɔspɪtəlaɪz] VT ricoverare (in or all'ospedale)

host [həust] N ospite m; (TV, Radio) presentatore(-trice); (Rel) ostia; (large number): **a ~ of** una schiera di ▶ VT (TV programme, games) presentare

hostage ['hɔstɪdʒ] N ostaggio(-a)

host country N paese m ospite, paese che ospita

hostel ['hɔstl] N ostello; (for students, nurses etc) pensionato; (for homeless people) ospizio, ricovero; (also: **youth hostel**) ostello della gioventù

hostelling ['hɔstəlɪŋ] N: **to go (youth) ~** passare le vacanze negli ostelli della gioventù

hostess ['həustɪs] N ospite f; (BRIT Aviat) hostess f inv; (in nightclub) entraineuse f inv

hostile ['hɔstaɪl] ADJ ostile

hostility [hɔ'stɪlɪtɪ] N ostilità f inv

hot [hɔt] ADJ caldo(-a); (as opposed to only warm) molto caldo(-a); (spicy) piccante; (fig) accanito(-a); ardente; violento(-a), focoso(-a); **to be ~** (person) aver caldo; (thing) essere caldo(-a); (Meteor) far caldo

▶ **hot up** (BRIT col) VI (situation) farsi più teso(-a); (party) scaldarsi ▶ VT (pace) affrettare; (engine) scaldare

hot-air balloon [hɔt'ɛə-] N mongolfiera

hotbed ['hɔtbɛd] N (fig) focolaio

hotchpotch ['hɔtʃpɔtʃ] N (BRIT) pot-pourri m

hot dog N hot dog m inv

hotel [həu'tɛl] N albergo

hotelier [həu'tɛljeɪ] N albergatore(-trice)

hotel industry N industria alberghiera

hotel room N camera d'albergo

hot flush N (BRIT) scalmana, caldana

hotfoot ['hɔtfut] ADV di gran carriera

hothead ['hɔthɛd] N (fig) testa calda

hotheaded [hɔt'hɛdɪd] ADJ focoso(-a), eccitabile

hothouse ['hɔthaus] N serra

hot line N (Pol) telefono rosso

hotly ['hɔtlɪ] ADV violentemente

hotplate ['hɔtpleɪt] N fornello; piastra riscaldante

hotpot ['hɔtpɔt] N (BRIT Culin) stufato

hot potato N (BRIT col) patata bollente; **to drop sb/sth like a ~** mollare subito qn/qc

hot seat N (fig) posto che scotta

hotspot ['hɔtspɔt] N (*Comput: also:* **wireless hotspot**) hotspot *m inv* Wi-Fi
hot spot N (*fig*) zona calda
hot spring N sorgente *f* termale
hot-tempered [hɔt'tɛmpəd] ADJ irascibile
hot-water bottle [hɔt'wɔ:tə-] N borsa dell'acqua calda
hot-wire ['hɔtwaɪəʳ] VT (*col: car*) avviare mettendo in contatto i fili dell'accensione
hound [haund] VT perseguitare ▶ N segugio; **the hounds** la muta
hour ['auəʳ] N ora; **at 30 miles an** ~ a 30 miglia all'ora; **lunch** ~ intervallo di pranzo; **to pay sb by the** ~ pagare qn a ore
hourly ['auəlɪ] ADJ (*ad*) ogni ora; (*rate*) orario(-a) ▶ ADV ogni ora; ~ **paid** *adj* pagato(-a) a ore
house (*pl* **houses** ['hauzɪz]) N [haus] casa; (*Pol*) camera; (*Theat*) sala; pubblico; spettacolo ▶ VT [hauz] (*person*) ospitare, alloggiare; **at** (*or* **to**) **my** ~ a casa mia; **the H~ (of Commons/Lords)** (*BRIT*) la Camera dei Comuni/Lords; **the H~ (of Representatives)** (*US*) ≈ la Camera dei Deputati; **on the** ~ (*fig*) offerto(-a) dalla casa
house arrest N arresti *mpl* domiciliari
houseboat ['hausbəut] N house boat *f inv*
housebound ['hausbaund] ADJ confinato(-a) in casa
housebreaking ['hausbreɪkɪŋ] N furto con scasso
house-broken ['hausbrəukn] ADJ (*US*) = **house-trained**
housecoat ['hauskəut] N vestaglia
household ['haushəuld] N famiglia; casa
householder ['haushəuldəʳ] N padrone(-a) di casa; (*head of house*) capofamiglia *mf*
household name N nome *m* che tutti conoscono
househunting ['haushʌntɪŋ] N: **to go** ~ mettersi a cercar casa
housekeeper ['hauski:pəʳ] N governante *f*
housekeeping ['hauski:pɪŋ] N (*work*) governo della casa; (*also:* **housekeeping money**) soldi *mpl* per le spese di casa; (: *Comput*) ausilio
houseman ['hausmən] N (*irreg*) (*BRIT Med*) ≈ interno
house-owner ['hausəunəʳ] N possessore *mf* di casa
house plant N pianta da appartamento
house-proud ['hauspraud] ADJ che è maniaco(-a) della pulizia
house-to-house ['haustə'haus] ADJ (*collection*) di porta in porta; (*search*) casa per casa
house-train ['haustreɪn] VT (*BRIT: pet animal*) addestrare a non sporcare in casa
house-trained ['haustreɪnd] ADJ (*BRIT: animal*) che non sporca in casa

house-warming party ['hauswɔ:mɪŋ-] N festa per inaugurare la casa nuova
housewife ['hauswaɪf] N (*irreg*) massaia, casalinga
house wine N vino della casa
housework ['hauswə:k] N faccende *fpl* domestiche
housing ['hauzɪŋ] N alloggio ▶ CPD (*problem, shortage*) degli alloggi
housing association N cooperativa edilizia
housing benefit N (*BRIT*) contributo abitativo (*ad affittuari e a coloro che comprano una casa*)
housing conditions NPL condizioni *fpl* di abitazione
housing development, (*BRIT*) **housing estate** N *zona residenziale con case popolari e/o private*
hovel ['hɔvl] N casupola
hover ['hɔvəʳ] VI (*bird*) librarsi; (*helicopter*) volare a punto fisso; **to** ~ **round sb** aggirarsi intorno a qn
hovercraft ['hɔvəkrɑ:ft] N hovercraft *m inv*
hoverport ['hɔvəpɔ:t] N porto per hovercraft
how [hau] ADV come; ~ **are you?** come sta?; ~ **do you do?** piacere!, molto lieto!; ~ **far is it to ...?** quanto è lontano ...?; ~ **long have you been here?** da quanto tempo è qui?; ~ **lovely!** che bello!; ~ **many?** quanti(-e)?; ~ **much?** quanto(-a)?; ~ **many people/much milk?** quante persone/quanto latte?; ~ **old are you?** quanti anni ha?; ~**'s life?** (*col*) come va (la vita)?; ~ **about a drink?** che ne diresti di andare a bere qualcosa?; ~ **is it that ...?** com'è che ...? +*sub*
however [hau'ɛvəʳ] ADV in qualsiasi modo *or* maniera che; (+*adjective*) per quanto +*sub*; (*in questions*) come ▶ CONJ comunque, però
howitzer ['hauɪtsəʳ] N (*Mil*) obice *m*
howl [haul] N ululato ▶ VI ululare; (*baby, person*) urlare
howler ['hauləʳ] N marronata
howling ['haulɪŋ] ADJ: **a** ~ **wind** *or* **gale** un vento terribile
HP N ABBR (*BRIT*) = **hire purchase**
hp ABBR (*Aut*) = **horsepower**
HQ N ABBR (= *headquarters*) Q.G.
HR N ABBR (*US*) = **House of Representatives**; (*human resources: department*) ufficio personale; (: *staff*) isorse umane
hr ABBR (= *hour*) h
HRH ABBR (= *His* (*or Her*) *Royal Highness*) S.A.R.
hrs ABBR (= *hours*) h
HRT N ABBR = **hormone replacement therapy**
HS ABBR (*US*) = **high school**
HST ABBR (= *Hawaiian Standard Time*) fuso orario
HT ABBR (= *high tension*) A.T.
HTML N ABBR (*Comput: = hypertext markup language*) HTML *m inv*

hub [hʌb] N (*of wheel*) mozzo; (*fig*) fulcro
hubbub ['hʌbʌb] N baccano
hubcap ['hʌbkæp] N (*Aut*) coprimozzo
HUD N ABBR (*US*) = **Department of Housing and Urban Development**
huddle ['hʌdl] VI: **to ~ together** rannicchiarsi l'uno contro l'altro
hue [hju:] N tinta; **~ and cry** n clamore m
huff [hʌf] N: **in a ~** stizzito(-a); **to take the ~** mettere il broncio
huffy ['hʌfɪ] ADJ (*col*) stizzito(-a), indispettito(-a)
hug [hʌg] VT abbracciare; (*shore, kerb*) stringere ▶ N abbraccio, stretta; **to give sb a ~** abbracciare qn
huge [hju:dʒ] ADJ enorme, immenso(-a)
hulk [hʌlk] N carcassa
hulking ['hʌlkɪŋ] ADJ: **~ (great)** grosso(-a) e goffo(-a)
hull [hʌl] N (*of ship*) scafo
hullabaloo [hʌləbə'lu:] N (*col: noise*) fracasso
hullo [hə'ləu] EXCL = **hello**
hum [hʌm] VT (*tune*) canticchiare ▶ VI canticchiare; (*insect, plane, tool*) ronzare ▶ N (*also Elec*) ronzio; (*of traffic, machines*) rumore m; (*of voices etc*) mormorio, brusio
human ['hju:mən] ADJ (*irreg*) umano(-a) ▶ N (*also:* **human being**) essere m umano
humane [hju:'meɪn] ADJ umanitario(-a)
humanism ['hju:mənɪzəm] N umanesimo
humanitarian [hju:mænɪ'tɛərɪən] ADJ umanitario(-a)
humanity [hju:'mænɪtɪ] N umanità; **the humanities** gli studi umanistici
humanly ['hju:mənlɪ] ADV umanamente
humanoid ['hju:mənɔɪd] ADJ che sembra umano(-a) ▶ N umanoide mf
human rights NPL diritti mpl dell'uomo
humble ['hʌmbl] ADJ umile, modesto(-a) ▶ VT umiliare
humbly ['hʌmblɪ] ADV umilmente, modestamente
humbug ['hʌmbʌg] N inganno; sciocchezze fpl; (*BRIT: sweet*) caramella alla menta
humdrum ['hʌmdrʌm] ADJ monotono(-a), tedioso(-a)
humid ['hju:mɪd] ADJ umido(-a)
humidifier [hju:'mɪdɪfaɪər] N umidificatore m
humidity [hju:'mɪdɪtɪ] N umidità
humiliate [hju:'mɪlɪeɪt] VT umiliare
humiliating ADJ umiliante
humiliation [hju:mɪlɪ'eɪʃən] N umiliazione f
humility [hju:'mɪlɪtɪ] N umiltà
hummus ['huməs] N purè di ceci
humorist ['hju:mərɪst] N umorista mf
humorous ['hju:mərəs] ADJ umoristico(-a); (*person*) buffo(-a)
humour, (*US*) **humor** ['hju:mər] N umore m

▶ VT (*person*) assecondare; **sense of ~** senso dell'umorismo; **to be in a good/bad ~** essere di buon/cattivo umore
humourless, (*US*) **humorless** ['hju:məlɪs] ADJ privo(-a) di umorismo
hump [hʌmp] N gobba
humpback ['hʌmpbæk] N schiena d'asino; (*BRIT: also:* **humpback bridge**) ponte m a schiena d'asino
humus ['hju:məs] N humus m
hunch [hʌntʃ] N gobba; (*premonition*) intuizione f; **I have a ~ that** ho la vaga impressione che
hunchback ['hʌntʃbæk] N gobbo(-a)
hunched [hʌntʃt] ADJ incurvato(-a)
hundred ['hʌndrəd] NUM cento; **about a ~ people** un centinaio di persone; **hundreds of people** centinaia fpl di persone; **I'm a ~ per cent sure** sono sicuro al cento per cento
hundredth [-ɪdθ] NUM centesimo(-a)
hundredweight ['hʌndrɪdweɪt] N (*BRIT*) = 50.8 kg; = 112 lb; (*US*) = 45.3 kg; = 100 lb
hung [hʌŋ] PT, PP *of* **hang**
Hungarian [hʌŋ'gɛərɪən] ADJ ungherese ▶ N ungherese mf; (*Ling*) ungherese m
Hungary ['hʌŋgərɪ] N Ungheria
hunger ['hʌŋgər] N fame f ▶ VI: **to ~ for** desiderare ardentemente
hunger strike N sciopero della fame
hungover [hʌŋ'əuvər] ADJ (*col*): **to be ~** avere i postumi della sbornia
hungrily ['hʌŋgrəlɪ] ADV voracemente; (*fig*) avidamente
hungry ['hʌŋgrɪ] ADJ affamato(-a); **to be ~** aver fame; **~ for** (*fig*) assetato di
hung up ADJ (*col*) complessato(-a)
hunk [hʌŋk] N bel pezzo
hunt [hʌnt] VT (*seek*) cercare; (*Sport*) cacciare ▶ VI: **to ~ (for)** andare a caccia (di) ▶ N caccia ▶ **hunt down** VT scovare
hunter ['hʌntər] N cacciatore m; (*BRIT: horse*) cavallo da caccia
hunting ['hʌntɪŋ] N caccia
hurdle ['hə:dl] N (*Sport, fig*) ostacolo
hurl [hə:l] VT lanciare con violenza
hurling ['hə:lɪŋ] N (*Sport*) hurling m
hurly-burly ['hə:lɪ'bə:lɪ] N chiasso, baccano
hurrah [hu'rɑ:], **hurray** [hu'reɪ] EXCL urra!, evviva!
hurricane ['hʌrɪkən] N uragano
hurried ['hʌrɪd] ADJ affrettato(-a); (*work*) fatto(-a) in fretta
hurriedly ['hʌrɪdlɪ] ADV in fretta
hurry ['hʌrɪ] N fretta ▶ VI (*also:* **hurry up**) affrettarsi ▶ VT (*also:* **hurry up**: *person*) affrettare; (: *work*) far in fretta; **to be in a ~** aver fretta; **to do sth in a ~** fare qc in fretta; **to ~ in/out** entrare/uscire in fretta; **to ~ back/ home** affrettarsi a tornare indietro/a casa

▶ **hurry along** VI camminare in fretta
▶ **hurry away, hurry off** VI andarsene in fretta
▶ **hurry up** VI sbrigarsi
hurt [həːt] (*pt*, *pp* ~) VT (*cause pain to*) far male a; (*injure*, *fig*) ferire; (*business*, *interests etc*) colpire, danneggiare ▶ VI far male ▶ ADJ ferito(-a); **I ~ my arm** mi sono fatto male al braccio; **where does it ~?** dove ti fa male?
hurtful ['həːtful] ADJ (*remark*) che ferisce
hurtle ['həːtl] VT scagliare ▶ VI: **to ~ past/down** passare/scendere a razzo
husband ['hʌzbənd] N marito
hush [hʌʃ] N silenzio, calma ▶ VT zittire; **~!** zitto(-a)!
▶ **hush up** VT (*fact*) cercare di far passare sotto silenzio
hush-hush ['hʌʃ'hʌʃ] ADJ (*col*) segretissimo(-a)
husk [hʌsk] N (*of wheat*) cartoccio; (*of rice*, *maize*) buccia
husky ['hʌski] ADJ roco(-a) ▶ N cane *m* eschimese
hustings ['hʌstiŋz] NPL (BRIT Pol) comizi *mpl* elettorali
hustle ['hʌsl] VT spingere, incalzare ▶ N pigia pigia *m inv*; **~ and bustle** trambusto
hut [hʌt] N rifugio; (*shed*) ripostiglio
hutch [hʌtʃ] N gabbia
hyacinth ['haiəsinθ] N giacinto
hybrid ['haibrid] ADJ ibrido(-a) ▶ N ibrido
hydrangea [hai'dreinʒə] N ortensia
hydrant ['haidrənt] N (*also*: **fire hydrant**) idrante *m*
hydraulic [hai'drɔlik] ADJ idraulico(-a)
hydraulics [hai'drɔliks] N idraulica
hydrochloric [haidrə'klɔrik] ADJ: **~ acid** acido cloridrico
hydroelectric [haidrəui'lektrik] ADJ idroelettrico(-a)
hydrofoil ['haidrəfɔil] N aliscafo
hydrogen ['haidrədʒən] N idrogeno
hydrogen bomb N bomba all'idrogeno
hydrophobia [haidrə'fəubiə] N idrofobia

hydroplane ['haidrəuplein] N idrovolante *m*
hyena [hai'iːnə] N iena
hygiene ['haidʒiːn] N igiene *f*
hygienic [hai'dʒiːnik] ADJ igienico(-a)
hymn [him] N inno; cantica
hype [haip] N (*col*) battage *m inv* pubblicitario
hyperactive [haipər'æktiv] ADJ iperattivo(-a)
hyperlink ['haipəliŋk] N link *m inv* ipertestuale
hypermarket ['haipəmɑːkit] N (BRIT) ipermercato
hypertension [haipə'tenʃən] N (Med) ipertensione *f*
hypertext ['haipətekst] N (Comput) ipertesto
hyphen ['haifn] N trattino
hypnosis [hip'nəusis] N ipnosi *f*
hypnotic [hip'nɔtik] ADJ ipnotico(-a)
hypnotism ['hipnətizəm] N ipnotismo
hypnotist ['hipnətist] N ipnotizzatore(-trice)
hypnotize ['hipnətaiz] VT ipnotizzare
hypoallergenic [haipəuæələ'dʒenik] ADJ ipoallergico(-a)
hypochondriac [haipə'kɔndriæk] N ipocondriaco(-a)
hypocrisy [hi'pɔkrisi] N ipocrisia
hypocrite ['hipəkrit] N ipocrita *mf*
hypocritical [hipə'kritikl] ADJ ipocrita
hypodermic [haipə'dəːmik] ADJ ipodermico(-a) ▶ N (*syringe*) siringa ipodermica
hypotenuse [hai'pɔtinjuːz] N ipotenusa
hypothermia [haipəu'θəːmiə] N ipotermia
hypothesis [hai'pɔθisis] (*pl* **hypotheses** [-siːz]) N ipotesi *f inv*
hypothetical [haipəu'θetikl] ADJ ipotetico(-a)
hysterectomy [histə'rektəmi] N isterectomia
hysteria [hi'stiəriə] N isteria
hysterical [hi'sterikl] ADJ isterico(-a); **to become ~** avere una crisi isterica
hysterics [hi'steriks] NPL accesso di isteria; (*laughter*) attacco di riso; **to have ~** avere una crisi isterica

I i

I, i [aɪ] N (letter) I, i f inv or m inv; **I for Isaac,** (US) **I for Item** = I come Imola

I [aɪ] PRON io ▶ ABBR (= island, isle) Is.

IA ABBR (US) = **Iowa**

IAEA N ABBR = **International Atomic Energy Agency**

ib. ['ɪb] ABBR (= ibidem: from the same source) ibid

Iberian [aɪ'bɪərɪən] ADJ iberico(-a)

Iberian Peninsula N: **the ~** la Penisola iberica

IBEW N ABBR (US: = International Brotherhood of Electrical Workers) associazione italiana degli elettrotecnici

ibid. ['ɪbɪd] ABBR (= ibidem: from the same source) ibid

i/c ABBR (BRIT) = **in charge**

ICBM N ABBR (= intercontinental ballistic missile) ICBM m inv

ICC N ABBR (= International Chamber of Commerce) C.C.I. f; (US: = Interstate Commerce Commission) commissione per il commercio tra gli stati degli USA

ice [aɪs] N ghiaccio; (on road) gelo ▶ VT (cake) glassare; (drink) mettere in fresco ▶ VI (also: **ice over**) ghiacciare; (also: **ice up**) gelare; **to keep sth on ~** (fig: plan, project) mettere da parte (per il momento), accantonare

Ice Age N era glaciale

ice axe N piccozza da ghiaccio

iceberg ['aɪsbəːg] N iceberg m inv; **tip of the ~** (also fig) punta dell'iceberg

icebox ['aɪsbɔks] N (US) frigorifero; (BRIT) reparto ghiaccio; (insulated box) frigo portatile

icebreaker ['aɪsbreɪkər] N rompighiaccio m inv

ice bucket N secchiello del ghiaccio

ice-cap ['aɪskæp] N calotta polare

ice-cold [aɪs'kəuld] ADJ gelato(-a)

ice cream N gelato

ice-cream soda N (gelato) affogato al seltz

ice cube N cubetto di ghiaccio

iced [aɪst] ADJ (drink) ghiacciato(-a); (coffee, tea) freddo(-a); (cake) glassato(-a)

ice hockey N hockey m su ghiaccio

Iceland ['aɪslənd] N Islanda

Icelander ['aɪsləndər] N islandese mf

Icelandic [aɪs'lændɪk] ADJ islandese ▶ N (Ling) islandese m

ice lolly N (BRIT) ghiacciolo

ice pick N piccone m per ghiaccio

ice rink N pista di pattinaggio

ice-skate ['aɪsskeɪt] N pattino da ghiaccio ▶ VI pattinare sul ghiaccio

ice skating ['aɪsskeɪtɪŋ] N pattinaggio sul ghiaccio

icicle ['aɪsɪkl] N ghiacciolo

icing ['aɪsɪŋ] N (Aviat etc) patina di ghiaccio; (Culin) glassa

icing sugar (BRIT) N zucchero a velo

ICJ N ABBR = **International Court of Justice**

icon ['aɪkɔn] N icona; (Comput) immagine f

ICR N ABBR (US) = **Institute for Cancer Research**

ICRC N ABBR (= International Committee of the Red Cross) CICR m

ICT N ABBR (BRIT Scol: = Information and Communications Technology) informatica

ICU N ABBR = **intensive care unit**

icy ['aɪsɪ] ADJ ghiacciato(-a); (weather, temperature) gelido(-a)

ID ABBR = **identification document**; (US) = **Idaho**

I'd [aɪd] = **I would; I had**

Ida. ABBR (US) = **Idaho**

ID card N = **identity card**

IDD N ABBR (BRIT Tel: = International direct dialling) teleselezione f internazionale

idea [aɪ'dɪə] N idea; **good ~!** buon'idea!; **to have an ~ that ...** aver l'impressione che ...; **I haven't the least ~** non ne ho la minima idea

ideal [aɪ'dɪəl] ADJ, N ideale (m)

idealist [aɪ'dɪəlɪst] N idealista mf

ideally [aɪ'dɪəlɪ] ADV perfettamente, assolutamente; **~ the book should have ...** l'ideale sarebbe che il libro avesse ...

identical [aɪ'dentɪkl] ADJ identico(-a)

identification [aɪdentɪfɪ'keɪʃən] N identificazione f; **means of ~** carta d'identità

identify [aɪ'dɛntɪfaɪ] VT identificare ▶ VI: **to ~ with** identificarsi con
Identikit® [aɪ'dɛntɪkɪt] N: ~ **(picture)** identikit *m inv*
identity [aɪ'dɛntɪtɪ] N identità *f inv*
identity card N carta d'identità
identity parade N (BRIT) confronto all'americana
identity theft N furto d'identità
ideological [aɪdɪə'lɔdʒɪkəl] ADJ ideologico(-a)
ideology [aɪdɪ'ɔlədʒɪ] N ideologia
idiocy ['ɪdɪəsɪ] N idiozia
idiom ['ɪdɪəm] N idioma *m*; (*phrase*) espressione *f* idiomatica
idiomatic [ɪdɪə'mætɪk] ADJ idiomatico(-a)
idiosyncrasy [ɪdɪəu'sɪŋkrəsɪ] N idiosincrasia
idiot ['ɪdɪət] N idiota *mf*
idiotic [ɪdɪ'ɔtɪk] ADJ idiota
idle ['aɪdl] ADJ inattivo(-a); (*lazy*) pigro(-a), ozioso(-a); (*unemployed*) disoccupato(-a); (*question, pleasures*) ozioso(-a) ▶ VI (*engine*) girare al minimo; **to lie ~** stare fermo, non funzionare
▶ **idle away** VT (*time*) sprecare, buttar via
idleness ['aɪdlnɪs] N ozio; pigrizia
idler ['aɪdləʳ] N ozioso(-a), fannullone(-a)
idle time N tempi *mpl* morti
idol ['aɪdl] N idolo
idolize ['aɪdəlaɪz] VT idoleggiare
idyllic [ɪ'dɪlɪk] ADJ idillico(-a)
i.e. ABBR = **id est** (*that is*) cioè
IED [aɪiː'diː] N (= *Improvised Explosive Device*) ordigno esplosivo improvvisato; IED *m inv*
if [ɪf] CONJ se ▶ N: **there are a lot of ifs and buts** ci sono molti se e ma; **I'd be pleased if you could do it** sarei molto contento se potesse farlo; **if I were you ...** se fossi in te ..., io al tuo posto ...; **if so** se è così; **if not** se no; **if necessary** se (è) necessario; **if only** se solo *or* soltanto; **if only he were here** se solo fosse qui; **if only to show him my gratitude** se non altro per esprimergli la mia gratitudine
iffy ['ɪfɪ] ADJ (*col*) incerto(-a)
igloo ['ɪgluː] N igloo *m inv*
ignite [ɪg'naɪt] VT accendere ▶ VI accendersi
ignition [ɪg'nɪʃən] N (*Aut*) accensione *f*; **to switch on/off the ~** accendere/spegnere il motore
ignition key N (*Aut*) chiave *f* dell'accensione
ignoble [ɪg'nəubl] ADJ ignobile
ignominious [ɪgnə'mɪnɪəs] ADJ vergognoso(-a), ignominioso(-a)
ignoramus [ɪgnə'reɪməs] N ignorante *mf*
ignorance ['ɪgnərəns] N ignoranza; **to keep sb in ~ of sth** tenere qn all'oscuro di qc
ignorant ['ɪgnərənt] ADJ ignorante; **to be ~ of** (*subject*) essere ignorante in; (*events*) essere ignaro(-a) di

ignore [ɪg'nɔːʳ] VT non tener conto di; (*person, fact*) ignorare
ikon ['aɪkɔn] N = **icon**
IL ABBR (US) = **Illinois**
ILA N ABBR (US: = *International Longshoremen's Association*) associazione internazionale degli scaricatori di porto
ill [ɪl] ADJ (*sick*) malato(-a); (*bad*) cattivo(-a) ▶ N male *m*; **to take** *or* **be taken ~** ammalarsi; **to feel ~** star male; **to speak/think ~ of sb** parlar/pensar male di qn
Ill. ABBR (US) = **Illinois**
I'll [aɪl] = **I will**; **I shall**
ill-advised [ɪləd'vaɪzd] ADJ (*decision*) poco giudizioso(-a); (*person*) mal consigliato(-a)
ill-at-ease [ɪlət'iːz] ADJ a disagio
ill-considered [ɪlkən'sɪdəd] ADJ (*plan*) avventato(-a)
ill-disposed [ɪldɪs'pəuzd] ADJ: **to be ~ towards sb/sth** essere maldisposto(-a) verso qn/qc *or* nei riguardi di qn/qc
illegal [ɪ'liːgl] ADJ illegale
illegally [ɪ'liːgəlɪ] ADV illegalmente
illegible [ɪ'lɛdʒɪbl] ADJ illeggibile
illegitimate [ɪlɪ'dʒɪtɪmət] ADJ illegittimo(-a)
ill-fated [ɪl'feɪtɪd] ADJ nefasto(-a)
ill-favoured, (US) **ill-favored** [ɪl'feɪvəd] ADJ sgraziato(-a), brutto(-a)
ill feeling N rancore *m*
ill-gotten ['ɪlgɔtn] ADJ: ~ **gains** maltolto
ill health N problemi *mpl* di salute
illicit [ɪ'lɪsɪt] ADJ illecito(-a)
ill-informed [ɪlɪn'fɔːmd] ADJ (*judgement, speech*) pieno(-a) di inesattezze; (*person*) male informato(-a)
illiterate [ɪ'lɪtərət] ADJ analfabeta, illetterato(-a); (*letter*) scorretto(-a)
ill-mannered [ɪl'mænəd] ADJ maleducato(-a), sgarbato(-a)
illness ['ɪlnɪs] N malattia
illogical [ɪ'lɔdʒɪkl] ADJ illogico(-a)
ill-suited [ɪl'suːtɪd] ADJ (*couple*) mal assortito(-a); **he is ~ to the job** è inadatto a quel lavoro
ill-timed [ɪl'taɪmd] ADJ intempestivo(-a), inopportuno(-a)
ill-treat [ɪl'triːt] VT maltrattare
ill-treatment [ɪl'triːtmənt] N maltrattamenti *mpl*
illuminate [ɪ'luːmɪneɪt] VT illuminare; **illuminated sign** insegna luminosa
illuminating [ɪ'luːmɪneɪtɪŋ] ADJ chiarificatore(-trice)
illumination [ɪluːmɪ'neɪʃən] N illuminazione *f*
illusion [ɪ'luːʒən] N illusione *f*; **to be under the ~ that** avere l'impressione che
illusive [ɪ'luːsɪv], **illusory** [ɪ'luːsərɪ] ADJ illusorio(-a)

illustrate ['ɪləstreɪt] vt illustrare
illustration [ɪlə'streɪʃən] N illustrazione f
illustrator ['ɪləstreɪtə'] N illustratore(-trice)
illustrious [ɪ'lʌstrɪəs] ADJ illustre
ill will N cattiva volontà
ILO N ABBR (= *International Labour Organization*)
OIL f
IM N (= *instant messaging*) messaggeria
istantanea
I'm [aɪm] = **I am**
image ['ɪmɪdʒ] N immagine f; (*public face*)
immagine (pubblica)
imagery ['ɪmɪdʒərɪ] N immagini fpl
imaginable [ɪ'mædʒɪnəbl] ADJ
immaginabile, che si possa immaginare
imaginary [ɪ'mædʒɪnərɪ] ADJ
immaginario(-a)
imagination [ɪmædʒɪ'neɪʃən] N
immaginazione f, fantasia
imaginative [ɪ'mædʒɪnətɪv] ADJ
immaginoso(-a)
imagine [ɪ'mædʒɪn] vt immaginare
imbalance [ɪm'bæləns] N squilibrio
imbecile ['ɪmbəsi:l] N imbecille mf
imbue [ɪm'bju:] vt: **to ~ sth with**
impregnare qc di
IMF N ABBR = **International Monetary Fund**
imitate ['ɪmɪteɪt] vt imitare
imitation [ɪmɪ'teɪʃən] N imitazione f
imitator ['ɪmɪteɪtə'] N imitatore(-trice)
immaculate [ɪ'mækjulət] ADJ immacolato(-a);
(*dress, appearance*) impeccabile
immaterial [ɪmə'tɪərɪəl] ADJ immateriale,
indifferente; **it is ~ whether** poco importa
se or che + sub
immature [ɪmə'tjuə'] ADJ immaturo(-a)
immaturity [ɪmə'tjuərɪtɪ] N immaturità,
mancanza di maturità
immeasurable [ɪ'mɛʒərəbl] ADJ
incommensurabile
immediacy [ɪ'mi:dɪəsɪ] N immediatezza
immediate [ɪ'mi:dɪət] ADJ immediato(-a)
immediately [ɪ'mi:dɪətlɪ] ADV (*at once*) subito,
immediatamente; **~ next to** proprio
accanto a
immense [ɪ'mɛns] ADJ immenso(-a); enorme
immensely ADV immensamente
immensity [ɪ'mɛnsɪtɪ] N (*of size, difference*)
enormità; (*of problem etc*) vastità
immerse [ɪ'mə:s] vt immergere
immersion heater [ɪ'mə:ʃən-] N (BRIT)
scaldaacqua m inv a immersione
immigrant ['ɪmɪgrənt] N immigrante mf;
(*already established*) immigrato(-a)
immigration [ɪmɪ'greɪʃən] N immigrazione f
immigration authorities NPL ufficio
stranieri
immigration laws NPL leggi fpl relative
all'immigrazione

imminent ['ɪmɪnənt] ADJ imminente
immobile [ɪ'məubaɪl] ADJ immobile
immobilize [ɪ'məubɪlaɪz] vt immobilizzare
immobilizer [ɪ'məubɪlaɪzə'] N (*Aut*)
immobilizer m inv, dispositivo di bloccaggio
del motore
immoderate [ɪ'mɔdərɪt] ADJ (*person*)
smodato(-a), sregolato(-a); (*opinion, reaction,
demand*) eccessivo(-a)
immodest [ɪ'mɔdɪst] ADJ (*indecent*) indecente,
impudico(-a); (*boasting*) presuntuoso(-a)
immoral [ɪ'mɔrl] ADJ immorale
immorality [ɪmə'rælɪtɪ] N immoralità
immortal [ɪ'mɔ:tl] ADJ, N immortale (mf)
immortalize [ɪ'mɔ:tələɪz] vt rendere
immortale
immovable [ɪ'mu:vəbl] ADJ (*object*) non
movibile; (*person*) irremovibile
immune [ɪ'mju:n] ADJ: **~ (to)** immune (da)
immune system N sistema m immunitario
immunity [ɪ'mju:nɪtɪ] N (*also fig: of diplomat*)
immunità; **diplomatic ~** immunità
diplomatica
immunization [ɪmjunaɪ'zeɪʃən] N
immunizzazione f
immunize ['ɪmjunaɪz] vt immunizzare
imp [ɪmp] N folletto, diavoletto; (*child*)
diavoletto
impact ['ɪmpækt] N impatto
impair [ɪm'pɛə'] vt danneggiare
impaired [ɪm'pɛəd] ADJ indebolito(-a)
-impaired [ɪm'pɛəd] SUFFIX: **visually~**
videoleso(-a)
impale [ɪm'peɪl] vt impalare
impart [ɪm'pɑ:t] vt (*make known*) comunicare;
(*bestow*) impartire
impartial [ɪm'pɑ:ʃl] ADJ imparziale
impartiality [ɪmpɑ:ʃɪ'ælɪtɪ] N imparzialità
impassable [ɪm'pɑ:səbl] ADJ insuperabile;
(*road*) impraticabile
impasse [æm'pɑ:s] N impasse f inv
impassioned [ɪm'pæʃənd] ADJ
appassionato(-a)
impassive [ɪm'pæsɪv] ADJ impassibile
impatience [ɪm'peɪʃəns] N impazienza
impatient [ɪm'peɪʃənt] ADJ impaziente;
to get or **grow ~** perdere la pazienza
impeach [ɪm'pi:tʃ] vt accusare, attaccare;
(*public official*) mettere sotto accusa
impeachment [ɪm'pi:tʃmənt] N (*Law*)
imputazione f
impeccable [ɪm'pɛkəbl] ADJ impeccabile
impecunious [ɪmpɪ'kju:nɪəs] ADJ povero(-a)
impede [ɪm'pi:d] vt impedire
impediment [ɪm'pɛdɪmənt] N
impedimento; (*also:* **speech impediment**)
difetto di pronuncia
impel [ɪm'pɛl] vt (*force*): **to ~ sb (to do sth)**
costringere or obbligare qn (a fare qc)

impending [ɪm'pɛndɪŋ] ADJ imminente
impenetrable [ɪm'pɛnɪtrəbl] ADJ
impenetrabile
imperative [ɪm'pɛrətɪv] ADJ imperativo(-a);
necessario(-a), urgente; (voice) imperioso(-a)
▶ N (Ling) imperativo
imperceptible [ɪmpə'sɛptɪbl] ADJ
impercettibile
imperfect [ɪm'pə:fɪkt] ADJ imperfetto(-a);
(goods etc) difettoso(-a) ▶ N (Ling: also:
imperfect tense) imperfetto
imperfection [ɪmpə:'fɛkʃən] N imperfezione
f; (flaw) difetto
imperial [ɪm'pɪərɪəl] ADJ imperiale; (measure)
legale
imperialism [ɪm'pɪərɪəlɪzəm] N
imperialismo
imperil [ɪm'pɛrɪl] VT mettere in pericolo
imperious [ɪm'pɪərɪəs] ADJ imperioso(-a)
impersonal [ɪm'pə:sənl] ADJ impersonale
impersonate [ɪm'pə:səneɪt] VT spacciarsi
per, fingersi; (Theat) imitare
impersonation [ɪmpə:sə'neɪʃən] N
(Law) usurpazione f d'identità; (Theat)
imitazione f
impersonator [ɪm'pə:səneɪtəʳ] N (gen, Theat)
imitatore(-trice)
impertinence [ɪm'pə:tɪnəns] N impertinenza
impertinent [ɪm'pə:tɪnənt] ADJ
impertinente
imperturbable [ɪmpə'tə:bəbl] ADJ
imperturbabile
impervious [ɪm'pə:vɪəs] ADJ impermeabile;
~ **to** (fig) insensibile a; impassibile di fronte a
impetuous [ɪm'pɛtjuəs] ADJ impetuoso(-a),
precipitoso(-a)
impetus ['ɪmpətəs] N impeto
impinge [ɪm'pɪndʒ]: **to ~ on** vt fus (person)
colpire; (rights) ledere
impish ['ɪmpɪʃ] ADJ malizioso(-a),
birichino(-a)
implacable [ɪm'plækəbl] ADJ implacabile
implant [ɪm'plɑ:nt] VT (Med) innestare; (fig:
idea, principle) inculcare
implausible [ɪm'plɔ:zɪbl] ADJ non plausibile
implement N ['ɪmplɪmənt] attrezzo; (for
cooking) utensile m ▶ VT ['ɪmplɪmɛnt]
effettuare
implicate ['ɪmplɪkeɪt] VT implicare
implication [ɪmplɪ'keɪʃən] N implicazione f;
by ~ implicitamente
implicit [ɪm'plɪsɪt] ADJ implicito(-a);
(complete) completo(-a)
implicitly [ɪm'plɪsɪtlɪ] ADV implicitamente
implore [ɪm'plɔ:ʳ] VT implorare
imply [ɪm'plaɪ] VT insinuare; suggerire
impolite [ɪmpə'laɪt] ADJ scortese
imponderable [ɪm'pɔndərəbl] ADJ
imponderabile

import VT [ɪm'pɔ:t] importare ▶ N ['ɪmpɔ:t]
(Comm) importazione f; (meaning) significato,
senso ▶ CPD (duty, licence etc) d'importazione
importance [ɪm'pɔ:tns] N importanza; **to
be of great/little ~** importare molto/poco,
essere molto/poco importante
important [ɪm'pɔ:tnt] ADJ importante; **it's
not ~** non ha importanza; **it is ~ that** è
importante che + sub
importantly [ɪm'pɔ:təntlɪ] ADV (pej) con
(un'aria d')importanza; **but, more ~, ...**
ma, quel che più conta or importa, ...
importation [ɪmpɔ:'teɪʃən] N importazione f
imported [ɪm'pɔ:tɪd] ADJ importato(-a)
importer [ɪm'pɔ:təʳ] N importatore(-trice)
impose [ɪm'pəuz] VT imporre ▶ VI: **to ~ on sb**
sfruttare la bontà di qn
imposing [ɪm'pəuzɪŋ] ADJ imponente
imposition [ɪmpə'zɪʃən] N imposizione f; **to
be an ~ on** (person) abusare della gentilezza
di
impossibility [ɪmpɔsə'bɪlɪtɪ] N impossibilità
impossible [ɪm'pɔsɪbl] ADJ impossibile; **it is
~ for me to leave now** mi è impossibile
venir via adesso
impostor [ɪm'pɔstəʳ] N impostore(-a)
impotence ['ɪmpətns] N impotenza
impotent ['ɪmpətnt] ADJ impotente
impound [ɪm'paund] VT confiscare
impoverished [ɪm'pɔvərɪʃt] ADJ
impoverito(-a)
impracticable [ɪm'præktɪkəbl] ADJ
impraticabile
impractical [ɪm'præktɪkl] ADJ non
pratico(-a)
imprecise [ɪmprɪ'saɪs] ADJ impreciso(-a)
impregnable [ɪm'prɛgnəbl] ADJ (fortress)
inespugnabile; (fig) inoppugnabile;
irrefutabile
impregnate ['ɪmprɛgneɪt] VT impregnare;
(fertilize) fecondare
impresario [ɪmprɪ'sɑ:rɪəu] N impresario(-a)
impress [ɪm'prɛs] VT impressionare; (mark)
imprimere, stampare; **to ~ sth on sb** far
capire qc a qn
impression [ɪm'prɛʃən] N impressione f; **to
be under the ~ that** avere l'impressione
che; **to make a good/bad ~ on sb** fare una
buona/cattiva impressione a or su qn
impressionable [ɪm'prɛʃnəbl] ADJ
impressionabile
impressionist [ɪm'prɛʃənɪst] N
impressionista mf
impressive [ɪm'prɛsɪv] ADJ notevole
imprint ['ɪmprɪnt] N (Publishing) sigla
editoriale
imprinted [ɪm'prɪntɪd] ADJ: **~ on**
impresso(-a) in
imprison [ɪm'prɪzn] VT imprigionare

imprisonment [ɪmˈprɪznmənt] N
imprigionamento
improbable [ɪmˈprɔbəbl] ADJ improbabile;
(*excuse*) inverosimile
impromptu [ɪmˈprɔmptjuː] ADJ
improvvisato(-a) ▶ ADV improvvisando, così
su due piedi
improper [ɪmˈprɔpəʳ] ADJ scorretto(-a);
(*unsuitable*) inadatto(-a), improprio(-a);
sconveniente, indecente
impropriety [ɪmprəˈpraɪətɪ] N sconvenienza;
(*of expression*) improprietà
improve [ɪmˈpruːv] VT migliorare ▶ VI
migliorare; (*pupil etc*) fare progressi
▶ **improve (up)on** VT FUS (*offer*) aumentare
improvement [ɪmˈpruːvmənt] N
miglioramento; progresso; **to make
improvements to** migliorare, apportare dei
miglioramenti a
improvisation [ɪmprəvaɪˈzeɪʃən] N
improvvisazione f
improvise [ˈɪmprəvaɪz] VT, VI improvvisare
imprudence [ɪmˈpruːdns] N imprudenza
imprudent [ɪmˈpruːdnt] ADJ imprudente
impudence [ˈɪmpjudns] N impudenza
impudent [ˈɪmpjudnt] ADJ impudente,
sfacciato(-a)
impugn [ɪmˈpjuːn] VT impugnare
impulse [ˈɪmpʌls] N impulso; **to act on ~**
agire d'impulso *or* impulsivamente
impulse buy N acquisto fatto d'impulso
impulsive [ɪmˈpʌlsɪv] ADJ impulsivo(-a)
impunity [ɪmˈpjuːnɪtɪ] N: **with ~**
impunemente
impure [ɪmˈpjuəʳ] ADJ impuro(-a)
impurity [ɪmˈpjuərɪtɪ] N impurità f inv
IN ABBR (*US*) = **Indiana**

(KEYWORD)

in [ɪn] PREP **1** (*indicating place, position*) in; **in
the house/garden** in casa/giardino; **in the
box** nella scatola; **in the fridge** nel
frigorifero; **I have it in my hand** ce l'ho in
mano; **in town/the country** in città/
campagna; **in school** a scuola; **in here/
there** qui/lì dentro
2 (*with place names: of town: region: country*): **in
London** a Londra; **in England** in
Inghilterra; **in the United States** negli
Stati Uniti; **in Yorkshire** nello Yorkshire
3 (*indicating time: during, in the space of*) in; **in
spring/summer** in primavera/estate; **in
1988** nel 1988; **in May** in *or* a maggio; **I'll see
you in July** ci vediamo a luglio; **in the
afternoon** nel pomeriggio; **at 4 o'clock in
the afternoon** alle 4 del pomeriggio; **I did
it in 3 hours/days** l'ho fatto in 3 ore/giorni;
I'll see you in 2 weeks *or* **in 2 weeks' time** ci
vediamo tra 2 settimane; **once in a**

hundred years una volta ogni cento anni
4 (*indicating manner etc*) a; **in a loud/soft voice**
a voce alta/bassa; **in pencil** a matita; **in
English/French** in inglese/francese; **in
writing** per iscritto; **the boy in the blue
shirt** il ragazzo con la camicia blu
5 (*indicating circumstances*): **in the sun** al sole;
in the shade all'ombra; **in the rain** sotto la
pioggia; **a rise in prices** un aumento dei
prezzi
6 (*indicating mood: state*): **in tears** in lacrime;
in anger per la rabbia; **in despair**
disperato(-a); **in good condition** in buono
stato, in buone condizioni; **to live in luxury**
vivere nel lusso
7 (*with ratios: numbers*): **1 in 10** 1 su 10; **20
pence in the pound** 20 pence per sterlina;
they lined up in twos si misero in fila per
due; **in hundreds** a centinaia
8 (*referring to people, works*) in; **the disease is
common in children** la malattia è comune
nei bambini; **in (the works of) Dickens** in
Dickens, nelle opere di Dickens
9 (*indicating profession etc*) in; **to be in
teaching** fare l'insegnante, insegnare; **to
be in publishing** lavorare nell'editoria
10 (*after superlative*) di; **the best in the class**
il migliore della classe
11 (*with present participle*): **in saying this**
dicendo questo, nel dire questo
12: **in that** conj poiché
▶ ADV: **to be in** (*person: at home, work*) esserci;
(*train, ship, plane*) essere arrivato(-a); (*in fashion*)
essere di moda; **their party is in** il loro
partito è al potere; **to ask sb in** invitare qn
ad entrare; **to run/limp** etc **in** entrare di
corsa/zoppicando etc
▶ N: **the ins and outs of the problem** tutti
gli aspetti del problema

in., ins ABBR = **inch**
inability [ɪnəˈbɪlɪtɪ] N inabilità, incapacità;
~ to pay impossibilità di pagare
inaccessible [ɪnækˈsɛsɪbl] ADJ inaccessibile
inaccuracy [ɪnˈækjurəsɪ] N inaccuratezza;
inesattezza; imprecisione f
inaccurate [ɪnˈækjurət] ADJ inaccurato(-a);
(*figures*) inesatto(-a); (*translation*)
impreciso(-a)
inaction [ɪnˈækʃən] N inazione f
inactivity [ɪnækˈtɪvɪtɪ] N inattività
inadequacy [ɪnˈædɪkwəsɪ] N insufficienza
inadequate [ɪnˈædɪkwət] ADJ insufficiente
inadmissible [ɪnədˈmɪsəbl] ADJ
inammissibile
inadvertent [ɪnədˈvəːtənt] ADJ
involontario(-a)
inadvertently [ɪnədˈvəːtntlɪ] ADV senza
volerlo

inadvisable [ɪnəd'vaɪzəbl] ADJ sconsigliabile
inane [ɪ'neɪn] ADJ vacuo(-a), stupido(-a)
inanimate [ɪn'ænɪmət] ADJ inanimato(-a)
inapplicable [ɪn'æplɪkəbl] ADJ inapplicabile
inappropriate [ɪnə'prəuprɪət] ADJ non
  adatto(-a); (word, expression) improprio(-a)
inapt [ɪn'æpt] ADJ maldestro(-a); fuori luogo
inaptitude [ɪn'æptɪtjuːd] N improprietà
inarticulate [ɪnɑː'tɪkjulət] ADJ (person) che si
  esprime male; (speech) inarticolato(-a)
inasmuch as [ɪnəz'mʌtʃæz] ADV in quanto
  che; (seeing that) poiché
inattention [ɪnə'tɛnʃən] N mancanza di
  attenzione
inattentive [ɪnə'tɛntɪv] ADJ disattento(-a),
  distratto(-a); negligente
inaudible [ɪn'ɔːdɪbl] ADJ che non si riesce a
  sentire
inaugural [ɪ'nɔːgjurəl] ADJ inaugurale
inaugurate [ɪ'nɔːgjureɪt] VT inaugurare;
  (president, official) insediare
inauguration [ɪnɔːgju'reɪʃən] N
  inaugurazione f; insediamento in carica
inauspicious [ɪnɔːs'pɪʃəs] ADJ poco
  propizio(-a)
in-between [ɪnbɪ'twiːn] ADJ fra i (or le) due
inborn [ɪn'bɔːn] ADJ (feeling) innato(-a);
  (defect) congenito(-a)
inbox ['ɪnbɔks] N (Comput) posta in arrivo;
  (US: intray) vaschetta della corrispondenza in
  arrivo
inbred [ɪn'brɛd] ADJ innato(-a); (family)
  connaturato(-a)
inbreeding [ɪn'briːdɪŋ] N incrocio ripetuto di
  animali consanguinei; unioni fpl fra
  consanguinei
Inc. ABBR (US: = incorporated) S.A.
Inca ['ɪŋkə] ADJ (also: **Incan**) inca inv
  ▶ N inca mf
incalculable [ɪn'kælkjuləbl] ADJ
  incalcolabile
incapability [ɪnkeɪpə'bɪlɪtɪ] N incapacità
incapable [ɪn'keɪpəbl] ADJ: ~ (of doing sth)
  incapace (di fare qc)
incapacitate [ɪnkə'pæsɪteɪt] VT: **to ~ sb
  from doing** rendere qn incapace di fare
incapacitated [ɪnkə'pæsɪteɪtɪd] ADJ (Law)
  inabilitato(-a)
incapacity [ɪnkə'pæsɪtɪ] N incapacità
incarcerate [ɪn'kɑːsəreɪt] VT imprigionare
incarnate ADJ [ɪn'kɑːnɪt] incarnato(-a) ▶ VT
  ['ɪnkɑːneɪt] incarnare
incarnation [ɪnkɑː'neɪʃən] N incarnazione f
incendiary [ɪn'sɛndɪərɪ] ADJ incendiario(-a)
  ▶ N (bomb) bomba incendiaria
incense N ['ɪnsɛns] incenso ▶ VT [ɪn'sɛns]
  (anger) infuriare
incense burner N incensiere m
incentive [ɪn'sɛntɪv] N incentivo

incentive scheme N piano di incentivazione
inception [ɪn'sɛpʃən] N inizio, principio
incessant [ɪn'sɛsnt] ADJ incessante
incessantly [ɪn'sɛsntlɪ] ADV di continuo,
  senza sosta
incest ['ɪnsɛst] N incesto
inch [ɪntʃ] N pollice m (= 25 mm; 12 in a foot);
  within an ~ of a un pelo da; **he wouldn't
  give an ~** (fig) non ha ceduto di un
  millimetro
  ▶ **inch forward** VI avanzare pian piano
inch tape N (BRIT) metro a nastro (da sarto)
incidence ['ɪnsɪdns] N (of crime, disease)
  incidenza
incident ['ɪnsɪdnt] N incidente m; (in book)
  episodio
incidental [ɪnsɪ'dɛntl] ADJ accessorio(-a),
  d'accompagnamento; (unplanned)
  incidentale; ~ **to** marginale a; ~ **expenses**
  npl spese fpl accessorie
incidentally [ɪnsɪ'dɛntəlɪ] ADV (by the way) a
  proposito
incidental music N sottofondo (musicale),
  musica di sottofondo
incident room N (Police) centrale f delle
  operazioni (per indagini)
incinerate [ɪn'sɪnəreɪt] VT incenerire
incinerator [ɪn'sɪnəreɪtər] N inceneritore m
incipient [ɪn'sɪpɪənt] ADJ incipiente
incision [ɪn'sɪʒən] N incisione f
incisive [ɪn'saɪsɪv] ADJ incisivo(-a); tagliante;
  acuto(-a)
incisor [ɪn'saɪzər] N incisivo
incite [ɪn'saɪt] VT incitare
incl. ABBR = **including; inclusive (of)**
inclement [ɪn'klɛmənt] ADJ inclemente
inclination [ɪnklɪ'neɪʃən] N inclinazione f
incline N ['ɪnklaɪn] pendenza, pendio ▶ VT
  [ɪn'klaɪn] inclinare ▶ VI (surface) essere
  inclinato(-a); **to ~ to** tendere a; **to be
  inclined to do** tendere a fare; essere
  propenso(-a) a fare; **to be well inclined
  towards sb** essere ben disposto(-a) verso qn
include [ɪn'kluːd] VT includere,
  comprendere; **the tip is/is not included** la
  mancia è compresa/esclusa
including [ɪn'kluːdɪŋ] PREP compreso(-a),
  incluso(-a); ~ **tip** mancia compresa,
  compresa la mancia
inclusion [ɪn'kluːʒən] N inclusione f
inclusive [ɪn'kluːsɪv] ADJ incluso(-a),
  compreso(-a); **£50, ~ of all surcharges** 50
  sterline, incluse tutte le soprattasse; ~ **of
  tax** etc tasse etc comprese
inclusive terms NPL (BRIT) prezzo tutto
  compreso
incognito [ɪnkɔg'niːtəu] ADV in incognito
incoherent [ɪnkəu'hɪərənt] ADJ incoerente
income ['ɪnkʌm] N reddito; **gross/net ~**

reddito lordo/netto; **~ and expenditure account** conto entrate ed uscite

income support N (BRIT) sussidio di indigenza or povertà

income tax N imposta sul reddito

income tax inspector N ispettore *m* delle imposte dirette

income tax return N dichiarazione *f* annuale dei redditi

incoming ['ɪnkʌmɪŋ] ADJ (*passengers, flight, mail*) in arrivo; (*government, tenant*) subentrante; **~ tide** marea montante

incommunicado [ɪnkəmjunɪ'ka:dəu] ADJ: **to hold sb ~** tenere qn in segregazione

incomparable [ɪn'kɔmpərəbl] ADJ incomparabile

incompatible [ɪnkəm'pætɪbl] ADJ incompatibile

incompetence [ɪn'kɔmpɪtns] N incompetenza, incapacità

incompetent [ɪn'kɔmpɪtnt] ADJ incompetente, incapace

incomplete [ɪnkəm'pli:t] ADJ incompleto(-a)

incomprehensible [ɪnkɔmprɪ'hɛnsɪbl] ADJ incomprensibile

inconceivable [ɪnkən'si:vəbl] ADJ inimmaginabile

inconclusive [ɪnkən'klu:sɪv] ADJ improduttivo(-a); (*argument*) poco convincente

incongruous [ɪn'kɔŋgruəs] ADJ poco appropriato(-a); (*remark, act*) incongruo(-a)

inconsequential [ɪnkɔnsɪ'kwɛnʃl] ADJ senza importanza

inconsiderable [ɪnkən'sɪdərəbl] ADJ: **not ~** non trascurabile

inconsiderate [ɪnkən'sɪdərət] ADJ sconsiderato(-a)

inconsistency [ɪnkən'sɪstənsɪ] N (*of actions etc*) incongruenza; (*of work*) irregolarità; (*of statement etc*) contraddizione *f*

inconsistent [ɪnkən'sɪstnt] ADJ incoerente; poco logico(-a); contraddittorio(-a); **~ with** in contraddizione con

inconsolable [ɪnkən'səuləbl] ADJ inconsolabile

inconspicuous [ɪnkən'spɪkjuəs] ADJ incospicuo(-a); (*colour*) poco appariscente; (*dress*) dimesso(-a); **to make o.s. ~** cercare di passare inosservato(-a)

inconstant [ɪn'kɔnstnt] ADJ incostante; mutevole

incontinence [ɪn'kɔntɪnəns] N incontinenza

incontinent [ɪn'kɔntɪnənt] ADJ incontinente

incontrovertible [ɪnkɔntrə'və:təbl] ADJ incontrovertibile

inconvenience [ɪnkən'vi:njəns] N inconveniente *m*; (*trouble*) disturbo ▶ VT disturbare; **to put sb to great ~** creare degli

inconvenienti a qn; **don't ~ yourself** non si disturbi

inconvenient [ɪnkən'vi:njənt] ADJ scomodo(-a); **that time is very ~ for me** quell'ora mi è molto scomoda, non è un'ora adatta per me

incorporate [ɪn'kɔ:pəreɪt] VT incorporare; (*contain*) contenere

incorporated [ɪn'kɔ:pəreɪtɪd] ADJ: **~ company** (US) società *f inv* registrata

incorrect [ɪnkə'rɛkt] ADJ scorretto(-a); (*statement*) inesatto(-a)

incorrigible [ɪn'kɔrɪdʒəbl] ADJ incorreggibile

incorruptible [ɪnkə'rʌptɪbl] ADJ incorruttibile

increase N ['ɪnkri:s] aumento ▶ VI [ɪn'kri:s] aumentare; **to be on the ~** essere in aumento; **an ~ of £5/10%** un aumento di 5 sterline/del 10%

increasing [ɪn'kri:sɪŋ] ADJ (*number*) crescente

increasingly [ɪn'kri:sɪŋlɪ] ADV sempre più

incredible [ɪn'krɛdɪbl] ADJ incredibile

incredibly ADV incredibilmente

incredulous [ɪn'krɛdjuləs] ADJ incredulo(-a)

increment ['ɪnkrɪmənt] N aumento, incremento

incriminate [ɪn'krɪmɪneɪt] VT compromettere

incriminating [ɪn'krɪmɪneɪtɪŋ] ADJ incriminante

incubate ['ɪnkjubeɪt] VT (*eggs*) covare ▶ VI (*egg*) essere in incubazione; (*disease*) avere un'incubazione

incubation [ɪnkju'beɪʃən] N incubazione *f*

incubation period N (periodo di) incubazione *f*

incubator ['ɪnkjubeɪtə'] N incubatrice *f*

inculcate ['ɪnkʌlkeɪt] VT: **to ~ sth in sb** inculcare qc a qn, instillare qc a qn

incumbent [ɪn'kʌmbənt] ADJ: **it is ~ on him to do ...** è suo dovere fare ... ▶ N titolare *mf*

incur [ɪn'kə:'] VT (*expenses*) incorrere; (*debt*) contrarre; (*loss*) subire; (*anger, risk*) esporsi a

incurable [ɪn'kjuərəbl] ADJ incurabile

incursion [ɪn'kə:ʃən] N incursione *f*

Ind. ABBR (US) = **Indiana**

indebted [ɪn'dɛtɪd] ADJ: **to be ~ to sb (for)** essere obbligato(-a) verso qn (per)

indecency [ɪn'di:snsɪ] N indecenza

indecent [ɪn'di:snt] ADJ indecente

indecent assault N (BRIT) aggressione *f* a scopo di violenza sessuale

indecent exposure N atti *mpl* osceni in luogo pubblico

indecipherable [ɪndɪ'saɪfərəbl] ADJ indecifrabile

indecision [ɪndɪ'sɪʒən] N indecisione *f*

indecisive [ɪndɪ'saɪsɪv] ADJ indeciso(-a); (*discussion*) non decisivo(-a)

indeed [ɪn'diːd] ADV infatti; veramente;
yes ~! certamente!
indefatigable [ɪndɪ'fætɪɡəbl] ADJ
infaticabile, instancabile
indefensible [ɪndɪ'fɛnsəbl] ADJ (conduct)
ingiustificabile
indefinable [ɪndɪ'faɪnəbl] ADJ indefinibile
indefinite [ɪn'dɛfɪnɪt] ADJ indefinito(-a);
(answer) vago(-a); (period, number)
indeterminato(-a)
indefinitely [ɪn'dɛfɪnɪtlɪ] ADV (wait)
indefinitamente
indelible [ɪn'dɛlɪbl] ADJ indelebile
indelicate [ɪn'dɛlɪkɪt] ADJ (tactless)
indelicato(-a), privo(-a) di tatto; (not polite)
sconveniente
indemnify [ɪn'dɛmnɪfaɪ] VT indennizzare
indemnity [ɪn'dɛmnɪtɪ] N (insurance)
assicurazione f; (compensation) indennità,
indennizzo
indent [ɪn'dɛnt] VT (Typ: text) far rientrare dal
margine
indentation [ɪndɛn'teɪʃən] N dentellatura;
(Typ) rientranza; (dent) tacca
indented [ɪn'dɛntɪd] ADJ (Typ) rientrante
indenture [ɪn'dɛntʃəʳ] N contratto m
formazione inv
independence [ɪndɪ'pɛndns] N
indipendenza
Independence Day N (US); vedi nota

> Negli Stati Uniti il 4 luglio si festeggia l'
> Independence Day, il giorno in cui è stata
> firmata, nel 1776, la Dichiarazione di
> Indipendenza con la quale tredici colonie
> britanniche dichiaravano la propria
> indipendenza dalla Gran Bretagna e la
> propria appartenenza agli Stati Uniti
> d'America.

independent [ɪndɪ'pɛndnt] ADJ
indipendente
independently [ɪndɪ'pɛndntlɪ] ADV
indipendentemente; separatamente; **~ of**
indipendentemente da
independent school N (BRIT) istituto
scolastico indipendente che si autofinanzia
in-depth ['ɪn'dɛpθ] ADJ approfondito(-a)
indescribable [ɪndɪ'skraɪbəbl] ADJ
indescrivibile
indestructible [ɪndɪ'strʌktəbl] ADJ
indistruttibile
indeterminate [ɪndɪ'təːmɪnɪt] ADJ
indeterminato(-a)
index ['ɪndɛks] N (pl **indexes**) (in book) indice
m; (in library etc) catalogo; (pl **indices**: ratio,
sign) indice m
index card N scheda
index finger N (dito) indice m
index-linked ['ɪndɛks'lɪŋkt], (US) **indexed**
['ɪndɛkst] ADJ legato(-a) al costo della vita

India ['ɪndɪə] N India
Indian ['ɪndɪən] ADJ, N indiano(-a)
Indian ink N inchiostro di china
Indian Ocean N: **the ~** l'Oceano Indiano
Indian Summer N (fig) estate f di San
Martino
India paper N carta d'India, carta bibbia
India rubber N caucciù m
indicate ['ɪndɪkeɪt] VT indicare ▶ VI (BRIT Aut):
to ~ left/right mettere la freccia a sinistra/a
destra
indication [ɪndɪ'keɪʃən] N indicazione f, segno
indicative [ɪn'dɪkətɪv] ADJ: **~ of** indicativo(-a)
di ▶ N (Ling) indicativo; **to be ~ of sth** essere
indicativo(-a) or un indice di qc
indicator ['ɪndɪkeɪtəʳ] N (sign) segno; (Aut)
indicatore m di direzione, freccia
indices ['ɪndɪsiːz] NPL of **index**
indict [ɪn'daɪt] VT accusare
indictable [ɪn'daɪtəbl] ADJ passibile di pena;
~ offence atto che costituisce reato
indictment [ɪn'daɪtmənt] N accusa
indifference [ɪn'dɪfrəns] N indifferenza
indifferent [ɪn'dɪfrənt] ADJ indifferente;
(poor) mediocre
indigenous [ɪn'dɪdʒɪnəs] ADJ indigeno(-a)
indigestible [ɪndɪ'dʒɛstɪbl] ADJ indigeribile
indigestion [ɪndɪ'dʒɛstʃən] N indigestione f
indignant [ɪn'dɪgnənt] ADJ: **~ (at sth/with sb)**
indignato(-a) (per qc/contro qn)
indignation [ɪndɪg'neɪʃən] N indignazione f
indignity [ɪn'dɪgnɪtɪ] N umiliazione f
indigo ['ɪndɪgəu] ADJ, N indaco (inv)
indirect [ɪndɪ'rɛkt] ADJ indiretto(-a)
indirectly [ɪndɪ'rɛktlɪ] ADV indirettamente
indiscreet [ɪndɪ'skriːt] ADJ indiscreto(-a);
(rash) imprudente
indiscretion [ɪndɪ'skrɛʃən] N indiscrezione f;
imprudenza
indiscriminate [ɪndɪ'skrɪmɪnət] ADJ (person)
che non sa discernere; (admiration) cieco(-a);
(killings) indiscriminato(-a)
indispensable [ɪndɪ'spɛnsəbl] ADJ
indispensabile
indisposed [ɪndɪ'spəuzd] ADJ (unwell)
indisposto(-a)
indisposition [ɪndɪspə'zɪʃən] N (illness)
indisposizione f
indisputable [ɪndɪ'spjuːtəbl] ADJ
incontestabile, indiscutibile
indistinct [ɪndɪ'stɪŋkt] ADJ indistinto(-a);
(memory, noise) vago(-a)
indistinguishable [ɪndɪ'stɪŋgwɪʃəbl] ADJ
indistinguibile
individual [ɪndɪ'vɪdjuəl] N individuo ▶ ADJ
individuale; (characteristic) particolare,
originale
individualist [ɪndɪ'vɪdjuəlɪst] N
individualista mf

individuality [ɪndɪvɪdjuˈælɪtɪ] N
individualità
individually [ɪndɪˈvɪdjuəlɪ] ADV
singolarmente, uno(-a) per uno(-a)
indivisible [ɪndɪˈvɪzɪbl] ADJ indivisibile
Indochina [ˈɪndəʊˈtʃaɪnə] N Indocina
indoctrinate [ɪnˈdɔktrɪneɪt] VT indottrinare
indoctrination [ɪndɔktrɪˈneɪʃən] N
indottrinamento
indolent [ˈɪndələnt] ADJ indolente
Indonesia [ɪndəʊˈniːzɪə] N Indonesia
Indonesian [ɪndəʊˈniːzɪən] ADJ, N
indonesiano(-a); (Ling) indonesiano
indoor [ˈɪndɔːʳ] ADJ da interno; (plant)
d'appartamento; (swimming pool) coperto(-a);
(sport, games) fatto(-a) al coperto
indoors [ɪnˈdɔːz] ADV all'interno; (at home) in
casa
indubitable [ɪnˈdjuːbɪtəbl] ADJ indubitabile
induce [ɪnˈdjuːs] VT persuadere; (bring about,
Med) provocare; **to ~ sb to do sth** persuadere
qn a fare qc
inducement [ɪnˈdjuːsmənt] N incitamento;
(incentive) stimolo, incentivo
induct [ɪnˈdʌkt] VT insediare; (fig) iniziare
induction [ɪnˈdʌkʃən] N (Med: of birth) parto
indotto
induction course N (BRIT) corso di
avviamento
indulge [ɪnˈdʌldʒ] VT (whim) compiacere,
soddisfare; (child) viziare ► VI: **to ~ in sth**
concedersi qc; abbandonarsi a qc
indulgence [ɪnˈdʌldʒəns] N lusso (che uno si
permette); (leniency) indulgenza
indulgent [ɪnˈdʌldʒənt] ADJ indulgente
industrial [ɪnˈdʌstrɪəl] ADJ industriale;
(injury) sul lavoro; (dispute) di lavoro
industrial action N azione f rivendicativa
industrial estate (BRIT) N zona industriale
industrialist [ɪnˈdʌstrɪəlɪst] N industriale m
industrialize [ɪnˈdʌstrɪəlaɪz] VT
industrializzare
industrial park N (US) zona industriale
industrial relations NPL relazioni fpl
industriali
industrial tribunal N (BRIT) ≈ Tribunale m
Amministrativo Regionale
industrial unrest N (BRIT) agitazione f
(sindacale)
industrious [ɪnˈdʌstrɪəs] ADJ industrioso(-a),
assiduo(-a)
industry [ˈɪndəstrɪ] N industria; (diligence)
operosità
inebriated [ɪˈniːbrɪeɪtɪd] ADJ ubriaco(-a)
inedible [ɪnˈɛdɪbl] ADJ immangiabile; non
commestibile
ineffective [ɪnɪˈfɛktɪv] ADJ inefficace
ineffectual [ɪnɪˈfɛktʃuəl] ADJ inefficace;
incompetente

inefficiency [ɪnɪˈfɪʃənsɪ] N inefficienza
inefficient [ɪnɪˈfɪʃənt] ADJ inefficiente
inelegant [ɪnˈɛlɪgənt] ADJ poco elegante
ineligible [ɪnˈɛlɪdʒɪbl] ADJ (candidate)
ineleggibile; **to be ~ for sth** non avere il
diritto a qc
inept [ɪˈnɛpt] ADJ inetto(-a)
ineptitude [ɪˈnɛptɪtjuːd] N inettitudine f,
stupidità
inequality [ɪnɪˈkwɔlɪtɪ] N ineguaglianza
inequitable [ɪnˈɛkwɪtəbl] ADJ iniquo(-a)
ineradicable [ɪnɪˈrædɪkəbl] ADJ inestirpabile
inert [ɪˈnəːt] ADJ inerte
inertia [ɪˈnəːʃə] N inerzia
inertia-reel seat belt [ɪˈnəːʃəˈriːl-] N cintura
di sicurezza con arrotolatore
inescapable [ɪnɪˈskeɪpəbl] ADJ inevitabile
inessential [ɪnɪˈsɛnʃl] ADJ non essenziale
inestimable [ɪnˈɛstɪməbl] ADJ inestimabile,
incalcolabile
inevitable [ɪnˈɛvɪtəbl] ADJ inevitabile
inevitably [ɪnˈɛvɪtəblɪ] ADV inevitabilmente;
as ~ happens … come immancabilmente
succede …
inexact [ɪnɪgˈzækt] ADJ inesatto(-a)
inexcusable [ɪnɪksˈkjuːzəbl] ADJ imperdonabile
inexhaustible [ɪnɪgˈzɔːstɪbl] ADJ
inesauribile; (person) instancabile
inexorable [ɪnˈɛksərəbl] ADJ inesorabile
inexpensive [ɪnɪkˈspɛnsɪv] ADJ poco
costoso(-a)
inexperience [ɪnɪkˈspɪərɪəns] N
inesperienza
inexperienced [ɪnɪkˈspɪərɪənst] ADJ
inesperto(-a), senza esperienza; **to be ~ in
sth** essere poco pratico di qc
inexplicable [ɪnɪkˈsplɪkəbl] ADJ inesplicabile
inexpressible [ɪnɪkˈsprɛsəbl] ADJ
inesprimibile
inextricable [ɪnɪkˈstrɪkəbl] ADJ inestricabile
infallibility [ɪnfæləˈbɪlɪtɪ] N infallibilità
infallible [ɪnˈfælɪbl] ADJ infallibile
infamous [ˈɪnfəməs] ADJ infame
infamy [ˈɪnfəmɪ] N infamia
infancy [ˈɪnfənsɪ] N infanzia
infant [ˈɪnfənt] N bambino(-a)
infantile [ˈɪnfəntaɪl] ADJ infantile
infant mortality N mortalità infantile
infantry [ˈɪnfəntrɪ] N fanteria
infantryman [ˈɪnfəntrɪmən] N (irreg) fante m
infant school N (BRIT) scuola elementare (per
bambini dall'età di 5 a 7 anni)
infatuated [ɪnˈfætjueɪtɪd] ADJ: **~ with**
infatuato(-a) di; **to become ~ (with sb)**
infatuarsi (di qn)
infatuation [ɪnfætjuˈeɪʃən] N infatuazione f
infect [ɪnˈfɛkt] VT infettare; **infected with**
(illness) affetto(-a) da; **to become infected**
(wound) infettarsi

infection [ɪnˈfɛkʃən] N infezione f
infectious [ɪnˈfɛkʃəs] ADJ (disease) infettivo(-a), contagioso(-a); (person, laughter, enthusiasm) contagioso(-a)
infer [ɪnˈfəːʳ] VT: **to ~ (from)** dedurre (da), concludere (da)
inference [ˈɪnfərəns] N deduzione f, conclusione f
inferior [ɪnˈfɪərɪəʳ] ADJ inferiore; (goods) di qualità scadente ▶ N inferiore mf; (in rank) subalterno(-a); **to feel ~** sentirsi inferiore
inferiority [ɪnfɪərɪˈɔrɪtɪ] N inferiorità
inferiority complex N complesso di inferiorità
infernal [ɪnˈfəːnl] ADJ infernale
inferno [ɪnˈfəːnəu] N inferno
infertile [ɪnˈfəːtaɪl] ADJ sterile
infertility [ɪnfəːˈtɪlɪtɪ] N sterilità
infested [ɪnˈfɛstɪd] ADJ: **~ (with)** infestato(-a) (di)
infidelity [ɪnfɪˈdɛlɪtɪ] N infedeltà
in-fighting [ˈɪnfaɪtɪŋ] N lotte fpl intestine
infiltrate [ˈɪnfɪltreɪt] VT (troops etc) far penetrare; (enemy line etc) infiltrare ▶ VI infiltrarsi
infinite [ˈɪnfɪnɪt] ADJ infinito(-a); **an ~ amount of time/money** un'illimitata quantità di tempo/denaro
infinitely [ˈɪnfɪnɪtlɪ] ADV infinitamente
infinitesimal [ɪnfɪnɪˈtɛsɪməl] ADJ infinitesimale
infinitive [ɪnˈfɪnɪtɪv] N infinito
infinity [ɪnˈfɪnɪtɪ] N infinità; (also Math) infinito
infirm [ɪnˈfəːm] ADJ infermo(-a)
infirmary [ɪnˈfəːmərɪ] N ospedale m; (in school, factory) infermeria
infirmity [ɪnˈfəːmɪtɪ] N infermità f inv
inflamed [ɪnˈfleɪmd] ADJ infiammato(-a)
inflammable [ɪnˈflæməbl] ADJ infiammabile
inflammation [ɪnfləˈmeɪʃən] N infiammazione f
inflammatory [ɪnˈflæmətərɪ] ADJ (speech) incendiario(-a)
inflatable [ɪnˈfleɪtəbl] ADJ gonfiabile
inflate [ɪnˈfleɪt] VT (tyre, balloon) gonfiare; (fig) esagerare; gonfiare; **to ~ the currency** far ricorso all'inflazione
inflated [ɪnˈfleɪtɪd] ADJ (style) gonfio(-a); (value) esagerato(-a)
inflation [ɪnˈfleɪʃən] N (Econ) inflazione f
inflationary [ɪnˈfleɪʃənərɪ] ADJ inflazionistico(-a)
inflexible [ɪnˈflɛksɪbl] ADJ inflessibile, rigido(-a)
inflict [ɪnˈflɪkt] VT: **to ~ on** infliggere a
infliction [ɪnˈflɪkʃən] N inflizione f; afflizione f
in-flight [ˈɪnflaɪt] ADJ a bordo

inflow [ˈɪnfləu] N afflusso
influence [ˈɪnfluəns] N influenza ▶ VT influenzare; **under the ~ of** sotto l'influenza di; **under the ~ of alcohol** sotto l'influenza or l'effetto dell'alcool
influential [ɪnfluˈɛnʃl] ADJ influente
influenza [ɪnfluˈɛnzə] N (Med) influenza
influx [ˈɪnflʌks] N afflusso
info [ˈɪnfəu] N (col) = **information**
inform [ɪnˈfɔːm] VT: **to ~ sb (of)** informare qn (di) ▶ VI: **to ~ on sb** denunciare qn; **to ~ sb about** mettere qn al corrente di
informal [ɪnˈfɔːml] ADJ (person, manner) alla buona, semplice; (visit, discussion) informale; (announcement, invitation) non ufficiale; **"dress ~"** "non è richiesto l'abito scuro"; **~ language** linguaggio colloquiale
informality [ɪnfɔːˈmælɪtɪ] N semplicità, informalità; carattere m non ufficiale
informally [ɪnˈfɔːməlɪ] ADV senza cerimonie; (invite) in modo non ufficiale
informant [ɪnˈfɔːmənt] N informatore(-trice)
informatics [ɪnfəˈmætɪks] N informatica
information [ɪnfəˈmeɪʃən] N informazioni fpl; particolari mpl; **to get ~ on** informarsi su; **a piece of ~** un'informazione; **for your ~** a titolo d'informazione, per sua informazione
information bureau N ufficio m informazioni inv
information office N ufficio m informazioni inv
information processing N elaborazione f delle informazioni
information retrieval N ricupero delle informazioni
information superhighway N autostrada informatica
information technology N informatica
informative [ɪnˈfɔːmətɪv] ADJ istruttivo(-a)
informed [ɪnˈfɔːmd] ADJ (observer) (ben) informato(-a); **an ~ guess** un'ipotesi fondata
informer [ɪnˈfɔːməʳ] N informatore(-trice)
infra dig [ˈɪnfrəˈdɪg] ADJ ABBR (col: = infra dignitatem: beneath one's dignity) indecoroso(-a)
infra-red [ɪnfrəˈrɛd] ADJ infrarosso(-a)
infrastructure [ˈɪnfrəstrʌktʃəʳ] N infrastruttura
infrequent [ɪnˈfriːkwənt] ADJ infrequente, raro(-a)
infringe [ɪnˈfrɪndʒ] VT infrangere ▶ VI: **to ~ on** calpestare
infringement [ɪnˈfrɪndʒmənt] N: **~ (of)** infrazione f (di)
infuriate [ɪnˈfjuərɪeɪt] VT rendere furioso(-a)
infuriating [ɪnˈfjuərɪeɪtɪŋ] ADJ molto irritante

infuse [ɪn'fjuːz] VT (with courage, enthusiasm): **to ~ sb with sth** infondere qc a qn, riempire qn di qc

infusion [ɪn'fjuːʒən] N (tea etc) infuso, infusione f

ingenious [ɪn'dʒiːnjəs] ADJ ingegnoso(-a)

ingenuity [ɪndʒɪ'njuːɪtɪ] N ingegnosità

ingenuous [ɪn'dʒənjuəs] ADJ ingenuo(-a)

ingot ['ɪŋgət] N lingotto

ingrained [ɪn'greɪnd] ADJ radicato(-a)

ingratiate [ɪn'greɪʃɪeɪt] VT: **to ~ o.s. with sb** ingraziarsi qn

ingratiating [ɪn'greɪʃɪeɪtɪŋ] ADJ (smile, speech) suadente, cattivante; (person) compiacente

ingratitude [ɪn'grætɪtjuːd] N ingratitudine f

ingredient [ɪn'griːdɪənt] N ingrediente m; elemento

ingrowing ['ɪngrəʊɪŋ], **ingrown** ['ɪngrəʊn] ADJ: **~ (toe)nail** unghia incarnita

inhabit [ɪn'hæbɪt] VT abitare

inhabitable [ɪn'hæbɪtəbl] ADJ abitabile

inhabitant [ɪn'hæbɪtnt] N abitante mf

inhale [ɪn'heɪl] VT inalare ▶ VI (in smoking) aspirare

inhaler [ɪn'heɪlər] N inalatore m

inherent [ɪn'hɪərənt] ADJ: **~ (in or to)** inerente (a)

inherently [ɪn'hɪərəntlɪ] ADV (easy, difficult) di per sé, di per se stesso(-a); **~ lazy** pigro di natura

inherit [ɪn'hɛrɪt] VT ereditare

inheritance [ɪn'hɛrɪtəns] N eredità

inhibit [ɪn'hɪbɪt] VT (Psych) inibire; **to ~ sb from doing** impedire a qn di fare

inhibited [ɪn'hɪbɪtɪd] ADJ (person) inibito(-a)

inhibiting [ɪn'hɪbɪtɪŋ] ADJ che inibisce

inhibition [ɪnhɪ'bɪʃən] N inibizione f

inhospitable [ɪnhɔs'pɪtəbl] ADJ inospitale

in-house ['ɪn'haus] ADJ effettuato(-a) da personale interno, interno(-a) ▶ ADV (training) all'interno dell'azienda

inhuman [ɪn'hjuːmən] ADJ inumano(-a), disumano(-a)

inhumane [ɪnhjuː'meɪn] ADJ inumano(-a), disumano(-a)

inimitable [ɪ'nɪmɪtəbl] ADJ inimitabile

iniquity [ɪ'nɪkwɪtɪ] N iniquità f inv

initial [ɪ'nɪʃl] ADJ iniziale ▶ N iniziale f ▶ VT siglare; **initials** NPL (of name) iniziali fpl; (as signature) sigla

initialize [ɪ'nɪʃəlaɪz] VT (Comput) inizializzare

initially [ɪ'nɪʃəlɪ] ADV inizialmente, all'inizio

initiate [ɪ'nɪʃɪeɪt] VT (start) avviare; intraprendere; iniziare; (person) iniziare; **to ~ sb into sth** iniziare qn a qc; **to ~ sb into a secret** mettere qn a parte di un segreto; **to ~ proceedings against sb** (Law) intentare causa a or contro qn

initiation [ɪnɪʃɪ'eɪʃən] N iniziazione f

initiative [ɪ'nɪʃətɪv] N iniziativa; **to take the ~** prendere l'iniziativa

inject [ɪn'dʒɛkt] VT (liquid) iniettare; (person) fare un'iniezione a; (fig: money): **to ~ sb with sth** fare a qn un'iniezione di qc; **to ~ into** immettere in

injection [ɪn'dʒɛkʃən] N iniezione f, puntura; **to have an ~** farsi fare un'iniezione or una puntura

injudicious [ɪndʒu'dɪʃəs] ADJ poco saggio(-a)

injunction [ɪn'dʒʌŋkʃən] N (Law) ingiunzione f, intimazione f

injure ['ɪndʒər] VT ferire; (wrong) fare male or torto a; (damage: reputation etc) nuocere a; (: feelings) offendere; **to ~ o.s.** farsi male

injured ['ɪndʒəd] ADJ (person, leg etc) ferito(-a); (tone, feelings) offeso(-a); **~ party** (Law) parte f lesa

injurious [ɪn'dʒuərɪəs] ADJ: **~ (to)** nocivo(-a) (a), pregiudizievole (per)

injury ['ɪndʒərɪ] N ferita; (wrong) torto; **to escape without ~** rimanere illeso

injury time N (Sport) tempo di recupero

injustice [ɪn'dʒʌstɪs] N ingiustizia; **you do me an ~** mi fa un torto, è ingiusto verso di me

ink [ɪŋk] N inchiostro

ink-jet printer ['ɪŋkdʒɛt-] N stampante f a getto d'inchiostro

inkling ['ɪŋklɪŋ] N sentore m, vaga idea

inkpad ['ɪŋkpæd] N tampone m, cuscinetto per timbri

inky ['ɪŋkɪ] ADJ macchiato(-a) or sporco(-a) d'inchiostro

inlaid ['ɪnleɪd] ADJ incrostato(-a); (table etc) intarsiato(-a)

inland ADJ ['ɪnlənd] interno(-a) ▶ ADV [ɪn'lænd] all'interno; **~ waterways** canali e fiumi mpl navigabili

Inland Revenue N (BRIT) Fisco

in-laws ['ɪnlɔːz] NPL suoceri mpl; famiglia del marito (or della moglie)

inlet ['ɪnlɛt] N (Geo) insenatura, baia

inlet pipe N (Tech) tubo d'immissione

inmate ['ɪnmeɪt] N (in prison) carcerato(-a); (in asylum) ricoverato(-a)

inmost ['ɪnməust] ADJ più profondo(-a), più intimo(-a)

inn [ɪn] N locanda

innards ['ɪnədz] NPL (col) interiora fpl, budella fpl

innate [ɪ'neɪt] ADJ innato(-a)

inner ['ɪnər] ADJ interno(-a), interiore

inner city N centro di una zona urbana

innermost ['ɪnəməust] ADJ = **inmost**

inner tube N camera d'aria

inning ['ɪnɪŋ] N (US Baseball) ripresa; **innings** (Cricket) turno di battuta; (BRIT fig) **he has had a good innings** ha avuto molto dalla vita

innocence ['ɪnəsns] N innocenza
innocent ['ɪnəsnt] ADJ innocente
innocuous [ɪ'nɔkjuəs] ADJ innocuo(-a)
innovation [ɪnəu'veɪʃən] N innovazione f
innovative ['ɪnəu'veɪtɪv] ADJ innovativo(-a)
innuendo [ɪnju'ɛndəu] (pl **innuendoes**) N
insinuazione f
innumerable [ɪ'nju:mrəbl] ADJ
innumerevole
inoculate [ɪ'nɔkjuleɪt] VT: **to ~ sb with sth/
against sth** inoculare qc a qn/qn contro qc
inoculation [ɪnɔkju'leɪʃən] N inoculazione f
inoffensive [ɪnə'fɛnsɪv] ADJ inoffensivo(-a),
innocuo(-a)
inopportune [ɪn'ɔpətjuːn] ADJ inopportuno(-a)
inordinate [ɪ'nɔːdɪnɪt] ADJ eccessivo(-a)
inordinately [ɪ'nɔːdɪnətlɪ] ADV
smoderatamente
inorganic [ɪnɔː'gænɪk] ADJ inorganico(-a)
in-patient ['ɪnpeɪʃənt] N ricoverato(-a)
input ['ɪnput] N (Elec) energia, potenza; (of
machine) alimentazione f; (of computer) input
m ▶ VT (Comput) inserire, introdurre
inquest ['ɪnkwɛst] N inchiesta
inquire [ɪn'kwaɪə'] VI informarsi ▶ VT
domandare, informarsi di or su; **to ~ about**
informarsi di or su, chiedere informazioni
su; **to ~ when/where/whether** informarsi
di quando/su dove/se
▶ **inquire after** VT FUS (person) chiedere di;
(sb's health) informarsi di
▶ **inquire into** VT FUS indagare su, fare delle
indagini or ricerche su
inquiring [ɪn'kwaɪərɪŋ] ADJ (mind)
inquisitivo(-a)
inquiry [ɪn'kwaɪərɪ] N domanda; (Law)
indagine f, investigazione f; **"inquiries"**
"informazioni"; **to hold an ~ into sth** fare
un'inchiesta su qc
inquiry desk N (BRIT) banco delle
informazioni
inquiry office N (BRIT) ufficio m
informazioni inv
inquisition [ɪnkwɪ'zɪʃən] N inquisizione f,
inchiesta; (Rel): **the I~** l'Inquisizione
inquisitive [ɪn'kwɪzɪtɪv] ADJ curioso(-a)
inroads ['ɪnrəudz] NPL: **to make ~ into**
(savings, supplies) intaccare (seriamente)
ins. ABBR = **inches**
insane [ɪn'seɪn] ADJ matto(-a), pazzo(-a);
(Med) alienato(-a)
insanitary [ɪn'sænɪtərɪ] ADJ insalubre
insanity [ɪn'sænɪtɪ] N follia; (Med)
alienazione f mentale
insatiable [ɪn'seɪʃəbl] ADJ insaziabile
inscribe [ɪn'skraɪb] VT iscrivere; (book etc): **to
~ (to sb)** dedicare (a qn)
inscription [ɪn'skrɪpʃən] N iscrizione f; (in
book) dedica

inscrutable [ɪn'skruːtəbl] ADJ
imperscrutabile
inseam ['ɪnsiːm] N (US): ~ **measurement**
lunghezza interna
insect ['ɪnsɛkt] N insetto
insect bite N puntura or morsicatura di
insetto
insecticide [ɪn'sɛktɪsaɪd] N insetticida m
insect repellent N insettifugo
insecure [ɪnsɪ'kjuə'] ADJ malsicuro(-a);
(person) insicuro(-a)
insecurity [ɪnsɪ'kjuərɪtɪ] N mancanza di
sicurezza
insensible [ɪn'sɛnsɪbl] ADJ insensibile;
(unconscious) privo(-a) di sensi
insensitive [ɪn'sɛnsɪtɪv] ADJ insensibile
insensitivity [ɪnsɛnsɪ'tɪvɪtɪ] N mancanza di
sensibilità
inseparable [ɪn'sɛprəbl] ADJ inseparabile
insert VT [ɪn'səːt] inserire, introdurre ▶ N
['ɪnsəːt] inserto
insertion [ɪn'səːʃən] N inserzione f
in-service ['ɪn'səːvɪs] ADJ (course, training) dopo
l'assunzione
inshore [ɪn'ʃɔː'] ADJ costiero(-a) ▶ ADV presso
la riva; verso la riva
inside ['ɪnsaɪd] N interno, parte f interiore;
(of road: BRIT) sinistra; (: US, in Europe etc)
destra ▶ ADJ interno(-a), interiore ▶ ADV
dentro, all'interno ▶ PREP dentro, all'interno
di; (of time): ~ **10 minutes** entro 10 minuti;
insides NPL (col) ventre m; ~ **out** adv alla
rovescia; **to turn sth ~ out** rivoltare qc; **to
know sth ~ out** conoscere qc a fondo;
~ **information** informazioni fpl riservate;
~ **story** storia segreta
inside forward N (Sport) mezzala, interno
inside lane N (Aut) corsia di marcia
inside leg measurement N (BRIT)
lunghezza interna
insider [ɪn'saɪdə'] N uno(-a) che ha le mani in
pasta
insider dealing, insider trading N (Stock
Exchange) insider trading m inv
insidious [ɪn'sɪdɪəs] ADJ insidioso(-a)
insight ['ɪnsaɪt] N acume m, perspicacia;
(glimpse, idea) percezione f; **to gain** or **get an ~
into sth** potersi render conto di qc
insignia [ɪn'sɪgnɪə] NPL insegne fpl
insignificant [ɪnsɪg'nɪfɪknt] ADJ
insignificante
insincere [ɪnsɪn'sɪə'] ADJ insincero(-a)
insincerity [ɪnsɪn'sɛrɪtɪ] N falsità, insincerità
insinuate [ɪn'sɪnjueɪt] VT insinuare
insinuation [ɪnsɪnju'eɪʃən] N insinuazione f
insipid [ɪn'sɪpɪd] ADJ insipido(-a), insulso(-a)
insist [ɪn'sɪst] VI insistere; **to ~ on doing**
insistere per fare; **to ~ that** insistere perché
+ sub; (claim) sostenere che

insistence [ɪn'sɪstəns] N insistenza
insistent [ɪn'sɪstənt] ADJ insistente
insofar [ɪnsəu'fɑːʳ] CONJ: ~ **as** in quanto
insole ['ɪnsəul] N soletta; (*fixed part of shoe*)
tramezza
insolence ['ɪnsələns] N insolenza
insolent ['ɪnsələnt] ADJ insolente
insoluble [ɪn'sɔljubl] ADJ insolubile
insolvency [ɪn'sɔlvənsɪ] N insolvenza
insolvent [ɪn'sɔlvənt] ADJ insolvente
insomnia [ɪn'sɔmnɪə] N insonnia
insomniac [ɪn'sɔmnɪæk] N chi soffre di
insonnia
inspect [ɪn'spɛkt] VT ispezionare; (*BRIT:
ticket*) controllare
inspection [ɪn'spɛkʃən] N ispezione f;
controllo
inspector [ɪn'spɛktəʳ] N ispettore(-trice);
(*BRIT: on buses, trains*) controllore m
inspiration [ɪnspə'reɪʃən] N ispirazione f
inspire [ɪn'spaɪəʳ] VT ispirare
inspired [ɪn'spaɪəd] ADJ (*writer, book etc*)
ispirato(-a); **in an ~ moment** in un
momento d'ispirazione
inspiring [ɪn'spaɪərɪŋ] ADJ stimolante
inst. [ɪnst] ABBR (*BRIT Comm: = instant*) c.m.
(*= corrente mese*)
instability [ɪnstə'bɪlɪtɪ] N instabilità
install [ɪn'stɔːl], (*US*) **instal** VT installare
installation [ɪnstə'leɪʃən] N installazione f
installment plan N (*US*) acquisto a rate
instalment, (*US*) **installment** [ɪn'stɔːlmənt]
N rata; (*of TV serial etc*) puntata; **in
instalments** (*pay*) a rate; (*receive*) una parte
per volta (: *publication*) a fascicoli
instance ['ɪnstəns] N esempio, caso; **for ~**
per *or* ad esempio; **in that ~** in quel caso; **in
the first ~** in primo luogo
instant ['ɪnstənt] N istante m, attimo ▶ ADJ
immediato(-a); urgente; (*coffee, food*) in
polvere; **the 10th ~** il 10 corrente (mese)
instantaneous [ɪnstən'teɪnɪəs] ADJ
istantaneo(-a)
instantly ['ɪnstəntlɪ] ADV immediatamente,
subito
instant message N messaggio istantaneo
instant messaging N messaggeria
istantanea
instant replay N (*US TV*) replay m inv
instead [ɪn'stɛd] ADV invece; ~ **of** invece di;
~ **of sb** al posto di qn
instep ['ɪnstɛp] N collo del piede; (*of shoe*)
collo della scarpa
instigate ['ɪnstɪgeɪt] VT (*rebellion, strike, crime*)
istigare a; (*new ideas etc*) promuovere
instigation [ɪnstɪ'geɪʃən] N istigazione f; **at
sb's ~** per *or* in seguito al suggerimento di qn
instil [ɪn'stɪl] VT: **to ~ (into)** inculcare (in)
instinct ['ɪnstɪŋkt] N istinto

instinctive [ɪn'stɪŋktɪv] ADJ istintivo(-a)
instinctively [ɪn'stɪŋktɪvlɪ] ADV per istinto
institute ['ɪnstɪtjuːt] N istituto ▶ VT istituire,
stabilire; (*inquiry*) avviare; (*proceedings*)
iniziare
institution [ɪnstɪ'tjuːʃən] N istituzione f;
istituto (d'istruzione); istituto (psichiatrico)
institutional [ɪnstɪ'tjuːʃənl] ADJ
istituzionale; ~ **care** assistenza presso un
istituto
instruct [ɪn'strʌkt] VT istruire; **to ~ sb in sth**
insegnare qc a qn; **to ~ sb to do** dare ordini a
qn di fare
instruction [ɪn'strʌkʃən] N istruzione f;
instructions (for use) istruzioni per l'uso
instruction book N libretto di istruzioni
instructive [ɪn'strʌktɪv] ADJ istruttivo(-a)
instructor [ɪn'strʌktəʳ] N istruttore(-trice);
(*for skiing*) maestro(-a)
instrument ['ɪnstrumənt] N strumento
instrumental [ɪnstru'mɛntl] ADJ (*Mus*)
strumentale; **to be ~ in sth/in doing sth**
contribuire fattivamente a qc/a fare qc
instrumentalist [ɪnstru'mɛntəlɪst] N
strumentista mf
instrument panel N quadro m,
portastrumenti inv
insubordinate [ɪnsə'bɔːdənɪt] ADJ
insubordinato(-a)
insubordination [ɪnsəbɔːdə'neɪʃən] N
insubordinazione f
insufferable [ɪn'sʌfrəbl] ADJ insopportabile
insufficient [ɪnsə'fɪʃənt] ADJ insufficiente
insufficiently [ɪnsə'fɪʃəntlɪ] ADV in modo
insufficiente
insular ['ɪnsjuləʳ] ADJ insulare; (*person*) di
mente ristretta
insulate ['ɪnsjuleɪt] VT isolare
insulating tape ['ɪnsjuleɪtɪŋ-] N nastro
isolante
insulation [ɪnsju'leɪʃən] N isolamento
insulin ['ɪnsjulɪn] N insulina
insult N ['ɪnsʌlt] insulto, affronto ▶ VT
[ɪn'sʌlt] insultare
insulting [ɪn'sʌltɪŋ] ADJ offensivo(-a),
ingiurioso(-a)
insuperable [ɪn'sjuːprəbl] ADJ
insormontabile, insuperabile
insurance [ɪn'ʃuərəns] N assicurazione f;
fire/life ~ assicurazione contro gli incendi/
sulla vita; **to take out ~ (against)** fare
un'assicurazione (contro), assicurarsi
(contro)
insurance agent N agente m d'assicurazioni
insurance broker N broker m inv
d'assicurazioni
insurance company N società di
assicurazioni
insurance policy N polizza d'assicurazione

insurance premium N premio assicurativo
insure [ɪnˈʃuəʳ] VT assicurare; **to ~ sb** or **sb's life** assicurare qn sulla vita; **to be insured for £5000** essere assicurato per 5000 sterline
insured [ɪnˈʃuəd] N: **the ~** l'assicurato(-a)
insurer [ɪnˈʃuərəʳ] N assicuratore(-trice)
insurgent [ɪnˈsəːdʒənt] ADJ ribelle ▶ N insorto(-a), rivoltoso(-a)
insurmountable [ɪnsəˈmauntəbl] ADJ insormontabile
insurrection [ɪnsəˈrɛkʃən] N insurrezione f
intact [ɪnˈtækt] ADJ intatto(-a)
intake [ˈɪnteɪk] N (Tech) immissione f; (of food) consumo; (Brit: of pupils etc) afflusso
intangible [ɪnˈtændʒɪbl] ADJ intangibile
integral [ˈɪntɪgrəl] ADJ integrale; (part) integrante
integrate [ˈɪntɪgreɪt] VT integrare ▶ VI integrarsi
integrated circuit N (Comput) circuito integrato
integration [ɪntɪˈgreɪʃən] N integrazione f; **racial ~** integrazione razziale
integrity [ɪnˈtɛgrɪtɪ] N integrità
intellect [ˈɪntəlɛkt] N intelletto
intellectual [ɪntəˈlɛktjuəl] ADJ, N intellettuale (mf)
intelligence [ɪnˈtɛlɪdʒəns] N intelligenza; (Mil etc) informazioni fpl
intelligence quotient N quoziente m d'intelligenza
Intelligence Service N servizio segreto
intelligence test N test m inv d'intelligenza
intelligent [ɪnˈtɛlɪdʒənt] ADJ intelligente
intelligible [ɪnˈtɛlɪdʒɪbl] ADJ intelligibile
intemperate [ɪnˈtɛmpərət] ADJ immoderato(-a); (drinking too much) intemperante nel bere
intend [ɪnˈtɛnd] VT (gift etc): **to ~ sth for** destinare qc a; **to ~ to do** aver l'intenzione di fare
intended [ɪnˈtɛndɪd] ADJ (insult) intenzionale; (effect) voluto(-a); (journey, route) progettato(-a)
intense [ɪnˈtɛns] ADJ intenso(-a); (person) di forti sentimenti
intensely [ɪnˈtɛnslɪ] ADV intensamente; profondamente
intensify [ɪnˈtɛnsɪfaɪ] VT intensificare
intensity [ɪnˈtɛnsɪtɪ] N intensità
intensive [ɪnˈtɛnsɪv] ADJ intensivo(-a)
intensive care N terapia intensiva; **~ unit** reparto terapia intensiva
intent [ɪnˈtɛnt] N intenzione f ▶ ADJ: **~ (on)** intento(-a) (a), immerso(-a) (in); **to all intents and purposes** a tutti gli effetti; **to be ~ on doing sth** essere deciso a fare qc
intention [ɪnˈtɛnʃən] N intenzione f

intentional [ɪnˈtɛnʃənl] ADJ intenzionale, deliberato(-a)
intentionally [ɪnˈtɛnʃənəlɪ] ADV apposta
intently [ɪnˈtɛntlɪ] ADV attentamente
inter [ɪnˈtəːʳ] VT sotterrare
interact [ɪntərˈækt] VI agire reciprocamente, interagire
interaction [ɪntərˈækʃən] N azione f reciproca, interazione f
interactive [ɪntərˈæktɪv] ADJ (Comput) interattivo(-a)
intercede [ɪntəˈsiːd] VI: **to ~ (with sb/on behalf of sb)** intercedere (presso qn/a favore di qn)
intercept [ɪntəˈsɛpt] VT intercettare; (person) fermare
interception [ɪntəˈsɛpʃən] N intercettamento
interchange N [ˈɪntətʃeɪndʒ] (exchange) scambio; (on motorway) incrocio pluridirezionale ▶ VT [ɪntəˈtʃeɪndʒ] scambiare; sostituire l'uno(-a) per l'altro(-a)
interchangeable [ɪntəˈtʃeɪndʒəbl] ADJ intercambiabile
intercity [ɪntəˈsɪtɪ] ADJ: **~ (train)** ≈ (treno) rapido
intercom [ˈɪntəkɔm] N interfono
interconnect [ɪntəkəˈnɛkt] VI (rooms) essere in comunicazione
intercontinental [ˈɪntəkɔntɪˈnɛntl] ADJ intercontinentale
intercourse [ˈɪntəkɔːs] N rapporti mpl; (sexual intercourse) rapporti sessuali
interdependent [ɪntədɪˈpɛndənt] ADJ interdipendente
interest [ˈɪntrɪst] N interesse m; (Comm: stake, share) interessi mpl ▶ VT interessare; **compound/simple ~** interesse composto/semplice; **business interests** attività fpl commerciali; **British interests in the Middle East** gli interessi (commerciali) britannici nel Medio Oriente
interested [ˈɪntrɪstɪd] ADJ interessato(-a); **to be ~ in** interessarsi di
interest-free [ˈɪntrɪstˈfriː] ADJ senza interesse
interesting [ˈɪntrɪstɪŋ] ADJ interessante
interest rate N tasso di interesse
interface [ˈɪntəfeɪs] N (Comput) interfaccia
interfere [ɪntəˈfɪəʳ] VI: **to ~ (in)** (quarrel, other people's business) immischiarsi (in); **to ~ with** (object) toccare; (plans, duty) interferire con
interference [ɪntəˈfɪərəns] N interferenza
interfering [ɪntəˈfɪərɪŋ] ADJ invadente
interim [ˈɪntərɪm] ADJ provvisorio(-a) ▶ N: **in the ~** nel frattempo; **~ dividend** (Comm) acconto di dividendo
interior [ɪnˈtɪərɪəʳ] N interno; (of country) entroterra ▶ ADJ interiore, interno(-a); (minister) degli Interni

interior decorator, interior designer N decoratore(-trice) (d'interni)

interior design N architettura d'interni

interjection [ɪntə'dʒɛkʃən] N interiezione f

interlock [ɪntə'lɔk] VI ingranarsi ▶ VT ingranare

interloper ['ɪntələupəʳ] N intruso(-a)

interlude ['ɪntəluːd] N intervallo; (Theat) intermezzo

intermarry [ɪntə'mærɪ] VI imparentarsi per mezzo di matrimonio; sposarsi tra parenti

intermediary [ɪntə'miːdɪərɪ] N intermediario(-a)

intermediate [ɪntə'miːdɪət] ADJ intermedio(-a); (Scol: course, level) medio(-a)

interment [ɪn'təːmənt] N (formal) inumazione f

interminable [ɪn'təːmɪnəbl] ADJ interminabile

intermission [ɪntə'mɪʃən] N pausa; (Theat, Cine) intermissione f, intervallo

intermittent [ɪntə'mɪtnt] ADJ intermittente

intermittently [ɪntə'mɪtntlɪ] ADV a intermittenza

intern VT [ɪn'təːn] internare ▶ N ['ɪntəːn] (US) medico interno

internal [ɪn'təːnl] ADJ interno(-a); ~ **injuries** lesioni fpl interne

internally [ɪn'təːnəlɪ] ADV all'interno; "**not to be taken ~**" "per uso esterno"

Internal Revenue, Internal Revenue Service N (US) Fisco

international [ɪntə'næʃənl] ADJ internazionale ▶ N (BRIT Sport) incontro internazionale

International Atomic Energy Agency N Agenzia Internazionale per l'Energia Atomica

International Court of Justice N Corte f Internazionale di Giustizia

international date line N linea del cambiamento di data

internationally [ɪntə'næʃnəlɪ] ADV a livello internazionale

International Monetary Fund N Fondo monetario internazionale

international relations NPL rapporti mpl internazionali

internecine [ɪntə'niːsaɪn] ADJ sanguinoso(-a)

internee [ɪntə'niː] N internato(-a)

Internet ['ɪntənɛt] N: **the ~** Internet f

Internet café N cybercaffè m inv

Internet Service Provider N Provider m inv

Internet user N utente mf Internet

internment [ɪn'təːnmənt] N internamento

interplay ['ɪntəpleɪ] N azione e reazione f

Interpol ['ɪntəpɔl] N Interpol f

interpret [ɪn'təːprɪt] VT interpretare ▶ VI fare da interprete

interpretation [ɪntəːprɪ'teɪʃən] N interpretazione f

interpreter [ɪn'təːprɪtəʳ] N interprete mf

interpreting [ɪn'təːprɪtɪŋ] N (profession) interpretariato

interrelated [ɪntərɪ'leɪtɪd] ADJ correlato(-a)

interrogate [ɪn'tɛrəugeɪt] VT interrogare

interrogation [ɪntɛrəu'geɪʃən] N interrogazione f; (of suspect etc) interrogatorio

interrogative [ɪntə'rɔgətɪv] ADJ interrogativo(-a) ▶ N (Ling) interrogativo

interrogator [ɪn'tɛrəgeɪtəʳ] N interrogante mf

interrupt [ɪntə'rʌpt] VT, VI interrompere

interruption [ɪntə'rʌpʃən] N interruzione f

intersect [ɪntə'sɛkt] VT intersecare ▶ VI (roads) intersecarsi

intersection [ɪntə'sɛkʃən] N intersezione f; (of roads) incrocio

intersperse [ɪntə'spəːs] VT: **to ~ with** costellare di

interstate ['ɪntəsteɪt] (US) N fra stati

intertwine [ɪntə'twaɪn] VT intrecciare ▶ VI intrecciarsi

interval ['ɪntəvl] N intervallo; (BRIT Scol) ricreazione f, intervallo; **bright intervals** (in weather) schiarite fpl; **at intervals** a intervalli

intervene [ɪntə'viːn] VI (time) intercorrere; (event, person) intervenire

intervention [ɪntə'vɛnʃən] N intervento

interview ['ɪntəvjuː] N (Radio, TV etc) intervista; (for job) colloquio ▶ VT intervistare; avere un colloquio con

interviewee [ɪntəvjuː'iː] N (TV) intervistato(-a); (for job) chi si presenta ad un colloquio di lavoro

interviewer ['ɪntəvjuːəʳ] N intervistatore(-trice)

intestate [ɪn'tɛsteɪt] ADJ intestato(-a)

intestinal [ɪn'tɛstɪnl] ADJ intestinale

intestine [ɪn'tɛstɪn] N intestino; **large/small ~** intestino crasso/tenue

intimacy ['ɪntɪməsɪ] N intimità

intimate ADJ ['ɪntɪmət] intimo(-a); (knowledge) profondo(-a) ▶ VT ['ɪntɪmeɪt] lasciar capire

intimately ['ɪntɪmɪtlɪ] ADV intimamente

intimation [ɪntɪ'meɪʃən] N annuncio

intimidate [ɪn'tɪmɪdeɪt] VT intimidire, intimorire

intimidating [ɪn'tɪmɪdeɪtɪŋ] ADJ (sight) spaventoso(-a); (appearance, figure) minaccioso(-a)

intimidation [ɪntɪmɪ'deɪʃən] N intimidazione f

into ['ɪntu] PREP dentro, in; **come ~ the house** entra in casa; **he worked late ~ the night** lavorò fino a tarda notte; **~ pieces**

a pezzi; ~ **Italian** in italiano; **to change pounds ~ dollars** cambiare delle sterline in dollari

intolerable [ɪn'tɔlərəbl] ADJ intollerabile

intolerance [ɪn'tɔlərns] N intolleranza

intolerant [ɪn'tɔlərnt] ADJ: ~ **(of)** intollerante (di)

intonation [ɪntəu'neɪʃən] N intonazione f

intoxicate [ɪn'tɔksɪkeɪt] VT inebriare

intoxicated [ɪn'tɔksɪkeɪtɪd] ADJ inebriato(-a)

intoxication [ɪntɔksɪ'keɪʃən] N ebbrezza

intractable [ɪn'træktəbl] ADJ intrattabile; (*illness*) difficile da curare; (*problem*) insolubile

intranet ['ɪntrənɛt] N Intranet f

intransigence [ɪn'trænsɪdʒəns] N intransigenza

intransigent [ɪn'trænsɪdʒənt] ADJ intransigente

intransitive [ɪn'trænsɪtɪv] ADJ intransitivo(-a)

intra-uterine device [ɪntrə'ju:təraɪn-] N dispositivo intrauterino

intravenous [ɪntrə'vi:nəs] ADJ endovenoso(-a)

in-tray ['ɪntreɪ] N raccoglitore m per le carte in arrivo

intrepid [ɪn'trɛpɪd] ADJ intrepido(-a)

intricacy ['ɪntrɪkəsɪ] N complessità f inv

intricate ['ɪntrɪkət] ADJ intricato(-a), complicato(-a)

intrigue [ɪn'tri:g] N intrigo ▶ VT affascinare ▶ VI complottare, tramare

intriguing [ɪn'tri:gɪŋ] ADJ affascinante

intrinsic [ɪn'trɪnsɪk] ADJ intrinseco(-a)

introduce [ɪntrə'dju:s] VT introdurre; **to ~ sb (to sb)** presentare qn (a qn); **to ~ sb to** (*pastime, technique*) iniziare qn a; **may I ~ ...?** permette che le presenti ...?

introduction [ɪntrə'dʌkʃən] N introduzione f; (*of person*) presentazione f; (*to new experience*) iniziazione f; **a letter of ~** una lettera di presentazione

introductory [ɪntrə'dʌktərɪ] ADJ introduttivo(-a); **an ~ offer** un'offerta di lancio; ~ **remarks** osservazioni fpl preliminari

introspection [ɪntrəu'spɛkʃən] N introspezione f

introspective [ɪntrəu'spɛktɪv] ADJ introspettivo(-a)

introvert ['ɪntrəuvə:t] ADJ, N introverso(-a)

intrude [ɪn'tru:d] VI (*person*) intromettersi; **to ~ on** (*person*) importunare; ~ **on** or **into** (*conversation*) intromettersi in; **am I intruding?** disturbo?

intruder [ɪn'tru:də^r] N intruso(-a)

intrusion [ɪn'tru:ʒən] N intrusione f

intrusive [ɪn'tru:sɪv] ADJ importuno(-a)

intuition [ɪntju:'ɪʃən] N intuizione f

intuitive [ɪn'tju:ɪtɪv] ADJ intuitivo(-a); dotato(-a) di intuito

inundate ['ɪnʌndeɪt] VT: **to ~ with** inondare di

inure [ɪn'juə^r] VT: **to ~ (to)** assuefare (a)

invade [ɪn'veɪd] VT invadere

invader [ɪn'veɪdə^r] N invasore m

invalid N ['ɪnvəlɪd] malato(-a); (*with disability*) invalido(-a) ▶ ADJ [ɪn'vælɪd] (*not valid*) invalido(-a), non valido(-a)

invalidate [ɪn'vælɪdeɪt] VT invalidare

invalid chair N (BRIT) sedia a rotelle

invaluable [ɪn'væljuəbl] ADJ prezioso(-a); inestimabile

invariable [ɪn'vɛərɪəbl] ADJ costante, invariabile

invariably [ɪn'vɛərɪəblɪ] ADV invariabilmente; sempre; **she is ~ late** è immancabilmente in ritardo

invasion [ɪn'veɪʒən] N invasione f

invective [ɪn'vɛktɪv] N invettiva

inveigle [ɪn'vi:gl] VT: **to ~ sb into (doing) sth** circuire qn per (fargli fare) qc

invent [ɪn'vɛnt] VT inventare

invention [ɪn'vɛnʃən] N invenzione f

inventive [ɪn'vɛntɪv] ADJ inventivo(-a)

inventiveness [ɪn'vɛntɪvnɪs] N inventiva

inventor [ɪn'vɛntə^r] N inventore m

inventory ['ɪnvəntrɪ] N inventario

inventory control N (Comm) controllo delle giacenze

inverse [ɪn'və:s] ADJ inverso(-a) ▶ N inverso, contrario; **in ~ proportion (to)** in modo inversamente proporzionale (a)

inversely [ɪn'və:slɪ] ADV inversamente

invert [ɪn'və:t] VT invertire; (*object*) rovesciare

invertebrate [ɪn'və:tɪbrɪt] N invertebrato

inverted commas [ɪn'və:tɪd-] NPL (BRIT) virgolette fpl

invest [ɪn'vɛst] VT investire; (fig: time, effort) impiegare; (*endow*): **to ~ sb with sth** investire qn di qc ▶ VI fare investimenti; **to ~ in** investire in, fare (degli) investimenti in; (*acquire*) comprarsi

investigate [ɪn'vɛstɪgeɪt] VT investigare, indagare; (*crime*) fare indagini su

investigation [ɪnvɛstɪ'geɪʃən] N investigazione f; (of crime) indagine f

investigative [ɪn'vɛstɪgətɪv] ADJ: ~ **journalism** giornalismo investigativo

investigator [ɪn'vɛstɪgeɪtə^r] N investigatore(-trice); **a private ~** un investigatore privato, un detective

investiture [ɪn'vɛstɪtʃə^r] N investitura

investment [ɪn'vɛstmənt] N investimento

investment income N reddito da investimenti

investment trust N fondo comune di investimento

investor [ɪn'vɛstə^r] N investitore(-trice); (*shareholder*) azionista *mf*

inveterate [ɪn'vɛtərət] ADJ inveterato(-a)

invidious [ɪn'vɪdɪəs] ADJ odioso(-a); (*task*) spiacevole

invigilate [ɪn'vɪdʒɪleɪt] VT, VI (BRIT Scol) sorvegliare

invigilator [ɪn'vɪdʒɪleɪtə^r] N (BRIT) chi sorveglia agli esami

invigorating [ɪn'vɪgəreɪtɪŋ] ADJ stimolante; vivificante

invincible [ɪn'vɪnsɪbl] ADJ invincibile

inviolate [ɪn'vaɪələt] ADJ inviolato(-a)

invisible [ɪn'vɪzɪbl] ADJ invisibile

invisible assets NPL (BRIT) beni *mpl* immateriali

invisible ink N inchiostro simpatico

invisible mending N rammendo invisibile

invitation [ɪnvɪ'teɪʃən] N invito; **by ~ only** esclusivamente su *or* per invito; **at sb's ~** dietro invito di qn

invite [ɪn'vaɪt] VT invitare; (*opinions etc*) sollecitare; (*trouble*) provocare; **to ~ sb (to do)** invitare qn (a fare); **to ~ sb to dinner** invitare qn a cena
  ▶ **invite out** VT invitare fuori
  ▶ **invite over** VT invitare (a casa)

inviting [ɪn'vaɪtɪŋ] ADJ invitante, attraente

invoice ['ɪnvɔɪs] N fattura ▶ VT fatturare; **to ~ sb for goods** inviare a qn la fattura per le *or* delle merci

invoke [ɪn'vəuk] VT invocare

involuntary [ɪn'vɔləntrɪ] ADJ involontario(-a)

involve [ɪn'vɔlv] VT (*entail*) richiedere, comportare; (*associate*): **to ~ sb (in)** implicare qn (in); coinvolgere qn (in); **to ~ o.s. in sth** (*politics etc*) impegnarsi in qc

involved [ɪn'vɔlvd] ADJ involuto(-a), complesso(-a); **to feel ~** sentirsi coinvolto(-a); **to be ~ in** essere coinvolto(-a) in; **to become ~ with sb** (*socially*) legarsi a qn; (*emotionally*) legarsi sentimentalmente a qn

involvement [ɪn'vɔlvmənt] N implicazione *f*; coinvolgimento; impegno; partecipazione *f*

invulnerable [ɪn'vʌlnərəbl] ADJ invulnerabile

inward ['ɪnwəd] ADJ (*movement*) verso l'interno; (*thought, feeling*) interiore, intimo(-a) ▶ ADV verso l'interno

inwardly ['ɪnwədlɪ] ADV (*feel, think etc*) nell'intimo, entro di sé

inwards ['ɪnwədz] ADV verso l'interno

I/O ABBR (*Comput*: = *input/output*) I/O

IOC N ABBR (= *International Olympic Committee*) CIO *m* (= *Comitato Internazionale Olimpico*)

iodine ['aɪəudiːn] N iodio

IOM ABBR (BRIT) = **Isle of Man**

ion ['aɪən] N ione *m*

Ionian Sea [aɪ'əunɪən-] N: **the ~** il mare Ionio

ioniser ['aɪənaɪzə^r] N ionizzatore *m*

iota [aɪ'əutə] N (*fig*) briciolo

IOU N ABBR (= *I owe you*) pagherò *m inv*

IOW ABBR (BRIT) = **Isle of Wight**

IPA N ABBR (= *International Phonetic Alphabet*) I.P.A. *m*

iPad® ['aɪˌpæd] N iPad® *m inv*

IP address N (*Comput*) indirizzo IP

iPhone® ['aɪˌfəun] N iPhone® *m inv*

iPod® ['aɪpɔd] N iPod® *m inv*, lettore *m* MP3

IQ N ABBR (= *intelligence quotient*) quoziente *m* d'intelligenza

IRA N ABBR (= *Irish Republican Army*) I.R.A. *f*; (*US*) = **individual retirement account**

Iran [ɪ'rɑːn] N Iran *m*

Iranian [ɪ'reɪnɪən] ADJ iraniano(-a) ▶ N iraniano(-a); (*Ling*) iranico

Iraq [ɪ'rɑːk] N Iraq *m*

Iraqi [ɪ'rɑːkɪ] ADJ iracheno(-a) ▶ N iracheno(-a)

irascible [ɪ'ræsɪbl] ADJ irascibile

irate [aɪ'reɪt] ADJ irato(-a)

Ireland ['aɪələnd] N Irlanda; **Republic of ~** Repubblica d'Irlanda, Eire *f*

iris ['aɪrɪs] (*pl* **irises** [-ɪz]) N iride *f*; (*Bot*) giaggiolo, iride

Irish ['aɪrɪʃ] ADJ irlandese ▶ NPL: **the ~** gli Irlandesi

Irishman ['aɪrɪʃmən] N (*irreg*) irlandese *m*

Irish Sea N: **the ~** il mar d'Irlanda

Irishwoman ['aɪrɪʃwumən] N (*irreg*) irlandese *f*

irk [əːk] VT seccare

irksome ['əːksəm] ADJ seccante

IRN N ABBR (= *Independent Radio News*) agenzia d'informazioni per la radio

IRO N ABBR (= *International Refugee Organization*) O.I.R. *f* (= *Organizzazione Internazionale per i Rifugiati*)

iron ['aɪən] N ferro; (*for clothes*) ferro da stiro ▶ ADJ di *or* in ferro ▶ VT (*clothes*) stirare; *see also* **irons**
  ▶ **iron out** VT (*crease*) appianare; (*fig*) spianare; far sparire

Iron Curtain N: **the ~** la cortina di ferro

iron foundry N fonderia

ironic [aɪ'rɔnɪk], **ironical** [aɪ'rɔnɪkl] ADJ ironico(-a)

ironically [aɪ'rɔnɪklɪ] ADV ironicamente

ironing ['aɪənɪŋ] N (*act*) stirare *m*; (*clothes*) roba da stirare

ironing board N asse *f* da stiro

iron lung N (*Med*) polmone *m* d'acciaio

ironmonger [ˈaɪənmʌŋgəʳ] N (BRIT)
negoziante m in ferramenta; ~'s (shop) n
negozio di ferramenta

iron ore N minerale m di ferro

irons [ˈaɪənz] NPL (chains) catene fpl

ironworks [ˈaɪənwəːks] N ferriera

irony [ˈaɪrənɪ] N ironia

irrational [ɪˈræʃənl] ADJ irrazionale;
irragionevole; illogico(-a)

irreconcilable [ɪrɛkənˈsaɪləbl] ADJ
irreconciliabile; (opinion): ~ with
inconciliabile con

irredeemable [ɪrɪˈdiːməbl] ADJ (Comm)
irredimibile

irrefutable [ɪrɪˈfjuːtəbl] ADJ irrefutabile

irregular [ɪˈrɛgjuləʳ] ADJ irregolare

irregularity [ɪrɛgjuˈlærɪtɪ] N irregolarità f inv

irrelevance [ɪˈrɛləvəns] N inappropriatezza

irrelevant [ɪˈrɛləvənt] ADJ non pertinente

irreligious [ɪrɪˈlɪdʒəs] ADJ irreligioso(-a)

irreparable [ɪˈrɛprəbl] ADJ irreparabile

irreplaceable [ɪrɪˈpleɪsəbl] ADJ insostituibile

irrepressible [ɪrɪˈprɛsəbl] ADJ irrefrenabile

irreproachable [ɪrɪˈprəutʃəbl] ADJ
irreprensibile

irresistible [ɪrɪˈzɪstɪbl] ADJ irresistibile

irresolute [ɪˈrɛzəluːt] ADJ irresoluto(-a),
indeciso(-a)

irrespective [ɪrɪˈspɛktɪv]: ~ of prep senza
riguardo a

irresponsible [ɪrɪˈspɔnsɪbl] ADJ
irresponsabile

irretrievable [ɪrɪˈtriːvəbl] ADJ (object)
irrecuperabile; (loss, damage) irreparabile

irreverent [ɪˈrɛvərnt] ADJ irriverente

irrevocable [ɪˈrɛvəkəbl] ADJ irrevocabile

irrigate [ˈɪrɪgeɪt] VT irrigare

irrigation [ɪrɪˈgeɪʃən] N irrigazione f

irritable [ˈɪrɪtəbl] ADJ irritabile

irritant [ˈɪrɪtənt] N sostanza irritante

irritate [ˈɪrɪteɪt] VT irritare

irritating ADJ (person, sound etc) irritante

irritation [ɪrɪˈteɪʃən] N irritazione f

IRS N ABBR (US) = **Internal Revenue Service**

is [ɪz] VB see **be**

ISA [ˈaɪsə] N ABBR (= individual savings account)
forma di investimento detassata

ISBN N ABBR (= International Standard Book
Number) ISBN m

ISDN N ABBR (= Integrated Services Digital
Network) ISDN f

Islam [ˈɪzlɑːm] N Islam m

Islamic [ɪzˈlæmɪk] ADJ islamico(-a)

island [ˈaɪlənd] N isola; (also: **traffic island**)
salvagente m

islander [ˈaɪləndəʳ] N isolano(-a)

isle [aɪl] N isola

isn't [ˈɪznt]= **is not**

isolate [ˈaɪsəleɪt] VT isolare

isolated [ˈaɪsəleɪtɪd] ADJ isolato(-a)

isolation [aɪsəˈleɪʃən] N isolamento

isolationism [aɪsəˈleɪʃənɪzəm] N
isolazionismo

isotope [ˈaɪsəutəup] N isotopo

ISP N ABBR (Comput: = internet service provider)
provider m inv

Israel [ˈɪzreɪl] N Israele m

Israeli [ɪzˈreɪlɪ] ADJ, N israeliano(-a)

issue [ˈɪʃuː] N questione f, problema m;
(outcome) esito, risultato; (of banknotes etc)
emissione f; (of newspaper etc) numero;
(offspring) discendenza ▶ VT (statement)
rilasciare; (rations, equipment) distribuire;
(orders) dare; (book) pubblicare; (banknotes,
cheques, stamps) emettere ▶ VI: **to ~ (from)**
uscire (da), venir fuori (da); **at ~** in gioco, in
discussione; **to avoid the ~** evitare la
discussione; **to take ~ with sb (over sth)**
prendere posizione contro qn (riguardo a
qc); **to confuse** or **obscure the ~** confondere
le cose; **to make an ~ of sth** fare un
problema di qc; **to ~ sth to sb, ~ sb with sth**
consegnare qc a qn

Istanbul [ɪstænˈbuːl] N Istanbul f

isthmus [ˈɪsməs] N istmo

IT N ABBR = **information technology**

(KEYWORD)

it [ɪt] PRON **1** (specific: subject) esso(-a) (mostly
omitted in Italian); (: direct object) lo (la), l';
(: indirect object) gli (le); **where's my book?
— it's on the table** dov'è il mio libro? — è
sulla tavola; **what is it?** che cos'è?; (what's the
matter?) cosa c'è?; **where is it?** dov'è?; **I can't
find it** non lo (or la) trovo; **give it to me**
dammelo (or dammela); **about/from/of it**
ne; **I spoke to him about it** gliene ho
parlato; **what did you learn from it?** quale
insegnamento ne hai tratto?; **I'm proud of
it** ne sono fiero; **in/to/at it** ci; **put the book
in it** mettici il libro; **did you go to it?** ci sei
andato?; **I wasn't at it** non c'ero; **above/
over it** sopra; **below/under it** sotto; **in
front of/behind it** lì davanti/dietro

2 (impers): **it's raining** piove; **it's Friday
tomorrow** domani è venerdì; **it's 6 o'clock**
sono le 6; **it's 2 hours on the train** sono or ci
vogliono 2 ore di treno; **who is it? — it's me**
chi è? — sono io

ITA N ABBR (BRIT: = initial teaching alphabet)
alfabeto fonetico semplificato per insegnare a
leggere

Italian [ɪˈtæljən] ADJ italiano(-a) ▶ N
italiano(-a); (Ling) italiano; **the Italians** gli
Italiani

italic [ɪˈtælɪk] ADJ corsivo(-a); **italics** NPL
corsivo

Italy ['ɪtəlɪ] N Italia

ITC N ABBR (*BRIT:* = *Independent Television Commission*) *organo di controllo sulle reti televisive*

itch [ɪtʃ] N prurito ▶ VI (*person*) avere il prurito; (*part of body*) prudere; **to be itching to do** avere una gran voglia di fare

itchy ['ɪtʃɪ] ADJ che prude; **my back is ~** ho prurito alla schiena

it'd ['ɪtd] = **it would; it had**

item ['aɪtəm] N articolo; (*on agenda*) punto; (*in programme*) numero; (*also:* **news item**) notizia; **items of clothing** capi *mpl* di abbigliamento

itemize ['aɪtəmaɪz] VT specificare, dettagliare

itemized bill ['aɪtəmaɪzd-] N conto dettagliato

itinerant [ɪ'tɪnərənt] ADJ ambulante

itinerary [aɪ'tɪnərərɪ] N itinerario

it'll ['ɪtl] = **it will; it shall**

ITN N ABBR (*BRIT:* = *Independent Television News*) *agenzia d'informazioni per la televisione*

its [ɪts] ADJ, PRON il (la) suo(-a), i (le) suoi (sue)

it's [ɪts] = **it is; it has**

itself [ɪt'sɛlf] PRON (*emphatic*) esso(-a) stesso(-a); (*reflexive*) si

ITV N ABBR (*BRIT:* = *Independent Television*) *rete televisiva indipendente; vedi nota*

> La ITV è un'azienda televisiva privata che comprende una serie di emittenti regionali, la prima delle quali è stata aperta nel 1955. Si autofinanzia tramite la pubblicità ed è sottoposta al controllo di un ente ufficiale, la *Ofcom; vedi anche* **BBC**.

IUD N ABBR = **intra-uterine device**

I've [aɪv] = **I have**

ivory ['aɪvərɪ] N avorio

Ivory Coast N Costa d'Avorio

ivory tower N torre *f* d'avorio

ivy ['aɪvɪ] N edera

Ivy League N (*US*); *vedi nota*

> *Ivy League* è il termine usato per indicare le otto università più prestigiose degli Stati Uniti nordorientali (Brown, Columbia, Cornell, Dartmouth College, Harvard, Princeton, University of Pennsylvania e Yale).

Jj

J, j [dʒeɪ] N (*letter*) J, j f *inv or* m *inv*; **J for Jack**, (*US*) **J for Jig** ≈ J come Jersey

JA N ABBR = **judge advocate**

J/A ABBR = **joint account**

jab [dʒæb] VT dare colpetti a; **to ~ sth into** affondare *or* piantare qc dentro ▶ VI: **to ~ at** dare colpi a ▶ N colpo; (*Med: col*) puntura

jabber ['dʒæbəʳ] VT, VI borbottare

jack [dʒæk] N (*Aut*) cricco; (*Bowls*) boccino, pallino; (*Cards*) fante m
   ▶ **jack in** VT (*col*) mollare
   ▶ **jack up** VT sollevare sul cricco; (*raise: prices etc*) alzare

jackal ['dʒækl] N sciacallo

jackass ['dʒækæs] N (*also fig*) asino, somaro

jackdaw ['dʒækdɔ:] N taccola

jacket ['dʒækɪt] N giacca; (*of book*) copertura; **potatoes in their jackets** (*BRIT*) patate *fpl* con la buccia

jacket potato N *patata cotta al forno con la buccia*

jack-in-the-box ['dʒækɪnðəbɔks] N scatola a sorpresa (con pupazzo a molla)

jack-knife ['dʒæknaɪf] VI: **the lorry jack-knifed** l'autotreno si è piegato su se stesso

jack-of-all-trades [dʒækəv'ɔ:ltreɪdz] N uno che fa un po' di tutto

jack plug N (*BRIT*) jack plug f *inv*

jackpot ['dʒækpɔt] N primo premio (in denaro)

Jacuzzi® [dʒə'ku:zɪ] N vasca per idromassaggio Jacuzzi®

jade [dʒeɪd] N (*stone*) giada

jaded ['dʒeɪdɪd] ADJ sfinito(-a), spossato(-a)

jagged ['dʒægɪd] ADJ seghettato(-a); (*cliffs etc*) frastagliato(-a)

jaguar ['dʒægjuəʳ] N giaguaro

jail [dʒeɪl] N prigione f ▶ VT mandare in prigione

jailbird ['dʒeɪlbə:d] N avanzo di galera

jailbreak ['dʒeɪlbreɪk] N evasione f

jailer ['dʒeɪləʳ] N custode m del carcere

jail sentence N condanna al carcere

jalopy [dʒə'lɔpɪ] N (*col*) macinino

jam [dʒæm] N marmellata; (*of shoppers etc*) ressa; (*also:* **traffic jam**) ingorgo; (: *col*) pasticcio ▶ VT (*passage etc*) ingombrare, ostacolare; (*mechanism, drawer etc*) bloccare; (*Radio*) disturbare con interferenze ▶ VI (*mechanism, sliding part*) incepparsi, bloccarsi; (*gun*) incepparsi; **to get sb out of a ~** tirare qn fuori dai pasticci; **to ~ sth into** forzare qc dentro; infilare qc a forza dentro; **the telephone lines are jammed** le linee sono sovraccariche

Jamaica [dʒə'meɪkə] N Giamaica

Jamaican [dʒə'meɪkən] ADJ, N giamaicano(-a)

jamb [dʒæm] N stipite m

jammed [dʒæmd] ADJ (*door*) bloccato(-a); (*rifle, printer*) inceppato(-a)

jam-packed [dʒæm'pækt] ADJ: **~ (with)** pieno(-a) zeppo(-a) (di), strapieno(-a) (di)

jam session N improvvisazione f jazzistica

Jan. ABBR (= *January*) gen., genn.

jangle ['dʒæŋgl] VI risuonare; (*bracelet*) tintinnare

janitor ['dʒænɪtəʳ] N (*caretaker*) portiere m; (: *Scol*) bidello

January ['dʒænjuərɪ] N gennaio; *see also* **July**

Japan [dʒə'pæn] N Giappone m

Japanese [dʒæpə'ni:z] ADJ giapponese ▶ N (*pl inv*) giapponese mf; (*Ling*) giapponese m

jar [dʒɑ:ʳ] N (*container*) barattolo, vasetto ▶ VI (*sound*) stridere; (*colours etc*) stonare ▶ VT (*shake*) scuotere

jargon ['dʒɑ:gən] N gergo

jarring ['dʒɑ:rɪŋ] ADJ (*sound, colour*) stonato(-a)

Jas. ABBR = **James**

jasmin, jasmine ['dʒæzmɪn] N gelsomino

jaundice ['dʒɔ:ndɪs] N itterizia

jaundiced ['dʒɔ:ndɪst] ADJ (*fig*) invidioso(-a) e critico(-a)

jaunt [dʒɔ:nt] N gita

jaunty ['dʒɔ:ntɪ] ADJ vivace; disinvolto(-a), spigliato(-a)

Java ['dʒɑ:və] N Giava

javelin ['dʒævlɪn] N giavellotto
jaw [dʒɔ:] N mascella; **jaws** NPL (Tech: of vice etc) morsa
jawbone ['dʒɔ:bəun] N mandibola
jay [dʒeɪ] N ghiandaia
jaywalker ['dʒeɪwɔ:kə^r] N pedone(-a) indisciplinato(-a)
jazz [dʒæz] N jazz m
  ▶ **jazz up** VT rendere vivace
jazz band N banda f jazz inv
jazzy ['dʒæzɪ] ADJ vistoso(-a), chiassoso(-a)
JCB® N scavatrice f
JCS N ABBR (US) = **Joint Chiefs of Staff**
JD N ABBR (US: = Doctor of Laws) titolo di studio; (= Justice Department) ministero della Giustizia
jealous ['dʒɛləs] ADJ geloso(-a)
jealously ['dʒɛləslɪ] ADV (enviously) con gelosia; (watchfully) gelosamente
jealousy ['dʒɛləsɪ] N gelosia
jeans [dʒi:nz] NPL (blue-)jeans mpl
Jeep® [dʒi:p] N jeep m inv
jeer [dʒɪə^r] VI: **to ~ (at)** fischiare; beffeggiare; see also **jeers**
jeering ['dʒɪərɪŋ] ADJ (crowd) che urla e fischia
  ▶ N fischi mpl; parole fpl di scherno
jeers ['dʒɪəz] NPL fischi mpl
Jello® ['dʒɛləu] N (US) gelatina di frutta
jelly ['dʒɛlɪ] N gelatina
jellyfish ['dʒɛlɪfɪʃ] N medusa
jeopardize ['dʒɛpədaɪz] VT mettere in pericolo
jeopardy ['dʒɛpədɪ] N: **in ~** in pericolo
jerk [dʒə:k] N sobbalzo, scossa; sussulto; (col) povero(-a) scemo(-a) ▶ VT dare una scossa a
  ▶ VI (vehicles) sobbalzare
jerkin ['dʒə:kɪn] N giubbotto
jerky ['dʒə:kɪ] ADJ a scatti; a sobbalzi
jerry-built ['dʒɛrɪbɪlt] ADJ fatto(-a) di cartapesta
jerry can ['dʒɛrɪ-] N tanica
Jersey ['dʒə:zɪ] N Jersey m
jersey ['dʒə:zɪ] N maglia; (fabric) jersey m
Jerusalem [dʒə'ru:sələm] N Gerusalemme f
jest [dʒɛst] N scherzo; **in ~** per scherzo
jester ['dʒɛstə^r] N (Hist) buffone m
Jesus ['dʒi:zəs] N Gesù m; **~ Christ** Gesù Cristo
jet [dʒɛt] N (of gas, liquid) getto; (Aut) spruzzatore m; (Aviat) aviogetto
jet-black ['dʒɛt'blæk] ADJ nero(-a) come l'ebano, corvino(-a)
jet engine N motore m a reazione
jet lag N (problemi mpl dovuti allo) sbalzo dei fusi orari
jetsam ['dʒɛtsəm] N relitti mpl di mare
jet-setter ['dʒɛtsɛtə^r] N membro del jet set
jet-ski VI acquascooter m inv
jettison ['dʒɛtɪsn] VT gettare in mare
jetty ['dʒɛtɪ] N molo

Jew [dʒu:] N ebreo
jewel ['dʒu:əl] N gioiello
jeweller, (US) **jeweler** ['dʒu:ələ^r] N orefice m, gioielliere(-a); **~'s shop** oreficeria, gioielleria
jewellery, (US) **jewelry** ['dʒu:əlrɪ] N gioielli mpl; **jewelry store** (US) oreficeria, gioielleria
Jewess ['dʒu:ɪs] N ebrea
Jewish ['dʒu:ɪʃ] ADJ ebreo(-a), ebraico(-a)
JFK N ABBR (US) = **John Fitzgerald Kennedy International Airport**
jib [dʒɪb] N (Naut) fiocco; (of crane) braccio ▶ VI (horse) impennarsi; **to ~ at doing sth** essere restio a fare qc
jibe [dʒaɪb] N beffa
jiffy ['dʒɪfɪ] N (col): **in a ~** in un batter d'occhio
jig [dʒɪg] N (dance, tune) giga
jigsaw ['dʒɪgsɔ:] N (tool) sega da traforo; (also: **jigsaw puzzle**) puzzle m inv
jilt [dʒɪlt] VT piantare in asso
jingle ['dʒɪŋgl] N (advert) sigla pubblicitaria
  ▶ VI tintinnare, scampanellare
jingoism ['dʒɪŋgəuɪzəm] N sciovinismo
jinx [dʒɪŋks] N (col) iettatura; (person) iettatore(-trice)
jitters ['dʒɪtəz] NPL (col): **to get the ~** aver fifa
jittery ['dʒɪtərɪ] ADJ (col) teso(-a), agitato(-a); **to be ~** aver fifa
jiujitsu [dʒu:'dʒɪtsu:] N jujitsu m
job [dʒɔb] N lavoro; (employment) impiego, posto; **a part-time/full-time ~** un lavoro a mezza giornata/a tempo pieno; **that's not my ~** non è compito mio; **he's only doing his ~** non fa che il suo dovere; **it's a good ~ that ...** meno male che ...; **just the ~!** proprio quello che ci vuole!
jobber ['dʒɔbə^r] N (Brit Stock Exchange) intermediario tra agenti di cambio
jobbing ['dʒɔbɪŋ] ADJ (Brit: workman) a ore, a giornata
job centre (Brit) N ufficio di collocamento
job creation scheme N progetto per la creazione di nuovi posti di lavoro
job description N caratteristiche fpl (di un lavoro)
jobless ['dʒɔblɪs] ADJ senza lavoro, disoccupato(-a) ▶ NPL: **the ~** i senza lavoro
job lot N partita di articoli disparati
job satisfaction N soddisfazione f nel lavoro
job security N sicurezza del posto di lavoro
job share VI fare un lavoro ripartito ▶ N lavoro ripartito
job specification N caratteristiche fpl (di un lavoro)
Jock [dʒɔk] N (col) termine colloquiale per chiamare uno scozzese
jockey ['dʒɔkɪ] N fantino, jockey m inv ▶ VI: **to ~ for position** manovrare per una posizione di vantaggio

jockey box N (US Aut) vano portaoggetti
jockstrap ['dʒɔkstræp] N conchiglia (per atleti)
jocular ['dʒɔkjuləʳ] ADJ gioviale; scherzoso(-a)
jog [dʒɔg] VT urtare ▶ VI (Sport) fare footing, fare jogging; **to ~ along** trottare; (fig) andare avanti pian piano; **to ~ sb's memory** rinfrescare la memoria di qn
jogger ['dʒɔgəʳ] N persona che fa footing or jogging
jogging ['dʒɔgɪŋ] N footing m, jogging m
john [dʒɔn] N (US col): **the ~** il gabinetto
join [dʒɔɪn] VT unire, congiungere; (become member of) iscriversi a; (meet) raggiungere; riunirsi a ▶ VI (roads, rivers) confluire ▶ N giuntura; **to ~ forces (with)** allearsi (con or a); (fig) mettersi insieme (a); **will you ~ us for dinner?** viene a cena con noi?; **I'll ~ you later** vi raggiungo più tardi
▶ **join in** VT FUS unirsi a, prendere parte a, partecipare a ▶ VI partecipare
▶ **join up** VI incontrarsi; (Mil) arruolarsi
joiner ['dʒɔɪnəʳ] N (BRIT) falegname m
joinery ['dʒɔɪnəri] N falegnameria
joint [dʒɔɪnt] N (Tech) giuntura; giunto; (Anat) articolazione f, giuntura; (BRIT Culin) arrosto; (col: place) locale m; (: of cannabis) spinello ▶ ADJ comune; (responsibility) collettivo(-a); (committee) misto(-a)
joint account N (at bank etc) conto comune
jointly ['dʒɔɪntlɪ] ADV in comune, insieme
joint ownership N comproprietà
joint-stock company ['dʒɔɪntstɔk-] N società f inv per azioni
joist [dʒɔɪst] N trave f
joke [dʒəuk] N scherzo; (funny story) barzelletta; (also: **practical joke**) beffa ▶ VI scherzare; **to play a ~ on** fare uno scherzo a
joker ['dʒəukəʳ] N buffone(-a), burlone(-a); (Cards) matta, jolly m inv
joking ['dʒəukɪŋ] N scherzi mpl
jollity ['dʒɔlɪtɪ] N allegria
jolly ['dʒɔlɪ] ADJ allegro(-a), gioioso(-a) ▶ ADV (BRIT col) veramente, proprio ▶ VT (BRIT): **to ~ sb along** cercare di tenere qn su (di morale); **~ good!** (BRIT) benissimo!
jolt [dʒəult] N scossa, sobbalzo ▶ VT urtare
Jordan ['dʒɔːdən] N (country) Giordania; (river) Giordano
Jordanian [dʒɔːˈdeɪnɪən] ADJ, N giordano(-a)
joss stick ['dʒɔs-] N bastoncino d'incenso
jostle ['dʒɔsl] VT spingere coi gomiti ▶ VI farsi spazio coi gomiti
jot [dʒɔt] N: **not one ~** nemmeno un po'
▶ **jot down** VT annotare in fretta, buttare giù
jotter ['dʒɔtəʳ] N (BRIT) quaderno; blocco
journal ['dʒəːnl] N (newspaper) giornale m; (periodical) rivista; (diary) diario

journalese [dʒəːnəˈliːz] N (pej) stile m giornalistico
journalism ['dʒəːnəlɪzəm] N giornalismo
journalist ['dʒəːnəlɪst] N giornalista mf
journey ['dʒəːnɪ] N viaggio; (distance covered) tragitto; **how was your ~?** com'è andato il viaggio?; **the ~ takes two hours** il viaggio dura due ore; **a 5-hour ~** un viaggio or un tragitto di 5 ore
jovial ['dʒəuvɪəl] ADJ gioviale, allegro(-a)
jowl [dʒaul] N mandibola; guancia
joy [dʒɔɪ] N gioia
joyful ['dʒɔɪful], **joyous** ['dʒɔɪəs] ADJ gioioso(-a), allegro(-a)
joyride ['dʒɔɪraɪd] N: **to go for a ~** rubare una macchina per farsi un giro
joyrider ['dʒɔɪraɪdəʳ] N chi ruba una macchina per andare a farsi un giro
joy stick ['dʒɔɪstɪk] N (Aviat) barra di comando; (Comput) joystick m inv
JP N ABBR = **Justice of the Peace**
Jr. ABBR = **junior**
jubilant ['dʒuːbɪlnt] ADJ giubilante; trionfante
jubilation [dʒuːbɪˈleɪʃən] N giubilo
jubilee ['dʒuːbɪliː] N giubileo; **silver ~** venticinquesimo anniversario
judge [dʒʌdʒ] N giudice mf ▶ VT giudicare; (consider) ritenere; (estimate: weight, size etc) calcolare, valutare ▶ VI: **judging** or **to ~ by his expression** a giudicare dalla sua espressione; **as far as I can ~** a mio giudizio; **I judged it necessary to inform him** ho ritenuto necessario informarlo
judge advocate N (Mil) magistrato militare
judgment, judgement ['dʒʌdʒmənt] N giudizio; (punishment) punizione f; **in my judg(e)ment** a mio giudizio; **to pass judg(e)ment (on)** (Law) pronunciare un giudizio (su); (fig) dare giudizi affrettati (su)
judicial [dʒuːˈdɪʃl] ADJ giudiziale, giudiziario(-a)
judiciary [dʒuːˈdɪʃɪərɪ] N magistratura
judicious [dʒuːˈdɪʃəs] ADJ giudizioso(-a)
judo ['dʒuːdəu] N judo
jug [dʒʌg] N brocca, bricco
jugged hare [dʒʌgd-] N (BRIT) lepre f in salmì
juggernaut ['dʒʌgənɔːt] N (BRIT: huge truck) bestione m
juggle ['dʒʌgl] VI fare giochi di destrezza
juggler ['dʒʌgləʳ] N giocoliere(-a)
Jugoslav ['juːgəuˈslɑːv] ADJ, N = **Yugoslav**
jugular ['dʒʌgjuləʳ] ADJ: **~ (vein)** vena giugulare
juice [dʒuːs] N succo; (of meat) sugo; **we've run out of ~** (col: petrol) siamo rimasti a secco
juicy ['dʒuːsɪ] ADJ succoso(-a)
jukebox ['dʒuːkbɔks] N juke-box m inv
Jul. ABBR (= July) lug., lu.

July [dʒuːˈlaɪ] N luglio; **the first of** ~ il primo luglio; **(on) the eleventh of** ~ l'undici luglio; **in the month of** ~ nel mese di luglio; **at the beginning/end of** ~ all'inizio/alla fine di luglio; **in the middle of** ~ a metà luglio; **during** ~ durante (il mese di) luglio; **in** ~ **of next year** a luglio dell'anno prossimo; **each** *or* **every** ~ ogni anno a luglio; ~ **was wet this year** ha piovuto molto a luglio quest'anno

jumble ['dʒʌmbl] N miscuglio ▶ VT (*also:* **jumble up, jumble together**) mischiare, mettere alla rinfusa

jumble sale (*BRIT*) N ≈ vendita di beneficenza; *vedi nota*

> La *jumble sale* è un mercatino dove vengono venduti vari oggetti, per lo più di seconda mano; viene organizzata in chiese, scuole o circoli ricreativi. I proventi delle vendite vengono devoluti in beneficenza o usati per una giusta causa.

jumbo ['dʒʌmbəu] ADJ: ~ **jet** jumbo-jet *m inv*; ~ **size** formato gigante

jump [dʒʌmp] VI saltare, balzare; (*start*) sobbalzare; (*increase*) rincarare ▶ VT saltare ▶ N salto, balzo; sobbalzo; (*Showjumping*) salto; (*fence*) ostacolo; **to** ~ **the queue** (*BRIT*) passare davanti agli altri (*in una coda*)
  ▶ **jump about** VI fare salti, saltellare
  ▶ **jump at** VT FUS (*fig*) cogliere *or* afferrare al volo; **he jumped at the offer** si affrettò ad accettare l'offerta
  ▶ **jump down** VI saltare giù
  ▶ **jump up** VI saltare in piedi

jumped-up ['dʒʌmptʌp] ADJ (*BRIT pej*) presuntuoso(-a)

jumper ['dʒʌmpəʳ] N (*BRIT: pullover*) maglione *m*; (*US: pinafore dress*) scamiciato; (*Sport*) saltatore(-trice)

jump leads, (*US*) **jumper cables** NPL cavi *mpl* per batteria

jump-start ['dʒʌmpstɑːt] VT (*car*) far partire spingendo; (*fig*) dare una spinta a, rimettere in moto

jump suit N tuta

jumpy ['dʒʌmpɪ] ADJ nervoso(-a), agitato(-a)

Jun. ABBR (= *June*) giu.

Jun., Junr ABBR = **junior**

junction ['dʒʌŋkʃən] N (*BRIT: of roads*) incrocio; (*of rails*) nodo ferroviario

juncture ['dʒʌŋktʃəʳ] N: **at this** ~ in questa congiuntura

June [dʒuːn] N giugno; *see also* **July**

jungle ['dʒʌŋgl] N giungla

junior ['dʒuːnɪəʳ] ADJ, N: **he's** ~ **to me (by 2 years),** **he's my** ~ **(by 2 years)** è più giovane di me (di 2 anni); **he's** ~ **to me** (*seniority*) è al di sotto di me, ho più anzianità di lui

junior executive N giovane dirigente *m*

junior high school N (*US*) scuola media (*da 12 a 15 anni*)

junior minister N (*BRIT Pol*) ministro che non fa parte del Cabinet

junior partner N socio meno anziano

junior school N (*BRIT*) scuola elementare (*da 8 a 11 anni*)

junior sizes NPL (*Comm*) taglie *fpl* per ragazzi

juniper ['dʒuːnɪpəʳ] N: ~ **berry** bacca di ginepro

junk [dʒʌŋk] N (*rubbish*) cianfrusaglie *fpl*; (*cheap goods*) robaccia; (*ship*) giunca ▶ VT disfarsi di

junk bond N (*Comm*) titolo *m* spazzatura *inv*

junk dealer N rigattiere *m*

junket ['dʒʌŋkɪt] N (*Culin*) giuncata; (*BRIT col*): **to go on a** ~ fare bisboccia

junk food N porcherie *fpl*, cibo a scarso valore nutritivo

junkie ['dʒʌŋkɪ] N (*col*) drogato(-a)

junk mail N pubblicità *f inv* in cassetta

junk room N (*US*) ripostiglio

junk shop N chincaglieria

junta ['dʒʌntə] N giunta

Jupiter ['dʒuːpɪtəʳ] N (*planet*) Giove *m*

jurisdiction [dʒuərɪsˈdɪkʃən] N giurisdizione *f*; **it falls** *or* **comes within/outside our** ~ è/ non è di nostra competenza

jurisprudence [dʒuərɪsˈpruːdəns] N giurisprudenza

juror ['dʒuərəʳ] N giurato(-a)

jury ['dʒuərɪ] N giuria

jury box N banco della giuria

juryman ['dʒuərɪmən] N (*irreg*) = **juror**

just [dʒʌst] ADJ giusto(-a) ▶ ADV: **he's** ~ **done it/left** lo ha appena fatto/è appena partito; ~ **as I expected** proprio come me lo aspettavo; ~ **right** proprio giusto; ~ **2 o'clock** le 2 precise; **she's** ~ **as clever as you** è in gamba proprio quanto te; ~ **as I arrived** proprio mentre arrivavo; **we were** ~ **going** stavamo proprio per telefonare; **I was** ~ **about to phone** stavo proprio per telefonare; ~ **as he was leaving** proprio mentre se ne stava andando; **it was** ~ **before/enough/here** era poco prima/appena assai/proprio qui; **it's** ~ **me** sono solo io; **it's** ~ **a mistake** non è che uno sbaglio; ~ **missed/caught** appena perso/ preso; ~ **listen to this!** senta un po' questo!; ~ **ask someone the way** basta che tu chieda la strada a qualcuno; **it's** ~ **as good** è altrettanto buono; **it's** ~ **as well you didn't go** meno male che non ci sei andato; **not** ~ **now** non proprio adesso; ~ **a minute!,** ~ **one moment!** un attimo!

justice ['dʒʌstɪs] N giustizia; **Lord Chief J~** (*BRIT*) presidente *m* della Corte d'Appello; **this photo doesn't do you** ~ questa foto non ti fa giustizia

Justice of the Peace N giudice m conciliatore

justifiable [dʒʌstɪˈfaɪəbl] ADJ giustificabile

justifiably [dʒʌstɪˈfaɪəblɪ] ADV legittimamente, con ragione

justification [dʒʌstɪfɪˈkeɪʃən] N giustificazione f; (Typ) giustezza

justify [ˈdʒʌstɪfaɪ] VT giustificare; (Typ etc) allineare, giustificare; **to be justified in doing sth** avere ragione di fare qc

justly [ˈdʒʌstlɪ] ADV giustamente

justness [ˈdʒʌstnɪs] N giustezza

jut [dʒʌt] VI (also: **jut out**) sporgersi

jute [dʒuːt] N iuta

juvenile [ˈdʒuːvənaɪl] ADJ giovane, giovanile; (court) dei minorenni; (books) per ragazzi ▶ N giovane mf, minorenne mf

juvenile delinquency N delinquenza minorile

juvenile delinquent N delinquente mf minorenne

juxtapose [ˈdʒʌkstəpəuz] VT giustapporre

juxtaposition [dʒʌkstəpəˈzɪʃən] N giustapposizione f

Kk

K, k [keɪ] N (*letter*) K, k *f inv or m inv*; **K for King** ≈ K come Kursaal

K N ABBR (= *one thousand*) mille ▶ ABBR (BRIT: = *Knight*) titolo; (= *kilobyte*) K

kaftan ['kæftæn] N caffettano

Kalahari Desert [kælə'hɑːrɪ-] N Deserto di Calahari

kale [keɪl] N cavolo verde

kaleidoscope [kə'laɪdəskəup] N caleidoscopio

kamikaze [kæmɪ'kɑːzɪ] ADJ da kamikaze

Kampala [kæm'pɑːlə] N Kampala *f*

Kampuchea [kæmpu'tʃɪə] N Kampuchea *f*

kangaroo [kæŋgə'ruː] N canguro

Kans. ABBR (US) = **Kansas**

kaput [kə'put] ADJ (*col*) kaputt *inv*

karaoke [kɑːrə'əukɪ] N karaoke *m inv*

karate [kə'rɑːtɪ] N karate *m*

Kashmir [kæʃ'mɪəʳ] N Kashmir *m*

Kazakhstan [kæzæk'stɑːn] N Kazakistan *m*

KC N ABBR (BRIT *Law*: = *King's Counsel*) avvocato della Corona; *see also* **QC**

kebab [kə'bæb] N spiedino

keel [kiːl] N chiglia; **on an even ~** (*fig*) in uno stato normale

▶ **keel over** VI (*Naut*) capovolgersi; (*person*) crollare

keen [kiːn] ADJ (*interest, desire*) vivo(-a); (*eye, intelligence*) acuto(-a); (*competition*) serrato(-a); (*edge*) affilato(-a); (*eager*) entusiasta; **to be ~ to do** *or* **on doing sth** avere una gran voglia di fare qc; **to be ~ on sth** essere appassionato(-a) di qc; **to be ~ on sb** avere un debole per qn; **I'm not ~ on going** non mi va di andare

keenly ['kiːnlɪ] ADV (*enthusiastically*) con entusiasmo; (*acutely*) vivamente; in modo penetrante

keenness ['kiːnnɪs] N (*eagerness*) entusiasmo

keep [kiːp] (*pt, pp* **kept** [kɛpt]) VT tenere; (*hold back*) trattenere; (*feed: one's family etc*) mantenere, sostentare; (*a promise*) mantenere; (*chickens, bees, pigs etc*) allevare ▶ VI (*food*) mantenersi; (*remain: in a certain state or place*) restare ▶ N (*of castle*) maschio; (*food etc*): **enough for his ~** abbastanza per vitto e alloggio; **to ~ doing sth** continuare a fare qc; fare qc di continuo; **to ~ sb from doing/sth from happening** impedire a qn di fare/che qc succeda; **to ~ sb busy/a place tidy** tenere qn occupato(-a)/un luogo in ordine; **to ~ sb waiting** far aspettare qn; **to ~ an appointment** andare ad un appuntamento; **to ~ a record** *or* **note of sth** prendere nota di qc; **to ~ sth to o.s.** tenere qc per sé; **to ~ sth (back) from sb** celare qc a qn; **to ~ time** (*clock*) andar bene; **~ the change** tenga il resto; *see also* **keeps**

▶ **keep away** VT: **to ~ sth/sb away from sb** tenere qc/qn lontano da qn ▶ VI: **to ~ away (from)** stare lontano (da)

▶ **keep back** VT (*crowds, tears, money*) trattenere ▶ VI tenersi indietro

▶ **keep down** VT (*control: prices, spending*) contenere, ridurre; (*retain: food*) trattenere, ritenere ▶ VI tenersi giù, stare giù

▶ **keep in** VT (*invalid, child*) tenere a casa; (*Scol*) trattenere a scuola ▶ VI (*col*): **to ~ in with sb** tenersi buono qn

▶ **keep off** VT (*dog, person*) tenere lontano da ▶ VI stare alla larga; **~ your hands off!** non toccare!, giù le mani!; **"~ off the grass"** "non calpestare l'erba"

▶ **keep on** VI continuare; **to ~ on doing** continuare a fare; **to ~ on (about sth)** continuare a insistere (su qc)

▶ **keep out** VT tener fuori ▶ VI restare fuori; **"~ out"** "vietato l'accesso"

▶ **keep up** VT continuare, mantenere ▶ VI mantenersi; **to ~ up with** tenere dietro a, andare di pari passo con; (*work etc*) farcela a seguire; **to ~ up with sb** (*in race etc*) mantenersi al passo con qn

keeper ['kiːpəʳ] N custode *mf*, guardiano(-a)

keep-fit [kiːp'fɪt] N ginnastica

keeping ['kiːpɪŋ] N (*care*) custodia; **in ~ with** in armonia con; in accordo con

keeps [kiːps] N: **for ~** (*col*) per sempre

keepsake ['ki:pseɪk] N ricordo
keg [kɛg] N barilotto
Ken. ABBR (US) = **Kentucky**
kennel ['kɛnl] N canile m; **kennels** NPL canile m; **to put a dog in kennels** mettere un cane al canile
Kenya ['kɛnjə] N Kenia m
Kenyan ['kɛnjən] ADJ, N Keniano(-a), Keniota (mf)
kept [kɛpt] PT, PP of **keep**
kerb [kə:b] N (BRIT) orlo del marciapiede
kerb crawler [-'krɔːlər] N chi va in macchina in cerca di una prostituta
kernel ['kə:nl] N nocciolo
kerosene ['kɛrəsi:n] N cherosene m
ketchup ['kɛtʃəp] N ketchup m inv
kettle ['kɛtl] N bollitore m
kettle drum N timpano
kettling ['kɛtəlɪŋ] N tecnica di contenimento forzato impiegata dalla polizia per accerchiare i manifestanti
key [ki:] N (gen, Mus) chiave f; (of piano, typewriter) tasto; (on map) leg(g)enda ▶ CPD (vital: position, industry etc) chiave inv
   ▶ **key in** VT (text) digitare
keyboard ['ki:bɔ:d] N tastiera ▶ VT (text) comporre su tastiera
keyboarder ['ki:bɔ:dər] N dattilografo(-a)
keyed up [ki:d'ʌp] ADJ: **to be ~** essere agitato(-a)
keyhole ['ki:həul] N buco della serratura
keyhole surgery N chirurgia mininvasiva
keynote ['ki:nəut] N (Mus) tonica; (fig) nota dominante
keypad ['ki:pæd] N tastierino numerico
key ring N portachiavi m inv
keystroke ['ki:strəuk] N battuta (di un tasto)
kg ABBR (= kilogram) Kg
KGB N ABBR KGB m
khaki ['kɑ:kɪ] ADJ, N cachi (m)
kibbutz [kɪ'buts] N kibbutz m inv
kick [kɪk] VT calciare, dare calci a; (col: habit etc) liberarsi di ▶ VI (horse) tirar calci
   ▶ N calcio; (of rifle) contraccolpo; (col: thrill): **he does it for kicks** lo fa giusto per il piacere di farlo
   ▶ **kick around** VI (col) essere in giro
   ▶ **kick off** VI (Sport) dare il primo calcio
kick-off ['kɪkɔf] N (Sport) calcio d'inizio
kick-start ['kɪkstɑ:t] N (also: **kick-starter**) pedale m d'avviamento
kid [kɪd] N (col: child) ragazzino(-a); (animal, leather) capretto ▶ VI (col) scherzare ▶ VT (col) prendere in giro
kid gloves NPL: **to treat sb with ~** trattare qn coi guanti
kidnap ['kɪdnæp] VT rapire, sequestrare
kidnapper ['kɪdnæpər] N rapitore(-trice)

kidnapping ['kɪdnæpɪŋ] N sequestro (di persona)
kidney ['kɪdnɪ] N (Anat) rene m; (Culin) rognone m
kidney bean N fagiolo borlotto
kidney machine N rene m artificiale
Kilimanjaro [kɪlɪmən'dʒɑ:rəu] N: **Mount ~** il monte Kilimangiaro
kill [kɪl] VT uccidere, ammazzare; (fig) sopprimere; soppraffare; ammazzare ▶ N uccisione f; **to ~ time** ammazzare il tempo
   ▶ **kill off** VT sterminare; (fig) eliminare, soffocare
killer ['kɪlər] N uccisore m, killer m inv; assassino(-a)
killer instinct N: **to have a/the ~** essere spietato(-a)
killing ['kɪlɪŋ] N assassinio; (massacre) strage f; (col): **to make a ~** fare un bel colpo
kill-joy ['kɪldʒɔɪ] N guastafeste mf
kiln [kɪln] N forno
kilo ['ki:ləu] N ABBR (= kilogram) chilo
kilobyte ['kɪləbaɪt] N (Comput) kilobyte m inv
kilogram, kilogramme ['kɪləugræm] N chilogrammo
kilometre, (US) kilometer ['kɪləmi:tər] N chilometro
kilowatt ['kɪləuwɔt] N chilowatt m inv
kilt [kɪlt] N gonnellino scozzese
kilter ['kɪltər] N: **out of ~** fuori fase
kimono [kɪ'məunəu] N chimono
kin [kɪn] N see **next of kin**; **kith**
kind [kaɪnd] ADJ gentile, buono(-a) ▶ N sorta, specie f; (species) genere m; **what ~ of ...?** che tipo di ...?; **to be two of a ~** essere molto simili; **would you be ~ enough to ...?**, **would you be so ~ as to ...?** sarebbe così gentile da ...?; **it's very ~ of you (to do)** è molto gentile da parte sua (di fare); **in ~** (Comm) in natura; (fig) **to repay sb in ~** ripagare qn della stessa moneta
kindergarten ['kɪndəgɑ:tn] N giardino d'infanzia
kind-hearted [kaɪnd'hɑ:tɪd] ADJ di buon cuore
Kindle® ['kɪndl] N Kindle® m inv
kindle ['kɪndl] VT accendere, infiammare
kindling ['kɪndlɪŋ] N frasche fpl, ramoscelli mpl
kindly ['kaɪndlɪ] ADJ pieno(-a) di bontà, benevolo(-a) ▶ ADV con bontà, gentilmente; **will you ... ?** vuole ... per favore; **he didn't take it ~** se l'è presa a male
kindness ['kaɪndnɪs] N bontà, gentilezza
kindred ['kɪndrɪd] ADJ imparentato(-a); **~ spirit** spirito affine
kinetic [kɪ'nɛtɪk] ADJ cinetico(-a)
king [kɪŋ] N re m inv
kingdom ['kɪŋdəm] N regno, reame m

kingfisher ['kɪŋfɪʃə^r] N martin m inv pescatore
kingpin ['kɪŋpɪn] N (Tech, fig) perno
king-size ['kɪŋsaɪz], **king-sized** ['kɪŋsaɪzd] ADJ super inv; gigante; (cigarette) extra lungo(-a)
king-size bed, king-sized bed N letto king-size
kink [kɪŋk] N (of rope) attorcigliamento; (in hair) ondina; (fig) aberrazione f
kinky ['kɪŋkɪ] ADJ (fig) eccentrico(-a); dai gusti particolari
kinship ['kɪnʃɪp] N parentela
kinsman ['kɪnzmən] N (irreg) parente m
kinswoman ['kɪnzwumən] N (irreg) parente f
kiosk ['kiːɔsk] N edicola, chiosco; (BRIT: also: **telephone kiosk**) cabina (telefonica); (also: **newspaper kiosk**) edicola
kipper ['kɪpə^r] N aringa affumicata
Kirghizia [kəːˈgɪzɪə] N Kirghizistan
kiss [kɪs] N bacio ▸ VT baciare; **to ~ (each other)** baciarsi; **to ~ sb goodbye** congedarsi da qn con un bacio; **~ of life** (BRIT) respirazione f bocca a bocca
kissagram ['kɪsəgræm] N servizio di recapito a domicilio di messaggi e baci augurali
kit [kɪt] N equipaggiamento, corredo; (set of tools etc) attrezzi mpl; (for assembly) scatola di montaggio; **tool ~** cassetta or borsa degli attrezzi
▸ **kit out** VT (BRIT) attrezzare, equipaggiare
kitbag ['kɪtbæg] N zaino; sacco militare
kitchen ['kɪtʃɪn] N cucina
kitchen garden N orto
kitchen sink N acquaio
kitchen unit N (BRIT) elemento da cucina
kitchenware ['kɪtʃɪnwɛə^r] N stoviglie fpl; utensili mpl da cucina
kite [kaɪt] N (toy) aquilone m; (Zool) nibbio
kith [kɪθ] N: **~ and kin** amici e parenti mpl
kitten ['kɪtn] N gattino(-a), micino(-a)
kitty ['kɪtɪ] N (money) fondo comune
kiwi ['kiːwiː], **kiwi fruit** N kiwi m inv
KKK N ABBR (US) = **Ku Klux Klan**
Kleenex® ['kliːnɛks] N fazzolettino di carta
kleptomaniac [klɛptəuˈmeɪnɪæk] N cleptomane mf
km ABBR (= kilometre) km
km/h ABBR (= kilometres per hour) km/h
knack [næk] N: **to have a ~ (for doing)** avere una pratica (per fare); **to have the ~ of** avere l'abilità di; **there's a ~ to doing this** c'è un trucco per fare questo
knackered ['nækəd] ADJ (col) fuso(-a)
knapsack ['næpsæk] N zaino, sacco da montagna
knave [neɪv] N (Cards) fante m
knead [niːd] VT impastare
knee [niː] N ginocchio
kneecap ['niːkæp] N rotula ▸ VT gambizzare

knee-deep ['niːˈdiːp] ADJ: **the water was ~** l'acqua ci arrivava alle ginocchia
kneel [niːl] (pt, pp **knelt** [nɛlt]) VI (also: **kneel down**) inginocchiarsi
kneepad ['niːpæd] N ginocchiera
knell [nɛl] N rintocco
knelt [nɛlt] PT, PP of **kneel**
knew [njuː] PT of **know**
knickers ['nɪkəz] NPL (BRIT) mutandine fpl
knick-knack ['nɪknæk] N ninnolo
knife [naɪf] (pl **knives**) N coltello ▸ VT accoltellare, dare una coltellata a; **~, fork and spoon** coperto
knife edge N: **to be on a ~** (fig) essere appeso(-a) a un filo
knight [naɪt] N cavaliere m; (Chess) cavallo
knighthood ['naɪthud] N cavalleria; (title): **to get a ~** essere fatto cavaliere
knit [nɪt] VT fare a maglia; (fig): **to ~ together** unire ▸ VI lavorare a maglia; (broken bones) saldarsi; **to ~ one's brows** aggrottare le sopracciglia
knitted ['nɪtɪd] ADJ lavorato(-a) a maglia
knitting ['nɪtɪŋ] N lavoro a maglia
knitting machine N macchina per maglieria
knitting needle N ferro (da calza)
knitting pattern N modello (per maglia)
knitwear ['nɪtwɛə^r] N maglieria
knives [naɪvz] NPL of **knife**
knob [nɔb] N bottone m; manopola; (BRIT): **a ~ of butter** una noce di burro
knobbly ['nɔblɪ], (US) **knobby** ['nɔbɪ] ADJ (wood, surface) nodoso(-a); (knee) ossuto(-a)
knock [nɔk] VT (strike) colpire; urtare; (fig: col) criticare ▸ VI (engine) battere; (at door etc): **to ~ at/on** bussare a ▸ N bussata; colpo, botta; **he knocked at the door** ha bussato alla porta; **to ~ a nail into sth** conficcare un chiodo in qc
▸ **knock down** VT abbattere; (pedestrian) investire; (price) abbassare
▸ **knock off** VI (col: finish) smettere (di lavorare) ▸ VT (strike off) far cadere; (from price) far abbassare; (col: steal) sgraffignare, grattare; **to ~ off £10** fare uno sconto di 10 sterline
▸ **knock out** VT stendere; (Boxing) mettere K.O., mettere fuori combattimento; (defeat) battere
▸ **knock over** VT (object) far cadere; (pedestrian) investire
knockdown ['nɔkdaun] ADJ (price) fortemente scontato(-a)
knocker ['nɔkə^r] N (on door) battente m
knocking ['nɔkɪŋ] N colpi mpl
knock-kneed [nɔkˈniːd] ADJ che ha le gambe ad x
knockout ['nɔkaut] N (Boxing) knock out m inv
▸ CPD a eliminazione

k

knockout competition N (BRIT) gara ad
eliminazione
knock-up ['nɔkʌp] N (Tennis etc) palleggio;
to have a ~ palleggiare
knot [nɔt] N nodo ▶ VT annodare; **to tie a ~**
fare un nodo
knotty ['nɔtɪ] ADJ (fig) spinoso(-a)
know [nəu] (pt **knew** [njuː], pp **known** [nəun])
VT sapere; (person, author, place) conoscere ▶ VI
sapere; **to ~ that** ... sapere che ...; **to ~ how
to do** sapere fare; **to get to ~ sth** venire a
sapere qc; **I ~ nothing about it** non ne so
niente; **I don't ~ him** non lo conosco; **to ~
right from wrong** distinguere il bene dal
male; **as far as I ~** ... che io sappia ..., per
quanto io ne sappia ...; **yes, I ~**, lo so; **I
don't ~** non lo so; **to ~ about** or **of sth/sb**
conoscere qc/qn
know-all ['nəuɔːl] N (BRIT pej) sapientone(-a)
know-how ['nəuhau] N tecnica; pratica
knowing ['nəuɪŋ] ADJ (look etc) d'intesa
knowingly ['nəuɪŋlɪ] ADV (purposely)
consapevolmente; di complicità; (smile, look)
con aria d'intesa
know-it-all ['nəuɪtɔːl] N (US) = **know-all**
knowledge ['nɔlɪdʒ] N consapevolezza;
(learning) conoscenza, sapere m; **to have no ~
of** ignorare, non sapere; **not to my ~** che io
sappia, no; **to have a working ~ of Italian**
avere una conoscenza pratica dell'italiano;
without my ~ a mia insaputa; **it is common
~ that** ... è risaputo che ...; **it has come to
my ~ that** ... sono venuto a sapere che ...
knowledgeable ['nɔlɪdʒəbl] ADJ ben
informato(-a)

known [nəun] PP of **know** ▶ ADJ (thief, facts)
noto(-a); (expert) riconosciuto(-a)
knuckle ['nʌkl] N nocca
▶ **knuckle down** VI (col): **to ~ down to some
hard work** mettersi sotto a lavorare
▶ **knuckle under** VI (col) cedere
knuckleduster ['nʌkldʌstər] N tirapugni
m inv
KO ABBR = **knock out** ▶ N K.O. m ▶ VT
mettere K.O.
koala [kəu'ɑːlə] N (also: **koala bear**) koala
m inv
kook [kuːk] N (US col) svitato(-a)
Koran [kɔ'rɑːn] N Corano
Korea [kə'riːə] N Corea; **North/South ~**
Corea del Nord/Sud
Korean [kə'riːən] ADJ, N coreano(-a)
kosher ['kəuʃər] ADJ kasher inv
Kosovar, Kosovan ['kɔsəvɑːr, 'kɔsəvən] ADJ
kosovaro(-a)
Kosovo ['kusəvəu] N Kosovo
kowtow ['kau'tau] VI: **to ~ to sb** mostrarsi
ossequioso(-a) verso qn
Kremlin ['krɛmlɪn] N: **the ~** il Cremlino
KS ABBR (US) = **Kansas**
Kt ABBR (BRIT: = Knight) titolo
Kuala Lumpur ['kwɑːlə'lumpuər] N Kuala
Lumpur f
kudos ['kjuːdɔs] N gloria, fama
Kurd [kəːd] N curdo(-a)
Kuwait [ku'weɪt] N Kuwait m
Kuwaiti [ku'weɪtɪ] ADJ, N
kuwaitiano(-a)
kW ABBR (= kilowatt) kw
KY, Ky. ABBR (US) = **Kentucky**

Ll

L, l [ɛl] N (letter) L, l f inv or m inv; **L for Lucy,** (US) **L for Love** ≈ L come Livorno

L ABBR (= lake) l; (= large) taglia grande; (= left) sin.; (BRIT Aut) = **learner**

l ABBR (= litre) l

LA N ABBR (US) = **Los Angeles** ▶ ABBR (US) = **Louisiana**

La. ABBR (US) = **Louisiana**

lab [læb] N ABBR (= laboratory) laboratorio

Lab. ABBR (CANADA) = **Labrador**

label ['leɪbl] N etichetta, cartellino; (brand: of record) casa ▶ VT etichettare; classificare

labor etc ['leɪbər] (US) = **labour** etc

laboratory [lə'bɔrətərɪ] N laboratorio

Labor Day N (US) festa del lavoro; vedi nota

> Negli Stati Uniti e nel Canada il Labor Day, la festa del lavoro, cade il primo lunedì di settembre, contrariamente a quanto accade nella maggior parte dei paesi europei dove tale celebrazione ha luogo il primo maggio.

laborious [lə'bɔːrɪəs] ADJ laborioso(-a)

labor union N (US) sindacato

Labour ['leɪbər] N (BRIT Pol: also: **the Labour Party**) il partito laburista, i laburisti

labour, (US) **labor** ['leɪbər] N (task) lavoro; (workmen) manodopera; (Med) travaglio del parto, doglie fpl ▶ VI: **to ~ (at)** lavorare duro(a); **to be in ~** (Med) avere le doglie; **hard ~** lavori mpl forzati

labour camp, (US) **labor camp** N campo dei lavori forzati

labour cost, (US) **labor cost** N costo del lavoro

labour dispute, (US) **labor dispute** N conflitto tra lavoratori e datori di lavoro

laboured, (US) **labored** ['leɪbəd] ADJ (breathing) affaticato(-a), affannoso(-a); (style) elaborato(-a), pesante

labourer, (US) **laborer** ['leɪbərər] N manovale m; **farm ~** lavoratore m agricolo

labour force, (US) **labor force** N manodopera

labour-intensive, (US) **labor-intensive** [leɪbərɪn'tɛnsɪv] ADJ che assorbe molta manodopera

labour market, (US) **labor market** N mercato del lavoro

labour pains, (US) **labor pains** NPL doglie fpl

labour relations, (US) **labor relations** NPL relazioni fpl industriali

labour-saving, (US) **labor-saving** ['leɪbəseɪvɪŋ] ADJ che fa risparmiare fatica o lavoro

labour unrest, (US) **labor unrest** N agitazioni fpl degli operai

labyrinth ['læbɪrɪnθ] N labirinto

lace [leɪs] N merletto, pizzo; (of shoe etc) laccio ▶ VT (shoe: also: **lace up**) allacciare; (: drink: fortify with spirits) correggere

lacemaking ['leɪsmeɪkɪŋ] N fabbricazione f dei pizzi or dei merletti

laceration [læsə'reɪʃən] N lacerazione f

lace-up ['leɪsʌp] ADJ (shoes etc) con i lacci, con le stringhe

lack [læk] N mancanza, scarsità ▶ VT mancare di; **through** or **for ~ of** per mancanza di; **to be lacking** mancare; **to be lacking in** mancare di

lackadaisical [lækə'deɪzɪkl] ADJ disinteressato(-a), noncurante

lackey ['lækɪ] N (also fig) lacchè m inv

lacklustre, (US) **lackluster** ['læklʌstər] ADJ (surface) opaco(-a); (style) scialbo(-a); (eyes) spento(-a)

laconic [lə'kɔnɪk] ADJ laconico(-a)

lacquer ['lækər] N lacca; **hair ~** lacca per (i) capelli

lacy ['leɪsɪ] ADJ (like lace) che sembra un pizzo

lad [læd] N ragazzo, giovanotto; (BRIT: in stable etc) mozzo or garzone m di stalla

ladder ['lædər] N scala; (BRIT: in tights) smagliatura ▶ VT smagliare ▶ VI smagliarsi

laden ['leɪdn] ADJ: **~ (with)** carico(-a) or caricato(-a) (di); **fully ~** (truck, ship) a pieno carico

ladle ['leɪdl] N mestolo

lady ['leɪdɪ] N signora; dama; **L~ Smith**

lady Smith; **the ladies' (toilets)** i gabinetti per signore; **a ~ doctor** una dottoressa

ladybird ['leɪdɪbəːd], (US) **ladybug** ['leɪdɪbʌg] N coccinella

lady-in-waiting ['leɪdɪɪn'weɪtɪŋ] N dama di compagnia

ladykiller ['leɪdɪkɪləʳ] N dongiovanni *m inv*

ladylike ['leɪdɪlaɪk] ADJ da signora, distinto(-a)

ladyship ['leɪdɪʃɪp] N: **your L~** signora contessa *etc*

lag [læg] N (*of time*) lasso, intervallo ▶ VI (*also*: **lag behind**) trascinarsi ▶ VT (*pipes*) rivestire di materiale isolante

lager ['lɑːgəʳ] N lager *m inv*

lager lout N (BRIT col) giovinastro ubriaco

lagging ['lægɪŋ] N rivestimento di materiale isolante

lagoon [lə'guːn] N laguna

Lagos ['leɪgɔs] N Lagos *f*

laid [leɪd] PT, PP *of* **lay**

laid-back [leɪd'bæk] ADJ (*col*) rilassato(-a), tranquillo(-a)

lain [leɪn] PP *of* **lie**

lair [lɛəʳ] N covo, tana

laissez-faire [lɛseɪ'fɛəʳ] N liberismo

laity ['leɪətɪ] N laici *mpl*

lake [leɪk] N lago

Lake District N: **the ~** (BRIT) la regione dei laghi

lamb [læm] N agnello

lamb chop N cotoletta d'agnello

lambskin ['læmskɪn] N (pelle *f* d')agnello

lambswool ['læmzwuːl] N lamb's wool *m*

lame [leɪm] ADJ zoppo(-a); (*excuse etc*) zoppicante; **~ duck** (*fig*: *person*) persona inetta; (*firm*) azienda traballante

lamely ['leɪmlɪ] ADV (*fig*) in modo poco convincente

lament [lə'mɛnt] N lamento ▶ VT lamentare, piangere

lamentable ['læməntəbl] ADJ doloroso(-a); deplorevole

laminated ['læmɪneɪtɪd] ADJ laminato(-a)

lamp [læmp] N lampada

lamplight ['læmplaɪt] N: **by ~** a lume della lampada

lampoon [læm'puːn] N satira

lamppost ['læmppəust] (BRIT) N lampione *m*

lampshade ['læmpʃeɪd] N paralume *m*

lance [lɑːns] N lancia ▶ VT (*Med*) incidere

lance corporal N (BRIT) caporale *m*

lancet ['lɑːnsɪt] N (*Med*) bisturi *m inv*

Lancs [læŋks] ABBR (BRIT) = **Lancashire**

land [lænd] N (*as opposed to sea*) terra (ferma); (*country*) paese *m*; (*soil*) terreno; suolo; (*estate*) terreni *mpl*, terre *fpl* ▶ VI (*from ship*) sbarcare; (*Aviat*) atterrare; (*fig: fall*) cadere ▶ VT (*obtain*) acchiappare; (*passengers*) sbarcare; (*goods*)

scaricare; **to go/travel by ~** andare/ viaggiare per via di terra; **to own ~** possedere dei terreni, avere delle proprietà (terriere); **to ~ sb with sth** affibbiare qc a qn; **to ~ on one's feet** cadere in piedi; (*fig: to be lucky*) cascar bene

▶ **land up** VI andare a finire

landed gentry ['lændɪd-] N proprietari *mpl* terrieri

landfill site ['lændfɪl-] N discarica dove i rifiuti vengono sepolti

landing ['lændɪŋ] N (*from ship*) sbarco; (*Aviat*) atterraggio; (*of staircase*) pianerottolo

landing card N carta di sbarco

landing craft N mezzo da sbarco

landing gear N (*Aviat*) carrello d'atterraggio

landing stage N pontile *m* da sbarco

landing strip N pista d'atterraggio

landlady ['lændleɪdɪ] N padrona or proprietaria di casa

landline ['lændlaɪn] N telefono fisso

landlocked ['lændlɔkt] ADJ senza sbocco sul mare

landlord ['lændlɔːd] N padrone *m* or proprietario di casa; (*of pub etc*) padrone *m*

landlubber ['lændlʌbəʳ] N marinaio d'acqua dolce

landmark ['lændmɑːk] N punto di riferimento; (*fig*) pietra miliare

landowner ['lændəunəʳ] N proprietario(-a) terriero(-a)

landscape ['lænskeɪp] N paesaggio

landscape architect, landscape gardener N paesaggista *mf*

landscape painting N (*Art*) paesaggistica

landslide ['lændslaɪd] N (*Geo*) frana; (*fig: Pol*) valanga

lane [leɪn] N (*in country*) viottolo; (*in town*) stradina; (*Aut, in race*) corsia; **shipping ~** rotta (marittima); **"get in ~"** "immettersi in corsia"

language ['læŋgwɪdʒ] N lingua; (*way one speaks*) linguaggio; **bad ~** linguaggio volgare

language laboratory N laboratorio linguistico

language school N scuola di lingue

languid ['læŋgwɪd] ADJ languente, languido(-a)

languish ['læŋgwɪʃ] VI languire

lank [læŋk] ADJ (*hair*) liscio(-a) e opaco(-a)

lanky ['læŋkɪ] ADJ allampanato(-a)

lanolin, lanoline ['lænəlɪn] N lanolina

lantern ['læntn] N lanterna

Laos [lauz] N Laos *m*

lap [læp] N (*of track*) giro; **in** or **on one's ~** in grembo ▶ VT (*also*: **lap up**) papparsi, leccare ▶ VI (*waves*) sciabordare

▶ **lap up** VT (*fig: compliments, attention*) bearsi di

La Paz [læ'pæz] N La Paz f
lapdog ['læpdɔg] N cane m da grembo
lapel [lə'pɛl] N risvolto
Lapland ['læplænd] N Lapponia
Lapp [læp] ADJ lappone ▶ N lappone mf; (Ling) lappone m
lapse [læps] N lapsus m inv; (longer) caduta; (fault) mancanza; (in behaviour) scorrettezza ▶ VI (law, act) cadere; (ticket, passport, membership, contract) scadere; **to ~ into bad habits** pigliare cattive abitudini; **~ of time** spazio di tempo; **a ~ of memory** un vuoto di memoria
laptop ['læptɔp] N (also: **laptop computer**) laptop m inv
larceny ['lɑːsənɪ] N furto
lard [lɑːd] N lardo
larder ['lɑːdəʳ] N dispensa
large [lɑːdʒ] ADJ grande; (person, animal) grosso(-a) ▶ ADV: **by and ~** generalmente; **at ~** (free) in libertà; (generally) in generale; nell'insieme; **to make larger** ingrandire; **a ~ number of people** molta gente; **on a ~ scale** su vasta scala
largely ['lɑːdʒlɪ] ADV in gran parte
large-scale ['lɑːdʒ'skeɪl] ADJ (map, drawing etc) in grande scala; (reforms, business activities) su vasta scala
lark [lɑːk] N (bird) allodola; (joke) scherzo, gioco
  ▶ **lark about** VI fare lo stupido
larrikin ['lærɪkɪn] N (AUSTRALIA, NEW ZEALAND col) furfante mf
larva ['lɑːvə] (pl **larvae** [-iː]) N larva
laryngitis [lærɪn'dʒaɪtɪs] N laringite f
larynx ['lærɪŋks] N laringe f
lasagne [lə'zænjə] N lasagne fpl
lascivious [lə'sɪvɪəs] ADJ lascivo(-a)
laser ['leɪzəʳ] N laser m
laser beam N raggio m laser inv
laser printer N stampante f laser inv
lash [læʃ] N frustata; (also: **eyelash**) ciglio
  ▶ VT frustare; (tie) legare; **to ~ to/together** legare a insieme
  ▶ **lash down** VT assicurare (con corde) ▶ VI (rain) scrosciare
  ▶ **lash out** VI: **to ~ out (at or against sb/sth)** attaccare violentemente (qn/qc); **to ~ out (on sth)** (col: spend) spendere un sacco di soldi (per qc)
lashing ['læʃɪŋ] N (beating) frustata, sferzata; **lashings of** (BRIT col) un mucchio di, una montagna di
lass [læs] N ragazza
lasso [læ'suː] N laccio ▶ VT acchiappare con il laccio
last [lɑːst] ADJ ultimo(-a); (week, month, year) scorso(-a), passato(-a) ▶ ADV per ultimo ▶ VI durare; **~ week** la settimana scorsa; **~ night**

ieri sera, la notte scorsa; **at ~** finalmente, alla fine; **~ but one** penultimo(-a); **the ~ time** l'ultima volta; **it lasts (for) 2 hours** dura 2 ore
last-ditch ['lɑːst'dɪtʃ] ADJ ultimo(-a) e disperato(-a)
lasting ['lɑːstɪŋ] ADJ durevole
lastly ['lɑːstlɪ] ADV infine, per finire, per ultimo ·
last-minute ['lɑːstmɪnɪt] ADJ fatto(-a) (or preso(-a) etc) all'ultimo momento
latch [lætʃ] N chiavistello; (automatic lock) serratura a scatto
  ▶ **latch on to** VT FUS (cling to: person) attaccarsi a, appiccicarsi a; (: idea) afferrare, capire
latchkey ['lætʃkiː] N chiave f di casa
late [leɪt] ADJ (not on time) in ritardo; (far on in day etc) tardi inv; tardo(-a); (recent) recente, ultimo(-a); (former) ex; (dead) defunto(-a) ▶ ADV tardi; (behind time, schedule) in ritardo; **to be (10 minutes) ~** essere in ritardo (di 10 minuti); **to work ~** lavorare fino a tardi; **~ in life** in età avanzata; **sorry I'm ~** scusi il ritardo; **the flight is two hours ~** il volo ha due ore di ritardo; **it's too ~** è troppo tardi; **of ~** di recente; **in the ~ afternoon** nel tardo pomeriggio; **in ~ May** verso la fine di maggio; **the ~ Mr X** il defunto Signor X
latecomer ['leɪtkʌməʳ] N ritardatario(-a)
lately ['leɪtlɪ] ADV recentemente
lateness ['leɪtnɪs] N (of person) ritardo; (of event) tardezza, ora tarda
latent ['leɪtnt] ADJ latente; **~ defect** vizio occulto
later ['leɪtəʳ] ADJ (date etc) posteriore; (version etc) successivo(-a) ▶ ADV più tardi; **~ on today** oggi più tardi
lateral ['lætərl] ADJ laterale
latest ['leɪtɪst] ADJ ultimo(-a), più recente; **at the ~** al più tardi; **the ~ news** le ultime notizie
latex ['leɪtɛks] N latice m
lath [læθ] N (pl **laths** [læðz]) assicella
lathe [leɪð] N tornio
lather ['lɑːðəʳ] N schiuma di sapone ▶ VT insaponare ▶ VI far schiuma
Latin ['lætɪn] N latino ▶ ADJ latino(-a)
Latin America N America Latina
Latin American ADJ sudamericano(-a)
latitude ['lætɪtjuːd] N latitudine f; (fig: freedom) libertà d'azione
latrine [lə'triːn] N latrina
latter ['lætəʳ] ADJ secondo(-a); più recente
  ▶ N: **the ~** quest'ultimo, il secondo
latterly ['lætəlɪ] ADV recentemente, negli ultimi tempi
lattice ['lætɪs] N traliccio; graticolato
lattice window N finestra con vetrata a losanghe

Latvia ['lætvɪə] N Lettonia
Latvian ['lætvɪən] ADJ lettone *inv* ▶ N lettone *mf*; (*Ling*) lettone *m*
laudable ['lɔːdəbl] ADJ lodevole
laudatory ['lɔːdətrɪ] ADJ elogiativo(-a)
laugh [lɑːf] N risata ▶ VI ridere
▶ **laugh at** VT FUS (*misfortune etc*) ridere di; **I laughed at his joke** la sua barzelletta mi fece ridere
▶ **laugh off** VT prendere alla leggera
laughable ['lɑːfəbl] ADJ ridicolo(-a)
laughing ['lɑːfɪŋ] ADJ (*face*) ridente; **this is no ~ matter** non è una cosa da ridere
laughing gas N gas *m* esilarante
laughing stock N: **the ~ of** lo zimbello di
laughter ['lɑːftər] N riso; risate *fpl*
launch [lɔːntʃ] N (*of rocket, product etc*) lancio; (*of new ship*) varo; (*boat*) scialuppa; (*also:* **motor launch**) lancia ▶ VT (*rocket, product*) lanciare; (*ship, plan*) varare
▶ **launch into** VT FUS lanciarsi in
▶ **launch out** VI: **to ~ out (into)** lanciarsi (in)
launching ['lɔːntʃɪŋ] N lancio; varo
launch pad, launching pad N rampa di lancio
launder ['lɔːndər] VT lavare e stirare
Launderette® [lɔːn'drɛt] (*US*), **Laundromat®** ['lɔːndrəmæt] N lavanderia (automatica)
laundry ['lɔːndrɪ] N lavanderia; (*clothes*) biancheria; (: *dirty*) panni *mpl* da lavare; **to do the ~** fare il bucato
laureate ['lɔːrɪət] ADJ *see* **poet laureate**
laurel ['lɔrl] N lauro, alloro; **to rest on one's laurels** riposare *or* dormire sugli allori
Lausanne [ləʊ'zæn] N Losanna
lava ['lɑːvə] N lava
lavatory ['lævətərɪ] N gabinetto
lavatory paper N (*BRIT*) carta igienica
lavender ['lævəndər] N lavanda
lavish ['lævɪʃ] ADJ copioso(-a), abbondante; sontuoso(-a); (*giving freely*): **~ with** prodigo(-a) di, largo(-a) in ▶ VT: **to ~ sth on sb/sth** colmare qn/qc di qc
lavishly ['lævɪʃlɪ] ADV (*give, spend*) generosamente; (*furnished*) sontuosamente, lussuosamente
law [lɔː] N legge *f*; **against the ~** contro la legge; **to study ~** studiare diritto; **to go to ~** (*BRIT*) ricorrere alle vie legali; **civil/criminal ~** diritto civile/penale
law-abiding ['lɔːəbaɪdɪŋ] ADJ ubbidiente alla legge
law and order N l'ordine *m* pubblico
lawbreaker ['lɔːbreɪkər] N violatore(-trice) della legge
law court N tribunale *m*, corte *f* di giustizia
lawful ['lɔːful] ADJ legale, lecito(-a)
lawfully ['lɔːfəlɪ] ADV legalmente

lawless ['lɔːlɪs] ADJ senza legge; illegale
Law Lords NPL ≈ Corte *f* Suprema
lawmaker ['lɔːmeɪkər] N legislatore *m*
lawn [lɔːn] N tappeto erboso
lawnmower ['lɔːnməʊər] N tosaerba *m inv or f inv*
lawn tennis N tennis *m* su prato
law school N facoltà *f inv* di legge
law student N studente(-essa) di legge
lawsuit ['lɔːsuːt] N processo, causa; **to bring a ~ against** intentare causa a
lawyer ['lɔːjər] N (*consultant, with company*) giurista *mf*; (*for sales, wills etc*) ≈ notaio; (*partner, in court*) ≈ avvocato(-essa)
lax [læks] ADJ (*conduct*) rilassato(-a); (*person: careless*) negligente; (: *on discipline*) permissivo(-a)
laxative ['læksətɪv] N lassativo
laxity ['læksɪtɪ] N rilassatezza; negligenza
lay [leɪ] PT *of* **lie** ▶ ADJ laico(-a); secolare; (*not expert*) profano(-a) ▶ VT (*pt, pp* **laid** [leɪd]) posare, mettere; (*eggs*) fare; (*trap*) tendere; (*plans*) fare, elaborare; **to ~ the table** apparecchiare la tavola; **to ~ the facts/one's proposals before sb** presentare i fatti/delle proposte a qn; **to get laid** (*col!*) scopare (!), essere scopato(-a) (!)
▶ **lay aside, lay by** VT mettere da parte
▶ **lay down** VT mettere giù; (*rules etc*) formulare, fissare; **to ~ down the law** (*fig*) dettar legge; **to ~ down one's life** dare la propria vita
▶ **lay in** VT fare una scorta di
▶ **lay into** VT FUS (*col: attack, scold*) aggredire
▶ **lay off** VT (*workers*) licenziare
▶ **lay on** VT (*water, gas*) installare, mettere; (*provide: meal etc*) fornire; (: *paint*) applicare
▶ **lay out** VT (*design*) progettare; (*display*) presentare; (*spend*) sborsare
▶ **lay up** VT (*to store*) accumulare; (*ship*) mettere in disarmo; (*illness*) costringere a letto
layabout ['leɪəbaut] N sfaccendato(-a), fannullone(-a)
lay-by ['leɪbaɪ] N (*BRIT*) piazzola (di sosta)
lay days NPL (*Naut*) stallie *fpl*
layer ['leɪər] N strato
layette [leɪ'ɛt] N corredino (per neonato)
layman ['leɪmən] N (*irreg*) laico; profano
lay-off ['leɪɔf] N sospensione *f*, licenziamento
layout ['leɪaut] N lay-out *m inv*, disposizione *f*; (*Press*) impaginazione *f*
laze [leɪz] VI oziare
laziness ['leɪzɪnɪs] N pigrizia
lazy ['leɪzɪ] ADJ pigro(-a)
lb. ABBR (*pound: = pound (weight)*) lb.
lbw ABBR (*Cricket: = leg before wicket*) fallo dovuto al fatto che il giocatore ha la gamba davanti alla porta

LC N ABBR (*US*) = **Library of Congress**
lc ABBR (*Typ*) = **lower case**
L/C ABBR = **letter of credit**
LCD N ABBR = **liquid crystal display**
Ld ABBR (*BRIT*: = *lord*) titolo
LDS N ABBR (*BRIT*: = *Licentiate in Dental Surgery*) *specializzazione dopo la laurea*; (= *Latter-day Saints*) *Chiesa di Gesù Cristo dei Santi dell'Ultimo Giorno*
LEA N ABBR (*BRIT*: = *local education authority*) ≈ Provveditorato degli Studi
lead¹ [li:d] (*pt, pp* **led** [lɛd]) N (*front position*) posizione *f* di testa; (*distance, time ahead*) vantaggio; (*clue*) indizio; (*Elec*) filo (elettrico); (*for dog*) guinzaglio; (*Theat*) parte *f* principale ▶ VT menare, guidare, condurre; (*induce*) indurre; (*be leader of*) essere a capo di; (: *orchestra*: *BRIT*) essere il primo violino di; (: *US*) dirigere; (*Sport*) essere in testa a ▶ VI condurre; (*Sport*) essere in testa; **in the** ~ in testa; **to** ~ **the way** fare strada; **to take the** ~ (*Sport*) passare in testa; (*fig*) prendere l'iniziativa; **to** ~ **to** menare a; condurre a; portare a; **to** ~ **astray** sviare; **to** ~ **sb to believe that …** far credere a qn che …; **to** ~ **sb to do sth** portare qn a fare qc
  ▶ **lead away** VT condurre via
  ▶ **lead back** VT riportare, ricondurre
  ▶ **lead off** VT portare ▶ VI partire da
  ▶ **lead on** VT (*tease*) tenere sulla corda
  ▶ **lead on to** VT (*induce*) portare a
  ▶ **lead up to** VT FUS portare a; (*fig*) preparare la strada per
lead² [lɛd] N (*metal*) piombo; (*in pencil*) mina
leaded ['lɛdɪd] ADJ (*petrol*) con piombo; ~ **windows** vetrate *fpl* (artistiche)
leaden ['lɛdn] ADJ di piombo
leader ['li:dəʳ] N capo; leader *m inv*; (*in newspaper*) articolo di fondo; (*Sport*) chi è in testa; **they are leaders in their field** (*fig*) sono all'avanguardia nel loro campo; **the L~ of the House** (*BRIT*) il capo della maggioranza ministeriale
leadership ['li:dəʃɪp] N direzione *f*; capacità di comando; **under the** ~ **of …** sotto la direzione *or* guida di …; **qualities of** ~ qualità *fpl* di un capo
lead-free ['lɛdfri:] ADJ senza piombo
leading ['li:dɪŋ] ADJ primo(-a), principale; **a** ~ **question** una domanda tendenziosa; ~ **role** ruolo principale
leading lady N (*Theat*) prima attrice
leading light N (*person*) personaggio di primo piano
leading man N (*irreg*) (*Theat*) primo attore
lead pencil [lɛd-] N matita con la mina di grafite
lead poisoning [lɛd-] N saturnismo
lead singer N cantante alla testa di un gruppo

lead time [li:d-] N (*Comm*) tempo di consegna
lead weight [lɛd-] N piombino, piombo
leaf [li:f] (*pl* **leaves**) N foglia; (*of table*) ribalta; **to turn over a new** ~ (*fig*) cambiar vita; **to take a** ~ **out of sb's book** (*fig*) prendere esempio da qn
  ▶ **leaf through** VT (*book*) sfogliare
leaflet ['li:flɪt] N dépliant *m inv*; (*Pol, Rel*) volantino
leafy ['li:fɪ] ADJ ricco(-a) di foglie
league [li:g] N lega; (*Football*) campionato; **to be in** ~ **with** essere in lega con
league table N classifica
leak [li:k] N (*out*) fuga; (*in*) infiltrazione *f*; (*fig: of information*) fuga di notizie; (*security leak*) fuga d'informazioni ▶ VI (*roof, bucket*) perdere; (*liquid*) uscire; (*shoes*) lasciar passare l'acqua ▶ VT (*liquid*) spandere; (*information*) divulgare
  ▶ **leak out** VI uscire; (*information*) trapelare
leakage ['li:kɪdʒ] N (*of water, gas etc*) perdita
leaky ['li:kɪ] ADJ (*pipe, bucket, roof*) che perde; (*shoe*) che lascia passare l'acqua; (*boat*) che fa acqua
lean [li:n] (*pt, pp* **leaned, leant** [lɛnt]) ADJ magro(-a) ▶ N (*of meat*) carne *f* magra
  ▶ VT: **to** ~ **sth on** appoggiare qc su ▶ VI (*slope*) pendere; (*rest*): **to** ~ **against** appoggiarsi contro; essere appoggiato(-a) a; **to** ~ **on** appoggiarsi a
  ▶ **lean back** VT sporgersi indietro
  ▶ **lean forward** VI sporgersi in avanti
  ▶ **lean out** VI: **to** ~ **out (of)** sporgersi (da)
  ▶ **lean over** VI inclinarsi
leaning ['li:nɪŋ] N: ~ **(towards)** propensione *f* (per) ▶ ADJ inclinato(-a), pendente; **the L~ Tower of Pisa** la torre (pendente) di Pisa
leant [lɛnt] PT, PP *of* **lean**
lean-to ['li:ntu:] N (*roof*) tettoia; (*building*) edificio con tetto appoggiato ad altro edificio
leap [li:p] (*pt, pp* **leaped** *or* **leapt** [lɛpt]) N salto, balzo ▶ VI saltare, balzare; **to** ~ **at an offer** afferrare al volo una proposta
  ▶ **leap up** VI (*person*) alzarsi d'un balzo, balzare su
leapfrog ['li:pfrɔg] N gioco della cavallina
  ▶ VI: **to** ~ **over sb/sth** saltare (alla cavallina) qn/qc
leapt [lɛpt] PT, PP *of* **leap**
leap year N anno bisestile
learn [lə:n] (*pt, pp* **learned, learnt** [-t]) VT, VI imparare; **to** ~ **(how) to do sth** imparare a fare qc; **to** ~ **that …** apprendere che …; **to** ~ **about sth** (*Scol*) studiare qc; (*hear*) apprendere qc; **we were sorry to** ~ **that it was closing down** la notizia della chiusura ci ha fatto dispiacere
learned ['lə:nɪd] ADJ erudito(-a), dotto(-a)
learner ['lə:nəʳ] N principiante *mf*;

639

apprendista *mf*; **he's a ~ (driver)** (*BRIT*) sta imparando a guidare

learning ['lə:nɪŋ] N erudizione *f*, sapienza

learnt [lə:nt] PT, PP *of* **learn**

lease [li:s] N contratto d'affitto ▸ VT affittare; **on ~** in affitto
▸ **lease back** VT effettuare un lease-back *inv*

leaseback ['li:sbæk] N lease-back *m inv*

leasehold ['li:shəuld] N (*contract*) contratto di affitto (*a lungo termine con responsabilità simili a quelle di un proprietario*) ▸ ADJ in affitto

leash [li:ʃ] N guinzaglio

least [li:st] ADJ: **the ~** (*+noun*) il (la) più piccolo(-a), il (la) minimo(-a); (*smallest amount of*) il (la) meno ▸ ADV (*+verb*) meno; **the ~** (*+adjective*): **the ~ beautiful girl** la ragazza meno bella; **the ~ expensive** il (la) meno caro(-a); **the ~ possible effort** il minimo sforzo possibile; **I have the ~ money** ho meno denaro di tutti; **at ~** almeno; **not in the ~** affatto, per nulla

leather ['lɛðəʳ] N (*soft*) pelle *f*; (*hard*) cuoio
▸ CPD di *or* in pelle; di cuoio; **~ goods** pelletteria, pelletterie *fpl*

leave [li:v] (*pt, pp* **left** [lɛft]) VT lasciare; (*go away from*) partire da ▸ VI partire, andarsene; (*bus, train*) partire ▸ N (*time off*) congedo; (*Mil, consent*) licenza; **to be left** rimanere; **there's some milk left over** c'è rimasto del latte; **to take one's ~ of** congedarsi di; **he's already left for the airport** è già uscito per andare all'aeroporto; **to ~ school** finire la scuola; **~ it to me!** ci penso io!, lascia fare a me!; **on ~** in congedo; **on ~ of absence** in permesso; (*public employee*) in congedo; (*Mil*) in licenza
▸ **leave behind** VT (*also fig*) lasciare; (*forget*) dimenticare
▸ **leave off** VT non mettere; (*BRIT col*: *stop*): **to ~ off doing sth** smetterla *or* piantarla di fare qc
▸ **leave on** VT lasciare su; (*light, fire, cooker*) lasciare acceso(-a)
▸ **leave out** VT omettere, tralasciare

leaves [li:vz] NPL *of* **leaf**

leavetaking ['li:vteɪkɪŋ] N commiato, addio

Lebanese [lɛbə'ni:z] ADJ, N (*pl inv*) libanese (*mf*)

Lebanon ['lɛbənən] N Libano

lecherous ['lɛtʃərəs] ADJ lascivo(-a), lubrico(-a)

lectern ['lɛktə:n] N leggio

lecture ['lɛktʃəʳ] N conferenza; (*Scol*) lezione *f*
▸ VI fare conferenze; fare lezioni; (*reprove*) rimproverare, fare una ramanzina a ▸ VT (*scold*): **to ~ sb on** *or* **about sth** rimproverare qn *or* fare una ramanzina a qn per qc; **to ~ on** fare una conferenza su; **to give a ~ (on)** (*BRIT*) fare una conferenza (su); fare lezione (su)

lecture hall N aula magna

lecturer ['lɛktʃərəʳ] N (*speaker*) conferenziere(-a); (*BRIT*: *at university*) professore(-essa), docente *mf*; **assistant ~** (*BRIT*) ≈ professore(-essa) associato(-a); **senior ~** (*BRIT*) ≈ professore(-essa) ordinario(-a)

lecture theatre N = **lecture hall**

LED N ABBR (*Elec*: = *light-emitting diode*) diodo a emissione luminosa

led [lɛd] PT, PP *of* **lead¹**

ledge [lɛdʒ] N (*of window*) davanzale *m*; (*on wall etc*) sporgenza; (*of mountain*) cornice *f*, cengia

ledger ['lɛdʒəʳ] N libro maestro, registro

lee [li:] N lato sottovento; **in the ~ of** a ridosso di, al riparo di

leech [li:tʃ] N sanguisuga

leek [li:k] N porro

leer [lɪəʳ] VI: **to ~ at sb** gettare uno sguardo voglioso (*or* maligno) su qn

leeward ['li:wəd] ADJ sottovento *inv* ▸ N lato sottovento; **to ~** sottovento

leeway ['li:weɪ] N (*fig*): **to have some ~** avere una certa libertà di agire

left [lɛft] PT, PP *of* **leave** ▸ ADJ sinistro(-a)
▸ ADV a sinistra ▸ N sinistra; **on the ~**, **to the ~** a sinistra; **the L~** (*Pol*) la sinistra

left-click ['lɛftklɪk] VI (*Comput*): **to ~ on** cliccare con il pulsante sinistro del mouse su

left-hand ADJ: **the ~ side** il lato sinistro

left-hand drive ['lɛfthænd-] N, ADJ (*BRIT*) guida a sinistra

left-handed [lɛft'hændɪd] ADJ mancino(-a); **~ scissors** forbici *fpl* per mancini

left-hand side ['lɛfthænd-] N lato *or* fianco sinistro

leftie ['lɛftɪ] N: **a ~** (*col*) uno(-a) di sinistra

leftist ['lɛftɪst] ADJ (*Pol*) di sinistra

left-luggage [lɛft'lʌgɪdʒ], (*BRIT*) **left-luggage office** [lɛft'lʌgɪdʒ-] N deposito *m* bagagli *inv*

left-luggage locker N armadietto per deposito bagagli

left-overs ['lɛftəuvəz] NPL avanzi *mpl*, resti *mpl*

left wing N (*Mil, Sport*) ala sinistra; (*Pol*) sinistra ▸ ADJ: **left-wing** (*Pol*) di sinistra

left-winger [lɛft'wɪŋəʳ] N (*Pol*) uno(-a) di sinistra; (*Sport*) ala sinistra

lefty ['lɛftɪ] N = **leftie**

leg [lɛg] N gamba; (*of animal*) zampa; (*of furniture*) piede *m*; (*Culin*: *of chicken*) coscia; (*of journey*) tappa; **1st/2nd ~** (*Sport*) partita di andata/ritorno; **~ of lamb** (*Culin*) cosciotto d'agnello; **to stretch one's legs** sgranchirsi le gambe

legacy ['lɛgəsɪ] N eredità *f inv*; (*fig*) retaggio

legal ['li:gl] ADJ legale; **to take ~ action** *or* **proceedings against sb** intentare un'azione legale contro qn, far causa a qn

legal adviser N consulente *mf* legale

legal holiday N (*US*) giorno festivo, festa nazionale

legality [lɪ'gælɪtɪ] N legalità

legalize ['li:gəlaɪz] VT legalizzare

legally ['li:gəlɪ] ADV legalmente; ~ **binding** legalmente vincolante

legal tender N moneta legale

legation [lɪ'geɪʃən] N legazione *f*

legend ['lɛdʒənd] N leggenda

legendary ['lɛdʒəndərɪ] ADJ leggendario(-a)

-legged ['lɛgɪd] SUFFIX: **two**~ a due gambe (*or* zampe), bipede

leggings ['lɛgɪŋz] NPL ghette *fpl*

leggy ['lɛgɪ] ADJ dalle gambe lunghe

legibility [lɛdʒɪ'bɪlɪtɪ] N leggibilità

legible ['lɛdʒəbl] ADJ leggibile

legibly ['lɛdʒəblɪ] ADV in modo leggibile

legion ['li:dʒən] N legione *f*

legionnaire [li:dʒə'nɛəʳ] N legionario; ~**'s disease** morbo del legionario

legislate ['lɛdʒɪsleɪt] VI legiferare

legislation [lɛdʒɪs'leɪʃən] N legislazione *f*; **a piece of** ~ una legge

legislative ['lɛdʒɪslətɪv] ADJ legislativo(-a)

legislator ['lɛdʒɪsleɪtəʳ] N legislatore(-trice)

legislature ['lɛdʒɪslətʃəʳ] N corpo legislativo

legitimacy [lɪ'dʒɪtɪməsɪ] N legittimità

legitimate [lɪ'dʒɪtɪmət] ADJ legittimo(-a)

legitimize [lɪ'dʒɪtɪmaɪz] VT (*gen*) legalizzare, rendere legale; (*child*) legittimare

legless ['lɛglɪs] ADJ (*BRIT col*) sbronzo(-a), fatto(-a)

leg-room ['lɛgru:m] N spazio per le gambe

Leics ABBR (*BRIT*) = **Leicestershire**

leisure ['lɛʒəʳ] N agio, tempo libero; ricreazioni *fpl*; **at** ~ con comodo

leisure centre N centro di ricreazione

leisurely ['lɛʒəlɪ] ADJ tranquillo(-a), fatto(-a) con comodo *or* senza fretta

leisure suit N (*BRIT*) tuta (da ginnastica)

lemon ['lɛmən] N limone *m*

lemonade [lɛmə'neɪd] N limonata

lemon cheese, lemon curd N crema di limone (*che si spalma sul pane ecc*)

lemon juice N succo di limone

lemon squeezer N spremiagrumi *m inv*

lemon tea N tè *m inv* al limone

lend [lɛnd] (*pt, pp* **lent** [lɛnt]) VT: **to ~ sth (to sb)** prestare qc (a qn); **to ~ a hand** dare una mano

lender ['lɛndəʳ] N prestatore(-trice)

lending library ['lɛndɪŋ-] N biblioteca circolante

length [lɛŋθ] N lunghezza; (*distance*) distanza; (*section: of road, pipe etc*) pezzo, tratto; ~ **of time** periodo (di tempo); **what ~ is it?** quant'è lungo?; **it is 2 metres in ~** è

lungo 2 metri; **to fall full** ~ cadere lungo disteso; **at** ~ (*at last*) finalmente, alla fine; (*lengthily*) a lungo; **to go to any ~(s) to do sth** fare qualsiasi cosa pur di *or* per fare qc

lengthen ['lɛŋθən] VT allungare, prolungare ▶ VI allungarsi

lengthways ['lɛŋθweɪz] ADV per il lungo

lengthy ['lɛŋθɪ] ADJ molto lungo(-a)

leniency ['li:nɪənsɪ] N indulgenza, clemenza

lenient ['li:nɪənt] ADJ indulgente, clemente

leniently ['li:nɪəntlɪ] ADV con indulgenza

lens [lɛnz] N lente *f*; (*of camera*) obiettivo

Lent [lɛnt] N Quaresima

lent [lɛnt] PT, PP *of* **lend**

lentil ['lɛntl] N lenticchia

Leo ['li:əu] N Leone *m*; **to be** ~ essere del Leone

leopard ['lɛpəd] N leopardo

leotard ['li:ətɑ:d] N calzamaglia

leper ['lɛpəʳ] N lebbroso(-a)

leper colony N lebbrosario

leprosy ['lɛprəsɪ] N lebbra

lesbian ['lɛzbɪən] N lesbica ▶ ADJ lesbico(-a)

lesion ['li:ʒən] N (*Med*) lesione *f*

Lesotho [lɪ'su:tu] N Lesotho *m*

less [lɛs] ADJ, PRON, ADV, PREP meno; ~ **tax/10% discount** meno tasse/il 10% di sconto; ~ **than you/ever** meno di lei/che mai; ~ **than half** meno della metà; ~ **and** ~ sempre meno; **the** ~ **he works** ... meno lavora ...; ~ **than £1/a kilo/3 metres** meno di una sterlina/un chilo/3 metri

lessee [lɛ'si:] N affittuario(-a), locatario(-a)

lessen ['lɛsn] VI diminuire, attenuarsi ▶ VT diminuire, ridurre

lesser ['lɛsəʳ] ADJ minore, più piccolo(-a); **to a** ~ **extent** *or* **degree** in grado *or* misura minore

lesson ['lɛsn] N lezione *f*; **a maths** ~ una lezione di matematica; **to give lessons in** dare *or* impartire lezioni di; **to teach sb a** ~ dare una lezione a qn; **it taught him a** ~ (*fig*) gli è servito di lezione

lessor ['lɛsɔ:ʳ, lɛ'sɔ:ʳ] N locatore(-trice)

lest [lɛst] CONJ per paura di + *infinitive*, per paura che + *sub*

let [lɛt] VT (*pt, pp* ~) lasciare; (*BRIT: lease*) dare in affitto; **to ~ sb do sth** lasciar fare qc a qn, lasciare che qn faccia qc; **to ~ sb know sth** far sapere qc a qn; **to ~ sb have sth** dare qc a qn; **he ~ me go** mi ha lasciato andare; ~ **the water boil and** ... fate bollire l'acqua e ...; ~**'s go** andiamo; ~ **him come** lo lasci venire; **"to ~"** "affittasi"

▶ **let down** VT (*lower*) abbassare; (*dress*) allungare; (*hair*) sciogliere; (*disappoint*) deludere; (*BRIT: tyre*) sgonfiare

▶ **let go** VI mollare ▶ VT mollare; (*allow to go*) lasciare andare

▶ **let in** VT lasciare entrare; (*visitor etc*) far entrare; **what have you ~ yourself in for?** in che guai *or* pasticci sei andato a cacciarti?

▶ **let off** VT (*allow to go*) lasciare andare; (*firework etc*) far partire; (*smell etc*) emettere; (*taxi driver, bus driver*) far scendere; **to ~ off steam** (*fig: col*) sfogarsi, scaricarsi

▶ **let on** VI (*col*): **to ~ on that ...** lasciar capire che ...

▶ **let out** VT lasciare uscire; (*dress*) allargare; (*scream*) emettere; (*rent out*) affittare, dare in affitto

▶ **let up** VI diminuire

let-down ['lɛtdaun] N (*disappointment*) delusione *f*

lethal ['li:θl] ADJ letale, mortale

lethargic [lɛ'θɑ:dʒɪk] ADJ letargico(-a)

lethargy ['lɛθədʒɪ] N letargia

letter ['lɛtə^r] N lettera; **letters** NPL (*Literature*) lettere; **small/capital ~** lettera minuscola/maiuscola; **~ of credit** lettera di credito; **documentary ~ of credit** lettera di credito documentata

letter bomb N lettera esplosiva

letterbox ['lɛtəbɔks] (*BRIT*) N buca delle lettere

letterhead ['lɛtəhɛd] N intestazione *f*

lettering ['lɛtərɪŋ] N iscrizione *f*; caratteri *mpl*

letter-opener ['lɛtərəupnə^r] N tagliacarte *m inv*

letterpress ['lɛtəprɛs] N (*method*) rilievografia

letter quality N (*of printer*) qualità di stampa

letters patent NPL brevetto di invenzione

lettuce ['lɛtɪs] N lattuga, insalata

let-up ['lɛtʌp] N (*col*) interruzione *f*

leukaemia, (*US*) **leukemia** [lu:'ki:mɪə] N leucemia

level ['lɛvl] ADJ piatto(-a), piano(-a); orizzontale ▶ N livello; (*also*: **spirit level**) livella (a bolla d'aria) ▶ VT livellare, spianare; (*gun*) puntare (verso); (*accusation*): **to ~ (against)** lanciare (a *or* contro) ▶ VI (*col*): **to ~ with sb** essere franco(-a) con qn; **to be ~ with** essere alla pari di; **a ~ spoonful** (*Culin*) un cucchiaio raso; **to draw ~ with** (*team*) mettersi alla pari di; (*runner, car*) affiancarsi a; **A levels** *npl* (*BRIT*) ≈ esami *mpl* di maturità; **O levels** *npl* (*BRIT formerly*) *diploma di istruzione secondaria conseguito a 16 anni in Inghilterra e Galles, ora sostituito dal GCSE*; **on the ~** piatto(-a); (*fig*) onesto(-a)

▶ **level off, level out** VI (*prices etc*) stabilizzarsi; (*ground*) diventare pianeggiante; (*aircraft*) volare in quota

level crossing N (*BRIT*) passaggio a livello

level-headed [lɛvl'hɛdɪd] ADJ equilibrato(-a)

levelling, (*US*) **leveling** ['lɛvlɪŋ] ADJ (*process, effect*) di livellamento

level playing field N: **to compete on a ~** (*fig*) competere ad armi pari

lever ['li:və^r] N leva ▶ VT: **to ~ up/out** sollevare/estrarre con una leva

leverage ['li:vərɪdʒ] N: ~ **(on** *or* **with)** forza (su); (*fig*) ascendente *m* (su)

levity ['lɛvɪtɪ] N leggerezza, frivolità

levy ['lɛvɪ] N tassa, imposta ▶ VT imporre

lewd [lu:d] ADJ osceno(-a), lascivo(-a)

lexicographer [lɛksɪ'kɔgrəfə^r] N lessicografo(-a)

lexicography [lɛksɪ'kɔgrəfɪ] N lessicografia

LGBT N LGBT *mpl*, *persone lesbiche, gay, bisessuali e transessuali*

LGV N ABBR (*BRIT*: = *Large Goods Vehicle*) automezzo pesante

LI ABBR (*US*) = **Long Island**

liabilities [laɪə'bɪlətɪz] NPL debiti *mpl*; (*on balance sheet*) passivo

liability [laɪə'bɪlɪtɪ] N responsabilità *f inv*; (*handicap*) peso

liable ['laɪəbl] ADJ (*subject*): **~ to** soggetto(-a) a; passibile di; (*responsible*) **~ (for)** responsabile (di); (*likely*) **~ to do** propenso(-a) a fare; **to be ~ to a fine** essere passibile di multa

liaise [li:'eɪz] VI: **to ~ (with)** mantenere i contatti (con)

liaison [li:'eɪzɔn] N relazione *f*; (*Mil*) collegamento

liar ['laɪə^r] N bugiardo(-a)

libel ['laɪbl] N libello, diffamazione *f* ▶ VT diffamare

libellous, (*US*) **libelous** ['laɪbləs] ADJ diffamatorio(-a)

liberal ['lɪbərl] ADJ liberale; (*generous*): **to be ~ with** distribuire liberalmente ▶ N (*Pol*): **L~** liberale *mf*

Liberal Democrat N liberaldemocratico(-a)

liberality [lɪbə'rælɪtɪ] N (*generosity*) generosità, liberalità

liberalize ['lɪbərəlaɪz] VT liberalizzare

liberal-minded [lɪbərl'maɪndɪd] ADJ tollerante

liberate ['lɪbəreɪt] VT liberare

liberation [lɪbə'reɪʃən] N liberazione *f*

liberation theology N teologia della liberazione

Liberia [laɪ'bɪərɪə] N Liberia

Liberian [laɪ'bɪərɪən] ADJ, N liberiano(-a)

liberty ['lɪbətɪ] N libertà *f inv*; **at ~** (*criminal*) in libertà; **at ~ to do** libero(-a) di fare; **to take the ~ of** prendersi la libertà di, permettersi di

libido [lɪ'bi:dəu] N libido *f*

Libra ['li:brə] N Bilancia; **to be ~** essere della Bilancia

librarian [laɪ'brɛərɪən] N bibliotecario(-a)

library ['laɪbrərɪ] N biblioteca

library book N libro della biblioteca

libretto [lɪˈbrɛtəu] N libretto
Libya [ˈlɪbɪə] N Libia
Libyan [ˈlɪbɪən] ADJ, N libico(-a)
lice [laɪs] NPL of **louse**
licence, (US) **license** [ˈlaɪsns] N
autorizzazione f, permesso; (Comm) licenza;
(Radio, TV) canone m, abbonamento; (also:
driving licence, US **driver's license**) patente f
di guida; (excessive freedom) licenza; **import ~**
licenza di importazione; **produced under ~**
prodotto su licenza
licence number N (BRIT Aut) numero di targa
license [ˈlaɪsns] N (US) = **licence** ▶ VT dare una
licenza a; (car) pagare la tassa di circolazione
or il bollo di
licensed [ˈlaɪsnst] ADJ (for alcohol) che ha la
licenza di vendere bibite alcoliche
licensed trade N commercio di bevande
alcoliche con licenza speciale
licensee [laɪsənˈsiː] N (BRIT: of pub)
detentore(-trice) di autorizzazione alla
vendita di bevande alcoliche
license plate N (esp US Aut) targa
(automobilistica)
licensing hours (BRIT) NPL orario d'apertura
(di un pub)
licentious [laɪˈsɛnʃəs] ADJ licenzioso(-a)
lichen [ˈlaɪkən] N lichene m
lick [lɪk] VT leccare; (col: defeat) suonarle a,
stracciare ▶ N leccata; **a ~ of paint** una
passata di vernice; **to ~ one's lips** (fig)
leccarsi i baffi
licorice [ˈlɪkərɪs] N = **liquorice**
lid [lɪd] N coperchio; (eyelid) palpebra; **to take
the ~ off sth** (fig) smascherare qc
lido [ˈlaɪdəu] N piscina all'aperto; (part of the
beach) lido, stabilimento balneare
lie [laɪ] N bugia, menzogna ▶ VI (pt, pp **lied**)
mentire, dire bugie; (pt **lay** [leɪ], pp **lain**
[leɪn]: rest) giacere, star disteso(-a); (in grave)
giacere, riposare; (object: be situated) trovarsi,
essere; **to tell lies** raccontare or dire bugie;
to ~ low (fig) latitare
▶ **lie about, lie around** VI (things) essere in
giro; (person) bighellonare
▶ **lie back** VI stendersi
▶ **lie down** VI stendersi, sdraiarsi
▶ **lie up** VI (hide) nascondersi
Liechtenstein [ˈlɪktənstaɪn] N
Liechtenstein m
lie detector N macchina della verità
lie-down [ˈlaɪdaun] N (BRIT): **to have a ~**
sdraiarsi, riposarsi
lie-in [ˈlaɪɪn] N (BRIT): **to have a ~** rimanere a
letto
lieu [luː] N: **in ~ of** invece di, al posto di
Lieut. ABBR (= lieutenant) Ten.
lieutenant [lɛfˈtɛnənt, (US) luːˈtɛnənt] N
tenente m

lieutenant-colonel [lɛfˈtɛnəntˈkəːnl, (US)
luːˈtɛnəntˈkəːnl] N tenente colonnello
life [laɪf] N (pl **lives**) vita ▶ CPD di vita; della
vita; a vita; **to come to ~** rianimarsi;
country/city ~ vita di campagna/di città;
to be sent to prison for ~ essere condannato
all'ergastolo; **true to ~** fedele alla realtà;
to paint from ~ dipingere dal vero
life annuity N rendita vitalizia
life assurance N (BRIT) = **life insurance**
lifebelt [ˈlaɪfbɛlt] N (BRIT) salvagente m
lifeblood [ˈlaɪfblʌd] N (fig) linfa vitale
lifeboat [ˈlaɪfbəut] N scialuppa di
salvataggio
life expectancy N durata media della vita
lifeguard [ˈlaɪfgɑːd] N bagnino
life imprisonment N ergastolo
life insurance N assicurazione f sulla vita
life jacket N giubbotto di salvataggio
lifeless [ˈlaɪflɪs] ADJ senza vita
lifelike [ˈlaɪflaɪk] ADJ che sembra vero(-a);
rassomigliante
lifeline [ˈlaɪflaɪn] N cavo di salvataggio
lifelong [ˈlaɪflɔŋ] ADJ per tutta la vita
life preserver [-prɪˈzəːvəʳ] N (US)
salvagente m; giubbotto di salvataggio;
(BRIT) sfollagente m inv
lifer [ˈlaɪfəʳ] N (col) ergastolano(-a)
life-raft [ˈlaɪfrɑːft] N zattera di salvataggio
life-saver [ˈlaɪfseɪvəʳ] N bagnino
life sentence N (condanna all')ergastolo
life-sized [ˈlaɪfsaɪzd] ADJ a grandezza
naturale
life span N (durata della) vita
life style N stile m di vita
life support system N (Med) respiratore m
automatico
lifetime [ˈlaɪftaɪm] N: **in his ~** durante la sua
vita; **in a ~** nell'arco della vita; in tutta la
vita; **the chance of a ~** un'occasione unica
lift [lɪft] VT sollevare; (ban, rule) levare; (steal)
prendere, rubare ▶ VI (fog) alzarsi ▶ N (BRIT:
elevator) ascensore m; **to give sb a ~** (BRIT)
dare un passaggio a qn
▶ **lift off** VT togliere ▶ VI (rocket) partire;
(helicopter) decollare
▶ **lift out** VT tirar fuori; (troops, evacuees etc) far
evacuare per mezzo di elicotteri (or aerei)
▶ **lift up** VT sollevare, alzare
lift-off [ˈlɪftɔf] N decollo
ligament [ˈlɪgəmənt] N legamento
light [laɪt] (pt, pp **lighted,** pt, pp **lit** [lɪt]) N luce
f, lume m; (daylight) luce, giorno; (lamp)
lampada; (Aut: rear light) luce f di posizione;
(: headlamp) fanale m; (for cigarette etc): **have
you got a ~?** ha da accendere? ▶ VT (candle,
cigarette, fire) accendere; (room) illuminare
▶ ADJ (room, colour) chiaro(-a); (not heavy, also fig)
leggero(-a) ▶ ADV (travel) con poco bagaglio;

lights NPL (Aut: traffic lights) semaforo; **in the ~ of** alla luce di; **to turn the ~ on/off** accendere/spegnere la luce; **to come to ~** venire alla luce, emergere; **to cast** or **shed** or **throw ~ on** gettare luce su; **to make ~ of sth** (fig) prendere alla leggera qc, non dar peso a qc; **to be lit by** essere illuminato(-a) da ▶ **light up** VI illuminarsi ▶ VT illuminare

light bulb N lampadina

lighten ['laitn] VI schiarirsi ▶ VT (give light to) illuminare; (make lighter) schiarire; (make less heavy) alleggerire

lighter ['laitə^r] N (also: **cigarette lighter**) accendino (boat) chiatta

light-fingered [lait'fiŋgəd] ADJ lesto(-a) di mano

light-headed ['lait'hɛdid] ADJ stordito(-a)

light-hearted ['lait'hɑːtid] ADJ gioioso(-a), gaio(-a)

lighthouse ['laithaus] N faro

lighting ['laitiŋ] N illuminazione f

lighting-up time ['laitiŋʌp-] N (BRIT) orario per l'accensione delle luci

lightly ['laitli] ADV leggermente; **to get off ~** cavarsela a buon mercato

light meter N (Phot) esposimetro

lightness ['laitnis] N chiarezza; (in weight) leggerezza

lightning ['laitniŋ] N lampo, fulmine m; **a flash of ~** un lampo, un fulmine

lightning conductor, (US) **lightning rod** N parafulmine m

lightning strike N (BRIT) sciopero m lampo inv

light pen N penna luminosa

lightship ['laitʃip] N battello m faro inv

lightweight ['laitweit] ADJ (suit) leggero(-a) ▶ N (Boxing) peso leggero

light year ['laitjiə^r] N anno m luce inv

Ligurian [li'gjuəriən] ADJ, N ligure (mf)

like [laik] VT (person) volere bene a; (activity, object, food): **I ~ swimming/that book/chocolate** mi piace nuotare/quel libro/il cioccolato ▶ PREP come ▶ ADJ simile, uguale ▶ N: **the ~** uno(-a) uguale; **I would ~**, **I'd ~** mi piacerebbe, vorrei; **would you ~ a coffee?** gradirebbe un caffè?; **if you ~** se vuoi; **to be/look ~ sb/sth** somigliare a qn/qc; **what does it look/taste ~?** che aspetto/gusto ha?; **what does it sound ~?** come fa?; **what's he ~?** che tipo è?, com'è?; **what's the weather ~?** che tempo fa?; **that's just ~ him** è proprio da lui; **something ~ that** qualcosa del genere; **do it ~ this** fallo così; **I feel ~ a drink** avrei voglia di bere qualcosa; **there's nothing ~ ...** non c'è niente di meglio di or niente come ...; **it is nothing ~ ...** non è affatto come ...; **his likes and dislikes** i suoi gusti

likeable ['laikəbl] ADJ simpatico(-a)

likelihood ['laiklihud] N probabilità; **in all ~** con ogni probabilità, molto probabilmente

likely ['laikli] ADJ probabile; plausibile; **he's ~ to leave** probabilmente partirà, è probabile che parta; **not ~!** (col) neanche per sogno!

like-minded ['laik'maindid] ADJ che pensa allo stesso modo

liken ['laikən] VT: **to ~ sth to** paragonare qc a

likeness ['laiknis] N (similarity) somiglianza

likewise ['laikwaiz] ADV similmente, nello stesso modo

liking ['laikiŋ] N: **~ (for)** simpatia (per); debole m (per); **to be to sb's ~** piacere a qn; **to take a ~ to sb** prendere qn in simpatia

lilac ['lailək] N lilla m inv ▶ ADJ lilla inv

Lilo® ['lailəu] N materassino gonfiabile

lilt [lilt] N cadenza

lilting ['liltiŋ] ADJ melodioso(-a)

lily ['lili] N giglio; **~ of the valley** mughetto

Lima ['liːmə] N Lima

limb [lim] N arto; **to be out on a ~** (fig) sentirsi spaesato(-a) or tagliato(-a) fuori

limber ['limbə^r]: **to ~ up** VI riscaldarsi i muscoli

limbo ['limbəu] N: **to be in ~** (fig) essere lasciato(-a) nel dimenticatoio

lime [laim] N (tree) tiglio; (fruit) limetta; (Geo) calce f

lime juice N succo di limetta

limelight ['laimlait] N: **in the ~** (fig) alla ribalta, in vista

limerick ['limərik] N poesiola umoristica di cinque versi

limestone ['laimstəun] N pietra calcarea; (Geo) calcare m

limit ['limit] N limite m ▶ VT limitare; **weight/speed ~** limite di peso/di velocità; **within limits** entro certi limiti

limitation [limi'teiʃən] N limitazione f, limite m

limited ['limitid] ADJ limitato(-a), ristretto(-a); **~ edition** edizione f a bassa tiratura; **to be ~ to** limitarsi a

limited company, limited liability company N (BRIT) ≈ società f inv a responsabilità limitata (S.r.l.)

limitless ['limitlis] ADJ illimitato(-a)

limousine ['liməziːn] N limousine f inv

limp [limp] N: **to have a ~** zoppicare ▶ VI zoppicare ▶ ADJ floscio(-a), flaccido(-a)

limpet ['limpit] N patella

limpid ['limpid] ADJ (poet) limpido(-a)

linchpin ['lintʃpin] N acciarino, bietta; (fig) perno

Lincs ABBR (BRIT) = **Lincolnshire**

line [lain] N (gen, Comm) linea; (rope) corda; (for fishing) lenza; (wire) filo; (of poem) verso;

(*row, series*) fila, riga; coda; (*on face*) ruga ▶ VT
(*trees, crowd*) fiancheggiare; **to ~ (with)**
(*clothes*) foderare (di); (*box*) rivestire *or*
foderare (di); **to cut in ~** (*US*) passare avanti;
in his ~ of business nel suo ramo; **on the
right lines** sulla buona strada; **a new ~ in
cosmetics** una nuova linea di cosmetici;
hold the ~ please (*BRIT Tel*) resti in linea per
cortesia; **to be in ~ for sth** (*fig*) essere in lista
per qc; **in ~ with** d'accordo con, in linea con;
to bring sth into ~ with sth mettere qc al
passo con qc; **to draw the ~ at (doing) sth**
(*fig*) rifiutarsi di fare qc; **to take the ~ that**
... essere del parere che ...
▶ **line up** VI allinearsi, mettersi in fila ▶ VT
mettere in fila; (*event, celebration*) preparare;
to have sth lined up avere qc in
programma; **to have sb lined up** avere qn
in mente

linear ['lɪnɪər] ADJ lineare
lined [laɪnd] ADJ (*paper*) a righe, rigato(-a);
(*face*) rugoso(-a); (*clothes*) foderato(-a)
line feed N (*Comput*) avanzamento di una
interlinea
linen ['lɪnɪn] N biancheria, panni *mpl*; (*cloth*)
tela di lino
line printer N stampante *f* parallela
liner ['laɪnər] N nave *f* di linea; **dustbin ~**
sacchetto per la pattumiera
linesman ['laɪnzmən] N (*irreg*) guardalinee *m
inv*, segnalinee *m inv*
line-up ['laɪnʌp] N allineamento, fila; (*also:*
police line-up) confronto all'americana;
(: *Sport*) formazione *f* di gioco
linger ['lɪŋgər] VI attardarsi; indugiare;
(*smell, tradition*) persistere
lingerie ['lænʒəri:] N biancheria intima
(femminile)
lingering ['lɪŋgərɪŋ] ADJ lungo(-a),
persistente; (*death*) lento(-a)
lingo ['lɪŋgəu] N (*pl* **lingoes**) (*pej*) gergo
linguist ['lɪŋgwɪst] N linguista *mf*; poliglotta
mf
linguistic [lɪŋ'gwɪstɪk] ADJ linguistico(-a)
linguistics [lɪŋ'gwɪstɪks] N linguistica
lining ['laɪnɪŋ] N fodera; (*Tech*) rivestimento
(interno); (*of brake*) guarnizione *f*
link [lɪŋk] N (*of a chain*) anello; (*relationship*)
legame *m*; (*connection*) legame *m*,
collegamento; (*Comput*) link, collegamento
▶ VT collegare, unire, congiungere; (*Comput*)
creare un collegamento con; (*associate*): **to ~
with** *or* **to** collegare a ▶ VI (*Comput*): **to ~ to a
site** creare un collegamento con un sitio;
rail ~ collegamento ferroviario; *see also* **links**
▶ **link up** VT collegare, unire ▶ VI riunirsi;
associarsi
links [lɪŋks] NPL pista *or* terreno da golf
link-up ['lɪŋkʌp] N legame *m*; (*of roads*) nodo;

(*of spaceships*) aggancio; (*Radio, TV*)
collegamento
linoleum [lɪ'nəulɪəm] N linoleum *m inv*
linseed oil ['lɪnsi:d-] N olio di semi di lino
lint [lɪnt] N garza
lintel ['lɪntl] N architrave *f*
lion ['laɪən] N leone *m*
lion cub N leoncino
lioness ['laɪənɪs] N leonessa
lip [lɪp] N labbro; (*of cup etc*) orlo; (*insolence*)
sfacciataggine *f*
liposuction ['lɪpəusʌkʃən] N liposuzione *f*
lipread ['lɪpri:d] VI leggere sulle labbra
lip salve [-sælv] N burro di cacao
lip service N: **to pay ~ to sth** essere
favorevole a qc solo a parole
lipstick ['lɪpstɪk] N rossetto
liquefy ['lɪkwɪfaɪ] VT liquefare ▶ VI liquefarsi
liqueur [lɪ'kjuər] N liquore *m*
liquid ['lɪkwɪd] N liquido ▶ ADJ liquido(-a)
liquid assets NPL attività *fpl* liquide, crediti
mpl liquidi
liquidate ['lɪkwɪdeɪt] VT liquidare
liquidation [lɪkwɪ'deɪʃən] N liquidazione *f*;
to go into ~ andare in liquidazione
liquidator ['lɪkwɪdeɪtər] N liquidatore *m*
liquid crystal display N visualizzazione *f* a
cristalli liquidi
liquidity [lɪ'kwɪdɪtɪ] N (*Comm*) liquidità
liquidize ['lɪkwɪdaɪz] VT (*BRIT Culin*) passare al
frullatore
liquidizer ['lɪkwɪdaɪzər] N (*BRIT Culin*)
frullatore *m* (a brocca)
liquor ['lɪkər] N alcool *m*
liquorice ['lɪkərɪs] N liquirizia
liquor store N (*US*) negozio di liquori
Lisbon ['lɪzbən] N Lisbona
lisp [lɪsp] N pronuncia blesa della "s"
lissom ['lɪsəm] ADJ leggiadro(-a)
list [lɪst] N lista, elenco; (*of ship*)
sbandamento ▶ VT (*write down*) mettere in
lista; fare una lista di; (*enumerate*) elencare;
(*Comput*) stampare (un prospetto di) ▶ VI
(*ship*) sbandare; **shopping ~** lista *or* nota
della spesa
listed building ['lɪstəd-] N (*Archit*) edificio
sotto la protezione delle Belle Arti
listed company N società quotata in Borsa
listen ['lɪsn] VI ascoltare; **to ~ to** ascoltare
listener ['lɪsnər] N ascoltatore(-trice)
listeria [lɪs'tɪərɪə] N listeria
listing ['lɪstɪŋ] N (*Comput*) lista stampata
listless ['lɪstlɪs] ADJ svogliato(-a); apatico(-a)
listlessly ['lɪstlɪslɪ] ADV svogliatamente;
apaticamente
list price N prezzo di listino
lit [lɪt] PT, PP *of* **light**
litany ['lɪtənɪ] N litania
liter ['li:tər] N (*US*) = **litre**

literacy ['lɪtərəsɪ] N il sapere leggere e scrivere

literacy campaign N lotta contro l'analfabetismo

literal ['lɪtərl] ADJ letterale

literally ['lɪtərəlɪ] ADV alla lettera, letteralmente

literary ['lɪtərərɪ] ADJ letterario(-a)

literate ['lɪtərɪt] ADJ che sa leggere e scrivere

literature ['lɪtərɪtʃəʳ] N letteratura; (*brochures etc*) materiale *m*

lithe [laɪð] ADJ agile, snello(-a)

lithography [lɪ'θɔgrəfɪ] N litografia

Lithuania [lɪθju'eɪnɪə] N Lituania

Lithuanian [lɪθju'eɪnɪən] ADJ lituano(-a) ▶ N lituano(-a); (*Ling*) lituano

litigate ['lɪtɪgeɪt] VT muovere causa a ▶ VI litigare

litigation [lɪtɪ'geɪʃən] N causa

litmus ['lɪtməs] N: ~ **paper** cartina di tornasole

litre, (*US*) **liter** ['li:təʳ] N litro

litter ['lɪtəʳ] N (*rubbish*) rifiuti *mpl*; (*young animals*) figliata ▶ VT sparpagliare; lasciare rifiuti in; **littered with** coperto(-a) di

litter bin N (*BRIT*) cestino per rifiuti

littered ADJ: ~ **with** coperto(-a) di

litter lout, (*US*) **litterbug** ['lɪtəbʌg] N *persona che butta per terra le cartacce o i rifiuti*

little ['lɪtl] ADJ (*small*) piccolo(-a); (*not much*) poco(-a) ▶ ADV poco; **a ~** un po' (di); **a ~ milk** un po' di latte; **a ~ bit** un pochino; **with ~ difficulty** senza fatica *or* difficoltà; **~ by ~** a poco a poco; **as ~ as possible** il meno possibile; **for a ~ while** per un po'; **to make ~ of** dare poca importanza a

little finger N mignolo

little-known ['lɪtl'nəun] ADJ poco noto(-a)

liturgy ['lɪtədʒɪ] N liturgia

live¹ [lɪv] VI vivere; (*reside*) vivere, abitare; **where do you ~?** dove abita?; **to ~ in London** abitare a Londra

▶ **live down** VT far dimenticare (alla gente)

▶ **live in** VI essere interno(-a); avere vitto e alloggio

▶ **live off** VI (*land, fish etc*) vivere di; (*pej: parents etc*) vivere alle spalle *or* a spese di

▶ **live on** VT FUS (*food*) vivere di ▶ VI sopravvivere, continuare a vivere; **to ~ on £50 a week** vivere con 50 sterline la settimana

▶ **live out** VI (*BRIT: students*) essere esterno(-a)

▶ VT: **to ~ out one's days** *or* **life** trascorrere gli ultimi anni

▶ **live together** VI vivere insieme, convivere

▶ **live up** VT: **to ~ it up** (*col*) fare la bella vita

▶ **live up to** VT FUS tener fede a, non venir meno a

live² [laɪv] ADJ (*animal*) vivo(-a); (*issue*) scottante, d'attualità; (*wire*) sotto tensione; (*broadcast*) diretto(-a); (*ammunition: not blank*) carico(-a); (: *unexploded*) inesploso(-a); (*performance*) dal vivo

live-in ['lɪvɪn] ADJ (*partner*) convivente; (*servant*) che vive in casa; **he has a ~ girlfriend** la sua ragazza vive con lui

livelihood ['laɪvlɪhud] N mezzi *mpl* di sostentamento

liveliness ['laɪvlɪnəs] N vivacità

lively ['laɪvlɪ] ADJ vivace, vivo(-a)

liven up ['laɪvn-] VT (*room etc*) ravvivare; (*discussion, evening*) animare ▶ VI ravvivarsi

liver ['lɪvəʳ] N fegato

liverish ['lɪvərɪʃ] ADJ che soffre di mal di fegato; (*fig*) scontroso(-a)

Liverpudlian [lɪvə'pʌdlɪən] ADJ di Liverpool ▶ N abitante *mf* di Liverpool; originario(-a) di Liverpool

livery ['lɪvərɪ] N livrea

lives [laɪvz] NPL *of* **life**

livestock ['laɪvstɔk] N bestiame *m*

live wire [laɪv-] N (*col: fig*): **to be a ~** essere pieno(-a) di vitalità

livid ['lɪvɪd] ADJ livido(-a); (*furious*) livido(-a) di rabbia, furibondo(-a)

living ['lɪvɪŋ] ADJ vivo(-a), vivente ▶ N: **to earn** *or* **make a ~** guadagnarsi la vita; **cost of ~** costo della vita, carovita *m*; **within ~ memory** a memoria d'uomo

living conditions NPL condizioni *fpl* di vita

living expenses NPL spese *fpl* di mantenimento

living room N soggiorno

living standards NPL tenore *m* di vita

living wage N salario sufficiente per vivere

living will N testamento biologico

lizard ['lɪzəd] N lucertola

llama ['lɑːmə] N lama *m inv*

LLB N ABBR (= *Bachelor of Laws*) ≈ laurea in legge

LLD N ABBR (= *Doctor of Laws*) titolo di studio

LMT ABBR (*US*: = *Local Mean Time*) tempo medio locale

load [ləud] N (*weight*) peso; (*Elec, Tech, thing carried*) carico ▶ VT (*also*: **load up**): **to ~ (with)** (*lorry, ship*) caricare (di); (*gun, camera*) caricare (con); **a ~ of, loads of** (*fig*) un sacco di; **to ~ a program** (*Comput*) caricare un programma

loaded ['ləudɪd] ADJ (*dice*) falsato(-a); (*question, word*) capzioso(-a); (*col: rich*) pieno(-a) di soldi; **~ (with)** (*vehicle*) carico(-a) (di)

loading bay ['ləudɪŋ-] N piazzola di carico

loaf [ləuf] (*pl* **loaves**) N pane *m*, pagnotta ▶ VI (*also*: **loaf about, loaf around**) bighellonare

loam [ləum] N terra di marna

loan [ləun] N prestito ▶ VT dare in prestito; **on ~** in prestito

loan account N conto dei prestiti

loan capital N capitale m di prestito
loan shark N (col, pej) strozzino(-a)
loath [ləuθ] ADJ: **to be ~ to do** essere
restio(-a) a fare
loathe [ləuð] VT detestare, aborrire
loathing ['ləuðɪŋ] N aborrimento, disgusto
loathsome ['ləuðsəm] ADJ (gen) ripugnante;
(person) detestabile, odioso(-a)
loaves [ləuvz] NPL of **loaf**
lob [lɔb] VT (ball) lanciare
lobby ['lɔbɪ] N atrio, vestibolo; (Pol: pressure
group) gruppo di pressione ▶ VT fare
pressione su
lobbyist ['lɔbɪɪst] N appartenente mf ad un
gruppo di pressione
lobe [ləub] N lobo
lobster ['lɔbstə^r] N aragosta
lobster pot N nassa per aragoste
local ['ləukl] ADJ locale ▶ N (BRIT: pub) ≈ bar m
inv all'angolo; **the locals** NPL la gente della
zona
local anaesthetic N anestesia locale
local authority N ente m locale
local call N (Tel) telefonata urbana
local government N amministrazione f
locale
locality [ləu'kælɪtɪ] N località f inv; (position)
posto, luogo
localize ['ləukəlaɪz] VT localizzare
locally ['ləukəlɪ] ADV da queste parti; nel
vicinato
locate [ləu'keɪt] VT (find) trovare; (situate)
collocare; situare
location [ləu'keɪʃən] N posizione f; **on ~** (Cine)
all'esterno
loch [lɔx] N lago
lock [lɔk] N (of door, box) serratura; (of canal)
chiusa; (of hair) ciocca, riccio ▶ VT (with key)
chiudere a chiave; (immobilize) bloccare ▶ VI
(door etc) chiudersi; (wheels) bloccarsi,
incepparsi; **~ stock and barrel** (fig) in
blocco; **on full ~** (BRIT Aut) a tutto sterzo
▶ **lock away** VT (valuables) tenere
(rinchiuso(-a)) al sicuro; (criminal) metter
dentro
▶ **lock in** VT chiudere dentro (a chiave)
▶ **lock out** VT chiudere fuori; **to ~ workers
out** fare una serrata
▶ **lock up** VT (criminal, mental patient)
rinchiudere; (house) chiudere (a chiave) ▶ VI
chiudere tutto (a chiave)
locker ['lɔkə^r] N armadietto
locker-room N (US Sport) spogliatoio
locket ['lɔkɪt] N medaglione m
lockjaw ['lɔkdʒɔː] N tetano
lockout ['lɔkaut] N (Industry) serrata
locksmith ['lɔksmɪθ] N magnano
lock-up ['lɔkʌp] N (prison) prigione f; (cell)
guardina; (also: **lock-up garage**) box m inv

locomotive [ləukə'məutɪv] N locomotiva
locum ['ləukəm] N (Med) medico sostituto
locust ['ləukəst] N locusta
lodge [lɔdʒ] N casetta, portineria; (hunting
lodge) casino di caccia; (Freemasonry) loggia
▶ VI (person): **to ~ (with)** essere a pensione
(presso or da); (bullet etc) conficcarsi ▶ VT
(appeal etc) presentare, fare; **to ~ a
complaint** presentare un reclamo; **to ~
(itself) in/between** piantarsi dentro/fra
lodger ['lɔdʒə^r] N affittuario(-a); (with room
and meals) pensionante mf
lodging ['lɔdʒɪŋ] N alloggio; see also **board**;
lodgings
lodging house N (BRIT) casa con camere in
affitto
lodgings ['lɔdʒɪŋz] NPL camera d'affitto;
camera ammobiliata
loft [lɔft] N solaio, soffitta; (Agr) granaio;
(US) appartamento ricavato da solaio (or
granaio etc)
lofty ['lɔftɪ] ADJ alto(-a); (haughty)
altezzoso(-a); (sentiments, aims) nobile
log [lɔg] N (of wood) ceppo; (also: **logbook**:
Naut, Aviat) diario di bordo; (Aut) libretto di
circolazione ▶ N ABBR = **logarithm** ▶ VT
registrare
▶ **log in, log on** VI (Comput) aprire una
sessione (con codice di riconoscimento)
▶ **log off, log out** VI (Comput) terminare una
sessione
logarithm ['lɔgərɪðm] N logaritmo
logbook ['lɔgbuk] N (Naut, Aviat) diario di
bordo; (Aut) libretto di circolazione; (of lorry
driver) registro di viaggio; (of events, movement
of goods etc) registro
log cabin N capanna di tronchi
log fire N fuoco di legna
logger ['lɔgə^r] N boscaiolo, taglialegna m inv
loggerheads ['lɔgəhɛdz] NPL: **at ~ (with)** ai
ferri corti (con)
logic ['lɔdʒɪk] N logica
logical ['lɔdʒɪkəl] ADJ logico(-a)
logically ['lɔdʒɪkəlɪ] ADV logicamente
login ['lɔgɪn] N (Comput) nome m utente inv
logistics [lɔ'dʒɪstɪks] N logistica
logjam ['lɔgdʒæm] N: **to break the ~**
superare l'impasse
logo ['ləugəu] N logo m inv
loin [lɔɪn] N (Culin) lombata; **loins** NPL
reni fpl
loin cloth N perizoma m
loiter ['lɔɪtə^r] VI attardarsi; **to ~ (about)**
indugiare, bighellonare
LOL ABBR (col: = laugh out loud) LOL, grandi
risate (nel gergo di Internet)
loll [lɔl] VI (also: **loll about**) essere
stravaccato(-a)
lollipop ['lɔlɪpɔp] N lecca lecca m inv

lollipop man, lollipop lady N (*irreg*) (BRIT); *vedi nota*

In Gran Bretagna il *lollipop man* e la *lollipop lady* sono persone incaricate di regolare il traffico in prossimità delle scuole e di aiutare i bambini ad attraversare la strada usano una paletta la cui forma ricorda quella di un lecca lecca, in inglese, appunto, *lollipop*.

lollop ['lɔləp] VI (BRIT) camminare (*or* correre) goffamente

lolly ['lɔlɪ] N (*col*) lecca lecca *m inv*; (*also*: **ice lolly**) ghiacciolo; (: *money*) grana

Lombardy ['lɔmbədɪ] N Lombardia

London ['lʌndən] N Londra

Londoner ['lʌndənəʳ] N londinese *mf*

lone [ləun] ADJ solitario(-a)

loneliness ['ləunlɪnɪs] N solitudine *f*, isolamento

lonely ['ləunlɪ] ADJ solo(-a); solitario(-a); (*place*) isolato(-a); **to feel ~** sentirsi solo(-a)

lonely hearts ADJ: **~ ads**, **~ column** messaggi *mpl* personali; **~ club** club *m inv* dei cuori solitari

lone parent N (*unmarried: mother*) ragazza madre; (: *father*) ragazzo padre; (*divorced*) genitore *m* divorziato(-a); (*widowed*) genitore rimasto vedovo

loner ['ləunəʳ] N solitario(-a)

lonesome ['ləunsəm] ADJ solo(-a)

long [lɔŋ] ADJ lungo(-a) ▶ ADV a lungo, per molto tempo ▶ N: **the ~ and the short of it is that …** (*fig*) a farla breve … ▶ VI: **to ~ for sth/to do** desiderare qc/di fare; non veder l'ora di aver qc/di fare; **he had ~ understood that …** aveva capito da molto tempo che …; **how ~ is this river/course?** quanto è lungo questo fiume/corso?; **6 metres ~** lungo 6 metri; **6 months ~** che dura 6 mesi, di 6 mesi; **all night ~** tutta la notte; **he no longer comes** non viene più; **~ before** molto tempo prima; **before ~** (*+future*) presto, fra poco; (*+past*) poco tempo dopo; **~ ago** molto tempo fa; **don't be ~!** faccia presto!; **I shan't be ~** non ne avrò per molto; **at ~ last** finalmente; **in the ~ run** alla fin fine; **so** *or* **as ~ as** (*while*) finché; (*provided that*) sempre che +*sub*

long-distance [lɔŋ'dɪstəns] ADJ (*race*) di fondo; (*call*) interurbano(-a)

long-haired ['lɔŋ'hɛəd] ADJ (*person*) dai capelli lunghi; (*animal*) dal pelo lungo

longhand ['lɔŋhænd] N scrittura normale

long-haul ['lɔŋhɔːl] ADJ (*flight*) a lunga percorrenza *inv*

longing ['lɔŋɪŋ] N desiderio, voglia, brama ▶ ADJ di desiderio; pieno(-a) di nostalgia

longingly ['lɔŋɪŋlɪ] ADV con desiderio (*or* nostalgia)

longitude ['lɔŋgɪtjuːd] N longitudine *f*

long johns [-dʒɔnz] NPL mutande *fpl* lunghe

long jump N salto in lungo

long-life ADJ (*milk*) a lunga conservazione; (*batteries*) di lunga durata

long-lost ['lɔŋlɔst] ADJ perduto(-a) da tempo

long-playing ['lɔŋpleɪɪŋ] ADJ: **~ record (LP)** (*disco*) 33 giri *m inv*

long-range [lɔŋ'reɪndʒ] ADJ a lunga portata; (*weather forecast*) a lungo termine

longshoreman ['lɔŋʃɔːmən] N (*irreg*) (US) scaricatore *m* (di porto), portuale *m*

long-sighted [lɔŋ'saɪtɪd] ADJ (BRIT) presbite; (*fig*) lungimirante

long-standing ['lɔŋstændɪŋ] ADJ di vecchia data

long-suffering [lɔŋ'sʌfərɪŋ] ADJ estremamente paziente; infinitamente tollerante

long-term ['lɔŋtəːm] ADJ a lungo termine

long wave N (*Radio*) onde *fpl* lunghe

long-winded [lɔŋ'wɪndɪd] ADJ prolisso(-a), interminabile

loo [luː] N (BRIT *col*) W.C. *m inv*, cesso

loofah ['luːfə] N luffa

look [luk] VI guardare; (*seem*) sembrare, parere; (*building etc*): **to ~ south/on to the sea** dare a sud/sul mare ▶ N sguardo; (*appearance*) aspetto, aria; **looks** NPL aspetto; (*good looks*) bellezza; **to ~ like** assomigliare a; **to ~ ahead** guardare avanti; **it looks about 4 metres long** sarà lungo un 4 metri; **it looks all right to me** a me pare che vada bene; **to have a ~ at sth** dare un'occhiata a qc; **to have a ~ for sth** cercare qc
▶ **look after** VT FUS occuparsi di, prendersi cura di; (*keep an eye on*) guardare, badare a
▶ **look around** VI guardarsi intorno
▶ **look at** VT FUS guardare
▶ **look back** VI: **to ~ back at sth/sb** voltarsi a guardare qc/qn; **to ~ back on** (*event, period*) ripensare a
▶ **look down on** VT FUS (*fig*) guardare dall'alto, disprezzare
▶ **look for** VT FUS cercare
▶ **look forward to** VT FUS non veder l'ora di; **I'm not looking forward to it** non ne ho nessuna voglia; **looking forward to hearing from you** (*in letter: to a friend*); aspettando tue notizie; (: *more formal*) in attesa di una vostra gentile risposta
▶ **look in** VI: **to ~ in on sb** (*visit*) fare un salto da qn
▶ **look into** VT FUS (*matter, possibility*) esaminare
▶ **look on** VI fare da spettatore
▶ **look out** VI (*beware*): **to ~ out (for)** stare in guardia (per)
▶ **look out for** VT FUS cercare; (*watch out for*):

to ~ out for sb/sth guardare se arriva qn/qc
▶ **look over** VT (*essay*) dare un'occhiata a, riguardare; (*town, building*) vedere; (*person*) esaminare
▶ **look round** VI (*turn*) girarsi, voltarsi; (*in shops*) dare un'occhiata; **to ~ round for sth** guardarsi intorno cercando qc
▶ **look through** VT FUS (*papers, book*) scorrere; (*telescope*) guardare attraverso
▶ **look to** VT FUS stare attento(-a) a; (*rely on*) contare su
▶ **look up** VI alzare gli occhi; (*improve*) migliorare ▶ VT (*word*) cercare; (*friend*) andare a trovare
▶ **look up to** VT FUS avere rispetto per
lookout ['lukaut] N posto d'osservazione; guardia; **to be on the look-out (for)** stare in guardia (per)
look-up table ['lukʌp-] N (*Comput*) tabella di consultazione
loom [lu:m] N telaio ▶ VI sorgere; (*fig*) incombere
loony ['lu:nɪ] ADJ, N (*col*) pazzo(-a)
loop [lu:p] N cappio; (*Comput*) anello ▶ VT: **to ~ sth round sth** passare qc intorno a qc
loophole ['lu:phəul] N via d'uscita; scappatoia
loose [lu:s] ADJ (*knot*) sciolto(-a); (*screw*) allentato(-a); (*stone*) cadente; (*clothes*) ampio(-a), largo(-a); (*animal*) in libertà, scappato(-a); (*life, morals*) dissoluto(-a); (*discipline*) allentato(-a); (*thinking*) poco rigoroso(-a), vago(-a) ▶ N: **to be on the ~** essere in libertà ▶ VT (*untie*) sciogliere; (*slacken*) allentare; (*free*) liberare; (*BRIT: arrow*) scoccare; **~ connection** (*Elec*) filo che fa contatto; **to be at a ~ end** *or* (*US*) **at ~ ends** (*fig*) non saper che fare; **to tie up ~ ends** (*fig*) avere ancora qualcosa da sistemare
loose change N spiccioli *mpl*, moneta
loose-fitting ['lu:sfɪtɪŋ] ADJ ampio(-a)
loose-leaf ['lu:sli:f] ADJ: **~ binder** *or* **folder** raccoglitore *m*
loose-limbed [lu:s'lɪmd] ADJ snodato(-a), agile
loosely ['lu:slɪ] ADV senza stringere; approssimativamente
loosely-knit ['lu:slɪ'nɪt] ADJ non rigidamente strutturato(-a)
loosen ['lu:sn] VT sciogliere; (*belt etc*) allentare
▶ **loosen up** VI (*before game*) sciogliere i muscoli, scaldarsi; (*col: relax*) rilassarsi
loot [lu:t] N bottino ▶ VT saccheggiare
looter ['lu:tər] N saccheggiatore(-trice)
looting ['lu:tɪŋ] N saccheggio
lop [lɔp] VT (*also*: **lop off**) tagliare via, recidere
lop-sided ['lɔp'saɪdɪd] ADJ non equilibrato(-a), asimmetrico(-a)

lord [lɔ:d] N signore *m*; **L~ Smith** lord Smith; **the L~** (*Rel*) il Signore; **good L~!** buon Dio!; **the (House of) Lords** (*BRIT*) la Camera dei Lord
lordly ['lɔ:dlɪ] ADJ nobile, maestoso(-a); (*arrogant*) altero(-a)
lordship ['lɔ:dʃɪp] N (*BRIT*): **your L~** Sua Eccellenza
lore [lɔ:ʳ] N tradizioni *fpl*
lorry ['lɔrɪ] N (*BRIT*) camion *m inv*
lorry driver N (*BRIT*) camionista *m*
lose [lu:z] (*pt, pp* **lost** [lɔst]) VT perdere; (*pursuers*) distanziare ▶ VI perdere; **to ~ (time)** (*clock*) ritardare; **to ~ no time (in doing sth)** non perdere tempo (a fare qc); **to get lost** (*person*) perdersi, smarrirsi; (*object*) andare perso *or* perduto
▶ **lose out** VI rimetterci
loser ['lu:zər] N perdente *mf*; **to be a good/bad ~** saper/non saper perdere
loss [lɔs] N perdita; **to cut one's losses** rimetterci il meno possibile; **to make a ~** subire una perdita; **to sell sth at a ~** vendere qc in perdita; **to be at a ~** essere perplesso(-a); **to be at a ~ to explain sth** non saper come fare a spiegare qc
loss adjuster N (*Insurance*) responsabile *mf* della valutazione dei danni
loss leader N (*Comm*) articolo a prezzo ridottissimo per attirare la clientela
lost [lɔst] PT, PP *of* **lose** ▶ ADJ perduto(-a); **~ in thought** immerso *or* perso nei propri pensieri; **~ and found property** *n* (*US*) oggetti *mpl* smarriti; **~ and found** *n* (*US*) ufficio oggetti smarriti
lost property, (*US*) **lost and found** N (*BRIT*) oggetti *mpl* smarriti; **~ office** *or* **department** ufficio oggetti smarriti
lot [lɔt] N (*at auctions*) lotto; (*destiny*) destino, sorte *f*; **the ~** tutto(-a) quanto(-a); tutti(-e) quanti(-e); **a ~** molto; **a ~ of** una gran quantità di, un sacco di; **lots of** molto(-a); **to draw lots (for sth)** tirare a sorte (per qc)
lotion ['ləuʃən] N lozione *f*
lottery ['lɔtərɪ] N lotteria
loud [laud] ADJ forte, alto(-a); (*gaudy*) vistoso(-a), sgargiante ▶ ADV (*speak etc*) forte; **out ~** (*read etc*) ad alta voce
loudhailer [laud'heɪləʳ] N (*BRIT*) portavoce *m inv*
loudly ['laudlɪ] ADV fortemente, ad alta voce
loudspeaker [laud'spi:kəʳ] N altoparlante *m*
lounge [laundʒ] N salotto, soggiorno; (*of hotel*) salone *m*; (*of airport*) sala d'attesa; (*BRIT: also*: **lounge bar**) bar *m inv* con servizio a tavolino ▶ VI oziare; starsene colle mani in mano
lounge bar N bar *m inv* con servizio a tavolino
lounge suit N (*BRIT*) completo da uomo

louse [laus] (*pl* **lice**) N pidocchio
▶ **louse up** VT (*col*) rovinare
lousy ['lauzɪ] ADJ (*col: fig*) orrendo(-a),
schifoso(-a); **to feel ~** stare da cani
lout [laut] N zoticone *m*
louvre, (*US*) **louver** ['luːvər] ADJ (*door, window*)
con apertura a gelosia
lovable ['lʌvəbl] ADJ simpatico(-a), carino(-a);
amabile
love [lʌv] N amore *m* ▶ VT amare; voler bene
a; **I ~ you** ti amo; **to ~ to do: I ~ to do** mi
piace fare; **I'd ~ to come** mi piacerebbe
molto venire; **to be in ~ with** essere
innamorato(-a) di; **to fall in ~ with**
innamorarsi di; **to make ~** fare l'amore;
~ at first sight amore a prima vista, colpo di
fulmine; **to send one's ~ to sb** mandare i
propri saluti a qn; **~ from Anne, ~, Anne**
con affetto, Anne; "**15 ~**" (*Tennis*) "15 a zero"
love affair N relazione *f*
love child N (*irreg*) figlio(-a) dell'amore
loved ones [lʌvd-] NPL: **my ~** i miei cari
love-hate relationship ['lʌv'heɪt-] N
rapporto amore-odio *inv*
love letter N lettera d'amore
love life N vita sentimentale
lovely ['lʌvlɪ] ADJ bello(-a); (*delicious: smell,
meal*) buono(-a); **we had a ~ time** ci siamo
divertiti molto
lover ['lʌvər] N amante *mf*; (*person in love*)
innamorato(-a); (*amateur*): **a ~ of** un (un')
amante di; un (un') appassionato(-a) di
lovesick ['lʌvsɪk] ADJ malato(-a) d'amore
lovesong ['lʌvsɔŋ] N canzone *f* d'amore
loving ['lʌvɪŋ] ADJ affettuoso(-a),
amoroso(-a), tenero(-a)
low [ləu] ADJ basso(-a) ▶ ADV in basso ▶ N
(*Meteor*) depressione *f* ▶ VI (*cow*) muggire; **to
be ~ on** (*supplies etc*) avere scarsità di; **to feel
~ sentirsi giù; he's very ~** (*ill*) è molto debole;
to reach a new *or* **an all-time ~** toccare il
livello più basso *or* il minimo; **to turn
(down)** ▶ *vt* abbassare
low-alcohol [ləu'ælkəhɔl] ADJ a basso
contenuto alcolico
lowbrow ['ləubrau] ADJ (*person*) senza pretese
intellettuali
low-calorie ['ləu'kælərɪ] ADJ a basso
contenuto calorico
low-carb [ləu'kɑːb] ADJ (*col*) a basso
contenuto di carboidrati
low-cut ['ləukʌt] ADJ (*dress*) scollato(-a)
low-down ['ləudaun] ADJ (*mean*) ignobile ▶ N
(*col*): **he gave me the ~ on it** mi ha messo al
corrente dei fatti
lower ['ləuər] ADJ, ADV COMPARATIVE (*bottom: of
2 things*) più basso; (*less important*) meno
importante ▶ VT (*gen*) calare; (*reduce: price,
eyes, voice*) abbassare, ridurre; (: *resistance*)

indebolire ▶ VI ['lauər] (*sky*) minacciare; **to ~
(at sb)** (*person*) dare un'occhiataccia (a qn)
lower case N minuscolo
low-fat ['ləu'fæt] ADJ magro(-a)
low-key ['ləu'kiː] ADJ moderato(-a); (*operation*)
condotto(-a) con discrezione
lowland ['ləulənd] N bassopiano, pianura
low-level ['ləulɛvl] ADJ a basso livello; (*flying*)
a bassa quota
low-loader ['ləuləudər] N camion *m* a
pianale basso
lowly ['ləulɪ] ADJ umile, modesto(-a)
low-lying [ləu'laɪɪŋ] ADJ a basso livello
low-paid [ləu'peɪd] ADJ mal pagato(-a)
low-rise ['ləuraɪz] ADJ di altezza contenuta
low-tech ['ləu'tɛk] ADJ a basso contenuto
tecnologico
loyal ['lɔɪəl] ADJ fedele, leale
loyalist ['lɔɪəlɪst] N lealista *mf*
loyalty ['lɔɪəltɪ] N fedeltà, lealtà
loyalty card N carta che offre sconti a clienti
abituali
lozenge ['lɔzɪndʒ] N (*Med*) pastiglia; (*Geom*)
losanga
LP N ABBR (= *long-playing record*) LP *m*
LPG N ABBR (= *liquefied petroleum gas*) GPL *m*
(= *gas di petrolio liquefatto*)
L-plate ['ɛlpleɪt] (*BRIT*) N ≈ contrassegno P
principiante; *vedi nota*

> Le *L-plates* sono delle tabelle bianche con
> una L rossa che in Gran Bretagna i
> guidatori principianti, *learners*, in
> possesso di una *provisional licence*, che
> corrisponde al nostro foglio rosa, devono
> applicare davanti e dietro alla loro
> autovettura finché non ottengono la
> patente.

L-plates ['ɛlpleɪts] NPL *targhette con la lettera L
(per 'learner') da esporre davanti e dietro ai veicoli
guidati da principianti*
LPN N ABBR (*US*: = *Licensed Practical Nurse*)
≈ infermiera diplomata
LRAM N ABBR (*BRIT*: = *Licentiate of the Royal
Academy of Music*) specializzazione dopo la laurea
LSD N ABBR (= *lysergic acid diethylamide*) L.S.D. *m*;
(*BRIT*: = *pounds, shillings and pence*) sistema
monetario in vigore in Gran Bretagna fino al 1971
LSE N ABBR = **London School of Economics**
LT ABBR (*Elec*: = *low tension*) B.T.
Lt. ABBR (= *lieutenant*) Ten.
Ltd ABBR (*Comm*: = *limited*) ≈ S.r.l.
lubricant ['luːbrɪkənt] N lubrificante *m*
lubricate ['luːbrɪkeɪt] VT lubrificare
lucid ['luːsɪd] ADJ lucido(-a)
lucidity [luːˈsɪdɪtɪ] N lucidità
luck [lʌk] N fortuna, sorte *f*; **bad ~** sfortuna,
mala sorte; **good ~** (buona) fortuna; **to be in
~** essere fortunato(-a); **to be out of ~** essere
sfortunato(-a)

luckily ['lʌkɪlɪ] ADV fortunatamente, per fortuna

luckless ['lʌklɪs] ADJ sventurato(-a)

lucky ['lʌkɪ] ADJ fortunato(-a); (number etc) che porta fortuna

lucrative ['lu:krətɪv] ADJ lucrativo(-a), lucroso(-a), profittevole

ludicrous ['lu:dɪkrəs] ADJ ridicolo(-a), assurdo(-a)

ludo ['lu:dəu] N ≈ gioco dell'oca

lug [lʌg] VT trascinare

luggage ['lʌgɪdʒ] N bagagli mpl

luggage rack N portabagagli m inv

luggage van, (US) **luggage car** N (Rail) bagagliaio

lugubrious [lu'gu:brɪəs] ADJ lugubre

lukewarm ['lu:kwɔːm] ADJ tiepido(-a)

lull [lʌl] N intervallo di calma ▶ VT (child) cullare; (person, fear) acquietare, calmare; **to ~ sb to sleep** cullare qn finché si addormenta

lullaby ['lʌləbaɪ] N ninnananna

lumbago [lʌm'beɪgəu] N lombaggine f

lumber ['lʌmbəʳ] N (wood) legname m; (junk) roba vecchia ▶ VT (BRIT col): **to ~ sb with sth/sb** affibbiare or rifilare qc/qn a qn ▶ VI (also: **lumber about, lumber along**) muoversi pesantemente

lumberjack ['lʌmbədʒæk] N boscaiolo

lumber room N (BRIT) sgabuzzino

lumber yard N segheria

luminous ['lu:mɪnəs] ADJ luminoso(-a)

lump [lʌmp] N pezzo; (in sauce) grumo; (swelling) gonfiore m; (also: **sugar lump**) zolletta ▶ VT (also: **lump together**) riunire, mettere insieme

lump sum N somma globale

lumpy ['lʌmpɪ] ADJ (sauce) pieno(-a) di grumi; (bed) bitorzoluto(-a)

lunacy ['lu:nəsɪ] N demenza, follia, pazzia

lunar ['lu:nəʳ] ADJ lunare

lunatic ['lu:nətɪk] ADJ, N pazzo(-a), matto(-a)

lunatic asylum N manicomio

lunch [lʌntʃ] N pranzo, colazione f; **to invite sb to** or **for ~** invitare qn a pranzo or a colazione

lunch break N intervallo del pranzo

luncheon ['lʌntʃən] N pranzo

luncheon meat N ≈ mortadella

luncheon voucher N buono m pasto inv

lunch hour N = **lunch break**

lunchtime ['lʌntʃtaɪm] N ora di pranzo

lung [lʌŋ] N polmone m

lung cancer N cancro del polmone

lunge [lʌndʒ] VI (also: **lunge forward**) fare un balzo in avanti; **to ~ at sb** balzare su qn

lupin ['lu:pɪn] N lupino

lurch [lə:tʃ] VI vacillare, barcollare ▶ N scatto improvviso; **to leave sb in the ~** piantare in asso qn

lure [luəʳ] N richiamo; lusinga ▶ VT attirare (con l'inganno)

lurid ['luərɪd] ADJ sgargiante; (details etc) impressionante

lurk [lə:k] VI stare in agguato

luscious ['lʌʃəs] ADJ succulento(-a); delizioso(-a)

lush [lʌʃ] ADJ lussureggiante

lust [lʌst] N lussuria; cupidigia; desiderio; (fig): **~ for** sete f di
▶ **lust after** VT FUS bramare, desiderare

luster ['lʌstəʳ] N (US) = **lustre**

lustful ['lʌstful] ADJ lascivo(-a), voglioso(-a)

lustre, (US) **luster** ['lʌstəʳ] N lustro, splendore m

lusty ['lʌstɪ] ADJ vigoroso(-a), robusto(-a)

lute [lu:t] N liuto

Luxembourg ['lʌksəmbə:g] N (state) Lussemburgo m; (city) Lussemburgo f

luxuriant [lʌg'zjuərɪənt] ADJ lussureggiante

luxurious [lʌg'zjuərɪəs] ADJ sontuoso(-a), di lusso

luxury ['lʌkʃərɪ] N lusso ▶ CPD di lusso

LV N ABBR (BRIT) = **luncheon voucher**

LW ABBR (Radio: = long wave) O.L.

Lycra® ['laɪkrə] N lycra® f inv

lying ['laɪɪŋ] N bugie fpl, menzogne fpl
▶ ADJ (statement, story) falso(-a); (person) bugiardo(-a)

lynch [lɪntʃ] VT linciare

lynx [lɪŋks] N lince f

Lyons ['laɪənz] N Lione f

lyre ['laɪəʳ] N lira

lyric ['lɪrɪk] ADJ lirico(-a); **lyrics** NPL (of song) parole fpl

lyrical ['lɪrɪkl] ADJ lirico(-a)

lyricism ['lɪrɪsɪzəm] N lirismo

Mm

M, m [ɛm] N (letter) M, m f inv or m inv; **M for Mary**, (US) **M for Mike** ≈ M come Milano

M N ABBR (BRIT) = **motorway** ▶ ABBR (= medium) taglia media; **the M8** ≈ l'A8

m ABBR (= metre) m; = **mile; million**

MA N ABBR (Scol) = **Master of Arts**; (US) = **military academy** ▶ ABBR (US) = **Massachusetts**

ma [mɑː] N (col) mamma

mac [mæk] N (BRIT) impermeabile m

macabre [mə'kɑːbrə] ADJ macabro(-a)

macaroni [mækə'rəunɪ] N maccheroni mpl

macaroon [mækə'ruːn] N amaretto (biscotto)

mace [meɪs] N mazza; (spice) macis m or f

Macedonia [mæsɪ'dəunɪə] N Macedonia

Macedonian [mæsɪ'dəunɪən] ADJ macedone ▶ N macedone mf; (Ling) macedone m

machinations [mækɪ'neɪʃənz] NPL macchinazioni fpl, intrighi mpl

machine [mə'ʃiːn] N macchina ▶ VT (dress etc) cucire a macchina; (Tech) lavorare (a macchina)

machine code N (Comput) codice m di macchina, codice assoluto

machine gun N mitragliatrice f

machine language N (Comput) linguaggio m macchina inv

machine-readable [mə'ʃiːnriːdəbl] ADJ (Comput) leggibile dalla macchina

machinery [mə'ʃiːnərɪ] N macchinario, macchine fpl; (fig) macchina

machine shop N officina meccanica

machine tool N macchina utensile

machine washable ADJ lavabile in lavatrice

machinist [mə'ʃiːnɪst] N macchinista mf

macho ['mætʃəu] ADJ macho inv

mackerel ['mækrəl] N (pl inv) sgombro

mackintosh ['mækɪntɔʃ] N (BRIT) impermeabile m

macro... ['mækrəu] PREFIX macro...

macroeconomics ['mækrəuiːkə'nɔmɪks] N macroeconomia

mad [mæd] ADJ matto(-a), pazzo(-a); (foolish) sciocco(-a); (angry) furioso(-a); **to go ~**

impazzire, diventar matto; **~ (at or with sb)** furibondo(-a) (con qn); **to be ~ (keen) about** or **on sth** (col) andar matto(-a) per qc

Madagascar [mædə'gæskər] N Madagascar m

madam ['mædəm] N signora; **M~ Chairman** Signora Presidentessa

madcap ['mædkæp] ADJ (col) senza senso, assurdo(-a)

mad cow disease N encefalite f bovina spongiforme

madden ['mædn] VT fare infuriare

maddening ['mædnɪŋ] ADJ esasperante

made [meɪd] PT, PP of **make**

Madeira [mə'dɪərə] N (Geo) Madera; (wine) madera m

made-to-measure ['meɪdtə'mɛʒər] ADJ (BRIT) fatto(-a) su misura

made-up ['meɪdʌp] ADJ (story) inventato(-a)

madhouse ['mædhaus] N (also fig) manicomio

madly ['mædlɪ] ADV follemente; (love) alla follia

madman ['mædmən] N (irreg) pazzo, alienato

madness ['mædnɪs] N pazzia

Madrid [mə'drɪd] N Madrid f

Mafia ['mæfɪə] N mafia f

mag. [mæg] N ABBR (BRIT col: Press) = **magazine**

magazine [mægə'ziːn] N (Press) rivista; (Radio, TV) rubrica; (Mil: store) magazzino, deposito; (of firearm) caricatore m

maggot ['mægət] N baco, verme m

magic ['mædʒɪk] N magia ▶ ADJ magico(-a)

magical ['mædʒɪkəl] ADJ magico(-a)

magician [mə'dʒɪʃən] N mago(-a)

magistrate ['mædʒɪstreɪt] N magistrato; giudice mf

magistrates' court N see **crown**

magnanimous [mæg'nænɪməs] ADJ magnanimo(-a)

magnate ['mægneɪt] N magnate m

magnesium [mæg'niːzɪəm] N magnesio

magnet ['mægnɪt] N magnete m, calamita

magnetic [mæg'nɛtɪk] ADJ magnetico(-a)
magnetic disk N (Comput) disco magnetico
magnetic tape N nastro magnetico
magnetism ['mægnɪtɪzəm] N magnetismo
magnification [mægnɪfɪ'keɪʃən] N
ingrandimento
magnificence [mæg'nɪfɪsns] N magnificenza
magnificent [mæg'nɪfɪsnt] ADJ
magnifico(-a)
magnify ['mægnɪfaɪ] VT ingrandire
magnifying glass ['mægnɪfaɪɪŋ-] N lente f
d'ingrandimento
magnitude ['mægnɪtjuːd] N grandezza;
importanza
magnolia [mæg'nəʊlɪə] N magnolia
magpie ['mægpaɪ] N gazza
mahogany [mə'hɒgənɪ] N mogano ▶ CPD di
or in mogano
maid [meɪd] N domestica; (in hotel)
cameriera; **old ~** (pej) vecchia zitella
maiden ['meɪdn] N fanciulla ▶ ADJ (aunt etc)
nubile; (speech, voyage) inaugurale
maiden name ['meɪdn-] N nome da m nubile
or da ragazza
mail [meɪl] N posta ▶ VT spedire (per posta);
by ~ per posta
mailbox ['meɪlbɒks] N (US) cassetta delle
lettere; (Comput) mailbox f inv
mailing list ['meɪlɪŋ-] N elenco d'indirizzi
mailman ['meɪlmæn] N (irreg) (US)
portalettere m inv, postino
mail-order ['meɪlɔːdər] N vendita (or
acquisto) per corrispondenza ▶ CPD: **~ firm**
or **house** ditta di vendita per corrispondenza
mailshot ['meɪlʃɒt] N mailing m inv
mail train N treno postale
mail truck N (US Aut) = **mail van**
mail van N (BRIT: Aut) furgone m postale;
(: Rail) vagone m postale
maim [meɪm] VT mutilare
main [meɪn] ADJ principale ▶ N (pipe)
conduttura principale; **the mains** (Elec) la
linea principale; **mains operated** adj che
funziona a elettricità; **in the ~** nel
complesso, nell'insieme
main course N (Culin) piatto principale,
piatto forte
mainframe ['meɪnfreɪm] N (also: **mainframe
computer**) mainframe m inv
mainland ['meɪnlənd] N continente m
mainline ['meɪnlaɪn] ADJ (Rail) della linea
principale ▶ VT (drugs slang) bucarsi di ▶ VI
(drugs slang) bucarsi
main line N (Rail) linea principale
mainly ['meɪnlɪ] ADV principalmente,
soprattutto
main road N strada principale
mainstay ['meɪnsteɪ] N (fig) sostegno
principale

mainstream ['meɪnstriːm] N (fig) corrente f
principale
main street N strada principale
maintain [meɪn'teɪn] VT mantenere;
(affirm) sostenere; **to ~ that ...** sostenere
che ...
maintenance ['meɪntənəns] N
manutenzione f; (alimony) alimenti mpl
maintenance contract N contratto di
manutenzione
maintenance order N (Law) obbligo degli
alimenti
maisonette [meɪzə'nɛt] N (BRIT)
appartamento a due piani
maize [meɪz] N granturco, mais m
Maj. ABBR (Mil) = **major**
majestic [mə'dʒɛstɪk] ADJ maestoso(-a)
majesty ['mædʒɪstɪ] N maestà f inv
major ['meɪdʒər] N (Mil) maggiore m ▶ ADJ
(greater, Mus) maggiore; (in importance)
principale, importante ▶ VI (US Scol): **to ~ (in)**
specializzarsi (in); **a ~ operation** (Med) una
grossa operazione
Majorca [mə'jɔːkə] N Maiorca
major general N (Mil) generale m di
divisione
majority [mə'dʒɒrɪtɪ] N maggioranza ▶ CPD
(verdict) maggioritario(-a)
majority holding N (Comm): **to have a ~**
essere maggiore azionista
make [meɪk] (pt, pp made [meɪd]) VT fare;
(manufacture) fare, fabbricare; (cause to be): **to
~ sb sad** etc rendere qn triste etc; (force): **to ~
sb do sth** costringere qn a fare qc, far fare qc
a qn; (equal): **2 and 2 ~ 4** 2 più 2 fa 4 ▶ N
fabbricazione f; (brand) marca; **to ~ a fool of
sb** far fare a qn la figura dello scemo; **to ~ a
profit** realizzare un profitto; **to ~ a loss**
subire una perdita; **to ~ it** (in time etc)
arrivare; (succeed) farcela; **what time do you
~ it?** che ora fai?; **to ~ good** vi (succeed) aver
successo; vt (deficit) colmare; (losses)
compensare; **to ~ do with** arrangiarsi con
▶ **make for** VT FUS (place) avviarsi verso
▶ **make off** VI svignarsela
▶ **make out** VT (write out) scrivere; (: cheque)
emettere; (understand) capire; (see)
distinguere; (: numbers) decifrare; (claim,
imply): **to ~ out (that)** voler far credere (che);
to ~ out a case for sth presentare delle
valide ragioni in favore di qc
▶ **make over** VT (assign): **to ~ over (to)**
passare (a), trasferire (a)
▶ **make up** VT (constitute) formare; (invent)
inventare; (parcel) fare ▶ VI conciliarsi; (with
cosmetics) truccarsi; **to be made up of** essere
composto di or formato da
▶ **make up for** VT FUS compensare;
ricuperare

m

make-believe ['meɪkbɪliːv] N: **a world of ~** un mondo di favole; **it's just ~** è tutta un'invenzione

makeover ['meɪkəʊvəʳ] N cambio di immagine; **to give sb a ~** far cambiare immagine a qn

maker ['meɪkəʳ] N (of programme etc) creatore(-trice); (manufacturer) fabbricante m

makeshift ['meɪkʃɪft] ADJ improvvisato(-a)

make-up ['meɪkʌp] N trucco

make-up bag N borsa del trucco

make-up remover N struccatore m

making ['meɪkɪŋ] N (fig): **in the ~** in formazione; **he has the makings of an actor** ha la stoffa dell'attore

maladjusted [mælə'dʒʌstɪd] ADJ disadattato(-a)

maladroit [mælə'drɔɪt] ADJ maldestro(-a)

malaise [mæ'leɪz] N malessere m

malaria [mə'lɛərɪə] N malaria

Malawi [mə'lɑːwɪ] N Malawi m

Malay [mə'leɪ] ADJ malese ▸ N malese mf; (Ling) malese m

Malaya [mə'leɪə] N Malesia

Malayan [mə'leɪən] ADJ, N = **Malay**

Malaysia [mə'leɪzɪə] N Malaysia

Malaysian [mə'leɪzɪən] ADJ, N malaysiano(-a)

Maldives ['mɔːldaɪvz] NPL: **the ~** le (isole) Maldive

male [meɪl] N (Biol, Elec) maschio ▸ ADJ (gen, sex) maschile; (animal, child) maschio(-a); **~ and female students** studenti e studentesse

male chauvinist N maschilista m

male nurse N infermiere m

malevolence [mə'lɛvələns] N malevolenza

malevolent [mə'lɛvələnt] ADJ malevolo(-a)

malfunction [mæl'fʌŋkʃən] N funzione f difettosa

malice ['mælɪs] N malevolenza

malicious [mə'lɪʃəs] ADJ malevolo(-a); (Law) doloso(-a)

malign [mə'laɪn] VT malignare su; calunniare

malignant [mə'lɪgnənt] ADJ (Med) maligno(-a)

malingerer [mə'lɪŋgərəʳ] N scansafatiche mf

mall [mɔːl] N (also: **shopping mall**) centro commerciale

malleable ['mælɪəbl] ADJ malleabile

mallet ['mælɪt] N maglio

malnutrition [mælnjuː'trɪʃən] N denutrizione f

malpractice [mæl'præktɪs] N prevaricazione f; negligenza

malt [mɔːlt] N malto ▸ CPD (whisky) di malto

Malta ['mɔːltə] N Malta

Maltese [mɔːl'tiːz] ADJ, N (pl inv) maltese (mf); (Ling) maltese m

maltreat [mæl'triːt] VT maltrattare

malware ['mælwɛəʳ] N (Comput) malware mpl, software mpl maligni

mammal ['mæml] N mammifero

mammoth ['mæməθ] N mammut m inv ▸ ADJ enorme, gigantesco(-a)

man [mæn] (pl **men**) N uomo; (Chess) pezzo; (Draughts) pedina ▸ VT fornire d'uomini; stare a; essere di servizio a; **an old ~** un vecchio; **~ and wife** marito e moglie

Man. ABBR (CANADA) = **Manitoba**

manacles ['mænəklz] NPL manette fpl

manage ['mænɪdʒ] VI farcela ▸ VT (be in charge of) occuparsi di; (shop, restaurant) gestire; **to ~ without sth/sb** fare a meno di qc/qn; **to ~ to do sth** riuscire a far qc

manageable ['mænɪdʒəbl] ADJ maneggevole; (task etc) fattibile

management ['mænɪdʒmənt] N amministrazione f, direzione f; gestione f; (persons: of business, firm) dirigenti mpl; (: of hotel, shop, theatre) direzione f; **"under new ~"** "sotto nuova gestione"

management accounting N contabilità di gestione

management buyout N acquisto di una società da parte dei suoi dirigenti

management consultant N consulente mf aziendale

manager ['mænɪdʒəʳ] N direttore m; (of shop, restaurant) gerente m; (of artist, Sport) manager m inv; **sales ~** direttore m delle vendite

manageress [mænɪdʒə'rɛs] N direttrice f; gerente f

managerial [mænə'dʒɪərɪəl] ADJ dirigenziale

managing director ['mænɪdʒɪŋ-] N amministratore m delegato

Mancunian [mæŋ'kjuːnɪən] ADJ di Manchester ▸ N abitante mf di Manchester; originario(-a) di Manchester

mandarin ['mændərɪn] N (person, fruit) mandarino

mandate ['mændeɪt] N mandato

mandatory ['mændətərɪ] ADJ obbligatorio(-a); ingiuntivo(-a)

mandolin, mandoline ['mændəlɪn] N mandolino

mane [meɪn] N criniera

maneuver etc [mə'nuːvəʳ] (US) = **manoeuvre** etc

manful ['mænful] ADJ coraggioso(-a), valoroso(-a)

manfully ['mænfəlɪ] ADV valorosamente

manganese [mæŋgə'niːz] N manganese m

mangetout ['mɔnʒ'tuː] N pisello dolce, taccola

mangle ['mæŋgl] VT straziare; mutilare ▸ N strizzatoio

mango ['mæŋgəʊ] (pl **mangoes**) N mango

mangrove ['mæŋgrəʊv] N mangrovia

mangy ['meɪndʒɪ] ADJ rognoso(-a)

manhandle ['mænhændl] VT (treat roughly) malmenare; (move by hand: goods) spostare a mano

manhole ['mænhəʊl] N botola stradale

manhood ['mænhʊd] N età virile; virilità

man-hour ['mænaʊəʳ] N ora di lavoro

manhunt ['mænhʌnt] N caccia all'uomo

mania ['meɪnɪə] N mania

maniac ['meɪnɪæk] N maniaco(-a)

manic ['mænɪk] ADJ (behaviour, activity) maniacale

manic-depressive ['mænɪkdɪ'presɪv] ADJ maniaco-depressivo(-a) ▶ N persona affetta da mania depressiva

manicure ['mænɪkjʊəʳ] N manicure f inv

manicure set N trousse f inv della manicure

manifest ['mænɪfest] VT manifestare ▶ ADJ manifesto(-a), palese ▶ N (Aviat, Naut) manifesto

manifestation [mænɪfes'teɪʃən] N manifestazione f

manifesto [mænɪ'festəʊ] N manifesto

manifold ['mænɪfəʊld] ADJ molteplice ▶ N (Aut etc): **exhaust ~** collettore m di scarico

Manila [mə'nɪlə] N Manila

manila, manilla [mə'nɪlə] ADJ (paper, envelope) manilla inv

manipulate [mə'nɪpjʊleɪt] VT (tool) maneggiare; (controls) azionare; (limb, facts) manipolare

manipulation [mənɪpju'leɪʃən] N maneggiare m; capacità di azionare; manipolazione f

mankind [mæn'kaɪnd] N umanità, genere m umano

manliness ['mænlɪnɪs] N virilità

manly ['mænlɪ] ADJ virile; coraggioso(-a)

man-made ['mæn'meɪd] ADJ sintetico(-a); artificiale

manna ['mænə] N manna

mannequin ['mænɪkɪn] N (dummy) manichino; (fashion model) indossatrice f

manner ['mænəʳ] N maniera, modo; (behaviour) modo di fare; (type, sort): **all ~ of things** ogni genere di cosa; **manners** NPL (conduct) maniere fpl; (**good**) **manners** buona educazione f, buone maniere; **bad manners** maleducazione f; **all ~ of** ogni sorta di

mannerism ['mænərɪzəm] N vezzo, tic m inv

mannerly ['mænəlɪ] ADJ educato(-a), civile

manoeuvrable, (US) **maneuverable** [mə'nu:vrəbl] ADJ facile da manovrare; (car) maneggevole

manoeuvre, (US) **maneuver** [mə'nu:vəʳ] VT manovrare ▶ VI far manovre ▶ N manovra; **to ~ sb into doing sth** costringere abilmente qn a fare qc

manor ['mænəʳ] N (also: **manor house**) maniero

manpower ['mænpaʊəʳ] N manodopera

Manpower Services Commission N (BRIT) ente nazionale per l'occupazione

manservant ['mænsə:vənt] (pl **menservants** ['men-]) N domestico

mansion ['mænʃən] N casa signorile

manslaughter ['mænslɔ:təʳ] N omicidio preterintenzionale

mantelpiece ['mæntlpi:s] N mensola del caminetto

mantle ['mæntl] N mantello

man-to-man ['mæntə'mæn] ADJ, ADV da uomo a uomo

Mantua ['mæntjuə] N Mantova

manual ['mænjuəl] ADJ, N manuale (m)

manual worker N manovale m

manufacture [mænju'fæktʃəʳ] VT fabbricare ▶ N fabbricazione f, manifattura

manufactured goods NPL manufatti mpl

manufacturer [mænju'fæktʃərəʳ] N fabbricante m

manufacturing industries [mænju'fæktʃərɪŋ-] NPL industrie fpl manifatturiere

manure [mə'njuəʳ] N concime m

manuscript ['mænjuskrɪpt] N manoscritto

many ['menɪ] ADJ molti(-e) ▶ PRON molti(-e), un gran numero; **a great ~** moltissimi(-e), un gran numero (di); **~ a ...** molti(-e) ..., più di un(-a) ...; **too ~ difficulties** troppe difficoltà; **twice as ~** due volte tanto; **how ~?** quanti(-e)?

Maori ['maʊrɪ] ADJ, N maori (mf) inv

map [mæp] N carta (geografica); (of city) cartina ▶ VT fare una carta di ▶ **map out** VT tracciare un piano di; (fig: career, holiday, essay) pianificare

maple ['meɪpl] N acero

mar [mɑ:ʳ] VT sciupare

Mar. ABBR (= March) mar.

marathon ['mærəθən] N maratona ▶ ADJ: **a ~ session** una seduta fiume

marathon runner N maratoneta mf

marauder [mə'rɔ:dəʳ] N saccheggiatore m; predatore m

marble ['mɑ:bl] N marmo; (toy) pallina, bilia; **marbles** N (game) palline, bilie

March [mɑ:tʃ] N marzo; see also **July**

march [mɑ:tʃ] VI marciare; sfilare ▶ N marcia; (demonstration) dimostrazione f; **to ~ into a room** entrare a passo deciso in una stanza

marcher ['mɑ:tʃəʳ] N dimostrante mf

marching ['mɑ:tʃɪŋ] N: **to give sb his ~ orders** (fig) dare il benservito a qn

march-past ['mɑ:tʃpɑ:st] N sfilata

mare [mɛəʳ] N giumenta

marg [mɑːdʒ] N ABBR (col) = **margarine**
margarine [mɑːdʒəˈriːn] N margarina
marge [mɑːdʒ] N ABBR (col) = **margarine**
margin [ˈmɑːdʒɪn] N margine m
marginal [ˈmɑːdʒɪnl] ADJ marginale; ~ **seat** (Pol) seggio elettorale ottenuto con una stretta maggioranza
marginally [ˈmɑːdʒɪnəlɪ] ADV (bigger, better) lievemente, di poco; (different) un po'
marigold [ˈmærɪɡəʊld] N calendola
marijuana [mærɪˈwɑːnə] N marijuana
marina [məˈriːnə] N marina
marinade N [mærɪˈneɪd] marinata ▶ VT [ˈmærɪneɪd] = **marinate**
marinate [ˈmærɪneɪt] VT marinare
marine [məˈriːn] ADJ (animal, plant) marino(-a); (forces, engineering) marittimo(-a) ▶ N (BRIT) fante m di marina; (US) marine m inv
marine insurance N assicurazione f marittima
marital [ˈmærɪtl] ADJ maritale, coniugale; ~ **status** stato coniugale
maritime [ˈmærɪtaɪm] ADJ marittimo(-a)
maritime law N diritto marittimo
marjoram [ˈmɑːdʒərəm] N maggiorana
mark [mɑːk] N segno; (stain) macchia; (of skid etc) traccia; (BRIT Scol) voto; (Sport) bersaglio; (Hist: currency) marco; (BRIT Tech): **M~ 2/3** 1a/2a serie f ▶ VT segnare; (stain) macchiare; (indicate) indicare; (BRIT Scol) dare un voto a; correggere; (Sport: player) marcare; **punctuation marks** segni di punteggiatura; **to be quick off the ~ (in doing)** (fig) non perdere tempo (per fare); **up to the ~** (in efficiency) all'altezza; **to ~ time** segnare il passo
▶ **mark down** VT (reduce: prices, goods) ribassare, ridurre
▶ **mark off** VT (tick off) spuntare, cancellare
▶ **mark out** VT delimitare
▶ **mark up** VT (price) aumentare
marked [mɑːkt] ADJ spiccato(-a), chiaro(-a)
markedly [ˈmɑːkɪdlɪ] ADV visibilmente, notevolmente
marker [ˈmɑːkər] N (sign) segno; (bookmark) segnalibro
market [ˈmɑːkɪt] N mercato ▶ VT (Comm) mettere in vendita; (promote) lanciare sul mercato; **to play the ~** giocare or speculare in borsa; **to be on the ~** essere (messo) in vendita or in commercio; **open ~** mercato libero
marketable [ˈmɑːkɪtəbl] ADJ commercializzabile
market analysis N analisi f di mercato
market day N giorno di mercato
market demand N domanda del mercato
market economy N economia di mercato

market forces NPL forze fpl di mercato
market garden N (BRIT) orto industriale
marketing [ˈmɑːkɪtɪŋ] N marketing m
marketplace [ˈmɑːkɪtpleɪs] N (piazza del) mercato; (world of trade) piazza, mercato
market price N prezzo di mercato
market research N indagine f or ricerca di mercato
market value N valore m di mercato
marking [ˈmɑːkɪŋ] N (on animal) marcatura di colore; (on road) segnaletica orizzontale
marksman [ˈmɑːksmən] N (irreg) tiratore m scelto
marksmanship [ˈmɑːksmənʃɪp] N abilità nel tiro
mark-up [ˈmɑːkʌp] N (Comm: margin) margine m di vendita; (: increase) aumento
marmalade [ˈmɑːməleɪd] N marmellata d'arance
maroon [məˈruːn] VT (fig): **to be marooned (in or at)** essere abbandonato(-a) (in) ▶ ADJ bordeaux inv
marquee [mɑːˈkiː] N padiglione m
marquess, marquis [ˈmɑːkwɪs] N marchese m
Marrakech, Marrakesh [mærəˈkeʃ] N Marrakesh f
marriage [ˈmærɪdʒ] N matrimonio
marriage bureau N agenzia matrimoniale
marriage certificate N certificato di matrimonio
marriage guidance, (US) marriage counseling N consulenza matrimoniale
marriage of convenience N matrimonio di convenienza
married [ˈmærɪd] ADJ sposato(-a); (life, love) coniugale, matrimoniale
marrow [ˈmærəʊ] N midollo; (vegetable) zucca
marry [ˈmærɪ] VT sposare, sposarsi con; (father, priest etc) dare in matrimonio ▶ VI (also: **get married**) sposarsi
Mars [mɑːz] N (planet) Marte m
Marseilles [mɑːˈseɪlz] N Marsiglia
marsh [mɑːʃ] N palude f
marshal [ˈmɑːʃl] N maresciallo; (US: fire marshal) capo; (: police marshal) capitano; (for demonstration, meeting) membro del servizio d'ordine ▶ VT (thoughts, support) ordinare; (soldiers) adunare
marshalling yard [ˈmɑːʃlɪŋ-] N scalo smistamento
marshmallow [mɑːʃˈmæləʊ] N (Bot) altea; (sweet) caramella soffice e gommosa
marshy [ˈmɑːʃɪ] ADJ paludoso(-a)
marsupial [mɑːˈsuːpɪəl] ADJ, N marsupiale (m)
martial [ˈmɑːʃl] ADJ marziale
martial arts NPL arti fpl marziali
martial law N legge f marziale

Martian ['mɑːʃən] N marziano(-a)
martin ['mɑːtɪn] N (also: **house martin**)
  balestruccio
martyr ['mɑːtər] N martire mf ▶ VT
  martirizzare
martyrdom ['mɑːtədəm] N martirio
marvel ['mɑːvl] N meraviglia ▶ VI: **to ~ (at)**
  meravigliarsi (di)
marvellous, (US) **marvelous** ['mɑːvələs] ADJ
  meraviglioso(-a)
Marxism ['mɑːksɪzəm] N marxismo
Marxist ['mɑːksɪst] ADJ, N marxista (mf)
marzipan ['mɑːzɪpæn] N marzapane m
mascara [mæs'kɑːrə] N mascara m inv
mascot ['mæskət] N mascotte f inv
masculine ['mæskjulɪn] ADJ maschile;
  (woman) mascolino(-a) ▶ N genere m
  maschile
masculinity [mæskju'lɪnɪtɪ] N mascolinità
MASH [mæʃ] N ABBR (US Mil: = mobile army
  surgical hospital) ospedale di campo di unità mobile
  dell'esercito
mash [mæʃ] VT (Culin) passare, schiacciare
mashed [mæʃt] ADJ: **~ potatoes** purè m di
  patate
mask [mɑːsk] N (gen, Elec) maschera ▶ VT
  mascherare
masochism ['mæsəkɪzəm] N masochismo
masochist ['mæsəkɪst] N masochista mf
mason ['meɪsn] N (also: **stonemason**)
  scalpellino; (also: **freemason**) massone m
masonic [mə'sɔnɪk] ADJ massonico(-a)
masonry ['meɪsnrɪ] N muratura
masquerade [mæskə'reɪd] N ballo in
  maschera; (fig) mascherata ▶ VI: **to ~ as** farsi
  passare per
mass [mæs] N moltitudine f, massa; (Physics)
  massa; (Rel) messa ▶ CPD di massa ▶ VI
  ammassarsi; **the masses** (ordinary people) le
  masse; **masses of** (col) una montagna di; **to
  go to ~** andare a or alla messa
Mass. ABBR (US) = **Massachusetts**
massacre ['mæsəkər] N massacro ▶ VT
  massacrare
massage ['mæsɑːʒ] N massaggio ▶ VT
  massaggiare
masseur [mæ'səːr] N massaggiatore m
masseuse [mæ'səːz] N massaggiatrice f
massive ['mæsɪv] ADJ enorme, massiccio(-a)
mass market N mercato di massa
mass media NPL mass media mpl
mass meeting N (of everyone concerned)
  riunione f generale; (huge) adunata popolare
mass-produce ['mæsprə'djuːs] VT produrre
  in serie
mass production N produzione f in serie
mast [mɑːst] N albero; (Radio, TV) pilone m
  (a traliccio)
mastectomy [mæs'tɛktəmɪ] N mastectomia

master ['mɑːstər] N padrone m; (teacher: in
  primary school, Art etc) maestro; (: in secondary
  school) professore m; (title for boys): **M~ X**
  Signorino X ▶ VT domare; (learn) imparare a
  fondo; (understand) conoscere a fondo; **~ of
  ceremonies** n maestro di cerimonie; **M~'s
  degree** n vedi nota

> Il Master's degree è il riconoscimento che
> viene conferito a chi segue un corso di
> specializzazione dopo aver conseguito
> un Bachelor's degree. Vi sono diversi tipi di
> Master's Degree; i più comuni sono il Master
> of Arts (MA) e il Master of Science (MSc) che si
> ottengono dopo aver seguito un corso e
> aver presentato una tesi originale. Per il
> Master of Letters (MLitt) e il Master of
> Philosophy (MPhil) è invece sufficiente
> presentare la tesi; vedi anche **doctorate**.

master disk N (Comput) disco m master inv,
  disco principale
masterful ['mɑːstəful] ADJ autoritario(-a),
  imperioso(-a)
master key N chiave f maestra
masterly ['mɑːstəlɪ] ADJ magistrale
mastermind ['mɑːstəmaɪnd] N mente f
  superiore ▶ VT essere il cervello di
Master of Arts/Science N Master m inv in
  lettere/scienze
masterpiece ['mɑːstəpiːs] N capolavoro
master plan N piano generale
master stroke N colpo maestro
mastery ['mɑːstərɪ] N dominio; padronanza
mastiff ['mæstɪf] N mastino inglese
masturbate ['mæstəbeɪt] VI masturbare
masturbation [mæstə'beɪʃən] N
  masturbazione f
mat [mæt] N stuoia; (also: **doormat**) stoino,
  zerbino; (also: **table mat**) sottopiatto ▶ ADJ
  = **matt**
match [mætʃ] N fiammifero; (game) partita,
  incontro; (fig) uguale mf; matrimonio;
  partito ▶ VT intonare; (go well with) andare
  benissimo con; (equal) uguagliare; (correspond
  to) corrispondere a; (pair: also: **match up**)
  accoppiare ▶ VI intonarsi; **to be a good ~**
  andare bene
  ▶ **match up** VT intonare
matchbox ['mætʃbɔks] N scatola per
  fiammiferi
matching ['mætʃɪŋ] ADJ ben assortito(-a)
matchless ['mætʃlɪs] ADJ senza pari
mate [meɪt] N compagno(-a) di lavoro; (col:
  friend) amico(-a); (animal) compagno(-a); (in
  merchant navy) secondo ▶ VI accoppiarsi ▶ VT
  accoppiare
material [mə'tɪərɪəl] N (substance) materiale
  m, materia; (cloth) stoffa ▶ ADJ materiale;
  (important) essenziale; **materials** NPL
  (equipment etc) materiali mpl; occorrente m

m

materialistic [mətɪərɪə'lɪstɪk] ADJ materialistico(-a)

materialize [mə'tɪərɪəlaɪz] VI materializzarsi, realizzarsi

materially [mə'tɪərɪəlɪ] ADV dal punto di vista materiale; sostanzialmente

maternal [mə'təːnl] ADJ materno(-a)

maternity [mə'təːnɪtɪ] N maternità ▸ CPD di maternità; (clothes) pre-maman inv

maternity benefit N sussidio di maternità

maternity hospital N ≈ clinica ostetrica

maternity leave N congedo di maternità

matey ['meɪtɪ] ADJ (BRIT col) amicone(-a)

math [mæθ] N ABBR (US) = **mathematics**

mathematical [mæθə'mætɪkl] ADJ matematico(-a)

mathematician [mæθəmə'tɪʃən] N matematico(-a)

mathematics [mæθə'mætɪks] N matematica

maths [mæθs] N ABBR (BRIT) = **mathematics**

matinée ['mætɪneɪ] N matinée f inv

mating ['meɪtɪŋ] N accoppiamento

mating call N chiamata all'accoppiamento

mating season N stagione f degli amori

matriarchal [meɪtrɪ'ɑːkl] ADJ matriarcale

matrices ['meɪtrɪsiːz] NPL of **matrix**

matriculation [mətrɪkju'leɪʃən] N immatricolazione f

matrimonial [mætrɪ'məunɪəl] ADJ matrimoniale, coniugale

matrimony ['mætrɪmənɪ] N matrimonio

matrix ['meɪtrɪks] (pl **matrices** ['meɪtrɪsiːz]) N matrice f

matron ['meɪtrən] N (in hospital) capoinfermiera; (in school) infermiera

matronly ['meɪtrənlɪ] ADJ da matrona

matt [mæt] ADJ opaco(-a)

matted ['mætɪd] ADJ ingarbugliato(-a)

matter ['mætə^r] N questione f; (Physics) materia, sostanza; (content) contenuto; (Med: pus) pus m ▸ VI importare; **matters** NPL (affairs) questioni; **it doesn't ~** non importa; (I don't mind) non fa niente; **what's the ~?** che cosa c'è?; **no ~ what** qualsiasi cosa accada; **that's another ~** quello è un altro affare; **as a ~ of course** come cosa naturale; **as a ~ of fact** in verità; **it's a ~ of habit** è una questione di abitudine; **printed ~** stampe fpl; **reading ~** (BRIT) qualcosa da leggere

matter-of-fact [mætərəv'fækt] ADJ prosaico(-a)

matting ['mætɪŋ] N stuoia

mattress ['mætrɪs] N materasso

mature [mə'tjuə^r] ADJ maturo(-a); (cheese) stagionato(-a) ▸ VI maturare; stagionare; (Comm) scadere

mature student N studente universitario che ha più di 25 anni

maturity [mə'tjuərɪtɪ] N maturità

maudlin ['mɔːdlɪn] ADJ lacrimoso(-a)

maul [mɔːl] VT lacerare

Mauritania [mɔrɪ'teɪnɪə] N Mauritania

Mauritius [mə'rɪʃəs] N Maurizio

mausoleum [mɔːsə'lɪəm] N mausoleo

mauve [məuv] ADJ malva inv

maverick ['mævərɪk] N (fig) chi sta fuori del branco

mawkish ['mɔːkɪʃ] ADJ sdolcinato(-a); insipido(-a)

max. ABBR = **maximum**

maxim ['mæksɪm] N massima

maxima ['mæksɪmə] NPL of **maximum**

maximize ['mæksɪmaɪz] VT (profits etc) massimizzare; (chances) aumentare al massimo

maximum ['mæksɪməm] (pl **maxima**) ADJ massimo(-a) ▸ N massimo

May [meɪ] N maggio; see also **July**

may [meɪ] (conditional **might**) VI (indicating possibility): **he ~ come** può darsi che venga; (be allowed to) **~ I smoke?** posso fumare?; **~ I sit here?** le dispiace se mi siedo qua?; (wishes) **~ God bless you!** Dio la benedica!; **he might be there** può darsi che ci sia; **he might come** potrebbe venire, può anche darsi che venga; **I might as well go** potrei anche andarmene; **you might like to try** forse le piacerebbe provare

maybe ['meɪbiː] ADV forse, può darsi; **~ he'll ...** può darsi che lui ... + sub, forse lui ...; **~ not** forse no, può darsi di no

mayday ['meɪdeɪ] N S.O.S. m, mayday m inv

May Day N il primo maggio

mayhem ['meɪhɛm] N cagnara

mayonnaise [meɪə'neɪz] N maionese f

mayor [mɛə^r] N sindaco

mayoress ['mɛərɛs] N sindaco (donna); moglie f del sindaco

maypole ['meɪpəul] N palo ornato di fiori attorno a cui si danza durante la festa di maggio

maze [meɪz] N labirinto, dedalo

MB ABBR (Comput) = **megabyte**; (CANADA) = **Manitoba**

MBA N ABBR (= Master of Business Administration) titolo di studio

MBE N ABBR (BRIT: = Member of the Order of the British Empire) titolo

MBO N ABBR = **management buyout**

MC N ABBR = **master of ceremonies**; (US: = Member of Congress) membro del Congresso

MCAT N ABBR (US: = Medical College Admissions Test) esame di ammissione a studi superiori di medicina

MD N ABBR (= Doctor of Medicine) titolo di studio; (Comm) = **managing director** ▸ ABBR (US) = **Maryland**

Md. ABBR (US) = **Maryland**

MDT ABBR (US: = Mountain Daylight Time) ora legale delle Montagne Rocciose

ME ABBR (US) = **Maine** ▶ N ABBR (Med: = myalgic encephalomyelitis) sindrome f da affaticamento cronico; (US) = **medical examiner**

me [mi:] PRON mi, m' + vowel or silent "h"; (stressed, after prep) me; **he heard me** mi ha or m'ha sentito; **give me a book** dammi (or mi dia) un libro; **it's me** sono io; **it's for me** è per me; **with me** con me; **without me** senza di me

meadow ['mɛdəu] N prato

meagre, (US) **meager** ['mi:gəʳ] ADJ magro(-a)

meal [mi:l] N pasto; (flour) farina; **to go out for a ~** mangiare fuori

meals on wheels N (BRIT) distribuzione f di pasti caldi a domicilio (per persone malate o anziane)

mealtime ['mi:ltaɪm] N l'ora di mangiare

mealy-mouthed ['mi:lɪmauðd] ADJ che parla attraverso eufemismi

mean [mi:n] (pt, pp **meant** [mɛnt]) ADJ (with money) avaro(-a), gretto(-a); (unkind) meschino(-a), maligno(-a); (US: vicious: animal) cattivo(-a); (: person) perfido(-a); (shabby) misero(-a); (average) medio(-a) ▶ VT (signify) significare, voler dire; (intend): **to ~ to do** aver l'intenzione di fare ▶ N mezzo; (Math) media; **to be meant for** essere destinato(-a) a; **do you ~ it?** dice sul serio?; **what do you ~?** che cosa vuol dire?; see also **means**

meander [mɪ'ændəʳ] VI far meandri; (fig) divagare

meaning ['mi:nɪŋ] N significato, senso

meaningful ['mi:nɪŋful] ADJ significativo(-a); (relationship) valido(-a)

meaningless ['mi:nɪŋlɪs] ADJ senza senso

meanness ['mi:nnɪs] N avarizia; meschinità

means [mi:nz] NPL (way, money) mezzi mpl; **by ~ of** per mezzo di; (person) a mezzo di; **by all ~** ma certo, prego

means test N (Admin) accertamento dei redditi (per una persona che ha chiesto un aiuto finanziario)

meant [mɛnt] PT, PP of **mean**

meantime ['mi:ntaɪm], **meanwhile** ['mi:nwaɪl] ADV (also: **in the meantime**) nel frattempo

measles ['mi:zlz] N morbillo

measly ['mi:zlɪ] ADJ (col) miserabile

measurable ['mɛʒərəbl] ADJ misurabile

measure ['mɛʒəʳ] VT, VI misurare ▶ N misura; (ruler) metro; **a litre ~** una misura da un litro; **some ~ of success** un certo successo; **to take measures to do sth** prendere provvedimenti per fare qc
▶ **measure up** VI: **to ~ up (to)** dimostrarsi or essere all'altezza (di)

measured ['mɛʒəd] ADJ misurato(-a)

measurement ['mɛʒəmənt] N (act) misurazione f; (measure) misura; **chest/hip ~** giro petto/fianchi; **to take sb's measurements** prendere le misure di qn

meat [mi:t] N carne f; **cold meats** (BRIT) affettati mpl; **crab ~** polpa di granchio

meatball ['mi:tbɔ:l] N polpetta di carne

meat pie N torta salata in pasta frolla con ripieno di carne

meaty ['mi:tɪ] ADJ che sa di carne; (fig) sostanzioso(-a); (person) corpulento(-a); (part of body) carnoso(-a); **~ meal** pasto a base di carne

Mecca ['mɛkə] N La Mecca; (fig): **a ~ (for)** la Mecca (di)

mechanic [mɪ'kænɪk] N meccanico; see also **mechanics**

mechanical [mɪ'kænɪkəl] ADJ meccanico(-a)

mechanical engineering N (science) ingegneria meccanica; (industry) costruzioni fpl meccaniche

mechanics [mə'kænɪks] N meccanica ▶ NPL meccanismo

mechanism ['mɛkənɪzəm] N meccanismo

mechanization [mɛkənaɪ'zeɪʃən] N meccanizzazione f

MEd N ABBR (= Master of Education) titolo di studio

medal ['mɛdl] N medaglia

medallion [mɪ'dælɪən] N medaglione m

medallist, (US) **medalist** ['mɛdəlɪst] N (Sport) vincitore(-trice) di medaglia; **to be a gold ~** essere medaglia d'oro

meddle ['mɛdl] VI: **to ~ in** immischiarsi in, mettere le mani in; **to ~ with** toccare

meddlesome ['mɛdlsəm], **meddling** ['mɛdlɪŋ] ADJ (interfering) che mette il naso dappertutto; (touching things) che tocca tutto

media ['mi:dɪə] NPL (Press, Radio, TV) media mpl

media circus N carrozzone m dell'informazione

mediaeval [mɛdɪ'i:vl] ADJ = **medieval**

median ['mi:dɪən] N (US: also: **median strip**) banchina f spartitraffico inv

media research N sondaggio tra gli utenti dei mass media

mediate ['mi:dɪeɪt] VI interporsi; fare da mediatore(-trice)

mediation [mi:dɪ'eɪʃən] N mediazione f

mediator ['mi:dɪeɪtəʳ] N mediatore(-trice)

Medicaid ['mɛdɪkeɪd] N (US) assistenza medica ai poveri

medical ['mɛdɪkl] ADJ medico(-a); **~ (examination)** n visita medica

medical certificate N certificato medico

medical examiner N (US) medico incaricato di indagare la causa di morte in circostanze sospette

medical student N studente(-essa) di medicina

Medicare ['mɛdɪkɛəʳ] N (US) assistenza medica agli anziani
medicated ['mɛdɪkeɪtɪd] ADJ medicato(-a)
medication [mɛdɪ'keɪʃən] N (drugs etc) medicinali mpl, farmaci mpl
medicinal [mɛ'dɪsɪnl] ADJ medicinale
medicine ['mɛdsɪn] N medicina
medicine chest N armadietto farmaceutico
medicine man N (irreg) stregone m
medieval [mɛdɪ'iːvl] ADJ medievale
mediocre [miːdɪ'əukəʳ] ADJ mediocre
mediocrity [miːdɪ'ɔkrɪtɪ] N mediocrità
meditate ['mɛdɪteɪt] VI: **to ~ (on)** meditare (su)
meditation [mɛdɪ'teɪʃən] N meditazione f
Mediterranean [mɛdɪtə'reɪnɪən] ADJ mediterraneo(-a); **the ~ (Sea)** il (mare) Mediterraneo
medium ['miːdɪəm] ADJ medio(-a) ▶ N (pl **media**: means) mezzo; (pl **mediums**: person) medium m inv; **the happy ~** una giusta via di mezzo; see also **media**
medium-dry ['miːdɪəm'draɪ] ADJ demisec inv
medium-sized ['miːdɪəmsaɪzd] ADJ (tin etc) di grandezza media; (clothes) di taglia media
medium wave N (Radio) onde fpl medie
medley ['mɛdlɪ] N selezione f
meek [miːk] ADJ dolce, umile
meet [miːt] (pt, pp **met** [mɛt]) VT incontrare; (for the first time) fare la conoscenza di; (go and fetch) andare a prendere; (fig) affrontare; far fronte a; soddisfare; raggiungere ▶ VI incontrarsi; (in session) riunirsi; (join: objects) unirsi ▶ N (BRIT Hunting) raduno (dei partecipanti alla caccia alla volpe); (US Sport) raduno (sportivo); **I'll ~ you at the station** verrò a prenderla alla stazione; **pleased to ~ you!** piacere (di conoscerla)!
▶ **meet up** VI: **to ~ up with sb** incontrare qn
▶ **meet with** VT FUS incontrare; **he met with an accident** ha avuto un incidente
meeting ['miːtɪŋ] N incontro; (session: of club etc) riunione f; (interview) intervista; (formal) colloquio; (Sport: rally) raduno; **she's at a ~** (Comm) è in riunione; **to call a ~** convocare una riunione
meeting place N luogo d'incontro
megabyte ['mɛgəbaɪt] N (Comput) megabyte m inv
megalomaniac [mɛgələu'meɪnɪæk] N megalomane mf
megaphone ['mɛgəfəun] N megafono
megapixel ['mɛgəpɪksl] N megapixel m inv
megawatt ['mɛgəwɔt] N megawatt m inv
melancholy ['mɛlənkəlɪ] N malinconia ▶ ADJ malinconico(-a)
mellow ['mɛləu] ADJ (wine, sound) ricco(-a); (person, light) dolce; (colour) caldo(-a); (fruit) maturo(-a) ▶ VI (person) addolcirsi

melodious [mɪ'ləudɪəs] ADJ melodioso(-a)
melodrama ['mɛləudrɑːmə] N melodramma m
melodramatic [mɛlədrə'mætɪk] ADJ melodrammatico(-a)
melody ['mɛlədɪ] N melodia
melon ['mɛlən] N melone m
melt [mɛlt] VI (gen) sciogliersi, struggersi; (metals) fondersi; (fig) intenerirsi ▶ VT sciogliere, struggere; fondere; (person) commuovere; **melted butter** burro fuso
▶ **melt away** VI sciogliersi completamente
▶ **melt down** VT fondere
meltdown ['mɛltdaun] N melt-down m inv
melting point ['mɛltɪŋ-] N punto di fusione
melting pot ['mɛltɪŋ-] N (fig) crogiolo; **to be in the ~** essere ancora in discussione
member ['mɛmbəʳ] N membro; (of club) socio(-a), iscritto(-a); (of political party) iscritto(-a); **~ country/state** n paese m/stato membro
Member of Congress (US) N membro del Congresso
Member of Parliament (BRIT) N deputato(-a)
Member of the European Parliament (BRIT) N eurodeputato(-a)
Member of the House of Representatives (US) N membro della Camera dei Rappresentanti
Member of the Scottish Parliament (BRIT) N deputato(-a) del Parlamento scozzese
membership ['mɛmbəʃɪp] N iscrizione f; (numero d')iscritti mpl, membri mpl
membership card N tessera (di iscrizione)
membrane ['mɛmbreɪn] N membrana
memento [mə'mɛntəu] N ricordo, souvenir m inv
memo ['mɛməu] N appunto; (Comm etc) comunicazione f di servizio
memoir ['mɛmwɑːʳ] N memoria; **memoirs** NPL memorie fpl, ricordi mpl
memo pad N blocchetto per appunti
memorable ['mɛmərəbl] ADJ memorabile
memorandum [mɛmə'rændəm] (pl **memoranda** [-də]) N appunto; (Comm etc) comunicazione f di servizio; (Diplomacy) memorandum m inv
memorial [mɪ'mɔːrɪəl] N monumento commemorativo ▶ ADJ commemorativo(-a)
Memorial Day N (US); vedi nota

Negli Stati Uniti il Memorial Day è una festa nazionale per la commemorazione di tutti i soldati americani caduti in guerra. Le celebrazioni sono tenute ogni anno l'ultimo lunedì di maggio.

memorize ['mɛməraɪz] VT memorizzare
memory ['mɛmərɪ] N (gen, Comput) memoria; (recollection) ricordo; **in ~ of** in memoria di;

to have a good/bad ~ aver buona/cattiva memoria; **loss of** ~ amnesia

memory card N (*for digital camera*) scheda di memoria

memory stick N (*Comput*) stick *m inv* di memoria

men [mɛn] NPL *of* **man**

menace ['mɛnɪs] N minaccia; (*col: nuisance*) peste *f* ▶ VT minacciare; **a public** ~ un pericolo pubblico

menacing ['mɛnɪsɪŋ] ADJ minaccioso(-a)

menagerie [mɪ'nædʒərɪ] N serraglio

mend [mɛnd] VT aggiustare, riparare; (*darn*) rammendare ▶ N rammendo; **on the** ~ in via di guarigione

mending ['mɛndɪŋ] N rammendo; (*items to be mended*) roba da rammendare

menial ['miːnɪəl] ADJ da servo, domestico(-a); umile

meningitis [mɛnɪn'dʒaɪtɪs] N meningite *f*

menopause ['mɛnəupɔːz] N menopausa

menservants ['mɛnsəːvənts] NPL *of* **manservant**

men's room N: **the** ~ (*esp US*) la toilette degli uomini

menstruate ['mɛnstrueɪt] VI mestruare

menstruation [mɛnstru'eɪʃən] N mestruazione *f*

menswear ['mɛnzwɛər] N abbigliamento maschile

mental ['mɛntl] ADJ mentale; ~ **illness** malattia mentale

mental hospital N ospedale *m* psichiatrico

mentality [mɛn'tælɪtɪ] N mentalità *f inv*

mentally ['mɛntlɪ] ADV: **to be** ~ **handicapped** essere minorato psichico

menthol ['mɛnθɔl] N mentolo

mention ['mɛnʃən] N menzione *f* ▶ VT menzionare, far menzione di; **don't** ~ **it!** non c'è di che!, prego!; **I need hardly** ~ **that** … inutile dire che …; **not to** ~, **without mentioning** per non parlare di, senza contare

mentor ['mɛntɔːr] N mentore *m*

menu ['mɛnjuː] N (*set menu, Comput*) menù *m inv*; (*printed*) carta

menu-driven ['mɛnjuːdrɪvn] ADJ (*Comput*) guidato(-a) da menù

MEP N ABBR = **Member of the European Parliament**

mercantile ['məːkəntaɪl] ADJ mercantile; (*law*) commerciale

mercenary ['məːsɪnərɪ] ADJ venale ▶ N mercenario

merchandise ['məːtʃəndaɪz] N merci *fpl* ▶ VT commercializzare

merchandiser ['məːtʃəndaɪzər] N merchandiser *m inv*

merchant ['məːtʃənt] N (*trader*) mercante *m*,

commerciante *m*; (*shopkeeper*) negoziante *m*; **timber/wine** ~ negoziante di legno/vino

merchant bank N (*BRIT*) banca d'affari

merchantman ['məːtʃəntmən] N (*irreg*) mercantile *m*

merchant navy, (*US*) **merchant marine** N marina mercantile

merciful ['məːsɪful] ADJ pietoso(-a), clemente

mercifully ['məːsɪflɪ] ADV con clemenza; (*fortunately*) per fortuna

merciless ['məːsɪlɪs] ADJ spietato(-a)

mercurial [məː'kjuərɪəl] ADJ (*unpredictable*) volubile

mercury ['məːkjurɪ] N mercurio

mercy ['məːsɪ] N pietà; (*Rel*) misericordia; **to have** ~ **on sb** aver pietà di qn; **at the** ~ **of** alla mercè di

mercy killing N eutanasia

mere [mɪər] ADJ semplice; **by a** ~ **chance** per mero caso

merely ['mɪəlɪ] ADV semplicemente, non … che

merge [məːdʒ] VT unire; (*Comput: files, text*) fondere ▶ VI fondersi, unirsi; (*Comm*) fondersi

merger ['məːdʒər] N (*Comm*) fusione *f*

meridian [mə'rɪdɪən] N meridiano

meringue [mə'ræŋ] N meringa

merit ['mɛrɪt] N merito, valore *m* ▶ VT meritare

meritocracy [mɛrɪ'tɔkrəsɪ] N meritocrazia

mermaid ['məːmeɪd] N sirena

merriment ['mɛrɪmənt] N gaiezza, allegria

merry ['mɛrɪ] ADJ gaio(-a), allegro(-a); **M~ Christmas!** Buon Natale!

merry-go-round ['mɛrɪgəuraund] N carosello

mesh [mɛʃ] N maglia; rete *f* ▶ VI (*gears*) ingranarsi; **wire** ~ rete metallica

mesmerize ['mɛzməraɪz] VT ipnotizzare; affascinare

mess [mɛs] N confusione *f*, disordine *m*; (*fig*) pasticcio; (*dirt*) sporcizia; (*Mil*) mensa; **to be (in) a** ~ (*house, room*) essere in disordine (*or* molto sporco); (*fig: marriage, life*) essere un caos; **to be/get o.s. in a** ~ (*fig*) essere/cacciarsi in un pasticcio

▶ **mess about, mess around** VI (*col*) trastullarsi

▶ **mess about with, mess around with, mess with** VT FUS (*col*) gingillarsi con; (: *plans*) fare un pasticcio di; (: *challenge, confront*) litigare con (*col*); (: *drugs, drinks*) abusare di

▶ **mess up** VT sporcare; fare un pasticcio di; rovinare

message ['mɛsɪdʒ] N messaggio ▶ VT messaggiare; (*col*) messaggiare; **to get the** ~ (*fig: col*) capire l'antifona; **she messaged me on Facebook**® mi ha messaggiato su Facebook®

message board N (*Comput*) bacheca elettronica

message switching N (*Comput*) smistamento messaggi

messenger ['mɛsɪndʒəʳ] N messaggero(-a)

Messiah [mɪ'saɪə] N Messia *m*

Messrs, Messrs. ['mɛsəz] ABBR (*on letters*: = *messieurs*) Spett.

messy ['mɛsɪ] ADJ sporco(-a); disordinato(-a); (*confused: situation etc*) ingarbugliato(-a)

Met [mɛt] N ABBR (*US*) = **Metropolitan Opera**

met [mɛt] PT, PP *of* **meet ▶** ADJ ABBR = **meteorological; the M~ Office** l'Ufficio Meteorologico

metabolism [mɛ'tæbəlɪzəm] N metabolismo

metal ['mɛtl] N metallo ▶ VT massicciare

metallic [mɛ'tælɪk] ADJ metallico(-a)

metallurgy [mɛ'tælədʒɪ] N metallurgia

metalwork ['mɛtlwə:k] N (*craft*) lavorazione *f* del metallo

metamorphosis [mɛtə'mɔ:fəsɪs] (*pl* -**phoses** [-i:z]) N metamorfosi *f inv*

metaphor ['mɛtəfəʳ] N metafora

metaphysics [mɛtə'fɪzɪks] N metafisica

mete [mi:t]: **to ~ out** *vt fus* infliggere

meteor ['mi:tɪəʳ] N meteora

meteoric [mi:tɪ'ɔrɪk] ADJ (*fig*) fulmineo(-a)

meteorite ['mi:tɪəraɪt] N meteorite *m*

meteorological [mi:tɪərə'lɔdʒɪkl] ADJ meteorologico(-a)

meteorology [mi:tɪə'rɔlədʒɪ] N meteorologia

meter ['mi:təʳ] N (*instrument*) contatore *m*; (*parking meter*) parchimetro; (*US: unit*) = **metre**

methane ['mi:θeɪn] N metano

method ['mɛθəd] N metodo; **~ of payment** modo *or* modalità *f inv* di pagamento

methodical [mɪ'θɔdɪkl] ADJ metodico(-a)

Methodist ['mɛθədɪst] ADJ, N metodista (*mf*)

meths [mɛθs] (*BRIT*) N = **methylated spirit**

methylated spirits ['mɛθɪleɪtɪd-] N (*BRIT: also*: **meths**) alcool *m* denaturato

meticulous [mɛ'tɪkjuləs] ADJ meticoloso(-a)

metre, (*US*) **meter** ['mi:təʳ] N metro

metric ['mɛtrɪk] ADJ metrico(-a); **to go ~** adottare il sistema metrico decimale

metrical ['mɛtrɪkl] ADJ metrico(-a)

metrication [mɛtrɪ'keɪʃən] N conversione *f* al sistema metrico

metric system N sistema *m* metrico decimale

metric ton N tonnellata

metro ['mɛtrəu] N metro *m inv*

metronome ['mɛtrənəum] N metronomo

metropolis [mɪ'trɔpəlɪs] N metropoli *f inv*

metropolitan [mɛtrə'pɔlɪtən] ADJ metropolitano(-a)

Metropolitan Police N (*BRIT*): **the ~** la polizia di Londra

mettle ['mɛtl] N coraggio

mew [mju:] VI (*cat*) miagolare

mews [mju:z] N (*BRIT*): **~ flat** appartamentino ricavato da una vecchia scuderia

Mexican ['mɛksɪkən] ADJ, N messicano(-a)

Mexico ['mɛksɪkəu] N Messico

Mexico City N Città del Messico

mezzanine ['mɛtsəni:n] N mezzanino

MFA N ABBR (*US*: = *Master of Fine Arts*) titolo di studio

mfr ABBR = **manufacture; manufacturer**

mg ABBR (= *milligram*) mg

Mgr ABBR (= *Monseigneur; Monsignor*) mons.; (*Comm*) = **manager**

MHR N ABBR (*US*) = **Member of the House of Representatives**

MHz ABBR (= *megahertz*) MHz

MI ABBR (*US*) = **Michigan**

MI5 N ABBR (*BRIT*: = *Military Intelligence, section five*) agenzia di controspionaggio

MI6 N ABBR (*BRIT*: = *Military Intelligence, section six*) agenzia di spionaggio

MIA ABBR = **missing in action**

miaow [mi:'au] VI miagolare

mice [maɪs] NPL *of* **mouse**

Mich. ABBR (*US*) = **Michigan**

micro... ['maɪkrəu] PREFIX micro...

microbe ['maɪkrəub] N microbio

microbiology [maɪkrəubaɪ'ɔlədʒɪ] N microbiologia

microblog ['maɪkrəublɔg] N microblog *m inv*

microchip ['maɪkrəutʃɪp] N microcircuito integrato, chip *m inv*

microcomputer [maɪkrəukəm'pju:təʳ] N microcomputer *m inv*

microcosm ['maɪkrəukɔzəm] N microcosmo

microeconomics [maɪkrəui:kə'nɔmɪks] N microeconomia

microfiche ['maɪkrəufi:ʃ] N microfiche *f inv*

microfilm ['maɪkrəufɪlm] N microfilm *m inv* ▶ VT microfilmare

microlight ['maɪkrəulaɪt] N aereo *m* biposto *inv*

micrometer [maɪ'krɔmɪtəʳ] N micrometro, palmer *m inv*

microphone ['maɪkrəfəun] N microfono

microprocessor [maɪkrəu'prəusɛsəʳ] N microprocessore *m*

micro-scooter ['maɪkrəusku:təʳ] N monopattino

microscope ['maɪkrəskəup] N microscopio; **under the ~** al microscopio

microscopic [maɪkrə'skɔpɪk] ADJ microscopico(-a)

microwavable, microwaveable ['maɪkrəuweɪvəbl] ADJ adatto(-a) al forno a microonde

microwave ['maɪkrəuweɪv] N (*also*: **microwave oven**) forno a microonde

mid [mɪd] ADJ: ~ **May** metà maggio;
~ **afternoon** metà pomeriggio; **in ~ air** a
mezz'aria; **he's in his ~ thirties** avrà circa
trentacinque anni

midday [mɪd'deɪ] N mezzogiorno

middle ['mɪdl] N mezzo; centro; (waist) vita
▶ ADJ di mezzo; **I'm in the ~ of reading it** sto
proprio leggendolo ora; **in the ~ of the
night** nel cuore della notte

middle age N mezza età

middle-aged [mɪdl'eɪdʒd] ADJ di mezza età

Middle Ages NPL: **the ~** il Medioevo

middle class ADJ (also: **middle-class**)
≈ borghese ▶ N: **the ~(es)** ≈ la borghesia

Middle East N: **the ~** il Medio Oriente

middleman ['mɪdlmæn] N (irreg)
intermediario; agente m rivenditore

middle management N quadri mpl
intermedi

middle name N secondo nome m

middle-of-the-road ['mɪdləvðə'rəud] ADJ
moderato(-a)

middle school N (US) scuola media per ragazzi
dagli 11 ai 14 anni; (BRIT) scuola media per ragazzi
dagli 8 o 9 ai 12 o 13 anni

middleweight ['mɪdlweɪt] N (Boxing) peso
medio

middling ['mɪdlɪŋ] ADJ medio(-a)

midge [mɪdʒ] N moscerino

midget ['mɪdʒɪt] N nano(-a)

midi system ['mɪdɪ-] N (hi-fi) compatto

Midlands ['mɪdləndz] NPL contee del centro
dell'Inghilterra

midnight ['mɪdnaɪt] N mezzanotte f; **at ~** a
mezzanotte

midriff ['mɪdrɪf] N diaframma m

midst [mɪdst] N: **in the ~ of** in mezzo a

midsummer [mɪd'sʌmər] N mezza or piena
estate f

midway [mɪd'weɪ] ADJ, ADV: ~ **(between)** a
mezza strada (fra); ~ **(through)** a metà (di)

midweek [mɪd'wiːk] ADV, ADJ a metà
settimana

midwife ['mɪdwaɪf] (pl **midwives** [-vz]) N
levatrice f

midwifery ['mɪdwɪfərɪ] N ostetrica

midwinter [mɪd'wɪntər] N pieno inverno

miffed [mɪft] ADJ (col) seccato(-a), stizzito(-a)

might [maɪt] VB see **may** ▶ N potere m, forza

mighty ['maɪtɪ] ADJ forte, potente ▶ ADV (col)
molto

migraine ['miːɡreɪn] N emicrania

migrant ['maɪɡrənt] N (bird, animal)
migratore m; (person) migrante mf; nomade
mf ▶ ADJ (bird) migratore(-trice), nomade;
(worker) emigrato(-a)

migrate [maɪ'ɡreɪt] VI (bird) migrare; (person)
emigrare

migration [maɪ'ɡreɪʃən] N migrazione f

mike [maɪk] N ABBR (= microphone) microfono

Milan [mɪ'læn] N Milano f

mild [maɪld] ADJ mite; (person, voice) dolce;
(flavour) delicato(-a); (illness) leggero(-a);
(interest) blando(-a) ▶ N (beer) birra leggera

mildew ['mɪldjuː] N muffa

mildly ['maɪldlɪ] ADV mitemente;
dolcemente; delicatamente; leggermente;
blandamente; **to put it ~** a dire poco

mildness ['maɪldnɪs] N mitezza; dolcezza;
delicatezza; non gravità

mile [maɪl] N miglio; **to do 20 miles per
gallon** ≈ usare 14 litri per cento chilometri

mileage ['maɪlɪdʒ] N distanza in miglia,
≈ chilometraggio

mileage allowance N rimborso per miglio

mileometer [maɪ'lɒmɪtər] N (BRIT)
= **milometer**

milestone ['maɪlstəun] N pietra miliare

milieu ['miːljəː] N ambiente m

militant ['mɪlɪtnt] ADJ, N militante (mf)

militarism ['mɪlɪtərɪzəm] N militarismo

militaristic [mɪlɪtə'rɪstɪk] ADJ
militaristico(-a)

military ['mɪlɪtərɪ] ADJ militare ▶ N: **the ~**
i militari, l'esercito

military service N servizio militare

militate ['mɪlɪteɪt] VI: **to ~ against** essere
d'ostacolo a

militia [mɪ'lɪʃə] N milizia

milk [mɪlk] N latte m ▶ VT (cow) mungere;
(fig) sfruttare

milk chocolate N cioccolato al latte

milk float N (BRIT) furgone m del lattaio

milking ['mɪlkɪŋ] N mungitura

milkman ['mɪlkmən] N (irreg) lattaio

milk shake N frappé m inv

milk tooth N dente m di latte

milk truck N (US) = **milk float**

milky ['mɪlkɪ] ADJ lattiginoso(-a); (colour)
latteo(-a)

Milky Way N Via Lattea

mill [mɪl] N mulino; (small: for coffee, pepper etc)
macinino; (factory) fabbrica; (spinning mill)
filatura ▶ VT macinare ▶ VI (also: **mill about**)
brulicare

millennium [mɪ'lɛnɪəm] (pl **millenniums** or
millennia [-'lɛnɪə]) N millennio

millennium bug N baco di fine millennio

miller ['mɪlər] N mugnaio

millet ['mɪlɪt] N miglio

milli... ['mɪlɪ] PREFIX milli...

milligram, milligramme ['mɪlɪɡræm] N
milligrammo

millilitre, (US) **milliliter** ['mɪlɪliːtər] N
millilitro

millimetre, (US) **millimeter** ['mɪlɪmiːtər] N
millimetro

milliner ['mɪlɪnər] N modista

millinery ['mɪlɪnərɪ] N modisteria
million ['mɪljən] NUM milione *m*
millionaire [mɪljə'nɛəʳ] N milionario, ≈ miliardario
millionth NUM milionesimo(-a)
millipede ['mɪlɪpiːd] N millepiedi *m inv*
millstone ['mɪlstəʊn] N macina
millwheel ['mɪlwiːl] N ruota di mulino
milometer [maɪ'lɒmɪtəʳ] N ≈ contachilometri *m inv*
mime [maɪm] N mimo ▶ VT, VI mimare
mimic ['mɪmɪk] N imitatore(-trice) ▶ VT (*comedian*) imitare; (*animal, person*) scimmiottare
mimicry ['mɪmɪkrɪ] N imitazioni *fpl*; (*Zool*) mimetismo
Min. ABBR (*Brit Pol*: = *ministry*) Min.
min. ABBR = *minute*; (= *minimum*) min.
minaret [mɪnə'rɛt] N minareto
mince [mɪns] VT tritare, macinare ▶ VI (*in walking*) camminare a passettini ▶ N (*Brit Culin*) carne *f* tritata *or* macinata; **he does not ~ (his) words** parla chiaro e tondo
mincemeat ['mɪnsmiːt] N frutta secca tritata per uso in pasticceria; (*US*) carne *f* tritata *or* macinata
mince pie N specie di torta con frutta secca
mincer ['mɪnsəʳ] N tritacarne *m inv*
mincing ['mɪnsɪŋ] ADJ lezioso(-a)
mind [maɪnd] N mente *f* ▶ VT (*attend to, look after*) badare a, occuparsi di; (*be careful*) fare attenzione a, stare attento(-a) a; (*object to*): **I don't ~ the noise** il rumore non mi dà alcun fastidio; **do you ~ if …?** le dispiace se …?; **I don't ~** non m'importa; **~ you, … sì**, però va detto che …; **never ~** non importa, non fa niente; (*don't worry*) non preoccuparti; **it is on my ~** mi preoccupa; **to change one's ~** cambiare idea; **to be in two minds about sth** essere incerto su qc; **to my ~** secondo me, a mio parere; **to be out of one's ~** essere uscito(-a) di mente; **to keep sth in ~** non dimenticare qc; **to bear sth in ~** tener presente qc; **to have sb/sth in ~** avere in mente qn/qc; **to have in ~ to do** aver l'intenzione di fare; **it went right out of my ~** mi è completamente passato di mente, me ne sono completamente dimenticato; **to bring** *or* **call sth to ~** riportare *or* richiamare qc alla mente; **to make up one's ~** decidersi; **"~ the step"** "attenzione allo scalino"
mind-boggling ['maɪndbɒglɪŋ] ADJ (*col*) sconcertante
-minded ['maɪndɪd] ADJ: **fair~** imparziale; **an industrially~ nation** una nazione orientata verso l'industria
minder ['maɪndəʳ] N (*child minder*) bambinaia; (*bodyguard*) guardia del corpo

mindful ['maɪndfʊl] ADJ: **~ of** attento(-a) a; memore di
mindless ['maɪndlɪs] ADJ idiota; (*violence, crime*) insensato(-a)
mine[1] [maɪn] PRON il (la) mio(-a); (*pl*) i (le) miei (mie); **this book is ~** questo libro è mio; **yours is red, ~ is green** il tuo è rosso, il mio è verde; **a friend of ~** un mio amico
mine[2] [maɪn] N miniera; (*explosive*) mina ▶ VT (*coal*) estrarre; (*ship, beach*) minare
mine detector N rivelatore *m* di mine
minefield ['maɪnfiːld] N campo minato
miner ['maɪnəʳ] N minatore *m*
mineral ['mɪnərəl] ADJ minerale ▶ N minerale *m*; **minerals** NPL (*Brit: soft drinks*) bevande *fpl* gasate
mineralogy [mɪnə'rælədʒɪ] N mineralogia
mineral water N acqua minerale
minesweeper ['maɪnswiːpəʳ] N dragamine *m inv*
mingle ['mɪŋgl] VT mescolare, mischiare ▶ VI: **to ~ with** mescolarsi a, mischiarsi con
mingy ['mɪndʒɪ] ADJ (*col: amount*) misero(-a); (: *person*) spilorcio(-a)
miniature ['mɪnətʃəʳ] ADJ in miniatura ▶ N miniatura
minibar ['mɪnɪbɑːʳ] N minibar *m inv*
minibus ['mɪnɪbʌs] N minibus *m inv*
minicab ['mɪnɪkæb] N (*Brit*) ≈ taxi *m inv*
minicomputer ['mɪnɪkəm'pjuːtəʳ] N minicomputer *m inv*
Minidisc® ['mɪnɪdɪsk] N minidisc *m inv*
minim ['mɪnɪm] N (*Mus*) minima
minima ['mɪnɪmə] NPL *of* **minimum**
minimal ['mɪnɪml] ADJ minimo(-a)
minimalist ['mɪnɪməlɪst] ADJ, N minimalista (*mf*)
minimize ['mɪnɪmaɪz] VT minimizzare
minimum ['mɪnɪməm] (*pl* **minima**) N minimo ▶ ADJ minimo(-a); **to reduce to a ~** ridurre al minimo; **~ wage** salario minimo garantito
minimum lending rate N (*Brit*) ≈ tasso ufficiale di sconto
mining ['maɪnɪŋ] N industria mineraria ▶ ADJ minerario(-a); di minatori
minion ['mɪnjən] N (*pej*) caudatario; favorito(-a)
mini-series ['mɪnɪsɪəriːz] N miniserie *f inv*
miniskirt ['mɪnɪskəːt] N minigonna
minister ['mɪnɪstəʳ] N (*Brit Pol*) ministro; (*Rel*) pastore *m* ▶ VI: **to ~ to sb** assistere qn; **to ~ to sb's needs** provvedere ai bisogni di qn
ministerial [mɪnɪs'tɪərɪəl] ADJ (*Brit Pol*) ministeriale
ministry ['mɪnɪstrɪ] N (*Brit Pol*) ministero; (*Rel*): **to go into the ~** diventare pastore
mink [mɪŋk] N visone *m*

mink coat N pelliccia di visone
Minn. ABBR (US) = **Minnesota**
minnow ['mɪnəʊ] N pesciolino d'acqua dolce
minor ['maɪnəʳ] ADJ minore, di poca
  importanza; (Mus) minore ▶ N (Law)
  minorenne mf
Minorca [mɪ'nɔːkə] N Minorca
minority [maɪ'nɔrɪtɪ] N minoranza; **to be
  in a ~** essere in minoranza
minster ['mɪnstəʳ] N cattedrale f (annessa a
  monastero)
minstrel ['mɪnstrəl] N giullare m, menestrello
mint [mɪnt] N (plant) menta; (sweet) pasticca
  di menta ▶ VT (coins) battere; **the (Royal) M~**
  (BRIT), **the (US) M~** (US) la Zecca; **in ~
  condition** come nuovo(-a) di zecca
mint sauce N salsa di menta
minuet [mɪnju'ɛt] N minuetto
minus ['maɪnəs] N (also: **minus sign**) segno
  meno ▶ PREP meno
minuscule ['mɪnəskjuːl] ADJ minuscolo(-a)
minute¹ ['mɪnɪt] N minuto; (official record)
  processo verbale, resoconto sommario;
  minutes NPL (of meeting) verbale m, verbali
  mpl; **it is 5 minutes past 3** sono le 3 e 5
  (minuti); **wait a ~!** (aspetta) un momento!;
  at the last ~ all'ultimo momento; **up to
  the ~** ultimissimo; modernissimo
minute² [maɪ'njuːt] ADJ minuscolo(-a);
  (detail) minuzioso(-a); **in ~ detail**
  minuziosamente
minute book N libro dei verbali
minute hand N lancetta dei minuti
minutely [maɪ'njuːtlɪ] ADV (by a small amount)
  di poco; (in detail) minuziosamente
minutiae [mɪ'njuːʃiː] NPL minuzie fpl
miracle ['mɪrəkl] N miracolo
miraculous [mɪ'rækjuləs] ADJ miracoloso(-a)
mirage ['mɪrɑːʒ] N miraggio
mire ['maɪəʳ] N pantano, melma
mirror ['mɪrəʳ] N specchio; (in car) specchietto
  ▶ VT rispecchiare, riflettere
mirror image N immagine f speculare
mirth [mɜːθ] N gaiezza
misadventure [mɪsəd'vɛntʃəʳ] N
  disavventura; **death by ~** (BRIT) morte f
  accidentale
misanthropist [mɪ'zænθrəpɪst] N
  misantropo(-a)
misapply [mɪsə'plaɪ] VT impiegare male
misapprehension ['mɪsæprɪ'hɛnʃən] N
  malinteso
misappropriate [mɪsə'prəʊprɪeɪt] VT
  appropriarsi indebitamente di
misappropriation ['mɪsəprəʊprɪ'eɪʃən] N
  appropriazione f indebita
misbehave [mɪsbɪ'heɪv] VI comportarsi male
misbehaviour, (US) **misbehavior**
  [mɪsbɪ'heɪvjəʳ] N comportamento scorretto

misc. ABBR = **miscellaneous**
miscalculate [mɪs'kælkjuleɪt] VT calcolare
  male
miscalculation ['mɪskælkju'leɪʃən] N errore
  m di calcolo
miscarriage ['mɪskærɪdʒ] N (Med) aborto
  spontaneo; **~ of justice** errore m giudiziario
miscarry [mɪs'kærɪ] VI (Med) abortire; (fail:
  plans) andare a monte, fallire
miscellaneous [mɪsɪ'leɪnɪəs] ADJ (items)
  vario(-a); (selection) misto(-a); **~ expenses**
  spese varie
miscellany [mɪ'sɛlənɪ] N raccolta
mischance [mɪs'tʃɑːns] N: **by (some) ~** per
  sfortuna
mischief ['mɪstʃɪf] N (naughtiness)
  birichineria; (harm) male m, danno;
  (maliciousness) malizia
mischievous ['mɪstʃɪvəs] ADJ (naughty)
  birichino(-a); (harmful) dannoso(-a)
misconception [mɪskən'sɛpʃən] N idea
  sbagliata
misconduct [mɪs'kɔndʌkt] N cattiva
  condotta; **professional ~** reato
  professionale
misconstrue [mɪskən'struː] VT
  interpretare male
miscount [mɪs'kaunt] VT, VI contare male
misdeed [mɪs'diːd] N (old) misfatto
misdemeanour, (US) **misdemeanor**
  [mɪsdɪ'miːnəʳ] N misfatto; infrazione f
misdirect [mɪsdɪ'rɛkt] VT mal indirizzare
miser ['maɪzəʳ] N avaro
miserable ['mɪzərəbl] ADJ infelice; (wretched)
  miserabile; (weather) deprimente; (offer,
  failure) misero(-a); **to feel ~** sentirsi avvilito
  or giù di morale
miserably ['mɪzərəblɪ] ADV (fail, live, pay)
  miseramente; (smile, answer) tristemente
miserly ['maɪzəlɪ] ADJ avaro(-a)
misery ['mɪzərɪ] N (unhappiness) tristezza;
  (pain) sofferenza; (wretchedness) miseria
misfire [mɪs'faɪəʳ] VI far cilecca; (car engine)
  perdere colpi
misfit ['mɪsfɪt] N (person) spostato(-a)
misfortune [mɪs'fɔːtʃən] N sfortuna
misgiving [mɪs'gɪvɪŋ] N, **misgivings**
  [mɪs'gɪvɪŋz] NPL dubbi mpl; **to have
  misgivings about sth** essere diffidente or
  avere dei dubbi per quanto riguarda qc
misguided [mɪs'gaɪdɪd] ADJ sbagliato(-a);
  poco giudizioso(-a)
mishandle [mɪs'hændl] VT (treat roughly)
  maltrattare; (mismanage) trattare male
mishap ['mɪshæp] N disgrazia
mishear [mɪs'hɪəʳ] VT, VI (irreg: like **hear**)
  capire male
mishmash ['mɪʃmæʃ] N (col) minestrone m,
  guazzabuglio

m

misinform [mɪsɪnˈfɔːm] VT informare male
misinterpret [mɪsɪnˈtəːprɪt] VT interpretare male
misinterpretation [ˈmɪsɪntəːprɪˈteɪʃən] N errata interpretazione f
misjudge [mɪsˈdʒʌdʒ] VT giudicare male
mislay [mɪsˈleɪ] VT (*irreg: like* **lay**) smarrire
mislead [mɪsˈliːd] VT (*irreg: like* **lead**[1]) sviare
misleading [mɪsˈliːdɪŋ] ADJ ingannevole
misled [mɪsˈlɛd] PT, PP *of* **mislead**
mismanage [mɪsˈmænɪdʒ] VT gestire male; trattare male
mismanagement [mɪsˈmænɪdʒmənt] N cattiva amministrazione f
misnomer [mɪsˈnəumər] N termine m sbagliato or improprio
misogynist [mɪˈsɔdʒɪnɪst] N misogino
misplace [mɪsˈpleɪs] VT smarrire; collocare fuori posto; **to be misplaced** (*trust etc*) essere malriposto(-a)
misprint [ˈmɪsprɪnt] N errore m di stampa
mispronounce [mɪsprəˈnauns] VT pronunziare male
misquote [mɪsˈkwəut] VT citare erroneamente
misread [mɪsˈriːd] VT (*irreg: like* **read**) leggere male
misrepresent [mɪsrɛprɪˈzɛnt] VT travisare
Miss [mɪs] N Signorina; **Dear ~ Smith** Cara Signorina; (*formal*) Gentile Signorina
miss [mɪs] VT (*fail to get*) perdere; (*fail to hit*) mancare; (*appointment, class*) mancare a; (*escape, avoid*) evitare; (*notice loss of: money etc*) accorgersi di non avere più; (*fail to see*): **you can't ~ it** non puoi non vederlo; (*regret the absence of*): **I ~ him/it** sento la sua mancanza, lui/esso mi manca ▶ VI mancare ▶ N (*shot*) colpo mancato; (*fig*): **that was a near ~** c'è mancato poco; **the bus just missed the wall** l'autobus per un pelo non è andato a finire contro il muro; **we missed our train** abbiamo perso il treno; **you're missing the point** non capisce
▶ **miss out** VT (*BRIT*) omettere
▶ **miss out on** VT FUS (*fun, party*) perdersi; (*chance, bargain*) lasciarsi sfuggire
Miss. ABBR (*US*) = **Mississippi**
missal [ˈmɪsl] N messale m
misshapen [mɪsˈʃeɪpən] ADJ deforme
missile [ˈmɪsaɪl] N (*Aviat*) missile m; (*object thrown*) proiettile m
missile base N base f missilistica
missile launcher N lancia-missili m inv
missing [ˈmɪsɪŋ] ADJ perso(-a), smarrito(-a); (*removed*) mancante; **to go ~** sparire; **~ person** scomparso(-a); (*after disaster*) disperso(-a); **~ in action** (*Mil*) disperso(-a); **to be ~** mancare
mission [ˈmɪʃən] N missione f; **on a ~ to sb** in missione da qn
missionary [ˈmɪʃənrɪ] N missionario(-a)
misspell [mɪsˈspɛl] VT (*irreg: like* **spell**) sbagliare l'ortografia di
misspent [mɪsˈspent] ADJ: **his ~ youth** la sua gioventù sciupata
mist [mɪst] N nebbia, foschia ▶ VI (*also:* **mist over, mist up**) annebbiarsi; (: *BRIT: windows*) appannarsi
mistake [mɪsˈteɪk] N sbaglio, errore m ▶ VT (*irreg: like* **take**) sbagliarsi di; fraintendere; **to ~ for** prendere per; **by ~** per sbaglio; **to make a ~** (*in writing, calculating etc*) fare uno sbaglio *or* un errore, sbagliare; **to make a ~ about sb/sth** sbagliarsi sul conto di qn/su qc; **there must be some ~** ci dev'essere un errore
mistaken [mɪsˈteɪkən] PP *of* **mistake** ▶ ADJ (*idea etc*) sbagliato(-a); **to be ~** sbagliarsi
mistaken identity N errore m di persona
mistakenly [mɪsˈteɪkənlɪ] ADV per errore
mister [ˈmɪstər] N (*col*) signore m; *see* **Mr**
mistletoe [ˈmɪsltəu] N vischio
mistook [mɪsˈtuk] PT *of* **mistake**
mistranslation [mɪstrænsˈleɪʃən] N traduzione f errata
mistreat [mɪsˈtriːt] VT maltrattare
mistress [ˈmɪstrɪs] N padrona; (*lover*) amante f; (*BRIT Scol*) insegnante f
mistrust [mɪsˈtrʌst] VT diffidare di ▶ N: **~ (of)** diffidenza (nei confronti di)
mistrustful [mɪsˈtrʌstful] ADJ: **~ (of)** diffidente (nei confronti di)
misty [ˈmɪstɪ] ADJ nebbioso(-a), brumoso(-a)
misty-eyed [ˈmɪstɪaɪd] ADJ trasognato(-a)
misunderstand [mɪsʌndəˈstænd] VT, VI (*irreg: like* **stand**) capire male, fraintendere
misunderstanding [mɪsʌndəˈstændɪŋ] N malinteso, equivoco; **there's been a ~** c'è stato un malinteso
misunderstood [mɪsʌndəˈstud] PT, PP *of* **misunderstand**
misuse N [mɪsˈjuːs] cattivo uso; (*of power*) abuso ▶ VT [mɪsˈjuːz] far cattivo uso di; abusare di
MIT N ABBR (*US*) = **Massachusetts Institute of Technology**
mite [maɪt] N (*small quantity*) briciolo; (*BRIT: small child*): **poor ~!** povera creaturina!
miter [ˈmaɪtər] N (*US*) = **mitre**
mitigate [ˈmɪtɪgeɪt] VT mitigare; (*suffering*) alleviare; **mitigating circumstances** circostanze fpl attenuanti
mitigation [mɪtɪˈgeɪʃən] N mitigazione f; alleviamento
mitre, (*US*) **miter** [ˈmaɪtər] N mitra; (*Carpentry*) giunto ad angolo retto
mitt [ˈmɪt], **mitten** [ˈmɪtn] N mezzo guanto; manopola

mix [mɪks] VT mescolare ▸ VI mescolarsi;
(*people*): **to ~ with** avere a che fare con ▸ N
mescolanza; preparato; **to ~ sth with sth**
mischiare qc a qc; **to ~ business with
pleasure** unire l'utile al dilettevole; **cake ~**
preparato per torta
▸ **mix in** VT (*eggs etc*) incorporare
▸ **mix up** VT mescolare; (*confuse*) confondere;
to be mixed up in sth essere coinvolto in qc
mixed [mɪkst] ADJ misto(-a)
mixed-ability ['mɪkstə'bɪlɪtɪ] ADJ (*class etc*)
con alunni di capacità diverse
mixed bag N miscuglio, accozzaglia; **it's a ~**
c'è un po' di tutto
mixed blessing N: **it's a ~** ha i suoi lati
positivi e negativi
mixed doubles NPL (*Sport*) doppio misto
mixed economy N economia mista
mixed grill N (*BRIT*) misto alla griglia
mixed marriage N matrimonio misto
mixed salad N insalata mista
mixed-up [mɪkst'ʌp] ADJ (*confused*)
confuso(-a)
mixer ['mɪksə^r] N (*for food: electric*) frullatore *m*;
(*: hand*) frullino; **he is a good ~** è molto
socievole
mixer tap N miscelatore *m*
mixture ['mɪkstʃə^r] N mescolanza; (*blend: of
tobacco etc*) miscela; (*Med*) sciroppo
mix-up ['mɪksʌp] N confusione *f*
MK ABBR (*BRIT Tech*) = **mark**
mk ABBR (*Hist: currency*) = **mark**
mkt ABBR = **market**
ml ABBR (= *millilitre(s)*) ml
MLitt N ABBR = **Master of Literature**;
(= *Master of Letters*) titolo di studio
MLR N ABBR (*BRIT*) = **minimum lending rate**
mm ABBR (= *millimetre*) mm
MMS N ABBR (= *multimedia messaging service*)
mms *m inv* (*servizio*); **~ message** mms *m inv*
MN ABBR (*BRIT*) = **merchant navy**; (*US*)
= **Minnesota**
MO N ABBR = **medical officer**; (*US: col*: = *modus
operandi*) modo d'agire ▸ ABBR (*US*) = **Missouri**
m.o. ABBR = **money order**
moan [məʊn] N gemito ▸ VI gemere; (*col:
complain*): **to ~ (about)** lamentarsi (di)
moaner ['məʊnə^r] N (*col*) uno(-a) che si
lamenta sempre
moaning ['məʊnɪŋ] N gemiti *mpl*
moat [məʊt] N fossato
mob [mɔb] N folla; (*disorderly*) calca; (*pej*): **the
~** la plebaglia ▸ VT accalcarsi intorno a
mobile ['məʊbaɪl] ADJ mobile ▸ N (*phone*)
telefonino, cellulare *m*; (*Art*) mobile *m inv*;
applicants must be ~ (*BRIT*) i candidati
devono essere disposti a viaggiare
mobile home N grande roulotte *f inv*
(*utilizzata come domicilio*)

mobile phone N telefono portatile,
telefonino
mobile shop N (*BRIT*) negozio ambulante
mobility [məʊ'bɪlɪtɪ] N mobilità; (*of applicant*)
disponibilità a viaggiare
mobilize ['məʊbɪlaɪz] VT mobilitare ▸ VI
mobilitarsi
moccasin ['mɔkəsɪn] N mocassino
mock [mɔk] VT deridere, burlarsi di ▸ ADJ
falso(-a); **mocks** NPL (*BRIT col: Scol*)
simulazione *f* degli esami
mockery ['mɔkərɪ] N derisione *f*; **to make
a ~ of** burlarsi di; (*exam*) rendere una farsa
mocking ['mɔkɪŋ] ADJ derisorio(-a)
mockingbird ['mɔkɪŋbəːd] N mimo
(*uccello*)
mock-up ['mɔkʌp] N modello dimostrativo;
abbozzo
MOD N ABBR (*BRIT*) = **Ministry of Defence**; *see*
defence
mod cons ['mɔd'kɔnz] NPL ABBR (*BRIT*)
= **modern conveniences**
mode [məʊd] N modo; (*of transport*) mezzo;
(*Comput*) modalità *f inv*
model ['mɔdl] N modello; (*person: for fashion*)
indossatore(-trice); (*: for artist*) modello(-a)
▸ VT modellare ▸ VI fare l'indossatore (*or*
l'indossatrice) ▸ ADJ (*small-scale: railway etc*) in
miniatura; (*child, factory*) modello *inv*; **to ~
clothes** presentare degli abiti; **to ~ sb/sth
on** modellare qn/qc su
modem ['məʊdem] N modem *m inv*
moderate ADJ ['mɔdərɪt] moderato(-a)
▸ N (*Pol*) moderato(-a) ▸ VI ['mɔdəreɪt]
moderarsi, placarsi ▸ VT moderare
moderately ['mɔdərɪtlɪ] ADV (*act*) con
moderazione; (*expensive, difficult*) non troppo;
(*pleased, happy*) abbastanza, discretamente;
~ priced a prezzo modico
moderation [mɔdə'reɪʃən] N moderazione *f*,
misura; **in ~** in quantità moderata, con
moderazione
moderator ['mɔdəreɪtə^r] N
moderatore(-trice); (*Rel*) *moderatore in
importanti riunioni ecclesiastiche*
modern ['mɔdən] ADJ moderno(-a);
~ conveniences comodità *fpl* moderne;
~ languages lingue *fpl* moderne
modernization [mɔdənaɪ'zeɪʃən] N
rimodernamento, modernizzazione *f*
modernize ['mɔdənaɪz] VT modernizzare
modest ['mɔdɪst] ADJ modesto(-a)
modesty ['mɔdɪstɪ] N modestia
modicum ['mɔdɪkəm] N: **a ~ of** un minimo di
modification [mɔdɪfɪ'keɪʃən] N
modificazione *f*; **to make modifications**
fare *or* apportare delle modifiche
modify ['mɔdɪfaɪ] VT modificare
modish ['məʊdɪʃ] ADJ (*literary*) à la page *inv*

Mods [mɔdz] N ABBR (BRIT: = (Honour) Moderations) esame all'università di Oxford

modular ['mɔdjulə'] ADJ (filing, unit) modulare

modulate ['mɔdjuleɪt] VT modulare

modulation [mɔdju'leɪʃən] N modulazione f

module ['mɔdju:l] N modulo

Mogadishu [mɔgə'dɪʃu:] N Mogadiscio f

mogul ['məugl] N (fig) magnate m, pezzo grosso; (Ski) cunetta

MOH N ABBR (BRIT: = Medical Officer of Health) ≈ ufficiale m sanitario

mohair ['məuhɛə'] N mohair m

Mohammed [məu'hæmɪd] N Maometto

moist [mɔɪst] ADJ umido(-a)

moisten ['mɔɪsn] VT inumidire

moisture ['mɔɪstʃə'] N umidità; (on glass) goccioline fpl di vapore

moisturize ['mɔɪstʃəraɪz] VT (skin) idratare

moisturizer ['mɔɪstʃəraɪzə'] N idratante f

molar ['məulə'] N molare m

molasses [məu'læsɪz] N molassa

mold etc [məuld] (US) = **mould** etc

Moldavia [mɔl'deɪvɪə], **Moldova** [mɔl'dəuvə] N Moldavia

Moldavian [mɔl'deɪvɪən], **Moldovan** [mɔl'dəuvən] ADJ moldavo(-a)

mole [məul] N (animal, fig) talpa; (spot) neo

molecule ['mɔlɪkju:l] N molecola

molehill ['məulhɪl] N cumulo di terra sulla tana di una talpa

molest [məu'lɛst] VT molestare

mollusc, (US) **mollusk** ['mɔləsk] N mollusco

mollycoddle ['mɔlɪkɔdl] VT coccolare, vezzeggiare

Molotov cocktail ['mɔlətɔf-] N (bottiglia) Molotov f inv

molt [məult] VI (US) = **moult**

molten ['məultən] ADJ fuso(-a)

mom [mɔm] N (US) = **mum**

moment ['məumənt] N momento, istante m; importanza; **at that ~** in quel momento; **at the ~** al momento, in questo momento; **for the ~** per il momento, per ora; **in a ~** tra un momento; **"one ~ please"** (Tel) "attenda, prego"

momentarily ['məuməntərɪlɪ] ADV per un momento; (US: very soon) da un momento all'altro

momentary ['məuməntərɪ] ADJ momentaneo(-a), passeggero(-a)

momentous [məu'mɛntəs] ADJ di grande importanza

momentum [məu'mɛntəm] N velocità acquisita, slancio; (Physics) momento; (fig) impeto; **to gather ~** aumentare di velocità; (fig) prendere or guadagnare terreno

mommy ['mɔmɪ] N (US) mamma

Mon. ABBR (= Monday) lun.

Monaco ['mɔnəkəu] N Monaco f

monarch ['mɔnək] N monarca m

monarchist ['mɔnəkɪst] N monarchico(-a)

monarchy ['mɔnəkɪ] N monarchia

monastery ['mɔnəstərɪ] N monastero

monastic [mə'næstɪk] ADJ monastico(-a)

Monday ['mʌndɪ] N lunedì m inv; see also **Tuesday**

Monegasque [mɔnə'gæsk] ADJ, N monegasco(-a)

monetarist ['mʌnɪtərɪst] N monetarista mf

monetary ['mʌnɪtərɪ] ADJ monetario(-a)

money ['mʌnɪ] N denaro, soldi mpl; **to make ~** (person) fare (i) soldi; (business) rendere; **danger ~** (BRIT) indennità di rischio; **I've got no ~ left** non ho più neanche una lira

money belt N marsupio (per soldi)

moneyed ['mʌnɪd] ADJ ricco(-a)

moneylender ['mʌnɪlɛndə'] N prestatore m di denaro

moneymaker ['mʌnɪmeɪkə'] N (BRIT col: business) affare m d'oro

moneymaking ['mʌnɪmeɪkɪŋ] ADJ che rende (bene or molto), lucrativo(-a)

money market N mercato monetario

money order N vaglia m inv

money-spinner ['mʌnɪspɪnə'] N (col) miniera d'oro (fig)

money supply N liquidità monetaria

Mongol ['mɔŋgəl] N mongolo(-a); (Ling) mongolo

mongol ['mɔŋgəl] ADJ, N (Med) mongoloide (mf)

Mongolia [mɔŋ'gəulɪə] N Mongolia

Mongolian [mɔŋ'gəulɪən] ADJ mongolico(-a) ▶ N mongolo(-a); (Ling) mongolo

mongoose ['mɔŋgu:s] N mangusta

mongrel ['mʌŋgrəl] N (dog) cane m bastardo

monitor ['mɔnɪtə'] N (BRIT Scol) capoclasse mf; (US Scol) chi sorveglia agli esami; (TV, Comput) monitor m inv ▶ VT controllare; (foreign station) ascoltare le trasmissioni di

monk [mʌŋk] N monaco

monkey ['mʌŋkɪ] N scimmia

monkey business N (col) scherzi mpl

monkey nut N (BRIT) nocciolina americana

monkey wrench N chiave f a rullino

mono ['mɔnəu] ADJ mono inv; (broadcast) in mono

mono... ['mɔnəu] PREFIX mono...

monochrome ['mɔnəkrəum] ADJ monocromo(-a)

monocle ['mɔnəkl] N monocolo

monogamous [mə'nɔgəməs] ADJ monogamo(-a)

monogamy [mə'nɔgəmɪ] N monogamia

monogram ['mɔnəgræm] N monogramma m

monolith ['mɔnəlɪθ] N monolito

monologue ['mɔnəlɔg] N monologo

monoplane ['mɒnəupleɪn] N monoplano
monopolize [mə'nɔpəlaɪz] VT
monopolizzare
monopoly [mə'nɔpəlɪ] N monopolio;
Monopolies and Mergers Commission
(BRIT) commissione f antimonopoli
monorail ['mɒnəureɪl] N monorotaia
monosodium glutamate
[mɒnə'səudɪəm'glu:təmeɪt] N glutammato
di sodio
monosyllabic [mɒnəsɪ'læbɪk] ADJ
monosillabico(-a); (person) che parla a
monosillabi
monosyllable ['mɒnəsɪləbl] N monosillabo
monotone ['mɒnətəun] N pronunzia (or voce
f) monotona; **to speak in a** ~ parlare con
voce monotona
monotonous [mə'nɔtənəs] ADJ
monotono(-a)
monotony [mə'nɔtənɪ] N monotonia
monoxide [mɔ'nɔksaɪd] N: **carbon** ~ ossido
di carbonio
monsoon [mɔn'su:n] N monsone m
monster ['mɔnstəʳ] N mostro
monstrosity [mɔn'strɔsɪtɪ] N mostruosità
f inv
monstrous ['mɔnstrəs] ADJ mostruoso(-a)
Mont. ABBR (US) = **Montana**
montage [mɔn'tɑ:ʒ] N montaggio
Mont Blanc [mɔ̃blɑ̃] N Monte m Bianco
month [mʌnθ] N mese m; **300 dollars a** ~
300 dollari al mese; **every** ~ (happen) tutti i
mesi; (pay) mensilmente, ogni mese
monthly ['mʌnθlɪ] ADJ mensile ▸ ADV al
mese; ogni mese ▸ N (magazine) rivista
mensile; **twice** ~ due volte al mese
monument ['mɔnjumənt] N monumento
monumental [mɔnju'mɛntl] ADJ
monumentale; (fig) colossale
monumental mason N lapidario
moo [mu:] VI muggire, mugghiare
mood [mu:d] N umore m; **to be in a good/
bad** ~ essere di buon/cattivo umore; **to be in
the** ~ **for** essere disposto(-a) a, aver voglia di
moody ['mu:dɪ] ADJ (variable) capriccioso(-a),
lunatico(-a); (sullen) imbronciato(-a)
moon [mu:n] N luna
moonbeam ['mu:nbi:m] N raggio di luna
moon landing N allunaggio
moonlight ['mu:nlaɪt] N chiaro di luna ▸ VI
fare del lavoro nero
moonlighting ['mu:nlaɪtɪŋ] N lavoro nero
moonlit ['mu:nlɪt] ADJ illuminato(-a) dalla
luna; **a** ~ **night** una notte rischiarata dalla
luna
moonshot ['mu:nʃɔt] N lancio sulla luna
moonstruck ['mu:nstrʌk] ADJ lunatico(-a)
moony ['mu:nɪ] ADJ (eyes) sognante
Moor [muəʳ] N moro(-a)

moor [muəʳ] N brughiera ▸ VT (ship)
ormeggiare ▸ VI ormeggiarsi
moorings ['muərɪŋz] NPL (chains) ormeggi
mpl; (place) ormeggio
Moorish ['muərɪʃ] ADJ moresco(-a)
moorland ['muələnd] N brughiera
moose [mu:s] N (pl inv) alce m
moot [mu:t] VT sollevare ▸ ADJ: ~ **point**
punto discutibile
mop [mɔp] N lavapavimenti m inv; (also: **mop
of hair**) zazzera ▸ VT lavare con lo straccio;
(face) asciugare; **to** ~ **one's brow** asciugarsi
la fronte
▸ **mop up** VT asciugare con uno straccio
mope [məup] VI fare il broncio
▸ **mope about, mope around** VI trascinarsi
or aggirarsi con aria avvilita
moped ['məupɛd] N (BRIT) ciclomotore m
MOR ADJ ABBR (Mus) = **middle-of-the-road**;
~ **music** musica leggera
moral ['mɔrəl] ADJ morale ▸ N morale f;
morals NPL (principles) moralità
morale [mɔ'rɑ:l] N morale m
morality [mə'rælɪtɪ] N moralità
moralize ['mɔrəlaɪz] VI: **to** ~ **(about)** fare il
(or la) moralista (riguardo), moraleggiare
(riguardo)
morally ['mɔrəlɪ] ADV moralmente
moral victory N vittoria morale
morass [mə'ræs] N palude f, pantano
moratorium [mɔrə'tɔ:rɪəm] N moratoria
morbid ['mɔ:bɪd] ADJ morboso(-a)

(KEYWORD)

more [mɔ:ʳ] ADJ **1** (greater in number etc) più;
more people/letters than we expected più
persone/lettere di quante ne aspettavamo; **I
have more wine/money than you** ho più
vino/soldi di te; **I have more wine than
beer** ho più vino che birra
2 (additional) altro(-a), ancora; **do you want
(some) more tea?** vuole dell'altro tè?, vuole
ancora del tè?; **I have no** or **I don't have any
more money** non ho più soldi
▸ PRON **1** (greater amount) più; **more than 10**
più di 10; **it cost more than we expected** è
costato più di quanto ci aspettassimo; **and
what's more ...** e per di più ...
2 (further or additional amount) ancora; **is there
any more?** ce n'è ancora?; **there's no more**
non ce n'è più; **a little more** ancora un po';
many/much more molti(-e)/molto(-a) di
più
▸ ADV: **more dangerous/easily (than)** più
pericoloso/facilmente (di); **more and more**
sempre di più; **more and more difficult**
sempre più difficile; **more or less** più o
meno; **more than ever** più che mai; **once
more** ancora (una volta), un'altra volta; **no**

m

more, not any more non … più; **I have no more money, I haven't any more money** non ho più soldi

moreover [mɔː'rəuvəʳ] ADV inoltre, di più

morgue [mɔːg] N obitorio

MORI ['mɔːrɪ] N ABBR (BRIT: = Market & Opinion Research Institute) istituto di sondaggio

moribund ['mɔrɪbʌnd] ADJ moribondo(-a)

morning ['mɔːnɪŋ] N mattina, mattino; (duration) mattinata ▶ CPD del mattino; **in the ~** la mattina; **this ~** stamattina; **7 o'clock in the ~** le 7 di or della mattina

morning-after pill ['mɔːnɪŋ'ɑːftə-] N pillola del giorno dopo

morning sickness N nausee fpl mattutine

Moroccan [mə'rɔkən] ADJ, N marocchino(-a)

Morocco [mə'rɔkəu] N Marocco

moron ['mɔːrɔn] N (col) deficiente mf

moronic [mə'rɔnɪk] ADJ deficiente

morose [mə'rəus] ADJ cupo(-a), tetro(-a)

morphine ['mɔːfiːn] N morfina

morris dancing ['mɔrɪs-] N vedi nota

> Il morris dancing è una danza folcloristica inglese tradizionalmente riservata agli uomini. Vestiti di bianco e con dei campanelli attaccati alle caviglie, i ballerini eseguono una danza tenendo in mano dei fazzoletti bianchi e lunghi bastoni. Questa danza è molto popolare nelle feste paesane.

Morse [mɔːs] N (also: **Morse code**) alfabeto Morse

morsel ['mɔːsl] N boccone m

mortal ['mɔːtl] ADJ, N mortale (m)

mortality [mɔː'tælɪtɪ] N mortalità

mortality rate N tasso di mortalità

mortar ['mɔːtəʳ] N (Constr) malta; (dish) mortaio

mortgage ['mɔːgɪdʒ] N ipoteca; (loan) prestito ipotecario ▶ VT ipotecare; **to take out a ~** contrarre un mutuo (or un'ipoteca)

mortgage company N (US) società f inv immobiliare

mortgagee [mɔːgɪ'dʒiː] N creditore m ipotecario

mortgagor ['mɔːgɪdʒəʳ] N debitore m ipotecario

mortician [mɔː'tɪʃən] N (US) impresario di pompe funebri

mortified ['mɔːtɪfaɪd] ADJ umiliato(-a)

mortise lock ['mɔːtɪs-] N serratura incastrata

mortuary ['mɔːtjuərɪ] N camera mortuaria; obitorio

mosaic [məu'zeɪɪk] N mosaico

Moscow ['mɔskəu] N Mosca

Moslem ['mɔzləm] ADJ, N = **Muslim**

mosque [mɔsk] N moschea

mosquito [mɔs'kiːtəu] (pl **mosquitoes**) N zanzara

mosquito net N zanzariera

moss [mɔs] N muschio

mossy ['mɔsɪ] ADJ muscoso(-a)

most [məust] (almost all) la maggior parte di; il più di; (largest, greatest): **who has (the) ~ money?** chi ha più soldi di tutti? ▶ PRON la maggior parte ▶ ADV più; (work, sleep etc) di più; (very) molto, estremamente; **the ~** (also: + adjective) il (la) più; **~ fish** la maggior parte dei pesci; **~ of** la maggior parte di; **~ of them** quasi tutti; **I saw ~** ho visto più io; **at the (very) ~** al massimo; **to make the ~ of** trarre il massimo vantaggio da; **a ~ interesting book** un libro estremamente interessante

mostly ['məustlɪ] ADV per lo più

MOT N ABBR (BRIT) = Ministry of Transport; **the ~ (test)** revisione obbligatoria degli autoveicoli

motel [məu'tɛl] N motel m inv

moth [mɔθ] N farfalla notturna; tarma

mothball ['mɔθbɔːl] N pallina di naftalina

moth-eaten ['mɔθiːtn] ADJ tarmato(-a)

mother ['mʌðəʳ] N madre f ▶ VT (care for) fare da madre a

mother board N (Comput) scheda madre

motherhood ['mʌðəhud] N maternità

mother-in-law ['mʌðərɪnlɔː] N suocera

mother-of-pearl [mʌðərəv'pəːl] N madreperla

Mother's Day N la festa della mamma

mother's help N bambinaia

mother-to-be [mʌðətə'biː] N futura mamma

mother tongue N madrelingua

mothproof ['mɔθpruːf] ADJ antitarmico(-a)

motif [məu'tiːf] N motivo

motion ['məuʃən] N movimento, moto; (gesture) gesto; (at meeting) mozione f; (BRIT: also: **bowel motion**) evacuazione f ▶ VT, VI: **to ~ (to) sb to do** fare cenno a qn di fare; **to be in ~** (vehicle) essere in moto; **to set in ~** avviare; **to go through the motions of doing sth** (fig) fare qc pro forma

motionless ['məuʃənlɪs] ADJ immobile

motion picture N film m inv

motivate ['məutɪveɪt] VT (act, decision) dare origine a, motivare; (person) spingere

motivated ['məutɪveɪtɪd] ADJ motivato(-a)

motivation [məutɪ'veɪʃən] N motivazione f

motive ['məutɪv] N motivo ▶ ADJ motore(-trice); **from the best motives** con le migliori intenzioni

motley ['mɔtlɪ] ADJ eterogeneo(-a), molto vario(-a)

motor ['məutəʳ] N motore m; (BRIT col: vehicle) macchina ▶ ADJ (industry, accident) automobilistico(-a); **~ vehicle** autoveicolo

motorbike ['məʊtəbaɪk] N moto f inv
motorboat ['məʊtəbəʊt] N motoscafo
motorcade ['məʊtəkeɪd] N corteo di macchine
motorcar ['məʊtəkɑː] N (BRIT) automobile f
motorcoach ['məʊtəkəʊtʃ] N (BRIT) pullman m inv
motorcycle ['məʊtəsaɪkl] N motocicletta
motorcyclist ['məʊtəsaɪklɪst] N motociclista mf
motoring ['məʊtərɪŋ] N (BRIT) turismo automobilistico ▶ ADJ (accident) d'auto, automobilistico(-a); (offence) di guida; ~ **holiday** vacanza in macchina
motorist ['məʊtərɪst] N automobilista mf
motorize ['məʊtəraɪz] VT motorizzare
motor oil N olio lubrificante
motor racing N (BRIT) corse f pl automobilistiche
motor scooter N motorscooter m inv
motor vehicle N autoveicolo
motorway ['məʊtəweɪ] N (BRIT) autostrada
mottled ['mɔtld] ADJ chiazzato(-a), marezzato(-a)
motto ['mɔtəʊ] (pl **mottoes**) N motto
mould, (US) **mold** [məʊld] N forma, stampo; (mildew) muffa ▶ VT formare; (fig) foggiare
moulder, (US) **molder** ['məʊldə'] VI (decay) ammuffire
moulding, (US) **molding** ['məʊldɪŋ] N (Archit) modanatura
mouldy, (US) **moldy** ['məʊldɪ] ADJ ammuffito(-a); (smell) di muffa
moult, (US) **molt** [məʊlt] VI far la muta
mound [maʊnd] N rialzo, collinetta; (heap) mucchio
mount [maʊnt] N (Geo) monte m, montagna; (horse) cavalcatura; (for jewel etc) montatura ▶ VT montare; (horse) montare a; (exhibition) organizzare; (attack) sferrare, condurre; (picture, stamp) sistemare ▶ VI salire; (get on a horse) montare a cavallo
▶ **mount up** VI (build up) accumularsi
mountain ['maʊntɪn] N montagna ▶ CPD di montagna; **to make a ~ out of a molehill** fare di una mosca un elefante
mountain bike N mountain bike f inv
mountaineer [maʊntɪ'nɪə'] N alpinista mf
mountaineering [maʊntɪ'nɪərɪŋ] N alpinismo; **to go ~** fare dell'alpinismo
mountainous ['maʊntɪnəs] ADJ montagnoso(-a)
mountain range N catena montuosa
mountain rescue team N ≈ squadra di soccorso alpino
mountainside ['maʊntɪnsaɪd] N fianco della montagna
mounted ['maʊntɪd] ADJ a cavallo

mourn [mɔːn] VT piangere, lamentare
▶ VI: **to ~ (for sb)** piangere (la morte di qn)
mourner ['mɔːnə'] N parente mf (or amico(-a)) del defunto
mourning ['mɔːnɪŋ] N lutto ▶ CPD (dress) da lutto; **in ~** in lutto
mouse [maʊs] (pl **mice** [maɪs]) N topo; (Comput) mouse m inv
mouse mat, mouse pad N (Comput) tappetino del mouse
mousetrap ['maʊstræp] N trappola per i topi
moussaka [mu'sɑːkə] N moussaka
mousse [muːs] N mousse f inv
moustache, (US) **mustache** [məs'tɑːʃ] N baffi mpl
mousy ['maʊsɪ] ADJ (person) timido(-a); (hair) né chiaro(-a) né scuro(-a)
mouth [maʊθ] (pl **mouths** [-ðz]) N bocca; (of river) bocca, foce f; (opening) orifizio
mouthful ['maʊθful] N boccata
mouth organ N armonica
mouthpiece ['maʊθpiːs] N (Mus) imboccatura, bocchino; (Tel) microfono; (of breathing apparatus) boccaglio; (person) portavoce mf
mouth-to-mouth ['maʊθtə'maʊθ] ADJ: **~ resuscitation** respirazione f bocca a bocca
mouthwash ['maʊθwɔʃ] N collutorio
mouth-watering ['maʊθwɔːtərɪŋ] ADJ che fa venire l'acquolina in bocca
movable ['muːvəbl] ADJ mobile
move [muːv] N (movement) movimento; (in game) mossa; (: turn to play) turno; (change: of house) trasloco; (: of job) cambiamento ▶ VT muovere; (change position of) spostare; (emotionally) commuovere; (Pol: resolution etc) proporre ▶ VI (gen) muoversi, spostarsi; (traffic) circolare; (also: **move house**) cambiar casa, traslocare; **to ~ towards** andare verso; **to ~ sb to do sth** indurre or spingere qn a fare qc; **to get a ~ on** affrettarsi, sbrigarsi; **to be moved** (emotionally) essere commosso(-a)
▶ **move about, move around** VI (fidget) agitarsi; (travel) viaggiare
▶ **move along** VI muoversi avanti
▶ **move away** VI allontanarsi, andarsene
▶ **move back** VI indietreggiare; (return) ritornare
▶ **move forward** VI avanzare ▶ VT avanzare, spostare in avanti; (people) far avanzare
▶ **move in** VI (to a house) entrare (in una nuova casa); (police etc) intervenire
▶ **move off** VI partire
▶ **move on** VI riprendere la strada ▶ VT (onlookers) far circolare
▶ **move out** VI (of house) sgombrare
▶ **move over** VI spostarsi
▶ **move up** VI avanzare

m

movement ['mu:vmənt] N (gen) movimento; (gesture) gesto; (of stars, water, physical) moto; **~ (of the bowels)** (Med) evacuazione f

mover ['mu:və^r] N proponente mf

movie ['mu:vɪ] N film m inv; **the movies** il cinema

movie camera N cinepresa

moviegoer ['mu:vɪgəuə^r] N (US) frequentatore(-trice) di cinema

movie theater (US) N cinema m inv

moving ['mu:vɪŋ] ADJ mobile; (causing emotion) commovente; (instigating) animatore(-trice)

mow [məu] (pt **mowed**, pp **mowed** or **mown** [məun]) VT falciare; (grass) tagliare; (corn) mietere
▶ **mow down** VT falciare

mower ['məuə^r] N (also: **lawn mower**) tagliaerba m inv

mown [məun] PP of **mow**

Mozambique [məuzəm'bi:k] N Mozambico

MP N ABBR = **Military Police**; (BRIT) = **Member of Parliament**; (CANADA) = **Mounted Police**

MP3 N MP3 m inv

MP3 player N lettore m MP3

mpg N ABBR = **miles per gallon**

mph N ABBR = **miles per hour**

MPhil N ABBR (= Master of Philosophy) titolo di studio

MPS N ABBR (BRIT) = **Member of the Pharmaceutical Society**

Mr, (US) **Mr.** ['mɪstə^r] N: **Mr X** Signor X, Sig. X

MRC N ABBR (BRIT: = Medical Research Council) ufficio governativo per la ricerca medica in Gran Bretagna e nel Commonwealth

MRCP N ABBR (BRIT) = **Member of the Royal College of Physicians**

MRCS N ABBR (BRIT) = **Member of the Royal College of Surgeons**

MRCVS N ABBR (BRIT) = **Member of the Royal College of Veterinary Surgeons**

Mrs, (US) **Mrs.** ['mɪsɪz] N: **~ X** Signora X, Sig. ra X

MS N ABBR (US: = Master of Science) titolo di studio; (Med) = **multiple sclerosis**; (= manuscript) ms
▶ ABBR (US) = **Mississippi**

Ms, (US) **Ms.** [mɪz] N = **Miss**; **Mrs**; **Ms X** ≈ Signora X, ≈ Sig.ra X

> In inglese si usa Ms al posto di Mrs (Signora) o Miss (Signorina) per evitare la distinzione tradizionale tra le donne sposate e quelle nubili.

MSA N ABBR (US: = Master of Science in Agriculture) titolo di studio

MSc N ABBR = **Master of Science**

MSG ABBR = **monosodium glutamate**

MSP N ABBR (BRIT) = **Member of the Scottish Parliament**

MST ABBR (US: = Mountain Standard Time)

ora invernale delle Montagne Rocciose

MSW N ABBR (US: = Master of Social Work) titolo di studio

MT N ABBR = **machine translation** ▶ ABBR (US) = **Montana**

Mt ABBR (Geo: = mount) M

mth ABBR (= month) m

MTV N ABBR = **music television**

(KEYWORD)

much [mʌtʃ] ADJ, PRON molto(-a); **he's done so much work** ha lavorato così tanto; **I have as much money as you** ho tanti soldi quanti ne hai tu; **how much is it?** quant'è?; **it's not much** non è tanto; **it costs too much** costa troppo; **as much as you want** quanto vuoi
▶ ADV **1** (greatly) molto, tanto; **thank you very much** molte grazie; **I like it very/so much** mi piace moltissimo/così tanto; **much to my amazement** con mio enorme stupore; **he's very much the gentleman** è il vero gentiluomo; **I read as much as I can** leggo quanto posso; **as much as you** tanto quanto te
2 (by far) molto; **it's much the biggest company in Europe** è di gran lunga la più grossa società in Europa
3 (almost) grossomodo, praticamente; **they're much the same** sono praticamente uguali

muck [mʌk] N (mud) fango; (dirt) sporcizia
▶ **muck about, muck around** VI (col) fare lo stupido; (waste time) gingillarsi; (tinker) armeggiare
▶ **muck in** VI (BRIT col) mettersi insieme
▶ **muck out** VT (stable) pulire
▶ **muck up** VT (col: dirty) sporcare; (spoil) rovinare

muckraking ['mʌkreɪkɪŋ] N (fig: col) caccia agli scandali ▶ ADJ scandalistico(-a)

mucky ['mʌkɪ] ADJ (dirty) sporco(-a), lordo(-a)

mucus ['mju:kəs] N muco

mud [mʌd] N fango

muddle ['mʌdl] N confusione f, disordine m; pasticcio ▶ VT (also: **muddle up**) mettere sottosopra; confondere; **to be in a ~** (person) non riuscire a raccapezzarsi; **to get in a ~** (while explaining etc) imbrogliarsi
▶ **muddle along** VI andare avanti a casaccio
▶ **muddle through** VI cavarsela alla meno peggio

muddle-headed [mʌdl'hɛdɪd] ADJ (person) confusionario(-a)

muddy ['mʌdɪ] ADJ fangoso(-a)

mud flats NPL distesa fangosa

mudguard ['mʌdgɑ:d] N parafango

mudpack ['mʌdpæk] N maschera di fango

mud-slinging ['mʌdslɪŋɪŋ] N (fig) infangamento

muesli ['mjuːzlɪ] N muesli m inv

muff [mʌf] N manicotto ▶ VT (shot, catch etc) mancare, sbagliare; **to ~ it** sbagliare tutto

muffin ['mʌfɪn] N specie di pasticcino soffice da tè

muffle ['mʌfl] VT (sound) smorzare, attutire; (against cold) imbacuccare

muffled ['mʌfld] ADJ smorzato(-a), attutito(-a)

muffler ['mʌflər] N (scarf) sciarpa (pesante); (US: Aut) marmitta; (: on motorbike) silenziatore m

mufti ['mʌftɪ] N: **in ~** in borghese

mug [mʌg] N (cup) tazzone m; (for beer) boccale m; (col: face) muso; (: fool) scemo(-a) ▶ VT (assault) assalire; **it's a ~'s game** (BRIT) è proprio (una cosa) da fessi
▶ **mug up** VT (BRIT col: also: **mug up on**) studiare bene

mugger ['mʌgər] N aggressore m

mugging ['mʌgɪŋ] N aggressione f (a scopo di rapina)

muggins ['mʌgɪnz] N (col) semplicione(-a), sprovveduto(-a)

muggy ['mʌgɪ] ADJ afoso(-a)

mug shot N (col) foto f inv segnaletica

mulatto [mjuːˈlætəu] (pl **mulattoes**) N mulatto(-a)

mulberry ['mʌlbərɪ] N (fruit) mora (di gelso); (tree) gelso, moro

mule [mjuːl] N mulo

mull [mʌl]: **to ~ over** VT rimuginare

mulled [mʌld] ADJ: **~ wine** vino caldo

multi... ['mʌltɪ] PREFIX multi...

multi-access [mʌltɪ'æksɛs] ADJ (Comput) ad accesso multiplo

multicoloured, (US) **multicolored** ['mʌltɪkʌləd] ADJ multicolore, variopinto(-a)

multifarious [mʌltɪ'fɛərɪəs] ADJ molteplice, svariato(-a)

multilateral [mʌltɪ'lætərəl] ADJ (Pol) multilaterale

multi-level ['mʌltɪlɛvl] ADJ (US) = **multistorey**

multimedia ['mʌltɪ'miːdɪə] ADJ multimedia inv

multimillionaire [mʌltɪmɪljə'nɛər] N multimiliardario(-a)

multinational [mʌltɪ'næʃənl] ADJ, N multinazionale (f)

multiple ['mʌltɪpl] ADJ multiplo(-a); molteplice ▶ N multiplo; (BRIT: also: **multiple store**) grande magazzino che fa parte di una catena

multiple choice (test) N esercizi mpl a scelta multipla

multiple crash N serie f inv di incidenti a catena

multiple sclerosis [-sklɪ'rəusɪs] N sclerosi f a placche

multiplex ['mʌltɪplɛks] N (also: **multiplex cinema**) cinema m inv multisale inv

multiplication [mʌltɪplɪ'keɪʃən] N moltiplicazione f

multiplication table N tavola pitagorica

multiplicity [mʌltɪ'plɪsɪtɪ] N molteplicità

multiply ['mʌltɪplaɪ] VT moltiplicare ▶ VI moltiplicarsi

multiracial [mʌltɪ'reɪʃəl] ADJ multirazziale

multistorey ['mʌltɪ'stɔːrɪ] ADJ (BRIT: building, car park) a più piani

multitude ['mʌltɪtjuːd] N moltitudine f

mum [mʌm] N (BRIT col) mamma ▶ ADJ: **to keep ~** non aprire bocca; **~'s the word!** acqua in bocca!

mumble ['mʌmbl] VT, VI borbottare

mumbo jumbo ['mʌmbəu-] N (col) parole fpl incomprensibili

mummify ['mʌmɪfaɪ] VT mummificare

mummy ['mʌmɪ] N (BRIT: mother) mamma; (embalmed) mummia

mumps [mʌmps] N orecchioni mpl

munch [mʌntʃ] VT, VI sgranocchiare

mundane [mʌn'deɪn] ADJ terra a terra inv

Munich ['mjuːnɪk] N Monaco f (di Baviera)

municipal [mjuː'nɪsɪpl] ADJ municipale

municipality [mjuːnɪsɪ'pælɪtɪ] N municipio

munitions [mjuː'nɪʃənz] NPL munizioni fpl

mural ['mjuərəl] N dipinto murale

murder ['məːdər] N assassinio, omicidio ▶ VT assassinare; **to commit ~** commettere un omicidio

murderer ['məːdərər] N omicida m, assassino

murderess ['məːdərɪs] N omicida f, assassina

murderous ['məːdərəs] ADJ micidiale

murk [məːk] N oscurità, buio

murky ['məːkɪ] ADJ tenebroso(-a), buio(-a)

murmur ['məːmər] N mormorio ▶ VT, VI mormorare; **heart ~** (Med) soffio al cuore

MusB, MusBac N ABBR (= Bachelor of Music) titolo di studio

muscle ['mʌsl] N muscolo; (fig) forza ▶ **muscle in** VI immischiarsi

muscular ['mʌskjulər] ADJ muscolare; (person, arm) muscoloso(-a)

muscular dystrophy N distrofia muscolare

MusD, MusDoc N ABBR (= Doctor of Music) titolo di studio

muse [mjuːz] VI meditare, sognare ▶ N musa

museum [mjuː'zɪəm] N museo

mush [mʌʃ] N pappa

mushroom ['mʌʃrum] N fungo ▶ VI (fig) svilupparsi rapidamente

mushy ['mʌʃɪ] ADJ (food) spappolato(-a); (sentimental) sdolcinato(-a)

music ['mjuːzɪk] N musica

musical ['mjuːzɪkəl] ADJ musicale; (person) portato(-a) per la musica ▶ N (show) commedia musicale

musical box N carillon *m inv*
musical chairs N gioco delle sedie (*in cui bisogna sedersi non appena cessa la musica*); (*fig*) scambio delle poltrone
musical instrument N strumento musicale
music box N carillon *m inv*
music centre N impianto *m* stereo *inv* monoblocco *inv*
music hall N teatro di varietà
musician [mjuːˈzɪʃən] N musicista *mf*
music stand N leggio
musk [mʌsk] N muschio
musket [ˈmʌskɪt] N moschetto
muskrat [ˈmʌskræt] N topo muschiato
musk rose N (*Bot*) rosa muschiata
Muslim [ˈmʌzlɪm] ADJ, N musulmano(-a)
muslin [ˈmʌzlɪn] N mussola
musquash [ˈmʌskwɔʃ] N (*fur*) rat musqué *m inv*
mussel [ˈmʌsl] N cozza
must [mʌst] AUX VB (*obligation*): **I ~ do it** devo farlo; (*probability*): **he ~ be there by now** dovrebbe essere arrivato ormai; **I ~ have made a mistake** devo essermi sbagliato
  ▶ N: **this programme/trip is a ~** è un programma/viaggio da non perdersi
mustache [ˈmʌstæʃ] N (*US*) = **moustache**
mustard [ˈmʌstəd] N senape *f*, mostarda
mustard gas N iprite *f*
muster [ˈmʌstəʳ] VT radunare; (*also: **muster up**: strength, courage*) fare appello a
mustiness [ˈmʌstɪnɪs] N odor di muffa *or* di stantio
mustn't [ˈmʌsnt]= **must not**
musty [ˈmʌstɪ] ADJ che sa di muffa *or* di rinchiuso
mutant [ˈmjuːtənt] ADJ, N mutante (*m*)
mutate [mjuːˈteɪt] VI subire una mutazione
mutation [mjuːˈteɪʃən] N mutazione *f*
mute [mjuːt] ADJ, N muto(-a)
muted [ˈmjuːtɪd] ADJ (*noise*) attutito(-a), smorzato(-a); (*criticism*) attenuato(-a); (*Mus*) in sordina; (*: trumpet*) con sordina
mutilate [ˈmjuːtɪleɪt] VT mutilare

mutilation [mjuːtɪˈleɪʃən] N mutilazione *f*
mutinous [ˈmjuːtɪnəs] ADJ (*troops*) ammutinato(-a); (*attitude*) ribelle
mutiny [ˈmjuːtɪnɪ] N ammutinamento
  ▶ VI ammutinarsi
mutter [ˈmʌtəʳ] VT, VI borbottare, brontolare
mutton [ˈmʌtn] N carne *f* di montone
mutual [ˈmjuːtʃuəl] ADJ mutuo(-a), reciproco(-a)
mutually [ˈmjuːtʃuəlɪ] ADV reciprocamente
Muzak® [ˈmjuːzæk] N (*often pej*) musica di sottofondo
muzzle [ˈmʌzl] N muso; (*protective device*) museruola; (*of gun*) bocca ▶ VT mettere la museruola a
MV ABBR (= *motor vessel*) M/N, m/n
MVP N ABBR (*US Sport*: = *most valuable player*) titolo ottenuto da sportivo
MW ABBR (*Radio*: = *medium wave*) O.M.; = **megawatt**
my [maɪ] ADJ il (la) mio(-a); (*pl*) i (le) miei (mie); **my house** la mia casa; **my books** i miei libri; **my brother** mio fratello; **I've washed my hair/cut my finger** mi sono lavato i capelli/tagliato
Myanmar [ˈmaɪænmɑːʳ] N Myanma
myopic [maɪˈɔpɪk] ADJ miope
myriad [ˈmɪrɪəd] N miriade *f*
myself [maɪˈsɛlf] PRON (*reflexive*) mi; (*emphatic*) io stesso(-a); (*after prep*) me; *see also* **oneself**
mysterious [mɪsˈtɪərɪəs] ADJ misterioso(-a)
mystery [ˈmɪstərɪ] N mistero
mystery story N racconto del mistero
mystic [ˈmɪstɪk] ADJ, N mistico(-a)
mystical [ˈmɪstɪkəl] ADJ mistico(-a)
mystify [ˈmɪstɪfaɪ] VT mistificare; (*puzzle*) confondere
mystique [mɪsˈtiːk] N fascino
myth [mɪθ] N mito
mythical [ˈmɪθɪkl] ADJ mitico(-a)
mythological [mɪθəˈlɔdʒɪkl] ADJ mitologico(-a)
mythology [mɪˈθɔlədʒɪ] N mitologia

Nn

N, n [ɛn] N (letter) N, n f inv or m inv; **N for Nellie**, (US) **N for Nan** ≈ N come Napoli

N ABBR (= north) N

NA N ABBR (US: = Narcotics Anonymous) associazione in aiuto dei tossicodipendenti; (US) = **National Academy**

n/a ABBR (= not applicable) non pertinente

NAACP N ABBR (US) = **National Association for the Advancement of Colored People**

NAAFI ['næfɪ] N ABBR (BRIT: = Navy, Army, & Air Force Institutes) organizzazione che gestisce negozi, mense ecc. per il personale militare

nab [næb] VT (col) beccare, acchiappare

NACU N ABBR (US) = **National Association of Colleges and Universities**

nadir ['neɪdɪəʳ] N (Astron) nadir m; (fig) punto più basso

nag [næg] N (pej: horse) ronzino; (person) brontolone(-a) ▶ VT tormentare ▶ VI brontolare in continuazione

nagging ['nægɪŋ] ADJ (doubt, pain) persistente ▶ N brontolii mpl, osservazioni fpl continue

nail [neɪl] N (human) unghia; (metal) chiodo ▶ VT inchiodare; **to ~ sb down to a date/price** costringere qn a un appuntamento/ad accettare un prezzo; **to pay cash on the ~** (BRIT) pagare a tamburo battente

nailbrush ['neɪlbrʌʃ] N spazzolino da or per unghie

nailfile ['neɪlfaɪl] N lima da or per unghie

nail polish N smalto da or per unghie

nail polish remover N acetone m, solvente m

nail scissors NPL forbici fpl da or per unghie

nail varnish N (BRIT) = **nail polish**

Nairobi [naɪ'rəubɪ] N Nairobi f

naïve [naɪ'iːv] ADJ ingenuo(-a)

naïveté [nɑːiːv'teɪ], **naivety** [naɪ'iːvtɪ] N ingenuità f inv

naked ['neɪkɪd] ADJ nudo(-a); **with the ~ eye** a occhio nudo

nakedness ['neɪkɪdnɪs] N nudità

NAM N ABBR (US) = **National Association of Manufacturers**

name [neɪm] N nome m; (reputation) nome, reputazione f ▶ VT (baby etc) chiamare; (plant, illness) nominare; (person, object) identificare; (price, date) fissare; **by ~** di nome; **she knows them all by ~** li conosce tutti per nome; **in the ~ of** in nome di; **what's your ~?** come si chiama?; **my ~ is Peter** mi chiamo Peter; **to take sb's ~ and address** prendere nome e indirizzo di qn; **to make a ~ for o.s.** farsi un nome; **to get (o.s.) a bad ~** farsi una cattiva fama or una brutta reputazione; **to call sb names** insultare qn

name dropping N menzionare qualcuno per fare bella figura

nameless ['neɪmlɪs] ADJ senza nome

namely ['neɪmlɪ] ADV cioè

nameplate ['neɪmpleɪt] N (on door etc) targa

namesake ['neɪmseɪk] N omonimo

nan bread [nɑː-] N tipo di pane indiano poco lievitato di forma allungata

nanny ['nænɪ] N bambinaia

nanny goat N capra

nap [næp] N (sleep) pisolino; (of cloth) peluria ▶ VI: **to be caught napping** essere preso alla sprovvista; **to have a ~** schiacciare un pisolino

NAPA N ABBR (US: = National Association of Performing Artists) associazione nazionale degli artisti di palcoscenico

napalm ['neɪpɑːm] N napalm m

nape [neɪp] N: **~ of the neck** nuca

napkin ['næpkɪn] N tovagliolo; (BRIT: for baby) pannolino

Naples ['neɪplz] N Napoli f

Napoleonic [nəpəʊlɪ'ɔnɪk] ADJ napoleonico(-a)

nappy ['næpɪ] N (BRIT) pannolino

nappy liner N (BRIT) fogliettino igienico

narcissistic [nɑː'sɪsɪstɪk] ADJ narcisistico(-a)

narcissus [nɑː'sɪsəs] (pl **narcissi** [-saɪ]) N narciso

narcotic [nɑː'kɔtɪk] N (Med) narcotico; **narcotics** NPL (drugs) narcotici, stupefacenti mpl

nark [nɑːk] VT (BRIT col) scocciare

n

narrate [nə'reɪt] VT raccontare, narrare
narration [nə'reɪʃən] N narrazione f
narrative ['nærətɪv] N narrativa ▶ ADJ narrativo(-a)
narrator [nə'reɪtəʳ] N narratore(-trice)
narrow ['nærəʊ] ADJ stretto(-a); (*resources, means*) limitato(-a), modesto(-a); (*fig*): **to take a ~ view** of avere una visione limitata di ▶ VI restringersi; **to have a ~ escape** farcela per un pelo
  ▶ **narrow down** VT (*search, investigation, possibilities*) restringere; (*list*) ridurre; **to ~ sth down to** ridurre qc a
narrow gauge ADJ (*Rail*) a scartamento ridotto
narrowly ['nærəʊlɪ] ADV per un pelo; (*time*) per poco; **Maria ~ escaped drowning** per un pelo Maria non è affogata; **he ~ missed hitting the cyclist** per poco non ha investito il ciclista
narrow-minded [nærəʊ'maɪndɪd] ADJ meschino(-a)
NAS N ABBR (*US*) = **National Academy of Sciences**
NASA ['næsə] N ABBR (*US*: = *National Aeronautics and Space Administration*) N.A.S.A. f
nasal ['neɪzl] ADJ nasale
Nassau ['næsɔ:] N Nassau f
nastily ['nɑ:stɪlɪ] ADV con cattiveria
nastiness ['nɑ:stɪnɪs] N (*of person, remark*) cattiveria; (: *spitefulness*) malignità
nasturtium [nəs'tə:ʃəm] N cappuccina, nasturzio (indiano)
nasty ['nɑ:stɪ] ADJ (*unpleasant: person, remark*) cattivo(-a); (: *spiteful*) maligno(-a); (*rude*) villano(-a); (*smell, wound, situation*) brutto(-a); **to turn ~** (*situation*) mettersi male; (*weather*) guastarsi; (*person*) incattivirsi; **it's a ~ business** è una brutta faccenda, è un brutto affare
NAS/UWT N ABBR (*BRIT*: = *National Association of Schoolmasters/Union of Women Teachers*) *sindacato di insegnanti in Inghilterra e Galles*
nation ['neɪʃən] N nazione f
national ['næʃənl] ADJ nazionale ▶ N cittadino(-a)
national anthem N inno nazionale
National Curriculum N (*BRIT*) ≈ programma m scolastico ministeriale (*in Inghilterra e Galles*)
national debt N debito pubblico
national dress N costume m nazionale
National Guard N (*US*) milizia nazionale (*volontaria, in ogni stato*)
National Health Service N (*BRIT*) ≈ Servizio sanitario nazionale
National Insurance N (*BRIT*) ≈ Previdenza Sociale
nationalism ['næʃnəlɪzəm] N nazionalismo

nationalist ['næʃnəlɪst] ADJ, N nazionalista (*mf*)
nationality [næʃə'nælɪtɪ] N nazionalità f inv
nationalization [næʃnəlaɪ'zeɪʃən] N nazionalizzazione f
nationalize ['næʃnəlaɪz] VT nazionalizzare
nationally ['næʃnəlɪ] ADV a livello nazionale
national park N parco nazionale
national press N stampa a diffusione nazionale
National Security Council N (*US*) consiglio nazionale di sicurezza
national service N (*Mil*) servizio militare
National Trust N sovrintendenza ai beni culturali e ambientali; *vedi nota*

> Fondato nel 1895, il *National Trust* è un'organizzazione che si occupa della tutela e salvaguardia di edifici e monumenti di interesse storico e di territori di interesse ambientale nel Regno Unito.

nationwide ['neɪʃənwaɪd] ADJ diffuso(-a) in tutto il paese ▶ ADV in tutto il paese
native ['neɪtɪv] N abitante *mf* del paese; (*in colonies*) indigeno(-a) ▶ ADJ indigeno(-a); (*country*) natio(-a); (*ability*) innato(-a); **a ~ of Russia** un nativo della Russia; **a ~ speaker of French** una persona di madrelingua francese; **~ language** madrelingua
Native American N *discendente di tribù dell'America settentrionale*
Nativity [nə'tɪvɪtɪ] N (*Rel*): **the ~** la Natività
nativity play N recita sulla Natività
NATO ['neɪtəʊ] N ABBR (= *North Atlantic Treaty Organization*) N.A.T.O. f
natter ['nætəʳ] (*BRIT col*) VI chiacchierare ▶ N chiacchierata
natural ['nætʃrəl] ADJ naturale; (*ability*) innato(-a); (*manner*) semplice; **death from ~ causes** (*Law*) morte f per cause naturali
natural childbirth N parto indolore
natural gas N gas m metano
natural history N storia naturale
naturalist ['nætʃrəlɪst] N naturalista *mf*
naturalization [nætʃrəlaɪ'zeɪʃən] N naturalizzazione f; acclimatazione f
naturalize ['nætʃrəlaɪz] VT: **to be naturalized** (*person*) naturalizzarsi; **to become naturalized** (*animal, plant*) acclimatarsi
naturally ['nætʃrəlɪ] ADV naturalmente; (*by nature: gifted*) di natura
naturalness ['nætʃrəlnɪs] N naturalezza
natural resources NPL risorse *fpl* naturali
natural selection N selezione f naturale
natural wastage N (*Industry*) diminuzione f di manodopera (*per pensionamento decesso ecc*)
nature ['neɪtʃəʳ] N natura; (*character*) natura, indole f; **by ~** di natura; **documents of a**

confidential ~ documenti *mpl* di natura privata

-natured ['neɪtʃəd] SUFFIX: **ill~** maldisposto(-a)

nature reserve N (*BRIT*) parco naturale

nature trail N *percorso tracciato in parchi nazionali ecc con scopi educativi*

naturist ['neɪtʃərɪst] N naturista *mf*, nudista *mf*

naught [nɔːt] N = **nought**

naughtiness ['nɔːtɪnɪs] N cattiveria

naughty ['nɔːtɪ] ADJ (*child*) birichino(-a), cattivello(-a); (*story, film*) spinto(-a)

nausea ['nɔːsɪə] N (*Med*) nausea; (*fig: disgust*) schifo

nauseate ['nɔːsɪeɪt] VT nauseare; far schifo a

nauseating ['nɔːsɪeɪtɪŋ] ADJ nauseante; (*fig*) disgustoso(-a)

nauseous ['nɔːsɪəs] ADJ nauseabondo(-a); (*feeling sick*): **to be** ~ avere la nausea

nautical ['nɔːtɪkl] ADJ nautico(-a)

nautical mile N miglio nautico *or* marino

naval ['neɪvl] ADJ navale

naval officer N ufficiale *m* di marina

nave [neɪv] N navata centrale

navel ['neɪvl] N ombelico

navigable ['nævɪgəbl] ADJ navigabile

navigate ['nævɪgeɪt] VT percorrere navigando ▶ VI navigare; (*Aut*) fare da navigatore

navigation [nævɪ'geɪʃən] N navigazione *f*

navigator ['nævɪgeɪtər] N (*Naut, Aviat*) ufficiale *m* di rotta; (*explorer*) navigatore *m*; (*Aut*) copilota *mf*

navvy ['nævɪ] N manovale *m*

navy ['neɪvɪ] N marina; **Department of the N~** (*US*) Ministero della Marina ▶ ADJ blu scuro *inv*

navy-blue ['neɪvɪ'bluː] ADJ blu scuro *inv*

Nazareth ['næzərɪθ] N Nazareth *f*

Nazi ['nɑːtsɪ] ADJ, N nazista (*mf*)

NB ABBR (= *nota bene*) N.B.; (*CANADA*) = **New Brunswick**

NBA N ABBR (*US*: = *National Basketball Association*) ≈ F.I.P. *f* (= *Federazione Italiana Pallacanestro*); = **National Boxing Association**

NBC N ABBR (*US*: = *National Broadcasting Company*) compagnia nazionale di radiodiffusione

NBS N ABBR (*US*: = *National Bureau of Standards*) ufficio per la normalizzazione

NC ABBR (*Comm etc*: = *no charge*) gratis; (*US*) = **North Carolina**

NCC N ABBR (*US*) = **National Council of Churches**

NCO N ABBR = **non-commissioned officer**

ND, N. Dak. ABBR (*US*) = **North Dakota**

NE ABBR (*US*) = **Nebraska; New England**

NEA N ABBR (*US*) = **National Education Association**

neap [niːp] N (*also*: **neaptide**) marea di quadratura

Neapolitan [nɪə'pɔlɪtən] ADJ, N napoletano(-a)

near [nɪər] ADJ vicino(-a); (*relation*) prossimo(-a) ▶ ADV vicino ▶ PREP (*also*: **near to**) vicino a, presso; (: *in time*) verso ▶ VT avvicinarsi a; **to come** ~ avvicinarsi; **~ here/ there** qui/lì vicino; **£25,000 or nearest offer** (*BRIT*) 25.000 sterline trattabili; **in the ~ future** in un prossimo futuro; **the building is nearing completion** il palazzo è quasi terminato *or* ultimato

nearby [nɪə'baɪ] ADJ vicino(-a) ▶ ADV vicino

Near East N: **the** ~ il Medio Oriente

nearer ['nɪərər] ADJ più vicino(-a) ▶ ADV più vicino

nearly ['nɪəlɪ] ADV quasi; **not** ~ non … affatto; **I** ~ **lost it** per poco non lo perdevo; **she was** ~ **crying** era lì lì per piangere

near miss N: **that was a** ~ c'è mancato poco

nearness ['nɪənɪs] N vicinanza

nearside ['nɪəsaɪd] N (*right-hand drive*) lato sinistro; (*left-hand drive*) lato destro ▶ ADJ sinistro(-a); destro(-a)

near-sighted [nɪə'saɪtɪd] ADJ miope

neat [niːt] ADJ (*person, room*) ordinato(-a); (*work*) pulito(-a); (*solution, plan*) ben indovinato(-a), azzeccato(-a); (*spirits*) liscio(-a)

neatly ['niːtlɪ] ADV con ordine; (*skilfully*) abilmente

neatness ['niːtnɪs] N (*tidiness*) ordine *m*; (*skilfulness*) abilità

Nebr. ABBR (*US*) = **Nebraska**

nebulous ['nɛbjuləs] ADJ nebuloso(-a); (*fig*) vago(-a)

necessarily ['nɛsɪsrɪlɪ] ADV necessariamente; **not** ~ non è detto, non necessariamente

necessary ['nɛsɪsrɪ] ADJ necessario(-a); **if** ~ se necessario

necessitate [nɪ'sɛsɪteɪt] VT rendere necessario(-a)

necessity [nɪ'sɛsɪtɪ] N necessità *f inv*; **in case of** ~ in caso di necessità

neck [nɛk] N collo; (*of garment*) colletto ▶ VI (*col*) pomiciare, sbaciucchiarsi; ~ **and** ~ testa a testa; **to stick one's** ~ **out** (*col*) rischiare (forte)

necklace ['nɛklɪs] N collana

neckline ['nɛklaɪn] N scollatura

necktie ['nɛktaɪ] N (*esp US*) cravatta

nectar ['nɛktər] N nettare *m*

nectarine ['nɛktərɪn] N nocepesca

née [neɪ] ADJ: ~ **Scott** nata Scott

need [niːd] N bisogno ▶ VT aver bisogno di; **do you** ~ **anything?** ha bisogno di qualcosa?; **I** ~ **to do it** lo devo fare, bisogna che io lo faccia; **you don't** ~ **to go** non deve andare, non c'è bisogno che lei vada; **a signature is needed** occorre or ci vuole una firma; **to be in ~ of, have ~ of** aver bisogno di; **£10 will meet my immediate needs** 10 sterline mi basteranno per le necessità più urgenti; **in case of ~** in caso di bisogno or necessità; **there's no ~ for ...** non c'è bisogno or non occorre che ...; **there's no ~ to do ...** non occorre fare ...; **the needs of industry** le esigenze dell'industria

needle ['niːdl] N ago; (on record player) puntina ▶ VT punzecchiare

needlecord ['niːdlkɔːd] N (BRIT) velluto a coste sottili

needless ['niːdlɪs] ADJ inutile; **~ to say, ...** inutile dire che ...

needlessly ['niːdlɪslɪ] ADV inutilmente

needlework ['niːdlwəːk] N cucito

needn't ['niːdnt]= **need not**

needy ['niːdɪ] ADJ bisognoso(-a)

negation [nɪ'ɡeɪʃən] N negazione f

negative ['nɛɡətɪv] N (Phot) negativa, negativo; (Elec) polo negativo; (Ling) negazione f ▶ ADJ negativo(-a); **to answer in the ~** rispondere negativamente or di no

negative equity N situazione in cui l'ammontare del mutuo su un immobile supera il suo valore sul mercato

neglect [nɪ'ɡlɛkt] VT trascurare ▶ N (of person, duty) negligenza; (of child, house etc) scarsa cura; **state of ~** stato di abbandono; **to ~ to do sth** trascurare or tralasciare di fare qc

neglected [nɪ'ɡlɛktɪd] ADJ trascurato(-a)

neglectful [nɪ'ɡlɛktful] ADJ (gen) negligente; **to be ~ of sb/sth** trascurare qn/qc

negligee ['nɛɡlɪʒeɪ] N négligé m inv

negligence ['nɛɡlɪdʒəns] N negligenza

negligent ['nɛɡlɪdʒənt] ADJ negligente

negligently ['nɛɡlɪdʒəntlɪ] ADV con negligenza

negligible ['nɛɡlɪdʒɪbl] ADJ insignificante, trascurabile

negotiable [nɪ'ɡəuʃɪəbl] ADJ negoziabile; (cheque) trasferibile; (road) transitabile

negotiate [nɪ'ɡəuʃɪeɪt] VI negoziare ▶ VT (Comm) negoziare; (obstacle) superare; (bend in road) prendere; **to ~ with sb for sth** trattare con qn per ottenere qc

negotiating table [nɪ'ɡəuʃɪeɪtɪŋ-] N tavolo delle trattative

negotiation [nɪɡəuʃɪ'eɪʃən] N trattativa; (Pol) negoziato; **to enter into negotiations with sb** entrare in trattative (or intavolare i negoziati) con qn

negotiator [nɪ'ɡəuʃɪeɪtə^r] N negoziatore(-trice)

Negress ['niːɡrɪs] N negra

Negro ['niːɡrəu] (pl **Negroes**) ADJ, N negro(-a)

neigh [neɪ] VI nitrire

neighbour, (US) **neighbor** ['neɪbə^r] N vicino(-a)

neighbourhood, (US) **neighborhood** ['neɪbəhud] N vicinato

neighbourhood watch N (BRIT: also: **neighbourhood watch scheme**) sistema di vigilanza reciproca in un quartiere

neighbouring, (US) **neighboring** ['neɪbərɪŋ] ADJ vicino(-a)

neighbourly, (US) **neighborly** ['neɪbəlɪ] ADJ: **he is a neighbo(u)rly person** è un buon vicino

neither ['naɪðə^r] ADJ, PRON né l'uno(-a) né l'altro(-a), nessuno(-a) dei due ▶ CONJ neanche, nemmeno, neppure ▶ ADV: **~ good nor bad** né buono né cattivo; **I didn't move and ~ did Claude** io non mi mossi e nemmeno Claude; **... ~ did I refuse ...**, ma non ho nemmeno rifiutato

neo... ['niːəu] PREFIX neo...

neolithic [niːəu'lɪθɪk] ADJ neolitico(-a)

neologism [nɪ'ɔlədʒɪzəm] N neologismo

neon ['niːɔn] N neon m

neon light N luce f al neon

neon sign N insegna al neon

Nepal [nɪ'pɔːl] N Nepal m

nephew ['nɛvjuː] N nipote m

nepotism ['nɛpətɪzəm] N nepotismo

nerd [nəːd] N (col) sfigato(-a), povero(-a) fesso(-a)

nerve [nəːv] N nervo; (fig) coraggio; (impudence) faccia tosta; **he gets on my nerves** mi dà ai nervi, mi fa venire i nervi; **a fit of nerves** una crisi di nervi; **to lose one's ~** (self-confidence) perdere fiducia in se stesso; **I lost my ~** (courage) mi è mancato il coraggio

nerve centre N (Anat) centro nervoso; (fig) cervello, centro vitale

nerve gas N gas m nervino

nerve-racking ['nəːvrækɪŋ] ADJ che spezza i nervi

nervous ['nəːvəs] ADJ nervoso(-a); (anxious) agitato(-a), in apprensione

nervous breakdown N esaurimento nervoso

nervously ['nəːvəslɪ] ADV nervosamente

nervousness ['nəːvəsnɪs] N nervosismo

nervous wreck N: **to be a ~** (col) essere nevrastenico(-a)

nervy ['nəːvɪ] ADJ agitato(-a), nervoso(-a)

nest [nɛst] N nido; **~ of tables** tavolini mpl cicogna inv ▶ VI fare il nido, nidificare

nest egg N (fig) gruzzolo

nestle ['nɛsl] VI accoccolarsi

nestling ['nɛslɪŋ] N uccellino di nido

net [nɛt] N rete f; (fabric) tulle m ▶ ADJ netto(-a) ▶ VT (person, profit) ricavare un utile netto di; (fish etc) prendere con la rete; (deal, *sale*) dare un utile netto di; **the N~** (*Internet*) Internet *f*; **~ of tax** netto, al netto di tasse; **he earns £10,000 ~ per year** guadagna 10.000 sterline nette all'anno

netball ['nɛtbɔ:l] N *specie di pallacanestro*

net curtains NPL tende *fpl* di tulle

Netherlands ['nɛðələndz] NPL: **the ~** i Paesi Bassi

netiquette ['nɛtɪkɛt] N netiquette *f inv*

net profit N utile *m* netto

netsurfer ['nɛtsə:fə^r] N navigatore(-trice) in Internet

nett [nɛt] ADJ **= net**

netting ['nɛtɪŋ] N (*for fence etc*) reticolato; (*fabric*) tulle *m*

nettle ['nɛtl] N ortica

network ['nɛtwə:k] N rete *f*

neuralgia [njuə'rældʒə] N nevralgia

neurological [njuərə'lɔdʒɪkl] ADJ neurologico(-a)

neurosis [njuə'rəusɪs] (*pl* **neuroses** [-si:z]) N nevrosi *f inv*

neurotic [njuə'rɔtɪk] ADJ, N nevrotico(-a)

neuter ['nju:tə^r] ADJ neutro(-a) ▶ N neutro ▶ VT (*cat etc*) castrare

neutral ['nju:trəl] ADJ neutro(-a); (*person, nation*) neutrale ▶ N (*Aut*): **in ~** in folle

neutrality [nju:'trælɪtɪ] N neutralità

neutralize ['nju:trəlaɪz] VT neutralizzare

neutron bomb ['nju:trɔn-] N bomba al neutrone

Nev. ABBR (*US*) **= Nevada**

never ['nɛvə^r] ADV (non...) mai; **~ again** mai più; **I'll ~ go there again** non ci vado più; **~ in my life** mai in vita mia; *see also* **mind**

never-ending [nɛvər'ɛndɪŋ] ADJ interminabile

nevertheless [nɛvəðə'lɛs] ADV tuttavia, ciò nonostante, ciò nondimeno

new [nju:] ADJ nuovo(-a); (*brand new*) nuovo(-a) di zecca; **as good as ~** come nuovo

New Age ADJ, N New Age *f inv*

newbie ['nju:bɪ] N (*Comput, Tech*) utilizzatore(-trice) inesperto(-a); (*to a job or group*) nuovo(-a) arrivato(-a); (*to a hobby or experience*) neofita *mf*

newborn ['nju:bɔ:n] ADJ neonato(-a)

newcomer ['nju:kʌmə^r] N nuovo(-a) venuto(-a)

new-fangled ['nju:fæŋgld] ADJ (*pej*) stramoderno(-a)

new-found ['nju:faund] ADJ nuovo(-a)

Newfoundland ['nju:fənlənd] N Terranova

New Guinea N Nuova Guinea

newly ['nju:lɪ] ADV di recente

newly-weds ['nju:lɪwɛdz] NPL sposini *mpl*, sposi *mpl* novelli

new moon N luna nuova

newness ['nju:nɪs] N novità

news [nju:z] N notizie *fpl*; (*Radio*) giornale *m* radio; (*TV*) telegiornale *m*; **a piece of ~** una notizia; **good/bad ~** buone/cattive notizie; **financial ~** (*Press*) pagina economica e finanziaria; (*Radio, TV*) notiziario economico

news agency N agenzia di stampa

newsagent ['nju:zeɪdʒənt] N (*BRIT*) giornalaio

news bulletin N (*Radio, TV*) notiziario

newscaster ['nju:zka:stə^r] N (*Radio, TV*) annunciatore(-trice)

newsdealer ['nju:zdi:lə^r] N (*US*) **= newsagent**

newsflash ['nju:zflæʃ] N notizia *f* lampo *inv*

newsletter ['nju:zlɛtə^r] N bollettino (*di ditta, associazione*)

newspaper ['nju:zpeɪpə^r] N giornale *m*; **daily ~** quotidiano; **weekly ~** settimanale *m*

newsprint ['nju:zprɪnt] N carta da giornale

newsreader ['nju:zri:də^r] N **= newscaster**

newsreel ['nju:zri:l] N cinegiornale *m*

newsroom ['nju:zrum] N (*Press*) redazione *f*; (*Radio, TV*) studio

news stand N edicola

newsworthy ['nju:zwə:ðɪ] ADJ degno(-a) di menzione (*per radio, TV ecc*); **to be ~** fare notizia

newt [nju:t] N tritone *m*

new town N (*BRIT*) *nuovo centro urbano creato con fondi pubblici*

New Year N Anno Nuovo; **Happy ~!** Buon Anno!; **to wish sb a happy ~** augurare Buon Anno a qn

New Year's Day N il Capodanno

New Year's Eve N la vigilia di Capodanno

New York [-'jɔ:k] N New York *f*, Nuova York *f*; (*also:* **New York State**) stato di New York

New Zealand [-'zi:lənd] N Nuova Zelanda ▶ ADJ neozelandese

New Zealander [-'zi:ləndə^r] N neozelandese *mf*

next [nɛkst] ADJ prossimo(-a) ▶ ADV accanto; (*in time*) dopo; **~ to** prep accanto a; **~ to nothing** quasi niente; **~ please!** (*avanti*) il prossimo!; **~ time** *adv* la prossima volta; **~ week** la settimana prossima; **the ~ week** la settimana dopo *or* seguente; **the week after** fra due settimane; **the ~ day** il giorno dopo, l'indomani; **~ year** l'anno prossimo *or* venturo; **"turn to the ~ page"** "vedi pagina seguente"; **who's ~?** a chi tocca?; **when do we meet ~?** quando ci rincontriamo?

next door ADV, ADJ accanto *inv*

next of kin N parente *mf* prossimo(-a)

NF N ABBR (*BRIT Pol*: *= National Front*) partito di estrema destra ▶ ABBR (*CANADA*) **= Newfoundland**

NFL N ABBR (*US*) **= National Football League**

Nfld. ABBR (*CANADA*) **= Newfoundland**

NG ABBR (US) = **National Guard**
NGO N ABBR = **non-governmental organization**
NH ABBR (US) = **New Hampshire**
NHL N ABBR (US: = National Hockey League) ≈ F.I.H.P. f (= Federazione Italiana Hockey e Pattinaggio)
NHS N ABBR (BRIT) = **National Health Service**
NI ABBR = **Northern Ireland**; (BRIT) = **National Insurance**
Niagara Falls [naɪˈægərə-] NPL: **the ~** le cascate del Niagara
nib [nɪb] N (of pen) pennino
nibble [ˈnɪbl] VT mordicchiare
Nicaragua [nɪkəˈrægjuə] N Nicaragua m
Nicaraguan [nɪkəˈrægjuən] ADJ, N nicaraguense (mf)
Nice [niːs] N Nizza
nice [naɪs] ADJ (holiday, trip) piacevole; (flat, picture) bello(-a); (person) simpatico(-a), gentile; (taste, smell, meal) buono(-a); (distinction, point) sottile
nice-looking [ˈnaɪslukɪŋ] ADJ bello(-a)
nicely [ˈnaɪslɪ] ADV bene; **that will do ~** andrà benissimo
niceties [ˈnaɪsɪtɪz] NPL finezze fpl
niche [niːʃ] N (Archit) nicchia
nick [nɪk] N taglietto; tacca ▶ VT intaccare; tagliare; (col: steal) rubare; (: BRIT: arrest) beccare; **in the ~ of time** appena in tempo; **in good ~** (BRIT col) decente, in buono stato; **to ~ o.s.** farsi un taglietto
nickel [ˈnɪkl] N nichel m; (US) moneta da cinque centesimi di dollaro
nickname [ˈnɪkneɪm] N soprannome m ▶ VT soprannominare
Nicosia [nɪkəˈsiːə] N Nicosia
nicotine [ˈnɪkətiːn] N nicotina
nicotine patch N cerotto antifumo (a base di nicotina)
niece [niːs] N nipote f
nifty [ˈnɪftɪ] ADJ (col: car, jacket) chic inv; (: gadget, tool) ingegnoso(-a)
Niger [ˈnaɪdʒəʳ] N Niger m
Nigeria [naɪˈdʒɪərɪə] N Nigeria
Nigerian [naɪˈdʒɪərɪən] ADJ, N nigeriano(-a)
niggardly [ˈnɪɡədlɪ] ADJ (person) tirchio(-a), spilorcio(-a); (allowance, amount) misero(-a)
nigger [ˈnɪɡəʳ] N (col!) negro(-a)
niggle [ˈnɪɡl] VT assillare ▶ VI fare il pignolo(-a)
niggling [ˈnɪɡlɪŋ] ADJ pignolo(-a); (detail) insignificante; (doubt, pain) persistente
night [naɪt] N notte f; (evening) sera; **at ~** la notte; la sera; **by ~** di notte; **in the ~**, **during the ~** durante la notte; **the ~ before last** l'altro ieri notte; l'altro ieri sera
night-bird [ˈnaɪtbəːd] N uccello notturno; (fig) nottambulo(-a)

nightcap [ˈnaɪtkæp] N bicchierino prima di andare a letto
night club N locale m notturno
nightdress [ˈnaɪtdrɛs] N camicia da notte
nightfall [ˈnaɪtfɔːl] N crepuscolo
nightie [ˈnaɪtɪ] N camicia da notte
nightingale [ˈnaɪtɪŋɡeɪl] N usignolo
night life [ˈnaɪtlaɪf] N vita notturna
nightly [ˈnaɪtlɪ] ADJ di ogni notte or sera; (by night) notturno(-a) ▶ ADV ogni notte or sera
nightmare [ˈnaɪtmɛəʳ] N incubo
night porter N portiere m di notte
night safe N cassa continua
night school N scuola serale
nightshade [ˈnaɪtʃeɪd] N: **deadly ~** (Bot) belladonna
nightshift [ˈnaɪtʃɪft] N turno di notte
night-time [ˈnaɪttaɪm] N notte f
night watchman N (irreg) guardiano notturno
nihilism [ˈnaɪɪlɪzəm] N nichilismo
nil [nɪl] N nulla m; (BRIT Sport) zero
Nile [naɪl] N: **the ~** il Nilo
nimble [ˈnɪmbl] ADJ agile
nine [naɪn] NUM nove
9-11 N 11 settembre
nineteen [naɪnˈtiːn] NUM diciannove
nineteenth [naɪnˈtiːnθ] NUM diciannovesimo(-a)
ninetieth [ˈnaɪntɪɪθ] NUM novantesimo(-a)
ninety [ˈnaɪntɪ] NUM novanta
ninth [naɪnθ] NUM nono(-a)
nip [nɪp] VT pizzicare; (bite) mordere ▶ VI (BRIT col): **to ~ out/down/up** fare un salto fuori/giù/di sopra ▶ N (pinch) pizzico; (drink) goccio, bicchierino
nipple [ˈnɪpl] N (Anat) capezzolo
nippy [ˈnɪpɪ] ADJ (weather) pungente; (BRIT: car, person) svelto(-a)
nit [nɪt] N (of louse) lendine m; (col: idiot) cretino(-a), scemo(-a)
nit-pick [ˈnɪtpɪk] VI (col) cercare il pelo nell'uovo
nitrogen [ˈnaɪtrədʒən] N azoto
nitroglycerin, nitroglycerine [naɪtrəuˈɡlɪsəriːn] N nitroglicerina
nitty-gritty [ˈnɪtɪˈɡrɪtɪ] N (col): **to get down to the ~** venire al sodo
nitwit [ˈnɪtwɪt] N (col) scemo(-a)
NJ ABBR (US) = **New Jersey**
NLF N ABBR (= National Liberation Front) ≈ F.L.N. m
NLRB N ABBR (US: = National Labor Relations Board) organismo per la tutela dei lavoratori
NM, N. Mex. ABBR (US) = **New Mexico**

KEYWORD

no [nəu] ADV (opposite of "yes") no; **are you coming? — no (I'm not)** viene? — no (non

vengo); **would you like some more? — no
thank you** ne vuole ancora un po'? — no,
grazie; **I have no more wine** non ho più
vino
▶ ADJ *(not any)* nessuno(-a); **I have no money/
time/books** non ho soldi/tempo/libri; **no
student would have done it** nessuno
studente lo avrebbe fatto; **there is no
reason to believe ...** non c'è nessuna
ragione per credere ...; **"no parking"**
"divieto di sosta"; **"no smoking"** "vietato
fumare"; **"no entry"** "ingresso vietato";
"no dogs" "vietato l'accesso ai cani"
▶ N *(pl* **noes)** no *m inv*; **I won't take no for an
answer** non accetterò un rifiuto

no. ABBR *(= number)* n.
nobble ['nɔbl] VT *(BRIT col: bribe: person)*
comprare, corrompere; *(person to speak to,
criminal)* bloccare, beccare; *(Racing: horse, dog)*
drogare
Nobel prize [nəu'bɛl-] N premio Nobel
nobility [nəu'bɪlɪtɪ] N nobiltà
noble ['nəubl] ADJ, N nobile *m*
nobleman ['nəublmən] N *(irreg)* nobile *m*,
nobiluomo
nobly ['nəublɪ] ADV *(selflessly)* generosamente
nobody ['nəubədɪ] PRON nessuno
no-claims bonus ['nəukleɪmz-] N bonus
malus *m inv*
nocturnal [nɔk'tə:nl] ADJ notturno(-a)
nod [nɔd] VI accennare col capo, fare un
cenno; *(in agreement)* annuire con un cenno
del capo; *(sleep)* sonnecchiare ▶ VT: **to ~
one's head** fare di sì col capo ▶ N cenno;
they nodded their agreement
accennarono di sì (col capo)
▶ **nod off** VI assopirsi
no-fly zone [nəu'flaɪ-] N zona di
interdizione aerea
noise [nɔɪz] N rumore *m*; *(din, racket)* chiasso
noiseless ['nɔɪzlɪs] ADJ silenzioso(-a)
noisily ['nɔɪzɪlɪ] ADV rumorosamente
noisy ['nɔɪzɪ] ADJ *(street, car)* rumoroso(-a);
(person) chiassoso(-a)
nomad ['nəumæd] N nomade *mf*
nomadic [nəu'mædɪk] ADJ nomade
no man's land N terra di nessuno
nominal ['nɔmɪnl] ADJ nominale; *(rent)*
simbolico(-a)
nominate ['nɔmɪneɪt] VT *(propose)* proporre
come candidato; *(elect)* nominare
nomination [nɔmɪ'neɪʃən] N nomina;
candidatura
nominee [nɔmɪ'ni:] N persona nominata;
candidato(-a)
non... [nɔn] PREFIX non...
non-alcoholic ['nɔnælkə'hɔlɪk] ADJ
analcolico(-a)

non-breakable [nɔn'breɪkəbl] ADJ
infrangibile
nonce word ['nɔns-] N parola coniata per
l'occasione
nonchalant ['nɔnʃələnt] ADJ incurante,
indifferente
non-commissioned [nɔnkə'mɪʃnd] ADJ:
~ officer sottufficiale *m*
non-committal [nɔnkə'mɪtl] ADJ evasivo(-a)
nonconformist [nɔnkən'fɔ:mɪst] N
anticonformista *mf*; *(BRIT Rel)* dissidente *mf*
▶ ADJ anticonformista
non-contributory [nɔnkən'trɪbjutərɪ] ADJ:
~ pension scheme *or* *(US)* **plan** *sistema di
pensionamento con i contributi interamente a carico
del datore di lavoro*
non-cooperation ['nɔnkəuɔpə'reɪʃən] N non
cooperazione *f*, non collaborazione *f*
nondescript ['nɔndɪskrɪpt] ADJ qualunque
inv
none [nʌn] PRON *(not one thing)* niente; *(not one
person)* nessuno(-a); **~ of you** nessuno(-a) di
voi; **I have ~** non ne ho nemmeno uno; **I
have ~ left** non ne ho più; **~ at all** proprio
niente; *(not one)* nemmeno uno; **he's ~ the
worse for it** non ne ha risentito
nonentity [nɔ'nɛntɪtɪ] N persona
insignificante
non-essential [nɔnɪ'sɛnʃl] ADJ non
essenziale ▶ N: **non-essentials** superfluo,
cose *fpl* superflue
nonetheless ['nʌnðə'lɛs] ADV nondimeno
non-event [nɔnɪ'vɛnt] N delusione *f*
non-executive [nɔnɪg'zɛkjutɪv] ADJ:
~ director direttore *m* senza potere esecutivo
non-existent [nɔnɪg'zɪstənt] ADJ inesistente
non-fiction [nɔn'fɪkʃən] N saggistica
non-flammable [nɔn'flæməbl] ADJ
ininfiammabile
non-intervention ['nɔnɪntə'vɛnʃən] N non
intervento
no-no ['nəunəu] N: **it's a ~!** *(undesirable)* è
inaccettabile!; *(forbidden)* non si può fare!
non obst. ABBR *(notwithstanding: = non obstante)*
nonostante
no-nonsense [nəu'nɔnsəns] ADJ che va al
sodo
non-payment [nɔn'peɪmənt] N mancato
pagamento
nonplussed [nɔn'plʌst] ADJ sconcertato(-a)
non-profit-making [nɔn'prɔfɪtmeɪkɪŋ] ADJ
senza scopo di lucro
nonsense ['nɔnsəns] N sciocchezze *fpl*; **~!** che
sciocchezze!, che assurdità!; **it is ~ to say
that ...** è un'assurdità *or* non ha senso dire
che ...
nonsensical [nɔn'sɛnsɪkl] ADJ assurdo(-a),
ridicolo(-a)
non-shrink [nɔn'ʃrɪŋk] ADJ *(BRIT)* irrestringibile

non-skid [nɒn'skɪd] ADJ antisdrucciolo(-a)

non-smoker ['nɒn'sməukəʳ] N non fumatore(-trice)

non-smoking ADJ (person) che non fuma; (area, section) per non fumatori

non-starter [nɒn'stɑːtəʳ] N: **it's a ~** è fallito in partenza

non-stick ['nɒn'stɪk] ADJ antiaderente, antiadesivo(-a)

non-stop ['nɒn'stɒp] ADJ continuo(-a); (train, bus) direttissimo(-a) ▶ ADV senza sosta

non-taxable [nɒn'tæksəbl] ADJ: **~ income** reddito non imponibile

non-U [nɒn'juː] ADJ ABBR (BRIT col) = **non-upper class**

non-volatile [nɒn'vɒlətaɪl] ADJ: **~ memory** (Comput) memoria permanente

non-voting [nɒn'vəutɪŋ] ADJ: **~ shares** azioni fpl senza diritto di voto

non-white ['nɒn'waɪt] ADJ di colore ▶ N persona di colore

noodles ['nuːdlz] NPL taglierini mpl

nook [nuk] N: **nooks and crannies** angoli mpl

noon [nuːn] N mezzogiorno

no one ['nəuwʌn] PRON = **nobody**

noose [nuːs] N nodo scorsoio, cappio; (hangman's) cappio

nor [nɔːʳ] CONJ = **neither** ▶ ADV see **neither**

norm [nɔːm] N norma

normal ['nɔːml] ADJ normale ▶ N: **to return to ~** tornare alla normalità

normality [nɔː'mælɪtɪ] N normalità

normally ['nɔːməlɪ] ADV normalmente

Normandy ['nɔːməndɪ] N Normandia

north [nɔːθ] N nord m, settentrione m ▶ ADJ nord inv, del nord, settentrionale ▶ ADV verso nord

North Africa N Africa del Nord

North African ADJ, N nordafricano(-a)

North America N America del Nord

North American ADJ, N nordamericano(-a)

Northants [nɔː'θænts] ABBR (BRIT) = **Northamptonshire**

northbound ['nɔːθbaund] ADJ (traffic) diretto(-a) a nord; (carriageway) nord inv

north-east [nɔːθ'iːst] N nord-est m

northeastern ADJ nordorientale

northerly ['nɔːðəlɪ] ADJ (wind) del nord; (direction) verso nord

northern ['nɔːðən] ADJ del nord, settentrionale

Northern Ireland N Irlanda del Nord

North Korea N Corea del Nord

North Pole N: **the ~** il Polo Nord

North Sea N: **the ~** il mare del Nord

North Sea oil N petrolio del mare del Nord

northward ['nɔːθwəd], **northwards** ['nɔːθwədz] ADV verso nord

north-west [nɔːθ'wɛst] N nord-ovest m

northwestern ADJ nordoccidentale

Norway ['nɔːweɪ] N Norvegia

Norwegian [nɔː'wiːdʒən] ADJ norvegese ▶ N norvegese mf; (Ling) norvegese m

nos. ABBR (= numbers) nn.

nose [nəuz] N naso; (of animal) muso ▶ VI (also: **nose one's way**) avanzare cautamente; **to pay through the ~ (for sth)** (col) pagare (qc) un occhio della testa ▶ **nose about, nose around** VI aggirarsi

nosebleed ['nəuzbliːd] N emorragia nasale

nose-dive ['nəuzdaɪv] N picchiata

nose drops NPL gocce fpl per il naso

nosey ['nəuzɪ] ADJ curioso(-a)

nostalgia [nɒs'tældʒɪə] N nostalgia

nostalgic [nɒs'tældʒɪk] ADJ nostalgico(-a)

nostril ['nɒstrɪl] N narice f; (of horse) frogia

nosy ['nəuzɪ] ADJ = **nosey**

not [nɒt] ADV non; **~ at all** niente affatto; (after thanks) prego, s'immagini; **you must ~** or **mustn't do this** non deve fare questo; **it's too late, isn't it** or **is it ~?** è troppo tardi, vero?; **he is ~** or **isn't here** non è qui, non c'è; **I hope ~** spero di no; **~ that I don't like him** non che (lui) non mi piaccia; **~ yet/now** non ancora/ora

notable ['nəutbl] ADJ notevole

notably ['nəutəblɪ] ADV notevolmente; (in particular) in particolare

notary ['nəutərɪ] N (also: **notary public**) notaio

notation [nəu'teɪʃən] N notazione f

notch [nɒtʃ] N tacca; (in saw) dente m ▶ **notch up** VT (score, victory) marcare, segnare

note [nəut] N nota; (letter, banknote) biglietto ▶ VT prendere nota di; **to take ~ of** prendere nota di; **to take notes** prendere appunti; **to compare notes** (fig) scambiarsi le impressioni; **of ~** eminente, importante; **just a quick ~ to let you know ...** ti scrivo solo due righe per informarti ...

notebook ['nəutbuk] N taccuino; (for shorthand) bloc-notes m inv

note-case ['nəutkeɪs] N (BRIT) portafoglio

noted ['nəutɪd] ADJ celebre

notepad ['nəutpæd] N bloc-notes m inv, blocchetto

notepaper ['nəutpeɪpəʳ] N carta da lettere

noteworthy ['nəutwəːðɪ] ADJ degno(-a) di nota, importante

nothing ['nʌθɪŋ] N nulla m, niente m; (zero) zero; **he does ~** non fa niente; **~ new** niente di nuovo; **for ~** (free) per niente; **~ at all** proprio niente

notice ['nəutɪs] N avviso; (of leaving) preavviso; (BRIT: review: of play etc) critica, recensione f ▶ VT notare, accorgersi di; **to take ~ of** fare attenzione a; **to bring sth to**

sb's ~ far notare qc a qn; **to give sb ~ of sth**
avvisare qn di qc; **to hand in one's ~, give ~**
(employee) licenziarsi; **without ~** senza
preavviso; **at short ~** con un breve
preavviso; **until further ~** fino a nuovo
avviso; **advance ~** preavviso; **to escape** or
avoid ~ passare inosservato; **it has come
to my ~ that ...** sono venuto a sapere che ...
noticeable ['nəutɪsəbl] ADJ evidente
notice board N (BRIT) tabellone m per affissi
notification [nəutɪfɪ'keɪʃən] N annuncio;
notifica; denuncia
notify ['nəutɪfaɪ] VT: **to ~ sth to sb** notificare
qc a qn; **to ~ sb of sth** avvisare qn di qc;
(police) denunciare qc a qn
notion ['nəuʃən] N idea; (concept) nozione f
notions ['nəuʃənz] NPL (US: haberdashery)
merceria
notoriety [nəutə'raɪətɪ] N notorietà
notorious [nəu'tɔːrɪəs] ADJ famigerato(-a)
notoriously [nəu'tɔːrɪəslɪ] ADV
notoriamente
Notts [nɔts] ABBR (BRIT) = **Nottinghamshire**
notwithstanding [nɔtwɪθ'stændɪŋ] ADV
nondimeno ▶ PREP nonostante, malgrado
nougat ['nuːgaː] N torrone m
nought [nɔːt] N zero
noun [naun] N nome m, sostantivo
nourish ['nʌrɪʃ] VT nutrire
nourishing ['nʌrɪʃɪŋ] ADJ nutriente
nourishment ['nʌrɪʃmənt] N nutrimento
Nov. ABBR (= November) nov.
Nova Scotia ['nəuvə'skəuʃə] N Nuova Scozia
novel ['nɔvl] N romanzo ▶ ADJ nuovo(-a)
novelist ['nɔvəlɪst] N romanziere(-a)
novelty ['nɔvəltɪ] N novità f inv
November [nəu'vɛmbər] N novembre m;
see also **July**
novice ['nɔvɪs] N principiante mf; (Rel)
novizio(-a)
NOW [nau] N ABBR (US: = National Organization
for Women) ≈ U.D.I. f (= Unione Donne Italiane)
now [nau] ADV ora, adesso ▶ CONJ: **~ (that)**
adesso che, ora che; **right ~** subito; **by ~**
ormai; **just ~** proprio ora; **that's the
fashion just ~** è la moda del momento;
I saw her just ~ l'ho vista proprio adesso;
I'll read it just ~ lo leggo subito; **~ and
then, ~ and again** ogni tanto; **from ~ on**
da ora in poi; **in 3 days from ~** fra 3 giorni;
between ~ and Monday da qui a lunedì,
entro lunedì; **that's all for ~** per ora basta
nowadays ['nauədeɪz] ADV oggidì
nowhere ['nəuwɛər] ADV in nessun luogo,
da nessuna parte; **~ else** in nessun altro
posto
no-win situation [nəu'wɪn-] N: **to be in a ~**
aver perso in partenza
noxious ['nɔkʃəs] ADJ nocivo(-a)

nozzle ['nɔzl] N (of hose etc) boccaglio;
(of fire extinguisher) lancia
NP N ABBR = **notary public**
nr ABBR (BRIT) = **near**
NS ABBR (CANADA) = **Nova Scotia**
NSC N ABBR (US) = **National Security Council**
NSF N ABBR (US) = **National Science
Foundation**
NSPCC N ABBR (BRIT) = **National Society for
the Prevention of Cruelty to Children**
NSW ABBR (AUSTRALIA) = **New South Wales**
NT N ABBR (= New Testament) N.T. ▶ ABBR
(CANADA) = **Northwest Territories**
nth [ɛnθ] ADJ: **for the ~ time** (col) per
l'ennesima volta
nuance ['njuːɑːns] N sfumatura
nubile ['njuːbaɪl] ADJ nubile; (attractive)
giovane e desiderabile
nuclear ['njuːklɪər] ADJ nucleare; (warfare)
atomico(-a)
nuclear disarmament N disarmo nucleare
nuclear family N famiglia nucleare
nuclear-free zone ['njuːklɪə'friː-] N zona
denuclearizzata
nucleus ['njuːklɪəs] (pl **nuclei** ['njuːklɪaɪ]) N
nucleo
NUCPS N ABBR (BRIT) = **National Union of
Civil and Public Servants**
nude [njuːd] ADJ nudo(-a) ▶ N (Art) nudo;
in the ~ tutto(-a) nudo(-a)
nudge [nʌdʒ] VT dare una gomitata a
nudist ['njuːdɪst] N nudista mf
nudity ['njuːdɪtɪ] N nudità
nugget ['nʌgɪt] N pepita
nuisance ['njuːsns] N: **it's a ~** è una
seccatura; **he's a ~** dà fastidio; **what a ~!**
che seccatura!
NUJ N ABBR (BRIT: = National Union of Journalists)
sindacato nazionale dei giornalisti
nuke [njuːk] N (col) bomba atomica
null [nʌl] ADJ: **~ and void** nullo(-a)
nullify ['nʌlɪfaɪ] VT annullare
NUM N ABBR (BRIT: = National Union of
Mineworkers) sindacato nazionale dei dipendenti
delle miniere
numb [nʌm] ADJ intorpidito(-a) ▶ VT
intorpidire; **~ with** (fear, grief) paralizzato(-a)
da, impietrito(-a) da; **~ with cold**
intirizzito(-a) (dal freddo)
number ['nʌmbər] N numero ▶ VT numerare;
(include) contare; **a ~ of** un certo numero di;
to be numbered among venire
annoverato(-a) tra; **telephone ~** numero di
telefono; **wrong ~** (Tel) numero sbagliato;
the staff numbers 20 gli impiegati sono in
20; **they were 10 in ~** erano in tutto 10
numbered account ['nʌmbəd-] N (in bank)
conto numerato
number plate N (BRIT Aut) targa

n

Number Ten N (*BRIT*: = 10 *Downing Street*) *residenza del Primo Ministro del Regno Unito*

numbness ['nʌmnɪs] N intorpidimento; (*due to cold*) intirizzimento

numbskull ['nʌmskʌl] N (*col*) imbecille *mf*, idiota *mf*

numeral ['nju:mərəl] N numero, cifra

numerate ['nju:mərɪt] ADJ (*BRIT*): **to be ~** saper far di conto

numerical [nju:'mɛrɪkl] ADJ numerico(-a)

numerous ['nju:mərəs] ADJ numeroso(-a)

nun [nʌn] N suora, monaca

nunnery ['nʌnərɪ] N convento

nuptial ['nʌpʃəl] ADJ nuziale

nurse [nə:s] N infermiere(-a); (*also:* **nursemaid**) bambinaia ▶ VT (*patient, cold*) curare; (*baby: BRIT*) cullare; (: *US*) allattare, dare il latte a; (*hope*) nutrire

nursery ['nə:sərɪ] N (*room*) camera dei bambini; (*institution*) asilo; (*for plants*) vivaio

nursery rhyme N filastrocca

nursery school N scuola materna

nursery slope N (*BRIT Ski*) pista per principianti

nursing ['nə:sɪŋ] N (*profession*) professione *f* di infermiere (*or* di infermiera); (*care*) cura ▶ ADJ (*mother*) che allatta

nursing home N casa di cura

nurture ['nə:tʃə'] VT allevare; nutrire

NUS N ABBR (*BRIT*: = *National Union of Students*) *sindacato nazionale degli studenti*

NUT N ABBR (*BRIT*: = *National Union of Teachers*) *sindacato nazionale degli insegnanti*

nut [nʌt] N (*of metal*) dado; (*fruit*) noce *f* (*or* nocciola *or* mandorla *etc*) ▶ ADJ (*chocolate etc*) alla nocciola *etc*; **he's nuts** (*col*) è matto

nutcase ['nʌtkeɪs] N (*col*) mattarello(-a)

nutcrackers ['nʌtkrækəz] NPL schiaccianoci *m inv*

nutmeg ['nʌtmɛg] N noce *f* moscata

nutrient ['nju:trɪənt] ADJ nutriente ▶ N sostanza nutritiva

nutrition [nju:'trɪʃən] N nutrizione *f*

nutritionist [nju:'trɪʃənɪst] N nutrizionista *mf*

nutritious [nju:'trɪʃəs] ADJ nutriente

nutshell ['nʌtʃɛl] N guscio di noce; **in a ~** in poche parole

nutty ['nʌtɪ] ADJ di noce (*or* nocciola *or* mandorla *etc*); (*BRIT col*) tocco(-a), matto(-a)

nuzzle ['nʌzl] VI: **to ~ up to** strofinare il muso contro

NV ABBR (*US*) = **Nevada**

NVQ N ABBR *BRIT*: = **National Vocational Qualification**

NWT ABBR (*CANADA*) = **Northwest Territories**

NY ABBR (*US*) = **New York**

NYC ABBR (*US*) = **New York City**

nylon ['naɪlɔn] N nailon *m* ▶ ADJ di nailon; **nylons** NPL calze *fpl* di nailon

nymph [nɪmf] N ninfa

nymphomaniac [nɪmfəu'meɪnɪæk] ADJ, N ninfomane (*f*)

NYSE ABBR (*US*) = **New York Stock Exchange**

Oo

O, o [əu] N (*letter*) O, o *f inv or m inv*; (*US Scol:* = *outstanding*) ≈ ottimo; (*number: Tel etc*) zero; **O for Oliver**, (*US*) **O for Oboe** ≈ O come Otranto

oaf [əuf] N zoticone *m*

oak [əuk] N quercia ▶ CPD di quercia

OAP N ABBR (*BRIT*) = **old-age pensioner**

oar [ɔːʳ] N remo; **to put** *or* **shove one's ~ in** (*fig: col*) intromettersi

oarsman ['ɔːzmən], **oarswoman** ['ɔːzwumən] N (*irreg*) rematore(-trice)

OAS N ABBR (= *Organization of American States*) O.S.A. *f* (= *Organizzazione degli Stati Americani*)

oasis [əu'eɪsɪs] (*pl* **oases** [əu'eɪsiːz]) N oasi *f inv*

oath [əuθ] N giuramento; (*swear word*) bestemmia; **to take the ~** giurare; **on ~** (*BRIT*) *or* **under ~** sotto giuramento

oatmeal ['əutmiːl] N farina d'avena

oats [əuts] NPL avena

obdurate ['ɔbdjurɪt] ADJ testardo(-a); incallito(-a); ostinato(-a), irremovibile

OBE N ABBR (*BRIT*: = *Order of the British Empire*) titolo

obedience [ə'biːdɪəns] N ubbidienza; **in ~ to** conformemente a

obedient [ə'biːdɪənt] ADJ ubbidiente; **to be ~ to sb/sth** ubbidire a qn/qc

obelisk ['ɔbɪlɪsk] N obelisco

obese [əu'biːs] ADJ obeso(-a)

obesity [əu'biːsɪtɪ] N obesità

obey [ə'beɪ] VT ubbidire a; (*instructions, regulations*) osservare ▶ VI ubbidire

obituary [ə'bɪtjuərɪ] N necrologia

object N ['ɔbdʒɪkt] oggetto; (*purpose*) scopo, intento; (*Ling*) complemento oggetto ▶ VI [əb'dʒɛkt]: **to ~ to** (*attitude*) disapprovare; (*proposal*) protestare contro, sollevare delle obiezioni contro; **I ~!** mi oppongo!; **he objected that ...** obiettò che ...; **do you ~ to my smoking?** la disturba se fumo?; **what's the ~ of doing that?** a che serve farlo?; **expense is no ~** non si bada a spese

objection [əb'dʒɛkʃən] N obiezione *f*; (*drawback*) inconveniente *m*; **if you have no ~** se non ha obiezioni; **to make** *or* **raise an ~** sollevare un'obiezione

objectionable [əb'dʒɛkʃənəbl] ADJ antipatico(-a); (*smell*) sgradevole; (*language*) scostumato(-a)

objective [əb'dʒɛktɪv] N obiettivo ▶ ADJ obiettivo(-a)

objectivity [ɔbdʒɪk'tɪvɪtɪ] N obiettività

object lesson N: **~ (in)** dimostrazione *f* (di)

objector [əb'dʒɛktəʳ] N oppositore(-trice)

obligation [ɔblɪ'geɪʃən] N obbligo, dovere *m*; (*debt*) obbligo (di riconoscenza); **"without ~"** "senza impegno"; **to be under an ~ to sb/to do sth** essere in dovere verso qn/di fare qc

obligatory [ə'blɪgətərɪ] ADJ obbligatorio(-a)

oblige [ə'blaɪdʒ] VT (*do a favour*) fare una cortesia a; (*force*): **to ~ sb to do** costringere qn a fare; **to be obliged to sb for sth** essere grato a qn per qc; **anything to ~!** (*col*) questo e altro!

obliging [ə'blaɪdʒɪŋ] ADJ servizievole, compiacente

oblique [ə'bliːk] ADJ obliquo(-a); (*allusion*) indiretto(-a) ▶ N (*BRIT Typ*): **~ (stroke)** barra

obliterate [ə'blɪtəreɪt] VT cancellare

oblivion [ə'blɪvɪən] N oblio

oblivious [ə'blɪvɪəs] ADJ: **~ of** incurante di; inconscio(-a) di

oblong ['ɔblɔŋ] ADJ oblungo(-a) ▶ N rettangolo

obnoxious [əb'nɔkʃəs] ADJ odioso(-a); (*smell*) disgustoso(-a), ripugnante

oboe ['əubəu] N oboe *m*

obscene [əb'siːn] ADJ osceno(-a)

obscenity [əb'sɛnɪtɪ] N oscenità *f inv*

obscure [əb'skjuəʳ] ADJ oscuro(-a) ▶ VT oscurare; (*hide: sun*) nascondere

obscurity [əb'skjuərɪtɪ] N oscurità; (*obscure point*) punto oscuro; (*lack of fame*) anonimato

obsequious [əb'siːkwɪəs] ADJ ossequioso(-a)

observable [əb'zəːvəbl] ADJ osservabile; (*appreciable*) notevole

o

observance [əb'zə:vns] N osservanza;
  religious observances pratiche *fpl* religiose
observant [əb'zə:vnt] ADJ attento(-a)
observation [ɔbzə'veɪʃən] N osservazione *f*;
  (by police etc) sorveglianza
observation post N *(Mil)* osservatorio
observatory [əb'zə:vətrɪ] N osservatorio
observe [əb'zə:v] VT osservare; *(remark)* fare
  osservare
observer [əb'zə:və'] N osservatore(-trice)
obsess [əb'sɛs] VT ossessionare; **to be**
  obsessed by *or* **with sb/sth** essere
  ossessionato da qn/qc
obsession [əb'sɛʃən] N ossessione *f*
obsessive [əb'sɛsɪv] ADJ ossessivo(-a)
obsolescence [ɔbsə'lɛsns] N obsolescenza;
  built-in *or* **planned ~** *(Comm)* obsolescenza
  programmata
obsolescent [ɔbsə'lɛsnt] ADJ obsolescente
obsolete ['ɔbsəli:t] ADJ obsoleto(-a); *(word)*
  desueto(-a)
obstacle ['ɔbstəkl] N ostacolo
obstacle race N corsa agli ostacoli
obstetrician [ɔbstə'trɪʃən] N ostetrico(-a)
obstetrics [ɔb'stɛtrɪks] N ostetrica
obstinacy ['ɔbstɪnəsɪ] N ostinatezza
obstinate ['ɔbstɪnɪt] ADJ ostinato(-a)
obstreperous [əb'strɛpərəs] ADJ
  turbolento(-a)
obstruct [əb'strʌkt] VT *(block)* ostruire,
  ostacolare; *(halt)* fermare; *(hinder)* impedire
obstruction [əb'strʌkʃən] N ostruzione *f*;
  ostacolo
obstructive [əb'strʌktɪv] ADJ ostruttivo(-a);
  che crea impedimenti
obtain [əb'teɪn] VT ottenere ▶ VI essere in
  uso; **to ~ sth (for o.s.)** procurarsi qc
obtainable [əb'teɪnəbl] ADJ ottenibile
obtrusive [əb'tru:sɪv] ADJ *(person)*
  importuno(-a); *(smell)* invadente; *(building*
  etc) imponente e invadente
obtuse [əb'tju:s] ADJ ottuso(-a)
obverse ['ɔbvə:s] N opposto, inverso
obviate ['ɔbvɪeɪt] VT ovviare a, evitare
obvious ['ɔbvɪəs] ADJ ovvio(-a), evidente
obviously ['ɔbvɪəslɪ] ADV ovviamente; **~!**
  certo!; **~ not!** certo che no!; **he was ~ not**
  drunk si vedeva che non era ubriaco; **he**
  was not ~ drunk non si vedeva che era
  ubriaco
OCAS N ABBR = **Organization of Central**
  American States
occasion [ə'keɪʒən] N occasione *f*; *(event)*
  avvenimento ▶ VT cagionare; **on that ~** in
  quell'occasione, quella volta; **to rise to the**
  ~ mostrarsi all'altezza della situazione
occasional [ə'keɪʒənl] ADJ occasionale; **I**
  smoke an ~ cigarette ogni tanto fumo una
  sigaretta

occasionally [ə'keɪʒənəlɪ] ADV ogni tanto;
  very ~ molto raramente
occasional table N tavolino
occult [ɔ'kʌlt] ADJ occulto(-a) ▶ N: **the ~**
  l'occulto
occupancy ['ɔkjupənsɪ] N occupazione *f*
occupant ['ɔkjupənt] N occupante *mf*; *(of*
  boat, car etc) persona a bordo
occupation [ɔkju'peɪʃən] N occupazione *f*;
  (job) mestiere *m*, professione *f*; **unfit for ~**
  (house) inabitabile
occupational [ɔkju'peɪʃənl] ADJ *(disease)*
  professionale; *(hazard)* del mestiere;
  ~ accident infortunio sul lavoro
occupational guidance N *(BRIT)*
  orientamento professionale
occupational pension scheme N *sistema*
  pensionistico programmato dal datore di lavoro
occupational therapy N ergoterapia
occupier ['ɔkjupaɪə'] N occupante *mf*
occupy ['ɔkjupaɪ] VT occupare; **to ~ o.s. by**
  doing occuparsi a fare; **to be occupied with**
  sth/in doing sth essere preso da qc/
  occupato a fare qc
occur [ə'kə:'] VI accadere; *(difficulty,*
  opportunity) capitare; *(phenomenon, error)*
  trovarsi; **to ~ to sb** venire in mente a qn
occurrence [ə'kʌrəns] N caso, fatto; presenza
ocean ['əuʃən] N oceano; **oceans of** *(col)* un
  sacco di
ocean bed N fondale *m* oceanico
ocean-going ['əuʃəngəuɪŋ] ADJ d'alto mare
Oceania [əuʃɪ'ɑ:nɪə] N Oceania
ocean liner N transatlantico
ochre, *(US)* **ocher** ['əukə'] ADJ ocra *inv*
o'clock [ə'klɔk] ADV: **it is one ~** è l'una; **it is**
  5 ~ sono le 5
OCR N ABBR = **optical character reader;**
  optical character recognition
Oct. ABBR (= *October*) ott.
octagonal [ɔk'tægənl] ADJ ottagonale
octane ['ɔkteɪn] N ottano; **high-~ petrol** *or*
  (US) **gas** benzina ad alto numero di ottani
octave ['ɔktɪv] N ottava
October [ɔk'təubə'] N ottobre *m*; *see also* **July**
octogenarian [ɔktəudʒɪ'nɛərɪən] N
  ottuagenario(-a)
octopus ['ɔktəpəs] N polpo, piovra
odd [ɔd] ADJ *(strange)* strano(-a), bizzarro(-a);
  (number) dispari *inv*; *(left over)* in più; *(not of a*
  set) spaiato(-a); **60-~** 60 e oltre; **at ~ times** di
  tanto in tanto; **the ~ one out** l'eccezione *f*
oddball ['ɔdbɔ:l] N *(col)* eccentrico(-a)
oddity ['ɔdɪtɪ] N bizzarria; *(person)* originale
  mf
odd-job man [ɔd'dʒɔb-] N *(irreg)* tuttofare *m*
  inv
odd jobs NPL lavori *mpl* occasionali
oddly ['ɔdlɪ] ADV stranamente

oddments ['ɔdmənts] NPL (*Brit Comm*)
rimanenze *fpl*

odds [ɔdz] NPL (*in betting*) quota; **the ~ are
against his coming** c'è poca probabilità che
venga; **it makes no ~** non importa; **at ~** in
contesa; **to succeed against all the ~**
riuscire contro ogni aspettativa; **~ and ends**
avanzi *mpl*

odds-on [ɔdz'ɔn] ADJ (*col*) probabile;
~ favourite (*Racing*) favorito(-a)

ode [əud] N ode *f*

odious ['əudɪəs] ADJ odioso(-a), ripugnante

odometer [ɔ'dɔmɪtər] N odometro

odour, (*US*) **odor** ['əudər] N odore *m*;
(*unpleasant*) cattivo odore

odourless, (*US*) **odorless** ['əudəlɪs] ADJ
inodoro(-a)

OECD N ABBR (= *Organization for Economic
Cooperation and Development*) O.C.S.E. *f*
(= *Organizzazione per la Cooperazione e lo Sviluppo
Economico*)

oesophagus, (*US*) **esophagus** [iː'sɔfəgəs] N
esofago

oestrogen, (*US*) **estrogen** ['iːstrəudʒən] N
estrogeno

KEYWORD

of [ɔv, əv] PREP **1** (*gen*) di; **a boy of 10** un
ragazzo di 10 anni; **a friend of ours** un
nostro amico; **that was kind of you** è stato
molto gentile da parte sua

2 (*expressing quantity, amount, dates etc*) di; **a kilo
of flour** un chilo di farina; **how much of
this do you need?** quanto gliene serve?;
there were four of them (*people*) erano in
quattro; (*objects*) ce n'erano quattro; **three of
us went** tre di noi sono andati; **the 5th of
July** il 5 luglio; **a quarter of 4** (*US*) le 4 meno
un quarto

3 (*from, out of*) di, in; **made of wood** (*fatto*) di
or in legno

Ofcom ['ɔfkɔm] N ABBR (*Brit*: = *Office of
Communications*) *organismo di regolamentazione
delle telecomunicazioni*

KEYWORD

off [ɔf] ADV **1** (*distance: time*): **it's a long way
off** è lontano; **the game is 3 days off** la
partita è tra 3 giorni

2 (*departure, removal*) via; **to go off to Paris**
andarsene a Parigi; **I must be off** devo
andare via; **to take off one's coat** togliersi
il cappotto; **the button came off** il bottone
è venuto via *or* si è staccato; **10% off** con lo
sconto del 10%

3 (*not at work*): **to have a day off** avere un
giorno libero; **to be off sick** essere assente
per malattia

▶ ADJ (*engine*) spento(-a); (*tap*) chiuso(-a);
(*cancelled*) sospeso(-a); (*Brit*: *food*) andato(-a) a
male; **to be well/badly off** essere/non
essere benestante; **the lid was off** non c'era
il coperchio; **I'm afraid the chicken is off**
(*Brit*: *not available*) purtroppo il pollo è finito;
on the off chance nel caso; **to have an off
day** non essere in forma; **that's a bit off,
isn't it?** (*fig*: *col*) non è molto carino, vero?

▶ PREP **1** (*motion, removal etc*) da; (: *distant from*)
a poca distanza da; **a street off the square**
una strada che parte dalla piazza; **5km off
the road** a 5km dalla strada; **off the coast**
al largo della costa; **a house off the main
road** una casa che non è sulla strada
principale

2: **to be off meat** non mangiare più la carne

---

offal ['ɔfl] N (*Culin*) frattaglie *fpl*

offbeat ['ɔfbiːt] ADJ eccentrico(-a)

off-centre, (*US*) **off-center** [ɔf'sɛntər] ADJ
storto(-a), fuori centro

off-colour ['ɔf'kʌlər] ADJ (*Brit*: *ill*) malato(-a),
indisposto(-a); **to feel ~** sentirsi poco bene

offence, (*US*) **offense** [ə'fɛns] N (*Law*)
contravvenzione *f*; (: *more serious*) reato; **to
give ~ to** offendere; **to take ~ at** offendersi
per; **to commit an ~** commettere un reato

offend [ə'fɛnd] VT (*person*) offendere ▶ VI:
to ~ against (*law, rule*) trasgredire

offender [ə'fɛndər] N delinquente *mf*;
(*against regulations*) contravventore(-trice)

offending [ə'fɛndɪŋ] ADJ (*often humorous*): **the
~ word/object** la parola
incriminata/l'oggetto incriminato

offense [ə'fɛns] N (*US*) = **offence**

offensive [ə'fɛnsɪv] ADJ offensivo(-a); (*smell etc*)
sgradevole, ripugnante ▶ N (*Mil*) offensiva

offer ['ɔfər] N offerta, proposta ▶ VT offrire;
"on ~" (*Comm*) "in offerta speciale"; **to
make an ~ for sth** fare un'offerta per qc;
to ~ sth to sb, **~ sb sth** offrire qc a qn; **to ~
to do sth** offrirsi di fare qc

offering ['ɔfərɪŋ] N offerta

off-grid [ɔf'grɪd] ADJ *autonomo non allacciato
alla rete elettrica (o dell'acqua, del gas, ecc.)*

offhand [ɔf'hænd] ADJ disinvolto(-a),
noncurante ▶ ADV all'improvvo; **I can't tell
you ~** non posso dirglielo su due piedi

office ['ɔfɪs] N (*place*) ufficio; (*position*) carica;
doctor's ~ (*US*) ambulatorio; **to take ~**
entrare in carica; **through his good offices**
con il suo prezioso aiuto; **O~ of Fair Trading**
(*Brit*) *organismo di protezione contro le pratiche
commerciali abusive*

office automation N automazione *f*
d'ufficio, burotica

office bearer N (*of club etc*) membro
dell'amministrazione

o

office block, (US) **office building** N complesso di uffici

office boy N garzone m

office hours NPL orario d'ufficio; (US Med) orario di visite

office manager N capoufficio mf

officer ['ɔfɪsəʳ] N (Mil etc) ufficiale m; (of organization) funzionario; (also: **police officer**) agente m di polizia

office work N lavoro d'ufficio

office worker N impiegato(-a) d'ufficio

official [ə'fɪʃl] ADJ (authorized) ufficiale ▶ N ufficiale m; (civil servant) impiegato(-a) statale; funzionario

officialdom [ə'fɪʃəldəm] N burocrazia

officially [ə'fɪʃəlɪ] ADV ufficialmente

official receiver N curatore m fallimentare

officiate [ə'fɪʃɪeɪt] VI (Rel) ufficiare; **to ~ as Mayor** esplicare le funzioni di sindaco; **to ~ at a marriage** celebrare un matrimonio

officious [ə'fɪʃəs] ADJ invadente

offing ['ɔfɪŋ] N: **in the ~** (fig) in vista

off-key [ɔf'kiː] ADJ stonato(-a) ▶ ADV fuori tono

off-licence ['ɔflaɪsns] N (BRIT) spaccio di bevande alcoliche; vedi nota

> In Gran Bretagna e in Irlanda, gli off-licences sono esercizi pubblici specializzati nella vendita strettamente regolamentata di bevande alcoliche, per la quale è necessario avere un'apposita licenza. In genere sono aperti fino a tarda sera.

off-limits [ɔf'lɪmɪts] ADJ (esp US) in cui vige il divieto d'accesso

off-line ADJ, ADV (Comput) off-line inv, non in linea; (: switched off) spento(-a)

off-load ['ɔfləud] VT scaricare

off-peak ['ɔf'piːk] ADJ (ticket etc) a tariffa ridotta; (time) non di punta

off-putting ['ɔfputɪŋ] ADJ (BRIT) sgradevole

off-season ['ɔfsiːzn] ADJ, ADV fuori stagione

offset ['ɔfsɛt] VT (irreg: like **set**) (counteract) controbilanciare, compensare ▶ N (also: **offset printing**) offset m

offshoot ['ɔfʃuːt] N (fig) diramazione f

offshore [ɔf'ʃɔːʳ] ADJ (breeze) di terra; (island) vicino alla costa; (fishing) costiero(-a); **~ oilfield** giacimento petrolifero in mare aperto

offside [ɔf'saɪd] ADJ (Sport) fuori gioco; (Aut: with right-hand drive) destro(-a); (: with left-hand drive) sinistro(-a) ▶ N destra; sinistra

offspring ['ɔfsprɪŋ] N prole f, discendenza

offstage [ɔf'steɪdʒ] ADV dietro le quinte

off-the-cuff [ɔfðə'kʌf] ADV improvvisando

off-the-job ['ɔfðə'dʒɔb] ADJ: **~ training** addestramento fuori sede

off-the-peg ['ɔfðə'pɛg], (US) **off-the-rack** ['ɔfðə'ræk] ADV prêt-à-porter

off-the-record ['ɔfðə'rɛkɔːd] ADJ ufficioso(-a) ▶ ADV in via ufficiosa

off-white ['ɔfwaɪt] ADJ bianco sporco inv

Ofgem ['ɔfdʒɛm] N ABBR (BRIT: = Office of Gas and Electricity Markets) organo indipendente di controllo per la tutela dei consumatori

often ['ɔfn] ADV spesso; **how ~ do you go?** quanto spesso ci va?; **as ~ as not** quasi sempre

Ofwat ['ɔfwɔt] N ABBR (BRIT: = Office of Water Services) in Inghilterra e Galles, organo indipendente di controllo per la tutela dei consumatori

ogle ['əugl] VT occhieggiare

ogre ['əugəʳ] N orco

OH ABBR (US) = **Ohio**

oh [əu] EXCL oh!

OHMS ABBR (BRIT) = **On His Majesty's Service**; **On Her Majesty's Service**

oil [ɔɪl] N olio; (petroleum) petrolio; (for central heating) nafta ▶ VT (machine) lubrificare

oilcan ['ɔɪlkæn] N oliatore m a mano; (for storing) latta da olio

oil change N cambio dell'olio

oilfield ['ɔɪlfiːld] N giacimento, petrolifero

oil filter N (Aut) filtro dell'olio

oil-fired ['ɔɪlfaɪəd] ADJ a nafta

oil gauge N indicatore m del livello dell'olio

oil industry N industria del petrolio

oil level N livello dell'olio

oil painting N quadro a olio

oil refinery N raffineria di petrolio

oil rig N derrick m inv; (at sea) piattaforma per trivellazioni subacquee

oilskins ['ɔɪlskɪnz] NPL indumenti mpl di tela cerata

oil slick N chiazza d'olio

oil tanker N (ship) petroliera; (truck) autocisterna per petrolio

oil well N pozzo petrolifero

oily ['ɔɪlɪ] ADJ unto(-a), oleoso(-a); (food) grasso(-a)

ointment ['ɔɪntmənt] N unguento

OK ABBR (US) = **Oklahoma**

O.K., okay [əu'keɪ] EXCL d'accordo! ▶ VT approvare ▶ N: **to give sth one's O.K.** approvare qc ▶ ADJ non male inv; **is it O.K.?**, **are you O.K.?** tutto bene?; **it's O.K. with** or **by me** per me va bene; **are you O.K. for money?** sei a posto coi soldi?

Okla. ABBR (US) = **Oklahoma**

old [əuld] ADJ vecchio(-a); (ancient) antico(-a), vecchio(-a); (person) vecchio(-a), anziano(-a); **how ~ are you?** quanti anni ha?; **he's 10 years ~** ha 10 anni; **older brother/sister** fratello/sorella maggiore; **any ~ thing will do** va bene qualsiasi cosa

old age N vecchiaia

old-age pension ['əuldeɪdʒ-] N (BRIT) pensione f di vecchiaia

old-age pensioner ['əuldeɪdʒ-] N (BRIT) pensionato(-a)

old-fashioned ['əuld'fæʃnd] ADJ antiquato(-a), fuori moda; (person) all'antica

old maid N zitella

old people's home N ricovero per anziani

old-style ['əuldstaɪl] ADJ (di) vecchio stampo inv

old-time ['əuldtaɪm] ADJ di una volta

old-timer [əuld'taɪmə'] N veterano(-a)

old wives' tale N vecchia superstizione f

O levels NPL (BRIT formerly) diploma di istruzione secondaria conseguito a 16 anni in Inghilterra e Galles, ora sostituito dal GCSE

olive ['ɔlɪv] N (fruit) oliva; (tree) olivo ▶ ADJ (also: **olive-green**) verde oliva inv

olive oil N olio d'oliva

Olympic [əu'lɪmpɪk] ADJ olimpico(-a); **the ~ Games, the Olympics** i giochi olimpici, le Olimpiadi

OM N ABBR (BRIT: = Order of Merit) titolo

Oman [əu'mɑːn] N Oman m

OMB N ABBR (US: = Office of Management and Budget) servizio di consulenza al Presidente in materia di bilancio

omelet, omelette ['ɔmlɪt] N omelette f inv; **ham/cheese ~(te)** omelette al prosciutto/al formaggio

omen ['əumən] N presagio, augurio

OMG ABBR (col) nel linguaggio degli SMS, esprime sorpresa o entusiasmo

ominous ['ɔmɪnəs] ADJ minaccioso(-a); (event) di malaugurio

omission [əu'mɪʃən] N omissione f

omit [əu'mɪt] VT omettere; **to ~ to do sth** tralasciare or trascurare di fare qc

omnivorous [ɔm'nɪvərəs] ADJ onnivoro(-a)

ON ABBR (CANADA) = **Ontario**

KEYWORD

on [ɔn] PREP 1 (indicating position) su; **on the wall** sulla parete; **on the left** a or sulla sinistra; **I haven't any money on me** non ho soldi con me

2 (indicating means: method: condition etc): **on foot** a piedi; **on the train/plane** in treno/aereo; **on the telephone** al telefono; **on the radio/television** alla radio/televisione; **to be on drugs** drogarsi; **on holiday** in vacanza; **he's on £16,000 a year** guadagna 16.000 sterline all'anno; **this round's on me** questo giro lo offro io

3 (referring to time): **on Friday** venerdì; **on Fridays** il or di venerdì; **on June 20th** il 20 giugno; **on Friday, June 20th** venerdì, 20 giugno; **a week on Friday** venerdì a otto; **on his arrival** al suo arrivo; **on seeing this** vedendo ciò

4 (about, concerning) su, di; **information on**

train services informazioni sui collegamenti ferroviari; **a book on Goldoni/physics** un libro su Goldoni/di or sulla fisica

▶ ADV 1 (referring to dress: covering): **to have one's coat on** avere indosso il cappotto; **to put one's coat on** mettersi il cappotto; **what's she got on?** cosa indossa?; **she put her boots/gloves/hat on** si mise gli stivali/i guanti/il cappello; **screw the lid on tightly** avvita bene il coperchio

2 (further, continuously): **to walk on, go on** etc continuare, proseguire; **to read on** continuare a leggere; **on and off** ogni tanto; **from that day on** da quel giorno in poi; **it was well on in the evening** era sera inoltrata

▶ ADJ 1 (in operation: machine, TV, light) acceso(-a); (tap) aperto(-a); (brake) inserito(-a); **is the meeting still on?** (in progress) la riunione è ancora in corso?; (not cancelled) è confermato l'incontro?; **there's a good film on at the cinema** danno un buon film al cinema; **when is the film on?** quando c'è questo film?; **my father's always on at me to get a job** (col) mio padre mi tormenta sempre perché trovi un lavoro

2 (col): **that's not on!** (not acceptable) non si fa così!; (not possible) non se ne parla neanche!

O

once [wʌns] ADV una volta ▶ CONJ non appena, quando; **~ he had left/it was done** dopo che se n'era andato/fu fatto; **at ~** subito; (simultaneously) a un tempo; **all at ~** (tutto) ad un tratto; **~ a week** una volta alla settimana; **~ more** ancora una volta; **I knew him ~** un tempo or in passato lo conoscevo; **~ and for all** una volta per sempre; **~ upon a time there was …** c'era una volta …

oncoming ['ɔnkʌmɪŋ] ADJ (traffic) che viene in senso opposto

KEYWORD

one [wʌn] NUM uno(-a); **one hundred and fifty** centocinquanta; **one day** un giorno; **it's one (o'clock)** è l'una; **to be one up on sb** essere avvantaggiato(-a) rispetto a qn; **to be at one (with sb)** andare d'accordo (con qn)

▶ ADJ 1 (sole) unico(-a); **the one book which** l'unico libro che; **the one man who** l'unico che

2 (same) stesso(-a); **they came in the one car** sono venuti nella stessa macchina

▶ PRON 1: **this one** questo(-a); **that one** quello(-a); **which one do you want?** quale vuole?; **I've already got one/a red one** ne ho già uno/uno rosso; **one by one** uno per uno

2: **one another** l'un l'altro; **to look at one another** guardarsi; **to help one another** aiutarsi l'un l'altro *or* a vicenda
3 (*impersonal*) si; **one never knows** non si sa mai; **to cut one's finger** tagliarsi un dito; **to express one's opinion** esprimere la propria opinione; **one needs to eat** bisogna mangiare

one-armed bandit ['wʌnɑːmd-] N slot-machine *f inv*
one-day excursion ['wʌndeɪ-] N (US) biglietto giornaliero di andata e ritorno
One-hundred share index ['wʌnhʌndrəd-] N *indice borsistico del Financial Times*
one-man ['wʌn'mæn] ADJ (*business*) diretto(-a) *etc* da un solo uomo
one-man band N *suonatore ambulante con vari strumenti*
one-off [wʌn'ɔf] (BRIT col) N fatto eccezionale ▶ ADJ eccezionale
one-parent family ['wʌnpɛərənt-] N famiglia monogenitore
one-piece ['wʌnpiːs] ADJ (*bathing suit*) intero(-a)
onerous ['ɔnərəs] ADJ (*task, duty*) gravoso(-a); (*responsibility*) pesante
oneself [wʌn'sɛlf] PRON (*reflexive*) si; (*after prep*) sé, se stesso(-a); **to do sth (by) ~** fare qc da sé; **to hurt ~** farsi male; **to keep sth for ~** tenere qc per sé; **to talk to ~** parlare da solo
one-shot [wʌn'ʃɔt] N (US) = **one-off**
one-sided [wʌn'saɪdɪd] ADJ (*decision, view, argument*) unilaterale; (*judgement, account*) parziale; (*game, contest*) impari *inv*
one-time ['wʌntaɪm] ADJ ex *inv*
one-to-one ['wʌntəwʌn] ADJ (*relationship*) univoco(-a)
one-upmanship [wʌn'ʌpmənʃɪp] N: **the art of ~** l'arte *f* di primeggiare
one-way ['wʌnweɪ] ADJ (*street, traffic*) a senso unico
ongoing ['ɔŋgəuɪŋ] ADJ in corso; in attuazione
onion ['ʌnjən] N cipolla
on-line ['ɔnlaɪn] ADJ, ADV (*Comput*) on-line *inv*, in linea; (: *switched on*) acceso(-a)
onlooker ['ɔnlukə^r] N spettatore(-trice)
only ['əunlɪ] ADV solo, soltanto ▶ ADJ solo(-a), unico(-a) ▶ CONJ solo che, ma; **an ~ child** un figlio unico; **not ~** non solo; **I ~ took one** ne ho preso soltanto uno, non ne ho preso che uno; **I saw her ~ yesterday** l'ho vista appena ieri; **I'd be ~ too pleased to help** sarei proprio felice di essere d'aiuto; **I would come, ~ I'm very busy** verrei volentieri, solo che sono molto occupato
ono ABBR = **or nearest offer**; *see* **near**
on-screen [ɔn'skriːn] ADJ sullo schermo *inv*
onset ['ɔnsɛt] N inizio; (*of winter*) arrivo

onshore ['ɔnʃɔː^r] ADJ (*wind*) di mare
onslaught ['ɔnslɔːt] N attacco, assalto
Ont. ABBR (CANADA) = **Ontario**
on-the-job ['ɔnðə'dʒɔb] ADJ: **~ training** addestramento in sede
onto ['ɔntu] PREP su, sopra
onus ['əunəs] N onere *m*, peso; **the ~ is upon him to prove it** sta a lui dimostrarlo
onward ['ɔnwəd], **onwards** ['ɔnwədz] ADV (*move*) in avanti; **from this time ~(s)** d'ora in poi
onyx ['ɔnɪks] N onice *f*
oops [ups] EXCL ops! (*esprime rincrescimento per un piccolo contrattempo*); **~-a-daisy!** oplà!
ooze [uːz] VI stillare
opacity [əu'pæsɪtɪ] N opacità
opal ['əupl] N opale *m or f*
opaque [əu'peɪk] ADJ opaco(-a)
OPEC ['əupɛk] N ABBR (= *Organization of Petroleum-Exporting Countries*) O.P.E.C. *f*
open ['əupn] ADJ aperto(-a); (*road*) libero(-a); (*meeting*) pubblico(-a); (*admiration*) evidente, franco(-a); (*question*) insoluto(-a); (*enemy*) dichiarato(-a) ▶ VT aprire ▶ VI (*eyes, door, debate*) aprirsi; (*flower*) sbocciare; (*shop, bank, museum*) aprire; (*book etc: commence*) cominciare; **in the ~ (air)** all'aperto; **the ~ sea** il mare aperto, l'alto mare; **~ ground** (*among trees*) radura; (*waste ground*) terreno non edificato; **to have an ~ mind (on sth)** non avere ancora deciso (su qc); **is it ~ to the public?** è aperto al pubblico?; **what time do you ~?** a che ora aprite?
▶ **open on to** VT FUS (*room, door*) dare su
▶ **open out** VT aprire ▶ VI aprirsi
▶ **open up** VT aprire; (*blocked road*) sgombrare ▶ VI aprirsi; (*shop, business*) aprire
open-air [əupn'ɛə^r] ADJ all'aperto
open-and-shut ['əupnən'ʃʌt] ADJ: **~ case** caso indubbio
open day N (BRIT) giornata di apertura al pubblico
open-ended [əupn'ɛndɪd] ADJ (*fig*) aperto(-a), senza limiti
c⸺er ['əupnə^r] N (*also*: **can opener, tin opener**) apriscatole *m inv*
o⸺-heart [əupn'hɑːt] ADJ: **~ surgery** chirurgia a cuore aperto
opening ['əupnɪŋ] N apertura; (*opportunity*) occasione *f*, opportunità *f inv*; (*job*) posto vacante ▶ ADJ (*speech*) di apertura
opening hours NPL orario d'apertura
opening night N (*Theat*) prima
open learning N *sistema educativo secondo il quale lo studente ha maggior controllo e gestione delle modalità di apprendimento*
openly ['əupnlɪ] ADV apertamente
open-minded [əupn'maɪndɪd] ADJ che ha la mente aperta

open-necked ['əupnnɛk] ADJ col collo slacciato

openness ['əupnnɪs] N (*frankness*) franchezza, sincerità

open-plan ['əupn'plæn] ADJ senza pareti divisorie

open prison N *istituto di pena dove viene data maggiore libertà ai detenuti*

open sandwich N canapè *m inv*

open shop N *fabbrica o ditta dove sono accolti anche operai non iscritti ai sindacati*

Open University N (BRIT); *vedi nota*

La *Open University* (*OU*), fondata in Gran Bretagna nel 1969, organizza corsi universitari per corrispondenza o via Internet, basati anche su lezioni che vengono trasmesse dalla BBC per radio e per televisione e su corsi estivi.

opera ['ɔpərə] N opera

opera glasses NPL binocolo da teatro

opera house N opera

opera singer N cantante *mf* d'opera *or* lirico(-a)

operate ['ɔpəreɪt] VT (*machine*) azionare, far funzionare; (*system*) usare ▶ VI funzionare; (*drug, person*) agire; **to ~ on sb (for)** (*Med*) operare qn (di)

operatic [ɔpə'rætɪk] ADJ dell'opera, lirico(-a)

operating ['ɔpəreɪtɪŋ] ADJ (*Comm: costs etc*) di gestione; (*Med*) operatorio(-a)

operating room N (*US*) = **operating theatre**

operating system N (*Comput*) sistema *m* operativo

operating theatre N (*Med*) sala operatoria

operation [ɔpə'reɪʃən] N operazione *f*; **to be in ~** (*machine*) essere in azione *or* funzionamento; (*system*) essere in vigore; **to have an ~ (for)** (*Med*) essere operato(-a) (di)

operational [ɔpə'reɪʃənl] ADJ operativo(-a); (*Comm*) di gestione, d'esercizio; (*ready for use or action*) in attività, in funzione; **when the service is fully ~** quando il servizio sarà completamente in funzione

operative ['ɔpərətɪv] ADJ (*measure*) operativo(-a) ▶ N (*in factory*) operaio(-a); **the ~ word** la parola chiave

operator ['ɔpəreɪtər] N (*of machine*) operatore(-trice); (*Tel*) centralinista *mf*

operetta [ɔpə'rɛtə] N operetta

ophthalmologist [ɔfθæl'mɔlədʒɪst] N oftalmologo(-a)

opinion [ə'pɪnjən] N opinione *f*, parere *m*; **in my ~** secondo me, a mio avviso; **to seek a second ~** (*Med etc*) consultarsi con un altro medico *etc*

opinionated [ə'pɪnjəneɪtɪd] ADJ dogmatico(-a)

opinion poll N sondaggio di opinioni

opium ['əupɪəm] N oppio

opponent [ə'pəunənt] N avversario(-a)

opportune ['ɔpətju:n] ADJ opportuno(-a)

opportunist [ɔpə'tju:nɪst] N opportunista *mf*

opportunity [ɔpə'tju:nɪtɪ] N opportunità *f inv*, occasione *f*; **to take the ~ to do** *or* **of doing** cogliere l'occasione per fare

oppose [ə'pəuz] VT opporsi a; **opposed to** contrario(-a) a; **as opposed to** in contrasto con

opposing [ə'pəuzɪŋ] ADJ opposto(-a); (*team*) avversario(-a)

opposite ['ɔpəzɪt] ADJ opposto(-a); (*house etc*) di fronte ▶ ADV di fronte, dirimpetto ▶ PREP di fronte a ▶ N opposto, contrario; (*of word*) contrario; **"see ~ page"** "vedere pagina a fronte"; **the ~ sex** l'altro sesso

opposite number N controparte *f*, corrispondente *mf*

opposite sex N: **the ~** l'altro sesso

opposition [ɔpə'zɪʃən] N opposizione *f*

oppress [ə'prɛs] VT opprimere

oppression [ə'prɛʃən] N oppressione *f*

oppressive [ə'prɛsɪv] ADJ oppressivo(-a)

opprobrium [ə'prəubrɪəm] N (*formal*) obbrobrio

opt [ɔpt] VI: **to ~ for** optare per; **to ~ to do** scegliere di fare

▶ **opt out** VI: **to ~ out of** ritirarsi da; (*of NHS*) scegliere di non far più parte di; (*of agreement, arrangement*) scegliere di non partecipare a

optical ['ɔptɪkl] ADJ ottico(-a)

optical character reader N lettore *m* ottico

optical character recognition N lettura ottica di caratteri

optical fibre N fibra ottica

optician [ɔp'tɪʃən] N ottico

optics ['ɔptɪks] N ottica

optimism ['ɔptɪmɪzəm] N ottimismo

optimist ['ɔptɪmɪst] N ottimista *mf*

optimistic [ɔptɪ'mɪstɪk] ADJ ottimistico(-a)

optimum ['ɔptɪməm] ADJ ottimale

option ['ɔpʃən] N scelta; (*Scol*) materia facoltativa; (*Comm*) opzione *f*; **to keep one's options open** (*fig*) non impegnarsi; **I have no ~** non ho scelta

optional ['ɔpʃənl] ADJ facoltativo(-a); (*Comm*) a scelta; **~ extra** optional *m inv*

opulence ['ɔpjuləns] N opulenza

opulent ['ɔpjulənt] ADJ opulento(-a)

OR ABBR (*US*) = **Oregon**

or [ɔ:r] CONJ o, oppure; (*with negative*): **he hasn't seen or heard anything** non ha visto né sentito niente; **or else** se no, altrimenti; oppure

oracle ['ɔrəkl] N oracolo

oral ['ɔ:rəl] ADJ orale ▶ N esame *m* orale

orange ['ɔrɪndʒ] N (*fruit*) arancia ▶ ADJ arancione

orangeade [ɔrɪndʒ'eɪd] N aranciata

orange juice N succo d'arancia

orange squash N succo d'arancia (*da diluire con l'acqua*)

oration [ɔːˈreɪʃən] N orazione *f*

orator [ˈɔrətəʳ] N oratore(-trice)

oratorio [ɔrəˈtɔːrɪəu] N oratorio

orb [ɔːb] N orbe *m*

orbit [ˈɔːbɪt] N orbita ▶ VT orbitare intorno a; **to be in/go into ~ (round)** essere/entrare in orbita (attorno a)

orbital [ˈɔːbɪtl] N (*also:* **orbital motorway**) raccordo anulare

orchard [ˈɔːtʃəd] N frutteto; **apple ~** meleto

orchestra [ˈɔːkɪstrə] N orchestra; (US: *seating*) platea

orchestral [ɔːˈkɛstrəl] ADJ orchestrale; (*concert*) sinfonico(-a)

orchestrate [ˈɔːkɪstreɪt] VT (*Mus: fig*) orchestrare

orchid [ˈɔːkɪd] N orchidea

ordain [ɔːˈdeɪn] VT (*Rel*) ordinare; (*decide*) decretare

ordeal [ɔːˈdiːl] N prova, travaglio

order [ˈɔːdəʳ] N ordine *m*; (*Comm*) ordinazione *f* ▶ VT ordinare; **to ~ sb to do** ordinare a qn di fare; **in ~** in ordine; (*document*) in regola; **in ~ of size** in ordine di grandezza; **in ~ to do** per fare; **in ~ that** affinché + *sub*; **a machine in working ~** una macchina che funziona bene; **out of ~** non in ordine; **to be out of ~** (*machine, toilets*) essere guasto(-a); (*telephone*) essere fuori servizio; **to place an ~ for sth with sb** ordinare qc a qn; **to the ~ of** (*Banking*) all'ordine di; **to be under orders to do sth** avere l'ordine di fare qc; **a point of ~** una questione di procedura; **to be on ~** essere stato ordinato; **made to ~** fatto su commissione; **the lower orders** (*pej*) i ceti inferiori

order book N copiacommissioni *m inv*

order form N modulo d'ordinazione

orderly [ˈɔːdəlɪ] N (*Mil*) attendente *m*; (*Med*) inserviente *m* ▶ ADJ (*room*) in ordine; (*mind*) metodico(-a); (*person*) ordinato(-a), metodico(-a)

order number N numero di ordinazione

ordinal [ˈɔːdɪnl] ADJ (*number*) ordinale

ordinary [ˈɔːdnrɪ] ADJ normale, comune; (*pej*) mediocre ▶ N: **out of the ~** diverso dal solito, fuori dell'ordinario

ordinary degree N laurea; *vedi nota*

> Il corso universitario di studi che porta al conferimento del *Bachelor's degree* può avere una durata diversa, a seconda del profitto dello studente. Chi non è interessato a proseguire gli studi oltre tre anni di corso può optare per l' *ordinary degree*; *vedi anche* **honours degree**.

ordinary seaman N (*irreg*) (BRIT) marinaio semplice

ordinary shares NPL azioni *fpl* ordinarie

ordination [ɔːdɪˈneɪʃən] N ordinazione *f*

ordnance [ˈɔːdnəns] N (*Mil: unit*) (reparto di) sussistenza

Ordnance Survey map N (BRIT) ≈ carta topografica dell'IGM

ore [ɔːʳ] N minerale *m* grezzo

Ore., Oreg. ABBR (US) = **Oregon**

oregano [ɔrɪˈɡɑːnəu] N origano

organ [ˈɔːɡən] N organo

organic [ɔːˈɡænɪk] ADJ organico(-a); (*food, produce*) biologico(-a)

organism [ˈɔːɡənɪzəm] N organismo

organist [ˈɔːɡənɪst] N organista *mf*

organization [ɔːɡənaɪˈzeɪʃən] N organizzazione *f*

organization chart N organigramma *m*

organize [ˈɔːɡənaɪz] VT organizzare; **to get organized** organizzarsi

organized [ˈɔːɡənaɪzd] ADJ organizzato(-a)

organized crime [ˈɔːɡənaɪzd-] N criminalità organizzata

organized labour [ˈɔːɡənaɪzd-] N manodopera organizzata

organizer [ˈɔːɡənaɪzəʳ] N organizzatore(-trice)

orgasm [ˈɔːɡæzəm] N orgasmo

orgy [ˈɔːdʒɪ] N orgia

Orient [ˈɔːrɪənt] N: **the ~** l'Oriente *m*

oriental [ɔːrɪˈɛntl] ADJ, N orientale (*mf*)

orientate [ˈɔːrɪənteɪt] VT orientare

orientation [ɔːrɪɛnˈteɪʃən] N orientamento

orifice [ˈɔrɪfɪs] N orifizio

origin [ˈɔrɪdʒɪn] N origine *f*; **country of ~** paese *m* d'origine

original [əˈrɪdʒɪnl] ADJ originale; (*earliest*) originario(-a) ▶ N originale *m*

originality [ərɪdʒɪˈnælɪtɪ] N originalità

originally [əˈrɪdʒɪnəlɪ] ADV (*at first*) all'inizio

originate [əˈrɪdʒɪneɪt] VI: **to ~ from** venire da, essere originario(-a) di; (*suggestion*) provenire da; **to ~ in** nascere in; (*custom*) avere origine in

originator [əˈrɪdʒɪneɪtəʳ] N iniziatore(-trice)

Orkneys [ˈɔːknɪz] NPL: **the ~** (*also:* **the Orkney Islands**) le (isole) Orcadi

ornament [ˈɔːnəmənt] N ornamento; (*trinket*) ninnolo

ornamental [ɔːnəˈmɛntl] ADJ ornamentale

ornamentation [ɔːnəmɛnˈteɪʃən] N decorazione *f*, ornamento

ornate [ɔːˈneɪt] ADJ molto ornato(-a)

ornithologist [ɔːnɪˈθɔlədʒɪst] N ornitologo(-a)

ornithology [ɔːnɪˈθɔlədʒɪ] N ornitologia

orphan [ˈɔːfn] N orfano(-a) ▶ VT: **to be orphaned** diventare orfano

orphanage [ˈɔːfənɪdʒ] N orfanotrofio

orthodox [ˈɔːθədɔks] ADJ ortodosso(-a)

orthopaedic, (*US*) **orthopedic** [ɔ:θə'pi:dɪk] ADJ ortopedico(-a)

OS ABBR (*BRIT*: = *Ordnance Survey*) ≈ IGM *m* = **Istituto Geografico Militare**; (*Naut*) = **ordinary seaman**; (*Dress*) = **outsize**

O.S. ABBR = **out of stock**

Oscar ['ɔskəʳ] N Oscar *m inv*

oscillate ['ɔsɪleɪt] VI oscillare

OSHA N ABBR (*US*: = *Occupational Safety and Health Administration*) amministrazione per la sicurezza e la salute sul lavoro

Oslo ['ɔzləu] N Oslo *f*

ostensible [ɔs'tɛnsɪbl] ADJ preteso(-a); apparente

ostensibly [ɔs'tɛnsɪblɪ] ADV all'apparenza

ostentation [ɔstɛn'teɪʃən] N ostentazione *f*

ostentatious [ɔstɛn'teɪʃəs] ADJ pretenzioso(-a); ostentato(-a)

osteopath ['ɔstɪəpæθ] N specialista *mf* di osteopatia

ostracize ['ɔstrəsaɪz] VT dare l'ostracismo a

ostrich ['ɔstrɪtʃ] N struzzo

OT ABBR (= *Old Testament*) V.T.

OTB N ABBR (*US*: = *off-track betting*) puntate effettuate fuori dagli ippodromi

OTE ABBR (= *on-target earnings*) stipendio compreso le commissioni

other ['ʌðəʳ] ADJ altro(-a) ▶ PRON: **the ~** l'altro(-a); **the others** gli altri; **the ~ day** l'altro giorno; **some ~ people have still to arrive** (alcuni) altri devono ancora arrivare; **some actor or ~** un certo attore; **somebody or ~** qualcuno; **~ than** altro che; a parte; **the car was none ~ than Roberta's** la macchina era proprio di Roberta

otherwise ['ʌðəwaɪz] ADV, CONJ altrimenti; **an ~ good piece of work** un lavoro comunque buono

OTT ABBR (*col*) = **over the top**; *see* **top**

otter ['ɔtəʳ] N lontra

OU N ABBR (*BRIT*) = **Open University**

ouch [autʃ] EXCL ohi!, ahi!

ought [ɔ:t] AUX VB: **I ~ to do it** dovrei farlo; **this ~ to have been corrected** questo avrebbe dovuto essere corretto; **he ~ to win** dovrebbe vincere; **you ~ to go and see it** dovreste andare a vederlo, fareste bene ad andarlo a vedere

ounce [auns] N oncia (= *28.35 g; 16 in a pound*)

our [auəʳ] ADJ il nostro(-a); (*pl*) i nostri(-e)

ours [auəz] PRON il nostro(-a); (*pl*) i nostri(-e); *see also* **mine¹**

ourselves [auə'sɛlvz] PL PRON (*reflexive*) ci; (*after preposition*) noi; (*emphatic*) noi stessi(-e); **we did it (all) by ~** l'abbiamo fatto (tutto) da soli; *see also* **oneself**

oust [aust] VT cacciare, espellere

out [aut] ADV (*gen*) fuori; **out here/there** qui/là fuori; **to speak out loud** parlare forte; **to have a night out** uscire una sera; **to be out and about** or (*US*) **around again** essere di nuovo in piedi; **the boat was 10 km out** la barca era a 10 km dalla costa; **the journey out** l'andata; **3 days out from Plymouth** a 3 giorni da Plymouth

▶ ADJ: **to be out** (*gen*) essere fuori; (*unconscious*) aver perso i sensi; (*style, singer*) essere fuori moda; **before the week was out** prima che la settimana fosse finita; **to be out to do sth** avere intenzione di fare qc; **he's out for all he can get** sta cercando di trarne il massimo profitto; **to be out in one's calculations** aver sbagliato i calcoli

▶ PREP: **out of** (*outside, beyond*) fuori di; (*because of*) per; (*origin*) da; (*without*) senza; **out of 10** (*from among*) su 10; **to go out of the house** uscire di casa; **to look out of the window** guardare fuori dalla finestra; **out of pity** per pietà; **out of boredom** per noia; **made out of wood** (fatto) di or in legno; **to drink out of a cup** bere da una tazza; **out of petrol** senza benzina; **it's out of stock** (*Comm*) è esaurito

outage ['autɪdʒ] N (*esp US: power failure*) interruzione *f* or mancanza di corrente elettrica

out-and-out ['autəndaut] ADJ vero(-a) e proprio(-a)

outback ['autbæk] N zona isolata; (*in Australia*) interno, entroterra

outbid [aut'bɪd] (*pt, pp* **~**) VT fare un'offerta più alta di

outboard ['autbɔ:d] N: **~ (motor)** (motore *m*) fuoribordo

outbound ['autbaund] ADJ: **~ (for** or **from)** in partenza (per or da)

outbox ['autbɔks] N (*Comput*) posta in uscita; (*US: out-tray*) vaschetta della corrispondenza in uscita

outbreak ['autbreɪk] N scoppio; epidemia

outbuilding ['autbɪldɪŋ] N dipendenza

outburst ['autbə:st] N scoppio

outcast ['autkɑ:st] N esule *mf*; (*socially*) paria *m inv*

outclass [aut'klɑ:s] VT surclassare

outcome ['autkʌm] N esito, risultato

outcrop ['autkrɔp] N affioramento

outcry ['autkraɪ] N protesta, clamore *m*

outdated [aut'deɪtɪd] ADJ (*custom, clothes*) fuori moda; (*idea*) sorpassato(-a)

outdistance [aut'dɪstəns] VT distanziare

outdo [aut'du:] VT (*irreg: like* **do**) sorpassare

outdoor [aut'dɔ:ʳ] ADJ all'aperto

outdoors [aut'dɔ:z] ADV fuori; all'aria aperta

outer ['autə^r] ADJ esteriore; **~ suburbs** estrema periferia

outer space N spazio cosmico

outfit ['autfɪt] N equipaggiamento; (clothes) completo; (: for sport) tenuta; (col: organization) organizzazione f

outfitter ['autfɪtə^r] N (BRIT): **"(gent's) outfitters"** "confezioni da uomo"

outgoing ['autɡəuɪŋ] ADJ (president, tenant) uscente; (means of transport) in partenza; (character) socievole

outgoings ['autɡəuɪŋz] NPL (BRIT: expenses) spese fpl, uscite fpl

outgrow [aut'ɡrəu] VT (irreg: like **grow**) (clothes) diventare troppo grande per

outhouse ['authaus] N costruzione f annessa

outing ['autɪŋ] N gita; escursione f

outlandish [aut'lændɪʃ] ADJ strano(-a)

outlast [aut'lɑːst] VT sopravvivere a

outlaw ['autlɔː] N fuorilegge mf ▶ VT (person) mettere fuori della legge; (practice) bandire

outlay ['autleɪ] N spese fpl; (investment) sborsa, spesa

outlet ['autlɛt] N (for liquid etc) sbocco, scarico; (for emotion) sfogo; (for goods) sbocco, mercato; (also: **retail outlet**) punto di vendita; (: US Elec) presa di corrente

outline ['autlaɪn] N contorno, profilo; (summary) abbozzo, grandi linee fpl ▶ VT (fig) descrivere a grandi linee

outlive [aut'lɪv] VT sopravvivere a

outlook ['autluk] N prospettiva, vista

outlying ['autlaɪɪŋ] ADJ periferico(-a)

outmanoeuvre, (US) **outmaneuver** [autmə'nuːvə^r] VT (rival etc) superare in strategia

outmoded [aut'məudɪd] ADJ passato(-a) di moda; antiquato(-a)

outnumber [aut'nʌmbə^r] VT superare in numero

out-of-court [autə'kɔːt] ADJ extragiudiziale ▶ ADV (settle) senza ricorrere al tribunale

out-of-date [autəv'deɪt] ADJ (passport, ticket) scaduto(-a); (theory, idea) sorpassato(-a), superato(-a); (custom) antiquato(-a); (clothes) fuori moda inv

out-of-doors [autəv'dɔːz] ADV all'aperto

out-of-the-way ['autəvðə'weɪ] ADJ (remote) fuori mano; (unusual) originale, insolito(-a)

out-of-town [autə'taun] ADJ (shopping centre etc) inv uori città

outpatient ['autpeɪʃənt] N paziente mf esterno(-a)

outpost ['autpəust] N avamposto

outpouring ['autpɔːrɪŋ] N (fig) torrente m

output ['autput] N produzione f; (Comput) output m inv ▶ VT emettere

outrage ['autreɪdʒ] N oltraggio; scandalo ▶ VT oltraggiare

outrageous [aut'reɪdʒəs] ADJ oltraggioso(-a); scandaloso(-a)

outrider ['autraɪdə^r] N (on motorcycle) battistrada m inv

outright ADV [aut'raɪt] completamente; schiettamente; apertamente; sul colpo ▶ ADJ ['autraɪt] completo(-a); schietto(-a) e netto(-a)

outrun [aut'rʌn] VT (irreg: like **run**) superare (nella corsa)

outset ['autsɛt] N inizio

outshine [aut'ʃaɪn] VT (irreg: like **shine**) (fig) eclissare

outside [aut'saɪd] N esterno, esteriore m ▶ ADJ esterno(-a), esteriore; (remote, unlikely): **an ~ chance** una vaga possibilità ▶ ADV fuori, all'esterno ▶ PREP fuori di, all'esterno di; **at the ~** (fig) al massimo; **~ left/right** n (Football) ala sinistra/destra

outside broadcast N (Radio, TV) trasmissione f in esterno

outside lane N (Aut) corsia di sorpasso

outside line N (Tel) linea esterna

outsider [aut'saɪdə^r] N (in race etc) outsider m inv; (stranger) straniero(-a)

outsize ['autsaɪz] ADJ enorme; (clothes) per taglie forti

outskirts ['autskəːts] NPL sobborghi mpl

outsmart [aut'smɑːt] VT superare in astuzia

outspoken [aut'spəukən] ADJ molto franco(-a)

outspread ['autsprɛd] ADJ (wings) aperto(-a), spiegato(-a)

outstanding [aut'stændɪŋ] ADJ eccezionale, di rilievo; (unfinished) non completo(-a); non evaso(-a); non regolato(-a); **your account is still ~** deve ancora saldare il conto

outstay [aut'steɪ] VT: **to ~ one's welcome** diventare un ospite sgradito

outstretched [aut'strɛtʃt] ADJ (hand) teso(-a); (body) disteso(-a)

outstrip [aut'strɪp] VT (also fig) superare

out-tray ['auttreɪ] N raccoglitore m per le carte da spedire

outvote [aut'vəut] VT: **to ~ sb (by)** avere la maggioranza rispetto a qn (per); **to ~ sth (by)** respingere qc (per)

outward ['autwəd] ADJ (sign, appearances) esteriore; (journey) d'andata

outwardly ['autwədlɪ] ADV esteriormente; in apparenza

outwards ['autwədz] ADV (esp BRIT) = **outward**

outweigh [aut'weɪ] VT avere maggior peso di

outwit [aut'wɪt] VT superare in astuzia

oval ['əuvl] ADJ, N ovale (m)

Oval Office N (US); vedi nota

L' Oval Office è una grande stanza di forma ovale nella White House, la Casa Bianca, dove ha sede l'ufficio del Presidente degli Stati Uniti. Spesso il termine è usato per indicare la stessa presidenza degli Stati Uniti.

ovarian [əu'vɛərɪən] ADJ ovarico(-a)
ovary ['əuvərɪ] N ovaia
ovation [əu'veɪʃən] N ovazione f
oven ['ʌvn] N forno
oven glove N guanto da forno
ovenproof ['ʌvnpru:f] da forno
oven-ready ['ʌvnrɛdɪ] ADJ pronto(-a) da
  infornare
ovenware ['ʌvnwɛəʳ] N vasellame m da
  mettere in forno
over ['əuvəʳ] ADV al di sopra; (excessively)
  molto, troppo ▸ ADJ, ADV (finished) finito(-a),
  terminato(-a); (too much) troppo; (remaining)
  che avanza ▸ PREP su; sopra; (above) al di
  sopra di; (on the other side of) di là di; (more
  than) più di; (during) durante; **~ here** qui;
  ~ there là; **all ~** (everywhere) dappertutto;
  (finished) tutto(-a) finito(-a); **~ and ~ (again)**
  più e più volte; **~ and above** oltre (a); **to ask
  ~** invitare qn (a passare); **now ~ to our
  Rome correspondent** diamo ora la linea al
  nostro corrispondente da Roma; **the world
  ~** in tutto il mondo; **she's not ~ intelligent**
  (BRIT) non è troppo intelligente; **they fell
  out ~ money** litigarono per una questione
  di denaro
over... ['əuvəʳ] PREFIX: **overabundant**
  sovrabbondante
overact [əuvər'ækt] VI (Theat) esagerare or
  strafare la propria parte
overall ADJ ['əuvərɔ:l] totale ▸ N ['əuvərɔ:l]
  (BRIT) grembiule m ▸ ADV [əuvər'ɔ:l]
  nell'insieme, complessivamente; **overalls**
  NPL tuta (da lavoro)
overall majority N maggioranza assoluta
overanxious [əuvər'æŋkʃəs] ADJ troppo
  ansioso(-a)
overawe [əuvər'ɔ:] VT intimidire
overbalance [əuvə'bæləns] VI perdere
  l'equilibrio
overbearing [əuvə'bɛərɪŋ] ADJ imperioso(-a),
  prepotente
overboard ['əuvəbɔ:d] ADV (Naut) fuori bordo,
  in acqua; **to go ~ for sth** (fig) impazzire per qc
overbook [əuvə'buk] VT sovrapprenotare
overcame [əuvə'keɪm] PT of **overcome**
overcapitalize [əuvə'kæpɪtəlaɪz] VT
  sovraccapitalizzare
overcast ['əuvəkɑ:st] ADJ (sky) coperto(-a)
overcharge [əuvə'tʃɑ:dʒ] VT: **to ~ sb for sth**
  far pagare troppo caro a qn per qc
overcoat ['əuvəkəut] N soprabito, cappotto
overcome [əuvə'kʌm] VT (irreg: like **come**)
  superare; sopraffare; **~ with grief**
  sopraffatto(-a) dal dolore
overconfident [əuvə'kɔnfɪdənt] ADJ troppo
  sicuro(-a) (di sé), presuntuoso(-a)
overcrowded [əuvə'kraudɪd] ADJ
  sovraffollato(-a)

overcrowding [əuvə'kraudɪŋ] N
  sovraffollamento; (in bus) calca
overdo [əuvə'du:] VT (irreg: like **do**) esagerare;
  (overcook) cuocere troppo; **to ~ it, to ~ things**
  (work too hard) lavorare troppo
overdone [əuvə'dʌn] ADJ troppo cotto(-a)
overdose ['əuvədəus] N dose f eccessiva
overdraft ['əuvədrɑ:ft] N scoperto (di conto)
overdrawn [əuvə'drɔ:n] ADJ (account)
  scoperto(-a)
overdrive ['əuvədraɪv] N (Aut) overdrive m inv
overdue [əuvə'dju:] ADJ in ritardo;
  (recognition) tardivo(-a); (bill) insoluto(-a);
  that change was long ~ quel cambiamento
  ci voleva da tempo
overemphasis [əuvər'ɛmfəsɪs] N: **~ on sth**
  importanza eccessiva data a qc
overemphasize [əuvər'ɛmfəsaɪz] VT dare
  un'importanza eccessiva a
overestimate [əuvər'ɛstɪmeɪt] VT
  sopravvalutare
overexcited [əuvərɪk'saɪtɪd] ADJ
  sovraeccitato(-a)
overexertion [əuvərɪg'zə:ʃən] N logorio
  (fisico)
overexpose [əuvərɪk'spəuz] VT (Phot)
  sovraesporre
overflow VI [əuvə'fləu] traboccare ▸ N
  ['əuvəfləu] eccesso; (also: **overflow pipe**)
  troppopieno
overfly [əuvə'flaɪ] VT (irreg: like **fly**) sorvolare
overgenerous [əuvə'dʒɛnərəs] ADJ troppo
  generoso(-a)
overgrown [əuvə'grəun] ADJ (garden)
  ricoperto(-a) di vegetazione; **he's just an ~
  schoolboy** è proprio un bambinone
overhang [əuvə'hæŋ] VT (irreg: like **hang**)
  sporgere da ▸ VI sporgere
overhaul VT [əuvə'hɔ:l] revisionare ▸ N
  ['əuvəhɔ:l] revisione f
overhead ADV [əuvə'hɛd] di sopra ▸ ADJ
  ['əuvəhɛd] aereo(-a); (lighting) verticale ▸ N
  ['əuvəhɛd] (US) = **overheads**
overhead projector N lavagna luminosa
overheads ['əuvəhɛdz] NPL (BRIT) spese fpl
  generali
overhear [əuvə'hɪəʳ] VT (irreg: like **hear**)
  sentire (per caso)
overheat [əuvə'hi:t] VI surriscaldarsi
overjoyed [əuvə'dʒɔɪd] ADJ pazzo(-a) di gioia
overkill ['əuvəkɪl] N (fig) strafare m
overland ['əuvəlænd] ADJ, ADV per via di terra
overlap VI [əuvə'læp] sovrapporsi ▸ N
  ['əuvəlæp] sovrapposizione f
overleaf [əuvə'li:f] ADV a tergo
overload [əuvə'ləud] VT sovraccaricare
overlook [əuvə'luk] VT (have view of) dare su;
  (miss) trascurare; (forgive) passare sopra a
overlord ['əuvəlɔ:d] N capo supremo

o

overmanning [əuvəˈmænɪŋ] N eccedenza di manodopera

overnight ADV [əuvəˈnaɪt] (*happen*) durante la notte; (*fig*) tutto ad un tratto ▸ ADJ [ˈəuvənaɪt] di notte; fulmineo(-a); **he stayed there ~** ci ha passato la notte; **if you travel ~ ...** se viaggia di notte ...; **he'll be away ~** passerà la notte fuori

overnight bag N borsa da viaggio

overpass [ˈəuvəpɑːs] N cavalcavia *m inv*

overpay [əuvəˈpeɪ] VT (*irreg: like* **pay**): **to ~ sb by £50** pagare 50 sterline in più a qn

overplay [əuvəˈpleɪ] VT dare troppa importanza a; **to ~ one's hand** sopravvalutare la propria posizione

overpower [əuvəˈpauəʳ] VT sopraffare

overpowering [əuvəˈpauərɪŋ] ADJ irresistibile; (*heat, stench*) soffocante

overproduction [ˈəuvəprəˈdʌkʃən] N sovrapproduzione *f*

overrate [əuvəˈreɪt] VT sopravvalutare

overreach [əuvəˈriːtʃ] VT: **to ~ o.s.** volere strafare

overreact [əuvəriːˈækt] VI reagire in modo esagerato

override [əuvəˈraɪd] VT (*irreg: like* **ride**) (*order, objection*) passar sopra a; (*decision*) annullare

overriding [əuvəˈraɪdɪŋ] ADJ preponderante

overrule [əuvəˈruːl] VT (*decision*) annullare; (*claim*) respingere

overrun [əuvəˈrʌn] VT (*irreg: like* **run**) (*Mil: country etc*) invadere; (: *time limit etc*) superare, andare al di là di ▸ VI protrarsi; **the town is ~ with tourists** la città è invasa dai turisti

overseas [əuvəˈsiːz] ADV oltremare; (*abroad*) all'estero ▸ ADJ (*trade*) estero(-a); (*visitor*) straniero(-a)

oversee [əuvəˈsiː] VT (*irreg: like* **see**) sorvegliare

overseer [ˈəuvəsɪəʳ] N (*in factory*) caposquadra *m*

overshadow [əuvəˈʃædəu] VT far ombra su; (*fig*) eclissare

overshoot [əuvəˈʃuːt] VT (*irreg: like* **shoot**) superare

oversight [ˈəuvəsaɪt] N omissione *f*, svista; **due to an ~** per una svista

oversimplify [əuvəˈsɪmplɪfaɪ] VT rendere troppo semplice

oversleep [əuvəˈsliːp] VI (*irreg: like* **sleep**) dormire troppo a lungo

overspend [əuvəˈspɛnd] VI (*irreg: like* **spend**) spendere troppo; **we have overspent by 5000 dollars** abbiamo speso 5000 dollari di troppo

overspill [ˈəuvəspɪl] N eccedenza di popolazione

overstaffed [əuvəˈstɑːft] ADJ: **to be ~** avere troppo personale

overstate [əuvəˈsteɪt] VT esagerare

overstatement [əuvəˈsteɪtmənt] N esagerazione *f*

overstay [əuvəˈsteɪ] VT: **to ~ one's welcome** trattenersi troppo a lungo (come ospite)

overstep [əuvəˈstɛp] VT: **to ~ the mark** superare ogni limite

overstock [əuvəˈstɔk] VT sovrapprovvigionare, sovraimmagazzinare

overstretched [əuvəˈstrɛtʃt] ADJ sovraccarico(-a); (*budget*) arrivato(-a) al limite

overstrike N [ˈəuvəstraɪk] (*on printer*) sovrapposizione *f* (di caratteri) ▸ VT [əuvəˈstraɪk] (*irreg: like* **strike**) sovrapporre

overt [əuˈvəːt] ADJ palese

overtake [əuvəˈteɪk] VT (*irreg: like* **take**) sorpassare

overtaking [əuvəˈteɪkɪŋ] N (*Aut*) sorpasso

overtax [əuvəˈtæks] VT (*Econ*) imporre tasse eccessive a, tassare eccessivamente; (*fig: strength, patience*) mettere alla prova, abusare di; **to ~ o.s.** chiedere troppo alle proprie forze

overthrow [əuvəˈθrəu] VT (*irreg: like* **throw**) (*government*) rovesciare

overtime [ˈəuvətaɪm] N (*lavoro*) straordinario; **to do** *or* **work ~** fare lo straordinario

overtime ban N rifiuto sindacale a fare gli straordinari

overtone [ˈəuvətəun] N (*also:* **overtones**) sfumatura

overtook [əuvəˈtuk] PT *of* **overtake**

overture [ˈəuvətʃuəʳ] N (*Mus*) ouverture *f inv*; (*fig*) approccio

overturn [əuvəˈtəːn] VT rovesciare ▸ VI rovesciarsi

overview [ˈəuvəvjuː] N visione *f* d'insieme

overweight [əuvəˈweɪt] ADJ (*person*) troppo grasso(-a); (*luggage*) troppo pesante

overwhelm [əuvəˈwɛlm] VT sopraffare; sommergere; schiacciare

overwhelming [əuvəˈwɛlmɪŋ] ADJ (*victory, defeat*) schiacciante; (*heat, desire*) intenso(-a); **one's ~ impression is of heat** l'impressione dominante è quella di caldo

overwhelmingly [əuvəˈwɛlmɪŋlɪ] ADV in massa

overwork [əuvəˈwəːk] VT far lavorare troppo ▸ VI lavorare troppo, strapazzarsi

overwrite [əuvəˈraɪt] VT (*irreg: like* **write**) (*Comput*) ricoprire

overwrought [əuvəˈrɔːt] ADJ molto agitato(-a)

ovulation [ɔvjuˈleɪʃən] N ovulazione *f*

ow [au] EXCL ahi!

owe [əu] VT dovere; **to ~ sb sth, to ~ sth to sb** dovere qc a qn

owing to [ˈəuɪŋtuː] PREP a causa di

owl [aul] N gufo

own [əun] ADJ proprio(-a) ▸ VT possedere ▸ VI (*BRIT*): **to ~ to sth** ammettere qc; **to ~ to**

having done sth ammettere di aver fatto qc; **a room of my ~** la mia propria camera; **to get one's ~ back** vendicarsi; **on one's ~** tutto(-a) solo(-a); **can I have it for my (very) ~?** posso averlo tutto per me?; **to come into one's ~** mostrare le proprie qualità
▶ **own up** VI confessare
own brand N (*Comm*) etichetta propria
owner ['əunə^r] N proprietario(-a)
owner-occupier ['əunər'ɔkjupaɪə^r] N *proprietario/a della casa in cui abita*
ownership ['əunəʃɪp] N possesso; **it's under new ~** ha un nuovo proprietario
own goal N (*also fig*) autogol *m inv*
ox [ɔks] (*pl* **oxen** ['ɔksn]) N bue *m*
Oxbridge ['ɔksbrɪdʒ] N *le università di Oxford e/o Cambridge*; *vedi nota*

> La parola *Oxbridge* deriva dalla fusione dei nomi Ox(ford) e (Cam)bridge e fa riferimento a queste due antiche università.

oxen ['ɔksn] NPL *of* **ox**
Oxfam ['ɔksfæm] N ABBR (*Brit*: = *Oxford Committee for Famine Relief*) *organizzazione per aiuti al terzo mondo*
oxide ['ɔksaɪd] N ossido
Oxon. ['ɔksn] ABBR (*Brit*: *of Oxford*) = **Oxoniensis**
oxtail ['ɔksteɪl] N: **~ soup** minestra di coda di bue
oxyacetylene ['ɔksɪə'sɛtɪliːn] ADJ ossiacetilenico(-a); **~ burner, ~ lamp** cannello ossiacetilenico
oxygen ['ɔksɪdʒən] N ossigeno
oxygen mask N maschera ad ossigeno
oxygen tent N tenda ad ossigeno
oyster ['ɔɪstə^r] N ostrica
oz. ABBR = **ounce**
ozone ['əuzəun] N ozono
ozone-friendly ['əuzəun'frɛndlɪ] ADJ che non danneggia lo strato d'ozono
ozone layer N fascia d'ozono

O

Pp

P, p [pi:] N (letter) P, p f inv or m inv; **P for Peter** ≈ P come Padova

P ABBR = **president; prince**

p [pi:] ABBR (= page) p; (BRIT) = **penny; pence**

PA N ABBR = **personal assistant; public address system** ▶ ABBR (US) = **Pennsylvania**

pa [pɑ:] N (col) papà m inv, babbo

p.a. ABBR = **per annum**

PAC N ABBR (US) = **political action committee**

pace [peɪs] N passo; (speed) passo; velocità ▶ VI: **to ~ up and down** camminare su e giù; **to keep ~ with** camminare di pari passo a; (events) tenersi al corrente di; **to put sb through his paces** (fig) mettere qn alla prova; **to set the ~** (running) fare l'andatura; (fig) dare il la or il tono

pacemaker ['peɪsmeɪkə^r] N (Med) pacemaker m inv, stimolatore m cardiaco; (Sport) chi fa l'andatura

Pacific [pə'sɪfɪk] ADJ pacifico(-a) ▶ N: **the ~ (Ocean)** il Pacifico, l'Oceano Pacifico

pacification [pæsɪfɪ'keɪʃən] N pacificazione f

pacifier ['pæsɪfaɪə^r] N (US: dummy) succhiotto, ciuccio (col)

pacifist ['pæsɪfɪst] N pacifista mf

pacify ['pæsɪfaɪ] VT pacificare; (soothe) calmare

pack [pæk] N (packet) pacco; (Comm) confezione f; (US: of cigarettes) pacchetto; (of goods) balla; (of hounds) muta; (of wolves) branco; (of thieves etc) banda; (of cards) mazzo ▶ VT (goods) impaccare, imballare; (in suitcase etc) mettere; (box) riempire; (cram) stipare, pigiare; (press down) tamponare; turare; (Comput) comprimere, impaccare ▶ VI: **to ~ one's bags** fare la valigia; **to send sb packing** (col) spedire via qn

▶ **pack in** (BRIT col) VI (watch, car) guastarsi ▶ VT mollare, piantare; **~ it in!** piantala!, dacci un taglio!

▶ **pack off** VT (col: person) spedire; **to ~ sb off** spedire via qn

▶ **pack up** VI (BRIT col: machine) guastarsi; (person) far fagotto ▶ VT (belongings, clothes) mettere in una valigia; (goods, presents) imballare

package ['pækɪdʒ] N pacco; balla; (also: **package deal**) pacchetto; forfait m inv ▶ VT (goods) confezionare

package holiday N (BRIT) vacanza organizzata

package tour N viaggio organizzato

packaging ['pækɪdʒɪŋ] N confezione f, imballo

packed [pækt] ADJ (crowded) affollato(-a); **~ lunch** (BRIT) pranzo al sacco

packer ['pækə^r] N (person) imballatore(-trice)

packet ['pækɪt] N pacchetto

packet switching [-swɪtʃɪŋ] N (Comput) commutazione f di pacchetto

pack ice ['pækaɪs] N banchisa

packing ['pækɪŋ] N imballaggio

packing case N cassa da imballaggio

pact [pækt] N patto, accordo; trattato

pad [pæd] N blocco; (for inking) tampone m; (to prevent friction) cuscinetto; (col: flat) appartamentino ▶ VT imbottire ▶ VI: **to ~ about/in** etc camminare/entrare etc a passi felpati

padded ADJ imbottito(-a)

padded cell ['pædɪd-] N cella imbottita

padding ['pædɪŋ] N imbottitura; (fig) riempitivo

paddle ['pædl] N (oar) pagaia; (US: for table tennis) racchetta da ping-pong ▶ VI sguazzare ▶ VT (boat) fare andare a colpi di pagaia

paddle steamer N battello a ruote

paddling pool ['pædlɪŋ-] N (BRIT) piscina per bambini

paddock ['pædək] N prato recintato; (at racecourse) paddock m inv

paddy ['pædɪ] N (also: **paddy field**) risaia

padlock ['pædlɔk] N lucchetto ▶ VT chiudere con il lucchetto

padre ['pɑ:drɪ] N cappellano

Padua ['pædʒuə] N Padova

paediatrician, (US) **pediatrician** [pi:dɪə'trɪʃən] N pediatra mf

paediatrics, (US) **pediatrics** [piːdɪˈætrɪks] N pediatria

paedophile, (US) **pedophile** [ˈpiːdəufaɪl] ADJ, N pedofilo(-a)

pagan [ˈpeɪgən] ADJ, N pagano(-a)

page [peɪdʒ] N pagina; (also: **page boy**) fattorino; (: at wedding) paggio ▶ VT (in hotel etc) (far) chiamare

pageant [ˈpædʒənt] N spettacolo storico; grande cerimonia

pageantry [ˈpædʒəntrɪ] N pompa

page break N interruzione f di pagina

pager [ˈpeɪdʒər] N (Tel) cicalino, cercapersone m inv

paginate [ˈpædʒɪneɪt] VT impaginare

pagination [pædʒɪˈneɪʃən] N impaginazione f

pagoda [pəˈgəudə] N pagoda

paid [peɪd] PT, PP of **pay** ▶ ADJ (work, official) rimunerato(-a); **to put ~ to** (BRIT) mettere fine a

paid-up [ˈpeɪdʌp], (US) **paid in** [ˈpeɪdɪn] ADJ (member) che ha pagato la sua quota; (share) interamente pagato(-a); **~ capital** capitale m interamente versato

pail [peɪl] N secchio

pain [peɪn] N dolore m; **to be in ~** soffrire, aver male; **to have a ~ in** aver male or un dolore a; **to take pains to do** mettercela tutta per fare; **on ~ of death** sotto pena di morte

pained [peɪnd] ADJ addolorato(-a), afflitto(-a)

painful [ˈpeɪnful] ADJ doloroso(-a), che fa male; (difficult) difficile, penoso(-a)

painfully [ˈpeɪnfəlɪ] ADV (fig: very) fin troppo

painkiller [ˈpeɪnkɪlər] N antalgico, antidolorifico

painstaking [ˈpeɪnzteɪkɪŋ] ADJ (person) sollecito(-a); (work) accurato(-a)

paint [peɪnt] N (for house etc) tinta, vernice f; (Art) colore m ▶ VT (Art: walls) dipingere; (: door etc) verniciare; **a tin of ~** un barattolo di tinta or vernice; **to ~ the door blue** verniciare la porta di azzurro; **to ~ in oils** dipingere a olio

paintbox [ˈpeɪntbɔks] N scatola di colori

paintbrush [ˈpeɪntbrʌʃ] N pennello

painter [ˈpeɪntər] N (artist) pittore m; (decorator) imbianchino

painting [ˈpeɪntɪŋ] N (activity: of artist) pittura; (: of decorator) imbiancatura; verniciatura; (picture) dipinto, quadro

paint-stripper [ˈpeɪntstrɪpər] N prodotto sverniciante

paintwork [ˈpeɪntwəːk] N (BRIT) tinta; (: of car) vernice f

pair [peər] N (of shoes, gloves etc) paio; (of people) coppia; duo m inv; **a ~ of scissors/trousers** un paio di forbici/pantaloni

▶ **pair off** VI: **to ~ off (with sb)** fare coppia (con qn)

pajamas [pəˈdʒɑːməz] NPL (US) pigiama m

Pakistan [pɑːkɪˈstɑːn] N Pakistan m

Pakistani [pɑːkɪˈstɑːnɪ] ADJ, N pakistano(-a)

PAL [pæl] N ABBR (TV: = phase alternation line) PAL m

pal [pæl] N (col) amico(-a), compagno(-a)

palace [ˈpæləs] N palazzo

palatable [ˈpælɪtəbl] ADJ gustoso(-a)

palate [ˈpælɪt] N palato

palatial [pəˈleɪʃəl] ADJ sontuoso(-a), sfarzoso(-a)

palaver [pəˈlɑːvər] N chiacchiere fpl; storie fpl

pale [peɪl] ADJ pallido(-a) ▶ VI impallidire ▶ N: **to be beyond the ~** aver oltrepassato ogni limite; **to grow** or **turn ~** (person) diventare pallido(-a), impallidire; **to ~ into insignificance (beside)** perdere d'importanza (nei confronti di); **~ blue** azzurro or blu pallido inv

paleness [ˈpeɪlnɪs] N pallore m

Palestine [ˈpælɪstaɪn] N Palestina

Palestinian [pælɪsˈtɪnɪən] ADJ, N palestinese (mf)

palette [ˈpælɪt] N tavolozza

paling [ˈpeɪlɪŋ] N (stake) palo; (fence) palizzata

palisade [pælɪˈseɪd] N palizzata

pall [pɔːl] N (of smoke) cappa ▶ VI: **to ~ (on)** diventare noioso(-a) (a)

pallet [ˈpælɪt] N (for goods) paletta

pallid [ˈpælɪd] ADJ pallido(-a), smorto(-a)

pallor [ˈpælər] N pallore m

pally [ˈpælɪ] ADJ (col) amichevole

palm [pɑːm] N (Anat) palma, palmo; (also: **palm tree**) palma ▶ VT: **to ~ sth off on sb** (col) rifilare qc a qn

palmist [ˈpɑːmɪst] N chiromante mf

Palm Sunday N Domenica delle Palme

palpable [ˈpælpəbl] ADJ palpabile

palpitation [pælpɪˈteɪʃən] N palpitazione f; **to have palpitations** avere le palpitazioni

paltry [ˈpɔːltrɪ] ADJ derisorio(-a), insignificante

pamper [ˈpæmpər] VT viziare, coccolare

pamphlet [ˈpæmflət] N dépliant m inv; (political etc) volantino, manifestino

pan [pæn] N (also: **saucepan**) casseruola; (also: **frying pan**) padella ▶ VI (Cine) fare una panoramica; **to ~ for gold** (lavare le sabbie aurifere per) cercare l'oro

panacea [pænəˈsɪə] N panacea

panache [pəˈnæʃ] N stile m

Panama [ˈpænəmɑː] N Panama m

Panama Canal N canale m di Panama

Panamanian [pænəˈmeɪnɪən] ADJ, N panamense (mf)

pancake [ˈpænkeɪk] N frittella

Pancake Day N (BRIT) martedì m grasso

P

pancake roll N *crêpe ripiena di verdure alla cinese*
pancreas ['pæŋkrɪəs] N pancreas *m inv*
panda ['pændə] N panda *m inv*
panda car N (*BRIT*) auto *f* della polizia
pandemic [pæn dɛmɪk] N pandemia
pandemonium [pændɪ'məunɪəm] N pandemonio
pander ['pændə^r] VI: **to ~ to** lusingare; concedere tutto a
p & h ABBR (*US: = postage and handling*) affrancatura e trasporto
P & L ABBR (*= profit and loss*) P.P.
p & p ABBR (*BRIT: = postage and packing*) affrancatura ed imballaggio
pane [peɪn] N vetro
panel ['pænl] N (*of wood, cloth etc*) pannello; (*Radio, TV*) giuria
panel game N (*BRIT*) quiz *m inv* a squadre
panelling, (*US*) **paneling** ['pænəlɪŋ] N rivestimento a pannelli
panellist, (*US*) **panelist** ['pænəlɪst] N partecipante *mf* (al quiz, alla tavola rotonda *etc*)
pang [pæŋ] N: **to feel pangs of remorse** essere torturato(-a) dal rimorso; **pangs of hunger** spasimi *mpl* della fame; **pangs of conscience** morsi *mpl* di coscienza
panhandler ['pænhændlə^r] N (*US col*) accattone(-a)
panic ['pænɪk] N panico ▶ VI perdere il sangue freddo
panic buying [-baɪɪŋ] N accaparramento (*di generi alimentari ecc*)
panicky ['pænɪkɪ] ADJ (*person*) pauroso(-a)
panic-stricken ['pænɪkstrɪkən] ADJ (*person*) preso(-a) dal panico, in preda al panico; (*look*) terrorizzato(-a)
pannier ['pænɪə^r] N (*on animal*) bisaccia; (*on bicycle*) borsa
panorama [pænə'rɑːmə] N panorama *m*
panoramic [pænə'ræmɪk] ADJ panoramico(-a)
pansy ['pænzɪ] N (*Bot*) viola del pensiero, pensée *f inv*; (*col, pej*) femminuccia
pant [pænt] VI ansare
pantechnicon [pæn'tɛknɪkən] N (*BRIT*) grosso furgone *m* per traslochi
panther ['pænθə^r] N pantera
panties ['pæntɪz] NPL slip *m*, mutandine *fpl*
pantihose ['pæntɪhəuz] N (*US*) collant *m inv*
panto ['pæntəu] N (*BRIT col*) see **pantomime**
pantomime ['pæntəmaɪm] N (*BRIT: at Christmas*) spettacolo natalizio; (*tecnica*) pantomima; *vedi nota*

In Gran Bretagna la *pantomime* (abbreviata in *panto*) è una sorta di libera interpretazione delle favole più conosciute che vengono messe in scena nei teatri durante il periodo natalizio.

Gli attori principali sono la dama, *dame*, che è un uomo vestito da donna, il protagonista, *principal boy*, che è una donna travestita da uomo, e il cattivo, *villain*. È uno spettacolo per tutta la famiglia, che prevede la partecipazione del pubblico.

pantry ['pæntrɪ] N dispensa
pants [pænts] NPL (*BRIT*) mutande *fpl*, slip *m*; (*US: trousers*) pantaloni *mpl*
pantsuit ['pæntsuːt] N (*US*) completo *m* or tailleur *m inv* pantalone *inv*
papacy ['peɪpəsɪ] N papato
papal ['peɪpəl] ADJ papale, pontificio(-a)
paparazzi [pæpə'rætsiː] NPL paparazzi *mpl*
paper ['peɪpə^r] N carta; (*also:* **wallpaper**) carta da parati, tappezzeria; (*also:* **newspaper**) giornale *m*; (: *study, article*) saggio; (: *exam*) prova scritta ▶ ADJ di carta ▶ VT tappezzare; **a piece of ~** (*odd bit*) un pezzo di carta; (*sheet*) un foglio (di carta); **to put sth down on ~** mettere qc per iscritto; *see also* **papers**
paper advance N (*on printer*) avanzamento della carta
paperback ['peɪpəbæk] N tascabile *m*; edizione *f* economica ▶ ADJ: **~ edition** edizione *f* tascabile
paper bag N sacchetto di carta
paperboy ['peɪpəbɔɪ] N (*selling*) strillone *m*; (*delivering*) ragazzo che recapita i giornali
paper clip N graffetta, clip *f inv*
paper handkerchief N fazzolettino di carta
paper mill N cartiera
paper money N cartamoneta, moneta cartacea
paper profit N utile *m* teorico
papers ['peɪpəz] NPL (*also:* **identity papers**) carte *fpl*, documenti *mpl*
paper shop N (*BRIT*) giornalaio (*negozio*)
paperweight ['peɪpəweɪt] N fermacarte *m inv*
paperwork ['peɪpəwəːk] N lavoro amministrativo
papier-mâché ['pæpɪeɪ'mæʃeɪ] N cartapesta
paprika ['pæprɪkə] N paprica
Pap test, Pap smear ['pæp-] N (*Med*) pap-test *m inv*
par [pɑː^r] N parità, pari *f*; (*Golf*) norma; **on a ~ with** alla pari con; **at/above/below ~** (*Comm*) alla/sopra la/sotto la pari; **above/below ~** (*gen, Golf*) al di sopra/al di sotto della norma; **to feel below** *or* **under** *or* **not up to ~** non sentirsi in forma
parable ['pærəbl] N parabola (*Rel*)
parabola [pə'ræbələ] N parabola (*Math*)
paracetamol [pærə'siːtəmɔl] N (*BRIT*) paracetamolo
parachute ['pærəʃuːt] N paracadute *m inv* ▶ VI scendere col paracadute

parachute jump N lancio col paracadute
parachutist ['pærəʃuːtɪst] N paracadutista
mf
parade [pə'reɪd] N parata; (*inspection*) rivista,
rassegna ▶ VT (*fig*) fare sfoggio di ▶ VI sfilare
in parata; **a fashion ~** (*BRIT*) una sfilata di
moda
parade ground N piazza d'armi
paradise ['pærədaɪs] N paradiso
paradox ['pærədɔks] N paradosso
paradoxical [pærə'dɔksɪkl] ADJ paradossale
paradoxically [pærə'dɔksɪklɪ] ADV
paradossalmente
paraffin ['pærəfɪn] N (*BRIT*): **~ (oil)** paraffina;
liquid ~ olio di paraffina
paraffin heater N (*BRIT*) stufa al cherosene
paraffin lamp N (*BRIT*) lampada al cherosene
paragon ['pærəgən] N modello di perfezione
or di virtù
paragraph ['pærəgrɑːf] N paragrafo; **to
begin a new ~** andare a capo
Paraguay ['pærəgwaɪ] N Paraguay *m*
Paraguayan [pærə'gwaɪən] ADJ, N
paraguaiano(-a)
parallel ['pærəlɛl] ADJ (*also Comput*)
parallelo(-a); (*fig*) analogo(-a) ▶ N (*line*)
parallela; (*fig, Geo*) parallelo; **~ (with *or* to)**
parallelo(-a) (a)
paralysed ['pærəlaɪzd] ADJ paralizzato(-a)
paralysis [pə'rælɪsɪs] (*pl* **paralyses** [-siːz]) N
paralisi *f inv*
paralytic [pærə'lɪtɪk] ADJ paralitico(-a); (*BRIT
col: drunk*) ubriaco(-a) fradicio(-a)
paralyze ['pærəlaɪz] VT paralizzare
paramedic [pærə'mɛdɪk] N paramedico
parameter [pə'ræmɪtəʳ] N parametro
paramilitary [pærə'mɪlɪtərɪ] ADJ
paramilitare
paramount ['pærəmaunt] ADJ: **of ~
importance** di capitale importanza
paranoia [pærə'nɔɪə] N paranoia
paranoid ['pærənɔɪd] ADJ paranoico(-a)
paranormal [pærə'nɔːml] ADJ paranormale
paraphernalia [pærəfə'neɪlɪə] N attrezzi
mpl, roba
paraphrase ['pærəfreɪz] VT parafrasare
paraplegic [pærə'pliːdʒɪk] N paraplegico(-a)
parapsychology [pærəsaɪ'kɔlədʒɪ] N
parapsicologia
parasite ['pærəsaɪt] N parassita *m*
parasol ['pærəsɔl] N parasole *m inv*
paratrooper ['pærətruːpəʳ] N paracadutista
m (*soldato*)
parcel ['pɑːsl] N pacco, pacchetto ▶ VT (*also:*
parcel up) impaccare
▶ **parcel out** VT spartire
parcel bomb N (*BRIT*) pacchetto esplosivo
parcel post N servizio pacchi
parch [pɑːtʃ] VT riardere

parched ['pɑːtʃt] ADJ (*person*) assetato(-a)
parchment ['pɑːtʃmənt] N pergamena
pardon ['pɑːdn] N perdono; grazia ▶ VT
perdonare; (*Law*) graziare; **~!** scusi!; **~ me!**
mi scusi!; **I beg your ~!** scusi!; (**I beg your)
~?**, (*US*) **~ me?** prego?
pare [pɛəʳ] VT (*BRIT: nails*) tagliarsi; (: *fruit etc*)
sbucciare, pelare
parent ['pɛərənt] N padre *m* (*or* madre *f*);
parents NPL genitori *mpl*
parentage ['pɛərəntɪdʒ] N natali *mpl*; **of
unknown ~** di genitori sconosciuti
parental [pə'rɛntl] ADJ dei genitori
parent company N società madre *f inv*
parenthesis [pə'rɛnθɪsɪs] (*pl* **parentheses**
[-siːz]) N parentesi *f inv*; **in parentheses**
fra parentesi
parenthood ['pɛərənthud] N paternità *or*
maternità
parenting ['pɛərəntɪŋ] N mestiere *m* di
genitore
Paris ['pærɪs] N Parigi *f*
parish ['pærɪʃ] N parrocchia; (*BRIT: civil*)
≈ municipio ▶ ADJ parrocchiale
parish council N (*BRIT*) ≈ consiglio comunale
parishioner [pə'rɪʃənəʳ] N parrocchiano(-a)
Parisian [pə'rɪzɪən] ADJ, N parigino(-a)
parity ['pærɪtɪ] N parità
park [pɑːk] N parco; (*public*) giardino
pubblico ▶ VT, VI parcheggiare
parka ['pɑːkə] N eskimo
park and ride N parcheggio di interscambio
parking ['pɑːkɪŋ] N parcheggio; **"no ~"**
"sosta vietata"
parking lights NPL luci *fpl* di posizione
parking lot N (*US*) posteggio, parcheggio
parking meter N parchimetro
parking offence N (*BRIT*) infrazione *f* al
divieto di sosta
parking place N posto di parcheggio
parking ticket N multa per sosta vietata
parking violation N (*US*) = **parking offence**
Parkinson's ['pɑːkɪnsənz] N (*also:*
Parkinson's disease) morbo di Parkinson
parkway ['pɑːkweɪ] N (*US*) viale *m*
parlance ['pɑːləns] N: **in common/modern
~** nel gergo *or* linguaggio comune/moderno
parliament ['pɑːləmənt] N parlamento;
vedi nota

Nel Regno Unito il Parlamento, *Parliament*,
è formato da due camere: la *House of
Commons*, e la *House of Lords*. Nella *House
of Commons* siedono 650 parlamentari,
chiamati *MPs*, eletti per votazione diretta
del popolo nelle rispettive circoscrizioni
elettorali, le *constituencies*. Le sessioni del
Parlamento sono presiedute e moderate
dal presidente della Camera, lo *Speaker*.
Alla *House of Lords*, i cui poteri sono più

limitati, in passato si accedeva per nomina o per carica ereditaria mentre ora le cariche ereditarie sono state ridotte e in futuro verranno abolite.

parliamentary [pɑːlə'mɛntərɪ] ADJ parlamentare

parlour, (US) **parlor** ['pɑːləʳ] N salotto

parlous ['pɑːləs] ADJ periglioso(-a)

Parmesan [pɑːmɪ'zæn] N (also: **Parmesan cheese**) parmigiano

parochial [pə'rəukɪəl] ADJ parrocchiale; (pej) provinciale

parody ['pærədɪ] N parodia

parole [pə'rəul] N: **on** ~ in libertà per buona condotta

paroxysm ['pærəksɪzəm] N (Med) parossismo; (of anger, laughter, coughing) convulso; (of grief) attacco

parquet ['pɑːkeɪ] N: ~ **floor(ing)** parquet m

parrot ['pærət] N pappagallo

parrot fashion ADV in modo pappagallesco

parry ['pærɪ] VT parare

parsimonious [pɑːsɪ'məunɪəs] ADJ parsimonioso(-a)

parsley ['pɑːslɪ] N prezzemolo

parsnip ['pɑːsnɪp] N pastinaca

parson ['pɑːsn] N prete m; (Church of England) parroco

part [pɑːt] N parte f; (of machine) pezzo; (Theat etc) parte, ruolo; (Mus) voce f; parte; (US: in hair) scriminatura ▶ ADJ in parte ▶ ADV = **partly** ▶ VT separare ▶ VI (people) separarsi; (roads) dividersi; **to take** ~ **in** prendere parte a; **to take sb's** ~ parteggiare per qn, prendere le parti di qn; **on his** ~ da parte sua; **for my** ~ per parte mia; **for the most** ~ in generale; nella maggior parte dei casi; **for the better** ~ **of the day** per la maggior parte della giornata; **to be** ~ **and parcel of** essere parte integrante di; **to take sth in good/ bad** ~ prendere bene/male qc; ~ **of speech** (Ling) parte del discorso

▶ **part with** VT FUS separarsi da; rinunciare a

partake [pɑː'teɪk] VI (irreg: like **take**) (formal): **to** ~ **of sth** consumare qc, prendere qc

part exchange N (BRIT): **in** ~ in pagamento parziale

partial ['pɑːʃl] ADJ parziale; **to be** ~ **to** avere un debole per

partially ['pɑːʃəlɪ] ADV in parte, parzialmente

participant [pɑː'tɪsɪpənt] N: ~ **(in)** partecipante mf (a)

participate [pɑː'tɪsɪpeɪt] VI: **to** ~ **(in)** prendere parte (a), partecipare (a)

participation [pɑːtɪsɪ'peɪʃən] N partecipazione f

participle ['pɑːtɪsɪpl] N participio

particle ['pɑːtɪkl] N particella

particular [pə'tɪkjuləʳ] ADJ particolare;

speciale; (fussy) difficile; meticoloso(-a); **particulars** N PL particolari mpl, dettagli mpl; (information) informazioni fpl; **in** ~ in particolare, particolarmente; **to be very** ~ **about** essere molto pignolo(-a) su; **I'm not** ~ per me va bene tutto

particularly [pə'tɪkjulǝlɪ] ADV particolarmente; in particolare

parting ['pɑːtɪŋ] N separazione f; (BRIT: in hair) scriminatura ▶ ADJ d'addio; ~ **shot** (fig) battuta finale

partisan [pɑːtɪ'zæn] N partigiano(-a) ▶ ADJ partigiano(-a); di parte

partition [pɑː'tɪʃən] N (Pol) partizione f; (wall) tramezzo

partly ['pɑːtlɪ] ADV parzialmente; in parte

partner ['pɑːtnəʳ] N (Comm) socio(-a); (wife, husband etc, Sport) compagno(-a); (at dance) cavaliere (dama)

partnership ['pɑːtnəʃɪp] N associazione f; (Comm) società f inv; **to go into** ~ **(with)**, **form a** ~ **(with)** mettersi in società (con), associarsi (a)

part payment N acconto

partridge ['pɑːtrɪdʒ] N pernice f

part-time ['pɑːt'taɪm] ADJ, ADV a orario ridotto, part-time (inv)

part-timer ['pɑːt'taɪməʳ] N (also: **part-time worker**) lavoratore(-trice) part-time

party ['pɑːtɪ] N (Pol) partito; (team) squadra; gruppo; (Law) parte f; (celebration) ricevimento; serata; festa ▶ ADJ (Pol) del partito, di partito; **dinner** ~ cena; **to give** or **throw a** ~ dare una festa or un party; **to be a** ~ **to a crime** essere coinvolto in un reato

party line N (Pol) linea del partito; (Tel) duplex m inv

party piece N: **to do one's** ~ (BRIT col) esibirsi nel proprio pezzo forte a una festa, cena ecc

party political broadcast N comunicato radiotelevisivo di propaganda

pass [pɑːs] VT (gen) passare; (place) passare davanti a; (exam) passare, superare; (candidate) promuovere; (overtake, surpass) sorpassare, superare; (approve) approvare ▶ VI passare; (Scol) essere promosso(-a) ▶ N (permit) lasciapassare m inv; permesso; (in mountains) passo, gola; (Sport) passaggio; (Scol: also: **pass mark**): **to get a** ~ prendere la sufficienza; **to** ~ **for** passare per; **could you** ~ **the vegetables round?** potrebbe far passare i contorni?; **to** ~ **sth through a hole** etc far passare qc attraverso un buco etc; **to make a** ~ **at sb** (col) fare delle proposte or delle avances a qn; **things have come to a pretty** ~ (BRIT) ecco a cosa siamo arrivati

▶ **pass away** VI morire

▶ **pass by** VI passare ▶ VT trascurare

▶ **pass down** VT (customs, inheritance)

tramandare, trasmettere
▶ **pass on** VI (*die*) spegnersi, mancare ▶ VT (*hand on*): **to ~ on (to)** (*news, information, object*) passare (a); (*cold, illness*) attaccare (a); (*benefits*) trasmettere (a); (*price rises*) riversare (su)
▶ **pass out** VI svenire; (*BRIT Mil*) uscire dall'accademia
▶ **pass over** VI (*die*) spirare ▶ VT lasciare da parte
▶ **pass up** VT (*opportunity*) lasciarsi sfuggire, perdere
passable ['pɑːsəbl] ADJ (*road*) praticabile; (*work*) accettabile
passage ['pæsɪdʒ] N (*gen*) passaggio; (*also:* **passageway**) corridoio; (: *in book*) brano, passo; (: *by boat*) traversata
passenger ['pæsɪndʒəʳ] N passeggero(-a)
passer-by [pɑːsə'baɪ] N passante *mf*
passing ['pɑːsɪŋ] ADJ (*fig*) fuggevole; **to mention sth in ~** accennare a qc di sfuggita
passing place N (*Aut*) piazzola (di sosta)
passion ['pæʃən] N passione *f*; amore *m*; **to have a ~ for sth** aver la passione di *or* per qc
passionate ['pæʃənɪt] ADJ appassionato(-a)
passion fruit N frutto della passione
passion play N rappresentazione *f* della Passione di Cristo
passive ['pæsɪv] ADJ (*also Ling*) passivo(-a)
passive smoking N fumo passivo
passkey ['pɑːskiː] N passe-partout *m inv*
Passover ['pɑːsəʊvəʳ] N Pasqua ebraica
passport ['pɑːspɔːt] N passaporto
passport control N controllo *m* passaporti *inv*
passport office N ufficio *m* passaporti *inv*
password ['pɑːswɜːd] N parola d'ordine
past [pɑːst] PREP (*further than*) oltre, di là di; dopo; (*later than*) dopo ▶ ADV: **to run ~** passare di corsa; **to walk ~** passare ▶ ADJ passato(-a); (*president etc*) ex *inv* ▶ N passato; **quarter/half ~ four** le quattro e un quarto/e mezzo; **ten/twenty ~ four** le quattro e dieci/venti; **he's ~ forty** ha più di quarant'anni; **it's ~ midnight** è mezzanotte passata; **ten ~ eight** le otto e dieci; **for the ~ few days** da qualche giorno; in questi ultimi giorni; **for the ~ 3 days** negli ultimi 3 giorni; **in the ~** in *or* nel passato; (*Ling*) al passato; **I'm ~ caring** non me ne importa più nulla; **to be ~ it** (*BRIT col*: *person*) essere finito(-a)
pasta ['pæstə] N pasta
paste [peɪst] N (*glue*) colla; (*Culin*) pâté *m inv*; pasta ▶ VT collare; **tomato ~** concentrato di pomodoro
pastel ['pæstl] ADJ pastello *inv*
pasteurized ['pæstəraɪzd] ADJ pastorizzato(-a)
pastille ['pæstl] N pastiglia
pastime ['pɑːstaɪm] N passatempo

past master N (*BRIT*): **to be a ~ at** essere molto esperto(-a) in
pastor ['pɑːstəʳ] N pastore *m*
pastoral ['pɑːstərl] ADJ pastorale
past participle [-'pɑːtɪsɪpl] N (*Ling*) participio passato
pastry ['peɪstrɪ] N pasta
pasture ['pɑːstʃəʳ] N pascolo
pasty¹ ['pæstɪ] N pasticcio di carne
pasty² ['peɪstɪ] ADJ pastoso(-a); (*complexion*) pallido(-a), smorto(-a)
pat [pæt] VT accarezzare, dare un colpetto (affettuoso) a ▶ N: **a ~ of butter** un panetto di burro; **to give sb/o.s. a ~ on the back** (*fig*) congratularsi *or* compiacersi con qn/se stesso; **he knows it (off) ~**, (*US*) **he has it down ~** lo conosce *or* sa a menadito
patch [pætʃ] N (*of material*) toppa; (*eye patch*) benda; (*spot*) macchia; (*of land*) pezzo ▶ VT (*clothes*) rattoppare; **a bad ~** (*BRIT*) un brutto periodo
▶ **patch up** VT rappezzare
patchwork ['pætʃwɜːk] N patchwork *m*
patchy ['pætʃɪ] ADJ irregolare
pate [peɪt] N: **a bald ~** una testa pelata
pâté ['pæteɪ] N pâté *m inv*
patent ['peɪtnt] N brevetto ▶ VT brevettare ▶ ADJ patente, manifesto(-a)
patent leather N cuoio verniciato
patently ['peɪtntlɪ] ADV palesemente
patent medicine N specialità *f inv* medicinale
patent office N ufficio brevetti
paternal [pə'tɜːnl] ADJ paterno(-a)
paternity [pə'tɜːnɪtɪ] N paternità
paternity leave [pə'tɜːnɪtɪ-] N congedo di paternità
paternity suit N (*Law*) causa di riconoscimento della paternità
path [pɑːθ] N sentiero, viottolo; viale *m*; (*fig*) via, strada; (*of planet, missile*) traiettoria
pathetic [pə'θetɪk] ADJ (*pitiful*) patetico(-a); (*very bad*) penoso(-a)
pathological [pæθə'lɒdʒɪkl] ADJ patologico(-a)
pathologist [pə'θɒlədʒɪst] N patologo(-a)
pathology [pə'θɒlədʒɪ] N patologia
pathos ['peɪθɒs] N pathos *m*
pathway ['pɑːθweɪ] N sentiero, viottolo
patience ['peɪʃns] N pazienza; (*BRIT Cards*) solitario; **to lose one's ~** spazientirsi
patient ['peɪʃnt] N paziente *mf*; malato(-a) ▶ ADJ paziente; **to be ~ with sb** essere paziente *or* aver pazienza con qn
patiently ['peɪʃntlɪ] ADV pazientemente
patio ['pætɪəu] N terrazza
patriot ['peɪtrɪət] N patriota *mf*
patriotic [pætrɪ'ɒtɪk] ADJ patriottico(-a)
patriotism ['pætrɪətɪzəm] N patriottismo

patrol [pə'trəʊl] N pattuglia ▶ VT pattugliare;
to be on ~ fare la ronda; essere in
ricognizione; essere in perlustrazione
patrol boat N guardacoste m inv
patrol car N autoradio f inv (della polizia)
patrolman [pə'trəʊlmən] N (irreg) (US)
poliziotto
patron ['peɪtrən] N (in shop) cliente mf; (of
charity) benefattore(-trice); **~ of the arts**
mecenate mf
patronage ['pætrənɪdʒ] N patronato
patronize ['pætrənaɪz] VT essere cliente
abituale di; (fig) trattare con condiscendenza
patronizing ['pætrənaɪzɪŋ] ADJ
condiscendente
patron saint N patrono
patter ['pætər] N picchiettio; (sales talk)
propaganda di vendita ▶ VI picchiettare
pattern ['pætən] N modello; (Sewing etc)
modello (di carta), cartamodello; (design)
disegno, motivo; (sample) campione m;
behaviour patterns tipi mpl di
comportamento
patterned ['pætənd] ADJ a disegni, a motivi;
(material) fantasia inv
paucity ['pɔːsɪtɪ] N scarsità
paunch [pɔːntʃ] N pancione m
pauper ['pɔːpər] N indigente mf; **~'s grave**
fossa comune
pause [pɔːz] N pausa ▶ VI fare una pausa,
arrestarsi; **to ~ for breath** fermarsi un
attimo per riprender fiato
pave [peɪv] VT pavimentare; **to ~ the way for**
aprire la via a
pavement ['peɪvmənt] N (BRIT) marciapiede
m; (US) pavimentazione f stradale
pavilion [pə'vɪlɪən] N padiglione m; tendone
m; (Sport) edificio annesso ad un campo sportivo
paving ['peɪvɪŋ] N pavimentazione f
paving stone N lastra di pietra
paw [pɔː] N zampa ▶ VT dare una zampata a;
(person: pej) palpare
pawn [pɔːn] N pegno; (Chess) pedone m; (fig)
pedina ▶ VT dare in pegno
pawnbroker ['pɔːnbrəʊkər] N prestatore m su
pegno
pawnshop ['pɔːnʃɔp] N monte m di pietà
pay [peɪ] (pt, pp **paid** [peɪd]) N stipendio; paga
▶ VT pagare; (be profitable to: also fig) convenire
a ▶ VI pagare; (be profitable) rendere; **to ~
attention (to)** fare attenzione (a); **to ~ sb a
visit** far visita a qn; **to ~ one's respects to
sb** porgere i propri rispetti a qn; **I paid £5 for
that record** quel disco l'ho pagato 5 sterline;
how much did you ~ for it? quanto l'ha
pagato?; **to ~ one's way** pagare la propria
parte; (company) coprire le spese; **to ~
dividends** (fig) dare buoni frutti
▶ **pay back** VT rimborsare

▶ **pay for** VT FUS pagare
▶ **pay in** VT versare
▶ **pay off** VT (debts) saldare; (creditor) pagare;
(mortgage) estinguere; (workers) licenziare ▶ VI
(scheme) funzionare; (patience) dare dei frutti;
to ~ sth off in instalments pagare qc a rate
▶ **pay out** VT (money) sborsare, tirar fuori;
(rope) far allentare
▶ **pay up** VT saldare
payable ['peɪəbl] ADJ pagabile; **to make a
cheque ~ to sb** intestare un assegno a
(nome di) qn
pay-as-you-go ['peɪəzjə'gəʊ] ADJ (mobile
phone) con scheda prepagata
pay award N aumento salariale
pay day N giorno di paga
PAYE N ABBR (BRIT: = pay as you earn) pagamento
di imposte tramite ritenute alla fonte
payee [peɪ'iː] N beneficiario(-a)
pay envelope N (US) busta f paga inv
paying ['peɪɪŋ] ADJ: **~ guest** ospite mf
pagante, pensionante mf
payload ['peɪləʊd] N carico utile
payment ['peɪmənt] N pagamento;
versamento; saldo; **advance ~** (part sum)
anticipo, acconto; (total sum) pagamento
anticipato; **deferred ~, ~ by instalments**
pagamento dilazionato or a rate; **in ~ for, in
~ of** in pagamento di; **on ~ of £5** dietro
pagamento di 5 sterline
payout N pagamento; (in competition) premio
pay packet N (BRIT) busta f paga inv
payphone ['peɪfəʊn] N cabina telefonica
payroll ['peɪrəʊl] N ruolo (organico); **to be
on a firm's ~** far parte del personale di una
ditta
pay slip N (BRIT) foglio m paga inv
pay station N (US) cabina telefonica
pay television N televisione f a pagamento,
pay-tv f inv
paywall ['peɪwɔːl] N (Comput) paywall m inv
PBS N ABBR (US: = Public Broadcasting Service)
servizio che collabora alla realizzazione di
programmi per la rete televisiva nazionale
PBX ABBR (= private branch exchange) sistema
telefonico con centralino
PC N ABBR = **personal computer**; (BRIT)
= **police constable** ▶ ABBR (BRIT) = **Privy
Councillor** ▶ ADJ ABBR = **politically correct**
pc ABBR = **per cent**; (= postcard) C.P.
p/c ABBR = **petty cash**
PCB N ABBR = **printed circuit board**
pcm ABBR = **per calendar month**
PD N ABBR (US) = **police department**
pd ABBR = **paid**
PDA N ABBR (= personal digital assistant) PDA
m inv
PDQ ABBR (col) = **pretty damn quick**
PDSA N ABBR (BRIT: = People's Dispensary for Sick

Animals) assistenza veterinaria gratuita
PDT ABBR (*US*: = *Pacific Daylight Time*) *ora legale
del Pacifico*
PE N ABBR (= *physical education*) ed. fisica ▶ ABBR
(*CANADA*) = **Prince Edward Island**
pea [pi:] N pisello
peace [pi:s] N pace *f*; (*calm*) calma,
tranquillità; **to be at ~ with sb/sth** essere
in pace con qn/qc; **to keep the ~** (*policeman*)
mantenere l'ordine pubblico; (*citizen*)
rispettare l'ordine pubblico
peaceable ['pi:səbl] ADJ pacifico(-a)
peaceful ['pi:sful] ADJ pacifico(-a), calmo(-a)
peacekeeping ['pi:ski:pɪŋ] N mantenimento
della pace; **~ force** forza di pace
peace offering N (*fig*) dono in segno di
riconciliazione
peach [pi:tʃ] N pesca
peacock ['pi:kɔk] N pavone *m*
peak [pi:k] N (*of mountain*) cima, vetta;
(*mountain itself*) picco; (*of cap*) visiera; (*fig*)
massimo; (: *of career*) apice *m*
peak-hour ['pi:kauəʳ] ADJ (*traffic etc*) delle ore
di punta
peak hours NPL ore *fpl* di punta
peak period N periodo di punta
peak rate N tariffa massima
peaky ['pi:kɪ] ADJ (*BRIT col*) sbattuto(-a)
peal [pi:l] N (*of bells*) scampanio, carillon *m
inv*; **peals of laughter** scoppi *mpl* di risa
peanut ['pi:nʌt] N arachide *f*, nocciolina
americana
peanut butter N burro di arachidi
pear [pɛəʳ] N pera
pearl [pə:l] N perla
peasant ['pɛznt] N contadino(-a)
peat [pi:t] N torba
pebble ['pɛbl] N ciottolo
peck [pɛk] VT (*also*: **peck at**) beccare; (: *food*)
mangiucchiare ▶ N colpo di becco; (*kiss*)
bacetto
pecking order ['pɛkɪŋ-] N (*fig*) ordine *m*
gerarchico
peckish ['pɛkɪʃ] ADJ (*BRIT col*): **I feel ~** ho un
languorino
peculiar [pɪ'kju:lɪəʳ] ADJ strano(-a),
bizzarro(-a); (*particular: importance, qualities*)
particolare; **~ to** tipico(-a) di,
caratteristico(-a) di
peculiarity [pɪkju:lɪ'ærɪtɪ] N peculiarità *f inv*;
(*oddity*) bizzarria
pecuniary [pɪ'kju:nɪərɪ] ADJ pecuniario(-a)
pedal ['pɛdl] N pedale *m* ▶ VI pedalare
pedal bin N (*BRIT*) pattumiera a pedale
pedalo ['pɛdələu] N pedalò *m inv*
pedantic [pɪ'dæntɪk] ADJ pedantesco(-a)
peddle ['pɛdl] VT (*goods*) andare in giro a
vendere; (*drugs*) spacciare; (*gossip*) mettere in
giro

peddler ['pɛdləʳ] N venditore *m* ambulante
pedestal ['pɛdəstl] N piedestallo
pedestrian [pɪ'dɛstrɪən] N pedone(-a) ▶ ADJ
pedonale; (*fig*) prosaico(-a), pedestre
pedestrian crossing N (*BRIT*) passaggio
pedonale
pedestrianized ADJ: **a ~ street** una zona
pedonalizzata
pedestrian mall N (*US*) zona pedonale
pedestrian precinct, (*US*) **pedestrian zone**
N zona pedonale
pediatrics [pi:dɪ'ætrɪks] N (*US*) = **paediatrics**
pedigree ['pɛdɪgri:] N stirpe *f*; (*of animal*)
pedigree *m inv*; (*fig*) background *m inv* ▶ CPD
(*animal*) di razza
pedlar ['pɛdləʳ] N = **peddler**
pedophile ['pi:dəufaɪl] (*US*) N = **paedophile**
pee [pi:] VI (*col*) pisciare
peek [pi:k] VI guardare furtivamente
peel [pi:l] N buccia; (*of orange, lemon*) scorza
▶ VT sbucciare ▶ VI (*paint etc*) staccarsi
▶ **peel back** VT togliere, levare
peeler [pi:ləʳ] N: **potato ~** sbucciapatate *m inv*
peelings ['pi:lɪŋz] NPL bucce *fpl*
peep [pi:p] N (*look*) sguardo furtivo, sbirciata;
(*sound*) pigolio ▶ VI guardare furtivamente
▶ **peep out** VI mostrarsi furtivamente
peephole ['pi:phəul] N spioncino
peer [pɪəʳ] VI: **to ~ at** scrutare ▶ N (*noble*) pari
m inv; (*equal*) pari *mf*, uguale *mf*; (*contemporary*)
contemporaneo(-a)
peerage ['pɪərɪdʒ] N dignità di pari; pari *mpl*
peerless ['pɪəlɪs] ADJ impareggiabile, senza
pari
peeved [pi:vd] ADJ stizzito(-a)
peevish ['pi:vɪʃ] ADJ stizzoso(-a)
peg [pɛg] N caviglia; (*tent peg*) picchetto;
(*for coat etc*) attaccapanni *m inv*; (*BRIT: also*:
clothes peg) molletta ▶ VT (*clothes*)
appendere con le mollette; (*BRIT: groundsheet*)
fissare con i picchetti; (*fig: prices, wages*)
fissare, stabilizzare; **off the ~**
confezionato(-a)
pejorative [pɪ'dʒɔrətɪv] ADJ peggiorativo(-a)
Pekin [pi:'kɪn], **Peking** [pi:'kɪŋ] N Pechino *f*
pekinese, pekingese [pi:kɪ'ni:z] N
pechinese *m*
pelican ['pɛlɪkən] N pellicano
pelican crossing N (*BRIT Aut*) attraversamento
pedonale con semaforo a controllo manuale
pellet ['pɛlɪt] N pallottola, pallina
pell-mell ['pɛl'mɛl] ADV disordinatamente,
alla rinfusa
pelmet ['pɛlmɪt] N mantovana; cassonetto
pelt [pɛlt] VT: **to ~ sb (with)** bombardare qn
(con) ▶ VI (*rain*) piovere a dirotto; (*col: run*)
filare ▶ N pelle *f*
pelvis ['pɛlvɪs] N pelvi *f inv*, bacino
pen [pɛn] N penna; (*for sheep*) recinto; (*US col*:

prison) galera; **to put ~ to paper** prendere la penna in mano

penal ['pi:nl] ADJ penale

penalize ['pi:nəlaɪz] VT punire; (*Sport*) penalizzare; (*fig*) svantaggiare

penal servitude [-'sə:vɪtju:d] N lavori *mpl* forzati

penalty ['pɛnltɪ] N penalità *f inv*; sanzione *f* penale; (*fine*) ammenda; (*Sport*) penalizzazione *f*; (*Football: also*: **penalty kick**) calcio di rigore

penalty area N (*BRIT Sport*) area di rigore

penalty clause N penale *f*

penalty kick N (*Football*) calcio di rigore

penalty shoot-out [-'ʃu:taut] N (*Football*) rigori *mpl*; **to beat a team in a ~** battere una squadra ai rigori

penance ['pɛnəns] N penitenza

pence [pɛns] NPL (*BRIT*) *of* **penny**

penchant ['pɑ̃:ʃɑ̃:ŋ] N debole *m*

pencil ['pɛnsl] N matita ▶ VT (*also*: **pencil in**) scrivere a matita

pencil case N astuccio per matite

pencil sharpener N temperamatite *m inv*

pendant ['pɛndnt] N pendaglio

pending ['pɛndɪŋ] PREP in attesa di ▶ ADJ in sospeso

pendulum ['pɛndjuləm] N pendolo

penetrate ['pɛnɪtreɪt] VT penetrare

penetrating ['pɛnɪtreɪtɪŋ] ADJ penetrante

penetration [pɛnɪ'treɪʃən] N penetrazione *f*

penfriend ['pɛnfrɛnd] N (*BRIT*) corrispondente *mf*

penguin ['pɛŋgwɪn] N pinguino

penicillin [pɛnɪ'sɪlɪn] N penicillina

peninsula [pə'nɪnsjulə] N penisola

penis ['pi:nɪs] N pene *m*

penitence ['pɛnɪtns] N penitenza

penitent ['pɛnɪtnt] ADJ penitente

penitentiary [pɛnɪ'tɛnʃərɪ] N (*US*) carcere *m*

penknife ['pɛnnaɪf] N temperino

Penn., Penna. ABBR (*US*) = **Pennsylvania**

pen name N pseudonimo

pennant ['pɛnənt] N banderuola

penniless ['pɛnɪlɪs] ADJ senza un soldo

Pennines ['pɛnaɪnz] NPL: **the ~** i Pennini

penny ['pɛnɪ] (*pl* **pennies** ['pɛnɪz] *or* **pence** [pɛns]) N (*BRIT*) penny *m* (*pl* = pence); (*US*) centesimo

penpal ['pɛnpæl] N corrispondente *mf*

penpusher ['pɛnpuʃə^r] N (*pej*) scribacchino(-a)

pension ['pɛnʃən] N pensione *f*
▶ **pension off** VT mandare in pensione

pensionable ['pɛnʃənəbl] ADJ (*person*) che ha diritto a una pensione, pensionabile; (*age*) pensionabile

pensioner ['pɛnʃənə^r] N (*BRIT*) pensionato(-a)

pension fund N fondo pensioni

pensive ['pɛnsɪv] ADJ pensoso(-a)

pentagon ['pɛntəgən] N pentagono; **the P~** (*US Pol*) il Pentagono; *vedi nota*

Il *Pentagon* è un edificio a pianta pentagonale che si trova ad Arlington, in Virginia, nel quale hanno sede gli uffici del Ministero della Difesa degli Stati Uniti. Il termine *Pentagon* è usato anche per indicare la dirigenza militare del paese.

Pentecost ['pɛntɪkɔst] N Pentecoste *f*

penthouse ['pɛnthaus] N appartamento (di lusso) nell'attico

pent-up ['pɛntʌp] ADJ (*feelings*) represso(-a)

penultimate [pɪ'nʌltɪmət] ADJ penultimo(-a)

penury ['pɛnjurɪ] N indigenza

people ['pi:pl] NPL gente *f*; persone *fpl*; (*citizens*) popolo ▶ N (*nation, race*) popolo ▶ VT popolare; **old** ~ i vecchi; **young** ~ i giovani; ~ **at large** il grande pubblico; **a man of the** ~ un uomo del popolo; **4/several** ~ **came** 4/ parecchie persone sono venute; **the room was full of** ~ la stanza era piena di gente; ~ **say that …** si dice *or* la gente dice che …

PEP [pɛp] N ABBR = **personal equity plan**

pep [pɛp] N (*col*) dinamismo
▶ **pep up** VT vivacizzare; (*food*) rendere più gustoso(-a)

pepper ['pɛpə^r] N pepe *m*; (*vegetable*) peperone *m* ▶ VT pepare; (*fig*): **to** ~ **with** spruzzare di

peppermint ['pɛpəmɪnt] N (*plant*) menta peperita; (*sweet*) pasticca di menta

pepperoni [pɛpə'rəunɪ] N salsiccia piccante

pepperpot ['pɛpəpɔt] N pepaiola

peptalk ['pɛptɔ:k] N (*col*) discorso di incoraggiamento

per [pə:^r] PREP per; a; ~ **hour** all'ora; ~ **kilo** *etc* il chilo *etc*; ~ **day** al giorno; ~ **week** alla settimana; ~ **person** a testa, a *or* per persona; **as** ~ **your instructions** secondo le vostre istruzioni

per annum ADV all'anno

per capita ADJ, ADV pro capite

perceive [pə'si:v] VT percepire; (*notice*) accorgersi di

per cent ADV per cento; **a 20** ~ **discount** uno sconto del 20 per cento

percentage [pə'sɛntɪdʒ] N percentuale *f*; **on a** ~ **basis** a percentuale

percentage point N punto percentuale

perceptible [pə'sɛptɪbl] ADJ percettibile

perception [pə'sɛpʃən] N percezione *f*; sensibilità; perspicacia

perceptive [pə'sɛptɪv] ADJ percettivo(-a); perspicace

perch [pə:tʃ] N (*fish*) pesce *m* persico; (*for bird*) sostegno, ramo ▶ VI appollaiarsi

percolate ['pə:kəleɪt] VT filtrare

percolator ['pə:kəleɪtə^r] N caffettiera a

pressione; caffettiera elettrica

percussion [pə'kʌʃən] N percussione f; (Mus) strumenti mpl a percussione

peremptory [pə'rɛmptərɪ] ADJ perentorio(-a)

perennial [pə'rɛnɪəl] ADJ perenne ▶ N pianta perenne

perfect ['pə:fɪkt] ADJ perfetto(-a) ▶ N (also: **perfect tense**) perfetto, passato prossimo ▶ VT [pə'fɛkt] perfezionare; mettere a punto; **he's a ~ stranger to me** mi è completamente sconosciuto

perfection [pə'fɛkʃən] N perfezione f

perfectionist [pə'fɛkʃənɪst] N perfezionista mf

perfectly ['pə:fɪktlɪ] ADV perfettamente, alla perfezione; **I'm ~ happy with the situation** sono completamente soddisfatta della situazione; **you know ~ well** sa benissimo

perforate ['pə:fəreɪt] VT perforare

perforated ulcer ['pə:fəreɪtɪd-] N (Med) ulcera perforata

perforation [pə:fə'reɪʃən] N perforazione f; (line of holes) dentellatura

perform [pə'fɔ:m] VT (carry out) eseguire, fare; (symphony etc) suonare; (play, ballet) dare; (opera) fare ▶ VI suonare; recitare

performance [pə'fɔ:məns] N esecuzione f; (at theatre etc) rappresentazione f, spettacolo; (of an artist) interpretazione f; (of player etc) performance f; (of car, engine) prestazione f; **the team put up a good ~** la squadra ha giocato una bella partita

performer [pə'fɔ:mə'] N artista mf

performing [pə'fɔ:mɪŋ] ADJ (animal) ammaestrato(-a)

performing arts NPL: **the ~** le arti dello spettacolo

perfume ['pə:fju:m] N profumo ▶ VT profumare

perfunctory [pə'fʌŋktərɪ] ADJ superficiale, per la forma

perhaps [pə'hæps] ADV forse; **~ he'll come** forse verrà, può darsi che venga; **~ so/not** forse sì/no, può darsi di sì/di no

peril ['pɛrɪl] N pericolo

perilous ['pɛrɪləs] ADJ pericoloso(-a)

perilously ['pɛrɪləslɪ] ADV: **they came ~ close to being caught** sono stati a un pelo dall'esser presi

perimeter [pə'rɪmɪtə'] N perimetro

perimeter wall N muro di cinta

period ['pɪərɪəd] N periodo; (Hist) epoca; (Scol) lezione f; (full stop) punto; (US Football) tempo; (Med) mestruazioni fpl ▶ ADJ (costume, furniture) d'epoca; **for a ~ of three weeks** per un periodo di or per la durata di tre settimane; **the holiday ~** (BRIT) il periodo delle vacanze

periodic [pɪərɪ'ɔdɪk] ADJ periodico(-a)

periodical [pɪərɪ'ɔdɪkl] ADJ periodico(-a) ▶ N periodico

periodically [pɪərɪ'ɔdɪklɪ] ADV periodicamente

period pains NPL (BRIT) dolori mpl mestruali

peripatetic [pɛrɪpə'tɛtɪk] ADJ (salesman) ambulante; (BRIT: teacher) peripatetico(-a)

peripheral [pə'rɪfərəl] ADJ periferico(-a) ▶ N (Comput) unità f inv periferica

periphery [pə'rɪfərɪ] N periferia

periscope ['pɛrɪskəup] N periscopio

perish ['pɛrɪʃ] VI perire, morire; (decay) deteriorarsi

perishable ['pɛrɪʃəbl] ADJ deperibile

perishables ['pɛrɪʃəblz] NPL merci fpl deperibili

perishing ['pɛrɪʃɪŋ] ADJ (BRIT col): **it's ~ (cold)** fa un freddo da morire

peritonitis [pɛrɪtə'naɪtɪs] N peritonite f

perjure ['pə:dʒə'] VT: **to ~ o.s.** spergiurare

perjury ['pə:dʒərɪ] N (Law: in court) falso giuramento; (breach of oath) spergiuro

perk [pə:k] N (col) vantaggio
▶ **perk up** VI (cheer up) rianimarsi

perky ['pə:kɪ] ADJ (cheerful) vivace, allegro(-a)

perm [pə:m] N (for hair) permanente f ▶ VT: **to have one's hair permed** farsi fare la permanente

permanence ['pə:mənəns] N permanenza

permanent ['pə:mənənt] ADJ permanente; (job, position) fisso(-a); (dye, ink) indelebile; **~ address** residenza fissa; **I'm not ~ here** non sono fisso qui

permanently ['pə:mənəntlɪ] ADV definitivamente

permeable ['pə:mɪəbl] ADJ permeabile

permeate ['pə:mɪeɪt] VI penetrare ▶ VT permeare

permissible [pə'mɪsɪbl] ADJ permissibile, ammissibile

permission [pə'mɪʃən] N permesso; **to give sb ~ to do sth** dare a qn il permesso di fare qc

permissive [pə'mɪsɪv] ADJ tollerante; **the ~ society** la società permissiva

permit N ['pə:mɪt] permesso; (entrance pass) lasciapassare m ▶ VT, VI [pə'mɪt] permettere; **fishing ~** licenza di pesca; **to ~ sb to do** permettere a qn di fare, dare il permesso a qn di fare; **weather permitting** tempo permettendo

permutation [pə:mju'teɪʃən] N permutazione f

pernicious [pə:'nɪʃəs] ADJ pernicioso(-a), nocivo(-a)

pernickety [pə'nɪkɪtɪ] ADJ (col: person) pignolo(-a); (task) da certosino

perpendicular [pə:pən'dɪkjulə'] ADJ, N perpendicolare (f)

perpetrate ['pə:pɪtreɪt] VT perpetrare, commettere

P

perpetual [pə'pɛtjuəl] ADJ perpetuo(-a)
perpetuate [pə'pɛtjueɪt] VT perpetuare
perpetuity [pɜ:pɪ'tju:ɪtɪ] N: **in ~** in perpetuo
perplex [pə'plɛks] VT lasciare perplesso(-a)
perplexing [pə'plɛksɪŋ] ADJ che lascia
perplesso(-a)
perquisites ['pɜ:kwɪzɪts] NPL (*also:* **perks**)
benefici *mpl* collaterali
persecute ['pɜ:sɪkju:t] VT perseguitare
persecution [pɜ:sɪ'kju:ʃən] N persecuzione *f*
perseverance [pɜ:sɪ'vɪərəns] N perseveranza
persevere [pɜ:sɪ'vɪə'] VI perseverare
Persia ['pɜ:ʃə] N Persia
Persian ['pɜ:ʃən] ADJ persiano(-a) ▶ N (*Ling*)
persiano; **the ~ Gulf** *n* il Golfo Persico
Persian cat N gatto persiano
persist [pə'sɪst] VI: **to ~ (in doing)** persistere
(nel fare); ostinarsi (a fare)
persistence [pə'sɪstəns] N persistenza;
ostinazione *f*
persistent [pə'sɪstənt] ADJ persistente;
ostinato(-a); (*lateness, rain*) continuo(-a);
~ offender (*Law*) delinquente *mf* abituale
persnickety [pə'snɪkɪtɪ] ADJ (*US col*)
= **pernickety**
person ['pɜ:sn] N persona; **in ~** di *or* in
persona, personalmente; **on** *or* **about one's
~** (*weapon*) su di sé; (*money*) con sé; **a ~ to ~ call**
(*Tel*) una chiamata con preavviso
personable ['pɜ:snəbl] ADJ di bell'aspetto
personal ['pɜ:snl] ADJ personale;
individuale; **~ belongings, ~ effects** oggetti
mpl d'uso personale; **a ~ interview** un
incontro privato
personal allowance N (*Tax*) quota del
reddito non imponibile
personal assistant N segretaria personale
personal call N (*Tel*) chiamata con preavviso
personal column N messaggi *mpl* personali
personal computer N personal computer
m inv
personal details NPL dati *mpl* personali
personal equity plan N (*Finance*) fondo di
investimento azionario con agevolazioni fiscali
destinato al piccolo risparmiatore
personal identification number N (*Comput,
Banking*) numero di codice segreto
personality [pɜ:sə'nælɪtɪ] N personalità *f inv*
personally ['pɜ:snəlɪ] ADV personalmente;
to take sth ~ prendere qc come una critica
personale
personal organizer N agenda; (*electronic*)
agenda elettronica
personal property N beni *mpl* personali
personal stereo N walkman® *m inv*
personify [pɜ:'sɔnɪfaɪ] VT personificare
personnel [pɜ:sə'nɛl] N personale *m*
personnel department N ufficio
del personale

personnel manager N direttore(-trice) del
personale
perspective [pə'spɛktɪv] N prospettiva; **to
get sth into ~** ridimensionare qc
Perspex® ['pə:spɛks] N (*BRIT*) *tipo di resina
termoplastica*
perspicacity [pə:spɪ'kæsɪtɪ] N perspicacia
perspiration [pə:spɪ'reɪʃən] N traspirazione *f*,
sudore *m*
perspire [pə'spaɪə'] VI traspirare
persuade [pə'sweɪd] VT: **to ~ sb to do sth**
persuadere qn a fare qc; **to ~ sb of sth/that**
persuadere qn di qc/che
persuasion [pə'sweɪʒən] N persuasione *f*;
(*creed*) convinzione *f*, credo
persuasive [pə'sweɪsɪv] ADJ persuasivo(-a)
pert [pə:t] ADJ (*bold*) sfacciato(-a),
impertinente; (*hat*) spiritoso(-a)
pertaining [pə:'teɪnɪŋ]: **~ to** *prep* che riguarda
pertinent ['pə:tɪnənt] ADJ pertinente
perturb [pə'tə:b] VT turbare
perturbing [pə'tə:bɪŋ] ADJ inquietante
Peru [pə'ru:] N Perù *m*
perusal [pə'ru:zl] N attenta lettura
Peruvian [pə'ru:vjən] ADJ, N peruviano(-a)
pervade [pə'veɪd] VT pervadere
pervasive [pə:'veɪsɪv] ADJ (*smell*) penetrante;
(*influence*) dilagante; (*gloom, feelings*) diffuso(-a)
perverse [pə'və:s] ADJ perverso(-a)
perversion [pə'və:ʃən] N pervertimento,
perversione *f*
perversity [pə'və:sɪtɪ] N perversità
pervert N ['pə:və:t] pervertito(-a) ▶ VT
[pə'və:t] pervertire
pessimism ['pɛsɪmɪzəm] N pessimismo
pessimist ['pɛsɪmɪst] N pessimista *mf*
pessimistic [pɛsɪ'mɪstɪk] ADJ
pessimistico(-a)
pest [pɛst] N animale *m* (*or* insetto) pestifero;
(*fig*) peste *f*
pest control N disinfestazione *f*
pester ['pɛstə'] VT tormentare, molestare
pesticide ['pɛstɪsaɪd] N pesticida *m*
pestilence ['pɛstɪləns] N pestilenza
pestle ['pɛsl] N pestello
pet [pɛt] N animale *m* domestico; (*favourite*)
favorito(-a) ▶ VT accarezzare ▶ VI (*col*) fare il
petting; **~ lion** *etc* leone *m etc* ammaestrato;
teacher's ~ favorito(-a) del maestro
petal ['pɛtl] N petalo
peter ['pi:tə']: **to ~ out** *vi* esaurirsi;
estinguersi
petite [pə'ti:t] ADJ piccolo(-a) e aggraziato(-a)
petition [pə'tɪʃən] N petizione *f* ▶ VI
richiedere; **to ~ for divorce** presentare
un'istanza di divorzio
pet name N (*BRIT*) nomignolo
petrified ['pɛtrɪfaɪd] ADJ (*fig*) morto(-a)
di paura

petrify ['pɛtrɪfaɪ] VT pietrificare; (fig) terrorizzare
petrochemical [pɛtrə'kɛmɪkl] ADJ petrolchimico(-a)
petrodollars ['pɛtrəudɔləz] NPL petrodollari mpl
petrol ['pɛtrəl] N (BRIT) benzina; **two/four-star ~** = benzina normale/super
petrol bomb N (BRIT) (bottiglia) molotov f inv
petrol can N (BRIT) tanica per benzina
petrol engine N (BRIT) motore m a benzina
petroleum [pə'trəulɪəm] N petrolio
petroleum jelly N vaselina
petrol pump N (BRIT: in car, at garage) pompa di benzina
petrol station N (BRIT) stazione f di rifornimento
petrol tank N (BRIT) serbatoio della benzina
petticoat ['pɛtɪkəut] N sottana
pettifogging ['pɛtɪfɔgɪŋ] ADJ cavilloso(-a)
pettiness ['pɛtɪnɪs] N meschinità
petty ['pɛtɪ] ADJ (mean) meschino(-a); (unimportant) insignificante
petty cash N piccola cassa
petty officer N sottufficiale m di marina
petulant ['pɛtjulənt] ADJ irritabile
pew [pju:] N panca (di chiesa)
pewter ['pju:tər] N peltro
Pfc ABBR (US Mil) = **private first class**
PG N ABBR (Cine: = parental guidance) consenso dei genitori richiesto
PG 13 ABBR (US Cine: = Parental Guidance 13) vietato ai minori di 13 anni non accompagnati dai genitori
PGA N ABBR (= Professional Golfers Association) associazione dei giocatori di golf professionisti
PH N ABBR (US Mil: = Purple Heart) decorazione per ferite riportate in guerra
PHA N ABBR (US: = Public Housing Administration) amministrazione per l'edilizia pubblica
phallic ['fælɪk] ADJ fallico(-a)
phantom ['fæntəm] N fantasma m
Pharaoh ['fɛərəu] N faraone m
pharmaceutical [fɑːmə'sju:tɪkl] ADJ farmaceutico(-a) ▶ N: **pharmaceuticals** prodotti mpl farmaceutici
pharmacist ['fɑːməsɪst] N farmacista mf
pharmacy ['fɑːməsɪ] N farmacia
phase [feɪz] N fase f, periodo
  ▶ **phase in** VT introdurre gradualmente
  ▶ **phase out** VT (machinery) eliminare gradualmente; (product) ritirare gradualmente; (job, subsidy) abolire gradualmente
PhD N ABBR = **Doctor of Philosophy**
pheasant ['fɛznt] N fagiano
phenomena [fə'nɔmɪnə] NPL of **phenomenon**
phenomenal [fɪ'nɔmɪnl] ADJ fenomenale
phenomenon [fə'nɔmɪnən] (pl **phenomena** [-nə]) N fenomeno

phew [fju:] EXCL uff!
phial ['faɪəl] N fiala
philanderer [fɪ'lændərər] N donnaiolo
philanthropic [fɪlən'θrɔpɪk] ADJ filantropico(-a)
philanthropist [fɪ'lænθrəpɪst] N filantropo
philatelist [fɪ'lætəlɪst] N filatelico(-a)
philately [fɪ'lætəlɪ] N filatelia
Philippines ['fɪlɪpi:nz] NPL (also: **Philippine Islands**): **the ~** le Filippine
philosopher [fɪ'lɔsəfər] N filosofo(-a)
philosophical [fɪlə'sofɪkl] ADJ filosofico(-a)
philosophy [fɪ'lɔsəfɪ] N filosofia
phlegm [flɛm] N flemma
phlegmatic [flɛg'mætɪk] ADJ flemmatico(-a)
phobia ['fəubjə] N fobia
phone [fəun] N telefono ▶ VT telefonare a
  ▶ VI telefonare; **to be on the ~** avere il telefono; (be calling) essere al telefono
  ▶ **phone back** VT, VI richiamare
  ▶ **phone up** VT telefonare a ▶ VI telefonare
phone book N guida del telefono, elenco telefonico
phone box, (US) **phone booth** N cabina telefonica
phone call N telefonata
phonecard ['fəunkɑːd] N scheda telefonica
phone-in ['fəunɪn] N (BRIT Radio, TV) trasmissione radiofonica o televisiva con intervento telefonico degli ascoltatori
phone number N numero di telefono
phone tapping [-tæpɪŋ] N intercettazioni fpl telefoniche
phonetics [fə'nɛtɪks] N fonetica
phoney ['fəunɪ] ADJ falso(-a), fasullo(-a) ▶ N (person) ciarlatano
phonograph ['fəunəgrɑːf] N (US) giradischi m inv
phony ['fəunɪ] ADJ, N = **phoney**
phosphate ['fosfeɪt] N fosfato
phosphorus ['fosfərəs] N fosforo
photo ['fəutəu] N foto f inv
photo... ['fəutəu] PREFIX foto...
photo album N (new) album m inv per fotografie; (containing photos) album m inv delle fotografie
photocall ['fəutəukɔːl] N convocazione di fotoreporter a scopo pubblicitario
photocopier ['fəutəukɔpɪər] N fotocopiatrice f
photocopy ['fəutəukɔpɪ] N fotocopia ▶ VT fotocopiare
photoelectric [fəutəu'lɛktrɪk] ADJ: **~ cell** cellula fotoelettrica
Photofit® ['fəutəufɪt] N photofit m inv
photogenic [fəutəu'dʒɛnɪk] ADJ fotogenico(-a)
photograph ['fəutəgræf] N fotografia ▶ VT fotografare; **to take a ~ of sb** fare una fotografia a or fotografare qn

p

photographer [fə'tɔgrəfəʳ] N fotografo
photographic [fəutə'græfɪk] ADJ
fotografico(-a)
photography [fə'tɔgrəfɪ] N fotografia
photo opportunity N opportunità di scattare
delle foto ad un personaggio importante
Photoshop® ['fəutəuʃɔp] N Photoshop® m
Photostat® ['fəutəustæt] N fotocopia
photosynthesis [fəutəu'sɪnθəsɪs] N
fotosintesi f
phrase [freɪz] N espressione f; (Ling)
locuzione f; (Mus) frase f ▶ VT esprimere;
(letter) redigere
phrasebook ['freɪzbuk] N vocabolarietto
physical ['fɪzɪkl] ADJ fisico(-a);
~ **examination** visita medica; ~ **education**
educazione f fisica; ~ **exercises** ginnastica
physically ['fɪzɪklɪ] ADV fisicamente
physician [fɪ'zɪʃən] N medico
physicist ['fɪzɪsɪst] N fisico
physics ['fɪzɪks] N fisica
physiological [fɪzɪə'lɔdʒɪkəl] ADJ
fisiologico(-a)
physiology [fɪzɪ'ɔlədʒɪ] N fisiologia
physiotherapist [fɪzɪəu'θɛrəpɪst] N
fisioterapista mf
physiotherapy [fɪzɪəu'θɛrəpɪ] N fisioterapia
physique [fɪ'zi:k] N fisico; costituzione f
pianist ['pi:ənɪst] N pianista mf
piano [pɪ'ænəu] N pianoforte m
piano accordion N (BRIT) fisarmonica (a
tastiera)
piccolo ['pɪkələu] N ottavino
pick [pɪk] N (tool: also: **pick-axe**) piccone m
▶ VT scegliere; (gather) cogliere; (remove)
togliere; (lock) far scattare; (scab, spot)
grattarsi ▶ VI: **to ~ and choose** scegliere con
cura; **take your ~** scelga; **the ~ of** il fior fiore
di; **to ~ one's nose** mettersi le dita nel naso;
to ~ one's teeth pulirsi i denti con lo
stuzzicadenti; **to ~ sb's brains** farsi dare dei
suggerimenti da qn; **to ~ pockets**
borseggiare; **to ~ a fight/quarrel with sb**
attaccar rissa/briga con qn; **to ~ one's way
through** attraversare stando ben attento a
dove mettere i piedi
▶ **pick off** VT (kill) abbattere
▶ **pick on** VT FUS (person) avercela con
▶ **pick out** VT scegliere; (distinguish)
distinguere
▶ **pick up** VI (improve) migliorarsi ▶ VT
raccogliere; (Police) prendere; (collect)
passare a prendere; (Aut: give lift to) far salire;
(person: for sexual encounter) rimorchiare; (learn)
imparare; (Radio, TV, Tel) ricevere; **to ~ o.s.
up** rialzarsi; **to ~ up where one left off**
riprendere dal punto in cui ci si era fermati;
to ~ up speed acquistare velocità
pickaxe, (US) **pickax** ['pɪkæks] N piccone m

picket ['pɪkɪt] N (in strike) scioperante mf che
fa parte di un picchetto; picchetto ▶ VT
picchettare
picket line N cordone m degli scioperanti
pickings ['pɪkɪŋz] NPL (pilferings): **there are
good ~ to be had here** qui ci sono buone
possibilità di intascare qualcosa sottobanco
pickle ['pɪkl] N (as condiment: also: **pickles**)
sottaceti mpl; (fig): **in a ~** nei pasticci ▶ VT
mettere sottaceto; mettere in salamoia
pick-me-up ['pɪkmi:ʌp] N tiramisù m inv
pickpocket ['pɪkpɔkɪt] N borsaiolo
pickup ['pɪkʌp] N (BRIT: on record player) pick-up
m inv; (small truck: also: **pickup truck, pickup
van**) camioncino
picnic ['pɪknɪk] N picnic m inv ▶ VI fare un
picnic
picnic area N area per il picnic
picnicker ['pɪknɪkəʳ] N chi partecipa a un
picnic
pictorial [pɪk'tɔ:rɪəl] ADJ illustrato(-a)
picture ['pɪktʃəʳ] N quadro; (painting) pittura;
(photograph) foto(grafia); (drawing) disegno;
(TV) immagine f; (film) film m inv ▶ VT
raffigurarsi; **the pictures** (BRIT) il cinema;
to take a ~ of sb/sth fare una foto a qn/di qc;
we get a good ~ here (TV) la ricezione qui è
buona; **the overall ~** il quadro generale; **to
put sb in the ~** mettere qn al corrente
picture book N libro illustrato
picture frame N cornice m inv
picture messaging N picture messaging m,
invio di messaggini con immagini
picturesque [pɪktʃə'rɛsk] ADJ pittoresco(-a)
picture window N finestra panoramica
piddling ['pɪdlɪŋ] ADJ (col) insignificante
pidgin English ['pɪdʒɪn-] N inglese semplificato
misto ad elementi indigeni
pie [paɪ] N torta; (of meat) pasticcio
piebald ['paɪbɔ:ld] ADJ pezzato(-a)
piece [pi:s] N pezzo; (of land) appezzamento;
(Draughts etc) pedina; (item): **a ~ of furniture/
advice** un mobile/consiglio ▶ VT: **to ~
together** mettere insieme; **in pieces**
(broken) in pezzi; (not yet assembled)
smontato(-a); **to take to pieces** smontare;
~ by ~ poco alla volta; **a 10p ~** (BRIT) una
moneta da 10 pence; **a six-~ band** un
complesso di sei strumentisti; **in one ~**
(object) intatto; **to get back all in one ~**
(person) tornare a casa incolume or sano e
salvo; **to say one's ~** dire la propria
piecemeal ['pi:smi:l] ADV pezzo a pezzo, a
spizzico
piece rate N tariffa a cottimo
piecework ['pi:swə:k] N (lavoro a) cottimo
pie chart N grafico a torta
Piedmont ['pi:dmɔnt] N Piemonte m
pier [pɪəʳ] N molo; (of bridge etc) pila

pierce [pɪəs] VT forare; (with arrow etc)
trafiggere; **to have one's ears pierced** farsi
fare i buchi per gli orecchini

pierced ADJ: **I've got ~ ears** ho i buchi per gli
orecchini

piercing ['pɪəsɪŋ] ADJ (cry) acuto(-a)

piety ['paɪətɪ] N pietà, devozione f

piffling ['pɪflɪŋ] ADJ insignificante

pig [pɪg] N maiale m, porco

pigeon ['pɪdʒən] N piccione m

pigeonhole ['pɪdʒənhəul] N casella ▶ VT
classificare

pigeon-toed ['pɪdʒən'təud] ADJ che
cammina con i piedi in dentro

piggy bank ['pɪgɪ-] N salvadanaio

pigheaded ['pɪg'hɛdɪd] ADJ caparbio(-a),
cocciuto(-a)

piglet ['pɪglɪt] N porcellino

pigment ['pɪgmənt] N pigmento

pigmentation [pɪgmən'teɪʃən] N
pigmentazione f

pigmy ['pɪgmɪ] N = **pygmy**

pigskin ['pɪgskɪn] N cinghiale m

pigsty ['pɪgstaɪ] N porcile m

pigtail ['pɪgteɪl] N treccina

pike [paɪk] N (spear) picca; (fish) luccio

pilchard ['pɪltʃəd] N specie di sardina

pile [paɪl] N (pillar, of books) pila; (heap)
mucchio; (of carpet) pelo; **to ~ into** (car)
stiparsi or ammucchiarsi in
▶ **pile up** VT ammucchiare ▶ VI
ammucchiarsi; **in a ~** ammucchiato;
see also **piles**
▶ **pile on** VT: **to ~ it on** (col) esagerare,
drammatizzare

piles [paɪlz] NPL (Med) emorroidi fpl

pileup ['paɪlʌp] N (Aut) tamponamento a
catena

pilfer ['pɪlfər] VT rubacchiare ▶ VI fare dei
furtarelli

pilfering ['pɪlfərɪŋ] N rubacchiare m

pilgrim ['pɪlgrɪm] N pellegrino(-a)

pilgrimage ['pɪlgrɪmɪdʒ] N pellegrinaggio

pill [pɪl] N pillola; **to be on the ~** prendere
la pillola

pillage ['pɪlɪdʒ] VT saccheggiare

pillar ['pɪlər] N colonna

pillar box N (Brit) cassetta delle lettere (a
colonnina)

pillion ['pɪljən] N (of motor cycle) sellino
posteriore; **to ride ~** viaggiare dietro

pillory ['pɪlərɪ] N berlina ▶ VT mettere alla
berlina

pillow ['pɪləu] N guanciale m

pillowcase ['pɪləukeɪs], **pillowslip**
['pɪləuslɪp] N federa

pilot ['paɪlət] N pilota mf ▶ CPD (scheme etc)
pilota inv ▶ VT pilotare

pilot boat N pilotina

pilot light N fiamma pilota

pimento [pɪ'mɛntəu] N peperoncino

pimp [pɪmp] N mezzano

pimple ['pɪmpl] N foruncolo

pimply ['pɪmplɪ] ADJ foruncoloso(-a)

PIN N ABBR (= personal identification number)
codice m segreto, PIN m inv

pin [pɪn] N spillo; (Tech) perno; (Brit: drawing
pin) puntina da disegno; (Brit Elec: of plug)
spinotto ▶ VT attaccare con uno spillo; **pins
and needles** formicolio; **to ~ sb against/to**
inchiodare qn contro/a; **to ~ sth on sb** (fig)
addossare la colpa di qc a qn
▶ **pin down** VT (fig): **to ~ sb down** obbligare
qn a pronunziarsi; **there's something
strange here but I can't quite ~ it down**
c'è qualcosa di strano qua ma non riesco a
capire cos'è

pinafore ['pɪnəfɔːr] N (also: **pinafore dress**)
scamiciato

pinball ['pɪnbɔːl] N flipper m inv

pincers ['pɪnsəz] NPL pinzette fpl

pinch [pɪntʃ] N pizzicotto, pizzico ▶ VT
pizzicare; (col: steal) grattare ▶ VI (shoe)
stringere; **at a ~** in caso di bisogno; **to feel
the ~** (fig) trovarsi nelle ristrettezze

pinched [pɪntʃt] ADJ (drawn) dai lineamenti
tirati; (short): ~ **for money/space** a corto di
soldi/di spazio; ~ **with cold** raggrinzito dal
freddo

pincushion ['pɪnkuʃən] N puntaspilli m inv

pine [paɪn] N (also: **pine tree**) pino ▶ VI: **to ~
for** struggersi dal desiderio di
▶ **pine away** VI languire

pineapple ['paɪnæpl] N ananas m inv

pine cone N pigna

pine needles NPL aghi mpl di pino

ping [pɪŋ] N (noise) tintinnio

Ping-Pong® ['pɪŋpɔŋ] N ping-pong® m

pink [pɪŋk] ADJ rosa inv ▶ N (colour) rosa m inv;
(Bot) garofano

pinking shears ['pɪŋkɪŋ-] N forbici fpl a
zigzag

pin money N (Brit) denaro per le piccole spese

pinnacle ['pɪnəkl] N pinnacolo

pinpoint ['pɪnpɔɪnt] VT indicare con
precisione

pinstripe ['pɪnstraɪp] N stoffa gessata; (also:
pinstripe suit) gessato

pint [paɪnt] N pinta (Brit = 0.57 l; US = 0.47 l);
(Brit col: of beer) ≈ birra grande

pinup ['pɪnʌp] N pin-up girl f inv

pioneer [paɪə'nɪər] N pioniere(-a) ▶ VT essere
un pioniere in

pious ['paɪəs] ADJ pio(-a)

pip [pɪp] N (seed) seme m; (Brit: time signal on
radio) segnale m orario

pipe [paɪp] N tubo; (for smoking) pipa; (Mus)
piffero ▶ VT portare per mezzo di tubazione;

pipes NPL (*also*: **bagpipes**) cornamusa (scozzese)
▶ **pipe down** VI (*col*) calmarsi
pipe cleaner N scovolino
piped music [paɪpt-] N musica di sottofondo
pipe dream N vana speranza
pipeline ['paɪplaɪn] N conduttura; (*for oil*) oleodotto; (*for natural gas*) metanodotto; **it is in the ~** (*fig*) è in arrivo
piper ['paɪpəʳ] N piffero; suonatore(-trice) di cornamusa
pipe tobacco N tabacco da pipa
piping ['paɪpɪŋ] ADV: **~ hot** bollente
piquant ['piːkənt] ADJ (*sauce*) piccante; (*conversation*) stimolante
pique [piːk] N picca
piracy ['paɪərəsɪ] N pirateria
pirate ['paɪərət] N pirata *m* ▶ VT (*record, video, book*) riprodurre abusivamente
pirate radio N radio pirata *f inv*
pirouette [pɪru'ɛt] N piroetta ▶ VI piroettare
Pisces ['paɪsiːz] N Pesci *mpl*; **to be ~** essere dei Pesci
piss [pɪs] VI (*col!*) pisciare; **~ off!** vaffanculo! (!)
pissed [pɪst] ADJ (BRIT *col: drunk*) ubriaco(-a) fradicio(-a)
pistol ['pɪstl] N pistola
piston ['pɪstən] N pistone *m*
pit [pɪt] N buca, fossa; (*also*: **coal pit**) miniera; (*also*: **orchestra pit**) orchestra; (: *quarry*) cava ▶ VT: **to ~ sb against sb** opporre qn a qn; **pits** NPL (*Aut*) box *m*; **to ~ o.s. against** opporsi a
pitapat ['pɪtə'pæt] ADV (BRIT): **to go ~** (*heart*) palpitare, battere forte; (*rain*) picchiettare
pitch [pɪtʃ] N (*throw*) lancia; (*Mus*) tono; (*of voice*) altezza; (*fig: degree*) grado, punto; (*also*: **sales pitch**) discorso di vendita, imbonimento; (: BRIT *Sport*) campo; (: *Naut*) beccheggio; (: *tar*) pece *f* ▶ VT (*throw*) lanciare ▶ VI (*fall*) cascare; (*Naut*) beccheggiare; **to ~ a tent** piantare una tenda; **at this ~** a questo ritmo
pitch-black [pɪtʃ'blæk] ADJ nero(-a) come la pece
pitched battle [pɪtʃt-] N battaglia campale
pitcher ['pɪtʃəʳ] N brocca
pitchfork ['pɪtʃfɔːk] N forcone *m*
piteous ['pɪtɪəs] ADJ pietoso(-a)
pitfall ['pɪtfɔːl] N trappola
pith [pɪθ] N (*of plant*) midollo; (*of orange*) parte *f* interna della scorza; (*fig*) essenza, succo; vigore *m*
pithead ['pɪthɛd] N (BRIT) imbocco della miniera
pithy ['pɪθɪ] ADJ conciso(-a); vigoroso(-a)
pitiable ['pɪtɪəbl] ADJ pietoso(-a)
pitiful ['pɪtɪful] ADJ (*touching*) pietoso(-a); (*contemptible*) miserabile

pitifully ['pɪtɪfəlɪ] ADV pietosamente; **it's ~ obvious** è penosamente chiaro
pitiless ['pɪtɪlɪs] ADJ spietato(-a)
pittance ['pɪtns] N miseria, magro salario
pitted ['pɪtɪd] ADJ: **~ with** (*potholes*) pieno(-a) di; (*chickenpox*) butterato(-a) da
pity ['pɪtɪ] N pietà ▶ VT aver pietà di, compatire, commiserare; **to have** *or* **take on sb** aver pietà di qn; **it is a ~ that you can't come** è un peccato che non possa venire; **what a ~!** che peccato!
pitying ['pɪtɪɪŋ] ADJ compassionevole
pivot ['pɪvət] N perno ▶ VI imperniarsi
pixel ['pɪksl] N (*Comput*) pixel *m inv*
pixie ['pɪksɪ] N folletto
pizza ['piːtsə] N pizza
placard ['plækaːd] N affisso
placate [plə'keɪt] VT placare, calmare
placatory [plə'keɪtərɪ] ADJ conciliante
place [pleɪs] N posto, luogo; (*proper position, rank, seat*) posto; (*house*) casa, alloggio; (*home*): **at/to his ~** a casa sua; (*in street names*): **Laurel P~** via dei Lauri ▶ VT (*object*) posare, mettere; (*identify*) riconoscere; individuare; (*goods*) piazzare; **to take ~** aver luogo; succedere; **out of ~** (*not suitable*) inopportuno(-a); **I feel rather out of ~ here** qui mi sento un po' fuori posto; **in the first ~** in primo luogo; **change places with sb** scambiare il posto con qn; **to put sb in his ~** (*fig*) mettere a posto qn, mettere qn al suo posto; **from ~ to ~** da un posto all'altro; **all over the ~** dappertutto; **he's going places** (*fig: col*) si sta facendo strada; **it is not my ~ to do it** non sta a me farlo; **how are you placed next week?** com'è messo la settimana prossima?; **to ~ an order with sb (for)** (*Comm*) fare un'ordinazione a qn (di); **to be placed** (*in race, exam*) classificarsi
placebo [plə'siːbəu] N placebo *m inv*
place mat N sottopiatto; (*in linen etc*) tovaglietta
placement ['pleɪsmənt] N collocamento; (*job*) lavoro
place name N toponimo
placenta [plə'sɛntə] N placenta
placid ['plæsɪd] ADJ placido(-a), calmo(-a)
placidity [plə'sɪdɪtɪ] N placidità
plagiarism ['pleɪdʒərɪzəm] N plagio
plagiarist ['pleɪdʒərɪst] N plagiario(-a)
plagiarize ['pleɪdʒəraɪz] VT plagiare
plague [pleɪg] N peste *f* ▶ VT tormentare; **to ~ sb with questions** assillare qn di domande
plaice [pleɪs] N (*pl inv*) pianuzza
plaid [plæd] N plaid *m inv*
plain [pleɪn] ADJ (*clear*) chiaro(-a), palese; (*simple*) semplice; (*frank*) franco(-a), aperto(-a); (*not handsome*) bruttino(-a); (*without seasoning etc*) scondito(-a); naturale;

(*in one colour*) tinta unita *inv* ▶ ADV
francamente, chiaramente ▶ N pianura; **to
make sth ~ to sb** far capire chiaramente qc
a qn; **in ~ clothes** (*police*) in borghese
plain chocolate N cioccolato fondente
plainly ['pleɪnlɪ] ADV chiaramente; (*frankly*)
francamente
plainness ['pleɪnnɪs] N semplicità
plain speaking N: **there has been some ~
between the two leaders** i due leader si
sono parlati chiaro
plaintiff ['pleɪntɪf] N attore(-trice)
plaintive ['pleɪntɪv] ADJ (*voice, song*)
lamentoso(-a); (*look*) struggente
plait [plæt] N treccia ▶ VT intrecciare; **to ~
one's hair** farsi una treccia (*or* le trecce)
plan [plæn] N pianta; (*scheme*) progetto,
piano ▶ VT (*think in advance*) progettare;
(*prepare*) organizzare; (*intend*) avere in
progetto ▶ VI: **to ~ (for)** far piani *or* progetti
(per); **to ~ to do** progettare di fare, avere
l'intenzione di fare; **how long do you ~ to
stay?** quanto conta di restare?
plane [pleɪn] N (*Aviat*) aereo; (*tree*) platano;
(*tool*) pialla; (*Art, Math etc*) piano ▶ ADJ
piano(-a), piatto(-a) ▶ VT (*with tool*) piallare
planet ['plænɪt] N pianeta *m*
planetarium [plænɪ'tɛərɪəm] N planetario
plank [plæŋk] N tavola, asse *f*
plankton ['plæŋktən] N plancton *m*
planned economy [plænd-] N economia
pianificata
planner ['plænər] N pianificatore(-trice);
(*chart*) calendario; **town** *or* (US) **city ~**
urbanista *mf*
planning ['plænɪŋ] N progettazione *f*; (*Pol,
Econ*) pianificazione *f*; **family ~**
pianificazione delle nascite
planning permission N (*Brit*) permesso di
costruzione
plant [plɑ:nt] N pianta; (*machinery*) impianto;
(*factory*) fabbrica ▶ VT piantare; (*bomb*)
mettere
plantation [plæn'teɪʃən] N piantagione *f*
plant pot N (*Brit*) vaso (di fiori)
plaque [plæk] N placca
plasma ['plæzmə] N plasma *m*
plasma TV N TV *f inv* al plasma
plaster ['plɑ:stər] N intonaco; (*also:* **plaster
of Paris**) gesso; (*Brit: also:* **sticking plaster**)
cerotto ▶ VT intonacare; ingessare; (*col: mud
etc*) impiastricciare; (*cover*): **to ~ with** coprire
di; **in ~** (*Brit: leg etc*) ingessato(-a)
plasterboard ['plɑ:stəbɔ:d] N lastra di
cartone ingessato
plaster cast N (*Med*) ingessatura, gesso;
(*model, statue*) modello in gesso
plastered ['plɑ:stəd] ADJ (*col*) ubriaco(-a)
fradicio(-a)

plasterer ['plɑ:stərər] N intonacatore *m*
plastic ['plæstɪk] N plastica ▶ ADJ (*made of
plastic*) di *or* in plastica; (*flexible*) plastico(-a),
malleabile; (*art*) plastico(-a)
plastic bag N sacchetto di plastica
plastic bullet N pallottola di plastica
plastic explosive N esplosivo al plastico
plasticine® ['plæstɪsi:n] N plastilina®
plastic surgery N chirurgia plastica
plate [pleɪt] N (*dish*) piatto; (*sheet of metal*)
lamiera; (*Phot*) lastra; (*Typ*) cliché *m inv*; (*in
book*) tavola; (*on door*) targa, targhetta; (*Aut:
number plate*) targa; (*dental plate*) dentiera;
(*dishes*): **gold/silver ~** vasellame *m*
d'oro/d'argento
plateau ['plætəu] (*pl* **plateaus** *or* **plateaux**
[-z]) N altipiano
plateful ['pleɪtful] N piatto
plate glass N vetro piano
platen ['plætən] N (*on typewriter, printer*) rullo
plate rack N scolapiatti *m inv*
platform ['plætfɔ:m] N (*stage, at meeting*)
palco; (*Brit: on bus*) piattaforma; (*Rail*)
marciapiede *m*; **the train leaves from ~ 7**
il treno parte dal binario 7
platform ticket N (*Brit*) biglietto d'ingresso
ai binari
platinum ['plætɪnəm] N platino
platitude ['plætɪtju:d] N luogo comune
platoon [plə'tu:n] N plotone *m*
platter ['plætər] N piatto
plaudits ['plɔ:dɪts] NPL plauso
plausible ['plɔ:zɪbl] ADJ plausibile, credibile;
(*person*) convincente
play [pleɪ] N gioco; (*Theat*) commedia ▶ VT
(*game*) giocare a; (*team, opponent*) giocare
contro; (*instrument, piece of music*) suonare;
(*record, tape*) ascoltare; (*play, part*) interpretare
▶ VI giocare; suonare; recitare; **to ~ safe**
giocare sul sicuro; **to bring** *or* **call into ~**
(*plan*) mettere in azione; (*emotions*) esprimere;
~ on words gioco di parole; **to ~ a trick on
sb** fare uno scherzo a qn; **they're playing at
soldiers** stanno giocando ai soldati; **to ~ for
time** (*fig*) cercare di guadagnar tempo; **to ~
into sb's hands** (*fig*) fare il gioco di qn
▶ **play about, play around** VI (*person*)
divertirsi; **to ~ about** *or* **around with** (*fiddle
with*) giocherellare con; (*idea*) accarezzare
▶ **play along** VI: **to ~ along with** (*fig: person*)
stare al gioco di; (*plan, idea*) fingere di
assecondare ▶ VT (*fig*): **to ~ sb along** tenere
qn in sospeso
▶ **play back** VT riascoltare, risentire
▶ **play down** VT minimizzare
▶ **play on** VT FUS (*sb's feelings, credulity*) giocare
su; **to ~ on sb's nerves** dare sui nervi a qn
▶ **play up** VI (*cause trouble*) fare i capricci
playact ['pleɪækt] VI fare la commedia

p

playboy ['pleɪbɔɪ] N playboy *m inv*
played-out ['pleɪd'aut] ADJ spossato(-a)
player ['pleɪə'] N giocatore(-trice); (*Theat*) attore(-trice); (*Mus*) musicista *mf*
playful ['pleɪful] ADJ giocoso(-a)
playgoer ['pleɪgəuə'] N assiduo(-a) frequentatore(-a) di teatri
playground ['pleɪgraund] N (*in school*) cortile *m* per la ricreazione; (*in park*) parco *m* giochi *inv*
playgroup ['pleɪgru:p] N giardino d'infanzia
playing card ['pleɪɪŋ-] N carta da gioco
playing field ['pleɪɪŋ-] N campo sportivo
playmaker ['pleɪmeɪkə'] N (*Sport*) playmaker *m inv*
playmate ['pleɪmeɪt] N compagno(-a) di gioco
play-off ['pleɪɔf] N (*Sport*) bella
playpen ['pleɪpɛn] N box *m inv*
playroom ['pleɪru:m] N stanza dei giochi
playschool N = **playgroup**
plaything ['pleɪθɪŋ] N giocattolo
playtime ['pleɪtaɪm] N (*Scol*) ricreazione *f*
playwright ['pleɪraɪt] N drammaturgo(-a)
plc ABBR (*Brit*: = *public limited company*) società per azioni a responsabilità limitata quotata in borsa
plea [pli:] N (*request*) preghiera, domanda; (*excuse*) scusa; (*Law*) (argomento di) difesa
plea bargaining N (*Law*) patteggiamento
plead [pli:d] VT patrocinare; (*give as excuse*) addurre a pretesto ▶ VI (*Law*) perorare la causa; (*beg*): **to ~ with sb** implorare qn; **to ~ for sth** implorare qc; **to ~ guilty/not guilty** (*defendant*) dichiararsi colpevole/innocente
pleasant ['plɛznt] ADJ piacevole, gradevole
pleasantly ['plɛzntlɪ] ADV piacevolmente
pleasantry ['plɛzntrɪ] N (*joke*) scherzo; (*polite remark*): **to exchange pleasantries** scambiarsi i convenevoli
please [pli:z] VT piacere a ▶ VI (*think fit*): **do as you ~** faccia come le pare; **~!** per piacere!, per favore!; (*acceptance*) **yes, ~** sì, grazie; **my bill, ~** il conto, per piacere; **~ yourself!** come ti (*or* le) pare!; **~ don't cry!** ti prego, non piangere!
pleased [pli:zd] ADJ (*happy*) felice, lieto(-a); **~ (with)** (*satisfied*) contento(-a) (di); **we are ~ to inform you that …** abbiamo il piacere di informarla che …; **~ to meet you!** piacere!
pleasing ['pli:zɪŋ] ADJ piacevole, che fa piacere
pleasurable ['plɛʒərəbl] ADJ molto piacevole, molto gradevole
pleasure ['plɛʒə'] N piacere *m*; **with ~** con piacere, volentieri; **"it's a ~"** "prego"; **is this trip for business or ~?** è un viaggio d'affari o di piacere?
pleasure cruise N crociera
pleat [pli:t] N piega
plebiscite ['plɛbɪsɪt] N plebiscito

plebs [plɛbz] NPL (*pej*) plebe *f*
plectrum ['plɛktrəm] N plettro
pledge [plɛdʒ] N pegno; (*promise*) promessa ▶ VT impegnare; promettere; **to ~ support for sb** impegnarsi a sostenere qn; **to ~ sb to secrecy** far promettere a qn di mantenere il segreto
plenary ['pli:nərɪ] ADJ plenario(-a); **in ~ session** in seduta plenaria
plentiful ['plɛntɪful] ADJ abbondante, copioso(-a)
plenty ['plɛntɪ] N abbondanza; **~ of** tanto(-a), molto(-a); un'abbondanza di; **we've got ~ of time to get there** abbiamo un sacco di tempo per arrivarci
pleurisy ['pluərɪsɪ] N pleurite *f*
Plexiglas® ['plɛksɪglɑ:s] N (*US*) plexiglas® *m*
pliable ['plaɪəbl] ADJ flessibile; (*person*) malleabile
pliers ['plaɪəz] NPL pinza
plight [plaɪt] N situazione *f* critica
plimsolls ['plɪmsəlz] NPL (*Brit*) scarpe *fpl* da tennis
plinth [plɪnθ] N plinto; piedistallo
PLO N ABBR (= *Palestine Liberation Organization*) O.L.P. *f*
plod [plɔd] VI camminare a stento; (*fig*) sgobbare
plodder ['plɔdə'] N sgobbone *m*
plodding ['plɔdɪŋ] ADJ lento(-a) e pesante
plonk [plɔŋk] (*col*) N (*Brit*: *wine*) vino da poco ▶ VT: **to ~ sth down** buttare giù qc bruscamente
plot [plɔt] N congiura, cospirazione *f*; (*of story, play*) trama; (*of land*) lotto ▶ VT (*mark out*) fare la pianta di; rilevare; (: *diagram etc*) tracciare; (*conspire*) congiurare, cospirare ▶ VI congiurare; **a vegetable ~** (*Brit*) un orticello
plotter ['plɔtə'] N cospiratore(-trice); (*Comput*) plotter *m inv*, tracciatore *m* di curve
plough, (*US*) **plow** [plau] N aratro ▶ VT (*earth*) arare; **to ~ money into** (*company etc*) investire danaro in
▶ **plough back** VT (*Comm*) reinvestire
▶ **plough through** VT FUS (*snow etc*) procedere a fatica in
ploughing, (*US*) **plowing** ['plauɪŋ] N aratura
ploughman, (*US*) **plowman** ['plaumən] N (*irreg*) aratore *m*; **~'s lunch** *n* (*Brit*) semplice pasto a base di pane e formaggio
plow *etc* [plau] (*US*) = **plough** *etc*
ploy [plɔɪ] N stratagemma *m*
pls ABBR = **please**
pluck [plʌk] VT (*fruit*) cogliere; (*musical instrument*) pizzicare; (*bird*) spennare; (*hairs*) togliere ▶ N coraggio, fegato; **to ~ one's eyebrows** depilarsi le sopracciglia; **to ~ up courage** farsi coraggio
plucky ['plʌkɪ] ADJ coraggioso(-a)

plug [plʌg] N tappo; (Elec) spina; (Aut: also: **spark(ing) plug**) candela ▶ VT (hole) tappare; (col: advertise) spingere; **to give sb/sth a ~** fare pubblicità a qn/qc
 ▶ **plug in** (Elec) VI inserire la spina ▶ VT attaccare a una presa
plughole ['plʌghəul] N (BRIT) scarico
plug-in ['plʌgɪn] N (Comput) plug-in m inv
plum [plʌm] N (fruit) susina ▶ CPD: **~ job** (col) impiego ottimo or favoloso
plumage ['pluːmɪdʒ] N piume fpl, piumaggio
plumb [plʌm] ADJ verticale ▶ N piombo ▶ ADV (exactly) esattamente ▶ VT sondare
 ▶ **plumb in** VT (washing machine) collegare all'impianto idraulico
plumber ['plʌmər] N idraulico
plumbing ['plʌmɪŋ] N (trade) lavoro di idraulico; (piping) tubature fpl
plumbline ['plʌmlaɪn] N filo a piombo
plume [pluːm] N piuma, penna; (decorative) pennacchio
plummet ['plʌmɪt] VI: **to ~ (down)** cadere a piombo
plump [plʌmp] ADJ grassoccio(-a) ▶ VT: **to ~ sth (down) on** lasciar cadere qc di peso su
 ▶ **plump for** VT FUS (col: choose) decidersi per
 ▶ **plump up** VT sprimacciare
plunder ['plʌndər] N saccheggio ▶ VT saccheggiare
plunge [plʌndʒ] N tuffo; (fig) caduta ▶ VT immergere ▶ VI (dive) tuffarsi; (fall) cadere, precipitare; **to take the ~** (fig) saltare il fosso; **to ~ a room into darkness** far piombare una stanza nel buio
plunger ['plʌndʒər] N (for blocked sink) sturalavandini m inv
plunging ['plʌndʒɪŋ] ADJ (neckline) profondo(-a)
pluperfect [pluː'pəːfɪkt] N piuccheperfetto
plural ['pluərl] ADJ, N plurale (m)
plus [plʌs] N (also: **plus sign**) segno più ▶ PREP più ▶ ADJ (Math, Elec) positivo(-a); **ten/ twenty ~** più di dieci/venti; **it's a ~** (fig) è un vantaggio
plus fours NPL calzoni mpl alla zuava
plush [plʌʃ] ADJ lussuoso(-a) ▶ N felpa
plus-one ['plʌs'wʌn] N accompagnatore(-trice)
plutonium [pluː'təunɪəm] N plutonio
ply [plaɪ] N (of wool) capo; (of wood) strato ▶ VT (tool) maneggiare; (a trade) esercitare ▶ VI (ship) fare il servizio; **three ~ (wool)** lana a tre capi; **to ~ sb with drink** dare da bere continuamente a qn
plywood ['plaɪwud] N legno compensato
PM N ABBR (BRIT) = **prime minister**
p.m. ADV ABBR (= post meridiem) del pomeriggio
PMS N ABBR (= premenstrual syndrome) sindrome f premestruale

PMT N ABBR (= premenstrual tension) sindrome f premestruale
pneumatic [njuː'mætɪk] ADJ pneumatico(-a); **~ drill** martello pneumatico
pneumonia [njuː'məunɪə] N polmonite f
PO N ABBR (= Post Office) ≈ P.T. (= Poste e Telegrafi)
 ▶ ABBR (Naut) = **petty officer**
po ABBR = **postal order**
POA N ABBR (BRIT: = Prison Officers' Association) sindacato delle guardie carcerarie
poach [pəutʃ] VT (cook: egg) affogare; (: fish) cuocere in bianco; (steal) cacciare (or pescare) di frodo ▶ VI fare il bracconiere
poached [pəutʃt] ADJ (egg) affogato(-a)
poacher ['pəutʃər] N bracconiere m
poaching ['pəutʃɪŋ] N caccia (or pesca) di frodo
PO box N ABBR = **post office box**
pocket ['pɔkɪt] N tasca ▶ VT intascare; **to be out of ~** (BRIT) rimetterci; **to be £5 in/out of ~** (BRIT) trovarsi con 5 sterline in più/in meno; **air ~** vuoto d'aria
pocketbook ['pɔkɪtbuk] N (US: wallet) portafoglio; (notebook) taccuino; (handbag) busta
pocket knife N temperino
pocket money N paghetta, settimana
pockmarked ['pɔkmaːkt] ADJ (face) butterato(-a)
pod [pɔd] N guscio ▶ VT sgusciare
podcast ['pɔdkaːst] N podcast m inv
podgy ['pɔdʒɪ] ADJ grassoccio(-a)
podiatrist [pɔ'diːətrɪst] N (US) callista mf, pedicure mf
podiatry [pɔ'diːətrɪ] N (US) mestiere m di callista
podium ['pəudɪəm] N podio
POE N ABBR = **port of embarkation; port of entry**
poem ['pəuɪm] N poesia
poet ['pəuɪt] N poeta(-essa)
poetic [pəu'ɛtɪk] ADJ poetico(-a)
poet laureate N (BRIT) poeta m laureato; _vedi nota_

> In Gran Bretagna il poet laureate è un poeta che riceve un vitalizio dalla casa reale britannica e che ha l'incarico di scrivere delle poesie commemorative in occasione delle festività ufficiali.

poetry ['pəuɪtrɪ] N poesia
poignant ['pɔɪnjənt] ADJ struggente
point [pɔɪnt] N (gen) punto; (tip: of needle etc) punta; (BRIT Elec: also: **power point**) presa (di corrente); (in time) punto, momento; (Scol) voto; (main idea, important part) nocciolo; (also: **decimal point**): **2 ~ 3 (2.3)** 2 virgola 3 (2,3) ▶ VT (show) indicare; (gun etc): **to ~ sth at** puntare qc contro ▶ VI: **to ~ at** mostrare a dito; **to ~ to**

p

indicare; (fig) dimostrare; **points** NPL (Aut)
puntine fpl; (Rail) scambio; **to make a ~** fare
un'osservazione; **to get/miss the ~** capire/
non capire; **to come to the ~** venire al fatto;
when it comes to the ~ quando si arriva al
dunque; **to be on the ~ of doing sth** essere
sul punto di or stare (proprio) per fare qc; **to
be beside the ~** non entrarci; **to make a ~ of
doing sth** non mancare di fare qc; **there's
no ~ (in doing)** è inutile (fare); **in ~ of fact** a
dire il vero; **that's the whole ~!**
precisamente!, sta tutto lì!; **you've got a ~
there!** giusto!, ha ragione!; **the train stops
at Carlisle and all points south** il treno
ferma a Carlisle e in tutte le stazioni a sud di
Carlisle; **good points** vantaggi mpl; (of person)
qualità fpl; **~ of departure** (also fig) punto di
partenza; **~ of order** mozione f d'ordine;
~ of sale (Comm) punto di vendita; **~ of view**
punto di vista
  ▶ **point out** VT far notare
point-blank ['pɔɪnt'blæŋk] ADV (also: **at
point-blank range**) a bruciapelo; (: fig)
categoricamente
point duty N (BRIT): **to be on ~** dirigere il
traffico
pointed ['pɔɪntɪd] ADJ (shape) aguzzo(-a),
appuntito(-a); (remark) specifico(-a)
pointedly ['pɔɪntɪdlɪ] ADV in maniera
inequivocabile
pointer ['pɔɪntəʳ] N (stick) bacchetta; (needle)
lancetta; (clue) indicazione f; (advice)
consiglio; (dog) pointer m, cane m da punta
pointless ['pɔɪntlɪs] ADJ inutile, vano(-a)
poise [pɔɪz] N (balance) equilibrio; (of head,
body) portamento; (calmness) calma ▶ VT
tenere in equilibrio; **to be poised for** (fig)
essere pronto(-a) a
poison ['pɔɪzn] N veleno ▶ VT avvelenare
poisoning ['pɔɪznɪŋ] N avvelenamento
poisonous ['pɔɪznəs] ADJ velenoso(-a);
(fumes) venefico(-a), tossico(-a); (ideas,
literature) pernicioso(-a); (rumours, individual)
perfido(-a)
poke [pəuk] VT (fire) attizzare; (jab with finger,
stick etc) punzecchiare; (put): **to ~ sth in(to)**
spingere qc dentro ▶ N (jab) colpetto; (with
elbow) gomitata; **to ~ one's head out of the
window** mettere la testa fuori dalla finestra;
to ~ fun at sb prendere in giro qn
  ▶ **poke about, poke around** VI frugare
  ▶ **poke out** VI (stick out) sporgere fuori
poker ['pəukəʳ] N attizzatoio; (Cards) poker m
poker-faced ['pəukə'feɪst] ADJ dal viso
impassibile
poky ['pəukɪ] ADJ piccolo(-a) e stretto(-a)
Poland ['pəulənd] N Polonia
polar ['pəuləʳ] ADJ polare
polar bear N orso bianco

polarize ['pəulərazɪz] VT polarizzare
Pole [pəul] N polacco(-a)
pole [pəul] N (of wood) palo; (Elec, Geo) polo
poleaxe, (US) **poleax** ['pəulæks] VT (fig)
stendere
pole bean N (US: runner bean) fagiolino
polecat ['pəulkæt] N puzzola; (US) moffetta
Pol. Econ. ['pɔlɪkɔn] N ABBR = **political
economy**
polemic [pɔ'lɛmɪk] N polemica
pole star N stella polare
pole vault N salto con l'asta
police [pə'liːs] N polizia ▶ VT mantenere
l'ordine in; (streets, city, frontier) presidiare; **a
large number of ~ were hurt** molti
poliziotti sono rimasti feriti
police car N macchina della polizia
police constable N (BRIT) agente m di polizia
police department N (US) dipartimento di
polizia
police force N corpo di polizia, polizia
policeman [pə'liːsmən] N (irreg) poliziotto,
agente m di polizia
police officer N = **police constable**
police record N: **to have a ~** avere precedenti
penali
police state N stato di polizia
police station N posto di polizia
policewoman [pə'liːswumən] N (irreg) donna
f poliziotto inv
policy ['pɔlɪsɪ] N politica; (of newspaper,
company) linea di condotta, prassi f inv; (also:
insurance policy) polizza (d'assicurazione);
to take out a ~ (Insurance) stipulare una
polizza di assicurazione
policy holder N assicurato(-a)
policy-making ['pɔlɪsɪmeɪkɪŋ] N messa a
punto dei programmi
polio ['pəulɪəu] N polio f
Polish ['pəulɪʃ] ADJ polacco(-a) ▶ N (Ling)
polacco
polish ['pɔlɪʃ] N (for shoes) lucido; (for floor)
cera; (for nails) smalto; (shine) lucentezza,
lustro; (fig: refinement) raffinatezza ▶ VT
lucidare; (fig: improve) raffinare
  ▶ **polish off** VT (work) sbrigare; (food)
mangiarsi
polished ['pɔlɪʃt] ADJ (fig) raffinato(-a)
polite [pə'laɪt] ADJ cortese; **it's not ~ to do
that** non è educato or buona educazione fare
questo
politely [pə'laɪtlɪ] ADV cortesemente
politeness [pə'laɪtnɪs] N cortesia
politic ['pɔlɪtɪk] ADJ diplomatico(-a)
political [pə'lɪtɪkl] ADJ politico(-a)
political asylum N asilo politico
politically [pə'lɪtɪklɪ] ADV politicamente
politically correct ADJ politicamente
corretto(-a)

politician [pɔlɪ'tɪʃən] N politico
politics ['pɔlɪtɪks] N politica ▶ NPL (*views, policies*) idee *fpl* politiche
polka ['pɔlkə] N polca
polka dot N pois *m inv*
poll [pəul] N scrutinio; (*votes cast*) voti *mpl*; (*also*: **opinion poll**) sondaggio (d'opinioni) ▶ VT ottenere; **to go to the polls** (*voters*) andare alle urne; (*government*) indire le elezioni
pollen ['pɔlən] N polline *m*
pollen count N tasso di polline nell'aria
pollination [pɔlɪ'neɪʃən] N impollinazione *f*
polling ['pəulɪŋ] N (*Pol*) votazione *f*, votazioni *fpl*; (*Tel*) interrogazione *f* ciclica
polling booth N (*BRIT*) cabina elettorale
polling day N (*BRIT*) giorno delle elezioni
polling station ['pəulɪŋ-] N (*BRIT*) sezione *f* elettorale
pollster ['pəulstər] N chi esegue sondaggi d'opinione
poll tax N (*BRIT*) *imposta locale sulla persona fisica (non più in vigore)*
pollutant [pə'lu:tənt] N sostanza inquinante
pollute [pə'lu:t] VT inquinare
pollution [pə'lu:ʃən] N inquinamento
polo ['pəuləu] N polo
polo neck N collo alto; (*also*: **polo neck sweater**) dolcevita ▶ ADJ a collo alto
polo shirt N polo *f inv*
poly ['pɔlɪ] N ABBR (*BRIT*) = **polytechnic**
poly bag N (*BRIT col*) borsa di plastica
polyester [pɔlɪ'ɛstər] N poliestere *m*
polygamy [pə'lɪgəmɪ] N poligamia
polygraph ['pɔlɪgrɑːf] N macchina della verità
Polynesia [pɔlɪ'niːzɪə] N Polinesia
Polynesian [pɔlɪ'niːzɪən] ADJ, N polinesiano(-a)
polyp ['pɔlɪp] N (*Med*) polipo
polystyrene [pɔlɪ'staɪriːn] N polistirolo
polytechnic [pɔlɪ'tɛknɪk] N (*college*) *istituto superiore ad indirizzo tecnologico*
polythene ['pɔlɪθiːn] N politene *m*
polythene bag N sacchetto di plastica
polyurethane ['pɔlɪ'juərɪθeɪn] N poliuretano
pomegranate ['pɔmɪgrænɪt] N melagrana
pommel ['pɔml] N pomo ▶ VT = **pummel**
pomp [pɔmp] N pompa, fasto
pompom ['pɔmpɔm] N pompon *m inv*
pompous ['pɔmpəs] ADJ pomposo(-a); (*person*) pieno(-a) di boria
pond [pɔnd] N pozza; stagno; (*in park*) laghetto
ponder ['pɔndər] VI riflettere, meditare ▶ VT ponderare, riflettere su
ponderous ['pɔndərəs] ADJ ponderoso(-a), pesante
pong [pɔŋ] (*BRIT col*) N puzzo ▶ VI puzzare

pontiff ['pɔntɪf] N pontefice *m*
pontificate [pɔn'tɪfɪkeɪt] VI (*fig*): **to ~ (about)** pontificare (su)
pontoon [pɔn'tuːn] N pontone *m*; (*BRIT Cards*) ventuno
pony ['pəunɪ] N pony *m inv*
ponytail ['pəunɪteɪl] N coda di cavallo
pony trekking [-trɛkɪŋ] N (*BRIT*) escursione *f* a cavallo
poodle ['puːdl] N barboncino, barbone *m*
pooh-pooh [puː'puː] VT deridere
pool [puːl] N (*of rain*) pozza; (*pond*) stagno; (*artificial*) vasca; (*also*: **swimming pool**) piscina; (*fig: of light*) cerchio; (*sth shared*) fondo comune; (*Comm: consortium*) pool *m inv*; (*US: monopoly trust*) trust *m inv*; (*billiards*) *specie di biliardo a buca* ▶ VT mettere in comune; **typing ~**, (*US*) **secretary ~** servizio comune di dattilografia; **to do the (football) pools** ≈ fare la schedina, ≈ giocare al totocalcio
poor [puər] ADJ povero(-a); (*mediocre*) mediocre, cattivo(-a) ▶ NPL: **the ~** i poveri; **~ in** povero(-a) di
poorly ['puəlɪ] ADV poveramente; (*badly*) male ▶ ADJ indisposto(-a), malato(-a)
pop [pɔp] N (*noise*) schiocco; (*Mus*) musica pop; (*US col: father*) babbo; (*col: drink*) bevanda gasata ▶ VT (*put*) mettere (in fretta) ▶ VI scoppiare; (*cork*) schioccare; **she popped her head out** (*of the window*) sporse fuori la testa
▶ **pop in** VI passare
▶ **pop out** VI fare un salto fuori
▶ **pop up** VI apparire, sorgere
pop concert N concerto *m* pop *inv*
popcorn ['pɔpkɔːn] N pop-corn *m*
pope [pəup] N papa *m*
poplar ['pɔplər] N pioppo
poplin ['pɔplɪn] N popeline *f*
popper ['pɔpər] N (*BRIT*) bottone *m* a pressione, bottone *m* automatico
poppy ['pɔpɪ] N papavero
poppycock ['pɔpɪkɔk] N (*col*) scempiaggini *fpl*
Popsicle® ['pɔpsɪkl] N (*US: ice lolly*) ghiacciolo
pop star N pop star *f inv*
populace ['pɔpjuləs] N popolo
popular ['pɔpjulər] ADJ popolare; (*fashionable*) in voga; **to be ~ (with)** (*person*) essere benvoluto(-a) *or* ben visto(-a) (da); (*decision*) essere gradito(-a); **a ~ song** una canzone di successo
popularity [pɔpju'lærɪtɪ] N popolarità
popularize ['pɔpjuləraɪz] VT divulgare; (*science*) volgarizzare
populate ['pɔpjuleɪt] VT popolare
population [pɔpju'leɪʃən] N popolazione *f*
population explosion N forte espansione *f* demografica

717

populous ['pɔpjuləs] ADJ popolato(-a)

pop-up ADJ (*Comput: menu, window*) a comparsa

porcelain ['pɔːslɪn] N porcellana

porch [pɔːtʃ] N veranda

porcupine ['pɔːkjupaɪn] N porcospino

pore [pɔːʳ] N poro ▶ VI: **to ~ over** essere immerso(-a) in

pork [pɔːk] N carne *f* di maiale

pork chop N braciola *or* costoletta di maiale

pork pie N (*BRIT Culin*) pasticcio di maiale in crosta

porn [pɔːn] (*col*) N pornografia ▶ ADJ porno *inv*

pornographic [pɔːnə'græfɪk] ADJ pornografico(-a)

pornography [pɔː'nɔgrəfɪ] N pornografia

porous ['pɔːrəs] ADJ poroso(-a)

porpoise ['pɔːpəs] N focena

porridge ['pɔrɪdʒ] N porridge *m*

port¹ [pɔːt] N porto; (*opening in ship*) portello; (*Naut: left side*) babordo; (*Comput*) porta; **to ~** (*Naut*) a babordo; **~ of call** (porto di) scalo

port² [pɔːt] N (*wine*) porto

portable ['pɔːtəbl] ADJ portatile

portal ['pɔːtl] N portale *m*

portcullis [pɔːt'kʌlɪs] N saracinesca

portent ['pɔːtɛnt] N presagio

porter ['pɔːtəʳ] N (*for luggage*) facchino, portabagagli *m inv*; (*doorkeeper*) portiere *m*, portinaio; (*US Rail*) addetto ai vagoni letto

portfolio [pɔːt'fəʊlɪəu] N (*case*) cartella; (*Pol: office: Econ*) portafoglio; (*of artist*) raccolta dei propri lavori

porthole ['pɔːthəul] N oblò *m inv*

portico ['pɔːtɪkəu] N portico

portion ['pɔːʃən] N porzione *f*

portly ['pɔːtlɪ] ADJ corpulento(-a)

portrait ['pɔːtreɪt] N ritratto

portray [pɔː'treɪ] VT fare il ritratto di; (*character on stage*) rappresentare; (*in writing*) ritrarre

portrayal ['pɔːtreɪəl] N ritratto; rappresentazione *f*

Portugal ['pɔːtjugl] N Portogallo

Portuguese [pɔːtju'giːz] ADJ portoghese ▶ N (*pl inv*) portoghese *mf*; (*Ling*) portoghese *m*

Portuguese man-of-war [-mænəv'wɔːʳ] N (*jellyfish*) medusa

pose [pəuz] N posa ▶ VI posare; (*pretend*): **to ~ as** atteggiarsi a, posare a ▶ VT porre; **to strike a ~** mettersi in posa

poser ['pəuzəʳ] N (*person*) domanda difficile; = **poseur**

poseur [pəu'zɜːʳ] N (*pej*) persona affettata

posh [pɔʃ] ADJ (*col*) elegante; (*family*) per bene ▶ ADV (*col*): **to talk ~** parlare in modo snob

position [pə'zɪʃən] N posizione *f*; (*job*) posto ▶ VT sistemare, collocare; **to be in a ~ to do sth** essere nella posizione di fare qc

positive ['pɔzɪtɪv] ADJ positivo(-a); (*certain*) sicuro(-a), certo(-a); (*definite*) preciso(-a); definitivo(-a)

positively ADV (*affirmatively, enthusiastically*) positivamente; (*decisively*) decisamente; (*really*) assolutamente

posse ['pɔsɪ] N (*US*) drappello

possess [pə'zɛs] VT possedere; **like one possessed** come un ossesso; **whatever can have possessed you?** cosa ti ha preso?

possession [pə'zɛʃən] N possesso; (*object*) bene *m*; **to take ~ of sth** impossessarsi *or* impadronirsi di qc; **possessions** NPL (*belongings*) beni *mpl*

possessive [pə'zɛsɪv] ADJ possessivo(-a)

possessiveness [pə'zɛsɪvnɪs] N possessività

possessor [pə'zɛsəʳ] N possessore (posseditrice)

possibility [pɔsɪ'bɪlɪtɪ] N possibilità *f inv*; **he's a ~ for the part** è uno dei candidati per la parte

possible ['pɔsɪbl] ADJ possibile; **it is ~ to do it** è possibile farlo; **if ~** se possibile; **as big as ~** il più grande possibile; **as far as ~** nei limiti del possibile

possibly ['pɔsɪblɪ] ADV (*perhaps*) forse; **if you ~ can** se le è possibile; **I cannot ~ come** proprio non posso venire

post [pəust] N (*BRIT: mail, letters, delivery*) posta; (*: collection*) levata; (*job, situation*) posto; (*Mil*) postazione *f*; (*pole*) palo; (*trading post*) stazione *f* commerciale; (*on blog, social network*) post *m inv*, commento ▶ VT (*BRIT: send by post*) impostare; (*Mil*) appostare; (*notice*) affiggere; (*to internet: video*) caricare; (*: comment*) mandare; (*BRIT*): (*appoint*) **to ~ to** assegnare a; **by ~** (*BRIT*) per posta; **by return of ~** (*BRIT*) a giro di posta; **to keep sb posted** tenere qn al corrente

post... [pəust] PREFIX post...; **post-1990** dopo il 1990

postage ['pəustɪdʒ] N affrancatura

postage stamp N francobollo

postal ['pəustəl] ADJ postale

postal order N vaglia *m inv* postale

postbag ['pəustbæg] N (*BRIT*) sacco postale, sacco della posta

postbox ['pəustbɔks] (*BRIT*) N cassetta delle lettere

postcard ['pəustkɑːd] N cartolina

postcode ['pəustkəud] N (*BRIT*) codice *m* (di avviamento) postale

postdate ['pəust'deɪt] VT (*cheque*) postdatare

poster ['pəustəʳ] N manifesto, affisso

poste restante [pəust'rɛstɑːnt] N (*BRIT*) fermo posta *m*

posterior [pɔs'tɪərɪəʳ] N (*col*) deretano, didietro

posterity [pɔs'tɛrɪtɪ] N posterità

poster paint N tempera

post exchange N (US Mil) spaccio militare

post-free [pəust'fri:] ADJ, ADV (BRIT) franco di porto

postgraduate ['pəust'grædjuət] N laureato/a che continua gli studi

posthumous ['pɔstjuməs] ADJ postumo(-a)

posthumously ['pɔstjuməslɪ] ADV dopo la mia (or sua etc) morte

posting ['pəustɪŋ] N (BRIT) incarico

postman ['pəustmən] N (irreg) postino

postmark ['pəustmɑ:k] N bollo or timbro postale

postmaster ['pəustmɑ:stər] N direttore m di un ufficio postale

Postmaster General N ≈ ministro delle Poste

postmistress ['pəustmɪstrɪs] N direttrice f di un ufficio postale

post-mortem [pəust'mɔ:təm] N autopsia; (fig) analisi f inv a posteriori

postnatal ['pəust'neɪtl] ADJ post-parto inv

post office N (building) ufficio postale; (organization) poste fpl; **the Post Office** ≈ le Poste e Telecomunicazioni

post office box N casella postale

post-paid ['pəust'peɪd] ADJ già affrancato(-a)

postpone [pəust'pəun] VT rinviare

postponement [pəust'pəunmənt] N rinvio

postscript ['pəustskrɪpt] N poscritto

postulate ['pɔstjuleɪt] VT postulare

posture ['pɔstʃər] N portamento; (pose) posa, atteggiamento ▶ VI posare

postwar ['pəust'wɔ:r] ADJ del dopoguerra

postwoman ['pəustwumən] N (irreg) (BRIT) postina

posy ['pəuzɪ] N mazzetto di fiori

pot [pɔt] N (for cooking) pentola; casseruola; (teapot) teiera; (coffeepot) caffettiera; (for plants, jam) vaso; (piece of pottery) ceramica; (col: marijuana) erba ▶ VT (plant) piantare in vaso; **a ~ of tea for two** tè per due; **to go to ~** (col: work, performance) andare in malora; **pots of** (BRIT col) un sacco di

potash ['pɔtæʃ] N potassa

potassium [pə'tæsɪəm] N potassio

potato [pə'teɪtəu] (pl **potatoes**) N patata

potato crisps, (US) **potato chips** NPL patatine fpl

potato flour N fecola di patate

potato peeler N sbucciapatate m inv

potbellied ['pɔtbelɪd] ADJ (from overeating) panciuto(-a); (from malnutrition) dal ventre gonfio

potency ['pəutnsɪ] N potenza; (of drink) forza

potent ['pəutnt] ADJ potente, forte

potentate ['pəutnteɪt] N potentato

potential [pə'tɛnʃl] ADJ potenziale ▶ N possibilità fpl; **to have ~** essere promettente

potentially [pə'tɛnʃəlɪ] ADV potenzialmente

pothole ['pɔthəul] N (in road) buca; (BRIT: underground) caverna

potholer ['pɔthəulər] N (BRIT) speleologo(-a)

potholing ['pɔthəulɪŋ] N (BRIT): **to go ~** fare la speleologia

potion ['pəuʃən] N pozione f

potluck [pɔt'lʌk] N: **to take ~** tentare la sorte

pot plant N pianta in vaso

potpourri [pəu'purɪ] N (dried petals etc) miscuglio di petali essiccati profumati; (fig) pot-pourri m inv

pot roast N brasato

potshot ['pɔtʃɔt] N: **to take potshots at** tirare a casaccio contro

potted ['pɔtɪd] ADJ (food) in conserva; (plant) in vaso; (fig: shortened) condensato(-a)

potter ['pɔtər] N vasaio ▶ VI (BRIT): **to ~ around, ~ about** lavoracchiare; **to ~ round the house** sbrigare con calma le faccende di casa; **~'s wheel** tornio (da vasaio)

pottery ['pɔtərɪ] N ceramiche fpl; (factory) fabbrica di ceramiche; **a piece of ~** una ceramica

potty ['pɔtɪ] ADJ (BRIT col: mad) tocco(-a) ▶ N (child's) vasino

potty-trained ['pɔtɪtreɪnd] ADJ che ha imparato a farla nel vasino

pouch [pautʃ] N borsa; (Zool) marsupio

pouf, pouffe [pu:f] N (stool) pouf m inv

poultice ['pəultɪs] N impiastro, cataplasma m

poultry ['pəultrɪ] N pollame m

poultry farm N azienda avicola

poultry farmer N pollicoltore(-trice)

pounce [pauns] VI: **to ~ (on)** balzare addosso (a), piombare (su) ▶ N balzo

pound [paund] N (weight) libbra (= 453g, 16 ounces); (money) (lira) sterlina (= 100 pence); (for dogs) canile m municipale ▶ VT (beat) battere; (crush) pestare, polverizzare ▶ VI (beat) battere, martellare; **half a ~** mezza libbra; **a five-~ note** una banconota da cinque sterline

pounding ['paundɪŋ] N: **to take a ~** (fig) prendere una batosta

pound sterling N sterlina

pour [pɔ:r] VT versare ▶ VI riversarsi; (rain) piovere a dirotto
  ▶ **pour away, pour off** VT vuotare
  ▶ **pour in** VI (people) entrare in fiotto; **to come pouring in** (water) entrare a fiotti; (letters) arrivare a valanghe; (cars, people) affluire in gran quantità
  ▶ **pour out** VI (people) riversarsi fuori ▶ VT vuotare; versare; (fig) sfogare

pouring ['pɔ:rɪŋ] ADJ: **~ rain** pioggia torrenziale

pout [paut] VI sporgere le labbra; fare il broncio

poverty ['pɔvətɪ] N povertà, miseria

poverty line N soglia di povertà
poverty-stricken ['pɒvətɪstrɪkən] ADJ molto povero(-a), misero(-a)
poverty trap N (BRIT) circolo vizioso della povertà
POW N ABBR = **prisoner of war**
powder ['paudə'] N polvere f ▶ VT spolverizzare; (face) incipriare; **powdered milk** latte m in polvere; **to ~ one's nose** incipriarsi il naso; (euphemism) andare alla toilette
powder compact N portacipria m inv
powder keg N (fig: area) polveriera; (: situation) situazione f esplosiva
powder puff N piumino della cipria
powder room N toilette f inv (per signore)
powdery ['paudərı] ADJ polveroso(-a)
power ['pauə'] N (strength) potenza, forza; (ability, Pol: of party, leader) potere m; (Math) potenza; (Elec) corrente f ▶ VT fornire di energia; azionare; **to be in ~** essere al potere; **to do all in one's ~ to help sb** fare tutto quello che si può per aiutare qn; **the world powers** le grandi potenze; **mental powers** capacità fpl mentali
powerboat ['pauəbəut] N (BRIT) motobarca, imbarcazione f a motore
power cut N (BRIT) interruzione f or mancanza di corrente
powered ['pauəd] ADJ: **~ by** azionato(-a) da; **nuclear-~ submarine** sottomarino a propulsione atomica
power failure N interruzione f della corrente elettrica
powerful ['pauəful] ADJ potente, forte
powerhouse ['pauəhaus] N (fig: person) persona molto dinamica; **a ~ of ideas** una miniera di idee
powerless ['pauəlıs] ADJ impotente, senza potere; **~ to do** impossibilitato(-a) a fare
power line N linea elettrica
power of attorney N procura
power point N (BRIT) presa di corrente
power station N centrale f elettrica
power steering N (Aut: also: **power-assisted steering**) servosterzo
powwow ['pauwau] N riunione f
pp ABBR (= pages) pp; (per procurationem): **pp J. Smith** per il Signor J. Smith
PPE N ABBR (BRIT Scol: = philosophy, politics, and economics) corso di laurea
PPS N ABBR (BRIT: = parliamentary private secretary) parlamentare che assiste un ministro; = **post postscriptum**
PQ ABBR (CANADA) = **Province of Quebec**
PR N ABBR = **proportional representation**; **public relations** ▶ ABBR (US) = **Puerto Rico**
Pr. ABBR = **prince**

practicability [præktıkə'bılıtı] N praticabilità
practicable ['præktıkəbl] ADJ (scheme) praticabile
practical ['præktıkl] ADJ pratico(-a)
practicality [præktı'kælıtı] N (of plan) fattibilità; (of person) senso pratico; **practicalities** NPL dettagli mpl pratici
practical joke N beffa
practically ['præktıklı] ADV (almost) quasi, praticamente
practice ['præktıs] N pratica; (of profession) esercizio; (at football etc) allenamento; (business) gabinetto; clientela ▶ VT, VI (US) = **practise**; **in ~** (in reality) in pratica; **out of ~** fuori esercizio; **2 hours' piano ~** 2 ore di esercizio al pianoforte; **it's common ~** è d'uso; **to put sth into ~** mettere qc in pratica; **target ~** pratica di tiro
practice match N partita di allenamento
practise, (US) **practice** ['præktıs] VT (work at: piano, one's backhand etc) esercitarsi a; (train for: skiing, running etc) allenarsi a; (a sport, religion) praticare; (method) usare; (profession) esercitare ▶ VI esercitarsi; (train) allenarsi; (lawyer, doctor) esercitare; **to ~ for a match** allenarsi per una partita
practised ['præktıst] ADJ (BRIT: person) esperto(-a); (: performance) da virtuoso(-a); (: liar) matricolato(-a); **with a ~ eye** con occhio esperto
practising ['præktısıŋ] ADJ (Christian etc) praticante; (lawyer) che esercita la professione; (homosexual) attivo(-a)
practitioner [præk'tıʃənə'] N professionista mf; (Med) medico
pragmatic [præg'mætık] ADJ pragmatico(-a)
Prague [prɑːg] N Praga
prairie ['prɛərı] N prateria
praise [preız] N elogio, lode f ▶ VT elogiare, lodare
praiseworthy ['preızwə:ðı] ADJ lodevole
pram [præm] N (BRIT) carrozzina
prance [prɑːns] VI (horse) impennarsi
prank [præŋk] N burla
prat [præt] N (BRIT col) cretino(-a)
prattle ['prætl] VI cinguettare
prawn [prɔːn] N gamberetto
prawn cocktail N cocktail m inv di gamberetti
pray [preı] VI pregare
prayer [prɛə'] N preghiera
prayer book N libro di preghiere
pre... [priː] PREFIX pre...; **pre-1970** prima del 1970
preach [priːtʃ] VT, VI predicare; **to ~ at sb** fare la predica a qn
preacher ['priːtʃə'] N predicatore(-trice); (US: minister) pastore m
preamble [prı'æmbl] N preambolo

prearranged [ˌpriːəˈreɪndʒd] ADJ organizzato(-a) in anticipo
precarious [prɪˈkɛərɪəs] ADJ precario(-a)
precaution [prɪˈkɔːʃən] N precauzione f
precautionary [prɪˈkɔːʃənərɪ] ADJ *(measure)* precauzionale
precede [prɪˈsiːd] VT, VI precedere
precedence [ˈprɛsɪdəns] N precedenza; **to take ~ over** avere la precedenza su
precedent [ˈprɛsɪdənt] N precedente m; **to establish** *or* **set a ~** creare un precedente
preceding [prɪˈsiːdɪŋ] ADJ precedente
precept [ˈpriːsɛpt] N precetto
precinct [ˈpriːsɪŋkt] N *(round cathedral)* recinto; *(US: district)* circoscrizione f; **precincts** NPL *(neighbourhood)* dintorni *mpl*, vicinanze *fpl*; **pedestrian ~** zona pedonale; **shopping ~** *(BRIT)* centro commerciale
precious [ˈprɛʃəs] ADJ prezioso(-a) ▶ ADV *(col)*: **~ little/few** ben poco/pochi; **your ~ dog** *(ironic)* il suo amatissimo cane
precipice [ˈprɛsɪpɪs] N precipizio
precipitate ADJ [prɪˈsɪpɪtɪt] *(hasty)* precipitoso(-a) ▶ VT [prɪˈsɪpɪteɪt] accelerare
precipitation [prɪsɪpɪˈteɪʃən] N precipitazione f
precipitous [prɪˈsɪpɪtəs] ADJ *(steep)* erto(-a), ripido(-a)
précis [ˈpreɪsiː] (*pl* **~** [-z]) N riassunto
precise [prɪˈsaɪs] ADJ preciso(-a)
precisely [prɪˈsaɪslɪ] ADV precisamente; **~!** appunto!
precision [prɪˈsɪʒən] N precisione f
preclude [prɪˈkluːd] VT precludere, impedire; **to ~ sb from doing** impedire a qn di fare
precocious [prɪˈkəuʃəs] ADJ precoce
preconceived [ˌpriːkənˈsiːvd] ADJ *(idea)* preconcetto(-a)
preconception [ˌpriːkənˈsɛpʃən] N preconcetto
precondition [ˌpriːkənˈdɪʃən] N condizione f necessaria
precursor [priːˈkəːsəʳ] N precursore m
predate [ˌpriːˈdeɪt] VT *(precede)* precedere
predator [ˈprɛdətəʳ] N predatore m
predatory [ˈprɛdətərɪ] ADJ predatore(-trice)
predecessor [ˈpriːdɪsɛsəʳ] N predecessore(-a)
predestination [priːdɛstɪˈneɪʃən] N predestinazione f
predetermine [ˌpriːdɪˈtəːmɪn] VT predeterminare
predicament [prɪˈdɪkəmənt] N situazione f difficile
predicate [ˈprɛdɪkɪt] N *(Ling)* predicativo
predict [prɪˈdɪkt] VT predire
predictable [prɪˈdɪktəbl] ADJ prevedibile
predictably [prɪˈdɪktəblɪ] ADV *(behave, react)* in modo prevedibile; **~ she didn't arrive** come era da prevedere, non è arrivata

prediction [prɪˈdɪkʃən] N predizione f
predispose [ˌpriːdɪsˈpəuz] VT predisporre
predominance [prɪˈdɔmɪnəns] N predominanza
predominant [prɪˈdɔmɪnənt] ADJ predominante
predominantly [prɪˈdɔmɪnəntlɪ] ADV in maggior parte; soprattutto
predominate [prɪˈdɔmɪneɪt] VI predominare
pre-eminent [priːˈɛmɪnənt] ADJ preminente
pre-empt [prɪˈɛmpt] VT acquistare per diritto di prelazione; *(fig)* anticipare
pre-emptive [prɪˈɛmptɪv] ADJ: **~ strike** azione f preventiva
preen [priːn] VT: **to ~ itself** *(bird)* lisciarsi le penne; **to ~ o.s.** agghindarsi
prefab [ˈpriːfæb] N casa prefabbricata
prefabricated [priːˈfæbrɪkeɪtɪd] ADJ prefabbricato(-a)
preface [ˈprɛfəs] N prefazione f
prefect [ˈpriːfɛkt] N *(BRIT: in school)* studente/essa con funzioni disciplinari; *(Admin: in Italy)* prefetto
prefer [prɪˈfəːʳ] VT preferire; *(Law: charges, complaint)* sporgere; *(: action)* intentare; **to ~ coffee to tea** preferire il caffè al tè; **to ~ doing** *or* **to do** preferire fare
preferable [ˈprɛfrəbl] ADJ preferibile
preferably [ˈprɛfrəblɪ] ADV preferibilmente
preference [ˈprɛfrəns] N preferenza; **in ~ to sth** piuttosto che qc
preference shares NPL *(BRIT)* azioni *fpl* privilegiate
preferential [ˌprɛfəˈrɛnʃəl] ADJ preferenziale; **~ treatment** trattamento di favore
preferred stock [prɪˈfəːd-] NPL *(US)* = **preference shares**
prefix [ˈpriːfɪks] N prefisso
pregnancy [ˈprɛɡnənsɪ] N gravidanza
pregnancy test N test *m inv* di gravidanza
pregnant [ˈprɛɡnənt] ADJ incinta *adj f*; *(animal)* gravido(-a); *(fig: remark, pause)* significativo(-a); **3 months ~** incinta di 3 mesi
prehistoric [ˌpriːhɪsˈtɔrɪk] ADJ preistorico(-a)
prehistory [priːˈhɪstərɪ] N preistoria
prejudge [ˌpriːˈdʒʌdʒ] VT pregiudicare
prejudice [ˈprɛdʒudɪs] N pregiudizio; *(harm)* torto, danno ▶ VT pregiudicare, ledere; *(bias)*: **to ~ sb in favour of/against** disporre bene/male qn verso
prejudiced [ˈprɛdʒudɪst] ADJ *(person)* pieno(-a) di pregiudizi; *(view)* prevenuto(-a); **to be ~ against sb/sth** essere prevenuto contro qn/qc; **~ (in favour of)** ben disposto(-a) (verso)
prelate [ˈprɛlət] N prelato
preliminaries [prɪˈlɪmɪnərɪz] NPL preliminari *mpl*
preliminary [prɪˈlɪmɪnərɪ] ADJ preliminare

P

prelude ['prɛlju:d] N preludio
premarital ['pri:'mærɪtl] ADJ prematrimoniale
premature ['prɛmətʃuəʳ] ADJ prematuro(-a); *(arrival)* (molto) anticipato(-a); **you are being a little ~** è un po' troppo precipitoso
premeditated [pri:'mɛdɪteɪtɪd] ADJ premeditato(-a)
premeditation [pri:mɛdɪ'teɪʃən] N premeditazione f
premenstrual tension [pri:'mɛnstruəl-] N *(Med)* tensione f premestruale
premier ['prɛmɪəʳ] ADJ primo(-a) ▶ N *(Pol)* primo ministro
première ['prɛmɪɛəʳ] N prima
Premier League [prɛmɪə'li:g] N ≈ serie A
premise ['prɛmɪs] N premessa
premises ['prɛmɪsɪz] NPL locale m; **on the ~** sul posto; **business ~** locali commerciali
premium ['pri:mɪəm] N premio; **to be at a ~** *(fig: housing etc)* essere ricercatissimo; **to sell at a ~** *(shares)* vendere sopra la pari
premium bond N *(Brit)* obbligazione f a premio
premium deal N *(Comm)* offerta speciale
premium gasoline N *(US)* super f
premonition [prɛmə'nɪʃən] N premonizione f
preoccupation [pri:ɔkju'peɪʃən] N preoccupazione f
preoccupied [pri:'ɔkjupaɪd] ADJ preoccupato(-a)
pre-owned [pri:'əund] ADJ di seconda mano
prepackaged [pri:'pækɪdʒd] ADJ già impacchettato(-a)
prepaid [pri:'peɪd] ADJ pagato(-a) in anticipo; *(envelope)* affrancato(-a)
preparation [prɛpə'reɪʃən] N preparazione f; **preparations** NPL *(for trip, war)* preparativi mpl; **in ~ for sth** in vista di qc
preparatory [prɪ'pærətərɪ] ADJ preparatorio(-a); **~ to sth/to doing sth** prima di qc/di fare qc
preparatory school [prɪ'pærətərɪ-] N *(Brit)* scuola elementare privata; *(US)* scuola superiore privata; *vedi nota*

> In Gran Bretagna, la *prep(aratory) school* è una scuola privata frequentata da bambini dai 7 ai 13 anni in vista dell'iscrizione alla *public school*. Negli Stati Uniti, invece, è una scuola superiore privata che prepara i ragazzi che si iscriveranno al *college*.

prepare [prɪ'pɛəʳ] VT preparare ▶ VI: **to ~ for** prepararsi a
prepared [prɪ'pɛəd] ADJ: **~ for** preparato(-a) a; **~ to** pronto(-a) a; **to be ~ to help sb** *(willing)* essere disposto or pronto ad aiutare qn

preponderance [prɪ'pɔndərns] N preponderanza
preposition [prɛpə'zɪʃən] N preposizione f
prepossessing [pri:pə'zɛsɪŋ] ADJ simpatico(-a), attraente
preposterous [prɪ'pɔstərəs] ADJ assurdo(-a)
prep school [prɛp-] N = **preparatory school**
prerecord ['pri:rɪ'kɔ:d] VT registrare in anticipo; **prerecorded broadcast** trasmissione f registrata; **prerecorded cassette** (musi)cassetta
prerequisite [pri:'rɛkwɪzɪt] N requisito indispensabile
prerogative [prɪ'rɔgətɪv] N prerogativa
presbyterian [prɛzbɪ'tɪərɪən] ADJ, N presbiteriano(-a)
presbytery ['prɛzbɪtərɪ] N presbiterio
preschool ['pri:'sku:l] ADJ *(age)* prescolastico(-a); *(child)* in età prescolastica
prescribe [prɪ'skraɪb] VT *(Med)* prescrivere, ordinare; **prescribed books** *(Brit Scol)* testi mpl in programma
prescription [prɪ'skrɪpʃən] N prescrizione f; *(Med)* ricetta; **to make up** *or (US)* **fill a ~** preparare *or* fare una ricetta; **"only available on ~"** "ottenibile solo dietro presentazione di ricetta medica"
prescription charges NPL *(Brit)* ticket m inv
prescriptive [prɪ'skrɪptɪv] ADJ normativo(-a)
presence ['prɛzns] N presenza; **~ of mind** presenza di spirito
present ['prɛznt] ADJ presente; *(wife, residence, job)* attuale ▶ N *(gift)* regalo; *(also:* **present tense)** tempo presente; **the ~** il presente ▶ VT [prɪ'zɛnt] presentare; *(give)*: **to ~ sb with sth** offrire qc a qn; **to be ~ at** essere presente a; **those ~** i presenti; **at ~** al momento; **to give sb a ~** fare un regalo a qn; **to make sb a ~ of sth** regalare qc a qn
presentable [prɪ'zɛntəbl] ADJ presentabile
presentation [prɛzn'teɪʃən] N presentazione f; *(gift)* regalo, dono; *(ceremony)* consegna ufficiale; **on ~ of the voucher** dietro presentazione del buono
present-day ['prɛzntdeɪ] ADJ attuale, d'oggigiorno
presenter [prɪ'zɛntəʳ] N *(Brit Radio, TV)* presentatore(-trice)
presently ['prɛzntlɪ] ADV *(soon)* fra poco, presto; *(at present)* al momento; *(US: now)* adesso, ora
present participle N participio presente
preservation [prɛzə'veɪʃən] N preservazione f, conservazione f
preservative [prɪ'zə:vətɪv] N conservante m
preserve [prɪ'zə:v] VT *(keep safe)* preservare, proteggere; *(maintain)* conservare; *(food)* mettere in conserva ▶ N *(for game, fish)*

riserva; (*often pl: jam*) marmellata; (: *fruit*) frutta sciroppata

preshrunk [priː'ʃrʌŋk] ADJ irrestringibile

preside [prɪ'zaɪd] VI: **to ~ (over)** presiedere (a)

presidency ['prezɪdənsɪ] N presidenza; (*US: of company*) direzione *f*

president ['prezɪdənt] N presidente *m*; (*US: of company*) direttore(-trice) generale

presidential [prezɪ'dɛnʃl] ADJ presidenziale

press [pres] N (*tool, machine*) pressa; (*for wine*) torchio; (*newspapers*) stampa; (*crowd*) folla ▶ VT (*push*) premere, pigiare; (*doorbell*) suonare; (*squeeze*) spremere; (: *hand*) stringere; (*clothes: iron*) stirare; (*pursue*) incalzare; (*insist*): **to ~ sth on sb** far accettare qc da qn; (*urge, entreat*): **to ~ sb to do** *or* **into doing sth** fare pressione su qn affinché faccia qc ▶ VI premere; accalcare; **to go to ~** (*newspaper*) andare in macchina; **to be in the ~** (*in the newspapers*) essere sui giornali; **we are pressed for time** ci manca il tempo; **to ~ for sth** insistere per avere qc; **to ~ sb for an answer** insistere perché qn risponda; **to ~ charges against sb** (*Law*) sporgere una denuncia contro qn
▶ **press ahead** VI: **to ~ ahead (with)** andare avanti (con)
▶ **press on** VI continuare

press agency N agenzia di stampa

press clipping N ritaglio di giornale

press conference N conferenza stampa

press cutting N = **press clipping**

press-gang ['presgæŋ] VT: **to ~ sb into doing sth** costringere qn a viva forza a fare qc

pressing ['presɪŋ] ADJ urgente ▶ N stiratura

press officer N addetto(-a) stampa *inv*

press release N comunicato stampa

press stud N (*BRIT*) bottone *m* a pressione

press-up ['presʌp] N (*BRIT*) flessione *f* sulle braccia

pressure ['preʃə'] N pressione *f* ▶ VT: **to put ~ on sb (to do)** mettere qn sotto pressione (affinché faccia); **high/low ~** alta/bassa pressione; **to put ~ on sb** fare pressione su qn

pressure cooker N pentola a pressione

pressure gauge N manometro

pressure group N gruppo di pressione

pressurize ['preʃəraɪz] VT pressurizzare; (*fig*): **to ~ sb (into doing sth)** fare delle pressioni su qn (per costringerlo a fare qc)

pressurized ['preʃəraɪzd] ADJ pressurizzato(-a)

Prestel® ['prestel] N Videotel® *m inv*

prestige [pres'tiːʒ] N prestigio

prestigious [pres'tɪdʒəs] ADJ prestigioso(-a)

presumably [prɪ'zjuːməblɪ] ADV presumibilmente; **~ he did it** penso *or* presumo che l'abbia fatto

presume [prɪ'zjuːm] VT supporre; **to ~ to do** (*dare*) permettersi di fare

presumption [prɪ'zʌmpʃən] N presunzione *f*; (*boldness*) audacia

presumptuous [prɪ'zʌmpʃəs] ADJ presuntuoso(-a)

presuppose [priːsə'pəuz] VT presupporre

pre-tax [priː'tæks] ADJ al lordo d'imposta

pretence, (*US*) **pretense** [prɪ'tens] N (*claim*) pretesa; (*pretext*) pretesto, scusa; **to make a ~ of doing** far finta di fare; **on** *or* **under the ~ of doing sth** con il pretesto *or* la scusa di fare qc; **she is devoid of all ~** non si nasconde dietro false apparenze; **under false pretences** con l'inganno

pretend [prɪ'tend] VT (*feign*) fingere ▶ VI far finta; (*claim*): **to ~ to sth** pretendere a qc; **to ~ to do** far finta di fare

pretense [prɪ'tens] N (*US*) = **pretence**

pretension [prɪ'tenʃən] N (*claim*) pretesa; **to have no pretensions to sth/to being sth** non avere la pretesa di avere qc/di essere qc

pretentious [prɪ'tenʃəs] ADJ pretenzioso(-a)

preterite ['pretərɪt] N preterito

pretext ['priːtekst] N pretesto; **on** *or* **under the ~ of doing sth** col pretesto di fare qc

pretty ['prɪtɪ] ADJ grazioso(-a), carino(-a) ▶ ADV abbastanza, assai

prevail [prɪ'veɪl] VI (*win, be usual*) prevalere; (*persuade*): **to ~ (up)on sb to do** persuadere qn a fare

prevailing [prɪ'veɪlɪŋ] ADJ dominante

prevalent ['prevələnt] ADJ (*belief*) predominante; (*customs*) diffuso(-a); (*fashion*) corrente; (*disease*) comune

prevarication [prɪværɪ'keɪʃən] N tergiversazione *f*

prevent [prɪ'vent] VT prevenire; **to ~ sb from doing** impedire a qn di fare; **to ~ sth from happening** impedire che qc succeda

preventable [prɪ'ventəbl] ADJ evitabile

preventative [prɪ'ventətɪv] ADJ preventivo(-a)

prevention [prɪ'venʃən] N prevenzione *f*

preventive [prɪ'ventɪv] ADJ preventivo(-a)

preview ['priːvjuː] N (*of film*) anteprima

previous ['priːvɪəs] ADJ precedente; anteriore; **I have a ~ engagement** ho già (preso) un impegno; **~ to doing** prima di fare

previously ['priːvɪəslɪ] ADV prima

prewar ['priː'wɔː'] ADJ anteguerra *inv*

prey [preɪ] N preda ▶ VI: **to ~ on** far preda di; **it was preying on his mind** lo stava ossessionando

price [praɪs] N prezzo; (*Betting: odds*) quotazione *f* ▶ VT (*goods*) fissare il prezzo di; valutare; **what is the ~ of ...?** quanto costa ...?; **to go up** *or* **rise in ~** salire *or* aumentare di prezzo; **to put a ~ on sth** valutare *or* stimare qc; **he regained his freedom, but at a ~** ha riconquistato la sua libertà, ma a caro prezzo; **what ~ his promises now?** (*BRIT*) a che valgono ora le sue promesse?; **to be priced out of the market** (*article*) essere così caro da diventare invendibile; (*producer, nation*) non poter sostenere la concorrenza

price control N controllo dei prezzi

price-cutting ['praɪskʌtɪŋ] N riduzione *f* dei prezzi

priceless ['praɪslɪs] ADJ di valore inestimabile; (*col: amusing*) impagabile, spassosissimo(-a)

price list N listino (dei) prezzi

price range N gamma di prezzi; **it's within my ~** rientra nelle mie possibilità

price tag N cartellino del prezzo

price war N guerra dei prezzi

pricey ['praɪsɪ] ADJ (*col*) caruccio(-a)

prick [prɪk] N puntura ▶ VT pungere; **to ~ up one's ears** drizzare gli orecchi

prickle ['prɪkl] N (*of plant*) spina; (*sensation*) pizzicore *m*

prickly ['prɪklɪ] ADJ spinoso(-a); (*fig: person*) permaloso(-a)

prickly heat N sudamina

prickly pear N fico d'India

pride [praɪd] N orgoglio; superbia ▶ VT: **to ~ o.s. on** essere orgoglioso(-a) di; vantarsi di; **to take (a) ~ in** tenere molto a; essere orgoglioso di; **to take a ~ in doing** andare orgoglioso di fare; **to have ~ of place** (*BRIT*) essere al primo posto

priest [priːst] N prete *m*, sacerdote *m*

priestess ['priːstɪs] N sacerdotessa

priesthood ['priːsthud] N sacerdozio

prig [prɪg] N: **he's a ~** è compiaciuto di se stesso

prim [prɪm] ADJ pudico(-a); contegnoso(-a)

primacy ['praɪməsɪ] N primato

prima facie ['praɪmə'feɪʃɪ] ADJ: **to have a ~ case** (*Law*) presentare una causa in apparenza fondata

primal ['praɪməl] ADJ primitivo(-a), originario(-a)

primarily ['praɪmərɪlɪ] ADV principalmente, essenzialmente

primary ['praɪmərɪ] ADJ primario(-a); (*first in importance*) primo(-a) ▶ N (*US: election*) primarie *fpl*; *vedi nota*

Negli Stati Uniti, attraverso le *primaries* viene fatta una prima scrematura dei candidati dei partiti alle elezioni presidenziali. La scelta definitiva del candidato da presentare alla presidenza si basa sui risultati delle *primaries* e ha luogo durante le *Conventions* dei partiti, che si tengono in luglio e in agosto.

primary colour N colore *m* fondamentale

primary school N (*BRIT*) scuola elementare; *vedi nota*

In Gran Bretagna la *primary school* è la scuola elementare, frequentata dai bambini dai 5 agli 11 anni di età. È suddivisa in *infant school* (5-7 anni) e *junior school* (7-11 anni); *vedi anche* **secondary school**.

primate N (*Rel*) ['praɪmɪt] primate *m*; (*Zool*) ['praɪmeɪt] primate *m*

prime [praɪm] ADJ primario(-a), fondamentale; (*excellent*) di prima qualità ▶ N: **in the ~ of life** nel fiore della vita ▶ VT (*gun*) innescare; (*pump*) adescare; (*wood*) preparare; (*fig*) mettere al corrente

prime minister N primo ministro

primer ['praɪmə^r] N (*book*) testo elementare; (*paint*) vernice *f* base *inv*

prime time N (*Radio, TV*) fascia di massimo ascolto

primeval [praɪ'miːvl] ADJ primitivo(-a)

primitive ['prɪmɪtɪv] ADJ primitivo(-a)

primrose ['prɪmrəuz] N primavera

primus® ['praɪməs], **primus stove**® N (*BRIT*) fornello a petrolio

prince [prɪns] N principe *m*

prince charming N principe *m* azzurro

princess [prɪn'sɛs] N principessa

principal ['prɪnsɪpl] ADJ principale ▶ N (*of school, college etc*) preside *mf*; (*money*) capitale *m*; (*in play*) protagonista *mf*

principality [prɪnsɪ'pælɪtɪ] N principato

principally ['prɪnsɪplɪ] ADV principalmente

principle ['prɪnsɪpl] N principio; **in ~** in linea di principio; **on ~** per principio

print [prɪnt] N (*mark*) impronta; (*letters*) caratteri *mpl*; (*fabric*) tessuto stampato; (*Art, Phot*) stampa ▶ VT imprimere; (*publish*) stampare, pubblicare; (*write in capitals*) scrivere in stampatello; **out of ~** esaurito(-a) ▶ **print out** VT (*Comput*) stampare

printed circuit board [prɪntɪd-] N circuito stampato

printed matter [prɪntɪd-] N stampe *fpl*

printer ['prɪntə^r] N tipografo; (*machine*) stampante *f*

printhead ['prɪnthɛd] N testa di stampa

printing ['prɪntɪŋ] N stampa

printing press N macchina tipografica

print-out ['prɪntaut] N tabulato

print wheel N margherita

prior ['praɪə^r] ADJ precedente; (*claim etc*) più importante ▶ N (*Rel*) priore *m*; **~ to doing** prima di fare; **without ~ notice** senza preavviso; **to have a ~ claim to sth** avere un diritto di precedenza su qc

priority [praɪ'ɔrɪtɪ] N priorità *f inv*; precedenza; **to have** *or* **take ~ over sth**

avere la precedenza su qc
priory ['praɪərɪ] N monastero
prise [praɪz] VT: **to ~ open** forzare
prism ['prɪzəm] N prisma m
prison ['prɪzn] N prigione f ▶ CPD (system) carcerario(-a); (conditions, food) nelle or delle prigioni
prison camp N campo di prigionia
prisoner ['prɪznər] N prigioniero(-a); **to take sb ~** far prigioniero qn; **the ~ at the bar** l'accusato, l'imputato; **~ of war** prigioniero(-a) di guerra
prissy ['prɪsɪ] ADJ per benino
pristine ['prɪstiːn] ADJ originario(-a); intatto(-a); immacolato(-a)
privacy ['prɪvəsɪ] N solitudine f, intimità
private ['praɪvɪt] ADJ privato(-a); personale ▶ N soldato semplice; **"~"** (on envelope) "riservata"; (on door) "privato"; **in ~** in privato; **in (his) ~ life** nella vita privata; **he is a very ~ person** è una persona molto riservata; **~ hearing** (Law) udienza a porte chiuse; **to be in ~ practice** essere medico non convenzionato (con la mutua)
private enterprise N iniziativa privata
private eye N investigatore m privato
private limited company N (BRIT) società per azioni non quotata in Borsa
privately ['praɪvɪtlɪ] ADV in privato; (within o.s.) dentro di sé
private parts NPL (Anat) parti fpl intime
private property N proprietà privata
private school N scuola privata
privation [praɪ'veɪʃən] N (state) privazione f; (hardship) privazioni fpl, stenti mpl
privatize ['praɪvɪtaɪz] VT privatizzare
privet ['prɪvɪt] N ligustro
privilege ['prɪvɪlɪdʒ] N privilegio
privileged ['prɪvɪlɪdʒd] ADJ privilegiato(-a); **to be ~ to do sth** avere il privilegio or l'onore di fare qc
privy ['prɪvɪ] ADJ: **to be ~ to** essere al corrente di
Privy Council N (BRIT) Consiglio della Corona; vedi nota

Il Privy Council, un gruppo di consiglieri del re, era il principale organo di governo durante il regno dei Tudor e degli Stuart. Col tempo ha perso la sua importanza e oggi è un organo senza potere effettivo formato da ministri e altre personalità politiche ed ecclesiastiche.

Privy Councillor N (BRIT) Consigliere m della Corona
prize [praɪz] N premio ▶ ADJ (example, idiot) perfetto(-a); (bull, novel) premiato(-a) ▶ VT apprezzare, pregiare
prize-fighter ['praɪzfaɪtər] N pugile m (che si batte per conquistare un premio)

prize giving N premiazione f
prize money N soldi mpl del premio
prizewinner ['praɪzwɪnər] N premiato(-a)
prizewinning ['praɪzwɪnɪŋ] ADJ vincente; (novel, essay etc) premiato(-a)
PRO N ABBR = **public relations officer**
pro [prəu] N (Sport) professionista mf ▶ PREP pro; **the pros and cons** il pro e il contro
pro- [prəu] PREFIX (in favour of) filo...; **~Soviet** adj filosovietico(-a)
pro-active [prəu'æktɪv] ADJ: **to be ~** agire d'iniziativa
probability [prɔbə'bɪlɪtɪ] N probabilità f inv; **in all ~** con ogni probabilità
probable ['prɔbəbl] ADJ probabile; **it is ~/hardly ~ that ...** è probabile/poco probabile che ... + sub
probably ['prɔbəblɪ] ADV probabilmente
probate ['prəubɪt] N (Law) omologazione f (di un testamento)
probation [prə'beɪʃən] N (in employment) periodo di prova; (Law) libertà vigilata; (Rel) probandato; **on ~** (employee) in prova; (Law) in libertà vigilata
probationary [prəu'beɪʃənərɪ] ADJ: **~ period** periodo di prova
probe [prəub] N (Med, Space) sonda; (enquiry) indagine f, investigazione f ▶ VT sondare, esplorare; indagare
probity ['prəubɪtɪ] N probità
problem ['prɔbləm] N problema m; **to have problems with the car** avere dei problemi con la macchina; **what's the ~?** che cosa c'è?; **I had no ~ in finding her** non mi è stato difficile trovarla; **no ~!** ma certamente!, non c'è problema!
problematic [prɔblə'mætɪk] ADJ problematico(-a)
problem-solving ['prɔbləmsɔlvɪŋ] N risoluzione f di problemi
procedure [prə'siːdʒər] N (Admin, Law) procedura; (method) metodo, procedimento
proceed [prə'siːd] VI (go forward) avanzare, andare avanti; (go about it) procedere; (continue): **to ~ (with)** continuare; **to ~ to** andare a; passare a; **to ~ to do** mettersi a fare; **to ~ against sb** (Law) procedere contro qn; **I am not sure how to ~** non so bene come fare
proceedings [prə'siːdɪŋz] NPL misure fpl; (Law) procedimento; (meeting) riunione f; (records) rendiconti mpl; atti mpl
proceeds ['prəusiːdz] NPL profitto, incasso
process ['prəusɛs] N processo; (method) metodo, sistema m ▶ VT trattare; (information) elaborare ▶ VI [prə'sɛs] (BRIT formal: go in procession) sfilare, procedere in corteo; **we are in the ~ of moving to ...** stiamo per trasferirci a ...

P

725

processed cheese, (US) **process cheese** N formaggio fuso

processing ['prəusɛsɪŋ] N trattamento; elaborazione f

procession [prə'sɛʃən] N processione f, corteo; **funeral ~** corteo funebre

pro-choice [prəu'tʃɔɪs] ADJ per la libertà di scelta di gravidanza

proclaim [prə'kleɪm] VT proclamare, dichiarare

proclamation [prɔklə'meɪʃən] N proclamazione f

proclivity [prə'klɪvɪtɪ] N tendenza, propensione f

procrastination [prəukræstɪ'neɪʃən] N procrastinazione f

procreation [prəukrɪ'eɪʃən] N procreazione f

Procurator Fiscal ['prɔkjureɪtə-] N (SCOTTISH) procuratore m

procure [prə'kjuər] VT (for o.s.) procurarsi; (for sb) procurare

procurement [prə'kjuəmənt] N approvvigionamento

prod [prɔd] VT dare un colpetto a; pungolare ▶ N (push, jab) colpetto

prodigal ['prɔdɪgl] ADJ prodigo(-a)

prodigious [prə'dɪdʒəs] ADJ prodigioso(-a)

prodigy ['prɔdɪdʒɪ] N prodigio

produce N ['prɔdju:s] (Agr) prodotto, prodotti mpl ▶ VT [prə'dju:s] produrre; (show) esibire, mostrare; (proof of identity) produrre, fornire; (cause) cagionare, causare; (Theat) mettere in scena

producer [prə'dju:sər] N (Theat, Cine, Agr) produttore m

product ['prɔdʌkt] N prodotto

production [prə'dʌkʃən] N produzione f; (Theat) messa in scena; **to put into ~** mettere in produzione

production agreement N (US) accordo sui tempi di produzione

production line N catena di lavorazione

production manager N production manager m inv, direttore m della produzione

productive [prə'dʌktɪv] ADJ produttivo(-a)

productivity [prɔdʌk'tɪvɪtɪ] N produttività

productivity agreement N (BRIT) accordo sui tempi di produzione

productivity bonus N premio di produzione

Prof. ABBR (= professor) Prof.

profane [prə'feɪn] ADJ profano(-a); (language) empio(-a)

profess [prə'fɛs] VT professare; **I do not ~ to be an expert** non pretendo di essere un esperto

professed [prə'fɛst] ADJ (self-declared) dichiarato(-a)

profession [prə'fɛʃən] N professione f; **the professions** le professioni liberali

professional [prə'fɛʃənl] N (Sport) professionista mf ▶ ADJ professionale; (work) da professionista; **he's a ~ man** è un professionista; **to take ~ advice** consultare un esperto

professionalism [prə'fɛʃnəlɪzəm] N professionismo

professionally [prə'fɛʃnəlɪ] ADV professionalmente, in modo professionale; (Sport: play) come professionista; **I only know him ~** con lui ho solo rapporti di lavoro

professor [prə'fɛsər] N professore m (titolare di una cattedra); (US: teacher) professore(-essa)

professorship [prə'fɛsəʃɪp] N cattedra

proffer ['prɔfər] VT (remark) profferire; (apologies) porgere, presentare; (one's hand) porgere

proficiency [prə'fɪʃənsɪ] N competenza, abilità

proficient [prə'fɪʃənt] ADJ competente, abile

profile ['prəufaɪl] N profilo; **to keep a low ~** (fig) cercare di passare inosservato or di non farsi notare troppo; **to maintain a high ~** mettersi in mostra

profit ['prɔfɪt] N profitto; beneficio ▶ VI: **to ~ (by or from)** approfittare (di); **~ and loss account** conto perdite e profitti; **to make a ~** realizzare un profitto; **to sell sth at a ~** vendere qc con un utile

profitability [prɔfɪtə'bɪlɪtɪ] N redditività

profitable ['prɔfɪtəbl] ADJ redditizio(-a); (fig: beneficial) vantaggioso(-a); (: meeting, visit) fruttuoso(-a)

profit centre N centro di profitto

profiteering [prɔfɪ'tɪərɪŋ] N (pej) affarismo

profit-making ['prɔfɪtmeɪkɪŋ] ADJ a scopo di lucro

profit margin N margine m di profitto

profit-sharing ['prɔfɪtʃɛərɪŋ] N compartecipazione f agli utili

profits tax N (BRIT) imposta sugli utili

profligate ['prɔflɪgɪt] ADJ (dissolute: behaviour) dissipato(-a); (: person) debosciato(-a); (extravagant): **he's very ~ with his money** è uno che sperpera i suoi soldi

pro forma ['prəu'fɔ:mə] ADV: **~ invoice** fattura proforma

profound [prə'faund] ADJ profondo(-a)

profuse [prə'fju:s] ADJ infinito(-a), abbondante

profusely [prə'fju:slɪ] ADV con grande effusione

profusion [prə'fju:ʒən] N profusione f, abbondanza

progeny ['prɔdʒɪnɪ] N progenie f; discendenti mpl

programme, (US) **program** ['prəugræm] N programma m ▶ VT programmare

programmer, (US) **programer**
['prəʊgræmə^r] N programmatore(-trice)
programming, (US) **programing**
['prəʊgræmɪŋ] N programmazione f
**programming language, programming
language** N linguaggio di programmazione
progress N ['prəʊgrɛs] progresso ▸ VI
[prə'grɛs] (go forward) avanzare, procedere; (in
time) procedere; (also: **make progress**) far
progressi; **in ~** in corso
progression [prə'grɛʃən] N progressione f
progressive [prə'grɛsɪv] ADJ progressivo(-a);
(person) progressista
progressively [prə'grɛsɪvlɪ] ADV
progressivamente
progress report N (Med) bollettino medico;
(Admin) rendiconto dei lavori
prohibit [prə'hɪbɪt] VT proibire, vietare; **to ~
sb from doing sth** vietare or proibire a qn di
fare qc; **"smoking prohibited"** "vietato
fumare"
prohibition [prəʊɪ'bɪʃən] N (US)
proibizionismo
prohibitive [prə'hɪbɪtɪv] ADJ (price etc)
proibitivo(-a)
project N ['prɔdʒɛkt] (plan) piano; (venture)
progetto; (Scol) studio, ricerca ▸ VT
[prə'dʒɛkt] proiettare ▸ VI (stick out) sporgere
projectile [prə'dʒɛktaɪl] N proiettile m
projection [prə'dʒɛkʃən] N proiezione f;
sporgenza
projectionist [prə'dʒɛkʃənɪst] N (Cine)
proiezionista mf
projection room N (Cine) cabina or sala di
proiezione
projector [prə'dʒɛktə^r] N proiettore m
proletarian [prəʊlɪ'tɛərɪən] ADJ, N
proletario(-a)
proletariat [prəʊlɪ'tɛərɪət] N proletariato
pro-life [prəʊ'laɪf] ADJ per il diritto alla, vita
proliferate [prə'lɪfəreɪt] VI proliferare
proliferation [prəlɪfə'reɪʃən] N
proliferazione f
prolific [prə'lɪfɪk] ADJ prolifico(-a); (artist etc)
fecondo(-a)
prologue, (US) **prolog** ['prəʊlɔg] N prologo
prolong [prə'lɔŋ] VT prolungare
prom [prɔm] N ABBR = **promenade**;
promenade concert; (US: ball) ballo
studentesco; vedi nota

> In Gran Bretagna i Proms (= promenade
> concerts) sono concerti di musica classica,
> i più noti dei quali sono quelli eseguiti
> nella Royal Albert Hall a Londra.
> Prendono il nome dal fatto che in origine
> il pubblico li ascoltava stando in piedi o
> passeggiando. Negli Stati Uniti, invece,
> con prom si intende il ballo studentesco di
> un'università o di un college.

promenade [prɔmə'nɑːd] N (by sea)
lungomare m
promenade concert N concerto (con posti in
piedi)
promenade deck N (Naut) ponte m di
passeggiata
prominence ['prɔmɪnəns] N prominenza;
importanza
prominent ['prɔmɪnənt] ADJ (standing out)
prominente; (important) importante; **he is ~
in the field of …** è un'autorità nel campo
di …
prominently ['prɔmɪnəntlɪ] ADV (display, set)
ben in vista; **he figured ~ in the case** ha
avuto una parte di primo piano nella
faccenda
promiscuity [prɔmɪs'kjuːɪtɪ] N (sexual)
rapporti mpl multipli
promiscuous [prə'mɪskjuəs] ADJ (sexually) di
facili costumi
promise ['prɔmɪs] N promessa ▸ VT, VI
promettere; **to make sb a ~** fare una
promessa a qn; **to ~ sb sth, to ~ sth to sb**
promettere qc a qn; **a young man of ~** un
giovane promettente; **to ~ (sb) that/to do
sth** promettere (a qn) che/di fare qc
promising ['prɔmɪsɪŋ] ADJ promettente
promissory note ['prɔmɪsərɪ-] N pagherò
m inv
promontory ['prɔməntrɪ] N promontorio
promote [prə'məʊt] VT promuovere;
(venture, event) organizzare; (product) lanciare,
reclamizzare; **the team was promoted to
the second division** (BRIT Football) la
squadra è stata promossa in serie B
promoter [prə'məʊtə^r] N (of sporting event)
organizzatore(-trice); (of cause etc)
sostenitore(-trice)
promotion [prə'məʊʃən] N promozione f
prompt [prɔmpt] ADJ rapido(-a), svelto(-a);
puntuale; (reply) sollecito(-a) ▸ ADV
(punctually) in punto ▸ N (Comput) prompt m
inv ▸ VT incitare; provocare; (Theat)
suggerire a; **at 8 o'clock ~** alle 8 in punto;
to be ~ to do sth essere sollecito nel fare qc;
to ~ sb to do spingere qn a fare
prompter ['prɔmptə^r] N (Theat) suggeritore m
promptly ['prɔmptlɪ] ADV prontamente;
puntualmente
promptness ['prɔmptnɪs] N prontezza;
puntualità
prone [prəʊn] ADJ (lying) prono(-a); **~ to**
propenso(-a) a, incline a; **to be ~ to illness**
essere soggetto(-a) a malattie; **she is ~ to
burst into tears if …** può facilmente
scoppiare in lacrime se …
prong [prɔŋ] N rebbio, punta
pronoun ['prəʊnaun] N pronome m
pronounce [prə'nauns] VT pronunciare

p

▸ VI: **to ~ (up)on** pronunciare su; **they pronounced him unfit to drive** lo hanno dichiarato inabile alla guida; **how do you ~ it?** come si pronuncia?
pronounced [prə'naunst] ADJ (*marked*) spiccato(-a)
pronouncement [prə'naunsmənt] N dichiarazione *f*
pronunciation [prənʌnsɪ'eɪʃən] N pronuncia
proof [pru:f] N prova; (*of book*) bozza; (*Phot*) provino; **70% ~** ≈ 40° in volume ▸ VT (*tent, anorak*) impermeabilizzare ▸ ADJ: **~ against** a prova di
proofreader ['pru:fri:dəʳ] N correttore(-trice) di bozze
prop [prɔp] N sostegno, appoggio ▸ VT (*also*: **prop up**) sostenere, appoggiare; (*lean*): **to ~ sth against** appoggiare qc contro *or* a; **props** oggetti *m inv* di scena
Prop. ABBR (*Comm*) = **proprietor**
propaganda [prɔpə'gændə] N propaganda
propagation [prɔpə'geɪʃən] N propagazione *f*
propel [prə'pɛl] VT spingere (in avanti), muovere
propeller [prə'pɛləʳ] N elica
propelling pencil [prə'pɛlɪŋ-] N (BRIT) matita a mina
propensity [prə'pɛnsɪtɪ] N tendenza
proper ['prɔpəʳ] ADJ (*suited, right*) adatto(-a), appropriato(-a); (*seemly*) decente; (*authentic*) vero(-a); (*col: real*) 'n' + vero(-a) e proprio(-a); **to go through the ~ channels** (*Admin*) seguire la regolare procedura
properly ['prɔpəlɪ] ADV decentemente; (*really, thoroughly*) veramente; (*eat, study*) bene; (*behave*) come si deve
proper noun N nome *m* proprio
property ['prɔpətɪ] N (*things owned*) beni *mpl*; (*land, building, Chem etc: quality*) proprietà *f inv*
property developer N (BRIT) costruttore *m* edile
property owner N proprietario(-a)
property tax N imposta patrimoniale
prophecy ['prɔfɪsɪ] N profezia
prophesy ['prɔfɪsaɪ] VT predire, profetizzare
prophet ['prɔfɪt] N profeta *m*
prophetic [prə'fɛtɪk] ADJ profetico(-a)
proportion [prə'pɔ:ʃən] N proporzione *f*; (*share*) parte *f* ▸ VT proporzionare, commisurare; **proportions** NPL (*size*) proporzioni *fpl*; **to be in/out of ~ to** *or* **with sth** essere in proporzione/sproporzionato rispetto a qc; **to see sth in ~** (*fig*) dare il giusto peso a qc
proportional [prə'pɔ:ʃənl] ADJ proporzionale
proportional representation N rappresentanza proporzionale
proportionate [prə'pɔ:ʃənɪt] ADJ proporzionato(-a)
proposal [prə'pəuzl] N proposta; (*plan*) progetto; (*of marriage*) proposta di matrimonio
propose [prə'pəuz] VT proporre, suggerire ▸ VI fare una proposta di matrimonio; **to ~ to do** proporsi di fare, aver l'intenzione di fare
proposer [prə'pəuzəʳ] N (BRIT: *of motion*) proponente *mf*
proposition [prɔpə'zɪʃən] N proposizione *f*; (*proposal*) proposta; **to make sb a ~** proporre qualcosa a qn
propound [prə'paund] VT proporre, presentare
proprietary [prə'praɪətərɪ] ADJ: **~ article** prodotto con marchio depositato; **~ brand** marchio di fabbrica
proprietor [prə'praɪətəʳ] N proprietario(-a)
propriety [prə'praɪətɪ] N (*seemliness*) decoro, rispetto delle convenienze sociali
propulsion [prə'pʌlʃən] N propulsione *f*
pro rata [prəu'rɑ:tə] ADV in proporzione
prosaic [prəu'zeɪɪk] ADJ prosaico(-a)
Pros. Atty. ABBR (*US*) = **prosecuting attorney**
proscribe [prə'skraɪb] VT proscrivere
prose [prəuz] N prosa; (*Scol: translation*) traduzione *f* dalla madrelingua
prosecute ['prɔsɪkju:t] VT (*Law*) perseguire
prosecuting attorney ['prɔsɪkju:tɪŋ-] N (*US*) ≈ procuratore *m*
prosecution [prɔsɪ'kju:ʃən] N (*Law*) procedimento giudiziario; (*accusing side*) accusa
prosecutor ['prɔsɪkju:təʳ] N (*also*: **public prosecutor**) ≈ procuratore *m* della Repubblica
prospect N ['prɔspɛkt] prospettiva; (*hope*) speranza ▸ VT [prə'spɛkt] esplorare ▸ VI: **to ~ for gold** cercare l'oro; **there is every ~ of an early victory** tutto lascia prevedere una rapida vittoria; *see also* **prospects**
prospecting [prə'spɛktɪŋ] N prospezione *f*
prospective [prə'spɛktɪv] ADJ (*buyer*) potenziale; (*legislation, son-in-law*) futuro(-a)
prospector [prə'spɛktəʳ] N prospettore *m*; **gold ~** cercatore *m* d'oro
prospects ['prɔspɛkts] NPL (*for work etc*) prospettive *fpl*
prospectus [prə'spɛktəs] N prospetto, programma *m*
prosper ['prɔspəʳ] VI prosperare
prosperity [prɔ'spɛrɪtɪ] N prosperità
prosperous ['prɔspərəs] ADJ prospero(-a)
prostate ['prɔsteɪt] N (*also*: **prostate gland**) prostata, ghiandola prostatica
prostitute ['prɔstɪtju:t] N prostituta; **male ~** uomo che si prostituisce
prostitution [prɔstɪ'tju:ʃən] N prostituzione *f*

prostrate ADJ ['prɔstreɪt] prostrato(-a) ▶ VT [prɔ'streɪt]: **to ~ o.s.** (before sb) prostrarsi

protagonist [prə'tægənɪst] N protagonista mf

protect [prə'tɛkt] VT proteggere, salvaguardare

protection [prə'tɛkʃən] N protezione f; **to be under sb's ~** essere sotto la protezione di qn

protectionism [prə'tɛkʃənɪzəm] N protezionismo

protection racket N racket m inv

protective [prə'tɛktɪv] ADJ protettivo(-a); **~ custody** (Law) protezione f

protector [prə'tɛktər] N protettore(-trice)

protégé ['prəutɪʒeɪ] N protetto

protégée ['prəutɪʒeɪ] N protetta

protein ['prəuti:n] N proteina

pro tem [prəu'tɛm] ADV ABBR (for the time being: = pro tempore) pro tempore

protest N ['prəutɛst] protesta ▶ VT, VI [prə'tɛst] protestare; **to do sth under ~** fare qc protestando; **to ~ against/about** protestare contro/per

Protestant ['prɔtɪstənt] ADJ, N protestante (mf)

protester, protestor [prə'tɛstər] N (in demonstration) dimostrante mf

protest march N marcia di protesta

protocol ['prəutəkɔl] N protocollo

prototype ['prəutətaɪp] N prototipo

protracted [prə'træktɪd] ADJ tirato(-a) per le lunghe

protractor [prə'træktər] N (Geom) goniometro

protrude [prə'tru:d] VI sporgere

protuberance [prə'tju:bərəns] N sporgenza

proud [praud] ADJ fiero(-a), orgoglioso(-a); (pej) superbo(-a); **to be ~ to do sth** essere onorato(-a) di fare qc; **to do sb ~** non far mancare nulla a qn; **to do o.s. ~** trattarsi bene

proudly ['praudlɪ] ADV con orgoglio, fieramente

prove [pru:v] VT provare, dimostrare ▶ VI: **to ~ (to be) correct** etc risultare vero(-a) etc; **to ~ o.s.** mostrare le proprie capacità; **to ~ o.s./ itself (to be) useful** etc mostrarsi or rivelarsi utile etc; **he was proved right in the end** alla fine i fatti gli hanno dato ragione

Provence [prɔvɑ̃s] N Provenza

proverb ['prɔvə:b] N proverbio

proverbial [prə'və:bɪəl] ADJ proverbiale

provide [prə'vaɪd] VT fornire, provvedere; **to ~ sb with sth** fornire or provvedere qn di qc; **to be provided with** essere dotato or munito di

▶ **provide for** VT FUS provvedere a; (future event) prevedere

provided [prə'vaɪdɪd] CONJ: **~ (that)** purché + sub, a condizione che + sub

Providence ['prɔvɪdəns] N Provvidenza

providing [prə'vaɪdɪŋ] CONJ purché + sub, a condizione che + sub

province ['prɔvɪns] N provincia

provincial [prə'vɪnʃəl] ADJ provinciale

provision [prə'vɪʒən] N (supply) riserva; (supplying) provvista; rifornimento; (stipulation) condizione f; **provisions** NPL (food) provviste fpl; **to make ~ for** (one's family, future) pensare a; **there's no ~ for this in the contract** il contratto non lo prevede

provisional [prə'vɪʒənl] ADJ provvisorio(-a) ▶ N: **P~** (IRISH Pol) provisional m inv

provisional licence N (BRIT Aut) ≈ foglio m rosa inv

provisionally [prə'vɪʒnəlɪ] ADV provvisoriamente; (appoint) a titolo provvisorio

proviso [prə'vaɪzəu] N condizione f; **with the ~ that** a condizione che + sub, a patto che + sub

Provo ['prɔvəu] N ABBR (col) = **Provisional**

provocation [prɔvə'keɪʃən] N provocazione f

provocative [prə'vɔkətɪv] ADJ (aggressive) provocatorio(-a); (thought-provoking) stimolante; (seductive) provocante

provoke [prə'vəuk] VT provocare; incitare; **to ~ sb to sth/to do** or **into doing sth** spingere qn a qc/a fare qc

provoking [prə'vəukɪŋ] ADJ irritante, esasperante

provost ['prɔvəst] N (BRIT: of university) rettore m; (SCOTTISH) sindaco

prow [prau] N prua

prowess ['prauɪs] N prodezza; **his ~ as a footballer** le sue capacità di calciatore

prowl [praul] VI (also: **prowl about, prowl around**) aggirarsi furtivamente ▶ N: **on the ~** in caccia

prowler ['praulər] N tipo sospetto (che s'aggira con l'intenzione di rubare, aggredire ecc)

proximity [prɔk'sɪmɪtɪ] N prossimità

proxy ['prɔksɪ] N procura; **by ~** per procura

PRP N ABBR (= performance related pay) retribuzione f commensurata al rendimento

prude [pru:d] N puritano(-a)

prudence ['pru:dns] N prudenza

prudent ['pru:dnt] ADJ prudente

prudish ['pru:dɪʃ] ADJ puritano(-a)

prune [pru:n] N prugna secca ▶ VT potare

pry [praɪ] VI: **to ~ into** ficcare il naso in

PS N ABBR (= postscript) P.S.

psalm [sɑ:m] N salmo

PSAT® N ABBR (US) = **Preliminary Scholastic Aptitude Test**

PSBR N ABBR (BRIT: = public sector borrowing requirement) fabbisogno di prestiti per il settore pubblico

pseud ['sjuːd] N (BRIT: col: intellectually) intellettualoide mf; (: socially) snob mf

pseudo- ['sjuːdəʊ] PREFIX pseudo...

pseudonym ['sjuːdənɪm] N pseudonimo

PSHE N ABBR (BRIT Scol: = personal, social and health education) formazione di formazione sociale e sanitaria

PST ABBR (US: = Pacific Standard Time) ora invernale del Pacifico

psyche ['saɪkɪ] N psiche f

psychedelic [saɪkɪ'delɪk] ADJ psichedelico(-a)

psychiatric [saɪkɪ'ætrɪk] ADJ psichiatrico(-a)

psychiatrist [saɪ'kaɪətrɪst] N psichiatra mf

psychiatry [saɪ'kaɪətrɪ] N psichiatria

psychic ['saɪkɪk] ADJ (also: **psychical**) psichico(-a); (: person) dotato(-a) di qualità telepatiche

psycho ['saɪkəʊ] N (col) folle mf, psicopatico(-a)

psychoanalyse [saɪkəʊ'ænəlaɪz] VT psicanalizzare

psychoanalysis [saɪkəʊə'nælɪsɪs] (pl **-ses** [-siːz]) N psicanalisi f inv

psychoanalyst [saɪkəʊ'ænəlɪst] N psicanalista m f

psychological [saɪkə'lɒdʒɪkl] ADJ psicologico(-a)

psychologist [saɪ'kɒlədʒɪst] N psicologo(-a)

psychology [saɪ'kɒlədʒɪ] N psicologia

psychopath ['saɪkəʊpæθ] N psicopatico(-a)

psychosis [saɪ'kəʊsɪs] (pl **psychoses** [-siːz]) N psicosi f inv

psychosomatic [saɪkəʊsə'mætɪk] ADJ psicosomatico(-a)

psychotherapy [saɪkəʊ'θɛrəpɪ] N psicoterapia

psychotic [saɪ'kɒtɪk] ADJ, N psicotico(-a)

PT N ABBR (BRIT: = physical training) ed. fisica

pt ABBR = **pint**; (= point) pt

Pt. ABBR (in place names: = Point) Pt.

PTA N ABBR (= Parent-Teacher Association) associazione genitori e insegnanti

Pte. ABBR (BRIT Mil) = **private**

PTO ABBR (= please turn over) v.r. (= vedi retro)

PTV N ABBR (US) = **pay television; public television**

pub [pʌb] N ABBR (= public house) pub m inv; vedi nota

> In Gran Bretagna e in Irlanda i pubs sono locali dove vengono servite bibite alcoliche ed analcoliche e dove è anche possibile mangiare. Sono punti di ritrovo dove spesso si può giocare a biliardo, a freccette o guardare la televisione. Le leggi che regolano la vendita degli alcolici sono molto severe in Gran Bretagna e quindi gli orari di apertura e di chiusura vengono osservati scrupolosamente.

pub crawl N: **to go on a ~** (BRIT col) fare il giro dei pub

puberty ['pjuːbətɪ] N pubertà

pubic ['pjuːbɪk] ADJ pubico(-a), del pube

public ['pʌblɪk] ADJ pubblico(-a) ▶ N pubblico; **in ~** in pubblico; **the general ~** il pubblico; **to make sth ~** render noto or di pubblico dominio qc; **to be ~ knowledge** essere di dominio pubblico; **to go ~** (Comm) emettere le azioni sul mercato

public address system N impianto di amplificazione

publican ['pʌblɪkən] N (BRIT) gestore m (or proprietario) di un pub

publication [pʌblɪ'keɪʃən] N pubblicazione f

public company N ≈ società f inv per azioni (costituita tramite pubblica sottoscrizione)

public convenience N (BRIT) gabinetti mpl

public holiday N (BRIT) giorno festivo, festa nazionale

public house N (BRIT) pub m inv

publicity [pʌb'lɪsɪtɪ] N pubblicità

publicize ['pʌblɪsaɪz] VT rendere pubblico(-a), pubblicizzare

public limited company N ≈ società per azioni a responsabilità limitata (quotata in Borsa)

publicly ['pʌblɪklɪ] ADV pubblicamente

public opinion N opinione f pubblica

public ownership N proprietà pubblica or sociale; **to be taken into ~** essere statalizzato(-a)

public prosecutor N pubblico ministero; **~'s office** ufficio del pubblico ministero

public relations N pubbliche relazioni fpl

public relations officer N addetto(-a) alle pubbliche relazioni

public school N (BRIT) scuola privata; (US) scuola statale; vedi nota

> In Inghilterra le public schools sono scuole o collegi privati di istruzione secondaria, spesso di un certo prestigio. In Scozia e negli Stati Uniti, invece, le public schools sono scuole pubbliche gratuite amministrate dallo stato.

public sector N settore m pubblico

public service vehicle N (BRIT) mezzo pubblico

public-spirited [pʌblɪk'spɪrɪtɪd] ADJ che ha senso civico

public transport, (US) **public transportation** N mezzi mpl pubblici

public utility N servizio pubblico

public works NPL lavori mpl pubblici

publish ['pʌblɪʃ] VT pubblicare

publisher ['pʌblɪʃər] N editore m; (firm) casa editrice

publishing ['pʌblɪʃɪŋ] N (industry) editoria; (of a book) pubblicazione f

publishing company N casa or società editrice
pub lunch N: **to go for a ~** andare a mangiare al pub
puce [pjuːs] ADJ color pulce inv
puck [pʌk] N (Ice Hockey) disco
pucker ['pʌkə^r] VT corrugare
pudding ['pudɪŋ] N budino; (BRIT: dessert) dolce m; **black ~**, (US) **blood ~** sanguinaccio; **rice ~** budino di riso
puddle ['pʌdl] N pozza, pozzanghera
puerile ['pjuəraɪl] ADJ puerile
Puerto Rico ['pwəːtəu'riːkəu] N Portorico
puff [pʌf] N sbuffo; (also: **powder puff**) piumino ▶ VT (also: **puff out**: sails, cheeks) gonfiare ▶ VI uscire a sbuffi; (pant) ansare; **to ~ out smoke** mandar fuori sbuffi di fumo; **to ~ one's pipe** tirare sboccate di fumo
puffed [pʌft] ADJ (col: out of breath) senza fiato
puffin ['pʌfɪn] N puffino
puff pastry, (US) **puff paste** N pasta sfoglia
puffy ['pʌfɪ] ADJ gonfio(-a)
pugnacious [pʌg'neɪʃəs] ADJ combattivo(-a)
pull [pul] N (tug) strattone m, tirata; (of moon, magnet, the sea etc) attrazione f; (fig) influenza ▶ VT tirare; (muscle) strappare, farsi uno strappo a; (trigger) premere ▶ VI tirare; **to give sth a ~** tirare su qc; **to ~ a face** fare una smorfia; **to ~ to pieces** fare a pezzi; **to ~ one's punches** (Boxing) risparmiare l'avversario; **not to ~ one's punches** (fig) non avere peli sulla lingua; **to ~ one's weight** dare il proprio contributo; **to ~ o.s. together** ricomporsi, riprendersi; **to ~ sb's leg** prendere in giro qn; **to ~ strings (for sb)** muovere qualche pedina (per qn)
  ▶ **pull about** VT (BRIT: handle roughly: object) strapazzare; (: person) malmenare
  ▶ **pull apart** VT (break) fare a pezzi
  ▶ **pull away** VI (move off: vehicle) muoversi, partire; (: boat) staccarsi dal molo, salpare; (draw back: person) indietreggiare
  ▶ **pull back** VT (lever etc) tirare indietro; (curtains) aprire ▶ VI (from confrontation etc) tirarsi indietro; (Mil: withdraw) ritirarsi
  ▶ **pull down** VT (house) demolire; (tree) abbattere
  ▶ **pull in** VI (Aut: at the kerb) accostarsi; (Rail) entrare in stazione
  ▶ **pull off** VT (clothes) togliere; (deal etc) portare a compimento
  ▶ **pull out** VI partire; (withdraw) ritirarsi; (Aut: come out of line) spostarsi sulla mezzeria ▶ VT staccare; far uscire; (withdraw) ritirare
  ▶ **pull over** VI (Aut) accostare
  ▶ **pull round** VI (unconscious person) rinvenire; (sick person) ristabilirsi
  ▶ **pull through** VI farcela

  ▶ **pull up** VI (stop) fermarsi ▶ VT (uproot) sradicare; (stop) fermare; (raise) sollevare
pulley ['pulɪ] N puleggia, carrucola
pull-out ['pulaut] N inserto ▶ CPD staccabile
pullover ['puləuvə^r] N pullover m inv
pulp [pʌlp] N (of fruit) polpa; (for paper) pasta per carta; (magazines, books) stampa di qualità e di tono scadenti; **to reduce sth to ~** spappolare qc
pulpit ['pulpɪt] N pulpito
pulsate [pʌl'seɪt] VI battere, palpitare
pulse [pʌls] N polso; (Bot) legume m; **to feel** or **take sb's ~** sentire or tastare il polso a qn
pulses ['pʌlsəz] NPL (Culin) legumi mpl
pulverize ['pʌlvəraɪz] VT polverizzare
puma ['pjuːmə] N puma m inv
pumice ['pʌmɪs], **pumice stone** ['pʌmɪs-] N (pietra) pomice f
pummel ['pʌml] VT dare pugni a
pump [pʌmp] N pompa; (shoe) scarpetta ▶ VT pompare; (fig: col) far parlare; **to ~ sb for information** cercare di strappare delle informazioni a qn
  ▶ **pump up** VT gonfiare
pumpkin ['pʌmpkɪn] N zucca
pun [pʌn] N gioco di parole
punch [pʌntʃ] N (blow) pugno; (fig: force) forza; (tool) punzone m; (drink) ponce m ▶ VT (hit): **to ~ sb/sth** dare un pugno a qn/qc; **to ~ a hole (in)** fare un buco (in)
  ▶ **punch in** VI (US) timbrare il cartellino (all'entrata)
  ▶ **punch out** VI (US) timbrare il cortellino (all'uscita)
punch card, punched card ['pʌntʃt-] N scheda perforata
punch-drunk ['pʌntʃdrʌŋk] ADJ (BRIT) stordito(-a)
punch line N (of joke) battuta finale
punch-up ['pʌntʃʌp] N (BRIT col) rissa
punctual ['pʌŋktjuəl] ADJ puntuale
punctuality [pʌŋktju'ælɪtɪ] N puntualità
punctually ['pʌŋktjuəlɪ] ADV puntualmente; **it will start ~ at 6** comincerà alle 6 precise or in punto
punctuate ['pʌŋktjueɪt] VT punteggiare
punctuation [pʌŋktju'eɪʃən] N interpunzione f, punteggiatura
punctuation mark N segno d'interpunzione
puncture ['pʌŋktʃə^r] N (BRIT) foratura ▶ VT forare; **to have a ~** (Aut) forare (una gomma)
pundit ['pʌndɪt] N sapientone(-a)
pungent ['pʌndʒənt] ADJ piccante; (fig) mordace, caustico(-a)
punish ['pʌnɪʃ] VT punire; **to ~ sb for sth/for doing sth** punire qn per qc/per aver fatto qc
punishable ['pʌnɪʃəbl] ADJ punibile
punishing ['pʌnɪʃɪŋ] ADJ (fig: exhausting) sfiancante

punishment ['pʌnɪʃmənt] N punizione f; **to take a lot of** ~ (col: boxer) incassare parecchi colpi; (car) essere messo(-a) a dura prova

punk [pʌŋk] N (person: also: **punk rocker**) punk mf; (music: also: **punk rock**) musica punk, punk rock m; (US col: hoodlum) teppista m

punt [pʌnt] N (boat) barchino; (Football) colpo a volo; (IRISH) sterlina irlandese ▶ VI (BRIT: bet) scommettere

punter ['pʌntə'] N (BRIT: gambler) scommettitore(-trice)

puny ['pju:nɪ] ADJ gracile

pup [pʌp] N cucciolo(-a)

pupil ['pju:pl] N allievo(-a); (Anat) pupilla

puppet ['pʌpɪt] N burattino

puppet government N governo fantoccio

puppy ['pʌpɪ] N cucciolo(-a), cagnolino(-a)

purchase ['pə:tʃɪs] N acquisto, compera; (grip) presa ▶ VT comprare; **to get a ~ on** (grip) trovare un appoggio su

purchase order N ordine m d'acquisto, ordinazione f

purchase price N prezzo d'acquisto

purchaser ['pə:tʃɪsə'] N compratore(-trice)

purchase tax N (BRIT) tassa d'acquisto

purchasing power ['pə:tʃɪsɪŋ-] N potere m d'acquisto

pure [pjuə'] ADJ puro(-a); **a ~ wool jumper** un golf di pura lana; **it's laziness ~ and simple** è pura pigrizia

purebred ['pjuəbred] ADJ di razza pura

purée ['pjuəreɪ] N purè m inv

purely ['pjuəlɪ] ADV puramente

purge [pə:dʒ] N (Med) purga; (Pol) epurazione f ▶ VT purgare; (fig) epurare

purification [pjuərɪfɪ'keɪʃən] N purificazione f

purify ['pjuərɪfaɪ] VT purificare

purist ['pjuərɪst] N purista mf

puritan ['pjuərɪtən] ADJ, N puritano(-a)

puritanical [pjuərɪ'tænɪkl] ADJ puritano(-a)

purity ['pjuərɪtɪ] N purezza

purl [pə:l] N punto rovescio ▶ VT lavorare a rovescio

purloin [pə:'lɔɪn] VT rubare

purple ['pə:pl] ADJ di porpora; viola inv

purport [pə:'pɔ:t] VI: **to ~ to be/do** pretendere di essere/fare

purpose ['pə:pəs] N intenzione f, scopo; **on ~** apposta, di proposito; **for illustrative purposes** a titolo illustrativo; **for teaching purposes** per l'insegnamento; **for the purposes of this meeting** agli effetti di questa riunione; **to no ~** senza nessun risultato, inutilmente

purpose-built ['pə:pəs'bɪlt] ADJ (BRIT) costruito(-a) allo scopo

purposeful ['pə:pəsful] ADJ deciso(-a), risoluto(-a)

purposely ['pə:pəslɪ] ADV apposta

purr [pə:'] N fusa fpl ▶ VI fare le fusa

purse [pə:s] N (BRIT) borsellino; (US: handbag) borsetta, borsa ▶ VT contrarre

purser ['pə:sə'] N (Naut) commissario di bordo

purse snatcher [-'snætʃə'] N (US) scippatore m

pursue [pə'sju:] VT inseguire; essere alla ricerca di; (inquiry, matter) approfondire; (fig: activity etc) continuare con; (: aim etc) perseguire

pursuer [pə'sju:ə'] N inseguitore(-trice)

pursuit [pə'sju:t] N inseguimento; (occupation) occupazione f, attività f inv; (fig) ricerca; (pastime) passatempo; **in (the) ~ of sth** alla ricerca di qc; **scientific pursuits** ricerche fpl scientifiche

purveyor [pə'veɪə'] N fornitore(-trice)

pus [pʌs] N pus m

push [puʃ] N spinta; (effort) grande sforzo; (drive) energia ▶ VT spingere; (button) premere; (fig) fare pubblicità a; (thrust): **to ~ sth (into)** ficcare qc (in) ▶ VI spingere; premere; **to ~ a door open/shut** aprire/chiudere una porta con una spinta or spingendola; **to be pushed for time/ money** essere a corto di tempo/soldi; **she is pushing 50** (col) va per i 50; **to ~ for** (better pay, conditions etc) insistere per ottenere; **"~"** (on door) "spingere"; (on bell) "suonare"; **at a ~** (BRIT col) in caso di necessità

▶ **push aside** VT scostare

▶ **push in** VI introdursi a forza

▶ **push off** VI (col) filare

▶ **push on** VI (continue) continuare

▶ **push over** VT far cadere

▶ **push through** VI farsi largo spingendo ▶ VT (measure) far approvare

▶ **push up** VT (total, prices) far salire

push-bike ['puʃbaɪk] N (BRIT) bicicletta

push-button ['puʃbʌtn] ADJ a pulsante

pushchair ['puʃtʃeə'] N (BRIT) passeggino

pusher ['puʃə'] N (also: **drug pusher**) spacciatore(-trice) (di droga)

pushover ['puʃəuvə'] N (col): **it's a ~** è un lavoro da bambini

push-up ['puʃʌp] N (US: press-up) flessione f sulle braccia

pushy ['puʃɪ] ADJ (pej) troppo intraprendente

puss [pus], **pussy(-cat)** ['pusɪ-] N micio

put [put] (pt, pp ~) VT mettere, porre; (say) dire, esprimere; (a question) fare; (estimate) stimare ▶ ADV: **to stay** ~ non muoversi; **to ~ sb to bed** mettere qn a letto; **to ~ sb in a good/bad mood** mettere qn di buon/cattivo umore; **to ~ sb to a lot of trouble** scomodare qn; **to ~ a lot of time into sth** dedicare molto tempo a qc; **to ~ money on a horse** scommettere su un cavallo; **how**

shall I ~ it? come dire?; **I ~ it to you that ...** (BRIT) io sostengo che ...
▶ **put about** VI (Naut) virare di bordo ▶ VT (rumour) diffondere
▶ **put across** VT (ideas etc) comunicare, far capire
▶ **put aside** VT (lay down: book etc) mettere da una parte, posare; (save) mettere da parte; (in shop) tenere da parte
▶ **put away** VT (clothes, toys etc) mettere via; (return) mettere a posto
▶ **put back** VT (replace) rimettere (a posto); (postpone) rinviare; (delay) ritardare; (set back: watch, clock) mettere indietro; **this will ~ us back 10 years** questo ci farà tornare indietro di 10 anni
▶ **put by** VT (money) mettere da parte
▶ **put down** VT (parcel etc) posare, mettere giù; (pay) versare; (in writing) mettere per iscritto; (suppress: revolt etc) reprimere, sopprimere; (attribute) attribuire
▶ **put forward** VT (ideas) avanzare, proporre; (date) anticipare
▶ **put in** VT (application, complaint) presentare; (time, effort) mettere
▶ **put in for** VT FUS (job) far domanda per; (promotion) far domanda di
▶ **put off** VT (postpone) rimandare, rinviare; (discourage) dissuadere
▶ **put on** VT (clothes, lipstick etc) mettere; (light etc) accendere; (play etc) mettere in scena; (concert, exhibition etc) allestire, organizzare; (extra bus, train etc) mettere in servizio; (food, meal) mettere su; (brake) mettere; (assume: accent, manner) affettare; (col: tease) prendere in giro; (inform, indicate): **to ~ sb on to sb/sth** indicare qn/qc a qn; **to ~ on weight** ingrassare; **to ~ on airs** darsi delle arie
▶ **put out** VT mettere fuori; (one's hand) porgere; (light etc) spegnere; (inconvenience: person) scomodare; (dislocate: shoulder, knee) lussarsi; (: back) farsi uno strappo a ▶ VI (Naut): **to ~ out to sea** prendere il largo; **to ~ out from Plymouth** partire da Plymouth
▶ **put through** VT (Tel: caller) mettere in comunicazione; (: call) passare; (plan) far approvare; **~ me through to Miss Blair** mi passi la signorina Blair

▶ **put together** VT mettere insieme, riunire; (assemble: furniture) montare; (: meal) improvvisare
▶ **put up** VT (raise) sollevare, alzare; (: umbrella) aprire; (: tent) montare; (pin up) affiggere; (hang) appendere; (build) costruire, erigere; (increase) aumentare; (accommodate) alloggiare; (incite): **to ~ sb up to doing sth** istigare qn a fare qc; **to ~ sth up for sale** mettere in vendita qc
▶ **put upon** VT FUS: **to be ~ upon** (imposed on) farsi mettere sotto i piedi
▶ **put up with** VT FUS sopportare
putrid ['pju:trɪd] ADJ putrido(-a)
putt [pʌt] VT (ball) colpire leggermente ▶ N colpo leggero
putter ['pʌtə^r] N (Golf) putter m inv ▶ VI (US) = **potter**
putting green ['pʌtɪŋ-] N green m inv; campo da putting
putty ['pʌtɪ] N stucco
put-up ['putʌp] ADJ: **~ job** montatura
puzzle ['pʌzl] N enigma m, mistero; (jigsaw) puzzle m; (also: **crossword puzzle**) parole fpl incrociate, cruciverba m inv ▶ VT confondere, rendere perplesso(-a) ▶ VI scervellarsi; **to ~ over** (sb's actions) cercare di capire; (mystery, problem) cercare di risolvere
puzzled ADJ perplesso(-a); **to be ~ about sth** domandarsi il perché di qc
puzzling ['pʌzlɪŋ] ADJ (question) poco chiaro(-a); (attitude, set of instructions) incomprensibile
PVC N ABBR (= polyvinyl chloride) P.V.C. m
Pvt. ABBR (US Mil) = **private**
PW N ABBR (US) = **prisoner of war**
pw ABBR = **per week**
PX N ABBR (US Mil) = **post exchange**
pygmy ['pɪgmɪ] N pigmeo(-a)
pyjamas (BRIT), (US) **pajamas** [pə'dʒɑ:məz] NPL pigiama m; **a pair of ~** un pigiama
pylon ['paɪlən] N pilone m
pyramid ['pɪrəmɪd] N piramide f
Pyrenean [pɪrə'ni:ən] ADJ pirenaico(-a)
Pyrenees [pɪrə'ni:z] NPL: **the ~** i Pirenei
Pyrex® ['paɪrɛks] N Pirex® m inv ▶ CPD: **~ dish** pirofila
python ['paɪθən] N pitone m

p

Qq

Q, q [kjuː] N (letter) Q, q f inv or m inv; **Q for Queen** ≈ Q come Quarto

Qatar [kæ'tɑːʳ] N Qatar m

QC N ABBR (BRIT: = Queen's Counsel) avvocato della Corona

QED ABBR (= quod erat demonstrandum) qed

QM N ABBR = **quartermaster**

q.t. N ABBR col: = **quiet; on the q.t.** di nascosto

qty ABBR = **quantity**

quack [kwæk] N (of duck) qua qua m inv; (pej: doctor) ciarlatano(-a)

quad [kwɔd] N ABBR = **quadrangle; quadruple; quadruplet**

quadrangle ['kwɔdræŋgl] N (Math) quadrilatero; (courtyard) cortile m

quadruped ['kwɔdrupɛd] N quadrupede m

quadruple [kwɔ'drupl] ADJ quadruplo(-a) ▶ N quadruplo ▶ VT quadruplicare ▶ VI quadruplicarsi

quadruplet [kwɔ'druːplɪt] N uno(-a) di quattro gemelli

quagmire ['kwægmaɪəʳ] N pantano

quail [kweɪl] N (Zool) quaglia ▶ VI (person): **to ~ at** or **before** perdersi d'animo davanti a

quaint [kweɪnt] ADJ bizzarro(-a); (old-fashioned) antiquato(-a) e pittoresco(-a)

quake [kweɪk] VI tremare ▶ N ABBR = **earthquake**

Quaker ['kweɪkəʳ] N quacchero(-a)

qualification [kwɔlɪfɪ'keɪʃən] N (degree etc) qualifica, titolo; (ability) competenza, qualificazione f; (limitation) riserva, restrizione f; **what are your qualifications?** quali sono le sue qualifiche?

qualified ['kwɔlɪfaɪd] ADJ qualificato(-a); (able) competente, qualificato(-a); (limited) condizionato(-a); **~ for/to do** qualificato(-a) per/per fare; **he's not ~ for the job** non ha i requisiti necessari per questo lavoro; **it was a ~ success** è stato un successo parziale

qualify ['kwɔlɪfaɪ] VT abilitare; (limit: statement) modificare, precisare ▶ VI: **to ~ (as)** qualificarsi (come); **to ~ (for)** acquistare i requisiti necessari (per); (Sport) qualificarsi (per or a); **to ~ as an engineer** diventare un perito tecnico

qualifying ['kwɔlɪfaɪɪŋ] ADJ (exam) di ammissione; (round) eliminatorio(-a)

qualitative ['kwɔlɪtətɪv] ADJ qualitativo(-a)

quality ['kwɔlɪtɪ] N qualità f inv ▶ CPD di qualità; **of good ~** di buona qualità; **of poor ~** scadente; **~ of life** qualità della vita

quality control N controllo di qualità

quality papers NPL, **quality press** N (BRIT): **the ~** la stampa d'informazione; vedi nota

> Il termine quality press si riferisce ai quotidiani o ai settimanali che offrono un'informazione seria ed approfondita. Questi giornali si differenziano da quelli popolari, i tabloid, per formato e contenuti. Questa divisione tra tipi di giornali riflette il tradizionale divario tra classi sociali nella società britannica; vedi anche **tabloid press**.

qualm [kwɑːm] N dubbio; scrupolo; **to have qualms about sth** avere degli scrupoli per qc

quandary ['kwɔndrɪ] N: **in a ~** in un dilemma

quango ['kwæŋgəu] N ABBR (BRIT: = quasi-autonomous non-governmental organization) commissione consultiva di nomina governativa

quantifiable ['kwɔntɪfaɪəbl] ADJ quantificabile

quantify ['kwɔntɪfaɪ] VT quantificare

quantitative ['kwɔntɪtətɪv] ADJ quantitativo(-a)

quantity ['kwɔntɪtɪ] N quantità f inv; **in ~** in grande quantità

quantity surveyor N (BRIT) geometra m (specializzato nel calcolare la quantità e il costo del materiale da costruzione)

quantum leap ['kwɔntəm-] N (fig) enorme cambiamento

quarantine ['kwɔrntiːn] N quarantena

quark [kwɑːk] N quark m inv

quarrel ['kwɔrl] N lite f, disputa ▶ VI litigare; **to have a ~ with sb** litigare con qn; **I've no ~**

with him non ho niente contro di lui; **I can't ~ with that** non ho niente da ridire su questo

quarrelsome ['kwɔrəlsəm] ADJ litigioso(-a)

quarry ['kwɔrɪ] N (for stone) cava; (animal) preda ▶ VT (marble etc) estrarre

quart [kwɔːt] N due pinte fpl, ≈ litro

quarter ['kwɔːtəʳ] N quarto f; (of year) trimestre m; (district) quartiere m; (US, CANADA: 25 cents) quarto di dollaro, 25 centesimi ▶ VT dividere in quattro; (Mil) alloggiare; **quarters** NPL (living quarters) alloggio; (Mil) alloggi mpl, quadrato; **to pay by the ~** pagare trimestralmente; **a ~ of an hour** un quarto d'ora; **it's a ~ to 3,** (US) **it's a ~ of 3** sono le 3 meno un quarto, manca un quarto alle 3; **it's a ~ past 3,** (US) **it's a ~ after 3** sono le 3 e un quarto; **from all quarters** da tutte le parti or direzioni; **at close quarters** a distanza ravvicinata

quarterback ['kwɔːtəbæk] N (US Football) quarterback m inv

quarter-deck ['kwɔːtədɛk] N (Naut) cassero

quarter final N quarto di finale

quarterly ['kwɔːtəlɪ] ADJ trimestrale ▶ ADV trimestralmente ▶ N periodico trimestrale

quartermaster ['kwɔːtəmɑːstəʳ] N (Mil) furiere m

quartet, quartette [kwɔːˈtɛt] N quartetto

quarto ['kwɔːtəu] ADJ, N in quarto m inv

quartz [kwɔːts] N quarzo ▶ CPD di quarzo; (watch, clock) al quarzo

quash [kwɔʃ] VT (verdict) annullare

quasi- ['kweɪzaɪ] PREFIX quasi + noun; quasi, pressoché + adjective

quaver ['kweɪvəʳ] N (BRIT Mus) croma ▶ VI tremolare

quay [kiː] N (also: **quayside**) banchina

Que. ABBR (CANADA) = **Quebec**

queasy ['kwiːzɪ] ADJ (stomach) delicato(-a); **to feel ~** aver la nausea

Quebec [kwɪˈbɛk] N Quebec m

queen [kwiːn] N (gen) regina; (Cards etc) regina, donna

queen mother N regina madre

Queen's speech N (BRIT); vedi nota

Durante la sessione di apertura del Parlamento britannico il sovrano legge un discorso redatto dal primo ministro, il Queen's speech (se si tratta della regina), che contiene le linee generali del nuovo programma politico.

queer [kwɪəʳ] ADJ strano(-a), curioso(-a); (suspicious) dubbio(-a), sospetto(-a); (BRIT: sick): **I feel ~** mi sento poco bene ▶ N (col) finocchio

quell [kwɛl] VT domare

quench [kwɛntʃ] VT (flames) spegnere; **to ~ one's thirst** dissetarsi

querulous ['kwɛruləs] ADJ querulo(-a)

query ['kwɪərɪ] N domanda, questione f; (doubt) dubbio ▶ VT mettere in questione; (disagree with, dispute) contestare

quest [kwɛst] N cerca, ricerca

question ['kwɛstʃən] N domanda, questione f ▶ VT (person) interrogare; (plan, idea) mettere in questione or in dubbio; **to ask sb a ~, put a ~ to sb** fare una domanda a qn; **to bring or call sth into ~** mettere in dubbio qc; **the ~ is …** il problema è …; **it's a ~ of doing** si tratta di fare; **there's some ~ of doing** c'è chi suggerisce di fare; **beyond ~** fuori di dubbio; **out of the ~** fuori discussione, impossibile

questionable ['kwɛstʃənəbl] ADJ discutibile

questioner ['kwɛstʃənəʳ] N interrogante mf

questioning ['kwɛstʃənɪŋ] ADJ interrogativo(-a) ▶ N interrogatorio

question mark N punto interrogativo

questionnaire [kwɛstʃəˈnɛəʳ] N questionario

queue [kjuː] (BRIT) N coda, fila ▶ VI fare la coda; **to jump the ~** passare davanti agli altri (in una coda)

quibble ['kwɪbl] VI cavillare

quiche [kiːʃ] N torta salata a base di uova, formaggio, prosciutto o altro

quick [kwɪk] ADJ rapido(-a), veloce; (reply) pronto(-a); (mind) pronto(-a), acuto(-a) ▶ ADV rapidamente, presto ▶ N: **cut to the ~** (fig) toccato(-a) sul vivo; **be ~!** fa presto!; **to be ~ to act** agire prontamente; **she was ~ to see that …** ha visto subito che …

quicken ['kwɪkn] VT accelerare, affrettare; (rouse) animare, stimolare ▶ VI accelerare, affrettarsi

quick fix N soluzione f tampone inv

quicklime ['kwɪklaɪm] N calce f viva

quickly ['kwɪklɪ] ADV rapidamente, velocemente; **we must act ~** dobbiamo agire tempestivamente

quickness ['kwɪknɪs] N rapidità; prontezza; acutezza

quicksand ['kwɪksænd] N sabbie fpl mobili

quickstep ['kwɪkstɛp] N tipo di ballo simile al fox-trot

quick-tempered [kwɪkˈtɛmpəd] ADJ che si arrabbia facilmente

quick-witted [kwɪkˈwɪtɪd] ADJ pronto(-a) d'ingegno

quid [kwɪd] N (pl inv: BRIT col) sterlina

quid pro quo ['kwɪdprəuˈkwəu] N contraccambio

quiet ['kwaɪət] ADJ tranquillo(-a), quieto(-a); (reserved) quieto(-a), taciturno(-a); (ceremony) semplice; (not noisy: engine) silenzioso(-a); (not busy: day) calmo(-a), tranquillo(-a); (: colour) discreto(-a) ▶ N tranquillità, calma ▶ VT, VI (US) = **quieten; keep ~!** sta zitto!; **on the ~** di nascosto; **I'll have a ~ word with**

q

him gli dirò due parole in privato; **business is ~ at this time of year** questa è la stagione morta

quieten ['kwaɪətn] vɪ (BRIT: also: **quieten down**) calmarsi, chetarsi ▸ vт calmare, chetare

quietly ['kwaɪətlɪ] ADV tranquillamente, calmamente; silenziosamente

quietness ['kwaɪətnɪs] N tranquillità, calma; silenzio

quill [kwɪl] N penna d'oca

quilt [kwɪlt] N trapunta; **continental ~** piumino

quin [kwɪn] N ABBR = **quintuplet**

quince [kwɪns] N (mela) cotogna; (tree) cotogno

quinine [kwɪˈniːn] N chinino

quintet, quintette [kwɪnˈtɛt] N quintetto

quintuplet [kwɪnˈtjuːplɪt] N uno(-a) di cinque gemelli

quip [kwɪp] N battuta di spirito

quire ['kwaɪəʳ] N ventesima parte di una risma

quirk [kwəːk] N ghiribizzo; **by some ~ of fate** per un capriccio della sorte

quirky ['kwəːkɪ] ADJ stravagante

quit [kwɪt] (pt, pp **~ or quitted**) vт mollare; (premises) lasciare, partire da ▸ vɪ (give up) mollare; (resign) dimettersi; **to ~ doing** smettere di fare; **~ stalling!** (US col) non tirarla per le lunghe!; **notice to ~** (BRIT) preavviso (dato all'inquilino)

quite [kwaɪt] ADV (rather) assai; (entirely) completamente, del tutto; **I ~ understand** capisco perfettamente; **~ a few of them** non pochi di loro; **~ (so)!** esatto!; **~ new** proprio nuovo; **that's not ~ right** non è proprio esatto; **she's ~ pretty** è piuttosto carina

Quito ['kiːtəu] N Quito m

quits [kwɪts] ADJ: **~ (with)** pari (con); **let's call it ~** adesso siamo pari

quiver ['kwɪvəʳ] vɪ tremare, fremere ▸ N (for arrows) faretra

quiz [kwɪz] N (game) quiz m inv; indovinello ▸ vт interrogare

quizzical ['kwɪzɪkəl] ADJ enigmatico(-a)

quoits [kwɔɪts] NPL gioco degli anelli

quorum ['kwɔːrəm] N quorum m

quota ['kwəutə] N quota

quotation [kwəuˈteɪʃən] N citazione f; (of shares etc) quotazione f; (estimate) preventivo

quotation marks NPL virgolette fpl

quote [kwəut] N citazione f ▸ vт (sentence) citare; (price) dare, indicare, fissare; (shares) quotare ▸ vɪ: **to ~ from** citare; **to ~ for a job** dare un preventivo per un lavoro; **quotes** NPL (col) = **quotation marks**; **in quotes** tra virgolette; **~ ... unquote** (in dictation) aprire le virgolette ... chiudere le virgolette

quotient ['kwəuʃənt] N quoziente m

qv ABBR (= quod vide: which see) v

qwerty keyboard ['kwəːtɪ-] N tastiera qwerty inv

Rr

R, r [ɑːʳ] N (*letter*) R, r f *inv or m inv*; **R for Robert,** (*US*) **R for Roger** ≈ R come Roma
R ABBR (= *Réaumur (scale)*) R; (= *river*) F; (= *right*) D; (*US Cine:* = *restricted*) ≈ vietato; (*US Pol*) = **republican**; (*BRIT*) = **Rex; Regina**
RA N ABBR (*BRIT*) = **Royal Academy; Royal Academician** ▶ ABBR = **rear admiral**
RAAF N ABBR = **Royal Australian Air Force**
Rabat [rə'bɑːt] N Rabat f
rabbi ['ræbaɪ] N rabbino
rabbit ['ræbɪt] N coniglio ▶ VI: **to ~ (on)** (*BRIT*) blaterare
rabbit hole N tana di coniglio
rabbit hutch N conigliera
rabble ['ræbl] N (*pej*) canaglia, plebaglia
rabid ['ræbɪd] ADJ rabbioso(-a); (*fig*) fanatico(-a)
rabies ['reɪbiːz] N rabbia
RAC N ABBR (*BRIT:* = *Royal Automobile Club*) ≈ A.C.I. m (= *Automobile Club d'Italia*)
raccoon, racoon [rə'kuːn] N procione m
race [reɪs] N razza; (*competition, rush*) corsa ▶ VT (*person*) gareggiare (in corsa) con; (*horse*) far correre; (*engine*) imballare ▶ VI correre; (*engine*) imballarsi; **the human ~** la razza umana; **he raced across the road** ha attraversato la strada di corsa; **to ~ in/out** *etc* precipitarsi dentro/fuori *etc*
race car N (*US*) = **racing car**
race car driver N (*US*) = **racing driver**
racecourse ['reɪskɔːs] N campo di corse, ippodromo
racehorse ['reɪshɔːs] N cavallo da corsa
race relations NPL rapporti razziali
racetrack ['reɪstræk] N pista
racial ['reɪʃl] ADJ razziale
racial discrimination N discriminazione f razziale
racialism ['reɪʃəlɪzəm] N razzismo
racialist ['reɪʃəlɪst] ADJ, N razzista mf
racing ['reɪsɪŋ] N corsa
racing car N (*BRIT*) macchina da corsa
racing driver N (*BRIT*) corridore m automobilista

racism ['reɪsɪzəm] N razzismo
racist ['reɪsɪst] ADJ, N (*pej*) razzista mf
rack [ræk] N rastrelliera; (*also:* **luggage rack**) rete f, portabagagli m inv; (*also:* **roof rack**) portabagagli; (*: dish rack*) scolapiatti m inv ▶ VT torturare, tormentare; **magazine ~** portariviste m inv; **shoe ~** scarpiera; **toast ~** portatoast m inv; **to go to ~ and ruin** (*building*) andare in rovina; (*business*) andare in malora *or* a catafascio; **to ~ one's brains** scervellarsi; **racked by** torturato(-a) da ▶ **rack up** VT accumulare
racket ['rækɪt] N (*for tennis*) racchetta; (*noise*) fracasso; baccano; (*swindle*) imbroglio, truffa; (*organized crime*) racket m inv
racketeer [rækɪ'tɪəʳ] N (*US*) trafficante mf
racoon [rə'kuːn] N = **raccoon**
racquet ['rækɪt] N racchetta
racy ['reɪsɪ] ADJ brioso(-a); piccante
RADA ['rɑːdə] N ABBR (*BRIT*) = **Royal Academy of Dramatic Art**
radar ['reɪdɑːʳ] N radar m ▶ CPD radar inv
radar trap N controllo della velocità con radar
radial ['reɪdɪəl] ADJ (*also:* **radial-ply**) radiale
radiance ['reɪdɪəns] N splendore m, radiosità
radiant ['reɪdɪənt] ADJ raggiante; (*Physics*) radiante
radiate ['reɪdɪeɪt] VT (*heat*) irraggiare, irradiare ▶ VI (*lines*) irradiarsi
radiation [reɪdɪ'eɪʃən] N irradiamento; (*radioactive*) radiazione f
radiation sickness N malattia da radiazioni
radiator ['reɪdɪeɪtəʳ] N radiatore m
radiator cap N tappo del radiatore
radiator grill N (*Aut*) mascherina, calandra
radical ['rædɪkl] ADJ radicale
radii ['reɪdɪaɪ] NPL *of* **radius**
radio ['reɪdɪəu] N radio f inv ▶ VT (*information*) trasmettere per radio; (*one's position*) comunicare via radio; (*person*) chiamare via radio ▶ VI: **to ~ to sb** comunicare via radio con qn; **on the ~** alla radio
radio... ['reɪdɪəu] PREFIX radio...

radioactive ['reɪdɪəu'æktɪv] ADJ
radioattivo(-a)
radioactivity ['reɪdɪəuæk'tɪvɪtɪ] N
radioattività
radio announcer N annunciatore/trice della
radio
radio-controlled ['reɪdɪəukən'trəuld] ADJ
radiocomandato(-a), radioguidato(-a)
radiographer [reɪdɪ'ɔgrəfəʳ] N (tecnico)
radiologo(-a)
radiography [reɪdɪ'ɔgrəfɪ] N radiografia
radiologist [reɪdɪ'ɔlədʒɪst] N (medico)
radiologo(-a)
radiology [reɪdɪ'ɔlədʒɪ] N radiologia
radio station N stazione f radio inv
radio taxi N radiotaxi m inv
radiotelephone ['reɪdɪəu'tɛlɪfəun] N
radiotelefono
radiotherapist ['reɪdɪəu'θɛrəpɪst] N
radioterapista mf
radiotherapy ['reɪdɪəu'θɛrəpɪ] N
radioterapia
radish ['rædɪʃ] N ravanello
radium ['reɪdɪəm] N radio
radius ['reɪdɪəs] (pl **radii** [-ɪaɪ]) N raggio;
(Anat) radio; **within a ~ of 50 miles** in un
raggio di 50 miglia
RAF N ABBR (BRIT) = **Royal Air Force**
raffia ['ræfɪə] N rafia
raffish ['ræfɪʃ] ADJ dal look trasandato
raffle ['ræfl] N lotteria ▶ VT (object) mettere in
palio
raft [rɑːft] N zattera; (also: **life raft**) zattera di
salvataggio
rafter ['rɑːftəʳ] N trave f
rag [ræg] N straccio, cencio; (pej: newspaper)
giornalaccio, bandiera; (for charity) iniziativa
studentesca a scopo benefico ▶ VT (BRIT)
prendere in giro; **rags** NPL (torn clothes)
stracci mpl, brandelli mpl; **in rags** stracciato
rag-and-bone man ['rægən'bəun-] N (irreg)
straccivendolo
ragbag ['rægbæg] N (fig) guazzabuglio
rag doll N bambola di pezza
rage [reɪdʒ] N (fury) collera, furia ▶ VI (person)
andare su tutte le furie; (storm) infuriare;
it's all the ~ fa furore; **to fly into a ~** andare
or montare su tutte le furie
ragged ['rægɪd] ADJ (edge) irregolare; (cuff)
logoro(-a); (appearance) pezzente
raging ['reɪdʒɪŋ] ADJ (all senses) furioso(-a);
in a ~ temper su tutte le furie
rag trade N (col): **the ~** l'abbigliamento
rag week N (BRIT); vedi nota

Durante il rag week, gli studenti
universitari organizzano vari spettacoli e
manifestazioni i cui proventi vengono
devoluti in beneficenza.

raid [reɪd] N (Mil) incursione f; (criminal)

rapina; (by police) irruzione f ▶ VT fare
un'incursione in; rapinare; fare irruzione
in
raider ['reɪdəʳ] N rapinatore(-trice); (plane)
aeroplano da incursione
rail [reɪl] N (on stair) ringhiera; (on bridge,
balcony) parapetto; (of ship) battagliola; (for
train) rotaia; **rails** NPL binario, rotaie fpl; **by ~**
per ferrovia, in treno
railcard ['reɪlkɑːd] N (BRIT) tessera di
riduzione ferroviaria
railing ['reɪlɪŋ] N, **railings** ['reɪlɪŋz] NPL
ringhiere fpl
railroad (US) N = **railway**
railway (BRIT) ['reɪlweɪ], (US) **railroad**
['reɪlrəud] N ferrovia
railway engine N (BRIT) locomotiva
railway line N (BRIT) linea ferroviaria
railwayman ['reɪlweɪmən] N (irreg) (BRIT)
ferroviere m
railway station N (BRIT) stazione f
ferroviaria
rain [reɪn] N pioggia ▶ VI piovere; **in the ~**
sotto la pioggia; **it's raining** piove; **it's
raining cats and dogs** piove a catinelle
rainbow ['reɪnbəu] N arcobaleno
raincoat ['reɪnkəut] N impermeabile m
raindrop ['reɪndrɔp] N goccia di pioggia
rainfall ['reɪnfɔːl] N pioggia; (measurement)
piovosità
rainforest ['reɪnfɔrɪst] N foresta pluviale or
equatoriale
rainproof ['reɪnpruːf] ADJ impermeabile
rainstorm ['reɪnstɔːm] N pioggia torrenziale
rainwater ['reɪnwɔːtəʳ] N acqua piovana
rainy ['reɪnɪ] ADJ piovoso(-a)
raise [reɪz] N aumento ▶ VT (lift) alzare;
sollevare; (build) erigere; (increase)
aumentare; (a protest, doubt, question)
sollevare; (cattle, family) allevare; (crop)
coltivare; (army, funds) raccogliere; (loan)
ottenere; (end: siege, embargo) togliere; **to ~
one's voice** alzare la voce; **to ~ sb's hopes**
accendere le speranze di qn; **to ~ one's glass
to sb/sth** brindare a qn/qc; **to ~ a laugh/a
smile** far ridere/sorridere
raisin ['reɪzn] N uva secca
Raj [rɑːdʒ] N: **the ~** l'impero britannico
(in India)
rajah ['rɑːdʒə] N ragià m inv
rake [reɪk] N (tool) rastrello; (person) libertino
▶ VT (garden) rastrellare; (with machine gun)
spazzare ▶ VI: **to ~ through** (fig: search)
frugare tra
rake-off ['reɪkɔf] N (col) parte f percentuale,
fetta
rakish ['reɪkɪʃ] ADJ dissoluto(-a);
disinvolto(-a)
rally ['rælɪ] N (Pol etc) riunione f; (Aut) rally

m inv; *(Tennis)* scambio ▶ VT riunire, radunare ▶ VI raccogliersi, radunarsi; *(sick person, Stock Exchange)* riprendersi

▶ **rally round** VT FUS raggrupparsi intorno a; venire in aiuto di

rallying point ['rælɪŋ-] N *(Pol, Mil)* punto di riunione, punto di raduno

RAM [ræm] N ABBR *(Comput: = random access memory)* RAM *f*

ram [ræm] N montone *m*, ariete *m*; *(device)* ariete ▶ VT conficcare; *(crash into)* cozzare, sbattere contro; percuotere; speronare

Ramadan [ræmə'dæn] N Ramadan *m inv*

ramble ['ræmbl] N escursione *f* ▶ VI *(pej: also:* **ramble on**) divagare

rambler ['ræmblə'] N escursionista *mf*; *(Bot)* rosa rampicante

rambling ['ræmblɪŋ] ADJ *(speech)* sconnesso(-a); *(Bot)* rampicante; *(house)* tutto(-a) nicchie e corridoi

rambunctious [ræm'bʌŋkʃəs] ADJ *(US)* = **rumbustious**

RAMC N ABBR *(Brit)* = **Royal Army Medical Corps**

ramification [ræmɪfɪ'keɪʃən] N ramificazione *f*

ramp [ræmp] N rampa; **on/off** ~ *(US Aut)* raccordo di entrata/uscita

rampage [ræm'peɪdʒ] N: **to go on the** ~ scatenarsi in modo violento ▶ VI: **they went rampaging through the town** si sono scatenati in modo violento per la città

rampant ['ræmpənt] ADJ *(disease etc)* che infierisce

rampart ['ræmpɑːt] N bastione *m*

ram raiding [-reɪdɪŋ] N *il rapinare un negozio sfondandone la vetrina con un veicolo rubato*

ramshackle ['ræmʃækl] ADJ *(house)* cadente; *(car etc)* sgangherato(-a)

RAN N ABBR = **Royal Australian Navy**

ran [ræn] PT *of* **run**

ranch [rɑːntʃ] N ranch *m inv*

rancher ['rɑːntʃə'] N *(owner)* proprietario di un ranch; *(ranch hand)* cowboy *m inv*

rancid ['rænsɪd] ADJ rancido(-a)

rancour, *(US)* **rancor** ['ræŋkə'] N rancore *m*

R & B N ABBR = **rhythm and blues**

R & D N ABBR = **research and development**

random ['rændəm] ADJ fatto(-a) *or* detto(-a) per caso; *(Comput, Math)* casuale ▶ N: **at** ~ a casaccio

random access N *(Comput)* accesso casuale

R & R N ABBR *(= rest and recreation)* ricreazione *f*; *(US Mil)* permesso per militari

randy ['rændɪ] ADJ *(col)* arrapato(-a); lascivo(-a)

rang [ræŋ] PT *of* **ring**

range [reɪndʒ] N *(of mountains)* catena; *(of missile, voice)* portata; *(of products)* gamma;

(Mil: also: **shooting range**) campo di tiro; *(also:* **kitchen range**) fornello, cucina economica ▶ VT *(place)* disporre, allineare; *(roam)* vagare per ▶ VI: **to** ~ **over** coprire; **to** ~ **from ... to** andare da ... a; **price** ~ gamma di prezzi; **do you have anything else in this price** ~? ha nient'altro su *or* di questo prezzo?; **within (firing)** ~ a portata di tiro; **ranged left/right** *(text)* allineato(-a) a destra/sinistra

ranger ['reɪndʒə'] N guardia forestale

Rangoon [ræŋ'guːn] N Rangun *m*

rank [ræŋk] N fila; *(status, Mil)* grado; *(Brit: also:* **taxi rank**) posteggio di taxi ▶ VI: **to** ~ **among** essere tra ▶ ADJ *(smell)* puzzolente; *(hypocrisy, injustice)* vero(-a) e proprio(-a); **the ranks** *(Mil)* la truppa; **the** ~ **and file** *(fig)* la gran massa; **to close ranks** *(Mil: fig)* serrare i ranghi; **I** ~ **him sixth** gli do il sesto posto, lo metto al sesto posto

rankle ['ræŋkl] VI: **to** ~ **with sb** bruciare (a qn)

rank outsider N outsider *mf*

ransack ['rænsæk] VT rovistare; *(plunder)* saccheggiare

ransom ['rænsəm] N riscatto; **to hold sb to** ~ *(fig)* esercitare pressione su qn

rant [rænt] VI vociare

ranting ['ræntɪŋ] N vociare *m*

rap [ræp] N *(noise)* colpetti *mpl*; *(at a door)* bussata; *(music)* rap *m inv* ▶ VT dare dei colpetti a; bussare a

rape [reɪp] N violenza carnale, stupro; *(Bot)* ravizzone *m* ▶ VT violentare

rape oil, rapeseed oil ['reɪpsiːd-] N olio di ravizzone

rapid ['ræpɪd] ADJ rapido(-a)

rapidity [rə'pɪdɪtɪ] N rapidità

rapidly ['ræpɪdlɪ] ADV rapidamente

rapids ['ræpɪdz] NPL *(Geo)* rapida

rapist ['reɪpɪst] N violentatore *m*

rapport [ræ'pɔː'] N rapporto

rapt [ræpt] ADJ *(attention)* rapito(-a), profondo(-a); **to be** ~ **in contemplation** essere in estatica contemplazione

rapture ['ræptʃə'] N estasi *f inv*; **to go into raptures over** andare in sollucchero per

rapturous ['ræptʃərəs] ADJ estatico(-a)

rare [rɛə'] ADJ raro(-a); *(Culin: steak)* al sangue; **it is** ~ **to find that ...** capita di rado *or* raramente che ... + *sub*

rarebit ['rɛəbɪt] N *see* **Welsh rarebit**

rarefied ['rɛərɪfaɪd] ADJ *(air, atmosphere)* rarefatto(-a)

rarely ['rɛəlɪ] ADV raramente

raring ['rɛərɪŋ] ADJ: **to be** ~ **to go** *(col)* non veder l'ora di cominciare

rarity ['rɛərɪtɪ] N rarità *f inv*

rascal ['rɑːskl] N mascalzone *m*

r

rash [ræʃ] ADJ imprudente, sconsiderato(-a)
▶ N (Med) eruzione f; (of events etc) scoppio;
to come out in a ~ avere uno sfogo

rasher ['ræʃər] N fetta sottile (di lardo or
prosciutto)

rasp [rɑːsp] N (tool) lima ▶ VT (speak: also:
rasp out) gracchiare

raspberry ['rɑːzbərɪ] N lampone m

raspberry bush N lampone m (pianta)

rasping ['rɑːspɪŋ] ADJ stridulo(-a)

Rastafarian [ræstə'fɛərɪən] ADJ, N
rastafariano(-a)

rat [ræt] N ratto

ratable ['reɪtəbl] ADJ = **rateable**

ratchet ['rætʃɪt] N: **~ wheel** ruota dentata

rate [reɪt] N (proportion) tasso, percentuale f;
(speed) velocità f inv; (price) tariffa ▶ VT
valutare; stimare; **to ~ sb/sth as** valutare
qn/qc come; **to ~ sb/sth among** annoverare
qn/qc tra; **to ~ sb/sth highly** stimare molto
qn/qc; **at a ~ of 60 kph** alla velocità di 60 km
all'ora; **~ of exchange** tasso di cambio; **~ of
flow** flusso medio; **~ of growth** tasso di
crescita; **~ of return** tasso di rendimento;
pulse ~ frequenza delle pulsazioni; see also
rates

rateable value ['reɪtəbl-] N (BRIT) valore m
imponibile (agli effetti delle imposte
comunali)

ratepayer ['reɪtpeɪər] N (BRIT) contribuente
mf (che paga le imposte comunali)

rates [reɪts] NPL (BRIT: property tax) imposte fpl
comunali; (fees) tariffe fpl

rather ['rɑːðər] ADV piuttosto; (somewhat)
abbastanza; (to some extent) un po'; **it's ~
expensive** è piuttosto caro; (too much) è un
po' caro; **there's ~ a lot** ce n'è parecchio;
I would or **I'd ~ go** preferirei andare;
I had ~ go farei meglio ad andare; **I'd ~
not leave** preferirei non partire; **or ~**
(more accurately) anzi, per essere (più) precisi;
I ~ think he won't come credo proprio che
non verrà

ratification [rætɪfɪ'keɪʃən] N ratificazione f

ratify ['rætɪfaɪ] VT ratificare

rating ['reɪtɪŋ] N classificazione f;
(assessment) valutazione f; (score) punteggio di
merito; (Naut: category) classe f; (: BRIT: sailor)
marinaio semplice

ratings ['reɪtɪŋz] NPL (Radio, TV) indice m di
ascolto

ratio ['reɪʃɪəʊ] N proporzione f; **in the ~ of 2
to 1** in rapporto di 2 a 1

ration ['ræʃən] N razione f ▶ VT razionare;
rations NPL razioni fpl

rational ['ræʃənl] ADJ razionale, ragionevole;
(solution, reasoning) logico(-a)

rationale [ræʃə'nɑːl] N fondamento logico;
giustificazione f

rationalization [ræʃnəlaɪ'zeɪʃən] N
razionalizzazione f

rationalize ['ræʃnəlaɪz] VT razionalizzare

rationally ['ræʃnəlɪ] ADV razionalmente;
logicamente

rationing ['ræʃnɪŋ] N razionamento

ratpack ['rætpæk] N (BRIT col) stampa
scandalistica

rat poison N veleno per topi

rat race N carrierismo, corsa al successo

rattan [ræ'tæn] N malacca

rattle ['rætl] N tintinnio; (louder) rumore m di
ferraglia; (object: of baby) sonaglino; (: of sports
fan) raganella ▶ VI risuonare, tintinnare;
fare un rumore di ferraglia ▶ VT far
tintinnare; (col: disconcert) sconcertare

rattlesnake ['rætlsneɪk] N serpente m a
sonagli

ratty ['rætɪ] ADJ (col) incavolato(-a)

raucous ['rɔːkəs] ADJ sguaiato(-a)

raucously ['rɔːkəslɪ] ADV sguaiatamente

raunchy ['rɔːntʃɪ] ADJ (col: person) allupato(-a);
(voice, song) libidinoso(-a)

ravage ['rævɪdʒ] VT devastare

ravages ['rævɪdʒɪz] NPL danni mpl

rave [reɪv] VI (in anger) infuriarsi; (with
enthusiasm) andare in estasi; (Med) delirare
▶ N (BRIT): **a ~ (party)** un rave ▶ ADJ (scene,
culture, music) del fenomeno rave ▶ CPD:
~ review (col) critica entusiastica

raven ['reɪvən] N corvo

ravenous ['rævənəs] ADJ affamato(-a)

ravine [rə'viːn] N burrone m

raving ['reɪvɪŋ] ADJ: **~ lunatic** pazzo(-a)
furioso(-a)

ravings ['reɪvɪŋz] NPL vaneggiamenti mpl

ravioli [rævɪ'əʊlɪ] N ravioli mpl

ravish ['rævɪʃ] VT (delight) estasiare

ravishing ['rævɪʃɪŋ] ADJ incantevole

raw [rɔː] ADJ (uncooked) crudo(-a); (not
processed) greggio(-a); (sore) vivo(-a);
(inexperienced) inesperto(-a); (weather, day)
gelido(-a); **to get a ~ deal** (col: bad bargain)
prendere un bidone; (: harsh treatment) venire
trattato ingiustamente

Rawalpindi [rɔːl'pɪndɪ] N Rawalpindi f

raw material N materia prima

ray [reɪ] N raggio; **a ~ of hope** un barlume di
speranza

rayon ['reɪɔn] N raion m

raze [reɪz] VT radere, distruggere; (also: **raze
to the ground**) radere al suolo

razor ['reɪzər] N rasoio

razor blade N lama di rasoio

razzle ['ræzl], **razzle-dazzle** ['ræzl'dæzl] N
(BRIT col): **to be/go on the ~(-dazzle)** darsi
alla pazza gioia

razzmatazz ['ræzmə'tæz] N (col) clamore m

RC ABBR = **Roman Catholic**

RCAF N ABBR = **Royal Canadian Air Force**
RCMP N ABBR = **Royal Canadian Mounted Police**
RCN N ABBR = **Royal Canadian Navy**
RD ABBR (US Post) = **rural delivery**
Rd ABBR = **road**
RDC N ABBR (BRIT) = **rural district council**
RE N ABBR (BRIT Mil: = Royal Engineers) = G.M. (= Genio Militare); (BRIT) = **religious education**
re [riː] PREP con riferimento a
reach [riːtʃ] N portata; (of river etc) tratto ▶ VT raggiungere; arrivare a ▶ VI stendersi; (stretch out hand: also: **reach down, reach over, reach across** etc) allungare una mano; **out of/within ~** (object) fuori/a portata di mano; **within easy ~ (of)** (place) a breve distanza (di), vicino (a); **to ~ sb by phone** contattare qn per telefono; **can I ~ you at your hotel?** la posso contattare al suo albergo?
▶ **reach out** VT (hand) allungare ▶ VI: **to ~ out for** stendere la mano per prendere
react [riːˈækt] VI reagire
reaction [riːˈækʃən] N reazione f
reactionary [riːˈækʃənrɪ] ADJ, N reazionario(-a)
reactor [riːˈæktər] N reattore m
read [riːd] (pt, pp ~ [rɛd]) VI leggere ▶ VT leggere; (understand) intendere, interpretare; (study) studiare; **do you ~ me?** (Tel) mi ricevete?; **to take sth as ~** (fig) dare qc per scontato
▶ **read out** VT leggere ad alta voce
▶ **read over** VT rileggere attentamente
▶ **read through** VT (quickly) dare una scorsa a; (thoroughly) leggere da cima a fondo
▶ **read up, read up on** VT studiare bene
readable [ˈriːdəbl] ADJ leggibile; che si legge volentieri
reader [ˈriːdər] N lettore(-trice); (book) libro di lettura; (BRIT: at university) professore con funzioni preminenti di ricerca
readership [ˈriːdəʃɪp] N (of paper etc) numero di lettori
readily [ˈrɛdɪlɪ] ADV volentieri; (easily) facilmente; (quickly) prontamente
readiness [ˈrɛdɪnɪs] N prontezza; **in ~** (prepared) pronto(-a)
reading [ˈriːdɪŋ] N lettura; (understanding) interpretazione f; (on instrument) indicazione f
reading lamp N lampada da studio
reading room N sala di lettura
readjust [riːəˈdʒʌst] VT raggiustare ▶ VI (person): **to ~ (to)** riadattarsi (a)
ready [ˈrɛdɪ] ADJ pronto(-a); (willing) pronto(-a), disposto(-a); (quick) rapido(-a); (available) disponibile ▶ N: **at the ~** (Mil) pronto a sparare; (fig) tutto(-a) pronto(-a)
▶ VT preparare; **~ for use** pronto per l'uso; **to**

be ~ to do sth essere pronto a fare qc; **to get ~** VI prepararsi
ready cash N denaro in contanti
ready-cooked [ˈrɛdɪˈkukt] ADJ già cotto(-a)
ready-made [ˈrɛdɪˈmeɪd] ADJ prefabbricato(-a); (clothes) confezionato(-a)
ready reckoner [-ˈrɛkənər] N (BRIT) prontuario di calcolo
ready-to-wear [ˈrɛdɪtəˈwɛər] ADJ prêt-à-porter inv
reagent [riːˈeɪdʒənt] N: **chemical ~** reagente m chimico
real [rɪəl] ADJ reale; vero(-a) ▶ ADV (US col: very) veramente, proprio; **in ~ terms** in realtà; **in ~ life** nella realtà
real ale N birra ad effervescenza naturale
real estate N beni mpl immobili
realism [ˈrɪəlɪzəm] N (Art) realismo
realist [ˈrɪəlɪst] N realista mf
realistic [rɪəˈlɪstɪk] ADJ realistico(-a)
reality [riːˈælɪtɪ] N realtà f inv; **in ~** in realtà, in effetti
reality TV N reality TV f
realization [rɪəlaɪˈzeɪʃən] N (awareness) presa di coscienza; (of hopes, project etc) realizzazione f
realize [ˈrɪəlaɪz] VT (understand) rendersi conto di; (a project, Comm: asset) realizzare; **I ~ that ...** mi rendo conto or capisco che ...
really [ˈrɪəlɪ] ADV veramente, davvero; **~!** (indicating annoyance) oh, insomma!
realm [rɛlm] N reame m, regno
real time N (Comput) tempo reale
Realtor® [ˈrɪəltɔːr] N (US) agente m immobiliare
ream [riːm] N risma; **reams** (fig: col) pagine e pagine fpl
reap [riːp] VT mietere; (fig) raccogliere
reaper [ˈriːpər] N (machine) mietitrice f
reappear [riːəˈpɪər] VI ricomparire, riapparire
reappearance [riːəˈpɪərəns] N riapparizione f
reapply [riːəˈplaɪ] VI: **to ~ for** fare un'altra domanda per
reappraisal [riːəˈpreɪzl] N riesame m
rear [rɪər] ADJ di dietro; (Aut: wheel etc) posteriore ▶ N didietro, parte f posteriore ▶ VT (cattle, family) allevare ▶ VI (also: **rear up**: animal) impennarsi
rear admiral N contrammiraglio
rear-engined [ˈrɪərˈɛndʒɪnd] ADJ (Aut) con motore posteriore
rearguard [ˈrɪəɡɑːd] N retroguardia
rearm [riːˈɑːm] VT, VI riarmare
rearmament [riːˈɑːməmənt] N riarmo
rearrange [riːəˈreɪndʒ] VT riordinare
rear-view mirror [ˈrɪəvjuː-] N (Aut) specchio retrovisivo

r

rear-wheel drive N trazione *fpl* posteriore
reason ['ri:zn] N ragione *f*; (*cause, motive*) ragione, motivo ▶ VI: **to ~ with sb** far ragionare qn; **to have ~ to think** avere motivi per pensare; **it stands to ~ that** è ovvio che; **the ~ for/why** la ragione *or* il motivo di/per cui; **with good ~** a ragione; **all the more ~ why you should not sell it** ragione di più per non venderlo
reasonable ['ri:znəbl] ADJ ragionevole; (*not bad*) accettabile
reasonably ['ri:znəblɪ] ADV ragionevolmente; **one can ~ assume that ...** uno può facilmente supporre che ...
reasoned ['ri:znd] ADJ (*argument*) ponderato(-a)
reasoning ['ri:znɪŋ] N ragionamento
reassemble [ri:ə'sɛmbl] VT riunire; (*machine*) rimontare
reassert [ri:ə'sə:t] VT riaffermare
reassurance [ri:ə'ʃuərəns] N rassicurazione *f*
reassure [ri:ə'ʃuə^r] VT rassicurare; **to ~ sb of** rassicurare qn di *or* su
reassuring [ri:ə'ʃuərɪŋ] ADJ rassicurante
reawakening [ri:ə'weɪknɪŋ] N risveglio
rebate ['ri:beɪt] N rimborso; (*on tax etc*) sgravio
rebel N ['rɛbl] ribelle *mf* ▶ VI [rɪ'bɛl] ribellarsi
rebellion [rɪ'bɛljən] N ribellione *f*
rebellious [rɪ'bɛljəs] ADJ ribelle
rebirth [ri:'bə:θ] N rinascita
rebound VI [rɪ'baund] (*ball*) rimbalzare ▶ N ['ri:baund] rimbalzo
rebuff [rɪ'bʌf] N secco rifiuto ▶ VT respingere
rebuild [ri:'bɪld] VT (*irreg: like* **build**) ricostruire
rebuke [rɪ'bju:k] N rimprovero ▶ VT rimproverare
rebut [rɪ'bʌt] VT rifiutare
rebuttal [rɪ'bʌtl] N rifiuto
recalcitrant [rɪ'kælsɪtrənt] ADJ recalcitrante
recall [rɪ'kɔ:l] VT (*gen, Comput*) richiamare; (*remember*) ricordare, richiamare alla mente ▶ N ['ri:kɔl] richiamo; **beyond ~** irrevocabile
recant [rɪ'kænt] VI ritrattarsi; (*Rel*) fare abiura
recap ['ri:kæp] N ricapitolazione *f* ▶ VT ricapitolare ▶ VI riassumere
recapture [ri:'kæptʃə^r] VT riprendere; (*atmosphere*) ricreare
recd. ABBR = **received**
recede [rɪ'si:d] VI allontanarsi; ritirarsi; calare
receding [rɪ'si:dɪŋ] ADJ (*forehead, chin*) sfuggente; **he's got a ~ hairline** è stempiato
receipt [rɪ'si:t] N (*document*) ricevuta; (*act of receiving*) ricevimento; **to acknowledge ~ of** accusare ricevuta di; **we are in ~ of ...** abbiamo ricevuto ...
receipts [rɪ'si:ts] NPL (*Comm*) introiti *mpl*

receivable [rɪ'si:vəbl] ADJ (*Comm*) esigibile; (*: owed*) dovuto(-a)
receive [rɪ'si:v] VT ricevere; (*guest*) ricevere, accogliere; **"received with thanks"** (*Comm*) "per quietanza"
Received Pronunciation N (*Brit*); *vedi nota*

Si chiama *Received Pronunciation* (RP) l'accento dell'inglese parlato in alcune parti del sud-est dell'Inghilterra. In esso si identifica l'inglese *standard* delle classi colte, privo di inflessioni regionali e adottato tradizionalmente dagli annunciatori della BBC. È anche l'accento standard dell'inglese insegnato come lingua straniera.

receiver [rɪ'si:və^r] N (*Tel*) ricevitore *m*; (*Radio*) apparecchio ricevente; (*of stolen goods*) ricettatore(-trice); (*Law, Comm*) curatore *m* fallimentare
receivership [rɪ'si:vəʃɪp] N curatela; **to go into ~** andare in amministrazione controllata
recent ['ri:snt] ADJ recente; **in ~ years** negli ultimi anni
recently ['ri:sntlɪ] ADV recentemente; **as ~ as ...** soltanto ...; **until ~** fino a poco tempo fa
receptacle [rɪ'sɛptɪkl] N recipiente *m*
reception [rɪ'sɛpʃən] N (*gen*) ricevimento; (*welcome*) accoglienza; (*TV etc*) ricezione *f*
reception centre N (*Brit*) centro di raccolta
reception desk N (*in hotel*) reception *f inv*; (*in hospital, at doctor's*) accettazione *f*; (*in large building, offices*) portineria
receptionist [rɪ'sɛpʃənɪst] N receptionist *mf*
receptive [rɪ'sɛptɪv] ADJ ricettivo(-a)
recess [rɪ'sɛs] N (*in room*) alcova; (*Pol etc: holiday*) vacanze *fpl*; (*US Law: short break*) sospensione *f*; (*US Scol*) intervallo
recession [rɪ'sɛʃən] N (*Econ*) recessione *f*
recessionista [rɪsɛʃə'nɪstə] N recessionista *mf*
recharge [ri:'tʃɑ:dʒ] VT (*battery*) ricaricare
rechargeable [ri:'tʃɑ:dʒəbl] ADJ ricaricabile
recipe ['rɛsɪpɪ] N ricetta
recipient [rɪ'sɪpɪənt] N beneficiario(-a); (*of letter*) destinatario(-a)
reciprocal [rɪ'sɪprəkl] ADJ reciproco(-a)
reciprocate [rɪ'sɪprəkeɪt] VT ricambiare, contraccambiare
recital [rɪ'saɪtl] N recital *m inv*; concerto (di solista)
recite [rɪ'saɪt] VT (*poem*) recitare
reckless ['rɛkləs] ADJ (*driver etc*) spericolato(-a); (*spender*) incosciente; (*spending*) folle
recklessly ['rɛkləslɪ] ADV in modo spericolato; da incosciente
reckon ['rɛkən] VT (*count*) calcolare; (*consider*) considerare, stimare; (*think*): **I ~ that ...**

penso che .. ▶ VI contare, calcolare; **to ~ without sb/sth** non tener conto di qn/qc; **he is somebody to be reckoned with** è uno da non sottovalutare
▶ **reckon on** VT FUS contare su

reckoning ['rɛknɪŋ] N conto; stima; **the day of ~** il giorno del giudizio

reclaim [rɪ'kleɪm] VT (land) bonificare; (demand back) richiedere, reclamare; (materials) recuperare

reclamation [rɛklə'meɪʃən] N bonifica

recline [rɪ'klaɪn] VI stare sdraiato(-a)

reclining [rɪ'klaɪnɪŋ] ADJ (seat) ribaltabile

recluse [rɪ'kluːs] N eremita m, recluso(-a)

recognition [rɛkəg'nɪʃən] N riconoscimento; **to gain ~** essere riconosciuto(-a); **in ~ of** in or come segno di riconoscimento per; **transformed beyond ~** irriconoscibile

recognizable ['rɛkəgnaɪzəbl] ADJ: **~ (by)** riconoscibile (a or da)

recognize ['rɛkəgnaɪz] VT: **to ~ (by/as)** riconoscere (a or da/come)

recoil [rɪ'kɔɪl] VI (gun) rinculare; (spring) balzare indietro; (person): **to ~ (from)** indietreggiare (davanti a) ▶ N (gun) rinculo

recollect [rɛkə'lɛkt] VT ricordare

recollection [rɛkə'lɛkʃən] N ricordo; **to the best of my ~** per quello che mi ricordo

recommend [rɛkə'mɛnd] VT raccomandare; (advise) consigliare; **she has a lot to ~ her** ha molti elementi a suo favore

recommendation [rɛkəmɛn'deɪʃən] N raccomandazione f; consiglio

recommended retail price [rɛkə'mɛndɪd-] N (BRIT) prezzo raccomandato al dettaglio

recompense ['rɛkəmpɛns] VT ricompensare; (compensate) risarcire ▶ N ricompensa; risarcimento

reconcilable ['rɛkənsaɪləbl] ADJ conciliabile

reconcile ['rɛkənsaɪl] VT (two people) riconciliare; (two facts) conciliare, quadrare; **to ~ o.s. to** rassegnarsi a

reconciliation [rɛkənsɪlɪ'eɪʃən] N riconciliazione f; conciliazione f

recondite [rɪ'kɔndaɪt] ADJ recondito(-a)

recondition [riːkən'dɪʃən] VT rimettere a nuovo; rifare

reconnaissance [rɪ'kɔnɪsns] N (Mil) ricognizione f

reconnoitre, (US) reconnoiter (Mil) [rɛkə'nɔɪtər] VT fare una ricognizione di ▶ VI fare una ricognizione

reconsider [riːkən'sɪdər] VT riconsiderare

reconstitute [riː'kɔnstɪtjuːt] VT ricostituire

reconstruct [riːkən'strʌkt] VT ricostruire

reconstruction [riːkən'strʌkʃən] N ricostruzione f

reconvene [riːkən'viːn] VT riconvocare ▶ VI radunarsi

record N ['rɛkɔːd] ricordo, documento; (of meeting etc) nota, verbale m; (register) registro; (file) pratica, dossier m inv; (Comput) record m inv, registrazione f; (also: **police record**) fedina penale sporca; (Mus: disc) disco; (Sport) record m inv, primato ▶ VT [rɪ'kɔːd] (set down) prendere nota di, registrare; (relate) raccontare; (Comput, Mus: song etc) registrare; **off the ~** adj ufficioso(-a); adv ufficiosamente; **public records** archivi mpl; **Italy's excellent ~** i brillanti successi italiani; **in ~ time** a tempo di record; **to keep a ~ of** tener nota di; **to set the ~ straight** mettere le cose in chiaro; **he is on ~ as saying that ...** ha dichiarato pubblicamente che ...

record card N (in file) scheda

recorded delivery letter [rɪ'kɔːdɪd-] N (BRIT Post) lettera raccomandata

recorder [rɪ'kɔːdər] N (Law) avvocato che funge da giudice; (Mus) flauto diritto

record holder N (Sport) primatista mf

recording [rɪ'kɔːdɪŋ] N (Mus) registrazione f

recording studio N studio di registrazione

record library N discoteca

record player N giradischi m inv

recount [rɪ'kaunt] VT raccontare, narrare

re-count N ['riːkaunt] (Pol: of votes) nuovo conteggio ▶ VT [riː'kaunt] ricontare

recoup [rɪ'kuːp] VT ricuperare; **to ~ one's losses** ricuperare le perdite, rifarsi

recourse [rɪ'kɔːs] N: **to have ~ to** ricorrere a

recover [rɪ'kʌvər] VT ricuperare ▶ VI (from illness) rimettersi (in salute), ristabilirsi; **to ~ (from)** (country, person: from shock) riprendersi (da)

re-cover [riː'kʌvər] VT (chair etc) ricoprire

recovery [rɪ'kʌvərɪ] N ricupero; ristabilimento; ripresa

recreate [riːkrɪ'eɪt] VT ricreare

recreation [rɛkrɪ'eɪʃən] N ricreazione f; svago

recreational [rɛkrɪ'eɪʃənəl] ADJ ricreativo(-a)

recreational drug [rɛkrɪ'eɪʃnl-] N droga usata saltuariamente

recreational vehicle N (US) camper m inv

recrimination [rɪkrɪmɪ'neɪʃən] N recriminazione f

recruit [rɪ'kruːt] N recluta; (in company) nuovo(-a) assunto(-a) ▶ VT reclutare

recruiting office [rɪ'kruːtɪŋ-] N ufficio di reclutamento

recruitment [rɪ'kruːtmənt] N reclutamento

rectangle ['rɛktæŋgl] N rettangolo

rectangular [rɛk'tæŋgjulər] ADJ rettangolare

rectify ['rɛktɪfaɪ] VT (error) rettificare; (omission) riparare

rector ['rɛktər] N (Rel) parroco (anglicano); (in Scottish universities) personalità eletta dagli studenti per rappresentarli

rectory ['rɛktərɪ] N presbiterio
rectum ['rɛktəm] N (Anat) retto
recuperate [rɪ'kju:pəreɪt] VI ristabilirsi
recur [rɪ'kə:ʳ] VI riaccadere; (idea, opportunity) riapparire; (symptoms) ripresentarsi
recurrence [rɪ'kʌrəns] N ripresentarsi m; riapparizione f
recurrent [rɪ'kʌrənt] ADJ ricorrente, periodico(-a)
recurring [rɪ'kʌrɪŋ] ADJ (Math) periodico(-a)
recyclable [ri:'saɪkləbl] ADJ riciclabile
recycle [ri:'saɪkl] VT riciclare
recycling [ri:'saɪklɪŋ] N riciclaggio
red [rɛd] N rosso; (Pol: pej) rosso(-a) ▸ ADJ rosso(-a); **in the ~** (account) scoperto; (business) in deficit
red alert N allarme m rosso
red-blooded ['rɛd'blʌdɪd] ADJ (col) gagliardo(-a)
red-brick university ['rɛdbrɪk-] N (BRIT) università di recente formazione; vedi nota

> In Gran Bretagna, con red-brick university (letteralmente, università di mattoni rossi) si indicano le università istituite tra la fine dell'Ottocento e i primi del Novecento, per contraddistinguerle dalle università più antiche, i cui edifici sono di pietra; vedi anche **Oxbridge**.

red carpet treatment N cerimonia col gran pavese
Red Cross N Croce f Rossa
redcurrant ['rɛdkʌrənt] N ribes m inv
redden ['rɛdn] VT arrossare ▸ VI arrossire
reddish ['rɛdɪʃ] ADJ rossiccio(-a)
redecorate [ri:'dɛkəreɪt] VT tinteggiare (e tappezzare) di nuovo
redeem [rɪ'di:m] VT (debt) riscattare; (sth in pawn) ritirare; (fig, also Rel) redimere
redeemable [rɪ'di:məbl] ADJ con diritto di riscatto; redimibile
redeeming [rɪ'di:mɪŋ] ADJ (feature) che salva
redefine [ri:dɪ'faɪn] VT ridefinire
redemption [rɪ'dɛmpʃən] N (Rel) redenzione f; (also: **past** or **beyond redemption**) irrecuperabile
redeploy [ri:dɪ'plɔɪ] VT (Mil) riorganizzare lo schieramento di; (resources) riorganizzare
redeployment [ri:dɪ'plɔɪmənt] N riorganizzazione f
redevelop [ri:dɪ'vɛləp] VT ristrutturare
redevelopment [ri:dɪ'vɛləpmənt] N ristrutturazione f
red-haired [-'hɛəd] ADJ dai capelli rossi
red-handed [rɛd'hændɪd] ADJ: **to be caught ~** essere preso(-a) in flagrante or con le mani nel sacco
redhead ['rɛdhɛd] N rosso(-a)
red herring N (fig) falsa pista
red-hot [rɛd'hɔt] ADJ arroventato(-a)

redirect [ri:daɪ'rɛkt] VT (mail) far seguire
redistribute [ri:dɪ'strɪbju:t] VT ridistribuire
red-letter day ['rɛdlɛtə-] N giorno memorabile
red light N: **to go through a ~** (Aut) passare col rosso
red-light district [rɛd'laɪt-] N quartiere m a luci rosse
red meat N carne f rossa
redness ['rɛdnɪs] N rossore m; (of hair) rosso
redo [ri:'du:] VT (irreg: like **do**) rifare
redolent ['rɛdələnt] ADJ: **~ of** che sa di; (fig) che ricorda
redouble [ri:'dʌbl] VT: **to ~ one's efforts** raddoppiare gli sforzi
redraft [ri:'drɑ:ft] VT fare una nuova stesura di
redress [rɪ'drɛs] N riparazione f ▸ VT riparare; **to ~ the balance** ristabilire l'equilibrio
Red Sea N: **the ~** il mar Rosso
redskin ['rɛdskɪn] N pellerossa mf
red tape N (fig) burocrazia
reduce [rɪ'dju:s] VT ridurre; (lower) ridurre, abbassare; **"~ speed now"** (Aut) "rallentare"; **to ~ sth by/to** ridurre qc di/a; **to ~ sb to silence/despair/tears** ridurre qn al silenzio/alla disperazione/in lacrime; **at a reduced price** scontato(-a)
reduced [rɪ'dju:st] ADJ (decreased) ridotto(-a); **at a ~ price** a prezzo ribassato or ridotto; **"greatly ~ prices"** "grandi ribassi"
reduction [rɪ'dʌkʃən] N riduzione f; (of price) ribasso; (discount) sconto
redundancy [rɪ'dʌndənsɪ] N licenziamento (per eccesso di personale); **compulsory ~** licenziamento; **voluntary ~** forma di cassa integrazione volontaria
redundancy payment N (BRIT) indennità f inv di licenziamento
redundant [rɪ'dʌndnt] ADJ (BRIT: worker) licenziato(-a); (detail, object) superfluo(-a); **to be made ~** (BRIT) essere licenziato (per eccesso di personale)
reed [ri:d] N (Bot) canna; (Mus: of clarinet etc) ancia
re-educate [ri:'ɛdjukeɪt] VT rieducare
reedy ['ri:dɪ] ADJ (voice, instrument) acuto(-a)
reef [ri:f] N (at sea) scogliera; **coral ~** barriera corallina
reek [ri:k] VI: **to ~ (of)** puzzare (di)
reel [ri:l] N bobina, rocchetto; (Tech) aspo; (Fishing) mulinello; (Cine) rotolo; (dance) danza veloce scozzese ▸ VT (Tech) annaspare; (also: **reel up**) avvolgere ▸ VI (sway) barcollare, vacillare; **my head is reeling** mi gira la testa
▸ **reel off** VT snocciolare
re-election [ri:ɪ'lɛkʃən] N rielezione f
re-enter [ri:'ɛntəʳ] VT rientrare in

re-entry [riːˈɛntrɪ] N rientro
re-export VT [riːˈɪkˈspɔːt] riesportare ▸ N [riːˈɛkspɔːt] merce f riesportata, riesportazione f
ref [rɛf] N ABBR (col: = referee) arbitro
ref. ABBR (Comm: = with reference to) sogg
refectory [rɪˈfɛktərɪ] N refettorio
refer [rɪˈfəːʳ] VT: **to ~ sth to** (dispute, decision) deferire qc a; **to ~ sb to** (inquirer, Med: patient) indirizzare qn a; (: reader: to text) rimandare qn a; **he referred me to the manager** mi ha detto di rivolgermi al direttore
▸ **refer to** VT FUS (allude to) accennare a; (apply to) riferire a; (consult) rivolgersi a; **referring to your letter** (Comm) in riferimento alla Vostra lettera
referee [rɛfəˈriː] N arbitro; (Tennis) giudice m di gara; (BRIT: for job application) referenza ▸ VT arbitrare
reference [ˈrɛfrəns] N riferimento; (mention) menzione f, allusione f; (for job application: letter) referenza; lettera di raccomandazione; (: person) referenza; (in book) rimando; **with ~ to** riguardo a; (Comm: in letter) in or con riferimento a; **"please quote this ~"** (Comm) "si prega di far riferimento al numero di protocollo"
reference book N libro di consultazione
reference library N biblioteca per la consultazione
reference number N (Comm) numero di riferimento
referendum [rɛfəˈrɛndəm] (pl **referenda** [-də]) N referendum m inv
referral [rɪˈfəːrəl] N deferimento; (Med) richiesta (di visita specialistica)
refill VT [riːˈfɪl] riempire di nuovo; (pen, lighter etc) ricaricare ▸ N [ˈriːfɪl] (for pen etc) ricambio
refine [rɪˈfaɪn] VT raffinare
refined [rɪˈfaɪnd] ADJ (person, taste) raffinato(-a)
refinement [rɪˈfaɪnmənt] N (of person) raffinatezza
refinery [rɪˈfaɪnərɪ] N raffineria
refit N [ˈriːfɪt] (Naut) raddobbo ▸ VT [riːˈfɪt] (ship) raddobbare
reflate [riːˈfleɪt] VT (economy) rilanciare
reflation [riːˈfleɪʃən] N rilancio
reflationary [riːˈfleɪʃənərɪ] ADJ nuovamente inflazionario(-a)
reflect [rɪˈflɛkt] VT (light, image) riflettere; (fig) rispecchiare ▸ VI (think) riflettere, considerare; **it reflects badly/well on him** si ripercuote su di lui in senso negativo/positivo
▸ **reflect on** VT FUS (discredit) rispecchiarsi su
reflection [rɪˈflɛkʃən] N riflessione f; (image) riflesso; (criticism): **~ on** giudizio su; attacco a; **on ~** pensandoci sopra

reflector [rɪˈflɛktəʳ] N (also Aut) catarifrangente m
reflex [ˈriːflɛks] ADJ riflesso(-a) ▸ N riflesso
reflexive [rɪˈflɛksɪv] ADJ (Ling) riflessivo(-a)
reform [rɪˈfɔːm] N (of sinner etc) correzione f; (of law etc) riforma ▸ VT correggere; riformare
reformat [rɪˈfɔːmæt] VT (Comput) riformattare
Reformation [rɛfəˈmeɪʃən] N: **the ~** la Riforma
reformatory [rɪˈfɔːmətərɪ] N (US) riformatorio
reformed [rɪˈfɔːmd] ADJ cambiato(-a) (per il meglio)
reformer [rɪˈfɔːməʳ] N riformatore(-trice)
refrain [rɪˈfreɪn] VI: **to ~ from doing** trattenersi dal fare ▸ N ritornello
refresh [rɪˈfrɛʃ] VT rinfrescare; (food, sleep) ristorare
refresher course [rɪˈfrɛʃə-] N (BRIT) corso di aggiornamento
refreshing [rɪˈfrɛʃɪŋ] ADJ (drink) rinfrescante; (sleep) riposante, ristoratore(-trice); (change etc) piacevole; (idea, point of view) originale
refreshment [rɪˈfrɛʃmənt] N (eating, resting etc) ristoro; **~(s)** rinfreschi mpl
refrigeration [rɪfrɪdʒəˈreɪʃən] N refrigerazione f
refrigerator [rɪˈfrɪdʒəreɪtəʳ] N frigorifero
refuel [riːˈfjuəl] VT rifornire (di carburante) ▸ VI far rifornimento (di carburante)
refuge [ˈrɛfjuːdʒ] N rifugio; **to take ~ in** rifugiarsi in
refugee [rɛfjuˈdʒiː] N rifugiato(-a), profugo(-a)
refugee camp N campo (di) profughi
refund N [ˈriːfʌnd] rimborso ▸ VT [rɪˈfʌnd] rimborsare
refurbish [riːˈfəːbɪʃ] VT rimettere a nuovo
refurnish [riːˈfəːnɪʃ] VT ammobiliare di nuovo
refusal [rɪˈfjuːzəl] N rifiuto; **to have first ~ on sth** avere il diritto d'opzione su qc
refuse¹ [ˈrɛfjuːs] N rifiuti mpl
refuse² [rɪˈfjuːz] VT, VI rifiutare; **to ~ to do sth** rifiutare or rifiutarsi di fare qc
refuse collection N raccolta di rifiuti
refuse disposal N sistema m di scarico dei rifiuti
refusenik [rɪˈfjuːznɪk] N ebreo a cui il governo sovietico impediva di lasciare il paese
refute [rɪˈfjuːt] VT confutare
regain [rɪˈɡeɪn] VT riguadagnare; riacquistare, ricuperare
regal [ˈriːɡl] ADJ regale
regale [rɪˈɡeɪl] VT: **to ~ sb with sth** intrattenere qn con qc
regalia [rɪˈɡeɪlɪə] N insegne fpl reali

r

regard [rɪ'gɑːd] N riguardo, stima ▶ VT
considerare, stimare; **to give one's regards
to** porgere i suoi saluti a; **(kind) regards**
cordiali saluti; **as regards, with ~ to**
riguardo a

regarding [rɪ'gɑːdɪŋ] PREP riguardo a, per
quanto riguarda

regardless [rɪ'gɑːdlɪs] ADV lo stesso; **~ of**
a dispetto di, nonostante

regatta [rɪ'gætə] N regata

regency ['riːdʒənsɪ] N reggenza

regenerate [rɪ'dʒɛnəreɪt] VT rigenerare;
(feelings, enthusiasm) far rinascere ▶ VI
rigenerarsi; rinascere

regent ['riːdʒənt] N reggente m

reggae ['rɛgeɪ] N reggae m

régime [reɪ'ʒiːm] N regime m

regiment N ['rɛdʒɪmənt] reggimento ▶ VT
['rɛdʒɪmɛnt] irreggimentare

regimental [rɛdʒɪ'mɛntl] ADJ reggimentale

regimentation [rɛdʒɪmɛn'teɪʃən] N
irreggimentazione f

region ['riːdʒən] N regione f; **in the ~ of** *(fig)*
all'incirca di

regional ['riːdʒənl] ADJ regionale

regional development N sviluppo
regionale

register ['rɛdʒɪstər] N registro; *(also:*
electoral register) lista elettorale ▶ VT
registrare; *(vehicle)* immatricolare; *(luggage)*
spedire assicurato(-a); *(letter)* assicurare;
(instrument) segnare ▶ VI iscriversi; *(at hotel)*
firmare il registro; *(make impression)* entrare
in testa; **to ~ a protest** fare un esposto; **to ~
for a course** iscriversi a un corso

registered ['rɛdʒɪstəd] ADJ *(design)*
depositato(-a); *(BRIT: letter)* assicurato(-a);
(student, voter) iscritto(-a)

registered company N società iscritta al
registro

registered nurse N *(US)* infermiere(-a)
diplomato(-a)

registered office N sede f legale

registered trademark N marchio depositato

registrar ['rɛdʒɪstrɑːr] N ufficiale m di stato
civile; segretario

registration [rɛdʒɪs'treɪʃən] N *(act)*
registrazione f; iscrizione f; *(Aut: also:*
registration number) numero di targa

registry ['rɛdʒɪstrɪ] N ufficio del registro

registry office N *(BRIT)* anagrafe f; **to get
married in a ~** ≈ sposarsi in municipio

regret [rɪ'grɛt] N rimpianto, rincrescimento
▶ VT rimpiangere; **I ~ that I/he cannot help**
mi rincresce di non poter aiutare/che lui
non possa aiutare; **we ~ to inform you that
…** siamo spiacenti di informarla che …

regretfully [rɪ'grɛtfəlɪ] ADV con
rincrescimento

regrettable [rɪ'grɛtəbl] ADJ deplorevole

regrettably [rɪ'grɛtəblɪ] ADV purtroppo,
sfortunatamente

regroup [riː'gruːp] VT raggruppare ▶ VI
raggrupparsi

regt ABBR (= *regiment*) Reg

regular ['rɛgjulər] ADJ regolare; *(usual)*
abituale, normale; *(listener, reader)* fedele;
(soldier) dell'esercito regolare; *(Comm: size)*
normale ▶ N *(client etc)* cliente mf abituale

regularity [rɛgju'lærɪtɪ] N regolarità f inv

regularly ['rɛgjulərlɪ] ADV regolarmente

regulate ['rɛgjuleɪt] VT regolare

regulation [rɛgju'leɪʃən] N *(rule)* regola,
regolamento; *(adjustment)* regolazione f
▶ CPD *(Mil)* di ordinanza

rehabilitate [riːə'bɪlɪteɪt] VT *(criminal, drug
addict, invalid)* ricuperare, reinserire

rehabilitation ['riːəbɪlɪ'teɪʃən] N *(see vb)*
ricupero, reinserimento; *(of offender)*
riabilitazione f; *(of disabled)* riadattamento

rehash [riː'hæʃ] VT *(col)* rimaneggiare

rehearsal [rɪ'həːsəl] N prova; **dress ~** prova
generale

rehearse [rɪ'həːs] VT provare

rehouse [riː'hauz] VT rialloggiare

reign [reɪn] N regno ▶ VI regnare

reigning ['reɪnɪŋ] ADJ *(monarch)* regnante;
(champion) attuale

reimburse [riːɪm'bəːs] VT rimborsare

rein [reɪn] N *(for horse)* briglia; **to give sb free
~** *(fig)* lasciare completa libertà a qn

reincarnation [riːɪnkɑː'neɪʃən] N
reincarnazione f

reindeer ['reɪndɪər] N pl inv renna

reinforce [riːɪn'fɔːs] VT rinforzare

reinforced concrete [riːɪn'fɔːst-] N cemento
armato

reinforcement [riːɪn'fɔːsmənt] N *(action)*
rinforzamento; **reinforcements** NPL *(Mil)*
rinforzi mpl

reinstate [riːɪn'steɪt] VT reintegrare

reinstatement [riːɪn'steɪtmənt] N
reintegrazione f

reissue [riː'ɪʃjuː] VT *(book)* ristampare,
ripubblicare; *(film)* distribuire di nuovo

reiterate [riː'ɪtəreɪt] VT reiterare, ripetere

reject N ['riːdʒɛkt] *(Comm)* scarto ▶ VT
[rɪ'dʒɛkt] rifiutare, respingere; *(Comm: goods)*
scartare

rejection [rɪ'dʒɛkʃən] N rifiuto

rejoice [rɪ'dʒɔɪs] VI: **to ~ (at or over)** provare
diletto (in)

rejoinder [rɪ'dʒɔɪndər] N *(retort)* replica

rejuvenate [rɪ'dʒuːvəneɪt] VT ringiovanire

rekindle [riː'kɪndl] VT riaccendere

relapse [rɪ'læps] N *(Med)* ricaduta

relate [rɪ'leɪt] VT *(tell)* raccontare; *(connect)*
collegare ▶ VI: **to ~ to** *(refer to)* riferirsi a; *(get*

on with) stabilire un rapporto con;
relating to che riguarda, rispetto a
related [rɪ'leɪtɪd] ADJ imparentato(-a);
collegato(-a), connesso(-a); **~ to**
imparentato(-a) con; collegato(-a) *or*
connesso(-a) con
relating [rɪ'leɪtɪŋ]: **~ to** *prep* che riguarda,
rispetto a
relation [rɪ'leɪʃən] N (*person*) parente *mf*;
(*link*) rapporto, relazione *f*; **relations** NPL
(*relatives*) parenti *mpl*; **in ~ to** con riferimento
a; **diplomatic/international relations**
rapporti diplomatici/internazionali;
to bear a ~ to corrispondere a
relationship [rɪ'leɪʃənʃɪp] N rapporto;
(*personal ties*) rapporti *mpl*, relazioni *fpl*;
(*also*: **family relationship**) legami *mpl* di
parentela; (: *affair*) relazione *f*; **they have
a good ~** vanno molto d'accordo
relative ['rɛlətɪv] N parente *mf* ▶ ADJ
relativo(-a); (*respective*) rispettivo(-a)
relatively ['rɛlətɪvlɪ] ADV relativamente;
(*fairly, rather*) abbastanza
relax [rɪ'læks] VI rilasciarsi; (*person: unwind*)
rilassarsi ▶ VT rilasciare; (*mind, person*)
rilassare; **~!** (*calm down*) calma!
relaxation [ri:læk'seɪʃən] N rilasciamento;
rilassamento; (*entertainment*) ricreazione *f*,
svago
relaxed [rɪ'lækst] ADJ rilasciato(-a);
rilassato(-a)
relaxing [rɪ'læksɪŋ] ADJ rilassante
relay ['ri:leɪ] N (*Sport*) corsa a staffetta ▶ VT
(*message*) trasmettere
release [rɪ'li:s] N (*from prison*) rilascio; (*from
obligation*) liberazione *f*; (*of gas etc*) emissione
f; (*of film etc*) distribuzione *f*; (*record*) disco;
(*device*) disinnesto ▶ VT (*prisoner*) rilasciare;
(*from obligation, wreckage etc*) liberare; (*book,
film*) fare uscire; (*news*) rendere pubblico(-a);
(*gas etc*) emettere; (*Tech: catch, spring etc*)
disinnestare; (*let go*) rilasciare; lasciar
andare; sciogliere; **to ~ one's grip** mollare
la presa; **to ~ the clutch** (*Aut*) staccare la
frizione
relegate ['rɛləgeɪt] VT relegare; (*BRIT Sport*):
to be relegated essere retrocesso(-a)
relent [rɪ'lɛnt] VI cedere
relentless [rɪ'lɛntlɪs] ADJ implacabile
relevance ['rɛləvəns] N pertinenza; **~ of sth
to sth** rapporto tra qc e qc
relevant ['rɛləvənt] ADJ pertinente; (*chapter*)
in questione; **~ to** pertinente a
reliability [rɪlaɪə'bɪlɪtɪ] N (*of person*) serietà;
(*of machine*) affidabilità
reliable [rɪ'laɪəbl] ADJ (*person, firm*) fidato(-a),
che dà affidamento; (*method*) sicuro(-a);
(*machine*) affidabile
reliably [rɪ'laɪəblɪ] ADV: **to be ~ informed**

sapere da fonti sicure
reliance [rɪ'laɪəns] N: **~ (on)** dipendenza (da)
reliant [rɪ'laɪənt] ADJ: **to be ~ on sth/sb**
dipendere da qc/qn
relic ['rɛlɪk] N (*Rel*) reliquia; (*of the past*) resto
relief [rɪ'li:f] N (*from pain, anxiety*) sollievo;
(*help, supplies*) soccorsi *mpl*; (*of guard*) cambio;
(*Art, Geo*) rilievo; **by way of light ~** come
diversivo
relief map N carta in rilievo
relief road N (*BRIT*) circonvallazione *f*
relieve [rɪ'li:v] VT (*pain, patient*) sollevare;
(*bring help*) soccorrere; (*take over from: gen*)
sostituire; (: *guard*) rilevare; **to ~ sb of sth**
(*load*) alleggerire qn di qc; **to ~ sb of his
command** (*Mil*) esonerare qn dal comando;
to ~ o.s. (*euphemism*) fare i propri bisogni
relieved [rɪ'li:vd] ADJ sollevato(-a); **to be ~
that ...** essere sollevato(-a) (dal fatto) che ...;
I'm ~ to hear it mi hai tolto un peso con
questa notizia
religion [rɪ'lɪdʒən] N religione *f*
religious [rɪ'lɪdʒəs] ADJ religioso(-a)
religious education N religione *f*
relinquish [rɪ'lɪŋkwɪʃ] VT abbandonare;
(*plan, habit*) rinunziare a
relish ['rɛlɪʃ] N (*Culin*) condimento; (*enjoyment*)
gran piacere *m* ▶ VT (*food etc*) godere; **to ~
doing** adorare fare
relive [ri:'lɪv] VT rivivere
reload [ri:'ləud] VT ricaricare
relocate [ri:ləu'keɪt] VT (*business*) trasferire
▶ VI trasferirsi; **to ~ in** trasferire la propria
sede a
reluctance [rɪ'lʌktəns] N riluttanza
reluctant [rɪ'lʌktənt] ADJ riluttante, mal
disposto(-a); **to be ~ to do sth** essere restio a
fare qc
reluctantly [rɪ'lʌktəntlɪ] ADV di mala voglia,
a malincuore
rely [rɪ'laɪ]: **to ~ on** *vt fus* contare su; (*be
dependent*) dipendere da
remain [rɪ'meɪn] VI restare, rimanere;
to ~ silent restare in silenzio; **I ~, yours
faithfully** (*BRIT: in letters*) distinti saluti
remainder [rɪ'meɪndər] N resto; (*Comm*)
rimanenza
remaining [rɪ'meɪnɪŋ] ADJ che rimane
remains [rɪ'meɪnz] NPL resti *mpl*
remand [rɪ'mɑːnd] N: **on ~** in detenzione
preventiva ▶ VT: **to ~ in custody** rinviare in
carcere; trattenere a disposizione della legge
remand home N (*BRIT*) riformatorio, casa di
correzione
remark [rɪ'mɑːk] N osservazione *f* ▶ VT
osservare, dire; (*notice*) notare ▶ VI: **to ~ on
sth** fare dei commenti su qc
remarkable [rɪ'mɑːkəbl] ADJ notevole;
eccezionale

r

remarry [riːˈmærɪ] vɪ risposarsi
remedial [rɪˈmiːdɪəl] ADJ (*tuition, classes*) di riparazione
remedy [ˈrɛmədɪ] N: ~ **(for)** rimedio (per) ▶ vᴛ rimediare a
remember [rɪˈmɛmbəʳ] vᴛ ricordare, ricordarsi di; **I ~ seeing it, I ~ having seen it** (mi) ricordo di averlo visto; **she remembered to do it** si è ricordata di farlo; **~ me to your wife and children!** saluti sua moglie e i bambini da parte mia!
remembrance [rɪˈmɛmbrəns] N memoria; ricordo
Remembrance Day, (*Brit*) **Remembrance Sunday** N; *vedi nota*

> Nel Regno Unito, la domenica più vicina all'11 di novembre, data in cui fu firmato l'armistizio con la Germania nel 1918, ricorre il *Remembrance Day* o *Remembrance Sunday*, giorno in cui vengono commemorati i caduti in guerra. In questa occasione molti portano un papavero di carta appuntato al petto in segno di rispetto.

remind [rɪˈmaɪnd] vᴛ: **to ~ sb of sth** ricordare qc a qn; **to ~ sb to do** ricordare a qn di fare; **that reminds me!** a proposito!
reminder [rɪˈmaɪndəʳ] N richiamo; (*note etc*) promemoria *m inv*
reminisce [rɛmɪˈnɪs] vɪ: **to ~ (about)** abbandonarsi ai ricordi (di)
reminiscences [rɛmɪˈnɪsnsɪz] NPL reminiscenze *fpl*, memorie *fpl*
reminiscent [rɛmɪˈnɪsnt] ADJ: ~ **of** che fa pensare a, che richiama
remiss [rɪˈmɪs] ADJ negligente; **it was ~ of me** è stata una negligenza da parte mia
remission [rɪˈmɪʃən] N remissione *f*; (*of fee*) esonero
remit [rɪˈmɪt] vᴛ rimettere
remittance [rɪˈmɪtəns] N rimessa
remnant [ˈrɛmnənt] N resto, avanzo; **remnants** NPL (*Comm*) scampoli *mpl*; fine *f* serie
remonstrate [ˈrɛmənstreɪt] vɪ protestare; **to ~ with sb about sth** fare le proprie rimostranze a qn circa qc
remorse [rɪˈmɔːs] N rimorso
remorseful [rɪˈmɔːsful] ADJ pieno(-a) di rimorsi
remorseless [rɪˈmɔːslɪs] ADJ (*fig*) spietato(-a)
remote [rɪˈməut] ADJ remoto(-a), lontano(-a); (*person*) distaccato(-a); **there is a ~ possibility that …** c'è una vaga possibilità che … +*sub*
remote control N telecomando
remote-controlled [rɪˈməutkən'trəuld] ADJ telecomandato(-a)

remotely [rɪˈməutlɪ] ADV remotamente; (*slightly*) vagamente
remoteness [rɪˈməutnɪs] N lontananza
remould [ˈriːməuld] N (*Brit: tyre*) gomma rivestita
removable [rɪˈmuːvəbl] ADJ (*detachable*) staccabile
removal [rɪˈmuːvəl] N (*taking away*) rimozione *f*; soppressione *f*; (*Brit: from house*) trasloco; (*from office: sacking*) destituzione *f*; (*Med*) ablazione *f*
removal man N (*irreg*) (*Brit*) addetto ai traslochi
removal van N (*Brit*) furgone *m* per traslochi
remove [rɪˈmuːv] vᴛ togliere, rimuovere; (*employee*) destituire; (*stain*) far sparire; (*doubt, abuse*) sopprimere, eliminare; **first cousin once removed** cugino di secondo grado
remover [rɪˈmuːvəʳ] N (*for paint*) prodotto sverniciante; (*for varnish*) solvente *m*; **make-up ~** struccatore *m*
remunerate [rɪˈmjuːnəreɪt] vᴛ rimunerare
remuneration [rɪmjuːnəˈreɪʃən] N rimunerazione *f*
Renaissance [rəˈneɪsəns] N: **the ~** il Rinascimento
rename [riːˈneɪm] vᴛ ribattezzare
rend [rɛnd] (*pt, pp* **rent** [rɛnt]) vᴛ lacerare
render [ˈrɛndəʳ] vᴛ rendere; (*Culin: fat*) struggere
rendering [ˈrɛndərɪŋ] N (*Mus etc*) interpretazione *f*
rendez-vous [ˈrɔndɪvuː] N appuntamento; (*place*) luogo d'incontro; (*meeting*) incontro ▶ vɪ ritrovarsi; (*spaceship*) effettuare un rendez-vous
rendition [rɛnˈdɪʃən] N (*Mus*) interpretazione *f*
renegade [ˈrɛnɪgeɪd] N rinnegato(-a)
renew [rɪˈnjuː] vᴛ rinnovare; (*negotiations*) riprendere
renewable [rɪˈnjuːəbl] ADJ riutilizzabile; (*contract*) rinnovabile; ~ **energy, renewables** fonti *mpl* di energia rinnovabile
renewal [rɪˈnjuːəl] N rinnovamento; ripresa
renounce [rɪˈnauns] vᴛ rinunziare a; (*disown*) ripudiare
renovate [ˈrɛnəveɪt] vᴛ rinnovare; (*art work*) restaurare
renovation [rɛnəˈveɪʃən] N rinnovamento; restauro
renown [rɪˈnaun] N rinomanza
renowned [rɪˈnaund] ADJ rinomato(-a)
rent [rɛnt] PT, PP *of* **rend** ▶ N affitto ▶ vᴛ (*take for rent*) prendere in affitto; (*car, TV*) noleggiare, prendere a noleggio; (*also:* **rent out**) dare in affitto; (*: car, TV*) noleggiare, dare a noleggio

rental ['rɛntl] N (cost: on TV, telephone) abbonamento; (: on car) noleggio

rent boy N (BRIT col) giovane prostituto

renunciation [rɪnʌnsɪ'eɪʃən] N rinnegamento; (self-denial) rinunzia

reopen [riː'əupən] VT riaprire

reopening [riː'əupnɪŋ] N riapertura

reorder [riː'ɔːdə^r] VT ordinare di nuovo; (rearrange) riorganizzare

reorganize [riː'ɔːgənaɪz] VT riorganizzare

Rep ABBR (US Pol) = **representative**; **republican**

rep [rɛp] N ABBR (Comm: = representative) rappresentante mf; (Theat: repertory) teatro di repertorio

repair [rɪ'pɛə^r] N riparazione f ▶ VT riparare; **in good/bad ~** in buono/cattivo stato; **under ~** in riparazione

repair kit N kit m inv per riparazioni

repair man N (irreg) riparatore m

repair shop N (Aut etc) officina

repartee [rɛpɑː'tiː] N risposta pronta

repast [rɪ'pɑːst] N (formal) pranzo

repatriate [riː'pætrɪeɪt] VT rimpatriare

repay [riː'peɪ] VT (irreg: like **pay**) (money, creditor) rimborsare, ripagare; (sb's efforts) ricompensare; (favour) ricambiare

repayment [riː'peɪmənt] N rimborso

repeal [rɪ'piːl] N (of law) abrogazione f; (of sentence) annullamento ▶ VT abrogare; annullare

repeat [rɪ'piːt] N (Radio, TV) replica ▶ VT ripetere; (pattern) riprodurre; (promise, attack, also Comm: order) rinnovare ▶ VI ripetere

repeatedly [rɪ'piːtɪdlɪ] ADV ripetutamente, spesso

repeat order N (Comm): **to place a ~ (for)** rinnovare l'ordinazione (di)

repeat prescription N (BRIT) ricetta ripetibile

repel [rɪ'pɛl] VT respingere

repellent [rɪ'pɛlənt] ADJ repellente ▶ N: **insect ~** prodotto m anti-insetti inv; **moth ~** anti-tarmico

repent [rɪ'pɛnt] VI: **to ~ (of)** pentirsi (di)

repentance [rɪ'pɛntəns] N pentimento

repercussion [riːpə'kʌʃən] N (consequence) ripercussione f

repertoire ['rɛpətwɑː^r] N repertorio

repertory ['rɛpətərɪ] N (also: **repertory theatre**) teatro di repertorio

repertory company N compagnia di repertorio

repetition [rɛpɪ'tɪʃən] N ripetizione f; (Comm: of order etc) rinnovo

repetitious [rɛpɪ'tɪʃəs] ADJ (speech) pieno(-a) di ripetizioni

repetitive [rɪ'pɛtɪtɪv] ADJ (movement) che si ripete; (work) monotono(-a); (speech) pieno(-a) di ripetizioni

replace [rɪ'pleɪs] VT (put back) rimettere a posto; (take the place of) sostituire; (Tel): **"~ the receiver"** "riattaccare"

replacement [rɪ'pleɪsmənt] N rimessa; sostituzione f; (person) sostituto(-a)

replacement part N pezzo di ricambio

replay ['riːpleɪ] N (of match) partita ripetuta; (of tape, film) replay m inv

replenish [rɪ'plɛnɪʃ] VT (glass) riempire; (stock etc) rifornire

replete [rɪ'pliːt] ADJ: ~ **(with)** ripieno(-a) (di); (well-fed) sazio(-a) (di)

replica ['rɛplɪkə] N replica, copia

reply [rɪ'plaɪ] N risposta ▶ VI rispondere; **in ~** in risposta; **there's no ~** (Tel) non risponde (nessuno)

reply coupon N buono di risposta

report [rɪ'pɔːt] N rapporto; (Press etc) cronaca f; (BRIT: also: **school report**) pagella; (of gun) sparo ▶ VT riportare; (Press etc) fare una cronaca su; (bring to notice: occurrence) segnalare; (: person) denunciare ▶ VI (make a report) fare un rapporto (or una cronaca); (present o.s.): **to ~ (to sb)** presentarsi (a qn); **to ~ (on)** fare un rapporto (su); **it is reported that** si dice che; **it is reported from Berlin that ...** ci è stato riferito da Berlino che ...

report card N (US, SCOTTISH) pagella

reportedly [rɪ'pɔːtɪdlɪ] ADV stando a quanto si dice; **he ~ told them to ...** avrebbe detto loro di ...; **she is ~ living in Spain** si dice che vive in Spagna

reported speech [rɪ'pɔːtɪd-] N (Ling) discorso indiretto

reporter [rɪ'pɔːtə^r] N (Press) cronista mf, reporter m inv; (Radio) radiocronista mf; (TV) telecronista mf

repose [rɪ'pəuz] N: **in ~** in riposo

repossess [riːpə'zɛs] VT rientrare in possesso di

repossession order [riːpə'zɛʃən-] N ordine m di espropriazione

reprehensible [rɛprɪ'hɛnsɪbl] ADJ riprensibile

represent [rɛprɪ'zɛnt] VT rappresentare

representation [rɛprɪzɛn'teɪʃən] N rappresentazione f; (petition) rappresentanza; **representations** NPL (protest) protesta

representative [rɛprɪ'zɛntətɪv] N rappresentativo(-a); (Comm) rappresentante m (di commercio); (US Pol) deputato(-a) ▶ ADJ: ~ **(of)** rappresentativo(-a) (di)

repress [rɪ'prɛs] VT reprimere

repression [rɪ'prɛʃən] N repressione f

repressive [rɪ'prɛsɪv] ADJ repressivo(-a)

reprieve [rɪ'priːv] N (Law) sospensione f

r

dell'esecuzione della condanna; *(fig)* dilazione *f* ▶ vt sospendere l'esecuzione della condanna a; accordare una dilazione a

reprimand ['rεprɪmɑːnd] N rimprovero ▶ vt rimproverare, redarguire

reprint ['riːprɪnt] N ristampa ▶ vt ristampare

reprisal [rɪ'praɪzl] N rappresaglia; **to take reprisals** fare delle rappresaglie

reproach [rɪ'prəutʃ] N rimprovero ▶ vt: **to ~ sb with sth** rimproverare qn di qc; **beyond ~** irreprensibile

reproachful [rɪ'prəutʃful] ADJ di rimprovero

reproduce [riːprə'djuːs] vt riprodurre ▶ vi riprodursi

reproduction [riːprə'dʌkʃən] N riproduzione *f*

reproductive [riːprə'dʌktɪv] ADJ riproduttore(-trice); riproduttivo(-a)

reproof [rɪ'pruːf] N riprovazione *f*

reprove [rɪ'pruːv] vt *(action)* disapprovare; *(person)*: **to ~ (for)** biasimare (per)

reproving [rɪ'pruːvɪŋ] ADJ di disapprovazione

reptile ['rεptaɪl] N rettile *m*

Repub. ABBR *(US Pol)* = **republican**

republic [rɪ'pʌblɪk] N repubblica

republican [rɪ'pʌblɪkən] ADJ, N repubblicano(-a)

repudiate [rɪ'pjuːdɪeɪt] vt ripudiare

repugnant [rɪ'pʌgnənt] ADJ ripugnante

repulse [rɪ'pʌls] vt respingere

repulsion [rɪ'pʌlʃən] N ripulsione *f*

repulsive [rɪ'pʌlsɪv] ADJ ripugnante, ripulsivo(-a)

reputable ['rεpjutəbl] ADJ di buona reputazione; *(occupation)* rispettabile

reputation [rεpju'teɪʃən] N reputazione *f*; **he has a ~ for being awkward** ha la fama di essere un tipo difficile

repute [rɪ'pjuːt] N reputazione *f*

reputed [rɪ'pjuːtɪd] ADJ reputato(-a); **to be ~ to be rich/intelligent** *etc* essere ritenuto(-a) ricco(-a)/intelligente *etc*

reputedly [rɪ'pjuːtɪdlɪ] ADV secondo quanto si dice

request [rɪ'kwεst] N domanda; *(formal)* richiesta ▶ vt: **to ~ (of** or **from sb)** chiedere (a qn); **at the ~ of** su richiesta di; **"you are requested not to smoke"** "si prega di non fumare"

request stop N *(BRIT: for bus)* fermata facoltativa *or* a richiesta

requiem ['rεkwɪəm] N requiem *m inv or f inv*

require [rɪ'kwaɪəʳ] vt *(need: person)* aver bisogno di; *(: thing, situation)* richiedere; *(want)* volere; esigere; *(order)* obbligare; **to ~ sb to do sth/sth of sb** esigere che qn faccia qc/qc da qn; **what qualifications are required?** che requisiti ci vogliono?;

required by law prescritto dalla legge; **if required** in caso di bisogno

required [rɪ'kwaɪəd] ADJ richiesto(-a)

requirement [rɪ'kwaɪəmənt] N *(need)* esigenza; bisogno; *(condition)* requisito; **to meet sb's requirements** soddisfare le esigenze di qn

requisite ['rεkwɪzɪt] N cosa necessaria ▶ ADJ necessario(-a); **toilet requisites** articoli *mpl* da toletta

requisition [rεkwɪ'zɪʃən] N: **~ (for)** richiesta (di) ▶ vt *(Mil)* requisire

reroute [riː'ruːt] vt *(train etc)* deviare

resale ['riːseɪl] N rivendita

resale price maintenance N prezzo minimo di vendita imposto

resat [riː'sæt] PT, PP *of* **resit**

rescind [rɪ'sɪnd] vt annullare; *(law)* abrogare; *(judgement)* rescindere

rescue ['rεskjuː] N salvataggio; *(help)* soccorso ▶ vt salvare; **to come/go to sb's ~** venire/andare in aiuto a *or* di qn

rescue party N squadra di salvataggio

rescuer ['rεskjuəʳ] N salvatore(-trice)

research [rɪ'səːtʃ] N ricerca, ricerche *fpl* ▶ vt fare ricerche su ▶ vi: **to ~ (into sth)** fare ricerca (su qc); **a piece of ~** un lavoro di ricerca; **~ and development** ricerca e sviluppo

researcher [rɪ'səːtʃəʳ] N ricercatore(-trice)

research work N ricerche *fpl*

resell [riː'sεl] vt *(irreg: like* **sell)** rivendere

resemblance [rɪ'zεmbləns] N somiglianza; **to bear a strong ~ to** somigliare moltissimo a

resemble [rɪ'zεmbl] vt assomigliare a

resent [rɪ'zεnt] vt risentirsi di

resentful [rɪ'zεntful] ADJ pieno(-a) di risentimento

resentment [rɪ'zεntmənt] N risentimento

reservation [rεzə'veɪʃən] N *(booking)* prenotazione *f*; *(doubt)* dubbio; *(protected area)* riserva; *(BRIT Aut: also:* **central reservation)** spartitraffico *m inv*; **to make a ~ (in an hotel/a restaurant/on a plane)** prenotare (una camera/una tavola/un posto); **with reservations** *(doubts)* con le dovute riserve

reservation desk N *(US: in hotel)* reception *f inv*

reserve [rɪ'zəːv] N riserva ▶ vt *(seats etc)* prenotare; **reserves** NPL *(Mil)* riserve *fpl*; **in ~** in serbo

reserve currency N valuta di riserva

reserved [rɪ'zəːvd] ADJ *(shy)* riservato(-a); *(seat)* prenotato(-a)

reserve price N *(BRIT)* prezzo di riserva, prezzo *m* base *inv*

reserve team N *(BRIT Sport)* seconda squadra

reservist [rɪ'zəːvɪst] N *(Mil)* riservista *m*

reservoir ['rɛzəvwɑːʳ] N serbatoio; (*artificial lake*) bacino idrico

reset [riː'sɛt] VT (*irreg: like* **set**) (*Comput*) azzerare

reshape [riː'ʃeɪp] VT (*policy*) ristrutturare

reshuffle [riː'ʃʌfl] N: **Cabinet** ~ (*Pol*) rimpasto governativo

reside [rɪ'zaɪd] VI risiedere

residence ['rɛzɪdəns] N residenza; **to take up** ~ prendere residenza; **in** ~ (*queen etc*) in sede; (*doctor*) fisso

residence permit N (*BRIT*) permesso di soggiorno

resident ['rɛzɪdənt] N (*gen, Comput*) residente *mf*; (*in hotel*) cliente *mf* fisso(-a) ▶ ADJ residente; (*doctor*) fisso(-a); (*course, college*) a tempo pieno con pernottamento

residential [rɛzɪ'dɛnʃəl] ADJ di residenza; (*area*) residenziale

residue ['rɛzɪdjuː] N resto; (*Chem, Physics*) residuo

resign [rɪ'zaɪn] VT (*one's post*) dimettersi da ▶ VI: **to** ~ (**from**) dimettersi (da), dare le dimissioni (da); **to** ~ **o.s. to** rassegnarsi a

resignation [rɛzɪg'neɪʃən] N dimissioni *fpl*; rassegnazione *f*; **to tender one's** ~ dare le dimissioni

resilience [rɪ'zɪlɪəns] N (*of material*) elasticità, resilienza; (*of person*) capacità di recupero

resilient [rɪ'zɪlɪənt] ADJ elastico(-a); (*person*) che si riprende facilmente

resin ['rɛzɪn] N resina

resist [rɪ'zɪst] VT resistere a

resistance [rɪ'zɪstəns] N resistenza

resistant [rɪ'zɪstənt] ADJ: ~ (**to**) resistente (a)

resit ['riːsɪt] (*BRIT*) VT (*irreg: like* **sit**) (*exam*) ripresentarsi a; (*subject*) ridare l'esame di ▶ N: **he's got his French** ~ **on Friday** deve ridare l'esame di francese venerdì

resolute ['rɛzəluːt] ADJ risoluto(-a)

resolution [rɛzə'luːʃən] N (*resolve*) fermo proposito, risoluzione *f*; (*determination*) risolutezza; (*on screen*) risoluzione *f*; **to make a** ~ fare un proposito

resolve [rɪ'zɔlv] N risoluzione *f* ▶ VI (*decide*): **to** ~ **to do** decidere di fare ▶ VT (*problem*) risolvere

resolved [rɪ'zɔlvd] ADJ risoluto(-a)

resonance ['rɛzənəns] N risonanza

resonant ['rɛzənənt] ADJ risonante

resort [rɪ'zɔːt] N (*town*) stazione *f*; (*place*) località *f inv*; (*recourse*) ricorso ▶ VI: **to** ~ **to** far ricorso a; **seaside/winter sports** ~ stazione *f* balneare/di sport invernali; **as a last** ~ come ultima risorsa

resound [rɪ'zaund] VI: **to** ~ (**with**) risonare (di)

resounding [rɪ'zaundɪŋ] ADJ risonante

resource [rɪ'sɔːs] N risorsa; **resources** NPL risorse *fpl*; **natural resources** risorse naturali; **to leave sb to his** (*or* **her**) **own resources** (*fig*) lasciare che qn si arrangi (per conto suo)

resourceful [rɪ'sɔːsful] ADJ pieno(-a) di risorse, intraprendente

resourcefulness [rɪ'sɔːsfəlnɪs] N intraprendenza

respect [rɪs'pɛkt] N rispetto; (*point, detail*): **in some respects** sotto certi aspetti ▶ VT rispettare; **respects** NPL ossequi *mpl*; **to have** *or* **show** ~ **for** aver rispetto per; **out of** ~ **for** per rispetto *or* riguardo a; **with** ~ **to** rispetto a, riguardo a; **in** ~ **of** quanto a; **in this** ~ per questo riguardo; **with (all) due** ~ **I …** con rispetto parlando, io …

respectability [rɪspɛktə'bɪlɪtɪ] N rispettabilità

respectable [rɪs'pɛktəbl] ADJ rispettabile; (*quite big: amount etc*) considerevole; (*quite good: player, result etc*) niente male *inv*

respectful [rɪs'pɛktful] ADJ rispettoso(-a)

respective [rɪs'pɛktɪv] ADJ rispettivo(-a)

respectively [rɪs'pɛktɪvlɪ] ADV rispettivamente

respiration [rɛspɪ'reɪʃən] N respirazione *f*

respirator ['rɛspɪreɪtəʳ] N respiratore *m*

respiratory ['rɛspərətərɪ] ADJ respiratorio(-a)

respite ['rɛspaɪt] N respiro, tregua

resplendent [rɪs'plɛndənt] ADJ risplendente

respond [rɪs'pɔnd] VI rispondere

respondent [rɪs'pɔndənt] N (*Law*) convenuto(-a)

response [rɪs'pɔns] N risposta; **in** ~ **to** in risposta a

responsibility [rɪspɔnsɪ'bɪlɪtɪ] N responsabilità *f inv*; **to take** ~ **for sth/sb** assumersi *or* prendersi la responsabilità di qc/per qn

responsible [rɪs'pɔnsɪbl] ADJ (*liable*): ~ (**for**) responsabile (di); (*trustworthy*) fidato(-a); (*job*) di (grande) responsabilità; **to be** ~ **to sb** (**for sth**) dover rispondere a qn (di qc)

responsibly [rɪs'pɔnsəblɪ] ADV responsabilmente

responsive [rɪs'pɔnsɪv] ADJ che reagisce

rest [rɛst] N riposo; (*stop*) sosta, pausa; (*Mus*) pausa; (*support*) appoggio, sostegno; (*remainder*) resto, avanzi *mpl* ▶ VI riposarsi; (*remain*) rimanere, restare; (*be supported*): **to** ~ **on** appoggiarsi su ▶ VT (far) riposare; (*lean*): **to** ~ **sth on/against** appoggiare qc su/ contro; **to set sb's mind at** ~ tranquillizzare qn; **the** ~ **of them** gli altri; **to** ~ **one's eyes** *or* **gaze on** posare lo sguardo su; ~ **assured that …** stia tranquillo che …; **it rests with him to decide** sta a lui decidere

restart [riː'stɑːt] VT (*engine*) rimettere in marcia; (*work*) ricominciare

restaurant ['rɛstərɔŋ] N ristorante m
restaurant car N (BRIT) vagone m ristorante
rest cure N cura del riposo
restful ['rɛstful] ADJ riposante
rest home N casa di riposo
restitution [rɛstɪ'tju:ʃən] N (act) restituzione f; (reparation) riparazione f
restive ['rɛstɪv] ADJ agitato(-a), impaziente; (horse) restio(-a)
restless ['rɛstlɪs] ADJ agitato(-a), irrequieto(-a); **to get ~** spazientirsi
restlessly ['rɛstlɪslɪ] ADV in preda all'agitazione
restock [ri:'stɔk] VT rifornire
restoration [rɛstə'reɪʃən] N restauro; restituzione f
restorative [rɪ'stɔrətɪv] ADJ corroborante, ristorativo(-a) ▶ N ricostituente m
restore [rɪ'stɔ:ʳ] VT (building) restaurare; (sth stolen) restituire; (peace, health) ristorare
restorer [rɪs'tɔ:rəʳ] N (Art etc) restauratore(-trice)
restrain [rɪs'treɪn] VT (feeling) contenere, frenare; (person): **to ~ (from doing)** trattenere (dal fare)
restrained [rɪs'treɪnd] ADJ (style) contenuto(-a), sobrio(-a); (manner) riservato(-a)
restraint [rɪs'treɪnt] N (restriction) limitazione f; (moderation) ritegno; (of style) contenutezza; **wage ~** restrizioni fpl salariali
restrict [rɪs'trɪkt] VT restringere, limitare
restricted area [rɪs'trɪktɪd-] N (Aut) zona a velocità limitata
restriction [rɪs'trɪkʃən] N: **~ (on)** restrizione f (di), limitazione f (di)
restrictive [rɪs'trɪktɪv] ADJ restrittivo(-a)
restrictive practices NPL (Industry) pratiche restrittive di produzione
rest room N (US) toletta
restructure [ri:'strʌktʃəʳ] VT ristrutturare
result [rɪ'zʌlt] N risultato ▶ VI: **to ~ in** avere per risultato; **as a ~ (of)** in or di conseguenza (a), in seguito (a); **to ~ (from)** essere una conseguenza (di), essere causato(-a) (da)
resultant [rɪ'zʌltənt] ADJ risultante, conseguente
resume [rɪ'zju:m] VT, VI (work, journey) riprendere; (sum up) riassumere
résumé ['reɪzju:meɪ] N riassunto; (US: curriculum vitae) curriculum vitae m inv
resumption [rɪ'zʌmpʃən] N ripresa
resurgence [rɪ'sə:dʒəns] N rinascita
resurrection [rɛzə'rɛkʃən] N risurrezione f
resuscitate [rɪ'sʌsɪteɪt] VT (Med) risuscitare
resuscitation [rɪsʌsɪ'teɪʃən] N rianimazione f
retail ['ri:teɪl] N (vendita al) minuto ▶ CPD al minuto ▶ VT vendere al minuto ▶ VI: **to ~ at**

essere in vendita al pubblico al prezzo di
retailer ['ri:teɪləʳ] N commerciante mf al minuto, dettagliante mf
retail outlet N punto di vendita al dettaglio
retail price N prezzo al minuto
retail price index N indice m dei prezzi al consumo
retain [rɪ'teɪn] VT (keep) tenere, serbare
retainer [rɪ'teɪnəʳ] N (servant) servitore m; (fee) onorario
retaliate [rɪ'tælɪeɪt] VI: **to ~ (against)** vendicarsi (di); **to ~ on sb** fare una rappresaglia contro qn
retaliation [rɪtælɪ'eɪʃən] N rappresaglie fpl; **in ~ for** per vendicarsi di
retaliatory [rɪ'tælɪətərɪ] ADJ di rappresaglia, di ritorsione
retarded [rɪ'tɑ:dɪd] ADJ ritardato(-a); (also: **mentally retarded**) tardo(-a) (di mente)
retch [rɛtʃ] VI aver conati di vomito
retentive [rɪ'tɛntɪv] ADJ ritentivo(-a)
rethink ['ri:'θɪŋk] VT ripensare
reticence ['rɛtɪsns] N reticenza
reticent ['rɛtɪsnt] ADJ reticente
retina ['rɛtɪnə] N retina
retinue ['rɛtɪnju:] N seguito, scorta
retire [rɪ'taɪəʳ] VI (give up work) andare in pensione; (withdraw) ritirarsi, andarsene; (go to bed) andare a letto, ritirarsi
retired [rɪ'taɪəd] ADJ (person) pensionato(-a)
retirement [rɪ'taɪəmənt] N pensione f; (act) pensionamento
retirement age N età del pensionamento
retiring [rɪ'taɪərɪŋ] ADJ (person) riservato(-a); (departing: chairman) uscente
retort [rɪ'tɔ:t] N (reply) rimbecco; (container) storta ▶ VI rimbeccare
retrace [ri:'treɪs] VT ricostruire; **to ~ one's steps** tornare sui propri passi
retract [rɪ'trækt] VT (statement) ritrattare; (claws, undercarriage, aerial) ritrarre, ritirare ▶ VI ritrarsi
retractable [rɪ'træktəbl] ADJ retrattile
retrain [ri:'treɪn] VT (worker) riaddestrare
retraining [ri:'treɪnɪŋ] N riaddestramento
retread VT [ri:'trɛd] (Aut: tyre) rigenerare ▶ N ['ri:trɛd] gomma rigenerata
retreat [rɪ'tri:t] N ritirata; (place) rifugio ▶ VI battere in ritirata; (flood) ritirarsi; **to beat a hasty ~** (fig) battersela
retrial [ri:'traɪəl] N nuovo processo
retribution [rɛtrɪ'bju:ʃən] N castigo
retrieval [rɪ'tri:vəl] N ricupero
retrieve [rɪ'tri:v] VT (sth lost) ricuperare, ritrovare; (situation, honour) salvare; (error, loss) rimediare a; (Comput) ricuperare
retriever [rɪ'tri:vəʳ] N cane m da riporto
retroactive [rɛtrəu'æktɪv] ADJ retroattivo(-a)
retrograde ['rɛtrəugreɪd] ADJ retrogrado(-a)

retrospect ['rɛtrəspɛkt] N: **in ~** guardando indietro

retrospective [rɛtrə'spɛktɪv] ADJ retrospettivo(-a); (law) retroattivo(-a) ▶ N (Art) retrospettiva

return [rɪ'tə:n] N (going or coming back) ritorno; (of sth stolen etc) restituzione f; (Comm: from land, shares) profitto, reddito; (: of merchandise) resa; (report) rapporto; (reward): **in ~ (for)** in cambio (di) ▶ CPD (journey, match) di ritorno; (BRIT: ticket) di andata e ritorno ▶ VI tornare, ritornare ▶ VT rendere, restituire; (bring back) riportare; (send back) mandare indietro; (put back) rimettere; (Pol: candidate) eleggere; **returns** NPL (Comm) incassi mpl; profitti mpl; **by ~ of post** a stretto giro di posta; **many happy returns (of the day)!** cento di questi giorni!

returnable [rɪ'tə:nəbl] ADJ: **~ bottle** vuoto a rendere

returner [rɪ'tə:nəʳ] N donna che ritorna al lavoro dopo la maternità

returning officer [rɪ'tə:nɪŋ-] N (BRIT Pol) funzionario addetto all'organizzazione delle elezioni in un distretto

return key N (Comput) tasto di ritorno

return ticket N (esp BRIT) biglietto di andata e ritorno

retweet [ri:'twi:t] N (on Twitter) retweet m inv ▶ VT ritwittare

reunion [ri:'ju:nɪən] N riunione f

reunite [ri:ju:'naɪt] VT riunire

rev [rɛv] N ABBR (Aut: = revolution) giro ▶ VT (also: **rev up**) imballare ▶ VI (also: **rev up**) imballarsi

Rev., Revd. ABBR = **Reverend**

revaluation [ri:vælju'eɪʃən] N rivalutazione f

revamp ['ri:'væmp] VT rinnovare; (firm) riorganizzare

rev counter N contagiri m inv

reveal [rɪ'vi:l] VT (make known) rivelare, svelare; (display) rivelare, mostrare

revealing [rɪ'vi:lɪŋ] ADJ rivelatore(-trice); (dress) scollato(-a)

reveille [rɪ'vælɪ] N (Mil) sveglia

revel ['rɛvl] VI: **to ~ in sth/in doing** dilettarsi di qc/a fare

revelation [rɛvə'leɪʃən] N rivelazione f

reveller ['rɛvləʳ] N festaiolo(-a)

revelry ['rɛvlrɪ] N baldoria

revenge [rɪ'vɛndʒ] N vendetta; (in game etc) rivincita ▶ VT vendicare; **to take ~ on** vendicarsi di; **to get one's ~ (for sth)** vendicarsi (di qc)

revengeful [rɪ'vɛndʒful] ADJ vendicatore(-trice); vendicativo(-a)

revenue ['rɛvənju:] N reddito

reverberate [rɪ'və:bəreɪt] VI (sound) rimbombare; (light) riverberarsi

reverberation [rɪvə:bə'reɪʃən] N (of light, sound) riverberazione f

revere [rɪ'vɪəʳ] VT venerare

reverence ['rɛvərəns] N venerazione f, riverenza

Reverend ['rɛvərənd] ADJ (in titles) reverendo(-a)

reverent ['rɛvərənt] ADJ riverente

reverie ['rɛvərɪ] N fantasticheria

reversal [rɪ'və:sl] N capovolgimento

reverse [rɪ'və:s] N contrario, opposto; (back) rovescio; (Aut: also: **reverse gear**) marcia indietro ▶ ADJ (order) inverso(-a); (direction) opposto(-a) ▶ VT (turn) invertire, rivoltare; (change) capovolgere, rovesciare; (Law: judgement) cassare; (car) fare marcia indietro con ▶ VI (BRIT Aut, person etc) fare marcia indietro; **in ~ order** in ordine inverso; **to go into ~** fare marcia indietro

reverse-charge call [rɪ'və:stʃɑ:dʒ-] N (BRIT Tel) telefonata con addebito al ricevente

reverse video N reverse video m

reversible [rɪ'və:səbl] ADJ (garment) double-face inv; (procedure) reversibile

reversing lights [rɪ'və:sɪŋ-] NPL (BRIT Aut) luci fpl per la retromarcia

reversion [rɪ'və:ʃən] N ritorno

revert [rɪ'və:t] VI: **to ~ to** tornare a

review [rɪ'vju:] N rivista; (of book, film) recensione f; (of situation) esame m ▶ VT passare in rivista; fare la recensione di; fare il punto di; **to come under ~** essere preso in esame

reviewer [rɪ'vju:əʳ] N recensore(-a)

revile [rɪ'vaɪl] VT insultare

revise [rɪ'vaɪz] VT (manuscript) rivedere, correggere; (opinion) emendare, modificare; (study: subject, notes) ripassare; **revised edition** edizione riveduta

revision [rɪ'vɪʒən] N revisione f; ripasso; (revised version) versione riveduta e corretta

revitalize [ri:'vaɪtəlaɪz] VT ravvivare

revival [rɪ'vaɪvəl] N ripresa; ristabilimento; (of faith) risveglio

revive [rɪ'vaɪv] VT (person) rianimare; (custom) far rivivere; (hope, courage, economy) ravvivare; (play, fashion) riesumare ▶ VI (person) rianimarsi; (hope) ravvivarsi; (activity) riprendersi

revoke [rɪ'vəuk] VT revocare; (promise, decision) rinvenire su

revolt [rɪ'vəult] N rivolta, ribellione f ▶ VI rivoltarsi, ribellarsi; **to ~ (against sb/sth)** ribellarsi (a qn/qc) ▶ VT (far) rivoltare

revolting [rɪ'vəultɪŋ] ADJ ripugnante

revolution [rɛvə'lu:ʃən] N rivoluzione f; (of wheel etc) rivoluzione, giro

revolutionary [rɛvə'lu:ʃənrɪ] ADJ, N rivoluzionario(-a)

r

753

revolutionize [rɛvə'lu:ʃənaɪz] VT rivoluzionare

revolve [rɪ'vɔlv] VI girare

revolver [rɪ'vɔlvəʳ] N rivoltella

revolving [rɪ'vɔlvɪŋ] ADJ girevole

revolving door N porta girevole

revue [rɪ'vju:] N (Theat) rivista

revulsion [rɪ'vʌlʃən] N ripugnanza

reward [rɪ'wɔːd] N ricompensa, premio ▶ VT: **to ~ (for)** ricompensare (per)

rewarding [rɪ'wɔːdɪŋ] ADJ (fig) soddisfacente; **financially ~** conveniente dal punto di vista economico

rewind [ri:'waɪnd] VT (irreg: like **wind²**) (watch) ricaricare; (ribbon etc) riavvolgere

rewire [ri:'waɪəʳ] VT (house) rifare l'impianto elettrico di

reword [ri:'wəːd] VT formulare or esprimere con altre parole

rewritable [ri:'raɪtəbl] ADJ (CD, DVD) riscrivibile

rewrite [ri:'raɪt] VT (irreg: like **write**) riscrivere

Reykjavik ['reɪkjəvi:k] N Reykjavik f

RFD ABBR (US Post) = **rural free delivery**

RGN N ABBR (BRIT: = Registered General Nurse) infermiera diplomata (dopo corso triennale)

Rh ABBR (= rhesus) Rh

rhapsody ['ræpsədɪ] N (Mus) rapsodia; (fig) elogio stravagante

rhesus negative ['ri:səs-] ADJ (Med) Rh-negativo(-a)

rhesus positive ADJ (Med) Rh-positivo(-a)

rhetoric ['rɛtərɪk] N retorica

rhetorical [rɪ'tɔrɪkl] ADJ retorico(-a)

rheumatic [ru:'mætɪk] ADJ reumatico(-a)

rheumatism ['ru:mətɪzəm] N reumatismo

rheumatoid arthritis ['ru:mətɔɪd-] N artrite f reumatoide

Rhine [raɪn] N: **the ~** il Reno

rhinestone ['raɪnstəun] N diamante m falso

rhinoceros [raɪ'nɔsərəs] N rinoceronte m

Rhodes [rəudz] N Rodi f

Rhodesia [rəu'di:ʒə] N Rhodesia

Rhodesian [rəu'di:ʒən] ADJ, N Rhodesiano(-a)

rhododendron [rəudə'dɛndrn] N rododendro

Rhone [rəun] N: **the ~** il Rodano

rhubarb ['ru:bɑːb] N rabarbaro

rhyme [raɪm] N rima; (verse) poesia ▶ VI: **to ~ (with)** fare rima (con); **without ~ or reason** senza capo né coda

rhythm ['rɪðm] N ritmo

rhythmic ['rɪðmɪk], **rhythmical** ['rɪðmɪkəl] ADJ ritmico(-a)

rhythmically ['rɪðmɪkəlɪ] ADV con ritmo

rhythm method N metodo Ogino-Knauss

RI ABBR (US) = **Rhode Island** ▶ N ABBR (BRIT) = **religious instruction**

rib [rɪb] N (Anat) costola ▶ VT (tease) punzecchiare

ribald ['rɪbəld] ADJ licenzioso(-a), volgare

ribbed [rɪbd] ADJ (knitting) a coste

ribbon ['rɪbən] N nastro; **in ribbons** (torn) a brandelli

rice [raɪs] N riso

ricefield ['raɪsfi:ld] N risaia

rice pudding N budino di riso

rich [rɪtʃ] ADJ ricco(-a); (clothes) sontuoso(-a); **the ~** npl i ricchi; **riches** NPL ricchezze fpl; **to be ~ in sth** essere ricco di qc

richly ['rɪtʃlɪ] ADV riccamente; (dressed) sontuosamente; (deserved) pienamente

rickets ['rɪkɪts] N rachitismo

rickety ['rɪkɪtɪ] ADJ zoppicante

rickshaw ['rɪkʃɔː] N risciò m inv

ricochet ['rɪkəʃeɪ] N rimbalzo ▶ VI rimbalzare

rid [rɪd] (pt, pp ~) VT: **to ~ sb of** sbarazzare or liberare qn di; **to get ~ of** sbarazzarsi di

riddance ['rɪdns] N: **good ~!** che liberazione!

ridden ['rɪdn] PP of **ride**

riddle ['rɪdl] N (puzzle) indovinello ▶ VT: **to be riddled with** (holes) essere crivellato(-a) di; (doubts) essere pieno(-a) di

ride [raɪd] (pt **rode** [rəud], pp **ridden** ['rɪdn]) N (on horse) cavalcata; (outing) passeggiata; (distance covered) cavalcata; corsa ▶ VI (as sport) cavalcare; (go somewhere: on horse, bicycle) andare a cavallo or in bicicletta etc); (journey: on bicycle, motorcycle, bus) andare, viaggiare ▶ VT (a horse) montare, cavalcare; **to go for a ~** andare a fare una cavalcata; andare a fare un giro; **can you ~ a bike?** sai andare in bicicletta?; **we rode all day/all the way** abbiamo cavalcato tutto il giorno/per tutto il tragitto; **to ~ a horse/bicycle/camel** montare a cavallo/in bicicletta/in groppa a un cammello; **to ~ at anchor** (Naut) essere alla fonda; **horse ~** cavalcata; **car ~** passeggiata in macchina; **to take sb for a ~** (fig) prendere in giro qn; fregare qn

▶ **ride out** VT: **to ~ out the storm** (fig) mantenersi a galla

rider ['raɪdəʳ] N cavalcatore(-trice); (jockey) fantino; (on bicycle) ciclista mf; (on motorcycle) motociclista mf; (in document) clausola addizionale, aggiunta

ridge [rɪdʒ] N (of hill) cresta; (of roof) colmo; (of mountain) giogo; (on object) riga (in rilievo)

ridicule ['rɪdɪkju:l] N ridicolo; scherno ▶ VT mettere in ridicolo; **to hold sb/sth up to ~** mettere in ridicolo qn/qc

ridiculous [rɪ'dɪkjuləs] ADJ ridicolo(-a)

riding ['raɪdɪŋ] N equitazione f

riding school N scuola d'equitazione

rife [raɪf] ADJ diffuso(-a); **to be ~ with** abbondare di

riffraff ['rɪfræf] N canaglia, gentaglia

rifle ['raɪfl] N carabina ▶ VT vuotare
▶ **rifle through** VT FUS frugare
rifle range N campo di tiro; (*at fair*) tiro a
segno
rift [rɪft] N fessura, crepatura; (*fig:
disagreement*) incrinatura, disaccordo
rig [rɪg] N (*also:* **oil rig**: *on land*) derrick *m inv*;
(*: at sea*) piattaforma di trivellazione ▶ VT
(*election etc*) truccare
▶ **rig out** VT (*BRIT*) attrezzare; (*pej*) abbigliare,
agghindare
▶ **rig up** VT allestire
rigging ['rɪgɪŋ] N (*Naut*) attrezzatura
right [raɪt] ADJ giusto(-a); (*suitable*)
appropriato(-a); (*not left*) destro(-a) ▶ N
giusto; (*title, claim*) diritto; (*not left*) destra
▶ ADV (*answer*) correttamente; (*not on the left*) a
destra ▶ VT raddrizzare; (*fig*) riparare ▶ EXCL
bene!; **the ~ time** l'ora esatta; **to be ~**
(*person*) aver ragione; (*answer*) essere
giusto(-a) *or* corretto(-a); **to get sth ~** far
giusto qc; **you did the ~ thing** ha fatto bene;
let's get it ~ this time! cerchiamo di farlo
bene stavolta!; **to put a mistake ~** (*BRIT*)
correggere un errore; **~ now** proprio adesso;
subito; **~ away** subito; **~ before/after** subito
prima/dopo; **to go ~ to the end of sth**
andare fino in fondo a qc; **~ against the
wall** proprio contro il muro; **~ ahead** sempre
diritto; proprio davanti; **~ in the middle**
proprio nel mezzo; **by rights** di diritto; **on
the ~, to the ~** a destra; **to be in the ~** aver
ragione, essere nel giusto; **~ and wrong** il
bene e il male; **to have a ~ to sth** aver diritto
a qc; **film rights** diritti di riproduzione
cinematografica
right angle N angolo retto
right-click ['raɪtklɪk] VI (*Comput*): **to ~ on**
cliccare con il pulsante destro del mouse su
righteous ['raɪtʃəs] ADJ retto(-a), virtuoso(-a);
(*anger*) giusto(-a), giustificato(-a)
righteousness ['raɪtʃəsnɪs] N rettitudine *f*,
virtù *f*
rightful ['raɪtful] ADJ (*heir*) legittimo(-a)
rightfully ['raɪtfəlɪ] ADV legittimamente
right-hand ADJ: **~ drive** guida a destra; **the ~
side** il lato destro; **~ man** braccio destro (*fig*)
right-handed [raɪt'hændɪd] ADJ (*person*) che
adopera la mano destra
rightly ['raɪtlɪ] ADV bene, correttamente;
(*with reason*) a ragione; **if I remember ~** se mi
ricordo bene
right-minded [raɪt'maɪndɪd] ADJ sensato(-a)
right of way N diritto di passaggio; (*Aut*)
precedenza
rights issue N (*Stock Exchange*) emissione *f* di
azioni riservate agli azionisti
right wing N (*Mil, Sport*) ala destra; (*Pol*)
destra ▶ ADJ: **right-wing** (*Pol*) di destra

right-winger [raɪt'wɪŋəʳ] N (*Pol*) uno(-a) di
destra; (*Sport*) ala destra
rigid ['rɪdʒɪd] ADJ rigido(-a); (*principle*)
rigoroso(-a)
rigidity [rɪ'dʒɪdɪtɪ] N rigidità
rigidly ['rɪdʒɪdlɪ] ADV rigidamente
rigmarole ['rɪgmərəul] N tiritera; commedia
rigor ['rɪgəʳ] N (*US*) = **rigour**
rigor mortis ['rɪgə'mɔːtɪs] N rigidità
cadaverica
rigorous ['rɪgərəs] ADJ rigoroso(-a)
rigorously ['rɪgərəslɪ] ADV rigorosamente
rigour, (*US*) **rigor** ['rɪgəʳ] N rigore *m*
rig-out ['rɪgaut] N (*BRIT col*) tenuta
rile [raɪl] VT irritare, seccare
rim [rɪm] N orlo; (*of spectacles*) montatura;
(*of wheel*) cerchione *m*
rimless ['rɪmlɪs] ADJ (*spectacles*) senza
montatura
rimmed [rɪmd] ADJ bordato(-a); cerchiato(-a)
rind [raɪnd] N (*of bacon*) cotenna; (*of lemon etc*)
scorza
ring [rɪŋ] (*pt* **rang**, *pp* **rung**) N anello;
(*also:* **wedding ring**) fede *f*; (*of people, objects*)
cerchio; (*of spies*) giro; (*of smoke etc*) spirale *f*;
(*arena*) pista, arena; (*for boxing*) ring *m inv*; (*sound
of bell*) scampanio; (*telephone call*) colpo di
telefono ▶ VI (*person, bell, telephone*) suonare;
(*also:* **ring out**: *voice, words*) risuonare; (*Tel*)
telefonare; (*ears*) fischiare ▶ VT (*BRIT Tel: also:*
ring up) telefonare a; (*bell, doorbell*) suonare; **to
give sb a ~** (*BRIT Tel*) dare un colpo di telefono a
qn; **that has the ~ of truth about it** questo
ha l'aria d'essere vero; **to ~ the bell** suonare
il campanello; **the name doesn't ~ a bell
(with me)** questo nome non mi dice niente
▶ **ring back** VT, VI (*BRIT Tel*) richiamare
▶ **ring off** VI (*BRIT Tel*) mettere giù, riattaccare
ring binder N classificatore *m* a anelli
ring-fence [rɪŋ'fɛns] VT isolare
ring finger N anulare *m*
ringing ['rɪŋɪŋ] N (*of bell*) scampanio; (*: louder*)
scampanellata; (*of telephone*) squillo; (*in ears*)
fischio, ronzio
ringing tone N (*BRIT Tel*) segnale *m* di libero
ringleader ['rɪŋliːdəʳ] N (*of gang*) capobanda *m*
ringlets ['rɪŋlɪts] NPL boccoli *mpl*
ring road N (*BRIT*) raccordo anulare
ringtone N (*Tel*) suoneria
rink [rɪŋk] N (*also:* **ice rink**) pista di
pattinaggio; (*: for roller-skating*) pista di
pattinaggio (a rotelle)
rinse [rɪns] N risciacquatura; (*hair tint*) cachet
m inv ▶ VT sciacquare
Rio ['riːəu], **Rio de Janeiro**
['riːəudədʒə'nɪərəu] N Rio de Janeiro *f*
riot ['raɪət] N sommossa, tumulto ▶ VI
tumultuare; **a ~ of colours** un'orgia di
colori; **to run ~** creare disordine

r

rioter ['raɪətə'] N dimostrante mf (durante dei disordini)

riot gear N: **in** ~ in assetto di guerra

riotous ['raɪətəs] ADJ tumultuoso(-a); che fa crepare dal ridere

riotously ['raɪətəslɪ] ADV: ~ **funny** che fa crepare dal ridere

riot police N = la Celere

RIP ABBR (= requiescat or requiescant in pace) R.I.P.

rip [rɪp] N strappo ▶ VT strappare ▶ VI strapparsi
  ▶ **rip off** VT (col: cheat) fregare
  ▶ **rip up** VT stracciare

ripcord ['rɪpkɔːd] N cavo di spiegamento

ripe [raɪp] ADJ (fruit, grain) maturo(-a); (cheese) stagionato(-a)

ripen ['raɪpən] VT maturare ▶ VI maturarsi; stagionarsi

ripeness ['raɪpnɪs] N maturità

rip-off ['rɪpɔf] N (col): **it's a** ~! è un furto!

riposte [rɪ'pɔst] N risposta per le rime

ripple ['rɪpl] N increspamento, ondulazione f; mormorio ▶ VI incresparsi ▶ VT increspare

rise [raɪz] (pt **rose** [rəuz], pp **risen** ['rɪzn]) N (slope) salita, pendio; (hill) altura; (increase: in wages: BRIT) aumento; (: in prices, temperature) rialzo, aumento; (fig: to power etc) ascesa ▶ VI alzarsi, levarsi; (prices) aumentare; (waters, river) crescere; (sun, wind, person: from chair, bed) levarsi; (building: also: **rise up**) ergersi; (rebel) insorgere; ribellarsi; (in rank) salire; **to give** ~ **to** provocare, dare origine a; **to** ~ **to the occasion** dimostrarsi all'altezza della situazione

risen ['rɪzn] PP of **rise**

rising ['raɪzɪŋ] ADJ (increasing: number) sempre crescente; (: prices) in aumento; (tide) montante; (sun, moon) nascente, che sorge ▶ N (uprising) sommossa

rising damp N infiltrazioni fpl d'umidità

rising star N (also fig) astro nascente

risk [rɪsk] N rischio; pericolo ▶ VT rischiare; **to take** or **run the** ~ **of doing** correre il rischio di fare; **at** ~ in pericolo; **at one's own** ~ a proprio rischio e pericolo; **fire/health** ~ rischio d'incendio/per la salute; **I'll** ~ **it** ci proverò lo stesso

risk capital N capitale m di rischio

risky ['rɪskɪ] ADJ rischioso(-a)

risqué ['riːskeɪ] ADJ (joke) spinto(-a)

rissole ['rɪsəul] N crocchetta

rite [raɪt] N rito; **last rites** l'estrema unzione

ritual ['rɪtjuəl] ADJ, N rituale (m)

rival ['raɪvl] N rivale mf; (in business) concorrente mf ▶ ADJ rivale; che fa concorrenza ▶ VT essere in concorrenza con; **to** ~ **sb/sth in** competere con qn/qc in

rivalry ['raɪvəlrɪ] N rivalità; concorrenza

river ['rɪvə'] N fiume m ▶ CPD (port, traffic) fluviale; **up/down** ~ a monte/valle

riverbank ['rɪvəbæŋk] N argine m

riverbed ['rɪvəbɛd] N alveo (fluviale)

riverside ['rɪəsaɪd] N sponda del fiume

rivet ['rɪvɪt] N ribattino, rivetto ▶ VT ribadire; (fig) concentrare, fissare

riveting ['rɪvɪtɪŋ] ADJ (fig) avvincente

Riviera [rɪvɪ'ɛərə] N: **the (French)** ~ la Costa Azzurra; **the Italian** ~ la Riviera

Riyadh [rɪ'jɑːd] N Riad f

RMT N ABBR (= National Union of Rail, Maritime and Transport Workers) sindacato dei Ferrovieri, Marittimi e Trasportatori

RN N ABBR (BRIT) = **Royal Navy**; (US) = **registered nurse**

RNA N ABBR (= ribonucleic acid) R.N.A. m

RNLI N ABBR (BRIT: = Royal National Lifeboat Institution) associazione volontaria che organizza e dispone di scialuppe di salvataggio

RNZAF N ABBR = **Royal New Zealand Air Force**

RNZN N ABBR = **Royal New Zealand Navy**

road [rəud] N strada; (small) cammino; (in town) via ▶ CPD stradale; **main** ~ strada principale; **major/minor** ~ strada con/senza diritto di precedenza; **it takes 4 hours by** ~ sono 4 ore di macchina (or in camion etc); **on the** ~ **to success** sulla via del successo; "~ **up**" (BRIT) "attenzione: lavori in corso"

road accident N incidente m stradale

roadblock ['rəudblɔk] N blocco stradale

road haulage N autotrasporti mpl

roadhog ['rəudhɔg] N pirata m della strada

road map N carta stradale

road rage N comportamento aggressivo al volante

road safety N sicurezza sulle strade

roadside ['rəudsaɪd] N margine m della strada; **by the** ~ a lato della strada

roadsign ['rəudsaɪn] N cartello stradale

roadsweeper ['rəudswiːpə'] N (BRIT: person) spazzino

road tax N (BRIT) tassa di circolazione

road user N utente mf della strada

roadway ['rəudweɪ] N carreggiata

roadworks ['rəudwəːks] NPL lavori mpl stradali

roadworthy ['rəudwəːðɪ] ADJ in buono stato di marcia

roam [rəum] VI errare, vagabondare ▶ VT vagare per

roar [rɔː'] N ruggito; (of crowd) tumulto; (of thunder, storm) muggito; (of laughter) scoppio ▶ VI ruggire; tumultuare; muggire; **to** ~ **with laughter** scoppiare dalle risa; **to do a roaring trade** fare affari d'oro

roaring ['rɔːrɪŋ] ADJ: **a** ~ **fire** un bel fuoco; **to do a** ~ **trade** fare affari d'oro; **a** ~ **success** un successo strepitoso

roast [rəust] N arrosto ▶ VT (*meat*) arrostire; (*coffee*) tostare, torrefare

roast beef N arrosto di manzo

roasting ['rəustɪŋ] N (*col*): **to give sb a ~** dare una lavata di capo a qn

rob [rɔb] VT (*person*) rubare; (*bank*) svaligiare; **to ~ sb of sth** derubare qn di qc; (*fig: deprive*) privare qn di qc

robber ['rɔbəʳ] N ladro; (*armed*) rapinatore *m*

robbery ['rɔbərɪ] N furto; rapina

robe [rəub] N (*for ceremony etc*) abito; (*also:* **bathrobe**) accappatoio; (*US: also:* **lap robe**) coperta ▶ VT vestire

robin ['rɔbɪn] N pettirosso

robot ['rəubɔt] N robot *m inv*

robotics ['rəubɔtɪks] N robotica

robust [rəu'bʌst] ADJ robusto(-a); (*material, economy*) solido(-a)

rock [rɔk] N (*substance*) roccia; (*boulder*) masso; roccia; (*in sea*) scoglio; (*US: pebble*) ciottolo; (*BRIT: sweet*) zucchero candito ▶ VT (*swing gently: cradle*) dondolare; (*: child*) cullare; (*shake*) scrollare, far tremare ▶ VI dondolarsi; oscillare; **on the rocks** (*drink*) col ghiaccio; (*ship*) sugli scogli; (*marriage etc*) in crisi; **to ~ the boat** (*fig*) piantare grane

rock and roll N rock and roll *m*

rock-bottom ['rɔk'bɔtəm] N (*fig*) stremo; **to reach** *or* **touch ~** (*price*) raggiungere il livello più basso; (*person*) toccare il fondo

rock climber N rocciatore(-trice), scalatore(-trice)

rock climbing N roccia

rockery ['rɔkərɪ] N giardino roccioso

rocket ['rɔkɪt] N razzo; (*Mil*) razzo, missile *m* ▶ VI (*prices*) salire alle stelle

rocket launcher [-lɔːntʃəʳ] N lanciarazzi *m inv*

rock face N parete *f* della roccia

rock fall N caduta di massi

rocking chair ['rɔkɪŋ-] N sedia a dondolo

rocking horse N cavallo a dondolo

rocky ['rɔkɪ] ADJ (*hill*) roccioso(-a); (*path*) sassoso(-a); (*unsteady: table*) traballante; (*: marriage etc*) instabile

Rocky Mountains NPL: **the ~** le Montagne Rocciose

rod [rɔd] N (*metallic, Tech*) asta; (*wooden*) bacchetta; (*also:* **fishing rod**) canna da pesca

rode [rəud] PT *of* **ride**

rodent ['rəudnt] N roditore *m*

rodeo ['rəudɪəu] N rodeo

roe [rəu] N (*species: also:* **roe deer**) capriolo; (*of fish: also:* **hard roe**) uova *fpl* di pesce; **soft ~** latte *m* di pesce

roe deer N (*species*) capriolo; (*female deer: pl inv*) capriolo femmina

rogue [rəug] N mascalzone *m*

roguish ['rəugɪʃ] ADJ birbantesco(-a)

role [rəul] N ruolo

role model N modello (di comportamento)

role-play ['rəulpleɪ], **role-playing** ['rəulpleɪɪŋ] N il recitare un ruolo, role-playing *m inv*

roll [rəul] N rotolo; (*of banknotes*) mazzo; (*also:* **bread roll**) panino; (*register*) lista; (*sound, of drums etc*) rullo; (*movement, of ship*) rullio ▶ VT rotolare; (*also:* **roll up**: *string*) aggomitolare; (*: sleeves*) rimboccare; (*cigarettes*) arrotolare; (*eyes*) roteare; (*pastry: also:* **roll out**) stendere; (*lawn, road etc*) spianare ▶ VI rotolare; (*wheel*) girare; (*drum*) rullare; (*vehicle: also:* **roll along**) avanzare; (*ship*) rollare; **cheese ~** panino al formaggio

▶ **roll about, roll around** VI rotolare qua e là; (*person*) rotolarsi

▶ **roll by** VI (*time*) passare

▶ **roll in** VI (*mail, cash*) arrivare a bizzeffe

▶ **roll over** VI rivoltarsi

▶ **roll up** VI (*col: arrive*) arrivare ▶ VT (*carpet, cloth, map*) arrotolare; (*sleeves*) rimboccare; **to ~ o.s. up into a ball** raggomitolarsi

roll call N appello

rolled gold [rəuld-] ADJ d'oro laminato

roller ['rəuləʳ] N rullo; (*wheel*) rotella; (*for hair*) bigodino

rollerblades® ['rəuləbleɪdz] NPL pattini *mpl* in linea

roller blind N (*BRIT*) avvolgibile *m*

roller coaster [-'kəustəʳ] N montagne *fpl* russe

roller skates NPL pattini *mpl* a rotelle

roller-skating N pattinaggio a rotelle; **to go ~** andare a pattinare (*con i pattini a rotelle*)

rollicking ['rɔlɪkɪŋ] ADJ allegro(-a) e chiassoso(-a); **to have a ~ time** divertirsi pazzamente

rolling ['rəulɪŋ] ADJ (*landscape*) ondulato(-a)

rolling mill N fabbrica di laminati

rolling pin N matterello

rolling stock N (*Rail*) materiale *m* rotabile

roll-on-roll-off ['rəulɔn'rəulɔf] ADJ (*BRIT: ferry*) roll-on roll-off *inv*

roly-poly ['rəulɪ'pəulɪ] N (*BRIT Culin*) rotolo di pasta con ripieno di marmellata

ROM [rɔm] N ABBR (*Comput: = read-only memory*) ROM *f*

Roman ['rəumən] ADJ, N romano(-a)

Roman Catholic ADJ, N cattolico(-a)

romance [rə'mæns] N storia (*or* avventura *or* film *m inv*) romantico(-a); (*charm*) poesia; (*love affair*) idillio

Romanesque [rəumə'nɛsk] ADJ romanico(-a)

Romania [rəu'meɪnɪə] N Romania

Romanian [rəu'meɪnɪən] ADJ romeno(-a) ▶ N romeno(-a); (*Ling*) romeno

Roman numeral N numero romano

romantic [rə'mæntɪk] ADJ romantico(-a); sentimentale

romanticism [rə'mæntɪsɪzəm] N romanticismo

Romany ['rɔmənɪ] ADJ zingaresco(-a) ▶ N (person) zingaro(-a); (Ling) lingua degli zingari

Rome [rəum] N Roma

romp [rɔmp] N gioco chiassoso ▶ VI (also: **romp about**) giocare chiassosamente; **to ~ home** (horse) vincere senza difficoltà, stravincere

rompers ['rɔmpəz] NPL pagliaccetto

rondo ['rɔndəu] N (Mus) rondò m inv

roof [ru:f] N tetto; (of tunnel, cave) volta ▶ VT coprire (con un tetto); **~ of the mouth** palato

roof garden N giardino pensile

roofing ['ru:fɪŋ] N materiale m per copertura

roof rack N (Aut) portabagagli m inv

rook [ruk] N (bird) corvo nero; (Chess) torre f ▶ VT (cheat) truffare, spennare

rookie ['rukɪ] N (col: esp Mil) pivellino(-a)

room [ru:m] N (in house) stanza; (bedroom, in hotel) camera; (in school etc) sala; (space) posto, spazio; **rooms** NPL (lodging) alloggio; **"rooms to let"**, (US) **"rooms for rent"** "si affittano camere"; **is there ~ for this?** c'è spazio per questo?, ci sta anche questo?; **to make ~ for sb** far posto a qn; **there is ~ for improvement** si potrebbe migliorare

rooming house ['ru:mɪŋ-] N (US) casa in cui si affittano camere o appartamenti ammobiliati

roommate ['ru:mmeɪt] N compagno(-a) di stanza

room service N servizio da camera

room temperature N temperatura ambiente

roomy ['ru:mɪ] ADJ spazioso(-a); (garment) ampio(-a)

roost [ru:st] N appollaiato ▶ VI appollaiarsi

rooster ['ru:stər] N gallo

root [ru:t] N radice f ▶ VI (plant, belief) attecchire ▶ VT (plant, belief) far radicare; **to take ~** (plant) attecchire, prendere; (idea) far presa; **the ~ of the problem is that ...** il problema deriva dal fatto che ...
  ▶ **root about** VI (fig) frugare
  ▶ **root for** VT FUS (col) fare il tifo per
  ▶ **root out** VT estirpare

root beer N (US) bibita dolce a base di estratti di erbe e radici

rope [rəup] N corda, fune f; (Naut) cavo ▶ VT (box) legare; (climbers) legare in cordata; **to ~ sb in** (fig) coinvolgere qn; **to know the ropes** (fig) conoscere i trucchi del mestiere

rope ladder N scala di corda

ropey ['rəupɪ] ADJ (col) scadente, da quattro soldi; **to feel ~** (ill) sentirsi male

rort [rɔ:t] N (Australia, New Zealand col) truffa ▶ VT fregare

rosary ['rəuzərɪ] N rosario; roseto

rose [rəuz] PT of **rise** ▶ N rosa; (also: **rose bush**) rosaio; (: on watering can) rosetta ▶ ADJ rosa inv

rosé ['rəuzeɪ] N vino rosato

rosebed ['rəuzbɛd] N roseto

rosebud ['rəuzbʌd] N bocciolo di rosa

rosebush ['rəuzbuʃ] N rosaio

rosemary ['rəuzmərɪ] N rosmarino

rosette [rəu'zɛt] N coccarda

ROSPA ['rɔspə] N ABBR (Brit: = Royal Society for the Prevention of Accidents) ≈ E.N.P.I. m (= Ente Nazionale Prevenzione Infortuni)

roster ['rɔstər] N: **duty ~** ruolino di servizio

rostrum ['rɔstrəm] N tribuna

rosy ['rəuzɪ] ADJ roseo(-a)

rot [rɔt] N (decay) putrefazione f; (col: nonsense) stupidaggini fpl ▶ VT, VI imputridire, marcire; **dry/wet ~** funghi parassiti del legno; **to stop the ~** (Brit fig) salvare la situazione

rota ['rəutə] N tabella dei turni; **on a ~ basis** a turno

rotary ['rəutərɪ] ADJ rotante

rotate [rəu'teɪt] VT (revolve) far girare; (change round: jobs) fare a turno; (: crops) avvicendare ▶ VI (revolve) girare

rotating [rəu'teɪtɪŋ] ADJ (movement) rotante

rotation [rəu'teɪʃən] N rotazione f; **in ~** a turno, in rotazione

rote [rəut] N: **to learn sth by ~** imparare qc a memoria

rotor ['rəutər] N rotore m

rotten ['rɔtn] ADJ (decayed) putrido(-a), marcio(-a); (: teeth) cariato(-a); (dishonest) corrotto(-a); (col: bad) brutto(-a); (: action) vigliacco(-a); **to feel ~** (ill) sentirsi a pezzi

rotting ['rɔtɪŋ] ADJ in putrefazione

rotund [rəu'tʌnd] ADJ grassoccio(-a); tondo(-a)

rouble, (US) **ruble** ['ru:bl] N rublo

rouge [ru:ʒ] N belletto

rough [rʌf] ADJ (skin, surface) ruvido(-a); (terrain, road) accidentato(-a); (voice) rauco(-a); (person, manner: coarse) rozzo(-a), aspro(-a); (: violent) brutale; (district) malfamato(-a); (weather) cattivo(-a); (sea) mosso(-a); (plan) abbozzato(-a); (guess) approssimativo(-a) ▶ N (Golf) macchia; **~ estimate** approssimazione f; **to ~ it** far vita dura; **to play ~** far il gioco pesante; **to sleep ~** (Brit) dormire all'addiaccio; **to feel ~** (Brit) sentirsi male; **to have a ~ time (of it)** passare un periodaccio; **the sea is ~ today** c'è mare grosso oggi
  ▶ **rough out** VT (draft) abbozzare

roughage ['rʌfɪdʒ] N alimenti mpl ricchi di cellulosa

rough-and-ready ['rʌfən'rɛdɪ] ADJ rudimentale

rough-and-tumble ['rʌfən'tʌmbl] N zuffa

roughcast ['rʌfkɑːst] N intonaco grezzo

rough copy, rough draft N brutta copia

roughen ['rʌfn] VT (a surface) rendere ruvido(-a)

rough justice N giustizia sommaria

roughly ['rʌflɪ] ADV (handle) rudemente, brutalmente; (make) grossolanamente; (speak) bruscamente; (approximately) approssimativamente; ~ **speaking** grosso modo, ad occhio e croce

roughness ['rʌfnɪs] N asprezza; rozzezza; brutalità

roughshod ['rʌfʃɔd] ADV: **to ride ~ over** (person) mettere sotto i piedi; (objection) passare sopra a

rough work N (at school etc) brutta copia

roulette [ruː'lɛt] N roulette f

Roumania etc [ruː'meɪnɪə] = **Romania** etc

round [raund] ADJ rotondo(-a) ▶ N tondo, cerchio; (BRIT: of toast) fetta; (duty: of policeman, milkman etc) giro; (: of doctor) visite fpl; (game: of cards, golf, in competition) partita; (Boxing) round m inv; (of talks) serie f inv ▶ VT (corner) girare; (bend) prendere; (cape) doppiare ▶ PREP intorno a ▶ ADV: **right ~, all ~** tutt'attorno; **the long way ~** il giro più lungo; **all the year ~** tutto l'anno; **in ~ figures** in cifra tonda; **it's just ~ the corner** (also fig) è dietro l'angolo; **to ask sb ~** invitare qn (a casa propria); **I'll be ~ at 6 o'clock** ci sarò alle 6; **to go ~** fare il giro; **to go ~ to sb's (house)** andare da qn; **to go ~ an obstacle** aggirare un ostacolo; **go ~ the back** passi da dietro; **to go ~ a house** visitare una casa; **enough to go ~** abbastanza per tutti; **she arrived ~ (about) noon** è arrivata intorno a mezzogiorno; **~ the clock** 24 ore su 24, ininterrottamente; **to go the rounds** (illness) diffondersi; (story) circolare, passare di bocca in bocca; **the daily ~** (fig) la routine quotidiana; **~ of ammunition** cartuccia; **~ of applause** applausi mpl; **~ of drinks** giro di bibite; **~ of sandwiches** (BRIT) sandwich m inv

▶ **round off** VT (speech etc) finire

▶ **round up** VT radunare; (criminals) fare una retata di; (prices) arrotondare

roundabout ['raundəbaut] N (BRIT: Aut) rotatoria; (: at fair) giostra ▶ ADJ (route, means) indiretto(-a)

rounded ['raundɪd] ADJ arrotondato(-a); (style) armonioso(-a)

rounders ['raundəz] NPL (game) gioco simile al baseball

roundly ['raundlɪ] ADV (fig) chiaro e tondo

round robin N (Sport: also: **round robin**

tournament) ≈ torneo all'italiana

round-shouldered [raund'ʃəuldəd] ADJ dalle spalle tonde

round trip N (viaggio di) andata e ritorno

roundup ['raundʌp] N raduno; (of criminals) retata; **a ~ of the latest news** un sommario or riepilogo delle ultime notizie

rouse [rauz] VT (wake up) svegliare; (stir up) destare; provocare; risvegliare

rousing ['rauzɪŋ] ADJ (speech, applause) entusiastico(-a)

rout [raut] N (Mil) rotta ▶ VT mettere in rotta

route² [ruːt] N itinerario; (of bus) percorso; (of trade, shipping) rotta; **"all routes"** (Aut) "tutte le direzioni"; **the best ~ to London** la strada migliore per andare a Londra; **en ~ for** in viaggio verso; **en ~ from ... to** viaggiando da ... a

route map N (BRIT: for journey) cartina di itinerario; (for trains etc) pianta dei collegamenti

routine [ruː'tiːn] ADJ (work) corrente, abituale; (procedure) solito(-a) ▶ N (pej) routine f, tran tran m; (Theat) numero; (Comput) sottoprogramma m; **daily ~** orario quotidiano; **~ procedure** prassi f

roving ['rəuvɪŋ] ADJ (life) itinerante

roving reporter N reporter m inv volante

row¹ [rəu] N (line) riga, fila; (Knitting) ferro; (behind one another: of cars, people) fila; (in boat) remata ▶ VI (in boat) remare; (as sport) vogare ▶ VT (boat) manovrare a remi; **in a ~** (fig) in fila

row² [rau] N (noise) baccano, chiasso; (dispute) lite f; (scolding) sgridata ▶ VI (argue) litigare; **to make a ~** far baccano; **to have a ~** litigare

rowboat ['rəubəut] N (US) barca a remi

rowdiness ['raudɪnɪs] N baccano; (fighting) zuffa

rowdy ['raudɪ] ADJ chiassoso(-a), turbolento(-a) ▶ N teppista mf

rowdyism ['raudɪɪzəm] N teppismo

rowing ['rəuɪŋ] N canottaggio

rowing boat N (BRIT) barca a remi

rowlock ['rɔlək] N scalmo

royal ['rɔɪəl] ADJ reale

Royal Academy N (BRIT); vedi nota

L'Accademia Reale d'Arte britannica, Royal Academy (of the Arts), è un'istituzione fondata nel 1768 al fine di incoraggiare la pittura, la scultura e l'architettura. Ogni anno organizza una mostra estiva d'arte contemporanea.

Royal Air Force N (BRIT) aeronautica militare britannica

royal blue ADJ blu reale inv

royalist ['rɔɪəlɪst] ADJ, N realista mf

Royal Navy N (BRIT) marina militare britannica

royalty ['rɔɪəltɪ] N (royal persons) (membri mpl della) famiglia reale; (payment: to author)

r

diritti mpl d'autore; (: *to inventor*) diritti di brevetto

RP N ABBR (BRIT: = *received pronunciation*) pronuncia standard

RPI ABBR (BRIT) = **retail price index**

rpm ABBR (= *revolutions per minute*) giri/min

RR ABBR (US: = *railroad*) Ferr

RRP N ABBR (BRIT) = **recommended retail price**

RSA N ABBR (BRIT) = **Royal Society of Arts**; **Royal Scottish Academy**

RSI N ABBR (Med: = *repetitive strain injury*) lesione al braccio tipica di violinisti e terminalisti

RSPB N ABBR (BRIT: = *Royal Society for the Protection of Birds*) ≈ L.I.P.U. f (= *Lega Italiana Protezione Uccelli*)

RSPCA N ABBR (BRIT: = *Royal Society for the Prevention of Cruelty to Animals*) ≈ E.N.P.A. m (= *Ente Nazionale per la Protezione degli Animali*)

RSVP ABBR (= *répondez s'il vous plaît*) R.S.V.P.

RTA N ABBR (= *road traffic accident*) incidente m stradale

Rt. Hon. ABBR (BRIT: = *Right Honourable*) ≈ On. (= *Onorevole*)

Rt Rev. ABBR (= *Right Reverend*) Rev.

rub [rʌb] N (*with cloth*) fregata, strofinata; (*on person*) frizione f, massaggio; **to give sth a ~** strofinare qc; (*sore place*) massaggiare qc ▶ VT fregare, strofinare; frizionare; massaggiare; (*hands: also*: **rub together**) sfregarsi; **to ~ sb up** *or* (US) **~ sb the wrong way** lisciare qn contro pelo

▶ **rub down** VT (*body*) strofinare, frizionare; (*horse*) strigliare

▶ **rub in** VT (*ointment*) far penetrare (massaggiando *or* frizionando)

▶ **rub off** VI andare via; **to ~ off on** lasciare una traccia su

▶ **rub out** VT cancellare ▶ VI cancellarsi

rubber ['rʌbəʳ] N gomma

rubber band N elastico

rubber bullet N pallottola di gomma

rubber gloves NPL guanti mpl di gomma

rubber plant N ficus m inv

rubber ring N (*for swimming*) ciambella

rubber stamp N timbro di gomma

rubber-stamp [rʌbə'stæmp] VT (*fig*) approvare senza discussione

rubbery ['rʌbərɪ] ADJ gommoso(-a)

rubbish ['rʌbɪʃ] N (*from household*) immondizie fpl, rifiuti mpl; (*fig, pej*) cose fpl senza valore; robaccia; (*nonsense*) sciocchezze fpl ▶ VT (*col*) sputtanare; **what you've just said is ~** quello che ha appena detto è una sciocchezza

rubbish bin N (BRIT) pattumiera

rubbish dump N discarica

rubbishy ['rʌbɪʃɪ] ADJ (BRIT col) scadente, che non vale niente

rubble ['rʌbl] N macerie fpl; (*smaller*) pietrisco

ruble ['ruːbl] N (US) = **rouble**

ruby ['ruːbɪ] N rubino

RUC N ABBR (BRIT: = *Royal Ulster Constabulary*) forza di polizia dell'Irlanda del Nord

rucksack ['rʌksæk] N zaino

ructions ['rʌkʃənz] NPL putiferio, finimondo

rudder ['rʌdəʳ] N timone m

ruddy ['rʌdɪ] ADJ (*face*) fresco(-a); (*col: damned*) maledetto(-a)

rude [ruːd] ADJ (*impolite: person*) scortese, rozzo(-a); (: *word, manners*) grossolano(-a), rozzo(-a); (*shocking*) indecente; **to be ~ to sb** essere maleducato con qn

rudely ['ruːdlɪ] ADV scortesemente; grossolanamente

rudeness ['ruːdnɪs] N scortesia; grossolanità

rudiment ['ruːdɪmənt] N rudimento

rudimentary [ruːdɪ'mɛntərɪ] ADJ rudimentale

rue [ruː] VT pentirsi amaramente di

rueful ['ruːful] ADJ mesto(-a), triste

ruff [rʌf] N gorgiera

ruffian ['rʌfɪən] N briccone m, furfante m

ruffle ['rʌfl] VT (*hair*) scompigliare; (*clothes, water*) increspare; (*fig: person*) turbare

rug [rʌg] N tappeto; (BRIT: *for knees*) coperta

rugby ['rʌgbɪ] N (*also*: **rugby football**) rugby m

rugged ['rʌgɪd] ADJ (*landscape*) aspro(-a); (*features, determination*) duro(-a); (*character*) brusco(-a)

rugger ['rʌgəʳ] N (*col*) rugby m

ruin ['ruːɪn] N rovina ▶ VT rovinare; (*spoil: clothes*) sciupare; **ruins** NPL (*of building, castle etc*) rovine fpl, ruderi mpl; **in ruins** in rovina

ruination [ruːɪ'neɪʃən] N rovina

ruinous ['ruːɪnəs] ADJ rovinoso(-a); (*expenditure*) inverosimile

rule [ruːl] N (*gen*) regola; (*regulation*) regolamento, regola; (*government*) governo; (*ruler*) riga; (*dominion etc*): **under British ~** sotto la sovranità britannica ▶ VT (*country*) governare; (*person*) dominare; (*decide*) decidere ▶ VI regnare; decidere; (Law) dichiarare; **to ~ against/in favour of/on** (Law) pronunciarsi a sfavore di/in favore di/su; **it's against the rules** è contro le regole *or* il regolamento; **by ~ of thumb** a lume di naso; **as a ~** normalmente, di regola

▶ **rule out** VT escludere; **murder cannot be ruled out** non si esclude che si tratti di omicidio

ruled [ruːld] ADJ (*paper*) vergato(-a)

ruler ['ruːləʳ] N (*sovereign*) sovrano(-a); (*leader*) capo (dello Stato); (*for measuring*) regolo, riga

ruling ['ruːlɪŋ] ADJ (*party*) al potere; (*class*) dirigente ▶ N (Law) decisione f

rum [rʌm] N rum m ▶ ADJ (BRIT col) strano(-a)

Rumania etc [ruː'meɪnɪə] = **Romania** etc

rumble ['rʌmbl] N rimbombo; brontolio ▶ VI rimbombare; (*stomach, pipe*) brontolare

rumbustious [rʌmˈbʌstʃəs] ADJ (*person*): **to be ~** essere un terremoto

rummage ['rʌmɪdʒ] VI frugare

rumour, (US) **rumor** ['ruːməʳ] N voce *f* ▶ VT: **it is rumoured that** corre voce che

rump [rʌmp] N (*of animal*) groppa

rumple ['rʌmpl] VT (*hair*) arruffare, scompigliare; (*clothes*) spiegazzare, sgualcire

rump steak [rʌmp-] N bistecca di girello

rumpus ['rʌmpəs] N (*col*) baccano; (*quarrel*) rissa; **to kick up a ~** fare un putiferio

run [rʌn] (*pt* **ran**, *pp* **~**) N corsa; (*outing*) gita (in macchina); (*distance travelled*) percorso, tragitto; (*series*) serie *f inv*; (*Theat*) periodo di rappresentazione; (*Ski*) pista; (*Cricket, Baseball*) meta; (*in tights, stockings*) smagliatura ▶ VT (*distance*) correre; (*operate: business*) gestire, dirigere; (*: competition, course*) organizzare; (*: hotel*) gestire; (*: house*) governare; (*Comput: program*) eseguire; (*water, bath*) far scorrere; (*force through*): (*rope, pipe*) **to ~ sth through** far passare qc attraverso; (*pass*): (*hand, finger*) **to ~ sth over** passare qc su; (*Press: feature*) presentare ▶ VI correre; (*flee*) scappare; (*pass: road etc*) passare; (*work: machine, factory*) funzionare, andare; (*bus, train: operate*) far servizio; (*: travel*) circolare; (*continue: play, contract*) durare; (*slide: drawer; flow: river, bath*) scorrere; (*colours, washing*) stemperarsi; (*in election*) presentarsi come candidato; (*nose*) colare; **to go for a ~** andare a correre; (*in car*) fare un giro (in macchina); **to break into a ~** mettersi a correre; **a ~ of luck** un periodo di fortuna; **to have the ~ of sb's house** essere libero di andare e venire in casa di qn; **there was a ~ on ...** c'era una corsa a ...; **in the long ~** a lungo andare; **in the short ~** sulle prime; **on the ~** in fuga; **to make a ~ for it** scappare, tagliare la corda; **to ~ a race** participare ad una gara; **I'll ~ you to the station** la porto alla stazione; **to ~ a risk** correre un rischio; **to ~ errands** andare a fare commissioni; **the train runs between Gatwick and Victoria** il treno collega Gatwick alla stazione Victoria; **the bus runs every 20 minutes** c'è un autobus ogni 20 minuti; **it's very cheap to ~** comporta poche spese; **to ~ on petrol** or (US) **gas/on diesel/off batteries** andare a benzina/a diesel/a batterie; **to ~ for the bus** fare una corsa per prendere l'autobus; **to ~ for president** presentarsi come candidato per la presidenza; **their losses ran into millions** le loro perdite hanno raggiunto i milioni; **to be ~ off one's feet** (BRIT) doversi fare in quattro

▶ **run about** VI (*children*) correre qua e là

▶ **run across** VT FUS (*find*) trovare per caso

▶ **run after** VT FUS (*to catch up*) rincorrere; (*chase*) correre dietro a

▶ **run away** VI fuggire

▶ **run down** VI (*clock*) scaricarsi ▶ VT (*Aut*) investire; (*criticize*) criticare; (BRIT: *reduce: production*) ridurre gradualmente; (*: factory, shop*) rallentare l'attività di; **to be ~ down** (*battery*) essere scarico(-a); (*person*) essere spossato(-a)

▶ **run in** VT (BRIT: *car*) rodare, fare il rodaggio di

▶ **run into** VT FUS (*meet: person*) incontrare per caso; (*: trouble*) incontrare, trovare; (*collide with*) andare a sbattere contro; **to ~ into debt** trovarsi nei debiti

▶ **run off** VI fuggire ▶ VT (*water*) far defluire; (*copies*) fare

▶ **run out** VI (*person*) uscire di corsa; (*liquid*) colare; (*lease*) scadere; (*money*) esaurirsi

▶ **run out of** VT FUS rimanere a corto di; **I've ~ out of petrol** or (US) **gas** sono rimasto senza benzina

▶ **run over** VT (*Aut*) investire, mettere sotto ▶ VT FUS (*revise*) rivedere

▶ **run through** VT FUS (*instructions*) dare una scorsa a; (*rehearse: play*) riprovare, ripetere

▶ **run up** VT (*debt*) lasciar accumulare; **to ~ up against** (*difficulties*) incontrare

runaround ['rʌnəraund] N (*col*): **to give sb the ~** far girare a vuoto qn

runaway ['rʌnəwei] ADJ (*person*) fuggiasco(-a); (*horse*) in libertà; (*truck*) fuori controllo; (*inflation*) galoppante

rundown ['rʌndaun] N (BRIT: *of industry etc*) riduzione *f* graduale dell'attività di

rung [rʌŋ] PP *of* **ring** ▶ N (*of ladder*) piolo

run-in ['rʌnɪn] N (*col*) scontro

runner ['rʌnəʳ] N (*in race*) corridore *m*; (*: horse*) partente *mf*; (*on sledge*) pattino; (*for drawer etc, carpet*) guida

runner bean N (BRIT) fagiolino

runner-up [rʌnərˈʌp] N secondo(-a) arrivato(-a)

running ['rʌnɪŋ] N corsa; direzione *f*; organizzazione *f*; funzionamento ▶ ADJ (*water*) corrente; (*commentary*) simultaneo(-a); **6 days ~** 6 giorni di seguito; **to be in/out of the ~ for sth** essere/non essere più in lizza per qc

running costs NPL (*of business*) costi *mpl* d'esercizio; (*of car*) spese *fpl* di mantenimento

running head N (*Typ*) testata, titolo corrente

running mate N (US Pol) candidato alla vicepresidenza

runny ['rʌnɪ] ADJ che cola

run-off ['rʌnɔf] N (*in contest, election*) confronto

definitivo; (*extra race*) spareggio

run-of-the-mill ['rʌnəvðə'mɪl] ADJ solito(-a), banale

runt [rʌnt] N omuncolo; (*Zool*) animale *m* più piccolo del normale

run-through ['rʌnθru:] N prova

run-up ['rʌnʌp] N (*BRIT*): ~ **to sth** (*election etc*) periodo che precede qc

runway ['rʌnweɪ] N (*Aviat*) pista (di decollo)

rupture ['rʌptʃər] N (*Med*) ernia ▶ VT: **to ~ o.s.** farsi venire un'ernia

rural ['ruərl] ADJ rurale

rural district council N (*BRIT*) consiglio (amministrativo) di distretto rurale

ruse [ru:z] N trucco

rush [rʌʃ] N corsa precipitosa; (*of crowd*) afflusso; (*hurry*) furia, fretta; (*of emotion*) impeto; (*Bot*) giunco; (*sudden demand*): ~ **for** corsa a; (*current*) flusso ▶ VT mandare *or* spedire velocemente; (*attack: town etc*) prendere d'assalto ▶ VI precipitarsi; **is there any ~ for this?** è urgente?; **we've had a ~ of orders** abbiamo avuto una valanga di ordinazioni; **I'm in a ~ (to do)** ho fretta *or* premura (di fare); **gold ~** corsa all'oro; **to ~ sth off** spedire con urgenza qc; **don't ~ me!** non farmi fretta!

▶ **rush through** VT (*meal*) mangiare in fretta; (*book*) dare una scorsa frettolosa a; (*town*) attraversare in fretta; (*Comm: order*) eseguire d'urgenza ▶ VT FUS (*work*) sbrigare frettolosamente

rush hour N ora di punta

rush job N (*urgent*) lavoro urgente

rush matting N stuoia

rusk [rʌsk] N fetta biscottata

Russia ['rʌʃə] N Russia

Russian ['rʌʃən] ADJ russo(-a) ▶ N russo(-a); (*Ling*) russo

rust [rʌst] N ruggine *f* ▶ VI arrugginirsi

rustic ['rʌstɪk] ADJ rustico(-a) ▶ N (*pej*) cafone(-a)

rustle ['rʌsl] VI frusciare ▶ VT (*paper*) far frusciare; (*US: cattle*) rubare

rustproof ['rʌstpru:f] ADJ inossidabile

rustproofing ['rʌstpru:fɪŋ] N trattamento antiruggine

rusty ['rʌstɪ] ADJ arrugginito(-a)

rut [rʌt] N solco; (*Zool*) fregola; **to be in a ~** (*fig*) essersi fossilizzato(-a)

rutabaga [ru:tə'beɪgə] N (*US*) rapa svedese

ruthless ['ru:θlɪs] ADJ spietato(-a)

ruthlessness ['ru:θlɪsnɪs] N spietatezza

RV ABBR (= *revised version*) *versione riveduta della Bibbia* ▶ N ABBR (*US*) = **recreational vehicle**

rye [raɪ] N segale *f*

Ss

S, s [ɛs] N (letter) S, s f inv or m inv; (US Scol:
= satisfactory) = sufficiente; **S for Sugar** ≈ S
come Savona
S ABBR (= saint) S.; (on clothes) = **small**; (= south) S
SA ABBR = **South Africa; South America**
Sabbath ['sæbəθ] N (Jewish) sabato; (Christian)
domenica
sabbatical [sə'bætɪkl] ADJ: **~ year** anno
sabbatico
sabotage ['sæbətɑːʒ] N sabotaggio ▶ VT
sabotare
saccharin, saccharine ['sækərɪn] N
saccarina
sachet ['sæʃeɪ] N bustina
sack [sæk] N (bag) sacco ▶ VT (dismiss)
licenziare, mandare a spasso; (plunder)
saccheggiare; **to get the ~** essere mandato
a spasso; **to give sb the ~** licenziare qn,
mandare qn a spasso
sackful ['sækful] N: **a ~ of** un sacco di
sacking ['sækɪŋ] N tela di sacco; (dismissal)
licenziamento
sacrament ['sækrəmənt] N sacramento
sacred ['seɪkrɪd] ADJ sacro(-a)
sacred cow N (fig: person) intoccabile mf;
(: institution) caposaldo; (: idea, belief) dogma m
sacrifice ['sækrɪfaɪs] N sacrificio ▶ VT
sacrificare; **to make sacrifices (for sb)** fare
(dei) sacrifici (per qn)
sacrilege ['sækrɪlɪdʒ] N sacrilegio
sacrosanct ['sækrəusæŋkt] ADJ sacrosanto(-a)
sad [sæd] ADJ triste; (deplorable) deplorevole
sadden ['sædn] VT rattristare
saddle ['sædl] N sella ▶ VT (horse) sellare;
to be saddled with sth (col) avere qc sulle
spalle
saddlebag ['sædlbæg] N bisaccia; (on bicycle)
borsa
sadism ['seɪdɪzəm] N sadismo
sadist ['seɪdɪst] N sadico(-a)
sadistic [sə'dɪstɪk] ADJ sadico(-a)
sadly ['sædlɪ] ADV tristemente; (regrettably)
sfortunatamente; **~ lacking in**
penosamente privo di

sadness ['sædnɪs] N tristezza
sadomasochism [seɪdəu'mæsəkɪzəm] N
sadomasochismo
sae ABBR (BRIT: = stamped addressed envelope)
busta affrancata e con indirizzo
safari [sə'fɑːrɪ] N safari m inv
safari park N zoosafari m inv
safe [seɪf] ADJ sicuro(-a); (out of danger)
salvo(-a), al sicuro; (cautious) prudente
▶ N cassaforte f; **~ from** al sicuro da; **~ and
sound** sano(-a) e salvo(-a); **~ journey!** buon
viaggio!; **(just) to be on the ~ side** per non
correre rischi; **to play ~** giocare sul sicuro;
it is ~ to say that ... si può affermare con
sicurezza che ...
safe bet N: **it's a ~** è una cosa sicura
safe-breaker ['seɪfbreɪkər] N (BRIT)
scassinatore m
safe-conduct [seɪf'kɒndʌkt] N
salvacondotto
safe-cracker ['seɪfkrækər] N = **safe-breaker**
safe-deposit ['seɪfdɪpɒzɪt] N (vault) caveau
m inv; (box) cassetta di sicurezza
safeguard ['seɪfgɑːd] N salvaguardia ▶ VT
salvaguardare
safe haven N zona sicura or protetta
safekeeping ['seɪf'kiːpɪŋ] N custodia
safely ['seɪflɪ] ADV sicuramente; sano(-a) e
salvo(-a) prudentemente; prudentemente;
I can ~ say ... posso tranquillamente
asserire ...
safe passage N passaggio sicuro
safe sex N sesso sicuro
safety ['seɪftɪ] N sicurezza; **~ first!** la
prudenza innanzitutto!
safety belt N cintura di sicurezza
safety catch N sicura
safety net N rete f di protezione
safety pin N spilla di sicurezza
safety valve N valvola di sicurezza
saffron ['sæfrən] N zafferano
sag [sæg] VI incurvarsi; afflosciarsi
saga ['sɑːgə] N saga; (fig) odissea
sage [seɪdʒ] N (herb) salvia; (man) saggio

S

Sagittarius [sædʒɪ'tɛərɪəs] N Sagittario; **to be** ~ essere del Sagittario

sago ['seɪgəʊ] N sagù m

Sahara [sə'hɑ:rə] N: **the ~ Desert** il Deserto del Sahara

Sahel [sæ'hɛl] N Sahel m

said [sɛd] PT, PP of **say**

Saigon [saɪ'gɔn] N Saigon f

sail [seɪl] N (on boat) vela; (trip): **to go for a ~** fare un giro in barca a vela ▸ VT (boat) condurre, governare ▸ VI (travel: ship) navigare; (: passenger) viaggiare per mare; (set off) salpare; (Sport) fare della vela; **they sailed into Genoa** entrarono nel porto di Genova
  ▸ **sail through** VT FUS (fig) superare senza difficoltà ▸ VI farcela senza difficoltà

sailboat ['seɪlbəʊt] N (US) barca a vela

sailing ['seɪlɪŋ] N (sport) vela; **to go ~** fare della vela

sailing boat N barca a vela

sailing ship N veliero

sailor ['seɪlə^r] N marinaio

saint [seɪnt] N santo(-a)

saintly ['seɪntlɪ] ADJ da santo(-a); santo(-a)

sake [seɪk] N: **for the ~ of** per, per amore di; **for pity's ~** per pietà; **for the ~ of argument** tanto per fare un esempio; **art for art's** ~ l'arte per l'arte

salad ['sæləd] N insalata; **tomato ~** insalata di pomodori

salad bowl N insalatiera

salad cream N (BRIT) (tipo di) maionese f

salad dressing N condimento per insalata

salad oil N olio da tavola

salami [sə'lɑ:mɪ] N salame m

salaried ['sælərɪd] ADJ stipendiato(-a)

salary ['sælərɪ] N stipendio

salary scale N scala dei salari

sale [seɪl] N vendita; (at reduced prices) svendita, liquidazione f; (auction) vendita all'asta; **sales** NPL (total amount sold) vendite fpl; **"for ~"** "in vendita"; **on ~** in vendita; **on ~ or return** da vendere o rimandare; **a closing-down** or (US) **liquidation ~** una liquidazione; ~ **and lease back** n lease back m inv

saleroom ['seɪlrʊm] N sala delle aste

sales assistant, (US) **sales clerk** N commesso(-a)

sales clerk N (US) commesso(-a)

sales conference N riunione f marketing e vendite

sales drive N campagna di vendita, sforzo promozionale

sales force N personale m addetto alle vendite

salesman ['seɪlzmən] N (irreg) commesso; (representative) rappresentante m

sales manager N direttore m commerciale

salesmanship ['seɪlzmənʃɪp] N arte f del vendere

salesperson N (irreg) (in shop) commesso(-a); (representative) rappresentante mf di commercio

sales rep N rappresentante mf di commercio

sales tax N (US) imposta sulle vendite

saleswoman ['seɪlzwʊmən] N (irreg) commessa; (representative) rappresentante f

salient ['seɪlɪənt] ADJ saliente

saline ['seɪlaɪn] ADJ salino(-a)

saliva [sə'laɪvə] N saliva

sallow ['sæləʊ] ADJ giallastro(-a)

sally forth, sally out ['sælɪ-] VI uscire di gran carriera

salmon ['sæmən] N (pl inv) salmone m

salmon trout N trota (di mare)

salon ['sælɔn] N (hairdressing salon) parrucchiere(-a); (beauty salon) salone m di bellezza

saloon [sə'lu:n] N (US) saloon m inv, bar m inv; (BRIT Aut) berlina; (ship's lounge) salone m

SALT [sɔ:lt] N ABBR (= Strategic Arms Limitation Talks/Treaty) S.A.L.T. m

salt [sɔ:lt] N sale m ▸ VT salare ▸ CPD di sale; (Culin) salato(-a); **an old ~** un lupo di mare
  ▸ **salt away** VT ammucchiare, mettere via

salt cellar N saliera

salt-free ['sɔ:lt'fri:] ADJ senza sale

saltwater ['sɔ:ltwɔ:tə^r] ADJ (fish etc) di mare

salty ['sɔ:ltɪ] ADJ salato(-a)

salubrious [sə'lu:brɪəs] ADJ salubre; (fig: district etc) raccomandabile

salutary ['sæljutərɪ] ADJ salutare

salute [sə'lu:t] N saluto ▸ VT salutare

salvage ['sælvɪdʒ] N (saving) salvataggio; (things saved) beni mpl salvati or recuperati ▸ VT salvare, mettere in salvo

salvage vessel N scialuppa di salvataggio

salvation [sæl'veɪʃən] N salvezza

Salvation Army [sæl'veɪʃən-] N Esercito della Salvezza

salver ['sælvə^r] N vassoio

salvo, salvoes ['sælvəʊ] N salva

Samaritan [sə'mærɪtən] N: **the Samaritans** (organization) ≈ telefono amico

same [seɪm] ADJ stesso(-a), medesimo(-a) ▸ PRON: **the ~** lo (la) stesso(-a), gli (le) stessi(-e); **the ~ book as** lo stesso libro di (or che); **on the ~ day** lo stesso giorno; **at the ~ time** allo stesso tempo; **all** or **just the ~** tuttavia; **to do the ~** fare la stessa cosa; **to do the ~ as sb** fare come qn; **the ~ again** (in bar etc) un altro; **they're one and the ~** (person/thing) sono la stessa persona/cosa; **and the ~ to you!** altrettanto a lei!; ~ **here!** anch'io!

sample ['sɑ:mpl] N campione m ▸ VT (food) assaggiare; (wine) degustare; **to take a ~**

prelevare un campione; **free** ~ campione omaggio

sanatorium [sænəˈtɔːrɪəm] (pl **sanatoria** [-rɪə]) N sanatorio

sanctify [ˈsæŋktɪfaɪ] VT santificare

sanctimonious [sæŋktɪˈməʊnɪəs] ADJ bigotto(-a), bacchettone(-a)

sanction [ˈsæŋkʃən] N sanzione f ▶ VT sancire, sanzionare; **sanctions** NPL (Pol) sanzioni fpl; **to impose economic sanctions on** or **against** adottare sanzioni economiche contro

sanctity [ˈsæŋktɪtɪ] N santità

sanctuary [ˈsæŋktjʊərɪ] N (holy place) santuario; (refuge) rifugio; (for wildlife) riserva

sand [sænd] N sabbia ▶ VT cospargere di sabbia; (also: **sand down**: wood etc) cartavetrare; see also **sands**

sandal [ˈsændl] N sandalo

sandbag [ˈsændbæg] N sacco di sabbia

sandblast [ˈsændblɑːst] VT sabbiare

sandbox [ˈsændbɒks] N (US: for children) buca di sabbia

sandcastle [ˈsændkɑːsl] N castello di sabbia

sand dune N duna di sabbia

sander [ˈsændər] N levigatrice f

sandpaper [ˈsændpeɪpər] N carta vetrata

sandpit [ˈsændpɪt] N (BRIT: for children) buca di sabbia

sands [sændz] NPL spiaggia

sandstone [ˈsændstəʊn] N arenaria

sandstorm [ˈsændstɔːm] N tempesta di sabbia

sandwich [ˈsændwɪtʃ] N tramezzino, panino, sandwich m inv ▶ VT (also: **sandwich in**) infilare; **cheese/ham** ~ sandwich al formaggio/prosciutto; **to be sandwiched between** essere incastrato(-a) fra

sandwich board N cartello pubblicitario (portato da un uomo sandwich)

sandwich course N (BRIT) corso di formazione professionale

sandwich man N uomo m sandwich inv

sandy [ˈsændɪ] ADJ sabbioso(-a); (colour) color sabbia inv, biondo(-a) rossiccio(-a)

sane [seɪn] ADJ (person) sano(-a) di mente; (outlook) sensato(-a)

sang [sæŋ] PT of **sing**

sanguine [ˈsæŋgwɪn] ADJ ottimista

sanitarium [sænɪˈtɛərɪəm] (pl **sanitaria** [-rɪə]) N (US) = **sanatorium**

sanitary [ˈsænɪtərɪ] ADJ (system, arrangements) sanitario(-a); (clean) igienico(-a)

sanitary towel [ˈsænɪtərɪ-], (US) **sanitary napkin** N assorbente m (igienico)

sanitation [sænɪˈteɪʃən] N (in house) impianti mpl sanitari; (in town) fognature fpl

sanitation department N (US) nettezza urbana

sanity [ˈsænɪtɪ] N sanità mentale; (common sense) buon senso

sank [sæŋk] PT of **sink**

San Marino [sænməˈriːnəʊ] N San Marino f

Santa Claus [sæntəˈklɔːz] N Babbo Natale

Santiago [sæntɪˈɑːgəʊ] N (also: **Santiago de Chile**) Santiago (del Cile) f

sap [sæp] N (of plants) linfa ▶ VT (strength) fiaccare

sapling [ˈsæplɪŋ] N alberello

sapphire [ˈsæfaɪər] N zaffiro

sarcasm [ˈsɑːkæzm] N sarcasmo

sarcastic [sɑːˈkæstɪk] ADJ sarcastico(-a); **to be** ~ fare del sarcasmo

sarcophagus [sɑːˈkɒfəgəs] (pl **sarcophagi** [-gaɪ]) N sarcofago

sardine [sɑːˈdiːn] N sardina

Sardinia [sɑːˈdɪnɪə] N Sardegna

Sardinian [sɑːˈdɪnɪən] ADJ, N sardo(-a)

sardonic [sɑːˈdɒnɪk] ADJ sardonico(-a)

sari [ˈsɑːrɪ] N sari m inv

SARS [sɑːz] N ABBR (= severe acute respiratory syndrome) SARS f, polmonite atipica

sartorial [sɑːˈtɔːrɪəl] ADJ di sartoria

SAS N ABBR (BRIT Mil: = Special Air Service) reparto dell'esercito britannico specializzato in operazioni clandestine

SASE N ABBR (US: = self-addressed stamped envelope) busta affrancata e con indirizzo

sash [sæʃ] N fascia

sash window N finestra a ghigliottina

Sask. ABBR (CANADA) = **Saskatchewan**

SAT N ABBR (US) = **Scholastic Aptitude Test**

sat [sæt] PT, PP of **sit**

Sat. ABBR (= Saturday) sab.

Satan [ˈseɪtən] N Satana m

satanic [səˈtænɪk] ADJ satanico(-a)

satchel [ˈsætʃl] N cartella

sated [ˈseɪtɪd] ADJ soddisfatto(-a); sazio(-a)

satellite [ˈsætəlaɪt] ADJ, N satellite m

satellite dish N antenna parabolica

satellite television N televisione f via satellite

satiate [ˈseɪʃɪeɪt] VT saziare

satin [ˈsætɪn] N raso, satin m ▶ ADJ di or in raso, di or in satin; **with a** ~ **finish** satinato(-a)

satire [ˈsætaɪər] N satira

satirical [səˈtɪrɪkl] ADJ satirico(-a)

satirist [ˈsætərɪst] N (writer etc) scrittore(-trice) etc satirico(-a); (cartoonist) caricaturista mf

satirize [ˈsætɪraɪz] VT satireggiare

satisfaction [sætɪsˈfækʃən] N soddisfazione f; **has it been done to your** ~? ne è rimasto soddisfatto?

satisfactory [sætɪsˈfæktərɪ] ADJ soddisfacente

satisfied [ˈsætɪsfaɪd] ADJ (customer)

S

soddisfatto(-a); **to be ~ (with sth)** essere soddisfatto(-a) (di qc)

satisfy ['sætɪsfaɪ] VT soddisfare; (convince) convincere; **to ~ the requirements** rispondere ai requisiti; **to ~ sb (that)** convincere qn (che), persuadere qn (che); **to ~ o.s. of sth** accertarsi di qc

satisfying ['sætɪsfaɪɪŋ] ADJ soddisfacente

satnav ['sætnæv] N ABBR (= satellite navigation) navigatore m satellitare

SATs N ABBR (BRIT: = standard assessment tasks or tests) esame di fine anno sostenuto dagli allievi delle scuole pubbliche inglesi a 7, 11 o 14 anni

satsuma [sæt'suːmə] N agrume di provenienza giapponese

saturate ['sætʃəreɪt] VT: **to ~ (with)** saturare (di)

saturated fat ['sætʃəreɪtɪd-] N grassi mpl saturi

saturation [sætʃə'reɪʃən] N saturazione f

Saturday ['sætədɪ] N sabato; see also **Tuesday**

sauce [sɔːs] N salsa; (containing meat, fish) sugo

saucepan ['sɔːspən] N casseruola

saucer ['sɔːsər] N sottocoppa m, piattino

saucy ['sɔːsɪ] ADJ impertinente

Saudi ['saʊdɪ], **Saudi Arabian** ['saʊdɪ-] ADJ, N saudita mf

Saudi Arabia ['saʊdɪ-] N Arabia Saudita

sauna ['sɔːnə] N sauna

saunter ['sɔːntər] VI andare a zonzo, bighellonare

sausage ['sɒsɪdʒ] N salsiccia; (salami etc) salame m

sausage roll N rotolo di pasta sfoglia ripieno di salsiccia

sauté ['səʊteɪ] ADJ (Culin: potatoes) saltato(-a); (: onions) soffritto(-a) ▶ VT far saltare; far soffriggere

sautéed ['səʊteɪd] ADJ saltato(-a)

savage ['sævɪdʒ] ADJ (cruel, fierce) selvaggio(-a), feroce; (primitive) primitivo(-a) ▶ N selvaggio(-a) ▶ VT attaccare selvaggiamente

savagery ['sævɪdʒrɪ] N crudeltà, ferocia

save [seɪv] VT (person, belongings, Comput) salvare; (money) risparmiare, mettere da parte; (time) risparmiare; (food) conservare; (avoid: trouble) evitare; (Sport) parare ▶ VI (also: **save up**) economizzare ▶ N (Sport) parata ▶ PREP salvo, a eccezione di; **it will ~ me an hour** mi farà risparmiare un'ora; **to ~ face** salvare la faccia; **God ~ the Queen!** Dio salvi la Regina!

saving ['seɪvɪŋ] N risparmio ▶ ADJ: **the ~ grace of** l'unica cosa buona di; **savings** NPL risparmi mpl; **to make savings** fare economia

savings account N (US) libretto di risparmio

savings and loan association N (US) ≈ società di credito immobiliare

savings bank N cassa di risparmio

saviour, (US) **savior** ['seɪvjər] N salvatore m

savour, (US) **savor** ['seɪvər] N sapore m, gusto ▶ VT gustare

savoury, (US) **savory** ['seɪvərɪ] ADJ saporito(-a); (dish: not sweet) salato(-a)

savvy ['sævɪ] N (col) arguzia

saw [sɔː] PT of **see** ▶ N (tool) sega ▶ VT (pt **sawed**, pp **sawed** or **sawn** [sɔːn]) segare; **to ~ sth up** fare a pezzi qc con la sega

sawdust ['sɔːdʌst] N segatura

sawmill ['sɔːmɪl] N segheria

sawn [sɔːn] PP of **saw**

sawn-off ['sɔːnɔf], (US) **sawed-off** ['sɔːdɔf] ADJ: ~ **shotgun** fucile m a canne mozze

saxophone ['sæksəfəʊn] N sassofono

say [seɪ] (pt, pp **said** [sɛd]) N: **to have one's ~** fare sentire il proprio parere; **to have a** or **some ~** avere voce in capitolo ▶ VT dire; **could you ~ that again?** potrebbe ripeterlo?; **to ~ yes/no** dire di sì/di no; **she said (that) I was to give you this** ha detto di darle questo; **my watch says 3 o'clock** il mio orologio fa le 3; **shall we ~ Tuesday?** facciamo martedì?; **that doesn't ~ much for him** non torna a suo credito; **when all is said and done** a conti fatti; **there is something** or **a lot to be said for it** ha i suoi lati positivi; **that is to ~** cioè, vale a dire; **to ~ nothing of** per non parlare di; **~ that ...** mettiamo or diciamo che ...; **that goes without saying** va da sé

saying ['seɪɪŋ] N proverbio, detto

SBA N ABBR (US: = Small Business Administration) organismo ausiliario per piccole imprese

SC N ABBR (US) = **supreme court** ▶ ABBR (US) = **South Carolina**

s/c ABBR (= self-contained) indipendente

scab [skæb] N crosta; (pej) crumiro(-a)

scabby ['skæbɪ] ADJ crostoso(-a)

scaffold ['skæfəʊld] N impalcatura; (gallows) patibolo

scaffolding ['skæfəldɪŋ] N impalcatura

scald [skɔːld] N scottatura ▶ VT scottare

scalding ['skɔːldɪŋ] ADJ (also: **scalding hot**) bollente

scale [skeɪl] N scala; (of fish) squama ▶ VT (mountain) scalare; **pay ~** scala dei salari; **~ of charges** tariffa; **on a large ~** su vasta scala; **to draw sth to ~** disegnare qc in scala; **small-~ model** modello in scala ridotta; see also **scales**

▶ **scale down** VT ridurre (proporzionalmente)

scaled-down [skeɪld'daʊn] ADJ su scala ridotta

scale drawing N disegno in scala

scale model N modello in scala

scales [skeɪlz] NPL *(for weighing)* bilancia
scallion ['skæljən] N cipolla; *(US: shallot)* scalogna; *(: leek)* porro
scallop ['skɔləp] N *(Zool)* pettine *m*; *(Sewing)* smerlo
scalp [skælp] N cuoio capelluto ▶ VT scotennare
scalpel ['skælpl] N bisturi *m inv*
scalper ['skælpə'] N *(US col: of tickets)* bagarino
scam [skæm] N *(col)* truffa
scamp [skæmp] N *(col: child)* peste *f*
scamper ['skæmpə'] VI: **to ~ away, ~ off** darsela a gambe
scampi ['skæmpɪ] NPL scampi *mpl*
scan [skæn] VT scrutare; *(glance at quickly)* scorrere, dare un'occhiata a; *(poetry)* scandire; *(TV)* analizzare; *(Radar)* esplorare ▶ N *(Med)* ecografia
scandal ['skændl] N scandalo; *(gossip)* pettegolezzi *mpl*
scandalize ['skændəlaɪz] VT scandalizzare
scandalous ['skændələs] ADJ scandaloso(-a)
Scandinavia [skændɪ'neɪvɪə] N Scandinavia
Scandinavian [skændɪ'neɪvɪən] ADJ, N scandinavo(-a)
scanner ['skænə'] N *(Radar, Med)* scanner *m inv*
scant [skænt] ADJ scarso(-a)
scantily ['skæntɪlɪ] ADV: **~ clad** *or* **dressed** succintamente vestito(-a)
scanty ['skæntɪ] ADJ insufficiente; *(swimsuit)* ridotto(-a)
scapegoat ['skeɪpgəut] N capro espiatorio
scar [skɑ:'] N cicatrice *f* ▶ VT sfregiare
scarce [skɛəs] ADJ scarso(-a); *(copy, edition)* raro(-a); **to make o.s. ~** *(col)* squagliarsela
scarcely ['skɛəslɪ] ADV appena; **~ anybody** quasi nessuno; **I can ~ believe it** faccio fatica a crederci
scarcity ['skɛəsɪtɪ] N scarsità, mancanza
scarcity value N valore *m* di rarità
scare [skɛə'] N spavento, paura; panico ▶ VT spaventare, atterrire; **to ~ sb stiff** spaventare a morte qn; **bomb ~** evacuazione *f* per sospetta presenza di un ordigno esplosivo; **there was a bomb ~ at the bank** hanno evacuato la banca per paura di un attentato dinamitardo
▶ **scare away, scare off** VT mettere in fuga
scarecrow ['skɛəkrəu] N spaventapasseri *m inv*
scared [skɛəd] ADJ: **to be ~** aver paura
scaremonger ['skɛəmʌŋgə'] N allarmista *mf*
scarf [skɑ:f] *(pl* **scarves** [skɑ:vz]) N *(long)* sciarpa; *(square)* fazzoletto da testa, foulard *m inv*
scarlet ['skɑ:lɪt] ADJ scarlatto(-a)
scarlet fever N scarlattina
scarper ['skɑ:pə'] VI *(BRIT col)* darsela a gambe

SCART socket ['skɑ:t-] N presa *f* SCART *inv*
scarves [skɑ:vz] NPL *of* **scarf**
scary ['skɛərɪ] ADJ *(col)* che fa paura
scathing ['skeɪðɪŋ] ADJ aspro(-a); **to be ~ about sth** essere molto critico rispetto a qc
scatter ['skætə'] VT spargere; *(crowd)* disperdere ▶ VI disperdersi
scatterbrained ['skætəbreɪnd] ADJ scervellato(-a), sbadato(-a)
scattered ['skætəd] ADJ sparso(-a), sparpagliato(-a)
scatty ['skætɪ] ADJ *(col)* scervellato(-a), sbadato(-a)
scavenge ['skævɪndʒ] VI *(person)*: **to ~ (for)** frugare tra i rifiuti (alla ricerca di); *(hyenas etc)* nutrirsi di carogne
scavenger ['skævəndʒə'] N spazzino
SCE N ABBR = **Scottish Certificate of Education**
scenario [sɪ'nɑ:rɪəu] N *(Theat, Cine)* copione *m*; *(fig)* situazione *f*
scene [si:n] N *(Theat, fig etc)* scena; *(of crime, accident)* scena, luogo; *(sight, view)* vista, veduta; **behind the scenes** *(also fig)* dietro le quinte; **to appear** *or* **come on the ~** *(also fig)* entrare in scena; **the political ~ in Italy** il quadro politico in Italia; **to make a ~** *(col: fuss)* fare una scenata
scenery ['si:nərɪ] N *(Theat)* scenario; *(landscape)* panorama *m*
scenic ['si:nɪk] ADJ scenico(-a); panoramico(-a)
scent [sɛnt] N odore *m*, profumo; *(sense of smell)* olfatto, odorato; *(fig: track)* pista; **to put** *or* **throw sb off the ~** *(fig)* far perdere le tracce a qn, sviare qn
sceptic, *(US)* **skeptic** ['skɛptɪk] N scettico(-a)
sceptical, *(US)* **skeptical** ['skɛptɪkl] ADJ scettico(-a)
scepticism, *(US)* **skepticism** ['skɛptɪsɪzm] N scetticismo
sceptre, *(US)* **scepter** ['sɛptə'] N scettro
schedule ['ʃɛdju:l, *(US)* 'skɛdju:l] N programma *m*, piano; *(of trains)* orario; *(of prices etc)* lista, tabella ▶ VT fissare; **as scheduled** come stabilito; **on ~** in orario; **to be ahead of/behind ~** essere in anticipo/ritardo sul previsto; **we are working to a very tight ~** il nostro programma di lavoro è molto intenso; **everything went according to ~** tutto è andato secondo i piani *or* secondo il previsto
scheduled flight ['ʃɛdju:ld, *(US)* 'skɛdju:ld] N *(date, time)* fissato(-a); *(visit, event)* programmato(-a); *(train, bus, stop)* previsto(-a) (sull'orario); **~ volo di linea**
schematic [skɪ'mætɪk] ADJ schematico(-a)
scheme [ski:m] N piano, progetto; *(method)* sistema *m*; *(dishonest plan, plot)* intrigo, trama;

S

767

(*arrangement*) disposizione *f*, sistemazione *f*; (*pension scheme etc*) programma *m* ▶ VT progettare; (*plot*) ordire ▶ VI fare progetti; (*intrigue*) complottare; **colour ~** combinazione *f* di colori

scheming ['ski:mɪŋ] ADJ intrigante ▶ N intrighi *mpl*, macchinazioni *fpl*

schism ['skɪzəm] N scisma *m*

schizophrenia [skɪtsə'fri:nɪə] N schizofrenia

schizophrenic [skɪtsə'frɛnɪk] ADJ, N schizofrenico(-a)

scholar ['skɔlər] N studioso(-a)

scholarly ['skɔləlɪ] ADJ dotto(-a), erudito(-a)

scholarship ['skɔləʃɪp] N erudizione *f*; (*grant*) borsa di studio

school [sku:l] N (*primary, secondary*) scuola; (*in university: US*) scuola, facoltà *f inv* ▶ CPD scolare, scolastico(-a) ▶ VT (*animal*) addestrare

school age N età scolare

schoolbook ['sku:lbuk] N libro scolastico

schoolboy ['sku:lbɔɪ] N scolaro

schoolchild ['sku:ltʃaɪld] (*pl* **-children** [-'tʃɪldrən]) N scolaro(-a)

schooldays ['sku:ldeɪz] NPL giorni *mpl* di scuola

schoolgirl ['sku:lgə:l] N scolara

schooling ['sku:lɪŋ] N istruzione *f*

school-leaver ['sku:lli:vər] N (*BRIT*) ≈ neodiplomato(-a)

schoolmaster ['sku:lmɑ:stər] N (*primary*) maestro; (*secondary*) insegnante *m*

schoolmistress ['sku:lmɪstrɪs] N (*primary*) maestra; (*secondary*) insegnante *f*

school report N (*BRIT*) pagella

schoolroom ['sku:lru:m] N classe *f*, aula

schoolteacher ['sku:lti:tʃər] N insegnante *mf*, docente *mf*; (*primary*) maestro(-a)

schoolyard ['sku:ljɑ:d] N (*US*) cortile *m* della scuola

schooner ['sku:nər] N (*ship*) goletta, schooner *m inv*; (*glass*) bicchiere *m* alto da sherry

sciatica [saɪ'ætɪkə] N sciatica

science ['saɪəns] N scienza; **the sciences** le scienze; (*Scol*) le materie scientifiche

science fiction N fantascienza

scientific [saɪən'tɪfɪk] ADJ scientifico(-a)

scientist ['saɪəntɪst] N scienziato(-a)

sci-fi ['saɪfaɪ] N ABBR (*col*) = **science fiction**

Scilly Isles ['sɪlɪ'aɪlz] NPL, **Scillies** ['sɪlɪz] NPL: **the ~** le isole Scilly

scintillating ['sɪntɪleɪtɪŋ] ADJ scintillante; (*wit, conversation, company*) brillante

scissors ['sɪzəz] NPL forbici *fpl*; **a pair of ~** un paio di forbici

sclerosis [sklɪ'rəusɪs] N sclerosi *f*

scoff [skɔf] VT (*BRIT col: eat*) tranguggiare, ingozzare ▶ VI: **to ~ (at)** (*mock*) farsi beffe (di)

scold [skəuld] VT rimproverare

scolding ['skəuldɪŋ] N lavata di capo, sgridata

scone [skɔn] N focaccina da tè

scoop [sku:p] N mestolo; (*for ice cream*) cucchiaio dosatore; (*Press*) colpo giornalistico, notizia (in) esclusiva
▶ **scoop out** VT scavare
▶ **scoop up** VT tirare su, sollevare

scooter ['sku:tər] N (*motorcycle*) motoretta, scooter *m inv*; (*toy*) monopattino

scope [skəup] N (*capacity: of plan, undertaking*) portata; (: *of person*) capacità *fpl*; (*opportunity*) possibilità *fpl*; **to be within the ~ of** rientrare nei limiti di; **it's well within his ~ to …** è perfettamente in grado di …; **there is plenty of ~ for improvement** (*BRIT*) ci sono notevoli possibilità di miglioramento

scorch [skɔ:tʃ] VT (*clothes*) strinare, bruciacchiare; (*earth, grass*) seccare, bruciare

scorched earth policy [skɔ:tʃt-] N tattica della terra bruciata

scorcher ['skɔ:tʃər] N (*col: hot day*) giornata torrida

scorching ['skɔ:tʃɪŋ] ADJ cocente, scottante

score [skɔ:r] N punti *mpl*, punteggio; (*Mus*) partitura, spartito; (*twenty*): **a ~** venti ▶ VT (*goal, point*) segnare, fare; (*success*) ottenere; (*cut: leather, wood, card*) incidere ▶ VI segnare; (*Football*) fare un goal; (*keep score*) segnare i punti; **on that ~** a questo riguardo; **to have an old ~ to settle with sb** (*fig*) avere un vecchio conto da saldare con qn; **scores of people** (*fig*) un sacco di gente; **to ~ 6 out of 10** prendere 6 su 10
▶ **score out** VT cancellare con un segno

scoreboard ['skɔ:bɔ:d] N tabellone *m* segnapunti

scorecard ['skɔ:kɑ:d] N cartoncino segnapunti

scoreline ['skɔ:laɪn] N (*Sport*) risultato

scorer ['skɔ:rər] N marcatore(-trice); (*keeping score*) segnapunti *m inv*

scorn [skɔ:n] N disprezzo ▶ VT disprezzare

scornful ['skɔ:nful] ADJ sprezzante

Scorpio ['skɔ:pɪəu] N Scorpione *m*; **to be ~** essere dello Scorpione

scorpion ['skɔ:pɪən] N scorpione *m*

Scot [skɔt] N scozzese *mf*

Scotch [skɔtʃ] N whisky *m* scozzese, scotch *m*

scotch [skɔtʃ] VT (*rumour etc*) soffocare

Scotch tape® ['skɔtʃ-] N scotch® *m*

scot-free ['skɔt'fri:] ADJ impunito(-a); **to get off ~** (*unpunished*) farla franca; (*unhurt*) uscire illeso(-a)

Scotland ['skɔtlənd] N Scozia

Scots [skɔts] ADJ scozzese

Scotsman ['skɔtsmən] N (*irreg*) scozzese *m*

Scotswoman ['skɔtswumən] N (*irreg*) scozzese *f*

Scottish ['skɔtɪʃ] ADJ scozzese; **the ~ National Party** il partito nazionalista scozzese; **the ~ Parliament** il Parlamento scozzese

scoundrel ['skaundrl] N farabutto(-a); (*child*) furfantello(-a)

scour ['skauə^r] VT (*clean*) pulire strofinando; raschiare via; ripulire; (*search*) battere, perlustrare

scourer ['skauərə^r] N (*pad*) paglietta; (*powder*) (detersivo) abrasivo

scourge [skə:dʒ] N flagello

scout [skaut] N (*Mil*) esploratore *m*; (*also:* **boy scout**) giovane esploratore, scout *m inv* ▸ **scout around** VI cercare in giro

scowl [skaul] VI accigliarsi, aggrottare le sopracciglia; **to ~ at** guardare torvo

scrabble ['skræbl] VI (*claw*): **to ~ (at)** graffiare, grattare; **to ~ about** *or* **around for sth** cercare affannosamente qc ▸ N: **S~®** Scarabeo®

scraggy ['skrægɪ] ADJ scarno(-a), molto magro(-a)

scram [skræm] VI (*col*) filare via

scramble ['skræmbl] N arrampicata ▸ VI inerpicarsi; **to ~ out** *etc* uscire *etc* in fretta; **to ~ for** azzuffarsi per; **to go scrambling** (*Sport*) fare il motocross

scrambled eggs NPL uova *fpl* strapazzate

scrap [skræp] N pezzo, pezzetto; (*fight*) zuffa; (*also:* **scrap iron**) rottami *mpl* di ferro, ferraglia ▸ VT demolire; (*fig*) scartare ▸ VI: **to ~ (with sb)** fare a botte (con qn); **scraps** NPL (*waste*) scarti *mpl*; **to sell sth for ~** vendere qc come ferro vecchio

scrapbook ['skræpbuk] N album *m inv* di ritagli

scrap dealer N commerciante *m* di ferraglia

scrape [skreɪp] VT, VI raschiare, grattare ▸ N: **to get into a ~** cacciarsi in un guaio ▸ **scrape through** VI (*succeed*) farcela per un pelo, cavarsela ▸ VT FUS (*exam*) passare per miracolo, passare per il rotto della cuffia

scraper ['skreɪpə^r] N raschietto

scrap heap N mucchio di rottami; **to throw sth on the ~** (*fig*) mettere qc nel dimenticatoio

scrap merchant N (*Brit*) commerciante *m* di ferraglia

scrap metal N ferraglia

scrap paper N cartaccia

scrappy ['skræpɪ] ADJ frammentario(-a), sconnesso(-a)

scrap yard N deposito di rottami; (*for cars*) cimitero delle macchine

scratch [skrætʃ] N graffio ▸ CPD: **~ team** squadra raccogliticcia ▸ VT graffiare, rigare; (*Comput*) cancellare ▸ VI grattare; (*paint, car*) graffiare; **to start from ~** cominciare *or* partire da zero; **to be up to ~** essere all'altezza

scratch card N (*Brit*) cartolina *f* gratta e vinci

scratch pad N (*US*) notes *m inv*, blocchetto

scrawl [skrɔ:l] N scarabocchio ▸ VI scarabocchiare

scrawny ['skrɔ:nɪ] ADJ scarno(-a), pelle e ossa *inv*

scream [skri:m] N grido, urlo ▸ VI urlare, gridare; **to ~ at sb (to do sth)** gridare a qn (di fare qc); **it was a ~** (*fig: col*) era da crepar dal ridere; **he's a ~** (*fig: col*) è una sagoma, è uno spasso

scree [skri:] N ghiaione *m*

screech [skri:tʃ] N strido; (*of tyres, brakes*) stridore *m* ▸ VI stridere

screen [skri:n] N schermo; (*fig*) muro, cortina, velo ▸ VT schermare, fare schermo a; (*from the wind etc*) riparare; (*film*) proiettare; (*book*) adattare per lo schermo; (*candidates etc*) passare al vaglio; (*for illness*) sottoporre a controlli medici

screen editing [-ɛdɪtɪŋ] N (*Comput*) correzione *f* e modifica su schermo

screening ['skri:nɪŋ] N (*Med*) dépistage *m inv*; (*of film*) proiezione *f*; (*for security*) controlli *mpl* (di sicurezza)

screen memory N (*Comput*) memoria di schermo

screenplay ['skri:npleɪ] N sceneggiatura

screensaver N (*Comput*) screen saver *m inv*

screenshot ['skri:nʃɔt] N (*Comput*) schermata

screen test N provino (cinematografico)

screw [skru:] N vite *f*; (*propeller*) elica ▸ VT avvitare; **to ~ sth to the wall** fissare qc al muro con viti ▸ **screw up** VT (*paper, material*) spiegazzare; (*col: ruin*) mandare a monte; **to ~ up one's face** fare una smorfia; **to ~ up one's eyes** strizzare gli occhi

screwdriver ['skru:draɪvə^r] N cacciavite *m*

screwed-up ['skru:d'ʌp] ADJ (*col*): **she's totally ~** è nel pallone

screwy ['skru:ɪ] ADJ (*col*) svitato(-a)

scribble ['skrɪbl] N scarabocchio ▸ VT scribacchiare ▸ VI scarabocchiare; **to ~ sth down** scribacchiare qc

scribe [skraɪb] N scriba *m*

script [skrɪpt] N (*Cine etc*) copione *m*; (*in exam*) elaborato *or* compito d'esame; (*writing*) scrittura

scripted ['skrɪptɪd] ADJ (*Radio, TV*) preparato(-a)

Scripture ['skrɪptʃə^r] N Sacre Scritture *fpl*

scriptwriter ['skrɪptraɪtə^r] N soggettista *mf*

scroll [skrəul] N rotolo di carta ▸ VT (*Comput*) scorrere

scroll bar N (*Comput*) barra di scorrimento
scrotum ['skrəʊtəm] N scroto
scrounge [skraʊndʒ] VT (*col*): **to ~ sth (off** or **from sb)** scroccare qc (a qn) ▶ VI: **to ~ on sb** vivere alle spalle di qn
scrounger ['skraʊndʒə'] N scroccone(-a)
scrub [skrʌb] N (*clean*) strofinata; (*land*) boscaglia ▶ VT pulire strofinando; (*reject*) annullare
scrubbing brush ['skrʌbɪŋ-] N spazzolone *m*
scruff [skrʌf] N: **by the ~ of the neck** per la collottola
scruffy ['skrʌfɪ] ADJ sciatto(-a)
scrum ['skrʌm], **scrummage** ['skrʌmɪdʒ] N mischia
scruple ['skru:pl] N scrupolo; **to have no scruples about doing sth** non avere scrupoli a fare qc
scrupulous ['skru:pjuləs] ADJ scrupoloso(-a)
scrupulously ['skru:pjuləslɪ] ADV scrupolosamente; **he tries to be ~ fair/honest** cerca di essere più imparziale/onesto che può
scrutinize ['skru:tɪnaɪz] VT scrutare, esaminare attentamente
scrutiny ['skru:tɪnɪ] N esame *m* accurato; **under the ~ of sb** sotto la sorveglianza di qn
scuba ['sku:bə] N autorespiratore *m*
scuba diving ['sku:bə-] N immersioni *fpl* subacquee
scuff [skʌf] VT (*shoes*) consumare strascicando
scuffle ['skʌfl] N baruffa, tafferuglio
scullery ['skʌlərɪ] N retrocucina *m* or *f*
sculptor ['skʌlptə'] N scultore *m*
sculpture ['skʌlptʃə'] N scultura
scum [skʌm] N schiuma; (*pej: people*) feccia
scupper ['skʌpə'] VT autoaffondare; (*BRIT fig*) far naufragare
scurrilous ['skʌrɪləs] ADJ scurrile, volgare
scurry ['skʌrɪ] VI sgambare, affrettarsi
scurvy ['skə:vɪ] N scorbuto
scuttle ['skʌtl] N (*Naut*) portellino; (*also:* **coal scuttle**) secchio del carbone ▶ VT (*ship*) autoaffondare ▶ VI (*scamper*): **to ~ away, ~ off** darsela a gambe, scappare
scythe [saɪð] N falce *f*
SD, S. Dak. ABBR (*US*) = **South Dakota**
SDI N ABBR (= *Strategic Defense Initiative*) S.D.I. *f*
SDLP N ABBR (*BRIT Pol*) = **Social Democratic and Labour Party**
sea [si:] N mare *m* ▶ CPD marino(-a), del mare; (*ship, port, route, transport*) marittimo(-a); (*bird, fish*) di mare; **on the ~** (*boat*) in mare; (*town*) di mare; **to go by ~** andare per mare; **by** or **beside the ~** (*holiday*) al mare; (*village*) sul mare; **to look out to ~** guardare il mare; **out to ~** al largo; **(out) at ~** in mare; **heavy** or **rough ~(s)** mare grosso

or agitato; **a ~ of faces** (*fig*) una marea di gente; **to be all at ~** (*fig*) non sapere che pesci pigliare
sea bed N fondo marino
sea bird N uccello di mare
seaboard ['si:bɔ:d] N costa
sea breeze N brezza di mare
seafarer ['si:fɛərə'] N navigante *m*
seafaring ['si:fɛərɪŋ] ADJ (*community*) marinaro(-a); (*life*) da marinaio
seafood ['si:fu:d] N frutti *mpl* di mare
sea front N lungomare *m*
seagoing ['si:gəʊɪŋ] ADJ (*ship*) d'alto mare
seagull ['si:gʌl] N gabbiano
seal [si:l] N (*animal*) foca; (*stamp*) sigillo; (*impression*) impronta del sigillo ▶ VT sigillare; (*decide: sb's fate*) segnare; (*: bargain*) concludere; **~ of approval** beneplacito ▶ **seal off** VT (*close*) sigillare; (*forbid entry to*) bloccare l'accesso a
sea level N livello del mare
sealing wax ['si:lɪŋ-] N ceralacca
sea lion N leone *m* marino
sealskin ['si:lskɪn] N pelle *f* di foca
seam [si:m] N cucitura; (*of coal*) filone *m*; **the hall was bursting at the seams** l'aula era piena zeppa
seaman ['si:mən] N (*irreg*) marinaio
seamanship ['si:mənʃɪp] N tecnica di navigazione
seamless ['si:mlɪs] ADJ senza cucitura
seamy ['si:mɪ] ADJ malfamato(-a); squallido(-a)
seance ['seɪɔns] N seduta spiritica
seaplane ['si:pleɪn] N idrovolante *m*
seaport ['si:pɔ:t] N porto di mare
search [sə:tʃ] N (*for person, thing*) ricerca; (*of drawer, pockets*) esame *m* accurato; (*Law: at sb's home*) perquisizione *f* ▶ VT perlustrare, frugare; (*scan, examine*) esaminare minuziosamente; (*Comput*) ricercare ▶ VI: **to ~ for** ricercare; **in ~ of** alla ricerca di; **"~ and replace"** (*Comput*) "ricercare e sostituire" ▶ **search through** VT FUS frugare
search engine N (*Comput*) motore *m* di ricerca
searcher ['sə:tʃə'] N chi cerca
searching ['sə:tʃɪŋ] ADJ minuzioso(-a); penetrante; (*question*) pressante
searchlight ['sə:tʃlaɪt] N proiettore *m*
search party N squadra di soccorso
search warrant N mandato di perquisizione
searing ['sɪərɪŋ] ADJ (*heat*) rovente; (*pain*) acuto(-a)
seashore ['si:ʃɔ:'] N spiaggia; **on the ~** sulla riva del mare
seasick ['si:sɪk] ADJ che soffre il mal di mare; **to be ~** avere il mal di mare
seaside ['si:saɪd] N spiaggia; **to go to the ~** andare al mare

seaside resort N stazione *f* balneare
season ['si:zn] N stagione *f* ▶ VT condire,
insaporire; **to be in/out of** ~ essere di/fuori
stagione; **the busy** ~ *(for shops)* il periodo di
punta; *(for hotels etc)* l'alta stagione; **the
open** ~ *(Hunting)* la stagione della caccia
seasonal ['si:zənl] ADJ stagionale
seasoned ['si:znd] ADJ *(wood)* stagionato(-a);
(fig: worker, actor, troops) con esperienza; **a** ~
campaigner un veterano
seasoning ['si:znıŋ] N condimento
season ticket N abbonamento
seat [si:t] N sedile *m*; *(in bus, train: place)* posto;
(Parliament) seggio; *(centre: of government etc, of
infection)* sede *f*; *(buttocks)* didietro; *(of trousers)*
fondo ▶ VT far sedere; *(have room for)* avere or
essere fornito(-a) di posti a sedere per; **are
there any seats left?** ci sono posti?; **to take
one's** ~ prendere posto; **to be seated** essere
seduto(-a); **please be seated** accomodatevi
per favore
seat belt N cintura di sicurezza
seating N posti *mpl* a sedere
seating arrangements ['si:tıŋ-] NPL
sistemazione *f* or disposizione *f* dei posti
seating capacity N posti *mpl* a sedere
SEATO ['si:təu] N ABBR (= Southeast Asia Treaty
Organization) SEATO *f*
sea water N acqua di mare
seaweed ['si:wi:d] N alghe *fpl*
seaworthy ['si:wə:ðı] ADJ atto(-a) alla
navigazione
SEC N ABBR (US: = Securities and Exchange
Commission) commissione di controllo sulle
operazioni in Borsa
sec. ABBR = **second¹**
secateurs [sɛkə'tə:z] NPL forbici *fpl* per
potare
secede [sı'si:d] VI: **to** ~ **(from)** ritirarsi (da)
secluded [sı'klu:dıd] ADJ isolato(-a),
appartato(-a)
seclusion [sı'klu:ʒən] N isolamento
second¹ ['sɛkənd] NUM secondo(-a) ▶ ADV *(in
race etc)* al secondo posto; *(Rail)* in seconda
▶ N *(unit of time)* secondo; *(in series, position)*
secondo(-a); *(Brit Scol: degree)* laurea con
punteggio discreto; *(Aut: also:* **second gear***)*
seconda; *(Comm: imperfect)* scarto ▶ VT *(motion)*
appoggiare; **Charles the S~** Carlo Secondo;
just a ~! un attimo!; ~ **floor** *(Brit)* secondo
piano; *(US)* primo piano; **to ask for a ~
opinion** *(Med)* chiedere un altro or ulteriore
parere; ~ **thoughts** ripensamenti *mpl*; **to
have ~ thoughts (about doing sth)** avere
dei ripensamenti (quanto a fare qc); **on ~
thoughts** *(Brit)* or **thought** *(US)* a
ripensarci, ripensandoci bene
second² [sı'kɔnd] VT *(employee)* distaccare
secondary ['sɛkəndərı] ADJ secondario(-a)

secondary school N scuola secondaria;
vedi nota

> In Gran Bretagna la *secondary school* è la
> scuola frequentata dai ragazzi dagli 11 ai
> 18 anni. Nel paese è obbligatorio andare a
> scuola fino a 16 anni; *vedi anche* **primary
> school**.

second-best [sɛkənd'bɛst] N ripiego; **as a** ~
in mancanza di meglio
second-class [sɛkənd'klɑ:s] ADJ di seconda
classe ▶ ADV: **to travel** ~ viaggiare in
seconda (classe); **to send sth** ~ spedire qc
per posta ordinaria; ~ **citizen** cittadino di
second'ordine
second cousin N cugino di secondo grado
seconder ['sɛkəndə'] N sostenitore(-trice)
second-guess [sɛkənd'gɛs] VT *(predict)*
anticipare; *(after the event)* giudicare col
senno di poi
second hand N *(on clock)* lancetta dei secondi
second-hand [sɛkənd'hænd] ADJ di seconda
mano, usato(-a) ▶ ADV *(buy)* di seconda mano;
to hear sth ~ venire a sapere qc da terze
persone
second-in-command ['sɛkəndınkə'mɑ:nd]
N *(Mil)* comandante *m* in seconda; *(Admin)*
aggiunto
secondly ['sɛkəndlı] ADV in secondo luogo
secondment [sı'kɔndmənt] N *(Brit)*
distaccamento
second-rate [sɛkənd'reıt] ADJ scadente
Second World War N: **the** ~ la seconda
guerra mondiale
secrecy ['si:krəsı] N segretezza
secret ['si:krıt] ADJ segreto(-a) ▶ N segreto;
in ~ in segreto, segretamente; **to keep sth** ~
(from sb) tenere qc segreto (a qn), tenere qc
nascosto (a qn); **keep it** ~ che rimanga un
segreto; **to make no** ~ **of sth** non far
mistero di qc
secret agent N agente *m* segreto
secretarial [sɛkrı'tɛərıəl] ADJ *(work)* da
segretario(-a); *(college, course)* di segretariato
secretariat [sɛkrı'tɛərıət] N segretariato
secretary ['sɛkrətrı] N segretario(-a); **S~ of
State** *(US Pol)* ≈ Ministro degli Esteri; **S~ of
State (for)** *(Brit Pol)* ministro (di)
secretary-general ['sɛkrətrı'dʒɛnərl] N
segretario generale
secrete [sı'kri:t] VT *(Med, Anat, Biol)* secernere;
(hide) nascondere
secretion [sı'kri:ʃən] N secrezione *f*
secretive ['si:krətıv] ADJ riservato(-a)
secretly ['si:krıtlı] ADV in segreto,
segretamente
secret police N polizia segreta
secret service N servizi *mpl* segreti
sect [sɛkt] N setta
sectarian [sɛk'tɛərıən] ADJ settario(-a)

S

section ['sɛkʃən] N sezione f; (of document) articolo ▸ VT sezionare, dividere in sezioni; **the business ~** (Press) la pagina economica

sector ['sɛktər] N settore m

secular ['sɛkjulər] ADJ secolare

secure [sɪ'kjuər] ADJ (free from anxiety) sicuro(-a); (firmly fixed) assicurato(-a), ben fermato(-a); (in safe place) al sicuro ▸ VT (fix) fissare, assicurare; (get) ottenere, assicurarsi; (Comm: loan) garantire; **to make sth ~** fissare bene qc; **to ~ sth for sb** procurare qc per or a qn

secured creditor [sɪ'kjuəd-] N creditore m privilegiato

security [sɪ'kjuərɪtɪ] N sicurezza; (for loan) garanzia; **securities** NPL (Stock Exchange) titoli mpl; **to increase/tighten ~** aumentare/intensificare la sorveglianza; **~ of tenure** garanzia del posto di lavoro, garanzia di titolo or di godimento

Security Council N: **the ~** il Consiglio di Sicurezza

security forces NPL forze fpl dell'ordine

security guard N guardia giurata

security risk N rischio per la sicurezza

secy. ABBR = **secretary**

sedan [sə'dæn] N (US Aut) berlina

sedate [sɪ'deɪt] ADJ posato(-a); calmo(-a) ▸ VT calmare

sedation [sɪ'deɪʃən] N (Med): **to be under ~** essere sotto l'azione di sedativi

sedative ['sɛdɪtɪv] N sedativo, calmante m

sedentary ['sɛdntrɪ] ADJ sedentario(-a)

sediment ['sɛdɪmənt] N sedimento

sedition [sɪ'dɪʃən] N sedizione f

seduce [sɪ'djuːs] VT sedurre

seduction [sɪ'dʌkʃən] N seduzione f

seductive [sɪ'dʌktɪv] ADJ seducente

see [siː] (pt **saw**, pp **seen**) VT vedere; (accompany): **to ~ sb to the door** accompagnare qn alla porta ▸ VI vedere; (understand) capire ▸ N sede f vescovile; **to ~ that** (ensure) badare che + sub, fare in modo che + sub; **to go and ~ sb** andare a trovare qn; **~ you soon/later/tomorrow!** a presto/più tardi/domani!; **as far as I can ~** da quanto posso vedere; **there was nobody to be seen** non c'era anima viva; **let me ~** (show me) fammi vedere; (let me think) vediamo (un po'); **~ for yourself** vai a vedere con i tuoi occhi; **I don't know what she sees in him** non so che cosa ci trovi in lui

▸ **see about** VT FUS (deal with) occuparsi di

▸ **see off** VT salutare alla partenza

▸ **see out** VT (take to the door) accompagnare alla porta

▸ **see through** VT portare a termine ▸ VT FUS non lasciarsi ingannare da

▸ **see to** VT FUS occuparsi di

seed [siːd] N seme m; (fig) germe m; (Tennis) testa di serie; **to go to ~** fare seme; (fig) scadere

seedless ['siːdlɪs] ADJ senza semi

seedling ['siːdlɪŋ] N piantina di semenzaio

seedy ['siːdɪ] ADJ (shabby: person) sciatto(-a); (: place) cadente

seeing ['siːɪŋ] CONJ: **~ (that)** visto che

seek [siːk] (pt, pp **sought**) VT cercare; **to ~ advice/help from sb** chiedere consiglio/aiuto a qn

▸ **seek out** VT (person) andare a cercare

seem [siːm] VI sembrare, parere; **there seems to be ...** sembra che ci sia ...; **it seems (that) ...** sembra or pare che ... + sub; **what seems to be the trouble?** cosa c'è che non va?

seemingly ['siːmɪŋlɪ] ADV apparentemente

seen [siːn] PP of **see**

seep [siːp] VI filtrare, trapelare

seer [sɪər] N profeta(-essa), veggente mf

seersucker ['sɪəsʌkər] N cotone m indiano

seesaw ['siːsɔː] N altalena a bilico

seethe [siːð] VI ribollire; **to ~ with anger** fremere di rabbia

see-through ['siːθruː] ADJ trasparente

segment ['sɛgmənt] N segmento

segregate ['sɛgrɪgeɪt] VT segregare, isolare

segregation [sɛgrɪ'geɪʃən] N segregazione f

Seine [seɪn] N Senna

seismic ['saɪzmɪk] ADJ sismico(-a)

seize [siːz] VT (grasp) afferrare; (take possession of) impadronirsi di; (Law) sequestrare

▸ **seize up** VI (Tech) grippare

▸ **seize (up)on** VT FUS ricorrere a

seizure ['siːʒər] N (Med) attacco; (Law) confisca, sequestro

seldom ['sɛldəm] ADV raramente

select [sɪ'lɛkt] ADJ scelto(-a); (hotel, restaurant) chic inv; (club) esclusivo(-a) ▸ VT scegliere, selezionare; **a ~ few** pochi eletti mpl

selection [sɪ'lɛkʃən] N selezione f, scelta

selection committee N comitato di selezione

selective [sɪ'lɛktɪv] ADJ selettivo(-a)

selector [sɪ'lɛktər] N (person) selezionatore(-trice); (Tech) selettore m

self [sɛlf] (pl **selves** [sɛlvz]) N: **the ~** l'io m

▸ PREFIX auto...

self-addressed ['sɛlfə'drɛst] ADJ: **~ envelope** busta col proprio nome e indirizzo

self-adhesive [sɛlfəd'hiːzɪv] ADJ autoadesivo(-a)

self-assertive [sɛlfə'səːtɪv] ADJ autoritario(-a)

self-assurance [sɛlfə'ʃuərəns] N sicurezza di sé

self-assured [sɛlfə'ʃuəd] ADJ sicuro(-a) di sé

self-catering [sɛlf'keɪtərɪŋ] ADJ (BRIT) in cui ci si cucina da sé; ~ **apartment** appartamento (per le vacanze)
self-centred, (US) **self-centered** [sɛlf'sɛntəd] ADJ egocentrico(-a)
self-cleaning [sɛlf'kli:nɪŋ] ADJ autopulente
self-confessed [sɛlfkən'fɛst] ADJ (alcoholic etc) dichiarato(-a)
self-confidence [sɛlf'kɔnfɪdəns] N sicurezza di sé
self-confident ADJ sicuro(-a) di sé
self-conscious [sɛlf'kɔnʃəs] ADJ timido(-a)
self-contained [sɛlfkən'teɪnd] ADJ (BRIT: flat) indipendente
self-control [sɛlfkən'trəul] N autocontrollo
self-defeating [sɛlfdɪ'fi:tɪŋ] ADJ futile
self-defence, (US) **self-defense** [sɛlfdɪ'fɛns] N autodifesa; (Law) legittima difesa
self-discipline [sɛlf'dɪsɪplɪn] N autodisciplina
self-drive ADJ (BRIT: rented car) senza autista
self-employed [sɛlfɪm'plɔɪd] ADJ che lavora in proprio
self-esteem [sɛlfɪ'sti:m] N amor proprio m
self-evident [sɛlf'ɛvɪdənt] ADJ evidente
self-explanatory [sɛlfɪk'splænətərɪ] ADJ ovvio(-a)
self-governing [sɛlf'gʌvənɪŋ] ADJ autonomo(-a)
self-harm [sɛlf'hɑːm] N autolesionismo ▶ VI farsi del male intenzionalmente
self-help ['sɛlf'hɛlp] N iniziativa individuale
self-importance [sɛlfɪm'pɔːtns] N sufficienza
self-indulgent [sɛlfɪn'dʌldʒənt] ADJ indulgente verso se stesso(-a)
self-inflicted [sɛlfɪn'flɪktɪd] ADJ autoinflitto(-a)
self-interest [sɛlf'ɪntrɪst] N interesse m personale
selfish ['sɛlfɪʃ] ADJ egoista
selfishly ['sɛlfɪʃlɪ] ADV egoisticamente
selfishness ['sɛlfɪʃnɪs] N egoismo
selfless ['sɛlflɪs] ADJ altruista
selflessly ['sɛlflɪslɪ] ADV altruisticamente
selflessness ['sɛlflɪsnɪs] N altruismo
self-made man ['sɛlfmeɪd-] N (irreg) self-made man m inv, uomo che si è fatto da sé
self-pity [sɛlf'pɪtɪ] N autocommiserazione f
self-portrait [sɛlf'pɔːtrɪt] N autoritratto
self-possessed [sɛlfpə'zɛst] ADJ controllato(-a)
self-preservation ['sɛlfprɛzə'veɪʃən] N istinto di conservazione
self-raising [sɛlf'reɪzɪŋ], (US) **self-rising** [sɛlf'raɪzɪŋ] ADJ: ~ **flour** miscela di farina e lievito
self-reliant [sɛlfrɪ'laɪənt] ADJ indipendente

self-respect [sɛlfrɪs'pɛkt] N rispetto di sé, amor proprio
self-respecting [sɛlfrɪs'pɛktɪŋ] ADJ che ha rispetto di sé
self-righteous [sɛlf'raɪtʃəs] ADJ soddisfatto(-a) di sé
self-rising [sɛlf'raɪzɪŋ] ADJ (US) = **self-raising**
self-sacrifice [sɛlf'sækrɪfaɪs] N abnegazione f
self-same ['sɛlfseɪm] ADJ stesso(-a)
self-satisfied [sɛlf'sætɪsfaɪd] ADJ compiaciuto(-a) di sé
self-sealing [sɛlf'si:lɪŋ] ADJ autosigillante
self-service [sɛlf'sə:vɪs] N autoservizio, self-service m
self-styled [sɛlf'staɪld] ADJ sedicente
self-sufficient [sɛlfsə'fɪʃənt] ADJ autosufficiente
self-supporting [sɛlfsə'pɔːtɪŋ] ADJ economicamente indipendente
self-taught [sɛlf'tɔːt] ADJ autodidatta
self-test ['sɛlftɛst] N (Comput) autoverifica
sell [sɛl] (pt, pp **sold** [səuld]) VT vendere ▶ VI vendersi; **to ~ at** or **for 100 euros** essere in vendita a 100 euro; **to ~ sb an idea** (fig) far accettare un'idea a qn
▶ **sell off** VT svendere, liquidare
▶ **sell out** VI: **to ~ out (to sb/sth)** (Comm) vendere (tutto) (a qn/qc) ▶ VT esaurire; **the tickets are all sold out** i biglietti sono esauriti
▶ **sell up** VI vendere (tutto)
sell-by date ['sɛlbaɪ-] N data di scadenza
seller ['sɛlər] N venditore(-trice); **~'s market** mercato favorevole ai venditori
selling price ['sɛlɪŋ-] N prezzo di vendita
Sellotape® ['sɛləuteɪp] N (BRIT) nastro adesivo, scotch® m
sellout ['sɛlaut] N (betrayal) tradimento; **it was a ~** registrò un tutto esaurito
selves [sɛlvz] NPL of **self**
semantic [sɪ'mæntɪk] ADJ semantico(-a)
semantics [sɪ'mæntɪks] N semantica
semaphore ['sɛməfɔ:ʳ] N segnali mpl con bandiere; (Rail) semaforo
semblance ['sɛmbləns] N parvenza, apparenza
semen ['si:mən] N sperma m
semester [sɪ'mɛstəʳ] N (US) semestre m
semi... ['sɛmɪ] PREFIX semi... ▶ N: **semi** = **semidetached (house)**
semi-breve ['sɛmɪbri:v] N (BRIT) semibreve f
semicircle ['sɛmɪsə:kl] N semicerchio
semicircular ['sɛmɪ'sə:kjuləʳ] ADJ semicircolare
semicolon [sɛmɪ'kəulən] N punto e virgola
semiconductor [sɛmɪkən'dʌktəʳ] N semiconduttore m
semiconscious [sɛmɪ'kɔnʃəs] ADJ parzialmente cosciente

S

semidetached (house) [sɛmɪdɪ'tætʃt-] N (BRIT) casa gemella
semifinal [sɛmɪ'faɪnl] N semifinale f
seminar ['sɛmɪnɑːʳ] N seminario
seminary ['sɛmɪnərɪ] N (Rel: for priests) seminario
semiprecious [sɛmɪ'prɛʃəs] ADJ semiprezioso(-a)
semiquaver ['sɛmɪkweɪvəʳ] N (BRIT) semicroma
semiskilled ['sɛmɪ'skɪld] ADJ: ~ **worker** operaio(-a) non specializzato(-a)
semi-skimmed ['sɛmɪ'skɪmd] ADJ (milk) parzialmente scremato(-a)
semitone ['sɛmɪtəun] N (Mus) semitono
semolina [sɛmə'liːnə] N semolino
Sen., sen. ABBR = **senator; senior**
senate ['sɛnɪt] N senato
senator ['sɛnɪtəʳ] N senatore(-trice)
send [sɛnd] (pt, pp **sent**) VT mandare; **to ~ by post** or (US) **mail** spedire per posta; **to ~ sb for sth** mandare qn a prendere qc; **to ~ word that ...** mandare a dire che ...; **she sends (you) her love** ti saluta affettuosamente; **to ~ sb to Coventry** (BRIT) dare l'ostracismo a qn; **to ~ sb to sleep/into fits of laughter** far addormentare/scoppiare dal ridere qn; **to ~ sth flying** far volare via qc
▸ **send away** VT (letter, goods) spedire; (person) mandare via
▸ **send away for** VT FUS richiedere per posta, farsi spedire
▸ **send back** VT rimandare
▸ **send for** VT FUS mandare a chiamare, far venire; (by post) ordinare per posta
▸ **send in** VT (report, application, resignation) presentare
▸ **send off** VT (goods) spedire; (BRIT Sport: player) espellere
▸ **send on** VT (BRIT: letter) inoltrare; (luggage etc: in advance) spedire in anticipo
▸ **send out** VT (invitation) diramare; (emit: light, heat) mandare, emanare; (: signals) emettere
▸ **send round** VT (letter, document etc) far circolare
▸ **send up** VT (person, price) far salire; (BRIT: parody) mettere in ridicolo
sender ['sɛndəʳ] N mittente mf
send-off ['sɛndɔf] N: **to give sb a good ~** festeggiare la partenza di qn
Senegal [sɛnɪ'gɔːl] N Senegal m
Senegalese [sɛnɪgə'liːz] ADJ, N senegalese mf
senile ['siːnaɪl] ADJ senile
senility [sɪ'nɪlɪtɪ] N senilità f
senior ['siːnɪəʳ] ADJ (older) più vecchio(-a); (of higher rank) di grado più elevato ▸ N persona più anziana; (in service) persona

con maggiore anzianità; **P. Jones ~** P. Jones senior, P. Jones padre
senior citizen N persona anziana
senior high school N (US) ≈ liceo
seniority [siːnɪ'ɔrɪtɪ] N anzianità; (in rank) superiorità
sensation [sɛn'seɪʃən] N sensazione f; **to create a ~** fare scalpore
sensational [sɛn'seɪʃənl] ADJ sensazionale; (marvellous) eccezionale
sense [sɛns] N senso; (feeling) sensazione f, senso; (meaning) senso, significato; (wisdom) buonsenso ▸ VT sentire, percepire; **senses** NPL (sanity) ragione f; **it makes ~** ha senso; **there is no ~ in (doing) that** non ha senso (farlo); **~ of humour** (senso dell')umorismo; **to come to one's senses** (regain consciousness) riprendere i sensi; (become reasonable) tornare in sé; **to take leave of one's senses** perdere il lume or l'uso della ragione
senseless ['sɛnslɪs] ADJ sciocco(-a); (unconscious) privo(-a) di sensi
sensibilities [sɛnsɪ'bɪlɪtɪz] NPL sensibilità fsg
sensible ['sɛnsɪbl] ADJ sensato(-a), ragionevole
sensitive ['sɛnsɪtɪv] ADJ sensibile; (skin, question) delicato(-a); **~ (to)** sensibile (a); **he is very ~ about it** è un tasto che è meglio non toccare con lui
sensitivity [sɛnsɪ'tɪvɪtɪ] N sensibilità
sensual ['sɛnsjuəl] ADJ sensuale
sensuous ['sɛnsjuəs] ADJ sensuale
sent [sɛnt] PT, PP of **send**
sentence ['sɛntns] N (Ling) frase f; (Law: judgement) sentenza; (: punishment) condanna
▸ VT: **to ~ sb to death/to 5 years** condannare qn a morte/a 5 anni; **to pass ~ on sb** condannare qn
sentiment ['sɛntɪmənt] N sentimento; (opinion) opinione f
sentimental [sɛntɪ'mɛntl] ADJ sentimentale
sentimentality [sɛntɪmɛn'tælɪtɪ] N sentimentalità, sentimentalismo
sentry ['sɛntrɪ] N sentinella
sentry duty N: **to be on ~** essere di sentinella
Seoul [səul] N Seul f
Sep. ABBR (= September) Sett.
separable ['sɛprəbl] ADJ separabile
separate ADJ ['sɛprɪt] separato(-a) ▸ VT ['sɛpəreɪt] separare ▸ VI ['sɛpəreɪt] separarsi; **~ from** separato da; **under ~ cover** (Comm) in plico a parte; **to ~ into** dividere in; see also **separates**
separately ['sɛprɪtlɪ] ADV separatamente
separates ['sɛprɪts] NPL (clothes) coordinati mpl
separation [sɛpə'reɪʃən] N separazione f
Sept. ABBR (= September) sett., set.
September [sɛp'tɛmbəʳ] N settembre m; see also **July**

septic ['sɛptɪk] ADJ settico(-a); (*wound*) infettato(-a); **to go ~** infettarsi

septicaemia, (*US*) **septicemia** [sɛptɪ'si:mɪə] N setticemia

septic tank N fossa settica

sequel ['si:kwl] N conseguenza; (*of story*) seguito; (*of film*) sequenza

sequence ['si:kwəns] N (*series*) serie f inv; (*order*) ordine m; **in ~** in ordine, di seguito; **~ of tenses** concordanza dei tempi

sequential [sɪ'kwɛnʃəl] ADJ: **~ access** (*Comput*) accesso sequenziale

sequin ['si:kwɪn] N lustrino, paillette f inv

Serb [sə:b] ADJ, N = **Serbian**

Serbia ['sə:bɪə] N Serbia

Serbian ['sə:bɪən] ADJ serbo(-a) ▶ N serbo(-a); (*Ling*) serbo

Serbo-Croat ['sə:bəu'krəuæt] N (*Ling*) serbocroato

serenade [sɛrə'neɪd] N serenata ▶ VT fare la serenata a

serene [sɪ'ri:n] ADJ sereno(-a), calmo(-a)

serenity [sɪ'rɛnɪtɪ] N serenità, tranquillità

sergeant ['sa:dʒənt] N sergente m; (*Police*) brigadiere m

sergeant major N maresciallo

serial ['sɪərɪəl] N (*Press*) romanzo a puntate; (*Radio, TV*) trasmissione f a puntate, serial m inv ▶ CPD (*number*) di serie; (*Comput*) seriale

serialize ['sɪərɪəlaɪz] VT pubblicare a puntate; trasmettere a puntate

serial killer N serial killer mf

serial number N numero di serie

series ['sɪəri:z] N (*pl inv*) serie f inv; (*Publishing*) collana

serious ['sɪərɪəs] ADJ serio(-a), grave; **are you ~ (about it)?** parla sul serio?

seriously ['sɪərɪəslɪ] ADV seriamente; **he's ~ rich** (*col: extremely*) ha un casino di soldi; **to take sth/sb ~** prendere qc/qn sul serio

seriousness ['sɪərɪəsnɪs] N serietà, gravità

sermon ['sə:mən] N sermone m

serrated [sɪ'reɪtɪd] ADJ seghettato(-a)

serum ['sɪərəm] N siero

servant ['sə:vənt] N domestico(-a)

serve [sə:v] VT (*employer etc*) servire, essere a servizio di; (*purpose*) servire a; (*customer, food, meal*) servire; (*apprenticeship*) fare; (*prison term*) scontare ▶ VI (*also Tennis*) servire; (*soldier etc*) prestare servizio; (*be useful*): **to ~ as/for/to do** servire da/per/per fare ▶ N (*Tennis*) servizio; **are you being served?** la stanno servendo?; **to ~ on a committee/jury** far parte di un comitato/una giuria; **it serves him right** ben gli sta, se l'è meritata; **it serves my purpose** fa al caso mio, serve al mio scopo

▶ **serve out, serve up** VT (*food*) servire

server ['sə:vər] N (*Comput*) server m inv

service ['sə:vɪs] N servizio; (*Aut: maintenance*) assistenza, revisione f; (*Rel*) funzione f ▶ VT (*car, washing machine*) revisionare; **services** NPL (*BRIT: on motorway*) stazione f di servizio; (*Mil*): **the Services** le forze armate; **to be of ~ to sb, to do sb a ~** essere d'aiuto a qn; **to put one's car in for (a) ~** portare la macchina in officina per una revisione; **dinner ~** servizio da tavola; **~ included/not included** servizio compreso/escluso

serviceable ['sə:vɪsəbl] ADJ pratico(-a), utile; (*usable, working*) usabile

service area N (*on motorway*) area di servizio

service charge N (*BRIT*) servizio

service industries NPL settore m terziario

serviceman ['sə:vɪsmən] N (*irreg*) militare m

service provider N (*Comput*) provider m inv

service station N stazione f di servizio

serviette [sə:vɪ'ɛt] N (*BRIT*) tovagliolo

servile ['sə:vaɪl] ADJ servile

session ['sɛʃən] N (*sitting*) seduta, sessione f; (*Scol*) anno scolastico (*or* accademico); **to be in ~** essere in seduta

session musician N musicista mf di studio

set [sɛt] (*pt, pp ~*) N serie f inv; (*of cutlery etc*) servizio; (*Radio, TV*) apparecchio; (*Tennis*) set m inv; (*group of people*) mondo, ambiente m; (*Cine*) scenario; (*Theat: stage*) scene fpl; (*: scenery*) scenario; (*Math*) insieme m; (*Hairdressing*) messa in piega ▶ ADJ (*fixed*) stabilito(-a), determinato(-a); (*ready*) pronto(-a) ▶ VT (*place*) posare, mettere; (*arrange*) sistemare; (*fix*) fissare; (*assign: task, homework*) dare, assegnare; (*adjust*) regolare; (*decide: rules etc*) stabilire, fissare; (*Typ*) comporre ▶ VI (*sun*) tramontare; (*jam, jelly*) rapprendersi; (*concrete*) fare presa; **to be ~ on doing** essere deciso a fare; **to be all ~ to do sth** essere pronto fare qc; **to be (dead) ~ against** essere completamente contrario a; **~ in one's ways** abitudinario; **a novel ~ in Rome** un romanzo ambientato a Roma; **to ~ to music** mettere in musica; **to ~ on fire** dare fuoco a; **to ~ free** liberare; **to ~ sth going** mettere in moto qc; **to ~ sail** prendere il mare; **a ~ phrase** una frase fatta; **a ~ of false teeth** una dentiera; **a ~ of dining-room furniture** una camera da pranzo

▶ **set about** VT FUS (*task*) intraprendere, mettersi a; **to ~ about doing sth** mettersi a fare qc

▶ **set aside** VT mettere da parte

▶ **set back** VT (*progress*) ritardare; **to ~ back (by)** (*in time*) mettere indietro (di); **a house ~ back from the road** una casa a una certa distanza dalla strada

▶ **set down** VT (*bus, train*) lasciare

▶ **set in** VI (*infection*) svilupparsi; (*complications*) intervenire; **the rain has ~ in for the day** ormai pioverà tutto il giorno

S

▶ **set off** vi partire ▶ vt (*bomb*) far scoppiare; (*cause to start*) mettere in moto; (*show up well*) dare risalto a

▶ **set out** vi partire; (*aim*): **to ~ out to do** proporsi di fare ▶ vt (*arrange*) disporre; (*state*) esporre, presentare

▶ **set up** vt (*organization*) fondare, costituire; (*record*) stabilire; (*monument*) innalzare

setback ['sɛtbæk] N (*hitch*) contrattempo, inconveniente *m*; (*in health*) ricaduta

set menu N menù *m inv* fisso

set square N squadra

settee [sɛ'tiː] N divano, sofà *m inv*

setting ['sɛtɪŋ] N (*background*) ambiente *m*; (*of controls*) posizione *f*; (*of sun*) tramonto; (*scenery*) sfondo; (*of jewel*) montatura

setting lotion N fissatore *m*

settle ['sɛtl] vt (*argument, matter*) appianare; (*problem*) risolvere; (*pay: bill, account*) regolare, saldare; (*Med: calm*) calmare; (*: colonize: land*) colonizzare ▶ vi (*bird, dust etc*) posarsi; (*sediment*) depositarsi; (*also*: **settle down**) sistemarsi, stabilirsi; (*: become calmer*) calmarsi; **to ~ to sth** applicarsi a qc; **to ~ for sth** accontentarsi di qc; **to ~ on sth** decidersi per qc; **that's settled then** allora è deciso; **to ~ one's stomach** calmare il mal di stomaco

▶ **settle in** vi sistemarsi

▶ **settle up** vi: **to ~ up with sb** regolare i conti con qn

settlement ['sɛtlmənt] N (*payment*) pagamento, saldo; (*agreement*) accordo; (*colony*) colonia; (*village etc*) villaggio, comunità *f inv*; **in ~ of our account** (*Comm*) a saldo del nostro conto

settler ['sɛtlə*] N colonizzatore(-trice)

setup ['sɛtʌp] N (*arrangement*) sistemazione *f*; (*situation*) situazione *f*; (*Comput*) setup *m inv*, installazione *f*

seven ['sɛvn] NUM sette

seventeen [sɛvn'tiːn] NUM diciassette

seventeenth [sɛvn'tiːnθ] NUM diciassettesimo(-a)

seventh ['sɛvnθ] NUM settimo(-a)

seventieth ['sɛvntɪɪθ] NUM settantesimo(-a)

seventy ['sɛvntɪ] NUM settanta

sever ['sɛvə*] vt recidere, tagliare; (*relations*) troncare

several ['sɛvərl] ADJ, PRON alcuni(-e), diversi(-e); **~ of us** alcuni di noi; **~ times** diverse volte

severance ['sɛvərəns] N (*of relations*) rottura

severance pay N indennità di licenziamento

severe [sɪ'vɪə*] ADJ severo(-a); (*serious*) serio(-a), grave; (*hard*) duro(-a); (*plain*) semplice, sobrio(-a)

severely [sɪ'vɪəlɪ] ADV (*gen*) severamente; (*wounded, ill*) gravemente

severity [sɪ'vɛrɪtɪ] N severità; gravità; (*of weather*) rigore *m*

sew [səu] (*pt* **sewed**, *pp* **sewn**) VT, VI cucire

▶ **sew up** VT ricucire; **it is all sewn up** (*fig*) è tutto apposto

sewage ['suːɪdʒ] N acque *fpl* di scolo

sewage works N stabilimento per la depurazione dei liquami

sewer ['suːə*] N fogna

sewing ['səuɪŋ] N cucitura; cucito

sewing machine N macchina da cucire

sewn [səun] PP *of* **sew**

sex [sɛks] N sesso; **to have ~ with** avere rapporti sessuali con

sex act N atto sessuale

sex appeal N sex appeal *m inv*

sex education N educazione *f* sessuale

sexism ['sɛksɪzəm] N sessismo

sexist ['sɛksɪst] ADJ, N sessista (*mf*)

sex life N vita sessuale

sex object N oggetto sessuale; **to be treated like a ~** (*woman*) essere trattata da donna oggetto

sextet [sɛks'tɛt] N sestetto

sexual ['sɛksjuəl] ADJ sessuale; **~ assault** violenza carnale; **~ harassment** molestie *fpl* sessuali; **~ intercourse** rapporti *mpl* sessuali

sexuality [sɛksju'ælɪtɪ] N sessualità

sexy ['sɛksɪ] ADJ provocante, sexy *inv*

Seychelles [seɪ'fɛlz] NPL: **the ~** le Seicelle

SF N ABBR = **science fiction**

SG N ABBR (*US*) = **Surgeon General**

Sgt. ABBR (= *sergeant*) serg.

shabbiness ['ʃæbɪnɪs] N trasandatezza; squallore *m*; meschinità

shabby ['ʃæbɪ] ADJ trasandato(-a); (*building*) squallido(-a), malandato(-a); (*behaviour*) meschino(-a)

shack [ʃæk] N baracca, capanna

shackles ['ʃæklz] NPL ferri *mpl*, catene *fpl*

shade [ʃeɪd] N ombra; (*for lamp*) paralume *m*; (*of colour*) tonalità *f inv*; (*US: window shade*) veneziana; (*small quantity*): **a ~ (more/too large)** un po' (di più/troppo grande); **a ~ smaller** un tantino più piccolo ▶ vt ombreggiare, fare ombra a; **shades** NPL (*US: sunglasses*) occhiali *mpl* da sole; **in the ~** all'ombra

shadow ['ʃædəu] N ombra ▶ vt (*follow*) pedinare; **without** *or* **beyond a ~ of doubt** senz'ombra di dubbio

shadow cabinet N (*Brit Pol*) governo *m* ombra *inv*

shadowy ['ʃædəuɪ] ADJ ombreggiato(-a), ombroso(-a); (*dim*) vago(-a), indistinto(-a)

shady ['ʃeɪdɪ] ADJ ombroso(-a); (*fig: dishonest*) losco(-a), equivoco(-a)

shaft [ʃɑːft] N (*of arrow, spear*) asta; (*Aut, Tech*)

albero; (*of mine*) pozzo; (*of lift*) tromba; (*of light*) raggio; **ventilator** ~ condotto di ventilazione

shaggy ['ʃægɪ] ADJ ispido(-a)

shake [ʃeɪk] (*pt* **shook**, *pp* **shaken**) VT scuotere; (*bottle, cocktail*) agitare ▶ VI tremare ▶ N scossa; **to** ~ **one's head** (*in refusal, dismay*) scuotere la testa; **to** ~ **hands with sb** stringere *or* dare la mano a qn
  ▶ **shake off** VT scrollare (via); (*fig*) sbarazzarsi di
  ▶ **shake up** VT scuotere

shake-up ['ʃeɪkʌp] N riorganizzazione *f* drastica

shakily ['ʃeɪkɪlɪ] ADV (*reply*) con voce tremante; (*walk*) con passo malfermo; (*write*) con mano tremante

shaky ['ʃeɪkɪ] ADJ (*hand, voice*) tremante; (*memory*) labile; (*knowledge*) incerto(-a); (*building*) traballante

shale [ʃeɪl] N roccia scistosa

shall [ʃæl] AUX VB: **I** ~ **go** andrò; ~ **I open the door?** apro io la porta?; **I'll get some,** ~ **I?** ne prendo un po', va bene?

shallot [ʃə'lɔt] N (BRIT) scalogna

shallow ['ʃæləʊ] ADJ poco profondo(-a); (*fig*) superficiale

sham [ʃæm] N finzione *f*, messinscena; (*jewellery, furniture*) imitazione *f* ▶ ADJ finto(-a) ▶ VT fingere, simulare

shambles ['ʃæmblz] N confusione *f*, baraonda, scompiglio; **the economy is (in) a complete** ~ l'economia è nel caos più totale

shambolic [ʃæm'bɔlɪk] ADJ (*col*) incasinato(-a)

shame [ʃeɪm] N vergogna ▶ VT far vergognare; **it is a** ~ **(that/to do)** è un peccato (che+*sub*/fare); **what a** ~! che peccato!; **to put sb/sth to** ~ (*fig*) far sfigurare qn/qc

shamefaced ['ʃeɪmfeɪst] ADJ vergognoso(-a)

shameful ['ʃeɪmful] ADJ vergognoso(-a)

shameless ['ʃeɪmlɪs] ADJ sfrontato(-a); (*immodest*) spudorato(-a)

shampoo [ʃæm'puː] N shampoo *m inv* ▶ VT fare lo shampoo a; ~ **and set** shampoo e messa in piega

shamrock ['ʃæmrɔk] N trifoglio (*simbolo nazionale dell'Irlanda*)

shandy ['ʃændɪ] N birra con gassosa

shan't [ʃɑːnt] = **shall not**

shanty town ['ʃæntɪ-] N bidonville *f inv*

SHAPE [ʃeɪp] N ABBR (= *Supreme Headquarters Allied Powers, Europe*) supremo quartier generale delle Potenze Alleate in Europa

shape [ʃeɪp] N forma ▶ VT (*clay, stone*) dar forma a; (*fig: ideas, character*) formare; (: *course of events*) determinare, condizionare;

(*statement*) formulare; (*sb's ideas*) condizionare ▶ VI (*also*: **shape up**: *events*) andare, mettersi; (: *person*) cavarsela; **to take** ~ prendere forma; **in the** ~ **of a heart** a forma di cuore; **to get o.s. into** ~ rimettersi in forma; **I can't bear gardening in any** ~ **or form** detesto il giardinaggio d'ogni genere e specie

-shaped [ʃeɪpt] SUFFIX: **heart~** a forma di cuore

shapeless ['ʃeɪplɪs] ADJ senza forma, informe

shapely ['ʃeɪplɪ] ADJ ben proporzionato(-a)

share [ʃeəʳ] N (*thing received, contribution*) parte *f*; (*Comm*) azione *f* ▶ VT dividere; (*have in common*) condividere, avere in comune; **to** ~ **out (among** *or* **between)** dividere (tra); **to** ~ **in** partecipare a

share capital N capitale *m* azionario

share certificate N certificato azionario

shareholder ['ʃeəhəʊldəʳ] N azionista *mf*

share index N listino di Borsa

shark [ʃɑːk] N squalo, pescecane *m*

sharp [ʃɑːp] ADJ (*razor, knife*) affilato(-a); (*point*) acuto(-a), acuminato(-a); (*nose, chin*) aguzzo(-a); (*outline*) netto(-a); (*curve, bend*) stretto(-a), accentuato(-a); (*cold, pain*) pungente; (*voice*) stridulo(-a); (*person: quick-witted*) sveglio(-a); (: *unscrupulous*) disonesto(-a); (*Mus*): **C** ~ do diesis ▶ N (*Mus*) diesis *m inv* ▶ ADV: **at 2 o'clock** ~ alle due in punto; **turn** ~ **left** giri tutto a sinistra; **to be** ~ **with sb** rimproverare qn; **look** ~! sbrigati!

sharpen ['ʃɑːpən] VT affilare; (*pencil*) fare la punta a; (*fig*) acuire

sharpener ['ʃɑːpnəʳ] N (*also*: **pencil sharpener**) temperamatite *m inv*; (*also*: **knife sharpener**) affilacoltelli *m inv*

sharp-eyed [ʃɑːp'aɪd] ADJ dalla vista acuta

sharpish ['ʃɑːpɪʃ] ADV (BRIT *col*: *quickly*) subito

sharply ['ʃɑːplɪ] ADV (*abruptly*) bruscamente; (*clearly*) nettamente; (*harshly*) duramente, aspramente

sharp-tempered [ʃɑːp'tɛmpəd] ADJ irascibile

shatter ['ʃætəʳ] VT mandare in frantumi, frantumare; (*fig: upset*) distruggere; (: *ruin*) rovinare ▶ VI frantumarsi, andare in pezzi

shattered ['ʃætəd] ADJ (*grief-stricken*) sconvolto(-a); (*exhausted*) a pezzi, distrutto(-a)

shatterproof ['ʃætəpruːf] ADJ infrangibile

shave [ʃeɪv] VT radere, rasare ▶ VI radersi, farsi la barba ▶ N: **to have a** ~ farsi la barba

shaven ['ʃeɪvn] ADJ (*head*) rasato(-a), tonsurato(-a)

shaver ['ʃeɪvəʳ] N (*also*: **electric shaver**) rasoio elettrico

shaving ['ʃeɪvɪŋ] N (*action*) rasatura; **shavings** NPL (*of wood etc*) trucioli *mpl*

shaving brush N pennello da barba

shaving cream N crema da barba
shaving foam N = **shaving cream**
shaving soap N sapone m da barba
shawl [ʃɔːl] N scialle m
she [ʃiː] PRON ella, lei; **there ~ is** eccola;
~-bear orsa; **~-cat** gatta; **~-elephant**
elefantessa, *for ships, countries follow the gender
of your translation*
sheaf [ʃiːf] (*pl* **sheaves**) N covone m
shear [ʃɪəʳ] (*pt* **sheared**, *pp* **sheared** *or* **shorn**
[ʃɔːn]) VT (*sheep*) tosare
▸ **shear off** VI (*break off*) spezzarsi
shears [ʃɪəz] NPL (*for hedge*) cesoie fpl
sheath [ʃiːθ] N fodero, guaina; (*contraceptive*)
preservativo
sheathe [ʃiːð] VT rivestire; (*sword*)
rinfoderare
sheath knife N coltello (con fodero)
sheaves [ʃiːvz] NPL *of* **sheaf**
shed [ʃɛd] (*pt, pp* **~**) N capannone m ▸ VT
(*leaves, fur etc*) perdere; (*tears, blood*) versare;
(*workers*) liberarsi di; **to ~ light on** (*problem,
mystery*) far luce su
she'd [ʃiːd] = **she had**; **she would**
sheen [ʃiːn] N lucentezza
sheep [ʃiːp] N (*pl inv*) pecora
sheepdog [ˈʃiːpdɔg] N cane m da pastore
sheep farmer N allevatore m di pecore
sheepish [ˈʃiːpɪʃ] ADJ vergognoso(-a),
timido(-a)
sheepskin [ˈʃiːpskɪn] N pelle f di pecora
sheepskin jacket N (giacca di) montone m
sheer [ʃɪəʳ] ADJ (*utter*) vero(-a) (e proprio(-a));
(*steep*) a picco, perpendicolare; (*transparent*)
trasparente; (*almost transparent*) sottile ▸ ADV
a picco; **by ~ chance** per puro caso
sheet [ʃiːt] N (*on bed*) lenzuolo; (*of paper*)
foglio; (*of glass*) lastra; (*of metal*) foglio,
lamina
sheet feed N (*on printer*) alimentazione f di
fogli
sheet lightning N lampo diffuso
sheet metal N lamiera
sheet music N fogli mpl di musica
sheik, sheikh [ʃeɪk] N sceicco
shelf [ʃɛlf] (*pl* **shelves** [ʃɛlvz]) N scaffale m,
mensola
shelf life N (*Comm*) durata di conservazione
shell [ʃɛl] N (*on beach*) conchiglia; (*of egg, nut
etc*) guscio; (*explosive*) granata; (*of building*)
scheletro, struttura ▸ VT (*peas*) sgranare;
(*Mil*) bombardare, cannoneggiare
▸ **shell out** VI (*col*): **to ~ out (for)** sganciare
soldi (per)
she'll [ʃiːl] = **she will**; **she shall**
shellfish [ˈʃɛlfɪʃ] N (*pl inv*: *crab etc*) crostaceo;
(*scallop etc*) mollusco; (*pl*: *as food*) crostacei;
molluschi
shellsuit [ˈʃɛlsuːt] N tuta di acetato

shelter [ˈʃɛltəʳ] N riparo, rifugio ▸ VT
riparare, proteggere; (*give lodging to*) dare
rifugio *or* asilo a ▸ VI ripararsi, mettersi al
riparo; **to take ~ (from)** mettersi al
riparo (da)
sheltered [ˈʃɛltəd] ADJ (*life*) ritirato(-a); (*spot*)
riparato(-a), protetto(-a)
shelve [ʃɛlv] VT (*fig*) accantonare, rimandare
shelves [ʃɛlvz] NPL *of* **shelf**
shelving [ˈʃɛlvɪŋ] N scaffalature fpl
shepherd [ˈʃɛpəd] N pastore m ▸ VT (*guide*)
guidare
shepherdess [ˈʃɛpədɪs] N pastora
shepherd's pie (BRIT) N timballo di carne
macinata e purè di patate
sherbet [ˈʃəːbət] N (BRIT: *powder*) polvere
effervescente al gusto di frutta; (US: *water ice*)
sorbetto
sheriff [ˈʃɛrɪf] (US) N sceriffo
sherry [ˈʃɛrɪ] N sherry m inv
she's [ʃiːz] = **she is**; **she has**
Shetland [ˈʃɛtlənd] N (*also*: **the Shetlands,
the Shetland Isles**) le (isole) Shetland
Shetland pony N pony m inv delle Shetland
shield [ʃiːld] N scudo; (*trophy*) scudetto;
(*protection*) schermo ▸ VT: **to ~ (from)**
riparare (da), proteggere (da *or* contro)
shift [ʃɪft] N (*change*) cambiamento; (*of
workers*) turno ▸ VT spostare, muovere;
(*remove*) rimuovere ▸ VI spostarsi, muoversi;
~ in demand (*Comm*) variazione f della
domanda; **the wind has shifted to the
south** il vento si è girato e soffia da sud
shift key N (*on typewriter*) tasto delle
maiuscole
shiftless [ˈʃɪftlɪs] ADJ fannullone(-a)
shift work N lavoro a squadre; **to do ~** fare i
turni
shifty [ˈʃɪftɪ] ADJ ambiguo(-a); (*eyes*)
sfuggente
Shiite [ˈʃiːaɪt] ADJ, N sciita mf
shilling [ˈʃɪlɪŋ] N (BRIT) scellino (12 *old pence*; 20
in a pound)
shilly-shally [ˈʃɪlɪʃælɪ] VI tentennare, esitare
shimmer [ˈʃɪməʳ] VI brillare, luccicare
shimmering [ˈʃɪmərɪŋ] ADJ (*gen*) luccicante,
scintillante; (*haze*) tremolante; (*satin etc*)
cangiante
shin [ʃɪn] N tibia ▸ VI: **to ~ up/down a tree**
arrampicarsi in cima a/scivolare giù da un
albero
shindig [ˈʃɪndɪg] N (*col*) festa chiassosa
shine [ʃaɪn] (*pt, pp* **shone**) N splendore m,
lucentezza ▸ VI (ri)splendere, brillare ▸ VT
far brillare, far risplendere; (*torch*): **to ~ sth
on** puntare qc verso
shingle [ˈʃɪŋgl] N (*on beach*) ciottoli mpl; (*on
roof*) assicella di copertura
shingles [ˈʃɪŋglz] N (*Med*) herpes zoster m

shining ['ʃaɪnɪŋ] ADJ (*surface, hair*) lucente; (*light*) brillante

shiny ['ʃaɪnɪ] ADJ lucente, lucido(-a)

ship [ʃɪp] N nave *f* ▶ VT trasportare (via mare); (*send*) spedire (via mare); (*load*) imbarcare, caricare; **on board** ~ a bordo

shipbuilder ['ʃɪpbɪldə^r] N costruttore *m* navale

shipbuilding ['ʃɪpbɪldɪŋ] N costruzione *f* navale

ship chandler [-'tʃɑːndlə^r] N fornitore *m* marittimo

shipment ['ʃɪpmənt] N carico

shipowner ['ʃɪpəʊnə^r] N armatore *m*

shipper ['ʃɪpə^r] N spedizioniere *m* (marittimo)

shipping ['ʃɪpɪŋ] N (*ships*) naviglio; (*traffic*) navigazione *f*

shipping agent N agente *m* marittimo

shipping company N compagnia di navigazione

shipping lane N rotta (di navigazione)

shipping line N = **shipping company**

shipshape ['ʃɪpʃeɪp] ADJ in perfetto ordine

shipwreck ['ʃɪprɛk] N relitto; (*event*) naufragio ▶ VT: **to be shipwrecked** naufragare, fare naufragio

shipyard ['ʃɪpjɑːd] N cantiere *m* navale

shire ['ʃaɪə^r] (*BRIT*) contea

shirk [ʃəːk] VT sottrarsi a, evitare

shirt [ʃəːt] N (*man's*) camicia; **in ~ sleeves** in maniche di camicia

shirty ['ʃəːtɪ] ADJ (*BRIT col*) incavolato(-a)

shit [ʃɪt] EXCL (*col!*) merda (!)

shiver ['ʃɪvə^r] N brivido ▶ VI rabbrividire, tremare

shoal [ʃəʊl] N (*of fish*) banco

shock [ʃɔk] N (*impact*) urto, colpo; (*Elec*) scossa; (*emotional*) colpo, shock *m inv*; (*Med*) shock ▶ VT colpire, scioccare; scandalizzare; **to give sb a ~** far venire un colpo a qn; **to be suffering from ~** essere in stato di shock; **it came as a ~ to hear that ...** è stata una grossa sorpresa sentire che ...

shock absorber N ammortizzatore *m*

shocker ['ʃɔkə^r] N: **it was a real ~** (*col*) è stata una vera bomba

shocking ['ʃɔkɪŋ] ADJ scioccante, traumatizzante; (*scandalous*) scandaloso(-a); (*very bad: weather, handwriting*) orribile; (: *results*) disastroso(-a)

shockproof ['ʃɔkpruːf] ADJ antiurto *inv*

shock therapy, shock treatment N (*Med*) shockterapia

shock wave N onda d'urto; (*fig: usually pl*) impatto *msg*

shod [ʃɔd] PT, PP *of* **shoe**

shoddy ['ʃɔdɪ] ADJ scadente

shoe [ʃuː] (*pt, pp* **shod** [ʃɔd]) N scarpa;

(*also*: **horseshoe**) ferro di cavallo; (: **brake shoe**) ganascia (del freno) ▶ VT (*horse*) ferrare

shoebrush ['ʃuːbrʌʃ] N spazzola per le scarpe

shoehorn ['ʃuːhɔːn] N calzante *m*

shoelace ['ʃuːleɪs] N stringa

shoemaker ['ʃuːmeɪkə^r] N calzolaio

shoe polish N lucido per scarpe

shoeshop ['ʃuːʃɔp] N calzoleria

shoestring ['ʃuːstrɪŋ] N stringa (delle scarpe); **on a ~** (*fig: do sth*) con quattro soldi

shoetree ['ʃuːtriː] N forma per scarpe

shone [ʃɔn] PT, PP *of* **shine**

shonky ['ʃɔŋkɪ] ADJ (*AUSTRALIA, NEW ZEALAND col: untrustworthy*) sospetto(-a)

shoo [ʃuː] EXCL sciò!, via! ▶ VT (*also*: **shoo away, shoo off**) cacciare (via)

shook [ʃʊk] PT *of* **shake**

shoot [ʃuːt] (*pt, pp* **shot** [ʃɔt]) N (*on branch, seedling*) germoglio; (*shooting party*) partita di caccia; (*competition*) gara di tiro ▶ VT (*game: BRIT*) cacciare, andare a caccia di; (*person*) sparare a; (*execute*) fucilare; (*film*) girare ▶ VI (*Football*) sparare, tirare (forte); **to ~ (at)** (*with gun*) sparare (a), fare fuoco (su); (*with bow*) tirare (su); **to ~ past sb** passare vicino a qn come un fulmine; **to ~ in/out** entrare/uscire come una freccia

▶ **shoot down** VT (*plane*) abbattere

▶ **shoot up** VI (*fig*) salire alle stelle

shooting ['ʃuːtɪŋ] N (*shots*) sparatoria; (*murder*) uccisione *f* (a colpi d'arma da fuoco); (*Hunting*) caccia; (*Cine*) riprese *fpl*

shooting range N poligono (di tiro), tirassegno

shooting star N stella cadente

shop [ʃɔp] N negozio; (*workshop*) officina ▶ VI (*also*: **go shopping**) fare spese; **repair ~** officina di riparazione; **to talk ~** (*fig*) parlare di lavoro

▶ **shop around** VI fare il giro dei negozi

shopaholic ['ʃɔpə'hɔlɪk] N (*col*) maniaco(-a) dello shopping

shop assistant N (*BRIT*) commesso(-a)

shop floor N (*BRIT fig*) operai *mpl*, maestranze *fpl*

shopkeeper ['ʃɔpkiːpə^r] N negoziante *mf*, bottegaio(-a)

shoplift ['ʃɔplɪft] VI taccheggiare

shoplifter ['ʃɔplɪftə^r] N taccheggiatore(-trice)

shoplifting ['ʃɔplɪftɪŋ] N taccheggio

shopper ['ʃɔpə^r] N compratore(-trice)

shopping ['ʃɔpɪŋ] N (*goods*) spesa, acquisti *mpl*

shopping bag N borsa per la spesa

shopping cart N (*US Comput: shopping trolley*) carrello

shopping centre, (*US*) **shopping center** N centro commerciale

shopping mall N centro commerciale

S

shopping trolley N (BRIT) carrello del supermercato

shop-soiled ['ʃɒpsɔɪld] ADJ sciupato(-a) a forza di stare in vetrina

shop steward N (BRIT Industry) rappresentante m sindacale

shop window N vetrina

shore [ʃɔːʳ] N (of sea) riva, spiaggia; (of lake) riva ▶ VT: **to ~ (up)** puntellare; **on ~** a riva

shore leave N (Naut) franchigia

shorn [ʃɔːn] PP of **shear**

short [ʃɔːt] ADJ (not long) corto(-a); (soon finished) breve; (person) basso(-a); (curt) brusco(-a), secco(-a); (insufficient) insufficiente ▶ N (also: **short film**) cortometraggio; **it is ~ for** è l'abbreviazione or il diminutivo di; **a ~ time ago** poco tempo fa; **in the ~ term** nell'immediato futuro; **to be ~ of sth** essere a corto di or mancare di qc; **to run ~ of sth** rimanere senza qc; **to be in ~ supply** scarseggiare; **I'm 3 ~** me ne mancano 3; **in ~** in breve; **~ of doing** a meno che non si faccia; **everything ~ of** tutto fuorché; **to cut ~** (speech, visit) accorciare, abbreviare; (person) interrompere; **to fall ~ of** venire meno a; non soddisfare; **to stop ~** fermarsi di colpo; **to stop ~ of** non arrivare fino a; see also **shorts**

shortage ['ʃɔːtɪdʒ] N scarsezza, carenza

shortbread ['ʃɔːtbrɛd] N biscotto di pasta frolla

short-change [ʃɔːt'tʃeɪndʒ] VT: **to ~ sb** imbrogliare qn sul resto

short-circuit [ʃɔːt'səːkɪt] N cortocircuito ▶ VT cortocircuitare ▶ VI fare cortocircuito

shortcoming ['ʃɔːtkʌmɪŋ] N difetto

shortcrust pastry ['ʃɔːtkrʌst-], **short pastry** ['ʃɔːt-] (BRIT) pasta frolla

shortcut ['ʃɔːtkʌt] N scorciatoia

shorten ['ʃɔːtn] VT accorciare, ridurre

shortening ['ʃɔːtnɪŋ] N grasso per pasticceria

shortfall ['ʃɔːtfɔːl] N deficit m inv

shorthand ['ʃɔːthænd] N (BRIT) stenografia; **to take sth down in ~** stenografare qc

shorthand notebook N (BRIT) bloc-notes m inv per stenografia

shorthand typist N (BRIT) stenodattilografo(-a)

short list N (BRIT: for job) rosa dei candidati

short-lived ['ʃɔːt'lɪvd] ADJ effimero(-a), di breve durata

shortly ['ʃɔːtlɪ] ADV fra poco

shortness ['ʃɔːtnɪs] N brevità; insufficienza

shorts [ʃɔːts] NPL (also: **a pair of shorts**) i calzoncini

short-sighted [ʃɔːt'saɪtɪd] ADJ (BRIT) miope; (fig) poco avveduto(-a)

short-sleeved ['ʃɔːtsliːvd] ADJ a maniche corte

short-staffed [ʃɔːt'stɑːft] ADJ a corto di personale

short story N racconto, novella

short-tempered [ʃɔːt'tɛmpəd] ADJ irascibile

short-term ['ʃɔːttəːm] ADJ (effect) di or a breve durata; (borrowing) a breve scadenza

short time N (Industry): **to work ~, be on ~** essere or lavorare a orario ridotto

short wave N (Radio) onde fpl corte

shot [ʃɒt] PT, PP of **shoot** ▶ N sparo, colpo; (shotgun pellets) pallottole fpl; (person) tiratore m; (try) prova; (Football) tiro; (injection) iniezione f; (Phot) foto f inv; **like a ~** come un razzo; (very readily) immediatamente; **to fire a ~ at sb/sth** sparare un colpo a qn/qc; **to have a ~ at sth/doing sth** provarci con qc/a fare qc; **a big ~** (col) un pezzo grosso, un papavero; **to get ~ of sb/sth** (col) sbarazzarsi di qn/qc

shotgun ['ʃɒtgʌn] N fucile m da caccia

should [ʃud] AUX VB: **I ~ go now** dovrei andare ora; **he ~ be there now** dovrebbe essere arrivato ora; **I ~ go if I were you** se fossi in lei andrei; **I ~ like to** mi piacerebbe; **~ he phone ...** se telefonasse ...

shoulder ['ʃəuldəʳ] N spalla; **hard ~** corsia d'emergenza ▶ VT (fig) addossarsi, prendere sulle proprie spalle; **to look over one's ~** guardarsi alle spalle; **to rub shoulders with sb** (fig) essere a contatto con qn; **to give sb the cold ~** (fig) trattare qn con freddezza

shoulder bag N borsa a tracolla

shoulder blade N scapola

shoulder strap N bretella, spallina

shouldn't ['ʃudnt]= **should not**

shout [ʃaut] N urlo, grido ▶ VT gridare ▶ VI (also: **shout out**) urlare, gridare; **to give sb a ~** chiamare qn gridando
▶ **shout down** VT zittire gridando

shouting ['ʃautɪŋ] N urli mpl

shouting match N (col) vivace scambio di opinioni

shove [ʃʌv] VT spingere; (col: put): **to ~ sth in** ficcare qc in ▶ N spintone m; **he shoved me out of the way** mi ha spinto da parte
▶ **shove off** VI (Naut) scostarsi

shovel ['ʃʌvl] N pala ▶ VT spalare

show [ʃəu] (pt **showed**, pp **shown** [ʃəun]) N (of emotion) dimostrazione f, manifestazione f; (semblance) apparenza; (exhibition) mostra, esposizione f; (Theat, Cine) spettacolo; (Comm, Tech) salone m, fiera ▶ VT far vedere, mostrare; (courage etc) dimostrare, dar prova di; (exhibit) esporre ▶ VI vedersi, essere visibile; **to ~ sb to his seat/to the door** accompagnare qn al suo posto/alla porta; **to ~ a profit/loss** (Comm) registrare un utile/una perdita; **it just goes to ~ that ...** il che sta a dimostrare che ...; **to ask for a ~ of**

hands chiedere che si voti per alzata di mano; **to be on ~** essere esposto; **it's just for ~** è solo per far scena; **who's running the ~ here?** (col) chi è il padrone qui?
▶ **show in** VT (person) far entrare
▶ **show off** VI (pej) esibirsi, mettersi in mostra ▶ VT (display) mettere in risalto; (pej) mettere in mostra
▶ **show out** VT (person) accompagnare alla porta
▶ **show up** VI (stand out) essere ben visibile; (col: turn up) farsi vedere ▶ VT mettere in risalto; (unmask) smascherare
showbiz ['ʃəubɪz] N (col) = **show business**
show business N industria dello spettacolo
showcase ['ʃəukeɪs] N vetrina, bacheca
showdown ['ʃəudaun] N prova di forza
shower ['ʃauəʳ] N doccia; (rain) acquazzone m; (of stones etc) pioggia; (US: party) festa in cui si fanno regali alla persona festeggiata (di fidanzamento ecc) ▶ VI fare la doccia ▶ VT: **to ~ sb with** (gifts, abuse etc) coprire qn di; (missiles) lanciare contro qn una pioggia di; **to have** or **take a ~** fare la doccia
shower cap N cuffia da doccia
shower gel N gel m doccia inv
showerproof ['ʃauəpruːf] ADJ impermeabile
showery ['ʃauərɪ] ADJ (weather) con piogge intermittenti
showground ['ʃəugraund] N terreno d'esposizione
showing ['ʃəuɪŋ] N (of film) proiezione f
show jumping N concorso ippico (di salto ad ostacoli)
showman ['ʃəumən] N (irreg) (at fair, circus) impresario; (fig) attore m
showmanship ['ʃəumənʃɪp] N abilità d'impresario
shown [ʃəun] PP of **show**
show-off ['ʃəuɔf] N (col: person) esibizionista mf
showpiece ['ʃəupiːs] N (of exhibition) pezzo forte; **that hospital is a ~** è un ospedale modello
showroom ['ʃəurum] N sala d'esposizione
show trial N processo a scopo dimostrativo (spesso ideologico)
showy ['ʃəuɪ] ADJ vistoso(-a), appariscente
shrank [ʃræŋk] PT of **shrink**
shrapnel ['ʃræpnl] N shrapnel m
shred [ʃred] N (gen pl) brandello; (fig: of truth, evidence) briciolo ▶ VT fare a brandelli; (Culin) sminuzzare, tagliuzzare; (documents) distruggere, sminuzzare
shredder ['ʃredəʳ] N (for documents, papers) distruttore m di documenti, sminuzzatrice f
shrew [ʃruː] N (Zool) toporagno; (fig: pej: woman) strega
shrewd [ʃruːd] ADJ astuto(-a), scaltro(-a)

shrewdness ['ʃruːdnɪs] N astuzia
shriek [ʃriːk] N strillo ▶ VT, VI strillare
shrift [ʃrɪft] N: **to give sb short ~** sbrigare qn
shrill [ʃrɪl] ADJ acuto(-a), stridulo(-a), stridente
shrimp [ʃrɪmp] N gamberetto
shrine [ʃraɪn] N reliquario; (place) santuario
shrink [ʃrɪŋk] (pt **shrank** [ʃræŋk], pp **shrunk** [ʃrʌŋk]) VI restringersi; (fig) ridursi; (also: **shrink away**) ritrarsi ▶ VT (wool) far restringere ▶ N (col, pej) psicanalista mf; **to ~ from doing sth** rifuggire dal fare qc
shrinkage ['ʃrɪŋkɪdʒ] N restringimento
shrink-wrap ['ʃrɪŋkræp] VT confezionare con plastica sottile
shrivel ['ʃrɪvl], **shrivel up** VT raggrinzare, avvizzire ▶ VI raggrinzirsi, avvizzire
shroud [ʃraud] N lenzuolo funebre ▶ VT: **shrouded in mystery** avvolto(-a) nel mistero
Shrove Tuesday ['ʃrəuv-] N martedì m grasso
shrub [ʃrʌb] N arbusto
shrubbery ['ʃrʌbərɪ] N arbusti mpl
shrug [ʃrʌg] N scrollata di spalle ▶ VT, VI: **to ~ (one's shoulders)** alzare le spalle, fare spallucce
▶ **shrug off** VT passare sopra a; (cold, illness) sbarazzarsi di
shrunk [ʃrʌŋk] PP of **shrink**
shrunken ['ʃrʌŋkən] ADJ rattrappito(-a)
shudder ['ʃʌdəʳ] N brivido ▶ VI rabbrividire
shuffle ['ʃʌfl] VT (cards) mescolare; **to ~ (one's feet)** strascicare i piedi
shun [ʃʌn] VT sfuggire, evitare
shunt [ʃʌnt] VT (Rail: direct) smistare; (: divert) deviare ▶ VI: **to ~ (to and fro)** fare la spola
shunting yard N fascio di smistamento
shush [ʃuʃ] EXCL zitto(-a)!
shut [ʃʌt] (pt, pp **~**) VT chiudere ▶ VI chiudersi, chiudere
▶ **shut down** VT, VI chiudere definitivamente
▶ **shut off** VT (stop: power) staccare; (: water) chiudere; (: engine) spegnere; (isolate) isolare
▶ **shut out** VT (person, noise, cold) non far entrare; (block: view) impedire, bloccare; (: memory) scacciare
▶ **shut up** VI (col: keep quiet) stare zitto(-a), fare silenzio ▶ VT (close) chiudere; (silence) far tacere
shutdown ['ʃʌtdaun] N chiusura
shutter ['ʃʌtəʳ] N imposta; (Phot) otturatore m
shuttle ['ʃʌtl] N spola, navetta; (space shuttle) navetta (spaziale); (also: **shuttle service**) servizio m navetta inv ▶ VI (vehicle, person) fare la spola ▶ VT (to and fro: passengers) portare (avanti e indietro)
shuttlecock ['ʃʌtlkɔk] N volano
shuttle diplomacy N frequenti mediazioni fpl diplomatiche

S

shy [ʃaɪ] ADJ timido(-a) ▶ VI: **to ~ away from doing sth** (fig) rifuggire dal fare qc; **to fight ~ of** tenersi alla larga da; **to be ~ of doing sth** essere restio a fare qc

shyness ['ʃaɪnɪs] N timidezza

Siam [saɪ'æm] N Siam m

Siamese [saɪə'miːz] ADJ: **~ cat** gatto siamese; **~ twins** fratelli mpl (or sorelle fpl) siamesi

Siberia [saɪ'bɪərɪə] N Siberia

sibling ['sɪblɪŋ] N (formal) fratello/sorella

Sicilian [sɪ'sɪlɪən] ADJ, N siciliano(-a)

Sicily ['sɪsɪlɪ] N Sicilia

sick [sɪk] ADJ (ill) malato(-a); (humour) macabro(-a); **to be ~** (vomiting) vomitare; **to feel ~** avere la nausea; **to be ~ of** (fig) averne abbastanza di; **a ~ person** un malato; **to be (off) ~** essere assente perché malato; **to fall** or **take ~** ammalarsi

sickbag ['sɪkbæg] N sacchetto (da usarsi in caso di malessere)

sick bay N infermeria

sick building syndrome N malattia causata da mancanza di ventilazione e luce naturale

sicken ['sɪkn] VT nauseare ▶ VI: **to be sickening for sth** (cold, flu etc) covare qc

sickening ['sɪknɪŋ] ADJ (fig) disgustoso(-a), rivoltante

sickle ['sɪkl] N falcetto

sick leave N congedo per malattia

sickle-cell anaemia ['sɪklsɛl-] N anemia drepanocitica

sickly ['sɪklɪ] ADJ malaticcio(-a); (causing nausea) nauseante

sickness ['sɪknɪs] N malattia; (vomiting) vomito

sickness benefit N indennità di malattia

sick pay N sussidio per malattia

sickroom ['sɪkruːm] N stanza di malato

side [saɪd] N (gen) lato; (of person, animal) fianco; (of lake) riva; (face, surface: gen) faccia; (: of paper) facciata; (fig: aspect) aspetto, lato; (team: Sport) squadra; (: Pol etc) parte f ▶ CPD (door, entrance) laterale ▶ VI: **to ~ with sb** parteggiare per qn, prendere le parti di qn; **by the ~ of** a fianco di; (road) sul ciglio di; **~ by ~** fianco a fianco; **to take sides (with)** schierarsi (con); **the right/wrong ~** il dritto/rovescio; **from ~ to ~** da una parte all'altra; **~ of beef** quarto di bue

sideboard ['saɪdbɔːd] N credenza

sideboards ['saɪdbɔːdz], (US) **sideburns** ['saɪdbəːnz] NPL (whiskers) basette fpl

sidecar ['saɪdkɑːʳ] N sidecar m inv

side dish N contorno

side drum N (Mus) piccolo tamburo

side effect N (Med) effetto collaterale

sidekick ['saɪdkɪk] N (col) compagno(-a)

sidelight ['saɪdlaɪt] N (Aut) luce f di posizione

sideline ['saɪdlaɪn] N (Sport) linea laterale;

(fig) attività secondaria

sidelong ['saɪdlɔŋ] ADJ obliquo(-a); **to give a ~ glance at sth** guardare qc con la coda dell'occhio

side order N contorno (pietanza)

side plate N piattino

side road N strada secondaria

sidesaddle ['saɪdsædl] ADV all'amazzone

side show N attrazione f

sidestep ['saɪdstɛp] VT (question) eludere; (problem) scavalcare ▶ VI (Boxing etc) spostarsi di lato

side street N traversa

sidetrack ['saɪdtræk] VT (fig) distrarre

sidewalk ['saɪdwɔːk] N (US) marciapiede m

sideways ['saɪdweɪz] ADV (move) di lato, di fianco; (look) con la coda dell'occhio

siding ['saɪdɪŋ] N (Rail) binario di raccordo

sidle ['saɪdl] VI: **to ~ up (to)** avvicinarsi furtivamente (a)

SIDS N (= sudden infant death syndrome) = **cot death**

siege [siːdʒ] N assedio; **to lay ~ to** porre l'assedio a

siege economy N economia da stato d'assedio

Sierra Leone [sɪ'ɛrəlɪ'əun] N Sierra Leone f

sieve [sɪv] N setaccio ▶ VT setacciare

sift [sɪft] VT passare al crivello; (fig) vagliare ▶ VI: **to ~ through** esaminare minuziosamente

sigh [saɪ] N sospiro ▶ VI sospirare

sight [saɪt] N (faculty) vista; (spectacle) spettacolo; (on gun) mira ▶ VT avvistare; **in ~** in vista; **on ~** a vista; **out of ~** non visibile; **at first ~** a prima vista; **to catch ~ of sth/sb** scorgere qc/qn; **to lose ~ of sb/sth** perdere di vista qn/qc; **to set one's sights on sth/on doing sth** mirare a qc/a fare qc; **at ~** a vista; **I know her by ~** la conosco di vista

sighted ['saɪtɪd] ADJ che ha il dono della vista; **partially ~** parzialmente cieco

sightseeing ['saɪtsiːɪŋ] N giro turistico; **to go ~** visitare una località

sightseer ['saɪtsiːəʳ] N turista mf

sign [saɪn] N segno; (with hand etc) segno, gesto; (notice) insegna, cartello; (road sign) segnale m ▶ VT firmare; (player) ingaggiare; **as a ~ of** in segno di; **it's a good/bad ~** è buon/brutto segno; **to show signs/no ~ of doing sth** accennare/non accennare a fare qc; **plus/minus ~** segno del più/meno; **to ~ one's name** firmare, apporre la propria firma

▶ **sign away** VT (rights etc) cedere (con una firma)

▶ **sign for** VT FUS (item) firmare per l'accettazione di

▶ **sign in** VI firmare il registro (all'arrivo)

▸ **sign off** VI (*Radio*, *TV*) chiudere le trasmissioni

▸ **sign on** VI (*Mil etc: enlist*) arruolarsi; (*as unemployed*) iscriversi sulla lista (dell'ufficio di collocamento); (*begin work*) prendere servizio; (*enrol*): **to ~ on for a course** iscriversi a un corso ▸ VT (*Mil*) arruolare; (*employee*) assumere

▸ **sign out** VI firmare il registro (alla partenza)

▸ **sign over** VT: **to ~ sth over to sb** cedere qc con scrittura legale a qn

▸ **sign up** (*Mil*) VT arruolare; (*player*) ingaggiare; (*recruits*) reclutare ▸ VI arruolarsi; (*for course*) iscriversi

signal ['sɪgnl] N segnale *m* ▸ VT (*person*) fare segno a; (*message*) comunicare per mezzo di segnali ▸ VI (*Aut*) segnalare, mettere la freccia; **to ~ to sb (to do sth)** far segno a qn (di fare qc); **to ~ a left/right turn** (*Aut*) segnalare un cambiamento di direzione a sinistra/destra

signal box N (*Rail*) cabina di manovra

signalman ['sɪgnlmən] N (*irreg*) (*Rail*) deviatore *m*

signatory ['sɪgnətərɪ] N firmatario(-a)

signature ['sɪgnətʃə^r] N firma

signature tune N sigla musicale

signet ring ['sɪgnət-] N anello con sigillo

significance [sɪg'nɪfɪkəns] N (*of remark*) significato; (*of event*) importanza; **that is of no ~** ciò non ha importanza

significant [sɪg'nɪfɪkənt] ADJ (*improvement, amount*) notevole; (*discovery, event*) importante; (*evidence, smile*) significativo(-a); **it is ~ that ...** è significativo che ...

significantly [sɪg'nɪfɪkəntlɪ] ADV (*smile*) in modo eloquente; (*improve, increase*) considerevolmente, decisamente

signify ['sɪgnɪfaɪ] VT significare

sign language N linguaggio dei muti

signpost ['saɪnpəust] N cartello indicatore

Sikh [si:k] ADJ, N sikh *mf*

silage ['saɪlɪdʒ] N insilato

silence ['saɪlns] N silenzio ▸ VT far tacere, ridurre al silenzio

silencer ['saɪlənsə^r] N (*on gun*, *BRIT Aut*) silenziatore *m*

silent ['saɪlnt] ADJ silenzioso(-a); (*film*) muto(-a); **to keep** *or* **remain ~** tacere, stare zitto(-a)

silently ['saɪlntlɪ] ADV silenziosamente, in silenzio

silent partner N (*Comm*) socio accomandante

silhouette [sɪlu:'ɛt] N silhouette *f inv* ▸ VT: **to be silhouetted against** stagliarsi contro

silicon ['sɪlɪkən] N silicio

silicon chip ['sɪlɪkən-] N chip *m inv* (al silicio)

silicone ['sɪlɪkəun] N silicone *m*

silk [sɪlk] N seta ▸ CPD di seta

silky ['sɪlkɪ] ADJ di seta, come la seta

sill [sɪl] N (*windowsill*) davanzale *m*; (*Aut*) predellino

silly ['sɪlɪ] ADJ stupido(-a), sciocco(-a); **to do something ~** fare una sciocchezza

silo ['saɪləu] N silo

silt [sɪlt] N limo

silver ['sɪlvə^r] N argento; (*money*) monete da 5, 10, 20 o 50 pence; (*also*: **silverware**) argenteria ▸ CPD d'argento

silver foil, (*BRIT*) **silver paper** N carta argentata, (carta) stagnola

silver-plated [sɪlvə'pleɪtɪd] ADJ argentato(-a)

silversmith ['sɪlvəsmɪθ] N argentiere *m*

silverware ['sɪlvəwɛə^r] N argenteria, argento

silvery ['sɪlvərɪ] ADJ (*colour*) argenteo(-a); (*sound*) argentino(-a)

SIM card ['sɪm-] N (*Tel:* = *Subscriber Identity Module card*) SIM card *f inv*

similar ['sɪmɪlə^r] ADJ: **~ (to)** simile (a)

similarity [sɪmɪ'lærɪtɪ] N somiglianza, rassomiglianza

similarly ['sɪmɪləlɪ] ADV (*in a similar way*) allo stesso modo; (*as is similar*) così pure

simile ['sɪmɪlɪ] N similitudine *f*

simmer ['sɪmə^r] VI cuocere a fuoco lento

▸ **simmer down** VI (*fig: col*) calmarsi

simper ['sɪmpə^r] VI fare lo(la) smorfioso(-a)

simpering ['sɪmpərɪŋ] ADJ lezioso(-a), smorfioso(-a)

simple ['sɪmpl] ADJ semplice; **the ~ truth** la pura verità

simple interest N (*Math, Comm*) interesse *m* semplice

simple-minded [sɪmpl'maɪndɪd] ADJ sempliciotto(-a)

simpleton ['sɪmpltən] N semplicione(-a), sempliciotto(-a)

simplicity [sɪm'plɪsɪtɪ] N semplicità

simplification [sɪmplɪfɪ'keɪʃən] N semplificazione *f*

simplify ['sɪmplɪfaɪ] VT semplificare

simply ['sɪmplɪ] ADV semplicemente

simulate ['sɪmjuleɪt] VT fingere, simulare

simulation [sɪmju'leɪʃən] N simulazione *f*

simultaneous [sɪməl'teɪnɪəs] ADJ simultaneo(-a)

simultaneously [sɪməl'teɪnɪəslɪ] ADV simultaneamente, contemporaneamente

sin [sɪn] N peccato ▸ VI peccare

Sinai ['saɪnaɪ] N Sinai *m*

since [sɪns] ADV da allora ▸ PREP da ▸ CONJ (*time*) da quando; (*because*) poiché, dato che; **~ then**, **ever ~** da allora; **~ Monday** da lunedì; **(ever) ~ I arrived** (fin) da quando sono arrivato

sincere [sɪn'sɪə^r] ADJ sincero(-a)

sincerely [sɪn'sɪəlɪ] ADV sinceramente;

S

Yours ~ (*at end of letter*) distinti saluti
sincerity [sɪn'sɛrɪtɪ] N sincerità
sine [saɪn] N (*Math*) seno
sinew ['sɪnju:] N tendine *m*; **sinews** NPL (*muscles*) muscoli *mpl*
sinful ['sɪnful] ADJ peccaminoso(-a)
sing [sɪŋ] (*pt* **sang**, *pp* **sung**) VT, VI cantare
Singapore [sɪŋgə'pɔːʳ] N Singapore *f*
singe [sɪndʒ] VT bruciacchiare
singer ['sɪŋəʳ] N cantante *mf*
Singhalese [sɪŋə'liːz] ADJ = **Sinhalese**
singing ['sɪŋɪŋ] N (*of person, bird*) canto; (*of kettle, bullet, in ears*) fischio
single ['sɪŋgl] ADJ solo(-a), unico(-a); (*unmarried: man*) celibe; (: *woman*) nubile; (*not double*) semplice ▶ N (*BRIT: also:* **single ticket**) biglietto di (sola) andata; (*record*) 45 giri *m inv*; **not a ~ one was left** non ne è rimasto nemmeno uno; **every ~ day** tutti i santi giorni; *see also* **singles**
▶ **single out** VT scegliere; (*distinguish*) distinguere
single bed N letto a una piazza
single-breasted ['sɪŋglbrɛstɪd] ADJ a un petto
Single European Market N: **the ~** il Mercato Unico
single file N: **in ~** in fila indiana
single-handed [sɪŋgl'hændɪd] ADV senza aiuto, da solo(-a)
single-minded [sɪŋgl'maɪndɪd] ADJ tenace, risoluto(-a)
single parent N ragazzo padre/ragazza madre; genitore *m* separato; **~ family** famiglia monoparentale
single room N camera singola
singles ['sɪŋglz] NPL (*Tennis*) singolo; (*US: single people*) single *mf*
singles bar N (*esp US*) bar *m inv* per single
single-sex school ['sɪŋgl'sɛks-] N (*for boys*) scuola maschile; (*for girls*) scuola femminile
singlet ['sɪŋglɪt] N canottiera
singly ['sɪŋglɪ] ADV separatamente
singsong ['sɪŋsɔŋ] ADJ (*tone*) cantilenante
▶ N (*songs*): **to have a ~** farsi una cantata
singular ['sɪŋgjuləʳ] ADJ (*Ling*) singolare; (*unusual*) strano(-a), singolare ▶ N (*Ling*) singolare *m*; **in the feminine ~** al femminile singolare
singularly ['sɪŋgjuləlɪ] ADV stranamente
Sinhalese [sɪnhə'liːz] ADJ singalese
sinister ['sɪnɪstəʳ] ADJ sinistro(-a)
sink [sɪŋk] (*pt* **sank**, *pp* **sunk**) N lavandino, acquaio ▶ VT (*ship*) (fare) affondare, colare a picco; (*foundations*) scavare; (*piles etc*): **to ~ sth into** conficcare qc in ▶ VI affondare, andare a fondo; (*ground etc*) cedere, avvallarsi; **my heart sank** mi sentii venir meno; **he sank into a chair/the mud** sprofondò in una

poltrona/nel fango
▶ **sink in** VI penetrare; **it took a long time to ~ in** ci ho (*or* ha *etc*) messo molto a capirlo
sinking ['sɪŋkɪŋ] ADJ: **that ~ feeling** una stretta allo stomaco
sinking fund N (*Comm*) fondo d'ammortamento
sink unit N blocco lavello
sinner ['sɪnəʳ] N peccatore(-trice)
Sinn Féin [ʃɪn'feɪn] N movimento separatista irlandese
sinuous ['sɪnjuəs] ADJ sinuoso(-a)
sinus ['saɪnəs] N (*Anat*) seno
sip [sɪp] N sorso ▶ VT sorseggiare
siphon ['saɪfən] N sifone *m* ▶ VT (*funds*) trasferire
▶ **siphon off** VT travasare (con un sifone)
sir [səʳ] N signore *m*; **S~ John Smith** Sir John Smith; **yes ~** sì, signore; **Dear S~** (*in letter*) Egregio signor (*followed by name*); **Dear Sirs** Spettabile ditta
siren ['saɪərn] N sirena
sirloin ['səːlɔɪn] N controfiletto
sirloin steak N bistecca di controfiletto
sirocco [sɪ'rɔkəu] N scirocco
sisal ['saɪsəl] N sisal *f inv*
sissy ['sɪsɪ] N (*col*) femminuccia
sister ['sɪstəʳ] N sorella; (*nun*) suora; (*BRIT: nurse*) infermiera *f* caposala *inv* ▶ CPD:
~ organization organizzazione *f* affine;
~ ship nave *f* gemella
sister-in-law ['sɪstərɪnlɔː] N cognata
sit [sɪt] (*pt, pp* **sat**) VI sedere, sedersi; (*dress etc*) cadere; (*assembly*) essere in seduta; (*for painter*) posare ▶ VT (*exam*) sostenere, dare; **to ~ on a committee** far parte di una commissione
▶ **sit about, sit around** VI star seduto(-a) (senza far nulla)
▶ **sit back** VI (*in seat*) appoggiarsi allo schienale
▶ **sit down** VI sedersi; **to be sitting down** essere seduto(-a)
▶ **sit in** VI: **to ~ in on a discussion** assistere ad una discussione
▶ **sit on** VT FUS (*jury, committee*) far parte di
▶ **sit up** VI tirarsi su a sedere; (*not go to bed*) stare alzato(-a) fino a tardi
sitcom ['sɪtkɔm] N ABBR (*TV: = situation comedy*) sceneggiato a episodi (*comico*)
sit-down ['sɪtdaun] ADJ: **~ strike** sciopero bianco (con occupazione della fabbrica); **a ~ meal** un pranzo
site [saɪt] N posto; (*also:* **building site**) cantiere *m*; (: *Comput*) sito ▶ VT situare
sit-in ['sɪtɪn] N (*demonstration*) sit-in *m inv*
siting ['saɪtɪŋ] N ubicazione *f*
sitter ['sɪtəʳ] N (*for painter*) modello(-a); (*also:* **baby sitter**) babysitter *mf*

sitting ['sɪtɪŋ] N (*of assembly etc*) seduta; (*in canteen*) turno
sitting member N (*Pol*) deputato(-a) in carica
sitting room N soggiorno
sitting tenant N (*BRIT*) attuale affittuario
situate ['sɪtjueɪt] VT collocare
situated ['sɪtjueɪtɪd] ADJ situato(-a)
situation [sɪtju'eɪʃən] N situazione f; (*job*) lavoro; (*location*) posizione f; **"situations vacant/wanted"** (*BRIT*) "offerte/domande di impiego"
situation comedy N (*Theat*) commedia di situazione
six [sɪks] NUM sei
six-pack ['sɪkspæk] N (*esp US*) confezione f da sei
sixteen [sɪks'ti:n] NUM sedici
sixteenth [sɪks'ti:nθ] NUM sedicesimo(-a)
sixth [sɪksθ] NUM sesto(-a) ▶ N: **the upper/lower ~** (*BRIT Scol*) l'ultimo/il penultimo anno di scuola superiore
sixth form N (*BRIT*) *ultimo biennio delle scuole superiori*
sixth-form college N *istituto che offre corsi di preparazione all'esame di maturità per ragazzi dai 16 ai 18 anni*
sixtieth ['sɪkstɪɪθ] NUM sessantesimo(-a) ▶ PRON (*in series*) sessantesimo(-a); (*fraction*) sessantesimo
sixty ['sɪkstɪ] NUM sessanta
size [saɪz] N dimensioni fpl; (*of clothing*) taglia, misura; (*of shoes*) numero; (*glue*) colla; **I take ~ 14 in a dress** ≈ porto la 44 di vestiti; **I'd like the small/large ~** (*of soap powder etc*) vorrei la confezione piccola/grande
▶ **size up** VT giudicare, farsi un'idea di
sizeable ['saɪzəbl] ADJ considerevole
sizzle ['sɪzl] VI sfrigolare
SK ABBR (*CANADA*) = **Saskatchewan**
skate [skeɪt] N pattino; (*fish: pl inv*) razza ▶ VI pattinare
▶ **skate over, skate around** VT (*problem, issue*) prendere alla leggera, prendere sottogamba
skateboard ['skeɪtbɔ:d] N skateboard m inv
skateboarding N skateboard m inv
skater ['skeɪtə^r] N pattinatore(-trice)
skating ['skeɪtɪŋ] N pattinaggio
skating rink N pista di pattinaggio
skeleton ['skɛlɪtn] N scheletro
skeleton key N passe-partout m inv
skeleton staff N personale m ridotto
skeptic etc ['skɛptɪk] (*US*) = **sceptic** etc
skeptical ['skɛptɪkl] (*US*) ADJ = **sceptical**
sketch [skɛtʃ] N (*drawing*) schizzo, abbozzo; (*Theat etc*) scenetta comica, sketch m inv ▶ VT abbozzare, schizzare
sketch book N album m inv per schizzi
sketch pad N blocco per schizzi

sketchy ['skɛtʃɪ] ADJ incompleto(-a), lacunoso(-a)
skew [skju:] N (*BRIT*): **on the ~** di traverso
skewer ['skju:ə^r] N spiedo
ski [ski:] N sci m inv ▶ VI sciare
ski boot N scarpone m da sci
skid [skɪd] N slittamento; (*sideways slip*) sbandamento ▶ VI slittare; sbandare; **to go into a ~** slittare; sbandare
skid mark N segno della frenata
skier ['ski:ə^r] N sciatore(-trice)
skiing ['ski:ɪŋ] N sci m
ski instructor N maestro(-a) di sci
ski jump N (*ramp*) trampolino; (*event*) salto con gli sci
skilful, (*US*) **skillful** ['skɪlful] ADJ abile
skilfully, (*US*) **skillfully** ['skɪlfəlɪ] ADV abilmente
ski lift N sciovia
skill [skɪl] N abilità f inv, capacità f inv; (*technique*) tecnica
skilled [skɪld] ADJ esperto(-a); (*worker*) qualificato(-a), specializzato(-a)
skillet ['skɪlɪt] N padella
skillful ['skɪlful] ADJ (*US*) = **skilful**
skillfully ['skɪlfəlɪ] ADV (*US*) = **skilfully**
skim [skɪm] VT (*milk*) scremare; (*soup*) schiumare; (*glide over*) sfiorare ▶ VI: **to ~ through** (*fig*) scorrere, dare una scorsa a
skimmed milk, (*US*) **skim milk** N latte m scremato
skimp [skɪmp] VI: **to ~ on** (*work*) fare alla carlona; (*cloth etc*) lesinare su
skimpy ['skɪmpɪ] ADJ misero(-a); striminzito(-a); frugale
skin [skɪn] N pelle f; (*of fruit, vegetable*) buccia; (*on pudding, paint*) crosta ▶ VT (*fruit etc*) sbucciare; (*animal*) scuoiare, spellare; **wet or soaked to the ~** bagnato fino al midollo
skin cancer N cancro alla pelle
skin-deep [skɪn'di:p] ADJ superficiale
skin diver N subacqueo
skin diving N nuoto subacqueo
skinflint ['skɪnflɪnt] N taccagno(-a), tirchio(-a)
skin graft N innesto epidermico
skinhead ['skɪnhɛd] N skinhead mf
skinny ['skɪnɪ] ADJ molto magro(-a), pelle e ossa inv
skin test N prova di reazione cutanea
skintight ['skɪntaɪt] ADJ aderente
skip [skɪp] N saltello; (*BRIT*) balzo; (*container*) benna ▶ VI saltare; (*with rope*) saltare la corda ▶ VT (*pass over*) saltare; **to ~ school** (*US*) marinare la scuola
ski pants NPL pantaloni mpl da sci
ski pass N ski pass m inv
ski pole N racchetta (da sci)
skipper ['skɪpə^r] N (*Naut, Sport*) capitano

S

skipping rope ['skɪpɪŋ-], (US) **skip rope** N corda per saltare

ski resort N località *f* inv sciistica

skirmish ['skə:mɪʃ] N scaramuccia

skirt [skə:t] N gonna, sottana ▶ VT fiancheggiare, costeggiare

skirting board ['skə:tɪŋ-] N (BRIT) zoccolo

ski run N pista (da sci)

ski slope N pista da sci

ski suit N tuta da sci

skit [skɪt] N parodia; scenetta satirica

ski tow N = **ski lift**

skittle ['skɪtl] N birillo; **skittles** N (game) (gioco dei) birilli *mpl*

skive [skaɪv] VI (BRIT col) fare il lavativo

skulk [skʌlk] VI muoversi furtivamente

skull [skʌl] N cranio, teschio

skullcap ['skʌlkæp] N (worn by Jews) zucchetto; (worn by Pope) papalina

skunk [skʌŋk] N moffetta

sky [skaɪ] N cielo; **to praise sb to the skies** portare alle stelle qn

sky-blue [skaɪ'blu:] ADJ azzurro(-a), celeste

sky-diving ['skaɪdaɪvɪŋ] N caduta libera, paracadutismo acrobatico

sky-high [skaɪ'haɪ] ADV (throw) molto in alto ▶ ADJ (col) esorbitante; **prices have gone ~** (col) i prezzi sono saliti alle stelle

skylark ['skaɪlɑ:k] N allodola

skylight ['skaɪlaɪt] N lucernario

skyline ['skaɪlaɪn] N (horizon) orizzonte *m*; (of city) profilo

sky marshal N agente *mf* a bordo

Skype® [skaɪp] (Internet, Tel) N Skype® *m* ▶ VT: **to ~ sb** chiamare qn con Skype

skyscraper ['skaɪskreɪpə'] N grattacielo

slab [slæb] N lastra; (of wood) tavola; (of meat, cheese) fetta

slack [slæk] ADJ (loose) allentato(-a); (slow) lento(-a); (careless) negligente; (Comm: market) stagnante; (: demand) scarso(-a); (period) morto(-a) ▶ N (in rope etc) parte *f* non tesa; **business is ~** l'attività commerciale è scarsa; see also **slacks**

slacken ['slækn], **slacken off** VI rallentare, diminuire ▶ VT allentare; (pressure) diminuire

slacks [slæks] NPL (trousers) pantaloni *mpl*

slag [slæg] N scorie *fpl*

slag heap N ammasso di scorie

slain [sleɪn] PP of **slay**

slake [sleɪk] VT (one's thirst) spegnere

slalom ['slɑ:ləm] N slalom *m*

slam [slæm] VT (door) sbattere; (throw) scaraventare; (criticize) stroncare ▶ VI sbattere

slammer ['slæmə'] N: **the ~** (col) la gattabuia

slander ['slɑ:ndə'] N calunnia; (Law) diffamazione *f* ▶ VT calunniare; diffamare

slanderous ['slɑ:ndrəs] ADJ calunnioso(-a); diffamatorio(-a)

slang [slæŋ] N gergo, slang *m*

slanging match ['slæŋɪŋ-] N (BRIT col) rissa verbale

slant [slɑ:nt] N pendenza, inclinazione *f*; (fig) angolazione *f*, punto di vista

slanted ['slɑ:ntɪd] ADJ tendenzioso(-a)

slanting ['slɑ:ntɪŋ] ADJ in pendenza, inclinato(-a)

slap [slæp] N manata, pacca; (on face) schiaffo ▶ VT dare una manata a; schiaffeggiare ▶ ADV (directly) in pieno; **it fell ~ in the middle** cadde proprio nel mezzo; **~ a coat of paint on it** dagli una mano di vernice

slapdash ['slæpdæʃ] ADJ abborracciato(-a)

slaphead ['slæphɛd] N (BRIT col) imbecille *mf*

slapstick ['slæpstɪk] N (comedy) farsa grossolana

slap-up ['slæpʌp] ADJ (BRIT): **a ~ meal** un pranzo (or una cena) coi fiocchi

slash [slæʃ] VT tagliare; (face) sfregiare; (fig: prices) ridurre drasticamente, tagliare

slat [slæt] N (of wood) stecca

slate [sleɪt] N ardesia; (piece) lastra di ardesia ▶ VT (fig: criticize) stroncare, distruggere

slaughter ['slɔ:tə'] N (of animals) macellazione *f*; (of people) strage *f*, massacro ▶ VT (animal) macellare; (people) trucidare, massacrare

slaughterhouse ['slɔ:təhaus] N macello, mattatoio

Slav [slɑ:v] ADJ, N slavo(-a)

slave [sleɪv] N schiavo(-a) ▶ VI (also: **slave away**) lavorare come uno schiavo; **to ~ (away) at sth/at doing sth** ammazzarsi di fatica or sgobbare per qc/per fare qc

slave driver N (col, pej) schiavista *mf*

slave labour N lavoro degli schiavi; (fig): **we're just ~ here** siamo solamente sfruttati qui dentro

slaver ['slævə'] VI (dribble) sbavare

slavery ['sleɪvərɪ] N schiavitù *f*

Slavic ['slɑ:vɪk] ADJ slavo(-a)

slavish ['sleɪvɪʃ] ADJ servile; pedissequo(-a)

slavishly ['sleɪvɪʃlɪ] ADV (copy) pedissequamente

Slavonic [slə'vɔnɪk] ADJ slavo(-a)

slay [sleɪ] (pt **slew** [slu:], pp **slain** [sleɪn]) VT (formal) uccidere

sleazy ['sli:zɪ] ADJ trasandato(-a)

sled [slɛd] (US) = **sledge**

sledge [slɛdʒ] N slitta

sledgehammer ['slɛdʒhæmə'] N martello da fabbro

sleek [sli:k] ADJ (hair, fur) lucido(-a), lucente; (car, boat) slanciato(-a), affusolato(-a)

sleep [sli:p] (pt, pp **slept** [slɛpt]) N sonno ▶ VI dormire ▶ VT: **we can ~ 4** abbiamo 4 posti

letto, possiamo alloggiare 4 persone;
to have a good night's ~ farsi una bella
dormita; **to go to** ~ addormentarsi; **to** ~
lightly avere il sonno leggero; **to put to** ~
(*patient*) far addormentare; (*animal*:
euphemism: *kill*) abbattere; **to** ~ **with sb**
(*euphemism*: *have sex*) andare a letto con qn
▶ **sleep in** VI (*lie late*) alzarsi tardi; (*oversleep*)
dormire fino a tardi

▶ **sleep together** VI (*have sex*) andare a letto
insieme

sleeper ['sli:pə^r] N (*person*) dormiente *mf*;
(BRIT: *Rail*: *on track*) traversina; (: *train*) treno di
vagoni letto

sleepily ['sli:pɪlɪ] ADV con aria assonnata

sleeping ['sli:pɪŋ] ADJ addormentato(-a)

sleeping bag N sacco a pelo

sleeping car N vagone *m* letto *inv*, carrozza *f*
letto *inv*

sleeping partner N (BRIT *Comm*) = **silent
partner**

sleeping pill N sonnifero

sleeping sickness N malattia del sonno

sleepless ['sli:plɪs] ADJ (*person*) insonne;
a ~ **night** una notte in bianco

sleeplessness ['sli:plɪsnɪs] N insonnia

sleepover ['sli:pəʊvə^r] N *il dormire a casa di
amici, usato in riferimento a bambini*

sleepwalk ['sli:pwɔ:k] VI camminare nel
sonno; (*as a habit*) essere sonnambulo(-a)

sleepwalker ['sli:pwɔ:kə^r] N sonnambulo(-a)

sleepy ['sli:pɪ] ADJ assonnato(-a),
sonnolento(-a); (*fig*) addormentato(-a);
to be or **feel** ~ avere sonno

sleet [sli:t] N nevischio

sleeve [sli:v] N manica; (*of record*) copertina

sleeveless ['sli:vlɪs] ADJ (*garment*) senza
maniche

sleigh [sleɪ] N slitta

sleight [slaɪt] N: ~ **of hand** gioco di destrezza

slender ['slɛndə^r] ADJ snello(-a), sottile; (*not
enough*) scarso(-a), esiguo(-a)

slept [slɛpt] PT, PP *of* **sleep**

sleuth [slu:θ] N (*col*) segugio

slew [slu:] VI (BRIT: *also*: **slew round**) girare
▶ PT *of* **slay**

slice [slaɪs] N fetta ▶ VT affettare, tagliare a
fette; **sliced bread** pane *m* a cassetta

slick [slɪk] ADJ (*skilful*) brillante; (*insincere*)
untuoso(-a), falso(-a) ▶ N (*also*: **oil slick**)
chiazza di petrolio

slid [slɪd] PT, PP *of* **slide**

slide [slaɪd] (*pt, pp* **slid** [slɪd]) N scivolone *m*;
(*in playground*) scivolo; (*Phot*) diapositiva;
(*microscope slide*) vetrino; (BRIT: *also*: **hair slide**)
fermaglio (per capelli); (*in prices*) caduta ▶ VT
far scivolare ▶ VI scivolare; **to let things** ~
(*fig*) lasciare andare tutto, trascurare tutto

slide projector N proiettore *m* per diapositive

slide rule N regolo calcolatore

slide show N (*Comput*) diaporama *m*

sliding ['slaɪdɪŋ] ADJ (*door*) scorrevole; ~ **roof**
(*Aut*) capotte *f inv*

sliding scale N scala mobile

slight [slaɪt] ADJ (*slim*) snello(-a), sottile; (*frail*)
delicato(-a), fragile; (*trivial*) insignificante;
(*small*) piccolo(-a) ▶ N offesa, affronto ▶ VT
(*offend*) offendere, fare un affronto a; **the
slightest** il minimo (or la minima); **not in
the slightest** affatto, neppure per sogno

slightly ['slaɪtlɪ] ADV lievemente, un po';
~ **built** esile

slim [slɪm] ADJ magro(-a), snello(-a) ▶ VI
dimagrire; fare or seguire) una dieta
dimagrante

slime [slaɪm] N limo, melma; viscidume *m*

slimming ['slɪmɪŋ] ADJ (*diet, pills*) dimagrante;
(*food*) ipocalorico(-a)

slimy ['slaɪmɪ] ADJ (*also fig*: *person*) viscido(-a);
(*covered with mud*) melmoso(-a)

sling [slɪŋ] (*pt, pp* **slung** [slʌŋ]) N (*Med*) fascia
al collo; (*for baby*) marsupio ▶ VT lanciare,
tirare; **to have one's arm in a** ~ avere un
braccio al collo

slink [slɪŋk] (*pt, pp* **slunk**) VI: **to** ~ **away**, ~ **off**
svignarsela

slinky ['slɪŋkɪ] ADJ (*clothing*) aderente,
attillato(-a)

slip [slɪp] N scivolata, scivolone *m*; (*mistake*)
errore *m*, sbaglio; (*underskirt*) sottoveste *f*;
(*paper*) foglietto; tagliando, scontrino ▶ VT
(*slide*) far scivolare ▶ VI (*slide*) scivolare;
(*decline*) declinare; **to** ~ **into/out of** (*move
smoothly*) scivolare in/fuori da; **to give sb the**
~ sfuggire qn; **a** ~ **of paper** un foglietto; **a** ~
of the tongue un lapsus linguae; **to** ~ **sth
on/off** infilarsi/togliersi qc; **to let a chance**
~ **by** lasciarsi scappare un'occasione; **it
slipped from her hand** le sfuggì di mano
▶ **slip away** VI svignarsela

▶ **slip in** VT introdurre casualmente

▶ **slip out** VI uscire furtivamente

▶ **slip up** VI sbagliarsi

slip-on ['slɪpɔn] ADJ (*gen*) comodo(-a) da
mettere; (*shoes*) senza allacciatura

slipped disc ['slɪpt-] N spostamento delle
vertebre

slipper ['slɪpə^r] N pantofola

slippery ['slɪpərɪ] ADJ scivoloso(-a); **it's** ~ si
scivola

slip road N (BRIT: *to motorway*) rampa di accesso

slipshod ['slɪpʃɔd] ADJ sciatto(-a),
trasandato(-a)

slip-up ['slɪpʌp] N granchio (*fig*)

slipway ['slɪpweɪ] N scalo di costruzione

slit [slɪt] (*pt, pp* ~) N fessura, fenditura; (*cut*)
taglio; (*tear*) strappo ▶ VT fendere; tagliare;
to ~ **sb's throat** tagliare la gola a qn

S

slither ['slɪðə^r] VI scivolare, sdrucciolare

sliver ['slɪvə^r] N (of glass, wood) scheggia; (of cheese, sausage) fettina

slob [slɔb] N (col) sciattone(-a)

slog [slɔg] (BRIT) N faticata ▶ VI lavorare con accanimento, sgobbare

slogan ['sləʊgən] N motto, slogan m inv

slop [slɔp] VI (also: **slop over**) traboccare; versarsi ▶ VT spandere; versare ▶ NPL: **slops** acqua sporca, sbobba

slope [sləʊp] N pendio; (side of mountain) versante m; (ski slope) pista; (of roof) pendenza; (of floor) inclinazione f ▶ VI: **to ~ down** declinare; **to ~ up** essere in salita

sloping ['sləʊpɪŋ] ADJ inclinato(-a)

sloppy ['slɔpɪ] ADJ (work) tirato(-a) via; (appearance) sciatto(-a); (film etc) sdolcinato(-a)

slosh [slɔʃ] VI (col): **to ~ about** or **around** (person) sguazzare; (liquid) guazzare

sloshed [slɔʃt] ADJ (col: drunk) sbronzo(-a)

slot [slɔt] N fessura; (fig: in timetable, Radio, TV) spazio ▶ VT: **to ~ into** infilare in

sloth [sləʊθ] N (vice) pigrizia, accidia; (Zool) bradipo

slot machine N (BRIT: vending machine) distributore m automatico; (for amusement) slot-machine f inv

slot meter N contatore m a gettoni

slouch [slaʊtʃ] VI (when walking) camminare dinoccolato(-a); **she was slouched in a chair** era sprofondata in una poltrona ▶ **slouch about, slouch around** VI (laze) oziare

Slovak ['sləʊvæk] ADJ slovacco(-a) ▶ N slovacco(-a); (Ling) slovacco; **the ~ Republic** la Repubblica Slovacca

Slovakia [sləʊ'vækɪə] N Slovacchia

Slovakian [sləʊ'vækɪən] ADJ, N = **Slovak**

Slovene ['sləʊviːn] ADJ sloveno(-a) ▶ N sloveno(-a); (Ling) sloveno

Slovenia [sləʊ'viːnɪə] N Slovenia

Slovenian [sləʊ'viːnɪən] ADJ, N = **Slovene**

slovenly ['slʌvənlɪ] ADJ sciatto(-a), trasandato(-a)

slow [sləʊ] ADJ lento(-a); (watch): **to be ~** essere indietro ▶ ADV lentamente ▶ VT, VI (also: **slow down, slow up**) rallentare; **"~"** (road sign) "rallentare"; **at a ~ speed** a bassa velocità; **to be ~ to act/decide** essere lento ad agire/a decidere; **my watch is 20 minutes ~** il mio orologio è indietro di 20 minuti; **business is ~** (Comm) gli affari procedono a rilento; **to go ~** (driver) andare piano; (in industrial dispute) fare uno sciopero bianco

slow-acting ['sləʊ'æktɪŋ] ADJ che agisce lentamente, ad azione lenta

slowly ['sləʊlɪ] ADV lentamente; **to drive ~** andare piano

slow motion N: **in ~** al rallentatore

slowness ['sləʊnɪs] N lentezza

sludge [slʌdʒ] N fanghiglia

slug [slʌg] N lumaca; (bullet) pallottola

sluggish ['slʌgɪʃ] ADJ lento(-a); (business, market, sales) stagnante, fiacco(-a)

sluice [sluːs] N chiusa ▶ VT: **to ~ down** or **out** lavare (con abbondante acqua)

slum [slʌm] N catapecchia

slumber ['slʌmbə^r] N sonno

slump [slʌmp] N crollo, caduta; (economic) depressione f, crisi f inv ▶ VI crollare; **he was slumped over the wheel** era curvo sul volante

slung [slʌŋ] PT, PP of **sling**

slunk [slʌŋk] PT, PP of **slink**

slur [sləː^r] N pronuncia indistinta; (stigma) diffamazione f, calunnia; (Mus) legatura; (smear): **~ (on)** macchia (su) ▶ VT pronunciare in modo indistinto; **to cast a ~ on sb** calunniare qn

slurp [sləːp] VT, VI bere rumorosamente ▶ N rumore fatto bevendo

slurred [sləːd] ADJ (pronunciation) inarticolato(-a), disarticolato(-a)

slush [slʌʃ] N neve f mista a fango

slush fund N fondi mpl neri

slushy ['slʌʃɪ] ADJ (snow) che si scioglie; (BRIT fig) sdolcinato(-a)

slut [slʌt] N donna trasandata, sciattona

sly [slaɪ] ADJ (smile, remark) sornione(-a); (person) furbo(-a), scaltro(-a); **on the ~** di soppiatto

SM N ABBR (= sadomasochism) sadomasochismo

smack [smæk] N (slap) pacca; (on face) schiaffo ▶ VT schiaffeggiare; (child) picchiare ▶ VI: **to ~ of** puzzare di; **to ~ one's lips** fare uno schiocco con le labbra

smacker ['smækə^r] N (col: kiss) bacio; (: BRIT: pound note) sterlina; (: US: dollar bill) dollaro

small [smɔːl] ADJ piccolo(-a); (in height) basso(-a); (letter) minuscolo(-a) ▶ N: **the ~ of the back** le reni; **to get** or **grow smaller** (stain, town) rimpicciolire; (debt, organization, numbers) ridursi; **to make smaller** (amount, income) ridurre; (garden, object, garment) rimpicciolire; **in the ~ hours** alle ore piccole; **a ~ shopkeeper** un piccolo negoziante

small ads NPL (BRIT) piccoli annunci mpl

small arms NPL armi fpl portatili or leggere

small business N piccola impresa

small change N moneta, spiccioli mpl

smallholder ['smɔːlhəʊldə^r] N (BRIT) piccolo proprietario

smallholding ['smɔːlhəʊldɪŋ] N (BRIT) piccola tenuta

smallish ['smɔːlɪʃ] ADJ piccolino(-a)

small-minded [smɔːl'maɪndɪd] ADJ meschino(-a)

smallpox ['smɔːlpɔks] N vaiolo
small print N caratteri mpl piccoli; (on document) parte scritta in piccolo
small-scale ['smɔːlskeɪl] ADJ (map, model) in scala ridotta; (business, farming) modesto(-a)
small talk N chiacchiere fpl
small-time ['smɔːltaɪm] ADJ (col) da poco; **a ~ thief** un ladro di polli
small-town ['smɔːltaun] ADJ (pej) provinciale, di paese
smarmy ['smɑːmɪ] ADJ (BRIT pej) untuoso(-a), strisciante
smart [smɑːt] ADJ elegante; (fashionable) alla moda; (clever) intelligente; (quick) sveglio(-a)
▶ VI bruciare; **the ~ set** il bel mondo; **to look ~** essere elegante; **my eyes are smarting** mi bruciano gli occhi
smartcard ['smɑːtkɑːd] N smartcard f inv, carta intelligente
smarten up ['smɑːtn-] VI farsi bello(-a) ▶ VT (people) fare bello(-a); (things) abbellire
smash [smæʃ] N (also: **smash-up**) scontro, collisione f; (: sound) fracasso; (: smash hit) successone m ▶ VT frantumare, fracassare; (opponent) annientare, schiacciare; (hopes) distruggere; (Sport: record) battere ▶ VI frantumarsi, andare in pezzi
▶ **smash up** VT (car) sfasciare; (room) distruggere
smash-hit [smæʃ'hɪt] N successone m
smashing ['smæʃɪŋ] ADJ (col) favoloso(-a), formidabile
smattering ['smætərɪŋ] N: **a ~ of** un'infarinatura di
SME NPL ABBR (= small and medium-sized enterprises) PMI fpl inv (= Piccole e Medie Imprese)
smear [smɪəʳ] N macchia; (Med) striscio; (insult) calunnia ▶ VT ungere; (make dirty) sporcare; (fig) denigrare, diffamare; **his hands were smeared with oil/ink** aveva le mani sporche di olio/inchiostro
smear campaign N campagna diffamatoria
smear test N (BRIT Med) Pap-test m inv
smell [smɛl] (pt, pp smelt [smɛlt], smelled [smɛld]) N odore m; (sense) olfatto, odorato ▶ VT sentire (l')odore di ▶ VI (food etc): **to ~ (of)** avere odore (di); (pej) puzzare, avere un cattivo odore; **it smells good** ha un buon odore
smelly ['smɛlɪ] ADJ puzzolente
smelt [smɛlt] PT, PP of **smell** ▶ VT (ore) fondere
smile [smaɪl] N sorriso ▶ VI sorridere
smiling ['smaɪlɪŋ] ADJ sorridente
smirk [smə:k] N sorriso furbo; sorriso compiaciuto
smith [smɪθ] N fabbro
smithy ['smɪðɪ] N fucina
smitten ['smɪtn] ADJ: **~ with** colpito(-a) da
smock [smɔk] N grembiule m, camice m

smog [smɔg] N smog m
smoke [sməuk] N fumo ▶ VT, VI fumare; **to have a ~** fumarsi una sigaretta; **do you ~?** fumi?; **to go up in ~** (house etc) bruciare, andare distrutto dalle fiamme; (fig) andare in fumo
smoke alarm N rivelatore f di fumo
smoked [sməukt] ADJ (bacon, glass) affumicato(-a)
smokeless fuel ['sməuklɪs-] N carburante m che non da fumo
smokeless zone N (BRIT) zona dove sono vietati gli scarichi di fumo
smoker ['sməukəʳ] N (person) fumatore(-trice); (Rail) carrozza per fumatori
smoke screen N cortina fumogena or di fumo; (fig) copertura
smoke shop N (US) tabaccheria
smoking ['sməukɪŋ] N fumo; **"no ~"** (sign) "vietato fumare"; **he's given up ~** ha smesso di fumare
smoking compartment, (US) **smoking car** N carrozza (per) fumatori
smoky ['sməukɪ] ADJ fumoso(-a); (taste, surface) affumicato(-a)
smolder ['sməuldəʳ] VI (US) = **smoulder**
smoochy ['smuːtʃɪ] ADJ (col) romantico(-a)
smooth [smuːð] ADJ liscio(-a); (sauce) omogeneo(-a); (flavour, whisky) amabile; (cigarette) leggero(-a); (movement) regolare; (person) mellifluo(-a); (landing, takeoff, flight) senza scosse ▶ VT lisciare, spianare; (also: **smooth out**: difficulties) appianare
▶ **smooth over** VT: **to ~ things over** (fig) sistemare le cose
smoothly ['smuːðlɪ] ADV (easily) liscio; **everything went ~** tutto andò liscio
smother ['smʌðəʳ] VT soffocare
smoulder, (US) **smolder** ['sməuldəʳ] VI covare sotto la cenere
SMS N ABBR (= short message service) SMS m (servizio)
SMS message N SMS m inv, messaggino
smudge [smʌdʒ] N macchia; sbavatura ▶ VT imbrattare, sporcare
smug [smʌg] ADJ soddisfatto(-a), compiaciuto(-a)
smuggle ['smʌgl] VT contrabbandare; **to ~ in/out** (goods etc) far entrare/uscire di contrabbando
smuggler ['smʌgləʳ] N contrabbandiere(-a)
smuggling ['smʌglɪŋ] N contrabbando
smut [smʌt] N (grain of soot) granello di fuliggine; (mark) segno nero; (in conversation etc) sconcezze fpl
smutty ['smʌtɪ] ADJ (fig) osceno(-a), indecente
snack [snæk] N spuntino; **to have a ~** fare uno spuntino

S

snack bar N tavola calda, snack bar *m inv*
snag [snæg] N intoppo, ostacolo imprevisto
snail [sneɪl] N chiocciola
snake [sneɪk] N serpente *m*
snap [snæp] N (*sound*) schianto, colpo secco; (*photograph*) istantanea; (*game*) rubamazzo ▶ ADJ improvviso(-a) ▶ VT (*far*) schioccare; (*break*) spezzare di netto; (*photograph*) scattare un'istantanea di ▶ VI spezzarsi con un rumore secco; (*fig: person*) crollare; **to ~ at sb** rivolgersi a qn con tono brusco; (*dog*) cercare di mordere qn; **to ~ open/shut** aprirsi/chiudersi di scatto; **to ~ one's fingers at** (*fig*) infischiarsi di; ~ **a cold** – (*of weather*) un'improvvisa ondata di freddo
  ▶ **snap off** VT (*break*) schiantare
  ▶ **snap up** VT afferrare
snap fastener N bottone *m* automatico
snappy ['snæpɪ] ADJ rapido(-a); **make it ~!** (*col: hurry up*) sbrigati!, svelto!
snapshot ['snæpʃɔt] N istantanea
snare [snɛəʳ] N trappola
snarl [snɑːl] VI ringhiare ▶ VT: **to get snarled up** (*wool, plans*) ingarbugliarsi; (*traffic*) intasarsi
snatch [snætʃ] N (*fig*) furto; (*BRIT: small amount*): **snatches of** frammenti *mpl* di ▶ VT strappare (con violenza); (*steal*) rubare ▶ VI: **don't ~!** non strappare le cose di mano!; **to ~ a sandwich** mangiarsi in fretta un panino; **to ~ some sleep** riuscire a dormire un po'
  ▶ **snatch up** VT raccogliere in fretta
snazzy ['snæzɪ] ADJ (*col: clothes*) sciccoso(-a)
sneak [sniːk] (*US pt* **snuck**) VI: **to ~ in/out** entrare/uscire di nascosto ▶ N spione(-a); **to ~ up on sb** avvicinarsi quatto quatto a qn ▶ VT: **to ~ a look at sth** guardare di sottecchi qc
sneakers ['sniːkəz] NPL scarpe *fpl* da ginnastica
sneaking ['sniːkɪŋ] ADJ: **to have a ~ feeling/ suspicion that ...** avere la vaga impressione/il vago sospetto che ...
sneaky ['sniːkɪ] ADJ falso(-a), disonesto(-a)
sneer [snɪəʳ] N ghigno, sogghigno ▶ VI ghignare, sogghignare; **to ~ at sb/sth** farsi beffe di qn/qc
sneeze [sniːz] N starnuto ▶ VI starnutire
snide [snaɪd] ADJ maligno(-a)
sniff [snɪf] N fiutata, annusata ▶ VI fiutare, annusare; tirare su col naso; (*in contempt*) arricciare il naso ▶ VT fiutare, annusare; (*glue, drug*) sniffare
  ▶ **sniff at** VT FUS: **it's not to be sniffed at** non è da disprezzare
sniffer dog ['snɪfə-] N cane *m* poliziotto (*per stupefacenti o esplosivi*)
snigger ['snɪɡəʳ] N riso represso ▶ VI ridacchiare, ridere sotto i baffi

snip [snɪp] N pezzetto; (*bargain*) (buon) affare *m*, occasione *f* ▶ VT tagliare
sniper ['snaɪpəʳ] N (*marksman*) franco tiratore *m*, cecchino
snippet ['snɪpɪt] N frammento
snivelling ['snɪvlɪŋ] ADJ piagnucoloso(-a)
snob [snɔb] N snob *mf*
snobbery ['snɔbərɪ] N snobismo
snobbish ['snɔbɪʃ] ADJ snob *inv*
snog [snɔɡ] VI (*col*) pomiciare
snooker ['snuːkəʳ] N tipo di gioco del biliardo
snoop [snuːp] VI: **to ~ on sb** spiare qn; **to ~ about** curiosare
snooper ['snuːpəʳ] N ficcanaso *mf*
snooty ['snuːtɪ] ADJ borioso(-a), snob *inv*
snooze [snuːz] N sonnellino, pisolino ▶ VI fare un sonnellino
snore [snɔːʳ] VI russare
snoring ['snɔːrɪŋ] N russare *m*
snorkel ['snɔːkl] N (*of swimmer*) respiratore *m* a tubo
snort [snɔːt] N sbuffo ▶ VI sbuffare ▶ VT (*drugs slang*) sniffare
snotty ['snɔtɪ] ADJ moccioso(-a)
snout [snaut] N muso
snow [snəu] N neve *f* ▶ VI nevicare ▶ VT: **to be snowed under with work** essere sommerso di lavoro
snowball ['snəubɔːl] N palla di neve ▶ VI (*fig*) crescere a vista d'occhio
snowboard ['snəubɔːd] N snowboard *m inv*; **to go snowboarding** fare snowboard
snowbound ['snəubaund] ADJ bloccato(-a) dalla neve
snow-capped ['snəukæpt] ADJ (*mountain*) con la cima coperta di neve; (*peak*) coperto(-a) di neve
snowdrift ['snəudrɪft] N cumulo di neve (*ammucchiato dal vento*)
snowdrop ['snəudrɔp] N bucaneve *m inv*
snowfall ['snəufɔːl] N nevicata
snowflake ['snəufleɪk] N fiocco di neve
snowman ['snəumæn] N (*irreg*) pupazzo di neve
snowplough, (*US*) **snowplow** ['snəuplau] N spazzaneve *m inv*
snowshoe ['snəuʃuː] N racchetta da neve
snowstorm ['snəustɔːm] N tormenta
snowy ['snəuɪ] ADJ nevoso(-a)
SNP N ABBR (*BRIT Pol*) = **Scottish National Party**
snub [snʌb] VT snobbare ▶ N offesa, affronto
snub-nosed [snʌb'nəuzd] ADJ dal naso camuso
snuff [snʌf] N tabacco da fiuto ▶ VT (*also:* **snuff out**: *candle*) spegnere
snuff movie N (*col*) film porno dove una persona viene uccisa realmente
snug [snʌɡ] ADJ comodo(-a); (*room, house*)

accogliente, comodo(-a); **it's a ~ fit** è attillato

snuggle ['snʌgl] vi: **to ~ down in bed** accovacciarsi a letto; **to ~ up to sb** stringersi a qn

snugly ['snʌglɪ] ADV comodamente; **it fits ~** (object in pocket etc) entra giusto giusto; (garment) sta ben attillato

SO ABBR (Banking) = **standing order**

(KEYWORD)

so [səu] ADV **1** (thus, likewise) così; **if so** se è così, quand'è così; **I didn't do it — you did so!** non l'ho fatto io — sì che l'hai fatto!; **so do I, so am I** anch'io; **it's 5 o'clock — so it is!** sono le 5 — davvero!; **I hope so** lo spero; **I think so** penso di sì; **quite so!** esattamente!; **even so** comunque; **so far** finora, fin qui; (in past) fino ad allora

2 (in comparisons etc: to such a degree) così; **so big (that)** così grande (che); **she's not so clever as her brother** lei non è (così) intelligente come suo fratello

3: **so much** adj tanto(-a); adv tanto; **I've got so much work/money** ho tanto lavoro/tanti soldi; **I love you so much** ti amo tanto; **so many** tanti(-e)

4 (phrases): **10 or so** circa 10; **so long!** (col: goodbye) ciao!, ci vediamo!; **so to speak** per così dire; **so what?** (col) e allora?, e con questo?

▶ CONJ **1** (expressing purpose): **so as to do** in modo or così da fare; **we hurried so as not to be late** ci affrettammo per non fare tardi; **so (that)** affinché + sub, perché + sub

2 (expressing result): **he didn't arrive so I left** non è venuto così me ne sono andata; **so you see, I could have gone** vedi, sarei potuto andare; **so that's the reason!** allora è questo il motivo!, ecco perché!

soak [səuk] vt inzuppare; (clothes) mettere a mollo ▶ vi inzupparsi; (clothes) essere a mollo; **to be soaked through** essere fradicio
▶ **soak in** vi penetrare
▶ **soak up** vt assorbire

soaking ['səukɪŋ] ADJ (also: **soaking wet**) fradicio(-a)

so-and-so ['səuənsəu] N (somebody) un tale; **Mr/Mrs ~** signor/signora tal dei tali

soap [səup] N sapone m

soapbox ['səupbɔks] N palco improvvisato (per orazioni pubbliche)

soapflakes ['səupfleɪks] NPL sapone m in scaglie

soap opera N soap opera f inv

soap powder N detersivo

soapsuds ['səupsʌdz] NPL saponata

soapy ['səupɪ] ADJ insaponato(-a)

soar [sɔːʳ] vi volare in alto; (price, morale, spirits) salire alle stelle; (building) ergersi

sob [sɔb] N singhiozzo ▶ vi singhiozzare

s.o.b. N ABBR (US: col!: = son of a bitch) figlio di puttana (!)

sober ['səubəʳ] ADJ non ubriaco(-a); (sedate) serio(-a); (moderate) moderato(-a); (colour, style) sobrio(-a)
▶ **sober up** vt far passare la sbornia a ▶ vi farsi passare la sbornia

sobriety [səu'braɪətɪ] N (not being drunk) sobrietà; (seriousness, sedateness) sobrietà, pacatezza

sob story N (col, pej) storia lacrimosa

Soc. ABBR (= society) Soc

so-called ['səu'kɔːld] ADJ cosiddetto(-a)

soccer ['sɔkəʳ] N calcio

soccer pitch N campo di calcio

soccer player N calciatore m

sociable ['səuʃəbl] ADJ socievole

social ['səuʃl] ADJ sociale ▶ N festa, serata

social climber N arrampicatore(-trice) sociale, arrivista mf

social club N club m inv sociale

Social Democrat N socialdemocratico(-a)

social insurance N (US) assicurazione f sociale

socialism ['səuʃəlɪzəm] N socialismo

socialist ['səuʃəlɪst] ADJ, N socialista mf

socialite ['səuʃəlaɪt] N persona in vista nel bel mondo

socialize ['səuʃəlaɪz] vi frequentare la gente; farsi degli amici; **to ~ with** socializzare con

social life N vita sociale

socially ['səuʃəlɪ] ADV socialmente, in società

social media NPL social media mpl

social network ['sɔʃəl 'netwɜːk] N social network m inv, rete f sociale

social networking N il comunicare tramite social network

social networking site N social network m

social science N scienze fpl sociali

social security N previdenza sociale; **Department of Social Security** (BRIT) = Istituto di Previdenza Sociale

social services NPL servizi mpl sociali

social welfare N assistenza sociale

social work N servizio sociale

social worker N assistente mf sociale

society [sə'saɪətɪ] N società f inv; (club) società, associazione f; (also: **high society**) alta società ▶ CPD (party, column) mondano(-a)

socioeconomic ['səusɪəui:kə'nɔmɪk] ADJ socio-economico(-a)

sociological [səusɪə'lɔdʒɪkl] ADJ sociologico(-a)

sociologist [səusɪ'ɔlədʒɪst] N sociologo(-a)

sociology [səusɪ'ɔlədʒɪ] N sociologia

S

sock [sɔk] N calzino ▸ VT (*hit*) dare un pugno a; **to pull one's socks up** (*fig*) darsi una regolata

socket ['sɔkɪt] N cavità *f inv*; (*of eye*) orbita; (BRIT Elec: *also*: **wall socket**) presa di corrente; (: *for light bulb*) portalampada *m inv*

sod [sɔd] N (*of earth*) zolla erbosa; (BRIT col!) bastardo(-a) (!)
▸ **sod off** VI: ~ **off!** (BRIT col!) levati dalle palle! (!)

soda ['səʊdə] N (Chem) soda; (*also*: **soda water**) acqua di seltz; (US: *also*: **soda pop**) gassosa

sodden ['sɔdn] ADJ fradicio(-a)

sodium ['səʊdɪəm] N sodio

sodium chloride N cloruro di sodio

sofa ['səʊfə] N sofà *m inv*

sofa bed N divano *m* letto *inv*

Sofia ['səʊfɪə] N Sofia

soft [sɔft] ADJ (*not rough*) morbido(-a); (*not hard*) soffice; (*not loud*) sommesso(-a); (*not bright*) tenue; (*kind*) gentile; (: *look, smile*) dolce; (*not strict*) indulgente; (*weak*) debole; (*stupid*) stupido(-a)

soft-boiled ['sɔftbɔɪld] ADJ (*egg*) alla coque

soft drink N analcolico

soft drugs NPL droghe *fpl* leggere

soften ['sɔfn] VT ammorbidire; addolcire; attenuare ▸ VI ammorbidirsi; addolcirsi; attenuarsi

softener ['sɔfnər] N ammorbidente *m*

soft fruit N (BRIT) ≈ frutti *mpl* di bosco

soft furnishings NPL tessuti *mpl* d'arredo

soft-hearted [sɔft'hɑːtɪd] ADJ sensibile

softly ['sɔftlɪ] ADV dolcemente; morbidamente

softness ['sɔftnɪs] N dolcezza; morbidezza

soft option N soluzione *f* (più) facile

soft sell N persuasione *f* all'acquisto

soft target N obiettivo civile (*e quindi facile da colpire*)

soft touch N (*col*): **to be a ~** lasciarsi spillare facilmente denaro

soft toy N giocattolo di peluche

software ['sɔftwɛər] N (Comput) software *m*

software package N pacchetto di software

soft water N acqua non calcarea

soggy ['sɔgɪ] ADJ inzuppato(-a)

soil [sɔɪl] N (*earth*) terreno, suolo ▸ VT sporcare; (*fig*) macchiare

soiled [sɔɪld] ADJ sporco(-a), sudicio(-a)

sojourn ['sɔdʒəːn] N (*formal*) soggiorno

solace ['sɔlɪs] N consolazione *f*

solar ['səʊlər] ADJ solare

solarium [sə'lɛərɪəm] (*pl* **solaria** [-rɪə]) N solarium *m inv*

solar panel N pannello solare

solar plexus [-'plɛksəs] N (Anat) plesso solare

solar power N energia solare

solar system N sistema *m* solare

sold [səʊld] PT, PP *of* **sell**

solder ['səʊldər] VT saldare ▸ N saldatura

soldier ['səʊldʒər] N soldato, militare *m* ▸ VI: **to ~ on** perseverare; **toy ~** soldatino

sold out ADJ (Comm) esaurito(-a)

sole [səʊl] N (*of foot*) pianta (del piede); (*of shoe*) suola; (*fish*: *pl inv*) sogliola ▸ ADJ solo(-a), unico(-a); (*exclusive*) esclusivo(-a)

solely ['səʊllɪ] ADV solamente, unicamente; **I will hold you ~ responsible** la considererò il solo responsabile

solemn ['sɔləm] ADJ solenne; grave; serio(-a)

sole trader N (Comm) commerciante *m* in proprio

solicit [sə'lɪsɪt] VT (*request*) richiedere, sollecitare ▸ VI (*prostitute*) adescare i passanti

solicitor [sə'lɪsɪtər] N (BRIT: *for wills etc*) ≈ notaio; (*in court*) ≈ avvocato; *vedi nota*

Il *solicitor* appartiene a una delle due branche della professione legale britannica (*vedi anche* **barrister**). È compito dei *solicitors* agire come consulenti in materia legale, redarre documenti legali, preparare i casi per i *barristers*. Contrariamente a questi ultimi, i *solicitors* non sono qualificati a rappresentare una parte nelle corti investite della potestà di decidere sui reati più gravi.

solid ['sɔlɪd] ADJ (*not hollow*) pieno(-a); (*strong, sound, reliable, not liquid*) solido(-a); (*meal*) sostanzioso(-a); (*line*) ininterrotto(-a); (*vote*) unanime ▸ N solido; **to be on ~ ground** essere su terraferma; (*fig*) muoversi su terreno sicuro; **we waited 2 ~ hours** abbiamo aspettato due ore buone

solidarity [sɔlɪ'dærɪtɪ] N solidarietà

solid fuel N combustibile *m* solido

solidify [sə'lɪdɪfaɪ] VI solidificarsi ▸ VT solidificare

solidity [sə'lɪdɪtɪ] N solidità

solid-state ['sɔlɪdsteɪt] ADJ (Elec) a transistor

soliloquy [sə'lɪləkwɪ] N soliloquio

solitaire [sɔlɪ'tɛər] N (*game, gem*) solitario

solitary ['sɔlɪtərɪ] ADJ solitario(-a)

solitary confinement N (Law): **to be in ~** essere in cella d'isolamento

solitude ['sɔlɪtjuːd] N solitudine *f*

solo ['səʊləʊ] N (Mus) assolo

soloist ['səʊləʊɪst] N solista *mf*

Solomon Islands ['sɔləmən-] N: **the ~** le isole Salomone

solstice ['sɔlstɪs] N solstizio

soluble ['sɔljʊbl] ADJ solubile

solution [sə'luːʃən] N soluzione *f*

solve [sɔlv] VT risolvere

solvency ['sɔlvənsɪ] N (Comm) solvenza, solvibilità

solvent ['sɔlvənt] ADJ (*Comm*) solvibile
▶ N (*Chem*) solvente *m*
solvent abuse N abuso di colle e, solventi
Somali [sə'mɑːlɪ] ADJ somalo(-a)
Somalia [səu'mɑːlɪə] N Somalia
Somaliland [səu'mɑːlɪlænd] N paesi *mpl* del corno d'Africa
sombre, (*US*) **somber** ['sɔmbəʳ] ADJ scuro(-a); (*mood, person*) triste

KEYWORD

some [sʌm] ADJ **1** (*a certain amount or number of*): **some tea/water/cream** del tè/dell'acqua/ della panna; **there's some milk in the fridge** c'è (del) latte nel frigo; **some children/apples** dei bambini/delle mele; **after some time** dopo un po'; **at some length** a lungo
2 (*certain: in contrasts*) certo(-a); **some people say that …** alcuni dicono che …, certa gente dice che …
3 (*unspecified*) un(-a) certo(-a), qualche; **some woman was asking for you** una tale chiedeva di lei; **some day** un giorno; **some day next week** un giorno della prossima settimana; **in some form or other** in una forma o nell'altra
▶ PRON **1** (*a certain number*) alcuni(-e), certi(-e); **I've got some** (*books etc*) ne ho alcuni; **some (of them) have been sold** alcuni sono stati venduti
2 (*a certain amount*) un po'; **I've got some** (*money, milk*) ne ho un po'; **I've read some of the book** ho letto parte del libro; **some (of it) was left** ne è rimasto un po'; **could I have some of that cheese?** potrei avere un po' di quel formaggio?
▶ ADV: **some 10 people** circa 10 persone

somebody ['sʌmbədɪ] PRON qualcuno; **~ or other** qualcuno
someday ['sʌmdeɪ] ADV uno di questi giorni, un giorno o l'altro
somehow ['sʌmhʌu] ADV in un modo o nell'altro, in qualche modo; (*for some reason*) per qualche ragione
someone ['sʌmwʌn] PRON = **somebody**
someplace ['sʌmpleɪs] ADV (*US*) = **somewhere**
somersault ['sʌməsɔːlt] N capriola; (*in air*) salto mortale ▶ VI fare una capriola (*or* un salto mortale); (*car*) cappottare
something ['sʌmθɪŋ] PRON qualcosa, qualche cosa; **~ nice** qualcosa di bello; **~ to do** qualcosa da fare; **he's ~ like me** mi assomiglia un po'; **it's ~ of a problem** è un bel problema
sometime ['sʌmtaɪm] ADV (*in future*) una volta o l'altra; (*in past*): **~ last month**

durante il mese scorso; **I'll finish it ~** lo finirò prima o poi
sometimes ['sʌmtaɪmz] ADV qualche volta
somewhat ['sʌmwɔt] ADV piuttosto
somewhere ['sʌmwɛəʳ] ADV in *or* da qualche parte; **~ else** da qualche altra parte
son [sʌn] N figlio
sonar ['səunɑːʳ] N sonar *m*
sonata [sə'nɑːtə] N sonata
song [sɔŋ] N canzone *f*
songbook ['sɔŋbuk] N canzoniere *m*
songwriter ['sɔŋraɪtəʳ] N compositore(-trice) di canzoni
sonic ['sɔnɪk] ADJ (*boom*) sonico(-a)
son-in-law ['sʌnɪnlɔː] N genero
sonnet ['sɔnɪt] N sonetto
sonny ['sʌnɪ] N (*col*) ragazzo mio
soon [suːn] ADV presto, fra poco; (*early*) presto; **~ afterwards** poco dopo; **very/quite ~** molto/abbastanza presto; **as ~ as possible** prima possibile; **I'll do it as ~ as I can** lo farò appena posso; **how ~ can you be ready?** fra quanto tempo sarà pronto?; **see you ~!** a presto!
sooner ['suːnəʳ] ADV (*time*) prima; (*preference*): **I would ~ do** preferirei fare; **~ or later** prima o poi; **no ~ said than done** detto fatto; **the ~ the better** prima è meglio è; **no ~ had we left than …** eravamo appena partiti, quando …
soot [sut] N fuliggine *f*
soothe [suːð] VT calmare
soothing ['suːðɪŋ] ADJ (*ointment etc*) calmante; (*tone, words etc*) rassicurante
SOP N ABBR = **standard operating procedure**
sop [sɔp] N: **that's only a ~** è soltanto un contentino
sophisticated [sə'fɪstɪkeɪtɪd] ADJ sofisticato(-a); raffinato(-a); complesso(-a); (*film, mind*) sottile
sophistication [səfɪstɪ'keɪʃən] N raffinatezza; (*of machine*) complessità; (*of argument etc*) sottigliezza
sophomore ['sɔfəmɔːʳ] N (*US*) studente(-essa) del secondo anno
soporific [sɔpə'rɪfɪk] ADJ soporifero(-a)
sopping ['sɔpɪŋ] ADJ (*also*: **sopping wet**) bagnato(-a) fradicio(-a)
soppy ['sɔpɪ] ADJ (*pej*) sentimentale
soprano [sə'prɑːnəu] N (*voice*) soprano *m*; (*singer*) soprano *mf*
sorbet ['sɔːbeɪ] N sorbetto
sorcerer ['sɔːsərəʳ] N stregone *m*, mago
sordid ['sɔːdɪd] ADJ sordido(-a)
sore [sɔːʳ] ADJ (*painful*) dolorante; (*col: offended*) offeso(-a) ▶ N piaga; **my eyes are ~, I have ~ eyes** mi fanno male gli occhi; **~ throat** mal *m* di gola; **it's a ~ point** (*fig*) è un punto delicato

S

sorely ['sɔːlɪ] ADV (tempted) fortemente
sorrel ['sɔrəl] N acetosa
sorrow ['sɔrəu] N dolore m
sorrowful ['sɔrəuful] ADJ triste
sorry ['sɔrɪ] ADJ spiacente; (condition, excuse) misero(-a), pietoso(-a); (sight, failure) triste; ~! scusa! (or scusi! or scusate!); **to feel ~ for sb** rincrescersi per qn; **I'm ~ to hear that ...** mi dispiace (sentire) che ...; **to be ~ about sth** essere dispiaciuto or spiacente di qc
sort [sɔːt] N specie f, genere m; (make: of coffee, car etc) tipo ▶ VT (also: **sort out**: papers) classificare; ordinare; (: letters etc) smistare; (: problems) risolvere; (Comput) ordinare; **what ~ of car?** che tipo di macchina?; **I shall do nothing of the ~!** nemmeno per sogno!; **it's ~ of awkward** (col) è piuttosto difficile
sortie ['sɔːtɪ] N sortita
sorting office ['sɔːtɪŋ-] N ufficio m smistamento inv
SOS N S.O.S. m inv
so-so ['səusəu] ADV così così
soufflé ['suːfleɪ] N soufflé m inv
sought [sɔːt] PT, PP of **seek**
sought-after ['sɔːtɑːftə'] ADJ richiesto(-a)
soul [səul] N anima; **the poor ~ had nowhere to sleep** il poveraccio non aveva dove dormire; **I didn't see a ~** non ho visto anima viva
soul-destroying ['səuldɪ'strɔɪŋ] ADJ demoralizzante
soulful ['səulful] ADJ pieno(-a) di sentimento
soulless ['səullɪs] ADJ senz'anima, inumano(-a)
soul mate N anima gemella
soul-searching ['səulsə:tʃɪŋ] N: **after much ~** dopo un profondo esame di coscienza
sound [saund] ADJ (healthy) sano(-a); (safe, not damaged) solido(-a), in buono stato; (reliable, not superficial) solido(-a); (sensible) giudizioso(-a), di buon senso; (valid: argument, policy, claim) valido(-a) ▶ ADV: **~ asleep** profondamente addormentato ▶ N (noise) suono; rumore m; (Geo) stretto ▶ VT (alarm) suonare; (also: **sound out**: opinions) sondare ▶ VI suonare; (fig: seem) sembrare; **to ~ like** rassomigliare a; **to be of ~ mind** essere sano di mente; **I don't like the ~ of it** (fig: film etc) non mi dice niente (: news) è preoccupante; **it sounds as if ...** ho l'impressione che ...; **it sounds like French** somiglia al francese; **that sounds like them arriving** mi sembra di sentirli arrivare
▶ **sound off** VI (col): **to ~ off (about)** (give one's opinions) fare dei grandi discorsi (su)
sound barrier N muro del suono
soundbite ['saundbaɪt] N frase f incisiva
sound effects NPL effetti mpl sonori

sound engineer N tecnico del suono
sounding ['saundɪŋ] N (Naut etc) scandagliamento
sounding board N (Mus) cassa di risonanza; (fig): **to use sb as a ~ for one's ideas** provare le proprie idee su qn
soundly ['saundlɪ] ADV (sleep) profondamente; (beat) duramente
soundproof ['saundpruːf] VT insonorizzare, isolare acusticamente ▶ ADJ insonorizzato(-a), isolato(-a) acusticamente
sound system N impianto m, audio inv
soundtrack ['saundtræk] N (of film) colonna sonora
soup [suːp] N minestra; (clear) brodo; (thick) zuppa; **in the ~** (fig) nei guai
soup course N minestra
soup kitchen N mensa per i poveri
soup plate N piatto fondo
soupspoon ['suːpspuːn] N cucchiaio da minestra
sour ['sauə'] ADJ aspro(-a); (fruit) acerbo(-a); (milk) acido(-a), fermentato(-a); (fig) arcigno(-a), acido(-a); **to go** or **turn ~** (milk, wine) inacidirsi; (fig: relationship, plans) guastarsi; **it's ~ grapes** (fig) è soltanto invidia
source [sɔːs] N fonte f, sorgente f; (fig) fonte; **I have it from a reliable ~ that ...** ho saputo da fonte sicura che ...
south [sauθ] N sud m, meridione m, mezzogiorno ▶ ADJ del sud, sud inv, meridionale ▶ ADV verso sud; (to the) ~ of a sud di; **the S~ of France** il sud della Francia; **to travel ~** viaggiare verso sud
South Africa N Sudafrica m
South African ADJ, N sudafricano(-a)
South America N Sudamerica m, America del sud
South American ADJ, N sudamericano(-a)
southbound ['sauθbaund] ADJ (gen) diretto(-a) a sud; (carriageway) sud inv
south-east [sauθ'iːst] N sud-est m
South-East Asia N Asia sudorientale
southeastern [sauθ'iːstən] ADJ sudorientale
southerly ['sʌðəlɪ] ADJ del sud
southern ['sʌðən] ADJ del sud, meridionale; (wall) esposto(-a) a sud; **the ~ hemisphere** l'emisfero australe
South Korea N Corea f del Sud
South Pole N Polo Sud
South Sea Islands NPL: **the ~** le isole dei Mari del Sud
South Seas NPL: **the ~** i Mari del Sud
South Vietnam N Vietnam m del Sud
southward ['sauθwəd], **southwards** ['sauθwədz] ADV verso sud
south-west [sauθ'wɛst] N sud-ovest m
southwestern [sauθ'wɛstən] ADJ sudoccidentale

souvenir [suːvəˈnɪər] N ricordo, souvenir m inv

sovereign [ˈsɒvrɪn] ADJ, N sovrano(-a)

sovereignty [ˈsɒvrəntɪ] N sovranità

soviet [ˈsəuvɪət] ADJ sovietico(-a)

Soviet Union N: **the** ~ l'Unione f Sovietica

sow¹ [səu] (pt **sowed**, pp **sown** [səun]) VT seminare

sow² [sau] N scrofa

soya [ˈsɔɪə], (US) **soy** [sɔɪ] N: ~ **bean** seme m di soia; ~ **sauce** salsa di soia

sozzled [ˈsɒzld] ADJ (BRIT col) sbronzo(-a)

spa [spaː] N (resort) stazione f termale; (US: also: **health spa**) centro di cure estetiche

space [speɪs] N spazio; (room) posto; spazio; (length of time) intervallo ▶ CPD spaziale ▶ VT (also: **space out**) distanziare; **in a confined** ~ in un luogo chiuso; **to clear a** ~ **for sth** fare posto per qc; **in a short** ~ **of time** in breve tempo; **(with)in the** ~ **of an hour/three generations** nell'arco di un'ora/di tre generazioni

space bar N (on typewriter) barra spaziatrice

spacecraft [ˈspeɪskrɑːft] N (pl inv) veicolo spaziale

spaceman [ˈspeɪsmæn] N (irreg) astronauta m, cosmonauta m

spaceship [ˈspeɪsʃɪp] N astronave f, navicella spaziale

space shuttle N shuttle m inv

spacesuit [ˈspeɪssuːt] N tuta spaziale

spacewoman [ˈspeɪswumən] N (irreg) astronauta f, cosmonauta f

spacing [ˈspeɪsɪŋ] N spaziatura; **single/double** ~ (Typ etc) spaziatura singola/doppia

spacious [ˈspeɪʃəs] ADJ spazioso(-a), ampio(-a)

spade [speɪd] N (tool) vanga; pala; (child's) paletta; **spades** NPL (Cards) picche fpl

spadework [ˈspeɪdwəːk] N (fig) duro lavoro preparatorio

spaghetti [spəˈgɛtɪ] N spaghetti mpl

Spain [speɪn] N Spagna

spam [spæm] (Comput) N spamming m ▶ VT: **to** ~ **sb** inviare a qn messaggi pubblicitari non richiesti via email

span [spæn] N (of bird, plane) apertura alare; (of arch) campata; (in time) periodo; durata ▶ VT attraversare; (fig) abbracciare

Spaniard [ˈspænjəd] N spagnolo(-a)

spaniel [ˈspænjəl] N spaniel m inv

Spanish [ˈspænɪʃ] ADJ spagnolo(-a) ▶ N (Ling) spagnolo; **the** ~ npl gli Spagnoli; ~ **omelette** frittata di cipolle, pomodori e peperoni

spank [spæŋk] VT sculacciare

spanner [ˈspænər] N (BRIT) chiave f inglese

spar [spɑːr] N asta, palo ▶ VI (Boxing) allenarsi

spare [spɛər] ADJ di riserva, di scorta; (surplus) in più, d'avanzo ▶ N (part) pezzo di ricambio ▶ VT (do without) fare a meno di; (afford to give)

concedere; (refrain from hurting, using) risparmiare; **to** ~ (surplus) d'avanzo; **there are 2 going** ~ (BRIT) ce ne sono 2 in più; **to** ~ **no expense** non badare a spese; **can you** ~ **the time?** ha tempo?; **I've a few minutes to** ~ ho un attimino di tempo; **there is no time to** ~ non c'è tempo da perdere; **can you** ~ **(me) £10?** puoi prestarmi 10 sterline?

spare part N pezzo di ricambio

spare room N stanza degli ospiti

spare time N tempo libero

spare tyre, (US) **spare tire** N (Aut) gomma di scorta

spare wheel N (Aut) ruota di scorta

sparing [ˈspɛərɪŋ] ADJ (amount) scarso(-a); (use) parsimonioso(-a); **to be** ~ **with** essere avaro(-a) di

sparingly [ˈspɛərɪŋlɪ] ADV moderatamente

spark [spɑːk] N scintilla

sparkle [ˈspɑːkl] N scintillio, sfavillio ▶ VI scintillare, sfavillare; (bubble) spumeggiare, frizzare

sparkler [ˈspɑːklər] N fuoco d'artificio

sparkling [ˈspɑːklɪŋ] ADJ scintillante, sfavillante; (wine) spumante

spark plug N candela

sparring partner [ˈspɑːrɪŋ-] N sparring partner m inv; (fig) interlocutore abituale in discussioni, dibattiti, tavole rotonde ecc

sparrow [ˈspærəu] N passero

sparse [spɑːs] ADJ sparso(-a), rado(-a)

spartan [ˈspɑːtən] ADJ (fig) spartano(-a)

spasm [ˈspæzəm] N (Med) spasmo; (fig) accesso, attacco

spasmodic [spæzˈmɔdɪk] ADJ spasmodico(-a); (fig) intermittente

spastic [ˈspæstɪk] N spastico(-a)

spat [spæt] PT, PP of **spit** ▶ N (US) battibecco

spate [speɪt] N (fig): ~ **of** diluvio or fiume m di; **in** ~ (river) in piena

spatial [ˈspeɪʃəl] ADJ spaziale

spatter [ˈspætər] VT, VI schizzare

spatula [ˈspætjulə] N spatola

spawn [spɔːn] VT deporre; (pej) produrre ▶ VI deporre le uova ▶ N uova fpl

SPCA N ABBR (US: = Society for the Prevention of Cruelty to Animals) ≈ E.N.P.A. m (= Ente Nazionale per la Protezione degli Animali)

SPCC N ABBR (US) = **Society for the Prevention of Cruelty to Children**

speak [spiːk] (pt **spoke** [spəuk], pp **spoken** [ˈspəukn]) VT (language) parlare; (truth) dire ▶ VI parlare; **to** ~ **to sb/of** or **about sth** parlare a qn/di qc; ~ **up!** parli più forte!; **to** ~ **at a conference/in a debate** partecipare ad una conferenza/ad un dibattito; **speaking!** (on telephone) sono io!; **to** ~ **one's mind** dire quello che si pensa; **he has no money to** ~ **of** non si può proprio dire che sia ricco

795

▶ **speak for** VT FUS: **to ~ for sb** parlare a nome di qn; **that picture is already spoken for** (*in shop*) quel quadro è già stato venduto

speaker ['spiːkəʳ] N (*in public*) oratore(-trice); (*also:* **loudspeaker**) altoparlante *m*; (*Pol*) **the S~** il presidente della Camera dei Comuni *or* (*US*) dei Rappresentanti; **are you a Welsh ~?** parla gallese?

speaking ['spiːkɪŋ] ADJ parlante; **Italian-~ people** persone che parlano italiano; **to be on ~ terms** parlarsi

spear [spɪəʳ] N lancia ▶ VT infilzare

spearhead ['spɪəhɛd] N punta di lancia; (*Mil*) reparto d'assalto ▶ VT (*attack etc*) condurre

spearmint ['spɪəmɪnt] N (*Bot etc*) menta verde

spec [spɛk] N (*Brit col*): **on ~** sperando bene; **to buy sth on ~** comprare qc sperando di fare un affare

special ['spɛʃl] ADJ speciale ▶ N (*train*) treno supplementare; **nothing ~** niente di speciale; **take ~ care** siate particolarmente prudenti

special agent N agente *m* segreto

special correspondent N inviato speciale

special delivery N (*Post*): **by ~** per espresso

special effects NPL (*Cine*) effetti *mpl* speciali

specialist ['spɛʃəlɪst] N specialista *mf*; **a heart ~** (*Med*) un cardiologo

speciality [spɛʃɪˈælɪtɪ], (*esp US*) **specialty** ['spɛʃəltɪ] N specialità *f inv*

specialize ['spɛʃəlaɪz] VI: **to ~ (in)** specializzarsi (in)

specially ['spɛʃəlɪ] ADV specialmente, particolarmente

special needs ADJ: **~ children** bambini *mpl* con difficoltà di apprendimento

special offer N (*Comm*) offerta speciale

special school N (*Brit*) scuola speciale (*per portatori di handicap*)

specialty ['spɛʃəltɪ] N (*esp US*) = **speciality**

species ['spiːʃiːz] N (*pl inv*) specie *f inv*

specific [spəˈsɪfɪk] ADJ specifico(-a); preciso(-a); **to be ~ to** avere un legame specifico con

specifically [spəˈsɪfɪklɪ] ADV (*explicitly: state, warn*) chiaramente, esplicitamente; (*especially: design, intend*) appositamente

specification [spɛsɪfɪˈkeɪʃən] N specificazione *f*; **specifications** NPL (*of car, machine*) dati *mpl* caratteristici; (*for building*) dettagli *mpl*

specify ['spɛsɪfaɪ] VT specificare, precisare; **unless otherwise specified** salvo indicazioni contrarie

specimen ['spɛsɪmən] N esemplare *m*, modello; (*Med*) campione *m*

specimen copy N campione *m*

specimen signature N firma depositata

speck [spɛk] N puntino, macchiolina; (*particle*) granello

speckled ['spɛkld] ADJ macchiettato(-a)

specs [spɛks] NPL (*col*) occhiali *mpl*

spectacle ['spɛktəkl] N spettacolo; *see also* **spectacles**

spectacle case N (*Brit*) fodero per gli occhiali

spectacles ['spɛktəklz] NPL (*Brit*) occhiali *mpl*

spectacular [spɛkˈtækjuləʳ] ADJ spettacolare ▶ N (*Cine etc*) film *m inv etc* spettacolare

spectator [spɛkˈteɪtəʳ] N spettatore(-trice)

spectator sport N sport *m inv* come spettacolo

spectra ['spɛktrə] NPL *of* **spectrum**

spectre, (*US*) **specter** ['spɛktəʳ] N spettro

spectrum ['spɛktrəm] (*pl* **spectra** [-rə]) N spettro; (*fig*) gamma

speculate ['spɛkjuleɪt] VI speculare; (*try to guess*): **to ~ about** fare ipotesi su

speculation [spɛkjuˈleɪʃən] N speculazione *f*; congetture *fpl*

speculative ['spɛkjulətɪv] ADJ speculativo(-a)

speculator ['spɛkjuleɪtəʳ] N speculatore(-trice)

sped [spɛd] PT, PP *of* **speed**

speech [spiːtʃ] N (*faculty*) parola; (*talk, Theat*) discorso; (*manner of speaking*) parlata; (*language*) linguaggio; (*enunciation*) elocuzione *f*

speech day N (*Brit Scol*) giorno della premiazione

speech impediment N difetto di pronuncia

speechless ['spiːtʃlɪs] ADJ ammutolito(-a), muto(-a)

speech therapy N cura dei disturbi del linguaggio

speed [spiːd] (*pt, pp* **sped** [spɛd]) N velocità *f inv*; (*promptness*) prontezza; (*Aut: gear*) marcia ▶ VI: **to ~ along** procedere velocemente; **the years sped by** gli anni sono volati; (*Aut: exceed speed limit*) andare a velocità eccessiva; **at ~** (*Brit*) velocemente; **at full** *or* **top ~** a tutta velocità; **at a ~ of 70 km/h** a una velocità di 70 km l'ora; **shorthand/typing speeds** numero di parole al minuto in stenografia/dattilografia; **a five-~ gearbox** un cambio a cinque marce

▶ **speed up** (*pt, pp* **speeded up**) VI, VT accelerare

speedboat ['spiːdbəut] N motoscafo; fuoribordo *m inv*

speed camera N Autovelox *m inv*

speed dating [-deɪtɪŋ] N *sistema di appuntamenti grazie al quale si possono incontrare in pochissimo tempo diverse persone e scegliere eventualmente chi frequentare*

speedily ['spi:dɪlɪ] ADV velocemente; prontamente

speeding ['spi:dɪŋ] N (Aut) eccesso di velocità

speed limit N limite m di velocità

speedometer [spɪ'dɔmɪtə^r] N tachimetro

speed trap N (Aut) tratto di strada sul quale la polizia controlla la velocità dei veicoli

speedway ['spi:dweɪ] N (Sport) pista per motociclismo

speedy ['spi:dɪ] ADJ veloce, rapido(-a); (reply) pronto(-a)

speleologist [spɛlɪ'ɔlədʒɪst] N speleologo(-a)

spell [spɛl] (pt, pp **spelt** [spɛlt] or **spelled** [spɛld]) N (also: **magic spell**) incantesimo; (period of time) (breve) periodo ▶ VT (in writing) scrivere (lettera per lettera); (aloud) dire lettera per lettera; (fig) significare; **to cast a ~ on sb** fare un incantesimo a qn; **he can't ~** fa errori di ortografia; **how do you ~ your name?** come si scrive il suo nome?; **can you ~ it for me?** me lo può dettare lettera per lettera?
▶ **spell out** VT (letter by letter) dettare lettera per lettera; (explain): **to ~ sth out for sb** spiegare qc a qn per filo e per segno

spellbound ['spɛlbaund] ADJ incantato(-a), affascinato(-a)

spellchecker ['spɛltʃekə^r] N correttore m ortografico

spelling ['spɛlɪŋ] N ortografia

spelt [spɛlt] PT, PP of **spell**

spend [spɛnd] (pt, pp **spent** [spɛnt]) VT (money) spendere; (time, life) passare; **to ~ time/money/effort on sth** dedicare tempo/soldi/energie a qc

spending ['spɛndɪŋ] N: **government ~** spesa pubblica

spending money N denaro per le piccole spese

spending power N potere m d'acquisto

spendthrift ['spɛndθrɪft] N spendaccione(-a)

spent [spɛnt] PT, PP of **spend** ▶ ADJ (patience) esaurito(-a); (cartridge, bullets, match) usato(-a)

sperm [spə:m] N sperma m

sperm bank N banca dello sperma

sperm whale N capodoglio

spew [spju:] VT vomitare

sphere [sfɪə^r] N sfera

spherical ['sfɛrɪkl] ADJ sferico(-a)

sphinx [sfɪŋks] N sfinge f

spice [spaɪs] N spezia ▶ VT aromatizzare

spick-and-span ['spɪkən'spæn] ADJ impeccabile

spicy ['spaɪsɪ] ADJ piccante

spider ['spaɪdə^r] N ragno; **~'s web** ragnatela

spiel [spi:l] N (col) tiritera

spike [spaɪk] N punta; **spikes** NPL (Sport) scarpe fpl chiodate

spike heel N (US) tacco a spillo

spiky ['spaɪkɪ] ADJ (bush, branch) spinoso(-a); (animal) ricoperto(-a) di aculei

spill [spɪl] (pt, pp **spilt** [-t], **spilled** [-d]) VT versare, rovesciare ▶ VI versarsi, rovesciarsi; **to ~ the beans** (col) vuotare il sacco
▶ **spill out** VI riversarsi fuori
▶ **spill over** VI: **to ~ over (into)** (liquid) versarsi (in); (crowd) riversarsi (in)

spillage ['spɪlɪdʒ] N (event) fuoriuscita; (substance) sostanza fuoriuscita

spin [spɪn] (pt, pp **spun** [spʌn]) N (revolution of wheel) rotazione f; (Aviat) avvitamento; (trip in car) giretto ▶ VT (wool etc) filare; (wheel) far girare; (BRIT: clothes) mettere nella centrifuga ▶ VI girare; **to ~ a yarn** raccontare una storia; **to ~ a coin** (BRIT) lanciare in aria una moneta
▶ **spin out** VT far durare

spina bifida ['spaɪnə'bɪfɪdə] N spina bifida

spinach ['spɪnɪtʃ] N spinacio; (as food) spinaci mpl

spinal ['spaɪnl] ADJ spinale

spinal column N colonna vertebrale, spina dorsale

spinal cord N midollo spinale

spindly ['spɪndlɪ] ADJ lungo(-a) e sottile, filiforme

spin doctor N (col) esperto di comunicazioni responsabile dell'immagine di un partito politico

spin-dry ['spɪn'draɪ] VT asciugare con la centrifuga

spin-dryer [spɪn'draɪə^r] N (BRIT) centrifuga

spine [spaɪn] N spina dorsale; (thorn) spina

spine-chilling ['spaɪntʃɪlɪŋ] ADJ agghiacciante

spineless ['spaɪnlɪs] ADJ invertebrato(-a), senza spina dorsale; (fig) smidollato(-a)

spinner ['spɪnə^r] N (of thread) tessitore(-trice)

spinning ['spɪnɪŋ] N filatura

spinning top N trottola

spinning wheel N filatoio

spin-off ['spɪnɔf] N applicazione f secondaria

spinster ['spɪnstə^r] N nubile f; zitella

spiral ['spaɪərl] N spirale f ▶ ADJ a spirale
▶ VI (prices) salire vertiginosamente; **the inflationary ~** la spirale dell'inflazione

spiral staircase N scala a chiocciola

spire ['spaɪə^r] N guglia

spirit ['spɪrɪt] N (soul) spirito, anima; (ghost) spirito, fantasma m; (mood) stato d'animo, umore m; (courage) coraggio; **spirits** NPL (drink) alcolici mpl; **in good spirits** di buon umore; **in low spirits** triste, abbattuto(-a); **community ~, public ~** senso civico

spirit duplicator N duplicatore m a spirito

spirited ['spɪrɪtɪd] ADJ vivace, vigoroso(-a); (horse) focoso(-a)

spirit level N livella a bolla (d'aria)

spiritual ['spɪrɪtjuəl] ADJ spirituale ▶ N (also: **Negro spiritual**) spiritual m inv

spiritualism ['spɪrɪtjuəlɪzəm] N spiritismo
spit [spɪt] (*pt, pp* **spat** [spæt]) N (*for roasting*) spiedo; (*spittle*) sputo; (*saliva*) ▶ VI sputare; (*fire, fat*) scoppiettare
spite [spaɪt] N dispetto ▶ VT contrariare, far dispetto a; **in ~ of** nonostante, malgrado
spiteful ['spaɪtful] ADJ dispettoso(-a); (*tongue, remark*) maligno(-a), velenoso(-a)
spitroast ['spɪt'rəust] VT cuocere allo spiedo
spitting ['spɪtɪŋ] N: **"~ prohibited"** "vietato sputare" ▶ ADJ: **to be the ~ image of sb** essere il ritratto vivente *or* sputato di qn
spittle ['spɪtl] N saliva; sputo
spiv [spɪv] N (*Brit col*) imbroglione *m*
splash [splæʃ] N spruzzo; (*sound*) tonfo; (*of colour*) schizzo ▶ VT spruzzare ▶ VI (*also:* **splash about**) sguazzare; **to ~ paint on the floor** schizzare il pavimento di vernice ▶ **splash out** VI (*col: Brit*) fare spese folli
splashdown ['splæʃdaun] N ammaraggio
splay [spleɪ] ADJ: **~ footed** che ha i piedi piatti
spleen [spli:n] N (*Anat*) milza
splendid ['splendɪd] ADJ splendido(-a), magnifico(-a)
splendour, (*US*) **splendor** ['splendər] N splendore *m*
splice [splaɪs] VT (*rope*) impiombare; (*wood*) calettare
splint [splɪnt] N (*Med*) stecca
splinter ['splɪntər] N scheggia ▶ VI scheggiarsi
splinter group N gruppo dissidente
split [splɪt] (*pt, pp* **~**) N spaccatura; (*fig: division, quarrel*) scissione *f* ▶ VT spaccare; (*party*) dividere; (*work, profits*) spartire, ripartire ▶ VI (*divide*) dividersi; **to do the splits** fare la spaccata; **to ~ the difference** dividersi la differenza ▶ **split up** VI (*couple*) separarsi, rompere; (*meeting*) sciogliersi
split-level ['splɪtlevl] ADJ (*house*) a piani sfalsati
split peas NPL piselli *mpl* secchi spaccati
split personality N doppia personalità
split second N frazione *f* di secondo
splitting ['splɪtɪŋ] ADJ: **a ~ headache** un mal di testa da impazzire
splutter ['splʌtər] VI farfugliare; sputacchiare
spoil [spɔɪl] (*pt, pp* **spoilt** [-t], **spoiled** [-d]) VT (*damage*) rovinare, guastare; (*mar*) sciupare; (*child*) viziare; (*ballot paper*) rendere nullo(-a), invalidare; **to be spoiling for a fight** morire dalla voglia di litigare
spoils [spɔɪlz] NPL bottino
spoilsport ['spɔɪlspɔːt] N guastafeste *mf*
spoilt [spɔɪlt] PT, PP *of* **spoil** ▶ ADJ (*child*) viziato(-a); (*ballot paper*) nullo(-a)
spoke [spəuk] PT *of* **speak** ▶ N raggio

spoken ['spəukn] PP *of* **speak**
spokesman ['spəuksmən] N (*irreg*) portavoce *m inv*
spokesperson ['spəukspə:sn] N portavoce *mf*
spokeswoman ['spəukswumən] N (*irreg*) portavoce *f inv*
sponge [spʌndʒ] N spugna; (*Culin: also:* **sponge cake**) pan *m* di Spagna ▶ VT spugnare, pulire con una spugna ▶ VI: **to ~ on** *or* **off** scroccare a
sponge bag N (*Brit*) nécessaire *m inv*
sponge cake N pan *m* di Spagna
sponger ['spʌndʒər] N (*pej*) parassita *mf*, scroccone(-a)
spongy ['spʌndʒɪ] ADJ spugnoso(-a)
sponsor ['spɔnsər] N (*Radio, TV, Sport etc*) sponsor *m inv*; (*of enterprise, bill, for fund-raising*) promotore(-trice) ▶ VT sponsorizzare; patrocinare; (*Pol: bill*) presentare; **I sponsored him at 3p a mile** (*in fund-raising race*) ho offerto in beneficenza 3 penny per ogni miglio che fa
sponsorship ['spɔnsəʃɪp] N sponsorizzazione *f*; patrocinio
spontaneity [spɔntə'neɪɪtɪ] N spontaneità
spontaneous [spɔn'teɪnɪəs] ADJ spontaneo(-a)
spoof [spu:f] N presa in giro, parodia
spooky ['spu:kɪ] ADJ (*col*) che fa accapponare la pelle
spool [spu:l] N bobina
spoon [spu:n] N cucchiaio
spoon-feed ['spu:nfi:d] VT nutrire con il cucchiaio; (*fig*) imboccare
spoonful ['spu:nful] N cucchiaiata
sporadic [spə'rædɪk] ADJ sporadico(-a)
sport [spɔːt] N sport *m inv*; (*person*) persona di spirito; (*amusement*) divertimento ▶ VT sfoggiare; **indoor/outdoor sports** sport *mpl* al chiuso/all'aria aperta; **to say sth in ~** dire qc per scherzo
sporting ['spɔːtɪŋ] ADJ sportivo(-a); **to give sb a ~ chance** dare a qn una possibilità (di vincere)
sport jacket N (*US*) = **sports jacket**
sports car N automobile *f* sportiva
sports centre N (*Brit*) centro sportivo
sports drink N sport drink *m inv*
sports ground N campo sportivo
sports jacket N (*Brit*) giacca sportiva
sportsman ['spɔːtsmən] N (*irreg*) sportivo
sportsmanship ['spɔːtsmənʃɪp] N spirito sportivo
sports page N pagina sportiva
sports utility vehicle N (*esp US*) SUV *m inv*
sportswear ['spɔːtswɛər] N abiti *mpl* sportivi
sportswoman ['spɔːtswumən] N (*irreg*) sportiva
sporty ['spɔːtɪ] ADJ sportivo(-a)

spot [spɔt] N punto; (*mark*) macchia; (*dot: on pattern*) pallino; (*pimple*) foruncolo; (*place*) posto; (*Radio, TV: also:* **spot advertisement**) spot *m inv*; (*small amount*): **a ~ of** un po' di ▶ VT (*notice*) individuare, distinguere; **on the ~** sul posto; **to do sth on the ~** fare qc immediatamente *or* su due piedi; **to put sb on the ~** mettere qn in difficoltà; **to come out in spots** coprirsi di foruncoli

spot check N controllo senza preavviso

spotless ['spɔtlɪs] ADJ immacolato(-a)

spotlight ['spɔtlaɪt] N proiettore *m*; (*Aut*) faro ausiliario

spot-on [spɔt'ɔn] ADJ (*BRIT*) esatto(-a)

spot price N (*Comm*) prezzo del pronto

spotted ['spɔtɪd] ADJ macchiato(-a); a puntini, a pallini; **~ with** punteggiato(-a) di

spotty ['spɔtɪ] ADJ (*face*) foruncoloso(-a)

spouse [spauz] N sposo(-a)

spout [spaut] N (*of jug*) beccuccio; (*of liquid*) zampillo, getto ▶ VI zampillare

sprain [spreɪn] N storta, distorsione *f* ▶ VT: **to ~ one's ankle** storcersi una caviglia

sprang [spræŋ] PT *of* **spring**

sprawl [sprɔːl] VI sdraiarsi (in modo scomposto); (*place*) estendersi (disordinatamente) ▶ N: **urban ~** sviluppo urbanistico incontrollato; **to send sb sprawling** mandare qn a gambe all'aria

spray [spreɪ] N spruzzo; (*container*) nebulizzatore *m*, spray *m inv*; (*of flowers*) mazzetto ▶ CPD (*deodorant*) spray *inv* ▶ VT spruzzare; (*crops*) irrorare

spread [sprɛd] (*pt, pp* ~) N diffusione *f*; (*distribution*) distribuzione *f*; (*Press, Typ: two pages*) doppia pagina; (: *across columns*) articolo a più colonne; (*Culin*) pasta (da spalmare); (*col: food*) banchetto ▶ VT (*cloth*) stendere, distendere; (*butter etc*) spalmare; (*disease, knowledge*) propagare, diffondere ▶ VI stendersi, distendersi; spalmarsi; propagarsi, diffondersi; **middle-age ~** pancetta; **repayments will be ~ over 18 months** i versamenti saranno scaglionati lungo un periodo di 18 mesi

▶ **spread out** VI (*move apart*) separarsi

spread-eagled ['sprɛdɪːgld] ADJ: **to be** *or* **lie ~** essere disteso(-a) a gambe e braccia aperte

spreadsheet ['sprɛdʃiːt] N (*Comput*) foglio elettronico

spree [spriː] N: **to go on a ~** fare baldoria

sprig [sprɪg] N ramoscello

sprightly ['spraɪtlɪ] ADJ vivace

spring [sprɪŋ] (*pt* **sprang** [spræŋ], *pp* **sprung** [sprʌŋ]) N (*leap*) salto, balzo; (*bounciness*) elasticità; (*coiled metal*) molla; (*season*) primavera; (*of water*) sorgente *f* ▶ VI saltare, balzare ▶ VT: **to ~ a leak** (*pipe etc*) cominciare a perdere; **to walk with a ~ in one's step**

camminare con passo elastico; **in ~, in the ~** in primavera; **to ~ from** provenire da; **to ~ into action** entrare (rapidamente) in azione; **he sprang the news on me** mi ha sorpreso con quella notizia

▶ **spring up** VI (*problem*) presentarsi

springboard ['sprɪŋbɔːd] N trampolino

spring-clean [sprɪŋ'kliːn] N (*also:* **spring-cleaning**) grandi pulizie *fpl* di primavera

spring onion N (*BRIT*) cipollina

spring roll N involtino fritto di verdure o carne tipico della cucina cinese

springtime ['sprɪŋtaɪm] N primavera

springy ['sprɪŋɪ] ADJ elastico(-a)

sprinkle ['sprɪŋkl] VT spruzzare; spargere; **to ~ water** *etc* **on, ~ with water** *etc* spruzzare dell'acqua *etc* su; **to ~ sugar** *etc* **on, ~ with sugar** *etc* spolverizzare di zucchero *etc*; **sprinkled with** (*fig*) cosparso(-a) di

sprinkler ['sprɪŋklə^r] N (*for lawn etc*) irrigatore *m*; (*for fire-fighting*) sprinkler *m inv*

sprinkling ['sprɪŋklɪŋ] N (*of water*) qualche goccia; (*of salt, sugar*) pizzico

sprint [sprɪnt] N scatto ▶ VI scattare; **the 200-metres ~** i 200 metri piani

sprinter ['sprɪntə^r] N velocista *mf*

sprite [spraɪt] N elfo, folletto

spritzer ['sprɪtsə^r] N spritz *m inv*

sprocket ['sprɔkɪt] N (*on printer etc*) dente *m*, rocchetto

sprout [spraut] VI germogliare

sprouts [sprauts] NPL (*also:* **Brussels sprouts**) cavolini *mpl* di Bruxelles

spruce [spruːs] N abete *m* rosso ▶ ADJ lindo(-a); azzimato(-a)

▶ **spruce up** VT (*tidy*) mettere in ordine; (*smarten up: room etc*) abbellire; **to ~ o.s. up** farsi bello(-a)

sprung [sprʌŋ] PP *of* **spring**

spry [spraɪ] ADJ arzillo(-a), sveglio(-a)

SPUC N ABBR (= *Society for the Protection of Unborn Children*) associazione anti-abortista

spun [spʌn] PT, PP *of* **spin**

spur [spə:^r] N sperone *m*; (*fig*) sprone *m*, incentivo ▶ VT (*also:* **spur on**) spronare; **on the ~ of the moment** lì per lì

spurious ['spjuərɪəs] ADJ falso(-a)

spurn [spə:n] VT rifiutare con disprezzo, sdegnare

spurt [spə:t] N (*of water*) getto; (*of energy*) esplosione *f* ▶ VI sgorgare; zampillare; **to put in** *or* **on a ~** (*runner*) fare uno scatto; (*fig: in work etc*) affrettarsi, sbrigarsi

sputter ['spʌtə^r] VI = **splutter**

spy [spaɪ] N spia ▶ CPD (*film, story*) di spionaggio ▶ VI: **to ~ on** spiare ▶ VT (*see*) scorgere

spying ['spaɪɪŋ] N spionaggio

spyware ['spaɪwɛə^r] N (*Comput*) spyware *mpl*

Sq. ABBR (*in address*) = **square**

sq. ABBR (*Math etc*) = **square**

squabble ['skwɔbl] N battibecco ▶ VI bisticciarsi

squad [skwɔd] N (*Mil*) plotone *m*; (*Police*) squadra; **flying ~** (*Police*) volante *f*

squad car N (*BRIT Police*) automobile *f* della polizia

squaddie ['skwɔdɪ] N (*Mil: col*) burba

squadron ['skwɔdrn] N (*Mil*) squadrone *m*; (*Aviat, Naut*) squadriglia

squalid ['skwɔlɪd] ADJ sordido(-a)

squall [skwɔ:l] N burrasca

squalor ['skwɔləʳ] N squallore *m*

squander ['skwɔndəʳ] VT dissipare

square [skwɛəʳ] N quadrato; (*in town*) piazza; (*US: block of houses*) blocco, isolato; (*instrument*) squadra ▶ ADJ quadrato(-a); (*honest*) onesto(-a); (*col: ideas, person*) di vecchio stampo ▶ VT (*arrange*) regolare; (*Math*) elevare al quadrato; (*reconcile*) conciliare ▶ VI (*agree*) accordarsi; **a ~ meal** un pasto abbondante; **2 metres ~** di 2 metri per 2; **1 ~ metre** 1 metro quadrato; **we're back to ~ one** (*fig*) siamo al punto di partenza; **all ~** pari; **to get one's accounts ~** mettere in ordine i propri conti; **I'll ~ it with him** (*col*) sistemo le cose con lui; **can you ~ it with your conscience?** (*reconcile*) puoi conciliarlo con la tua coscienza?

▶ **square up** VI (*BRIT: settle*) saldare, pagare; **to ~ up with sb** regolare i conti con qn

square bracket N (*Typ*) parentesi *f inv* quadra

squarely ['skwɛəlɪ] ADV (*directly*) direttamente; (*honestly, fairly*) onestamente

square root N radice *f* quadrata

squash [skwɔʃ] N (*vegetable*) zucca; (*Sport*) squash *m*; **lemon/orange ~** (*BRIT*) sciroppo di limone/arancia ▶ VT schiacciare

squat [skwɔt] ADJ tarchiato(-a), tozzo(-a) ▶ VI accovacciarsi; (*on property*) occupare abusivamente

squatter ['skwɔtəʳ] N occupante *mf* abusivo(-a)

squawk [skwɔ:k] VI emettere strida rauche

squeak [skwi:k] VI squittire ▶ N (*of hinge, wheel etc*) cigolio; (*of shoes*) scricchiolio; (*of mouse etc*) squittio

squeaky ['skwi:kɪ] ADJ (*col*) cigolante; **to be ~ clean** (*fig*) avere un'immagine pulita

squeal [skwi:l] VI strillare

squeamish ['skwi:mɪʃ] ADJ schizzinoso(-a); disgustato(-a)

squeeze [skwi:z] N pressione *f*; (*also Econ*) stretta; (*credit squeeze*) stretta creditizia ▶ VT premere; (*hand, arm*) stringere ▶ VI (*also*: **squeeze in**) infilarsi; **to ~ past/under sth** passare vicino/sotto a qc con difficoltà; **a ~ of lemon** una spruzzata di limone

▶ **squeeze out** VT spremere

squelch [skwɛltʃ] VI fare ciac; sguazzare

squib [skwɪb] N petardo

squid [skwɪd] N calamaro

squint [skwɪnt] VI essere strabico(-a); (*in the sunlight*) strizzare gli occhi ▶ N: **he has a ~** è strabico; **to ~ at sth** guardare qc di traverso; (*quickly*) dare un'occhiata a qc

squire ['skwaɪəʳ] N (*BRIT*) proprietario terriero

squirm [skwə:m] VI contorcersi

squirrel ['skwɪrəl] N scoiattolo

squirt [skwə:t] N schizzo ▶ VI schizzare; zampillare ▶ VT spruzzare

Sr ABBR = **senior; sister**

SRC N ABBR (*BRIT*: = *Students' Representative Council*) comitato di rappresentanza studenti

Sri Lanka [srɪ'læŋkə] N Sri Lanka *m*

SRO ABBR (*US*: = *standing room only*) solo posti in piedi

SS ABBR = **steamship**

SSA N ABBR (*US*: = *Social Security Administration*) ≈ Previdenza Sociale

SST N ABBR (*US*) = **supersonic transport**

ST ABBR (*US*: = *Standard Time*) ora ufficiale

St ABBR = **saint; street**

stab [stæb] N (*with knife etc*) pugnalata; (*of pain*) fitta; (*col: try*): **to have a ~ at (doing) sth** provare a fare qc ▶ VT pugnalare; **to ~ sb to death** uccidere qn a coltellate

stabbing ['stæbɪŋ] N: **there's been a ~** qualcuno è stato pugnalato ▶ ADJ (*pain, ache*) lancinante

stability [stə'bɪlɪtɪ] N stabilità

stabilization [steɪbəlaɪ'zeɪʃən] N stabilizzazione *f*

stabilize ['steɪbəlaɪz] VT stabilizzare ▶ VI stabilizzarsi

stabilizer ['steɪbəlaɪzəʳ] N (*Aviat, Naut*) stabilizzatore *m*

stable ['steɪbl] N (*for horses*) scuderia; (*for cattle*) stalla ▶ ADJ stabile; **riding stables** maneggio

staccato [stə'kɑ:təu] ADV in modo staccato ▶ ADJ (*Mus*) staccato(-a); (*sound*) scandito(-a)

stack [stæk] N catasta, pila; (*col*) mucchio, sacco ▶ VT accatastare, ammucchiare; **there's stacks of time to finish it** (*BRIT col*) abbiamo un sacco di tempo per finirlo

stadium ['steɪdɪəm] N stadio

staff [stɑ:f] N (*work force: gen*) personale *m*; (: *BRIT Scol*) personale insegnante; (: *servants*) personale di servizio; (*Mil*) stato maggiore; (*stick*) bastone *m* ▶ VT fornire di personale

staffroom ['stɑ:fru:m] N sala dei professori

Staffs ABBR (*BRIT*) = **Staffordshire**

stag [stæg] N cervo; (*BRIT Stock Exchange*) rialzista *mf* su nuove emissioni

stage [steɪdʒ] N (*platform*) palco; (*in theatre*)

palcoscenico; **the ~** il teatro, la scena; (*point*) fase *f*, stadio ▶ VT (*play*) allestire, mettere in scena; (*demonstration*) organizzare; (*fig*: *perform: recovery etc*) effettuare; **in stages** per gradi; a tappe; **in the early/final stages** negli stadi iniziali/finali; **to go through a difficult ~** attraversare un periodo difficile

stagecoach ['steɪdʒkəʊtʃ] N diligenza

stage door N ingresso degli artisti

stage fright N paura del pubblico

stagehand ['steɪdʒhænd] N macchinista *m*

stage-manage ['steɪdʒmænɪdʒ] VT allestire le scene per; montare

stage manager N direttore *m* di scena

stagger ['stægə'] VI barcollare ▶ VT (*person*) sbalordire; (*hours, holidays*) scaglionare

staggering ['stægərɪŋ] ADJ (*amazing*) incredibile, sbalorditivo(-a)

staging post ['steɪdʒɪŋ-] N passaggio obbligato

stagnant ['stægnənt] ADJ stagnante

stagnate [stæg'neɪt] VI (*also fig*) stagnare

stagnation [stæg'neɪʃən] N stagnazione *f*, ristagno

stag night, stag party N festa di addio al celibato

staid [steɪd] ADJ posato(-a), serio(-a)

stain [steɪn] N macchia; (*colouring*) colorante *m* ▶ VT macchiare; (*wood*) tingere

stained glass [ˌsteɪnd'glɑːs] N vetro colorato

stained glass window ['steɪnd-] N vetrata

stainless ['steɪnlɪs] ADJ (*steel*) inossidabile

stain remover N smacchiatore *m*

stair [stɛə'] N (*step*) gradino; **stairs** NPL (*flight of stairs*) scale *fpl*, scala

staircase ['stɛəkeɪs], **stairway** ['stɛəweɪ] N scale *fpl*, scala

stairwell ['stɛəwɛl] N tromba delle scale

stake [steɪk] N palo, piolo; (*Comm*) interesse *m*; (*Betting*) puntata, scommessa ▶ VT (*bet*) scommettere; (*risk*) rischiare; (*also*: **stake out**: *area*) delimitare con paletti; **to be at ~** essere in gioco; **to have a ~ in sth** avere un interesse in qc; **to ~ a claim (to sth)** rivendicare (qc)

stakeout ['steɪkaʊt] N sorveglianza

stalactite ['stæləktaɪt] N stalattite *f*

stalagmite ['stæləgmaɪt] N stalagmite *f*

stale [steɪl] ADJ (*bread*) raffermo(-a); (*food*) stantio(-a); (*air*) viziato(-a); (*beer*) svaporato(-a); (*smell*) di chiuso

stalemate ['steɪlmeɪt] N stallo; (*fig*) punto morto

stalk [stɔːk] N gambo, stelo ▶ VT inseguire ▶ VI camminare impettito(-a)

stall [stɔːl] N (*in street, market etc*) bancarella; (*in stable*) box *m inv* di stalla ▶ VT (*Aut*) far spegnere; (*fig*) bloccare ▶ VI (*Aut*) spegnersi, fermarsi; (*fig*) temporeggiare; **stalls** NPL

(BRIT: *in cinema, theatre*) platea; **newspaper/ flower ~** chiosco del giornalaio/del fioraio

stallholder ['stɔːlhəʊldə'] N (BRIT) bancarellista *mf*

stallion ['stæljən] N stallone *m*

stalwart ['stɔːlwət] N membro fidato

stamen ['steɪmen] N stame *m*

stamina ['stæmɪnə] N vigore *m*, resistenza

stammer ['stæmə'] N balbuzie *f* ▶ VI balbettare

stamp [stæmp] N (*postage stamp*) francobollo; (*implement*) timbro; (*mark, also fig*) marchio, impronta; (*on document*) bollo; timbro ▶ VI (*also*: **stamp one's foot**) battere il piede ▶ VT battere; (*letter*) affrancare; (*mark with a stamp*) timbrare; **stamped addressed envelope** busta affrancata per la risposta

▶ **stamp out** VT (*fire*) estinguere; (*crime*) eliminare; (*opposition*) soffocare

stamp album N album *m inv* per francobolli

stamp collecting N filatelia

stamp duty N (BRIT) bollo

stampede [stæm'piːd] N fuggi fuggi *m inv*; (*of cattle*) fuga precipitosa

stamp machine N distributore *m* automatico di francobolli

stance [stæns] N posizione *f*

stand [stænd] (*pt, pp* **stood** [stud]) N (*position*) posizione *f*; (*Mil*) resistenza; (*for taxis*) posteggio; (*structure*) supporto, sostegno; (*at exhibition*) stand *m inv*; (*in shop*) banco; (*at market*) bancarella; (*booth*) chiosco; (*Sport*) tribuna; (*also*: **music stand**) leggio *m* ▶ VI stare in piedi; (*rise*) alzarsi in piedi; (*be placed*) trovarsi ▶ VT (*place*) mettere, porre; (*tolerate, withstand*) resistere, sopportare; **to make a ~** prendere posizione; **to take a ~ on an issue** prendere posizione su un problema; **to ~ for parliament** (BRIT) presentarsi come candidato (per il parlamento); **to ~ guard** or **watch** (*Mil*) essere di guardia; **it stands to reason** è logico; **as things ~** stando così le cose; **to ~ sb a drink/meal** offrire da bere/ un pranzo a qn; **I can't ~ him** non lo sopporto

▶ **stand aside** VI farsi da parte, scostarsi

▶ **stand back** VI prendere le distanze

▶ **stand by** VI (*be ready*) tenersi pronto(-a) ▶ VT FUS (*opinion*) sostenere

▶ **stand down** VI (*withdraw*) ritirarsi; (*Law*) lasciare il banco dei testimoni

▶ **stand for** VT FUS (*signify*) rappresentare, significare; (*tolerate*) sopportare, tollerare

▶ **stand in for** VT FUS sostituire

▶ **stand out** VI (*be prominent*) spiccare

▶ **stand up** VI (*rise*) alzarsi in piedi

▶ **stand up for** VT FUS difendere

▶ **stand up to** VT FUS tener testa a, resistere a

stand-alone ['stændələʊn] ADJ (*Comput*) stand-alone *inv*

standard ['stændəd] N modello, standard m inv; (*level*) livello; (*flag*) stendardo ▶ ADJ (*size etc*) normale, standard inv; (*practice*) normale; (*model*) di serie; **standards** NPL (*morals*) principi mpl, valori mpl; **to be** or **come up to** ~ rispondere ai requisiti; **below** or **not up to** ~ (*work*) mediocre; **to apply a double** ~ usare metri diversi (nel giudicare or fare *etc*); ~ **of living** livello di vita

standardization [stændədaɪ'zeɪʃən] N standardizzazione f

standardize ['stændədaɪz] VT normalizzare, standardizzare

standard lamp N (*BRIT*) lampada a stelo

standard time N ora ufficiale

stand-by ['stændbaɪ] N riserva, sostituto; **to be on** ~ (*gen*) tenersi pronto(-a); (*doctor*) essere di guardia; **a** ~ **ticket** un biglietto standby; **to fly** ~ essere in lista d'attesa per un volo

stand-by generator N generatore m d'emergenza

stand-by passenger N (*Aviat*) passeggero(-a) in lista d'attesa

stand-by ticket N (*Aviat*) biglietto senza garanzia

stand-in ['stændɪn] N sostituto(-a); (*Cine*) controfigura

standing ['stændɪŋ] ADJ diritto(-a), in piedi; (*permanent: committee*) permanente; (: *rule*) fisso(-a); (: *army*) regolare; (*grievance*) continuo(-a) ▶ N rango, condizione f, posizione f; (*duration*): **of 6 months'** ~ che dura da 6 mesi; **of many years'** ~ che esiste da molti anni; **it's a** ~ **joke** è diventato proverbiale; **he was given a** ~ **ovation** tutti si alzarono per applaudirlo; **a man of some** ~ un uomo di una certa importanza

standing committee N commissione f permanente

standing order N (*BRIT: at bank*) ordine m di pagamento (permanente); **standing orders** NPL (*Mil*) regolamento

standing room N posto all'impiedi

stand-off ['stændɔf] N (*esp US: stalemate*) situazione f di stallo

standoffish [stænd'ɔfɪʃ] ADJ scostante, freddo(-a)

standpat ['stændpæt] ADJ (*US*) irremovibile

standpipe ['stændpaɪp] N fontanella

standpoint ['stændpɔɪnt] N punto di vista

standstill ['stændstɪl] N: **at a** ~ fermo(-a); (*fig*) a un punto morto; **to come to a** ~ fermarsi; giungere a un punto morto

stank [stæŋk] PT of **stink**

stanza ['stænzə] N stanza (*poesia*)

staple ['steɪpl] N (*for papers*) graffetta; (*chief product*) prodotto principale ▶ ADJ (*food etc*) di base; (*crop, industry*) principale ▶ VT cucire

stapler ['steɪplə^r] N cucitrice f

star [stɑː^r] N stella; (*celebrity*) divo(-a); (*principal actor*) vedette f inv ▶ VI: **to** ~ **(in)** essere il (or la) protagonista (di) ▶ VT (*Cine*) essere interpretato(-a) da; **the stars** NPL (*Astrology*) le stelle; **four-~ hotel** ≈ albergo di prima categoria; **2-~ petrol** (*BRIT*) ≈ benzina normale; **4-~ petrol** (*BRIT*) ≈ super f

star attraction N numero principale

starboard ['stɑːbəd] N dritta; **to** ~ a dritta

starch [stɑːtʃ] N amido

starched ['stɑːtʃt] ADJ (*collar*) inamidato(-a)

starchy ['stɑːtʃɪ] ADJ (*food*) ricco(-a) di amido

stardom ['stɑːdəm] N celebrità

stare [stɛə^r] N sguardo fisso ▶ VI: **to** ~ **at** fissare

starfish ['stɑːfɪʃ] N stella di mare

stark [stɑːk] ADJ (*bleak*) desolato(-a); (*simplicity, colour*) austero(-a); (*reality, poverty, truth*) crudo(-a) ▶ ADV: ~ **naked** completamente nudo(-a)

starkers ['stɑːkəz] ADJ: **to be** ~ (*BRIT col*) essere nudo(-a) come un verme

starlet ['stɑːlɪt] N (*Cine*) stellina

starlight ['stɑːlaɪt] N: **by** ~ alla luce delle stelle

starling ['stɑːlɪŋ] N storno

starlit ['stɑːlɪt] ADJ stellato(-a)

starry ['stɑːrɪ] ADJ stellato(-a)

starry-eyed [stɑːrɪ'aɪd] ADJ (*idealistic, gullible*) ingenuo(-a); (*from wonder*) meravigliato(-a)

Stars and Stripes NPL: **the** ~ la bandiera a stelle e strisce

star sign N segno zodiacale

star-studded ['stɑːstʌdɪd] ADJ: **a** ~ **cast** un cast di attori famosi

start [stɑːt] N inizio; (*of race*) partenza; (*sudden movement*) sobbalzo; (*advantage*) vantaggio ▶ VT cominciare, iniziare; (*found: business, newspaper*) fondare, creare; (: *car*) mettere in moto ▶ VI cominciare; (*on journey*) partire, mettersi in viaggio; (*jump*) sobbalzare; **to** ~ **doing sth** (in)cominciare a fare qc; **at the** ~ all'inizio; **for a** ~ tanto per cominciare; **to make an early** ~ partire di buon'ora; **to** ~ **(off) with ...** (*firstly*) per prima cosa ...; (*at the beginning*) all'inizio; **to** ~ **a fire** provocare un incendio

▶ **start off** VI cominciare; (*leave*) partire

▶ **start out** VI (*begin*) cominciare; (*set out*) partire

▶ **start over** VI (*US*) ricominciare

▶ **start up** VI cominciare; (*car*) avviarsi ▶ VT iniziare; (*car*) avviare

starter ['stɑːtə^r] N (*Aut*) motorino d'avviamento; (*Sport: official*) starter m inv; (: *runner, horse*) partente mf; (*BRIT Culin*) primo piatto

starting handle ['stɑːtɪŋ-] N (*BRIT*) manovella d'avviamento

starting point N punto di partenza
starting price N prezzo *m* base *inv*
startle ['stɑːtl] VT far trasalire
startling ['stɑːtlɪŋ] ADJ sorprendente, sbalorditivo(-a)
star turn N (*BRIT*) attrazione *f* principale
starvation [stɑːˈveɪʃən] N fame *f*, inedia; **to die of** ~ morire d'inedia
starve [stɑːv] VI morire di fame; soffrire la fame ▶ VT far morire di fame, affamare; **I'm starving** muoio di fame
stash [stæʃ] VT: **to** ~ **sth away** (*col*) nascondere qc
state [steɪt] N stato; (*pomp*): **in** ~ in pompa ▶ VT dichiarare, affermare; annunciare; **to be in a** ~ essere agitato(-a); **the** ~ **of the art** il livello di tecnologia (*or* cultura *etc*); ~ **of emergency** stato di emergenza; ~ **of mind** stato d'animo
state control N controllo statale
stated ['steɪtɪd] ADJ fissato(-a), stabilito(-a)
State Department N (*US*) Dipartimento di Stato, ≈ Ministero degli Esteri
state education N (*BRIT*) istruzione *f* pubblica *or* statale
stateless ['steɪtlɪs] ADJ apolide
stately ['steɪtlɪ] ADJ maestoso(-a), imponente
stately home N residenza nobiliare (*d'interesse storico o artistico spesso aperta al pubblico*)
statement ['steɪtmənt] N dichiarazione *f*; (*Law*) deposizione *f*; (*Finance*) rendiconto; **official** ~ comunicato ufficiale; ~ **of account**, **bank** ~ estratto conto
state-owned ['steɪt'əund] ADJ statalizzato(-a)
States [steɪts] NPL: **the** ~ (*USA*) gli Stati Uniti
state school N scuola statale
statesman ['steɪtsmən] N (*irreg*) statista *m*
statesmanship ['steɪtsmənʃɪp] N abilità politica
static ['stætɪk] N (*Radio*) scariche *fpl* ▶ ADJ statico(-a); ~ **electricity** elettricità statica
station ['steɪʃən] N stazione *f*; (*rank*) rango, condizione *f* ▶ VT collocare, disporre; **action stations** posti *mpl* di combattimento; **to be stationed in** (*Mil*) essere di stanza in
stationary ['steɪʃənərɪ] ADJ fermo(-a), immobile
stationer ['steɪʃənəʳ] N cartolaio(-a); ~**'s shop** cartoleria
stationery ['steɪʃənərɪ] N articoli *mpl* di cancelleria; (*writing paper*) carta da lettere
station master N (*Rail*) capostazione *m*
station wagon N (*US*) giardinetta
statistic [stəˈtɪstɪk] N statistica; *see also* **statistics**
statistical [stəˈtɪstɪkəl] ADJ statistico(-a)
statistics [stəˈtɪstɪks] N (*science*) statistica

statue ['stætjuː] N statua
statuesque [stætjuˈɛsk] ADJ statuario(-a)
statuette [stætjuˈɛt] N statuetta
stature ['stætʃəʳ] N statura
status ['steɪtəs] N posizione *f*, condizione *f* sociale; (*prestige*) prestigio; (*legal, marital*) stato
status quo [-'kwəu] N: **the** ~ lo statu quo
status symbol N simbolo di prestigio
statute ['stætjuːt] N legge *f*; **statutes** NPL (*of club etc*) statuto
statute book N codice *m*
statutory ['stætjutərɪ] ADJ stabilito(-a) dalla legge, statutario(-a); ~ **meeting** (*Comm*) assemblea ordinaria
staunch [stɔːntʃ] ADJ fidato(-a), leale ▶ VT (*flow*) arrestare; (*blood*) arrestare il flusso di
stave [steɪv] N (*Mus*) rigo ▶ VT: **to** ~ **off** (*attack*) respingere; (*threat*) evitare
stay [steɪ] N (*period of time*) soggiorno, permanenza ▶ VI rimanere; (*reside*) alloggiare, stare; (*spend some time*) trattenersi, soggiornare; ~ **of execution** (*Law*) sospensione *f* dell'esecuzione; **to** ~ **put** non muoversi; **to** ~ **with friends** stare presso amici; **to** ~ **the night** passare la notte
▶ **stay away** VI (*from person, building*) stare lontano (*from event*) non andare
▶ **stay behind** VI restare indietro
▶ **stay in** VI (*at home*) stare in casa
▶ **stay on** VI restare, rimanere
▶ **stay out** VI (*of house*) rimanere fuori (di casa); (*strikers*) continuare lo sciopero
▶ **stay up** VI (*at night*) rimanere alzato(-a)
staying power ['steɪɪŋ-] N capacità di resistenza
STD N ABBR (*BRIT*: = *subscriber trunk dialling*) teleselezione *f*; (= *sexually transmitted disease*) malattia venerea
stead [stɛd] N (*BRIT*): **in sb's** ~ al posto di qn; **to stand sb in good** ~ essere utile a qn
steadfast ['stɛdfɑːst] ADJ fermo(-a), risoluto(-a)
steadily ['stɛdɪlɪ] ADV (*firmly*) saldamente; (*constantly*) continuamente; (*fixedly*) fisso; (*walk*) con passo sicuro
steady ['stɛdɪ] ADJ (*not wobbling*) stabile, solido(-a), fermo(-a); (*regular*) costante; (*boyfriend etc*) fisso(-a); (*person, character*) serio(-a); (: *calm*) calmo(-a), tranquillo(-a) ▶ VT stabilizzare; calmare; **to** ~ **o.s.** ritrovare l'equilibrio
steak [steɪk] N (*meat*) bistecca; (*fish*) trancia
steakhouse ['steɪkhaus] N ristorante specializzato in bistecche
steal [stiːl] N (*pt* **stole** [stəul], *pp* **stolen** ['stəuln]) VT rubare ▶ VI (*thieve*) rubare; (*move*) muoversi furtivamente
▶ **steal away**, **steal off** VI svignarsela, andarsene alla chetichella

S

stealth [stɛlθ] N: **by ~** furtivamente

stealthy ['stɛlθɪ] ADJ furtivo(-a)

steam [sti:m] N vapore m ▶ VT trattare con vapore; (Culin) cuocere a vapore ▶ VI fumare; (ship): **to ~ along** filare; **to let off ~** (fig) sfogarsi; **under one's own ~** (fig) da solo, con i propri mezzi; **to run out of ~** (fig: person) non farcela più
▶ **steam up** VI (window) appannarsi; **to get steamed up about sth** (fig) andare in bestia per qc

steam engine N macchina a vapore; (Rail) locomotiva a vapore

steamer ['sti:məᵊ] N piroscafo, vapore m; (Culin) pentola a vapore

steam iron N ferro a vapore

steamroller ['sti:mrəʊləᵊ] N rullo compressore

steamship ['sti:mʃɪp] N piroscafo, vapore m

steamy ['sti:mɪ] ADJ (room) pieno(-a) di vapore; (window) appannato(-a)

steed [sti:d] N (literary) corsiero, destriero

steel [sti:l] N acciaio ▶ CPD di acciaio

steel band N banda di strumenti a percussione (tipica dei Caribi)

steel industry N industria dell'acciaio

steel mill N acciaieria

steelworks ['sti:lwə:ks] N acciaieria

steely ['sti:lɪ] ADJ (determination) inflessibile; (gaze) duro(-a); (eyes) freddo(-a) come l'acciaio

steep [sti:p] ADJ ripido(-a), scosceso(-a); (price) eccessivo(-a) ▶ VT inzuppare; (washing) mettere a mollo

steeple ['sti:pl] N campanile m

steeplechase ['sti:pltʃeɪs] N corsa a ostacoli, steeplechase m inv

steeplejack ['sti:pldʒæk] N chi ripara campanili e ciminiere

steer [stɪəᵊ] N manzo ▶ VT (ship) governare; (car) guidare ▶ VI (Naut: person) governare; (: ship) rispondere al timone; (car) guidarsi; **to ~ clear of sb/sth** (fig) tenersi alla larga da qn/qc

steering ['stɪərɪŋ] N (Aut) sterzo

steering column N piantone m dello sterzo

steering committee N comitato direttivo

steering wheel N volante m

stem [stɛm] N (of flower, plant) stelo; (of tree) fusto; (of glass) gambo; (of fruit, leaf) picciolo
▶ VT contenere, arginare
▶ **stem from** VT FUS provenire da, derivare da

stem cell N cellula staminale

stench [stɛntʃ] N puzzo, fetore m

stencil ['stɛnsl] N (of metal, cardboard) stampino, mascherina; (in typing) matrice f

stenographer [stɛ'nɔɡrəfəᵊ] N (US) stenografo(-a)

stenography [stɛ'nɔɡrəfɪ] N (US) stenografia

step [stɛp] N passo; (stair) gradino, scalino; (action) mossa, azione f ▶ VI: **to ~ forward/back** fare un passo avanti/indietro; **steps** NPL (BRIT) = **stepladder**; **~ by ~** un passo dietro l'altro; (fig) poco a poco; **to be in/out of ~ with** (also fig) stare/non stare al passo con
▶ **step down** VI (fig) ritirarsi
▶ **step in** VI fare il proprio ingresso
▶ **step off** VT FUS scendere da
▶ **step over** VT FUS scavalcare
▶ **step up** VT aumentare; intensificare

step aerobics N step m inv

stepbrother ['stɛpbrʌðəᵊ] N fratellastro

stepchild ['stɛptʃaɪld] N (irreg) figliastro(-a)

stepdaughter ['stɛpdɔ:təᵊ] N figliastra

stepfather ['stɛpfɑ:ðəᵊ] N patrigno

stepladder ['stɛplædəᵊ] N scala a libretto

stepmother ['stɛpmʌðəᵊ] N matrigna

stepping stone ['stɛpɪŋ-] N pietra di un guado; (fig) trampolino

step Reebok® [-'ri:bɔk] N step m inv

stepsister ['stɛpsɪstəᵊ] N sorellastra

stepson ['stɛpsʌn] N figliastro

stereo ['stɛrɪəʊ] N (system) sistema m stereofonico; (record player) stereo m inv ▶ ADJ (also: **stereophonic**) stereofonico(-a); **in ~** in stereofonia

stereotype ['stɪərɪətaɪp] N stereotipo

sterile ['stɛraɪl] ADJ sterile

sterility [stɛ'rɪlɪtɪ] N sterilità

sterilization [stɛrɪlaɪ'zeɪʃən] N sterilizzazione f

sterilize ['stɛrɪlaɪz] VT sterilizzare

sterling ['stə:lɪŋ] ADJ (gold, silver) di buona lega; (fig) autentico(-a), genuino(-a) ▶ N (Econ) (lira) sterlina; **a pound ~** una lira sterlina

sterling area N area della sterlina

stern [stə:n] ADJ severo(-a) ▶ N (Naut) poppa

sternum ['stə:nəm] N sterno

steroid ['stɛrɔɪd] N steroide m

stethoscope ['stɛθəskəʊp] N stetoscopio

stevedore ['sti:vɪdɔ:ᵊ] N scaricatore m di porto

stew [stju:] N stufato ▶ VT, VI cuocere in umido; **stewed tea** tè lasciato troppo in infusione; **stewed fruit** frutta cotta

steward ['stju:əd] N (Aviat, Naut, Rail) steward m inv; (in club etc) dispensiere m; (shop steward) rappresentante mf sindacale

stewardess ['stju:ədɛs] N assistente f di volo, hostess f inv

stewardship ['stju:ədʃɪp] N amministrazione f

stewing steak ['stju:ɪŋ-], (US) **stew meat** N carne f (di manzo) per stufato

St. Ex. ABBR = **stock exchange**

stg ABBR = **sterling**

stick [stɪk] (*pt, pp* **stuck** [stʌk]) N bastone *m*; (*of rhubarb, celery*) gambo; (*of dynamite*) candelotto ▶ VT (*glue*) attaccare; (*thrust*): **to ~ sth into** conficcare *or* piantare *or* infiggere qc in; (*col: put*) ficcare; (*: tolerate*) sopportare ▶ VI attaccarsi; tenere; (*remain*) restare, rimanere; (*get jammed: door, lift*) bloccarsi; **to ~ to** (*one's word, promise*) mantenere; (*principles*) tener fede a; **to get hold of the wrong end of the ~** (*fig*) capire male; **it stuck in my mind** mi è rimasto in mente
▶ **stick around** VI (*col*) restare, fermarsi
▶ **stick out** VI sporgere, spuntare ▶ VT: **to ~ it out** (*col*) tener duro
▶ **stick up** VI sporgere, spuntare
▶ **stick up for** VT FUS difendere

sticker ['stɪkəʳ] N cartellino adesivo
sticking plaster ['stɪkɪŋ-] N cerotto adesivo
sticking point N (*fig*) punto di stallo, impasse *f inv*
stick insect N insetto *m* stecco *inv*
stickleback ['stɪklbæk] N spinarello
stickler ['stɪkləʳ] N: **to be a ~ for** essere pignolo(-a) su, tenere molto a
stick-on ['stɪkɔn] ADJ (*label*) adesivo(-a)
stick shift N (*US Aut*) cambio manuale
stick-up ['stɪkʌp] N (*col*) rapina a mano armata
sticky ['stɪkɪ] ADJ attaccaticcio(-a), vischioso(-a); (*label*) adesivo(-a); (*fig: situation*) difficile
stiff [stɪf] ADJ rigido(-a), duro(-a); (*muscle*) legato(-a), indolenzito(-a); (*difficult*) difficile, arduo(-a); (*cold: manner etc*) freddo(-a), formale; (*strong*) forte; (*high: price*) molto alto(-a) ▶ ADV: **bored ~** annoiato(-a) a morte; **to be** *or* **feel ~** (*person*) essere *or* sentirsi indolenzito; **to have a ~ neck/back** avere il torcicollo/mal di schiena; **to keep a ~ upper lip** (*BRIT fig*) conservare il sangue freddo
stiffen ['stɪfn] VT irrigidire; rinforzare ▶ VI irrigidirsi; indurirsi
stiffness ['stɪfnɪs] N rigidità; indolenzimento; difficoltà; freddezza
stifle ['staɪfl] VT soffocare
stifling ['staɪflɪŋ] ADJ (*heat*) soffocante
stigma ['stɪgmə] N (*pl Bot, Med*) **stigmata** [stɪg'mɑ:tə], *pl* (*fig*) **stigmas**) stigma *m*
stigmata [stɪg'mɑ:tə] NPL (*Rel*) stigmate *fpl*
stile [staɪl] N cavalcasiepe *m*; cavalcasteccato
stiletto [stɪ'lɛtəu] N (*BRIT: also:* **stiletto heel**) tacco a spillo
still [stɪl] ADJ fermo(-a); (*quiet*) silenzioso(-a); (*orange juice etc*) non gassato(-a) ▶ ADV (*up to this time, even*) ancora; (*nonetheless*) tuttavia, ciò nonostante ▶ N (*Cine*) fotogramma *m*; **keep ~!** stai fermo!; **he ~ hasn't arrived** non è ancora arrivato
stillborn ['stɪlbɔ:n] ADJ nato(-a) morto(-a)

still life N natura morta
stilt [stɪlt] N trampolo; (*pile*) palo
stilted ['stɪltɪd] ADJ freddo(-a), formale; artificiale
stimulant ['stɪmjulənt] N stimolante *m*
stimulate ['stɪmjuleɪt] VT stimolare
stimulating ['stɪmjuleɪtɪŋ] ADJ stimolante
stimulation [stɪmju'leɪʃən] N stimolazione *f*
stimulus ['stɪmjuləs] (*pl* **stimuli** ['stɪmjulaɪ]) N stimolo
sting [stɪŋ] (*pt, pp* **stung**) N puntura; (*organ*) pungiglione *m*; (*col*) trucco ▶ VT pungere ▶ VI bruciare; **my eyes are stinging** mi bruciano gli occhi
stingy ['stɪndʒɪ] ADJ spilorcio(-a), tirchio(-a)
stink [stɪŋk] (*pt* **stank** [stæŋk], *pp* **stunk** [stʌŋk]) N fetore *m*, puzzo ▶ VI puzzare
stinker ['stɪŋkəʳ] N (*col*) porcheria; (*person*) fetente *mf*
stinking ['stɪŋkɪŋ] ADJ (*col*): **a ~ ...** uno schifo di ..., un(-a) maledetto(-a) ...; **~ rich** ricco(-a) da far paura
stint [stɪnt] N lavoro, compito ▶ VI: **to ~ on** lesinare su
stipend ['staɪpɛnd] N stipendio, congrua
stipendiary [staɪ'pɛndɪərɪ] ADJ: **~ magistrate** magistrato stipendiato
stipulate ['stɪpjuleɪt] VT stipulare
stipulation [stɪpju'leɪʃən] N stipulazione *f*
stir [stə:ʳ] N agitazione *f*, clamore *m* ▶ VT mescolare; (*move*) smuovere, agitare; (*fig*) risvegliare ▶ VI muoversi; **to give sth a ~** mescolare qc; **to cause a ~** fare scalpore
▶ **stir up** VT provocare, suscitare
stir-fry ['stə:'fraɪ] VT saltare in padella ▶ N pietanza al salto
stirring ['stə:rɪŋ] ADJ eccitante; commovente
stirrup ['stɪrəp] N staffa
stitch [stɪtʃ] N (*Sewing*) punto; (*Knitting*) maglia; (*Med*) punto (di sutura); (*pain*) fitta ▶ VT cucire, attaccare; suturare
stoat [stəut] N ermellino
stock [stɔk] N riserva, provvista; (*Comm*) giacenza, stock *m inv*; (*Agr*) bestiame *m*; (*Culin*) brodo; (*Finance*) titoli *mpl*, azioni *fpl*; (*Rail: also:* **rolling stock**) materiale *m* rotabile; (*: descent, origin*) stirpe *f* ▶ ADJ (*fig: reply etc*) consueto(-a), solito(-a), classico(-a); (*greeting*) usuale; (*Comm: goods, size*) standard *inv* ▶ VT (*have in stock*) avere, vendere; **well-stocked** ben fornito(-a); **to have sth in ~** avere qc in magazzino; **out of ~** esaurito(-a); **to take ~** (*fig*) fare il punto; **stocks and shares** valori *mpl* di borsa; **government ~** titoli di Stato
▶ **stock up** VI: **to ~ up (with)** fare provvista (di)
stockade [stɔ'keɪd] N palizzata
stockbroker ['stɔkbrəukəʳ] N agente *m* di cambio

S

stock control N gestione f magazzino
stock cube N (BRIT Culin) dado
stock exchange N Borsa (valori)
stockholder ['stɔkhəʊldə^r] N (Finance) azionista mf
Stockholm ['stɔkhəʊm] N Stoccolma
stocking ['stɔkɪŋ] N calza
stock-in-trade ['stɔkɪn'treɪd] N (fig): **it's his ~** è la sua specialità
stockist ['stɔkɪst] N (BRIT) fornitore m
stock market N (BRIT) Borsa, mercato finanziario
stock phrase N cliché m inv
stockpile ['stɔkpaɪl] N riserva ▸ VT accumulare riserve di
stockroom ['stɔkrum] N magazzino
stocktaking ['stɔkteɪkɪŋ] N (BRIT Comm) inventario
stocky ['stɔkɪ] ADJ tarchiato(-a), tozzo(-a)
stodgy ['stɔdʒɪ] ADJ pesante, indigesto(-a)
stoic ['stəʊɪk] N stoico(-a)
stoical ['stəʊɪkəl] ADJ stoico(-a)
stoke [stəʊk] VT alimentare
stoker ['stəʊkə^r] N fochista m
stole [stəʊl] PT of **steal** ▸ N stola
stolen ['stəʊln] PP of **steal**
stolid ['stɔlɪd] ADJ impassibile
stomach ['stʌmək] N stomaco; (abdomen) ventre m; (belly) pancia ▸ VT sopportare, digerire
stomach ache N mal m di stomaco
stomach pump N pompa gastrica
stomach ulcer N ulcera allo stomaco
stomp [stɔmp] VI: **to ~ in/out** etc entrare/uscire etc con passo pesante
stone [stəʊn] N pietra; (pebble) sasso, ciottolo; (in fruit) nocciolo; (Med) calcolo; (BRIT: weight) 6.348 kg., 14 libbre ▸ CPD di pietra ▸ VT lapidare; (fruit) togliere il nocciolo a; **within a ~'s throw of the station** a due passi dalla stazione
Stone Age N: **the ~** l'età della pietra
stone-cold [stəʊn'kəʊld] ADJ gelido(-a)
stoned [stəʊnd] ADJ (col: drunk) sbronzo(-a); (on drugs) fuori inv
stone-deaf [stəʊn'dɛf] ADJ sordo(-a) come una campana
stonemason ['stəʊnmeɪsn] N scalpellino
stonewall [stəʊn'wɔːl] VI fare ostruzionismo ▸ VT ostacolare
stonework ['stəʊnwɜːk] N muratura
stony ['stəʊnɪ] ADJ pietroso(-a), sassoso(-a)
stood [stud] PT, PP of **stand**
stooge [stuːdʒ] N (col) tirapiedi mf
stool [stuːl] N sgabello
stoop [stuːp] VI (also: **have a stoop**) avere una curvatura; (also: **stoop down**: bend) chinarsi, curvarsi; **to ~ to sth/doing sth** abbassarsi a qc/a fare qc

stop [stɔp] N arresto; (stopping place) fermata; (in punctuation) punto ▸ VT arrestare, fermare; (break off) interrompere; (also: **put a stop to**) porre fine a; (: prevent) impedire ▸ VI fermarsi; (rain, noise etc) cessare, finire; **to ~ doing sth** cessare or finire di fare qc; **to ~ sb (from) doing sth** impedire a qn di fare qc; **to ~ dead** fermarsi di colpo; **~ it!** smettila!, basta!
  ▸ **stop by** VI passare, fare un salto
  ▸ **stop off** VI sostare brevemente
  ▸ **stop up** VT (hole) chiudere, turare
stopcock ['stɔpkɔk] N rubinetto di arresto
stopgap ['stɔpgæp] N (person) tappabuchi mf; (measure) ripiego ▸ CPD (measures, solution) di fortuna
stoplights ['stɔplaɪts] NPL (Aut) stop mpl
stopover ['stɔpəʊvə^r] N breve sosta; (Aviat) scalo
stoppage ['stɔpɪdʒ] N arresto, fermata; (of pay) trattenuta; (strike) interruzione f del lavoro
stopper ['stɔpə^r] N tappo
stop press N ultimissime fpl
stopwatch ['stɔpwɔtʃ] N cronometro
storage ['stɔːrɪdʒ] N immagazzinamento; (Comput) memoria
storage heater N (BRIT) radiatore m elettrico che accumula calore
store [stɔː^r] N provvista, riserva; (depot) deposito; (BRIT: department store) grande magazzino; (US: shop) negozio ▸ VT mettere da parte; conservare; (grain, goods) immagazzinare; (Comput) registrare; **to set great/little ~ by sth** dare molta/poca importanza a qc; **in ~ di riserva; in serbo; who knows what is in ~ for us?** chissà cosa ci riserva il futuro?
  ▸ **store up** VT mettere in serbo, conservare
storehouse ['stɔːhaus] N magazzino, deposito
storekeeper ['stɔːkiːpə^r] N (US) negoziante mf
storeroom ['stɔːrum] N dispensa
storey, (US) story ['stɔːrɪ] N piano
stork [stɔːk] N cicogna
storm [stɔːm] N tempesta; (also: **thunderstorm**) temporale m, burrasca; uragano; (fig) infuriarsi ▸ VT prendere d'assalto
storm cloud N nube f temporalesca
storm door N controporta
stormy ['stɔːmɪ] ADJ tempestoso(-a), burrascoso(-a)
story ['stɔːrɪ] N storia; favola; racconto; (Press) articolo; (US) = **storey**
storybook ['stɔːrɪbuk] N libro di racconti
storyteller ['stɔːrɪtɛlə^r] N narratore(-trice)
stout [staut] ADJ solido(-a), robusto(-a); (brave) coraggioso(-a); (supporter) tenace; (fat)

corpulento(-a), grasso(-a) ▶ N birra scura

stove [stəuv] N (for cooking) fornello; (: small) fornelletto; (for heating) stufa; **gas/electric ~** cucina a gas/elettrica

stow [stəu] VT mettere via

stowaway ['stəuəweɪ] N passeggero(-a) clandestino(-a)

straddle ['strædl] VT stare a cavalcioni di

strafe [strɑːf] VT mitragliare

straggle ['strægl] VI crescere (or estendersi) disordinatamente; trascinarsi; rimanere indietro; **straggled along the coast** disseminati(-e) lungo la costa

straggler ['stræglər] N sbandato(-a)

straggling ['stræglɪŋ], **straggly** ['stræglɪ] ADJ in disordine

straight [streɪt] ADJ (continuous, direct) dritto(-a); (frank) onesto(-a), franco(-a); (plain, uncomplicated) semplice; (Theat: part, play) serio(-a); (col: heterosexual) eterosessuale ▶ ADV diritto; (drink) liscio ▶ N: **the ~** la linea retta; (Rail) il rettilineo; (Sport) la dirittura d'arrivo; **to put** or **get ~** mettere in ordine, mettere ordine in; **to be (all) ~** (tidy) essere a posto, essere sistemato; (clarified) essere chiaro; **ten ~ wins** dieci vittorie di fila; **~ away**, **~ off** (at once) immediatamente; **~ off**, **~ out** senza esitare; **I went ~ home** sono andato direttamente a casa

straighten ['streɪtn] VT (also: **straighten out**) raddrizzare; **to ~ things out** mettere le cose a posto

straighteners ['streɪtnəz] NPL (for hair) piastra f per capelli

straight-faced [streɪt'feɪst] ADJ impassibile, imperturbabile ▶ ADV con il viso serio

straightforward [streɪt'fɔːwəd] ADJ semplice; (frank) onesto(-a), franco(-a)

strain [streɪn] N (Tech) sollecitazione f; (physical) sforzo; (mental) tensione f; (Med) strappo; distorsione f; (streak, trace) tendenza; elemento; (breed) razza; (of virus) tipo ▶ VT tendere; (muscle) stirare; (ankle) slogar; (friendship, marriage) mettere a dura prova; (filter) colare, filtrare; (resources) pesare su; (food) colare; passare ▶ VI sforzarsi; **strains** NPL (Mus) note fpl; **she's under a lot of ~** è molto tesa, è sotto pressione

strained [streɪnd] ADJ (muscle) stirato(-a); (laugh etc) forzato(-a); (relations) teso(-a)

strainer ['streɪnər] N passino, colino

strait [streɪt] N (Geo) stretto; **straits** NPL: **to be in dire straits** (fig) essere nei guai

straitjacket ['streɪtdʒækɪt] N camicia di forza

strait-laced [streɪt'leɪst] ADJ puritano(-a)

strand [strænd] N (of thread) filo

stranded ADJ nei guai; senza mezzi di trasporto

strange [streɪndʒ] ADJ (not known) sconosciuto(-a); (odd) strano(-a), bizzarro(-a)

strangely ['streɪndʒlɪ] ADV stranamente

stranger ['streɪndʒər] N (unknown) sconosciuto(-a); (from another place) estraneo(-a); **I'm a ~ here** non sono del posto

strangle ['stræŋgl] VT strangolare

stranglehold ['stræŋglhəuld] N (fig) stretta (mortale)

strangulation [stræŋgju'leɪʃən] N strangolamento

strap [stræp] N cinghia; (of slip, dress) spallina, bretella ▶ VT legare con una cinghia; (child etc) punire (con una cinghia)

straphanging ['stræphæŋɪŋ] N viaggiare m in piedi (su mezzi pubblici reggendosi a un sostegno)

strapless ['stræplɪs] ADJ (bra, dress) senza spalline

strapped [stræpt] ADJ: **~ for cash** a corto di soldi; **financially ~** finanziariamente a terra

strapping ['stræpɪŋ] ADJ ben piantato(-a)

Strasbourg ['stræzbəːg] N Strasburgo f

strata ['strɑːtə] NPL of **stratum**

stratagem ['strætɪdʒəm] N stratagemma m

strategic [strə'tiːdʒɪk] ADJ strategico(-a)

strategist ['strætɪdʒɪst] N stratega m

strategy ['strætɪdʒɪ] N strategia

stratosphere ['strætəsfɪər] N stratosfera

stratum ['strɑːtəm] (pl **strata** ['strɑːtə]) N strato

straw [strɔː] N paglia; (drinking straw) cannuccia; **that's the last ~!** è la goccia che fa traboccare il vaso!

strawberry ['strɔːbərɪ] N fragola

stray [streɪ] ADJ (animal) randagio(-a); (bullet) vagante; (scattered) sparso(-a) ▶ VI perdersi; allontanarsi, staccarsi (dal gruppo); **~ bullet** proiettile m vagante

streak [striːk] N striscia; (of hair) mèche f inv; **a ~ of** una vena di ▶ VT striare, screziare ▶ VI: **to ~ past** passare come un fulmine; **to have streaks in one's hair** avere le mèche nei capelli; **a winning/losing ~** un periodo fortunato/sfortunato

streaker ['striːkər] N streaker mf

streaky ['striːkɪ] ADJ screziato(-a), striato(-a)

streaky bacon (BRIT) N pancetta

stream [striːm] N ruscello; corrente f; (of people, smoke etc) fiume m ▶ VT (Scol) dividere in livelli di rendimento ▶ VI scorrere; **to ~ in/out** entrare/uscire a fiotti; **against the ~** controcorrente; **on ~** (new power plant etc) in funzione, in produzione

streamer ['striːmər] N (of paper) stella filante

stream feed N (on photocopier etc) alimentazione f continua

streamline ['striːmlaɪn] VT dare una linea aerodinamica a; (fig) razionalizzare

streamlined ['stri:mlaɪnd] ADJ aerodinamico(-a), affusolato(-a); (fig) razionalizzato(-a)

street [stri:t] N strada, via; **the back streets** le strade secondarie; **to be on the streets** (homeless) essere senza tetto; (as prostitute) battere il marciapiede

streetcar ['stri:tkɑːʳ] N (US) tram m inv

street cred [-krɛd] N (col) credibilità presso i giovani

street lamp N lampione m

street light N lampione m

street lighting N illuminazione f stradale

street map N pianta (di una città)

street market N mercato all'aperto

street plan N pianta (di una città)

streetwise ['stri:twaɪz] ADJ (col) esperto(-a) dei bassifondi

strength [strɛŋθ] N forza; (of girder, knot etc) resistenza, solidità; (of chemical solution) concentrazione f; (of wine) gradazione f alcolica; **on the ~ of** sulla base di, in virtù di; **below/at full ~** con gli effettivi ridotti/al completo

strengthen ['strɛŋθən] VT rinforzare; (muscles) irrobustire; fortificare; (economy, currency) consolidare

strenuous ['strɛnjuəs] ADJ vigoroso(-a), energico(-a); (tiring) duro(-a), pesante

stress [strɛs] N (force, pressure) pressione f; (mental strain) tensione f; (accent) accento; (emphasis) enfasi f ▶ VT insistere su, sottolineare; accentare; **to be under ~** essere sotto tensione; **to lay great ~ on sth** dare grande importanza a qc

stressed ADJ (tense: person) stressato(-a); (Ling, Poetry: syllable) accentato(-a)

stressful ['strɛsful] ADJ (job) difficile, stressante

stretch [strɛtʃ] N (of sand etc) distesa; (of time) periodo ▶ VI stirarsi; (extend): **to ~ to** or **as far as** estendersi fino a; (be enough: money, food): **to ~ (to)** bastare (per) ▶ VT tendere, allungare; (spread) distendere; (fig) spingere (al massimo); **at a ~** ininterrottamente; **to ~ a muscle** tendere un muscolo; **to ~ one's legs** sgranchirsi le gambe
▶ **stretch out** VI allungarsi, estendersi ▶ VT (arm etc) allungare, tendere; (spread) distendere; **to ~ out for sth** allungare la mano per prendere qc

stretcher ['strɛtʃəʳ] N barella, lettiga

stretcher-bearer ['strɛtʃəbɛərəʳ] N barelliere m

stretch marks NPL smagliature fpl

strewn [struːn] ADJ: **~ with** cosparso(-a) di

stricken ['strɪkən] ADJ provato(-a), affranto(-a); **~ with** colpito(-a) da

strict [strɪkt] ADJ (severe) rigido(-a), severo(-a); (: order, rule) rigoroso(-a); (: supervision) stretto(-a); (precise) preciso(-a), stretto(-a); **in ~ confidence** in assoluta confidenza

strictly ['strɪktlɪ] ADV severamente; rigorosamente; strettamente; **~ confidential** strettamente confidenziale; **~ speaking** a rigor di termini; **~ between ourselves ...** detto fra noi ...

stride [straɪd] (pt **strode** [strəud], pp **stridden** ['strɪdn]) N passo lungo ▶ VI camminare a grandi passi; **to take in one's ~** (fig: changes etc) prendere con tranquillità

strident ['straɪdnt] ADJ stridente

strife [straɪf] N conflitto; litigi mpl

strike [straɪk] (pt, pp **struck** [strʌk]) N sciopero; (of oil etc) scoperta; (attack) attacco ▶ VT colpire; (oil etc) scoprire, trovare; (produce, make: coin, medal) coniare; (: agreement, deal) concludere; (bargain) fare; (fig): **the thought** or **it strikes me that ...** mi viene in mente che ... ▶ VI far sciopero, scioperare; (attack) attaccare; (clock) suonare; **on ~** (workers) in sciopero; **to go on** or **come out on ~** mettersi in sciopero; **to ~ a match** accendere un fiammifero; **to ~ a balance** (fig) trovare il giusto mezzo
▶ **strike back** VI (Mil) fare rappresaglie; (fig) reagire
▶ **strike down** VT (fig) atterrare
▶ **strike off** VT (from list) cancellare; (: doctor etc) radiare
▶ **strike out** VT depennare
▶ **strike up** VT (Mus) attaccare; **to ~ up a friendship with** fare amicizia con

strikebreaker ['straɪkbreɪkəʳ] N crumiro(-a)

striker ['straɪkəʳ] N scioperante mf; (Sport) attaccante m

striking ['straɪkɪŋ] ADJ impressionante

Strimmer® ['strɪməʳ] N tagliabordi m inv

string [strɪŋ] (pt, pp **strung** [strʌŋ]) N spago; (row) fila; sequenza; catena; (Comput) stringa, sequenza; (Mus) corda ▶ VT: **to ~ out** disporre di fianco; **to ~ together** (words, ideas) mettere insieme; **the strings** NPL (Mus) gli archi; **~ of pearls** filo di perle; **with no strings attached** (fig) senza vincoli, senza obblighi; **to pull strings for sb** (fig) raccomandare qn

string bean N fagiolino

stringed instrument, string instrument N (Mus) strumento a corda

stringent ['strɪndʒənt] ADJ rigoroso(-a); (reasons, arguments) stringente, impellente

string quartet N quartetto d'archi

strip [strɪp] N striscia; (Sport): **wearing the Celtic ~** con la divisa del Celtic ▶ VT spogliare; (paint) togliere; (also: **strip down**: machine) smontare ▶ VI spogliarsi
▶ **strip off** VT (paint etc) staccare ▶ VI (person) spogliarsi

strip cartoon N fumetto

stripe [straɪp] N striscia, riga; (Mil, Police) gallone m

striped ['straɪpt] ADJ a strisce or righe

strip light N (BRIT) tubo al neon

stripper ['strɪpəʳ] N spogliarellista mf

strip-search ['strɪpsəːtʃ] VT: **to ~ sb** perquisire qn facendo(-a) spogliare ▶ N perquisizione f (facendo spogliare il perquisito)

striptease ['strɪptiːz] N spogliarello

strive [straɪv] (pt **strove** [strəuv], pp **striven** ['strɪvn]) VI: **to ~ to do** sforzarsi di fare

strobe [strəub] N (also: **strobe light**) luce f stroboscopica

strode [strəud] PT of **stride**

stroke [strəuk] N colpo; (of piston) corsa; (Med) colpo apoplettico; (Swimming) bracciata; (: style) stile m; (caress) carezza ▶ VT accarezzare; **at a ~** in un attimo; **on the ~ of 5** alle 5 in punto, allo scoccare delle 5; **a ~ of luck** un colpo di fortuna; **two-~ engine** motore a due tempi

stroll [strəul] N giretto, passeggiata ▶ VI andare a spasso; **to go for a ~, have** or **take a ~** andare a fare un giretto or due passi

stroller ['strəuləʳ] N (US) passeggino

strong [strɔŋ] ADJ (gen) forte; (sturdy: table, fabric etc) robusto(-a); (concentrated, intense: bleach, acid) concentrato(-a); (: protest, letter, measures) energico(-a) ▶ ADV: **to be going ~** (company) andare a gonfie vele; (person) essere attivo(-a); **they are 50 ~** sono in 50; **~ language** (swearing) linguaggio volgare

strong-arm ['strɔŋɑːm] ADJ (tactics, methods) energico(-a)

strongbox ['strɔŋbɔks] N cassaforte f

stronghold ['strɔŋhəuld] N fortezza; (also fig) roccaforte f

strongly ['strɔŋlɪ] ADV fortemente, con forza; solidamente; energicamente; **to feel ~ about sth** avere molto a cuore qc

strongman ['strɔŋmæn] N (irreg) personaggio di spicco

strongroom ['strɔŋruːm] N camera di sicurezza

stroppy ['strɔpɪ] ADJ (BRIT col) scontroso(-a), indisponente

strove [strəuv] PT of **strive**

struck [strʌk] PT, PP of **strike**

structural ['strʌktʃərəl] ADJ strutturale; (Constr) di costruzione; di struttura

structurally ['strʌktʃrəlɪ] ADV dal punto di vista della struttura

structure ['strʌktʃəʳ] N struttura; (building) costruzione f, fabbricato

struggle ['strʌgl] N lotta ▶ VI lottare; **to have a ~ to do sth** avere dei problemi per fare qc

strum [strʌm] VT (guitar) strimpellare

strung [strʌŋ] PT, PP of **string**

strut [strʌt] N sostegno, supporto ▶ VI pavoneggiarsi

strychnine ['strɪkniːn] N stricnina

stub [stʌb] N mozzicone m; (of ticket etc) matrice f, talloncino ▶ VT: **to ~ one's toe (on sth)** urtare or sbattere il dito del piede (contro qc)
▶ **stub out** VT schiacciare; **to ~ out a cigarette** spegnere una sigaretta

stubble ['stʌbl] N stoppia; (on chin) barba ispida

stubborn ['stʌbən] ADJ testardo(-a), ostinato(-a)

stubby ['stʌbɪ] ADJ tozzo(-a)

stucco ['stʌkəu] N stucco

stuck [stʌk] PT, PP of **stick** ▶ ADJ (jammed) bloccato(-a); **to get ~** bloccarsi

stuck-up [stʌk'ʌp] ADJ presuntuoso(-a)

stud [stʌd] N bottoncino; borchia; (also: **stud earring**) orecchino a pressione (of horses) scuderia, allevamento di cavalli; (also: **stud horse**) stallone m ▶ VT (fig): **studded with** tempestato(-a) di

student ['stjuːdənt] N studente(-essa) ▶ CPD studentesco(-a); universitario(-a); degli studenti; **a law/medical ~** uno studente di legge/di medicina

student driver N (US) conducente mf principiante

students' union N (BRIT: association) circolo universitario; (: building) sede f del circolo universitario

studied ['stʌdɪd] ADJ studiato(-a), calcolato(-a)

studio ['stjuːdɪəu] N studio

studio flat, (US) **studio apartment** N monolocale m

studious ['stjuːdɪəs] ADJ studioso(-a); (studied) studiato(-a), voluto(-a)

studiously ['stjuːdɪəslɪ] ADV (carefully) deliberatamente, di proposito

study ['stʌdɪ] N studio ▶ VT studiare; esaminare ▶ VI studiare; **to make a ~ of sth** fare uno studio su qc; **to ~ for an exam** prepararsi a un esame

stuff [stʌf] N (substance) materiale m; (belongings) cose fpl, roba ▶ VT imbottire; (animal: for exhibition) impagliare; (Culin) farcire; (col: push) ficcare; **my nose is stuffed up** ho il naso chiuso; **get stuffed!** (col!) va' a farti fottere! (!); **stuffed toy** giocattolo di peluche

stuffing ['stʌfɪŋ] N imbottitura; (Culin) ripieno

stuffy ['stʌfɪ] ADJ (room) mal ventilato(-a), senz'aria; (ideas) antiquato(-a)

stumble ['stʌmbl] VI inciampare; **to ~ across** (fig) imbattersi in

stumbling block ['stʌmblɪŋ-] N ostacolo, scoglio

S

stump [stʌmp] N ceppo; *(of limb)* moncone *m*
▸ VT: **to be stumped** essere sconcertato(-a);
to be stumped for an answer essere
incapace di rispondere
stun [stʌn] VT stordire; *(amaze)* sbalordire
stung [stʌŋ] PT, PP *of* **sting**
stunk [stʌŋk] PP *of* **stink**
stunned [stʌnd] ADJ *(from blow)* stordito(-a);
(amazed, shocked) sbalordito(-a)
stunning ['stʌnɪŋ] ADJ *(piece of news etc)*
sbalorditivo(-a); *(girl, dress)* stupendo(-a),
favoloso(-a)
stunt [stʌnt] N bravata; trucco pubblicitario;
(Aviat) acrobazia ▸ VT arrestare
stunted ['stʌntɪd] ADJ stentato(-a),
rachitico(-a)
stuntman ['stʌntmæn] N *(irreg)* cascatore *m*
stupefaction [stjuːpɪ'fækʃən] N
stupefazione *f*, stupore *m*
stupefy ['stjuːpɪfaɪ] VT stordire; intontire;
(fig) stupire
stupendous [stjuː'pɛndəs] ADJ stupendo(-a),
meraviglioso(-a)
stupid ['stjuːpɪd] ADJ stupido(-a)
stupidity [stjuː'pɪdɪtɪ] N stupidità *f inv*,
stupidaggine *f*
stupidly ['stjuːpɪdlɪ] ADV stupidamente
stupor ['stjuːpər] N torpore *m*
sturdy ['stəːdɪ] ADJ robusto(-a), vigoroso(-a);
solido(-a)
sturgeon ['stəːdʒən] N storione *m*
stutter ['stʌtər] N balbuzie *f* ▸ VI balbettare
Stuttgart ['ʃtutgart] N Stoccarda
sty [staɪ] N *(of pigs)* porcile *m*
stye [staɪ] N *(Med)* orzaiolo
style [staɪl] N stile *m*; *(distinction)* eleganza,
classe *f*; *(hair style)* pettinatura; *(of dress etc)*
modello, linea; **in the latest ~** all'ultima
moda
styli ['staɪlaɪ] NPL *of* **stylus**
stylish ['staɪlɪʃ] ADJ elegante
stylist ['staɪlɪst] N: **hair ~** parrucchiere(-a)
stylized ['staɪlaɪzd] ADJ stilizzato(-a)
stylus ['staɪləs] *(pl* **styluses** *or* **styli** [-laɪ]*)* N *(of
record player)* puntina
Styrofoam® ['staɪrəfəum] N *(US)*
= **polystyrene** ▸ ADJ *(cup)* di polistirene
suave [swɑːv] ADJ untuoso(-a)
sub [sʌb] N ABBR = **submarine**; **subscription**
sub... [sʌb] PREFIX sub..., sotto...
subcommittee ['sʌbkəmɪtɪ] N sottocomitato
subconscious [sʌb'kɔnʃəs] ADJ, N
subcosciente *m*
subcontinent [sʌb'kɔntɪnənt] N: **the
(Indian) ~** il subcontinente (indiano)
subcontract N [sʌb'kɔntrækt] subappalto
▸ VT [sʌbkən'trækt] subappaltare
subcontractor ['sʌbkən'træktər] N
subappaltatore(-trice)

subdivide [sʌbdɪ'vaɪd] VT suddividere
subdivision ['sʌbdɪvɪʒən] N suddivisione *f*
subdue [səb'djuː] VT sottomettere,
soggiogare
subdued [səb'djuːd] ADJ pacato(-a); *(light)*
attenuato(-a); *(person)* poco esuberante
sub-editor ['sʌb'ɛdɪtər] N *(Brit)* redattore(-a)
aggiunto(-a)
subject N ['sʌbdʒɪkt] soggetto; *(citizen etc)*
cittadino(-a); *(Scol)* materia ▸ VT [səb'dʒɛkt]:
to ~ to sottomettere a; esporre a; **to be ~ to**
(law) essere sottomesso(-a) a; *(disease)* essere
soggetto(-a) a; **~ to confirmation in
writing** a condizione di ricevere conferma
scritta; **to change the ~** cambiare discorso
subjection [səb'dʒɛkʃən] N sottomissione *f*,
soggezione *f*
subjective [səb'dʒɛktɪv] ADJ soggettivo(-a)
subject matter N argomento; contenuto
sub judice [sʌb'dʒuːdɪsɪ] ADJ *(Law)* sub iudice
subjugate ['sʌbdʒugeɪt] VT sottomettere,
soggiogare
subjunctive [səb'dʒʌŋktɪv] ADJ
congiuntivo(-a) ▸ N congiuntivo
sublet [sʌb'lɛt] VT, VI *(irreg)* subaffittare
sublime [sə'blaɪm] ADJ sublime
subliminal [sʌb'lɪmɪnl] ADJ subliminale
submachine gun ['sʌbmə'ʃiːn-] N mitra *m inv*
submarine [sʌbmə'riːn] N sommergibile *m*
submerge [səb'məːdʒ] VT sommergere;
immergere ▸ VI immergersi
submersion [səb'məːʃən] N sommersione *f*;
immersione *f*
submission [səb'mɪʃən] N sottomissione *f*;
(to committee etc) richiesta, domanda
submissive [səb'mɪsɪv] ADJ remissivo(-a)
submit [səb'mɪt] VT sottomettere; *(proposal,
claim)* presentare ▸ VI sottomettersi
subnormal [sʌb'nɔːməl] ADJ subnormale
subordinate [sə'bɔːdɪnət] ADJ, N
subordinato(-a)
subpoena [səb'piːnə] N *(Law)* citazione *f*,
mandato di comparizione ▸ VT *(Law)* citare
in giudizio
subprime ['sʌbpraɪm] ADJ *(Finance)* subprime
inv; **~ mortgage** mutuo subprime
subroutine ['sʌbruːtiːn] N *(Comput)*
sottoprogramma *m*
subscribe [səb'skraɪb] VI contribuire; **to ~ to**
(opinion) approvare, condividere; *(fund)*
sottoscrivere a; *(newspaper)* abbonarsi a;
essere abbonato(-a) a
subscriber [səb'skraɪbər] N *(to periodical,
telephone)* abbonato(-a)
subscript ['sʌbskrɪpt] N deponente *m*
subscription [səb'skrɪpʃən] N sottoscrizione
f; abbonamento; **to take out a ~ to**
abbonarsi a
subsequent ['sʌbsɪkwənt] ADJ *(later)*

successivo(-a), seguente; conseguente;
(*further*) ulteriore; ~ **to** in seguito a
subsequently ['sʌbsɪkwəntlɪ] ADV in
seguito, successivamente
subservient [səb'sə:vɪənt] ADJ: ~ **(to)**
remissivo(-a) (a), sottomesso(-a) (a)
subside [səb'saɪd] VI cedere, abbassarsi;
(*flood*) decrescere; (*wind*) calmarsi
subsidence [səb'saɪdns] N cedimento,
abbassamento
subsidiarity [səbsɪdɪ'ærɪtɪ] N (*Pol*) principio del
decentramento del potere
subsidiary [səb'sɪdɪərɪ] ADJ sussidiario(-a);
accessorio(-a); (*BRIT Scol: subject*)
complementare ▶ N filiale f
subsidize ['sʌbsɪdaɪz] VT sovvenzionare
subsidy ['sʌbsɪdɪ] N sovvenzione f
subsist [səb'sɪst] VI: **to** ~ **on sth** vivere di qc
subsistence [səb'sɪstəns] N esistenza; mezzi
mpl di sostentamento
subsistence allowance N indennità f inv di
trasferta
subsistence level N livello minimo di vita
substance ['sʌbstəns] N sostanza; (*fig*)
essenza; **to lack** ~ (*argument*) essere debole
substance abuse N abuso di sostanze
tossiche
substandard [sʌb'stændəd] ADJ (*goods,
housing*) di qualità scadente
substantial [səb'stænʃl] ADJ solido(-a);
(*amount, progress etc*) notevole; (*meal*)
sostanzioso(-a)
substantially [səb'stænʃəlɪ] ADV
sostanzialmente; ~ **bigger** molto più grande
substantiate [səb'stænʃɪeɪt] VT comprovare
substitute ['sʌbstɪtju:t] N (*person*)
sostituto(-a); (*thing*) succedaneo, surrogato
▶ VT: **to** ~ **sth/sb for** sostituire qc/qn a
substitute teacher N (*US*) supplente *mf*
substitution [sʌbstɪ'tju:ʃən] N sostituzione f
subterfuge ['sʌbtəfju:dʒ] N sotterfugio
subterranean [sʌbtə'reɪnɪən] ADJ
sotterraneo(-a)
subtitle ['sʌbtaɪtl] N (*Cine*) sottotitolo
subtle ['sʌtl] ADJ sottile; (*flavour, perfume*)
delicato(-a)
subtlety ['sʌtltɪ] N sottigliezza
subtly ['sʌtlɪ] ADV sottilmente;
delicatamente
subtotal [sʌb'təutl] N somma parziale
subtract [səb'trækt] VT sottrarre
subtraction [səb'trækʃən] N sottrazione f
suburb ['sʌbə:b] N sobborgo; **the suburbs** la
periferia
suburban [sə'bə:bən] ADJ suburbano(-a)
suburbia [sə'bə:bɪə] N periferia, sobborghi
mpl
subversion [səb'və:ʃən] N sovversione f
subversive [səb'və:sɪv] ADJ sovversivo(-a)

subway ['sʌbweɪ] N (*US: underground*)
metropolitana; (*BRIT: underpass*)
sottopassaggio
subzero [sʌb'zɪərəu] ADJ: ~ **temperatures**
temperature fpl sotto zero
succeed [sək'si:d] VI riuscire; avere successo
▶ VT succedere a; **to** ~ **in doing** riuscire a fare
succeeding [sək'si:dɪŋ] ADJ (*following*)
successivo(-a); ~ **generations** generazioni
fpl future
success [sək'sɛs] N successo
successful [sək'sɛsful] ADJ (*venture*)
coronato(-a) da successo, riuscito(-a); **to be** ~
(in doing) riuscire (a fare)
successfully [sək'sɛsfəlɪ] ADV con successo
succession [sək'sɛʃən] N successione f; **in** ~
di seguito
successive [sək'sɛsɪv] ADJ successivo(-a);
consecutivo(-a); **on 3** ~ **days** per 3 giorni
consecutivi or di seguito
successor [sək'sɛsəʳ] N successore m
succinct [sək'sɪŋkt] ADJ succinto(-a), breve
succulent ['sʌkjulənt] ADJ succulento(-a) ▶ N
(*Bot*): **succulents** piante fpl grasse
succumb [sə'kʌm] VI soccombere
such [sʌtʃ] ADJ tale; ~ **books** tali libri, libri del
genere; (*so much*): ~ **courage** tanto coraggio;
(*of that kind*): ~ **a book** un tale libro, un libro
del genere ▶ ADV talmente, così; ~ **a long
trip** un viaggio così lungo; ~ **good books**
libri così buoni; ~ **a lot of** talmente or così
tanto(-a); **making** ~ **a noise that** facendo
un rumore tale che; ~ **a long time ago** tanto
tempo fa; ~ **as** (*like*) come; **a noise** ~ **as to** un
rumore tale da; ~ **books as I have** quei pochi
libri che ho; **as** ~ come or in quanto tale;
I said no ~ **thing** non ho detto niente del
genere
such-and-such ['sʌtʃənsʌtʃ] ADJ tale (*after
noun*)
suchlike ['sʌtʃlaɪk] PRON (*col*): **and** ~ e così via
suck [sʌk] VT succhiare; (*baby*) poppare;
(*pump, machine*) aspirare
sucker ['sʌkəʳ] N (*Zool, Tech*) ventosa; (*Bot*)
pollone m; (*col*) gonzo(-a), babbeo(-a)
suckle ['sʌkl] VT allattare
sucrose ['su:krəuz] N saccarosio
suction ['sʌkʃən] N succhiamento; (*Tech*)
aspirazione f
suction pump N pompa aspirante
Sudan [su:'dɑːn] N Sudan m
Sudanese [su:də'niːz] ADJ, N sudanese *mf*
sudden ['sʌdn] ADJ improvviso(-a); **all of a** ~
improvvisamente, all'improvviso
sudden-death [sʌdn'dɛθ] N (*also:* **sudden-
death playoff:** *Sport*) spareggio, bella
suddenly ['sʌdnlɪ] ADV bruscamente,
improvvisamente, di colpo
sudoku [su'dəuku:] N sudoku m inv

S

811

suds [sʌdz] NPL schiuma (di sapone)
sue [su:] VT citare in giudizio ▸ VI: **to ~ (for)**
intentare causa (per); **to ~ for divorce**
intentare causa di divorzio; **to ~ sb for**
damages citare qn per danni
suede [sweɪd] N pelle f scamosciata ▸ CPD
scamosciato(-a)
suet ['suɪt] N grasso di rognone
Suez ['suːɪz] N: **the ~ Canal** il Canale
di Suez
suffer ['sʌfər] VT soffrire, patire; (bear)
sopportare, tollerare; (undergo: loss, setback)
subire ▸ VI soffrire; **to ~ from** soffrire di;
to ~ from the effects of alcohol/a fall
risentire degli effetti dell'alcool/di una
caduta
sufferance ['sʌfərəns] N: **he was only there**
on ~ era più che altro sopportato lì
sufferer ['sʌfərər] N (Med): **~ (from)**
malato(-a) (di)
suffering ['sʌfərɪŋ] N sofferenza; (hardship,
deprivation) privazione f
suffice [sə'faɪs] VI essere sufficiente, bastare
sufficient [sə'fɪʃənt] ADJ sufficiente;
~ money abbastanza soldi
sufficiently [sə'fɪʃəntlɪ] ADV
sufficientemente, abbastanza
suffix ['sʌfɪks] N suffisso
suffocate ['sʌfəkeɪt] VI (have difficulty
breathing) soffocare; (die through lack of air)
asfissiare
suffocation [sʌfə'keɪʃən] N soffocamento;
(Med) asfissia
suffrage ['sʌfrɪdʒ] N suffragio
suffuse [sə'fjuːz] VT: **to ~ (with)** (colour)
tingere (di); (light) soffondere (di); **her face**
was suffused with joy la gioia si dipingeva
sul suo volto
sugar ['ʃugər] N zucchero ▸ VT zuccherare
sugar beet N barbabietola da zucchero
sugar bowl N zuccheriera
sugar cane N canna da zucchero
sugar-coated ['ʃugəkəutɪd] ADJ ricoperto(-a)
di zucchero
sugar lump N zolletta di zucchero
sugar refinery N raffineria di zucchero
sugary ['ʃugərɪ] ADJ zuccherino(-a), dolce;
(fig) sdolcinato(-a)
suggest [sə'dʒɛst] VT proporre, suggerire;
(indicate) indicare; **what do you ~ I do?** cosa
mi suggerisce di fare?
suggestion [sə'dʒɛstʃən] N suggerimento,
proposta; indicazione f
suggestive [sə'dʒɛstɪv] ADJ suggestivo(-a);
(indecent) spinto(-a), indecente
suicidal [suɪ'saɪdl] ADJ suicida inv; (fig) fatale,
disastroso(-a)
suicide ['suɪsaɪd] N (person) suicida mf; (act)
suicidio; **to commit ~** suicidarsi

suicide attempt, suicide bid N tentato
suicidio
suicide bomber N kamikaze mf,
attentatore(-trice) suicida
suicide bombing N attentato suicida
suit [suːt] N (man's) vestito; (woman's)
completo, tailleur m inv; (lawsuit) causa;
(Cards) seme m, colore m ▸ VT andar bene a or
per; essere adatto(-a) a or per; (adapt): **to ~**
sth to adattare qc a; **to be suited to sth**
(suitable for) essere adatto a qc; **well suited**
(couple) ben assortito(-a); **to bring a ~**
against sb intentare causa a qn; **to follow ~**
(fig) fare altrettanto
suitable ['suːtəbl] ADJ adatto(-a);
appropriato(-a); **would tomorrow be ~?**
andrebbe bene domani?; **we found**
somebody ~ abbiamo trovato la persona
adatta
suitably ['suːtəblɪ] ADV (dress) in modo adatto;
(thank) adeguatamente
suitcase ['suːtkeɪs] N valigia
suite [swiːt] N (of rooms) appartamento; (Mus)
suite f inv; (furniture): **bedroom/dining room**
~ arredo or mobilia per la camera da letto/
sala da pranzo; **a three-piece ~** un salotto
comprendente un divano e due poltrone
suitor ['suːtər] N corteggiatore m,
spasimante m
sulfate ['sʌlfeɪt] N (US) = **sulphate**
sulfur etc ['sʌlfər] (US) = **sulphur** etc
sulk [sʌlk] VI fare il broncio
sulky ['sʌlkɪ] ADJ imbronciato(-a)
sullen ['sʌlən] ADJ scontroso(-a); cupo(-a)
sulphate, (US) **sulfate** ['sʌlfeɪt] N solfato;
copper ~ solfato di rame
sulphur, (US) **sulfur** ['sʌlfər] N zolfo
sulphur dioxide N biossido di zolfo
sulphuric, (US) **sulfuric** [sʌl'fjuərɪk] ADJ:
~ acid acido solforico
sultan ['sʌltən] N sultano
sultana [sʌl'tɑːnə] N (fruit) uva (secca)
sultanina
sultry ['sʌltrɪ] ADJ afoso(-a)
sum [sʌm] N somma; (Scol etc) addizione f
▸ **sum up** VT riassumere; (evaluate rapidly)
valutare, giudicare ▸ VI riassumere
Sumatra [su'mɑːtrə] N Sumatra
summarize ['sʌmәraɪz] VT riassumere,
riepilogare
summary ['sʌmәrɪ] N riassunto ▸ ADJ (justice)
sommario(-a)
summer ['sʌmər] N estate f ▸ CPD d'estate,
estivo(-a); **in (the) ~** d'estate
summer camp N (US) colonia (estiva)
summer holidays NPL vacanze fpl estive
summerhouse ['sʌmәhaus] N (in garden)
padiglione m
summertime ['sʌmәtaɪm] N (season) estate f

summer time N (by clock) ora legale (estiva)
summery ['sʌmərɪ] ADJ estivo(-a)
summing-up [sʌmɪŋ'ʌp] N (Law) ricapitolazione f del processo
summit ['sʌmɪt] N cima, sommità; (Pol) vertice m
summit conference N conferenza al vertice
summon ['sʌmən] VT chiamare, convocare; **to ~ a witness** citare un testimone
▶ **summon up** VT raccogliere, fare appello a
summons N ordine m di comparizione ▶ VT citare; **to serve a ~ on sb** notificare una citazione a qn
sumo ['suːməʊ] N (also: **sumo wrestling**) sumo
sump [sʌmp] N (Aut) coppa dell'olio
sumptuous ['sʌmptjuəs] ADJ sontuoso(-a)
sun [sʌn] N sole m; **in the ~** al sole; **to catch the ~** prendere sole; **they have everything under the ~** hanno tutto ciò che possono desiderare
Sun. ABBR (= Sunday) dom.
sunbathe ['sʌnbeɪð] VI prendere un bagno di sole
sunbeam ['sʌnbiːm] N raggio di sole
sunbed ['sʌnbɛd] N lettino solare
sunblock ['sʌnblɔk] N crema solare a protezione totale
sunburn ['sʌnbəːn] N (tan) abbronzatura; (painful) scottatura
sunburnt ['sʌnbəːnt], **sunburned** ['sʌnbəːnd] ADJ abbronzato(-a); (painfully) scottato(-a) dal sole
sun cream N crema solare
sundae ['sʌndeɪ] N coppa di gelato guarnita
Sunday ['sʌndɪ] N domenica; see also **Tuesday**
Sunday paper N giornale m della domenica; vedi nota

I Sunday papers sono i giornali che escono di domenica. Sono generalmente corredati da supplementi e riviste di argomento culturale, sportivo e di attualità ed hanno un'alta tiratura.

Sunday school N ≈ scuola di catechismo
sundial ['sʌndaɪəl] N meridiana
sundown ['sʌndaʊn] N tramonto
sundries ['sʌndrɪz] NPL articoli diversi, cose diverse
sundry ['sʌndrɪ] ADJ vari(-e), diversi(-e); **all and ~** tutti quanti
sunflower ['sʌnflaʊər] N girasole m
sung [sʌŋ] PP of **sing**
sunglasses ['sʌnglɑːsɪz] NPL occhiali mpl da sole
sunk [sʌŋk] PP of **sink**
sunken ['sʌŋkən] ADJ sommerso(-a); (eyes, cheeks) infossato(-a); (bath) incassato(-a)
sunlamp ['sʌnlæmp] N lampada a raggi ultravioletti

sunlight ['sʌnlaɪt] N (luce f del) sole m
sunlit ['sʌnlɪt] ADJ assolato(-a), soleggiato(-a)
sun lounger N sedia a sdraio
sunny ['sʌnɪ] ADJ assolato(-a), soleggiato(-a); (fig) allegro(-a), felice; **it is ~** c'è il sole
sunrise ['sʌnraɪz] N levata del sole, alba
sunroof ['sʌnruːf] N (on building) tetto a terrazzo; (Aut) tetto apribile
sunscreen ['sʌnskriːn] N (protective ingredient) filtro solare; (cream) crema solare protettiva
sunset ['sʌnsɛt] N tramonto
sunshade ['sʌnʃeɪd] N parasole m
sunshine ['sʌnʃaɪn] N (luce f del) sole m
sunspot ['sʌnspɔt] N macchia solare
sunstroke ['sʌnstrəʊk] N insolazione f, colpo di sole
suntan ['sʌntæn] N abbronzatura
suntan lotion N lozione f solare
suntanned ['sʌntænd] ADJ abbronzato(-a)
suntan oil N olio solare
suntrap ['sʌntræp] N luogo molto assolato, angolo pieno di sole
super ['suːpər] ADJ (col) fantastico(-a)
superannuation [suːpərænju'eɪʃən] N contributi mpl pensionistici, pensione f
superb [suː'pəːb] ADJ magnifico(-a)
Super Bowl N (US Sport) Super Bowl m inv
supercilious [suːpə'sɪlɪəs] ADJ sprezzante, sdegnoso(-a)
superconductor [suːpəkən'dʌktər] N superconduttore m
superficial [suːpə'fɪʃəl] ADJ superficiale
superficially [suːpə'fɪʃəlɪ] ADV superficialmente
superfluous [suː'pəːfluəs] ADJ superfluo(-a)
superglue ['suːpəgluː] N colla a presa rapida
superhighway ['suːpəhaɪweɪ] N (US) autostrada; **the information ~** l'autostrada telematica
superhuman [suːpə'hjuːmən] ADJ sovrumano(-a)
superimpose ['suːpərɪm'pəʊz] VT sovrapporre
superintend [suːpərɪn'tɛnd] VT dirigere, sovraintendere
superintendent [suːpərɪn'tɛndənt] N direttore(-trice); (Police) ≈ commissario (capo)
superior [suː'pɪərɪər] ADJ superiore; (Comm: goods, quality) di prim'ordine, superiore; (smug: person) che fa il superiore ▶ N superiore mf; **Mother S~** (Rel) Madre f Superiora, Superiora
superiority [supɪərɪ'ɔrɪtɪ] N superiorità
superlative [suː'pəːlətɪv] ADJ superlativo(-a), supremo(-a) ▶ N (Ling) superlativo
superman ['suːpəmæn] N (irreg) superuomo
supermarket ['suːpəmɑːkɪt] N supermercato
supermodel ['suːpəmɔdl] N top model mf

S

supernatural [suːpəˈnætʃərəl] ADJ, N soprannaturale m

supernova [suːpəˈnəuvə] N supernova

superpower [ˈsuːpəpauəʳ] N (Pol) superpotenza

superscript [ˈsuːpəskrɪpt] N esponente m

supersede [suːpəˈsiːd] VT sostituire, soppiantare

supersonic [ˈsuːpəˈsɒnɪk] ADJ supersonico(-a)

superstar [ˈsuːpəstɑːʳ] ADJ, N superstar f inv

superstition [suːpəˈstɪʃən] N superstizione f

superstitious [suːpəˈstɪʃəs] ADJ superstizioso(-a)

superstore [ˈsuːpəstɔːʳ] N (BRIT) grande supermercato

supertanker [ˈsuːpətæŋkəʳ] N superpetroliera

supertax [ˈsuːpətæks] N soprattassa

supervise [ˈsuːpəvaɪz] VT (person etc) sorvegliare; (organization) soprintendere a

supervision [suːpəˈvɪʒən] N sorveglianza; supervisione f; **under medical ~** sotto controllo medico

supervisor [ˈsuːpəvaɪzəʳ] N sorvegliante mf; soprintendente mf; (in shop) capocommesso(-a); (at university) relatore(-trice)

supervisory [suːpəvaɪzərɪ] ADJ di sorveglianza

supine [ˈsuːpaɪn] ADJ supino(-a)

supper [ˈsʌpəʳ] N cena; **to have ~** cenare

supplant [səˈplɑːnt] VT soppiantare

supple [ˈsʌpl] ADJ flessibile; agile

supplement N [ˈsʌplɪmənt] supplemento ▶ VT [sʌplɪˈmɛnt] completare, integrare

supplementary [sʌplɪˈmɛntərɪ] ADJ supplementare

supplementary benefit N (BRIT) forma di indennità assistenziale

supplier [səˈplaɪəʳ] N fornitore m

supply [səˈplaɪ] VT (a need) soddisfare; **to ~ sth (to sb)** (goods) fornire qc (a qn); **to ~ sb (with sth)** (people, organization) fornire a qn (qc); **to ~ sth (with sth)** (system, machine) alimentare qc (con qc) ▶ N riserva, provvista; (supplying) approvvigionamento; (Tech) alimentazione f; **supplies** NPL (food) viveri mpl; (Mil) sussistenza; **office supplies** forniture fpl per ufficio; **to be in short ~** scarseggiare, essere scarso(-a); **the electricity/water/gas ~** l'erogazione f di corrente/d'acqua/di gas; **~ and demand** la domanda e l'offerta; **the car comes supplied with a radio** l'auto viene fornita completa di radio

supply teacher N (BRIT) supplente mf

support [səˈpɔːt] N (moral, financial etc) sostegno, appoggio; (Tech) supporto ▶ VT sostenere; (financially) mantenere; (uphold) sostenere, difendere; (Sport: team) fare il tifo per; **they stopped work in ~ (of)** hanno smesso di lavorare per solidarietà (con); **to ~ o.s.** (financially) mantenersi

supporter [səˈpɔːtəʳ] N (Pol etc) sostenitore(-trice), fautore(-trice); (Sport) tifoso(-a)

supporting [səˈpɔːtɪŋ] ADJ (wall) di sostegno

supporting actor N attore m non protagonista

supporting actress N attrice f non protagonista

supporting role N ruolo non protagonista

supportive [səˈpɔːtɪv] ADJ d'appoggio; **I have a ~ wife/family** mia moglie/la mia famiglia mi appoggia

suppose [səˈpəuz] VT, VI supporre; immaginare; **to be supposed to do** essere tenuto(-a) a fare; **always supposing (that) he comes** ammesso e non concesso che venga; **I don't ~ she'll come** non credo che venga; **he's supposed to be an expert** dicono che sia un esperto, passa per un esperto

supposedly [səˈpəuzɪdlɪ] ADV presumibilmente; (seemingly) apparentemente

supposing [səˈpəuzɪŋ] CONJ se, ammesso che + sub

supposition [sʌpəˈzɪʃən] N supposizione f, ipotesi f inv

suppository [səˈpɒzɪtərɪ] N supposta, suppositorio

suppress [səˈprɛs] VT reprimere; sopprimere; tenere segreto(-a); occultare

suppression [səˈprɛʃən] N repressione f; soppressione f

suppressor [səˈprɛsəʳ] N (Elec etc) soppressore m

supremacy [suˈprɛməsɪ] N supremazia

supreme [suˈpriːm] ADJ supremo(-a)

Supreme Court N (US) Corte f suprema; **~ of Judicature** corte di giudizio suprema dell'Inghilterra e del Galles

supremo [suˈpriːməu] N autorità f inv massima

Supt. ABBR (Police) = **superintendent**

surcharge [ˈsəːtʃɑːdʒ] N supplemento; (extra tax) soprattassa

sure [ʃuəʳ] ADJ sicuro(-a); (definite, convinced) sicuro(-a), certo(-a) ▶ ADV (col: US): **that ~ is pretty, that's ~ pretty** è veramente or davvero carino; **~!** (of course) senz'altro!, certo!; **~ enough** infatti; **to make ~ of** assicurarsi di; **to be ~ of sth** essere sicuro di qc; **to be ~ of o.s.** essere sicuro di sé; **I'm not ~ how/why/when** non so bene come/perché/quando + sub

sure-fire [ˈʃuəfaɪəʳ] ADJ (col) infallibile

sure-footed [ʃuəˈfutɪd] ADJ dal passo sicuro
surely [ˈʃuəlɪ] ADV sicuramente; certamente; ~ **you don't mean that!** non parlerà sul serio!
surety [ˈʃuərətɪ] N garanzia; **to go** or **stand ~ for sb** farsi garante per qn
surf [sə:f] N (waves) cavalloni mpl; (foam) spuma ▶ VT: **to ~ the Net** navigare in Internet
surface [ˈsə:fɪs] N superficie f ▶ VT (road) asfaltare ▶ VI risalire alla superficie; (fig: person, news, feeling) venire a galla, farsi vivo(-a); **on the ~ it seems that ...** (fig) superficialmente sembra che ...
surface area N superficie f
surface mail N posta ordinaria
surface-to-surface [ˈsə:fɪstəˈsə:fɪs] ADJ (Mil) terra-terra inv
surfboard [ˈsə:fbɔ:d] N tavola per surfing
surfeit [ˈsə:fɪt] N: **a ~ of** un eccesso di; un'indigestione di
surfer [ˈsə:fəʳ] N (in sea) surfista mf; (on the Internet) navigatore(-trice)
surfing [ˈsə:fɪŋ] N surfing m
surge [sə:dʒ] N (strong movement) ondata; (of feeling) impeto; (Elec) sovracorrente f transitoria ▶ VI (waves) gonfiarsi; (people) riversarsi; (Elec: power) aumentare improvvisamente; **to ~ forward** buttarsi avanti
surgeon [ˈsə:dʒən] N chirurgo
Surgeon General N (US) ≈ Ministro della Sanità
surgery [ˈsə:dʒərɪ] N chirurgia; (BRIT Med: room) studio or gabinetto medico, ambulatorio; (: session) visita ambulatoriale; (BRIT: of MP etc) incontri mpl con gli elettori; (also: **surgery hours**) orario delle visite or di consultazione; **to undergo ~** subire un intervento chirurgico
surgery hours NPL (BRIT) orario delle visite or di consultazione
surgical [ˈsə:dʒɪkl] ADJ chirurgico(-a)
surgical spirit N (BRIT) alcool denaturato
surly [ˈsə:lɪ] ADJ scontroso(-a), burbero(-a)
surmise [sə:ˈmaɪz] VT supporre, congetturare
surmount [sə:ˈmaunt] VT sormontare
surname [ˈsə:neɪm] N cognome m
surpass [sə:ˈpɑ:s] VT superare
surplus [ˈsə:pləs] N eccedenza; (Econ) surplus m inv ▶ ADJ eccedente, d'avanzo; **it is ~ to our requirements** eccede i nostri bisogni; ~ **stock** merce f in sovrappiù
surprise [sə:ˈpraɪz] N sorpresa; (astonishment) stupore m ▶ VT sorprendere; stupire; **to take by ~** (person) cogliere di sorpresa; (Mil: town, fort) attaccare di sorpresa
surprised [sə:ˈpraɪzd] ADJ (look, smile) sorpreso(-a); **to be ~** essere sorpreso, sorprendersi

surprising [sə:ˈpraɪzɪŋ] ADJ sorprendente, stupefacente
surprisingly [sə:ˈpraɪzɪŋlɪ] ADV (easy, helpful) sorprendentemente; (**somewhat**) ~, **he agreed** cosa (alquanto) sorprendente, ha accettato
surrealism [səˈrɪəlɪzəm] N surrealismo
surrealist [səˈrɪəlɪst] ADJ, N surrealista mf
surrender [səˈrɛndəʳ] N resa, capitolazione f ▶ VI arrendersi ▶ VT (claim, right) rinunciare a
surrender value N (Comm) valore m di riscatto
surreptitious [sʌrəpˈtɪʃəs] ADJ furtivo(-a)
surrogate [ˈsʌrəgɪt] N (BRIT: substitute) surrogato ▶ ADJ surrogato(-a)
surrogate mother N madre f sostitutiva
surround [səˈraund] VT circondare; (Mil etc) accerchiare
surrounding [səˈraundɪŋ] ADJ circostante
surroundings [səˈraundɪŋz] NPL dintorni mpl; (fig) ambiente m
surtax [ˈsə:tæks] N soprattassa
surveillance [sə:ˈveɪləns] N sorveglianza, controllo
survey N [ˈsə:veɪ] (comprehensive view: of situation, development) quadro generale; (study) indagine f, studio; (in housebuying etc) perizia; (of land) rilevamento, rilievo topografico ▶ VT [sə:ˈveɪ] osservare; esaminare; (Surveying: building) fare una perizia di; (: land) fare il rilevamento di
surveying [səˈveɪɪŋ] N (of land) agrimensura
surveyor [səˈveɪəʳ] N perito; geometra m; (of land) agrimensore m
survival [səˈvaɪvl] N sopravvivenza; (relic) reliquia, vestigio
survival course N corso di sopravvivenza
survival kit N equipaggiamento di prima necessità
survive [səˈvaɪv] VI sopravvivere ▶ VT sopravvivere a
survivor [səˈvaɪvəʳ] N superstite mf, sopravvissuto(-a)
susceptible [səˈsɛptəbl] ADJ: ~ (**to**) sensibile (a); (disease) predisposto(-a) (a)
suspect ADJ [ˈsʌspɛkt] sospetto(-a) ▶ N [ˈsʌspɛkt] persona sospetta ▶ VT [səsˈpɛkt] sospettare; (think likely) supporre; (doubt) dubitare di
suspected [səsˈpɛktɪd] ADJ presunto(-a); **to have a ~ facture** avere una sospetta frattura
suspend [səsˈpɛnd] VT sospendere
suspended animation N: **in a state of ~** in stato comatoso
suspended sentence N condanna con la condizionale
suspender belt [səsˈpɛndəʳ-] N (BRIT) reggicalze m inv
suspenders [səsˈpɛndəz] NPL (BRIT) giarrettiere fpl; (US) bretelle fpl

S

suspense [səs'pɛns] N apprensione f; (in film etc) suspense m; **to keep sb in ~** tenere qn in sospeso

suspension [səs'pɛnʃən] N (gen, Aut) sospensione f; (of driving licence) ritiro temporaneo

suspension bridge N ponte m sospeso

suspicion [səs'pɪʃən] N sospetto; **to be under ~** essere sospettato; **arrested on ~ of murder** arrestato come presunto omicida

suspicious [səs'pɪʃəs] ADJ (suspecting) sospettoso(-a); (causing suspicion) sospetto(-a); **to be ~ of** or **about sb/sth** nutrire sospetti nei riguardi di qn/qc

suss out VT (BRIT col): **I've sussed it/him out** ho capito come stanno le cose/che tipo è

sustain [səs'teɪn] VT sostenere; sopportare; (Law: charge) confermare; (suffer) subire

sustainable [səs'teɪnəbl] ADJ sostenibile

sustained [sə'steɪnd] ADJ (effort) prolungato(-a)

sustenance ['sʌstɪnəns] N nutrimento; mezzi mpl di sostentamento

suture ['suːtʃər] N sutura

SUV N ABBR (= sports utility vehicle) SUV m inv

SW ABBR (Radio: = short wave) O.C.

swab [swɔb] N (Med) tampone m ▶ VT (Naut: also: **swab down**) radazzare

swagger ['swægər] VI pavoneggiarsi

swallow ['swɔləu] N (bird) rondine f; (of food) boccone m; (of drink) sorso ▶ VT inghiottire; (fig: story) bere
▶ **swallow up** VT inghiottire

swam [swæm] PT of **swim**

swamp [swɔmp] N palude f ▶ VT sommergere

swampy ['swɔmpɪ] ADJ palludoso(-a), pantanoso(-a)

swan [swɔn] N cigno

swank [swæŋk] VI (col: talk boastfully) fare lo spaccone; (: show off) mettersi in mostra

swan song N (fig) canto del cigno

swap [swɔp] N scambio ▶ VT: **to ~ (for)** scambiare (con)

SWAPO ['swɑːpəu] N ABBR = **South-West Africa People's Organization**

swarm [swɔːm] N sciame m ▶ VI formicolare; (bees) sciamare; (people) brulicare; (place): **to be swarming with** brulicare di

swarthy ['swɔːðɪ] ADJ di carnagione scura

swashbuckling ['swɔʃbʌklɪŋ] ADJ (role, hero) spericolato(-a)

swastika ['swɔstɪkə] N croce f uncinata, svastica

SWAT [swɔt] N ABBR (US: = Special Weapons and Tactics) reparto speciale di polizia; (= a SWAT team) uno squadrone del reparto speciale (di polizia)

swat [swɔt] VT schiacciare ▶ N (BRIT: also: **fly swat**) ammazzamosche m inv

swathe [sweɪð] N fascio ▶ VT: **to ~ in** (bandages, blankets) avvolgere in

swatter ['swɔtər] N (also: **fly swatter**) ammazzamosche m inv

sway [sweɪ] VI (building) oscillare; (tree) ondeggiare; (person) barcollare ▶ VT (influence) influenzare, dominare ▶ N (rule, power): **~ (over)** influenza (su); **to hold ~ over sb** dominare qn

Swaziland ['swɑːzɪlænd] N Swaziland m

swear [sweər] (pt **swore**, pp **sworn**) VI (witness etc) giurare; (curse) bestemmiare, imprecare ▶ VT: **to ~ an oath** prestare giuramento; **to ~ to sth** giurare qc
▶ **swear in** VT prestare giuramento a

swearword ['sweəwəːd] N parolaccia

sweat [swɛt] N sudore m, traspirazione f ▶ VI sudare; **in a ~** in un bagno di sudore

sweatband ['swɛtbænd] N (Sport) fascia elastica (per assorbire il sudore)

sweater ['swɛtər] N maglione m

sweatshirt ['swɛtʃəːt] N felpa f

sweatshop ['swɛtʃɔp] N azienda o fabbrica dove i dipendenti sono sfruttati

sweaty ['swɛtɪ] ADJ sudato(-a); bagnato(-a) di sudore

Swede [swiːd] N svedese mf

swede [swiːd] N (BRIT) rapa svedese

Sweden ['swiːdn] N Svezia

Swedish ['swiːdɪʃ] ADJ svedese ▶ N (Ling) svedese m

sweep [swiːp] (pt, pp **swept**) N spazzata; (curve) curva; (expanse) distesa; (range) portata; (also: **chimney sweep**) spazzacamino ▶ VT spazzare, scopare; (fashion, craze) invadere; (current) spazzare ▶ VI camminare maestosamente; precipitarsi, lanciarsi; (e)stendersi; (hand) muoversi con gesto ampio; (wind) infuriare
▶ **sweep away** VT spazzare via; trascinare via
▶ **sweep past** VI sfrecciare accanto; passare accanto maestosamente
▶ **sweep up** VT, VI spazzare

sweeper ['swiːpər] N (person) spazzino(-a); (machine) spazzatrice f; (Football) libero

sweeping ['swiːpɪŋ] ADJ (gesture) ampio(-a); (changes, reforms) ampio(-a), radicale; **a ~ statement** un'affermazione generica

sweepstake ['swiːpsteɪk] N lotteria (spesso abbinata alle corse dei cavalli)

sweet [swiːt] N (BRIT: pudding) dolce m; (candy) caramella ▶ ADJ dolce; (fresh) fresco(-a); (fig) piacevole; delicato(-a), grazioso(-a); (kind) gentile; (cute) carino(-a) ▶ ADV: **to smell/ taste ~** avere un odore/sapore dolce; **~ and sour** adj agrodolce

sweetbread ['swiːtbrɛd] N animella

sweetcorn ['swiːtkɔːn] N granturco dolce

sweeten ['swiːtn] VT addolcire; zuccherare

sweetener ['swiːtnər] N (Culin) dolcificante m

sweetheart ['swiːthɑːt] N innamorato(-a)

sweetly ['swiːtlɪ] ADV dolcemente

sweetness ['swiːtnɪs] N sapore m dolce; dolcezza

sweet pea N pisello odoroso

sweet potato N patata americana, patata dolce

sweetshop ['swiːtʃɔp] N (BRIT) ≈ pasticceria

sweet tooth N: **to have a ~** avere un debole per i dolci

swell [swɛl] (pt **swelled**, pp **swollen** ['swəulən] or **swelled**) N (of sea) mare m lungo ▶ ADJ (US col: excellent) favoloso(-a) ▶ VT gonfiare, ingrossare; (numbers, sales etc) aumentare ▶ VI gonfiarsi, ingrossarsi; (sound) crescere; (Med: also: **swell up**) gonfiarsi

swelling ['swɛlɪŋ] N (Med) tumefazione f, gonfiore m

sweltering ['swɛltərɪŋ] ADJ soffocante

swept [swɛpt] PT, PP of **sweep**

swerve [swəːv] VI deviare; (driver) sterzare; (boxer) scartare

swift [swɪft] N (bird) rondone m ▶ ADJ rapido(-a), veloce

swiftly ['swɪftlɪ] ADV rapidamente, velocemente

swiftness ['swɪftnɪs] N rapidità, velocità

swig [swɪg] N (col: drink) sorsata

swill [swɪl] N broda ▶ VT (also: **swill out, swill down**) risciacquare

swim [swɪm] (pt **swam** [swæm], pp **swum** [swʌm]) N: **to go for a ~** andare a fare una nuotata ▶ VI nuotare; (Sport) fare del nuoto; (head, room) girare ▶ VT (river, channel) attraversare or percorrere a nuoto; (length) nuotare; **to go swimming** andare a nuotare; **to ~ a length** fare una vasca (a nuoto)

swimmer ['swɪmər] N nuotatore(-trice)

swimming ['swɪmɪŋ] N nuoto

swimming baths NPL (BRIT) piscina

swimming cap N cuffia

swimming costume N (BRIT) costume m da bagno

swimmingly ['swɪmɪŋlɪ] ADV: **to go ~** (wonderfully) andare a gonfie vele

swimming pool N piscina

swimming trunks NPL costume m da bagno (da uomo)

swimsuit ['swɪmsuːt] N costume m da bagno

swindle ['swɪndl] N truffa ▶ VT truffare

swindler ['swɪndlər] N truffatore(-trice)

swine [swaɪn] N (pl inv) maiale m, porco; (col!) porco (!)

swine flu N influenza suina

swing [swɪŋ] (pt, pp **swung** [swʌŋ]) N altalena; (movement) oscillazione f; (Mus) ritmo; (also: **swing music**) swing m ▶ VT dondolare, far oscillare; (also: **swing round**) far girare ▶ VI oscillare, dondolare; (also: **swing round**: object) roteare; (: person) girarsi, voltarsi; (: activity) essere in piena attività; (party etc) essere nel pieno; **a ~ to the left** (Pol) una svolta a sinistra; **to get into the ~ of things** entrare nel pieno delle cose; **the road swings south** la strada prende la direzione sud

swing bridge N ponte m girevole

swing door N (BRIT) porta battente

swingeing ['swɪndʒɪŋ] ADJ (BRIT: defeat) violento(-a); (: price increase) enorme

swinging ['swɪŋɪŋ] ADJ (step) cadenzato(-a), ritmico(-a); (rhythm, music) trascinante; **~ door** (US) porta battente

swipe [swaɪp] N forte colpo; schiaffo ▶ VT (hit) colpire con forza; dare uno schiaffo a; (col: steal) sgraffignare; (credit card etc) far passare (nell'apposita macchinetta)

swipe card N tessera magnetica

swirl [swəːl] N turbine m, mulinello ▶ VI turbinare, far mulinello

swish [swɪʃ] ADJ (col: smart) all'ultimo grido, alla moda ▶ N (sound, of whip) sibilo; (: of skirts, grass) fruscio ▶ VI sibilare

Swiss [swɪs] ADJ, N (pl inv) svizzero(-a)

Swiss French ADJ svizzero(-a) francese

Swiss German ADJ svizzero(-a) tedesco(-a)

switch [swɪtʃ] N (for light, radio etc) interruttore m; (change) cambiamento ▶ VT (also: **switch round, switch over**) cambiare; scambiare
▶ **switch off** VT spegnere
▶ **switch on** VT accendere; (engine, machine) mettere in moto, avviare; (Aut: ignition) inserire; (BRIT: water supply) aprire

switchback ['swɪtʃbæk] N (BRIT) montagne fpl russe

switchblade ['swɪtʃbleɪd] N (also: **switchblade knife**) coltello a scatto

switchboard ['swɪtʃbɔːd] N (Tel) centralino

switchboard operator N centralinista mf

Switzerland ['swɪtsələnd] N Svizzera

swivel ['swɪvl] VI (also: **swivel round**) girare

swollen ['swəulən] PP of **swell** ▶ ADJ (ankle etc) gonfio(-a)

swoon [swuːn] VI svenire

swoop [swuːp] N (by police etc) incursione f; (of bird etc) picchiata ▶ VI (also: **swoop down**) scendere in picchiata, piombare; (police) **to ~ (on)** fare un'incursione (in)

swop [swɔp] N, VT = **swap**

sword [sɔːd] N spada

swordfish ['sɔːdfɪʃ] N pesce m spada inv

swore [swɔːr] PT of **swear**

sworn [swɔːn] PP of **swear** ▶ ADJ giurato(-a)

swot [swɔt] VT sgobbare su ▶ VI sgobbare

swum [swʌm] PP of **swim**

S

swung [swʌŋ] PT, PP of **swing**
sycamore ['sɪkəmɔːʳ] N sicomoro
sycophant ['sɪkəfənt] N leccapiedi *mf*
sycophantic [sɪkə'fæntɪk] ADJ
ossequioso(-a), adulatore(-trice)
Sydney ['sɪdnɪ] N Sydney *f*
syllable ['sɪləbl] N sillaba
syllabus ['sɪləbəs] N programma *m*; **on the ~**
in programma d'esame
symbol ['sɪmbl] N simbolo
ADJ simbolico(-a); **to be ~ of sth**
simboleggiare qc
symbolism ['sɪmbəlɪzəm] N simbolismo
symbolize ['sɪmbəlaɪz] VT simbolizzare
symmetrical [sɪ'mɛtrɪkl] ADJ simmetrico(-a)
symmetry ['sɪmɪtrɪ] N simmetria
sympathetic [sɪmpə'θɛtɪk] ADJ (*showing pity*)
compassionevole; (*kind*) comprensivo(-a);
~ towards ben disposto(-a) verso; **to be ~ to
a cause** (*well-disposed*) simpatizzare per una
causa
sympathetically [sɪmpə'θɛtɪklɪ] ADV in
modo compassionevole; con comprensione
sympathize ['sɪmpəθaɪz] VI: **to ~ with sb**
compatire qn; partecipare al dolore di qn;
(*understand*) capire qn; **to ~ with a cause**
simpatizzare per una causa
sympathizer ['sɪmpəθaɪzəʳ] N (*Pol*)
simpatizzante *mf*
sympathy ['sɪmpəθɪ] N compassione *f*; **in ~
with** d'accordo con; (*strike*) per solidarietà
con; **with our deepest ~** con le nostre più
sincere condoglianze
symphonic [sɪm'fɒnɪk] ADJ sinfonico(-a)
symphony ['sɪmfənɪ] N sinfonia
symphony orchestra N orchestra sinfonica
symposium [sɪm'pəuzɪəm] N simposio
symptom ['sɪmptəm] N sintomo; indizio
symptomatic [sɪmptə'mætɪk] ADJ: **~ (of)**
sintomatico(-a) (di)
synagogue ['sɪnəgɔg] N sinagoga

sync [sɪŋk] N (*col*): **in/out of ~** in/fuori
sincronia; (*fig: people*): **they are in ~** sono in
sintonia
synchromesh [sɪŋkrəu'mɛʃ] N cambio
sincronizzato
synchronize ['sɪŋkrənaɪz] VT sincronizzare
▶ VI: **to ~ with** essere contemporaneo(-a) a
synchronized swimming N nuoto
sincronizzato
syncopated ['sɪŋkəpeɪtɪd] ADJ sincopato(-a)
syndicate ['sɪndɪkɪt] N sindacato; (*Press*)
agenzia di stampa
syndrome ['sɪndrəum] N sindrome *f*
synonym ['sɪnənɪm] N sinonimo
synonymous [sɪ'nɒnɪməs] ADJ: **~ (with)**
sinonimo(-a) (di)
synopsis [sɪ'nɒpsɪs] (*pl* **synopses** [-siːz]) N
sommario, sinossi *f inv*
syntax ['sɪntæks] N sintassi *f inv*
synthesis ['sɪnθəsɪs] (*pl* **syntheses** [-siːz]) N
sintesi *f inv*
synthesizer ['sɪnθəsaɪzəʳ] N (*Mus*)
sintetizzatore *m*
synthetic [sɪn'θɛtɪk] ADJ sintetico(-a) ▶ N
prodotto sintetico; (*Textiles*) fibra sintetica
syphilis ['sɪfɪlɪs] N sifilide *f*
syphon ['saɪfən] = **siphon**
Syria ['sɪrɪə] N Siria
Syrian ['sɪrɪən] ADJ, N siriano(-a)
syringe [sɪ'rɪndʒ] N siringa
syrup ['sɪrəp] N sciroppo; (*also:* **golden syrup**)
melassa raffinata
syrupy ['sɪrəpɪ] ADJ sciropposo(-a)
system ['sɪstəm] N sistema *m*; (*network*) rete *f*;
(*order*) metodo; (*Anat*) apparato; **it was a
shock to his ~** è stato uno shock per il suo
organismo
systematic [sɪstə'mætɪk] ADJ
sistematico(-a); metodico(-a)
system disk N (*Comput*) disco del sistema
systems analyst N analista *mf* di sistemi

Tt

T, t [tiː] N *(letter)* T, t *m inv or f inv*; **T for Tommy** ≈ T come Taranto

TA N ABBR *(BRIT)* = **Territorial Army**

ta [tɑː] EXCL *(BRIT col)* grazie!

tab [tæb] N ABBR = **tabulator** ▶ N *(loop: on coat etc)* laccetto; *(label)* etichetta; **to keep tabs on** *(fig)* tenere d'occhio

tabby ['tæbɪ] N *(also: **tabby cat**)* (gatto) soriano, gatto tigrato

tabernacle ['tæbənækl] N tabernacolo

table ['teɪbl] N tavolo, tavola; *(Math, Chem etc)* tavola; *(chart)* tabella ▶ VT *(BRIT: motion etc)* presentare; **to lay** *or* **set the ~** apparecchiare *or* preparare la tavola; **to clear the ~** sparecchiare; **league ~** *(Football, Rugby)* classifica; **~ of contents** indice *m*

tablecloth ['teɪblklɔθ] N tovaglia

table d'hôte [tɑːblˈdəut] ADJ *(meal)* a prezzo fisso

table lamp N lampada da tavolo

tablemat ['teɪblmæt] N sottopiatto

table salt N sale *m* fino *or* da tavola

tablespoon ['teɪblspuːn] N cucchiaio da tavola; *(also: **tablespoonful**: as measurement)* cucchiaiata

tablet ['tæblɪt] N *(Med)* compressa; *(: for sucking)* pastiglia; *(for writing)* blocco; *(of stone)* targa; **~ of soap** *(BRIT)* saponetta

table tennis N tennis *m* da tavolo, ping-pong® *m*

table wine N vino da tavola

tabloid ['tæblɔɪd] N *(newspaper)* tabloid *m inv* *(giornale illustrato di formato ridotto)*; **the tabloids, the ~ press** i giornali popolari; *vedi nota*

> Il termine *tabloid press* si riferisce ai quotidiani o ai settimanali popolari che, rispetto ai *quality papers* hanno un formato ridotto e presentano le notizie in modo più sensazionalistico e meno approfondito; *vedi anche* **quality press**.

taboo [təˈbuː] ADJ, N tabù *m inv*

tabulate ['tæbjuleɪt] VT *(data, figures)* tabulare, disporre in tabelle

tabulator ['tæbjuleɪtər] N tabulatore *m*

tachograph ['tækəgrɑːf] N tachigrafo

tachometer [tæˈkɔmɪtər] N tachimetro

tacit ['tæsɪt] ADJ tacito(-a)

taciturn ['tæsɪtəːn] ADJ taciturno(-a)

tack [tæk] N *(nail)* bulletta; *(stitch)* punto d'imbastitura; *(Naut)* bordo, bordata; *(fig)* approccio ▶ VT imbullettare; imbastire ▶ VI bordeggiare; **to change ~** virare di bordo; **on the wrong ~** *(fig)* sulla strada sbagliata; **to ~ sth on to (the end of) sth** *(of letter, book)* aggiungere qc alla fine di qc

tackle ['tækl] N *(equipment)* attrezzatura, equipaggiamento; *(for lifting)* paranco; *(Rugby)* placcaggio; *(Football)* contrasto ▶ VT *(difficulty)* affrontare; *(Rugby)* placcare; *(Football)* contrastare

tacky ['tækɪ] ADJ colloso(-a), appiccicaticcio(-a); ancora bagnato(-a); *(pej: shabby)* scadente

tact [tækt] N tatto

tactful ['tæktful] ADJ delicato(-a), discreto(-a); **to be ~** avere tatto

tactfully ['tæktfəlɪ] ADV con tatto

tactical ['tæktɪkl] ADJ tattico(-a)

tactical voting N voto tattico

tactician [tækˈtɪʃən] N tattico(-a)

tactics ['tæktɪks] N, NPL tattica

tactless ['tæktlɪs] ADJ che manca di tatto

tactlessly ['tæktlɪslɪ] ADV senza tatto

tadpole ['tædpəul] N girino

taffy ['tæfɪ] N *(US)* caramella *f* mou *inv*

tag [tæg] N etichetta; **price/name ~** etichetta del prezzo/con il nome
▶ **tag along** VI seguire

Tahiti [təˈhiːti] N Tahiti *f*

tail [teɪl] N coda; *(of shirt)* falda ▶ VT *(follow)* seguire, pedinare; **to turn ~** voltare la schiena; **tails** NPL *(formal suit)* frac *m inv*; *see also* **head**
▶ **tail away, tail off** VI *(in size, quality etc)* diminuire gradatamente

tailback ['teɪlbæk] N *(BRIT)* ingorgo

tail coat N marsina

t

tail end N (*of train, procession etc*) coda; (*of meeting etc*) fine f

tailgate ['teɪlgeɪt] N (*Aut*) portellone m posteriore

tail light N (*Aut*) fanalino di coda

tailor ['teɪlə^r] N sarto ▶ VT: **to ~ sth (to)** adattare qc (alle esigenze di); **~'s (shop)** sartoria (da uomo)

tailoring ['teɪlərɪŋ] N (*cut*) taglio

tailor-made ['teɪlə'meɪd] ADJ (*also fig*) fatto(-a) su misura

tailwind ['teɪlwɪnd] N vento di coda

taint [teɪnt] VT (*meat, food*) far avariare; (*fig: reputation*) infangare

tainted ['teɪntɪd] ADJ (*food*) guasto(-a); (*water, air*) infetto(-a); (*fig*) corrotto(-a)

Taiwan [taɪ'wɑ:n] N Taiwan m

Taiwanese [taɪwə'ni:z] ADJ, N taiwanese

Tajikistan [tɑ:dʒɪkɪ'stɑ:n] N Tagikistan m

take [teɪk] (*pt* **took**, *pp* **taken**) VT prendere; (*gain: prize*) ottenere, vincere; (*require: effort, courage*) occorrere, volerci; (*tolerate*) accettare, sopportare; (*hold: passengers etc*) contenere; (*accompany*) accompagnare; (*bring, carry*) portare; (*conduct: meeting*) condurre; (*exam*) sostenere, presentarsi a; **to ~ a photo/a shower** fare una fotografia/una doccia ▶ VI (*dye, fire etc*) prendere; (*injection*) fare effetto; (*plant*) attecchire ▶ N (*Cine*) ripresa; **I ~ it that** suppongo che; **to ~ for a walk** (*child, dog*) portare a fare una passeggiata; **to ~ sb's hand** prendere qn per mano; **to ~ it upon o.s. to do sth** prendersi la responsabilità di fare qc; **to be taken ill** avere un malore; **to be taken with sb/sth** (*attracted*) essere tutto preso da qn/qc; **it won't ~ long** non ci vorrà molto tempo; **it takes a lot of time/ courage** occorre *or* ci vuole molto tempo/ coraggio; **it will ~ at least 5 litres** contiene almeno 5 litri; **~ the first on the left** prenda la prima a sinistra; **to ~ Russian at university** fare russo all'università; **I took him for a doctor** l'ho preso per un dottore

▶ **take after** VT FUS assomigliare a

▶ **take apart** VT smontare

▶ **take away** VT portare via; togliere; **to ~ away (from)** sottrarre (da)

▶ **take back** VT (*return*) restituire; riportare; (*one's words*) ritirare

▶ **take down** VT (*building*) demolire; (*dismantle: scaffolding*) smontare; (: *letter etc*) scrivere

▶ **take in** VT (*lodger*) prendere, ospitare; (*orphan*) accogliere; (*stray dog*) raccogliere; (*Sewing*) stringere; (*deceive*) imbrogliare, abbindolare; (*understand*) capire; (*include*) comprendere, includere

▶ **take off** VI (*Aviat*) decollare; (*go away*) andarsene ▶ VT (*remove*) togliere; (*imitate*) imitare

▶ **take on** VT (*work*) accettare, intraprendere; (*employee*) assumere; (*opponent*) sfidare, affrontare

▶ **take out** VT portare fuori; (*remove*) togliere; (*licence*) prendere, ottenere; **to ~ sth out of** (*drawer, pocket etc*) tirare qc fuori da; estrarre qc da; **don't ~ it out on me!** non prendertela con me!

▶ **take over** VT (*business*) rilevare ▶ VI: **to ~ over from sb** prendere le consegne *or* il controllo da qn

▶ **take to** VT FUS (*person*) prendere in simpatia; (*activity*) prendere gusto a; (*form habit of*): **to ~ to doing sth** prendere *or* cominciare a fare qc

▶ **take up** VT (*one's story*) riprendere; (*dress*) accorciare; (*absorb: liquids*) assorbire; (*accept: offer, challenge*) accettare; (*occupy: time, space*) occupare; (*engage in: hobby etc*) mettersi a; **to ~ up with sb** fare amicizia con qn; **to ~ sb up on sth** accettare qc da qn

takeaway ['teɪkəweɪ] (*BRIT*) ADJ (*food*) da portar via ▶ N (*shop etc*) ≈ rosticceria; (*food*) pasto per asporto

take-home pay ['teɪkhəum-] N stipendio netto

taken ['teɪkn] PP *of* **take**

takeoff ['teɪkɔf] N (*Aviat*) decollo

takeout ['teɪkaut] ADJ, N (*US*) = **takeaway**

takeover ['teɪkəuvə^r] N (*Comm*) assorbimento

takeover bid N offerta di assorbimento

takings ['teɪkɪŋz] NPL (*Comm*) incasso

talc [tælk] N (*also:* **talcum powder**) talco

tale [teɪl] N racconto, storia; (*pej*) fandonia; **to tell tales** (*fig: to teacher, parent etc*) fare la spia

talent ['tælənt] N talento

talented ['tæləntɪd] ADJ di talento

talent scout N talent scout mf

talisman ['tælɪzmən] N talismano

talk [tɔ:k] N discorso; (*gossip*) chiacchiere fpl; (*conversation*) conversazione f; (*interview*) discussione f ▶ VI parlare; (*chatter*) chiacchierare; **talks** NPL (*Pol etc*) colloqui mpl; **to give a ~** tenere una conferenza; **to ~ about** parlare di; (*converse*) discorrere *or* conversare su; **to ~ sb out of/into doing** dissuadere qn da/convincere qn a fare; **to ~ shop** parlare di lavoro *or* di affari; **talking of films, have you seen …?** a proposito di film, ha visto …?

▶ **talk over** VT discutere

talkative ['tɔ:kətɪv] ADJ loquace, ciarliero(-a)

talking point ['tɔ:kɪŋ-] N argomento di conversazione

talking-to ['tɔ:kɪŋtu:] N: **to give sb a good ~** fare una bella paternale a qn

talk show N (TV, Radio) talk show m inv
tall [tɔːl] ADJ alto(-a); **to be 6 feet ~** ≈ essere alto 1 metro e 80; **how ~ are you?** quanto è alto?
tallboy ['tɔːlbɔɪ] N (BRIT) cassettone m alto
tallness ['tɔːlnɪs] N altezza
tall story N panzana, frottola
tally ['tælɪ] N conto, conteggio ▶ VI: **to ~ (with)** corrispondere (a); **to keep a ~ of sth** tener il conto di qc
talon ['tælən] N artiglio
tambourine [tæmbə'riːn] N tamburello
tame [teɪm] ADJ addomesticato(-a); (fig: story, style) insipido(-a), scialbo(-a)
Tamil ['tæmɪl] ADJ tamil inv ▶ N tamil mf; (Ling) tamil m
tamper ['tæmpər] VI: **to ~ with** manomettere
tampon ['tæmpɔn] N tampone m
tan [tæn] N (also: **suntan**) abbronzatura ▶ VT abbronzare ▶ VI abbronzarsi ▶ ADJ (colour) marrone rossiccio inv; **to get a ~** abbronzarsi
tandem ['tændəm] N tandem m inv
tandoori [tæn'duərɪ] ADJ nella cucina indiana, detto di carni o verdure cucinate allo spiedo in particolari forni
tang [tæŋ] N odore m penetrante; sapore m piccante
tangent ['tændʒənt] N (Math) tangente f; **to go off at a ~** (fig) partire per la tangente
tangerine [tændʒə'riːn] N mandarino
tangible ['tændʒəbl] ADJ tangibile; **~ assets** patrimonio reale
Tangier [tæn'dʒɪər] N Tangeri f
tangle ['tæŋgl] N groviglio ▶ VT aggrovigliare; **to get in(to) a ~** aggrovigliarsi; (fig) combinare un pasticcio
tango ['tæŋgəu] N tango
tank [tæŋk] N serbatoio; (for processing) vasca; (for fish) acquario; (Mil) carro armato
tankard ['tæŋkəd] N boccale m
tanker ['tæŋkər] N (ship) nave f cisterna inv; (for oil) petroliera; (truck) autobotte f, autocisterna
tankini [tæn'kiːnɪ] N tankini m inv
tanned [tænd] ADJ abbronzato(-a)
tannin ['tænɪn] N tannino
tanning ['tænɪŋ] N (of leather) conciatura
tannoy® ['tænɔɪ] N (BRIT) altoparlante m; **over the ~** per altoparlante
tantalizing ['tæntəlaɪzɪŋ] ADJ allettante
tantamount ['tæntəmaunt] ADJ: **~ to** equivalente a
tantrum ['tæntrəm] N accesso di collera; **to throw a ~** fare le bizze
Tanzania [tænzə'nɪə] N Tanzania
Tanzanian [tænzə'nɪən] ADJ, N tanzaniano(-a)
tap [tæp] N (on sink etc) rubinetto; (gentle blow) colpetto ▶ VT dare un colpetto a; (resources) sfruttare, utilizzare; (telephone conversation) intercettare; (telephone) mettere sotto controllo; **on ~** (beer) alla spina; (fig: resources) a disposizione
tap-dancing ['tæpdɑːnsɪŋ] N tip tap m
tape [teɪp] N nastro; (also: **magnetic tape**) nastro (magnetico); (: sticky tape) nastro adesivo ▶ VT (record) registrare (su nastro); (stick) attaccare con nastro adesivo; **on ~** (song etc) su nastro
tape deck N piastra di registrazione
tape measure N metro a nastro
taper ['teɪpər] N candelina ▶ VI assottigliarsi
tape-record ['teɪprɪkɔːd] VT registrare (su nastro)
tape recorder N registratore m (a nastro)
tape recording N registrazione f
tapered ['teɪpəd], **tapering** ['teɪpərɪŋ] ADJ affusolato(-a)
tapestry ['tæpɪstrɪ] N arazzo; tappezzeria
tape-worm ['teɪpwəːm] N tenia, verme m solitario
tapioca [tæpɪ'əukə] N tapioca
tappet ['tæpɪt] N punteria
tar [tɑːr] N catrame m; **low-/middle-~ cigarettes** sigarette a basso/medio contenuto di nicotina
tarantula [tə'ræntjulə] N tarantola
tardy ['tɑːdɪ] ADJ tardo(-a); tardivo(-a)
target ['tɑːgɪt] N bersaglio; (fig: objective) obiettivo; **to be on ~** (project) essere nei tempi (di lavorazione)
target practice N tiro al bersaglio
tariff ['tærɪf] N tariffa
tarmac ['tɑːmæk] N (BRIT: on road) macadam m al catrame; (Aviat) pista di decollo ▶ VT (BRIT) macadamizzare
tarnish ['tɑːnɪʃ] VT offuscare, annerire; (fig) macchiare
tarot ['tærəu] N tarocco
tarpaulin [tɑː'pɔːlɪn] N tela incatramata
tarragon ['tærəgən] N dragoncello
tart [tɑːt] N (Culin) crostata; (BRIT col, pej: woman) sgualdrina ▶ ADJ (flavour) aspro(-a), agro(-a)
▶ **tart up** VT (col): **to ~ o.s. up** farsi bello(-a); (pej) agghindarsi
tartan ['tɑːtn] N tartan m inv
tartar ['tɑːtər] N (on teeth) tartaro
tartar sauce, tartare sauce N salsa tartara
task [tɑːsk] N compito; **to take to ~** rimproverare
task force N (Mil, Police) unità operativa
taskmaster ['tɑːskmɑːstər] N: **he's a hard ~** è un vero tiranno
Tasmania [tæz'meɪnɪə] N Tasmania
tassel ['tæsl] N fiocco
taste [teɪst] N gusto; (flavour) sapore m, gusto; (sample) assaggio; (fig: glimpse, idea) idea ▶ VT

gustare; (*sample*) assaggiare ▶ vi: **to ~ of** *or*
like (*fish etc*) sapere di, avere sapore di; **what
does it ~ like?** che sapore *or* gusto ha?; **it
tastes like fish** sa di pesce; **in good/bad ~** di
buon/cattivo gusto; **you can ~ the garlic (in
it)** (ci) si sente il sapore dell'aglio; **can I
have a ~?** posso assaggiarlo?; **can I have a ~
of this wine?** posso assaggiare un po' di
questo vino?; **to have a ~ of sth** assaggiare
qc; **to have a ~ for sth** avere un'inclinazione
per qc; **to be in bad** *or* **poor ~** essere di
cattivo gusto

taste bud N papilla gustativa
tasteful ['teɪstful] ADJ di buon gusto
tastefully ['teɪstfəlɪ] ADV con gusto
tasteless ['teɪstlɪs] ADJ (*food*) insipido(-a);
(*remark*) di cattivo gusto
tasty ['teɪstɪ] ADJ saporito(-a), gustoso(-a)
tattered ['tætəd] ADJ *see* **tatters**
tatters ['tætəz] NPL: **in ~** (*also:* **tattered**) a
brandelli, sbrindellato(-a)
tattoo [tə'tuː] N tatuaggio; (*spectacle*) parata
militare ▶ vt tatuare
tatty ['tætɪ] ADJ (*Brit col*) malandato(-a)
taught [tɔːt] PT, PP *of* **teach**
taunt [tɔːnt] N scherno ▶ vt schernire
Taurus ['tɔːrəs] N Toro; **to be ~** essere del Toro
taut [tɔːt] ADJ teso(-a)
tavern ['tævən] N taverna
tawdry ['tɔːdrɪ] ADJ pacchiano(-a)
tawny ['tɔːnɪ] ADJ fulvo(-a)
tax [tæks] N (*on goods*) imposta; (*on services*)
tassa; (*on income*) imposte *fpl*, tasse *fpl* ▶ vt
tassare; (*fig: strain: patience etc*) mettere alla
prova; **free of ~** esentasse *inv*, esente da
imposte; **before/after ~** al lordo/netto delle
tasse
taxable ['tæksəbl] ADJ imponibile
tax allowance N detrazione *f* d'imposta
taxation [tæk'seɪʃən] N tassazione *f*; tasse
fpl, imposte *fpl*; **system of ~** sistema *m*
fiscale
tax avoidance N *l'evitare legalmente il
pagamento di imposte*
tax collector ·N esattore *m* delle imposte
tax disc N (*Brit Aut*) ≈ bollo
tax evasion N evasione *f* fiscale
tax exemption N esenzione *f* fiscale
tax exile N *chi ripara all'estero per evadere le
imposte*
tax-free [tæks'friː] ADJ esente da imposte
tax haven N paradiso fiscale
taxi ['tæksɪ] N taxi *m inv* ▶ vi (*Aviat*) rullare
taxidermist ['tæksɪdəːmɪst] N tassidermista
mf
taxi driver N tassista *mf*
tax inspector N (*Brit*) ispettore *m* delle tasse
taxi rank, (*US*) **taxi stand** N posteggio dei
taxi

taxi stand (*US*) N = **taxi rank**
tax payer N contribuente *mf*
tax rebate N rimborso fiscale
tax relief N sgravio fiscale
tax return N dichiarazione *f* dei redditi
tax shelter N paradiso fiscale
tax year N anno fiscale
TB N ABBR (= *tuberculosis*) TBC *f*
tbc ABBR (= *to be confirmed*) da confermarsi
TD N ABBR (*US*) = **Treasury Department**;
(*Football*) = **touchdown**
tea [tiː] N tè *m inv*; (*Brit: snack: for children*)
merenda; **high ~** (*Brit*) cena leggera (*presa nel
tardo pomeriggio*)
tea bag N bustina di tè
tea break N (*Brit*) intervallo per il tè
teacake ['tiːkeɪk] N (*Brit*) panino dolce
all'uva
teach [tiːtʃ] (*pt, pp* **taught** [tɔːt]) vt: **to ~ sb
sth, ~ sth to sb** insegnare qc a qn ▶ vi
insegnare; **it taught him a lesson** (*fig*) gli è
servito da lezione
teacher ['tiːtʃəʳ] N (*gen*) insegnante *mf*; (*in
secondary school*) professore(-essa); (*in primary
school*) maestro(-a); **French ~** insegnante di
francese
teacher training college N (*for primary
schools*) ≈ istituto magistrale; (*for secondary
schools*) scuola universitaria per l'abilitazione
all'insegnamento nelle medie superiori
teaching ['tiːtʃɪŋ] N insegnamento
teaching aids NPL materiali *mpl* per
l'insegnamento
teaching hospital N (*Brit*) clinica
universitaria
teaching staff N (*Brit*) insegnanti *mpl*,
personale *m* insegnante
tea cloth N (*for dishes*) strofinaccio; (*Brit: for
trolley*) tovaglietta da tè
tea cosy N copriteiera *m inv*
teacup ['tiːkʌp] N tazza da tè
teak [tiːk] N teak *m*
tea leaves NPL foglie *fpl* di tè
team [tiːm] N (*of animals*) tiro
▶ **team up** vi: **to ~ up (with)** mettersi
insieme (a)
team games NPL giochi *mpl* di squadra
teamwork ['tiːmwəːk] N lavoro di squadra
tea party N tè *m inv* (*ricevimento*)
teapot ['tiːpɔt] N teiera
tear[1] [tɪəʳ] N lacrima; **in tears** in lacrime;
to burst into tears scoppiare in lacrime
tear[2] [tɛəʳ] (*pt* **tore** [tɔːʳ], *pp* **torn** [tɔːn]) N
strappo ▶ vt strappare ▶ vi strapparsi; **to ~
to pieces** *or* **to bits** *or* **to shreds** (*also fig*) fare
a pezzi *or* a brandelli
▶ **tear along** vi (*rush*) correre all'impazzata
▶ **tear apart** vt (*also fig*) distruggere
▶ **tear away** vt: **to ~ o.s. away (from sth)**

(*fig*) staccarsi (da qc)
▶ **tear down** VT (*building, statue*) demolire;
(*poster, flag*) tirare giù
▶ **tear off** VT (*sheet of paper etc*) strappare;
(*one's clothes*) togliersi di dosso
▶ **tear out** VT (*sheet of paper, cheque*) staccare
▶ **tear up** VT (*sheet of paper etc*) strappare
tearaway ['tɛərəweɪ] N (*col*) monello(-a)
teardrop ['tɪədrɔp] N lacrima
tearful ['tɪəful] ADJ piangente, lacrimoso(-a)
tear gas N gas *m* lacrimogeno
tearoom ['tiːruːm] N sala da tè
tease [tiːz] VT canzonare; (*unkindly*)
tormentare
tea set N servizio da tè
teashop ['tiːʃɔp] N (*BRIT*) sala da tè
Teasmaid® ['tiːzmeɪd] N macchinetta per
fare il tè
teaspoon ['tiːspuːn] N cucchiaino da tè;
(*also*: **teaspoonful**: *as measurement*) cucchiaino
tea strainer N colino da tè
teat [tiːt] N capezzolo; (*of bottle*) tettarella
teatime ['tiːtaɪm] N ora del tè
tea towel N (*BRIT*) strofinaccio (per i piatti)
tea urn N bollitore *m* per il tè
tech [tɛk] N ABBR (*col*) (= *technical college*)
= **technical college**; **technology**
technical ['tɛknɪkl] ADJ tecnico(-a)
technical college N ≈ istituto tecnico
technicality [tɛknɪ'kælɪtɪ] N tecnicità;
(*detail*) dettaglio tecnico; **on a legal ~** grazie
a un cavillo legale
technically ['tɛknɪklɪ] ADV dal punto di vista
tecnico
technician [tɛk'nɪʃən] N tecnico(-a)
technique [tɛk'niːk] N tecnica
techno ['tɛknəu] N (*Mus*) techno *f inv*
technocrat ['tɛknəkræt] N tecnocrate *mf*
technological [tɛknə'lɔdʒɪkl] ADJ
tecnologico(-a)
technologist [tɛk'nɔlədʒɪst] N tecnologo(-a)
technology [tɛk'nɔlədʒɪ] N tecnologia
teddy ['tɛdɪ], **teddy bear** ['tɛdɪ-] N
orsacchiotto
tedious ['tiːdɪəs] ADJ noioso(-a), tedioso(-a)
tedium ['tiːdɪəm] N noia, tedio
tee [tiː] N (*Golf*) tee *m inv*
teem [tiːm] VI abbondare, brulicare; **to ~**
with brulicare di; **it is teeming (with rain)**
piove a dirotto
teen [tiːn] ADJ = **teenage** ▶ N (*US*) = **teenager**
teenage ['tiːneɪdʒ] ADJ (*fashions etc*) per
giovani, per adolescenti
teenager ['tiːneɪdʒə'] N adolescente *mf*
teens [tiːnz] NPL: **to be in one's ~** essere
adolescente
tee-shirt ['tiːʃəːt] N = **T-shirt**
teeter ['tiːtə'] VI barcollare, vacillare
teeth [tiːθ] NPL *of* **tooth**

teethe [tiːð] VI mettere i denti
teething ring ['tiːðɪŋ-] N dentaruolo
teething troubles NPL (*fig*) difficoltà *fpl*
iniziali
teetotal ['tiːˈtəutl] ADJ astemio(-a)
teetotaller, (*US*) **teetotaler** ['tiːˈtəutlə'] N
astemio(-a)
TEFL ['tɛfl] N ABBR = **Teaching of English as a
Foreign Language**
Teflon® ['tɛflɔn] N teflon® *m*
Tehran [tɛəˈrɑːn] N Tehran *f*
tel. ABBR (= *telephone*) tel
Tel Aviv ['tɛləˈviːv] N Tel Aviv *f*
telecast ['tɛlɪkɑːst] VT, VI teletrasmettere
telecommunications
['tɛlɪkəmjuːnɪˈkeɪʃənz] N telecomunicazioni
fpl
teleconferencing ['tɛlɪkɔnfərnsɪŋ] N
teleconferenza
telegram ['tɛlɪgræm] N telegramma *m*
telegraph ['tɛlɪgrɑːf] N telegrafo
telegraphic [tɛlɪ'græfɪk] ADJ telegrafico(-a)
telegraph pole N palo del telegrafo
telegraph wire N filo del telegrafo
telepathic [tɛlɪ'pæθɪk] ADJ telepatico(-a)
telepathy [tə'lɛpəθɪ] N telepatia
telephone ['tɛlɪfəun] N telefono ▶ VT (*person*)
telefonare a; (*message*) comunicare per
telefono; **to have a ~**, (*BRIT*) **to be on the ~**
(*subscriber*) avere il telefono; **to be on the ~**
(*be speaking*) essere al telefono
telephone book N elenco telefonico
telephone box, (*US*) **telephone booth** N
cabina telefonica
telephone call N telefonata
telephone directory N elenco telefonico
telephone exchange N centralino
telefonico
telephone number N numero di telefono
telephone operator N centralinista *mf*
telephone tapping N intercettazione *f*
telefonica
telephonist [tə'lɛfənɪst] N (*BRIT*) telefonista
mf
telephoto lens ['tɛlɪfəutəu-] N teleobiettivo
teleprinter ['tɛlɪprɪntə'] N telescrivente *f*
Teleprompter® ['tɛlɪprɔmptə'] N (*US*) gobbo
telesales ['tɛlɪseɪlz] N vendita per telefono
telescope ['tɛlɪskəup] N telescopio ▶ VI
chiudersi a telescopio; (*fig: vehicles*)
accartocciarsi
telescopic [tɛlɪs'kɔpɪk] ADJ telescopico(-a);
(*umbrella*) pieghevole
Teletext® ['tɛlɪtɛkst] N (*system*) teletext *m inv*;
(*in Italy*) televideo
telethon ['tɛlɪθɔn] N maratona televisiva
televise ['tɛlɪvaɪz] VT teletrasmettere
television ['tɛlɪvɪʒən] N televisione *f*; **on ~**
alla televisione

t

television licence N (*Brit*) abbonamento alla televisione

television programme N programma *m* televisivo

television set N televisore *m*

teleworking ['tɛlɪwəːkɪŋ] N telelavoro

telex ['tɛlɛks] N telex *m inv* ▶ VT trasmettere per telex ▶ VI mandare un telex; **to ~ sb (about sth)** informare qn via telex (di qc)

tell [tɛl] (*pt, pp* **told**) VT dire; (*relate: story*) raccontare; (*distinguish*): **to ~ sth from** distinguere qc da ▶ VI (*talk*): **to ~ (of)** parlare (di); (*have effect*) farsi sentire, avere effetto; **to ~ sb to do** dire a qn di fare; **to ~ sb about sth** dire a qn di qc; raccontare qc a qn; **to ~ the time** leggere l'ora; **can you ~ me the time?** può dirmi l'ora?; **(I) ~ you what ...** so io che cosa fare ...; **I couldn't ~ them apart** non riuscivo a distinguerli
▶ **tell off** VT rimproverare, sgridare
▶ **tell on** VT FUS (*inform against*) denunciare

teller ['tɛlə^r] N (*in bank*) cassiere(-a)

telling ['tɛlɪŋ] ADJ (*remark, detail*) rivelatore(-trice)

telltale ['tɛlteɪl] ADJ (*sign*) rivelatore(-trice) ▶ N malalingua, pettegolo(-a)

telly ['tɛlɪ] N ABBR (*Brit: col: = television*) tivù *f inv*

temerity [tə'mɛrɪtɪ] N temerarietà

temp [tɛmp] ABBR (*Brit col*) = **temporary** ▶ N impiegato(-a) interinale ▶ VI lavorare come impiegato(-a) interinale

temper ['tɛmpə^r] N (*nature*) carattere *m*; (*mood*) umore *m*; (*fit of anger*) collera ▶ VT (*moderate*) temperare, moderare; **to be in a ~** essere in collera; **to keep one's ~** restare calmo; **to lose one's ~** andare in collera

temperament ['tɛmprəmənt] N (*nature*) temperamento

temperamental [tɛmprə'mɛntl] ADJ capriccioso(-a)

temperance ['tɛmpərns] N moderazione *f*; (*in drinking*) temperanza nel bere

temperate ['tɛmprət] ADJ moderato(-a); (*climate*) temperato(-a)

temperature ['tɛmprətʃə^r] N temperatura; **to have** *or* **run a ~** avere la febbre

tempered ['tɛmpəd] ADJ (*steel*) temprato(-a)

tempest ['tɛmpɪst] N tempesta

tempestuous [tɛm'pɛstjuəs] ADJ (*relationship, meeting*) burrascoso(-a)

tempi ['tɛmpiː] NPL *of* **tempo**

template, (*US*) **templet** ['tɛmplɪt] N sagoma

temple ['tɛmpl] N (*building*) tempio; (*Anat*) tempia

templet ['tɛmplɪt] N (*US*) = **template**

tempo ['tɛmpəu] (*pl* **tempos, tempi**) N tempo; (*fig: of life etc*) ritmo

temporal ['tɛmpərl] ADJ temporale

temporarily ['tɛmpərərɪlɪ] ADV temporaneamente

temporary ['tɛmpərərɪ] ADJ temporaneo(-a); (*job, worker*) avventizio(-a), temporaneo(-a); **~ secretary** segretaria temporanea; **~ teacher** supplente *mf*

temporize ['tɛmpəraɪz] VI temporeggiare

tempt [tɛmpt] VT tentare; **to ~ sb into doing** indurre qn a fare; **to be tempted to do sth** essere tentato di fare qc

temptation [tɛmp'teɪʃən] N tentazione *f*

tempting ['tɛmptɪŋ] ADJ allettante, seducente

ten [tɛn] NUM dieci ▶ N dieci; **tens of thousands** decine di migliaia

tenable ['tɛnəbl] ADJ sostenibile

tenacious [tə'neɪʃəs] ADJ tenace

tenacity [tə'næsɪtɪ] N tenacia

tenancy ['tɛnənsɪ] N affitto; condizione *f* di inquilino

tenant ['tɛnənt] N inquilino(-a)

tend [tɛnd] VT badare a, occuparsi di; (*sick etc*) prendersi cura di ▶ VI: **to ~ to do** tendere a fare; **to ~ to** (*colour*) tendere a

tendency ['tɛndənsɪ] N tendenza

tender ['tɛndə^r] ADJ tenero(-a); (*sore*) dolorante; (*fig: subject*) delicato(-a) ▶ N (*Comm: offer*) offerta; (*money*): **legal ~** moneta in corso legale ▶ VT offrire; **to put in a ~ (for)** fare un'offerta (per); **to put work out to ~** (*Brit*) dare lavoro in appalto; **to ~ one's resignation** presentare le proprie dimissioni

tenderize ['tɛndəraɪz] VT (*Culin*) far intenerire

tenderly ['tɛndəlɪ] ADV teneramente

tenderness ['tɛndənɪs] N tenerezza; sensibilità

tendon ['tɛndən] N tendine *m*

tenement ['tɛnəmənt] N casamento

Tenerife [tɛnə'riːf] N Tenerife *f*

tenet ['tɛnət] N principio

Tenn. ABBR (*US*) = **Tennessee**

tenner ['tɛnə^r] N (*Brit col*) (banconota da) dieci sterline *fpl*

tennis ['tɛnɪs] N tennis *m*

tennis ball N palla da tennis

tennis court N campo da tennis

tennis elbow N (*Med*) gomito del tennista

tennis match N partita di tennis

tennis player N tennista *mf*

tennis racket N racchetta da tennis

tennis shoes NPL scarpe *fpl* da tennis

tenor ['tɛnə^r] N (*Mus, of speech etc*) tenore *m*

tenpin bowling ['tɛnpɪn-] N (*Brit*) bowling *m*

tense [tɛns] ADJ teso(-a) ▶ N (*Ling*) tempo ▶ VT (*tighten: muscles*) tendere

tenseness ['tɛnsnɪs] N tensione *f*

tension ['tɛnʃən] N tensione f

tent [tɛnt] N tenda

tentacle ['tɛntəkl] N tentacolo

tentative ['tɛntətɪv] ADJ esitante, incerto(-a); (*conclusion*) provvisorio(-a)

tenterhooks ['tɛntəhuks] NPL: **on ~** sulle spine

tenth [tɛnθ] NUM decimo(-a)

tent peg N picchetto da tenda

tent pole N palo da tenda, montante m

tenuous ['tɛnjuəs] ADJ tenue

tenure ['tɛnjuəʳ] N (*of property*) possesso; (*of job*) incarico; (*guaranteed employment*): **to have ~** essere di ruolo

tepid ['tɛpɪd] ADJ tiepido(-a)

Ter. ABBR = **terrace**

term [tə:m] N (*limit*) termine m; (*word*) vocabolo, termine; (*Scol*) trimestre m; (*Law*) sessione f ▶ VT chiamare, definire; **terms** NPL (*conditions*) condizioni fpl; (*Comm*) prezzi mpl, tariffe fpl; **~ of imprisonment** periodo di prigionia; **during his ~ of office** durante il suo incarico; **in the short/long ~** a breve/ lunga scadenza; **"easy terms"** (*Comm*) "facilitazioni di pagamento"; **to be on good terms with** essere in buoni rapporti con; **to come to terms with** (*person*) arrivare a un accordo con; (*problem*) affrontare

terminal ['tə:mɪnl] ADJ finale, terminale; (*disease*) terminale ▶ N (*Elec, Comput*) morsetto; (*Aviat, for oil, ore etc*) terminal m inv; (*BRIT: also*: **coach terminal**) capolinea m

terminate ['tə:mɪneɪt] VT mettere fine a ▶ VI: **to ~ in** finire in or con

termination [tə:mɪ'neɪʃən] N fine f; (*of contract*) rescissione f; **~ of pregnancy** (*Med*) interruzione f della gravidanza

termini ['tə:mɪnaɪ] NPL of **terminus**

terminology [tə:mɪ'nɔlədʒɪ] N terminologia

terminus ['tə:mɪnəs] (*pl* **termini** ['tə:mɪnaɪ]) N (*for buses*) capolinea m; (*for trains*) stazione f terminale

termite ['tə:maɪt] N termite f

term paper N (*US Univ*) saggio scritto da consegnare a fine trimestre

Terr. ABBR = **terrace**

terrace ['tɛrəs] N terrazza; (*BRIT: row of houses*) fila di case a schiera; **the terraces** NPL (*BRIT Sport*) le gradinate

terraced ['tɛrɪst] ADJ (*garden*) a terrazze; (*in a row: house, cottage etc*) a schiera

terrain [tɛ'reɪn] N terreno

terrestrial [tɪ'rɛstrɪəl] ADJ (*life*) terrestre; (*BRIT: channel*) terrestre

terrible ['tɛrɪbl] ADJ terribile; (*weather*) bruttissimo(-a); (*performance, report*) pessimo(-a)

terribly ['tɛrəblɪ] ADV terribilmente; (*very badly*) malissimo

terrier ['tɛrɪəʳ] N terrier m inv

terrific [tə'rɪfɪk] ADJ incredibile, fantastico(-a); (*wonderful*) formidabile, eccezionale

terrified ['tɛrɪfaɪd] ADJ atterrito(-a)

terrify ['tɛrɪfaɪ] VT terrorizzare; **to be terrified** essere atterrito(-a)

terrifying ADJ terrificante

territorial [tɛrɪ'tɔ:rɪəl] ADJ territoriale

territorial waters NPL acque fpl territoriali

territory ['tɛrɪtərɪ] N territorio

terror ['tɛrəʳ] N terrore m

terror attack N attentato terroristico

terrorism ['tɛrərɪzəm] N terrorismo

terrorist ['tɛrərɪst] N terrorista mf

terrorize ['tɛrəraɪz] VT terrorizzare

terse [tə:s] ADJ (*style*) conciso(-a); (*reply*) laconico(-a)

tertiary ['tə:ʃərɪ] ADJ (*gen*) terziario(-a); **~ education** (*BRIT*) educazione f superiore post-scolastica

Terylene® ['tɛrəli:n] N (*BRIT*) terital® m, terilene® m

TESL ['tɛsl] N ABBR = **Teaching of English as a Second Language**

TESSA ['tɛsə] N ABBR (*BRIT*: = *Tax Exempt Special Savings Account*) deposito a risparmio esente da tasse

test [tɛst] N (*trial, check: of courage etc*) prova; (*: of goods in factory*) controllo, collaudo; (*Med*) esame m; (*Chem*) analisi f inv; (*exam: of intelligence etc*) test m inv; (*: in school*) compito in classe; (*also*: **driving test**) esame m di guida ▶ VT provare; controllare, collaudare; esaminare; analizzare; sottoporre ad esame; **to put sth to the ~** mettere qc alla prova; **to ~ sth for sth** analizzare qc alla ricerca di qc; **to ~ sb in history** esaminare qn in storia

testament ['tɛstəmənt] N testamento; **the Old/New T~** il Vecchio/Nuovo testamento

test ban N (*also*: **nuclear test ban**) divieto di esperimenti nucleari

test case N (*Law, fig*) caso che farà testo

testes ['tɛsti:z] NPL testicoli mpl

test flight N volo di prova

testicle ['tɛstɪkl] N testicolo

testify ['tɛstɪfaɪ] VI (*Law*) testimoniare, deporre; **to ~ to sth** (*Law*) testimoniare qc; (*gen*) comprovare or dimostrare qc; (*be sign of*) essere una prova di qc

testimonial [tɛstɪ'məunɪəl] N (*reference*) benservito; (*gift*) testimonianza di stima

testimony ['tɛstɪmənɪ] N (*Law*) testimonianza, deposizione f

testing ['tɛstɪŋ] ADJ (*difficult: time*) duro(-a)

test match N (*Cricket, Rugby*) partita internazionale

testosterone [tɛs'tɔstərəun] N testosterone m

t

test paper N (*Scol*) interrogazione *f* scritta
test pilot N pilota *m* collaudatore
test tube N provetta
test-tube baby ['tɛsttjuːb-] N bambino(-a) concepito(-a) in provetta
testy ['tɛstɪ] ADJ irritabile
tetanus ['tɛtənəs] N tetano
tetchy ['tɛtʃɪ] ADJ irritabile, irascibile
tether ['tɛðəʳ] VT legare ▶ N: **at the end of one's ~** al limite (della pazienza)
Tex. ABBR (*US*) = **Texas**
text [tɛkst] N testo; (*Tel*) sms *m inv*, messaggino ▶ VT: **to ~ sb** (*col*) mandare un sms a ▶ VI messaggiarsi
textbook ['tɛkstbuk] N libro di testo
textile ['tɛkstaɪl] N tessile *m*; **textiles** NPL tessuti *mpl*
texting ['tɛkstɪŋ] N invio di sms
text message N (*Tel*) sms *m inv*, messaggino
text messaging [-'mɛsɪdʒɪŋ] N il mandarsi sms
textual ['tɛkstjuəl] ADJ testuale, del testo
texture ['tɛkstʃəʳ] N tessitura; (*of skin, paper etc*) struttura
TGIF ABBR (*col*) = **thank God it's Friday**
TGWU N ABBR (*BRIT*: = *Transport and General Workers' Union*) sindacato degli operai dei trasporti e non specializzati
Thai [taɪ] ADJ tailandese ▶ N tailandese *mf*; (*Ling*) tailandese *m*
Thailand ['taɪlænd] N Tailandia
thalidomide® [θə'lɪdəmaɪd] N talidomide® *m*
Thames [tɛmz] N: **the ~** il Tamigi
than [ðæn, ðən] CONJ (*in comparisons*) che; (*with numerals, pronouns, proper names*) di; **more ~ 10/Maria/once** più di 10/Maria/una volta; **I have more/less ~ you** ne ho più/meno di te; **you know her better ~ I do** la conosce meglio di me *or* di quanto non la conosca io; **she has more apples ~ pears** ha più mele che pere; **it is better to phone ~ to write** è meglio telefonare che scrivere; **no sooner did he leave ~ the phone rang** non appena uscì il telefono suonò; **she is older ~ you think** è più vecchia di quanto tu (non) pensi
thank [θæŋk] VT ringraziare; **~ you (very much)** grazie (tante); **~ heavens/God!** grazie al cielo/a Dio!; *see also* **thanks**
thankful ['θæŋkful] ADJ: **~ (for)** riconoscente (per); **~ for/that** (*relieved*) sollevato(a) da/dal fatto che
thankfully ['θæŋkfəlɪ] ADV con riconoscenza; con sollievo; **~ there were few victims** grazie al cielo ci sono state poche vittime
thankless ['θæŋklɪs] ADJ ingrato(-a)
thanks [θæŋks] NPL ringraziamenti *mpl*, grazie *fpl* ▶ EXCL grazie!; **~ to** *prep* grazie a
Thanksgiving (Day) ['θæŋksgɪvɪŋ-] N (*US*) giorno del ringraziamento; *vedi nota*

Negli Stati Uniti il quarto giovedì di novembre ricorre il *Thanksgiving (Day)*, festa nazionale in ricordo della celebrazione con cui i Padri Pellegrini, i puritani inglesi che fondarono la colonia di Plymouth nel Massachusetts, ringraziarono Dio del buon raccolto del 1621.

(KEYWORD)

that [ðæt] (*pl* **those**) ADJ (*demonstrative*) quel (quell', quello) *m*; quella (quell') *f*; **that man/ woman/book** quell'uomo/quella donna/ quel libro; (*not "this"*) quell'uomo/quella donna/quel libro là; **that one** quello(-a) là ▶ PRON **1** (*demonstrative*) ciò; (: *not "this one"*) quello(-a); **who's that?** chi è?; **what's that?** cos'è quello?; **is that you?** sei tu?; **I prefer this to that** preferisco questo a quello; **that's what he said** questo è ciò che ha detto; **after that** dopo; **what happened after that?** che è successo dopo?; **that is (to say)** cioè; **at** *or* **with that she …** con ciò lei …; **do it like that** fallo così
2 (*relative: direct*) che; (: *indirect*) cui; **the book (that) I read** il libro che ho letto; **the box (that) I put it in** la scatola in cui l'ho messo; **the people (that) I spoke to** le persone con cui *or* con le quali ho parlato; **not that I know of** non che io sappia
3 (*relative: of time*) in cui; **the day (that) he came** il giorno in cui è venuto
▶ CONJ che; **he thought that I was ill** pensava che io fossi malato
▶ ADV (*demonstrative*) così; **I can't work that much** non posso lavorare (così) tanto; **that high** così alto; **the wall's about that high and that thick** il muro è alto circa così e spesso circa così

thatched [θætʃt] ADJ (*roof*) di paglia; **~ cottage** cottage *m inv* col tetto di paglia
Thatcherism ['θætʃərɪzəm] N thatcherismo
thaw [θɔː] N disgelo ▶ VI (*ice*) sciogliersi; (*food*) scongelarsi ▶ VT (*food*) (fare) scongelare; **it's thawing** (*weather*) sta sgelando

(KEYWORD)

the [ðiː, ðə] DEF ART **1** (*gen*) il (lo, l') *m*; la (l') *f*; i (gli) *mpl*; le *fpl*; **the boy/girl/ink** il ragazzo/la ragazza/l'inchiostro; **the books/pencils** i libri/le matite; **the history of the world** la storia del mondo; **give it to the postman** dallo al postino; **I haven't the time/money** non ho tempo/soldi; **the rich and the poor** i ricchi e i poveri; **1.5 euros to the dollar** 1.5 euro per un dollaro; **paid by the hour** pagato a ore

2 (*in titles*): **Elizabeth the First** Elisabetta prima; **Peter the Great** Pietro il Grande
3 (*in comparisons*): **the more he works, the more he earns** più lavora più guadagna; **the sooner the better** prima è meglio è

theatre, (*US*) **theater** ['θɪətər] N teatro; (*also:* **lecture theatre**) aula magna; (*also:* **operating theatre**) sala operatoria
theatre-goer ['θɪətəgəuər] N frequentatore(-trice) di teatri
theatrical [θɪ'ætrɪkl] ADJ teatrale
theft [θɛft] N furto
their [ðɛər] ADJ il (la) loro *pl* i (le) loro
theirs [ðɛəz] PRON il (la) loro *pl* i (le) loro; **it is ~** è loro; **a friend of ~** un loro amico; *see also* **my; mine**[1]
them [ðɛm, ðəm] PRON (*direct*) li(le); (*indirect*) gli, loro (*after vb*); (*stressed, after prep: people*) loro; (: *people, things*) essi(-e); **I see ~** li vedo; **give ~ the book** dà loro *or* dagli il libro; **give me a few of ~** dammene un po' *or* qualcuno; *see also* **me**
theme [θiːm] N tema *m*
theme park N parco a tema
theme song, theme tune N tema musicale
themselves [ðəm'sɛlvz] PL PRON (*reflexive*) si; (*emphatic*) loro stessi(-e); (*after prep*) se stessi(-e); **between ~** tra (di) loro
then [ðɛn] ADV (*at that time*) allora; (*next*) poi, dopo; (*and also*) e poi ▶ CONJ (*therefore*) perciò, dunque, quindi ▶ ADJ: **the ~ president** il presidente di allora; **by ~** allora; **from ~ on** da allora in poi; **until ~** fino ad allora; **and ~ what?** e poi?, e allora?; **what do you want me to do ~?** allora cosa vuole che faccia?
theologian [θɪə'ləudʒən] N teologo(-a)
theological [θɪə'lɔdʒɪkl] ADJ teologico(-a)
theology [θɪ'ɔlədʒɪ] N teologia
theorem ['θɪərəm] N teorema *m*
theoretical [θɪə'rɛtɪkl] ADJ teorico(-a)
theorize ['θɪəraɪz] VI teorizzare
theory ['θɪərɪ] N teoria; **in ~** in teoria
therapeutic [θɛrə'pjuːtɪk], **therapeutical** [θɛrə'pjuːtɪkl] ADJ terapeutico(-a)
therapist ['θɛrəpɪst] N terapista *mf*
therapy ['θɛrəpɪ] N terapia

(KEYWORD)

there [ðɛər] ADV **1: there is** c'è; **there are** ci sono; **there are 3 of them** (*people*) sono in 3; (*things*) ce ne sono 3; **there is no-one here** non c'è nessuno qui; **there has been an accident** c'è stato un incidente
2 (*referring to place*) là, lì; **it's there** è là *or* lì; **up/in/down there** lassù/là dentro/laggiù; **back there** là dietro; **on there** lassù; **over there** là; **through there** di là; **he went there on Friday** ci è andato venerdì; **it**

takes two hours to go there and back ci vogliono due ore per andare e tornare; **I want that book there** voglio quel libro là *or* lì; **there he is!** eccolo!
3: there, there (*esp to child*) su, su

thereabouts ['ðɛərəbauts] ADV (*place*) nei pressi, da quelle parti; (*amount*) giù di lì, all'incirca
thereafter [ðɛər'ɑːftər] ADV da allora in poi
thereby [ðɛə'baɪ] ADV con ciò
therefore ['ðɛəfɔːr] ADV perciò, quindi
there's [ðɛəz] = **there is; there has**
thereupon [ðɛərə'pɔn] ADV (*at that point*) a quel punto; (*formal: on that subject*) in merito
thermal ['θəːml] ADJ (*currents, spring*) termale; (*underwear, printer*) termico(-a); (*paper*) termosensibile
thermodynamics [θəː'məudaɪ'næmɪks] N termodinamica
thermometer [θə'mɔmɪtər] N termometro
thermonuclear ['θəːməu'njuːklɪər] ADJ termonucleare
Thermos® ['θəːməs] N (*also:* **Thermos flask**) thermos® *m inv*
thermostat ['θəːməstæt] N termostato
thesaurus [θɪ'sɔːrəs] N dizionario dei sinonimi
these [ðiːz] PL PRON, ADJ questi(-e)
thesis ['θiːsɪs] (*pl* **theses** ['θiːsiːz]) N tesi *f inv*
they [ðeɪ] PL PRON essi(esse); (*people only*) loro; **~ say that ...** (*it is said that*) si dice che ...
they'd [ðeɪd] = **they would; they had**
they'll [ðeɪl] = **they will; they shall**
they're [ðɛər] = **they are**
they've [ðeɪv] = **they have**
thick [θɪk] ADJ spesso(-a); (*crowd*) compatto(-a); (*stupid*) ottuso(-a), lento(-a) ▶ N: **in the ~ of** nel folto di; **it's 20 cm ~** ha uno spessore di 20 cm
thicken ['θɪkən] VI ispessire ▶ VT (*sauce etc*) ispessire, rendere più denso(-a)
thicket ['θɪkɪt] N boscaglia
thickly ['θɪklɪ] ADV (*spread*) a strati spessi; (*cut*) a fette grosse; (*populated*) densamente
thickness ['θɪknɪs] N spessore *m*
thickset [θɪk'sɛt] ADJ tarchiato(-a), tozzo(-a)
thickskinned [θɪk'skɪnd] ADJ (*fig*) insensibile
thief [θiːf] (*pl* **thieves** [θiːvz]) N ladro(-a)
thieving ['θiːvɪŋ] N furti *mpl*
thigh [θaɪ] N coscia
thighbone ['θaɪbəun] N femore *m*
thimble ['θɪmbl] N ditale *m*
thin [θɪn] ADJ sottile; (*person*) magro(-a); (*soup*) poco denso(-a); (*hair, crowd*) rado(-a); (*fog*) leggero(-a) ▶ VT (*hair*) sfoltire ▶ VI (*fog*) diradarsi; (*also:* **thin out**: *crowd*) disperdersi; **to ~ (down)** (*sauce, paint*) diluire; **his hair is thinning** sta perdendo i capelli

t

thing [θɪŋ] N cosa; (object) oggetto; (contraption) aggeggio; (mania): **to have a ~ about** essere fissato(-a) con; **things** NPL (belongings) cose fpl; **for one ~** tanto per cominciare; **the best ~ would be to** la cosa migliore sarebbe di; **the ~ is …** il fatto è che …; **the main ~ is to …** la cosa più importante è di …; **first ~ (in the morning)** come or per prima cosa (di mattina); **last ~ (at night)** come or per ultima cosa (di sera); **poor ~** poveretto(-a); **she's got a ~ about mice** è terrorizzata dai topi; **how are things?** come va?

think [θɪŋk] (pt, pp thought [θɔːt]) VI pensare, riflettere ▶ VT pensare, credere; (imagine) immaginare; **to ~ of** pensare a; **what did you ~ of them?** cosa ne ha pensato?; **to ~ about sth/sb** pensare a qc/qn; **I'll ~ about it** ci penserò; **to ~ of doing** pensare di fare; **I ~ so/not** penso or credo di sì/no; **to ~ well of** avere una buona opinione di; **to ~ aloud** pensare ad alta voce; **~ again!** rifletti!, pensaci su!

▶ **think out** VT (plan) elaborare; (solution) trovare

▶ **think over** VT riflettere su; **I'd like to ~ things over** vorrei pensarci su

▶ **think through** VT riflettere a fondo su

▶ **think up** VT ideare

thinking [ˈθɪŋkɪŋ] N: **to my (way of) ~** a mio parere

think tank N gruppo di esperti

thinly [ˈθɪnlɪ] ADV (cut) a fette sottili; (spread) in uno strato sottile

thinness [ˈθɪnnɪs] N sottigliezza; magrezza

third [θəːd] N terzo(-a) ▶ N terzo(-a); (fraction) terzo, terza parte f; (Aut) terza; (BRIT Scol: degree) laurea col minimo dei voti

third-degree burns [ˈθəːdɪˈgriː-] NPL ustioni fpl di terzo grado

thirdly [ˈθəːdlɪ] ADV in terzo luogo

third party insurance N (BRIT) assicurazione f contro terzi

third-rate [θəːdˈreɪt] ADJ di qualità scadente

Third World N: **the ~** il Terzo Mondo

thirst [θəːst] N sete f

thirsty [ˈθəːstɪ] ADJ (person) assetato(-a), che ha sete; **to be ~** aver sete

thirteen [θəːˈtiːn] NUM tredici

thirteenth [-ˈtiːnθ] NUM tredicesmo(-a)

thirtieth [ˈθəːtɪɪθ] NUM trentesimo(-a)

thirty [ˈθəːtɪ] NUM trenta

KEYWORD

this [ðɪs ʃ] (pl these) ADJ (demonstrative) questo(-a); **this man/woman/book** quest'uomo/questa donna/questo libro; (not "that") quest'uomo/questa donna/questo libro qui; **this one** questo(-a) qui; **this time** questa volta; **this time last year** l'anno scorso in questo periodo; **this way** (in this direction) da questa parte; (in this fashion) così ▶ PRON (demonstrative) questo(-a); (: not "that one") questo(-a) qui; **who/what is this?** chi è/che cos'è questo?; **I prefer this to that** preferisco questo a quello; **this is where I live** io abito qui; **this is what he said** questo è ciò che ha detto; **they were talking of this and that** stavano parlando del più e del meno; **this is Mr Brown** (in introductions, photo) questo è il signor Brown; (on telephone) sono il signor Brown

▶ ADV (demonstrative): **this high/long** etc alto/lungo etc così; **it's about this high** è alto circa così; **I didn't know things were this bad** non sapevo andasse così male

thistle [ˈθɪsl] N cardo

thong [θɒŋ] N cinghia

thorn [θɔːn] N spina

thorny [ˈθɔːnɪ] ADJ spinoso(-a)

thorough [ˈθʌrə] ADJ (person) preciso(-a), accurato(-a); (search) minuzioso(-a); (knowledge, research) approfondito(-a), profondo(-a); (person) coscienzioso(-a); (cleaning) a fondo

thoroughbred [ˈθʌrəbred] N (horse) purosangue mf

thoroughfare [ˈθʌrəfɛər] N strada transitabile; **"no ~"** (BRIT) "divieto di transito"

thoroughgoing [ˈθʌrəgəʊɪŋ] ADJ (analysis) approfondito(-a); (reform) totale

thoroughly [ˈθʌrəlɪ] ADV accuratamente; (search) minuziosamente, in profondità; (wash, study) a fondo; (very) assolutamente; **he ~ agreed** fu completamente d'accordo

thoroughness [ˈθʌrənɪs] N precisione f

those [ðəʊz] PL PRON quelli(-e) ▶ PL ADJ quei (quegli) mpl; quelle fpl

though [ðəʊ] CONJ benché, sebbene ▶ ADV comunque, tuttavia; **even ~** anche se; **it's not so easy, ~** tuttavia non è così facile

thought [θɔːt] PT, PP of think ▶ N pensiero; (opinion) opinione f; (intention) intenzione f; **after much ~** dopo molti ripensamenti; **I've just had a ~** mi è appena venuta un'idea; **to give sth some ~** prendere qc in considerazione, riflettere su qc

thoughtful [ˈθɔːtful] ADJ pensieroso(-a), pensoso(-a); ponderato(-a); (considerate) premuroso(-a)

thoughtfully [ˈθɔːtfəlɪ] ADV (pensively) con aria pensierosa

thoughtless [ˈθɔːtlɪs] ADJ sconsiderato(-a); (behaviour) scortese

thoughtlessly [ˈθɔːtlɪslɪ] ADV sconsideratamente; scortesemente

thought-provoking [ˈθɔːtprəvəukɪŋ] ADJ stimolante

thousand [ˈθauzənd] NUM mille; **one ~** mille; **thousands of** migliaia di

thousandth [ˈθauzəntθ] NUM millesimo(-a)

thrash [θræʃ] VT picchiare; bastonare; (defeat) battere
▶ **thrash about** VI dibattersi
▶ **thrash out** VT dibattere, sviscerare

thrashing [ˈθræʃɪŋ] N: **to give sb a ~** picchiare qn di santa ragione

thread [θrɛd] N filo; (of screw) filetto ▶ VT (needle) infilare; **to ~ one's way between** infilarsi tra

threadbare [ˈθrɛdbɛəʳ] ADJ consumato(-a), logoro(-a)

threat [θrɛt] N minaccia; **to be under ~ of** (closure, extinction) rischiare di; (exposure) essere minacciato(-a) di

threaten [ˈθrɛtn] VI (storm) minacciare ▶ VT: **to ~ sb with sth/to do** minacciare qn con qc/di fare

threatening [ˈθrɛtnɪŋ] ADJ minaccioso(-a)

three [θriː] NUM tre

three-dimensional [θriːdaɪˈmɛnʃənl] ADJ tridimensionale; (film) stereoscopico(-a)

three-piece [ˈθriːpiːs] CPD: **~ suit** n completo (con gilè); **~ suite** n salotto comprendente un divano e due poltrone

three-ply [θriːˈplaɪ] ADJ (wood) a tre strati; (wool) a tre fili

three-quarters [θriːˈkwɔːtəz] NPL tre quarti mpl; **~ full** pieno per tre quarti

three-wheeler [θriːˈwiːləʳ] N (car) veicolo a tre ruote

thresh [θrɛʃ] VT (Agr) trebbiare

threshing machine [ˈθrɛʃɪŋ-] N trebbiatrice f

threshold [ˈθrɛʃhəuld] N soglia; **to be on the ~ of** (fig) essere sulla soglia di

threshold agreement N (Econ) ≈ scala mobile

threw [θruː] PT of **throw**

thrift [θrɪft] N parsimonia

thrifty [ˈθrɪftɪ] ADJ economico(-a), parsimonioso(-a)

thrill [θrɪl] N brivido ▶ VI eccitarsi, tremare ▶ VT (audience) elettrizzare; **to be thrilled** (with gift etc) essere elettrizzato(-a)

thrilled ADJ: **I was ~ to get your letter** la tua lettera mi ha fatto veramente piacere

thriller [ˈθrɪləʳ] N thriller m inv

thrilling [ˈθrɪlɪŋ] ADJ (book, play etc) pieno(-a) di suspense; (news, discovery) elettrizzante

thrive [θraɪv] (pt **thrived** or **throve** [θrəuv], pp **thrived** or **thriven** [ˈθrɪvn]) VI crescere or svilupparsi bene; (business) prosperare; **he thrives on it** gli fa bene, ne gode

thriving [ˈθraɪvɪŋ] ADJ (industry etc) fiorente

throat [θrəut] N gola; **to have a sore ~** avere (un or il) mal di gola

throb [θrɔb] N (of heart) battito; (of engine) vibrazione f; (of pain) fitta ▶ VI (heart) palpitare; (engine) vibrare; (with pain) pulsare; **my head is throbbing** mi martellano le tempie

throes [θrəuz] NPL: **in the ~ of** alle prese con; in preda a; **in the ~ of death** in agonia

thrombosis [θrɔmˈbəusɪs] N trombosi f

throne [θrəun] N trono

throng [θrɔŋ] N moltitudine f ▶ VT affollare

throttle [ˈθrɔtl] N (Aut) valvola a farfalla; (on motorcycle) (manopola del) gas ▶ VT strangolare

through [θruː] PREP attraverso; (time) per, durante; (by means of) per mezzo di; (owing to) a causa di ▶ ADJ (ticket, train, passage) diretto(-a) ▶ ADV attraverso; **(from) Monday ~ Friday** (US) da lunedì a venerdì; **I am halfway ~ the book** sono a metà libro; **to let sb ~** lasciar passare qn; **to put sb ~ to sb** (Tel) passare qn a qn; **to be ~** (Tel) ottenere la comunicazione; (have finished) avere finito; **"no ~ traffic"** (US) "divieto d'accesso"; **"no ~ road"** (BRIT) "strada senza sbocco"

throughout [θruːˈaut] PREP (place) dappertutto in; (time) per or durante tutto(-a) ▶ ADV dappertutto; sempre

throughput [ˈθruːput] N (of goods, materials) materiale m in lavorazione; (Comput) volume m di dati immessi

throve [θrəuv] PT of **thrive**

throw [θrəu] (pt **threw**, pp **thrown**) N tiro, getto; (Sport) lancio ▶ VT tirare, gettare; (Sport) lanciare; (rider) disarcionare; (fig) confondere; (pottery) formare al tornio; **to ~ a party** dare una festa; **to ~ open** (doors, windows) spalancare; (house, gardens etc) aprire al pubblico; (competition, race) aprire a tutti
▶ **throw about, throw around** VT (litter etc) spargere
▶ **throw away** VT gettare or buttare via
▶ **throw in** VT (Sport: ball) rimettere in gioco; (include) aggiungere
▶ **throw off** VT sbarazzarsi di
▶ **throw out** VT buttare fuori; (reject) respingere
▶ **throw together** VT (clothes, meal etc) mettere insieme; (essay) buttar giù
▶ **throw up** VI vomitare

throwaway [ˈθrəuəweɪ] ADJ da buttare

throwback [ˈθrəubæk] N: **it's a ~ to** (fig) ciò risale a

throw-in [ˈθrəuɪn] N (Sport) rimessa in gioco

thrown [θrəun] PP of **throw**

thru [θruː] PREP, ADJ, ADV (US) = **through**

thrush [θrʌʃ] N (Zool) tordo; (Med: esp in children) mughetto; (: BRIT: in women) candida

thrust [θrʌst] (pt, pp **~**) N (Tech) spinta ▶ VT spingere con forza; (push in) conficcare

t

829

thrusting ['θrʌstɪŋ] ADJ (troppo) intraprendente

thud [θʌd] N tonfo

thug [θʌg] N delinquente m

thumb [θʌm] N (Anat) pollice m ▶ VT (book) sfogliare; **to ~ a lift** fare l'autostop; **to give sb/sth the thumbs up/down** approvare/ disapprovare qn/qc

thumb index N indice m a rubrica

thumbnail ['θʌmneɪl] N unghia del pollice

thumbnail sketch N descrizione f breve

thumbtack ['θʌmtæk] N (US) puntina da disegno

thump [θʌmp] N colpo forte; (sound) tonfo ▶ VT (person) picchiare; (object) battere su ▶ VI picchiare; battere

thunder ['θʌndə^r] N tuono ▶ VI tuonare; (train etc): **to ~ past** passare con un rombo

thunderbolt ['θʌndəbəult] N fulmine m

thunderclap ['θʌndəklæp] N rombo di tuono

thunderous ['θʌndərəs] ADJ fragoroso(-a)

thunderstorm ['θʌndəstɔ:m] N temporale m

thunderstruck ['θʌndəstrʌk] ADJ (fig) sbigottito(-a)

thundery ['θʌndəri] ADJ temporalesco(-a)

Thur(s). ABBR (= Thursday) gio.

Thursday ['θə:zdɪ] N giovedì m inv; see also **Tuesday**

thus [ðʌs] ADV così

thwart [θwɔ:t] VT contrastare

thyme [taɪm] N timo

thyroid ['θaɪrɔɪd] N tiroide f

tiara [tɪ'ɑ:rə] N (woman's) diadema m

Tiber ['taɪbə^r] N: **the ~** il Tevere

Tibet [tɪ'bɛt] N Tibet m

Tibetan [tɪ'bɛtən] ADJ tibetano(-a) ▶ N (person) tibetano(-a); (Ling) tibetano

tibia ['tɪbɪə] N tibia

tic [tɪk] N tic m inv

tick [tɪk] N (sound, of clock) tic tac m inv; (mark) segno; spunta; (Zool) zecca; (BRIT col): **in a ~** in un attimo; (: credit): **to buy sth on ~** comprare qc a credito ▶ VI fare tic tac ▶ VT spuntare; **to put a ~ against sth** fare un segno di fianco a qc
▶ **tick off** VT spuntare; (person) sgridare
▶ **tick over** VI (BRIT: engine) andare al minimo

ticker tape ['tɪkə-] N nastro di telescrivente; (US: in celebrations) stelle fpl filanti

ticket ['tɪkɪt] N biglietto; (in shop: on goods) etichetta; (: from cash register) scontrino; (for library) scheda; (US Pol) lista dei candidati; **to get a (parking) ~** (Aut) prendere una multa (per sosta vietata); **a single/return ~ to ...** un biglietto di sola andata/di andata e ritorno per...

ticket agency N (Theat) agenzia di vendita di biglietti

ticket barrier N (BRIT Rail) cancelletto d'ingresso

ticket collector N bigliettaio

ticket holder N persona munita di biglietto

ticket inspector N controllore m

ticket machine N distributore m di biglietti

ticket office N biglietteria

tickle ['tɪkl] N solletico ▶ VT fare il solletico a; (fig) stuzzicare; piacere a; far ridere ▶ VI: **it tickles** mi (or gli etc) fa il solletico

ticklish ['tɪklɪʃ] ADJ che soffre il solletico; (which tickles: blanket, cough) che provoca prurito; (problem) delicato(-a)

tidal ['taɪdl] ADJ di marea

tidal wave N onda anomala

tidbit ['tɪdbɪt] N (US) = **titbit**

tiddlywinks ['tɪdlɪwɪŋks] N gioco della pulce

tide [taɪd] N marea; (fig: of events) corso ▶ VT: **will £20 ~ you over till Monday?** ti basteranno 20 sterline fino a lunedì?; **high/ low ~** alta/bassa marea; **the ~ of public opinion** l'orientamento dell'opinione pubblica

tidily ['taɪdɪlɪ] ADV in modo ordinato; **to arrange ~** sistemare; **to dress ~** vestirsi per benino

tidiness ['taɪdɪnɪs] N ordine m

tidy ['taɪdɪ] ADJ (room) ordinato(-a), lindo(-a); (dress, work) curato(-a), in ordine; (person) ordinato(-a); (mind) organizzato(-a) ▶ VT (also: **tidy up**) riordinare, mettere in ordine; **to ~ o.s. up** rassettarsi

tie [taɪ] N (string etc) legaccio; (BRIT: also: **necktie**) cravatta; (fig: link) legame m; (Sport: match) incontro; (: draw) pareggio; (US Rail) traversina ▶ VT (parcel) legare; (ribbon) annodare ▶ VI (Sport) pareggiare; **"black/ white ~"** "smoking/abito di rigore"; **family ties** legami familiari; **to ~ sth in a bow** annodare qc; **to ~ a knot in sth** fare un nodo a qc
▶ **tie down** VT legare, assicurare con una corda; (fig): **to ~ sb down to** (price etc) costringere qn ad accettare
▶ **tie in** VI: **to ~ in (with)** (correspond) corrispondere (a)
▶ **tie on** VT (BRIT: label etc) attaccare
▶ **tie up** VT (parcel, dog) legare; (boat) ormeggiare; (arrangements) concludere; **to be tied up** (busy) essere occupato or preso

tie-break ['taɪbreɪk], **tie-breaker** ['taɪbreɪkə^r] N (Tennis) tie-break m inv; (in quiz) spareggio

tie-on ['taɪɔn] ADJ (BRIT: label) volante

tie-pin ['taɪpɪn] N (BRIT) fermacravatta m inv

tier [tɪə^r] N fila; (of cake) piano, strato

Tierra del Fuego [tɪ'ɛrədɛl'fweɪgəu] N Terra del Fuoco

tie tack N (US) fermacravatta m inv

tiff [tɪf] N battibecco

tiger ['taɪgə^r] N tigre f

tight [taɪt] ADJ (*rope*) teso(-a), tirato(-a); (*money*) poco(-a); (*clothes, budget, programme, bend*) stretto(-a); (*control*) severo(-a), fermo(-a); (*col: drunk*) sbronzo(-a) ▶ ADV (*squeeze*) fortemente; (*shut*) ermeticamente; **to be packed ~** (*suitcase*) essere pieno zeppo; (*people*) essere pigiati; **everybody hold ~!** tenetevi stretti!; *see also* **tights**

tighten ['taɪtn] VT (*rope*) tendere; (*screw*) stringere; (*control*) rinforzare ▶ VI tendersi; stringersi

tight-fisted [taɪt'fɪstɪd] ADJ avaro(-a)

tight-lipped ['taɪt'lɪpt] ADJ: **to be ~** essere reticente; (*angry*) tenere le labbra serrate

tightly ['taɪtlɪ] ADV (*grasp*) bene, saldamente

tightrope ['taɪtrəʊp] N corda (da acrobata)

tightrope walker N funambolo(-a)

tights [taɪts] NPL (BRIT) collant *m inv*

tigress ['taɪɡrɪs] N tigre *f* (femmina)

tilde ['tɪldə] N tilde *f*

tile [taɪl] N (*on roof*) tegola; (*on floor, wall*) mattonella, piastrella ▶ VT (*floor, bathroom etc*) piastrellare

tiled [taɪld] ADJ rivestito(-a) di tegole; a mattonelle; a piastrelle

till [tɪl] N registratore *m* di cassa ▶ VT (*land*) coltivare ▶ PREP, CONJ = **until**

tiller ['tɪlər] N (*Naut*) barra del timone

tilt [tɪlt] VT inclinare, far pendere ▶ VI inclinarsi, pendere ▶ N (*slope*) pendio; **to wear one's hat at a ~** portare il cappello sulle ventitré; **(at) full ~** a tutta velocità

timber ['tɪmbər] N (*material*) legname *m*; (*trees*) alberi *mpl* da legname

time [taɪm] N tempo; (*epoch: often pl*) epoca, tempo; (*by clock*) ora; (*moment*) momento; (*occasion, also Math*) volta; (*Mus*) tempo ▶ VT (*race*) cronometrare; (*programme*) calcolare la durata di; (*fix moment for*) programmare; (*remark etc*): **to ~ sth well/badly** scegliere il momento più/meno opportuno per qc; **a long ~** molto tempo; **for the ~ being** per il momento; **4 at a ~** 4 per or alla volta; **from ~ to ~** ogni tanto; **~ after ~, ~ and again** mille volte; **in ~** (*soon enough*) in tempo; (*after some time*) col tempo; (*Mus*) a tempo; **at times** a volte; **to take one's ~** prenderla con calma; **in a week's ~** fra una settimana; **in no ~** in un attimo; **any ~** in qualsiasi momento; **on ~** puntualmente; **to be 30 minutes behind/ahead of ~** avere 30 minuti di ritardo/anticipo; **by the ~ he arrived** quando è arrivato; **5 times 5** 5 volte 5, 5 per 5; **what ~ is it?** che ora è?, che ore sono?; **what ~ do you make it?** che ora fa?; **to have a good ~** divertirsi; **they had a hard ~ of it** è stato duro per loro; **~'s up!** è (l')ora!; **to be behind the times** vivere nel passato; **I've no ~ for it** (*fig*) non ho tempo da perdere con cose del genere; **he'll do it in his own (good) ~** (*without being hurried*) lo farà quando avrà (un minuto di) tempo; **he'll do it in** or (US) **on his own ~** (*out of working hours*) lo farà nel suo tempo libero; **the bomb was timed to explode 5 minutes later** la bomba era stata regolata in modo da esplodere 5 minuti più tardi

time-and-motion study ['taɪmənd'məʊʃən-] N analisi *f inv* dei tempi e dei movimenti

time bomb N bomba a orologeria

time card N cartellino (da timbrare)

time clock N orologio *m* marcatempo *inv*

time-consuming ['taɪmkənsju:mɪŋ] ADJ che richiede molto tempo

time difference N differenza di fuso orario

time frame N tempi *mpl*

time-honoured, (US) **time-honored** ['taɪmɒnəd] ADJ consacrato(-a) dal tempo

timekeeper ['taɪmki:pər] N (*Sport*) cronometrista *mf*

time lag N intervallo, ritardo; (*in travel*) differenza di fuso orario

timeless ['taɪmlɪs] ADJ eterno(-a)

time limit N limite *m* di tempo

timely ['taɪmlɪ] ADJ opportuno(-a)

time off N tempo libero

timer ['taɪmər] N (*in kitchen*) contaminuti *m inv*; (*Tech: time switch*) timer *m inv*, temporizzatore *m*

time-saving ['taɪmseɪvɪŋ] ADJ che fa risparmiare tempo

time scale N tempi *mpl* d'esecuzione

time-share ADJ: **~ apartment/villa** appartamento/villa in multiproprietà

time-sharing ['taɪmʃɛərɪŋ] N (*Comput*) divisione *f* di tempo

time sheet N = **time card**

time signal N segnale *m* orario

time switch N interruttore *m* a tempo

timetable ['taɪmteɪbl] N orario; (*programme of events etc*) programma *m*

time zone N fuso orario

timid ['tɪmɪd] ADJ timido(-a); (*easily scared*) pauroso(-a)

timidity [tɪ'mɪdɪtɪ] N timidezza

timing ['taɪmɪŋ] N sincronizzazione *f*; (*fig*) scelta del momento opportuno, tempismo; (*Sport*) cronometraggio

timing device N (*on bomb*) timer *m inv*

timpani ['tɪmpənɪ] NPL timpani *mpl*

tin [tɪn] N stagno; (*also*: **tin plate**) latta; (BRIT: *can*) barattolo (di latta), lattina; (*container*) scatola; (*for baking*) teglia; **a ~ of paint** un barattolo di tinta *or* vernice

tin foil N stagnola

tinge [tɪndʒ] N sfumatura ▶ VT: **tinged with** tinto(-a) di

t

tingle ['tɪŋgl] vɪ (*cheeks, skin: from cold*)
pungere, pizzicare; (: *from bad circulation*)
formicolare

tinker ['tɪŋkər] n stagnino ambulante; (*gipsy*)
zingaro(-a)
  ▶ **tinker with** vт fus armeggiare intorno a;
  cercare di riparare

tinkle ['tɪŋkl] vɪ tintinnare ▶ n (*col*): **to give
sb a ~** dare un colpo di telefono a qn

tin mine n miniera di stagno

tinned [tɪnd] adj (BRIT: *food*) in scatola

tinnitus [tɪ'naɪtəs] n (*Med*) ronzio auricolare

tinny ['tɪnɪ] adj metallico(-a)

tin-opener ['tɪnəupnər] n (BRIT) apriscatole
m inv

tinsel ['tɪnsl] n decorazioni *fpl* natalizie
(*argentate*)

tint [tɪnt] n tinta; (*for hair*) shampoo *m inv*
colorante ▶ vт (*hair*) fare uno shampoo
colorante a

tinted ['tɪntɪd] adj (*hair*) tinto(-a); (*spectacles,
glass*) colorato(-a)

tiny ['taɪnɪ] adj minuscolo(-a)

tip [tɪp] n (*end*) punta; (*protective: on umbrella
etc*) puntale *m*; (*gratuity*) mancia; (*for coal*)
discarica; (BRIT: *for rubbish*) immondezzaio;
(*advice*) suggerimento ▶ vт (*waiter*) dare la
mancia a; (*tilt*) inclinare; (*overturn: also*: **tip
over**) capovolgere; (*empty: also*: **tip out**)
scaricare; (*predict: winner*) pronosticare;
(: *horse*) dare vincente; **he tipped out the
contents of the box** ha rovesciato il
contenuto della scatola
  ▶ **tip off** vт fare una soffiata a

tip-off ['tɪpɔf] n (*hint*) soffiata

tipped [tɪpt] adj (BRIT: *cigarette*) col filtro;
steel-~ con la punta d'acciaio

Tipp-Ex® ['tɪpɛks] n (BRIT) liquido correttore

tipple ['tɪpl] (BRIT) vɪ sbevazzare ▶ n: **to have
a ~** prendere un bicchierino

tipster ['tɪpstər] n (*Racing*) chi vende informazioni
sulle corse e altre manifestazioni oggetto di

tipsy ['tɪpsɪ] adj brillo(-a)

tiptoe ['tɪptəu] n: **on ~** in punta di piedi

tiptop ['tɪptɔp] adj: **in ~ condition** in ottime
condizioni

tirade [taɪ'reɪd] n filippica

tire ['taɪər] vт stancare ▶ vɪ stancarsi ▶ n (US)
= tyre
  ▶ **tire out** vт sfinire, spossare

tired ['taɪəd] adj stanco(-a); **to be/feel/look ~**
essere/sentirsi/sembrare stanco; **to be ~ of**
essere stanco *or* stufo di

tiredness ['taɪədnɪs] n stanchezza

tireless ['taɪəlɪs] adj instancabile

tire pressure n (US) **= tyre pressure**

tiresome ['taɪəsəm] adj noioso(-a)

tiring ['taɪərɪŋ] adj faticoso(-a)

tissue ['tɪʃuː] n tessuto; (*paper handkerchief*)
fazzoletto di carta

tissue paper n carta velina

tit [tɪt] n (*bird*) cinciallegra; (*col: breast*) tetta;
to give ~ for tat rendere pan per focaccia

titanium [tɪ'teɪnɪəm] n titanio

titbit ['tɪtbɪt], (US) **tidbit** ['tɪdbɪt] n (*food*)
leccornia; (*news*) notizia, ghiotta

titillate ['tɪtɪleɪt] vт titillare

titivate ['tɪtɪveɪt] vт agghindare

title ['taɪtl] n titolo; (*Law: right*): **~ (to)**
diritto (a)

title deed n (*Law*) titolo di proprietà

title page n frontespizio

title role n ruolo *or* parte *f* principale

titter ['tɪtər] vɪ ridere scioccamente

tittle-tattle ['tɪtltætl] n chiacchiere *fpl*,
pettegolezzi *mpl*

titular ['tɪtjulər] adj (*in name only*) nominale

tizzy ['tɪzɪ] n (*col*): **to be in a ~** essere in
agitazione

T-junction ['tiː'dʒʌŋkʃən] n incrocio a T

TM n abbr (= *transcendental meditation*) M.T. *f*;
(*Comm*) **= trademark**

TN abbr (US) **= Tennessee**

TNT n abbr (= *trinitrotoluene*) T.N.T. *m*

(KEYWORD)

to [tuː, tə] prep **1** (*direction*) a; **to go to
France/London/school** andare in Francia/a
Londra/a scuola; **to go to town** andare in
città; **to go to Paul's/the doctor's** andare
da Paul/dal dottore; **the road to Edinburgh**
la strada per Edimburgo; **to the left/right** a
sinistra/destra

2 (*as far as*) (fino) a; **from here to London** da
qui a Londra; **to count to 10** contare fino a
10; **from 40 to 50 people** da 40 a 50 persone

3 (*with expressions of time*): **a quarter to 5** le 5
meno un quarto; **it's twenty to 3** sono le 3
meno venti

4 (*for, of*): **the key to the front door** la chiave
della porta d'ingresso; **a letter to his wife**
una lettera per la moglie

5 (*expressing indirect object*) a; **to give sth to sb**
dare qc a qn; **give it to me** dammelo; **to
talk to sb** parlare a qn; **it belongs to him**
gli appartiene, è suo; **to be a danger to sb/
sth** rappresentare un pericolo per qn/qc

6 (*in relation to*) a; **3 goals to 2** 3 goal a 2; **30
miles to the gallon** ≈ 11 chilometri con un
litro; **4 apples to the kilo** 4 mele in un chilo

7 (*purpose: result*): **to come to sb's aid** venire
in aiuto a qn; **to sentence sb to death**
condannare a morte qn; **to my surprise** con
mia sorpresa
  ▶ with vb **1** (*simple infinitive*): **to go/eat** etc
  andare/mangiare etc

2 (*following another vb*): **to want/try/start to
do** volere/cercare di/cominciare a fare

3 (*with vb omitted*): **I don't want to** non voglio (farlo); **you ought to** devi (farlo)
4 (*purpose, result*) per; **I did it to help you** l'ho fatto per aiutarti
5 (*equivalent to relative clause*): **I have things to do** ho da fare; **the main thing is to try** la cosa più importante è provare
6 (*after adjective etc*): **ready to go** pronto(-a) a partire; **too old/young to ...** troppo vecchio(-a)/giovane per ...
▶ ADV: **to push the door to** accostare la porta; **to go to and fro** andare e tornare

toad [təud] N rospo
toadstool ['təudstu:l] N fungo (velenoso)
toady ['təudɪ] VI adulare
toast [təust] N (*Culin*) pane m tostato; (*drink, speech*) brindisi m inv ▶ VT (*Culin*) tostare; (*drink to*) brindare a; **a piece** *or* **slice of ~** una fetta di pane tostato
toaster ['təustəʳ] N tostapane m inv
toastmaster ['təustmɑːstəʳ] N direttore m dei brindisi
toast rack N portatoast m inv
tobacco [tə'bækəu] N tabacco; **pipe ~** tabacco da pipa
tobacconist [tə'bækənɪst] N tabaccaio(-a); **~'s (shop)** tabaccheria
Tobago [tə'beɪgəu] N *see* **Trinidad and Tobago**
toboggan [tə'bɔgən] N toboga m inv; (*child's*) slitta
today [tə'deɪ] ADV, N (*also fig*) oggi m inv; **what day is it ~?** che giorno è oggi?; **what date is it ~?** quanti ne abbiamo oggi?; **~ is the 4th of March** (oggi) è il 4 di marzo; **~'s paper** il giornale di oggi; **a fortnight ~** quindici giorni a oggi
toddler ['tɔdləʳ] N bambino(-a) che impara a camminare
toddy ['tɔdɪ] N grog m inv
to-do [tə'du:] N (*fuss*) storie fpl
toe [təu] N dito del piede; (*of shoe*) punta ▶ VT: **to ~ the line** (*fig*) stare in riga, conformarsi; **big ~** alluce m; **little ~** mignolino
TOEFL ['təufl] N ABBR = **Test(ing) of English as a Foreign Language**
toehold ['təuhəuld] N punto d'appoggio
toenail ['təuneɪl] N unghia del piede
toffee ['tɔfɪ] N caramella
toffee apple N (*BRIT*) mela caramellata
tofu ['təufu:] N tofu m (*latte di soia non fermentato*)
toga ['təugə] N toga
together [tə'gɛðəʳ] ADV insieme; (*at same time*) allo stesso tempo; **~ with** insieme a
togetherness [tə'gɛðənɪs] N solidarietà; intimità
toggle switch ['tɔgl-] N (*Comput*) tasto bistabile

Togo ['təugəu] N Togo
togs [tɔgz] NPL (*col: clothes*) vestiti mpl
toil [tɔɪl] N travaglio, fatica ▶ VI affannarsi; sgobbare
toilet ['tɔɪlət] N (*BRIT: lavatory*) gabinetto ▶ CPD (*soap etc*) da toletta; **to go to the ~** andare al gabinetto *or* al bagno
toilet bag N (*BRIT*) nécessaire m inv da toilette
toilet bowl N vaso *or* tazza del gabinetto
toilet paper N carta igienica
toiletries ['tɔɪlɪtrɪz] NPL articoli mpl da toletta
toilet roll N rotolo di carta igienica
toilet water N acqua di colonia
to-ing and fro-ing ['tu:ɪŋən'frəuɪŋ] N (*BRIT*) andirivieni m inv
token ['təukən] N (*sign*) segno; (*voucher*) buono ▶ CPD (*fee, strike*) simbolico(-a); (*substitute coin*) gettone m; **book/record/gift ~** (*BRIT*) buono-libro/-disco/-regalo; **by the same ~** (*fig*) per lo stesso motivo
tokenism ['təukənɪzəm] N (*Pol*) concessione f pro forma inv
Tokyo ['təukjəu] N Tokyo f
told [təuld] PT, PP *of* **tell**
tolerable ['tɔlərəbl] ADJ (*bearable*) tollerabile; (*fairly good*) passabile
tolerably ['tɔlərəblɪ] ADV (*good, comfortable*) abbastanza
tolerance ['tɔlərns] N (*also Tech*) tolleranza
tolerant ['tɔlərnt] ADJ: **~ (of)** tollerante (nei confronti di)
tolerate ['tɔləreɪt] VT sopportare; (*Med, Tech*) tollerare
toleration [tɔlə'reɪʃən] N tolleranza
toll [təul] N (*tax, charge*) pedaggio ▶ VI (*bell*) suonare; **the accident ~ on the roads** il numero delle vittime della strada
tollbridge ['təulbrɪdʒ] N ponte m a pedaggio
toll call N (*US Tel*) (telefonata) interurbana
toll-free ['təul'fri:] (*US*) ADJ senza addebito, gratuito(-a) ▶ ADV gratuitamente; **~ number** ≈ numero verde
tomato [tə'mɑːtəu] (*pl* **tomatoes**) N pomodoro
tomato sauce N salsa di pomodoro
tomb [tu:m] N tomba
tombola [tɔm'bəulə] N tombola
tomboy ['tɔmbɔɪ] N maschiaccio
tombstone ['tu:mstəun] N pietra tombale
tomcat ['tɔmkæt] N gatto
tomorrow [tə'mɔrəu] ADV, N (*also fig*) domani m inv; **the day after ~** dopodomani; **a week ~** domani a otto; **~ morning** domani mattina
ton [tʌn] N tonnellata (*Brit* = 1016 kg; 20 cwt; *US* = 907 kg; *metric* = 1000 kg); (*Naut: also*: **register ton**) tonnellata di stazza (= 2.83 cu.m; 100 cu.ft); **tons of** (*col*) un mucchio *or* sacco di
tonal ['təunl] ADJ tonale

t

tone [təun] N tono; (of musical instrument) timbro ▶ VI (also: **tone in**) intonarsi
▶ **tone down** VT (colour, criticism, sound) attenuare
▶ **tone up** VT (muscles) tonificare

tone-deaf [təun'dɛf] ADJ che non ha orecchio (musicale)

toner ['təunər] N (for photocopier) colorante m organico, toner m

Tonga ['tɔŋgə] N isole fpl Tonga

tongs [tɔŋz] NPL tenaglie fpl; (for coal) molle fpl; (for hair) arricciacapelli m inv

tongue [tʌŋ] N lingua; ~ **in cheek** (fig: say, speak) ironicamente

tongue-tied ['tʌŋtaɪd] ADJ (fig) muto(-a)

tongue-twister ['tʌŋtwɪstər] N scioglilingua m inv

tonic ['tɔnɪk] N (Med) ricostituente m; (skin tonic) tonico; (Mus) nota tonica; (also: **tonic water**) acqua tonica

tonight [tə'naɪt] ADV stanotte; (this evening) stasera ▶ N questa notte; questa sera; **I'll see you ~** ci vediamo stasera

tonnage ['tʌnɪdʒ] N (Naut) tonnellaggio, stazza

tonne [tʌn] N (BRIT: metric ton) tonnellata

tonsil ['tɔnsl] N tonsilla; **to have one's tonsils out** farsi operare di tonsille

tonsillitis [tɔnsɪ'laɪtɪs] N tonsillite f; **to have ~** avere la tonsillite

too [tu:] ADV (excessively) troppo; (also) anche; **it's ~ sweet** è troppo dolce; **I went ~** ci sono andato anch'io; **~ much** adv troppo; adj troppo(-a); **~ many** adj troppi(-e); **~ bad!** tanto peggio!; peggio così!

took [tuk] PT of **take**

tool [tu:l] N utensile m, attrezzo; (fig: person) strumento ▶ VT lavorare con un attrezzo

tool box N cassetta f portautensili inv

tool kit N cassetta di attrezzi

toot [tu:t] VI suonare; (with car horn) suonare il clacson

tooth [tu:θ] (pl **teeth** [ti:θ]) N (Anat, Tech) dente m; **to clean one's teeth** lavarsi i denti; **to have a ~ out** or (US) **pulled** farsi togliere un dente; **by the skin of one's teeth** per il rotto della cuffia

toothache ['tu:θeɪk] N mal m di denti; **to have ~** avere il mal di denti

toothbrush N spazzolino da denti

tooth fairy N: **the ~** fatina che porta soldini in regalo a un bimbo quando perde un dentino di latte, ≈ topolino

toothpaste ['tu:θpeɪst] N dentifricio

toothpick ['tu:θpɪk] N stuzzicadenti m inv

tooth powder N dentifricio in polvere

top [tɔp] N (of mountain, page, ladder) cima f; (of box, cupboard, table) sopra m inv, parte f superiore; (lid: of box, jar) coperchio; (: of bottle) tappo; (toy) trottola; (Dress: blouse etc) camicia (or maglietta etc); (of pyjamas) giacca ▶ ADJ più alto(-a); (in rank) primo(-a); (best) migliore
▶ VT (exceed) superare; (be first in) essere in testa a; **on ~ of** sopra, in cima a; (in addition to) oltre a; **from ~ to toe** (BRIT) dalla testa ai piedi; **from ~ to bottom** da cima a fondo; **at the ~ of the stairs/page/street** in cima alle scale/alla pagina/alla strada; **the ~ of the milk** (BRIT) la panna; **at ~ speed** a tutta velocità; **at the ~ of one's voice** (fig) a squarciagola; **over the ~** (col: behaviour etc) eccessivo(-a); **to go over the ~** esagerare
▶ **top up**, (US) **top off** VT riempire; (salary) integrare

topaz ['təupæz] N topazio

top-class ['tɔp'klɑ:s] ADJ di prim'ordine

topcoat ['tɔpkəut] N soprabito

topflight ['tɔpflaɪt] ADJ di primaria importanza

top floor N ultimo piano

top hat N cilindro

top-heavy [tɔp'hɛvɪ] ADJ (object) con la parte superiore troppo pesante

topic ['tɔpɪk] N argomento

topical ['tɔpɪkəl] ADJ d'attualità

topless ['tɔplɪs] ADJ (bather etc) col seno scoperto; **~ swimsuit** topless m inv

top-level ['tɔplɛvl] ADJ (talks) ad alto livello

topmost ['tɔpməust] ADJ il(la) più alto(-a)

top-notch ['tɔp'nɔtʃ] ADJ (col: player, performer) di razza; (: school, car) eccellente

topography [tə'pɔgrəfɪ] N topografia

topping ['tɔpɪŋ] N (Culin) guarnizione f

topple ['tɔpl] VT rovesciare, far cadere ▶ VI cadere; traballare

top-ranking ['tɔp'ræŋkɪŋ] ADJ di massimo grado

top-secret ['tɔp'si:krɪt] ADJ segretissimo(-a)

top-security ['tɔpsɪ'kjuərɪtɪ] ADJ (BRIT) di massima sicurezza

topsy-turvy ['tɔpsɪ'tə:vɪ] ADJ, ADV sottosopra inv

top-up ['tɔpʌp] N (for mobile phone: also: **top-up card**) ricarica; **would you like a ~?** vuole che le riempia il bicchiere (or la tazza etc)?

top-up loan N (BRIT) prestito integrativo

torch [tɔ:tʃ] N torcia; (BRIT: electric) lampadina tascabile

tore [tɔ:r] PT of **tear²**

torment N ['tɔ:mɛnt] tormento ▶ VT [tɔ:'mɛnt] tormentare; (fig: annoy) infastidire

torn [tɔ:n] PP of **tear²** ▶ ADJ: **~ between** (fig) combattuto(-a) tra

tornado [tɔ:'neɪdəu] (pl **tornadoes**) N tornado

torpedo [tɔ:'pi:dəu] (pl **torpedoes**) N siluro

torpedo boat N motosilurante f

torpor ['tɔ:pər] N torpore m

torrent ['tɔrnt] N torrente m
torrential [tɔ'rɛnʃl] ADJ torrenziale
torrid ['tɔrɪd] ADJ torrido(-a); (fig) denso(-a) di passione
torso ['tɔ:səu] N torso
tortoise ['tɔ:təs] N tartaruga
tortoiseshell ['tɔ:təʃɛl] ADJ di tartaruga
tortuous ['tɔ:tjuəs] ADJ tortuoso(-a)
torture ['tɔ:tʃər] N tortura ▶ VT torturare
torturer ['tɔ:tʃərər] N torturatore(-trice)
Tory ['tɔ:rɪ] ADJ, N (BRIT Pol) tory mf, conservatore(-trice)
toss [tɔs] VT gettare, lanciare; (BRIT: pancake) far saltare; (head) scuotere ▶ N (movement, of head etc) movimento brusco; (of coin) lancio; **to win/lose the ~** vincere/perdere a testa o croce; (Sport) vincere/perdere il sorteggio; **to ~ a coin** fare a testa o croce; **to ~ up for sth** fare a testa o croce per qc; **to ~ and turn** (in bed) girarsi e rigirarsi
tot [tɔt] N (BRIT: drink) bicchierino; (child) bimbo(-a)
▶ **tot up** VT (BRIT: figures) sommare
total ['təutl] ADJ totale ▶ N totale m ▶ VT (add up) sommare; (amount to) ammontare a; **in ~** in tutto
totalitarian [təutælɪ'tɛərɪən] ADJ totalitario(-a)
totality [təu'tælɪtɪ] N totalità
totally ['təutəlɪ] ADV completamente
tote bag ['təut-] N sporta
totem pole ['təutəm-] N totem m inv
totter ['tɔtər] VI barcollare; (object, government) vacillare
touch [tʌtʃ] N tocco; (sense) tatto; (contact) contatto; (Football) fuori gioco m ▶ VT toccare; **a ~ of** (fig) un tocco di; un pizzico di; **to get in ~ with** mettersi in contatto con; **to lose ~** (friends) perdersi di vista; **I'll be in ~** mi farò sentire; **to be out of ~ with events** essere tagliato fuori; **the personal ~** una nota personale; **to put the finishing touches to sth** dare gli ultimi ritocchi a qc
▶ **touch down** VI (on land) atterrare
▶ **touch on** VT FUS (topic) sfiorare, accennare a
▶ **touch up** VT (improve) ritoccare
touch-and-go ['tʌtʃən'gəu] ADJ incerto(-a); **it was ~ with the sick man** il malato era tra la vita e la morte
touchdown ['tʌtʃdaun] N atterraggio; (on sea) ammaraggio; (US Football) meta
touched [tʌtʃt] ADJ commosso(-a); (col) tocco(-a), toccato(-a)
touching ['tʌtʃɪŋ] ADJ commovente
touchline ['tʌtʃlaɪn] N (Sport) linea laterale
touch screen N (Tech) schermo touch screen; **touch-screen mobile** telefono touch screen; **touch-screen technology**

tecnologia touch screen
touch-sensitive ['tʌtʃ'sɛnsɪtɪv] ADJ sensibile al tatto
touch-type ['tʌtʃtaɪp] VI dattilografare (senza guardare i tasti)
touchy ['tʌtʃɪ] ADJ (person) suscettibile
tough [tʌf] ADJ duro(-a); (resistant) resistente; (meat) duro(-a), tiglioso(-a); (journey) faticoso(-a), duro(-a); (person: rough) violento(-a), brutale ▶ N (gangster etc) delinquente m/f; **~ luck!** che sfortuna!
toughen ['tʌfn] VT indurire, rendere più resistente
toughness ['tʌfnɪs] N durezza; resistenza
toupee ['tu:peɪ] N parrucchino
tour [tuər] N viaggio; (also: **package tour**) viaggio organizzato or tutto compreso (of town, museum) visita; (by artist) tournée f inv ▶ VT visitare; **to go on a ~ of** (region, country) fare il giro di; (museum, castle) visitare; **to go on ~** andare in tournée
tour guide N guida turistica
touring ['tuərɪŋ] N turismo
tourism ['tuərɪzəm] N turismo
tourist ['tuərɪst] N turista m/f ▶ ADV (travel) in classe turistica ▶ CPD turistico(-a); **the ~ trade** il turismo
tourist class N (Aviat) classe f turistica
tourist office N pro loco f inv
tournament ['tuənəmənt] N torneo
tourniquet ['tuənɪkeɪ] N (Med) laccio emostatico, pinza emostatica
tour operator N (BRIT) operatore m turistico
tousled ['tauzld] ADJ (hair) arruffato(-a)
tout [taut] VI: **to ~ for** procacciare, raccogliere; cercare clienti per ▶ N (BRIT: also: **ticket tout**) bagarino; **to ~ sth (around)** (BRIT) cercare di (ri)vendere qc
tow [təu] VT rimorchiare ▶ N rimorchio; **"on ~"**, (US) **"in ~"** (Aut) "veicolo rimorchiato"; **to give sb a ~** rimorchiare qn
toward [tə'wɔ:d], **towards** [tə'wɔ:dz] PREP verso; (of attitude) nei confronti di; (of purpose) per; **~(s) noon/the end of the year** verso mezzogiorno/la fine dell'anno; **to feel friendly ~(s) sb** provare un sentimento d'amicizia per qn
towel ['tauəl] N asciugamano; (also: **tea towel**) strofinaccio; **to throw in the ~** (fig) gettare la spugna
towelling ['tauəlɪŋ] N (fabric) spugna
towel rail, (US) **towel rack** N portasciugamano
tower ['tauər] N torre f ▶ VI (building, mountain) innalzarsi; **to ~ above or over sb/sth** sovrastare qn/qc
tower block N (BRIT) palazzone m
towering ['tauərɪŋ] ADJ altissimo(-a), imponente

t

towline ['təulaın] N (cavo da) rimorchio
town [taun] N città f inv; **to go to ~** andare in città; (fig) mettercela tutta; **in (the) ~** in città; **to be out of ~** essere fuori città
town centre N centro (città)
town clerk N segretario comunale
town council N consiglio comunale
town crier [-'kraıəʳ] N (BRIT) banditore(-trice)
town hall N ≈ municipio
townie ['taunı] N (BRIT col) uno(-a) di città
town plan N pianta della città
town planner N urbanista mf
town planning N urbanistica
township ['taunʃıp] N township f inv
townspeople ['taunzpiːpl] NPL cittadinanza, cittadini mpl
towpath ['təupɑːθ] N alzaia
towrope ['təurəup] N (cavo da) rimorchio
tow truck N (US) carro m attrezzi inv
toxic ['tɔksık] ADJ tossico(-a)
toxic asset N (Econ) titolo tossico
toxic bank N (Econ) banca cattiva (che investe in titoli tossici)
toxin ['tɔksın] N tossina
toy [tɔı] N giocattolo
▶ **toy with** VT FUS giocare con; (idea) accarezzare, trastullarsi con
toyshop ['tɔıʃɔp] N negozio di giocattoli
trace [treıs] N traccia ▶ VT (draw) tracciare; (follow) seguire; (locate) rintracciare; **without ~** (disappear) senza lasciare traccia; **there was no ~ of it** non ne restava traccia
trace element N oligoelemento
trachea [trə'kıə] N (Anat) trachea
tracing paper ['treısıŋ-] N carta da ricalco
track [træk] N (mark: of person, animal) traccia; (on tape, Sport: path: gen) pista; (: of bullet etc) traiettoria; (: of suspect, animal) pista, tracce fpl; (Rail) binario, rotaie fpl; (Comput) traccia, pista ▶ VT seguire le tracce di; **to keep ~ of** seguire; **to be on the right ~** (fig) essere sulla buona strada
▶ **track down** VT (prey) scovare; snidare; (sth lost) rintracciare
tracker dog ['trækə-] N (BRIT) cane m poliziotto inv
track events NPL (Sport) prove fpl su pista
tracking station ['trækıŋ-] N (Space) osservatorio spaziale
track meet N (US) meeting m inv di atletica
track record N: **to have a good ~** (fig) avere un buon curriculum
tracksuit ['træksuːt] N tuta sportiva
tract [trækt] N (Geo) tratto, estensione f; (pamphlet) opuscolo, libretto; **respiratory ~** (Anat) apparato respiratorio
traction ['trækʃən] N trazione f
tractor ['træktəʳ] N trattore m
trade [treıd] N commercio; (skill, job)

mestiere m; (industry) industria, settore m
▶ VI commerciare; **to ~ with/in** commerciare con/in ▶ VT: **to ~ sth (for sth)** barattare qc (con qc); **foreign ~** commercio estero; **Department of T~ and Industry** (BRIT) ≈ Ministero del Commercio
▶ **trade in** VT (old car etc) dare come pagamento parziale
trade barrier N barriera commerciale
trade deficit N bilancio commerciale in deficit
Trade Descriptions Act N (BRIT) legge f a tutela del consumatore
trade discount N sconto sul listino
trade fair N fiera campionaria
trade-in ['treıdın] N: **to take as a ~** accettare in permuta
trade-in price N prezzo di permuta
trademark ['treıdmɑːk] N marchio di fabbrica
trade mission N missione f commerciale
trade name N marca, nome m depositato
trade-off ['treıdɔf] N compromesso, accomodamento
trader ['treıdəʳ] N commerciante mf
trade secret N segreto di fabbricazione
tradesman ['treıdzmən] N (irreg) fornitore m; (shopkeeper) negoziante m
trade union N sindacato
trade unionist [-'juːnjənıst] N sindacalista mf
trade wind N aliseo
trading ['treıdıŋ] N commercio
trading estate N (BRIT) zona industriale
trading stamp N bollo premio
tradition [trə'dıʃən] N tradizione f; **traditions** NPL tradizioni, usanze fpl
traditional [trə'dıʃənl] ADJ tradizionale
traffic ['træfık] N traffico ▶ VI: **to ~ in** (pej: liquor, drugs) trafficare in
traffic calming [-'kɑːmıŋ] N uso di accorgimenti per rallentare il traffico in zone abitate
traffic circle N (US) isola rotatoria
traffic island N salvagente m, isola f, spartitraffico inv
traffic jam N ingorgo (del traffico)
trafficker ['træfıkəʳ] N trafficante mf
traffic lights NPL semaforo
traffic offence N (BRIT) infrazione f al codice stradale
traffic sign N cartello stradale
traffic violation N (US) = **traffic offence**
traffic warden N addetto(-a) al controllo del traffico e del parcheggio
tragedy ['trædʒədı] N tragedia
tragic ['trædʒık] ADJ tragico(-a)
trail [treıl] N (tracks) tracce fpl, pista; (path) sentiero; (of smoke etc) scia ▶ VT trascinare, strascicare; (follow) seguire ▶ VI essere al traino; (dress etc) strusciare; (plant)

arrampicarsi; strusciare; (*in game*) essere in svantaggio; **to be on sb's** ~ essere sulle orme di qn
▶ **trail away, trail off** VI (*sound*) affievolirsi; (*interest, voice*) spegnersi a poco a poco
▶ **trail behind** VI essere al traino

trailer ['treɪləʳ] N (*Aut*) rimorchio; (*US*) roulotte *f inv*; (*Cine*) prossimamente *m inv*

trailer truck N (*US*) autoarticolato

train [treɪn] N treno; (*of dress*) coda, strascico; (*BRIT: series*): ~ **of events** serie *f* di avvenimenti a catena ▶ VT (*apprentice, doctor etc*) formare; (*sportsman*) allenare; (*dog*) addestrare; (*memory*) esercitare; (*point: gun etc*): **to** ~ **sth on** puntare qc contro ▶ VI formarsi; allenarsi; (*learn a skill*) fare pratica, fare tirocinio; **to go by** ~ andare in *or* col treno; **one's** ~ **of thought** il filo dei propri pensieri; **to** ~ **sb to do sth** preparare qn a fare qc

train attendant N (*US*) addetto(-a) ai vagoni letto

trained [treɪnd] ADJ qualificato(-a); allenato(-a), addestrato(-a)

trainee [treɪ'niː] N allievo(-a); (*in trade*) apprendista *mf*; **he's a** ~ **teacher** sta facendo tirocinio come insegnante

trainer ['treɪnəʳ] N (*Sport*) allenatore(-trice); (*of dogs etc*) addestratore(-trice); **trainers** NPL (*shoes*) scarpe *fpl* da ginnastica

training ['treɪnɪŋ] N formazione *f*; allenamento; addestramento; **in** ~ (*Sport*) in allenamento; (*fit*) in forma

training college N istituto professionale

training course N corso di formazione professionale

training shoes NPL scarpe *fpl* da ginnastica

train wreck N (*fig*) persona distrutta; (: *pej*) rottame *m*; **he's a complete** ~ è completamente distrutto, è un rottame

traipse [treɪps] VI: **to** ~ **in/out** *etc* entrare/uscire *etc* trascinandosi

trait [treɪt] N tratto

traitor ['treɪtəʳ] N traditore(-trice)

trajectory [trə'dʒɛktərɪ] N traiettoria

tram [træm] N (*BRIT: also:* **tramcar**) tram *m inv*

tramline ['træmlaɪn] N linea tranviaria

tramp [træmp] N (*person*) vagabondo(-a); (*col, pej: woman*) sgualdrina ▶ VI camminare con passo pesante ▶ VT (*walk through: town, streets*) percorrere a piedi

trample ['træmpl] VT: **to** ~ **(underfoot)** calpestare

trampoline ['træmpəliːn] N trampolino

trance [trɑːns] N trance *f inv*; (*Med*) catalessi *f inv*; **to go into a** ~ cadere in trance

tranquil ['træŋkwɪl] ADJ tranquillo(-a)

tranquillity, (*US*) **tranquility** [træŋ'kwɪlɪtɪ] N tranquillità

tranquillizer, (*US*) **tranquilizer** ['træŋkwɪlaɪzəʳ] N (*Med*) tranquillante *m*

transact [træn'zækt] VT (*business*) trattare

transaction [træn'zækʃən] N transazione *f*; **transactions** NPL (*minutes*) atti *mpl*; **cash** ~ operazione *f* in contanti

transatlantic ['trænzət'læntɪk] ADJ transatlantico(-a)

transcend [træn'sɛnd] VT trascendere; (*excel over*) superare

transcendental [trænsɛn'dɛntl] ADJ: ~ **meditation** meditazione *f* trascendentale

transcribe [træn'skraɪb] VT trascrivere

transcript ['trænskrɪpt] N trascrizione *f*

transcription [træn'skrɪpʃən] N trascrizione *f*

transept ['trænsɛpt] N transetto

transfer N ['trænsfəʳ] (*gen, also Sport*) trasferimento; (*Pol: of power*) passaggio; (*picture, design*) decalcomania; (: *stick-on*) autoadesivo ▶ VT [træns'fəːʳ] trasferire; passare; decalcare; **by bank** ~ tramite trasferimento bancario; **to** ~ **the charges** (*BRIT Tel*) fare una chiamata a carico del destinatario

transferable [træns'fəːrəbl] ADJ trasferibile; **not** ~ non cedibile, personale

transfix [træns'fɪks] VT trafiggere; (*fig*): **transfixed with fear** paralizzato dalla paura

transform [træns'fɔːm] VT trasformare

transformation [trænsfə'meɪʃən] N trasformazione *f*

transformer [træns'fɔːməʳ] N (*Elec*) trasformatore *m*

transfusion [træns'fjuːʒən] N trasfusione *f*

transgress [træns'grɛs] VT (*go beyond*) infrangere; (*violate*) trasgredire, infrangere

tranship [træn'ʃɪp] VT trasbordare

transient ['trænzɪənt] ADJ transitorio(-a), fugace

transistor [træn'zɪstəʳ] N (*Elec*) transistor *m inv*; (*also:* **transistor radio**) radio *f inv* a transistor

transit ['trænzɪt] N: **in** ~ in transito

transit camp N campo (di raccolta) profughi

transition [træn'zɪʃən] N passaggio, transizione *f*

transitional [træn'zɪʃənl] ADJ di transizione

transitive ['trænzɪtɪv] ADJ (*Ling*) transitivo(-a)

transit lounge N (*Aviat*) sala di transito

transitory ['trænzɪtərɪ] ADJ transitorio(-a)

translate [trænz'leɪt] VT tradurre; **to** ~ **(from/into)** tradurre (da/in)

translation [trænz'leɪʃən] N traduzione *f*; (*Scol: as opposed to prose*) versione *f*

translator [trænz'leɪtəʳ] N traduttore(-trice)

translucent [trænz'luːsnt] ADJ traslucido(-a)

t

transmission [trænz'mıʃən] N trasmissione f
transmit [trænz'mıt] VT trasmettere
transmitter [trænz'mıtər] N trasmettitore m
transparency [træns'pɛərnsɪ] N (Phot)
diapositiva
transparent [træns'pærnt] ADJ trasparente
transpire [træns'paɪər] VI (happen) succedere;
it finally transpired that ... alla fine si è
venuto a sapere che ...
transplant VT [træns'plɑ:nt] trapiantare
▶ N ['trænsplɑ:nt] (Med) trapianto; **to have
a heart ~** subire un trapianto cardiaco
transport N ['trænspɔ:t] trasporto ▶ VT
[træns'pɔ:t] trasportare; **public ~** mezzi mpl
pubblici; **Department of T~** (Brit)
Ministero dei Trasporti
transportation ['trænspɔ:'teɪʃən] N (mezzo
di) trasporto; (of prisoners) deportazione f;
Department of T~ (US) Ministero dei
Trasporti
transport café N (Brit) trattoria per
camionisti
transpose [træns'pəuz] VT trasporre
transsexual [trænz'sɛksjuəl] ADJ, N
transessuale mf
transverse ['trænzvə:s] ADJ trasversale
transvestite [trænz'vɛstaɪt] N travestito(-a)
trap [træp] N (snare, trick) trappola; (carriage)
calesse m ▶ VT prendere in trappola,
intrappolare; (immobilize) bloccare; (jam)
chiudere, schiacciare; **to set** or **lay a ~ (for
sb)** tendere una trappola (a qn); **to ~ one's
finger in the door** chiudersi il dito nella
porta; **shut your ~!** (col) chiudi quella
boccaccia!
trap door N botola
trapeze [trə'pi:z] N trapezio
trapper ['træpər] N cacciatore m di animali
da pelliccia
trappings ['træpɪŋz] NPL ornamenti mpl;
indoratura, sfarzo
trash [træʃ] N (col: goods) ciarpame m;
(: nonsense) sciocchezze fpl; (US: rubbish) rifiuti
mpl, spazzatura
trash can N (US) secchio della spazzatura
trashy ['træʃɪ] ADJ (col) scadente
trauma ['trɔ:mə] N trauma m
traumatic [trɔ:'mætɪk] ADJ (Psych: fig)
traumatico(-a), traumatizzante
travel ['trævl] N viaggio; viaggi mpl ▶ VI
viaggiare; (move) andare, spostarsi ▶ VT
(distance) percorrere; **this wine doesn't ~
well** questo vino non resiste agli
spostamenti
travel agency N agenzia (di) viaggi
travel agent N agente m di viaggio
travel brochure N dépliant m di viaggi
travel insurance N assicurazione f di
viaggio

traveller, (US) **traveler** ['trævlər] N
viaggiatore(-trice); (Comm) commesso
viaggiatore
traveller's cheque, (US) **traveler's check** N
assegno turistico
travelling, (US) **traveling** ['trævlɪŋ] N viaggi
mpl ▶ ADJ (circus, exhibition) itinerante ▶ CPD
(bag, clock) da viaggio; (expenses) di viaggio
travelling salesman, (US) **traveling
salesman** N (irreg) commesso viaggiatore
travelogue ['trævəlɔg] N (book, film) diario or
documentario di viaggio; (talk) conferenza
sui viaggi
travel-sick ADJ: **to get ~** (in vehicle) soffrire di
mal d'auto; (in aeroplane) soffrire di mal
d'aria; (in boat) soffrire di mal di mare
travel sickness N mal m d'auto (or di mare or
d'aria)
traverse ['trævəs] VT traversare, attraversare
travesty ['trævəstɪ] N parodia
trawler ['trɔ:lər] N peschereccio (a strascico)
tray [treɪ] N (for carrying) vassoio; (on desk)
vaschetta
treacherous ['trɛtʃərəs] ADJ infido(-a); **road
conditions today are ~** oggi il fondo
stradale è pericoloso
treachery ['trɛtʃərɪ] N tradimento
treacle ['tri:kl] N melassa
tread [trɛd] (pt **trod**, pp **trodden**) N passo;
(sound) rumore m di passi; (of stairs) pedata;
(of tyre) battistrada m inv ▶ VI camminare
▶ **tread on** VT FUS calpestare
treadle ['trɛdl] N pedale m
treas. ABBR = **treasurer**
treason ['tri:zn] N tradimento
treasure ['trɛʒər] N tesoro ▶ VT (value) tenere
in gran conto, apprezzare molto; (store)
custodire gelosamente
treasure hunt N caccia al tesoro
treasurer ['trɛʒərər] N tesoriere(-a)
treasury ['trɛʒərɪ] N tesoreria; (Pol): **the T~**
(Brit), **the T~ Department** (US) ≈ il
Ministero del Tesoro
treasury bill N buono del tesoro
treat [tri:t] N regalo ▶ VT trattare; (Med)
curare; (consider) considerare; **it was a ~** mi
(or ci etc) ha fatto veramente piacere; **to ~ sb
to sth** offrire qc a qn; **to ~ sth as a joke**
considerare qc uno scherzo
treatise ['tri:tɪz] N trattato
treatment ['tri:tmənt] N trattamento; **to
have ~ for sth** (Med) farsi curare qc
treaty ['tri:tɪ] N patto, trattato
treble ['trɛbl] ADJ triplo(-a), triplice ▶ N (Mus)
soprano mf ▶ VT triplicare ▶ VI triplicarsi
treble clef N chiave f di violino
tree [tri:] N albero
tree-lined ['tri:laɪnd] ADJ fiancheggiato(-a)
da alberi

treetop ['tri:tɔp] N cima di un albero

tree trunk N tronco d'albero

trek [trɛk] N (*hike*) escursione f a piedi; (*in car*) escursione f in macchina; (*tiring walk*) camminata sfiancante ▶ VI (*as holiday*) fare dell'escursionismo

trellis ['trɛlɪs] N graticcio, pergola

tremble ['trɛmbl] VI tremare; (*machine*) vibrare

trembling ['trɛmblɪŋ] N tremito ▶ ADJ tremante

tremendous [trɪ'mɛndəs] ADJ (*enormous*) enorme; (*excellent*) meraviglioso(-a), formidabile

tremendously [trɪ'mɛndəslɪ] ADV incredibilmente; **he enjoyed it** ~ gli è piaciuto da morire

tremor ['trɛmə'] N tremore m, tremito; (*also:* **earth tremor**) scossa sismica

trench [trɛntʃ] N trincea

trench coat N trench m inv

trench warfare N guerra di trincea

trend [trɛnd] N (*tendency*) tendenza; (*of events*) corso; (*fashion*) moda; ~ **towards/away from** tendenza a/ad allontanarsi da; **to set the** ~ essere all'avanguardia; **to set a** ~ lanciare una moda

trendy ['trɛndɪ] ADJ (*idea*) di moda; (*clothes*) all'ultima moda

trepidation [trɛpɪ'deɪʃən] N trepidazione f, agitazione f

trespass ['trɛspəs] VI: **to** ~ **on** entrare abusivamente in; (*fig*) abusare di; **"no trespassing"** "proprietà privata", "vietato l'accesso"

trespasser ['trɛspəsə'] N trasgressore m; **"trespassers will be prosecuted"** "i trasgressori saranno puniti secondo i termini di legge"

trestle ['trɛsl] N cavalletto

trestle table N tavola su cavalletti

trial ['traɪəl] N (*Law*) processo; (*test: of machine etc*) collaudo; (*hardship*) prova, difficoltà f inv; (*worry*) cruccio; **trials** NPL (*Athletics*) prove fpl di qualificazione; **horse trials** concorso ippico; **to be on** ~ (*Law*) essere sotto processo; ~ **by jury** processo penale con giuria; **to be sent for** ~ essere rinviato a giudizio; **to bring sb to** ~ (**for a crime**) portare qn in giudizio (per un reato); **by** ~ **and error** a tentoni

trial balance N (*Comm*) bilancio di verifica

trial basis N: **on a** ~ in prova

trial period N periodo di prova

trial run N periodo di prova

triangle ['traɪæŋgl] N (*Math, Mus*) triangolo

triangular [traɪ'æŋgjulə'] ADJ triangolare

triathlon [traɪ'æθlən] N triathlon m inv

tribal ['traɪbəl] ADJ tribale

tribe [traɪb] N tribù f inv

tribesman ['traɪbzmən] N (*irreg*) membro della tribù

tribulation [trɪbju'leɪʃən] N tribolazione f

tribunal [traɪ'bju:nl] N tribunale m

tributary ['trɪbju:tərɪ] N (*river*) tributario, affluente m

tribute ['trɪbju:t] N tributo, omaggio; **to pay** ~ **to** rendere omaggio a

trice [traɪs] N: **in a** ~ in un attimo

trick [trɪk] N trucco; (*clever act*) stratagemma m; (*joke*) tiro; (*Cards*) presa ▶ VT imbrogliare, ingannare; **to play a** ~ **on sb** giocare un tiro a qn; **it's a** ~ **of the light** è un effetto ottico; **that should do the** ~ (*col*) vedrai che funziona; **to** ~ **sb into doing sth** convincere qn a fare qc con l'inganno; **to** ~ **sb out of sth** fregare qc a qn

trickery ['trɪkərɪ] N inganno

trickle ['trɪkl] N (*of water etc*) rivolo; gocciolio ▶ VI gocciolare; **to** ~ **in/out** (*people*) entrare/uscire alla spicciolata

trick question N domanda f trabocchetto inv

trickster ['trɪkstə'] N imbroglione(-a)

tricky ['trɪkɪ] ADJ difficile, delicato(-a)

tricycle ['traɪsɪkl] N triciclo

trifle ['traɪfl] N sciocchezza; (*Brit Culin*) ≈ zuppa inglese ▶ ADV: **a** ~ **long** un po' lungo ▶ VI: **to** ~ **with** prendere alla leggera

trifling ['traɪflɪŋ] ADJ insignificante

trigger ['trɪgə'] N (*of gun*) grilletto ▶ **trigger off** VT dare l'avvio a

trigonometry [trɪgə'nɔmətrɪ] N trigonometria

trilby ['trɪlbɪ] N (*Brit: also:* **trilby hat**) cappello floscio di feltro

trill [trɪl] N (*of bird, Mus*) trillo

trilogy ['trɪlədʒɪ] N trilogia

trim [trɪm] ADJ ordinato(-a); (*house, garden*) ben tenuto(-a); (*figure*) snello(-a) ▶ N (*haircut etc*) spuntata, regolata; (*embellishment*) finiture fpl; (*on car*) guarnizioni fpl ▶ VT spuntare; (*Naut: a sail*) orientare; (*decorate*): **to** ~ (**with**) decorare (con); **to keep in (good)** ~ mantenersi in forma

trimmings ['trɪmɪŋz] NPL decorazioni fpl; (*extras: gen: Culin*) guarnizione f

Trinidad and Tobago ['trɪnɪdæd-] N Trinidad e Tobago m

Trinity ['trɪnɪtɪ] N: **the** ~ la Trinità

trinket ['trɪŋkɪt] N gingillo; (*piece of jewellery*) ciondolo

trio ['tri:əu] N trio

trip [trɪp] N viaggio; (*excursion*) gita, escursione f; (*stumble*) passo falso ▶ VI inciampare; (*go lightly*) camminare con passo leggero; **on a** ~ in viaggio ▶ **trip up** VI inciampare ▶ VT fare lo sgambetto a

t

tripartite [traɪˈpɑːtaɪt] ADJ (agreement) tripartito(-a); (talks) a tre

tripe [traɪp] N (Culin) trippa; (pej: rubbish) sciocchezze fpl, fesserie fpl

triple [ˈtrɪpl] ADJ triplo(-a) ▶ ADV: ~ **the distance/the speed** tre volte più lontano/ più veloce

triple jump N triplo salto

triplets [ˈtrɪplɪts] NPL bambini(-e) trigemini(-e)

triplicate [ˈtrɪplɪkət] N: **in** ~ in triplice copia

tripod [ˈtraɪpɔd] N treppiede m

Tripoli [ˈtrɪpəlɪ] N Tripoli f

tripper [ˈtrɪpəʳ] N (BRIT) gitante mf

tripwire [ˈtrɪpwaɪəʳ] N filo in tensione che fa scattare una trappola, allarme ecc

trite [traɪt] ADJ banale, trito(-a)

triumph [ˈtraɪʌmf] N trionfo ▶ VI: **to** ~ **(over)** trionfare (su)

triumphal [traɪˈʌmfl] ADJ trionfale

triumphant [traɪˈʌmfənt] ADJ trionfante

trivia [ˈtrɪvɪə] NPL banalità fpl

trivial [ˈtrɪvɪəl] ADJ insignificante; (matter) futile; (excuse, comment) banale; (amount) irrisorio(-a); (mistake) di poco conto

triviality [trɪvɪˈælɪtɪ] N frivolezza; (trivial detail) futilità

trivialize [ˈtrɪvɪəlaɪz] VT sminuire

trod [trɔd] PT of **tread**

trodden [ˈtrɔdn] PP of **tread**

troll [trɔl] N (also Comput) troll m inv

trolley [ˈtrɔlɪ] N carrello; (in hospital) lettiga

trolley bus N filobus m inv

trollop [ˈtrɔləp] N prostituta

trombone [trɔmˈbəun] N trombone m

troop [truːp] N gruppo; (Mil) squadrone m; **troops** NPL (Mil) truppe fpl; **trooping the colour** (BRIT: ceremony) sfilata della bandiera ▶ **troop in** VI entrare a frotte ▶ **troop out** VI uscire a frotte

troop carrier N (plane) aereo per il trasporto (di) truppe; (Naut: also: **troopship**) nave f per il trasporto (di) truppe

trooper [ˈtruːpəʳ] N (Mil) soldato di cavalleria; (US: policeman) poliziotto (della polizia di stato)

troopship [ˈtruːpʃɪp] N nave f per il trasporto (di) truppe

trophy [ˈtrəufɪ] N trofeo

tropic [ˈtrɔpɪk] N tropico; **in the tropics** ai tropici; **T~ of Cancer/Capricorn** tropico del Cancro/Capricorno

tropical [ˈtrɔpɪkəl] ADJ tropicale

trot [trɔt] N trotto ▶ VI trottare; **on the** ~ (BRIT fig) di fila, uno(-a) dopo l'altro(-a) ▶ **trot out** VT (excuse, reason) tirar fuori; (names, facts) recitare di fila

trouble [ˈtrʌbl] N difficoltà f inv, problema m; (problems) difficoltà fpl, problemi mpl; (worry) preoccupazione f; (bother, effort) sforzo; (with sth mechanical) noie fpl; (Pol) conflitti mpl, disordine m; (Med): **stomach** etc ~ disturbi mpl gastrici etc ▶ VT disturbare; (worry) preoccupare ▶ VI: **to** ~ **to do** disturbarsi a fare; **troubles** NPL (Pol etc) disordini mpl; **to be in** ~ avere dei problemi; (for doing wrong) essere nei guai; **to go to the** ~ **of doing** darsi la pena di fare; **it's no** ~! di niente!; **what's the** ~? cosa c'è che non va?; **the** ~ **is ...** c'è che ..., il guaio è che ...; **to have** ~ **doing sth** avere delle difficoltà a fare qc; **please don't** ~ **yourself** non si disturbi

troubled [ˈtrʌbld] ADJ (person) preoccupato(-a), inquieto(-a); (epoch, life) agitato(-a), difficile

trouble-free [ˈtrʌblfriː] ADJ senza problemi

troublemaker [ˈtrʌblmeɪkəʳ] N elemento disturbatore, agitatore(-trice); (child) disloco(-a)

troubleshooter [ˈtrʌblʃuːtəʳ] N (in conflict) conciliatore m

troublesome [ˈtrʌblsəm] ADJ fastidioso(-a), seccante

trouble spot N zona calda

troubling [ˈtrʌblɪŋ] ADJ (thought) preoccupante; **these are** ~ **times** questi sono tempi difficili

trough [trɔf] N (also: **drinking trough**) abbeveratoio; (also: **feeding trough**) trogolo, mangiatoia; (: channel) canale m; ~ **of low pressure** (Meteor) depressione f

trounce [trauns] VT (defeat) sgominare

troupe [truːp] N troupe f inv

trouser press N stirapantaloni m inv

trousers [ˈtrauzəz] NPL pantaloni mpl, calzoni mpl; **short** ~ (BRIT) calzoncini mpl

trouser suit N (BRIT) completo m or tailleur m inv pantalone inv

trousseau [ˈtruːsəu] N (pl **trousseaux** or **trousseaus** [-z]) N corredo da sposa

trout [traut] N (pl inv) trota

trowel [ˈtrauəl] N cazzuola

truant [ˈtruːənt] N: **to play** ~ (BRIT) marinare la scuola

truce [truːs] N tregua

truck [trʌk] N autocarro, camion m inv; (Rail) carro merci aperto; (for luggage) carrello m portabagagli inv

truck driver, (US) **trucker** [ˈtrʌkəʳ] N camionista mf

truck farm N (US) orto industriale

trucking [ˈtrʌkɪŋ] N (esp US) autotrasporto

trucking company N (esp US) impresa di trasporti

truculent [ˈtrʌkjulənt] ADJ aggressivo(-a), brutale

trudge [trʌdʒ] VI trascinarsi pesantemente

true [truː] ADJ vero(-a); (accurate) accurato(-a),

esatto(-a); (*genuine*) reale; (*faithful*) fedele; (*wall, beam*) a piombo; (*wheel*) centrato(-a); **to come ~** avverarsi; **~ to life** verosimile

truffle ['trʌfl] N tartufo

truly ['tru:lɪ] ADV veramente; (*truthfully*) sinceramente; (*faithfully*) fedelmente; **yours ~** (*in letter-writing*) distinti saluti

trump [trʌmp] N (*Cards*) atout *m inv*; **to turn up trumps** (*fig*) fare miracoli

trump card N atout *m inv*; (*fig*) asso nella manica

trumped-up ['trʌmpt'ʌp] ADJ inventato(-a)

trumpet ['trʌmpɪt] N tromba

truncated [trʌŋ'keɪtɪd] ADJ tronco(-a)

truncheon ['trʌntʃən] N sfollagente *m inv*

trundle ['trʌndl] VT, VI: **to ~ along** rotolare rumorosamente

trunk [trʌŋk] N (*of tree, person*) tronco; (*of elephant*) proboscide *f*; (*case*) baule *m*; (*US Aut*) bagagliaio

trunk call N (*Brit Tel*) (telefonata) interurbana

trunk road N (*Brit*) strada principale

trunks [trʌŋks] NPL (*also:* **swimming trunks**) calzoncini *mpl* da bagno

truss [trʌs] N (*Med*) cinto erniario ▶ VT: **to ~ (up)** (*Culin*) legare

trust [trʌst] N fiducia; (*Law*) amministrazione *f* fiduciaria; (*Comm*) trust *m inv* ▶ VT (*have confidence in*) fidarsi di; (*rely on*) contare su; (*entrust*): **to ~ sth to sb** affidare qc a qn; (*hope*): **to ~ (that)** sperare (che); **you'll have to take it on ~** deve credermi sulla parola; **in ~** (*Law*) in amministrazione fiduciaria

trust company N trust *m inv*

trusted ['trʌstɪd] ADJ fidato(-a)

trustee [trʌs'tiː] N (*Law*) amministratore(-a) fiduciario(-a); (*of school etc*) amministratore(-trice)

trustful ['trʌstful] ADJ fiducioso(-a)

trust fund N fondo fiduciario

trusting ['trʌstɪŋ] ADJ = **trustful**

trustworthy ['trʌstwəːðɪ] ADJ fidato(-a), degno(-a) di fiducia

trusty ['trʌstɪ] ADJ fidato(-a)

truth [truːθ] N (*pl* **truths** [truːðz]) N verità *f inv*

truthful ['truːθful] ADJ (*person*) sincero(-a); (*description*) veritiero(-a), esatto(-a)

truthfully ['truːθəlɪ] ADV sinceramente

truthfulness ['truːθəlnɪs] N veracità

try [traɪ] N prova, tentativo; (*Rugby*) meta ▶ VT (*Law*) giudicare; (*test: also:* **try out:** *sth new*) provare; (*strain: patience, person*) mettere alla prova ▶ VI provare; **to have a ~** fare un tentativo; **to ~ to do** provare a fare; (*seek*) cercare di fare; **to give sth a ~** provare qc; **to ~ one's (very) best** *or* **one's (very) hardest** mettercela tutta

▶ **try on** VT (*clothes*) provare, mettere alla prova; **to ~ it on** (*fig*) cercare di farla

▶ **try out** VT provare, mettere alla prova

trying ['traɪɪŋ] ADJ (*day, experience*) logorante, pesante; (*child*) difficile, insopportabile

tsar [zɑːʳ] N zar *m inv*

T-shirt ['tiːʃəːt] N maglietta

TSO N ABBR (*Brit*: = *The Stationery Office*) ≈ Poligrafici *mpl* dello Stato

T-square ['tiːskwɛəʳ] N riga a T

tsunami [tsuˈnɑːmɪ] N tsunami *m inv*

TT ADJ ABBR (*Brit col*) = **teetotal** ▶ ABBR (*US*) = **Trust Territory**

tub [tʌb] N tinozza; mastello; (*bath*) bagno

tuba ['tjuːbə] N tuba

tubby ['tʌbɪ] ADJ grassoccio(-a)

tube [tjuːb] N tubo; (*Brit: underground*) metropolitana, metrò *m inv*; (*for tyre*) camera d'aria; (*col: television*): **the ~** la tele

tubeless ['tjuːblɪs] ADJ (*tyre*) senza camera d'aria

tuber ['tjuːbəʳ] N (*Bot*) tubero

tuberculosis [tjubəːkjuˈləusɪs] N tubercolosi *f inv*

tube station N (*Brit*) stazione *f* della metropolitana

tubing ['tjuːbɪŋ] N tubazione *f*; **a piece of ~** un tubo

tubular ['tjuːbjuləʳ] ADJ tubolare

TUC N ABBR (*Brit*: = *Trades Union Congress*) confederazione *f* dei sindacati britannici

tuck [tʌk] N (*Sewing*) piega ▶ VT (*put*) mettere

▶ **tuck away** VT riporre; (*building*): **to be tucked away** essere in un luogo isolato

▶ **tuck in** VT mettere dentro; (*child*) rimboccare ▶ VI (*eat*) mangiare di buon appetito; abbuffarsi

▶ **tuck up** VT (*child*) rimboccare

tucker ['tʌkəʳ] N (*Australia, New Zealand col*) cibo

tuck shop N negozio di pasticceria (*in una scuola*)

Tue(s)., Tues. ABBR (= *Tuesday*) mar.

Tuesday ['tjuːzdɪ] N martedì *m inv*; (**the date**) **today is ~ 23 March** oggi è martedì 23 marzo; **on ~** martedì; **on Tuesdays** di martedì; **every ~** tutti i martedì; **every other ~** ogni due martedì; **last/next ~** martedì scorso/prossimo; **~ next** martedì prossimo; **the following ~** (*in past*) il martedì successivo; (*in future*) il martedì dopo; **a week/fortnight on ~**, **~ week/fortnight** martedì fra una settimana/quindici giorni; **the ~ before last** martedì di due settimane fa; **the ~ after next** non questo martedì ma il prossimo; **~ morning/lunchtime/afternoon/evening** martedì mattina/all'ora di pranzo/pomeriggio/sera; **~ night** martedì sera; (*overnight*) martedì notte; **~'s newspaper** il giornale di martedì

t

tuft [tʌft] N ciuffo
tug [tʌg] N (*ship*) rimorchiatore *m* ▶ VT tirare con forza
tug-of-love [tʌgəv'lʌv] N contesa per la custodia dei figli; ~ **children** bambini *mpl* coinvolti nella contesa per la custodia
tug-of-war [tʌgəv'wɔːʳ] N tiro alla fune
tuition [tjuːˈɪʃən] N (BRIT: *lessons*) lezioni *fpl*; (: *private tuition*) lezioni *fpl* private; (US: *fees*) tasse *fpl* scolastiche (*or* universitarie)
tulip [ˈtjuːlɪp] N tulipano
tumble [ˈtʌmbl] N (*fall*) capitombolo ▶ VI capitombolare, ruzzolare; (*somersault*) fare capriole ▶ VT far cadere; **to ~ to sth** (*col*) realizzare qc
tumbledown [ˈtʌmbldaun] N cadente, diroccato(-a)
tumble dryer N (BRIT) asciugatrice *f*
tumbler [ˈtʌmbləʳ] N bicchiere *m* senza stelo
tummy [ˈtʌmɪ] N (*col*) pancia
tumour, (US) **tumor** [ˈtjuːməʳ] N tumore *m*
tumult [ˈtjuːmʌlt] N tumulto
tumultuous [tjuːˈmʌltjuəs] ADJ tumultuoso(-a)
tuna [ˈtjuːnə] N (*pl inv*: *also*: **tuna fish**) tonno
tune [tjuːn] N (*melody*) melodia, aria ▶ VT (*Mus*) accordare; (*Radio, TV, Aut*) regolare, mettere a punto; **to be in/out of ~** (*instrument*) essere accordato(-a)/scordato(-a); (*singer*) essere intonato(-a)/stonato(-a); **to the ~ of** (*fig: amount*) per la modesta somma di; **in ~ with** (*fig*) in accordo con
  ▶ **tune in** VI (*Radio, TV*): **to ~ in (to)** sintonizzarsi (su)
  ▶ **tune up** VI (*musician*) accordare lo strumento
tuneful [ˈtjuːnful] ADJ melodioso(-a)
tuner [ˈtjuːnəʳ] N (*radio set*) sintonizzatore *m*; **piano ~** accordatore(-trice) di pianoforte
tuner amplifier N amplificatore *m* di sintonia
tungsten [ˈtʌŋstn] N tungsteno
tunic [ˈtjuːnɪk] N tunica
tuning [ˈtjuːnɪŋ] N messa a punto
tuning fork N diapason *m inv*
Tunis [ˈtjuːnɪs] N Tunisi *f*
Tunisia [tjuːˈnɪzɪə] N Tunisia
Tunisian [tjuːˈnɪzɪən] ADJ, N tunisino(-a)
tunnel [ˈtʌnl] N galleria ▶ VI scavare una galleria
tunnel vision N (*Med*) riduzione *f* del campo visivo; (*fig*) visuale *f* ristretta
tunny [ˈtʌnɪ] N tonno
turban [ˈtəːbən] N turbante *m*
turbid [ˈtəːbɪd] ADJ torbido(-a)
turbine [ˈtəːbaɪn] N turbina
turbo [ˈtəːbəu] N turbo *m inv*
turbojet [ˈtəːbəuˈdʒɛt] N turboreattore *m*
turboprop [ˈtəːbəuˈprɔp] N turboelica *m inv*

turbot [ˈtəːbət] N (*pl inv*) rombo gigante
turbulence [ˈtəːbjuləns] N (*Aviat*) turbolenza
turbulent [ˈtəːbjulənt] ADJ turbolento(-a); (*sea*) agitato(-a)
tureen [təˈriːn] N zuppiera
turf [təːf] N terreno erboso; (*clod*) zolla ▶ VT coprire di zolle erbose; **the T~** l'ippodromo
  ▶ **turf out** VT (*col*) buttar fuori
turf accountant N (BRIT) allibratore *m*
turgid [ˈtəːdʒɪd] ADJ (*speech*) ampolloso(-a), pomposo(-a)
Turin [tjuəˈrɪn] N Torino *f*
Turk [təːk] N turco(-a)
Turkey [ˈtəːkɪ] N Turchia
turkey [ˈtəːkɪ] N tacchino
Turkish [ˈtəːkɪʃ] ADJ turco(-a) ▶ N (*Ling*) turco
Turkish bath N bagno turco
Turkish delight N gelatine ricoperte di zucchero a velo
turmeric [ˈtəːmərɪk] N curcuma
turmoil [ˈtəːmɔɪl] N confusione *f*, tumulto
turn [təːn] N giro; (*change*) cambiamento; (*in road*) curva; (*tendency: of mind, events*) tendenza; (*performance*) numero; (*chance*) turno; (*Med*) crisi *f inv*, attacco ▶ VT girare, voltare; (*milk*) far andare a male; (*shape: wood, metal*) tornire; (*change*): **to ~ sth into** trasformare qc in ▶ VI girare; (*person: look back*) girarsi, voltarsi; (*reverse direction*) girarsi indietro; (*change*) cambiare; (*milk*) andare a male; (*become*) diventare; **to ~ into** trasformarsi in; **a good ~** un buon servizio; **a bad ~** un brutto tiro; **it gave me quite a ~** mi ha fatto prendere un bello spavento; **"no left ~"** (*Aut*) "divieto di svolta a sinistra"; **it's your ~** tocca a lei; **in ~** a sua volta; a turno; **to take turns (at sth)** fare (qc) a turno; **at the ~ of the year/century** alla fine dell'anno/del secolo; **to take a ~ for the worse** (*situation, events*) volgere al peggio; (*patient, health*) peggiorare; **to ~ left/right** girare a sinistra/destra
  ▶ **turn about** VI girarsi indietro
  ▶ **turn away** VI girarsi (dall'altra parte) ▶ VT (*reject: person*) mandar via; (: *business*) rifiutare
  ▶ **turn back** VI ritornare, tornare indietro
  ▶ VT far tornare indietro; (*clock*) spostare indietro
  ▶ **turn down** VT (*refuse*) rifiutare; (*reduce*) abbassare; (*fold*) ripiegare
  ▶ **turn in** VI (*col: go to bed*) andare a letto ▶ VT (*fold*) voltare in dentro
  ▶ **turn off** VI (*from road*) girare, voltare ▶ VT (*light, radio, engine etc*) spegnere
  ▶ **turn on** VT (*light, radio etc*) accendere; (*engine*) avviare
  ▶ **turn out** VT (*light, gas*) chiudere; spegnere; (*produce: goods*) produrre; (: *novel, good pupils*) creare ▶ VI (*appear, attend: troops, doctor, voters etc*)

presentarsi; **to ~ out to be** ... rivelarsi ..., risultare ...

▶ **turn over** vi (*person*) girarsi; (*car etc*) capovolgersi ▶ vt girare

▶ **turn round** vi girare; (*person*) girarsi

▶ **turn to** vt fus: **to ~ to sb** girarsi verso qn; **to ~ to sb for help** rivolgersi a qn per aiuto

▶ **turn up** vi (*person*) arrivare, presentarsi; (*lost object*) saltar fuori ▶ vt (*collar, sound, gas etc*) alzare

turnabout ['tə:nəbaut], **turnaround** ['tə:nəraund] N (*fig*) dietrofront *m inv*

turncoat ['tə:nkəut] N voltagabbana *mf*

turned-up ['tə:ndʌp] ADJ (*nose*) all'insù

turning ['tə:nɪŋ] N (*in road*) curva; (*side road*) strada laterale; **the first ~ on the right** la prima a destra

turning circle N (BRIT) diametro di sterzata

turning point N (*fig*) svolta decisiva

turning radius N (US) = **turning circle**

turnip ['tə:nɪp] N rapa

turnout ['tə:naut] N presenza, affluenza

turnover ['tə:nəuvəʳ] N (*Comm: amount of money*) giro di affari; (*: of goods*) smercio; (*Culin*): **apple** *etc* **~** sfogliatella alle mele *etc*; **there is a rapid ~ in staff** c'è un ricambio molto rapido di personale

turnpike ['tə:npaɪk] N (US) autostrada a pedaggio

turnstile ['tə:nstaɪl] N tornella

turntable ['tə:nteɪbl] N (*on record player*) piatto

turn-up ['tə:nʌp] N (BRIT: *on trousers*) risvolto

turpentine ['tə:pəntaɪn] N (*also:* **turps**) acqua ragia

turquoise [tə:kwɔɪz] N (*stone*) turchese *m* ▶ ADJ turchese; di turchese

turret ['tʌrɪt] N torretta

turtle ['tə:tl] N testuggine *f*

turtleneck (sweater) ['tə:tlnɛk-] N maglione *m* con il collo alto

Tuscan ['tʌskən] ADJ, N toscano(-a)

Tuscany ['tʌskənɪ] N Toscana

tusk [tʌsk] N zanna

tussle ['tʌsl] N baruffa, mischia

tutor ['tju:təʳ] N (*in college*) docente *mf* (*responsabile di un gruppo di studenti*); (*private teacher*) precettore *m*

tutorial [tju:'tɔ:rɪəl] N (Scol) lezione *f* con discussione (*a un gruppo limitato*)

tuxedo [tʌk'si:dəu] N (US) smoking *m inv*

TV [ti:'vi:] N ABBR (= *television*) tivù *f inv*

TV dinner N pasto surgelato pronto in due minuti

twaddle ['twɔdl] N scemenze *fpl*

twang [twæŋ] N (*of instrument*) suono vibrante; (*of voice*) accento nasale ▶ vi vibrare ▶ vt (*guitar*) pizzicare le corde di

tweak [twi:k] vt (*nose*) pizzicare; (*ear, hair*) tirare

tweed [twi:d] N tweed *m inv*

tweet [twi:t] N (*on Twitter*) post *m* su Twitter ▶ vt, vi (*on Twitter*) scrivere su Twitter

tweezers ['twi:zəz] NPL pinzette *fpl*

twelfth [twelfθ] NUM dodicesimo(-a)

Twelfth Night N la notte dell'Epifania

twelve [twelv] NUM dodici; **at ~** alle dodici, a mezzogiorno; (*midnight*) a mezzanotte

twentieth ['twentɪɪθ] NUM ventesimo(-a)

twenty ['twentɪ] NUM venti; **in ~ fourteen** nel duemilaquattordici

twerp [twə:p] N (*col*) idiota *mf*

twice [twaɪs] ADV due volte; **~ as much** due volte tanto; **~ a week** due volte alla settimana; **she is ~ your age** ha il doppio dei suoi anni

twiddle ['twɪdl] vt, vi: **to ~ (with) sth** giocherellare con qc; **to ~ one's thumbs** (*fig*) girarsi i pollici

twig [twɪg] N ramoscello ▶ vt, vi (*col*) capire

twilight ['twaɪlaɪt] N (*evening*) crepuscolo; (*morning*) alba; **in the ~** nella penombra

twill [twɪl] N spigato

twin [twɪn] ADJ, N gemello(-a) ▶ vt: **to ~ one town with another** fare il gemellaggio di una città con un'altra

twin-bedded room ['twɪn'bɛdɪd-] N stanza con letti gemelli

twin beds NPL letti *mpl* gemelli

twin-carburettor ['twɪnkɑ:bju'rɛtəʳ] ADJ a doppio carburatore

twine [twaɪn] N spago, cordicella ▶ vi (*plant*) attorcigliarsi; (*road*) serpeggiare

twin-engined ['twɪn'ɛndʒɪnd] ADJ a due motori; **~ aircraft** bimotore *m*

twinge [twɪndʒ] N (*of pain*) fitta; **a ~ of conscience/regret** un rimorso/rimpianto

twinkle ['twɪŋkl] N scintillio ▶ vi scintillare; (*eyes*) brillare

twin room N stanza con letti gemelli

twin town N città *f inv* gemella

twirl [twə:l] N piroetta ▶ vt far roteare ▶ vi roteare

twist [twɪst] N torsione *f*; (*in wire, flex*) piega; (*in story*) colpo di scena; (*bend*) svolta, piega; (*in road*) curva ▶ vt attorcigliare; (*ankle*) slogare; (*weave*) intrecciare; (*roll around*) arrotolare; (*fig*) distorcere ▶ vi attorcigliarsi; arrotolarsi; (*road*) serpeggiare; **to ~ one's ankle/wrist** (Med) slogarsi la caviglia/il polso

twisted ['twɪstɪd] ADJ (*wire, rope*) attorcigliato(-a); (*ankle, wrist*) slogato(-a); (*fig: logic, mind*) contorto(-a)

twit [twɪt] N (*col*) cretino(-a)

twitch [twɪtʃ] N tiratina; (*nervous*) tic *m inv* ▶ vi contrarsi; avere un tic

Twitter® ['twɪtəʳ] N Twitter® *m*

two [tu:] NUM due; **~ by ~**, **in twos** a due a due; **to put ~ and ~ together** (*fig*) fare uno più uno

t

two-bit [tuːˈbɪt] ADJ (*esp US col, pej*) da quattro soldi

two-door [tuːˈdɔːʳ] ADJ (*Aut*) a due porte

two-faced ['tuːˈfeɪst] ADJ (*pej: person*) falso(-a)

twofold ['tuːfəuld] ADV: **to increase ~** aumentare del doppio ▶ ADJ (*increase*) doppio(-a); (*reply*) in due punti

two-piece ['tuːˈpiːs] N (*also:* **two-piece suit**) due pezzi *m inv*; (*also:* **two-piece swimsuit**) (costume *m* da bagno a) due pezzi *m inv*

two-seater ['tuːˈsiːtəʳ] N (*plane*) biposto; (*car*) macchina a due posti

twosome ['tuːsəm] N (*people*) coppia

two-stroke ['tuːstrəuk] N (*engine*) due tempi *m inv* ▶ ADJ a due tempi

two-tone ['tuːtəun] ADJ (*colour*) bicolore

two-way ['tuːweɪ] ADJ (*traffic*) a due sensi; **~ radio** radio *f inv* ricetrasmittente

TX ABBR (*US*) = **Texas**

tycoon [taɪˈkuːn] N: **(business) ~** magnate *m*

type [taɪp] N (*category*) genere *m*; (*model*) modello; (*example*) tipo; (*Typ*) tipo, carattere *m* ▶ VT (*letter etc*) battere (a macchina), dattilografare; **what ~ do you want?** che tipo vuole?; **in bold/italic ~** in grassetto/corsivo

type-cast ['taɪpkɑːst] ADJ (*actor*) a ruolo fisso

typeface ['taɪpfeɪs] N carattere *m* tipografico

typescript ['taɪpskrɪpt] N dattiloscritto

typeset ['taɪpsɛt] VT (*irreg: like* **set**) comporre

typesetter ['taɪpsɛtəʳ] N compositore *m*

typewriter ['taɪpraɪtəʳ] N macchina da scrivere

typewritten ['taɪprɪtn] ADJ dattiloscritto(-a), battuto(-a) a macchina

typhoid ['taɪfɔɪd] N tifoidea

typhoon [taɪˈfuːn] N tifone *m*

typhus ['taɪfəs] N tifo

typical ['tɪpɪkl] ADJ tipico(-a)

typically ADV tipicamente; **~, he arrived late** come al solito è arrivato tardi

typify ['tɪpɪfaɪ] VT essere tipico(-a) di

typing ['taɪpɪŋ] N dattilografia

typing error N errore *m* di battitura

typing pool N ufficio *m*, dattilografia *inv*

typist ['taɪpɪst] N dattilografo(-a)

typo ['taɪpəu] N ABBR (*col:* = *typographical error*) refuso

typography [taɪˈpɔgrəfɪ] N tipografia

tyranny ['tɪrənɪ] N tirannia

tyrant ['taɪərnt] N tiranno

tyre, (*US*) **tire** ['taɪəʳ] N pneumatico, gomma; **I've got a flat ~** ho una gomma a terra

tyre pressure N pressione *f* (delle gomme)

Tyrol [tɪˈrəul] N Tirolo

Tyrolean [tɪrəˈliːən], **Tyrolese** [tɪrəˈliːz] ADJ, N tirolese *mf*

Tyrrhenian Sea [tɪˈriːnɪən-] N: **the ~** il mar Tirreno

Uu

U, u [ju:] N (*letter*) U, u *m inv or f inv*; **U for
Uncle** ≈ U come Udine
U N ABBR (*BRIT Cine*: = *universal*) per tutti
UAW N ABBR (*US*: = *United Automobile Workers*)
sindacato degli operai automobilistici
UB40 N ABBR (*BRIT*: = *unemployment benefit form
40*) modulo per la richiesta del sussidio di
disoccupazione
U-bend ['ju:bɛnd] N (*in pipe*) sifone *m*
ubiquitous [ju:'bɪkwɪtəs] ADJ onnipresente
UCAS ['ju:kæs] N ABBR (*BRIT*) = **Universities
and Colleges Admissions Service**
UDA N ABBR (*BRIT*: = *Ulster Defence Association*)
organizzazione paramilitare protestante
UDC N ABBR (*BRIT*) = **Urban District Council**
udder ['ʌdəʳ] N mammella
UDI ABBR (*BRIT Pol*) = **unilateral declaration of
independence**
UDR N ABBR (*BRIT*: = *Ulster Defence Regiment*)
*reggimento dell'esercito britannico in Irlanda del
Nord*
UEFA [ju:'eɪfə] N ABBR (= *Union of European
Football Associations*) UEFA *f*
UFO ['ju:fəu] N ABBR (= *unidentified flying object*)
UFO *m inv*
Uganda [ju:'gændə] N Uganda
Ugandan [ju:'gændən] ADJ, N ugandese *mf*
UGC N ABBR (*BRIT*: = *University Grants Committee*)
organo che autorizza sovvenzioni alle università
ugh [ə:h] EXCL puah!
ugliness ['ʌglɪnɪs] N bruttezza
ugly ['ʌglɪ] ADJ brutto(-a)
UHF ABBR = **ultra-high frequency**
UHT ADJ ABBR (= *ultra heat treated*) UHT *inv*, a
lunga conservazione; **~ milk** latte *m* UHT
UK N ABBR = **United Kingdom**
Ukraine [ju:'kreɪn] N Ucraina
Ukrainian [ju:'kreɪnɪən] ADJ ucraino(-a)
▶ N (*person*) ucraino(-a); (*Ling*) ucraino
ulcer ['ʌlsəʳ] N ulcera; **mouth ~** afta
Ulster ['ʌlstəʳ] N Ulster *m*
ulterior [ʌl'tɪərɪəʳ] ADJ ulteriore; **~ motive**
secondo fine *m*
ultimata [ʌltɪ'meɪtə] NPL *of* **ultimatum**

ultimate ['ʌltɪmɪt] ADJ ultimo(-a), finale;
(*authority*) massimo(-a), supremo(-a) ▶ N:
the ~ in luxury il non plus ultra del lusso
ultimately ['ʌltɪmɪtlɪ] ADV alla fine; in
definitiva, in fin dei conti
ultimatum [ʌltɪ'meɪtəm] (*pl* **ultimatums** or
ultimata [-tə]) N ultimatum *m inv*
ultrasonic [ʌltrə'sɔnɪk] ADJ ultrasonico(-a)
ultrasound [ʌltrə'saund] N ultrasuono;
(*Med*) ecografia
ultraviolet ['ʌltrə'vaɪəlɪt] ADJ ultravioletto(-a)
umbilical [ʌm'bɪlɪkl] ADJ: **~ cord** cordone *m*
ombelicale
umbrage ['ʌmbrɪdʒ] N: **to take ~** offendersi,
impermalirsi
umbrella [ʌm'brɛlə] N ombrello; **under the
~ of** (*fig*) sotto l'egida di
umlaut ['umlaut] N Umlaut *m inv*
umpire ['ʌmpaɪəʳ] N arbitro
umpteen [ʌmp'ti:n] ADJ non so quanti(-e);
for the umpteenth time per l'ennesima
volta
UMW N ABBR (= *United Mineworkers of America*)
unione dei minatori d'America
UN N ABBR (= *United Nations*) ONU *f*
unabashed [ʌnə'bæʃt] ADJ imperturbato(-a)
unabated [ʌnə'beɪtɪd] ADJ non diminuito(-a)
unable [ʌn'eɪbl] ADJ: **to be ~ to** non potere,
essere nell'impossibilità di; (*not to know how
to*) essere incapace di, non sapere
unabridged [ʌnə'brɪdʒd] ADJ integrale
unacceptable [ʌnək'sɛptəbl] ADJ (*proposal,
behaviour*) inaccettabile; (*price*) impossibile
unaccompanied [ʌnə'kʌmpənɪd] ADJ (*child,
lady*) non accompagnato(-a); (*singing, song*)
senza accompagnamento
unaccountably [ʌnə'kauntəblɪ] ADV
inesplicabilmente
unaccounted [ʌnə'kauntɪd] ADJ: **two
passengers are ~ for** due passeggeri
mancano all'appello
unaccustomed [ʌnə'kʌstəmd] ADJ
insolito(-a); **to be ~ to sth** non essere
abituato(-a) a qc

unacquainted [ˌʌnə'kweɪntɪd] ADJ: **to be ~ with** (*facts*) ignorare, non essere al corrente di

unadulterated [ˌʌnə'dʌltəreɪtɪd] ADJ (*gen*) puro(-a); (*wine*) non sofisticato(-a)

unaffected [ˌʌnə'fektɪd] ADJ (*person, behaviour*) naturale, spontaneo(-a); (*emotionally*): **to be ~ by** non essere toccato(-a) da

unafraid [ˌʌnə'freɪd] ADJ: **to be ~** non aver paura

unaided [ʌn'eɪdɪd] ADV senza aiuto

unanimity [ˌjuːnə'nɪmɪtɪ] N unanimità

unanimous [juː'nænɪməs] ADJ unanime

unanimously [juː'nænɪməslɪ] ADV all'unanimità

unanswered [ʌn'ɑːnsəd] ADJ (*question, letter*) senza risposta; (*criticism*) non confutato(-a)

unappetizing [ʌn'æpɪtaɪzɪŋ] ADJ poco appetitoso(-a)

unappreciative [ˌʌnə'priːʃɪətɪv] ADJ che non apprezza

unarmed [ʌn'ɑːmd] ADJ (*person*) disarmato(-a); (*combat*) senz'armi

unashamed [ˌʌnə'ʃeɪmd] ADJ sfacciato(-a), senza vergogna

unassisted [ˌʌnə'sɪstɪd] ADJ, ADV senza nessun aiuto

unassuming [ˌʌnə'sjuːmɪŋ] ADJ modesto(-a), senza pretese

unattached [ˌʌnə'tætʃt] ADJ senza legami, libero(-a)

unattended [ˌʌnə'tendɪd] ADJ (*car, child, luggage*) incustodito(-a)

unattractive [ˌʌnə'træktɪv] ADJ privo(-a) di attrattiva, poco attraente

unauthorized [ʌn'ɔːθəraɪzd] ADJ non autorizzato(-a)

unavailable [ˌʌnə'veɪləbl] ADJ (*article, room, book*) non disponibile; (*person*) impegnato(-a)

unavoidable [ˌʌnə'vɔɪdəbl] ADJ inevitabile

unavoidably [ˌʌnə'vɔɪdəblɪ] ADV (*detained*) per cause di forza maggiore

unaware [ˌʌnə'wɛəʳ] ADJ: **to be ~ of** non sapere, ignorare

unawares [ˌʌnə'wɛəz] ADV di sorpresa, alla sprovvista

unbalanced [ʌn'bælənst] ADJ squilibrato(-a)

unbearable [ʌn'bɛərəbl] ADJ insopportabile

unbeatable [ʌn'biːtəbl] ADJ imbattibile

unbeaten [ʌn'biːtn] ADJ (*team, army*) imbattuto(-a); (*record*) insuperato(-a)

unbecoming [ˌʌnbɪ'kʌmɪŋ] ADJ (*unseemly: language, behaviour*) sconveniente; (*unflattering: garment*) che non dona

unbeknown [ˌʌnbɪ'nəun], **unbeknownst** [ˌʌnbɪ'nəunst] ADV: **~(st) to** all'insaputa di

unbelief [ˌʌnbɪ'liːf] N incredulità

unbelievable [ˌʌnbɪ'liːvəbl] ADJ incredibile

unbelievingly [ˌʌnbɪ'liːvɪŋlɪ] ADV con aria incredula

unbend [ʌn'bend] VI (*irreg: like* **bend**) distendersi ▶ VT (*wire*) raddrizzare

unbending [ʌn'bendɪŋ] ADJ (*fig*) inflessibile, rigido(-a)

unbiased, unbiassed [ʌn'baɪəst] ADJ obiettivo(-a), imparziale

unblemished [ʌn'blemɪʃt] ADJ senza macchia

unblock [ʌn'blɔk] VT (*pipe, road*) sbloccare

unborn [ʌn'bɔːn] ADJ non ancora nato(-a)

unbounded [ʌn'baundɪd] ADJ sconfinato(-a), senza limite

unbreakable [ʌn'breɪkəbl] ADJ infrangibile

unbridled [ʌn'braɪdld] ADJ sbrigliato(-a)

unbroken [ʌn'brəukən] ADJ (*intact*) intero(-a); (*continuous*) continuo(-a); (*record*) insuperato(-a)

unbuckle [ʌn'bʌkl] VT slacciare

unburden [ʌn'bəːdn] VT: **to ~ o.s.** sfogarsi

unbutton [ʌn'bʌtn] VT sbottonare

uncalled-for [ʌn'kɔːldfɔːʳ] ADJ (*remark*) fuori luogo *inv*; (*action*) ingiustificato(-a)

uncanny [ʌn'kænɪ] ADJ misterioso(-a), strano(-a)

unceasing [ʌn'siːsɪŋ] ADJ incessante

unceremonious [ˌʌnserɪ'məunɪəs] ADJ (*abrupt, rude*) senza tante cerimonie

uncertain [ʌn'səːtn] ADJ incerto(-a); dubbio(-a); **it's ~ whether ...** non è sicuro se ...; **in no ~ terms** chiaro e tondo, senza mezzi termini

uncertainty [ʌn'səːtntɪ] N incertezza

unchallenged [ʌn'tʃælɪndʒd] ADJ incontestato(-a); **to go ~** non venire contestato, non trovare opposizione

unchanged [ʌn'tʃeɪndʒd] ADJ immutato(-a)

uncharitable [ʌn'tʃærɪtəbl] ADJ duro(-a), severo(-a)

uncharted [ʌn'tʃɑːtɪd] ADJ inesplorato(-a)

unchecked [ʌn'tʃekt] ADJ incontrollato(-a)

uncivilized [ʌn'sɪvɪlaɪzd] ADJ (*gen*) selvaggio(-a); (*fig*) incivile, barbaro(-a)

uncle ['ʌŋkl] N zio

unclear [ʌn'klɪəʳ] ADJ non chiaro(-a); **I'm still ~ about what I'm supposed to do** non ho ancora ben capito cosa dovrei fare

uncoil [ʌn'kɔɪl] VT srotolare ▶ VI srotolarsi, svolgersi

uncomfortable [ʌn'kʌmfətəbl] ADJ scomodo(-a); (*uneasy*) a disagio, agitato(-a); (*unpleasant*) fastidioso(-a); (*situation*) sgradevole

uncomfortably [ʌn'kʌmfətəblɪ] ADV scomodamente; (*uneasily: say*) con voce inquieta; (: *think*) con inquietudine

uncommitted [ˌʌnkə'mɪtɪd] ADJ (*attitude, country*) neutrale

uncommon [ʌn'kɔmən] ADJ raro(-a), insolito(-a), non comune

uncommunicative [ʌnkə'mjuːnɪkətɪv] ADJ poco comunicativo(-a), chiuso(-a)

uncomplicated [ʌn'kɒmplɪkeɪtɪd] ADJ semplice, poco complicato(-a)

uncompromising [ʌn'kɒmprəmaɪzɪŋ] ADJ intransigente, inflessibile

unconcerned [ʌnkən'səːnd] ADJ (*unworried*) tranquillo(-a); **to be ~ about** non darsi pensiero di, non preoccuparsi di *or* per

unconditional [ʌn'kən'dɪʃənl] ADJ incondizionato(-a), senza condizioni

uncongenial [ʌnkən'dʒiːnɪəl] ADJ (*work, surroundings*) poco piacevole

unconnected [ʌnkə'nɛktɪd] ADJ (*unrelated*) senza connessione, senza rapporto; **to be ~ with** essere estraneo(-a) a

unconscious [ʌn'kɒnʃəs] ADJ privo(-a) di sensi, svenuto(-a); (*unaware*) inconsapevole, inconscio(-a) ▶ N: **the ~** l'inconscio; **to knock sb ~** far perdere i sensi a qn con un pugno

unconsciously [ʌn'kɒnʃəslɪ] ADV inconsciamente

unconstitutional [ʌnkɒnstɪ'tjuːʃənl] ADJ incostituzionale

uncontested [ʌnkən'tɛstɪd] ADJ (*champion*) incontestato(-a); (*Pol: seat*) non disputato(-a)

uncontrollable [ʌnkən'trəuləbl] ADJ incontrollabile; indisciplinato(-a)

uncontrolled [ʌnkən'trəuld] ADJ (*child, dog, emotion*) sfrenato(-a); (*inflation, price rises*) che sfugge al controllo

unconventional [ʌnkən'vɛnʃənl] ADJ poco convenzionale

unconvinced [ʌnkən'vɪnst] ADJ: **to be** *or* **remain ~** non essere convinto(-a)

unconvincing [ʌnkən'vɪnsɪŋ] ADJ non convincente, poco persuasivo(-a)

uncork [ʌn'kɔːk] VT stappare

uncorroborated [ʌnkə'rɒbəreɪtɪd] ADJ non convalidato(-a)

uncouth [ʌn'kuːθ] ADJ maleducato(-a), grossolano(-a)

uncover [ʌn'kʌvər] VT scoprire

unctuous ['ʌŋktjuəs] ADJ untuoso(-a)

undamaged [ʌn'dæmɪdʒd] ADJ (*goods*) in buono stato; (*fig: reputation*) intatto(-a)

undaunted [ʌn'dɔːntɪd] ADJ intrepido(-a)

undecided [ʌndɪ'saɪdɪd] ADJ indeciso(-a)

undelivered [ʌndɪ'lɪvəd] ADJ non recapitato(-a); **if ~ return to sender** in caso di mancato recapito rispedire al mittente

undeniable [ʌndɪ'naɪəbl] ADJ innegabile, indiscutibile

under ['ʌndər] PREP sotto; (*less than*) meno di; al disotto di; (*according to*) secondo, in conformità a ▶ ADV (al) disotto; **from ~ sth** da sotto a *or* dal disotto di qc; **~ there** là sotto; **in ~ 2 hours** in meno di 2 ore;

~ anaesthetic sotto anestesia; **~ discussion** in discussione; **~ repair** in riparazione; **~ the circumstances** date le circostanze

under ... ['ʌndər] PREFIX sotto..., sub...

under-age [ʌndər'eɪdʒ] ADJ minorenne

underarm ['ʌndərɑːm] N ascella ▶ ADJ ascellare ▶ ADV da sotto in su

undercapitalized [ʌndə'kæpɪtəlaɪzd] ADJ carente di capitali

undercarriage ['ʌndəkærɪdʒ] N (*BRIT Aviat*) carrello (d'atterraggio)

undercharge [ʌndə'tʃɑːdʒ] VT far pagare di meno a

underclass ['ʌndəklɑːs] N sottoproletariato

underclothes ['ʌndəkləuðz] NPL biancheria (intima)

undercover ['ʌndəkʌvər] ADJ segreto(-a), clandestino(-a)

undercurrent ['ʌndəkʌrənt] N corrente f sottomarina

undercut [ʌndə'kʌt] VT (*irreg: like* **cut**) vendere a prezzo minore di

underdeveloped ['ʌndədɪ'vɛləpt] ADJ sottosviluppato(-a)

underdog ['ʌndədɒg] N oppresso(-a)

underdone [ʌndə'dʌn] ADJ (*Culin*) al sangue; (*pej*) poco cotto(-a)

under-employment [ʌndərɪm'plɔɪmənt] N sottoccupazione f

underestimate [ʌndər'ɛstɪmeɪt] VT sottovalutare

underexposed [ʌndərɪks'pəuzd] ADJ (*Phot*) sottoesposto(-a)

underfed [ʌndə'fɛd] ADJ denutrito(-a)

underfoot [ʌndə'fut] ADV sotto i piedi

under-funded ['ʌndə'fʌndɪd] ADJ insufficientemente sovvenzionato(-a)

undergo [ʌndə'gəu] VT (*irreg: like* **go**) subire; (*treatment*) sottoporsi a; **the car is undergoing repairs** la macchina è in riparazione

undergraduate [ʌndə'grædjuɪt] N studente(-essa) universitario(-a) ▶ CPD: **~ courses** corsi mpl di laurea

underground ['ʌndəgraund] N (*BRIT: railway*) metropolitana; (*Pol*) movimento clandestino ▶ ADJ sotterraneo(-a); (*fig*) clandestino(-a); (*Art, Cine*) underground *inv* ▶ ADV sottoterra; clandestinamente; **to go ~** (*fig*) darsi alla macchia

undergrowth ['ʌndəgrəuθ] N sottobosco

underhand [ʌndə'hænd], **underhanded** [ʌndə'hændɪd] ADJ (*fig*) furtivo(-a), subdolo(-a)

underinsured [ʌndərɪn'ʃuəd] ADJ non sufficientemente assicurato(-a)

underlie [ʌndə'laɪ] VT (*irreg: like* **lie**) essere alla base di; **the underlying cause** il motivo di fondo

u

847

underline [ʌndə'laɪn] VT sottolineare

underling ['ʌndəlɪŋ] N (pej) subalterno(-a), tirapiedi mf

undermanning [ʌndə'mænɪŋ] N carenza di personale

undermentioned [ʌndə'mɛnʃənd] ADJ (riportato(-a)) qui sotto or qui di seguito

undermine [ʌndə'maɪn] VT minare

underneath [ʌndə'niːθ] ADV sotto, disotto
▸ PREP sotto, al di sotto di

undernourished [ʌndə'nʌrɪʃt] ADJ denutrito(-a)

underpaid [ʌndə'peɪd] ADJ mal pagato(-a)

underpants ['ʌndəpænts] NPL (BRIT) mutande fpl, slip m inv

underpass ['ʌndəpɑːs] N (BRIT) sottopassaggio

underpin [ʌndə'pɪn] VT puntellare; (argument, case) corroborare

underplay [ʌndə'pleɪ] VT minimizzare

underpopulated [ʌndə'pɔpjuleɪtɪd] ADJ scarsamente popolato(-a), sottopopolato(-a)

underprice [ʌndə'praɪs] VT vendere a un prezzo inferiore al dovuto

underprivileged [ʌndə'prɪvɪlɪdʒd] ADJ svantaggiato(-a)

underrate [ʌndə'reɪt] VT sottovalutare

underscore [ʌndə'skɔːʳ] VT sottolineare

underseal ['ʌndəsiːl] VT rendere stagno il fondo di

undersecretary [ʌndə'sɛkrətrɪ] N sottosegretario

undersell ['ʌndə'sɛl] VT (irreg: like **sell**) (competitors) vendere a prezzi più bassi di

undershirt ['ʌndəʃəːt] N (US) maglietta

undershorts ['ʌndəʃɔːts] NPL (US) mutande fpl, slip m inv

underside ['ʌndəsaɪd] N disotto

undersigned ['ʌndəsaɪnd] ADJ, N sottoscritto(-a)

underskirt ['ʌndəskəːt] (BRIT) N sottoveste f

understaffed [ʌndə'stɑːft] ADJ a corto di personale

understand [ʌndə'stænd] VT, VI (irreg: like **stand**) capire, comprendere; **I don't ~** non capisco; **I ~ that ...** sento che ...; credo di capire che ...; **to make o.s. understood** farsi capire

understandable [ʌndə'stændəbl] ADJ comprensibile

understanding [ʌndə'stændɪŋ] ADJ comprensivo(-a) ▸ N comprensione f; (agreement) accordo; **on the ~ that ...** a patto che or a condizione che ...; **to come to an ~ with sb** giungere ad un accordo con qn

understate [ʌndə'steɪt] VT minimizzare, sminuire

understatement [ʌndə'steɪtmənt] N: **that's an ~!** a dire poco!

understood [ʌndə'stud] PT, PP of **understand**
▸ ADJ inteso(-a); (implied) sottinteso(-a)

understudy ['ʌndəstʌdɪ] N sostituto(-a), attore(-trice) supplente

undertake [ʌndə'teɪk] VT (irreg: like **take**) intraprendere; **to ~ to do sth** impegnarsi a fare qc

undertaker ['ʌndəteɪkəʳ] N impresario di pompe funebri

undertaking [ʌndə'teɪkɪŋ] N impresa; (promise) promessa

undertone ['ʌndətəun] N (low voice) tono sommesso; (of criticism etc) vena, sottofondo; **in an ~** sottovoce

undervalue [ʌndə'vælju:] VT svalutare, sottovalutare

underwater [ʌndə'wɔːtəʳ] ADV sott'acqua
▸ ADJ subacqueo(-a)

underway [ˌʌndə'weɪ] ADJ: **to be ~** essere in corso

underwear ['ʌndəwɛəʳ] N biancheria (intima)

underweight [ʌndə'weɪt] ADJ al di sotto del giusto peso; (person) sottopeso inv

underwent [ʌndə'wɛnt] VB see **undergo**

underworld ['ʌndəwəːld] N (of crime) malavita

underwrite ['ʌndəraɪt] VT (irreg: like **write**) (Finance) sottoscrivere; (Insurance) assicurare

underwriter ['ʌndəraɪtəʳ] N sottoscrittore(-trice); assicuratore(-trice)

undeserving [ʌndɪ'zəːvɪŋ] ADJ: **to be ~ of** non meritare, non essere degno di

undesirable [ʌndɪ'zaɪərəbl] ADJ indesiderato(-a)

undeveloped [ʌndɪ'vɛləpt] ADJ (land, resources) non sfruttato(-a)

undies ['ʌndɪz] NPL (col) robina, biancheria intima da donna

undiluted [ʌndaɪ'luːtɪd] ADJ non diluito(-a)

undiplomatic [ʌndɪplə'mætɪk] ADJ poco diplomatico(-a)

undischarged ['ʌndɪs'tʃɑːdʒd] ADJ: **~ bankrupt** fallito non riabilitato

undisciplined [ʌn'dɪsɪplɪnd] ADJ indisciplinato(-a)

undisguised [ʌndɪs'gaɪzd] ADJ (dislike, amusement etc) palese

undisputed [ʌndɪs'pjuːtɪd] ADJ indiscusso(-a)

undistinguished [ʌndɪs'tɪŋgwɪʃt] ADJ mediocre, qualunque

undisturbed [ʌndɪs'təːbd] ADJ tranquillo(-a); **to leave sth ~** lasciare qc così com'è

undivided [ʌndɪ'vaɪdɪd] ADJ: **I want your ~ attention** esigo tutta la sua attenzione

undo [ʌn'duː] VT (irreg: like **do**) disfare

undoing [ʌn'duːɪŋ] N rovina, perdita

undone [ʌn'dʌn] PP of **undo**; **to come ~** slacciarsi

undoubted [ʌn'dautɪd] ADJ sicuro(-a), certo(-a)

undoubtedly [ʌn'dautɪdlɪ] ADV senza alcun dubbio

undress [ʌn'drɛs] VI spogliarsi

undrinkable [ʌn'drɪŋkəbl] ADJ *(unpalatable)* imbevibile; *(poisonous)* non potabile

undue [ʌn'dju:] ADJ eccessivo(-a)

undulating ['ʌndjuleɪtɪŋ] ADJ ondeggiante, ondulato(-a)

unduly [ʌn'dju:lɪ] ADV eccessivamente

undying [ʌn'daɪɪŋ] ADJ imperituro(-a)

unearned [ʌn'ə:nd] ADJ *(praise, respect)* immeritato(-a); **~ income** rendita

unearth [ʌn'ə:θ] VT dissotterrare; *(fig)* scoprire

unearthly [ʌn'ə:θlɪ] ADJ soprannaturale; *(hour)* impossibile

uneasy [ʌn'i:zɪ] ADJ a disagio; *(worried)* preoccupato(-a); *(peace)* precario(-a); **to feel ~ about doing sth** non sentirsela di fare qc

uneconomic ['ʌni:kə'nɒmɪk],
uneconomical ['ʌni:kə'nɒmɪkl] ADJ non economico(-a), antieconomico(-a)

uneducated [ʌn'edjukeɪtɪd] ADJ senza istruzione, incolto(-a)

unemployed [ʌnɪm'plɔɪd] ADJ disoccupato(-a) ► NPL: **the ~** i disoccupati

unemployment [ʌnɪm'plɔɪmənt] N disoccupazione f

unemployment benefit, *(US)*
unemployment compensation N sussidio di disoccupazione

unending [ʌn'ɛndɪŋ] ADJ senza fine

unenviable [ʌn'ɛnvɪəbl] ADJ poco invidiabile

unequal [ʌn'i:kwəl] ADJ *(length, objects)* disuguale; *(amounts)* diverso(-a); *(division of labour)* ineguale

unequalled, *(US)* **unequaled** [ʌn'i:kwəld] ADJ senza pari, insuperato(-a)

unequivocal [ʌnɪ'kwɪvəkəl] ADJ *(answer)* inequivocabile; *(person)* esplicito(-a), chiaro(-a).

unerring [ʌn'ə:rɪŋ] ADJ infallibile

UNESCO [ju:'nɛskəu] N ABBR (= *United Nations Educational, Scientific and Cultural Organization*) U.N.E.S.C.O f

unethical [ʌn'ɛθɪkəl] ADJ *(methods)* poco ortodosso(-a), non moralmente accettabile; *(doctor's behaviour)* contrario(-a) all'etica professionale

uneven [ʌn'i:vn] ADJ ineguale; *(ground)* disuguale, accidentato(-a); *(heartbeat)* irregolare

uneventful [ʌnɪ'vɛntful] ADJ senza sorprese, tranquillo(-a)

unexceptional [ʌnɪk'sɛpʃənl] ADJ che non ha niente d'eccezionale

unexciting [ʌnɪk'saɪtɪŋ] ADJ *(news)* poco emozionante; *(film, evening)* poco interessante

unexpected [ʌnɪk'spɛktɪd] ADJ inatteso(-a), imprevisto(-a)

unexpectedly [ʌnɪk'spɛktɪdlɪ] ADV inaspettatamente

unexplained [ʌnɪk'spleɪnd] ADJ inspiegato(-a)

unexploded [ʌnɪk'spləudɪd] ADJ inesploso(-a)

unfailing [ʌn'feɪlɪŋ] ADJ *(supply, energy)* inesauribile; *(remedy)* infallibile

unfair [ʌn'fɛər] ADJ: **~ (to)** ingiusto(-a) (nei confronti di); **it's ~ that ...** non è giusto che ...+sub

unfair dismissal N licenziamento ingiustificato

unfairly [ʌn'fɛəlɪ] ADV ingiustamente

unfaithful [ʌn'feɪθful] ADJ infedele

unfamiliar [ʌnfə'mɪlɪər] ADJ sconosciuto(-a), strano(-a); **to be ~ with sth** non essere pratico di qc, non avere familiarità con qc

unfashionable [ʌn'fæʃnəbl] ADJ *(clothes)* fuori moda *inv*; *(district)* non alla moda

unfasten [ʌn'fɑ:sn] VT slacciare; sciogliere

unfathomable [ʌn'fæðəməbl] ADJ insondabile

unfavourable, *(US)* **unfavorable** [ʌn'feɪvərəbl] ADJ sfavorevole

unfavourably, *(US)* **unfavorably** [ʌn'feɪvərəblɪ] ADV: **to look ~ upon** vedere di malocchio

unfeeling [ʌn'fi:lɪŋ] ADJ insensibile, duro(-a)

unfinished [ʌn'fɪnɪʃt] ADJ incompiuto(-a)

unfit [ʌn'fɪt] ADJ inadatto(-a); *(ill)* non in forma; *(incompetent)*: **~ (for)** incompetente (in) *(work, Mil)* inabile (a); **~ for habitation** inabitabile

unflagging [ʌn'flægɪŋ] ADJ instancabile

unflappable [ʌn'flæpəbl] ADJ calmo(-a), composto(-a)

unflattering [ʌn'flætərɪŋ] ADJ *(dress, hairstyle)* che non dona

unflinching [ʌn'flɪntʃɪŋ] ADJ che non indietreggia, risoluto(-a)

unfold [ʌn'fəuld] VT spiegare; *(fig)* rivelare ► VI *(view)* distendersi; *(story)* svelarsi

unforeseeable ['ʌnfɔ:'si:əbl] ADJ imprevedibile

unforeseen [ʌnfɔ:'si:n] ADJ imprevisto(-a)

unforgettable [ʌnfə'gɛtəbl] ADJ indimenticabile

unforgivable [ʌnfə'gɪvəbl] ADJ imperdonabile

unformatted [ʌn'fɔ:mætɪd] ADJ *(disk, text)* non formattato(-a)

unfortunate [ʌn'fɔ:tʃnɪt] ADJ sfortunato(-a); *(event, remark)* infelice

unfortunately [ʌn'fɔ:tʃnɪtlɪ] ADV sfortunatamente, purtroppo

u

unfounded [ʌnˈfaʊndɪd] ADJ infondato(-a)

unfriend [ʌnˈfrɛnd] VT (*Internet*) cancellare dagli amici

unfriendly [ʌnˈfrɛndlɪ] ADJ poco amichevole, freddo(-a)

unfulfilled [ʌnfʊlˈfɪld] ADJ (*ambition*) non realizzato(-a); (*prophecy*) che non si è avverato(-a); (*desire*) insoddisfatto(-a); (*promise*) non mantenuto(-a); (*terms of contract*) non rispettato(-a); (*person*) frustrato(-a)

unfurl [ʌnˈfəːl] VT spiegare

unfurnished [ʌnˈfəːnɪʃt] ADJ non ammobiliato(-a)

ungainly [ʌnˈɡeɪnlɪ] ADJ goffo(-a), impacciato(-a)

ungodly [ʌnˈɡɔdlɪ] ADJ empio(-a); **at an ~ hour** a un'ora impossibile

ungrateful [ʌnˈɡreɪtful] ADJ ingrato(-a)

unguarded [ʌnˈɡɑːdɪd] ADJ: **in an ~ moment** in un momento di distrazione

unhappily [ʌnˈhæpɪlɪ] ADV (*unfortunately*) purtroppo, sfortunatamente

unhappiness [ʌnˈhæpɪnɪs] N infelicità

unhappy [ʌnˈhæpɪ] ADJ infelice; **~ about/ with** (*arrangements etc*) insoddisfatto(-a) di

unharmed [ʌnˈhɑːmd] ADJ incolume, sano(-a) e salvo(-a)

UNHCR N ABBR (= *United Nations High Commission for Refugees*) Alto Commissariato delle Nazioni Unite per Rifugiati

unhealthy [ʌnˈhɛlθɪ] ADJ (*gen*) malsano(-a); (*person*) malaticcio(-a)

unheard-of [ʌnˈhəːdɔv] ADJ inaudito(-a), senza precedenti

unhelpful [ʌnˈhɛlpful] ADJ poco disponibile

unhesitating [ʌnˈhɛzɪteɪtɪŋ] ADJ (*loyalty*) che non vacilla; (*reply, offer*) pronto(-a), immediato(-a)

unholy [ʌnˈhəʊlɪ] ADJ: **an ~ alliance** un'alleanza nefasta; **he returned at an ~ hour** è tornato ad un'ora indecente

unhook [ʌnˈhuk] VT sganciare; sfibbiare

unhurt [ʌnˈhəːt] ADJ incolume, illeso(-a)

unhygienic [ʌnhaɪˈdʒiːnɪk] ADJ non igienico(-a)

UNICEF [ˈjuːnɪsɛf] N ABBR (= *United Nations International Children's Emergency Fund*) UNICEF *m*

unicorn [ˈjuːnɪkɔːn] N unicorno

unidentified [ʌnaɪˈdɛntɪfaɪd] ADJ non identificato(-a)

uniform [ˈjuːnɪfɔːm] N uniforme *f*, divisa ▶ ADJ uniforme

uniformity [juːnɪˈfɔːmɪtɪ] N uniformità

unify [ˈjuːnɪfaɪ] VT unificare

unilateral [juːnɪˈlætərəl] ADJ unilaterale

unimaginable [ʌnɪˈmædʒɪnəbl] ADJ inimmaginabile, inconcepibile

unimaginative [ʌnɪˈmædʒɪnətɪv] ADJ privo(-a) di fantasia, a corto di idee

unimpaired [ʌnɪmˈpɛəd] ADJ intatto(-a), non danneggiato(-a)

unimportant [ʌnɪmˈpɔːtənt] ADJ senza importanza, di scarsa importanza

unimpressed [ʌnɪmˈprɛst] ADJ niente affatto impressionato(-a)

uninhabited [ʌnɪnˈhæbɪtɪd] ADJ disabitato(-a)

uninhibited [ʌnɪnˈhɪbɪtɪd] ADJ senza inibizioni; senza ritegno

uninjured [ʌnˈɪndʒəd] ADJ incolume

uninspiring [ʌnɪnˈspaɪərɪŋ] ADJ banale

uninstall [ʌnɪnˈstɔːl] VT (*Comput*) disinstallare

unintelligent [ʌnɪnˈtɛlɪdʒənt] ADJ poco intelligente

unintentional [ʌnɪnˈtɛnʃənəl] ADJ involontario(-a)

unintentionally [ʌnɪnˈtɛnʃnəlɪ] ADV senza volerlo, involontariamente

uninvited [ʌnɪnˈvaɪtɪd] ADJ non invitato(-a)

uninviting [ʌnɪnˈvaɪtɪŋ] ADJ (*place, food*) non invitante, poco invitante; (*offer*) poco allettante

union [ˈjuːnjən] N unione *f*; (*also*: **trade union**) sindacato ▶ CPD sindacale, dei sindacati; **the U~** (*US*) gli stati dell'Unione

unionize [ˈjuːnjənaɪz] VT sindacalizzare, organizzare in sindacato

Union Jack N bandiera nazionale britannica

Union of Soviet Socialist Republics N (*Hist*) Unione *f* delle Repubbliche Socialiste Sovietiche

union shop N stabilimento in cui tutti gli operai sono tenuti ad aderire ad un sindacato

unique [juːˈniːk] ADJ unico(-a)

unisex [ˈjuːnɪsɛks] ADJ unisex *inv*

Unison [ˈjuːnɪsn] N (*trade union*) sindacato generale dei funzionari

unison [ˈjuːnɪsn] N: **in ~** all'unisono

unit [ˈjuːnɪt] N unità *f inv*; (*section: of furniture etc*) elemento; (*team, squad*) reparto, squadra; **production ~** reparto *m*, produzione *inv*; **sink ~** blocco *m* lavello *inv*

unit cost N costo unitario

unite [juːˈnaɪt] VT unire ▶ VI unirsi

united [juːˈnaɪtɪd] ADJ unito(-a); unificato(-a); (*efforts*) congiunto(-a)

United Arab Emirates NPL Emirati *mpl* Arabi Uniti

United Kingdom N Regno Unito

United Nations (Organization) N (Organizzazione *f* delle) Nazioni Unite

United States (of America) N Stati *mpl* Uniti (d'America)

unit price N prezzo unitario

unit trust N (*BRIT Comm*) fondo d'investimento

unity ['ju:nɪtɪ] N unità
Univ. ABBR = **university**
universal [ju:nɪ'və:sl] ADJ universale
universe ['ju:nɪvə:s] N universo
university [ju:nɪ'və:sɪtɪ] N università f inv
▶ CPD (student, professor, education)
universitario(-a); (year) accademico(-a)
university degree N laurea
unjust [ʌn'dʒʌst] ADJ ingiusto(-a)
unjustifiable ['ʌndʒʌstɪ'faɪəbl] ADJ
ingiustificabile
unjustified [ʌn'dʒʌstɪfaɪd] ADJ
ingiustificato(-a); (Typ) non allineato(-a)
unkempt [ʌn'kɛmpt] ADJ trasandato(-a);
spettinato(-a)
unkind [ʌn'kaɪnd] ADJ poco gentile, scortese
unkindly [ʌn'kaɪndlɪ] ADV (speak) in modo
sgarbato; (treat) male
unknown [ʌn'nəun] ADJ sconosciuto(-a); ~ **to
me** ... a mia insaputa ...; ~ **quantity** (Math:
fig) incognita
unladen [ʌn'leɪdn] ADJ (ship, weight) a vuoto
unlawful [ʌn'lɔːful] ADJ illecito(-a), illegale
unleaded ['ʌn'lɛdɪd] ADJ senza piombo;
~ **petrol** benzina verde or senza piombo
unleash [ʌn'liːʃ] VT sguinzagliare; (fig)
scatenare
unleavened [ʌn'lɛvnd] ADJ non lievitato(-a),
azzimo(-a)
unless [ʌn'lɛs] CONJ a meno che (non) + sub;
~ **otherwise stated** salvo indicazione
contraria; ~ **I am mistaken** se non mi
sbaglio
unlicensed [ʌn'laɪsənst] ADJ (BRIT) senza
licenza per la vendita di alcolici
unlike [ʌn'laɪk] ADJ diverso(-a) ▶ PREP a
differenza di, contrariamente a
unlikelihood [ʌn'laɪklɪhud] N improbabilità
unlikely [ʌn'laɪklɪ] ADJ improbabile;
(explanation) inverosimile
unlimited [ʌn'lɪmɪtɪd] ADJ illimitato(-a)
unlisted [ʌn'lɪstɪd] ADJ (US Tel): **to be** ~ non
essere sull'elenco; (Stock Exchange) non
quotato(-a)
unlit [ʌn'lɪt] ADJ (room) senza luce; (road) non
illuminato(-a)
unload [ʌn'ləud] VT scaricare
unlock [ʌn'lɔk] VT aprire
unlucky [ʌn'lʌkɪ] ADJ sfortunato(-a); (object,
number) che porta sfortuna, di malaugurio;
to be ~ (person) essere sfortunato, non avere
fortuna
unmanageable [ʌn'mænɪdʒəbl] ADJ (tool,
vehicle) poco maneggevole; (situation)
impossibile
unmanned [ʌn'mænd] ADJ (spacecraft) senza
equipaggio
unmannerly [ʌn'mænəlɪ] ADJ
maleducato(-a)

unmarked [ʌn'mɑːkt] ADJ (unstained)
pulito(-a), senza macchie; ~ **police car**
civetta della polizia
unmarried [ʌn'mærɪd] ADJ non sposato(-a);
(man only) scapolo, celibe; (woman only) nubile
unmarried mother N ragazza f madre inv
unmask [ʌn'mɑːsk] VT smascherare
unmatched [ʌn'mætʃt] ADJ senza uguali
unmentionable [ʌn'mɛnʃnəbl] ADJ (vice,
topic) innominabile; (word) irripetibile
unmerciful [ʌn'mə:sɪful] ADJ spietato(-a)
unmistakable, unmistakeable
[ʌnmɪs'teɪkəbl] ADJ inconfondibile
unmitigated [ʌn'mɪtɪgeɪtɪd] ADJ (disaster etc)
totale, assoluto(-a)
unnamed [ʌn'neɪmd] ADJ (nameless) senza
nome; (anonymous) anonimo(-a)
unnatural [ʌn'nætʃrəl] ADJ innaturale;
contro natura
unnecessary [ʌn'nɛsəsərɪ] ADJ inutile,
superfluo(-a)
unnerve [ʌn'nə:v] VT (accident) sgomentare;
(hostile attitude) bloccare; (long wait, interview)
snervare
unnoticed [ʌn'nəutɪst] ADJ: **to go** or **pass** ~
passare inosservato(-a)
UNO ['ju:nəu] N ABBR (= United Nations
Organization) ONU f
unobservant [ʌnəb'zə:vənt] ADJ: **to be** ~ non
avere spirito di osservazione
unobtainable [ʌnəb'teɪnəbl] ADJ (Tel) non
ottenibile
unobtrusive [ʌnəb'tru:sɪv] ADJ discreto(-a)
unoccupied [ʌn'ɔkjupaɪd] ADJ (house)
vuoto(-a); (seat, Mil: zone) libero(-a), non
occupato(-a)
unofficial [ʌnə'fɪʃl] ADJ non ufficiale; (strike)
non dichiarato(-a) dal sindacato
unopened [ʌn'əupənd] ADJ (letter) non
aperto(-a); (present) ancora incartato(-a)
unopposed [ʌnə'pəuzd] ADJ senza
incontrare opposizione
unorthodox [ʌn'ɔ:θədɔks] ADJ non
ortodosso(-a)
unpack [ʌn'pæk] VI disfare la valigia (or le
valigie) ▶ VT disfare
unpaid [ʌn'peɪd] ADJ (holiday) non pagato(-a);
(work) non retribuito(-a); (bill, debt) da pagare
unpalatable [ʌn'pælətəbl] ADJ (food)
immangiabile; (drink) imbevibile; (truth)
sgradevole
unparalleled [ʌn'pærəlɛld] ADJ
incomparabile, impareggiabile
unpatriotic ['ʌnpætrɪ'ɔtɪk] ADJ (person) poco
patriottico(-a); (speech, attitude)
antipatriottico(-a)
unplanned [ʌn'plænd] ADJ (visit)
imprevisto(-a); (baby) non previsto(-a)
unpleasant [ʌn'plɛznt] ADJ spiacevole;

(*person, remark*) antipatico(-a); (*day, experience*) brutto(-a)

unplug [ʌn'plʌg] VT staccare

unpolluted [ʌnpə'lu:tɪd] ADJ non inquinato(-a)

unpopular [ʌn'pɒpjuləʳ] ADJ impopolare; **to make o.s. ~ (with)** rendersi antipatico (a); (*politician etc*) alienarsi le simpatie (di)

unprecedented [ʌn'prɛsɪdəntɪd] ADJ senza precedenti

unpredictable [ʌnprɪ'dɪktəbl] ADJ imprevedibile

unprejudiced [ʌn'prɛdʒudɪst] ADJ (*not biased*) obiettivo(-a), imparziale; (*having no prejudices*) senza pregiudizi

unprepared [ʌnprɪ'pɛəd] ADJ (*person*) impreparato(-a); (*speech*) improvvisato(-a)

unprepossessing [ʌnpri:pə'zɛsɪŋ] ADJ insulso(-a)

unpretentious [ʌnprɪ'tɛnʃəs] ADJ senza pretese

unprincipled [ʌn'prɪnsɪpld] ADJ senza scrupoli

unproductive [ʌnprə'dʌktɪv] ADJ improduttivo(-a); (*discussion*) sterile

unprofessional ['ʌnprə'fɛʃənl] ADJ: **~ conduct** scorrettezza professionale

unprofitable [ʌn'prɒfɪtəbl] ADJ (*financially*) non redditizio(-a); (*job, deal*) poco lucrativo(-a)

UNPROFOR ['ʌnprəfɔ:ʳ] N ABBR (= *United Nations Protection Force*) UNPROFOR *m*

unprotected ['ʌnprə'tɛktɪd] ADJ (*sex*) non protetto(-a)

unprovoked [ʌnprə'vəukt] ADJ non provocato(-a)

unpunished [ʌn'pʌnɪʃt] ADJ: **to go ~** restare impunito(-a)

unqualified [ʌn'kwɒlɪfaɪd] ADJ (*worker*) non qualificato(-a); (*in professions*) non abilitato(-a); (*success*) assoluto(-a), senza riserve

unquestionably [ʌn'kwɛstʃənəblɪ] ADV indiscutibilmente

unquestioning [ʌn'kwɛstʃənɪŋ] ADJ (*obedience, acceptance*) cieco(-a)

unravel [ʌn'rævl] VT dipanare, districare

unreal [ʌn'rɪəl] ADJ irreale

unrealistic [ʌnrɪə'lɪstɪk] ADJ (*idea*) illusorio(-a); (*estimate*) non realistico(-a)

unreasonable [ʌn'ri:znəbl] ADJ irragionevole; **to make ~ demands on sb** voler troppo da qn

unrecognizable [ʌn'rɛkəgnaɪzəbl] ADJ irriconoscibile

unrecognized [ʌn'rɛkəgnaɪzd] ADJ (*talent, genius*) misconosciuto(-a); (*Pol: regime*) non ufficialmente riconosciuto(-a)

unrecorded [ʌnrɪ'kɔ:dɪd] ADJ non documentato(-a), non registrato(-a)

unrefined [ʌnrɪ'faɪnd] ADJ (*sugar, petroleum*) greggio(-a); (*person*) rozzo(-a)

unrehearsed [ʌnrɪ'hə:st] ADJ (*Theat etc*) improvvisato(-a); (*spontaneous*) imprevisto(-a)

unrelated [ʌnrɪ'leɪtɪd] ADJ: **~ (to)** senza rapporto (con); (*by family*) non imparentato(-a) (con)

unrelenting [ʌnrɪ'lɛntɪŋ] ADJ implacabile; accanito(-a)

unreliable [ʌnrɪ'laɪəbl] ADJ (*person, machine*) che non dà affidamento; (*news, source of information*) inattendibile

unrelieved [ʌnrɪ'li:vd] ADJ (*monotony*) uniforme

unremitting [ʌnrɪ'mɪtɪŋ] ADJ incessante, infaticabile

unrepeatable [ʌnrɪ'pi:təbl] ADJ (*offer*) unico(-a)

unrepentant [ʌnrɪ'pɛntənt] ADJ impenitente

unrepresentative [ʌnrɛprɪ'zɛntətɪv] ADJ atipico(-a), poco rappresentativo(-a)

unreserved [ʌnrɪ'zə:vd] ADJ (*seat*) non prenotato(-a), non riservato(-a); (*approval, admiration*) senza riserve

unresponsive [ʌnrɪs'pɒnsɪv] ADJ che non reagisce

unrest [ʌn'rɛst] N agitazione *f*

unrestricted [ʌnrɪ'strɪktɪd] ADJ (*power, time*) illimitato(-a); (*access*) libero(-a)

unrewarded [ʌnrɪ'wɔ:dɪd] ADJ non ricompensato(-a)

unripe [ʌn'raɪp] ADJ acerbo(-a)

unrivalled, (*US*) **unrivaled** [ʌn'raɪvəld] ADJ senza pari

unroll [ʌn'rəul] VT srotolare

unruffled [ʌn'rʌfld] ADJ (*person*) calmo(-a) e tranquillo(-a), imperturbato(-a); (*hair*) a posto

unruly [ʌn'ru:lɪ] ADJ indisciplinato(-a)

unsafe [ʌn'seɪf] ADJ pericoloso(-a), rischioso(-a); **~ to drink** non potabile; **~ to eat** non commestibile

unsaid [ʌn'sɛd] ADJ: **to leave sth ~** passare qc sotto silenzio

unsaleable, (*US*) **unsalable** [ʌn'seɪləbl] ADJ invendibile

unsatisfactory ['ʌnsætɪs'fæktərɪ] ADJ che lascia a desiderare, insufficiente

unsavoury, (*US*) **unsavory** [ʌn'seɪvərɪ] ADJ (*fig: person*) losco(-a); (*: reputation, subject*) disgustoso(-a), ripugnante

unscathed [ʌn'skeɪðd] ADJ incolume

unscientific ['ʌnsaɪən'tɪfɪk] ADJ poco scientifico(-a)

unscrew [ʌn'skru:] VT svitare

unscrupulous [ʌn'skru:pjuləs] ADJ senza scrupoli

unseat [ʌn'siːt] VT (*rider*) disarcionare; (*fig: an official*) spodestare

unsecured [ʌnsɪ'kjuəd] ADJ: ~ **creditor** creditore *m* chirografario

unseeded [ʌn'siːdɪd] ADJ (*Sport*) che non è una testa di serie

unseemly [ʌn'siːmlɪ] ADJ sconveniente

unseen [ʌn'siːn] ADJ (*person*) inosservato(-a); (*danger*) nascosto(-a)

unselfish [ʌn'sɛlfɪʃ] ADJ (*person*) altruista; (*act*) disinteressato(-a)

unsettled [ʌn'sɛtld] ADJ (*person, future*) incerto(-a); indeciso(-a); turbato(-a); (*question*) non risolto(-a); (*weather, market*) instabile; **to feel ~** sentirsi disorientato(-a)

unsettling [ʌn'sɛtlɪŋ] ADJ inquietante

unshakable, unshakeable [ʌn'ʃeɪkəbl] ADJ irremovibile

unshaven [ʌn'ʃeɪvn] ADJ non rasato(-a)

unsightly [ʌn'saɪtlɪ] ADJ brutto(-a), sgradevole a vedersi

unskilled [ʌn'skɪld] ADJ: ~ **worker** operaio(-a) specializzato(-a)

unsociable [ʌn'səuʃəbl] ADJ (*person*) poco socievole; (*behaviour*) antipatico(-a)

unsocial [ʌn'səuʃəl] ADJ: ~ **hours** orario sconveniente

unsold [ʌn'səuld] ADJ invenduto(-a)

unsolicited [ʌnsə'lɪsɪtɪd] ADJ non richiesto(-a)

unsophisticated [ʌnsə'fɪstɪkeɪtɪd] ADJ semplice, naturale

unsound [ʌn'saund] ADJ (*health*) debole, cagionevole; (*in construction: floor, foundations*) debole, malsicuro(-a); (: *policy, advice*) poco sensato(-a); (: *judgment, investment*) poco sicuro(-a)

unspeakable [ʌn'spiːkəbl] ADJ (*bad*) abominevole

unspoiled ['ʌn'spɔɪld], **unspoilt** ['ʌn'spɔɪlt] ADJ (*place*) non deturpato(-a)

unspoken [ʌn'spəukən] ADJ (*words*) non detto(-a); (*agreement, approval*) tacito(-a)

unstable [ʌn'steɪbl] ADJ (*gen*) instabile; (*mentally*) squilibrato(-a)

unsteady [ʌn'stɛdɪ] ADJ instabile, malsicuro(-a)

unstinting [ʌn'stɪntɪŋ] ADJ (*support*) incondizionato(-a); (*generosity*) illimitato(-a); (*praise*) senza riserve

unstuck [ʌn'stʌk] ADJ: **to come ~** scollarsi; (*fig*) fare fiasco

unsubscribe [ʌnsʌb'skraɪb] VI (*Comput*) disdire l'abbonamento

unsubstantiated [ʌnsəb'stænʃɪeɪtɪd] ADJ (*rumour, accusation*) infondato(-a)

unsuccessful [ʌnsək'sɛsful] ADJ (*writer, proposal*) che non ha successo; (*marriage, attempt*) mal riuscito(-a), fallito(-a); **to be ~** (*in attempting sth*) non riuscire; non avere successo; (*application*) non essere considerato(-a)

unsuccessfully [ʌnsək'sɛsfəlɪ] ADV senza successo

unsuitable [ʌn'suːtəbl] ADJ inadatto(-a); (*moment*) inopportuno(-a); sconveniente

unsuited [ʌn'suːtɪd] ADJ: **to be ~ for** *or* **to** non essere fatto(-a) per

unsung ['ʌn'sʌŋ] ADJ: **an ~ hero** un eroe misconosciuto

unsupported [ʌnsə'pɔːtɪd] ADJ (*claim*) senza fondamento; (*theory*) non dimostrato(-a)

unsure [ʌn'ʃuəʳ] ADJ: ~ (**of** *or* **about**) incerto(-a) (su); **to be ~ of o.s.** essere insicuro(-a)

unsuspecting [ʌnsə'spɛktɪŋ] ADJ che non sospetta niente

unsweetened [ʌn'swiːtnd] ADJ senza zucchero

unswerving [ʌn'swəːvɪŋ] ADJ fermo(-a)

unsympathetic ['ʌnsɪmpə'θɛtɪk] ADJ (*attitude*) poco incoraggiante; (*person*) antipatico(-a); ~ (**to**) non solidale (verso)

untangle [ʌn'tæŋgl] VT sbrogliare

untapped [ʌn'tæpt] ADJ (*resources*) non sfruttato(-a)

untaxed [ʌn'tækst] ADJ (*goods*) esente da imposte; (*income*) non imponibile

unthinkable [ʌn'θɪŋkəbl] ADJ impensabile, inconcepibile

unthinkingly ['ʌn'θɪŋkɪŋlɪ] ADV senza pensare

untidy [ʌn'taɪdɪ] ADJ (*room*) in disordine; (*appearance, work*) trascurato(-a); (*person, writing*) disordinato(-a)

untie [ʌn'taɪ] VT (*knot, parcel*) disfare; (*prisoner, dog*) slegare

until [ʌn'tɪl] PREP fino a; (*after negative*) prima di ▶ CONJ finché, fino a quando; (*in past, after negative*) prima che + *sub*, prima di + *infinitive*; ~ **he comes** finché *or* fino a quando non arriva; ~ **now** finora; ~ **then** fino ad allora; **from morning ~ night** dalla mattina alla sera

untimely [ʌn'taɪmlɪ] ADJ intempestivo(-a), inopportuno(-a); (*death*) prematuro(-a)

untold [ʌn'təuld] ADJ incalcolabile; indescrivibile

untouched [ʌn'tʌtʃt] ADJ (*not used etc*) non toccato(-a), intatto(-a); (*safe: person*) incolume; (*unaffected*): ~ **by** insensibile a

untoward [ʌntə'wɔːd] ADJ sfortunato(-a), sconveniente

untrained ['ʌn'treɪnd] ADJ (*worker*) privo(-a) di formazione professionale; (*troops*) privo(-a) di addestramento; **to the ~ eye** ad un occhio inesperto

untrammelled [ʌn'træmld] ADJ illimitato(-a)

u

untranslatable [ˌʌntrænz'leɪtəbl] ADJ intraducibile

untrue [ʌn'truː] ADJ (statement) falso(-a), non vero(-a)

untrustworthy [ʌn'trʌstwəːðɪ] ADJ di cui non ci si può fidare

unusable [ʌn'juːzəbl] ADJ inservibile, inutilizzabile

unused¹ [ʌn'juːzd] ADJ (new) nuovo(-a); (not made use of) non usato(-a), non utilizzato(-a)

unused² [ʌn'juːst] ADJ: **to be ~ to sth/to doing sth** non essere abituato(-a) a qc/a fare qc

unusual [ʌn'juːʒuəl] ADJ insolito(-a), eccezionale raro(-a)

unusually [ʌn'juːʒuəlɪ] ADV insolitamente

unveil [ʌn'veɪl] VT scoprire; svelare

unwanted [ʌn'wɔntɪd] ADJ (clothing) smesso(-a); (child) non desiderato(-a)

unwarranted [ʌn'wɔrəntɪd] ADJ ingiustificato(-a)

unwary [ʌn'wɛərɪ] ADJ incauto(-a)

unwavering [ʌn'weɪvərɪŋ] ADJ fermo(-a), incrollabile

unwelcome [ʌn'wɛlkəm] ADJ (gen) non gradito(-a); **to feel ~** sentire che la propria presenza non è gradita

unwell [ʌn'wɛl] ADJ indisposto(-a); **to feel ~** non sentirsi bene

unwieldy [ʌn'wiːldɪ] ADJ poco maneggevole

unwilling [ʌn'wɪlɪŋ] ADJ: **to be ~ to do** non voler fare

unwillingly [ʌn'wɪlɪŋlɪ] ADV malvolentieri

unwind [ʌn'waɪnd] VT (irreg: like **wind²**) svolgere, srotolare ▸ VI (relax) rilassarsi

unwise [ʌn'waɪz] ADJ (decision, act) poco saggio(-a)

unwitting [ʌn'wɪtɪŋ] ADJ involontario(-a)

unwittingly [ʌn'wɪtɪŋlɪ] ADV senza volerlo

unworkable [ʌn'wəːkəbl] ADJ (plan etc) inattuabile

unworthy [ʌn'wəːðɪ] ADJ indegno(-a); **to be ~ of sth/to do sth** non essere degno di qc/di fare qc

unwrap [ʌn'ræp] VT disfare; (present) aprire

unwritten [ʌn'rɪtn] ADJ (agreement) tacito(-a)

unzip [ʌn'zɪp] VT aprire (la chiusura lampo di); (Comput) dezippare

(KEYWORD)

up [ʌp] PREP su; **he went up the stairs/the hill** è salito su per le scale/sulla collina; **the cat was up a tree** il gatto era su un albero; **they live further up the street** vivono un po' più su nella stessa strada

▸ ADV **1** (upwards, higher) su, in alto; **up in the sky/the mountains** su nel cielo/in montagna; **up there** lassù; **up above** su in alto; **up with Leeds United!** viva il Leeds United!

2: to be up (out of bed) essere alzato(-a); (prices, level) essere salito(-a); (building) essere terminato(-a); (tent) essere piantato(-a); (curtains, shutters, wallpaper) essere su; **"this side up"** "alto"; **to be up (by)** (in price, value) essere salito(-a) or aumentato(-a) (di); **when the year was up** (finished) finito l'anno; **time's up** il tempo è scaduto; **he's well up in or on politics** (BRIT) è molto informato di or sulla politica

3: up to (as far as) fino a; **up to now** finora

4: to be up to (depending on): **it's up to you** sta a lei, dipende da lei; (equal to): **he's not up to it** (job, task etc) non ne è all'altezza; (be doing: col): **what is he up to?** cosa sta combinando?; **what's up?** (col: wrong) che c'è?; **what's up with him?** che ha?, che gli prende?

▸ N: **ups and downs** alti e bassi mpl

▸ VI (col): **she upped and left** improvvisamente se ne andò

up-and-coming ['ʌpənd'kʌmɪŋ] ADJ pieno(-a) di promesse, promettente

upbeat ['ʌpbiːt] N (Mus) tempo in levare; (in economy, prosperity) incremento ▸ ADJ (col) ottimistico(-a)

upbraid [ʌp'breɪd] VT rimproverare

upbringing ['ʌpbrɪŋɪŋ] N educazione f

upcoming ['ʌpkʌmɪŋ] ADJ imminente, prossimo(-a)

update [ʌp'deɪt] VT aggiornare

upend [ʌp'ɛnd] VT rovesciare

upfront [ʌp'frʌnt] ADJ (col) franco(-a), aperto(-a) ▸ ADV (pay) subito

upgrade [ʌp'greɪd] VT promuovere; (job) rivalutare; (house) rimodernare; (employee) avanzare di grado; (Comput) fare un upgrade di

upheaval [ʌp'hiːvl] N sconvolgimento; tumulto

uphill [ʌp'hɪl] ADJ in salita; (fig: task) difficile ▸ ADV: **to go ~** andare in salita, salire

uphold [ʌp'həuld] VT (irreg: like **hold**) approvare; sostenere

upholstery [ʌp'həulstərɪ] N tappezzeria

upkeep ['ʌpkiːp] N manutenzione f

upload ['ʌpləud] VT caricare

up-market [ʌp'maːkɪt] ADJ (product) che si rivolge ad una fascia di mercato superiore

upon [ə'pɔn] PREP su

upper ['ʌpər] ADJ superiore ▸ N (of shoe) tomaia; **the ~ class** ≈ l'alta borghesia

upper case N maiuscolo

upper-class [ʌpə'klɑːs] ADJ dell'alta borghesia; (district) signorile; (accent) aristocratico(-a); (attitude) snob inv

uppercut ['ʌpəkʌt] N uppercut m inv, montante m

upper hand N: **to have the ~** avere il coltello dalla parte del manico
Upper House N: **the ~** (*in Britain*) la Camera Alta, la Camera dei Lords; (*in US etc*) il Senato
uppermost [ˈʌpəməust] ADJ il(la) più alto(-a); predominante; **it was ~ in my mind** è stata la mia prima preoccupazione
Upper Volta [-ˈvɔltə] N Alto Volta *m*
upright [ˈʌpraɪt] ADJ diritto(-a); verticale; (*fig*) diritto(-a), onesto(-a) ▶ N montante *m*
uprising [ˈʌpraɪzɪŋ] N insurrezione *f*, rivolta
uproar [ˈʌprɔːʳ] N tumulto, clamore *m*
uproarious [ʌpˈrɔːrɪəs] ADJ clamoroso(-a); (*hilarious*) esilarante; **~ laughter** risata sonora
uproot [ʌpˈruːt] VT sradicare
upset N [ˈʌpset] turbamento; (*to plan etc*) contrattempo ▶ VT [ʌpˈset] (*irreg: like* **set**) (*glass etc*) rovesciare; (*plan, stomach*) scombussolare; (*person: offend*) contrariare; (*: grieve*) addolorare; sconvolgere ▶ ADJ [ʌpˈset] contrariato(-a), addolorato(-a); (*stomach*) scombussolato(-a), disturbato(-a); **to have a stomach ~** (BRIT) avere lo stomaco in disordine *or* scombussolato; **to get ~** contrariarsi; addolorarsi
upset price N (US, SCOTTISH) prezzo di riserva
upsetting [ʌpˈsetɪŋ] ADJ (*saddening*) sconvolgente; (*offending*) offensivo(-a); (*annoying*) fastidioso(-a)
upshot [ˈʌpʃɔt] N risultato; **the ~ of it all was that …** la conclusione è stata che …
upside down [ˈʌpsaɪd-] ADV sottosopra; **to turn ~** capovolgere; (*fig*) mettere sottosopra
upstage [ˈʌpsteɪdʒ] VT: **to ~ sb** rubare la scena a qn
upstairs [ʌpˈsteəz] ADV, ADJ di sopra, al piano superiore ▶ N piano di sopra
upstart [ˈʌpstaːt] N parvenu *m inv*
upstream [ʌpˈstriːm] ADV a monte
upsurge [ˈʌpsəːdʒ] N (*of enthusiasm etc*) ondata
uptake [ˈʌpteɪk] N: **he is quick/slow on the ~** è pronto/lento di comprendonio
uptight [ʌpˈtaɪt] ADJ (*col*) teso(-a)
up-to-date [ˈʌptəˈdeɪt] ADJ moderno(-a); aggiornato(-a)
uptown [ˈʌptaun] (US) ADV verso i quartieri residenziali ▶ ADJ dei quartieri residenziali
upturn [ˈʌptəːn] N (*in luck*) svolta favorevole; (*in value of currency*) rialzo
upturned [ˈʌptəːnd] ADJ (*nose*) all'insù
upward [ˈʌpwəd] ADJ ascendente; verso l'alto ▶ ADV = **upwards**
upwardly-mobile [ˈʌpwədlɪˈməubaɪl] N: **to be ~** salire nella scala sociale
upwards [ˈʌpwədz] ADV in su, verso l'alto
URA N ABBR (US: = *Urban Renewal Administration*) amministrazione per il rinnovamento urbano
Ural Mountains [ˈjuərəl-] NPL: **the ~** (*also:*

the Urals) gli Urali, i Monti Urali
uranium [juəˈreɪnɪəm] N uranio
Uranus [juəˈreɪnəs] N (*planet*) Urano
urban [ˈəːbən] ADJ urbano(-a)
urbane [əːˈbeɪn] ADJ civile, urbano(-a), educato(-a)
urbanization [əːbənaɪˈzeɪʃən] N urbanizzazione *f*
urchin [ˈəːtʃɪn] N monello; **sea ~** riccio di mare
Urdu [ˈuəduː] N urdu *m inv*
urge [əːdʒ] N impulso; stimolo; forte desiderio ▶ VT (*caution etc*) raccomandare vivamente; **to ~ sb to do** esortare qn a fare, spingere qn a fare; raccomandare a qn di fare
▶ **urge on** VT spronare
urgency [ˈəːdʒənsɪ] N urgenza; (*of tone*) insistenza
urgent [ˈəːdʒənt] ADJ urgente; (*earnest, persistent: plea*) pressante; (*: tone, voice*) insistente, incalzante
urgently [ˈəːdʒəntlɪ] ADV d'urgenza, urgentemente; con insistenza
urinal [ˈjuərɪnl] N (BRIT: *building*) vespasiano; (*: vessel*) orinale *m*, pappagallo
urinate [ˈjuərɪneɪt] VI orinare
urine [ˈjuərɪn] N orina
URL N ABBR (= *uniform resource locator*) URL *m inv*, indirizzo Internet
urn [əːn] N urna; (*also:* **tea urn**) bollitore *m* per il tè
Uruguay [ˈjuərəgwaɪ] N Uruguay *m*
Uruguayan [juərəˈgwaɪən] ADJ, N uruguaiano(-a)
US N ABBR = **United States**
us [ʌs] PRON ci; (*stressed, after prep*) noi; *see also* **me**
USA N ABBR (*Geo*) = **United States of America**; (*Mil*) = **United States Army**
usable [ˈjuːzəbl] ADJ utilizzabile, usabile
USAF N ABBR = **United States Air Force**
usage [ˈjuːzɪdʒ] N uso
USB stick N pennetta USB
USCG N ABBR = **United States Coast Guard**
USDA N ABBR = **United States Department of Agriculture**
USDAW [ˈʌzdɔː] N ABBR (BRIT: = *Union of Shop, Distributive and Allied Workers*) sindacato dei dipendenti di negozi, reti di distribuzione e simili
USDI N ABBR = **United States Department of the Interior**
use N [juːs] uso; impiego, utilizzazione *f* ▶ VT [juːz] usare, utilizzare, servirsi di; **she used to do it** lo faceva (una volta), era solita farlo; **in ~** in uso; **out of ~** fuori uso; **to be of ~** essere utile, servire; **to make ~ of sth** far uso di qc, utilizzare qc; **ready for ~** pronto per l'uso; **it's no ~** non serve, è inutile; **to**

u

have the ~ of poter usare; **what's this used for?** a che serve?; **to be used to** avere l'abitudine di; **to get used to** abituarsi a, fare l'abitudine a
▸ **use up** vt finire; (*supplies*) dare fondo a; (*left-overs*) consumare
used [juːzd] ADJ (*car, object*) usato(-a)
useful ['juːsful] ADJ utile; **to come in ~** fare comodo, tornare utile
usefulness ['juːsfəlnɪs] N utilità
useless ['juːslɪs] ADJ inutile; (*unusable: object*) inservibile; (*: person*) inetto(-a)
user ['juːzə^r] N utente mf; (*of petrol, gas etc*) consumatore(-trice)
user-friendly ['juːzə'frɛndlɪ] ADJ orientato(-a) all'utente; (*computer*) di facile uso
username ['juːzəneɪm] N username m inv
USES N ABBR = **United States Employment Service**
usher ['ʌʃə^r] N usciere m; (*in cinema*) maschera
▸ VT: **to ~ sb in** far entrare qn
usherette [ʌʃə'rɛt] N (*in cinema*) maschera
USIA N ABBR = **United States Information Agency**
USM N ABBR = **United States Mint; United States Mail**
USN N ABBR = **United States Navy**
USP N ABBR = **unique selling point; unique selling proposition**
USPHS N ABBR = **United States Public Health Service**
USPO N ABBR = **United States Post Office**
USS ABBR = **United States Ship; United States Steamer**

USSR N ABBR (*Hist*) = **Union of Soviet Socialist Republics**
usu. ABBR = **usually**
usual ['juːʒuəl] ADJ solito(-a); **as ~** come al solito, come d'abitudine
usually ['juːʒuəlɪ] ADV di solito
usurer ['juːʒərə^r] N usuraio(-a)
usurp [juː'zəːp] VT usurpare
UT ABBR (*US*) = **Utah**
ute [juːt] N (*AUSTRALIA, NEW ZEALAND*) pick-up m inv
utensil [juː'tɛnsl] N utensile m; **kitchen utensils** utensili da cucina
uterus ['juːtərəs] N utero
utilitarian [juːtɪlɪ'tɛərɪən] ADJ utilitario(-a)
utility [juː'tɪlɪtɪ] N utilità; (*also:* **public utility**) servizio pubblico
utility room N locale adibito alla stiratura dei panni ecc
utilization [juːtɪlaɪ'zeɪʃən] N utilizzazione f
utilize ['juːtɪlaɪz] VT utilizzare; sfruttare
utmost ['ʌtməust] ADJ estremo(-a) ▸ N: **to do one's ~** fare il possibile or di tutto; **of the ~ importance** della massima importanza; **it is of the ~ importance that ...** è estremamente importante che ... +sub
utter ['ʌtə^r] ADJ assoluto(-a), totale ▸ VT pronunciare, proferire; emettere
utterance ['ʌtərəns] N espressione f; parole fpl
utterly ['ʌtəlɪ] ADV completamente, del tutto
U-turn ['juː'təːn] N inversione f a U; (*fig*) voltafaccia m inv
Uzbekistan [ʌzbɛkɪ'stɑːn] N Uzbekistan

Vv

V, v [viː] N (letter) V, v m inv or f inv; **V for Victor** ≈ V come Venezia

v ABBR (= verse) v.; (= vide) v., vedi; (= volt) V.; (= versus) contro

VA, Va. ABBR (US) = **Virginia**

vac [væk] N ABBR (BRIT col) = **vacation**

vacancy ['veɪkənsɪ] N (job) posto libero; (room) stanza libera; **"no vacancies"** "completo"; **have you any vacancies?** (office) avete bisogno di personale?; (hotel) avete una stanza?

vacant ['veɪkənt] ADJ (job, seat etc) libero(-a); (expression) assente

vacant lot N terreno non occupato; (for sale) terreno in vendita

vacate [və'keɪt] VT lasciare libero(-a)

vacation [və'keɪʃən] N (esp US) vacanze fpl; **to take a ~** prendere una vacanza, prendere le ferie; **on ~** in vacanza, in ferie

vacation course N corso estivo

vacationer, (US) vacationist N vacanziere(-a)

vaccinate ['væksɪneɪt] VT vaccinare

vaccination [væksɪ'neɪʃən] N vaccinazione f

vaccine ['væksiːn] N vaccino

vacuum ['vækjum] N vuoto

vacuum bottle N (US) = **vacuum flask**

vacuum cleaner N aspirapolvere m inv

vacuum flask N (BRIT) thermos® m inv

vacuum-packed ['vækjum'pækt] ADJ confezionato(-a) sottovuoto

vagabond ['vægəbɒnd] N vagabondo(-a)

vagary ['veɪgərɪ] N capriccio

vagina [və'dʒaɪnə] N vagina

vagrancy ['veɪgrənsɪ] N vagabondaggio

vagrant ['veɪgrənt] N vagabondo(-a)

vague [veɪg] ADJ vago(-a); (blurred: photo, memory) sfocato(-a); **I haven't the vaguest idea** non ho la minima or più pallida idea

vaguely ['veɪglɪ] ADV vagamente

vain [veɪn] ADJ (useless) inutile, vano(-a); (conceited) vanitoso(-a); **in ~** inutilmente, invano

valance ['væləns] N volant m inv, balza

valedictory [vælɪ'dɪktərɪ] ADJ di commiato

valentine ['væləntaɪn] N (also: **valentine card**) cartolina or biglietto di San Valentino

Valentine's Day ['væləntaɪnzdeɪ] N San Valentino m

valet ['vælɪt] N cameriere m personale

valet parking N parcheggio effettuato da un dipendente (dell'albergo ecc)

valet service N (for clothes) servizio di lavanderia; (for car) servizio completo di lavaggio

valiant ['vælɪənt] ADJ valoroso(-a), coraggioso(-a)

valid ['vælɪd] ADJ valido(-a), valevole; (excuse) valido(-a)

validate ['vælɪdeɪt] VT (contract, document) convalidare; (argument, claim) comprovare

validity [və'lɪdɪtɪ] N validità

valise [və'liːz] N borsa da viaggio

valley ['vælɪ] N valle f

valour, (US) valor ['vælər] N valore m

valuable ['væljuəbl] ADJ (jewel) di (grande) valore; (time, help) prezioso(-a); **valuables** NPL oggetti mpl di valore

valuation [vælju'eɪʃən] N valutazione f, stima

value ['væljuː] N valore m ▶ VT (fix price) valutare, dare un prezzo a; (cherish) apprezzare, tenere a; **values** NPL (principles) valori mpl; **to be of great ~ to sb** avere molta importanza per qn; **to lose (in) ~** (currency) svalutarsi; (property) perdere (di) valore; **to gain (in) ~** (currency) guadagnare; (property) aumentare di valore; **you get good ~ (for money) in that shop** si compra bene in quel negozio

value added tax N (BRIT) imposta sul valore aggiunto

valued ['væljuːd] ADJ (appreciated) stimato(-a), apprezzato(-a)

valuer ['væljuər] N stimatore(-trice)

valve [vælv] N valvola

vampire ['væmpaɪər] N vampiro

van [væn] N (Aut) furgone m; (BRIT Rail) vagone m

V and A N ABBR (*Brit*) = **Victoria and Albert Museum**
vandal ['vændl] N vandalo(-a)
vandalism ['vændəlɪzəm] N vandalismo
vandalize ['vændəlaɪz] VT vandalizzare
vanguard ['vængɑːd] N avanguardia
vanilla [və'nɪlə] N vaniglia ▸ CPD (*ice cream*) alla vaniglia
vanish ['vænɪʃ] VI svanire, scomparire
vanity ['vænɪtɪ] N vanità
vanity case N valigetta per cosmetici
vantage ['vɑːntɪdʒ] N: ~ **point** posizione *f or* punto di osservazione; (*fig*) posizione vantaggiosa
vaporize ['veɪpəraɪz] VT vaporizzare ▸ VI vaporizzarsi
vapour, (*US*) **vapor** ['veɪpər] N vapore *m*
variable ['vɛərɪəbl] ADJ variabile; (*mood*) mutevole ▸ N fattore *m* variabile, variabile *f*
variance ['vɛərɪəns] N: **to be at ~ (with)** essere in disaccordo (con); (*facts*) essere in contraddizione (con)
variant ['vɛərɪənt] N variante *f*
variation [vɛərɪ'eɪʃən] N variazione *f*; (*in opinion*) cambiamento
varicose ['værɪkəus] ADJ: ~ **veins** varici *fpl*
varied ['vɛərɪd] ADJ vario(-a), diverso(-a)
variety [və'raɪətɪ] N varietà *f inv*; (*quantity*) quantità, numero; **a wide ~ of ...** una vasta gamma di ...; **for a ~ of reasons** per una serie di motivi
variety show N spettacolo di varietà
various ['vɛərɪəs] ADJ vario(-a), diverso(-a); (*several*) parecchi(-e), molti(-e); **at ~ times** in momenti diversi; (*several*) diverse volte
varnish ['vɑːnɪʃ] N vernice *f*; (*nail varnish*) smalto ▸ VT verniciare; mettere lo smalto su; **to ~ one's nails** mettersi lo smalto sulle unghie
vary ['vɛərɪ] VT, VI variare, mutare; **to ~ (with** *or* **according to)** variare (con *or* a seconda di)
varying ['vɛərɪɪŋ] ADJ variabile
vase [vɑːz] N vaso
vasectomy [væ'sɛktəmɪ] N vasectomia
Vaseline® ['væsɪliːn] N vaselina
vast [vɑːst] ADJ vasto(-a); (*amount, success*) enorme
vastly ['vɑːstlɪ] ADV enormemente
vastness ['vɑːstnɪs] N vastità
VAT [væt] N ABBR (*Brit*: = *value added tax*) I.V.A. *f*
vat [væt] N tino
Vatican ['vætɪkən] N: **the ~** il Vaticano
vatman ['vætmæn] N (*irreg*) (*Brit col*): **the ~** ≈ l'ispettore *m* dell'IVA
vault [vɔːlt] N (*of roof*) volta; (*tomb*) tomba; (*in bank*) camera blindata; (*jump*) salto ▸ VT (*also*: **vault over**) saltare (d'un balzo)
vaunted ['vɔːntɪd] ADJ: **much-~** tanto celebrato(-a)

VC N ABBR (*Brit*: = *Victoria Cross*) medaglia al coraggio; = **vice-chairman**
VCR N ABBR = **video cassette recorder**
VD N ABBR = **venereal disease**
VDU N ABBR = **visual display unit**
veal [viːl] N vitello
veer [vɪər] VI girare; virare
veg. [vɛdʒ] N ABBR (*Brit*: *col*: = *vegetable(s)*) ≈ contorno
vegan ['viːgən] N (*Brit*) vegetaliano(-a)
vegeburger, veggieburger ['vɛdʒɪbəːgər] N hamburger *m inv* vegetariano
vegetable ['vɛdʒtəbl] N verdura, ortaggio ▸ ADJ vegetale
vegetable garden N orto
vegetarian [vɛdʒɪ'tɛərɪən] ADJ, N vegetariano(-a)
vegetate ['vɛdʒɪteɪt] VI vegetare
vegetation [vɛdʒɪ'teɪʃən] N vegetazione *f*
vegetative ['vɛdʒɪtətɪv] ADJ (*also Bot*) vegetativo(-a)
vehemence ['viːɪməns] N veemenza, violenza
vehement ['viːɪmənt] ADJ veemente, violento(-a); profondo(-a)
vehicle ['viːɪkl] N veicolo; (*fig*) mezzo
vehicular [vɪ'hɪkjulər] ADJ: **"no ~ traffic"** "chiuso al traffico di veicoli"
veil [veɪl] N velo ▸ VT velare; **under a ~ of secrecy** (*fig*) protetto da una cortina di segretezza
veiled [veɪld] ADJ (*also fig*) velato(-a)
vein [veɪn] N vena; (*on leaf*) nervatura; (*fig: mood*) vena, umore *m*
Velcro® ['vɛlkrəu] N velcro® *m inv*
vellum ['vɛləm] N (*writing paper*) carta patinata
velocity [vɪ'lɔsɪtɪ] N velocità *f inv*
velour [və'luər] N velours *m inv*
velvet ['vɛlvɪt] N velluto ▸ ADJ di velluto
vending machine ['vɛndɪŋ-] N distributore *m* automatico
vendor ['vɛndər] N venditore(-trice); **street ~** venditore ambulante
veneer [və'nɪər] N impiallacciatura; (*fig*) vernice *f*
venerable ['vɛnərəbl] ADJ venerabile
venereal disease [vɪ'nɪərɪəl-] N malattia venerea
Venetian [vɪ'niːʃən] ADJ, N veneziano(-a)
Venetian blind N (tenda alla) veneziana
Venezuela [vɛnɪ'zweɪlə] N Venezuela *m*
Venezuelan [vɛnɪ'zweɪlən] ADJ, N venezuelano(-a)
vengeance ['vɛndʒəns] N vendetta; **with a ~** (*fig*) davvero; furiosamente
vengeful ['vɛndʒful] ADJ vendicativo(-a)
Venice ['vɛnɪs] N Venezia

venison ['vɛnɪsn] N carne f di cervo

venom ['vɛnəm] N veleno

venomous ['vɛnəməs] ADJ velenoso(-a)

vent [vɛnt] N foro, apertura; (in dress, jacket) spacco ▶ VT (fig: one's feelings) sfogare, dare sfogo a

ventilate ['vɛntɪleɪt] VT (room) dare aria a, arieggiare

ventilation [vɛntɪ'leɪʃən] N ventilazione f

ventilation shaft N condotto di aerazione

ventilator ['vɛntɪleɪtəʳ] N ventilatore m

ventriloquist [vɛn'trɪləkwɪst] N ventriloquo(-a)

venture ['vɛntʃəʳ] N impresa (rischiosa) ▶ VT rischiare, azzardare ▶ VI arrischiarsi, azzardarsi; **a business** ~ un'iniziativa commerciale; **to ~ to do sth** azzardarsi a fare qc

venture capital N capitale m di rischio

venue ['vɛnjuː] N luogo di incontro; (Sport) luogo (designato) per l'incontro

Venus ['viːnəs] N (planet) Venere m

veracity [və'ræsɪtɪ] N veridicità

veranda, verandah [və'rændə] N veranda

verb [vəːb] N verbo

verbal ['vəːbəl] ADJ verbale; (translation) orale

verbally ['vəːbəlɪ] ADV a voce

verbatim [vəː'beɪtɪm] ADV, ADJ parola per parola

verbose [vəː'bəus] ADJ verboso(-a)

verdict ['vəːdɪkt] N verdetto; (opinion) giudizio, parere m; ~ **of guilty/not guilty** verdetto di colpevolezza/non colpevolezza

verge [vəːdʒ] N bordo, orlo; **"soft verges"** (BRIT) "banchina cedevole"; **on the ~ of doing** sul punto di fare
▶ **verge on** VT FUS rasentare

verger ['vəːdʒəʳ] N (Rel) sagrestano

verification [vɛrɪfɪ'keɪʃən] N verifica

verify ['vɛrɪfaɪ] VT verificare; (prove the truth of) confermare

veritable ['vɛrɪtəbl] ADJ vero(-a)

vermin ['vəːmɪn] NPL animali mpl nocivi; (insects) insetti mpl parassiti

vermouth ['vəːməθ] N vermut m inv

vernacular [və'nækjuləʳ] N vernacolo

versatile ['vəːsətaɪl] ADJ (person) versatile; (machine, tool etc) (che si presta) a molti usi

verse [vəːs] N (of poem) verso; (stanza) stanza, strofa; (in bible) versetto; (no pl: poetry) versi mpl; **in ~** in versi

versed [vəːst] ADJ: (**well-**)~ **in** versato(-a) in

version ['vəːʃən] N versione f

versus ['vəːsəs] PREP contro

vertebra ['vəːtɪbrə] (pl **vertebrae** [-briː]) N vertebra

vertebrate ['vəːtɪbrɪt] N vertebrato

vertical ['vəːtɪkl] ADJ, N verticale (m)

vertically ['vəːtɪklɪ] ADV verticalmente

vertigo ['vəːtɪgəu] N vertigine f; **to suffer from** ~ soffrire di vertigini

verve [vəːv] N brio; entusiasmo

very ['vɛrɪ] ADV molto ▶ ADJ: **the ~ book which** proprio il libro che; ~ **much** moltissimo; ~ **well** molto bene; ~ **little** molto poco; **at the ~ end** proprio alla fine; **the ~ last** proprio l'ultimo; **at the ~ least** almeno; **the ~ thought (of it) alarms me** il solo pensiero mi spaventa, sono spaventato solo al pensiero

vespers ['vɛspəz] NPL vespro

vessel ['vɛsl] N (Anat) vaso; (Naut) nave f; (container) recipiente m

vest [vɛst] N (BRIT) maglia; (: sleeveless) canottiera; (US: waistcoat) gilè m inv ▶ VT: **to ~ sb with sth, to ~ sth in sb** conferire qc a qn

vested interest N: **to have a ~ in doing** avere tutto l'interesse a fare; **vested interests** NPL (Comm) diritti mpl acquisiti

vestibule ['vɛstɪbjuːl] N vestibolo

vestige ['vɛstɪdʒ] N vestigio

vestment ['vɛstmənt] N (Rel) paramento liturgico

vestry ['vɛstrɪ] N sagrestia

Vesuvius [vɪ'suːvɪəs] N Vesuvio

vet [vɛt] N ABBR (BRIT: = veterinary surgeon) veterinario; (US col) = **veteran** ▶ VT esaminare minuziosamente; (text) rivedere; **to ~ sb for a job** raccogliere delle informazioni dettagliate su qn prima di offrirgli un posto

veteran ['vɛtərn] N veterano; (also: **war veteran**) veterano, reduce m ▶ ADJ: **she's a ~ campaigner for ...** lotta da sempre per ...

veteran car N auto f inv d'epoca (anteriore al 1919)

veterinarian [vɛtrɪ'nɛərɪən] N (US) = **veterinary surgeon**

veterinary ['vɛtrɪnərɪ] ADJ veterinario(-a)

veterinary surgeon, (US) **veterinarian** [vɛtrɪ'nɛərɪən] N veterinario

veto ['viːtəu] (pl **vetoes**) N veto ▶ VT opporre il veto a; **to put a ~ on** opporre il veto a

vetting ['vɛtɪŋ] N: **positive** ~ indagine per accertare l'idoneità di un aspirante ad una carica ufficiale

vex [vɛks] VT irritare, contrariare

vexed [vɛkst] ADJ (question) controverso(-a), dibattuto(-a)

VFD N ABBR (US) = **voluntary fire department**

VG ABBR (BRIT Scol etc: = very good) ottimo

VHF ABBR (= very high frequency) VHF

VI ABBR (US) = **Virgin Islands**

via ['vaɪə] PREP (by way of) via; (by means of) tramite

viability [vaɪə'bɪlɪtɪ] N attuabilità

viable ['vaɪəbl] ADJ attuabile; vitale

viaduct ['vaɪədʌkt] N viadotto

V

vial ['vaɪəl] N fiala

vibes [vaɪbz] NPL (col): **I got good/bad ~** ho trovato simpatica/antipatica l'atmosfera

vibrant ['vaɪbrənt] ADJ (sound) vibrante; (colour) vivace, vivo(-a)

vibraphone ['vaɪbrəfəun] N vibrafono

vibrate [vaɪ'breɪt] VI: **to ~ (with)** vibrare (di); (resound) risonare (di)

vibration [vaɪ'breɪʃən] N vibrazione f

vibrator [vaɪ'breɪtər] N vibratore m

vicar ['vɪkər] N pastore m

vicarage ['vɪkərɪdʒ] N presbiterio

vicarious [vɪ'kɛərɪəs] ADJ sofferto(-a) al posto di un altro; **to get ~ pleasure out of sth** trarre piacere indirettamente da qc

vice [vaɪs] N (evil) vizio; (Tech) morsa

vice- [vaɪs] PREFIX vice ...

vice-chairman [vaɪs'tʃɛəmən] N (irreg) vicepresidente m

vice-chancellor [vaɪs'tʃɑ:nsələr] N (BRIT Scol) rettore m (per elezione)

vice-president [vaɪs'prɛzɪdənt] N vicepresidente m

viceroy ['vaɪsrɔɪ] N viceré m inv

vice squad N (squadra del) buon costume f

vice versa ['vaɪsɪ'və:sə] ADV viceversa

vicinity [vɪ'sɪnɪtɪ] N vicinanze fpl

vicious ['vɪʃəs] ADJ (remark) maligno(-a), cattivo(-a); (dog) cattivo(-a); (blow) violento(-a); **a ~ circle** un circolo vizioso

viciousness ['vɪʃəsnɪs] N malignità, cattiveria; ferocia

vicissitudes [vɪ'sɪsɪtju:dz] NPL vicissitudini fpl

victim ['vɪktɪm] N vittima; **to be the ~ of** essere vittima di

victimization [vɪktɪmaɪ'zeɪʃən] N persecuzione f; rappresaglie fpl

victimize ['vɪktɪmaɪz] VT perseguitare; compiere delle rappresaglie contro

victor ['vɪktər] N vincitore m

Victorian [vɪk'tɔ:rɪən] ADJ vittoriano(-a)

victorious [vɪk'tɔ:rɪəs] ADJ vittorioso(-a)

victory ['vɪktərɪ] N vittoria; **to win a ~ over sb** riportare una vittoria su qn

video ['vɪdɪəu] CPD video... ▶ N (video film) video m inv; (also: **video cassette**) videocassetta; (also: **video recorder**) videoregistratore m

video call N videochiamata

video camera N videocamera

video cassette N videocassetta

video cassette recorder N videoregistratore m

videodisc ['vɪdɪəudɪsk] N disco ottico

video game N videogioco

video nasty N video estremamente violento o porno

videophone ['vɪdɪəufəun] N videotelefono

video recorder N videoregistratore m

video recording N registrazione f su video

video shop N videonoleggio

video tape N videotape m inv

video wall N schermo m multivideo inv

vie [vaɪ] VI: **to ~ with** competere con, rivaleggiare con

Vienna [vɪ'ɛnə] N Vienna

Vietnam, Viet Nam [vjɛt'næm] N Vietnam m

Vietnamese [vjɛtnə'mi:z] ADJ vietnamita ▶ N vietnamita mf; (Ling) vietnamita m

view [vju:] N vista, veduta; (opinion) opinione f ▶ VT (also fig: situation) considerare; (house) visitare; **on ~** (in museum etc) esposto(-a); **to be in** or **within ~ (of sth)** essere in vista (di qc); **in full ~ of sb** sotto gli occhi di qn; **an overall ~ of the situation** una visione globale della situazione; **in my ~** a mio parere, secondo me; **in ~ of the fact that** considerato che; **to take** or **hold the ~ that ...** essere dell'opinione che ...; **with a ~ to doing sth** con l'intenzione di fare qc

viewdata ['vju:deɪtə] N (BRIT) sistema di televideo

viewer ['vju:ər] N (viewfinder) mirino; (small projector) visore m; (TV) telespettatore(-trice)

viewfinder ['vju:faɪndər] N mirino

viewpoint ['vju:pɔɪnt] N punto di vista; (place) posizione f

vigil ['vɪdʒɪl] N veglia; **to keep ~** vegliare

vigilance ['vɪdʒɪləns] N vigilanza

vigilant ['vɪdʒɪlənt] ADJ vigile

vigilante [vɪdʒɪ'læntɪ] N cittadino che si fa giustizia da solo

vigorous ['vɪgərəs] ADJ vigoroso(-a)

vigour, (US) vigor [vɪgər] N vigore m

vile [vaɪl] ADJ (action) vile; (smell) disgustoso(-a), nauseante; (temper) pessimo(-a)

vilify ['vɪlɪfaɪ] VT diffamare

villa ['vɪlə] N villa

village ['vɪlɪdʒ] N villaggio

villager ['vɪlɪdʒər] N abitante mf di villaggio

villain ['vɪlən] N (scoundrel) canaglia; (BRIT: criminal) criminale m; (in novel etc) cattivo

VIN N ABBR (US) = **vehicle identification number**

vinaigrette [vɪneɪ'grɛt] N vinaigrette f inv

vindicate ['vɪndɪkeɪt] VT comprovare; giustificare

vindication [vɪndɪ'keɪʃən] N: **in ~ of** per giustificare; a discolpa di

vindictive [vɪn'dɪktɪv] ADJ vendicativo(-a)

vine [vaɪn] N vite f; (climbing plant) rampicante m

vinegar ['vɪnɪgər] N aceto

vine grower N viticoltore m

vine-growing ['vaɪngrəuɪŋ] ADJ viticolo(-a) ▶ N viticoltura

vineyard ['vɪnjɑːd] N vigna, vigneto
vintage ['vɪntɪdʒ] N (*year*) annata, produzione *f*; **the 1970 ~** il vino del 1970 ▶ CPD d'annata
vintage car N auto *f inv* d'epoca
vintage wine N vino d'annata
vinyl ['vaɪnl] N vinile *m*
viola [vɪ'əʊlə] N viola
violate ['vaɪəleɪt] VT violare
violation [vaɪə'leɪʃən] N violazione *f*; **in ~ of sth** violando qc
violence ['vaɪələns] N violenza; (*Pol etc*) incidenti *mpl* violenti
violent ['vaɪələnt] ADJ violento(-a); **a ~ dislike of sb/sth** una violenta avversione per qn/qc
violently ['vaɪələntlɪ] ADV violentemente; (*ill, angry*) terribilmente
violet ['vaɪələt] ADJ (*colour*) viola *inv*, violetto(-a) ▶ N (*plant*) violetta; (*colour*) violetto
violin [vaɪə'lɪn] N violino
violinist [vaɪə'lɪnɪst] N violinista *mf*
VIP N ABBR (= *very important person*) V.I.P. *mf*
viper ['vaɪpər] N vipera
viral ['vaɪərəl] ADJ virale
virgin ['vəːdʒɪn] N vergine *f* ▶ ADJ vergine *inv*; **she is a ~** lei è vergine; **the Blessed V~** la Beatissima Vergine
virginity [vəː'dʒɪnɪtɪ] N verginità
Virgo ['vəːgəʊ] N (*sign*) Vergine *f*; **to be ~** essere della Vergine
virile ['vɪraɪl] ADJ virile
virility [vɪ'rɪlɪtɪ] N virilità
virtual ['vəːtjuəl] ADJ effettivo(-a), vero(-a); (*Comput, Physics*) virtuale; (*in effect*): **it's a ~ impossibility** è praticamente impossibile; **the ~ leader** il capo all'atto pratico
virtually ['vəːtjuəlɪ] ADV (*almost*) praticamente; **it is ~ impossible** è praticamente impossibile
virtual reality N (*Comput*) realtà *f inv* virtuale
virtue ['vəːtjuː] N virtù *f inv*; (*advantage*) pregio, vantaggio; **by ~ of** grazie a
virtuosity [vəːtju'ɒsɪtɪ] N virtuosismo
virtuoso [vəːtju'əʊzəu] N virtuoso
virtuous ['vəːtjuəs] ADJ virtuoso(-a)
virulent ['vɪrulənt] ADJ virulento(-a)
virus ['vaɪərəs] N (*also Comput*) virus *m inv*
visa ['viːzə] N visto
vis-à-vis [viːzə'viː] PREP rispetto a, nei riguardi di
viscount ['vaɪkaunt] N visconte *m*
viscous ['vɪskəs] ADJ viscoso(-a)
vise [vaɪs] N (*US Tech*) = **vice**
visibility [vɪzɪ'bɪlɪtɪ] N visibilità
visible ['vɪzəbl] ADJ visibile; **~ exports/imports** esportazioni *fpl*/importazioni *fpl* visibili

visibly ['vɪzəblɪ] ADV visibilmente
vision ['vɪʒən] N (*sight*) vista; (*foresight, in dream*) visione *f*
visionary ['vɪʒənərɪ] N visionario(-a)
visit ['vɪzɪt] N visita; (*stay*) soggiorno ▶ VT (*person: US: also:* **visit with**) andare a trovare; (*place*) visitare; **to pay a ~ to** (*person*) fare una visita a; (*place*) andare a visitare; **on a private/official ~** in visita privata/ufficiale
visiting ['vɪzɪtɪŋ] ADJ (*speaker, professor, team*) ospite
visiting card N biglietto da visita
visiting hours NPL (*in hospital etc*) orario delle visite
visitor ['vɪzɪtər] N visitatore(-trice); (*guest*) ospite *mf*
visitor centre, (*US*) **visitor center** N centro informazioni per visitatori di museo, zoo, parco ecc
visitors' book N libro d'oro; (*in hotel*) registro
visor ['vaɪzər] N visiera
VISTA ['vɪstə] N ABBR (= *Volunteers in Service to America*) volontariato in zone depresse degli Stati Uniti
vista ['vɪstə] N vista, prospettiva
visual ['vɪzjuəl] ADJ visivo(-a); visuale; ottico(-a)
visual aid N sussidio visivo
visual arts NPL arti *fpl* figurative
visual display unit N unità *f inv* di visualizzazione
visualize ['vɪzjuəlaɪz] VT immaginare, figurarsi; (*foresee*) prevedere
visually ['vɪzjuəlɪ] ADV: **~ appealing** piacevole a vedersi; **~ handicapped** con una menomazione della vista
vital ['vaɪtl] ADJ vitale; **of ~ importance (to sb/sth)** di vitale importanza (per qn/qc)
vitality [vaɪ'tælɪtɪ] N vitalità
vitally ['vaɪtəlɪ] ADV estremamente
vital statistics NPL (*of population*) statistica demografica; (*col: woman's*) misure *fpl*
vitamin ['vɪtəmɪn] N vitamina
vitiate ['vɪʃɪeɪt] VT viziare
vitreous ['vɪtrɪəs] ADJ (*rock*) vetroso(-a); (*china, enamel*) vetrificato(-a)
vitriolic [vɪtrɪ'ɔlɪk] ADJ (*fig*) caustico(-a)
viva ['vaɪvə] N (*also:* **viva voce**) (*esame m*) orale
vivacious [vɪ'veɪʃəs] ADJ vivace
vivacity [vɪ'væsɪtɪ] N vivacità
vivid ['vɪvɪd] ADJ vivido(-a)
vividly ['vɪvɪdlɪ] ADV (*describe*) vividamente; (*remember*) con precisione
vivisection [vɪvɪ'sɛkʃən] N vivisezione *f*
vixen ['vɪksn] N volpe *f* femmina; (*pej: woman*) bisbetica
viz ABBR (= *vide licet: namely*) cioè
VLF ABBR (= *very low frequency*) bassissima frequenza

V

V-neck ['viːnɛk] N maglione *m* con lo scollo a V

VOA N ABBR (= *Voice of America*) voce *f* dell'America (*alla radio*)

vocabulary [vəu'kæbjuləri] N vocabolario

vocal ['vəukl] ADJ (*Mus*) vocale; (*communication*) verbale; (*noisy*) rumoroso(-a)

vocal cords NPL corde *fpl* vocali

vocalist ['vəukəlist] N cantante *mf* (*in un gruppo*)

vocation [vəu'keiʃən] N vocazione *f*

vocational [vəu'keiʃənl] ADJ professionale; ~ **guidance** orientamento professionale; ~ **training** formazione *f* professionale

vociferous [və'sifərəs] ADJ rumoroso(-a)

vodka ['vɔdkə] N vodka *f inv*

vogue [vəug] N moda; (*popularity*) popolarità, voga; **to be in ~**, **be the ~** essere di moda

voice [vɔis] N voce *f* ▶ VT (*opinion*) esprimere; **in a loud/soft** ~ a voce alta/bassa; **to give ~ to** esprimere

voice mail N servizio di segreteria telefonica

voice-over ['vɔisəuvə^r] N voce *f* fuori campo

void [vɔid] N vuoto ▶ ADJ (*invalid*) nullo(-a); (*empty*): ~ **of** privo(-a) di

voile [vɔil] N voile *m*

vol. ABBR (= *volume*) vol.

volatile ['vɔlətail] ADJ volatile; (*fig*) volubile

volcanic [vɔl'kænik] ADJ vulcanico(-a)

volcano [vɔl'keinəu] (*pl* **volcanoes**) N vulcano

volition [və'liʃən] N: **of one's own** ~ di propria volontà

volley ['vɔli] N (*of gunfire*) salva; (*of stones etc*) raffica, gragnola; (*Tennis etc*) volata

volleyball ['vɔlibɔːl] N pallavolo *f*

volt [vəult] N volt *m inv*

voltage ['vəultidʒ] N tensione *f*, voltaggio; **high/low** ~ alta/bassa tensione

voluble ['vɔljubl] ADJ loquace, ciarliero(-a)

volume ['vɔljuːm] N volume *m*; (*of tank*) capacità *f inv*; ~ **one/two** (*of book*) volume primo/secondo; **his expression spoke volumes** la sua espressione lasciava capire tutto

volume control N (*Radio, TV*) regolatore *m or* manopola del volume

volume discount N (*Comm*) vantaggio sul volume di vendita

voluminous [və'luːminəs] ADJ voluminoso(-a); (*notes etc*) abbondante

voluntarily ['vɔləntrili] ADV volontariamente; gratuitamente

voluntary ['vɔləntəri] ADJ volontario(-a); (*unpaid*) gratuito(-a), non retribuito(-a)

voluntary liquidation N (*Comm*) liquidazione *f* volontaria

volunteer [vɔlən'tiə^r] N volontario(-a) ▶ VT offrire volontariamente ▶ VI (*Mil*) arruolarsi volontario; **to ~ to do** offrire (volontariamente) di fare

voluptuous [və'lʌptjuəs] ADJ voluttuoso(-a)

vomit ['vɔmit] N vomito ▶ VT, VI vomitare

voracious [və'reiʃəs] ADJ (*appetite*) smisurato(-a); (*reader*) avido(-a)

vote [vəut] N voto, suffragio; (*cast*) voto; (*franchise*) diritto di voto ▶ VI votare ▶ VT (*gen*) votare; (*sum of money etc*) votare a favore di; (*propose*): **to ~ that** approvare la proposta che; **to ~ to do sth** votare a favore di fare qc; **he was voted secretary** è stato eletto segretario; **to put sth to the ~**, **to take a ~ on sth** mettere qc ai voti; ~ **for/against** voto a favore/contrario; **to pass a ~ of confidence/no confidence** dare il voto di fiducia/sfiducia; ~ **of thanks** discorso di ringraziamento

voter ['vəutə^r] N elettore(-trice)

voting ['vəutiŋ] N scrutinio

voting paper N (*Brit*) scheda elettorale

voting right N diritto di voto

vouch [vautʃ] : **to ~ for** *vt fus* farsi garante di

voucher ['vautʃə^r] N (*for meal, petrol*) buono; (*receipt*) ricevuta; **travel** ~ voucher *m inv*, tagliando

vow [vau] N voto, promessa solenne ▶ VI giurare; **to take** *or* **make a ~ to do sth** fare voto di fare qc ▶ VT: **to ~ to do/that** giurare di fare/che

vowel ['vauəl] N vocale *f*

voyage ['vɔiidʒ] N viaggio per mare, traversata

voyeur [vwɑː'jəː^r] N guardone(-a)

VP N ABBR (= *vice-president*) V.P.

vs ABBR (= *versus*) contro

VSO N ABBR (*Brit*: = *Voluntary Service Overseas*) *servizio volontario in paesi sottosviluppati*

VT, Vt. ABBR (*US*) = **Vermont**

vulgar ['vʌlgə^r] ADJ volgare

vulgarity [vʌl'gæriti] N volgarità

vulnerability [vʌlnərə'biliti] N vulnerabilità

vulnerable ['vʌlnərəbl] ADJ vulnerabile

vulture ['vʌltʃə^r] N avvoltoio

Ww

W, w ['dʌblju:] N (*letter*) W, w *m inv or f inv*;
W for William ≈ W come Washington
W ABBR (= *west*) O; (*Elec*: = *watt*) w
WA ABBR (*US*) = **Washington**
wad [wɔd] N (*of cotton wool, paper*) tampone *m*;
(*of banknotes etc*) fascio
wadding ['wɔdɪŋ] N imbottitura
waddle ['wɔdl] VI camminare come una
papera
wade [weɪd] VI: **to ~ through** camminare a
stento in; (*fig: book*) leggere con fatica ▶ VT
guadare
wafer ['weɪfəʳ] N (*Culin*) cialda; (*Rel*) ostia;
(*Comput*) wafer *m inv*
wafer-thin ['weɪfə'θɪn] ADJ molto sottile
waffle ['wɔfl] N (*Culin*) cialda; (*col*) ciance *fpl*;
riempitivo ▶ VI cianciare; parlare a vuoto
waffle iron N stampo per cialde
waft [wɔft] VT portare ▶ VI diffondersi
wag [wæg] VT agitare, muovere ▶ VI agitarsi;
the dog wagged its tail il cane scodinzolò
wage [weɪdʒ] N (*also*: **wages**) salario, paga
▶ VT: **to ~ war** fare la guerra; **a day's wages**
un giorno di paga
wage claim N rivendicazione *f* salariale
wage differential N differenza di salario
wage earner N salariato(-a)
wage freeze N blocco dei salari
wage packet N (*BRIT*) busta *f* paga *inv*
wager ['weɪdʒəʳ] N scommessa
waggle ['wægl] VT dimenare, agitare ▶ VI
dimenarsi, agitarsi
wagon, waggon ['wægən] N (*horse-drawn*)
carro; (*truck*) furgone *m*; (*BRIT Rail*) vagone *m*
(merci)
wail [weɪl] N gemito; (*of siren*) urlo ▶ VI
gemere; urlare
waist [weɪst] N vita, cintola
waistcoat ['weɪskəut] N (*BRIT*) panciotto,
gilè *m inv*
waistline ['weɪstlaɪn] N (giro di) vita
wait [weɪt] N attesa ▶ VI aspettare, attendere;
to ~ for aspettare; **~ for me, please**
aspettami, per favore; **to keep sb waiting**

far aspettare qn; **~ a moment!** (aspetti) un
momento!; **"repairs while you ~"**
"riparazioni lampo"; **I can't ~ to ...** (*fig*) non
vedo l'ora di ...; **to lie in ~ for** stare in
agguato a
▶ **wait behind** VI rimanere (ad aspettare)
▶ **wait on** VT FUS servire
▶ **wait up** VI restare alzato(-a) (ad aspettare);
don't ~ up for me non rimanere alzato per
me
waiter ['weɪtəʳ] N cameriere *m*
waiting ['weɪtɪŋ] N: **"no ~"** (*BRIT Aut*) "divieto
di sosta"
waiting list N lista d'attesa
waiting room N sala d'aspetto *or* d'attesa
waitress ['weɪtrɪs] N cameriera
waive [weɪv] VT rinunciare a, abbandonare
waiver ['weɪvəʳ] N rinuncia
wake [weɪk] (*pt* **woke** [wəuk] *or* **waked**, *pp*
woken ['wəukn] *or* **waked**) VT (*also*: **wake up**)
svegliare ▶ VI (*also*: **wake up**) svegliarsi ▶ N
(*for dead person*) veglia funebre; (*Naut*) scia; **to
~ up to sth** (*fig*) rendersi conto di qc; **in the ~
of** sulla scia di; **to follow in sb's ~** (*fig*)
seguire le tracce di qn
waken ['weɪkn] VT, VI = **wake**
Wales [weɪlz] N Galles *m*
walk [wɔ:k] N passeggiata; (*short*) giretto;
(*gait*) passo, andatura; (*path*) sentiero;
(*in park etc*) sentiero, vialetto ▶ VI camminare;
(*for pleasure, exercise*) passeggiare ▶ VT
(*distance*) fare *or* percorrere a piedi; (*dog*)
accompagnare, portare a passeggiare;
10 minutes' ~ from 10 minuti di cammino
or a piedi da; **to go for a ~** andare a fare
quattro passi; andare a fare una passeggiata;
from all walks of life di tutte le condizioni
sociali; **to ~ in one's sleep** essere
sonnambulo(-a); **I'll ~ you home** ti
accompagno a casa
▶ **walk out** VI (*go out*) uscire; (*as protest*) uscire
(in segno di protesta); (*audience*) andarsene;
(*strike*) scendere in sciopero; **to ~ out on sb**
piantare in asso qn

W

walkabout ['wɔːkəbaut] N: **to go (on a) ~** avere incontri informali col pubblico (*durante una visita ufficiale*)

walker ['wɔːkəʳ] N (*person*) camminatore(-trice)

walkie-talkie ['wɔːkɪ'tɔːkɪ] N walkie-talkie *m inv*

walking ['wɔːkɪŋ] N camminare *m*; **it's within ~ distance** ci si arriva a piedi

walking holiday N vacanza fatta di lunghe camminate

walking shoes NPL scarpe *fpl* da passeggio

walking stick N bastone *m* da passeggio

Walkman® ['wɔːkmən] N walkman® *m inv*

walk-on ['wɔːkɔn] ADJ (*Theat: part*) da comparsa

walkout ['wɔːkaut] N (*of workers*) sciopero senza preavviso *or* a sorpresa

walkover ['wɔːkəuvəʳ] N (*col*) vittoria facile, gioco da ragazzi

walkway ['wɔːkweɪ] N passaggio pedonale

wall [wɔːl] N muro; (*internal, of tunnel, cave*) parete *f*; **to go to the ~** (*fig: firm etc*) fallire ▸ **wall in** VT (*garden etc*) circondare con un muro

wall cupboard N pensile *m*

walled [wɔːld] ADJ (*city*) fortificato(-a)

wallet ['wɔlɪt] N portafoglio

wallflower ['wɔːlflauəʳ] N violacciocca; **to be a ~** (*fig*) fare da tappezzeria

wall hanging N tappezzeria

wallop ['wɔləp] VT (*col*) pestare

wallow ['wɔləu] VI sguazzare, rotolarsi; **to ~ in one's grief** crogiolarsi nel proprio dolore

wallpaper ['wɔːlpeɪpəʳ] N carta da parati; (*Comput*) sfondo ▸ VT (*room*) mettere la carta da parati in

wall-to-wall ['wɔːltə'wɔːl] ADJ: **~ carpeting** moquette *f*

walnut ['wɔːlnʌt] N noce *f*; (*tree*) noce *m*

walrus ['wɔːlrəs] (*pl ~ or* **walruses**) N tricheco

waltz [wɔːlts] N valzer *m inv* ▸ VI ballare il valzer

wan [wɔn] ADJ pallido(-a), smorto(-a); triste

wand [wɔnd] N (*also*: **magic wand**) bacchetta (*magica*)

wander ['wɔndəʳ] VI (*person*) girare senza meta, girovagare; (*thoughts*) vagare; (*river*) serpeggiare ▸ VT girovagare per

wanderer ['wɔndərəʳ] N vagabondo(-a)

wandering ['wɔndrɪŋ] ADJ (*tribe*) nomade; (*minstrel, actor*) girovago(-a); (*path, river*) tortuoso(-a); (*glance, mind*) distratto(-a)

wane [weɪn] VI (*moon*) calare; (*reputation*) declinare

wangle ['wæŋgl] (*BRIT col*) VT procurare (con l'astuzia) ▸ N astuzia

wanker ['wæŋkəʳ] N (*col!*) segaiolo (!); (*as insult*) coglione (!) *m*

want [wɔnt] VT volere; (*need*) aver bisogno di; (*lack*) mancare di ▸ N (*poverty*) miseria, povertà; **wants** NPL (*needs*) bisogni *mpl*; **for ~ of** per mancanza di; **to ~ to do** volere fare; **to ~ sb to do** volere che qn faccia; **you're wanted on the phone** la vogliono al telefono; **"cook wanted"** "cercasi cuoco"

want ads NPL (*US*) piccoli annunci *mpl*

wanted ADJ (*criminal*) ricercato(-a); **"~"** (*in adverts*) "cercasi"

wanting ['wɔntɪŋ] ADJ: **to be ~ (in)** mancare (di); **to be found ~** non risultare all'altezza

wanton ['wɔntn] ADJ sfrenato(-a); senza motivo

war [wɔːʳ] N guerra; **to go to ~** entrare in guerra; **to make ~ (on)** far guerra (a)

warble ['wɔːbl] N (*of bird*) trillo ▸ VI trillare

war cry N grido di guerra

ward [wɔːd] N (*in hospital: room*) corsia; (*: section*) reparto; (*Pol*) circoscrizione *f*; (*Law: child: also*: **ward of court**) pupillo(-a) ▸ **ward off** VT parare, schivare

warden ['wɔːdn] N (*of institution*) direttore(-trice); (*of park, game reserve*) guardiano(-a); (*BRIT: also*: **traffic warden**) addetto(-a) al controllo del traffico e del parcheggio

warder ['wɔːdəʳ] N (*BRIT*) guardia carceraria

wardrobe ['wɔːdrəub] N (*cupboard*) guardaroba *m inv*, armadio; (*clothes*) guardaroba; (*Theat*) costumi *mpl*

warehouse ['wεəhaus] N magazzino

wares [wεəz] NPL merci *fpl*

warfare ['wɔːfεəʳ] N guerra

war game N war game *m inv*

warhead ['wɔːhεd] N (*Mil*) testata, ogiva

warily ['wεərɪlɪ] ADV cautamente, con prudenza

warlike ['wɔːlaɪk] ADJ guerriero(-a)

warm [wɔːm] ADJ caldo(-a); (*welcome, applause*) caloroso(-a); (*person, greeting*) cordiale; (*heart*) d'oro; (*supporter*) convinto(-a); **it's ~** fa caldo; **I'm ~** ho caldo; **to keep sth ~** tenere qc al caldo; **with my warmest thanks** con i miei più sentiti ringraziamenti ▸ **warm up** VI scaldarsi, riscaldarsi; (*athlete, discussion*) riscaldarsi ▸ VT scaldare, riscaldare; (*engine*) far scaldare

warm-blooded ['wɔːm'blʌdɪd] ADJ a sangue caldo

war memorial N monumento ai caduti

warm-hearted [wɔːm'hɑːtɪd] ADJ affettuoso(-a)

warmly ['wɔːmlɪ] ADV caldamente; (*applaud, welcome*) calorosamente; vivamente; (*dress*) con abiti pesanti

warmonger ['wɔːmʌŋgəʳ] N guerrafondaio

warmongering ['wɔːmʌŋgrɪŋ] N bellicismo

warmth [wɔːmθ] N calore *m*

warm-up ['wɔ:mʌp] N (Sport) riscaldamento
warn [wɔ:n] VT avvertire, avvisare; **to ~ sb not to do sth** or **against doing sth** avvertire or avvisare qn di non fare qc; **to ~ sb that** avvertire or avvisare qn che
warning ['wɔ:nɪŋ] N avvertimento; (notice) avviso; (signal) segnalazione f; **without (any) ~** senza preavviso; **gale ~** avviso di burrasca
warning light N spia luminosa
warning triangle N (Aut) triangolo
warp [wɔ:p] N (Textiles) ordito ▶ VI deformarsi ▶ VT deformare; (fig) corrompere
warpath ['wɔ:pɑ:θ] N: **to be on the ~** (fig) essere sul sentiero di guerra
warped [wɔ:pt] ADJ (wood) curvo(-a); (fig: character, sense of humour etc) contorto(-a)
warrant ['wɔrnt] N (voucher) buono; (Law: to arrest) mandato di cattura; (: to search) mandato di perquisizione ▶ VT (justify, merit) giustificare
warrant officer N sottufficiale m
warranty ['wɔrəntɪ] N garanzia; **under ~** (Comm) in garanzia
warren ['wɔrən] N (of rabbits) tana
warring ['wɔ:rɪŋ] ADJ (interests etc) opposto(-a), in lotta; (nations) in guerra
warrior ['wɔrɪər] N guerriero(-a)
Warsaw ['wɔ:sɔ:] N Varsavia
warship ['wɔ:ʃɪp] N nave f da guerra
wart [wɔ:t] N verruca
wartime ['wɔ:taɪm] N: **in ~** in tempo di guerra
wary ['wɛərɪ] ADJ prudente; **to be ~ about** or **of doing sth** andare cauto nel fare qc
was [wɔz] PT of **be**
wash [wɔʃ] VT lavare; (sweep, carry: sea etc) portare, trascinare ▶ VI lavarsi; (sea): **to ~ over/against sth** infrangersi su/contro qc ▶ N lavaggio; (of ship) scia; **to give sth a ~** lavare qc, dare una lavata a qc; **to have a ~** lavarsi; **he was washed overboard** fu trascinato in mare (dalle onde)
▶ **wash away** VT (stain) togliere lavando; (river etc) trascinare via
▶ **wash down** VT lavare
▶ **wash off** VI andare via con il lavaggio
▶ **wash up** VI (BRIT) lavare i piatti; (US: have a wash) lavarsi
Wash. ABBR (US) = **Washington**
washable ['wɔʃəbl] ADJ lavabile
washbasin ['wɔʃbeɪsn], (US) **washbowl** N lavabo
washcloth ['wɔʃklɔθ] N (US) pezzuola (per lavarsi)
washer ['wɔʃər] N (Tech) rondella
washing ['wɔʃɪŋ] N (BRIT: linen etc) bucato; **dirty ~** biancheria da lavare
washing line N (BRIT) corda del bucato

washing machine N lavatrice f
washing powder N (BRIT) detersivo (in polvere)
Washington ['wɔʃɪŋtən] N Washington f
washing-up [wɔʃɪŋ'ʌp] N (dishes) piatti mpl sporchi; **to do the ~** lavare i piatti
washing-up liquid N (BRIT) detersivo liquido (per stoviglie)
wash-out ['wɔʃaut] N (col) disastro
washroom ['wɔʃrum] N gabinetto
wasn't ['wɔznt] = **was not**
Wasp, WASP [wɔsp] N ABBR (US: = White Anglo-Saxon Protestant) W.A.S.P. m (protestante bianco anglosassone)
wasp [wɔsp] N vespa
waspish ['wɔspɪʃ] ADJ litigioso(-a)
wastage ['weɪstɪdʒ] N spreco; (in manufacturing) scarti mpl
waste [weɪst] N spreco; (of time) perdita; (rubbish) rifiuti mpl; (also: **household waste**) immondizie fpl ▶ ADJ (material) di scarto; (food) avanzato(-a); (energy, heat) sprecato(-a); (land, ground: in city) abbandonato(-a); (: in country) incolto(-a) ▶ VT sprecare; (time, opportunity) perdere; **wastes** NPL distesa desolata; **it's a ~ of money** sono soldi sprecati; **to go to ~** andare sprecato; **to lay ~** devastare
▶ **waste away** VI deperire
wastebasket ['weɪstbɑ:skɪt] N = **wastepaper basket**
waste disposal, waste disposal unit N (BRIT) eliminatore m di rifiuti
wasteful ['weɪstful] ADJ sprecone(-a); (process) dispendioso(-a)
waste ground N (BRIT) terreno incolto or abbandonato
wasteland ['weɪstlænd] N terra desolata
wastepaper basket ['weɪstpeɪpə-] N cestino per la carta straccia
waste pipe N tubo di scarico
waste products NPL (Industry) materiali mpl di scarto
waster ['weɪstər] N (col) buono(-a) a nulla
watch [wɔtʃ] N (wristwatch) orologio (da polso); (act of watching, vigilance) sorveglianza; (guard: Mil, Naut) guardia; (: Naut: spell of duty) quarto ▶ VT (look at) osservare; (: match, programme) guardare; (spy on, guard) sorvegliare, tenere d'occhio; (be careful of) fare attenzione a ▶ VI osservare, guardare; (keep guard) fare or montare la guardia; **to keep a close ~ on sb/sth** tener bene d'occhio qn/qc; **~ how you drive/what you're doing** attento a come guidi/quel che fai
▶ **watch out** VI fare attenzione
watchband ['wɔtʃbænd] N (US) cinturino da orologio

w

watchdog ['wɔtʃdɒg] N cane m da guardia; (fig) sorvegliante mf

watchful ['wɔtʃful] ADJ attento(-a), vigile

watchmaker ['wɔtʃmeɪkəʳ] N orologiaio(-a)

watchman ['wɔtʃmən] N (irreg) guardiano; (also: **night watchman**) guardiano notturno

watch stem N (US) corona di carica

watch strap N cinturino da orologio

watchword ['wɔtʃwəːd] N parola d'ordine

water ['wɔːtəʳ] N acqua ▶ VT (plant) annaffiare ▶ VI (eyes) lacrimare; **in British waters** nelle acque territoriali britanniche; **I'd like a drink of** ~ vorrei un bicchier d'acqua; **to pass** ~ orinare; **to make sb's mouth** ~ far venire l'acquolina in bocca a qn
▶ **water down** VT (milk) diluire; (fig: story) edulcorare

water closet N (BRIT) W.C. m inv, gabinetto

watercolour, (US) **watercolor** ['wɔːtəkʌləʳ] N (picture) acquerello; **watercolours** NPL colori mpl per acquerelli

water-cooled ['wɔːtəkuːld] ADJ raffreddato(-a) ad acqua

watercress ['wɔːtəkrɛs] N crescione m

waterfall ['wɔːtəfɔːl] N cascata

waterfront ['wɔːtəfrʌnt] N (seafront) lungomare m; (at docks) banchina

water heater N scaldabagno

water hole N pozza d'acqua

water ice N (BRIT) sorbetto

watering can ['wɔːtərɪŋ-] N annaffiatoio

water level N livello dell'acqua; (of flood) livello delle acque

water lily N ninfea

waterline ['wɔːtəlaɪn] N (Naut) linea di galleggiamento

waterlogged ['wɔːtəlɒgd] ADJ saturo(-a) d'acqua; imbevuto(-a) d'acqua; (football pitch etc) allagato(-a)

watermark ['wɔːtəmɑːk] N (on paper) filigrana

watermelon ['wɔːtəmɛlən] N anguria, cocomero

water polo N pallanuoto f

waterproof ['wɔːtəpruːf] ADJ impermeabile

water-repellent ['wɔːtərɪ'pɛlənt] ADJ idrorepellente

watershed ['wɔːtəʃɛd] N (Geo, fig) spartiacque m

water-skiing ['wɔːtəskiːɪŋ] N sci m acquatico

water softener N addolcitore m; (substance) anti-calcare m

water tank N serbatoio d'acqua

watertight ['wɔːtətaɪt] ADJ stagno(-a)

water vapour N vapore m acqueo

waterway ['wɔːtəweɪ] N corso d'acqua navigabile

waterworks ['wɔːtəwəːks] NPL impianto idrico

watery ['wɔːtəri] ADJ (colour) slavato(-a); (coffee) acquoso(-a)

watt [wɔt] N watt m inv

wattage ['wɔtɪdʒ] N wattaggio

wattle ['wɔtl] N graticcio

wave [weɪv] N onda; (of hand) gesto, segno; (in hair) ondulazione f; (fig: of enthusiasm, strikes etc) ondata ▶ VI fare un cenno con la mano; (branches, grass) ondeggiare; (flag) sventolare ▶ VT (hand) fare un gesto con; (handkerchief) sventolare; (stick) brandire; (hair) ondulare; **short/medium/long** ~ (Radio) onde corte/medie/lunghe; **the new** ~ (Cine, Mus) la new wave; **to** ~ **sb goodbye, to** ~ **goodbye to sb** fare un cenno d'addio a qn; **he waved us over to his table** ci invitò con un cenno al suo tavolo
▶ **wave aside, wave away** VT (person): **to** ~ **sb aside** fare cenno a qn di spostarsi; (fig: suggestion, objection) respingere, rifiutare (: doubts) scacciare

waveband ['weɪvbænd] N gamma di lunghezze d'onda

wavelength ['weɪvlɛŋθ] N lunghezza d'onda

waver ['weɪvəʳ] VI esitare; (voice) tremolare

wavy ['weɪvi] ADJ ondulato(-a); ondeggiante

wax [wæks] N cera ▶ VT dare la cera a; (car) lucidare ▶ VI (moon) crescere

waxworks ['wækswəːks] NPL cere fpl; museo delle cere

way [weɪ] N via, strada; (path, access) passaggio; (distance) distanza; (direction) parte f, direzione f; (manner) modo, stile m; (habit) abitudine f; (condition) condizione f; **which** ~? — **this** ~ da che parte or in quale direzione? — da questa parte or per di qua; **to crawl one's** ~ **to ...** raggiungere ... strisciando; **he lied his** ~ **out of it** se l'è cavata mentendo; **to lose one's** ~ perdere la strada; **on the** ~ (en route) per strada; (expected) in arrivo; **you pass it on your** ~ **home** ci passi davanti andando a casa; **to be on one's** ~ essere in cammino or sulla strada; **to be in the** ~ bloccare il passaggio; (fig) essere tra i piedi or d'impiccio; **to keep out of sb's** ~ evitare qn; **it's a long** ~ **away** è molto lontano da qui; **the village is rather out of the** ~ il villaggio è abbastanza fuori mano; **to go out of one's** ~ **to do** (fig) mettercela tutta or fare di tutto per fare; **to be under** ~ (work, project) essere in corso; **to lose one's** ~ perdere la strada; **to make** ~ **(for sb/sth)** far strada (a qn/qc); (fig) lasciare il posto or far largo (a qn/qc); **to get one's own** ~ fare come si vuole; **put it the right** ~ **up** (BRIT) mettilo in piedi dalla parte giusta; **to be the wrong** ~ **round** essere al contrario; **he's in a bad** ~ è ridotto male; **in a** ~ in un certo senso; **in some ways** sotto certi aspetti; **in the ~ of** come; **by ~ of** (*through*) attraverso; (*as a sort of*) come; **"~ in"** (BRIT) "entrata", "ingresso"; **"~ out"** (BRIT) "uscita"; **the ~ back** la via del ritorno; **this ~ and that** di qua e di là; **"give ~"** (BRIT Aut) "dare la precedenza"; **no ~!** (*col*) neanche per idea!; **by the ~ ...** a proposito ...

waybill ['weɪbɪl] N (*Comm*) bolla di accompagnamento

waylay [weɪ'leɪ] VT (*irreg: like* **lay**) tendere un agguato a; attendere al passaggio; (*fig*): **I got waylaid** ho avuto un contrattempo

wayside ['weɪsaɪd] N bordo della strada; **to fall by the ~** (*fig*) perdersi lungo la strada

way station N (*US Rail*) stazione *f* secondaria; (*fig*) tappa

wayward ['weɪwəd] ADJ capriccioso(-a); testardo(-a)

WC ['dʌblju'si:] N ABBR (BRIT: = *water closet*) W.C. *m inv*, gabinetto

WCC N ABBR (= *World Council of Churches*) Consiglio Ecumenico delle Chiese

we [wi:] PL PRON noi; **here we are** eccoci

weak [wi:k] ADJ debole; (*health*) precario(-a); (*beam etc*) fragile; (*tea, coffee*) leggero(-a); **to grow ~(er)** indebolirsi

weaken ['wi:kən] VI indebolirsi ▶ VT indebolire

weak-kneed ['wi:k'ni:d] ADJ (*fig*) debole, codardo(-a)

weakling ['wi:klɪŋ] N smidollato(-a); debole *mf*

weakly ['wi:klɪ] ADJ deboluccio(-a), gracile ▶ ADV debolmente

weakness ['wi:knɪs] N debolezza; (*fault*) punto debole, difetto; **to have a ~ for** avere un debole per

wealth [wɛlθ] N (*money, resources*) ricchezza, ricchezze *fpl*; (*of details*) abbondanza, profusione *f*

wealth tax N imposta sul patrimonio

wealthy ['wɛlθɪ] ADJ ricco(-a)

wean [wi:n] VT svezzare

weapon ['wɛpən] N arma; **weapons of mass destruction** armi di distruzione di massa

wear [wɛə^r] (*pt* **wore** [wɔ:^r], *pp* **worn** [wɔ:n]) N (*use*) uso; (*deterioration through use*) logorio, usura; (*clothing*): **sports/baby ~** abbigliamento sportivo/per neonati ▶ VT (*clothes*) portare; (*put on*) mettersi; (*look, smile, beard etc*) avere; (*damage: through use*) consumare ▶ VI (*last*) durare; (*rub etc through*) consumarsi; **~ and tear** usura, consumo; **town/evening ~** abiti *mpl or* tenuta da città/sera; **to ~ a hole in sth** bucare qc a furia di usarlo

▶ **wear away** VT consumare; erodere ▶ VI consumarsi; essere eroso(-a)

▶ **wear down** VT consumare; (*strength*) esaurire

▶ **wear off** VI sparire lentamente

▶ **wear on** VI passare

▶ **wear out** VT consumare; (*person, strength*) esaurire

wearable ['wɛərəbl] ADJ indossabile

wearily ['wɪərɪlɪ] ADV stancamente

weariness ['wɪərɪnɪs] N stanchezza

wearisome ['wɪərɪsəm] ADJ (*tiring*) estenuante; (*boring*) noioso(-a)

weary ['wɪərɪ] ADJ stanco(-a); (*tiring*) faticoso(-a) ▶ VT stancare ▶ VI: **to ~ of** stancarsi di

weasel ['wi:zl] N (*Zool*) donnola

weather ['wɛðə^r] N tempo ▶ VT (*wood*) stagionare; (*storm, crisis*) superare; **what's the ~ like?** che tempo fa?; **under the ~** (*fig: ill*) poco bene

weather-beaten ['wɛðəbi:tn] ADJ (*person*) segnato(-a) dalle intemperie; (*building*) logorato(-a) dalle intemperie

weather forecast N previsioni *fpl* del tempo, bollettino meteorologico

weatherman ['wɛðəmæn] N (*irreg*) meteorologo

weatherproof ['wɛðəpru:f] ADJ (*garment*) impermeabile

weather report N bollettino meteorologico

weather vane N = **weather cock**

weave [wi:v] (*pt* **wove** [wəuv], *pp* **woven** ['wəuvn]) VT (*cloth*) tessere; (*basket*) intrecciare ▶ VI (*pt, pp* **weaved**) (*fig: move in and out*) zigzagare

weaver ['wi:və^r] N tessitore(-trice)

weaving ['wi:vɪŋ] N tessitura

web [wɛb] N (*of spider*) ragnatela; (*on foot*) palma; (*fabric, also fig*) tessuto; **the (World Wide) W~** la Rete

web address N indirizzo Internet

webbed [wɛbd] ADJ (*foot*) palmato(-a)

webbing ['wɛbɪŋ] N (*on chair*) cinghie *fpl*

webcam ['wɛbkæm] N webcam *f inv*

webinar ['wɛbɪnɑ:^r] N (*Comput*) webinar *m inv*

webmail ['wɛbmeɪl] N (*Comput*) webmail *f*

web page N (*Comput*) pagina *f* web *inv*

website ['wɛbsaɪt] N (*Comput*) sito (Internet)

wed [wɛd] (*pt, pp* **wedded**) VT sposare ▶ VI sposarsi ▶ N: **the newly-weds** gli sposi novelli

Wed. ABBR (= *Wednesday*) mer.

we'd [wi:d] = **we had; we would**

wedded ['wɛdɪd] PT, PP *of* **wed**

wedding ['wɛdɪŋ] N matrimonio; **silver/ golden ~** nozze *fpl* d'argento/d'oro

wedding anniversary N anniversario di matrimonio

wedding day N giorno delle nozze *or* del matrimonio

W

wedding dress N abito nuziale
wedding present N regalo di nozze
wedding ring N fede f
wedge [wɛdʒ] N (of wood etc) cuneo; (under door etc) zeppa; (of cake) spicchio, fetta ▶ VT mettere una zeppa sotto (or in); (fix) fissare con zeppe; (pack tightly) incastrare; **to ~ a door open** tenere aperta una porta con un fermo
wedge-heeled shoes ['wɛdʒhi:ld-] NPL scarpe fpl con tacco a zeppa
wedlock ['wɛdlɔk] N vincolo matrimoniale
Wednesday ['wɛnzdɪ] N mercoledì m inv; see also **Tuesday**
wee [wi:] ADJ (SCOTTISH) piccolo(-a)
weed [wi:d] N erbaccia ▶ VT diserbare
▶ **weed out** VT fare lo spoglio di
weed-killer ['wi:dkɪlər] N diserbante m
weedy ['wi:dɪ] ADJ (man) allampanato
week [wi:k] N settimana; **once/twice a ~** una volta/due volte alla settimana; **in 2 weeks' time** fra 2 settimane, fra 15 giorni; **Tuesday ~, a ~ on Tuesday** martedì a otto; **a ~ today** oggi a otto
weekday ['wi:kdeɪ] N giorno feriale; (Comm) giornata lavorativa; **on weekdays** durante la settimana
weekend [wi:k'ɛnd] N fine settimana m inv or f inv, weekend m inv
weekend case N borsa da viaggio
weekly ['wi:klɪ] ADV ogni settimana, settimanalmente ▶ ADJ, N settimanale (m)
weep [wi:p] (pt, pp **wept** [wɛpt]) VI (person) piangere; (Med: wound etc) essudare
weeping willow ['wi:pɪŋ-] N salice m piangente
weepy ['wi:pɪ] N (col) film m inv or storia strappalacrime
weft [wɛft] N (Textiles) trama
weigh [weɪ] VT, VI pesare; **to ~ anchor** salpare or levare l'ancora; **to ~ the pros and cons** valutare i pro e i contro
▶ **weigh down** VT (branch) piegare; (fig: with worry) opprimere, caricare
▶ **weigh out** VT (goods) pesare
▶ **weigh up** VT valutare
weighbridge ['weɪbrɪdʒ] N bascula
weighing machine ['weɪɪŋ-] N pesa
weight [weɪt] N peso; **sold by ~** venduto(-a) a peso; **weights and measures** pesi e misure; **to put on/lose ~** ingrassare/dimagrire
weighting ['weɪtɪŋ] N: **~ allowance** indennità f inv speciale (per carovita ecc)
weightlessness ['weɪtlɪsnɪs] N mancanza di peso
weightlifter ['weɪtlɪftər] N pesista m
weightlifting N sollevamento pesi
weight training N: **to do ~** allenarsi con i pesi

weighty ['weɪtɪ] ADJ pesante; (fig) importante, grave
weir [wɪər] N diga
weird [wɪəd] ADJ strano(-a), bizzarro(-a); (eerie) soprannaturale
weirdo ['wɪədəu] N (col) tipo(-a) allucinante
welcome ['wɛlkəm] ADJ benvenuto(-a) ▶ N accoglienza, benvenuto ▶ VT accogliere cordialmente; (also: **bid welcome**) dare il benvenuto a; (: be glad of) rallegrarsi di; **to be ~** essere il benvenuto(-a); **to make sb ~** accogliere bene qn; **you're ~** (after thanks) prego; **you're ~ to try** provi pure
welcoming ['wɛlkəmɪŋ] ADJ accogliente
weld [wɛld] N saldatura ▶ VT saldare
welder ['wɛldər] N (person) saldatore m
welding ['wɛldɪŋ] N saldatura (autogena)
welfare ['wɛlfɛər] N benessere m
welfare state N stato sociale
welfare work N assistenza sociale
well [wɛl] N pozzo ▶ ADV bene ▶ ADJ: **to be ~** (person) stare bene ▶ EXCL allora!; ma!; ebbene!; **~ done!** bravo(-a)!; **get ~ soon!** guarisci presto!; **to do ~** andare bene; **to do ~ in sth** riuscire in qc; **to be doing ~** stare bene; **to think ~ of sb** avere una buona opinione di qn; **I don't feel ~** non mi sento bene; **as ~** (in addition) anche; **X as ~ as Y** sia X che Y; **he did as ~ as he could** ha fatto come meglio poteva; **you might as ~ tell me** potresti anche dirmelo; **it would be as ~ to ask** sarebbe bene chiedere; **~, as I was saying ...** dunque, come stavo dicendo ...
▶ **well up** VI (tears, emotions) sgorgare
we'll [wi:l] = **we will**; **we shall**
well-behaved ['wɛlbɪ'heɪvd] ADJ ubbidiente
well-being ['wɛl'bi:ɪŋ] N benessere m
well-bred ['wɛl'brɛd] ADJ educato(-a), beneducato(-a)
well-built ['wɛl'bɪlt] ADJ (person) ben fatto(-a)
well-chosen ['wɛl'tʃəuzn] ADJ (remarks, words) ben scelto(-a), appropriato(-a)
well-developed ['wɛldɪ'vɛləpt] ADJ sviluppato(-a)
well-disposed ['wɛldɪs'pəuzd] ADJ: **~ to(wards)** bendisposto(-a) verso
well-dressed ['wɛl'drɛst] ADJ ben vestito(-a), vestito(-a) bene
well-earned ['wɛl'ə:nd] ADJ (rest) meritato(-a)
well-groomed ['wɛl'gru:md] ADJ curato(-a), azzimato(-a)
well-heeled ['wɛl'hi:ld] ADJ (col: wealthy) agiato(-a), facoltoso(-a)
wellies ['wɛlɪz] NPL (BRIT col) stivali mpl di gomma
well-informed ['wɛlɪn'fɔ:md] ADJ ben informato(-a)

Wellington ['wɛlɪŋtən] N Wellington f
wellingtons ['wɛlɪŋtənz] NPL (also:
wellington boots) stivali mpl di gomma
well-kept ['wɛl'kɛpt] ADJ (house, grounds,
secret) ben tenuto(-a); (hair, hands) ben
curato(-a)
well-known ['wɛl'nəun] ADJ noto(-a),
famoso(-a)
well-mannered ['wɛl'mænəd] ADJ ben
educato(-a)
well-meaning ['wɛl'mi:nɪŋ] ADJ ben
intenzionato(-a)
well-nigh ['wɛl'naɪ] ADV: **~ impossible**
quasi impossibile
well-off ['wɛl'ɔf] ADJ benestante,
danaroso(-a)
well-paid [wɛl'peɪd] ADJ ben pagato(-a)
well-read ['wɛl'rɛd] ADJ colto(-a)
well-spoken ['wɛl'spəukn] ADJ che parla
bene
well-stocked ['wɛl'stɔkt] ADJ (shop, larder)
ben fornito(-a)
well-timed ['wɛl'taɪmd] ADJ opportuno(-a)
well-to-do ['wɛltə'du:] ADJ abbiente,
benestante
well-wisher ['wɛlwɪʃəʳ] N
ammiratore(-trice); **letters from
well-wishers** lettere fpl di incoraggiamento
well-woman clinic ['wɛlwumən-] N
≈ consultorio (familiare)
Welsh [wɛlʃ] ADJ gallese ▶ N (Ling) gallese m;
the ~ npl i gallesi; **the ~ National Assembly**
il Parlamento gallese
Welshman ['wɛlʃmən] N (irreg) gallese m
Welsh rarebit N crostino al formaggio
Welshwoman ['wɛlʃwumən] N (irreg)
gallese f
welter ['wɛltəʳ] N massa, mucchio
went [wɛnt] PT of **go**
wept [wɛpt] PT, PP of **weep**
were [wəːʳ] PT of **be**
we're [wɪəʳ] = **we are**
weren't [wəːnt] = **were not**
werewolf ['wɪəwulf] (pl **-wolves** [-wulvz]) N
licantropo, lupo mannaro (col)
west [wɛst] N ovest m, occidente m, ponente
m ▶ ADJ (a) ovest inv, occidentale ▶ ADV verso
ovest; **the W~** l'Occidente
westbound ['wɛstbaund] ADJ (traffic)
diretto(-a) a ovest; (carriageway) ovest inv
West Country N: **the ~** il sud-ovest
dell'Inghilterra
westerly ['wɛstəlɪ] ADJ (wind) occidentale,
da ovest
western ['wɛstən] ADJ occidentale, dell'ovest
▶ N (Cine) western m inv
westerner ['wɛstənəʳ] N occidentale mf
westernized ['wɛstənaɪzd] ADJ
occidentalizzato(-a)

West German ADJ, N (formerly) tedesco(-a)
occidentale
West Germany N (formerly) Germania
Occidentale
West Indian ADJ delle Indie Occidentali
▶ N abitante mf (or originario(-a)) delle Indie
Occidentali
West Indies [-'ɪndɪz] NPL: **the ~** le Indie
Occidentali
Westminster ['wɛstmɪnstəʳ] N il
parlamento (britannico)
westward ['wɛstwəd], **westwards**
['wɛstwədz] ADV verso ovest
wet [wɛt] ADJ umido(-a), bagnato(-a); (soaked)
fradicio(-a); (rainy) piovoso(-a) ▶ N (Brit Pol)
politico moderato ▶ VT: **to ~ one's pants** or
o.s. farsi la pipì addosso; **to get ~** bagnarsi;
"~ paint" "vernice fresca"
wet blanket N (fig) guastafeste mf
wetness ['wɛtnɪs] N umidità
wet suit N tuta da sub
we've [wiːv] = **we have**
whack [wæk] VT picchiare, battere
whacked [wækt] ADJ (col: tired) sfinito(-a),
a pezzi
whale [weɪl] N (Zool) balena
whaler ['weɪləʳ] N (ship) baleniera
whaling ['weɪlɪŋ] N caccia alla balena
wharf [wɔːf] (pl **wharves** [wɔːvz]) N banchina

(KEYWORD)

what [wɔt] ADJ **1** (in direct/indirect questions) che;
quale; **what size is it?** che taglia è?; **what
colour is it?** di che colore è?; **what books do
you want?** quali or che libri vuole?; **for what
reason?** per quale motivo?
2 (in exclamations) che; **what a mess!** che
disordine!
▶ PRON **1** (interrogative) che cosa, cosa, che;
what's in there? cosa c'è lì dentro?; **what is
his address?** qual è il suo indirizzo?; **what
will it cost?** quanto costerà?; **what are you
doing?** che or (che) cosa fai?; **what are you
talking about?** di che cosa parli?; **what's
happening?** che or (che) cosa succede?;
what is it called? come si chiama?; **what
about me?** e io?; **what about doing ...?** e se
facessimo ...?
2 (relative) ciò che, quello che; **I saw what
you did** ho visto quello che hai fatto; **I saw
what was on the table** ho visto cosa c'era
sul tavolo; **what I want is a cup of tea** ciò
che voglio adesso è una tazza di tè
3 (indirect use) (che) cosa; **he asked me what
she had said** mi ha chiesto che cosa avesse
detto; **tell me what you're thinking about**
dimmi a cosa stai pensando; **I don't know
what to do** non so cosa fare
▶ EXCL (disbelieving) cosa!, come!

W

whatever [wɔt'ɛvə^r] ADJ: ~ **book** qualunque or qualsiasi libro +sub ▶ PRON: **do ~ is necessary/you want** faccia qualunque or qualsiasi cosa sia necessaria/lei voglia; ~ **happens** qualunque cosa accada; **no reason** ~ or **whatsoever** nessuna ragione affatto or al mondo; ~ **it costs** costi quello che costi; **nothing** ~ proprio niente

whatsoever [wɔtsəu'ɛvə^r] ADJ, PRON = **whatever**

wheat [wi:t] N grano, frumento

wheatgerm ['wi:tdʒə:m] N germe m di grano

wheatmeal ['wi:tmi:l] N farina integrale di frumento

wheedle ['wi:dl] VT: **to ~ sb into doing sth** convincere qn a fare qc (con lusinghe); **to ~ sth out of sb** ottenere qc da qn (con lusinghe)

wheel [wi:l] N ruota; (Aut: also: **steering wheel**) volante m; (Naut) (ruota del) timone m ▶ VT spingere ▶ VI (birds) roteare; (also: **wheel round**) girare

wheelbarrow ['wi:lbærəu] N carriola

wheelbase ['wi:lbeis] N interasse m

wheelchair ['wi:ltʃɛə^r] N sedia a rotelle

wheel clamp N (Aut): **wheel clamps** ganasce fpl (per vetture in sosta vietata)

wheeler-dealer ['wi:lə'di:lə^r] N trafficone m, maneggione m

wheelie-bin ['wi:lɪbɪn] N (BRIT) bidone m (della spazzatura) a rotelle

wheeling ['wi:lɪŋ] N: ~ **and dealing** maneggi mpl

wheeze [wi:z] N respiro affannoso ▶ VI ansimare

wheezy ['wi:zɪ] ADJ (person) che respira con affanno; (breath) sibilante

(KEYWORD)

when [wɛn] ADV quando; **when did it happen?** quando è successo?
▶ CONJ **1** (at, during, after the time that) quando; **she was reading when I came in** quando sono entrato lei leggeva; **that was when I needed you** era allora che avevo bisogno di te
2 (on, at which): **on the day when I met him** il giorno in cui l'ho incontrato; **one day when it was raining** un giorno che pioveva
3 (whereas) quando, mentre; **you said I was wrong when in fact I was right** mi hai detto che avevo torto, quando in realtà avevo ragione

whenever [wɛn'ɛvə^r] ADV quando mai ▶ CONJ quando; (every time that) ogni volta che; **I go ~ I can** ci vado ogni volta che posso

where [wɛə^r] ADV, CONJ dove; **this is ~** è qui che; ~ **are you from?** di dov'è?; ~ **possible**

quando è possibile, se possibile

whereabouts ['wɛərəbauts] ADV dove
▶ N: **sb's** ~ luogo dove qn si trova

whereas [wɛər'æz] CONJ mentre

whereby [wɛə'baɪ] ADV (formal) per cui

whereupon [wɛərə'pɔn] ADV al che

wherever [wɛər'ɛvə^r] ADV dove mai ▶ CONJ dovunque +sub; (interrogative) dove mai; **sit ~ you like** si sieda dove vuole

wherewithal ['wɛəwɪðɔ:l] N: **the ~ (to do sth)** i mezzi (per fare qc)

whet [wɛt] VT (tool) affilare; (appetite etc) stimolare

whether ['wɛðə^r] CONJ se; **I don't know ~ to accept or not** non so se accettare o no; **it's doubtful ~** è poco probabile che; ~ **you go or not** che lei vada o no

whey [weɪ] N siero

(KEYWORD)

which [wɪtʃ] ADJ **1** (interrogative: direct, indirect) quale; **which picture do you want?** quale quadro vuole?; **which one?** quale?; **which one of you did it?** chi di voi lo ha fatto?; **tell me which one you want** mi dica quale vuole
2: **in which case** nel qual caso; **by which time** e a quel punto
▶ PRON **1** (interrogative) quale; **which (of these) are yours?** quali di questi sono suoi?; **which of you are coming?** chi di voi viene?
2 (relative) che; (: indirect) cui, il (la) quale; **the apple which you ate/which is on the table** la mela che hai mangiato/che è sul tavolo; **the chair on which you are sitting** la sedia sulla quale or su cui sei seduto; **the book of which we were speaking** il libro del quale stavamo parlando; **he said he knew, which is true** ha detto che lo sapeva, il che è vero; **I don't mind which** non mi importa quale; **after which** dopo di che

whichever [wɪtʃ'ɛvə^r] ADJ: **take ~ book you prefer** prenda qualsiasi libro che preferisce; ~ **book you take** qualsiasi libro prenda; ~ **way you …** in qualunque modo lei … +sub

whiff [wɪf] N odore m; **to catch a ~ of sth** sentire l'odore di qc

while [waɪl] N momento ▶ CONJ mentre; (as long as) finché; (although) sebbene +sub; per quanto +sub; **for a ~** per un po'; **in a ~** tra poco; **all the ~** tutto il tempo; **we'll make it worth your ~** faremo in modo che le valga la pena
▶ **while away** VT (time) far passare

whilst [waɪlst] CONJ = **while**

whim [wɪm] N capriccio

whimper ['wɪmpə^r] N piagnucolio ▶ VI piagnucolare

whimsical ['wɪmzɪkl] ADJ (*person*) capriccioso(-a); (*look*) strano(-a)

whine [waɪn] N gemito ▶ VI gemere; uggiolare; piagnucolare

whip [wɪp] N frusta; (*for riding*) frustino; (*Pol: person*) capogruppo (*che sovrintende alla disciplina dei colleghi di partito*); *vedi nota* ▶ VT frustare; (*Culin: cream, eggs etc*) sbattere; (*snatch*) sollevare (*or* estrarre) bruscamente ▶ **whip up** VT (*cream*) montare, sbattere; (*col: meal*) improvvisare; (*: stir up: support, feeling*) suscitare, stimolare

> Nel Parlamento britannico i *whips* sono parlamentari incaricati di mantenere la disciplina tra i deputati del loro partito durante le votazioni e di verificare la loro presenza in aula.

whiplash ['wɪplæʃ] N (*Med: also:* **whiplash injury**) colpo di frusta

whipped cream ['wɪpt-] N panna montata

whipping boy ['wɪpɪŋ-] N (*fig*) capro espiatorio

whip-round ['wɪpraʊnd] N (*BRIT*) colletta

whirl [wə:l] N turbine *m* ▶ VT (*far*) girare rapidamente; (*far*) turbinare ▶ VI turbinare; (*dancers*) volteggiare; (*leaves, water, dust*) sollevarsi in un vortice

whirlpool ['wə:lpu:l] N mulinello

whirlwind ['wə:lwɪnd] N turbine *m*

whirr [wə:ʳ] VI ronzare

whisk [wɪsk] N (*Culin*) frusta; frullino ▶ VT sbattere, frullare; **to ~ sb away** *or* **off** portar via qn a tutta velocità

whiskers ['wɪskəz] NPL (*of animal*) baffi *mpl*; (*of man*) favoriti *mpl*

whisky, (*IRISH, US*) **whiskey** ['wɪskɪ] N whisky *m inv*

whisper ['wɪspəʳ] N bisbiglio, sussurro; (*rumour*) voce *f* ▶ VT, VI bisbigliare, sussurrare; **to ~ sth to sb** bisbigliare qc a qn

whispering ['wɪspərɪŋ] N bisbiglio

whist [wɪst] N (*BRIT*) whist *m*

whistle ['wɪsl] N (*sound*) fischio; (*object*) fischietto ▶ VI, VT fischiare; **to ~ a tune** fischiettare un motivetto

whistle-stop ['wɪslstɔp] ADJ: **~ tour** (*Pol, fig*) rapido giro

Whit [wɪt] N Pentecoste *f*

white [waɪt] ADJ bianco(-a); (*with fear*) pallido(-a) ▶ N bianco; (*person*) bianco(-a); **to turn** *or* **go ~** (*person*) sbiancare; (*hair*) diventare bianco; **the whites** (*washing*) i capi bianchi; **tennis whites** completo da tennis

whitebait ['waɪtbeɪt] N bianchetti *mpl*

whiteboard ['waɪtbɔ:d] N lavagna bianca; **interactive ~** lavagna interattiva

white-collar worker ['waɪtkɔlə-] N impiegato(-a)

white elephant N (*fig*) oggetto (*or* progetto) costoso ma inutile

white goods NPL (*appliances*) elettrodomestici *mpl*; (*linens*) biancheria per la casa

white-hot [waɪt'hɔt] ADJ (*metal*) incandescente

White House N: **the ~** la Casa Bianca; *vedi nota*

> La *White House* è la residenza ufficiale del presidente degli Stati Uniti e ha sede a Washington DC. Spesso il termine viene usato per indicare l'esecutivo del governo statunitense.

white lie N bugia pietosa

whiteness ['waɪtnɪs] N bianchezza

white noise N rumore *m* bianco

white paper N (*Pol*) libro bianco

whitewash ['waɪtwɔʃ] N (*paint*) bianco di calce ▶ VT imbiancare; (*fig*) coprire

whiting ['waɪtɪŋ] N (*pl inv: fish*) merlango

Whit Monday N lunedì *m inv* di Pentecoste

Whitsun ['wɪtsn] N Pentecoste *f*

whittle ['wɪtl] VT: **to ~ away, ~ down** ridurre, tagliare

whizz [wɪz] VI: **to ~ past** *or* **by** passare sfrecciando

whizz kid N (*col*) prodigio

WHO N ABBR (= *World Health Organization*) O.M.S. *f* (= *Organizzazione mondiale della sanità*)

(KEYWORD)

who [hu:] PRON **1** (*interrogative*) chi; **who is it?, who's there?** chi è?

2 (*relative*) che; **the man who spoke to me** l'uomo che ha parlato con me; **those who can swim** quelli che sanno nuotare

whodunit [hu:'dʌnɪt] N (*col*) giallo

whoever [hu:'ɛvəʳ] PRON: **~ finds it** chiunque lo trovi; **ask ~ you like** lo chieda a chiunque vuole; **~ she marries** chiunque sposerà, non importa chi sposerà; **~ told you that?** chi mai gliel'ha detto?

whole [həʊl] ADJ (*complete*) tutto(-a), completo(-a); (*not broken*) intero(-a), intatto(-a) ▶ N (*all*): **the ~ of** tutto(-a) il; (*not broken*) tutto; **the ~ lot (of it)** tutto; **the ~ lot (of them)** tutti; **the ~ of the time** tutto il tempo; **the ~ of the town** tutta la città, la città intera; **on the ~, as a ~** nel complesso, nell'insieme; **~ villages were destroyed** interi paesi furono distrutti

wholefood N, **wholefoods** NPL cibo integrale

wholehearted [həʊl'hɑ:tɪd] ADJ sincero(-a)

wholeheartedly [həʊl'hɑ:tɪdlɪ] ADV sentitamente, di tutto cuore

wholemeal ['həʊlmi:l] ADJ (*BRIT: flour, bread*) integrale

W

whole note N (US) semibreve f
wholesale ['həulseɪl] N commercio or vendita all'ingrosso ▶ ADJ all'ingrosso; (destruction) totale
wholesaler ['həulseɪləʳ] N grossista mf
wholesome ['həulsəm] ADJ sano(-a); (climate) salubre
wholewheat ['həulwi:t] ADJ = **wholemeal**
wholly ['həulɪ] ADV completamente, del tutto

(KEYWORD)

whom [hu:m] PRON **1** (interrogative) chi; **whom did you see?** chi hai visto?; **to whom did you give it?** a chi lo hai dato?
2 (relative) che, prep + il (la) quale; **the man whom I saw** l'uomo che ho visto; **the man to whom I spoke** l'uomo al or con il quale ho parlato; **those to whom I spoke** le persone alle or con le quali ho parlato

whooping cough ['hu:pɪŋ-] N pertosse f
whoops [wu:ps] EXCL: **~-a-daisy!** ops!
whoosh [wuʃ] N: **it came out with a ~** (sauce etc) è uscito di getto; (air) è uscito con un sibilo
whopper ['wɔpəʳ] N (col: lie) balla; (: large thing) cosa enorme
whopping ['wɔpɪŋ] ADJ (col: big) enorme
whore [hɔːʳ] N (col, pej) puttana

(KEYWORD)

whose [hu:z] ADJ **1** (possessive: interrogative) di chi; **whose book is this?**, **whose is this book?** di chi è questo libro?; **whose daughter are you?** di chi sei figlia?; **whose pencil have you taken?** di chi è la matita che hai preso?
2 (possessive: relative): **the man whose son you rescued** l'uomo il cui figlio hai salvato or a cui hai salvato il figlio; **the girl whose sister you were speaking to** la ragazza alla cui sorella stavi parlando
▶ PRON di chi; **whose is this?** di chi è questo?; **I know whose it is** so di chi è

Who's Who ['hu:z'hu:] N elenco di personalità

(KEYWORD)

why [waɪ] ADV perché; **why not?** perché no?; **why not do it now?** perché non farlo adesso?
▶ CONJ perché; **I wonder why he said that** mi chiedo perché l'abbia detto; **that's not why I'm here** non è questo il motivo per cui sono qui; **the reason why** il motivo per cui
▶ EXCL (surprise) ma guarda un po'!; (remonstrating) ma (via)!; (explaining) ebbene!

whyever [waɪ'ɛvəʳ] ADV perché mai

WI N ABBR (BRIT: = Women's Institute) circolo femminile ▶ ABBR (Geo) = **West Indies**; (US) = **Wisconsin**
wick [wɪk] N lucignolo, stoppino
wicked ['wɪkɪd] ADJ cattivo(-a), malvagio(-a); (mischievous) malizioso(-a); (terrible: prices, weather) terribile
wicker ['wɪkəʳ] N vimine m; (also: **wickerwork**) articoli mpl di vimini
wicket ['wɪkɪt] N (Cricket) porta; area tra le due porte
wicket keeper N (Cricket) ≈ portiere m
wide [waɪd] ADJ largo(-a); (region, knowledge) vasto(-a); (choice) ampio(-a) ▶ ADV: **to open ~** spalancare; **to shoot ~** tirare a vuoto or fuori bersaglio; **it is 3 metres ~** è largo 3 metri
wide-angle lens ['waɪdæŋgl-] N grandangolare m
wide-awake [waɪdə'weɪk] ADJ completamente sveglio(-a)
wide-eyed [waɪd'aɪd] ADJ con gli occhi spalancati
widely ['waɪdlɪ] ADV (different) molto, completamente; (believed) generalmente; **~ spaced** molto distanziati(-e); **to be ~ read** (author) essere molto letto; (reader) essere molto colto
widen ['waɪdn] VT allargare, ampliare
wideness ['waɪdnɪs] N larghezza; vastità; ampiezza
wide open ADJ spalancato(-a)
wide-ranging [waɪd'reɪndʒɪŋ] ADJ (survey, report) vasto(-a); (interests) svariato(-a)
widescreen ['waɪdskri:n] ADJ (television, TV) a schermo panoramico
widespread ['waɪdspred] ADJ (belief etc) molto or assai diffuso(-a)
widget ['wɪdʒɪt] N (Comput) widget m inv
widow ['wɪdəu] N vedova
widowed ['wɪdəud] ADJ (che è rimasto(-a)) vedovo(-a)
widower ['wɪdəuəʳ] N vedovo
width [wɪdθ] N larghezza; **it's 7 metres in ~** è largo 7 metri
widthways ['wɪdθweɪz] ADV trasversalmente
wield [wi:ld] VT (sword) maneggiare; (power) esercitare
wife [waɪf] (pl **wives** [waɪvz]) N moglie f
Wi-Fi ['waɪfaɪ] N WiFi m
wig [wɪg] N parrucca
wigging ['wɪgɪŋ] N (BRIT col) lavata di capo
wiggle ['wɪgl] VT dimenare, agitare ▶ VI (loose screw etc) traballare; (worm) torcersi
wiggly ['wɪglɪ] ADJ (line) ondulato(-a), sinuoso(-a)
wiki ['wɪkɪ] N (Internet) wiki m inv
wild [waɪld] ADJ (animal, plant) selvatico(-a); (countryside, appearance) selvaggio(-a); (sea, weather) tempestoso(-a); (idea, life) folle;

stravagante; (applause) frenetico(-a); (col: angry) arrabbiato(-a), furibondo(-a); (enthusiastic): **to be ~ about** andar pazzo(-a) per ▶ N: **the ~** la natura; **wilds** NPL regione f selvaggia

wild card N (Comput) carattere m jolly inv

wildcat ['waɪldkæt] N gatto(-a) selvatico(-a)

wildcat strike N ≈ sciopero selvaggio

wilderness ['wɪldənɪs] N deserto

wildfire ['waɪldfaɪə^r] N: **to spread like ~** propagarsi rapidamente

wild-goose chase [waɪld'guːs-] N (fig) pista falsa

wildlife ['waɪldlaɪf] N natura

wildly ['waɪldlɪ] ADV selvaggiamente; (applaud) freneticamente; (hit, guess) a casaccio; (happy) follemente

wiles [waɪlz] NPL astuzie fpl

wilful, (US) **willful** ['wɪlful] ADJ (person) testardo(-a); ostinato(-a); (action) intenzionale; (crime) premeditato(-a)

(KEYWORD)

will [wɪl] AUX VB **1** (forming future tense): **I will finish it tomorrow** lo finirò domani; **I will have finished it by tomorrow** lo finirò entro domani; **will you do it? — yes I will/ no I won't** lo farai? — sì (lo farò)/no (non lo farò); **the car won't start** la macchina non parte

2 (in conjectures: predictions): **he will** or **he'll be there by now** a quest'ora dovrebbe essere arrivato; **that will be the postman** sarà il postino

3 (in commands: requests: offers): **will you be quiet!** vuoi stare zitto?; **will you sit down?** (politely) prego, si accomodi; (angrily) vuoi metterti seduto?; **will you come?** vieni anche tu?; **will you help me?** mi aiuti?, mi puoi aiutare?; **you won't lose it, will you?** non lo perderai, vero?; **will you have a cup of tea?** vorrebbe una tazza di tè?; **I won't put up with it!** non lo accetterò!

▶ VT (pt, pp **willed**): **to will sb to do** volere che qn faccia; **he willed himself to go on** continuò grazie a un grande sforzo di volontà

▶ N **1** (desire) volontà; **against sb's will** contro la volontà or il volere di qn; **to do sth of one's own free will** fare qc di propria volontà

2 (Law) testamento; **to make a/one's will** fare testamento

willful ['wɪlful] ADJ (US) = **wilful**

willing ['wɪlɪŋ] ADJ volonteroso(-a) ▶ N: **to show ~** dare prova di buona volontà; **~ to do** disposto(-a) a fare

willingly ['wɪlɪŋlɪ] ADV volentieri

willingness ['wɪlɪŋnɪs] N buona volontà

will-o'-the-wisp [wɪləðə'wɪsp] N (also fig) fuoco fatuo

willow ['wɪləu] N salice m

willpower ['wɪlpauə^r] N forza di volontà

willy-nilly ['wɪlɪ'nɪlɪ] ADV volente o nolente

wilt [wɪlt] VI appassire

Wilts [wɪlts] ABBR (BRIT) = **Wiltshire**

wily ['waɪlɪ] ADJ furbo(-a)

wimp [wɪmp] N (col) mezza calzetta

win [wɪn] (pt, pp **won** [wʌn]) N (in sports etc) vittoria ▶ VT (battle, prize, money) vincere; (popularity) guadagnare; (contract) aggiudicarsi ▶ VI vincere

▶ **win over,** (BRIT) **win round** VT convincere

wince [wɪns] N trasalimento, sussulto ▶ VI trasalire

winch [wɪntʃ] N verricello, argano

Winchester disk ['wɪntʃɪstə-] N (Comput) disco Winchester

wind[1] [wɪnd] N vento; (Med) flatulenza, ventosità; (breath) respiro, fiato ▶ VT (take breath away) far restare senza fiato; **the ~(s)** (Mus) i fiati; **into** or **against the ~** controvento; **to get ~ of sth** venire a sapere qc; **to break ~** scoreggiare (col)

wind[2] [waɪnd] (pt, pp **wound** [waund]) VT attorcigliare; (wrap) avvolgere; (clock, toy) caricare ▶ VI (road, river) serpeggiare

▶ **wind down** VT (car window) abbassare; (fig: production, business) diminuire

▶ **wind up** VT (clock) caricare; (debate) concludere

windbreak ['wɪndbreɪk] N frangivento

windcheater ['wɪndtʃiːtə^r], (US) **windbreaker** ['wɪndbreɪkə^r] N giacca a vento

winder ['waɪndə^r] N (BRIT: on watch) corona di carica

windfall ['wɪndfɔːl] N (money) guadagno insperato

wind farm N centrale f eolica

winding ['waɪndɪŋ] ADJ (road) serpeggiante; (staircase) a chiocciola

wind instrument N (Mus) strumento a fiato

windmill ['wɪndmɪl] N mulino a vento

window ['wɪndəu] N (gen, Comput) finestra; (in car, train, plane) finestrino; (in shop etc) vetrina; (also: **window pane**) vetro

window box N cassetta da fiori

window cleaner N (person) pulitore m di finestre

window dressing N allestimento della vetrina

window envelope N busta a finestra

window frame N telaio di finestra

window ledge N davanzale m

window pane N vetro

window seat N posto finestrino

W

window-shopping ['wɪndəʊʃɔpɪŋ] N: **to go ~** andare a vedere le vetrine
windowsill ['wɪndəʊsɪl] N davanzale *m*
windpipe ['wɪndpaɪp] N trachea
wind power N energia eolica
windscreen ['wɪndskriːn], (US) **windshield** ['wɪndʃiːld] N parabrezza *m inv*
windscreen washer N lavacristallo
windscreen wiper, (US) **windshield wiper** N tergicristallo
windshield ['wɪndʃiːld] N (US) = **windscreen**
windsurfing ['wɪndsəːfɪŋ] N windsurf *m inv*
windswept ['wɪndswɛpt] ADJ spazzato(-a) dal vento
wind tunnel N galleria aerodinamica *or* del vento
wind turbine ['wɪndtəːbaɪn] N pala eolica
windy ['wɪndɪ] ADJ ventoso(-a); **it's ~** c'è vento
wine [waɪn] N vino ▶ VT: **to ~ and dine sb** offrire un ottimo pranzo a qn
wine bar N enoteca (*per degustazione*)
wine cellar N cantina
wine glass N bicchiere *m* da vino
wine list N lista dei vini
wine merchant N commerciante *m* di vino
wine tasting N degustazione *f* dei vini
wine waiter N sommelier *m inv*
wing [wɪŋ] N ala; (*Aut*) fiancata; **wings** NPL (*Theat*) quinte *fpl*
winger ['wɪŋər] N (*Sport*) ala
wing mirror N (*BRIT*) specchietto retrovisore esterno
wing nut N galletto
wingspan ['wɪŋspæn], **wingspread** ['wɪŋsprɛd] N apertura alare, apertura d'ali
wink [wɪŋk] N occhiolino, strizzatina d'occhi ▶ VI ammiccare, fare l'occhiolino; (*light*) baluginare
winkle ['wɪŋkl] N litorina
winner ['wɪnər] N vincitore(-trice)
winning ['wɪnɪŋ] ADJ (*team*) vincente; (*goal*) decisivo(-a); (*charming*) affascinante; *see also* **winnings**
winning post N traguardo
winnings ['wɪnɪŋz] NPL vincite *fpl*
winsome ['wɪnsəm] ADJ accattivante
winter ['wɪntər] N inverno; **in ~** d'inverno, in inverno
winter sports NPL sport *mpl* invernali
wintertime N inverno, stagione *f* invernale
wintry ['wɪntrɪ] ADJ invernale
wipe [waɪp] N pulita, passata ▶ VT pulire (strofinando); (*erase: tape*) cancellare; (: *dishes*) asciugare; **to give sth a ~** dare una pulita *or* una passata a qc; **to ~ one's nose** soffiarsi il naso
▶ **wipe off** VT cancellare; (*stains*) togliere strofinando

▶ **wipe out** VT (*debt*) pagare, liquidare; (*memory*) cancellare; (*destroy*) annientare
▶ **wipe up** VT asciugare
wire ['waɪər] N filo; (*Elec*) filo elettrico; (*Tel*) telegramma *m* ▶ VT (*Elec: house*) fare l'impianto elettrico di; (: *circuit*) installare; (*also*: **wire up**) collegare, allacciare; (: *person*) telegrafare a
wire brush N spazzola metallica
wire cutters [-kʌtəz] NPL tronchese *m or f*
wireless ['waɪəlɪs] N (*BRIT: set*) (apparecchio *m*) radio *f inv* ▶ ADJ wireless *inv*, senza fili
wireless technology N tecnologia wireless
wire netting N rete *f* metallica
wire service N (US) = **news agency**
wire-tapping ['waɪətæpɪŋ] N intercettazione *f* telefonica
wiring ['waɪərɪŋ] N (*Elec*) impianto elettrico
wiry ['waɪərɪ] ADJ magro(-a) e nerboruto(-a)
Wis., Wisc. ABBR (US) = **Wisconsin**
wisdom ['wɪzdəm] N saggezza; (*of action*) prudenza
wisdom tooth N dente *m* del giudizio
wise [waɪz] ADJ saggio(-a); (*advice, remark*) prudente; giudizioso(-a); **I'm none the wiser** ne so come prima
▶ **wise up** VI (*col*): **to ~ up to** divenire più consapevole di
...wise [waɪz] SUFFIX: **timewise** per quanto riguarda il tempo, in termini del tempo
wisecrack ['waɪzkræk] N battuta spiritosa
wish [wɪʃ] N (*desire*) desiderio; (*specific desire*) richiesta ▶ VT desiderare, volere; **best wishes** (*on birthday etc*) i migliori auguri; **with best wishes** (*in letter*) cordiali saluti, con i migliori saluti; **give her my best wishes** le faccia i migliori auguri da parte mia; **to ~ sb goodbye** dire arrivederci a qn; **he wished me well** mi augurò di riuscire; **to ~ to do/sb to do** desiderare *or* volere fare/che qn faccia; **to ~ for** desiderare; **to ~ sth on sb** rifilare qc a qn
wishbone ['wɪʃbəun] N forcella
wishful ['wɪʃful] ADJ: **it's ~ thinking** è prendere i desideri per realtà
wishy-washy ['wɪʃɪ'wɔʃɪ] ADJ insulso(-a)
wisp [wɪsp] N ciuffo, ciocca; (*of smoke, straw*) filo
wistful ['wɪstful] ADJ malinconico(-a); (*nostalgic*) nostalgico(-a)
wit [wɪt] N (*gen pl*) intelligenza; presenza di spirito; (*wittiness*) spirito, arguzia; (*person*) bello spirito; **to be at one's wits' end** (*fig*) non sapere più cosa fare; **to have** *or* **keep one's wits about one** avere presenza di spirito; **to ~** *adv* cioè
witch [wɪtʃ] N strega
witchcraft ['wɪtʃkrɑːft] N stregoneria
witch doctor N stregone *m*

witch-hunt ['wɪtʃhʌnt] N (fig) caccia alle streghe

(KEYWORD)

with [wɪð, wɪθ] PREP **1** (in the company of) con; **I was with him** ero con lui; **we stayed with friends** siamo stati da amici; **I'll be with you in a minute** vengo subito
2 (descriptive) con; **a room with a view** una camera con vista (sul mare or sulle montagne etc); **the man with the grey hat/ blue eyes** l'uomo con il cappello grigio/gli occhi blu
3 (indicating manner: means: cause): **with tears in her eyes** con le lacrime agli occhi; **red with anger** rosso(-a) dalla rabbia; **to shake with fear** tremare di paura; **covered with snow** coperto(-a) di neve
4: **I'm with you** (I understand) la seguo; **to be with it** (col: up-to-date) essere alla moda; (: alert) essere sveglio(-a); **I'm not really with it today** (col) oggi sono un po' fuori

withdraw [wɪθ'drɔː] VT (irreg: like **draw**) ritirare; (money from bank) ritirare; prelevare ▶ VI ritirarsi; **to ~ into o.s.** chiudersi in se stesso
withdrawal [wɪθ'drɔːəl] N ritiro; prelievo; (of army) ritirata; (Med) stato di privazione
withdrawal symptoms NPL (Med) crisi f di astinenza
withdrawn [wɪθ'drɔːn] PP of **withdraw** ▶ ADJ (person) distaccato(-a)
withdrew [wɪθ'druː] PT of **withdraw**
wither ['wɪðəʳ] VI appassire
withered ['wɪðəd] ADJ appassito(-a); (limb) atrofizzato(-a)
withhold [wɪθ'həuld] VT (irreg: like **hold**) (money) trattenere; (permission): **to ~ (from)** rifiutare (a); (information) nascondere (a)
within [wɪð'ɪn] PREP all'interno di; (in time, distances) entro ▶ ADV all'interno, dentro; **~ reach (of)** alla portata (di); **~ sight (of)** in vista (di); **~ a mile of** entro un miglio da; **~ the week** prima della fine della settimana; **~ an hour from now** da qui a un'ora; **to be ~ the law** restare nei limiti della legge
without [wɪð'aut] PREP senza; **to go** or **do ~ sth** fare a meno di qc; **~ anybody knowing** senza che nessuno lo sappia
withstand [wɪθ'stænd] VT (irreg: like **stand**) resistere a
witness ['wɪtnɪs] N (person, also Law) testimone mf ▶ VT (event) essere testimone di; (document) attestare l'autenticità di ▶ VI: **to ~ to sth/having seen sth** testimoniare qc/di aver visto qc; **to bear ~ to sth** testimoniare qc; **~ for the prosecution/defence** testimone a carico/discarico

witness box, (US) **witness stand** N banco dei testimoni
witticism ['wɪtɪsɪzəm] N spiritosaggine f
witty ['wɪtɪ] ADJ spiritoso(-a)
wives [waɪvz] NPL of **wife**
wizard ['wɪzəd] N mago
wizened ['wɪznd] ADJ raggrinzito(-a)
wk ABBR = **week**
Wm. ABBR = **William**
WMD N ABBR see **weapons of mass destruction**
WO N ABBR see **warrant officer**
wobble ['wɔbl] VI tremare; (chair) traballare
wobbly ['wɔblɪ] ADJ (hand, voice) tremante; (table, chair) traballante; (object about to fall) che oscilla pericolosamente
woe [wəu] N dolore m; disgrazia
woeful ['wəuful] ADJ (sad) triste; (deplorable) deplorevole
wok [wɔk] N wok m inv (padella concava usata nella cucina cinese)
woke [wəuk] PT of **wake**
woken ['wəukn] PP of **wake**
wolf [wulf] (pl **wolves** [wulvz]) N lupo
woman ['wumən] (pl **women** ['wɪmɪn]) N donna ▶ CPD: **~ doctor** n dottoressa; **~ friend** n amica; **~ teacher** n insegnante f; **women's page** n (Press) rubrica femminile
womanize ['wumənaɪz] VI essere un donnaiolo
womanly ['wumənlɪ] ADJ femminile
womb [wuːm] N (Anat) utero
women ['wɪmɪn] NPL of **woman**
Women's Movement, Women's Liberation Movement N (also: **Women's Lib**) Movimento per la Liberazione della Donna
won [wʌn] PT, PP of **win**
wonder ['wʌndəʳ] N meraviglia ▶ VI: **to ~ whether/why** domandarsi se/perché; **to ~ at** essere sorpreso(-a) di; meravigliarsi di; **to ~ about** domandarsi di; pensare a; **it's no ~ that** c'è poco or non c'è da meravigliarsi che + sub
wonderful ['wʌndəful] ADJ meraviglioso(-a)
wonderfully ['wʌndəfəlɪ] ADV (+ adjective) meravigliosamente; (+ verb) a meraviglia
wonky ['wɔŋkɪ] ADJ (BRIT col) traballante
wont [wəunt] N: **as is his/her ~** com'è solito/a fare
won't [wəunt] = **will not**
woo [wuː] VT (woman) fare la corte a
wood [wud] N legno; (timber) legname m; (forest) bosco ▶ CPD di bosco, silvestre
wood carving N scultura in legno, intaglio
wooded ['wudɪd] ADJ boschivo(-a); boscoso(-a)
wooden ['wudn] ADJ di legno; (fig) rigido(-a); inespressivo(-a)

W

woodland ['wʊdlənd] N zona boscosa

woodpecker ['wʊdpɛkəʳ] N picchio

wood pigeon N colombaccio, palomba

woodwind ['wʊdwɪnd] NPL (*Mus*): **the ~** i legni

woodwork ['wʊdwəːk] N parti *fpl* in legno; (*craft, subject*) falegnameria

woodworm ['wʊdwəːm] N tarlo del legno

woof [wʊf] N (*of dog*) bau bau *m* ▶ VI abbaiare; **~, ~!** bau bau!

wool [wʊl] N lana; **to pull the ~ over sb's eyes** (*fig*) gettare fumo negli occhi a qn

woollen, (*US*) **woolen** ['wʊlən] ADJ di lana; (*industry*) laniero(-a) ▶ N: **woollens** indumenti *mpl* di lana

woolly, (*US*) **wooly** ['wʊlɪ] ADJ di lana; (*fig: ideas*) confuso(-a)

woozy ['wuːzɪ] ADJ (*col*) stordito(-a)

word [wəːd] N parola; (*news*) notizie *fpl* ▶ VT esprimere, formulare; **~ for ~** parola per parola, testualmente; **what's the ~ for "pen" in Italian?** come si dice "pen" in italiano?; **to put sth into words** esprimere qc a parole; **in other words** in altre parole; **to have a ~ with sb** scambiare due parole con qn; **to have words with sb** (*quarrel with*) avere un diverbio con qn; **to break/keep one's ~** non mantenere/mantenere la propria parola; **I'll take your ~ for it** la crederò sulla parola; **to send ~** avvisare di; **to leave ~ (with** or **for sb) that ...** lasciare detto (a qn) che ...

wording ['wəːdɪŋ] N formulazione *f*

word of mouth N passaparola *m*; **I learned it by** or **through ~** lo so per sentito dire

word-perfect ['wəːd'pəːfɪkt] ADJ (*speech etc*) imparato(-a) a memoria

word processing N word processing *m*, elaborazione *f* testi

word processor N word processor *m inv*

wordwrap ['wəːdræp] N (*Comput*) ritorno carrello automatico

wordy ['wəːdɪ] ADJ verboso(-a), prolisso(-a)

wore [wɔːʳ] PT *of* **wear**

work [wəːk] N lavoro; (*Art, Literature*) opera ▶ VI lavorare; (*mechanism, plan etc*) funzionare; (*medicine*) essere efficace ▶ VT (*clay, wood etc*) lavorare; (*mine etc*) sfruttare; (*machine*) far funzionare; (*cause: effect, miracle*) fare; **to be at ~ (on sth)** lavorare (a qc); **to set to ~, to start ~** mettersi all'opera; **to go to ~** andare al lavoro; **to be out of ~** essere disoccupato(-a); **to ~ one's way through a book** riuscire a leggersi tutto un libro; **to ~ one's way through college** lavorare per pagarsi gli studi; **how does this ~?** come funziona?; **the TV isn't working** la TV non funziona; **to ~ hard** lavorare sodo; **to ~ loose** allentarsi; *see also* **works**

▶ **work on** VT FUS lavorare a; (*principle*) basarsi su; **he's working on the car** sta facendo dei lavori alla macchina

▶ **work out** VI (*plans etc*) riuscire, andare bene; (*Sport*) allenarsi ▶ VT (*problem*) risolvere; (*plan*) elaborare; **it works out at £100** fa 100 sterline

workable ['wəːkəbl] ADJ (*solution*) realizzabile

workaholic [wəːkə'hɔlɪk] N stacanovista *mf*

workbench ['wəːkbɛntʃ] N banco (da lavoro)

worked up ADJ: **to get ~** andare su tutte le furie; eccitarsi

worker ['wəːkəʳ] N lavoratore(-trice); (*esp Agr, Industry*) operaio(-a); **office ~** impiegato(-a)

work experience ['wəːkɪkspɪərɪəns] N (*previous jobs*) esperienze *fpl* lavorative; (*student training placement*) tirocinio

work force N forza lavoro

work-in ['wəːkɪn] N (*Brit*) sciopero alla rovescia

working ['wəːkɪŋ] ADJ (*day*) feriale; (*tools, conditions*) di lavoro; (*clothes*) da lavoro; (*wife*) che lavora; (*partner*) attivo(-a); **in ~ order** funzionante; **~ knowledge** conoscenza pratica

working capital N (*Comm*) capitale *m* d'esercizio

working class N classe *f* operaia or lavoratrice ▶ ADJ: **working-class** operaio(-a)

working man N (*irreg*) lavoratore *m*

working party N (*Brit*) commissione *f*

working week N settimana lavorativa

work-in-progress ['wəːkɪn'prəʊgrɛs] N (*products*) lavoro in corso; (*value*) valore *m* del manufatto in lavorazione

workload ['wəːkləʊd] N carico di lavoro

workman ['wəːkmən] N (*irreg*) operaio

workmanship ['wəːkmənʃɪp] N (*of worker*) abilità; (*of thing*) fattura

workmate ['wəːkmeɪt] N collega *mf*

work of art N opera d'arte

workout ['wəːkaʊt] N (*Sport*) allenamento

work permit N permesso di lavoro

workplace N posto di lavoro

works [wəːks] N (*Brit: factory*) fabbrica ▶ NPL (*of clock, machine*) meccanismo; **road ~** opere stradali

works council N consiglio aziendale

work sheet N (*Comput*) foglio col programma di lavoro

workshop ['wəːkʃɔp] N officina; (*practical session*) gruppo di lavoro

work station N stazione *f* di lavoro

work study N studio di organizzazione del lavoro

work surface N piano di lavoro

worktop ['wəːktɔp] N piano di lavoro

work-to-rule ['wəːktə'ruːl] N (*Brit*) sciopero bianco

world [wə:ld] N mondo ▶ CPD (*tour, champion*) del mondo; (*record, power, war*) mondiale; **all over the ~** in tutto il mondo; **to think the ~ of sb** (*fig*) pensare un gran bene di qn; **out of this ~** (*fig*) formidabile; **what in the ~ is he doing?** che cavolo sta facendo?; **to do sb a ~ of good** fare un gran bene a qn; **W~ War One/Two** la prima/seconda guerra mondiale

world champion N campione(-essa) mondiale

World Cup N (*Football*) Coppa del Mondo

world-famous [wə:ld'feɪməs] ADJ di fama mondiale

worldly ['wə:ldlɪ] ADJ di questo mondo

world music N musica etnica

World Series N: **the ~** (*US Baseball*) la finalissima di baseball

world-wide ['wə:ld'waɪd] ADJ universale

World-Wide Web N World Wide Web *m*

worm [wə:m] N (*also:* **earthworm**) verme *m*

worn [wɔ:n] PP *of* **wear** ▶ ADJ usato(-a)

worn-out ['wɔ:naut] ADJ (*object*) consumato(-a), logoro(-a); (*person*) sfinito(-a)

worried ['wʌrɪd] ADJ preoccupato(-a); **to be ~ about sth** essere preoccupato per qc

worrier ['wʌrɪər] N ansioso(-a)

worrisome ['wʌrɪsəm] ADJ preoccupante

worry ['wʌrɪ] N preoccupazione *f* ▶ VT preoccupare ▶ VI preoccuparsi; **to ~ about** *or* **over sth/sb** preoccuparsi di qc/per qn

worrying ['wʌrɪɪŋ] ADJ preoccupante

worse [wə:s] ADJ peggiore ▶ ADV, N peggio; **a change for the ~** un peggioramento; **to get ~, to grow ~** peggiorare; **he is none the ~ for it** non ha avuto brutte conseguenze; **so much the ~ for you!** tanto peggio per te!

worsen ['wə:sn] VT, VI peggiorare

worse off ADJ in condizioni (economiche) peggiori; (*fig*) **you'll be ~ this way** così sarà peggio per lei; **he is now ~ than before** ora è in condizioni peggiori di prima

worship ['wə:ʃɪp] N culto ▶ VT (*God*) adorare, venerare; (*person*) adorare; **Your W~** (*BRIT: to mayor*) signor sindaco; (: *to judge*) signor giudice

worshipper ['wə:ʃɪpər] N adoratore(-trice); (*in church*) fedele *mf*, devoto(-a)

worst [wə:st] ADJ il (la) peggiore ▶ ADV, N peggio; **at ~** al peggio, per male che vada; **to come off ~** avere la peggio; **if the ~ comes to the ~** nel peggior dei casi

worst-case ['wə:st'keɪs] ADJ: **the ~ scenario** la peggiore delle ipotesi

worsted ['wustɪd] N: (**wool**) **~** lana pettinata

worth [wə:θ] N valore *m* ▶ ADJ: **to be ~** valere; **how much is it ~?** quanto vale?; **it's ~ it** ne vale la pena; **it's not ~ the trouble** non ne vale la pena; **50 pence ~ of apples** 50 pence di mele

worthless ['wə:θlɪs] ADJ di nessun valore

worthwhile ['wə:θ'waɪl] ADJ (*activity*) utile; (*cause*) lodevole; **a ~ book** un libro che vale la pena leggere

worthy ['wə:ðɪ] ADJ (*person*) degno(-a); (*motive*) lodevole; **~ of** degno di

(KEYWORD)

would [wud] AUX VB **1** (*conditional tense*): **if you asked him he would do it** se glielo chiedessi lo farebbe; **if you had asked him he would have done it** se glielo avesse chiesto lo avrebbe fatto

2 (*in offers: invitations: requests*): **would you like a biscuit?** vorrebbe *or* vuole un biscotto?; **would you ask him to come in?** lo faccia entrare, per cortesia; **would you open the window please?** apra la finestra, per favore

3 (*in indirect speech*): **I said I would do it** ho detto che l'avrei fatto

4 (*emphatic*): **it WOULD have to snow today!** doveva proprio nevicare oggi!

5 (*insistence*): **she wouldn't do it** non ha voluto farlo

6 (*conjecture*): **it would have been midnight** sarà stata mezzanotte; **it would seem so** sembrerebbe proprio di sì

7 (*indicating habit*): **he would go there on Mondays** andava lì ogni lunedì

would-be ['wudbi:] ADJ (*pej*) sedicente

wouldn't ['wudnt] = **would not**

wound[1] [wu:nd] N ferita ▶ VT ferire; **wounded in the leg** ferito(-a) alla gamba

wound[2] [waund] PT, PP *of* **wind**[2]

wove [wəuv] PT *of* **weave**

woven ['wəuvn] PP *of* **weave**

WP ABBR (*BRIT: col: = weather permitting*) tempo permettendo ▶ N ABBR = **word processing**; **word processor**

WPC N ABBR (*BRIT: = woman police constable*) donna poliziotto

wpm ABBR (= *words per minute*) p.p.m.

WRAC N ABBR (*BRIT: = Women's Royal Army Corps*) ausiliarie dell'esercito

WRAF N ABBR (*BRIT: = Women's Royal Air Force*) ausiliarie dell'aeronautica militare

wrangle ['ræŋgl] N litigio ▶ VI litigare

wrap [ræp] N (*stole*) scialle *m*; (*cape*) mantellina ▶ VT (*also:* **wrap up**) avvolgere; (: *parcel*) incartare; **under wraps** segreto

wrapper ['ræpər] N (*on chocolate*) carta; (*BRIT: of book*) copertina

wrapping ['ræpɪŋ] N carta

wrapping paper ['ræpɪŋ-] N carta da pacchi; (*for gift*) carta da regali

wrath [rɔθ] N collera, ira

W

wreak [riːk] VT (*destruction*) portare, causare; **to ~ vengeance on** vendicarsi su; **to ~ havoc on** portare scompiglio in

wreath [riːθ] (*pl* **wreaths** [riːðz]) N corona

wreck [rɛk] N (*sea disaster*) naufragio; (*ship*) relitto; (*pej: person*) rottame *m* ▶ VT demolire; (*ship*) far naufragare; (*fig*) rovinare

wreckage ['rɛkɪdʒ] N rottami *mpl*; (*of building*) macerie *fpl*; (*of ship*) relitti *mpl*

wrecker ['rɛkəʳ] N (*US: breakdown van*) carro *m* attrezzi *inv*

WREN [rɛn] N ABBR (*Brit*) *membro del* WRNS

wren [rɛn] N (*Zool*) scricciolo

wrench [rɛntʃ] N (*Tech*) chiave *f*; (*tug*) torsione *f* brusca; (*fig*) strazio ▶ VT strappare; storcere; **to ~ sth from** strappare qc a *or* da

wrest [rɛst] VT: **to ~ sth from sb** strappare qc a qn

wrestle ['rɛsl] VI: **to ~ (with sb)** lottare (con qn); **to ~ with** (*fig*) combattere *or* lottare contro

wrestler ['rɛsləʳ] N lottatore(-trice)

wrestling ['rɛslɪŋ] N lotta; (*also:* **all-in wrestling**: *Brit*) catch *m*, lotta libera

wrestling match N incontro di lotta (*or* lotta libera)

wretch [rɛtʃ] N disgraziato(-a), sciagurato(-a); **little ~!** (*often humorous*) birbante!

wretched ['rɛtʃɪd] ADJ disgraziato(-a); (*col: weather, holiday*) orrendo(-a), orribile; (: *child, dog*) pestifero(-a)

wriggle ['rɪgl] N contorsione *f* ▶ VI (*also:* **wriggle about**) dimenarsi; (: *snake, worm*) serpeggiare, muoversi serpeggiando

wring [rɪŋ] (*pt, pp* **wrung** [rʌŋ]) VT torcere; (*wet clothes*) strizzare; (*fig*): **to ~ sth out of** strappare qc a

wringer ['rɪŋəʳ] N strizzatoio (manuale)

wringing ['rɪŋɪŋ] ADJ (*also:* **wringing wet**) bagnato(-a) fradicio(-a)

wrinkle ['rɪŋkl] N (*on skin*) ruga; (*on paper etc*) grinza ▶ VT (*nose*) torcere; (*forehead*) corrugare; raggrinzire ▶ VI corrugarsi; (*skin, paint*) raggrinzirsi

wrinkled ['rɪŋkld], **wrinkly** ['rɪŋklɪ] ADJ (*fabric, paper*) stropicciato(-a); (*surface*) corrugato(-a), increspato(-a); (*skin*) rugoso(-a)

wrist [rɪst] N polso

wristband ['rɪstbænd] N (*of shirt*) polsino; (*of watch*) cinturino

wrist watch N orologio da polso

writ [rɪt] N ordine *m*; mandato; **to issue a ~ against sb**, **serve a ~ on sb** notificare un mandato di comparizione a qn

write [raɪt] (*pt* **wrote** [rəut], *pp* **written** ['rɪtn]) VT, VI scrivere; **to ~ sb a letter** scrivere una lettera a qn

▶ **write away** VI: **to ~ away for** (*information*) richiedere per posta; (*goods*) ordinare per posta

▶ **write down** VT annotare; (*put in writing*) mettere per iscritto

▶ **write off** VT (*debt, plan*) cancellare; (*depreciate*) deprezzare; (*smash up: car*) distruggere

▶ **write out** VT mettere per iscritto; (*cheque, receipt*) scrivere; (*copy*) ricopiare

▶ **write up** VT redigere

write-off ['raɪtɔf] N perdita completa; **the car is a ~** la macchina va bene per il demolitore

write-protect ['raɪtprə'tɛkt] VT (*Comput*) proteggere contro scrittura

writer ['raɪtəʳ] N autore(-trice), scrittore(-trice)

write-up ['raɪtʌp] N (*review*) recensione *f*

writhe [raɪð] VI contorcersi

writing ['raɪtɪŋ] N scrittura; (*of author*) scritto, opera; **in ~** per iscritto; **in my own ~** scritto di mio pugno

writing case N nécessaire *m inv* per la corrispondenza

writing desk N scrivania, scrittoio

writing paper N carta da lettere

written ['rɪtn] PP *of* **write**

WRNS N ABBR (*Brit*: = *Women's Royal Naval Service*) ausiliarie della marina militare

wrong [rɔŋ] ADJ sbagliato(-a); (*not suitable*) inadatto(-a); (*wicked*) cattivo(-a); (*unfair*) ingiusto(-a) ▶ ADV in modo sbagliato, erroneamente ▶ N (*evil*) male *m*; (*injustice*) torto ▶ VT fare torto a; **to be ~** (*answer*) essere sbagliato; (*in doing, saying*) avere torto; **you are ~ to do it** ha torto a farlo; **you are ~ about that, you've got it ~** si sbaglia; **to be in the ~** avere torto; **what's ~?** cosa c'è che non va?; **there's nothing ~** va tutto bene; **what's ~ with the car?** cos'ha la macchina che non va?; **to go ~** (*person*) sbagliarsi; (*plan*) fallire, non riuscire; (*machine*) guastarsi; **it's ~ to steal, stealing is ~** è male rubare

wrongdoer ['rɔŋduːəʳ] N malfattore(-trice)

wrong-foot [rɔŋ'fut] VT (*Sport: also fig*) prendere in contropiede

wrongful ['rɔŋful] ADJ illegittimo(-a); ingiusto(-a); **~ dismissal** licenziamento ingiustificato

wrongly ['rɔŋlɪ] ADV (*incorrectly, by mistake*) in modo sbagliato; (*accuse, dismiss*) a torto; (*answer, do, count*) erroneamente; (*treat*) ingiustamente

wrong number N: **you have the ~** (*Tel*) ha sbagliato numero

wrong side N (*of cloth*) rovescio

wrote [rəut] PT *of* **write**

wrought [rɔ:t] ADJ: **~ iron** ferro battuto
wrung [rʌŋ] PT, PP of **wring**
WRVS N ABBR (*BRIT*) = **Women's Royal Voluntary Service**
wry [raɪ] ADJ storto(-a)
wt. ABBR = **weight**

WV, W. Va. ABBR (*US*) = **West Virginia**
WWW N ABBR = **World Wide Web**; **the ~** la Rete
WY, Wyo. ABBR (*US*) = **Wyoming**
WYSIWYG ['wɪzɪwɪg] ABBR (*Comput*) = **what you see is what you get**

Xx

X, x [ɛks] N (*letter*) X, x f *inv or* m *inv*; (BRIT *Cine:
old*) ≈ film vietato ai minori di 18 anni; **X for
Xmas** ≈ X come Xeres
Xerox® ['zɪərɔks] N (*also:* **Xerox machine**)
fotocopiatrice f; (: *photocopy*) fotocopia
▸ VT fotocopiare
XL ABBR = **extra large**

Xmas ['ɛksməs] N ABBR = **Christmas**
X-rated ['ɛks'reɪtɪd] ADJ (*US: film*) ≈ vietato ai
minori di 18 anni
X-ray ['ɛks'reɪ] N raggio X; (*photograph*)
radiografia ▸ VT radiografare; **to have an ~**
farsi fare una radiografia
xylophone ['zaɪləfəun] N xilofono

Yy

Y, y [waɪ] N (*letter*) Y, y f *inv or* m *inv*; **Y for Yellow**, (*US*) **Y for Yoke** ≈ Y come Yacht

yacht [jɔt] N panfilo, yacht m *inv*

yachting ['jɔtɪŋ] N yachting m, sport m della vela

yachtsman ['jɔtsmən] N (*irreg*) yachtsman m *inv*

yam [jæm] N igname m; (*sweet potato*) patata dolce

Yank [jæŋk], **Yankee** ['jæŋkɪ] N (*pej*) yankee mf, nordamericano(-a)

yank [jæŋk] N strattone m ▶ VT tirare, dare uno strattone a

yap [jæp] VI (*dog*) guaire

yard [jɑːd] N (*of house etc*) cortile m; (*US: garden*) giardino; (*measure*) iarda (= *914 mm; 3 feet*); **builder's ~** deposito di materiale da costruzione

yard sale (*US*) N *vendita di oggetti usati nel cortile di una casa privata*

yardstick ['jɑːdstɪk] N (*fig*) misura, criterio

yarn [jɑːn] N filato; (*tale*) lunga storia

yawn [jɔːn] N sbadiglio ▶ VI sbadigliare

yawning ['jɔːnɪŋ] ADJ (*gap*) spalancato(-a)

yd. ABBR = **yard**

yeah [jɛə] ADV (*col*) sì

year [jɪəʳ] N (*gen, Scol*) anno; (*referring to harvest, wine etc*) annata; **every ~** ogni anno, tutti gli anni; **this ~** quest'anno; **~ in, ~ out** anno dopo anno; **she's three years old** ha tre anni; **an eight-~-old child** un(a) bambino(-a) di otto anni; **a** *or* **per ~** all'anno

yearbook ['jɪəbuk] N annuario

yearly ['jɪəlɪ] ADJ annuale ▶ ADV annualmente; **twice-~** semestrale

yearn [jəːn] VI: **to ~ for sth/to do** desiderare ardentemente qc/di fare

yearning ['jəːnɪŋ] N desiderio intenso

yeast [jiːst] N lievito

yell [jɛl] N urlo ▶ VI urlare

yellow ['jɛləu] ADJ giallo(-a)

yellow fever N febbre f gialla

yellowish ['jɛləuɪʃ] ADJ giallastro(-a), giallognolo(-a)

Yellow Pages ® NPL pagine fpl gialle

Yellow Sea N: **the ~** il mar Giallo

yelp [jɛlp] N guaito, uggiolio ▶ VI guaire, uggiolare

Yemen ['jɛmən] N Yemen m

yen [jɛn] N (*currency*) yen m *inv*; (*craving*): **~ for/ to do** gran voglia di/di fare

yeoman ['jəumən] N (*irreg*): **Y~ of the Guard** guardiano della Torre di Londra

yes [jɛs] ADV, N sì (m *inv*); **to say ~ (to)** dire di sì(a)

yesterday ['jɛstədɪ] ADV, N ieri (m *inv*); **~ morning/evening** ieri mattina/sera; **the day before ~** l'altro ieri; **all day ~** ieri per tutta la giornata

yet [jɛt] ADV ancora; già ▶ CONJ ma, tuttavia; **it is not finished ~** non è ancora finito; **the best ~** finora il migliore finora; **as ~** finora; **~ again** di nuovo; **must you go just ~?** deve andarsene di già?; **a few days ~** ancora qualche giorno

yew [juː] N tasso (*albero*)

Y-fronts ® ['waɪfrʌnts] NPL (*BRIT*) slip m *inv* da uomo

YHA N ABBR (*BRIT*: = *Youth Hostels Association*) Y.H.A. f

Yiddish ['jɪdɪʃ] N yiddish m

yield [jiːld] N produzione f, resa; reddito; (*of crops etc*) raccolto ▶ VT produrre, rendere; (*surrender*) cedere ▶ VI cedere; (*US Aut*) dare la precedenza; **a ~ of 5%** un profitto *or* un interesse del 5%

YMCA N ABBR (= *Young Men's Christian Association*) Y.M.C.A. m

yob ['jɔb], **yobbo** ['jɔbəu] N (*BRIT col*) bullo

yodel ['jəudl] VI cantare lo jodel *or* alla tirolese

yoga ['jəugə] N yoga m

yoghurt, yogurt ['jəugət] N iogurt m *inv*

yoke [jəuk] N giogo ▶ VT (*also*: **yoke together**: *oxen*) aggiogare

yolk [jəuk] N tuorlo, rosso d'uovo

yonder ['jɔndəʳ] ADV là

yonks [jɔŋks] NPL: **for ~** (*col*) da una vita

y

Yorks [jɔ:ks] ABBR (*BRIT*) = **Yorkshire**

(KEYWORD)

you [ju:] PRON **1** (*subject*) tu; (: *polite form*) lei; (: *pl*) voi; (: *formal*) loro; **you Italians enjoy your food** a voi italiani piace mangiare bene; **you and I will go** andiamo io e te (*or* lei ed io); **if I was** *or* **were you** se fossi in te (*or* lei *etc*)
2 (*object: direct*) ti; la; vi; loro (*after vb*); (: *indirect*) ti; le; vi; loro (*after vb*); **I know you** ti (*or* la *or* vi) conosco; **I'll see you tomorrow** ci vediamo domani; **I gave it to you** te l'ho dato; gliel'ho dato; ve l'ho dato; l'ho dato loro
3 (*stressed, after prep, in comparisons*) te; lei; voi; loro; **I told YOU to do it** ho detto a TE (*or* a LEI *etc*) di farlo; **she's younger than you** è più giovane di te (*or* lei *etc*)
4 (*impers: one*) si; **fresh air does you good** l'aria fresca fa bene; **you never know** non si sa mai

you'd [ju:d] = **you had**; **you would**
you'll [ju:l] = **you will**; **you shall**
young [jʌŋ] ADJ giovane ▶ NPL (*of animal*) piccoli *mpl*; **the ~** i giovani, la gioventù; **a ~ man** un giovanotto; **a ~ lady** una signorina; **a ~ woman** una giovane donna; **the younger generation** la nuova generazione; **my younger brother** il mio fratello minore
youngish [ˈjʌŋɪʃ] ADJ abbastanza giovane
youngster [ˈjʌŋstəʳ] N giovanotto(-a), ragazzo(-a); (*child*) bambino(-a)
your [jɔ:ʳ] ADJ il (la) tuo(-a); (*pl*) i (le) tuoi (tue); (*polite form*) il (la) suo(-a); (*pl*) i (le) suoi (sue); (*pl*) il (la) vostro(-a); (*pl*) i (le) vostri(-e); (: *formal*) il (la) loro; (*pl*) i (le) loro
you're [juəʳ] = **you are**

yours [jɔ:z] PRON il (la) tuo(-a); (*pl*) i (le) tuoi (tue); (*polite form*) il (la) suo(-a); (*pl*) i (le) suoi (sue); (*pl*) il (la) vostro(-a); (*pl*) i (le) vostri(-e); (: *formal*) il (la) loro; (*pl*) i (le) loro; **~ sincerely/faithfully** (*in letter*) cordiali/distinti saluti; **a friend of ~** un tuo (*or* suo *etc*) amico; **is it ~?** è tuo (*or* suo *etc*)?; *see also* **mine¹**
yourself [jɔ:ˈsɛlf] PRON (*reflexive*) ti; (: *polite form*) si; (*after prep*) te; sé; (*emphatic*) tu stesso(-a); lei stesso(-a); **you ~ told me** me l'hai detto proprio tu, tu stesso me l'hai detto
yourselves [jɔ:ˈsɛlvz] PL PRON (*reflexive*) vi; (: *polite form*) si; (*after prep*) voi; loro; (*emphatic*) voi stessi(-e); loro stessi(-e); *see also* **oneself**
youth [ju:θ] N gioventù *f*; (*pl* **youths** [ju:ðz]: *young man*) giovane *m*, ragazzo; **in my ~** da giovane, quando ero giovane
youth club N centro giovanile
youthful [ˈju:θful] ADJ giovane; da giovane; giovanile
youthfulness [ˈju:θfəlnɪs] N giovinezza
youth hostel N ostello della gioventù
youth movement N movimento giovanile
you've [ju:v] = **you have**
yowl [jaul] N (*of dog, person*) urlo; (*of cat*) miagolio ▶ VI urlare; miagolare
yr ABBR = **year**
YT ABBR (*CANADA*) = **Yukon Territory**
Yugoslav [ˈju:gəuslɑ:v] ADJ, N (*formerly*) jugoslavo(-a)
Yugoslavia [ju:gəuˈslɑ:vɪə] N (*formerly*) Jugoslavia
Yugoslavian [ju:gəuˈslɑ:vɪən] ADJ, N (*formerly*) jugoslavo(-a)
Yule log [ju:l-] N ceppo nel caminetto a Natale
yuppie [ˈjʌpɪ] ADJ, N (*col*) yuppie *mf inv*
YWCA N ABBR (= *Young Women's Christian Association*) Y.W.C.A. *m*

Zz

Z, z [zɛd, (US) zi:] N (letter) Z, z f inv or m inv;
Z for Zebra ≈ Z come Zara
Zaire [zɑː'ɪər] N Zaire m
Zambia ['zæmbɪə] N Zambia m
Zambian ['zæmbɪən] ADJ, N zambiano(-a)
zany ['zeɪnɪ] ADJ un po' pazzo(-a)
zap [zæp] VT (Comput) cancellare
zeal [zi:l] N zelo; entusiasmo
zealot ['zɛlət] N zelota mf
zealous ['zɛləs] ADJ zelante; premuroso(-a)
zebra ['zi:brə] N zebra
zebra crossing N (BRIT) (passaggio pedonale
a) strisce fpl, zebre fpl
zenith ['zɛnɪθ] N zenit m inv; (fig) culmine m
zero ['zɪərəu] N zero; **5° below** ~ 5° sotto zero
zero hour N l'ora zero
zero option N (Pol) opzione f zero
zero-rated ['zɪərəu'reɪtɪd] ADJ (BRIT) ad
aliquota zero
zest [zɛst] N gusto; (Culin) buccia
zigzag ['zɪgzæg] N zigzag m inv ▶ VI zigzagare
Zimbabwe [zɪm'bɑːbwɪ] N Zimbabwe m
Zimbabwean [zɪm'bɑːbwɪən] ADJ dello
Zimbabwe
Zimmer® ['zɪmər] N (also: **Zimmer frame**)
deambulatore m
zinc [zɪŋk] N zinco

Zionism ['zaɪənɪzəm] N sionismo
Zionist ['zaɪənɪst] ADJ sionistico(-a) ▶ N
sionista mf
zip [zɪp] N (also: **zip fastener**) chiusura f or
cerniera f lampo inv; (: energy) energia, forza
▶ VT (Comput) zippare; (also: **zip up**) chiudere
con una cerniera lampo
zip code N (US) codice m di avviamento
postale
zipper (US) N cerniera f lampo inv
zit [zɪt] N brufolo
zither ['zɪðər] N cetra
zodiac ['zəudɪæk] N zodiaco
zombie ['zɒmbɪ] N (fig): **like a** ~ come un
morto che cammina
zone [zəun] N (also Mil) zona
zoo [zu:] N zoo m inv
zoological [zuə'lɒdʒɪkl] ADJ zoologico(-a)
zoologist [zu:'ɒlədʒɪst] N zoologo(-a)
zoology [zu:'ɒlədʒɪ] N zoologia
zoom [zu:m] VI: **to** ~ **past** sfrecciare; **to** ~ **in**
(on sb/sth) (Phot, Cine) zumare (su qn/qc)
zoom lens N zoom m inv, obiettivo a focale
variabile
zucchini [zu:'ki:nɪ] N (pl inv: US) zucchina
Zulu ['zu:lu:] ADJ, N zulù mf
Zürich ['zjuərɪk] N Zurigo f

Grammar
Grammatica

Using the grammar

The Grammar section deals systematically and comprehensively with all the information you will need in order to communicate accurately in Italian. The user-friendly layout explains the grammar point on a left-hand page, leaving the facing page free for illustrative examples. The numbers, → ❶ etc, direct you to the relevant example in every case.

The Grammar section also provides invaluable guidance on the danger of translating English structures by identical structures in Italian. Use of Numbers and Punctuation are important areas covered towards the end of the section. Finally, the index lists the main words and grammatical terms in both English and Italian.

Italic letters in Italian words show where stress does not follow the usual rules.

Abbreviations

fem.	feminine
infin.	infinitive
masc.	masculine
perf.	perfect
plur.	plural
sing.	singular
qc	qualcosa
qn	qualcuno
sb	somebody
sth	something

Contents

Simple Tenses: Formation

In English, tenses are either simple, which means they consist of one word, e.g. *I work*, or compound, which means they consist of more than one word, e.g. *I have worked, I have been working*. The same is true in Italian.

In Italian the simple tenses are:

Present → **①**
Imperfect → **②**
Future → **③**
Present Conditional → **④**
Past Historic → **⑤**
Present Subjunctive → **⑥**
Imperfect Subjunctive → **⑦**

They are formed by adding endings to a verb stem. The endings show the number and person of the subject of the verb → **⑧**

The stem and endings of regular verbs are totally predictable. The following sections show all the patterns for regular verbs. For irregular verbs see page 80 onwards.

Regular Verbs

There are three regular verb patterns (called conjugations), each identifiable by the ending of the infinitive:

First conjugation verbs end in **-are** e.g. **parlare** to speak

Second conjugation verbs end in **-ere** e.g. **credere** to believe

Third conjugation verbs end in **-ire** e.g. **finire** to finish

These three conjugations are treated in order on the following pages.

1	parlo	I speak
		I am speaking
	parlo?	do I speak?
2	parlavo	I spoke
		I was speaking
		I used to speak
3	parlerò	I shall/will/'ll speak
4	parlerei	I should/would/'d speak
5	parlai	I spoke
6	(che) parli	that I speak
7	(che) parlassi	that I should speak
8	parlo	I speak
	parliamo	we speak
	parlerei	I'd speak
	parleremmo	we'd speak

Simple Tenses: First Conjugation

The stem is formed by taking the -are ending off the infinitive. The stem of parlare is parl- .

Add the following endings to the stem:

		① PRESENT	② IMPERFECT	③ FUTURE
sing.	1st person	-o	-avo	-erò
	2nd person	-i	-avi	-erai
	3rd person	-a	-ava	-erà
plur.	1st person	-iamo	-avamo	-eremo
	2nd person	-ate	-avate	-erete
	3rd person	-ano	-avano	-eranno

		④ PRESENT CONDITIONAL	⑤ PAST HISTORIC
sing.	1st person	-erei	-ai
	2nd person	-eresti	-asti
	3rd person	-erebbe	-ò
plur.	1st person	-eremmo	-ammo
	2nd person	-ereste	-aste
	3rd person	-erebbero	-arono

		⑥ PRESENT SUBJUNCTIVE	⑦ IMPERFECT SUBJUNCTIVE
sing.	1st, 2nd person	-i	-assi
	3rd person	-i	-asse
plur.	1st person	-iamo	-assimmo
	2nd person	-iate	-aste
	3rd person	-ino	-assero

1 PRESENT
parlo
parli
parla
parliamo
parlate
parlano

2 IMPERFECT
parlavo
parlavi
parlava
parlavamo
parlavate
parlavano

3 FUTURE
parlerò
parlerai
parlerà
parleremo
parlerete
parleranno

4 PRESENT CONDITIONAL
parlerei
parleresti
parlerebbe
parleremmo
parlereste
parlerebbero

5 PAST HISTORIC
parlai
parlasti
parlò
parlammo
parlaste
parlarono

6 PRESENT SUBJUNCTIVE
parli
parli
parli
parliamo
parliate
parlino

7 IMPERFECT SUBJUNCTIVE
parlassi
parlassi
parlasse
parlassimo
parlaste
parlassero

Simple Tenses: Second Conjugation

The stem is formed by taking the **-ere** ending off the infinitive. The stem of **credere** is **cred-**.

Add the following endings to the stem:

		① PRESENT	② IMPERFECT	③ FUTURE
sing.	1st person	-o	-evo	-erò
	2nd person	-i	-evi	-erai
	3rd person	-e	-eva	-erà
plur.	1st person	-iamo	-evamo	-eremo
	2nd person	-ete	-evate	-erete
	3rd person	-ono	-evano	-eranno

		④ PRESENT CONDITIONAL	⑤ PAST HISTORIC
sing.	1st person	-erei	-ei or -etti
	2nd person	-eresti	-esti
	3rd person	-erebbe	-ette
plur.	1st person	-eremmo	-emmo
	2nd person	-ereste	-este
	3rd person	-erebbero	-ettero

		⑥ PRESENT SUBJUNCTIVE	⑦ IMPERFECT SUBJUNCTIVE
sing.	1st, 2nd persons	-a	-essi
	3rd person	-a	-esse
plur.	1st person	-iamo	-essimmo
	2nd person	-iate	-este
	3rd person	-ano	-essero

❶ PRESENT
credo
credi
crede
crediamo
credete
credono

❷ IMPERFECT
credevo
credevi
credeva
credevamo
credevate
credevano

❸ FUTURE
crederò
crederai
crederà
crederemo
crederete
crederanno

❹ PRESENT CONDITIONAL
crederei
crederesti
crederebbe
crederemmo
credereste
crederebbero

❺ PAST HISTORIC
credei *or* credetti
credesti
credette
credemmo
credeste
credettero

❻ PRESENT SUBJUNCTIVE
creda
creda
creda
crediamo
crediate
credano

❼ IMPERFECT SUBJUNCTIVE
credessi
credessi
credesse
credessimo
credeste
credessero

Simple Tenses: Third Conjugation

Generally, the stem is formed by taking the -ire ending off the infinitive. The stem for most tenses of finire is fin-.

However, in the present tense and present subjunctive, -isc- is added to the basic stem (except for the 1st and 2nd person plural):

EXCEPTIONS: servire to serve, dormire to sleep, soffrire to suffer, coprire to cover, sentire to feel, partire to leave, offrire to offer, aprire to offer

The present tenses of finire and dormire are as follows:

	1st person	finisco	dormo
sing.	2nd person	finisci	dormi
	3rd person	finisce	dorme
	1st person	finiamo	dormiamo
plur.	2nd person	finite	dormite
	3rd person	finiscono	dormono

Both types of verb take the following endings:

		① PRESENT	② IMPERFECT	③ FUTURE
	1st person	-o	-ivo	-irò
sing.	2nd person	-i	-ivi	-irai
	3rd person	-e	-iva	-irà
	1st person	-iamo	-ivamo	-iremo
plur.	2nd person	-ite	-ivate	-irete
	3rd person	-ono	-ivano	-iranno

		④ PRESENT CONDITIONAL	⑤ PAST HISTORIC
	1st person	-irei	-i
sing.	2nd person	-iresti	-isti
	3rd person	-irebbe	-ì
	1st person	-iremmo	-immo
plur.	2nd person	-ireste	-iste
	3rd person	-irebbero	-irono

		⑥ PRESENT SUBJUNCTIVE	⑦ IMPERFECT SUBJUNCTIVE
sing.	1st, 2nd persons	-a	-issi
	3rd person	-a	-isse
plur.	1st person	-iamo	-issimmo
	2nd person	-iate	-iste
	3rd person	-ano	-issero

① **PRESENT**
finisco
finisci
finisce
finiamo
finite
finiscono

② **IMPERFECT**
finivo
finivi
finiva
finivamo
finivate
finívano

③ **FUTURE**
finirò
finirai
finirà
finiremo
finirete
finiranno

④ **PRESENT SUBJUNCTIVE**
finirei
finiresti
finirebbe
finiremmo
finireste
finirebbero

⑤ **PAST HISTORIC**
finii
finisti
finì
finimmo
finiste
finirono

⑥ **PRESENT SUBJUNCTIVE**
finisca
finisca
finisca
finiamo
finiate
finiscano

⑦ **IMPERFECT SUBJUNCTIVE**
finissi
finissi
finisse
finissimo
finiste
finissero

13

First Conjugation Spelling Irregularities

Before certain endings, the stems of some -are verbs may change slightly.

Verbs ending:	-care
Change:	c becomes ch before e or i
Tenses affected:	Present, Future, Conditional, Present Subjunctive
Model:	cercare to look for → ❶

Why the change occurs: h is added to keep the c sound hard k.

Verbs ending:	-gare
Change:	g becomes gh before e or i
Tenses affected:	Present, Future, Conditional, Present Subjunctive
Model:	pagare to pay → ❷

Why the change occurs: h is added to keep the g sound hard g.

Examples

① INFINITIVE
cercare

PRESENT	FUTURE
cerco	cercherò
cerchi	cercherai
cerca	cercherà
cerchiamo	cercheremo
cercate	cercherete
cercano	cercheranno

CONDITIONAL	PRESENT SUBJUNCTIVE
cercherei	**cerchi**
cercheresti	**cerchi**
cercherebbe	**cerchi**
cercheremmo	**cerchiamo**
cerchereste	**cerchiate**
cercherebbero	**cerchino**

② INFINITIVE
pagare

PRESENT	FUTURE
pago	**pagherò**
paghi	**pagherai**
paga	**pagherà**
paghiamo	**pagheremo**
pagate	**pagherete**
pagano	**pagheranno**

CONDITIONAL	PRESENT SUBJUNCTIVE
pagherei	**paghi**
pagheresti	**paghi**
pagherebbe	**paghi**
pagheremmo	**paghiamo**
paghereste	**paghiate**
pagherebbero	**paghino**

First Conjugation Spelling Irregularities *continued*

Verbs ending: -ciare
Change: i is dropped before e or i
Tenses affected: Present, Future, Conditional, Present Subjunctive
Model: annunciare to announce → ❶

Why the change occurs: the i of the infinitive is needed to keep c soft
tʃ before a (before e and i, c is soft, so the i is
unnecessary).

Verbs ending: -giare
Change: i is dropped before e or i
Tenses affected: Present, Future, Conditional, Present Subjunctive
Model: mangiare to eat → ❷

Why the change occurs: the i of the infinitive is needed to keep g soft
dʒ before a (before e and i, g is soft, so the i is
unnecessary).

Examples

❶ INFINITIVE
annunciare

PRESENT	FUTURE
annuncio	annuncerò
annunci	annuncerai
annuncia	annuncerà
annunciamo	annunceremo
annunciate	annuncerete
annunciano	annunceranno

CONDITIONAL	PRESENT SUBJUNCTIVE
annuncerei	annunci
annunceresti	annunci
annuncerebbe	annunci
annunceremmo	annunciamo
annuncereste	annunciate
annuncerebbero	annuncino

❷ INFINITIVE
mangiare

PRESENT	FUTURE
mangio	mangerò
mangi	mangerai
mangia	mangerà
mangiamo	mangeremo
mangiate	mangerete
mangiano	mangeranno

CONDITIONAL	PRESENT SUBJUNCTIVE
mangerei	mangi
mangeresti	mangi
mangerebbe	mangi
mangeremmo	mangiamo
mangereste	mangiate
mangerebbero	mangino

First Conjugation Spelling Irregularities *continued*

Verbs ending:	**-iare**
Change:	i is not dropped before another i, which is what usually happens
Tenses affected:	Present, Present Subjunctive
Model:	**inviare** to send, **sciare** to ski → **❶**

Why the change occurs: The i has to be retained in forms where it is the stressed vowel.

Verbs ending:	**-gliare**
Change:	i is dropped before endings beginning with -i
Tenses affected:	Present, Present subjunctive, Imperfect Subjunctive, Imperative
Model:	**consigliare** to advise, **svegliare** to wake up → **❷**

Why the change occurs: There is no need to retain the i.

Examples

1 INFINITIVE
inviare

PRESENT
invio
invii
invia
inviamo
inviate
inviano

2 INFINITIVE
svegliare

PRESENT
sveglio
svegli
sveglia
svegliamo
svegliate
svegliano

The Imperative

The imperative is the form of the verb used to give commands or instructions. It can be used politely, as in English 'Please take a seat'. In Italian, the polite imperative is the 3rd person form, either singular or plural. The 1st person plural (we) is used to make suggestions, as in 'Let's go'.

The imperative is formed by adding endings to the stem of the verb. The endings for the 1st and 2nd persons plural are the same as those for the present tense, the others are different. → ①

			FIRST	SECOND	THIRD
sing.	2nd	person	-a	-i	-i
	3rd	person	-i	-a	-a
plur.	1st	person	-iamo	-iamo	-iamo
	2nd	person	-ate	-ete	-ite
	3rd	person	-ino	-ano	-ano

NB Third conjugation verbs which add isc to the stem in the present tense also do so in the imperative → ②

The imperative of irregular verbs is given in the verb tables page 80.

Position of object and reflexive pronouns with the imperative:
* they follow imperatives in the 2nd person and the -iamo form, and are joined on to make one word → ③
* they precede 3rd person polite imperatives, and are not joined on to them → ④

Changes to pronouns following the imperative:
* the first letter of the pronoun is doubled when the imperative is one syllable: mi becomes mmi, ti becomes tti, lo becomes llo etc → ⑤
* When the pronouns mi, ti, ci and vi are followed by another pronoun they become -me, -te, -ce and -ve, and gli and le become glie- → ⑥

Negative imperatives:
* non precedes the imperative to make it negative (except in the 2nd person singular) → ⑦
* non precedes the infinitive in the 2nd person singular) → ⑧
* in 2nd person singular negative commands, non is used with the infinitive instead of the imperative. Pronouns may be joined onto the infinitive, or precede it → ⑧

① **Compare:**

Aspetti, Maria?	Are you waiting, Maria?
and: Aspetta Maria!	Wait Maria!
Prende l'autobus	He gets the bus
and: Prenda l'autobus, signora!	Get the bus, madam!

②

Finisci l'esercizio, Marco!	Finish the exercise, Marco!
Finisca tutto, signore!	Finish it all, sir!
Finiamo tutto	Let's finish it all
Finite i compiti, ragazzi!	Finish your homework, children!
Finiscano tutto signori!	Finish it all, ladies and gentlemen!

③

Guardami, mamma!	Look at me, mum!
Aspettateli!	Wait for them!
Proviamolo!	Let's try it!

④

Mi dia un chilo d'uva, per favore	Give me a kilo of grapes please
Si accomodi!	Take a seat!
La prenda, signore	Take it, sir

⑤

Dimmi!	Tell me!
Fallo subito!	Do it immediately!

⑥

Mandameli	Send me them
Daglielo	Give it to him
Mandiamogliela!	Let's send it to them!

⑦

Non dimentichiamo	Don't let's forget
Non si preoccupi, signore	Don't worry, sir

⑧

Non dire bugie Andrea!	Don't tell lies Andrea!
Non dimenticare!	Don't forget!
Non toccarlo! *or* Non lo toccare!	Don't touch it!
Non glielo dire! *or* Non dirglielo	Don't tell him about it!
Non preoccuparti! *or* Non ti preoccupare!	Don't worry!

21

Compound Tenses

Continuous tenses

The simple tense of an Italian verb, e.g. **piove**, can have two meanings:
'it rains', or 'it's raining'; the continuous tense, **sta piovendo** is an
alternative way of expressing the English present continuous (it's raining).

The Present Continuous is used less in Italian than in English. It is formed
with the present tense of the verb **stare**, plus the gerund → ❶

The Past Continuous is formed with the imperfect tense of **stare**,
and the gerund → ❷

For information on how to form the gerund, see page 52.

The Past Continuous is also less used in Italian than in English,
as the imperfect tense can be used to express this meaning.

Examples

1 Ci sto pensando   I'm thinking about it
Stanno arrivando   They're coming
Cosa stai facendo?   What are you doing?

2 Stavo studiando   I was studying
Stava morendo   He was dying
Stavano lavorando   They were working

Compound Tenses *continued*

Formed with the past participle

These are:

Perfect → ❶
Pluperfect → ❷
Future Perfect → ❸
Perfect Conditional → ❹
Past Anterior → ❺
Perfect Subjunctive → ❻
Pluperfect Subjunctive → ❼

They consist of the past past participle and an auxiliary verb. Most verbs take the auxiliary avere, but some take essere (see page 30).

These tenses are formed in the same way for regular and irregular verbs, the only difference being that an irregular verb may have an irregular past participle.

The Past Participle

The past participle of regular verbs is formed as follows:

First conjugation: replace the -are of the infinitive with -ato → ❽

Second conjugation: replace the -ere of the infinitive with -uto → ❾

Third conjugation: replace the -ire of the infinitive with -ito → ❿

	with avere		with essere	
1	ho parlato	I spoke, have spoken	sono andato	I went, have gone
2	avevo parlato	I had spoken	ero andato	I had gone
3	avrò parlato	I will have spoken	sarò andato	I will have gone
4	avrei parlato	I would have spoken	sarei andato	I would have gone
5	ebbi parlato	I had spoken	fui andato	I had gone
6	abbia parlato	I spoke, have spoken	sia andato	I went, have gone
7	avessi parlato	I had spoken	fossi andato	I had gone

8 parlare to speak → parlato spoken

9 credere to believe → creduto believed

10 finire to finish → finito finished

Compound Tenses *continued*

Verbs taking the auxiliary avere

PERFECT TENSE
The present tense of **avere** plus the past participle → **①**

PLUPERFECT TENSE
The imperfect tense of **avere** plus the past participle → **②**

FUTURE PERFECT
The future tense of **avere** plus the past participle → **③**

PERFECT CONDITIONAL
The conditional of **avere** plus the past participle → **④**

PAST ANTERIOR
The past historic of **avere** plus the past participle → **⑤**

PERFECT SUBJUNCTIVE
The present subjunctive of **avere** plus the past participle → **⑥**

PLUPERFECT SUBJUNCTIVE
The imperfect subjunctive of **avere** plus the past participle → **⑦**

For how to form the past participle of regular verbs see page 24. The past participle of irregular verbs is given for each verb in the verb tables, page 80 onwards.

The past participle agrees in number and gender with a preceding direct object when it is **lo, la, li** or **le**, e.g.

Le matite? Le ho comprate ieri   The pencils? I bought them yesterday

Examples

① PERFECT

ho parlato	abbiamo parlato
hai parlato	avete parlato
ha parlato	hanno parlato

② PLUPERFECT

avevo parlato	avevamo parlato
avevi parlato	avevate parlato
aveva parlato	avevano parlato

③ FUTURE PERFECT

avrò parlato	avremo parlato
avrai parlato	avrete parlato
avrà parlato	avranno parlato

④ PERFECT CONDITIONAL

avrei parlato	avremmo parlato
avresti parlato	avreste parlato
avrebbe parlato	avrebbero parlato

⑤ PAST ANTERIOR

ebbi parlato	avemmo parlato
avesti parlato	aveste parlato
ebbe parlato	ebbero parlato

⑥ PERFECT SUBJUNCTIVE

abbia parlato	abbiamo parlato
abbia parlato	abbiate parlato
abbia parlato	abbiano parlato

⑦ PLUPERFECT SUBJUNCTIVE

avessi parlato	avessimo parlato
avessi parlato	aveste parlato
avesse parlato	avessero parlato

Compound Tenses *continued*

Verbs taking the auxiliary *essere*

PERFECT TENSE
The present tense of *essere* plus the past participle → ❶

PLUPERFECT TENSE
The imperfect tense of *essere* plus the past participle → ❷

FUTURE PERFECT
The future tense of *essere* plus the past participle → ❸

PERFECT CONDITIONAL
The conditional of *essere* plus the past participle → ❹

PAST ANTERIOR
The past historic of *essere* plus the past participle → ❺

PERFECT SUBJUNCTIVE
The present subjunctive of *essere* plus the past participle → ❻

PLUPERFECT SUBJUNCTIVE
The imperfect subjunctive of *essere* plus the past participle → ❼

For how to form the past participle of regular verbs see page 24. The past participle of irregular verbs is given for each verb in the verb tables, page 80 onwards.

For agreement of past participles see page 56.

For a list of verbs and verb types that take the auxiliary *essere*, see page 30.

① PERFECT

sono andato(a)	siamo andati(e)
sei andato(a)	siete andati(e)
è andato(a)	sono andati(e)

② PLUPERFECT

ero andato(a)	eravamo andati(e)
eri andato(a)	eravate andati(e)
era andato(a)	erano andati(e)

③ FUTURE PERFECT

sarò andato(a)	saremo andati(e)
sarai andato(a)	sarete andati(e)
sarà andato(a)	saranno andati(e)

④ PERFECT CONDITIONAL

sarei andato(a)	saremmo andati(e)
saresti andato(a)	sareste andati(e)
sarebbe andato(a)	sarebbero andati(e)

⑤ PAST ANTERIOR

fui andato(a)	fummo andati(e)
fosti andato(a)	foste andati(e)
fu andato(a)	furono andati(e)

⑥ PERFECT SUBJUNCTIVE

sia andato(a)	siamo andati(e)
sia andato(a)	siate andati(e)
sia andato(a)	siano andati(e)

⑦ PLUPERFECT SUBJUNCTIVE

fossi andato(a)	fossimo andati(e)
fossi andato(a)	foste andati(e)
fosse andato(a)	fossero andati(e)

Compound Tenses *continued*

The following verbs take the auxiliary *essere*
Reflexive verbs (see page 32) → ❶

Many intransitive verbs (i.e. verbs not taking a direct object),
including the following:

andare to go	partire to leave
apparire to appear	restare to stay
arrivare to arrive → ❷	rimanere to stay
bastare to be enough	ritornare to return → ❹
cadere to fall	riuscire to succeed/manage → ❺
costare to cost → ❸	salire to go up/get on
dipendere to depend	scadere to expire
divenire to become	scappare to get away
diventare to become	scendere to go down
durare to last	scivolare to slip
entrare to come in	sparire to disappear → ❻
esistere to exist	stare to be/stay
essere to be	succedere to happen
fuggire to escape	tornare to come back
intervenire to intervene	venire to come
morire to die	uscire to go out
nascere to be born	

The following verbs, often used in impersonal constructions:

bisognare	occorrere
convenire	parere → ❽
dispiacere	piacere → ❾
importare	sembrare
mancare → ❼	

Verbs that can be used both transitively and intransitively take the
auxiliary *essere* when intransitive and *avere* when transitive → ❿

Impersonal verbs which describe the weather are used with both *essere*
and *avere* → ⓫

ⓘ Note that the past participle agrees in gender and number with the
subject of verbs conjugated with *essere*.

1 Mi sono fatto male — I've hurt *or* I hurt myself
Si è rotta la gamba — She's broken *or* She broke her leg
Vi siete divertiti? — Did you have *or* Have you had a nice time?
Si sono addormentati — They've gone *or* They went to sleep

2 È arrivata — She's arrived *or* She arrived

3 È costato parecchio — It cost a lot *or* It has cost a lot

4 Siamo ritornati — We've returned *or* We returned

5 Sei riuscito? — Did you succeed? *or* Have you succeeded?

6 Sono spariti — They've disappeared

7 Ti sono mancata? — Did you miss me?

8 Mi è parso strano — It seemed strange to me

9 Vi è piaciuta la musica? — Did you like the music?

10 **passare**
Intransitive
Sono passati molti anni — Many years have passed
Transitive
Ho passato l'esame — I've passed the exam
saltare
Intransitive
Il gatto è saltato sul tavolo — The cat jumped on the table
Transitive
Ho saltato il pranzo — I skipped lunch

11 Ha piovuto *or*
È piovuto molto — It rained a lot
Ha nevicato! *or*
È nevicato! — It's snowed!

Reflexive Verbs

A reflexive verb is one accompanied by a reflexive pronoun, e.g. divertirsi to enjoy oneself; annoiarsi to get bored.
The reflexive pronouns are:

	SINGULAR	PLURAL
1st person	mi	ci
2nd person	ti	vi
3rd person	si	si

The Italian reflexive pronoun is often not translated in English → ❶

Plural reflexive pronouns can sometimes be translated as 'each other' → ❷

Simple tenses of reflexive verbs are conjugated in exactly the same way as other verbs, except that the reflexive pronoun is always used. Compound tenses are conjugated with the auxiliary essere. A sample reflexive verb is conjugated in full on pages 36 and 37.

Position of Reflexive Pronouns

The pronoun generally comes before the verb → ❸

However, in positive 2nd person commands the pronoun is joined onto the end of the imperative → ❹

In the infinitive, the final e is dropped and replaced by the reflexive pronoun → ❺

When the infinitive is used with non in negative commands, the reflexive pronoun ti either comes first, as a separate word, or is joined on at the end → ❻

Two alternatives also exist
- when the infinitive is used after another verb, the pronoun either goes before the main verb or joins onto the infinitive → ❼
- in continuous tenses the pronoun either goes before the main verb or joins onto the gerund → ❽

❶ Mi annoio — I'm getting bored
Ti fidi di lui? — Do you trust him?
Si vergogna — He's embarrassed
Non vi preoccupate! — Don't worry!

❷ Si odiano — They hate each other

❸ Mi diverto — I'm enjoying myself
Ci prepariamo — We're getting ready
Si accomodi! — Take a seat!

❹ Svegliati! — Wake up!
Divertitevi! — Enjoy yourselves!

❺ Compare:

ordinary infinitive	reflexive infinitive
lavare to wash	lavarsi to get washed, wash oneself
divertire to amuse	divertirsi to enjoy oneself

❻ Non ti bruciare! *or*
Non bruciarti! — Don't burn yourself!
Non ti preoccupare! *or*
Non preoccuparti! — Don't worry!

Mi voglio abbronzare *or*
Voglio abbronzarmi — I want to get a tan
Ti devi alzare *or*
Devi alzarti — You must get up
Vi dovreste preparare *or*
Dovreste preparavi — You ought to get ready

❼ Ti stai annoiando? *or*
Stai annoiandoti? — Are you getting bored?
Si stanno alzando? *or*
Stanno alzandosi? — Are they getting up?

Reflexive Verbs *continued*

Past Participle Agreement

The past participle used in compound tenses of reflexive verbs generally agrees with the subject of the verb → ❶

Here are some common reflexive verbs:

accomodarsi to sit down/take a seat
addormentarsi to go to sleep
alzarsi to get up
annoiarsi to get bored/be bored
arrabbiarsi to get angry
cambiarsi to get changed
chiamarsi to be called
chiedersi to wonder
divertirsi to enjoy oneself/have fun
farsi male to hurt oneself
fermarsi to stop
lavarsi to wash/get washed
perdersi to get lost
pettinarsi to comb one's hair
preoccuparsi to worry
prepararsi to get ready
ricordarsi to remember
sbrigarsi to hurry
sedersi to sit
svegliarsi to wake up
vestirsi to dress/get dressed

Examples

① Si è lavato le mani   He washed his hands
    Si è lavata le mani   She washed her hands
    I ragazzi si sono lavati le mani   The boys washed their hands
    Le ragazze si sono lavate le mani   The girls washed their hands

Reflexive Verbs *continued*

Conjugation of: **divertirsi** to enjoy oneself – SIMPLE TENSES

PRESENT

mi diverto	ci divertiamo
ti diverti	vi divertite
si diverte	si divertono

IMPERFECT

mi divertivo	ci divertivamo
ti divertivi	vi divertivate
si divertiva	si divertivano

FUTURE

mi divertirò	ci divertiremo
ti divertirai	vi divertirete
si divertirà	si divertiranno

CONDITIONAL

mi divertirei	ci divertiremmo
ti divertiresti	vi divertireste
si divertirebbe	si divertirebbero

PAST HISTORIC

mi divertii	ci divertimmo
ti divertisti	vi divertiste
si divertì	si divertirono

PRESENT SUBJUNCTIVE

mi diverta	ci divertiamo
ti diverta	vi divertiate
si diverta	si divertano

IMPERFECT SUBJUNCTIVE

mi divertissi	ci divertissimo
ti divertissi	vi divertiste
si divertisse	si divertissero

Conjugation of: divertirsi to enjoy oneself – COMPOUND TENSES

PRESENT CONTINUOUS

mi sto divertendo *or*
sto divertendomi
ti stai divertendo *or*
stai divertendoti
si sta divertendo *or*
sta divertendosi

ci stiamo divertendo *or*
stiamo divertendoci
vi state divertendo *or*
state divertendovi
si stanno divertendo *or*
stanno divertendosi

PERFECT

mi sono divertito(a)
ti sei divertito(a)
si è divertito(a)

ci siamo divertiti(e)
vi siete divertiti(e)
si sono divertiti(e)

PLUPERFECT

mi ero divertito(a)
ti eri divertito(a)
si era divertito(a)

ci eravamo divertiti(e)
vi eravate divertiti(e)
si erano divertiti(e)

FUTURE PERFECT

mi sarò divertito(a)
ti sarai divertito(a)
si sarà divertito(a)

ci saremo divertiti(e)
vi sarete divertiti(e)
si saranno divertiti(e)

PERFECT CONDITIONAL

mi sarei divertito(a)
ti saresti divertito(a)
si sarebbe divertito(a)

ci saremmo divertiti(e)
vi sareste divertiti(e)
si sarebbero divertiti(e)

PAST ANTERIOR

mi fui divertito(a)
ti fosti divertito(a)
si fu divertito(a)

ci fummo divertiti(e)
vi foste divertiti(e)
si furono divertiti(e)

PERFECT SUBJUNCTIVE

mi sia divertito(a)
ti sia divertito(a)
si sia divertito(a)

ci siamo divertiti(e)
vi siate divertiti(e)
si siano divertiti(e)

PLUPERFECT SUBJUNCTIVE

mi fossi divertito(a)
ti fossi divertito(a)
si fosse divertito(a)

ci fossimo divertiti(e)
vi foste divertiti(e)
si fossero divertiti(e)

37

The Passive

In the passive, the subject *receives* the action (e.g. I was hit) as opposed to *performing* it (e.g. I hit him). In English the passive is formed with the verb 'to be' and the past participle, and in Italian the passive is formed in exactly the same way, i.e. a tense of **essere** + *past participle*.

The past participle agrees in gender and number with the subject → ❶

A sample verb is conjugated in the passive on pages 40 and 41.

In English it is possible to make the indirect object of an active sentence into the subject of a passive sentence, e.g. Someone told me → I was told.

This is not possible in Italian; instead a 3ʳᵈ person plural can be used → ❷

The passive is used less overall in Italian. The following alternatives are used:
- active constructions → ❸
- the **si passivante** (preceding an active verb with **si**, to make it passive → ❹
- an impersonal construction with **si** → ❺

① È stato costretto a ritirarsi dalla gara — He was forced to withdraw from the competition

L'elettricità è stata tagliata ieri — The electricity was cut off yesterday

La partita è stata rinviata — The match has been postponed

Siamo invitati ad una festa a casa loro — We're invited to a party at their house

I ladri sono stati catturati — The thieves have been caught

Le finestre saranno riparate domani — The windows will be repaired tomorrow

② Mi hanno dato una chiave — I've been given a key

Gli diranno tutto — He'll be told everything

③ Due persone sono morte — Two people were killed

Mi hanno rubato la macchina la settimana scorsa — My car was stolen last week

C'erano delle microspie nella stanza — The room was bugged

Dicono che sia molto ambizioso — He's said to be very ambitious

④ Dove si trovano i vini migliori? — Where are the best wines to be found?

Non si accettano assegni — Cheques are not accepted

Queste parole non si usano più — These words are no longer used

Questo vino si beve a temperatura ambiente — This wine should be drunk at room temperature

⑤ Non si fa così — That's not how it's done

Si raccomanda la massima discrezione — The utmost discretion is called for

The Passive *continued*

Conjugation of: invitare to invite

PRESENT

sono invitato(a)

sei invitato(a)

è invitato(a)

siamo invitati(e)

siete invitati(e)

sono invitati(e)

IMPERFECT

ero invitato(a)

eri invitato(a)

era invitato(a)

ervamo invitati(e)

eravate invitati(e)

erano invitati(e)

FUTURE

sarò invitato(a)

sarai invitato(a)

sarà invitato(a)

saremo invitati(e)

sarete invitati(e)

saranno invitati(e)

CONDITIONAL

sarei invitato(a)

saresti invitato(a)

sarebbe invitato(a)

saremmo invitati(e)

sareste invitati(e)

sarebbero invitati(e)

PAST HISTORIC

fui invitato(a)

fosti invitato(a)

fu invitato(a)

fummo invitati(e)

foste invitati(e)

furono invitati(e)

PRESENT SUBJUNCTIVE

sia invitato(a)

sia invitato(a)

sia invitato(a)   ·

siamo invitati(e)

siate invitati(e)

siano invitati(e)

IMPERFECT SUBJUNCTIVE

fossi invitato(a)

fossi invitato(a)

fosse invitato(a)

fossimo invitati(e)

foste invitati(e)

fossero invitati(e)

The Passive *continued*

Conjugation of: **invitare** to invite

PERFECT

sono stato(a) invitato(a)

sei stato(a) invitato(a)

è stato(a) invitato(a)

siamo stati(e) invitati(e)

siete stati(e) invitati(e)

sono stati(e) invitati(e)

PLUPERFECT

ero stato(a) invitato(a)

eri stato(a) invitato(a)

era stato(a) invitato(a)

eravamo stati(e) invitati(e)

eravate stati(e) invitati(e)

erano stati(e) invitati(e)

FUTURE PERFECT

sarò stato(a) invitato(a)

sarai stato(a) invitato(a)

sarà stato(a) invitato(a)

saremo stati(e) invitati(e)

sarete stati(e) invitati(e)

saranno stati(e) invitati(e)

PERFECT CONDITIONAL

sarei stato(a) invitato(a)

saresti stato(a) invitato(a)

sarebbe stato(a) invitato(a)

saremmo stati(e) invitati(e)

sareste stati(e) invitati(e)

sarebbero stati(e) invitati(e)

PAST ANTERIOR

fui stato(a) invitato(a)

fosti stato(a) invitato(a)

fu stato(a) invitato(a)

fummo stati(e) invitati(e)

foste stati(e) invitati(e)

furono stati(e) invitati(e)

PERFECT SUBJUNCTIVE

sia stato(a) invitato(a)

sia stato(a) invitato(a)

sia stato(a) invitato(a)

siamo stati(e) invitati(e)

siate stati(e) invitati(e)

siano stati(e) invitati(e)

PLUPERFECT SUBJUNCTIVE

fossi stato(a) invitato(a)

fossi stato(a) invitato(a)

fosse stato(a) invitato(a)

fossimo stati(e) invitati(e)

foste stati(e) invitati(e)

fossero stati(e) invitati(e)

Impersonal Verbs

Any verb can be made impersonal by the use of si → ❶

si is often used to make the following verbs impersonal:

dire	si dice che → ❷
	it's said that
potere	si può → ❸
	it's possible to/you can
trattarsi	si tratta di → ❹
	it's about/it's a matter of

Impersonal verbs are used only in the infinitive, with a gerund and in third person singular simple tenses. No pronoun is used in Italian.

e.g. Ha iniziato a piovere.   It started to rain.
      Sta piovendo?   Is it raining?
      Nevicava da due giorni.   It had been snowing for two days.
      È facile capire che...   It's easy to see that...

Common impersonal verbs are:

diluviare	diluvia	it's pouring
gelare	gela	it's freezing
grandinare	grandina	it's hailing
nevicare	nevica	it's snowing
piovere	piove	it's raining
tuonare	tuona	it's thundering

Other verbs are often used impersonally:

bastare	basta	that's enough
importare	non importa	it doesn't matter

1. In quel ristorante si mangia bene e si spende pòco

   In that restaurant the food's good and it doesn't cost much

2. Si dice che sia una persona strana

   It's said that he's a strange person

3. Si può visitare il castello tutti i giorni dell'anno

   You can visit the castle every day of the year

4. Di cosa si tratta?
   Si tratta di poche ore

   What's it about?
   It's a matter of a few hours

Impersonal Verbs *continued*

The following verbs are used in impersonal constructions:

INFINITIVE	CONSTRUCTIONS
bastare	basta + *infinitive* → ❶ you just have to
bisognare	bisogna + *infinitive* → ❷ you have to
convenire	*indirect pronoun* + conviene + *infinitive* → ❸ it's best to
essere	è + *noun to do with time/season* → ❹
sono	+ *plural times of the clock* → ❺ it is è + *adjective* + *infinitive* → ❻ è + *adjective* + che → ❼ it is
fare	fa + *adjective describing weather* → ❽ it is fa + *noun to do with weather, time of day*
occorrere	occorre + *infinitive* → ❾ it would be best to
parere	pare + di + sì/no → ❿ it seems so/not pare + che → ⓫ it seems/apparently
sembrare	sembra + che → ⓬ it seems

❶	Basta chiedere a qualcuno	You just have to ask someone
❷	Bisogna prenotare?	Do you have to book?
	Bisogna arrivare un'ora prima	You have to get there an hour before
❸	Conviene partire presto	It's best to set off early
❹	È tardi.	It's late
	Era presto	It was early
	Era Pasqua	It was Easter
	È mezzogiorno	It's midday
❺	Sono le otto	It's eight o'clock
❻	È stato stupido buttarli via	It was stupid to throw them away
	Sarebbe bello andarci	It would be nice to go there
❼	È vero che sono stato impaziente	It's true that I've been impatient
	È possibile che abbia sbagliato tu	Maybe you made a mistake
❽	Fa caldo	It's hot
	Fa freddo	It's cold
	Faceva bel tempo	It was good weather or The weather was good
	Fa sempre brutto tempo	The weather's always bad
	Si sta facendo buio	It's getting dark
❾	Occorre farlo subito	It would be best to do it immediately
❿	Sono contenti? — Pare di sì.	Are they happy? — It seems so.
	L'ha creduto? — Pare di no.	Did he believe it? — Apparently not.
⑪	Pare che sia stato lui	Apparently it was him
⑫	Sembra che tu abbia ragione	It seems you're right

The Infinitive

The infinitive is the form of the verb found in dictionary entries, e.g. parlare to speak; finire to finish. The infinitive sometimes drops its final -e.

All regular verbs have infinitives ending in -are, -ere, or -ire.

A few irregular verbs have infinitives ending in -rre, e.g.

comporre	to compose	condurre	to lead
porre	to put	produrre	to produce
proporre	to propose	ridurre	to reduce
supporre	to suppose	tradurre	to translate

In Italian the infinitive is used in the following ways:
- after adjectives and nouns that are followed by di → ①
- after another verb → ②
- to give instructions and orders → ③
- in 2nd person negative imperatives → ④

See page 20 for negative imperatives

- after prepositions → ⑤

See pages 190-197 for prepositions

- as the subject or object of a sentence → ⑥

There are three main types of constructions when the infinitive follows another verb:
- no linking preposition → ⑦
- linking preposition a (see also pages 70-78) → ⑧
- linking preposition di (see also pages 70-78) → ⑨

Examples

1. Sono contento di vederti — I'm glad to see you
   Sono sorpreso di vederti qui — I'm surprised to see you here
   Sono stufo di studiare — I'm fed up of studying
   Non c'è bisogno di prenotare — There's no need to book

2. Non devi mangiare se non vuoi — You don't have to eat if you don't want to

   Posso entrare? — Can I come in?
   Cosa ti piacerebbe fare? — What would you like to do?

3. Rallentare — Slow down
   Spingere — Push

4. Non fare sciocchezze! — Don't do anything silly!
   Non toccarlo! — Don't touch it!

5. È andato via senza dire niente — He went away without saying anything

6. Camminare fa bene — Walking is good for you
   Mi piace cavalcare — I like riding

7. Devi aspettare — You must wait

8. Hanno cominciato a ridere — They started to laugh

9. Quando sono entrato hanno smesso di parlare — When I came in they stopped talking

The Infinitive *continued*

Verbs followed by the infinitive with no linking preposition

dovere, potere, sapere, volere (i.e. modal auxiliary verbs: page 58).

verbs of seeing and hearing, e.g. vedere to see; sentire to hear → ①

Verbs used impersonally such as piacere, dispiacere, occorrere and convenire → ②

fare → ③

lasciare to let, allow → ④

The following common verbs:

bisognare → ⑤	to be necessary
detestare	to hate
desiderare → ⑥	to want
odiare → ⑦	to hate
preferire → ⑧	to prefer

1. Ci ha visto arrivare — He saw us arriving
   Ti ho sentito cantare — I heard you singing

2. Mi piace andare in bici — I like cycling
   Ci dispiace andar via — We're sorry to be leaving
   Occorre farlo subito — It should be done immediately
   Ti conviene partire presto — You'd best set off early

3. Non mi far ridere! — Don't make me laugh!

4. Lascia fare a me — Let me do it

5. Bisogna prenotare — You need to book

6. Desiderava migliorare il suo inglese — He wanted to improve his English

7. Odio alzarmi presto al mattino — I hate getting up early in the morning

8. Preferisco non parlarne — I prefer not to talk about it

The Infinitive *continued*

Set expressions

The following are set in Italian with the meaning shown:

> far entrare to let in → ❶
> far sapere to inform/let someone know → ❷
> far fare to have done → ❸
> farsi fare to have done → ❹
> lasciare stare to leave alone → ❺
> sentir dire che to hear that → ❻
> sentir parlare di to hear about → ❼
> voler dire to mean → ❽

The Perfect Infinitive

The perfect infinitive is formed using the auxiliary verb **avere** or *essere* (as appropriate) with the past participle of the verb → ❾

The perfect infinitive is found:
- after modal verbs → ❿
- after prepositions → ⓫

❶	Non mi hanno fatto entrare	They wouldn't let me in
❷	Ti farò sapere prima possibile	I'll let you know as soon as possible
❸	Ho fatto riparare la macchina	I had the car repaired
❹	Mi sono fatta tagliare i capelli	I had my hair cut
❺	Lascia stare mia sorella!	Leave my sister alone!
❻	Ho sentito dire che è stato licenziato	I heard he's been sacked
❼	Non ho più sentito parlare di loro	I haven't heard any more about them
❽	Non so che cosa vuol dire	I don't know what it means
❾	aver(e) visto essere partito essersi fatto male	to have seen to have gone to have hurt oneself
❿	Può aver avuto un incidente Dev'essere successo ieri	He may have had an accident It must have happened yesterday
⓫	senza aver dato un esame dopo essere rimasto chiuso	without having done an exam after having been closed

The Gerund

Formation

First conjugation:

Replace the -are of the infinitive with -ando → ①

Second and Third conjugations:

Replace the -ere, or -ire of the infinitive with -endo → ②

Exceptions to these rules are:

fare and verbs made by adding a prefix to fare → ③
dire and verbs made by adding a prefix to dire → ④
porre and verbs made by adding a prefix to porre → ⑤
verbs with infinitives ending in -durre → ⑥

The gerund is invariable.*

*A word that is invariable never changes its ending.

① parlare **to speak** → parlando **speaking**
andare **to go** → andando **going**
dare **to give** → dando **giving**

② credere **to believe** → credendo **believing**
essere **to be** → essendo **being**
dovere **to have to** → dovendo **having to**
finire **to finish** → finendo **finishing**
dormire **to sleep** → dormendo **sleeping**

③ fare **to do** → facendo **doing**
rifare **to redo** → rifacendo **redoing**

④ dire **to say** → dicendo **saying**
contraddire **to contradict** → contraddicendo **contradicting**

⑤ porre **to put** → ponendo **putting**
comporre **to compose** → componendo **composing**
supporre **to suppose** → supponendo **supposing**

⑥ condurre **to lead** → conducendo **leading**
produrre **to produce** → producendo **producing**
ridurre **to reduce** → riducendo **reducing**

The Gerund *continued*

Uses

The gerund is used with the present tense of **stare** to make the present continuous tense → ①

The gerund is used with the imperfect tense of **stare** to make the past continuous tense → ②

ⓘ Note that the Italian past participle is sometimes used with the verbs *stare* or *essere* to make a continuous tense, e.g.

essere or stare **disteso**	to be lying → ③
essere or stare **seduto**	to be sitting → ③
essere or stare **appoggiato**	to be leaning → ③

The gerund can used adverbially, to indicate when or why something happens → ④

Pronouns are usually joined onto the end of the gerund → ⑤

When the gerund is part of a continuous tense the pronoun can either come before **stare** or be joined onto the gerund → ⑥

❶ Sto lavorando — I'm working
Cosa stai facendo? — What are you doing?

❷ Il bambino stava piangendo — The little boy was crying
Stavo lavando i piatti — I was washing the dishes

❸ Era disteso sul divano — He was lying on the sofa
Stava seduta accanto a me — She was sitting next to me
La scala era appoggiata al muro — The ladder was leaning against the wall

❹ Entrando ho sentito odore di pesce — When I came in I could smell fish
Ripensandoci, credo che non fosse colpa sua — Thinking back on it, I reckon it wasn't his fault
Vedendolo solo, è venuta a parlargli — Seeing that he was on his own, she came to speak to him
Sentendomi male, sono andato a letto — Because I felt ill I went to bed
Volendo, potremmo comprarne un altro — If we wanted to, we could buy another

❺ Vedendoli è scoppiata in lacrime — When she saw them she burst into tears
Mi sono addormentato ascoltandolo — As I listened to him I fell asleep
Sbagliando si impara — You learn by making mistakes

❻ Ti sto parlando *or*
Sto parlandoti — I'm talking to you
Si sta vestendo *or*
Sta vestendosi — He's getting dressed
Me lo stavano mostrando *or*
Stavano mostrandomelo — They were showing me it

Past Participle Agreement

For the formation of the past participle, see page 24.

Note that many Italian verbs have irregular past participles → ①

Past participles are sometimes like adjectives, and change their endings. For the rules of agreement, see below:

		MASCULINE	FEMININE
SING.	1st conj	andato	andata
SING.	2nd conj	caduto	caduta
SING.	3rd conj	uscito	uscita
PLUR.	1st conj	andati	andate
PLUR.	2nd conj	caduti	cadute
PLUR.	3rd conj	usciti	uscite

Rules of Agreement in Compound Tenses

When the auxiliary verb is avere:

The past participle generally remains in the masculine singular form → ②

EXCEPTION: When the object of the verb is la (*feminine*: her/it), li (*masculine plural*: them) or le (*feminine plural*: them), the participle agrees with la, li or le → ③

When the auxiliary verb is essere:

The past participle agrees in number and gender with the subject → ④

For the agreement of the past participle with reflexive verbs, see page 34.

The Past Participle as an adjective

When a past participles is used as an adjective it agrees in the normal way → ⑤

1 crescere **to grow**   cresciuto **grown**
dire **to say**   detto **said**
fare **to do**   fatto **done**
porre **to put**   posto **put**

2 Mio fratello ha comprato una macchina   My brother has bought a car

Mia sorella ha comprato una macchina   My sister has bought a car

I ragazzi hanno comprato dei gelati   The children bought ice creams

3 Dov'è Marco? L'hai visto?   Where's Marco? Have you seen him?

Dov'è Silvia? L'hai vista?   Where's Silvia? Have you seen her?

Dove sono i ragazzi? Li hai visti?   Where are the boys? Have you seen them?

Dove sone le ragazze? Le hai viste?   Where are the girls? Have you seen them?

4 È andato a casa   He's gone home
È andata a casa   She's gone home
I ragazzi sono usciti   The boys have gone out
Le ragazze sono uscite   The girls have gone out
Si è fatto male?   Has he hurt himself?
Si è fatta male?   Has she hurt herself?
Vi siete fatti male, ragazzi?   Have you hurt yourselves, boys?
Vi siete fatte male, ragazze?   Have you hurt yourselves, girls?

5 È chiuso il supermercato?   Is the supermarket closed?
È chiusa la banca?   Is the bank closed?
Sono chiuse le finestre?   Are the windows closed?

Modal Auxiliary Verbs

In Italian, the modal auxiliary verbs (i verbi servili) are: dovere, potere, sapere and volere.

They are followed by the infinitive (without a connecting preposition) and have the following meanings:

dovere	to have to, must → ❶
	to be going to, to be supposed to → ❷
	in the present conditional/perfect conditional:
	should/should have, ought/ought to have → ❸
potere	to be able to, can → ❹
	to be allowed to, can, may → ❺
	indicating possibility: may/might/could → ❻
sapere	to know how to, can → ❼
volere	to want/wish to → ❽
	with negative won't/wouldn't → ❾
	in polite phrases → ❿

Compound Tenses of dovere and potere

dovere and potere are conjugated with avere if the following verb is conjugated with avere, e.g. dare, risolvere → ⑪

dovere and potere are generally conjugated with essere if the following verb is conjugated with essere, e.g. andare, partire, alzarsi → ⑫

EXCEPTION: avere is used in compound tenses of dovere and potere when followed by *essere*, e.g. Avrebbe dovuto *essere* più freddo It should have been colder

1 Devi farlo proprio adesso? — Do you have to do it right now?
È dovuta partire — She had to leave
Dev'essere caro — It must be expensive

2 Deve scendere qui? — Are you going to get off here?
Dovevo venire, ma poi non ho avuto tempo — I was going to come, but then I didn't have time
Dovevano arrivare ieri sera — They were supposed to arrive yesterday evening

3 Dovresti parlargli — You should speak to him
Avrei dovuto stare più attento — I should have been more careful

4 Non potrò venire domani — I won't be able to come tomorrow
Cosa posso dire? — What can I say?

5 Posso entrare? — May I come in?
Non si può parcheggiare qui — You can't park here

6 Può anche essere vero — It may/might even be true
Potrebbe piovere — It may/might/could rain

7 Sai guidare? — Can you drive?
Non so fare gli gnocchi — I don't know how to make gnocchi

8 Vuole rimanere ancora un giorno — He wants to stay another day

9 Non vuole aiutarci — She won't help us
Non voleva ascoltarmi — He wouldn't listen to me

10 Vuole bere qualcosa? — Would you like something to drink?

11 Ho dovuto darglielo — I had to give it to him
Ho potuto risolvere il problema — I was able to sort out the problem

12 È dovuta partire subito — She had to leave immediately
Ci siamo dovuti alzare presto — We had to get up early
Lara è potuta venire — Lara was able to come
Non si sono potuti decidere — They couldn't decide
Si sarebbero potuti sbagliare — They could have been mistaken

Use of Tenses

The Present

The Italian simple present can be used to translate both the English simple present, e.g. I work, and the English present continuous, e.g. I'm working → ❶

The Italian present continuous tense is also used for continuous actions → ❷

Italian uses the present tense with the preposition da to describe an action that *has been continuing for* some time, or *has continued since* some time in the past → ❸

The Italian present is also used
- for the immediate future → ❹
- for offers → ❺
- for arrangements → ❻
- for predictions → ❼
- when asking for suggestions → ❽

The Future

The future is generally used as in English, but note the following:

> the future tense is used after quando, if the verb in the main clause is in the future → ❾

The Future Perfect

It is used as in English to mean 'shall/will have done' → ❿

It is also used in time clauses relating to the future, where English uses the perfect → ⓫

① Dove abitano?
　Dove abitano adesso?
　Piove molto qui
　Ora piove

Where do they live?
Where are they living now?
It rains a lot here
It's raining now

② Cosa stai facendo? *or* Cosa fai?
　Sta piovendo *or* Piove

What are you doing?
It's raining

③ Studio italiano da due anni

　Aspettiamo da un'ora
　Lavora qui da settembre

　Non lo vedo da un pezzo
　Vivono qui dal 2006

I've been learning Italian for two
　years
We've been waiting for an hour
She's been working here since
　September
I haven't seen him for a while
They've lived here since 2006

④ Prendo un espresso
　È rotto, lo butto via

I'll have an espresso
It's broken, I'm going to throw it
　away

⑤ Pago io!
　Devo tornare a casa — Ti porto io!

I'll pay!
I need to go home — I'll take you!

⑥ Parto alle due
　Domani gioco a tennis

I'm leaving at two
I'm playing tennis tomorrow

⑦ Se fai così lo rompi
　Se piove non viene nessuno

If you do that you'll break it
If it rains nobody will come

⑧ Dove lo metto?
　Cosa facciamo?

Where shall I put it?
What shall we do?

⑨ Quando finirò, verrò da te *or*
　Quando finisco, vengo da te
　Lo comprerò quando avrò
　　abbastanza soldi
　Quando verrà saremo già
　　in vacanza

When I finish I'll come to yours

I'll buy it when I've got enough
　money
When he comes we'll be on
　holiday

⑩ Avrò finito fra un'ora

I'll have finished in an hour

⑪ Quando l'avrai letto ritornamelo

　Partirò quando avrò finito

When you've read it let me have
　it back
I'll leave when I've finished

Use of Tenses *continued*

The Imperfect

The imperfect describes:
- an action (or state) in the past without definite time limits → ①
- habitual action(s) in the past (often translated by 'would' or 'used to') → ②

Italian uses the imperfect tense with the preposition **da** to describe an action that *had been continuing for* some time, or *had continued since* some time in the past → ③

The Perfect

The Italian perfect tense corresponds to both the English perfect tense and the English simple past → ④

The Past Historic

The past historic, used mainly in written Italian, and in the south of Italy, corresponds to the English simple past → ⑤

The Past Anterior

This tense is used instead of the pluperfect when a verb in another part of the sentence is in the past historic → ⑥

The Perfect Conditional

The perfect conditional, not the present conditional, is used in reported speech → ⑦

① Avevo la febbre — I had a temperature
Non ne sapeva niente — He didn't know anything about it
Guardavo la tivù — I was watching TV

② Ti prendevano in giro, vero? — They used to tease you, didn't they?
Facevamo lunghissime passeggiate — We would go for very long walks
Mi raccontava delle belle storie — She used to tell me lovely stories

③ Studiavo italiano da due anni — I had been learning Italian for two years
Aspettavamo da molto tempo — We had been waiting for a long time
Lavorava a Roma dal 2010 — She'd been working in Rome since 2010
Non lo vedevo da un pezzo — I hadn't seen him for a while

④ Non l'ho mai visto — I've never seen it
Non l'ho visto ieri — I didn't see it yesterday
Sono stata in città — I've been to town
Stamattina sono stata in città — I went to town this morning

⑤ Dormimmo profondamente e ci svegliammo riposati — We slept soundly and awoke refreshed

⑥ Mi addormentai dopo che se ne furono andati — I went to sleep after they had gone

⑦ Ha detto che mi avrebbe aiutato — He said he would help me
Ho detto che avrei pagato la metà — I said I'd pay half
Hanno promesso che sarebbero venuti — They promised they would come

The Subjunctive

When to use it

For how to form the subjunctive see page 8 onwards.

The subjunctive follows the conjunction che:

- when used with verbs expressing belief or hope, such as credere, pensare and sperare → ❶
- when used with verbs and expressions expressing uncertainty → ❷
- when it is used with volere. The Italian subjunctive + che corresponds to the infinitive construction in English → ❸
- following impersonal verbs → ❹
- after impersonal constructions which express necessity, possibility etc:

è meglio che	it's better (that) → ❺
è possibile che	it's possible (that) → ❻
è facile che	it's likely (that) → ❼
può darsi che	it's possible (that) → ❽
non è che	it's not that → ❾
sembra che	it seems (that) → ❿

1. Penso che sia giusto — I think it's fair
   Credo che partano domani — I think they're leaving tomorrow
   Spero che Luca arrivi in tempo — I hope Luca arrives in time

2. Non so se sia la risposta giusta — I don't know if it's the right answer
   Non sono sicura che tu abbia ragione — I'm not sure you're right

3. Voglio che i miei ragazzi siano felici — I want my children to be happy
   Vuole che la aiuti — She wants me to help her
   Non voglio che mi parlino — I don't want them to speak to me

4. Mi dispiace che non siano qui — I'm sorry they're not here

5. È meglio che tu te ne vada — You'd better leave

6. È possibile che siano stranieri — It's possible they're foreigners

7. È facile che scelgano quelli rossi — They'll probably choose those red ones

8. Può darsi che non venga — It's possible that he won't come

9. Non è che si debba sempre dire la verità — You don't always have to tell the truth

10. Sembra che abbiano vinto — It seems they've won

The Subjunctive *continued*

The subjunctive is used:

- after the following conjunctions:

prima che	before → ❶
affinché	so that → ❷
a meno che	unless → ❸
benché	although → ❹
nel caso che	in case → ❺
nonostante	even though → ❻
perché	so (that) → ❼
per quanto	however → ❽
purché	as long as → ❾
sebbene	even though → ❿

- after superlatives → ⑪
  la più grande che ci sia   the biggest there is

- after:
  chiunque whoever → ⑫
  qualunque + *noun* whatever → ⑬
  per quanto however → ⑭

Note that **che** is not always followed by the subjunctive.

The indicative follows **che** when it is used with positive uses of **sapere** to know, and with other expressions indicating certainty, such as **Sono sicuro** *I'm sure* → ⑮

① Vuoi parlargli prima che parta? Do you want to speak to him before he goes?

② Ti do venti euro affinché tu possa comprarlo I'll give you twenty euros so that you can buy it

③ Lo prendo io, a meno che lo voglia tu I'll take it, unless you want it

④ Mi aiutò a fare i compiti benché fosse molto stanca She helped me do my homework although she was very tired

⑤ Vi do il mio numero di telefono nel caso che veniate a Roma I'll give you my phone number in case you come to Rome

⑥ Vuole alzarsi, nonostante sia ancora malato He wants to get up even though he's still ill

⑦ Lo metto qui perché tutti possano usarlo I'll put it here so everyone can use it

⑧ Per quanto mi sforzi non riesco a capire I can't understand, however hard I try

⑨ Vengo anch'io, purché possa pagare la mia parte I'll come too as long as I can pay my share

⑩ Mi prestò il denaro sebbene non ne avesse molto She lent me the money even though she hadn't got much

⑪ È la persona più simpatica che conosca He's the nicest person I know

⑫ Chiunque sia, digli che non ci sono Whoever it is, tell them I'm not here

⑬ qualunque cosa accada whatever happens

⑭ per quanto bello sia however nice it may be

⑮ So che non è suo I know it's not hers
Sai che ti piace You know you like it
Sono sicura che l'ha preso lui I'm sure he took it
Sei sicuro che verranno? Are you sure they're coming?

The Subjunctive *continued*

The Perfect Subjunctive

The perfect subjunctive follows the conjunction che
- when it follows verbs such as credere, pensare and sperare relating to something in the past → ①
- when it follows an impersonal expression → ②
- when it follows a superlative → ③
- when it follows a conjunction ending in che → ④

The Imperfect Subjunctive

The imperfect subjunctive is used:
- following che, and other conjunctions, as above → ⑤
- with past tenses of volere + che → ⑥
- following se in conditional clauses describing hypothetical situations → ⑦

The Pluperfect Subjunctive

The pluperfect subjunctive is used:
- after che, in the same way as other tenses of the subjunctive → ⑧
- after other conjunctions → ⑨
- following se in conditional clauses describing past hypothetical situations → ⑩

1. Penso che sia stata una buona idea — I think it was a good idea
   Spero che non si sia fatta male — I hope she didn't hurt herself
   Spero che abbia detto la verità — I hope you told the truth

2. È possibile che abbiano cambiato idea — It's possible they've changed their minds
   Mi dispiace che abbia fatto brutto tempo — I'm sorry the weather was bad

3. la più bella che abbia mai visto — the most beautiful one I've ever seen

4. Sarà qui fra poco, a meno che abbia perso l'autobus — He'll be here soon, unless he's missed the bus

5. Voleva alzarsi nonostante fosse ancora malato — He wanted to get up, even though he was still ill

6. Voleva che fossimo pronti alle otto — He wanted us to be ready at eight
   Volevano che tutto fosse in ordine — They wanted everything to be tidy
   Volevo che andasse più veloce — I wanted him to go faster
   Non volevo che mi parlassero — I didn't want them to speak to me

7. Se tu ne avessi bisogno, te lo darei — If you needed it I'd give it to you
   Se potessi dormirei fino a tardi — If I could I'd have a lie-in
   Se lo sapesse sarebbe molto deluso — If he knew he'd be very disappointed
   Se solo avessi più denaro! — If only I had more money!

8. Non pensavo che l'avesse fatto — I didn't think he'd done it
   Credevo che fossero partiti — I thought they had left
   Ero sicuro che avesse perso il treno — I was sure he'd missed the train
   la più bella che avessi mai visto — the most beautiful one I had ever seen

9. Non ha detto niente nonostante si fosse fatto male — He didn't say anything even though he'd hurt himself

10. Se l'avessi saputo non l'avrei mai fatto — If I had known, I'd never have done it
    Se fosse stato più furbo non avrebbe detto niente — If he'd had more sense he wouldn't have said anything
    Se l'avessi visto mi crederesti — If you'd seen, it you'd believe me
    Se solo mi avessi creduto! — If only you'd believed me!

Verbs governing a and di

The following list (pages 70 to 78) contain common verbal constructions using the prepositions a and di

Note the following abbreviations:

infin.	*infinitive*
perf. infin.	*perfect infinitive*
qc	qualcosa
qn	qualcuno
sb	somebody
sth	something

Verbs governing a may be followed by the stressed pronouns me, te, lui, lei, noi, voi and loro → ①

More often, however, they are preceded by an unstressed indirect pronoun, without a → ②

For stressed and unstressed pronouns see page 162.

abituarse qn a qc/a + *infin.*	to accustom sb to sth/to doing
abituarsi a + *infin.*	to get used to doing → ③
acconsentire a qc/a + *infin.*	to agree to sth/to do → ④
accorgersi di qc	to notice sth → ⑤
accusare qn di qc/di + (*perf.*) *infin.*	to accuse sb of sth/of doing, having done → ⑥
affrettarsi a + *infin.*	to hurry to do
aiutare qn a + *infin.*	to help sb to do → ⑦
andare a + *infin.*	to go to do
approfittare di qc/di + *infin.*	to take advantage of sth/of doing
aspettarsi di + *infin.*	to expect to do → ⑧
assistere a qc	to attend sth, be at sth
assomigliare a qn/qc	to look/be like sb/sth → ⑨
aver bisogno di qc /di + *infin.*	to need sth/to do sth
aver paura di qc/di + *infin.*	to be afraid to do/of doing
aver voglia di qc/di + *infin.*	to want sth/to do
avvicinarsi a qn/qc	to approach sb/sth → ⑩
badare a qc/qn	to look after sth/sb
cambiarsi di qc	to change sth → ⑪
cercare di + *infin.*	to try to do → ⑫

Examples

1. Assomigli a lui, non a lei — You look like him, not like her

2. Gli ho chiesto i soldi — I asked him for the money

3. Si è abituato a bere di meno — He got used to drinking less

4. Non hanno acconsentito a venderlo — They haven't agreed to sell it

5. Non si è accorto del mio errore — He didn't notice my mistake

6. Mi ha accusato d'aver mentito — He accused me of lying

7. Aiutatemi a portare queste valigie — Help me to carry these cases

8. Si aspettava di vederlo? — Was she expecting to see him?

9. Sara assomiglia molto a sua madre — Sara looks very like her mother

10. Si è avvicinata a me — She came up to me

11. Mi sono cambiato d'abito — I changed my clothes

12. Ho cercato di capirla — I tried to understand her

Verbs governing a and di *continued*

cessare di + *infin.*	to stop doing → ①
chiedere qc a qn	to ask sb sth/for sth → ②
chiedere a qn di + *infin.*	to ask sb to do → ③
cominciare a + *infin.*	to begin to do, to start to do → ④
comprare qc a qn	to buy sth from sb/for sb → ⑤
consentire qc a qn	to allow sb sth
consentire a qn di + *infin.*	to allow sb to do
consigliare a qn di + *infin.*	to advise sb to do → ⑥
continuare a + *infin.*	to continue to do
convincere qn a + *infin.*	to persuade sb to do → ⑦
dare la colpa a qn di qc	to blame sb for sth
decidere di + *infin.*	to decide to → ⑧
decidersi a + *infin.*	to resolve to do, to make up one's mind to do
diffidare di qn	to distrust sb
dimenticare di + *infin.*	to forget to do → ⑨
dire a qn di + *infin.*	to tell sb to do → ⑩
discutere di qc	to discuss sth
disobbedire a qn	to disobey sb → ⑪
dispiacere a qn	to displease sb → ⑫
divertirsi a + *infin.*	to enjoy doing
domandare qc a qn	to ask sb sth/for sth
dubitare di qc	to doubt sth
esitare a + *infin.*	to hesitate to do
evitare di + *infin.*	to avoid doing → ⑬
far male a qn	to hurt sb
farcela a + *infin.*	to manage to do
fare a meno di qc	to do/go without sth → ⑭
fare finta di + *infin.*	to pretend to do → ⑮
fidarsi di qn	to trust sb → ⑯
fingere di + *infin.*	to pretend to do → ⑰
finire di + *infin.*	to finish doing → ⑱
forzare qn a + *infin.*	to force sb to do
giocare a (+ *sports, games*)	to play → ⑲
giurare di + *infin.*	to swear to do
godere di qc	to enjoy sth → ⑳

①	Ha cessato di piovere?	Has it stopped raining?
②	Ho chiesto a Paola che ora fosse	I asked Paola what time it was
③	Chiedi a Francesca di farlo	Ask Francesca to do it
④	Comincia a nevicare	It's starting to snow
⑤	Cristina ha comprato a Paolo due biglietti	Cristina bought two tickets for Paolo
⑥	Ha consigliato a Paolo di aspettare	He advised Paolo to wait
⑦	Ci ha convinti a restare	She persuaded us to stay
⑧	Cosa avete deciso di fare?	What have you decided to do?
⑨	Non dimenticarti di prendere l'ombrello	Don't forget to take your umbrella
⑩	Dì a Gigi di stare zitto	Tell Gigi to be quiet
⑪	Disobbediscono spesso ai genitori	They often disobey their parents
⑫	A me non dispiace il loro modo di fare	I quite like their attitude
⑬	Evita di parlarle	He avoids speaking to her
⑭	Ho fatto a meno dell'elettricità per diversi giorni	I did without electricity for several days
⑮	Ho fatto finta di non vederlo	I pretended not to see him
⑯	Non mi fido di quella gente	I don't trust those people
⑰	Finge di dormire	She's pretending to be asleep
⑱	Ha finito di leggere questo giornale?	Have you finished reading this newspaper?
⑲	Gioca a tennis	She plays tennis
⑳	Gode di buona salute	He enjoys good health

Verbs governing a and di *continued*

imparare a + *infin.*	to learn to do → ❶
impedire a qn di + *infin.*	to prevent sb from doing → ❷
impegnarsi a + *infin.*	to undertake to do
incaricarsi di qc/di + *infin.*	to see to sth/undertake to do
incoraggiare qn a + *infin.*	to encourage sb to do → ❸
iniziare a + *infin.*	to begin to do
insegnare qc a qn	to teach sb sth
insegnare a qn a + *infin.*	to teach sb to do → ❹
intendersi di qc	to know about sth
interessarsi a qn/qc	to be interested in sb/sth → ❺
invitare qn a + *infin.*	to invite sb to do → ❻
lagnarsi di qc	to complain about sth
lamentarsi di qc	to complain about sth
mancare a qn	to be missed by sb → ❼
mancare di qc	to lack sth
mancare di + *infin.*	to fail to do → ❽
meritare di + *infin.*	to deserve to do → ❾
mettersi a + *infin.*	to begin to do
minacciare di + *infin.*	to threaten to do → ❿
nascondere qc a qn	to hide sth from sb → ⓫
nuocere a qc	to harm sth, to damage sth → ⓬
obbligare qn a + *infin.*	to oblige/force sb to do → ⓭
occuparsi di qc/qn	to look after sth/sb → ⓮
offrirsi di + *infin.*	to offer to do → ⓯
omettere di + *infin.*	to fail to do
ordinare a qn di + *infin.*	to order sb to do → ⓰
partecipare a qc	to take part in sth
pensare a qn/qc	to think about sb/sth → ⓱
pentirsi di + *(perf.) infin.*	to regret doing, having done → ⓲
perdonare qc a qn	to forgive sb for sth
perdonare a qn di + *perf. infin.*	to forgive sb for doing → ⓳
permettere qc a qn	to allow sb sth
permettere a qn di + *infin.*	to allow sb to do → ⓴

Examples

1. Sta imparando a leggere — She's learning to read

2. Il rumore mi impedisce di lavorare — The noise is preventing me from working

3. Incoraggia i figli ad essere indipendenti — She encourages her children to be independent

4. Gli sto insegnando a nuotare — I'm teaching him to swim

5. Si interessa molto di sport — She's very interested in sport

6. Mi ha invitato a cenare da lui — He invited me for dinner at his house

7. Manchi molto ai tuoi genitori — Your parents miss you very much

8. Non mancherò di dirglielo — I'll be sure to tell him about it

9. Meritano di avere la promozione — They deserve to be promoted

10. Ha minacciato di dare le dimissioni — She threatened to resign

11. Nascondile il regalo! — Hide the present from her!

12. Il fumo nuoce alla salute di tutti — Smoking damages everybody's health

13. Li ha obbligati a farlo — He forced them to do it

14. Mi occupo di mia nipote — I'm looking after my niece

15. Marco si è offerto di venire con noi — Marco has offered to go with us

16. Ha ordinato loro di sparare — He ordered them to shoot

17. Penso spesso a te — I often think about you

18. Mi pento di averglielo detto — I'm sorry I told him

19. Hai perdonato Carlo di averti mentito? — Have you forgiven Carlo for lying to you?

20. Permettetemi di continuare, per favore — Allow me to go on, please

Verbs governing a and di *continued*

persuadere qn a + *infin.*	to persuade sb to do
piacere a qn	to please sb → ❶
portare via qc a qn	to take sth away from sb
pregare qn a + *infin.*	to beg sb to do
prendere qc a qn	to take sth from sb → ❷
prendersi gioco di qn/qc	to make fun of sb/sth
preparare qn a + *infin.*	to prepare sb to do
prepararsi a + *infin.*	to get ready to do
proibire a qn di + *infin.*	to forbid sb to do → ❸
promettere qc a qn	to promise sb sth
promettere a qn di + *infin.*	to promise sb to do → ❹
proporre di + *infin.*	to suggest doing → ❺
provare a + *infin.*	to try to do
rammaricarsi di + *(perf.) infin.*	to regret doing, having done
resistere a qc	to resist sth → ❻
ricordarsi di qn/qc/di + *(perf.) infin.*	to remember sb/sth/doing, having done → ❼
ridere di qn/qc	to laugh at sb/sth
rifiutarsi di + *infin.*	to refuse to do → ❽
rimpiangere di + *(perf.) infin.*	to regret doing, having done
rimproverare qc a qn	to reproach sb with/for sth → ❾
ringraziare qn di qc/di + *(perf.) infin.*	to thank sb for sth/for doing, having done → ❿
rinunciare a qc/a + *infin.*	to give up sth /give up doing
rischiare di + *infin.*	to risk doing → ⓫
rispondere a qn	to answer sb
riuscire a + *infin.*	to manage to do → ⓬
rivolgersi a qn	to ask sb
rubare qc a qn	to steal sth from sb
scordare di + *infin.*	to forget to do
scordarsi di + *infin.*	to forget to do
scusarsi di qc/di + *(perf.) infin.*	to apologize for sth/for doing, having done → ⓭
servire a qc/a + *infin.*	to be used for sth/for doing → ⓮
servirsi di qc	to use sth → ⓯
sforzarsi di + *infin.*	to make an effort to do
smettere di + *infin.*	to stop doing → ⓰
sognare di + *infin.*	to dream of doing

①	A lui piace questo genere di film	He likes this kind of film
②	Gli ho preso il cellulare	I took his mobile phone from him
③	Ho proibito loro di uscire	I've forbidden them to go out
④	Hanno promesso a Luca di venire	They promised Luca they would come
⑤	Ho proposto a mio fratello di invitarli	I suggested to my brother that he should invite them
⑥	Come riesci a resistere alla tentazione?	How do you manage to resist the temptation?
⑦	Vi ricordate di Luciana? Non si ricorda di averlo perso	Do you remember Luciana? He doesn't remember losing it
⑧	Si è rifiutato di cooperare	He has refused to cooperate
⑨	Rimproverano alla figlia la sua mancanza d'entusiasmo	They reproach their daughter for her lack of enthusiasm
⑩	Li abbiamo ringraziati della loro gentilezza	We thanked them for their kindness
⑪	Rischiate di perdere soldi	You risk losing money
⑫	Siete riusciti a convincermi	You've managed to convince me
⑬	Mi scuso del ritardo	I'm sorry I'm late
⑭	Questo pulsante serve a regolare il volume	This button is for adjusting the volume
⑮	Si è servito di un cacciavite per aprirlo	He used a screwdriver to open it
⑯	Smettete di fare rumore!	Stop making so much noise!

Verbs governing a and di *continued*

somigliare a qn/qc	to look/be like sb/sth
sopravvivere a qn	to outlive sb → ❶
spicciarsi a + *infin.*	to hurry to do
spingere qn a + *infin.*	to urge sb to do
strappare via qc a qn	to snatch sth from sb → ❷
stufarsi di qc/qn	to be fed up with sth/sb
stupirsi di qc	to be amazed at sth
succedere a qn	to succeed sb
tardare a + *infin.*	to delay doing → ❸
telefonare a qn	to phone sb
tendere a + *infin.*	to tend to do
tenere a + *infin.*	to be keen to do → ❹
tentare di + *infin.*	to try to do → ❺
togliere qc a qn	to take sth away from sb
trattare di qc	to be about sth
ubbidire a qn	to obey sb
vantarsi di qc	to boast about sth
venire a + *infin.*	to come to do
vietare a qn di + *infin.*	to forbid sb to do → ❻
vivere di qc	to live on sth

Verbs followed by a preposition in English but not in Italian.

ascoltare qc/qn	to listen to sth/sb → ❼
aspettare qc/qn	to wait for sth/sb → ❽
cercare qc/qn	to look for sth/sb → ❾
chiedere qc	to ask for sth → ❿
guardare qc/qn	to look at sth/sb → ⓫
pagare qc/qn	to pay for sth/sb → ⓬

1. È sopravvissuta a suo marito — She outlived her husband

2. Il ladro le ha strappato via la borsa — The thief snatched her bag

3. Non ha tardato a prendere una decisione — He didn't take long to make a decision

4. Ci tiene a farlo da sola — She's keen to do it by herself

5. Ho tentato di darlo ad Alessia — I tried to give it to Alessia

6. Ha vietato ai bambini di giocare con i fiammiferi — He's forbidden the children to play with matches

7. Mi stai ascoltando? — Are you listening to me?

8. Aspettami! — Wait for me!

9. Sto cercando la chiave — I'm looking for my key

10. Ha chiesto qualcosa da mangiare — He asked for something to eat

11. Guarda la sua faccia — Look at his face

12. Ho già pagato il biglietto — I've already paid for my ticket

Introduction

The Verb Tables in the following section contain tables of Italian verbs (some regular and some irregular) in alphabetical order. Each table shows you the following forms: Present, Present Subjunctive, Perfect, Imperfect, Future, Conditional, Past Historic, Pluperfect, Imperative and the Past Participle and Gerund.

In Italian there are regular verbs (their forms follow the regular patterns of -are, -ere or -ire verbs), and irregular verbs (their forms do not follow the normal rules). Examples of regular verbs in these tables are:

parlare (regular -are verb)
credere (regular -ere verb)
capire (regular -ire verb)

Some irregular verbs are irregular in most of their forms, while others may only have a couple of irregular forms.

accorgersi (to realize)

	PRESENT		IMPERFECT
io	mi accorgo	io	mi accorgevo
tu	ti accorgi	tu	ti accorgevi
lui/lei/Lei	si accorge	lui/lei/Lei	si accorgeva
noi	ci accorgiamo	noi	ci accorgevamo
voi	vi accorgete	voi	vi accorgevate
loro	si accorgono	loro	si accorgevano

	FUTURE		CONDITIONAL
io	mi accorgerò	io	mi accorgerei
tu	ti accorgerai	tu	ti accorgeresti
lui/lei/Lei	si accorgerà	lui/lei/Lei	si accorgerebbe
noi	ci accorgeremo	noi	ci accorgeremmo
voi	vi accorgerete	voi	vi accorgereste
loro	si accorgeranno	loro	si accorgerebbero

	PRESENT SUBJUNCTIVE		PAST HISTORIC
io	mi accorga	io	mi accorsi
tu	ti accorga	tu	ti accorgesti
lui/lei/Lei	si accorga	lui/lei/Lei	si accorse
noi	ci accorgiamo	noi	ci accorgemmo
voi	vi accorgiate	voi	vi accorgeste
loro	si accorgano	loro	si accorsero

PAST PARTICIPLE	IMPERATIVE
accorto	accorgiti
	accorgiamoci
	accorgetevi

GERUND	AUXILIARY
accorgendosi	essere

addormentarsi (to go to sleep)

	PRESENT		IMPERFECT
io	mi addormento	io	mi addormentavo
tu	ti addormenti	tu	ti addormentavi
lui/lei/Lei	si addormenta	lui/lei/Lei	si addormentava
noi	ci addormentiamo	noi	ci addormentavamo
voi	vi addormentate	voi	vi addormentavate
loro	si addormentano	loro	si addormentavano

	FUTURE		CONDITIONAL
io	mi addormenterò	io	mi addormenterei
tu	ti addormenterai	tu	ti addormenteresti
lui/lei/Lei	si addormenterà	lui/lei/Lei	si addormenterebbe
noi	ci addormenteremo	noi	ci addormenteremmo
voi	vi addormenterete	voi	vi addormentereste
loro	si addormenteranno	loro	si addormenterebbero

	PRESENT SUBJUNCTIVE		PAST HISTORIC
io	mi addormenti	io	mi addormentai
tu	ti addormenti	tu	ti addormentasti
lui/lei/Lei	si addormenti	lui/lei/Lei	si addormentò
noi	ci addormentiamo	noi	ci addormentammo
voi	vi addormentiate	voi	vi addormentaste
loro	si addormentino	loro	si addormentarono

PAST PARTICIPLE	IMPERATIVE
addormentato	addormentati
	addormentiamoci
	addormentatevi

GERUND	AUXILIARY
addormentandosi	essere

andare (to go)

	PRESENT		IMPERFECT
io	vado	io	andavo
tu	vai	tu	andavi
lui/lei/Lei	va	lui/lei/Lei	andava
noi	andiamo	noi	andavamo
voi	andate	voi	andavate
loro	vanno	loro	andavano

	FUTURE		CONDITIONAL
io	andrò	io	andrei
tu	andrai	tu	andresti
lui/lei/Lei	andrà	lui/lei/Lei	andrebbe
noi	andremo	noi	andremmo
voi	andrete	voi	andreste
loro	andranno	loro	andrebbero

	PRESENT SUBJUNCTIVE		PAST HISTORIC
io	vada	io	andai
tu	vada	tu	andasti
lui/lei/Lei	vada	lui/lei/Lei	andò
noi	andiamo	noi	andammo
voi	andiate	voi	andaste
loro	vadano	loro	andarono

PAST PARTICIPLE
andato

IMPERATIVE
vai
andiamo
andate

GERUND
andando

AUXILIARY
essere

aprire (to open)

	PRESENT			IMPERFECT
io	apro		io	aprivo
tu	apri		tu	aprivi
lui/lei/Lei	apre		lui/lei/Lei	apriva
noi	apriamo		noi	aprivamo
voi	aprite		voi	aprivate
loro	aprono		loro	aprivano

	FUTURE			CONDITIONAL
io	aprirò		io	aprirei
tu	aprirai		tu	apriresti
lui/lei/Lei	aprirà		lui/lei/Lei	aprirebbe
noi	apriremo		noi	apriremmo
voi	aprirete		voi	aprireste
loro	apriranno		loro	aprirebbero

	PRESENT SUBJUNCTIVE			PAST HISTORIC
io	apra		io	aprii
tu	apra		tu	apristi
lui/lei/Lei	apra		lui/lei/Lei	aprì
noi	apriamo		noi	aprimmo
voi	apriate		voi	apriste
loro	aprano		loro	aprirono

PAST PARTICIPLE	IMPERATIVE
aperto	apri
	apriamo
	aprite

GERUND	AUXILIARY
aprendo	avere

assumere (to take on, to employ)

	PRESENT		IMPERFECT
io	assumo	io	assumevo
tu	assumi	tu	assumevi
lui/lei/Lei	assume	lui/lei/Lei	assumeva
noi	assumiamo	noi	assumevamo
voi	assumete	voi	assumevate
loro	assumono	loro	assumevano

	FUTURE		CONDITIONAL
io	assumerò	io	assumerei
tu	assumerai	tu	assumeresti
lui/lei/Lei	assumerà	lui/lei/Lei	assumerebbe
noi	assumeremo	noi	assumeremmo
voi	assumerete	voi	assumereste
loro	assumeranno	loro	assumerebbero

	PRESENT SUBJUNCTIVE		PAST HISTORIC
io	assuma	io	assunsi
tu	assuma	tu	assumesti
lui/lei/Lei	assuma	lui/lei/Lei	assunse
noi	assumiamo	noi	assumemmo
voi	assumiate	voi	assumeste
loro	assumano	loro	assunsero

PAST PARTICIPLE
assunto

IMPERATIVE
assumi
assumiamo
assumete

GERUND
assumendo

AUXILIARY
avere

avere (to have)

	PRESENT		IMPERFECT
io	ho	io	avevo
tu	hai	tu	avevi
lui/lei/Lei	ha	lui/lei/Lei	aveva
noi	abbiamo	noi	avevamo
voi	avete	voi	avevate
loro	hanno	loro	avevano

	FUTURE		CONDITIONAL
io	avrò	io	avrei
tu	avrai	tu	avresti
lui/lei/Lei	avrà	lui/lei/Lei	avrebbe
noi	avremo	noi	avremmo
voi	avrete	voi	avreste
loro	avranno	loro	avrebbero

	PRESENT SUBJUNCTIVE		PAST HISTORIC
io	abbia	io	ebbi
tu	abbia	tu	avesti
lui/lei/Lei	abbia	lui/lei/Lei	ebbe
noi	abbiamo	noi	avemmo
voi	abbiate	voi	aveste
loro	abbiano	loro	ebbero

PAST PARTICIPLE	IMPERATIVE
avuto	abbi
	abbiamo
	abbiate

GERUND	AUXILIARY
avendo	avere

bere (to drink)

	PRESENT		IMPERFECT
io	bevo	io	bevevo
tu	bevi	tu	bevevi
lui/lei/Lei	beve	lui/lei/Lei	beveva
noi	beviamo	noi	bevevamo
voi	bevete	voi	bevevate
loro	bevono	loro	bevevano

	FUTURE		CONDITIONAL
io	berrò	io	berrei
tu	berrai	tu	berresti
lui/lei/Lei	berrà	lui/lei/Lei	berrebbe
noi	berremo	noi	berremmo
voi	berrete	voi	berreste
loro	berranno	loro	berrebbero

	PRESENT SUBJUNCTIVE		PAST HISTORIC
io	beva	io	bevvi
tu	beva	tu	bevesti
lui/lei/Lei	beva	lui/lei/Lei	bevve
noi	beviamo	noi	bevemmo
voi	beviate	voi	beveste
loro	bevano	loro	bevvero

PAST PARTICIPLE	IMPERATIVE
bevuto	bevi
	beviamo
	bevete

GERUND	AUXILIARY
bevendo	avere

cadere (to fall)

	PRESENT		IMPERFECT
io	cado	io	cadevo
tu	cadi	tu	cadevi
lui/lei/Lei	cade	lui/lei/Lei	cadeva
noi	cadiamo	noi	cadevamo
voi	cadete	voi	cadevate
loro	cadono	loro	cadevano

	FUTURE		CONDITIONAL
io	cadrò	io	cadrei
tu	cadrai	tu	cadresti
lui/lei/Lei	cadrà	lui/lei/Lei	cadrebbe
noi	cadremo	noi	cadremmo
voi	cadrete	voi	cadreste
loro	cadranno	loro	cadrebbero

	PRESENT SUBJUNCTIVE		PAST HISTORIC
io	cada	io	caddi
tu	cada	tu	cadesti
lui/lei/Lei	cada	lui/lei/Lei	cadde
noi	cadiamo	noi	cademmo
voi	cadiate	voi	cadeste
loro	cadano	loro	caddero

PAST PARTICIPLE	IMPERATIVE
caduto	cadi
	cadiamo
	cadete

GERUND	AUXILIARY
cadendo	essere

capire (to understand)

	PRESENT		IMPERFECT
io	capisco	io	capivo
tu	capisci	tu	capivi
lui/lei/Lei	capisce	lui/lei/Lei	capiva
noi	capiamo	noi	capivamo
voi	capite	voi	capivate
loro	capiscono	loro	capivano

	FUTURE		CONDITIONAL
io	capirò	io	capirei
tu	capirai	tu	capiresti
lui/lei/Lei	capirà	lui/lei/Lei	capirebbe
noi	capiremo	noi	capiremmo
voi	capirete	voi	capireste
loro	capiranno	loro	capirebbero

	PRESENT SUBJUNCTIVE		PAST HISTORIC
io	capisca	io	capii
tu	capisca	tu	capisti
lui/lei/Lei	capisca	lui/lei/Lei	capì
noi	capiamo	noi	capimmo
voi	capiate	voi	capiste
loro	capiscano	loro	capirono

PAST PARTICIPLE	IMPERATIVE
capito	capisci
	capiamo
	capite

GERUND	AUXILIARY
capendo	avere

cercare (to look for)

	PRESENT		IMPERFECT
io	cerco	io	cercavo
tu	cerchi	tu	cercavi
lui/lei/Lei	cerca	lui/lei/Lei	cercava
noi	cerchiamo	noi	cercavamo
voi	cercate	voi	cercavate
loro	cercano	loro	cercavano

	FUTURE		CONDITIONAL
io	cercherò	io	cercherei
tu	cercherai	tu	cercheresti
lui/lei/Lei	cercherà	lui/lei/Lei	cercherebbe
noi	cercheremo	noi	cercheremmo
voi	cercherete	voi	cerchereste
loro	cercheranno	loro	cercherebbero

	PRESENT SUBJUNCTIVE		PAST HISTORIC
io	cerchi	io	cercai
tu	cerchi	tu	cercasti
lui/lei/Lei	cerchi	lui/lei/Lei	cercò
noi	cerchiamo	noi	cercammo
voi	cerchiate	voi	cercaste
loro	cerchino	loro	cercarono

PAST PARTICIPLE	IMPERATIVE
cercato	cerca
	cerchiamo
	cercate

GERUND	AUXILIARY
cercando	avere

chiudere (to close)

	PRESENT		IMPERFECT
io	chiudo	io	chiudevo
tu	chiudi	tu	chiudevi
lui/lei/Lei	chiude	lui/lei/Lei	chiudeva
noi	chiudiamo	noi	chiudevamo
voi	chiudete	voi	chiudevate
loro	chiudono	loro	chiudevano

	FUTURE		CONDITIONAL
io	chiuderò	io	chiuderei
tu	chiuderai	tu	chiuderesti
lui/lei/Lei	chiuderà	lui/lei/Lei	chiuderebbe
noi	chiuderemo	noi	chiuderemmo
voi	chiuderete	voi	chiudereste
loro	chiuderanno	loro	chiuderebbero

	PRESENT SUBJUNCTIVE		PAST HISTORIC
io	chiuda	io	chiusi
tu	chiuda	tu	chiudesti
lui/lei/Lei	chiuda	lui/lei/Lei	chiuse
noi	chiudiamo	noi	chiudemmo
voi	chiudiate	voi	chiudeste
loro	chiudano	loro	chiusero

PAST PARTICIPLE	IMPERATIVE
chiuso	chiudi
	chiudiamo
	chiudete

GERUND	AUXILIARY
chiudendo	avere

correre (to run)

	PRESENT		IMPERFECT
io	corro	io	correvo
tu	corri	tu	correvi
lui/lei/Lei	corre	lui/lei/Lei	correva
noi	corriamo	noi	correvamo
voi	correte	voi	correvate
loro	corrono	loro	correvano

	FUTURE		CONDITIONAL
io	correrò	io	correrei
tu	correrai	tu	correresti
lui/lei/Lei	correrà	lui/lei/Lei	correrebbe
noi	correremo	noi	correremmo
voi	correrete	voi	correreste
loro	correranno	loro	correrebbero

	PRESENT SUBJUNCTIVE		PAST HISTORIC
io	corra	io	corsi
tu	corra	tu	corresti
lui/lei/Lei	corra	lui/lei/Lei	corse
noi	corriamo	noi	corremmo
voi	corriate	voi	correste
loro	corrano	loro	corsero

PAST PARTICIPLE	IMPERATIVE
corso	corri
	corriamo
	correte

GERUND	AUXILIARY
correndo	avere

credere (to believe)

	PRESENT		IMPERFECT
io	credo	io	credevo
tu	credi	tu	credevi
lui/lei/Lei	crede	lui/lei/Lei	credeva
noi	crediamo	noi	credevamo
voi	credete	voi	credevate
loro	credono	loro	credevano

	FUTURE		CONDITIONAL
io	crederò	io	crederei
tu	crederai	tu	crederesti
lui/lei/Lei	crederà	lui/lei/Lei	crederebbe
noi	crederemo	noi	crederemmo
voi	crederete	voi	credereste
loro	crederanno	loro	crederebbero

	PRESENT SUBJUNCTIVE		PAST HISTORIC
io	creda	io	credetti *or* credei
tu	creda	tu	credesti
lui/lei/Lei	creda	lui/lei/Lei	credette
noi	crediamo	noi	credemmo
voi	crediate	voi	credeste
loro	credano	loro	credettero

PAST PARTICIPLE	IMPERATIVE
creduto	credi
	crediamo
	credete

GERUND	AUXILIARY
credendo	avere

crescere (to grow)

	PRESENT		IMPERFECT
io	cresco	io	crescevo
tu	cresci	tu	crescevi
lui/lei/Lei	cresce	lui/lei/Lei	cresceva
noi	cresciamo	noi	crescevamo
voi	crescete	voi	crescevate
loro	crescono	loro	crescevano

	FUTURE		CONDITIONAL
io	crescerò	io	crescerei
tu	crescerai	tu	cresceresti
lui/lei/Lei	crescerà	lui/lei/Lei	crescerebbe
noi	cresceremo	noi	cresceremmo
voi	crescerete	voi	crescereste
loro	cresceranno	loro	crescerebbero

	PRESENT SUBJUNCTIVE		PAST HISTORIC
io	cresca	io	crebbi
tu	cresca	tu	crescesti
lui/lei/Lei	cresca	lui/lei/Lei	crebbe
noi	cresciamo	noi	crescemmo
voi	cresciate	voi	cresceste
loro	crescano	loro	crebbero

PAST PARTICIPLE
cresciuto

IMPERATIVE
cresci
cresciamo
crescete

GERUND
crescendo

AUXILIARY
essere

dare (to give)

	PRESENT		IMPERFECT
io	do	io	davo
tu	dai	tu	davi
lui/lei/Lei	dà	lui/lei/Lei	dava
noi	diamo	noi	davamo
voi	date	voi	davate
loro	danno	loro	davano

	FUTURE		CONDITIONAL
io	darò	io	darei
tu	darai	tu	daresti
lui/lei/Lei	darà	lui/lei/Lei	darebbe
noi	daremo	noi	daremmo
voi	darete	voi	dareste
loro	daranno	loro	darebbero

	PRESENT SUBJUNCTIVE		PAST HISTORIC
io	dia	io	dette
tu	dia	tu	desti
lui/lei/Lei	dia	lui/lei/Lei	diede *or* detti
noi	diamo	noi	demmo
voi	diate	voi	deste
loro	diano	loro	diedero *or* dettero

PAST PARTICIPLE
dato

IMPERATIVE
dai *or* da'
diamo
date

GERUND
dando

AUXILIARY
avere

dire (to say)

	PRESENT		IMPERFECT
io	dico	io	dicevo
tu	dici	tu	dicevi
lui/lei/Lei	dice	lui/lei/Lei	diceva
noi	diciamo	noi	dicevamo
voi	dite	voi	dicevate
loro	dicono	loro	dicevano

	FUTURE		CONDITIONAL
io	dirò	io	direi
tu	dirai	tu	diresti
lui/lei/Lei	dirà	lui/lei/Lei	direbbe
noi	diremo	noi	diremmo
voi	direte	voi	direste
loro	diranno	loro	direbbero

	PRESENT SUBJUNCTIVE		PAST HISTORIC
io	dica	io	dissi
tu	dica	tu	dicesti
lui/lei/Lei	dica	lui/lei/Lei	disse
noi	diciamo	noi	dicemmo
voi	diciate	voi	diceste
loro	dicano	loro	dissero

PAST PARTICIPLE	IMPERATIVE
detto	di'
	diciamo
	dite

GERUND	AUXILIARY
dicendo	avere

dirigere (to direct)

	PRESENT		**IMPERFECT**
io	dirigo	io	dirigevo
tu	dirigi	tu	dirigevi
lui/lei/Lei	dirige	lui/lei/Lei	dirigeva
noi	dirigiamo	noi	dirigevamo
voi	dirigete	voi	dirigevate
loro	dirigono	loro	dirigevano

	FUTURE		**CONDITIONAL**
io	dirigerò	io	dirigerei
tu	dirigerai	tu	dirigeresti
lui/lei/Lei	dirigerà	lui/lei/Lei	dirigerebbe
noi	dirigeremo	noi	dirigeremmo
voi	dirigerete	voi	dirigereste
loro	dirigeranno	loro	dirigerebbero

	PRESENT SUBJUNCTIVE		**PAST HISTORIC**
io	diriga	io	diressi
tu	diriga	tu	dirigesti
lui/lei/Lei	diriga	lui/lei/Lei	diresse
noi	dirigiamo	noi	dirigemmo
voi	dirigiate	voi	dirigeste
loro	dirigano	loro	diressero

PAST PARTICIPLE	**IMPERATIVE**
diretto	dirigi
	dirigiamo
	dirigete

GERUND	**AUXILIARY**
dirigendo	avere

dormire (to sleep)

	PRESENT		IMPERFECT
io	dormo	io	dormivo
tu	dormi	tu	dormivi
lui/lei/Lei	dorme	lui/lei/Lei	dormiva
noi	dormiamo	noi	dormivamo
voi	dormite	voi	dormivate
loro	dormono	loro	dormivano

	FUTURE		CONDITIONAL
io	dormirò	io	dormirei
tu	dormirai	tu	dormiresti
lui/lei/Lei	dormirà	lui/lei/Lei	dormirebbe
noi	dormiremo	noi	dormiremmo
voi	dormirete	voi	dormireste
loro	dormiranno	loro	dormirebbero

	PRESENT SUBJUNCTIVE		PAST HISTORIC
io	dorma	io	dormii
tu	dorma	tu	dormisti
lui/lei/Lei	dorma	lui/lei/Lei	dormì
noi	dormiamo	noi	dormimmo
voi	dormiate	voi	dormiste
loro	dormano	loro	dormirono

PAST PARTICIPLE
dormito

IMPERATIVE
dormi
dormiamo
dormite

GERUND
dormendo

AUXILIARY
avere

dovere (to have to)

	PRESENT		IMPERFECT
io	devo	io	dovevo
tu	devi	tu	dovevi
lui/lei/Lei	deve	lui/lei/Lei	doveva
noi	dobbiamo	noi	dovevamo
voi	dovete	voi	dovevate
loro	devono	loro	dovevano

	FUTURE		CONDITIONAL
io	dovrò	io	dovrei
tu	dovrai	tu	dovresti
lui/lei/Lei	dovrà	lui/lei/Lei	dovrebbe
noi	dovremo	noi	dovremmo
voi	dovrete	voi	dovreste
loro	dovranno	loro	dovrebbero

	PRESENT SUBJUNCTIVE		PAST HISTORIC
io	debba	io	dovetti
tu	debba	tu	dovesti
lui/lei/Lei	debba	lui/lei/Lei	dovette
noi	dobbiamo	noi	dovemmo
voi	dobbiate	voi	doveste
loro	debbano	loro	dovettero

PAST PARTICIPLE	IMPERATIVE
dovuto	–

GERUND	AUXILIARY
dovendo	avere

essere (to be)

	PRESENT		IMPERFECT
io	sono	io	ero
tu	sei	tu	eri
lui/lei/Lei	è	lui/lei/Lei	era
noi	siamo	noi	eravamo
voi	siete	voi	eravate
loro	sono	loro	erano

	FUTURE		CONDITIONAL
io	sarò	io	sarei
tu	sarai	tu	saresti
lui/lei/Lei	sarà	lui/lei/Lei	sarebbe
noi	saremo	noi	saremmo
voi	sarete	voi	sareste
loro	saranno	loro	sarebbero

	PRESENT SUBJUNCTIVE		PAST HISTORIC
io	sia	io	fui
tu	sia	tu	fosti
lui/lei/Lei	sia	lui/lei/Lei	fu
noi	siamo	noi	fummo
voi	siate	voi	foste
loro	siano	loro	furono

PAST PARTICIPLE
stato

IMPERATIVE
sii
siamo
siate

GERUND
essendo

AUXILIARY
essere

fare (to do, to make)

	PRESENT		**IMPERFECT**
io	faccio	io	facevo
tu	fai	tu	facevi
lui/lei/Lei	fa	lui/lei/Lei	faceva
noi	facciamo	noi	facevamo
voi	fate	voi	facevate
loro	fanno	loro	facevano

	FUTURE		**CONDITIONAL**
io	farò	io	farei
tu	farai	tu	faresti
lui/lei/Lei	farà	lui/lei/Lei	farebbe
noi	faremo	noi	faremmo
voi	farete	voi	fareste
loro	faranno	loro	farebbero

	PRESENT SUBJUNCTIVE		**PAST HISTORIC**
io	faccia	io	feci
tu	faccia	tu	facesti
lui/lei/Lei	faccia	lui/lei/Lei	fece
noi	facciamo	noi	facemmo
voi	facciate	voi	faceste
loro	facciano	loro	fecero

PAST PARTICIPLE
fatto

IMPERATIVE
fai *or* fa'
facciamo
fate

GERUND
facendo

AUXILIARY
avere

leggere (to read)

	PRESENT		IMPERFECT
io	leggo	io	leggevo
tu	leggi	tu	leggevi
lui/lei/Lei	legge	lui/lei/Lei	leggeva
noi	leggiamo	noi	leggevamo
voi	leggete	voi	leggevate
loro	leggono	loro	leggevano

	FUTURE		CONDITIONAL
io	leggerò	io	leggerei
tu	leggerai	tu	leggeresti
lui/lei/Lei	leggerà	lui/lei/Lei	leggerebbe
noi	leggeremo	noi	leggeremmo
voi	leggerete	voi	leggereste
loro	leggeranno	loro	leggerebbero

	PRESENT SUBJUNCTIVE		PAST HISTORIC
io	legga	io	lessi
tu	legga	tu	leggesti
lui/lei/Lei	legga	lui/lei/Lei	lesse
noi	leggiamo	noi	leggemmo
voi	leggiate	voi	leggeste
loro	leggano	loro	lessero

PAST PARTICIPLE	IMPERATIVE
letto	leggi
	leggiamo
	leggete

GERUND	AUXILIARY
leggendo	avere

mettere (to put)

	PRESENT		IMPERFECT
io	metto	io	mettevo
tu	metti	tu	mettevi
lui/lei/Lei	mette	lui/lei/Lei	metteva
noi	mettiamo	noi	mettevamo
voi	mettete	voi	mettevate
loro	mettono	loro	mettevano

	FUTURE		CONDITIONAL
io	metterò	io	metterei
tu	metterai	tu	metteresti
lui/lei/Lei	metterà	lui/lei/Lei	metterebbe
noi	metteremo	noi	metteremmo
voi	metterete	voi	mettereste
loro	metteranno	loro	metterebbero

	PRESENT SUBJUNCTIVE		PAST HISTORIC
io	metta	io	misi
tu	metta	tu	mettesti
lui/lei/Lei	metta	lui/lei/Lei	mise
noi	mettiamo	noi	mettemmo
voi	mettiate	voi	metteste
loro	mettano	loro	misero

PAST PARTICIPLE	IMPERATIVE
messo	metti
	mettiamo
	mettete

GERUND	AUXILIARY
mettendo	avere

morire (to die)

	PRESENT		IMPERFECT
io	muoio	io	morivo
tu	muori	tu	morivi
lui/lei/Lei	muore	lui/lei/Lei	moriva
noi	moriamo	noi	morivamo
voi	morite	voi	morivate
loro	muoiono	loro	morivano

	FUTURE		CONDITIONAL
io	morirò	io	morirei
tu	morirai	tu	moriresti
lui/lei/Lei	morirà	lui/lei/Lei	morirebbe
noi	moriremo	noi	moriremmo
voi	morirete	voi	morireste
loro	moriranno	loro	morirebbero

	PRESENT SUBJUNCTIVE		PAST HISTORIC
io	muoia	io	morii
tu	muoia	tu	moristi
lui/lei/Lei	muoia	lui/lei/Lei	morì
noi	moriamo	noi	morimmo
voi	moriate	voi	moriste
loro	muoiano	loro	morirono

PAST PARTICIPLE	IMPERATIVE
morto	muori
	moriamo
	morite

GERUND	AUXILIARY
morendo	essere

muovere (to move)

	PRESENT		IMPERFECT
io	muovo	io	muovevo
tu	muovi	tu	muovevi
lui/lei/Lei	muove	lui/lei/Lei	muoveva
noi	muoviamo	noi	muovevamo
voi	muovete	voi	muovevate
loro	muovono	loro	muovevano

	FUTURE		CONDITIONAL
io	muoverò	io	muoverei
tu	muoverai	tu	muoveresti
lui/lei/Lei	muoverà	lui/lei/Lei	muoverebbe
noi	muoveremo	noi	muoveremmo
voi	muoverete	voi	muovereste
loro	muoveranno	loro	muoverebbero

	PRESENT SUBJUNCTIVE		PAST HISTORIC
io	muova	io	mossi
tu	muova	tu	muovesti
lui/lei/Lei	muova	lui/lei/Lei	mosse
noi	muoviamo	noi	muovemmo
voi	muoviate	voi	muoveste
loro	muovano	loro	mossero

PAST PARTICIPLE	IMPERATIVE
mosso	muovi
	muoviamo
	muovete

GERUND	AUXILIARY
muovendo	avere

nascere (to be born)

	PRESENT		IMPERFECT
io	nasco	io	nascevo
tu	nasci	tu	nascevi
lui/lei/Lei	nasce	lui/lei/Lei	nasceva
noi	nasciamo	noi	nascevamo
voi	nascete	voi	nascevate
loro	nascono	loro	nascevano

	FUTURE		CONDITIONAL
io	nascerò	io	nascerei
tu	nascerai	tu	nasceresti
lui/lei/Lei	nascerà	lui/lei/Lei	nascerebbe
noi	nasceremo	noi	nasceremmo
voi	nascerete	voi	nascereste
loro	nasceranno	loro	nascerebbero

	PRESENT SUBJUNCTIVE		PAST HISTORIC
io	nasca	io	nacqui
tu	nasca	tu	nascesti
lui/lei/Lei	nasca	lui/lei/Lei	nacque
noi	nasciamo	noi	nascemmo
voi	nasciate	voi	nasceste
loro	nascano	loro	nacquero

PAST PARTICIPLE
nato

IMPERATIVE
nasci
nasciamo
nascete

GERUND
nascendo

AUXILIARY
essere

parlare (to speak)

	PRESENT		IMPERFECT
io	parlo	io	parlavo
tu	parli	tu	parlavi
lui/lei/Lei	parla	lui/lei/Lei	parlava
noi	parliamo	noi	parlavamo
voi	parlate	voi	parlavate
loro	parlano	loro	parlavano

	FUTURE		CONDITIONAL
io	parlerò	io	parlerei
tu	parlerai	tu	parleresti
lui/lei/Lei	parlerà	lui/lei/Lei	parlerebbe
noi	parleremo	noi	parleremmo
voi	parlerete	voi	parlereste
loro	parleranno	loro	parlerebbero

	PRESENT SUBJUNCTIVE		PAST HISTORIC
io	parli	io	parlai
tu	parli	tu	parlasti
lui/lei/Lei	parli	lui/lei/Lei	parlò
noi	parliamo	noi	parlammo
voi	parliate	voi	parlaste
loro	parlino	loro	parlarono

PAST PARTICIPLE
parlato

IMPERATIVE
parla
parliamo
parlate

GERUND
parlando

AUXILIARY
avere

piacere (to be pleasing)

	PRESENT		IMPERFECT
io	piaccio	io	piacevo
tu	piaci	tu	piacevi
lui/lei/Lei	piace	lui/lei/Lei	piaceva
noi	piacciamo	noi	piacevamo
voi	piacete	voi	piacevate
loro	piacciono	loro	piacevano

	FUTURE		CONDITIONAL
io	piacerò	io	piacerei
tu	piacerai	tu	piaceresti
lui/lei/Lei	piacerà	lui/lei/Lei	piacerebbe
noi	piaceremo	noi	piaceremmo
voi	piacerete	voi	piacereste
loro	piaceranno	loro	piacerebbero

	PRESENT SUBJUNCTIVE		PAST HISTORIC
io	piaccia	io	piacqui
tu	piaccia	tu	piacesti
lui/lei/Lei	piaccia	lui/lei/Lei	piacque
noi	piacciamo	noi	piacemmo
voi	piacciate	voi	piaceste
loro	piacciano	loro	piacquero

PAST PARTICIPLE
piaciuto

IMPERATIVE
piaci
piacciamo
piacciate

GERUND
piacendo

AUXILIARY
essere

piovere (to rain)

PRESENT
piove

IMPERFECT
pioveva

FUTURE
pioverà

CONDITIONAL
pioverebbe

PRESENT SUBJUNCTIVE
piova

PAST HISTORIC
piovve

PAST PARTICIPLE
piovuto

IMPERATIVE
–

GERUND
piovendo

AUXILIARY
essere

potere (to be able)

	PRESENT		IMPERFECT
io	posso	io	potevo
tu	puoi	tu	potevi
lui/lei/Lei	può	lui/lei/Lei	poteva
noi	possiamo	noi	potevamo
voi	potete	voi	potevate
loro	possono	loro	potevano

	FUTURE		CONDITIONAL
io	potrò	io	potrei
tu	potrai	tu	potresti
lui/lei/Lei	potrà	lui/lei/Lei	potrebbe
noi	potremo	noi	potremmo
voi	potrete	voi	potreste
loro	potranno	loro	potrebbero

	PRESENT SUBJUNCTIVE		PAST HISTORIC
io	possa	io	potei
tu	possa	tu	potesti
lui/lei/Lei	possa	lui/lei/Lei	poté
noi	possiamo	noi	potemmo
voi	possiate	voi	poteste
loro	possano	loro	poterono

PAST PARTICIPLE	IMPERATIVE
potuto	–

GERUND	AUXILIARY
potendo	avere

prendere (to take)

	PRESENT		IMPERFECT
io	prendo	io	prendevo
tu	prendi	tu	prendevi
lui/lei/Lei	prende	lui/lei/Lei	prendeva
noi	prendiamo	noi	prendevamo
voi	prendete	voi	prendevate
loro	prendono	loro	prendevano

	FUTURE		CONDITIONAL
io	prenderò	io	prenderei
tu	prenderai	tu	prenderesti
lui/lei/Lei	prenderà	lui/lei/Lei	prenderebbe
noi	prenderemo	noi	prenderemmo
voi	prenderete	voi	prendereste
loro	prenderanno	loro	prenderebbero

	PRESENT SUBJUNCTIVE		PAST HISTORIC
io	prenda	io	presi
tu	prenda	tu	prendesti
lui/lei/Lei	prenda	lui/lei/Lei	prese
noi	prendiamo	noi	prendemmo
voi	prendiate	voi	prendeste
loro	prendano	loro	presero

PAST PARTICIPLE	IMPERATIVE
preso	prendi
	prendiamo
	prendete

GERUND	AUXILIARY
prendendo	avere

rompere (to break)

	PRESENT		IMPERFECT
io	rompo	io	rompevo
tu	rompi	tu	rompevi
lui/lei/Lei	rompe	lui/lei/Lei	rompeva
noi	rompiamo	noi	rompevamo
voi	rompete	voi	rompevate
loro	rompono	loro	rompevano

	FUTURE		CONDITIONAL
io	romperò	io	romperei
tu	romperai	tu	romperesti
lui/lei/Lei	romperà	lui/lei/Lei	romperebbe
noi	romperemo	noi	romperemmo
voi	romperete	voi	rompereste
loro	romperanno	loro	romperebbero

	PRESENT SUBJUNCTIVE		PAST HISTORIC
io	rompa	io	ruppi
tu	rompa	tu	rompesti
lui/lei/Lei	rompa	lui/lei/Lei	ruppe
noi	rompiamo	noi	rompemmo
voi	rompiate	voi	rompeste
loro	rompano	loro	ruppero

PAST PARTICIPLE	IMPERATIVE
rotto	rompi
	rompiamo
	rompete

GERUND	AUXILIARY
rompendo	avere

salire (to go up)

	PRESENT		IMPERFECT
io	salgo	io	salivo
tu	sali	tu	salivi
lui/lei/Lei	sale	lui/lei/Lei	saliva
noi	saliamo	noi	salivamo
voi	salite	voi	salivate
loro	salgono	loro	salivano

	FUTURE		CONDITIONAL
io	salirò	io	salirei
tu	salirai	tu	saliresti
lui/lei/Lei	salirà	lui/lei/Lei	salirebbe
noi	saliremo	noi	saliremmo
voi	salirete	voi	salireste
loro	saliranno	loro	salirebbero

	PRESENT SUBJUNCTIVE		PAST HISTORIC
io	salga	io	salii
tu	salga	tu	salisti
lui/lei/Lei	salga	lui/lei/Lei	salì
noi	saliamo	noi	salimmo
voi	saliate	voi	saliste
loro	salgano	loro	salirono

PAST PARTICIPLE	IMPERATIVE
salito	sali
	saliamo
	salite

GERUND	AUXILIARY
salendo	essere

sapere (to know)

	PRESENT		IMPERFECT
io	so	io	sapevo
tu	sai	tu	sapevi
lui/lei/Lei	sa	lui/lei/Lei	sapeva
noi	sappiamo	noi	sapevamo
voi	sapete	voi	sapevate
loro	sanno	loro	sapevano

	FUTURE		CONDITIONAL
io	saprò	io	saprei
tu	saprai	tu	sapresti
lui/lei/Lei	saprà	lui/lei/Lei	saprebbe
noi	sapremo	noi	sapremmo
voi	saprete	voi	sapreste
loro	sapranno	loro	saprebbero

	PRESENT SUBJUNCTIVE		PAST HISTORIC
io	sappia	io	seppi
tu	sappia	tu	sapesti
lui/lei/Lei	sappia	lui/lei/Lei	seppe
noi	sappiamo	noi	sapemmo
voi	sappiate	voi	sapeste
loro	sappiano	loro	seppero

PAST PARTICIPLE	IMPERATIVE
saputo	sappi
	sappiamo
	sappiate

GERUND	AUXILIARY
sapendo	avere

scrivere (to write)

	PRESENT		**IMPERFECT**
io	scrivo	io	scrivevo
tu	scrivi	tu	scrivevi
lui/lei/Lei	scrive	lui/lei/Lei	scriveva
noi	scriviamo	noi	scrivevamo
voi	scrivete	voi	scrivevate
loro	scrivono	loro	scrivevano

	FUTURE		**CONDITIONAL**
io	scriverò	io	scriverei
tu	scriverai	tu	scriveresti
lui/lei/Lei	scriverà	lui/lei/Lei	scriverebbe
noi	scriveremo	noi	scriveremmo
voi	scriverete	voi	scrivereste
loro	scriveranno	loro	scriverebbero

	PRESENT SUBJUNCTIVE		**PAST HISTORIC**
io	scriva	io	scrissi
tu	scriva	tu	scrivesti
lui/lei/Lei	scriva	lui/lei/Lei	scrisse
noi	scriviamo	noi	scrivemmo
voi	scriviate	voi	scriveste
loro	scrivano	loro	scrissero

PAST PARTICIPLE	**IMPERATIVE**
scritto	scrivi
	scriviamo
	scrivete

GERUND	**AUXILIARY**
scrivendo	avere

sedere (to sit)

	PRESENT		IMPERFECT
io	siedo	io	sedevo
tu	siedi	tu	sedevi
lui/lei/Lei	siede	lui/lei/Lei	sedeva
noi	sediamo	noi	sedevamo
voi	sedete	voi	sedevate
loro	siedono	loro	sedevano

	FUTURE		CONDITIONAL
io	sederò	io	sederei
tu	sederai	tu	sederesti
lui/lei/Lei	sederà	lui/lei/Lei	sederebbe
noi	sederemo	noi	sederemmo
voi	sederete	voi	sedereste
loro	sederanno	loro	sederebbero

	PRESENT SUBJUNCTIVE		PAST HISTORIC
io	sieda	io	sedetti
tu	sieda	tu	sedesti
lui/lei/Lei	sieda	lui/lei/Lei	sedette
noi	sediamo	noi	sedemmo
voi	sediate	voi	sedeste
loro	siedano	loro	sedettero

PAST PARTICIPLE	IMPERATIVE
seduto	siedi
	sediamo
	sedete

GERUND	AUXILIARY
sedendo	essere

stare (to be)

	PRESENT		IMPERFECT
io	sto	io	stavo
tu	stai	tu	stavi
lui/lei/Lei	sta	lui/lei/Lei	stava
noi	stiamo	noi	stavamo
voi	state	voi	stavate
loro	stanno	loro	stavano

	FUTURE		CONDITIONAL
io	starò	io	starei
tu	starai	tu	staresti
lui/lei/Lei	starà	lui/lei/Lei	starebbe
noi	staremo	noi	staremmo
voi	starete	voi	stareste
loro	staranno	loro	starebbero

	PRESENT SUBJUNCTIVE		PAST HISTORIC
io	stia	io	stetti
tu	stia	tu	stesti
lui/lei/Lei	stia	lui/lei/Lei	stette
noi	stiamo	noi	stemmo
voi	stiate	voi	steste
loro	stiano	loro	stettero

PAST PARTICIPLE	IMPERATIVE
stato	stai
	stiamo
	state

GERUND	AUXILIARY
stando	essere

succedere (to happen)

	PRESENT			IMPERFECT
sing.	succede		*sing.*	succedeva
plur.	succedono		*plur.*	succedevano

	FUTURE			CONDITIONAL
sing.	succederà		*sing.*	succederebbe
plur.	succederanno		*plur.*	succederebbero

	PRESENT SUBJUNCTIVE			PAST HISTORIC
sing.	succeda		*sing.*	successe
plur.	succedano		*plur.*	successero

PAST PARTICIPLE	IMPERATIVE
successo	–

GERUND	AUXILIARY
succedendo	essere

tenere (to hold)

	PRESENT		IMPERFECT
io	tengo	io	tenevo
tu	tieni	tu	tenevi
lui/lei/Lei	tiene	lui/lei/Lei	teneva
noi	teniamo	noi	tenevamo
voi	tenete	voi	tenevate
loro	tengono	loro	tenevano

	FUTURE		CONDITIONAL
io	terrò	io	terrei
tu	terrai	tu	terresti
lui/lei/Lei	terrà	lui/lei/Lei	terrebbe
noi	terremo	noi	terremmo
voi	terrete	voi	terreste
loro	terranno	loro	terrebbero

	PRESENT SUBJUNCTIVE		PAST HISTORIC
io	tenga	io	tenni
tu	tenga	tu	tenesti
lui/lei/Lei	tenga	lui/lei/Lei	tenne
noi	teniamo	noi	tenemmo
voi	teniate	voi	teneste
loro	tengano	loro	tennero

PAST PARTICIPLE
tenuto

IMPERATIVE
tieni
teniamo
tenete

GERUND
tenendo

AUXILIARY
avere

uscire (to go out)

	PRESENT			IMPERFECT
io	esco		io	uscivo
tu	esci		tu	uscivi
lui/lei/Lei	esce		lui/lei/Lei	usciva
noi	usciamo		noi	uscivamo
voi	uscite		voi	uscivate
loro	escono		loro	uscivano

	FUTURE			CONDITIONAL
io	uscirò		io	uscirei
tu	uscirai		tu	usciresti
lui/lei/Lei	uscirà		lui/lei/Lei	uscirebbe
noi	usciremo		noi	usciremmo
voi	uscirete		voi	uscireste
loro	usciranno		loro	uscirebbero

	PRESENT SUBJUNCTIVE			PAST HISTORIC
io	esca		io	uscii
tu	esca		tu	uscisti
lui/lei/Lei	esca		lui/lei/Lei	uscì
noi	usciamo		noi	uscimmo
voi	usciate		voi	usciste
loro	escano		loro	uscirono

PAST PARTICIPLE	IMPERATIVE
uscito	esci
	usciamo
	uscite

GERUND	AUXILIARY
uscendo	essere

vedere (to see)

	PRESENT		IMPERFECT
io	vedo	io	vedevo
tu	vedi	tu	vedevi
lui/lei/Lei	vede	lui/lei/Lei	vedeva
noi	vediamo	noi	vedevamo
voi	vedete	voi	vedevate
loro	vedono	loro	vedevano

	FUTURE		CONDITIONAL
io	vedrò	io	vedrei
tu	vedrai	tu	vedresti
lui/lei/Lei	vedrà	lui/lei/Lei	vedrebbe
noi	vedremo	noi	vedremmo
voi	vedrete	voi	vedreste
loro	vedranno	loro	vedrebbero

	PRESENT SUBJUNCTIVE		PAST HISTORIC
io	veda	io	vidi
tu	veda	tu	vedesti
lui/lei/Lei	veda	lui/lei/Lei	vide
noi	vediamo	noi	vedemmo
voi	vediate	voi	vedeste
loro	vedano	loro	videro

PAST PARTICIPLE	IMPERATIVE
visto	vedi
	vediamo
	vedete

GERUND	AUXILIARY
vedendo	avere

venire (to come)

	PRESENT		IMPERFECT
io	vengo	io	venivo
tu	vieni	tu	venivi
lui/lei/Lei	viene	lui/lei/Lei	veniva
noi	veniamo	noi	venivamo
voi	venite	voi	venivate
loro	vengono	loro	venivano

	FUTURE		CONDITIONAL
io	verrò	io	verrei
tu	verrai	tu	verresti
lui/lei/Lei	verrà	lui/lei/Lei	verrebbe
noi	verremo	noi	verremmo
voi	verrete	voi	verreste
loro	verranno	loro	verrebbero

	PRESENT SUBJUNCTIVE		PAST HISTORIC
io	venga	io	venni
tu	venga	tu	venisti
lui/lei/Lei	venga	lui/lei/Lei	venne
noi	veniamo	noi	venimmo
voi	veniate	voi	veniste
loro	vengano	loro	vennero

PAST PARTICIPLE	IMPERATIVE
venuto	vieni
	veniamo
	venite

GERUND	AUXILIARY
venendo	essere

vincere (to defeat)

	PRESENT		IMPERFECT
io	vinco	io	vincevo
tu	vinci	tu	vincevi
lui/lei/Lei	vince	lui/lei/Lei	vinceva
noi	vinciamo	noi	vincevamo
voi	vincete	voi	vincevate
loro	vincono	loro	vincevano

	FUTURE		CONDITIONAL
io	vincerò	io	vincerei
tu	vincerai	tu	vinceresti
lui/lei/Lei	vincerà	lui/lei/Lei	vincerebbe
noi	vinceremo	noi	vinceremmo
voi	vincerete	voi	vincereste
loro	vinceranno	loro	vincerebbero

	PRESENT SUBJUNCTIVE		PAST HISTORIC
io	vinca	io	vinsi
tu	vinca	tu	vincesti
lui/lei/Lei	vinca	lui/lei/Lei	vinse
noi	vinciamo	noi	vincemmo
voi	vinciate	voi	vinceste
loro	vincano	loro	vinsero

PAST PARTICIPLE	IMPERATIVE
vinto	vinci
	vinciamo
	vincete

GERUND	AUXILIARY
vincendo	avere

vivere (to live)

	PRESENT		IMPERFECT
io	vivo	io	vivevo
tu	vivi	tu	vivevi
lui/lei/Lei	vive	lui/lei/Lei	viveva
noi	viviamo	noi	vivevamo
voi	vivete	voi	vivevate
loro	vivono	loro	vivevano

	FUTURE		CONDITIONAL
io	vivrò	io	vivrei
tu	vivrai	tu	vivresti
lui/lei/Lei	vivrà	lui/lei/Lei	vivrebbe
noi	vivremo	noi	vivremmo
voi	vivrete	voi	vivreste
loro	vivranno	loro	vivrebbero

	PRESENT SUBJUNCTIVE		PAST HISTORIC
io	viva	io	vissi
tu	viva	tu	vivesti
lui/lei/Lei	viva	lui/lei/Lei	visse
noi	viviamo	noi	vivemmo
voi	viviate	voi	viveste
loro	vivano	loro	vissero

PAST PARTICIPLE	IMPERATIVE
vissuto	vivi
	viviamo
	vivete

GERUND	AUXILIARY
vivendo	avere

volere (to want)

	PRESENT		IMPERFECT
io	voglio	io	volevo
tu	vuoi	tu	volevi
lui/lei/Lei	vuole	lui/lei/Lei	voleva
noi	vogliamo	noi	volevamo
voi	volete	voi	volevate
loro	vogliono	loro	volevano

	FUTURE		CONDITIONAL
io	vorrò	io	vorrei
tu	vorrai	tu	vorresti
lui/lei/Lei	vorrà	lui/lei/Lei	vorrebbe
noi	vorremo	noi	vorremmo
voi	vorrete	voi	vorreste
loro	vorranno	loro	vorrebbero

	PRESENT SUBJUNCTIVE		PAST HISTORIC
io	voglia	io	volli
tu	voglia	tu	volesti
lui/lei/Lei	voglia	lui/lei/Lei	volle
noi	vogliamo	noi	volemmo
voi	vogliate	voi	voleste
loro	vogliano	loro	vollero

PAST PARTICIPLE	IMPERATIVE
voluto	–

GERUND	AUXILIARY
volendo	avere

The Gender of Nouns

In Italian, all nouns are either masculine or feminine, whether they denote people, animals or things.

The gender of a noun is often indicated by its final letter. Here are some guidelines to help you determine what gender a noun is:

Nearly all nouns ending in -o are masculine, e.g.
il treno the train
l'uomo the man
un topo a mouse
un gatto a (tom)cat
un italiano an Italian (man)

EXCEPTIONS:
la mano the hand
una foto a photo
la radio the radio
una moto a motorbike

Very many nouns ending in -a are feminine, e.g.
la casa the house
una donna a woman
una gatta a (she) cat
un'italiana an Italian woman

There are, however, numerous exceptions, e.g.
il dramma the drama
il papa the pope
il problema the problem

A few nouns ending in -a are feminine, but can refer to a man or a woman, e.g.
una guida a guide (male or female)
una persona a person (male or female)
una vittima a victim (male or female)

Nouns ending in -ista denoting people, can be masculine or feminine, e.g.
un giornalista a (male) journalist
una giornalista a (female) journalist

The Gender of Nouns *continued*

un pessimista a (male) pessimist
una pessimista a (female) pessimist

Nearly all words ending in -à, -sione and -zione are feminine, e.g.
una difficoltà a difficulty
un'occasione an opportunity
una conversazione a conversation

Nouns ending in a consonant are nearly always masculine, e.g.
un film a film
un computer a computer
un box a garage

EXCEPTIONS:
una jeep a jeep
una star a star

Nouns ending in -e or -i can be masculine or feminine, e.g.
un mese a month
la mente the mind
un brindisi a toast
una crisi a crisis

The names of languages, and all months, are masculine, whether they
end in -o or -e, e.g.
il tedesco German
il francese French
lo scorso febbraio last February
il prossimo dicembre next December

Suffixes that differentiate between male and female are shown on page 128.

Some words have different meanings depending on their gender, e.g.

il fine the objective	la fine the end
un posto a place	la posta the mail
il manico the handle	la manica the sleeve
un modo a way	la moda the fashion
un mostro a monster	una mostra an exhibition
il capitale capital (money)	una capitale a capital city

The Formation of Feminines

As in English, male and female are sometimes differentiated by the use of quite different words, e.g.

> un fratello a brother
> una sorella a sister
> un toro a bull
> una mucca a cow

More often, however, words in Italian show gender by their ending:

> Many Italian nouns ending in -o can be made feminine by changing the ending to -a → ①
>
> Some nouns ending in -e also change the ending to -a for the feminine → ②
>
> Some nouns ending in -a or -e have no change of ending for the feminine → ③
>
> Nouns ending in -ese that describe nationality are the same for masculine and feminine → ④
>
> Nouns ending in -ante are the same for masculine and feminine → ⑤
>
> Nouns ending in -tore make the the feminine by substituting the ending -trice → ⑥
>
> Some nouns ending in -e have feminine forms ending in -essa → ⑦

① un cuoco — a (*male*) cook
una cuoca — a (*female*) cook
uno zio — an uncle
una zia — an aunt
una ragazzo — a boy
una ragazza — a girl
un italiano — an Italian (man)
un'italiana — an Italian (woman)

② un signore — a gentleman
una signora — a lady
un infermiere — a (*male*) nurse
un'infermiera — a (*female*) nurse
un parrucchiere — a (*male*) hairdresser
una parrucchiera — a (*female*) hairdresser

③ un collega — a (*male*) colleague
una collega — a (*female*) colleague
il mio dentista — my dentist (*male*)
la mia dentista — my dentist (*female*)
un nipote — a grandson
una nipote — a granddaughter

④ un irlandese — an Irishman
un'irlandese — an Irishwoman
uno scozzese — a Scotsman
una scozzese — a Scotswoman

⑤ un cantante — a (*male*) singer
una cantante — a (*female*) singer
un amante — a (*male*) lover
un'amante — a (*female*) lover
un principiante — a (*male*) beginner
una principiante — a (*female*) beginner

⑥ un attore — an actor
un'attrice — a (*female*) actor
un pittore — a (*male*) painter
una pittrice — a (*female*) painter

⑦ il professore — the (*male*) teacher
la professoressa — the (*female*) teacher
uno studente — a (*male*) student
una studentessa — a (*female*) student

129

The Formation of Plurals

Masculine nouns, whether they end in -o, -a or -e, nearly always take the ending -i in the plural → ❶

Feminine nouns ending in -a take the ending -e in the plural → ❷

Feminine nouns ending in -e take the ending -i in the plural → ❸

Nouns that have no change of ending in the plural

Nouns ending in an accented vowel do not change the ending in the plural → ❹

Nouns ending in -i and -ie do not change in the plural → ❺

Words ending with a consonant remain unchanged in the plural → ❻

Other common words that do not change in the plural are:

il cinema	cinema	i cinema
la radio	radio	le radio
la moto	motorbike	le moto
l'auto	car	le auto
la foto	photo	le foto

❶

un anno	one year
due anni	two years
un ragazzo	a boy
i ragazzi	the boys
un ciclista	a (*male*) cyclist
due ciclisti	two cyclists
un problema	a problem
molti problemi	lots of problems
un mese	one month
due mesi	two months
un francese	a Frenchman
due francesi	two Frenchmen

❷

una settimana	one week
due settimane	two weeks
una ragazza	one girl
due ragazze	two girls

❸

un'inglese	an Englishwoman
due inglesi	two Englishwomen
la vite	the vine
le viti	the vines

❹

la città	the city
le città	the cities
la loro università	their university
le loro università	their universities
un caffè	a coffee
due caffè	two coffees
una virtù	a virtue
le sue virtù	her virtues

❺

un'analisi	an analysis
delle analisi	analyses
una serie	a series
due serie	two series
una specie	a sort
varie specie	various sorts

❻

il film	the film
i film	the films
il manager	the manager
i manager	the managers
il computer	the computer
i computer	the computers
la jeep	the jeep
le jeep	the jeeps

Irregular Plural Forms

Some masculine nouns become feminine in the plural, and take the ending -a → ❶

The plural of uomo man is uomini. The plural of la mano hand is le mani.

Nouns ending in -ca and -ga add an h before the plural ending, to keep the sound of the c and g hard → ❷

Some nouns ending in -co and -go also add an h before the plural ending, to keep the sound of the c and g hard → ❸

There are numerous exceptions. You can check the plural of such nouns in the dictionary.

> EXCEPTIONS:
> amico friend (*plural* amici)
> nemico enemy (*plural* nemici)
> psicologo psychologist (*plural* psicologi)
> geologo geologist (*plural* geologi)

The plurals of compound nouns such as pescespada (*swordfish*), capolavoro (*masterpiece*), or apriscatole (*tin opener*) do not always follow the usual rules. You can find them in the dictionary.

1 il dito — the finger
le dita — the fingers
un uovo — an egg
le uova — the eggs
il lenzuolo — the sheet
le lenzuola — the sheets

2 amica — (*female*) friend
amiche — (*female*) friends
buca — hole
buche — holes
riga — line
righe — lines
casalinga — housewife
casalinghe — housewives

3 gioco — game
giochi — games
fuoco — fire
fuochi — fires
luogo — place
luoghi — places
borgo — district
borghi — districts

The Definite Article

il (l')/lo, la(l'), i/gli;le

	MASCULINE	FEMININE
SING.	il	la
	lo	
	l'	l'
PLUR.	i	le
	gli	

The form of the Italian article depends on the gender and number of the noun it accompanies. It also depends on the letter the noun starts with.

il is used with masculine nouns starting with most consonants, except for z, gn, pn, ps, x, y and impure s*; lo is used with these. l' is used before vowels → **1**

i is used with masculine plural nouns starting with most consonants; gli is used before vowels and z, gn, pn, ps, x, y and impure s*. → **2**

la is used before feminine singular nouns beginning with a consonant, and l' is used before a vowel → **3**

le is used with all feminine plural nouns → **4**

If the article is separated from the noun by an adjective, the first letter of the adjective determines the choice of article → **5**

For uses of the definite article see page 138.

*Impure s means s + another consonant.

1

il ragazzo	the boy
il cellulare	the mobile phone
lo zio	the uncle
lo studente	the student
lo pneumatico	the tyre
lo psichiatra	the psychiatrist
lo yogurt	the yoghurt
l'ospedale	the hospital
l'albergo	the hotel

2

i fratelli	the brothers
i cellulari	the mobile phones
gli studenti	the students
gli zii	the uncles
gli gnocchi	the gnocchi
gli pneumatici	the tyres
gli yogurt	the yoghurts
gli amici	the friends
gli orari	the timetables

3

la ragazza	the girl
la macchina	the car
l'amica	the (girl) friend
l'arancia	the orange

4

le ragazze	the girls
le amiche	the (girl) friends

5

l'amico **the friend**	il migliore amico **the best friend**
lo studente **the student**	il migliore studente **the best student**
gli studenti **the students**	i migliori studenti **the best students**

The Definite Article *continued*

The prepositions a, da, di, in and su combine with the article to form one word.

a + article → ❶

SING.
a + il = ai   a + la = alla
a + l' = all'   a + l' = all'
a + lo = allo

PLUR.
a + i = ai   a + le = alle
a + gli = agli

da + article → ❷

SING.
da + il = dal   da + la = dalla
da + l' = dall'   da + l' = dall'
da + lo = dallo

PLUR.
da + i = dai   da + le = dalle
da + gli = dagli

di + article → ❸

SING.
di + il = del   di + la = della
di + l' = dell'   di + l' = dell'
di + lo = dello

PLUR.
di + i = dei   di + le = delle
di + gli = degli

in + article → ❹

SING.
in + il = nel   in + la = nella
in + l' = nell'   in + l' = nell'
in + lo = nello

PLUR.
in + i = nei   in + le = nelle
in + gli = negli

su + article → ❺

SING.
su + il = sul   su + la = sulla
su + l' = sull'   su + l' = sull'
su + lo = sullo

PLUR.
su + i = sui   su + le = sulle
su + gli = sugli

Examples

1 al cinema — to the cinema
allo stadio — at *or* to the stadium
ai concerti — at *or* to the concerts
alle partite — at *or* to the matches

2 dall'albergo — from the hotel
dalla stazione — from the station
dagli aeroporti — from the airports
della squadra — of the team
degli studenti — of the students

3 nel giardino — in the garden
nell'appartamento — in the flat

4 nei dintorni — in the surroundings

5 sullo scoglio — on the rock
sulla spiaggia — on the beach

The Definite Article *continued*

Uses of the Definite Article

The definite article is used much more in Italian than it is in English. It generally translates the English definite article, but is also used in many contexts where English has no article:

> with possessive pronouns → ①

> with plurals and uncountable* nouns → ②

> in generalizations → ③

> with the names of regions and countries → ④
> EXCEPTIONS: no article with countries following the Italian preposition in *in/to* → ⑤

> with parts of the body, replacing the English possessive adjective → ⑥

> 'Ownership' of parts of the body, and of clothes, is often indicated by an indirect object pronoun or a reflexive pronoun → ⑦

> with the time, dates and years → ⑧

> in expressions of quantity/rate/price → ⑨

> with titles, ranks, professions followed by a proper name, and colloquially, with female names → ⑩

---

* An uncountable noun is one which cannot be used in the plural or with an indefinite article, e.g. *milk*.

1 la mia casa — my house
le sue figlie — her daughters
i vostri amici — your friends

2 I bambini soffrono — Children are suffering
Mi piacciono gli animali — I like animals
Le cose vanno meglio — Things are going better
Il nuoto è il mio sport preferito — Swimming is my favourite sport
Non mi piace il riso — I don't like rice

3 Lo zucchero non fa bene — Sugar isn't good for you
La povertà è un grande problema — Poverty is a big problem

4 L'Australia è molto grande — Australia is very big
La Calabria è bella — Calabria is beautiful

5 Vado in Francia a giugno — I'm going to France in June
Lavorano in Germania — They work in Germany

6 Dammi la mano — Give me your hand
Attento alla testa! — Mind your head!

7 Mi fa male il piede — My foot is hurting
Soffiati il naso! — Blow your nose!
Si è tolto il cappotto — He took off his coat
Mettiti le scarpe — Put your shoes on

8 all'una — at one o'clock
alle due — at two o'clock
Era l'una — It was one o'clock
Sono le due — It's two o'clock
Sono nata il primo maggio 1990 — I was born on May 1, 1990
Verranno nel 2015 — They're coming in 2015

9 Costano 3 euro al chilo — They cost 3 euro a kilo
70 km all'ora — 70 km an hour
50.000 dollari al mese — 50,000 dollars per month
due volte alla settimana — twice a week

10 La signora Rossi è qui — Mrs. Rossi is here
Il dottor Gentile — Doctor Gentile
la regina Elisabetta — Queen Elizabeth
Ecco la Silvia! — Here's Silvia!

The Partitive Article

The partitive article has the sense of 'some' or 'any', although the Italian is not always translated in English.

Forms of the partitive

	WITH MASC. NOUN	WITH FEM. NOUN
SING.	del	della
	dell'	dell'
	dello	
PLUR.	dei	delle
	degli	

del burro	some butter
dell'olio	some oil
della carta	some paper
dei fiammiferi	some matches
delle uova	some eggs
Hanno rotto dei bicchieri	They broke some glasses
Mi ha fatto vedere delle foto	He showed me some photos
Ci vuole del sale	It needs (some) salt
Aggiungi della farina	Add (some) flour

The Indefinite Article

MASCULINE	FEMININE
un	una
uno	un'

The form of the indefinite article depends on the gender of the noun it accompanies. It also depends on the letter the noun starts with.

un is used with masculine nouns starting with vowels and most consonants, except for z, gn, pn, ps, x, y and impure s* → ❶

uno is used with these → ❷

una is used before feminine nouns beginning with a consonant, and un' is used before a vowel → ❸

If the article is separated from the noun by an adjective, the first letter of the adjective determines the choice of article → ❹

The indefinite article is used in Italian largely as it is in English except: → ❺

- with the words cento and mille
- when translating *a few* or *a lot*
- in exclamations with che

The indefinite article is not used when speaking of someone's profession – either the verb essere is used, with no article, or fare is used with the definite article → ❻

* impure s means s + another consonant.

① un cellulare   a mobile phone
   un uomo   a man

② uno studente   a student
   uno zio   an uncle
   uno psichiatra   a psychiatrist

③ una ragazza   a girl
   una mela   an apple
   un'ora   an hour
   un'amica   a (girl) friend
   un albergo   a hotel

④ uno splendido albergo   a magnificent hotel
   uno scultore   a sculptor
   un bravo scultore   a good sculptor

⑤ cento volte   a hundred times
   mille sterline   a thousand pounds
   qualche parola   a few words
   molti soldi   a lot of money
   Che sorpresa!   What a surprise!
   Che peccato!   What a pity!

⑥ È medico   He's a doctor
   Sono professori   They're teachers
   Faccio l'ingegnere   I'm an engineer
   Fa l'avvocato   She's a lawyer

The formation of feminines and plurals

Most adjectives agree in number and gender with the noun or pronoun.

The formation of feminines

If the masculine singular form of the adjective ends in -o, the feminine ends in -a → **1**

If the adjective ends in -e, the ending does not change for the feminine → **2**

The formation of plurals

If the masculine singular of the adjective ends in -o, the ending changes to -i for the masculine plural, and to -e for the feminine plural → **3**

If the adjective ends in -e, the ending changes to -i for both masculine and feminine plural → **4**

Invariable adjectives

Some adjectives have no change of ending either for the feminine or the plural → **5**

❶ un ragazzo alto — a tall boy
una ragazza alta — a tall girl
un film italiano — an Italian film
una squadra italiana — an Italian team

❷ un libro inglese — an English book
una famiglia inglese — an English family
un treno veloce — a fast train
una macchina veloce — a fast car

❸ un fiore rosso — a red flower
dei fiori rossi — red flowers
un computer nuovo — a new computer
dei computer nuovi — new computers
una strada pericolosa — a dangerous road
delle strade pericolose — dangerous roads
una moto nera — a black motorbike
delle moto nere — black motorbikes

❹ un esercizio difficile — a difficult exercise
degli esercizi difficili — difficult exercises
un sito web interessante — an interesting website
dei siti web interessanti — interesting websites
una storia triste — a sad story
delle storie tristi — sad stories
una valigia pesante — a heavy case
delle valigie pesanti — heavy cases

❺ un calzino rosa — a pink sock
una maglietta rosa — a pink T-shirt
un paio di guanti rosa — a pair of pink gloves

un tappeto blu — a blue rug
una macchina blu — a blue car
delle tende blu — blue curtains

un gruppo pop — a pop group
la musica pop — pop music
dei gruppi pop — pop groups

Irregular Adjectives

When **bello** *beautiful* is used in front of a masculine noun it has different forms depending on which letter follows it.

MASC. SING.	MASC. PLUR.	EXAMPLES
bel	bei	before most consonants → ❶
bell'	begli	before vowels → ❷
bello	begli	before z, gn, pn, ps, x and impure s* → ❸

When used after a verb, **bello** has the same endings as any other adjective ending in -o → ❹

buono *good* is becomes **buon** when used before a masculine singular noun, unless the noun starts with z, gn, pn, ps, x or impure s* → ❺

grande *big, great* is often shortened to **gran** when it comes before a singular noun starting with a consonant → ❻

*Impure s means s + another consonant.

1. bel tempo   beautiful weather
   bei nomi   beautiful names

2. un bell'*a*lbero   a beautiful tree
   dei begli *a*lberi   beautiful trees

3. un bello strumento   a beautiful instrument
   dei begli strumenti   beautiful instruments

4. Il tempo era bello   The weather was beautiful
   I fiori sono belli   The flowers are beautiful

5. Buon vi*a*ggio!   Have a good journey!
   un buon uomo   a good man
   un buono studente   a good student

6. la Gran Bretagna   Great Britain
   un gran n*u*mero di m*a*cchine a large number of cars

Comparatives and Superlatives

Comparatives are formed using the following constructions:

> più ... (di) more ... (than) → ❶
> meno ... (di) less ... (than) → ❷
> (così) .... come as ... as → ❸
> (tanto) .... quanto as ... as → ❹

Superlatives are formed using the following constructions:

> il/la/i/le più ... (che) the most ... (that) → ❺
> il/la/i/le meno ... (che) the least ... (that) → ❻

After a superlative the preposition di is often translated as 'in' → ❼

If a clause follows a superlative the verb is in the subjunctive → ❽

Adjectives with irregular comparatives/superlatives

ADJECTIVE	COMPARATIVE	SUPERLATIVE
buono	migliore	il migliore
good	better	the best
cattivo	peggiore	il peggiore
bad	worse	worst
grande	maggiore	il maggiore
big	bigger/older	the biggest/oldest
piccolo	minore	il minore
small	smaller/younger	the smallest/youngest
alto	superiore	il superiore
high	higher	the highest
basso	inferiore	l'inferiore
low	lower	the lowest

The above words also have regular comparatives/superlatives → ❾

Emphatic adjectives

For added emphasis, the final vowel of an adjective can be replaced with the ending -issimo, or -issima → ❿

Examples

1 una macchina più grande — a bigger car
Sono più alto di te — I'm taller than you

2 un computer meno caro — a less expensive computer
i suoi film meno interessanti — his less interesting films
Quello verde è meno caro del nero — The green one is less expensive than the black one

3 È alta come sua sorella — She's as tall as her sister
La mia borsa non è pesante come la tua — My bag's not as heavy as yours
Non è così lontano come credi — It's not as far as you think

4 Sono stanca quanto te — I'm just as tired as you are
Ha tanto lavoro quanto ne hai tu — He's got as much work as you have
Non ho tanti soldi quanti ne hai tu — I haven't got as much money as you

5 il più alto — the tallest
Queste sono le scarpe più comode — These shoes are the most comfortable

6 il meno interessante — the least interesting
Gianni è il meno ambizioso — Gianni is the least ambitious

7 lo stadio più grande d'Italia — the biggest stadium in Italy
il ristorante più caro della città — the most expensive restaurant in the town

8 la persona più pigra che conosca — the laziest person I know
È una delle cose più belle che ci siano — It's one of the nicest things there is

9 Il libro è migliore del film — The book is better than the film
Questo è più buono — This one's better
la loro sorella minore — their younger sister
il loro fratello più piccolo — their younger brother

10 Il tempo era bellissimo — The weather was really beautiful
Anna è sempre elegantissima — Anna is always terribly smart
Sono educatissimi — They're extremely polite

Demonstrative Adjectives

questo/questa/questi/queste → ①

	MASCULINE	FEMININE	
SING.	questo	questa	this
PLUR.	questi	queste	these

quello has different forms, depending on the gender of the following noun, and the letter it starts with.

	MASCULINE	FEMININE	
SING.	quel	quella	that
	quello		
	quell'	quell'	
PLUR.	quei	quelle	those
	quegli		

quel is used before most consonants, except for z, gn, pn, ps, x and impure s. quello is used before these letters. quell' is used before vowels. quei is used before most consonants; quegli is used before vowels and z, gn, pn, ps, x and impure s*.

quella is used before feminine singular nouns beginning with a consonant, with quell' used before a vowel → ②

*Impure s means s + another consonant.

❶ Questa gonna è troppo stretta   This skirt is too tight
Questi pantaloni mi piacciono   I like these trousers
Queste scarpe sono comode   These shoes are comfortable

❷ quel ragazzo   that boy
quello zaino   that rucksack
quello studente   that student
quell'albero   that tree
quei cani   those dogs
quegli uomini   those men
quegli studenti   those students
quella ragazza   that girl
quell'amica   that friend
quelle macchine   those cars

Interrogative Adjectives

che? what?

che is invariable → ❶

quale/quali? → ❷

	MASCULINE/FEMININE	
SING.	quale	what?; which?
PLUR.	quali	what?; which?

quanto/quanta/quanti/quante? → ❸

	MASCULINE	FEMININE	
SING.	quanto	quanta	how much?
PLUR.	quanti	quante	how many?

Interrogative adjectives are often preceded by prepositions → ❹

Exclamatory Adjectives

che and quanto are used with nouns in exclamations → ❺

che is also used with other adjectives → ❻

1 Che giorno è oggi? — What day is it today?
Che ore sono? — What time is it?
Che gusto preferisci? — Which flavour do you like best?
Che film hai visto? — Which film did you see?
Che programmi hai? — What plans have you got?

2 Quale tipo vuoi? — What kind do you want?

3 Quanto pane hai comprato? — How much bread did you buy?
Quanta minestra vuoi? — How much soup do you want?
Quanti bicchieri ci sono? — How many glasses are there?
Quante uova vuoi? — How many eggs do you want?

4 A che ora ti alzi? — What time do you get up?
Di che colore è? — What colour is it?
Per quale squadra tifi? — Which team do you support?

5 Che peccato! — What a pity!
Che disordine! — What a mess!
Che bella giornata! — What a lovely day!
Che brutto tempo! — What awful weather!
Quanto tempo sprecato! — What a waste of time!
Quanta gente! — What a lot of people!
Quanti soldi! — What a lot of money!
Quante storie! — What a fuss!

6 Che carino! — Isn't he sweet!
Che brutti! — They're horrible!

Possessive Adjectives

WITH SING. NOUN		WITH PLUR. NOUN		
MASC.	FEM.	MASC.	FEM.	
il mio	la mia	i miei	le mie	my
il tuo	la tua	i tuoi	le tue	your
il suo	la sua	i suoi	le sue	his; her; its; your
il nostro	la nostra	i nostri	le nostre	our
il vostro	la vostra	i vostri	le vostre	your
il loro	la loro	i loro	le loro	their

Possessive adjectives are generally preceded by the article → ➊

Possessive adjectives agree in number and gender with the noun they describe (i.e. the thing which is owned), not with the owner → ➋

il suo/la sua/i suoi/le sue can mean either 'his' or 'her'. To make clear which is meant, di lui can be used for 'his', and di lei for 'her' → ➌

The article is not used with any possessive adjective except loro when referring to singular family members → ➍

EXCEPTIONS: mamma, babbo and papà

Examples

1 Dove sono le mie chiavi? — Where are my keys?
Luca ha perso il suo portafoglio — Luca has lost his wallet
Ecco i nostri passaporti — Here are our passports
Qual è la vostra camera? — Which is your room?
Il tuo amico ti aspetta — Your friend is waiting for you

2 Anna ha perso il suo cellulare — Anna has lost her mobile phone
Le ragazze hanno i loro biglietti — The girls have got their tickets

3 Le scarpe di lui sono eleganti — His shoes are smart
Le scarpe di lei non mi piacciono — I don't like her shoes

4 con mia madre — with my mother
Dov'è tuo padre? — Where's your father?
lei e suo marito — she and her husband
È sua moglie — She's his wife
mia sorella ed io — my sister and I
Non è il loro padre — He's not their father
Maria e il suo papà — Maria and her dad

Position of Adjectives

Italian adjectives usually follow the noun → ❶

Adjectives of colour or nationality *always* follow the noun → ❷

As in English, demonstrative, possessive, numerical and interrogative adjectives precede the noun → ❸

The adjectives ogni, qualche and nessuno always precede the noun → ❹

The following common adjectives can precede the noun:

ottimo very good	pessimo very bad
bello beautiful	brutto bad, ugly
bravo good	buono good
prossimo next	ultimo last
povero poor	grande big, great
nuovo new	vecchio old
breve short	piccolo small

The meaning of the following adjectives can be affected by their position:

	AFTER NOUN	BEFORE NOUN
grande	big	great → ❺
povero	poor	unfortunate → ❻
vecchio	old	long-standing → ❼

Adjectives following the noun are linked by e → ❽

1. un gesto spont*a*neo   a spontaneous gesture
   una partita importante   an important match

2. capelli biondi   blonde hair
   pantaloni neri   black trousers
   una parola italiana   an Italian word

3. questo cellulare   this mobile phone
   la mia mamma   my mum
   il primo piano   the first floor
   Quale gusto?   What flavour?

4. ogni giorno   every day
   qualche volta   some times
   Non c'è nessun bisogno di andarci   There's no need to go

5. un uomo grande   a big man
   una grande sorpresa   a great surprise

6. gente povera   poor people
   Povera Anna!   Poor Anna!

7. una casa vecchia   an old house
   un mio vecchio amico   an old friend of mine

8. un libro lungo e noioso   a long, boring book
   ragazze antipatiche e maleducate   nasty rude girls

Personal Pronouns

	SUBJECT PRONOUNS	
	SINGULAR	PLURAL
1st person	io I	noi we
2nd person	tu you	voi you
3rd person (*masc.*)	lui he	loro they
(*fem.*)	lei she	
(*used as polite 'you'*)	lei/Lei you	

Italian verbs are frequently used without subject pronouns → ❶

tu/lei
Lei, as well as being the 3rd person singular feminine, is used when addressing someone politely. As a general rule, use tu only when addressing a friend, a child, a fellow student, someone you know very well, or when invited to do so. In other cases use lei, which is occasionally spelled with a capital when used to mean *you* ❷

loro
Loro is used only to refer to people, not to things → ❸

Loro is occasionally used as a very formal alternative to voi → ❹

1 Conosci Paolo?
Parlo italiano
Costa troppo

Do you know Paul?
I speak Italian
It costs too much

2 Tu cara, cosa prendi?

Lei, signora, cosa prende?

What are you going to have,
dear?
What are you going to have,
madam?

3 Loro chi sono?
Cosa sono? — Sono noci.

Who are they?
What are they? — They're
walnuts.

4 Loro cosa prendono?

What will you have, ladies and
gentlemen?

Personal Pronouns *continued*

3rd Person Pronouns

lui, lei and **loro** are the subject pronouns normally used in spoken Italian. In older written Italian you may find **egli** (masc. sing.), **ella** (fem. sing.), **essi** (masc. plur.) and **esse** (fem. plur.).

esso and **essa** are subject pronouns meaning *it*, but they are very rarely used. In Italian there is normally no pronoun corresponding to *it* at the start of a sentence → ❶

Subject pronouns often follow the verb → ❷

Subject pronouns are used:
- to add emphasis, for clarity, or to attract someone's attention → ❸
- after **anche** *too*, **neanche** *neither* and **pure** *as well* → ❹
- when the verb in Italian is understood → ❺

	UNSTRESSED DIRECT OBJECT PRONOUNS	
	SINGULAR	PLURAL
1ˢᵗ person	mi me	ci us
2ⁿᵈ person	ti you	vi you
3ʳᵈ person (*masc.*)	lo (l') him; it	li them
(*fem.*)	la (l') her; it	le them
(*used as polite 'you'*)	la/La (l') you	le you

mi, ti, ci and **vi** can (but do not have to) become **m', t', c'** and **v'** before a vowel or mute h → ❻

lo and **la** change to **l'** before a vowel or mute h → ❼

For information on past participle agreement see page 56.

lo/la /li/le
lo means *him*, or *it*, when the object referred to is masculine → ❽

la means *her*, or *it*, when the object referred to is feminine → ❾

li refers to people, or objects that are masculine → ❿

le refers to females, or objects that are feminine → ⓫

1 Fa caldo | It's hot
Sono le tre | It's three o'clock
È tardi | It's late

2 Pago io | I'll pay
Ci pensiamo noi | We'll see to it

3 Tu cosa dici? | What do <u>you</u> think?
No, l'ha fatto lui | No, <u>he</u> did it
Lei, signore, cosa prende? | And you sir, what will you have?

4 Prendi un gelato anche tu? | Are you going to have an ice cream too?

Non so perché. — Neanch'io | I don't know why. — Neither do I
È venuto pure lui | He came as well

5 Chi è il più bravo? — Lui. | Who's the best? — He is.
Viene lui, ma lei no | He's coming, but she isn't

6 Non c'hanno visto *or* | They didn't see us
Non ci hanno visto

7 Non l'ho visto più | I didn't see him again
L'ho incontrata ieri | I met her yesterday

8 Gianni? Non lo vedo mai | Gianni? I never see him
Dov'è il mio cellulare? Non lo vedo | Where's my mobile phone? I can't see it

9 Chiara? Non la vedo mai | Chiara? I never see her
La birra? Non la bevo mai. | Beer? I never drink it.

10 Marco e Sara — li conosci? | Marco and Sara — do you know them?

Hai i biglietti? Sì, li ho nel portafoglio | Have you got the tickets? Yes, I've got them in my wallet

11 Le sue sorelle? Non le conosco | His sisters? I don't know them
Hai le chiavi? Sì, le ho in tasca | Have you got the keys? Yes, I've got them in my pocket

Personal Pronouns *continued*

Position of unstressed direct object pronouns

The pronoun generally comes before the verb → ❶

Unstressed direct pronouns come after the verb

- in imperatives, with the pronoun joined onto the verb → ❷

ⓘ If the verb consists of a single syllable, the initial consonant of the pronoun is doubled, except in the case of gli → ❸

- in infinitive constructions, when the final -e of the infinitive is dropped, and replaced by the pronoun → ❹

Stressed direct object pronouns

	STRESSED DIRECT OBJECT PRONOUNS	
	SINGULAR	PLURAL
1ˢᵗ person	me	noi
2ⁿᵈ person	te	voi
3ʳᵈ person (*masc.*)	lui	loro
(*fem.*)	lei	loro
(*used as polite 'you'*)	lei/Lei	loro

Stressed direct object pronouns are used:
- for emphasis or contrast → ❺
- after prepositions → ❻
- in comparisons → ❼

For further information, see Order of Object Pronouns, page 166.

Reflexive Pronouns

These are dealt with under reflexive verbs, page 32.

1. Ti amo — I love you
   Lo invito alla festa — I'm inviting him to the party
   Non lo mangio — I'm not going to eat it
   La guardava — He was looking at her
   Vi cercavo — I was looking for you
   Li conosciamo — We know them

2. Aiutami! — Help me!
   Lasciala stare — Leave her alone

3. Fallo subito! — Do it right away!

4. Potresti venire a prendermi? — Could you come and get me?
   Non posso aiutarvi — I can't help you
   Devo proprio farlo? — Do I really have to do it?

5. Amo solo te — I love only you
   Invito lui alla festa, ma lei no — I'm inviting him to the party but not her

   Non guardava me, guardava lei — He wasn't looking at me, he was looking at her

6. Vengo con te — I'll come with you
   Sono arrivati dopo di noi — They arrived after us

7. Sei più alto di me — You're taller than me
   Sono più ricchi di lui — They're richer than him

Personal Pronouns *continued*

	UNSTRESSED INDIRECT OBJECT PRONOUNS	
	SINGULAR	PLURAL
1st person	mi	ci
2nd person	ti	vi
3rd person (*masc.*)	gli	gli *or* loro
(*fem.*)	le	gli *or* loro
(*used as polite 'you'*)	le	loro

The pronouns in the above table replace the preposition a + *noun*, where the noun is a person or an animal → ①

Indirect object pronouns are used with verbs governing a → ②

Unstressed indirect pronouns are also used with impersonal verbs which govern a → ③

Position of unstressed indirect object pronouns

Unstressed indirect pronouns generally come before the verb → ④

Unstressed indirect pronouns come after the verb:
- in imperatives, with the pronoun joined onto the verb → ⑤

ⓘ If the verb consists of a single syllable, the initial consonant of the pronoun is doubled, except in the case of gli → ⑥

- in infinitive constructions. The final -e of the infinitive is dropped, and replaced by the pronoun → ⑦

① Ho detto la verità a Paola — I told Paola the truth
Le ho detto la verità — I told her the truth
Hai dato del latte al gatto? — Have you given the cat some milk?

Gli hai dato del latte? — Have you given him some milk?
Potresti dare qualche consiglio ai signori? — Could you give the lady and gentleman some advice?
Potresti dar loro *or* dargli qualche consiglio? — Could you give them some advice?

② telefonare a qn — to phone sb
Non le ho telefonato — I didn't phone her
promettere qc a qn — to promise sb sth
Mi ha promesso un regalo — He promised me a present
consigliare a qn di fare qc — to advise sb to do sth
Ci ha consigliato di aspettare — He advised us to wait

③ Le piacciono i gatti — She likes cats
Non gli importa il prezzo, sono ricchi — They don't care about the price, they're rich
Se gli interessa può venire con me — If he's interested he can come with me

④ Mi assomiglia? — Does she look like me?
Ti piace? — Do you like it?

⑤ Rispondigli! — Answer him!
Mandami un SMS — Send me a text

⑥ Dimmi dov'è — Tell me where it is
Dacci una mano — Give us a hand

⑦ Dovresti scriverle — You ought to write to her
Luigi? Non voglio parlargli — Luigi? I don't want to talk to him

Personal Pronouns *continued*

Stressed Indirect Pronouns

		STRESSED INDIRECT OBJECT PRONOUNS	
		SINGULAR	PLURAL
1st	person	a me	a noi
2nd	person	a te	a voi
3rd	person (*masc.*)	a lui	a loro
	(*fem.*)	a lei	a loro
	(*used as polite 'you'*)	a lei	a loro

The above forms are used for special emphasis, either before or after the verb → ①

For further information, see Order of Object Pronouns, below.

Reflexive Pronouns

These are dealt with under reflexive verbs, page 32.

Order of Object Pronouns

If direct and indirect unstressed pronouns occur together, the indirect pronoun always comes first.

mi/ti/ci/vi when followed by a direct object pronoun become me, te, ce and ve → ②

gli and le when followed by a direct object pronoun both become glie-, and add the pronoun to make one word: glielo, gliela, glieli or gliele → ③

When an indirect pronoun and a direct pronoun follow an imperative, or an infinitive, they join on to it to make one word → ④

When a stressed indirect object pronoun and an unstressed direct object pronoun occur together the above rules do not apply → ⑤

Examples

1. Ho scritto a lei, a lui no
   A me piace, ma Luca preferisce l'altro

   I wrote to her, but not to him
   I like it, but Luca would rather have the other one

2. Me la dai?
   È mia – non te la do

   Will you give me it?
   It's mine, I'm not going to give it to you

   Ce l'hanno promesso
   Ve lo mando domani

   They promised it to us
   I'll send it to you tomorrow

3. Glieli hai promessi
   Gliel'ha spedite
   Carlo? Glielo dirò domani

   You promised them to her
   He sent them to them
   Carlo? I'll tell him tomorrow

4. Mi piacciono, ma non vuole comprarmeli
   Ecco la lettera di Rita, puoi dargliela?
   Ecco le chiavi. Dagliele

   I like them but she won't buy me them
   Here's Rita's letter, can you give it to her?
   Here are the keys. Give them to her.

   Non abbiamo i biglietti – può mandarceli?

   We haven't got the tickets – can you send us them?

5. Mandale a lui, non a me

   Send them to him, not to me

The pronoun ne

ne replaces the preposition di + *noun* → ❶

There may be no preposition in the English translation of verbal constructions with di/ne → ❷

ne also replaces the partitive article (English = some, any) + *noun* → ❸

When used with amounts or numbers, ne represents the noun → ❹

Position: ne always follows another pronoun and comes before all verbs except imperatives and infinitives → ❺

Pronouns which precede ne change their form:
mi/ti/si/ci/vi before ne become me/te/se/ce/ve → ❻

ne follows the imperative and joins onto to it to make one word → ❼

ne joins onto the infinitive, which drops the final -e → ❽

Pronouns which come between the imperative or infinitive and ne change their form: mi, ti, ci, vi become me, te, ce and ve.
gli and le become glie → ❾

Examples

① Sono conscio del pericolo — I'm aware of the danger
Ne sono conscio — I'm aware of it
Sono sicura del fatto — I'm sure of the fact
Ne sono sicura — I'm sure of it
Ha scritto della guerra sul giornale — She's written about the war in the paper
Ne ha scritto sul giornale — She's written about it in the paper
Parliamo del futuro. — Sì, parliamone. — Let's talk about the future. — Yes, let's talk about it.

② accorgersi di qc — to realize sth
Non se ne accorge — He doesn't realize it
aver bisogno di qc — to need sth
Hai bisogno della chiave? — No, non ne ho più bisogno. — Do you need the key? — No, I don't need it any more.

③ Perché non prendi delle fragole? — Why aren't you having any strawberries?
Perché non ne prendi? — Why aren't you having any?
Vuoi del pane? — Would you like some bread?
Ne vuoi? — Would you like some?

④ Hai due figli? — No, ne ho tre. — Have you got two children? — No, I've got three.
Hai dello zucchero? — Ne ho un poco. — Have you got any sugar? — I've got a bit.

⑤ Ne hai paura? — Are you afraid of it?

⑥ Ti ricordi di quel giorno? — Do you remember that day?
Te ne ricordi? — Do you remember it?
Non si accorge degli errori — He doesn't notice mistakes
Non se ne accorge — He doesn't notice them

⑦ Assaggiane un po' — Try a bit

⑧ Non voglio parlarne — I don't want to talk about it

⑨ Dammene uno per favore — Give me one of them please
Dagliene due rossi — Give him two red ones
Non posso dartene uno — I can't give you one
Non posso dargliene due rossi — I can't give him two red ones

169

The pronoun ci

ci replaces the preposition a + *noun* → ①

There may be no preposition in the English translation of verbal constructions with a/ci → ②

Position: like ne, ci comes before the verb, unless it is an imperative, infinitive, or the gerund → ③

For ci as a personal pronoun see page 164.

Note that ci is also an adverb meaning 'there' → ④

①

Credi ai fantasmi?	Do you believe in ghosts?
Ci credi?	Do you believe in them?
Non pensa al futuro	She doesn't think about the future
Non ci pensa	She doesn't think about it

②

far caso a qc	to notice sth
Non ci ho fatto caso	I didn't notice it
avvicinarsi a qc	to approach sth
Ci si avvicinò	He approached it

③

Ci penso io	I'll see to it
BUT	
Pensaci un po'	Think about it a bit
Non so che farci	I don't know what to do about it
Ripensandoci mi sono pentito	When I thought it over I was sorry

④

Non voglio andarci	I don't want to go there
Ci sono molti turisti	There are a lot of tourists

Indefinite Pronouns

The following are indefinite pronouns:

alcuni(e) some → ①

altro(a, i, e) the other one; another one; other people → ②

chiunque anyone → ③

ciascuno(a) each → ④

molto(a, i, e) a lot, lots → ⑤

nessuno(a) nobody, anybody; none → ⑥

niente nothing → ⑦

nulla nothing → ⑧

ognuno(a) each → ⑨

parecchio, parecchia, parecchi, parecchie quite a lot → ⑩

poco, poca, pochi, poche not much, not many → ⑪

qualcosa something, anything → ⑫

qualcuno(a) somebody; any → ⑬

tanto(a, i, e) lots, so much, so many → ⑭

troppo(a, i, e) too much, too many → ⑮

tutti(e) everybody, all → ⑯

tutto everything, all → ⑰

uno(a) somebody → ⑱

Examples

1. Ci sono posti liberi? — Sì, alcuni.

   Ci sono ancora delle fragole?
      — Sì, alcune.

2. L'altro è meno caro
   Non m'interessa quello che
      dicono gli altri
   Prendine un altro

3. Attacca discorso con chiunque

4. Ne avevamo uno per ciascuno
   Le torte costano due euro ciascuna

5. Ne ha molto
   molti di noi

6. Non è venuto nessuno
   Nessuna delle ragazze è venuta

7. Cosa c'è? — Niente.

8. Che cos'hai comprato? — Nulla.

9. ognuno di voi

10. C'è ancora del pane? — Sì,
       parecchio.
    Avete avuto problemi?
       — Sì, parecchi.

11. C'è pane? — Poco.
    Ci sono turisti? — Pochi.

12. Ho qualcosa da dirti
    Ha bisogno di qualcosa?

13. Ha telefonato qualcuno
    Conosci qualcuna delle ragazze?

14. Hai mangiato? — Sì, tanto!

15. Ci sono errori? — Sì, troppi.

16. Vengono tutti
    Sono arrivate tutte

17. Va tutto bene?
    L'ho finito tutto

18. Ho incontrato uno che ti conosce

Are there any empty seats?
   — Yes, some.

Are there any strawberries left?
   — Yes, some.

The other one is cheaper
I don't care what other people
   say
Take another one

She'll talk to anyone

We had one each
The cakes cost two euros each

He's got lots
a lot of us

Nobody came
None of the girls came

What's wrong? — Nothing.

What did you buy? — Nothing.

each of you

Is there any bread left? — Yes,
   quite a lot.
Did you have problems?
   — Yes, a lot.

Is there any bread? — Not much.
Are there any tourists? —
   Not many.

I've got something to tell you
Do you need anything?

Somebody phoned
Do you know any of the girls?

Have you eaten? — Yes, lots!

Are there any mistakes? — Yes,
   too many.

Everybody is coming
They've all arrived

Is everything okay?
I've finished it all

I met somebody who knows you

Relative Pronouns

che who; whom; which; that
che is an invariable pronoun that can be the subject or object of a relative clause, and can refer to people or things → **①**

The Italian object pronoun cannot be omitted, though it need not be translated in English → **②**

After a preposition use **cui** → **③**

il che which
This is used to refer to a fact or situation that's just been mentioned → **④**

il quale, la quale, i quali, le quali who; whom; which; that
These are more formal relative pronouns, which agree in number and gender with the noun → **⑤**

il quale, la quale, i quali and **le quali** are used most often with prepositions.
The prepositions di, da, a, in and su combine with the articles il, la, i and le → **⑥**

Article + preposition combinations are dealt with on page 136

il cui, la cui, i cui, le cui whose
These agree in number and gender with the thing possessed → **⑦**

Use **cui** instead of **che** with a preposition → **⑧**

quello che, ciò che what, the thing which

These can be used as the subject or object of a relative clause. Literally they mean 'that which' → **⑨**

In combination with **di**, **quello** *or* **ciò che** become **quello di cui** *or* **ciò di cui** → **⑩**

Examples

1. quella signora che ha un piccolo cane nero — that lady who has a little black dog
   una persona che detesto — a person whom I detest
   l'uomo che hanno arrestato — the man that they've arrested
   la squadra che ha vinto — the team which won

2. la persona che ammiro di più — the person (whom) I admire most
   il dolce che hai fatto — the pudding (that) you made

3. la ragazza di cui ti ho parlato — the girl that I told you about
   gli amici con cui andiamo in vacanza — the friends we go on holiday with
   la persona a cui si riferiva — the person he was referring to
   il quartiere in cui abito — the area in which I live

4. Non pagano nulla, il che non mi sembra giusto — They don't pay anything, which doesn't seem fair to me
   Dice che non è colpa sua, il che è vero — She says it's not her fault, which is true

5. suo padre, il quale è avvocato — his father, who is a lawyer
   le sue sorelle, le quali studiano a Roma — his sisters, who study in Rome

6. l'albergo nel quale ci siamo fermati — the hotel that we stayed at
   la borsa di studio sulla quale contava — the grant he was counting on
   gli amici dai quali ho avuto questo regalo — the friends I had this present from
   la medicina della quale ho bisogno — the medicine I need

7. una persona il cui nome mi sfugge — a person whose name escapes me
   la persona i cui bagagli sono qui — the person whose bags are here

8. È quello con cui parlavo — He's the one I was talking to

9. Ho visto quello *or* ciò che c'era sul tavolo — I saw what was on the table
   Quello *or* ciò che mi preoccupa è che... — The thing which worries me is that...
   Quello *or* ciò che dici non ha senso — What you say doesn't make sense
   Ho fatto quello *or* ciò che potevo — I did what I could

10. Non è quello *or* ciò di cui si tratta — That's not what it's about
    Non è quello *or* ciò che mi aspettavo — That's not what I was expecting

Interrogative Pronouns

These pronouns are used in direct questions:
    chi? who? whom?
    che? what?
    cosa? what?
    che cosa? what?

These pronouns are invariable, and can be the subject or object of the verb → ❶

che cos'è/cos'è? what is it?
This is used to ask for something to be explained or identified → ❷

Prepositions come before the interrogative pronoun, and never at the end of the question → ❸

di chi? whose → ❹

quale? which? which one? what?
quale is the singular form (qual before a vowel), and quali the plural → ❺

qual è?/quali sono? what is/what are?
These are used to ask about a particular detail, name, number etc → ❻

quanto(a)? How much? → ❼

quanti(e)? How many? → ❽

All the pronouns used in direct questions can be used in indirect questions → ❾

1 Chi è? — Who is it?
Chi cerca? — Who(m) are you looking for?
Che vuoi? — What do you want?
Cosa vuole? — What does he want?
Che cosa vogliono? — What do they want?

2 Che cos'è? — È un regalo. — What is it? — It's a present.

3 A chi l'hai dato? — Who did you give it to?
Con chi parlavi? — Who were you talking to?
Di che cosa hai bisogno? — What do you need?
Cosa ti aspettavi? — What were you expecting?

4 Di chi è questa borsa? — Whose is this bag?
Di chi sono queste chiavi? — Whose are these keys?

5 Conosco sua sorella. — Quale? — I know his sister. — Which one?
Ho rotto dei bicchieri. — Quali? — I broke some glasses. — Which ones?

6 Qual è il suo indirizzo? — What's her address?
Qual è la capitale della Finlandia? — What's the capital of Finland?
Quali sono i loro nomi? — What are their names?

7 Farina? Quanta ce ne vuole? — Flour? How much is needed?

8 Quante di loro passano la sera a leggere? — How many of them spend the evening reading?

9 Dimmi chi è — Tell me who it is
Non so cosa vuol dire — I don't know what it means
Ho chiesto di chi era — I asked whose it was
Può dirmi di che cosa si tratta? — Can you tell me what it's about?

Possessive Pronouns

Singular:

MASCULINE	FEMININE	
il mio	la mia	mine
il tuo	la tua	yours
il suo	la sua	his; hers; its; yours
il nostro	la nostra	ours
il vostro	la vostra	yours
il loro	la loro	theirs

Plural:

MASCULINE	FEMININE	
i miei	le mie	mine
i tuoi	le tue	yours
i suoi	le sue	his; hers; its; yours
i nostri	le nostre	ours
i vostri	le vostre	yours
i loro	le loro	theirs

The pronoun agrees in number and gender with the noun it replaces, not with the owner → ❶

di/da/a/su/in + *possessive pronoun*
These prepositions combine with the article → ❷

1 Paolo, questa borsa non è la mia, è la tua

Paolo, this bag's not mine, it's yours

La nostra casa è piccola, la vostra è grande

Our house is small, yours is big

I miei genitori e i suoi si conoscono

My parents and hers know each other

2 La mia macchina è più vecchia della sua

My car is older than his

Preferisco il nostro giardino al loro

I prefer our garden to theirs

Demonstrative Pronouns

questo/questa/questi/queste
quello/quella/quelli/quelle

	MASCULINE	FEMININE	
SING.	questo	questa	this, this one
	quello	quella	that, that one, that man/that woman
PLUR.	questi	queste	these, these ones
	quelli	quelle	those, those ones, those people

The pronoun agrees in number and gender with the noun it replaces → ❶

quello/a used to mean that man/woman is pejorative → ❷

quello(a, i, e) che the one(s) who/which → ❸

quello(a, i, e) di the one(s) belonging to/the one(s) of
This use is often translated by apostrophe s ('s), or s apostrophe (s') → ❹

questo(a, i, e) qui/qua
qui or qua can be used with questo for emphasis or to distinguish
between two things → ❺

quello(a, i, e) lì/là
lì or là can be used with quello for emphasis or to distinguish between
two things → ❻

① Questo è mio marito
This is my husband

Questa è camera mia
This is my bedroom

Questi sono i miei fratelli
These are my brothers

Quali scarpe ti metti? — Queste
Which shoes are you going to wear? — These ones

Qual è la sua borsa? — Quella
Which bag is yours? — That one

Quelli quanto costano?
How much do those cost?

② Dice sempre bugie quello
That man is always telling lies

Quelle non sono mai contente
Those women are never happy

③ È quello che preferisco
That's the one (that) I prefer

È quella che parla di più
She's the one who talks most

Sono quelli che sono partiti senza pagare
They're the ones who left without paying

Queste scarpe sono quelle che ha ordinato
These shoes are the ones (that) you ordered

④ Questo giardino è più grande di quello di Giulia
This garden is bigger than Giulia's

Preferisco la mia macchina a quella di mio marito
I prefer my car to my husband's

Le mie scarpe sono più belle di quelle di Lucia
My shoes are nicer than Lucia's

i miei genitori e quelli delle mie amiche
my parents and those of my friends

le montagne della Svizzera e quelle della Scozia
the mountains of Switzerland and those of Scotland

⑤ Non quello, questo qui
Not that one, this one here

Voglio queste qua
I want these ones here

⑥ Questa gonna non ti sta bene, prova quella là
This skirt doesn't look good on you, try that one

Quali prendi? — Quelli lì
Which ones are you going to have? — Those over there

Formation

Some adverbs are formed by adding -mente to an adjective.

-mente is added to the feminine form, (which ends in -a) of an adjective ending in -o → ❶

-mente is added to the basic form when an adjective ends in -e for both masculine and feminine → ❷

Adjectives ending in -le and -re drop the final e → ❸

Irregular Adverbs

ADJECTIVE	ADVERB
buono good	bene well → ❹
cattivo bad	male badly → ❺
migliore better	meglio better → ❻
peggiore worse	peggio worse → ❼

Adjectives used as adverbs

Certain adjectives are used adverbially. These include: giusto, vicino, diritto, certo, solo, forte, molto, poco → ❽

1   MASC./FEM. ADJECTIVE   ADVERB
lento/lenta slow   lentamente slowly
fortunato/fortunata lucky   fortunatamente luckily

2   MASC./FEM. ADJECTIVE   ADVERB
veloce quick, fast   velocemente quickly, fast
corrente fluent   correntemente fluently

3   -le/-re ADJECTIVE   ADVERB
facile easy   facilmente easily
particolare particular   particolarmente particularly

4   Parlano bene l'italiano   They speak Italian well

5   Ho giocato male   I played badly

6   Sto meglio   I'm better

7   Mi sento peggio   I'm feeling worse

8   Ha risposto giusto   She answered correctly
Abitano vicino   They live nearby
Siamo andati sempre diritto   We kept straight on
Vieni stasera? — Certo!   Are you coming tonight?
    — Of course!

L'ho incontrata solo due volte   I've only met her twice
Correva forte   He was running fast
Quel quadro mi piace molto   I like that picture a lot
Vengo in ufficio poco spesso   I don't come into the office very often

Position of Adverbs

When the adverb accompanies a verb in a simple tense, it generally follows the verb → ❶

For emphasis the adverb can come at the beginning of the sentence → ❷

When adverbs such as mai, sempre, già and appena accompany a verb in a compound tense, they come between the auxilary verb and the past participle → ❸

When the adverb accompanies an adjective or another adverb it generally precedes the adjective/adverb → ❹

Comparatives of Adverbs

These are formed as follows:
> più ... (di) more ... (than) → ❺
> meno ... (di) less ... (than) → ❻

sempre più is used with the adjective to mean *more and more* → ❼

Superlatives of Adverbs

più ... and meno ... are also used to express the superlative → ❽
più ... di tutti/meno di tutti can be used to emphasize the superlative → ❾

Examples

1 Viene sempre — He always comes
Parli bene l'italiano — You speak Italian well

2 Ora non posso — I can't do it just now
Prima non lo sapevo — I didn't know that before

3 Non sono mai stata a Milano — I've never been to Milan
È sempre venuto con me — He always came with me
L'ho già letto — I've already read it
Se n'è appena andato — He's just left

4 Fa troppo freddo — It's too cold
Vai più piano — Go more slowly

5 più spesso — more often
più lentamente — more slowly
Correva più forte di me — He was running faster than me

6 meno velocemente — less quickly
Costa meno — It costs less
Vengo meno spesso di lui — I come less often than he does

7 Le cose vanno sempre meglio — Things are going better and better
Mio nonno sta sempre peggio — My grandfather's getting worse and worse
Cammina sempre più lento — He's walking slower and slower

8 È Carlo che viene più spesso — It's Carlo who comes most often
Sono loro che lavorano meno volontieri — They're the ones who work least willingly

9 Cammina più piano di tutti — She walks the slowest (of all)
L'ha fatto meno volentieri di tutti — He did it the least willingly

Adverbs with irregular comparatives/superlatives

ADVERB	COMPARATIVE/SUPERLATIVE
bene well	meglio better/best
male badly	peggio worse/worst
molto a lot	più more/most
poco not much	meno less/least

Emphatic Adverbs

For added emphasis the ending -issimamente can be used. It replaces the endings -amente, -emente or -mente → ❶

bene and male have irregular emphatic forms: benissimo and malissimo → ❷

Adverbial phrases

di più and di meno are used to say what you do most/least → ❸

❶ lentamente — slowly
lentissimamente — very slowly
velocemente — quickly
velocissimamente — very quickly

❷ Hai fatto benissimo — You did very well

❸ la cosa che temeva di più — the thing she feared most
quello che mi piace di meno — the one I like least
Sono quelli che guadagnano di meno — They're the ones who earn least

Some common adverbs and their usage

Some common adverbs:

> abbastanza quite; enough → ❶
>
> anche too → ❷
>
> ancora still; yet → ❸
>
> appena just; only just → ❹
>
> certo certainly; of course → ❺
>
> così so; like this; like that → ❻
>
> ecco here → ❼
>
> forse perhaps, maybe → ❽
>
> già already → ❾
>
> mai never; ever → ❿
>
> molto very; very much; much → ⓫
>
> piuttosto quite; rather → ⓬
>
> poco not very; not at all → ⓭
>
> presto soon; early → ⓮
>
> quasi nearly → ⓯
>
> spesso often → ⓰
>
> tanto so; so much → ⓱
>
> troppo too; too much → ⓲

1. È abbastanza alta — She's quite tall
   Non studia abbastanza — He doesn't study enough

2. È venuta anche mia sorella — My sister came too

3. Sei ancora a letto? — Are you still in bed?
   Silvia non è ancora arrivata — Silvia's not here yet

4. L'ho appena fatto — I've just done it
   L'indirizzo era appena leggibile — The address was only just legible

5. Certo che puoi — Of course you can
   Certo che sì — Certainly

6. È così simpatica! — She's so nice!
   Si apre così — It opens like this
   Non si fa così — You don't do it like that

7. Ecco l'autobus! — Here's the bus!
   Dov'è Carla? — Eccola! — Where's Carla? — Here she is!

8. Forse hanno ragione — Maybe they're right

9. Te l'ho già detto — I've already told you

10. Non sono mai stato in America — I've never been to America
    Sei mai stato in America? — Have you ever been to America?

11. Sono molto stanca — I'm very tired
    Ti piace? — Sì, molto. — Do you like it? — Yes, very much
    Ora mi sento molto meglio — I feel much better now

12. Fa piuttosto caldo oggi — It's quite warm today
    È piuttosto lontano — It's rather a long way

13. Mi sento poco bene — I don't feel at all well
    Mi piacciono poco — I don't like them at all

14. Arriverà presto — He'll be here soon
    Mi alzo sempre presto — I always get up early

15. Sono quasi pronta — I'm nearly ready

16. Vanno spesso in centro — They often go into town

17. Questo libro è tanto noioso — This book is so boring
    Mi manchi tanto — I miss you so much

18. È troppo caro — It's too expensive
    Parlano troppo — They talk too much

On the following pages you will find some of the most frequent uses of prepositions in Italian. Particular attention is paid to cases where usage differs greatly from English. It is often difficult to give an English equivalent for Italian prepositions, since usage varies so much between the two languages.

In the list below, the broad meaning of the preposition is given on the left, with examples of usage following.

Prepositions are given in alphabetical order, except for a, di, da and in. These prepositions, shown first, combine with the definite article to make one word.

For combinations of a, di, da, in and su with the definite article, see page 136.

a

at	**alla porta** at the door
	a casa at home
	alla prossima fermata at the next stop
	a 50 chilometri all'ora at 50 km an hour
in	**a Londra** in London
	al sole in the sun
	Sta a letto He's in bed
on	**al terzo piano** on the third floor
	alla radio on the radio
to	**Andiamo al cinema?** Shall we go to the cinema?
	Vai a letto? Are you going to bed?
	Sei mai stato a New York?
	Have you ever been to New York?
	dare qc a qn to give sth to sb
	A chi l'hai dato? Who did you give it to?
	promettere qc a qn to promise sth to sb
	il primo/l'ultimo a fare qc the first/last to do sth
from	**comprare qc a qn** to buy sth from sb

	nascondere qc a qn to hide sth from sb
	prendere qc a qn to take sth from sb
	rubare qc a qn to steal sth from sb

| see you | a presto see you soon |
| | a domani see you tomorrow |

manner	a piedi on foot
	a mano by hand
	a poco a poco little by little
	all'antica in the old-fashioned way
	alla milanese in the Milanese way

(made) with	un gelato alla fragola a strawberry ice cream
	una torta al cioccolato a chocolate cake
	gli spaghetti al pomodoro
	spaghetti with tomato sauce

time: at	alle due at two o'clock
	a mezzanotte at midnight
	a Pasqua at Easter

| *with month*: in | a maggio in May |

distance	a tre chilometri da qui three kilometres from here
	a due ore di distanza in macchina
	two hours away by car

purpose	Sono uscita a fare due passi I went out for a little walk
	Sono andati a fare il bagno
	They've gone to have a swim

| *after certain verbs* | See pages 70-79 |

di

of, belonging to	un amico di famiglia a friend of the family
	il padre di Marco Marco's father
	la casa dei miei amici my friends' house
	Di chi è? Whose is it?
	il periodo delle vacanze the holiday season
	il professore di francese the French teacher
	il campione del mondo the world champion

(made) by	un quadro di Picasso a picture by Picasso
	una commedia di Shakespeare
	a play by Shakespeare

| from | È di Firenze He's from Florence |
| | Di dove sei? Where are you from? |

| *comparisons* | È più alto di me He's taller than me |
| | È più brava di lui She's better than him |

| in (*after superlative*) | il più grande del mondo the biggest in the world |
| | il migliore d'Italia the best in Italy |

time	di domenica on Sundays
	di notte at night
	d'inverno in winter

contents, composition, material, colour	una bottiglia di vino a bottle of wine
	un gruppo di turisti a group of tourists
	una maglietta di cotone a cotton T-shirt
	Di che colore è? What colour is it?

| *manner* | di rado rarely |
| | di solito usually |

after certain numbers	un milione di dollari a million dollars
	un migliaio di persone about a thousand people
	una ventina di macchine about twenty cars

after certain adjectives	Le arance sono ricche di vitamina C Oranges are rich in vitamin C Era pieno di gente It was full of people
after certain verbs	see pages 70-79

da

from	a tre chilometri da qui three kilometres from here Viene da Roma He comes from Rome da cima a fondo from top to bottom
off, out of	Isobel è scesa dal treno Isobel got off the train È scesa dalla macchina She got out of the car
at/to the home of	Sono da Anna I'm at Anna's house Andiamo da Gabriele? Shall we go to Gabriele's house?
at/to (*shop, workplace*)	Laura è dal parrucchiere Laura's at the hairdresser's È andato dal dentista He's gone to the dentist's
for	Vivo qui da un anno I've been living here for a year (*note tense*)
since	da allora since then Ti aspetto dalle tre I've been waiting for you since three o'clock (*note tense*)
by (*with passive agent*)	dipinto da un grande artista painted by a great artist Sono stati catturati dalla polizia They were caught by the police
to (*with infinitive*)	C'è molto da fare There's lots to do È un film da vedere It's a film that you've got to see
as	Da bambino avevo paura del buio As a child I was afraid of the dark

descriptive	**una ragazza dagli occhi azzurri** a girl with blue eyes
	un vestito da cento euro
	a dress costing a hundred euros
purpose/use	**un nuovo paio di scarpe da corsa**
	a new pair of running shoes
	Non ho il costume da bagno
	I haven't got my swimming costume

in

to, in (*place*)	**in centro** in/to the town centre
	in Italia in/to Italy
into	**Su! Sali in macchina** Come on! get into the car
on, at (*state*)	**in vacanza** on holiday
	in pace at peace
in (*years, seasons, months*)	**nel duemilasei** in two thousand and six
	in estate in summer
	in ottobre in October
in (*time taken*)	**L'ha fatto in sei mesi** He did it in six months
transport	**in treno** by train
	in bici by bike
language	**in italiano** in Italian

con

with	**Con chi sei stata?** Who were you with?
to	**Hai parlato con lui?** Have you spoken to him?
manner	**con calma** without hurrying
	con la forza by force

Prepositions

davanti a

in front of   Erano seduti davanti a me nell' *a*utobus
              They were sitting in front of me in the bus
opposite   la casa davanti alla mia the house opposite mine

dopo

after   dopo cena after dinner
+ *pronoun* (add di)   dopo di loro after them

fra/tra

in (*time*)   Torno fra *or* tra un'ora I'll be back in an hour

between   fra *or* tra la cucina ed il soggiorno
                        between the kitchen and the living room

+ *pronoun* (add di)   fra *or* tra di noi between/among us

per

for   Questo è per te This is for you
                È troppo difficile per lui It's too difficult for him
                L'ho comprato per trenta cent*e*simi
                 I bought it for thirty cents
                Ho guidato per trecento chilometri
                 I drove for three hundred kilometres
                una *c*amera per due notti a room for two nights
                Parte per Milano She's leaving for Milan

(going) to   il volo per Londra the flight to London
                il treno per Roma the train to Rome

through   I ladri sono entrati per la finestra
                 The burglars got in through the window
                Siamo passati per Crewe We went through Crewe

by (means of)	per posta by post
	per via aerea by airmail
	per posta elettronica by email
	per ferrovia by rail
	per telefono by phone
	per errore by mistake

(so as) to	L'ho fatto per aiutarti I did it to help you
	Si è chinato per prenderlo He bent down to get it

out of	Ci sono andato per abitudine I went out of habit
	Non l'ho fatto per pigrizia
	I didn't do it out of laziness

distribution	uno per uno one by one
	giorno per giorno day by day
	una per volta one at a time
	due per tre two times three

prima di

before (+noun, pronoun)	prima delle sette before seven
	prima di me before me

+ infin	prima di cominciare before starting

until	Non sarà pronto prima delle otto
	It won't be ready until eight o'clock

senza

without	Esci senza cappotto?
	Are you going out without a coat?

+ pronoun (add di)	senza di te without you

+ infinitive	È uscito senza dire niente
	He went out without saying anything

Prepositions

sopra

over	le donne sopra i sessant'anni women over sixty
above	cento metri sopra il livello del mare a hundred metres above sea level
on top of	sopra l'armadio on top of the cupboard

su*

on	sul pavimento on the floor sulla sinistra on the left un libro sugli animali a book on animals
in	sul giornale in the paper
out of (*ratio*)	in tre casi su dieci in three cases out of ten due giorni su tre two days out of three
approximation	sui cinquecento euro around five hundred euros È sulla trentina She's about thirty

*su combines with the definite article to make one word

verso

| towards (*place*) | Correva verso l'uscita
 He was running towards the exit |
| about | Arriverò verso le sette I'll arrive about seven |

Conjunctions

Some conjunctions introduce a main clause, e.g. e (and), ma (but), o (or). Others introduce subordinate clauses, e.g. perché (because), mentre (while), quando (when), se (if). Conjunctions also link single words. Most are used in much the same way as in English, but note the following:

e and
When followed by a vowel, e often becomes ed → ①

Some Italian conjunctions have to be followed by the subjunctive, see page 66

Some conjunctions are split in Italian, like 'both ... and', 'either ... or' in English.
o ... o either ... or → ②
né ... né neither ... nor, either ... or → ③
sia ... che both ... and → ④

In Italian, sentences with split conjunctions can have a singular or a plural verb → ⑤

che that
  • is followed by the indicative in statements → ⑥
  • is followed by the subjunctive after verbs expressing uncertainty, see page 64

perché because, so that
When perché means 'because' it is followed by the indicative → ⑦
When it means 'so that', it is followed by the subjunctive → ⑧

Note that perché? can also be used as an adverb with the meaning 'why?'

se if, whether
When used in conditional clauses se is followed by the subjunctive → ⑨
Followed by the infinitive, se means 'whether to' → ⑩
Followed by the indicative se expresses doubt → ⑪

Conjunctions are sometimes used in phrases where a verb is understood → ⑫

1 mia sorella ed io — my sister and I
È venuto qui ed è rimasto mezzora — He came here and stayed for half an hour

2 o oggi o domani — either today or tomorrow

3 Non mi hanno chiamato né Claudio né Luca — Neither Claudio nor Luca has phoned me
Non avevo né guanti né scarponi — I didn't have either gloves or boots

4 Verranno sia Luigi che suo fratello — Both Luigi and his brother are coming

5 Non vengono *or* Non viene né lui né sua moglie — Neither he nor his wife is coming

6 Ha detto che farà tardi — He said that he'll be late

7 Sono uscita perché faceva bel tempo — I went out because it was nice weather

8 Gliel'ho dato perché lo leggesse — I gave it him so that he could read it

9 se fosse qui — if he was here
Se avessi studiato avresti passato l'esame — If you'd worked you would have passed the exam

10 Non so se andarci o no — I don't know whether to go or not

11 Mi chiedo se avresti accettato — I wonder if you would have accepted

12 Ti dispiace? — Ma no! — Do you mind? — Of course I don't!
Ho fame. — Anch'io! — I'm hungry. — So am I!
Sì, lo so — strano però — Yes, I know — it's odd though

Word Order

Word order in Italian is very flexible, but:

- unstressed object pronouns always come before the verb, except when attached to the end of an infinitive or an imperative → ❶
  For details see pages 166

- most adjectives come after the noun → ❷
  For details see pages 156

- Adverbs of frequency accompanying verbs in a simple tense usually follow the verb, and those used with a compound tense follow the auxiliary verb → ❸
  For details see pages 184

Other parts of speech, however, may be positioned to give emphasis, or make a contrast:

- the noun which is the object of a verb generally follows the verb, but for emphasis it may come first → ❹

- a question word generally comes first, but for emphasis, a noun subject or object can precede it → ❺

- adjectives generally follow the verb essere, but may precede it for emphasis → ❻

- unstressed object pronouns generally precede the verb, but stressed pronouns can be used instead, and these follow the verb → ❼
  For details see pages 166

- subject pronouns are not normally used, but when added for emphasis they may come before or after the verb → ❽

1 Li vedo! — I can see them!
Me l'ha dato — He gave it to me

2 la squadra italiana — the Italian team
un vino rosso — a red wine

3 Ci vado spesso — I often go there
Non ci sono mai stato — I've never been there

4 **Normal order:**
Non posso soffrire quel cane — I can't stand that dog
Emphatic order:
Quel cane non lo posso soffrire
note object pronoun added before the verb

5 **Normal order:**
Dov'è Lidia? — Where's Lidia?
Di chi sono queste scarpe? — Whose are these shoes?
Dove metto questa borsa? — Where shall I put this bag?
Emphatic order:
Lidia, dov'è?
Queste scarpe di chi sono?
Questa borsa dove la metto?
note added object pronoun

6 **Normal order**
Sono belli — They're lovely
Sei pazza — You're mad
Emphatic order:
Belli sono! — They're lovely!
Pazza sei! — You're mad!

7 **Order with unstressed pronoun:**
Me l'ha dato — He gave it to me
Order with stressed pronoun:
L'ha dato a me (non a te) — He gave it to me (not to you)

8 **Unemphatic:**
Cosa pensi? — What do you think?
Emphatic:
Tu cosa pensi?/Cosa pensi tu?

Negatives

In Italian, sentences are generally made negative by adding **non** before the verb → ①

di no is used after verbs such as **dire**, **credere**, **pensare** and **sperare** → ②

o no? is used to mean 'or not' → ③

noun/pronoun + **no**
no is used when making a distinction between people or things → ④

non is used in combination with other negative words such as **niente** *nothing*, **nessuno** *nobody*, **mai** *never* → ⑤

When **mai** is used with a compound tense, it usually comes between the auxiliary verb and the past participle → ⑥

When **niente** or **nessuno** are the subject of the verb they can come first, or they can follow the verb. If they come first, **non** is not used → ⑦

More than one negative word can follow a negative verb → ⑧

nessuno, nessuna no
These negative adjectives change their endings according to the letter that follows them, like the indefinite article **uno** → ⑨

non ... né .... né neither ... nor/not ... either ... or
A plural verb is required if there are two subjects → ⑩

1. Non posso venire — I can't come
   Non l'ho visto — I didn't see it
   Non è qui — It's not here

2. Ha detto di no — He said not
   Credo di no — I don't think so
   Pensa di no — He doesn't think so
   Speriamo di no — Let's hope not

3. Vieni o no? — Are you coming or not?
   che ti piaccia o no — whether you like it or not

4. Invito lui, lei no — I'm going to invite him, but not her
   Loro hanno finito, noi no — They've finished, but we haven't
   Lei è brava, io no — She's good, but I'm not
   Prendo un dolce, il caffè no — I'll have a sweet, but not a coffee

5. Non ho niente — I haven't got anything/I've got nothing
   Non l'ho detto a nessuno — I haven't told anyone/I've told nobody
   Non ci vado mai — I never go there

6. Non l'ho mai vista — I've never seen her
   Non ci siamo mai stati — We've never been there

7. Niente è cambiato — Nothing has changed
   BUT
   Non è cambiato niente
   Nessuno vuole andarci — Nobody wants to go
   BUT
   Non vuole andarci nessuno

8. Non fanno mai niente — They never do anything
   Non si confida mai con nessuno — He never confides in anyone
   Non vendiamo più niente — We no longer sell anything

9. Nessun tipo di pianta può viverci — No type of plant can live there
   Non ho nessuna voglia di farlo — I have no desire to do it
   Non hanno fatto nessuno sforzo — They didn't make any effort

10. Non verranno né Anna né Maria — Neither Anna nor Maria is coming
    BUT
    Non invito né Anna né Maria — I'm not inviting either Anna or Maria

Question Forms

In Italian, questions differ from statements in intonation, or the use of a question mark in writing. Unlike in English, the verb forms in questions are no different from those in statements → **1**

Word order

When the subject of the question is a noun, it comes either before or after the verb → **2**

When the object of the question is a noun, it either comes after the verb, or comes first. In this case an object pronoun agreeing with the noun is added before the verb → **3**

A subject pronoun may also be added at the end of a question, for special emphasis → **4**

When answering a question, either say sì or no, or sì or no with a full statement. There is no Italian equivalent for short answers such as Yes I do, or No I don't → **5**

Question words such as dove? where?, chi? who? cosa? what? generally come first → **6**

However, note the following:
- a noun subject can either follow the verb, or precede the question word → **7**
- a noun object can follow the verb, or precede the question word. In this case an object pronoun agreeing with the noun is added before the verb → **8**
- prepositions such as di, con and a, must precede question words → **9**

1 **STATEMENT**

Basta **That's enough**
Sono di qui **They're from here**
L'ha fatto lui **He did it**
Va bene **That's okay**

QUESTION

Basta? **Is that enough?**
Sono di qui? **Are they from here?**
L'ha fatto lui? **Did he do it?**
Va bene? **Is that okay?**

2 Tua sorella è partita? *or*
  È partita tua sorella?
La Calabria è bella? *or*
  È bella la Calabria?
Gli spaghetti sono buoni? *or*
Sono buoni gli spaghetti?

Has your sister gone?

Is Calabria beautiful?

Is the spaghetti nice?

3 Vuoi un gelato? *or*
  Un gelato lo vuoi?
Vuoi del latte *or*
  Un po' di latte lo vuoi?

Do you want an ice cream?

Do you want some milk?

4 **Contrast**
Fai il bucato?
with
Il bucato lo fai tu?

Are you doing the washing?

Will you do the washing?

5 Piove? Sì, piove
Capisci? No *or* No, non capisco

Is it raining? Yes *or* **Yes, it's raining**
Do you understand? No *or*
  No, I don't

6 Dove vai?
Chi parla?

Where are you going?
Who's speaking?

7 Quanto costano queste scarpe? *or*
Queste scarpe, quanto costano?
Chi è quella signora? *or*
Quella signora, chi è?

How much are these shoes?

Who is that lady?

8 Chi pagherà il conto? *or*
Il conto, chi lo pagherà?

Who will pay the bill?

9 Di che colore è?
Con chi parlavi?
A cosa stai pensando?

What colour is it?
Who were you talking to?
What are you thinking about?

Question Forms *continued*

no?, vero?
no? or vero? is used to check that what you've said is correct, like 'isn't it?'
or 'haven't you?' in English → ❶

vero is used to check a negative statement → ❷

Indirect Questions

Word order in Italian indirect questions is no different from that of
statements → ❸

Tenses in indirect questions are generally the same as in English, except
for the use of the perfect conditional where the present conditional is used
in English → ❹

1 Hai finito, no?
    Questa è la tua macchina, vero?

You've finished, haven't you?
This is your car, isn't it?

2 Non sono partiti, vero?
    Non fa molto male, vero?

They haven't gone, have they?
It doesn't hurt much, does it?

3 Vorrei sapere quanto costa

I'd like to know how much it
    costs

    Mi domando cosa pensano

I wonder what they think

4 Ha detto che non era colpa sua
    Ha detto che verrà
    Aveva detto che sarebbe venuto

He said it wasn't his fault
He said he'll come
He'd said he'd come

Cardinal
(one, two *etc*)

Ordinal
(first, second *etc*)

Cardinal		Ordinal	
zero	0		
uno (una, un)	1	primo	1°
due	2	secondo	2°
tre	3	terzo	3°
quattro	4	quarto	4°
cinque	5	quinto	5°
sei	6	sesto	6°
sette	7	settimo	7°
otto	8	ottavo	8°
nove	9	nono	9°
dieci	10	decimo	10°
undici	11	undicesimo	11°
dodici	12	dodicesimo	12°
tredici	13	tredicesimo	13°
quattordici	14	quattordicesimo	14°
quindici	15	quindicesimo	15°
sedici	16	sedicesimo	16°
diciassette	17	diciassettesimo	17°
diciotto	18	diciottesimo	18°
diciannove	19	diciannovesimo	19°
venti	20	ventesimo	20°
ventuno	21	ventunesimo	21°
ventidue	22	ventiduesimo	22°
ventitré	23	ventitreesimo	23°
trenta	30	trentesimo	30°
quaranta	40	quarantesimo	40°
cinquanta	50	cinquantesimo	50°
sessanta	60	sessantesimo	60°
settanta	70	settantesimo	70°
ottanta	80	ottantesimo	80°
novanta	90	novantesimo	90°
novantanove	99	novantanovesimo	99°

Use of numbers

Cardinal		Ordinal	
cento	100	centesimo	100°
centouno	101	centunesimo	101°
(centouna, centoun)			
centodue	102	centoduesimo	102°
centotré	103	centotreesimo	103°
centodieci	110	centodecimo	110°
centoquarantadue	142	centoquarantaduesimo	142°
duecento	200	duecentesimo	200°
duecentouno	201	duecentunesimo	201°
duecentotré	203	duecentotreesimo	203°
trecento	300	trecentesimo	300°
quattrocento	400	quattrocentesimo	400°
cinquecento	500	cinquecentesimo	500°
seicento	600	seicentesimo	600°
settecento	700	settecentesimo	700°
ottocento	800	ottocentesimo	800°
novecento	900	novecentesimo	900°
mille	1000	millesimo	1000°
milleuno	1001	millunesimo	1001°
milleduecentodue	1202	milleduecentoduesimo	1202°
duemila	2000	duemillesimo	2000°
cinquemilatrecento	5300	cinquemilatrecentesimo	5300°
un milione	1.000.000	milionesimo	1.000.000°
due milioni	2.000.000	duemilionesimo	2.000.000°

Ordinal numbers are adjectives which tell you the order in which the noun occurs (first, third, etc). They end with either o, or a, depending on whether the noun is masculine or feminine:

il 15° piano	the 15th floor	la 24ª giornata	the 24th day

Fractions		Other numerical expressions	
un mezzo	a half	zero virgola cinque (0,5)	0.5
un terzo	a third	uno virgola tre (1,3)	1.3
due terzi	two thirds	dieci per cento	10%
un quarto	a quarter	sei più due	6 + 2
tre quarti	three quarters	sei meno due	6 − 2
un quinto	a fifth	due volte sei	2 × 6
un sesto	a sixth	sei diviso due	6 ÷ 2

ⓘ Note the use of commas in decimal numbers, and full stops with millions.

Other Uses

Approximate numbers
- ending in **-ina**

una ventina di DVD	about twenty DVDs
Eravamo una trentina	There were about thirty of us
È sulla quarantina	He's about forty
gente sulla cinquantina	people of around fifty

- ending in **-aio**

un centinaio di persone	about a hundred people
centinaia di volte	hundreds of times
un migliaio di casi	about a thousand cases
due miglaia di macchine	about two thousand cars

Measurements

venti metri quadri	20 square metres
venti metri cubi	20 cubic metres
un ponte lungo cento metri	a bridge 100 metres long
essere largo/alto tre metri	to be 3 metres wide/long

Miscellaneous

Abitano al numero dieci	They live at number 10
nel capitolo sei	in chapter 6
Sono a pagina tre	They're on page 3
Abitano al terzo piano	They live on the 3rd floor
Sono arrivata seconda nella gara	I came second in the competition
su una scala da uno a dieci	on a scale of one to ten

Telephone numbers

The digits in a telephone number are spoken individually:

zero zero tre nove zero sei quattro due otto uno sette sei zero due
(0039 0642817602)

tre quattro sette sette zero tre quattro nove zero cinque
(3477034905)

Calendar

Che data è oggi?/ Quanti ne abbiamo oggi?	What's the date today?
È il primo maggio	It's May 1st
È il due maggio	It's May 2nd
È il ventotto febbraio	It's February 28th
Arrivano il diciannove luglio	They're arriving on July 19th

ⓘ Use cardinal numbers except for the first of the month.

Years

È nata nel 1993	She was born in 1993
il dodici febbraio duemilatredici	(on) 12th February 2013

Other expressions

negli anni sessanta	in the sixties
nel ventunesimo secolo	in the twenty-first century
in *or* a maggio	in May
lunedì (quindici)	on Monday (the fifteenth)
di lunedì	on Mondays
fra *or* tra dieci giorni	in 10 days' time
otto giorni fa	8 days ago

The time

Che ore sono?	What time is it?
È l'una	It's one o'clock
Sono le due	It's two o'clock

ⓘ Use **sono** for all times except one o'clock.

00.00	mezzanotte **midnight, twelve o'clock**
00.10	mezzanotte e dieci **ten past midnight**
00.15	mezzanotte e un quarto, mezzanotte e quindici
00.30	mezzanotte e mezza, mezzanotte e trenta
00.45	l'una meno un quarto, l'una meno quindici, mezzanotte e quarantacinque
01.00	l'una di mattina **one a.m., one o'clock in the morning**
01.10	l'una e dieci (di mattina)
01.15	l'una e un quarto, l'una e quindici
01.30	l'una e mezza, l'una e trenta
01.45	l'una e quarantacinque; le due meno un quarto, le due meno quindici
01.50	l'una e cinquanta, le due meno dieci
01.59	l'una e cinquantanove, le due meno un minuto
12.00	mezzogiorno, le dodici **noon, twelve o'clock**
12.30	mezzogiorno e mezza, mezzogiorno e trenta, le dododici e mezza
13.00	l'una (del pomeriggio), le tredici, le ore tredici
01.30	l'una e mezza/trenta (del pomeriggio), le tredici e trenta, le ore tredici e trenta
19.00	le sette (di sera), le diciannove, le ore diciannove
19.30	le sette e mezza/trenta, le diciannove e trenta, le ore diciannove e trenta

ⓘ The twenty-four hour clock is widely used in Italy.

alle diciannove or	at nineteen hours
alle ore diciannove	at nineteen hundred hours

A che ora venite? — Alle sette

L'ufficio è chiuso da mezzogiorno
  alle due
alle due di notte/del
pomeriggio

alle otto di sera

alle cinque in punto
verso le nove
poco dopo mezzogiorno
fra le otto e le nove
Erano le tre e mezza passate
Devi esserci entro le nove
Ci vogliono tre ore
Ci metto una mezz'ora
È rimasta in bagno per un'ora

Li aspetto da quaranta minuti

Sono partiti qualche minuto fa
L'ho fatto in venti minuti
Il treno arriva fra un quarto d'ora

Per quanto tempo dovremo
  aspettare?

What time are you coming?
  — At seven

The office is closed from twelve
  to two
at two o'clock in the morning/
  afternoon; at two a.m./p.m.

at eight in the evening;
  at eight p.m.
at five o'clock sharp
at around nine
shortly after noon
between eight and nine o'clock
It was after half past three
You have to be there by nine
It takes three hours
It takes me half an hour
She was in the bathroom for an
  hour

I've been waiting for them for
  forty minutes

They left a few minutes ago
I did it in twenty minutes
The train arrives in a quarter of
  an hour
How long will we have to wait?

Beware of translating word for word. The following are examples of where Italian tends to differ from English:

> English phrasal verbs (i.e. verbs such as 'to look for'; 'to fall down') are often translated by one word in Italian → ❶

> English verbs often require a preposition where there is none in Italian, or vice versa → ❷

> Different English prepositions may be translated by the one Italian preposition → ❸

> A word which is singular in English may be plural in Italian, or vice versa → ❹

> There is no Italian equivalent for the apostrophe s and s apostrophe possessive → ❺

See also at/in/to, page 220.

The following pages look at some specific problems.

❶
scappare	to run away
cadere	to fall down
rendere	to give back

❷
pagare qc	to pay for sth
guardare qc/qn	to look at sth/sb
ascoltare qc/qn	to listen to sth/sb
dire a qn	to tell sb
ubbedire a qn	to obey sb
ricordarsi di qc/qn	to remember sth/sb

❸
meravigliarsi di	to be surprised at
stufo di	fed up of/with
rubare qc a	to steal sth from
restio a	reluctant to

❹
gli affari	business
i suoi capelli	his/her hair
Le lasagne sono ...	Lasagne is...
i bagagli	luggage

❺
la macchina di mia sorella	my sister's car (*literally*: ... of my sister)
la camera delle ragazze	the girls' bedroom (*literally*... of the girls)

-ing

This is translated by the gerund in Italian:

> 'to be ...-ing' is sometimes translated by **stare** + *gerund*, when the verb describes something at the moment, but a simple tense is often used. A simple tense must be used when the verb refers to the future. → ①

The past participle, not the gerund, is used for physical positions such as lying and sitting → ②

> to see/hear sb ...-ing, use an infinitive or **che** + *verb* → ③

'-ing' can also be translated by:

- an infinitive, see page 46 → ④
- a perfect infinitive, see page 50 → ⑤
- the gerund, when used abverbially, see page 52 → ⑥
- a noun → ⑦

to be

'to be' is generally translated by *essere* → ⑧

Examples

1. Che fai *or* stai facendo? — What are you doing?
   Che fai domani sera? — What are you doing tomorrow evening?

   Partono *or* Stanno partendo — They're leaving
   Partono alle sette — They're leaving at seven

2. Erano seduti in prima fila — They were sitting in the front row
   Era sdraiata sulla sabbia — She was lying on the sand

3. L'ho visto partire — I saw him leaving
   L'ho visto che partiva
   L'ho sentita piangere — I heard her crying
   L'ho sentita che piangeva

4. Mi piace cucinare — I like cooking
   invece di rispondere — instead of answering
   prima di partire — before leaving
   Iniziò a piovere — It started raining

5. dopo aver perso molti soldi — after losing a lot of money

6. Essendo più timida di me, non ha gli ha parlato — Being shyer than me, she didn't speak to him

7. Il fumo fa molto male — Smoking is very bad for you

8. È tardi — It's late
   Sono loro — It's them
   Siamo stanchi — We're tired

stare is used

- with the gerund to make continuous tenses → **1**
- in perfect and pluperfect tenses of *essere*, which consist of the present/imperfect tense of *essere* + past participle of stare → **2**
- interchangeably with *essere* when talking about locations → **3**
- when talking about health → **4**

In various set expressions *avere* is used (with the final e dropped):

aver caldo/freddo	to be hot/cold
aver fame/sete	to be hungry/thirsty
aver paura	to be afraid
aver torto/ragione	to be wrong/right

fare is used to talk about the weather → **5**

avere is used for ages → **6**

it is, it's

These are never translated by a pronoun in Italian → **7**

In expressions of time, use sono, except for one o'clock → **8**

To describe the weather, see above.

When 'it's' is followed by a pronoun, such as 'me', 'her' or 'them', the form of *essere* agrees with the person referred to → **9**

can, be able

Ability is generally expressed by potere → **10**

If the meaning is 'to know how to' use sapere → **11**

'can' with verbs of seeing and hearing is not translated in Italian → **12**

1. Ci sto pensando — I'm thinking about it
   Stavano chiacchierando — They were chatting

2. Non ci sono mai stata — I've never been there
   Ero stato malato — I had been ill

3. La casa sta *or* è sulla collina — The house is on the hill
   Sta *or* è fuori — It's outside

4. Sto bene, grazie — I'm fine thanks
   Sta male — He's not well

5. Che tempo fa? — What's the weather like?
   Fa caldo/freddo — It's hot/cold
   Fa bel/brutto tempo — It's nice/bad weather

6. Quanti anni hai? — How old are you?
   Ho quindici anni — I'm fifteen

7. Dammelo, è mio — Give it me, it's mine
   È molto lontano — It's a long way

8. Sono le nove — It's nine o'clock
   È l'una meno un quarto — It's a quarter to one

9. Sono io — It's me
   È lei — It's her
   Sono loro — It's them

10. Puoi venire? — Can you come?

11. Non so come spiegarlo — I can't explain it

12. Si vede il mare — You can see the sea
    Non ti sento — I can't hear you

to like

piacere, the Italian verb used to translate 'to like', means 'to be pleasing', so **Mi piace l'Italia** literally means 'Italy is pleasing to me', and **Gli animali piacciono ai bambini** means 'Animals are pleasing to children'.

Remember the following when using **piacere**:
- the thing(s) liked is/are the subject of the Italian verb → ❶
- if the thing liked is singular, the verb is singular (**piace/è piaciuto** etc): if the things liked are plural, the verb is plural (**piacciono/sono piaciuti** etc) → ❷
- **piacere** is used with **a**, or an indirect object pronoun → ❸

to

'to' is often translated by **a**, see page 190 → ❹

When telling the time, e.g. ten to six, use **meno** → ❺

When the meaning is 'in order to' use **per** → ❻

When 'to' is part of the infinitive following an adjective such as 'easy', 'difficult', 'impossible', use the Italian infinitive with **da** → ❼

unless the infinitive has an object → ❽

at/in/to

For 'in' or 'to' + a country, use the Italian preposition **in** → ❾

For 'in' or 'to' + a town, use the Italian preposition **a** → ❿

When the meaning is 'to'/'at' + someone's house/place of business use **da** → ⑪

1 Il cane piace a mio figlio — My son likes the dog
I cani piacciono a mio figlio — My son likes dogs

2 Il concerto è piaciuto a tutti — Everyone liked the concert
I cioccolatini piaceranno a tutti — Everyone will like the chocolates

3 A mia madre piace molto il giardinaggio — My mother likes gardening very much
Ti piace questa canzone? — Do you like this song?
Non gli piacciono i pomodori — He doesn't like tomatoes

4 Dallo a Patrizia — Give it to Patrizia

5 le sei meno un quarto — a quarter to six
l'una meno tre minuti — three minutes to one

6 L'ho fatto per rassicurarti — I did it to reassure you
Si è fermato per guardarlo — He stopped to look at it

7 facile da capire — easy to understand
impossibile da dimenticare — impossible to forget

8 È facile capirlo — It's easy to understand it
È impossibile crederci — It's impossible to believe it

9 Abitano negli Stati Uniti — They live in the United States
Andiamo in Germania il quattro maggio — We're going to Germany on May 4
una città in Cina — a city in China

10 È andato a Parigi — He's gone to Paris
Vive a Bologna — He lives in Bologna

11 Andiamo da Anna — Let's go to Anna's house
È dal parucchiere — She's at the hairdresser's

General Points

Vowels and consonants are always clearly pronounced in Italian, and each syllable of a word is audible, unlike in English, where letters, and sometimes whole syllables, are often not pronounced. Compare, for example:

lettera (both es are equally clear, audible r)

letter (2nd e indistinct, r usually not pronounced)

interessante, (5 syllables)

interesting (3 syllables)

Diphthongs

A diphthong is a glide between two vowel sounds in the same syllable. The vowels in 'say', 'go' and 'might' are diphthongs. Diphthongs are very common in English, but much less so in Italian, where most vowels are a single sound, as they are in English words such as 'top', 'back' and 'set' The diphthongs found in Italian are vowels preceded by a y, or a w sound:

ia [ja] - chiaro	ua [wa] - sguardo
ie [je] - pieno	ue [we] - guerra
io [jo] - pioggia	ui [wi] - guidare
iu [ju] - chiuso	uo [wo] - fuoco

Stress

Italian words are generally stressed on the next to the last syllable, (so two-syllable words are stressed on the first syllable, three-syllable words on the second syllable, and so on):

ca sa	set ti **ma** na
ra **gaz** zo	ge ne ral **men** te

For more details see page 180.

If the stress comes on the last vowel of a word with more than one syllable, the vowel is always written with an accent:

per **ché**

par le **rò**

un i ver si **tà**

For more details see page 180.

Pronunciation of Consonants

Most consonants are pronounced as in English, except that they are always clear, and double consonants are audible. Thus, in **sabbia** *sand*, for example, the **b** sound ending the first syllable carries on to start the second syllable: sab-bya.

Note the following:

		PRONOUNCED	EXAMPLES
c before a, o, u	[k]	like k in kiss	camera, come, cubo
c before e or i	[tʃ]	like ch in China	certo, cinese
ch	[k]	like k in kiss	chiesa
g before a, o, u	[g]	like g in good	gara, largo, gusto
g before e or i	[dʒ]	like g in rage	gelato, giro
gh	[g]	like g in good	laghi, ghiaccio
gl before i	[ʎ]	like ll in million	meglio, gli
gl before other vowels	[gl]	like gl in piglet	sigla
gn	[ɲ]	like ny in canyon	gnocchi, ragno
h is not pronounced		like h in honest	hanno
r	[r]	like r in zero	raro, rapido
sc before e or i	[ʃ]	like sh in ship	scena, sci
z	[dz]	like ds in lids	zanzara
z	[ts]	like ts in bits	ragazzo

Pronunciation of Vowels

		PRONOUNCED	EXAMPLES
a	[a]	like a in apple	animale
e	[ɛ]	like e in set	schema
e	[e]	like ay in day	stella
i	[i]	like ee in sheep	clima
i before a vowel often	[j]	like y in yoghurt	Lidia, negozio
o	[o]	like o in pot	ora
u	[u]	like oo in soot	puro
u before a vowel often	[w]	like w in win	usuale

Stress: Cases where the normal rule does not apply

In cases where the last syllable of a word is stressed, this is shown by an accent. Most of these are:

- nouns ending in **-tà**, many of which have counterparts in English ending in -ty, such as 'reality' and 'university'

re al tà	reality	u ni ver si tà	university
fe li ci tà	happiness, felicity	fe del tà	fidelity
cu rio si tà	curiosity	fa col tà	faculty
bon tà	goodness	cit tà	city
cru del tà	cruelty	e tà	age
me tà	half		

- 1ˢᵗ and 3ʳᵈ person singular future verbs , and 3ʳᵈ person singular past historics:

sa rò	I will be
fi ni rà	it will finish
as pet te rà	she'll wait
par lò	he spoke
an dò	she went

- adverbs and conjunctions such as

perché	why
però	however
così	so

In cases where the stress is on an unexpected syllable other than the last, there is no accent to show this. In this book, such vowels are shown in italics, e.g.

m*a*cchina	car
*u*tile	useful
port*a*tile	laptop

Stress in present tense verb forms

All present tense forms except the 3rd person plural follow the rule, and stress the next to the last syllable, e.g. *parlo* I speak; *considera* he considers

In the 3rd person plural form the stress is not on the next to the last syllable, but matches that of the 1st person singular:

1st person singular		3rd person plural	
par lo	I speak	par la no	they speak
con si de ro	I consider	con si de ra no	they consider
mi al le no	I'm training	si al le na no	they're training

Stress in 2nd conjugation infinitives

Stress is regular for the infinitives of all 1st and 3^{rd,} and many 2nd conjugation verbs, e.g. **parlare** *to speak*, **finire** *to finish*, **vedere** *to see*. However, there are also many 2nd conjugation infinitives which do not stress the 1st e of the **-ere** ending, eg:

essere *to be*, **vendere** *to sell*, **permettere** *to allow*, **dividere** *to divide*.

When learning 2nd conjugation verbs, note which syllable of the infinitive is stressed.

From Sounds to Spelling

Apart from the occasional problem of unexpected stress, the way Italian is spelled is a good guide to how it should be pronounced. See page 180.

It is also easy to know how to spell words, if the following points are remembered:

-care/-gare verbs

Verbs with infinitives ending -care, or -gare, for example cercare and pagare, add an h to keep the c or g hard in front of endings starting with e or i:

Vowel that follows c/g	Present of cercare		Present of pagare	
o	cerco	I look for	pago	I pay
i	cerchi	you look for	paghi	you pay
a	cerca	he/she looks for	paga	he/she pays
i	cerchiamo	we look for	paghiamo	we pay
a	cercate	you look for	pagate	you pay
a	cercano	they look for	pagano	they pay

Vowel that follows c/g	Future of cercare		Future of pagare	
e	cercherò	I'll look for	pagherò	I'll pay
e	cercherai	you'll look for	pagherai	you'll pay
e	cercherà	he/she will look for	pagherà	he/she will pay
e	cercheremo	we'll look for	pagheremo	we'll pay
e	cercherete	you'll look for	pagherete	you'll pay
e	cercheranno	they'll look for	pagheranno	they'll pay

-ca/-ga nouns and adjectives

Nouns and adjectives ending in -ca and -ga always keep the hard sound of the consonant in the plural, so h is added before the plural ending -e:

Singular		Plural	
amica	friend	amiche	friends
riga	line	righe	lines
ricca	rich	ricche	rich
lunga	long	lunghe	long

-co/-go nouns and adjectives

Some nouns and adjectives ending in -co and -go keep the hard sound of the consonant in the plural, so h is added before the plural ending -i, e.g.:

Singular		Plural	
fuoco	fire	fuochi	fires
albergo	hotel	alberghi	hotels
ricco	rich	ricchi	rich
lungo	long	lunghi	long

Other nouns nouns and adjectives ending in -co and -go change the sound of the consonant in the plural from hard [k] or [g] to soft [tʃ] or [dʒ], so no h is added, e.g.:

Singular		Plural	
amico	friend	amici	friends
astrologo	astrologer	astrologi	astrologers
greco	Greek	greci	Greek
psicologico	psychological	psicologici	psychological

-io nouns

The plural of nouns ending -io is spelled -ii if the i of the -io ending is a stressed vowel, e.g. zio *uncle* plural: zii, and invio *dispatch* plural: invii.

In cases where the i of the -io is not a stressed vowel, but is pronounced [j], the plural is spelled with a single i, e.g. occhio *eye* plural occhi; figlio *son* plural: figli.

227

-cia/-gia nouns

Generally, if the i of the -cia/-gia ending of a noun is a stressed vowel, the i is retained in the plural, eg farmacia *chemist* plural: farmacie; bugia *lie* plural: bugie. If the i of the ending serves to keep the c/g soft, and is not pronounced as a vowel, there is no i in the plural: faccia *face*, plural: facce; spiaggia *beach*, plural: spiagge.

Accents

Use an accent when a word is stressed on the final syllable, e.g. città, cercherò, università. See page 180.

Accents are also used on certain one-syllable words to distinguish them from words that are spelled the same (homophones):

da	from	dà	he/she gives
e	and	è	is
la	the/it	là	there
li	them	lì	there
ne	of it/them	né	neither
se	if	sé	himself
si	himself/herself/one	sì	yes
te	you	tè	tea

The grave accent (à, è, ì, ò ,ù) is used on most words. The acute accent is used to spell conjunctions ending in che, such as benché *although*, and perché *because*. It is also used on né and sé (except in the phrases se stesso and se stessa *himself; herself*).

può, già, ciò, più and giù are spelled with an accent, for no obvious reason.

The Alphabet

A,a	a	J,j	[i'lunga]	S,s	['ɛsse]
B,b	[bi]	K,k	['kappa]	T,t	[ti]
C,c	[tʃi]	L,l	['ɛlle]	U,u	u
D,d	[di]	M,m	['ɛmme]	V,v	[vi, vu]
E,e	e	N,n	['ɛnne]	W,w	['dɔppjovu]
F,f	['ɛffe]	O,o	[ɔ]	X,x	[iks]
G,g	[dʒi]	P,p	[pi]	Y,y	['ipsilon]
H,h	['akka]	Q,q	[ku]	Z,z	[dzɛta]
I,i	i	R,r	['ɛrre]		

Capital letters are used as in English except for the following:

adjectives of nationality

e.g. una città tedesca   a German town

una scrittrice italiana   an Italian writer

languages

e.g. Parla inglese?   Do you speak English?

Parlo francese ed italiano   I speak French and Italian

days of the week:

lunedì Monday

martedì Tuesday

mercoledì Wednesday

giovedì Thursday

venerdì Friday

sabato Saturday

domenica Sunday

months of the year:

gennaio January   luglio July

febbraio February   agosto August

marzo March   settembre September

aprile April   ottobre October

maggio May   novembre November

giugno June   dicembre December

The following index lists comprehensively both grammatical terms and key words in English and Italian.

Index

Index